Metric Equivalency Tables

Linear Measure

1 millimeter (mm) ...... 0.03937 inch
1 centimeter (cm) .... 0.3937 inch

Volume Measure

1 milliliter .... 0.061 cubic inch
1 centiliter .... 0.338 fluid ounce
1 deciliter .... 3.38 fluid ounces or
0.1057 liquid quart
1 liter .... 1.0567 liquid quarts or
0.9081 dry quart or
61.024 cubic inches
1 dekaliter .... 2.64 gallons or
0.284 bushel
1 hectoliter .... 26.418 gallons or
2838 bushels
1 kiloliter .... 264.18 gallons or
35.315 cubic feet
1 ounce (liquid) .... 29.573 milliliters
1 cup .... 0.2366 liter
1 gallon .... 3.785 liters
1 bushel .... 35.238 liters
1 peck .... 8.810 liters
1 pint (dry) .... 0.551 liter
1 pint (liquid) .... 0.473 liter
1 quart (dry) .... 1.101 liters
1 quart (liquid) .... 0.946 liter

Weights

1 decagram .... 0.3527 ounce
1 hectogram .... 3.5274 ounces
1 kilogram .... 2.2046 pounds
1 metric ton .... 2,204.6 pounds
1 ounce .... 28.349 grams
1 pound .... 0.453 kilogram
1 short ton .... 0.907 metric ton
1 long ton .... 1.016 metric tons

Cubic Measure

1 cubic centimeter (cm^3)..0.06102 cubic inch
1 cubic decimeter (dm^3)..61.023 cubic inches or
0.0353 cubic foot
1 cubic meter (m^3) .... 1.308 cubic yards or
35.314 cubic feet
1 cubic inch (in^3) .... 16.387 cubic centimeters
1 cubic foot (ft^3) .... 28.317 cubic decimeters
1 cubic yard (yd^3) .... 0.765 cubic meter
9 square feet .... 1 square yard (yd^2) or
1,296 square inches
30½ square yards .... 1 square rod (rd^2) or
272¼ square feet
160 square rods .... 1 acre or 4,840 yards or
43,560 square feet
640 acres .... 1 square mile (mi^2)
1 mile square .... 1 section (of land)
6 miles square .... 1 township or
36 sections or
36 square miles

Cubic Measure

1,728 cubic inches (in^3) . 1 cubic foot (ft^3)
27 cubic feet .... 1 cubic yard (yd^3)

Dry Measure

When necessary to distinguish the dry pint or quart from the liquid pint or quart, the word "dry" should be used in combination with the name or abbreviation of the dry unit.

2 pints .... 1 quart (qt)
8 quarts .... 1 peck (pk) or 16 pints
4 pecks .... 1 bushel (bu) or
32 quarts

Liquid Measure

When necessary to distinguish the liquid pint or quart from the dry pint or quart, the word "liquid" or the abbreviation "liq" should be used in combination with the name or abbreviation of the liquid unit.

4 gills .... 1 pint (pt) or
28.875 cubic inches
2 pints .... 1 quart (qt) or
57.75 cubic inches
4 quarts .... 1 gallon (gal) or
231 cubic inches or
8 pints or 32 gills

WEBSTER'S DICTIONARY OF MODERN ENGLISH

Abbreviations used in the Dictionary

a.	adjective
abbrev.	abbreviation
Acc.	Accounting
adv.	adverb
Aeron.	Aeronautics
Afr.	Africa(n)
Amer.	America(n)
Anat.	Anatomy
Archaeol.	Archaeology
Archit.	Architecture
Arith.	Arithmetic
Astrol.	Astrology
Astron.	Astronomy
Aust.	Australia(n)
Biochem.	Biochemistry
Biol.	Biology
Bot.	Botany
Brit.	Britain, British
Bus.	Business
Canad.	Canada, Canadian
cent.	century
Ch.	Church
Chem.	Chemistry
Cine.	Cinema
Class. lit.	Classical literature
Class. myth.	Classical mythology
cm.	centimeter(s)
Comm.	Commerce
comp.	comparative
Comp.	Computers
conj.	conjunction
cu.	cubic
dial.	dialect
dim.	diminutive
E	East
Eccles.	Ecclesiastical
Ecol.	Ecology
Econ.	Economics
Educ.	Education
eg	for example
Elec.	Electricity
Electron.	Electronics
esp.	especially
fem.	feminine
fig.	figuratively
Fin.	Finance
Fr.	French
g	gram(s)
Geog.	Geography
Ger.	German
Gr.	Greek
Gram.	Grammar
Her.	Heraldry
Hist.	History
Hort.	Horticulture
ie	that is
impers.	impersonal
ind.	indicative
inf.	informal
interj.	interjection
It.	Italian
k	kilogram(s)
km	kilometer(s)
l	liter(s)
Lat.	Latin
Linguis.	Linguistics
lit.	literally
Lit.	Literary, Literature
m	meter(s)
masc.	masculine
Math.	Mathematics
Mech.	Mechanics
Med.	Medicine
Met.	Meteorology
Mil.	Military
Min.	Mineralogy
mm	millimeter(s)
Mus.	Music
Myth.	Mythology
n.	noun
N	North
Naut.	Nautical
N.T.	New Testament
N.Z.	New Zealand
obs.	obsolete, obsolescent
offens.	offensive
oft.	often
orig.	originally
O.T.	Old Testament
Pathol.	Pathology
pers.	person
pert.	pertaining
Philos.	Philosophy
Phonet.	Phonetics
Photog.	Photography
Phys.	Physics
Phys. Ed.	Physical Education
Physiol.	Physiology
pl.	plural
pl.n.	plural noun
Poet.	Poetic, Poetry
Pol.	Politics
poss.	possessive
pp.	past participle
prep.	preposition
pres.t.	present tense
Print.	Printing
pron.	pronoun
pr.p.	present participle
Psych.	Psychiatry
Psychoanal.	Psychoanalysis
Psychol.	Psychology
pt.	past tense
Rad.	Radio
R.C.	Roman Catholic
refl.	reflexive
Rel.	Religion
S	South
Sc.	Science
Scot.	Scottish
sing.	singular
sl.	slang
Sociol.	Sociology
Sp.	Spanish
sq.	square
St.Ex.	Stock Exchange
sup.	superlative
Surg.	Surgery
Surv.	Surveying
Theat.	Theater
Trig.	Trigonometry
T.V.	Television
usu.	usually
v.	verb
v.aux.	auxiliary verb
Vet.	Veterinary Medicine
vi.	intransitive verb
vt.	transitive verb
W	West
Zool.	Zoology

A	**Australian**
C	**Canadian**
NZ	**New Zealand**
SA	**South African**
UK	**United Kingdom**

Pronunciation Key

Stress is shown by placing a mark, ', *before* the syllable that carries the main stress in a word.

Most of the letters used in the phonetic respelling are pronounced in the usual way; but the following special symbols are also used.

ə as in *above* (ə'buv), *butter* ('butər), *nation* ('nāshən), *bird* (bərd)
ä as in *calm* (käm), *father* ('fädhər), *farm* (färm)
ā as in *fate* (fāt), *neigh* (nā), *explain* (ik'splān)
ē as in *keep* (kēp), *deceive* (di'sēv), *machine* (mə'shēn)
ī as in *thigh* (thī), *dive* (dīv), *guy* (gī)
ö as in *all* (öl), *crawl* (kröl), *drawer* ('dröər)
ō as in *code* (kōd), *road* (rōd), *beau* (bō)
o͝o as in *book* (bo͝ok), *woman* ('wo͝omən), *should* (sho͝od)
o͞o as in *food* (fo͞od), *queue* (kyo͞o), *you* (yo͞o)
ow as in *bow* (bow), *out* (owt), *bough* (bow)
oi as in *boy* (boi), *oil* (oil), *employment* (im'ploimənt)
zh as in *pleasure* ('plezhər), *invasion* (in'vāzhən)
dh as in *those* (dhōz), *bathe* (bādh), *lather* ('ladhər)

Foreign Sounds

ü as in French *tu* (tü)
œ as in French *deux* (dœ)
˜ is placed over a nasal vowel, as in French *bon* (bõ), *vin* (vẽ), *sans* (sã), *un* (œ̃)
kh as in Scots *loch* (lokh), German *Buch* (bo͝okh)

Note: Though the pronunciaton of words like *where, why, when* is shown with a simple 'w' sound, many speakers use 'hw' in such words. Both versions are equally acceptable and such variation is to be assumed in these cases.

About the Dictionary

This Dictionary has been specially prepared to provide concise but wide-ranging coverage of the contemporary American language in a format that is convenient to handle and easy to use. The coverage is up-to-date and the emphasis is on today's written and spoken language. With 50,000 entries and over 61,000 definitions, it is a compact all-purpose dictionary that will serve the everyday needs of most people.

All main entries are given in a single alphabetical listing that includes abbreviations, foreign words, and prefixes and suffixes (combining forms). These last enable the reader to construct for himself the meanings of hundreds of additional terms.

Within each main entry different meanings are clearly marked off from each other by bold numbers. After the meanings of the main headword come *derived words* as subentries in smaller bold type, in alphabetical order. These in turn are followed by *compounds* (if any) and then by *phrases*, again in alphabetical order within the paragraph.

Words that can function as more than one part of speech are printed out only once, the change of function being shown by a second (or subsequent) part-of-speech label, thus: **advance** (əd'väns) *vt.* **1**. bring forward ... —*vi.* **5**. go forward ... —*n.* **7**. forward movement ... —*a.* **11**. (*with* of) ahead in time ... In the case of very short, simple entries, two parts of speech may be combined, thus: **agape** (ə'gāp) *a./adv.* open-mouthed ... Spelling of verb parts is indicated as necessary in brackets after the definition of the verb, thus: **jab** ... stab abruptly (-**bb**-).

First Published 1987

NOTE

Entered words that we have reason to believe constitute trademarks have been designated as such. However, neither the presence nor absence of such designation should be regarded as affecting the legal status of any trademark.

Library of Congress Cataloging-in-publication Data

Webster's dictionary of modern English.

1. English language — Dictionaries.
PE1628.W55612 1987 423 87-1589
ISBN 0-8407-3180-9

WEBSTER'S DICTIONARY OF MODERN ENGLISH

Managing Editor
William T. McLeod

Editorial Staff
Mary Pauson

Alice Grandison, Danielle McGrath, Marian Makins

THOMAS NELSON PUBLISHERS
NASHVILLE

cavity of the body between chest and pelvis **2.** in arthropods, the hindmost part of the body —**abdominal** (ab'dominəl) *a.*

abduct (ab'dukt) *vt.* carry off, kidnap —**ab'duction** *n.*

abeam (ə'bēm) *adv.* abreast, in line

Abel ('ābəl) *n.* in O.T., son of Adam and Eve, murdered by his brother Cain

abele (ə'bēl, 'ābəl) *n.* white poplar

Aberdeen Angus ('abərdēn 'anggəs) breed of cattle, *orig.* Scottish

aberration (abə'rāshən) *n.* **1.** failure of lens or mirror to form exact image **2.** deviation from what is normal **3.** flaw **4.** lapse —**a'berrant** *a.*

abet (ə'bet) *vt.* assist, encourage, *esp.* in doing wrong (**-tt-**) —**a'bettor** *or* **a'better** *n.*

abeyance (ə'bāəns) *n.* condition of not being in use or action

abhor (əb'hōr) *vt.* dislike strongly, loathe —**ab'horrence** *n.* —**ab'horrent** *a.* hateful

abide (ə'bīd) *vt.* **1.** endure, put up with —*vi.* **2.** *obs.* stay, reside (**a'bode** *or* **a'bided** *pt./pp.*, **a'biding** *pr.p.*) —**abide by** obey

ability (ə'biliti) *n.* **1.** competence, power **2.** talent

ab initio (ab i'nishiō) *Lat.* from the start

abject ('abjekt) *a.* **1.** humiliated, wretched **2.** despicable —**ab'jection** *or* **'abjectness** *n.*

abjure (əb'jōōər) *vt.* give up by oath, renounce —**abju'ration** *n.*

ablation (ab'lāshən) *n.* **1.** surgical removal of organ or part **2.** *Astrophysics* melting or wearing away of part **3.** wearing away of rock or glacier

ablative ('ablətiv) *n.* case in (*esp.* Latin) nouns indicating source, agent, instrument of action

ablaut ('ablowt) *n.* vowel change within word, indicating modification of use, *eg sink, sank, sunk*

ablaze (ə'blāz) *a.* burning

able ('ābəl) *a.* capable, competent —**'ably** *adv.* —**able-bodied** *a.* —**able-bodied seaman** seaman, *esp.* one in merchant navy, trained in certain skills (*also* **able seaman**)

-able (*a. comb. form*) **1.** capable of or deserving of (being acted upon as indicated), as in *enjoyable, washable* **2.** inclined to; able to; causing, as in *comfortable, variable* —**-ably** (*adv. comb. form*) —**-ability** (*n. comb. form*)

ablution (ə'blōōshən) *n.* (*usu. pl.*) act of washing (oneself)

ABM antiballistic missile

Abnaki (ab'näki) *n.* confederacy of more than 20 Amerindian tribes of Maine, New Brunswick and southern Quebec, including Penobscots, Malacites and Passamaquoddies

abnegate ('abnigāt) *vt.* give up, renounce —**abne'gation** *n.*

abnormal (ab'nōrməl) *a.* **1.** irregular **2.** not usual or typical **3.** freakish, odd —**abnor'mality** *n.* —**ab'normally** *adv.*

aboard (ə'bōrd) *adv.* on board, on ship, train or aircraft

abode (ə'bōd) *n.* **1.** home **2.** dwelling —*v.* **3.** *pt./pp. of* ABIDE

ABO group the classification of human blood into the groups A, B, AB and O according to the reactions to each other

abolish (ə'bolish) *vt.* do away with —**abo'lition** *n.* —**abo'litionist** *n.* one who wishes to do away with something, *esp.* slavery

A-bomb *n.* atomic bomb

abominate (ə'bomināt) *vt.* detest —**a'bominable** *a.* —**a'bominably** *adv.* —**abomi'nation** *n.* **1.** loathing **2.** the object loathed —**abominable snowman** large legendary apelike creature said to inhabit the Himalayas (*also* **yeti**)

aborigine (abə'rijini) *n.* **1.** original inhabitant of region **2.** Australian aborigine —*pl.* **3.** native flora and fauna —**abo'riginal** *a.* **1.** of, relating to the aborigines of Aust. **2.** indigenous, earliest

abort (ə'bōrt) *v.* **1.** (cause to) end prematurely (*esp.* pregnancy) —*vi.* **2.** give birth to dead fetus **3.** fail —**aborti'facient** *n./a.* (drug or agent) inducing abortion —**a'bortion** *n.* **1.** operation to terminate pregnancy **2.** something deformed —**a'bortionist** *n.* one who performs abortion, *esp.* illegally —**a'bortive** *a.* unsuccessful —**a'bortively** *adv.*

abound (ə'bownd) *vi.* **1.** be plentiful **2.** overflow —**a'bounding** *a.*

about (ə'bowt) *adv.* **1.** on all sides **2.** nearly **3.** up and down **4.** out, astir —*prep.* **5.** round **6.** near **7.** concerning —**about to** ready to —**about-turn** *n.* reversal, complete change

above (ə'buv) *adv.* **1.** higher up —*prep.* **2.** over **3.** higher than, more than **4.** beyond

abracadabra (abrəkə'dabrə) *n.* supposedly magic word

abrade (ə'brād) *vt.* rub off, scrape away

Abraham ('ābrəham) *n.* in O.T., founder of the nation of Israel, and its first patriarch —**Abraham's bosom** repose of the happy in death —**Abraham's covenant 1.** covenant made by God with Abraham that Messiah should spring from his seed **2.** rite of circumcision

abrasion (ə'brāzhən) *n.* **1.** place scraped or worn by rubbing (*eg* on skin) **2.** scraping, rubbing —**a'brasive** *n.* **1.** substance for grinding, polishing *etc.* —*a.* **2.** causing abrasion **3.** grating

abreast (ə'brest) *adv.* side by side —**abreast of** keeping up with

abridge (ə'brij) *vt.* cut short, abbreviate —**a'bridgment** *or* **a'bridgement** *n.*

abroad (ə'brōd) *adv.* **1.** to or in a foreign country **2.** at large

abrogate ('abrōgāt) *vt.* cancel, repeal —**abro'gation** *n.*

a *or* **A** (ā) *n.* **1.** first letter of English alphabet **2.** any of several speech sounds represented by this letter, as in *take, calm* **3.** first in series, *esp.* grade rating student as superior (*pl.* **a's, A's,** *or* **As**) —**from A to Z** from start to finish

a (ə; *emphatic* ā) *a.* the indefinite article meaning one; *an* is used before vowel sounds, and sometimes before unaccented syllables beginning with *h* aspirate

a. 1. absent **2.** acceleration **3.** acre **4.** adult **5.** alto **6.** ampere **7.** anode **8.** answer **9.** ante **10.** anterior **11.** are **12.** area **13.** author

A 1. *Mus.* sixth note of scale of C major; major or minor key having this note as its tonic **2.** human blood type of ABO group **3.** ampere **4.** absolute (temperature) **5.** area **6.** alto **7.** (*comb. form*) atomic, as in *A-bomb, A-plant*

Å angstrom unit

a-[1] *or before vowel* **an-** (*comb. form*) not; without; opposite to, as in *atonal, asocial, anesthetic*

a-[2] (*comb. form*) **1.** on; in; toward, as in *aground, aback* **2.** in state of, as in *afloat, asleep*

A1, A-1, *or* **A-one** ('ā'wun) *a.* **1.** physically fit **2.** *inf.* first-class; excellent **3.** (of vessel) in first-class condition

AA 1. Alcoholics Anonymous **2.** anti-aircraft **3.** associate in arts

A.A.A. American Automobile Association

aardvark

A and M agricultural and mechanical

aardvark ('ärdvärk) *n.* nocturnal Afr. mammal which feeds on termites

Aaron ('arən) *n.* in O.T., brother and helper of Moses —**Aaron's beard** popular name for many wild plants including rose of Sharon, ivy-leaved toadflax, meadowsweet *etc.* —**Aaron's rod** popular name for goldenrod, great mullein

AAU Amateur Athletic Union of the United States

ab about

AB Alberta

A.B. 1. able-bodied seaman **2.** bachelor of arts

ab-[1] (*comb. form*) away from; opposite to, as in *abnormal*

ab-[2] (*comb. form*) cgs unit of measurement in electromagnetic system, as in *abampere, abvolt*

ABA American Bar Association

aback (ə'bak) *adv.* —**taken aback** startled

abacus ('abəkəs) *n.* **1.** counting device of frame holding rods designating place value on which counters are free to slide **2.** flat tablet at top of column

abaft (ə'baft) *Naut. adv./a.* **1.** toward rear of vessel —*prep.* **2.** behind; aft of

abalone (abə'lōni) *n.* edible gastropod, yielding mother-of-pearl

abandon (ə'bandən) *vt.* **1.** desert **2.** give up altogether —*n.* **3.** freedom from inhibitions *etc.* —**a'bandoned** *a.* **1.** deserted, forsaken **2.** uninhibited **3.** wicked —**a'bandonment** *n.*

abase (ə'bās) *vt.* humiliate, degrade —**a'basement** *n.*

abash (ə'bash) *vt.* (*usu. passive*) confuse, make ashamed —**a'bashment** *n.*

abate (ə'bāt) *v.* make or become less, diminish —**a'batement** *n.*

abattoir ('abətwär) *n.* slaughterhouse

abbé ('abā) *n.* **1.** French abbot **2.** title used in addressing any French cleric

abbess ('abis) *n.* head of convent

abbey ('abi) *n.* **1.** dwelling place of community of monks or nuns **2.** church of an abbey

abbot ('abət) *n.* head of abbey or monastery —**'abbacy** *n.* office, rights of abbot

abbr. *or* **abbrev.** abbreviation

abbreviate (ə'brēviāt) *vt.* shorten, abridge —**abbrevi'ation** *n.* shortened form of word or phrase

ABC[1] *n.* **1.** (*oft. pl.*) the alphabet **2.** (*pl.*) rudiments of subject

ABC[2] **1.** American Bowling Congress **2.** American Broadcasting Company

Abdias (ab'dīəs) *n.* *Bible* Obadiah in the Douay Version of the O.T.

abdicate ('abdikāt) *v.* formally give up (throne *etc.*) —**abdi'cation** *n.*

abdomen ('abdəmən) *n.* **1.** in mammals,

abrupt (ə'brupt) *a.* **1.** sudden **2.** blunt **3.** hasty **4.** steep —**a'bruptly** *adv.* —**a'bruptness** *n.*

abscess ('abses) *n.* gathering of pus in any part of the body

abscissa (ab'sisə) *n. Math.* distance of point from the axis of coordinates (*pl.* **-s, -sae** (-sē))

abscond (əb'skond) *vi.* leave secretly, *esp.* having stolen something

abseil ('absīl) *vi.* descend vertical slope by means of rope

absent ('absənt) *a.* **1.** away **2.** not attentive —*vt.* (ab'sent) **3.** keep away —'**absence** *n.* —**absen'tee** *n.* one who stays away, *esp.* habitually —**absen'teeism** *n.* persistent absence from work *etc.* —'**absently** *adv.* —**absentee ballot** ballot submitted in advance of election by voter unable to be present at the polls —**absent-minded** *a.*

absinthe *or* **absinth** ('absinth) *n.* potent aniseed-flavored liqueur

absolute ('absəlōōt) *a.* **1.** complete **2.** not limited, unconditional **3.** pure (as **absolute alcohol**) —*n.* **4.** something that is absolute —'**absolutely** *adv.* **1.** completely —*interj.* **2.** certainly —'**absoluteness** *n.* —'**absolutism** *n.* political system in which unrestricted power is vested in dictator *etc.*; despotism —'**absolutist** *n.* —**absolute pitch** ability to identify immediately a musical sound by name or to sing any tone at will —**absolute zero** lowest temperature theoretically attainable

absolve (əb'zolv) *vt.* free, pardon, acquit —**absolution** (absə'lōōshən) *n.*

absorb (əb'sörb) *vt.* **1.** suck up, drink in **2.** engage, occupy (attention *etc.*) **3.** receive (impact) —**ab'sorbent** *a.* —**ab'sorption** *n.* —**ab'sorptive** *a.*

abstain (əb'stān) *vi.* (*usu. with* from) keep (from), refrain (from drinking alcohol, voting *etc.*) —**ab'stainer** *n.* —**abstention** (əb'stenchən) *n.* —**abstinence** ('abstinəns) *n.* —**abstinent** ('abstinənt) *a.*

abstemious (əb'stēmiəs) *a.* sparing in food or *esp.* drink, temperate —**ab'stemiously** *adv.* —**ab'stemiousness** *n.*

abstract ('abstrakt) *a.* **1.** existing only in the mind **2.** not concrete **3.** not representational —*n.* **4.** summary, abridgment —*vt.* (ab'strakt) **5.** draw (from), remove **6.** deduct —**ab'stracted** *a.* preoccupied —**ab'straction** *n.* —'**abstractly** *adv.* —**abstract expressionism** direction in abstract art of 1940s and 1950s of which the essence was the spontaneous assertion of the artist in a nonobjective visual expression

abstruse (əb'strōōs) *a.* obscure, difficult to understand, profound —**ab'strusely** *adv.*

absurd (əb'sərd) *a.* contrary to reason —**ab'surdity** *n.* —**ab'surdly** *adv.*

abundance (ə'bundəns) *n.* great amount —**a'bundant** *a.* plentiful —**a'bundantly** *adv.*

abuse (ə'byōōz) *vt.* **1.** misuse **2.** address rudely —*n.* (ə'byōōs) **3.** improper use **4.** insulting speech —**a'busive** *a.* —**a'busively** *adv.* —**a'busiveness** *n.*

abut (ə'but) *vi.* adjoin, border (on) (**-tt-**) —**a'butment** *n.* support, *esp.* of bridge or arch

abuzz (ə'buz) *a.* noisy, busy with activity *etc.*

abysmal (ə'bizməl) *a.* **1.** immeasurable, very great **2.** *inf.* extremely bad —**a'bysmally** *adv.*

abyss (ə'bis) *n.* very deep gulf or pit

Abyssinian (abi'siniən) *n.* purebred short-haired domestic cat with slender body and brownish coat marked with darker-color bands

ac 1. account **2.** money of account

Ac *Chem.* actinium

AC 1. air-conditioning **2.** alternating current **3.** athletic club **4.** (on prescription) before meals **5.** area code **6.** ante Christum: before Christ

acacia (ə'kāshə) *n.* **1.** genus of deciduous or evergreen shrubs or trees of the pea family grown in warm regions (*also* **wattle**) **2.** *see* **gum arabic** *at* GUM[2]

academy (ə'kadəmi) *n.* **1.** society to advance arts or sciences **2.** institution for specialized training **3.** secondary school **4.** (**A-**) Greek school of philosophy founded by Plato —**academic** (akə'demik) *a.* **1.** of academy **2.** belonging to University *etc.* **3.** theoretical —**academically** (akə'demikəli) *adv.* —**acade'mician** *n.*

Acadia (ə'kādiə) *n.* former name for Nova Scotia

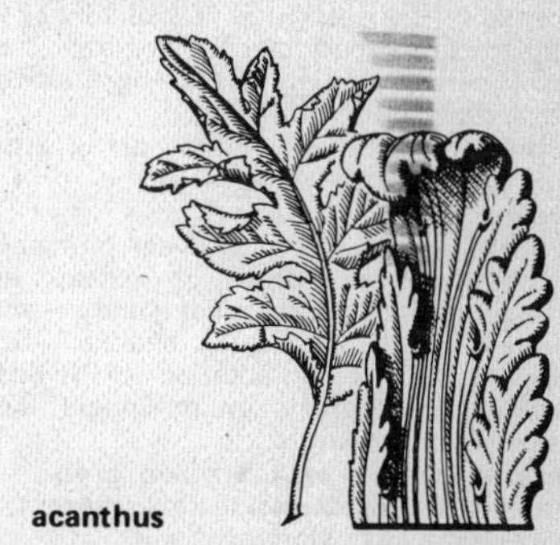
acanthus

acanthus (ə'kanthəs) *n.* **1.** prickly plant **2.** architectural ornament like leaf of acanthus plant (*pl.* **-es, -thi** (-thī))

a cappella (ä kə'pelə) (of choral music) without instrumental accompaniment

acc. accusative

accede (ak'sēd) *vi.* (*usu. with* to) **1.** agree, consent **2.** attain (office, right *etc.*)

accelerando (akselə'randō) *a./adv. Mus.* becoming faster

accelerate (ak'selərāt) *v.* (cause to) increase speed, hasten —**accele'ration** *n.* —**ac'celerative** *a.* —**ac'celerator** *n.* mechanism to increase speed, *esp.* in motor vehicle

accent ('aksent) *n.* **1.** stress or pitch in speaking **2.** mark to show such stress **3.** local or national style of pronunciation **4.** particular attention or emphasis **5.** *Mus.* stress on one tone or chord —*vt.* **6.** stress **7.** mark with accent

accentor (ak'sentər) *n.* member of family of sparrowlike songbirds found in Europe and north Asia

accentuate (ak'senchōōāt) *vt.* stress, emphasize —**ac'centual** *a.* —**accentu'ation** *n.*

accept (ək'sept) *vt.* **1.** take, receive **2.** admit, believe **3.** agree to —**accepta'bility** *n.* —**ac'ceptable** *a.* —**ac'ceptably** *adv.* —**ac'ceptance** *n.* —**accep'tation** *n.* common or accepted meaning of word *etc.* —**ac'cepter** *n.* —**ac'ceptor** *n.* **1.** *Comm.* person or organization on which bill of exchange is drawn **2.** *Electron.* impurity added to semiconductor to increase its p-type conductivity

access ('akses) *n.* **1.** act, right or means of entry —*vt. Comp.* **2.** obtain or retrieve (information) from storage device **3.** place (information) in storage device —**accessi'bility** *n.* —**ac'cessible** *a.* easy to approach —**ac'cessibly** *adv.* —**access time** *Comp.* time required to retrieve stored information

accessary (ək'sesəri) *see* ACCESSORY

accession (ək'seshən) *n.* **1.** attaining of office, right *etc.* **2.** increase, addition

accessory (ək'sesəri) *n.* **1.** additional or supplementary part of car, woman's dress *etc.* **2.** person inciting or assisting in crime —*a.* **3.** contributory, assisting

accidence ('aksidəns) *n.* the part of grammar dealing with changes in the form of words

accident ('aksidənt) *n.* **1.** event happening by chance **2.** misfortune or mishap, *esp.* causing injury **3.** nonessential quality —**acci'dental** *a.* **1.** happening by chance —*n.* **2.** *Mus.* sign used in notation to indicate chromatic alterations or to cancel them —**acci'dentally** *adv.*

acclaim (ə'klām) *vt.* **1.** applaud, praise —*n.* **2.** applause —**acclamation** (aklə'māshən) *n.* —**acclamatory** (ə'klamətōri) *a.*

acclimatize (ə'klīmətīz) *vt.* accustom to new climate or environment —**acclimati'zation** *n.*

accolade ('akəlād) *n.* **1.** praise, public approval **2.** award, honor **3.** token of award of knighthood

accommodate (ə'komədāt) *vt.* **1.** supply, *esp.* with board and lodging **2.** oblige **3.** harmonize, adapt —**ac'commodating** *a.* obliging —**accommo'dation** *n.* **1.** lodging **2.** agreement **3.** adjustment of lens of eye **4.** loan

accompany (ə'kumpəni) *vt.* **1.** go with **2.** supplement **3.** occur with **4.** provide a musical accompaniment for (**-panied, -panying**) —**ac'companiment** *n.* that which accompanies, *esp.* in music, part which goes with solos *etc.* —**ac'companist** *n.*

accomplice (ə'komplis, ə'kum-) *n.* one assisting another in criminal deed

accomplish (ə'komplish, ə'kum-) *vt.* **1.** carry out **2.** finish —**ac'complished** *a.* **1.** complete, perfect **2.** proficient —**ac'complishment** *n.* **1.** completion **2.** personal ability

accord (ə'kōrd) *n.* **1.** agreement, harmony (*esp. in* **in accord with**) —*v.* **2.** (cause to) be in accord —*vt.* **3.** grant —**ac'cordance** *n.* —**ac'cordant** *a.* —**ac'cordingly** *adv.* **1.** as the circumstances suggest **2.** therefore —**according to 1.** in proportion to **2.** as stated by **3.** in conformity with

accordion (ə'kōrdiən) *n.* portable musical instrument with keys, metal reeds and a bellows. The right hand plays piano-like keyboard —**ac'cordionist** *n.*

accost (ə'kost) *vt.* approach and speak to, ask question *etc.*

account (ə'kownt) *n.* **1.** report, description **2.** importance, value **3.** statement of moneys received, paid or owed **4.** person's money held in bank **5.** credit available to person at store *etc.* —*vt.* **6.** reckon **7.** judge —*vi.* **8.** give reason, answer (for) —**accounta'bility** *n.* —**ac'countable** *a.* responsible —**ac'countancy** *n.* keeping, preparation of business accounts, financial records *etc.* —**ac'countant** *n.* one practicing accountancy —**ac'counting** *n.* skill or practice of keeping and preparing business accounts

accouter (ə'kōōtər) *vt.* equip —**ac'couterments** *pl.n.* **1.** equipment, *esp.* military **2.** trappings

accredit (ə'kredit) *vt.* **1.** ascribe, attribute **2.** give official recognition to **3.** certify as meeting required standards **4.** (*oft. with* at, to) send (envoy *etc.*) with official credentials; appoint as envoy *etc.* **5.** believe —**ac'credited** *a.*

accretion (ə'krēshən) *n.* **1.** growth **2.** something added on

accrue (ə'krōō) *vi.* **1.** be added **2.** result

acct. 1. account **2.** accountant

acculturate (ə'kulchərāt) *vi.* assimilate traits of another cultural group —**accultur'ation** *n.*

accumulate (ə'kyōōmyōōlāt) *v.* **1.** gather, become gathered in increasing quantity **2.** collect —**accumu'lation** *n.* —**ac'cumulator** *n.* (in computer) part where numbers are totaled or stored

accurate ('akyərit) *a.* exact, correct, without errors —**'accuracy** *n.* —**'accurately** *adv.*

accursed (ə'kərsid, ə'kərst) *or* **accurst** (ə'kərst) *a.* **1.** under a curse **2.** hateful, detestable

accuse (ə'kyōōz) *vt.* **1.** charge with wrongdoing 2. blame —**accu'sation** *n.* —**ac'cusative** *n.* grammatical case indicating the direct object —**ac'cusatory** *a.* —**ac'cuser** *n.*

accustom (ə'kustəm) *vt.* make used (to), familiarize —**ac'customed** *a.* **1.** usual **2.** used (to) **3.** in the habit (of)

ace (ās) *n.* **1.** the one at dice, cards, dominoes **2.** *Tennis* winning serve, *esp.* one untouched by opponent **3.** *Golf* hole made in one shot **4.** very successful fighter pilot **5.** *inf.* person expert at anything —*a.* **6.** *inf.* excellent —**ace up one's sleeve** something effective kept secretly in reserve

-aceous (*comb. form*) relating to, having the nature of, or resembling, as in *herbaceous*

acerbate ('asərbāt) *vt.* **1.** make worse **2.** make sour, bitter —**a'cerbity** *n.* **1.** severity, sharpness **2.** sourness, bitterness

acetate ('asitāt) *n.* **1.** fiber made from cellulose **2.** salt of acetic acid

acetic (ə'sētik) *a.* derived from or having the nature of vinegar —**acetic acid** acid which gives vinegar its characteristic taste, also important industrial chemical

aceto- *or before vowel* **acet-** (*comb. form*) containing acetyl group or derived from acetic acid, as in *acetone*

acetone ('asitōn) *n.* colorless liquid used as solvent

acetylcholine (asətil'kōlēn) *n.* derivative of choline involved in transmission of nerve impulses

acetylene (ə'setilēn) *n.* colorless, flammable gas used *esp.* in welding metals

acetylsalicylic acid (ə'sētilsalisilik) aspirin

Acey Deucy ('āsi 'dyōōsi, -'dōōsi) variation of backgammon

ache (āk) *n.* **1.** continuous pain —*vi.* **2.** be painful **3.** be in pain —**'aching** *a.*

achieve (ə'chēv) *vt.* **1.** accomplish, perform successfully **2.** gain —**a'chievement** *n.* something accomplished

Achilles (ə'kilēz) *n.* greatest warrior among the Greeks at the siege of Troy, and slayer of Hector —**Achilles' heel** vulnerable point —**Achilles tendon** fibrous cord connecting muscles of calf to heelbone

achlorhydria (āklōr'hidriə) *n.* lack of production of hydrochloric acid in the stomach

achromatic (akrə'matik) *a.* **1.** free from or not showing color, as of a lens **2.** colorless **3.** (of musical scale) without accidentals or modulations

acid ('asid) *a.* **1.** sharp, sour —*n.* **2.** sour substance **3.** *Chem.* one of a class of compounds which combines with bases (alkalis, oxides *etc.*) to form salts —**a'cidic** *a.* —**a'cidify** *v.* (**-fied, -fying**) —**a'cidity** *n.* —**aci'dosis** *n.* condition when the ability of the blood to neutralize acidic substances decreases —**a'cidulate** *vt.* make slightly acid —**a'cidulous** *a.* —**'acidhead** *n.* person who uses LSD —**acid rain** rain acidified by atmospheric pollution —**acid test** conclusive test of value

acidophilus milk (asi'dofiləs) milk fermented by bacteria used therapeutically to modify intestinal flora

ack-ack ('akak) *n.* anti-aircraft guns or gunfire

acknowledge (ək'nolij) *vt.* **1.** admit, own, recognize **2.** say one has received —**ac'knowledgment** *or* **ac'knowledgement** *n.*

aclinic (ā'klinik) *a.* without inclination, said of the magnetic equator, on which the magnetic needle has no dip

ACLU American Civil Liberties Union

acme ('akmi) *n.* highest point

acne ('akni) *n.* pimply skin disease

acolyte ('akəlīt) *n.* follower or attendant, *esp.* of priest

aconite ('akənīt) *n.* **1.** genus of plants related to the buttercup, including monkshood **2.** drug, poison obtained from such

acorn ('ākörn) *n.* nut or fruit of the oak tree —**acorn squash** acorn-shaped dark green winter squash with sweet yellowish-to-orange flesh

acoustic (ə'kōōstik) *or* **acoustical** *a.* pert. to sound and to hearing —**a'coustics** *pl.n.* **1.** (*with sing. v.*) science of sound **2.** features of room or building as regards sounds heard within it —**acoustic guitar** ordinary guitar, not amplified

acquaint (ə'kwānt) *vt.* make familiar, inform —**ac'quaintance** *n.* **1.** person known **2.** personal knowledge —**ac'quaintanceship** *n.*

acquiesce (akwi'es) *vi.* agree, consent without complaint —**acqui'escence** *n.* —**acqui'escent** *a.*

acquire (ə'kwīər) *vt.* gain, get —**ac'quirement** *n.* —**acquisition** (akwi'zishən) *n.* **1.** act of getting **2.** material gain —**acquisitive** (ə'kwizitiv) *a.* desirous of gaining —**acquisitiveness** (ə'kwizitivnis) *n.* —**acquired immuno-deficiency syndrome** disease that breaks down the body's natural immunity, oft. resulting in fatal infection (*also* **AIDS**)

acquit (ə'kwit) *vt.* **1.** declare innocent **2.** settle, discharge, as a debt **3.** behave (oneself) (**-tt-**) —**ac'quittal** *n.* declaration of innocence in court —**ac'quittance** *n.* discharge of debts

acre ('ākər) *n.* **1.** measure of land, 4840 square yards, 4047 square meters —*pl.* **2.** lands, estates **3.** *inf.* large area or plenty —**'acreage** *n.* extent of land in acres

acrid ('akrid) *a.* **1.** pungent, sharp **2.** irritating —**a'cridity** *n.*

acrimony ('akrimōni) *n.* bitterness of feeling or language —**acri'monious** *a.*

acrobat ('akrəbat) *n.* one skilled in gymnastic feats, *esp.* as entertainer in circus *etc.* —**acro'batic** *a.* —**acro'batics** *pl.n.* (*with sing. v.*) any activity requiring agility

acromegaly (akrō'megəli) *n.* rare disease of

adult life in which enlargement of many parts of the body occurs

acronym ('akrənim) *n.* word formed from initial letters of other words, *eg* UNESCO, ANZUS, NATO

acrophobia (akrə'fōbiə) *n.* abnormal fear of being at great height —**acro'phobic** *a.*

acropolis (ə'kropəlis) *n.* citadel, *esp.* in ancient Greece

across (ə'kros) *adv./prep.* **1.** crosswise **2.** from side to side **3.** on or to the other side —**get** (*or* **put**) **something across** explain something, make something understood

acrostic (ə'krostik) *n.* word puzzle in which the first, middle, or last letters of each line spell a word or words

acrylic (ə'krilik) *n.* variety of synthetic materials, *esp.* textiles, derived from an organic acid —**acrylic resin** any of group of polymers of acrylic acid, its esters or amides, used as paints, plastics *etc.*

act (akt) *n.* **1.** thing done, deed **2.** doing **3.** law, decree **4.** section of a play —*v.* **5.** perform, as in a play —*vi.* **6.** exert force, work, as mechanism **7.** behave —**'acting** *n.* **1.** performance of a part —*a.* **2.** temporarily performing the duties of another —**'action** *n.* **1.** operation **2.** deed **3.** gesture **4.** expenditure of energy **5.** battle **6.** lawsuit —**'actionable** *a.* subject to lawsuit —**'activate** *vt.* **1.** make active, put into operation **2.** make radioactive **3.** make chemically active —**acti'vation** *n.* —**'activator** *n.* —**'active** *a.* **1.** moving, working **2.** brisk, energetic —**'actively** *adv.* —**'activism** *n.* —**'activist** *n.* one who takes (direct) action to achieve political or social ends —**ac'tivity** *n.* —**'actor** *n.* person who acts in a play, motion picture *etc.* (**-tress** *fem.*) —**action painting** type of abstract painting characterized by smeared or spattered paint (*also* **'tachism**) —**activated sludge** aerated sewage added to untreated sewage to hasten bacterial decomposition —**active service** full-time service in the armed forces —**Act of God** *Law* unavoidable occurrence, such as earthquake, caused by natural forces

A.C.T. Australian Capital Territory

ACTH adrenocorticotrophic hormone: protein hormone of pituitary gland

actinide series ('aktinīd) series of 15 radioactive elements with increasing atomic numbers from actinium to lawrencium

actinism ('aktinizəm) *n.* chemical action of sun's rays —**ac'tinic** *a.*

actinium (ak'tiniəm) *n. Chem.* radioactive element discovered in 1899 in pitchblende *Symbol* Ac, at. wt. 227, at. no. 89

actinomycetes (aktinō'mīsēts) *pl.n.* mold-like bacteria sometimes called ray fungi, some of which excrete antibiotic substances

Acts (akts) *pl.n.* (*with sing. v.*) *Bible* 5th book of the N.T., written by Luke in about 63 A.D., describing the beginnings of the early Church

actual ('akchōōəl) *a.* **1.** existing in the present **2.** real —**actu'ality** *n.* —**'actually** *adv.* really, indeed

actuary ('akchōōeri) *n.* statistician who calculates insurance risks, premiums *etc.* —**actu'arial** *a.*

actuate ('akchōōāt) *vt.* **1.** activate **2.** motivate —**actu'ation** *n.*

acuity (ə'kyōōiti) *n.* keenness, *esp.* in vision or thought

acumen (ə'kyōōmən) *n.* sharpness of wit, perception, penetration

acupuncture ('akyōōpungkchər) *n. orig.* Chinese treatment involving insertion of needles at various points on the body to cure disease or relieve pain —**'acupuncturist** *n.*

acute (ə'kyōōt) *a.* **1.** keen, shrewd **2.** sharp **3.** severe **4.** less than 90° —*n.* **5.** accent (´) over a letter to indicate the quality or length of its sound, *eg* abbé —**a'cutely** *adv.* —**a'cuteness** *n.*

ad (ad) *n.* advertisement —**'adman** *n. inf.* man who works in advertising

A.D. anno Domini

ad- (*comb. form*) **1.** to; toward, as in *adverb* **2.** near; next to, as in *adrenal*

ADA **1.** average daily attendance **2.** Americans for Democratic Action **3.** American Dental Association

adage ('adij) *n.* much-used wise saying, proverb

adagio (ə'däjiō) *a./adv./n. Mus.* **1.** slow (tempo), between andante and largo —*n.* **2.** composition in this tempo, often second movement of sonata (*pl.* **-s**)

Adam[1] ('adəm) *n.* in O.T., the first man —**Adam's ale** water —**Adam's apple** projecting part at front of the throat, the thyroid cartilage —**Adam's needle** popular name for plant furnishing needle-like leaves, *eg* yucca

Adam[2] ('adəm) *a.* in neoclassical style made popular by Robert Adam (1728–92), Scottish architect and furniture designer

adamant ('adəmənt) *a.* very hard, unyielding —**ada'mantine** *a.*

Adams[1] ('adəmz) *n.* **John.** the 2nd President of the U.S. (1797-1801)

Adams[2] ('adəmz) *n.* **John Quincy.** the 6th President of the U.S. (1825-29)

adapt (ə'dapt) *v.* **1.** alter for new use **2.** fit, modify **3.** change —**adapta'bility** *n.* —**a'daptable** *a.* —**adap'tation** *n.* —**a'dapter** *or* **a'daptor** *n. esp.* appliance for connecting two parts (*eg* electrical)

A.D.C. **1.** aide-de-camp **2.** analog-digital converter **3.** Aid to Dependent Children **4.** Air Defense Command **5.** assistant division commander

add (ad) *v.* **1.** join **2.** increase by **3.** say further —**ad'dition** *n.* —**ad'ditional** *a.*

addax ('adaks) *n.* large light-colored antelope of N Afr., Arabia and Syria

addendum (ə'dendəm) *n.* thing to be added (*pl.* **-da** (-də)) —**'addend** *n.* any of set of numbers that form sum

adder ('adər) *n.* small poisonous snake

addict ('adikt) *n.* **1.** one who has become dependent on something, *eg* drugs (*drug addict*) —*vt.* (ə'dikt) **2.** (*usu. passive*) cause to become dependent (on something, *esp.* drug) —**ad'dicted** *a.* —**ad'diction** *n.* —**ad'dictive** *a.* causing addiction

Addison's disease ('adisənz) disease characterized by deep bronzing of skin, anemia and extreme weakness, caused by underactivity of adrenal glands

additive ('aditiv) *n.* **1.** something added to another substance, *esp.*food, to improve it or to suppress unwanted properties —*a.* **2.** of, relating to or characterized by addition

addle ('adəl) *v.* make or become rotten or muddled

address (ə'dres) *n.* **1.** direction on letter **2.** place where one lives **3.** speech —*pl.* **4.** courtship —*vt.* **5.** mark destination on **6.** speak to **7.** direct **8.** dispatch —**addressee** (adre'sē) *n.* person addressed

adduce (ə'dyo͞os, -'do͞os) *vt.* **1.** offer as proof **2.** cite —**ad'ducible** *a.* —**adduction** (ə'dukshən) *n.*

-ade (*comb. form*) sweetened drink made of fruit, as in *lemonade*

adenoids ('adinoidz) *pl.n.* tissue at back of nose —**ade'noidal** *a.*

adept (ə'dept) *a.* **1.** skilled —*n.* ('adept) **2.** expert

adequate ('adikwit) *a.* **1.** sufficient, enough, suitable **2.** not outstanding —**'adequacy** *n.* —**'adequately** *adv.*

à deux (a 'dœ) *Fr.* of or for two persons

adhere (əd'hēər) *vi.* **1.** stick **2.** be firm in opinion *etc.* —**ad'herent** *n./a.* —**ad'hesion** *n.* band of scar tissue formed within the body in response to inflammation or injury —**ad'hesive** *a./n.* (substance) capable of holding materials together by surface attachment

ad hoc (ad 'hok) **1.** for a particular occasion only **2.** improvised

ad hominem (ad 'hominem) *Lat.* directed against person rather than his arguments

adieu (ə'dyo͞o, -'do͞o) *interj.* **1.** farewell —*n.* **2.** act of taking leave (*pl.* **-s, adieux** (ə'dyo͞oz, -'do͞oz))

ad infinitum (ad infi'nītəm) *Lat.* endlessly

ad interim (ad 'intərim) *Lat.* for the meantime

adipose ('adipōs) *a.* of fat, fatty

adit ('adit) *n.* almost horizontal entrance into a mine

adj. **1.** adjective **2.** adjourned **3.** adjutant

adjacent (ə'jāsənt) *a.* lying near, next (to) —**ad'jacency** *n.*

adjective ('ajiktiv) *n.* word which qualifies or limits a noun —**adjectival** (ajik'tīvəl) *a.* of adjective

adjoin (ə'join) *v.* **1.** be next (to) **2.** join —**ad'joining** *a.* next (to), near

adjourn (ə'jərn) *vt.* **1.** postpone temporarily, as meeting —*vi.* **2.** *inf.* move elsewhere —**ad'journment** *n.*

adjudge (ə'juj) *vt.* **1.** declare **2.** decide **3.** award —**ad'judgment** *or* **ad'judgement** *n.*

adjudicate (ə'jo͞odikāt) *v.* **1.** try, judge —*vi.* **2.** sit in judgment —**adjudi'cation** *n.* —**ad'judicator** *n.*

adjunct ('ajungkt) *a.* **1.** joined, added —*n.* **2.** person or thing added or subordinate —**ad'junctive** *a.* —**adjunct professor** temporary or honorary professor at college or university

adjure (ə'jo͝oər) *vt.* beg, entreat earnestly —**adju'ration** *n.*

adjust (ə'just) *v.* **1.** make suitable, adapt **2.** alter slightly, regulate —**ad'justable** *a.* —**ad'juster** *or* **ad'justor** *n.* one that adjusts, *esp.* insurance agent assessing damage —**ad'justment** *n.*

adjutant ('ajətənt) *n.* military officer who assists superiors —**'adjutancy** *n.* his office, rank

ad-lib (ad'lib) *v.* **1.** improvise, speak *etc.* without previous preparation (**-bb-**) —*n.* **2.** such speech *etc.* —*a.* **3.** improvised —**ad lib** without preparation; freely

ad libitum (ad 'libitəm) *Mus.* at performer's discretion

Adm. Admiral

admin ('admin) *n. inf.* administration

administer (əd'ministər) *vt.* **1.** manage, look after **2.** dispense, as justice *etc.* **3.** apply —**ad'ministrate** *v.* manage (business, institution, government department *etc.*) —**admini'stration** *n.* —**ad'ministrative** *a.* —**ad'ministrator** *n.* (**admini'stratrix** *fem.*)

admiral ('admərəl) *n.* **1.** commissioned officer in navy or coastguard ranking above vice admiral and whose insignia is four stars **2.** any of several brightly colored butterflies

admire (əd'mīər) *vt.* **1.** look on with wonder and pleasure **2.** respect highly —**admirable** ('admərəbəl) *a.* —**admirably** ('admərəbli) *adv.* —**admiration** (admə'rāshən) *n.* —**ad'mirer** *n.* —**ad'miringly** *adv.*

admit (əd'mit) *vt.* **1.** confess **2.** accept as true **3.** allow **4.** let in (**-tt-**) —**ad'missible** *a.* —**ad'missibly** *adv.* —**ad'mission** *n.* **1.** permission to enter **2.** entrance fee **3.** confession —**ad'mittance** *n.* permission to enter —**ad'mittedly** *adv.* willingly conceded

admixture (ad'mikschər) *n.* **1.** mixture **2.** ingredient —**ad'mix** *vt.*

admonish (əd'monish) *vt.* **1.** reprove **2.** advise **3.** warn **4.** exhort —**admo'nition** *n.* —**ad'monitory** *a.*

ad nauseam (ad 'nöziəm) *Lat.* to a boring or disgusting extent

ado (ə'do͞o) *n.* fuss

adobe (ə'dōbi) *n.* sun-dried brick

adolescence (adə'lesəns) *n.* period of life

just before maturity —**ado'lescent** *n.* **1.** a youth —*a.* **2.** of adolescence **3.** immature

Adonis (ə'dōnis) *n.* a beautiful youth beloved by Aphrodite

adopt (ə'dopt) *vt.* **1.** take into relationship, *esp.* as one's child **2.** take up, as belief, principle, resolution —**a'doption** *n.* —**a'doptive** *a.* due to adoption

adore (ə'dör) *vt.* **1.** love intensely —*v.* **2.** worship —**a'dorable** *a.* —**ado'ration** *n.* —**a'dorer** *n.* lover

adorn (ə'dörn) *vt.* beautify, embellish, deck —**a'dornment** *n.* ornament, decoration

A.D.P. automatic data processing

ad rem (ad 'rem) *Lat.* to the point

adrenal (ə'drēnəl) *a.* near the kidney —**adrenal gland** either of pair of thumbnail-sized glands above the kidneys secreting sex hormones and hormones affecting metabolism —**Adrenalin** (ə'drenəlin) *n.* trade name for preparation of adrenaline —**adrenaline** (ə'drenəlin) *n.* epinephrine

Adriatic (ādri'atik) *n.* arm of the Mediterranean Sea, between Italy and Yugoslavia (*also* **Adriatic Sea**)

adrift (ə'drift) *a./adv.* **1.** drifting free **2.** *inf.* detached **3.** *inf.* off course

adroit (ə'droit) *a.* **1.** skillful, expert **2.** clever —**a'droitly** *adv.* —**a'droitness** *n.* dexterity

adsorb (əd'sörb) *v.* (of gas, vapor) condense and form thin film on surface —**ad'sorbent** *a./n.* —**ad'sorption** *n.*

adulation (ajə'lāshən) *n.* flattery —**'adulate** *vt.* flatter —**'adulator** *n.* —**'adulatory** *a.*

adult ('adult, ə'dult) *a.* **1.** grown-up, mature —*n.* **2.** grown-up person **3.** full-grown animal or plant

adulterate (ə'dultərāt) *vt.* make impure by addition —**a'dulterant** *n./a.* —**a'dulterated** *a.* —**adulter'ation** *n.* —**a'dulterator** *n.*

adultery (ə'dultəri) *n.* sexual unfaithfulness of a husband or wife —**a'dulterer** *n.* (**a'dulteress** *fem.*) —**a'dulterous** *a.*

adumbrate ('adumbrāt) *vt.* **1.** outline **2.** give indication of —**a'dumbrant** *or* **a'dumbrative** *a.* —**adum'bration** *n.*

adv. 1. adverb(ial) **2.** advertisement

ad valorem (ad və'lörəm) *Lat.* in proportion to the value of goods in question

advance (əd'väns) *vt.* **1.** bring forward **2.** suggest **3.** encourage **4.** pay beforehand —*vi.* **5.** go forward **6.** improve in position or value —*n.* **7.** forward movement **8.** improvement **9.** loan —*pl.* **10.** personal approach(es) to gain favor *etc.* —*a.* **11.** (*with* of) ahead in time or position —**ad'vanced** *a.* **1.** at a late stage **2.** not elementary **3.** ahead of the times —**ad'vancement** *n.* promotion

advantage (əd'väntij) *n.* **1.** superiority **2.** more favorable position or state **3.** benefit —**advan'tageous** *a.* —**advan'tageously** *adv.*

advent ('advent) *n.* **1.** a coming, arrival **2.** (**A-**) the four weeks before Christmas **3.** (**A-**) the coming of Christ —**Ad'ventist** *n.* one of number of Christian sects believing in imminent return of Christ and the end of the world

adventitious (adven'tishəs) *a.* **1.** added, artificial **2.** accidental, occurring by chance

adventure (əd'venchər) *n.* **1.** risk **2.** bold exploit **3.** remarkable happening **4.** enterprise **5.** commercial speculation —*v.* **6.** (take) risk —**ad'venturer** *n.* **1.** one who seeks adventures **2.** one who lives on his wits (**ad'venturess** *fem.*) —**ad'venturism** *n.* recklessness, *esp.* in politics and finance —**ad'venturous** *a.* —**ad'venturously** *adv.* —**ad'venturousness** *n.*

adverb ('advərb) *n.* word added to verb, adjective or other adverb to modify meaning —**ad'verbial** *a.* —**ad'verbially** *adv.*

adverse (ad'vərs, 'advərs) *a.* **1.** opposed **2.** hostile **3.** unfavorable, bringing harm —**'adversary** *n.* enemy —**ad'versative** *a.* —**ad'versely** *adv.* —**ad'versity** *n.* distress, misfortune

advert (əd'vərt) *vi.* **1.** turn the mind or attention **2.** refer —**ad'vertence** *n.* —**ad'vertently** *adv.*

advertise ('advərtīz) *vt.* **1.** publicize **2.** make known **3.** give notice of, *esp.* in newspapers *etc.* —*vi.* **4.** make public request (for) —**adver'tisement** *n.* —**'advertiser** *n.* —**'advertising** *a./n.*

advice (əd'vīs) *n.* **1.** opinion given **2.** counsel **3.** information **4.** (formal) notification

advise (əd'vīz) *vt.* **1.** offer advice **2.** recommend a line of conduct **3.** give notice (of) —**ad'visable** *a.* expedient —**ad'vised** *a.* considered, as in *well-advised* —**advisedly** (əd'vīzidli) *adv.* —**ad'viser** *or* **ad'visor** *n.* —**ad'visory** *a.*

advocaat ('advōkä) *n.* liqueur made with egg yolk and brandy

advocate ('advəkit) *n.* **1.** one who pleads the cause of another, *esp.* in court of law —*vt.* ('advəkāt) **2.** uphold, recommend —**'advocacy** *n.* —**advo'cation** *n.*

adz *or* **adze** (adz) *n.* carpenter's tool, like ax, but with arched blade set at right angles to handle

AEC Atomic Energy Commission

AEF American Expeditionary Force

aegis ('ējis) *n.* sponsorship, protection (*orig.* shield of Zeus)

Aeolian (ē'ōliən) *a.* acted on by the wind, as **Aeolian harp** open narrow box with strings tuned in unison

aerate ('āərāt) *vt.* **1.** charge liquid with gas, as effervescent drink **2.** expose to air —**aer'ation** *n.* —**'aerator** *n.* apparatus for charging liquid with gas

aerial ('āəriəl) *a.* **1.** of the air **2.** operating in the air **3.** pertaining to aircraft —*n.* **4.** antenna —**'aerialist** *n.* trapeze artist

aerie *or* **aery** ('āəri) *n.* **1.** nest of bird of prey, *esp.* eagle **2.** high dwelling place

aero-, aeri-, *or before vowel* **aer-** (*comb. form*) air or aircraft, as in *aero engine*

aerobatics (āərō'batiks) *pl.n.* stunt flying

aerobic (āə'rōbik) *a.* **1.** taking place in the presence of oxygen —*pl.n.* **2.** (*with sing. or pl.v.*) system of exercises designed to improve respiratory and circulatory functions of body

aerodynamics (āərōdī'namiks) *pl.n.* (*with sing. v.*) study of air flow, *esp.* round moving solid bodies

aero engine engine for powering aircraft

aerofoil ('āərōfoil) *n.* surfaces of wing *etc.* of aircraft designed to give lift

aerolite ('āərəlīt) *n.* meteoric stone

aerometry (āə'romitri) *n.* measurement of weight or density of gases

aeronaut ('āərənōt) *n.* pilot or navigator of lighter-than-air craft —**aero'nautical** *a.* —**aero'nautics** *pl.n.* (*with sing. v.*) science of air navigation and flying in general

aerosol ('āərəsol) *n.* (substance dispensed as fine spray from) pressurized can

aerospace ('āərəspās) *n.* **1.** earth's atmosphere and space beyond —*a.* **2.** of missiles, space vehicles *etc.*

aerostatics (āərə'statiks) *pl.n.* (*with sing. v.*) **1.** study of gases in equilibrium and bodies held in equilibrium in gases **2.** study of lighter-than-air craft

aesthetic (es'thetik, is-) *or* **aesthetical** *a.* relating to principles of beauty, taste and art —**aesthete** ('esthēt) *n.* one who affects extravagant love of art —**aes'thetically** *adv.* —**aes'theticism** *n.* —**aes'thetics** *pl.n.* (*with sing. v.*) study of art, taste *etc.*

AF **1.** air force **2.** audio frequency

afar (ə'fär) *adv.* from, at, or to, a great distance

AFB air force base

A.F.C. **1.** American Football Conference **2.** automatic frequency control

affable ('afəbəl) *a.* easy to speak to, polite and friendly —**affa'bility** *n.* —**'affably** *adv.*

affair (ə'fāər) *n.* **1.** thing done or attended to **2.** business **3.** happening **4.** sexual liaison —*pl.* **5.** personal or business interests **6.** matters of public interest

affect (ə'fekt) *vt.* **1.** act on, influence **2.** move feelings of **3.** make show, pretense of **4.** assume **5.** have liking for —**affec'tation** *n.* show, pretense —**af'fected** *a.* **1.** making a pretense **2.** moved **3.** acted upon —**af'fectedly** *adv.* —**af'fecting** *a.* moving the feelings of —**af'fectingly** *adv.* —**af'fection** *n.* fondness, love —**af'fectionate** *a.* —**af'fectionately** *adv.*

affenpinscher ('afənpinchər) *n.* purebred toy dog with hard wiry black coat, pointed ears, bushy eyebrows, chin tuft and mustache

afferent ('afərənt) *a.* bringing to, *esp.* describing nerves which carry sensation to the brain

affiance (ə'fīəns) *vt.* betroth —**af'fianced** *a./n.* (one) promised in marriage

affidavit (afi'dāvit) *n.* written statement on oath

affiliate (ə'filiāt) *vt.* (*with* to *or* with) **1.** connect, attach (with larger body, organization) **2.** adopt —**affili'ation** *n.*

affinity (ə'finiti) *n.* **1.** natural liking **2.** resemblance **3.** relationship by marriage **4.** chemical attraction —**af'finitive** *a.*

affirm (ə'fərm) *v.* **1.** assert positively, declare **2.** maintain (statement) —*vi.* **3.** make solemn declaration —**affir'mation** *n.* —**af'firmative** *a.* **1.** asserting —*n.* **2.** word of assent —**af'firmatively** *adv.*

affix (ə'fiks) *vt.* **1.** fasten **2.** attach, append —*n.* ('afiks) **3.** addition, *esp.* to word, as suffix, prefix

afflatus (ə'flātəs) *n.* impulse of creative power or inspiration

afflict (ə'flikt) *vt.* **1.** give pain or grief to, distress **2.** trouble, vex —**af'fliction** *n.* —**af'flictive** *a.*

affluent ('aflōōənt) *a.* **1.** wealthy **2.** abundant —*n.* **3.** tributary stream —**'affluence** *n.* wealth, abundance

afford (ə'fōrd) *vt.* **1.** be able to buy **2.** be able to spare (the time *etc.*) **3.** produce, yield, furnish

afforest (ə'forist) *vt.* turn into forest, plant trees on —**affores'tation** *n.*

affray (ə'frā) *n.* fight, brawl

affront (ə'frunt) *vt.* **1.** insult openly —*n.* **2.** insult **3.** offense

Afghanistan (af'ganistan) *n.* country in southern Asia, bounded north by the U.S.S.R., east and south by Pakistan and west by Iran —**'Afghan** *n.* **1.** native or inhabitant of Afghanistan **2.** Pashto **3.** (**a-**) knitted or crocheted blanket or shawl made up of squares or stripes **4.** (**a-**) large Turkoman carpet with long pile woven in geometric designs —**Afghan hound** purebred dog with long narrow head with topknot and long thick silky coat

aficionado (əfishiə'nädō) *n.* **1.** ardent supporter or devotee **2.** devotee of bullfighting (*pl.* **-s**)

afield (ə'fēld) *adv.* **1.** away from home **2.** in or on the field

afire (ə'fīər) *adv.* on fire

aflame (ə'flām) *adv.* burning

AFL-CIO American Federation of Labor and Congress of Industrial Organizations

afloat (ə'flōt) *adv.* **1.** floating **2.** at sea **3.** in circulation

afoot (ə'fōōt) *adv.* **1.** astir **2.** on foot

afore (ə'fōr) *prep./adv.* before, usu. in compounds —**a'fore'mentioned** *a.* chiefly in legal documents, stated or mentioned before —**a'forethought** *a.* premeditated (*esp. in* **malice aforethought**)

a fortiori (ā fōrti'ōrī) *adv.* for a stronger reason

afoul (ə'fowl) *a./adv.* into difficulty
Afr. Africa(n)
afraid (ə'frād) *a.* **1.** frightened **2.** sorry
A-frame ('āfrām) *n.* a building with steeply angled sides meeting at the top like the shape of the letter A
afresh (ə'fresh) *adv.* again, anew
Africa ('afrikə) *n.* continent in eastern hemisphere south of Europe, between the Atlantic and Indian oceans —'**African** *a.* **1.** belonging to Africa —*n.* **2.** native of Africa —**Afri'cana** *pl.n.* objects of cultural or historical interest of southern Afr. origin —**African lily** S Afr. plant with funnel-shaped flowers —**African violet** house plant with pink, white or purple flowers and hairy leaves
Africander (afri'kandər) *n.* breed of humpbacked S Afr. cattle
Afrikaans (afri'käns, -'känz) *n.* language used in S Afr., derived from 17th-cent. Dutch —**Afri'kaner** *n.* White native of S Afr. with Afrikaans as mother tongue
Afro ('afrō) *n.* fuzzy, bushy hairstyle
Afro- (*comb. form*) Africa or African, as in *Afro-Asiatic*
Afro-American *n./a.* American of African and *esp.* of Negroid descent
Afro-Asian *n.* language phylum comprising Semitic, Berber, Cushitic and Chadic families
afrormosia (afrör'mōzhiə) *n.* hard teaklike wood obtained from tropical Afr. tree
aft (äft) *adv.* toward rear of ship
after ('äftər) *adv.* **1.** later **2.** behind —*prep.* **3.** behind **4.** later than **5.** on the model of **6.** pursuing —*conj.* **7.** at a later time than that at which —*a.* **8.** nearer ship's rear —'**afterward** *or* '**afterwards** *adv.* later
afterbirth ('äftərbərth) *n.* membrane expelled after a birth (*also* **placenta**)
aftercare ('äftərkāər) *n.* care, *esp.* medical, bestowed on person after period of treatment, and *esp.* after childbirth
aftereffect ('äftərifekt) *n.* subsequent effect of deed, event *etc.*
afterglow ('äftərglō) *n.* light after sunset
afterlife ('äftərlīf) *n.* life after death or at later time in person's lifetime
aftermath ('äftərmath) *n.* result, consequence, *esp.* difficult one
afternoon (äftər'nōōn) *n.* time from noon to evening
afterpains ('äftərpānz) *pl.n.* pains caused by contraction of uterus after childbirth
aftershave (lotion) ('äftərshāv) *n.* lotion applied to face after shaving
afterthought ('äftərthôt) *n.* idea occurring later
Ag *Chem.* silver
AG **1.** adjutant general **2.** attorney general
Agada (ə'gädə) *n.* fables, folklore and anecdotes in the Talmud
again (ə'gen, ə'gin) *adv.* **1.** once more **2.** in addition **3.** back, in return **4.** besides
against (ə'genst, ə'ginst) *prep.* **1.** in opposition to **2.** in contact with **3.** opposite **4.** in readiness for
Aga Khan ('ägə 'kän) the spiritual leader of Ismaili Muslims
Agamemnon (agə'memnon) *n.* in Greek legend, the King of Mycenae and leader of the Greeks at the siege of Troy
agape (ə'gāp) *a./adv.* open-mouthed as in wonder *etc.*
agar ('ägär) *n.* gelatinous carbohydrate obtained from seaweeds, used as culture medium for bacteria in food *etc.* (*also* **agar-agar**)
agaric ('agərik) *n.* **1.** any of various fungi, *eg* mushroom —*a.* **2.** fungoid
agate ('agit) *n.* **1.** colored, semiprecious, decorative form of quartz **2.** playing marble of agate **3.** size of type approximately 5½ point —**agate line** unit of measurement used in classified advertising
agave (ə'gävi) *n.* any of genus of plants native to tropical Amer., with spiny-margined leaves cultivated for fiber or for ornament
age (āj) *n.* **1.** length of time person or thing has existed **2.** time of life **3.** period of history **4.** maturity **5.** long time —*v.* **6.** make or grow old —**aged** ('ājid) *a.* **1.** old —*pl.n.* **2.** old people —'**ageism** *n.* discrimination against the old —'**ageless** *a.* —**age-old** *a.*
-age (*comb. form*) **1.** collection, set or group, as in *baggage* **2.** process or action or result of action, as in *breakage* **3.** state or relationship, as in *bondage* **4.** house or place, as in *orphanage* **5.** charge or fee, as in *postage* **6.** rate, as in *dosage*
agenda (ə'jendə) *pl.n.* (*with sing. v.*) **1.** things to be done **2.** program of business meeting
agent ('ājənt) *n.* **1.** one authorized to carry on business or affairs for another **2.** person or thing producing effect **3.** cause **4.** natural force —'**agency** *n.* **1.** instrumentality **2.** business, place of business of agent
agent provocateur (a'zhā provoka'tœr) *Fr.* police spy who tries to provoke persons to act illegally
Aggeus (a'gēəs) *n. Bible* Haggai in the Douay Version of the O.T.
agglomerate (ə'glomərāt) *v.* **1.** gather into a mass —*n.* (ə'glomərit, -rāt) **2.** confused mass **3.** rock consisting of volcanic fragments —*a.* (ə'glomərit, -rāt) **4.** formed into a mass —**agglomer'ation** *n.* —**ag'glomerative** *a.*
agglutinate (ə'glōōtināt) *vt.* **1.** unite with glue *etc.* **2.** form (words) into compounds —*a.* (ə'glōōtinit, -nāt) **3.** united, as by glue —**aggluti'nation** *n.* —**ag'glutinative** *a.*
aggrandize (ə'grandīz) *vt.* make greater in size, power or rank —**aggrandizement** (ə'grandizmənt) *n.*
aggravate ('agrəvāt) *vt.* **1.** make worse or

more severe **2.** *inf.* annoy —**'aggravating** *a.* —**aggra'vation** *n.*

aggregate ('agrigāt) *vt.* **1.** gather into mass —*a.* ('agrigit) **2.** gathered thus —*n.* ('agrigit, -gāt) **3.** mass, sum total **4.** rock consisting of mixture of minerals **5.** mixture of gravel *etc.* for concrete —**aggre'gation** *n.*

aggression (ə'greshən) *n.* **1.** unprovoked attack **2.** hostile activity —**ag'gress** *vi.* —**ag'gressive** *a.* —**ag'gressiveness** *n.* —**ag'gressor** *n.*

aggrieve (ə'grēv) *vt.* inflict pain on, injure —**ag'grieved** *a.*

aghast (ə'gäst) *a.* overcome with horror or amazement

agile ('ajil) *a.* **1.** nimble **2.** active **3.** quick —**'agilely** *adv.* —**a'gility** *n.*

Agilon ('ajilon) *n.* trade name for stretch yarn

agin (ə'gin) *prep. inf., dial.* against

agitate ('ajitāt) *vt.* **1.** disturb, excite **2.** keep in motion, stir, shake up **3.** trouble —*vi.* **4.** stir up public opinion (for or against something) —**agi'tation** *n.* —**'agitator** *n.*

agitprop ('ajitprop) *n.* political agitation and propaganda, *esp.* of Communist nature

agley (ə'glā, ə'glē, ə'glī) *a. Scot.* awry

aglitter (ə'glitər) *a.* sparkling; glittering

aglow (ə'glō) *a.* glowing

agnostic (ag'nostik) *n.* **1.** one who holds that we know nothing of things outside the material world —*a.* **2.** of this theory —**ag'nosticism** *n.*

Agnus Dei ('agnōōs 'dāi) **1.** figure of a lamb emblematic of Christ **2.** part of Mass beginning with these words

ago (ə'gō) *adv.* in the past

agog (ə'gog) *a.* eager, astir

agony ('agəni) *n.* extreme suffering of mind or body, violent struggle —**'agonize** *vi.* **1.** suffer agony **2.** worry greatly —**'agonizing** *a.* —**agony column** newspaper column containing personal advertisements relating to lost relatives, pets *etc.*

agoraphobia (agərə'fōbiə) *n.* fear of open spaces —**agora'phobic** *a.*

agouti (ə'gōōti) *n.* **1.** rabbit-sized tropical American rodent **2.** barred pattern as result of alternating light and dark bands of fur **3.** animal with fur of this pattern

agrarian (ə'greriən, -'grar-) *a.* of agriculture, land, or its management —**a'grarianism** *n.*

agree (ə'grē) *v.* **1.** be of same opinion **2.** consent **3.** harmonize **4.** determine, settle **5.** suit (**a'greed, a'greeing**) —**agreea'bility** *n.* —**a'greeable** *a.* **1.** willing **2.** pleasant —**a'greeableness** *n.* —**a'greeably** *adv.* —**a'greement** *n.* **1.** concord **2.** contract

agriculture ('agrikulchər) *n.* art, practice of cultivating land —**agri'cultural** *a.* —**agri'culturist** *n.*

agrimony ('agrimōni) *n.* yellow-flowered plant with bitter taste

agronomy (ə'gronəmi) *n.* study of management of land and scientific cultivation of crops —**a'gronomist** *n.*

aground (ə'grownd) *adv./a.* (of boat) touching bottom

agt. agent

ague ('āgyōō) *n. obs.* **1.** malarial fever with periodic attacks of chills and sweating **2.** fit of shivering

ah (ä) *interj.* exclamation of pleasure, pain *etc.*

A.H. **1.** (indicating years in Muslim system of dating, numbered from Hegira (622 A.D.)) anno hegirae **2.** ampere-hour **3.** arts and humanities

aha (ä'hä) *interj.* exclamation of triumph, surprise *etc.*

Ahab ('āhab) *n.* in O.T., king of Israel whose name is a byword for wickedness

ahead (ə'hed) *adv.* **1.** in front **2.** onward

ahem (ə'hem) *interj.* clearing of throat to attract attention *etc.*

ahoy (ə'hoi) *interj.* shout used at sea for hailing

A.I. **1.** artificial insemination **2.** artificial intelligence **3.** ad interim

aid (ād) *vt.* **1.** to help —*n.* **2.** help, support, assistance

AID Agency for International Development

A.I.D. artificial insemination by donor

aide (ād) *or* **aide-de-camp** ('āddə'kamp) *n.* military officer personally assisting superior (*pl.* **aides(-de-camp)**)

AIDS (ādz) acquired immuno-deficiency syndrome

aigrette (ā'gret, 'āgret) *n.* **1.** long plume worn on hats or as headdress, *esp.* one of egret feathers **2.** ornament in imitation of plume of feathers

aiguille (ā'gwēl) *n.* **1.** sharp, slender peak **2.** blasting drill

A.I.H. artificial insemination by husband

ail (āl) *vt.* **1.** trouble, afflict, disturb —*vi.* **2.** be ill —**'ailing** *a.* sickly —**'ailment** *n.* illness

aileron ('āləron) *n.* movable section of wing of aircraft which gives lateral control

aim (ām) *v.* **1.** give direction to (weapon *etc.*) **2.** direct effort (toward) —*n.* **3.** direction **4.** object, purpose —**'aimless** *a.* without purpose

A.I.M. American Indian Movement

ain't (ānt) *nonstandard* **1.** am not **2.** is not **3.** are not **4.** has not **5.** have not

Ainu ('īnōō) *n.* **1.** member of indigenous Caucasoid people of Japan (*pl.* **Ainu** *or* **-s**) **2.** their language

air (āər) *n.* **1.** mixture of gases we breathe, the atmosphere **2.** breeze **3.** tune **4.** manner —*pl.* **5.** affected manners —*vt.* **6.** expose to air to dry or ventilate —**'airily** *adv.* —**'airiness** *n.* —**'airing** *n.* **1.** exposure to open air or heat for drying or freshening **2.** exercise in open air **3.** exposure to public view **4.** radio or television broadcast —**'airy**

a. **1.** of or relating to air **2.** unreal, illusory **3.** open to air circulation **4.** carelessly condescending —**air bag** automatically inflating bag in front of automobile passengers to protect them from impact in case of accident —**air base** military airfield —**air bladder** sac containing gas and air, *esp.* present in most fishes serving as accessory to respiration —**'airborne** *a.* flying in the air —**air brake 1.** brake operated by compressed air **2.** structure for lowering speed of airplane —**'airbrush** *n.* **1.** atomizer, *esp.* for applying paint —*vt.* **2.** paint with airbrush —**air-condition** *vt.* —**air conditioner** —**air-conditioning** *n.* apparatus for controlling temperature and humidity of air —**air-cool** *vt.* cool (engine) by flow of air —**'aircraft** *n.* **1.** collective name for flying machines **2.** airplane —**aircraft carrier** warship with flight deck on which airplanes can be launched and landed —**air cushion** pocket of air supporting hovercraft —**air-cushion vehicle** *see* **ground-effect machine** *at* GROUND[1] —**'airfield** *n.* **1.** landing field for aircraft **2.** airport —**air force 1.** military organization of nation for air warfare **2.** unit of U.S. Air Force higher than division and lower than command —**air gun 1.** gun from which projectile is propelled by compressed air **2.** hand tool operated by compressed air —**air lane** path usu. followed by airplanes —**air letter** airmail letter —**'airlift** *n.* system of transporting goods and persons by aircraft to or from otherwise inaccessible area —**'airline** *n.* air transportation system including equipment, routes and personnel —**'airliner** *n.* large passenger aircraft —**air lock 1.** intermediate chamber between places of unequal atmospheric pressure or temperature **2.** stoppage of flow caused by air being in a part where water ought to circulate —**'airmail** *n.* **1.** system of transporting mail by aircraft **2.** mail so transported —**'airman** *n.* **1.** pilot, aviator or aviation technician **2.** enlisted man in U.S. Air Force ranking above airman basic and below airman first class —**airman basic** enlisted man of lowest rank in U.S. Air Force —**airman first class** enlisted man above airman and below sergeant —**'airplane** *n.* fixed-wing aircraft heavier than air, driven by propeller or by high-velocity jet, supported by the dynamic reaction of the air against its wings —**air plant 1.** epiphyte **2.** bryophyllum —**air pocket** condition of local atmosphere causing airplane to drop suddenly —**air pollution** waste products in the form of extraneous gases and small suspended particles in the atmosphere —**'airport** *n.* place maintained for landing and take-off of aircraft and receiving and discharging passengers and cargo, with facilities for shelter, supply and repair of aircraft —**air pump** machine to extract, compress or supply air —**air raid** attack by armed aircraft —**air rifle** rifle whose projectile is propelled by compressed air or carbon dioxide —**air sac 1.** air-filled space in body of bird, connected to lungs **2.** air cell of the lungs of mammals —**air screw 1.** screw propeller designed to operate in air **2. UK** airplane propeller —**air shaft** well-like ventilating passage —**'airship** *n.* lighter-than-air aircraft with propulsion and steering control —**'airsickness** *n. see* **motion sickness** *at* MOTION —**'airspace** *n.* space above the earth, *esp.* that lying above a country and under its jurisdiction —**'airspeed** *n.* speed of aircraft relative to air —**'airstrip** *n.* runway lacking airport facilities —**'airtight** *a.* **1.** impermeable to air or nearly so **2.** (of argument) without weakness or loophole —**air-to-air** *a.* relating to aircraft in flight —**air trap** device to prevent escape of foul gases —**air valve** —**'airwave** *n.* **1.** medium of radio and television transmission **2.** channel of designated radio frequency for communication —**'airway** *n.* **1.** passage for current of air **2.** designated route for aircraft —**'airworthiness** *n.* —**'airworthy** *a.* fit for operation in the air

Airedale ('āərdāl) *n.* purebred large rough-coated terrier

aisle (īl) *n.* passageway separating seating areas in church, theater *etc.*

aitch (āch) *n.* letter *h* or sound represented by it

aitchbone ('āchbōn) *n.* **1.** hip bone in cattle **2.** cut of beef containing this bone

ajar[1] (ə'jär) *a./adv.* partly open

ajar[2] (ə'jär) *a.* (*with* with) in contradiction (to), at variance (with)

AK Alaska

AKA *or* **a.k.a.** also known as

AKC American Kennel Club

akialoa (äkiə'lōə) *n.* Hawaiian honeycreeper: songbird found only in Hawaiian Islands, having long thin beak and tubular tongue with brushlike tip

akimbo (ə'kimbō) *adv.* with hands on hips and elbows outward

akin (ə'kin) *a.* **1.** related by blood **2.** alike, having like qualities

akita (ə'kētə) *n.* purebred working dog resembling a spitz, orig. from Japan

Al *Chem.* aluminum

AL 1. Alabama **2.** American League **3.** American Legion

-al[1] (*a. comb. form*) of; related to, as in *functional, sectional*

-al[2] (*n. comb. form*) act or process of, as in *renewal*

-al[3] (*n. comb. form*) **1.** aldehyde, as in *salicylal* **2.** pharmaceutical product, as in *phenobarbital*

à la (ä lä) **1.** in the manner of **2.** as prepared in, by or for

ALA 1. American Legal Association 2. American Library Association

Ala. Alabama

Alabama (alə'bamə) *n.* East South Central state of the U.S., admitted to the Union in 1819. Abbrev.: **Ala., AL** (with ZIP code)

alabaster ('aləbästər) *n.* soft, white, semi-transparent stone —**ala'bastrine** *a.* of, like this

à la carte (ä lä 'kärt) (of menu) pricing each item separately

alack (ə'lak) *or* **alackaday** (ə'lakədā) *interj. obs., poet.* cry of sorrow

alacrity (ə'lakriti) *n.* quickness, briskness, readiness

à la mode *or* **a la mode** (ä lä 'mōd) 1. in fashion 2. topped with ice cream

alarm (ə'lärm) *n.* 1. sudden fright 2. apprehension 3. notice of danger 4. bell, buzzer 5. call to arms —*vt.* 6. frighten 7. warn of danger —**a'larming** *a.* —**a'larmist** *n.* one given to prophesying danger or exciting alarm *esp.* needlessly —**alarm clock** clock which sounds a buzzer or bell at a set time —**alarm reaction** initial response (as increased hormonal activity) of an organism to stress

alas (ə'las) *interj.* cry of grief

Alaska (ə'laskə) *n.* Pacific state of the U.S., admitted to the Union in 1959. Abbrev.: **AK** (with ZIP code) —**Alaskan malamute** purebred working dog with heavy coat, erect ears, heavily cushioned feet and plumy tail

alate ('ālāt) *a.* having wings

alb (alb) *n.* long white priestly vestment, worn at Mass

albacore ('albəkōr) *n.* any of several tunas

Albania (al'bāniə) *n.* country of eastern Europe bounded north and east by Yugoslavia, south by Greece and west by Adriatic Sea —**Al'banian** *n./a.* 1. (native or inhabitant) of Albania —*n.* 2. language of Albania, which is the only member of its branch

albatross

albatross ('albətrōs) *n.* member of family of sea-living birds found from the Antarctic to the tropics, about the size of a goose or swan, except for the wandering albatross with an 11-12ft. wingspan

albeit (ōl'bēit) *conj.* although

Alberta (al'bərtə) *n.* western province of Canada, bounded south by the U.S., west by British Columbia, north by Northwest Territory and east by Saskatchewan

albino (al'bīnō) *n.* person or animal with white skin and hair, and pinkish eyes, due to lack of coloring matter (*pl.* **-s**) —**albinism** ('albinizəm) *n.*

Albion ('albiən) *n. obs., poet.* 1. Britain 2. England

album ('albəm) *n.* 1. book of blank leaves, for photographs, stamps, autographs *etc.* 2. one or more long-playing records released as single item

albumen *or* **albumin** (al'byōōmin) *n.* egg white

albumin (al'byōōmin) *n.* constituent of animal and vegetable matter, found nearly pure in white of egg —**al'buminous** *a.*

alchemy ('alkəmi) *n.* medieval chemistry, *esp.* attempts to turn base metals into gold and find elixir of life —**'alchemist** *n.*

alcohol ('alkəhōl) *n.* 1. intoxicating fermented liquor 2. class of organic chemical substances —**alco'holic** *a.* 1. of alcohol —*n.* 2. one addicted to alcoholic drink —**'alcoholism** *n.* (disease caused by) habitual heavy consumption of alcoholic drink

alcove ('alkōv) *n.* recess

aldehyde ('aldihīd) *n.* one of the class of chemical compounds with the general formula RCHO, where R is an organic group, the simplest aldehyde being formaldehyde

alder ('ōldər) *n.* tree related to the birch

alderman ('ōldərmən) *n.* member of governing body of a municipality —**alder'manic** *a.*

ale (āl) *n.* fermented malt liquor, type of beer, *orig.* without hops —**'alehouse** *n. obs.* public house

aleatory ('āliətōri) *or* **aleatoric** (āliə'tōrik) *a.* 1. dependent on chance 2. *Mus.* involving elements chosen at random

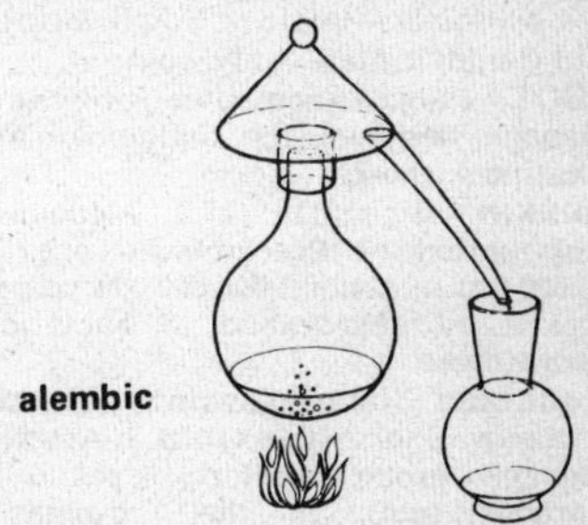

alembic

alembic (ə'lembik) *n.* 1. formerly, retort used for distillation 2. anything that distills or purifies

alert (ə'lərt) *a.* 1. watchful 2. brisk, active —*n.* 3. warning of sudden attack or surprise —*vt.* 4. warn, *esp.* of danger 5. draw (someone's) attention to something —**a'lertness** *n.* —**on the alert** watchful

Aleut (ali'o͞ot) *n.* **1.** member of Amerindian people inhabiting Kenai and Alaska peninsula and the Aleutian Islands **2.** language of this people —**Aleutian Islands** (ə'lo͞oshən) archipelago extending southwest from the Alaska peninsula in the north Pacific Ocean (*also* **Aleutians**)

Alexander the Great (alig'zandər) (356-323 B.C.) conqueror of the civilized world who extended Greek civilization to the East

Alexandrine (alig'zandrin) *n.* **1.** verse of six iambic feet **2.** verse of 12 syllables containing four accents

alexandrite (alig'zandrīt) *n.* variety of chrysoberyl, green by daylight and red-violet by artificial light, used as gemstone

alexia (ə'leksiə) *n.* impaired ability to read

Alfa ('alfə) *n.* word used in communications for the letter *a*

alfalfa (al'falfə) *n.* plant of Europe and Asia used as fodder (*also* **lu'cerne**)

alfresco (al'freskō) *adv./a.* in the open air

alg. algebra

alga ('algə) *n.* lower plant classified according to color: blue-green, green, brown or red, which may be microscopic unicellular organisms, sometimes colonial, to multicellular seaweed (*pl.* **algae** ('aljē)) —**al'gologist** *n.* specialist in study of algae

algebra ('aljibrə) *n.* **1.** branch of mathematics dealing with the properties and relations of numbers **2.** the generalization and extension of arithmetic —**algebraic(al)** (alji'brāik(əl)) *a.* —**algebraist** (alji'brāist) *n.*

Algeria (al'jēəriə) *n.* country in north Africa, bounded west by Morocco and Western Sahara, southwest by Mauritania and Mali, southeast by Niger, east by Libya and Tunisia, and north by the Mediterranean Sea —**Al'gerian** *a./n.*

-algia (*n. comb. form*) pain in part specified, as in *neuralgia* —**-algic** (*a. comb. form*)

algid ('aljid) *a. Med.* chilly, cold

ALGOL ('algol) computer programming language designed for mathematical and scientific purposes

Algonkin (al'gongkin) *n.* **1.** Algonquian **2.** *Geol.* period of Precambrian era, about 600 000 000 to about 1 000 000 000 years ago, marked by appearance of bacteria and marine algae

Algonquian (al'gongkwiən), **Algonquin** (al'gonkwin), *or* **Algonkin** *n.* **1.** Amerindian language group formerly spoken from Labrador south to the Carolinas and westward to the Rockies **2.** a people of Ottawa River Valley **3.** speaker of any of Algonquian dialects

algorism ('algərizəm) *or* **algorithm** ('algəridhəm) *n.* **1.** any method or procedure for computation **2.** formerly, operations with the decimal system using placement notation

Alhambra (al'hambrə) *n.* citadel and palace built at Granada, Spain, by Moorish kings in 13th century

alias ('āliəs) *adv.* **1.** otherwise —*n.* **2.** assumed name (*pl.* **-es**)

alibi ('alibī) *n.* **1.** plea of being somewhere else when crime was committed **2.** *inf.* excuse (*pl.* **-s**)

alien ('āliən) *a.* **1.** foreign **2.** different in nature **3.** repugnant —*n.* **4.** foreigner —**aliena'bility** *n.* —**'alienable** *a.* able to be transferred to another owner —**'alienate** *vt.* **1.** estrange **2.** transfer —**alie'nation** *n.* —**'alienist** *n.* psychiatrist, *esp.* one who specializes in legal aspects of mental illness

alight[1] (ə'līt) *vi.* **1.** get down **2.** land, settle

alight[2] (ə'līt) *a.* **1.** burning **2.** lit up

align (ə'līn) *vt.* **1.** bring into line or agreement —*vi.* **2.** be in or come into correct relative position —**a'lignment** *n.*

alike (ə'līk) *a.* **1.** like, similar —*adv.* **2.** in the same way

aliment ('alimənt) *n.* something that nourishes or sustains body or mind —**ali'mentary** *a.* of food —**alimentary canal** tubular passage extending from mouth to anus, whose function is to ingest food and eliminate residual waste

alimony ('alimōni) *n.* allowance paid under court order to separated or divorced spouse

A-line ('ālīn) *a.* (of garments) flaring out slightly from waist or shoulders

aliped ('aliped) *a.* **1.** wing-footed —*n.* **2.** animal, like the bat, whose toes are joined by membrane that serves as wing

aliphatic (ali'fatik) *a. Chem.* of any organic compound having open chain structure

aliquant ('alikwənt) *a. Math.* (of quantity or number) that is not exact divisor of given quantity or number

aliquot ('alikwot) *a. Math.* of or signifying an exact divisor of a quantity or number

alive (ə'līv) *a.* **1.** living **2.** active **3.** aware **4.** swarming

aliyah *or* **aliya** (ä'lēyä) *n.* the immigration of Jews to Israel

alizarin (ə'lizərin) *n.* red dye formerly obtained from madder

alkali ('alkəlī) *n.* one of a class of substances that neutralize or are neutralized by acids and form corrosive solutions in water, *eg* caustic soda, ammonia (*pl.* **-s, -es**) —**alkaline** ('alkəlin) *a.* —**alka'linity** *n.* —**'alkalize** *vt.* —**'alkaloid** *n./a.* —**alka'losis** *n.* condition caused by excess of alkaline substances or shortage of acidic substances in the body fluids —**alkali metal** *Chem.* any of group of elements comprising lithium, sodium, potassium, rubidium, cesium and francium (so-called because their hydroxides are strongly alkaline)

Alkoran *or* **Alcoran** (alko'ran) *n.* see KORAN

all (ōl) *a.* **1.** the whole of, every one of —*adv.* **2.** wholly, entirely —*n.* **3.** the whole **4.**

everything, everyone —**all-American** *a.* **1.** comprising wholly American elements **2.** typical of the U.S. **3.** (*esp.* of athlete) selected as one of the best in U.S. in category at particular time —*n.* **4.** such a person —**all around 1.** competent in many fields **2.** having general usefulness or merit —**all fours 1.** all limbs of quadruped **2.** legs and arms of person when crawling —**all get-out** utmost conceivable degree —**all in** tired —**all in all** on the whole —**all out** with enthusiasm —**all over 1.** over whole extent **2.** everywhere **3.** thoroughly —**all-over** *a.* covering whole surface —**'allover** *a.* consisting of repeated pattern —**all right** *a.* **1.** adequate; satisfactory **2.** unharmed; safe —*adv.* **3.** very well **4.** satisfactorily **5.** without doubt (*also* (*nonstandard*) **al'right**) —**All Saints' Day** Christian festival celebrated on Nov. 1st to honor all saints —**all set** ready to begin —**All Souls' Day** *R.C.* day of prayer (Nov. 2nd) for the dead —**all there** mentally alert

alla breve ('alə brēv) *Mus. a./adv.* **1.** in quick duple time with half note rather than quarter note as the beat, *ie* 2/2 instead of 4/4 —*n.* **2.** mark indicating this

Allah ('alə, ä'lä) *n.* Muslim name for the Supreme Deity

allay (ə'lā) *vt.* lighten, relieve, calm, soothe

allege (ə'lej) *vt.* **1.** state without or before proof **2.** produce as argument —**allegation** (ali'gāshən) *n.* —**al'leged** *a.* —**allegedly** (ə'lejidli) *adv.*

Allegheny (ali'gāni) *n.* river flowing south from southwest New York through western Pennsylvania, joining Monongahela at Pittsburgh to form Ohio River —**Allegheny Mountains** mountain range in Pennsylvania, Maryland, West Virginia and Virginia: part of the Appalachian Mountains —**Allegheny spurge** (spərj) low perennial of the box family widely grown as ground cover

allegiance (ə'lējəns) *n.* duty of a subject to his sovereign or state, loyalty

allegory ('aligōri) *n.* **1.** story with a meaning other than literal one **2.** description of one thing under image of another —**alle'goric(al)** *a.* —**alle'gorically** *adv.* —**'allegorist** *n.* —**'allegorize** *vt.*

allegretto (ali'gretō) *Mus. adv./a./n.* **1.** (in) tempo between allegro and andante —*n.* **2.** short piece in lively tempo (*pl.* **-s**)

allegro (ə'lāgrō, -'leg-) *Mus. adv./a./n.* **1.** (in) fast tempo —*n.* **2.** title for movement or composition in fast tempo (*pl.* **-s**)

alleluia (ali'lo͞oyə) *interj.* praise the Lord (*also* **hallelujah**)

allemande ('alimand) *n. Mus.* **1.** first dance movement in suites of pre-18th-cent. composers **2.** in late 18th cent., quick waltzlike dance in 3/4 or 3/8 time

allentando (alen'tandō) *a./adv. Mus.* slowing down

allergy ('alərji) *n.* abnormal sensitivity to some food or substance innocuous to most people —**'allergen** *n.* substance capable of inducing an allergy —**aller'genic** *a.* —**al'lergic** *a.* **1.** having or caused by an allergy **2.** *inf.* having an aversion (to)

alleviate (ə'lēviāt) *vt.* **1.** ease, lessen, mitigate **2.** make light —**allevi'ation** *n.* —**al'leviator** *n.*

alley ('ali) *n.* **1.** narrow street, *esp.* through middle of block giving rear access to buildings **2.** walk, path **3.** enclosure for skittles **4.** hardwood lane for bowling **5.** building housing group of such lanes **6.** playing marble (*pl.* **-s**)

alliance (ə'līəns) *n.* **1.** state of being allied **2.** union between families by marriage, and states by treaty **3.** confederation

alligator ('aligātər) *n.* **1.** reptile of crocodile family of southern U.S. and northern Central America —*a.* **2.** (of article) made from skin of alligator —**alligator clip** spring-loaded clip with jaws resembling alligator's, used for temporary electrical connections —**alligator pear** avocado

alliteration (əlitə'rāshən) *n.* beginning two or more words in close succession with same sound, *eg* Sing a Song of Sixpence —**al'literate** *v.* —**al'literative** *a.*

allo- (*comb. form*) other, as in *allogamy, allopathy*

allocate ('aləkāt) *vt.* **1.** assign as a share **2.** place —**allo'cation** *n.*

allocution (alə'kyo͞oshən) *n.* formal address

allogamy (ə'logəmi) *n.* cross-fertilization

allomorphism (alə'mōrfizəm) *n.* **1.** variation of form without change in essential nature **2.** variation of crystalline form of chemical compound

allopathy (ə'lopəthi) *n.* orthodox practice of medicine: opposite of homeopathy

allot (ə'lot) *vt.* **1.** distribute as shares **2.** give out (**-tt-**) —**al'lotment** *n.* **1.** distribution **2.** portion of land rented for cultivation **3.** portion allotted

allotropy (ə'lotrəpi) *or* **allotropism** *n.* property of some elements of existing in more than one form, *eg* carbon in the form of diamond and graphite —**'allotrope** *n.* —**allo'tropic** *a.*

allow (ə'low) *vt.* **1.** permit **2.** acknowledge **3.** set aside —*vi.* (*usu. with* for) **4.** take into account —**al'lowable** *a.* —**al'lowably** *adv.* —**al'lowance** *n.* —**allowedly** (ə'lowidli) *adv.* **1.** by general agreement **2.** admittedly

alloy ('aloi, ə'loi) *n.* **1.** mixture of two or more metals —*vt.* (ə'loi) **2.** mix (metals) to form an alloy **3.** debase by mixing with something inferior

allspice ('ōlspīs) *n.* **1.** (berry of) W Indian tree **2.** spice made from this berry

allude (ə'lo͞od) *vi.* **1.** mention lightly, hint (at), make indirect reference (to) **2.** refer (to) —**al'lusion** *n.* —**al'lusive** *a.* —**al'lusively** *adv.*

allure (ə'lŏŏər) *vt.* **1.** entice, win over, fascinate —*n.* **2.** attractiveness —**al'lurement** *n.* —**al'luring** *a.* charming, seductive —**al'luringly** *adv.*

alluvial (ə'lŏŏviəl) *a.* deposited by rivers —**al'luvion** *n.* land formed by washed-up deposit —**al'luvium** *n.* water-borne matter deposited by rivers, floods *etc.* (*pl.* **-s, -via** (-viə))

ally (ə'lī) *vt.* **1.** join in relationship by treaty, marriage or friendship *etc.* (**al'lied, al'lying**) —*n.* ('alī) **2.** state or sovereign bound to another by treaty **3.** confederate (*pl.* **'allies**) —**allied** (ə'līd, 'alīd) *a.* —**'Allies** *pl.n.* **1.** (in World War I) powers of the Triple Entente (France, Russia and Britain) together with nations allied with them **2.** (in World War II) countries that fought against the Axis, *esp.* Britain and Commonwealth countries, U.S., Soviet Union and France

alma mater ('almə 'mätər) *Lat.* **1.** one's school, university or college **2.** song or hymn of school, university or college

almanac ('ôlmənak) *n.* **1.** yearly calendar with detailed information on year's tides, events *etc.* **2.** annual publication containing astronomical or meteorological data **3.** compendium of useful facts

almighty (ôl'mīti) *a.* **1.** having all power, omnipotent **2.** *inf.* very great —**the Almighty** God

almond ('ämənd) *n.* **1.** edible kernel of the fruit of a tree related to the peach **2.** tree bearing this fruit —**almond paste** edible paste made from ground almonds

almost ('ôlmōst) *adv.* very nearly, all but

alms (ämz) *pl.n.* gifts to the poor

aloe ('alō) *n.* **1.** genus of succulent plants of the lily family, with basal leaves and spikelike flowers grown for ornament —*pl.n.* (*with sing. v.*) **2.** bitter drug made from plant

aloft (ə'loft) *adv.* **1.** on high **2.** overhead **3.** in ship's rigging

alone (ə'lōn) *a.* **1.** single, solitary —*adv.* **2.** separately, only

along (ə'long) *adv.* **1.** in a line **2.** together with one **3.** forward —*prep.* **4.** over the length of —**a'long'side** *adv./prep.* beside (something)

aloof (ə'lŏŏf) *a.* **1.** withdrawn **2.** distant **3.** uninvolved —**a'loofness** *n.*

alopecia (alə'pēshiə) *n.* baldness

aloud (ə'lowd) *adv.* **1.** loudly **2.** audibly

alp (alp) *n.* high mountain —**alpine** ('alpīn) *a.* **1.** of the Alps **2.** of high mountains —*n.* **3.** mountain plant —**alpinist** ('alpinist) *n.* mountain climber —**'alpenstock** *n.* iron-shod staff used by climbers —**alpine horn** primitive wind instrument used by herdsmen in the Alps for calling cattle and rendering simple melodies —**the Alps** high mountain range in S central Europe

alpaca (al'pakə) *n.* **1.** Peruvian llama **2.** its wool **3.** cloth made from this

alpaca

alpha ('alfə) *n.* **1.** first letter in Greek alphabet (Α, α) —*a.* **2.** involving helium nuclei; denoting isomeric or allotropic form of substance —**alpha particle** helium nucleus emitted during some radioactive transformations —**alpha ray** ionizing radiation consisting of stream of alpha particles —**alpha and omega** the first and last

alphabet ('alfəbet) *n.* **1.** the set of letters used in writing a language **2.** system of signs or signals substituting for alphabet —**alpha'betic(al)** *a.* in the standard order of the letters —**alpha'betically** *adv.* —**'alphabetize** *vt.* **1.** arrange in alphabetical order **2.** express by alphabet

alphanumeric (alfənyŏŏ'merik, -nŏŏ-) *or* **alphanumerical** *a.* consisting of alphabetical and numerical symbols

already (ôl'redi) *adv.* **1.** before, previously **2.** sooner than expected

alright (ôl'rīt) *adv. nonstandard see* **all right** *at* ALL

Alsatian (al'sāshən) *n. see* **German shepherd** *at* GERMAN

also ('ôlsō) *adv.* **1.** as well, too **2.** besides, moreover —**also-ran** *n.* **1.** contestant *etc.* failing to finish among first three **2.** *inf.* loser

alt. **1.** alternate **2.** altitude **3.** alto

Alta. Alberta

altar ('ôltər) *n.* **1.** raised place, stone *etc.*, on which sacrifices are offered **2.** in Christian church, table on which priest consecrates the Eucharist —**altar boy** boy serving as an acolyte —**'altarcloth** *n.* —**'altarpiece** *n.*

alter ('ôltər) *v.* change, make or become different —**altera'bility** *n.* —**'alterable** *a.* —**'alterably** *adv.* —**alte'ration** *n.* —**'alterative** *a.*

altercation (ôltər'kāshən) *n.* dispute, wrangling, controversy —**'altercate** *vi.*

alter ego ('ôltər 'ēgō, 'egō) *Lat.* **1.** second self **2.** close friend

alternate ('ôltərnāt) *v.* **1.** occur or cause to occur by turns —*a.* ('ôltərnit) **2.** one after the other, by turns —*n.* ('ôltərnit) **3.** one that substitutes for another —**'alternately** *adv.* —**alter'nation** *n.* **1.** in algebra and geometry, one of the properties of proportion **2.** in symbolic logic, one of several names given to the relation 'either-or-both' —**al'ternative** *n.* **1.** one of two choices —*a.* **2.** presenting choice, *esp.* between two possibilities only **3.** (of two things) mutually exclusive **4.** denoting life style *etc.* regarded as preferable to that of contemporary society because it is less conventional, materialistic or institutionalized —**al'ternatively** *adv.* —**'alternator** *n.* electric generator for producing alternating current —**alternating current** electric current that reverses direction with a frequency independent of characteristics of circuit —**alternative society** group of people who agree in rejecting traditional values of society around them

althaea *or* **althea** (al'thēə) *n.* hollyhock

althorn ('alt-hörn) *n.* alto saxhorn

although (ōl'dhō) *conj.* despite the fact that

altimeter (al'timitər, 'altimētər) *n.* instrument for measuring height

altitude ('altityōōd, -tōōd) *n.* height, eminence, elevation, loftiness

alto ('altō) *n. Mus.* **1.** contralto **2.** male singing voice or instrument above tenor (*pl.* **-s**) —*a.* **3.** of an alto —**alto clef** clef that establishes middle C as being on third line of staff

altogether (ōltə'gedhər) *adv.* **1.** entirely **2.** on the whole **3.** in total —*n.* **4.** (*with* the) nude

altruism ('altrōōizəm) *n.* principle of living and acting for good of others —**altru'istic** *a.* —**altru'istically** *adv.*

alum ('aləm) *n.* mineral salt, double sulfate of aluminum and potassium, used as astringent and styptic —**aluminous** (ə'lōōminəs) *a.*

aluminum (ə'lōōminəm) *n. Chem.* metallic element noted for its lightness and resistance to oxidation *Symbol* Al, at. wt. 27.0, at. no. 13 —**a'lumina** *n.* oxide of aluminum —**a'luminize** *vt.* coat with aluminum —**a'luminous** *a.*

alumnus (ə'lumnəs) *or* (*fem.*) **alumna** (ə'lumnə) *n.* one who has attended or graduated from a particular school, college or university (*pl.* **-ni** (-nī) *or* **-nae** (-nē))

alumroot ('aləmrōōt) *n.* heuchera with an astringent root

always ('ōlwāz) *adv.* **1.** at all times **2.** for ever

alyssum (ə'lisəm) *n.* genus of hardy annuals, herbaceous perennials and evergreen subshrubs of the cabbage family, widely grown as ornamentals

Alzheimer's disease ('älts-hīmərz) disease characterized by loss of memory for recent events and inability to store new memories

am (am; *unstressed* əm) *first person sing. pres. ind. of* BE

Am 1. *Chem.* americium **2.** America(n)

AM *or* **am** amplitude modulation

a.m. *or* **A.M.** ante meridiem

AMA American Medical Association

amah ('ämä) *n.* Chinese nursemaid or maidservant

amain (ə'mān) *adv. obs., poet.* with great strength or haste

amalgam (ə'malgəm) *n.* **1.** compound of mercury and another metal **2.** soft, plastic mixture **3.** combination of elements

amalgamate (ə'malgəmāt) *v.* mix, combine or cause to combine —**amalga'mation** *n.*

amanuensis (əmanyōō'ensis) *n.* **1.** person employed to take dictation **2.** copyist **3.** secretary (*pl.* **-ses** (-sēz))

amaranth ('amərənth) *n.* **1.** imaginary purple everlasting flower **2.** genus of flowering plants —**ama'ranthine** *a.* never fading

amaryllis (amə'rilis) *n.* **1.** genus comprising single bulbous species of lily family (*also* **belladonna lily**) **2.** hippeastrum **3.** (**A-**) rustic sweetheart

amass (ə'mas) *vt.* collect in quantity —**a'massable** *a.*

amateur ('amətər) *n.* **1.** one who carries on an art, study, game *etc.* for pleasure rather than for financial gain **2.** unskilled practitioner —*a.* **3.** not professional or expert —**ama'teurish** *a.* imperfect, untrained —**ama'teurishly** *adv.* —**'amateurism** *n.*

Amati (ə'mäti) *n.* member of family of violin-makers of Cremona from about 1535 to 1684 who brought the art of violin-making to its peak, and teachers of Stradivarius and Guarnerius (*pl.* **-s**)

amatol ('amətōl) *n.* high explosive consisting of ammonium nitrate and trinitrotoluene (TNT)

amatory ('amətōri) *or* **amatorial** (amə'tōriəl) *a.* relating to love

amaze (ə'māz) *vt.* surprise greatly, astound —**a'mazement** *n.* —**a'mazing** *a.* —**a'mazingly** *adv.*

Amazon ('aməzən) *n.* **1.** female warrior of legend **2.** tall, strong woman —**Ama'zonian** *a.*

ambassador (am'basədər) *n.* **1.** official envoy, *esp.* person accredited to a foreign state as representative of own country **2.** authorized representative **3.** unofficial representative —**ambassa'dorial** *a.* —**am'bassadorship** *n.* —**ambassador-at-large** *n.* person performing same duties as ambassador, but not accredited to a particular state

amber ('ambər) *n.* **1.** yellowish, translucent fossil resin —*a.* **2.** made of, colored like amber

ambergris ('ambərgrēs, -gris) *n.* waxy substance secreted by the sperm whale, used in making perfumes

ambi- (*comb. form*) both, as in *ambidextrous, ambivalence*

ambidextrous (ambi'dekstrəs) *a.* able to use both hands with equal ease —**ambidex'terity** *n.*

ambience *or* **ambiance** ('ambiəns) *n.* atmosphere of a place

ambient ('ambiənt) *a.* surrounding

ambiguous (am'bigyŏŏəs) *a.* **1.** having more than one meaning **2.** obscure —**ambi'guity** *n.* —**am'biguously** *adv.*

ambit ('ambit) *n.* **1.** circuit **2.** compass

ambition (am'bishən) *n.* **1.** desire for power, fame, honor *etc.* **2.** the object of that desire —**am'bitious** *a.* —**am'bitiously** *adv.* —**am'bitiousness** *n.*

ambivalence (am'bivələns) *n.* simultaneous existence of two conflicting desires, opinions *etc.* —**am'bivalent** *a.*

amble ('ambəl) *vi.* **1.** move along easily and gently **2.** move at an easy pace —*n.* **3.** this movement or pace —'**ambler** *n.*

ambrosia (am'brōzhiə) *n.* **1.** *Myth.* food of the gods **2.** anything smelling or tasting particularly good

ambulance ('ambyŏŏləns) *n.* conveyance for sick or injured —**ambulance chaser** lawyer or agent who incites accident victim to sue for damages

ambulatory ('ambyŏŏlətōri) *a.* **1.** of or for walking **2.** not fixed **3.** able to walk (*also* '**ambulant**) —*n.* **4.** place for walking, such as cloister

ambuscade (ambə'skād) *n.* **1.** act of hiding to launch surprise attack **2.** ambush

ambush ('ambŏŏsh) *n.* **1.** act of lying in wait —*vt.* **2.** waylay, attack from hiding, lie in wait for

ameliorate (ə'mēlyərāt) *v.* make better, improve —**amelio'ration** *n.* —**a'meliorative** *a.*

amen (ā'men, ä'men) *interj.* **1.** surely **2.** so let it be

amenable (ə'mēnəbəl) *a.* easy to be led or controlled —**amena'bility** *or* **a'menableness** *n.* —**a'menably** *adv.* —**amenable to 1.** likely to respond to **2.** answerable to

amend (ə'mend) *vt.* **1.** correct **2.** improve **3.** alter in detail, as bill in parliament *etc.* —**a'mendment** *n.* —**a'mends** *pl.n.* reparation

amenity (ə'meniti, -'mē-) *n.* (*oft. pl.*) useful or pleasant facility or service

amenorrhea (āmenə'rēə, ä-) *n.* abnormal absence of menstruation

Amer. America(n)

America (ə'merikə) *n.* **1.** continent in western hemisphere between the Atlantic and Pacific Oceans **2.** the U.S. —**A'merican** *n./a.* (native or inhabitant) of the American continent or the U.S. —**Ameri'cana** *pl.n.* **1.** artifacts typical of American civilization **2.** American culture —**A'mericanism** *n.* characteristic of American English, *esp.* in contrast to British English —**A'mericanist** *n.* **1.** anthropologist specializing in Amerindian languages or cultures **2.** specialist in American culture or history —**Americani'zation** *n.* —**A'mericanize** *v.* **1.** make or become American in character —*vt.* **2.** naturalize as an American —**American Civil War** war (1861-65) between the U.S. and 11 Southern states which seceded from the Union and formed the Confederate States of America (*also* **War Between the States**) —**American English** native language of most U.S. inhabitants, distinguishable from British English in vocabulary and syntax but not sufficiently so as to make it a separate language —**American foxhound** purebred hound smaller than English foxhound but with longer ears and a dense hard glossy coat, usu. black, tan and white —**American Indian** Amerindian —**American Legion** organization of veterans of U.S. wars, founded in 1919 —**American leopard** jaguar —**American plan** hotel plan in which rates cover the cost of meals —**American Revolution** war (1775-83) for independence, waged by the 13 American colonies against Great Britain —**American saddle horse** 3- or 5-gaited horse of breed developed from thoroughbreds and native stock, mainly in Kentucky —**American shorthair** purebred domestic cat with short plushy coat —**American water spaniel** purebred medium-sized sporting dog of Amer. origin with curly chocolate- or liver-colored coat —**American wirehair** purebred domestic cat with short-haired woolly coat —**America's Cup** an international yachting trophy first won by the schooner *America* in 1851 —**the Americas** North and South America considered together

americium (amə'risiəm) *n. Chem.* transuranic element *Symbol* Am, at. wt. 243, at. no. 95

Amerindian (amə'rindiən) *n./a.* (of) member of any of the aboriginal peoples of the western hemisphere (*also* **American Indian**) —'**Amerind** *n.*

amethyst ('amithist) *n.* bluish-violet semiprecious stone

Amharic (am'harik) *n.* **1.** official language of Ethiopia —*a.* **2.** denoting this language

amiable ('āmiəbəl) *a.* friendly, kindly —**amia'bility** *or* '**amiableness** *n.* —'**amiably** *adv.*

amicable ('amikəbəl) *a.* friendly —**amica'bility** *n.* —'**amicably** *adv.*

amid (ə'mid) *or* **amidst** *prep.* in the middle of, among

amidships (ə'midships) *adv.* near, toward middle of ship

amino acid (ə'mēnō) any of group of nitrogen-containing organic compounds that form the proteins from which plants and animals are made

Amish ('ämish) *n./a.* (of or relating to) strict sect of Mennonites that settled in eastern Pennsylvania in 18th century

amiss (ə'mis) *a.* **1.** wrong —*adv.* **2.** faultily, badly —**take amiss** be offended by

amity ('amiti) *n.* friendship

ammeter ('amētər) *n.* instrument for measuring electric current

ammo ('amō) *n. inf.* ammunition

ammonia (ə'mōnyə) *n.* **1.** pungent alkaline gas containing hydrogen and nitrogen **2.** its solution in water —**am'moniac** *or* **ammoniacal** (amə'nīəkəl) *a.* —**am'moniated** *a.* —**am'monium** *n.*

ammonite ('amənīt) *n.* whorled fossil shell like ram's horn

ammunition (amyōō'nishən) *n.* **1.** any projectiles (bullets, rockets *etc.*) that can be discharged from a weapon **2.** any means of defense or attack, as in argument

amnesia (am'nēzhə) *n.* loss of memory

amnestic confabulatory syndrome (am'nestik kən'fabyələtōri) Korsakoff's psychosis

amnesty ('amnisti) *n.* **1.** general pardon —*vt.* **2.** grant amnesty to

amnion ('amniən) *n.* innermost of two membranes enclosing embryonic reptile, bird or mammal (*pl.* **-s, amnia** ('amniə)) —**amni'otic** *a.* —**amniotic fluid** fluid surrounding baby in womb

amoeba (ə'mēbə) *n.* one-celled microorganism found in water, damp soil, and digestive tracts of animals (*pl.* **-s, -bae** (-bē)) —**a'moebic** *a.* —**amoebic dysentery** destruction of the intestinal lining by amoeba

amok *or* **amuck** (ə'muk) *adv.* possessed with murderous frenzy

among (ə'mung) *or* **amongst** *prep.* mixed with, in the midst of, of the number of, between

amoral (ā'mōrəl) *a.* nonmoral, having no moral qualities —**amo'rality** *n.*

amorous ('amərəs) *a.* **1.** inclined to love **2.** in love —**'amorously** *adv.* —**'amorousness** *n.*

amorphous (ə'mōrfəs) *a.* without distinct shape —**a'morphism** *n.*

amortize (ə'mōrtīz) *vt.* pay off (a debt) by a sinking fund

Amos ('āməs) *n.* **1.** *Bible* 30th book of the O.T. **2.** author of this book, 8th-cent. B.C. prophet, who pled for social justice

amount (ə'mownt) *vi.* **1.** come (to), be equal (to) —*n.* **2.** quantity **3.** sum total

amour (ə'mōōər) *n.* (illicit) love affair

amour-propre (amōōr'propr) *Fr.* self-respect

amp ampere

ampere ('ampēər) *n.* unit of electric current —**amperage** ('ampərij) *n.* strength of electric current measured in amperes —**ampere-hour** *n.* practical unit of quantity of electricity

ampersand ('ampərsand) *n.* the sign & (and)

amphetamine (am'fetəmēn) *n.* synthetic liquid used medicinally mainly for its stimulant action on central nervous system

amphi- (*comb. form*) **1.** on both sides; at both ends; of both kinds, as in *amphipod, amphibious* **2.** around, as in *amphibole*

amphibious (am'fibiəs) *a.* living or operating both on land and in water —**am'phibian** *n.* **1.** cold-blooded egg-laying vertebrate with soft skin, gills at tadpole stage when aquatic, replaced by lungs as land-living adults, *eg* frogs, salamanders, toads **2.** vehicle able to travel on land or water **3.** aircraft that can alight on land or water

amphitheater ('amfithēətər) *n.* building with tiers of seats rising round an arena

amphora ('amfərə) *n.* two-handled jar of ancient Greece and Rome (*pl.* **-rae** (-rē), **-s**)

amp hr ampere-hour

ampicillin (ampi'silin) *n.* form of penicillin used to treat infections of respiratory, intestinal and urinary tracts

ample ('ampəl) *a.* **1.** big enough **2.** large, spacious —**'amply** *adv.*

amplify ('amplifī) *vt.* **1.** increase **2.** make bigger, louder *etc.* (**-fied, -fying**) —**amplifi'cation** *n.* —**'amplifier** *n.*

amplitude ('amplityōōd, -tōōd) *n.* spaciousness, width, magnitude —**amplitude modulation** *Rad.* method of transmitting information in which amplitude of carrier wave is varied

ampoule, ampule, *or* **ampul** ('ampyōōl, -pōōl) *n.* container for hypodermic dose

ampulla (am'pōōlə) *n.* **1.** *Anat.* dilated end part of duct or canal **2.** *Christianity* vessel for wine and water used at the Eucharist; small flask for consecrated oil **3.** Roman two-handled bottle (*pl.* **ampullae** (-'pōōlē))

amputate ('ampyōōtāt) *v.* cut off (limb *etc.*) —**ampu'tation** *n.*

amt amount

Amtrak ('amtrak) *n.* railroad system in U.S.

amuck (ə'muk) *adv. see* AMOK

amulet ('amyōōlit) *n.* something carried or worn as a charm

amuse (ə'myōōz) *vt.* **1.** divert **2.** occupy pleasantly **3.** cause to laugh or smile —**a'musement** *n.* entertainment, pastime —**a'musing** *a.* —**a'musingly** *adv.*

AMVETS ('amvets) American Veterans of World War II

amylase ('amilās, -lāz) *n.* enzyme that hydrolyzes starch and glycogen to simple sugar

amylum ('amiləm) *n. see* STARCH

an (an; *unstressed* ən) *see* A

an- *or before consonant* **a-** (*comb. form*) not; without, as in *anaphrodisiac*

-an, -ean, *or* **-ian** (*comb. form*) **1.** belonging to; coming from; typical of; adhering to, as in *European, Elizabethan, Christian* **2.** person who specializes or is expert in, as in *dietician*

Anabaptist (anə'baptist) *n.* member of Protestant movement that rejected infant baptism and insisted adults be rebaptized

anabolism (ə'nabəlizəm) *n.* metabolic process in which complex molecules are synthesized from simpler ones with storage of energy —**ana'bolic** *a.* —**anabolic steroid** any of various hormones that encourage muscle and bone growth

anabranch ('ănəbrănch) *n.* stream that leaves a river and re-enters it further downstream

anachronism (ə'nakrənizəm) *n.* **1.** mistake of time, by which something is put in wrong historical period **2.** something out of date —**anachro'nistic** *a.*

anacoluthon (anəkə'lo͞othon) *n.* a sentence or words faulty in grammatical sequence (*pl.* **-tha** (-thə))

anaconda (anə'kondə) *n.* large snake which kills by constriction

anadromous (ə'nadrəməs) *a.* (of salmon *etc.*) migrating up rivers to breed

anaerobe (an'āərōb) *n.* organism that can live without oxygen —**anaer'obic** *a.*

anaesthetic (anis'thetik) *n./a.* *see* ANESTHETIC

anagram ('anəgram) *n.* word or words made by arranging in different order the letters of another word or words, *eg ant* from *tan* —**anagram'matical** *a.* —**ana'grammatist** *n.*

anal ('ānəl) *a. see* ANUS

analects ('anəlekts) *or* **analecta** (anə'lektə) *pl.n.* selected literary passages from one or more works, usu. by one author

analgesia (anəl'jēzhə) *n.* absence of pain —**anal'gesic** *a./n.* pain-relieving (agent)

analog ('anəlog) *n.* **1.** something analogous to something else **2.** *Biol.* analogous part or organ —*a.* **3.** using analog (such as dial and pointer) to represent data or information —**analog computer** computer that uses voltages to represent numbers of physical quantities

analogy (ə'naləji) *n.* **1.** agreement or likeness in certain respects **2.** correspondence —**ana'logical** *a.* —**ana'logically** *adv.* —**a'nalogist** *n.* —**a'nalogize** *v.* explain by analogy —**analogous** (ə'naləgəs) *a.* **1.** similar **2.** parallel —**analogously** (ə'naləgəsli) *adv.*

analysis (ə'nalisis) *n.* separation of something into its elements or components (*pl.* **-yses** (-isēz)) —**a'nalysand** *n.* person undergoing psychoanalysis —**'analyst** *n.* one skilled in analysis, *esp.* chemical or psychiatric analysis —**ana'lytic(al)** *a.* **1.** relating to analysis **2.** capable of or given to analyzing —**ana'lytically** *adv.* —**'analyze** *vt.* **1.** examine critically **2.** determine the constituent parts of —**analytic geometry** technique of using algebra to deal with geometry

anapest ('anəpest) *n.* metrical foot of two short syllables followed by one long syllable or two unstressed syllables followed by one stressed syllable

anaphora (ə'nafərə) *n.* **1.** *Rhetoric* repetition of word or phrase at beginning of successive clauses **2.** *Gram.* use of word such as pronoun to avoid repetition

anaphylaxis (anəfi'laksis) *n.* phenomenon of severe allergic reaction —**anaphy'lactic** *a.* —**anaphylactic shock** shock produced by ingesting allergen

anarchy ('anərki) *n.* **1.** lawlessness **2.** lack of government in a state **3.** confusion —**an'archic(al)** *a.* —**an'archically** *adv.* —**'anarchism** *n.* —**'anarchist** *n.* one who opposes all forms of government

anastigmat (a'nastigmat, anə'stigmat) *n.* lens corrected for astigmatism —**anastig'matic** *a.* (of lens) not astigmatic

anastomosis (ənastə'mōsis) *n.* interconnection of branches (streams, blood vessels, leaf veins) (*pl.* **-ses** (-sēz))

anat. **1.** anatomical **2.** anatomy

anathema (ə'nathəmə) *n.* **1.** anything detested, hateful **2.** ban of the church **3.** curse —**a'nathematize** *v.*

anatomy (ə'natəmi) *n.* **1.** science of structure of organisms **2.** detailed analysis **3.** the body —**ana'tomical** *a.* —**ana'tomically** *adv.* —**a'natomist** *n.* —**a'natomize** *vt.*

-ance *or* **-ancy** (*comb. form*) action, state or condition, or quality, as in *utterance, resemblance*

ancestor ('ansestər) *n.* **1.** person from whom another is descended **2.** early type of later form or product —**an'cestral** *a.* —**'ancestry** *n.*

anchor ('angkər) *n.* **1.** heavy (*usu.* hooked) implement dropped on cable, chain *etc.* to bottom of sea to secure vessel **2.** source of stability or security —*vt.* **3.** fasten by or as by anchor —**'anchorage** *n.* act of, place of anchoring —**anchor man** **1.** *Sport* last competitor in relay team **2.** broadcaster who usu. introduces other reporters and reads the news **3.** one with lowest standing in a graduating class —**weigh anchor** haul up anchor and set sail

anchorite ('angkərīt) *n.* hermit, recluse ('**anchoress** *fem.*)

anchovy ('anchōvi) *n.* small savory fish of herring family

anchusa (ang'kyo͞osə) *n.* plant with hairy leaves and blue flowers

ancien régime (ãsyẽ rā'zhēm) **1.** *Fr.* political and social system of France before the Revolution of 1789 **2.** the old order of things (*pl.* ***anciens régimes*** (ãsyẽ rā'zhēm))

ancient ('ānshənt) *a.* **1.** belonging to former age **2.** old **3.** timeworn —*n.* **4.** (*oft. pl.*) one who lived in an earlier age —**'anciently** *adv.* —**ancient history** **1.** history of ancient times **2.** common knowledge

ancillary (an'siləri) *a.* subordinate, subservient, auxiliary

-ancy (*comb. form*) condition or quality, as in *poignancy* (*see also* -ANCE)

and (and; *unstressed* ənd, ən) *conj.* connecting word, used to join words and sentences, to introduce a consequence *etc.* —**and/or**

conj. used to join terms when either one or other or both is indicated

andante (an'danti) *Mus. a./adv.* **1.** at moderately slow tempo, between allegretto and adagio —*n.* **2.** passage or piece performed in this manner

andantino (andan'tēnō) *a./adv. Mus.* slightly faster than andante

Andean ('andiən) *a.* of the Andes, range of mountains in western S Amer. —**andesine** ('andizēn) *n.* mineral of feldspar group having play of colors, usu. found as crystals in igneous rock —**andesite** ('andizīt) *n.* volcanic rock, usu. dark gray

andiron ('andīərn) *n.* iron bar or bracket for supporting logs in fireplace

Andorra (an'dōrə) *n.* country in southern Europe, situated in eastern Pyrenees on the French-Spanish border —**An'dorran** *a./n.*

andro- *or before vowel* **andr-** (*comb. form*) **1.** male; masculine **2.** in botany, stamen or anther

androgen ('andrəjən) *n.* steroid that promotes development of male sexual characteristics

androgynous (an'drojinəs) *a.* **1.** *Bot.* having male and female flowers in same inflorescence **2.** hermaphrodite

android ('android) *n.* **1.** in science fiction, robot resembling human being —*a.* **2.** resembling human being

Andromeda (an'droməde) *n.* **1.** in Greek legend, princess rescued from monster by her future husband Perseus **2.** northern constellation directly south of Cassiopeia, between Pegasus and Perseus

anecdote ('anikdōt) *n.* very short story dealing with single incident —**anec'dotal** *or* **anec'dotic** *a.*

anemia (ə'nēmiə) *n.* deficiency in number of red blood cells —**a'nemic** *a.* **1.** suffering from anemia **2.** pale, sickly, lacking vitality

anemograph (ə'neməgraf) *n.* recording anemometer

anemometer (ani'momitər) *n.* instrument for recording force and direction of wind —**anemo'metric** *or* **anemo'metrical** *a.* —**ane'mometry** *n.*

anemone (ə'neməni) *n.* flower related to buttercup —**sea anemone** plantlike sea animal

anent (ə'nent) *prep. obs.* concerning

aneroid ('anəroid) *a.* without liquid —**aneroid barometer** barometer in which pointer is actuated by atmospheric pressure bending a metallic surface

anesthetic (anis'thetik) *n./a.* (agent) causing loss of sensation —**anesthesia** (anis'thēzhə) *n.* loss of sensation —**anes'thetically** *adv.* —**anesthetist** (ə'nesthətist) *n.* expert in use of anesthetics —**anesthetize** (ə'nesthətīz) *vt.*

aneurysm ('anyərizəm) *n.* swelling out of a part of an artery

anew (ə'nyōō, -'nōō) *adv.* afresh, again

angel ('ānjəl) *n.* **1.** divine messenger **2.** ministering or attendant spirit **3.** person with the qualities of such a spirit, as gentleness, purity *etc.* **4.** financial backer, *esp.* of theatrical production —**angelic** (an'jelik) *a.* —**angelically** (an'jelikəli) *adv.* —**angel dust** drug used illicitly as hallucinogen —**'angelfish** *n.* **1.** small tropical marine fish which has brightly colored body **2.** S Amer. freshwater fish which has large dorsal and anal fins **3.** shark with flattened pectoral fins (*pl.* **-fish, -fishes**) —**angel food cake** light sponge cake made without egg yolks

Angeleno (anjə'lēnō) *n.* inhabitant or native of Los Angeles, California (*pl.* **-s**)

angelica (an'jelikə) *n.* **1.** aromatic plant **2.** the candied stalks of this plant used in cookery **3.** (**A-**) white dessert wine of Californian origin

Angelus ('anjiləs) *n.* devotional service in R.C. Church in memory of the Incarnation, said at morning, noon and sunset

anger ('anggər) *n.* **1.** strong emotion excited by a real or supposed injury **2.** wrath **3.** rage —*vt.* **4.** excite to wrath **5.** enrage —**'angrily** *adv.* —**'angry** *a.* **1.** full of anger **2.** inflamed

angina pectoris (an'jīnə 'pektəris) severe pain accompanying heart disease

angiosperm ('anjiəspərm) *n.* a flowering plant

angle[1] ('anggəl) *vi.* fish with hook and line —**'angler** *n.* **1.** fisherman **2.** sea fish with spiny dorsal fin (*also* **angler fish**) —**'angling** *n.*

angle[2] ('anggəl) *n.* **1.** meeting of two lines or surfaces **2.** sharp corner **3.** point of view **4.** *inf.* devious motive —*vt.* **5.** bend at an angle —**angle of incidence 1.** angle of line or beam of radiation to line perpendicular to surface at point of incidence **2.** angle between chord line of aircraft wing or tailplane and longitudinal axis

Anglican ('angglikən) *a./n.* (member) of the Church of England —**'Anglicanism** *n.*

anglicize ('angglisīz) *vt.* express in English, turn into English form —**'Anglicism** *n.* English idiom or peculiarity

Anglo ('anggl ō) *n.* **1.** (among Hispanics and Indians) person of Caucasian descent **2.** C English-speaking Canadian (*pl.* **-s**)

Anglo- (*comb. form*) English, as in *Anglo-American*

Anglo-French *a.* **1.** of England and France **2.** of Anglo-French —*n.* **3.** Norman-French language of medieval England

Anglo-Norman *a.* **1.** relating to Norman conquerors of England or their language —*n.* **2.** Norman inhabitant of England after 1066 **3.** Anglo-French language

Anglophile ('angglōfīl) *or* **Anglophil** *n.* person having admiration for England or the English

Anglophobia (angglō'fōbiə) *n.* dislike of England *etc.*

Anglo-Saxon *n.* **1.** member of West Germanic tribes that settled in Britain from 5th cent. A.D. **2.** language of these tribes (*see* **Old English** *at* OLD) **3.** White person whose native language is English **4.** *inf.* plain blunt English —*a.* **5.** forming part of Germanic element in Modern English **6.** of Anglo-Saxons or Old English language **7.** of White Protestant culture of Britain and Amer.

Angola (ang'gōlə) *n.* country in west Africa, bounded by Congo on the north, Zaïre on the north and northeast, Zambia on the east, Namibia on the south and the Atlantic Ocean on the west —**An'golan** *a./n.*

angora (ang'gōrə) *n.* (*sometimes* **A-**) **1.** goat with long white silky hair which is used in the making of mohair **2.** cloth or wool made from this hair —**angora cat** *or* **rabbit** purebred varieties of cat and rabbit with long, silky fur

angostura bitters (anggə'styōōərə, -'stōōə-) (*oft.* **A-**) trade name for bitter tonic used as flavoring in alcoholic drinks

angstrom ('angstrəm) *n.* unit of length equal to one ten-billionth of a meter for measuring wavelengths of light

Anguilla (ang'gwilə) *n.* country comprising the most northerly of the Leeward Islands in the Caribbean Sea

anguish ('anggwish) *n.* great mental or physical pain

angular ('anggyōōlər) *a.* **1.** (of people) bony, awkward **2.** having angles **3.** measured by an angle —**angu'larity** *n.*

anhydrous (an'hīdrəs) *a.* (of chemical substances) free from water

anil ('anil) *n.* leguminous West Indian shrub (*also* **'indigo**)

aniline ('anilin) *n.* product of coal tar or indigo, which yields dyes

animadvert (animad'vərt) *vi.* (*usu. with* on *or* upon) criticize, pass censure —**animad'version** *n.* criticism, censure

animal ('animəl) *n.* **1.** living creature, having sensation and power of voluntary motion **2.** beast —*a.* **3.** of, pert. to animals **4.** sensual —**ani'malcular** *a.* —**ani'malcule** *n.* very small animal, *esp.* one which cannot be seen by naked eye —**'animalism** *n.* —**'animally** *adv.* —**animal husbandry** science of breeding and rearing farm animals —**animal kingdom** the animal species of the world collectively —**animal magnetism 1.** quality of being attractive, *esp.* to opposite sex **2.** *obs.* hypnotism

animate ('animāt) *vt.* **1.** give life to **2.** enliven **3.** inspire **4.** actuate **5.** make cartoon film of —**'animated** *a.* **1.** lively **2.** in form of cartoons —**ani'mation** *n.* **1.** life, vigor **2.** cartoon film —**'animator** *n.*

animato (ani'mätō) *a./adv. Mus.* lively; animated

animism ('animizəm) *n.* belief that natural effects are due to spirits or that inanimate things have spirits —**'animist** *n.* —**ani'mistic** *a.*

animosity (ani'mositi) *n.* hostility, enmity

animus ('animəs) *n.* **1.** intense dislike; hatred **2.** animosity

anion ('anīən) *n.* ion with negative charge

anise ('anis) *n.* annual herb related to carrot, with licorice-flavored seeds (**'aniseed**) —**ani'sette** *n.* sweet liqueur flavored with aniseed

ankh (ängk) *n.* cross with loop for its upper vertical arm, serving as an emblem of life

ankle ('angkəl) *n.* joint between foot and leg —**'anklet** *n.* ornamental chain *etc.* worn around ankle

ankylosis (angki'lōsis) *n.* abnormal adhesion or immobility of bones in joint, by disease or by surgery

anna ('anə) *n.* **1.** formerly, monetary unit of Burma, India and Pakistan **2.** coin representing one anna

annals ('anəlz) *pl.n.* historical records of events —**'annalist** *n.*

Annapolis (ə'napəlis) *n.* U.S. Naval Academy

anneal (ə'nēl) *vt.* **1.** toughen (metal or glass) by heating and slow cooling **2.** temper (determination, will *etc.*) —**an'nealing** *n.*

annelid ('anəlid) *n.* any member of a phylum of invertebrate animals with segmented cylindrical bodies, including earthworms, lugworms and leeches

annex (a'neks) *vt.* **1.** add, append, attach **2.** take possession of (*esp.* territory) —*n.* ('aneks) **3.** supplementary building **4.** something added —**annex'ation** *n.*

Annie Oakley ('ani 'ōkli) a free ticket

annihilate (ə'nīəlāt) *vt.* reduce to nothing, destroy utterly —**annihi'lation** *n.* —**an'nihilative** *a.* —**an'nihilator** *n.*

anniversary (ani'vərsəri) *n.* **1.** yearly recurrence of a date of notable event **2.** celebration of this

anno Domini ('anō 'dominī, -nē) *Lat.* in the year of our Lord

annotate ('anōtāt, 'anə-) *vt.* provide notes for (literary work *etc.*), comment —**anno'tation** *n.* —**'annotator** *n.*

announce (ə'nowns) *vt.* make known, proclaim —**an'nouncement** *n.* —**an'nouncer** *n.* broadcaster who announces items in program, introduces speakers *etc.*

annoy (ə'noi) *vt.* **1.** vex **2.** make slightly angry **3.** tease —**an'noyance** *n.*

annual ('anyōōəl) *a.* **1.** yearly **2.** of, for a year —*n.* **3.** plant which completes its life cycle in a year **4.** book published each year —**'annually** *adv.*

annuity (ə'nyōōiti, -'nōō-) *n.* sum or grant paid every year —**an'nuitant** *n.* holder of annuity

annul (ə'nul) *vt.* make void, cancel, abolish (**-ll-**) —**an'nulment** *n.*

annular ('anyələr) *a.* ring-shaped —'**annulate** *a.* having or marked with rings —'**annulated** *a.* formed in rings —**annu'lation** *n.* —'**annulet** *n.* small ring or fillet —'**annulus** *n. Math.* the area between two circles when one is inside the other

Annunciation (ənunsi'āshən) *n.* **1.** angel's announcement to the Virgin Mary, commemorated on March 25th as a church festival **2.** (**a-**) announcing —**an'nunciate** *vt.* proclaim, announce

anode ('anōd) *n. Elec.* the positive pole, or point of entry of current —'**anodize** *vt.* cover (metal object) with protective film by using it for anode in electrolysis

anodyne ('anədīn) a. **1.** relieving pain, soothing —*n.* **2.** pain-relieving drug

anoint (ə'noint) *vt.* **1.** smear with oil or ointment **2.** consecrate with oil —**a'nointment** *n.* —**the Anointed** the Messiah

anomalous (ə'noməlәs) *a.* irregular, abnormal —**a'nomaly** *n.* **1.** irregularity **2.** deviation from rule

anomie *or* **anomy** ('anəmi) *n. Sociol.* lack of social or moral standards of person or group

anon (ə'non) *adv. obs.* **1.** in a short time, soon **2.** now and then

anon. anonymous(ly)

anonymous (ə'nonimәs) *a.* nameless, *esp.* without an author's name —**ano'nymity** *n.* —**a'nonymously** *adv.*

anopheles (ə'nofilēz) *n.* genus including all mosquitoes which transmit malaria to man

anorexia (anə'reksiə) *n.* loss of appetite —**anorexia nervosa** (nər'vōsə) psychological condition characterized by refusal to eat

another (ə'nudhər) *pron./a.* **1.** one other **2.** a different (one) **3.** one more

anoxia (an'oksiə) *n.* decrease in supply of oxygen to the tissues of the body

anserine ('ansərīn) *a.* **1.** of or like goose **2.** silly

answer ('ansər) *v.* **1.** reply (to) **2.** be accountable (for, to) —*vt.* **3.** solve; reply correctly **4.** meet **5.** match **6.** satisfy, suit —*n.* **7.** reply **8.** solution —'**answerable** *a.* accountable

ant (ant) *n.* small social insect, proverbial for industry —**ant bear** *see* AARDVARK —**ant hill** mound raised by ants

Ant. Antarctica

-ant (*comb. form*) causing or performing action or existing in certain condition, as in *pleasant, deodorant, servant*

Antabuse ('antəbyōōs) *n.* trade name for disulfiram: used to treat alcoholism

antacid (ant'asid) *n.* **1.** substance used to treat acidity, *esp.* in stomach —*a.* **2.** having properties of this substance

antagonist (an'tagənist) *n.* opponent, adversary —**an'tagonism** *n.* —**antago'nistic** *a.* —**antago'nistically** *adv.* —**an'tagonize** *vt.* arouse hostility in

Antarctic (ant'ärktik) *a.* **1.** of south polar regions —*n.* **2.** region round South Pole —**An'tarctica** *n.* continent surrounding South Pole —**Antarctic Circle** imaginary circle around earth at latitude 66° 32′ S —**Antarctic Ocean** seas surrounding Antarctica, comprising southernmost parts of Pacific, Atlantic and Indian Oceans

ante ('anti) *n.* **1.** player's stake in poker —*v.* **2.** place stake

ante- (*comb. form*) before, as in *antechamber.* Such words are not given here where the meaning may easily be inferred from the simple word

anteater ('antētər) *n.* any of several mammals that feed entirely on ants or termites, *eg* aardvark, echidna

antebellum (anti'beləm) *a.* existing before a war, *esp.* the American Civil War

antecedent (anti'sēdənt) *a./n.* (event, person or thing) going before

antedate ('antidāt) *vt.* **1.** be or occur at earlier date than **2.** affix or assign date to (document *etc.*) earlier than actual date **3.** cause to occur sooner —*n.* **4.** earlier date

antediluvian (antidi'lōōviən) *a.* **1.** before the Flood **2.** ancient

antelope ('antilōp) *n.* deerlike ruminant animal, remarkable for grace and speed

ante meridiem (mə'ridiəm) *Lat.* before noon

antenatal (anti'nātəl) *a.* prenatal

antenna (an'tenə) *n.* **1.** movable segmented organ of sensation on head of insects, myriapods and crustaceans **2.** part of radio *etc.* receiving or sending radio waves (*pl.* **-ae** (-ē))

antepenultimate (antipi'nultimit) *a.* **1.** third last —*n.* **2.** anything third last

anterior (an'tēəriər) *a.* **1.** to the front **2.** earlier

anteroom ('antirōōm, -rŏŏm) *n.* room giving entrance to larger room, oft. used as waiting room

anthem ('anthəm) *n.* **1.** song of loyalty, *esp.* to a country **2.** Scripture passage set to music **3.** piece of sacred music, orig. sung in alternate parts by two choirs

anther ('anthər) *n.* sac in flower, containing pollen, at top of stamen —'**antheral** *a.*

anthology (an'tholəji) *n.* collection of poems, literary extracts *etc.* —**an'thologist** *n.* maker of such —**an'thologize** *vt.* include (poem *etc.*) in anthology

anthracite ('anthrəsīt) *n.* hard coal that burns slowly almost without flame or smoke

anthrax ('anthraks) *n.* **1.** bacterial disease of sheep and cattle, communicable to man **2.** sore caused by this

anthropo- (*comb. form*) man, human, as in *anthropology*

anthropocentric (anthrəpō'sentrik) *a.* regarding man as central factor in universe

anthropoid ('anthrəpoid) *a.* **1.** like man —*n.* **2.** ape resembling man

anthropology (anthrə'poləji) *n.* **1.** science of human beings, their origins, distribution, physical attributes and culture **2.** aspect of Christian teaching dealing with the origin, nature and destiny of human beings —**anthropo'logical** *a.* —**anthro'pologist** *n.*

anthropomorphize (anthrəpə'mörfīz) *vt.* ascribe human attributes to (God or an animal) —**anthropo'morphic** *a.* —**anthropo'morphism** *n.* —**anthropo'morphous** *a.* shaped like human being

anti ('antī, 'anti) *inf. a.* **1.** opposed to party *etc.* —*n.* **2.** opponent

anti- (*comb. form*) against, as in *antiaircraft, antispasmodic.* Such words are not given here where meaning may easily be inferred from simple word

antibiosis (antibī'ōsis, antī-) *n.* association between two organisms that is harmful to one of them

antibiotic (antibī'otik, antī-) *n.* **1.** any of various chemical, fungal or synthetic substances, *esp.* penicillin, used against bacterial or fungal infection —*a.* **2.** of antibiotics

antibody ('antibodi) *n.* substance produced by the body in response to the presence of antigens

Antichrist ('antikrīst) *n.* **1.** *Bible* the antagonist of Christ **2.** (*sometimes* **a-**) an enemy of Christ or Christianity

anticipate (an'tisipāt) *vt.* **1.** expect **2.** take or consider beforehand **3.** foresee **4.** enjoy in advance —**antici'pation** *n.* —**an'ticipative** *or* **an'ticipatory** *a.*

anticlerical (anti'klerikəl, antī-) *a.* **1.** opposed to influence of clergy, *esp.* in politics —*n.* **2.** supporter of anticlerical party

anticlimax (anti'klīmaks) *n.* **1.** disappointing conclusion to series of events *etc.* **2.** sudden descent to the trivial or ludicrous

anticline ('antiklīn) *n.* formation of stratified rock folded into broad arch so that strata slope down on both sides from common crest

anticoagulant (antikō'agyələnt, antī-) *n.* substance that inhibits blood clotting

antics ('antiks) *pl.n.* absurd or grotesque movements or acts

anticyclone (anti'sīklōn) *n.* system of winds moving round center of high barometric pressure

antidote ('antidōt) *n.* counteracting remedy

antifreeze ('antifrēz) *n.* liquid added to water to lower its freezing point, as in automobile radiators

antigen ('antijən) *n.* substance stimulating production of antibodies in the blood

Antigone (an'tigəni) *n.* in Greek legend, daughter of Oedipus by his mother Jocasta, famed for her heroic attachment to her father and brothers

Antigua and Barbuda (an'tēgə; bär'bōōdə) country comprising three islands of the Lesser Antilles in the eastern Caribbean

antihero ('antihēərō, 'antī-) *n.* central character in novel *etc.*, who lacks traditional heroic virtues

antihistamine (anti'histəmēn, antī-; -min) *n.* drug used *esp.* to treat allergies

antiknock (anti'nok) *n.* compound added to gasoline to reduce knocking in engine

antilogarithm (anti'logəridhəm, antī-) *n.* number whose logarithm is the given number (*also* **'antilog**)

antimacassar (antimə'kasər) *n.* cover to protect back or arms of furniture

antimatter ('antimatər) *n.* hypothetical form of matter composed of antiparticles

antimony ('antimōni) *n. Chem.* metallic element used in alloys, drugs and dyes *Symbol* Sb, at. wt. 121.8, at. no. 51

antinomy (an'tinəmi) *n.* **1.** opposition of one law *etc.* to another **2.** *Philos.* contradiction between two conclusions correctly derived from two laws both assumed to be correct

antinovel ('antinovəl, 'antī-) *n.* prose fiction in which conventional novelistic elements are rejected

antiparticle ('antipärtikəl, 'antī-) *n.* any of group of elementary particles that have same mass as corresponding particle but have charge of equal magnitude but opposite sign

antipasto (anti'pastō, -'päs-) *n.* course of hors d'œuvres in Italian meal (*pl.* **-s**)

antipathy (an'tipəthi) *n.* dislike, aversion —**antipa'thetic** *a.*

antiperspirant (anti'pərspərənt) *n.* substance used to reduce sweating

antiphon ('antifən) *n.* **1.** composition in which verses, lines are sung alternately by two choirs **2.** anthem —**an'tiphonal** *a.*

antipodes (an'tipədēz) *pl.n.* countries, peoples on opposite side of the globe (oft. refers to Aust. and N.Z.) —**an'tipodal** *or* **antipo'dean** *a.*

antipope ('antipōp) *n.* pope elected in opposition to the one regularly chosen

antipyretic (antipī'retik, antī-) *n./a.* (remedy) effective against fever

antique (an'tēk) *n.* **1.** relic of former times, usu. piece of furniture *etc.* that is collected —*a.* **2.** ancient **3.** old-fashioned —**antiquary** ('antikweri) *or* **antiquarian** (anti'kweriən) *n.* student or collector of old things —**antiquated** ('antikwātid) *a.* out-of-date —**antiquity** (an'tikwiti) *n.* **1.** former times **2.** age of Greek and Roman civilization ending with fall of Roman Empire in 5th cent. A.D.

antirrhinum (anti'rīnəm) *n.* genus of plants including snapdragon

antiscorbutic (antiskör'byōōtik, antī-) *n./a.* (agent) preventing or curing scurvy

anti-Semitic *a.* discriminating against Jews —**anti-Semitism** (-'semitizəm) *n.*

antiseptic (anti'septik) *n./a.* **1.** (substance) destroying or preventing the growth of disease-producing microorganisms —*a.* **2.** free from infection

antisocial (anti'sōshəl, antī-) *a.* **1.** avoiding company of other people; unsociable **2.** contrary to interests of society in general

antistatic (anti'statik, antī-) *a.* (of textile *etc.*) retaining sufficient moisture to provide conducting path, thus avoiding effects of static electricity

antithesis (an'tithisis) *n.* **1.** direct opposite **2.** contrast **3.** opposition of ideas (*pl.* **-eses** (-isēz)) —**anti'thetical** *a.* —**anti'thetically** *adv.*

antitoxin (anti'toksin) *n.* serum used to neutralize bacterial poisons

antitrades ('antitrādz, 'antī-) *pl.n.* winds blowing in opposite direction from and above trade winds

antitrust (anti'trust, antī-) *a.* regulating or opposing trusts or similar organizations

antitype ('antitīp) *n.* **1.** person or thing foreshadowed or represented by type or symbol **2.** opposite type

antivenin (anti'venin, antī-) *n.* antitoxin to a venom

antler ('antlər) *n.* branching horn of certain deer —**'antlered** *a.*

antonym ('antənim) *n.* word of opposite meaning to another, *eg cold* is an antonym of *hot*

Antron ('antron) *n.* trade name for a type of nylon

antrum ('antrəm) *n. Anat.* natural cavity or sinus, *esp.* in bone (*pl.* **-tra** (-trə))

anuresis (anyōō'rēsis) *n.* inability to urinate

anus ('ānəs) *n.* the posterior opening of the alimentary canal —**'anal** *a.* of or near the anus

anvil ('anvil) *n.* heavy iron block on which a smith hammers metal into shape

anxious ('angkshəs, 'angshəs) *a.* **1.** troubled, uneasy **2.** concerned —**anxiety** (ang'zīiti) *n. Psych.* emotional reaction of fear to indiscernible source of danger —**'anxiously** *adv.*

any ('eni) *a./pron.* **1.** one indefinitely **2.** some **3.** whatever, whichever —**'anybody** *pron.* any person —**'anyhow** *adv.* in any manner —**any'more** *adv.* any longer; still; nowadays —**'anyone** *pron.* any person at all —**'anything** *pron.* any thing whatever —**'anyway** *adv.* —**'anywhere** *adv.* in or to any place

Anzac ('anzak) *a.* **1.** of Australian-New Zealand Army Corps in WWI —*n.* **2.** soldier of that corps, Gallipoli veteran

ANZUS ('anzəs) Aust., N.Z. and U.S., with reference to security alliance between them

AO 1. account of **2.** and others

aorist ('āərist) *n. Gram.* tense of verb, *esp.* in classical Greek, indicating past action without reference to whether action involved was momentary or continuous

aorta (ā'örtə) *n.* main artery of the body —**a'ortal** *a.* —**aor'titis** *n.* inflammation of the aorta

aoudad ('owdad, 'äōōdad) *n.* a wild sheep of N Afr.

AP 1. additional premium **2.** Associated Press

apace (ə'pās) *adv.* swiftly

Apache (ə'pachi) *n.* **1.** group or member of Amerindian peoples of SW U.S. (*pl.* **A'pache, -s**) **2.** language of these peoples **3.** (ə'pash) (**a-**) member of gang of criminals in Paris

apart (ə'pärt) *adv.* **1.** separately, aside **2.** in pieces

apartheid (ə'pärtīt, -āt) *n. esp.* in S Afr., official government policy of racial segregation

apartment (ə'pärtmənt) *n.* room or rooms, furnished with housekeeping equipment and usu. leased —**apartment building** *or* **house** building containing separate apartments —**apartment hotel** hotel containing apartments as well as accommodation for transients

apathy ('apəthi) *n.* **1.** indifference **2.** lack of emotion —**apa'thetic** *a.* —**apa'thetically** *adv.*

apatite ('apətīt) *n.* common mineral consisting basically of calcium fluorophosphate

APB all points bulletin

ape (āp) *n.* **1.** tailless primate (*eg* chimpanzee, gorilla) **2.** coarse, clumsy person **3.** imitator —*vt.* **4.** imitate —**'apish** *a.* —**'apishly** *adv.* —**'apeman** *n.* apelike primate thought to have been forerunner of modern man

aperient (ə'pēəriənt) *a.* **1.** mildly laxative —*n.* **2.** any mild laxative

aperiodic (āpēəri'odik) *a. Elec.* having no natural period or frequency

apéritif (əperi'tēf) *n.* alcoholic appetizer

aperture ('apərchər) *n.* opening, hole

apex ('āpeks) *n.* **1.** top, peak **2.** vertex (*pl.* **-es, 'apices**) —**'apical** *a.* of, at, or being apex

aphasia (ə'fāzhiə) *n.* dumbness or loss of speech control, due to disease of brain

aphelion (a'fēlyən) *n.* point of planet's orbit farthest from sun (*pl.* **-lia** (-lyə))

aphis ('āfis) *n.* any of various sap-sucking insects (*pl.* **aphides** ('āfidēz)) —**'aphid** *n.* an aphis

aphorism ('afərizəm) *n.* maxim, pithy saying —**'aphorist** *n.* —**apho'ristic** *a.*

aphrodisiac (afrə'diziak) *a.* **1.** exciting sexual desire —*n.* **2.** substance believed to excite sexual desire

apiary ('āpieri) *n.* place where bees are kept —**api'arian** *or* **'apian** *a.* —**'apiarist** *n.* beekeeper —**'apiculture** *n.* breeding and care of bees

apices ('āpisēz, 'a-) *n., pl. of* APEX

apiece (ə'pēs) *adv.* for each

APL computer-programming language designed for the concise representation of algorisms

aplastic anemia (ā'plastik) anemia characterized by defective function of blood-forming organs, caused by toxic agents or arising spontaneously

aplomb (ə'plom) *n.* self-possession, coolness, assurance

APO army post office

apo- *or* **ap-** (*comb. form*) **1.** away from; off, as in *apogee* **2.** separation of, as in *apocarpous*

apocalypse (ə'pokəlips) *n.* **1.** prophetic revelation, of Jewish and Christian writing of 200 B.C. to 150 A.D. **2.** (**A-**) *Bible* Revelation in the Douay Version of the N.T. —**apoca'lyptic** *a.* —**apoca'lyptically** *adv.* —**Apocalypse of Baruch** noncanonical apocalyptic sacred scripture

apocrypha (ə'pokrifə) *n.* religious writing of doubtful authenticity —**a'pocryphal** *a.* spurious —**the Apocrypha** collective name for 14 books orig. in Old Testament

apodosis (ə'podəsis) *n.* consequent clause in conditional sentence, as distinct from protasis or *if* clause (*pl.* **-oses** (-əsēz))

apogee ('apəjē) *n.* **1.** point of moon's or satellite's orbit farthest from the earth **2.** climax

apolitical (āpə'litikəl) *a.* politically neutral

apologia (apə'lōjiə) *n.* written defense of one's beliefs, conduct *etc.*

apologue ('apəlog) *n.* allegory, moral fable

apology (ə'poləji) *n.* **1.** acknowledgment of offense and expression of regret **2.** written or spoken defense **3.** (*with* for) poor substitute —**apolo'getic** *a.* —**apolo'getically** *adv.* —**apolo'getics** *pl.n.* (*with sing. v.*) branch of theology charged with defense of Christianity —**a'pologist** *n.* —**a'pologize** *vi.*

apoplexy ('apəpleksi) *n.* loss of sense and oft. paralysis caused by broken or blocked blood vessel in brain —**apo'plectic** *a.*

apostasy (ə'postəsi) *n.* abandonment of one's religious or other faith —**a'postate** *n./a.*

a posteriori (ā postēəri'ōrī, ā; -rē) **1.** denoting form of inductive reasoning which arrives at causes from effects **2.** empirical

apostle (ə'posəl) *n.* **1.** (*oft.* **A-**) one sent to preach the Gospel, *esp.* one of the first disciples of Jesus **2.** founder of Christian church in a country **3.** leader of reform —**a'postleship** *n.* —**apostolic(al)** (apə'stolik(əl)) *a.* —**Apostles' Creed** concise statement of Christian beliefs —**Apostolic See** see of pope

apostrophe (ə'postrəfi) *n.* **1.** mark (') showing omission of letter or letters in word **2.** digression to appeal to someone dead or absent —**a'postrophize** *v.*

apothecary (ə'pothikeri) *n.* **1.** one who prepares and sells drugs for medical purposes **2.** pharmacy —**apothecaries' measure** system of measurement in which the pound equals 12 ounces (0.373 kilogram)

apothegm ('apəthem) *n.* startling or paradoxical aphorism —**apothegmatic** (apətheg'matik) *a.*

apothem ('apəthem) *n.* perpendicular from center of regular polygon to any of its sides

apotheosis (əpothi'ōsis) *n.* deification, act of raising any person or thing to status of a god (*pl.* **-ses** (-sēz)) —**apo'theosize** *vt.* **1.** deify **2.** glorify, idealize

Appalachian (apə'lāchən) *a.* **1.** of mountain range extending from southern Quebec to northern Alabama —*n.* **2.** Caucasian native or resident of this mountain area —**Appalachian trail** hiking trail through these mountains from central Maine to northern Georgia

appall (ə'pōl) *vt.* dismay, terrify —**ap'palling** *a.* dreadful, terrible

Appaloosa (apə'lōōsə) *n.* rugged saddle horse bred in western N Amer. with a mottled hide, striped hoofs and patches of white hair over the rump and loins

appanage *or* **apanage** ('apənij) *n.* **1.** land or other provision granted by king for support of *esp.* younger son **2.** customary perquisite

apparatus (apə'ratəs, -'rātəs) *n.* **1.** equipment, instruments, for performing any experiment, operation *etc.* **2.** means by which something operates

apparel (ə'parəl) *n.* **1.** clothing —*vt.* **2.** clothe

apparent (ə'parənt) *a.* **1.** seeming **2.** obvious **3.** acknowledged, as in *heir apparent* —**ap'parently** *adv.*

apparition (apə'rishən) *n.* unexpected appearance, *esp.* of ghost

appeal (ə'pēl) *vi.* **1.** make earnest request **2.** be attractive **3.** refer, have recourse **4.** apply to higher court —*n.* **5.** request **6.** reference **7.** supplication —**ap'pealable** *a.* —**ap'pealing** *a.* **1.** making appeal **2.** pleasant, attractive —**ap'pealingly** *adv.* —**ap'pellant** *n.* one who appeals to higher court —**appellate** (ə'pelit) *a.* of appeals

appear (ə'pēər) *vi.* **1.** become visible or present **2.** seem, be plain **3.** be seen in public —**ap'pearance** *n.* **1.** an appearing **2.** aspect **3.** pretense

appease (ə'pēz) *vt.* pacify, quiet, allay, satisfy —**ap'peasable** *a.* —**ap'peasement** *n.*

appellant (ə'pelənt) *n. see* APPEAL

appellation (api'lāshən) *n.* name or title —**ap'pellative** *a./n.*

append (ə'pend) *vt.* join on, add —**ap'pendage** *n.*

appendix (ə'pendiks) *n.* **1.** subsidiary addition to book *etc.* **2.** *Anat.* projection, *esp.* small worm-shaped part of intestine (*pl.* **-dices** (-disēz), **-es**) —**appen'dectomy** *n.* surgical removal of any appendage, *esp.* vermiform appendix —**appendi'citis** *n.* inflammation of vermiform appendix

apperception (apər'sepshən) *n.* **1.** perception **2.** apprehension **3.** the mind's perception of itself as a conscious agent —**apper'ceive** *vt.*

appertain (apər'tān) *vi.* belong, relate, be appropriate

appetence ('apitəns) *or* **appetency** *n.* **1.** desire, craving **2.** sexual appetite —'**appetent** *a.*

appetite ('apitīt) *n.* desire, inclination, *esp.* desire for food —**ap'petitive** *a.* —'**appetizer** *n.* something stimulating to appetite —'**appetizing** *a.* —'**appetizingly** *adv.*

applaud (ə'plöd) *v.* **1.** express approval (of) by hand-clapping —*vt.* **2.** praise; approve —**ap'plauder** *n.* —**ap'plause** *n.* loud approval

apple ('apəl) *n.* **1.** round, firm, fleshy fruit **2.** tree bearing it —'**applejack** *n.* liquor distilled from fermented cider —**apple-pie order** *inf.* perfect order —**apple of one's eye** person or thing very much loved

appliance (ə'plīəns) *n.* piece of equipment, *esp.* electrical

appliqué

appliqué ('aplikā) *n.* **1.** ornaments, embroidery *etc.*, secured to surface of material —*vt.* **2.** ornament thus

apply (ə'plī) *vt.* **1.** utilize, employ **2.** lay or place on **3.** administer, devote —*vi.* **4.** have reference (to) **5.** make request (to) (**-lied, -lying**) —**applicability** (aplikə'biliti) *n.* —**applicable** ('aplikəbəl, ə'plikə-) *a.* relevant —**applicably** ('aplikəbli, ə'plikə-) *adv.* —**applicant** ('aplikənt) *n.* —**application** (apli'kāshən) *n.* **1.** applying something for a particular use **2.** relevance **3.** request for job *etc.* **4.** concentration, diligence —**applicator** ('aplikātər) *n.* device, such as spatula, for applying medicine, glue *etc.* —**ap'plied** *a.* (of skill, science *etc.*) put to practical use

appoint (ə'point) *vt.* **1.** name for, assign to job or position **2.** fix, settle **3.** equip —**ap'pointment** *n.* **1.** engagement to meet **2.** (selection for a) job —*pl.* **3.** fittings

apportion (ə'pörshən) *vt.* divide out in shares —**ap'portionment** *n.*

appose (ə'pōz) *vt.* **1.** place side by side **2.** place (something) near or against another thing

apposite ('apəzit) *a.* suitable, apt —'**appositely** *adv.* —'**appositeness** *n.* —**appo'sition** *n.* **1.** proximity **2.** the placing of one word beside another

appraise (ə'prāz) *vt.* set price on, estimate value of —**ap'praisable** *a.* —**ap'praisal** *or* **ap'praisement** *n.* —**ap'praiser** *n.*

appreciate (ə'prēshiāt) *vt.* **1.** value at true worth **2.** be grateful for **3.** understand **4.** enjoy —*vi.* **5.** rise in value —**ap'preciable** *a.* **1.** estimable **2.** substantial —**ap'preciably** *adv.* —**appreci'ation** *n.* —**ap'preciative** *or* **ap'preciatory** *a.* capable of expressing pleasurable recognition —**ap'preciator** *n.*

apprehend (apri'hend) *vt.* **1.** seize by authority **2.** take hold of **3.** recognize, understand **4.** dread —**apprehensi'bility** *n.* —**appre'hensible** *a.* —**appre'hension** *n.* **1.** dread, anxiety **2.** arrest **3.** conception **4.** ability to understand —**appre'hensive** *a.*

apprentice (ə'prentis) *n.* **1.** person learning a trade under specified conditions **2.** novice —*vt.* **3.** bind as apprentice —**ap'prenticeship** *n.*

apprise (ə'prīz) *vt.* inform

approach (ə'prōch) *v.* **1.** draw near (to) —*vt.* **2.** set about **3.** address request to **4.** approximate to —*n.* **5.** a drawing near **6.** means of reaching or doing **7.** approximation **8.** (*oft. pl.*) friendly overture(s) —**approacha'bility** *n.* —**ap'proachable** *a.*

approbation (aprə'bāshən) *n.* approval

appropriate (ə'prōpriāt) *vt.* **1.** take for oneself **2.** put aside for particular purpose —*a.* (ə'prōpriit) **3.** suitable, fitting —**ap'propriately** *adv.* —**ap'propriateness** *n.* —**appropri'ation** *n.* **1.** act of setting apart for purpose **2.** money set aside by formal action for particular use —**ap'propriative** *a.* —**ap'propriator** *n.*

approve (ə'prōōv) *vt.* **1.** think well of, commend **2.** authorize, agree to —*vi.* **3.** (*usu. with* of) take favorable view —**ap'proval** *n.* —**ap'prover** *n.* —**ap'provingly** *adv.*

approx. approximate(ly)

approximate (ə'proksimit) *a.* **1.** very near, nearly correct **2.** inexact, imprecise —*vt.* (ə'proksimāt) **3.** bring close **4.** be almost the same as —*vi.* (ə'proksimāt) **5.** come near —**ap'proximately** *adv.* —**approxi'mation** *n.* —**ap'proximative** *a.*

appurtenance (ə'pərtinəns) *n.* **1.** less significant thing or part **2.** accessory

Apr. April

après-ski (aprā'skē) *n.* social activities after day's skiing

apricot ('aprikot, 'āpri-) *n.* **1.** orange-colored stone-fruit related to plum —*a.* **2.** of the color of the fruit

April ('āprəl) *n.* fourth month —**April fool** victim of practical joke performed on Apr. 1st (**April Fools' Day** *or* **All Fools' Day**)

a priori (ā prī'ōrī, ä pri'ōri) **1.** denoting deductive reasoning from general principle to expected facts or effects **2.** denoting knowledge gained independently of experience

apron ('āprən) *n.* **1.** cloth, piece of leather *etc.*, worn in front of body to protect clothes, or as part of official dress **2.** in theater, strip of stage before curtain **3.** on airfield, tarmac area where aircraft stand, are loaded *etc.* **4.** *fig.* any of a variety of things resembling these —**apron strings** symbol of dominance or complete control

apropos (aprə'pō) *adv.* **1.** to the purpose **2.** by the way —*a.* **3.** apt, appropriate —**apropos of** concerning

apse (aps) *n.* arched recess, *esp.* in church —'**apsidal** *a.*

apsis ('apsis) *n.* either of two points lying at extremities of eccentric orbit of satellite *etc.* (*pl.* **apsides** ('apsidēz)) (*also* **apse**)

apso ('apsō) *n. see* LHASA APSO (*pl.* **-s**)

apt (apt) *a.* **1.** suitable **2.** likely **3.** prompt, quick-witted **4.** dexterous —'**aptitude** *n.* capacity, fitness —'**aptly** *adv.* —'**aptness** *n.*

apteryx ('aptəriks) *n. see* KIWI (sense 1)

aqua ('akwə) *n.* **1.** water (*pl.* **aquae** ('akwē), **-s**) —*a.* **2.** *see* AQUAMARINE (sense 2) —**aqua regia** ('rējiə) mixture of nitric and hydrochloric acids that dissolves gold and platinum

aquaculture ('akwəkulchər) *n.* hydroponics

Aqualung ('akwəlung) *n.* trade name for apparatus enabling swimmer to breathe underwater

aquamarine (akwəmə'rēn) *n.* **1.** variety of beryl used as gemstone —*a.* **2.** greenish-blue, sea-colored

aquanaut ('akwənöt) *n.* person who works or swims underwater

aquaplane ('akwəplān) *n.* **1.** plank or boat towed by fast motorboat —*vi.* **2.** ride on aquaplane **3.** (of automobile) be in contact with water on road, not with road surface —'**aquaplaning** *n.*

aquarelle (akwə'rel) *n.* picture executed with transparent watercolors

aquarium (ə'kwariəm, -'kwer-) *n.* tank or pond for keeping aquatic animals or plants (*pl.* **-s, -ria** (-riə))

Aquarius (ə'kwariəs, -'kwer-) *n.* (the water-bearer) 11th sign of zodiac, operative c. Jan. 20th–Feb. 18th

aquatic (ə'kwotik, -'kwat-) *a.* living, growing, done in or on water —**a'quatics** *pl.n.* water sports

aquatint ('akwətint) *n.* etching, engraving imitating drawings *etc.*

aqua vitae ('vītē) *Lat. obs.* brandy

aqueduct ('akwidukt) *n.* **1.** artificial channel for water, *esp.* one like bridge **2.** conduit

aqueous ('ākwiəs) *a.* of, like, containing water —**aqueous humor** *Physiol.* fluid between cornea and lens of eye

aquilegia (akwi'lējiə) *n.* columbine

aquiline ('akwilīn) *a.* **1.** relating to eagle **2.** hooked like eagle's beak

Ar *Chem.* argon

AR Arkansas

ar. 1. arrival **2.** arrive(s)

Ar. 1. Arabic **2.** Aramaic

Arab ('arəb) *n.* **1.** native of Arabia **2.** general term for inhabitants of Middle Eastern countries **3.** Arabian horse (small breed used for riding) —**Arabia** (ə'rābiə) *n.* peninsula in southwest Asia, including Saudi Arabia, Yemen, Oman and Aden —**A'rabian** *a.* **1.** of Arabia —*n.* **2.** Arab —'**Arabic** *n.* **1.** language of Arabs —*a.* **2.** of Arabia or Arabs —**Arabian Sea** northwest arm of Indian Ocean, between India and Arabia —**Arabic numeral** one of numbers 1,2,3,4,5,6,7,8,9,0 —**Arab League** regional organization of sovereign states within framework of United Nations

arabesque (arə'besk) *n.* **1.** classical ballet position **2.** fanciful painted or carved ornament of Arabian origin —*a.* **3.** (in style) of arabesque

arabis ('arəbis) *n.* genus of low-growing annual or evergreen perennial garden plants of the cabbage family, with white or pink flowers

arable ('arəbəl) *a.* suitable for plowing or planting crops

Araby ('arəbi) *n. obs., poet.* Arabia

arachnid (ə'raknid) *n.* land-living arthropod with four pairs of legs, *eg* scorpion, spider, mite and tick —**a'rachnoid** *a.* —**arach'nology** *n.*

Aramaic (arə'māik) *n.* **1.** ancient Semitic language of Middle East —*a.* **2.** of, relating to or using this language

Aran ('arən) *a.* (of sweaters *etc.*) made with naturally oily, unbleached wool, oft. with complicated pattern

Arapaho (ə'rapəhō) *n.* member of Amerindian people of Algonquian linguistic stock, orig. of Plains, now living in Montana and Wyoming (*pl.* **Arapaho, -s**)

Araucanian (ərow'käniən) *n.* **1.** American Indian of central Chile and Argentina **2.** language of Araucanians, which constitutes a language family

Arawak ('arəwäk) *n.* **1.** member of American Indian people of Arawakan group now living chiefly along the coast of Guyana **2.** their language —**Ara'wakan** *n.* **1.** member of group of American Indian people of S Amer. and the W Indies **2.** their language, which constitutes a language family

arbiter ('ärbitər) *n.* judge, umpire —**ar'bitrament** *n.* —**arbi'trarily** *adv.* —'**arbitrary** *a.* **1.** not bound by rules, despotic **2.** random —'**arbitrate** *vt.* **1.** decide (dispute) **2.** submit to, settle by arbitration —*vi.* **3.** act as umpire —**arbi'tration** *n.* hearing, settling of disputes, *esp.* industrial and legal, by impartial referee(s) —'**arbitrator** *n.*

arbor[1] ('ärbər) *n.* **1.** rotating shaft in machine on which grinding wheel is fitted **2.** rotating shaft

arbor[2] ('ärbər) *n.* leafy glade *etc.*, sheltered by trees —**Arbor Day** day designated for planting trees

arboreal (är'böriəl) *a.* relating to trees

—**arbo'rescent** *a.* having characteristics of tree —**arbo'retum** *n.* place for cultivating specimens of trees (*pl.* **-s, -ta** (-tə)) —**'arboriculture** *n.* forestry, cultivation of trees

arbutus (är'byōōtəs) *n.* genus of half-hardy and hardy shrubs or trees of the heather family, with edible fruits (*pl.* **-es**)

arc (ärk) *n.* **1.** part of circumference of circle or similar curve **2.** luminous electric discharge between two conductors —*vi.* **3.** form an arc —**arc lamp** —**arc light**

ARC American Red Cross

arcade (är'kād) *n.* **1.** row of arches on pillars **2.** covered walk or avenue, *esp.* lined by shops

Arcadian (är'kādiən) *a.* **1.** of idealized Arcadia of pastoral poetry **2.** rustic, bucolic —*n.* **3.** person who leads simple rural life

arcane (är'kān) *a.* **1.** mysterious **2.** esoteric

arch[1] (ärch) *n.* **1.** curved structure in building, supporting itself over open space by pressure of stones one against the other **2.** any similar structure **3.** curved shape **4.** curved part of sole of foot —*v.* **5.** form, make into, an arch —**arched** *a.* —**'archway** *n.*

arch[2] (ärch) *a.* **1.** chief **2.** experienced, expert **3.** superior, knowing; coyly playful —**'archly** *adv.* —**'archness** *n.*

arch. **1.** archaic **2.** architecture

arch- *or* **archi-** (*comb. form*) chief, as in *archenemy.* Such words are not given here where the meaning may easily be inferred from the simple word

-arch (*comb. form*) leader; ruler; chief, as in *patriarch, monarch, matriarch*

archaeology *or* **archeology** (ärki'oləji) *n.* study of ancient times from remains of art, implements *etc.* —**archaeo'logical** *or* **archeo'logical** *a.* —**archae'ologist** *or* **arche'ologist** *n.*

archaeopteryx (ärki'optəriks) *n.* extinct bird of Jurassic times, with teeth, long tail and well-developed wings

archaic (är'kāik) *a.* old, primitive —**ar'chaically** *adv.* —**'archaism** *n.* the use of obsolete words or syntax for deliberate effect

archangel ('ärkānjəl) *n.* **1.** chief angel, in Christianity Michael, in Islam Gabriel, Michael, Azrael and Israfel **2.** in celestial hierarchy, order higher than angel, lower than principality

archduke (ärch'dyōōk, -'dōōk) *n.* **1.** sovereign prince **2.** prince of imperial family of Austria (**arch'duchess** *fem.*) —**arch'ducal** *a.* —**arch'duchy** *n.*

archery ('ärchəri) *n.* skill, sport of shooting with bow and arrow (*also* **tox'ophily**) —**'archer** *n.*

archetype ('ärkitīp) *n.* **1.** prototype **2.** perfect specimen —**arche'typal** *a.*

archfiend (ärch'fēnd) *n.* (*oft.* **A-**) the devil; Satan

archiepiscopal (ärkii'piskəpəl) *a.* of archbishop —**archie'piscopate** *n.*

archimandrite (ärki'mandrīt) *n.* dignitary in Eastern Catholic Church ranking below bishop, *esp.* head of monastery or group of monasteries

Archimedes (ärki'mēdēz) *n.* Sicilian mathematician and physical scientist (287-212 B.C.) who made many discoveries, *esp.* the principle of the lever —**Archi'medean** *a.* —**Archimedean solid** polyhedron whose faces are all regular polygons not congruent to one another —**Archimedes' screw** device used to raise water

archipelago (ärki'peləgō) *n.* **1.** group of islands **2.** sea full of small islands, *esp.* Aegean (*pl.* **-es, -s**) —**archipelagic** (ärkipə'lajik) *a.*

architect ('ärkitekt) *n.* **1.** one qualified to design and supervise construction of buildings **2.** contriver —**architec'tonic** *a.* of or resembling architecture —**archi'tectural** *a.* —**'architecture** *n.*

architrave ('ärkitrāv) *n. Archit.* **1.** lowest division of entablature **2.** ornamental band round door or window opening

archives ('ärkīvz) *pl.n.* **1.** collection of records, documents *etc.* about institution, family *etc.* **2.** place where these are kept —**ar'chival** *a.* —**archivist** ('ärkivist) *n.*

archpriest (ärch'prēst) *n.* **1.** formerly, chief assistant to bishop **2.** senior priest

Arctic ('ärktik) *a.* **1.** of northern polar regions **2.** (**a-**) very cold —*n.* **3.** region round North Pole —**Arctic Circle** imaginary circle around earth at latitude 66° 32′ N

ardent ('ärdənt) *a.* **1.** fiery **2.** passionate —**'ardency** *n.* —**'ardently** *adv.* —**'ardor** *n.* **1.** enthusiasm **2.** zeal

arduous ('ärjōōəs) *a.* **1.** hard to accomplish, difficult **2.** strenuous; laborious —**'arduously** *adv.* —**'arduousness** *n.*

are[1] (är; *unstressed* ər) *pres. ind. pl. of* BE

are[2] (āər, är) *n.* unit of measure, 100 square meters

area ('āəriə) *n.* **1.** extent, expanse of any surface **2.** two-dimensional expanse enclosed by boundary (area of square, circle *etc.*) **3.** region **4.** part, section **5.** subject, field of activity **6.** small sunken yard —**area code** 3-digit number identifying telephone service area in a country

areca ('arikə, ə'rēkə) *n.* genus of palms, including betel palm

arena (ə'rēnə) *n.* **1.** enclosure for sports events *etc.* **2.** space in middle of amphitheater or stadium **3.** sphere, scene of conflict

arenaceous (ari'nāshəs) *a.* **1.** composed of sand **2.** growing in sandy soil

aren't (ärnt) **1.** *contraction of* are not **2.** *inf., chiefly* **UK** (used in interrogative sentences) *contraction of* am not

areola (ə'rēələ) *n.* **1.** *Biol.* space outlined on surface, such as area between veins on leaf **2.** *Anat.* any small circular area, such as pigmented ring around human nipple (*pl.* **-lae** (-lē), **-s**)

arête (əˈrāt) *n.* sharp ridge that separates glacial valleys

argent (ˈärjənt) *n.* **1.** silver —*a.* **2.** silver, silvery-white, *esp.* in heraldry

Argentina (ärjənˈtēnə) *n.* country in South America bounded north by Bolivia, northeast by Paraguay, east by Brazil, Uruguay and the Atlantic Ocean, and west by Chile —**Argentinian** (ärjənˈtiniən) *a./n.*

argon (ˈärgon) *n. Chem.* noble gas used for filling fluorescent and incandescent lamps *Symbol* Ar, at. wt. 39.944, at. no. 18

argosy (ˈärgəsi) *n. Poet.* large richly-laden merchant ship

argot (ˈärgət, -gō) *n.* special vocabulary of any set cf persons

argue (ˈärgyōō) *vi.* **1.** quarrel, dispute **2.** offer reasons —*vt.* **3.** prove by reasoning **4.** discuss —ˈ**arguable** *a.* —ˈ**arguably** *adv.* as can be argued —ˈ**arguer** *n.* —ˈ**argument** *n.* **1.** quarrel **2.** reasoning **3.** discussion **4.** theme —**argumenˈtation** *n.* —**arguˈmentative** *a.*

Argus (ˈärgəs) *n.* fabulous being with a hundred eyes —**Argus-eyed** *a.* watchful

aria (ˈäriə) *n.* composition for solo voice with instrumental accompaniment in opera, oratorio or cantata

arid (ˈarid) *a.* **1.** parched with heat, dry **2.** dull —**aˈridity** *n.*

Aries (ˈariēz, ˈer-) *n.* (the ram) 1st sign of zodiac, operative c. Mar. 21st–Apr. 21st

aright (əˈrīt) *adv.* rightly

arise (əˈrīz) *vi.* **1.** come about **2.** get up **3.** rise (up), ascend (**aˈrose, arisen** (əˈrizən), **aˈrising**)

aristocracy (ariˈstokrəsi) *n.* **1.** nobility **2.** upper classes **3.** government by the best in birth or fortune —**aˈristocrat** *n.* —**aristoˈcratic** *a.* **1.** noble **2.** elegant —**aristoˈcratically** *adv.*

Aristotle (ˈaristotəl) *n.* Greek philosopher (384-322 B.C.), master of every field of learning known, pupil of Plato and tutor to Alexander the Great —**Aristotelian** *or* **Aristotelean** (aristəˈtēlyən) *a./n.* —**Aristotelian elements** fire, air, earth and water —**Aristotelian theory** notion that these elements formed all matter in the world

arithmetic (əˈrithmətik) *n.* **1.** science of numbers **2.** art of reckoning by figures —**arithˈmetic(al)** *a.* —**arithˈmetically** *adv.* —**arithmeˈtician** *n.* —**arithmetic mean** average value of set of terms or quantities, expressed as their sum divided by their number (*also* ˈ**average**) —**arithmetic progression** sequence, each term of which differs from succeeding term by constant amount

Arizona (ariˈzōnə) *n.* Mountain state of the U.S., admitted to the Union in 1912. Abbrev.: **Ariz., AZ** (with ZIP code)

ark (ärk) *n.* **1.** Noah's vessel **2.** structure giving protection and safety

Ark (ärk) *n. Judaism* **1.** most sacred symbol of God's presence among Hebrew people, carried in their journey from Sinai to Promised Land (*also* **Ark of the Covenant**) **2.** receptacle for the scrolls of the Law (*also* **Holy Ark**)

Arkansas (ˈärkənsö) *n.* West South Central state of the U.S., admitted to the Union in 1836. Abbrev.: **Ark., AR** (with ZIP code)

arm[1] (ärm) *n.* **1.** limb extending from shoulder to wrist **2.** anything projecting from main body, as branch of sea, supporting rail of chair *etc.* **3.** sleeve —ˈ**armlet** *n.* band worn round arm —ˈ**armchair** *n.* —ˈ**armful** *n.* —ˈ**armhole** *n.* —ˈ**armpit** *n.* hollow under arm at shoulder

arm[2] (ärm) *vt.* **1.** supply with weapons, furnish **2.** prepare (bomb *etc.*) for use —*vi.* **3.** take up arms —*n.* **4.** weapon **5.** branch of army **6.** power, *esp.* of law —*pl.* **7.** weapons **8.** war, military exploits **9.** official heraldic symbols —ˈ**armament** *n.* —**armed forces** military, naval and air forces of a nation —**arms race** competition among nations in accumulating weapons

armada (ärˈmädə) *n.* large number of ships or aircraft

armadillo (ärməˈdilō) *n.* any of several small Amer. nocturnal burrowing mammals protected by bands of bony plates (*pl.* **-s**)

Armageddon (ärməˈgedən) *n.* **1.** *Bible* place designated as scene of final battle at end of world **2.** catastrophic and extremely destructive conflict

armature (ˈärməchōōər) *n.* **1.** part of electric machine, *esp.* revolving structure in electric motor, generator **2.** rigid framework used by sculptor as foundation for moldable substance

Armenia (ärˈmēniə) *n.* **1.** ancient country in west Asia **2.** popular name for Armenian Soviet Socialist Republic —**Arˈmenian** *a.* **1.** of, relating to Armenia, its inhabitants or language —*n.* **2.** native or inhabitant of Armenia **3.** the Indo-European language of Armenians, which is the only member of its branch

armistice (ˈärmistis) *n.* truce, suspension of fighting —**Armistice Day** anniversary of signing of armistice that ended World War I (Nov. 11th)

armoire (ärmˈwär) *n.* large cabinet, orig. used for storing weapons

armor (ˈärmər) *n.* **1.** defensive covering or dress **2.** plating of tanks, warships *etc.* **3.** armored fighting vehicles, as tanks —ˈ**armorer** *n.* —**arˈmorial** *a.* relating to heraldic arms —ˈ**armory** *n.* —**armor plate** tough heavy steel oft. hardened on surface, used for protecting warships *etc.*

army (ˈärmi) *n.* **1.** large body of men armed for warfare and under military command **2.**

host, great number —**army corps** military unit of U.S. Army comprising at least two divisions and commanded by a lieutenant general

arnica ('ärnikə) *n. Bot.* genus of hardy perennials. A tincture of *Arnica montana* is used for sprains and bruises

aroma (ə'rōmə) *n.* **1.** sweet smell, fragrance **2.** peculiar charm —**aro'matic** *a. Chem.* of the class of cyclic organic compounds derived from or having similar properties to benzene —**a'romatize** *vt.*

arose (ə'rōz) *pt. of* ARISE

around (ə'rownd) *prep.* **1.** on all sides of **2.** somewhere in or near **3.** approximately (of time) —*adv.* **4.** on every side **5.** in a circle **6.** here and there, nowhere in particular **7.** *inf.* present in or at some place

arouse (ə'rowz) *vt.* **1.** awaken **2.** stimulate

arpeggio (är'pejiō) *n. Mus.* playing of a chord with its notes sounded in succession (*pl.* **-s**)

arquebus ('ärkwibəs) *n. see* HARQUEBUS

arr. 1. arranged **2.** arrival **3.** arrive(d)

arrack ('arək) *n.* coarse spirit distilled from rice *etc.*

arraign (ə'rān) *vt.* accuse, indict, put on trial —**ar'raigner** *n.* —**ar'raignment** *n.*

arrange (ə'rānj) *vt.* **1.** set in order **2.** arrive at agreement about **3.** plan **4.** adapt, as music **5.** settle, as dispute —**ar'rangement** *n.*

arrant ('arənt) *a.* downright, notorious —**'arrantly** *adv.*

arras ('arəs) *n.* tapestry

array (ə'rā) *n.* **1.** order, *esp.* military order **2.** dress **3.** imposing show, splendor —*vt.* **4.** set in order **5.** dress, equip, adorn

arrears (ə'rēərz) *pl.n.* amount unpaid or undone

arrest (ə'rest) *vt.* **1.** detain by legal authority **2.** stop **3.** catch (attention) —*n.* **4.** seizure by warrant **5.** making prisoner —**ar'resting** *a.* attracting attention, striking —**ar'restor** *n.* **1.** person who arrests **2.** mechanism to stop or slow moving object

arrière-pensée (aryerpā'sā) *Fr.* hidden meaning or purpose

arris ('aris) *n.* sharp ridge or edge

arrive (ə'rīv) *vi.* **1.** reach destination **2.** (*with* at) reach, attain **3.** *inf.* succeed —**ar'rival** *n.*

arriviste (arē'vēst) *n.* person who is a new and uncertain arrival

arrogance ('arəgəns) *n.* aggressive conceit —**'arrogant** *a.* **1.** proud **2.** overbearing —**'arrogantly** *adv.*

arrogate ('arəgāt) *vt.* **1.** claim for oneself without justification **2.** attribute to another without justification

arrow ('arō) *n.* pointed shaft shot from bow —**'arrowhead** *n.* **1.** head of arrow **2.** any triangular shape

arrowroot ('arōroot) *n.* nutritious starch from W Indian plant, used as a food

arroyo (ə'roiō) *n.* **1.** watercourse in arid region **2.** water-carved channel (*pl.*-**s**)

ARS Agricultural Research Service

arsenal ('ärsnəl) *n.* magazine of stores for warfare, guns, ammunition

arsenic ('ärsnik) *n. Chem.* metalloid element, solid, brittle, and highly poisonous *Symbol* As, at. wt. 74.9, at. no. 33 —**arsenical** (är'senikəl) *a.* —**arsenious** (är'sēniəs) *a.*

arson ('ärsən) *n.* crime of intentionally setting property on fire

art (ärt) *n.* **1.** skill **2.** human skill as opposed to nature **3.** creative skill in painting, poetry, music *etc.* **4.** any of the works produced thus **5.** profession, craft **6.** knack **7.** contrivance, cunning, trick **8.** system of rules —*pl.* **9.** certain branches of learning, languages, history *etc.*, as distinct from natural science **10.** wiles —**'artful** *a.* wily —**'artfully** *adv.* —**'artfulness** *n.* —**'artist** *n.* **1.** one who practices fine art, *esp.* painting **2.** one who makes his craft a fine art —**ar'tiste** *n.* professional entertainer, singer, dancer *etc.* —**ar'tistic** *a.* —**ar'tistically** *adv.* —**'artistry** *n.* —**'artless** *a.* natural, frank —**'artlessly** *adv.* —**'artlessness** *n.* —**'arty** *a.* ostentatiously artistic —**art therapy** practice of painting, modeling, craftwork *etc.* as curative activity of patients

art. 1. article **2.** artificial

arteriosclerosis (ärtēəriōskli'rōsis) *n.* hardening of the arteries (*pl.* **-ses** (-sēz))

artery ('ärtəri) *n.* **1.** one of tubes carrying blood from heart **2.** any main channel of communications —**ar'terial** *a.* **1.** pert. to an artery **2.** of or relating to through-traffic facilities

artesian well (är'tēzhən) **1.** deep well in which water rises by internal pressure **2.** deep-bored well

arthritis (är'thrītis) *n.* painful inflammation of joint(s) —**arthritic** (är'thritik) *a./n.*

arthropod ('ärthrəpod) *n.* any member of a phylum of invertebrate animals with segmented bodies and paired jointed legs such as insects, spiders and centipedes

Arthur[1] ('ärthər) *n.* **1.** hero of a great cycle of medieval romance **2.** 6th-cent. Welsh chieftain —**Arthurian** (är'thyooəriən, -'thoo͝ə-) *a.* —**Arthurian legend** body of literature from 6th cent. to present, based on the combined mythical and historical Arthur

Arthur[2] ('ärthər) *n.* **Chester Alan.** the 21st President of the U.S. (1881-85)

artichoke ('ärtichōk) *n.* **1.** thistlelike perennial **2.** its edible flower —**Jerusalem artichoke** sunflower with edible tubers like potato

article ('ärtikəl) *n.* **1.** item, object **2.** short written piece **3.** paragraph, section **4.** *Gram.* words *the, a, an* **5.** clause in contract **6.** rule, condition —*vt.* **7.** bind as apprentice

articular (är'tikyələr) *a.* of joints or structural components in joint

articulate (är'tikyəlit) *a.* **1.** able to express oneself fluently **2.** jointed **3.** (of speech) clear, distinct —*vt.* (är'tikyəlāt) **4.** joint **5.** utter distinctly —*vi.* (är'tikyəlāt) **6.** speak —**ar'ticulated** *a.* jointed —**ar'ticulately** *adv.* —**ar'ticulateness** *n.* —**articu'lation** *n.*

artifact ('ärtifakt) *n.* something made by man, *esp.* by hand

artifice ('ärtifis) *n.* **1.** contrivance **2.** trick **3.** cunning; skill —**ar'tificer** *n.* craftsman —**arti'ficial** *a.* **1.** manufactured, synthetic **2.** insincere —**artifici'ality** *n.* —**arti'ficially** *adv.* —**artificial respiration** method of restarting person's breathing after it has stopped

artillery (är'tiləri) *n.* **1.** large guns on wheels **2.** troops who use them

artisan ('ärtizən) *n.* craftsman; skilled mechanic; manual worker

artiste (är'tēst) *n. see* ART

Art Nouveau ('är nōō'vō; *Fr.* ar nōō'vō) style of art and architecture of 1890s, characterized by sinuous outlines and stylized natural forms

arum lily ('arəm, 'er-) plant with large white flower

ARV *Bible* American Revised Version

-ary (*comb. form*) **1.** of; related to; belonging to, as in *cautionary* **2.** person or thing connected with, as in *missionary, aviary*

Aryan ('ariən, 'er-) *a.* **1.** relating to Indo-European family of languages **2.** non-Jewish and Caucasian, *esp.* Nordic —*n.* **3.** member or descendant of prehistoric people who spoke Indo-European **4.** (in Nazi doctrine) non-Jewish Caucasian, *esp.* of Nordic stock

as (az; əz) *adv./conj. denoting* **1.** comparison **2.** similarity **3.** equality **4.** identity **5.** concurrence **6.** reason

As *Chem.* arsenic

AS **1.** Anglo-Saxon (*also* **A.S.**) **2.** antisubmarine

A.S.A. American Standards Association

asafetida *or* **asafoetida** (asə'fetidə) *n.* bitter resin with unpleasant smell, obtained from roots of some umbelliferous plants, formerly used medicinally

asap as soon as possible

asbestos (as'bestəs) *n.* fibrous mineral which does not burn —**asbestosis** (asbes'tōsis) *n.* lung disease caused by inhalation of asbestos fiber

ASCAP ('askap) American Society of Composers, Authors and Publishers

ascariasis (askə'rīəsis) *n.* infestation with the giant intestinal roundworm

ascend (ə'send) *vi.* **1.** climb, rise —*vt.* **2.** walk up, climb, mount —**as'cendancy** *or* **as'cendency** *n.* control, dominance —**as'cendant** *or* **as'cendent** *a.* rising —**as'cension** *n.* —**as'cent** *n.* rise

Ascension Day (ə'senchən) 40th day after Easter, when Ascension of Christ into heaven is celebrated

ascertain (asər'tān) *vt.* get to know, find out, determine —**ascer'tainable** *a.* —**ascer'tainment** *n.*

ascetic (ə'setik) *n.* **1.** one who practices severe self-denial —*a.* **2.** rigidly abstinent, austere —**as'cetically** *adv.* —**as'ceticism** *n.*

ascites (ə'sītēz) *n.* accumulation of large amounts of fluid in the abdomen (*pl.* **ascites**)

ascorbic acid (ə'skörbik) vitamin C

ascot ('askət) *n.* **1.** broad neck scarf looped under the chin —*n./a.* **2.** (**A-**) (of the) racecourse and horse races at Ascot Heath in Berkshire, England

ascribe (ə'skrīb) *vt.* attribute, impute, assign —**as'cribable** *a.* —**ascription** (ə'skripshən) *n.*

aseptic (ā'septik, ə-) *a.* germ-free —**a'sepsis** *n.*

asexual (ā'sekshōōəl) *a.* without sex

ash[1] (ash) *n.* **1.** dust or remains of anything burnt —*pl.* **2.** ruins **3.** remains, *eg* of cremated body —**'ashen** *a.* **1.** like ashes **2.** pale —**'ashy** *a.* —**ash can** metal receptacle for refuse (*also* **garbage can, trash can**) —**Ashcan school** early 20th-century group of American realist painters whose subject was urban life —**'ashtray** *n.* receptacle for tobacco ash, cigarette butts *etc.* —**Ash Wednesday** first day of Lent —**the Ashes** symbol of victory in cricket test-match series between England and Australia

ash[2] (ash) *n.* **1.** any of a genus (*Fraxinus*) of deciduous trees of the olive family with opposite compound leaves, catkin-like flowers and winged seeds in drooping clusters **2.** its tough fine-grained elastic wood

ashamed (ə'shāmd) *a.* affected with shame, abashed

Ashkenazi (ashkə'nazi) *n.* **1.** Jew in or from central eastern Europe (*pl.* **-zim** (-zim)) —*a.* **2.** of Ashkenazim

ashlar ('ashlər) *n.* hewn or squared building stone

ashore (ə'shör) *adv.* to or on shore

ashram ('äshrəm) *n.* religious retreat or community where Hindu holy man lives

Asia ('āzhə) *n.* continent in eastern hemisphere bounded by Europe and the Arctic, Pacific and Indian oceans —**'Asian** *a.* **1.** of Asia —*n.* **2.** native of Asia or descendant of one **3.** **UK** person orig. from Bangladesh, India or Pakistan —**Asi'atic** *a.* —**Asia Minor** the peninsula in west Asia between the Black and Mediterranean Seas

aside (ə'sīd) *adv.* **1.** to or on one side **2.** privately —*n.* **3.** words spoken in an undertone not to be heard by some person present

asinine ('asinīn) *a.* of or like an ass, silly —**asininity** (asi'niniti) *n.*

ask (äsk) *vt.* **1.** request, require, question, invite —*vi.* **2.** make inquiry or request

askance (ə'skans) *or* **askant** (ə'skant) *adv.*

1. sideways, awry 2. with a side look or meaning —**look askance** view with suspicion

askew (ə'skyōō) *adv.* awry

aslant (ə'slänt) *adv.* on the slant, obliquely, athwart

asleep (ə'slēp) *a.* sleeping, at rest

asocial (ā'sōshəl) *a.* 1. avoiding contact 2. unconcerned about welfare of others 3. hostile to society

asp (asp) *n.* small venomous snake of Egypt

asparagus (ə'sparəgəs) *n.* perennial plant of lily family, cultivated for edible shoot (*also* **sparrow grass**)

aspect ('aspekt) *n.* 1. look 2. view 3. appearance 4. expression

aspen ('aspən) *n.* any of several N Amer. poplars with leaves that flutter in the slightest breeze

aspergillosis (aspərji'lōsis) *n.* fungus disease attacking the skin, ear, nose, lungs and other parts of body

asperity (a'speriti) *n.* 1. roughness 2. harshness 3. coldness

aspersion (ə'spərzhən, -shən) *n.* 1. (*usu. in pl.*) malicious remarks 2. slanderous attack

asphalt ('asfölt) *n.* 1. brown-to-black bituminous substance found in natural beds and also obtained as residue in refining petroleum 2. asphaltic composition used for pavements and as waterproof coating —**as'phaltic** *a.* —**asphalt jungle** big city

asphodel ('asfədel) *n.* plant with clusters of yellow or white flowers

asphyxia (as'fiksiə) *n.* suffocation —**as'phyxiate** *v.* —**as'phyxiated** *a.* —**asphyxi'ation** *n.*

aspic ('aspik) *n.* 1. jelly used to coat meat, eggs, fish *etc.* 2. *Bot.* species of lavender

aspidistra (aspi'distrə) *n.* plant with broad tapered leaves (*also* **cast-iron plant**)

aspire (ə'spīər) *vi.* 1. desire eagerly 2. rise to great height —**aspirant** ('aspirənt) *n.* 1. one who aspires 2. candidate —**aspirate** ('aspirāt) *vt.* pronounce with full breathing, as 'h' —**aspiration** (aspi'rāshən) *n.* —**aspirator** ('aspirātər) *n.* device employing suction, such as jet pump or one for removing fluids from body cavity —**as'piring** *a.* —**as'piringly** *adv.*

aspirin ('asprin) *n.* (a tablet of) drug used to allay pain and fever

ass[1] (as) *n.* 1. quadruped of horse family 2. contemptible person

ass[2] (as) *n. offens.* 1. buttocks 2. anus 3. sexual intercourse —**smart ass** *see* **smart aleck** *at* SMART

assagai ('asəgī) *n. see* ASSEGAI

assail (ə'sāl) *vt.* attack, assault —**as'sailable** *a.* —**as'sailant** *n.*

Assamese (asə'mēz) *n./a.* 1. (native or inhabitant) of Assam, India (*pl.* **-ese**) —*n.* 2. the Indic language of the Assamese, one of the languages of the constitution of India

assassin (ə'sasin) *n.* 1. one who kills, *esp.* prominent person, by treacherous violence 2. murderer —**as'sassinate** *vt.* —**assassi'nation** *n.*

assault (ə'sölt) *n.* 1. attack, *esp.* sudden —*vt.* 2. attack —**assault and battery** *Law* threat of attack to person followed by actual attack

assay (ə'sā, 'asā) *v.* 1. test (*esp.* proportions of metals) in alloy or ore —*n.* ('asā, ə'sā) 2. analysis, *esp.* of metals 3. trial, test —**as'sayer** *n.*

assegai *or* **assagai** ('asəgī) *n.* slender spear of S Afr. tribes

assemble (ə'sembəl) *v.* 1. meet, bring together 2. collect —*vt.* 3. put together (of machinery *etc.*) —**as'semblage** *n.* —**as'sembly** *n.* 1. gathering, meeting 2. assembling —**assembly line** sequence of machines, workers in factory assembling product

assent (ə'sent) *vi.* 1. concur, agree —*n.* 2. acquiescence, agreement, compliance

assert (ə'sərt) *vt.* 1. declare strongly 2. insist upon —**as'sertion** *n.* —**as'sertive** *a.* —**as'sertively** *adv.*

assess (ə'ses) *vt.* 1. fix value of 2. evaluate, estimate, *esp.* for taxation 3. fix amount of (tax or fine) 4. impose tax or fine on (a person *etc.*) —**as'sessable** *a.* —**as'sessment** *n.* —**as'sessor** *n.*

asset ('aset) *n.* 1. valuable or useful person, thing —*pl.* 2. property available to pay debts, *esp.* of insolvent debtor

asseverate (ə'sevərāt) *vt.* assert solemnly —**asseve'ration** *n.*

assiduous (ə'sijōōəs) *a.* persevering, attentive, diligent —**assiduity** (asi'dyōōiti, -'dōō-) *n.* —**as'siduously** *adv.*

assign (ə'sīn) *vt.* 1. appoint to job *etc.* 2. allot, apportion, fix 3. ascribe 4. transfer —*n.* 5. assignee —**as'signable** *a.* —**assignation** (asig'nāshən) *n.* 1. secret meeting 2. appointment to meet —**assignee** (asi'nē) *n. Law* person to whom property *etc.* is transferred —**as'signment** *n.* 1. act of assigning 2. allotted duty —**assignor** (asi'nör) *n.*

assimilate (ə'similāt) *vt.* 1. learn and understand 2. make similar 3. absorb into the system —**as'similable** *a.* —**assimi'lation** *n.* —**as'similative** *a.*

assist (ə'sist) *v.* 1. give help 2. work as assistant (to) —**as'sistance** *n.* —**as'sistant** *n.* helper —**assistant professor** member of college or university faculty who ranks above instructor and below associate professor

assize (ə'sīz) *n.* 1. enactment made by legislature 2. statute regulating weights and measures 3. fixed or customary standard 4. judicial inquest

assn. association

assoc. 1. associate 2. associated 3. association

associate (ə'sōshiāt, -si-) *vt.* 1. link, connect, *esp.* as ideas in mind 2. join —*vi.* 3. keep company 4. combine, unite —*n.* (ə'sōshiit, -si-) 5. companion, partner 6. friend, ally 7.

subordinate member of association —*a.* (ə'sōshiit, -si-) 8. affiliated —**associ'ation** *n.* society, club —**associate professor** member of college or university faculty who ranks above assistant professor and below professor —**association football** soccer

assonance ('asənəns) *n.* **1.** likeness in sound **2.** rhyming of vowels only —**'assonant** *a.*

assort (ə'sŏrt) *vt.* **1.** classify, arrange —*vi.* **2.** match, agree, harmonize —**as'sorted** *a.* mixed —**as'sortment** *n.*

ASSR Autonomous Soviet Socialist Republic

asst. assistant

assuage (ə'swāj) *vt.* **1.** soften, pacify **2.** soothe —**as'suagement** *n.*

assume (ə'sōōm) *vt.* **1.** take for granted **2.** pretend to **3.** take upon oneself **4.** claim —**assumption** (ə'sumpshən) *n.* —**assumptive** (ə'sumptiv) *a.* —**Assumption of Moses** noncanonical apocalyptic sacred scripture

assure (ə'shōōər) *vt.* **1.** tell positively, promise **2.** make sure **3.** insure against loss **4.** affirm —**as'surance** *n.* —**as'sured** *a.* sure —**assuredly** (ə'shōōəridli) *adv.*

A.S.T. Atlantic Standard Time

astatic (ā'statik) *a. Phys.* having no tendency to take fixed position

astatine ('astətēn) *n. Chem.* highly unstable radioactive element of the halogen group *Symbol* At, at. wt. 210, at. no. 85

aster ('astər) *n.* **1.** any of various fall-blooming perennials of the daisy family with showy radiated flowers **2.** structure formed in cell radiating around centrosome during meiosis or mitosis

asterisk ('astərisk) *n.* **1.** star (*) used in printing —*vt.* **2.** mark thus —**'asterism** *n.*

astern (ə'stərn) *adv.* **1.** in or toward the rear of ship **2.** backward

asteroid ('astəroid) *n.* **1.** small planet —*a.* **2.** star-shaped

asthma ('azmə) *n.* condition in which bronchial tubes go into spasm resulting in labored breathing and wheezing —**asth'matic** *a./n.* —**asth'matically** *adv.*

astigmatism (ə'stigmətizəm) *n.* inability of lens to focus clearly all portions of horizontal, diagonal or vertical lines —**astig'matic** *a.*

astilbe (ə'stilbi) *n.* genus of herbaceous perennials of the saxifrage family with spirelike clusters of white, pink or red flowers

astir (ə'stər) *a.* **1.** on the move **2.** out of bed **3.** in excitement

astonish (ə'stonish) *vt.* amaze, surprise —**a'stonishing** *a.* —**a'stonishment** *n.*

astound (ə'stownd) *vt.* **1.** astonish greatly **2.** stun with amazement —**a'stounding** *a.* startling

astraddle (ə'stradəl) *a.* **1.** with a leg on either side of something —*prep.* **2.** astride

astrakhan ('astrəkən) *n.* **1.** karakul **2.** cloth imitating this

astral ('astrəl) *a.* of the stars or spirit world —**astral body**

astray (ə'strā) *adv.* **1.** off the right path **2.** in error

astride (ə'strīd) *adv.* **1.** with the legs apart —*prep.* **2.** straddling

astringent (ə'strinjənt) *a.* **1.** severe, harsh **2.** sharp **3.** constricting (body tissues, blood vessels *etc.*) —*n.* **4.** astringent substance —**as'tringency** *n.*

astro- (*comb. form*) indicating star or star-shaped structure

astrol. astrology

astrolabe ('astrəlāb) *n.* instrument used by early astronomers to measure altitude of stars *etc.*

astrology (ə'stroləji) *n.* **1.** foretelling of events by stars **2.** medieval astronomy —**as'trologer** *n.* —**astro'logical** *a.*

astrometry (ə'stromitri) *n.* determination of apparent magnitudes of fixed stars

astron. astronomy

astronaut ('astrənŏt) *n.* one trained for travel in space —**astro'nautics** *pl.n.* (*with sing. v.*) science and technology of space flight

astronomy (ə'stronəmi) *n.* scientific study of heavenly bodies —**as'tronomer** *n.* —**astro'nomical** *a.* **1.** very large **2.** of astronomy —**astronomical unit** unit of distance used in astronomy equal to the mean distance between the earth and the sun

astrophysics (astrō'fiziks) *n.* the science of the chemical and physical characteristics of heavenly bodies —**astro'physical** *a.* —**astro'physicist** *n.*

astute (ə'styōōt, -'stōōt) *a.* perceptive, shrewd —**as'tutely** *adv.* —**as'tuteness** *n.*

asunder (ə'sundər) *adv.* **1.** apart **2.** in pieces

ASV *Bible* American Standard Version (published 1901)

asylum (ə'sīləm) *n.* **1.** refuge, sanctuary, place of safety **2.** home for care of the unfortunate, *esp.* of mentally ill

asymmetry (ā'simitri) *n.* **1.** lack of symmetry **2.** *Chem.* condition of not being superimposable on a mirror image —**asym'metric(al)** *a.*

asymptote ('asimtōt) *n.* straight line that continually approaches a curve, but never meets it

asyndeton (ə'sinditon) *n.* omission of conjunctions between parts of sentence (*pl.* **-deta** (-ditə)) —**asyn'detic** *a.* without conjunctions or cross-references

at (at) *prep./adv. denoting* **1.** location in space or time **2.** rate **3.** condition or state **4.** amount **5.** direction **6.** cause

At *Chem.* astatine

at. **1.** atmosphere **2.** atomic

Atabrine ('atəbrin) *n.* trade name for yellow dye used in the treatment of malaria

ataractic (atə'raktik) *or* **ataraxic** (atə'rak-sik) *n.* drug that induces calmness or emotional tranquillity

atavism ('atəvizəm) *n.* appearance of ancestral, not parental, characteristics in human beings, animals or plants —**ata'vistic** *a.*

ataxia (ə'taksiə) *or* **ataxy** (ə'taksi) *n.* lack of muscular coordination

ate (āt) *pt. of* EAT

-ate[1] (*comb. form*) **1.** having appearance or characteristics of, as in *fortunate* **2.** chemical compound, *esp.* salt or ester of acid, as in *carbonate* **3.** product of process, as in *condensate* **4.** forming verbs from nouns and adjectives, as in *hyphenate*

-ate[2] (*comb. form*) office, rank or group having certain function, as in *episcopate*

atelier (atəl'yā) *n.* **1.** artist's studio **2.** workshop

Athabaskan (athə'baskən) *n./a.* (of) Amerindian people inhabiting central Alaska, closely related to Navaho, Apache and Hupas of southwest U.S.

Athapaskan (athə'paskən) *n.* Amerindian language family found in Pacific Northwest and Alaska and in southwest U.S.

atheism ('āthiizəm) *n.* belief that there is no God —**'atheist** *n.* —**athe'istic(al)** *a.*

athenaeum *or* **atheneum** (athi'nēəm) *n.* **1.** institution for promotion of learning **2.** building containing reading room or library

atherosclerosis (athərōskli'rōsis) *n.* degenerative disease of arteries characterized by thickening of arterial walls, caused by deposits of fatty material (*pl.* **-oses** (-ōsēz))

athlete ('athlēt) *n.* **1.** one trained for physical exercises, feats or contests of strength **2.** one good at sports —**athletic** (ath'letik) *a.* —**athletically** (ath'letikəli) *adv.* —**athleticism** (ath'letisizəm) *n.* —**athletics** (ath'letiks) *pl.n.* (*with sing. v.*) term for all competitive individual and team games and sports depending upon feats of physical strength or skill —**athlete's foot** fungal infection of skin of foot, *esp.* between toes and on soles —**athletic supporter** jockstrap

at-home *n.* **1.** social gathering in person's home —*a.* **2.** suitable for one's home

athwart (ə'thwört) *prep.* **1.** across —*adv.* **2.** across, *esp.* obliquely

Atlantic (ət'lantik) *n.* **1.** (*short for* **Atlantic Ocean**) world's second largest ocean —*a.* **2.** of or bordering Atlantic Ocean **3.** of Atlas or Atlas Mountains

Atlantis (ət'lantis) *n.* in ancient legend, continent said to have sunk beneath Atlantic west of Gibraltar

atlas ('atləs) *n.* **1.** bound volume of maps **2.** bound collection of tables, charts or plates **3.** (**A-**) titan condemned to support sky on his shoulders **4.** (**A-**) mountains in northwest Africa ranging through Morocco, Algeria and Tunisia

atm. 1. atmosphere **2.** atmospheric

atmosphere ('atməsfēər) *n.* **1.** mass of gas surrounding heavenly body, *esp.* the earth **2.** prevailing tone or mood (of place *etc.*) **3.** unit of pressure in cgs system —**atmospheric** (atməs'ferik) *a.* —**atmospherics** (atməs'feriks) *pl.n.* noises in radio reception due to electrical disturbance in the atmosphere —**atmospheric perspective** effect of distance in a painting, created by using color (*also* **aerial perspective, color perspective**)

at. no. atomic number

atoll ('atöl) *n.* ring-shaped coral island enclosing lagoon

atom ('atəm) *n.* **1.** smallest unit of an element which can enter into chemical combination **2.** any very small particle —**a'tomic** *a.* of, arising from atoms —**ato'micity** *n.* number of atoms in molecule of an element —**'atomize** *vt.* reduce to atoms or small particles —**'atomizer** *n.* instrument for discharging liquids in fine spray —**atom bomb** *or* **atomic bomb** bomb whose immense power derives from nuclear fission or fusion, nuclear bomb —**atomic energy** nuclear energy —**atomic number** the number of protons in the nucleus of an atom —**atomic pile** *see* **nuclear reactor** *at* REACT —**atomic theory 1.** any theory in which matter is regarded as consisting of atoms **2.** current concept of atom as entity with definite structure —**atomic weight** the weight of an atom of an element relative to that of carbon 12 —**atom smasher** *see* **particle accelerator** *at* PARTICLE

atonality (ātō'naliti) *n.* **1.** absence of or disregard for established musical key in composition **2.** principles of composition embodying this

atone (ə'tōn) *vi.* **1.** make reparation, amends **2.** give satisfaction —**a'tonement** *n.*

atonic (ā'tonik, a-) *a.* unaccented

atop (ə'top) *adv.* **1.** at or on the top —*prep.* **2.** above

atracurium (atrə'kyōōriəm) *n.* drug used as muscle relaxant during surgery

atrium ('ātriəm) *n.* open central court in Greek and Roman dwellings (*pl.* **'atria, -s**) —**atrium house** house built around a courtyard

atrocious (ə'trōshəs) *a.* **1.** extremely cruel or wicked **2.** horrifying **3.** *inf.* very bad —**a'trociously** *adv.* —**atrocity** (ə'trositi) *n.* wickedness

atrophy ('atrəfi) *n.* **1.** wasting away, emaciation —*vi.* **2.** waste away, become useless

atropine ('atrəpēn) *n.* poisonous alkaloid obtained from deadly nightshade, used medicinally: main ingredient of belladonna

att. 1. attached **2.** attention **3.** attorney

attach (ə'tach) *v.* **1.** join, fasten **2.** unite **3.** be connected **4.** attribute **5.** appoint **6.** seize by law —**at'tached** *a.* (*with* to) fond (of) —**at'tachment** *n.*

attaché (atə'shā) *n.* specialist attached to

diplomatic mission —**attaché case** (ə'tashā) small thin suitcase for papers

attack (ə'tak) *vt.* **1.** take action against (in war, sport *etc.*) **2.** criticize **3.** set about with vigor **4.** affect adversely —*n.* **5.** attacking action **6.** bout

attain (ə'tān) *vt.* **1.** arrive at **2.** reach, gain by effort, accomplish —**attaina'bility** *n.* —**at'tainable** *a.* —**at'tainment** *n. esp.* personal accomplishment

attainder (ə'tāndər) *n. Hist.* loss of rights through conviction of high treason

attar ('atər) *n.* fragrant oil made *esp.* from rose petals

attempt (ə'tempt) *vt.* **1.** try, endeavor —*n.* **2.** trial, effort

attend (ə'tend) *vt.* **1.** be present at **2.** accompany —*vi.* (*with* to) **3.** take care (of) **4.** give the mind (to), pay attention (to) —**at'tendance** *n.* **1.** an attending **2.** presence **3.** persons attending —**at'tendant** *n./a.* —**at'tention** *n.* **1.** notice **2.** heed **3.** act of attending **4.** care **5.** courtesy **6.** alert position in military drill —**at'tentive** *a.* —**at'tentively** *adv.* —**at'tentiveness** *n.*

attenuate (ə'tenyōōāt) *v.* **1.** weaken or become weak **2.** make or become thin —**at'tenuated** *a.* —**attenu'ation** *n.* reduction of intensity

attest (ə'test) *vt.* bear witness to, certify —**atte'station** *n.* formal confirmation by oath *etc.*

attic ('atik) *n.* space within roof where ceiling follows line of roof

Attic ('atik) *a.* **1.** of Athens **2.** classically pure —*n.* **3.** literary language of the Greek-speaking world

Attila (ə'tilə) *n.* king of the Huns (died 453), noted for his cruelty and vandalism

attire (ə'tīər) *vt.* **1.** dress, array —*n.* **2.** dress, clothing

attitude ('atityōōd, -tōōd) *n.* **1.** mental view, opinion **2.** posture, pose **3.** disposition, behavior —**atti'tudinize** *vi.* assume affected attitudes

attorney (ə'tərni) *n.* one legally appointed to act for another, *esp.* a lawyer (*pl.* **-s**) —**attorney-at-law** *n.* legally qualified practitioner who may act for clients in court —**attorney general** the chief law officer of the U.S. or State who represents the government in litigation and is chief legal adviser to the State

attract (ə'trakt) *vt.* **1.** draw (attention *etc.*) **2.** arouse interest of **3.** cause to come closer (as magnet *etc.*) —**at'traction** *n.* **1.** power to attract **2.** something offered so as to interest, please —**at'tractive** *a.* —**at'tractively** *adv.* —**at'tractiveness** *n.*

attribute (ə'tribyət) *vt.* **1.** (*usu. with* to) regard as belonging (to) or produced (by) —*n.* ('atribyōōt) **2.** quality, property or characteristic of anything —**at'tributable** *a.* —**attri'bution** *n.* —**at'tributive** *a./n.* (of) word or phrase used as adjective —**at'tributively** *adv.*

attrition (ə'trishən) *n.* **1.** wearing away of strength *etc.* **2.** rubbing away, friction

attune (ə'tyōōn, -'tōōn) *vt.* **1.** tune, harmonize **2.** make accordant

at. wt. atomic weight

atypical (ā'tipikəl) *a.* not typical

Au *Chem.* gold

aubergine ('ōbərzhēn) *n.* **UK** eggplant

aubrietia (ō'brēshə) *n.* genus of low-growing or trailing evergreen perennials of the cabbage family grown in rock and wall gardens

auburn ('ōbərn) *a.* **1.** reddish-brown —*n.* **2.** this color

au courant (ō kōō'rā) *Fr.* **1.** up-to-date **2.** acquainted

auction ('ōkshən) *n.* **1.** public sale in which bidder offers increase of price over another and what is sold goes to one who bids highest —*vt.* **2.** (*oft. with* off) sell by auction —**auctio'neer** *n.* —**auction bridge** *see* BRIDGE[2]

audacious (ō'dāshəs) *a.* **1.** bold **2.** daring, impudent —**audacity** (ō'dasiti) *n.*

audible ('ōdibəl) *a.* able to be heard —**audi'bility** *n.* —**'audibly** *adv.*

audience ('ōdiəns) *n.* **1.** assembly of hearers **2.** act of hearing **3.** judicial hearing **4.** formal interview

audio ('ōdiō) *n.* frequency in audible range of 50 hertz to 20 000 hertz

audio- (*comb. form*) relating to sound or hearing

audiometer (ōdi'omitər) *n.* instrument for testing hearing

audiotape ('ōdiōtāp) *n.* tape recording of sound

audiovisual (ōdiō'vizhōōəl) *a.* (*esp.* of teaching aids) involving, directed at, both sight and hearing, as film *etc.*

audit ('ōdit) *n.* **1.** formal examination or settlement of accounts —*vt.* **2.** examine (accounts) —**'auditor** *n.*

audition (ō'dishən) *n.* **1.** screen or other test of prospective performer **2.** hearing —*v.* **3.** conduct or be tested in such a test —**audi'torium** *n.* **1.** place where audience sits **2.** hall (*pl.* **-s, -ia** (-iə)) —**'auditory** *a.* pert. to sense of hearing

Audubon Society ('ōdəbon) society founded in 1905 for the preservation of wildlife, *esp.* birds

au fait (ō 'fā) *Fr.* **1.** fully informed **2.** expert

auf Wiedersehen (owf 'vēdərzāən) *Ger.* goodbye

Aug. August

Augean stable (ō'jēən) extremely dirty place

auger ('ōgər) *n.* carpenter's tool for boring holes, large gimlet

aught (ōt) *n.* **1.** *Lit., obs.* anything **2.** zero, cipher

augment (ōg'ment) *v.* increase, enlarge —**augmen'tation** *n.* —**aug'mentative** *a.* increasing in force

au gratin (ō gra'tē) *Fr.* covered with breadcrumbs or grated cheese and browned under broiler

augur ('ōgər) *n.* **1.** among the Romans, soothsayer —*v.* **2.** be a sign of future events, foretell —**augural** ('ōgyərəl) *a.* —**augury** ('ōgyəri) *n.*

august (ō'gust) *a.* majestic, dignified

August ('ōgəst) *n.* eighth month

Augustan (ō'gustən) *a.* **1.** of Augustus, the Roman Emperor **2.** classic, distinguished, as applied to a period of literature, *esp.* in 18th-century England

auk (ōk) *n.* family of black-and-white diving marine birds found from Arctic southward to California, western Europe and Japan

au lait (ō 'lā) with milk

auld lang syne (ōld lang 'zīn) times past, *esp.* those remembered with nostalgia

au naturel (ō natü'rel) *Fr.* **1.** naked; nude **2.** uncooked or plainly cooked

aunt (änt) *n.* **1.** father's or mother's sister **2.** uncle's wife —**'auntie** *or* **'aunty** *n. inf.* aunt

au pair (ō 'pāər) young foreigner who receives free board and lodging in return for housework *etc.*

aura ('ōrə) *n.* **1.** quality, air, atmosphere considered distinctive of person or thing **2.** medical symptom warning of impending epileptic fit *etc.*

aural ('ōrəl) *a.* of, by ear —**'aurally** *adv.*

aureate ('ōriit) *a.* **1.** covered with gold; gilded **2.** (of style of writing or speaking) excessively elaborate

aureole ('ōriōl) *or* **aureola** (ō'rēələ) *n.* **1.** gold disk round head in sacred pictures **2.** halo

au revoir (ō rə'vwär) *Fr.* goodbye

auricle ('ōrikəl) *n.* **1.** outside ear **2.** upper cavity of heart —**au'ricular** *a.* **1.** of the auricle **2.** aural

auricula (ō'rikyələ) *n.* **1. UK** alpine primrose with leaves shaped like bear's ear **2.** *Biol.* ear-shaped part (*also* **'auricle**) (*pl.* **-lae** (-lē), **-s**)

auriferous (ō'rifərəs) *a.* gold-bearing

aurochs ('owroks) *n.* species of wild ox, now extinct (*also* **wisent**)

aurora (ō'rōrə) *n.* **1.** lights in the atmosphere seen radiating from regions of the poles. The northern is called **aurora borealis** and the southern **aurora australis** **2.** *Poet.* dawn

AUS Army of the United States

auscultation (ōskəl'tāshən) *n.* listening to movement of heart and lungs with stethoscope —**'auscultator** *n.* —**aus'cultatory** *a.*

auspice ('ōspis) *n.* **1.** omen, augury —*pl.* **2.** patronage —**aus'picious** *a.* of good omen, favorable —**aus'piciously** *adv.*

Aussie ('ōsi) *n./a. inf.* Australian

austere (o'stēər) *a.* **1.** harsh, strict, severe **2.** without luxury —**aus'terely** *adv.* —**austerity** (o'steriti) *n.*

austral ('ōstrəl) *a.* southern

Australasia (ōstrə'lāzhə) *n.* Australia, New Zealand and adjacent islands —**Austral'asian** *a./n.*

Australia (ō'strālyə) *n.* **1.** continent in eastern hemisphere, southeast of Asia, between the Indian and Pacific oceans **2.** (*also* **Commonwealth of Australia**) federation of former British colonies of New South Wales, Victoria, Queensland, South Australia, Western Australia and Tasmania —**Aus'tralian** *n./a.* —**Australian Rules** game resembling rugby football, played in Aust. between teams of 18 men on oval pitch with oval ball

Austria ('ōstriə) *n.* country in central Europe bounded north by Germany and Czechoslovakia, east by Hungary, south by Yugoslavia and Italy, and west by Switzerland —**'Austrian** *a./n.*

Austro-[1] (*comb. form*) southern, as in *Austro-Asiatic*

Austro-[2] (*comb. form*) Austrian, as in *Austro-Hungarian*

autarchy ('ōtärki) *n.* **1.** absolute sovereignty **2.** absolute or autocratic rule **3.** autarky

autarky ('ōtärki) *n.* (*esp.* of political unit) policy of economic self-sufficiency

auth. **1.** author **2.** authentic **3.** authorized

authentic (ō'thentik) *a.* **1.** real, genuine, true **2.** trustworthy —**au'thentically** *adv.* —**au'thenticate** *vt.* **1.** make valid, confirm **2.** establish truth, authorship *etc.* of —**authenti'cation** *or* **authenticity** (ōthen'tisiti) *n.*

author ('ōthər) *n.* **1.** writer of book **2.** originator, constructor (**-ess** *fem.*) —**'authorship** *n.*

authority (ō'thoriti) *n.* **1.** legal power or right **2.** delegated power **3.** influence **4.** permission **5.** expert **6.** (*oft. pl.*) body or board in control —**authori'tarian** *a.* **1.** favoring or characterized by strict obedience to authority or government by small elite **2.** dictatorial —*n.* **3.** person who favors or practices authoritarian policies —**au'thoritative** *a.* —**au'thoritatively** *adv.* —**authori'zation** *n.* —**'authorize** *vt.* **1.** empower **2.** permit, sanction —**Authorized Version** English translation of the Bible published in 1611 under James I (*also* **King James Version**)

autism ('ōtizəm) *n.* tendency to see world in terms of one's own needs and wishes —**au'tistic** *a.*

auto- *or sometimes before vowel* **aut-** (*comb. form*) self, as in *autograph, autosuggestion.* Such words are not given here where the meaning may easily be inferred from the simple word

autobahn (ˈötəbän) *n.* German motorway
autobiography (ötōbīˈogrəfi) *n.* life story of person written by himself —**autobiˈographer** *n.* —**autobioˈgraphical** *a.* —**autobioˈgraphically** *adv.*
autochthon (öˈtokthən) *n.* original inhabitant (person, plant or animal) —**auˈtochthonous** *a.*
autocrat (ˈötəkrat) *n.* **1.** absolute ruler **2.** despotic person —**auˈtocracy** *n.* —**autoˈcratic** *a.* —**autoˈcratically** *adv.*
autocross (ˈötōkros) *n.* motor-racing sport over rough course
auto-da-fé (ötōdəˈfā) *n.* **1.** *Hist.* ceremony of Spanish Inquisition including pronouncement and execution of sentences passed on heretics **2.** burning to death of people condemned as heretics by Inquisition (*pl.* **autos-da-fé**)
autoeroticism (ötōiˈrotisizəm) *or* **autoerotism** (ötōˈerətizəm) *n.* self-produced sexual arousal
autogamy (öˈtogəmi) *n.* self-fertilization
autogenous (öˈtojinəs) *a.* self-generated
autogiro *or* **autogyro** (ötōˈjīrō) *n.* aircraft like helicopter using horizontal airscrew for vertical ascent and descent
autograph (ˈötəgraf) *n.* **1.** handwritten signature **2.** person's handwriting —*vt.* **3.** sign —**autoˈgraphic** *a.*
autogyro (ötōˈjīrō) *n.* *see* AUTOGIRO
Autoharp (ˈötōhärp) *n.* trade name for zither with button-controlled dampers
autointoxication (ötōintoksiˈkāshən) *n.* poisoning of tissues of the body as a result of internally produced toxic substances
Automat (ˈötəmat) *n.* trade name for cafeteria in which food is usu. dispensed from vending machines
automate (ˈötəmāt) *vt.* make (manufacturing process *etc.*) automatic
automatic (ötəˈmatik) *a.* **1.** operated or controlled mechanically **2.** done without conscious thought —*a./n.* **3.** self-loading (weapon) —**autoˈmatically** *adv.* —**automation** (ötəˈmāshən) *n.* use of automatic devices in industrial production —**auˈtomatism** *n.* involuntary action —**auˈtomaton** *n.* self-acting machine, *esp.* simulating a human being (*pl.* **-ata** (-ətə)) —**automatic transmission** transmission system in motor vehicle, in which gears change automatically
automobile (ötəmōˈbēl) *n.* self-propelling (usu. by internal-combustion engine) vehicle for passenger transportation on streets and roadways —**automoˈbilist** *n.* motorist —**automobile racing 1.** speed competition among racing cars **2.** racing against clock for individual performance records
automotive (ötəˈmōtiv) *a.* **1.** relating to motor vehicles **2.** self-propelling
autonomy (öˈtonəmi) *n.* self-government —**auˈtonomous** *a.*
autopsy (ˈötopsi, -təp-) *n.* **1.** post-mortem examination to determine cause of death **2.** critical analysis —**auˈtoptic(al)** *a.*
autoroute (ˈötōrōōt) *n.* French motorway
autostrada (ˈötōsträdə) *n.* Italian motorway
autosuggestion (ötōsəˈjeschən) *n.* process of influencing the mind (toward health *etc.*), conducted by the subject himself
autumn (ˈötəm) *n./a.* (typical of) the season after summer —**autumnal** (öˈtumnəl) *a.* typical of the onset of winter —**autumnally** (öˈtumnəli) *adv.*
aux. auxiliary
auxiliary (ögˈzilyəri, -ˈzilə-) *a.* **1.** helping, subsidiary —*n.* **2.** helper **3.** something subsidiary, as troops **4.** verb used to form tenses of others
av 1. avenue **2.** average **3.** avoirdupois
AV 1. *Bible* Authorized Version (King James) **2.** ad valorem **3.** audiovisual
avail (əˈvāl) *v.* **1.** be of use, advantage, value (to) —*n.* **2.** benefit (*esp. in* **of no avail, to little avail**) —**availaˈbility** *n.* —**aˈvailable** *a.* **1.** obtainable **2.** accessible —**avail oneself of** make use of
avalanche (ˈavələnch) *n.* **1.** mass of snow, ice, sliding down mountain **2.** sudden overwhelming quantity of anything
avant-garde (äväntˈgärd) *a.* markedly experimental or in advance, *esp.* in the arts
avarice (ˈavəris) *n.* greed for wealth —**avaˈricious** *a.* —**avaˈriciously** *adv.*
avast (əˈväst) *interj. Naut.* stop
avatar (ˈavətär) *n.* **1.** *Hinduism* manifestation of deity in human or animal form **2.** visible manifestation of abstract concept
avaunt (əˈvönt) *interj. obs.* go away, depart
avdp. avoirdupois
Ave. *or* **ave.** Avenue
Ave Maria (ˈävā məˈrēə) *see* **Hail Mary** *at* HAIL[2]
avenge (əˈvenj) *vt.* take vengeance on behalf of (person) or on account of (thing) —**aˈvenger** *n.*
avenue (ˈavinyōō, -nōō) *n.* **1.** wide street, oft. lined with trees **2.** approach **3.** double row of trees
aver (əˈvər) *vt.* affirm, assert (**-rr-**) —**aˈverment** *n.*
average (ˈavərij, ˈavrij) *n.* **1.** the mean value or quantity of a number of values or quantities —*a.* **2.** calculated as an average **3.** medium, ordinary —*vt.* **4.** fix or calculate an average of —*vi.* **5.** exist in or form a mean
averse (əˈvərs) *a.* disinclined, unwilling —**aˈversion** *n.* (*usu. with* to *or* for) dislike, person or thing disliked —**aversion therapy** *Psych.* way of suppressing undesirable habit by associating unpleasant effect, such as electric shock, with it
avert (əˈvərt) *vt.* **1.** turn away **2.** ward off
avg average
aviary (ˈāvieri) *n.* enclosure for birds —**ˈaviarist** *n.*

aviation (āvi'āshən) *n.* **1.** art of flying aircraft **2.** design, production and maintenance of aircraft —**'aviator** *n.*

avid ('avid) *a.* **1.** keen, enthusiastic **2.** (*oft. with* for) greedy —**a'vidity** *n.*

avn aviation

avocado (avə'kädō) *n.* **1.** tropical tree **2.** its green-skinned edible fruit

avocation (avə'kāshən) *n.* **1.** vocation **2.** employment, business

avocet ('avəset) *n.* wading bird of snipe family with upward-curving bill

Avogadro number (avə'gädrō) number of atoms in one gram-atom —**Avogadro's law** law stating that gases at the same temperature and pressure have same number of molecules per unit volume

avoid (ə'void) *vt.* **1.** keep away from **2.** refrain from **3.** not allow to happen —**a'voidable** *a.* —**a'voidance** *n.*

avoirdupois *or* **avoirdupois weight** (avərdə'poiz) *n./a.* (of) system of weights based on 16 ounces to pound and 16 drams to ounce

avouch (ə'vowch) *vt. obs.* affirm, maintain, attest, own —**a'vouchment** *n.*

avow (ə'vow) *vt.* **1.** declare **2.** admit —**a'vowable** *a.* —**a'vowal** *n.* —**a'vowed** *a.* —**avowedly** (ə'vowidli) *adv.*

avuncular (ə'vungkyələr) *a.* of or resembling an uncle, genial

await (ə'wāt) *vt.* **1.** wait or stay for **2.** be in store for

awake (ə'wāk) *v.* **1.** emerge or rouse from sleep **2.** become or cause to become alert (**a'woke** *or* **a'waked, a'woken** *or* **a'waked, a'waking**) —*a.* **3.** not sleeping **4.** alert —**a'wakening** *n.*

award (ə'wörd) *vt.* **1.** give formally (*esp.* prize or punishment) —*n.* **2.** prize **3.** judicial decision

aware (ə'wāər) *a.* informed, conscious —**a'wareness** *n.*

awash (ə'wosh) *a.* **1.** level with surface of water **2.** filled or overflowing with water

away (ə'wā) *a.* **1.** absent, apart, at a distance, out of the way —*n.* **2.** *Sport* game played on opponent's ground

awe (ö) *n.* dread mingled with reverence —**'awesome** *a.*

aweigh (ə'wā) *a. Naut.* (of anchor) no longer hooked into bottom; hanging by its rope or chain

awful ('öfəl) *a.* **1.** very bad, unpleasant **2.** *obs.* impressive **3.** *inf.* very great —**'awfully** *adv.* **1.** in an unpleasant way **2.** *inf.* very much

awhile (ə'wīl) *adv.* for a time

awkward ('ökwərd) *a.* **1.** clumsy, ungainly **2.** difficult **3.** inconvenient **4.** embarrassed —**'awkwardly** *adv.* —**'awkwardness** *n.*

awl (öl) *n.* pointed tool for boring wood, leather *etc.*

awn (ön) *n.* any of bristles growing from flowering parts of certain grasses and cereals

awning ('öning) *n.* (canvas) roof or shelter, to protect from weather

awoke (ə'wōk) *pt. of* AWAKE —**a'woken** *pp. of* AWAKE

A.W.O.L. *or* **AWOL** (*when acronym* 'āwöl) absent without leave

awry (ə'rī) *adv.* **1.** crookedly **2.** amiss **3.** at a slant —*a.* **4.** crooked, distorted **5.** wrong

ax *or* **axe** (aks) *n.* **1.** tool with sharp blade for chopping **2.** *inf.* dismissal from employment *etc.* —*vt.* **3.** remove (from job, budget, agenda *etc.*)

axel ('aksəl) *n. Skating* jump of one and a half turns, taking off from forward outside edge of one skate and landing on backward outside edge of other

axes[1] ('aksēz) *n., pl. of* AXIS

axes[2] ('aksiz) *n., pl. of* AX

axil ('aksil) *n.* upper angle between branch or leaf stalk and stem

axiom ('aksiəm) *n.* **1.** received or accepted principle from which secondary ones are derived **2.** self-evident truth —**axio'matic** *a.*

axis ('aksis) *n.* **1.** (imaginary) line round which body spins **2.** line or column around which parts of thing, system *etc.* are arranged (*pl.* **'axes**) —**'axial** *a.* —**'axially** *adv.* —**'Axis** *n.* coalition of Germany, Italy and Japan, 1936–45

axle ('aksəl) *n.* rod on which wheel turns

axolotl ('aksəlotəl) *n.* aquatic salamander of N Amer. capable of breeding in larval state

ay *or* **aye** (ā) *adv. Poet., obs.* always

ayah ('Iə) *n.* Indian maidservant or nursemaid

ayatollah (Iə'tolə) *n.* one of class of Islamic religious leaders

aye *or* **ay** (I) *adv.* **1.** yes —*n.* **2.** affirmative answer or vote —*pl.* **3.** those voting for motion

AYH American Youth Hostels

Aymara (Imə'rä) *n.* Amerindian language spoken in Bolivia and Peru

AZ Arizona

azalea (ə'zālyə) *n.* gardening term for genus (*Azalea*) of rhododendron

Azazel (ə'zāzəl) *n. Judaism* evil spirit living in the wilderness, associated with scapegoat

azimuth ('azimәth) *n.* **1.** vertical arc from zenith to horizon **2.** angular distance of this from meridian

Azores ('āzörz, ə'zörz) *pl.n.* autonomous division of Portugal situated in the Atlantic at 40° N latitude and 30° E latitude

Azrael ('azrāl) *n. Islam* the angel of death

Aztec ('aztek) *a./n.* **1.** (member) of Indian race ruling Mexico before Spanish conquest —*n.* **2.** language of this people

azure ('azhər) *n.* **1.** sky-blue color **2.** sky —*a.* **3.** sky-blue

B

b *or* **B** (bē) *n.* **1.** second letter of English alphabet **2.** speech sound represented by this letter, as in *bell* **3.** second in series, class or rank (*also* **ˈbeta**) (*pl.* **b's, B's,** *or* **Bs**)

b 1. bachelor **2.** bass(o) **3.** bishop **4.** book **5.** born

B 1. *Mus.* seventh note of scale of C major; major or minor key having this note as its tonic **2.** less important of two things **3.** human blood type of ABO group **4.** rating of student's work as better than average **5.** *Chem.* boron **6.** magnetic flux density **7.** (of pencils) softness of graphite **8.** *Phys.* bel (*also* **b**) **9.** *Phys.* baryon number

b. *or* **B. 1.** (on maps *etc.*) bay **2.** (**B.**) Bible **3.** (**b.**) *Cricket* bowled; bye **4.** breadth **5.** black

Ba *Chem.* barium

B.A. 1. Bachelor of Arts **2.** batting averages **3.** Buenos Aires

baa (bä) *vi.* **1.** make cry of sheep; bleat (**ˈbaaing, baaed**) —*n.* **2.** cry made by sheep

baas (bäs) *n.* **SA** boss

baba (ˈbäbä) *n.* small cake, usu. soaked in rum

babble (ˈbabəl) *vi.* **1.** speak foolishly, incoherently, or childishly —*n.* **2.** foolish, confused talk —**ˈbabbler** *n.* **1.** one who babbles **2.** tropical bird with incessant song —**ˈbabbling** *n./a.*

babe (bāb) *n.* **1.** *old-fashioned* baby **2.** guileless person

babel (ˈbābəl) *n.* confused noise or scene, uproar

baboon (baˈbo͞on) *n.* any of several large African or Asian terrestrial monkeys with cheek pouches, doglike muzzles and usu. short tails —**baˈboonish** *a.*

baby (ˈbābi) *n.* very young child, infant —**ˈbabyhood** *n.* —**ˈbabyish** *a.* —**baby carriage** cotlike four-wheeled carriage for baby (*also* **baby buggy**) —**baby grand** small grand piano —**baby-sit** *vi.* —**baby-sitter** *n.* one who cares for children when parents are out

baccarat (băkəˈrä) *n.* gambling card game in which object is to hold a combination of cards totaling 9, differing from chemin de fer in that players bet against the house

bacchanal (ˈbakənəl) *n.* **1.** follower of Bacchus **2.** (participant in) drunken, riotous celebration

bacchanalia (bakəˈnālyə) *pl.n.* **1.** (*oft.* **B-**) orgiastic rites associated with Bacchus **2.** drunken revelry —**bacchaˈnalian** *a./n.*

bacchant (ˈbakənt) *or* (*fem.*) **bacchante** (bəˈkanti) *n.* **1.** priest or priestess of Bacchus **2.** drunken reveler

bachelor (ˈbachələr, ˈbachlər) *n.* **1.** unmarried man **2.** holder of university degree **3.** *Hist.* young knight —**ˈbachelorhood** *or* **ˈbachelorship** *n.* —**bachelor girl** young unmarried woman, *esp.* one who is self-supporting

bacillus (bəˈsiləs) *n.* any rod-shaped bacterium (*pl.* **-cilli** (-ˈsilī)) —**baˈcilliform** *a.*

back (bak) *n.* **1.** hinder part of anything, *eg* human body **2.** part opposite front **3.** part or side of something further away or less used **4.** (position of) player in ball games behind other (forward) players —*a.* **5.** situated behind **6.** earlier —*adv.* **7.** at, to the back **8.** in, into the past **9.** in return —*vi.* **10.** move backwards —*vt.* **11.** support **12.** put wager on **13.** provide with back or backing —**ˈbacker** *n.* **1.** one supporting another, *esp.* in contest **2.** one betting on horse *etc.* in race —**ˈbacking** *n.* **1.** support **2.** material to protect the back of something **3.** musical accompaniment, *esp.* for pop singer —**ˈbackward** *a.* **1.** directed toward the rear **2.** behind in education **3.** reluctant, bashful —*adv.* **4.** backwards —**ˈbackwardness** *n.* —**ˈbackwards** *adv.* **1.** to the rear **2.** to the past **3.** into a worse state (*also* **ˈbackward**) —**ˈbackache** *n.* lumbago —**ˈbackˈbencher** *n.* member of parliament not holding office in government or opposition —**ˈbackbite** *v.* slander (absent person) —**ˈbackbiter** *n.* —**ˈbackbiting** *n.* —**ˈbackboard** *n.* **1.** board that is placed behind something to form or support its back **2.** board worn to support back, as after surgery **3.** *Basketball* flat upright surface under which basket is attached —**ˈbackbone** *n.* **1.** spinal column **2.** strength of character —**ˈbackbreaking** *a.* exhausting —**ˈbackcomb** *v.* comb under layers of (hair) toward roots to add bulk to hairstyle (*also* **tease**) —**backˈdate** *vt.* make effective from earlier date —**back door 1.** door at rear or side of building **2.** means of entry to job *etc.* that is secret or obtained through influence —**ˈbackdrop** *n.* painted cloth at back of stage —**backˈfire** *vi.* **1.** ignite at wrong time, as fuel in cylinder of internal-combustion engine **2.** (of plan, scheme *etc.*) fail to work, *esp.* to the cost of the instigator **3.** ignite wrongly, as gas burner *etc.* —*n.* **4.** explosion in exhaust of internal-combustion engine —**ˈbackgammon** *n.* game for two players played on a board with pieces called stones or men whose moves toward 'home' are governed by throwing dice —'**background** *n.* **1.** space behind chief figures of picture *etc.* **2.** past history of person —'**backhand** *n. Tennis etc.* stroke with hand turned backwards —**back'handed** *a.* (of compliment) with second, uncomplimentary meaning —'**backhander** *n.* **1.** blow with back of hand **2.** *inf.* a bribe —'**backlash** *n.* sudden and adverse reaction —'**backlog** *n.* **1.** large log at back of hearth **2.** accumulation of work *etc.* to be dealt with —**back number 1.** issue of newspaper *etc.* that appeared on a previous date **2.** *inf.* person or thing considered old-fashioned —**back pack** *n.* **1.** type of knapsack —*vi.* **2.** travel with knapsack —**back-pedal** *vi.* **1.** turn pedals backward **2.** retract previous opinion *etc.* —**back room** place where important and usu. secret research is done —**back seat 1.** seat at back, *esp.* of vehicle **2.** *inf.* subordinate or inconspicuous position (*esp. in* **take a back seat**) —**back-seat driver** *inf.* **1.** passenger who offers unwanted advice to driver **2.** person who offers advice on matters that are not his concern —**back'side** *n.* rump —'**backslide** *vi.* fall back in faith or morals —**back'stage** *adv.* **1.** behind part of theater in view of audience —*a.* **2.** situated backstage —'**back'stairs** *pl.n.* **1.** secondary staircase in house —*a.* **2.** underhand (*also* '**back'stair**) —'**backstroke** *n. Swimming* stroke performed on the back —'**backtrack** *vi.* **1.** return by same route by which one has come **2.** retract or reverse one's opinion *etc.* —'**backup** *n.* **1.** support; reinforcement **2.** reserve; substitute —'**backwash** *n.* **1.** water thrown back by ship's propellers *etc.* **2.** a backward current **3.** a reaction —'**backwater** *n.* **1.** remote place **2.** still water fed by back flow of stream —'**backwoods** *pl.n.* remote forest areas —**back yard** yard at back of house *etc.* —**back up 1.** support **2.** (of water) accumulate **3.** *Comp.* make copy of (data file) —**in one's own back yard** close at hand

bacon ('bākən) *n.* cured pig's flesh

Baconian (bā'kōniən) *a.* **1.** pert. to English philosopher Francis Bacon (1561–1626) or his inductive method of reasoning —*n.* **2.** follower of Bacon's philosophy **3.** person believing that Bacon is the author of the works of Shakespeare

bacteria (bak'tēəriə) *pl.n.* microscopic unicellular organisms (*sing.* **-rium** (-riəm)) —**bacter'emia** *n.* invasion of blood by bacteria without giving rise to symptoms of disease, but resulting in boils or sore throats —**bac'terial** *a.* —**bacteri'ologist** *n.* —**bacteri'ology** *n.* study of bacteria —**bacteriophage** (bak'tēəriəfāj) *n.* virus that infects bacteria —**bacterial endocarditis** bacterial infection of the lining of the heart, *esp.* the valves

Bactrian camel ('baktriən) two-humped camel, used in deserts of central Asia

bad (bad) *a.* **1.** of poor quality **2.** faulty **3.** evil **4.** immoral **5.** offensive **6.** severe **7.** rotten, decayed (**worse** *comp.*, **worst** *sup.*) —'**badly** *adv.* —'**badness** *n.* —**bad blood** feeling of intense hatred or hostility; enmity —**bad debt** debt which is not collectable

bade *or* **bad** (bad) *pt. of* BID

badge (baj) *n.* distinguishing emblem or sign

badger ('bajər) *n.* **1.** any of various carnivorous burrowing mammals —*vt.* **2.** pester, worry —**badger game** method of extortion in which the victim is lured into a compromising sexual situation and then threatened with exposure unless money is paid

badinage (badi'näzh) *n.* playful talk, banter

badminton ('badmintən) *n.* court game for two or four players played with light rackets and a shuttlecock volleyed over a net

baffle ('bafəl) *vt.* **1.** check **2.** frustrate **3.** bewilder —'**baffler** *n.* —'**baffling** *a.* —**baffle plate** device to regulate or divert flow of liquid, gas, sound waves *etc.*

bag (bag) *n.* **1.** sack, pouch **2.** measure of quantity **3.** woman's handbag **4.** *offens.* unattractive woman —*pl.* **5.** *inf.* lots (of) —*vi.* **6.** swell out **7.** bulge **8.** sag —*vt.* **9.** put in bag **10.** kill as game *etc.* (**-gg-**) —'**bagging** *n.* cloth —'**baggy** *a.* loose, drooping —'**bagman** *n.* agent who collects bribe, extortion or kidnaping money

bagasse (bə'gas) *n.* sugar cane refuse

bagatelle (bagə'tel) *n.* **1.** trifle **2.** game like pinball played with nine balls and cue on a board

bagel ('bāgəl) *n.* ring-shaped bread roll, hard and glazed on the outside, soft in the center

baggage ('bagij) *n.* **1.** suitcases *etc.*, packed for journey **2.** portable equipment

bagpipe ('bagpīp) *n.* musical instrument comprising reed pipes and a windbag, the chanter pipes producing the melody and the drone pipes the one-tone accompaniment —'**bagpiper** *n.*

bah (bä, ba) *interj.* expression of contempt or disgust

Bahaism (bä'häizəm) *n.* religious movement founded in 1863 stressing unity of all faiths, education, sexual equality, monogamy and the attainment of world peace —**Ba'ha'i** *a.* —**Ba'haist** *n.*

Bahamas (bə'hämǝz) *pl.n.* country in Atlantic Ocean consisting of 700 islands and more than 1000 cays off the southeastern coast of Florida —**Bahamian** (bə'hāmiən, -'hä-) *or* **Bahaman** (bə'hāmən, -'hä-) *n./a.*

Bahrain *or* **Bahrein** (bä'rān) *n.* country comprising an archipelago in the Arabian Gulf between the Qatar peninsula and the mainland of Saudi Arabia —**Bah'raini** *or* **Bah'reini** *n./a.*

bail[1] (bāl) *n.* **1.** *Law* security given for person's reappearance in court **2.** one giving such security —*vt.* **3.** release, or obtain release of, on security —**bail out** *inf.* help (person, firm *etc.*) out of trouble

bail[2] (bāl) *n.* **1.** *Cricket* crosspiece on wicket **2.** bar separating horses in stable

bail[3] (bāl) *vt.* empty out (water) from boat —**bail out** leave aircraft by parachute

bailey (ˈbāli) *n.* outermost wall of castle

Bailey bridge (ˈbāli) bridge composed of prefabricated sections

bailiff (ˈbālif) *n.* **1.** land steward, agent **2.** sheriff's officer

bailiwick (ˈbāliwik) *n.* jurisdiction of bailiff

bain-marie (bĕmaˈrē) *Fr.* vessel for holding hot water, in which sauces *etc.* are gently cooked or kept warm (*pl.* ***bains-marie*** (bĕmaˈrē))

bairn (bāərn) *n. Scot.* infant, child

bait (bāt) *n.* **1.** food to entice fish **2.** any lure or enticement —*vt.* **3.** set a lure for **4.** annoy, persecute

baize (bāz) *n.* smooth woolen or cotton cloth resembling felt

bake (bāk) *vt.* **1.** cook or harden by dry heat —*vi.* **2.** make bread, cakes *etc.* **3.** be scorched or tanned —ˈ**baker** *n.* —ˈ**bakery** *or* ˈ**bakehouse** *n.* —ˈ**baking** *n.* —**baked beans** navy beans, baked in tomato sauce —**baker's dozen** thirteen —**baking powder** raising agent containing sodium bicarbonate and cream of tartar used in baking —**baking soda** common name for sodium hydrogen carbonate (*also* **sodium bicarbonate**)

Bakelite (ˈbākəlīt) *n.* trade name for hard nonflammable synthetic resin, used for dishes, trays, electrical insulators *etc.*

baksheesh *or* **backsheesh** (ˈbakshēsh) *n.* in some Eastern countries, *esp.* formerly, money given as tip

bal. balance

Balaclava helmet (baləˈklävə) close-fitting woolen helmet covering head and neck

balalaika (baləˈlīkə) *n.* Russian guitar of variable size with triangular body, long neck with frets, and usu. three gut strings tuned in fourths

balance (ˈbaləns) *n.* **1.** pair of scales **2.** equilibrium **3.** surplus **4.** sum due on an account **5.** difference between two sums —*vt.* **6.** weigh **7.** bring to equilibrium —**balance of payments** difference over given time between total payments to and receipts from foreign nations —**balance of power** distribution of power among countries so that no nation can seriously threaten another —**balance sheet** tabular statement of assets and liabilities —**balance wheel** regulating wheel of watch

balcony (ˈbalkəni) *n.* **1.** railed platform outside window **2.** upper seats in theater

bald (böld) *a.* **1.** hairless **2.** plain **3.** bare —ˈ**balding** *a.* becoming bald —ˈ**baldly** *adv.* —ˈ**baldness** *n.*

balderdash (ˈböldərdash) *n.* idle, senseless talk

baldric (ˈböldrik) *n.* shoulder belt for sword *etc.*

bale (bāl) *n.* **1.** bundle or package —*vt.* **2.** make into bundles or pack into cartons —ˈ**baler** *n.* machine which makes bales of hay *etc.*

baleen (bəˈlēn) *n.* whalebone

baleful (ˈbālfəl) *a.* menacing —ˈ**balefully** *adv.*

balk (bök) *vi.* **1.** swerve, pull up —*vt.* **2.** thwart, hinder —*n.* **3.** hindrance **4.** square timber, beam **5.** *Baseball* illegal pitching motion while one or more runners are on base —**balk at 1.** recoil from **2.** stop short at

Balkan (ˈbölkən) *a.* of or denoting large peninsula in SE Europe, its inhabitants, countries *etc.* —ˈ**Balkanize** *vt.* divide (region, territory) into small, ineffective countries

ball[1] (böl) *n.* **1.** anything round **2.** globe, sphere, *esp.* as used in games **3.** *Baseball* ball as delivered **4.** bullet —*vi.* **5.** clog, gather into a mass —**ball-and-socket joint** *Anat.* joint in which rounded head fits into rounded cavity —**ball bearings** steel balls used to lessen friction on bearings —**ball boy** *esp.* in tennis, person who retrieves balls that go out of play —**ball cock** device for regulating flow of liquid into cistern *etc.*, consisting of floating ball and a valve —**ball game 1.** any game played with a ball **2.** game of baseball **3.** *inf.* any activity —**ball-park figure** rough estimate; guess —ˈ**ballpoint** *or* **ballpoint pen** *n.* pen with tiny ball bearing as nib

ball[2] (böl) *n.* assembly for dancing —ˈ**ballroom** *n.*

ballad (ˈbaləd) *n.* **1.** narrative poem **2.** simple song

ballade (baˈläd) *n.* **1.** short poem with refrain and envoy **2.** piece of music

ballast (ˈbaləst) *n.* **1.** heavy material put in ship to give steadiness **2.** that which renders anything steady —*vt.* **3.** load with ballast, steady

ballet (ˈbalā, baˈlā) *n.* theatrical presentation of dancing and miming —**balleˈrina** *n.* female ballet dancer

balletomania (baletōˈmāniə) *n.* enthusiasm for ballet —**balˈletomane** *n.*

ballista (bəˈlistə) *n.* ancient catapult for hurling stones *etc.* (*pl.* **-tae** (-tē)) —**balˈlistic** *a.* moving as, or pertaining to motion of a projectile —**balˈlistics** *pl.n.* (*with sing. v.*) scientific study of ballistic motion —**ballistic missile** missile that follows ballistic trajectory when propulsive power is discontinued

balloon (bəˈlo͞on) *n.* **1.** large, airtight bag that rises when filled with air or gas —*vi.* **2.** puff out —**balˈlooning** *n.* —**balˈloonist** *n.*

ballot (ˈbalət) *n.* **1.** method of voting secretly, usu. by marking ballot paper and putting it into box —*v.* **2.** vote or elicit a vote from —**ballot box 1.** sealed receptacle for completed ballot papers **2.** *fig.* the democratic process

ballyhoo ('balihōō) *n.* **1.** noisy confusion or uproar **2.** vulgar, exaggerated publicity or advertisement

balm (bäm) *n.* **1.** aromatic substance obtained from certain trees, used for healing or soothing **2.** anything soothing —'**balminess** *n.* —'**balmy** *a.* **1.** mild **2.** silly

baloney (bə'lōni) *n. inf.* foolish talk; nonsense

balsa ('bölsə) *n.* tropical Amer. tree with light but strong wood

balsam ('bölsəm) *n.* **1.** resinous aromatic substance obtained from various trees and shrubs **2.** soothing ointment —**bal'samic** *a.*

Baltic ('böltik) *a.* **1.** denoting or relating to the Baltic Sea or the states bordering it **2.** of or relating to group of Indo-European languages comprising Lithuanian and Latvian —**Baltic Sea** sea in northern Europe bounded by Sweden, Finland, U.S.S.R., Poland, East Germany, West Germany and Denmark

Balto-Slavic (böltō'slavik, -'släv-) *n.* branch of Indo-European languages spoken from eastern Europe to the Pacific comprising the Baltic and Slavic groups

baluster ('baləstər) *n.* short pillar used as support to rail of staircase *etc.* —'**balustrade** *n.* row of short pillars surmounted by rail

bamboo (bam'bōō) *n.* any of various usu. tropical woody grasses ranging in size from a foot to that of a tall tree —**bamboo curtain** barrier of secrecy in Asian countries —**bamboo shoot** edible rhizome of certain bamboos

bamboozle (bam'bōōzəl) *vt.* **1.** mystify **2.** hoax

ban (ban) *vt.* **1.** prohibit, forbid, outlaw (**-nn-**) —*n.* **2.** prohibition **3.** proclamation

banal (bə'näl) *a.* commonplace, trivial, trite —**ba'nality** *n.*

banana (bə'nanə) *n.* **1.** tropical treelike plant **2.** its fruit —**banana republic** *inf.* small country, *esp.* in Central Amer., that is politically unstable and has economy dominated by foreign interest

band¹ (band) *n.* **1.** strip used to bind **2.** range of values, frequencies *etc.*, between two limits —'**bandage** *n.* strip of cloth for binding wound —**band saw** power-operated saw consisting of endless toothed metal band running over two wheels

band² (band) *n.* **1.** company, group **2.** company of musicians —*v.* **3.** (*with* together) bind together —'**bandmaster** *n.* —'**bandsman** *n.* —'**bandstand** *n.*

bandanna *or* **bandana** (ban'danə) *n.* large figured colored silk or cotton handkerchief

B and B bed-and-breakfast

bandbox ('bandboks) *n.* light box of cardboard for hats *etc.*

B and E breaking and entering

bandeau (ban'dō) *n.* **1.** band, ribbon for the hair **2.** lightweight brassiere (*pl.* **-deaux** (-'dōz))

bandicoot ('bandikōōt) *n.* ratlike Aust. marsupial

bandit ('bandit) *n.* **1.** outlaw **2.** robber, brigand (*pl.* **-s, banditti** (ban'diti))

bandolier *or* **bandoleer** (bandə'lēər) *n.* **1.** shoulder belt for cartridges **2.** band worn for ornament or part of ceremonial dress

b and w black-and-white

bandwagon ('bandwagən) *n.* —**climb, jump, get on the bandwagon** join something that seems assured of success

bandy ('bandi) *vt.* **1.** beat to and fro **2.** toss from one to another ('**bandied,** '**bandying**) —'**bandy** *or* **bandy-legged** *a.* having legs curving outward (*also* **bow-legged**)

bane (bān) *n.* person or thing causing misery or distress —'**baneful** *a.* —'**banefully** *adv.*

bang¹ (bang) *n.* **1.** sudden loud noise, explosion **2.** heavy blow —*vi.* **3.** make loud noise —*vt.* **4.** beat, strike violently **5.** slam

bang² (bang) *n.* (*usu. pl.*) fringe of hair cut straight across forehead

Bangladesh (bänggla'desh) *n.* country in Asia bounded west, northwest and north by India, east by India and Burma and south by the Bay of Bengal —**Bangla'deshi** *n./a.*

bangle ('banggəl) *n.* ring worn on arm or leg

banish ('banish) *vt.* **1.** condemn to exile **2.** drive away **3.** dismiss —'**banishment** *n.* exile

banister *or* **bannister** ('banistər) *n.* railing and supporting balusters on staircase

banjo ('banjō) *n.* stringed musical instrument with body like shallow drum, long fretted neck and usu. six strings (*pl.* **-s, -es**) —'**banjoist** *n.*

bank¹ (bangk) *n.* **1.** establishment for keeping, lending, exchanging *etc.* money **2.** any supply or store for future use, as blood bank —*vt.* **3.** put in bank —*vi.* **4.** transact business with bank —'**banker** *n.* —'**banking** *n.* —**bank account** account created by deposit of money at bank by customer —'**bankbook** *n.* book held by depositor, in which bank enters record of deposits, withdrawals *etc.* (*also* '**passbook**) —**bank note** written promise of payment —**bank on** rely on

bank² (bangk) *n.* **1.** mound or ridge of earth **2.** edge of river, lake *etc.* **3.** rising ground in sea —*vt.* **4.** enclose with ridge —*v.* **5.** pile up **6.** (of aircraft) tilt inward in turning

bank³ (bangk) *n.* **1.** tier **2.** row of oars

bankrupt ('bangkrupt, -rəpt) *n.* **1.** one who fails in business, insolvent debtor —*a.* **2.** financially ruined —*vt.* **3.** make, cause to be, bankrupt —'**bankruptcy** *n.*

banksia ('bangksiə) *n.* genus of Aust. shrubs with dense, usu. yellow, cylindrical heads of flowers

Banlon ('banlon) *n.* trade name for method

of stretching and bulking thermoplastic fibers

banner (ˈbanər) *n.* **1.** long strip with slogan *etc.* **2.** placard **3.** flag used as ensign

bannister (ˈbanistər) *n. see* BANISTER

banns (banz) *pl.n.* announcement, usu. in church, of intention to marry

banquet (ˈbangkwit) *n.* **1.** feast —*vi.* **2.** hold or take part in banquet —*vt.* **3.** treat with feast —ˈ**banqueter** *n.*

banquette (bangˈket) *n.* **1.** raised firing step behind parapet **2.** upholstered bench

banshee (ˈbanshē, banˈshē) *n.* Irish fairy with a wail portending death

bantam (ˈbantəm) *n.* dwarf variety of domestic fowl —ˈ**bantamweight** *n.* **1.** professional boxer weighing 112-118 lbs. (51-53.5 kg); amateur boxer weighing 112-119 lbs. (51-54 kg) **2.** wrestler weighing usu. 115-126 lbs. (52-57 kg)

banter (ˈbantər) *v.* **1.** speak or tease lightly or jokingly —*n.* **2.** light, teasing language

Bantu (ˈbäntōō) *n.* **1.** member of a group of Negroid peoples in equatorial and southern Africa (*pl.* **-tu, -s**) **2.** (*also* ˈ**Bantic**) group of languages of the Niger-Congo group of which Swahili has the largest number of speakers —*a.* **3.** of the Bantu

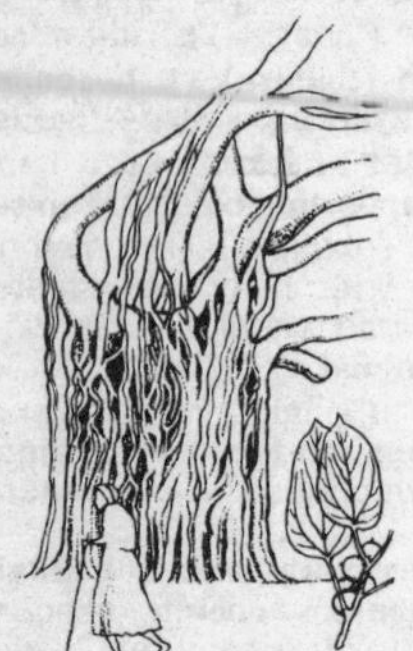

banyan

banyan (ˈbanyən) *n.* Indian fig tree with spreading branches which take root

baobab (ˈbāōbab) *n.* Afr. tree with thick trunk and angular branches

Bap *or* **Bapt** Baptist

baptize (bapˈtīz) *vt.* **1.** immerse in, sprinkle with water ceremoniously **2.** christen —ˈ**baptism** *n.* —**bapˈtismal** *a.* —**bapˈtismally** *adv.* —ˈ**Baptist** *n.* member of Protestant Christian denomination holding that true church is of believers only, who are all equal, and the only authority the Bible —ˈ**baptistery** *or* ˈ**baptistry** *n.* place where baptism is performed —**baptism of fire 1.** soldier's first experience of battle; any initiating ordeal **2.** spiritual baptism

bar[1] (bär) *n.* **1.** rod or block of any substance **2.** obstacle **3.** bank of sand at mouth of river **4.** rail in law court **5.** body of lawyers **6.** counter where drinks are served, *esp.* in hotel *etc.* **7.** unit of music —*vt.* **8.** fasten **9.** obstruct **10.** exclude (**-rr-**) —*prep.* **11.** except —ˈ**barring** *prep.* excepting —**bar code** arrangement of parallel lines, readable by computer, printed on, and giving details of, merchandise in shop *etc.* —**bar graph** graph consisting of bars whose lengths are proportional to quantities —ˈ**barmaid** *n.* —**bar sinister 1.** erroneous term for bend sinister or baton sinister **2.** condition of being of illegitimate birth —ˈ**bartender** *n.*

bar[2] (bär) *n.* unit of pressure

bar. 1. barometer **2.** barrel

barathea (barəˈthēə) *n.* **1.** fine woolen cloth, usu. black **2.** imitation of this in cotton and rayon

barb (bärb) *n.* **1.** sharp point curving backwards behind main point of spear, fish hook *etc.* **2.** cutting remark —**barbed** *a.* —**barbed wire** fencing wire with barbs at close intervals

Barbados (bärˈbādəs) *n.* country in the Windward Islands of the Caribbean Sea —**Barˈbadian** *n./a.*

barbarous (ˈbärbərəs) *a.* **1.** savage, brutal **2.** uncivilized —**barbarian** (bärˈberiən, -ˈbar-) *n.* —**barbaric** (bärˈbarik) *a.* —ˈ**barbarism** *n.* —**barbarity** (bärˈbariti) *n.* —ˈ**barbarously** *adv.*

Barbary ape (ˈbärbəri) tailless macaque that inhabits NW Afr. and Gibraltar

barbecue (ˈbärbikyōō) *n.* **1.** meal cooked outdoors over open fire **2.** fireplace or grill used for this —*vt.* **3.** cook (meat *etc.*) in this manner (**-cued, -cuing**)

barbel (ˈbärbəl) *n.* **1.** spine or bristle that hangs from jaws of certain fishes **2.** any of several European fishes resembling carp

barbell (ˈbärbel) *n.* metal rod to which heavy disks are attached at each end used for weightlifting exercises

barber (ˈbärbər) *n.* one who shaves beards and cuts hair

Barbera (bärˈberə) *n.* **1.** red table wine **2.** grape used to make this wine

barberry (ˈbärberi) *n.* any spiny Asian shrub, having yellow flowers and orange or red berries

barbican (ˈbärbikən) *n.* **1.** outwork of fortified place, *esp.* to defend drawbridge **2.** watchtower projecting from fortification

barbital (ˈbärbitôl) *n. see* BARBITURATE

barbiturate (bärˈbityŏŏrit, -rāt) *n.* derivative of barbituric acid used as sedative, anesthetic, and to induce sleep, *eg* barbital, Veronal —**barbiˈturic** *a.* —**barbituric acid** crystalline solid used in preparation of barbiturate drugs

barcarole *or* **barcarolle** (ˈbärkərōl) *n.* **1.** gondolier's song **2.** composition imitating gondolier's song, written in 6/8 or 12/8 meter

bard (bärd) *n.* **1.** formerly, Celtic poet **2.** wandering minstrel —**'bardic** *a.* —**the Bard** Shakespeare

bare (bāər) *a.* **1.** uncovered **2.** naked **3.** plain **4.** scanty —*vt.* **5.** make bare —**'barely** *adv.* only just, scarcely —**'bareness** *n.* —**'barebacked** *a.* on unsaddled horse —**'barefaced** *a.* shameless

bargain ('bärgin) *n.* **1.** something bought at price favorable to purchaser **2.** contract, agreement —*vi.* **3.** haggle, negotiate **4.** make bargain

barge (bärj) *n.* **1.** flat-bottomed freight boat **2.** state or pleasure boat —*vi. inf.* **3.** (*with* into *or* in) interrupt **4.** (*with* into) bump (into), push —**'bargeman** *n.* —**'bargepole** *n.* long pole used to propel barge

baritone ('baritōn) *n.* **1.** (singer with) second lowest adult male voice **2.** musical instrument larger than cornet with the bell pointing upwards, used in a brass band —*a.* **3.** written for or possessing baritone voice

barium ('bāəriəm) *n. Chem.* metallic element *Symbol* Ba, at. wt. 137.3, at. no. 56 —**barium meal** preparation of barium sulfate —**barium sulfate** white insoluble fine heavy powder which is opaque to x-rays: swallowed by patient before x-ray of alimentary canal

bark[1] (bärk) *n.* **1.** sharp loud cry of dog *etc.* —*v.* **2.** make, utter with such sound —**'barker** *n.* crier outside fair booth *etc.*

bark[2] (bärk) *n.* **1.** outer layer of trunk, branches of tree —*vt.* **2.** strip bark from **3.** rub off (skin), graze (shins *etc.*)

bark[3] (bärk) *n.* **1.** sailing ship, *esp.* large, three-masted one (*also* **barque, 'barkentine, 'barquentine**) **2.** craft propelled by sails or oars

barley ('bärli) *n.* grain used for food and in making malt —**'barleycorn** *n.* **1.** (grain of) barley **2.** *obs.* unit of length equal to a third of an inch

barm (bärm) *n.* **1.** yeast **2.** froth —**'barmy** *a.* *see* **balmy** (sense 2) *at* BALM

bar mitzvah (bär 'mitsvə) (*sometimes* **B-M-**) *Judaism* **1.** ceremony marking 13th birthday of boy, who then assumes full religious obligations **2.** the boy himself

barn (bärn) *n.* farm building, used to store grain, hay *etc.* —**barn dance** (party with) country dancing —**barn owl** owl with pale brown-and-white plumage —**'barnstorm** *vi.* tour rural districts putting on shows or making speeches in political campaign —**'barnstormer** *n.* —**'barnyard** *n.* farmyard

barnacle ('bärnəkəl) *n.* marine crustacean which adheres to rocks and ships' bottoms —**barnacle goose** N European goose that has black-and-white head and body

barograph ('barəgraf) *n.* recording barometer

barometer (bə'romitər) *n.* instrument to measure pressure of atmosphere —**baro'metric** *a.* —**ba'rometry** *n.*

baron ('barən) *n.* **1.** member of lowest rank of British peerage **2.** powerful businessman **3.** indeterminate rank of European nobleman —**'baronage** *n.* —**'baroness** *n.* **1.** wife, ex-wife or widow of baron **2.** woman holding baronial rank in own right —**ba'ronial** *a.* —**'barony** *n.*

baronet ('barənit) *n.* lowest British hereditary title, below baron but above knight —**'baronetage** *n.* —**'baronetcy** *n.*

baroque (bə'rok, bə'rōk) *a.* extravagantly ornamented, *esp.* in architecture and art

baroscope ('barəskōp) *n.* any instrument for measuring atmospheric pressure —**baroscopic** (barə'skopik) *a.*

barouche (bə'ro͞osh) *n.* four-wheeled carriage with folding top over rear seat

barrack ('barək) *n.* **1.** (*usu. pl.*) building for lodging soldiers **2.** huge bare building

barracouta (barə'ko͞otə) *n.* marine food fish of southern hemisphere

barracuda (barə'ko͞odə) *n.* any of several voracious, pikelike marine fishes, some caught as food, others dangerous or poisonous

barrage (bə'räzh) *n.* **1.** heavy artillery fire **2.** continuous and heavy delivery, *esp.* of questions *etc.* **3.** ('bärij) dam across river —**barrage balloon** one of number of tethered balloons with cables or net suspended from them, used to deter low-flying air attack

barratry ('barətri) *n.* **1.** fraudulent breach of duty by master of ship **2.** stirring up of law suits —**'barrator** *n.* —**'barratrous** *a.*

barre (bar) *Fr.* rail used for ballet practice

barrel ('barəl) *n.* **1.** round wooden vessel, made of curved staves bound with hoops **2.** amount that barrel can hold (*also* **'barrelful**) **3.** anything long and hollow, as tube of gun *etc.* —*vt.* **4.** put in barrel —**'barreled** *a.* —**barrel organ** instrument consisting of cylinder turned by handle, having pins that interrupt air flow to certain pipes or pluck strings, thereby playing tunes —**barrel vault** *Archit.* vault in form of half cylinder

barren ('barən) *a.* **1.** unfruitful, sterile **2.** unprofitable **3.** dull —**'barrenness** *n.* —**Barren Lands** *or* **Grounds** sparsely inhabited tundra region in N Canada

barricade (bari'kād, 'barikād) *n.* **1.** improvised fortification, barrier —*vt.* **2.** protect by building barrier **3.** block

barrier ('bariər) *n.* fence, obstruction, obstacle, boundary —**barrier cream** cream to protect skin —**barrier reef** coral reef lying parallel to shore

barrister ('baristər) *n.* advocate in the higher law courts of England

barrow[1] ('barō) *n.* **1.** small wheeled handcart **2.** wheelbarrow

barrow[2] ('barō) *n.* **1.** burial mound **2.** tumulus

Bart. Baronet

barter (ˈbärtər) *v.* **1.** trade by exchange of goods —*n.* **2.** practice of bartering

Baruch (bəˈrōōk, ˈbärōōk) *n. Bible* 30th book in the Douay Version of the O.T.

baryon (ˈbarion) *n. Phys.* elementary particle of matter

baryta (bəˈrītə) *n.* **1.** barium oxide **2.** barium hydroxide

barytes (bəˈrītēz) *n.* barium sulfate

basalt (bəˈsölt) *n.* dark-colored, hard, compact, igneous rock —**baˈsaltic** *a.*

bascule (ˈbaskyōōl) *n.* **1.** lever apparatus **2.** drawbridge on counterpoise principle

base[1] (bās) *n.* **1.** bottom, foundation **2.** starting point **3.** center of operations **4.** fixed point **5.** *Chem.* compound that combines with an acid to form a salt **6.** medium into which other substances are mixed **7.** *Math.* in arithmetic, the number which raised to various powers, forms the main counting unit of a system; in logarithms, the number which when raised to a certain power will produce a certain number —*vt.* **8.** found, establish —ˈ**basal** *a.* of base —ˈ**baseless** *a.* —**basal metabolism rate** measure of body energy output at rest and in the fasting state —ˈ**baseline** *n.* **1.** *Surv.* measured line through survey area from which triangulations are made **2.** line at each end of games court that marks limit of play —ˈ**basement** *n.* lowest level of building

base[2] (bās) *a.* **1.** low, mean **2.** despicable —ˈ**basely** *adv.* —ˈ**baseness** *n.* —ˈ**baseborn** *a.* illegitimate

baseball (ˈbāsböl) *n.* **1.** outdoor game played with bat and ball by two teams with nine players each on a field with four bases arranged in a diamond in which the object is to score runs **2.** the ball used in this game

bases (ˈbāsēz) *n., pl. of* BASIS

bash (bash) *inf. vt.* **1.** strike violently —*n.* **2.** blow **3.** attempt

bashful (ˈbashfəl) *a.* shy, modest —ˈ**bashfully** *adv.* —ˈ**bashfulness** *n.*

basic (ˈbāsik) *a.* **1.** relating to, serving as base **2.** fundamental **3.** necessary —**basic slag** slag produced in steel-making, containing calcium phosphate

BASIC (ˈbāsik) *Comp. B*eginners' *A*ll-purpose *S*ymbolic *I*nstruction *C*ode

basil (ˈbazəl) *n.* annual plant of the mint family, the leaves of which are used in cooking

basilica (bəˈsilikə, -ˈzil-) *n.* type of church with long hall and pillars —**baˈsilican** *a.*

basilisk (ˈbazilisk) *n.* legendary small fire-breathing dragon

basin (ˈbāsən) *n.* **1.** deep circular dish **2.** harbor **3.** land drained by river

basis (ˈbāsis) *n.* **1.** foundation **2.** principal constituent (*pl.* ˈ**bases**)

bask (bäsk) *vi.* lie in warmth and sunshine —**basking shark** large plankton-eating shark

basket (ˈbäskit) *n.* vessel made of woven cane, straw *etc.* —ˈ**basketry** *or* ˈ**basketwork** *n.* —ˈ**basketball** *n.* indoor or outdoor game played by two teams of five players each whose object is to score points by tossing a ball into the opposing team's basket —**basket chair** wickerwork chair —**basket weave** weave where two or more warp or weft threads are interlaced

basque (bask) *n.* tight-fitting bodice for women

Basque (bask) *n.* **1.** one of race from W Pyrenees **2.** their language which is a relic of a non-Indo-European language

bas-relief (bäriˈlēf) *n.* sculpture with figures standing out slightly from background

bass[1] (bās) *n.* **1.** lowest part in music **2.** bass singer or voice —*a.* **3.** relating to or denoting the bass —**bass clef** clef that establishes F a fifth below middle C on fourth line of staff

bass[2] (bas) *n.* any of numerous freshwater food and game fishes of N Amer.

basset (ˈbasit) *n.* type of smooth-haired dog

basset horn forerunner of clarinet

bassinet (basiˈnet) *n.* wickerwork or wooden cradle, usu. hooded

bassoon (bəˈsōōn) *n.* orchestral woodwind instrument of the oboe family pitched two octaves below the oboe with a tube bent back on account of its great length —**basˈsoonist** *n.* —**double bassoon** instrument with range an octave lower than bassoon, with a tube doubled on itself four times

bast (bast) *n.* fibrous material obtained from phloem of jute, flax *etc.* used for making rope *etc.*

bastard (ˈbastərd) *n.* **1.** child born of unmarried parents **2.** *inf.* person, as in *lucky bastard* —*a.* **3.** illegitimate **4.** spurious —ˈ**bastardize** *vt.* **1.** debase **2.** declare illegitimate —ˈ**bastardy** *n.*

baste[1] (bāst) *vt.* **1.** moisten (meat) during cooking with hot fat **2.** beat with stick —ˈ**basting** *n.*

baste[2] (bāst) *vt.* sew loosely, tack

bastinado (bastiˈnādō) *n.* **1.** beating with stick, *esp.* on soles of feet (*pl.* **-es**) —*vt.* **2.** inflict a bastinado on (**-doing, -doed**)

bastion (ˈbaschən) *n.* **1.** projecting part of fortification, tower **2.** strong defense or bulwark

bat[1] (bat) *n.* **1.** any of various types of club used to hit ball in certain sports, *eg* cricket, baseball —*v.* **2.** strike with bat or use bat in sport (**-tt-**) —**'batting** *n.* performance with bat —**'batsman** *n.*

bat[2] (bat) *n.* nocturnal mouselike flying animal

bat[3] (bat) *vt.* flutter (one's eyelids) (**-tt-**)

batch (bach) *n.* group or set of similar objects, *esp.* cakes *etc.* baked together

bated ('bātid) *a.* —**with bated breath** anxiously

bath (băth) *n.* **1.** vessel or place to bathe in **2.** water for bathing **3.** act of bathing —**bath cube** cube of soluble scented material for use in bath —**'bathrobe** *n.* loose-fitting garment of toweling, for wear before or after bath or swimming —**'bathroom** *n.* **1.** room containing bath and usu. washbowl and toilet **2.** toilet —**bath salts** soluble scented salts for use in bath

Bath chair (băth) **UK** invalid chair

bathe (bādh) *vi.* **1.** swim —*vt.* **2.** apply liquid to —*v.* **3.** wash **4.** immerse or be immersed in water (**bathed, 'bathing**) —*n.* **5.** a swim or paddle —**'bather** *n.*

bathometer (bə'thomitər) *n.* instrument for measuring depth of water —**batho'metric** *a.*

bathos ('bāthos) *n.* ludicrous descent from the elevated to the ordinary in writing or speech

bathyscaphe ('bathiskāf, -skaf) *or* **bathyscaph** ('bathiskaf) *n.* vessel for deep-sea observation

bathysphere ('bathisfēər) *n.* strong steel deep-sea diving sphere, lowered by cable

batik (bə'tēk, 'batik) *n.* dyeing process using wax to cover parts not to be dyed

batiste (ba'tēst) *n.* **1.** fine sheer cotton or linen fabric **2.** imitation made of rayon or wool

baton (bə'ton) *n.* **1.** slender stick used by conductor of an orchestra **2.** policeman's truncheon **3.** staff serving as symbol of office

batrachian (bə'trākiən) *n.* any vertebrate amphibian, *esp.* frog or toad

battalion (bə'talyən) *n.* **1.** U.S. Army unit consisting of four or more companies usu. commanded by a lieutenant colonel **2.** large group

batten[1] ('batən) *n.* **1.** narrow piece of board, strip of wood —*vt.* **2.** (*esp. with* down) fasten, make secure

batten[2] ('batən) *vi.* (*usu. with* on) thrive, *esp.* at someone else's expense

batter ('batər) *vt.* **1.** strike continuously —*n.* **2.** mixture of flour, eggs, milk, used in cooking —**battered baby** young child who has sustained serious injuries through violence of parent or other adult —**battering ram** *esp.* formerly, large beam used to break down fortifications

battery ('batəri) *n.* **1.** connected group of electrical cells **2.** any electrical cell or accumulator **3.** number of similar things occurring together **4.** *Law* assault by beating **5.** number of guns **6.** place where they are mounted **7.** unit of artillery **8.** pitcher and catcher of baseball team

batting ('bating) *n.* fiber, used as stuffing

battle ('batəl) *n.* **1.** fight between armies, combat —*vi.* **2.** fight **3.** struggle —**'battlement** *n.* wall, parapet on fortification with openings or embrasures —**battle-ax** *n. inf.* domineering woman —**battle cruiser** high-speed heavily armed warship of battleship size but with light armor —**battle dress** ordinary uniform of soldier —**'battlefield** *or* **'battleground** *n.* place where battle is fought —**battle royal 1.** fight involving more than two combatants **2.** long violent argument —**'battleship** *n.* heavily armed and armored fighting ship

battledore ('batəldôr) *n.* **1.** ancient racket game (*also* **battledore and shuttlecock**) **2.** light racket used in this game

batty ('bati) *a. inf.* crazy, silly

bauble ('bôbəl) *n.* showy trinket

Bauhaus ('bowhows) *n.* center for research and teaching architecture, art and industrial design whose practitioners created the prevailing international style in architecture

bauxite ('bôksīt) *n.* chief ore of aluminum

bawd (bôd) *n.* **1.** prostitute **2.** brothel keeper —**'bawdy** *a.* obscene, lewd

bawl (bôl) *v.* **1.** cry **2.** shout —*n.* **3.** loud cry or shout

bay[1] (bā) *n.* **1.** wide inlet of sea **2.** space between two columns **3.** recess —**bay window 1.** window projecting to exterior thus forming recess in room **2.** potbelly

bay[2] (bā) *n.* **1.** bark **2.** cry of hounds in pursuit —*vi.* **3.** bark —**at bay 1.** cornered **2.** at a distance

bay[3] (bā) *n.* **1.** laurel tree —*pl.* **2.** honorary crown of victory —**'bayberry** *n.* tropical Amer. tree that yields oil —**bay rum** aromatic liquid, used in medicines *etc.*, orig. obtained by distilling leaves of bayberry tree with rum

bay[4] (bā) *a.* (of horse) reddish-brown

bayonet ('bāənit) *n.* **1.** stabbing weapon fixed to rifle —*vt.* **2.** stab with this (**'bayoneted, 'bayoneting**)

bazaar (bə'zär) *n.* **1.** market, *esp.* in Orient **2.** department store **3.** sale of goods for charity

bazooka (bə'zōōkə) *n.* antitank rocket launcher

B.B. 1. ball bearing **2.** base on balls **3.** B'nai Brith

BBB Better Business Bureau

B.B.C. British Broadcasting Corporation

bbl barrel(s)

BC British Columbia

B.C. before Christ

BCD binary code decimal

B.C.E. *Judaism* before Common Era

BCG Bacillus Calmette-Guérin (antituberculosis vaccine)

B.Com. *or* **B.Comm.** Bachelor of Commerce

bd **1.** barrels per day **2.** bound **3.** bundle

BD **1.** Bachelor of Divinity **2.** bills discounted **3.** bomb disposal

bd ft board foot

bdrm bedroom

be (bē; *unstressed* bi) *vi.* **1.** live **2.** exist **3.** have a state or quality (I **am**, he **is**; we, you, they **are**, *pr. ind.* —**was**, *pl.* **were**, *pt.* —**been** *pp.* —ˈ**being** *pr.p.*)

Be *Chem.* beryllium

be- (*comb. form*) **1.** surround; cover, as in *befog* **2.** affect completely, as in *bedazzle* **3.** consider as; cause to be, as in *befriend* **4.** at, for, against, on, or over, as in *bewail, berate*

B.E. **1.** bill of exchange **2.** Bachelor of Engineering

beach (bēch) *n.* **1.** shore of sea —*vt.* **2.** run (boat) on shore —ˈ**beachcomber** *n.* **1.** loafer who lives on casual earnings, *esp.* in S Pacific **2.** one who habitually searches shore debris for items of value —ˈ**beachhead** *n.* **1.** area on beach captured from enemy **2.** base for operations

beacon (ˈbēkən) *n.* **1.** signal fire **2.** lighthouse, buoy **3.** (radio) signal used for navigation

bead (bēd) *n.* **1.** little ball pierced for threading on string of necklace, rosary *etc.* **2.** drop of liquid **3.** narrow molding —ˈ**beaded** *a.* —ˈ**beading** *n.* —ˈ**beady** *a.* small and bright

beadle (ˈbēdəl) *n. Hist.* church or parish officer

beagle (ˈbēgəl) *n.* small short-legged smooth-coated hound

beak (bēk) *n.* **1.** projecting horny jaws of bird **2.** anything pointed or projecting

beaker (ˈbēkər) *n.* **1.** large drinking cup **2.** glass vessel used by chemists and pharmacists

beam (bēm) *n.* **1.** long squared piece of wood **2.** ship's cross timber, side or width **3.** ray of light *etc.* **4.** broad smile **5.** bar of a balance —*vt.* **6.** aim (light, radio waves *etc.*) in a certain direction —*vi.* **7.** shine **8.** smile benignly —**on her beam-ends** (of vessel) heeled over through angle of 90°

bean (bēn) *n.* any of various leguminous plants and their seeds —ˈ**beanery** *n.* restaurant —ˈ**beanbag** *n.* **1.** small cloth bag filled with dried beans and thrown in games **2.** pellet-filled cushion used as furniture —**bean-ball** *n.* baseball pitched at batter's head —**bean curd** soft cheese made from soybean milk (*also* **tofu**) —**bean-eater** *n.* inhabitant of Boston, Massachusetts —**bean pole** tall, skinny person —**bean sprout** shoot of mung bean, eaten raw or cooked —**know one's beans** be informed in or be skillful in one's field of endeavor

bear[1] (bāər) *vt.* **1.** carry **2.** support **3.** produce **4.** endure —*vi.* **5.** (*with* upon) press (upon) (**bore** *pt.*, **born** *or* **borne** *pp.*, ˈ**bearing** *pr.p.*) —ˈ**bearable** *a.* endurable; tolerable —ˈ**bearer** *n.*

bear[2] (bāər) *n.* **1.** any of a family of massive mammals with coarse fur, short legs, plantigrade feet and rudimentary tail and feeding mainly on fruit and insects **2.** any of various other bearlike animals, *eg* ant bear, koala bear **3.** gruff, shambling person **4.** *Fin.* someone who believes the market will decline —**bear garden** scene of tumult —**bear hug** **1.** wrestling hold in which arms are locked round opponent's chest and arms **2.** any similar tight embrace —ˈ**bearskin** *n.* Guards' tall fur helmet

beard (bēərd) *n.* **1.** hair on chin —*vt.* **2.** oppose boldly

bearing (ˈbāəring) *n.* **1.** support or guide for mechanical part, *esp.* one reducing friction **2.** relevance **3.** behavior **4.** direction **5.** relative position **6.** device on shield

beast (bēst) *n.* **1.** animal **2.** four-footed animal **3.** brutal man —ˈ**beastliness** *n.* —ˈ**beastly** *a.*

beat (bēt) *vt.* **1.** strike repeatedly **2.** overcome **3.** surpass **4.** stir vigorously with striking action **5.** flap (wings) **6.** make, wear (path) —*vi.* **7.** throb **8.** sail against wind (**beat** *pt.*, ˈ**beaten, beat** *pp.*) —*n.* **9.** stroke **10.** pulsation **11.** appointed course **12.** basic rhythmic unit in piece of music —*a.* **13.** *sl.* exhausted —ˈ**beater** *n.* **1.** instrument for beating **2.** one who rouses game for shooters

beatify (biˈatifī) *vt.* **1.** make happy **2.** *R.C.Ch.* pronounce in eternal happiness (first step in canonization) (**-fied, -fying**) —**beaˈtific** *a.* —**beatifiˈcation** *n.* —**beˈatitude** *n.* blessedness

beatnik (ˈbētnik) *n.* **1.** member of Beat Generation of 1950s, rebelling against conventional attitudes **2.** *inf.* person with long hair and shabby clothes

beau (bō) *n.* suitor (*pl.* **-s, beaux** (bōz))

Beaufort scale (ˈbōfərt) system of indicating wind strength (from 0, calm, to 12, hurricane)

beaujolais (bōzhōˈlā) *n.* (*sometimes* **B-**) red or white wine from southern Burgundy, France

beauty (ˈbyōōti) *n.* **1.** loveliness, grace **2.** beautiful person or thing —ˈ**beauteous** *a.* —**beauˈtician** *n.* one who works in beauty parlor —ˈ**beautiful** *a.* —ˈ**beautifully** *adv.* —ˈ**beautify** *vt.* —**beauty parlor** *or* **salon** establishment offering hairdressing, manicure *etc.* —**beauty sleep** *inf.* sleep, *esp.* before midnight —**beauty spot** **1.** small dark-colored patch worn on lady's face as adornment **2.** mole or similar natural mark on skin **3.** place of outstanding beauty

beaver (ˈbēvər) *n.* **1.** any of two semiaquatic rodents with webbed hind feet and broad flat tail **2.** fur or pelt of the beaver **3.** hat with plush finish **4.** beard **5.** *offens.* female genitalia —**beaver away** work hard

bebop (ˈbēbop) *n. see* BOP (sense 1)

becalmed (bi'kämd, -'kälmd) *a.* (of ship) motionless through lack of wind
became (bi'kām) *pt. of* BECOME
because (bi'koz, -'kəz) *conj.* since —**because of** on account of
béchamel sauce (bāshə'mel) thick white sauce
bêche-de-mer (beshdə'māər) *n.* edible sea slug
beck (bek) *n.* —**at someone's beck and call** subject to someone's slightest whim
beckon ('bekən) *v.* (*sometimes with* to) summon or lure by silent signal
become (bi'kum) *vi.* **1.** come to be —*vt.* **2.** suit (**be'came** *pt.*, **be'come** *pp.*, **be'coming** *pr.p.*) —**be'coming** *a.* **1.** suitable **2.** proper
bed (bed) *n.* **1.** piece of furniture for sleeping on **2.** garden plot **3.** place in which anything rests **4.** bottom of river **5.** layer, stratum —*vt.* **6.** lay in a bed **7.** plant (**-dd-**) —**'bedding** *n.* —**bed-and-breakfast** *a.* offering overnight accommodation and breakfast —**'bedbug** *n.* blood-sucking small wingless insect with flattened body and characteristic unpleasant odor living in mattresses or cracks of furniture or houses —**'bedclothes** *pl.n.* sheets, blankets and other bed coverings —**bed linen** sheets, pillowcases *etc.* —**'bedpan** *n.* container used as toilet by bedridden people —**'bedridden** *a.* confined to bed by age or sickness —**'bedrock** *n.* —**'bedroom** *n.* —**'bedsitter** *n.* one-roomed apartment —**'bedsore** *n.* chronic ulcer on skin of bedridden person, caused by prolonged pressure —**'bedspread** *n.* top cover on bed —**'bedstead** *n.* —**bed-wetting** *n. see* ENURESIS
B.Ed. Bachelor of Education
bedaub (bi'döb) *vt.* **1.** smear with something thick, sticky or dirty **2.** ornament in gaudy or vulgar fashion
bedeck (bi'dek) *vt.* cover with decorations; adorn
bedevil (bi'devəl) *vt.* **1.** confuse **2.** torment —**be'devilment** *n.*
bedew (bi'dyōō, -'dōō) *vt.* wet as with dew
Bedford cord ('bedfərd) very strong fabric with prominent rib weave made of cotton, wool or rayon
bedizen (bi'dīzən, -'dizən) *vt. obs.* dress gaudily or tastelessly —**be'dizenment** *n.*
bedlam ('bedləm) *n.* noisy confused scene
Bedlington terrier ('bedlingtən) woolly-coated terrier with convex head profile
bedouin *or* **beduin** ('bedŏŏin) *n.* **1.** member of nomadic Arab race —*a.* **2.** nomadic
bedraggle (bi'dragəl) *vt.* dirty by trailing in wet or mud —**be'draggled** *a.*
bee[1] (bē) *n.* social insect that makes honey from nectar gathered from flowers —**bee-eater** *n.* insect-eating bird found in warm regions of Europe, Asia, Afr. and Aust. —**'beehive** *n.* —**'beeline** *n.* shortest route —**'beeswax** *n.* wax secreted by bees —**'beeswing** *n.* filmy crust of tartar that forms in some wines after long keeping in bottle
bee[2] (bē) *n.* social gathering for specific purpose —**spelling bee** competition to test proficiency in spelling
beech (bēch) *n.* **1.** any of family of N Amer. woodland trees common east of the Mississippi with smooth gray bark and triangular nuts eaten by birds and mammals **2.** its wood **3.** any of several European varieties, *eg* copper beech and weeping beech grown as ornamentals —**'beechen** *a.*
beef (bēf) *n.* **1.** flesh of cattle raised and killed for eating **2.** *inf.* complaint —*vi.* **3.** *inf.* complain —**'beefy** *a.* fleshy, stolid —**beeves** *pl.n.* cattle —**'beefburger** *n.* hamburger —**'beefcake** *n.* photographs, usu. in magazines, displaying muscle development of male physique —**'beefeater** *n.* **1.** yeoman of the guard **2.** warder of Tower of London —**beef tea** drink made by boiling pieces of lean beef
Beelzebub (bi'elzibub) *n.* Satan or any devil
been (bēn, bin) *pp. of* BE
beep (bēp) *n.* **1.** short, loud sound of automobile horn *etc.* —*vi.* **2.** make this sound
beer (bēər) *n.* fermented alcoholic drink made from hops and malt —**'beery** *a.* —**beer parlor C** licensed place where beer is sold to the public —**beer and skittles** *inf.* enjoyment or pleasure
beestings ('bēstingz) *pl.n.* (*with sing. v.*) first milk secreted by cow
beet (bēt) *n.* any of various plants with root used for food or extraction of sugar
beetle[1] ('bētəl) *n.* class of insect with hard upper-wing cases closed over the back for protection —**beetle-browed** *a.* with prominent brows
beetle[2] ('bētəl) *vi.* **1.** overhang; jut —*a.* **2.** overhanging; prominent
bef before
befall (bi'föl) *v.* happen (to) (**be'fell, be'fallen**)
befit (bi'fit) *vt.* be suitable to (**-tt-**) —**be'fittingly** *adv.*
befog (bi'fog) *vt.* perplex, confuse (**-gg-**)
before (bi'fōr) *prep.* **1.** in front of **2.** in presence of **3.** in preference to **4.** earlier than —*adv.* **5.** earlier **6.** in front —*conj.* **7.** sooner than —**be'forehand** *adv.* previously
befoul (bi'fowl) *vt.* make filthy
befriend (bi'frend) *vt.* make friend of
befuddle (bi'fudəl) *vt.* **1.** confuse **2.** make stupid with drink —**be'fuddlement** *n.*
beg[1] (beg) *vt.* **1.** ask earnestly, beseech —*vi.* **2.** ask for or live on alms (**-gg-**) —**'beggar** *n.* —**'beggarly** *a.*
beg[2] begin(ning)
began (bi'gan) *pt. of* BEGIN
beget (bi'get) *vt.* produce, generate (**be'got, be'gat** *pt.*, **be'gotten, be'got** *pp.*, **be'getting** *pr.p.*) —**be'getter** *n.*
begin (bi'gin) *v.* **1.** (cause to) start —*vt.* **2.**

originate **3.** initiate (**be'gan, be'gun, be'ginning**) —**be'ginner** *n.* novice —**be'ginning** *n.*

begone (bi'gon) *interj.* go away

begonia (bi'gōnyə) *n.* any of a large genus of tender perennial evergreen and deciduous plants grown for their flowers and foliage

begot (bi'got) *pt./pp. of* BEGET

begrudge (bi'gruj) *vt.* grudge, envy (someone) the possession of

beguile (bi'gīl) *vt.* **1.** charm, fascinate **2.** amuse **3.** deceive —**be'guiler** *n.*

beguine (bi'gēn) *n.* **1.** dance of S Amer. origin **2.** music in rhythm of this dance

begum ('bāgəm) *n. esp.* in India, Muslim woman of high rank

begun (bi'gun) *pp. of* BEGIN

behalf (bi'hăf) *n.* favor, benefit, interest (*esp. in* **in behalf of**)

behave (bi'hāv) *vi.* act, function in particular way —**be'havior** *n.* conduct —**be'haviorism** *n.* school of psychology that regards observable behavior as the only valid subject for study —**behave oneself** conduct oneself (well)

behead (bi'hed) *vt.* cut off head of

beheld (bi'held) *pt./pp. of* BEHOLD

behemoth (bi'hēməth) *n.* **1.** *Bible* gigantic beast described in Job **2.** huge person or thing

behest (bi'hest) *n.* charge, command

behind (bi'hīnd) *prep.* **1.** further back or earlier than **2.** in support of —*adv.* **3.** in the rear —**be'hindhand** *a./adv.* **1.** in arrears **2.** tardy

behold (bi'hōld) *vt.* watch, see (**be'held** *pt.*, **be'held, be'holden** *pp.*) —**be'holder** *n.*

beholden (bi'hōldən) *a.* bound in gratitude

behove (bi'hōv) *vt.* (*only impers.*) be fit, necessary for

beige (bāzh) *n.* **1.** undyed woolen cloth **2.** its color

being ('bēing) *n.* **1.** existence **2.** that which exists **3.** creature —*v.* **4.** *pr.p. of* BE

bejewel (bi'jōōəl) *vt.* decorate as with jewels

bel (bel) *n.* ten decibels

belabor (bi'lābər) *vt.* beat soundly

belated (bi'lātid) *a.* **1.** late **2.** too late

belay (bi'lā) *vt.* fasten (rope) to peg, pin *etc.*

belch (belch) *vi.* **1.** void wind by mouth —*vt.* **2.** eject violently **3.** cast up —*n.* **4.** emission of wind *etc.*

beldam *or* **beldame** ('beldəm) *n. obs.* old woman

beleaguer (bi'lēgər) *vt.* besiege

belfry ('belfri) *n.* bell tower

Belgium ('beljəm) *n.* country in Europe bounded north by the Netherlands, northwest by the North Sea, west and south by France, east by Federal Republic of Germany and Luxembourg —'**Belgian** *n./a.*

Belial ('bēliəl) *n.* the devil, Satan

belie (bi'lī) *vt.* **1.** contradict **2.** misrepresent (**be'lied** *pt./pp.*, **be'lying** *pr.p.*)

believe (bi'lēv) *vt.* **1.** regard as true or real —*vi.* **2.** have faith —**be'lief** *n.* —**be'lievable** *a.* credible —**be'liever** *n. esp.* one of same religious faith

belittle (bi'litəl) *vt.* regard, speak of, as having little worth or value —**be'littlement** *n.*

Belize (bə'lēz) *n.* country in Central America bounded north by Mexico, west by Guatemala and south and east by the Caribbean Sea —**Be'lizean** *n./a.*

bell (bel) *n.* **1.** hollow metal instrument giving ringing sound when struck **2.** electrical device emitting ring or buzz as signal **3.** the sound of this, *esp.* as a signal on a ship to mark the passing of the half hour of each watch: thus eight bells marks the end of each watch —**bell-bottomed** *a.* —**bell-bottoms** *pl.n.* pants that flare from knee —'**bellboy** *n.* page boy in hotel —**bell jar** bell-shaped glass cover to protect flower arrangements *etc.* or to cover apparatus in experiments (*also* **bell glass**) —**bell metal** alloy of copper and tin, used in casting bells —'**bellwether** *n.* **1.** sheep that leads flock, oft. bearing bell **2.** leader, *esp.* one followed blindly

belladonna (belə'donə) *n.* deadly nightshade —**belladonna lily** *see* AMARYLLIS (sense 1)

belle (bel) *n.* beautiful woman, reigning beauty

belles-lettres (*Fr.* bel'letr) *pl.n.* (*with sing. v*) literary works, *esp.* essays and poetry —**bel'letrist** *n.*

bellicose ('belikōs) *a.* warlike

belligerent (bi'lijərənt) *a.* **1.** hostile, aggressive **2.** making war —*n.* **3.** warring person or nation —**bel'ligerence** *n.*

bellow ('belō) *v.* **1.** roar like bull **2.** shout —*n.* **3.** roar of bull **4.** any deep cry or shout

bellows ('belōz) *pl.n.* instrument for creating stream of air

Bell's palsy (belz) paralysis of one side of the face produced by degeneration of the nerve that supplies the muscles of the face

belly ('beli) *n.* **1.** part of body which contains intestines **2.** stomach —*v.* **3.** swell out ('**bellied,** '**bellying**) —**belly ache** *inf.* ache in stomach —'**bellyache** *vi. sl.* complain repeatedly —'**bellybutton** *n. inf.* navel —**belly dance** sensuous dance performed by women, with undulating movements of abdomen —**belly-dance** *vi.* perform belly dance —**belly flop** dive into water in which body lands horizontally —**belly-flop** *vi.* perform belly flop —'**bellyful** *n.* **1.** as much as one wants or can eat **2.** *sl.* more than one can tolerate —**belly laugh** *inf.* hearty laugh

belong (bi'long) *vi.* **1.** (*with* to) be the property or attribute (of) **2.** (*with* to) be a member or inhabitant (of) **3.** have an allotted place **4.** pertain —**be'longings** *pl.n.* personal possessions

beloved (bi'luvid, -'luvd) *a.* **1.** much loved —*n.* **2.** dear one

below (bi'lō) *adv.* **1.** beneath —*prep.* **2.** lower than

Bel Paese (bel pä'äzi) semihard, mold-ripened, rich, creamy cheese with a mild flavor, orig. made in Italy

belt (belt) *n.* **1.** band **2.** girdle **3.** zone or district —*vt.* **4.** surround, fasten with belt **5.** mark with band **6.** *inf.* thrash

beluga (bi'lōōgə) *n.* large white sturgeon

belvedere ('belvidēər) *n.* building, such as summerhouse, sited to command fine view

Bemberg ('bembərg) *n.* trade name for rayon cloth

bemoan (bi'mōn) *vt.* grieve over (loss *etc.*)

bemuse (bi'myōōz) *vt.* confuse, bewilder

ben (ben) *n. Scot., Irish* mountain peak

bench (bench) *n.* **1.** long seat **2.** seat or body of judges *etc.* —*vt.* **3.** provide with benches —**bench mark** fixed point, criterion

bend (bend) *v.* **1.** (cause to) form a curve (**bent** *pt./pp.*) —*n.* **2.** curve —*pl.* **3.** decompression sickness —'**bender** *n. inf.* drinking bout —**bend sinister** *Her.* diagonal line on shield, typically indicating bastard line

beneath (bi'nēth) *prep.* **1.** under, lower than —*adv.* **2.** below

Benedictine (beni'diktin, -tēn) *n.* **1.** monk or nun of order of Saint Benedict **2.** liqueur first made at Benedictine monastery

benediction (beni'dikshən) *n.* invocation of divine blessing

benefit ('benifit) *n.* **1.** advantage, favor, profit, good **2.** fund-raising event, usu. entertainment, for a person or cause —*vt.* **3.** do good to —*vi.* **4.** receive good ('**benefited,** '**benefiting**) —**bene'faction** *n.* —'**benefactor** *n.* **1.** one who helps or does good to others **2.** patron ('**benefactress** *fem.*) —'**benefice** *n.* an ecclesiastical living —**be'neficence** *n.* —**be'neficent** *a.* **1.** doing good **2.** kind —**be'neficently** *adv.* —**bene'ficial** *a.* advantageous, helpful —**bene'ficially** *adv.* —**bene'ficiary** *n.* —**benefit society** association of persons to create a fund for the assistance of its members in case of sudden need

Benelux nations ('beniluks) Belgium, Netherlands and Luxembourg

benevolent (bi'nevələnt) *a.* **1.** kindly **2.** charitable —**be'nevolence** *n.* —**be'nevolently** *adv.*

Bengali (ben'gōli, beng-) *n.* **1.** member of people living chiefly in Bangladesh and West Bengal in India **2.** their language —*a.* **3.** of Bengal, Bengalis or their language —**bengaline** ('benggəlēn) *n.* crosswise-ribbed fabric made of rayon, silk, wool or cotton

benighted (bi'nītid) *a.* ignorant, uncultured

benign (bi'nīn) *a.* **1.** kindly **2.** mild **3.** favorable **4.** (of tumor *etc.*) not malignant —**benignancy** (bi'nignənsi) *n.* —**benignant** (bi'nignənt) *a.* —**benignantly** (bi'nignəntli) *adv.* —**benignity** (bi'nigniti) *n.* —**be'nignly** *adv.*

Benin (bə'nin, -'nēn, 'benin) *n.* country in Africa bounded east by Nigeria, north by Niger and Burkina-Faso, west by Togo and south by the Gulf of Guinea —**Benin'ese** *n./a.*

benison ('benizən, -sən) *n. obs.* blessing

bent (bent) *v.* **1.** *pt./pp. of* BEND —*a.* **2.** curved **3.** resolved (on) **4.** *inf.* corrupt **5.** *inf.* deviant **6.** *inf.* crazy —*n.* **7.** inclination, personal propensity —'**bentwood** *a.* of furniture permanently bent into various forms by heat, moisture and pressure

bentwood chair

bent grass low-growing perennial grass which spreads by rhizomes and is used widely as a fine lawn grass

benumb (bi'num) *vt.* make numb, deaden

Benzedrine ('benzidrēn) *n.* trade name for amphetamine

benzene ('benzēn) *n.* volatile, flammable, carcinogenic cyclic hydrocarbon, the simplest member of the class of aromatic compounds —**benzene ring** planar ring of six carbon atoms arranged in a regular hexagon

benzoin ('benzoin, -zōin) *n.* gum resin obtained from various tropical Asian trees, used in ointments, perfume *etc.*

bequeath (bi'kwēdh, -'kwēth) *vt.* leave (property *etc.*) by will —**bequest** (bi'kwest) *n.* **1.** bequeathing **2.** legacy

berate (bi'rāt) *vt.* scold harshly

Berber ('bərbər) *n.* **1.** member of various Caucasoid peoples of N Afr. **2.** any of the 24 languages of the Afro-Asiatic group of these peoples —*a.* **3.** of these peoples or their languages

berceuse (*Fr.* ber'sœz) *n.* **1.** lullaby **2.** instrumental piece suggestive of this

berdache (bər'dash) *n.* (in some Amerindian tribes) man adopting dress and social role of woman

bereave (bi'rēv) *vt.* (*usu. with* of) deprive (of), *esp.* by death (-'**reaved,** -'**reft** *pt./pp.*) —**be'reavement** *n.* loss, *esp.* by death

beret (bə'rā) *n.* round, close-fitting hat

berg (bərg) *n.* **1.** large mass of ice **2.** SA mountain

bergamot ('bərgəmot) *n.* **1.** ornamental plant of the mint family the leaves of which are dried and used for flavoring and to make Oswego tea **2.** pear-shaped orange cultivated for oil of bergamot obtained from its rind which is also used in confectionery and cooking **3.** type of English pear

beriberi (beri'beri) *n.* disease caused by vitamin B deficiency

berk (bərk) *n. sl.* stupid person

berkelium ('bərkliəm) *n. Chem.* transuranic element *Symbol* Bk, at. wt. 249, at. no. 97

Bermuda (bər'myōōdə) *n.* country consisting of about 150 small islands in the western Atlantic Ocean, 570 miles from Cape Hatteras, North Carolina, and 690 miles from New York —**Ber'mudian** *or* **Ber'mudan** *n./a.* —**Bermuda shorts** close-fitting shorts that come down to knees

berry ('beri) *n.* **1.** small juicy stoneless fruit **2.** *Bot.* fruit in which seeds are imbedded in pulp, *eg* tomato, melon, orange, grape —*vi.* **3.** look for or pick berries

berserk (bər'zərk, -'sərk) *a.* frenzied

berth (bərth) *n.* **1.** ship's mooring place **2.** place to sleep in ship or train —*vt.* **3.** moor

beryl ('beril) *n.* variety of crystalline mineral including aquamarine and emerald

beryllium (be'riliəm) *n. Chem.* metallic element *Symbol* Be, at. wt. 9.0, at. no. 4 —**beryli'osis** *n.* beryllium poisoning

beseech (bi'sēch) *vt.* entreat, implore (**be'sought** *pt./pp.*)

beset (bi'set) *vt.* assail, surround with danger, problems (**be'set, be'setting**)

beside (bi'sīd) *prep.* **1.** by the side of, near **2.** distinct from —**be'sides** *adv./prep.* in addition (to)

besiege (bi'sēj) *vt.* surround (with armed forces *etc.*)

besmirch (bi'smərch) *vt.* **1.** make dirty; soil **2.** reduce brightness of **3.** sully

besom ('bēzəm) *n.* broom, *esp.* one made of bundle of twigs tied to handle

besotted (bi'sotid) *a.* **1.** drunk **2.** foolish **3.** infatuated

besought (bi'sôt) *pt./pp. of* BESEECH

bespangle (bi'spanggəl) *vt.* cover with or as if with spangles

bespatter (bi'spatər) *vt.* **1.** splash, as with dirty water **2.** defile; besmirch

bespeak (bi'spēk) *vt.* engage beforehand (**be'spoke** *pt.*, **be'spoke, be'spoken** *pp.*) —**be'spoke** *a.* **1.** (of garments) made to order **2.** selling such garments

Bessemer process ('besimər) process for producing steel by blowing air through molten pig iron in refractory-lined furnace to remove impurities

best (best) *a./adv.* **1.** *sup. of* GOOD *and* WELL —*vt.* **2.** defeat —**best man** (male) attendant of bridegroom at wedding —**best seller 1.** book or other product that has sold in great numbers **2.** author of one or more such books *etc.*

bestial ('beschəl) *a.* like a beast, brutish —**besti'ality** *n.*

bestiary ('beschəri) *n.* moralizing medieval collection of descriptions of real and/or mythical animals

bestir (bi'stər) *vt.* rouse to activity

bestow (bi'stō) *vt.* give, confer —**be'stowal** *n.*

bestrew (bi'strōō) *vt.* scatter over (surface)

bestride (bi'strīd) *vt.* **1.** sit or stand over with legs apart **2.** mount (horse) (**be'strode, be'stridden, be'striding**)

bet[1] (bet) *v.* **1.** agree to pay (money *etc.*) if wrong (or win if right) in guessing result of contest *etc.* (**bet** *or* **'betted** *pt./pp.*, **'betting** *pr.p.*) —*n.* **2.** money risked in this way

bet[2] between

beta ('bātə) *n.* **1.** second letter in Gr. alphabet (Β or β) **2.** second in group or series

betake (bi'tāk) *vt.* —**betake oneself** go; move

beta particle electron or positron emitted by nucleus during radioactive decay

betatron ('bātətron) *n.* particle accelerator for producing high-energy beams of electrons by magnetic induction

betel ('bētəl) *n.* pepper whose leaves are chewed in parts of Asia as a narcotic —**betel nut** the nut of the areca palm

bête noire (bet 'nwar) *Fr.* pet aversion

bethink (bi'thingk) *obs., dial. v.* **1.** cause (oneself) to consider or meditate —*vt.* **2.** (*oft. with* of) remind (oneself)

betide (bi'tīd) *v.* happen (to)

betimes (bi'tīmz) *adv. obs.* **1.** in good time; early **2.** soon

betoken (bi'tōkən) *vt.* be a sign of

betony ('betəni) *n.* garden perennial grown for its white, silky leaves and reddish-purple flower spike

betray (bi'trā) *vt.* **1.** be disloyal to, *esp.* by assisting an enemy **2.** reveal, divulge **3.** show signs of —**be'trayal** *n.* —**be'trayer** *n.*

betroth (bi'trōdh) *vt.* promise to marry —**be'trothal** *n.* —**be'trothed** *n./a.*

better ('betər) *a./adv.* **1.** *comp. of* GOOD *and* WELL —*v.* **2.** improve —**'betterment** *n.*

between (bi'twēn) *prep./adv.* **1.** in the intermediate part, in space or time **2.** indicating reciprocal relation or comparison

betwixt (bi'twikst) *prep./adv. obs.* between

bevel ('bevəl) *n.* **1.** surface not at right angle to another **2.** slant —*vi.* **3.** slope, slant —*vt.* **4.** cut on slant —*a.* **5.** slanted —**bevel gear** gear having teeth cut into conical surface

beverage ('bevərij, 'bevrij) *n.* drink

bevy ('bevi) *n.* flock or group

bewail (bi'wāl) *vt.* lament

beware (bi'wāər) *v.* be on one's guard (against), be wary (of)

bewilder (bi'wildər) *vt.* puzzle, confuse —**be'wildering** *a.* —**be'wilderingly** *adv.* —**be'wilderment** *n.*

bewitch (bi'wich) *vt.* **1.** cast spell over **2.** charm, fascinate —**be'witching** *a.* —**be'witchingly** *adv.*

bey (bā) *n.* **1.** in Ottoman Empire, title given to provincial governors **2.** in modern Turkey, title of address, corresponding to *Mr.* (*also* **beg**)

beyond (bi'yond) *adv.* **1.** farther away **2.** besides —*prep.* **3.** on the farther side of **4.** later than **5.** surpassing, out of reach of

bezel ('bezəl) *n.* **1.** sloping face adjacent to working edge of cutting tool **2.** oblique faces of cut gem **3.** grooved ring or part holding watch crystal *etc.*

bezique (bi'zēk) *n.* **1.** card game for two players played with a 64-card deck made up of two standard decks with sixes and cards below that rank omitted. The object is to score points by melding and taking tricks **2.** meld of queen of spades and jack of diamonds

b.f. *Print.* boldface

BF **1.** board foot **2.** brought forward **3.** *inf.* boyfriend

BG *or* **B. Gen** brigadier general

Bhagavad Gita ('bägəväd 'gētə) 'The Song of the Lord', the most popular book of Hindu scripture which conveys the message that there are many ways to salvation

bhang (bang) *n.* preparation of leaves and flower tops of Indian hemp, much used as narcotic in India

b.h.p. brake horsepower

Bhutan (bōō'tan, -'tän) *n.* country in Asia situated in the eastern Himalaya Mountains bordered on the north and east by Tibet and India, on the west by Sikkim and on the south by India —**Bhutan'ese** *n./a.*

Bi *Chem.* bismuth

bi- *or sometimes before vowel* **bin-** (*comb. form*) **1.** two; having two, as in *bifocal* **2.** occurring every two, as in *biennial* **3.** on both sides *etc.*, as in *bilateral* **4.** occurring twice during, as in *biweekly* **5.** indicating acid salt of dibasic acid, as in *sodium bicarbonate*

B.I.A. **1.** Bureau of Indian Affairs **2.** Braille Institute of America

biannual (bī'anyōōəl) *a.* occurring twice a year —**bi'annually** *adv.*

bias ('bīəs) *n.* **1.** slant **2.** personal inclination or preference **3.** one-sided inclination (*pl.* **-es**) —*vt.* **4.** influence, affect (**-s-**, **-ss-**) —**'biased** *a.* prejudiced —**bias binding** strip of material cut on bias, used for binding hems or for decoration

biathlon (bī'athlən, -lon) *n.* athletic event comprising skiing and rifle shooting

biaxial (bī'aksiəl) *a.* (*esp.* of crystal) having two axes

bib (bib) *n.* **1.** cloth put under child's chin to protect clothes when eating **2.** top of apron or overalls —**best bib and tucker** best clothes

Bibb lettuce (bib) variety of lettuce with small head and dark green leaves

bibcock ('bibkok) *n.* faucet with nozzle bent downward

bibelot ('bēbəlō) *n.* attractive or curious trinket

bibl. **1.** bibliographical **2.** bibliography

Bibl. Biblical

Bible ('bībəl) *n.* the sacred writings of the Christian religion —**biblical** ('biblikəl) *a.* —**biblicist** ('biblisist) *n.*

biblio- (*comb. form*) book or books, as in *bibliography*

bibliography (bibli'ogrəfi) *n.* **1.** list of books on a subject **2.** history and description of books —**bibli'ographer** *n.* —**biblio'graphical** *a.*

bibliomania (bibliō'māniə) *n.* extreme fondness for books —**biblio'maniac** *n./a.*

bibliophile ('bibliəfīl) *or* **bibliophil** ('bibliəfil) *n.* lover, collector of books —**bibli'ophily** *n.*

bibliotherapy (bibliō'therəpi) *n.* the treatment of illness by using books and other reading materials

bibulous ('bibyōōləs) *a.* given to drinking

bicameral (bī'kamərəl) *a.* (of legislature) consisting of two chambers —**bi'cameralism** *n.*

bicarbonate (bī'kärbənit, -nāt) *n.* chemical compound releasing carbon dioxide when mixed with acid —**bicarbonate of soda** sodium bicarbonate

bicentennial (bīsen'teniəl) *or* **bicentenary** (bīsen'tēnəri) *n.* **1.** two hundredth anniversary **2.** its celebration

biceps ('bīseps) *n.* two-headed muscle, *esp.* muscle of upper arm

bicker ('bikər) *vi./n.* quarrel over petty things —**'bickering** *n.*

bicolor ('bīkulər) *or* **bicolored** ('bīkulərd) *a.* two-colored

bicuspid (bī'kuspid) *a.* **1.** having two points —*n.* **2.** bicuspid tooth; premolar

bicycle ('bīsikəl) *n.* vehicle with two wheels, one in front of other, pedaled by rider —**'bicyclist** *n.*

bid (bid) *vt.* **1.** offer **2.** say **3.** command **4.** invite (**bade** *or* **bid, 'bidden**) —*n.* **5.** offer, *esp.* of price **6.** try **7.** *Cards* call —**'biddable** *a.* **1.** having sufficient value to be bid on **2.** docile; obedient —**'biddableness** *n.* —**'bidder** *n.* —**'bidding** *n.*

biddy ('bidi) *n. dial.* young chicken or hen

bide (bīd) *vi.* **1.** remain **2.** dwell —*vt.* **3.** await (**'bided** *or* **bode, 'bided**) —**'biding** *n.*

bidet (bē'dā) *n.* low basin for washing genital area and posterior of body

Biedermeier ('bēdərmīər) *a.* of German and Austrian form of empire style ca. 1815-48, *esp.* in furniture

biennial (bī'eniəl) *a.* **1.** happening every two years **2.** lasting two years —*n.* **3.** plant living two years —**bi'ennially** *adv.*

bier (bēər) *n.* **1.** coffin and its stand **2.** frame for bearing dead to grave

biff (bif) *sl. n.* **1.** blow with fist —*vt.* **2.** give (someone) such a blow

bifid (ˈbīfid) *a.* divided into two lobes by median cleft —**biˈfidity** *n.*

bifocal (bīˈfōkəl) *a.* having two different focal lengths —**biˈfocals** *pl.n.* eyeglasses having bifocal lenses for near and distant vision

bifurcate (ˈbīfərkāt) *vi.* **1.** divide into two branches —*a.* (ˈbīfərkāt, -kit) **2.** forked or divided into two branches —**bifurˈcation** *n.*

big (big) *a.* of great or considerable size, height, number, power *etc.* (ˈ**bigger** *comp.*, ˈ**biggest** *sup.*) —ˈ**bigness** *n.* —**Big Board** the New York Stock Exchange —**Big Brother** person or organization that exercises total dictatorial control —**big deal!** *sl.* you can't impress me! —**Big Dipper** the seven main stars in the constellation of Ursa Major which are arranged in the form of a dipper —**big league 1.** league of highest division in baseball **2.** highest level of enterprise —**big name** famous person —**big shot** *sl.* important person —**big stick** *inf.* force or threat of force —**big time** *sl.* highest level of profession, *esp.* entertainment —**big-timer** *n.* —**big top** *inf.* **1.** main tent of circus **2.** circus itself —ˈ**bigwig** *n. sl.* important person

bigamy (ˈbigəmi) *n.* crime of marrying a person while one is still legally married to someone else —ˈ**bigamist** *n.* —ˈ**bigamous** *a.*

bight (bīt) *n.* **1.** curve or loop in rope **2.** long curved shoreline or water bounded by it

bigot (ˈbigət) *n.* person intolerant or not receptive to ideas of others, *esp.* on religion *etc.* —ˈ**bigoted** *a.* —ˈ**bigotry** *n.*

bijou (ˈbēzho͞o) *n.* **1.** something small and delicately worked (*pl.* **-joux** (-zho͞oz)) —*a.* **2.** small but tasteful

bike (bīk) *n.* **1.** bicycle **2.** motorbike

bikini (biˈkēni) *n.* **1.** woman's brief two-piece bathing suit **2.** man or woman's low-cut briefs

bilateral (bīˈlatərəl) *a.* two-sided

bile (bīl) *n.* **1.** fluid secreted by the liver **2.** anger, ill temper —**biliary** (ˈbilieri) *a.* of bile, ducts that convey bile, or gall bladder —**bilious** (ˈbilyəs) *a.* nauseous, nauseating —**biliousness** (ˈbilyəsnis) *n.* —**biliary calculus** gallstone

bilge (bilj) *n.* **1.** bottom of ship's hull **2.** dirty water that collects in vessel's bilge (*also* **bilge water**) **3.** *inf.* nonsense —*vi.* **4.** spring a leak

bilharzia (bilˈhärziə) *n.* schistosomiasis

bilingual (bīˈlinggwəl) *a.* speaking, or written in, two languages —**biˈlingualism** *n.* equal competence in two languages

bilk (bilk) *vt.* **1.** balk; thwart **2.** (*oft. with* of) cheat, deceive **3.** escape from; elude —*n.* **4.** swindle, cheat **5.** person who swindles or cheats —ˈ**bilker** *n.*

bill[1] (bil) *n.* **1.** written account of charges **2.** draft of law presented for enactment by legislative assembly **3.** poster **4.** commercial document **5.** piece of paper money —*vt.* **6.** present account of charges to **7.** announce by advertisement —ˈ**billing** *n.* degree of importance, *esp.* in theater *etc.* —ˈ**billboard** *n.* **1.** large board for displaying advertisements **2.** ledge on vessel on which anchor rests —**bill of exchange** written order to pay designated sum to a nominated person —**bill of fare** menu, program —**bill of health 1.** certificate of freedom from disease, usu. of ship's company **2.** favorable account of person's or company's financial position —**bill of indictment** indictment before it is presented to a grand jury —**bill of lading** list giving details of ship's cargo —**Bill of Rights** statement of people's rights and privileges as guaranteed in the first 10 amendments to U.S. Constitution —**bill of sale** document transferring ownership of personal property

bill[2] (bil) *n.* **1.** bird's beak —*vi.* **2.** touch bills, as doves **3.** caress

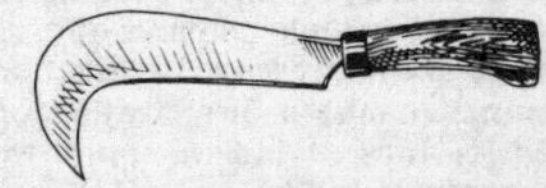
billhook

bill[3] (bil) *n.* **1.** tool for pruning **2.** hooked weapon —ˈ**billhook** *n.* hatchet with hook at end of cutting edge

billabong (ˈbiləbong) *n.* **A** pool in intermittent stream

billet[1] (ˈbilit) *n.* **1.** civilian quarters for troops **2.** resting place —*vt.* **3.** quarter, as troops

billet[2] (ˈbilit) *n.* **1.** chunk of wood, *esp.* for fuel **2.** small bar of iron or steel

billet-doux (bilāˈdo͞o) *Fr.* love letter

billiards (ˈbilyərdz) *pl.n.* (*with sing. v.*) **1.** indoor game played with ivory or composition balls and a cue on felt-covered rectangular table whose object is to propel the cue ball to hit the two object balls in succession (*also* **carom billiards**) **2.** game played on billiard table with pockets when the object is to drive a number of colored balls into pockets (*also* **pocket billiards, pool**)

billion (ˈbilyən) *n.* in U.S. and France, the numeral 1 followed by 9 zeros, a thousand millions; in U.K. and Germany, the numeral 1 followed by 12 zeros, a million millions

billow (ˈbilō) *n.* **1.** great swelling wave —*pl.* **2.** the sea —*vi.* **3.** surge **4.** swell out

billy (ˈbili) *n.* policeman's club

billy goat male goat

Biloxi (biˈloksi) *n.* (member of) Siouan-speaking Amerindian people of Mississippi (*pl.* **Biloxi, -s**)

biltong (ˈbiltong) *n.* **SA** thin strips of meat dried in sun

bimetallism (bīˈmetəlizəm) *n.* use of two

metals, *esp.* gold and silver, in fixed relative values as standard of value and currency

bimonthly (bī'munthli) *adv./a.* **1.** every two months **2.** twice a month

bin (bin) *n.* **1.** receptacle for corn, refuse *etc.* **2.** one particular bottling of wine

binary ('bīnəri) *a.* **1.** composed of, characterized by, two **2.** dual —**binary star** double star system containing two associated stars revolving around common center of gravity

bind (bīnd) *vt.* **1.** tie fast **2.** tie round, gird **3.** tie together **4.** oblige **5.** seal **6.** constrain **7.** bandage **8.** unite **9.** put (book) into cover —*v.* **10.** (cause to) cohere (**bound** *pt./pp.*) —'**binder** *n.* one who, or that which binds —'**bindery** *n.* —'**binding** *n.* **1.** cover of book **2.** tape for hem *etc.* —'**bindweed** *n.* convolvulus

bine (bīn) *n.* climbing or twining stem of any of various plants, such as woodbine

binge (binj) *n. inf.* **1.** excessive indulgence in eating or drinking **2.** spree

bingo ('binggō) *n.* game of chance in which numbers drawn are matched with those on a card

binnacle ('binəkəl) *n.* box holding ship's compass

binocular (bi'nokyōōlər, bī-) *a.* seeing with, made for both eyes —**bi'noculars** *pl.n.* telescope made for both eyes

binomial (bī'nōmiəl) *a./n.* (denoting) mathematical expression consisting of two terms connected by a plus sign or a minus sign —**binomial nomenclature** system for naming plants and animals giving every species an official scientific name accepted internationally —**binomial theorem** general formula that expresses any power of binomial

bio- *or before vowel* **bi-** (*comb. form*) life, living, as in *biochemistry.* Such words are not given here where the meaning may easily be inferred from the simple word

bioastronautics (bīōastrə'nōtiks) *pl.n.* (*with sing. v.*) study of effects of space flight on living organisms

biocenosis (bīōsi'nōsis) *n.* relationships between animals and plants subsisting together

biochemistry (bīō'kemistri) *n.* science concerned with the chemistry of plants and animals

biodegradable (bīōdi'grādəbəl) *a.* capable of decomposition by natural means

bioengineering (bīōenji'nēəring) *n.* **1.** design and manufacture of aids to rectify defective body functions **2.** design, manufacture and maintenance of engineering equipment used in biosynthetic processes —**bioengi'neer** *n.*

biofeedback (bīō'fēdbak) *n.* the mechanical monitoring of bodily functions for the purpose of gaining control over the functions monitored

biog. **1.** biographer **2.** biographical **3.** biography

biogenesis (bīō'jenisis) *n.* principle that living organism must originate from similar parent organism —**bioge'netic(al)** *a.*

biography (bī'ogrəfi) *n.* story of one person's life —**bi'ographer** *n.* —**bio'graphical** *a.* —**bio'graphically** *adv.*

biol. **1.** biological **2.** biology

biology (bī'oləji) *n.* study of living organisms —**bio'logical** *a.* —**bio'logically** *adv.* —**bi'ologist** *n.* —**biological clock** means by which living organisms can time their rhythmic periods without external cues —**biological control** control of destructive organisms by nonchemical means —**biological warfare** use of living organisms or their toxic products as weapon of war

biomass ('bīōmas) *n.* the various forms of plant and animal life on the earth

biomedicine (bīō'medisin) *n.* medical and biological study of effects of unusual environmental stress

bionics (bī'oniks) *pl.n.* (*with sing. v.*) study of relation of biological and electronic processes —**bi'onic** *a.* having physical functions augmented by electronic equipment

biophysics (bīō'fiziks) *pl.n.* (*with sing. v.*) physics of biological processes and application of methods used in physics to biology —**bio'physical** *a.* —**biophysicist** (bīō'fizisist) *n.*

biopolymer (bīō'polimər) *n.* polymeric substance found in living organisms, *esp.* proteins, carbohydrates and nucleic acids

biopsy ('bīopsi) *n.* examination of tissue removed surgically from a living body

biorhythm ('bīōridhəm) *n.* complex repeated pattern of physiological states, believed to affect physical, emotional, or mental states

bioscope ('bīəskōp) *n.* **SA** cinema

bioscopy (bī'oskəpi) *n.* examination of body to determine whether it is alive

biosphere ('bīəsfēər) *n.* part of earth's surface and atmosphere inhabited by living things

biosynthesis (bīō'sinthisis) *n.* formation of chemical compounds by living organisms —**biosynthetic** (bīōsin'thetik) *a.*

biotin ('bīətin) *n.* vitamin of B complex, abundant in egg yolk and liver

bipartisan (bī'pärtizən) *a.* consisting of or supported by two political parties

bipartite (bī'pärtīt) *a.* consisting of two parts or parties

biped ('bīped) *n.* two-footed animal —**bi'pedal** *a.*

biplane ('bīplān) *n.* airplane with two pairs of wings

bipolar (bī'pōlər) *a.* **1.** having two poles **2.** of North and South Poles **3.** having two opposed opinions *etc.*—**bipo'larity** *n.*

birch (bərch) *n.* **1.** tree with silvery bark —*vt.* **2.** flog —'**birchen** *a.* —'**birchbark** *n.*

canoe made of birch bark —**birch beer** carbonated or fermented drink flavored with extract of birch bark

bird (bərd) *n.* **1.** warm-blooded egg-laying vertebrate with a feathered body, scaly legs, and forelimbs modified to form wings **2.** *inf.* a person **3.** shuttlecock —**'birder** *n.* **1.** birdwatcher **2.** one who catches or hunts birds to sell —**'birdbrain** *n.* **1.** stupid person **2.** scatterbrain —**'birdlime** *n.* **1.** sticky substance smeared on twigs to catch birds —*vt.* **2.** smear with birdlime —**bird of paradise 1.** any of various brilliantly plumed birds of the New Guinea area **2.** perennial house plant with flower resembling bird's head —**bird of passage 1.** transient person **2.** migratory bird —**bird's eye** fabric or wood marked with spots resembling bird's eye —**bird's-eye** *a.* seen from above, summarizing (*esp. in* **bird's-eye view**) —**'birdwatcher** *n.* person who observes or identifies birds in their natural habitat —**get the bird** *sl.* be rejected —**strictly for the birds** *sl.* trivial, to be regarded with contempt

birdie ('bərdi) *n.* **1.** *Golf* score of one stroke under par for hole **2.** *inf.* bird, *esp.* small bird

biretta (bi'retə) *n.* square cap worn by Catholic clergy

birth (bərth) *n.* **1.** bearing, or the being born, of offspring **2.** parentage, origin **3.** noble descent —**birth control** limitation of child bearing usu. by artificial means —**'birthday** *n.* —**birthday suit** state of nakedness —**'birthmark** *n.* blemish, usu. dark, formed on skin before birth —**birth rate** ratio of live births in specified area *etc.* to population, usu. expressed per 1000 population per year —**'birthright** *n.* **1.** privileges that person is entitled to as soon as he is born **2.** privileges of first-born son **3.** inheritance —**'birthstone** *n.* precious or semiprecious stone associated with month or sign of zodiac and thought to bring luck if worn by person born in that month

biscuit ('biskit) *n.* **1.** dry, small, thin variety of bread **2.** unglazed porcelain or pottery

bisect (bī'sekt) *vt.* divide into two equal parts —**bi'sector** *n.*

bisexual (bī'sekshŏŏəl) *a.* **1.** sexually attracted to both men and women **2.** of both sexes

bishop ('bishəp) *n.* **1.** clergyman governing diocese **2.** chessman —**'bishopric** *n.* diocese or office of a bishop

bismuth ('bizməth) *n.* *Chem.* metallic element *Symbol* Bi, at. wt. 209.0, at. no. 83

bison ('bīsən) *n.* **1.** large wild ox **2.** Amer. buffalo

bisque[1] (bisk) *n.* thick rich soup made from shellfish

bisque[2] (bisk) *n.* **1.** pink to yellowish tan color **2.** earthenware or porcelain that has been fired but not glazed

bister *or* **bistre** ('bistər) *n.* **1.** transparent water-soluble brownish-yellow pigment made by boiling soot of wood **2.** yellowish-brown to dark brown color

bistro ('bēstrō) *n.* small restaurant

bit[1] (bit) *n.* **1.** fragment, piece **2.** biting, cutting part of tool **3.** mouthpiece of horse's bridle —**'bitty** *a.* **1.** lacking unity; disjointed **2.** containing bits, sediment *etc.*

bit[2] (bit) *pt./pp. of* BITE

bit[3] (bit) *n.* *Comp.* smallest unit of information

bitch (bich) *n.* **1.** female dog, fox or wolf **2.** *offens. sl.* spiteful woman **3.** *inf.* complaint —*vi.* **4.** *inf.* complain —**'bitchy** *a.*

bite (bīt) *vt.* **1.** cut into, *esp.* with teeth **2.** grip —*vi.* **3.** rise to bait —*v.* **4.** (of corrosive material) eat away or into (**bit** *pt.*, **bit, 'bitten** *pp.*, **'biting** *pr.p.*) —*n.* **5.** act of biting **6.** wound so made **7.** mouthful —**'biter** *n.* —**'biting** *a.* **1.** piercing; keen **2.** sarcastic; incisive —**'bitingly** *adv.*

bitter ('bitər) *a.* **1.** sharp, sour-tasting **2.** unpleasant **3.** (of person) angry or resentful **4.** sarcastic —**'bitterly** *adv.* —**'bitterness** *n.* —**'bitters** *pl.n.* essence of bitter herbs —**bitter end** final extremity —**'bittersweet** *n.* **1.** N Amer. climbing plant **2.** woody nightshade —*a.* **3.** being a mixture of bitterness and sweetness **4.** pleasant but tinged with sadness

bittern ('bitərn) *n.* any of various nocturnal herons noted for their booming cry

bitumen (bi'tyōōmin, -'tōō-) *n.* viscous substance occurring in asphalt, tar *etc.* —**bi'tuminous** *a.*

bivalent (bī'vālənt) *a.* **1.** *Chem. see* DIVALENT **2.** (of homologous chromosomes) associated together in pairs —**bi'valency** *n.*

bivalve ('bīvalv) *a.* **1.** having a double shell —*n.* **2.** mollusk with such shell

bivouac ('bivŏŏak, 'bivwak) *n.* **1.** temporary encampment of soldiers, hikers *etc.* —*vi.* **2.** pass the night in temporary camp (**'bivouacked, 'bivouacking**)

bizarre (bi'zär) *a.* unusual, weird

bk 1. bank **2.** book **3.** brook

Bk berkelium

bkgd background

bks barracks

bl 1. bale **2.** barrel **3.** black **4.** block **5.** blue

blab (blab) *v.* **1.** reveal (secrets) —*vi.* **2.**

chatter idly (**-bb-**) —*n.* **3.** telltale **4.** gossip —**'blabber** *n.* **1.** person who blabs **2.** idle chatter —*vi.* **3.** talk without thinking; chatter

black (blak) *a.* **1.** of the darkest color **2.** without light **3.** dark **4.** evil **5.** somber **6.** dishonorable —*n.* **7.** darkest color **8.** black dye, clothing *etc.* **9.** (**B-**) person of dark-skinned race —*vt.* **10.** boycott (specified goods *etc.*) in industrial dispute —**'blacken** *v.* —**'blacking** *n.* substance used for blacking and cleaning leather *etc.* —**'blackamoor** *n. obs.* Negro or other person with dark skin —**black-and-blue** *a.* **1.** (of skin) discolored, as from bruise **2.** feeling pain, as from beating —**black-and-white** *n.* photograph *etc.* in black, white, and shades of gray rather than in color —**black art** black magic —**'blackball** *vt.* vote against, exclude —**black belt 1.** (*oft.* **B- B-**) region or area occupied by Blacks **2.** highest ranking in judo and karate; person of this rank —**'blackberry** *n.* plant with thorny stems and dark juicy berries, bramble —**'blackbird** *n.* common European and Asian songbird —**'blackboard** *n.* dark-colored surface for writing on with chalk —**black book** book containing names of people to be punished, blacklisted *etc.* —**black box** *inf.* flight recorder —**'blackcap** *n.* European warbler —**'blackcock** *n.* male of the black grouse —**black'currant** *n.* **1.** N temperate shrub having edible black berries **2.** its fruit —**black eye** *inf.* bruising round eye —**black gum** woodland tree of eastern N Amer. of the dogwood family characterized by sharp horizontal twigs and branches (*also* **sour gum, pepperidge, 'tupelo**) —**'blackhead** *n.* dark, fatty plug blocking pore in skin —**black hole** *Astron.* region of space resulting from collapse of star, and surrounded by gravitational field that neither matter nor radiation could escape from —**'blackjack** *n.* **1.** flexible loaded club **2.** card game in which the object is to hold a combination of cards higher than dealer but totaling less than 21 (*also* **twenty-one**) —**'blackleg** *n.* **1.** swindling gambler **2.** disease of cattle —**'blacklist** *n.* **1.** list of people, organizations considered suspicious, untrustworthy *etc.* —*vt.* **2.** put on blacklist —**black magic** magic used for evil purposes —**'blackmail** *vt.* **1.** extort money from (a person) by threats —*n.* **2.** act of blackmailing **3.** money extorted thus —**'blackmailer** *n.* —**Black Maria** (mə'rīə) patrol wagon —**black mark** indication of disapproval *etc.* —**black market** illegal buying and selling of goods —**black mass** travesty of Christian Mass performed by practitioners of black magic —**Black Muslim** member of Amer. Muslim sect advocating establishment of separate Black nation in U.S. —**'blackout** *n.* **1.** complete failure of electricity supply **2.** sudden cutting off of all stage lights **3.** state of temporary unconsciousness **4.** obscuring of all lights as precaution against night air attack —**Black Power** social, economic, and political movement of Black people to obtain equality with Whites —**black sheep** person regarded as disgrace or failure by his family or group —**'Blackshirt** *n.* member of fascist organization, *esp.* It. Fascist party before and during World War II —**'blacksmith** *n.* smith who works in iron —**black spot** any of several plant diseases —**'blackthorn** *n.* shrub with black twigs —**black tie** *n.* **1.** black bow tie worn with dinner jacket —*a.* **2.** denoting occasion when dinner jacket should be worn —**black widow** poisonous spider, female having red hourglass spot on abdomen —**black out 1.** obliterate or extinguish (lights) **2.** create a blackout in (a city *etc.*) **3.** lose consciousness, vision or memory temporarily —**in black and white** in print or writing; in extremes —**the Black Death** name given to bubonic plague pandemic in Europe during 14th cent.

Blackfoot ('blakfo͝ot) *n.* **1.** confederacy of Amerindians of Montana, Alberta and Saskatchewan **2.** member of the Blackfoot (*pl.* **Blackfoot, 'Blackfeet**) **3.** the Algonquian language of the Blackfoot

blackguard ('blagärd, -gərd) *n.* **1.** scoundrel —*a.* **2.** unprincipled, wicked —*vt.* **3.** revile —**'blackguardism** *n.* —**'blackguardly** *a.*

bladder ('bladər) *n.* membranous bag to contain liquid, *esp.* urinary bladder

blade (blād) *n.* **1.** edge, cutting part of knife or tool **2.** leaf of grass *etc.* **3.** sword **4.** *obs.* dashing fellow **5.** flat of oar

blain (blān) *n.* **1.** inflamed swelling **2.** pimple, blister

blame (blām) *n.* **1.** censure **2.** culpability —*vt.* **3.** find fault with **4.** censure —**'blamable** *or* **'blameable** *a.* —**'blameless** *a.* —**'blameworthy** *a.*

blanch (blanch) *vt.* **1.** whiten, bleach, take color out of **2.** (of foodstuffs) briefly boil or fry —*v.* **3.** turn pale

blancmange (blə'monzh) *n.* Jello-like dessert made with milk

bland (bland) *a.* **1.** devoid of distinctive characteristics **2.** smooth in manner

blandish ('blandish) *vt.* **1.** coax **2.** flatter —**'blandishments** *pl.n.*

blank (blangk) *a.* **1.** without marks or writing **2.** empty **3.** vacant, confused **4.** (of verse) without rhyme —*n.* **5.** empty space **6.** void **7.** cartridge containing no bullet —**'blankly** *adv.* —**blank check 1.** check that has been signed but on which amount payable has not been specified **2.** complete freedom of action —**blank verse** unrhymed verse, *esp.* in iambic pentameters

blanket ('blangkit) *n.* **1.** thick (woolen) covering for bed **2.** concealing cover —*vt.* **3.** cover with blanket **4.** cover, stifle —**blanket stitch** strong reinforcing stitch for edges of blankets and other thick material

blare (blāər) *v.* **1.** sound loudly and harshly —*n.* **2.** such sound

blarney ('blärni) *n.* flattering talk —**Blarney stone** stone at Blarney Castle in Ireland said to confer a skillful tongue on those who kiss it

blasé (blä'zā) *a.* **1.** indifferent through familiarity **2.** bored

blaspheme (blas'fēm) *v.* show contempt for (God or sacred things, *esp.* in speech) —**blas'phemer** *n.* —**blasphemous** ('blasfiməs) *a.* —**blasphemously** ('blasfiməsli) *adv.* —**blasphemy** ('blasfimi) *n.*

blast (bläst) *n.* **1.** explosion **2.** high-pressure wave of air coming from an explosion **3.** current of air **4.** gust of wind or air **5.** loud sound **6.** *sl.* reprimand —*vt.* **7.** blow up **8.** remove, open *etc.* by explosion **9.** blight **10.** ruin —'**blasted** *a.* **1.** blighted, withered **2.** damned —**blast furnace** furnace for smelting ore, using preheated blast of air —'**blastoff** *n.* **1.** launching of rocket **2.** time at which this occurs —**blast off** be launched

blastomycosis (blastōmī'kōsis) *n.* fungus disease, apparently limited to N Amer. continent affecting the skin and internal organs (*also* **Gilchrist's disease**)

blatant ('blātənt) *a.* obvious —'**blatancy** *n.*

blather ('bladhər) *vi.* **1.** speak foolishly —*n.* **2.** foolish talk; nonsense

Blaue Reiter ('blowə 'rītər) *Ger.* —**der Blaue Reiter** (dər). group of Munich-based artists formed in 1911 to attest to liveliness of modern art

blaze[1] (blāz) *n.* **1.** strong fire or flame **2.** brightness **3.** outburst —*vi.* **4.** burn strongly **5.** be very angry

blaze[2] (blāz) *v.* **1.** mark (trees) to establish trail —*n.* **2.** mark on tree **3.** white mark on horse's face

blaze[3] (blāz) *vt.* **1.** proclaim, publish (as with trumpet) —*n.* **2.** wide publicity

blazer ('blāzər) *n.* type of jacket, worn *esp.* for sports

blazon ('blāzən) *vt.* **1.** make public, proclaim **2.** describe, depict (arms) —*n.* **3.** coat of arms

bldg building

bleach (blēch) *v.* **1.** make or become white —*n.* **2.** bleaching substance

bleak[1] (blēk) *a.* **1.** cold and cheerless **2.** exposed —'**bleakly** *adv.*

bleak[2] (blēk) *n.* European river fish of the carp family

bleary ('blēəri) *a.* with eyes dimmed, as by tears or tiredness —**bleary-eyed** *or* **blear-eyed** *a.* having bleary eyes

bleat (blēt) *vi.* **1.** cry, as sheep —*v.* **2.** say, speak plaintively —*n.* **3.** sheep's cry

bleed (blēd) *vi.* **1.** lose blood —*vt.* **2.** draw blood or liquid from **3.** extort money from (**bled** *pt./pp.*)

bleep (blēp) *n.* short high-pitched sound —'**bleeper** *n.* small portable electronic signaling device

blemish ('blemish) *n.* **1.** defect **2.** stain —*vt.* **3.** make (something) defective, dirty *etc.* —'**blemished** *a.*

blench (blench) *vi.* start back, flinch

blend (blend) *vt.* **1.** mix —*n.* **2.** mixture —'**blender** *n.* one who, that which blends, *esp.* electrical kitchen appliance for mixing food (*also* **liquidizer**)

blende (blend) *n.* **1.** a zinc ore **2.** any of several sulfide ores

blenny ('bleni) *n.* any of several small fishes of rocky shores, with tapering scaleless body

blesbok ('blesbok) *n.* S Afr. antelope

bless (bles) *vt.* **1.** consecrate **2.** give thanks to **3.** ask God's favor for **4.** (*usu. pass.*) endow (with) **5.** glorify **6.** make happy (**blessed, blest** *pp.*) —**blessed** ('blesid) *a.* **1.** made holy **2.** worthy of deep reverence **3.** *R.C.Ch.* (of person) beatified by pope **4.** characterized by happiness **5.** bringing great happiness **6.** damned —**blessedness** ('blesidnis) *n.* —'**blessing** *n.* **1.** (ceremony asking for) God's protection, aid **2.** short prayer **3.** approval **4.** welcome event, benefit

Bleu cheese (bloo͞) *see* **blue cheese** *at* BLUE

blew (bloo͞) *pt. of* BLOW[1]

blight (blīt) *n.* **1.** plant disease **2.** harmful influence —*vt.* **3.** injure as with blight

blimp (blimp) *n.* small, nonrigid airship used for observing

blind (blīnd) *a.* **1.** unable to see **2.** heedless, random **3.** dim **4.** closed at one end **5.** *sl.* very drunk —*vt.* **6.** deprive of sight —*n.* **7.** something cutting off light **8.** window screen **9.** pretext —'**blindly** *adv.* —'**blindness** *n.* —**blind alley 1.** alley open at one end only; cul-de-sac **2.** *inf.* situation in which no further progress can be made —**blind date** *inf.* social meeting between man and woman who have not met before —'**blindfold** *vt.* **1.** cover the eyes of, so as to prevent vision —*n.* **2.** piece of cloth *etc.* used to cover eyes —**blindman's buff** game in which one player is blindfolded —**blind spot 1.** small area of retina, where optic nerve enters, in which vision is not experienced **2.** area where vision is obscured **3.** subject about which person is ignorant or prejudiced —**blind trust** arrangement made by person, usu. politician, to relinquish control of his financial affairs by placing it in the hands of an agent during his period of office

blink (blingk) *vi.* **1.** wink **2.** twinkle **3.** shine intermittently —*n.* **4.** gleam —'**blinkers** *pl.n.* leather flaps to prevent horse from seeing to the side —**blink at** see, know about, but ignore —**on the blink** *inf.* not working (properly)

blintz (blints) *n.* pancake folded around a filling of cottage cheese or fruit and covered with sour cream

blip (blip) *n.* repetitive sound or visible pulse, *eg* on radar screen

bliss (blis) *n.* perfect happiness —**'blissful** *a.* —**'blissfully** *adv.* —**'blissfulness** *n.*

blister ('blistər) *n.* **1.** bubble on skin **2.** surface swelling, *eg* on paint —*v.* **3.** form blisters (on) —**'blistering** *a.* (of verbal attack) bitter —**blister pack** package for goods with hard, raised, transparent cover

blithe (blīdh) *a.* happy, gay —**'blithely** *adv.* —**'blitheness** *n.*

blithering ('blidhəring) *a.* **1.** talking foolishly; jabbering **2.** *inf.* stupid; foolish

blitz (blits) *n.* sudden, concentrated attack —**blitzkrieg** ('blitskrēg) *n.* intensive military attack designed to defeat opposition quickly

blizzard ('blizərd) *n.* blinding storm of wind and snow

blk 1. black **2.** block **3.** bulk

bloat (blōt) *v.* **1.** puff or swell out —*n.* **2.** distension of stomach of cow *etc.* by gas —**'bloated** *a.* swollen —**'bloater** *n.* smoked herring

blob (blob) *n.* **1.** soft mass, *esp.* drop of liquid **2.** shapeless form

bloc (blok) *n.* (political) grouping of people or countries

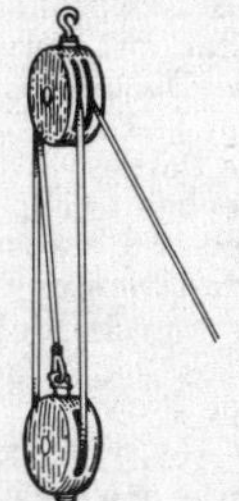

block and tackle

block (blok) *n.* **1.** solid (rectangular) piece of wood, stone *etc.*, *esp. Hist.* that on which people were beheaded **2.** obstacle **3.** stoppage **4.** pulley with frame **5.** main part of internal-combustion engine, *ie* the cylinders and valves **6.** large portion of shares, seats *etc.* as a unit **7.** area enclosed by intersecting streets —*vt.* **8.** obstruct, stop up **9.** shape on block —**'blockage** *n.* obstruction —**block and tackle** hoisting device in which rope or chain is passed around pair of blocks containing one or more pulleys —**'blockbuster** *n. inf.* **1.** large bomb used to demolish extensive areas **2.** very forceful person, thing *etc.* —**'blockbusting** *n.* inducing owners to sell their homes at a low price by the threat of a fall in value as the result of predicted change in neighborhood racial pattern —**'blockflute** *n. see* **recorder** (sense 2) *at* RECORD —**'blockhead** *n. derogatory* fool, simpleton —**'blockhouse** *n.* **1.** formerly, wooden fortification with ports for defensive fire *etc.* **2.** concrete structure strengthened for protection against enemy fire, with apertures for defensive gunfire **3.** building constructed of logs or squared timber —**block letters** written capital letters —**block in** sketch in

blockade (blo'kād) *n.* **1.** physical prevention of access, *esp.* to port *etc.* —*vt.* **2.** subject to blockade

blond (blond) *a.* **1.** (of hair) light-colored —*n.* **2.** someone with blond hair (**blonde** *fem.*)

blood (blud) *n.* **1.** red body fluid **2.** race **3.** kindred **4.** parental heritage **5.** temperament **6.** passion —*vt.* **7.** initiate (into hunting, war *etc.*) —**'bloodily** *adv.* —**'bloodless** *a.* —**'bloody** *a.* **1.** covered in blood **2.** slaughterous —*a./adv.* **3.** *sl.* common intensifier —*vt.* **4.** make bloody —**blood bank** (institution managing) store of human blood preserved for transfusion —**blood bath** indiscriminate slaughter; massacre —**blood count** determination of number of red and white blood corpuscles in sample of blood —**'bloodcurdling** *a.* terrifying; horrifying —**blood group** any of various groups into which human blood is classified (*also* **blood type**) —**'bloodhound** *n.* breed of large hound noted for its keen powers of scent —**'bloodletting** *n.* **1.** therapeutic removal of blood (*also* **phlebotomy**) **2.** bloodshed, *esp.* in feud —**blood money 1.** compensation paid to relatives of murdered person **2.** money paid to hired murderer —**blood poisoning** condition in which blood is invaded by bacteria leading to bacteremia or septicemia —**blood pressure** pressure exerted by blood on inner walls of arteries —**blood relation** *or* **relative** person related by birth —**'bloodshed** *n.* slaughter, killing —**'bloodshot** *a.* (of eyes) inflamed —**blood sport** sport in which animals are killed —**'bloodstone** *n.* green variety of chalcedony spotted or streaked with red, used as a gem —**'bloodstream** *n.* flow of blood through vessels of living body —**'bloodsucker** *n.* **1.** parasite (*eg* mosquito) living on host's blood **2.** parasitic person —**blood test** examination of sample of blood —**'bloodthirsty** *a.* murderous, cruel —**blood transfusion** replacement of blood loss —**blood vessel** artery, capillary or vein —**Bloody Mary** ('māəri) cocktail consisting of vodka and tomato juice —**bloody-minded** *a. inf.* deliberately obstructive and unhelpful —**in cold blood** cruelly and ruthlessly; deliberately and calmly —**make one's blood boil** cause one to be angry —**make one's blood run cold** fill one with horror

bloom[1] (bloom) *n.* **1.** flower of plant **2.** blossoming **3.** prime, perfection **4.** glow **5.** powdery deposit on fruit —*vi.* **6.** be in flower **7.** flourish —**'blooming** *a.*

bloom[2] (bloom) *n.* rectangular mass of metal obtained by rolling or forging cast ingot

bloomers ('blo͞omərz) *pl.n.* wide, baggy underpants

blooper ('blo͞opər) *n.* **1.** ludicrous public mistake **2.** high baseball pitch lobbed to batter **3.** baseball hit high into infield

blossom ('blosəm) *n.* **1.** flower **2.** flower bud —*vi.* **3.** flower **4.** develop

blot (blot) *n.* **1.** spot, stain **2.** disgrace **3.** backgammon counter exposed to capture —*vt.* **4.** spot, stain **5.** obliterate **6.** detract from **7.** soak up (ink *etc.*) from (**-tt-**) —**blotting paper** absorbent paper, used *esp.* for soaking up surplus ink

blotch (bloch) *n.* **1.** dark spot on skin —*vt.* **2.** make spotted —'**blotchy** *a.*

blotto ('blotō) *a. sl.* drunk

blouse (blows) *n.* light, loose upper garment

blouson ('blo͞ozon) *n.* loosely fitting but tight-waisted jacket

blow[1] (blō) *vi.* **1.** make a current of air **2.** pant **3.** make sound by blowing **4.** (of whale) spout —*vt.* **5.** drive air upon or into **6.** drive by current of air **7.** sound **8.** fan **9.** *sl.* squander (**blew, blown**) —*n.* **10.** blast **11.** gale —'**blower** *n.* —'**blowy** *a.* windy —**blow-by-blow** *a.* explained in great detail —**blow-dry** *vt.* **1.** style (hair) after washing, using hand-held hair dryer —*n.* **2.** this method of drying hair —'**blowfly** *n.* fly which infects food *etc.* (*also* '**bluebottle**) —'**blowhole** *n.* **1.** nostril of whales, situated far back on skull **2.** hole in ice through which seals *etc.* breathe **3.** vent for air or gas —**blow-out** *n.* **1.** sudden puncture in tire **2.** uncontrolled escape of oil or gas from well —'**blowpipe** *n.* **1.** small tubular device used for directing jet of air on to flame to intensify and to concentrate the heat **2.** dart tube —**blow torch** small burner with very hot flame, for removing paint *etc.* —**blow out 1.** extinguish **2.** (of tire) puncture suddenly **3.** (of fuse) melt —**blow hot and cold** be for and then against something or someone —**blow one's mind 1.** astound one **2.** induce hallucinations in one with drugs —**blow one's own trumpet** praise oneself —**blow the whistle on** reveal —**blow up 1.** explode **2.** inflate **3.** enlarge (photograph) **4.** *inf.* lose one's temper

blow[2] (blō) *n.* **1.** stroke, knock **2.** sudden misfortune, loss

blown (blōn) *pp. of* BLOW[1]

blowsy *or* **blowzy** ('blowzi) *a.* **1.** slovenly, sluttish **2.** red-faced

BLS Bureau of Labor Statistics

BLT bacon, lettuce and tomato (sandwich)

blubber ('blubər) *vi.* **1.** weep —*n.* **2.** fat of whales **3.** weeping

bludgeon ('blujən) *n.* **1.** short thick club —*vt.* **2.** strike (as) with bludgeon **3.** coerce

blue (blo͞o) *a.* **1.** of color of sky or shades of that color **2.** depressed **3.** indecent —*n.* **4.** the color **5.** dye or pigment **6.** clothing, *esp.* of police force —*vt.* **7.** make blue **8.** dip in blue liquid (**blued** *pt./pp.*) —**blues** *pl.n. inf.* (*oft. with sing. v.*) **1.** depression **2.** form of Amer. Negro folk song in slow tempo, employed in jazz music —'**bluish** *a.* —**blue baby** baby born with bluish skin caused by heart defect —'**bluebell** *n.* wild spring flower —'**blueberry** *n.* N Amer. shrub with blue-black edible berries —'**bluebird** *n.* common songbird related to robin of eastern N Amer. —**blue blood** royal or aristocratic descent —'**bluebook** *n.* **1.** volume of specialized information, *esp.* that published by government **2.** directory of socially prominent persons **3.** booklet in which students write examination papers **4.** the examination itself —'**bluebottle** *n.* blowfly —**blue cheese** any of various semihard cheeses with blue veins —**blue chip** *Fin.* reliable stock —**blue-collar** *a.* denoting manual industrial workers —**Blue Cross Plans** U.S. and Canad. nonprofit organizations providing hospital care to subscribers —**Blue Dorset** Dorset vinny —**blue nose** *sl.* puritanical person —**blue-pencil** *vt.* alter, delete parts of, *esp.* to censor —**blue peter** signal flag of blue with white square at center, displayed by vessel about to leave port —'**bluepoint** *n.* edible oyster —'**blueprint** *n.* **1.** copy of drawing **2.** original plan —**blue ribbon 1.** honor or award for excellence **2.** badge awarded as first prize in competition —**Blue Shield Plans** U.S. and Canad. nonprofit organizations providing medical and surgical care to subscribers —'**bluestocking** *n.* scholarly, intellectual woman —**Blue vinny** Dorset vinny —**blue whale** largest living mammal: bluish-gray whalebone whale —**blue in the face** furious —**once in a blue moon** very rarely —**out of the blue** unexpectedly —**true blue** loyal

bluff[1] (bluf) *n.* **1.** cliff, steep bank **2. C** clump of trees —*a.* **3.** hearty **4.** blunt **5.** steep **6.** abrupt

bluff[2] (bluf) *v.* **1.** deceive (someone) by pretense of strength —*n.* **2.** pretense

blunder ('blundər) *n.* **1.** clumsy mistake —*vi.* **2.** make stupid mistake **3.** act clumsily

blunderbuss ('blundərbus) *n.* obsolete short gun with wide bore

blunt (blunt) *a.* **1.** not sharp **2.** (of speech) abrupt —*vt.* **3.** make blunt —'**bluntly** *adv.* —'**bluntness** *n.*

blur (blər) *v.* **1.** make, become less distinct (**-rr-**) —*n.* **2.** something vague, indistinct —'**blurry** *a.*

blurb (blərb) *n.* statement, advertising or recommending book *etc.*

blurt (blərt) *vt.* (*oft. with* out) utter suddenly or unadvisedly

blush (blush) *vi.* **1.** become red in face **2.** be ashamed **3.** redden —*n.* **4.** this effect —'**blusher** *n.* cosmetic applied to cheeks to give rosy color

bluster ('blustər) *vi./n.* (indulge in) noisy, aggressive behavior —'**blustering** *or* '**blustery** *a.* (of wind *etc.*) noisy and gusty

blvd boulevard

bm beam

BM **1.** basal metabolism **2.** bill of material **3.** board measure **4.** bowel movement

BMOC big man on campus

BMR basal metabolism rate

BNDD Bureau of Narcotics and Dangerous Drugs

B.O. **1.** back order **2.** body odor **3.** box office

boa (ˈbōə) *n.* **1.** any of family of nonvenomous snakes ranging in size from 15 inches to 33 feet that kill prey by crushing **2.** long scarf of fur or feathers —**boa constrictor** boa native to tropical S Amer. that reaches 15 feet in length

boar (bōr) *n.* **1.** male pig **2.** wild pig

board (bōrd) *n.* **1.** broad, flat piece of wood **2.** sheet of rigid material for specific purpose **3.** table **4.** meals **5.** group of people who administer company **6.** governing body **7.** thick, stiff paper —*pl.* **8.** theater, stage **9.** C wooden enclosure where ice hockey, box lacrosse is played —*vt.* **10.** cover with planks **11.** supply with regular meals **12.** enter (ship *etc.*) —*vi.* **13.** take daily meals —ˈ**boarder** *n.* —**boarding house** lodging house where meals may be had —**boarding school** school providing living accommodation for pupils —ˈ**boardroom** *n.* room where board of company meets —**above board** beyond suspicion —**board up** cover with boards —**on board** in or into ship

boast (bōst) *vi.* **1.** speak too much in praise of oneself, one's possessions *etc.* —*n.* **2.** something boasted (of) —ˈ**boaster** *n.* —ˈ**boastful** *a.* —ˈ**boastfully** *adv.* —ˈ**boastfulness** *n.* —**boast of** **1.** brag of **2.** have to show

boat (bōt) *n.* **1.** small open vessel **2.** ship —*vi.* **3.** sail about in boat —ˈ**boater** *n.* flat straw hat —ˈ**boating** *n.* —ˈ**boathook** *n.* —ˈ**boathouse** *n.* —ˈ**boatman** *n.* —**boatswain** (ˈbōsən) *n.* ship's officer in charge of boats, sails *etc.* —**in the same boat** having identical troubles

bob (bob) *vi.* **1.** move up and down —*vt.* **2.** move jerkily **3.** cut (hair) short (**-bb-**) —*n.* **4.** short, jerking motion **5.** short hair style **6.** weight on pendulum *etc.* **7.** *inf.* formerly, shilling —**bobbed** *a.*

bobbin (ˈbobin) *n.* cylinder on which thread is wound

bobble (ˈbobəl) *n.* small, tufted ball for decoration

bobby (ˈbobi) *n.* **UK** *inf.* policeman

bobcat (ˈbobkat) *n.* medium-sized feline with black-spotted reddish-brown coat of eastern N Amer. (*also* **wildcat**)

bobolink (ˈbobəlingk) *n.* Amer. songbird

bobsled (ˈbobsled) *n.* large four-runner sled with steering wheel and hand brake capable of carrying two to four persons —ˈ**bobsledding** *n.* competitive downhill racing in a bobsled over specially constructed course covered with ice or snow

bobtail (ˈbobtāl) *n.* **1.** docked or diminutive tail **2.** animal with such tail —*a.* **3.** having tail cut short (*also* ˈ**bobtailed**) —*vt.* **4.** dock tail of **5.** cut short; curtail

boccie, bocci, *or* **bocce** (ˈbochē) *n.* grass court game played by two players or teams of two to four players in which the object is to bowl eight wooden balls close to the jack ball

bock beer (bok) special brew of beer, usu. strong, dark and sweet, brewed in winter for use in spring

bode[1] (bōd) *vt.* be an omen of

bode[2] (bōd) *pt.* *of* BIDE

bodega (bōˈdāgə) *n.* shop selling wine, *esp.* in Spanish-speaking country

bodge (boj) *vt.* *inf.* make mess of; botch

bodice (ˈbodis) *n.* upper part of woman's dress

bodkin (ˈbodkin) *n.* **1.** large blunt needle **2.** tool for piercing holes

body (ˈbodi) *n.* **1.** whole frame of man or animal **2.** main part of such frame **3.** corpse **4.** main part of anything **5.** substance **6.** mass **7.** person **8.** number of persons united or organized **9.** matter, opposed to spirit —ˈ**bodiless** *a.* —ˈ**bodily** *a./adv.* —**body colors** pigments with opacity in contrast to transparent pigments —ˈ**bodyguard** *n.* escort to protect important person —**body politic** people of nation or nation itself considered as political entity —**body stocking** one-piece undergarment, usu. of nylon, covering torso —**body types** categories of human physique based on major anatomical characteristics developed by theories relating body type and personality —ˈ**bodywork** *n.* shell of motor vehicle

Boer (bōōər) *n.* a S Afr. of Dutch or Huguenot descent

bog (bog) *n.* wet, soft ground —ˈ**boggy** *a.* marshy —**bog down** stick as in a bog

bogan (ˈbōgən) *n.* C sluggish side stream

bogey *or* **bogy** (ˈbōgi) *n.* **1.** evil or mischievous spirit **2.** *Golf* par, popularly one stroke above par —ˈ**bogeyman** *n.*

boggle (ˈbogəl) *vi.* stare, be surprised

bogie *or* **bogy** (ˈbōgi) *n.* **1.** low truck on four wheels **2.** pivoted undercarriage, as on railway rolling stock

bogus (ˈbōgəs) *a.* sham, false

Bohemian (bōˈhēmiən) *a.* **1.** unconventional —*n.* **2.** (*oft.* **b-**) one who leads an unsettled life —**Boˈhemianism** *n.*

boil[1] (boil) *vi.* **1.** change from liquid to gas, *esp.* by heating **2.** become cooked by boiling **3.** bubble **4.** be agitated **5.** seethe **6.** *inf.* be hot **7.** *inf.* be angry —*vt.* **8.** cause to boil **9.** cook by boiling —*n.* **10.** boiling state —ˈ**boiler** *n.* vessel for boiling —**boiler suit** garment covering whole body —**boiling point** temperature at which boiling occurs (212°F, 100°C for water)

boil[2] (boil) *n.* inflamed suppurating swelling on skin

boisterous ('boistərəs, -strəs) *a.* **1.** wild **2.** noisy **3.** turbulent —'**boisterously** *adv.* —'**boisterousness** *n.*

bola ('bōlə) *or* **bolas** ('bōləs) *n.* weapon used for hunting consisting of weights joined by cords or thongs

bold (bōld) *a.* **1.** daring, fearless **2.** presumptuous **3.** striking, prominent —'**boldly** *adv.* —'**boldness** *n.* —'**boldface** *a.* —**bold face** *Print.* type with thick heavy lines

bole (bōl) *n.* trunk of tree

bolero (bə'lāərō) *n.* **1.** Spanish dance **2.** short loose jacket

Bolivia (bə'liviə) *n.* country in South America landlocked by Brazil to the north and east, Paraguay to the southeast, Argentina to the south, and Chile and Peru to the west —**Bo'livian** *n./a.*

boll (bōl) *n.* seed capsule of cotton, flax *etc.*

bollard ('boləd) *n.* **1.** post on quay or ship to secure mooring lines **2.** short post in road or footpath as barrier or marker

Bolshevik ('bolshivik) *n.* member of Russian Social Democratic Party that seized power in the revolution of November 1917

bolster ('bōlstər) *vt.* **1.** support, uphold —*n.* **2.** long pillow **3.** pad, support

bolt[1] (bōlt) *n.* **1.** bar or pin, *esp.* with thread for nut **2.** rush **3.** discharge of lightning **4.** roll of cloth —*vt.* **5.** fasten with bolt **6.** swallow hastily —*vi.* **7.** rush away **8.** break from control

bolt[2] (bōlt) *vt.* **1.** pass (flour *etc.*) through sieve **2.** examine and separate —'**bolter** *n.*

bomb (bom) *n.* **1.** explosive projectile **2.** any explosive device **3.** small pressurized dispenser (*also* **aerosol**) —*vt.* **4.** attack with bombs —**bom'bard** *vt.* **1.** shell **2.** attack (verbally) —**bombardier** (bombər'dēər) *n.* artillery noncommissioned officer —**bom'bardment** *n.* —'**bomber** *n.* aircraft capable of carrying bombs —'**bombshell** *n.* **1.** shell of bomb **2.** surprise —**the bomb** nuclear bomb

bombast ('bombast) *n.* **1.** pompous language **2.** pomposity —**bom'bastic** *a.*

Bombay duck (bom'bā) salty dried fish eaten with curry dishes (*also* '**bummalo**)

bombazine (bombə'zēn) *n.* twilled fabric, *esp.* one of silk and worsted

bona fide ('bōnə fīd, 'bōnə 'fīdi) *Lat.* **1.** genuine(ly) **2.** sincere(ly) —**bona fides** ('fīdēz) good faith, sincerity

bonanza (bə'nanzə) *n.* sudden good luck or wealth

bonbon ('bonbon) *n.* candy with chocolate or fondant coating and with any of various fillings

bond (bond) *n.* **1.** that which binds **2.** link, union **3.** written promise to pay money or carry out contract —*vt.* **4.** bind **5.** store (goods) until duty is paid on them —'**bonded** *a.* **1.** placed in bond **2.** mortgaged —'**bondsman** *n.* **1.** *Law* person bound by bond to act as surety for another **2.** serf, slave (*also* '**bondservant**)

bondage ('bondij) *n.* slavery

bone (bōn) *n.* **1.** hard substance forming animal's skeleton **2.** piece of this —*pl.* **3.** essentials —*vt.* **4.** remove bones from —*vi.* **5.** *inf.* (*with* up) study hard —'**boneless** *a.* —'**bony** *a.* —**bone china** porcelain containing bone ash —**bone-dry** *a. inf.* completely dry —**bone graft** section of bone used to repair injured or diseased bone —'**bonehead** *n. inf.* stupid person —'**bonemeal** *n.* dried and ground animal bones, used as fertilizer —'**boneshaker** *n.* **1.** early type of bicycle having solid tires **2.** *sl.* any rickety vehicle

bonfire ('bonfīər) *n.* large outdoor fire

bongo ('bonggō) *n.* small drum, usu. one of pair, played with fingers (*pl.* **-s, -es**)

bonhomie (bonə'mē) *Fr.* good humor, geniality

bonkers ('bongkərz) *a. sl.* crazy

bon mot (*Fr.* bõ 'mō) clever and fitting remark (*pl.* **bons mots** (bõ 'mō))

bonnet ('bonit) *n.* **1.** hat with strings **2.** cap

bonny ('boni) *a.* beautiful, handsome —'**bonnily** *adv.*

bonsai (bōn'sī) *n.* (art of growing) dwarf trees, shrubs

bontebok ('bontibuk) *n.* S Afr. antelope

bonus ('bōnəs) *n.* extra (unexpected) payment or gift

bon vivant (bõ vē'vã) *Fr.* person who enjoys luxuries, *esp.* good food and drink (*pl.* ***bons vivants*** (bõ vē'vã))

bon voyage (*Fr.* bõ vwa'yazh) phrase used to wish traveler pleasant journey

bonze (bonz) *n.* Buddhist monk

boo (bo͞o) *interj.* **1.** expression of disapproval or contempt **2.** exclamation to surprise *esp.* child —*v.* **3.** make this sound (at)

boob (bo͞ob) *n. sl.* **1.** awkward person **2.** simpleton **3.** female breast

booby ('bo͞obi) *n.* **1.** fool **2.** tropical marine bird —**booby prize** mock prize for poor performance —**booby trap 1.** harmless-looking object which explodes when disturbed **2.** trap for the unwary

boodle ('bo͞odəl) *n. sl.* money

boogie-woogie ('bo͝ogi'wo͝ogi, 'bo͞ogi'wo͞ogi) *n.* kind of jazz piano playing, emphasizing a rolling bass in syncopated eighth notes

book (bo͝ok) *n.* **1.** collection of sheets of paper bound together **2.** literary work **3.** main division of this —*v.* **4.** reserve (room, ticket *etc.*) —*vt.* **5.** charge with legal offense **6.** enter name in book —'**booking** *n.* reservation —'**bookish** *a.* studious, fond of reading —'**booklet** *n.* —'**bookbinder** *n.* —'**bookcase** *n.* —**book club** club that sells books at low prices to members —**book end** one of pair of ornamental supports for holding row of books upright —**book-keeping** *n.* systematic recording of business transactions —'**bookmaker** *n.* person whose work is taking bets (*also* (*inf.*) ˈ**bookie**) —ˈ**bookmark** *or* ˈ**bookmarker** *n.* strip of material put between pages of book to mark place —**book of hours** late medieval book of prayers for private devotions often sumptuously decorated —ˈ**bookplate** *n.* label bearing owner's name and design, pasted into book —**book value 1.** value of asset of business according to its books **2.** net capital value of enterprise as shown by excess of book assets over book liabilities —ˈ**bookworm** *n.* **1.** insect that eats holes in books **2.** great reader

boom[1] (bo͞om) *n.* **1.** sudden commercial activity **2.** prosperity —*vi.* **3.** become active, prosperous

boom[2] (bo͞om) *vi./n.* (make) loud, deep sound

boom[3] (bo͞om) *n.* **1.** long spar, as for stretching the bottom of a sail **2.** barrier across harbor **3.** pole carrying overhead microphone *etc.*

boomerang (ˈbo͞omərang) *n.* **1.** curved wooden missile of Aust. Aborigines, which returns to the thrower —*vi.* **2.** recoil **3.** return unexpectedly **4.** backfire

boon (bo͞on) *n.* something helpful, favor

boor (bo͞oər) *n.* rude person —ˈ**boorish** *a.*

boost (bo͞ost) *n.* **1.** encouragement, help **2.** upward push **3.** increase —*vt.* **4.** encourage, assist or improve —ˈ**booster** *n.* person or thing that supports, increases power *etc.* —**booster shot** *inf.* supplementary injection of vaccine given to maintain immunization

boot[1] (bo͞ot) *n.* **1.** shoe covering the foot and ankle or leg **2.** *inf.* kick —*vt.* **3.** *inf.* kick —ˈ**booted** *a.* —ˈ**bootee** *n.* baby's soft shoe —**boot camp** training base for recruits to U.S. Navy or Marine Corps

boot[2] (bo͞ot) *n.* profit, use —ˈ**bootless** *a.* fruitless, vain —**to boot** in addition

booth (bo͞oth) *n.* **1.** stall **2.** cubicle

bootleg (ˈbo͞otleg) *v.* **1.** make, carry, sell (illicit goods, *esp.* liquor) (**-gg-**) —*a.* **2.** produced, distributed or sold illicitly —ˈ**bootlegger** *n.*

booty (ˈbo͞oti) *n.* plunder, spoil

booze (bo͞oz) *n./vi. inf.* (consume) alcoholic drink —ˈ**boozer** *n. inf.* person fond of drinking —ˈ**boozy** *a. inf.* inclined to or involving excessive consumption of alcohol —**booze-up** *n. inf.* drinking spree

bop (bop) *n.* **1.** form of jazz characterized by rhythmic and harmonic complexity (*also* **bebop**) —*vi.* **2.** *inf.* dance to pop music (**-pp-**) —ˈ**bopper** *n.*

BOQ bachelor officers' quarters

bor borough

borage (ˈborij) *n.* hardy annual culinary herb with flavor resembling cucumber

borax (ˈböraks) *n.* white soluble substance, compound of boron used to make glass, enamels and detergents

Bordeaux (börˈdō) *n.* any of several red, white or rosé wines produced around Bordeaux in SW France

border (ˈbördər) *n.* **1.** margin **2.** frontier **3.** limit **4.** flower bed —*vt.* **5.** provide with border **6.** adjoin —ˈ**borderline** *n.* **1.** border; dividing line **2.** indeterminate position between two conditions —*a.* **3.** on edge of one category and verging on another

bore[1] (bör) *vt.* **1.** pierce —*vi.* **2.** make a hole —*n.* **3.** hole **4.** caliber of gun —ˈ**borer** *n.* **1.** instrument for making holes **2.** insect which bores holes

bore[2] (bör) *vt.* **1.** make weary by repetition *etc.* —*n.* **2.** tiresome person or thing —ˈ**boredom** *n.* —ˈ**boring** *a.*

bore[3] (bör) *n.* tidal wave which rushes up river estuary

bore[4] (bör) *pt. of* BEAR[1]

born (börn) *pp. of* BEAR[1] —**born again Christian** person having undergone a conversion to Christianity —**not born yesterday** difficult to deceive

borne (börn) *pp. of* BEAR[1] —**be borne in on** *or* **upon** (of fact *etc.*) be realized by

boron (ˈböron) *n. Chem.* metalloid element *Symbol* B, at. wt. 10.8, at. no. 5 —ˈ**boric** *a.* of or containing boron (*also* **boˈracic**) —**boric acid** white crystalline boron compound formerly in wide use as antiseptic, before the discovery of its poisonous properties

borough (ˈburə) *n.* town

borrow (ˈborō) *vt.* **1.** obtain on loan or trust **2.** appropriate —ˈ**borrower** *n.*

borscht (börsht) *or* **borsch** (börsh) *n.* soup made from beets and served hot or cold with or without sour cream —**borscht belt** *or* **circuit** resort area in the Catskill Mountains of New York

borzoi (ˈbörzoi) *n.* breed of tall hound with long, silky coat and narrow head (*also* **Russian wolfhound**)

bosh (bosh) *n. inf.* nonsense

bo's'n (ˈbōsən) *n. Naut. see* **boatswain** *at* BOAT

bosom (ˈbo͞ozəm) *n.* **1.** human breast **2.** seat of passions and feelings

boss[1] (bos) *n.* **1.** person in charge of or employing others —*vt.* **2.** be in charge of **3.** be domineering over —ˈ**bossy** *a.* overbearing

boss[2] (bos) *n.* **1.** knob or stud **2.** raised ornament —*vt.* **3.** emboss

bosun (ˈbōsən) *n. Naut. see* **boatswain** *at* BOAT

bot. 1. botanical **2.** botany **3.** bottle

botany[1] (ˈbotəni) *n.* branch of biology concerned with plant life —**boˈtanic(al)** *a.* —ˈ**botanist** *n.* —**botanical garden** garden, usu. public, where plants are grown for scientific study

botany[2] (ˈbotəni) *a.* of fine wool from merino sheep

botch (boch) *vt.* (*oft. with* up) spoil by clumsiness

botfly (ˈbotflī) *n.* fly, larvae of which are parasites of man, sheep and horses

both (bōth) *a./pron.* **1.** the two —*adv./conj.* **2.** as well

bother (ˈbodhər) *vt.* **1.** pester **2.** perplex —*vi./n.* **3.** fuss, trouble —**botheˈration** *n.* **1.** state of worry, trouble or confusion —*interj.* **2.** exclamation of slight annoyance —**ˈbothersome** *a.* causing bother; troublesome

Bothnia (ˈbothniə) *n.* —**Gulf of Bothnia** arm of the Baltic Sea separating Sweden and Finland

bo tree (bō) Indian fig tree sacred to Buddhists

Botswana (botˈswänə) *n.* country in Africa lying between the Molopo River on the south and the Zambesi on the north, extending from the Transvaal Province and Zimbabwe on the east to Namibia on the west

Botticelli (botiˈcheli) *n.* parlor game in which players attempt to discover the identity selected by person who is 'it'

bottle (ˈbotəl) *n.* **1.** vessel for holding liquid **2.** its contents —*vt.* **3.** put into bottle —**ˈbottler** *n.* —**ˈbottlebrush** *n.* **1.** cylindrical brush for cleaning bottle **2.** any of various Aust. shrubs with brushlike flowers —**bottled gas** pressurized gas in portable cylinders —**ˈbottleneck** *n.* narrow outlet which impedes smooth flow of traffic or production of goods —**bottle party** party to which guests bring drink —**bottle up 1.** restrain (powerful emotion) **2.** *inf.* keep (army or other force) contained or trapped

bottom (ˈbotəm) *n.* **1.** lowest part of anything **2.** bed of sea, river *etc.* **3.** buttocks —*vt.* **4.** put bottom to **5.** base **6.** get to bottom of —**ˈbottomless** *a.* —**bottom line** last line of financial statement that shows net profit or loss of company *etc.* —**bottom out** reach lowest point

botulism (ˈbotyŏŏlizəm) *n.* food poisoning caused by contamination by anaerobic soil bacillus

bouclé (bōōˈklā) *n.* looped yarn giving knobbly effect

boudoir (ˈbōōdwär) *n.* **1.** lady's private sitting room **2.** bedroom

bouffant (bōōˈfänt) *a.* **1.** (of hairstyle) having extra height through backcombing **2.** (of skirts *etc.*) puffed out

bougainvillea (bōōgənˈvilyə) *n.* (sub)tropical climbing plant with red or purple bracts

bough (bow) *n.* branch of tree

bought (bôt) *pt./pp. of* BUY

bouillabaisse (bōōyəˈbās) *n.* rich stew or soup of fish and vegetables

bouillon (ˈbōōyon) *n.* plain unclarified broth or stock

boulder (ˈbōldər) *n.* large weatherworn rounded stone —**boulder clay** unstratified glacial deposit consisting of fine clay, boulders and pebbles

boulevard (ˈbōōləvärd) *n.* broad street or promenade

boulle (bōōl) *n.* ornamental furniture inlay of silver, brass, mother-of-pearl, tortoiseshell *etc.* (*also* **buhl**)

bounce (bowns) *v.* **1.** (cause to) rebound (repeatedly) on impact, as a ball —*n.* **2.** rebounding **3.** quality in object causing this **4.** *inf.* vitality, vigor —**ˈbouncer** *n. sl.* man, *esp.* one employed at club *etc.* to evict undesirables (forcibly) —**ˈbouncing** *a.* vigorous, robust —**ˈbouncy** *a.* lively

bound[1] (bownd) *n./vt.* limit —**ˈboundary** *n.* —**ˈbounded** *a.* —**ˈboundless** *a.*

bound[2] (bownd) *vi./n.* spring, leap

bound[3] (bownd) *a.* on a specified course, as *outward bound*

bound[4] (bownd) *v.* **1.** *pt./pp. of* BIND —*a.* **2.** committed **3.** certain **4.** tied

bounden (ˈbowndən) *a.* morally obligatory (*obs. except in* **bounden duty**)

bounty (ˈbownti) *n.* **1.** liberality **2.** gift **3.** premium —**ˈbounteous** *or* **ˈbountiful** *a.* liberal, generous

bouquet (bōˈkā, bōō-) *n.* **1.** bunch of flowers **2.** fragrance of wine **3.** compliment —**bouquet garni** (gärˈnē) bunch of herbs tied together and used for flavoring stews *etc.* (*pl.* **bouquets garnis** (gärˈnē))

bourbon (ˈbərbən) *n.* whiskey made from corn mash

bourgeois (ˈbōōərzhwä) *n./a. oft. disparaging* **1.** middle class **2.** smugly conventional (person) —**bourgeoiˈsie** *n.* **1.** middle classes **2.** in Marxist thought, capitalist ruling class

bourn *or* **bourne** (bōrn) *n. obs.* **1.** destination; goal **2.** boundary

Bourse (bōōərs) *n.* stock exchange of continental Europe, *esp.* Paris

bout (bowt) *n.* **1.** period of time spent doing something **2.** contest, fight

boutique (bōōˈtēk) *n.* small shop, *esp.* one selling clothes

bouzouki (bōōˈzōōki) *n.* Greek stringed musical instrument resembling mandolin

bovine (ˈbōvīn) *a.* **1.** of the ox or cow **2.** oxlike **3.** stolid, dull

bow[1] (bō) *n.* **1.** weapon for shooting arrows **2.** implement for playing violin *etc.* **3.** ornamental knot of ribbon *etc.* **4.** bend, bent line **5.** rainbow —*v.* **6.** bend —**bow-legged** *a.* bandy —**bow tie** tie tied in bow —**bow window** window with outward curve

bow[2] (bow) *vi.* **1.** bend body in respect, assent *etc.* **2.** submit —*vt.* **3.** bend downward **4.** cause to stoop **5.** crush —*n.* **6.** bowing of head or body

bow[3] (bow) *n.* **1.** fore end of ship, prow **2.** rower nearest bow —**bowline** (ˈbōlin) *n. Naut.* **1.** line for controlling weather leech of square sail when vessel is close-hauled **2.** knot for securing loop —**bowsprit** (ˈbōsprit) *n.* spar projecting from ship's bow

bowdlerize (ˈbowdlərīz) *vt.* expurgate

bowel (ˈbowəl) *n.* (*oft. pl.*) **1.** part of intestine (*esp.* with reference to defecation) **2.** inside of anything

bower ('bowər) *n.* **1.** shady retreat **2.** inner room —'**bowerbird** *n.* Aust. bird that hoards decorative but useless things

bowie knife ('bōōi, 'bōi) stout hunting knife with short hilt and guard for hand

bowl[1] (bōl) *n.* **1.** round vessel, deep basin **2.** drinking cup **3.** hollow

bowl[2] (bōl) *n.* **1.** composition or wooden ball —*pl.* **2.** game for two, three, or four players in which such balls are rolled toward a smaller ball called a jack in which the object is to get as close as possible to the jack —*v.* **3.** roll or throw (ball) in various ways —'**bowler** *n.* —'**bowling** *n.* **1.** indoor game in which players roll solid composition balls down wooden alleys toward groups of ten wooden pins trying to knock all of the pins down in one or two attempts **2.** game of bowls —**bowling alley** —**bowling green**

bowler ('bōlər) *n.* **UK** man's low-crowned stiff felt hat; derby

bowser ('bowzər) *n.* fuel tanker

box[1] (boks) *n.* **1.** (wooden) container, usu. rectangular with lid **2.** its contents **3.** small enclosure **4.** any boxlike cubicle, shelter or receptacle, *eg* letter box —*vt.* **5.** put in box **6.** confine —**box girder** girder that is hollow and square or rectangular in shape —**Boxing Day UK** first weekday after Christmas —**box lacrosse C** indoor lacrosse —**box lunch** packed lunch —**box number** number given to newspaper advertisements to which replies may be sent —**box office 1.** office at theater *etc.* where tickets are sold **2.** public appeal of actor or production —**box pleat** double pleat made by folding under fabric on either side of it —**box score** printed score of baseball or basketball game recording names of players, their positions and activity for each phase of the game —**box seat 1.** seat in the box of a theater or grandstand **2.** any favorable position for viewing something —**box social** fund-raising event at which box lunches are auctioned —**box turtle** *or* **tortoise** any of several N Amer. land turtles with ability to withdraw completely into shell —**box the compass 1.** name 32 points of compass in order **2.** make complete turn

box[2] (boks) *v.* **1.** fight with fists, *esp.* wearing padded gloves —*vt.* **2.** strike —*n.* **3.** blow —'**boxer** *n.* **1.** one who boxes **2.** breed of large dog resembling bulldog —'**boxing** *n.* art or profession of fighting with fists

box[3] (boks) *n.* evergreen shrub used for hedges

boy (boi) *n.* **1.** male child **2.** young man —*interj.* **3.** exclamation of surprise —'**boyhood** *n.* —'**boyfriend** *n.* male friend with whom person is romantically or sexually involved —**Boy Scout** member of Boy Scouts of America, an organization for boys aged 11 to 17, whose aim is to develop character, self-reliance and usefulness to others

boycott ('boikot) *vt.* **1.** refuse to deal with or participate in —*n.* **2.** act of boycotting

boysenberry ('boizənberi) *n.* **1.** type of bramble, cross of loganberry, various blackberries and raspberries **2.** edible fruit of this plant

BP 1. beautiful people **2.** before the present **3.** blood pressure **4.** boiling point

BPD barrels per day

bpi 1. bits per inch **2.** bytes per inch

BPOE Benevolent and Protective Order of Elks

BPW 1. Board of Public Works **2.** Business and Professional Women's Clubs

Br *Chem.* bromine

br. 1. branch **2.** bronze **3.** brother

Br. 1. Britain **2.** British

bra (brä) *n. short for* BRASSIERE

brace (brās) *n.* **1.** tool for boring **2.** clasp, clamp **3.** pair, couple **4.** strut, support —*pl.* **5.** straps worn over shoulders to hold up trousers **6.** dental appliance for straightening teeth —*vt.* **7.** steady (oneself), as before a blow **8.** support, make firm —'**bracelet** *n.* **1.** ornament for the arm —*pl.* **2.** *sl.* handcuffs —'**bracing** *a.* invigorating

brachiopod ('brākiəpod) *n.* any marine invertebrate animal having ciliated feeding organ and shell consisting of dorsal and ventral valves

bracken ('brakən) *n.* large fern

bracket ('brakit) *n.* **1.** support for shelf *etc.* **2.** group —*pl.* **3.** marks [ ], ( ) used to enclose words *etc.* —*vt.* **4.** enclose in brackets **5.** connect

brackish ('brakish) *a.* (of water) slightly salty

bract (brakt) *n.* leaflike structure at base of flower stalk which may be large and brightly colored as in the poinsettia

brad (brad) *n.* small nail —'**bradawl** *n.* small boring tool

brae (brā) *n. Scot.* hill(side); slope

brag (brag) *vi.* **1.** boast (**-gg-**) —*n.* **2.** boastful talk —'**braggart** *n.*

braggadocio (bragə'dōshiō) *n.* **1.** vain empty boasting **2.** braggart (*pl.* **-s**)

Brahma ('brämə) *n.* **1.** Hindu god, the Creator **2.** *Hinduism* ultimate and impersonal divine reality of universe (*also* '**Brahman**)

Brahman ('brämən) *n.* **1.** member of priestly Hindu caste (*also esp.* (*formerly*) '**Brahmin**) **2.** breed of beef cattle

braid (brād) *vt.* **1.** interweave **2.** trim with braid —*n.* **3.** length of anything interwoven or plaited **4.** ornamental tape

Braille (brāl) *n.* system of printing for the blind, with arrangements of raised dots instead of letters

brain (brān) *n.* **1.** mass of nerve tissue in head **2.** intellect —*vt.* **3.** kill by hitting on head —'**brainless** *a.* —'**brainy** *a.* —'**brainchild** *n.* invention —**brain death** irreversible cessation of respiration due to irreparable brain damage —'**brainpicking** *n.* act of getting information from another person —'**brainstorm** *vi.* **1.** engage in conference with aim of problem-solving through spontaneous contribution of participants resulting in bright idea(s) —*n.* **2.** the bright idea(s) so generated —**brain trust** unofficial and sometimes unacknowledged panel of experts and advisers, *esp.* to president —'**brainwash** *vt.* change, distort ideas or beliefs of —**brain wave** sudden, clever idea

braise (brāz) *vt.* cook slowly in small amount of fat and water usu. in covered pan

brake[1] (brāk) *n.* **1.** instrument for retarding motion of wheel on vehicle —*vt.* **2.** apply brake to —**brake horsepower** rate at which engine does work, expressed in horsepower, measured by a dynamometer —**brake shoe** curved metal casting to which brake lining is riveted in drum brake

brake[2] (brāk) *n.* **1.** fern **2.** bracken **3.** thicket **4.** brushwood

bramble ('brambəl) *n.* **1.** prickly shrub **2.** blackberry —'**brambly** *a.*

brambling ('brambling) *n.* an Old World finch

bran (bran) *n.* sifted husks of cereal grain

branch (bränch) *n.* **1.** limb of tree **2.** offshoot or subsidiary part of something larger or primary —*vi.* **3.** bear branches **4.** diverge **5.** spread —**branched** *a.* —'**branchy** *a.*

brand (brand) *n.* **1.** trademark **2.** class of goods **3.** particular kind, sort **4.** mark made by hot iron **5.** burning piece of wood **6.** sword **7.** mark of infamy —*vt.* **8.** burn with iron **9.** mark **10.** stigmatize —**brand-new** *a.* absolutely new

brandish ('brandish) *vt.* flourish, wave (weapon *etc.*)

brandy ('brandi) *n.* spirit distilled from wine —**brandy snap** crisp, sweet cookie

brant (brant) *n.* small goose of eastern N Amer. with black head, neck and breast which flies in irregular formation

brash (brash) *a.* bold, impudent

brass (bräs) *n.* **1.** alloy of copper and zinc **2.** group of brass wind instruments forming part of orchestra or band **3.** *inf.* money **4.** *inf.* (army) officers —*a.* **5.** made of brass —'**brassy** *a.* **1.** showy **2.** harsh —**brass hat** *inf.* top-ranking official, *esp.* military officer —**brass tacks** *inf.* basic realities; hard facts (*esp. in* **get down to brass tacks**)

brasserie (brasə'rē) *n.* restaurant specializing in food and beer

brassica ('brasikə) *n.* plant of cabbage family

brassiere (brə'zēər) *n.* woman's undergarment for supporting the breasts

brat (brat) *n. disparaging* child

bravado (brə'vädō) *n.* showy display of boldness

brave (brāv) *a.* **1.** bold, courageous **2.** splendid, fine —*n.* **3.** warrior, *esp.* Amerindian —*vt.* **4.** defy, meet boldly —'**bravely** *adv.* —'**bravery** *n.*

bravo (brä'vō) *interj.* well done

Bravo ('brävō) *n.* word used in communications for the letter *b*

bravura (brə'vyŏŏərə, -'vŏŏərə) *n.* **1.** display of boldness or daring **2.** *Mus.* passage requiring great spirit and skill by performer

brawl (brōl) *vi.* **1.** fight noisily —*n.* **2.** noisy disagreement or fight —'**brawler** *n.*

brawn (brōn) *n.* **1.** muscle **2.** strength —'**brawny** *a.* muscular

bray (brā) *n.* **1.** donkey's cry —*vi.* **2.** utter this sound **3.** give out harsh or loud sounds

braze[1] (brāz) *vt.* decorate with or make of brass

braze[2] (brāz) *vt.* make joint between (two metal surfaces) by fusing layer of high-melting solder between them —'**brazer** *n.*

brazen ('brāzən) *a.* **1.** of, like brass **2.** impudent, shameless —*vt.* **3.** (*usu. with* out) face, carry through with impudence —'**brazenness** *n.* effrontery

brazier[1] *or* **brasier** ('brāzhər) *n.* brass worker

brazier[2] *or* **brasier** ('brāzhər) *n.* pan for burning charcoal or coals

Brazil (brə'zil) *n.* country in South America bounded east by the Atlantic and on its northwest and southern borders by all the countries of South America except Chile and Ecuador —**Bra'zilian** *n./a.* —**brazil nut 1.** tropical S Amer. tree producing globular capsules, each containing several triangular nuts **2.** its nut

brazil nut

breach (brēch) *n.* **1.** break, opening **2.** breaking of rule, duty *etc.* **3.** quarrel —*vt.* **4.** make a gap in

bread (bred) *n.* **1.** food made of flour or meal and then baked **2.** food **3.** *sl.* money —'**breaded** *a.* coated with bread crumbs —'**breadbasket** *n.* **1.** stomach **2.** important cereal-producing region —'**breadfruit** *n.* breadlike fruit found in Pacific Islands —'**breadwinner** *n.* person supporting dependants by his earnings —**bread and butter** *inf.* means of support or subsistence; livelihood —**bread and circuses** palliative for the masses —**cast one's bread upon the waters** perform charitable deeds without expectation of return —**on the breadline** *inf.* living at subsistence level

breadth (bredth, bretth) *n.* **1.** extent across, width **2.** largeness of view, mind

break (brāk) *vt.* **1.** part by force **2.** shatter **3.** burst, destroy **4.** fail to observe **5.** disclose **6.** interrupt **7.** surpass **8.** make bankrupt **9.** relax **10.** mitigate **11.** accustom (horse) to being ridden **12.** decipher (code) —*vi.* **13.** become broken, shattered, divided **14.** open, appear **15.** come suddenly **16.** crack, give way **17.** part, fall out **18.** (of voice) change in tone, pitch (**broke, 'broken**) —*n.* **19.** fracture **20.** gap **21.** opening **22.** separation **23.** interruption **24.** respite **25.** interval **26.** *inf.* opportunity **27.** dawn **28.** *Billiards* consecutive series of successful strokes **29.** *Boxing* separation after a clinch —**'breakable** *a.* —**'breakage** *n.* —**'breaker** *n.* **1.** one that breaks, *eg* electrical circuit breaker **2.** wave beating on rocks or shore —**'breakaway** *n.* loss or withdrawal of group of members from association, club *etc.* —**breakbone fever** dengue fever —**'breakdown** *n.* **1.** collapse, as nervous breakdown **2.** failure to function effectively **3.** analysis —**break-even point** point when sales have covered costs in an enterprise —**breakfast** ('brekfəst) *n.* first meal of the day —**break-in** *n.* illegal entering of building, *esp.* by thieves —**'breakneck** *a.* dangerous —**break-out** *n.* escape, *esp.* from prison —**'breakthrough** *n.* important advance —**break-up** *n.* **1.** separation or disintegration **2.** in Canad. north, breaking up of ice on body of water that marks beginning of spring **3.** this season —**'breakwater** *n.* barrier to break force of waves —**break a leg** good luck expression made to performer —**break away** (*oft. with* from) **1.** leave hastily; escape **2.** withdraw, secede —**break camp** pack up camp site —**break (new) ground** pioneer —**break out** **1.** begin suddenly **2.** make escape, *esp.* from prison **3.** (*with* in) (of skin) erupt (in rash *etc.*) —**break up** **1.** (cause to) separate **2.** put an end to (a relationship) or (of a relationship) to come to an end **3.** dissolve or cause to dissolve **4.** *sl.* lose control of emotions —**break wind** expel gas from anus

bream (brim, brēm) *n.* **1.** small game fish of eastern N Amer. ponds and streams **2.** European or Aust. marine food fish

breast (brest) *n.* **1.** human chest **2.** milk-secreting gland on chest of human female **3.** seat of the affections **4.** any protuberance —*vt.* **5.** face, oppose **6.** reach summit of —**'breastbone** *n.* thin flat structure of bone to which most of ribs are attached in front of chest (*also* **'sternum**) —**breast-feed** *v.* feed (baby) with milk from breast —**'breastplate** *n.* piece of armor covering chest —**'breaststroke** *n.* stroke in swimming —**'breastwork** *n.* temporary defensive work, usu. breast-high

breath (breth) *n.* **1.** air used by lungs **2.** life **3.** respiration **4.** slight breeze —**breathe** (brēdh) *vi.* **1.** inhale and exhale air from lungs **2.** live **3.** pause, rest —*vt.* **4.** inhale and exhale **5.** utter softly, whisper —**breather** ('brēdhər) *n.* short rest —**breathing** ('brēdhing) *n.* —**'breathless** *a.* —**'breathtaking** *a.* causing awe or excitement

bred (bred) *pt./pp. of* BREED

breech (brēch) *n.* **1.** buttocks **2.** hinder part of anything, *esp.* gun —**breeches** ('brichiz, 'brē-) *pl.n.* trousers —**breech delivery** birth of baby with feet or buttocks appearing first —**breeches buoy** ring-shaped life buoy with support in form of pair of breeches —**'breechloader** *n.*

breed (brēd) *vt.* **1.** generate, bring forth, give rise to **2.** rear —*vi.* **3.** be produced **4.** be with young (**bred** *pt./pp.*) —*n.* **5.** offspring produced **6.** race, kind —**'breeder** *n.* —**'breeding** *n.* **1.** producing **2.** manners **3.** ancestry —**breeder reactor** nuclear reactor that produces more fissionable material than it consumes

breeze (brēz) *n.* gentle wind —**'breezily** *adv.* —**'breezy** *a.* **1.** windy **2.** jovial, lively **3.** casual

Bren gun (bren) air-cooled gas-operated sub-machine gun, used by Brit. in World War II

brethren ('bredhrin) *n., pl. of* BROTHER, *obs.* except in religious contexts

Breton ('bretən) *a.* **1.** of Brittany, its people or their Celtic language —*n.* **2.** native or inhabitant of Brittany

breviary ('brēvyəri) *n.* book of daily prayers of R.C. Church

brevity ('breviti) *n.* **1.** conciseness of expression **2.** short duration

brew (bro͞o) *vt.* **1.** prepare (liquor, as beer) from malt *etc.* **2.** make (drink, as tea) by infusion **3.** plot, contrive —*vi.* **4.** be in preparation —*n.* **5.** beverage produced by brewing —**'brewer** *n.* —**'brewery** *n.* —**'brewing** *n.*

briar ('brīər) *n.* tobacco pipe made from root of brier

bribe (brīb) *n.* **1.** anything offered or given to someone to gain favor, influence —*vt.* **2.** influence by bribe —**'briber** *n.* —**'bribery** *n.*

bric-a-brac ('brikəbrak) *n.* miscellaneous small objects, used for ornament

brick (brik) *n.* **1.** oblong mass of hardened clay used in building —*vt.* **2.** build, block *etc.* with bricks —**'brickbat** *n.* **1.** piece of brick *etc., esp.* used as weapon **2.** *inf.* blunt criticism —**brick cheese** semihard, whole-milk cheese produced in brick form with a yellowish-brown surface originating in Amer. —**'bricklayer** *n.*

bride (brīd) *n.* woman about to be, or just, married —**'bridal** *a.* of, relating to, a bride or wedding —**'bridegroom** *n.* man about to be, or just, married —**'bridesmaid** *n.*

bridge[1] (brij) *n.* **1.** structure for crossing river *etc.* **2.** something joining or supporting other parts **3.** raised narrow platform on ship **4.** upper part of nose **5.** part of violin *etc.* supporting strings —*vt.* **6.** make bridge over, span —ˈ**bridgehead** *n.* advanced position established on enemy territory

bridge[2] (brij) *n.* card game of whist family in which winner of the auction (declarer) nominates the trump suit or no-trump and plays his partner's hand —**auction bridge** form of bridge in which tricks made are scored toward game —**Chicago bridge** four-deal contract bridge —**contract bridge** form of bridge in which only tricks bid are scored toward game (*also* **rubber bridge**) —**duplicate bridge** contract bridge played in competition

bridle (ˈbrīdəl) *n.* **1.** headgear of horse harness **2.** curb —*vt.* **3.** put bridle on **4.** restrain —*vi.* **5.** show resentment —**bridle path** path suitable for riding horses

Brie (brē) *n.* flat, round cheese with an edible crust made from fermented, mold-inoculated whole milk, originally from France

brief (brēf) *a.* **1.** short in duration **2.** concise **3.** scanty —*n.* **4.** summary of case for counsel's use **5.** papal letter **6.** instructions —*pl.* **7.** underpants **8.** panties —*vt.* **9.** give instructions —ˈ**briefly** *adv.* —ˈ**briefness** *n.* —ˈ**briefcase** *n.* hand case for carrying papers

brier (ˈbrīər) *n.* plant, *esp.* rose, with prickly stem

brig (brig) *n.* two-masted, square-rigged ship

brigade (briˈgād) *n.* **1.** U.S. army unit consisting of three or more battalions and usu. commanded by a colonel **2.** organized band —**brigadier general** (brigəˈdēər) commissioned officer in the army, air force or marine corps ranking above a colonel and below a major general whose insignia is one star

brigand (ˈbrigənd) *n.* bandit, *esp.* member of gang in mountainous areas

brigantine (ˈbrigəntēn) *n.* two-masted vessel with square-rigged foremast and fore-and-aft mainmast

bright (brīt) *a.* **1.** shining **2.** full of light **3.** cheerful **4.** clever —ˈ**brighten** *v.* —ˈ**brightly** *adv.* —ˈ**brightness** *n.*

Bright's disease (brīts) chronic inflammation of kidneys; chronic nephritis

brill (bril) *n.* European food fish

brilliant (ˈbrilyənt) *a.* **1.** shining **2.** sparkling **3.** splendid **4.** very clever **5.** distinguished —ˈ**brilliance** *or* ˈ**brilliancy** *n.* —ˈ**brilliantly** *adv.*

brilliantine (ˈbrilyəntēn) *n.* **1.** perfumed hair oil **2.** light lustrous fabric resembling alpaca and with a cotton warp and worsted weft

brim (brim) *n.* margin, edge, *esp.* of river, cup, hat —**brimˈful** *a.* —ˈ**brimless** *a.* —ˈ**brimming** *a.*

brimstone (ˈbrimstōn) *n.* sulfur

brindled (ˈbrindəld) *a.* spotted and streaked

brine (brīn) *n.* **1.** salt water **2.** pickle —ˈ**briny** *a.* **1.** very salty —*n.* **2.** *inf.* the sea

bring (bring) *vt.* **1.** fetch **2.** carry with one **3.** cause to come (**brought** *pt./pp.*)

brink (bringk) *n.* **1.** edge of steep place **2.** verge, margin —ˈ**brinkmanship** *n.* practice of pressing dangerous situation, *esp.* in international affairs, to limit of safety in order to win advantage

briquette *or* **briquet** (briˈket) *n.* block of compressed coal dust

bris (bris) *or* **brith** (brith) *n.* *Judaism* ceremony of circumcision

brisk (brisk) *a.* active, vigorous —ˈ**briskly** *adv.* —ˈ**briskness** *n.*

brisket (ˈbriskit) *n.* meat from breast or lower chest of animal

brisling *or* **bristling** (ˈbrizling, ˈbris-) *n.* *see* SPRAT

bristle (ˈbrisəl) *n.* **1.** short stiff hair —*vi.* **2.** stand erect **3.** show temper —ˈ**bristliness** *n.* —ˈ**bristly** *a.*

Brit (brit) *n. inf.* British person

Brit. **1.** Britain **2.** British

Britannia (briˈtaniə) *n.* **1.** female warrior carrying trident, personifying Great Britain or British Empire **2.** in ancient Roman Empire, southern part of Great Britain —**Britannia metal** alloy of tin with antimony and copper, used for decorative purposes and for bearings

Britannic (briˈtanik) *a.* of Britain; British (*esp. in* **His** *or* **Her Britannic Majesty**)

britches (ˈbrichiz) *pl.n. inf.* trousers

British (ˈbritish) *a.* **1.** of Great Britain or the British Commonwealth **2.** relating to English language as spoken in Britain —*n.* **3.** natives or inhabitants of Britain —**Briticism** (ˈbritisizəm) *n.* word or idiom used in Great Britain but not in the U.S. —ˈ**Briton** *n.* native or inhabitant of Britain —**British Antarctic Territory** colony consisting of the Graham Land peninsula, certain parts of the Antarctic mainland and the archipelagoes, the South Shetland Islands and South Orkney Islands —**British Indian Ocean Territory** colony comprising the Chagos Archipelago, lying 1180 miles (1899 km) northwest of Mauritius —**British thermal unit** amount of heat required to raise the temperature of one pound of water through one degree Fahrenheit (1055 joules)

brittle (ˈbritəl) *a.* **1.** easily broken, fragile **2.** curt, irritable —ˈ**brittleness** *n.*

broach (brōch) *vt.* **1.** pierce (cask) **2.** open, begin —*vi.* **3.** *Naut.* turn beam-on to wind and waves

broad (brōd) *a.* **1.** wide, spacious, open **2.** plain, obvious **3.** coarse **4.** general **5.** tolerant **6.** (of pronunciation) dialectal —ˈ**broaden** *v.* —ˈ**broadly** *adv.* —ˈ**broadness** *n.* —**broad bean** **1.** Eurasian plant cultivated for its large edible seeds **2.** its seed —ˈ**broadcast** *v.*

1. transmit (broadcast) by radio or television —*vt.* 2. make widely known 3. scatter, as seed —*n.* 4. radio or television program —'**broadcaster** *n.* —'**broadcloth** *n.* 1. fabric woven on wide loom 2. closely woven fabric of wool *etc.* with lustrous finish —**broad-minded** *a.* 1. tolerant 2. generous —'**broadsheet** *n.* 1. newspaper with large format 2. ballad or popular song printed on one side of sheet of paper, *esp.* in 16th-cent. England (*also* **broadside (ballad)**) —'**broadside** *n.* 1. discharge of all guns on one side of ship 2. strong (verbal) attack —'**broadsword** *n.* broad-bladed sword for cutting rather than stabbing

brocade (brō'kād) *n.* rich woven fabric with raised design

broccoli ('brokəli) *n.* type of cauliflower with densely packed green florets

brochure (brō'shōōər) *n.* pamphlet, booklet

brogue (brōg) *n.* 1. stout shoe with perforated wingtip band at toe 2. dialect, *esp.* Irish accent

broil[1] (broil) *n.* noisy quarrel

broil[2] (broil) *vt.* 1. cook over hot coals 2. cook under direct heat —*vi.* 3. be heated —'**broiler** *n.*

broke (brōk) *v.* 1. *pt. of* BREAK —*a.* 2. *inf.* penniless —'**broken** *pp. of* BREAK —**broken chord** arpeggio —**broken-down** *a.* 1. worn out, as by age; dilapidated 2. not in working order —**broken'hearted** *a.* overwhelmed by grief or disappointment

broker ('brōkər) *n.* 1. one employed to buy and sell for others 2. dealer —'**brokerage** *n.* payment to broker

bromeliad (brō'mēliad) *n.* any of various plants of the pineapple family, which have many forms and mainly warm habitats. Terrestrial forms are widely grown as house plants for their decorative flowers and leaves

bromide ('brōmīd) *n.* 1. chemical compound used in medicine and photography 2. commonplace or soothing remark —**bromide paper** fast-printing photographic printing paper

bromine ('brōmēn) *n. Chem.* nonmetallic element *Symbol* Br, at. wt. 79.9, at. no. 35 —'**bromic** *a.*

bronchus ('brongkəs) *n.* either of two main branches of trachea (*pl.* **bronchi** ('brongkī)) —'**bronchial** *a.* —**bronchiectasis** (brongki'ektəsis) *n.* disease of the air passages marked by weakening and stretching of the walls of the bronchi —**bron'chitis** *n.* inflammation of bronchi —'**bronchoscope** *n.* tube with light at one end used to inspect the bronchi

bronco *or* **broncho** ('brongkō) *n.* half-tamed horse (*pl.* **-s**)

brontosaurus (brontə'sörəs) *or* **brontosaur** ('brontəsör) *n.* very large herbivorous dinosaur

Bronx (brongks) *n.* —**Bronx cheer** *inf.* rude sound made with lips, raspberry —**the Bronx** borough of New York City

bronze (bronz) *n.* 1. alloy of copper and tin —*a.* 2. made of, or colored like, bronze —*vt.* 3. give appearance of bronze to —**bronzed** *a.* 1. coated with bronze 2. sunburnt —**Bronze Age** era of bronze implements beginning in Europe from about 2000 B.C. to 500 B.C. ending with the coming of iron

brooch (brōch) *n.* ornamental pin or fastening

brood (brōōd) *n.* 1. family of young, *esp.* of birds 2. tribe, race —*vi.* 3. sit, as hen on eggs 4. meditate, fret —'**broody** *a.* moody, sullen

brook[1] (brŏŏk) *n.* small stream —'**brooklet** *n.*

brook[2] (brŏŏk) *vt.* put up with, endure, tolerate

Brooklyn ('brŏŏklin) *n.* borough of New York City

broom (brōōm, brŏŏm) *n.* 1. brush for sweeping 2. any shrub of the pea family with long slender branches, small leaves and usu. showy yellow or cream flowers —'**broomstick** *n.* handle of a broom

bros. *or* **Bros.** brothers

broth (broth) *n.* thick soup

brothel ('brothəl) *n.* house of prostitution

brother ('brudhər) *n.* 1. son of same parents as another person 2. one closely united with another —'**brotherhood** *n.* 1. relationship 2. fraternity, company —'**brotherliness** *n.* —'**brotherly** *a.* —**brother-in-law** *n.* 1. brother of husband or wife 2. husband of sister

brougham ('brōōəm, brōōm) *n.* 1. four-wheeled horse-drawn closed carriage having raised open driver's seat in front 2. *obs.* early electric automobile

brought (bröt) *pt./pp. of* BRING

brouhaha (brōō'hähä) *n.* loud confused noise; uproar

brow (brow) *n.* 1. ridge over eyes 2. forehead 3. eyebrow 4. edge of hill —'**browbeat** *vt.* bully

brown (brown) *a.* 1. of dark color inclining to red or yellow —*n.* 2. brown color, pigment or dye —*v.* 3. make, become brown —'**brownie** *n.* 1. in folklore, elf said to do helpful work at night, *esp.* household chores 2. flat, nutty chocolate cake 3. **(B-)** junior Girl Scout —**brown bagging** 1. bringing lunch to work from home 2. carrying alcoholic drink to club or restaurant —**Brownie points** credit, *esp.* with superior —**brown rice** unpolished rice —**brown study** mood of deep absorption; reverie —**brown sugar** unrefined or partially refined sugar

browse (browz) *vi.* 1. look (through book, articles for sale *etc.*) in a casual manner 2. feed on shoots and leaves

brucellosis (brōōsi'lōsis) *n.* bacterial disease occurring in goats, cattle, hogs and man (*also* **Malta fever, undulant fever, Mediterranean fever**)

Brücke (ˈbrükə) *Ger.* —**die Brücke** (dē). group of German expressionist painters in Dresden about 1905

bruin (ˈbrōōin) *n.* name for a bear, used in children's tales *etc.*

bruise (brōōz) *vt.* **1.** injure without breaking skin —*n.* **2.** contusion, discoloration caused by blow —ˈ**bruiser** *n.* strong, tough person

brumby (ˈbrumbi) *n.* Aust. wild horse

brunch (brunch) *n. inf.* breakfast and lunch combined

Brunei (ˈbrōōnī) *n.* country in the Indian Ocean on the northwest coast of Borneo bounded on all sides by Sarawak territory

brunette (brōōˈnet) *n.* **1.** woman of dark complexion and hair —*a.* **2.** dark brown

brunt (brunt) *n.* **1.** shock of attack, chief stress **2.** first blow

brush (brush) *n.* **1.** device with bristles, hairs, wires *etc.* used for cleaning, painting *etc.* **2.** act, instance of brushing **3.** brief contact **4.** skirmish, fight **5.** bushy tail **6.** brushwood **7.** (carbon) device taking electric current from moving to stationary parts of generator *etc.* —*vt.* **8.** apply, remove, clean, with brush —*v.* **9.** touch lightly —ˈ**brushoff** *n. inf.* **1.** dismissal **2.** refusal **3.** snub **4.** rebuff —ˈ**brushwood** *n.* **1.** broken-off branches **2.** land covered with scrub —**brush up** *inf.* **1.** (*oft. with* on) refresh one's knowledge, memory of (subject) **2.** make person or oneself clean or neat as after journey

brusque (brusk) *a.* rough in manner, curt, blunt

Brussels sprout (ˈbrusəlz) **1.** variety of cabbage, having stem with heads resembling tiny cabbages **2.** head of this plant, eaten as vegetable

brute (brōōt) *n.* **1.** any animal except man **2.** crude, vicious person —*a.* **3.** animal **4.** sensual, stupid **5.** physical —ˈ**brutal** *a.* —**bruˈtality** *n.* —ˈ**brutalize** *vt.* —ˈ**brutally** *adv.* —ˈ**brutish** *a.* bestial, gross

bryony (ˈbrīəni) *n.* wild climbing hedge plant

bryophyllum (brīōˈfiləm) *n.* any of various kalanchoes grown as foliage plants that propagate new plants from leaves

bryophyte (ˈbrīəfīt) *n.* plant phylum comprising mosses and liverworts —**bryophytic** (brīəˈfitik) *a.*

B.Sc. Bachelor of Science

BSI British Standards Institution

Bt. Baronet

B.t.u. British thermal unit

bubble (ˈbubəl) *n.* **1.** hollow globe of liquid, blown out with air **2.** something insubstantial, not serious **3.** transparent dome —*vi.* **4.** rise in bubbles **5.** make gurgling sound —ˈ**bubbly** *a.* —**bubble and squeak UK** dish of cabbage and potatoes fried together —**bubble gum** chewing gum that can be blown into bubbles

bubonic plague (byōōˈbonik) acute infectious disease characterized by swellings and fever

buccaneer (bukəˈnēər) *n.* pirate, sea rover —**buccaˈneering** *n.*

Buchanan (byōōˈkanən) *n.* **James.** the 15th President of the U.S. (1857-61)

buck[1] (buk) *n.* **1.** male deer, or other male animal **2.** act of bucking **3.** *sl.* dollar —*vt.* **4.** (of horse) attempt to throw rider by jumping upward *etc.* **5.** resist, oppose —ˈ**buckshot** *n.* lead shot in shotgun shell —ˈ**buckskin** *n.* **1.** skin of male deer **2.** strong grayish-yellow leather —*pl.* **3.** buckskin breeches —ˈ**buckteeth** *pl.n.* projecting upper teeth

buck[2] (buk) *n. Poker* marker in jackpot to remind winner of some obligation when his turn to deal —**pass the buck** *inf.* shift blame or responsibility

buck[3] (buk) *n.* small vaulting horse used in gymnastics

buckboard (ˈbukbörd) *n.* open four-wheeled horse-drawn carriage with seat attached to flexible board between front and rear axles

bucket (ˈbukit) *n.* **1.** vessel, round with arched handle, for water *etc.* **2.** anything resembling this —*vt.* **3.** put, carry, in bucket —ˈ**bucketful** *n.* —**bucket seat** seat with back shaped to occupier's figure

buckle (ˈbukəl) *n.* **1.** metal clasp for fastening belt, strap *etc.* —*vt.* **2.** fasten with buckle —*vi.* **3.** warp, bend —ˈ**buckler** *n.* shield —**buckle down** start work

buckram (ˈbukrəm) *n.* coarse cloth stiffened with size

bucolic (byōōˈkolik) *a.* rustic

bud (bud) *n.* **1.** embryo shoot, flower or flower cluster of plant —*vi.* **2.** begin to grow —*vt.* **3.** graft (**-dd-**)

Buddha (ˈbōōdə) *n.* **1.** the state of perfect enlightenment **2.** image of Siddhartha Gautama (about 563-483 B.C.), founder of Buddhism —ˈ**Buddhism** *n.* system of ethics and philosophy based on belief that purpose of life is to attain enlightenment, which has manifestations in many forms, *eg* Lamaism, Zen *etc.* —ˈ**Buddhist** *n./a.* —**Budˈdhistic** *a.*

buddleia (ˈbudliə) *n.* shrub with mauve flower spikes

buddy (ˈbudi) *n.* companion, friend —**buddy system** arrangement where two persons are mutually responsible for each other, *esp.* in potentially dangerous situations

budge (buj) *v.* move, stir

budgerigar (ˈbujərigär) *n.* small Aust. parakeet (*also* ˈ**budgie**)

budget (ˈbujit) *n.* **1.** annual financial statement **2.** plan of systematic spending —*vi.* **3.** prepare financial statement —*v.* **4.** plan financially

Buerger's disease (ˈbərgərz) circulatory disease of unknown cause which gradually closes off blood vessels in the arms and legs (*also* **thromboangiitis obliterans**)

buff[1] (buf) *n.* **1.** leather made from buffalo or

ox hide **2.** light yellow color **3.** bare skin **4.** polishing pad —*vt.* **5.** polish

buff[2] (buf) *n. inf.* expert on some subject

buffalo ('bufəlō) *n.* **1.** type of ox found in Asia and S Afr. **2.** domesticated ox of Asia (*also* **water buffalo**) **3.** N Amer. bison (*pl.* **-es, -s, -lo**) —*vt. sl.* **4.** intimidate **5.** mystify (**-loed, -loing**)

buffer ('bufər) *n.* contrivance to lessen shock of concussion —**buffer state** small, usu. neutral state between two rival powers —**buffer zone** neutral territory between two hostile powers

buffet[1] (bu'fā, bo͞o-) *n.* **1.** refreshment bar **2.** meal at which guests serve themselves **3.** sideboard

buffet[2] ('bufit) *n.* **1.** blow, slap **2.** misfortune —*vt.* **3.** strike with blows **4.** contend against —'**buffeting** *n.*

buffoon (bə'fo͞on) *n.* **1.** clown **2.** fool —**buf'foonery** *n.* clowning

bug (bug) *n.* **1.** any small insect **2.** *inf.* germ or virus infection **3.** *inf.* concealed listening device —*vt. inf.* **4.** install secret microphone *etc.* in **5.** irritate (**-gg-**)

bugbear ('bugbāər) *n.* **1.** object of needless terror **2.** nuisance

buggy ('bugi) *n.* **1.** light horse-drawn carriage having two or four wheels **2.** *see* **baby carriage** *at* BABY

bugle ('byo͞ogəl) *n.* brass military musical instrument shaped like a trumpet without valves —'**bugler** *n.*

buhl (bo͞ol) *n. see* BOULLE

build (bild) *v.* **1.** make, construct, by putting together parts or materials (**built** *pt./pp.*) —*n.* **2.** make, form —'**builder** *n.* —'**building** *n.* —**build-up** *n.* **1.** progressive increase in number *etc.* **2.** extravagant publicity or praise **3.** *Mil.* process of attaining required strength of forces and equipment —**built-in** *a.* **1.** made as integral part **2.** essential; inherent —**built-up** *a.* having many buildings —**build up 1.** construct gradually **2.** increase, *esp.* by degrees **3.** improve health of **4.** prepare for climax, as in story

bulb (bulb) *n.* **1.** modified bud with fleshy scales usu. formed underground sometimes used as food **2.** any plant with fleshy rootstock *eg* corms, tubers and rhizomes **3.** globe surrounding filament of electric light —'**bulbous** *a.*

bulbul ('bo͝olbo͝ol) *n.* any of several songbirds of Afr. and southern Asia

Bulgaria (bul'gariə, -'ger-) *n.* country in Europe bounded in the north by Romania, east by the Black Sea, south by Turkey and Greece and west by Yugoslavia —**Bul'garian** *n./a.* **1.** (native or inhabitant) of Bulgaria —*n.* **2.** language of Bulgaria which is a Balto-Slavic language and is written in the Cyrillic alphabet

bulge (bulj) *n.* **1.** swelling, protuberance **2.** temporary increase —*vi.* **3.** swell out —'**bulginess** *n.* —'**bulgy** *a.*

bulk (bulk) *n.* **1.** size, volume **2.** greater part **3.** cargo —*vi.* **4.** be of weight or importance —'**bulkiness** *n.* —'**bulking** *n.* process for fluffing up surface of man-made yarns to give extra absorbency, lightness and springiness —'**bulky** *a.*

bulkhead ('bulk-hed) *n.* **1.** interior partition in ship, aircraft or vehicle **2.** retaining wall at harbor **3.** frame with sloping doors giving outside access to cellar —**bulkhead door** such a door opening on to a stairway

bull[1] (bo͝ol) *n.* **1.** male of cattle **2.** male of various other animals **3.** *Fin.* someone who believes the market will rise —'**bullock** *n.* castrated bull —'**bulldog** *n.* thickset breed of dog —'**bulldoze** *vt.* —'**bulldozer** *n.* powerful tractor with blade for excavating *etc.* —'**bullfight** *n.* spectacle pitting matador against the bull in an arena for the diversion of an audience —'**bullfighter** *n.* —'**bullfighting** *n.* —'**bullfinch** *n.* **1.** European finch, male of which has bright red throat and breast **2.** any of similar finches —**bullheaded** *a.* blindly obstinate; stupid —'**bullpen** *n. Baseball* area where pitchers warm up before game —'**bullring** *n.* arena for bullfighting —**bull's-eye** *n.* middle part of target —**bull terrier** breed of terrier developed by crossing bulldog with English terrier

bull[2] (bo͝ol) *n.* papal edict

bull[3] (bo͝ol) *n. sl.* nonsense

bull[4] bulletin

bullet ('bo͝olit) *n.* projectile discharged from rifle, pistol *etc.*

bulletin ('bo͝olitin) *n.* official report

bullion ('bo͝olyən) *n.* **1.** gold or silver in bars or ingots **2.** garment decoration in gold or silver threads

bully ('bo͝oli) *n.* **1.** one who hurts, persecutes or intimidates weaker people —*vt.* **2.** intimidate, overawe **3.** ill-treat ('**bullied,** '**bullying**) —**bully beef** corned beef

bully-off *n. Hockey* method of starting play, in which two players strike sticks together and against ground three times before trying to hit ball (*also* '**bully**) —**bully off** *Hockey* start play with bully-off (*also* '**bully**)

bulrush ('bo͝olrush) *n.* tall reedlike marsh plant with brown velvety spike

bulwark ('bo͝olwərk) *n.* **1.** rampart **2.** any defense or means of security **3.** raised side of ship **4.** breakwater

bum (bum) *sl. n.* **1.** loafer, scrounger —*vt.* **2.** get by scrounging (**-mm-**) —*a.* **3.** useless

bumble ('bumbəl) *vi.* speak or proceed clumsily —'**bumbler** *n.*

bumblebee ('bumbəlbē) *n.* large hairy social bee

bump (bump) *n.* **1.** heavy blow, dull in sound **2.** swelling caused by blow **3.** protuberance **4.** sudden movement —*vt.* **5.** strike or push against —'**bumper** *n.* **1.** horizontal bar at front and rear of automobile to protect against damage **2.** full glass —*a.* **3.** full, abundant —**bump off** *sl.* murder

bumpkin ('bumpkin) *n.* rustic

bumptious ('bumpshəs) *a.* offensively self-assertive

bun (bun) *n.* **1.** small, round cake **2.** round knot of hair

bunch (bunch) *n.* **1.** number of things tied or growing together **2.** cluster **3.** tuft, knot **4.** group, party —*vt.* **5.** put together in bunch —*vi.* **6.** gather together —'**bunchy** *a.* —**like (someone** *or* **something) a bunch** be enthusiastic about (someone *or* something)

bundle ('bundəl) *n.* **1.** package **2.** number of things tied together **3.** *sl.* lot of money —*vt.* **4.** tie in bundle **5.** send (off) without ceremony

bung (bung) *n.* **1.** stopper for cask, large cork —*vt.* **2.** stop up, seal, close **3.** *inf.* throw, sling —'**bunghole** *n.*

bungalow ('bunggəlō) *n.* one-storied house

bungle ('bunggəl) *vt.* **1.** do badly from lack of skill, botch —*vi.* **2.** act clumsily, awkwardly —*n.* **3.** blunder, muddle —'**bungled** *a.* —'**bungler** *n.* —'**bungling** *a./n.*

bunion ('bunyən) *n.* deformity of the great toe

bunk[1] (bungk) *n.* narrow, shelflike bed —**bunk bed** one of pair of beds constructed one above the other

bunk[2] (bungk) *n.* bunkum

bunker ('bungkər) *n.* **1.** large storage container for oil, coal *etc.* **2.** sandy hollow on golf course **3.** (military) underground defensive position

bunkum *or* **buncombe** ('bungkəm) *n.* nonsensical talk

bunny ('buni) *n. inf.* rabbit

Bunsen burner ('bunsən) gas burner, producing great heat, used for chemical experiments

bunt (bunt) *v.* attempt to hit (baseball) with shortened grip so that infielder cannot reach it in time

bunting[1] ('bunting) *n.* material for flags

bunting[2] ('bunting) *n.* bird with short, stout bill

buoy ('bōōi) *n.* **1.** floating marker anchored in sea **2.** lifebuoy —*vt.* **3.** mark with buoy **4.** keep from sinking **5.** support —**buoyancy** ('boiənsi) *n.* —**buoyant** ('boiənt) *a.*

bur[1] (bər) *n.* **1.** rough prickly envelope of fruit **2.** plant bearing burs

bur[2] bureau

Burberry ('bərbəri) *n.* **1.** trade name for a light raincoat made of water-resistant fabric (*pl.* **-ries**) **2.** plaid pattern used for lining, scarves, hats and luggage

burble ('bərbəl) *vi.* **1.** gurgle, as stream or baby **2.** talk idly

burden[1] ('bərdən) *n.* **1.** load, weight **2.** cargo **3.** anything difficult to bear —*vt.* **4.** load, encumber —'**burdensome** *a.*

burden[2] ('bərdən) *n.* **1.** chorus of a song **2.** chief theme

burdock ('bərdok) *n.* plant with prickly burs

bureau ('byōōərō) *n.* **1.** writing desk **2.** office **3.** government department (*pl.* **-s, -reaux** (-rōz)) —**bureaucracy** (byōō'rokrəsi) *n.* **1.** government by officials **2.** body of officials —'**bureaucrat** *n.* —**bureau'cratic** *a.*

burette *or* **buret** (byōō'ret) *n.* graduated glass tube with stopcock on one end, for dispensing known volumes of fluids

burgee (bər'jē, 'bərjē) *n.* small nautical flag

burgeon ('bərjən) *vi.* **1.** bud **2.** develop rapidly

burgess ('bərjis) *n.* inhabitant of borough, *esp.* citizen with full municipal rights

burgh ('bərō) *n.* Scottish borough —**burgher** ('bərgər) *n.* citizen

burglar ('bərglər) *n.* one who enters building to commit crime, *esp.* theft —'**burglary** *n.* —'**burgle** *or* '**burglarize** *vt.*

burgundy ('bərgəndi) *n.* name of various red or white wines produced in the Burgundy region of France

burin ('byōōrin) *n.* chisel of tempered steel used for engraving metal, wood or marble

Burkina-Faso (bər'kēnə'fasō) *n.* country in Africa bounded north and west by Mali, east by Niger and south by Benin, Togo, Ghana and the Ivory Coast

burlap ('bərlap) *n.* coarse plain-weave fabric of jute or hemp

burlesque (bər'lesk) *n.* **1.** (artistic) caricature **2.** ludicrous imitation —*vt.* **3.** caricature

burly ('bərli) *a.* sturdy, stout, robust —'**burliness** *n.*

Burma ('bərmə) *n.* country in Asia bounded east by China, Laos and Thailand, west by the Indian Ocean, Bangladesh and India —'**Burman** *n./a.* (denoting) native or inhabitant of Burma —**Bur'mese** *n.* the language of Burma which is a member of the Sino-Tibetan family

burn (bərn) *vt.* **1.** destroy or injure by fire —*vi.* **2.** be on fire (*lit.* or *fig.*) **3.** be consumed by fire (**burned** *or* **burnt** *pt./pp.*) —*n.* **4.** wound caused by action of heat, caustic chemicals or electricity —'**burner** *n.* **1.** part of stove *etc.* that produces flame **2.** apparatus for burning fuel, refuse *etc.* —'**burning** *a.* —**burning glass** convex lens for concentrating sun's rays to produce fire

burnish ('bərnish) *vt.* **1.** make bright by rubbing, polish —*n.* **2.** gloss, luster —'**burnisher** *n.*

burnoose *or* **burnous** (bər'nōōs) *n.* long circular cloak with hood, worn *esp.* by Arabs

burnt (bərnt) *v.* **1.** *pt./pp. of* BURN —*a.* **2.** affected as if by burning; charred

burp (bərp) *n./v. inf.* (*esp.* of baby) belch

burr[1] (bər) *n.* soft trilling sound given to letter *r* in some dialects

burr[2] (bər) *n.* rough edge left after cutting, drilling *etc.*

burro ('bo͞orō) *n.* donkey (*pl.* **-s**)

burrow ('burō) *n.* **1.** hole dug by rabbit *etc.* —*v.* **2.** make holes in (ground) —*vt.* **3.** bore **4.** conceal

bursar ('bərsər) *n.* official managing finances of college, school *etc.*

burst (bərst) *vi.* **1.** fly asunder **2.** break into pieces **3.** rend **4.** break suddenly into some expression of feeling —*vt.* **5.** shatter, break violently (**burst** *pt./pp.*) —*n.* **6.** bursting **7.** explosion **8.** outbreak **9.** spurt

Burundi (bə'ro͞ondi) *n.* country in east Africa lying astride the main Nile-Congo dividing crest bounded on the west by the Ruzizi River and Lake Tanganyika

bury ('beri) *vt.* **1.** put underground, inter **2.** conceal (**'buried, 'burying**) —**'burial** *n./a.* —**bury the hatchet** become reconciled

bus (bus) *n.* **1.** large motor-driven vehicle for passengers (*orig.* omnibus) —*v.* **2.** travel or transport by bus (**bused** *or* **bussed** *pt.*, **'busing** *or* **'bussing** *pr.p.*) —**bus boy** assistant to waiter who removes dirty dishes to kitchen —**bus lane** strip of road for use by buses only —**busman's holiday** *inf.* holiday spent doing same as one does at work

bus. business

busby ('buzbi) *n.* tall fur hat worn by certain soldiers

bush[1] (bo͞osh) *n.* **1.** shrub **2.** woodland, thicket **3. A, SA** *etc.* uncleared country, backwoods, interior —**bushed** *a.* **1.** tired out **2. A** lost, bewildered —**'bushy** *a.* shaggy —**'bushbaby** *n.* tree-living, nocturnal Afr. animal —**bush fire** widespread destructive fire in the bush —**bush-league** *a.* mediocre of its kind —**bush line C** airline operating in bush country —**'Bushman** *n.* member of hunting and gathering people of southern Afr. —**bush pilot** —**bush telegraph** *inf.* means of spreading rumor *etc.*

bush[2] (bo͞osh) *n.* **1.** thin metal sleeve or tubular lining serving as bearing —*v.* **2.** fit bush to (casing *etc.*)

bushel ('bo͞oshəl) *n.* unit of dry capacity equal to 4 pecks: 2150.42 cubic inches or 35.239 liters

business ('biznis) *n.* **1.** profession, occupation **2.** commercial or industrial establishment **3.** commerce, trade **4.** responsibility, affair, matter **5.** work —**'businesslike** *a.* —**'businessman** *n.* person engaged in business, *esp.* as owner or executive (**'businesswoman** *fem.*)

busker ('buskər) *n.* one who makes money by singing, dancing *etc.* in the street —**busk** *vi.*

buskin ('buskin) *n.* **1.** formerly, sandal-like covering for foot and leg, reaching calf **2.** thick-soled laced half boot worn *esp.* by actors of ancient Greece **3.** (*usu. with* the) tragic drama

bust[1] (bust) *n.* **1.** sculpture of head and shoulders of human body **2.** woman's breasts

bust[2] (bust) *inf. v.* **1.** burst **2.** make, become bankrupt —*vt.* **3.** raid **4.** arrest —*a.* **5.** broken **6.** bankrupt —*n.* **7.** police raid or arrest

bustard ('bustərd) *n.* any of several swift-running birds of Afr. related to cranes

bustle[1] ('busəl) *vi.* **1.** be noisily busy, active —*n.* **2.** fuss, commotion

bustle[2] ('busəl) *n. Hist.* pad worn by ladies to support back of skirt

busy ('bizi) *a.* **1.** actively employed **2.** full of activity —*vt.* **3.** occupy (**'busied, 'busying**) —**'busily** *adv.* —**'busybody** *n.* meddler —**'busywork** *n.* inessential activity performed to keep one occupied

but (but; *unstressed* bət) *prep./conj.* **1.** without **2.** except **3.** only **4.** yet **5.** still **6.** besides

butane ('byo͞otān) *n.* gas used for fuel

butch (bo͞och) *a./n. sl.* **1.** markedly or aggressively masculine (person) **2.** (woman) assuming male role in lesbian relationship

butcher ('bo͞ochər) *n.* **1.** one who kills animals for food, or sells meat **2.** ruthless or brutal murderer —*vt.* **3.** slaughter, murder **4.** spoil (work) —**'butchery** *n.*

butler ('butlər) *n.* chief male servant

butt[1] (but) *n.* **1.** the thick end **2.** target **3.** object of ridicule **4.** bottom or unused end of anything —*v.* **5.** lie, be placed end-on to

butt[2] (but) *vt.* **1.** strike with head **2.** push —*n.* **3.** blow with head, as of sheep —**butt in** interfere, meddle

butt[3] (but) *n.* large cask

butter ('butər) *n.* **1.** fatty substance made from cream by churning —*vt.* **2.** spread with butter —**butter bean** lima bean with large pale edible seeds —**'butterfingered** *a.* —**'butterfingers** *n. inf.* person who drops things inadvertently —**'buttermilk** *n.* milk that remains after churning —**'butterscotch** *n.* kind of hard, brittle toffee or flavoring —**butter up** *inf.* flatter

buttercup ('butərkup) *n.* wild plant with glossy, yellow flowers

butterfly ('butərflī) *n.* **1.** insect with large wings **2.** inconstant person **3.** stroke in swimming —**have butterflies in the stomach** feel nervous

buttock ('butək) *n.* (*usu. pl.*) rump, protruding hinder part

button ('butən) *n.* **1.** knob, stud for fastening —*vt.* **2.** fasten with buttons —**'buttonhole** *n.* **1.** slit in garment to pass button through as fastening —*vt.* **2.** detain (reluctant listener) in conversation

buttress ('butris) *n.* **1.** structure to support wall **2.** prop —*vt.* **3.** support (wall) with buttress

buxom ('buksəm) *a.* **1.** full of health, plump, gay **2.** large-breasted

buy (bī) *vt.* **1.** get by payment, purchase **2.** bribe (**bought** *pt./pp.*) —**'buyer** *n.*

buzz (buz) *vi.* **1.** make humming sound —*n.* **2.** humming sound of bees **3.** *inf.* telephone call

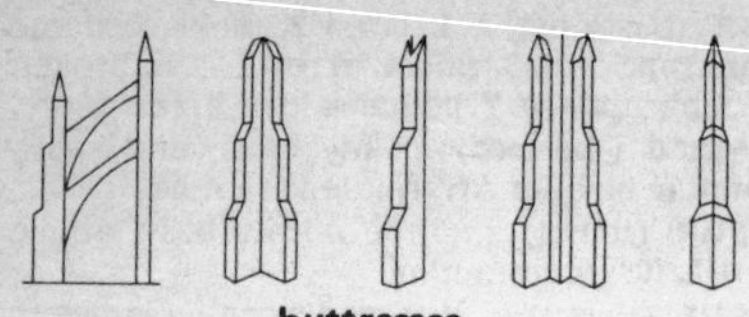

buttresses

—'**buzzer** *n.* any apparatus that makes buzzing sound —**buzz saw** circular saw —'**buzzword** *n.* catch phrase used to impress —**buzz off** *sl.* go away

buzzard ('buzərd) *n.* bird of prey of hawk family

BV Blessed Virgin

BW **1.** bacteriological warfare **2.** biological warfare **3.** black-and-white **4.** bread and water

bwana ('bwänə) *n.* in E Afr., master, oft. used as form of address corresponding to *sir*

B.W.I. British West Indies

BWOC big woman on campus

bx box

BX base exchange

by[1] (bī) *prep.* **1.** near **2.** along **3.** across **4.** past **5.** during **6.** not later than **7.** through use or agency of **8.** in units of —*adv.* **9.** near **10.** away, aside **11.** past —**by and by** soon, in the future —**by and large 1.** on the whole **2.** speaking generally —**come by** obtain

by[2] billion years

by- *or* **bye-** (*comb. form*) subsidiary, incidental, out-of-the-way, near, as in *bypath, by-product, bystander*

bye (bī) *n. Sport* situation where player, team advances in a tournament without playing a given round

bygone ('bīgon) *a.* **1.** past, former —*n.* **2.** (*oft. pl.*) past occurrence **3.** small antique

bylaw *or* **bye-law** ('bīlö) *n.* standing rule adopted by organization to govern its internal affairs

by-line *n.* line under title of newspaper or magazine article giving author's name

BYO bring your own

BYOB bring your own bottle

byp bypass

bypass ('bīpäs) *n.* **1.** road around a town **2.** secondary channel connected to a main passage —**bypass surgery** operation on blood vessels of heart

by-play *n.* diversion, action apart from main action of play

byre (bīər) *n.* cowshed

bystander ('bīstandər) *n.* person present but not involved; spectator

byte (bīt) *n. Comp.* sequence of bits processed as single unit of information

byway ('bīwā) *n.* **1.** seldom-traveled side road **2.** area, field of study *etc.* that is of secondary importance

byword ('bīwərd) *n.* well-known name, saying

Byzantine ('bizəntēn, 'bī-; -tīn; bi'zan-, bī-) *a.* **1.** of the eastern Roman Empire at Byzantium (later Constantinople, now Istanbul) **2.** (*oft.* **b-**) complicated, devious, underhand **3.** of style of art and architecture of which high points were in early 6th cent. and 9th cent. **4.** of the eastern Catholic churches in communion with the Patriarch of Constantinople

C

c *or* **C** (sē) *n.* **1.** third letter of English alphabet **2.** speech sound represented by this letter, usu. either as in *cigar* or as in *case* **3.** third in series, *esp.* third highest grade in examination **4.** something shaped like C (*pl.* **c's, C's** *or* **Cs**)

C 1. *Mus.* first degree of major scale containing no sharps or flats (**C major**); major or minor key having this note as tonic; time signature denoting four quarter notes to bar (*see also* ALLA BREVE (sense 2), **common time** *at* COMMON) **2.** *Chem.* carbon **3.** capacitance **4.** heat capacity **5.** cold (water) **6.** *Phys.* compliance **7.** Celsius **8.** centigrade **9.** Conservative **10.** century, as in *C20* **11.** Roman numeral, 100

c. 1. carat **2.** cent **3.** circa **4.** copyright

Ca *Chem.* calcium

CA California

ca. circa

C.A. chartered accountant

cab (kab) *n.* **1.** taxi **2.** driver's enclosed compartment on locomotive, truck *etc.* —**'cabman** *or* **'cabby** *n.* taxi driver

CAB Civil Aeronautics Board

cabal (kə'bal) *n.* **1.** small group of intriguers **2.** secret plot

cabala, cabbala, *or* **cabbalah** (kə'bälə) *n.* **1.** ancient Jewish mystical tradition **2.** any secret or occult doctrine —**'cabalist** *n.* —**caba'listic** *a.*

cabaret (kabə'rā, 'kabərā) *n.* floor show at nightclub or restaurant

cabbage ('kabij) *n.* vegetable with large head of green or reddish leaves

caber ('kābər) *n.* heavy wooden pole tossed as trial of strength at Highland games

Cabernet ('kabərnā) *n.* red table wine

cabin ('kabin) *n.* **1.** hut, shed **2.** small room, *esp.* in ship —*vt.* **3.** cramp, confine —**cabin boy** boy who waits on officers and passengers of ship —**cabin cruiser** power boat with cabin, bunks *etc.*

cabinet ('kabinit) *n.* **1.** piece of furniture with drawers or shelves **2.** outer case of television, radio *etc.* **3.** (*oft.* **C-**) body of advisers to a head of state **4.** in parliamentary system, committee of politicians governing country **5.** *obs.* small room —**cabinetmaker** *n.* craftsman who makes fine furniture

cable ('kābəl) *n.* **1.** strong rope **2.** wire or bundle of wires conveying electric power, telegraph signals *etc.* **3.** message sent by this **4.** nautical unit of measurement (100–120 fathoms) —*v.* **5.** telegraph by cable —**cable car** passenger car on cable railway, drawn by strong cable operated by motor —**'cablegram** *n.* cabled message

cabochon ('kabəshon) *n.* **1.** convex oval or round decoration used on furniture and articles made in metal **2.** unfaceted, highly polished gemstone in this form

caboodle (kə'bōōdəl) *n. inf.* entity, group or lot —**the whole (kit and) caboodle** the whole lot

caboose (kə'bōōs) *n.* **1.** ship's galley **2.** freight-train car for use of train crew **3.** one that brings up the rear

cabriolet (kabriō'lā) *n.* early type of hansom cab

cacao (kə'kow, -'kāō) *n.* tropical tree from the seeds of which chocolate and cocoa are made

Cacciocavallo (kachiōkə'valō) *n.* a hard, whole-cream cheese with a salty, smoky flavor orig. from Italy

cachalot ('kashəlot) *n.* sperm whale

cache (kash) *n.* **1.** secret hiding place **2.** store of food *etc.*

cachet (ka'shā) *n.* **1.** mark, stamp **2.** mark of authenticity **3.** prestige, distinction

cachinnate ('kakināt) *vi.* laugh loudly —**cachin'nation** *n.*

cachou ('kashōō, ka'shōō) *n.* **1.** lozenge eaten to sweeten breath **2.** substance obtained from certain tropical plants and used in medicine *etc.* (*also* **'catechu, cutch**)

cackle ('kakəl) *vi.* **1.** make chattering noise, as hen —*n.* **2.** cackling noise or laughter **3.** empty chatter —**'cackler** *n.*

caco- (*comb. form*) bad, unpleasant, incorrect, as in *cacophony*

cacophony (kə'kofəni) *n.* **1.** disagreeable sound **2.** discord of sounds —**ca'cophonous** *a.*

cactus ('kaktəs) *n.* spiny succulent plant (*pl.* **-es, cacti** ('kaktī))

cad (kad) *n.* dishonorable, unchivalrous person —**'caddish** *a.*

cadaver (kə'davər) *n.* corpse —**ca'daverous** *a.* **1.** corpselike **2.** sickly-looking **3.** gaunt

caddie *or* **caddy** ('kadi) *n.* **1.** golfer's attendant **2.** small cart used by golfers to carry clubs (*also* **caddie cart**) —*vi.* **3.** act as caddie

caddis fly ('kadis) small mothlike insect having two pairs of hairy wings —**caddis worm** *or* **'caddis** *n.* aquatic larva of caddis fly, which constructs protective case around itself made of silk *etc.* (*also* **'caseworm, 'strawworm**)

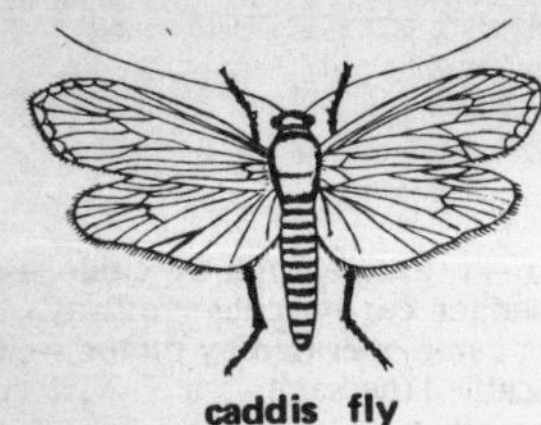

caddis fly

caddy ('kadi) *n.* small box for tea
cadence ('kādəns) *or* **cadency** *n.* fall or modulation of voice in music or verse
cadenza (kə'denzə) *n. Mus.* elaborate passage for solo instrument or singer
cadet (kə'det) *n.* youth in training, *esp.* for officer status in armed forces
cadge (kaj) *v.* get (food, money *etc.*) by sponging or begging —**'cadger** *n.* sponger
cadi *or* **kadi** ('kădi, 'kādi) *n.* judge in Muslim community (*pl.* **-s**)
cadmium ('kadmiəm) *n. Chem.* metallic element *Symbol* Cd, at. wt. 112.4, at. no. 48
cadre ('kadri) *n.* **1.** nucleus or framework, *esp.* of indoctrinated personnel **2.** member of a cadre, *esp.* in China
caduceus (kə'dyōōsləs, -'dōō-) *n.* **1.** *Class. myth.* winged staff entwined with two serpents carried by Hermes (Mercury) **2.** insignia resembling this, used as emblem of medical profession (*pl.* **-cei** (-sīī))
Caenozoic (sēnō'zōik) *see* CENOZOIC
Caerphilly (kär'fili) *n.* creamy white mild-flavored cheese
caesura *or* **cesura** (si'zhōōrə) *n.* **1.** in modern prosody, pause, *esp.* for sense, usu. near middle of verse line **2.** in classical prosody, break between words within metrical foot (*pl.* **-s, -rae** (-rē))
café (ka'fā) *n.* small or inexpensive restaurant serving light refreshments —**cafe'teria** *n.* restaurant designed for self-service
caff (kaf) *n. sl.* café
caffeine ('kafēn) *n.* naturally occurring chemical found in the coffee bean, tea leaf, cocoa bean and kola nut used in high dose to stimulate the nervous system
caftan ('kaftan) *n.* ankle-length garment with long loose sleeves based on open-sleeved overtunic worn since Biblical times in the Levant
cage (kāj) *n.* **1.** enclosure, box with bars or wires, *esp.* for keeping animals or birds **2.** place of confinement **3.** enclosed platform of lift, *esp.* in mine —*vt.* **4.** put in cage, confine —**'cagey** *or* **'cagy** *a.* wary, not communicative
cahoots (kə'hōōts) *pl.n. sl.* partnership (*esp. in* **in cahoots with**)
caiman *or* **cayman** ('kāmən) *n.* any of several tropical Amer. crocodilians related to alligator
cairn (kāərn) *n.* heap of stones, *esp.* as monument or landmark —**cairn terrier** small rough-haired terrier orig. from Scotland
cairngorm ('kāərngörm) *n.* yellow or brownish-colored gem
caisson ('kāson) *n.* **1.** chamber for working under water **2.** apparatus for lifting vessel out of water **3.** ammunition wagon
caitiff ('kātif) *obs. n.* **1.** mean, despicable fellow —*a.* **2.** base, mean
cajole (kə'jōl) *vt.* persuade by flattery, wheedle —**ca'jolement** *n.* —**ca'joler** *n.* —**ca'jolery** *n.*
Cajun *or* **Cajan** ('kājən) *n.* **1.** inhabitant of Louisiana descended from 18th-cent. French-Canadian immigrants **2.** the dialect spoken by Cajuns
cake (kāk) *n.* **1.** baked, sweetened, breadlike food **2.** compact mass —*vt.* **3.** make into cake —*vi.* **4.** harden (as of mud) —**'cakewalk** *n.* **1.** dance orig. performed by Amer. Negroes for prize of cake **2.** piece of music for this dance
cal. **1.** calendar **2.** caliber **3.** (small) calorie
Cal. (large) Calorie
calabash ('kaləbash) *n.* **1.** tree with large hard-shelled fruit **2.** this fruit **3.** drinking, cooking vessel made from gourd
calaboose ('kaləbōōs) *n. inf.* prison
calamine ('kaləmīn) *n.* mixture of zinc oxide and ferric oxide used in soothing lotion or ointment
calamity (kə'lamiti) *n.* **1.** great misfortune **2.** deep distress, disaster —**ca'lamitous** *a.*
calceolaria (kalsiə'leriə) *n.* Amer. plant with speckled, slipper-shaped flowers (*also* **slipperwort**)
calces ('kalsēz) *n., pl. of* CALX
calcicole ('kalsikōl) *n.* plant requiring a chalky soil
calciferol (kal'sifərol) *n.* fat-soluble steroid, found *esp.* in fish-liver oils and used in treatment of rickets (*also* **vitamin D_2**)
calcifuge ('kalsifyōōj) *n.* plant requiring an acid soil
calcium ('kalsiəm) *n. Chem.* metallic element *Symbol* Ca, at. wt. 40.1, at. no. 20 —**calcareous** (kal'kariəs, -'ker-) *a.* containing lime —**cal'ciferous** *a.* producing salts of calcium, *esp.* calcium carbonate —**'calcify** *v.* convert, be converted, to lime —**'calcine** *vt.* **1.** reduce to quicklime **2.** burn to ashes —**'calcite** *n.* crystalline calcium carbonate —**calcium carbonate** white crystalline salt occurring in limestone, chalk *etc.*
calculate ('kalkyōōlāt) *vt.* **1.** estimate **2.** compute —*vi.* **3.** make reckonings —**'calculable** *a.* —**'calculated** *a.* **1.** undertaken after considering likelihood of success **2.** premeditated —**'calculating** *a.* **1.** able to perform calculations **2.** shrewd, designing, scheming

—**calcu'lation** *n.* —**'calculator** *n.* electronic device for making calculations —**'calculus** *n.* **1.** *Math.* any system of operations involving the use of symbols, *esp.* infinitesimal calculus, a system of mathematical analysis **2.** stone in body formed by mineral deposit around an organic core (*pl.* **calculi** ('kalkyŏŏlī))

caldron ('köldrən) *n.* kettle or pot used for boiling

calèche (*Fr.* ka'lesh) *n.* **C** horse-drawn carriage for taking tourists around

Caledonian (kali'dōniən) *a.* **1.** relating to Scotland —*n.* **2.** *Lit.* native of Scotland

calendar ('kalindər) *n.* **1.** table of months and days in the year **2.** list of events, documents, register —*vt.* **3.** enter in list **4.** index

calender ('kalindər) *n.* **1.** machine in which paper or cloth is smoothed by passing between rollers —*vt.* **2.** subject to such process

calends ('kalindz) *pl.n.* first day of each month in ancient Roman calendar

calendula (ka'lenjələ) *n.* marigold

calf[1] (käf) *n.* **1.** young of cow and of other animals **2.** leather made of calf's skin (*pl.* **calves**) —**calve** *vi.* give birth to calf —**calf love** infatuation of adolescent for member of opposite sex

calf[2] (käf) *n.* fleshy back part of leg below knee (*pl.* **calves**)

caliber ('kalibər) *n.* **1.** size of bore of gun **2.** capacity, character —**'calibrate** *vt.* mark (scale of measuring instrument) so that readings can be made in appropriate units —**cali'bration** *n.*

calices ('kalisēz) *n., pl. of* CALIX

calico ('kalikō) *n.* cheap cotton cloth

California (kali'förniə) *n.* Pacific state of the U.S., admitted to the Union in 1850. Abbrev.: **Calif., CA** (with ZIP code)

californium (kali'förniəm) *n. Chem.* transuranic element *Symbol* Cf, at. wt. 251, at. no. 98

caliper ('kalipər) *n.* **1.** metal or plastic splint for leg —*pl.* **2.** measuring implement with two adjustable legs used to determine distance on a surface **3.** instrument for measuring diameters

caliph, calif *or* **khalif** ('kālif, 'kal-) *n. Islam* title of successors of Mohammed as rulers of Islamic world —**'caliphate, 'califate** *or* **'khalifate** *n.* office or reign of caliph

calix ('kāliks, 'ka-) *n.* cup; chalice (*pl.* **'calices**)

calk[1] (kök) *vt. see* CAULK

calk[2] (kök) *or* **calkin** ('kökin) *n.* **1.** metal projection on horse's shoe to prevent slipping —*vt.* **2.** provide with calks

call (köl) *vt.* **1.** speak loudly to attract attention of **2.** summon **3.** (*oft. with* up) telephone **4.** name —*vi.* **5.** shout **6.** pay visit —*n.* **7.** shout **8.** animal's cry **9.** visit **10.** inner urge, summons, as to be priest *etc.* **11.** need, demand —**'caller** *n.* —**'calling** *n.* vocation, profession —**call box** kiosk for public telephone—**call girl** prostitute with whom appointments are made by telephone —**call up 1.** summon to serve in army **2.** imagine

calligraphy (kə'ligrəfi) *n.* handwriting, penmanship —**calli'graphic** *a.*

callisthenics *or* **calisthenics** (kalis'theniks) *pl.n.* light gymnastic exercises —**callis'thenic** *or* **calis'thenic** *a.*

callosity (kə'lositi) *n.* **1.** hardheartedness **2.** callus

callous ('kaləs) *a.* hardened, unfeeling —**'callously** *adv.* —**'callousness** *n.*

callow ('kalō) *a.* inexperienced, immature

callus ('kaləs) *n.* area of thick, hardened skin

calm (käm, kälm) *a.* **1.** still **2.** quiet **3.** tranquil —*n.* **4.** stillness **5.** tranquillity **6.** absence of wind —*v.* **7.** become, make, still or quiet —**'calmly** *adv.* —**'calmness** *n.*

calomel ('kaləmel, -məl) *n.* colorless, tasteless powder used medicinally, *esp.* as cathartic

calorie *or* **calory** ('kaləri) *n.* **1.** unit of heat **2.** unit of energy obtained from foods —**ca'loric** *a.* **1.** of heat or calories —*n.* **2.** *obs.* hypothetical elastic fluid, embodiment of heat —**calo'rific** *a.* heat-making —**calo'rimeter** *n.*

calumet ('kalyŏŏmet) *n.* long, ornamented tobacco pipe of Amerindians used at ceremonies, *esp.* as token of peace

calumny ('kaləmni) *n.* slander, false accusation —**ca'lumniate** *vt.* —**calumni'ation** *n.* —**ca'lumniator** *n.* —**ca'lumnious** *a.*

Calvary ('kalvəri) *n.* place outside walls of Jerusalem where Jesus was crucified (*also* **Gol'gotha**)

calves (kävz) *n., pl. of* CALF[1], CALF[2]

Calvinism ('kalvinizəm) *n.* theological system of Calvin, characterized by emphasis on predestination and justification by faith —**'Calvinist** *n./a.* —**Calvin'istic(al)** *a.*

calx (kalks) *n.* **1.** powdery metallic oxide formed when ore or mineral is roasted **2.** calcium oxide (*pl.* **-es, 'calces**)

calypso (kə'lipsō) *n.* W Indian improvised song on topical subject

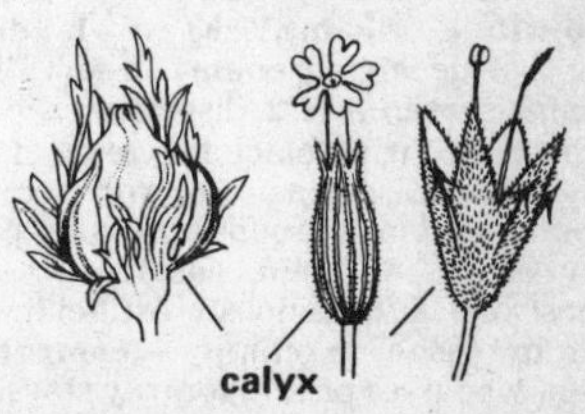

calyx ('kāliks, 'kaliks) *n.* covering of bud (*pl.* **-es, calyces** ('kalisēz, 'kāli-))

cam (kam) *n.* device to change rotary to reciprocating motion —'**camshaft** *n.* in motoring, rotating shaft to which cams are fixed to lift valves

camaraderie (kamə'rädəri) *n.* spirit of comradeship, trust

camber ('kambər) *n.* **1.** convexity on upper surface of road, bridge *etc.* **2.** curvature of aircraft wing

cambium ('kambiəm) *n.* layer of cells between the xylem and phloem that retains the power of growth

Cambodia (kam'bōdiə) *n. former name of* KAMPUCHEA

Cambrian ('kambriən) *a.* **1.** of first 100 million years of Paleozoic era **2.** of Wales —*n.* **3.** Cambrian period or rock system **4.** Welshman

cambric ('kāmbrik) *n.* fine white linen or cotton cloth

came (kām) *pt. of* COME

camel ('kaməl) *n.* animal of Asia and Afr., with humped back, used as beast of burden —**camel's hair** *or* '**camelhair** *n.* **1.** hair of camel, used in rugs *etc.* **2.** soft cloth made of this hair, usu. tan in color —*a.* **3.** (of painter's brush) made from tail hairs of squirrels

camellia (kə'mēlyə) *n.* ornamental shrub

camelopard (kə'meləpärd) *n. obs.* giraffe

Camembert ('kaməmbāər) *n.* a rich, soft cheese from cow's milk with an edible crust, orig. from France

cameo ('kamiō) *n.* **1.** medallion, brooch *etc.* with profile head or design carved in relief **2.** single brief scene or appearance in film *etc.* by (well-known) actor

camera ('kamərə) *n.* apparatus used to take photographs —'**cameraman** *n.* photographer, *esp.* for television or cinema —**camera obscura** (əb'skyŏŏrə) darkened chamber in which views of surrounding country are shown on sheet by means of lenses —**in camera** (of legal proceedings *etc.*) conducted in private

Cameroon (kamə'rōōn) *n.* country in Africa bounded west by the Gulf of Guinea, northwest by Nigeria, east by Chad and the Central African Republic, and south by Congo, Gabon and Equatorial Guinea

camisole ('kamisōl) *n.* underbodice

camomile ('kaməmīl) *n. see* CHAMOMILE

camouflage ('kaməfläzh) *n.* **1.** disguise, means of deceiving enemy observation, *eg* by paint, screen —*vt.* **2.** disguise

camp (kamp) *n.* **1.** (place for) tents of hikers, army *etc.* **2.** cabins *etc.* for temporary accommodation **3.** group supporting political party *etc.* **4.** **SA** field, pasture —*a. inf.* **5.** homosexual **6.** consciously artificial —*vi.* **7.** form or lodge in camp —'**camper** *n.* **1.** person who lives or temporarily stays in tent *etc.* **2.** vehicle equipped for camping out —'**camping** *n.* —**Camp Fire Girl** member of national organization for girls aged 7 to 18 —**camp follower** **1.** civilian, *esp.* prostitute, who unofficially provides services to military personnel **2.** nonmember who is sympathetic to group *etc.*

campaign (kam'pān) *n.* **1.** series of coordinated activities for some purpose, *eg* political or military campaign —*vi.* **2.** serve in campaign —**cam'paigner** *n.*

campanile (kampə'nēli) *n. esp.* in Italy, bell tower, not usu. attached to another building

campanology (kampə'noləji) *n.* art of ringing bells

campanula (kam'panyŏŏlə) *n.* plant with blue or white bell-shaped flowers

camphor ('kamfər) *n.* crystalline highly odorous substance from the wood and bark of the camphor tree used as antiseptic and irritant —**camphorated oil** liniment consisting of camphor and peanut oil, used as irritant —**camphorated opium tincture** paregoric —**camphor tree** evergreen Asian tree which yields camphor

campion ('kampiən) *n.* white or pink wild flower

campus ('kampəs) *n.* grounds and buildings of school, college or university

can[1] (kan; *unstressed* kən) *vi.* **1.** be able to **2.** have the power to **3.** be allowed to (**could** *pt.*)

can[2] (kan) *n.* **1.** container, usu. metal, for liquids, foods —*vt.* **2.** put in can (**-nn-**) —**canned** *a.* **1.** preserved in can **2.** (of music, programs *etc.*) previously recorded —'**cannery** *n.* factory where food is canned

Can. **1.** Canada **2.** Canadian

Canada ('kanədə) *n.* country in N Amer. bounded south by U.S., west by Pacific Ocean, north by Arctic Ocean and east by Atlantic Ocean —**Canadian** (kə'nādiən) *n./a.* (native) of Canada —**Ca'nadianize** *v.* make or become Canadian —**Canada balsam** **1.** yellow transparent resin obtained from balsam fir **2.** balsam fir —**Canada Day** Jul. 1st, anniversary of day in 1867 when Canad. received dominion status —**Canada goose** large grayish-brown N Amer. goose —**Canada lynx** medium-sized feline of northern N Amer. with long, loose, mottled gray body —**Canadian Shield** wide area of rock extending over most of E and Central Canad.: rich in minerals (*also* **Laurentian Shield**)

canaille (kə'nī) *Fr.* masses; mob; rabble

canal (kə'nal) *n.* **1.** artificial watercourse **2.** duct in body —**canali'zation** *n.* —'**canalize** *vt.* **1.** convert into canal **2.** direct (thoughts, energies *etc.*) into one channel

canapé ('kanəpi, -pā) *n.* small piece of toast *etc.* with savory topping

canard (kə'närd) *n.* **1.** false report; rumor, hoax **2.** aircraft in which tailplane is mounted in front of wing

canary (kə'nāəri) *n.* small usu. yellow finch, noted for singing

canasta (kə'nastə) *n.* form of rummy played

with two standard 52-card decks and four jokers for four players (two partnerships) with variations for two players, three players and six players using three decks and six jokers

cancan ('kankan) *n.* high-kicking (orig. Fr. music-hall) dance

cancel ('kansəl) *vt.* **1.** cross out **2.** annul **3.** call off —**cancel'lation** *n.*

cancer ('kansər) *n.* abnormal and uncontrolled growth of the cells of living organisms —'**cancerous** *a.*

Cancer ('kansər) *n.* **1.** (crab) 4th sign of zodiac, operative c. Jun. 21st-Jul. 21st **2.** constellation —**tropic of Cancer** parallel of latitude 23½° N of the equator

candela (kan'dēlə, -'delə) *n.* basic SI unit of luminous intensity

candid ('kandid) *a.* **1.** frank, open **2.** impartial —'**candidly** *adv.* —'**candidness** *or* '**candor** *n.* frankness —**candid camera** small camera used to take informal photographs of people

candidate ('kandidāt) *n.* **1.** one who seeks office, appointment *etc.* **2.** person taking examination or test —'**candidacy** *or* '**candidature** *n.*

candle ('kandəl) *n.* **1.** stick of wax with wick **2.** light —**candelabrum** (kandi'labrəm) *n.* large, branched candle holder (*pl.* **-bra** (-brə)) —'**candlepower** *n.* unit for measuring light —'**candlestick** *n.* —'**candlewick** *n.* cotton fabric with tufted surface

Candlemas ('kandəlməs) *n. Christianity* Feb. 2nd, Feast of Purification of Virgin Mary and presentation of Christ in Temple

candy ('kandi) *n.* **1.** crystallized sugar **2.** confectionery in general —*vt.* **3.** preserve with sugar —*vi.* **4.** become encrusted with sugar ('**candied,** '**candying**) —'**candied** *a.*

candytuft ('kandituft) *n.* garden plant with clusters of white, pink or purple flowers

cane (kān) *n.* **1.** stem of small palm or large grass **2.** walking stick —*vt.* **3.** beat with cane —**cane sugar 1.** sucrose obtained from sugar cane **2.** *see* SUCROSE

canine ('kānīn) *a.* like, pert. to, dog —**canine tooth** one of four sharp, pointed teeth, two in each jaw

canister ('kanistər) *n.* container, *usu.* of metal, *esp.* for storing dry food

canker ('kangkər) *n.* **1.** eating sore **2.** thing that eats away, destroys, corrupts —*vt.* **3.** infect, corrupt —*vi.* **4.** decay —'**cankered** *or* '**cankerous** *a.* —'**cankerworm** *n.*

canna ('kanə) *n.* tropical flowering plant

cannabis ('kanəbis) *n.* **1.** hemp plant **2.** drug derived from this

cannel coal ('kanəl) dull coal burning with smoky luminous flame

cannelloni (kani'lōni) *pl.n.* tubular pieces of pasta filled with meat *etc.*

cannibal ('kanibəl) *n.* **1.** one who eats human flesh —*a.* **2.** relating to this practice —'**cannibalism** *n.* —**cannibal'istic** *a.* —'**cannibalize** *vt.* use parts from (one machine *etc.*) to repair another

cannon[1] ('kanən) *n.* large gun (*pl.* **-s,** '**cannon**) —**canno'nade** *n./vt.* attack with cannon —'**cannonball** *n.* —**cannon bone** horse's leg bone —**cannon fodder** men regarded as expendable in war because they are part of huge army

cannon[2] ('kanən) *n.* **1.** billiard stroke, hitting both object balls with one's own —*vi.* **2.** make this stroke **3.** rebound, collide

cannot ('kanot, ka'not) *negative form of* CAN[1]

canoe (kə'nōō) *n.* **1.** light narrow boat with pointed ends propelled by paddling —*vi.* **2.** travel in canoe —*vt.* **3.** transport in canoe —**ca'noeist** *n.*

canon[1] ('kanən) *n.* **1.** law or rule, *esp.* of church **2.** standard **3.** body of books accepted as genuine **4.** list of saints —**canoni'zation** *n.* —'**canonize** *vt.* enroll in list of saints

canon[2] ('kanən) *n.* church dignitary, member of cathedral chapter —**ca'nonical** *a.* —**ca'nonicals** *pl.n.* vestments worn by clergy when officiating —**canon'istic** *a.* —**canonical hour 1.** *R.C.Ch.* one of seven prayer times appointed for each day by canon law **2.** *Ch. of England* any time at which marriages may lawfully be celebrated —**canon law** body of laws enacted by supreme authorities of Christian Church

canopy ('kanəpi) *n.* **1.** covering over throne, bed *etc.* **2.** any overhanging shelter —*vt.* **3.** cover with canopy (**-opied, -opying**)

can't (känt) *v.* cannot

cant[1] (kant) *n.* **1.** hypocritical speech **2.** whining **3.** language of a sect **4.** technical jargon **5.** slang, *esp.* of thieves —*vi.* **6.** use cant

cant[2] (kant) *vt.* **1.** tilt, slope **2.** bevel —*n.* **3.** inclination from vertical or horizontal plane

Cant. *Bible* Canticle of Canticles

cantabile (kan'tabili) *Mus. a./adv.* **1.** singing —*n.* **2.** piece or passage performed in this way

cantaloupe *or* **cantaloup** ('kantəlōp) *n.* variety of muskmelon with netted rind and orange flesh

cantankerous (kan'tangkərəs) *a.* ill-natured, quarrelsome

cantata (kan'tätə) *n.* choral work like, but shorter than, oratorio

canteen (kan'tēn) *n.* **1.** flask for carrying liquid used by hikers *etc.* **2.** small shop in military camp

canter ('kantər) *n.* **1.** 3-beat gait slower than gallop —*v.* **2.** move at, make to canter —**at a canter** with ease

Canterbury bell ('kantərberi) cultivated campanula

cantharides (kan'tharidēz) *pl.n.* diuretic and urogenital stimulant prepared from dried bodies of Spanish fly (*sing.* '**cantharis**) (*also* **Spanish fly**)

canticle (ˈkantikəl) *n.* short hymn —**Canticle of Canticles** *Bible* Song of Solomon in the Douay Version of the O.T.
cantilever (ˈkantilēvər, -levər) *n.* beam, girder *etc.* fixed at one end only
canto (ˈkantō) *n.* division of poem (*pl.* **-s**)
canton (ˈkantən, -ton) *n.* division of country, *esp.* Swiss federal state
Cantonese (kantəˈnēz) *n.* **1.** dialect of Chinese spoken in Canton **2.** native or inhabitant of Canton (*pl.* **-ese**) —*a.* **3.** of Canton or Chinese language spoken there
cantonment (kənˈtōnmənt) *n.* quarters for troops
cantor (ˈkantər) *n.* **1.** *Judaism* leading singer in synagogue liturgy **2.** *Christianity* leader of singing in church choir
Cantrece (kanˈtrēs) *n.* trade name for self-crimping nylon yarn used for stockings and panty hose
Canuck (kəˈnuk) *n./a.* **C** *inf.* Canadian
canvas (ˈkanvəs) *n.* **1.** coarse cloth used for sails, painting on *etc.* **2.** sails of ship **3.** picture —**under canvas** in tents
canvass (ˈkanvəs) *vt.* **1.** solicit votes, contributions *etc.* from **2.** discuss, examine —*n.* **3.** solicitation
canyon (ˈkanyən) *n.* deep gorge
caoutchouc (ˈkowcho͝ok) *n. see* RUBBER[1] (sense 1)
cap (kap) *n.* **1.** covering for head **2.** lid, top or other covering —*vt.* **3.** put cap on **4.** outdo **5.** select for a team (**-pp-**)
CAP Civil Air Patrol
cap. 1. capacity **2.** capital **3.** capitalize **4.** capital letter
capable (ˈkāpəbəl) *a.* **1.** able, gifted, competent **2.** having the capacity, power —**capaˈbility** *n.*
capacity (kəˈpasiti) *n.* **1.** power of holding or grasping **2.** room **3.** volume **4.** character **5.** ability, power of mind —**capacious** (kəˈpāshəs) *a.* roomy —**caˈpacitance** *n.* (measure of) ability of system to store electric charge —**caˈpacitor** *n.*
caparison (kəˈparisən) *n.* **1.** ornamental covering, equipment for horse —*vt.* **2.** adorn thus
CAPD continuous ambulatory peritoneal dialysis
cape[1] (kāp) *n.* covering for shoulders
cape[2] (kāp) *n.* point of land running into sea, headland —**Cape Colored SA** *see* **Colored** (sense 2) *at* COLOR —**Cape pigeon** pied petrel of southern oceans —**Cape salmon SA** geelbek —**Cape sparrow** common S Afr. bird
caper[1] (ˈkāpər) *n.* **1.** skip **2.** frolic **3.** escapade —*vi.* **4.** skip, dance
caper[2] (ˈkāpər) *n.* pickled flower bud of Sicilian shrub
capercaillie *or* **capercailzie** (kapərˈkālyi) *n.* large black old world grouse
Cape Verde (vərd) country in the Atlantic Ocean 385 miles west-northwest of Senegal consisting of 10 islands and 5 islets
capillary (ˈkapileri) *a.* **1.** hairlike **2.** of capillarity —*n.* **3.** extremely small blood vessel connecting arteries with veins and the point of interaction between the blood and body tissues —**capilˈlarity** *n.* phenomenon caused by surface tension and resulting in elevation or depression of surface of liquid in contact with solid (*also* **capillary action**)
capital (ˈkapitəl) *n.* **1.** chief town **2.** money, stock, funds **3.** large-sized letter **4.** headpiece of column —*a.* **5.** involving or punishable by death **6.** serious **7.** chief, leading **8.** excellent —**ˈcapitalism** *n.* economic system which is based on private ownership of industry —**ˈcapitalist** *n.* **1.** owner of capital **2.** supporter of capitalism —*a.* **3.** run by, possessing, capital —**ˈcapitalize** *vt.* **1.** convert into capital —*vi.* **2.** (*with* on) turn to advantage —**ˈcapitally** *adv.* —**capital gain** amount by which selling price of financial asset exceeds cost —**capital levy** tax on capital or property as contrasted with tax on income —**capital punishment** punishment of death for crime; death penalty —**capital stock 1.** par value of total share capital a company is authorized to issue **2.** total physical capital existing in economy at any time
capitation (kapiˈtāshən) *n.* **1.** tax or grant per head **2.** census
Capitol Hill (ˈkapitəl) the legislative branch of the U.S. government
capitulate (kəˈpichəlāt) *vi.* surrender on terms, give in —**capituˈlation** *n.*
capo (ˈkapō) *n.* device fitted across all strings of guitar *etc.* to raise pitch of each string simultaneously (*pl.* **-s**) (*also* **capo tasto** (ˈtastō))
capon (ˈkāpən) *n.* castrated cock fowl fattened for eating —**ˈcaponize** *vt.*
cappuccino (kapo͝oˈchēnō) *n.* coffee with steamed milk
caprice (kəˈprēs) *n.* whim —**capricious** (kəˈprishəs) *a.* —**capriciousness** (kəˈprishəsnis) *n.*
Capricorn (ˈkaprikôrn) *n.* **1.** (sea-goat) 10th sign of zodiac, operative c. Dec. 21st–Jan. 19th **2.** constellation —**tropic of Capricorn** parallel of latitude 23½° S of the equator
capriole (ˈkapriōl) *Dressage n.* **1.** upward but not forward leap made by horse with all four feet off ground —*vi.* **2.** perform capriole
caps. 1. capital letters **2.** capsule
capsicum (ˈkapsikəm) *n.* tropical vegetable with mild peppery flavor, sweet pepper
capsize (kapˈsīz) *vt.* **1.** (of boat) upset —*vi.* **2.** be overturned —**capˈsizal** *n.*
capstan (ˈkapstən) *n.* machine to wind cable, *esp.* to hoist anchor
capsule (ˈkapsyəl, -so͞ol) *n.* **1.** gelatin case for dose of medicine or drug **2.** any small enclosed area or container **3.** seed vessel of

plant —'**capsulize** *vt.* **1.** state in highly condensed form **2.** enclose in capsule

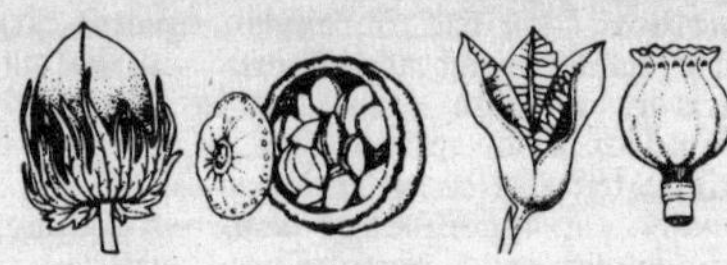

capsules

Capt. Captain

captain ('kaptin) *n.* **1.** commander of vessel or company of soldiers **2.** leader, chief —*vt.* **3.** be captain of

caption ('kapshən) *n.* heading, title of article, picture *etc.*

captious ('kapshəs) *a.* ready to find fault, critical, peevish —'**captiously** *adv.* —'**captiousness** *n.*

captive ('kaptiv) *n.* **1.** prisoner —*a.* **2.** taken, imprisoned **3.** unable to avoid speeches *etc.* —'**captivate** *vt.* fascinate —'**captivating** *a.* delightful —**cap'tivity** *n.*

capture ('kapchər) *vt.* **1.** seize, make prisoner —*n.* **2.** seizure, taking —'**captor** *n.*

Capuchin ('kapyəshin, 'kapə-) *n.* friar belonging to branch of Franciscan Order

capybara (kapi'barə) *n.* largest rodent, found in S Amer.

car (kär) *n.* **1.** self-propelled road vehicle **2.** passenger compartment, as in cable car **3.** railroad carriage of specified type —**car park** *esp.* **UK** area, building where vehicles may be left for a time —'**carport** *n.* shelter for automobile usu. consisting of roof supported by posts —'**carsickness** *n. see* **motion sickness** *at* MOTION

carabineer *or* **carabinier** (karəbi'nēər) *n. see* **carbineer** *at* CARBINE

caracal ('karəkal) *n.* **1.** lynxlike feline mammal inhabiting deserts of N Afr. and S Asia, having smooth coat of reddish fur **2.** this fur

caracole ('karəkōl) *or* **caracol** ('karəkol) *Dressage n.* **1.** half turn to right or left —*vi.* **2.** execute half turn

caracul ('karəkul) *n. see* KARAKUL

carafe (kə'raf, -'räf) *n.* glass water bottle for table, decanter

caramel ('karəməl) *n.* **1.** burnt sugar for cooking **2.** type of confectionery

carapace ('karəpās) *n.* thick hard shield that covers part of body of tortoise *etc.*

carat ('karət) *n. see* KARAT

caravan ('karəvan) *n.* group of vehicles traveling together in single file —**caravanserai** (karə'vansərī) *or* **caravansary** (karə'vansəri) *n.* in some Eastern countries, large inn enclosing courtyard, providing accommodation for caravans

caravel ('karəvel) *n.* two- or three-masted sailing ship in 15th and 16th centuries

caraway ('karəwā) *n.* plant of which the seeds are used as spice in cakes *etc.*

carbide ('kärbīd) *n.* compound of carbon with an element, *esp.* calcium carbide

carbine ('kärbēn, -bīn) *n.* short rifle —**carbineer** (kärbi'nēər), **carabi'neer** *or* **carabi'nier** *n.* formerly, soldier equipped with carbine

carbo- *or before vowel* **carb-** (*comb. form*) carbon, as in *carbohydrate, carbonate*

carbohydrate (kärbō'hīdrāt) *n.* any of large group of compounds containing carbon, hydrogen and oxygen, *esp.* sugars and starches as components of food

carbolic acid (kär'bolik) disinfectant derived from coal tar —'**carbolated** *a.* containing carbolic acid

carbon ('kärbən) *n. Chem.* nonmetallic element occurring in nature as diamond and graphite and a constituent of all organic matter *Symbol* C, at. wt. 12.0, at. no. 6 —**carbo'naceous** *a.* of, resembling or containing carbon —'**carbonate** *n.* salt of carbonic acid —**car'bonic** *a.* —**carbo'niferous** *a.* —'**carbonize** *v.* —**carbon black** finely divided carbon produced by incomplete combustion of natural gas or petroleum: used in pigments and ink —**carbon dating** technique for determining age of wood *etc.*, based on its content of radioisotope ^{14}C acquired from atmosphere when it formed part of living plant —**carbon dioxide** colorless gas exhaled in respiration of animals —**carbonic acid 1.** carbon dioxide **2.** compound formed by carbon dioxide and water —**carbon monoxide** colorless, odorless poisonous gas formed when carbon compounds burn in insufficient air —**carbon paper** paper coated with a dark, waxy pigment, used for duplicating written or typed matter, producing **carbon copy** —**carbon tetrachloride** colorless volatile nonflammable liquid made from chlorine and used as solvent *etc.*

Carboniferous (kärbə'nifərəs) *a.* **1.** of fifth period of Paleozoic era during which coal measures were formed —*n.* **2.** Carboniferous period or rock system divided into **Upper Carboniferous** and **Lower Carboniferous** periods

Carborundum (kärbə'rundəm) *n.* trade name for various abrasives

carboy ('kärboi) *n.* glass, plastic or metal container for liquids of about 5 to 15 gallons in capacity usu. in protective cushion

carbuncle ('kärbungkəl) *n.* **1.** inflamed ulcer, boil or tumor **2.** fiery-red precious stone

carburetor ('kärbyərātər, -bə-) *n.* device for vaporizing and mixing fuel with air in internal-combustion engine

carcass ('kärkəs) *n.* **1.** dead animal body **2.** skeleton **3.** basic structure of object

carcinoma (kärsi'nōmə) *n.* a malignant

tumor —**car'cinogen** *n.* substance producing cancer —**'carcinoid** *a.* —**carcinoid syndrome** disease caused by cancerous tumor of glandular tissue

card[1] (kärd) *n.* **1.** thick, stiff paper **2.** piece of this giving identification *etc.* **3.** illustrated card sending greetings *etc.* **4.** one of the 52 playing cards making up a deck **5.** *inf.* a character, eccentric —*pl.* **6.** any card game —**'cardboard** *n.* thin, stiff board made of paper pulp —**card index** index in which each entry is made on separate card —**'cardsharp** *or* **'cardsharper** *n.* professional card player who cheats

card[2] (kärd) *n.* **1.** instrument for combing wool *etc.* —*vt.* **2.** comb —**'carder** *n.*

cardamom ('kärdəməm) *n.* **1.** tropical Asian plant with large hairy leaves **2.** seeds of this plant, used *esp.* as spice or condiment

cardiac ('kärdiak) *a.* **1.** pert. to the heart —*n.* **2.** person with heart disorder —**'cardiogram** *n.* tracing made by cardiograph —**'cardiograph** *n.* instrument which records movements of the heart —**'cardioid** *a.* heart-shaped —**cardi'ologist** *n.* —**cardi'ology** *n.* branch of medical science concerned with heart and its diseases

cardigan ('kärdigən) *n.* knitted jacket

cardinal ('kärdinəl) *a.* **1.** chief, principal —*n.* **2.** highest rank, next to the Pope in R.C. Church **3.** bright red N Amer. bunting (*also* **'redbird**) —**'cardinalate** *n.* —**cardinal numbers** 1, 2, 3, *etc.* —**cardinal points** north, south, east and west

cardio- *or before vowel* **cardi-** (*comb. form*) heart, as in *cardiogram*

cardiolipin test (kärdiō'lipin) Wassermann test

care (kāər) *vi.* **1.** be anxious —*n.* **2.** attention **3.** pains, heed **4.** charge, protection **5.** anxiety **6.** caution —**'carefree** *a.* —**'careful** *a.* —**'carefully** *adv.* —**'carefulness** *n.* —**'careless** *a.* —**'carelessness** *n.* —**'caretaker** *n.* **1.** person in charge of premises —*a.* **2.** temporary, interim —**'careworn** *a.* showing signs of care, stress *etc.* —**care for 1.** have regard or liking for **2.** look after **3.** be disposed to

careen (kə'rēn) *vt.* **1.** lay (ship) over on her side for cleaning and repair —*vi.* **2.** keel over **3.** sway dangerously

career (kə'rēər) *n.* **1.** course through life **2.** profession **3.** rapid motion —*vi.* **4.** run or move at full speed —**ca'reerist** *n.* person who seeks to advance his career by any possible means

caress (kə'res) *vt.* **1.** fondle, embrace, treat with affection —*n.* **2.** act or expression of affection

caret ('karit) *n.* mark (⋏) showing where to insert something omitted

cargo ('kärgō) *n.* load, freight, carried by ship, plane *etc.* (*pl.* **-es**)

Carib ('karib) *n.* **1.** member of group of Amer. Indian peoples of NE South Amer. and Lesser Antilles (*pl.* **-s, 'Carib**) **2.** family of languages spoken by these peoples

caribou ('karibōō) *n.* any of several large deer of N Amer. and Siberia with palmate antlers in both sexes and grouped with reindeer in one species

caricature ('karikətyōōər, -tōōər) *n.* **1.** likeness exaggerated or distorted to appear ridiculous —*vt.* **2.** portray in this way

caries ('kāərēz) *n.* decay of tooth or bone —**'carious** *a.* (of teeth or bone) affected with caries; decayed

carillon ('karilon) *n.* **1.** set of bells *usu.* hung in tower and played by means of a keyboard or other mechanism **2.** the orchestral glockenspiel —**carillonneur** (karilə'nər) *n.*

Carmelite ('kärməlīt) *n. R.C.Ch.* **1.** member of order of mendicant friars **2.** member of corresponding order of nuns

carminative (kär'minətiv) *n.* **1.** medicine to remedy flatulence —*a.* **2.** acting as this

carmine ('kärmīn) *n.* **1.** brilliant red color (prepared from cochineal) —*a.* **2.** of this color

carnage ('kärnij) *n.* slaughter

carnal ('kärnəl) *a.* **1.** fleshly, sensual **2.** worldly —**'carnalism** *n.* —**car'nality** *n.* —**'carnally** *adv.* —**carnal knowledge** *chiefly law* sexual intercourse

carnation (kär'nāshən) *n.* **1.** cultivated flower **2.** flesh color

carnelian (kär'nēlyən) *n.* reddish-yellow translucent chalcedony, used as gemstone

carnival ('kärnivəl) *n.* **1.** festive occasion **2.** traveling fair **3.** show or display for amusement

carnivorous (kär'nivərəs) *a.* flesh-eating —**'carnivore** *n.*

carob ('karəb) *n.* **1.** evergreen Mediterranean tree with edible pods **2.** long blackish sugary pod of this tree, used for fodder and sometimes human food

carol ('karəl) *n.* **1.** song or hymn of joy or praise (*esp.* Christmas carol) —*vi.* **2.** sing carols

Caroline ('karəlīn) *or* **Carolean** (karə'lēən) *a.* of Charles I or Charles II (kings of England, Scotland and Ireland), society over which they ruled or their government (*also* **Caro'linian**)

Carolingian (karə'linjiən) *Hist. a.* **1.** of Frankish dynasty founded by Pepin the Short —*n.* **2.** member of dynasty of Carolingian Franks (*also* **Carlo'vingian, Caro'linian**) —**Carolingian art** European art from end of 8th cent. to beginning of 10th cent.

carom billiards ('karəm) *see* BILLIARDS

carotid (kə'rotid) *n.* **1.** either of two principal arteries that supply blood to head and neck —*a.* **2.** of either of these arteries

carouse (kə'rowz) *vi.* **1.** have merry drinking spree —*n.* **2.** merry drinking party (*also* **ca'rousal**) —**ca'rouser** *n.*

carousel (karə'sel, -'zel) *n.* merry-go-round
carp[1] (kärp) *n.* freshwater fish
carp[2] (kärp) *vi.* complain about small faults or errors; nag —'**carper** *n.* —'**carping** *a.* —'**carpingly** *adv.*
carpal ('kärpəl) *n.* any bone of wrist

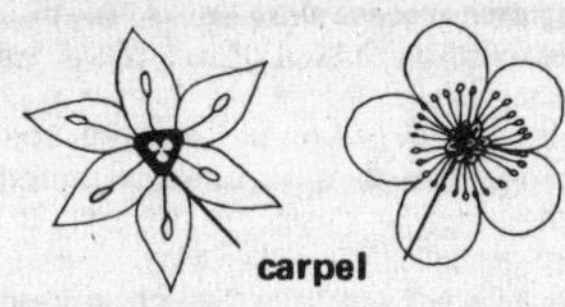

carpel ('kärpəl) *n.* female reproductive organ of flowering plants, consisting of ovary, style and stigma
carpenter ('kärpəntər) *n.* person who builds or repairs wooden structures or their constituent parts —'**carpentry** *n.* art of carpenter —**carpenter ant** ant that gnaws tunnels in dead wood —**carpenter bee** solitary bee that gnaws galleries in sound wood
carpet ('kärpit) *n.* **1.** heavy fabric for covering floor —*vt.* **2.** cover (floor) with carpet **3.** *inf.* call up for censure —'**carpetbag** *n.* traveling bag —'**carpetbagger** *n.* political adventurer, *esp.* Northerner in southern states after Civil War —**carpet slipper** slipper orig. made with woolen upper resembling carpeting
carpus ('kärpəs) *n.* **1.** wrist **2.** eight small bones of human wrist (*pl.* **carpi** ('kärpī))
carrageen *or* **carragheen** ('karəgēn) *n.* edible red seaweed of N Amer. and N Europe, used to make jelly *etc.* (*also* **Irish moss**)
carriage ('karij) *n.* **1.** railway coach **2.** bearing, conduct **3.** horse-drawn vehicle **4.** act, cost, of carrying —**carriage clock** portable clock, usu. in rectangular case, orig. used by travelers —**carriage forward** charge for conveying, to be paid by receiver —**carriage paid** charge for conveying, to be paid by sender —'**carriageway** *n.* part of road along which traffic passes in single line
carrion ('kariən) *n.* rotting dead flesh —**carrion crow** scavenging European crow
carrot ('karət) *n.* **1.** plant with orange-red edible root **2.** inducement —'**carroty** *a.* red, reddish
carry ('kari) *vt.* **1.** convey, transport **2.** capture, win **3.** effect **4.** conduct (oneself) in specified manner —*vi.* **5.** (of projectile, sound) reach or penetrate to distance ('**carried,** '**carrying**) —*n.* **6.** range —'**carrier** *n.* **1.** one that carries goods **2.** one who, himself immune, communicates a disease to others **3.** aircraft carrier —**carrier pigeon** homing pigeon, *esp.* for carrying messages —**carrier wave** *Rad.* wave of fixed amplitude and frequency, modulated to carry signal in radio transmission *etc.* (*also* '**carrier**) —**carry-out** *n. chiefly Scot.* **1.** alcohol bought at liquor store *etc.* for consumption elsewhere **2.** shop which sells hot cooked food for consumption away from premises —**carry on 1.** continue **2.** *inf.* fuss unnecessarily **3.** *inf.* have an affair —**carry out 1.** perform; cause to be implemented **2.** accomplish
cart (kärt) *n.* **1.** open (two-wheeled) vehicle, *esp.* pulled by horse —*vt.* **2.** convey in cart **3.** carry with effort —'**cartage** *n.* —'**carter** *n.* —'**carthorse** *n.* —'**cartwheel** *n.* **1.** large, spoked wheel **2.** sideways somersault —'**cartwright** *n.* maker of carts
carte blanche ('kärt 'blänch) *Fr.* complete discretion or authority
cartel (kär'tel) *n.* **1.** industrial combination for the purpose of fixing prices, output *etc.* **2.** alliance of political parties *etc.* to further common aims
Carter ('kärtər) *n.* **James Earl.** the 39th President of the U.S. (1977-81)
Cartesian (kär'tēzhən) *a.* **1.** pert. to French philosopher René Descartes (1596–1650) or his system of coordinates —*n.* **2.** adherent of his philosophy —**Cartesian coordinates** system of coordinates that defines location of point in terms of perpendicular distance from each of set of mutually perpendicular axes
Carthusian (kär'thyo͞ozhən, -'tho͞o-) *n.* *R.C.Ch.* member of monastic order founded by Saint Bruno
cartilage ('kärtilij) *n.* **1.** firm elastic tissue in the body lacking blood vessels and nerves **2.** gristle —**cartilaginous** (kärti'lajinəs) *a.*
cartogram ('kärtəgram) *n.* map showing statistical information in diagrammatic form
cartography (kär'togrəfi) *n.* mapmaking —**car'tographer** *n.* —**carto'graphic(al)** *a.*
carton ('kärtən) *n.* cardboard or plastic container
cartoon (kär'to͞on) *n.* **1.** drawing, *esp.* humorous or satirical **2.** sequence of drawings telling story **3.** preliminary design for painting —**car'toonist** *n.*
cartouche *or* **cartouch** (kär'to͞osh) *n.* **1.** carved or cast ornamental tablet or panel in form of scroll **2.** oblong figure enclosing characters expressing royal or divine names in Egyptian hieroglyphics
cartridge ('kärtrij) *n.* **1.** case containing charge for gun **2.** container for film, magnetic tape *etc.* **3.** unit in head of phonograph pick-up —**cartridge paper** strong, thick paper
carve (kärv) *vt.* **1.** cut, hew **2.** sculpture **3.** engrave **4.** cut (meat) in pieces or slices —'**carver** *n.* —'**carving** *n.*
caryatid (kari'atid) *n.* supporting column in shape of female figure
Casanova (kasə'nōvə) *n.* any man noted for amorous adventures

casbah ('kazbä) *n.* (*sometimes* **C-**) **1.** citadel of various N Afr. cities **2.** quarter where casbah is located (*also* '**kasbah**)

cascade (kas'kād) *n.* **1.** waterfall **2.** anything resembling this —*vi.* **3.** fall in cascades

cascara (kas'kärə) *n.* **1.** dried bark of cascara buckthorn, used as laxative and stimulant (*also* **cascara sagrada**) **2.** shrub or small tree of NW North Amer. (*also* **cascara buckthorn**)

case[1] (kās) *n.* **1.** instance **2.** event, circumstance **3.** question at issue **4.** state of affairs, condition **5.** arguments supporting particular action *etc.* **6.** *Med.* patient under treatment **7.** lawsuit **8.** grounds for suit **9.** grammatical relation of words in sentence —**case history** record of person's background, medical history *etc.* —**case law** law established by following judicial decisions given in earlier cases

case[2] (kās) *n.* **1.** box, sheath, covering **2.** receptacle **3.** box and contents —*vt.* **4.** put in a case —'**casing** *n.* **1.** protective cover **2.** material for cover **3.** frame containing door or window (*also* **case**) —**case-harden** *vt.* **1.** harden by carbonizing the surface of (iron) by converting into steel **2.** make hard, callous

casein (kā'sēn, 'kāsiin) *n.* protein in milk and its products —'**caseous** *a.* like cheese —**casein paint** alkaline paint based on casein producing effects ranging from transparency to thick-textured opacity

casement ('kāsmənt) *n.* window opening on hinges

cash (kash) *n.* **1.** money, bank notes and coins —*vt.* **2.** turn into or exchange for money —**ca'shier** *n.* one in charge of receiving and paying of money —**cash-and-carry** *a./adv.* sold on basis of cash payment for merchandise that is taken away by buyer —'**cashbook** *n.* —**cash crop** crop grown for sale rather than subsistence —**cash flow** movement of money into and out of a business —**cash register** till that records amount of money put in —**cash on delivery** service entailing cash payment to carrier on delivery of merchandise

cashew ('kashōō, kə'shōō) *n.* **1.** tropical tree bearing kidney-shaped nuts **2.** nut of this tree (*also* **cashew nut**)

cashier (ka'shēər) *vt.* dismiss from office or service

cashmere ('kazhmēər, 'kash-) *n.* **1.** fine soft fabric **2.** shawl made from goat's wool

casino (kə'sēnō) *n.* building, institution for gambling (*pl.* **-s**)

cask (kask) *n.* **1.** barrel **2.** container for wine

casket ('kaskit) *n.* **1.** small case for jewels *etc.* **2.** coffin

casque (kask) *n.* *Zool.* helmet or helmetlike structure, as on bill of most hornbills

Cassandra (kə'sandrə) *n.* **1.** *Gr. myth.* daughter of Priam and Hecuba, endowed with gift of prophecy but fated never to be believed **2.** anyone whose prophecies of doom are unheeded

cassata (kə'sätə) *n.* ice cream, *esp.* containing fruit and nuts

cassava (kə'sävə) *n.* **1.** any of various tropical plants, *esp.* Amer. species (**bitter cassava, sweet cassava**) (*also* '**manioc**) **2.** starch derived from root of this plant: source of tapioca

casserole ('kasərōl) *n.* **1.** fireproof cooking and serving dish **2.** kind of stew cooked in this dish —*v.* **3.** cook or be cooked in casserole

cassette (ka'set) *n.* plastic container for film, magnetic tape *etc.*

cassia ('kashə) *n.* **1.** tropical plant whose pods yield **cassia pulp,** mild laxative (*see also* SENNA) **2.** lauraceous tree of tropical Asia —**cassia bark** cinnamonlike bark of this tree, used as spice

cassis (kä'sēs) *n.* blackcurrant cordial

cassock ('kasək) *n.* long tunic worn by clergymen

cassowary ('kasəweri) *n.* large flightless bird of NE Aust., New Guinea and adjacent islands

cast (kast) *v.* **1.** throw, fling **2.** shed **3.** throw down **4.** deposit (a vote) **5.** allot, as parts in play **6.** mold, as metal (**cast** *pt./pp.*) —*n.* **7.** throw **8.** distance thrown **9.** squint **10.** mold **11.** that which is shed or ejected **12.** set of actors **13.** type, quality —'**caster** *n.* machine that casts type —'**casting** *n.* —'**castaway** *n./a.* shipwrecked (person) —**casting vote** decisive vote —**cast iron** iron containing so much carbon that it must be cast into shape —**cast-iron** *a.* **1.** made of cast iron **2.** rigid, unyielding —**cast-off** *a.* abandoned —'**cast-off** *n.* **1.** person or thing discarded or abandoned **2.** *Print.* estimate of amount of space a piece of copy will occupy —**cast steel** steel containing varying amounts of carbon *etc.,* that is cast into shape —**cast off** **1.** remove (mooring lines) that hold (vessel) to dock **2.** knot (row of stitches, *esp.* final row) in finishing off knitted or woven material **3.** *Print.* estimate amount of space that will be taken up by (book *etc.*)

castanets (kastə'nets) *pl.n.* **1.** percussion instrument consisting of two shell-shaped pieces of hard wood hinged together used by Spanish dancers **2.** orchestral castanets with springs and handles

caste (kast) *n.* **1.** section of society in India **2.** social rank

castellated ('kastilātid) *a.* **1.** having turrets and battlements, like castle **2.** having indentations similar to battlements —**castel'lation** *n.*

castigate ('kastigāt) *vt.* **1.** punish, rebuke severely, correct **2.** chastise —**casti'gation** *n.* —'**castigator** *n.* —'**castigatory** *a.*

castle ('kasəl) *n.* **1.** fortress **2.** country

mansion **3.** chessman (*also* **rook**) —**castle in the air** *or* **in Spain** hope or desire unlikely to be realized; daydream

castor ('kastər) *n.* **1.** bottle with perforated top **2.** small swiveled wheel on table leg *etc.*

castor oil vegetable medicinal oil

castrate (ka'strāt) *vt.* **1.** remove testicles of, deprive of power of generation **2.** deprive of vigor, masculinity *etc.* —**cas'tration** *n.*

casual ('kazhōōəl) *a.* **1.** accidental **2.** unforeseen **3.** occasional **4.** unconcerned **5.** informal —**'casually** *adv.* —**'casualty** *n.* **1.** person killed or injured in accident, war *etc.* **2.** thing lost, destroyed, in accident *etc.*

casuarina (kashōōə'rēnə) *n.* tree of Aust. and E Indies, having jointed leafless branches

casuist ('kazhōōist) *n.* **1.** one who studies and solves moral problems **2.** quibbler —**casu'istical** *a.* —**'casuistry** *n.*

cat (kat) *n.* any of various feline animals, including small domesticated furred animal, and lions, tigers *etc.* —**'catkin** *n.* drooping flower spike —**'catty** *a.* spiteful —**'catcall** *n.* derisive cry —**'catfish** *n.* mainly freshwater fish with catlike whiskers —**'catgut** *n.* strong cord made from dried intestines of sheep *etc.*, used for stringing musical instruments and sports rackets —**'catmint** *n.* scented plant —**'catnap** *vi./n.* doze —**cat-o'-nine-tails** *n.* whip consisting of nine knotted thongs, used formerly to flog prisoners (*pl.* **-tails**) (*also* **cat**) —**cat's cradle** game played by making patterns with loop of string between fingers —**cat's-paw** *n.* **1.** person used by another as tool; dupe **2.** pattern of ripples on surface of water caused by light wind —**'catwalk** *n.* narrow, raised path or plank

catabolism (kə'tabəlizəm) *n.* breaking down of complex molecules, destructive metabolism

cataclysm ('katəklizəm) *n.* **1.** (disastrous) upheaval **2.** deluge —**cata'clysmal** *a.*

catacomb ('katəkōm) *n.* **1.** underground gallery for burial —*pl.* **2.** series of underground tunnels and caves

catafalque ('katəfalk) *n.* temporary raised platform on which body lies in state before or during funeral

Catalan ('katəlan) *n.* **1.** language of Catalonia, closely related to Provençal **2.** native of Catalonia —*a.* **3.** of Catalonia

catalepsy ('katəlepsi) *n.* condition of unconsciousness with rigidity of muscles —**cata'leptic** *a.*

catalog *or* **catalogue** ('katəlog) *n.* **1.** descriptive list —*vt.* **2.** make such list of **3.** enter in catalog

catalyst ('katəlist) *n.* substance causing or assisting a chemical reaction without taking part in it —**ca'talysis** *n.* —**'catalyze** *vt.*

catamaran (katəmə'ran) *n.* **1.** type of sailing boat with twin hulls **2.** raft of logs

cataplexy ('katəpleksi) *n.* **1.** sudden loss of muscle tone causing victim to collapse **2.** state assumed by animals shamming death —**cata'plectic** *a.*

catapult ('katəpult) *n.* **1.** small forked stick with elastic sling used for throwing stones **2.** *Hist.* engine of war for hurling arrows, stones *etc.* **3.** launching device —*vt.* **4.** shoot forth (as) from catapult —*v.* **5.** move precipitately

cataract ('katərakt) *n.* **1.** waterfall **2.** downpour **3.** disease of eye marked by opacity of the lens

catarrh (kə'tär) *n.* inflammation of a mucous membrane —**ca'tarrhal** *a.*

catastrophe (kə'tastrəfi) *n.* **1.** great disaster, calamity **2.** culmination of a tragedy —**cata'strophic** *a.*

catatonia (katə'tōniə) *n.* form of schizophrenia characterized by stupor, with outbreaks of excitement —**catatonic** (katə'tonik) *a./n.*

Catawba (kə'töbə) *n.* **1.** (member of) Siouan-speaking Amerindian people of South Carolina (*pl.* **-ba, -s**) **2.** dry or semisweet white table wine

catch (kach) *vt.* **1.** take hold of, seize **2.** understand **3.** hear **4.** contract (disease) **5.** be in time for **6.** surprise, detect —*vi.* **7.** be contagious **8.** get entangled **9.** begin to burn (**caught** *pt./pp.*) —*n.* **10.** seizure **11.** thing that holds, stops *etc.* **12.** what is caught **13.** *inf.* snag, disadvantage **14.** form of musical composition **15.** thing, person worth catching —**'catcher** *n.* —**'catching** *a.* —**'catchy** *a.* **1.** pleasant, memorable **2.** tricky —**catchment area 1.** area in which rainfall collects to form the supply of river *etc.* **2.** area from which people are allocated to a particular school, hospital *etc.* —**'catchpenny** *a.* **1.** worthless **2.** made to sell quickly —**catch phrase** frequently used phrase, *esp.* associated with particular group *etc.* —**'catchword** *n.* popular phrase or idea

catechize ('katikīz) *vt.* **1.** instruct by question and answer **2.** question —**cate'chetical** *a.* —**'catechism** *n.* —**'catechist** *n.* —**cate'chumen** *n.* one under instruction in Christianity

catechu ('katichōō) *n.* astringent resinous substance obtained from certain tropical plants, and used in dyeing *etc.*

category ('katigöri) *n.* class, order, division —**cate'gorical** *a.* **1.** positive **2.** of category —**cate'gorically** *adv.* —**'categorize** *vt.*

catenary ('katəneri) *n.* **1.** curve formed by heavy flexible cord hanging from two points **2.** hanging cable between pylons along railway track, from which trolley wire is suspended —*a.* **3.** of catenary or suspended chain

catenation (kati'nāshən) *n.* chain, or series as links of chain

cater ('kātər) *vi.* provide what is required or desired, *esp.* food *etc.* —**'caterer** *n.*

caterpillar ('katərpilər) *n.* **1.** hairy grub of

moth or butterfly **2.** type of tractor fitted with caterpillar wheels —**caterpillar wheel** articulated belt revolving round two or more wheels to propel heavy vehicle over difficult ground

caterwaul (ˈkatərwöl) *vi.* wail, howl

catharsis (kəˈthärsis) *n.* **1.** purging of emotions through evocation of pity and fear, as in tragedy **2.** *Psychoanal.* bringing repressed ideas or experiences to consciousness, by means of free association *etc.* **3.** purgation, *esp.* of bowels (*pl.* **catharses** (kəˈthärsēz)) —**caˈthartic** *a.* **1.** purgative **2.** effecting catharsis —*n.* **3.** purgative drug or agent

Cathay (kaˈthā) *n. Lit., obs.* China

cathedral (kəˈthēdrəl) *n.* **1.** principal church of diocese —*a.* **2.** pert. to, containing cathedral

catherine wheel (ˈkathrin) wheel with spikes around rim

catheter (ˈkathitər) *n. Med.* long slender flexible tube for inserting into bodily cavity for introducing or withdrawing fluid

cathode (ˈkathōd) *n.* negative electrode —**cathode rays** stream of electrons —**cathode-ray tube** vacuum tube in which beam of electrons is focused on to fluorescent screen to give visible spot of light

catholic (ˈkathəlik, ˈkathlik) *a.* **1.** universal **2.** including whole body of Christians **3.** (**C-**) relating to R.C. Church —*n.* **4.** (**C-**) adherent of R.C. Church —**Caˈtholicism** *n.* —**cathoˈlicity** *n.* —**caˈtholicize** *v.*

cation (ˈkatīən) *n.* positively charged ion; ion attracted to cathode during electrolysis —**catiˈonic** *a.*

catsup (ˈkechəp, ˈkach-, ˈkatsəp) *or* **ketchup** *n.* tomato purée seasoned with vinegar and spices

cattle (ˈkatəl) *pl.n.* beasts of pasture, *esp.* oxen, cows —**cattle-grid** *n.* heavy grid over ditch in road to prevent passage of livestock —ˈ**cattleman** *n.*

Caucasian (köˈkāzhən) *a.* **1.** of or pert. to White racial group of mankind **2.** of Caucasus in SW U.S.S.R. —*n.* **3.** member of Caucasian race; White person **4.** native of Caucasus —ˈ**Caucasoid** *a./n.* Caucasian

caucus (ˈkökəs) *n.* group, meeting, *esp.* of members of political party, with power to decide policy *etc.*

caudal (ˈködəl) *a.* **1.** *Anat.* of posterior part of body **2.** *Zool.* resembling or in position of tail —ˈ**caudate** *or* ˈ**caudated** *a.* having tail

caudle (ˈködəl) *n.* hot spiced wine drink made with gruel, formerly used medicinally

caught (köt) *pt./pp. of* CATCH

caul (köl) *n. Anat.* portion of amniotic sac sometimes covering child's head at birth

cauliflower (ˈkoliflowər) *n.* variety of cabbage with flowering head —**cauliflower ear** permanent distortion of ear

caulk *or* **calk** (kök) *vt.* stop up (cracks) with waterproof filler —ˈ**caulker** *n.* —ˈ**caulking** *n.*

cause (köz) *n.* **1.** that which produces an effect **2.** reason, origin **3.** motive, purpose **4.** charity, movement **5.** lawsuit —*vt.* **6.** bring about, make happen —ˈ**causal** *a.* —**cauˈsality** *n.* —**cauˈsation** *n.* —ˈ**causative** *a.* **1.** *Gram.* relating to form or class of verbs that express causation **2.** (*oft. with* of) producing effect —*n.* **3.** causative form or class of verbs —ˈ**causeless** *a.* groundless

cause célèbre (köz səˈlebrə) *Fr.* famous case

causerie (kōzəˈrē) *n.* **1.** informal talk **2.** conversational piece of writing

causeway (ˈközwā) *n.* **1.** raised way over marsh *etc.* **2.** paved street

caustic (ˈköstik) *a.* **1.** burning **2.** bitter, severe —*n.* **3.** corrosive substance —ˈ**caustically** *adv.* —**caustic soda** *see* **sodium hydroxide** *at* SODIUM

cauterize (ˈkötərīz) *vt.* burn with caustic or hot iron —**cauteriˈzation** *n.* —ˈ**cautery** *n.*

caution (ˈköshən) *n.* **1.** heedfulness, care **2.** warning —*vt.* **3.** warn —ˈ**cautionary** *a.* containing warning or precept —ˈ**cautious** *a.* —ˈ**cautiously** *adv.* —ˈ**cautiousness** *n.*

cavalcade (kavəlˈkād) *n.* column or procession of riders

cavalier (kavəˈlēər) *a.* **1.** careless, disdainful —*n.* **2.** courtly gentleman **3.** *obs.* horseman **4.** (**C-**) adherent of Charles I in English Civil War —**cavaˈlierly** *adv.*

cavalry (ˈkavəlri) *n.* mounted troops

cave (kāv) *n.* **1.** hollow place in the earth **2.** den —**cavern** (ˈkavərn) *n.* deep cave —**cavernous** (ˈkavərnəs) *a.* —**cavernously** (ˈkavərnəsli) *adv.* —ˈ**caving** *n.* sport of exploring caves —**cavity** (ˈkaviti) *n.* hollow —ˈ**caveman** *n.* prehistoric cave dweller —**cave in 1.** fall in **2.** submit, give in

caveat (ˈkaviät, ˈkāv-) *n.* **1.** *Law* formal notice requesting court not to take action without warning person lodging caveat **2.** a caution

caviar *or* **caviare** (ˈkaviär) *n.* salted sturgeon roe

cavil (ˈkavil) *vi.* find fault without sufficient reason, make trifling objections —ˈ**caviler** *n.* —ˈ**caviling** *a./n.*

cavort (kəˈvört) *vi.* prance, frisk

cavy (ˈkāvi) *n.* small S Amer. rodent

caw (kö) *n.* **1.** crow's cry —*vi.* **2.** cry so

cay (kē, kā) *n.* low island or bank composed of sand and coral fragments (*also* **key**)

cayenne pepper (kīˈen, kā-) pungent red pepper

cayman (ˈkāmən) *n. see* CAIMAN

Cayman Islands country in the Caribbean Sea comprising three islands about 200 miles northwest of Jamaica

Cayuga (kēˈo͞ogə, ˈkyo͞o-) *n.* (member of)

Iroquoian-speaking Amerindian people of upper New York state (*pl.* **-ga, -s**)

Cb *Chem.* columbium

CB citizens band

CBC Canadian Broadcasting Corporation

cc *or* **c.c.** **1.** carbon copy or copies **2.** cubic centimeter

cc. chapters

C.C. **1.** City Council **2.** County Council **3.** Cricket Club

CCC Commodity Credit Corporation

cd candela

Cd *Chem.* cadmium

C.D. **1.** Civil Defense (Corps) **2.** Corps Diplomatique (Diplomatic Corps)

CDMB Civil and Defense Mobilization Board

Cdr. *Mil.* Commander

Ce *Chem.* cerium

C.E. *Judaism* Common Era

CEA Council of Economic Advisers

cease (sēs) *v.* bring or come to an end —**'ceaseless** *a.* —**'ceaselessly** *adv.*

cecum ('sēkəm) *n. Anat.* pouch, *esp.* at beginning of large intestine (*pl.* **-ca** (-kə))

cedar ('sēdər) *n.* **1.** large evergreen tree **2.** its wood

cede (sēd) *v.* yield, give up, transfer, *esp.* of territory

cedilla (si'dilə) *n.* hooklike mark (¸) placed under a letter *c* to show the sound of *s*

ceiling ('sēling) *n.* **1.** inner, upper surface of a room **2.** maximum price, wage *etc.* **3.** *Met.* lower level of clouds **4.** *Aviation* limit of height to which aircraft can climb —**ceil** *vt.* line (room), *esp.* with plaster

celadon ('selədon) *n.* Chinese or Japanese porcelain ware with a grayish or greenish glaze

celandine ('seləndīn) *n.* yellow wild flower

Celanese (selə'nēz) *n.* trade name for viscose rayon

celebrate ('selibrāt) *v.* **1.** rejoice or have festivities to mark (happy day, event *etc.*) —*vt.* **2.** observe (birthday *etc.*) **3.** perform (religious ceremony *etc.*) **4.** praise publicly —**'celebrant** *n.* —**'celebrated** *a.* famous —**cele'bration** *n.* —**ce'lebrity** *n.* **1.** famous person **2.** fame

celeriac (si'leriak) *n.* variety of celery with large turniplike root, used as vegetable

celerity (si'leriti) *n.* swiftness

celery ('seləri) *n.* vegetable with long juicy edible stalks

celesta (sə'lestə) *n.* orchestral percussion instrument resembling a small piano, with its hammers operating on steel bars

celestial (si'leschəl) *a.* **1.** heavenly, divine **2.** of the sky —**celestial equator** great circle lying on celestial sphere, plane of which is perpendicular to line joining north and south celestial poles (*also* **equi'noctial, equinoctial circle**) —**celestial sphere** imaginary sphere of infinitely large radius enclosing universe

celiac ('sēliak) *a.* pertaining to abdominal cavity —**celiac disease** chronic disease of young children marked by inability to digest fats

celibacy ('selibəsi) *n.* single life, unmarried state —**'celibate** *n./a.*

cell (sel) *n.* **1.** small room, *esp.* in prison **2.** small cavity **3.** minute, basic unit of living matter **4.** device converting chemical energy into electrical energy **5.** small local group operating as nucleus of larger political or religious organization —**'cellular** *a.* —**'cellule** *n.* small cell

cellar ('selər) *n.* **1.** underground room for storage **2.** stock of wine —**'cellarage** *n.* —**'cellarer** *n.* monastic official responsible for food *etc.* —**cella'ret** *n.* cabinet for wine

cello ('chelō) *n.* popular name for violoncello, musical instrument of the violin family larger (thus lower in pitch) than the viola and smaller than the double bass

cellophane ('seləfān) *n.* regenerated cellulose in thin transparent sheets used *esp.* in packing and making adhesive tape

cellulite ('selyo͝olīt) *n.* subcutaneous fat alleged to resist dieting

celluloid ('selyo͝oloid) *n.* **1.** synthetic plastic substance with wide range of uses **2.** coating of photographic film **3.** a motion-picture film

cellulose ('selyo͝olōs, -lōz) *n.* **1.** substance of vegetable cell wall **2.** group of carbohydrates **3.** varnish

Celsius ('selsiəs) *a./n.* (of) scale of temperature from 0° (melting point of ice) to 100° (boiling point of water) divided into 100 equal degrees

Celtic ('keltik, 'sel-) *or* **Keltic** ('keltik) *n.* **1.** branch of languages including Gaelic and Welsh —*a.* **2.** of Celtic peoples or languages —**Celt** *or* **Kelt** *n.* **1.** person who speaks a Celtic language **2.** member of Indo-European people who in pre-Roman times inhabited Brit., Gaul and Spain

cement (si'ment) *n.* **1.** fine mortar **2.** adhesive, glue —*vt.* **3.** unite with cement **4.** join firmly

cemetery ('semiteri) *n.* burial ground, *esp.* other than churchyard

cenotaph ('senətaf) *n.* monument to person buried elsewhere

Cenozoic (sēnō'zōik) *a.* **1.** of most recent geological era characterized by appearance of hominids —*n.* **2.** this era

censer ('sensər) *n.* pan in which incense is burned

censor ('sensər) *n.* **1.** one authorized to examine films, books *etc.* and suppress all or part if considered morally or otherwise unacceptable —*vt.* **2.** ban or cut portions of (film *etc.*) **3.** act as censor of (behavior *etc.*) —**cen'sorial** *a.* of censor —**cen'sorious** *a.*

fault-finding —**cen'soriousness** *n.* —**'censorship** *n.*

censure ('senchər) *n.* **1.** blame; harsh criticism —*vt.* **2.** blame; criticize harshly

census ('sensəs) *n.* official counting of people, things *etc.*

cent (sent) *n.* **1.** monetary unit equal to $^1/_{100}$ of a basic unit **2.** piece of metal or paper money representing this **3.** the fen of the People's Republic of China

cent. 1. centigrade **2.** central **3.** century

centaur ('sentôr) *n.* mythical creature, half man, half horse

centenary (sen'tenəri) *n.* **1.** 100 years **2.** celebration of hundredth anniversary —*a.* **3.** pert. to a hundred —**cente'narian** *n.* one a hundred years old —**cen'tennial** *a.* lasting, happening every hundred years

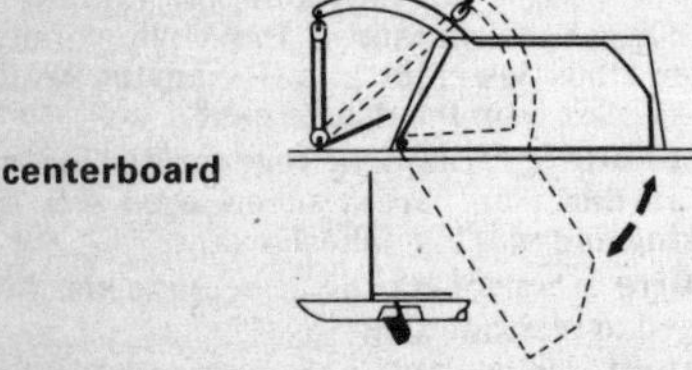

center ('sentər) *n.* **1.** midpoint **2.** pivot, axis **3.** point to or from which things move or are drawn **4.** place for specific organization or activity —**'central** *a.* —**cen'trality** *n.* —**centrali'zation** *n.* —**'centralize** *vt.* **1.** bring to a center **2.** concentrate under one control —**'centrally** *adv.* —**'centric** *a.* —**cen'trifugal** *a.* tending from center —**'centrifuge** *n.* **1.** rotating machine that separates liquids from solids or other liquids by centrifugal force **2.** rotating device for subjecting human beings or animals to varying accelerations —*vt.* **3.** subject to action of centrifuge —**cen'tripetal** *a.* tending toward center —**'centrist** *n.* person holding moderate political views —**'centerboard** *n.* supplementary keel for sailing vessel —**'centerfold** *n.* large colored illustration folded to form central spread of magazine —**center forward** *Soccer, hockey etc.* central forward in attack —**center half** *Soccer* defender in middle of defense —**center of gravity** point through which resultant of gravitational forces on body always acts —**'centerpiece** *n.* object used as center of something, *esp.* for decoration —**central bank** national bank that does business mainly with government and other banks —**central heating** method of heating building from one central source —**central processing unit** part of computer that performs logical and arithmetical operations on data —**Central Standard Time** time reckoned from the 90th to 105th meridians west of Greenwich

centi- *or before vowel* **cent-** (*comb. form*) **1.** one hundredth, as in *centimeter* **2.** *rare* hundred, as in *centipede*

centigrade ('sentigrād) *a.* **1.** Celsius **2.** having one hundred degrees

centigram ('sentigram) *n.* hundredth part of gram

centiliter ('sentilētər) *n.* hundredth part of liter

centime ('sontēm; *Fr.* sã'tēm) *n.* monetary unit of France *etc.*, worth one hundredth of standard unit of currency

centimeter ('sentimētər) *n.* hundredth part of meter —**centimeter-gram-second** *n. see* CGS UNITS

centipede ('sentipēd) *n.* small segmented animal with many legs

CENTO ('sentō) Central Treaty Organization

Central African Republic country in Africa bounded north by Chad, east by Sudan, south by Zaïre and Congo, and west by Cameroon

centrosome ('sentrəsōm) *n.* minute, protoplasmic body regarded as active center of cell division in mitosis

centuplicate (sen'tyo͞oplikāt, -'to͞o-) *vt.* **1.** increase 100 times —*a.* (sen'tyo͞oplikit, -'to͞o-) **2.** increased hundredfold —*n.* (sen'tyo͞oplikit, -'to͞o-) **3.** one hundredfold (*also* **'centuple**)

centurion (sen'tyo͝orion, -'to͝oə-) *n.* Roman commander of 100 men

century ('senchəri) *n.* **1.** 100 years **2.** any set of 100

cephalic (si'falik) *a.* **1.** of head **2.** situated in, on or near head

cephalopod ('sefələpod) *n.* any of various marine mollusks characterized by well-developed head and eyes and ring of sucker-bearing tentacles, including octopus

ceramic (si'ramik) *n.* **1.** hard brittle material of baked clay **2.** object made of this —*pl.* **3.** (*with sing. v.*) art, techniques of making ceramic objects **4.** such objects —*a.* **5.** of ceramic or ceramics

cere (sēər) *n.* soft waxy swelling, containing nostrils, at base of upper beak, as in parrot

cereal ('sēəriəl) *n.* **1.** any edible grain, *eg* wheat, rice *etc.* **2.** (breakfast) food made from grain —*a.* **3.** of cereal

cerebellum (seri'beləm) *n.* one of major divisions of vertebrate brain whose function is coordination of voluntary movements (*pl.* **-s, -la** (-lə))

cerebrum (sə'rēbrəm) *n.* **1.** anterior portion of brain of vertebrates: dominant part of brain in man, associated with intellectual function *etc.* **2.** brain as whole (*pl.* **-s, -bra** (-brə)) —**ce'rebral** *a.* pert. to brain —**cerebrate** ('seribrāt) *vi. usu. jocular* use the mind; think; ponder; consider —**cerebration** (seri'brāshən) *n.* —**cerebro'spinal** *a.* of brain and spinal cord —**cerebro'vascular** *a.* of blood vessels and blood supply of brain —**cerebral atherosclerosis** hardening of the arteries of the brain —**cerebral embolism** *or* **hemorrhage** *see* STROKE —**cerebral palsy** impairment of muscular function and weakness of limbs, caused by damage to brain —**cerebral thrombosis** *see* STROKE

cerecloth ('sēərkloth) *n.* waxed waterproof cloth formerly used for shrouds

ceremony ('serimōni) *n.* **1.** formal observance **2.** sacred rite **3.** courteous act —**cere'monial** *a./n.* —**cere'monially** *adv.* —**cere'monious** *a.* —**cere'moniously** *adv.* —**cere'moniousness** *n.*

cerise (sə'rēs, -'rēz) *n./a.* clear, pinkish red

cerium ('sēəriəm) *n. Chem.* metallic element *Symbol* Ce, at. wt. 140.1, at. no. 58

CERN (sərn) Conseil Européen pour la Recherche Nucléaire; organization of European states with center in Geneva, for research in high-energy particle physics

cert (sərt) *n. inf.* something certain (*esp. in* **a dead cert**)

cert. 1. certificate **2.** certification **3.** certified

certain ('sərtən) *a.* **1.** sure **2.** settled, inevitable **3.** some, one **4.** of moderate (quantity, degree *etc.*) —**'certainly** *adv.* —**'certainty** *n.* —**'certitude** *n.* confidence

certes ('sərtiz) *adv. obs.* with certainty; truly

certify ('sərtifī) *vt.* **1.** declare formally **2.** endorse, guarantee **3.** declare legally insane (**-fied, -fying**) —**certificate** (sər'tifikit) *n.* **1.** written declaration —*vt.* (sər'tifikāt) **2.** authorize by or present with official document —**certifi'cation** *n.* —**'certified** *a.* **1.** holding or guaranteed by certificate **2.** endorsed, guaranteed **3.** (of person) declared legally insane —**'certifier** *n.*

cerulean (si'rōōliən) *a.* sky-blue

cervix ('sərviks) *n.* neck, *esp.* of womb —**'cervical** *a.* —**cervical smear** *Med.* smear taken from neck of uterus for detection of cancer (*see also* PAP SMEAR)

Cesarean *or* **Cesarian** (si'zariən, -'zer-) *a.* **1.** of any of Caesars, *esp.* Julius Caesar —*n.* **2.** (*sometimes* **c-**) *Surg.* Cesarean section —**Cesarean section** surgical incision through abdominal wall to deliver baby

cesium ('sēziəm) *n. Chem.* metallic element *Symbol* Cs, at. wt. 132.9, at. no. 55

cessation (se'sāshən) *n.* ceasing, stopping; pause

cession ('seshən) *n.* yielding up

cesspool ('sespōōl) *or* **cesspit** ('sespit) *n.* pit in which filthy water collects, receptacle for sewage

cestus[1] ('sestəs) *n.* woman's belt, *esp.* that worn by bride

cestus[2] ('sestəs) *n.* in classical Roman boxing, pugilist's gauntlet of bull's hide studded with metal (*pl.* **-tus, -es**)

cesura (si'zhōōrə) *n. Prosody see* CAESURA

cetacean (si'tāshən) *a.* **1.** of order of aquatic mammals having no hind limbs and blowhole for breathing: includes toothed and whalebone whales (*also* **ce'taceous**) —*n.* **2.** whale

cetane ('sētān) *n.* colorless liquid hydrocarbon used in determination of cetane number of diesel fuel (*also* **'hexadecane**) —**cetane number** measure of quality of diesel fuel expressed as percentage of cetane (*also* **cetane rating**)

ceteris paribus ('kātəris 'paribəs) *Lat.* all things being equal

Ceylon (si'lon) *n. former name of* SRI LANKA

Cf *Chem.* californium

cf. confer (*Lat.*, compare)

c/f carried forward

CFL Canadian Football League

cg centigram

cgs units metric system of units based on *centimeter, gram, second*

ch. 1. chapter **2.** church

Chablis (sha'blē) *n.* dry white table wine

cha-cha ('chächä) *n.* **1.** fast ballroom dance from Latin Amer. **2.** music composed for this dance —*vi.* **3.** perform this dance

Chad (chad) *n.* country in central Africa bounded west by Cameroon, Nigeria and Niger, north by Libya, east by Sudan and south by Central African Republic

chafe (chāf) *vt.* **1.** make sore or worn by rubbing **2.** make warm by rubbing **3.** vex, irritate —**chafing dish** vessel with heating apparatus beneath it, for cooking or keeping food warm at table

chafer ('chāfər) *n.* any of various beetles, such as cockchafer

chaff (chaf) *n.* **1.** husks of grain **2.** worthless matter **3.** banter —*vt.* **4.** tease good-naturedly

chaffer ('chafər) *vi.* **1.** haggle, bargain —*n.* **2.** bargaining

chaffinch ('chafinch) *n.* small songbird

Chagas' disease ('shägəs) tropical infection with a parasite transmitted by insects, *esp.* bedbugs

chagrin (shə'grin) *n.* **1.** vexation, disappointment —*vt.* **2.** embarrass **3.** annoy **4.** disappoint

chain (chān) *n.* **1.** series of connected links or rings **2.** thing that binds **3.** connected series of things or events **4.** surveyor's measure —*vt.* **5.** fasten with chain **6.** confine **7.** restrain —**chain armor** —**chain gang** group of prisoners chained together —**chain mail** —**chain reaction** —**chain smoker** one who smokes cigarettes *etc.* continuously, *esp.* lighting one from preceding one —**chain stitch** —**chain store**

chair (chāər) *n.* **1.** movable seat, with back, for one person **2.** seat of authority **3.** professorship **4.** iron support for rail on railway —*vt.* **5.** preside over **6.** carry in triumph —**'chairlift** *n.* series of chairs fixed to cable for conveying people (*esp.* skiers) up mountain —**'chairman** *n.* one who presides over meeting —**'chairmanship** *n.*

chaise (shāz) *n.* light horse-drawn carriage —**chaise longue** (long) sofa

chalcedony (kalˈsedəni) *n.* translucent variety of quartz, often milky or grayish, used as gem

chalet (shaˈlā) *n.* Swiss wooden house

chalice (ˈchalis) *n.* **1.** *Poet.* cup; bowl **2.** communion cup

chalk (chök) *n.* **1.** white substance, carbonate of lime **2.** crayon —*v.* **3.** rub, draw, mark with chalk —ˈ**chalkiness** *n.* —ˈ**chalky** *a.*

challa (ˈhälə) *n.* braided white bread glazed with egg white

challenge (ˈchalinj) *vt.* **1.** call to fight or account **2.** dispute **3.** stimulate **4.** object to **5.** claim —*n.* **6.** call to engage in fight *etc.* **7.** questioning of statement *etc.* **8.** demanding situation *etc.* **9.** demand by sentry *etc.* for identification or password —ˈ**challenger** *n.* —ˈ**challenging** *a.* difficult but stimulating

challis (ˈshali) *n.* soft lightweight woven fabric made of worsted wool

chamber (ˈchāmbər) *n.* **1.** room for assembly **2.** assembly, body of men **3.** compartment **4.** cavity **5.** *obs.* room —**chamberlain** (ˈchāmbərlin) *n.* official at court of a monarch having charge of domestic and ceremonial affairs —ˈ**chambermaid** *n.* servant with care of bedrooms —**chamber music** music for performance by a few instruments —**chamber of commerce** organization composed mainly of local businessmen to promote and protect their interests —**chamber pot** vessel for urine

chambray (ˈshambrā) *n.* fine-quality cotton fabric made with white weft threads and colored warp threads

chameleon (kəˈmēlyən) *n.* **1.** small lizard famous for its power of changing color **2.** changeable person

chamfer (ˈchamfər) *vt.* **1.** groove **2.** bevel **3.** flute —*n.* **4.** groove

chamois (ˈshami) *n.* **1.** goatlike mountain antelope **2.** soft pliable leather

chamomile *or* **camomile** (ˈkaməmīl) *n.* aromatic creeping plant of the daisy family, used medicinally

champ[1] (champ) *v.* **1.** munch (food) noisily, as horse **2.** be nervous, impatient

champ[2] (champ) *n. inf.* champion

champagne (shamˈpān) *n.* **1.** light, sparkling white wine made in a strictly defined area in France **2.** wine resembling this made elsewhere **3.** a pale yellowish-brown color

champion (ˈchampiən) *n.* **1.** one that excels all others **2.** defender of a cause **3.** one who fights for another **4.** hero —*vt.* **5.** fight for, maintain —ˈ**championship** *n.*

chance (chans) *n.* **1.** unpredictable course of events **2.** fortune, luck **3.** opportunity **4.** possibility **5.** risk **6.** probability —*vt.* **7.** risk —*vi.* **8.** happen —*a.* **9.** casual, unexpected —ˈ**chancy** *a.* risky

chancel (ˈchansəl) *n.* part of church where altar is

chancellor (ˈchansələr) *n.* **1.** high officer of state **2.** chief officer of university or state college system —ˈ**chancellery** *or* ˈ**chancellory** *n.* —ˈ**chancellorship** *n.* —**Chancellor of the Exchequer UK** cabinet minister responsible for finance

chancery (ˈchansəri) *n.* the office of an embassy

chancre (ˈshangkər) *n.* small hard growth: first sign of syphilis —ˈ**chancrous** *a.*

chandelier (shandiˈlēər) *n.* hanging frame with branches for holding lights

chandler (ˈchandlər) *n.* dealer in ropes, ships' supplies *etc.*

Chanel-line (shaˈnel-) *a.* of loose cardigan-type jacket worn with straight or slightly flared skirt, usu. worn with mass of necklaces in gold

change (chānj) *v.* **1.** alter, make or become different **2.** put on (different clothes, fresh coverings) —*vt.* **3.** put or give for another **4.** exchange, interchange —*n.* **5.** alteration, variation **6.** variety **7.** conversion of money **8.** small money, coins **9.** balance received on payment —**changeaˈbility** *n.* —ˈ**changeable** *a.* —ˈ**changeably** *adv.* —ˈ**changeful** *a.* —ˈ**changeless** *a.* —ˈ**changeling** *n.* child believed substituted for another by fairies —**change of life** menopause

channel (ˈchanəl) *n.* **1.** bed of stream **2.** strait **3.** deeper part of strait, bay, harbor **4.** groove **5.** means of passing or conveying **6.** band of radio frequencies **7.** television broadcasting station —*vt.* **8.** groove, furrow **9.** guide, convey

chant (chant) *n.* **1.** simple song or melody **2.** rhythmic or repetitious slogan —*vi.* **3.** sing or utter chant **4.** speak monotonously or repetitiously

Chantelle (shanˈtel) *n.* a red-coated semi-hard cheese with open texture and a mild flavor

chanticleer (chantiˈklēər) *n.* rooster

chantry (ˈchantri) *n. Christianity* **1.** endowment for singing of Masses for soul of founder **2.** chapel or altar so endowed

chanty (ˈshanti, ˈchan-) *n. see* SHANTY[2]

Chanuka, Channuka, *or* **Hanuka** (ˈhänəkə) *n. Judaism* the Feast of Lights, an eight-day holiday in December memorializing the successful rebellion against Greco-Syrian despots

chaos (ˈkāos) *n.* **1.** disorder, confusion **2.** state of universe before Creation —**chaˈotic** *a.*

chap[1] (chap) *v.* (of skin) become dry, raw and cracked, *esp.* by exposure to cold and wind (**-pp-**) —**chapped** *a.*

chap[2] (chap) *n. inf.* fellow, man

chapatti *or* **chapati** (chəˈpati, -ˈpäti) *n.* in Indian cookery, flat unleavened bread resembling pancake (*pl.* **-ti, -s, -es**)

chapel ('chapəl) *n.* **1.** private church **2.** subordinate place of worship **3.** division of church with its own altar **4.** organization of the union printers in a printing house

chaperon *or* **chaperone** ('shapərōn) *n.* **1.** one who attends young unmarried lady in public as protector —*vt.* **2.** attend in this way

chaplain ('chaplin) *n.* clergyman attached to chapel, regiment, warship, institution *etc.* —'**chaplaincy** *n.* his office

chaplet ('chaplit) *n.* **1.** ornamental wreath of flowers worn on head **2.** string of beads **3.** *R.C.Ch.* string of prayer beads constituting one third of rosary; prayers counted on this string **4.** narrow molding in form of string of beads

chapman ('chapmən) *n.* *obs.* trader, *esp.* itinerant peddler

chappie ('chapi) *n.* *inf.* *see* CHAP[2]

chaps (chaps, shaps) *pl.n.* cowboy's leggings of thick leather

chapter ('chaptər) *n.* **1.** division of book **2.** section, heading **3.** assembly of clergy, bishop's council *etc.* **4.** organized branch of society, fraternity, sorority —'**chapterhouse** *n.*

char[1] (chär) *vt.* scorch, burn to charcoal (**-rr-**) —**charred** *a.*

char[2] *or* **charr** (chär) *n.* troutlike small fish

character ('kariktər) *n.* **1.** nature **2.** total of qualities making up individuality **3.** moral qualities **4.** reputation, *esp.* good one **5.** statement of qualities of person **6.** an eccentric **7.** personality in play or novel **8.** letter, sign or any distinctive mark **9.** essential feature —**character'istic** *n./a.* —**character'istically** *adv.* —**characteri'zation** *n.* —'**characterize** *vt.* **1.** mark out, distinguish **2.** describe by peculiar qualities —'**characterless** *a.*

charade (shə'räd) *n.* **1.** absurd act **2.** travesty —*pl.* **3.** word-guessing parlor game with syllables of word acted

charcoal ('chärkōl) *n.* **1.** black residue of wood, bones *etc.*, produced by smothered burning **2.** charred wood —**charcoal-burner** *n.*

chard (chärd) *n.* beet with large succulent leaves and thick stalks, used as vegetable (*also* **Swiss chard**)

charge (chärj) *vt.* **1.** ask as price **2.** bring accusation against **3.** lay task on **4.** command **5.** attack **6.** deliver injunction against **7.** fill with electricity **8.** fill, load —*vi.* **9.** make onrush, attack —*n.* **10.** cost, price **11.** accusation **12.** attack, onrush **13.** command, exhortation **14.** accumulation of electricity —*pl.* **15.** expenses —'**chargeable** *a.* —'**charger** *n.* **1.** strong, fast battle horse **2.** that which charges, *esp.* electrically

chargé d'affaires ('shärzhā da'fāər) **1.** temporary head of diplomatic mission in absence of ambassador or minister **2.** head of diplomatic mission of lowest level (*pl.* **chargés d'affaires** ('shärzhā, -zhāz))

chariot ('chariət) *n.* **1.** two-wheeled car used in ancient fighting **2.** state carriage —**chario'teer** *n.*

charisma (kə'rizmə) *or* **charism** ('karizəm) *n.* special power of individual to inspire fascination, loyalty *etc.* (*pl.* **cha'rismata**) —**charis'matic** *a.*

charity ('chariti) *n.* **1.** the giving of help, money *etc.* to those in need **2.** organization for doing this **3.** the money *etc.* given **4.** love, kindness **5.** disposition to think kindly of others —'**charitable** *a.* —'**charitably** *adv.*

charlatan ('shärlətən) *n.* quack, impostor —'**charlatanry** *n.*

charleston ('chärlstən) *n.* fast, rhythmic dance of 1920s

Charlie ('chärli) *n.* word used in communications for the letter *c*

charlock ('chärlok) *n.* weedy Eurasian plant with yellow flowers (*also* **wild mustard**)

charlotte ('shärlət) *n.* **1.** dessert made with fruit and bread or cake crumbs, sponge cake *etc.* **2.** cold dessert made with sponge fingers, cream *etc.* (*also* **charlotte russe**)

charm (chärm) *n.* **1.** attractiveness **2.** anything that fascinates **3.** amulet **4.** magic spell —*vt.* **5.** bewitch **6.** delight, attract —**charmed** *a.* —'**charmer** *n.* —'**charming** *a.*

charnel house ('chärnəl) *esp.* formerly, vault for bones of the dead

chart (chärt) *n.* **1.** map of sea **2.** diagram or tabulated statement —*vt.* **3.** map **4.** represent on chart —**the charts** *inf.* lists produced weekly of best-selling pop records

charter ('chärtər) *n.* **1.** document granting privileges *etc.* **2.** patent —*vt.* **3.** let or hire **4.** establish by charter

chartreuse (shär'trōōz; *Fr.* shar'trœz) *n.* **1.** either of two liqueurs, green or yellow, made from herbs **2.** yellowish-green color

chary ('chāəri) *a.* cautious, sparing —'**charily** *adv.* —'**chariness** *n.* caution

Charybdis (kə'ribdis) *n.* ship-devouring monster in classical mythology, identified with whirlpool off coast of Sicily

chase[1] (chās) *vt.* **1.** hunt, pursue **2.** drive (from, away, into *etc.*) —*n.* **3.** pursuit, hunting **4.** the hunted **5.** hunting ground —'**chaser** *n.* drink of beer, soda *etc.* taken after spirit

chase[2] (chās) *vt.* engrave —'**chaser** *n.* —'**chasing** *n.*

chase[3] (chās) *n.* **1.** *Letterpress print.* rectangular steel frame into which metal type and blocks are locked for printing **2.** part of cannon enclosing bore **3.** groove or channel, *esp.* to take pipe *etc.* —*vt.* **4.** cut groove, furrow or flute in (surface *etc.*) (*also* '**chamfer**)

chasm ('kazəm) *n.* **1.** deep cleft, fissure **2.** abyss

chassé (sha'sā) *n.* **1.** rapid gliding step used in dancing —*vi.* **2.** perform the step

chassis ('chasi) *n.* **1.** framework, wheels and machinery of motor vehicle excluding body and coachwork **2.** underframe of aircraft (*pl.* **-sis** (-siz))

chaste (chāst) *a.* **1.** virginal **2.** pure **3.** modest **4.** virtuous —'**chastely** *adv.* —**chastity** ('chastiti) *n.*

chasten ('chāsən) *vt.* **1.** correct by punishment **2.** restrain, subdue —'**chastened** *a.* —**chastise** (chas'tīz) *vt.* inflict punishment on —**chastisement** (chas'tīzmənt) *n.*

chasuble ('chazhŏŏbəl) *n.* priest's long sleeveless outer vestment

chat[1] (chat) *vi.* **1.** talk idly or familiarly (**-tt-**) —*n.* **2.** familiar idle talk —'**chattily** *adv.* —'**chatty** *a.*

chat[2] (chat) *n.* any of various European songbirds, Amer. warblers, Aust. wrens

château (sha'tō) *n.* *esp.* in France, castle, country house (*pl.* **-teaux** (-'tō, -'tōz), **-s**)

chateaubriand (shatōbrē'än) *n.* broiled tenderloin steak served with a sauce

chatelaine ('shatəlān; *Fr.* shat'len) *n.* **1.** *esp.* formerly, mistress of castle or large household **2.** chain or clasp worn at waist by women in 16th to 19th century, with handkerchief *etc.* attached

chattel ('chatəl) *n.* (*usu. pl.*) any movable property

chatter ('chatər) *vi.* **1.** talk idly or rapidly **2.** (of teeth) click rapidly —*n.* **3.** idle talk —'**chatterer** *n.* —'**chattering** *n.* —'**chatterbox** *n.* one who chatters incessantly

chauffeur ('shōfər, shō'fər) *n.* paid driver motor vehicle (**chauf'feuse** *fem.*)

chauvinism ('shōvinizəm) *n.* **1.** assertive patriotism **2.** smug sense of superiority —'**chauvinist** *or* **chauvin'istic** *a.*

cheap (chēp) *a.* **1.** low in price, inexpensive **2.** easily obtained **3.** of little value or estimation **4.** mean, inferior —'**cheapen** *vt.* —'**cheaply** *adv.* —'**cheapness** *n.* —**cheapjack** *inf. n.* **1.** person who sells cheap and shoddy goods —*a.* **2.** shoddy, inferior —'**cheapskate** *n. inf.* miserly person

cheat (chēt) *vt.* **1.** deceive, defraud, swindle, impose upon —*vi.* **2.** practice deceit to gain advantage —*n.* **3.** fraud

check[1] (check) *n.* **1.** written order to banker to pay money from one's account **2.** printed slip of paper used for this —'**checkbook** *n.* book of blank checks

check[2] (chek) *vt.* **1.** stop **2.** restrain **3.** hinder **4.** repress **5.** control **6.** examine for accuracy, quality *etc.* **7.** leave or receive for temporary safekeeping —*n.* **8.** repulse **9.** stoppage **10.** restraint **11.** brief examination for correctness or accuracy **12.** pattern of squares on fabric **13.** threat to king at chess —'**checker** *n.* **1.** person who examines for accuracy **2.** person who receives coats, parcels *etc.* for temporary safekeeping **3.** cashier at supermarket or restaurant —'**checkmate** *n.* **1.** *Chess* final winning move **2.** any overthrow, defeat —*vt.* **3.** *Chess* place (opponent's king) in checkmate **4.** defeat —'**checkout** *n.* counter in supermarket where customers pay —'**checkroom** *n.* room where items may be temporarily stored, *esp.* in restaurant —'**checkup** *n.* examination (*esp.* medical) to see if all is in order

checked (chekt) *a.* having pattern of small squares

checker ('chekər) *n.* man in checkers

checkers ('chekərz) *pl.n.* (*with sing. v.*) board game for two players played with 12 thick disks called checkers or men —'**checkerboard** *n.* board with 64 squares of alternating colors for playing checkers —**Chinese checkers** board game for two or three players in which the player who first succeeds in moving his pieces across the board wins

Cheddar ('chedər) *n.* a hard cheese made from cow's milk with a mild-to-sharp flavor depending on age, orig. from England

cheek (chēk) *n.* **1.** side of face below eye **2.** *inf.* impudence —*vt.* **3.** *inf.* address impudently —'**cheeky** *a.*

cheep (chēp) *vi./n.* (utter) high-pitched cry, as of young bird

cheer (chēər) *vt.* **1.** comfort **2.** gladden **3.** encourage by shouts —*vi.* **4.** shout applause —*n.* **5.** shout of approval **6.** happiness, good spirits **7.** mood **8.** *obs.* rich food —'**cheerful** *a.* —'**cheerfully** *adv.* —'**cheerfulness** *n.* —'**cheerily** *adv.* —'**cheerless** *a.* —'**cheerlessness** *n.* —**cheers** *interj. inf., chiefly* **UK** **1.** drinking toast **2.** goodbye, cheerio **3.** thanks —'**cheery** *a.*

cheerio (chēəri'ō) *inf. interj.* **1.** *chiefly* **UK** farewell greeting **2.** *chiefly* **UK** drinking toast —*n.* **3. NZ** small sausage

cheese (chēz) *n.* food derived from milk, usu. made by separating curd from whey by mechanical means or by action of rennet, and then ripened and molded —'**cheesiness** *n.* —'**cheesy** *a.* —'**cheeseburger** *n.* hamburger cooked with cheese on top —'**cheesecake** *n.* **1.** pastry shell filled with cheese, *esp.* cream cheese, cream, sugar *etc.* **2.** *sl.* women displayed for their sex appeal, as in photographs or films —'**cheesecloth** *n.* loosely woven cotton cloth —'**cheeseparing** *a.* stingy

cheetah ('chētə) *n.* large, swift, spotted feline animal

chef (shef) *n.* head cook, *esp.* in restaurant

chef-d'œuvre (she'dœvr) *Fr.* masterpiece

chem. **1.** chemical **2.** chemistry

chemin de fer (shə'man də 'fāər) gambling game, variation of baccarat

chemise (shə'mēz) *n.* loose-fitting dress hanging straight from shoulders; loose shirtlike undergarment (*also* **shift**)

chemistry ('kemistri) *n.* science concerned

with composition, properties and reactions of matter —'**chemical** *n./a.* —'**chemically** *adv.* —'**chemist** *n.* person trained in chemistry —**chemical engineer** —**chemical engineering** engineering concerned with design and manufacture of plant used in industrial chemical processes —**chemical reaction** process in which substances are converted to other substances with different sets of properties —**chemical warfare** warfare using asphyxiating gases, poisons *etc.*

chemotherapy (kēmō'therəpi) *n.* treatment of disease by chemical agent

chemurgy ('kemərji) *n.* branch of applied chemistry devoted to the development of agricultural products —**che'murgic(al)** *a.*

chenille (shə'nēl) *n.* woven fabric with tufted pile —**chenille yarn** yarn with soft fluffy finish

cheongsam ('chöngsäm) *n.* tight dress with mandarin collar and slits at each side of skirt

cherish ('cherish) *vt.* **1.** treat with affection **2.** protect **3.** foster

Cherokee ('cherəkē) *n.* **1.** member of Amerindian people orig. of Tennessee and North Carolina (*pl.* **-kee, -s**) **2.** Iroquoian language of this people

cheroot (shə'rōōt) *n.* cigar with both ends open

cherry ('cheri) *n.* **1.** small red or yellow fruit with stone **2.** tree bearing it —*a.* **3.** ruddy, bright red

cherub ('cherəb) *n.* **1.** winged creature with human face **2.** angel (*pl.* **'cherubim, -s**) —**che'rubic** *a.*

chervil ('chərvil) *n.* a herb

Cheshire ('cheshər) *n.* a hard cheese made from cow's milk, blue-veined, with a mild-to-rich flavor, orig. from England where it is the oldest cheese known

chess (ches) *n.* universal game for two players played on board with 16 pieces each: king, queen, two rooks or castles, two bishops, two knights and eight pawns —'**chessboard** *n.* board with 64 squares of alternating colors for playing chess —'**chessman** *n.* one of the pieces for playing chess

chest (chest) *n.* **1.** upper part of trunk of body **2.** large, strong box —**chest of drawers** piece of furniture containing drawers

chesterfield ('chestərfēld) *n.* overcoat

chestnut ('chesnut) *n.* **1.** large reddish-brown nut growing in prickly husk **2.** tree bearing it **3.** *inf.* old joke **4.** horse of golden-brown color —*a.* **5.** reddish-brown

cheval glass (shə'val) full-length mirror mounted to swivel within frame

chevalier (shevə'lēər) *n.* **1.** member of order of merit, such as French Legion of Honor **2.** lowest title of rank in old French nobility **3.** *obs.* knight **4.** chivalrous man; gallant

Cheviot ('sheviət) *n.* **1.** Brit. sheep reared for its wool **2.** (*oft.* **c-**) rough woolen fabric

chevron ('shevrən) *n. Mil.* V-shaped band of braid worn on sleeve to designate rank

chew (chōō) *v.* **1.** grind with teeth —*n.* **2.** act of chewing **3.** something that is chewed —'**chewy** *a.* firm, sticky when chewed —**chewing gum** —**chew the fat** *sl.* **1.** argue over a point **2.** talk idly; gossip

Cheyenne (shī'an) *n.* **1.** member of Amerindian people of western plains (*pl.* **-enne, -s**) **2.** Algonquian language of this people

chi (kī) *n.* 22nd letter in Gr. alphabet (χ, X)

chianti (ki'anti) *n.* It. wine

chiaroscuro (kiärə'skyōōərō, -'skōōə-) *n.* **1.** treatment of light and shade in a painting **2.** formerly, line-block woodcut printed in several colors (*pl.* **-s**)

chic (shēk) *a.* **1.** stylish, elegant —*n.* **2.** stylishness, *esp.* in dress

chicane (shi'kān) *n.* **1.** bridge or whist hand without trumps **2.** *Motor racing* barrier placed before dangerous corner to reduce speeds **3.** *rare* chicanery —*vt.* **4.** deceive or trick by chicanery —*vi.* **5.** use chicanery —**chi'canery** *n.* **1.** quibbling **2.** trick, artifice

chicano (chi'käno) *n.* American of Mexican descent (*pl.* **-s**)

chick (chik) *n.* **1.** young of birds, *esp.* of hen **2.** *sl.* girl, young woman —'**chicken** *n.* **1.** domestic fowl bred for flesh or eggs **2.** its flesh as food **3.** *sl.* cowardly person —*a.* **4.** *sl.* easily scared; cowardly; timid —**chicken feed** trifling amount (of money) —**chicken-hearted** *a.* cowardly —'**chickenpox** *n.* highly contagious virus disease (*also* **varicella**) —'**chickpea** *n.* dwarf pea —'**chickweed** *n.* weed with small white flowers

Chickahominy (chikə'homini) *n.* (member of) Amerindian people of Virginia (*pl.* **-ny, -nies**)

chicle ('chikəl) *n.* substance obtained from sapodilla; main ingredient of chewing gum

chicory ('chikəri) *n.* salad plant of which the root is ground and used with, or instead of, coffee

chide (chīd) *vt.* scold, reprove, censure (**chid** *pt.*, **'chidden, chid** *pp.*, **'chiding** *pr.p.*)

chief (chēf) *n.* **1.** head or principal person —*a.* **2.** principal, foremost, leading —'**chiefly** *adv.* —**chieftain** ('chēftən, -tin) *n.* leader, chief of clan or tribe —**chief petty officer** senior naval rank for personnel without commissioned or warrant rank

chiffchaff ('chifchaf) *n.* common European warbler

chiffon (shi'fon, 'shifon) *n.* thin gauzy material —**chiffo'nier** *n.* ornamental cupboard

chigger ('chigər) *n.* any of various small mites in their larval stage which attack man

chignon ('shēnyon) *n.* roll, knot of hair worn at back of head

chigoe ('chigō) *n.* tropical flea, female of

which burrows into skin of man *etc.* (*also* **'chigger**)

Chihuahua (chi'wäwä, -wə) *n.* breed of tiny dog, *orig.* from Mexico

chilblain ('chilblān) *n.* inflamed sore on hands, legs *etc.*, due to cold (*also* **pernio**)

child (chīld) *n.* **1.** young human being **2.** offspring (*pl.* **children** ('childrən)) —**'childhood** *n.* period between birth and puberty —**'childish** *a.* **1.** of or like a child **2.** silly **3.** trifling —**'childishly** *adv.* —**'childless** *a.* —**'childlike** *a.* **1.** of or like a child **2.** innocent **3.** frank **4.** docile —**'childbed** *n.* state of giving birth to child —**'childbirth** *n.* act of giving birth: in humans, takes place about 280 days after the last menstrual period —**child's play** very easy task

Chile ('chili) *n.* country in South America bounded north by Peru, east by Bolivia and Argentina, and south and west by the Pacific Ocean

chili ('chili) *n.* **1.** small red hot-tasting seed pod **2.** plant producing it

chiliad ('kiliad) *n.* **1.** group of one thousand **2.** thousand years —**chili'astic** *a.*

chill (chil) *n.* **1.** coldness **2.** cold with shivering **3.** anything that damps, discourages —*v.* **4.** make, become cold (*esp.* food, drink) —**chilled** *a.* —**'chilliness** *n.* —**'chilly** *a.*

chime (chīm) *n.* **1.** sound of bell **2.** harmonious, ringing sound —*pl.* **3.** orchestral percussion instrument consisting of a set of about eighteen metal tubes suspended from a frame and struck with a hammer —*vi.* **4.** ring harmoniously **5.** agree —*vt.* **6.** strike (bells) —**chime in** come into conversation with agreement

chimera *or* **chimaera** (kī'mēərə, ki-) *n.* **1.** fabled monster, made up of parts of various animals **2.** wild fancy **3.** living organism in which two separate kinds of tissue exist —**chimeric(al)** (kī'merik(əl), ki-) *a.* fanciful

chimney ('chimni) *n.* **1.** a passage for smoke **2.** narrow vertical cleft in rock (*pl.* **-s**)

chimp (chimp) *n. inf.* chimpanzee

chimpanzee (chimpan'zē) *n.* gregarious, intelligent ape of Afr.

chin (chin) *n.* part of face below mouth

china ('chīnə) *n.* **1.** fine earthenware, porcelain **2.** cups, saucers *etc.* collectively —**china clay** kaolin

China ('chīnə) *n.* **1. People's Republic of China.** country in Asia bounded north by the U.S.S.R. and Mongolia, east by Korea, the Yellow Sea and the East China Sea, with Hong Kong and Macao as enclaves on the southeast coast, south by Vietnam, Laos, Burma, India, Bhutan and Nepal, west by India, Pakistan, Afghanistan and the U.S.S.R. **2. Republic of China.** *see* TAIWAN

chincherinchee (chinchərin'chē) *n.* S Afr. plant with white or yellow flower spikes

chinchilla (chin'chilə) *n.* S Amer. rodent with soft, gray fur —**chinchilla cloth** durable fabric with small balls and loops on surface —**chinchilla rabbit** breed of rabbit with bluish-white black-tipped pelt

chine (chīn) *n.* **1.** backbone **2.** joint of meat **3.** ridge or crest of land **4.** intersection of bottom and sides of flat-bottom boat

Chinese (chī'nēz) *a.* **1.** of China, its people or their languages —*n.* **2.** native of China or descendant of one (*pl.* **-ese**) **3.** any of languages of China —**Chinese checkers** *see* CHECKERS —**Chinese lantern** Asian plant cultivated for its orange-red inflated calyx

chink[1] (chingk) *n.* cleft, crack

chink[2] (chingk) *n.* **1.** light metallic sound —*v.* **2.** (cause to) make this sound

chino ('chēnō) *n.* tan-colored cotton fabric used for men's trousers and summer army uniforms

chinoiserie (shēnwäzə'rē, -'wäzəri) *n.* **1.** style of decorative art based on imitations of Chinese motifs **2.** object or objects in this style

Chinook (shi'nŏŏk, -'nŏŏk) *n.* **1.** member of Amerindian people of Oregon (*pl.* **-nook, -s**) **2.** (**c-**) warm moist SW wind of W coast of U.S.A. from Oregon northward or warm dry wind descending eastern slopes of the Rocky Mountains —**Chi'nookan** *n.* language of the Chinook —**Chinook salmon** large red-fleshed salmon occurring in N Pacific Ocean

chintz (chints) *n.* cotton cloth printed in colored designs with glazed finish

chip (chip) *n.* **1.** splinter **2.** place where piece has been broken off **3.** thin strip of potato, fried **4.** tiny wafer of silicon or other semiconductor forming integrated circuit in computer *etc.* —*vt.* **5.** chop into small pieces **6.** break small pieces from **7.** shape by cutting off pieces —*vi.* **8.** break off (**-pp-**) —**chip-based** *a.* using microchips in electronic equipment —**'chipboard** *n.* paperboard made from waste paper —**chip in 1.** interrupt **2.** contribute

chipmunk ('chipmungk) *n.* small, striped N Amer. squirrel

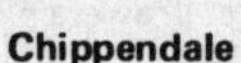

Chippendale

Chippendale ('chipəndāl) *a.* (of furniture) in

style of Thomas Chippendale (1718–79), characterized by use of Chinese and Gothic motifs *etc.*

Chippewa (ˈchipiwŏ, -wä) *n. see* OJIBWA (*pl.* **-wa, -s**)

chirography (kīˈrogrəfi) *n.* penmanship

chiromancy (ˈkīrəmansi) *n.* palmistry —ˈ**chiromancer** *n.*

chiropodist (kiˈropədist) *n.* one who treats disorders of feet —**chiˈropody** *n.* podiatry

chiropractor (ˈkīrəpraktər) *n.* one skilled in treating bodily disorders by manipulation, massage *etc.* —**chiroˈpractic** *n.* the principle and method of drugless healing

chirp (chərp) *n.* **1.** short, sharp cry of bird —*vi.* **2.** make this sound —ˈ**chirpy** *a. inf.* happy

chisel (ˈchizəl) *n.* **1.** cutting tool, usu. bar of steel with edge across main axis —*vt.* **2.** cut, carve with chisel **3.** *sl.* cheat

chit[1] (chit) *n.* informal note, memorandum

chit[2] (chit) *n.* child, young girl

chitchat (ˈchitchat) *n.* **1.** gossip —*vi.* **2.** gossip

chitin (ˈkītin) *n.* polysaccharide that is principal component of outer coverings of arthropods *etc.* —ˈ**chitinous** *a.*

chivalry (ˈshivəlri) *n.* **1.** bravery and courtesy **2.** medieval system of knighthood —ˈ**chivalrous** *a.* —ˈ**chivalrously** *adv.*

chive (chīv) *n.* herb with mild onion flavor

chivy, chivvy (ˈchivi), *or* **chevy** (ˈchevi) **UK** *vt.* **1.** harass; nag **2.** hunt —*vi.* **3.** run about (ˈ**chivied,** ˈ**chivying,** ˈ**chivvied,** ˈ**chivvying** *or* ˈ**chevied,** ˈ**chevying**) —*n.* **4.** hunt **5.** *obs.* hunting cry

chloral hydrate (ˈklŏrəl) colorless crystalline soluble solid produced by reaction of chloral with water and used as sedative

chloramphenicol (klŏramˈfenikol) *n.* broad-spectrum antibiotic derived from a soil microorganism or prepared synthetically

chlorine (ˈklŏrēn) *n. Chem.* nonmetallic element *Symbol* Cl, at. wt. 35.5, at. no. 17 —ˈ**chlorate** *n.* salt of chloric acid —ˈ**chloric** *a.* —ˈ**chloride** *n.* **1.** compound of chlorine **2.** bleaching agent —ˈ**chlorinate** *vt.* **1.** disinfect **2.** purify with chlorine

chloroform (ˈklŏrəfŏrm) *n.* **1.** compound of carbon, hydrogen and chlorine used as anesthetic, liniment, cleansing agent, solvent for fats and oils, and antifreeze —*vt.* **2.** render insensible with it

Chloromycetin (klŏrōmīˈsētin) *n.* trade name for chloramphenicol

chlorophyll (ˈklŏrəfil) *n.* green coloring matter in plants

Chloroquine (ˈklŏrōkwēn) *n.* antimalarial drug

chlorpromazine (klŏrˈproməzēn) *n.* tranquilizing drug used to treat anxiety, as pain reliever, antiemetic and treatment for hiccups (trade name Thorazine)

chlorpropamide (klŏrˈpropəmīd) *n.* drug taken by mouth as pill to control diabetes

chock (chok) *n.* block or wedge to prevent heavy object rolling or sliding —**chock-full** *or* **chock-a-block** *a.* packed full

chocolate (ˈchokəlit, ˈchoklit, -lət) *n.* **1.** paste from ground cacao seeds **2.** confectionery, drink made from this —*a.* **3.** dark brown —**choc-ice** *n.* chocolate-covered slice of ice cream —**chocolate-box** *a. inf.* sentimentally pretty or appealing

Choctaw (ˈchoktŏ) *n.* **1.** member of Amerindian people of Mississippi, Alabama and Louisiana (*pl.* **-taw, -s**) **2.** the Muskogean language of the Choctaw people

choice (chois) *n.* **1.** act or power of choosing **2.** alternative **3.** thing or person chosen —*a.* **4.** select, fine, worthy of being chosen —ˈ**choicely** *adv.*

choir (ˈkwīər) *n.* **1.** band of singers, *esp.* in church **2.** part of church set aside for them

choke (chōk) *vt.* **1.** hinder, stop the breathing of **2.** smother, stifle **3.** obstruct —*vi.* **4.** suffer choking —*n.* **5.** act, noise of choking **6.** device in carburetor to increase richness of fuel-air mixture —**choked** *a.* —ˈ**choker** *n.* **1.** woman's high collar **2.** neckband or necklace worn tightly around throat **3.** high clerical collar; stock **4.** person or thing that chokes —ˈ**chokebore** *n.* gun with bore narrowed toward muzzle —ˈ**chokedamp** *n.* carbon dioxide gas in coal mines

cholecystectomy (kolisisˈtektəmi) *n.* surgical removal of the gall bladder

choler (ˈkolər) *n.* bile, anger —ˈ**choleric** *a.* bad-tempered

cholera (ˈkolərə) *n.* acute bacterial infection of the gastrointestinal tract caused by contaminated water

cholesterol (kəˈlestərol) *n.* organic compound found in all tissues of the human body *esp.* the brain and spinal cord

chomp (chomp) *v.* chew noisily

choose (chōōz) *vt.* **1.** pick out, select **2.** take by preference —*vi.* **3.** decide, think fit (**chose,** ˈ**chosen,** ˈ**choosing**) —ˈ**chooser** *n.* —ˈ**choosy** *a.* fussy

chop[1] (chop) *vt.* **1.** cut with blow **2.** hack (**-pp-**) —*n.* **3.** hewing blow **4.** slice of meat containing rib or other bone —ˈ**chopper** *n.* **1.** short ax **2.** *inf.* helicopter **3.** *inf.* customized motorcycle **4.** high-bouncing batted baseball —ˈ**choppy** *a.* (of sea) having short, broken waves

chop[2] (chop) *vt.* exchange, bandy (*esp. in* **chop logic, chop and change**) (**-pp-**)

chops (chops) *pl.n. inf.* jaws, cheeks

chopsticks (ˈchopstiks) *pl.n.* implements used for eating food, orig. Chinese

chop suey (ˈsōōi) dish of stir-fried vegetables and meat or fish served with rice

choral (ˈkŏrəl) *a.* of, for, sung by, a choir

chorale *or* **choral** (kəˈral) *n.* slow, stately hymn tune

chord (körd) *n.* **1.** emotional response, *esp.* of sympathy **2.** simultaneous sounding of musical notes **3.** straight line joining ends of arc

chordotomy (kör'dotəmi) *n.* surgical severance of pain-carrying nerve fibers in the spinal cord

chore (chör) *n.* **1.** (unpleasant) task **2.** odd job

chorea (kə'rēə) *n.* disorder of central nervous system characterized by uncontrollable jerky movements (*also* **Saint Vitus's dance, Sydenham's chorea**)

choreography (köri'ogrəfi) *n.* art of arranging dances, *esp.* ballet —**chore'ographer** *n.* —**choreo'graphic** *a.*

choreology (köri'oləji) *n.* notation of ballet dancing

chorography (kə'rogrəfi) *n.* art of describing and making maps of particular regions —**choro'graphic** *a.*

choroid ('köroid) *or* **chorioid** ('körioid) *n.* vascular membrane of eyeball between sclera and retina

chorology (kə'roləji) *n.* science of geographical distribution of plants and animals —**cho'rologist** *n.*

chortle ('chörtəl) *vi.* **1.** chuckle happily —*n.* **2.** gleeful chuckle

chorus ('körəs) *n.* **1.** band of singers **2.** combination of voices singing together **3.** refrain —*vt.* **4.** sing or say together —**choric** ('korik) *a.* —**chorister** ('koristər) *n.*

chose (chōz) *pt. of* CHOOSE —**'chosen** *pp. of* CHOOSE

chough (chuf) *n.* black passerine bird of Europe, Asia and Afr., with red bill

choux pastry (sho͞o) very light pastry made with eggs

chow (chow) *n. inf.* food

chow-chow *n.* thick-coated dog with curled tail, *orig.* from China (*also* **chow**)

chowder ('chowdər) *n.* thick soup or stew containing clams or fish

chow mein (mān) Chinese dish consisting of sliced vegetables and meat, poultry or shellfish on a noodle base

chrism ('krizəm) *n.* mixture of olive oil and balsam used for sacramental anointing

Christ (krīst) *n.* **1.** Jesus of Nazareth, regarded by Christians as fulfilling Old Testament prophecies of Messiah **2.** Messiah as subject of Old Testament prophecies **3.** image of Christ —*interj.* **4.** *offens. sl.* oath expressing annoyance *etc.* (*see also* JESUS)

Christian ('krischən) *n.* **1.** follower of Christ —*a.* **2.** following Christ **3.** relating to Christ or his religion **4.** exhibiting kindness or goodness —**christen** ('krisən) *vt.* baptize, give name to —**Christendom** ('krisəndəm) *n.* all the Christian world —**Christi'anity** *n.* religion of Christ —**'christianize** *vt.* —**Christian name** name given at baptism —**Christian Science** religious system of Church of Christ, Scientist, emphasizing spiritual healing and unreality of matter

christie *or* **christy** ('kristi) *n. Skiing* turn in which body is swung sharply round with skis parallel

Christmas ('krisməs) *n.* festival of birth of Christ —**'Christmassy** *a.* —**Christmas card** —**Christmas Day** Dec. 25th, U.S. national holiday —**Christmas rose** evergreen plant of S Europe and W Asia, with white or pinkish winter-blooming flowers (*also* **'hellebore, winter rose**) —**Christmas tree**

chromatic (krə'matik) *a.* **1.** of color **2.** *Mus.* of raised or lowered notes instead of normal degrees of the scale

chromatin ('krōmətin) *n.* part of protoplasmic substance in nucleus of cells which takes color in staining tests

chromatography (krōmə'togrəfi) *n.* technique of separating and analyzing components of mixture by selective adsorption in column of powder or on strip of paper

chrome (krōm) *n.* metal used in alloys and for plating

chromium ('krōmiəm) *n. Chem.* metallic element *Symbol* Cr, at. wt. 52.0, at. no. 24

chromosome ('krōməsōm) *n.* body found in the nucleus of all plant and animal cells, always occurring in pairs and incorporating genes

chromosphere ('krōməsfēər) *n.* layer of incandescent gas surrounding the sun

Chron. Chronicles

chronic ('kronik) *a.* **1.** lasting a long time **2.** habitual **3.** *inf.* serious **4.** *inf.* of bad quality

chronicle ('kronikəl) *n.* **1.** record of events in order of time **2.** account —*vt.* **3.** record —**'chronicler** *n.*

Chronicles ('kronikəlz) *pl.n.* (*with sing. v.*) *Bible* 13th and 14th books of the O.T., which record the genealogies of Adam, Saul's life and David's victory over Philistines, reign of Solomon, kings of Judah

chronology (krə'noləji) *n.* **1.** determination of sequence of past events **2.** arrangement in order of occurrence —**chrono'logical** *a.* arranged in order of time —**chrono'logically** *adv.* —**chro'nologist** *n.*

chronometer (krə'nomitər) *n.* **1.** instrument for measuring time exactly **2.** watch —**chrono'metrical** *a.* —**chro'nometry** *n.*

chrysalis ('krisəlis) *n.* **1.** resting state of insect between grub and butterfly *etc.* **2.** case enclosing it (*pl.* **-es, chrysalides** (kri'salidēz))

chrysanthemum (kri'santhəməm) *n.* garden flower of various colors

chrysoberyl ('krisəberil) *n.* yellowish mineral consisting of an aluminum-iron compound used as a gem

chrysolite ('krisəlīt) *n.* an olive-green semiprecious stone

chub (chub) *n.* **1.** European freshwater fish **2.**

any of various N Amer. fishes, *esp.* whitefishes and minnows

chubby ('chubi) *a.* plump

chuck[1] (chuk) *vt.* **1.** *inf.* throw **2.** pat affectionately (under chin) **3.** *inf.* give up, reject

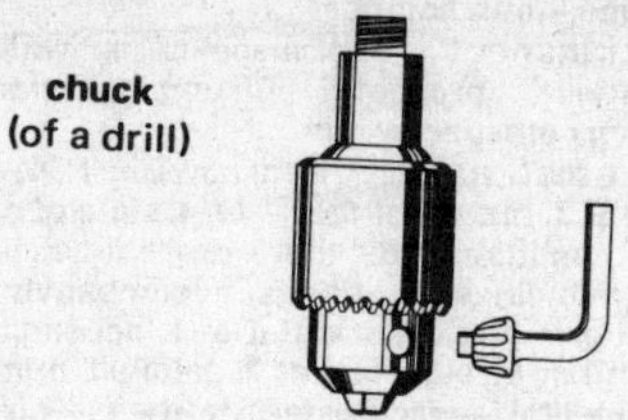

chuck[2] (chuk) *n.* **1.** cut of beef **2.** device for gripping, adjusting bit in power drill *etc.*

chuckle ('chukəl) *vi.* **1.** laugh softly —*n.* **2.** such laugh —'**chucklehead** *n. inf.* stupid person; blockhead; dolt

chuff (chuf) *n.* **1.** puffing sound as of steam engine —*vi.* **2.** move while emitting such sounds

chug (chug) *n.* **1.** short dull sound, such as that made by engine —*vi.* **2.** (of engine *etc.*) operate while making such sounds (**-gg-**)

chukker, chukkar ('chukər), *or* **chukka** ('chukə) *n.* period of play in game of polo

chum (chum) *n. inf.* close friend —'**chummy** *a.*

chump (chump) *n.* **1.** *inf.* stupid person **2.** heavy block of wood **3.** thick blunt end of anything, *esp.* meat

chunk (chungk) *n.* thick, solid piece —'**chunky** *a.*

church (chərch) *n.* **1.** building for Christian worship **2.** (**C-**) whole body or sect of Christians **3.** clergy —'**churchman** *n.* —**Church of Christ** Protestant Christian denomination whose doctrine is based on basic New Testament faith and is highly tolerant in doctrinal and religious matters —**Church of England** reformed state Church in England, with Sovereign as temporal head —'**churchwarden** *n.* **1.** officer who represents interests of parish **2.** long clay pipe —'**churchyard** *n.*

churl (chərl) *n.* **1.** rustic **2.** ill-bred fellow —'**churlish** *a.* —'**churlishly** *adv.* —'**churlishness** *n.*

churn (chərn) *n.* **1.** large container for milk **2.** vessel for making butter —*v.* **3.** shake up, stir (liquid) violently

chute (sho͞ot) *n.* **1.** slide for sending down parcels, coal *etc.* **2.** channel **3.** slide into swimming pool **4.** narrow passageway, *eg* for spraying, counting cattle, sheep *etc.* **5.** *inf.* parachute

chutney ('chutni) *n.* pickle of fruit, spices *etc.*

chutzpa *or* **chutzpah** ('ho͝otspə) *n.* shameless audacity, presumption or gall

chyle (kīl) *n.* milky fluid composed of lymph and emulsified fat globules, formed in small intestine during digestion

chyme (kīm) *n.* thick fluid mass of partially digested food that leaves stomach

C.I.A. Central Intelligence Agency

cicada (si'kādə) *or* **cicala** (si'kälə) *n.* cricketlike insect

cicatrix ('sikətriks) *n.* scar of healed wound —**cicatri'zation** *n.* —'**cicatrize** *v.* heal

cicely ('sisəli) *n.* perennial plant similar to chervil, used as herb (*also* **sweet cicely**)

cicerone (sisə'rōni, chēch-) *n.* person who conducts and informs sightseers (*pl.* **-s, -ni** (-ni))

C.I.D. Criminal Investigation Department

-cide (*n. comb. form*) **1.** person or thing that kills, as in *insecticide* **2.** killing; murder, as in *homicide* —**-cidal** (*a. comb. form*)

cider ('sīdər) *n.* drink made from apples

c.i.f. *or* **C.I.F.** cost, insurance and freight (included in price quoted)

cigar (si'gär) *n.* roll of tobacco leaves for smoking —**ciga'rette** *n.* finely-cut tobacco rolled in paper for smoking

cilium ('siliəm) *n.* **1.** short thread projecting from surface of cell *etc.*, whose rhythmic beating causes movement **2.** eyelash (*pl.* **cilia** ('siliə)) —'**ciliary** *a.* of cilia —'**ciliate** *or* '**ciliated** *a.* —**ciliary body** part of eye that joins choroid to iris

C in C *or* **C.-in-C.** Commander-in-Chief

cinch (sinch) *n. inf.* easy task, certainty

cinchona (sing'kōnə) *n.* **1.** tree or shrub of S Amer. having medicinal bark **2.** dried bark of this tree, which yields quinine **3.** any of drugs derived from cinchona bark

cincture ('singkchər) *n.* something that encircles, *esp.* belt or girdle

cinder ('sindər) *n.* remains of burned coal

Cinderella (sində'relə) *n.* **1.** girl who achieves fame after being obscure **2.** poor, neglected or unsuccessful person or thing

cine- (*comb. form*) relating to motion pictures

cinema ('sinimə) *n.* **1.** motion picture **2.** motion-picture theater **3.** motion pictures generally or collectively —**cine'matograph** *n.* combined camera, printer and projector —**cinema'tography** *n.*

cineraria (sinə'reriə, -'rar-) *n.* garden plant with daisylike flowers

cinerarium (sinə'reriəm, -'rar-) *n.* place for keeping ashes of dead after cremation (*pl.* **-ria** (-riə))

cinerary ('sinəreri) *a.* pert. to ashes

cinnabar ('sinəbär) *n.* **1.** heavy red mineral consisting of mercuric sulfide: chief ore of mercury **2.** red form of mercuric sulfide, *esp.* when used as pigment **3.** bright red;

vermilion **4.** large red-and-black European moth

cinnamon ('sinəmən) *n.* **1.** spice got from bark of Asian tree **2.** the tree —*a.* **3.** of light-brown color

cinque (singk) *n.* number five in cards, dice *etc.* —**cinquecento** (chingkwi'chentō) *n.* the 16th cent. *esp.* when referring to Italian art and literature —'**cinquefoil** *n.* plant with five-lobed leaves

cipher ('sīfər) *n.* **1.** secret writing **2.** arithmetical symbol **3.** person of no importance **4.** monogram —*vt.* **5.** write in cipher

circa ('sərkə) *Lat.* about, approximately

circadian (sər'kādiən) *a.* of biological processes that occur at 24-hour intervals

circle ('sərkəl) *n.* **1.** perfectly round plane figure **2.** line enclosing it with every point on the line the same distance from the center **3.** ring **4.** group, society with common interest **5.** spiritualist seance **6.** class of society —*vt.* **7.** surround —*vi.* **8.** move round —'**circular** *a.* **1.** round **2.** moving round —*n.* **3.** letter sent to several persons —**circulari'zation** *n.* —'**circularize** *vt.* **1.** distribute circulars to **2.** canvass or petition, as for votes *etc.* by distributing letters *etc.* **3.** make circular —'**circulate** *vi.* **1.** move round **2.** pass from hand to hand or place to place —*vt.* **3.** send round —**circu'lation** *n.* **1.** flow of blood from, and back to, heart **2.** act of moving round **3.** extent of sale of periodical —'**circulatory** *a.* —**circular saw** saw in which circular disk with toothed edge is rotated at high speed —**circulating library** lending library —**circulatory system** system of blood vessels, heart *etc.* involved in the circulation of blood and lymph

circuit ('sərkit) *n.* **1.** complete round or course **2.** area **3.** path of electric current **4.** round of visitation, *esp.* of judges **5.** series of sporting events **6.** district —**circuitous** (sər'kyōōitəs) *a.* roundabout, indirect —**circuitously** (sər'kyōōitəsli) *adv.* —'**circuitry** *n.* electrical circuit(s) —**circuit breaker** device that under abnormal conditions stops flow of current in electrical circuit

circum- (*comb. form*) around; surrounding; on all sides, as in *circumlocution, circumpolar.* Such compounds are not given here where the meaning may easily be found from the simple word

circumambient (sərkəm'ambiənt) *a.* surrounding

circumcise ('sərkəmsīz) *vt.* cut off foreskin of —**circum'cision** *n.*

circumference (sər'kumfərəns) *n.* boundary line, *esp.* of circle

circumflex ('sərkəmfleks) *n.* **1.** mark (^) placed over vowel to show it is pronounced with rising and falling pitch or as long vowel —*a.* **2.** (of nerves *etc.*) bending or curving around

circumlocution (sərkəmlə'kyōōshən) *n.* roundabout speech

circumnavigate (sərkəm'navigāt) *vt.* sail or fly right round —**circumnavi'gation** *n.* —**circum'navigator** *n.*

circumscribe ('sərkəmskrīb) *vt.* confine, bound, limit, hamper

circumspect ('sərkəmspekt) *a.* watchful, cautious, prudent —**circum'spection** *n.* —'**circumspectly** *adv.*

circumstance ('sərkəmstans) *n.* **1.** detail **2.** event **3.** matter of fact —*pl.* **4.** state of affairs **5.** condition in life, *esp.* financial **6.** surroundings or things accompanying an action —**circum'stantial** *a.* **1.** depending on detail or circumstances **2.** detailed, minute **3.** incidental —**circumstanti'ality** *n.* —**circum'stantially** *adv.* —**circum'stantiate** *vt.* **1.** prove by details **2.** describe exactly —**circumstantial evidence** indirect evidence that tends to establish conclusion by inference

circumvent (sərkəm'vent) *vt.* outwit, evade, get round —**circum'vention** *n.*

circus ('sərkəs) *n.* **1.** (performance of) traveling group of acrobats, clowns, performing animals *etc.* **2.** circular structure for public shows

ciré ('sērā) *n.* **1.** any supple fabric with highly lustrous and smooth finish **2.** satin treated with surface wax

cirque (sərk) *n.* steep-sided semicircular depression found in mountainous regions

cirrhosis (si'rōsis) *n.* any of various chronic progressive diseases of liver —**cirrhotic** (si'rotik) *a.*

cirrus ('sirəs) *n.* high wispy cloud (*pl.* **cirri** ('sirī)) —**cirro'cumulus** *n.* high cloud of ice crystals grouped into small separate globular masses (*pl.* **-li** (-lī)) —**cirro'stratus** *n.* uniform layer of cloud above about 6000 meters (*pl.* **-tai** (-tī))

cisco ('siskō) *n.* N Amer. whitefish (*pl.* **-s, -es**)

cist (sist) *n.* neolithic burial chamber made from stone slabs

Cistercian (si'stərshən) *n.* member of Christian order of monks and nuns, which follows strict form of Benedictine rule (*also* **White Monk**)

cistern ('sistərn) *n.* water tank

cistus ('sistəs) *n.* any of various shrubs or herbaceous plants cultivated for yellow-white or reddish roselike flowers (*also* '**rockrose**)

citadel ('sitədəl, -del) *n.* fortress in, near or commanding a city

cite (sīt) *vt.* **1.** quote **2.** bring forward as proof **3.** commend (soldier *etc.*) for outstanding bravery *etc.* **4.** summon to appear before court of law —**ci'tation** *n.* **1.** quoting **2.** commendation for bravery *etc.*

cithara ('sithərə, 'kith-) *n.* *see* KITHARA

citizen ('sitizən) *n.* **1.** native, naturalized member of state, nation *etc.* **2.** inhabitant of city —'**citizenry** *n.* citizens collectively —'**citizenship** *n.* —**citizens band** range of radio frequencies assigned officially for use by public for private communication

citron ('sitrən) *n.* **1.** fruit like a lemon **2.** the tree —'**citric** *a.* of the acid of lemon or citron —**citric acid cycle** *see* KREBS CYCLE —**citrus fruit** fruit covered by leathery rind with acidic juicy pulp divided into segments by a membrane

citronella (sitrə'nelə) *n.* **1.** tropical Asian grass with bluish-green lemon-scented leaves **2.** aromatic oil obtained from this grass, used in perfumes *etc.* (*also* **citronella oil**)

cittern ('sitərn), **cither** ('sidhər), *or* **cithern** ('sidhərn) *n.* medieval stringed instrument resembling lute but having wire strings and flat back

city ('siti) *n.* large town —**city editor** (on newspaper) editor in charge of local news —**city father** person who is prominent in public affairs of city —**the City 1.** area in central London where United Kingdom's major financial business is transacted **2.** financial institutions located in this area

civet ('sivit) *n.* strong, musky perfume —**civet-cat** *n.* catlike animal producing it

civic ('sivik) *a.* pert. to city or citizen —'**civics** *pl.n.* (*with sing. v.*) study of the rights and responsibilities of citizenship

civil ('sivəl) *a.* **1.** relating to citizens of state **2.** not military **3.** refined, polite **4.** *Law* not criminal —**ci'vilian** *n.* nonmilitary person —**ci'vility** *n.* —'**civilly** *adv.* —**civil defense** organizing of civilians to deal with enemy attacks —**civil disobedience** refusal to obey laws, pay taxes *etc.*: nonviolent means of protesting —**civil engineer** person qualified to design and construct roads, bridges *etc.* —**civil engineering** —**civil law 1.** law of state relating to private affairs **2.** body of law in ancient Rome, *esp.* as applicable to private citizens **3.** law based on Roman system —**civil liberty** right of individual to freedom of speech and action —**civil marriage** *Law* marriage performed by official other than clergyman —**civil rights** *pl.n.* **1.** personal rights of individual citizen —*a.* **2.** of equality in social, economic and political rights —**civil service** service responsible for public administration of government of a country —**civil war** war between factions within same nation

civilize ('sivilīz) *vt.* **1.** bring out of barbarism **2.** refine —**civili'zation** *n.* —'**civilized** *a.*

civvy ('sivi) *sl. n.* **1.** civilian —*pl.* **2.** civilian clothing —**civvy street** civilian life

cl centiliter

Cl *Chem.* chlorine

clack (klak) *n.* **1.** sound, as of two pieces of wood striking together —*v.* **2.** make such sound **3.** jabber

clad (klad) *pt./pp. of* **clothe** (*see* CLOTH)

cladding ('klading) *n.* material used for outside facing of building *etc.*

claim (klām) *vt.* **1.** demand as right **2.** assert **3.** call for —*n.* **4.** demand for thing supposed due **5.** right **6.** thing claimed **7.** plot of mining land marked out by stakes as required by law —'**claimant** *n.*

clairvoyance (klāər'voiəns) *n.* power of seeing things not present to senses, second sight —**clair'voyant** *n./a.*

clam (klam) *n.* edible mollusk

clamber ('klambər) *vi.* climb with difficulty or awkwardly

clammy ('klami) *a.* moist and sticky —'**clamminess** *n.*

clamor ('klamər) *n.* **1.** loud shouting, outcry, noise —*vi.* **2.** shout, call noisily —'**clamorous** *a.* —'**clamorously** *adv.*

clamp[1] (klamp) *n.* **1.** tool for holding or compressing —*vt.* **2.** fasten, strengthen with or as with clamp

clamp[2] (klamp) *n.* **1.** mound of harvested root crop, covered with straw and earth to protect it from winter weather —*vt.* **2.** enclose in mound

clan (klan) *n.* **1.** tribe or collection of families under chief and of common ancestry **2.** faction, group —'**clannish** *a.* —'**clannishly** *adv.* —'**clannishness** *n.*

clandestine (klan'destin) *a.* **1.** secret **2.** sly

clang (klang) *v.* **1.** (cause to) make loud ringing sound —*n.* **2.** loud ringing sound —'**clanger** *n.* **1.** *inf.* conspicuous mistake **2.** that which clangs

clangor ('klangər, 'klanggər) *n.* **1.** loud resonant noise **2.** uproar —*vi.* **3.** make loud resonant noise —'**clangorous** *a.*

clank (klangk) *n.* **1.** short sound as of pieces of metal struck together —*v.* **2.** cause, move with, such sound

clap[1] (klap) *v.* **1.** (cause to) strike with noise **2.** strike (hands) together **3.** applaud —*vt.* **4.** pat **5.** place or put quickly (**-pp-**) —*n.* **6.** hard, explosive sound **7.** slap —'**clapper** *n.* —'**clapping** *n.* —'**claptrap** *n. inf.* empty words

clap[2] (klap) *n. sl.* gonorrhea

claque (klak) *n.* **1.** group of people hired to applaud **2.** group of fawning admirers

claret ('klarət) *n.* a dry dark red wine of Bordeaux

clarify ('klarifī) *v.* make or become clear, pure or more easily understood (**-fied, -fying**) —**clarifi'cation** *n.* —'**clarity** *n.* clearness

clarinet (klari'net) *n.* orchestral woodwind musical instrument formed like a cylindrical pipe with holes closed by keys ending in a bell, with a mouthpiece which has a single reed fixed to its back, available in many sizes and types

clarion ('klariən) *n.* **1.** clear-sounding trumpet **2.** rousing sound

clary ('klāəri) *n.* herb

clash (klash) *n.* **1.** loud noise, as of weapons striking **2.** conflict, collision —*vi.* **3.** make clash **4.** come into conflict **5.** (of events) coincide **6.** (of colors) look ugly together —*vt.* **7.** strike together to make clash

clasp (klasp) *n.* **1.** hook or other means of fastening **2.** embrace —*vt.* **3.** fasten **4.** embrace, grasp —**clasp knife** large knife with one or more blades or other devices folding into handle

class (klas) *n.* **1.** any division, order, kind, sort **2.** rank **3.** group of persons taught together **4.** persons graduating in same year **5.** *Biol.* taxonomic category of plants and animals below phylum and above order **6.** division by merit **7.** quality **8.** *inf.* excellence; elegance —*vt.* **9.** assign to proper division —**classifi'cation** *n.* —**'classified** *a.* **1.** arranged in classes **2.** secret **3.** (of advertisements) arranged under headings in newspapers —**'classify** *vt.* arrange methodically in classes (**-fied, -fying**) —**'classy** *a. inf.* stylish, elegant —**class-conscious** *a.* aware of belonging to particular social rank —**class-consciousness** *n.*

classic ('klasik) *a.* **1.** of first rank **2.** of highest rank generally, but *esp.* of art **3.** (of clothing) in simple style based on excellence of cut, proportion and color **4.** refined **5.** typical **6.** famous —*n.* **7.** (literary) work of recognized excellence —*pl.* **8.** ancient Latin and Greek literature —**'classical** *a.* **1.** of Greek and Roman literature, art, culture **2.** of classic quality **3.** *Mus.* of established standards of form, complexity *etc.* —**'classically** *adv.* —**'classicism** *n.* —**'classicist** *n.*

clatter ('klatər) *n.* **1.** rattling noise **2.** noisy conversation —*v.* **3.** (cause to) make clatter

clause (klöz) *n.* **1.** part of sentence, containing verb **2.** article in formal document as treaty, contract *etc.*

claustrophobia (klöstrə'fōbiə) *n.* abnormal fear of confined spaces

clavichord ('klavikörd) *n.* earliest type of stringed keyboard musical instrument made of small rectangular wooden box with keyboard of three octaves and strings running parallel to keyboard

clavicle ('klavikəl) *n.* collarbone —**cla'vicular** *a.* pert. to this

clavier (klə'vēər, 'klavēər) *n.* generic name for the stringed keyboard instruments: clavichord, harpsichord and pianoforte

claw (klö) *n.* **1.** sharp hooked nail of bird or beast **2.** foot of bird of prey **3.** clawlike article —*vt.* **4.** tear with claws **5.** grip

clay (klā) *n.* **1.** fine-grained earth, plastic when wet, hardening when baked **2.** earth —**'clayey** *a.* —**clay pigeon** disk of baked clay hurled into air as target to be shot at

claymore ('klāmör) *n.* ancient Highland two-edged sword

CLC Canadian Labor Congress

clean (klēn) *a.* **1.** free from dirt, stain or defilement **2.** pure **3.** guiltless **4.** trim, shapely —*adv.* **5.** so as to leave no dirt **6.** entirely —*vt.* **7.** free from dirt —**'cleaner** *n.* —**cleanliness** ('klenlinis) *n.* —**cleanly** ('klēnli) *adv.* **1.** in a clean manner —*a.* ('klenli) **2.** clean —**'cleanness** *n.* —**cleanse** (klenz) *vt.* make clean —**cleanser** ('klenzər) *n.* preparation used for cleaning —**clean-cut** *a.* **1.** clearly outlined; neat **2.** definite —**come clean** *inf.* confess

clear (klēər) *a.* **1.** pure, undimmed, bright **2.** free from cloud **3.** transparent **4.** plain, distinct **5.** without defect or drawback **6.** unimpeded —*adv.* **7.** brightly **8.** wholly, quite —*vt.* **9.** make clear **10.** acquit **11.** pass over or through **12.** make as profit **13.** free from obstruction, difficulty **14.** free by payment of dues —*vi.* **15.** become clear, bright, free, transparent —**'clearance** *n.* **1.** making clear **2.** removal of obstructions, surplus stock *etc.* **3.** certificate that ship has been cleared at customhouse **4.** space for moving part, vehicle, to pass within, through or past something —**'clearing** *n.* land cleared of trees —**'clearly** *adv.* —**'clearness** *n.* —**clear-cut** *a.* **1.** definite; not vague **2.** clearly outlined —**clearing house 1.** *Banking* institution where checks *etc.* drawn on member banks are canceled against each other **2.** central agency for collection and distribution of information —**clear-sighted** *a.* discerning

clearstory ('klēərstöri) *n. see* CLERESTORY

cleat (klēt) *n.* **1.** wedge **2.** piece of wood or iron with two projecting ends around which ropes are made fast

cleave[1] (klēv) *vt.* **1.** split asunder —*vi.* **2.** crack, part asunder (**clove, cleft** *pt.*, **'cloven, cleft** *pp.*, **'cleaving** *pr.p.*) —**'cleavage** *n.* **1.** separation between woman's breasts, *esp.* as revealed by low-cut dress **2.** division, split —**'cleaver** *n.* short chopper

cleave[2] (klēv) *vi.* **1.** stick, adhere **2.** be loyal (**cleaved, 'cleaving**)

clef (klef) *n. Mus.* mark to show pitch of staff

cleft (kleft) *n.* **1.** crack, fissure, chasm **2.** opening made by cleaving —*v.* **3.** *pt./pp. of* CLEAVE[1] —**cleft lip** *see* **harelip** *at* HARE —**cleft palate** congenital fissure in midline of hard palate, oft. associated with harelip —**cleft stick** situation involving choice between two equally unsatisfactory alternatives

cleg (kleg) *n.* horsefly

clematis ('klemətis) *n.* flowering climbing perennial plant

clement ('klemənt) *a.* **1.** merciful **2.** gentle **3.** mild —**'clemency** *n.* —**'clemently** *adv.*

clench (klench) *vt.* **1.** set firmly together **2.** grasp, close (fist)

clerestory *or* **clearstory** ('klēərstöri) *n.* **1.** outside wall of room or building that rises above an adjoining roof and contains windows **2.** row of windows in upper part of church above the nave —'**clerestoried** *or* '**clearstoried** *a.*

clergy ('klərji) *n.* body of appointed ministers of Christian Church —'**clergyman** *n.*

clerical ('klerikəl) *a.* **1.** of clergy **2.** of, connected with, office work —'**cleric** *n.* clergyman —'**clericalism** *n.*

clerk (klərk) *n.* **1.** subordinate who keeps files *etc.* in an office **2.** officer in charge of records, correspondence *etc.*, of department or corporation **3.** salesperson —'**clerkly** *a.* —'**clerkship** *n.* —**clerk of the works** employee who supervises building work

Cleveland ('klēvlənd) *n.* **Grover.** the 22nd and 24th President of the U.S. (1885-89 and 1893-97)

clever ('klevər) *a.* **1.** intelligent **2.** able, skillful, adroit —'**cleverly** *adv.* —'**cleverness** *n.*

clew (kloo) *n.* **1.** ball of thread or yarn **2.** *Naut.* lower corner of sail —*vt.* **3.** coil into ball

cliché (klē'shā) *n.* hackneyed phrase

click[1] (klik) *n.* **1.** short, sharp sound, as of latch in door **2.** catch —*v.* **3.** (cause to) make short, sharp sound

click[2] (klik) *vi.* **1.** *sl.* be a success **2.** *inf.* become clear **3.** *inf.* strike up friendship

client ('klīənt) *n.* **1.** customer **2.** one who employs professional person —**clientele** (klīən'tel) *n.* body of clients

cliff (klif) *n.* steep rock face —'**cliffhanger** *n.* tense situation, *esp.* in film *etc.*

climacteric (klī'maktərik, klīmak'terik) *n.* **1.** critical event or period **2.** *see* MENOPAUSE **3.** period in life of man corresponding to menopause, characterized by diminished sexual activity —*a.* (*also* **climac'terical**) **4.** involving crucial event or period

climate ('klīmit) *n.* **1.** condition of country with regard to weather **2.** prevailing feeling, atmosphere —**cli'matic** *a.* of climate

climax ('klīmaks) *n.* **1.** highest point, culmination **2.** point of greatest excitement, tension in story *etc.* —**cli'mactic** *a.*

climb (klīm) *v.* **1.** go up or ascend **2.** progress with difficulty **3.** creep up, mount **4.** slope upward —'**climber** *n.* —'**climbing** *n.*

clime (klīm) *n.* **1.** region, country **2.** climate

clinch (klinch) *vt.* **1.** *see* CLENCH **2.** settle, conclude (an agreement) —'**clincher** *n. inf.* something decisive

cling (kling) *vi.* **1.** adhere **2.** be firmly attached **3.** be dependent (on) (**clung** *pt./pp.*)

clinic ('klinik) *n.* place for medical examination, advice or treatment —'**clinical** *a.* **1.** relating to clinic, care of sick *etc.* **2.** objective, unemotional **3.** bare, plain —'**clinically** *adv.* —**clinical thermometer** thermometer used for taking body temperature

clink[1] (klingk) *n.* **1.** sharp metallic sound —*v.* **2.** (cause to) make this sound

clink[2] (klingk) *n. sl.* prison

clinker ('klingkər) *n.* **1.** fused coal residues from fire or furnace **2.** hard brick

clinker-built *a.* (of boat) with outer boards or plates overlapping

Clio ('klīō, 'klēō) *n.* statuette awarded annually for notable achievements in radio and television by a professional organization (*pl.* **-s**)

clip[1] (klip) *vt.* **1.** cut with scissors **2.** cut short (**-pp-**) —*n.* **3.** *inf.* sharp blow —'**clipper** *n.* —'**clipping** *n.* something cut out, *esp.* article from newspaper; cutting —**clip joint** *sl.* nightclub *etc.* in which customers are overcharged

clip[2] (klip) *n.* device for gripping or holding together, *esp.* hair, clothing *etc.* —'**clipboard** *n.* portable writing board with clip at top for holding paper

clipper ('klipər) *n.* fast sailing ship

clippie ('klipi) *n.* **UK** *inf.* bus conductress

clique (klēk, klik) *n.* **1.** small exclusive set **2.** faction, group of people —'**cliquish** *a.*

clitoris ('klitəris, kli'tōris) *n.* small erectile part of female genitals

cloak (klōk) *n.* **1.** loose outer garment **2.** disguise, pretext —*vt.* **3.** cover with cloak **4.** disguise, conceal —**cloak-and-dagger** *a.* concerned with intrigue and espionage —'**cloakroom** *n.* place for keeping coats, hats, luggage

clobber ('klobər) *vt. inf.* **1.** beat, batter **2.** defeat utterly

cloche (klōsh) *n.* woman's close-fitting hat

clock (klok) *n.* **1.** instrument for measuring time **2.** device with dial for recording or measuring —'**clockwise** *adv./a.* in the direction that the hands of a clock rotate —'**clockwork** *n.* mechanism similar to that of a clock, as in a wind-up toy —**clock in** *or* **on, out** *or* **off** record arrival or departure on automatic time recorder

clod (klod) *n.* **1.** lump of earth **2.** blockhead —'**cloddish** *a.* —'**clodhopper** *n. inf.* **1.** clumsy person; lout **2.** (*usu. pl.*) large heavy shoe

clog (klog) *vt.* **1.** hamper, impede, choke up (**-gg-**) —*n.* **2.** obstruction, impediment **3.** wooden-soled shoe —**clog dance**

cloisonné (kloizə'nā) *n.* **1.** enamel decoration in compartments formed by small fillets of metal —*a.* **2.** of cloisonné

cloister ('kloistər) *n.* **1.** covered pillared arcade **2.** monastery or convent —'**cloistered** *a.* confined, secluded, sheltered

clomp (klomp) *see* CLUMP[2]

clone (klōn) *n.* **1.** any living organism produced by division from one parent with the result being genetically identical —*v.* **2.** (cause to) produce clone

clop (klop) *vi.* move, sound, as horse's hooves (**-pp-**)

cloqué (klō'kā) *n.* fabric with a blistered finish

close[1] (klōs) *a.* **1.** adjacent, near **2.** compact **3.** crowded **4.** affectionate, intimate **5.** almost equal **6.** careful, searching **7.** confined **8.** secret **9.** unventilated, stifling **10.** reticent **11.** niggardly **12.** strict, restricted —*adv.* **13.** nearly **14.** tightly —*n.* **15.** shut-in place **16.** precinct of cathedral —**'closely** *adv.* —**'closeness** *n.* —**close-fisted** *a.* mean; avaricious —**close harmony** singing in which all parts except bass lie close together —**close quarters** cramped space or position —**close season** time when it is illegal to kill certain kinds of game and fish —**close shave** *inf.* narrow escape —**'closeup** *n.* close view, *esp.* portion of motion picture —**at close quarters** engaged in hand-to-hand combat; in close proximity; very near together

close² (klōz) *vt.* **1.** shut **2.** stop up **3.** prevent access to **4.** finish —*vi.* **5.** come together **6.** grapple —*n.* **7.** end —**closed circuit** complete electrical circuit through which current can flow —**closed shop** place of work in which all workers must belong to a union

closet ('klozit) *n.* **1.** cupboard **2.** small private room **3.** water closet, toilet —*a.* **4.** private, secret —*vt.* **5.** shut up in private room, *esp.* for conference **6.** conceal

closure ('klōzhər) *n.* **1.** act of closing **2.** ending of debate by majority vote or other authority

clot (klot) *n.* **1.** mass or lump **2.** *inf.* fool **3.** *Med.* coagulated mass of blood —*vt.* **4.** form into lumps —*vi.* **5.** coagulate (**-tt-**)

cloth (kloth) *n.* fabric made by weaving, knitting, netting or compressing filaments —**clothe** (klōdh) *vt.* put clothes on (**clothed** *or* **clad** *pt./pp.*) —**clothes** (klōdhz) *pl.n.* **1.** dress **2.** bed coverings —**clothier** ('klōdhiər) *n.* —**clothing** ('klōdhing) *n.* —**clotheshorse** ('klōdhz-hōrs) *n.* **1.** frame on which to hang laundry for drying or airing **2.** *inf.* excessively fashionable person

cloud (klowd) *n.* **1.** condensed water vapor floating in air **2.** state of gloom **3.** multitude —*vt.* **4.** overshadow, dim, darken —*vi.* **5.** become cloudy —**'cloudless** *a.* —**'cloudy** *a.* —**'cloudburst** *n.* heavy downpour

clout (klowt) *n.* **1.** *inf.* blow **2.** influence, power —*vt.* **3.** *inf.* strike

clove¹ (klōv) *n.* **1.** dried flower bud of tropical tree, used as spice **2.** one of small bulbs making up compound bulb

clove² (klōv) *pt. of* CLEAVE¹ —**'cloven** *pp. of* CLEAVE¹ —**cloven hoof** *or* **foot 1.** divided hoof of cow, deer *etc.* **2.** symbol of Satan

clove hitch knot for securing rope to spar, post or larger rope

clover ('klōvər) *n.* low-growing forage plant, trefoil —**'cloverleaf** *n.* **1.** arrangement of connecting roads, resembling four-leaf clover, that joins two intersecting main roads —*a.* **2.** in shape of leaf of clover —**be in clover** be in luxury

clown (klown) *n.* **1.** comic entertainer in circus **2.** jester, fool —*vi.* **3.** play jokes or tricks **4.** act foolishly —**'clownish** *a.*

cloy (kloi) *vt.* weary by sweetness, sameness *etc.*

CLU chartered life underwriter

club (klub) *n.* **1.** thick stick **2.** bat, stick used in some games **3.** association for pursuance of common interest **4.** building used by such association **5.** one of the suits at cards —*vt.* **6.** strike with club —*vi.* **7.** join for a common object (**-bb-**) —**club foot** deformed foot —**club moss** any primitive plant with trailing, branching stems at free ends —**club root** fungal disease of cabbages *etc.*, in which roots become thickened and distorted

cluck (kluk) *vi./n.* (make) noise of hen

clue *or* **clew** (klo͞o) *n.* **1.** indication, *esp.* of solution of mystery or puzzle —*vt.* **2.** (*usu. with* up) provide with helpful information

clump¹ (klump) *n.* **1.** cluster of trees or plants **2.** compact mass

clump² (klump) *vi.* **1.** walk, tread heavily —*n.* **2.** dull, heavy tread or similar sound

clumsy ('klumzi) *a.* **1.** awkward, unwieldy, ungainly **2.** badly made or arranged —**'clumsily** *adv.* —**'clumsiness** *n.*

clung (klung) *pt./pp. of* CLING

clunk (klungk) *n.* (sound of) blow or something falling

cluster ('klustər) *n.* **1.** group, bunch —*v.* **2.** gather, grow in cluster

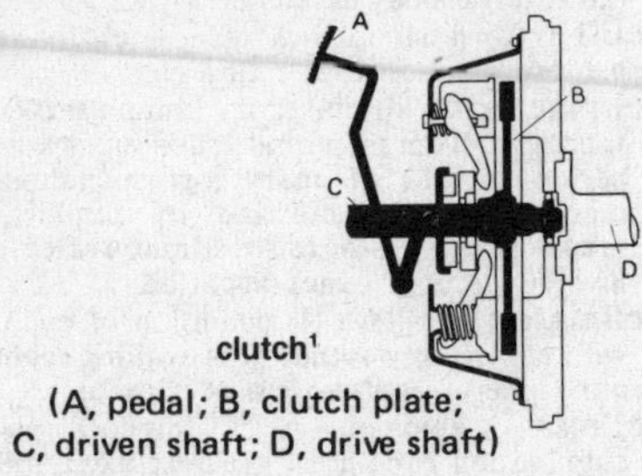

clutch¹
(A, pedal; B, clutch plate; C, driven shaft; D, drive shaft)

clutch¹ (kluch) *v.* **1.** grasp eagerly **2.** snatch (at) —*n.* **3.** grasp, tight grip **4.** device enabling two revolving shafts to be connected and disconnected at will

clutch² (kluch) *n.* **1.** set of eggs hatched at one time **2.** brood of chickens

clutter ('klutər) *v.* **1.** strew **2.** crowd together in disorder —*n.* **3.** disordered, obstructive mass of objects

Clydesdale ('klīdzdāl) *n.* heavy powerful carthorse, orig. from Scotland

cm *or* **cm.** centimeter

Cm *Chem.* curium

Cmdr. *Mil.* Commander

cml commercial

CN credit note

C.N.D. UK Campaign for Nuclear Disarmament

Co *Chem.* cobalt

CO 1. Colorado 2. cash order

Co. *or* **co.** Company

Co. County

C.O. 1. Commanding Officer 2. conscientious objector

co- (*comb. form*) 1. together, as in *coproduction* 2. partnership or equality, as in *costar, copilot* 3. to similar degree, as in *coextend* 4. *Math., astron.* of complement of angle, as in *cosecant*

c/o care of

coach (kōch) *n.* 1. long-distance or touring bus 2. large four-wheeled carriage 3. railroad carriage 4. tutor, instructor —*vt.* 5. instruct —**coach-builder** *n.* —ˈ**coachman** *n.*

coadjutor (kōˈajōōtər) *n.* 1. bishop appointed as assistant to diocesan bishop 2. *rare* assistant

coagulate (kōˈagyōōlāt) *v.* 1. curdle, clot, form into a mass 2. congeal, solidify —**coaguˈlation** *n.*

coal (kōl) *n.* 1. rock consisting of carbonized vegetable matter, used as fuel 2. glowing ember —*v.* 3. supply with or take in coal —ˈ**coalface** *n.* exposed seam of coal in mine —ˈ**coalfield** *n.* district in which coal is found —**coal gas** mixture of gases produced by distillation of bituminous coal and used for heating and lighting —**coal tar** black tar, produced by distillation of bituminous coal, that can be further distilled to yield benzene *etc.* —**coal tit** small songbird having black head with white patch on nape

coalesce (kōəˈles) *vi.* unite, merge —**coaˈlescence** *n.*

coalfish (ˈkōlfish) *n.* food fish with dark-colored skin

coalition (kōəˈlishən) *n.* alliance, *esp.* of political parties

coaming (ˈkōming) *n.* raised frame round ship's hatchway for keeping out water

coarse (kōrs) *a.* 1. rough, harsh 2. unrefined 3. indecent —ˈ**coarsely** *adv.* —ˈ**coarsen** *v.* make or become coarse —ˈ**coarseness** *n.* —**coarse fish** freshwater fish not of salmon family —**coarse fishing**

coast (kōst) *n.* 1. sea shore —*v.* 2. move under momentum 3. sail along (coast) —*vi.* 4. proceed without making much effort —ˈ**coaster** *n.* 1. small ship 2. that which, one who, coasts 3. small table mat for glasses *etc.* —ˈ**coastguard** *n.* 1. maritime force which aids shipping, prevents smuggling *etc.* 2. member of such force (*also* ˈ**coastguardsman**)

coat (kōt) *n.* 1. sleeved outer garment 2. animal's fur or feathers 3. covering layer —*vt.* 4. cover with layer 5. clothe —ˈ**coating** *n.* 1. outer layer 2. fabric for making coats —**coat of arms** armorial bearings

coax (kōks) *vt.* wheedle, cajole, persuade, force gently

coaxial (kōˈaksiəl) *a.* having the same axis —**coaxial cable** high-frequency cable with outer conductor tube surrounding insulated central conductor (*also* **coaxial line**)

cob (kob) *n.* 1. short-legged stout horse 2. male swan 3. corncob

cobalt (ˈkōbölt) *n.* 1. *Chem.* metallic element *Symbol* Co, at. wt. 58.9, at. no. 27 2. blue pigment from it —**cobalt bomb** 1. cobalt-60 device used in radiotherapy 2. nuclear weapon consisting of hydrogen bomb encased in cobalt

cobber (ˈkobər) *n.* **A, NZ** friend: used as term of address to males

cobble (ˈkobəl) *vt.* 1. patch roughly 2. mend (shoes) —*n.* 3. round stone —ˈ**cobbler** *n.* shoe mender —ˈ**cobblestone** *n.* rounded stone used for paving (*also* ˈ**cobble**)

cobbler (ˈkoblər) *n.* 1. sweetened iced drink, usu. made from fruit and wine 2. deep-dish fruit pie

COBOL (ˈkōböl) computer-programming language for general commercial use

cobra (ˈkōbrə) *n.* venomous, hooded snake of Asia and Afr.

cobweb (ˈkobweb) *n.* spider's web

coca (ˈkōkə) *n.* either of two shrubs, native to Andes, whose dried leaves contain cocaine

cocaine (kōˈkān) *n.* addictive narcotic drug obtained from leaves of certain S Amer. trees

coccidioidomycosis (koksidioidōmīˈkōsis) *n.* fungus disease found principally in southern U.S.

coccus (ˈkokəs) *n.* spherical or nearly spherical bacterium, such as staphylococcus (*pl.* **-ci** (-sī))

coccyx (ˈkoksiks) *n.* small triangular bone at end of spinal column (*pl.* **coccyges** (ˈkoksijēz))

cochineal (ˈkochinēl) *n.* scarlet dye from Mexican insect

cochlea (ˈkōkliə) *n.* spiral tube that forms part of internal ear, converting sound vibrations into nerve impulses (*pl.* **-leae** (-liē))

cock (kok) *n.* 1. male bird, *esp.* of domestic fowl 2. tap for liquids 3. hammer of gun 4. its position drawn back —*vt.* 5. draw back (gun hammer) to firing position 6. raise, turn in alert or jaunty manner —ˈ**cockerel** *n.* young rooster —**cock-a-hoop** *a.* 1. in very high spirits 2. boastful 3. askew; confused —**cock-and-bull story** *inf.* obviously improbable story, *esp.* one used as excuse —ˈ**cockcrow** *or* ˈ**cockcrowing** *n.* daybreak —**cocked hat** hat with brims turned up and caught together to give two or three points —ˈ**cockeyed** *a.* 1. cross-eyed 2. with a squint 3. askew —ˈ**cockfight** *n.* —ˈ**cockfighting** *n.* sport, illegal in U.S. and many other countries, in which two gamecocks fight until one is acknowledged winner —ˈ**cockscomb** *or* ˈ**coxcomb** *n.* 1. comb of domestic cock 2. garden plant with flowers in broad spike resembling comb of cock 3. *inf.*

conceited dandy —**cock'sure** *a.* overconfident; arrogant —**knock into a cocked hat** *sl.* outdo, defeat

cockade (ko'kād) *n.* rosette, badge for hat

cockatoo ('kokətōō) *n.* Aust., New Guinea, crested parrot

cockatrice ('kokətris, -trīs) *n.* fabulous animal similar to basilisk

cockchafer ('kokchāfər) *n.* large, flying beetle

cocker spaniel ('kokər) small compact spaniel

cockle[1] ('kokəl) *n.* shellfish —**'cockleshell** *n.* **1.** shell of cockle **2.** shell of certain other mollusks **3.** small light boat

cockle[2] ('kokəl) *v.* wrinkle, pucker

cockney ('kokni) *n.* (*oft.* **C-**) native of London, *esp.* of East End (*pl.* **-s**)

cockpit ('kokpit) *n.* **1.** pilot's seat, compartment in small aircraft **2.** driver's seat in racing car **3.** orig. enclosure for cockfights

cockroach ('kokrōch) *n.* kind of insect, household pest

cocktail ('koktāl) *n.* **1.** short drink of spirits with flavorings *etc.* **2.** appetizer

cocky ('koki) *a.* conceited, pert

cocoa ('kōkō) *n.* **1.** powder made from seed of cacao (tropical) tree **2.** drink made from the powder

coconut ('kōkənut) *n.* **1.** tropical palm **2.** very large, hard nut from this palm —**coconut matting** coarse matting made from fibrous husk of coconut —**coconut milk** liquid extracted from grated flesh of fresh mature coconut or from reconstituted dried shredded coconut

cocoon (kə'kōōn) *n.* **1.** sheath of insect in chrysalis stage **2.** any protective covering

cocotte (ko'kot) *n.* **1.** small fireproof dish in which individual portions of food are cooked and served **2.** prostitute; promiscuous woman

cod (kod) *n.* food fish of northern Atlantic (*also* **'codfish**) —**cod-liver oil** oil extracted from fresh codfish livers, rich in vitamins A and D

C.O.D. cash on delivery

coda ('kōdə) *n. Mus.* final part of musical composition

coddle ('kodəl) *vt.* overprotect, pamper

code (kōd) *n.* **1.** system of letters, symbols and rules for their association to transmit messages secretly or briefly **2.** scheme of conduct **3.** collection of laws —**codifi'cation** *n.* —**'codify** *vt.*

codeine ('kōdēn) *n.* narcotic derived from opium used to relieve pain and to control coughing

codex ('kōdeks) *n.* ancient manuscript volume, *esp.* of Bible *etc.* (*pl.* **codices** ('kōdisēz, 'kodi-))

codger ('kojər) *n. inf.* odd old man

codicil ('kodisil) *n.* addition to will —**codi'cillary** *a.*

codpiece ('kodpēs) *n.* bag covering male genitals, attached to breeches: worn in 15th and 16th centuries

coeducation (kōejə'kāshən) *n.* instruction in schools *etc.* attended by both sexes —**co-ed** *n.* **1.** female student in such an institution —*a.* **2.** coeducational —**coedu'cational** *a.* of education of boys and girls together in mixed classes

coefficient (kōi'fishənt) *n. Math.* numerical or constant factor

coelenterate (si'lentərāt, -rit) *n.* any member of a phylum (*Coelenterata*) of invertebrate animals including the corals, sea anemones, jellyfishes and hydroids

coequal (kō'ēkwəl) *a.* **1.** of same size, rank *etc.* —*n.* **2.** person or thing equal with another —**coe'quality** *n.*

coerce (kō'ərs) *vt.* compel, force —**co'ercion** *n.* forcible compulsion or restraint —**co'ercive** *or* **co'ercible** *a.*

coeval (kō'ēvəl) *a.* of same age or generation

coexist (kōig'zist) *vi.* exist together —**coex'istence** *n.* —**coex'istent** *a.*

coextend (kōik'stend) *v.* extend or cause to extend equally in space or time —**coex'tension** *n.* —**coex'tensive** *a.*

coffee ('kofi) *n.* **1.** seeds of tropical shrub **2.** drink made from roasting and grinding these —**coffee mill** machine for grinding roasted coffee beans —**coffee shop** informal restaurant —**coffee table** low table on which coffee may be served

coffer ('kofər) *n.* **1.** chest for valuables **2.** treasury, funds

cofferdam ('kofərdam) *n.* watertight structure enabling construction work to be done under water

coffin ('kofin) *n.* box in which corpse is buried or cremated

cog (kog) *n.* **1.** one of series of teeth on rim of wheel **2.** person, thing forming small part of big process, organization *etc.* —**'cogwheel** *n.*

cogent ('kōjənt) *a.* convincing, compelling, persuasive —**'cogency** *n.* —**'cogently** *adv.*

cogitate ('kojitāt) *vi.* think, reflect, ponder —**cogi'tation** *n.* —**'cogitative** *a.*

Cognac ('konyak) *n.* French brandy

cognate ('kognāt) *a.* of same stock, related, kindred —**cog'nation** *n.*

cognition (kog'nishən) *n.* act or faculty of knowing —**cog'nitional** *a.*

cognizance ('kognizəns) *n.* knowledge, perception —**'cognizable** *a.* —**'cognizant** *a.*

cognomen (kog'nōmən) *n.* surname, nickname (*pl.* **-s, -nomina** (-'nominə, -'nō-))

cognoscenti (konyō'shenti, kognə-) *or* **conoscenti** (konō'shenti) *pl.n.* people with knowledge in particular field, *esp.* arts (*sing.* **-te** (-tē))

cohabit (kō'habit) *vi.* live together as husband and wife

coheir (kō'āər) *n.* a joint heir (**co'heiress** *fem.*)

cohere (kō'hēər) *vi.* stick together, be consistent —**co'herence** *n.* —**co'herent** *a.* **1.** capable of logical speech, thought **2.** connected, making sense **3.** sticking together —**co'herently** *adv.* —**co'hesion** *n.* cohering —**co'hesive** *a.*

cohort ('kōhôrt) *n.* **1.** troop **2.** associate

coif (koif) *n.* **1.** close-fitting cap worn under veil in Middle Ages **2.** leather cap worn under chainmail hood **3.** (kwäf) *rare* coiffure —*vt.* **4.** cover with or as if with coif **5.** (kwäf) arrange (hair) (**-ff-**)

coiffure (kwä'fyōōər) *n.* hairstyle —**coiffeur** (kwä'fər) *n.* hairdresser

coign of vantage (koin) advantageous position for observation or action

coil (koil) *vt.* **1.** lay in rings **2.** twist into winding shape —*vi.* **3.** twist, take up a winding shape or spiral —*n.* **4.** series of rings **5.** device in vehicle *etc.* to transform low-tension current to higher voltage for ignition purposes **6.** contraceptive device inserted in womb

coin (koin) *n.* **1.** piece of money **2.** money —*vt.* **3.** make into money, stamp **4.** invent —'**coinage** *n.* **1.** coining **2.** coins collectively —'**coiner** *n.* maker of counterfeit money —**coin silver** silver alloy containing about 900 parts silver and 100 parts base metal

coincide (kōin'sīd) *vi.* **1.** happen together **2.** agree exactly —**co'incidence** *n.* —**co'incident** *a.* coinciding —**coinci'dental** *a.*

Cointreau ('kwäntrō) *n.* trade name for colorless liqueur with orange flavoring

coir ('koiər) *n.* fiber of coconut husk

coitus ('kōitəs) *or* **coition** (kō'ishən) *n.* sexual intercourse

coke[1] (kōk) *n.* residue left from distillation of coal, used as fuel

coke[2] (kōk) *n. sl.* cocaine

Coke (kōk) *n.* trade name for a carbonated cola drink

col (kol) *n.* high mountain pass

Col. 1. Colonel **2.** Colossians

cola ('kōlə) *n.* **1.** tropical tree **2.** its nut, used to flavor drink

colander ('kuləndər, 'kol-) *n.* culinary strainer perforated with small holes

cold (kōld) *a.* **1.** lacking heat **2.** indifferent, unmoved, apathetic **3.** dispiriting **4.** reserved or unfriendly **5.** (of colors) giving an impression of coldness —*n.* **6.** lack of heat **7.** illness, marked by runny nose *etc.* —'**coldly** *adv.* —'**coldness** *n.* —**cold-blooded** *a.* **1.** lacking pity, mercy **2.** having body temperature that varies with that of the surroundings —**cold chisel** toughened steel chisel —**cold cream** emulsion of water and fat for softening and cleansing skin —**cold feet** *sl.* loss of confidence —**cold frame** unheated wooden frame with glass top, used to protect young plants —**cold front** *Met.* boundary line between warm air mass and cold air pushing it —**cold-hearted** *a.* lacking in feeling or warmth; unkind —**cold-heartedness** *n.* —**cold shoulder** *inf.* show of indifference; slight —**cold-shoulder** *vt. inf.* treat with indifference —**cold sore** cluster of blisters caused by virus infection which may appear anywhere in the body (*also* **fever blisters**) —**cold storage 1.** method of preserving perishable foods *etc.* by keeping them at artificially reduced temperature **2.** *inf.* state of temporary suspension —**cold sweat** *inf.* bodily reaction to fear or nervousness, characterized by chill and moist skin —**cold war** economic, diplomatic but nonmilitary hostility —**(out) in the cold** *inf.* neglected; ignored

cole (kōl) *n.* any of various plants such as cabbage and rape (*also* '**colewort**)

coleopteran (kōli'optərən) *n.* **1.** any of order of insects, including beetles, in which forewings form shell-like protective elytra (*also* **cole'opteron**) —*a.* **2.** of this order (*also* **cole'opterous**)

coleslaw ('kōlslô) *n.* salad dish based on shredded cabbage

coleus ('kōliəs) *n.* plant of the mint family cultivated for its variegated leaves

colic ('kolik) *n.* severe pains in the intestines —**co'litis** *n.* inflammation of the colon

coliseum (koli'sēəm) *or* **colosseum** (kolə'sēəm) *n.* large building, such as stadium, used for entertainments *etc.*

collaborate (kə'labərāt) *vi.* work with another on a project —**collabo'ration** *n.* —**col'laborator** *n.* one who works with another, *esp.* one who aids an enemy in occupation of his own country

collage (kə'läzh, kō-) *n.* picture or design made up of flat everyday materials *esp.* paper, fixed to a background

collagen ('koləjən) *n.* fibrous protein of connective tissue and bones that yields gelatin on boiling —**collagen diseases** group of ailments characterized by inflammation of the collagen tissue, *eg* rheumatoid arthritis

collapse (kə'laps) *vi.* **1.** fall **2.** give way **3.** lose strength, fail —*n.* **4.** act of collapsing **5.** breakdown —**col'lapsible** *or* **col'lapsable** *a.*

collar ('kolər) *n.* **1.** band, part of garment, worn round neck —*vt.* **2.** seize by collar **3.** *inf.* capture, seize —'**collarbone** *n.* bone from shoulder to breastbone

collate (ko'lāt, kə-) *vt.* **1.** compare carefully **2.** place in order (as printed sheets for binding) —**col'lation** *n.* **1.** collating **2.** light meal

collateral (kə'latərəl) *n.* **1.** security pledged for repayment of loan —*a.* **2.** accompanying **3.** side by side **4.** of same stock but different line **5.** subordinate

colleague ('kolēg) *n.* associate, companion in office or employment, fellow worker

collect[1] (kə'lekt) *vt.* **1.** gather, bring together —*vi.* **2.** come together **3.** *inf.* receive money

—*adv./a.* **4.** (of telephone calls *etc.*) paid for by the receiver —**col'lected** *a.* **1.** calm **2.** gathered —**col'lection** *n.* —**col'lective** *n.* **1.** factory, farm *etc.*, run on principles of collectivism —*a.* **2.** formed or assembled by collection **3.** forming whole or aggregate **4.** of individuals acting in cooperation —**col'lectively** *adv.* —**col'lectivism** *n.* theory that the state should own all means of production —**col'lector** *n.* —**collective bargaining** negotiation between labor union and employer or employers' organization on incomes and working conditions of employees —**collector's item** any rare or beautiful object thought worthy of collection

collect[2] ('kolekt) *n.* short prayer

colleen (ko'lēn, 'kolēn) *n. Irish name for* girl

college ('kolij) *n.* **1.** place of higher education **2.** society of scholars **3.** association —**collegi'ality** *n.* participation of bishops in governance of R.C. Church —**col'legian** *n.* student —**col'legiate** *a.* —**college boards** set of examinations taken by aspirants to certain colleges

collide (kə'līd) *vi.* **1.** strike or dash together **2.** come into conflict —**collision** (kə'lizhən) *n.* colliding

collie ('koli) *n.* any of several breeds of dog orig. bred to herd sheep

collier ('kolyər) *n.* **1.** coal miner **2.** coal ship —**'colliery** *n.* coal mine

collimate ('kolimāt) *vt.* **1.** adjust line of sight of (optical instrument) **2.** make parallel or bring into line —**colli'mation** *n.*

collocate ('koləkāt) *vt.* group, place together —**collo'cation** *n.*

collodion (kə'lōdiən) *n.* chemical solution used in photography and medicine

colloid ('koloid) *n.* suspension of particles in a solution

collop ('koləp) *n.* **1.** slice of meat **2.** small piece of anything

colloquial (kə'lōkwiəl) *a.* pert. to, or used in, informal conversation —**col'loquialism** *n.* —**'colloquy** *n.* **1.** conversation **2.** dialogue

colloquium (kə'lōkwiəm) *n.* **1.** gathering for discussion **2.** academic seminar (*pl.* **-s, -quia** (-kwiə))

collotype ('kolōtīp) *n.* printing process used for fine illustration work (*also* **photogelatin**)

collusion (kə'lo͞ozhən) *n.* secret agreement for a fraudulent purpose, *esp.* in legal proceedings —**col'lusive** *a.*

Colo. Colorado

cologne (kə'lōn) *n.* perfumed liquid (*also* **eau de cologne**)

Colombia (kə'lumbiə) *n.* country in South America bounded north by the Caribbean Sea, northwest by Panama, west by the Pacific Ocean, southwest by Ecuador and Peru, northwest by Venezuela and southeast by Brazil

colon[1] ('kōlən) *n.* mark (:) indicating break in sentence

colon[2] ('kōlən) *n.* part of large intestine from cecum to rectum

colonel ('kərnəl) *n.* commander of regiment or battalion —**'colonelcy** *n.*

colonnade (kolə'nād) *n.* row of columns

colony ('koləni) *n.* **1.** body of people who settle in new country but remain subject to parent state **2.** country so settled **3.** distinctive group living together —**co'lonial** *a.* of colony —**co'lonialism** *n.* policy and practice of extending control over weaker peoples or areas (*also* **im'perialism**) —**co'lonialist** *n./a.* —**'colonist** *n.* —**coloni'zation** *n.* —**'colonize** *v.*

colophon ('koləfən, -fon) *n.* publisher's imprint or device

color ('kulər) *n.* **1.** hue, tint **2.** complexion **3.** paint **4.** pigment **5.** *fig.* semblance, pretext **6.** *fig.* timber, quality **7.** *fig.* mood —*pl.* **8.** flag **9.** *Sport* distinguishing badge, symbol —*vt.* **10.** stain, dye, paint, give color to **11.** *fig.* disguise **12.** *fig.* influence or distort —*vi.* **13.** become colored **14.** blush —**'colorable** *a.* **1.** capable of being colored **2.** appearing to be true; plausible **3.** pretended; feigned —**colo'ration** *n.* —**'colored** *a.* **1.** possessing color **2.** having strong element of fiction or fantasy; distorted (*esp. in* **highly colored**) —**'Colored** *a.* **1.** non-White **2.** in S Afr., of mixed descent —**'colorful** *a.* **1.** with bright or varied colors **2.** distinctive —**'coloring** *n.* **1.** process or art of applying color **2.** anything used to give color, such as paint **3.** appearance with regard to shade and color **4.** arrangements of colors, as in markings of birds **5.** color of complexion **6.** false appearance —**'colorless** *a.* **1.** without color **2.** lacking interest **3.** gray; pallid **4.** without prejudice; neutral —**color bar** discrimination against people of different race, *esp.* as practiced by Whites against Blacks —**color blindness** **1.** inability to distinguish one or more colors **2.** nonrecognition of racial differences —**'colorfast** *a.* (of fabric) having colors that are able to resist fading —**color perspective** *see* **atmospheric perspective** *at* ATMOSPHERE

Colorado (kolə'radō) *n.* Mountain state of the U.S., admitted to the Union in 1876. Abbrev.: **Colo., CO** (with ZIP code) —**Colorado beetle** black-and-yellow beetle that is serious pest of potatoes

coloratura (kolərə'tyo͞oərə, -'to͞oərə) *n. Mus.* **1.** florid virtuoso passage **2.** soprano who specializes in such music (*also* **coloratura soprano**)

Colossians (kə'losiənz) *pl.n.* (*with sing. v.*) *Bible* 12th book of the N.T., epistle written by St. Paul to Christians of Colossae and Laodicea

colossus (kə'losəs) *n.* **1.** huge statue **2.** something, somebody very large (*pl.* **colossi** (kə'losī), **-es**) —**co'lossal** *a.* huge, gigantic

colostomy (kə'lostəmi) *n.* surgical formation

of opening from colon on to surface of body, which functions as anus

colostrum (kə'lostrəm) *n.* thin milky secretion from nipples that precedes and follows true lactation

colt (kōlt) *n.* young male horse —**'coltish** *a.* **1.** inexperienced; unruly **2.** playful and lively

coltsfoot ('kōltsfo͝ot) *n.* wild plant with heart-shaped leaves and yellow flowers (*pl.* **-s**)

columbine ('koləmbīn) *n.* flower with five spurred petals

columbium (kə'lumbiəm) *n. see* NIOBIUM

Columbus Day (kə'lumbəs) Oct. 12th, legal holiday in most U.S. states: date of Columbus's landing in West Indies in 1492 (*also* **Discovery Day**)

column ('koləm) *n.* **1.** long vertical cylinder, pillar **2.** support **3.** division of page **4.** *Journalism* regular feature in paper **5.** body of troops —**columnar** (kə'lumnər) *a.* —**'columnist** *n.* journalist writing regular feature for newspaper

colza oil ('kolzə, 'kōl-) *see* RAPE[2]

com- *or* **con-** (*comb. form*) together; with; jointly, as in *commingle*

coma ('kōmə) *n.* state of unconsciousness —**'comatose** *a.*

Comanche (kə'manchi) *n.* **1.** member of Amerindian people ranging from Wyoming and Nebraska into New Mexico and Texas (*pl.* **-che, -s**) **2.** the Uto-Aztecan language of the Comanche

comb (kōm) *n.* **1.** toothed instrument for tidying, arranging, ornamenting hair **2.** cock's crest **3.** mass of honey cells —*vt.* **4.** use comb on **5.** search with great care —**'comber** *n.* **1.** person, tool or machine that combs wool, flax *etc.* **2.** long curling wave; roller —**'combing** *n.* method of separating long from short fibers

combat ('kombat) *vt./n.* fight, contest —**'combatant** *n.* —**'combative** *a.* —**combat fatigue** form of nervous breakdown that appears under stress of battle (*also* **combat neurosis, combat exhaustion, shell shock**)

combine (kəm'bīn) *v.* **1.** join together **2.** ally —*n.* ('kombīn) **3.** trust, syndicate, *esp.* of businesses, trade organizations *etc.* —**combination** (kombi'nāshən) *n.* —**combinative** ('kombinātiv) *a.* —**combination lock** lock that can only be opened when set of dials is turned to show specific sequence of numbers —**combine harvester** machine to harvest and thresh grain in one operation —**combining form** linguistic element that occurs only as part of compound word, such as *anthropo-* in *anthropology*

combo ('kombō) *n.* **1.** small group of jazz musicians **2.** *inf.* any combination (*pl.* **-s**)

combustion (kəm'buschən) *n.* process of burning —**combusti'bility** *n.* —**com'bustible** *a.*

come (kum) *vi.* **1.** approach, arrive, move toward something or someone nearer **2.** reach **3.** happen as a result **4.** occur **5.** be available **6.** originate **7.** become, turn out to be (**came, come, 'coming**) —**'coming** *a.* **1.** (of time *etc.*) approaching; next **2.** promising (*esp. in* **up and coming**) —*n.* **3.** arrival; approach —**'comeback** *n. inf.* **1.** return to active life after retirement **2.** retort —**'comedown** *n.* **1.** setback **2.** descent in social status —**come-hither** *a. inf.* alluring; seductive —**come-on** *n. inf.* anything that serves as lure —**come'uppance** *n. sl.* just retribution —**come on 1.** (of power *etc.*) start functioning **2.** progress **3.** advance, *esp.* in battle **4.** begin **5.** make entrance on stage —**come on strong** make forceful or exaggerated impression —**have it coming to one** *inf.* deserve what one is about to suffer

Comecon ('komikon) *n.* association of Soviet-oriented Communist nations, founded in 1949 to coordinate economic development *etc.*

comedy ('komidi) *n.* **1.** dramatic or other work of light, amusing character **2.** humor **3.** *Class. lit.* play in which main characters triumph over adversity —**co'median** *n.* **1.** entertainer who tells jokes *etc.* **2.** actor in comedy (**comedi'enne** *fem.*)

comely ('kumli) *a.* fair, pretty, good-looking —**'comeliness** *n.*

comestible (kə'mestibəl) *n.* (*usu. pl.*) food

comet ('komit) *n.* luminous heavenly body consisting of diffuse head, nucleus and long tail —**'cometary** *a.*

comfit ('kumfit, 'kom-) *n.* candy

comfort ('kumfərt) *n.* **1.** wellbeing **2.** ease **3.** consolation **4.** means of consolation or satisfaction —*vt.* **5.** soothe **6.** cheer, gladden, console —**comfortable** ('kumftəbəl) *a.* **1.** free from pain *etc.* **2.** *inf.* well-off financially —**comfortably** ('kumftəbli) *adv.* —**'comforter** *n.* **1.** one who comforts **2.** long narrow knitted scarf —**'comfy** *a. inf.* comfortable

comfrey ('kumfri) *n.* wild plant with hairy leaves

comic ('komik) *a.* **1.** relating to comedy **2.** funny, laughable —*n.* **3.** comedian **4.** magazine consisting of strip cartoons —**'comical** *a.* —**'comically** *adv.* —**comic strip** sequence of drawings in newspaper *etc.*, relating comic or adventurous situation

comity ('komiti) *n.* **1.** mutual civility; courtesy **2.** friendly recognition accorded by nation to laws and usages of another (*also* **comity of nations**)

comm. 1. commonwealth **2.** communist

comma ('komə) *n.* punctuation mark (,) separating parts of sentence

command (kə'mand) *vt.* **1.** order **2.** rule **3.** compel **4.** have in one's power **5.** overlook, dominate **6.** receive as due —*vi.* **7.** exercise rule —*n.* **8.** order **9.** power of controlling, ruling, dominating, overlooking **10.** knowledge, mastery **11.** post of one commanding

12. district commanded, jurisdiction —'**commandant** *n.* —**comman'deer** *vt.* seize for military use, appropriate —**com'mander** *n.* —**com'manding** *a.* **1.** in command **2.** with air of authority —**com'mandment** *n.*

commando (kə'mandō) *n.* (member of) special military unit trained for airborne, amphibious attack (*pl.* **-s**)

commedia dell'arte (kom'medya dāl'lartā) *It.* form of improvised comedy in Italy in 16th to 18th cent., with stock characters such as Punchinello, Harlequin *etc.*

commemorate (kə'meməràt) *vt.* **1.** celebrate, keep in memory by ceremony **2.** be a memorial of —**commemo'ration** *n.* —**com'memorative** *a.*

commence (kə'mens) *v.* begin —**com'mencement** *n.*

commend (kə'mend) *vt.* **1.** praise **2.** commit, entrust —**com'mendable** *a.* —**com'mendably** *adv.* —**commen'dation** *n.* —**com'mendatory** *a.*

commensurate (kə'mensərit, -chə-) *a.* **1.** equal in size or length of time **2.** in proportion, adequate —**com'mensurable** *a.* **1.** *Math.* having common factor; having units of same dimensions and being related by whole numbers **2.** proportionate

comment ('koment) *n.* **1.** remark, criticism **2.** gossip **3.** note, explanation —*vi.* **4.** remark, note **5.** write notes explaining or criticizing a text —'**commentary** *n.* **1.** explanatory notes or comments **2.** spoken accompaniment to film *etc.* —'**commentate** *vi.* —'**commentator** *n.* author, speaker of commentary

commerce ('komərs) *n.* **1.** buying and selling **2.** dealings **3.** trade —**com'mercial** *a.* **1.** of, concerning, business, trade, profit *etc.* —*n.* **2.** advertisement, *esp.* on radio or television —**com'mercialize** *vt.* **1.** make commercial **2.** exploit for profit, *esp.* at expense of quality

commie ('komi) *n./a. inf., offens.* communist

commination (komi'nāshən) *n.* act of threatening punishment or vengeance —'**comminatory** *a.*

commingle (ko'minggəl) *v.* mix or be mixed

comminute ('kominyōōt, -nōōt) *vt.* **1.** break (bone) into small fragments **2.** divide (property) into small lots —**commi'nution** *n.*

commiserate (kə'mizərāt) *vi.* (*usu. with* with) pity, condole, sympathize —**commiser'ation** *n.*

commissar ('komisär) *n.* official of Communist Party responsible for political education

commissariat (komi'seriət, -'sar-) *n.* military department of food supplies and transport

commissary ('komiseri) *n.* **1.** shop supplying food or equipment, as in military camp **2.** army officer responsible for supplies **3.** restaurant in film studio **4.** representative or deputy, *esp.* of bishop

commission (kə'mishən) *n.* **1.** something entrusted to be done **2.** delegated authority **3.** body entrusted with some special duty **4.** payment by percentage for doing something **5.** warrant giving authority **6.** document appointing soldier, sailor or airman to officer's rank **7.** doing, committing —*vt.* **8.** charge with duty or task **9.** *Mil.* confer a rank on **10.** give order for —**com'missioner** *n.* **1.** one empowered to act by commission or warrant **2.** member of commission or government board —**commissioned officer** officer in armed forces holding commission, such as second lieutenant in air force, army or marine corps or ensign in coastguard or navy, or officer senior to these ranks

commit (kə'mit) *vt.* **1.** entrust, give in charge **2.** perpetrate, be guilty of **3.** pledge, promise **4.** compromise, entangle **5.** send for trial (**-tt-**) —**com'mitment** *n.* —**com'mittal** *n.*

committee (kə'miti) *n.* body appointed, elected for special business usu. from larger body

commode (kə'mōd) *n.* **1.** chest of drawers **2.** stool containing chamber pot

commodious (kə'mōdiəs) *a.* roomy

commodity (kə'moditi) *n.* **1.** article of trade **2.** anything useful

commodore ('komədör) *n.* **1.** presiding officer of yacht club or boating society **2.** ranking officer in convoy of merchant ships

common ('komən) *a.* **1.** shared by or belonging to all, or to several **2.** public, general **3.** ordinary, usual, frequent **4.** inferior **5.** vulgar —*n.* **6.** land belonging to community —*pl.* **7.** ordinary people **8.** (**C-**) lower House of British Parliament, House of Commons —**commo'nality** *n.* **1.** fact of being common **2.** commonalty —'**commonalty** *n.* general body of people —'**commoner** *n.* one of the common people, *ie* not of the nobility —'**commonly** *adv.* —**common fraction** fraction whose numerator and denominator are both whole numbers —**common law** body of law based on judicial decisions and custom —**common-law marriage** state of marriage deemed to exist between man and woman after years of cohabitation —**Common Market** European Economic Community —'**commonplace** *a.* **1.** ordinary, everyday —*n.* **2.** trite remark **3.** anything occurring frequently —**common room** sitting room in schools *etc.* —**common sense** sound, practical understanding —**common time** *Mus.* time signature indicating four quarter notes to bar; 4/4 time —'**commonwealth** *n.* **1.** republic **2.** (**C-**) federation of self-governing states

commotion (kə'mōshən) *n.* stir, disturbance, tumult

commune[1] (kə'myōōn) *vi.* converse together intimately —**com'munion** *n.* **1.** sharing of thoughts, feelings *etc.* **2.** fellowship **3.** body with common faith **4.** (**C-**) participation in sacrament of the Lord's Supper **5.** (**C-**) that sacrament, Eucharist

commune[2] ('komyōōn) *n.* group of families, individuals living together and sharing property, responsibility *etc.* —'**communal** *a.* for common use

communicate (kə'myōōnikāt) *vt.* **1.** impart, convey **2.** reveal —*vi.* **3.** give or exchange information **4.** have connecting passage, door **5.** receive Communion —**com'municable** *a.* —**com'municant** *n.* one who receives Communion —**communi'cation** *n.* **1.** act of giving, *esp.* information **2.** information, message **3.** (*usu. pl.*) passage (road, railroad *etc.*) or means of exchanging messages (radio, mail *etc.*) between places —*pl.* **4.** connections between military base and front —**com'municative** *a.* free with information

communiqué (kə'myōōnikā) *n.* official announcement

communism ('komyōōnizəm) *n.* **1.** doctrine that all goods, means of production *etc.* should be property of community and each member should work for common benefit **2.** (**C-**) political movement seeking to overthrow capitalism and to establish form of communism dominated by totalitarian bureaucracy —'**communist** *n./a.* —**commu'nistic** *a.*

community (kə'myōōniti) *n.* **1.** body of people with something in common, *eg* district of residence, religion *etc.* **2.** society, the public **3.** joint ownership **4.** similarity, agreement —**community center** place for community to participate in recreational and educational activities —**community chest** (*oft.* **C- C-**) fund of individual contributions distributed by community —**community college** tax-supported nonresidential two-year college —**community property** assets held jointly by husband and wife —**community sing** concert by large crowd singing in unison

commute (kə'myōōt) *vi.* **1.** travel daily some distance to work —*vt.* **2.** exchange **3.** change (punishment *etc.*) into something less severe **4.** change (duty *etc.*) for money payment —**commu'tation** *n.* —**com'mutative** *a.* relating to or involving substitution —'**commutator** *n.* —**commutative law** *Math.* principle in addition and multiplication of numbers that the end product is not affected by the order in which the terms are manipulated

Comoros ('komərōz) *pl.n.* country in the Indian Ocean consisting of three islands between the Afr. mainland and Madagascar

compact[1] (kəm'pakt) *a.* **1.** neatly arranged or packed **2.** solid, concentrated **3.** terse —*v.* **4.** make, become compact —*vt.* **5.** compress —**com'pactly** *adv.* —**com'pactness** *n.* —**compact disk** small audio disk read by optical laser system

compact[2] ('kompakt) *n.* small case to hold face powder, powder puff and mirror

compact[3] ('kompakt) *n.* agreement, covenant, treaty, contract

companion[1] (kəm'panyən) *n.* **1.** fellow, comrade, associate **2.** person employed to live with another —**com'panionable** *a.* —**com'panionship** *n.*

companion[2] (kəm'panyən) *n.* **1.** raised cover over staircase from deck to cabin of ship **2.** deck skylight —**com'panionway** *n.* staircase from deck to cabin

company ('kumpəni) *n.* **1.** gathering of persons **2.** companionship, fellowship **3.** guests **4.** business firm **5.** subdivision of military battalion **6.** crew of ship **7.** actors in play —**company man** person identifying completely with firm he works for —**company town** town whose residents are completely dependent on one company for employment, housing *etc.*

compare (kəm'pāər) *vt.* **1.** notice or point out likenesses and differences of **2.** liken **3.** make comparative and superlative of (adjective or adverb) —*vi.* **4.** compete —**comparability** (kompərə'biliti) *n.* —**comparable** ('kompərəbəl) *a.* —**comparative** (kəm'parətiv) *a.* **1.** that may be compared **2.** not absolute **3.** relative, partial **4.** *Gram.* denoting form of adjective, adverb, indicating 'more' —*n.* **5.** comparative form of adjective or adverb —**comparatively** (kəm'parətivli) *adv.* —**comparison** (kəm'parisən) *n.* act of comparing —**compare with** be like

compartment (kəm'pärtmənt) *n.* **1.** division or part divided off, *eg* in railway carriage **2.** section —**compart'mentalize** *vt.* put into categories *etc., esp.* to excessive degree

compass ('kumpəs) *n.* **1.** instrument for showing the north **2.** (*usu. pl.*) instrument for drawing circles **3.** circumference, measurement round **4.** space, area **5.** scope, reach —*vt.* **6.** surround **7.** comprehend **8.** attain, accomplish

compassion (kəm'pashən) *n.* pity, sympathy —**com'passionate** *a.* —**com'passionately** *adv.*

compatible (kəm'patəbəl) *a.* **1.** capable of harmonious existence **2.** consistent, agreeing —**compati'bility** *n.* —**com'patibly** *adv.*

compatriot (kəm'pātriət) *n.* fellow countryman

compel (kəm'pel) *vt.* **1.** force, oblige **2.** bring about by force (**-ll-**)

compendium (kəm'pendiəm) *n.* **1.** collection of different games **2.** abridgment, summary (*pl.* **-s, -ia** (-iə)) —**com'pendious** *a.* brief but inclusive —**com'pendiously** *adv.*

compensate ('kompənsāt) *vt.* **1.** make up for **2.** recompense suitably **3.** reward —*vi.* **4.** (*with* for) supply an equivalent —**compen'sation** *n.* **1.** act or process of compensating **2.** *Psych., psychol.* psychological mechanism whereby deficiency in one area is counterbalanced by achievement in another —**com'pensatory** *a.*

compete (kəm'pēt) *vi.* (*oft. with* with) strive in rivalry, contend, vie —**competition** (kompi'tishən) *n.* —**competitive** (kəm'petitiv) *a.* —**competitor** (kəm'petitər) *n.*

competent ('kompitənt) *a.* **1.** able, skillful **2.** properly qualified **3.** proper, due, legitimate **4.** suitable, sufficient —'**competence** *n.* efficiency —'**competently** *adv.*

compile (kəm'pīl) *vt.* **1.** make up (*eg* book) from various sources or materials **2.** gather, put together —**compilation** (kompi'lāshən) *n.* —**com'piler** *n.*

complacent (kəm'plāsənt) *a.* **1.** self-satisfied **2.** pleased, gratified —**com'placence** *or* **com'placency** *n.* —**com'placently** *adv.*

complain (kəm'plān) *vi.* **1.** protest **2.** bring charge, make known a grievance **3.** (*with* of) make known that one is suffering (from) —**com'plainant** *n.* —**com'plaint** *n.* **1.** statement of a wrong, grievance **2.** ailment, illness

complaisant (kəm'plāzənt) *a.* obliging, willing to please, compliant —**com'plaisance** *n.* **1.** act of pleasing **2.** affability

complement ('kompliment) *n.* **1.** person or thing that completes something **2.** full allowance, equipment *etc.* —*vt.* ('kompliment) **3.** add to, make complete —**comple'mentary** *a./n.* —**complementary color** color with maximum contrast to another color. Complementary of a primary color is the mixture of the other 2 primary colors, *eg* green (blue and yellow mixed) is the complementary of red

complete (kəm'plēt) *a.* **1.** full, perfect **2.** finished, ended **3.** entire **4.** thorough —*vt.* **5.** make whole, perfect **6.** finish —**com'pletely** *adv.* —**com'pleteness** *n.* —**com'pletion** *n.*

complex ('kompleks) *a.* **1.** intricate, compound, involved —*n.* **2.** complicated whole **3.** group of related buildings **4.** psychological abnormality, obsession —**com'plexity** *n.* —**complex fraction** *Math.* fraction in which numerator or denominator or both contain fractions (*also* **compound fraction**) —**complex number** number of form $a + bi$, where a and b are real numbers and $i = \sqrt{-1}$

complexion (kəm'plekshən) *n.* **1.** look, color, of skin, *esp.* of face, appearance **2.** aspect, character **3.** disposition

compliant (kəm'plīənt) *a. see* COMPLY

complicate ('komplikāt) *vt.* make intricate, involved, difficult, mix up —**compli'cation** *n.*

complicity (kəm'plisiti) *n.* partnership in wrongdoing

compliment ('komplimənt) *n.* **1.** expression of regard, praise **2.** flattering speech —*pl.* **3.** expression of courtesy, formal greetings —*vt.* ('kompliment) **4.** praise, congratulate —**compli'mentary** *a.* **1.** expressing praise **2.** free of charge

compline ('komplin, -plīn) *n. Eccles.* last service of day

comply (kəm'plī) *vi.* consent, yield, do as asked (**com'plied, com'plying**) —**com'pliance** *n.* —**com'pliant** *a.*

component (kəm'pōnənt) *n.* **1.** part, element, constituent of whole —*a.* **2.** composing, making up

comport (kəm'pōrt) *vi.* **1.** agree —*vt.* **2.** behave

compose (kəm'pōz) *vt.* **1.** arrange, put in order **2.** write, invent **3.** make up **4.** calm **5.** settle, adjust —**com'posed** *a.* calm —**com'poser** *n.* one who composes, *esp.* music —'**composite** *a.* **1.** made up of distinct parts —*n.* **2.** any member of the daisy family in which many small individual flowers are united in one head —**compo'sition** *n.* —**compositor** (kəm'pozitər) *n.* typesetter, one who arranges type for printing —**com'posure** *n.* calmness —**composite school C** school offering both academic and nonacademic courses

compos mentis ('kompəs 'mentis) *Lat.* of sound mind

compost ('kompōst) *n.* fertilizing mixture of decayed vegetable matter for soil

compote ('kompōt) *n.* **1.** fruit stewed or preserved in syrup **2.** bowl with stem and base

compound[1] ('kompownd) *n.* **1.** mixture, joining **2.** substance, word, made up of parts **3.** *Chem.* substance that can be decomposed into simpler substances —*a.* **4.** not simple **5.** composite, mixed —*vt.* (kom'pownd) **6.** mix, make up, put together **7.** intensify, make worse **8.** *Law* agree not to prosecute in return for a consideration —*v.* **9.** compromise, settle (debt) by partial payment —**compound eye** convex eye of insects and some crustaceans, consisting of numerous separate units —**compound fracture** fracture in which broken bone pierces skin —**compound interest** interest calculated on both principal and its accrued interest —**compound sentence** sentence containing at least two coordinate clauses —**compound time** *Mus.* time in which number of beats per bar is multiple of three

compound[2] ('kompownd) *n.* (fenced or walled) enclosure containing houses *etc.*

comprehend (kompri'hend) *vt.* **1.** understand, take in **2.** include, comprise —**compre'hensible** *a.* —**compre'hension** *n.* —**compre'hensive** *a.* **1.** wide, full **2.** taking in much —**compre'hensively** *adv.* —**compre'hensiveness** *n.*

compress (kəm'pres) *vt.* **1.** squeeze together **2.** make smaller in size, bulk —*n.* ('kompres) **3.** pad of lint applied to wound, inflamed part *etc.* —**com'pressible** *a.* —**com'pression** *n.* in internal-combustion engine, squeezing of explosive charge before ignition, to give additional force —**com'pressor** *n. esp.* machine to compress air, gas

comprise (kəm'prīz) *vt.* include, contain —**com'prisable** *a.*

compromise ('komprəmīz) *n.* **1.** meeting halfway, coming to terms by giving up part of claim **2.** middle course —*v.* **3.** settle (dispute) by making concessions —*vt.* **4.** expose to risk or suspicion

Comptometer (komp'tomitər) *n.* trade name for office machine used for arithmetical calculations

comptroller (kən'trōlər) *n.* controller (in some titles)

compulsion (kəm'pulshən) *n.* **1.** act of compelling **2.** irresistible impulse —**com'pulsive** *a.* —**com'pulsorily** *adv.* —**com'pulsory** *a.* not optional

compunction (kəm'pungkshən) *n.* regret for wrongdoing

compute (kəm'pyo͞ot) *v.* reckon, calculate, *esp.* using computer —**compu'tation** *n.* reckoning, estimate —**com'puter** *n.* electronic machine for storing, retrieving information and performing calculations —**com'puterize** *v.* equip with, perform by computer

comrade ('komrad, -rid) *n.* companion, friend —**'comradeship** *n.*

con[1] (kon) *vt. inf.* swindle, defraud after winning victim's confidence (**-nn-**) —**con game** *sl. see* **confidence game** *at* CONFIDE —**con man** person who swindles another by means of confidence game

con[2] (kon) *n.* argument against —**pros and cons** arguments for and against

con[3] (kon) *see* CONN (**-nn-**)

con[4] (kon) *vt.* commit (something) to memory, study (**-nn-**)

con[5] (kon) *n. sl.* convict

concatenate (kon'katināt) *vt.* link together —**concate'nation** *n.* connected chain (as of circumstances)

concave (kon'kāv, 'konkāv) *a.* hollow, rounded inward —**concavity** (kon'kaviti) *n.*

conceal (kən'sēl) *vt.* hide, keep secret —**con'cealment** *n.*

concede (kən'sēd) *vt.* **1.** admit, admit truth of **2.** grant, allow —*vi.* **3.** yield

conceit (kən'sēt) *n.* **1.** vanity, overweening opinion of oneself **2.** far-fetched comparison —**con'ceited** *a.*

conceive (kən'sēv) *vt.* **1.** believe **2.** form conception of **3.** become pregnant with —*vi.* **4.** become pregnant —**con'ceivable** *a.* —**con'ceivably** *adv.* —**conceive of** have an idea of; imagine; think of

concentrate ('konsəntrāt) *vt.* **1.** focus (one's efforts *etc.*) **2.** increase in strength **3.** reduce to small space —*vi.* **4.** devote all attention **5.** come together —*n.* **6.** concentrated material or solution —**concen'tration** *n.* —**concentration camp** detention camp where civilian political prisoners are confined

concentric (kən'sentrik) *a.* having the same center, as of circles or spheres one inside another

concept ('konsept) *n.* **1.** abstract idea **2.** mental expression —**con'ceptual** *a.* —**con'ceptualize** *v.*

conception (kən'sepshən) *n.* **1.** idea, notion **2.** act of conceiving

concern (kən'sərn) *vt.* **1.** relate or apply to **2.** interest, affect, trouble **3.** (*with* in *or* with) involve (oneself) —*n.* **4.** affair **5.** regard, worry **6.** importance **7.** business enterprise —**con'cerned** *a.* **1.** connected **2.** interested **3.** worried **4.** involved —**con'cerning** *prep.* respecting, about

concert ('konsərt) *n.* **1.** musical entertainment **2.** harmony, agreement —*v.* (kən'sərt) **3.** arrange, plan together —**con'certed** *a.* **1.** mutually arranged, planned **2.** determined —**concert grand** the largest-size grand piano, adapted to concert use —**concer'tina** *n.* **1.** musical instrument of hexagonal shape, resembling accordion —*vi.* **2.** fold, collapse, as bellows —**'concertmaster** *n.* the first violinist of an orchestra, who sits closest to the conductor and occasionally substitutes for him —**concerto** (kən'chertō) *n.* musical composition for solo instrument and orchestra (*pl.* **-s**) —**concert pitch 1.** international pitch **2.** *inf.* state of extreme readiness

concession (kən'seshən) *n.* **1.** act of conceding **2.** thing conceded **3.** grant **4.** special privilege **5.** **C** land division in township survey —**concession'aire** *or* **con'cessioner** *n.* someone who holds or operates concession —**con'cessive** *a.*

conch (kongk, konch) *n.* large spiral-shelled gastropod —**conchology** (kong'koləji) *n.* branch of zoology concerned with shells

concierge (kōn'syerzh) *n.* in France, caretaker, doorkeeper

conciliate (kən'siliāt) *vt.* pacify, win over from hostility —**concili'ation** *n.* —**con'ciliator** *n.* —**con'ciliatory** *a.*

concise (kən'sīs) *a.* brief, terse —**con'cisely** *adv.* —**con'ciseness** *n.* —**concision** (kən'sizhən) *n.*

conclave ('konklāv) *n.* **1.** private meeting **2.** assembly for election of Pope

conclude (kən'klo͞od) *vt.* **1.** end, finish **2.** deduce **3.** settle **4.** decide —*vi.* **5.** come to an end —**con'clusion** *n.* —**con'clusive** *a.* decisive, convincing —**con'clusively** *adv.*

concoct (kən'kokt) *vt.* **1.** make (mixture), with various ingredients **2.** make up **3.** contrive, plan —**con'coction** *n.*

concomitant (kən'komitənt) *a.* accompanying —**con'comitance** *n.* existence

concord ('konkörd) *n.* **1.** agreement **2.** harmony —**con'cordance** *n.* **1.** agreement **2.** index to words of book (*esp.* Bible) —**con'cordant** *a.* —**con'cordat** *n.* pact or treaty, *esp.* between Vatican and another state concerning interests of religion in that state

concourse ('konkörs) *n.* **1.** crowd **2.** large, open place in public area

concrete ('konkrēt) *n.* **1.** mixture of sand,

cement *etc.*, used in building —*a.* **2.** made of concrete **3.** particular, specific **4.** perceptible, actual **5.** solid —**'concretely** *adv.* —**con'cretion** *n.* **1.** mass of compressed particles **2.** stonelike growth in body

concubine ('kongkjoobIn) *n.* **1.** woman living as secondary wife in society where polygamy is sanctioned **2.** (*also* **mistress**) woman living with man as his wife, but not married to him —**concubinage** (kon'kyoobinij) *n.*

concupiscence (kən'kyoopisəns) *n.* lust

concur (kən'kər) *vi.* **1.** agree, express agreement **2.** happen together **3.** coincide (**-rr-**) —**con'currence** *n.* —**con'current** *a.* —**con'currently** *adv.* at the same time

concuss (kən'kus) *vt.* injure (brain) by blow, fall *etc.* —**con'cussion** *n.* temporary paralysis of brain function occurring immediately after injury to brain

condemn (kən'dem) *vt.* **1.** blame **2.** find guilty **3.** doom **4.** find, declare unfit for use —**condemnation** (kondem'nāshən) *n.* —**condemnatory** (kon'demnətōri) *a.*

condense (kən'dens) *vt.* **1.** concentrate, make more solid **2.** turn from gas into liquid **3.** pack into few words —*vi.* **4.** turn from gas to liquid —**conden'sation** *n.* —**con'denser** *n.* **1.** *Elec.* apparatus for storing electrical energy, a capacitor **2.** apparatus for reducing vapors to liquid form **3.** a lens or mirror for focusing light —**condensed milk** milk reduced by evaporation to thick concentration, with sugar added

condescend (kondi'send) *vi.* **1.** treat graciously one regarded as inferior **2.** do something below one's dignity —**conde'scending** *a.* —**conde'scension** *n.*

condign (kən'dIn) *a.* (*esp.* of punishment) fitting; deserved

condiment ('kondimənt) *n.* relish, seasoning for food

condition (kən'dishən) *n.* **1.** state or circumstances of anything **2.** thing on which statement or happening or existing depends **3.** stipulation, prerequisite **4.** health, physical fitness **5.** rank —*vt.* **6.** accustom **7.** regulate **8.** make fit, healthy **9.** be essential to happening or existence of —**con'ditional** *a.* **1.** dependent on circumstances or events —*n.* **2.** *Gram.* conditional verb form, clause *etc.* —**conditioned reflex** in psychology and physiology, automatic response induced by stimulus

condo ('kondō) *n. see* CONDOMINIUM (senses 1, 2)

condole (kən'dōl) *vi.* **1.** grieve (with), offer sympathy **2.** commiserate (with) —**con'dolence** *n.*

condom ('kondəm) *n.* sheathlike rubber contraceptive device worn by man

condominium (kondə'miniəm) *n.* **1.** building in which apartments are individually owned **2.** an apartment in such a building **3.** sovereignty over a territory by at least two states **4.** a territory so administered

condone (kən'dōn) *vt.* overlook, forgive, treat as not existing

condor

condor ('kondər) *n.* large vulture found in the Andes

conduce (kən'dyoos, -'doos) *vi.* (*with* to) **1.** help, promote **2.** tend (toward) —**con'ducive** *a.*

conduct ('kondukt) *n.* **1.** behavior **2.** management —*vt.* (kən'dukt) **3.** escort, guide **4.** lead, direct **5.** manage **6.** transmit (heat, electricity) —**con'ductance** *n.* ability of system to conduct electricity —**con'duction** *n.* —**con'ductive** *a.* —**conduc'tivity** *n.* —**con'ductor** *n.* **1.** director of orchestra **2.** one who leads, guides **3.** substance capable of transmitting heat, electricity *etc.* **4.** person who collects fares in a public conveyance

conduit ('kondyooit, -dooit) *n.* channel or pipe for conveying water, electric cables *etc.*

cone (kōn) *n.* **1.** solid figure with circular base, tapering to a point **2.** fruit of pine, fir *etc.* —**'conic(al)** *a.* of or like cone —**conic section** one of group of curves formed by intersection of plane and right circular cone

Conestoga (koni'stōgə) *n.* covered wagon used by settlers of Amer. traveling across prairies

confabulate (kən'fabyoolāt) *vi.* chat —**'confab** *n. inf.* shortened form of **confabu'lation** *n.* confidential conversation

confection (kən'fekshən) *n.* prepared delicacy, *esp.* something sweet —**con'fectioner** *n.* manufacturer of or dealer in confectionery —**con'fectionery** *n.* sweet foods, *eg* candy, pastry

confederate (kən'fedərit) *n.* **1.** ally **2.** accomplice —*v.* (kən'fedərāt) **3.** unite —**con'federacy** *n.* —**confede'ration** *n.* alliance of political units

confer (kən'fər) *vt.* **1.** grant, give **2.** bestow **3.** award —*vi.* **4.** consult together (**-rr-**) —**'conference** *n.* meeting for consultation or deliberation —**con'ferment** *n.*

confess (kən'fes) *vt.* **1.** admit, own **2.** (of priest) hear sins of —*vi.* **3.** acknowledge **4.** declare one's sins orally to priest —**con'fession** *n.* —**con'fessional** *n.* confessor's stall or box —**con'fessor** *n.* priest who hears confessions

confetti (kən'feti) *n.* small bits of colored paper for throwing *esp.* at weddings

confide (kən'fīd) *vi.* **1.** (*with* in) tell secrets, trust —*vt.* **2.** entrust —**confidant** ('konfidant) *n.* one entrusted with secrets (-**e** *fem.*) —**confidence** ('konfidəns) *n.* **1.** trust **2.** boldness, assurance **3.** intimacy **4.** something confided, secret —**confident** ('konfidənt) *a.* **1.** having or showing certainty; sure **2.** sure of oneself **3.** presumptuous —**confidential** (konfi'denchəl) *a.* **1.** private **2.** secret **3.** entrusted with another's confidences —**confidentially** (konfi'denchəli) *adv.* —**confidently** ('konfidəntli) *adv.* —**con'fiding** *a.* unsuspicious; trustful —**confidence game** swindle in which victim entrusts money *etc.* to thief, believing him honest

configuration (kənfigyə'rāshən, -figə-) *n.* shape, aspect, conformation, arrangement

confine (kən'fīn) *vt.* **1.** keep within bounds **2.** keep in house, bed *etc.* **3.** shut up, imprison —**con'finement** *n.* **1.** act of confining or state of being confined **2.** period of birth of child —**'confines** *pl.n.* boundaries, limits

confirm (kən'fərm) *vt.* **1.** make certain of, verify **2.** strengthen, settle **3.** make valid, ratify **4.** administer confirmation to —**confir'mation** *n.* **1.** making strong, certain **2.** rite administered by bishop to confirm vows made at baptism —**con'firmatory** *a.* tending to confirm or establish, corroborative —**con'firmed** *a.* (of habit *etc.*) long-established

confiscate ('konfiskāt) *vt.* seize by authority —**confis'cation** *n.* —**con'fiscatory** *a.*

conflagration (konflə'grāshən) *n.* great destructive fire

conflate (kən'flāt) *vt.* combine, blend to form whole

conflict ('konflikt) *n.* **1.** struggle, trial of strength **2.** disagreement —*vi.* (kən'flikt) **3.** be at odds (with), be inconsistent (with) **4.** clash

confluence ('konflōōəns) *or* **conflux** ('konfluks) *n.* **1.** union of streams **2.** meeting place —**'confluent** *a.*

conform (kən'fôrm) *vi.* **1.** comply with accepted standards, conventions *etc.* —*v.* **2.** adapt to rule, pattern, custom *etc.* —**con'formable** *a.* —**con'formably** *adv.* —**confor'mation** *n.* structure, adaptation —**con'formist** *n.* one who conforms, *esp.* excessively —**con'formity** *n.* compliance

confound (kən'fownd) *vt.* **1.** baffle, perplex **2.** confuse **3.** defeat —**con'founded** *a. esp. inf.* damned

confrère ('konfrāər) *n.* fellow member of profession *etc.*

confront (kən'frunt) *vt.* **1.** face **2.** bring face to face (with) —**confron'tation** *n.*

Confucianism (kən'fyōōshənizəm) *n.* ethical system of Confucius (551-479 B.C.), Chinese philosopher, emphasizing devotion to family, peace and justice

confuse (kən'fyōōz) *vt.* **1.** bewilder **2.** jumble **3.** make unclear **4.** mistake (one thing) for another **5.** disconcert —**con'fusion** *n.*

confute (kən'fyōōt) *vt.* prove wrong; disprove —**confu'tation** *n.*

conga ('konggə) *n.* Latin American dance performed by number of people in single file

congé (kōn'zhā) *n.* **1.** permission to depart or dismissal, *esp.* when formal **2.** farewell

congeal (kən'jēl) *v.* solidify by cooling or freezing —**conge'lation** *n.*

congener ('konjinər, kən'jēnər) *n.* member of same genus as another plant or animal

congenial (kən'jēnyəl) *a.* **1.** pleasant, to one's liking **2.** of similar disposition, tastes *etc.* —**congeni'ality** *n.* —**con'genially** *adv.*

congenital (kən'jenitəl) *a.* **1.** existing at birth **2.** dating from birth

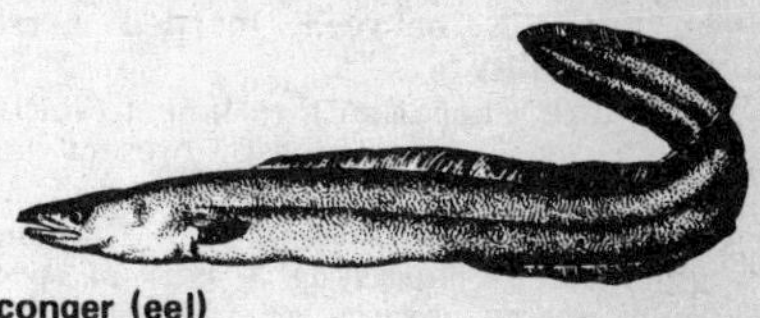

conger (eel)

conger ('konggər) *n.* large, voracious sea eel, important as food fish

congeries ('konjərēz) *n. sing. and pl.* collection or mass of small bodies, conglomeration

congest (kən'jest) *v.* overcrowd or clog —**con'gested** *a.* —**con'gestion** *n.* abnormal accumulation, overcrowding

conglomerate (kən'glomərit) *n.* **1.** thing, substance (*esp.* rock) composed of mixture of other, smaller elements or pieces **2.** business organization comprising many companies —*v.* (kən'glomərāt) **3.** gather together —*a.* **4.** made up of heterogeneous elements **5.** (of sedimentary rocks) consisting of rounded fragments within finer matrix —**conglomer'ation** *n.*

Congo ('konggō) *n.* **1.** country in Africa bounded by Cameroon and the Central African Republic to the north, Zaïre to the east and south, Angola and the Atlantic Ocean to the southwest and Gabon to the west **2.** *former name of* ZAÏRE

congratulate (kən'grachəlāt, -'graj-) *vt.* express pleasure at good fortune, success *etc.* —**congratu'lation** *n.* —**con'gratulatory** *a.*

congregate ('konggrigāt) *v.* **1.** assemble **2.** collect, flock together —**congre'gation** *n.* assembly, *esp.* for worship —**congre'gational** *a.* —**Congre'gationalism** *n.* system in which each separate church is self-governing —**Congre'gationalist** *n.*

congress ('konggris) *n.* **1.** meeting **2.** formal assembly for discussion **3.** legislative body —**con'gressional** *a.* —**'congressman** *n.* member of the U.S. House of Representatives

congruent ('konggrōōənt) *a.* **1.** suitable, accordant **2.** fitting together, *esp.* triangles —**'congruence** *n.* —**con'gruity** *n.* —**'congruous** *a.*

conic(al) ('konik(əl)) *a. see* CONE

conifer ('konifər, 'kōn-) *n.* **1.** order of mainly evergreen trees and shrubs including pine, fir, spruce and also yews and related species **2.** cone-bearing plant or other plant producing pollen in cones —**co'niferous** *a.*

conjecture (kən'jekchər) *n.* **1.** guess, guesswork —*v.* **2.** guess, surmise —**con'jectural** *a.*

conjoin (kən'join) *vt.* **1.** combine —*vi.* **2.** come, or act, together —**con'joint** *a.* concerted, united —**con'jointly** *adv.*

conjugal ('konjōōgəl) *a.* **1.** relating to marriage **2.** between married persons —**conju'gality** *n.*

conjugate ('konjōōgāt) *vt.* inflect (verb) in its various forms (past, present *etc.*) —**conju'gation** *n.*

conjunction (kən'jungkshən) *n.* **1.** union **2.** simultaneous happening **3.** part of speech joining words, phrases *etc.* —**con'junctive** *a.* —**con'juncture** *n.*

conjunctiva (konjungk'tīvə) *n.* mucous membrane lining eyelid —**conjuncti'vitis** *n.* inflammation of this

conjure ('konjər) *vi.* **1.** produce magic effects **2.** perform tricks by jugglery *etc.* **3.** invoke devils —*vt.* (kən'jōōər) **4.** implore earnestly —**conju'ration** *n.* —**'conjurer** *or* **'conjuror** *n.* —**conjure up 1.** present to the mind **2.** call up (spirit or devil) by incantation

conk (kongk) *inf. vt.* **1.** strike (*esp.* on head) —*n.* **2.** nose —**conk out** *inf.* **1.** break down **2.** tire suddenly; collapse

conn *or* **con** (kon) *vt.* **1.** direct steering of (ship) —*n.* **2.** the control of one who conns

Conn. Connecticut

connect (kə'nekt) *v.* **1.** join together, unite —*vt.* **2.** associate in the mind —**con'nection** *n.* **1.** association **2.** train *etc.* timed to enable passengers to transfer from another **3.** family relation —**con'nective** *a.* —**connecting rod** that part of engine which transfers motion from piston to crankshaft

Connecticut (kə'netikət) *n.* New England state of the U.S.: ratified the Constitution in 1788. Abbrev.: **Conn., CT** (with ZIP code)

conning tower ('koning) armored control position in submarine, battleship *etc.* (*see also* CONN)

connive (kə'nīv) *vi.* **1.** plot, conspire **2.** assent, refrain from preventing or forbidding —**con'nivance** *n.*

connoisseur (koni'sər) *n.* **1.** critical expert in matters of taste, *esp.* fine arts **2.** competent judge

connote (ko'nōt) *vt.* imply, mean in addition to primary meaning —**conno'tation** *n.*

connubial (kə'nyōōbiəl, -'nōō-) *a.* of marriage

conquer ('kongkər) *vt.* **1.** win by force of arms, overcome **2.** defeat —*vi.* **3.** be victorious —**'conqueror** *n.* —**'conquest** *n.*

conquistador (kon'kwistədōr) *n.* adventurer or conqueror, *esp.* one of Sp. conquerors of New World in 16th cent. (*pl.* **-s, -dores** (-dōrās))

consanguinity (konsan'gwiniti) *n.* kinship —**consan'guineous** *a.*

conscience ('konchəns) *n.* sense of right or wrong governing person's words and actions —**consci'entious** *a.* **1.** scrupulous **2.** obedient to the dictates of conscience —**consci'entiously** *adv.* —**conscience money** money paid voluntarily to compensate for dishonesty, *esp.* for taxes formerly evaded —**conscience-stricken** *a.* feeling anxious or guilty (*also* **conscience-smitten**) —**conscientious objector** one who refuses military service on moral or religious grounds

conscious ('konchəs) *a.* **1.** aware **2.** awake to one's surroundings and identity **3.** deliberate, intentional —**'consciously** *adv.* —**'consciousness** *n.* being conscious

conscript ('konskript) *n.* **1.** one compulsorily enlisted for military service —*vt* (kən'skript) **2.** enroll for compulsory military service —**con'scription** *n.*

consecrate ('konsikrāt) *vt.* make sacred —**conse'cration** *n.*

consecutive (kən'sekyətiv, -kə-) *a.* in unbroken succession —**con'secutively** *adv.*

consensus (kən'sensəs) *n.* widespread agreement, unanimity

consent (kən'sent) *vi.* **1.** agree, comply —*n.* **2.** acquiescence **3.** permission **4.** agreement —**con'sentient** *a.*

consequence ('konsikwəns) *n.* **1.** result, effect, outcome **2.** that which naturally follows **3.** significance, importance —**'consequent** *a.* —**conse'quential** *a.* important —**'consequently** *adv.* therefore, as a result

conservatoire (kən'sərvətwär) *n. see at* CONSERVE

conserve (kən'sərv) *vt.* **1.** keep from change or decay **2.** preserve **3.** maintain —*n.* ('konsərv) **4.** jam, preserved fruit *etc.* —**conser'vation** *n.* protection, careful management of natural resources and environment —**conser'vationist** *n./a.* —**con'servatism** *n.* —**con'servative** *a.* **1.** tending or wishing to conserve **2.** moderate —*n.* **3.** *Pol.* one who desires to preserve institutions of his country against change and innovation **4.** one opposed to hasty changes or innovations —**conservatoire** (kən'sərvətwär) *n.* an institution or school for instruction in music —**con'servatory** *n.* **1.** greenhouse **2.** conservatoire —**conservation of energy** principle that total energy of isolated system is constant and independent of changes occurring within system —**conservation of mass** principle that total mass of isolated system is constant and independent of chemical and physical changes taking place within system

consider (kən'sidər) *vt.* **1.** think over **2.** examine **3.** make allowance for **4.** have as opinion **5.** discuss —**con'siderable** *a.* **1.** important **2.** somewhat large —**con'siderably** *adv.* —**con'siderate** *a.* thoughtful for others' feelings, careful —**con'siderately** *adv.* —**conside'ration** *n.* **1.** deliberation **2.** point of importance **3.** thoughtfulness **4.** bribe, recompense —**con'sidered** *a.* **1.** presented or thought out with care **2.** esteemed —**con'sidering** *prep.* **1.** in view of —*adv.* **2.** *inf.* all in all; taking circumstances into account —*conj.* **3.** in view of the fact (that)

consign (kən'sīn) *vt.* **1.** commit, hand over **2.** entrust to carrier —**consign'ee** *n.* —**con'signment** *n.* goods consigned —**con'signor** *n.*

consist (kən'sist) *vi.* **1.** be composed (of) **2.** (*with* in) have as basis **3.** agree (with), be compatible (with) —**con'sistency** *or* **con'sistence** *n.* **1.** agreement **2.** harmony **3.** degree of firmness —**con'sistent** *a.* **1.** unchanging, constant **2.** agreeing (with) —**con'sistently** *adv.*

consistory (kən'sistəri) *n.* ecclesiastical court or council, *esp.* of Pope and Cardinals

console[1] (kən'sōl) *vt.* comfort, cheer in distress —**conso'lation** *n.* —**con'solatory** *a.*

console[2] ('konsōl) *n.* **1.** bracket supporting shelf **2.** keyboard, stops *etc.*, of organ **3.** cabinet for television, radio *etc.*

consolidate (kən'solidāt) *vt.* **1.** combine into connected whole **2.** make firm, secure —**consoli'dation** *n.*

consommé (konsə'mā) *n.* clear soup made from concentrated stock —**jellied consommé** consommé which has been chilled

consonant ('konsənənt) *n.* **1.** sound making a syllable only with vowel **2.** nonvowel —*a.* **3.** agreeing, in accord —'**consonance** *n.*

consort (kən'sört) *vi.* **1.** associate, keep company —*n.* ('konsört) **2.** husband, wife, *esp.* of ruler **3.** ship sailing with another —**con'sortium** *n.* association of banks, companies *etc.*

conspectus (kən'spektəs) *n.* **1.** a comprehensive view or survey of subject **2.** synopsis

conspicuous (kən'spikyōōəs) *a.* **1.** striking, noticeable, outstanding **2.** prominent **3.** eminent —**con'spicuously** *adv.*

conspire (kən'spīər) *vi.* **1.** combine for evil purpose **2.** plot, devise —**conspiracy** (kən'spirəsi) *n.* —**conspirator** (kən'spirətər) *n.* —**conspiratorial** (kənspirə'töriəl) *a.*

constable ('kunstəbəl, 'kon-) *n. Hist.* officer of the peace —**con'stabulary** *n.* police force

constant ('konstənt) *a.* **1.** fixed, unchanging **2.** steadfast **3.** always duly happening or continuing —*n.* **4.** quantity that does not vary —'**constancy** *n.* **1.** steadfastness **2.** loyalty —'**constantly** *adv.*

constellation (konsti'lāshən) *n.* **1.** any of 88 designated configurations of stars **2.** assembly of related persons or things

consternation (konstər'nāshən) *n.* alarm, dismay, panic —'**consternate** *vt.*

constipation (konsti'pāshən) *n.* difficulty in emptying bowels —'**constipate** *vt.* affect with this disorder

constituent (kən'stichōōənt) *a.* **1.** going toward making up whole **2.** having power to make, alter constitution of state **3.** electing representative —*n.* **4.** component part **5.** element **6.** elector —**con'stituency** *n.* **1.** residents of electoral district **2.** electoral district

constitute ('konstityōōt, -tōōt) *vt.* **1.** compose, set up, establish, form **2.** make into, found, give form to —**consti'tution** *n.* **1.** structure, composition **2.** health **3.** character, disposition **4.** principles on which state is governed —**consti'tutional** *a.* **1.** pert. to constitution **2.** in harmony with political constitution —*n.* **3.** walk taken for health's sake —**consti'tutionally** *adv.* —'**constitutive** *a.* **1.** having power to enact or establish **2.** *see* CONSTITUENT (sense 1)

constrain (kən'strān) *vt.* force, compel —**con'straint** *n.* **1.** compulsion **2.** restraint **3.** embarrassment, tension

constriction (kən'strikshən) *n.* compression, squeezing together —**con'strict** *vt.* —**con'strictive** *a.* —**con'strictor** *n.* that which constricts (*see also* BOA)

construct (kən'strukt) *vt.* **1.** make, build, form **2.** put together **3.** compose —*n.* ('konstrukt) **4.** something formulated systematically —**con'struction** *n.* —**con'structive** *a.* **1.** serving to improve **2.** positive —**con'structively** *adv.*

construe (kən'strōō) *vt.* **1.** interpret **2.** deduce **3.** analyze grammatically

consul ('konsəl) *n.* **1.** officer appointed by a government to represent it in a foreign country **2.** in ancient Rome, one of the chief magistrates —'**consular** *a.* —'**consulate** *n.* —'**consulship** *n.*

consult (kən'sult) *vt.* seek counsel, advice, information from —**con'sultant** *n.* **1.** specialist **2.** expert —**consul'tation** *n.* **1.** consulting **2.** appointment to seek professional advice, *esp.* of doctor, lawyer —**con'sultative** *a.* **1.** having privilege of consulting, but not of voting **2.** advisory

consume (kən'sōōm) *vt.* **1.** eat or drink **2.** engross, possess **3.** use up **4.** destroy —**con'sumer** *n.* **1.** buyer or user of commodity **2.** one who consumes —**con'sumerism** *n.* **1.** protection of interests of consumers **2.** advocacy of high rate of consumption as basis for sound economy —**consumption** (kən'sumpshən) *n.* **1.** using up **2.** destruction **3.** tuberculosis —**consumptive** (kən'sumptiv) *a./n.* —**consumptiveness** (kən'sumptivnis) *n.*

consummate ('konsəmāt) *vt.* **1.** perfect **2.** fulfill **3.** complete (*esp.* marriage by sexual intercourse) —*a.* (kən'sumit, 'konsəmit) **4.** of greatest perfection or completeness —**con'summately** *adv.* —**consum'mation** *n.*

cont. continued

contact ('kontakt) *n.* **1.** touching **2.** being in touch **3.** junction of two or more electrical conductors **4.** useful acquaintance —*vt.* ('kontakt, kən'takt) **5.** put, come or be in touch (with) —**contact lens** lens fitting over eyeball to correct defect of vision

contagion (kən'tājən) *n.* **1.** passing on of disease by touch, contact **2.** contagious disease **3.** harmful physical or moral influence —**con'tagious** *a.* communicable by contact, catching

contain (kən'tān) *vt.* **1.** hold **2.** have room for **3.** include, comprise **4.** restrain —**con'tainer** *n.* **1.** box *etc.* for holding **2.** large cargo-carrying standard-sized receptacle for different modes of transport —**containeri'zation** *n.* —**con'tainerize** *vt.* **1.** convey in standard-sized containers **2.** adapt to use of standard-sized containers —**con'tainment** *n.* act of containing, *esp.* of restraining power of hostile country or operations of hostile military force

contaminate (kən'taminat) *vt.* **1.** stain, pollute, infect **2.** make radioactive —**contami'nation** *n.* pollution

contemn (kən'tem) *vt.* regard with contempt; scorn

contemplate ('kontəmplāt) *vt.* **1.** reflect, meditate on **2.** gaze upon **3.** intend —**contem'plation** *n.* **1.** thoughtful consideration **2.** spiritual meditation —**con'templative** *a./n.* (one) given to contemplation

contemporary (kən'tempəreri) *a.* **1.** existing or lasting at same time **2.** of same age **3.** present-day —*n.* **4.** one existing at same time as another —**contempo'raneous** *a.*

contempt (kən'tempt) *n.* **1.** feeling that something is worthless, despicable *etc.* **2.** expression of this feeling **3.** state of being despised, disregarded **4.** willful disrespect of authority

contend (kən'tend) *vi.* **1.** strive, fight —*v.* **2.** dispute —*vt.* **3.** maintain —**con'tention** *n.* **1.** strife **2.** debate **3.** subject matter of dispute —**con'tentious** *a.* **1.** quarrelsome **2.** causing dispute —**con'tentiously** *adv.*

content[1] ('kontent) *n.* **1.** that contained **2.** holding capacity —*pl.* **3.** that contained **4.** index of topics in book

content[2] (kən'tent) *a.* **1.** satisfied **2.** willing —*vt.* **3.** satisfy —*n.* **4.** satisfaction —**con'tented** *a.* —**con'tentment** *n.*

conterminous (kən'tərminəs) *a.* **1.** of the same extent (in time *etc.*) **2.** meeting along a common boundary **3.** meeting end to end

contest ('kontest) *n.* **1.** competition **2.** conflict —*vt.* (kən'test) **3.** dispute, debate **4.** fight or compete for —**con'testable** *a.* —**con'testant** *n.* —**contes'tation** *n.*

context ('kontekst) *n.* **1.** words coming before, after a word or passage **2.** conditions and circumstances of event, fact *etc.* —**con'textual** *a.*

contiguous (kən'tigyōōəs) *a.* touching, near —**conti'guity** *n.*

continent[1] ('kontinənt) *n.* large continuous mass of land —**conti'nental** *a.* —**continental breakfast** light breakfast of coffee and rolls —**continental code** the International Morse Code —**continental drift** *Geol.* theory that earth's continents move gradually over surface of planet on substratum of magma —**continental shelf** submarine plain bordering continent and sloping eventually to a deep abyss

continent[2] ('kontinənt) *a.* **1.** able to control one's urination and defecation **2.** sexually chaste —'**continence** *n.*

contingent (kən'tinjənt) *a.* **1.** depending **2.** possible **3.** accidental —*n.* **4.** group (of troops, sportsmen *etc.*) part of or representative of a larger group —**con'tingency** *n.* —**con'tingently** *adv.*

continue (kən'tinyōō) *v.* **1.** remain, keep in existence **2.** carry on, last, go on **3.** resume **4.** prolong —**con'tinual** *a.* recurring frequently, *esp.* at regular intervals —**con'tinually** *adv.* —**con'tinuance** *n.* **1.** act of continuing **2.** duration of action *etc.* **3.** adjournment of legal proceeding —**continu'ation** *n.* **1.** extension, extra part **2.** resumption **3.** constant succession, prolongation —**conti'nuity** *n.* **1.** logical sequence **2.** state of being continuous —**con'tinuo** *n. Mus.* representation of keyboard part by bass notes only (*pl.* **-s**) (*also* **basso continuo, thorough bass**) —**con'tinuous** *a.* unceasing —**con'tinuously** *adv.* —**con'tinuum** *n.* continuous series or whole with no part perceptibly different from adjacent parts (*pl.* **-'tinua, -s**)

contort (kən'tôrt) *vt.* twist out of normal shape —**con'tortion** *n.* —**con'tortionist** *n.* one who contorts his body to entertain

contour ('kontōōər) *n.* outline, shape, *esp.* mountains, coast *etc.* —**contour line** line on map drawn through places of same height —**contour map**

contra- (*comb. form*) against, as in *contraposition.* Such words are omitted where the meaning may easily be inferred from the simple word

contraband ('kontrəband) *n.* **1.** smuggled goods **2.** illegal traffic in such goods —*a.* **3.** prohibited by law

contrabassoon (kontrəbə'sōōn) *n. see* **double bassoon** *at* BASSOON

contraception (kontrə'sepshən) *n.* prevention of conception usu. by artificial means, birth control —**contra'ceptive** *a./n.*

contract (kən'trakt) *v.* **1.** make or become smaller, shorter —*vi.* ('kontrakt) **2.** make a contract —*vt.* **3.** become affected by **4.** incur **5.** undertake by contract —*n.* ('kontrakt) **6.** bargain, agreement **7.** formal document recording agreement **8.** agreement enforceable by law —**con'tracted** *a.* drawn together —**con'tractile** *a.* tending to contract —**con'traction** *n.* —**'contractor** *n.* one making contract, *esp.* builder —**con'tractual** *a.* —**contract bridge** *see* BRIDGE[2]

contradict (kontrə'dikt) *vt.* **1.** deny **2.** be at variance or inconsistent with —**contra'diction** *n.* —**contra'dictious** *a.* —**contra'dictor** *n.* —**contra'dictory** *a.*

contradistinction (kontrədi'stingkshən) *n.* distinction made by contrasting different qualities

contralto (kən'traltō) *n.* **1.** singing voice with range between mezzosoprano and tenor **2.** person having this voice **3.** the part sung by a contralto (*pl.* **-s**)

contraption (kən'trapshən) *n.* **1.** gadget **2.** device **3.** construction, device oft. overelaborate or eccentric

contrapuntal (kontrə'puntəl) *a. Mus.* pert. to counterpoint

contrary ('kontreri) *a.* **1.** opposed **2.** opposite, other **3.** (kən'trāəri) perverse, obstinate —*n.* **4.** something the exact opposite of another —*adv.* **5.** in opposition —**contra'riety** *n.* —**'contrarily** *adv.* —**'contrariwise** *adv.* conversely

contrast (kən'träst) *vt.* **1.** distinguish by comparison of unlike or opposite qualities —*vi.* **2.** show great difference —*n.* ('konträst) **3.** striking difference **4.** *T.V.* sharpness of image

contravene (kontrə'vēn) *vt.* **1.** transgress, infringe **2.** conflict with **3.** contradict —**contra'vention** *n.*

contretemps ('kontrətän) *n.* unexpected and embarrassing situation or mishap

contribute (kən'tribyo͞ot) *v.* **1.** give, pay to common fund **2.** write (articles *etc.*) for the press —*vi.* **3.** help to occur —**contri'bution** *n.* —**con'tributive** *a.* —**con'tributor** *n.* **1.** one who writes articles for newspapers *etc.* **2.** one who donates —**con'tributory** *a.* **1.** partly responsible **2.** giving to pension fund *etc.*

contrite ('kontrīt, kən'trīt) *a.* remorseful for wrongdoing, penitent —**'contritely** *adv.* —**contrition** (kən'trishən) *n.*

contrive (kən'trīv) *vt.* **1.** manage **2.** devise, invent, design —*v.* **3.** plot, scheme —**con'trivance** *n.* artifice or device —**con'trived** *a.* obviously planned, artificial —**con'triver** *n.*

control (kən'trōl) *vt.* **1.** command, dominate **2.** regulate **3.** direct, check, test (**-ll-**) —*n.* **4.** power to direct or determine **5.** curb, check **6.** standard of comparison in experiment —*pl.* **7.** system of instruments to control car, aircraft *etc.* —**con'trollable** *a.* —**con'troller** *n.* **1.** one who controls **2.** official controlling expenditure —**control tower** tower in airfield from which take-offs and landings are directed

controversy ('kontrəvərsi) *n.* dispute, debate, *esp.* over public issues —**contro'versial** *a.* —**contro'versialist** *n.* —**'controvert** *vt.* **1.** deny **2.** argue about —**contro'vertible** *a.*

contumacy (kən'tyo͞oməsi, -'to͞o-) *n.* stubborn disobedience —**contu'macious** *a.*

contumely (kən'tyo͞omili, -'to͞o-) *n.* insulting language or treatment —**contumelious** (kontyə'mēliəs, -tə-) *a.* abusive, insolent

contusion (kən'tyo͞ozhən, -'to͞o-) *n.* bruise —**con'tuse** *vt.* bruise

conundrum (kə'nundrəm) *n.* riddle, *esp.* with punning answer

conurbation (konər'bāshən) *n.* densely populated urban sprawl formed by spreading of towns

convalesce (konvə'les) *vi.* recover health after illness, operation *etc.* —**conva'lescence** *n.* —**conva'lescent** *a./n.*

convection (kən'vekshən) *n.* transmission, *esp.* of heat, by currents in liquids or gases —**con'vector** *n.*

convene (kən'vēn) *vt.* call together, assemble, convoke —**convention** (kən'venchən) *n.* **1.** assembly **2.** treaty, agreement **3.** rule **4.** practice based on agreement **5.** accepted usage —**conventional** (kən'venchənəl) *a.* **1.** (slavishly) observing customs of society **2.** customary **3.** (of weapons, war *etc.*) not nuclear —**conventionality** (kənvenchə'nali ti) *n.* —**conventionally** (kən'venchənəli) *adv.*

convenient (kən'vēnyənt) *a.* **1.** handy **2.** favorable to needs, comfort **3.** well-adapted to one's purpose —**con'venience** *n.* **1.** ease, comfort, suitability **2.** toilet —*a.* **3.** (of food) quick to prepare —**con'veniently** *adv.*

convent ('konvənt) *n.* **1.** religious community, *esp.* of nuns **2.** their building **3.** school in which teachers are nuns (*also* **convent school**) —**con'ventual** *a.*

conventicle (kən'ventikəl) *n.* **1.** secret or unauthorized assembly for worship **2.** small meeting house or chapel, *esp.* of Dissenters

converge (kən'vərj) *vi.* **1.** move toward same point **2.** meet, join **3.** *Math.* (of infinite series) approach finite limit as number of terms increases —**con'vergence** *or* **con'vergency** *n.* —**con'vergent** *a.*

conversant (kən'vərsənt) *a.* acquainted, familiar, versed (in)

converse[1] (kən'vərs) *vi.* **1.** talk —*n.* ('konvərs) **2.** talk —**conver'sation** *n.* —**conver'sational** *a.* —**conver'sationalist** *n.*

converse[2] (kən'vərs, 'konvərs) *a.* **1.** opposite, turned round, reversed —*n.* **2.** the opposite, contrary

convert (kən'vərt) *vt.* **1.** apply to another purpose **2.** change **3.** transform **4.** cause to adopt (another) religion, opinion —*vi.* **5.** make successful try for point or free throw —*n.* (ˈkonvərt) **6.** converted person —**conˈversion** *n.* **1.** change of state **2.** unauthorized appropriation **3.** change of opinion, religion or party —**conˈverter** *n.* **1.** one who, that which converts **2.** electrical device for changing alternating current into direct current **3.** vessel in which molten metal is refined —**conˈvertible** *n.* **1.** automobile with folding roof —*a.* **2.** capable of being converted **3.** (of automobile) having folding or removable roof

convex (konˈveks, ˈkonveks) *a.* **1.** curved outward **2.** of a rounded form —**conˈvexity** *n.*

convey (kənˈvā) *vt.* **1.** carry, transport **2.** impart, communicate **3.** *Law* make over, transfer —**conˈveyance** *n.* **1.** carrying **2.** vehicle **3.** act by which title to property is transferred —**conˈveyancer** *n.* one skilled in legal forms of transferring property —**conˈveyancing** *n.* this work —**conveyor belt** continuous moving belt for transporting things, *esp.* in factory

convict (kənˈvikt) *vt.* **1.** prove or declare guilty —*n.* (ˈkonvikt) **2.** pérson found guilty of crime **3.** criminal serving prison sentence —**conˈviction** *n.* **1.** verdict of guilty **2.** being convinced, firm belief, state of being sure

convince (kənˈvins) *vt.* firmly persuade, satisfy by evidence or argument —**conˈvincing** *a.* capable of compelling belief, effective

convivial (kənˈviviəl) *a.* sociable, festive, jovial —**conviviˈality** *n.*

convoke (kənˈvōk) *vt.* call together —**convoˈcation** *n.* calling together, assembly, *esp.* of clergy, university graduates *etc.*

convolute (ˈkonvəlo͞ot) *vt.* twist, coil, tangle —ˈ**convoluted** *a.* —**convoˈlution** *n.*

convolvulus (kənˈvolvyo͞oləs) *n.* genus of plants with twining stems of the morning-glory family

convoy (ˈkonvoi) *n.* **1.** party of ships, troops, trucks *etc.* traveling together for protection —*vt.* **2.** escort for protection

convulse (kənˈvuls) *vt.* **1.** shake violently **2.** affect with violent involuntary contractions of muscles —**conˈvulsion** *n.* **1.** violent upheaval —*pl.* **2.** spasms **3.** fits of laughter or hysteria —**conˈvulsive** *a.* —**conˈvulsively** *adv.*

cony *or* **coney** (ˈkōni) *n.* rabbit

coo (ko͞o) *n.* **1.** cry of doves —*vi.* **2.** make such cry (**cooed, ˈcooing**)

cook (ko͝ok) *vt.* **1.** prepare (food) for table, *esp.* by heat **2.** *inf.* falsify (accounts *etc.*) —*vi.* **3.** undergo cooking **4.** act as cook —*n.* **5.** one who prepares food for table —ˈ**cooker** *n.* cooking apparatus —ˈ**cookery** *n.* —ˈ**cookie** *n.* **1.** small flat dry cake of sweet dough **2.** attractive woman **3.** *sl.* person —ˈ**cookbook** *n.* **1.** book of recipes and cooking directions **2.** book of detailed instructions —**cook one's goose** ruin one's chances —**cook up 1.** *inf.* invent, plan **2.** prepare (meal)

cool (ko͞ol) *a.* **1.** moderately cold **2.** unexcited, calm **3.** lacking friendliness or interest **4.** *inf.* calmly insolent **5.** *inf.* sophisticated, elegant —*v.* **6.** make, become cool —*n.* **7.** cool time, place *etc.* **8.** *inf.* calmness, composure —ˈ**coolant** *n.* fluid used for cooling tool, machinery *etc.* —ˈ**cooler** *n.* **1.** vessel in which liquids are cooled **2.** *sl.* prison **3.** tall iced alcoholic drink —ˈ**coolly** *adv.* —**cooling tower** structure used in industrial processes to cool hot water for reuse —**cool it** calm down

Coolidge (ˈko͞olij) *n.* **Calvin.** the 30th President of the U.S. (1925-29)

coolie (ˈko͞oli) *n.* cheaply hired oriental unskilled laborer

coon (ko͞on) *n. sl. offens.* Black person

coop (ko͞op) *n.* **1.** cage or pen for fowls —*vt.* (*oft. with* up) **2.** shut up in a coop **3.** confine

co-op (ˈkōop) *n.* cooperative society or shop run by one

cooper (ˈko͞opər) *n.* one who makes casks

cooperate (kōˈopərāt) *vi.* work together —**cooperˈation** *n.* —**coˈoperative** *a.* **1.** willing to cooperate **2.** (of an enterprise) owned collectively and managed for joint economic benefit —*n.* **3.** cooperative organization, such as farm —**coˈoperator** *n.*

co-opt (kōˈopt) *vt.* bring on (committee *etc.*) as member, colleague, without election by larger body choosing first members

coordinate (kōˈördināt) *vt.* **1.** bring into order as parts of whole **2.** place in same rank **3.** put into harmony —*n.* (kōˈördinit) **4.** *Math.* any of set of numbers defining location of point —*pl.* **5.** clothes of matching or harmonious colors and design, suitable for wearing together —*a.* (kōˈördinit) **6.** equal in degree, status *etc.* —**coordiˈnation** *n.* —**coˈordinative** *a.* —**coordinate geometry** *see* **analytic geometry** *at* ANALYSIS

coot (ko͞ot) *n.* **1.** small black water fowl **2.** *sl.* silly (old) person

cop (kop) *sl. vt.* **1.** catch **2.** (*usu. with* it) be punished (**-pp-**) —*n.* **3.** policeman **4.** a capture —**cop-out** *n. sl.* act of copping out —**cop out** *sl.* fail to assume responsibility, fail to perform

copal (ˈkōpəl, -pal) *n.* resin used in varnishes

copartner (kōˈpärtnər) *n.* joint partner —**coˈpartnership** *n.*

cope[1] (kōp) *vi.* deal successfully

cope[2] (kōp) *n.* ecclesiastical vestment like long cloak

Copernican (kəˈpərnikən) *a.* pert. to Copernicus, Polish astronomer (1473–1543), or to his system —**Copernican system** theory published by Copernicus, which stated that earth and planets rotated around sun

copestone (ˈkōpstōn) *n.* **1.** stone used to form coping **2.** stone at top of wall *etc.*

copier (ˈkopiər) *n. see* COPY

copilot ('kōpīlət) *n.* second or relief pilot of aircraft

coping ('kōping) *n.* top course of wall, usu. sloping to throw off rain

coping saw handsaw with U-shaped frame for cutting curves in wood

copious ('kōpiəs) *a.* **1.** abundant **2.** plentiful **3.** full, ample —'**copiously** *adv.* —'**copiousness** *n.*

copper[1] ('kopər) *n.* **1.** *Chem.* metallic element *Symbol* Cu, at. wt. 63.5, at. no. 29 **2.** bronze money, coin **3.** large washing vessel —*vt.* **4.** cover with copper —**copper-bottomed** *a.* reliable, *esp.* financially —'**copperplate** *n.* **1.** plate of copper for engraving, etching **2.** print from this **3.** copybook writing **4.** fine handwriting based upon that used on copperplate engravings —'**coppersmith** *n.* one who works with copper

copper[2] ('kopər) *n. sl.* policeman

coppice ('kopis) *n.* wood of small trees

copra ('kōprə) *n.* dried coconut kernels

Copt (kopt) *n.* **1.** member of Coptic Church **2.** Egyptian descended from ancient Egyptians —'**Coptic** *n.* **1.** Afro-Asiatic language, written in Greek alphabet but descended from ancient Egyptian —*a.* **2.** of this language **3.** of Copts —**Coptic art** Christian art in Egypt from the 3rd to 9th centuries

copula ('kopyŏŏlə) *n.* **1.** word, *esp.* verb acting as connecting link in sentence **2.** connection, tie

copulate ('kopyŏŏlāt) *vi.* unite sexually —**copu'lation** *n.* —'**copulative** *a.*

copy ('kopi) *n.* **1.** imitation **2.** single specimen of book **3.** matter for printing **4.** *Journalism inf.* suitable material for an article —*vt.* **5.** make copy of, imitate **6.** transcribe **7.** follow example of ('**copied,** '**copying**) —'**copier** *n.* person or device that copies —'**copyist** *n.* —'**copybook** *n.* **1.** book of specimens, *esp.* of penmanship, for imitation —*a.* **2.** trite, unoriginal —'**copycat** *n. inf.* person, *esp.* child, who imitates another —**copy editor 1.** editor who prepares copy for the printer **2.** person who edits and headlines newspaper copy —'**copyhold** *n. Law* formerly, tenure less than freehold of land in England evidenced by copy of Court roll —'**copyright** *n.* **1.** legal exclusive right to print and publish book, article, work of art *etc.* —*vt.* **2.** protect by copyright (*see also* **Universal Copyright Convention** *at* UNIVERSE) —'**copywriter** *n.* one who composes advertisements —**blot one's copybook** *inf.* sully one's reputation

coquette (kō'ket) *n.* woman who flirts —'**coquetry** *n.* —**co'quettish** *a.*

coracle ('korəkəl) *n.* boat of wicker covered with skins

coral ('korəl) *n.* **1.** hard substance made by sea polyps and forming growths, islands, reefs **2.** ornament of coral —*a.* **3.** made of coral **4.** of deep pink color —'**coralline** *a.*

cor anglais ('kör 'ängglā) **UK** English horn

corbel ('körbəl) *n.* stone or timber projection from wall to support something

corbie ('körbi) *n. Scot.* **1.** raven **2.** crow

cord (körd) *n.* **1.** thin rope or thick string **2.** rib on cloth **3.** ribbed fabric —*vt.* **4.** fasten with cord —'**cordage** *n.*

cordate ('kördāt) *a.* (of leaf) heart-shaped

cordial ('körjəl) *a.* **1.** hearty, sincere, warm —*n.* **2.** sweet, fruit-flavored drink —**cordi'ality** *n.* —'**cordially** *adv.*

cordite ('kördīt) *n.* explosive compound

cordon ('kördən) *n.* **1.** chain of troops or police **2.** fruit tree grown as single stem —*vt.* **3.** (*oft. with* off) form cordon around

cordon bleu (*Fr.* kordō 'blœ) (*esp.* of food preparation) of highest standard

cordovan ('kördəvən) *n.* fine leather now made principally from horsehide

corduroy ('kördəroi) *n.* cotton fabric with velvety, ribbed surface

cordwainer ('kördwānər) *n. obs.* shoemaker or worker in leather

core (kör) *n.* **1.** horny seed case of apple and other fruits **2.** central or innermost part of anything —*vt.* **3.** take out the core of

corespondent (kōri'spondənt) *n.* one cited in divorce case, alleged to have committed adultery with the respondent

corgi ('körgi) *n.* a small Welsh dog

coriaceous (kori'āshəs) *a.* of, like leather

coriander ('koriandər) *n.* type of herb

Corinthian (kə'rinthiən) *a.* **1.** of Corinth **2.** of Corinthian order of architecture, ornate Greek

Corinthians (kə'rinthiənz) *pl.n.* (*with sing. v.*) *Bible* 7th and 8th books of the N.T., epistles written to Christians at Corinth by St. Paul probably in 55 and 56 A.D.

cork (körk) *n.* **1.** bark of an evergreen Mediterranean oak tree **2.** piece of it or other material, *esp.* used as stopper for bottle *etc.* —*vt.* **3.** stop up with cork —'**corkage** *n.* charge for opening wine bottles in restaurant —**corked** *a.* tainted through having cork containing excess tannin —'**corker** *n. sl.* something, someone outstanding —'**corkscrew** *n.* tool for pulling out corks

corm (körm) *n.* storage organ of plant, a compact thickened stem resembling a bulb but without the separate scales

cormorant ('körmərənt) *n.* large voracious sea bird

corn[1] (körn) *n.* **1.** grain, fruit of cereals **2.** grain of all kinds **3.** maize **4.** oversentimental, trite quality in play, film *etc.* —*vt.* **5.** preserve (meat) with salt —'**corny** *a. inf.* trite, oversentimental, hackneyed —'**corncob** *n.* core of ear of Indian corn, to which kernels are attached —'**corncrake** *n.* brown bird with harsh call, land rail —'**cornflakes** *pl.n.* toasted flakes of corn meal eaten for breakfast —'**cornflower** *n.* bachelor's button —**corn snow** granular snow formed by

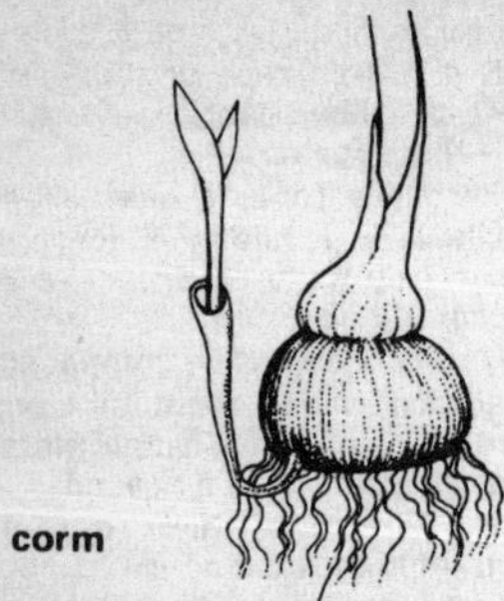

alternate freezing and thawing —'**cornstarch** *n.* starch made from corn, used as thickening agent in food and in many industrial processes —**corn syrup** sweetener obtained by partial hydrolysis of cornstarch

corn[2] (körn) *n.* painful horny growth on foot or toe

cornea ('körniə) *n.* transparent membrane covering front of eye —'**corneal** *a.* —**corneal transplant** cornea usu. obtained from deceased person used to replace diseased or deformed cornea of a blind or partially blind person —**corneal ulcer** patch of destroyed cornea resulting from injury or infection

cornel ('körnəl) *n.* any small tree with very hard wood, as the dogwood *etc.*

cornelian (kör'nēlyən) *n.* precious stone, kind of chalcedony

corner ('körnər) *n.* **1.** part of room where two sides meet **2.** remote or humble place **3.** point where two walls, streets *etc.* meet **4.** angle, projection **5.** *Business* buying up of whole existing stock of commodity **6.** *Sport* free kick or shot from corner of field —*vt.* **7.** drive into position of difficulty, or leaving no escape **8.** acquire enough of (commodity) to attain control of the market **9.** attain control of (market) in such a manner (*also* **en'gross**) —*vi.* **10.** move round corner —'**cornered** *a.* —'**cornerstone** *n.* indispensable part, basis

cornet (kör'net) *n.* musical instrument shorter than the trumpet usu. played in a brass band

cornice ('körnis) *n.* **1.** projection near top of wall **2.** ornamental, carved molding below ceiling

Cornish ('körnish) *a.* **1.** of Cornwall or its inhabitants —*n.* **2.** Celtic language of Cornwall: extinct by 1800 —*pl.* **3.** natives of Cornwall —'**Cornishman** *n.*

cornucopia (környə'kōpiə, -nə-) *n.* symbol of plenty, consisting of goat's horn, overflowing with fruit and flowers

corolla (kə'rolə) *n.* flower's inner envelope of petals

corollary ('korəleri) *n.* **1.** inference from a preceding statement **2.** deduction **3.** result

corona (kə'rōnə) *n.* **1.** halo around heavenly body **2.** flat projecting part of cornice **3.** top or crown (*pl.* **-s, -nae** (-nē)) —'**coronal** *a.*

coronary ('korəneri) *a.* **1.** of blood vessels surrounding heart —*n.* **2.** coronary thrombosis —**coronary thrombosis** formation of obstructing clot in coronary artery

coronation (korə'nāshən) *n.* ceremony of crowning a sovereign

coroner ('korənər) *n.* officer who holds inquests on bodies of persons supposed killed by violence, accident *etc.* —'**coronership** *n.*

coronet (korə'net) *n.* small crown

corporal[1] ('körpərəl) *a.* **1.** of the body **2.** material, not spiritual —**corporal punishment** punishment (flogging *etc.*) of physical nature

corporal[2] ('körpərəl, 'körprəl) *n.* noncommissioned officer in army ranking above private first class and below sergeant; in marine corps above lance corporal and below sergeant

corporation (körpə'rāshən) *n.* **1.** association, body of persons legally authorized to act as an individual **2.** authorities of town or city —'**corporate** *a.*

corporeal (kör'pōriəl) *a.* **1.** of the body, material **2.** tangible

corps (kör) *n.* **1.** military force, body of troops **2.** any organized body of persons (*pl.* **corps** (körz)) —**corps de ballet** members of ballet company who dance together in group —**corps diplomatique** (diplōma'tēk) body of diplomats accredited to state (*also* **diplomatic corps**)

corpse (körps) *n.* dead body

corpulent ('körpyŏŏlənt) *a.* fat —'**corpulence** *n.*

corpus ('körpəs) *n.* **1.** collection or body of works, *esp.* by single author **2.** main part or body of something (*pl.* **-pora** (-pərə))

corpuscle ('körpusəl) *n.* minute organism or particle, *esp.* red and white corpuscles of blood

corral (ko'ral) *n.* enclosure for cattle, or for defense

correct (kə'rekt) *vt.* **1.** set right **2.** indicate errors in **3.** rebuke, punish **4.** counteract, rectify —*a.* **5.** right, exact, accurate **6.** in accordance with facts or standards —**cor'rection** *n.* —**cor'rective** *n./a.* —**cor'rectly** *adv.* —**cor'rectness** *n.*

correlate ('korilāt) *vt.* **1.** bring into reciprocal relation —*n.* **2.** either of two things or words necessarily implying the other —**corre'lation** *n.* —**cor'relative** *a./n.*

correspond (kori'spond) *vi.* **1.** be in agreement, be consistent (with) **2.** be similar (to) **3.** exchange letters —**corre'spondence** *n.* **1.** agreement, corresponding **2.** similarity **3.** exchange of letters **4.** letters received —**corre'spondent** *n.* **1.** writer of letters **2.**

one employed by newspaper *etc.* to report on particular topic, country *etc.* —**correspondence school** educational institution that offers tuition by mail

corridor ('koridər) *n.* **1.** passage in building, railroad passenger car *etc.* **2.** strip of territory (or air route) not under control of state through which it passes

corrie ('kori) *n.* **1.** *Scot.* circular hollow on hillside **2.** *Geol.* cirque

corrigendum (kori'jendəm) *n.* thing to be corrected (*pl.* **-da** (-də))

corrigible ('korijibəl) *a.* **1.** capable of being corrected **2.** submissive

corroborate (kə'robərāt) *vt.* confirm, support (statement *etc.*) —**corrobo'ration** *n.* —**cor'roborative** *a.*

corroboree (kə'robəri) *n.* **A 1.** native assembly of sacred, festive or warlike character **2.** any noisy gathering

corrode (kə'rōd) *vt.* eat, wear away, eat into (by chemical action, disease *etc.*) —**cor'rosion** *n.* —**cor'rosive** *a.*

corrugate ('korəgāt) *v.* wrinkle, bend into wavy ridges —'**corrugated** *a.* —**corru'gation** *n.*

corrupt (kə'rupt) *a.* **1.** lacking integrity **2.** open to, or involving, bribery **3.** wicked **4.** spoilt by mistakes, altered for the worse (of words, literary passages *etc.*) —*vt.* **5.** make evil, pervert **6.** bribe **7.** make rotten —**corrupti'bility** *n.* —**cor'ruptible** *a.* —**cor'ruption** *n.* —**cor'ruptly** *adv.*

corsage (kör'säzh) *n.* (flower, spray, worn on) bodice of woman's dress

corsair ('körsāər) *n.* pirate

corselet ('körslit) *n.* **1.** piece of armor to cover the trunk **2.** (körsə'let) one-piece foundation garment

corset ('körsit) *n.* close-fitting undergarment stiffened to give support or shape to the body

cortege *or* **cortège** (kör'tezh) *n.* formal (funeral) procession

cortex ('körteks) *n.* **1.** *Anat.* outer layer **2.** bark **3.** sheath (*pl.* **cortices** ('körtisēz)) —'**cortical** *a.*

corticosteroid (körtikō'stēəroid) *n.* any of various adrenal cortex steroids (corticosterone, cortisone, aldosterone)

cortisone ('körtisōn, -zōn) *n.* product of the adrenal cortex or its synthesized equivalent used in medical treatment

corundum (kə'rundəm) *n.* native crystalline aluminum oxide, used as abrasive

coruscate ('korəskāt) *vi.* emit flashes of light; sparkle —**corus'cation** *n.*

corvette (kör'vet) *n.* lightly armed warship for escort and antisubmarine duties

corymb ('korimb, -rim) *n.* inflorescence in form of flat-topped flower cluster with oldest flowers at periphery

coryza (kə'rīzə) *n.* acute inflammation of mucous membrane of nose, with discharge of mucus; head cold

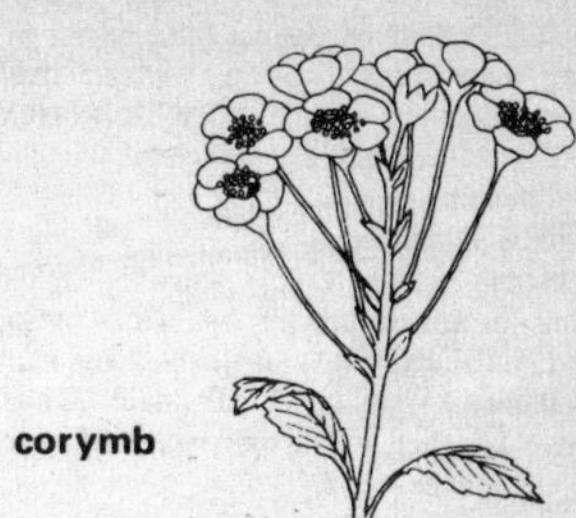

corymb

cos (koz) cosine

cosec ('kōsek) cosecant

cosecant (kō'sēkant) *n.* (of angle) trigonometric function that in right triangle is ratio of length of hypotenuse to that of opposite side

cosh (kosh) *n.* **1.** blunt weapon —*vt.* **2.** strike with one

cosignatory (kō'signətōri) *n.* **1.** person, country *etc.* that signs document jointly with others —*a.* **2.** signing jointly

cosine ('kōsīn) *n.* in a right triangle, the ratio of a side adjacent to a given angle and the hypotenuse

cos lettuce (kos) romaine

cosmetic (koz'metik) *n.* **1.** preparation to beautify or improve skin, hair *etc.* —*a.* **2.** designed to improve appearance only

cosmic ('kozmik) *a.* **1.** relating to the universe **2.** of the vastness of the universe —**cosmic rays** high-energy electromagnetic rays from space

cosmo- *or before vowel* **cosm-** (*comb. form*) world; universe, as in *cosmology, cosmonaut*

cosmopolitan (kozmə'politən) *n.* **1.** person who has lived and traveled in many countries —*a.* **2.** familiar with many countries **3.** sophisticated **4.** free from national prejudice —**cosmo'politanism** *n.* —**cos'mopolite** *n.*

cosmos[1] ('kozməs) *n.* the world or universe considered as an ordered system —**cos'mogony** *n.* study of origin and development of universe or system in universe —**cos'mographer** *n.* —**cosmo'graphic** *a.* —**cos'mography** *n.* description or mapping of the universe —**cosmo'logical** *a.* —**cos'mology** *n.* the science or study of the universe —'**cosmonaut** *n.* Soviet astronaut

cosmos[2] ('kozməs) *n.* plant cultivated for brightly colored flowers (*pl.* **-mos, -es**)

Cossack ('kosak) *n.* member of tribe in SE Russia

cosset ('kosit) *vt.* pamper, pet

cost (kost) *n.* **1.** price **2.** expenditure of time, labor *etc.* —*pl.* **3.** expenses of lawsuit —*vt.* **4.** have as price **5.** entail payment, loss or sacrifice of (**cost** *pt./pp.*) —'**costing** *n.* system of calculating cost of production

—'**costliness** *n.* —'**costly** *a.* **1.** valuable **2.** expensive —**cost of living** basic cost of food, clothing and shelter necessary to maintain life —**cost price** price at which article is bought by one intending to resell it

costal ('kostəl) *a.* pert. to side of body or ribs —'**costate** *a.* ribbed

Costa Rica (kostə 'rēkə) country in Central America bounded north by Nicaragua, east by the Caribbean Sea, southeast by Panama, and south and west by the Pacific Ocean

costive ('kostiv) *a.* **1.** constipated **2.** niggardly

costume ('kostyo͞om, -to͞om) *n.* **1.** style of dress of particular place or time, or for particular activity **2.** theatrical clothes —**cos'tumier** *n.* dealer in costumes —**costume jewelry** inexpensive jewelry set with imitation gemstones

cot[1] (kot) *n.* light collapsible bed, usu. canvas, stretched on a frame

cot[2] (kot) *n. Lit., obs.* small cottage

cot[3] (kot) cotangent

cotangent (kō'tanjənt) *n.* (of angle) trigonometric function that in right triangle is ratio of length of adjacent side to that of opposite side

cote (kōt) *n.* shelter, shed for animals or birds, *eg* dovecote

coterie ('kōtərē) *n.* **1.** exclusive group of people with common interests **2.** social clique

coterminous (kō'tərminəs) *a. see* CONTERMINOUS (sense 2)

cotillion (kō'tilyən) *n.* **1.** ballroom dance resembling quadrille **2.** formal ball

cotoneaster (kət'ōniastər) *n.* garden shrub with red berries

cottage ('kotij) *n.* small house —**cottage cheese** a soft cheese made by coagulating skim milk with a lactic acid culture, frequently flavored with fruit, spices *etc.* —**cottage industry** industry in which workers work in their own homes —**cottage pudding** plain cake covered with hot sauce

cotter ('kotər) *n.* pin, wedge *etc.* to prevent relative motion of two parts of machine *etc.*

cotton ('kotən) *n.* **1.** plant **2.** white downy fibrous covering of its seeds **3.** thread or cloth made of this —**cotton candy** candy made from spun sugar —**cotton gin** machine that separates debris from cotton —'**cottonmouth** *n.* water moccasin —**cotton-picking** *a.* damned —**cottonseed oil** oil obtained from seed of cotton plant —'**cottontail** *n.* any of several small sandy-brown N Amer. rabbits with white tufted tail —**cotton to** *or* **on to** understand (idea *etc.*)

cotyledon (koti'lēdən) *n.* seed leaf

couch (kowch) *n.* **1.** piece of furniture for reclining on by day, sofa —*vt.* **2.** express in a particular style of language **3.** cause to lie down —'**couchant** *a. Her.* lying down

couch grass *see* QUACK GRASS

cougar ('ko͞ogər) *n.* large tawny feline found throughout the New World (*also* **puma, painter, mountain lion**)

cough (kof) *vi.* **1.** expel air from lungs with sudden effort and noise, oft. to remove obstruction —*n.* **2.** act of coughing —**cough drop** lozenge to relieve cough —**cough syrup** medicine that relieves coughing

could (ko͝od) *pt. of* CAN[1]

coulomb ('ko͞olom) *n.* derived SI unit of electric charge; quantity of electricity transported in one second by current of one ampere

coulter ('kōltər) *n.* sharp blade or disk at front of plow

council ('kownsəl) *n.* **1.** deliberative or administrative body **2.** one of its meetings **3.** local governing authority of town *etc.* —'**councillor** *or* '**councilor** *n.* member of council

counsel ('kownsəl) *n.* **1.** advice, deliberation, debate **2.** lawyer; lawyers **3.** plan, policy —*vt.* **4.** advise, recommend —'**counselor** *or* '**counsellor** *n.* **1.** lawyer that manages cases for clients **2.** adviser **3.** person with supervisory duties at summer camp —**keep one's counsel** keep a secret

count[1] (kownt) *vt.* **1.** reckon, calculate, number **2.** include **3.** consider to be —*vi.* **4.** depend (on) **5.** be of importance —*n.* **6.** reckoning **7.** total number reached by counting **8.** item in list of charges or indictment **9.** act of counting —'**countless** *a.* too many to be counted —'**countdown** *n.* act of counting backwards to time critical operation exactly, such as launching of rocket —**counting house** room or building for book-keeping —**count down** count backwards to time critical operation exactly —**count out 1.** *inf.* leave out; exclude **2.** (of boxing referee) judge (floored boxer) to have failed to recover within specified time

count[2] (kownt) *n.* nobleman corresponding to British earl —'**countess** *n.* wife, ex-wife or widow of count or earl

countenance ('kowntinəns) *n.* **1.** face or its expression **2.** support, approval **3.** composure; self-control —*vt.* **4.** give support to, approve

counter[1] ('kowntər) *n.* **1.** horizontal surface in bank, shop *etc.*, over which business is transacted **2.** disk, token used for counting or scoring

counter[2] ('kowntər) *adv.* **1.** in opposite direction **2.** contrary —*vt.* **3.** oppose, contradict **4.** *Fencing* parry —*n.* **5.** parry

counter- (*comb. form*) reversed, opposite, rival, retaliatory, as in *counterclaim, counterclockwise, counterirritant, countermarch, countermeasure, countermine, counterrevolution.* Such words are not given here where the meaning may be inferred from the simple word

counteract (kowntər'akt) *vt.* neutralize, hinder —**counter'action** *n.*
counterattack ('kowntərətak) *v./n.* attack after enemy's advance
counterbalance ('kowntərbaləns) *n.* weight balancing or neutralizing another
counterfeit ('kowntərfit) *a.* **1.** sham, forged —*n.* **2.** imitation, forgery —*vt.* **3.** imitate with intent to deceive **4.** forge —'**counterfeiter** *n.* —'**counterfeitly** *adv.*
counterfoil ('kowntərfoil) *n.* part of check, receipt, money order, kept as record
counterintelligence (kowntərin'telijəns) *n.* activities designed to frustrate enemy espionage
countermand ('kowntərmand) *vt.* cancel (previous order)
counterpane ('kowntərpān) *n.* bedspread
counterpart ('kowntərpärt) *n.* **1.** thing so like another as to be mistaken for it **2.** something complementary to or correlative of another
counterpoint ('kowntərpoint) *n.* **1.** melody added as accompaniment to given melody **2.** art of so adding melodies
counterpoise ('kowntərpoiz) *n.* **1.** force, influence *etc.* that counterbalances another **2.** state of balance; equilibrium **3.** weight that balances another —*vt.* **4.** oppose with something of equal effect, weight or force; offset **5.** bring into equilibrium
counterproductive (kowntərprə'duktiv) *a.* tending to hinder achievement of aim; having effects contrary to those intended
Counter-Reformation (kowntərrefər'māshən) *n.* reform movement in Catholic Church in 16th and early 17th centuries
countersign ('kowntərsīn) *vt.* sign (document already signed by another), ratify
countersink ('kowntərsingk) *vt.* enlarge (upper part of hole drilled in timber *etc.*) to take head of screw, bolt *etc.* below surface
countertenor ('kowntərtenər) *n.* **1.** adult male voice with alto range **2.** singer with such voice
countervail (kowntər'vāl) *v.* **1.** act or act against with equal power or force —*vt.* **2.** make up for; compensate; offset
counterweight ('kowntərwāt) *n.* counterbalancing weight, influence or force
countess ('kowntis) *n. see* COUNT[2]
country ('kuntri) *n.* **1.** region, district **2.** territory of nation **3.** land of birth, residence *etc.* **4.** rural districts as opposed to town **5.** nation —'**countrified** *a.* rural in manner or appearance —**country-and-western** *n.* urban 20th-century White folk music of SE Amer. —**country club** club in the country, having sporting and social facilities —**country dance** folk dance in which couples face one another in line —'**countryman** *n.* **1.** rustic **2.** compatriot —'**countryside** *n.* **1.** rural district **2.** its inhabitants
county ('kownti) *n.* **1.** largest local government division within a state of the U.S. **2.** chief administrative division of most of the United Kingdom —*a.* **3. UK** *inf.* upper-class; of or like landed gentry
coup (ko͞o) *n.* **1.** successful stroke, move or gamble **2.** (*short for* **coup d'état**) sudden, violent seizure of government
coup de grâce (ko͞o də 'gräs) *Fr.* **1.** mortal or finishing blow, *esp.* delivered as act of mercy to sufferer **2.** final or decisive stroke (*pl.* ***coups de grâce*** (ko͞o də 'gräs))
coupé (ko͞o'pā) *or* **coupe** (ko͞o'pā, ko͞op) *n.* closed 2-door automobile usu. for two persons
couple ('kupəl) *n.* **1.** two, pair **2.** indefinite small number **3.** two people who regularly associate with each other or live together **4.** any two persons —*vt.* **5.** connect, fasten together **6.** associate, connect in the mind —*vi.* **7.** join —'**coupler** *n.* —'**couplet** *n.* two lines of verse, *esp.* rhyming and of equal length —'**coupling** *n.* act of coming together
coupon ('kyo͞opon, 'ko͞o-) *n.* **1.** ticket or voucher entitling holder to discount, gift *etc.* **2.** detachable slip used as order form **3.** (in betting *etc.*) printed form on which to forecast results
courage ('kurij) *n.* bravery, boldness —**cou'rageous** *a.* —**cou'rageously** *adv.*
courgette (ko͝oər'zhet) *n.* **UK** zucchini
courier ('ko͝oəriər) *n.* **1.** express messenger **2.** person who looks after, guides travelers
course (kōrs) *n.* **1.** movement in space or time **2.** direction of movement **3.** successive development, sequence **4.** line of conduct or action **5.** series of lectures, exercises *etc.* **6.** any of successive parts of meal **7.** continuous line of masonry at particular level in building **8.** area where golf is played **9.** track or ground on which a race is run —*vt.* **10.** hunt —*vi.* **11.** run swiftly, gallop about **12.** (of blood) circulate —'**courser** *n. Poet.* swift horse —'**coursing** *n.* **1.** (of hounds or dogs) hunting by sight **2.** sport in which hounds are matched against one another in pairs for hunting of hares by sight
court (kōrt) *n.* **1.** space enclosed by buildings, yard **2.** area marked off or enclosed for playing various games **3.** retinue and establishment of sovereign **4.** body with judicial powers, place where it meets, one of its sittings **5.** attention, homage, flattery —*vt.* **6.** woo, try to win or attract **7.** seek, invite —'**courtier** *n.* one who frequents royal court —'**courtliness** *n.* —'**courtly** *a.* **1.** ceremoniously polite **2.** characteristic of a court —'**courtship** *n.* wooing —'**courthouse** *n.* public building in which courts of law are held —**court martial** court of naval or military officers for trying naval or military offenses (*pl.* **court martials, courts martial**) —**court plaster** plaster, composed of isinglass on silk, formerly used as beauty spots —**court tennis** ancient form of tennis played

in four-walled indoor court —'**courtyard** *n.* paved space enclosed by buildings or walls

courtesan ('körtizən) *n. obs.* **1.** court mistress **2.** high-class prostitute

courtesy ('kərtisi) *n.* **1.** politeness, good manners **2.** act of civility —'**courteous** *a.* polite —'**courteously** *adv.* —**courtesy title** title accorded by usage usu. to heir of peer

cousin ('kuzən) *n.* **1.** son or daughter of uncle or aunt **2.** formerly, any kinsman —'**cousinly** *a.*

couture (ko͞o'to͞oər) *n.* high-fashion designing and dressmaking —**couturier** (ko͞o'to͞oriər) *n.* person who designs, makes and sells fashion clothes for women (**couturière** (ko͞o'to͞oriər) *fem.*)

cove[1] (kōv) *n.* small inlet of coast, sheltered bay

cove[2] (kōv) *vt.* make in concave form

coven ('kuvən) *n.* gathering of witches

covenant ('kuvənənt) *n.* **1.** contract, mutual agreement **2.** compact —*v.* **3.** agree to a covenant (concerning) —**Covenanter** ('kuvənəntər, kuvə'nantər) *n. Scot. hist.* person upholding either of two 17th-cent. Presbyterian covenants

Coventry ('kuvəntri) *n.* —**send to Coventry** ostracize; ignore

cover ('kuvər) *vt.* **1.** place or spread over **2.** extend over, spread over **3.** bring upon (oneself) **4.** screen, protect **5.** travel over **6.** include **7.** be sufficient to meet **8.** *Journalism* report on **9.** point a gun at —*n.* **10.** lid, wrapper, envelope, binding, screen, anything which covers —'**coverage** *n.* amount, extent covered —'**coverlet** *n.* bedspread —**cover charge** fixed charge added to cost of food in restaurant *etc.* —**covering letter** accompanying letter sent as explanation, introduction or record —**cover-up** *n.* concealment or attempted concealment of crime *etc.* —**cover up** **1.** cover completely **2.** attempt to conceal (mistake or crime)

covert ('kuvərt) *a.* **1.** secret, veiled, concealed, sly —*n.* **2.** thicket, place sheltering game **3.** worsted twill cloth once used for hunting clothes —'**covertly** *adv.*

covet ('kuvit) *vt.* long to possess, *esp.* what belongs to another —'**covetous** *a.* avaricious —'**covetousness** *n.*

covey ('kuvi) *n.* brood of partridges or quail (*pl.* **-s**)

cow[1] (kow) *n.* **1.** the female of the bovine and of certain other animals, *eg* elephant, whale **2.** *inf.* disagreeable woman —'**cowboy** *n.* **1.** herdsman in charge of cattle on western plains of U.S. **2.** *inf.* ruthless or unscrupulous operator in business *etc.* —**cow parsley** Eurasian umbelliferous hedgerow plant —'**cowpox** *n.* viral disease of cows. Same infection in man protects against smallpox

cow[2] (kow) *vt.* frighten into submission, overawe, subdue

coward ('kowərd) *n.* one who lacks courage, shrinks from danger —'**cowardice** *n.* —'**cowardly** *a.*

cower ('kowər) *vi.* crouch, shrink in fear

cowl (kowl) *n.* **1.** monk's hooded cloak **2.** its hood **3.** hooded top for chimney, ship's funnel *etc.*

cowling ('kowling) *n.* covering for aircraft engine

co-worker *n.* fellow worker; associate

cowrie *or* **cowry** ('kowri) *n.* brightly-marked glossy marine gastropod of warm seas

cowslip ('kowslip) *n.* wild species of primrose

coxcomb ('kokskōm) *n. obs.* one given to showing off

Coxsackie virus (kok'saki) any of several virus infections principally affecting children in late summer and fall

coxswain ('koksən, -swān) *n.* steersman of boat —**cox** *n.* **1.** coxswain —*v.* **2.** command or steer

coy (koi) *a.* (pretending to be) shy, modest —'**coyly** *adv.* —'**coyness** *n.*

coyote (kī'ōti) *n.* N Amer. prairie wolf

coypu ('koipo͞o) *n.* aquatic rodent, orig. from S Amer., yielding nutria fur

cozen ('kuzən) *vt.* flatter in order to cheat, beguile

cozy ('kōzi) *a.* **1.** snug, comfortable, sheltered —*n.* **2.** covering to keep teapot hot —'**cozily** *adv.*

cp. compare

C.P. **1.** Canadian Pacific **2.** Cape Province **3.** Communist Party

cpd. compound

Cpl. Corporal

C.P.U. central processing unit

CQ symbol transmitted by amateur radio operator requesting communication with any other amateur radio operator

Cr *Chem.* chromium

crab[1] (krab) *n.* **1.** edible crustacean with ten legs, noted for sidelong and backward walk **2.** type of louse —*vi.* **3.** catch crabs **4.** move sideways (**-bb-**) —**crabbed** ('krabid) *a.* (of handwriting) hard to read —'**crabby** *a.* bad-tempered —**crab louse** parasitic louse that infests pubic region in man —**catch a crab** *Rowing* dig oar too deeply for clean retrieval

crab[2] (krab) *inf. vi.* **1.** find fault; grumble (**-bb-**) —*n.* **2.** irritable person

crab apple wild sour apple

crack (krak) *vt.* **1.** break, split partially **2.** break with sharp noise **3.** cause to make sharp noise, as of whip, rifle *etc.* **4.** yield **5.** *inf.* tell (joke) **6.** solve, decipher —*vi.* **7.** make sharp noise **8.** split, fissure **9.** (of the voice) lose clearness when changing from boy's to man's —*n.* **10.** sharp explosive noise **11.** split, fissure **12.** flaw **13.** *inf.* joke, *esp.* sarcastic **14.** *dial.* chat **15.** a pure form of cocaine —*a.* **16.** *inf.* special, smart, of great reputation for skill *etc.* —**cracked** *a.* **1.** damaged by cracking **2.** *sl.* crazy —'**cracker** *n.* **1.** *see* **snapper** (sense 2) *at* SNAP **2.** explosive firework **3.** thin dry biscuit —'**cracking** *a.* **1.** *inf.* fast; vigorous —*n.* **2.** process of breaking down hydrocarbons by heat and pressure —'**crackle** *n.* **1.** sound of repeated small cracks **2.** network of fine cracks on the glaze of fine porcelain —*vi.* **3.** make crackling sound —'**crackling** *n.* **1.** crackle **2.** crisp skin of roast pork —'**crackbrained** *a.* insane, idiotic, crazy —'**crackerbarrel** *a.* of or suggesting rustic directness —'**crackerjack** *n./a.* (of) person or thing of exceptional merit —**Cracker Jack** trade name for candied popcorn and peanuts —'**crackpot** *inf. n.* **1.** eccentric person; crank —*a.* **2.** eccentric; crazy —'**cracksman** *n.* burglar, *esp.* safe-breaker —**crack-up** *n.* **1.** collision **2.** *inf.* nervous breakdown —**crack of dawn** daybreak —**crack the whip** *n.* **1.** game in which players in a line run, roller-skate or ice-skate until the leader suddenly changes direction, causing those at the tail of the line to fall or let go —*vi.* **2.** demand obedience from another —**crack up 1.** (cause to) laugh out loud **2.** smash up (vehicle) by losing control —**get cracking** *inf.* start doing something quickly or with increased speed

cradle ('krādəl) *n.* **1.** infant's bed (on rockers) **2.** *fig.* earliest resting-place or home **3.** supporting framework —*vt.* **4.** hold or rock as in a cradle **5.** cherish —'**cradling** *n.*

craft[1] (kraft) *n.* **1.** skill, ability, *esp.* manual ability **2.** cunning **3.** skilled trade **4.** members of a trade —'**craftily** *adv.* —'**craftsman** *n.* —'**craftsmanship** *n.* —'**crafty** *a.* cunning, shrewd

craft[2] (kraft) *n.* vessel, ship (*pl.* **craft**)

crag (krag) *n.* steep rugged rock —'**craggy** *a.* rugged

crake (krāk) *n.* any of various birds of rail family

cram (kram) *vt.* **1.** fill quite full **2.** stuff, force **3.** pack tightly **4.** feed to excess **5.** prepare quickly for examination —*vi.* **6.** study, *esp.* for examination, by hastily memorizing (**-mm-**) —*n.* **7.** act or condition of cramming **8.** crush

cramp (kramp) *n.* **1.** painful muscular contraction **2.** clamp for holding masonry, timber *etc.* together —*vt.* **3.** restrict, hamper **4.** hem in, keep within too narrow limits

crampon ('krampon) *n.* spike in shoe for mountain climbing, *esp.* on ice

cranberry ('kranberi, -bəri) *n.* edible red berry of dwarf evergreen shrub

crane (krān) *n.* **1.** wading bird with long legs, neck and bill **2.** machine for moving heavy weights —*v.* **3.** stretch (neck) to see

crane fly insect with long spindly legs (*also* **daddy longlegs**)

cranesbill ('krānzbil) *n.* plant with pink or purple flowers and beaked fruits

craniometry (krāni'omitri) *n.* the study of the measurements of the human head

cranium ('krāniəm) *n.* skull (*pl.* **-s, -nia** (-niə)) —'**cranial** *a.* —**cranio'logical** *a.*—**crani'ologist** *n.* —**crani'ology** *n.* branch of science concerned with shape and size of human skull —**cranial capacity** measurement of internal capacity or brain volume of the skull —**cranial nerves** nerves arising directly from brain of vertebrates that communicate with head and neck but do not pass through the spinal cord

crank (krangk) *n.* **1.** arm at right angles to axis, for turning main shaft, changing reciprocal into rotary motion *etc.* **2.** *inf.* eccentric person, faddist —*v.* **3.** start (engine) by turning crank —'**cranky** *a.* **1.** eccentric **2.** bad-tempered **3.** shaky —'**crankpin** *n.* short cylindrical surface fitted between two arms of crank parallel to main shaft of crankshaft —'**crankshaft** *n.* principal shaft of engine

cranny ('krani) *n.* small opening, chink —'**crannied** *a.*

crap[1] (krap) *n.* gambling game played with two dice (*also* **craps**)

crap[2] (krap) *n.* **1.** *sl.* nonsense, lies **2.** *offens.* excrement **3.** anything inferior

crape (krāp) *n.* crepe, *esp.* when used for mourning clothes

crapulous ('krapyələs) *a.* **1.** given to or resulting from intemperance **2.** suffering from intemperance; drunken

crash[1] (krash) *v.* **1.** (cause to) make loud noise **2.** (cause to) fall with crash **3.** cause (aircraft) to hit land or water or (of aircraft) land in this way **4.** (cause to) collide **5.** move noisily or violently —*vi.* **6.** break, smash **7.** collapse, fail, *esp.* financially —*n.* **8.** loud, violent fall or impact **9.** collision, wrecking **10.** sudden, uncontrolled descent of aircraft to land **11.** sudden collapse or downfall **12.** bankruptcy —*a.* **13.** requiring, using, great effort to achieve results quickly —'**crashing** *a. inf.* thorough (*esp. in* **crashing bore**) —**crash helmet** helmet worn by motorcyclists *etc.* to protect head —**crash-land** *v.* land (aircraft) in emergency, *esp.* with damage to craft

crash[2] (krash) *n.* fabric, usu. linen, with rough texture and coarse uneven yarns

crass (kras) *a.* grossly stupid —'**crassly** *adv.* —'**crassness** *n.*

crate (krāt) *n.* large (*usu.* wooden) container for packing goods

crater ('krātər) *n.* **1.** mouth of volcano **2.** bowl-shaped cavity, *esp.* one made by explosion of large shell, bomb, mine *etc.*

cravat (krə'vat) *n.* man's neckcloth

crave (krāv) *v.* **1.** have very strong desire (for), long (for) —*vt.* **2.** ask humbly **3.** beg —'**craving** *n.*

craven ('krāvən) *a.* **1.** cowardly, abject, spineless —*n.* **2.** coward

Cravenette (krāvə'net) *n.* trade name for rainproofing process applied to woolens and worsteds for making outer garments

craw (krō) *n.* **1.** bird's or animal's stomach **2.** bird's crop

crawfish ('krōfish) *n. see* CRAYFISH

crawl (krōl) *vi.* **1.** move on belly or on hands and knees **2.** move very slowly **3.** ingratiate oneself, cringe **4.** swim with crawl-stroke **5.** be overrun (with) —*n.* **6.** crawling motion **7.** very slow pace or motion **8.** racing stroke at swimming —'**crawler** *n.*

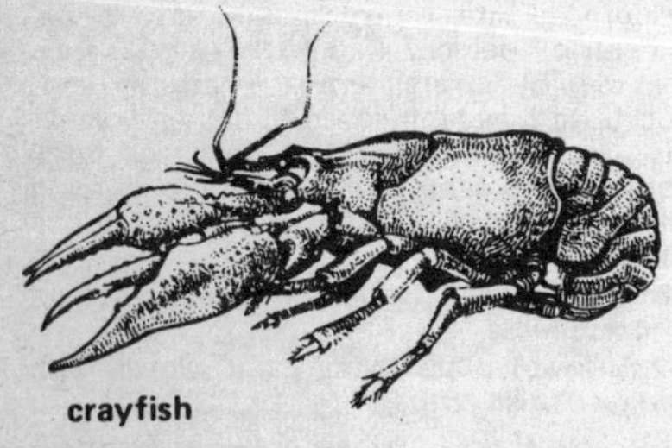

crayfish

crayfish ('krāfish) *or* **crawfish** *n.* edible freshwater crustacean like lobster

crayon ('kraon, -ən) *n.* stick or pencil of colored chalk, wax *etc.*

craze (krāz) *n.* **1.** short-lived current fashion **2.** strong desire or passion, mania **3.** madness —**crazed** *a.* **1.** demented **2.** (of porcelain) having fine cracks —'**crazy** *a.* **1.** insane **2.** very foolish **3.** (*with* about *or* over) madly eager (for)

CRC Civil Rights Commission

creak (krēk) *n.* **1.** harsh grating noise —*vi.* **2.** make creaking sound

cream (krēm) *n.* **1.** fatty part of milk **2.** various foods, dishes, resembling cream **3.** cosmetic *etc.* with creamlike consistency **4.** yellowish-white color **5.** best part of anything —*vt.* **6.** take cream from **7.** take best part from **8.** beat to creamy consistency —'**creamer** *n.* **1.** vessel or device for separating cream from milk **2.** powdered milk substitute for coffee —'**creamery** *n.* **1.** establishment where milk and cream are made into butter and cheese **2.** place where dairy products are sold —'**creamy** *a.* —**cream cheese** soft cheese made by draining superfluous moisture from whole milk —**cream of tartar** potassium hydrogen tartrate, used in baking powders

crease (krēs) *n.* **1.** line made by folding **2.** wrinkle **3.** superficial bullet wound —*v.* **4.** make, develop creases

create (krē'āt) *vt.* **1.** bring into being **2.** give rise to **3.** make —*vi.* **4.** *inf.* make a fuss —**cre'ation** *n.* —**cre'ative** *a.* —**cre'ator** *n.*

creatine ('krēətēn) *n.* nitrogenous substance found in muscles of vertebrates where it stores energy

creature ('krēchər) *n.* **1.** living being **2.** thing created **3.** dependant —**creature comforts** bodily comforts

crèche (kresh, krāsh) *n.* **1.** day nursery for very young children **2.** foundling home **3.** Nativity scene

credence ('krēdəns) *n.* **1.** belief, credit **2.** side-table for elements of the Eucharist before consecration

credentials (kri'denshəlz) *pl.n.* **1.** testimonials **2.** letters of introduction, *esp.* those given to ambassador

credible ('kredibəl) *a.* **1.** worthy of belief **2.** trustworthy —**credi'bility** *n.* —'**credibly** *adv.* —**credibility gap** disparity between claims or statements and facts

credit ('kredit) *n.* **1.** commendation, approval **2.** source, cause, of honor **3.** belief, trust **4.** good name **5.** influence, honor or power based on trust of others **6.** system of allowing customers to take goods for later payment **7.** money at one's disposal in bank *etc.* **8.** side of book on which such sums are entered **9.** reputation for financial reliability —*pl.* **10.** list of those responsible for production of film —*vt.* **11.** (*with* with) attribute **12.** believe **13.** put on credit side of account —'**creditable** *a.* bringing honor —'**creditably** *adv.* —'**creditor** *n.* one to whom debt is due —**credit card** card issued by banks *etc.* enabling holder to obtain goods and services on credit —**credit union** nonprofit organization, regulated by law, owned by its members, whose function is to make low-interest loans exclusively to members

credo ('krēdō, 'krā-) *n.* formal statement of beliefs, principles or opinions (*pl.* **-s**)

credulous ('krejələs) *a.* too easy of belief, easily deceived or imposed on, gullible —**cre'dulity** *n.* —'**credulousness** *n.*

Cree (krē) *n.* **1.** member of Amerindian people of Manitoba and Saskatchewan (*pl.* **Cree, -s**) **2.** the Algonquian language of this people

creed (krēd) *n.* **1.** formal statement of Christian beliefs **2.** statement, system of beliefs or principles

creek (krēk) *n.* natural stream of water smaller than a river —**up the creek** in a difficult situation

Creek (krēk) *n.* **1.** confederacy of Amerindian peoples of Alabama, Georgia and Florida **2.** member of any of these peoples **3.** Muskogean language of the Creek nation

creel (krēl) *n.* angler's fishing basket

creep (krēp) *vi.* **1.** make way along ground, as snake **2.** move with stealthy, slow movements **3.** crawl **4.** act in servile way **5.** (of skin or flesh) feel shrinking, shivering sensation, due to fear or repugnance (**crept** *pt./pp.*) —*n.* **6.** creeping **7.** *sl.* repulsive person —*pl.* **8.** *sl.* feeling of fear or repugnance —'**creeper** *n.* **1.** creeping or climbing plant, *eg* ivy **2.** one-piece garment for child at crawling stage —'**creepy** *a. inf.* **1.** uncanny, unpleasant **2.** causing flesh to creep

cremation (kri'māshən) *n.* burning as means of disposing of corpses —**cre'mate** *vt.* —**crema'torium** *n.* place for cremation

crème de la crème (krem də la 'krem) *n. Fr.* the very best

crème de menthe (krēm də 'mint, 'menth; krem də 'mänt) liqueur flavored with peppermint

crenate ('krēnāt) *or* **crenated** *a.* having scalloped margin, as certain leaves —**cre'nation** *n.*

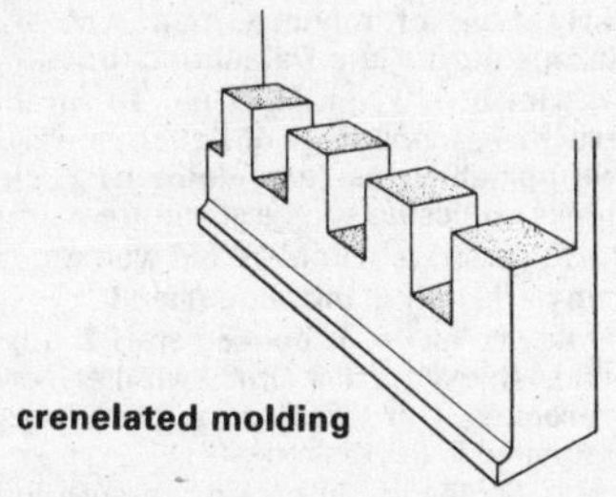

crenelated molding

crenelated ('krenilātid) *a.* having battlements

creole ('krēōl) *n.* **1.** hybrid language **2.** (**C-**) native-born W Indian, Latin American, of European descent

creosote ('krēəsōt) *n.* **1.** oily antiseptic liquid distilled from coal or wood tar, used for preserving wood —*vt.* **2.** coat or impregnate with creosote

crepe *or* **crêpe** (krāp) *n.* **1.** fabric with crimped surface **2.** very thin pancake, oft. folded round filling —**crepe de Chine** (də 'shēn) very thin crepe of silk or similar light fabric —**crepe paper** thin crinkled paper resembling crepe —**crepe rubber** rough-surfaced rubber used for soles of shoes

crepitate ('krepitāt) *vi.* make rattling or crackling sound

crepitus ('krepitəs) *n.* **1.** crackling chest sound heard in pneumonia *etc.* **2.** grating sound of two ends of broken bone rubbing together

crepon ('krāpon) *n.* crinkle-weave fabric heavier than crepe

crept (krept) *pt./pp. of* CREEP

crepuscular (kri'puskyŏŏlər) *a.* **1.** of or like twilight; dim **2.** (of creatures) active at twilight

Cres. Crescent

crescendo (kri'shendō) *n.* **1.** gradual increase of loudness, *esp.* in music —*adv.* **2.** with a crescendo

crescent ('kresənt) *n.* **1.** (shape of) moon as seen in first or last quarter **2.** any figure of this shape

cress (kres) *n.* any of various plants with edible pungent leaves

crest (krest) *n.* **1.** comb or tuft on bird's or animal's head **2.** plume on top of helmet **3.** top of mountain, ridge, wave *etc.* **4.** badge above shield of coat of arms, also used separately on seal, plate *etc.* —*vt.* **5.** crown **6.** reach top of —'**crestfallen** *a.* cast down by failure, dejected

cretaceous (kri'tāshəs) *a.* chalky

Cretaceous (kri'tāshəs) *a.* **1.** of last period of Mesozoic era, during which chalk deposits were formed —*n.* **2.** Cretaceous period or rock system

cretin ('krētin) *n.* **1.** person afflicted with cretinism **2.** *inf.* stupid person —'**cretinism** *n.* deficiency in thyroid gland causing physical and mental retardation

cretonne ('krēton, kri'ton) *n.* unglazed cotton cloth printed in colored patterns

crevasse (kri'vas) *n.* deep open chasm, *esp.* in glacier

crevice ('krevis) *n.* cleft, fissure, chink

crew (krōō) *n.* **1.** ship's, boat's or aircraft's company, excluding passengers **2.** *inf.* gang, set —*v.* **3.** serve as crew (on) —**crew cut** man's closely cropped haircut —**crew neck** round collarless neckline

crewel ('krōōil) *n.* fine worsted yarn, used in fancy work and embroidery

crib (krib) *n.* **1.** child's bed with enclosing sides **2.** barred rack used for fodder **3.** plagiarism **4.** something used to cheat in examination —*vt.* **5.** confine in small space **6.** copy unfairly (**-bb-**) —**crib death** unexplained death of healthy baby while asleep (*also* **sudden infant death syndrome**)

cribbage ('kribij) *n.* card game for 2 to 4 persons, in which players try to win a set number of points before their opponents

crick (krik) *n.* spasm or cramp in muscles, *esp.* in neck or back

cricket[1] ('krikit) *n.* chirping insect

cricket[2] ('krikit) *n.* outdoor game played with bats, ball and wickets by two teams of 11 players on a large grassy field in which object is to score runs —'**cricketer** *n.*

cri de coeur (krē də 'kœr) *Fr.* heartfelt or impassioned appeal (*pl.* **cris de coeur** (krē də 'kœr))

cried (krīd) *pt./pp. of* CRY

crier ('krīər) *n.* **1.** person or animal that cries **2.** formerly, official who made public announcements, *esp.* in town or court

crime (krīm) *n.* **1.** violation of law (usu. a serious offense) **2.** wicked or forbidden act **3.** *inf.* something to be regretted —**criminal** ('kriminəl) *a./n.* —**criminality** (krimi'naliti) *n.* —**criminally** ('kriminəli) *adv.* —**criminology** (krimi'noləji) *n.* study of crime and criminals

crimp (krimp) *vt.* **1.** make wavy or pleated **2.** pinch together to form seal, *esp.* pie crust —*n.* **3.** artificially waved hair **4.** curl in synthetic fiber —'**crimpy** *a.* frizzy

crimson ('krimzən) *a./n.* **1.** (of) rich deep red —*v.* **2.** turn crimson

cringe (krinj) *vi.* **1.** shrink, cower **2.** behave obsequiously

crinkle ('kringkəl) *v./n.* wrinkle

crinoline ('krinəlin) *n.* **1.** hooped petticoat or skirt **2.** stiff-sized fabric

cripple ('kripəl) *n.* **1.** one not having normal use of limbs, disabled or deformed person —*vt.* **2.** maim, disable, impair **3.** weaken, lessen efficiency of

crisis ('krīsiṣ) *n.* **1.** turning point or decisive moment, *esp.* in illness **2.** time of acute danger or difficulty (*pl.* **crises** ('krīsēz))

crisp (krisp) *a.* **1.** brittle but firm **2.** brisk, decided **3.** clear-cut **4.** fresh, invigorating **5.** (of hair) curly —'**crisper** *n.* refrigerator compartment for storing salads *etc.* —'**crispy** *a.*

crisscross ('kriskros) *v.* **1.** (cause to) move in crosswise pattern **2.** mark with or consist of pattern of crossing lines —*a.* **3.** (*esp.* of lines) crossing one another in different directions —*n.* **4.** pattern made of crossing lines —*adv.* **5.** in crosswise manner or pattern

criterion (krī'tēəriən) *n.* standard of judgment (*pl.* **-ria** (-riə))

critical ('kritikəl) *a.* **1.** fault-finding **2.** discerning **3.** skilled in or given to judging **4.** of great importance, crucial, decisive —'**critic** *n.* **1.** one who passes judgment **2.** writer expert in judging works of literature, art *etc.* —'**critically** *adv.* —'**criticism** *n.* —'**criticize** *v.* —**critique** (kri'tēk) *n.* critical essay, carefully written criticism —**critical path analysis** technique for planning projects with reference to critical path, which is sequence of stages requiring longest time

croak (krōk) *vi.* **1.** utter deep hoarse cry, as raven, frog **2.** talk dismally **3.** *sl.* die —*n.* **4.** deep hoarse cry —'**croaker** *n.* —'**croaky** *a.* hoarse

Croatian (krō'āshən) *a.* **1.** of Croatia in Yugoslavia, its people or their dialect of Serbo-Croatian —*n.* **2.** dialect of Croatia **3.** native or inhabitant of Croatia

crochet (krō'shā) *n.* **1.** handicraft in which item or fabric is formed by interlocking a single thread with a hooked needle —*vi.* **2.** do such work —*vt.* **3.** make (garment *etc.*) by such work

crock (krok) *n.* **1.** earthenware jar or pot **2.** broken piece of earthenware **3.** dye rubbed off from suede **4.** *inf.* cripple —**crocked** *a. sl.* drunk —'**crockery** *n.* earthenware dishes, utensils *etc.*

Crockpot ('krokpot) *n.* trade name for electric pot used for slow cooking

crocodile ('krokədīl) *n.* **1.** large amphibious reptile **2.** skin or hide of a crocodile —**crocodilian** (krokə'diliən) *n.* **1.** large predatory reptile, such as crocodile, alligator *etc.* —*a.* **2.** of crocodiles or crocodilians —**crocodile tears** insincere grief

crocus ('krōkəs) *n.* small bulbous plant with yellow, white or purple flowers

Croesus ('krēsəs) *n.* very rich man

croft (kroft) *n. Scot.* small piece of arable land, smallholding —'**crofter** *n.* one who works croft

Crohn's disease (krōnz) inflammatory disease of the small intestine giving rise to a wide range of symptoms

croissant (krəwä'sän, kwä-) *n.* crescent-shaped roll of rich flaky pastry

Cro-Magnon man (krō'magnən, -'manyən) early type of modern man who lived in Europe during late Paleolithic times

cromlech ('kromlek) *n.* **1.** prehistoric structure, monument of flat stone resting on two upright ones (*also* **dolmen**) **2.** circle of stones enclosing such a structure

crone (krōn) *n.* witchlike old woman

crony ('krōni) *n.* intimate friend

crook (krŏŏk) *n.* **1.** hooked staff **2.** any hook, bend, sharp turn **3.** *inf.* swindler, criminal —**crooked** ('krŏŏkid) *a.* **1.** bent, twisted **2.** deformed **3.** *inf.* dishonest

croon (krōōn) *v.* hum, sing in soft, low tone —'**crooner** *n.*

crop (krop) *n.* **1.** produce of cultivation of any plant or plants **2.** harvest (*lit. or fig.*) **3.** pouch in bird's gullet **4.** stock of whip **5.** hunting whip **6.** short haircut —*vt.* **7.** cut short **8.** poll, clip **9.** (of animals) bite, eat down —*vi.* **10.** raise, produce or occupy land with crop (**-pp-**) —'**cropper** *n. inf.* **1.** heavy fall **2.** disastrous failure —**crop-dusting** *n.* spreading fungicide *etc.* on crops from aircraft —**crop up** *inf.* happen unexpectedly

croquet (krō'kā) *n.* lawn game played with balls, wooden mallets and hoops where the object is to propel the ball through the hoops in a prescribed sequence

croquette (krō'ket) *n.* fried ball of minced meat, fish *etc.* in bread crumbs

crosier *or* **crozier** ('krōzhər) *n.* bishop's or abbot's staff

cross (kros) *n.* **1.** structure or symbol of two intersecting lines or pieces (at right angles) **2.** such a structure of wood as means of execution by tying or nailing victim to it **3.** symbol of Christian faith **4.** any thing or mark in the shape of cross **5.** misfortune, annoyance, affliction **6.** intermixture of breeds, hybrid —*v.* **7.** move or go across (something) **8.** intersect —*vi.* **9.** meet and pass —*vt.* **10.** mark with lines across **11.** (*with* out) delete **12.** place or put in form of cross **13.** make sign of cross on or over **14.** modify breed of animals or plants by intermixture **15.** thwart **16.** oppose —*a.* **17.** out of temper, angry **18.** peevish, perverse **19.** transverse **20.**

intersecting **21.** contrary **22.** adverse —ˈ**crossing** *n.* **1.** intersection of roads, rails *etc.* **2.** place or structure where pedestrians and vehicles cross —ˈ**crossly** *adv.* —ˈ**crosswise** *adv./a.* —ˈ**crossbar** *n.* **1.** horizontal bar, line, stripe *etc.* **2.** horizontal beam across pair of goal posts **3.** horizontal bar on man's bicycle —ˈ**crossbill** *n.* bird whose mandibles cross when closed —ˈ**crossbow** *n.* bow fixed across wooden shoulder stock —ˈ**crossbreed** *n.* breed produced from parents of different breeds —**crossˈcheck** *v.* **1.** verify (report *etc.*) by consulting other sources —*n.* **2.** act of crosschecking —**cross-country** *n.* long race held over open ground —**cross-examination** *n.* —**cross-examine** *vt.* examine (witness already examined by other side) —**cross-eyed** *a.* having eye(s) turning inward —**cross-fertilization** *n.* fertilization of one plant by pollen of another —ˈ**crossfire** *n.* **1.** *Mil.* converging fire from one or more positions **2.** lively exchange of ideas, opinions *etc.* —**cross-grained** *a.* perverse —ˈ**crosspatch** *n. inf.* bad-tempered person —**cross-ply** *a.* (of tire) having fabric cords in outer casing running diagonally —**cross-purpose** *n.* contrary aim or purpose —**cross-question** *vt.* **1.** cross-examine —*n.* **2.** question asked in cross-examination —**cross-refer** *v.* refer from one part to another —**cross-reference** *n.* reference within text to another part of text —ˈ**crossroads** *n.* —**cross section** **1.** transverse section **2.** group of people fully representative of a nation, community *etc.* —**cross-stitch** *n.* **1.** embroidery stitch made by two stitches forming cross —*v.* **2.** embroider (piece of needlework) with cross-stitch —**cross-talk** *n. Rad., telephony* unwanted sounds picked up on receiving channel —ˈ**crosswalk** *n.* place marked where pedestrians may cross road —**crossword (puzzle)** puzzle built up of intersecting words, of which some letters are common, the words being indicated by clues —**at cross-purposes** conflicting; opposed; disagreeing —**the Cross** **1.** cross on which Jesus Christ was executed **2.** model or picture of this

crosse (kros) *n.* light staff with triangular frame to which network is attached, used in playing lacrosse

crotch (kroch) *n.* **1.** angle between two legs, branches or members **2.** forked pole used as prop

crotchet (ˈkrochit) *n.* whimsical notion —ˈ**crotchety** *a.* peevish; irritable

croton (ˈkrōtən) *n.* any chiefly tropical shrub or tree, seeds of which yield croton oil, formerly used as purgative

crouch (krowch) *vi.* **1.** bend low **2.** huddle down close to ground **3.** stoop servilely, cringe —*n.* **4.** act of stooping or bending

croup[1] (kro͞op) *n.* group of symptoms *esp.* spasm of the larynx, hoarseness, cough *esp.* in infants

croup[2] (kro͞op) *n.* **1.** hindquarters of horse **2.** place behind saddle

croupier (ˈkro͞opiər) *n.* person dealing cards, collecting money *etc.* at gambling table

crouton (ˈkro͞oton, kro͞oˈton) *n.* small piece of fried or toasted bread, usu. served in soup

crow[1] (krō) *n.* large black carrion-eating bird —ˈ**crowfoot** *n.* any of several plants that have yellow or white flowers and leaves resembling foot of crow (*pl.* **-s**) —**crow's-foot** *n.* wrinkle at corner of eye —**crow's-nest** *n.* lookout platform high on ship's mast

crow[2] (krō) *vi.* **1.** utter cock's cry **2.** boast one's happiness or superiority —*n.* **3.** cock's cry

Crow (krō) *n.* **1.** member of Amerindian people of Montana **2.** the Siouan language of this people

crowbar (ˈkrōbär) *n.* iron bar, usu. flattened at working end for levering

crowd (krowd) *n.* **1.** throng, mass —*vi.* **2.** flock together —*vt.* **3.** cram, force, thrust, pack **4.** fill with people —**crowd out** exclude by excess already in

crown (krown) *n.* **1.** monarch's headdress **2.** wreath for head **3.** monarch **4.** monarchy **5.** royal power **6.** formerly, British coin of five shillings **7.** any of various foreign coins **8.** top of head **9.** summit, top **10.** completion or perfection of thing —*vt.* **11.** put crown on **12.** confer title upon **13.** occur as culmination of (series of events) **14.** *inf.* hit on head —**crown jewels** jewelry, including regalia, used by sovereign on state occasion —**crown prince** heir to throne

crozier (ˈkrōzhər) *n. see* CROSIER

CRT cathode-ray tube

crucial (ˈkro͞oshəl) *a.* **1.** decisive, critical **2.** *inf.* very important

cruciate (ˈkro͞oshiāt) *a.* cross-shaped

crucible (ˈkro͞osibəl) *n.* small melting pot

crucify (ˈkro͞osifī) *vt.* **1.** put to death on cross **2.** treat cruelly **3.** *inf.* ridicule (ˈ**crucified,** ˈ**crucifying**) —ˈ**crucifix** *n.* **1.** cross **2.** image of (Christ on the) Cross —**cruciˈfixion** *n.* —ˈ**cruciform** *a.*

crude (kro͞od) *a.* **1.** lacking taste, vulgar **2.** in natural or raw state, unrefined **3.** rough, unfinished —ˈ**crudely** *adv.* —ˈ**crudity** *n.*

cruel (ˈkro͞oəl) *a.* **1.** delighting in others' pain **2.** causing pain or suffering —ˈ**cruelly** *adv.* —ˈ**cruelty** *n.*

cruet (ˈkro͞oit) *n.* **1.** small container for salt, pepper, vinegar, oil *etc.* **2.** stand holding such containers **3.** vessel to hold wine and water for the Eucharist

cruise (kro͞oz) *vi.* **1.** travel about in a ship for pleasure *etc.* **2.** (of vehicle, aircraft) travel at safe, average speed —*n.* **3.** cruising voyage, *esp.* organized for holiday purposes —ˈ**cruiser** *n.* **1.** ship that cruises **2.** warship lighter and faster than battleship —ˈ**cruiserweight** *n. Boxing* light-heavyweight

crumb (krum) *n.* **1.** small particle, fragment,

esp. of bread —*vt.* **2.** reduce to, break into, cover with crumbs

crumble (ˈkrumbəl) *v.* **1.** break into small fragments, disintegrate, crush **2.** perish, decay —*vi.* **3.** fall apart or away —*n.* **4.** pudding covered with crumbly mixture —ˈ**crumbly** *a.*

crummy (ˈkrumi) *a. sl.* inferior, contemptible

crump (krump) *vi.* **1.** thud, explode with dull sound —*n.* **2.** crunching sound **3.** *inf.* shell, bomb

crumpet (ˈkrumpit) *n.* flat round bread baked on griddle usu. toasted before eating

crumple (ˈkrumpəl) *v.* **1.** (cause to) collapse **2.** make or become crushed, wrinkled, creased —ˈ**crumpled** *a.*

crunch (krunch) *n.* **1.** sound made by chewing crisp food, treading on gravel, hard snow *etc.* **2.** *inf.* critical moment or situation —*v.* **3.** (cause to) make crunching sound

crupper (ˈkrupər) *n.* **1.** strap holding back saddle in place by passing round horse's tail **2.** horse's hindquarters

crusade (kro͞oˈsād) *n.* **1.** medieval Christian war to recover Holy Land **2.** campaign against something believed to be evil **3.** concerted action to further a cause —*vi.* **4.** campaign vigorously for something **5.** go on crusade —**cruˈsader** *n.*

cruse (kro͞oz) *n.* small earthenware jug or pot

crush[1] (krush) *vt.* **1.** compress so as to break, bruise, crumple **2.** break to small pieces **3.** defeat utterly, overthrow —*n.* **4.** act of crushing **5.** crowd of people *etc.* **6.** drink prepared by or as if by crushing fruit

crush[2] (krush) *n. inf.* infatuation

crust (krust) *n.* **1.** hard outer part of bread **2.** similar hard outer casing on anything —*v.* **3.** cover with, form, crust —ˈ**crustily** *adv.* —ˈ**crusty** *a.* **1.** having, or like, crust **2.** short-tempered

crustacean (kruˈstāshən) *n.* hard-shelled animal, *eg* crab, lobster —**crusˈtaceous** *a.*

crutch (kruch) *n.* **1.** staff with crosspiece to go under armpit of lame person **2.** support **3.** groin, crotch

crux (kruks) *n.* **1.** that on which a decision turns **2.** anything that puzzles very much (*pl.* **-es, cruces** (ˈkro͞osēz))

cry (krī) *vi.* **1.** weep **2.** wail **3.** utter call **4.** shout **5.** clamor or beg (for) —*vt.* **6.** utter loudly, proclaim (**cried, ˈcrying**) —*n.* **7.** loud utterance **8.** scream, wail, shout **9.** call of animal **10.** fit of weeping **11.** watchword —ˈ**crying** *a.* notorious; lamentable (*esp. in* **crying shame**)

cryogenics (krīəˈjeniks) *n.* branch of physics concerned with phenomena at very low temperatures —**cryoˈgenic** *a.*

crypt (kript) *n.* vault, *esp.* under church —ˈ**cryptic** *a.* secret, mysterious —ˈ**cryptically** *adv.* —ˈ**cryptogram** *n.* piece of writing in code —**crypˈtography** *n.* art of writing, decoding ciphers

cryptococcosis (kriptōkoˈkōsis) *n.* fungus infection usu. attacking brain and meninges

cryptogam (ˈkriptōgam) *n.* nonflowering plant, *eg* fern, moss *etc.*

crystal (ˈkristəl) *n.* **1.** clear transparent mineral **2.** very clear glass **3.** cut-glass ware **4.** characteristic form assumed by many substances, with definite internal structure and external shape of symmetrically arranged plane surfaces —ˈ**crystalline** *or* ˈ**crystalloid** *a.* —**crystalliˈzation** *or* **-aliˈzation** *n.* —ˈ**crystallize** *or* **-alize** *v.* **1.** (cause to) form into crystals **2.** (cause to) become definite —**crystalˈlographer** *n.* —**crystalˈlography** *n.* science of the structure, forms and properties of crystals —**crystal gazer** —**crystal gazing 1.** act of staring into crystal ball supposedly to arouse visual perceptions of future *etc.* **2.** act of trying to foresee or predict

Cs *Chem.* cesium

CS gas gas causing tears, salivation and painful breathing, used in chemical warfare and civil disturbances

CST Central Standard Time

CT Connecticut

ct. 1. cent **2.** carat **3.** court

ctenophore (ˈtenəfōr) *n.* marine invertebrate whose body bears eight rows of fused cilia for locomotion

CTV Canadian Television (Network Ltd.)

cu *or* **cu.** cubic

Cu *Chem.* copper

cub (kub) *n.* **1.** young of fox and other animals **2.** (**C-**) Cub Scout —*v.* **3.** give birth to (cubs) (**-bb-**) —**Cub Scout** 8- to 10-year-old member of Boy Scouts of America

Cuba (ˈkyo͞obə) *n.* country in Caribbean comprising islands of the Greater Antilles group lying 135 miles south of the tip of Florida

cubbyhole (ˈkubihōl) *n.* small, enclosed space or room

cube (kyo͞ob) *n.* **1.** regular solid figure contained by six equal square sides **2.** cube-shaped block **3.** the third power of a quantity, the product of three equal factors —*vt.* **4.** multiply to produce this —ˈ**cubic(al)** *a.* —ˈ**cubism** *n.* movement of modern art led by Pablo Picasso and Georges Braque as reaction to impressionism flourishing between 1907 and 1915 —ˈ**cubist** *n./a.* —**cube root** a number which taken 3 times as a factor produces the cube of the given factor, *eg* 3 is the cube root of 27 —**cubic measure** system of units for measurement of volumes

cubicle (ˈkyo͞obikəl) *n.* partially or totally enclosed section of room, as in dormitory

cubit (ˈkyo͞obit) *n.* old measure of length, about 18 inches

cuckold (ˈkukəld) *n.* **1.** man whose wife has committed adultery —*vt.* **2.** make cuckold of

cuckoo ('ko͝oko͞o) *n.* **1.** migratory bird which deposits its eggs in nests of other birds **2.** its call —*a.* **3.** *sl.* crazy —**cuckoopint** ('ko͝oko͞o-pint) *n.* European plant with arrow-shaped leaves, pale purple spadix and scarlet berries (*also* **lords-and-ladies**) —**cuckoo spit** white frothy mass on plants, produced by froghopper larvae

cucumber ('kyo͞okumbər) *n.* **1.** plant with long fleshy green fruit **2.** the fruit, used in salad

cud (kud) *n.* food which ruminant animal brings back into mouth to chew again —**chew the cud** reflect, meditate

cuddle ('kudəl) *vt.* **1.** hug —*vi.* **2.** lie close and snug, nestle —*n.* **3.** close embrace, *esp.* when prolonged

cuddy ('kudi) *n.* small cabin in boat

cudgel ('kujəl) *n.* **1.** short thick stick —*vt.* **2.** beat with cudgel

cue[1] (kyo͞o) *n.* **1.** last words of actor's speech *etc.* as signal to another to act or speak **2.** signal, hint, example for action

cue[2] (kyo͞o) *n.* long tapering rod used in billiards *etc.* —**cue ball** ball struck by cue in billiards or pool

cuff[1] (kuf) *n.* **1.** ending of sleeve **2.** wristband —**cuff link** one pair of linked buttons to join buttonholes on shirt cuffs —**off the cuff** *inf.* without preparation

cuff[2] (kuf) *vt.* **1.** strike with open hand —*n.* **2.** blow of this kind

cuirass (kwi'ras) *n.* metal or leather armor of breastplate and backplate

Cuisenaire rod (kwizə'nāər) trade name for any of set of rods of various colors and lengths representing different numbers, used to teach arithmetic

cuisine (kwi'zēn) *n.* **1.** style of cooking **2.** menu, food offered by restaurant *etc.*

cul-de-sac (kuldə'sak, ko͝ol-) *n.* **1.** street, lane open only at one end **2.** blind pouch (*pl.* **culs-de-sac**)

culinary ('kulineri, 'kyo͞o-) *a.* of, for, suitable for, cooking or kitchen

cull (kul) *vt.* **1.** gather, select **2.** take out (selected animals) from herd —*n.* **3.** act of culling

culminate ('kulmināt) *vi.* **1.** reach highest point **2.** come to climax, to a head —**culmi'nation** *n.*

culottes ('ko͞olots, 'kyo͞o-; ko͝o'lots, kyo͝o-) *pl.n.* divided skirt

culpable ('kulpəbəl) *a.* blameworthy —**culpa'bility** *n.* —'**culpably** *adv.*

culprit ('kulprit) *n.* one guilty of usu. minor offense

cult (kult) *n.* **1.** system of religious worship **2.** pursuit of, devotion to, some person, thing, or activity

cultivate ('kultivāt) *vt.* **1.** till and prepare (ground) to raise crops **2.** develop, improve, refine **3.** devote attention to, cherish **4.** practice **5.** foster —'**cultivable** *or* '**cultivatable** *a.* (of land) capable of being cultivated —**culti'vation** *n.* —'**cultivator** *n.*

culture ('kulchər) *n.* **1.** state of manners, taste and intellectual development at a time or place **2.** cultivating **3.** artificial rearing **4.** set of bacteria so reared —'**cultural** *a.* —'**cultured** *a.* refined, showing culture —**cultured pearl** pearl artificially induced to grow in oyster shell

culvert ('kulvərt) *n.* tunneled drain for passage of water under road, railroad *etc.*

cum (ko͝om, kum) *Lat.* with —**cum laude** (ko͝om 'lowdə) with distinction, *esp.* of college or university degree

cumbersome ('kumbərsəm) *or* **cumbrous** ('kumbrəs) *a.* awkward, unwieldy —'**cumber** *vt.* **1.** obstruct; hinder **2.** *obs.* inconvenience —'**cumbrance** *n.* **1.** burden; obstacle; hindrance **2.** trouble; bother

cumin ('kumin) *n.* herb cultivated for aromatic seed used as spice

cummerbund ('kumərbund) *n.* broad sash worn round waist

cumulative ('kyo͞omyo͝olətiv) *a.* **1.** becoming greater by successive additions **2.** representing the sum of many items

cumulus ('kyo͞omyo͝oləs) *n.* cloud shaped in rounded white woolly masses (*pl.* **cumuli** ('ko͞omyo͝olī))

cuneiform (kyo͝o'nēifôrm, 'kyo͞oni-) *a.* wedge-shaped, *esp.* of ancient Babylonian writing

cunnilingus (kuni'linggəs) *n.* sexual activity in which female genitalia are stimulated by partner's lips and tongue

cunning ('kuning) *a.* **1.** crafty, sly **2.** ingenious —*n.* **3.** skill in deceit or evasion **4.** skill, ingenuity —'**cunningly** *adv.*

cup (kup) *n.* **1.** small drinking vessel with handle at one side **2.** any small drinking vessel **3.** contents of cup **4.** any of various cup-shaped formations, cavities, sockets *etc.* **5.** cup-shaped trophy as prize **6.** portion, lot **7.** iced drink of wine and other ingredients **8.** either of two cup-shaped parts of brassiere *etc.* —*vt.* **9.** shape as cup (hands *etc.*) (**-pp-**) —'**cupful** *n.* (*pl.* '**cupfuls,** '**cupsful**) —'**cupping** *n. Med.* formerly, use of evacuated glass cup to draw blood to surface of skin for bloodletting —**cupboard** ('kubərd) *n.* recess in room, with door, for storage —'**cupcake** *n.* small cake baked in cuplike mold —**in one's cups** drunk

cupel (kyo͝o'pel, 'kyo͞opəl) *n.* small vessel used in refining metals

Cupid ('kyo͞opid) *n.* god of love

cupidity (kyo͞o'piditi) *n.* **1.** greed for possessions **2.** covetousness

cupola ('kyo͞opələ) *n.* dome

cupreous ('kyo͞opriəs, 'ko͞o-) *a.* of, containing, copper

cupronickel (kyo͞oprō'nikəl, ko͞o-) *n.* copper alloy containing up to 40 per cent nickel

cur (kər) *n.* **1.** dog of mixed breed **2.** surly, contemptible or mean person

curaçao (kyŏŏərə'sō, kŏŏə-) *n.* liqueur flavored with bitter orange peel

curare (kyŏŏ'räri, kŏŏ-) *n.* poisonous resin of S Amer. tree, now used as muscle relaxant in medicine

curate ('kyŏŏərit) *n.* **1.** clergyman in charge of parish **2.** clergyman serving as assistant to rector —**'curacy** *n.* curate's office

curative ('kyŏŏərətiv) *a.* **1.** tending to cure disease —*n.* **2.** anything able to heal or cure

curator (kyŏŏə'rātər) *n.* custodian, *esp.* of museum, library *etc.* —**cura'torial** *a.* —**cu'ratorship** *n.*

curb (kərb) *n.* **1.** check, restraint **2.** chain or strap passing under horse's lower jaw and giving powerful control with reins **3.** stone edging along paved street —*vt.* **4.** restrain, apply curb to

curd (kərd) *n.* coagulated milk —**'curdle** *v.* turn into curd, coagulate —**'curdy** *a.*

cure (kyŏŏər) *vt.* **1.** heal, restore to health **2.** remedy **3.** preserve (fish, skins *etc.*) —*n.* **4.** remedy **5.** course of medical treatment **6.** successful treatment, restoration to health —**cura'bility** *n.* —**'curable** *a.* —**cure of souls** care of parish or congregation

curette (kyŏŏ'ret) *n.* spoon-shaped surgical instrument for removing dead tissue *etc.* from some body cavities —**curettage** (kyŏŏri'täzh) *n.* technique or act of using curette

curfew ('kərfyōō) *n.* **1.** official regulation restricting or prohibiting movement of people, *esp.* at night **2.** time set as deadline by such regulation

curia ('kyŏŏriə, 'kŏŏ-) *n.* **1.** papal court and government of Roman Catholic Church **2.** (in Middle Ages) court held in king's name (*pl.* **curiae** ('kyŏŏriē, 'kŏŏ-))

curie ('kyŏŏəri, -rē; 'kŏŏə-) *n.* standard unit of radium emanation

curio ('kyŏŏriō) *n.* rare or curious thing of the kind sought for collections (*pl.* **-s**)

curious ('kyŏŏriəs) *a.* **1.** eager to know, inquisitive **2.** prying **3.** puzzling, strange, odd —**curi'osity** *n.* **1.** eagerness to know **2.** inquisitiveness **3.** strange or rare thing —**'curiously** *adv.*

curium ('kyŏŏriəm) *n. Chem.* transuranic element *Symbol* Cm, at. wt. 248, at. no. 96

curl (kərl) *vi.* **1.** take spiral or curved shape or path —*vt.* **2.** bend into spiral or curved shape —*n.* **3.** spiral lock of hair **4.** spiral, curved state, form or motion —**'curler** *n.* **1.** pin, clasp *etc.* for curling hair **2.** person or thing that curls **3.** person who plays curling —**'curling** *n.* game like bowls, played with large rounded stones on ice by teams of four players each —**'curly** *a.* —**curling tongs** heated, metal, scissor-like device for curling hair

curlew ('kərlyōō, -lōō) *n.* large long-billed wading bird

curlicue ('kərlikyōō) *n.* intricate ornamental curl or twist

curmudgeon (kər'mujən) *n.* surly or miserly person

curragh *or* **currach** ('kurəkh, 'kurə) *n.* coracle with a keel

currant ('kurənt) *n.* **1.** dried type of grape **2.** fruit of various plants allied to gooseberry **3.** any of these plants

current ('kurənt) *a.* **1.** of immediate present, going on **2.** up-to-date, not yet superseded **3.** in circulation or general use —*n.* **4.** body of water or air in motion **5.** tendency, drift **6.** transmission of electricity through conductor —**'currency** *n.* **1.** money in use **2.** state of being in use **3.** time during which thing is current —**'currently** *adv.*

curricle ('kurikəl) *n.* two-wheeled open carriage drawn by two horses side by side

curriculum (kə'rikyələm) *n.* specified course of study (*pl.* **-s, -la** (-lə)) —**curriculum vitae** ('vītē) outline of person's educational and professional history, usu. for job applications (*pl.* **curricula vitae**)

curry[1] ('kuri) *n.* **1.** food or dish flavored with curry powder **2.** curry powder —*vt.* **3.** prepare, flavor dish with curry powder (**'curried, 'currying**) —**curry powder** condiment consisting of combination of various pungent aromatic ground spices

curry[2] ('kuri) *vt.* **1.** groom (horse) with comb **2.** dress (leather) (**'curried, 'currying**) —**curry comb** metal comb for grooming horse —**curry favor** try to win favor, ingratiate oneself

curse (kərs) *n.* **1.** profane or obscene expression of anger *etc.* **2.** utterance expressing extreme ill will towards some person or thing **3.** affliction, misfortune, scourge —*v.* **4.** utter curse, swear (at) —*vt.* **5.** afflict —**cursed** ('kərsid, kərst) *a.* **1.** hateful **2.** wicked **3.** deserving of, or under, a curse —**cursedly** ('kərsidli) *adv.* —**cursedness** ('kərsidnis) *n.*

cursive ('kərsiv) *a.* written in running script, with letters joined

cursor ('kərsər) *n.* **1.** sliding part of measuring instrument **2.** movable point of light *etc.* that identifies specific position on visual display unit

cursory ('kərsəri) *a.* rapid, hasty, not detailed, superficial —**'cursorily** *adv.*

curt (kərt) *a.* short, rudely brief, abrupt —**'curtly** *adv.* —**'curtness** *n.*

curtail (kər'tāl) *vt.* cut short, diminish —**cur'tailment** *n.*

curtain ('kərtən) *n.* **1.** hanging drapery at window *etc.* **2.** cloth hung as screen **3.** screen separating audience and stage in theater **4.** end to act or scene *etc.* —*pl.* **5.** *inf.* death or ruin; the end —*vt.* **6.** provide, cover with curtain —**curtain call** return to stage by performers to acknowledge applause —**curtain-raiser** *n.* **1.** short play coming before main one **2.** any preliminary event —**curtain wall** wall that divides space but does not bear structural weight

curtsy *or* **curtsey** ('kərtsi) *n.* **1.** woman's bow or respectful gesture made by bending knees and lowering body —*vi.* **2.** make a curtsy

curve (kərv) *n.* **1.** line of which no part is straight **2.** bent line or part —*v.* **3.** bend into curve —**cur'vaceous** *a. inf.* shapely —'**curvature** *n.* **1.** a bending **2.** bent shape —**curvi'linear** *a.* of bent lines

curvet (kər'vet) *n.* **1.** leap of horse in which forelegs touch the ground first —*vi.* **2.** prance or frisk about (**-tt-**)

Cushing's disease ('ko͝oshingz) tumor of the pituitary gland —**Cushing's syndrome** disease of the adrenal gland marked by excessive secretions from the gland

cushion ('ko͝oshən) *n.* **1.** bag filled with soft stuffing or air, to support or ease body **2.** any soft pad or support **3.** resilient rim of billiard table —*vt.* **4.** provide, protect with cushion **5.** lessen effects of

cushy ('ko͝oshi) *a. inf.* soft, comfortable, pleasant, light, well-paid

cusp (kusp) *n.* **1.** either end of crescent moon **2.** point on grinding surface of tooth **3.** point of transition from one astrological sign to another —'**cuspid** *n.* pointed tooth —'**cuspidal** *a.* **1.** ending in point **2.** of or like cusp

cuspidor ('kuspidŏr) *n.* spittoon

cuss (kus) *inf. n.* **1.** curse; oath **2.** person or animal, *esp.* annoying one —*v.* **3.** *see* CURSE (sense 4) —**cussed** ('kusid) *a. inf.* **1.** *see* **cursed** *at* CURSE **2.** obstinate **3.** annoying —'**cussedness** *n.*

custard ('kustərd) *n.* dish made of eggs and milk

custody ('kustədi) *n.* safekeeping, guardianship, imprisonment —**cus'todian** *n.* keeper, caretaker, curator

custom ('kustəm) *n.* **1.** habit **2.** practice **3.** fashion, usage **4.** business patronage **5.** toll, tax —*pl.* **6.** duties levied on imports **7.** government department which collects these **8.** area in airport *etc.* where customs officials examine luggage for dutiable goods —**custom'arily** *adv.* —'**customary** *a.* usual, habitual —'**customer** *n.* **1.** one who enters shop to buy, *esp.* regularly **2.** purchaser —**custom-built** *a.* (of automobiles, houses *etc.*) made to specifications of buyer —'**customhouse** *n.* building where customs are collected —**custom-made** *a.* (of suits *etc.*) made to specifications of buyer —**customs duties** taxes laid on imported or exported goods

cut (kut) *vt.* **1.** sever, penetrate, wound, divide, or separate with pressure of edge or edged instrument **2.** pare, detach, trim, or shape by cutting **3.** divide **4.** intersect **5.** reduce, decrease **6.** abridge **7.** *inf.* refuse to recognize (person) **8.** strike (with whip *etc.*) **9.** divide (deck of cards), *esp.* to decide dealer —*vi. Cine.* **10.** call a halt to shooting sequence **11.** (*with* to) move quickly to another scene (**cut, 'cutting**) —*n.* **12.** act of cutting **13.** stroke **14.** blow, wound (of knife, whip *etc.*) **15.** reduction, decrease **16.** fashion, shape **17.** incision **18.** engraving **19.** piece cut off **20.** division **21.** *inf.* share, *esp.* of profits —'**cutter** *n.* **1.** one who, that which, cuts **2.** warship's rowing and sailing boat **3.** small sloop-rigged vessel with straight running bowsprit —'**cutting** *n.* **1.** act of cutting, thing cut off or out, *esp.* excavation (for road, canal *etc.*) through high ground **2.** shoot, twig of plant **3.** *esp.* **UK** piece cut from newspaper *etc.*; clipping —*a.* **4.** sarcastic, unkind —'**cutaway** *n.* **1.** man's coat cut diagonally from front waist to back of knees **2.** drawing or model of machine *etc.* in which part of casing is omitted to reveal workings —'**cutback** *n.* decrease; reduction —**cut glass** glass, *esp.* vases *etc.*, decorated by facet cutting or grinding —**cut-rate** *a.* **1.** available at prices or rates below standard price or rate **2.** offering goods or services at prices below standard price —'**cutthroat** *a.* **1.** merciless **2.** (of partnership card games) characterized by players changing partners in order to attain highest personal scores —*n.* **3.** murderous person —**cut back 1.** shorten by cutting off end; prune **2.** reduce or make reduction (in) —**cut in 1.** intrude **2.** interrupt (in conversation) **3.** interrupt dancing couple and take one as one's partner **4.** mix (dried food ingredients) with chopping motion

cutaneous (kyo͞o'tāniəs) *a.* of skin

cute (kyo͞ot) *a.* appealing, attractive, pretty

cuticle ('kyo͞otikəl) *n.* **1.** the skin **2.** dead skin at edges of fingernail or toenail **3.** thin fatty film covering surface of many higher plants

cutis ('kyo͞otis) *n. Anat.* skin (*pl.* **-tes** (-tēz), **-es**)

cutlass ('kutləs) *n.* short broad-bladed sword

cutlery ('kutləri) *n.* implements for cutting food —'**cutler** *n.* one who makes, repairs, deals in knives and cutting implements

cutlet ('kutlit) *n.* small piece of meat broiled or fried

cuttlefish ('kutəlfish) *n.* marine mollusk resembling squid but with calcified internal shell (*also* '**cuttle**) —'**cuttlebone** *n.* internal shell of cuttlefish, used as mineral supplement to diet of cagebirds and as polishing agent

C.V. curriculum vitae

Cwlth. Commonwealth

cwm (ko͞om) *n.* **1.** in Wales, valley **2.** *Geol. see* CIRQUE

c.w.o. *or* **C.W.O.** cash with order

cwt. hundredweight

-cy (*comb. form*) **1.** state, quality, condition,

as in *plutocracy, lunacy* **2.** rank, office, as in *captaincy*

cyan ('sīan, 'sīən) *n.* **1.** green-blue color *—a.* **2.** of this color

cyanide ('sīənīd) *n.* extremely poisonous organic compound, used for fumigating buildings and soil —**cy'anogen** *n.* poisonous gas composed of nitrogen and carbon

cyanosis (sīə'nōsis) *n.* blueness of the skin

cybernetics (sībər'netiks) *pl.n.* (*with sing. v.*) comparative study of control mechanisms of electronic and biological systems

cyclamate ('sīkləmāt) *n.* compound formerly used as food additive and sugar substitute

cyclamen ('sīkləmən, 'sik-) *n.* plant with flowers having turned-back petals

cycle ('sīkəl) *n.* **1.** recurrent series or period **2.** rotation of events **3.** complete series or period **4.** development following course of stages **5.** series of poems *etc.* **6.** bicycle, tricycle or motorcycle *—vi.* **7.** move in cycles **8.** ride cycle —**'cyclic(al)** *a.* **1.** recurring or revolving in a cycle **2.** *Chem.* (of compound) having atoms which form a ring —**'cyclist** *n.* cycle rider —**cy'clometer** *n.* instrument for measuring circles or recording distance traveled by wheel, *esp.* of bicycle

cyclo- *or before vowel* **cycl-** (*comb. form*) **1.** indicating circle or ring, as in *cyclotron* **2.** denoting cyclic compound, as in *cyclopropane*

cyclone ('sīklōn) *n.* **1.** system of winds moving round centre of low pressure **2.** circular storm —**cyclonic** (sī'klonik) *a.*

cyclopedia *or* **cyclopaedia** (sīklō'pēdiə) *n.* *see* ENCYCLOPEDIA

cyclopropane (sīklō'prōpān) *n.* colorless gaseous hydrocarbon, used as anesthetic

Cyclops ('sīklops) *n. Class. myth.* one of race of giants having single eye in middle of forehead (*pl.* **Cyclopes** (sī'klōpēz), **-es**)

cyclorama (sīklō'rämə) *n.* **1.** picture on interior wall of cylindrical room, designed to appear in natural perspective to spectator **2.** *Theat.* curtain or wall curving along back of stage —**cycloramic** (sīklō'ramik) *a.*

cyclostyle ('sīkləstīl) *vt.* **1.** produce (pamphlets *etc.*) in large numbers for distribution *—a./n.* **2.** (of) machine, method for doing this

cyclotron ('sīklətron) *n.* powerful apparatus which accelerates the circular movement of subatomic particles in a magnetic field, used for work in nuclear disintegration *etc.*

cygnet ('signit) *n.* young swan

cylinder ('silindər) *n.* **1.** solid or hollow object with straight sides and circular ends **2.** piston chamber of engine —**cy'lindrical** *a.*

cymbal ('simbəl) *n.* one of pair of two brass plates struck together to produce ringing or clashing sound in orchestra

cyme (sīm) *n.* inflorescence in which first flower is terminal bud of main stem and subsequent flowers develop as terminal buds of lateral stems —**cy'miferous** *a.*

Cymric *or* **Kymric** ('kimrik) *a.* Welsh

cynic ('sinik) *n.* one who expects, believes, the worst about people, their motives, or outcome of events —**'cynical** *a.* —**'cynicism** *n.* being cynical

cynosure ('sīnəshōōər, 'sin-) *n.* center of attraction

cypress ('sīprəs) *n.* any of genus of mainly evergreen trees of pine family with overlapping leaves resembling scales

Cyprus ('sīprəs) *n.* country in eastern Mediterranean comprising one island lying 50 miles off the south coast of Turkey and 65 miles off the coast of Syria —**Cypriot** ('sipriət) *or* **Cypriote** ('sipriōt) *n.* **1.** native of Cyprus **2.** dialect of Greek spoken in Cyprus *—a.* **3.** relating to Cyprus

Cyrillic (si'rilik) *a.* **1.** relating to alphabet devised supposedly by Saint Cyril, for Slavonic languages *—n.* **2.** this alphabet

cyst (sist) *n.* **1.** abnormal sac formed in the body **2.** resistant cover surrounding a parasite produced by the parasite or host —**'cystic** *a.* **1.** of cysts **2.** of the bladder —**cys'titis** *n.* inflammation of bladder —**cystic fibrosis** congenital disease, usu. affecting children, characterized by chronic infection of respiratory tract and pancreatic insufficiency

cystocele ('sistōsēl) *n.* the protrusion of the urinary bladder into the vagina

cytochrome ('sītōkrōm) *n.* pigment found in plant and animal tissue enabling air-breathing organisms to utilize atmospheric oxygen

cytology (sī'toləji) *n.* branch of biology concerned with all aspects of plant or animal cells

cytoplasm ('sītōplazəm) *n.* protoplasm of cell excluding nucleus

cytoscope ('sītəskōp) *n.* slender tubular medical instrument for examining interior of urethra and urinary bladder —**cy'toscopy** *n.* visual examination of the urinary bladder with cytoscope

czar, tsar, *or* **tzar** (zär) *n.* **1.** emperor, king, *esp.* of Russia 1547–1917 **2.** one having great power —**cza'rina, cza'ritsa, tsa'ritsa** *or* **tza'ritsa** *n.* wife of czar

czardas ('chärdash) *n.* **1.** Hungarian national dance of alternating slow and fast sections **2.** music for this dance

Czechoslovakia (chekōslō'vakiə) *n.* country in central Europe bounded north by the German Democratic Republic and Poland, south by Hungary and Austria, and west by the Federal Republic of Germany —**Czech** *n.* member of western branch of Slavs —**Czecho'slovak** *or* **Czechoslo'vakian** *a.* **1.** of Czechoslovakia, its peoples or languages *—n.* **2.** (loosely) either of two languages of Czechoslovakia: Czech or Slovak

D

d *or* **D** (dē) *n.* **1.** fourth letter of English alphabet **2.** speech sound represented by this letter (*pl.* **d's, D's** *or* **Ds**)

d *Phys.* density

D 1. *Mus.* second note of scale of C major; major or minor key having this note as its tonic **2.** *Chem.* deuterium **3.** Roman numeral, 500

d. 1. day **2.** denarius (*Lat.*, penny) **3.** departs **4.** diameter **5.** died

D. Democratic

dab[1] (dab) *vt.* **1.** apply with momentary pressure (*esp.* anything wet and soft) **2.** strike feebly (**-bb-**) —*n.* **3.** smear **4.** slight blow or tap **5.** small mass —**'dabchick** *n.* small grebe —**dab hand** *inf.* someone good at something

dab[2] (dab) *n.* any of various small flatfishes, *esp.* flounder

dabble ('dabəl) *vi.* **1.** splash about **2.** be desultory student or amateur —**'dabbler** *n.*

da capo (dä 'käpō) *Mus.* repeat from beginning

dace (dās) *n.* any of various small European or N Amer. freshwater fishes (*pl.* **dace, -s**)

dachshund ('däks-ho͝ont) *n.* short-legged long-bodied dog

Dacron ('dākron, 'dak-) *n.* trade name for polyester fiber

dactyl ('daktil) *n.* metrical foot of one long followed by two short syllables

dad (dad) *or* **daddy** ('dadi) *n. inf.* father —**daddy longlegs** ('longlegz) *inf.* any of various insects or spiders with long slender legs

Dada ('dädä) *or* **Dadaism** ('dädäizəm) *n.* artistic movement of early 20th century, founded on principles of incongruity and irreverence toward accepted aesthetic criteria —**'Dadaist** *n./a.*

dado ('dādō) *n.* lower part of room wall when lined or painted separately (*pl.* **-es, -s**)

daemon ('dēmən) *or* **daimon** ('dīmon) *n.* **1.** demigod **2.** guardian spirit of place or person

daff (daf) *inf.* daffodil

daffodil ('dafədil) *n.* spring flower, yellow narcissus (*also* **Lent lily**)

daft (daft) *a.* foolish, crazy

dag (dag) *n.* **1.** daglock **2. A, NZ** *sl.* eccentric character —**'daglock** *n.* dung-caked locks of wool around hindquarters of sheep

dagga ('dakhə, 'dägə) *n.* **SA** hemp, smoked as narcotic

dagger ('dagər) *n.* short, edged stabbing weapon

dago ('dāgō) *n. offens.* person of Italian descent (*pl.* **-s, -es**)

daguerreotype (də'gerōtīp) *n.* **1.** early photographic process **2.** photograph formed by this process

dahlia ('dalyə) *n.* garden plant of various colors

Dáil Éireann ('doil 'āərən) *or* **Dáil** *n.* lower chamber of parliament in the Irish Republic

daily ('dāli) *a.* **1.** done, occurring, published every day —*adv.* **2.** every day —*n.* **3.** daily newspaper

dainty ('dānti) *a.* **1.** delicate **2.** elegant, choice **3.** pretty and neat **4.** fastidious —*n.* **5.** delicacy —**'daintily** *adv.* —**'daintiness** *n.*

daiquiri ('dīkiri, 'dak-) *n.* iced drink containing rum, lime juice and sugar (*pl.* **-s**)

dairy ('dāəri) *n.* place for processing milk and its products —**'dairying** *n.* —**dairy cattle** cows raised mainly for milk —**dairy farm** farm specializing in producing milk—**'dairymaid** *n.* —**'dairyman** *n.* —**dairy products** milk, cheese, butter *etc.*

dais ('dāis, 'dīis) *n.* raised platform, usu. at end of hall

daisy ('dāzi) *n.* flower with yellow center and white petals —**daisy-wheel** *n.* flat, wheel-shaped device with printing characters at end of spokes

Dakota (də'kōtə) *n.* **1.** member of Amerindian people of northern Mississippi Valley (*pl.* **-s, Dakota**) **2.** the Siouan language of this people (*also* **Sioux**)

Dalai Lama ('dälī 'lämə) head of Tibetan Buddhism

dale (dāl) *n.* valley —**'dalesman** *n.* native of dale, *esp.* of N England

dalles (dalz) *pl.n.* **C** river rapids flowing between high rock walls

dally ('dali) *vi.* **1.** trifle, spend time in idleness or amusement **2.** loiter (**'dallied, 'dallying**) —**'dalliance** *n.*

Dalmatian (dal'māshən) *n.* large dog, white with black spots

dal segno ('däl 'sānyō) *Mus.* repeat from point marked with sign to word *fine*

dam[1] (dam) *n.* **1.** barrier to hold back flow of waters **2.** water so collected —*vt.* **3.** hold with or as with dam (**-mm-**)

dam[2] (dam) *n.* female parent (used of animals)

damage ('damij) *n.* **1.** injury, harm, loss —*pl.*

2. sum claimed or adjudged in compensation for injury —*vt.* **3.** harm

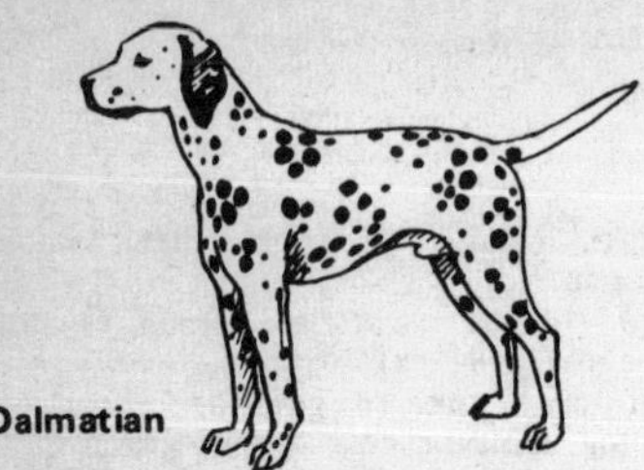
Dalmatian

damascene (ˈdaməsēn) *n.* **1.** technique of decorating iron and steel with inlaid patterns of gold and silver —*vt.* **2.** decorate (iron and steel) thus

damask (ˈdaməsk) *n.* **1.** figured woven material of silk or linen, *esp.* white table linen with design shown up by light **2.** color of damask rose, velvety red —**damask rose** fragrant rose used to make the perfume attar

dame (dām) *n.* **1.** *obs.* lady **2.** (**D-**) title of lady in Order of the British Empire **3.** *sl.* woman

damn (dam) *vt.* **1.** condemn to hell **2.** be the ruin of **3.** give hostile reception to —*vi.* **4.** curse (**damned, ˈdamning**) —*interj.* **5.** expression of annoyance, impatience *etc.* —**damnable** (ˈdamnəbəl) *a.* **1.** deserving damnation **2.** hateful, annoying —**damˈnation** *n.* —**damnatory** (ˈdamnətöri) *a.*

damp (damp) *a.* **1.** moist **2.** slightly moist —*n.* **3.** diffused moisture **4.** in coal mines, dangerous gas —*vt.* **5.** make damp **6.** (*oft. with* down) deaden, discourage —ˈ**dampen** *v.* **1.** make, become damp —*vt.* **2.** stifle, deaden —ˈ**damper** *n.* **1.** anything that discourages or depresses **2.** plate in flue to control draft

damsel (ˈdamzəl) *n. obs.* girl

damson (ˈdamzən) *n.* **1.** small dark purple plum **2.** tree bearing it **3.** its color

dan (dan) *n.* any one of 12 grades of proficiency in judo

Dan. *Bible* Daniel

dance (dans) *vi.* **1.** move with measured rhythmic steps, usu. to music **2.** be in lively movement **3.** bob up and down —*vt.* **4.** perform (dance) **5.** cause to dance —*n.* **6.** lively, rhythmical movement **7.** arrangement of such movements **8.** tune for them **9.** social gathering for the purpose of dancing —ˈ**dancer** *n.*

D and C dilation and curettage (of womb)

dandelion (ˈdandilīən) *n.* yellow-flowered wild plant

dander (ˈdandər) *n. inf.* temper, fighting spirit

dandle (ˈdandəl) *vt.* **1.** move (young child) up and down (on knee or in arms) **2.** pet; fondle

dandruff (ˈdandrəf) *n.* dead skin in small scales among the hair

dandy (ˈdandi) *n.* **1.** man excessively concerned with smartness of dress —*a.* **2.** *inf.* excellent —ˈ**dandify** *vt.* dress like or cause to resemble a dandy —ˈ**dandyism** *n.*

Dane (dān) *n. see* DENMARK

danger (ˈdānjər) *n.* **1.** liability or exposure to harm **2.** risk, peril —ˈ**dangerous** *a.* —ˈ**dangerously** *adv.*

dangle (ˈdanggəl) *vi.* **1.** hang loosely and swaying —*vt.* **2.** hold suspended **3.** tempt with

Daniel (ˈdanyəl) *n. Bible* 27th book of the O.T., written by the prophet Daniel, presenting Jerusalem under Gentile control

Danish (ˈdānish) *see* DENMARK

dank (dangk) *a.* unpleasantly damp and chilly —ˈ**dankness** *n.*

danseuse (dāˈsœz) *n.* female dancer

daphne (ˈdafni) *n.* ornamental shrub with bell-shaped flowers

dapper (ˈdapər) *a.* neat and precise, *esp.* in dress, spruce

dapple (ˈdapəl) *v.* mark or become marked with spots —ˈ**dappled** *a.* spotted, mottled, variegated —**dapple-gray** *a.* (of horse) gray marked with darker spots

DAR Daughters of the American Revolution

dare (dāər) *v.* **1.** venture, have courage (to) —*vt.* **2.** challenge —*n.* **3.** challenge —ˈ**daring** *a.* **1.** bold —*n.* **2.** adventurous courage —ˈ**daredevil** *a./n.* reckless (person)

dark (därk) *a.* **1.** without light **2.** gloomy **3.** deep in tint **4.** secret **5.** unenlightened **6.** wicked —*n.* **7.** absence of light, color or knowledge —ˈ**darken** *v.* —ˈ**darkly** *adv.* —ˈ**darkness** *n.* —**Dark Ages** *Hist.* period from about late 5th cent. A.D. to about 1000 A.D. —**Dark Continent** Africa when relatively unexplored —**dark horse** somebody, *esp.* competitor in race, about whom little is known —ˈ**darkroom** *n.* darkened room for processing film

darling (ˈdärling) *a./n.* much loved or very lovable (person)

darn[1] (därn) *vt.* **1.** mend by filling (hole) with interwoven yarn —*n.* **2.** place so mended —ˈ**darning** *n.*

darn[2] (därn) *interj.* mild expletive

darnel (ˈdärnəl) *n.* grass that grows as weed in grain fields

dart (därt) *n.* **1.** small light pointed missile **2.** darting motion **3.** tapering seam in garment —*pl.* **4.** indoor game played with numbered target and miniature darts —*vt.* **5.** cast, throw rapidly (glance *etc.*) —*vi.* **6.** go rapidly or abruptly —ˈ**dartboard** *n.* circular piece of wood *etc.* used as target in darts

Darwinian (därˈwiniən) *a.* pert. to Charles Darwin (1809–82) or his theory of evolution

dash (dash) *vt.* **1.** smash, throw, thrust, send with violence **2.** cast down **3.** tinge, flavor, mix —*vi.* **4.** move, go with great speed or violence —*n.* **5.** rush **6.** vigor **7.** smartness **8.**

small quantity, tinge **9.** stroke (-) between words —**'dasher** *n.* **C** ledge along top of boards at ice-hockey rink —**'dashing** *a.* spirited, showy —**'dashboard** *n.* in vehicle, instrument panel in front of driver

dastard ('dastərd) *n. obs.* contemptible, sneaking coward —**'dastardly** *a.*

data ('dātə, 'dätə) *pl.n.* (*oft. with sing. v.*) **1.** series of observations, measurements or facts **2.** information —**data bank** *or* **base** store of information, *esp.* in form that can be handled by computer —**data processing** sequence of operations performed on data, *esp.* by computer, to extract information *etc.*

DATA Defense Air Transportation Administration

date[1] (dāt) *n.* **1.** day of the month **2.** statement on document of its time of writing **3.** time of occurrence **4.** period of work of art *etc.* **5.** engagement, appointment —*vt.* **6.** mark with date **7.** refer to date of **8.** reveal age of **9.** *inf.* accompany on social outing —*vi.* **10.** exist (from) **11.** betray time or period of origin, become old-fashioned —**'dateless** *a.* **1.** without date **2.** immemorial —**'dateline** *n. Journalism* date and location of story, placed at top of article —**date line** (*oft.* **D- L-**) line (180° meridian) E of which is one day earlier than W of it —**date stamp 1.** adjustable rubber stamp for recording date **2.** inked impression made by this

date[2] (dāt) *n.* **1.** sweet, single-stone fruit of palm **2.** the palm

dative ('dātiv) *n.* noun case indicating indirect object

datum ('dātəm, 'dätəm) *n.* thing given, known or assumed as basis for reckoning, reasoning *etc.* (*pl.* **'data**)

daub (dôb) *vt.* **1.** coat, plaster, paint coarsely or roughly —*n.* **2.** rough picture **3.** smear —**'dauber** *n.*

daughter ('dôtər) *n.* **1.** one's female child —*a.* **2.** *Biol.* of cell or unicellular organism produced by division of one of its own kind. **3.** *Phys.* (of nuclide) formed from another nuclide by radioactive decay —**'daughterly** *a.* —**daughter-in-law** *n.* son's wife

daunt (dônt) *vt.* frighten, *esp.* into giving up purpose —**'dauntless** *a.* intrepid, fearless

dauphin ('dôfin; *Fr.* dō'fẽ) *n.* formerly, eldest son of French king

davenport ('davənpôrt) *n.* **1.** small writing table with drawers **2.** large couch or settee

davit ('dāvit, 'da-) *n.* crane, usu. one of pair, at ship's side for lowering and hoisting boats

Davy Jones's locker ('dāvi 'jōnziz) bottom of the sea; ships' or sailors' graveyard

daw (dô) *n. obs.* jackdaw

dawdle ('dôdəl) *vi.* idle, waste time, loiter —**'dawdler** *n.*

dawn (dôn) *n.* **1.** first light **2.** first gleam or beginning of anything —*vi.* **3.** begin to grow light **4.** appear, begin **5.** (begin to) be understood —**'dawning** *n.* —**dawn chorus** singing of birds at dawn

day (dā) *n.* **1.** period of 24 hours **2.** time when sun is above horizon **3.** point or unit of time **4.** daylight **5.** part of day occupied by certain activity, time period **6.** special or designated day —**day bed** couch intended for use as seat and as bed —**'daybook** *n.* diary —**'daybreak** *n.* dawn —**'daydream** *n.* **1.** idle fancy —*vi.* **2.** indulge in idle fantasy —**'daylight** *n.* **1.** natural light **2.** dawn —*pl.* **3.** consciousness, wits —**daylight robbery** *inf.* blatant overcharging —**daylight saving time** time set one hour ahead of local standard time (*also* **daylight time**) —**day room** communal living room in residential institution —**'dayspring** *n.* dawn —**'daystar** *n.* morning star —**'daytime** *n.* time between sunrise and sunset —**day-to-day** *a.* routine; everyday —**see daylight** begin to apprehend the solution to a problem or the end of a task

Dayak *or* **Dyak** ('dīak) *n.* **1.** member of any of the Indonesian peoples of Borneo **2.** the language of these peoples

Day-Glo ('dāglō) *n.* trade name for luminous printing ink

daze (dāz) *vt.* **1.** stupefy, stun, bewilder —*n.* **2.** stupefied or bewildered state —**dazed** *a.*

dazzle ('dazəl) *vt.* **1.** blind, confuse or overpower with brightness, light, brilliant display or prospects —*n.* **2.** brightness that dazzles the vision —**'dazzlement** *n.*

dB *or* **db** decibel(s)

DC 1. District of Columbia **2.** direct current **3.** *Mus.* da capo

DD Doctor of Divinity

D-day *n.* day selected for start of something, *esp.* Allied invasion of Europe in 1944

DDT dichlorodiphenyltrichloroethane, hydrocarbon compound used as an insecticide

DE Delaware

de- (*comb. form*) removal of, from, reversal of, as in *delouse, desegregate.* Such words are not given here where the meaning may be inferred from the simple word

deacon ('dēkən) *n.* **1.** clergyman ranking below priest in certain Christian denominations **2.** layman in charge of business matters in certain churches **3.** Mormon in lowest grade of priesthood (**'deaconess** *fem.*)

deactivate (dē'aktivāt) *vt.* **1.** make (bomb *etc.*) harmless or inoperative **2.** make less radioactive

dead (ded) *a.* **1.** no longer alive **2.** obsolete **3.** numb, without sensation **4.** no longer functioning, extinguished **5.** lacking luster, movement or vigor **6.** sure, complete —*pl. n.* **7.** dead persons —*adv.* **8.** utterly —**'deaden** *vt.* —**'deadly** *a.* **1.** fatal **2.** deathlike —*adv.* **3.** as if dead —**dead-and-alive** *a.* dull —**'deadbeat** *a./n. inf.* lazy, useless (person) —**dead duck** *sl.* person or thing doomed to death, failure *etc., esp.* because of mistake —**dead end 1.** cul-de-sac **2.** situation in which further progress is impossible —ˈ**deadhead** *n.* 1. one who has not paid for a ticket or contributed to the pot in a poker game. 2. log sticking out of water as hindrance to navigation —**dead heat** race in which competitors finish exactly even —**dead letter** 1. law no longer observed 2. letter which post office cannot deliver —ˈ**deadline** *n.* limit of time allowed —ˈ**deadlock** *n.* standstill —**dead loss** 1. complete loss for which no compensation is paid 2. *inf.* useless person or thing —**deadly nightshade** belladonna —**dead man's handle** *or* **pedal** safety switch on piece of machinery that allows operation only while depressed by operator —**dead march** solemn funeral music to accompany procession —ˈ**deadpan** *a.* expressionless —**dead reckoning** calculation of ship's position from log and compass, when observations cannot be taken —**dead set** *adv.* 1. absolutely —*n.* 2. resolute attack —**dead weight** 1. heavy weight or load 2. oppressive burden 3. difference between loaded and unloaded weights of ship 4. intrinsic invariable weight of structure —ˈ**deadwood** *n.* 1. dead trees or branches 2. *inf.* useless person; encumbrance —**dead of night** time of greatest stillness and darkness

deaf (def) *a.* 1. wholly or partly without hearing 2. unwilling to listen —ˈ**deafen** *vt.* make deaf —ˈ**deafness** *n.* —**deaf aid** hearing aid —**deaf-and-dumb** *a.* 1. unable to hear or speak 2. for use of deaf-mutes —**deaf-mute** *n.* 1. person unable to hear or speak —*a.* 2. unable to hear or speak

deal[1] (dēl) *vt.* 1. distribute, give out 2. inflict —*vi.* 3. act 4. treat 5. do business (with, in) (**dealt** *pt./pp.*) —*n.* 6. agreement 7. treatment 8. share 9. business transaction —ˈ**dealer** *n.* 1. one who deals (*esp.* cards) 2. trader —ˈ**dealings** *pl.n.* transactions or relations with others —**deal with** handle, act toward

deal[2] (dēl) *n.* (plank of) fir or pine wood

dealt (delt) *pt./pp. of* DEAL[1]

dean (dēn) *n.* 1. university or college official 2. head of cathedral chapter 3. secondary-school administrator in charge of discipline —ˈ**deanery** *n.* cathedral dean's house or appointment

dear (dēər) *a.* 1. beloved; precious 2. costly, expensive —*n.* 3. beloved one —*adv.* 4. at a high price —ˈ**dearly** *adv.* —ˈ**dearness** *n.*

dearth (dərth) *n.* scarcity

death (deth) *n.* 1. dying 2. end of life 3. end, extinction 4. annihilation 5. (**D-**) personification of death, as skeleton —ˈ**deathless** *a.* immortal —ˈ**deathly** *a./adv.* like death —ˈ**deathbed** *n.* bed in which person is about to die —ˈ**deathblow** *n.* thing or event that destroys life or hope, *esp.* suddenly —**death cap** kind of toadstool —**death certificate** legal document issued by doctor, certifying death of person and stating cause if known —**death mask** cast of person's face taken after death —**death penalty** capital punishment —**death rate** ratio of deaths in specified area *etc.* to population of that area *etc.* (*also* **mortality rate**) —**death's-head** *n.* human skull or representation of one —**death tax** tax on property left at death —**death trap** building *etc.* considered unsafe —**death warrant** official authorization for carrying out sentence of death —**deathwatch beetle** beetle that bores into wood —**sign one's (own) death warrant** cause one's own destruction

debacle (diˈbäkəl) *n.* utter collapse, rout, disaster

debar (diˈbär) *vt.* 1. shut out 2. stop 3. prohibit 4. preclude (**-rr-**)

debark (diˈbärk) *v.* disembark

debase (diˈbās) *vt.* 1. lower in value, quality or character 2. adulterate —**deˈbasement** *n.*

debate (diˈbāt) *v.* 1. argue, discuss, *esp.* in a formal assembly 2. consider (something) —*n.* 3. discussion 4. controversy —**deˈbatable** *a.* —**deˈbater** *n.*

debauch (diˈbŏch) *vt.* 1. lead into a life of depraved self-indulgence —*n.* 2. bout of sensual indulgence —**debauˈchee** *n.* dissipated person —**deˈbauchery** *n.*

debenture (diˈbenchər) *n.* bond of company or corporation secured by its general assets

debility (diˈbiliti) *n.* 1. feebleness, *esp.* of health 2. languor —**deˈbilitate** *vt.* weaken, enervate

debit (ˈdebit) *Accounting n.* 1. entry in account of sum owed 2. side of book in which such sums are entered —*vt.* 3. charge, enter as due

debonair (debəˈnāər) *a.* 1. suave 2. genial 3. affable

debouch (diˈbowch) *vi.* move out from narrow place to wider one —**deˈbouchment** *n.*

debrief (dēˈbrēf) *vt.* interrogate (pilot, agent) to obtain results of mission

debris (dəˈbrē, dā-; ˈdābrē) *n.* fragments of unwanted material

debt (det) *n.* 1. what is owed 2. state of owing —ˈ**debtor** *n.* —**debt of honor** debt that is morally but not legally binding

debug (dēˈbug) *vt. inf.* 1. remove concealed microphones from (room *etc.*) 2. remove defects in (device *etc.*) 3. remove insects from (**-gg-**)

debunk (dēˈbungk) *vt.* expose falseness, pretentiousness of, *esp.* by ridicule

debut (ˈdābyōō, dāˈbyōō) *n.* first appearance in public —**debutante** (ˈdebyōōtänt) *n.* girl making official debut into society

Dec. December

deca-, deka- *or before vowel* **dec-, dek-** (*comb. form*) ten, as in *decaliter*

decade (ˈdekād, deˈkād) *n.* 1. period of ten years 2. set of ten

decadent (ˈdekədənt) *a.* 1. declining, deteriorating 2. morally corrupt —ˈ**decadence** *or* ˈ**decadency** *n.*

decaffeinated (dē'kafinātid) *a.* (of coffee or tea) with caffeine removed
decagon ('dekəgon) *n.* figure of 10 angles —**de'cagonal** *a.*
decagram ('dekəgram) *n. see* DEKAGRAM
decahedron (dekə'hēdrən) *n.* solid of 10 faces —**deca'hedral** *a.*
decalcify (dē'kalsifī) *vt.* deprive of lime, as bones or teeth of their calcareous matter (**-fied, -fying**)
decaliter ('dekəlētər) *n. see* DEKALITER
Decalogue ('dekəlog) *n.* the Ten Commandments
decameter ('dekəmētər) *n. see* DEKAMETER
decamp (di'kamp) *vi.* **1.** make off **2.** break camp **3.** abscond
decanal (di'kānəl) *a.* of dean, deanery
decant (di'kant) *vt.* pour off (liquid, as wine) without disturbing sediment —**de'canter** *n.* stoppered bottle for wine or spirits
decapitate (di'kapitāt) *vt.* behead —**decapi'tation** *n.* —**de'capitator** *n.*

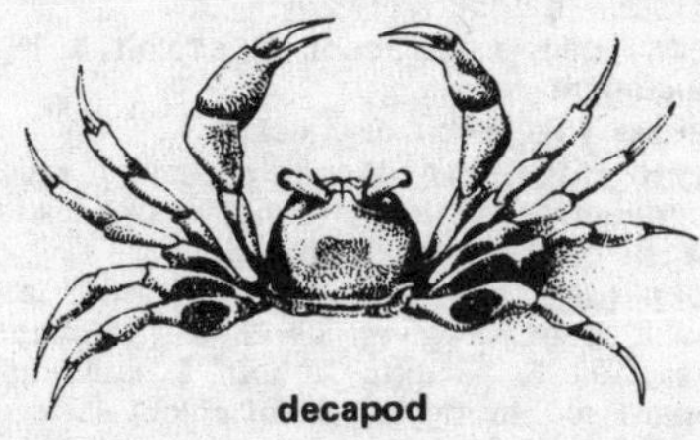

decapod

decapod ('dekəpod) *n.* **1.** crustacean having five pairs of walking limbs, as crab *etc.* **2.** cephalopod mollusk having eight short tentacles and two longer ones, as squid *etc.*
decarbonize (dē'kärbənīz) *vt.* remove (deposit of carbon) from, as from motor cylinder (*also* **decoke**) —**decarboni'zation** *n.*
decasyllable ('dekəsiləbəl) *n.* ten-syllabled line —**decasyl'labic** *a.*
decathlon (di'kathlən, -lon) *n.* athletic contest with ten events
decay (di'kā) *v.* **1.** rot, decompose **2.** (cause to) fall off, decline —*n.* **3.** rotting **4.** a falling away, break-up
decease (di'sēs) *n.* **1.** death —*vi.* **2.** die —**de'ceased** *n./a.*
deceive (di'sēv) *vt.* **1.** mislead **2.** delude **3.** cheat —**de'ceit** *n.* **1.** fraud **2.** duplicity —**de'ceitful** *a.* —**de'ceiver** *n.*
decelerate (dē'selərāt) *vi.* slow down
December (di'sembər) *n.* twelfth and last month of year
decennial (di'seniəl) *a.* of period of ten years —**de'cennially** *adv.*
decent ('dēsənt) *a.* **1.** respectable **2.** fitting, seemly **3.** not obscene **4.** adequate **5.** *inf.* kind —**'decency** *n.* —**'decently** *adv.*
decentralize (dē'sentrəlīz) *vt.* divide (government, organization) among local centers
deception (di'sepshən) *n.* **1.** deceiving **2.** illusion **3.** fraud **4.** trick —**de'ceptive** *a.* **1.** misleading **2.** apt to mislead
deci- (*comb. form*) one tenth, as in *decimeter*
decibel ('desibel) *n.* unit for measuring intensity of a sound
decide (di'sīd) *vt.* **1.** settle, determine, bring to resolution **2.** give judgment on —*vi.* **3.** come to a decision, conclusion —**de'cided** *a.* **1.** unmistakable **2.** settled **3.** resolute —**de'cidedly** *adv.* certainly, undoubtedly —**decision** (di'sizhən) *n.* —**de'cisive** *a.* —**de'cisively** *adv.*
deciduous (di'sijōōəs) *a.* **1.** (of trees) losing leaves annually **2.** (of antlers, teeth *etc.*) being shed at the end of a period of growth
decigram ('desigram) *n.* tenth of gram
deciliter ('desilētər) *n.* tenth of liter
decimal ('desiməl) *a.* **1.** relating to tenths **2.** proceeding by tens —*n.* **3.** decimal fraction —**decimali'zation** *n.* —**'decimalize** *vt.* convert into decimal fractions or system —**decimal number system** the ordinary system in use which denotes real numbers according to place values for multiples of 10 (plus the digits 0 through 9)
decimate ('desimāt) *vt.* kill a tenth or large proportion of —**deci'mation** *n.* —**'decimator** *n.*
decimeter ('desimētər) *n.* tenth of meter
decipher (di'sīfər) *vt.* **1.** make out meaning of **2.** decode —**de'cipherable** *a.*
deck (dek) *n.* **1.** platform or floor, *esp.* one covering whole or part of ship's hull **2.** turntable of record-player **3.** part of tape recorder supporting tapes —*vt.* **4.** array, decorate —**deck chair** folding chair made of canvas suspended in wooden frame —**deck hand 1.** seaman assigned duties on deck of ship **2.** helper aboard yacht
deckle edge ('dekəl) **1.** rough edge of paper oft. left as ornamentation **2.** imitation of this
declaim (di'klām) *vi.* **1.** speak dramatically, rhetorically or passionately **2.** protest loudly —**declamation** (deklə'māshən) *n.* —**declamatory** (di'klamətōri) *a.*
declare (di'klāər) *vt.* **1.** announce formally **2.** state emphatically **3.** show **4.** name (as liable to customs duty) —*vi.* **5.** take sides (for) —**declaration** (deklə'rāshən) *n.* —**declarative** (di'klarətiv) *or* **declaratory** (di'klarətōri) *a.* —**de'clarer** *n. Bridge* person who plays the hand
declassify (dē'klasifī) *vt.* release (document *etc.*) from security list (**-fying, -fied**) —**declassifi'cation** *n.*
decline (di'klīn) *v.* **1.** refuse **2.** list case endings of (nouns) —*vi.* **3.** slope, bend or sink downward **4.** deteriorate gradually **5.** grow smaller, diminish —*n.* **6.** gradual deterioration **7.** movement downward **8.** diminution **9.** downward slope —**declension** (di'klenshən) *n.* **1.** group of nouns **2.** falling off **3.** declining

—**de'clinable** *a.* —**declination** (dekli'nāshən) *n.* **1.** sloping away, deviation **2.** angle

declivity (di'kliviti) *n.* downward slope

declutch (di'kluch) *vi.* disengage clutch of car *etc.*

decoction (di'kokshən) *n.* **1.** extraction of essence by boiling down **2.** such essence —**de'coct** *vt.* boil down

decode (dē'kōd) *vt.* convert from code into intelligible language

decoke (dē'kōk) *vt.* decarbonize

décollage (dākə'läzh, -ko-) *n.* the tearing away of parts of posters *etc.* that have been applied in layers so that sections of the underlayers create the composition; the reverse of collage

décolleté (dākolə'tā) *a.* (of women's garment) having a low-cut neckline —**décolletage** (dākolə'täzh) *n.* low-cut dress or neckline

decommission (dēkə'mishən) *vt.* dismantle (industrial plant or nuclear reactor) to an extent such that it can be safely abandoned

decompose (dēkəm'pōz) *v.* **1.** separate into elements **2.** rot —**decompo'sition** *n.* decay

decompress (dēkəm'pres) *vt.* **1.** free from pressure **2.** return to condition of normal atmospheric pressure —**decom'pression** *n.* —**decompression sickness** *or* **illness** disorder characterized by severe pain *etc.*, caused by sudden change in atmospheric pressure

decongestant (dēkən'jestənt) *a./n.* (drug) relieving (*esp.* nasal) congestion

decontaminate (dēkən'taminät) *vt.* free from contamination, *eg* from poisons, radioactive substances *etc.* —**decontami'nation** *n.*

decontrol (dēkən'trōl) *vt.* release from state control (**-ll-**)

decor *or* **décor** (dā'kör) *n.* **1.** decorative scheme of room *etc.* **2.** stage decoration, scenery

decorate ('dekərāt) *vt.* **1.** beautify by additions **2.** paint or wallpaper (room *etc.*) **3.** invest (with an order, medal *etc.*) —**deco'ration** *n.* —**'decorative** *a.* —**'decorator** *n.* —**Decorated style** 14th-century style of English architecture characterized by geometrical tracery *etc.*

decorum (di'körəm) *n.* seemly behavior, propriety, decency —**'decorous** *a.* —**'decorously** *adv.*

decoy ('dēkoi, di'koi) *n.* **1.** something used to entrap others or to distract their attention **2.** bait, lure —*v.* (di'koi) **3.** lure, be lured as with decoy

decrease (di'krēs) *v.* **1.** diminish, lessen —*n.* ('dēkrēs, di'krēs) **2.** lessening

decree (di'krē) *n.* **1.** order having the force of law **2.** edict —*vt.* **3.** determine judicially **4.** order

decrement ('dekrimənt) *n.* **1.** act or state of decreasing **2.** quantity lost by decrease

decrepit (di'krepit) *a.* **1.** old and feeble **2.** broken-down, worn-out —**de'crepitude** *n.*

decrescendo (dākri'shendō) *a.* diminuendo

decretal (di'krētəl) *n.* **1.** *R.C.Ch.* papal decree; edict on doctrine or church law —*a.* **2.** of decree

decry (di'krī) *vt.* disparage (**de'cried, de'crying**)

dedicate ('dedikāt) *vt.* **1.** commit wholly to special purpose or cause **2.** inscribe or address (book *etc.*) **3.** devote to God's service —**'dedicated** *a.* **1.** devoted to particular purpose or cause **2.** *Comp.* designed to fulfill one function **3.** manufactured for specific purpose —**dedi'cation** *n.* —**'dedicator** *n.* —**'dedicatory** *a.*

deduce (di'dyōōs, -'dōōs) *vt.* draw as conclusion from facts —**de'duct** *vt.* take away, subtract —**de'ductible** *a.* capable of being deducted, esp. against income tax —**de'duction** *n.* **1.** deducting **2.** amount subtracted **3.** conclusion deduced **4.** inference from general to particular —**de'ductive** *a.* —**de'ductively** *adv.*

deed (dēd) *n.* **1.** action **2.** exploit **3.** legal document

deejay ('dē'jā) *inf.* disc jockey

deem (dēm) *vt.* judge, consider, regard —**'deemster** *n.* title of either of two justices in Isle of Man (*also* **'dempster**)

deep (dēp) *a.* **1.** extending far down, in or back **2.** at, of given depth **3.** profound **4.** heartfelt **5.** hard to fathom **6.** cunning **7.** engrossed, immersed **8.** (of color) dark and rich **9.** (of sound) low and full —*n.* **10.** deep place **11.** the sea —*adv.* **12.** far down *etc.* —**'deepen** *v.* —**'deeply** *adv.* —**deep-freeze** *vt.* quick-freeze —**deep-laid** *a.* (of plot or plan) carefully worked out and kept secret —**deep-rooted** *or* **deep-seated** *a.* (of ideas *etc.*) firmly fixed or held; ingrained

deer (dēər) *n.* family of ruminant animals typically with antlers in male (*pl.* **deer, -s**) —**'deerhound** *n.* large rough-coated dog —**'deerskin** *n.* hide of deer —**'deerstalker** *n.* **1.** one who stalks deer **2.** kind of cloth hat with peaks

deface (di'fās) *vt.* **1.** spoil or mar surface of **2.** disfigure —**de'facement** *n.*

de facto (dā 'faktō) *Lat.* existing in fact, whether legally recognized or not

defalcate (di'falkāt) *vi.* *Law* misuse or misappropriate property or funds entrusted to one

defame (di'fām) *vt.* speak ill of, dishonor by slander or rumor —**defamation** (defə'māshən) *n.* —**defamatory** (di'famətöri) *a.*

default (di'fölt) *n.* **1.** failure to act, appear or pay —*vi.* **2.** fail (to pay) —**de'faulter** *n. esp.* soldier guilty of military offense —**in default of** in the absence of

defeat (di'fēt) *vt.* **1.** overcome, vanquish **2.** thwart —*n.* **3.** overthrow **4.** lost battle or encounter **5.** frustration —**de'featism** *n.*

attitude tending to accept defeat —**de'featist** *n./a.*

defecate ('defikāt) *vi.* **1.** empty the bowels —*vt.* **2.** clear of impurities —**defe'cation** *n.*

defect ('dēfekt, di'fekt) *n.* **1.** lack **2.** blemish, failing —*vi.* (di'fekt) **3.** desert one's country, cause *etc., esp.* to join opponents —**de'fection** *n.* abandonment of duty or allegiance —**de'fective** *a.* **1.** incomplete **2.** faulty

defend (di'fend) *vt.* **1.** protect **2.** support by argument, evidence **3.** (try to) maintain (title *etc.*) against challenger —**de'fendant** *n.* person accused in court —**de'fender** *n.* —**de'fense** *n.* —**defensi'bility** *n.* —**de'fensible** *a.* —**de'fensive** *a.* **1.** serving for defense —*n.* **2.** position or attitude of defense

defer[1] (di'fər) *vt.* put off, postpone (**-rr-**) —**de'ferment** *n.*

defer[2] (di'fər) *vi.* submit to opinion or judgment of another (**-rr-**) —**deference** ('defərəns) *n.* respect for another inclining one to accept his views *etc.* —**deferential** (defə'renchəl) *a.* —**deferentially** (defə'renchəli) *adv.*

defiance (di'fīəns) *n. see* DEFY

deficient (di'fishənt) *a.* lacking or falling short in something, insufficient —**de'ficiency** *n.* —**deficit** ('defisit) *n.* amount by which sum of money is too small —**deficiency disease** any condition, such as pellagra, produced by lack of vitamins and minerals

defile[1] (di'fīl) *vt.* **1.** make dirty, pollute, soil **2.** sully **3.** desecrate —**de'filement** *n.*

defile[2] (di'fīl, 'dēfīl) *n.* **1.** narrow pass or valley —*vi.* **2.** march in file

define (di'fīn) *vt.* **1.** state contents or meaning of **2.** show clearly the form or outline of **3.** lay down clearly, fix **4.** mark out —**de'finable** *a.* —**definite** ('definit) *a.* **1.** exact, defined **2.** clear, specific **3.** certain, sure —**definitely** ('definitli) *adv.* —**definition** (defi'nishən) *n.* —**definitive** (di'finitiv) *a.* conclusive, to be looked on as final —**definitively** (di'finitivli) *adv.*

deflate (dē'flāt) *v.* **1.** (cause to) collapse by release of gas **2.** *Econ.* cause deflation of (an economy *etc.*) —*vt.* **3.** take away self-esteem from —**de'flation** *n.* **1.** deflating **2.** *Econ.* reduction of economic and industrial activity —**de'flationary** *a.*

deflect (di'flekt) *v.* (cause to) turn from straight course —**de'flection** *n.*

deflower (dē'flowər) *vt.* deprive of virginity, innocence *etc.* —**defloration** (dēflō'rāshən) *n.*

defoliate (dē'fōliāt) *v.* (cause to) lose leaves, *esp.* by action of chemicals —**de'foliant** *n.* —**defoli'ation** *n.*

deforest (dē'forist) *vt.* clear of trees —**deforest'ation** *n.*

deform (di'fōrm) *vt.* **1.** spoil shape of **2.** make ugly **3.** disfigure —**defor'mation** *n.* —**de'formed** *a.* —**de'formity** *n.*

defraud (di'frōd) *vt.* cheat, swindle

defray (di'frā) *vt.* provide money for (expenses *etc.*)

defrock (dē'frok) *vt.* deprive (priest, minister) of ecclesiastical status

defrost (dē'frost) *v.* **1.** make, become free of frost, ice **2.** thaw

deft (deft) *a.* skillful, adroit —**'deftly** *adv.* —**'deftness** *n.*

defunct (di'fungkt) *a.* **1.** dead **2.** obsolete

defuse (dē'fyōōz) *vt.* **1.** remove fuse of (bomb *etc.*) **2.** remove tension from (situation *etc.*)

defy (di'fī) *vt.* **1.** challenge, resist successfully **2.** disregard (**de'fied, de'fying**) —**de'fiance** *n.* resistance —**de'fiant** *a.* **1.** openly and aggressively hostile **2.** insolent —**de'fiantly** *adv.*

degauss (dē'gows) *vt.* equip (ship) with apparatus which prevents it detonating magnetic mines

degenerate (di'jenərāt) *vi.* **1.** deteriorate to lower mental, moral or physical level —*a.* (di'jenərit) **2.** fallen away in quality —*n.* (di'jenərit) **3.** degenerate person —**de'generacy** *n.* —**degene'ration** *n.* —**de'generative** *a.*

degrade (di'grād) *vt.* **1.** dishonor **2.** debase **3.** reduce to lower rank —*vi.* **4.** decompose chemically —**de'gradable** *a.* capable of chemical, biological decomposition —**degradation** (degrə'dāshən) *n.* —**de'graded** *a.* shamed, humiliated

degree (di'grē) *n.* **1.** step, stage in process, scale, relative rank, order, condition, manner, way **2.** university award **3.** unit of measurement of temperature or angle —**third degree** severe, lengthy examination, *esp.* of accused person by police, to extract information, confession

dehiscent (di'hisənt) *a.* opening, as capsule of plant —**de'hisce** *vi.* burst open —**de'hiscence** *n.*

dehumanize (dē'hyōōmənīz) *vt.* **1.** deprive of human qualities **2.** render mechanical, artificial or routine

dehumidify (dēhyōō'midifī) *vt.* extract moisture from

dehydrate (dē'hīdrāt) *vt.* remove moisture from —**dehy'dration** *n.* excessive loss of body fluid

de-ice (dē'īs) *vt.* dislodge ice from (*eg* windshield) or prevent its forming

deify ('dēifī, 'dā-) *vt.* make god of, treat, worship as god (**'deified, 'deifying**) —**deifi'cation** *n.* —**'deiform** *a.* godlike in form

deign (dān) *vi.* **1.** condescend, stoop **2.** think fit

deism ('dēizəm, 'dā-) *n.* belief in god but not in revelation —**'deist** *n.* —**de'istic** *a.* —**'deity** *n.* **1.** divine status or attributes **2.** a god

déjà vu ('dāzhä 'vōō, 'vyōō) *Fr.* experience of perceiving new situation as if it had occurred before

deject (di'jekt) *vt.* dishearten, cast down, depress —**de'jected** *a.* —**de'jection** *n.*

de jure (dā 'yōōərā) *Lat.* in law, by right

deka- *or before vowel* **dek-** *see* DECA-

dekagram *or* **decagram** ('dekəgram) *n.* measure of weight equal to 10 grams

dekaliter *or* **decaliter** ('dekəlētər) *n.* 10 liters

dekameter *or* **decameter** ('dekəmētər) *n.* 10 meters

Delaware[1] ('deləwāər) *n.* South Atlantic state of the U.S.: ratified the Constitution in 1787. Abbrev.: **Del., DE** (with ZIP code)

Delaware[2] ('deləwāər) *n.* **1.** member of Amerindian people orig. of Delaware Valley (*pl.* **-ware, -s**) **2.** Algonquian language of this people

Delaware[3] ('deləwāər) *n.* **1.** dry white table wine **2.** grape used to make this wine

delay (di'lā) *vt.* **1.** postpone, hold back —*vi.* **2.** be tardy, linger (**de'layed, de'laying**) —*n.* **3.** act or instance of delaying **4.** interval of time between events

delectable (di'lektəbəl) *a.* delightful —**delec'tation** *n.* pleasure

delegate ('deligit, -gāt) *n.* **1.** person chosen to represent another —*vt.* ('deligāt) **2.** send as deputy **3.** commit (authority, business *etc.*) to a deputy —'**delegacy** *n.* —**dele'gation** *n.*

delete (di'lēt) *vt.* remove, cancel, erase —**de'letion** *n.*

deleterious (deli'tēəriəs) *a.* harmful, injurious

Delft (delft) *n.* **1.** town in Netherlands **2.** tin-glazed earthenware orig. from Delft, usu. with blue decoration on white ground (*also* '**delftware**)

deliberate (di'libərit) *a.* **1.** intentional **2.** well-considered **3.** without haste, slow —*vt.* (di'libərāt) **4.** consider, debate —**de'liberately** *adv.* —**delibe'ration** *n.* —**de'liberative** *a.*

delicate ('delikit) *a.* **1.** exquisite **2.** not robust, fragile **3.** sensitive **4.** requiring tact **5.** deft —'**delicacy** *n.* —'**delicately** *adv.*

delicatessen (delikə'tesən) *n.* shop selling *esp.* imported or unusual foods

delicious (di'lishəs) *a.* delightful, pleasing to senses, *esp.* taste —**de'liciously** *adv.*

delight (di'līt) *vt.* **1.** please greatly —*vi.* **2.** take great pleasure (in) —*n.* **3.** great pleasure —**de'lightful** *a.* charming

delimitation (dēlimi'tāshən) *n.* assigning of boundaries —**de'limit** *vt.*

delineate (di'liniāt) *vt.* portray by drawing or description —**deline'ation** *n.* —**de'lineator** *n.*

delinquent (di'lingkwənt) *n.* someone, *esp.* young person, guilty of delinquency —**de'linquency** *n.* (minor) offense or misdeed

deliquesce (deli'kwes) *vi.* become liquid —**deli'quescence** *n.* —**deli'quescent** *a.*

delirium (di'liriəm) *n.* **1.** disorder of the mind, *esp.* in feverish illness **2.** violent excitement (*pl.* **-s, -liria** (-'liriə)) —**de'lirious** *a.* **1.** raving **2.** light-headed, wildly excited —**delirium tremens** ('tremenz, 'trē-) disordered mental state produced by advanced alcoholism (*also* **D.T.s**)

deliver (di'livər) *vt.* **1.** carry (goods *etc.*) to destination **2.** hand over **3.** release **4.** give birth (to) or assist in birth (of) **5.** utter or present (speech *etc.*) —**de'liverance** *n.* rescue —**de'liverer** *n.* —**de'livery** *n.*

dell (del) *n.* wooded hollow

Delphic ('delfik) *a.* pert. to Delphi or to the oracle of Apollo

delphinium (del'finiəm) *n.* garden plant with tall spikes of usu. blue flowers (*pl.* **-s, -ia** (-iə))

delta ('deltə) *n.* **1.** alluvial tract where river at mouth breaks into several streams **2.** fourth letter in Gr. alphabet (Δ or δ) **3.** shape of this letter —**delta wing** triangular swept-back aircraft wing —'**deltoid** *or* **deltoid muscle** triangular muscle covering front, side and rear portions of the shoulder joint

Delta ('deltə) *n.* word used in communications for the letter *d*

delude (di'lōōd) *vt.* **1.** deceive **2.** mislead —**de'lusion** *n.* —**de'lusive** *a.*

deluge ('delyōōj) *n.* **1.** flood, great flow **2.** rush **3.** downpour, cloudburst —*vt.* **4.** flood **5.** overwhelm

de luxe (də 'lŏŏks, 'luks) **1.** rich, sumptuous **2.** superior in quality

delve (delv) *v.* **1.** (*with* into) search intensively **2.** dig

demagnetize (dē'magnətīz) *vt.* deprive of magnetic polarity

demagogue *or* **demagog** ('deməgog) *n.* mob leader or agitator —**demagogic** (demə'gogik) *a.* —**demagogy** ('deməgogi) *n.*

demand (di'mand) *vt.* **1.** ask as giving an order **2.** ask as by right **3.** call for as due, right or necessary —*n.* **4.** urgent request, claim, requirement **5.** call (for specific commodity) —**de'manding** *a.* requiring great skill, patience *etc.*

demarcate (di'märkāt) *vt.* mark boundaries or limits of —**demar'cation** *or* **demar'kation** *n.*

demean (di'mēn) *vt.* degrade, lower, humiliate

demeanor (di'mēnər) *n.* **1.** conduct, behavior **2.** bearing

demented (di'mentid) *a.* **1.** mad, crazy **2.** beside oneself —**dementia** (di'menchə) *n.* deterioration of mental faculties

demerge (di'mərj) *v.* **1.** split (business concern) into two or more independent companies —*vi.* **2.** (of companies) be so split **3.** undo previous merger —**de'merger** *n.*

demerit (di'merit) *n.* **1.** bad point **2.** undesirable quality

Demerol ('demərōl) *n.* trade name for meperidine

demesne (di'mān, -'mēn) *n.* **1.** estate, territory **2.** sphere of action —**hold in demesne** have unrestricted possession of

demi- (*comb. form*) half, as in *demigod.* Such words are not given here where the meaning may be inferred from the simple word

demijohn ('demijon) *n.* narrow-necked bottle holding from one to 10 gallons

demilitarize (dē'militərīz) *vt.* prohibit military presence or function in (an area) —**demilitari'zation** *n.*

demimonde ('demimond) *n.* class of women of doubtful reputation

demise (di'mīz) *n.* **1.** death **2.** conveyance by will or lease **3.** transfer of sovereignty on death or abdication —*vt.* **4.** convey to another by will **5.** lease

demist (dē'mist) *v.* free or become free of condensation —**de'mister** *n.*

demiurge ('demiərj) *n.* name given in some philosophies (*esp.* Platonic) to the creator of the world and man

demo ('demō) *inf.* demonstration

demobilize (dē'mōbilīz) *vt.* **1.** disband (troops) **2.** discharge (soldier) —**demobili'zation** *n.*

democracy (di'mokrəsi) *n.* **1.** government by the people or their elected representatives **2.** state so governed —**'democrat** *n.* advocate of democracy —**demo'cratic** *a.* **1.** connected with democracy **2.** favoring popular rights —**demo'cratically** *adv.* —**democrati'zation** *n.* —**de'mocratize** *vt.*

demodulation (dēmojə'lāshən) *n. Electron.* process by which output wave or signal is obtained having characteristics of original modulating wave or signal

demography (di'mogrəfi) *n.* study of population statistics, as births, deaths, diseases —**de'mographer** *n.* —**demo'graphic** *a.*

demolish (di'molish) *vt.* **1.** knock down (buildings *etc.*) **2.** destroy utterly **3.** overthrow —**demo'lition** *n.*

demon ('dēmən) *n.* **1.** devil, evil spirit **2.** very cruel or malignant person **3.** person very good at or devoted to a given activity —**demoniac** (di'mōniak) *n.* one possessed with a devil —**demo'niacal** *a.* —**de'monic** *a.* of the nature of a devil —**demo'nology** *n.* study of demons

demonetize (dē'monitīz, -'mun-) *vt.* **1.** deprive (metal) of its capacity as monetary standard **2.** withdraw from use as currency —**demoneti'zation** *n.*

demonstrate ('demənstrāt) *vt.* **1.** show by reasoning, prove **2.** describe, explain by specimens or experiments —*vi.* **3.** make exhibition of support, protest *etc.* by public parade, rally **4.** make show of armed force —**de'monstrable** *a.* —**de'monstrably** *adv.* —**demon'stration** *n.* **1.** making clear, proving by evidence **2.** exhibition and description **3.** organized expression of public opinion **4.** display of armed force —**de'monstrative** *a.* **1.** expressing feelings, emotions easily and unreservedly **2.** pointing out **3.** conclusive —**'demonstrator** *n.* **1.** one who demonstrates equipment, products *etc.* **2.** one who takes part in a public demonstration

demoralize (di'morəlīz) *vt.* **1.** deprive of courage and discipline **2.** undermine morally —**demorali'zation** *n.*

demote (di'mōt) *vt.* reduce in status or rank —**de'motion** *n.*

demotic (di'motik) *a.* **1.** of common people; popular **2.** of simplified form of hieroglyphics used in ancient Egypt —*n.* **3.** demotic script of ancient Egypt

demur (di'mər) *vi.* **1.** make difficulties, object (**-rr-**) —*n.* **2.** raising of objection **3.** objection raised —**de'murrer** *n. Law* exception taken to opponent's point

demure (di'myŏŏər) *a.* reserved, quiet —**de'murely** *adv.*

demurrage (di'murij) *n.* charge for keeping ship *etc.* beyond time agreed for unloading

demystify (dē'mistifī) *vt.* remove mystery from; make clear —**demystifi'cation** *n.*

den (den) *n.* **1.** cave or hole of wild beast **2.** lair **3.** small room, *esp.* study **4.** site, haunt

denarius (di'nariəs, -'ner-) *n.* **1.** ancient Roman silver coin, oft. called penny in translation **2.** gold coin worth 25 silver denarii (*pl.* **-narii** (-'narīī, -'ner-))

denary ('dēnəri) *a.* **1.** calculated by tens; decimal **2.** containing ten parts; tenfold

denationalize (dē'nashənəlīz) *vt.* return (an industry) from public to private ownership —**denationali'zation** *n.*

denature (dē'nāchər) *or* **denaturize** (dē'nāchərīz) *vt.* deprive of essential qualities, adulterate —**denatured alcohol** alcohol made undrinkable

denazify (dē'nätsifī) *vt.* obliterate Nazi influence from (**-ified, -ifying**)

dendrology (den'droləji) *n.* natural history of trees

dengue fever ('denggi, -gā) virus disease of subtropical and tropical regions transmitted by the mosquito (*also* **breakbone fever**)

denial (di'nīəl) *n. see* DENY

denier ('denyər) *n.* gauge of yarn used for stockings and panty hose

denigrate ('denigrāt) *vt.* belittle or disparage character of

denim ('denim) *n.* strong cotton drill for trousers, overalls *etc.*

denizen ('denizən) *n.* inhabitant

Denmark ('denmärk) *n.* country in Europe occupying a peninsula between the North Sea to the west and the Baltic Sea to the east and bounded south by the Federal Republic of Germany —**Dane** *n.* native of Denmark —**'Danish** *a.* **1.** of Denmark —*n.* **2.** language of Denmark which is a Scandinavian language

denominate (di'nomināt) *vt.* give name to —**denomi'nation** *n.* **1.** distinctly named church or sect **2.** name, *esp.* of class or group —**denomi'national** *a.* —**de'nominator** *n.* divisor in common fraction

denote (di'nōt) *vt.* **1.** stand for, be the name of **2.** mark, indicate, show —**deno'tation** *n.*

denouement (dānōō'män) *or* **dénouement** (*Fr.* dānōō'mã) *n.* **1.** unraveling of dramatic plot **2.** final solution of mystery

denounce (di'nowns) *vt.* **1.** speak violently against **2.** accuse **3.** terminate (treaty) —**denunci'ation** *n.* denouncing —**denunciatory** (di'nunsiətōri) *a.*

dense (dens) *a.* **1.** thick, compact **2.** stupid —'**densely** *adv.* —'**density** *n.* mass per unit of volume

dent (dent) *n.* **1.** hollow or mark left by blow or pressure —*vt.* **2.** make dent in **3.** mark with dent

dental ('dentəl) *a.* **1.** of, pert. to teeth or dentistry **2.** pronounced by applying tongue to teeth —'**dentate** *a.* toothed —**dentifrice** ('dentifris) *n.* powder, paste or wash for cleaning teeth —'**dentist** *n.* surgeon who attends to teeth —'**dentistry** *n.* science concerned with diseases of teeth and mouth, *esp.* gums —**den'tition** *n.* **1.** teething **2.** arrangement of teeth —'**denture** *n.* (*usu. pl.*) set of false teeth —**dental floss** waxed thread for cleaning between teeth

dentin ('dentin) *or* **dentine** ('dentēn) *n.* the hard bonelike part of a tooth

denude (di'nyōōd, -'nōōd) *vt.* **1.** strip, make bare **2.** expose (rock) by erosion of plants, soil *etc.* —**denudation** (dēnyōō'dāshən, -nōō-) *n.*

denumerable (di'nyōōmərəbəl, -'nōō-) *a. Math.* capable of being counted by correspondence with positive integers; countable

denunciation (dinunsi'āshən) *n. see* DENOUNCE

deny (di'nī) *vt.* **1.** declare untrue **2.** contradict **3.** reject, disown **4.** refuse to give **5.** refuse **6.** (*refl.*) abstain from (**de'nied, de'nying**) —**de'niable** *a.* —**de'nial** *n.*

deodar ('dēədär) *n.* **1.** Himalayan cedar with drooping branches **2.** fragrant wood of this tree

deodorize (dē'ōdərīz) *vt.* rid of smell or mask smell of —**de'odorant** *n.* —**deodori'zation** *n.* —**de'odorizer** *n.*

deontology (dēon'toləji) *n.* science of ethics and moral obligations —**deon'tologist** *n.*

Deo volente ('dāō və'lenti) *Lat.* God willing

deoxidize (dē'oksidīz) *vt.* deprive of oxygen —**deoxidi'zation** *n.*

dep. 1. depart(s) **2.** departure **3.** deposed **4.** deposit **5.** deputy

depart (di'pärt) *vi.* **1.** go away **2.** start out, set forth **3.** deviate, vary **4.** die —**de'parture** *n.*

department (di'pärtmənt) *n.* **1.** division **2.** branch **3.** province —**depart'mental** *a.* —**depart'mentally** *adv.* —**department store** store selling all kinds of goods

depend (di'pend) *vi.* **1.** (*usu. with* on) rely entirely **2.** be contingent, await settlement or decision —**de'pendable** *a.* reliable —**de'pendant** *n.* one for whose maintenance another is responsible —**de'pendence** *n.* —**de'pendency** *n.* subject territory —**de'pendent** *a.* depending

depict (di'pikt) *vt.* **1.** give picture of **2.** describe in words —**de'piction** *n.* —**de'pictor** *n.*

depilatory (di'pilətōri) *n.* **1.** substance that removes hair —*a.* **2.** serving to remove hair

deplete (di'plēt) *vt.* **1.** empty **2.** reduce **3.** exhaust —**de'pletion** *n.*

deplore (di'plōr) *vt.* **1.** lament, regret **2.** deprecate, complain of —**de'plorable** *a.* **1.** lamentable **2.** disgraceful

deploy (di'ploi) *v.* **1.** (of troops, ships) (cause to) adopt battle formation —*vt.* **2.** arrange —**de'ployment** *n.*

depolarize (dē'pōlərīz) *vt.* deprive of polarity —**depolari'zation** *n.*

deponent (di'pōnənt) *a.* **1.** (of verb) having passive form but active meaning —*n.* **2.** deponent verb **3.** one who makes statement on oath **4.** deposition

depopulate (dē'popyōōlāt) *v.* (cause to) be reduced in population —**depopu'lation** *n.*

deport (di'pōrt) *vt.* expel from a country, banish —**depor'tation** *n.*

deportment (di'pōrtmənt) *n.* behavior, conduct, bearing —**de'port** *vt.* behave, carry (oneself)

depose (di'pōz) *vt.* **1.** remove from office, *esp.* of sovereign —*vi.* **2.** make statement on oath, give evidence —**de'posable** *a.* —**de'posal** *n.* **1.** removal from office **2.** statement made on oath

deposit (di'pozit) *vt.* **1.** set down, *esp.* carefully **2.** give into safekeeping, *esp.* in bank. **3.** let fall (as sediment) —*n.* **4.** thing deposited **5.** money given in part payment or as security **6.** sediment —**de'positary** *n.* person with whom thing is deposited —**deposition** (depə'zishən) *n.* **1.** statement written and attested **2.** act of deposing or depositing —**de'positor** *n.* —**de'pository** *n.* place for safekeeping

depot ('depō, 'dēpō) *n.* **1.** storehouse **2.** building for storage and servicing of buses, railway engines *etc.* **3.** railroad station

deprave (di'prāv) *vt.* make bad, corrupt, pervert —**depravity** (di'praviti) *n.* wickedness, viciousness

deprecate ('deprikāt) *vt.* **1.** express disapproval of **2.** advise against —**depre'cation** *n.* —'**deprecatory** *a.*

depreciate (di'prēshiāt) *vt.* **1.** lower price, value or purchasing power of **2.** belittle —*vi.* **3.** fall in value —**depreci'ation** *n.* —**de'preciator** *n.* —**de'preciatory** *a.*

depredation (depri'dāshən) *n.* plundering, pillage —'**depredate** *vt.* plunder, despoil —'**depredator** *n.*

depress (di'pres) *vt.* **1.** affect with low spirits

2. lower in level or activity —**de'pressant** *n.* —**de'pressed** *a.* 1. low in spirits; downcast 2. lower than surrounding surface 3. pressed down; flattened 4. characterized by economic hardship 5. lowered in force *etc.* 6. *Bot., zool.* flattened —**de'pression** *n.* 1. hollow 2. low spirits, dejection, despondency 3. low state of trade, slump —**de'pressive** *a.*

deprive (di'prīv) *vt.* strip, dispossess —**deprivation** (depri'vāshən) *n.* —**de'prived** *a.* lacking adequate food, care, amenities *etc.*

dept. department

depth (depth) *n.* 1. (degree of) deepness 2. deep place, abyss 3. intensity (of color, feeling) 4. profundity (of mind) —**depth charge** bomb for use against submarines

depute (di'pyōōt) *vt.* 1. allot 2. appoint as agent or substitute —**depu'tation** *n.* persons sent to speak for others —**'deputize** *vi.* 1. act for another —*vt.* 2. depute —**'deputy** *n.* 1. assistant 2. substitute, delegate

derail (di'rāl) *v.* (cause to) go off the rails, as train *etc.* —**de'railment** *n.*

derailleur (di'rālər) *a./n.* (of) gearshift mechanism for bicycles

derange (di'rānj) *vt.* 1. put out of place, out of order 2. upset 3. make insane —**de'rangement** *n.*

derby ('dərbi) *n.* 1. annual horse race at Churchill Downs, Kentucky and at Epsom, England 2. contest of any kind open to all 3. man's stiff felt hat with dome-shaped crown

deregulate (dē'regyəlāt) *v.* 1. cancel regulations (concerning an activity or process) —*vt.* 2. exempt (an activity) from regulations —**deregu'lation** *n.*

derelict ('derilikt) *a.* 1. abandoned, forsaken 2. falling into ruins, dilapidated —*n.* 3. social outcast, vagrant 4. abandoned property, ship *etc.* —**dere'liction** *n.* 1. neglect (of duty) 2. abandoning

derestrict (dēri'strikt) *vt.* render or leave free from restriction, *esp.* road from speed limits

deride (di'rīd) *vt.* speak of or treat with contempt, ridicule —**derision** (di'rizhən) *n.* ridicule —**de'risive** *a.* —**de'risory** *a.* mocking, ridiculing

de rigueur (də rē'gœr) *Fr.* required by etiquette or fashion

derive (di'rīv) *vt.* 1. deduce, get (from) 2. show origin of —*vi.* 3. issue, be descended (from) —**derivation** (deri'vāshən) *n.* —**derivative** (di'rivətiv) *a./n.*

dermatitis (dərmə'tītis) *n.* inflammation of skin

dermato-, derma- *or before vowel* **dermat-, derm-** (*comb. form*) skin, as in *dermatitis*

dermatology (dərmə'toləji) *n.* science of skin —**derma'tologist** *n.* physician specializing in skin diseases

dermatomyositis (dərmətōmīō'sītis) *n.* disease of unknown origin marked by inflammation and degeneration of muscles of the limbs and trunk

dermis ('dərmis) *n.* the fine skin, below the epidermis, containing blood vessels

derogate ('derəgāt) *vi.* 1. (*with* from) cause to seem inferior; detract 2. (*with* from) deviate in standard or quality —*vt.* 3. cause to seem inferior *etc.;* disparage —**dero'gation** *n.*

derogatory (di'rogətōri) *a.* disparaging, belittling, intentionally offensive

derrick ('derik) *n.* 1. hoisting machine 2. framework over oil well *etc.*

derring-do (dering'dōō) *n.* (act of) spirited bravery, boldness

derringer ('derinjər) *n.* small pistol with large bore

dervish ('dərvish) *n.* member of Muslim ascetic order, noted for frenzied, whirling dance

desalination (dēsali'nāshən) *or* **desalinization** *n.* process of removing salt, *esp.* from sea water

descant ('deskant) *n.* 1. *Mus.* decorative variation sung as accompaniment to basic melody —*vi.* (*with* on *or* upon) 2. talk in detail (about) 3. dwell (on) at length

descend (di'send) *vi.* 1. come or go down 2. slope down 3. stoop, condescend 4. spring (from ancestor *etc.*) 5. pass to heir, be transmitted 6. swoop on, attack —*vt.* 7. go or come down —**des'cendant** *n.* person descended from an ancestor —**des'cendent** *a.* 1. descending —*n.* 2. descendant —**des'cent** *n.*

describe (di'skrīb) *vt.* 1. give detailed account of 2. pronounce, label 3. trace out (geometrical figure *etc.*) —**description** (di'skripshən) *n.* 1. detailed account 2. marking out 3. kind, sort, species —**descriptive** (di'skriptiv) *a.*

descry (di'skrī) *vt.* make out, catch sight of, *esp.* at a distance, espy (**de'scried, de'scrying**)

desecrate ('desikrāt) *vt.* 1. violate sanctity of 2. profane 3. convert to evil use —**dese'cration** *n.*

desert[1] ('dezərt) *n.* 1. uninhabited and barren region —*a.* 2. barren, uninhabited, desolate

desert[2] (di'zərt) *vt.* 1. abandon, forsake, leave —*vi.* 2. (*esp.* of soldiers *etc.*) run away from service —**de'serter** *n.* —**de'sertion** *n.*

desert[3] (di'zərt) *n.* 1. (*usu. pl.*) what is due as reward or punishment 2. merit, virtue

deserve (di'zərv) *vt.* 1. show oneself worthy of 2. have by conduct a claim to —**de'served** *a.* rightfully earned; justified; warranted —**deservedly** (di'zərvidli) *adv.* —**deservedness** (di'zərvidnis) *n.* —**de'serving** *a.* worthy (of reward *etc.*)

deshabille (desə'bēl) *n. see* DISHABILLE

desiccate ('desikāt) *vt.* 1. dry 2. dry up —**'desiccant** *n.* drying agent —**desic'cation** *n.*

desideratum (disidə'rätəm, -zid-) *n.* something lacked and wanted (*pl.* **-ta** (-tə))

design (di'zīn) *vt.* **1.** make working drawings for **2.** sketch **3.** plan out **4.** intend, select for —*n.* **5.** outline sketch **6.** working plan **7.** art of making decorative patterns *etc.* **8.** project, purpose, mental plan —**designedly** (di'zīnidli) *adv.* on purpose —**de'signer** *n. esp.* one who draws designs for manufacturers —**de'signing** *a.* crafty, scheming

designate ('dezignāt) *vt.* **1.** name **2.** pick out **3.** appoint to office —*a.* ('dezignāt, -nit) **4.** appointed but not yet installed —**desig'nation** *n.* name, appellation

desire (di'zīər) *vt.* **1.** wish, long for **2.** ask for, entreat —*n.* **3.** longing, craving **4.** expressed wish, request **5.** sexual appetite **6.** something wished for or requested —**desira'bility** *n.* —**de'sirable** *a.* worth desiring —**de'sirous** *a.* filled with desire

desist (di'zist) *vi.* cease, stop

desk (desk) *n.* **1.** table or other piece of furniture designed for reading or writing at **2.** counter **3.** section of organization covering specific subject

desolate ('desəlit, 'dez-) *a.* **1.** uninhabited **2.** neglected, barren, ruinous **3.** solitary **4.** dreary, dismal, forlorn —*vt.* ('desəlāt, 'dez-) **5.** depopulate, lay waste **6.** overwhelm with grief —**deso'lation** *n.*

despair (di'spāər) *vi.* **1.** (*oft. with* of) lose hope —*n.* **2.** loss of all hope **3.** cause of this **4.** despondency

despatch (di'spach) *see* DISPATCH

desperate ('despərit, -prit) *a.* **1.** reckless from despair **2.** difficult; dangerous **3.** frantic **4.** hopelessly bad **5.** leaving no room for hope —**desperado** (despə'rädō) *n.* reckless, lawless person (*pl.* **-es, -s**) —**'desperately** *adv.* —**despe'ration** *n.*

despise (di'spīz) *vt.* look down on as contemptible, inferior —**despicable** (di'spikəbəl, 'despik-) *a.* base, contemptible, vile —**despicably** (di'spikəbli, 'despik-) *adv.*

despite (di'spīt) *prep.* in spite of

despoil (di'spoil) *vt.* plunder, rob, strip —**despoliation** (dispōli'āshən) *n.*

despondent (di'spondənt) *a.* dejected, depressed —**de'spond** *vi.* —**de'spondency** *n.* —**de'spondently** *adv.*

despot ('despət, -pot) *n.* tyrant, oppressor —**des'potic** *a.* —**des'potically** *adv.* —**'despotism** *n.* autocratic government, tyranny

despumate (di'spyōōmāt, 'despyōōmāt) *vi.* **1.** throw off impurities **2.** form scum

desquamate ('deskwəmāt) *vi.* (of skin) come off in scales —**desqua'mation** *n.*

dessert (di'zərt) *n.* sweet course, or fruit, served at end of meal

destination (desti'nāshən) *n.* **1.** place a person or thing is bound for **2.** goal **3.** purpose

destine ('destin) *vt.* **1.** ordain or fix beforehand **2.** set apart, devote

destiny ('destini) *n.* **1.** course of events; person's fate **2.** the power which foreordains

destitute ('destityōōt, -tōōt) *a.* **1.** in absolute want **2.** in great need, devoid (of) **3.** penniless —**desti'tution** *n.*

destroy (di'stroi) *vt.* **1.** ruin **2.** pull to pieces **3.** undo **4.** put an end to **5.** demolish **6.** annihilate —**de'stroyer** *n.* **1.** one who destroys **2.** small, swift, heavily armed warship —**de'struct** *vt.* destroy (one's own missile *etc.*) for safety —**de'structible** *a.* —**de'struction** *n.* **1.** ruin, overthrow **2.** death —**de'structive** *a.* **1.** destroying **2.** negative, not constructive —**de'structively** *adv.* —**de'structor** *n.* that which destroys, *esp.* incinerator

desuetude ('deswityōōd, di'sōōityōōd, -tōōd) *n.* disuse, discontinuance

desultory ('desəltōri, 'dez-) *a.* **1.** passing, changing fitfully from one thing to another **2.** aimless **3.** unmethodical

detach (di'tach) *vt.* unfasten, disconnect, separate —**de'tachable** *a.* —**de'tached** *a.* **1.** standing apart, isolated **2.** impersonal, disinterested —**de'tachment** *n.* **1.** aloofness **2.** detaching **3.** a body of troops detached for special duty

detail (di'tāl, 'dētāl) *n.* **1.** particular **2.** small or unimportant part **3.** treatment of anything item by item **4.** party or man assigned for duty in army —*vt.* **5.** relate in full **6.** appoint for duty

detain (di'tān) *vt.* **1.** keep under restraint **2.** hinder **3.** keep waiting —**de'tention** *n.* **1.** confinement **2.** arrest **3.** detaining

detect (di'tekt) *vt.* find out or discover existence, presence, nature or identity of —**de'tection** *n.* —**de'tective** *n.* **1.** policeman or private agent employed in detecting crime —*a.* **2.** employed in detection —**de'tector** *n. esp.* mechanical sensing device or device for detecting radio signals

détente (dā'tänt; *Fr.* dā'tāt) *n.* lessening of tension in political or international affairs

detention (di'tenchən) *n. see* DETAIN

deter (di'tər) *vt.* **1.** discourage, frighten **2.** hinder, prevent (**-rr-**) —**de'terrent** *a./n.*

detergent (di'tərjənt) *n.* **1.** cleansing, purifying substance —*a.* **2.** having cleansing power —**de'terge** *vt.*

deteriorate (di'tēəriərāt) *v.* become or make worse —**deterio'ration** *n.*

determine (di'tərmin) *vt.* **1.** make up one's mind on, decide **2.** fix as known **3.** bring to a decision **4.** be deciding factor in **5.** *Law* end —*vi.* **6.** come to an end **7.** come to decision —**de'terminable** *a.* —**de'terminant** *a./n.* —**de'terminate** *a.* fixed in scope or nature —**determi'nation** *n.* **1.** determining **2.** firm or resolute conduct or purpose **3.** resolve —**de'termined** *a.* resolute —**de'terminism** *n.* theory that human action is settled by forces independent of will —**de'terminist** *n./a.*

detest (di'test) *vt.* hate, loathe —**de'testable** *a.* —**de'testably** *adv.* —**detes'tation** *n.*

dethrone (di'thrōn) *vt.* remove from throne, depose —**de'thronement** *n.*

detonate ('detənāt) *vt.* **1.** cause (bomb, mine *etc.*) to explode —*vi.* **2.** (of bomb, mine *etc.*) explode —**deto'nation** *n.* —'**detonator** *n.* mechanical, electrical device, or small amount of explosive, used to set off main explosive charge

detour ('dētoōər) *n.* **1.** course which leaves main route to rejoin it later **2.** roundabout way —*vi.* **3.** make detour

detoxify (dē'toksifī) *vt.* remove poison from (**-fying, -fied**) —**detoxifi'cation** *n.*

detract (di'trakt) *v.* take away (a part) from, diminish —**de'traction** *n.* —**de'tractive** *a.* —**de'tractor** *n.*

detriment ('detrimənt) *n.* harm done, loss, damage —**detri'mental** *a.* damaging, injurious —**detri'mentally** *adv.*

detritus (di'trītəs) *n.* worn-down matter, such as gravel or rock debris —**de'trital** *a.* —**detrition** (di'trishən) *n.* wearing away from solid bodies by friction

de trop (də 'trō) *Fr.* not wanted, superfluous

detrude (di'trōōd) *vt.* thrust down —**de'trusion** *n.*

detumescence (detyōō'mesəns, -tōō-) *n.* subsidence of swelling

deuce (dyōōs, dōōs) *n.* **1.** two **2.** card with two spots **3.** *Tennis* forty all **4.** in exclamatory phrases, the devil —**deuced** ('dyōōsid, 'dōōsid) *a. inf.* excessive

Deut. Deuteronomy

deuterium (dyōō'tēəriəm, dōō-) *n.* form of hydrogen twice as heavy as normal gas —'**deuteron** *n.* nucleus of this gas

Deuteronomy (dyōōtə'ronəmi, dōō-) *n. Bible* 5th book of the O.T., last of the five books written by Moses, reinterpreting the law for the new generation

deutsch mark (doich) monetary unit of West Germany

deutzia ('dyōōtsiə, 'dōōtsiə) *n.* shrub with white or pink flower clusters

devalue (dē'valyōō) *or* **devaluate** (dē'valyōōāt) *v.* **1.** (of currency) reduce or be reduced in value —*vt.* **2.** reduce the value or worth of —**devalu'ation** *n.*

devastate ('devəstāt) *vt.* **1.** lay waste **2.** ravage **3.** *inf.* overwhelm —**devas'tation** *n.*

develop (di'veləp) *vt.* **1.** bring to maturity **2.** elaborate **3.** bring forth, bring out **4.** evolve **5.** treat (photographic plate or film) to bring out image **6.** improve value or change use of (land) by building *etc.* —*vi.* **7.** grow to maturer state (**de'veloped, de'veloping**) —**de'veloper** *n.* **1.** one who develops land **2.** chemical for developing film —**de'velopment** *n.* —**developing country** poor country seeking to develop its resources by industrialization

deviate ('dēviāt) *vi.* leave the way, turn aside, diverge —'**deviant** *n./a.* (person) deviating from normal, *esp.* in sexual practices —**devi'ation** *n.* —'**deviator** *n.* —'**devious** *a.* **1.** deceitful, underhand **2.** roundabout, rambling **3.** erring —**deviated septum** abnormal displacement of the bone and cartilage partition dividing the nasal cavity into two halves

device (di'vīs) *n.* **1.** contrivance, invention **2.** apparatus **3.** stratagem **4.** scheme, plot **5.** heraldic or emblematic figure or design

devil ('devəl) *n.* **1.** personified spirit of evil **2.** superhuman evil being **3.** person of great wickedness, cruelty *etc.* **4.** *inf.* fellow **5.** *inf.* something difficult or annoying **6.** energy, dash, unconquerable spirit **7.** *inf.* rogue, rascal —*vi.* **8.** do work that passes for employer's, as for lawyer or author —*vt.* **9.** season with hot condiments —'**devilish** *a.* **1.** like, of the devil **2.** evil —*adv.* **3.** *inf.* very, extremely —'**devilment** *n.* **1.** wickedness **2.** wild and reckless mischief, revelry, high spirits —'**devilry** *n.* —**devil-may-care** *a.* happy-go-lucky —**devil's advocate** one who advocates opposing, unpopular view, *usu.* for sake of argument —**devil to pay** trouble to be faced

devious ('dēviəs) *a. see* DEVIATE

devise (di'vīz) *vt.* **1.** plan, contrive **2.** invent **3.** plot **4.** leave by will —**devi'see** *n.* —**de'visor** *n.*

devitrification (dēvitrifi'kāshən) *n.* loss of glassy or vitreous condition —**de'vitrify** *vt.* deprive of character or appearance of glass (**-fied, -fying**)

devoid (di'void) *a.* (*usu. with* of) empty, lacking, free (from)

devolve (di'volv) *vi.* **1.** pass or fall (to, upon) —*vt.* **2.** throw (duty *etc.*) on to another —**devo'lution** *n.* devolving, *esp.* transfer of authority from central to regional government

Devonian (də'vōniən) *a.* **1.** of fourth period of Paleozoic era, between Silurian and Carboniferous periods **2.** of Devon, England —*n.* **3.** Devonian period or rock system

devote (di'vōt) *vt.* set apart, give up exclusively (to person, purpose *etc.*) —**de'voted** *a.* loving, attached —**devotee** (devə'tē) *n.* **1.** ardent enthusiast **2.** zealous worshipper —**de'votion** *n.* **1.** deep affection, loyalty **2.** dedication **3.** religious earnestness —*pl.* **4.** prayers, religious exercises —**de'votional** *a.*

devour (di'vowər) *vt.* **1.** eat greedily **2.** consume, destroy **3.** read, gaze at eagerly —**de'vourer** *n.*

devout (di'vowt) *a.* **1.** earnestly religious, pious **2.** sincere, heartfelt —**de'voutly** *adv.*

dew (dyōō, dōō) *n.* **1.** moisture from air deposited as small drops on cool surface between nightfall and morning **2.** any beaded moisture —*vt.* **3.** wet with or as with dew —'**dewiness** *n.* —'**dewy** *a.* —'**dewclaw** *n.*

partly developed inner toe of dogs —**'dewlap** *n.* fold of loose skin hanging from neck —**dew point** temperature at which dew begins to form —**dew pond** small natural pond —**dew-worm** *n.* C large earthworm used as bait —**dewy-eyed** *a.* naive, innocent

dewberry ('dyōōberi, 'dōō-) *n.* bramble with blue-black fruits

Dewey Decimal System ('dyōōi, 'dōōi) system of library book classification with ten main subject classes (*also* **decimal classification**)

DEW line (dyōō, dōō) distant early warning line, network of sensors situated in Arctic regions of N Amer.

Dexedrine ('deksədrēn) *n.* trade name for preparation of amphetamine

dexterity (dek'steriti) *n.* **1.** manual skill **2.** neatness **3.** deftness **4.** adroitness —**'dexter** *a. Her.* on the bearer's right-hand side of a shield —**'dexterous** *a.* showing dexterity, skillful

dextran ('dekstrən) *n.* gummy polysaccharide produced by certain bacteria from sucrose used as partial substitute for blood plasma

dextrin ('dekstrin) *or* **dextrine** ('dekstrēn, -trin) *n.* sticky substance obtained from starch, used as thickening agent in foods and as gum

dextrose ('dekstrōs, -trōz) *n.* white, soluble, sweet-tasting crystalline solid, occurring naturally in fruit, honey, animal tissue

D.F. Defender of the Faith

D.F.C. Distinguished Flying Cross

D.F.M. Distinguished Flying Medal

dg *or* **dg.** decigram

dharma ('därmə) *n.* **1.** *Hinduism* social custom regarded as religious and moral duty **2.** *Hinduism* essential principle of cosmos; natural law; conduct that conforms with this **3.** *Buddhism* ideal truth

dhow (dow) *n.* lateen-rigged Arab sailing vessel

di-[1] (*comb. form*) **1.** twice; two; double, as in *dicotyledon* **2.** containing two specified atoms or groups of atoms, as in *carbon dioxide*

di-[2] (*comb. form*) *see* DIA-

dia- *or before vowel* **di-** (*comb. form*) through

diabetes (dīə'bētēz, -tis) *n.* disorder characterized by excretion of abnormal amount of urine —**diabetes insipidus** (in'sipidəs) condition marked by discharge of large quantities of dilute urine —**diabetes mellitus** (mə'lītəs) disease marked by inability of the body to burn sugar as a fuel —**diabetic** (dīə'betik) *n./a.*

diabolic (dīə'bolik) *a.* devilish —**dia'bolical** *a. inf.* very bad —**dia'bolically** *adv.* —**di'abolism** *n.* devil-worship

diabolo (di'abəlō) *n.* game in which top is spun into air from string attached to two sticks

diaconal (dī'akənəl) *a.* pert. to deacon —**di'aconate** *n.* **1.** office, rank of deacon **2.** body of deacons

diacritic (dīə'kritik) *n.* **1.** sign above letter or character indicating special phonetic value *etc.* —*a.* **2.** diacritical —**dia'critical** *a.* **1.** of a diacritic **2.** showing a distinction (*also* **dia'critic**)

diadem ('dīədem) *n.* a crown

diaeresis *or* **dieresis** (dī'erisis) *n.* mark (¨) placed over vowel to show that it is sounded separately from preceding one, as in *Noël* (*pl.* **-ses** (-sēz))

diagnosis (dīəg'nōsis) *n.* identification of disease from symptoms (*pl.* **-ses** (-sēz)) —**'diagnose** *v.* —**diag'nostic** *a.*

diagonal (dī'agənəl) *a.* **1.** from corner to corner **2.** oblique —*n.* **3.** line from corner to corner —**di'agonally** *adv.*

diagram ('dīəgram) *n.* drawing, figure in lines, to illustrate something being expounded —**diagram'matic** *a.* —**diagram'matically** *adv.*

dial ('dīəl) *n.* **1.** face of clock *etc.* **2.** plate marked with graduations on which pointer moves (as on meter, weighing machine *etc.*) **3.** numbered disk on front of telephone **4.** *sl.* face —*vt.* **5.** operate (telephone) **6.** indicate on dial —**dial tone** continuous purring heard over telephone indicating that number can be dialed

dialect ('dīəlekt) *n.* **1.** characteristic speech of district **2.** local variety of a language —**dia'lectal** *a.*

dialectic (dīə'lektik) *n.* discovery of truth by systematic reasoning —**dia'lectical** *a.* —**dia'lectically** *adv.* —**dialec'tician** *n.* **1.** logician **2.** reasoner

dialogue ('dīəlog) *n.* **1.** conversation between two or more (persons) **2.** representation of such conversation in drama, novel *etc.* **3.** discussion between representatives of two states, countries *etc.*

dialysis (dī'alisis) *n. Med.* filtering of blood through membrane to remove waste products

diamagnetism (dīə'magnitizəm) *n.* phenomenon exhibited by substances that are repelled by both poles of magnet

diamanté (dēəmän'tā) *n.* (fabric covered with) glittering particles —**diamantine** (dīəman'tīn) *a.* like diamond

diameter (dī'amitər) *n.* **1.** (length of) straight line from side to side of figure or body (*esp.* circle) through center **2.** thickness —**dia'metrical** *a.* opposite —**dia'metrically** *adv.*

diamond ('dīəmənd) *n.* **1.** precious stone, usu. bluish-white, crystallized pure carbon, the hardest known substance, poorer grades of which are used as abrasives **2.** rhomboid figure **3.** suit at cards **4.** playing field in baseball —**diamond jubilee** *or* **wedding** 60th (sometimes 75th) anniversary

dianthus (dīˈanthōōs) *n.* genus of herbaceous flowers, *eg* pinks and carnations

diapason (dīəˈpāzən) *n.* **1.** fundamental organ stop **2.** compass of voice or instrument

diaper (ˈdīəpər) *n.* **1.** absorbent material worn by infant to retain excreta **2.** fabric with small diamond pattern **3.** pattern of that kind —ˈ**diapered** *a.* —**diaper rash** redness, maceration and erosion of the skin of the diaper area in infants

diaphanous (dīˈafənəs) *a.* transparent

diaphoretic (dīəfəˈretik) *n.* **1.** diaphoretic drug —*a.* **2.** relating to or causing perspiration

diaphragm (ˈdīəfram) *n.* **1.** muscular partition dividing two cavities of body, midriff **2.** plate or disk wholly or partly closing tube or opening **3.** any thin dividing or covering membrane **4.** contraceptive cap covering neck of womb —**diaphragmatic** (dīəfragˈmatik) *a.*

diapositive (dīəˈpozitiv) *n.* positive transparency; slide

diarrhea (dīəˈrēə) *n.* excessive looseness of the bowels

diary (ˈdīəri) *n.* **1.** daily record of events, engagements, thoughts *etc.* **2.** book for this —ˈ**diarist** *n.* writer of diary

Diaspora (dīˈaspərə) *n.* **1.** dispersion of Jews from Palestine after Babylonian captivity; Jewish communities that arose after this **2.** (*oft.* **d-**) dispersion, as of people orig. of one nation

diastase (ˈdīəstās, -stāz) *n.* enzyme that converts starch into sugar

diastole (dīˈastəli) *n.* dilation of chambers of heart

diathermy (ˈdīəthərmi) *n.* heating of body tissues with electric current for medical treatment

diatom (ˈdīətom) *n.* one of order of microscopic algae —**diaˈtomic** *a.* of two atoms

diatonic (dīəˈtonik) *a. Mus.* **1.** pert. to regular major and minor scales **2.** (of melody) composed in such a scale

diatribe (ˈdīətrīb) *n.* violently bitter verbal attack, invective, denunciation

dibble (ˈdibəl) *n.* **1.** small tool used to make holes in ground for bulbs *etc.* (*also* ˈ**dibber**) —*v.* **2.** make hole in (ground) with dibble **3.** plant (seeds *etc.*) with dibble

dice (dīs) *pl.n.* **1.** (*also functions as sing., orig. sing.* **die**) cubes each with six sides marked one to six for games of chance —*vi.* **2.** gamble with dice —*vt.* **3.** cut into small cubes —ˈ**dicer** *n.* —ˈ**dicey** *a. inf.* dangerous, risky

dicephalous (dīˈsefələs) *a.* two-headed

dichotomy (dīˈkotəmi) *n.* division into two parts

dichroism (ˈdīkrōizəm) *n.* property possessed by some crystals of exhibiting different colors when viewed from different directions —**diˈchroic** *a.*

dichromatic (dīkrōˈmatik) *a.* **1.** having two colors (*also* **diˈchroic**) **2.** (of animal species) having two different color varieties **3.** able to perceive only two colors

dick (dik) *n. sl.* **1.** fellow, person **2.** detective

Dickensian (diˈkenziən) *a.* **1.** of Charles Dickens (1820–70), English novelist, or his novels **2.** denoting poverty, distress and exploitation as depicted in Dickens's novels **3.** grotesquely comic, as some Dickens characters

dicker (ˈdikər) *v.* **1.** trade (goods) by bargaining; barter —*n.* **2.** petty bargain or barter

dickey *or* **dicky** (ˈdiki) *n.* detachable false shirt front (*pl.* ˈ**dickeys,** ˈ**dickies**) —ˈ**dickybird** *n. inf.* child's word for small bird

dicotyledon (dīkotiˈlēdən) *n.* flowering plant having two embryonic seed leaves

Dictaphone (ˈdiktəfōn) *n.* trade name for machine that records and plays back dictation

dictate (dikˈtāt) *v.* **1.** say or read for another to transcribe —*vt.* **2.** prescribe, lay down —*vi.* **3.** seek to impose one's will on others —*n.* (ˈdiktāt) **4.** bidding —**dicˈtation** *n.* —**dicˈtator** *n.* absolute ruler —**dictaˈtorial** *a.* **1.** despotic **2.** overbearing —**dictaˈtorially** *adv.* —**dicˈtatorship** *n.*

diction (ˈdikshən) *n.* **1.** choice and use of words **2.** enunciation

dictionary (ˈdikshəneri) *n.* **1.** book setting forth, alphabetically, words of language with meanings *etc.* **2.** reference book with items in alphabetical order

dictum (ˈdiktəm) *n.* **1.** pronouncement **2.** saying, maxim (*pl.* **-s, -ta** (-tə))

dicumarol (dīˈkyōōmərōl, -ˈkōō-; -rōl) *n.* drug used to prevent formation of blood clots in arteries and veins

did (did) *pt. of* DO[1]

didactic (dīˈdaktik, di-) *a.* **1.** designed to instruct **2.** (of people) opinionated, dictatorial —**diˈdacticism** *n.*

diddle (ˈdidəl) *vt. inf.* cheat

didgeridoo (dijəriˈdōō) *n. Mus.* native Aust. wind instrument

die[1] (dī) *vi.* **1.** cease to live **2.** come to an end **3.** stop functioning **4.** *inf.* be nearly overcome (with laughter *etc.*) (**died,** ˈ**dying**) —ˈ**diehard** *n.* one who resists (reform *etc.*) to the end —**be dying for** be looking eagerly forward to

die[2] (dī) *n. see* DICE

die[3] (dī) *n.* **1.** shaped block of hard material to form metal in forge, press *etc.* **2.** tool for cutting thread on pipe *etc.* —**die-cast** *vt.* shape or form (object) by introducing molten metal or plastic into reusable mold —**die-casting** *n.*

dieldrin (ˈdēldrin) *n.* highly toxic crystalline insecticide

dielectric (dīˈlektrik) *n.* **1.** substance through or across which electric induction takes place **2.** nonconductor **3.** insulator

dieresis (dīˈerisis) *n. see* DIAERESIS

diesel (ˈdēzəl) *a.* **1.** pert. to internal-combustion engine using oil as fuel —*n.* **2.** this engine **3.** diesel oil —**diesel-electric** *n.* **1.** locomotive fitted with diesel engine driving electric generator —*a.* **2.** of such locomotive or system —**diesel oil** fuel, distilled from petroleum, used in diesel engines

diet[1] (ˈdīət) *n.* **1.** restricted or regulated course of feeding **2.** kind of food lived on **3.** food —*vi.* **4.** follow a dietary regimen, as to lose weight —ˈ**dietary** *a.* **1.** relating to diet —*n.* **2.** a regulated diet **3.** system of dieting —**dieˈtetic** *a.* —**dieˈtetics** *pl.n.* (*with sing. v.*) science of diet —**dieˈtitian** *or* **dieˈtician** *n.* one skilled in dietetics

diet[2] (ˈdīət) *n.* **1.** legislature of some provinces or nations **2.** formal assembly

differ (ˈdifər) *vi.* **1.** be unlike **2.** disagree —ˈ**difference** *n.* **1.** unlikeness **2.** degree or point of unlikeness **3.** disagreement **4.** remainder left after subtraction —ˈ**different** *a.* unlike —ˈ**differently** *adv.*

differentia (difəˈrenchiə) *n. Logic* feature by which subclasses of same class of named objects can be distinguished (*pl.* **-tiae** (-chiē))

differential (difəˈrenchəl) *a.* **1.** varying with circumstances **2.** special **3.** *Math.* pert. to an infinitesimal change in variable quantity **4.** *Phys. etc.* relating to difference between sets of motions acting in the same direction or between pressures *etc.* —*n.* **5.** *Math.* infinitesimal difference between two consecutive states of variable quantity **6.** differential gear **7.** difference between rates of pay for different types of labor —**differˈentially** *adv.* —**differˈentiate** *vt.* **1.** serve to distinguish between, make different —*vi.* **2.** discriminate —**differentiˈation** *n.* —**differential calculus** method of calculating relative rate of change for continuously varying quantities —**differential gear** epicyclic gear mounted in driving axle of vehicle, that permits one driving wheel to rotate faster than the other, as when cornering

difficult (ˈdifikəlt) *a.* **1.** requiring effort, skill *etc.* to do or understand, not easy **2.** obscure —ˈ**difficulty** *n.* **1.** being difficult **2.** difficult task, problem **3.** embarrassment **4.** hindrance **5.** obscurity **6.** trouble

diffident (ˈdifidənt) *a.* lacking confidence, timid, shy —ˈ**diffidence** *n.* shyness —ˈ**diffidently** *adv.*

diffract (diˈfrakt) *vi.* break up, *esp.* of rays of light, sound waves —**difˈfraction** *n.* deflection of ray of light, electromagnetic wave caused by obstacle

diffuse (diˈfyo͞oz) *vt.* **1.** spread abroad —*a.* (diˈfyo͞os) **2.** widely spread **3.** loose, verbose, wordy —**diffusely** (diˈfyo͞osli) *adv.* **1.** loosely **2.** wordily —**difˈfusible** *a.* —**difˈfusion** *n.* process by which one substance mixes with another through the motion of its particles —**diffusive** (diˈfyo͞osiv, -ziv) *a.* —**diffusively** (diˈfyo͞osivli, -zivli) *adv.*

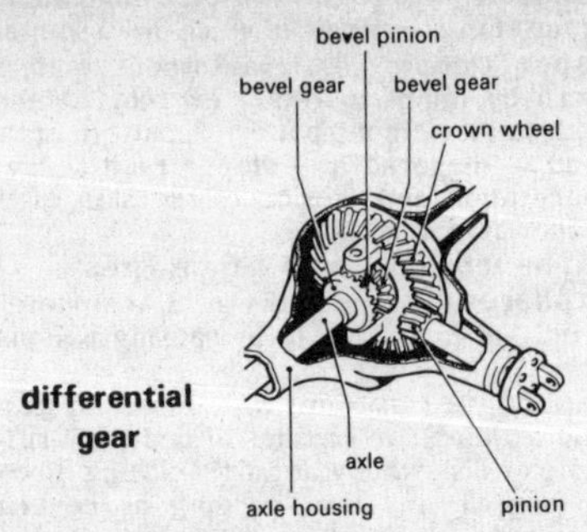

dig (dig) *vi.* **1.** work with spade **2.** search, investigate —*vt.* **3.** turn up with spade **4.** hollow out, make hole in **5.** excavate **6.** thrust **7.** (*oft. with* out *or* up) discover by searching (**dug,** ˈ**digging**) —*n.* **8.** piece of digging **9.** archaeological excavation **10.** thrust **11.** jibe, taunt —*pl.* **12.** *inf.* lodgings —ˈ**digger** *n.* **1.** one who digs **2.** gold miner **3.** Aust. or N.Z. soldier

digest (dīˈjest, di-) *vt.* **1.** prepare (food) in stomach *etc.* for assimilation **2.** bring into handy form by sorting, tabulating, summarizing **3.** reflect on **4.** absorb —*vi.* **5.** (of food) undergo digestion —*n.* (ˈdījest) **6.** methodical summary, *esp.* of laws **7.** magazine containing condensed version of articles *etc.* already published elsewhere —**diˈgestible** *a.* —**diˈgestion** *n.* digesting —**diˈgestive** *a.* **1.** relating to digestion —*n.* **2.** substance that aids digestion

digit (ˈdijit) *n.* **1.** finger or toe **2.** any of the numbers 0 to 9 —ˈ**digital** *a.* **1.** of, resembling digits **2.** performed with fingers **3.** displaying information (time *etc.*) by numbers rather than by pointer on dial —ˈ**digitate** *a.* having separate fingers, toes —**digital clock** *or* **watch** clock or watch in which time is indicated by digits rather than by hands on dial —**digital computer** electronic computer consisting of numbers, letters *etc.* that are represented internally in binary notation

digitalis (dijiˈtalis, -ˈtā-) *n.* group of chemically related drugs obtained from dried leaves of certain flowering plants, *esp.* foxgloves: used to treat heart disease

dignity (ˈdigniti) *n.* **1.** stateliness, gravity **2.** worthiness, excellence, repute **3.** honorable office or title —ˈ**dignified** *a.* stately, majestic —ˈ**dignify** *vt.* give dignity to (**-fied, -fying**) —ˈ**dignitary** *n.* holder of high office

digraph (ˈdīgraf) *n.* combination of two letters used to represent single sound such as *gh* in *tough*

digress (dīˈgres, di-) *vi.* turn from main course, *esp.* to deviate from subject in speaking or writing —**diˈgression** *n.* —**diˈgressive** *a.*

dihedral (dīˈhēdrəl) *a.* having two plane faces or sides

dik-dik (ˈdikdik) *n.* small Afr. antelope

dike *or* **dyke** (dīk) *n.* **1.** embankment to prevent flooding **2.** ditch

diktat (dikˈtät) *n.* arbitrary decree

dilapidate (diˈlapidāt) *v.* (cause to) fall into ruin —**diˈlapidated** *a.* **1.** in ruins **2.** decayed —**dilapiˈdation** *n.*

dilate (dīˈlāt, ˈdīlāt) *vt.* **1.** widen, expand —*vi.* **2.** expand **3.** talk or write at length (on) —**diˈlation** *or* **dilatation** (diləˈtāshən, dī-) *n.*

dilatory (ˈdilətōri) *a.* tardy, slow, belated —**ˈdilatorily** *adv.* —**ˈdilatoriness** *n.* delay

dilemma (diˈlemə, dī-) *n.* **1.** position in fact or argument offering choice only between unwelcome alternatives **2.** predicament

dilettante (ˈdilitänt) *n.* **1.** person with taste and knowledge of fine arts as pastime **2.** dabbler (*pl.* **dilettanti** (diliˈtänti)) —*a.* **3.** amateur, desultory —**ˈdilettantism** *n.*

diligent (ˈdilijənt) *a.* unremitting in effort, industrious, hard-working —**ˈdiligence** *n.*

dill (dil) *n.* yellow-flowered herb with medicinal seeds

dilly (ˈdili) *n. sl.* remarkable person or thing

dilly-dally (ˈdilidali) *vi. inf.* **1.** loiter **2.** vacillate

dilute (dīˈlo͞ot, di-) *vt.* **1.** reduce (liquid) in strength, *esp.* by adding water **2.** thin **3.** reduce in force, effect *etc.* —*a.* **4.** weakened thus —**diluent** (ˈdilyo͞oənt) *a./n.* —**diˈlution** *n.*

diluvial (diˈlo͞oviəl, dī-) *or* **diluvian** *a.* of, connected with, a deluge or flood, *esp.* the Flood of the book of Genesis

dim (dim) *a.* **1.** indistinct, faint, not bright **2.** mentally dull **3.** unfavorable (**ˈdimmer** *comp.*, **ˈdimmest** *sup.*) —*v.* **4.** make, grow dim (**-mm-**) —**ˈdimly** *adv.* —**ˈdimmer** *n.* device for dimming electric lights —**ˈdimness** *n.* —**ˈdimwit** *n. inf.* stupid or silly person —**dim-witted** *a.*

dime (dīm) *n.* 10-cent piece, coin of U.S. and Canad.

dimenhydrinate (dīmenˈhīdrināt) *n. see* DRAMAMINE

dimension (diˈmenchən, dī-) *n.* **1.** measurement, size **2.** aspect —**diˈmensional** *a.* —**dimensionˈality** *n.* —**fourth dimension 1.** *Phys.* time **2.** supranatural, fictional dimension additional to those of length, breadth, thickness

diminish (diˈminish) *v.* lessen —**dimiˈnution** *n.* —**diˈminutive** *a.* **1.** very small —*n.* **2.** derivative word, affix implying smallness

diminuendo (diminyo͞oˈendō) *a. Mus.* (of sound) dying away

dimity (ˈdimiti) *n.* strong cotton fabric

dimple (ˈdimpəl) *n.* **1.** small hollow in surface of skin, *esp.* of cheek **2.** any small hollow —*v.* **3.** mark with, show dimples

din (din) *n.* continuous roar of confused noises —**din into** instill into by constant repetition (**-nn-**)

dinar (diˈnär, ˈdēnär) *n.* **1.** standard monetary unit of Iraq, Jordan, Libya, Yugoslavia *etc.* **2.** an Iranian monetary unit

dine (dīn) *vi.* **1.** eat dinner —*vt.* **2.** give dinner to —**ˈdiner** *n.* **1.** one who dines **2.** small cheap restaurant —**dining car** railroad coach in which meals are served (*also* **restaurant car**) —**dining room** room where meals are eaten

ding (ding) *v.* **1.** ring (*esp.* with tedious repetition) —*vi.* **2.** make (imitation of) sound of bell —*n.* **3.** this sound —**ding-dong** *n.* **1.** sound of bell **2.** imitation of sound of bell **3.** violent exchange of blows or words —*a.* **4.** sounding or ringing repeatedly

dinghy (ˈdingi, ˈdinggi) *n.* **1.** small open boat **2.** collapsible rubber boat

dingle (ˈdinggəl) *n.* dell

dingo (ˈdinggō) *n.* Aust. wild dog

dingy (ˈdinji) *a.* dirty-looking, dull —**ˈdinginess** *n.*

dinkum (ˈdingkəm) *a.* **A, NZ** *inf.* genuine; right —**dinkum oil** truth

dinky (ˈdingki) *a. inf.* inconsequential; insignificant

dinner (ˈdinər) *n.* **1.** chief meal of the day **2.** official banquet —**dinner jacket** tuxedo

dinosaur (ˈdīnəsōr) *n.* extinct reptile, oft. of gigantic size —**dinoˈsaurian** *a.*

dint (dint) *n.* dent, mark —**by dint of** by means of

diocese (ˈdīəsis, -sēz, -sēs) *n.* district, jurisdiction of bishop —**diocesan** (dīˈosisən) *a.* **1.** of diocese —*n.* **2.** bishop of diocese

diode (ˈdīōd) *n.* **1.** semiconductor device for converting alternating current to direct current **2.** electronic valve having two electrodes between which current can flow in only one direction

dioecious (dīˈēshəs) *a.* (of plants) having male and female reproductive organs on separate plants

Dionysian (dīəˈniziən) *a.* **1.** of Dionysus, Gr. god of wine and revelry **2.** (*oft.* **d-**) wild; orgiastic

diopter (dīˈoptər) *n.* unit for measuring refractive power of lens —**diˈoptrics** *pl.n.* (*with sing. v.*) that part of the science of optics which deals with refraction of light

diorama (dīəˈrämə) *n.* **1.** miniature three-dimensional scene, *esp.* as museum exhibit **2.** device for producing changing effects in a partly translucent painting by manipulating direction, color and intensity of light

dioxide (dīˈoksīd) *n.* oxide with two parts of oxygen to one of the other constituents

dioxin (dīˈoksin) *n.* any of various by-products of manufacture of certain herbicides and bactericides

dip (dip) *vt.* **1.** put partly or briefly into liquid, *esp.* to coat **2.** immerse **3.** lower and raise again **4.** take up in ladle, bucket *etc.* **5.** direct (headlights of vehicle) downwards —*vi.* **6.** plunge partially or temporarily **7.** go down, sink **8.** slope downwards (**-pp-**) —*n.* **9.** act of dipping **10.** bathe **11.** liquid chemical in which livestock are immersed to treat insect pests *etc.* **12.** downward slope **13.** hollow **14.** creamy (savory) mixture in which crackers *etc.* are dipped before being eaten **15.** lottery —**'dipstick** *n.* graduated rod dipped into container to indicate fluid level —**dip switch** device for dipping car headlights —**dip into 1.** glance at **2.** make inroads into for funds

diphtheria (dif'thēəriə, dip-) *n.* infectious bacterial disease of throat *etc.* —**diphtheritic** (difthə'ritik, dip-) *a.*

diphthong ('difthong, 'dip-) *n.* union of two vowel sounds in single compound sound

diplococcus (diplō'kokəs) *n.* any of various spherical bacteria which occur in pairs including those causing pneumonia, gonorrhea and epidemic meningitis (*pl.* **-cocci** (-'koksī))

diploid ('diploid) *n.* single cell having basic chromosome number doubled

diploma (di'plōmə) *n.* **1.** document vouching for person's proficiency **2.** title to degree, honor *etc.*

diplomacy (di'plōməsi) *n.* **1.** management of international relations **2.** skill in negotiation **3.** tactful, adroit dealing —**'diplomat** *n.* one engaged in official diplomacy —**diplo'matic** *a.* —**diplo'matically** *adv.* —**di'plomatist** *n.* **1.** diplomat **2.** tactful person —**diplomatic corps** *see* **corps diplomatique** *at* CORPS —**diplomatic immunity** immunity from local jurisdiction *etc.* afforded to diplomatic staff abroad

diplopia (di'plōpiə) *n.* double vision

dipolar ('dīpōlər, di'pōlər) *a.* having two poles

dipole ('dīpōl) *n.* type of radio and television antenna

dipper ('dipər) *n.* **1.** ladle, bucket, scoop **2.** (*also* **water ouzel**) N Amer. swimming and diving songbird

dipsomania (dipsō'māniə) *n.* uncontrollable craving for alcohol —**dipso'maniac** *n.* victim of this

dipterous ('diptərəs) *a.* **1.** of order of insects having single pair of wings and sucking or piercing mouthparts (*also* **'dipteran**) **2.** *Bot.* having two winglike parts

diptych ('diptik) *n.* **1.** ancient tablet hinged in center, folding together like a book **2.** painting, carving on two hinged panels

dire ('dīər) *a.* **1.** terrible **2.** urgent

direct (di'rekt, dī-) *vt.* **1.** control, manage, order **2.** tell or show the way **3.** aim, point, turn **4.** address (letter *etc.*) **5.** supervise (actors *etc.*) in (play or motion picture) —*a.* **6.** frank, straightforward **7.** straight **8.** going straight to the point **9.** immediate **10.** lineal —**di'rection** *n.* **1.** directing **2.** aim, course of movement **3.** address, instruction —**di'rectional** *a.* **1.** of or relating to spatial direction **2.** *Electron.* having or relating to increased sensitivity to radio waves *etc.* coming from particular direction; (of antenna) transmitting or receiving radio waves more effectively in some directions than in others **3.** *Phys., electron.* concentrated in, following or producing motion in particular direction —**di'rective** *a./n.* —**di'rectly** *adv.* —**di'rectness** *n.* —**di'rector** *n.* **1.** one who directs, *esp.* a motion picture **2.** member of board managing company (**di'rectress** *fem.*) —**di'rectorate** *n.* **1.** body of directors **2.** office of director —**di'rectorship** *n.* —**di'rectory** *n.* **1.** alphabetical book of names, addresses, streets *etc.* **2.** (**D-**) French revolutionary government 1795–99 —**direct current** continuous electric current that flows in one direction —**direct election** election decided by voters, not by representatives —**direction finder** radio receiver that determines the direction of incoming waves —**direct mail** advertisements, requests for donations *etc.* addressed directly to individuals —**direct object** *Gram.* noun, pronoun or noun phrase whose referent receives direct action of verb

dirge (dərj) *n.* poem or song of mourning

dirigible ('dirijibəl, di'rij-) *a.* **1.** steerable —*n.* **2.** balloon; airship

dirk (dərk) *n.* short dagger orig. carried by Scottish clansmen

dirndl ('dərndəl) *n.* full, gathered skirt

dirt (dərt) *n.* **1.** filth **2.** soil, earth **3.** obscene or pornographic material **4.** contamination —**'dirtiness** *n.* —**'dirty** *a.* **1.** unclean, filthy **2.** obscene **3.** unfair **4.** dishonest —**dirt-cheap** *a./adv. inf.* at extremely low price —**dirt track** loose-surfaced track, *eg* for motorcycle racing

dis- (*comb. form*) negation, opposition, deprivation; in many verbs indicates undoing of the action of simple verb. See the list below

disable (dis'ābəl) *vt.* **1.** make unable **2.**

disappro'bation
disap'proval
disap'rove
disar'range
disa'vow
dis'band
disbe'lief
disbe'lieve
discom'pose
discom'posure
discon'nect
discon'tent
discon'tented
discon'tentment
discon'tinue
discon'tinuous
dis'courteous
dis'courtesy
disem'bark
disen'chant
disen'cumber
disen'tangle
disen'tanglement
disequi'librium
dises'tablish
dises'tablishment
dis'franchise
dis'harmony

cripple, maim —**disa'bility** *n.* **1.** incapacity **2.** drawback

disabuse (disə'byōōz) *vt.* **1.** undeceive, disillusion **2.** free from error

disadvantage (disəd'vantij) *n.* **1.** drawback **2.** hindrance **3.** detriment —*vt.* **4.** handicap —**disad'vantaged** *a.* deprived, discriminated against, underprivileged —**disadvan'tageous** *a.*

disaffected (disə'fektid) *a.* ill-disposed, alienated, estranged —**disaf'fection** *n.*

disagree (disə'grē) *vi.* (*oft. with* with) **1.** be at variance **2.** conflict **3.** (of food *etc.*) have bad effect (on) —**disa'greeable** *a.* unpleasant —**disa'greement** *n.* **1.** difference of opinion **2.** discord **3.** discrepancy

disallow (disə'low) *vt.* reject as untrue or invalid —**disal'lowance** *n.*

disappear (disə'pēər) *vi.* **1.** vanish **2.** cease to exist **3.** be lost —**disap'pearance** *n.*

disappoint (disə'point) *vt.* fail to fulfill (hope), frustrate —**disap'pointment** *n.*

disarm (dis'ärm) *vt.* **1.** deprive of arms or weapons **2.** reduce war weapons of (a country) **3.** win over —**dis'armament** *n.* —**dis'arming** *a.* removing hostility, suspicion

disarray (disə'rā) *vt.* **1.** throw into disorder, derange —*n.* **2.** disorderliness, *esp.* of clothing

disassociate (disə'sōshiāt) *v. see* DISSOCIATE

disaster (di'zastər) *n.* calamity, sudden or great misfortune —**dis'astrous** *a.* calamitous

disbar (dis'bär) *vt.* expel from the legal profession

disbud (dis'bud) *vt.* remove superfluous buds, shoots from (plants, cattle)

disburse (dis'bərs) *vt.* pay out —**dis'bursement** *n.*

disc (disk) *n. see* DISK —**disc brake** brake in which two pads rub against flat disc attached to wheel hub when brake is applied —**disc jockey** announcer playing records, oft. on radio

discard (dis'kärd) *vt.* **1.** reject **2.** give up **3.** cast off, dismiss

discern (di'sərn) *vt.* **1.** make out **2.** distinguish —**dis'cernible** *a.* —**dis'cerning** *a.* **1.** discriminating **2.** penetrating —**dis'cernment** *n.* insight

discharge (dis'chärj) *vt.* **1.** release **2.** dismiss **3.** emit **4.** perform (duties), fulfill (obligations) **5.** let go **6.** fire off **7.** unload **8.** pay —*n.* ('dischärj, dis'chärj) **9.** discharging **10.** being discharged **11.** release **12.** matter emitted **13.** document certifying release, payment *etc.*

disciple (di'sīpəl) *n.* follower, one who takes another as teacher and model —**dis'cipleship** *n.*

discipline ('disiplin) *n.* **1.** training that produces orderliness, obedience, self-control **2.** result of such training in order, conduct *etc.* **3.** system of rules *etc.* **4.** instrument of self-mortification, *eg* hair shirt —*vt.* **5.** train **6.** punish —**discipli'narian** *n.* one who enforces rigid discipline —**'disciplinary** *a.*

disclaim (dis'klām) *vt.* deny, renounce —**dis'claimer** *n.* repudiation, denial

disclose (dis'klōz) *vt.* **1.** allow to be seen **2.** make known —**dis'closure** *n.* revelation

disco ('diskō) discotheque

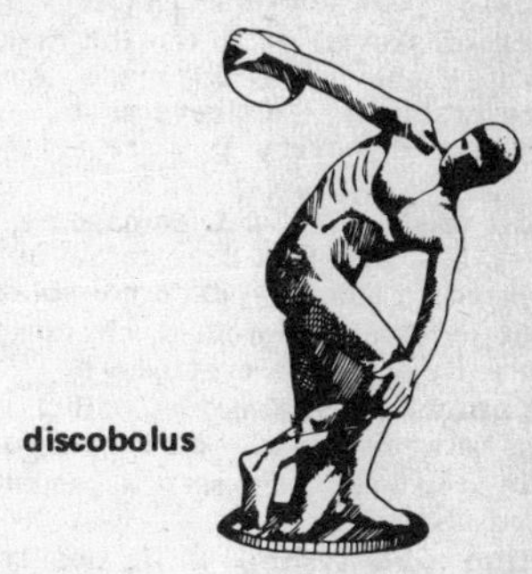
discobolus

discobolus (dis'kobələs) *n.* discus thrower (*pl.* **-li** (-lī))

discolor (dis'kulər) *vt.* alter color of, stain —**discolor'ation** *n.*

discomfit (dis'kumfit) *vt.* embarrass, disconcert, baffle —**dis'comfiture** *n.*

discomfort (dis'kumfərt) *n.* **1.** inconvenience, distress or mild pain **2.** something that disturbs or deprives of ease —*vt.* **3.** make uncomfortable or uneasy

discommode (diskə'mōd) *vt.* **1.** put to inconvenience **2.** disturb —**discom'modious** *a.*

disconcert (diskən'sərt) *vt.* **1.** ruffle, confuse **2.** upset, embarrass

disconsolate (dis'konsəlit) *a.* unhappy, downcast, forlorn

discord ('diskörd) *n.* **1.** strife **2.** difference, dissension **3.** disagreement of sounds —**dis'cordance** *n.* —**dis'cordant** *a.* —**dis'cordantly** *adv.*

discotheque ('diskətek) *n.* **1.** club *etc.* for dancing to recorded music **2.** mobile equipment for providing music for dancing

dis'hearten
dis'heartenment
dis'honest
dis'honesty
disin'ter
disin'terment
dis'join
dis'loyal
dis'loyalty
dis'mast
dis'mount
disorgani'zation
dis'organize
dispro'portion
dispro'portionate
disre'gard
dis'reputable
disre'pute
disre'spect
disre'spectful
dissatis'faction
dis'satisfy
dis'similar
dissimi'larity
dis'symmetry
dis'trust
dis'trustful
disu'nite

discount (dis'kownt, 'diskownt) *vt.* **1.** consider as possibility but reject as unsuitable, inappropriate *etc.* **2.** deduct (amount, percentage) from usual price **3.** sell at reduced price —*n.* ('diskownt) **4.** amount deducted from cost, expressed as cash amount or percentage

discountenance (dis'kowntinəns) *vt.* **1.** abash **2.** discourage **3.** frown upon

discourage (dis'kurij) *vt.* **1.** reduce confidence of **2.** deter **3.** show disapproval of —**dis'couragement** *n.*

discourse ('diskörs, dis'körs) *n.* **1.** conversation **2.** speech, treatise, sermon —*vi.* (dis'körs) **3.** speak, converse, lecture

discover (di'skuvər) *vt.* **1.** (be the first to) find out, light upon **2.** make known —**dis'coverable** *a.* —**dis'coverer** *n.* —**dis'covery** *n.* —**Discovery Day** *see* COLUMBUS DAY

discredit (dis'kredit) *vt.* **1.** damage reputation of **2.** cast doubt on **3.** reject as untrue —*n.* **4.** disgrace **5.** doubt —**dis'creditable** *a.*

discreet (di'skrēt) *a.* prudent, circumspect —**dis'creetly** *adv.* —**dis'creetness** *n.*

discrepancy (di'skrepənsi) *n.* conflict, variation, as between figures —**dis'crepant** *a.*

discrete (dis'krēt, 'diskrēt) *a.* separate, disunited, discontinuous

discretion (di'skreshən) *n.* **1.** quality of being discreet **2.** prudence **3.** freedom to act as one chooses —**dis'cretionary** *or* **dis'cretional** *a.*

discriminate (di'skriminãt) *vi.* **1.** single out particular person, group *etc.* for special favor or disfavor **2.** distinguish (between) **3.** be discerning —**discrimi'nation** *n.* —**dis'criminatory** *or* **dis'criminative** *a.* **1.** based on prejudice; biased **2.** capable of making fine distinctions

discursive (di'skərsiv) *a.* passing from subject to subject, rambling

discus ('diskəs) *n.* disk-shaped object thrown in athletic competition (*pl.* **-es, disci** ('diskī))

discuss (di'skus) *vt.* **1.** exchange opinions about **2.** debate —**dis'cussion** *n.*

disdain (dis'dān) *n.* **1.** scorn, contempt —*vt.* **2.** scorn —**dis'dainful** *a.* —**dis'dainfully** *adv.*

disease (di'zēz) *n.* illness, disorder of health —**dis'eased** *a.* —**disease vector** insect or other animal carrying infectious organism from infected to noninfected individual

disembodied (disim'bodid) *a.* (of spirit) released from bodily form

disembowel (disim'bowəl) *vt.* take out entrails of

disenchanted (disin'chantid) *a.* disillusioned

disengage (disin'gāj) *v.* **1.** release or become released from connection *etc.* **2.** *Mil.* withdraw (forces) from close action **3.** *Fencing* move (one's blade) from one side of opponent's blade to another in circular motion —**disen'gaged** *a.* —**disen'gagement** *n.*

disfavor (dis'fāvər) *n.* **1.** disapproval; dislike **2.** state of being disapproved of or disliked **3.** unkind act —*vt.* **4.** treat with disapproval or dislike

disfigure (dis'figyər) *vt.* mar appearance of —**disfigu'ration** *n.* —**dis'figurement** *n.* blemish, defect

disgorge (dis'gôrj) *vt.* **1.** vomit **2.** give up —**dis'gorgement** *n.*

disgrace (dis'grās) *n.* **1.** shame, loss of reputation, dishonor —*vt.* **2.** bring shame or discredit upon —**dis'graceful** *a.* shameful —**dis'gracefully** *adv.*

disgruntled (dis'gruntəld) *a.* vexed, put out

disguise (dis'gīz) *vt.* **1.** change appearance of, make unrecognizable **2.** conceal, cloak **3.** misrepresent —*n.* **4.** false appearance **5.** costume, mask *etc.* to conceal identity

disgust (dis'gust) *n.* **1.** violent distaste, loathing, repugnance —*vt.* **2.** affect with loathing

dish (dish) *n.* **1.** shallow vessel for food **2.** portion or variety of food **3.** contents of dish **4.** *sl.* attractive person —*vt.* **5.** put in dish —'**dishcloth** *n.* cloth for washing dishes —**dish out** *inf.* give generously —**dish up 1.** serve (meal *etc.*) **2.** *inf.* prepare or present, *esp.* attractively

dishabille (disa'bēl) *or* **deshabille** *n.* state of being partly or carelessly dressed

disheveled *or* **dishevelled** (di'shevəld) *a.* **1.** with disordered hair **2.** ruffled, untidy, unkempt

dishonor (dis'onər) *vt.* **1.** treat with disrespect **2.** fail or refuse to pay **3.** cause disgrace of (woman) by seduction or rape —*n.* **4.** lack of honor or respect **5.** state of shame or disgrace **6.** person or thing that causes loss of honor **7.** insult; affront **8.** refusal or failure to accept or pay a commercial paper —**dis'honorable** *a.* **1.** characterized by or causing dishonor or discredit **2.** having little or no integrity; unprincipled

disillusion (disi'lōōzhən) *vt.* **1.** destroy ideals, illusions, or false ideas of —*n.* **2.** act of disillusioning or being disillusioned (*also* **disil'lusionment**)

disincentive (disin'sentiv) *n.* **1.** something that acts as deterrent —*a.* **2.** acting as deterrent

disincline (disin'klīn) *v.* make or be unwilling, reluctant or averse —**disinclination** (disinkli'nāshən) *n.*

disinfectant (disin'fektənt) *n.* agent which kills disease-producing organisms —**disin'fect** *vt.*

disinformation (disinfər'māshən) *n.* deliberately leaked false information intended to mislead foreign agents

disingenuous (disin'jenyōōəs) *a.* not sincere or frank

disinherit (disin'herit) *vt.* deprive of inheritance

disintegrate (dis'intigrāt) *vi.* break up, fall to pieces —**disinte'gration** *n.*

disinterest (dis'intrist) *n.* freedom from bias or involvement —**dis'interested** *a.*

disjoint (dis'joint) *vt.* **1.** put out of joint **2.** break the natural order or logical arrangement of —**dis'jointed** *a.* **1.** (of discourse) incoherent **2.** disconnected

disjunctive (dis'jungktiv) *a.* **1.** serving to disconnect or separate **2.** *Gram.* denoting word, *esp.* conjunction, that serves to express opposition or contrast **3.** *Logic* characterizing, containing or included in disjunction —*n.* **4.** *Gram.* disjunctive word, *esp.* conjunction **5.** *Logic* disjunctive proposition

disk *or* **disc** (disk) *n.* **1.** thin, flat, circular object like a coin **2.** phonograph record

dislike (dis'līk) *vt.* **1.** consider unpleasant or disagreeable —*n.* **2.** aversion; antipathy —**dis'likable** *or* **dis'likeable** *a.*

dislocate ('disləkāt) *vt.* **1.** put out of joint **2.** disrupt, displace —**dislo'cation** *n.*

dislodge (dis'loj) *vt.* drive out or remove from hiding place or previous position —**dis'lodgement** *or* **dis'lodgment** *n.*

dismal ('dizməl) *a.* **1.** depressing **2.** depressed **3.** cheerless, dreary, gloomy —**'dismally** *adv.*

dismantle (dis'mantəl) *vt.* take apart —**dis'mantlement** *n.*

dismay (dis'mā) *vt.* **1.** dishearten, daunt —*n.* **2.** consternation, horrified amazement **3.** apprehension

dismember (dis'membər) *vt.* **1.** remove limbs or members of **2.** divide, partition —**dis'memberment** *n.*

dismiss (dis'mis) *vt.* **1.** remove, discharge from employment **2.** send away **3.** reject —**dis'missal** *n.*

disobey (disə'bā) *v.* refuse or fail to obey —**disobedience** (disə'bēdiəns) *n.* —**disobedient** (disə'bēdiənt) *a.*

disoblige (disə'blīj) *vt.* disregard the wishes, preferences of

disorder (dis'ördər) *n.* **1.** disarray, confusion, disturbance **2.** upset of health, ailment —*vt.* **3.** upset order of **4.** disturb health of —**dis'orderly** *a.* **1.** untidy **2.** unruly

disorient (dis'örient) *or* **disorientate** *vt.* cause (someone) to lose his bearings, confuse

disown (dis'ōn) *vt.* refuse to acknowledge

disparage (di'sparij) *vt.* **1.** speak slightingly of **2.** belittle —**dis'paragement** *n.*

disparate (di'sparit, 'dispərit) *a.* essentially different, unrelated —**dis'parity** *n.* **1.** inequality **2.** incongruity

dispassionate (dis'pashənit) *a.* **1.** unswayed by passion **2.** calm, impartial

dispatch *or* **despatch** (di'spach) *vt.* **1.** send off to destination or on an errand **2.** send off **3.** finish off, get done with speed **4.** *inf.* eat up **5.** kill —*n.* **6.** sending off **7.** efficient speed **8.** official message, report —**dispatch case** container for carrying official documents —**dispatch rider** horseman or motorcyclist who carries dispatches

dispel (di'spel) *vt.* clear, drive away, scatter (-ll-)

dispense (di'spens) *vt.* **1.** deal out **2.** make up (medicine) **3.** administer (justice) **4.** grant exemption from —**dis'pensable** *a.* —**dis'pensary** *n.* place where medicine is made up —**dispen'sation** *n.* **1.** act of dispensing **2.** license; exemption **3.** provision of nature or providence —**dis'penser** *n.* —**dispense with** **1.** do away with **2.** manage without

disperse (di'spərs) *v.* scatter —**dis'persal** *or* **dis'persion** *n.* —**dis'persed** *a.* **1.** scattered **2.** placed here and there

dispirited (di'spiritid) *a.* dejected, disheartened —**dis'piritedly** *adv.* —**dis'piriting** *a.*

displace (dis'plās) *vt.* **1.** move from the usual place **2.** remove from office **3.** take place of —**dis'placement** *n.* **1.** displacing **2.** weight of liquid displaced by a solid in a fluid —**displaced person** person forced from his home country, *esp.* by war *etc.*

display (di'splā) *vt.* **1.** spread out for show **2.** show, expose to view **3.** (of visual display unit *etc.*) represent (data) visually, as on cathode-ray tube screen —*n.* **4.** displaying **5.** parade **6.** show, exhibition **7.** ostentation **8.** *Electron.* device capable of representing data visually, as on cathode-ray tube screen

displease (dis'plēz) *v.* offend; annoy —**displeasure** (dis'plezhər) *n.* anger, vexation

disport (di'spört) *v.refl.* **1.** amuse oneself —*vi.* **2.** frolic, gambol

dispose (di'spōz) *vt.* **1.** arrange **2.** distribute **3.** incline **4.** adjust —*vi.* **5.** determine —**dis'posable** *a.* designed to be thrown away after use —**dis'posal** *n.* —**dis'posed** *a.* having inclination as specified (toward something) —**dispo'sition** *n.* **1.** inclination **2.** temperament **3.** arrangement **4.** plan —**dispose of** **1.** sell, get rid of **2.** have authority over **3.** deal with

dispossess (dispə'zes) *vt.* cause to give up possession (of)

disprove (dis'proōv) *vt.* to show (assertion, claim *etc.*) to be incorrect

dispute (di'spyoōt) *vi.* **1.** debate, discuss —*vt.* **2.** call in question **3.** debate, argue **4.** oppose, contest —**dis'putable** *a.* —**dis'putant** *n.* —**dispu'tation** *n.* —**dispu'tatious** *a.* argumentative, quarrelsome

disqualify (dis'kwolifī) *vt.* make ineligible, unfit for some special purpose

disquiet (dis'kwīət) *n.* **1.** anxiety, uneasiness —*vt.* **2.** cause (someone) to feel this —**dis'quietude** *n.* feeling of anxiety

disquisition (diskwi'zishən) *n.* learned or elaborate treatise, discourse or essay

disrepair (disri'pāər) *n.* state of bad repair, neglect
disrobe (dis'rōb) *v.* **1.** undress —*vt.* **2.** divest of robes
disrupt (dis'rupt) *vt.* **1.** interrupt **2.** throw into turmoil or disorder —**dis'ruption** *n.* —**dis'ruptive** *a.*
dissect (di'sekt, dī-) *vt.* **1.** cut up (body, organism) for detailed examination **2.** examine or criticize in detail —**dis'section** *n.* —**dis'sector** *n.* anatomist
dissemble (di'sembəl) *v.* **1.** conceal, disguise (feelings *etc.*) —*vt.* **2.** simulate —**dis'sembler** *n.*
disseminate (di'semināt) *vt.* spread abroad, scatter —**dissemi'nation** *n.* —**dis'seminator** *n.*
dissent (di'sent) *vi.* **1.** differ in opinion **2.** express such difference **3.** disagree with doctrine *etc.* of established church —*n.* **4.** such disagreement —**dis'sension** *n.* —**dis'senter** *n.* —**dis'sentient** *a./n.*
dissertation (disər'tāshən) *n.* **1.** written thesis **2.** formal discourse —**'dissertate** *vi.* hold forth
disservice (dis'sərvis) *n.* ill turn, wrong, injury
dissident ('disidənt) *n./a.* (one) not in agreement, *esp.* with government —**'dissidence** *n.* dissent; disagreement
dissimulate (di'simyo͞olāt) *v.* dissemble, practice deceit —**dissimu'lation** *n.* —**dis'simulator** *n.*
dissipate ('disipāt) *vt.* **1.** scatter **2.** waste, squander —**'dissipated** *a.* **1.** indulging in pleasure without restraint, dissolute **2.** scattered, wasted —**dissi'pation** *n.* **1.** scattering **2.** frivolous, dissolute way of life
dissociate (di'sōshiāt, -si-) *v.* **1.** separate —*vt.* **2.** disconnect, sever —**dissoci'ation** *n.*
dissolute ('disəlo͞ot) *a.* lax in morals
dissolution (disə'lo͞oshən) *n.* **1.** break-up **2.** termination of parliament, meeting or legal relationship **3.** destruction **4.** death
dissolve (di'zolv) *vt.* **1.** absorb or melt in fluid **2.** break up, put an end to, annul —*vi.* **3.** melt in fluid **4.** disappear, vanish **5.** break up, scatter —**dis'solvable** *a.* capable of being dissolved —**dis'solvent** *n.* thing with power to dissolve
dissonant ('disənənt) *a.* jarring, discordant —**'dissonance** *n.*
dissuade (di'swād) *vt.* advise to refrain, persuade not to do something —**dis'suasion** *n.* —**dis'suasive** *a.*
distaff ('distaf) *n.* cleft stick to hold wool *etc.* for spinning —**distaff side** maternal side, female line of family
distance ('distəns) *n.* **1.** amount of space between two things **2.** remoteness **3.** aloofness, reserve —*vt.* **4.** hold or place at distance —**'distant** *a.* **1.** far off, remote **2.** haughty, cold —**'distantly** *adv.*
distaste (dis'tāst) *n.* **1.** dislike of food or drink **2.** aversion, disgust —**dis'tasteful** *a.* unpleasant, displeasing to feelings —**dis'tastefully** *adv.* —**dis'tastefulness** *n.*
distemper (dis'tempər) *n.* **1.** disease of dogs **2.** method of painting on plaster without oil **3.** paint used for this —*vt.* **4.** paint with distemper
distend (di'stend) *v.* swell out by pressure from within, inflate —**dis'tensible** *a.* —**dis'tension** *n.*
distich ('distik) *n.* couplet
distill (dis'til) *vt.* **1.** vaporize and recondense (a liquid) **2.** purify, separate, concentrate (liquids) by this method **3.** *fig.* extract quality of —*vi.* **4.** trickle down —**'distillate** *n.* distilled liquid, *esp.* as fuel for some engines —**distil'lation** *n.* **1.** distilling **2.** process of evaporating or boiling liquid and condensing its vapor **3.** purification or separation of mixture by using different evaporation rates or boiling points of their components **4.** process of obtaining essence or extract of substance, usu. by heating in solvent **5.** distillate **6.** concentrated essence —**dis'tiller** *n.* one who distills, *esp.* manufacturer of alcoholic spirits —**dis'tillery** *n.*
distinct (di'stingkt) *a.* **1.** clear, easily seen **2.** definite **3.** separate, different —**dis'tinction** *n.* **1.** point of difference **2.** act of distinguishing **3.** eminence, repute, high honor, high quality —**dis'tinctive** *a.* characteristic —**dis'tinctly** *adv.* —**dis'tinctness** *n.*
distingué (dēstē'gā) *Fr.* distinguished; noble
distinguish (di'stinggwish) *vt.* **1.** make difference in **2.** recognize, make out **3.** honor **4.** make prominent or honored (*usu. refl.*) **5.** class —*vi.* **6.** (*usu. with* between *or* among) draw distinction, grasp difference —**dis'tinguishable** *a.* —**dis'tinguished** *a.* **1.** noble, dignified **2.** famous, eminent
distort (di'stört) *vt.* **1.** put out of shape, deform **2.** misrepresent **3.** garble, falsify —**dis'tortion** *n.*
distract (di'strakt) *vt.* **1.** draw attention of (someone) away from work *etc.* **2.** divert **3.** perplex, bewilder **4.** drive mad —**dis'traction** *n.*
distraint (di'strānt) *n.* legal seizure of goods to enforce payment —**dis'train** *vt.* —**dis'trainment** *n.*
distrait (di'strā; *Fr.* dē'stre) *a.* **1.** absent-minded **2.** abstracted
distraught (di'ströt) *a.* **1.** bewildered, crazed with grief **2.** frantic, distracted
distress (di'stres) *n.* **1.** severe trouble, mental pain **2.** severe pressure of hunger, fatigue or want **3.** *Law* distraint —*vt.* **4.** afflict, give mental pain —**dis'tressed** *a.* **1.** much troubled; upset; afflicted **2.** in financial straits; poor —**dis'tressful** *a.*
distribute (di'stribyət) *vt.* **1.** deal out, dispense **2.** spread, dispose at intervals **3.** classify —**distri'bution** *n.* —**dis'tributive** *a.* —**dis'tributor** *n.* rotary switch distributing

electricity in engine —**distributive law 1.** in arithmetic, the rule that permits the multiplier to be applied separately to each term **2.** the rule that conjunction ('and') can be applied separately to each of the 2 members of a disjunction ('either-or')

district ('distrikt) *n.* **1.** region, locality **2.** portion of territory —**District of Columbia** (kə'lumbiə) postal district of Washington, the U.S. capital. Abbrev.: **DC** (with ZIP code)

disturb (di'stərb) *vt.* trouble, agitate, unsettle, derange —**dis'turbance** *n.* —**dis'turbed** *a. Psych.* emotionally or mentally unstable —**dis'turber** *n.*

disuse (dis'yo͞os) *n.* state of being no longer used —**disused** (dis'yo͞ozd) *a.*

disyllable ('dīsiləbəl) *n.* word of two syllables —**disyl'labic** *a.*

ditch (dich) *n.* **1.** long narrow hollow dug in ground for drainage *etc.* —*v.* **2.** make ditch in **3.** run (car *etc.*) into ditch —*vt.* **4.** *sl.* abandon, discard

dither ('didhər) *vi.* **1.** be uncertain or indecisive —*n.* **2.** this state

dithyramb ('dithiram, -ramb) *n.* ancient Gr. hymn sung in honor of Dionysus —**dithy'rambic** *a.*

dittany ('ditəni) *n.* aromatic plant native to Greece

ditto ('ditō) *n.* **1.** the aforementioned; the above; the same: used in lists *etc.* to avoid repetition, and symbolized by two small marks („) placed under thing to be repeated **2.** *inf.* duplicate (*pl.* **-s**) —*adv.* **3.** in same way —*interj.* **4.** *inf.* used to avoid repeating or confirm agreement with preceding sentence —*vt.* **5.** copy; repeat (**-toing, -toed**)

ditty ('diti) *n.* simple song

diuretic (dīyə'retik) *a.* **1.** increasing the discharge of urine —*n.* **2.** substance with this property

diurnal (dī'ərnəl) *a.* **1.** daily **2.** in or of daytime **3.** taking a day

divalent (dī'vālənt) *a.* capable of combining with two atoms of hydrogen or their equivalent —**di'valency** *n.*

divan (di'van) *n.* **1.** bed, couch without back or head **2.** backless low cushioned seat

dive (dīv) *vi.* **1.** plunge under surface of water **2.** descend suddenly **3.** disappear **4.** go deep down **5.** rush or go quickly (**dove, dived, 'diving**) —*n.* **6.** act of diving **7.** *sl.* disreputable bar or club —**'diver** *n.* **1.** one who descends into deep water **2.** any of various kinds of diving bird —**dive bomber** aircraft which attacks after diving steeply —**diving bell** early diving submersible having open bottom and being supplied with compressed air —**diving board** platform or springboard from which swimmers may dive —**diving suit** waterproof suit used by divers, having heavy detachable helmet and air supply

diverge (di'vərj, dī-) *vi.* **1.** get farther apart **2.** separate —**di'vergence** *or* **di'vergency** *n.* —**di'vergent** *a.*

divers ('dīvərz) *a. obs.* some, various

diverse (dī'vərs, di-; 'dīvərs) *a.* different, varied —**di'versely** *adv.* —**diversifi'cation** *n.* —**di'versify** *vt.* **1.** make diverse or varied **2.** give variety to (**-ified, -ifying**) —**di'versity** *n.*

divert (di'vərt, dī-) *vt.* **1.** turn aside, ward off **2.** amuse, entertain —**di'version** *n.* **1.** a diverting **2.** official detour for traffic when main route is closed **3.** amusement —**di'verting** *a.*

diverticulosis (dīvərtikyoo'lōsis) *n.* the presence of pouches in the walls of the gastrointestinal tract

divertissement (di'vərtismənt) *n.* brief entertainment or diversion, usu. between acts of play

divest (dī'vest, di-) *vt.* **1.** unclothe, strip **2.** dispossess, deprive

divide (dī'vīd) *vt.* **1.** make into two or more parts, split up, separate **2.** distribute, share **3.** classify —*v.* **4.** diverge in opinion —*vi.* **5.** become separated **6.** part into two groups for voting —*n.* **7.** watershed —**dividend** ('dividend) *n.* **1.** share of profits, of money divided among creditors *etc.* **2.** number to be divided by another —**di'viders** *pl.n.* measuring compasses

divine (di'vīn) *a.* **1.** of, pert. to, proceeding from, God **2.** sacred **3.** heavenly —*n.* **4.** theologian **5.** clergyman —*vt.* **6.** guess **7.** predict, foresee, tell by inspiration or magic —**divination** (divi'nāshən) *n.* divining —**di'vinely** *adv.* —**di'viner** *n.* —**divinity** (di'viniti) *n.* **1.** quality of being divine **2.** god **3.** theology —**divining rod** forked stick said to move when held over ground where water is present (*also* **dowsing rod**)

division (di'vizhən) *n.* **1.** act of dividing **2.** part of whole **3.** barrier **4.** section **5.** political constituency **6.** difference in opinion *etc.* **7.** *Math.* method of finding how many times one number is contained in another **8.** army unit **9.** separation, disunion —**di'visible** *a.* capable of division —**di'visional** *a.* —**divisive** (di'vīsiv) *a.* causing disagreement —**divisor** (di'vīzər) *n. Math.* number which divides dividend —**division sign** symbol ÷, placed between dividend and divisor to indicate division, as in 12 ÷ 6 = 2

divorce (di'vörs) *n.* **1.** legal dissolution of marriage **2.** complete separation, disunion —*v.* **3.** separate or be separated by divorce —*vt.* **4.** separate **5.** sunder —**divorcée** *or* (*masc.*) **divorcé** (divör'sā) *n.*

divot ('divət) *n.* piece of turf

divulge (di'vulj, dī-) *vt.* reveal, let out (secret) —**di'vulgence** *n.*

divvy ('divi) *vt. inf.* (*esp. with* up) divide and share

dixie ('diksi) *n.* **1.** *inf.* (military) cooking utensil or mess tin **2.** (**D-**) southern states of

U.S.A. (*also* **'Dixieland**) —**'Dixieland** *n.* **1.** jazz derived from New Orleans tradition of playing, but with more emphasis on melody, regular rhythms *etc.* **2.** Dixie

D.I.Y. *or* **d.i.y.** do-it-yourself

dizzy ('dizi) *a.* **1.** feeling dazed, unsteady, as if about to fall **2.** causing or fit to cause dizziness, as speed *etc.* **3.** *inf.* silly —*vt.* **4.** make dizzy (**'dizzied, 'dizzying**) —**'dizzily** *adv.* —**'dizziness** *n.*

D.J. *or* **d.j.** disc jockey

djellaba *or* **djellabah** (jə'läbə) *n.* loose cloak with full sleeves and hood

Djibouti (ji'bōōti) *n.* country in Africa bounded northeast by the Gulf of Aden, southeast by Somalia and on all other sides by Ethiopia

djinni ('jēni), **djinn,** *or* **djin** (jin) *n. see* JINNI (*pl.* **djinn, djinns**)

dl deciliter

D.Litt. *or* **D.Lit.** **1.** Doctor of Letters **2.** Doctor of Literature

dm decimeter

D.Mus. *or* **DMus** Doctor of Music

DNA deoxyribonucleic acids, nucleic acids responsible for preserving the information which guides the synthesis of proteins

do[1] (dōō; *unstressed* dŏŏ, də) *vt.* **1.** perform, effect, transact, bring about, finish **2.** work at **3.** work out, solve **4.** suit **5.** cover (distance) **6.** provide, prepare **7.** *sl.* cheat, swindle **8.** frustrate —*vi.* **9.** (*oft. with* for) look after **10.** act **11.** manage **12.** work **13.** fare **14.** serve, suffice **15.** happen —*v. aux.* **16.** makes negative and interrogative sentences and expresses emphasis (**did, done, 'doing**) —*n.* **17.** *inf.* celebration, festivity —**'doer** *n.* active or energetic person —**do-gooder** *n. inf.* well-intentioned person, *esp.* naive or impractical one —**do-it-yourself** *n.* hobby of constructing and repairing things oneself —**do away with** destroy —**do up** **1.** fasten **2.** renovate —**do with** **1.** need **2.** make use of —**do without** deny oneself

do[2] (dō) *n. Mus.* **1.** in fixed system of solmization, the note C **2.** in movable do system, the first note of a major scale

do. ditto (*It.*, the same)

dobbin ('dobin) *n.* name for horse, *esp.* workhorse

Doberman pinscher ('dōbərmən 'pinchər) breed of working dog with glossy black-and-tan coat

doc (dok) *n. inf.* doctor

docile ('dosil) *a.* willing to obey, submissive —**do'cility** *n.*

dock[1] (dok) *n.* **1.** artificial enclosure near harbor for loading or repairing ships —*v.* **2.** (of vessel) put or go into dock **3.** (of spacecraft) link or be linked together in space —**'docker** *n.* one who works at docks, *esp.* loading *etc.* cargoes —**'dockyard** *n.* enclosure with docks, for building or repairing ships

dock[2] (dok) *n.* **1.** solid part of tail **2.** cut end, stump —*vt.* **3.** cut short (*esp.* tail) **4.** curtail, deduct (an amount) from

dock[3] (dok) *n.* enclosure in criminal court for prisoner

dock[4] (dok) *n.* coarse weed with broad leaves and long taproot used in folk medicine

docket ('dokit) *n.* **1.** piece of paper sent with package *etc.* with details of contents, delivery instructions *etc.* —*vt.* **2.** fix docket to

doctor ('doktər) *n.* **1.** medical practitioner **2.** one holding university's highest degree in any faculty —*vt.* **3.** treat medically **4.** repair, mend **5.** falsify (accounts *etc.*) **6.** *inf.* castrate, spay —**'doctoral** *a.* —**'doctorate** *n.*

doctrine ('doktrin) *n.* **1.** what is taught **2.** teaching of church, school or person **3.** belief, opinion, dogma —**doctri'naire** *n.* **1.** person who stubbornly applies theory without regard for circumstances —*a.* **2.** adhering to a doctrine in a stubborn, dogmatic way —**'doctrinal** *a.*

document ('dokyəmənt) *n.* **1.** piece of paper *etc.* providing information or evidence —*vt.* ('dokyəment) **2.** furnish with proofs, illustrations, certificates —**docu'mentary** *a./n. esp.* (of) type of film dealing with real life, not fiction —**documen'tation** *n.*

dodder[1] ('dodər) *vi.* totter or tremble, as with age —**'dodderer** *n.* feeble or inefficient person

dodder[2] ('dodər) *n.* any of genus of parasitic plants

dodecagon (dō'dekəgon) *n.* polygon having twelve sides

dodecahedron (dōdekə'hēdrən) *n.* solid figure having twelve plane faces

dodge (doj) *v.* **1.** avoid or attempt to avoid (blow, discovery *etc.*) as by moving quickly **2.** evade (questions) by cleverness —*n.* **3.** trick, artifice **4.** ingenious method **5.** act of dodging —**'dodger** *n.* shifty person —**'dodgy** *a. inf.* **1.** dangerous **2.** unreliable **3.** tricky

dodo ('dōdō) *n.* **1.** large extinct bird **2.** stupid or inept person (*pl.* **-s, -es**)

doe (dəʊ) *n.* female of deer, hare, rabbit —**'doeskin** *n.* **1.** skin of deer, lamb or sheep **2.** very supple leather made from this. **3.** heavy smooth cloth

doer ('dōōər) *n. see* DO[1]

does (duz) *third pers. sing., pres. ind. active of* DO[1]

doff (dof) *vt.* **1.** take off (hat, clothing) **2.** discard, lay aside

dog (dog) *n.* **1.** domestic mammal closely related to wolf with great differences in form **2.** male of wolf, fox and other animals **3.** person (in contempt, abuse or playfully) **4.** name given to various mechanical contrivances acting as holdfasts **5.** device with tooth which penetrates or grips object and detains it **6.** firedog —*vt.* **7.** follow steadily or closely (**-gg-**) —**dogged** ('dogid) *a.* persistent, resolute, tenacious —'**doggy** *a.* —'**doglike** *a.* —'**dogcart** *n.* open vehicle with crosswise back-to-back seats —**dog collar** **1.** collar for dog **2.** *inf.* clerical collar **3.** *inf.* tight-fitting necklace —**dog days** **1.** hot season of the rising of Dog Star **2.** period of inactivity —**dog-ear** *n.* **1.** turned-down corner of page in book —*vt.* **2.** turn down corners of (pages) —'**dogfight** *n.* **1.** skirmish between fighter planes **2.** savage contest characterized by disregard of rules —'**dogfish** *n.* very small species of shark —'**doghouse** *n.* **1.** kennel **2.** *inf.* disfavor (*esp. in* **in the doghouse**) —**dog in the manger** person who refuses to give up something that is of no use to him —'**dogleg** *n.* sharp bend or angle —**dog paddle** swimming stroke in which swimmer paddles his hands in imitation of swimming dog —**dog-paddle** *vi.* swim using dog paddle —**dog rose** European wild rose —**Dog Star** bright star in Sirius or Procyon —**dog tag** identification tag worn around neck by serviceperson —**dog-tired** *a. inf.* exhausted —**dog train** **C** sleigh drawn by dog team —'**dogwatch** *n.* in ships, short half-watch, 4-6, 6-8 p.m. —'**dogwood** *n.* any of various shrubs and trees —**go to the dogs** degenerate —**the dogs** greyhound race meeting

doge (dōj) *n.* formerly, chief magistrate in Venice

dogey ('dōgi) *n.* young calf

doggerel ('dogərəl) *n.* slipshod, unpoetic or trivial verse

doggo ('dogō) *adv.* —**lie doggo** *inf.* keep quiet, still, hidden

dogie ('dōgi) *n.* motherless calf (*pl.* **-gies**)

dogma ('dogmə) *n.* **1.** article of belief, *esp.* one laid down authoritatively by church **2.** body of beliefs (*pl.* **-s, -ata** (-ətə)) —**dog'matic(al)** *a.* **1.** asserting opinions with arrogance **2.** relating to dogma —**dog'matically** *adv.* —'**dogmatism** *n.* arrogant assertion of opinion —'**dogmatist** *n.* —'**dogmatize** *v.*

doily *or* **doyley** ('doili) *n.* small cloth, paper, piece of lace to place under cake, dish *etc.*

Dolby ('dolbi, 'dōl-) *n.* trade name for system used in tape recorders which reduces noise level on recorded or broadcast sound

dolce ('dōlchā) *a. Mus.* sweet

doldrums ('dōldrəmz, 'dol-) *pl.n.* **1.** state of depression, dumps **2.** region of light winds and calms near the equator

dole (dōl) *n.* **1.** charitable gift **2.** (*usu. with* the) *inf.* payment under unemployment insurance —*vt.* **3.** (*usu. with* out) deal out sparingly

doleful ('dōlfəl) *a.* dreary, mournful —'**dolefully** *adv.*

doll (dol) *n.* **1.** child's toy image of human being **2.** *sl.* attractive girl or woman —**doll up** dress up in latest fashion or smartly

dollar ('dolər) *n.* monetary unit of U.S. and many other countries —**dollar-a-year** *a.* earning token salary, usu. for public service —**dollar day** day on which seller offers goods for one dollar per item —**dollar diplomacy** the use of financial resources to enhance political transactions

dollop ('doləp) *n. inf.* semisolid lump

dolly ('doli) *n.* **1.** child's word for doll **2.** wheeled support for motion-picture or TV camera **3.** any of various metal devices used as aids in hammering, riveting

dolman sleeve ('dōlmən, 'dol-) sleeve that is wide at armhole and tapers to tight wrist

dolmen ('dōlmən, 'dol-) *n.* **1.** *see* CROMLECH (sense 1) **2.** stone table

dolomite ('dōləmīt, 'dol-) *n.* type of limestone

dolor ('dōlər, 'dol-) *n.* grief, sadness, distress —'**dolorous** *a.* —'**dolorously** *adv.*

dolphin ('dolfin) *n.* sea mammal, smaller than whale, with beaklike snout —**dolphi'narium** *n.* pool or aquarium for dolphins

dolt (dōlt) *n.* stupid fellow —'**doltish** *a.*

-dom (*comb. form*) **1.** state, condition, as in *freedom* **2.** rank, office or domain of, as in *earldom* **3.** collection of persons, as in *officialdom*

domain (də'mān) *n.* **1.** lands held or ruled over **2.** sphere, field of influence **3.** province

dome (dōm) *n.* **1.** rounded vault forming a roof **2.** something of this shape

Domesday Book ('do͞omzdā, 'dōmz-) record of survey of England in 1086

domestic (də'mestik) *a.* **1.** of, in the home **2.** home-loving **3.** (of animals) tamed, kept by man **4.** of, in one's own country, not foreign —*n.* **5.** house servant —**do'mesticate** *vt.* **1.** tame (animals) **2.** accustom to home life **3.** adapt to an environment —**domesti'cation** *n.* —**domes'ticity** *n.*

domicile ('domisīl) *n.* person's regular place of abode —'**domiciled** *a.* living —**domiciliary** (domi'silieri) *a.* of a dwelling place

dominate ('dominät) *vt.* **1.** rule, control, sway **2.** (of heights) overlook —*vi.* **3.** control, be the most powerful or influential member or part of something —'**dominant** *a./n.* —**domi'nation** *n.* —**domi'neer** *vi.* act imperiously, tyrannize

Dominica (domi'nēkə) *n.* country in Caribbean Sea in the Windward group of the West Indies located between Martinique and Guadeloupe

Dominican (də'minikən) *n.* **1.** friar or nun of the order of St. Dominic —*a.* **2.** pert. to this order

Dominican Republic country in the West Indies occupying the eastern portion of the island of Hispaniola (the western portion forming the Republic of Haiti)

dominion (də'minyən) *n.* **1.** sovereignty, rule **2.** territory of government

Dominion Day *see* **Canada Day** *at* CANADA

dominoes ('dominōz) *pl.n.* **1.** (*with sing. v.*) any of several games in which matching halves of dominoes are laid together —*sing.* **2.** small rectangular block used in dominoes, divided on one side into 2 equal areas, each either blank or marked with one to six dots **3.** cloak with eye mask for masquerading —**domino theory** theory that event in one place, *esp.* political takeover, will influence occurrence of similar events elsewhere

don[1] (don) *vt.* put on (clothes) (**-nn-**)

don[2] (don) *n.* **1.** fellow or tutor of college **2.** Sp. title, Sir —'**donnish** *a.* of or resembling university don, *esp.* denoting pedantry or fussiness

Doña ('donyə) *n.* Sp. title of address equivalent to *Mrs.* or *Madam*

donate (dō'nāt) *v.* give —**do'nation** *n.* gift to fund —'**donor** *n.*

done (dun) *pp. of* DO[1]

Donegal tweed ('donigöl) tweed with colored flecks woven into the fabric

dong (dong) *n.* **1.** imitation of sound of bell —*vi.* **2.** make such sound

Don Juan ('don 'hwän, 'wän, 'jo͞oən) **1.** legendary Sp. nobleman and philanderer **2.** successful seducer of women

donkey ('dongki) *n.* ass (*pl.* **-s**) —**donkey engine** auxiliary engine —**donkey jacket** short, thick jacket, oft. worn by workmen —**donkey's years** *inf.* a long time —**donkey-work** *n.* drudgery

Donna ('donə) *n.* It. title of address equivalent to *Madam*

Don Quixote ('don kē'hōtē, 'kwiksət) impractical idealist

doodad ('do͞odad) *n.* **1.** small item whose common name is unknown or forgotten **2.** trivial ornament

doodle ('do͞odəl) *v.* **1.** scribble absent-mindedly —*n.* **2.** picture *etc.* drawn aimlessly —'**doodlebug** *n.* **1.** *see* V-1 **2.** diviner's rod

doom (do͞om) *n.* **1.** fate, destiny **2.** ruin **3.** judicial sentence, condemnation **4.** the Last Judgment —*vt.* **5.** sentence, condemn **6.** destine to destruction or suffering —'**dooms-day** *n.* the day of the Last Judgment

door (dör) *n.* hinged or sliding barrier to close any entrance —'**doorjamb** *n.* one of two vertical members forming sides of door frame (*also* '**doorpost**) —'**doorman** *n.* man employed to attend doors of certain buildings —'**doormat** *n.* **1.** mat at entrance for wiping shoes on **2.** *sl.* person who offers little resistance to ill-treatment —'**doorstop** *n.* any device which prevents open door from moving —'**doorway** *n.* entrance with or without door —'**dooryard** *n.* yard next to house door —**door to door 1.** (of selling *etc.*) from one house to next **2.** (of journeys *etc.*) direct

dopa ('dōpə) *n.* amino acid found in the broad bean: used for the treatment of Parkinson's disease

dope (dōp) *n.* **1.** kind of varnish **2.** drug, *esp.* illegal, narcotic drug **3.** *inf.* information **4.** *inf.* stupid person —*vt.* **5.** drug (*esp.* racehorse) —'**dopey** *or* '**dopy** *a. inf.* **1.** foolish **2.** drugged **3.** half asleep —**dope out** figure out

Doppelgänger ('dopəlgengər) *n. Legend* ghostly duplicate of living person

Doppler effect ('doplər) change in apparent frequency of sound or light wave *etc.* as result of relative motion between observer and source (*also* **Doppler shift**)

Doric ('dorik) *a.* **1.** of the inhabitants of Doris, in ancient Greece, or their dialect —*n.* **2.** dialect of Dorians **3.** style of Gr. architecture **4.** rustic dialect —**Dorian** ('döriən) *a./n.* (member) of early Gr. race

dormant ('dörmənt) *a.* **1.** not active, in state of suspension **2.** sleeping —'**dormancy** *n.*

dormer ('dörmər) *n.* upright window set in sloping roof

dormitory ('dörmitöri) *n.* sleeping room with many beds —**dormitory town** town whose inhabitants travel elsewhere to work

dormouse ('dörmows) *n.* small hibernating mouselike rodent

dorp (dörp) *n.* **SA** small town

dorsal ('dörsəl) *a. Anat., zool.* of, on back

Dorset vinny ('dörsit 'vini), **Blue Dorset,** *or* **Blue vinny** hard, blue-veined cheese made from skimmed cow's milk orig. from England

dory ('döri) *n.* deep-bodied type of fish, *esp.* John Dory

dose (dōs) *n.* **1.** amount (of drug *etc.*) administered at one time **2.** *inf.* instance or period of something unpleasant, *esp.* disease —*vt.* **3.** give doses to —'**dosage** *n.* —**do'simeter** *n.* device for measuring radiation

doss (dos) *inf. n.* **1.** temporary bed —*vi.* **2.** sleep in dosshouse **3.** sleep —'**dosshouse** *n.* cheap lodging house

dossier ('dosyā) *n.* set of papers on some particular subject or event

dot[1] (dot) *n.* **1.** small spot, mark —*vt.* **2.** mark with dots **3.** sprinkle **4.** *sl.* hit (**-tt-**) —'**dotty** *a.* **1.** *sl.* crazy **2.** *sl.* (*with* about) extremely fond (of) **3.** marked with dots —**dotted swiss** sheer crisp cotton fabric with woven dots

dot[2] (dot) *n.* dowry

dote (dōt) *vi.* **1.** (*with* on *or* upon) be passionately fond (of) **2.** be silly or weak-minded —'**dotage** *n.* senility —'**dotard** *n.* —'**doting** *a.* blindly affectionate

dotterel ('dotərəl) *n.* kind of plover

dottle ('dotəl) *n.* plug of tobacco left in pipe after smoking

Douay Version (do͞o'ā) English translation of the Bible used by Roman Catholics

double ('dubəl) *a.* **1.** of two parts, layers *etc.,* folded **2.** twice as much or as many **3.** of two kinds **4.** designed for two users **5.** ambiguous **6.** deceitful —*adv.* **7.** twice **8.** to twice the amount or extent **9.** in a pair —*n.* **10.** person or thing exactly like, or mistakable for, another **11.** quantity twice as much as another **12.** sharp turn **13.** running pace *—pl.* **14.** game between 2 pairs of players *—v.* **15.** make, become double **16.** increase twofold **17.** fold in two **18.** get round, sail round (headland *etc.*) *—vi.* **19.** turn sharply **—'doubly** *adv.* **—double agent** spy employed simultaneously by two opposing sides **—double-barreled** *a.* **1.** (of gun) having two barrels **2.** serving two purposes; ambiguous **—double bass** largest and lowest-toned instrument of violin family **—double boiler** saucepan in two detachable parts in which food in upper part is cooked slowly by water boiling in lower part **—double-breasted** *a.* (of garment) having overlapping fronts **—double-check** *v.* check again; verify **—double check 1.** second examination or verification **2.** *Chess* simultaneous check from two pieces **—double chin** fold of fat under chin **—double-cross** *vt.* cheat; betray **—double-crosser** *n.* **—double dagger** character (‡) used in printing to indicate cross-reference **—double-dealing** *n.* artifice, duplicity **—double-decker** *n.* thing or structure having two decks, layers or levels **—double-edged** *a.* **1.** acting in two ways **2.** (of remark *etc.*) having two possible interpretations **3.** (of knife *etc.*) having cutting edge on either side of blade **—double entry** book-keeping system in which transaction is entered as debit in one account and as credit in another **—double exposure** accidental or deliberate repeat exposure of film, creating double image **—double helix** pair of parallel helices with common axis, *esp.* in structure of DNA molecule **—double indemnity** provision for payment of twice value of life-insurance policy in the event of accidental death **—double jeopardy** subjecting person to being tried twice for the same offense **—double-jointed** *a.* having unusually flexible joints permitting abnormal degree of motion **—double play** baseball play resulting in two players' being put out **—double pneumonia** pneumonia affecting both lungs **—double-quick** *a./adv.* very fast **—double standard** set of principles that allows greater freedom to one person or group than another **—double take** delayed reaction to a remark, situation *etc.* **—double talk 1.** rapid speech with mixture of nonsense syllables and real words; gibberish **2.** empty, deceptive or ambiguous talk **—'doublethink** *n.* accepting as true two different versions of a factual matter at the same time by disciplining the mind to ignore the inconsistency between them **—double time 1.** doubled wage rate for working on public holidays *etc.* **2.** *Mus.* two beats per bar **3.** *U.S. Army* fast march; slow running pace, keeping in step **—double or nothing** a gamble on paying twice the amount risked or nothing at all

double entendre (ăn'tăndrə) word or phrase with two meanings, one usu. indelicate

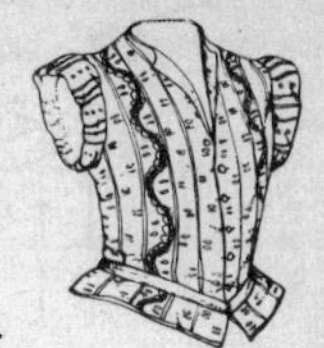

doublet

doublet ('dublit) *n.* **1.** close-fitting body garment formerly worn by men **2.** one of two words from same root but differing in form and usu. in meaning, as *warden* and *guardian* **3.** false gem of thin layer of gemstone fused on to base of glass *etc.*

doubloon (du'bloōn) *n.* ancient Sp. gold coin

doubt (dowt) *vt.* **1.** hesitate to believe **2.** call into question **3.** suspect *—vi.* **4.** be wavering or uncertain in belief or opinion *—n.* **5.** uncertainty, wavering in belief **6.** state of affairs giving cause for uncertainty **—'doubter** *n.* **—'doubtful** *a.* **—'doubtfully** *adv.* **—'doubtless** *adv./a.*

douche (dōōsh) *n.* **1.** jet or spray of water applied to (part of) body *—vt.* **2.** give douche to

dough (dō) *n.* **1.** flour or meal kneaded with water **2.** *sl.* money **—'doughy** *a.* **—'doughnut** *n.* sweetened and fried ball or ring-shaped piece of dough

doughty ('dowti) *a.* valiant **—'doughtily** *adv.* **—'doughtiness** *n.* boldness

dour (dōōər) *a.* grim, stubborn, severe

douse *or* **dowse** (dows, dowz) *vt.* **1.** thrust into water **2.** extinguish (light)

dovecote

dove (duv) *n.* bird of pigeon family **—dovecot** ('duvkot) *or* **dovecote** ('duvkōt, -kot) *n.* house for doves **—'dovetail** *n.* **1.** joint made with fan-shaped tenon *—v.* **2.** fit closely, neatly, firmly together

dowager ('dowəjər) *n.* widow with title or property derived from deceased husband

dowdy ('dowdi) *a.* **1.** unattractively or shabbily dressed *—n.* **2.** woman so dressed

dowel ('dowəl) *n.* wooden, metal peg, *esp.* joining two adjacent parts

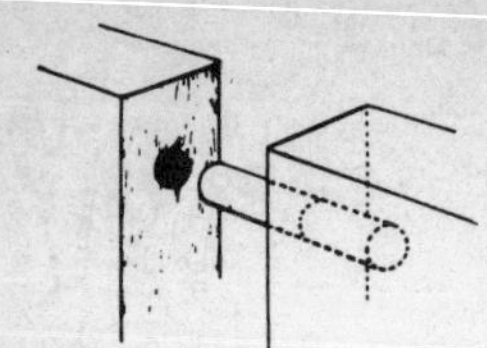

dower (ˈdowər) *n.* **1.** widow's share for life of husband's estate —*vt.* **2.** endow —ˈ**dowry** *n.* **1.** property wife brings to husband at marriage **2.** any endowment

Dow-Jones average (dowˈjōnz) *Fin.* index compiled from relative daily movement of prices of selected common stocks

down[1] (down) *adv.* **1.** to, in, or toward, lower position **2.** below the horizon **3.** (of payment) on the spot, immediate —*prep.* **4.** from higher to lower part of **5.** at lower part of **6.** along —*a.* **7.** depressed, miserable —*vt.* **8.** knock, pull, push down **9.** *inf.* drink, *esp.* quickly —ˈ**downward** *a./adv.* —ˈ**downwards** *adv.* —ˈ**downcast** *a.* **1.** dejected **2.** looking down —ˈ**downer** *n.* depressant, *esp.* barbiturate —ˈ**downfall** *n.* **1.** sudden loss of health, reputation *etc.* **2.** fall of rain, snow *etc., esp.* sudden heavy one —ˈ**downgrade** *vt.* **1.** reduce in importance or value, *esp.* to demote (person) to poorer job **2.** speak of disparagingly —*n.* **3.** *chiefly* **US** downward slope —**downˈhearted** *a.* discouraged; dejected —ˈ**downˈhill** *a.* **1.** going or sloping down —*adv.* **2.** toward bottom of hill; downward —*n.* **3.** downward slope of hill; descent **4.** skiing race downhill —**down payment** deposit paid on item purchased on hire-purchase *etc.* —ˈ**downpour** *n.* heavy fall of rain —ˈ**downright** *a.* **1.** plain, straightforward —*adv.* **2.** quite, thoroughly —ˈ**down-ˈstage** *a./adv.* at, to front of stage —ˈ**down-ˈstairs** *adv.* **1.** down the stairs; to or on lower floor —*n.* **2.** lower or ground floor **3. UK** *inf.* servants of household collectively —ˈ**down-ˈstream** *adv./a.* in or toward lower part of stream; with current —**down-to-earth** *a.* sensible; practical; realistic —ˈ**downtrodden** *a.* **1.** subjugated; oppressed **2.** trodden down —ˈ**downˈwind** *adv./a.* in same direction toward which wind is blowing; with wind from behind —**down and out** finished, defeated —**down under** *inf.* Australia and New Zealand —**go downhill** *inf.* decline; deteriorate —**have a down on** *inf.* have grudge against —**on the downgrade** waning in importance *etc.*

down[2] (down) *n.* **1.** soft underfeathers, hair or fiber **2.** fluff —ˈ**downy** *a.*

down[3] (down) *n. obs.* hill, *esp.* sand dune (*also* **downs**) —ˈ**downland** *n.* open high land (*also* **downs**)

Downing Street (ˈdowning) **1.** street in London: official residences of prime minister of Great Britain and chancellor of the exchequer **2.** *inf.* prime minister; British Government

Down's syndrome (downz) *Pathol.* chromosomal abnormality resulting in flat face and nose, short stubby fingers, vertical fold of skin at inner edge of eye and mental retardation (*also* **mongolism**)

dowry (ˈdowri) *n. see* DOWER

dowse (dowz) *vi.* use divining rod —ˈ**dowser** *n.* water diviner —**dowsing rod** divining rod

doxology (dokˈsoləji) *n.* short hymn of praise to God

doyen (ˈdoiən) *n.* senior member of a body or profession (**doyenne** (doiˈen) *fem.*)

doyley (ˈdoili) *n. see* DOILY

doz. dozen

doze (dōz) *vi.* **1.** sleep drowsily, be half-asleep —*n.* **2.** nap —ˈ**dozy** *a.* **1.** drowsy **2.** *inf.* stupid

dozen (ˈduzən) *n.* (set of) twelve

D.Phil., D.Ph., *or* **DPh** Doctor of Philosophy (*also* **Ph.D., PhD**)

Dr. 1. Doctor **2.** Drive

drab[1] (drab) *a.* **1.** dull, monotonous **2.** of a dingy brown color —*n.* **3.** mud color

drab[2] (drab) *obs. n.* **1.** slatternly woman **2.** whore —*vi.* **3.** consort with prostitutes (**-bb-**)

drachma (ˈdrakmə) *n.* monetary unit of Greece (*pl.* **-s, -mae** (-mē))

Draconian (drāˈkōniən) *a.* (*oft.* **d-**) **1.** like the laws of Draco **2.** very harsh, cruel

draft (draft, dräft) *n.* **1.** current of air between apertures in room *etc.* **2.** act or action of drawing **3.** dose of medicine **4.** act of drinking **5.** quantity drunk at once **6.** inhaling **7.** depth of ship in water **8.** the drawing in of, or fish taken in, net **9.** preliminary plan or layout for work to be executed **10.** design, sketch **11.** rough copy of document **12.** order for money **13.** detachment of men, *esp.* troops, reinforcements —*vt.* **14.** make sketch, plan or rough design of **15.** make rough copy of (writing *etc.*) **16.** select for compulsory military service —*v.* **17.** detach (military personnel) from one unit to another —*a.* **18.** for drawing **19.** drawn —ˈ**drafty** *a.* full of air currents —**draft horse** horse for vehicles carrying heavy loads —ˈ**draftsman** *n.* one who makes drawings, plans *etc.* —ˈ**draftsmanship** *n.*

drag (drag) *vt.* **1.** pull along with difficulty or friction **2.** trail on ground **3.** sweep with net or grapnels **4.** protract —*vi.* **5.** lag, trail **6.** (*oft. with* on *or* out) be tediously protracted (**-gg-**) —*n.* **7.** check on progress **8.** checked motion **9.** iron shoe to check wheel **10.** type of carriage **11.** lure for hounds to hunt **12.** kind of harrow **13.** sledge, net, grapnel, rake **14.** *inf.* tedious person or thing **15.** *sl.* women's clothes worn by man (*esp. in* **in drag**) —ˈ**dragnet** *n.* **1.** fishing net to be dragged along sea floor **2.** comprehensive search, *esp.* by police for criminal *etc.* —ˈ**dragster** *n.* automobile designed, modified for drag racing —**drag race** race where automobiles are timed over measured distance —**drag racing**

draggle (ˈdragəl) *v.* **1.** make or become wet or dirty by trailing on ground —*vi.* **2.** lag; dawdle

dragoman (ˈdragəmən) *n.* in some Middle Eastern countries, *esp.* formerly, professional interpreter or guide (*pl.* **-s, -men**)

dragon (ˈdragən) *n.* **1.** mythical fire-breathing monster, like winged crocodile **2.** type of large lizard —ˈ**dragonfly** *n.* long-bodied insect with gauzy wings

dragoon (drəˈgo͞on) *n.* **1.** cavalryman of certain regiments —*vt.* **2.** oppress **3.** coerce

drain (drān) *vt.* **1.** draw off (liquid) by pipes, ditches *etc.* **2.** dry **3.** drink to dregs **4.** empty, exhaust —*vi.* **5.** flow off or away **6.** become rid of liquid —*n.* **7.** channel for removing liquid **8.** sewer **9.** depletion, strain —ˈ**drainage** *n.* —ˈ**drainboard** *n.* sloping grooved surface at side of sink for draining washed dishes *etc.* (*also* ˈ**drainer**) —ˈ**drainpipe** *n.* pipe for carrying off rainwater *etc.* —**drainpipe trousers** *or* ˈ**drainpipes** *pl.n.* trousers with narrow legs

drake (drāk) *n.* male duck

Dralon (ˈdrālon) *n.* trade name for acrylic fiber, *esp.* as velvet for draperies and upholstery

dram (dram) *n.* **1.** small draft of strong drink **2.** *see* **fluid dram** *at* FLUID

drama (ˈdrämə) *n.* **1.** stage play **2.** art or literature of plays **3.** playlike series of events —**draˈmatic** *a.* **1.** pert. to drama **2.** suitable for stage representation **3.** with force and vividness of drama **4.** striking **5.** tense **6.** exciting —ˈ**dramatist** *n.* writer of plays —**dramatiˈzation** *n.* —ˈ**dramatize** *vt.* adapt (novel) for acting

Dramamine (ˈdraməmēn) *n.* trade name for dimenhydrinate, an antihistamine used to treat and prevent motion sickness

dramatis personae (ˈdrämətis pərˈsōnē) characters in play

dramaturgy (ˈdramətərji) *n.* technique of writing and producing plays —**dramaˈturgic(al)** *a.* —ˈ**dramaturge** *n.* playwright

Drambuie (dramˈbo͞oi) *n.* Scottish liqueur made from whisky and heather honey

drank (drangk) *pt. of* DRINK

drape (drāp) *vt.* **1.** cover, adorn with cloth **2.** arrange in graceful folds —ˈ**draper** *n.* dealer in cloth, linen *etc.* —ˈ**drapery** *n.*

drastic (ˈdrastik) *a.* **1.** extreme, forceful **2.** severe

draw (drö) *vt.* **1.** pull, pull along, haul **2.** inhale **3.** entice, attract **4.** delineate, portray with pencil *etc.* **5.** frame, compose, draft, write **6.** bring (upon, out *etc.*) **7.** get by lot **8.** (of ship) require (depth of water) **9.** take from (well, barrel *etc.*) **10.** receive (money) **11.** bend (bow) —*vi.* **12.** pull, shrink **13.** make, admit current of air **14.** make pictures with pencil *etc.* **15.** finish game with equal points, goals *etc.*, tie **16.** write orders for money **17.** come, approach (near) (**drew** *pt.*, **drawn** *pp.*) —*n.* **18.** act of drawing **19.** casting of lots **20.** game or contest ending in a tie —ˈ**drawable** *a.* —**drawer** (ˈdröər) *n.* **1.** one who or that which draws **2.** (drör) sliding box in table or chest —*pl.* (drörz) **3.** two-legged undergarment —ˈ**drawing** *n.* **1.** art of depicting in line **2.** sketch so done **3.** art of making drawings —ˈ**drawback** *n.* anything that takes away from satisfaction; snag —ˈ**drawbridge** *n.* hinged bridge that can be raised or lowered —**drawing account** money available in advance of actual earnings *esp.* for traveling expenses —**drawing room 1.** formal reception room in house **2.** private room in railroad car —ˈ**drawstring** *n.* cord *etc.* run through hem around opening, so that when it is pulled tighter, the opening closes —**draw near** approach —**draw out** lengthen —**draw up 1.** arrange **2.** stop

drawl (dröl) *v.* **1.** speak or utter (words) slowly —*n.* **2.** such speech —ˈ**drawlingly** *adv.*

drawn (drön) *v.* **1.** *pp. of* DRAW —*a.* **2.** haggard, tired or tense in appearance

dray (drā) *n.* low cart without sides for heavy loads

dread (dred) *vt.* **1.** fear greatly —*n.* **2.** awe, terror —*a.* **3.** feared, awful —ˈ**dreadful** *a.* disagreeable, shocking, bad —ˈ**dreadnought** *n.* large battleship mounting heavy guns

dream (drēm) *n.* **1.** vision during sleep **2.** fancy **3.** reverie **4.** aspiration **5.** very pleasant idea, person, thing —*vi.* **6.** have dreams —*vt.* **7.** see, imagine in dreams **8.** think of as possible (**dreamt** (dremt) *or* **dreamed** *pt./pp.*) —ˈ**dreamer** *n.* —ˈ**dreamless** *a.* —ˈ**dreamy** *a.* **1.** given to daydreams, unpractical, vague **2.** *inf.* wonderful

dreary (ˈdrēəri) *a.* dismal, dull —**drear** *a. Lit.* dreary —ˈ**drearily** *adv.* —ˈ**dreariness** *n.* gloom

dreck (drek) *n. inf.* cheap, worthless trash

dredge[1] (drej) *v.* **1.** bring up (mud *etc.*) from sea bottom **2.** deepen (channel) by dredge —*vt.* **3.** search for, produce (obscure, remote, unlikely material) —*n.* **4.** form of scoop or grab —ˈ**dredger** *n.* ship for dredging

dredge[2] (drej) *vt.* sprinkle with flour *etc.* —ˈ**dredger** *n.*

dregs (dregz) *pl.n.* **1.** sediment, grounds **2.** worthless part

drench (drench) *vt.* **1.** wet thoroughly, soak **2.** make (animal) take dose of medicine —*n.* **3.** soaking **4.** dose for animal

Dresden (ˈdrezdən) *n.* **1.** city in East Germany **2.** delicate and decorative porcelain ware made near Dresden (*also* **Dresden china**) —*a.* **3.** of Dresden china

dress (dres) *vt.* **1.** clothe **2.** array for show **3.** trim, smooth, prepare surface of **4.** prepare (food) for table **5.** put dressing on (wound) **6.** align (troops) —*vi.* **7.** put on one's clothes **8.**

form in proper line —*n.* **9.** one-piece garment for woman **10.** clothing **11.** clothing for ceremonial evening wear —'**dresser** *n.* **1.** one who dresses, *esp.* actors or actresses **2.** surgeon's assistant **3.** kitchen sideboard —'**dressing** *n.* **1.** something applied to something else, as sauce to food, ointment to wound, manure to land *etc.* **2.** *inf.* scolding, as in *dressing down* —'**dressy** *a.* **1.** stylish **2.** fond of dress —**dress coat** cutaway coat worn by men as evening dress —**dressing room** room, *esp.* one in theater for changing costumes and make-up —**dressing station** *Mil.* first-aid post close to combat area —**dressing table** —'**dressmaker** *n.* —**dress rehearsal 1.** last rehearsal of play *etc.* using costumes *etc.* as for first night **2.** any full-scale practice —**dress suit** man's evening suit, *esp.* tails

dressage (drə'säzh) *n.* method of training horse in special maneuvers to show obedience

drew (droo͞) *pt. of* DRAW

dribble ('dribəl) *v.* **1.** (allow to) flow in drops, trickle **2.** work (basketball) forward with continuous bounces —*vi.* **3.** run at the mouth —*n.* **4.** trickle, drop —'**driblet** *n.* small portion or installment

dried (drīd) *pt./pp. of* DRY

drier ('drīər) *comp. of* DRY

driest ('drīist) *sup. of* DRY

drift (drift) *vi.* **1.** be carried as by current of air, water **2.** move aimlessly or passively —*n.* **3.** process of being driven by current **4.** slow current or course **5.** deviation from course **6.** tendency **7.** meaning **8.** wind-heaped mass of snow, sand *etc.* **9.** material driven or carried by water —'**drifter** *n.* **1.** one who, that which drifts **2.** *inf.* aimless person with no fixed job *etc.* —'**driftwood** *n.* wood washed ashore by sea

drill[1] (dril) *n.* **1.** boring tool or machine **2.** exercise of soldiers or others in handling of arms and maneuvers **3.** routine teaching —*v.* **4.** bore, pierce (hole) in (material) (as if) with drill **5.** exercise in military and other routine —*vi.* **6.** practice routine

drill[2] (dril) *n.* **1.** machine for sowing seed **2.** small furrow for seed **3.** row of plants —*v.* **4.** sow (seed) in drills or furrows

drill[3] (dril) *n.* coarsely woven twilled fabric

drill[4] (dril) *n.* W Afr. monkey

drink (dringk) *v.* **1.** swallow (liquid) **2.** take (intoxicating liquor), *esp.* to excess —*vt.* **3.** absorb (**drank** *pt.*, **drunk** *pp.*) —*n.* **4.** liquid for drinking **5.** portion of this **6.** act of drinking **7.** intoxicating liquor or excessive consumption of it —'**drinkable** *a.* —'**drinker** *n.* —**drink to** *or* **drink the health of** express good wishes *etc.* by drinking a toast to

drip (drip) *v.* **1.** fall or let fall in drops (**-pp-**) —*n.* **2.** act of dripping **3.** drop **4.** *Med.* intravenous administration of solution **5.** *inf.* dull, insipid person —'**dripping** *n.* **1.** melted fat that drips from roasting meat —*a.* **2.** very wet —**drip-dry** *a.* (of fabric) drying free of creases if hung up while wet —'**dripstone** *n.* projection over window or door to stop dripping of water

drive (drīv) *vt.* **1.** urge in some direction **2.** make move and steer (vehicle, animal *etc.*) **3.** urge, impel **4.** fix by blows, as nail **5.** chase **6.** convey in vehicle **7.** hit (ball) with force as in golf, tennis —*vi.* **8.** keep machine, animal going, steer it **9.** be conveyed in vehicle **10.** rush, dash, drift fast (**drove, driven** ('drivən), '**driving**) —*n.* **11.** act, action of driving **12.** journey in vehicle **13.** private road leading to house **14.** capacity for getting things done **15.** united effort, campaign **16.** means by which automobile is propelled **17.** forceful stroke or sustained effort —'**driver** *n.* **1.** one that drives **2.** *Golf* club used for tee shots —**drive-in** *a.* **1.** denoting public facility or service designed for use by patrons in cars —*n.* **2.** establishment designed to be used in such a manner —**driver's license** official document authorizing person to drive motor vehicle —'**driveway** *n.* path for vehicles, oft. connecting house with public road —**driving belt** belt that communicates motion to machinery

drivel ('drivəl) *vi.* **1.** run at mouth or nose **2.** talk nonsense —*n.* **3.** silly or senseless talk —'**driveler** *n.*

drizzle ('drizəl) *vi.* **1.** rain in fine drops —*n.* **2.** fine, light rain

drogue (drōg) *n.* **1.** any funnel-like device, *esp.* of canvas, used as sea anchor **2.** small parachute **3.** wind indicator **4.** windsock towed behind target aircraft **5.** funnel-shaped device on end of refueling hose of tanker aircraft to receive probe of aircraft being refueled

droll (drōl) *a.* funny, odd, comical —'**drollery** *n.* —'**drolly** *adv.*

dromedary ('droməderi, 'drum-) *n.* one-humped camel bred *esp.* for racing

drone (drōn) *n.* **1.** male of honey bee **2.** lazy idler **3.** deep humming **4.** bass pipe of bagpipe **5.** its note —*vi.* **6.** hum **7.** talk in monotonous tone

drongo ('dronggō) *n.* black tropical bird

drool (droo͞l) *vi.* slaver, drivel

droop (droo͞p) *vi.* **1.** hang down **2.** wilt, flag —*vt.* **3.** let hang down —*n.* **4.** drooping condition —'**droopy** *a.*

drop (drop) *n.* **1.** globule of liquid **2.** very small quantity **3.** fall, descent **4.** distance through which thing falls **5.** thing that falls, as gallows platform —*vt.* **6.** let fall **7.** let fall in drops **8.** utter casually **9.** set down, unload **10.** discontinue —*vi.* **11.** fall **12.** fall in drops **13.** lapse **14.** come or go casually (**-pp-**) —'**droplet** *n.* —'**dropper** *n.* **1.** small tube having bulb at one end for dispensing drops of liquid **2.** person or thing that drops —'**droppings** *pl.n.* dung of rabbits, sheep, birds *etc.* —'**dropout** *n.* person who fails to complete course of study or one who rejects conventional society

dropsy ('dropsi) *n. see* EDEMA —'**dropsical** *a.*

droshky ('droshki) *or* **drosky** ('droski) *n.* open four-wheeled carriage, formerly used in Russia

dross (dros) *n.* **1.** scum of molten metal **2.** impurity, refuse **3.** anything of little or no value

drought (drowt) *n.* long spell of dry weather

drove[1] (drōv) *pt. of* DRIVE

drove[2] (drōv) *n.* **1.** herd, flock, crowd, *esp.* in motion —*v.* **2.** drive (cattle *etc.*) *esp.* a long distance —'**drover** *n.* driver of cattle

drown (drown) *v.* **1.** die from suffocation caused by water in the lungs —*vt.* **2.** get rid of as by submerging in liquid **3.** (*sometimes with* out) make (sound) inaudible by louder sound

drowsy ('drowzi) *a.* **1.** half asleep **2.** lulling **3.** dull —**drowse** *v.* —'**drowsily** *adv.* —'**drowsiness** *n.*

drub (drub) *vt.* thrash, beat (**-bb-**) —'**drubbing** *n.* beating

drudge (druj) *vi.* **1.** work at menial or distasteful tasks, slave —*n.* **2.** one who drudges, hack —'**drudgery** *n.*

drug (drug) *n.* **1.** substance used in the treatment of disease **2.** narcotic **3.** commodity which is unsalable because of overproduction —*vt.* **4.** mix drugs with **5.** administer drug to, *esp.* one inducing unconsciousness (**-gg-**) —**drug abuse** compulsive use of substances capable of causing harm, *esp.* narcotics, stimulants, chemical solvents —**drug addict** person abnormally dependent on drugs —'**drugstore** *n.* pharmacy where wide variety of goods is available

drugget ('drugit) *n.* coarse woolen fabric, *esp.* used for carpeting

druid ('drōōid) *n.* (*sometimes* **D-**) **1.** member of ancient order of Celtic priests **2.** Eisteddfod official —**dru'idic(al)** *a.* —'**druidism** *n.*

drum (drum) *n.* **1.** percussion instrument of skin stretched over round hollow frame, played by beating with sticks **2.** any of various things shaped like drum **3.** eardrum —*vi.* **4.** play drum —*v.* **5.** tap, thump continuously (**-mm-**) —'**drummer** *n.* one who plays drum —'**drumfire** *n.* heavy continuous rapid artillery fire —**drum major** leader of marching band —**drum majorette** (māje'ret) **1.** girl or woman who leads a marching band **2.** baton twirler accompanying a marching band —'**drumstick** *n.* **1.** stick for beating drum **2.** lower joint of cooked fowl's leg —**drum out** expel (from club *etc.*) —**drum up** obtain (support *etc.*) by solicitation or canvassing

drunk (drungk) *a.* **1.** overcome by strong drink **2.** *fig.* overwhelmed by strong emotion —*v.* **3.** *pp. of* DRINK —'**drunkard** *n.* one given to excessive drinking —'**drunken** *a.* **1.** intoxicated **2.** habitually drunk **3.** caused by, showing intoxication —'**drunkenness** *n.*

drupe (drōōp) *n.* fruit that has fleshy or fibrous part around stone that encloses seed, as peach *etc.*

dry (drī) *a.* **1.** without moisture **2.** rainless **3.** not yielding milk or other liquid **4.** cold, unfriendly **5.** caustically witty **6.** having prohibition of alcoholic drink **7.** uninteresting **8.** needing effort to study **9.** lacking sweetness (as wines) **10.** (of fruit) without fleshy walls, *eg* peas, beans, nuts —*vt.* **11.** remove water, moisture from —*vi.* **12.** become dry **13.** evaporate (**dried, 'drying**) —'**dryer** *or* '**drier** *n.* **1.** person or thing that dries **2.** apparatus for removing moisture —'**dryly** *or* '**drily** *adv.* —'**dryness** *n.* —**dry battery** electric battery without liquid —**dry cell** primary cell in which electrolyte is in form of paste or is treated in some way to prevent spilling —**dry-clean** *vt.* clean (clothes) with solvent other than water —**dry-cleaner** *n.* —**dry dock** dock that can be pumped dry for work on ship's bottom —**dry farming** methods of producing crops in areas of low rainfall —**dry fly** *Angling* artificial fly designed to be floated on surface of water —**dry ice** solid carbon dioxide —**dry measure** unit or system of units for measuring dry goods, such as grains *etc.* —**dry point 1.** needle for engraving without acid **2.** engraving so made —**dry rot** fungoid decay in wood —**dry run** practice, rehearsal in simulated conditions —**drystone** *a.* (of wall) made without mortar —**dry out 1.** make or become dry **2.** *inf.* (cause to) undergo treatment for alcoholism or drug addiction

dryad ('drīəd, -ad) *n.* wood nymph

dryly ('drīli) *adv. see* DRY

D.Sc. Doctor of Science

D.S.C. Distinguished Service Cross

D.S.M. *Mil.* Distinguished Service Medal

D.S.O. Distinguished Service Order

D.T.'s *inf.* delirium tremens

dual ('dyōōəl, 'dōō-) *a.* **1.** twofold **2.** of two, double, forming pair —'**dualism** *n.* recognition of two independent powers or principles, *eg* good and evil, mind and matter —**du'ality** *n.*

dub (dub) *vt.* **1.** confer knighthood on **2.** give title to **3.** provide (motion picture) with soundtrack not in original language **4.** smear with grease, dubbin (**-bb-**) —'**dubbin** *or* '**dubbing** *n.* grease for making leather supple

dubious ('dyōōbiəs, 'dōō-) *a.* **1.** causing doubt, not clear or decided **2.** of suspect character —**du'biety** *n.* uncertainty, doubt

ducal ('dyōōkəl, 'dōō-) *a.* of duke or duchy

ducat ('dukət) *n.* former gold coin of Italy *etc.*

duchess ('duchis) *n.* duke's wife, ex-wife or widow

duchy ('duchi) *n.* territory of duke, dukedom

duck[1] (duk) *n.* **1.** common swimming bird (**drake** *masc.*) —*v.* **2.** plunge (someone) under water **3.** bob down —'**duckling** *n.* —**duck-billed platypus** aquatic burrowing egg-laying mammal of Aust. and Tasmania with dense fur, bony ducklike beak and flattened tail —'**duckweed** *n.* plant that floats on ponds *etc.*

duck[2] (duk) *n.* **1.** strong linen or cotton fabric —*pl.* **2.** trousers made of this fabric

duck[3] (duk) *n.* amphibious vehicle used in World War II

duct (dukt) *n.* channel, tube —**ductile** ('duktil) *a.* **1.** capable of being drawn into wire **2.** flexible and tough **3.** docile —**duc'tility** *n.* —'**ductless** *a.* (of glands) secreting directly certain substances essential to health

dud (dud) *n.* **1.** futile, worthless person or thing **2.** shell that fails to explode —*a.* **3.** worthless

dude (dyōōd, dōōd) *n.* tourist, *esp.* in ranch district —**dude ranch** ranch serving as guesthouse and showplace

dudgeon ('dujən) *n.* anger, indignation, resentment

duds (dudz) *pl.n. inf.* clothes

due (dyōō, dōō) *a.* **1.** owing **2.** proper to be given, inflicted *etc.* **3.** adequate, fitting **4.** under engagement to arrive, be present **5.** timed (for) —*adv.* **6.** (with points of compass) exactly —*n.* **7.** person's right **8.** (*usu. pl.*) charge, fee *etc.* —'**duly** *adv.* **1.** properly **2.** fitly **3.** rightly **4.** punctually —**due to 1.** attributable to **2.** caused by

duel ('dyōōəl, 'dōōəl) *n.* **1.** arranged fight with deadly weapons, between two persons **2.** keen two-sided contest —*vi.* **3.** fight in duel —'**duelist** *or* '**duellist** *n.*

duenna (dyōō'enə, dōō-) *n.* older woman acting as companion and chaperone, *esp.* to younger woman in Spanish or Portuguese household

duet (dyōō'et, dōō-) *n.* piece of music for two performers —**du'ettist** *n.*

duff[1] (duf) *n.* kind of boiled pudding

duff[2] (duf) *vt.* **1.** manipulate, alter (article) so as to make it look like new **2.** mishit, *esp.* at golf —*a.* **3.** *sl.* bad, useless

duffel *or* **duffle** ('dufəl) *n.* **1.** coarse woolen cloth **2.** coat made of this —**duffel bag** large cylindrical cloth bag for clothing *etc.*

duffer ('dufər) *n.* stupid inefficient person

dug[1] (dug) *pt./pp. of* DIG

dug[2] (dug) *n.* udder, teat of animal

dugong ('dōōgong) *n.* whalelike mammal of tropical seas

dugout ('dugowt) *n.* **1.** covered excavation to provide shelter for troops *etc.* **2.** canoe of hollowed-out tree **3.** *Sport* covered enclosure where players wait when not on the field

duiker *or* **duyker** ('dīkər) *n.* small Afr. antelope (*also* '**duikerbok**)

duke (dyōōk, dōōk) *n.* **1.** nobleman of high rank **2.** sovereign of small state called duchy ('**duchess** *fem.*) —'**dukedom** *n.*

dukes (dyōōks, dōōks) *pl.n. sl.* fists

dulcet ('dulsit) *a.* (of sounds) sweet, melodious

dulcimer ('dulsimər) *n.* percussion instrument consisting of set of strings stretched over sounding board, played with two hammers

dull (dul) *a.* **1.** stupid **2.** insensible **3.** sluggish **4.** tedious **5.** lacking liveliness or variety **6.** gloomy, overcast —*v.* **7.** make or become dull —'**dullard** *n.* —'**dully** *adv.*

duly ('dyōōli, 'dōō-) *adv. see* DUE

dumb (dum) *a.* **1.** incapable of speech **2.** silent **3.** *inf.* stupid —'**dumbly** *adv.* —'**dumbness** *n.* —'**dumbbell** *n.* weight for exercises —**dumb'found** *vt.* confound into silence —**dumb show** acting without words —'**dumbwaiter** *n.* **1.** stand placed near dining table to hold food; revolving circular tray placed on table to hold food **2.** small elevator, usu. hand-operated, for conveying food and dishes between floors

dumdum ('dumdum) *n.* soft-nosed expanding bullet

dummy ('dumi) *n.* **1.** tailor's or dressmaker's model **2.** imitation object **3.** bridge hand exposed on table and played by partner **4.** one secretly acting for another **5.** figure used by football players for tackling practice **6.** prototype of book, indicating appearance of finished product; designer's layout of page —*a.* **7.** sham, bogus —**dummy run** experimental run; practice; rehearsal

dump (dump) *vt.* **1.** throw down in mass **2.** deposit **3.** unload **4.** send (low-priced goods) for sale abroad —*n.* **5.** refuse heap **6.** *inf.* dirty, unpleasant place **7.** temporary depot of stores or munitions —*pl.* **8.** low spirits, dejection

dumpling ('dumpling) *n.* small round pudding of dough, oft. fruity —'**dumpy** *a.* short, stout —**dumpy level** surveyor's leveling instrument

dun[1] (dun) *vt.* **1.** persistently press (debtor) for payment of debts (**-nn-**) —*n.* **2.** one who duns

dun[2] (dun) *a.* **1.** of dull grayish brown —*n.* **2.** this color **3.** horse of this color

dunce (duns) *n.* slow learner, stupid pupil

dunderhead ('dundərhed) *n.* blockhead —'**dunderheaded** *a.*

dune (dyōōn, dōōn) *n.* sand hill on coast or in desert

dung (dung) *n.* **1.** excrement of animals; manure —*vt.* **2.** manure (ground) —'**dunghill** *n.* **1.** heap of dung **2.** foul place, condition or person

dungaree (dunggə'rē) *n.* **1.** coarse cotton fabric —*pl.* **2.** overalls made of this material

dungeon (ˈdunjən) *n.* **1.** underground cell or vault for prisoners, donjon **2.** formerly, tower or keep of castle

dunk (dungk) *vt.* **1.** dip (bread *etc.*) in liquid before eating it **2.** submerge

dunlin (ˈdunlin) *n.* small sandpiper

dunnage (ˈdunij) *n.* material for packing cargo

dunnock (ˈdunək) *n.* hedge sparrow

duo (ˈdyo͞oō, ˈdo͞oō) *n.* pair of performers (*pl.* **-s, dui** (ˈdyo͞oē, ˈdo͞oē))

duodecimo (dyo͞oōˈdesimō, do͞oō-) *n.* **1.** size of book in which each sheet is folded into 12 leaves **2.** book of this size (*pl.* **-s**) *—a.* **3.** of this size —**duoˈdecimal** *a.* —**duodecimal system** numeration system whose base is 12, the numbers 10 and 11 being denoted by special symbols and regarded as digits

duodenum (dyo͞oōˈdēnəm, do͞oō-) *n.* upper part of small intestine —**duoˈdenal** *a.*

duologue (ˈdyo͞oəlog, ˈdo͞o-) *n.* **1.** part or all of play in which speaking roles are limited to two actors **2.** *rare* dialogue

dupe (dyo͞op, do͞op) *n.* **1.** victim of delusion or sharp practice *—vt.* **2.** deceive for advantage, impose upon

duple (ˈdyo͞opəl, ˈdo͞o-) *a.* **1.** *rare* double **2.** *Mus.* (of time or music) having two beats in bar

duplex (ˈdyo͞opleks, ˈdo͞o-) *a.* **1.** twofold *—n.* **2.** apartment on two floors

duplicate (ˈdyo͞oplikāt, ˈdo͞o-) *vt.* **1.** make exact copy of **2.** double *—a.* (ˈdyo͞oplikit, ˈdo͞o-) **3.** double **4.** exactly the same as something else *—n.* (ˈdyo͞oplikit, ˈdo͞o-) **5.** exact copy —**dupliˈcation** *n.* —ˈ**duplicator** *n.* machine for making copies —**duˈplicity** *n.* deceitfulness, double-dealing, bad faith

durable (ˈdyŏŏrəbəl, ˈdŏŏ-) *a.* lasting, resisting wear —**duraˈbility** *n.* —ˈ**durably** *adv.* —**durable goods** goods that require infrequent replacement (*also* ˈ**durables**)

dura mater (ˈdyŏŏrə ˈmātər, ˈdŏŏrə) outermost and toughest of three membranes covering brain and spinal cord (*also* ˈ**dura**)

durance (ˈdyŏŏrəns, ˈdŏŏ-) *n. obs.* imprisonment

duration (dyŏŏˈrāshən, dŏŏ-) *n.* length of time something lasts

durbar (ˈdərbär, dərˈbär) *n.* formerly, court of native ruler or governor in India or levée at such court

duress (dyŏŏˈres, dŏŏ-) *n.* compulsion by use of force or threats

during (ˈdyŏŏəring, ˈdŏŏ-) *prep.* throughout, in the time of, in the course of

durst (dərst) *obs. pt. of* DARE

dusk (dusk) *n.* **1.** darker stage of twilight **2.** partial darkness —ˈ**duskily** *adv.* —ˈ**dusky** *a.* **1.** dark **2.** dark-colored

dust (dust) *n.* **1.** fine particles, powder of earth or other matter, lying on surface or blown along by wind **2.** ashes of the dead *—vt.* **3.** sprinkle with powder **4.** rid of dust —ˈ**duster** *n.* **1.** cloth for removing dust **2.** woman's lightweight coat —ˈ**dusty** *a.* covered with dust —ˈ**dustbowl** *n.* region stripped of vegetation by drought and erosion —**dust cover 1.** large cloth used to protect furniture from dust (*also* ˈ**dustsheet**) **2.** removable paper cover to protect bound book (*also* **dust jacket**) —ˈ**dustpan** *n.* short-handled hooded shovel for sweepings —**dust-up** *n. inf.* fight; argument —**dust up** attack

Dutch (duch) *a.* pert. to the Netherlands, its inhabitants or its language —**Dutch auction** auction method in which item is offered at high price and gradually reduced until buyer is found —**Dutch courage** drunken bravado —**Dutch elm disease** fungal disease of elm trees characterized by withering of foliage and stems —**Dutch oven 1.** iron or earthenware container with cover, used for stews *etc.* **2.** metal box, open in front, for cooking in front of open fire —**Dutch treat** meal *etc.* where each person pays his own share —**Dutch uncle** *inf.* person who criticizes or reproves frankly and severely —**in Dutch** in trouble

duty (ˈdyo͞oti, ˈdo͞o-) *n.* **1.** moral or legal obligation **2.** that which is due **3.** tax on goods **4.** military service **5.** one's proper employment —ˈ**duteous** *a.* —ˈ**dutiable** *a.* liable to customs duty —ˈ**dutiful** *a.* —**duty-bound** *a.* morally obliged —**duty-free** *a./adv.* with exemption from customs or excise duties

D.V. *Deo volente*

dwarf (dwörf) *n.* **1.** very undersized person **2.** mythological, small, manlike creature (*pl.* **-s, dwarves**) *—a.* **3.** unusually small, stunted *—vt.* **4.** make seem small by contrast **5.** make stunted —ˈ**dwarfish** *a.* —ˈ**dwarfism** *n.* abnormally small stature, commonly caused by disease of bones or glands

dwell (dwel) *vi.* **1.** live, make one's abode (in) **2.** fix one's attention, write or speak at length (on) (**dwelt** *pt./pp.*) —ˈ**dweller** *n.* —ˈ**dwelling** *n.* house

dwindle (ˈdwindəl) *vi.* grow less, waste away, decline

Dy *Chem.* dysprosium

Dyak (ˈdīak) *n. see* DAYAK

dye (dī) *vt.* **1.** impregnate (cloth *etc.*) with coloring matter **2.** color thus (**dyed,** ˈ**dyeing**) *—n.* **3.** coloring matter in solution or which may be dissolved for dyeing **4.** tinge, color —ˈ**dyeing** *n.* process or industry of coloring yarns *etc.* —ˈ**dyer** *n.* —**dyed-in-the-wool** *a.* **1.** extreme or unchanging in opinion *etc.* **2.** (of fabric) made of dyed yarn

dying (ˈdīing) *v.* **1.** *pr.p. of* DIE[1] *—a.* **2.** relating to or occurring at moment of death

dyke[1] (dīk) *n. see* DIKE

dyke[2] (dīk) *n. offens.* lesbian

dynamics (dīˈnamiks) *pl.n.* **1.** (*with sing. v.*) branch of physics dealing with force as producing or affecting motion **2.** physical forces —**dyˈnamic** *a.* **1.** of, relating to motive force, force in operation **2.** energetic and forceful **—dy'namical** *a.* **—dy'namically** *adv.* **—'dynamism** *n.* **1.** *Philos.* theory that attempts to explain phenomena in terms of immanent force or energy **2.** forcefulness of energetic personality

dynamite ('dīnəmīt) *n.* **1.** high-explosive mixture *—vt.* **2.** blow up with this **—'dynamiter** *n.*

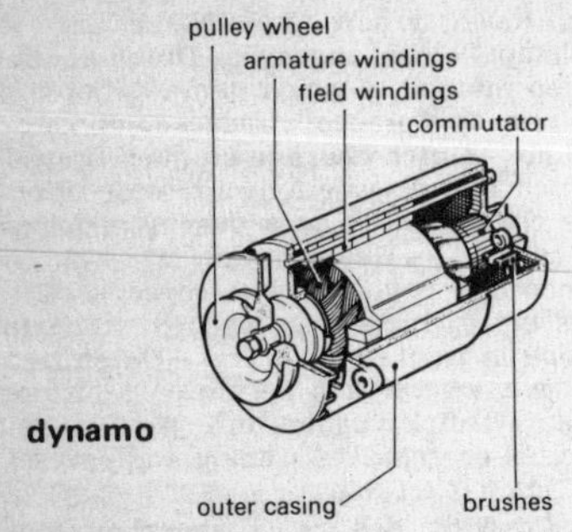

dynamo ('dīnəmō) *n.* **1.** machine to convert mechanical into electrical energy, generator of electricity **2.** *inf.* energetic, hard-working person (*pl.* **-s**) **—dyna'mometer** *n.* instrument to measure energy expended

dynasty ('dīnəsti) *n.* line, family, succession of hereditary rulers **—'dynast** *n.* **—dy'nastic** *a.* of dynasty

dyne (dīn) *n.* cgs unit of force

Dynel ('dīnəl) *n.* trade name for acrylic fiber

dys- (*comb. form*) **1.** diseased; abnormal **2.** difficult; painful **3.** bad

dysentery ('disənteri) *n.* painful inflammation of large intestine usu. with severe diarrhea

dysfunction (dis'fungkshən) *n.* abnormal, impaired functioning, *esp.* of bodily organ

dyslexia (dis'leksiə) *n.* impaired ability to read **—dys'lexic** *a.*

dysmenorrhea (dismenə'rēə) *n.* abnormally painful menstruation

dyspepsia (dis'pepsiə) *n.* indigestion **—dys'peptic** *a./n.*

dysprosium (dis'prōziəm) *n. Chem.* metallic element *Symbol* Dy, at. wt. 162.5, at. no. 66

dystrophy ('distrəfi) *n.* wasting of body tissues, *esp.* muscles

dz. dozen

Dzhudesmo (jōō'dezmō) *n.* *see* LADINO (sense 1)

E

e *or* **E** (ē) *n.* **1.** fifth letter of English alphabet **2.** any of several speech sounds represented by this letter, as in *he, bet* (*pl.* **e's, E's** *or* **Es**)

e 1. *Math.* transcendental number used as base of natural logarithms **2.** electron

E 1. *Mus.* third note of scale of C major; major or minor key having this note as its tonic **2.** *Phys.* energy; electromotive force **3.** East **4.** Eastern **5.** English **6.** Egypt(ian)

e. engineer(ing)

ea. each

each (ēch) *a./pron.* every (one) taken separately

eager ('ēgər) *a.* **1.** having a strong wish (for something) **2.** keen, anxious or impatient —'**eagerly** *adv.* —'**eagerness** *n.* —**eager beaver** *inf.* person who displays conspicuous diligence

eagle ('ēgəl) *n.* **1.** large bird with keen sight which preys on small birds and animals **2.** *Golf* score of two strokes under par for a hole —'**eaglet** *n.* young eagle —**eagle-eyed** *a.* having keen eyesight

ear[1] (ēər) *n.* **1.** organ of hearing and balance **2.** external part of it **3.** sense of hearing **4.** sensitiveness to sounds **5.** attention —'**earache** *n.* acute pain in ear —'**eardrum** *n. see* **tympanic membrane** *at* TYMPANUM —**ear duster** baseball pitched close to or at the batter's head —'**earmark** *vt.* **1.** assign, reserve for definite purpose **2.** make identification mark on ear of (sheep *etc.*) —*n.* **3.** any distinguishing mark —'**earmuffs** *pl.n.* ear coverings for protection against cold or noise —'**earphone** *n.* receiver for radio *etc.* held to or put in ear —'**earring** *n.* ornament for lobe of ear —'**earshot** *n.* hearing distance —'**earsplitting** *a.* piercingly loud —**ear trumpet** trumpet-shaped instrument formerly used as hearing aid —'**earwig** *n.* small insect with pincerlike tail —**be all ears** listen closely —**be up to the ears (in something)** *inf.* be deeply involved (in something) —**have one's ear to the ground** be alert to trends

ear[2] (ēər) *n.* spike, head of corn

earl (ərl) *n.* Brit. nobleman ranking next below marquis —'**earldom** *n.* his domain, title

early ('ərli) *a./adv.* **1.** before expected or usual time **2.** in first part, near or nearer beginning of some portion of time —**early bird** *inf.* one who arrives or rises early

earn (ərn) *vt.* **1.** obtain by work or merit **2.** gain —'**earnings** *pl.n.*

earnest[1] ('ərnist) *a.* **1.** serious, ardent **2.** sincere —'**earnestly** *adv.* —**in earnest** serious, determined

earnest[2] ('ərnist) *n.* **1.** money paid over in token to bind bargain, pledge **2.** pledge

earth (ərth) *n.* **1.** planet or world we live on **2.** ground, dry land **3.** mold, soil, mineral **4.** fox's hole **5.** wire connecting electrical apparatus to earth —*vt.* **6.** cover with earth **7.** connect electrically with earth —'**earthen** *a.* made of clay or earth —'**earthly** *a.* possible, feasible —'**earthy** *a.* **1.** of earth **2.** uninhibited **3.** vulgar —**earth closet** toilet in which earth is used to cover excreta —'**earthenware** *n.* porous white ceramic ware to which a shiny glaze is fused —'**earthquake** *n.* convulsion of earth's surface —**earth science** any of various sciences, such as geology, concerned with structure *etc.* of the earth —'**earthwork** *n.* bank of earth in fortification —'**earthworm** *n.* terrestrial annelid that burrows in soil —**come back** *or* **down to earth** return to reality from fantasy

ease (ēz) *n.* **1.** comfort **2.** freedom from constraint, annoyance, awkwardness, pain or trouble **3.** idleness —*v.* **4.** make or become less burdensome **5.** give bodily or mental ease to **6.** (cause to) move carefully or gradually —*vt.* **7.** slacken **8.** relieve of pain —'**easement** *n.* *Law* right of way *etc.* over another's land —'**easily** *adv.* —'**easiness** *n.* **1.** quality or condition of being easy to accomplish *etc.* **2.** ease or relaxation of manner —'**easy** *a.* **1.** not difficult **2.** free from pain, care, constraint or anxiety **3.** compliant **4.** characterized by low demand **5.** fitting loosely **6.** *inf.* having no preference for any particular course of action —**easy chair** comfortable upholstered armchair —**easy-going** *a.* **1.** not fussy **2.** indolent

easel ('ēzəl) *n.* frame to support artist's canvas *etc.*

east (ēst) *n.* **1.** part of horizon where sun rises **2.** eastern lands, orient —*a.* **3.** on, in or near east **4.** coming from east —*adv.* **5.** from or to east —'**easterly** *a./adv.* from or to east —'**eastern** *a.* of, dwelling in, east —'**easterner** *n.* —'**easting** *n.* distance eastwards of a point from a given meridian —'**eastward** *a./n.* —'**eastwards** *or* '**eastward** *adv.* —**Eastern Church 1.** any of Christian Churches of former Byzantine Empire **2.** any Church owing allegiance to Orthodox Church —**eastern hemisphere** (*oft.* **E- H-**) **1.** that half of the globe containing Europe, Asia,

Afr. and Aust. **2.** lands in this, *esp.* Asia —**Eastern Seaboard** states on the Atlantic shore: Maine, New Hampshire, Massachusetts, Rhode Island, Connecticut, New York, Pennsylvania, Delaware, Maryland, Virginia, North and South Carolina, and Georgia —**Eastern Standard Time** time as reckoned from 75th to 90th meridians west of Greenwich —**East Germany** *see* GERMAN DEMOCRATIC REPUBLIC

Easter (ˈēstər) *n.* movable festival of the Resurrection of Christ —**Easter egg** chocolate egg or hen's egg with its shell painted, given as gift at Easter —ˈ**Eastertide** *n.* Easter season

easy (ˈēzi) *a. see* EASE

eat (ēt) *v.* **1.** chew and swallow **2.** gnaw —*vt.* **3.** consume, destroy **4.** wear away (**ate** *pt.*, ˈ**eaten** *pp.*) —ˈ**eatable** *a.* —ˈ**eating** *n.* **1.** food, *esp.* in relation to quality or taste —*a.* **2.** suitable for eating —**eats** *pl.n. sl.* articles of food —**eat one's words** take back something said

eau de Cologne (ō də kəˈlōn) *Fr.* light perfume

eau de vie (ō də ˈvē) brandy

eaves (ēvz) *pl.n.* overhanging edges of roof —ˈ**eavesdrop** *vi.* listen secretly —ˈ**eavesdropper** *n.* —ˈ**eavesdropping** *n.*

ebb (eb) *vi.* **1.** flow back **2.** decay —*n.* **3.** flowing back of tide **4.** decline, decay —**ebb tide**

ebony (ˈebəni) *n.* **1.** hard black wood —*a.* **2.** made of, black as ebony —ˈ**ebonite** *n.* vulcanite —ˈ**ebonize** *vt.* make color of ebony

ebullient (iˈbo͝olyənt, iˈbul-) *a.* **1.** exuberant **2.** boiling —eˈ**bullience** *n.* —**ebullition** (ebəˈlishən) *n.* **1.** boiling **2.** effervescence **3.** outburst

eccentric (ikˈsentrik) *a.* **1.** odd, unconventional **2.** irregular **3.** not placed, or not having axis placed, centrally **4.** not circular (in orbit) —*n.* **5.** odd, unconventional person **6.** mechanical contrivance to change circular into to-and-fro movement —**ec**ˈ**centrically** *adv.* —**eccen**ˈ**tricity** *n.*

Eccles. *Bible* Ecclesiastes

Ecclesiastes (iklēziˈastēz) *n. Bible* 21st book of the O.T., authorship traditionally ascribed to Solomon, the theme of which is the excellence of wisdom

ecclesiastic (iklēziˈastik) *n.* **1.** clergyman —*a.* **2.** of, relating to the Christian Church —**ecclesi**ˈ**astical** *a.* —**ecclesi**ˈ**ology** *n.* science of church building and decoration

eccrinology (ekriˈnoləji) *n.* branch of physiology that relates to bodily secretions

E.C.G. **1.** electrocardiogram **2.** electrocardiograph

echelon (ˈeshəlon) *n.* **1.** level, grade, of responsibility or command **2.** formation of troops, planes *etc.* in parallel divisions, each slightly to left or right of the one in front

echidna (iˈkidnə) *n.* spine-covered mammal of Aust. and New Guinea (*pl.* **-s, -nae** (-nē)) (*also* **spiny anteater**)

echinoderm (iˈkīnōdərm) *n.* any member of a phylum of invertebrate animals with spiny skins and globular star-shaped bodies such as starfish, sea urchin and sea cucumber

echo (ˈekō) *n.* **1.** repetition of sounds by reflection **2.** close imitation (*pl.* **-es**) —*vt.* **3.** repeat as echo, send back the sound of **4.** imitate closely —*vi.* **5.** resound **6.** be repeated (ˈ**echoed,** ˈ**echoing**) —**echoic** (eˈkōik) *a.* **1.** characteristic of or resembling echo **2.** onomatopoeic —**echo chamber** room with walls that reflect sound, used to make acoustic measurements and in recording (*also* **reverberation chamber**) —**echo-lo**ˈ**cation** *n.* determination of position of object by measuring reflected sound —**echo sounder** —**echo sounding** system of ascertaining depth of water by measuring time required to receive echo from sea bottom or submerged object —**echo viruses** group of viruses infecting the gastrointestinal tract *esp.* of children

Echo (ˈekō) *n.* word used in communications for the letter *e*

éclair (āˈklāər, iˈklāər) *n.* finger-shaped, iced cake filled with cream or custard

eclampsia (iˈklampsiə) *n.* convulsions and comas in late pregnancy associated with group of disorders known as toxemia

éclat (āˈklä) *n.* **1.** splendor **2.** renown **3.** acclamation

eclectic (eˈklektik, iˈklek-) *a.* **1.** selecting **2.** borrowing one's philosophy from various sources **3.** catholic in views or taste —*n.* **4.** person who favors eclectic approach —**ec**ˈ**lecticism** *n.*

eclipse (iˈklips) *n.* **1.** blotting out of sun, moon *etc.* by another heavenly body **2.** obscurity —*vt.* **3.** obscure, hide **4.** surpass —**e**ˈ**cliptic** *a.* **1.** of eclipse —*n.* **2.** apparent path of sun

eclogue (ˈeklog) *n.* short poem, *esp.* pastoral dialogue

eco- (*comb. form*) ecology; ecological, as in *ecosphere*

ecology (iˈkoləji) *n.* science of plants and animals in relation to their environment —**eco**ˈ**logical** *a.* —**e**ˈ**cologist** *n.* specialist in or advocate of ecological studies

econ. **1.** economical **2.** economics **3.** economy

economy (iˈkonəmi) *n.* **1.** careful management of resources to avoid unnecessary expenditure or waste **2.** sparing, restrained or efficient use **3.** system of interrelationship of money, industry and employment in a country —**eco**ˈ**nomic** *a.* **1.** of economics **2.** profitable **3.** economical —**eco**ˈ**nomical** *a.* **1.** not wasteful of money, time, effort *etc.* **2.** frugal —**eco**ˈ**nomically** *adv.* —**eco**ˈ**nomics** *pl.n.* **1.** (*with sing. v.*) study of economies of nations **2.** (*with pl. v.*) financial aspects —**e**ˈ**conomist** *n.* specialist in economics

—e'**conomize** *v.* limit or reduce (expense, waste *etc.*)

ecosystem ('ēkōsistəm, 'ekō-) *n. Ecol.* system involving interactions between community and its nonliving environment

ecru ('ekrōō, 'ākrōō) *n./a.* (of) color of unbleached linen, beige

ecstasy ('ekstəsi) *n.* **1.** exalted state of feeling, mystic trance **2.** frenzy —**ec'static** *a.* —**ec'statically** *adv.*

E.C.T. electroconvulsive therapy

ecto- (*comb. form*) outer, outside, as in *ectoplasm*

-ectomy (*comb. form*) surgical excision of part, as in *appendectomy*

ectoplasm ('ektōplazəm) *n.* in spiritualism, supposedly a semiluminous plastic substance which exudes from medium's body

Ecuador ('ekwədōr) *n.* country in S Amer. bounded on the north by Colombia, on the east and south by Peru and on the west by the Pacific Ocean —**Ecua'doran** *or* **Ecua'dorian** *a./n.*

ecumenical (ekyōō'menikəl) *a.* of the Christian Church throughout the world, *esp.* with regard to its unity —**ecu'menicalism, ecu'menicism** *or* **ecu'menism** *n.*

eczema (ig'zēmə, 'eksimə) *n.* any of group of transient or chronic skin disorders characterized by redness, swelling, blisters and scaling

ed. **1.** edited **2.** edition (*pl.* **eds.**) **3.** editor (*pl.* **eds.**) **4.** education

-ed[1] (*comb. form*) forming past tense of most English verbs

-ed[2] (*comb. form*) forming past participle of most English verbs

-ed[3] (*comb. form*) possessing or having characteristics of, as in *salaried, red-blooded*

Edam ('ēdəm) *n.* firm cheese of mild flavor made from cow's milk, molded into a ball and covered with red wax, orig. from Holland

E.D.C. European Defence Community

Edda ('edə) *n.* collection of old Icelandic myths

eddy ('edi) *n.* **1.** small whirl in water, smoke *etc.* —*vi.* **2.** move in whirls (**'eddied, 'eddying**)

edelweiss ('ādəlwīs, -vīs) *n.* white-flowered alpine plant with woolly leaves

edema (i'dēmə) *n.* swelling in body tissues, due to accumulation of fluid (*pl.* **-mata** (-mətə))

Eden ('ēdən) *n.* **1.** garden in which Adam and Eve were placed at the Creation **2.** any delightful, happy place or state

edentate (ē'dentāt) *n.* **1.** any mammal of the order *Edentata,* which have few or no teeth, such as anteater —*a.* **2.** of the order *Edentata*

edge (ej) *n.* **1.** border, boundary **2.** cutting side of blade **3.** sharpness **4.** advantage **5.** acrimony, bitterness —*vt.* **6.** give edge or border to **7.** move gradually —*vi.* **8.** advance sideways or gradually —**'edgeways** *or* **'edgewise** *adv.* —**'edging** *n.* —**'edgy** *a.* irritable, sharp or keen in temper —**on edge** **1.** nervy, irritable **2.** excited

edelweiss

edible ('edibəl) *a.* eatable, fit for eating —**edi'bility** *n.*

edict ('ēdikt) *n.* order proclaimed by authority, decree

edifice ('edifis) *n.* building, *esp.* big one

edify ('edifī) *vt.* improve morally, instruct (**-fied, -fying**) —**edifi'cation** *n.* improvement of mind or morals

edit ('edit) *vt.* prepare (book, motion picture, tape *etc.*) for publication or broadcast —**e'dition** *n.* **1.** form in which something is published **2.** number of copies of new publication printed at one time —**'editor** *n.* —**edi'torial** *a.* **1.** of editor —*n.* **2.** article stating opinion of newspaper *etc.*

edit. **1.** edited **2.** edition **3.** editor

EDP emotionally disturbed person

E.D.P. electronic data processing

educate ('ejəkāt) *vt.* **1.** provide schooling for **2.** teach **3.** train mentally and morally **4.** train **5.** improve, develop —**educa'bility** *or* **educata'bility** *n.* —**'educable** *or* **'educatable** *a.* capable of being trained or educated —**'educated** *a.* **1.** having education, *esp.* a good one **2.** cultivated —**edu'cation** *n.* —**edu'cational** *a.* —**edu'cationally** *adv.* —**'educative** *a.* —**'educator** *n.* —**educated guess** guess based on experience or information

educe (i'dyōōs, -'dōōs) *vt.* **1.** bring out, elicit, develop **2.** infer, deduce —**e'ducible** *a.* —**eduction** (i'dukshən) *n.*

Edwardian (ed'wördiən) *a.* of reign (1901–10) of Edward VII, king of Great Britain and Ireland —**Ed'wardianism** *n.*

-ee (*comb. form*) **1.** recipient of action, as in *assignee* **2.** person in specified state or condition, as in *absentee*

EEC European Economic Community

EEG electroencephalogram

eel (ēl) *n.* snakelike fish

e'en (ēn) *adv./n. Poet., obs.* even, evening

-eer *or* **-ier** (*comb. form*) **1.** person who is concerned with something specified, as in *auctioneer, engineer, profiteer* **2.** be concerned with something specified, as in *electioneer*

e'er (āər) *adv. Poet., obs.* ever

eerie ('ēəri) *a.* **1.** weird, uncanny **2.** causing superstitious fear

efface (i'fās) *vt.* wipe or rub out —**ef'faceable** *a.* —**ef'facement** *n.*

effect (i'fekt) *n.* **1.** result, consequence **2.** efficacy **3.** impression **4.** condition of being operative —*pl.* **5.** property **6.** lighting, sounds *etc.* to accompany film, broadcast *etc.* —*vt.* **7.** bring about, accomplish —**ef'fective** *a.* **1.** having power to produce effects **2.** in effect, operative **3.** serviceable **4.** powerful **5.** striking —**ef'fectively** *adv.* —**ef'fectual** *a.* **1.** successful in producing desired effect **2.** satisfactory **3.** efficacious —**ef'fectually** *adv.* —**ef'fectuate** *vt.*

effeminate (i'feminit) *a.* (of man or boy) womanish, unmanly —**ef'feminacy** *n.*

efferent ('efərənt) *a.* conveying outward or away

effervesce (efər'ves) *vi.* **1.** give off bubbles **2.** be in high spirits —**effer'vescence** *n.* —**effer'vescent** *a.*

effete (e'fēt, i'fēt) *a.* worn-out, feeble

efficacious (efi'kāshəs) *a.* **1.** producing or sure to produce desired effect **2.** effective **3.** powerful **4.** adequate —**'efficacy** *n.* **1.** potency **2.** force **3.** efficiency

efficient (i'fishənt) *a.* capable, competent, producing effect —**ef'ficiency** *n.* —**ef'ficiently** *adv.*

effigy ('efiji) *n.* image, likeness

effloresce (eflō'res) *vi.* burst into flower —**efflo'rescence** *n.* —**efflo'rescent** *a.*

effluent ('eflo͞oənt) *n.* **1.** liquid discharged as waste **2.** stream flowing from larger stream, lake *etc.* —*a.* **3.** flowing out —**'effluence** *or* **efflux** ('efluks) *n.* —**ef'fluvium** *n.* something flowing out invisibly, *esp.* affecting lungs or sense of smell (*pl.* **-ia** (-iə))

effort ('efərt) *n.* **1.** exertion **2.** endeavor, attempt **3.** something achieved —**'effortless** *a.*

effrontery (i'fruntəri) *n.* brazen impudence

effulgent (i'fuljənt) *a.* radiant, shining brightly —**ef'fulgence** *n.*

effusion (i'fyo͞ozhən) *n.* (unrestrained) outpouring —**ef'fuse** *v.* pour out, shed —**ef'fusive** *a.* gushing, demonstrative —**ef'fusively** *adv.* —**ef'fusiveness** *n.*

eft (eft) *n. dial., obs.* newt

EFT electronic funds transfer

EFTA ('eftə) European Free Trade Association

e.g. exempli gratia (*Lat.*, for example)

egalitarian (igali'teriən) *a.* **1.** believing that all people should be equal **2.** promoting this ideal —*n.* **3.** adherent of egalitarian principles —**egali'tarianism** *n.*

egg[1] (eg) *n.* **1.** oval or round object produced by female of bird or reptile from which young emerge, *esp.* egg of domestic fowl, used as food **2.** ovum —**'eggbeater** *n.* **1.** hand-operated utensil for stirring or mixing eggs **2.** helicopter —**egg cup 1.** small cup for holding boiled egg to be eaten out of the shell **2.** cup composed of two small bowls joined at bottoms, one for holding upright a soft-boiled egg, the other larger bowl for holding a soft-boiled egg emptied into it —**egg foo young** (fo͞o yung) Chinese-American type of omelet filled with a chicken, shellfish or meat and vegetable mixture —**'egghead** *n. inf.* intellectual —**'eggnog** *n.* drink made of eggs, milk, sugar, spice, and brandy, rum *etc.* —**'eggplant** *n.* perennial plant yielding a large smooth dark purple egg-shaped fruit eaten as a vegetable —**egg roll** Chinese dish made of dough wrapped around chopped vegetables and meat or shellfish and deep-fried —**'eggshell** *n.* **1.** outer layer of bird's egg —*a.* **2.** (of paint) having mat finish —**good egg** friendly, helpful person

egg[2] (eg) *vt.* —**egg on 1.** encourage, urge **2.** incite

eglantine ('egləntīn) *n.* sweet brier

ego ('ēgō, 'egō) *n.* **1.** the self **2.** the conscious thinking subject **3.** one's image of oneself **4.** morale —**'egoism** *n.* **1.** systematic selfishness **2.** theory that bases morality on self-interest —**'egoist** *n.* —**ego'istic(al)** *a.* —**'egotism** *n.* **1.** selfishness **2.** self-conceit —**'egotist** *n.* —**ego'tistic(al)** *a.* —**ego'centric** *a.* **1.** self-centred **2.** egoistic **3.** centered in the ego —**ego trip** *inf.* something undertaken to boost person's own image or appraisal of himself

egregious (i'grējəs) *a.* **1.** outstandingly bad, blatant **2.** (*esp.* of mistake *etc.*) absurdly obvious

egress ('ēgres) *n.* **1.** way out **2.** departure

egret ('ēgrit) *n.* **1.** lesser white heron **2.** down of dandelion

Egypt ('ējipt) *n.* country in Africa bounded east by Israel, the Gulf of Aqaba and the Red Sea, south by Sudan, west by Libya and north by the Mediterranean —**Egyptian** (i'jipshən) *a./n.* —**Egyp'tologist** *n.* —**Egyp'tology** *n.* study of archaeology and language of ancient Egypt

eh (ā) *interj.* exclamation expressing surprise or inquiry, or to seek confirmation of statement or question

EHF extremely high frequency

eider *or* **eider duck** ('īdər) *n.* Arctic duck —**'eiderdown** *n.* **1.** its breast feathers **2.** quilt (stuffed with feathers)

eight (āt) *n.* **1.** cardinal number one above seven **2.** eight-oared boat **3.** its crew —*a.* **4.** amounting to eight —**eigh'teen** *a./n.* eight more than ten —**eigh'teenth** *a./n.* —**eigh'teenthly** *adv.* —'**eightfold** *a./adv.* —**eighth** *a./n.* ordinal number of eight —'**eighthly** *adv.* —'**eightieth** *a./n.* —'**eighty** *a./n.* ten times eight —**eightfold path** tenets of Buddhism —**eightsome reel** Scottish dance for eight people —**figure of eight** **1.** a skating figure **2.** any figure shaped as 8

einsteinium (īn'stīniəm) *n. Chem.* transuranic element *Symbol* E, at. wt. 254, at. no. 99

Eire ('erə) *n.* the Republic of Ireland

Eisenhower ('īzənhowər) *n.* **Dwight** (dwīt) **David.** the 34th President of the U.S. (1953-61)

eisteddfod (ī'stedhvod) *n.* **1.** annual congress of Welsh bards **2.** local gathering for competition in music and other performing arts

either ('ēdhər, 'īdhər) *a./pron.* **1.** one or the other **2.** one of two **3.** each —*adv./conj.* **4.** bringing in first of alternatives or strengthening an added negation

ejaculate (i'jakyəlāt) *v.* **1.** eject (semen) **2.** exclaim, utter suddenly —**ejacu'lation** *n.* —**e'jaculatory** *a.*

eject (i'jekt) *vt.* **1.** throw out **2.** expel, drive out —**e'jection** *n.* —**e'jectment** *n.* —**e'jector** *n.* —**ejection seat** seat, *esp.* in military aircraft, that ejects occupant in emergency

eke out (ēk) **1.** make (supply) last, *esp.* by frugal use **2.** supply deficiencies of **3.** make with difficulty (a living *etc.*)

elaborate (i'labərit) *a.* **1.** carefully worked out, detailed **2.** complicated —*vi.* (i'labərāt) **3.** expand —*vt.* (i'labərāt) **4.** work out in detail **5.** take pains with —**elabo'ration** *n.*

élan (ā'län) *n.* **1.** dash **2.** ardor **3.** impetuosity

eland ('ēlənd) *n.* largest S Afr. antelope, resembling elk

elapse (i'laps) *vi.* (of time) pass

elastic (i'lastik) *a.* **1.** resuming normal shape after distortion, springy **2.** flexible —*n.* **3.** tape, fabric, containing interwoven strands of flexible rubber —**e'lasticated** *a.* —**elas'ticity** *n.*

elation (i'lāshən) *n.* **1.** high spirits **2.** pride —**e'late** *vt.* (*usu. passive*) **1.** raise the spirits of **2.** make happy **3.** exhilarate

elbow ('elbō) *n.* **1.** joint between fore and upper parts of arm (*esp.* outer part of it) **2.** part of sleeve covering this —*vt.* **3.** shove, strike with elbow —**elbow grease** hard work —'**elbowroom** *n.* sufficient room

elder[1] ('eldər) *a. comp. of* OLD **1.** older, senior —*n.* **2.** person of greater age **3.** old person **4.** official of certain churches —'**elderly** *a.* growing old —'**eldest** *a. sup. of* OLD oldest

elder[2] ('eldər) *n.* white-flowered tree —'**elderberry** *n.* **1.** fruit of elder **2.** elder (tree)

El Dorado (el də'rädō) fictitious country rich in gold

eldritch ('eldrich) *a.* **1.** hideous **2.** weird **3.** uncanny **4.** haggish

elect (i'lekt) *vt.* **1.** choose by vote **2.** choose —*a.* **3.** appointed but not yet in office **4.** chosen, select, choice —**e'lection** *n.* choosing, *esp.* by voting —**election'eer** *vi.* busy oneself in political elections —**e'lective** *a.* appointed, filled or chosen by election —**e'lector** *n.* one who elects —**e'lectoral** *a.* —**e'lectorate** *n.* body of electors —**e'lectorship** *n.*

elect. *or* **elec. 1.** electric(al) **2.** electricity

electricity (ilek'trisiti) *n.* **1.** form of energy associated with stationary or moving electrons or other charged particles **2.** electric current or charge **3.** science dealing with electricity —**e'lectric** *a.* **1.** derived from, produced by, producing, transmitting or powered by electricity **2.** excited, emotionally charged —**e'lectrical** *a.* —**elec'trician** *n.* one trained in installation *etc.* of electrical devices —**electrifi'cation** *n.* —**e'lectrify** *vt.* —**electric blanket** blanket containing electric heating element —**electric chair** chair in which criminals sentenced to death are electrocuted —**electric eel** eel-like freshwater fish of N South Amer., having electric organs in body —**electric eye** *see* PHOTOCELL —**electric fire** appliance that supplies heat by means of electrically operated metal coil —**electric guitar** *see* GUITAR —**electric organ** *Mus.* organ in which sound is produced by electric devices instead of wind —**electric shock** effect of an electric current passing through body

electro- *or sometimes before vowel* **electr-** (*comb. form*) by, caused by electricity, as in *electrotherapy.* Such words are not given here where the meaning may easily be inferred from the simple word

electrocardiograph (ilektrō'kärdiōgraf) *n.* instrument for recording electrical activity of heart —**electro'cardiogram** *n.* tracing produced by this

electroconvulsive therapy (ilektrōkən'vulsiv) *see* **shock therapy** *at* SHOCK[1]

electrocute (i'lektrəkyōōt) *vt.* execute, kill by electricity —**electro'cution** *n.*

electrode (i'lektrōd) *n.* conductor by which electric current enters or leaves battery, vacuum tube *etc.*

electrodynamics (ilektrōdī'namiks) *pl.n.* (*with sing. v.*) dynamics of electricity

electroencephalograph (ilektrōin'sefələgraf) *n.* instrument for recording electrical activity of brain —**electroen'cephalogram** *n.* tracing produced by this

electrolyte (i'lektrōlīt) *n.* substance capable of furnishing ions when dissolved in water

electrolyze (i'lektrōlīz) *vt.* decompose by electricity —**elec'trolysis** *n.*

electromagnet (ilektrō'magnit) *n.* magnet containing coil of wire through which electric current is passed —**electromag'netic** *a.* —**electro'magnetism** *n.* **1.** magnetism produced by electric current **2.** branch of

electromagnet

physics concerned with interaction of electric and magnetic fields

electromotive (ilektrō'mōtiv) *a.* of, concerned with or producing electric current —**electromotive force** *Phys.* **1.** source of energy that can cause current to flow in electrical circuit **2.** rate at which energy is drawn from this source

electron (i'lektron) *n.* tiny bit of exceedingly small mass and negative electric charge —**elec'tronic** *a.* **1.** of electrons or electronics **2.** using devices, such as semiconductors, transistors or valves, dependent on action of electrons —**elec'tronics** *pl.n.* **1.** (*with sing. v.*) technology concerned with development of electronic devices and circuits **2.** science of behavior and control of electrons —**electronic brain** *inf.* electronic computer —**electronic data processing** data processing largely performed by electronic equipment —**electronic music** music consisting of sounds produced by electric currents prerecorded on magnetic tape —**electronic organ** *Mus.* keyboard instrument in which sounds are produced by electronic or electrical means —**electron microscope** microscope that uses electrons and electron lenses to produce magnified image —**electron tube** electrical device, such as valve, in which flow of electrons between electrodes takes place —**electron volt** unit of energy used in nuclear physics

electroplate (i'lektrōplāt) *vt.* **1.** coat with silver *etc.* by electrolysis —*n.* **2.** articles electroplated

electroscope (i'lektrōskōp) *n.* instrument to show presence or kind of electricity

electroshock therapy (i'lektrōshok) *see* **shock therapy** *at* SHOCK[1]

electrostatics (ilektrō'statiks) *n.* branch of physics concerned with static electricity —**electro'static** *a.*

electrotype (i'lektrōtīp) *n.* **1.** art of producing copies of type *etc.* by electric deposition of copper upon mould **2.** copy so produced

electrum (i'lektrəm) *n.* alloy of gold and silver used in jewelry *etc.*

eleemosynary (eli'mosineri) *a.* **1.** charitable **2.** dependent on charity

elegant ('eligənt) *a.* **1.** graceful, tasteful **2.** refined —'**elegance** *n.*

elegy ('eliji) *n.* lament for the dead in poem or song —**elegiac** (eli'jīək) *a.* **1.** suited to elegies **2.** plaintive —**elegiacs** (eli'jīəks) *pl.n.* elegiac verses

element ('elimənt) *n.* **1.** substance which cannot be separated into other substances by chemical techniques **2.** component part **3.** small amount, trace **4.** heating wire in electric kettle, stove *etc.* **5.** proper abode or sphere **6.** situation in which person is happiest or most effective (*esp. in* **in** *or* **out of one's element**) —*pl.* **7.** powers of atmosphere **8.** rudiments, first principles —**ele'mental** *a.* **1.** fundamental **2.** of powers of nature —**ele'mentary** *a.* rudimentary, simple —**elementary particle** any of several entities, such as electrons *etc.*, that are less complex than atoms —**elementary school** school comprising the first six or eight grades

elephant ('elifənt) *n.* huge four-footed, thick-skinned animal with ivory tusks and long trunk —**elephan'tiasis** *n.* disease with hardening of skin and enlargement of legs *etc.* —**ele'phantine** *a.* unwieldy, clumsy, heavily big

elevate ('elivāt) *vt.* raise, lift up, exalt —**ele'vation** *n.* **1.** raising **2.** height, *esp.* above sea level **3.** angle above horizon, as of gun **4.** drawing of one side of building *etc.* —'**elevator** *n.* platform, compartment *etc.* raised or lowered in vertical shaft to transport persons or goods in a building

eleven (i'levən) *n.* **1.** number next above 10 **2.** team of 11 persons —*a.* **3.** amounting to eleven —**e'levenfold** *a./adv.* —**e'levenses** *pl.n. inf.* light mid-morning snack —**e'leventh** *a.* ordinal number of eleven —**eleven-plus** *n.* **UK** *esp.* formerly, examination taken by children aged 11 or 12, that selects suitable candidates for grammar schools —**eleventh hour** latest possible time

elf (elf) *n.* **1.** fairy **2.** woodland sprite (*pl.* **elves**) —'**elfin,** '**elfish,** '**elvish** *or* '**elflike** *a.* roguish, mischievous

elicit (i'lisit) *vt.* **1.** draw out, evoke **2.** bring to light

elide (i'līd) *v.* omit (a vowel or syllable) at beginning or end of word—**e'lision** *n.*

eligible ('elijəbəl) *a.* **1.** fit or qualified to be chosen **2.** suitable, desirable —**eligi'bility** *n.*

eliminate (i'limināt) *vt.* remove, get rid of, set aside —**elimi'nation** *n.* —**e'liminator** *n.* one who, that which, eliminates

elision (i'lizhən) *n. see* ELIDE

elite (ā'lēt, i-) *n.* **1.** choice or select body **2.** the pick or best part of society **3.** typewriter typesize (12 letters to inch) —*a.* **4.** of or suitable for an elite —**e'litism** *n.* **1.** belief that society should be governed by an elite **2.** pride in being one of an elite group

elixir (i'liksər) *n.* **1.** preparation sought by alchemists to change base metals into gold, or to prolong life **2.** sovereign remedy

Elizabethan (ilizə'bēthən) *a.* **1.** of reigns of Elizabeth I (queen of England, 1558-1603) or Elizabeth II (queen of Great Britain and N Ireland since 1952) **2.** of style of architecture used in England during reign of Elizabeth I —*n.* **3.** person who lived in England during reign of Elizabeth I

elk (elk) *n.* **1.** N Amer. deer similar to European red deer (*also* **wapiti**) **2.** deer of Europe and Asia resembling moose **3.** (**E-**) member of a society called the Benevolent and Protective Order of Elks

ell (el) *n.* obsolete unit of length, approximately 45 inches

Ellice Islands ('elis) *former name for* TUVALU

ellipse (i'lips) *n.* oval —**el'lipsoid** *n.* **1.** geometric surface whose plane sections are ellipses or circles **2.** solid having this shape —**ellip'soidal** *a.* —**el'liptical** *a.* **1.** relating to or having the shape of an ellipse **2.** relating to or resulting from ellipsis **3.** (of speech *etc.*) very concise, obscure; circumlocutory (*also* **el'liptic**) —**el'liptically** *adv.*

ellipsis (i'lipsis) *n. Gram.* omission of parts of word or sentence (*pl.* **ellipses** (i'lipsēz))

elm (elm) *n.* **1.** tree with serrated leaves **2.** its wood

elocution (elə'kyōōshən) *n.* art of public speaking, voice management —**elo'cutionist** *n.* **1.** teacher of this **2.** specialist in verse speaking

elongate ('ēlonggāt) *vt.* lengthen, extend, prolong —**elon'gation** *n.*

elope (i'lōp) *vi.* run away from home with lover —**e'lopement** *n.*

eloquence ('eləkwəns) *n.* fluent, powerful use of language —**'eloquent** *a.* —**'eloquently** *adv.*

El Salvador (el 'salvədōr) country in Central America bounded south by the Pacific, west by Guatemala and north by Honduras —**Salva'doran, Salva'dorean,** *or* **Salva'dorian** *a./n.*

else (els) *adv.* **1.** besides, instead **2.** otherwise —**'elsewhere** *adv.* in or to some other place

elucidate (i'lōōsidāt) *vt.* throw light upon, explain —**eluci'dation** *n.* —**e'lucidatory** *a.*

elude (i'lōōd) *vt.* **1.** escape, slip away from, dodge **2.** baffle —**e'lusion** *n.* **1.** act of eluding **2.** evasion —**e'lusive** *a.* difficult to catch hold of, deceptive —**e'lusively** *adv.* —**e'lusory** *a.*

elver ('elvər) *n.* young eel

elves (elvz) *n., pl. of* ELF

Elysium (i'liziəm) *n.* **1.** *Gr. myth.* dwelling place of blessed after death (*also* **Elysian fields**) **2.** state or place of perfect bliss

em (em) *n. Print.* the square of any size of type

em- (*comb. form*) *see* EN-

'em (əm) *pron. inf.* them

emaciate (i'māsiāt) *v.* make or become abnormally thin —**emaci'ation** *n.*

emanate ('emənāt) *vi.* issue, proceed, originate —**ema'nation** *n.* —**emanative** ('emənātiv) *a.*

emancipate (i'mansipāt) *vt.* set free —**emanci'pation** *n.* **1.** act of setting free, *esp.* from social, legal restraint **2.** state of being set free —**emanci'pationist** *n.* advocate of emancipation, *esp.* of slaves or women —**e'mancipator** *n.* —**emancipatory** (i'mansipətōri) *a.*

emasculate (i'maskyəlāt) *vt.* **1.** castrate **2.** enfeeble, weaken —**emascu'lation** *n.* —**e'masculative** *a.*

embalm (im'bäm, -'bälm) *vt.* preserve (corpse) from decay by use of chemicals, herbs *etc.* —**em'balmment** *n.*

embankment (im'bangkmənt) *n.* artificial mound carrying road, railroad, or serving to dam water

embargo (em'bärgō) *n.* **1.** order stopping movement of ships **2.** suspension of commerce **3.** ban (*pl.* **-es**) —*vt.* **4.** put under embargo **5.** requisition

embark (em'bärk) *v.* **1.** put, go, on board ship, aircraft *etc.* **2.** (*with* on *or* upon) commence (new project, venture *etc.*) —**embar'kation** *n.*

embarrass (im'barəs) *vt.* **1.** perplex, disconcert **2.** abash **3.** confuse **4.** encumber **5.** involve in financial difficulties —**em'barrassment** *n.*

embassy ('embəsi) *n.* **1.** office, work or official residence of ambassador **2.** deputation

embattle (im'batəl) *vt.* **1.** deploy (troops) for battle **2.** fortify (position *etc.*)

embed *or* **imbed** (im'bed) *vt.* fix fast in something solid

embellish (im'belish) *vt.* adorn, enrich —**em'bellishment** *n.*

ember ('embər) *n.* **1.** glowing cinder —*pl.* **2.** red-hot ashes

Ember days days appointed by Church for fasting in each quarter

embezzle (im'bezəl) *vt.* divert fraudulently, misappropriate (money in trust *etc.*) —**em'bezzlement** *n.* —**em'bezzler** *n.*

embitter (im'bitər) *vt.* make bitter —**em'bitterment** *n.*

emblazon (im'blāzən) *vt.* adorn richly, *esp.* heraldically

emblem ('embləm) *n.* **1.** symbol **2.** badge, device —**emblem'atic** *a.* —**emblem'atically** *adv.*

embody (im'bodi) *vt.* **1.** give body, concrete expression to **2.** represent, include, be expression of (**em'bodied, em'bodying**) —**em'bodiment** *n.*

embolden (im'bōldən) *vt.* make bold

embolism ('embəlizəm) *n.* clot or other obstruction carried in the bloodstream until it becomes lodged in a vessel too narrow to permit passage

embolus ('embələs) *n.* material, such as

blood clot, that impedes circulation (*pl.* **-li** (-lī))

emboss (im'bos) *vt.* mold, stamp or carve in relief

embrace (im'brās) *vt.* **1.** clasp in arms, hug **2.** seize, avail oneself of, accept **3.** comprise —*n.* **4.** act of embracing

embrasure (im'brāzhər) *n.* **1.** opening in wall for cannon **2.** beveling of wall at sides of window

embrocation (embrō'kāshən) *n.* lotion for rubbing limbs *etc.* to relieve pain —'**embrocate** *vt.*

embroider (im'broidər) *vt.* **1.** ornament with needlework **2.** embellish, exaggerate (story) —**em'broidery** *n.*

embroil (im'broil) *vt.* **1.** bring into confusion **2.** involve in hostility —**em'broilment** *n.*

embryo ('embriō) *n.* **1.** unborn or undeveloped offspring, germ **2.** undeveloped thing (*pl.* **-s**) —**embry'ologist** *n.* —**embry'ology** *n.* study of development of the individual from the egg —**embry'onic** *a.*

embus (im'bus) *v.* (*esp.* of troops) put into, mount bus (**-ss-**)

emend (i'mend) *vt.* remove errors from, correct —**emen'dation** *n.* —'**emendator** *n.* —**e'mendatory** *a.*

emerald ('emərəld, 'emrəld) *n.* **1.** bright green precious stone —*a.* **2.** of the color of emerald —**Emerald Isle** *Poet.* Ireland

emerge (i'mərj) *vi.* **1.** come up, out **2.** rise to notice **3.** come into view **4.** come out on inquiry —**e'mergence** *n.* —**e'mergent** *a.* —**e'mersion** *n.* **1.** act or instance of emerging **2.** *Astron.* reappearance of celestial body after eclipse or occultation

emergency (i'mərjənsi) *n.* **1.** sudden unforeseen thing or event needing prompt action **2.** difficult situation **3.** exigency, crisis

emeritus (i'meritəs) *a.* retired, honorably discharged but retaining one's title (*eg* professor) on honorary basis

emery ('eməri) *n.* hard mineral used for polishing —**emery board** nail file of cardboard coated with crushed emery —**emery cloth** stiff paper coated with finely powdered emery

emetic (i'metik) *n./a.* (denoting) drug which causes vomiting

emf electromotive force

-emia *or* **-hemia** (*comb. form*) blood, *esp.* specified condition of blood in diseases, as in *leukemia*

emigrate ('emigrāt) *vi.* go and settle in another country —'**emigrant** *n.* —**emi'gration** *n.* —'**emigratory** *a.*

émigré ('emigrā) *n.* emigrant, *esp.* one forced to leave his country for political reasons

éminence grise (āmēnās 'grēz) *Fr.* person who wields power and influence unofficially (*pl.* ***éminences grises*** (āmēnās 'grēz))

eminent ('eminənt) *a.* distinguished, notable —'**eminence** *n.* **1.** distinction **2.** height **3.** rank **4.** fame **5.** rising ground **6.** (**E-**) title of cardinal —'**eminently** *adv.*

emir (i'mēər) *n.* (in Islamic world) **1.** independent ruler or chieftain **2.** military commander or governor **3.** male descendant of Mohammed —**e'mirate** *n.*

emissary ('emiseri) *n.* agent, representative (*esp.* of government) sent on mission

emit (i'mit) *vt.* give out, put forth (**-tt-**) —**e'mission** *n.* —**e'mitter** *n.*

Emmenthal ('eməntäl) *or* **Emmenthaler** ('eməntälər) *n.* hard cheese, pale yellow in color with large, shiny holes and a nutty, sweet flavor, orig. from Switzerland (*also* **Swiss cheese**)

emollient (i'molyənt) *a.* **1.** softening, soothing —*n.* **2.** ointment or other softening application

emolument (i'molyəmənt) *n.* salary, pay, profit from work

emotion (i'mōshən) *n.* mental agitation, excited state of feeling, as joy, fear *etc.* —**e'mote** *vi. inf.* display exaggerated emotion, as in acting —**e'moter** *n.* —**e'motional** *a.* **1.** given to emotion **2.** appealing to the emotions —**e'motive** *a.* tending to arouse emotion

Emp. **1.** Emperor **2.** Empire **3.** Empress

empanel *or* **impanel** (im'panəl) *vt. Law* **1.** enter on list (names of persons to be summoned for jury service) **2.** select (jury) from such list —**em'panelment** *or* **im'panelment** *n.*

empathy ('empəthi) *n.* power of understanding, imaginatively entering into, another's feelings —**em'pathic** *or* **empa'thetic** *a.*

emperor ('empərər) *n.* ruler of an empire ('**empress** *fem.*) —**emperor penguin** Antarctic penguin, the largest known, reaching a height of 1.3 m (4 ft.)

emphasis ('emfəsis) *n.* **1.** importance attached **2.** stress on words **3.** vigor of speech, expression (*pl.* **-ses** (-sēz)) —'**emphasize** *vt.* —**em'phatic** *a.* **1.** forceful, decided **2.** stressed —**em'phatically** *adv.*

emphysema (emfi'zēmə) *n.* distension of the terminal air sacs of the lungs

empire ('empīər) *n.* large territory, *esp.* aggregate of states under supreme ruler, supreme control —**empire-builder** *n. inf.* person who seeks extra power, *esp.* by increasing his staff —**empire-building** *n./a.* —**empire style** style of decorative arts of French First Empire (1804-14) characterized by clarity, balance and restraint, and motifs from classical antiquity

empirical (em'pirikəl) *a.* relying on experiment or experience, not on theory —**em'piric** *a.* **1.** empirical —*n.* **2.** one who relies solely on experience and observation —**em'pirically** *adv.* —**empiricism** (em'pirisizəm) *n.*

emplacement (im'plāsmənt) *n.* **1.** putting in position **2.** gun platform

emplane (im'plān) *v.* board or put on board airplane

employ (im'ploi) *vt.* **1.** provide work for (a person) in return for money, hire **2.** keep busy **3.** use (**em'ployed, em'ploying**) —**employ'ee** *n.* —**em'ployer** *n.* —**em'ployment** *n.* **1.** an employing, being employed **2.** work, trade **3.** occupation

emporium (em'pōriəm) *n.* **1.** large general shop **2.** centre of commerce (*pl.* **-s, -ria** (-riə))

empower (im'powər) *vt.* **1.** enable **2.** authorize

empress ('empris) *n. see* EMPEROR

empty ('empti) *a.* **1.** containing nothing **2.** unoccupied **3.** senseless **4.** vain, foolish —*v.* **5.** make, become devoid of content **6.** discharge (contents) (into) (**'emptied, 'emptying**) —**'empties** *pl.n.* empty boxes, bottles *etc.* —**'emptiness** *n.* —**empty-handed** *a.* **1.** carrying nothing in hands **2.** having gained nothing —**empty-headed** *a.* lacking sense

empyrean (empī'rēən) *n.* **1.** *obs.* in ancient cosmology, highest part of the heavens **2.** *Poet.* heavens; sky —*a., also* **empy'real** **3.** of sky **4.** heavenly, sublime

emu ('ēmyōō) *n.* large Aust. flightless bird like ostrich

emulate ('emyəlāt) *vt.* **1.** strive to equal or excel **2.** imitate —**emu'lation** *n.* **1.** rivalry **2.** competition —**'emulative** *a.* —**'emulator** *n.* —**'emulous** *a.* eager to equal or surpass another or his deeds

emulsion (i'mulshən) *n.* **1.** light-sensitive coating of film **2.** milky liquid with oily or resinous particles in suspension **3.** paint *etc.* in this form —**e'mulsifier** *n.* substance used to disperse particles of an oily, fatty or other substance in a liquid —**e'mulsify** *v.* (**e'mulsified, e'mulsifying**) —**e'mulsive** *a.*

en (en) *n. Print.* unit of measurement, half an em

en- *or* **em-** (*comb. form*) put in, into, on, as in *enrage.* Such words are not given here where the meaning may easily be inferred from the simple word

-en[1] (*comb. form*) cause to be; become; cause to have, as in *blacken, heighten*

-en[2] (*comb. form*) of; made of; resembling, as in *ashen, wooden*

enable (in'ābəl) *vt.* make able, authorize, empower, supply with means (to do something) —**enabling act** legislative act conferring certain powers on person or organization

enact (in'akt) *vt.* **1.** make law **2.** represent or perform as in a play —**en'actment** *n.*

enamel (i'naməl) *n.* **1.** glasslike coating applied to metal *etc.* to preserve surface **2.** coating of teeth **3.** any hard outer coating —*vt.* **4.** decorate with enamel **5.** ornament with glossy variegated colors, as if with enamel **6.** portray in enamel

enamor (in'amər) *vt.* **1.** inspire with love **2.** charm **3.** bewitch

en bloc (ã 'blok) *Fr.* **1.** in a lump or block **2.** all together

enc. **1.** enclosed **2.** enclosure

encamp (in'kamp) *v.* set up (in) camp —**en'campment** *n.* camp

encapsulate (in'kapsəlāt) *vt.* **1.** enclose in capsule **2.** put in concise or abridged form

encase (in'kās) *vt.* place or enclose as in case —**en'casement** *n.*

encaustic (in'kŏstik) *a.* **1.** with colors burnt in —*n.* **2.** art of ornament by burnt-in colors

-ence *or* **-ency** (*comb. form*) action, state, condition, quality, as in *benevolence, residence, patience, fluency, permanency*

enceinte (on'sant) *a.* pregnant

encephalitis (insefə'lītis) *n.* inflammation of brain —**encephalitic** (insefə'litik) *a.*

encephalo- *or before vowel* **encephal-** (*comb. form*) brain, as in *encephalogram, encephalitis*

encephalogram (in'sefələgram) *n.* x-ray photograph of brain

enchain (in'chān) *vt.* **1.** bind with chains **2.** hold fast or captivate (attention *etc.*) —**en'chainment** *n.*

enchant (in'chant) *vt.* **1.** bewitch **2.** delight —**en'chanter** *n.* (**-tress** *fem.*) —**en'chantment** *n.*

enchilada (enchi'lädə) *n.* Mexican dish of tortilla filled with meat, served with chili sauce

encircle (in'sərkəl) *vt.* **1.** surround **2.** enfold **3.** go round so as to encompass —**en'circlement** *n.*

enclave ('enklāv) *n.* portion of territory entirely surrounded by foreign land

enclitic (en'klitik) *a.* **1.** pronounced as part of another word —*n.* **2.** enclitic word or form

enclose *or* **inclose** (in'klōz) *vt.* **1.** shut in **2.** surround **3.** envelop **4.** place in with something else (in letter *etc.*) —**en'closure** *or* **in'closure** *n.* —**enclosed order** Christian religious order whose members do not go into the outside world

encomium (en'kōmiəm) *n.* **1.** formal praise **2.** eulogy —**en'comiast** *n.* one who composes encomiums —**encomi'astic** *a.* —**encomi'astically** *adv.*

encompass (in'kumpəs) *vt.* **1.** surround, encircle **2.** contain

encore ('ongkōr) *interj.* **1.** again, once more —*n.* **2.** call for repetition of song *etc.* **3.** the repetition —*vt.* **4.** ask to repeat

encounter (in'kowntər) *vt.* **1.** meet unexpectedly **2.** meet in conflict **3.** be faced with (difficulty) —*n.* **4.** casual or unexpected meeting **5.** hostile meeting; contest —**encounter group** group of people who meet to develop self-awareness and mutual understanding by openly expressing feelings *etc.*

encourage (in'kurij) *vt.* **1.** hearten, animate,

inspire with hope **2.** embolden —**en'couragement** *n.*

encroach (in'krōch) *vi.* **1.** intrude (on) as usurper **2.** trespass —**en'croachment** *n.*

encrust *or* **incrust** (in'krust) *v.* cover with or form a crust or hard covering

encumber *or* **incumber** (in'kumbər) *vt.* **1.** hamper **2.** burden —**en'cumbrance** *or* **in'cumbrance** *n.* impediment, burden

-ency (*comb. form*) *see* -ENCE

encyclical (en'siklikəl) *a.* **1.** sent to many persons or places —*n.* **2.** circular letter, *esp.* from Pope

encyclopedia *or* **encyclopaedia** (ensīklō'pēdiə) *n.* book, set of books of information on all subjects, or on every branch of subject, usu. arranged alphabetically —**encyclo'pedic** *or* **encyclo'paedic** *a.* —**encyclo'pedist** *or* **encyclo'paedist** *n.*

end (end) *n.* **1.** limit **2.** extremity **3.** conclusion, finishing **4.** fragment **5.** latter part **6.** death **7.** event, issue **8.** purpose, aim **9.** *Sport* either of the defended areas of a playing field *etc.* —*vt.* **10.** put an end to —*vi.* **11.** come to an end, finish —**'ending** *n.* —**'endless** *a.* —**'endmost** *a.* nearest end; most distant —**'endways** *adv.* —**'endpapers** *pl.n.* blank pages at beginning and end of book —**end product** final result of process *etc., esp.* in manufacturing —**end run** play in football in which the ball carrier tries to run wide of the opponents to reach the goal line —**end of steel** **C** (town at) point to which railroad tracks have been laid —**end it all** *inf.* commit suicide

endanger (in'dānjər) *vt.* put in danger or peril —**en'dangerment** *n.*

endear (in'dēər) *vt.* make dear or beloved —**en'dearing** *a.* —**en'dearingly** *adv.* —**en'dearment** *n.* **1.** loving word **2.** tender affection

endeavor (in'devər) *vi.* **1.** try, strive —*n.* **2.** attempt, effort

endemic (en'demik) *a.* **1.** regularly occurring in a country or district —*n.* **2.** endemic disease

endive ('endīv) *n.* curly-leaved chicory used as salad

endo- *or before vowel* **end-** (*comb. form*) within, as in *endocardium, endocrine.* Such words are not given here where the meaning may easily be inferred from the simple word

endocardium (endō'kärdiəm) *n.* lining membrane of the heart

endocrine ('endōkrin, -krīn) *a.* of those glands (thyroid, pituitary *etc.*) which secrete hormones directly into bloodstream

endogenous (en'dojinəs) *a. Biol.* developing or originating within an organism —**en'dogeny** *n.*

endorphin (en'dörfin) *n.* chemical occurring in brain, which has similar effect to morphine

endorse *or* **indorse** (in'dörs) *vt.* **1.** sanction **2.** confirm **3.** write (*esp.* sign name) on back of **4.** record (conviction) on (driver's license) —**endor'sation** *n.* **C** approval, support —**en'dorsement** *or* **in'dorsement** *n.*

endow (in'dow) *vt.* **1.** provide permanent income for **2.** furnish (with) —**en'dowment** *n.* —**endowment policy** life insurance that provides for payment of specified sum to policyholder at designated date or to his beneficiary should he die before this date

endue *or* **indue** (in'dyōō, -'dōō) *vt.* invest, furnish (with quality *etc.*)

endure (in'dyōōər, -'dōōər) *vt.* **1.** undergo **2.** tolerate, bear —*vi.* **3.** last —**en'durable** *a.* —**en'durance** *n.* act or power of enduring —**en'during** *a.* **1.** permanent **2.** having forbearance —**en'duringness** *n.*

enema ('enimə) *n.* medicine, liquid injected into rectum

enemy ('enəmi) *n.* **1.** hostile person **2.** opponent **3.** armed foe **4.** hostile force

energy ('enərji) *n.* **1.** capacity to do work *esp.* the capacity of a force to set a body of matter in motion **2.** source(s) of power, as oil, coal *etc.* **3.** capacity of machine, battery *etc.* for work or output of power —**ener'getic** *a.* —**ener'getically** *adv.* —**'energize** *vt.* give vigor to

enervate ('enərvāt) *vt.* weaken, deprive of vigor —**ener'vation** *n.* lassitude, weakness

enfant terrible (āfā te'rēbl) *Fr.* person given to unconventional conduct or indiscreet remarks (*pl.* ***enfants terribles*** (āfā te'rēbl))

enfeeble (in'fēbəl) *vt.* weaken, debilitate —**en'feeblement** *n.*

enfilade ('enfilād) *n.* fire from artillery, sweeping line from end to end

enfold *or* **infold** (in'fōld) *vt.* **1.** cover by enclosing **2.** embrace —**en'folder** *or* **in'folder** *n.*

enforce (in'förs) *vt.* **1.** compel obedience to **2.** impose (action) upon **3.** drive home —**en'forceable** *a.* —**en'forcement** *n.*

enfranchise (in'franchīz) *vt.* **1.** give right of voting to **2.** give parliamentary representation to **3.** set free —**en'franchisement** *n.*

Eng. **1.** England **2.** English

eng. **1.** engine **2.** engineer **3.** engineering

engage (in'gāj) *vt.* **1.** employ **2.** reserve, hire **3.** bind by contract or promise **4.** order **5.** pledge oneself **6.** betroth **7.** undertake **8.** attract **9.** occupy **10.** bring into conflict **11.** interlock —*vi.* **12.** employ oneself (in) **13.** promise **14.** begin to fight —**en'gaged** *a.* **1.** betrothed **2.** in use **3.** occupied, busy —**en'gagement** *n.* —**en'gaging** *a.* charming

engender (in'jendər) *vt.* **1.** give rise to **2.** beget **3.** rouse

engine ('enjin) *n.* **1.** any machine to convert energy into mechanical work, as steam engine **2.** railroad locomotive **3.** fire engine —**engi'neer** *n.* **1.** one who is in charge of engines, machinery *etc.* or construction work (*eg* roads, bridges) or installation of plant **2.** one who originates, organizes something **3.** driver of railroad locomotive —*vt.* **4.** construct as engineer **5.** contrive —**engi'neering** *n.*

England ('ingglənd) *n.* country in W Europe in S Great Britain bordered north by Scotland, east by the North Sea, south by the English Channel and west by Wales and the Irish Sea: part of United Kingdom —**'English** *n.* **1.** the language of Britain, the U.S.A., most parts of the Commonwealth and certain other countries **2.** (*with pl.v.*) the people of England —*a.* **3.** relating to England —**English horn** an alto oboe

engorge (in'görj) *vt.* **1.** *Pathol.* congest with blood **2.** eat (food) greedily **3.** gorge (oneself) —**en'gorgement** *n.*

engr. **1.** engineer **2.** engraved **3.** engraver **4.** engraving

engraft (in'graft) *vt.* **1.** graft on **2.** plant deeply **3.** incorporate

engrain (in'grān) *vt. see* INGRAIN

engrave (in'grāv) *vt.* **1.** cut in lines on metal for printing **2.** carve, incise **3.** impress deeply —**en'graver** *n.* —**en'graving** *n.* copy of picture printed from engraved plate

engross (in'grōs) *vt.* **1.** absorb (attention) **2.** occupy wholly **3.** write out in large letters or in legal form **4.** corner —**en'grossment** *n.*

engulf (in'gulf) *vt.* swallow up

enhance (in'hans) *vt.* heighten, intensify, increase value or attractiveness of —**en'hancement** *n.*

enigma (i'nigmə) *n.* **1.** puzzling thing or person **2.** riddle —**enig'matic(al)** *a.* —**enig'matically** *adv.*

enjambment *or* **enjambement** (in'jammənt) *n.* in verse, continuation of sentence beyond end of line

enjoin (in'join) *vt.* **1.** command **2.** forbid, prohibit

enjoy (in'joi) *vt.* **1.** delight in **2.** take pleasure in **3.** have use or benefit of —*v. refl.* **4.** be happy —**en'joyable** *a.* —**en'joyment** *n.*

enkindle (in'kindəl) *vt.* **1.** set on fire; kindle **2.** excite to activity or ardor; arouse

enlarge (in'lärj) *vt.* **1.** make bigger **2.** reproduce on larger scale, as photograph —*vi.* **3.** grow bigger **4.** talk, write in greater detail **5.** be capable of reproduction on larger scale —**en'largeable** *a.* —**en'largement** *n.* —**en'larger** *n.* optical instrument for enlarging photographs

enlighten (in'lītən) *vt.* **1.** give information to **2.** instruct, inform **3.** *Poet.* shed light on —**en'lightenment** *n.*

enlist (in'list) *v.* (persuade to) enter armed forces —**en'listment** *n.*

enliven (in'līvən) *vt.* brighten, make more lively, animate

en masse (*Fr.* ã 'mas) **1.** in a group, body **2.** all together

enmesh (in'mesh) *or* **immesh** *vt.* entangle

enmity ('enmiti) *n.* ill will, hostility

ennoble (i'nōbəl) *vt.* make noble, elevate —**en'noblement** *n.*

ennui ('on'wē) *n.* boredom

enormous (i'nörməs) *a.* very big, vast —**e'normity** *n.* **1.** a gross offense **2.** great wickedness **3.** *inf.* great size

enough (i'nuf) *a.* **1.** as much or as many as need be **2.** sufficient —*n.* **3.** sufficient quantity —*adv.* **4.** (just) sufficiently

enounce (i'nowns) *vt.* **1.** state **2.** enunciate, proclaim —**e'nouncement** *n.*

en passant (on pa'sän) *Fr.* in passing, by the way

enplane (in'plān) *vi.* board aircraft

enquire (in'kwīər) *v. see* INQUIRE

enrapture (in'rapchər) *vt.* **1.** delight excessively **2.** charm —**en'rapt** *or* **en'raptured** *a.* entranced

enrich (in'rich) *vt.* **1.** make rich **2.** add to —**en'richment** *n.*

enroll *or* **enrol** (in'rōl) *vt.* **1.** write name of on roll or list **2.** engage, enlist, take in as member **3.** enter, record —*vi.* **4.** become member —**en'rollment** *n.*

en route (on 'ro͞ot) *Fr.* on the way

ensconce (in'skons) *vt.* **1.** place snugly **2.** establish in safety

ensemble (on'sombəl) *n.* **1.** whole **2.** all parts taken together **3.** woman's complete outfit **4.** company of actors, dancers *etc.* **5.** *Mus.* group of soloists performing together **6.** *Mus.* concerted passage **7.** general effect —*adv.* **8.** all together or at once

enshrine (in'shrīn) *vt.* **1.** set in shrine **2.** preserve with great care and sacred affection

enshroud (in'shrowd) *vt.* cover or hide as with shroud

ensign ('ensīn) *n.* **1.** (*also* 'ensən) naval or military flag **2.** badge **3.** (in U.S. Navy and coastguard) commissioned officer ranking above chief warrant officer and below lieutenant junior grade

ensilage ('ensilij) *n.* the process of making silage

enslave (in'slāv) *vt.* make into slave —**en'slavement** *n.* bondage —**en'slaver** *n.*

ensnare *or* **insnare** (in'snāər) *vt.* **1.** capture in snare or trap **2.** trick into false position **3.** entangle

ensue (in'so͞o) *vi.* follow, happen after

en suite (ã 'swēt) forming a set or single unit

ensure (en'sho͝oər) *vt.* **1.** make safe or sure **2.** make certain to happen **3.** secure

E.N.T. *Med.* ear, nose and throat

-ent (*comb. form*) causing or performing action or existing in certain condition; agent that performs action, as in *astringent, dependent*

entablature (en'tabləcho͝oər) *n. Archit.* part of classical temple above columns, having architrave, frieze and cornice

entail (in'tāl) *vt.* **1.** involve as result, necessitate **2.** *Law* restrict (ownership of property) to designated line of heirs

entangle (in'tanggəl) *vt.* **1.** ensnare **2.** perplex —**en'tanglement** *n.*

entente (*Fr.* ā'tāt) *n.* friendly understanding between nations —**entente cordiale** (kor'dyal) **1.** friendly understanding between political powers **2.** (*oft.* **E- C-**) understanding reached by France and Britain in April 1904 over colonial disputes

enter ('entər) *vt.* **1.** go, come into **2.** penetrate **3.** join **4.** write in, register —*vi.* **5.** go, come in **6.** join a party *etc.* **7.** begin —'**entrance** *n.* **1.** going, coming in **2.** door, passage to enter **3.** right to enter **4.** fee paid for this —'**entrant** *n.* one who enters, *esp.* contest —'**entry** *n.* **1.** entrance **2.** entering **3.** item entered, *eg* in account, list

enteric (en'terik) *or* **enteral** ('entərəl) *a.* of intestines —**ente'ritis** *n.* bowel inflammation

enterprise ('entərprīz) *n.* **1.** bold or difficult undertaking **2.** bold spirit **3.** force of character in launching out **4.** business, company —'**enterprising** *a.*

entertain (entər'tān) *vt.* **1.** amuse, divert **2.** receive as guest **3.** maintain **4.** consider favorable **5.** take into consideration —**enter'tainer** *n.* —**enter'taining** *a.* serving to entertain; amusing —**enter'tainment** *n.*

enthrall *or* **enthral** (in'thrōl) *vt.* captivate, thrill, hold spellbound —**en'thrallment** *n.*

enthrone (en'thrōn) *vt.* **1.** place on throne **2.** honor; exalt **3.** assign authority to —**en'thronement** *n.*

enthusiasm (in'thyōōziazəm, -'thōō-) *n.* ardent eagerness, zeal —**en'thuse** *v.* (cause to) show enthusiasm —**en'thusiast** *n.* ardent supporter —**enthusi'astic** *a.* —**enthusi'astically** *adv.*

entice (in'tīs) *vt.* allure, attract, inveigle, tempt —**en'ticement** *n.* —**en'ticing** *a.* alluring

entire (in'tīər, 'entīər) *a.* **1.** whole, complete **2.** unbroken —**en'tirely** *adv.* —**entirety** (in'tīriti, -'tīərti) *n.*

entitle (in'tītəl) *vt.* **1.** give claim to **2.** qualify **3.** give title to **4.** style

entity ('entiti) *n.* **1.** thing's being or existence **2.** reality **3.** thing having real existence

entomb (in'tōōm) *vt.* **1.** place in or as if in tomb; bury **2.** serve as tomb for —**en'tombment** *n.*

entomology (entə'moləji) *n.* study of insects —**entomo'logical** *a.* —**ento'mologist** *n.* —**ento'mologize** *vi.*

entourage (ontōō'räzh) *n.* **1.** associates, retinue **2.** surroundings

entozoon (entō'zōon) *n.* internal parasite (*pl.* **-zoa** (-'zōə)) —**entozoic** (entō'zōik) *a.*

entr'acte ('ontrakt) *n.* **1.** interval between acts of play *etc.* **2.** *esp.* formerly, entertainment during such interval

entrails ('entrālz) *pl.n.* **1.** bowels, intestines **2.** inner parts

entrain (in'trān) *v.* board or put aboard train —**en'trainment** *n.*

entrance[1] ('entrəns) *n. see* ENTER

entrance[2] (in'trans) *vt.* **1.** delight **2.** throw into a trance

entrap (in'trap) *vt.* **1.** catch or snare as in trap **2.** trick into difficulty *etc.* (**-pp-**) —**en'trapment** *n.*

entreat (in'trēt) *vt.* **1.** ask earnestly **2.** beg, implore —**en'treaty** *n.* earnest request

entrée ('ontrā) *n.* **1.** (dish served before) main course of meal **2.** right of access, admission

entrench *or* **intrench** (in'trench) *vt.* **1.** establish in fortified position with trenches **2.** establish firmly —**en'trenchment** *or* **in'trenchment** *n.*

entrepreneur (ontrəprə'nər) *n.* person who attempts to profit by risk and initiative

entropy ('entrəpi) *n.* **1.** unavailability of the heat energy of a system for mechanical work **2.** measurement of this

entrust *or* **intrust** (in'trust) *vt.* **1.** commit, charge (with) **2.** (*oft. with* to) put into care or protection of

entwine (in'twīn) *vt.* **1.** plait, interweave **2.** wreathe **3.** embrace

enumerate (i'nyōōmərāt, -'nōō-) *vt.* **1.** mention one by one **2.** count —**enumer'ation** *n.* —**e'numerative** *a.* —**e'numerator** *n.*

enunciate (i'nunsiāt) *vt.* **1.** state clearly **2.** proclaim **3.** pronounce —**enunci'ation** *n.* —**e'nunciative** *a.* —**e'nunciator** *n.*

enure (in'yōōər, in'ōōər) *vt. see* INURE

enuresis (enyōō'rēsis) *n.* involuntary discharge of urine, *esp.* during sleep —**enuretic** (enyōō'retik) *a.*

envelop (in'veləp) *vt.* **1.** wrap up, enclose **2.** surround **3.** encircle —**en'velopment** *n.*

envelope ('envəlōp, 'on-) *n.* **1.** folded, gummed cover of letter **2.** covering, wrapper

envenom (in'venəm) *vt.* **1.** put poison, venom in **2.** embitter

environ (in'vīrən) *vt.* surround —**en'vironment** *n.* **1.** surroundings **2.** conditions of life or growth —**environ'mental** *a.* —**environ'mentalist** *n.* ecologist —**en'virons** *pl.n.* districts round town *etc.*, outskirts

envisage (in'vizij) *vt.* **1.** conceive of as possibility **2.** visualize

envoi *or* **envoy** ('envoi) *n.* concluding stanza in ballade

envoy ('envoi) *n.* **1.** messenger **2.** diplomatic representative of rank below ambassador

envy ('envi) *vt.* **1.** grudge (another's good fortune, success or qualities) **2.** feel jealous of ('**envied, 'envying**) —*n.* **3.** bitter contemplation of another's good fortune **4.** jealousy **5.** object of this feeling —'**enviable** *a.* arousing envy —'**envious** *a.* full of envy

enzyme ('enzīm) *n.* substance which catalyzes a reaction in a living system

Eocene ('ēəsēn) *a.* **1.** of second epoch of Tertiary period, during which hooved mammals appeared —*n.* **2.** Eocene epoch or rock series

eolith ('ēəlith) *n.* early flint implement —**Eo'lithic** *a.* of the period before Stone Age

eon ('ēən, 'ēon) *n.* **1.** age, very long period of time **2.** eternity

-eous (*comb. form*) relating to or having nature of, as in *gaseous*

EP **1.** extended-play **2.** electroplate

epaulet *or* **epaulette** (epə'let, 'epəlet) *n.* shoulder ornament formerly on uniform

épée ('epā) *n.* sword similar to foil but with heavier blade —**'épéeist** *n.*

epergne (i'pərn) *n.* ornamental centerpiece for table, holding flowers *etc.*

Eph. *Bible* Ephesians

ephedrine (i'fedrin) *n.* drug used to treat asthma, hay fever and other allergic disorders

ephemeral (i'femərəl) *a.* short-lived, transient —**e'phemeron** *n.* ephemeral thing (*pl.* **-s, -ra** (-rə)) (*also* **e'phemera** (*pl.* **-s, -rae** (-rē))) —**e'phemerous** *a.*

Ephesians (i'fēzhənz) *pl.n.* (*with sing. v.*) *Bible* 10th book of the N.T., epistle written by St. Paul to Christians of Ephesus from his captivity at Rome about 60 A.D.

epi-, eph-, *or before vowel* **ep-** (*comb. form*) **1.** upon; above, as in *epidermis* **2.** in addition to, as in *epiphenomenon* **3.** after, as in *epilogue* **4.** near, as in *epicalyx*

epic ('epik) *n.* **1.** long poem or story telling of achievements of hero or heroes **2.** film *etc.* about heroic deeds —*a.* **3.** of, like, an epic **4.** impressive, grand

epicene ('episēn) *a.* common to both sexes

epicenter ('episentər) *n.* focus of earthquake —**epi'central** *a.*

epicure ('epikyŏŏər) *n.* one delighting in eating and drinking —**epicu'rean** *a.* **1.** of Epicurus, who taught that pleasure, in the shape of practice of virtue, was highest good **2.** given to refined sensuous enjoyment —*n.* **3.** such person or philosopher —**epicu'reanism** *n.* —**'epicurism** *n.*

epicycle ('episīkəl) *n.* circle whose center moves on circumference of greater circle

epidemic (epi'demik) *a.* **1.** (*esp.* of disease) prevalent and spreading rapidly **2.** widespread —*n.* **3.** widespread occurrence of a disease **4.** rapid development, spread or growth of something —**epi'demical** *a.* —**epidemiological** (epidēmiə'lojikəl) *a.* —**epidemiologist** (epidēmi'oləjist) *n.* —**epidemiology** (epidēmi'oləji) *n.* branch of medical science concerned with epidemic diseases —**epidemic parotitis** (parō'tītis) mumps

epidermis (epi'dərmis) *n.* outer skin

epidiascope (epi'dīəskōp) *n.* optical device for projecting magnified image on to screen

epidural (epi'dyŏŏrəl, -'dŏŏrəl) *n./a.* (of) spinal anesthetic used for relief of pain during childbirth

epiglottis (epi'glotis) *n.* cartilage that covers opening of larynx in swallowing —**epi'glottic** *a.*

epigram ('epigram) *n.* concise, witty poem or saying —**epigram'matic(al)** *a.* —**epigram'matically** *adv.* —**epi'grammatist** *n.*

epigraph ('epigraf) *n.* inscription

epilepsy ('epilepsi) *n.* disorder of nervous system causing fits and convulsions —**epi'leptic** *n.* **1.** sufferer from this —*a.* **2.** of, subject to, this

epilogue ('epilog) *n.* short speech or poem at end, *esp.* of play

epinephrine *or* **epinephrin** (epi'nefrin) *n.* hormone secreted by medulla of the adrenal gland which mobilizes the body for strenuous or emergency activity, used medicinally as stimulant *etc.* (*also* **adrenaline**)

Epiphany (i'pifəni) *n.* festival of the announcement of Christ to the Magi, celebrated Jan. 6th

epiphysis (i'pifisis) *n.* pineal body

epiphyte ('epifīt) *n.* plant which grows on another without being parasitic

Epis. **1.** Episcopal; Episcopalian (*also* **Episc.**) **2.** Epistle

episcopal (i'piskəpəl) *a.* **1.** of bishop **2.** ruled by bishops —**e'piscopacy** *n.* government by body of bishops —**Episco'palian** *a.* **1.** of branch of Anglican Church in the U.S. —*n.* **2.** member or adherent of Protestant Christian denomination whose doctrine is based on the Apostles' Creed and in which practice ranges from rationalist to acceptance of most Roman Catholic dogma and is part of the Anglican Communion —**e'piscopate** *n.* **1.** bishop's office, see, or duration of office **2.** body of bishops

episode ('episōd) *n.* **1.** incident **2.** section of (serialized) book, television program *etc.* —**episodic(al)** (epi'sodik(əl)) *a.*

epistemology (ipisti'moləji) *n.* study of source, nature and limitations of knowledge —**epistemo'logical** *a.* —**episte'mologist** *n.*

epistle (i'pisəl) *n.* **1.** letter, *esp.* of apostle **2.** poem in letter form —**epistolary** (i'pistəleri) *a.* —**epistoler** (i'pistələr) *n.*

epitaph ('epitaf) *n.* memorial inscription on tomb

epithelium (epi'thēliəm) *n.* tissue covering external and internal surfaces of body (*pl.* **-s, -lia** (-liə)) —**epi'thelial** *or* **epi'thelioid** *a.*

epithet ('epithet) *n.* additional, descriptive word or name —**epi'thetic(al)** *a.*

epitome (i'pitəmi) *n.* **1.** typical example **2.** summary —**e'pitomist** *n.* —**e'pitomize** *vt.* typify

epoch ('epək, 'epok) *n.* **1.** beginning of period

2. period, era, *esp.* one of notable events —**'epochal** *a.*

epode ('epōd) *n.* third, or last, part of lyric ode

eponym ('epənim) *n.* **1.** name, *esp.* place name, derived from name of real or mythical person **2.** name of person from which such name is derived —**e'ponymous** *a.* —**e'ponymously** *adv.* —**e'ponymy** *n.*

epoxy ('epoksi, e'poksi) *a. Chem.* of, consisting of, or containing oxygen atom joined to two different groups that are themselves joined to other groups —**epoxy resin** any of various thermosetting synthetic resins containing epoxy groups: used in surface coatings, adhesives *etc.*

epsilon ('epsilon) *n.* fifth letter of Gr. alphabet (E, ϵ)

Epsom salts ('epsəm) medicinal preparation of hydrated magnesium sulfate, used as purgative *etc.*

equable ('ekwəbəl) *a.* **1.** even-tempered, placid **2.** uniform —**equa'bility** *n.* —**'equably** *adv.*

equal ('ēkwəl) *a.* **1.** the same in number, size, merit *etc.* **2.** identical **3.** fit or qualified **4.** evenly balanced —*n.* **5.** one equal to another —*vt.* **6.** be equal to —**equality** (i'kwoliti) *n.* **1.** state of being equal **2.** uniformity —**equali'zation** *n.* —**'equalize** *v.* make, become, equal —**'equally** *adv.*

equanimity (ēkwə'nimiti, ekwə-) *n.* calmness, composure, steadiness

equate (i'kwāt) *vt.* **1.** make equal **2.** bring to a common standard —**equation** (i'kwāzhən, -shən) *n.* in chemistry and mathematics, statement asserting the equality of two expressions or two numbers

equator (i'kwātər) *n.* imaginary circle round earth equidistant from the poles —**equa'torial** *a.*

Equatorial Guinea country in Africa bounded west by the Atlantic, north by Cameroon and east and south by Gabon

equerry ('ekwəri, i'kweri) *n.* **1.** officer in attendance on sovereign **2.** officer in royal household in charge of horses

equestrian (i'kwestriən) *a.* **1.** of, skilled in, horse-riding **2.** mounted on horse —*n.* **3.** rider

equi- (*comb. form*) equal, at equal, as in *equidistant.* Such words are not given here where the meaning can easily be inferred from the simple word

equiangular (ēkwi'anggyŏŏlər) *a.* having equal angles

equilateral (ēkwi'latərəl) *a.* having equal sides

equilibrium (ēkwi'libriəm) *n.* state of steadiness, equipoise or stability (*pl.* **-s, -ria** (-riə))

equine ('ekwīn) *a.* of, like a horse

equinox ('ēkwinoks) *n.* **1.** time when sun crosses equator and day and night are equal —*pl.* **2.** points at which sun crosses equator —**equinoctial** (ēkwi'nokshəl) *a.*

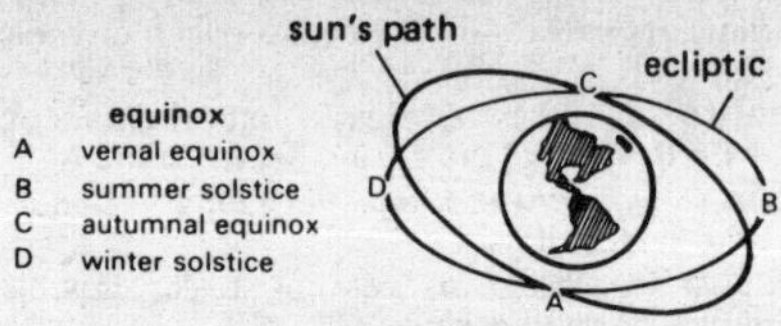

equip (i'kwip) *vt.* supply, fit out, array (**-pp-**) —**equipage** ('ekwipij) *n.* **1.** carriage, horses and attendants **2.** *obs.* outfit, requisites —**e'quipment** *n.*

equipoise ('ekwipoiz) *n.* **1.** perfect balance **2.** counterpoise **3.** equanimity —*vt.* **4.** counterbalance

equisetum (ekwi'sētəm) *n.* genus of primitive plant comprising the horsetail and scouring rush

equitation (ekwi'tāshən) *n.* study and practice of riding and horsemanship

equity ('ekwiti) *n.* **1.** fairness **2.** ownership right in property **3.** (**E-**) actors' union —**'equitable** *a.* fair, reasonable, just —**'equitably** *adv.* —**equity capital** corporate earnings or individual savings available for investment in new enterprise (*also* **venture capital**)

equiv. equivalent

equivalent (i'kwivələnt) *a.* **1.** equal in value **2.** having the same meaning or result **3.** tantamount **4.** corresponding —**e'quivalence** *or* **e'quivalency** *n.*

equivocal (i'kwivəkəl) *a.* **1.** of double or doubtful meaning **2.** questionable **3.** liable to suspicion —**equivo'cality** *n.* —**e'quivocate** *vi.* use equivocal words to mislead —**equivo'cation** *n.* —**e'quivocator** *n.*

er (ə, ər) *interj.* sound made when hesitating in speech

Er *Chem.* erbium

E.R. Elizabeth Regina (*Lat.,* Queen Elizabeth)

-er[1] (*comb. form*) **1.** person or thing that performs specified action, as in *reader* **2.** person engaged in profession *etc.,* as in *writer* **3.** native or inhabitant of, as in *Londoner* **4.** person or thing having certain characteristic, as in *newcomer*

-er[2] (*comb. form*) forming comparative degree of adjective or adverb, as in *deeper, faster*

era ('ēərə) *n.* **1.** system of time in which years are numbered from particular event **2.** time of the event **3.** memorable date, period

ERA 1. equal rights amendment **2.** *Baseball* earned run average

eradicate (i'radikāt) *vt.* **1.** wipe out, exterminate **2.** root out —**e'radicable** *a.*

—**eradi'cation** *n.* —**e'radicative** *a./n.* —**e'radicator** *n.*

erase (i'rās) *vt.* **1.** rub out **2.** remove, *eg* recording from magnetic tape —**e'raser** *n.* —**e'rasure** *n.*

erbium ('ərbiəm) *n. Chem.* metallic element *Symbol* Er, at. wt. 167.3, at. no. 68

ere (āər) *prep./conj.* **1.** *Poet.* before **2.** sooner than —**ere'long** *adv. obs., poet.* before long; soon

erect (i'rekt) *a.* **1.** upright —*vt.* **2.** set up **3.** build —**e'rectile** *a.* —**e'rection** *n. esp.* an erect penis —**e'rector** *n.*

eremite ('erimīt) *n.* Christian hermit or recluse —**eremitic(al)** (eri'mitik(əl)) *a.* —'**eremitism** *n.*

erg (ərg) *n.* cgs unit of work or energy

ergo ('ərgō) *adv.* therefore

ergonomics (ərgə'nomiks) *pl.n.* (*with sing. v.*) study of relationship between workers and their environment

ergot ('ərgət, -got) *n.* **1.** disease of grain *esp.* rye **2.** diseased seed used as drug —'**ergotism** *n.* disease caused by eating ergot-infested bread

erica ('erikə) *n.* genus of plants including heathers

Erin ('erin) *n. obs., poet.* Ireland

ermine ('ərmin) *n.* **1.** stoat in northern regions, *esp.* in winter **2.** its white winter fur

erne *or* **ern** (ərn) *n.* fish-eating sea eagle

erode (i'rōd) *v.* **1.** wear away —*vt.* **2.** eat into —**e'rosion** *n.* —**e'rosive** *a.*

erogenous (i'rojinəs) *a.* sensitive to sexual stimulation

erotic (i'rotik) *a.* relating to, or treating of, sexual pleasure —**e'rotica** *n.* sexual literature or art —**e'roticism** *n.*

err (er, ər) *vi.* **1.** make mistakes **2.** be wrong **3.** sin —**er'ratic** *a.* irregular in movement, conduct *etc.* —**er'ratically** *adv.* —**erratum** (e'rätəm) *n.* printing mistake noted for correction (*pl.* **-ta** (-tə)) —**er'roneous** *a.* mistaken, wrong —'**error** *n.* **1.** mistake **2.** wrong opinion **3.** sin

errand ('erənd) *n.* **1.** short journey for simple business **2.** purpose of such journey **3.** the business, mission of messenger —**errand boy**

errant ('erənt) *a.* **1.** wandering in search of adventure **2.** erring —'**errancy** *n.* erring state or conduct —'**errantry** *n.* state or conduct of knight errant

ersatz ('āərzats, 'erzats) *a.* substitute, imitation

Erse (ərs) *n.* **1.** *see* **Gaelic** *at* GAEL —*a.* **2.** of or relating to Gaelic language

erst (ərst) *adv.* of old, formerly

eruct (i'rukt) *v.* **1.** belch **2.** (of volcano) pour out (fumes or volcanic matter) —**eruc'tation** *n.*

erudite ('eryədīt, 'erə-) *a.* learned —**erudition** (eryə'dishən, erə-) *n.* learning

erupt (i'rupt) *vi.* burst out —**e'ruption** *n.* **1.** bursting out, *esp.* volcanic outbreak **2.** rash on the skin —**e'ruptive** *a.*

-ery *or* **-ry** (*comb. form*) **1.** place of business or activity, as in *bakery, refinery* **2.** class or collection of things, as in *cutlery* **3.** qualities, actions, as in *snobbery, trickery* **4.** practice, occupation, as in *husbandry* **5.** state, condition, as in *slavery*

erysipelas (eri'sipiləs) *n.* acute skin infection caused by streptococcus

erythema (eri'thēmə) *n.* patchy inflammation of skin —**erythematic** (erithi'matik) *or* **ery'thematous** *a.*

erythrocyte (i'rithrəsīt) *n.* red blood cell of vertebrates that transports oxygen and carbon dioxide —**erythrocytic** (irithrə'sitik) *a.*

Es *Chem.* einsteinium

escalate ('eskəlāt) *v.* increase, be increased, in extent, intensity *etc.*

escalator ('eskəlātər) *n.* moving staircase —**escalator clause** clause in contract stipulating adjustment in wages *etc.* in event of large rise in cost of living *etc.*

escallop (i'skoləp, i'skal-) *see* SCALLOP

escape (i'skāp) *vi.* **1.** get free **2.** get off safely **3.** go unpunished **4.** find way out —*vt.* **5.** elude **6.** be forgotten by —*n.* **7.** escaping —**escapade** ('eskəpād) *n.* wild (mischievous) adventure —**es'capement** *n.* **1.** mechanism consisting of toothed wheel and anchor, used in timepieces to provide periodic impulses to pendulum or balance **2.** any similar mechanism that regulates movement —**es'capism** *n.* taking refuge in fantasy to avoid facing disagreeable facts —**escapologist** (iskā'poləjist) *n.* entertainer specializing in freeing himself from confinement —**escape clause** clause releasing signatory to contract under certain conditions —**escape hatch** means of emergency exit from shop *etc.* —**escape velocity** minimum velocity necessary for a body to escape from the gravitational field of the earth *etc.*

escarp (i'skärp) *n.* steep bank under rampart —**es'carpment** *n.* **1.** steep hillside **2.** escarp

-escent (*a. comb. form*) beginning to be, do, show *etc.*, as in *convalescent, luminescent* —**-escence** (*n. comb. form*)

eschatology (eskə'toləji) *n.* study of death, judgment and last things —**eschato'logical** *a.*

escheat (is'chēt) *Law n.* **1.** reversion of property to state in absence of legal heirs **2.** property so reverting —*v.* **3.** take (land) by escheat or (of land) revert by escheat —**es'cheatable** *a.* —**es'cheatage** *n.*

eschew (is'chōō) *vt.* avoid, abstain from, shun

eschscholtzia (is'kolshə) *n.* garden plant with bright flowers, California poppy

escort ('eskört) *n.* **1.** armed guard for traveler *etc.* **2.** person or persons accompanying another —*vt.* (is'kört) **3.** accompany or attend as escort

escritoire ('eskritwär) *n.* type of writing desk

esculent ('eskyələnt) *a.* edible

escutcheon (i'skuchən) *n.* **1.** shield with coat of arms **2.** ornamental plate round keyhole *etc.* —**blot on one's escutcheon** stain on one's honor

Esdras ('ezdrəs) *n. Bible* Ezra and Nehemiah in the Douay Version of the O.T.

-ese (*comb. form*) place of origin, language, style, as in *Cantonese, Japanese, journalese*

Eskimo ('eskimō) *n.* **1.** one of aboriginal race inhabiting N Amer., Greenland *etc.* (*pl.* **-s**) **2.** their language **3.** *sl.* a Jew

esophagus

esophagus (i'sofəgəs) *n.* gullet, canal from mouth to stomach (*pl.* **-gi** (-gī, -jī)) —**esophageal** (isofə'jēəl) *a.*

esoteric (esə'terik) *a.* **1.** abstruse, obscure **2.** secret **3.** restricted to initiates

E.S.P. extrasensory perception

esp. especially

espadrille ('espədril) *n.* canvas shoe, *esp.* with braided cord sole

espalier (i'spalyər) *n.* **1.** shrub, (fruit) tree trained to grow flat, as against wall *etc.* **2.** trellis for this

esparto (i'spärtō) *n.* kind of grass yielding fiber used for making rope *etc.*

especial (i'speshəl) *a.* **1.** pre-eminent, more than ordinary **2.** particular —**es'pecially** *adv.*

Esperanto (espə'rantō) *n.* artificial language designed for universal use —**Espe'rantist** *n.* one who uses Esperanto

espionage ('espiənäzh) *n.* **1.** spying **2.** use of secret agents

esplanade ('esplənäd, -nād) *n.* level space, *esp.* one used as public promenade

espouse (i'spowz) *vt.* **1.** support, embrace (cause *etc.*) **2.** *obs.* marry —**es'pousal** *n.*

espresso (e'spresō) *n.* strong coffee made by forcing steam through ground coffee beans

esprit (i'sprē) *n.* **1.** spirit **2.** animation —**esprit de corps** (də 'kör) attachment, loyalty to the society *etc.* one belongs to

espy (i'spī) *vt.* catch sight of (**es'pied, es'pying**) —**es'pial** *n.* observation

Esq. Esquire

-esque (*comb. form*) specified character, manner, style or resemblance, as in *picturesque, Romanesque, statuesque*

esquire ('eskwīər, is'kwīər) *n.* **1.** gentleman's courtesy title used on letters **2.** formerly, squire

-ess (*comb. form*) female, as in *actress*

essay ('esā; *def. 3 also* e'sā) *n.* **1.** prose composition **2.** short treatise **3.** attempt —*vt.* (e'sā) **4.** try, attempt **5.** test (**es'sayed, es'saying**) —**'essayist** *n.*

essence ('esəns) *n.* **1.** all that makes thing what it is **2.** existence, being **3.** entity, reality **4.** extract got by distillation —**es'sential** *a.* **1.** necessary, indispensable **2.** inherent **3.** of, constituting essence of thing —*n.* **4.** indispensable element **5.** chief point —**essenti'ality** *n.* —**essential oil** any of various volatile oils in plants, having odor *etc.* of plant from which they are extracted

E.S.T. Eastern Standard Time

est. **1.** established **2.** estimate(d)

-est (*comb. form*) forming superlative degree of adjective or adverb, as in *fastest*

establish (i'stablish) *vt.* **1.** make secure **2.** set up **3.** settle **4.** prove —**es'tablishment** *n.* **1.** permanent organized body, full number of regiment *etc.* **2.** household **3.** business **4.** public institution —**the Establishment** group, class of people holding authority within a society

estate (i'stāt) *n.* **1.** landed property **2.** person's property **3.** area of property development, *esp.* of houses or factories **4.** class as part of nation **5.** rank, state, condition of life —**estate tax** tax levied on property of deceased before it is transferred to the heirs

esteem (i'stēm) *vt.* **1.** think highly of **2.** consider —*n.* **3.** favorable opinion, regard, respect

ester ('estər) *n. Chem.* organic compound produced by reaction between acid and alcohol

Esther ('estər) *n. Bible* 17th book of the O.T., telling the story of Esther who became queen to Xerxes and saved the Jews from massacre which is commemorated annually in the feast of Purim

estimate ('estimāt) *vt.* **1.** form approximate idea of (amounts, measurements *etc.*) **2.** form opinion of **3.** quote probable price for —*n.* ('estimit) **4.** approximate judgment of amounts *etc.* **5.** amount *etc.* arrived at **6.** opinion **7.** price quoted by contractor —**'estimable** *a.* worthy of regard —**esti'mation** *n.* **1.** opinion, judgment **2.** esteem

estivate ('estivāt) *vi.* spend the summer, *esp.* in dormant condition —**'estival** *a. rare* of summer —**esti'vation** *n.*

estrange (i'strānj) *vt.* **1.** lose affection of **2.** alienate —**es'trangement** *n.*

estrogen ('estrəjən) *n.* hormone in females *esp.* controlling changes, cycles in reproductive organs

estrus ('estrəs) *or* **estrum** ('estrəm) *n. see* HEAT (sense 5)

estuary ('eschōōəri) *n.* tidal mouth of river, inlet —'**estuarine** *a.*

-et (*comb. form*) small, lesser, as in *islet, baronet*

eta ('ātə, 'ētə) *n.* seventh letter in Gr. alphabet (H, η)

E.T.A. estimated time of arrival

et al. 1. et alibi (*Lat.*, and elsewhere) **2.** et alii (*Lat.*, and others)

etc. et cetera

et cetera (et 'setərə, 'setrə) *Lat.* and the rest, and other things —**et'ceteras** *pl.n.* miscellaneous extras

etch (ech) *v.* **1.** make (engraving) by eating away surface of metal plate with acids *etc.* —*vt.* **2.** imprint vividly —'**etcher** *n.* —'**etching** *n.*

eternal (i'tərnəl) *a.* **1.** without beginning or end **2.** everlasting **3.** changeless —**e'ternally** *adv.* —**e'ternity** *n.* —**eternal triangle** emotional relationship in which there are conflicts involving a man and two women or a woman and two men —**eternity ring** ring, *esp.* one set all around with stones to symbolize continuity —**the Eternal City** Rome

ethane ('ethān) *n.* odorless flammable gaseous alkane obtained from natural gas and petroleum

ether ('ēthər) *n.* **1.** colorless volatile liquid used as anesthetic **2.** intangible fluid formerly supposed to fill all space **3.** the clear sky, region above clouds —**ethereal** (i'thēəriəl) *a.* **1.** light, airy **2.** heavenly, spiritlike —**ethereality** (ithēəri'aliti) *n.* —**ethereali'zation** *n.* —**etherealize** (i'thēəriəlīz) *vt.* **1.** make or regard as being ethereal **2.** add ether to or make into ether

ethical ('ethikəl) *a.* relating to morals —'**ethically** *adv.* —'**ethics** *pl.n.* **1.** (*with sing. v.*) science of morals **2.** moral principles, rules of conduct —**ethical drug** drug which can only be bought on physician's prescription

Ethiopia (ēthi'ōpiə) *n.* country in Africa bounded northeast by the Red Sea, east by Djibouti and Somalia, south by Kenya and west by Sudan —**Ethi'opian** *a.* **1.** of Ethiopia —*n.* **2.** native of Ethiopia **3.** Amharic —*n./a.* **4.** *obs.* Negro

ethnic ('ethnik) *a.* of race or relating to classification of humans into social, cultural *etc.* groups —'**ethnics** *pl.n.* minority groups distinguished by culture —**ethno'graphic** *a.* —**eth'nography** *n.* description of races of men —**ethno'logical** *a.* —**eth'nology** *n.* the study of human races

ethology (ē'tholəji) *n.* scientific study of animal behavior in its natural state

ethos ('ēthos) *n.* distinctive character, spirit *etc.* of people, culture *etc.*

ethyl ('ethil) *n.* (C_2H_5) radical of ordinary alcohol and ether —'**ethylene** *n.* poisonous gas used as anesthetic and fuel —**ethyl alcohol** *see* ALCOHOL (sense 1)

etiolate ('ētiəlāt) *v.* **1.** *Bot.* whiten (green plant) through lack of sunlight **2.** (cause to) become pale and weak —**etio'lation** *n.*

etiology (ēti'oləji) *n.* study of causes, *esp.* inquiry into origin of disease —**etio'logical** *a.*

etiquette ('etikit, -ket) *n.* conventional code of conduct or behavior

Eton collar ('ētən) broad stiff white collar worn outside Eton jacket

Eton crop short mannish hair style worn by women in 1920s

Eton jacket waist-length jacket, open in front, formerly worn by pupils of Eton College, public school for boys in S England

Etruscan (i'truskən) *or* **Etrurian** (i'trōōriən) *n.* **1.** member of ancient people of Etruria in central Italy **2.** language of ancient Etruscans —*a.* **3.** of Etruria, Etruscans, their culture or their language —**Etruscan art** tomb painting and artifacts produced between 7th and 3rd centuries B.C. by Etruscans

et seq. 1. et sequens (*Lat.*, and the following) **2.** (*also* **et seqq.**) et sequentia (*Lat.*, and those that follow)

-ette (*comb. form*) **1.** small, as in *cigarette* **2.** female, as in *majorette* **3.** imitation, as in *Leatherette*

étude ('ātyōōd, -tōōd) *n.* short musical composition, study, intended often as technical exercise

ety., etym., *or* **etymol. 1.** etymological **2.** etymology

etymology (eti'moləji) *n.* **1.** tracing, account of, formation of word's origin, development **2.** science of this —**etymo'logical** *a.* —**etymo'logically** *adv.* —**ety'mologist** *n.*

Eu *Chem.* europium

eu- (*comb. form*) well, as in *eugenic, euphony*

eucalyptus (yōōkə'liptəs) *or* **eucalypt** ('yōōkəlipt) *n.* mostly Aust. genus of tree, the gum tree, yielding timber and oil, used medicinally from leaves

Eucharist ('yōōkərist) *n.* **1.** Christian sacrament of the Lord's Supper **2.** the consecrated elements —**Eucha'ristic** *a.*

euchre ('yōōkər) *n.* family of card games for four players (two partnerships) played usu. with 32 cards from a standard deck by omitting all cards below seven in which the object is to win tricks with a card of the highest rank in a plain suit or the trump suit

Euclidean (yōō'klidiən) *a.* denoting system of geometry based on axioms of Gr. mathematician Euclid —**Euclidean geometry** the study of three classes of objects, *ie* points, lines and planes (which are not defined) and their relations to each other

eugenic (yōō'jenik) *a.* relating to, or tending towards, production of fine offspring

—eu'genicist *n.* —eu'genics *pl.n.* (*with sing. v.*) this science
Euler circles ('oilər) concentric or enclosing circles used to show relations between sets and subsets
eulogy ('yo͞oləji) *n.* **1.** speech or writing in praise of person **2.** praise —'**eulogist** *n.* —**eulo'gistic** *a.* —**eulo'gistically** *adv.* —'**eulogize** *v.*
eunuch ('yo͞onək) *n.* castrated man, *esp.* formerly one employed in harem —'**eunuchoidism** *n.* glandular disturbance marked by development of female physical traits in men
euphemism ('yo͞ofimizəm) *n.* **1.** substitution of mild term for offensive or hurtful one **2.** instance of this —'**euphemist** *n.* —**euphe'mistic** *a.* —**euphe'mistically** *adv.* —'**euphemize** *v.*
euphonium (yo͞o'fōniəm) *n.* brass musical instrument larger than the cornet with the oval bell pointing backwards, used in brass bands
euphony ('yo͞ofəni) *n.* pleasantness of sound —**euphonic** (yo͞o'fonik) *or* **euphonious** (yo͞o'fōniəs) *a.* pleasing to ear
euphoria (yo͞o'fōriə) *n.* sense of wellbeing or elation —**euphoric** (yo͞o'forik) *a.*
euphuism ('yo͞ofyo͞oizəm) *n.* affected high-flown manner of writing, *esp.* in imitation of Lyly's *Euphues* (1580) —**euphu'istic** *a.*
Eur. Europe(an)
Eurasian (yo͝o'rāzhən, -shən) *a.* **1.** of mixed European and Asiatic descent **2.** of Europe and Asia —*n.* **3.** one of this descent
Euratom (yo͝o'ratəm) *n.* European Atomic Energy Commission
eureka (yo͝o'rēkə) *interj.* exclamation of triumph at finding something
eurhythmics *or* **eurythmics** (yo͞o'ridhmiks) *pl.n.* (*with sing. v.*) system of training through physical movement to music —**eu'rhythmy** *or* **eu'rythmy** *n.*
Euro- ('yo͝orō-) *or before vowel* **Eur-** (*comb. form*) Europe; European
Eurodollar ('yo͝orōdolər) *n.* U.S. dollar as part of European holding
European (yo͝orə'pēən) *n./a.* (native) of Europe —**European Atomic Energy Commission** authority established by Common Market to develop peaceful uses of nuclear energy —**European Economic Community** association of a number of European nations for trade
europium (yo͞o'rōpiəm) *n. Chem.* metallic element *Symbol* Eu, at. wt. 152.0, at. no. 63
eurythmics (yo͞o'ridhmiks) *n. see* EURHYTHMICS
Eustachian tube (yo͞o'stāshən) passage leading from pharynx to middle ear
euthanasia (yo͞othə'nāzhə) *n.* **1.** gentle, painless death **2.** putting to death in this way, *esp.* to relieve suffering
euthenics (yo͞o'theniks) *pl.n.* (*with sing. v.*) science of the relation of environment to human beings
eV electronvolt
evacuate (i'vakyo͞oāt) *vt.* **1.** empty **2.** cause to withdraw **3.** discharge —**evacu'ation** *n.* —**evacu'ee** *n.* person moved from danger area, *esp.* in time of war
evade (i'vād) *vt.* **1.** avoid, escape from **2.** elude —**e'vasion** *n.* **1.** subterfuge **2.** excuse **3.** equivocation —**e'vasive** *a.* elusive, not straightforward —**e'vasively** *adv.*
evaluate (i'valyo͞oāt) *vt.* find or judge value of —**evalu'ation** *n.*
evanesce (evə'nes) *vi.* fade away —**eva'nescence** *n.* —**eva'nescent** *a.* fleeting, transient
evangelical (ēvan'jelikəl) *a.* **1.** of, or according to, gospel teaching **2.** of Protestant sect which maintains salvation by faith —*n.* **3.** member of evangelical sect —**evan'gelicalism** *n.* —**e'vangelism** *n.* —**e'vangelist** *n.* **1.** writer of one of the four gospels **2.** ardent, zealous preacher of the gospel **3.** revivalist —**evangeli'zation** *n.* —**e'vangelize** *vt.* **1.** preach gospel to **2.** convert
evaporate (i'vapərāt) *vi.* **1.** turn into, pass off in, vapor —*vt.* **2.** turn into vapor —**evapo'ration** *n.* conversion of liquid into gaseous state at surface —**e'vaporative** *a.* —**e'vaporator** *n.* —**evaporated milk** milk from which some of the water has been evaporated
evasion (i'vāzhən) *n. see* EVADE
eve (ēv) *n.* **1.** evening before (festival *etc.*) **2.** time just before (event *etc.*) **3.** *obs.* evening
Eve (ēv) *n.* the first woman, and wife of Adam
even[1] ('ēvən) *a.* **1.** flat, smooth **2.** uniform in quality, equal in amount, balanced **3.** divisible by two **4.** impartial —*vt.* **5.** make even **6.** smooth **7.** equalize —*adv.* **8.** equally **9.** simply **10.** notwithstanding —'**evens** *a./adv.* **1.** (of bet) winning identical sum if successful **2.** (of runner) offered at such odds —**even-handed** *a.* fair; impartial —**even-handedly** *adv.* —**even-handedness** *n.*
even[2] ('ēvən) *n. obs.* eve; evening —'**evensong** *n.* evening prayer
evening ('ēvning) *n.* **1.** the close of day or early part of night **2.** decline, end —**evening dress** attire for formal occasion during evening —**evening paper** daily newspaper published at or after noon —**evening star** planet, usu. Venus, seen in west just after sunset
event (i'vent) *n.* **1.** happening **2.** notable occurrence **3.** issue, result **4.** any one contest in series in sporting program —**e'ventful** *a.* full of exciting events —**e'ventual** *a.* **1.** resulting in the end **2.** ultimate **3.** final —**eventu'ality** *n.* possible event —**e'ventually** *adv.* —**e'ventuate** *vi.* **1.** turn out **2.** happen **3.** end —**in the event that** if it should happen that
ever ('evər) *adv.* **1.** always **2.** constantly **3.** at any time —**ever'more** *adv.* —'**evergreen**

any time —ever'more *adv.* —'evergreen *n./a.* (tree or shrub) bearing foliage throughout year —ever'lasting *a.* 1. eternal 2. lasting for an indefinitely long period —ever'lastingly *adv.*

every ('evri) *a.* 1. each of all 2. all possible —'**everybody** *pron.* —'**every'day** *a.* usual, ordinary —'**Everyman** *n.* (*oft.* **e-**) ordinary person; common man —'**everyone** *pron.* —'**everything** *pron.* —'**everywhere** *adv.* to or in all places

evict (i'vikt) *vt.* expel by legal process, turn out —**e'viction** *n.* —**e'victor** *n.*

evident ('evidənt) *a.* plain, obvious —'**evidence** *n.* 1. ground of belief 2. sign, indication 3. testimony —*vt.* 4. indicate, prove —**evi'dential** *a.* —'**evidently** *adv.* —**in evidence** conspicuous

evil ('ēvəl) *a.* 1. bad, harmful —*n.* 2. what is bad or harmful 3. sin —'**evilly** *adv.* —**evil'doer** *n.* sinner —**evil-eyed** *a.* —**the evil eye** 1. look superstitiously supposed to have power of inflicting harm *etc.* 2. power to inflict harm *etc.* by such a look

evince (i'vins) *vt.* show, indicate

eviscerate (i'visərāt) *vt.* 1. remove internal organs of 2. deprive of meaning or significance —**eviscer'ation** *n.* —**e'viscerator** *n.*

evoke (i'vōk) *vt.* 1. draw forth 2. call to mind —**evocation** (evə'kāshən) *n.* —**evocative** (i'vokətiv) *a.*

evolve (i'volv) *v.* 1. develop or cause to develop gradually —*vi.* 2. undergo slow changes in process of growth —**evolution** (evə'lo͞oshən, ēvə-) *n.* 1. evolving 2. development of species from earlier forms —**evolutional** (evə'lo͞oshənəl, ēvə-) *a.* —**evolutionary** (evə'lo͞oshəneri, ēvə-) *a.* —**evolutionist** (evə'lo͞oshənist, ēvə-) *n.*

ewe (yo͞o) *n.* female sheep

ewer ('yo͞oər) *n.* pitcher, water jug with wide spout

ex[1] (eks) *prep.* 1. *Fin.* excluding; without 2. *Comm.* without charge to buyer until removed from —**ex cathedra** (kə'thēdrə) 1. with authority 2. (of papal pronouncements) defined as infallibly true —**ex gratia** ('grāshə) given as favor, *esp.* where no legal obligation exists —**ex hypothesi** (hī'pothəsi) in accordance with hypothesis stated —**ex libris** ('lēbris) from the library of —**ex officio** (ə'fishiō) by right of position or office —**ex post facto** ('faktō) having retrospective effect

ex[2] (eks) *n. inf.* ex-wife, ex-husband *etc.*

ex-, e-, *or* **ef-** (*comb. form*) out from, from, out of, formerly, as in *exclaim, evade, effusive, exodus.* Such words are not given here where the meaning may easily be inferred from the simple word

ex. 1. example 2. except(ed) 3. extra

exacerbate (ig'zasərbāt) *vt.* 1. aggravate, make worse 2. embitter —**exacer'bation** *n.*

exact (ig'zakt) *a.* 1. precise, accurate, strictly correct —*vt.* 2. demand, extort 3. insist upon 4. enforce —**ex'acting** *a.* making rigorous or excessive demands —**ex'action** *n.* 1. act of exacting 2. that which is exacted, as excessive work *etc.* 3. oppressive demand —**ex'actitude** *n.* —**ex'actly** *adv.* —**ex'actness** *n.* 1. accuracy 2. precision —**ex'actor** *n.*

exaggerate (ig'zajərāt) *vt.* 1. magnify beyond truth, overstate 2. enlarge 3. overestimate —**exagger'ation** *n.* —**ex'aggerative** *a.* —**ex'aggerator** *n.*

exalt (ig'zölt) *vt.* 1. raise up 2. praise 3. make noble, dignify —**exal'tation** *n.* 1. an exalting 2. elevation in rank, dignity or position 3. rapture

exam (ig'zam) examination

examine (ig'zamin) *vt.* 1. investigate 2. look at closely 3. ask questions of 4. test knowledge or proficiency of 5. inquire into —**exami'nation** *n.* —**exami'nee** *n.* —**ex'aminer** *n.*

example (ig'zampəl) *n.* 1. thing illustrating general rule 2. specimen 3. model 4. warning 5. precedent 6. instance

exasperate (ig'zaspərāt) *vt.* 1. irritate, enrage 2. intensify, make worse —**exasper'ation** *n.*

Excalibur (ek'skalibər) *n.* the sword of King Arthur

excavate ('ekskəvāt) *vt.* 1. hollow out 2. unearth 3. make (hole) by digging —**exca'vation** *n.* —'**excavator** *n.*

exceed (ik'sēd) *vt.* 1. be greater than 2. go beyond 3. surpass —**ex'ceeding** *a.* 1. very great; exceptional; excessive —*adv.* 2. *obs.* to a great or unusual degree —**ex'ceedingly** *adv.* 1. very 2. greatly

excel (ik'sel) *vt.* 1. surpass, be better than —*vi.* 2. be very good, pre-eminent (**-ll-**) —'**excellence** *n.* —'**Excellency** *n.* title borne by ambassadors and R.C. bishops and archbishops —'**excellent** *a.* very good

except (ik'sept) *prep.* 1. not including 2. but —*conj.* 3. *obs.* unless —*vt.* 4. leave or take out 5. exclude —**ex'cepting** *prep.* not including —**ex'ception** *n.* 1. thing excepted, not included in a rule 2. objection —**ex'ceptionable** *a.* open to objection —**ex'ceptional** *a.* not ordinary, *esp.* much above average —**ex'ceptionally** *adv.*

excerpt ('eksərpt, 'egzərpt) *n.* 1. quoted or extracted passage from book *etc.* —*vt.* (ek'sərpt, eg'zərpt) 2. extract, quote (passage from book *etc.*) —**ex'cerption** *n.*

excess (ik'ses, 'ekses) *n.* 1. an exceeding 2. amount by which thing exceeds 3. too great amount 4. intemperance, immoderate conduct —**ex'cessive** *a.* —**ex'cessively** *adv.*

exchange (iks'chānj) *vt.* 1. give (something) in return for something else 2. barter —*n.* 3. giving one thing and receiving another 4. thing given for another 5. building where merchants meet for business 6. central telephone office where connections are made *etc.* —**exchangea'bility** *n.* —**ex'changeable** *a.* —**exchange rate** rate at which currency unit of one country may be exchanged for that of another

exchequer (iks'chekər) *n.* **UK** government department in charge of revenue

excise[1] ('eksīz, -sīs) *n.* duty charged on goods during manufacture or before sale

excise[2] (ik'sīz) *vt.* cut out, cut away —**excision** (ik'sizhən) *n.*

excite (ik'sīt) *vt.* **1.** arouse to strong emotion, stimulate **2.** rouse up, set in motion **3.** *Elec.* magnetize poles of —**excita'bility** *n.* —**ex'citable** *a.* —**ex'citably** *adv.* —**exci'tation** *n.* —**ex'cited** *a.* emotionally or sexually aroused —**ex'citedness** *n.* —**ex'citement** *n.* —**ex'citing** *a.* **1.** thrilling **2.** rousing to action

exclaim (ik'sklām) *vi.* **1.** speak suddenly —*v.* **2.** cry out —**exclamation** (ekskləˈmāshən) *n.* —**exclamatory** (iks'klamətöri) *a.* —**exclamation point** punctuation mark **!** used after exclamations and vehement commands

exclude (ik'sklōōd) *vt.* **1.** shut out **2.** debar **3.** reject, not consider —**ex'clusion** *n.* —**ex'clusive** *a.* **1.** excluding **2.** inclined to keep out (from society *etc.*) **3.** sole, only **4.** select —*n.* **5.** something exclusive, *esp.* story appearing only in one newspaper —**ex'clusively** *adv.*

excommunicate (ekskəˈmyōōnikāt) *vt.* cut off from the sacraments of the Church —**excommuni'cation** *n.*

excoriate (ik'sköriāt) *vt.* **1.** strip (skin) from (person or animal) **2.** denounce vehemently —**excori'ation** *n.*

excrement ('ekskrimənt) *n.* **1.** waste matter from body, *esp.* from bowels **2.** dung —**excreta** (ik'skrētə) *pl.n.* excrement —**excrete** (ik'skrēt) *vt.* discharge from the system —**excretion** (ik'skrēshən) *n.* —**excretory** ('ekskrətöri) *a.* —**excretory system** structures collectively removing waste from the animal body

excrescent (ik'skresənt) *a.* **1.** growing out of something **2.** redundant —**ex'crescence** *n.* unnatural outgrowth

excruciate (ik'skrōōshiāt) *vt.* torment acutely, torture in body or mind —**ex'cruciating** *a.* —**excruci'ation** *n.*

exculpate ('ekskulpāt, ek'skulpāt) *vt.* free from blame, acquit —**excul'pation** *n.* —**ex'culpatory** *a.*

excursion (ik'skərzhən) *n.* **1.** journey, ramble, trip for pleasure **2.** digression —**ex'cursive** *a.* **1.** tending to digress **2.** involving detours —**ex'cursiveness** *n.* —**ex'cursus** *n.* digression (*pl.* **-es, -sus** (*rare*))

excuse (ik'skyōōz) *vt.* **1.** forgive, overlook **2.** try to clear from blame **3.** seek exemption for **4.** set free, remit —*n.* (ik'skyōōs) **5.** that which serves to excuse **6.** apology —**ex'cusable** *a.*

exec. **1.** executive **2.** executor

execrate ('eksikrāt) *vt.* **1.** loathe, detest **2.** denounce, deplore **3.** curse —**'execrable** *a.* abominable, hatefully bad —**exe'cration** *n.* —**'execrative** *or* **'execratory** *a.*

execute ('eksikyōōt) *vt.* **1.** inflict capital punishment on, kill **2.** carry out, perform **3.** make, produce **4.** sign (document) —**ex'ecutant** *n.* performer, *esp.* of music —**exe'cution** *n.* —**exe'cutioner** *n.* one employed to execute criminals —**ex'ecutive** *n.* **1.** person in administrative position **2.** executive body **3.** committee carrying on business of society *etc.* —*a.* **4.** carrying into effect, *esp.* of branch of government enforcing laws —**ex'ecutor** *n.* person appointed to carry out provisions of a will (**ex'ecutrix** *fem.*)

exegesis (eksi'jēsis) *n.* explanation, *esp.* of Scripture (*pl.* **-geses** (-'jēsēz)) —**exegetic(al)** (eksi'jetik(əl)) *a.*

exemplar (ig'zemplär, -plər) *n.* model type —**exem'plarily** *adv.* —**ex'emplary** *a.* **1.** fit to be imitated, serving as example **2.** commendable **3.** typical —**exemplifi'cation** *n.* —**ex'emplify** *vt.* **1.** serve as example of **2.** illustrate **3.** exhibit **4.** make attested copy of (**-fied, -fying**)

exempt (ig'zempt) *vt.* **1.** free **2.** excuse —*a.* **3.** freed (from), not liable (for) **4.** not affected (by) —**ex'emption** *n.*

exequies ('eksikwiz) *pl.n.* funeral rites or procession

exercise ('eksərsīz) *vt.* **1.** use, employ **2.** give exercise to **3.** carry out, discharge **4.** trouble, harass —*vi.* **5.** take exercise —*n.* **6.** use of limbs for health **7.** practice for training **8.** task for training **9.** lesson **10.** employment **11.** use (of limbs, faculty *etc.*)

exert (ig'zərt) *vt.* **1.** apply (oneself) diligently, make effort **2.** bring to bear —**ex'ertion** *n.* effort, physical activity

exeunt ('eksiunt) *Lat. Theat.* they leave the stage: stage direction —**exeunt omnes** ('omnāz) they all go out

exfoliate (eks'fōliāt) *v.* peel in scales, layers

exhale (eks'hāl) *v.* **1.** breathe out **2.** give, pass off as vapor

exhaust (ig'zöst) *vt.* **1.** tire out **2.** use up **3.** empty **4.** draw off **5.** treat, discuss thoroughly —*n.* **6.** used steam or fluid from engine **7.** waste gases from internal-combustion engine **8.** passage for, or coming out of this —**exhausti'bility** *n.* —**ex'haustible** *a.* —**ex'haustion** *n.* **1.** state of extreme fatigue **2.** limit of endurance —**ex'haustive** *a.* comprehensive

exhibit (ig'zibit) *vt.* **1.** show, display **2.** manifest **3.** show publicly (oft. in competition) —*n.* **4.** thing shown, *esp.* in competition or as evidence in court —**exhi'bition** *n.* **1.** display, act of displaying **2.** public show (of works of art *etc.*) —**exhi'bitionism** *n.* —**exhi'bitionist** *n.* one with compulsive desire to draw attention to himself or to expose genitals publicly —**exhibition'istic** *a.*

—ex'**hibitor** *n.* one who exhibits, *esp.* in show —ex'**hibitory** *a.*

exhilarate (ig'zilərāt) *vt.* enliven, gladden —**exhila'ration** *n.* high spirits, enlivenment

exhort (ig'zört) *vt.* urge, admonish earnestly —**exhor'tation** *n.* —**ex'horter** *n.*

exhume (ig'zyōōm, -'zōōm; iks'hyōōm, -'yōōm) *vt.* unearth (what has been buried), disinter —**exhu'mation** *n.*

exigent ('eksijənt) *a.* **1.** exacting **2.** urgent, pressing —'**exigence** *or* '**exigency** *n.* **1.** pressing need **2.** emergency —'**exigible** *a.* liable to be exacted or demanded

exiguous (ig'zigyōōəs) *a.* scanty, meager

exile ('egzīl, 'eksīl) *n.* **1.** banishment, expulsion from one's own country **2.** long absence abroad **3.** one banished or permanently living away from his home or country —*vt.* **4.** banish, expel

exist (ig'zist) *vi.* be, have being, live —**ex'istence** *n.* —**ex'istent** *a.*

existential (egzi'stenchəl, eksi-) *a.* **1.** of existence **2.** *Philos.* based on personal experience **3.** of existentialism —**exis'tentialism** *n.* theory which holds that man is free and responsible for his own acts

exit ('egzit, 'eksit) *n.* **1.** way out **2.** going out **3.** death **4.** actor's departure from stage —*vi.* **5.** go out

exo- (*comb. form*) external, outside, or beyond, as in *exothermal*

exocrine ('eksəkrin) *a.* of gland (*eg* salivary, sweat) secreting its products through ducts

Exod. *Bible* Exodus

exodus ('eksədəs) *n.* **1.** the departure of many people **2.** (**E-**) the departure of the Israelites from Egypt led by Moses **3.** (**E-**) *Bible* 2nd book of the O.T., account of the founding of the nation of Israel and the building of the tabernacle

exonerate (ig'zonərāt) *vt.* **1.** free, declare free, from blame **2.** exculpate **3.** acquit —**exoner'ation** *n.* —**ex'onerative** *a.*

exophthalmos (eksof'thalməs) *n.* protrusion of the eyeball

exorbitant (ig'zörbitənt) *a.* very excessive, inordinate, immoderate —**ex'orbitance** *n.* —**ex'orbitantly** *adv.*

exorcise *or* **-ize** ('eksörsīz) *vt.* **1.** cast out (evil spirits) by invocation **2.** free (person) of evil spirits —**exorcism** ('eksörsizəm) *n.* —**exorcist** ('eksörsist) *n.*

exordium (eg'zördiəm) *n.* introductory part of a speech or treatise (*pl.* **-s, -ia** (-iə)) —**ex'ordial** *a.*

exoteric (eksə'terik) *a.* **1.** understandable by the many **2.** ordinary, popular

exotic (ig'zotik) *a.* **1.** brought in from abroad, foreign **2.** rare, unusual, having strange or bizarre allure —*n.* **3.** exotic plant *etc.* —**ex'otica** *pl.n.* (collection of) exotic objects —**ex'oticism** *n.* —**exotic dancer** striptease or belly dancer

expand (ik'spand) *v.* **1.** increase **2.** spread out **3.** dilate **4.** develop —**ex'pandable** *or* **ex'pandible** *a.* —**ex'panse** *n.* **1.** wide space **2.** open stretch of land —**expansi'bility** *n.* —**ex'pansible** *a.* —**ex'pansion** *n.* —**ex'pansionism** *n.* practice of expanding economy or territory of country —**ex'pansionist** *n./a.* —**expansion'istic** *a.* —**ex'pansive** *a.* **1.** wide **2.** extensive **3.** friendly, talkative

expatiate (ek'spāshiāt) *vi.* **1.** speak or write at great length **2.** enlarge —**expati'ation** *n.*

expatriate (eks'patriāt) *vt.* **1.** banish, exile **2.** withdraw (oneself) from one's native land —*a./n.* (eks'patriāt, -it) **3.** (person) exiled or banished from his native country —**expatri'ation** *n.*

expect (ik'spekt) *vt.* **1.** regard as probable **2.** look forward to **3.** await **4.** hope for —**ex'pectancy** *n.* **1.** state or act of expecting **2.** that which is expected **3.** hope —**ex'pectant** *a.* looking or waiting for, *esp.* for birth of child —**ex'pectantly** *adv.* —**expec'tation** *n.* **1.** act or state of expecting **2.** prospect of future good **3.** what is expected **4.** promise **5.** value of something expected —*pl.* **6.** prospect of fortune or profit by will

expectorate (ik'spektərāt) *v.* spit out (phlegm *etc.*) —**ex'pectorant** *Med. a.* **1.** promoting secretion, liquefaction or expulsion of sputum from respiratory passages —*n.* **2.** expectorant drug or agent —**expecto'ration** *n.*

expedient (ik'spēdiənt) *a.* **1.** fitting, advisable, politic, suitable, convenient —*n.* **2.** something suitable, useful, *esp.* in emergency —**ex'pediency** *n.* —**ex'pediently** *adv.*

expedite ('ekspidīt) *vt.* **1.** help on, hasten **2.** dispatch —**expedition** (ekspi'dishən) *n.* **1.** journey for definite (oft. scientific or military) purpose **2.** people, equipment comprising expedition **3.** excursion **4.** promptness —**expeditionary** (ekspi'dishəneri) *a.* —**expeditious** (ekspi'dishəs) *a.* prompt, speedy

expel (ik'spel) *vt.* **1.** drive, cast out **2.** exclude **3.** discharge (**-ll-**) —**expulsion** (ik'spulshən) *n.* —**expulsive** (ik'spulsiv) *a.*

expend (ik'spend) *vt.* **1.** spend, pay out **2.** use up —**ex'pendable** *a.* likely, or meant, to be used up or destroyed —**ex'penditure** *n.* —**ex'pense** *n.* **1.** cost **2.** (cause of) spending —*pl.* **3.** charges, outlay incurred —**ex'pensive** *a.* high-priced, costly, dear —**expense account** **1.** arrangement by which expenses are refunded to employee by employer **2.** record of such expenses

experience (ik'spēəriəns) *n.* **1.** observation of facts as source of knowledge **2.** being affected consciously by event **3.** the event **4.** knowledge, skill, gained from life, by contact with facts and events —*vt.* **5.** undergo, suffer, meet with —**ex'perienced** *a.* skilled, expert, capable —**experi'ential** *a.*

experiment (ik'sperimənt) *n.* **1.** test, trial, something done in the hope that it may succeed, or to test theory —*vi.* (ik'speriment) **2.** make experiment —**experi'mental** *a.* —**experi'mentalist** *n.* —**experi'mentally** *adv.*

expert ('ekspərt) *n.* **1.** one skillful, knowledgeable, in something **2.** authority —*a.* **3.** practiced, skillful —**expertise** (ekspər'tēz) *n.*

expiate ('ekspiāt) *vt.* **1.** pay penalty for **2.** make amends for —**expi'ation** *n.* —**'expiator** *n.* —**'expiatory** *a.*

expire (ik'spīər) *vi.* **1.** come to an end **2.** give out breath **3.** die —*vt.* **4.** breathe out —**expiration** (ekspi'rāshən) *n.* —**ex'piratory** *a.* —**ex'piry** *n.* end

explain (ik'splān) *vt.* **1.** make clear, intelligible **2.** interpret **3.** elucidate **4.** give details of **5.** account for —**explanation** (eksplə'nāshən) *n.* —**explanatory** (iks'planətōri) *or* **explanative** (iks'planətiv) *a.*

expletive ('eskplətiv) *n.* **1.** exclamation **2.** oath —*a.* **3.** serving only to fill out sentence *etc.*

explicable (ek'splikəbəl, 'eksplik-) *a.* explainable —**'explicate** *vt.* develop, explain —**ex'plicative** *or* **ex'plicatory** *a.*

explicit (ik'splisit) *a.* **1.** stated in detail **2.** stated, not merely implied **3.** outspoken **4.** clear, plain **5.** unequivocal

explode (ik'splōd) *vi.* **1.** go off with bang **2.** burst violently **3.** (of population) increase rapidly —*vt.* **4.** make explode **5.** discredit, expose (a theory *etc.*) —**ex'plosion** *n.* —**ex'plosive** *a./n.*

exploit ('eksploit) *n.* **1.** brilliant feat, deed —*vt.* (ik'sploit) **2.** turn to advantage **3.** make use of for one's own ends —**exploi'tation** *n.* —**ex'ploiter** *n.*

explore (ik'splōr) *vt.* **1.** investigate **2.** examine **3.** scrutinize **4.** examine (country *etc.*) by going through it —**explo'ration** *n.* —**exploratory** (ik'splōrətōri) *a.* —**ex'plorer** *n.*

explosion (ik'splōzhən) *n. see* EXPLODE

expo ('ekspō) *n. inf.* exposition, large international exhibition

exponent (ik'spōnənt) *n. see* EXPOUND

export (ek'spōrt, 'ekspōrt) *vt.* **1.** send (goods) out of the country —*n./a.* ('ekspōrt) **2.** (of) goods or services sold to foreign country or countries —**expor'tation** *n.* —**ex'porter** *n.*

expose (ik'spōz) *vt.* **1.** exhibit **2.** disclose, reveal **3.** lay open **4.** leave unprotected **5.** subject (photographic plate or film) to light —**ex'posed** *a.* **1.** not concealed **2.** without shelter from the elements **3.** vulnerable —**ex'posure** *n.* **1.** act of exposing or condition of being exposed **2.** position or outlook of building **3.** lack of shelter from weather, *esp.* cold **4.** exposed surface **5.** *Photog.* act of exposing film or plate to light *etc.*; area on film or plate that has been exposed **6.** *Photog.* intensity of light falling on film or plate multiplied by time of exposure; combination of lens aperture and shutter speed used in taking photograph **7.** appearance before public, as on TV

exposé (ekspō'zā) *n.* newspaper article *etc.* disclosing scandal, crime *etc.*

exposition (ekspə'zishən) *n. see* EXPOUND

expostulate (ik'sposchəlāt) *vi.* **1.** remonstrate **2.** reason (in a kindly manner) —**expostu'lation** *n.* —**ex'postulatory** *a.*

expound (ik'spownd) *vt.* explain, interpret —**exponent** (ik'spōnənt) *n.* **1.** one who sets out facts or interprets something **2.** one favoring a particular policy **3.** *Math.* small, raised number showing the power of a factor —**expo'nential** *a.* —**expo'sition** *n.* **1.** explanation, description **2.** exhibition of goods *etc.* —**expositor** (ik'spozitər) *n.* one who explains, interpreter —**expository** (ik'spozitōri) *a.* explanatory

express (ik'spres) *vt.* **1.** put into words **2.** make known or understood by words, behavior *etc.* **3.** squeeze out —*a.* **4.** definitely stated **5.** specially designed **6.** clear **7.** positive **8.** speedy **9.** (of messenger) specially sent off **10.** (of train) fast and making few stops —*adv.* **11.** specially **12.** on purpose **13.** with speed —*n.* **14.** express train or messenger **15.** rapid parcel delivery service —**ex'pressible** *a.* —**ex'pression** *n.* **1.** expressing **2.** word, phrase **3.** look, aspect **4.** feeling **5.** utterance —**ex'pressionism** *n.* theory that art depends on expression of artist's creative self, not on mere reproduction —**ex'pressive** *a.* —**ex'pressly** *adv.* —**ex'pressway** *n.* urban highway usu. divided with controlled access and departure lanes

expresso (ik'spresō) *n. see* ESPRESSO

expropriate (eks'prōpriāt) *vt.* **1.** dispossess **2.** take out of owner's hands —**expropri'ation** *n.* —**ex'propriator** *n.*

expulsion (ik'spulshən) *n. see* EXPEL

expunge (ik'spunj) *vt.* strike out, erase —**ex'punction** *n.*

expurgate ('ekspərgāt) *vt.* remove objectionable parts from (book *etc.*), purge —**expur'gation** *n.* —**'expurgator** *n.* —**ex'purgatory** *a.*

exquisite (ek'skwizit, 'ekskwizit) *a.* **1.** of extreme beauty or delicacy **2.** keen, acute **3.** keenly sensitive —**ex'quisitely** *adv.*

ex-serviceman *n.* man who has served in the armed forces

extant ('ekstənt, ek'stant) *a.* still existing

extempore (ik'stempəri) *a./adv.* without previous thought or preparation —**extempo'raneous** *a.* —**ex'temporary** *a.* —**extempori'zation** *n.* —**ex'temporize** *vi.* **1.** speak without preparation —*vt.* **2.** devise for the occasion

extend (ik'stend) *vt.* **1.** stretch out, lengthen **2.** prolong in duration **3.** widen in area, scope **4.** accord, grant —*vi.* **5.** reach **6.** cover a certain area **7.** have a certain range or scope

8. become larger or wider —**ex'tendable, ex'tendible,** *or* **ex'tensible** *a.* that can be extended —**ex'tension** *n.* **1.** stretching out, prolongation, enlargement **2.** expansion **3.** continuation, additional part, as of telephone *etc.* —**ex'tensive** *a.* wide, large, comprehensive —**ex'tensor** *n.* straightening muscle —**ex'tent** *n.* **1.** space or degree to which thing is extended **2.** size **3.** compass **4.** volume —**extended family** nuclear family together with blood relatives, oft. spanning three or more generations —**extended-play** *a.* denoting phonograph record played at 45 r.p.m.

extenuate (ik'stenyōōāt) *vt.* make less blameworthy, mitigate —**extenu'ation** *n.* —**ex'tenuatory** *a.*

exterior (ik'stēəriər) *n.* **1.** the outside **2.** outward appearance —*a.* **3.** outer, outward, external —**exteriori'zation** *n. Surg.* temporary exposure of structure outside the body —**ex'teriorize** *vt.* —**exterior angle 1.** angle of polygon contained between one side extended and adjacent side **2.** any of four angles made by transversal that are outside region between two intersected lines

exterminate (ik'stərmināt) *vt.* destroy utterly, annihilate, root out, eliminate —**extermi'nation** *n.* —**ex'terminator** *n.* destroyer

external (ik'stərnəl) *a.* outside, outward —**externali'zation** *n.* —**ex'ternalize** *vt.* **1.** make external **2.** *Psychol.* attribute (one's feelings) to one's surroundings —**ex'ternally** *adv.*

extinct (ik'stingkt) *a.* **1.** having died out or come to an end **2.** no longer existing **3.** quenched, no longer burning —**ex'tinction** *n.*

extinguish (ik'stinggwish) *vt.* **1.** put out, quench **2.** wipe out —**ex'tinguishable** *a.* —**ex'tinguisher** *n.* device, *esp.* spraying liquid or foam, used to put out fires

extirpate ('ekstərpāt) *vt.* **1.** root out **2.** destroy utterly —**extir'pation** *n.* —**'extirpator** *n.*

extol *or* **extoll** (ik'stōl) *vt.* praise highly (**-ll-**)

extort (ik'stōrt) *vt.* **1.** get by force or threats **2.** wring out **3.** exact —**ex'tortion** *n.* —**ex'tortionate** *a.* (of prices *etc.*) excessive, exorbitant —**ex'tortioner** *n.*

extra ('ekstrə) *a.* **1.** additional **2.** larger, better, than usual —*adv.* **3.** additionally **4.** more than usually —*n.* **5.** extra thing **6.** something charged as additional **7.** *Cine.* person hired for crowd scenes

extra- (*comb. form*) beyond, as in *extradition, extramural, extraterritorial.* Such words are not given here where the meaning may easily be inferred from the simple word

extract (ik'strakt) *vt.* **1.** take out, *esp.* by force **2.** obtain against person's will **3.** get by pressure, distillation *etc.* **4.** deduce **5.** derive **6.** copy out, quote —*n.* ('ekstrakt) **7.** passage from book, motion picture *etc.* **8.** matter got by distillation **9.** concentrated solution —**ex'traction** *n.* **1.** extracting, *esp.* of tooth **2.** ancestry —**ex'tractor** *n.*

extracurricular (ekstrəkə'rikyələr) *a.* **1.** taking place outside normal school timetable **2.** beyond regular duties *etc.*

extradition (ekstrə'dishən) *n.* delivery, under treaty, of foreign fugitive from justice to authorities concerned —**extraditable** ('ekstrədītəbəl) *a.* —**extradite** ('ekstrədīt) *vt.* **1.** surrender (alleged offender) for trial to foreign state **2.** procure extradition of

extramural (ekstrə'myōōrəl) *a.* situated outside walls or boundaries of a place, *eg* sports, medical care

extraneous (ik'strāniəs) *a.* **1.** not essential **2.** irrelevant **3.** added from without, not belonging

extraordinary (ik'strōrdəneri) *a.* **1.** out of the usual course **2.** additional **3.** unusual, surprising, exceptional —**extraordi'narily** *adv.*

extrapolate (ik'strapəlāt) *v.* **1.** infer (something not known) from known facts **2.** *Math.* estimate (a value) beyond known values

extrasensory (ekstrə'sensəri) *a.* of perception apparently gained without use of known senses

extraterrestrial (ekstrəti'restriəl) *a.* of, or from outside the earth's atmosphere

extravagant (ik'stravigənt) *a.* **1.** wasteful **2.** exorbitant **3.** wild, absurd —**ex'travagance** *n.* —**ex'travagantly** *adv.* —**extrava'ganza** *n.* elaborate, lavish, entertainment, display *etc.*

extravert ('ekstrəvərt) *n. see* EXTROVERT

extreme (ik'strēm) *a.* **1.** of high or highest degree **2.** severe **3.** going beyond moderation **4.** at the end **5.** outermost —*n.* **6.** utmost degree **7.** thing at one end or the other, first and last of series —**ex'tremely** *adv.* —**ex'tremism** *n.* —**ex'tremist** *n.* **1.** advocate of extreme measures —*a.* **2.** of immoderate or excessive actions, opinions *etc.* —**extremity** (ik'stremiti) *n.* **1.** end —*pl.* **2.** hands and feet **3.** utmost distress **4.** extreme measures —**extreme unction** sacrament in which dying person is anointed by priest

extricate ('ekstrikāt) *vt.* disentangle, unravel, set free —**'extricable** *a.* —**extri'cation** *n.*

extrinsic (ek'strinzik, -sik) *a.* accessory, not belonging, not intrinsic —**ex'trinsically** *adv.*

extrovert *or* **extravert** ('ekstrəvərt) *n.* one who is interested in other people and things rather than his own feelings —**extro'version** *or* **extra'version** *n.*

extrude (ik'strōōd) *vt.* **1.** squeeze, force out **2.** (*esp.* of molten metal or plastic *etc.*) shape by squeezing through suitable nozzle or die

exuberant (ig'zōōbərənt) *a.* **1.** high-spirited, vivacious **2.** prolific, abundant, luxurious —**ex'uberance** *n.* —**ex'uberantly** *adv.*

exude (ig'zōōd) *vi.* **1.** ooze out —*vt.* **2.** give off (moisture) —**exudation** (eksyōō'dāshən, eksōō-) *n.* —**ex'udative** *a.*

exult (ig'zult) *vi.* **1.** rejoice **2.** triumph —**ex'ultancy** *n.* —**ex'ultant** *a.* triumphant —**exul'tation** *n.*

-ey (*comb. form*) *see* -Y[1], -Y[2]

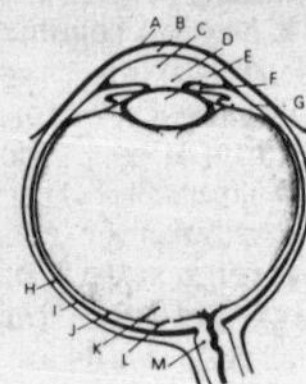

eye
(A, conjunctiva; B, cornea; C, aqueous humour; D, pupil; E, crystalline lens; F, iris; G, ciliary body; H, sclera; I, choroid; J, retina; K, vitreous body; L, forea centralis; M, optic nerve)

eye (ɪ) *n.* **1.** organ of sight **2.** look, glance **3.** attention **4.** aperture **5.** view **6.** judgment **7.** watch, vigilance **8.** thing, mark resembling eye **9.** slit in needle for thread —*vt.* **10.** look at **11.** observe —**'eyeless** *a.* —**'eyelet** *n.* **1.** small hole through which rope or cord is passed **2.** ring reinforcing this —**'eyeball** *n.* ball of eye —**eye bank** place for storage of corneas removed from the recently dead for transplanting to the eyes of those with corneal defects —**'eyebrow** *n.* ridge or fringe of hair above eye —**eye-catcher** *n.* —**eye-catching** *a.* striking —**'eyeful** *n. inf.* **1.** view, glance *etc.* **2.** beautiful sight, *esp.* a woman —**'eyeglasses** *pl.n.* lenses to assist sight —**'eyehole** *n.* **1.** hole through which rope *etc.* is passed **2.** *inf.* cavity containing eyeball **3.** peephole —**'eyelash** *n.* hair fringing eyelid —**eyelet embroidery** eyelets decorated with needlework to form a fabric —**'eyelid** *n.* either of two muscular folds of skin that can be moved to cover exposed portion of eyeball —**'eyeliner** *n.* cosmetic used to outline eyes —**eye-opener** *n. inf.* **1.** surprising news **2.** revealing statement —**'eyepiece** *n.* lens or lenses in optical instrument nearest eye of observer —**eye shadow** colored cosmetic put on around the eyes —**'eyeshot** *n.* range of vision —**'eyesight** *n.* ability to see —**'eyesore** *n.* thing that annoys one to see —**'eyestrain** *n.* fatigue of eyes —**'eyetooth** *n.* canine tooth —**'eyewash** *n. inf.* deceptive talk *etc.*, nonsense —**'eye'witness** *n.* one who saw something for himself —**an eye for an eye** retributive justice; retaliation —**eyeball to eyeball** confronting another closely —**up to the eyeballs (in something)** deeply occupied (with something)

eyrie ('ēəri, 'āəri) *n. see* AERIE

Ezech. *Bible* Ezechiel

Ezechiel (i'zēkyəl) *n. Bible* Ezekiel in the Douay Version of the O.T.

Ezekiel (i'zēkyəl) *n. Bible* 26th book of the O.T., written by the prophet Ezekiel concerning the fate of the nation of Israel after the Babylonian captivity

Ezra ('ezrə) *n. Bible* 15th book of the O.T., a postexilic book relating the experiences of the Jews as they reunited

F

f *or* **F** (ef) *n.* **1.** sixth letter of English alphabet **2.** speech sound represented by this letter, as in *fat* (*pl.* **f's, F's** *or* **Fs**)

f, f/, *or* **f:** f-number

f. *Mus.* forte

f. *or* **F. 1.** female **2.** *Gram.* feminine **3.** folio (*pl.* **ff.** *or* **FF.**) **4.** following (page) (*pl.* **ff.**) **5.** franc **6.** furlong

F 1. *Mus.* fourth note of scale of C major; major or minor key having this note as its tonic **2.** Fahrenheit **3.** *Chem.* fluorine **4.** *Phys.* force **5.** farad **6.** *Genetics* generation of filial offspring, F_1 being first generation **7.** Fellow

fa (fä) *n. Mus.* **1.** in fixed system of solmization, the note F **2.** in movable do system, the fourth note of a major scale

FAA Federal Aviation Agency

fable (ˈfābəl) *n.* **1.** short story with moral, *esp.* one with animals as characters **2.** tale **3.** legend **4.** fiction; lie —*v.* **5.** tell (fables) —*vi.* **6.** tell lies —*vt.* **7.** talk of in manner of fable —**fabulist** (ˈfabyəlist) *n.* writer of fables —**fabulous** (ˈfabyələs) *a.* **1.** amazing **2.** *inf.* extremely good **3.** told of in fables

fabric (ˈfabrik) *n.* **1.** cloth **2.** texture **3.** frame, structure —ˈ**fabricate** *vt.* **1.** build **2.** frame **3.** construct **4.** invent (lie *etc.*) **5.** forge (document) —**fabriˈcation** *n.* —ˈ**fabricator** *n.*

facade *or* **façade** (fəˈsäd) *n.* **1.** front of building **2.** *fig.* outward appearance

face (fās) *n.* **1.** front of head **2.** distorted expression **3.** outward appearance **4.** front, upper surface or chief side of anything **5.** dial of a clock *etc.* **6.** dignity **7.** *inf.* make-up (*esp. in* **put one's face on**) **8.** *Print.* printing surface of type character; style or design of character on type (*also* ˈ**typeface**) —*vt.* **9.** look or front toward **10.** meet (boldly) **11.** give a covering surface to —*vi.* **12.** turn —ˈ**faceless** *a.* **1.** without a face **2.** anonymous —ˈ**facer** *n.* person or thing that faces —**facet** (ˈfasit) *n.* **1.** one side of many-sided body, *esp.* cut gem **2.** one aspect —**facial** (ˈfāshəl) *a.* **1.** pert. to face —*n.* **2.** cosmetic treatment for face —ˈ**facing** *n.* **1.** piece of material used *esp.* to conceal seam and prevent fraying **2.** (*usu. pl.*) collar, cuffs *etc.* of military uniform jacket **3.** outer layer or coat of material applied to surface of wall —**face card** king, queen or jack at cards —**face-lift** *n.* **1.** operation to tighten skin of face to remove wrinkles **2.** improvement, renovation —**face-saving** *a.* maintaining dignity —**face value 1.** value on face of commercial paper or coin **2.** apparent value —**face the music** face unpleasant consequences bravely —**face up to** accept (unpleasant fact *etc.*) —**on the face of it** to all appearances

facetious (fəˈsēshəs) *a.* **1.** (sarcastically) witty **2.** humorous, given to jesting, *esp.* at inappropriate time

-facient (*comb. form*) state; quality, as in *absorbefacient*

facile (ˈfasil) *a.* **1.** easy **2.** working easily **3.** easy-going **4.** superficial, silly —**faˈcilitate** *vt.* make easy, help progress of —**faciliˈtation** *n.* —**faˈcility** *n.* **1.** easiness **2.** dexterity —*pl.* **3.** opportunities, good conditions **4.** means, equipment for doing something

facsimile (fakˈsimili) *n.* **1.** exact copy **2.** telegraphic system in which document is scanned photoelectrically and resulting signals are transmitted and reproduced photographically after reception **3.** image produced by this means

fact (fakt) *n.* **1.** thing known to be true **2.** deed **3.** reality —ˈ**factual** *a.* —**as a matter of fact, in (point of) fact** in reality or actuality —**fact of life** (*esp.* unpleasant) inescapable truth

faction[1] (ˈfakshən) *n.* **1.** (dissenting) minority group within larger body **2.** dissension —ˈ**factious** *a.* of or producing factions

faction[2] (ˈfakshən) *n.* dramatization of factual event

factitious (fakˈtishəs) *a.* **1.** artificial **2.** specially made up **3.** unreal

factor (ˈfaktər) *n.* **1.** something contributing to a result **2.** one of numbers which multiplied together give a given number **3.** agent, dealer —**facˈtorial** *Math. n.* **1.** product of all positive integers from one up to and including given integer —*a.* **2.** of factorials or factors —**facˈtotum** *n.* man-of-all-work

factory (ˈfaktəri) *n.* building where things are manufactured —**factory ship** fishing vessel that processes its catch before returning to port

faculty (ˈfakəlti) *n.* **1.** inherent power **2.** power of the mind **3.** ability, aptitude **4.** teaching staff and administrators with academic qualifications at an institution for learning **5.** members of profession **6.** authorization —ˈ**facultative** *a.* **1.** optional **2.** contingent

fad (fad) *n.* **1.** short-lived fashion **2.** whim —ˈ**faddish** *or* ˈ**faddy** *a.*

fade (fād) *vi.* **1.** lose color, strength **2.** wither **3.** grow dim **4.** disappear gradually —*vt.* **5.**

cause to fade —**'fadeless** *a.* —**fade-in, fade-out** *n.* **1.** *Rad.* variation in strength of signals **2.** *T.V., cine.* gradual appearance and disappearance of picture

faeces ('fēsēz) *pl.n. see* FECES

faerie *or* **faery** ('fāəri) *obs., poet. n.* **1.** fairyland —*a./n.* **2.** *see* FAIRY

Faeroe *or* **Faroe Islands** ('farō, 'fer-) self-governing region of kingdom of Denmark —**Faero'ese** *or* **Faro'ese** *a./n.*

fag (fag) *n.* **1.** *inf.* boring task **2.** *sl.* cigarette **3.** *sl.* male homosexual **4. UK** *esp.* formerly, young public school boy who performs menial chores for older boy or prefect —*v.* **5.** *inf.* (*esp. with* out) tire —*vi.* **6.** do menial tasks for a senior boy in school (**-gg-**) —**fag end** last part, inferior remnant

faggot ('fagət) *n. sl.* male homosexual

fagot *or* **faggot** ('fagət) *n.* bundle of sticks tied together —**'fagoting** *or* **'faggoting** *n.* fabric decoration in which threads are tied in bundles after crosswise threads have been withdrawn

Fah. *or* **Fahr.** Fahrenheit

Fahrenheit ('farənhīt) *a.* measured by thermometric scale with freezing point of water 32°, boiling point 212°

faïence (fā'äns, fī-) *n.* glazed earthenware or china

fail (fāl) *vi.* **1.** be unsuccessful **2.** stop operating or working **3.** be below the required standard **4.** be insufficient **5.** run short **6.** be wanting when in need **7.** lose power **8.** die away **9.** become bankrupt —*vt.* **10.** disappoint, give no help to **11.** neglect **12.** judge (candidate) to be below required standard —**'failing** *n.* **1.** deficiency **2.** fault —*prep.* **3.** in default of —**'failure** *n.* —**fail-safe** *a.* (of device) ensuring safety or remedy of malfunction in machine, weapon *etc.* —**without fail** certainly

faille (fīl, 'fīəl) *n.* ribbed silk or rayon fabric

fain (fān) *obs. a.* **1.** glad, willing; constrained —*adv.* **2.** gladly

faint (fānt) *a.* **1.** feeble, dim, pale **2.** weak **3.** dizzy, about to lose consciousness —*vi.* **4.** lose consciousness temporarily —*n.* **5.** an instance of this (*also* **syncope**) —**faint-hearted** *a.* timid

fair[1] (fāər) *a.* **1.** just, impartial **2.** according to rules, legitimate **3.** blond(e) **4.** beautiful **5.** ample **6.** of moderate quality or amount **7.** unblemished **8.** plausible **9.** middling **10.** (of weather) favorable —*adv.* **11.** honestly **12.** absolutely; quite —**'fairing** *n. Aviation* streamlined casing, or any part so shaped that it provides streamline form —**'fairly** *adv.* **1.** moderately **2.** as deserved; justly **3.** positively —**'fairness** *n.* —**fair copy** neat copy of corrected document —**fair-haired boy** boy or man favored by person or group —**Fair Isle** intricate multicolored pattern knitted with Shetland wool —**fair play** (abidance by) established standard of decency —**'fairway** *n.* **1.** navigable channel **2.** *Golf* trimmed turf between rough —**fair-weather** *a.* **1.** suitable for use in fair weather only **2.** unreliable in difficult situations —**the fair sex** women collectively

fair[2] (fāər) *n.* **1.** traveling entertainment with sideshows, amusements *etc.* **2.** large exhibition of commercial or industrial products **3.** periodical market often with amusements —**'fairground** *n.*

fairy ('fāəri) *n.* **1.** imaginary small creature with powers of magic **2.** *sl.* male homosexual —*a.* **3.** of fairies **4.** like fairy, beautiful and delicate —**fairy godmother** benefactress, *esp.* unknown —**'fairyland** *n.* —**fairy ring** circle of darker color in grass —**fairy tale 1.** story of imaginary beings and happenings, *esp.* as told to children **2.** highly improbable account

fait accompli (fe takō'plē) *Fr.* something already done that cannot be altered

faith (fāth) *n.* **1.** trust **2.** belief (without proof) **3.** religion **4.** promise **5.** loyalty, constancy —**'faithful** *a.* constant, true —**'faithfully** *adv.* —**'faithless** *a.* —**faith healing** method of treating illness by religious faith and prayer

fake (fāk) *vt.* **1.** conceal defects of by artifice **2.** touch up **3.** counterfeit **4.** sham —*n.* **5.** fraudulent object, person, act —*a.* **6.** not genuine —**'faker** *n.* **1.** one who deals in fakes **2.** swindler

fakir (fə'kēər) *n.* **1.** member of Islamic religious order **2.** Hindu ascetic

Falange ('falanj) *n.* Fascist movement in Spain —**Fa'langist** *n./a.*

falchion ('fölchən) *n.* broad curved medieval sword

falcon ('falkən, 'föl-) *n.* small bird of prey, *esp.* trained in hawking for sport —**'falconer** *n.* one who keeps, trains or hunts with falcons —**'falconry** *n.* hawking

falderal ('foldərol) *n. see* FOLDEROL

Falkland Islands ('fölklənd) crown colony of United Kingdom situated in S Atlantic Ocean about 480 miles northeast of Cape Horn

fall (föl) *vi.* **1.** drop, come down freely **2.** become lower **3.** decrease **4.** hang down **5.** come to the ground, cease to stand **6.** perish **7.** collapse **8.** be captured **9.** revert **10.** lapse **11.** be uttered **12.** become **13.** happen (**fell** *pt.*, **'fallen** *pp.*) —*n.* **14.** falling **15.** amount that falls **16.** amount of descent **17.** decrease **18.** collapse, ruin **19.** drop **20.** (*oft. pl.*) cascade **21.** cadence **22.** yielding to temptation **23.** autumn **24.** rope of hoisting tackle —**fall guy** *inf.* victim of confidence trick —**falling sickness** *or* **evil** *former name for* epilepsy —**falling star** *inf.* meteor —**'fallout** *n.* radioactive particles spread as result of nuclear explosion —**fall for** *inf.* **1.** fall in love with **2.** be taken in by —**fall out 1.** disagree **2.** leave place in rank

fallacy ('faləsi) *n.* **1.** incorrect, misleading opinion or argument **2.** flaw in logic **3.** illusion —**fallacious** (fə'lāshəs) *a.* —**falli'bility** *n.* —**'fallible** *a.* liable to error —**'fallibly** *adv.*

fallen ('fōlən) *v.* **1.** *pp. of* FALL —*a.* **2.** having sunk in reputation or honor **3.** killed in battle with glory —**fallen arch** collapse of arch formed by instep of foot, resulting in flat feet

Fallopian tube (fə'lōpiən) either of pair of tubes through which egg cells pass from ovary to womb (*also* **oviduct**)

fallow[1] ('falō) *a.* **1.** plowed and harrowed but left without crop **2.** uncultivated **3.** neglected

fallow[2] ('falō) *a.* brown or reddish-yellow —**fallow deer** deer of this color

false (fōls) *a.* **1.** wrong, erroneous **2.** deceptive **3.** faithless **4.** sham, artificial —**'falsehood** *n.* lie —**'falsely** *adv.* —**'falseness** *n.* faithlessness —**falsifi'cation** *n.* —**'falsify** *vt.* **1.** alter fraudulently **2.** misrepresent **3.** disappoint (hopes *etc.*) (**'falsified, 'falsifying**) —**'falsity** *n.* —**false pretenses** misrepresentation of facts to gain advantage (*esp. in* **under false pretenses**)

falsetto (fōl'setō) *n.* high-pitched voice above natural range (*pl.* **-s**)

Falstaffian (fōl'stafiən) *a.* like Shakespeare's Falstaff, fat, convivial and boasting

falter ('fōltər) *vi.* **1.** hesitate **2.** waver **3.** stumble —**'falteringly** *adv.*

fame (fām) *n.* **1.** reputation **2.** renown —**famed** *a.* —**'famous** *a.* **1.** widely known **2.** *inf.* excellent

familiar (fə'milyər) *a.* **1.** well-known **2.** frequent, customary **3.** intimate **4.** closely acquainted **5.** unceremonious **6.** impertinent, too friendly —*n.* **7.** familiar friend **8.** familiar demon —**famili'arity** *n.* —**familiari'zation** *n.* —**fa'miliarize** *vt.* —**fa'miliarly** *adv.*

family ('famili, 'famli) *n.* **1.** group of parents and children, or near relatives **2.** person's children **3.** all descendants of common ancestor **4.** household **5.** group of allied objects **6.** *Biol.* taxonomic division of plants and animals ranking above a genus and below an order —**fa'milial** *a.* —**family man** married man who has children, *esp.* one who is devoted to his family —**family name** surname, *esp.* representing family honor —**family planning** control of number of children in family, *esp.* by contraception —**family tree** chart showing relationships and lines of descent of family (*also* **genealogical tree**)

famine ('famin) *n.* **1.** extreme scarcity of food **2.** starvation **3.** acute shortage of anything —**'famished** *a.* very hungry

famous ('fāməs) *a. see* FAME

fan[1] (fan) *n.* **1.** instrument for producing current of air, *esp.* for ventilating or cooling **2.** folding object of paper *etc.* used, *esp.* formerly, for cooling the face **3.** outspread feathers of a bird's tail —*vt.* **4.** blow or cool with fan —*v.* **5.** spread out like fan (**-nn-**) —**fan belt** belt that drives cooling fan in internal-combustion engine —**'fanjet** *n. see* TURBOFAN —**'fanlight** *n.* (fan-shaped) window over door —**'fantail** *n.* kind of bird (*esp.* pigeon) with fan-shaped tail —**fan vaulting** *Archit.* vaulting having ribs that radiate, like those of fan, from top of capital (*also* **palm vaulting**)

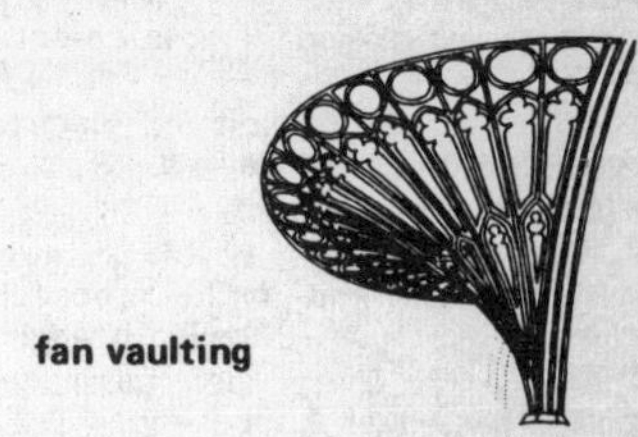

fan vaulting

fan[2] (fan) *n. inf.* **1.** devoted admirer **2.** enthusiast, particularly for sport *etc.*

fanatic (fə'natik) *a.* **1.** filled with abnormal enthusiasm, *esp.* in religion —*n.* **2.** fanatic person —**fa'natical** *a.* —**fa'natically** *adv.* —**fa'naticism** *n.*

fancy ('fansi) *a.* **1.** ornamental, not plain **2.** of whimsical or arbitrary kind —*n.* **3.** whim, caprice **4.** liking, inclination **5.** imagination **6.** mental image —*vt.* **7.** imagine **8.** be inclined to believe **9.** *inf.* have a liking for (**'fancied, 'fancying**) —*interj.* **10.** exclamation of surprise (*also* **fancy that**) —**'fancier** *n.* one with liking and expert knowledge (respecting some specific thing) —**'fanciful** *a.* —**'fancifully** *adv.* —**fancy dress** costume worn at masquerades *etc.* representing historical figure *etc.* —**fancy-free** *a.* having no commitments —**fancy goods** small decorative gifts —**fancy man** *sl.* **1.** woman's lover **2.** pimp —**fancy woman** *sl.* **1.** mistress **2.** prostitute

fandango (fan'danggō) *n.* **1.** lively Sp. dance with castanets **2.** music for this dance (*pl.* **-s**)

fanfare ('fanfāər) *n.* **1.** a flourish of trumpets or bugles **2.** ostentatious display

fang (fang) *n.* **1.** snake's poison tooth **2.** long, pointed tooth

fantasy ('fantəsi, -zi) *n.* **1.** power of imagination, *esp.* extravagant **2.** mental image **3.** fanciful invention or design —**fantasia** (fan'tāzhə) *n.* fanciful musical composition —**'fantasize** *v.* —**fan'tastic** *a.* **1.** quaint **2.** grotesque **3.** extremely fanciful, wild **4.** *inf.* very good **5.** *inf.* very large —**fan'tastically** *adv.*

FAO Food and Agriculture Organization (of the United Nations)

far (fär) *adv.* **1.** at or to a great distance or advanced point **2.** at or to a remote time **3.** by very much —*a.* **4.** distant **5.** more distant (**'farther, 'further** *comp.*, **'farthest, 'furthest** *sup.*) —**'faraway** *a.* **1.** distant **2.** absent-minded —**Far East** countries of E Asia, including China, Japan *etc.* —**Far Eastern** —**far-fetched** *a.* incredible —**far-flung** *a.* **1.** widely distributed **2.** far distant; remote —**Far North** Arctic and sub-Arctic regions —**far-off** *a.* remote; distant —**far-out** *a. sl.* **1.** bizarre, avant-garde **2.** wonderful —**far'sighted** *a.* possessing prudence and foresight —**far'sightedness** *n.* hypermetropia —**far and away** by a very great margin —**far out** *sl.* expression of amazement or delight

farad ('farad, -rəd) *n.* unit of electrical capacity —**faradaic** (farə'dāik) *a.*

farce[1] (färs) *n. see* FORCEMEAT

farce[2] (färs) *n.* **1.** comedy of boisterous humor **2.** absurd and futile proceeding —'**farcical** *a.* ludicrous —'**farcically** *adv.*

fare (fāər) *n.* **1.** charge for passenger's transport **2.** passenger **3.** food —*vi.* **4.** get on **5.** happen **6.** travel, progress —**fare'well** *interj.* **1.** goodbye —*n.* **2.** leave-taking

farina (fə'rēnə) *n.* **1.** flour or meal made from cereal grain **2.** any powdery or mealy substance —**farinaceous** (fari'nāshəs) *a.* **1.** mealy **2.** starchy

farm (färm) *n.* **1.** tract of land for cultivation or rearing livestock **2.** unit of land, water, for growing or rearing a particular crop, animal *etc.* —*v.* **3.** cultivate (land) **4.** rear (livestock) on farm —'**farmer** *n.* —**farm hand** person hired to work on farm —'**farmhouse** *n.* —'**farmstead** *n.* farm or part of farm consisting of main buildings together with adjacent grounds —'**farmyard** *n.* —**farm out** **1.** send (work) to be done by others **2.** put into care of others

faro ('fāərō) *n.* card game

farrago (fə'rägō) *n.* medley, hodgepodge (*pl.* **-s**)

farrier ('fariər) *n.* one who shoes, cares for horses —'**farriery** *n.* his art

farrow ('farō) *n.* **1.** litter of pigs —*v.* **2.** give birth to (litter)

fart (färt) *vulgar n.* **1.** (audible) emission of gas from anus —*vi.* **2.** break wind

farther ('färdhər) *adv./a. comp. of* FAR further —'**farthermost** *a.* most distant —'**farthest** *adv./a. sup. of* FAR furthest

farthing ('färdhing) *n.* **UK** formerly, coin worth quarter of penny

farthingale ('färdhin-gāl, 'färdhinggāl) *n. Hist.* hoop worn under skirts

fasces ('fasēz) *pl.n.* **1.** bundle of rods bound together round ax, forming Roman badge of authority **2.** emblem of It. fascists

fascia ('fāshiə) *n.* **1.** flat surface above shop window **2.** *Archit.* long flat surface between moldings under eaves **3.** face of wood or stone in a building **4.** dashboard (*pl.* **-ciae** (-shiē))

fascinate ('fasināt) *vt.* **1.** attract and delight by rousing interest and curiosity **2.** render motionless, as with a fixed stare —**fasci'nation** *n.*

farthingale

Fascism ('fashizəm) *n.* **1.** authoritarian political system opposed to democracy and liberalism **2.** (*oft.* **f-**) behavior (*esp.* by those in authority) supposedly typical of this system —'**Fascist** *a./n.*

fashion ('fashən) *n.* **1.** (latest) style, *esp.* of dress *etc.* **2.** manner, mode **3.** form, type —*vt.* **4.** shape, make —'**fashionable** *a.* —'**fashionably** *adv.*

fast[1] (fast) *a.* **1.** (capable of) moving quickly **2.** permitting, providing, rapid progress **3.** ahead of true time **4.** *obs.* dissipated **5.** firm, steady **6.** permanent —*adv.* **7.** rapidly **8.** tightly —'**fastness** *n.* **1.** fast state **2.** fortress, stronghold —'**fastback** *n.* automobile with back forming continuous slope from roof to rear —**fast-breeder reactor** nuclear reactor that uses little or no moderator and produces more fissionable material than it consumes —**fast food** food, *esp.* hamburgers *etc.*, prepared and served very quickly

fast[2] (fast) *vi.* **1.** go without food, or some kinds of food —*n.* **2.** act or period of fasting —'**fasting** *n.*

fasten ('fasən) *vt.* **1.** attach, fix, secure —*vi.* **2.** become joined **3.** (*usu. with* on) seize (upon) —'**fastening** *n.* something that fastens, such as clasp

fastidious (fa'stidiəs) *a.* **1.** hard to please **2.** discriminating, particular

fat (fat) *n.* **1.** oily edible substance **2.** fat part —*a.* **3.** having too much fat **4.** containing fat, greasy **5.** profitable **6.** fertile ('**fatter** *comp.*, '**fattest** *sup.*) —*vt.* **7.** feed (animals) for slaughter (-tt-) —'**fatness** *n.* —'**fatten** *v.* —'**fatty** *a./n.* —'**fathead** *n. inf.* dolt, idiot —**fat stock** livestock fattened and ready for market —**fatty acid** any of class of aliphatic carboxylic acids, such as palmitic acid

fate (fāt) *n.* **1.** power supposed to predetermine events **2.** goddess of destiny **3.** destiny **4.** person's appointed lot or condition **5.** death; destruction —*vt.* **6.** preordain —'**fatal** *a.* **1.** deadly, ending in death **2.** destructive **3.** disastrous **4.** inevitable —'**fatalism** *n.* **1.** belief that everything is predetermined **2.** submission to fate —'**fatalist** *n.* —**fatal'istic**

a. —**fatal'istically** *adv.* —**fatality** (fă'taliti, fə-) *n.* **1.** accident resulting in death **2.** person killed in war, accident —'**fatally** *adv.* —'**fateful** *a.* **1.** fraught with destiny **2.** prophetic

father ('fädhər) *n.* **1.** male parent **2.** forefather, ancestor **3.** (**F-**) God **4.** originator, early leader **5.** priest, confessor **6.** oldest member of a society —*vt.* **7.** beget **8.** originate **9.** pass as father or author of **10.** act as father to —'**fatherhood** *n.* —'**fatherless** *a.* —'**fatherly** *a.* —**father-in-law** *n.* husband's or wife's father —'**fatherland** *n.* **1.** person's native country **2.** country of person's ancestors —**Father's Day** day for honoring fathers *usu.* the 3rd Sunday in June

fathom ('fadhəm) *n.* **1.** measure of six feet of water —*vt.* **2.** sound (water) **3.** get to bottom of, understand —'**fathomable** *a.* —'**fathomless** *a.* too deep to fathom

fatigue (fə'tēg) *n.* **1.** weariness **2.** toil **3.** weakness of metals *etc.* subjected to stress **4.** soldier's nonmilitary duty —*pl.* **5.** special clothing worn by military personnel to carry out such duties —*vt.* **6.** weary

fatuous ('fachōōəs) *a.* very silly, idiotic —**fatuity** (fə'tyōōiti, -'tōō-) *n.*

faucet ('fôsit) *n.* device for allowing water to emerge from a pipe in a controlled flow

fault (fôlt) *n.* **1.** defect **2.** flaw **3.** misdeed **4.** blame, culpability **5.** blunder, mistake **6.** *Tennis* ball wrongly served **7.** *Geol.* break in strata —*vt.* **8.** find fault in —*v.* **9.** (cause to) undergo fault —*vi.* **10.** commit a fault —'**faultily** *adv.* —'**faultless** *a.* —'**faultlessly** *adv.* —'**faulty** *a.* —**to a fault** excessively

faun (fôn) *n.* mythological woodland being with tail and horns

fauna ('fônə) *n.* animals of region or period collectively (*pl.* **-s, -ae** (-ē))

Fauves (fōv) *pl.n.* —**les Fauves** (lā). orig. a contemptuous name for a group of French postimpressionist painters who showed their work at the Salon d'Automne in 1905 so-called because of their use of strident color, violent distortions and broad, bold brush strokes

faux pas ('fō 'pä) social blunder or indiscretion (*pl.* **faux pas** ('fō 'päz))

favor ('fāvər) *n.* **1.** goodwill **2.** approval **3.** especial kindness **4.** partiality **5.** small gift or toy given to guest at party *etc.* **6** *Hist.* badge or knot of ribbons —*vt.* **7.** regard or treat with favor **8.** oblige **9.** treat with partiality **10.** aid **11.** support **12.** resemble —'**favorable** *a.* **1.** advantageous, encouraging, promising **2.** giving consent —'**favorably** *adv.* —'**favored** *a.* **1.** treated with favor **2.** having appearance (as specified), as in *ill-favored* —**favorite** ('fāvərit) *n.* **1.** favored person or thing **2.** horse *etc.* expected to win race —*a.* **3.** chosen, preferred —**favoritism** ('fāvəritizəm) *n.* practice of showing undue preference

fawn[1] (fôn) *n.* **1.** young deer —*a.* **2.** light grayish-brown

fawn[2] (fôn) *vi.* **1.** (of person) cringe, court favor servilely **2.** (*esp.* of dog) show affection by wagging tail and groveling

Fax (faks) *n.* facsimile transmission device which transmits printed material by telephone

fay (fā) *n.* fairy, sprite

F.B.I. Federal Bureau of Investigation

FCA Farm Credit Administration

FCC Federal Communications Commission

FDA Food and Drug Administration

FDIC Federal Deposit Insurance Corporation

Fe *Chem.* iron

fealty ('fēəlti) *n.* **1.** fidelity of vassal to his lord **2.** loyalty

fear (fēər) *n.* **1.** dread, alarm, anxiety, unpleasant emotion caused by coming evil or danger —*vi.* **2.** have this feeling, be afraid —*vt.* **3.** regard with fear **4.** shrink from **5.** revere —'**fearful** *a.* **1.** afraid **2.** causing fear **3.** *inf.* very unpleasant —'**fearfully** *adv.* —'**fearless** *a.* intrepid —'**fearlessly** *adv.* —'**fearsome** *a.*

feasible ('fēzəbəl) *a.* **1.** able to be done **2.** likely —**feasi'bility** *n.* —'**feasibly** *adv.*

feast (fēst) *n.* **1.** banquet, lavish meal **2.** religious anniversary **3.** something very pleasant, sumptuous —*vi.* **4.** partake of banquet; fare sumptuously —*vt.* **5.** regale with feast **6.** provide delight for —'**feaster** *n.*

feat (fēt) *n.* **1.** notable deed **2.** surprising or striking trick

feather ('fedhər) *n.* **1.** one of the barbed shafts which form covering of birds **2.** anything resembling this —*vt.* **3.** provide, line with feathers —*vi.* **4.** grow feathers —*v.* **5.** turn (oar) edgeways —'**feathery** *a.* —**feather bed** mattress filled with feathers —**feather'bed** *vi.* require employer to hire more persons than needed to perform task —'**featherbrain** *or* '**featherhead** *n.* frivolous or forgetful person —'**featherbrained** *or* '**featherheaded** *a.* —'**featherstitch** *n.* embroidery stitch producing pattern of branches along a stem —'**featherweight** *n.* very light person or thing, *esp.* boxer (between bantamweight and lightweight) weighing not more than 126 lbs. —**feather one's nest** enrich oneself —**the white feather** cowardice

feature ('fēchər) *n.* **1.** (*usu. pl.*) part of face **2.** characteristic or notable part of anything **3.** main or special item —*vt.* **4.** portray **5.** *Cine.* present in leading role in a motion picture **6.** give prominence to —*vi.* **7.** be prominent —'**featureless** *a.* without striking features

Feb. February

febrile ('febril, 'fē-) *a.* of fever

February ('febyōōəri, -brōō-) *n.* second month of year (normally containing 28 days; in leap year, 29)

feces *or* **faeces** (ˈfēsēz) *pl.n.* excrement, bodily waste —**fecal** *or* **faecal** (ˈfēkəl) *a.*

feckless (ˈfeklis) *a.* spiritless; weak; irresponsible

feculent (ˈfekyələnt) *a.* full of sediment, turbid —ˈ**feculence** *n.*

fecund (ˈfekənd, ˈfēk-) *a.* fertile, fruitful, fertilizing —ˈ**fecundate** *vt.* fertilize, impregnate —**fecunˈdation** *n.* —**fecundity** (fiˈkunditi) *n.*

fed (fed) *pt./pp. of* FEED —**fed up** bored, dissatisfied

Fed. *or* **fed.** **1.** Federal **2.** Federation **3.** Federated

federal (ˈfedərəl) *a.* of or like the government of states which are united but retain internal independence —ˈ**federalism** *n.* —ˈ**federalist** *n./a.* —ˈ**federate** *v.* form into, become, a federation —**fedeˈration** *n.* **1.** league **2.** federal union —**federal style** American architectural style of about 1780–1820 characterized by symmetrical facades, smooth surfaces, and restrained classical ornament

fee (fē) *n.* payment for professional and other services

feeble (ˈfēbəl) *a.* **1.** weak **2.** lacking strength or effectiveness, insipid —ˈ**feebly** *adv.* —**feeble-minded** *a.* **1.** lacking in intelligence **2.** mentally defective

feed (fēd) *vt.* **1.** give food to **2.** supply, support —*vi.* **3.** take food (**fed** *pt./pp.*) —*n.* **4.** feeding **5.** fodder, pasturage **6.** allowance of fodder **7.** material supplied to machine **8.** part of machine taking in material —ˈ**feeder** *n.* **1.** one who or that which feeds **2.** child's bib **3.** tributary channel —ˈ**feedback** *n.* **1.** return of part of output of electrical circuit or loudspeakers. In **negative feedback** rise in output energy reduces input energy; in **positive feedback** increase in output energy reinforces input energy **2.** information received in response to inquiry *etc.* —ˈ**feedlot** *n.* area, building where cattle are fattened for market

feel (fēl) *vt.* **1.** perceive, examine by touch **2.** experience **3.** find (one's way) cautiously **4.** be sensitive to **5.** believe, consider —*vi.* **6.** have physical or emotional sensation of (something) (**felt** *pt./pp.*) —*n.* **7.** act or instance of feeling **8.** quality or impression of something perceived by feeling **9.** sense of touch —ˈ**feeler** *n.* **1.** special organ of touch in some animals **2.** proposal put forward to test others' opinion **3.** that which feels —ˈ**feeling** *n.* **1.** sense of touch **2.** ability to feel **3.** physical sensation **4.** emotion **5.** sympathy, tenderness **6.** conviction or opinion not solely based on reason —*pl.* **7.** susceptibilities —*a.* **8.** sensitive, sympathetic, heartfelt —**feel for** show sympathy or compassion toward —**feel like** have an inclination for

feet (fēt) *n., pl. of* FOOT

feign (fān) *v.* pretend, sham

feint[1] (fānt) *n.* **1.** sham attack or blow meant to deceive opponent **2.** semblance, pretense —*vi.* **3.** make feint

feint[2] (fānt) *n. Print.* narrowest rule used in production of ruled paper

feldspar (ˈfeldspär, ˈfelspär) *or* **felspar** *n.* crystalline mineral found in granite *etc.* —**feldspathic** (feldˈspathik, felˈspath-) *or* **felˈspathic** *a.*

felicity (fiˈlisiti) *n.* **1.** great happiness, bliss **2.** appropriate expression or style —**feˈlicitate** *vt.* congratulate —**feliciˈtation** *n.* (*usu. in pl.*) —**feˈlicitous** *a.* **1.** apt, well-chosen **2.** happy

feline (ˈfēlīn) *a./n.* (of, relating to) a member of the cat family —**felinity** (fiˈliniti) *n.*

fell[1] (fel) *pt. of* FALL

fell[2] (fel) *vt.* **1.** knock down **2.** cut down (tree) —ˈ**feller** *n.*

fell[3] (fel) *a. obs.* fierce, terrible —**one fell swoop** a single hasty action or occurrence

fell[4] (fel) *n.* skin or hide with hair

fell[5] (fel) *n.* mountain, stretch of moorland, *esp.* in N of England

fellatio (fiˈlāshiō) *n.* sexual activity in which penis is stimulated by partner's mouth

felloe (ˈfelō) *or* **felly** *n.* outer part (or section) of wheel

fellow (ˈfelō) *n.* **1.** man, boy **2.** person **3.** comrade, associate **4.** counterpart, like thing **5.** member (of society, college *etc.*) —*a.* **6.** of the same class, associated —ˈ**fellowship** *n.* **1.** fraternity **2.** friendship **3.** in university *etc.*, research post; special scholarship —**fellow traveler** **1.** companion on journey **2.** non-Communist who sympathizes with Communism

felon (ˈfelən) *n.* one guilty of felony —**feˈlonious** *a.* —ˈ**felony** *n.* serious crime

felspar (ˈfelspär) *n. see* FELDSPAR

felt[1] (felt) *pt./pp. of* FEEL

felt[2] (felt) *n.* **1.** soft, matted fabric made by bonding fibers chemically and by pressure **2.** thing made of this —*vt.* **3.** make into, or cover with, felt —*vi.* **4.** become matted like felt —**felt-tip pen** pen whose writing point is made from pressed fibers (*also* **fiber-tip pen**)

fem. feminine

female (ˈfēmāl) *a.* **1.** of sex which bears offspring **2.** relating to this sex —*n.* **3.** one of this sex

feminine (ˈfeminin) *a.* **1.** of women **2.** womanly **3.** denoting class or type of grammatical inflection in some languages —**femiˈninity** *n.* —ˈ**feminism** *n.* advocacy of equal rights for women —ˈ**feminist** *n./a.*

femur (ˈfēmər) *n.* thighbone —ˈ**femoral** *a.* of the thigh

fen[1] (fen) *n.* tract of marshy land, swamp —ˈ**fenny** *a.*

fen[2] (fen) *n.* monetary unit of the People's Republic of China, worth one hundredth of a yuan

fence (fens) *n.* **1.** structure of wire, wood *etc.* enclosing an area **2.** *Machinery* guard, guide **3.** *sl.* dealer in stolen property —*vt.* **4.** erect fence on or around **5.** (*with* in) enclose —*vi.* **6.** fight (as sport) with swords **7.** avoid question *etc.* **8.** *sl.* deal in stolen property —**'fencing** *n.* close-combat sport involving personal offense and defense between two persons using swords

fend (fend) *vt.* **1.** (*usu. with* off) ward off, repel —*vi.* **2.** provide (for oneself *etc.*) —**'fender** *n.* **1.** low metal frame in front of fireplace **2.** name for various protective devices **3.** frame **4.** edge **5.** buffer **6.** guard over wheel of automobile

fenestration (feni'strāshən) *n.* arrangement of windows in a building

Fenian ('fēniən) *n.* **1.** formerly, member of Irish revolutionary organization founded in U.S.A. in 19th century to fight for independent Ireland —*a.* **2.** of Fenians

fennel ('fenəl) *n.* yellow-flowered fragrant herb

fenugreek ('fenyəgrēk) *n.* heavily scented leguminous plant

-fer (*n. comb. form*) person or thing that bears something specified, as in *crucifer, conifer* —**-ferous** (*a. comb. form*) bearing, producing, as in *coniferous*

feral[1] ('fēərəl) *a.* wild, uncultivated

feral[2] ('fēərəl) *a. obs.* funereal, gloomy

fermata (fer'mätə) *n. Mus.* pause (*pl.* **-s, -te** (-ti))

ferment ('fərment) *n.* **1.** leaven, substance causing thing to ferment **2.** excitement, tumult —*v.* (fər'ment) **3.** (cause to) undergo chemical change with effervescence, liberation of heat and alteration of properties, *eg* process of wine-making and bread-making **4.** (cause to) become excited —**fermen'tation** *n.*

fermium ('fərmiəm) *n. Chem.* transuranic element *Symbol* Fm, at. wt. 253, at. no. 100

fern (fərn) *n.* class of pteridophytes of various sizes, distinguished by large leaves and complicated structure —**'fernery** *n.* place for growing ferns —**'ferny** *a.* full of ferns

ferocious (fə'rōshəs) *a.* fierce, savage, cruel —**ferocity** (fə'rositi) *n.*

ferret ('ferit) *n.* **1.** tamed animal like weasel, used to catch rabbits, rats *etc.* —*vt.* (*usu. with* out) **2.** drive out with ferrets **3.** search out —*vi.* **4.** search about, rummage

ferric ('ferik) *a.* pert. to, containing, iron —**fer'riferous** *a.* yielding iron —**'ferrous** *a.* of or containing iron in divalent state —**ferruginous** (fə'ro͞ojinəs, fe-) *a.* **1.** containing iron **2.** reddish-brown —**ferro'concrete** *n.* concrete strengthened by framework of metal

Ferris wheel ('feris) in fairground, large, vertical wheel with seats for riding

ferro- (*comb. form*) **1.** property or presence of iron, as in *ferromagnetism* **2.** presence of iron in divalent state, as in *ferrocyanide*

ferrocene ('ferōsēn) *n.* **1.** crystalline stable organometallic coordination compound **2.** analogous compound with heavy metal

ferrule ('ferəl) *n.* metal cap to strengthen end of stick *etc.*

ferry ('feri) *n.* **1.** boat *etc.* for transporting people, vehicles, across body of water, *esp.* as repeated or regular service **2.** place for ferrying —*v.* **3.** carry, travel, by ferry —*vt.* **4.** convey (passengers *etc.*) (**'ferried, 'ferrying**) —**'ferryman** *n.*

fertile ('fərtil) *a.* **1.** (capable of) producing offspring, bearing crops *etc.* **2.** fruitful, producing abundantly **3.** inventive —**fer'tility** *n.* —**fertili'zation** *n.* —**'fertilize** *vt.* make fertile —**'fertilizer** *n.*

ferule ('ferəl) *n.* **1.** flat piece of wood, such as ruler, formerly used in some schools to cane children on hand —*vt.* **2.** punish with ferule

fervent ('fərvənt) *a.* ardent, vehement, intense —**'fervency** *n.* —**'fervently** *adv.* —**'fervor** *n.*

fervid ('fərvid) *a.* **1.** very hot, burning **2.** fervent —**'fervidly** *adv.*

fescue ('feskyo͞o) *n.* grass used as pasture, with stiff narrow leaves

fess *or* **fesse** (fes) *n. Her.* horizontal band across shield

festal ('festəl) *a.* **1.** of feast or holiday **2.** merry, gay —**'festally** *adv.*

fester ('festər) *v.* **1.** (cause to) form pus —*vi.* **2.** rankle **3.** become embittered

festival ('festivəl) *n.* **1.** day, period set aside for celebration, *esp.* of religious feast **2.** organized series of events, performances *etc., usu.* in one place —**'festive** *a.* **1.** joyous, merry **2.** of feast —**fes'tivity** *n.* **1.** gaiety, mirth **2.** rejoicing —*pl.* **3.** festive proceedings

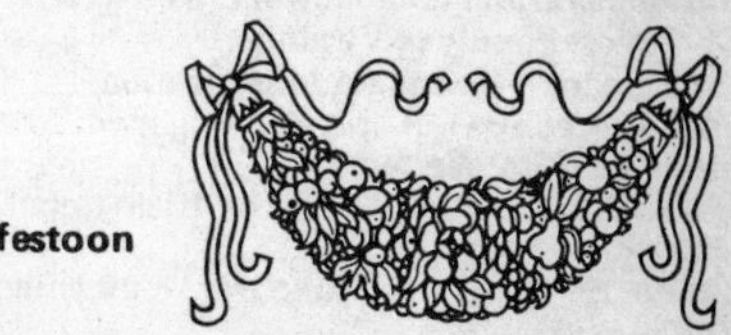
festoon

festoon (fe'sto͞on) *n.* **1.** chain of flowers, ribbons *etc.* hung in curve between two points —*vt.* **2.** form into, adorn with festoons

fetch[1] (fech) *vt.* **1.** go and bring **2.** draw forth **3.** be sold for —*n.* **4.** trick —**'fetching** *a.* attractive —**fetch up 1.** *inf.* arrive **2.** *sl.* vomit (food *etc.*)

fetch[2] (fech) *n.* ghost or apparition of living person

fete *or* **fête** (fāt, fet) *n.* **1.** gala, bazaar *etc., esp.* one held out of doors **2.** festival, holiday, celebration —*vt.* **3.** feast **4.** honor with festive entertainment

fetid *or* **foetid** (ˈfetid) *a.* stinking

fetish *or* **fetich** (ˈfetish, ˈfētish) *n.* **1.** (inanimate) object believed to have magical powers **2.** excessive attention to something **3.** object, activity, to which excessive devotion is paid

fetlock (ˈfetlok) *n.* projection behind and above horse's hoof, or tuft of hair on this

fetter (ˈfetər) *n.* **1.** chain or shackle for feet **2.** check, restraint —*pl.* **3.** captivity —*vt.* **4.** chain up **5.** restrain, hamper

fettle (ˈfetəl) *n.* condition, state of health

fetus *or* **foetus** (ˈfētəs) *n.* unborn or unhatched young of vertebrate, *esp.* human embryo three months after conception —ˈ**fetal** *or* ˈ**foetal** *a.*

feud (fyo͞od) *n.* **1.** bitter, lasting, mutual hostility, *esp.* between two families or tribes **2.** vendetta —*vi.* **3.** carry on feud

feudal (ˈfyo͞odəl) *a.* **1.** of, like, medieval social and economic system based on holding land from superior in return for service **2.** *inf.* very old-fashioned —ˈ**feudalism** *n.*

fever (ˈfēvər) *n.* **1.** elevation of body temperature above 98.6°F **2.** intense nervous excitement —ˈ**fevered** *a.* —ˈ**feverish** *a.* **1.** having fever **2.** accompanied by, caused by, fever **3.** in a state of restless excitement —ˈ**feverishly** *adv.* —**fever blisters** *see* **cold sore** *at* COLD —ˈ**feverfew** *n.* bushy plant with white flower heads —**fever pitch 1.** very fast pace **2.** intense excitement —**fever therapy** treatment of disease by elevating body temperature

few (fyo͞o) *a.* **1.** not many —*n.* **2.** small number —**a good few, quite a few** several

fey (fā) *a.* **1.** clairvoyant, visionary **2.** *esp. Scot.* fated to die

fez (fez) *n.* red, brimless, orig. Turkish tasseled cap (*pl.* ˈ**fezzes**)

ff *Mus.* fortissimo

ff. 1. folios **2.** and the following (pages *etc.*)

FFV First Family of Virginia

FHA Federal Housing Administration

fiancé (fēonˈsā) *n.* person engaged to be married (**fianˈcée** *fem.*)

Fianna Fáil (ˈfēənə ˈfāl) the Irish Republican Party

fiasco (fēˈäskō) *n.* breakdown, total failure (*pl.* **-s, -es**)

fiat (ˈfēət, -at, -ät; ˈfīət, -at) *n.* **1.** decree **2.** official permission

fib (fib) *n.* **1.** trivial lie, falsehood —*vi.* **2.** tell fib (**-bb-**) —ˈ**fibber** *n.*

fiber (ˈfībər) *n.* **1.** elongated, thick-walled cell which strengthens tissue in plants and animals **2.** substance that can be spun (*eg* wool, cotton) —ˈ**fibril** *n.* **1.** small fiber or part of fiber **2.** *Biol.* root hair —ˈ**fibroid** *a.* **1.** *Anat.* (of structures or tissues) containing or resembling fibers —*n.* **2.** benign tumor derived from fibrous connective tissue (*also* **fiˈbroma**) —**fiˈbrosis** *n.* formation of abnormal amount of fibrous tissue in organ *etc.* —**fibroˈsitis** *n.* rheumatic condition of the soft tissues —ˈ**fibrous** *a.* made of fiber —ˈ**fiberboard** *n.* building material of compressed plant fibers —ˈ**fiberglass** *n.* material made of fine glass fibers —**fiber optics** use of bundles of long transparent glass fibers in transmitting light

Fibonacci series (fēbəˈnächi) the series of numbers in which each term is the sum of the two preceding terms, *ie* 0, 1, 1, 2, 3, 5, 8, 13, 21

fibrin (ˈfibrin) *n.* insoluble protein in blood, causing coagulation —**fiˈbrinogen** *n.* globulin produced in the liver, present in blood plasma and converted into fibrin during clotting of blood

fibroma (fīˈbrōmə) *n. see* **fibroid** *at* FIBER

fibula (ˈfibyələ) *n.* slender outer bone of lower leg (*pl.* **-lae** (-lē), **-s**) —ˈ**fibular** *a.*

fickle (ˈfikəl) *a.* changeable, inconstant —ˈ**fickleness** *n.*

fiction (ˈfikshən) *n.* **1.** prose, literary works of the imagination **2.** invented statement or story —ˈ**fictional** *a.* —ˈ**fictionalize** *vt.* make into fiction —**ficˈtitious** *a.* **1.** not genuine, false **2.** imaginary **3.** assumed

fiddle (ˈfidəl) *n.* **1.** *inf.* violin **2.** triviality **3.** *inf.* illegal, fraudulent arrangement —*vi.* **4.** play fiddle **5.** make idle movements, fidget, trifle —*v.* **6.** *sl.* cheat, contrive —ˈ**fiddling** *a.* trivial —ˈ**fiddly** *a.* small, awkward to handle —**fiddler crab** burrowing crab of Amer. coastal regions, male of which has one pincerlike claw enlarged —ˈ**fiddlesticks** *interj.* nonsense

Fidei Defensor (ˈfīdiī diˈfensŏr) *Lat.* Defender of the Faith

fidelity (fiˈdeliti) *n.* **1.** faithfulness **2.** quality of sound reproduction

fidget (ˈfijit) *vi.* **1.** move restlessly **2.** be uneasy —*n.* **3.** (*oft. pl.*) nervous restlessness, restless mood **4.** one who fidgets —ˈ**fidgety** *a.*

fiduciary (fiˈdyo͞oshieri, -ˈdo͞o-) *a.* **1.** held, given in trust **2.** relating to trustee —*n.* **3.** trustee

fie (fī) *interj. obs., jocular* exclamation of distaste or mock dismay

field (fēld) *n.* **1.** area of (farming) land **2.** enclosed piece of land **3.** tract of land rich in specified product (*eg goldfield*) **4.** players in a game or sport collectively **5.** all competitors but the favorite **6.** battlefield **7.** area over which electric, gravitational, magnetic force can be exerted **8.** surface of shield, coin *etc.* **9.** sphere of knowledge **10.** range, area of operation —*vt.* **11.** *Sport* stop or return (ball) **12.** send (player, team) on to sportsfield —*vi.* **13.** *Sport* (of player or team) act or take turn as fielder(s) —ˈ**fielder** *n.* —**field day 1.** day of maneuvers, outdoor activities **2.** important occasion —**field event** any track-and-field activity except a race —ˈ**fieldfare** *n.* Eurasian thrush with pale gray head and rump —**field glasses** binoculars —**field hockey** game played on turf by two teams of 11 players using curved sticks to propel a small hard ball into opponents' goal —**field house** building enclosing area suitable for athletic events and usu. with facilities for dressing —**fielding average** measure of fielding ability of a baseball player, *eg* a player with 10 errors in 600 chances has a fielding average of .984 —**field judge** football official whose duties include timing intermission periods and time-outs —**field officer** officer holding rank of major, lieutenant colonel or colonel —**field trip** visit made by teacher and students to a place away from school for educational purposes —**field work 1.** work done in field by students to gain first-hand experience of subject **2.** gathering of anthropological and sociological data —**field of view** area visible through optical instrument

fiend (fēnd) *n.* **1.** demon, devil **2.** wicked person **3.** person very fond of or addicted to something, *eg fresh-air fiend, drug fiend* —**'fiendish** *a.* **1.** wicked **2.** *inf.* difficult; unpleasant

fierce (fēərs) *a.* **1.** savage, wild, violent **2.** rough **3.** severe **4.** intense —**'fiercely** *adv.* —**'fierceness** *n.*

fiery ('fīəri) *a.* **1.** consisting of fire **2.** blazing, glowing, flashing **3.** irritable **4.** spirited ('**fierier** *comp.*, '**fieriest** *sup.*) —**'fierily** *adv.*

fiesta (fi'estə) *n.* (*esp.* in Spain and Latin America) **1.** (religious) celebration **2.** carnival

FIFA ('fēfə) Fédération Internationale de Football Association

fife (fīf) *n.* small transverse flute with finger holes used in marching bands —**'fifer** *n.*

fifteen (fif'tēn) *see* FIVE

fig (fig) *n.* **1.** soft, pear-shaped fruit **2.** tree bearing it **3.** something of negligible value

fig. 1. figurative(ly) **2.** figure

fight (fīt) *v.* **1.** contend (with) in battle or in single combat **2.** maintain (cause *etc.*) against opponent —*vt.* **3.** resolve by combat (**fought** *pt./pp.*) —*n.* **4.** battle, struggle or physical combat **5.** quarrel, dispute, contest **6.** resistance **7.** boxing match —**'fighter** *n.* **1.** one who fights **2.** *Mil.* aircraft designed for destroying other aircraft —**fighting chance** chance of success dependent on struggle

figment ('figmənt) *n.* invention, purely imaginary thing

figure ('figyər) *n.* **1.** numerical symbol **2.** amount, number **3.** form, shape **4.** bodily shape **5.** appearance, *esp.* conspicuous appearance **6.** character, personage **7.** space enclosed by lines or surfaces **8.** diagram, illustration **9.** likeness, image **10.** pattern, movement in dancing, skating, *etc.* **11.** abnormal form of expression for effect in speech, *eg* metaphor —*vt.* **12.** calculate, estimate **13.** *inf.* consider **14.** represent by picture or diagram **15.** ornament —*vi.* **16.** (*oft.* *with* in) show, appear, be conspicuous, be included —**figu'ration** *n.* **1.** *Mus.* florid ornamentation of musical passage **2.** instance of representing figuratively, as by allegory **3.** figurative representation **4.** decorating with design —**'figurative** *a.* **1.** metaphorical **2.** full of figures of speech —**'figuratively** *adv.* —**figurine** (figyə'rēn, figə-) *n.* statuette —**'figurehead** *n.* **1.** nominal leader **2.** ornamental figure under bowsprit of ship —**figure of speech** expression of language by which literal meaning of word is not employed

figwort ('figwərt) *n.* plant related to foxglove, having small greenish flowers

Fiji ('fējē) *n.* country in S Pacific Ocean comprising about 332 islands and islets lying between 15° and 22° S latitude and 174° and 177° longitude

filament ('filəmənt) *n.* **1.** fine wire in electric light bulb and radio valve which is heated by electric current **2.** threadlike body

filariasis (filə'rīəsis) *n.* infection by any of a species of threadlike roundworms

filbert ('filbərt) *n.* **1.** N temperate shrub with edible nuts **2.** this nut (*also* **'hazelnut, 'cobnut**)

filch (filch) *vt.* steal, pilfer

file[1] (fīl) *n.* **1.** box, folder, clip *etc.* holding papers for reference **2.** papers so kept **3.** information about specific person, subject **4.** orderly line, as of soldiers, one behind the other —*vt.* **5.** arrange (papers *etc.*) and put them away for reference **6.** send (copy) to a newspaper **7.** bring (suit) in lawcourt —*vi.* **8.** register as candidate in primary election —**'filing** *n.* —**single** (*or* **Indian**) **file** single line of people one behind the other

file[2] (fīl) *n.* **1.** roughened tool for smoothing or shaping —*vt.* **2.** apply file to, smooth, polish —**'filing** *n.* **1.** action of using file **2.** scrap of metal removed by file

filial ('filiəl, 'filyəl) *a.* of, befitting, son or daughter —**'filially** *adv.*

filibuster ('filibustər) *n.* **1.** process of obstructing legislation by using delaying tactics —*v.* **2.** obstruct (legislation) with delaying tactics —*vi.* **3.** engage in unlawful military action

filigree ('filigrē) *or* **filagree** ('filəgrē) *n.* fine tracery or openwork of metal, usu. gold or silver wire

Filipino (fili'pēnō) *n.* **1.** native of the Philippines (*pl.* **-s**) —*a.* **2.** of the Philippines

fill (fil) *vt.* **1.** make full **2.** occupy completely **3.** hold, discharge duties of **4.** stop up **5.** satisfy, fulfill —*vi.* **6.** become full —*n.* **7.** full supply **8.** as much as desired **9.** soil *etc.* to bring area of ground up to required level —**'filler** *n.* **1.** person or thing that fills **2.** object or substance used to add weight *etc.* or to fill in gap **3.** paste used for filling in cracks *etc.* before painting **4.** inner portion of cigar **5.** *Journalism* space-filling item in newspaper *etc.* —**'filling** *n.* **1.** act or instance of filling **2.** something used to fill cavity or container **3.** food mixture to fill cake, pastry or sandwich **4.** yarn for shuttle or interlacing warp —**filling station** garage selling gasoline *etc.* —**fill in 1.** complete contents of (outlined drawing or writing) **2.** complete (form of application) **3.** *inf.* inform fully **4.** (*with* for) *inf.* substitute —**fill the bill** *inf.* supply all that is wanted

fillet ('filit) *n.* **1.** boneless slice of meat, fish **2.** narrow strip —*vt.* **3.** cut into fillets, bone —**'filleted** *a.*

fillip ('filip) *n.* **1.** stimulus **2.** sudden release of finger bent against thumb **3.** snap so produced —*vt.* **4.** stimulate **5.** give fillip to

Fillmore ('filmôr) *n.* **Millard.** the 13th President of the U.S. (1850-53)

filly ('fili) *n.* female horse under four years old

film (film) *n.* **1.** thin coating or covering layer **2.** (single roll of) light-sensitive strip or sheet used for taking photographs or making a motion picture **3.** a motion picture —*a.* **4.** connected with the motion-picture industry —*vt.* **5.** make motion picture of (a subject) **6.** photograph with motion-picture camera —*v.* **7.** cover or become covered with film —**'filmy** *a.* **1.** membranous **2.** gauzy —**film star** movie star —**film strip** strip of film composed of images projected separately as slides

filter ('filtər) *n.* **1.** cloth or other material, or a device, permitting fluid to pass but retaining solid particles **2.** anything performing similar function —*v.* **3.** (*oft. with* out) remove or separate (suspended particles *etc.*) from (liquid, gas *etc.*) by action of filter —*vi.* **4.** pass slowly (as if) through filter —**'filtrate** *n.* filtered gas or liquid —**filter paper** porous paper for filtering liquids —**filter tip 1.** attachment to mouth end of cigarette for trapping impurities **2.** cigarette having such attachment —**filter-tipped** *a.*

filth (filth) *n.* **1.** disgusting dirt **2.** pollution **3.** obscenity —**'filthily** *adv.* —**'filthiness** *n.* —**'filthy** *a.* **1.** unclean **2.** foul

fin (fin) *n.* **1.** propelling or steering organ of fish **2.** anything like this, *eg* stabilizing plane of airplane

fin. 1. finance **2.** financial

finagle (fi'nāgəl) *inf. vt.* **1.** get or achieve by craftiness —*v.* **2.** use trickery on (person) —**fi'nagler** *n.*

final ('fīnəl) *a.* **1.** at the end **2.** conclusive —*n.* **3.** game, heat, examination *etc.* coming at end of series —**finale** (fi'nali, -'näli) *n.* **1.** closing part of musical composition, opera *etc.* **2.** termination —**'finalist** *n.* contestant who has reached last stage of competition —**fi'nality** *n.* —**'finalize** *v.* —**'finally** *adv.*

finance (fi'nans, 'fīnans) *n.* **1.** management of money **2.** (*also pl.*) money resources —*vt.* **3.** find capital for —**fi'nancial** *a.* of finance —**fi'nancially** *adv.* —**fi'nancier** *n.*

finch (finch) *n.* one of family of small singing birds

find (fīnd) *vt.* **1.** come across, light upon **2.** obtain **3.** realize **4.** experience, discover **5.** discover by searching **6.** supply (as funds) **7.** *Law* give a verdict (upon) (**found** *pt./pp.*) —*n.* **8.** finding **9.** (valuable) thing found —**'finder** *n.* —**'finding** *n.* judicial verdict —**find out 1.** gain knowledge of (something); learn **2.** detect crime, deception *etc.* of (someone)

fine[1] (fīn) *a.* **1.** choice, of high quality, excellent **2.** delicate **3.** subtle **4.** pure **5.** in small particles **6.** slender **7.** handsome **8.** showy **9.** *inf.* healthy, at ease, comfortable **10.** free from rain —*vt.* **11.** make clear or pure **12.** refine **13.** thin —**'finely** *adv.* —**'fineness** *n.* —**'finery** *n.* showy dress —**finesse** (fi'nes) *n.* elegant, skillful management —**fine art** art produced for its aesthetic value —**fine-drawn** *a.* **1.** (of distinctions *etc.*) precise; subtle **2.** (of wire *etc.*) drawn out until very fine —**'fine'spun** *a.* **1.** spun out to fine thread **2.** excessively subtle or refined —**fine-tooth comb** comb with fine, closely set teeth —**go over** *or* **through with a fine-tooth comb** examine very thoroughly

fine[2] (fīn) *n.* **1.** sum fixed as penalty —*vt.* **2.** punish by fine —**in fine 1.** in conclusion **2.** in brief

fines herbes (*Fr.* fēn 'zerb) mixture of finely chopped herbs, used to flavor omelets *etc.*

finger ('finggər) *n.* **1.** one of the jointed branches of the hand **2.** any of various things like this —*vt.* **3.** touch or handle with fingers —**'fingering** *n.* **1.** *Mus.* technique of using one's fingers **2.** *Mus.* numerals in musical part indicating this **3.** fine wool yarn for manufacture of stockings *etc.* —**'fingerboard** *n.* part of musical instrument on which fingers are placed —**finger bowl** small bowl filled with water for rinsing fingers at table after meal —**finger plate** ornamental plate above door handle to prevent finger marks —**'fingerprint** *n.* impression of tip of finger, *esp.* as used for identifying criminals

finial ('fīniəl) *n. Archit.* ornament at apex of pinnacles, gables, spires *etc.*

finicky ('finiki) *or* **finicking** *a.* **1.** fastidious, fussy **2.** too fine

finis ('finis) *Lat.* end, *esp.* of book

finish ('finish) *v.* **1.** bring, come to an end, conclude —*vt.* **2.** complete **3.** perfect **4.** kill —*n.* **5.** end **6.** way in which thing is finished, as an *oak finish* of furniture **7.** final appearance —**'finisher** *n.* —**finishing school** private school for girls that teaches social graces

finite (ˈfīnīt) *a.* bounded, limited —**finite set** set containing a limited number of elements

Finland (ˈfinlənd) *n.* country in N Europe bounded east by the U.S.S.R., south by the Baltic Sea, west by the Gulf of Bothnia and Sweden and north by Norway —**Finn** *n.* native of Finland —ˈ**Finnish** *a.* **1.** of Finland —*n.* **2.** official language of Finland

finnan haddock (ˈfinən) *or* **haddie** (ˈhadi) smoked haddock

fiord (fēˈôrd) *n. see* FJORD

fipple (ˈfipəl) *n.* wooden plug forming flue in end of pipe —**fipple flute** generic name for musical instruments of the flageolet or recorder type

fir (fər) *n.* **1.** kind of coniferous resinous tree **2.** its wood

fire (ˈfīər) *n.* **1.** state of burning, combustion, flame, glow **2.** mass of burning fuel **3.** destructive burning, conflagration **4.** device for heating a room *etc.* **5.** ardor, keenness, spirit **6.** shooting of firearms —*vt.* **7.** discharge (firearm) **8.** propel from firearm **9.** *inf.* dismiss from employment **10.** bake **11.** make burn **12.** supply with fuel **13.** inspire **14.** explode —*vi.* **15.** discharge firearm **16.** begin to burn —ˈ**firing** *n.* **1.** process of baking ceramics *etc.* in kiln **2.** act of stoking fire or furnace **3.** discharge of firearm **4.** something used as fuel —**fire alarm** device to give warning of fire —ˈ**firearm** *n.* gun, rifle, pistol *etc.* —ˈ**fireball** *n.* **1.** ball-shaped discharge of lightning **2.** region of hot ionized gas at center of nuclear explosion **3.** *Astron.* large bright meteor **4.** *sl.* energetic person —ˈ**firebomb** *n. see* INCENDIARY (sense 6) —ˈ**firebrand** *n.* **1.** burning piece of wood **2.** energetic (troublesome) person —ˈ**firebreak** *n.* strip of cleared land to arrest progress of bush or grass fire —ˈ**firebrick** *n.* refractory brick made of fire clay, for lining furnaces *etc.* —ˈ**firebug** *n. inf.* person who intentionally sets fire to buildings *etc.* —**fire clay** heat-resistant clay used in making of firebricks *etc.* —ˈ**firecracker** *n.* small cardboard container filled with explosive powder —ˈ**firecrest** *n.* small European warbler —ˈ**firedamp** *n.* explosive hydrocarbon gas forming in mines —**fire department** organized, usu. municipal, body responsible for preventing and putting out fires —ˈ**firedog** *n.* either of pair of metal stands used to support logs in open fire —**fire drill** rehearsal of procedures for escape from fire —**fire-eater** *n.* **1.** performer who simulates swallowing of fire **2.** belligerent person —**fire engine** vehicle with apparatus for extinguishing fires —**fire escape** means, *esp.* outside metal stairs, for escaping from burning buildings —ˈ**firefly** *n.* insect giving off intermittent glow —ˈ**fireguard** *n.* **1.** fire screen **2.** one who watches for and extinguishes fires —**fire hall** fire station —**fire irons** tongs, poker and shovel —ˈ**fireman** *n.* **1.** member of fire department **2.** stoker **3.** assistant to locomotive driver —ˈ**fireplace** *n.* recess in room for fire —ˈ**fireplug** *n.* hydrant placed on sidewalk —**fire ship** burning vessel sent drifting against enemy ships —**fire station** building housing fire apparatus —ˈ**firetrap** *n.* building unsafe in case of fire —ˈ**firework** *n.* **1.** (*oft. pl.*) device to give spectacular effects by explosions and colored sparks —*pl.* **2.** outburst of temper, anger —**firing line 1.** *Mil.* positions from which fire is delivered **2.** leading position in an activity —**firing squad** detachment sent to fire volleys at military funeral, or to shoot criminal —**under fire 1.** under attack **2.** under criticism

firkin (ˈfərkin) *n.* **1.** small cask **2. UK** measure of 9 gallons

firm[1] (fərm) *a.* **1.** solid **2.** fixed, stable **3.** steadfast **4.** resolute **5.** settled —*v.* **6.** make, become firm

firm[2] (fərm) *n.* **1.** commercial enterprise **2.** partnership

firmament (ˈfərməmənt) *n.* expanse of sky, heavens

first (fərst) *a.* **1.** earliest in time or order **2.** foremost in rank or position **3.** most excellent **4.** highest, chief —*n.* **5.** beginning **6.** first occurrence of something **7.** highest place in competition —*adv.* **8.** before others in time, order *etc.* —ˈ**firstly** *adv.* —**first aid** help given to injured person before arrival of doctor —**first base 1.** base that must be touched first in order to score a run at baseball **2.** player defending this base **3.** first step in a course of action —**first class** *n.* **1.** class of highest value, quality *etc.* —*a.* **2.** of highest class **3.** excellent **4.** of most comfortable class of accommodation in hotel, train *etc.* —**first-class** *adv.* by first-class means of transportation *etc.* —**first cousin** son or daughter of one's aunt or uncle —**first-day cover** *Philately* envelope post-marked on first day of issue of its stamps —**first finger** finger next to thumb —**first fruits 1.** first results or profits of undertaking **2.** earliest fruits gathered and offered to Deity in gratitude for fruitfulness —**first-hand** *a.* obtained directly from the first source —**first lady** (*oft.* **F- L-**) wife or official hostess of state governor or U.S. president —**first mate** *or* **officer** officer of merchant vessel immediately below captain —**first name** personal or Christian name —**first night** first public performance of a play or opera —**first offender** person convicted of criminal offense for first time —**first person** grammatical category of pronouns and verbs used by speaker to refer to himself —**first-rate** *a.* of highest class or quality —**first string** the best players of an athletic team —**first water 1.** finest quality of precious stone **2.** best quality

firth (fərth) *or* **frith** *n. esp.* in Scotland, arm of the sea, river estuary

fiscal (ˈfiskəl) *a.* of finances —**fiscal year**

annual period at end of which firm's accounts are made up

fish (fish) *n.* **1.** cold-blooded egg-laying aquatic vertebrate with scaly skin, gills and paired fins **2.** its flesh as food (*pl.* **fish, -es**) —*vi.* **3.** (attempt to) catch fish **4.** search (for something) **5.** (*with* for) try to get information indirectly —**'fisher** *n.* —**'fishery** *n.* **1.** business of fishing **2.** fishing ground —**'fishy** *a.* **1.** of, like, or full of fish **2.** dubious, open to suspicion —**fish-and-chips** *pl.n. esp.* **UK** fried fish and French fries —**fish cake** fried flattened ball of flaked fish mixed with mashed potatoes —**'fisherman** *n.* one who catches fish for a living or for pleasure —**fish-eye lens** *Photog.* lens of small focal length, that covers almost 180° —**fish-kettle** *n.* oval pot for cooking fish —**fish meal** ground dried fish used as fertilizer *etc.* —**'fishmonger** *n.* seller of fish —**'fishskin** *n.* disease in which skin is coarse, dry and scaly (*also* **ichthy'osis**) —**fish slice 1.** fish carver **2.** flat-bladed utensil for turning or lifting food in frying —**fish story** unbelievable tale —**'fishwife** *n.* coarse, scolding woman —**have other fish to fry** have more important matters to attend to

fishplate ('fishplāt) *n.* piece of metal holding rails together

fission ('fishən, 'fizh-) *n.* splitting of an atomic nucleus into two approximately equal parts accompanied by the release of great amounts of energy —**'fissionable** *a.* capable of undergoing nuclear fission —**fis-siparous** (fi'sipərəs) *a.* reproducing by fission

fissure ('fishər) *n.* cleft, split, cleavage —**fissile** ('fisil) *a.* **1.** capable of splitting **2.** tending to split

fist (fist) *n.* clenched hand —**'fisticuffs** *pl.n.* fighting

fistula ('fischələ) *n.* pipelike ulcer (*pl.* **-s, -lae** (-lē))

fit[1] (fit) *vt.* **1.** be suited to **2.** be properly adjusted to **3.** arrange, adjust, apply, insert **4.** supply, furnish —*vi.* **5.** be correctly adjusted or adapted **6.** be of right size (**-tt-**) —*a.* **7.** well-suited, worthy **8.** qualified **9.** proper, becoming **10.** ready **11.** in good condition or health (**'fitter** *comp.*, **'fittest** *sup.*) —*n.* **12.** way anything fits, its style **13.** adjustment —**'fitly** *adv.* —**'fitment** *n.* piece of furniture —**'fitness** *n.* —**'fitted** *a.* **1.** designed for excellent fit **2.** (of carpet) cut to cover floor completely **3.** (of furniture) built to fit particular space —**'fitter** *n.* **1.** one who, that which, makes fit **2.** one who supervises making and fitting of garments **3.** mechanic skilled in fitting up metalwork —**'fitting** *a.* **1.** appropriate, suitable, proper —*n.* **2.** fixture **3.** apparatus **4.** action of fitting —**fit in 1.** give place or time to **2.** belong or conform, *esp.* after adjustment

fit[2] (fit) *n.* **1.** seizure with convulsions, spasms, loss of consciousness *etc.*, of epilepsy, hysteria *etc.* **2.** sudden passing attack of illness **3.** passing state, mood —**'fitful** *a.* spasmodic, capricious —**'fitfully** *adv.* —**have** *or* **throw a fit** *inf.* become very angry

five (fīv) *a./n.* cardinal number after four —**fif'teen** *a./n.* ten plus five —**fif'teenth** *a./n.* —**fifth** (fifth) *a./n.* ordinal number of five —**fifthly** ('fifthli) *adv.* —**fiftieth** ('fiftiith) *a./n.* —**fifty** ('fifti) *a./n.* five tens —**'fiver** *n. inf.* 5-dollar bill —**fifth column** organization spying for enemy within country at war —**fifty-fifty** *a./adv. inf.* in equal parts —**five-o'clock shadow** beard growth visible late in day on man's shaven face —**'fivepins** *pl.n.* bowling game played *esp.* in Canada —**five-star** *a.* of the highest class —**five-star general** a general of the army —**Five-Year Plan** in socialist economies, government plan for economic development over five-year period

fix (fiks) *vt.* **1.** fasten, make firm or stable **2.** set, establish **3.** appoint, assign, determine **4.** make fast **5.** repair **6.** *inf.* influence the outcome of unfairly or by deception **7.** *inf.* bribe **8.** *inf.* give (someone) his just deserts —*vi.* **9.** become firm or solidified **10.** determine —*n.* **11.** difficult situation **12.** position of ship, aircraft ascertained by radar, observation *etc.* **13.** *sl.* dose of narcotic drug —**fix'ation** *n.* **1.** act of fixing **2.** preoccupation, obsession **3.** situation of being set in some way of acting or thinking —**'fixative** *a.* **1.** capable of, or tending to fix —*n.* **2.** fluid sprayed over drawings to prevent smudging *etc.* **3.** substance added to liquid to make it less volatile —**fixed** *a.* **1.** attached so as to be immovable **2.** stable **3.** steadily directed **4.** established as to relative position **5.** always at same time **6.** (of ideas *etc.*) firmly maintained **7.** (of element) held in chemical combination **8.** (of substance) nonvolatile **9.** arranged **10.** *inf.* equipped; provided for **11.** *inf.* illegally arranged —**fixedly** ('fiksidli) *adv.* intently —**'fixity** *n.* —**'fixture** *n.* **1.** thing fixed in position **2.** thing attached to house **3.** date for sporting event **4.** the event —**fixed star** star whose position appears to be stationary over long period of time —**fix (someone) up** attend to (someone's) needs —**fix up** arrange

fizz (fiz) *vi.* **1.** hiss, splutter —*n.* **2.** hissing noise **3.** effervescent liquid, such as soda water, champagne —**'fizzle** *vi.* **1.** splutter weakly —*n.* **2.** fizzling noise **3.** fiasco —**'fizzy** *a.* effervescent —**fizzle out** *inf.* come to nothing, fail

fjord *or* **fiord** (fē'örd) *n. esp.* in Norway, long, narrow inlet of sea

FL Florida

fl. **1.** floor **2.** *floruit* (*Lat.*, (he or she) flourished) **3.** fluid

Fla. Florida

flabbergast ('flabərgast) *vt.* overwhelm with astonishment

flabby ('flabi) *a.* **1.** hanging loose, limp **2.** out of condition, too fat **3.** feeble **4.** yielding

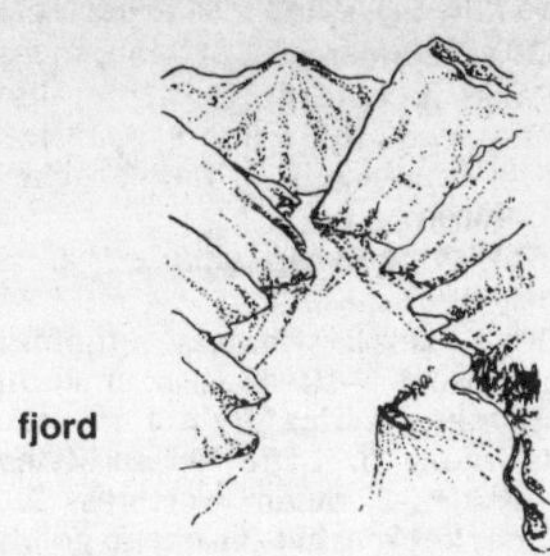

fjord

—**flab** *n. inf.* unsightly fat on the body —'**flabbiness** *n.*

flaccid ('flaksid, 'flasid) *a.* flabby, lacking firmness —**flac'cidity** *n.*

flag[1] (flag) *n.* **1.** banner, piece of bunting attached to staff or halyard as standard or signal **2.** small paper emblem sold on flag days —*vt.* **3.** decorate or mark with flag(s) **4.** send or communicate (messages *etc.*) by flag signals (**-gg-**) —**flag day** day on which small flags or emblems are sold in streets for charity —'**flagpole** *or* '**flagstaff** *n.* pole on which flag is hoisted and displayed (*pl.* **-poles** *or* **-staffs, -staves** (-stāvz)) —'**flagship** *n.* **1.** admiral's ship **2.** most important ship of fleet —**flag down** warn or signal (vehicle) to stop —**flag of convenience** national flag flown by ship registered in that country to gain financial or legal advantage —**flag of truce** white flag indicating invitation to enemy to negotiate

flag[2] (flag) *n.* any plant with sword-shaped leaves, *esp.* the iris —'**flaggy** *a.*

flag[3] (flag) *n.* **1.** flat slab of stone —*pl.* **2.** pavement of flags —*vt.* **3.** furnish (floor *etc.*) with flagstones (**-gg-**) —'**flagstone** *n.*

flag[4] (flag) *vi.* **1.** droop, fade **2.** lose vigor (**-gg-**)

flagellate[1] ('flajəlit) *n.* any microorganism having whiplike appendages

flagellate[2] ('flajilāt) *vt.* scourge, flog —'**flagellant** *n.* one who scourges himself, *esp.* in religious penance —**flagel'lation** *n.* —'**flagellator** *n.*

flagellum (flə'jeləm) *n.* **1.** *Biol.* whiplike outgrowth from cell that acts as organ of locomotion **2.** *Bot.* long thin shoot (*pl.* **-la** (-lə), **-s**)

flageolet (flajə'let) *n.* small musical instrument similar to the recorder with four finger holes in front and two thumb holes in back

flagon ('flagən) *n.* large bottle of wine *etc.*

flagrant ('flāgrənt) *a.* glaring, scandalous, blatant —'**flagrancy** *n.* —'**flagrantly** *adv.*

flail (flāl) *n.* **1.** instrument for threshing corn by hand —*v.* **2.** beat with, move as, flail

flair (flāər) *n.* **1.** natural ability **2.** elegance

flak *or* **flack** (flak) *n.* **1.** anti-aircraft fire **2.** *inf.* adverse criticism

flake (flāk) *n.* **1.** small, thin piece, *esp.* particle of snow **2.** piece chipped off —*v.* **3.** (cause to) peel off in flakes —'**flaky** *a.* —**flake out** *inf.* collapse, sleep from exhaustion

flambé (flām'bā) *a.* (of food) served in flaming brandy *etc.*

flamboyant (flam'boiənt) *a.* **1.** florid, gorgeous, showy **2.** exuberant, ostentatious

flame (flām) *n.* **1.** burning gas, *esp.* above fire **2.** visible burning **3.** passion, *esp.* love **4.** *inf.* sweetheart —*vi.* **5.** give out flames, blaze **6.** shine **7.** burst out —'**flaming** *a.* **1.** burning with flames **2.** glowing brightly **3.** ardent **4.** *inf.* a common intensifier —**flame-thrower** *n.* weapon that ejects stream of burning fluid

flamenco (flə'mengkō) *n.* Sp. dance to guitar (*pl.* **-s**)

flamingo (flə'minggō) *n.* large pink bird with long neck and legs (*pl.* **-s, -es**)

flammable ('flaməbəl) *a.* liable to catch fire

flange (flanj) *n.* **1.** projecting flat rim, collar or rib —*v.* **2.** provide with or take form of flange

flank (flangk) *n.* **1.** part of side between hips and ribs **2.** side of anything, *eg* body of troops —*vt.* **3.** guard or strengthen on flank **4.** attack flank of **5.** be at, move along either side of

flannel ('flanəl) *n.* **1.** soft woolen fabric for clothing, *esp.* trousers —*pl.* **2.** trousers *etc.* made of flannel —**flanne'lette** *n.* cotton fabric imitating flannel —'**flannelly** *a.* —**flannel-mouthed** *a.* speaking insincerely

flap (flap) *v.* **1.** move (wings, arms *etc.*) as bird flying **2.** (cause to) sway —*vt.* **3.** strike with flat object —*vi.* **4.** *inf.* be agitated, flustered (**-pp-**) —*n.* **5.** act of flapping **6.** broad piece of anything hanging from hinge or loosely from one side **7.** movable part of aircraft wing **8.** *inf.* state of excitement or panic —'**flapper** *n.* in 1920s, young woman, *esp.* one flaunting unconventional behavior —'**flapjack** *n.* pancake

flare (flāər) *vi.* **1.** blaze with unsteady flame **2.** *inf.* (*with* up) suddenly burst into anger **3.** spread outward, as bottom of skirt —*n.* **4.** instance of flaring **5.** signal light —**flare-path** *n.* area lit up to facilitate landing or takeoff of aircraft —**flare-up** *n.* **1.** sudden burst of fire **2.** *inf.* sudden burst of emotion —**flare up 1.** burst suddenly into fire **2.** *inf.* burst into anger

flash (flash) *n.* **1.** sudden burst of light or flame **2.** sudden short blaze **3.** very short time **4.** brief news item **5.** ribbon; badge **6.** display —*vi.* **7.** break into sudden flame **8.** gleam **9.** burst into view **10.** move very fast **11.** appear suddenly **12.** *sl.* expose oneself indecently —*vt.* **13.** cause to gleam **14.** emit (light *etc.*) suddenly —*a.* **15.** showy (*also* '**flashy**) **16.** sham —'**flasher** *n.* **1.** something which flashes **2.** *sl.* someone who indecently exposes himself —'**flashing** *n.* weatherproof material used to cover valleys between slopes of roof *etc.* —'**flashback** *n.* break in continuity of book, play or motion picture, to introduce what has taken place previously —'**flashbulb** *n. Photog.* small light bulb triggered, *usu.* electrically, to produce bright flash of light —'**flashcube** *n.* boxlike camera attachment, holding four flashbulbs, that turns so that each flashbulb can be used —'**flashlight** *n.* **1.** small battery-powered light **2.** *Photog.* brief bright light emitted by electronic flash (*also* **flash**) —**flash point** temperature at which a vapor ignites —**flash in the pan** person *etc.* that enjoys only short-lived success

flask (flask) *n.* narrow-necked bottle often fitted with top to be carried in a pocket

flat[1] (flat) *a.* **1.** level **2.** spread out **3.** at full length **4.** smooth **5.** downright **6.** dull, lifeless **7.** *Mus.* below pitch **8.** (of tire) deflated, punctured **9.** (of battery) fully discharged, dead ('**flatter** *comp.*, '**flattest** *sup.*) —*adv.* **10.** completely, utterly; absolutely —*n.* **11.** flat object, surface or part **12.** *Mus.* tone or note produced below pitch **13.** punctured tire **14.** shallow box for raising seedlings —'**flatly** *adv.* —'**flatness** *n.* —'**flatten** *v.* —'**flatfish** *n.* type of fish which swims along sea floor on one side of body with both eyes on uppermost side —'**flatfoot** *n.* **1.** condition in which instep arch of foot is flattened **2.** *sl.* policeman (*pl.* **-s, -feet**) —'**flatiron** *n.* iron for pressing clothes —**flat race** race over level ground with no jumps —**flat spin 1.** aircraft spin in which longitudinal axis is more nearly horizontal than vertical **2.** *inf.* state of confusion —'**flatware** *n.* **1.** table utensils such as knives, forks and spoons **2.** serving dishes, *esp.* silver, that are more or less flat —'**flatworm** *n.* any member of a phylum of invertebrate animals with flattened bodies including tapeworms and liver flukes —**flat out** at, with maximum speed or effort

flat[2] (flat) *n.* apartment on one floor of building

flatter ('flatər) *vt.* **1.** fawn on **2.** praise insincerely **3.** gratify vanity of **4.** represent too favorably —'**flatterer** *n.* —'**flattery** *n.*

flatulent ('flachələnt) *a.* **1.** suffering from, generating (excess) gases in intestines **2.** pretentious —'**flatulence** *n.* **1.** flatulent condition **2.** verbosity, emptiness

flaunt (flŏnt) *v.* **1.** show off **2.** wave proudly

flautist ('flŏtist) *n.* **UK** flute player

flavescent (flə'vesənt) *a.* yellowish; turning yellow

flavor ('flāvər) *n.* **1.** mixed sensation of smell and taste **2.** distinctive taste, savor **3.** undefinable characteristic, quality of anything —*vt.* **4.** give flavor to **5.** season —'**flavoring** *n.*

flaw[1] (flŏ) *n.* **1.** crack **2.** defect, blemish —*vt.* **3.** make flaw in —'**flawless** *a.* perfect

flaw[2] (flŏ) *n.* sudden gust of wind; squall

flax (flaks) *n.* **1.** plant grown for its textile fiber and seeds **2.** its fibers, spun into linen thread —'**flaxen** *a.* **1.** of flax **2.** light yellow, straw-colored

flay (flā) *vt.* **1.** strip skin off **2.** criticize severely

flea (flē) *n.* small, wingless, jumping, blood-sucking insect —'**fleabag** *n.* unkempt person, horse *etc.* —'**fleabite** *n.* **1.** insect's bite **2.** trifling injury **3.** trifle —**flea-bitten** *a.* **1.** bitten by flea **2.** mean, worthless **3.** scruffy —**flea market** market for cheap goods

fleck (flek) *n.* **1.** small mark, streak or particle —*vt.* **2.** mark with flecks

fled (fled) *pt./pp. of* FLEE

fledged (flejd) *a.* **1.** (of birds) able to fly **2.** experienced, trained —'**fledgling** *n.* **1.** young bird **2.** inexperienced person

flee (flē) *v.* run away (from) (**fled,** '**fleeing**)

fleece (flēs) *n.* **1.** whole sheep's wool —*vt.* **2.** rob —'**fleecy** *a.* —**fleece-lined** *a.* (of knitted fabric) napped on one side

fleet[1] (flēt) *n.* **1.** number of warships organized as unit **2.** number of ships, trucks *etc.* operating together

fleet[2] (flēt) *a.* swift, nimble —'**fleeting** *a.* passing, transient —'**fleetingly** *adv.*

Fleet Street (flēt) **1.** street in London where many newspaper offices are situated **2.** Brit. journalism or journalists collectively

Flemish ('flemish) *n.* **1.** language spoken by Flemings, almost identical to Dutch —*a.* **2.** of Flanders —'**Fleming** *n.* native of Flanders, medieval principality in the Low Countries, or of Flemish-speaking Belgium —**the Flemish** the Flemish people

flense (flens), **flench** (flench), *or* **flinch** (flinch) *vt.* strip (*esp.* whale) of flesh

flesh (flesh) *n.* **1.** soft part, muscular substance, between skin and bone **2.** in plants, pulp **3.** fat **4.** sensual appetites —'**fleshily** *adv.* —'**fleshly** *a.* **1.** carnal **2.** material —'**fleshy** *a.* **1.** plump **2.** pulpy —'**fleshpots** *pl.n.* (places catering for) self-indulgent living —**flesh wound** wound affecting superficial tissues —**in the flesh** in person; actually present

fleur-de-lis *or* **fleur-de-lys** (flərdə'lē) *n.* **1.** heraldic lily with three petals **2.** iris (*pl.* **fleurs-de-lis** *or* **fleurs-de-lys** (flərdə'lēz))

flew (flo͞o) *pt. of* FLY[1]

flews (flo͞oz) *pl.n.* fleshy hanging lip of bloodhound or similar dog

flex (fleks) *n.* **1.** instance or act of flexing —*v.* **2.** bend, be bent —**flexi'bility** *n.* —'**flexible** *a.* **1.** easily bent **2.** manageable **3.** adaptable —'**flexibly** *adv.* —'**flexion** *n.* **1.** bending **2.** bent state —'**flextime** *n.* system permitting variation in starting and finishing times of work, providing an agreed number of hours is worked over a specified period

flibbertigibbet (ˈflibərtijibit) *n.* flighty, gossiping person

flick (flik) *vt.* **1.** strike lightly, jerk —*n.* **2.** light blow **3.** jerk **4.** *sl.* motion picture —**flick knife** knife with retractable blade that springs out when button is pressed

flicker (ˈflikər) *vi.* **1.** burn, shine, unsteadily **2.** waver, quiver —*n.* **3.** unsteady light or movement

flight (flīt) *n.* **1.** act or manner of flying through air **2.** number flying together, as birds **3.** journey in aircraft **4.** smallest air force unit **5.** power of flying **6.** swift movement or passage **7.** sally **8.** distance flown **9.** feather *etc.* fitted to arrow or dart to give it stability in flight **10.** stairs between two landings **11.** running away —**flight attendant** person attending passengers on an airplane —**flight deck 1.** crew compartment in airliner **2.** upper deck of aircraft carrier where aircraft take off —**flight path** the planned course of something, *esp.* aircraft, in flight —**flight pay** extra allowance paid to military personnel on flight duty —**flight plan** statement of details of intended journey filed by a pilot with an authority —**flight recorder** electronic device in aircraft storing information about its flight

flighty (ˈflīti) *a.* **1.** frivolous **2.** erratic

flimsy (ˈflimzi) *a.* **1.** frail, weak **2.** thin **3.** easily destroyed —ˈ**flimsily** *adv.*

flinch (flinch) *vi.* shrink, draw back, wince

fling (fling) *v.* **1.** throw, send, move, with force (**flung** *pt./pp.*) —*n.* **2.** throw **3.** hasty attempt **4.** spell of indulgence **5.** vigorous dance

flint (flint) *n.* **1.** hard steel-gray stone **2.** piece of this **3.** hard substance used (as flint) for striking fire —ˈ**flintily** *adv.* —ˈ**flinty** *a.* **1.** like or consisting of flint **2.** hard, cruel —ˈ**flintlock** *n.* **1.** gunlock in which charge is ignited by spark produced by flint in hammer **2.** firearm having such lock

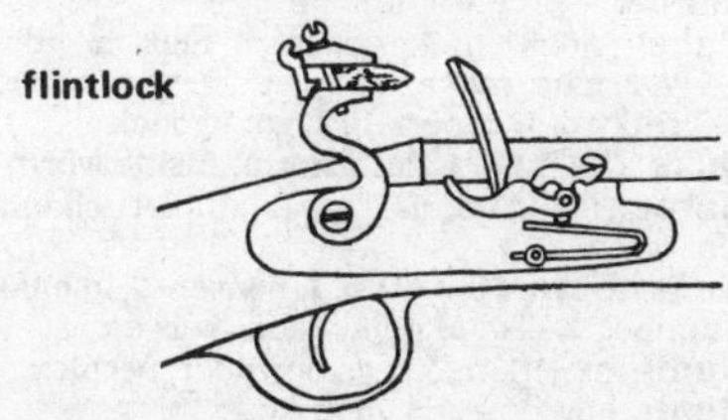

flip (flip) *vt.* **1.** throw or flick lightly **2.** turn over —*vi.* **3.** *sl.* fly into rage or emotional outburst (*also* **flip one's lid** *or* **top**) (**-pp-**) —*n.* **4.** instance, act, of flipping **5.** drink with beaten egg —*a.* **6.** *inf.* flippant; pert —ˈ**flippancy** *n.* —ˈ**flippant** *a.* treating serious things lightly —ˈ**flippantly** *adv.* —ˈ**flipper** *n.* **1.** limb, fin for swimming —*pl.* **2.** fin-shaped rubber devices worn on feet to help in swimming —**flip side** less important side of pop record

flirt (flərt) *vi.* **1.** toy, play with another's affections **2.** trifle, toy (with) —*n.* **3.** person who flirts —**flirˈtation** *n.* —**flirˈtatious** *a.*

flit (flit) *vi.* **1.** pass lightly and rapidly **2.** dart **3.** *inf.* go away hastily, secretly (**-tt-**)

flitch (flich) *n.* side of bacon

float (flōt) *vi.* **1.** rest, drift on surface of liquid **2.** be suspended freely **3.** move aimlessly —*vt.* **4.** (of liquid) support, bear alone **5.** in commerce, get (company) started **6.** *Fin.* allow (currency) to fluctuate against other currencies in accordance with market forces —*n.* **7.** anything small that floats (*esp.* to support something else, *eg* fishing net) **8.** motor vehicle carrying tableau *etc.* in parade **9.** sum of money used to provide change —ˈ**floating** *a.* **1.** having little or no attachment **2.** (of organ *etc.*) displaced and abnormally movable **3.** uncommitted, unfixed **4.** *Fin.* (of capital) available for current use; (of debt) short-term and unfunded; (of currency) free to fluctuate against other currencies in accordance with market forces —**floˈtation** *or* **floaˈtation** *n.* act of floating, *esp.* floating of company —**floating rib** any rib of lower two pairs of ribs, which are not attached to breastbone —**floating voter** voter of no fixed political allegiance

flocculent (ˈflokyələnt) *a.* like tufts of wool

flock[1] (flok) *n.* **1.** number of animals of one kind together **2.** body of people **3.** religious congregation —*vi.* **4.** gather in a crowd

flock[2] (flok) *n.* **1.** lock, tuft of wool *etc.* **2.** wool refuse for stuffing cushions *etc.* —ˈ**flocking** *n.* method of applying raised patterns to fabric, leather, paper *etc.* by adhesive —ˈ**flocky** *a.*

floe (flō) *n.* sheet of floating ice

flog (flog) *vt.* beat with whip, stick *etc.* (**-gg-**)

flood (flud) *n.* **1.** inundation, overflow of water **2.** rising of tide **3.** outpouring **4.** flowing water —*vt.* **5.** inundate **6.** cover, fill with water —*vi.* **7.** arrive, move *etc.* in great numbers —ˈ**floodgate** *n.* gate, sluice for letting water in or out —ˈ**floodlight** *n.* broad, intense beam of artificial light —ˈ**floodlit** *a.* —**flood tide 1.** the rising tide **2.** *fig.* peak of prosperity

floor (flōr) *n.* **1.** lower surface of room **2.** set of rooms on one level, story **3.** flat space **4.** (right to speak in) legislative hall or formal meeting —*vt.* **5.** supply with floor **6.** knock down **7.** confound —ˈ**flooring** *n.* material for floors —**floor leader** legislator chosen by political party to direct activities on legislative floor —**floor manager** person at political convention who coordinates support for his candidate —**floor plan** drawing to scale of arrangement of rooms on one floor of building —**floor sample** item offered at reduced price because store has used it for demonstration or display —**floor show** entertainment in nightclub *etc.*

floozy *or* **floozie** (ˈflo͞ozi) *n. sl.* disreputable woman

flop (flop) *vi.* **1.** bend, fall, collapse loosely, carelessly **2.** fall flat on floor, on water *etc.* **3.** *inf.* go to sleep **4.** *inf.* fail (**-pp-**) —*n.* **5.** flopping movement or sound **6.** *inf.* failure —ˈ**floppily** *adv.* —ˈ**floppiness** *n.* —ˈ**floppy** *a.* limp, unsteady —**floppy disk** flexible magnetic disk that stores information and can be used to store data in memory of digital computer

flora (ˈflörə) *n.* **1.** plants of a region **2.** list of them (*pl.* **-s, -rae** (-rē)) —ˈ**floral** *a.* of flowers —**floˈrescence** *n.* state or time of flowering —ˈ**floret** *n.* small flower forming part of composite flower —**floriˈbunda** *n.* type of rose whose flowers grow in large clusters —**floriˈcultural** *a.* —ˈ**floriculture** *n.* cultivation of flowers —**floriˈculturist** *n.* —**florist** (ˈflorist) *n.* dealer in flowers

Florentine (ˈflörəntēn) *a.* **1.** of Florence in Italy **2.** of dishes cooked with spinach —*n.* **3.** native of Florence —**Florence flask** (ˈflörəns) glass laboratory vessel

florid (ˈflorid) *a.* **1.** with red, flushed complexion **2.** ornate

Florida (ˈflöridə) *n.* South Atlantic state of the U.S.: ratified the Constitution in 1845. Abbrev.: **Fla., FL** (with ZIP code)

florin (ˈflorin) *n.* formerly, Brit. silver two-shilling piece

floss (flos) *n.* **1.** mass of fine, silky fibers, *eg* of cotton, silk **2.** fluff —ˈ**flossy** *a.* light and downy

flotation *or* **floatation** (flōˈtāshən) *n. see* FLOAT

flotilla (flōˈtilə) *n.* **1.** fleet of small vessels **2.** group of destroyers

flotsam (ˈflotsəm) *n.* **1.** floating wreckage **2.** discarded waste objects

flounce[1] (flowns) *vi.* **1.** go, move abruptly and impatiently —*n.* **2.** fling, jerk of body or limb

flounce[2] (flowns) *n.* ornamental gathered strip on woman's garment

flounder[1] (ˈflowndər) *vi.* **1.** plunge and struggle, *esp.* in water or mud **2.** proceed in bungling, hesitating manner —*n.* **3.** act of floundering

flounder[2] (ˈflowndər) *n.* flatfish

flour (ˈflowər) *n.* **1.** powder prepared by sifting and grinding wheat *etc.* **2.** fine soft powder —*vt.* **3.** sprinkle with flour —ˈ**flouriness** *n.* —ˈ**floury** *a.*

flourish (ˈflurish) *vi.* **1.** thrive **2.** be in the prime —*vt.* **3.** brandish, wave about **4.** display —*n.* **5.** ornamental curve **6.** showy gesture in speech *etc.* **7.** waving of hand, weapon *etc.* **8.** fanfare (of trumpets)

flout (flowt) *vt.* **1.** show contempt for, mock **2.** defy

flow (flō) *vi.* **1.** glide along as stream **2.** circulate, as the blood **3.** move easily **4.** move in waves **5.** hang loose **6.** be present in abundance —*n.* **7.** act, instance of flowing **8.** quantity that flows **9.** rise of tide **10.** ample supply —**flow chart** diagram showing sequence of operations in industrial *etc.* process

flower (ˈflowər) *n.* **1.** part of plant from which fruit is developed **2.** bloom, blossom **3.** ornamentation **4.** choicest part, pick —*pl.* **5.** chemical sublimate —*vi.* **6.** produce flowers **7.** bloom **8.** come to prime condition —*vt.* **9.** ornament with flowers —ˈ**flowered** *a.* **1.** having flowers **2.** decorated with floral design —ˈ**floweret** *n.* floret —ˈ**flowery** *a.* **1.** abounding in flowers **2.** full of fine words, ornamented with figures of speech —**flower girl** small girl attendant at wedding

flown (flōn) *pp.* *of* FLY[1]

fl. oz. fluid ounce(s)

flu (flo͞o) *n.* influenza

fluctuate (ˈflukcho͞oāt) *v.* **1.** vary —*vi.* **2.** rise and fall, undulate —**fluctuˈation** *n.*

flue (flo͞o) *n.* passage or pipe for smoke or hot air, chimney

fluent (ˈflo͞oənt) *a.* **1.** speaking, writing a given language easily and well **2.** easy, graceful

fluff (fluf) *n.* **1.** soft, feathery stuff **2.** down **3.** *inf.* mistake —*v.* **4.** make or become soft, light **5.** *inf.* make mistake (in) —ˈ**fluffy** *a.*

Fluflon (ˈfluflon) *n.* trade name for a stretch nylon yarn

flügelhorn (ˈflo͞ogəlhörn) *n.* musical instrument resembling the cornet, but with a wider bore, played in brass bands

fluid (ˈflo͞oid) *a.* **1.** flowing easily **2.** not solid —*n.* **3.** gas or liquid —**fluˈidity** *n.* —**fluid dram** ⅛ of fluid ounce —**fluid drive** automobile transmission using oil to transmit power —**fluid mechanics** branch of physics concerned with the properties of liquids and gases —**fluid ounce** unit of capacity $\frac{1}{16}$ of pint

fluke[1] (flo͞ok) *n.* **1.** flat triangular point of anchor —*pl.* **2.** whale's tail

fluke[2] (flo͞ok) *n.* **1.** stroke of luck, accident —*vt.* **2.** gain, make, hit by accident or by luck —ˈ**fluky** *a.* **1.** uncertain **2.** got by luck

fluke[3] (flo͞ok) *n.* **1.** flatfish **2.** parasitic worm

flume (flo͞om) *n.* narrow (artificial) channel for water

flummery (ˈflumәri) *n.* **1.** nonsense, idle talk, humbug **2.** dish of milk, flour, eggs *etc.*

flummox (ˈfluməks) *vt.* bewilder, perplex

flung (flung) *pt./pp.* *of* FLING

flunk (flungk) *inf.* *v.* **1.** (cause to) fail to reach required standard (in) —*vi.* **2.** (*with* out) be dismissed from school

flunky *or* **flunkey** (ˈflungki) *n.* **1.** servant, *esp.* liveried manservant **2.** servile person

fluorescence (flo͞oəˈresəns) *n.* emission of light or other radiation from substance when bombarded by particles (electrons *etc.*) or other radiation, as in fluorescent lamp

—**fluo'resce** *vi.* —**fluo'rescent** *a.* —**fluorescent lamp** lamp in which ultraviolet radiation from electrical gas discharge causes layer of phosphor on tube's inside surface to fluoresce —'**fluoroscope** *n.* device consisting of fluorescent screen and x-ray source that enables x-ray image of person *etc.* to be observed directly —**fluo'roscopy** *n.* examination of person *etc.* by means of fluoroscope

fluorite ('flōōərīt, 'flōōr-) *or* **fluorspar** ('flōōərspär, 'flōōr-) *n.* mineral containing fluorine —'**fluoridate** *vt.* —**fluori'dation** *n.* —'**fluoride** *n.* salt containing fluorine, *esp.* as added to domestic water supply as protection against tooth decay —'**fluorinate** *vt.* treat or cause to combine with fluorine —'**fluorine** *n. Chem.* nonmetallic element *Symbol* F, at. wt. 19.0, at. no. 9

fluorocarbon (flōōərō'kärbən, flōōrō-) *n.* substance containing both fluorine and carbon atoms used in refrigeration and air-conditioning units

flurry ('fluri) *n.* **1.** squall, gust **2.** bustle, commotion **3.** death struggle of whale **4.** fluttering (as of snowflakes) —*vt.* **5.** agitate, bewilder, fluster ('**flurried,** '**flurrying**)

flush[1] (flush) *vi.* **1.** blush **2.** (of skin) redden **3.** flow suddenly or violently —*vt.* **4.** cleanse (*eg* toilet) by rush of water **5.** excite —*n.* **6.** reddening, blush **7.** rush of water **8.** excitement **9.** elation **10.** glow of color **11.** freshness, vigor —*a.* **12.** full **13.** *inf.* having plenty of money **14.** *inf.* well supplied **15.** level with surrounding surface

flush[2] (flush) *vt.* cause to leave cover and take flight

flush[3] (flush) *n. Poker* hand of cards all of one suit —**royal flush** an ace-high straight flush —**straight flush** hand of five cards in sequence in the same suit

fluster ('flustər) *v.* **1.** make or become nervous, agitated —*n.* **2.** state of confusion or agitation

flute (flōōt) *n.* **1.** orchestral woodwind instrument in the form of a straight pipe, held horizontally and played through a hole located near one end. Toward the other end are a number of finger holes covered with keys **2.** groove, channel —*vi.* **3.** play on flute —*vt.* **4.** make grooves in —'**fluted** *a.* —'**fluting** *n.* —'**flutist** *or* '**flautist** *n.* flute player

flutter ('flutər) *v.* **1.** flap (as wings) rapidly without flight or in short flights **2.** be or make excited, agitated —*vi.* **3.** quiver —*n.* **4.** flapping movement **5.** nervous agitation **6.** *inf.* modest wager

fluvial ('flōōviəl) *a.* of rivers

flux (fluks) *n.* **1.** discharge **2.** constant succession of changes **3.** substance mixed with metal to clean, aid adhesion in soldering *etc.* **4.** measure of strength in magnetic field

fly[1] (flī) *vi.* **1.** move through air on wings or in aircraft **2.** pass quickly **3.** rush **4.** flee, run away —*vt.* **5.** operate (aircraft) **6.** cause to fly **7.** set flying —*v.* **8.** float loosely (**flew** *pt.,* **flown** *pp.*) —*n.* **9.** (zipper or buttons fastening) opening in trousers **10.** flap in garment or tent **11.** flying —'**flier** *or* '**flyer** *n.* **1.** person or thing that flies **2.** aviator, pilot **3.** *inf.* long, flying leap **4.** rectangular step in straight flight of stairs **5.** *Athletics inf.* flying start —'**flying** *a.* hurried, brief —'**flyaway** *a.* **1.** (of hair *etc.*) loose and fluttering **2.** frivolous, flighty; giddy —**fly ball** baseball batted up into the air (*also* **fly**) —**fly-by-night** *inf. a.* **1.** untrustworthy, *esp.* in finance —*n.* **2.** untrustworthy person —**fly-fish** *vi.* fish with artificial fly as lure —**fly front** flap of material at garment opening concealing fastening —**flying boat** airplane fitted with floats instead of landing wheels —**flying buttress** *Archit.* arched or slanting structure attached at only one point to a mass of masonry —**flying colors** conspicuous success —**flying doctor** (*esp.* Aust.) doctor visiting patients in outback areas by aircraft —**flying fish** fish with winglike fins used for gliding above the sea —**flying fox** large fruit-eating bat —**flying saucer** unidentified (disk-shaped) flying object, supposedly from outer space —**flying squad** special detachment of police, soldiers *etc.,* ready to act quickly —**flying start** start to race in which competitor is already traveling at speed as he passes starting line —**flying tackle** football tackle in which player hurls himself at ball carrier —'**flyleaf** *n.* blank leaf at beginning or end of book —'**flyover** *n.* low-altitude flight as demonstration by one or more airplanes —'**flypaper** *n.* paper with sticky and poisonous coating to trap flies —**fly sheet** sheet of instructions —**fly spray** liquid sprayed from aerosol to destroy flies —'**flytrap** *n.* **1.** insectivorous plant **2.** device for catching flies —'**flyweight** *n.* **1.** professional boxer weighing not more than 112 lbs. (51 kg); amateur boxer weighing 106-112 lbs. (48-51 kg) **2.** in Olympic wrestling, wrestler weighing not more than 115 lbs. (52 kg) —'**flywheel** *n.* heavy wheel regulating speed of machine —**fly in the face of** act in defiance of —**fly the coop** *sl.* leave secretly —**go fly a kite!** *sl.* go away!

flying fish

fly[2] (flī) *n.* two-winged insect, *esp.* common housefly —'**flyblown** *a.* infested with larvae of blowfly —ˈ**flycatcher** *n.* small insect-eating songbird

Fm *Chem.* fermium

FM frequency modulation

fm. 1. fathom (*also* **fm**) **2.** from

FMB Federal Maritime Board

FMCS Federal Mediation and Conciliation Service

f-number *or* **f number** *n. Photog.* numerical value of relative aperture

fo. folio

foal (fōl) *n.* **1.** young of horse, ass *etc.* —*v.* **2.** bear (foal)

foam (fōm) *n.* **1.** collection of small bubbles on liquid **2.** froth of saliva or sweat **3.** light cellular solid used for insulation, packing *etc.* —*v.* **4.** (cause to) produce foam —*vi.* **5.** be very angry (*esp. in* **foam at the mouth**) —ˈ**foamy** *a.* —**foam rubber** rubber treated to form firm, spongy foam

fob (fob) *n.* **1.** short watch chain **2.** small pocket in waistband of trousers or vest

f.o.b. *or* **F.O.B.** *Comm.* free on board

fob off 1. ignore, dismiss (someone or something) in offhand (insulting) manner **2.** dispose of (**-bb-**)

fo'c'sle (ˈfōksəl) *n. see* FORECASTLE

focus (ˈfōkəs) *n.* **1.** point at which rays meet after being reflected or refracted (*also* **focal point**) **2.** state of optical image when it is clearly defined **3.** state of instrument producing such image **4.** point of convergence **5.** point on which interest, activity is centered (*pl.* **-es, foci** (ˈfōsī)) —*vt.* **6.** bring to focus, adjust **7.** concentrate —*vi.* **8.** come to focus **9.** converge —ˈ**focal** *a.* of, at focus —**focal length** *or* **distance** distance from focal point of lens to reflecting surface

fodder (ˈfodər) *n.* bulk food for livestock

foe (fō) *n.* enemy

foetid (ˈfetid) *a. see* FETID

foetus (ˈfētəs) *n. see* FETUS

fog (fog) *n.* **1.** thick mist **2.** dense watery vapor in lower atmosphere **3.** cloud of anything reducing visibility —*vt.* **4.** cover in fog **5.** puzzle (**-gg-**) —ˈ**foggy** *a.* —ˈ**fogbound** *a.* prevented from operation by fog —ˈ**foghorn** *n.* instrument to warn ships in fog

Foggy Bottom the U.S. Department of State

fogy *or* **fogey** (ˈfōgi) *n.* old-fashioned person

foible (ˈfoibəl) *n.* minor weakness; idiosyncrasy

foil[1] (foil) *vt.* baffle, defeat, frustrate —ˈ**foilable** *a.*

foil[2] (foil) *n.* **1.** metal in thin sheet **2.** anything which sets off another thing to advantage **3.** *Archit.* small arc between cusps

foil[3] (foil) *n.* light, slender, flexible sword tipped by button

foist (foist) *vt.* (*usu. with* off *or* on) sell, pass off (inferior or unwanted thing) as valuable

fold[1] (fōld) *vt.* **1.** double up, bend part of **2.** interlace (arms) **3.** wrap up **4.** clasp (in arms) **5.** *Cooking* mix gently —*vi.* **6.** become folded **7.** admit of being folded **8.** *inf.* fail —*n.* **9.** folding **10.** coil **11.** winding **12.** line made by folding **13.** crease **14.** foldlike geological formation —ˈ**folder** *n.* binder, file for loose papers —ˈ**foldaway** *a.* (of bed *etc.*) able to be folded away when not in use —**folding door** door in form of hinged leaves that can be folded one against another

fold[2] (fōld) *n.* **1.** enclosure for sheep **2.** body of believers, church

-fold (*comb. form*) having so many parts; being so many times as much or as many, as in *hundredfold*

folderol *or* **falderal** (ˈfoldərol) *n.* **1.** showy but worthless trifle **2.** nonsense

foliage (ˈfōliij) *n.* leaves collectively, leafage —**foliˈaceous** *a.* of or like leaf —ˈ**foliate** *a.* leaflike, having leaves —**foliˈation** *n.* **1.** *Bot.* process of producing leaves; state of being in leaf; arrangement of leaves in leaf bud **2.** *Archit.* ornamentation consisting of cusps and foils **3.** consecutive numbering of leaves of book **4.** *Geol.* arrangement of constituents of rock in leaflike layers

folio (ˈfōliō) *n.* **1.** sheet of paper 19 × 25 inches folded in half to make two leaves of book **2.** book more than 12 inches in height **3.** page in an account book **4.** page number (*pl.* **-s**)

folk (fōk) *n.* **1.** race of people —*pl.* **2.** people in general **3.** family, relatives —ˈ**folksy** *a.* **1.** of or like ordinary people **2.** friendly; affable **3.** affectedly simple —**folk art** art of past and present peasant societies characterized by naive subject matter and lively style —**folk dance** —**folk etymology** gradual change in form of word through influence of more familiar word with which it becomes associated —ˈ**folklore** *n.* tradition, customs, beliefs popularly held —**folk music 1.** music passed on from generation to generation **2.** any music composed in this idiom —**folk song 1.** song handed down among common people **2.** modern song in folk idiom

Folle blanche (fol blänsh) dry white table wine

follicle (ˈfolikəl) *n.* **1.** small sac **2.** seed vessel —**folˈlicular** *a.*

follow (ˈfolō) *v.* **1.** go or come after —*vt.* **2.** accompany, attend on **3.** keep to (path *etc.*) **4.** take as guide, conform to **5.** engage in **6.** have a keen interest in **7.** be consequent on **8.** grasp meaning of —*vi.* **9.** come next **10.** result —ˈ**follower** *n.* **1.** disciple **2.** supporter —ˈ**following** *a.* **1.** about to be mentioned —*n.* **2.** body of supporters —**follow-through** *n.* in ball games, continuation of stroke after impact with ball —**follow-up** *n.* something done to reinforce initial action

folly (ˈfoli) *n.* **1.** foolishness **2.** foolish action, idea *etc.* **3.** useless, extravagant structure

foment (fōˈment) *vt.* **1.** foster, stir up **2.** bathe with hot lotions —**fomenˈtation** *n.*

fond (fond) *a.* **1.** tender, loving **2.** *obs.* credulous **3.** *obs.* foolish —**'fondly** *adv.* —**'fondness** *n.* —**fond of** having liking for

fondant ('fondənt) *n.* **1.** soft sugar mixture for candies **2.** candy made of this

fondle ('fondəl) *vt.* caress

fondue *or* **fondu** (fon'dyo͞o, -'do͞o; 'fondyo͞o, -do͞o) *n.* **1.** preparation of Swiss cheese flavored with wine used as hot dip for bread cubes **2.** cubes of meat or fruit cooked in a hot liquid —**fondue fork** long fork with identifying color used for dipping fondue —**fondue pan** receptacle usu. heated by alcohol lamp for preparing fondue

font (font) *n.* **1.** bowl for baptismal water, usu. on pedestal **2.** assortment of printing type of one size

fontanel *or* **fontanelle** (fontə'nel) *n.* soft, membranous gap between bones of baby's skull

food (fo͞od) *n.* **1.** any substance except water incorporated by a living organism for its maintenance **2.** what one eats **3.** mental or spiritual nourishment —**food chain** series of organisms each feeding on a lower member —**food poisoning** acute illness caused by food that is naturally poisonous or contaminated by bacteria —**food processor** kitchen appliance for preparing foods by grinding, shredding, liquidizing *etc.* —**food stamps** stamps distributed by federal government for purchasing food —**'foodstuff** *n.* food —**food value** nutritional power of food

fool (fo͞ol) *n.* **1.** silly, empty-headed person **2.** dupe **3.** simpleton **4.** *Hist.* jester, clown **5.** dessert of purḗed fruit mixed with cream *etc.* —*vt.* **6.** delude, dupe —*vi.* **7.** act as fool —**'foolery** *n.* **1.** habitual folly **2.** act of playing the fool **3.** absurdity —**'foolish** *a.* **1.** ill-considered, silly **2.** stupid —**'foolishly** *adv.* —**'foolhardiness** *n.* —**'foolhardy** *a.* foolishly adventurous —**'foolproof** *a.* proof against failure —**fool's cap 1.** jester's or dunce's cap **2.** this as watermark —**'foolscap** *n.* size of paper about 13 inches by eight inches which formerly had this mark —**fool's errand** fruitless undertaking —**fool's gold** any of various yellow minerals mistaken for gold —**fool's paradise** illusory happiness

foot (fo͝ot) *n.* **1.** lowest part of leg, from ankle down **2.** lowest part of anything, base, stand **3.** end of bed *etc.* **4.** infantry **5.** measure of twelve inches **6.** division of verse (*pl.* **feet**) —*v.* **7.** dance (*also* **foot it**) —*vt.* **8.** walk over (*esp. in* **foot it**) **9.** pay cost of (*esp. in* **foot the bill**) —**'footage** *n.* **1.** length in feet **2.** length, extent, of film used —**'footing** *n.* **1.** basis, foundation **2.** firm standing, relations, conditions —*pl.* **3.** (concrete) foundations for walls of buildings —**foot-and-mouth disease** infectious viral disease in sheep, cattle *etc.* —**'football** *n.* **1.** outdoor game played by two teams of usu. 11 players each, each team attempting to carry or kick a large inflated ball over the other team's goal line (*see* **Australian Rules** *at* AUSTRALIA, RUGBY, SOCCER) **2.** the ball —**'footballer** *n.* —**'footboard** *n.* **1.** treadle or foot-operated lever on machine **2.** vertical board at foot of bed —**foot brake** brake operated by pressure on foot pedal —**'footbridge** *n.* narrow bridge for pedestrians —**'footfall** *n.* sound of footstep —**foot fault** *Tennis* fault of overstepping baseline while serving —**'foothill** *n.* (*oft. pl.*) low hill at foot of mountain —**'foothold** *n.* **1.** place affording secure grip for the foot **2.** secure position from which progress may be made —**'footlights** *pl.n.* lights across front of stage —**'footloose** *a.* free from any ties —**'footman** *n.* liveried servant —**'footnote** *n.* note of reference or explanation printed at foot of page —**'footpad** *n. obs.* robber, highwayman —**'footpath** *n.* narrow path for pedestrians —**foot-pound** *n.* amount of energy required to raise weight of one pound to height of one foot —**'footprint** *n.* mark left by foot —**'footrest** *n.* something that provides support for feet —**'footsore** *a.* having sore feet, *esp.* from walking —**'footwear** *n.* anything worn to cover feet —**'footwork** *n.* skillful use of feet, as in sports *etc.*

fop (fop) *n.* man excessively concerned with fashion —**'foppery** *n.* —**'foppish** *a.* —**'foppishly** *adv.*

for (fŏr; *unstressed* fər) *prep.* **1.** intended to reach **2.** directed or belonging to **3.** because of **4.** instead of **5.** toward **6.** on account of **7.** in favor of **8.** respecting **9.** during **10.** in search of **11.** in payment of **12.** in the character of **13.** in spite of —*conj.* **14.** because —**for it** *inf.* liable for punishment or blame

for- (*comb. form*) from, away, against, as in *forswear, forbid.* Such words are not given here where the meaning may easily be inferred from the simple word

forage ('forij) *n.* **1.** food for cattle and horses —*vi.* **2.** collect forage **3.** make roving search

foramen (fə'rāmən) *n.* natural hole, *esp.* in bone (*pl.* **-ramina** (-'raminə), **-s**)

forasmuch as ('fŏrəzmuch) *conj.* seeing that

foray ('forā) *n.* **1.** raid, inroad —*vi.* **2.** make one —**'forayer** *n.*

forbear[1] ('fŏrbāər) *n. see* FOREBEAR

forbear[2] (fŏr'bāər) *v.* **1.** (*esp. with* from) cease; refrain (from) —*vi.* **2.** be patient (**for'bore** *pt.*, **for'borne** *pp.*) —**for'bearance** *n.* self-control; patience —**for'bearing** *a.*

forbid (fər'bid) *vt.* prohibit, refuse to allow (**forbade** (fər'bad, -'bād) *pt.*, **for'bidden** *pp.*, **for'bidding** *pr.p.*) —**for'bidding** *a.* **1.** uninviting **2.** threatening

force (fŏrs) *n.* **1.** strength, power **2.** compulsion **3.** that which is exerted on a motionless body of matter to put it in motion or to change the velocity of a body if it is already in motion **4.** mental or moral strength **5.** body of troops, police *etc.* **6.**

group of people organized for particular task or duty **7.** effectiveness, operative state **8.** violence *—vt.* **9.** constrain, compel **10.** produce by effort, strength **11.** break open **12.** urge, strain **13.** drive **14.** hasten maturity of **—forced** *a.* **1.** accomplished by great effort **2.** compulsory **3.** unnatural **4.** strained **—'forceful** *a.* **1.** powerful **2.** persuasive **—'forcible** *a.* **1.** done by force **2.** efficacious, compelling, impressive **3.** strong **—'forcibly** *adv.* **—force-feed** *vt.* force (person or animal) to eat or swallow (food)

forcemeat ('försmēt) *n.* mixture of chopped ingredients used for stuffing (*also* **farce**)

forceps ('försips) *pl.n.* surgical pincers

ford (förd) *n.* **1.** shallow place where river may be crossed *—vt.* **2.** cross (river *etc.*) over shallow area **—'fordable** *a.*

Ford (förd) *n.* **Gerald Rudolph.** the 38th President of the U.S. (1974-77)

fore[1] (för) *a.* **1.** in front (**'former, 'further** *comp.,* **'foremost, first, 'furthest** *sup.*) *—n.* **2.** front part

fore[2] (för) *interj.* golfer's warning

fore- (*comb. form*) previous, before, front

fore-and-aft *a.* placed in line from bow to rear of ship

forearm ('förärm) *n.* **1.** arm between wrist and elbow *—vt.* (för'ärm) **2.** arm by stockpiling weapons

forebear *or* **forbear** ('förbāər) *n.* ancestor

forebode (för'bōd) *vt.* indicate in advance **—fore'boding** *n.* anticipation of evil

forecast ('förkast) *vt.* **1.** estimate beforehand (*esp.* weather); prophesy *—n.* **2.** prediction

forecastle *or* **fo'c'sle** ('föksəl) *n.* **1.** forward raised part of ship **2.** sailors' quarters

foreclose (för'klōz) *vt.* **1.** take away power of redeeming (mortgage) **2.** prevent **3.** shut out, bar **—fore'closure** *n.*

forecourt ('förkört) *n.* courtyard, open space, in front of building

forefather ('förfädhər) *n.* ancestor

forefinger ('förfinggər) *n.* finger next to thumb

forefoot ('förfŏŏt) *n.* either of front feet of quadruped

forefront ('förfrunt) *n.* **1.** extreme front **2.** position of most prominence or action

foregather (för'gadhər) *vi. see* FORGATHER

forego[1] (för'gō) *vt.* precede in time, place (**-'went** *pt.,* **-'gone** *pp.,* **-'going** *pr.p.*) **—fore'going** *a.* going before, preceding **—fore'gone** *a.* **1.** determined beforehand **2.** preceding **—foregone conclusion** result that might have been foreseen

forego[2] (för'gō) *vt. see* FORGO

foreground ('förgrownd) *n.* part of view, *esp.* in picture, nearest observer

forehand ('förhand) *a.* (of stroke in racket games) made with inner side of wrist leading

forehead ('förid) *n.* part of face above eyebrows and between temples

foreign ('forin) *a.* **1.** not of, or in, one's own country **2.** relating to, or connected with other countries **3.** irrelevant **4.** coming from outside **5.** unfamiliar, strange **—'foreigner** *n.* **—foreign aid** economic assistance to another country **—foreign correspondent** person reporting news from another country **—foreign exchange 1.** process of settling debts between countries **2.** the currency of other countries **—Foreign Legion** body of foreign volunteers in an army, *esp.* the French army **—foreign service** field personnel of U.S. Department of State

foreknow (för'nō) *vt.* know in advance **—foreknowledge** (för'nolij) *n.*

foreland ('förlənd) *n.* **1.** headland, promontory **2.** land lying in front of something, such as water

foreleg ('förleg) *n.* either of front legs of horse or other quadruped

forelimb ('förlim) *n.* either of front limbs of vertebrate

forelock ('förlok) *n.* lock of hair above forehead

foreman ('förmən) *n.* **1.** one in charge of work **2.** leader of jury

foremast ('förmast; *Naut.* 'förməst) *n.* mast nearest bow

foremost ('förmōst) *a./adv.* first in time, place, importance *etc.*

forenoon ('förnōōn) *n.* morning

forensic (fə'rensik, -zik) *a.* of courts of law **—forensic medicine** application of medical knowledge in legal matters

foreordain (förör'dān) *vt.* determine (events *etc.*) in future **—foreordination** (förördi'nāshən) *n.*

forepaw ('förpö) *n.* either of front feet of most land mammals that do not have hooves

foreplay ('förplā) *n.* sexual stimulation before intercourse

forerunner ('förrunər) *n.* one who goes before, precursor

foresail ('försāl; *Naut.* 'försəl) *n. Naut.* **1.** aftermost headsail of fore-and-aft rigged vessel **2.** lowest sail set on foremast of square-rigged vessel

foresee (för'sē) *vt.* see beforehand (**-'saw** *pt.,* **-'seen** *pp.*)

foreshadow (för'shadō) *vt.* show, suggest beforehand

foreshore ('förshör) *n.* part of shore between high and low tide marks

foreshortening (för'shörtəning) *n.* the application of the rules of perspective to an individual form to create the illusion of depth and dimensionality

foresight ('försīt) *n.* **1.** foreseeing **2.** care for future

foreskin ('förskin) *n.* skin that covers tip of penis

forest ('forist) *n.* **1.** area with heavy growth

of trees and plants **2.** these trees **3.** *fig.* something resembling forest —*vt.* **4.** plant, create forest in (an area) —**fores'tation** *n.* planting of trees over wide area —**'forester** *n.* one skilled in forestry —**'forestry** *n.* study, management of forest planting and maintenance

forestall (fŏr'stŏl) *vt.* **1.** anticipate **2.** prevent, guard against in advance

foretaste ('fŏrtast) *n.* **1.** anticipation **2.** taste beforehand

foretell (fŏr'tel) *vt.* prophesy (**fore'told** *pt./pp.*)

forethought ('fŏrthŏt) *n.* thoughtful consideration of future events

foretoken ('fŏrtōkən) *n.* **1.** sign of future event —*vt.* (fŏr'tōkən) **2.** foreshadow

foretop ('fŏrtop; *Naut.* 'fŏrtəp) *n.* platform at top of foremast

for ever *or* **forever** (fə'revər, fŏ-) *adv.* **1.** always **2.** eternally —*n.* **3.** a long time

forewarn (fŏr'wŏrn) *vt.* warn, caution in advance

forewent (fŏr'went) *pt. of* FOREGO[1], FOREGO[2]

foreword ('fŏrwərd) *n.* preface

forfeit ('fŏrfit) *n.* **1.** thing lost by crime or fault **2.** penalty, fine —*a.* **3.** lost by crime or fault —*vt.* **4.** lose by penalty —**'forfeiture** *n.*

forgather *or* **foregather** (fŏr'gadhər) *vi.* **1.** meet together, assemble **2.** associate

forgave (fər'gāv) *pt. of* FORGIVE

forge[1] (fŏrj) *n.* **1.** place where metal is worked, smithy **2.** furnace, workshop for melting or refining metal —*vt.* **3.** shape (metal) by heating in fire and hammering **4.** make, shape **5.** invent **6.** make a fraudulent imitation of, counterfeit —**'forger** *n.* —**'forgery** *n.* **1.** forged document, bank note *etc.* **2.** the making of it

forge[2] (fŏrj) *vi.* advance steadily

forget (fər'get) *vt.* **1.** lose memory of **2.** neglect, overlook (**for'got** *pt.*, **for'gotten** *or* **for'got** *pp.*, **for'getting** *pr.p.*) —**for'getful** *a.* liable to forget —**for'getfully** *adv.* —**forget-me-not** *n.* plant with small blue flower

forgive (fər'giv) *v.* **1.** cease to blame or hold resentment (against) —*vt.* **2.** pardon —**for'giveness** *n.* —**for'giving** *a.* willing to forgive

forgo *or* **forego** (fŏr'gō) *vt.* go without, give up (**-'went** *pt.*, **-'gone** *pp.*, **-'going** *pr.p.*)

forgot (fər'got) *pt./pp. of* FORGET —**for'gotten** *pp. of* FORGET

fork (fŏrk) *n.* **1.** pronged instrument for eating food **2.** pronged tool for digging or lifting **3.** division into branches **4.** point of this division **5.** one of the branches —*vi.* **6.** branch —*vt.* **7.** dig, lift, throw with fork **8.** make fork-shaped —**forked** *a.* **1.** having fork or forklike parts **2.** zigzag —**'forklift** *n.* vehicle having two power-operated horizontal prongs that can be raised and lowered —**fork out, over** *or* **up** *inf.* pay out (money)

forlorn (fər'lŏrn) *a.* **1.** forsaken **2.** desperate —**forlorn hope** anything undertaken with little hope of success

form (fŏrm) *n.* **1.** shape **2.** visible appearance **3.** visible person or animal **4.** structure **5.** nature **6.** species, kind **7.** regularly drawn up document, *esp.* printed one with blanks for particulars **8.** condition, *esp.* good condition **9.** model for fitting clothes **10.** customary way of doing things **11.** set order of words **12.** long seat without back, bench **13.** hare's nest **14.** *Print.* frame for type —*vt.* **15.** shape, mold **16.** arrange, organize **17.** train **18.** shape in the mind, conceive **19.** go to make up, make part of —*vi.* **20.** come into existence or shape —**for'mation** *n.* **1.** forming **2.** thing formed **3.** structure, shape, arrangement **4.** military order —**'formative** *a.* **1.** of, relating to, development **2.** serving or tending to form **3.** used in forming —**'formless** *a.* —**form letter** standard letter for dealing with routine matters

-form (*comb. form*) having shape or form of; resembling, as in *cruciform, vermiform*

formal ('fŏrməl) *a.* **1.** ceremonial **2.** according to rule **3.** of outward form or routine **4.** of, for, formal occasions **5.** according to rule that does not matter **6.** precise; stiff —**'formalism** *n.* **1.** quality of being formal **2.** exclusive concern for form, structure, technique in an activity, *eg* art —**'formalist** *n.* —**for'mality** *n.* **1.** observance required by custom or etiquette **2.** condition or quality of being formal **3.** conformity to custom, conventionality, mere form **4.** in art, precision, stiffness, as opposed to originality —**formali'zation** *n.* —**'formalize** *vt.* **1.** make formal **2.** make official or valid **3.** give definite form to —**'formally** *adv.*

formaldehyde (fŏr'maldihīd) *n.* colorless, poisonous, pungent gas, used in making antiseptics and in chemistry —**'formalin** *n.* solution of formaldehyde in water, used as disinfectant, preservative *etc.*

format ('fŏrmat) *n.* **1.** size and shape of book **2.** organization of television show *etc.*

former ('fŏrmər) *a.* **1.** earlier in time **2.** of past times **3.** first named —*n.* **4.** first named thing, person or fact —**'formerly** *adv.* previously

Formica (fŏr'mīkə) *n.* trade name for type of laminated sheet used to make heat-resistant surfaces

formic acid ('fŏrmik) acid found in insects (*esp.* ants) and some plants used in textile manufacture

formidable ('fŏrmidəbəl, fŏr'mid-) *a.* **1.** to be feared **2.** overwhelming, terrible, redoubtable **3.** likely to be difficult, serious —**'formidably** *adv.*

Formosa (fŏr'mōsə) *n.* *former name for* TAIWAN

formula ('fŏrmyələ) *n.* **1.** set form of words setting forth principle, method or rule for doing, producing something **2.** human milk substitute for feeding infant **3.** specific category of car in motor racing **4.** recipe **5.** *Science, math.* rule, fact expressed in symbols and figures (*pl.* **-ulae** (-yəlē), **-s**) —**'formulary** *n.* collection of formulas —**'formulate** *vt.* **1.** reduce to, express in formula, or in definite form **2.** devise —**formu'lation** *n.* —**'formulator** *n.*

fornication (förni'kāshən) *n.* sexual intercourse outside marriage —**'fornicate** *vi.*

forsake (fə'rsāk) *vt.* **1.** abandon, desert **2.** give up (**for'sook, for'saken, for'saking**)

forsooth (fər'sōōth) *adv. obs.* in truth

forswear (för'swāər) *vt.* **1.** renounce **2.** deny —*v. refl.* **3.** perjure (-**'swore** *pt.*, -**'sworn** *pp.*)

forsythia (fər'sithiə) *n.* widely cultivated shrub with yellow flowers

fort (fört) *n.* fortified place, stronghold —**hold the fort** *inf.* guard something temporarily

forte[1] (fört, 'förtā) *n.* one's strong point, that in which one excels

forte[2] ('förti) *adv. Mus.* loudly (**for'tissimo** *sup.*)

forth (förth) *adv.* **1.** onward **2.** into view —**'forth'coming** *a.* **1.** about to come **2.** ready when wanted **3.** willing to talk, communicative —**forth'with** *adv.* at once, immediately

forthright ('förthrīt) *a.* direct, outspoken

fortieth ('förtiith) *see* FOUR

fortify ('förtifī) *vt.* **1.** strengthen **2.** provide with defensive works (**'fortified, 'fortifying**) —**fortifi'cation** *n.*

fortitude ('förtityōōd, -tōōd) *n.* courage in adversity or pain, endurance

fortnight ('förtnīt) *n.* two weeks —**'fortnightly** *a./adv.*

FORTRAN ('förtran) *Comp. formula translator*, high-level language for writing scientific programs

fortress ('förtris) *n.* fortified place, *eg* castle, stronghold

fortuitous (för'tyōōitəs, -'tōō-) *a.* accidental, by chance —**for'tuitously** *adv.* —**for'tuity** *n.*

fortune ('förchən) *n.* **1.** good luck **2.** prosperity, wealth **3.** chance, luck —**'fortunate** *a.* —**'fortunately** *adv.* —**fortune-hunter** *n.* person seeking fortune, *esp.* by marriage —**fortune-teller** *n.* one who predicts a person's future

forty ('förti) *see* FOUR —**forty winks** short sleep, nap

forum ('förəm) *n.* (place or medium for) meeting, assembly for open discussion or debate

forward ('förwərd) *a.* **1.** lying in front of something **2.** onward **3.** presumptuous, impudent **4.** advanced, progressive **5.** relating to the future —*n.* **6.** player placed in forward position in various team games, *eg* football —*adv.* **7.** toward the future **8.** toward the front, to the front **9.** into view **10.** ('förwərd; *Naut.* 'forərd) at, in fore part of ship **11.** onward, so as to make progress —*vt.* **12.** help forward **13.** send, dispatch —**'forwardly** *adv.* pertly —**'forwardness** *n.* —**'forwards** *adv.*

forwent (för'went) *pt. of* FORGO

fosse *or* **foss** (fos) *n.* ditch; moat

fossil ('fosəl) *n.* **1.** remnant or impression of animal or plant, *esp.* prehistoric one, preserved in earth **2.** *inf.* person, idea *etc.* that is outdated and incapable of change —*a.* **3.** of, like or forming fossil **4.** dug from earth **5.** *inf.* antiquated —**'fossilize** *v.* **1.** turn into fossil —*vt.* **2.** petrify —**fossil fuel** fuel derived from materials formed over a long period of time from the remains of living organisms, *eg* petroleum, natural gas and coal

foster ('fostər) *vt.* **1.** promote growth or development of **2.** bring up (child) *esp.* not one's own —**foster brother, sister, father, mother, parent, child** one related by upbringing, not blood

fought (föt) *pt./pp. of* FIGHT

foul (fowl) *a.* **1.** loathsome, offensive **2.** stinking **3.** dirty **4.** unfair **5.** (of weather) wet, rough **6.** obscene, disgustingly abusive **7.** charged with harmful matter, clogged, choked —*n.* **8.** act of unfair play **9.** the breaking of a rule —*adv.* **10.** unfairly —*v.* **11.** make, become foul **12.** jam —*vt.* **13.** collide with —**'foully** *adv.* —**foul ball** baseball hit outside the foul lines —**foul line 1.** in baseball, one of two lines extending from home plate marking the boundary **2.** in basketball, one of two lines on the court at which player stands to take foul shot —**foul play 1.** violent crime, *esp.* murder **2.** violation of rules in game —**foul shot** in basketball, a throw at the basket without interference by opponents, awarded as a penalty against them —**fall foul of 1.** get into trouble with **2.** (of ships) collide with

foulard (fōō'lärd) *n.* soft light fabric of silk or rayon

found[1] (fownd) *pt./pp. of* FIND —**found object** something found, not looked for, incorporated into works of art by the Dadaists and surrealists (*also* **objet trouvé**)

found[2] (fownd) *vt.* **1.** establish, institute **2.** lay base of **3.** base, ground —**foun'dation** *n.* **1.** basis **2.** base, lowest part of building **3.** founding **4.** endowed institution *etc.* **5.** cosmetic used as base for make-up —**'founder** *n.* —**foundation garment** woman's undergarment worn to shape and support figure (*also* **foun'dation**) —**foundation stone** one of stones forming foundation of building, *esp.* stone laid with public ceremony

found[3] (fownd) *vt.* **1.** melt and run into mold **2.** cast —**'founder** *n.* —**'foundry** *n.* **1.** place for casting **2.** art of this

founder ('fowndər) *vi.* **1.** collapse **2.** sink **3.** become stuck as in mud *etc.*

foundling ('fowndling) *n.* deserted infant

fount (fownt) *n.* fountain

fountain ('fowntin) *n.* **1.** jet of water, *esp.* ornamental one **2.** spring **3.** source —'**fountainhead** *n.* source —**fountain pen** pen with ink reservoir

four (för) *n./a.* cardinal number next after three —'**fortieth** *a./n.* —'**forty** *n./a.* four tens —**four'teen** *n./a.* four plus ten —**four'teenth** *a.* —**fourth** *a.* ordinal number of four —'**fourthly** *adv.* —**Four Freedoms** freedom of expression, of worship, from want, from fear —**Four-H** *or* **4-H club** club for *h*ead, *h*eart, *h*ands, and *h*ealth, organization sponsored by Deptartment of Agriculture for rural youth —**Four Hundred** formerly, the most exclusive social set in New York City —**four-in-hand** *n.* **1.** road vehicle drawn by four horses and driven by one driver **2.** four-horse team **3.** long narrow necktie tied in flat slipknot with ends dangling —**four-leaf clover** clover with four leaves rather than three, supposed to bring good luck —**four-letter word** any of several short English words referring to sex or excrement: regarded generally as offensive —**four-poster** *n.* bed with four posts for curtains *etc.* —'**four'score** *a./n. obs.* eighty —'**foursome** *n.* **1.** group of four people **2.** game or dance for four people —**four'square** *a.* firm, steady —**four-stroke** *n.* internal-combustion engine firing once every four strokes of piston —**fourth-class mail** class of mail sent at cheapest rate —**fourth estate** (*sometimes* **F-E-**) journalists; journalism —**on all fours** on hands and knees —**the Fourth** July 4th, Independence Day

fowl (fowl) *n.* **1.** domestic cock or hen **2.** bird, its flesh —*vi.* **3.** hunt wild birds —'**fowler** *n.* —**fowling piece** light gun

fox (foks) *n.* **1.** wild animal of the dog family related to wolf with pointed snout, reddish or gray fur and a bushy tail **2.** its pelt, *esp.* silver fox **3.** cunning person **4.** (**F-**) member of Amerindian people formerly living in Wisconsin —*vt.* **5.** perplex **6.** repair (shoe) by renewing top **7.** mislead —*vi.* **8.** act craftily —'**foxy** *a.* **1.** of or resembling fox, *esp.* in craftiness **2.** of reddish-brown color **3.** (of grapes) having sharp flavor **4.** (of woman) physically attractive —'**foxglove** *n.* genus of erect biennial or perennial plants grown for ornament and as a source of digitalis —'**foxhole** *n. sl.* in war, small trench giving protection —'**foxhound** *n.* dog bred for hunting foxes —**fox-hunting** *n.* —**fox terrier** small dog now mainly kept as pet —'**foxtrot** *n.* **1.** (music for) ballroom dance **2.** (**F-**) word used in communications for the letter *f* —*vi.* **3.** perform foxtrot

foyer ('foiər, 'foiā) *n.* entrance hall in theaters, hotels *etc.*

F.P. *or* **f.p.** **1.** freezing point (*also* **fp**) **2.** fully paid

FPC Federal Power Commission

f.p.s. **1.** feet per second **2.** foot-pound-second

Fr *Chem.* francium

fr. **1.** fragment **2.** franc **3.** from

Fr. **1.** Father **2.** Frater (*Lat.* brother) **3.** French **4.** Friday

fracas ('frākəs, 'fra-) *n.* noisy quarrel; uproar; brawl

fraction ('frakshən) *n.* **1.** any indicated quotient of two quantities, *esp.* any algebraic expression with a numerator and a denominator **2.** fragment, piece —'**fractional** *a.* **1.** constituting a fraction **2.** forming but a small part **3.** insignificant

fractious ('frakshəs) *a.* **1.** unruly **2.** irritable

fracture ('frakchər) *n.* **1.** breakage, part broken **2.** breaking of bone **3.** breach, rupture —*v.* **4.** break

fragile ('frajil) *a.* **1.** breakable **2.** frail, delicate —**fra'gility** *n.*

fragment ('fragmənt) *n.* **1.** piece broken off **2.** small portion **3.** incomplete part —*v.* ('fragment) **4.** (cause to) break into fragments —'**fragmentary** *a.*

fragrant ('frāgrənt) *a.* sweet-smelling —'**fragrance** *n.* scent —'**fragrantly** *adv.*

frail (frāl) *a.* **1.** fragile, delicate **2.** infirm, in weak health **3.** morally weak —'**frailly** *adv.* —'**frailty** *n.*

frambesia (fram'bēzhiə) *n.* yaws

frame (frām) *n.* **1.** that in which thing is set, as square of wood round picture *etc.* **2.** structure **3.** build of body **4.** constitution **5.** mood **6.** individual exposure on strip of film **7.** *Pool etc.* wooden triangle used to set up balls, balls when set up or single game finished when all balls have been potted —*vt.* **8.** put together, make **9.** adapt **10.** put into words **11.** put into frame **12.** *sl.* conspire to incriminate on false charge —**frame-up** *n. sl.* **1.** plot **2.** manufactured evidence —'**framework** *n.* **1.** structure into which completing parts can be fitted **2.** supporting work

franc (frangk; *Fr.* frã) *n.* monetary unit of France, Switzerland and other countries

France (frans) *n.* country in Europe bounded north by the English Channel, northeast by Belgium and Luxembourg, east by the Federal Republic of Germany, Switzerland and Italy, south by the Mediterranean (with Monaco as a coastal enclave), southwest by Spain and Andorra and west by the Atlantic Ocean

franchise ('franchīz) *n.* **1.** right of voting **2.** citizenship **3.** privilege or right, *esp.* right to sell certain goods

Franciscan (fran'siskən) *n.* monk or nun of the order founded by St. Francis of Assisi in 1209

francium ('fransiəm) *n. Chem.* radioactive element of alkali-metal group *Symbol* Fr, at. wt. 223, at. no. 87

Franco- ('frangkō-) (*comb. form*) France; French, as in *Franco-Prussian*

francolin ('frangkəlin) *n.* Afr. or Asian partridge

frangipani ('franji'pani, -'päni) *n.* tropical Amer. shrub (*pl.* **-s, -'pani**)

frank (frangk) *a.* **1.** candid, outspoken **2.** sincere —*n.* **3.** official mark on letter either canceling stamp or ensuring delivery without stamp —*vt.* **4.** mark letter thus —**'frankly** *adv.* candidly —**'frankness** *n.* —**franking machine** machine that prints marks on letters *etc.* indicating that postage has been paid

Frank (frangk) *n.* member of group of W Germanic peoples who gradually conquered most of Gaul and Germany in late 4th century A.D. —**'Frankish** *n.* **1.** ancient W Germanic language of Franks —*a.* **2.** of Franks or their language

Frankenstein's monster ('frangkinstīnz) creation or monster that brings disaster and is beyond the control of its creator

frankfurter *or* **frankforter** ('frangkfərtər) *n.* cured cooked sausage of beef or beef and pork (*also* **hot dog**)

frankincense ('frangkinsens) *n.* aromatic gum resin burned as incense

frantic ('frantik) *a.* **1.** distracted with rage, grief, joy *etc.* **2.** frenzied —**'frantically** *adv.*

frappé (fra'pā) *n.* **1.** drink consisting of liqueur *etc.* poured over crushed ice **2.** thick milk shake —*a.* **3.** (*esp.* of drinks) chilled

fraternal (frə'tərnəl) *a.* of brother; brotherly —**fra'ternally** *adv.* —**fra'ternity** *n.* **1.** brotherliness **2.** brotherhood **3.** men's student organization for usu. social purposes —**fraterni'zation** *n.* —**'fraternize** *vi.* associate, make friends —**fratri'cidal** *a.* —**'fratricide** *n.* killing, killer of brother or sister

Frau (frow) *n.* married German woman: usu. used as title equivalent to *Mrs.* (*pl.* **Frauen** ('frowən), **-s**)

fraud (frōd) *n.* **1.** criminal deception **2.** swindle, imposture **3.** *inf.* person who acts in false or deceitful way —**'fraudulence** *n.* —**'fraudulent** *a.*

fraught (frōt) *a.* —**fraught with** filled with, involving

fray[1] (frā) *n.* **1.** fight **2.** noisy quarrel

fray[2] (frā) *v.* **1.** wear through by rubbing **2.** make, become ragged at edge

frazil ('frāzil) *n.* C broken spikes of ice formed in turbulent water

frazzle ('frazəl) *inf.* *v.* **1.** make or become exhausted **2.** make or become irritated —*n.* **3.** exhausted state

freak (frēk) *n.* **1.** abnormal person, animal, thing —*a.* **2.** oddly different from what is normal —**'freakish** *or* (*inf.*) **'freaky** *a.* —**freak out** *inf.* (cause to) hallucinate, be wildly excited *etc.*

freckle ('frekəl) *n.* **1.** light brown spot on skin, *esp.* caused by sun **2.** any small spot —*v.* **3.** mark or become marked in freckles —**'freckled** *a.*

free (frē) *a.* **1.** able to act at will, not under compulsion or restraint **2.** (*with* from) not restricted or affected by **3.** not subject to cost or tax **4.** independent **5.** not exact or literal **6.** generous **7.** not in use **8.** (of person) not occupied, having no engagement **9.** loose, not fixed —*vt.* **10.** set at liberty **11.** (*with* of *or* from) remove (obstacles, pain *etc.*), rid (of) (**freed, 'freeing**) —**'freebie, 'freebee,** *or* **'freeby** *n. sl.* anything that is free of charge —**'freedom** *n.* —**'freely** *adv.* —**'freeboard** *n.* space between deck of vessel and waterline —**free enterprise** economic system in which commercial organizations compete for profit with little state control —**free flight** flight of rocket *etc.* when engine has ceased to produce thrust —**free-for-all** *n.* brawl —**'freehand** *a.* drawn without guiding instruments —**free kick** in football, place kick awarded for foul or infringement —**'freelance** *a./n.* **1.** (of) self-employed, unattached person —*vi.* **2.** work as freelance —*adv.* **3.** as freelance —**free-living** *a.* **1.** given to indulgence of appetites **2.** (of animals *etc.*) not parasitic —**free'load** *vi.* eat, drink *etc.* at another's expense —**free love** practice of sexual relationships without fidelity to single partner —**'freemartin** *n.* calf incapable of reproducing —**'Freemason** *n.* member of secret fraternity for mutual help —**free ride** something obtained without cost —**free speech** right to express opinions publicly —**free'standing** *a.* not attached to or supported by another object —**'freestyle** *n.* race, as in swimming, in which each participant may use style of his or her choice —**free'thinker** *n.* skeptic who forms his own opinions, *esp.* in religion —**free trade** international trade free of protective tariffs —**free verse** unrhymed verse without metrical pattern —**'freeway** *n.* **1.** expressway with controlled access **2.** toll-free highway —**free'wheel** *vi.* coast —**free will 1.** apparent human ability to make choices not externally determined **2.** doctrine that human beings have such freedom of choice **3.** ability to make choice without coercion —**free-will** *a.* voluntary; spontaneous —**free on board** (of shipment of goods) delivered on board ship *etc.* without charge to buyer —**the Free World** non-Communist countries collectively

freesia ('frēzhə) *n.* plant with fragrant, tubular flowers

freeze (frēz) *v.* **1.** change (by reduction of temperature) from liquid to solid, as water to ice —*vt.* **2.** preserve (food *etc.*) by extreme cold, as in freezer **3.** fix (prices *etc.*) —*vi.* **4.** feel very cold **5.** become rigid as with fear **6.** stop (**froze, 'frozen, 'freezing**) —**'freezer** *n.* insulated cabinet for long-term storage of perishable foodstuffs —**frozen** ('frōzən) *a.* (of credits *etc.*) unrealizable —**freeze-dry** *vt.* preserve (substance) by rapid freezing and subsequently drying in vacuum —**freezing point** temperature at which liquid becomes solid, 32°F or 0°C for water

freight (frāt) *n.* **1.** commercial transport (*esp.* by railroad, ship) **2.** cost of this **3.** goods so carried —*vt.* **4.** send as or by freight —'**freightage** *n.* money paid for freight —'**freighter** *n.*

French (french) *n.* **1.** Romance language spoken by people of France and some Canadians, Belgians and Swiss —*a.* **2.** of France —**French Canadian** Canadian citizen whose native language is French —**French-Canadian** *a.* of French Canadians —**French chalk** variety of talc used to mark cloth or remove grease stains —**French dressing** salad dressing of oil and vinegar —**French fries** potatoes cut into thin strips and fried in deep fat —**French horn** orchestral brass instrument with a narrow conical tube wound twice in a circle, funnel-shaped mouthpiece, and a flaring bell —**French leave** unauthorized leave —**French toast** sliced bread dipped in egg-and-milk batter and sautéed —**French window** pair of exterior windows reaching to the floor, opening in the middle and used as a door

frenetic (fri'netik) *a.* frenzied

frenzy ('frenzi) *n.* **1.** violent mental derangement **2.** wild excitement —'**frenzied** *a.*

frequent ('frēkwənt) *a.* **1.** happening often **2.** common **3.** numerous —*vt.* (frē'kwent) **4.** go often to —'**frequency** *n.* **1.** rate of occurrence **2.** in radio *etc.*, cycles per second of alternating current —**fre'quentative** *a.* expressing repetition —'**frequently** *adv.* —**frequency modulation** *Rad.* method of transmitting information in which frequency of carrier wave is varied

fresco ('freskō) *n.* **1.** method of painting in watercolor on plaster of wall before it dries **2.** painting done thus (*pl.* **-es, -s**)

fresh (fresh) *a.* **1.** not stale **2.** new **3.** additional **4.** different **5.** recent **6.** inexperienced **7.** pure **8.** not pickled, frozen *etc.* **9.** not faded or dimmed **10.** not tired **11.** (of wind) strong **12.** *inf.* impudent **13.** *inf.* arrogant —'**freshen** *v.* —'**freshet** *n.* **1.** rush of water at river mouth **2.** flood of river water —'**freshly** *adv.* —'**freshman** *n.* first-year student —'**freshness** *n.* —'**freshwater** *a.* **1.** of or living in fresh water **2.** (*esp.* of sailor who has not sailed on sea) inexperienced **3.** little known

fret[1] (fret) *v.* **1.** irritate or be irritated **2** worry (**-tt-**) —*n.* **3.** irritation —'**fretful** *a.* irritable, (easily) upset

fret[2] (fret) *n.* **1.** repetitive geometrical pattern **2.** small bar on fingerboard of guitar *etc.* —*vt.* **3.** ornament with carved pattern (**-tt-**) —**fret saw** saw with narrow blade and fine teeth, used for fretwork —'**fretwork** *n.* carved or open woodwork in ornamental patterns and devices

Freudian ('froidiən) *a.* pert. to Austrian psychologist Sigmund Freud, or his theories —**Freudian slip** any action, such as slip of tongue, that may reveal unconscious thought

Fri. Friday

friable ('frīəbəl) *a.* easily crumbled —**fria'bility** *or* '**friableness** *n.*

friar ('frīər) *n.* member of mendicant religious order —'**friary** *n.* house of friars

fricassee ('frikəsē, frikə'sē) *n.* **1.** dish of pieces of chicken or meat, fried or stewed and served with rich sauce —*vt.* **2.** cook thus

fricative ('frikətiv) *n.* **1.** consonant produced by partial occlusion of air stream, such as (f) or (z) —*a.* **2.** relating to fricative

friction ('frikshən) *n.* **1.** rubbing **2.** resistance met with by body moving over another **3.** clash of wills *etc.*, disagreement —'**frictional** *a.*

Friday ('frīdi) *n.* sixth day of week —**Good Friday** the Friday before Easter

fried (frīd) *pt./pp. of* FRY[1]

Friedman's disease ('frēdmənz) *see* NARCOLEPSY

friend (frend) *n.* **1.** one well known to another and regarded with affection and loyalty **2.** intimate associate **3.** supporter **4.** (**F-**) Quaker —'**friendless** *a.* —'**friendliness** *n.* —'**friendly** *a.* **1.** having disposition of a friend, kind **2.** favorable —'**friendship** *n.* —**Friends of the Earth** organization of environmentalists and conservationists

frier ('frīər) *n. see* **fryer** *at* FRY[1]

frieze[1] (frēz) *n.* ornamental band, strip (on wall)

frieze[2] (frēz) *n.* kind of coarse woolen cloth

frigate ('frigit) *n.* **1.** old (sailing) warship corresponding to modern cruiser **2.** fast destroyerlike warship equipped for escort and antisubmarine duties —**frigate bird** bird of tropical and subtropical seas, with wide wingspan

fright (frīt) *n.* **1.** sudden fear **2.** shock **3.** alarm **4.** grotesque or ludicrous person or thing —*vt.* **5.** *obs.* frighten —'**frighten** *vt.* cause fear, fright in —'**frightful** *a.* **1.** terrible, calamitous **2.** shocking **3.** *inf.* very great, very large —'**frightfully** *adv. inf.* **1.** terribly **2.** very —'**frightfulness** *n.*

frigid ('frijid) *a.* **1.** formal, dull **2.** (sexually) unfeeling **3.** cold —**fri'gidity** *n.* —'**frigidly** *adv.* —**frigid zone** cold region inside Arctic or Antarctic Circle

Frigidaire (friji'dāər) *n.* trade name, but used to refer to any domestic refrigerator

frill (fril) *n.* **1.** fluted strip of fabric gathered at one edge **2.** ruff of hair, feathers around neck of dog, bird *etc.* **3.** fringe **4.** (*oft. pl.*) unnecessary words, politeness; superfluous thing; adornment —*vt.* **5.** make into, decorate with frill

fringe (frinj) *n.* **1.** ornamental edge of hanging threads, tassels *etc.* **2.** anything like this **3.** edge, limit —*vt.* **4.** adorn with fringe **5.** be fringe for —*a.* **6.** (of theater *etc.*)

unofficial, unconventional, extra —**fringe benefit** benefit provided by employer to supplement employee's regular pay

frippery ('fripəri) *n.* **1.** finery **2.** trivia

Frisbee ('frizbē) *n.* trade name for plastic disk thrown with spinning motion for recreation

Frisian ('frizhən, 'frēzhən) *n.* **1.** language spoken in NW Netherlands and adjacent islands **2.** speaker of this language —*a.* **3.** of this language or its speakers

frisk (frisk) *vi.* **1.** move, leap playfully —*vt.* **2.** wave briskly **3.** *inf.* search (person) for concealed weapons *etc.* —*n.* **4.** playful antic or movement **5.** *inf.* instance of frisking a person —'**friskily** *adv.* —'**frisky** *a.*

fritillary ('fritileri) *n.* **1.** bulbous plant with purple or white bell-shaped flowers **2.** butterfly with black spots on orange wings

fritter[1] ('fritər) *vt.* (*usu. with* away) waste

fritter[2] ('fritər) *n.* piece of food fried in batter

frivolous ('frivələs) *a.* **1.** not serious, flippant **2.** unimportant —**fri'volity** *n.*

frizz (friz) *vt.* **1.** crisp, curl into small curls —*n.* **2.** frizzed hair —'**frizzy** *a.* crimped

frizzle ('frizəl) *v.* fry, toast or grill with sizzling sound

fro (frō) *adv.* away, from (*only in* **to and fro**)

frock (frok) *n.* **1.** long cloak worn by monks and friars **2.** woman's or girl's dress —*vt.* **3.** invest with office of priest —**frock coat** man's double-breasted skirted coat not cut away in front

frog[1] (frog) *n.* tailless amphibious animal developed from tadpole —'**frogman** *n.* swimmer equipped for swimming, working underwater —'**frogmarch** *n.* any method of moving person against his will

frog[2] (frog) *n.* **1.** fastening of knot or button and loop **2.** attachment to belt to carry sword

frolic ('frolik) *n.* **1.** merrymaking —*vi.* **2.** behave playfully ('**frolicked,** '**frolicking**) —'**frolicsome** *a.*

from (from; *unstressed* frəm) *prep.* expressing point of departure, source, distance, cause, change of state *etc.*

frond (frond) *n.* large leaf, finely divided *esp.* of fern and palm

front (frunt) *n.* **1.** fore part **2.** position directly before or ahead **3.** seaside promenade **4.** battle line or area **5.** *Met.* dividing line between two air masses of different characteristics **6.** outward aspect, bearing **7.** *inf.* something serving as a respectable cover for another, *usu.* criminal activity **8.** field of activity **9.** group with common goal —*v.* **10.** look, face (on to) —*vt.* **11.** *inf.* be a cover for —*a.* **12.** of, at the front —'**frontage** *n.* **1.** facade of building **2.** extent of front —'**frontal** *a.* —**fron'tier** *n.* part of country which borders on another —'**frontispiece** *n.* illustration facing title page of book —'**front-runner** *n. inf.* leader in race *etc.*

frost (frost) *n.* **1.** frozen dew or mist **2.** act or state of freezing **3.** weather in which temperature falls below point at which water turns to ice —*v.* **4.** cover, be covered with frost or something similar in appearance —*vt.* **5.** give slightly roughened surface to —'**frostily** *adv.* —'**frosting** *n.* **1.** icing **2.** rough or matt finish on glass *etc.* —'**frosty** *a.* **1.** accompanied by frost **2.** chilly, cold **3.** unfriendly —'**frostbite** *n.* destruction of tissue, *esp.* of fingers, ears *etc.*, by cold

froth (froth) *n.* **1.** collection of small bubbles, foam **2.** scum **3.** idle talk —*v.* **4.** (cause to) foam —'**frothily** *adv.* —'**frothy** *a.*

froward ('frōərd) *a.* obstinate; contrary

frown (frown) *vi.* **1.** wrinkle brows —*n.* **2.** act of frowning **3.** show of dislike or displeasure

frowsty ('frowsti) *a.* stale, musty

frowsy *or* **frowzy** ('frowzi) *a.* **1.** dirty **2.** unkempt

froze (frōz) *pt. of* FREEZE —'**frozen** *pp. of* FREEZE

FRS Federal Reserve System

fructify ('fruktifī) *v.* (cause to) bear fruit ('**fructified,** '**fructifying**) —**fructifi'cation** *n.*

fructose ('fruktōs) *n.* crystalline sugar occurring in many fruits (*also* **levulose**)

frugal ('froōgəl) *a.* **1.** sparing, thrifty, economical **2.** meager —**fru'gality** *n.* —'**frugally** *adv.*

fruit (froōt) *n.* **1.** seed and its envelope, *esp.* edible one **2.** vegetable products **3.** (*usu. in pl.*) result, benefit —*vi.* **4.** bear fruit —'**fruitful** *a.* **1.** bearing fruit in abundance **2.** productive, prolific **3.** producing results or profits —**fruition** (froō'ishən) *n.* **1.** enjoyment **2.** realization of hopes —'**fruitless** *a.* **1.** unproductive **2.** without fruit —'**fruity** *a.* **1.** of or resembling fruit **2.** (of voice) mellow, rich

frump (frump) *n.* dowdy woman —'**frumpish** *or* '**frumpy** *a.*

frustrate ('frustrāt) *vt.* **1.** thwart, balk **2.** disappoint —**frus'tration** *n.*

frustum ('frustəm) *n. Geom.* part of the solid between two parallel lines cutting the solid (*pl.* **-s, -ta** (-tə))

fry[1] (frī) *vt.* **1.** cook with fat —*vi.* **2.** be cooked thus (**fried,** '**frying**) —*n.* **3.** fried meat **4.** dish of anything fried —'**fryer** *or* '**frier** *n.* **1.** one that fries **2.** utensil for deep-frying foods —**frying pan** shallow pan for frying —**out of the frying pan into the fire** from bad situation to worse one

fry[2] (frī) *n.* young fishes —**small fry** young or insignificant beings

f-stop *n.* any of settings for f-number of camera

ft. **1.** feet **2.** foot **3.** fort

FTC Federal Trade Commission

fth. *or* **fthm.** fathom

fuchsia ('fyoōshə) *n.* ornamental shrub with purple-red flowers

fuddle (ˈfudəl) *v.* **1.** (cause to) be intoxicated, confused —*n.* **2.** this state

fuddy-duddy (ˈfudidudi) *n. inf.* (elderly) dull person

fudge[1] (fuj) *n.* soft, creamy candy made of milk, butter and sugar —**hot fudge** warm chocolate sauce served on ice cream

fudge[2] (fuj) *vt.* **1.** make, do carelessly or dishonestly **2.** fake

fuel (fyo͞oəl) *n.* **1.** material for burning as source of heat or power **2.** something which nourishes —*vt.* **3.** provide with fuel —**fuel cell** cell in which chemical energy is converted directly into electrical energy —**fuel injection** system for introducing fuel directly into the combustion chambers of internal-combustion engine without use of carburetor

fugitive (ˈfyo͞ojitiv) *n.* **1.** one who flees, *esp.* from arrest or pursuit —*a.* **2.** fleeing, elusive

fugue (fyo͞og) *n.* musical composition in which themes are repeated in different parts

führer *or* ***fuehrer*** (ˈfürər) *n.* leader, title of Ger. dictator, *esp.* Hitler

-ful (*comb. form*) **1.** full of; characterized by, as in *painful, restful* **2.** able or tending to, as in *useful* **3.** as much as will fill thing specified, as in *mouthful*

fulcrum (ˈfo͝olkrəm, ˈful-) *n.* point on which lever is placed for support (*pl.* **-cra** (-krə))

fulfill *or* **fulfil** (fo͝olˈfil) *vt.* **1.** satisfy **2.** carry out **3.** obey —**fulˈfillment** *n.*

full[1] (fo͝ol) *a.* **1.** containing as much as possible **2.** abundant **3.** complete **4.** ample **5.** plump **6.** (of garment) of ample cut —*adv.* **7.** very **8.** quite **9.** exactly —ˈ**fullness** *n.* —ˈ**fully** *adv.* —ˈ**fulsome** *a.* excessive —ˈ**fullback** *n.* *Football etc.* defensive player or position held by this player —**full-blooded** *a.* **1.** (*esp.* of horses) of unmixed ancestry **2.** having great vigor —**full-blown** *a.* **1.** characterized by fullest or best development **2.** in full bloom —**full-bodied** *a.* having full rich flavor or quality —**full-fledged** *a.* **1.** (of bird) having acquired adult feathers and being able to fly **2.** completely developed **3.** of full rank or status —**full house 1.** *Poker* hand with three cards of same value and another pair **2.** theater *etc.* filled to capacity **3.** in bingo *etc.*, set of numbers needed to win —**full-scale** *a.* **1.** (of plan *etc.*) of actual size **2.** using all resources —**full stop** *see* PERIOD (sense 6) —**full-time** *a.* for entire time appropriate to activity —**full time** *adv.* **1.** on full-time basis —*n.* **2.** end of match —**fully fashioned** (of stockings *etc.*) shaped so as to fit closely

full[2] (fo͝ol) *v.* become or make (cloth *etc.*) more compact during manufacture through shrinking and pressing —**fuller's earth** absorbent clay

fulmar (ˈfo͝olmər) *n.* Arctic sea bird

fulminate (ˈfo͝olminăt, ˈful-) *vi.* **1.** (*esp. with* against) criticize harshly —*n.* **2.** chemical compound exploding readily —**fulmiˈnation** *n.*

fulsome (ˈfo͝olsəm) *a. see* FULL[1]

fumble (ˈfumbəl) *vi.* **1.** grope about —*vt.* **2.** handle awkwardly —*n.* **3.** awkward attempt

fume (fyo͞om) *vi.* **1.** be angry **2.** emit smoke or vapor —*n.* **3.** smoke **4.** vapor —ˈ**fumigate** *vt.* apply fumes or smoke to, *esp.* for disinfection —**fumiˈgation** *n.* —ˈ**fumigator** *n.*

fumitory (ˈfyo͞omitŏri) *n.* plant with spurred flowers

fun (fun) *n.* anything enjoyable, amusing *etc.* —ˈ**funnily** *adv.* —ˈ**funny** *a.* **1.** comical **2.** odd, difficult to explain

function (ˈfungkshən) *n.* **1.** work a thing is designed to do **2.** (large) social event **3.** duty **4.** profession **5.** *Math.* quantity whose value depends on varying value of another —*vi.* **6.** operate, work —ˈ**functional** *a.* **1.** having a special purpose **2.** practical, necessary **3.** capable of operating —ˈ**functionary** *n.* official

fund (fund) *n.* **1.** stock or sum of money **2.** supply, store —*pl.* **3.** money resources —*vt.* **4.** in financial, business dealings, furnish money to in form of fund

fundamental (fundəˈmentəl) *a.* **1.** of, affecting, or serving as the base **2.** essential, primary —*n.* **3.** basic rule or fact —ˈ**fundament** *n.* **1.** buttocks **2.** foundation —**fundaˈmentalism** *n.* —**fundaˈmentalist** *n.* one laying stress on belief in literal and verbal inspiration of Bible and other traditional creeds —**fundamental particle** *see* **elementary particle** *at* ELEMENT

funeral (ˈfyo͞onərəl) *n.* (ceremony associated with) burial or cremation of dead —**funereal** (fyo͞oˈnēəriəl) *a.* **1.** like a funeral **2.** dark **3.** gloomy —**funeral director** undertaker —**funeral home** place where dead are prepared for burial or cremation and placed on view

fungus (ˈfunggəs) *n.* any of a large group of lower plants lacking chlorophyll and reproducing by spores, *eg* molds, yeasts, mushrooms (*pl.* **fungi** (ˈfunjī, ˈfunggī), **-es**) —ˈ**fungal** *or* ˈ**fungous** *a.* —**fungicide** (ˈfunjisīd) *n.* fungus destroyer —ˈ**fungoid** *a.* resembling fungus

funicular (fyo͞oˈnikyələr) *n.* cable railway on mountainside with two counterbalanced cars

funk (fungk) *n.* panic (*esp. in* **blue funk**)

funky (ˈfungki) *a. inf.* (of jazz, pop *etc.*) passionate and soulful, reminiscent of early blues

funnel (ˈfunəl) *n.* **1.** cone-shaped vessel or tube **2.** chimney of locomotive or ship **3.** ventilating shaft —*v.* **4.** (cause to) move as through funnel —*vt.* **5.** concentrate, focus

funny (ˈfuni) *a. see* FUN —**funny bone** area near elbow where sharp tingling sensation is experienced when struck

fur (fər) *n.* **1.** soft hair of animal **2.** garment *etc.* of dressed skins with such hair **3.** furlike coating —*vt.* **4.** cover with fur (**-rr-**)

—'**furrier** *n.* dealer in furs —'**furry** *a.* of, like fur

fur. furlong

furbelow ('fərbilō) *n.* **1.** flounce, ruffle **2.** (*oft. pl.*) showy ornamentation —*vt.* **3.** put furbelow on (garment *etc.*)

furbish ('fərbish) *vt.* clean up

furcate ('fərkāt) *a.* forked, branching

furious ('fyŏŏriəs) *a.* **1.** extremely angry **2.** violent —'**furiously** *adv.* —'**furiousness** *n.*

furl (fərl) *vt.* roll up and bind (sail, umbrella *etc.*)

furlong ('fərlong) *n.* unit of distance equal to 220 yards

furlough ('fərlō) *n.* leave of absence

furnace ('fərnis) *n.* **1.** apparatus for applying great heat to metals **2.** closed structure for producing heat **3.** hot place

furnish ('fərnish) *vt.* **1.** fit up (house) with furniture **2.** equip **3.** supply, yield —'**furnishings** *pl.n.* furniture, carpets *etc.* with which room is furnished —'**furniture** *n.* movable contents of a house or room

furor ('fyŏŏərōr) *n.* **1.** public outburst, *esp.* of protest **2.** sudden enthusiasm

furrow ('furō) *n.* **1.** trench as made by plow **2.** groove —*vt.* **3.** make furrows in

further ('fərdhər) *adv. comp. of* FAR *and* FORE[1] **1.** more **2.** in addition **3.** at or to a greater distance or extent —*a. comp. of* FAR *and* FORE[1] **4.** more distant **5.** additional —*vt.* **6.** help forward, promote —'**furtherance** *n.* —'**furtherer** *n.* —'**furthermore** *adv.* besides —'**furthermost** *a.* —'**furthest** *a./adv. sup. of* FAR, FORE[1]

furtive ('fərtiv) *a.* stealthy, sly, secretive —'**furtively** *adv.*

fury ('fyŏŏəri) *n.* **1.** wild rage, violent anger **2.** violence of storm *etc.* **3.** (*usu. pl.*) snake-haired avenging deity

furze (fərz) *n.* prickly shrub, gorse

fuscous ('fuskəs) *a.* dark-colored

fuse (fyŏŏz) *v.* **1.** blend by melting **2.** melt with heat **3.** amalgamate **4.** (cause to) fail as a result of blown fuse —*n.* **5.** soft wire, with low melting point, used as safety device in electrical systems **6.** device (*orig.* combustible cord) for igniting bomb *etc.* —**fusi'bility** *n.* —'**fusible** *a.* —'**fusion** *n.* **1.** melting **2.** state of being melted **3.** union of things, as atomic nuclei, as if melted together

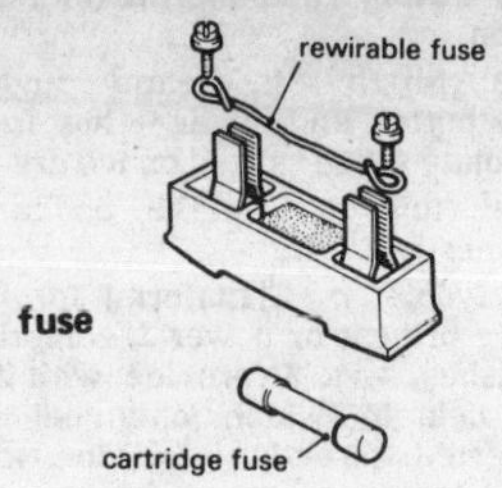

fuselage ('fyŏŏsilăzh, -zi-) *n.* body of aircraft

fusil ('fyŏŏzil) *n.* light flintlock musket —**fusi'lier** *n.* soldier of certain regiments —**fusil'lade** *n.* continuous discharge of firearms

fuss (fus) *n.* **1.** needless bustle or concern **2.** complaint, objection —*vi.* **3.** make fuss —'**fussily** *adv.* —'**fussiness** *n.* —'**fussy** *a.* **1.** particular **2.** faddy **3.** overmeticulous **4.** overelaborate

fustian ('fuschən) *n.* **1.** thick cotton cloth **2.** inflated language

fusty ('fusti) *a.* **1.** moldy **2.** smelling of damp **3.** old-fashioned —'**fustily** *adv.* —'**fustiness** *n.*

futile ('fyŏŏtil) *a.* **1.** useless, ineffectual **2.** trifling —**fu'tility** *n.*

future ('fyŏŏchər) *n.* **1.** time to come **2.** what will happen **3.** tense of verb indicating this **4.** likelihood of development —*a.* **5.** that will be **6.** of, relating to, time to come —'**futurism** *n.* movement in art marked by revolt against tradition —'**futurist** *n./a.* —**futur'istic** *a.* ultramodern —**fu'turity** *n.* —**future perfect** *Gram. a.* **1.** denoting tense of verbs describing action that will have been performed by certain time —*n.* **2.** future perfect tense; verb in this tense

fuze (fyŏŏz) *vt.* equip with a fuse

fuzz (fuz) *n.* **1.** fluff **2.** fluffy or frizzed hair **3.** blur **4.** *sl.* police(man) —'**fuzzy** *a.* **1.** fluffy **2.** frizzy **3.** blurred, indistinct

fwd. forward

-fy (*comb. form*) make; become, as in *beautify*

G

g *or* **G** (jē) *n.* **1.** seventh letter of English alphabet **2.** speech sound represented by this letter, usu. as in *grass,* or as in *page* (*pl.* **g's, G's** *or* **Gs**)

g 1. gram(s) **2.** (acceleration due to) gravity

G 1. *Mus.* fifth note of scale of C major; major or minor key having this note as its tonic **2.** gravitational constant **3.** *Phys.* conductance **4.** German **5.** giga **6.** good **7.** *sl.* grand (thousand dollars)

Ga *Chem.* gallium

GA Georgia

gabardine ('gabərdēn) *n.* **1.** fine twill cloth like serge used *esp.* for raincoats **2.** *Hist.* loose upper garment worn by Jews (*also* **gaberdine**)

gabble ('gabəl) *v.* **1.** talk, utter inarticulately or too fast (**'gabbled, 'gabbling**) *—n.* **2.** such talk **—gab** *vi.* **1.** talk excessively; chatter (**-bb-**) *—n.* **2.** idle or trivial talk **—'gabby** *a. inf.* talkative **—gift of the gab** eloquence, loquacity

gable ('gābəl) *n.* triangular upper part of wall at end of ridged roof (*also* **gable end**)

Gabon (ga'bōn) *n.* country in Africa bounded west by the Atlantic Ocean, north by Equatorial Guinea and Cameroon and east and south by Congo

gad (gad) *vi.* (*esp. with* about) go around in search of pleasure (**-dd-**) **—'gadabout** *n.* pleasure-seeker

gadfly ('gadflī) *n.* **1.** cattle-biting fly **2.** worrying person

gadget ('gajit) *n.* **1.** small mechanical device **2.** object valued for its novelty or ingenuity **—'gadgetry** *n.*

gadoid ('gādoid) *a.* **1.** of order of marine fishes typically having pectoral and pelvic fins close together and small cycloid scales *—n.* **2.** gadoid fish

gadolinium (gadə'liniəm) *n. Chem.* metallic element *Symbol* Gd, at. wt. 157.3, at. no. 64

gadroon (gə'drōōn) *n.* **1.** *Archit.* carved or indented convex molding **2.** decorative border formed by convex series of curves, *esp.* in furniture and silver ware

gadwall ('gadwöl) *n.* duck related to mallard

Gael (gāl) *n.* one who speaks Gaelic **—Gaelic** ('gālik, 'ga-) *n.* **1.** language of Ireland and Scottish Highlands *—a.* **2.** of Gaels, their language or customs

gaff (gaf) *n.* **1.** stick with iron hook for landing fish **2.** spar for top of fore-and-aft sail *—vt.* **3.** seize (fish) with gaff

gaffe (gaf) *n.* social blunder, *esp.* tactless remark

gaffer ('gafər) *n.* **1.** old man **2.** technician in charge of lighting in motion picture or television production

gag[1] (gag) *vt.* **1.** stop up (person's mouth) with cloth *etc.* *—vi.* **2.** *sl.* retch, choke (**-gg-**) *—n.* **3.** cloth *etc.* put into, tied across mouth

gag[2] (gag) *n.* joke, funny story, gimmick

gaga ('gägä) *a. sl.* **1.** senile **2.** crazy

gage[1] (gāj) *n.* **1.** pledge, thing given as security **2.** challenge, or something symbolizing one

gage[2] (gāj) *see* GAUGE

gaggle ('gagəl) *n.* **1.** flock of geese **2.** *inf.* disorderly crowd

gaiety ('gāəti) *n. see* GAY

gain (gān) *vt.* **1.** obtain, secure **2.** obtain as profit **3.** win **4.** earn **5.** reach *—v.* **6.** increase, improve *—vi.* **7.** (*usu. with* on *or* upon) get nearer **8.** (of watch, machine *etc.*) operate too fast *—n.* **9.** profit **10.** increase, improvement **—'gainful** *a.* profitable; lucrative **—'gainfully** *adv.*

gainsay (gān'sā) *vt.* deny; contradict (**gain'said, gain'saying**)

gait (gāt) *n.* **1.** manner of walking **2.** pace

gaiter ('gātər) *n.* covering of leather, cloth *etc.* for lower leg

gal *or* **gal.** gallon

Gal. *Bible* Galatians

gala ('gālə, 'galə, 'gälə) *n.* **1.** festive occasion **2.** show **3.** competitive sporting event

galah (gə'lä) *n.* Aust. gray cockatoo with reddish breast

galantine ('galəntēn) *n.* cold dish of meat or poultry, boned, cooked, then pressed and glazed

Galatians (gə'lāshənz) *pl.n.* (*with sing. v.*) *Bible* 9th book of the N.T., epistle written by St. Paul to Christians of central Asia Minor in Galatia

galaxy ('galəksi) *n.* **1.** system of stars bound by gravitational forces **2.** splendid gathering, *esp.* of famous people **—ga'lactic** *a.*

gale (gāl) *n.* **1.** strong wind **2.** *inf.* loud outburst, *esp.* of laughter

galena (gə'lēnə) *n.* bluish-gray or black mineral consisting of lead sulfide: principal ore of lead

gall[1] (göl) *n.* **1.** *inf.* impudence **2.** bitterness **—gall bladder** sac attached to liver, reservoir for bile **—'gallstone** *n.* hard secretion in gall bladder or ducts leading from it (*also* **biliary calculus**)

gall[2] (gôl) *n.* **1.** painful swelling, *esp.* on horse **2.** sore caused by chafing —*vt.* **3.** make sore by rubbing **4.** vex, irritate —**'galling** *a.* irritating, exasperating, humiliating

gall[3] (gôl) *n.* abnormal outgrowth on trees *etc.*

gallant ('galənt) *a.* **1.** fine, stately, brave **2.** (gə'lant, gə'länt) (of man) very attentive to women; chivalrous —*n.* (gə'lant, gə'länt, 'galənt) **3.** lover, suitor **4.** fashionable young man —**'gallantly** *adv.* —**'gallantry** *n.*

galleon ('galiən) *n.* large, high-built sailing ship of war

gallery ('galəri) *n.* **1.** covered walk with side openings, colonnade **2.** platform or projecting upper floor in church, theater *etc.* **3.** group of spectators **4.** long, narrow platform on outside of building **5.** room or rooms for special purposes, *eg* showing works of art **6.** passage in wall, open to interior of building **7.** horizontal passage, as in mine *etc.*

galley ('gali) *n.* **1.** one-decked vessel with sails and oars, usu. rowed by slaves or criminals **2.** kitchen of ship or aircraft **3.** large rowing boat **4.** *Print.* tray for holding composed type —**galley proof** printer's proof in long slip form —**galley slave 1.** one condemned to row in galley **2.** drudge

galliard ('galyərd) *n.* **1.** dance in triple time for two persons **2.** music for this dance

Gallic ('galik) *a.* **1.** of ancient Gaul **2.** French —**'Gallicism** *n.* French word or idiom

gallinaceous (gali'nāshəs) *a.* of order of birds, including domestic fowl, pheasants *etc.*, having heavy rounded body and strong legs

gallium ('galiəm) *n. Chem.* metallic element *Symbol* Ga, at. wt. 69.7, at. no. 31

gallivant ('galivant) *vi.* gad about

Gallo- ('galō-) (*comb. form*) Gaul; France, as in *Gallo-Roman*

gallon ('galən) *n.* unit of liquid measure comprising four quarts or 231 cubic inches

gallop ('galəp) *v.* **1.** go, ride at gallop —*vi.* **2.** move fast —*n.* **3.** horse's fastest pace with all four feet off the ground at once in each stride **4.** ride at this pace —**'galloper** *n.* —**'galloping** *a.* **1.** at a gallop **2.** speedy, swift

gallows ('galōz) *n.* structure, usu. of two upright beams and crossbar, *esp.* for hanging criminals

Gallup Poll ('galəp) method of finding out public opinion by questioning a cross section of the population

galoot (gə'lo͞ot) *n. inf.* silly, clumsy person

galore (gə'lōr) *adv.* in plenty

galoshes (gə'loshiz) *pl.n.* waterproof overshoes

galumph (gə'lumpf, -'lumf) *vi. inf.* leap or move about clumsily or joyfully

galvanic (gal'vanik) *a.* **1.** of, producing, concerning electric current, *esp.* when produced chemically **2.** *inf.* resembling effect of electric shock; startling —**'galvanize** *vt.* **1.** stimulate to action; excite; startle **2.** cover (iron *etc.*) with protective zinc coating —**galva'nometer** *n.* instrument for detecting or measuring small electric currents

Gamay (ga'mā) *n.* **1.** red, light-bodied table wine **2.** grape used to make this wine

Gambia ('gambia) *n.* —**The Gambia** country in Africa bounded west by the Atlantic Ocean and on all other sides by Senegal

gambit ('gambit) *n.* **1.** *Chess* opening involving offer of a pawn **2.** any opening maneuver, comment *etc.* intended to secure an advantage

gamble ('gambəl) *vi.* **1.** play games of chance to win money **2.** act on expectation of something —*n.* **3.** risky undertaking **4.** bet, wager —**'gambler** *n.*

gamboge (gam'bōj, -'bo͞ozh) *n.* gum resin used as yellow pigment

gambol ('gambəl) *vi.* **1.** skip, jump playfully —*n.* **2.** playful antic

game[1] (gām) *n.* **1.** diversion, pastime **2.** jest **3.** contest for amusement **4.** scheme, strategy **5.** animals or birds hunted **6.** their flesh —*a.* **7.** brave **8.** willing —*vi.* **9.** gamble —**'gamester** *n.* gambler —**'gaming** *n.* gambling —**'gamy** *or* **'gamey** *a.* **1.** having smell or flavor of game **2.** *inf.* spirited; plucky; brave —**'gamecock** *n.* fowl bred for fighting —**'gamekeeper** *n.* man employed to breed and take care of game —**game laws** laws governing hunting and preservation of game —**game plan** design for course of action —**game point** state in a game when one side needs only one point to win —**'gamesmanship** *n. inf.* art of winning games or defeating opponents by cunning practices without actually cheating

game[2] (gām) *a.* lame, crippled

gamete (gə'mēt, 'gamēt) *n. Biol.* sexual cell that unites with another for reproduction

gamin ('gamin) *n.* street urchin

gamine (ga'mēn) *n.* slim, boyish girl; elfish tomboy

gamma ('gamə) *n.* third letter of Gr. alphabet (Γ, γ) —**gamma globulin** group of proteins in blood plasma that includes most of the antibodies used by the body to combat disease —**gamma ray** invisible, highly penetrative, light ray emitted during radioactive disintegration

gammon ('gamən) *n.* **1.** double victory in backgammon in which player throws off all his pieces before his opponent throws any —*vt.* **2.** score such a victory over

gamut ('gamət) *n.* whole range or scale

gander ('gandər) *n.* **1.** male goose **2.** *inf.* a quick look (*esp. in* **take** (*or* **have**) **a gander**)

gang (gang) *n.* **1.** (criminal) group **2.** organized group of workmen —*vi.* **3.** (*esp.*

with together) form gang —**gang up on** *inf.* combine against

gangling (ˈganggling) *or* **gangly** *a.* lanky, awkward in movement

ganglion (ˈgangglìən) *n.* **1.** mass of nerve tissue outside brain and spinal cord **2.** cyst on tendon **3.** center of activity (*pl.* **-glia** (-gliə), **-s**)

gangplank (ˈgangplangk) *n.* portable bridge for boarding or leaving vessel

gangrene (ˈganggrēn) *n.* death of body tissue as result of inadequate blood supply —**gangrenous** (ˈganggrinəs) *a.*

gangster (ˈgangstər) *n.* **1.** member of criminal gang **2.** notorious or hardened criminal

gangue (gang) *n.* valueless and undesirable material in ore

gangway (ˈgangwā) *n.* **1.** gangplank **2.** passage between row of seats —*interj.* **3.** clear a path

gannet (ˈganit) *n.* predatory sea bird

ganoid (ˈganoid) *a./n.* (fish) with smooth, hard, enameled, bony scales, *eg* sturgeon

gantry (ˈgantri) *n.* **1.** structure to support crane, railroad signals *etc.* **2.** framework beside rocket on launching pad (*also* **gantry scaffold**)

GAO General Accounting Office

gap (gap) *n.* **1.** breach, opening, interval **2.** cleft **3.** empty space

gape (gāp) *vi.* **1.** stare in wonder **2.** open mouth wide, as in yawning **3.** be, become wide open —*n.* **4.** act of gaping

garage (gəˈräzh, -ˈräj) *n.* **1.** (part of) building to house motor vehicles **2.** refueling and repair center for motor vehicles —*vt.* **3.** leave (vehicle) in garage —**garage sale** sale of used objects held in or near family garage

garb (gärb) *n.* **1.** dress **2.** fashion of dress —*vt.* **3.** dress, clothe

garbage (ˈgärbij) *n.* **1.** food waste **2.** useless material —**garbage in, garbage out** *Comp.* faulty input results in faulty output

garbanzo (gärˈbanzō) *n.* chickpea (*pl.* **-s**)

garble (ˈgärbəl) *vt.* jumble or distort (story, account *etc.*)

garçon (*Fr.* garˈsõ) *n.* waiter, *esp.* French

garden (ˈgärdən) *n.* **1.** ground for growing flowers, fruit, or vegetables —*vi.* **2.** cultivate garden —ˈ**gardener** *n.* —ˈ**gardening** *n.* —**garden-variety** *a.* ordinary, everyday

gardenia (gärˈdēnyə) *n.* (sub)tropical shrub with fragrant white or yellow flowers

Garfield (ˈgärfēld) *n.* **James Abram.** the 20th President of the U.S. (Mar.–Sept. 1881)

garfish (ˈgärfish) *n.* elongated bony fish

garganey (ˈgärgəni) *n.* small Eurasian duck related to mallard

gargantuan (gärˈganchōōən) *a.* (*sometimes* **G-**) immense, enormous, huge

gargle (ˈgärgəl) *vi.* **1.** wash throat with liquid kept moving by the breath —*vt.* **2.** wash (throat) thus —*n.* **3.** gargling **4.** preparation for this purpose

gargoyle (ˈgärgoil) *n.* carved (grotesque) face on waterspout, *esp.* on Gothic church

garish (ˈgāərish) *a.* **1.** showy **2.** gaudy

garland (ˈgärlənd) *n.* **1.** wreath of flowers worn or hung as decoration —*vt.* **2.** decorate with garlands

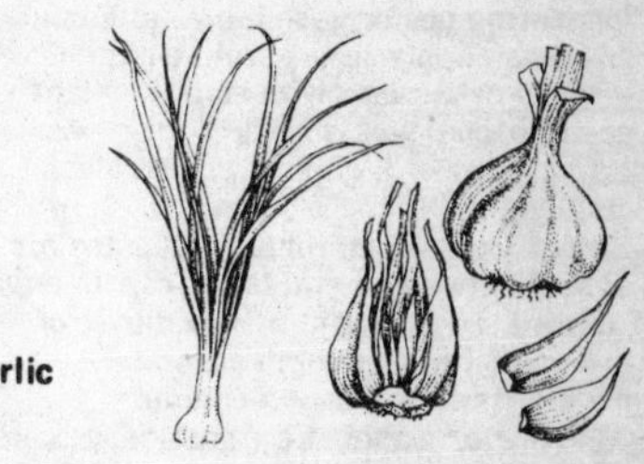
garlic

garlic (ˈgärlik) *n.* (bulb of) plant with strong smell and taste, used in cooking and seasoning

garment (ˈgärmənt) *n.* article of clothing —**Garment District** area in New York City where clothing is made and sold wholesale

garner (ˈgärnər) *vt.* store up, collect, as if in granary

garnet (ˈgärnit) *n.* red semiprecious stone

garnish (ˈgärnish) *vt.* **1.** adorn, decorate (*esp.* food) —*n.* **2.** material for this

garret (ˈgarit) *n.* room on top floor, attic

garrison (ˈgarisən) *n.* **1.** troops stationed in town, fort *etc.* **2.** fortified place —*vt.* **3.** station (troops) in (fort *etc.*) —**garrison cap** folding, wedge-shaped cap worn as part of soldier's uniform (*also* **overseas cap**)

garrotte *or* **garotte** (gəˈrot) *n.* **1.** Spanish capital punishment by strangling **2.** apparatus for this —*vt.* **3.** execute, kill thus —**garˈrotter** *or* **gaˈrotter** *n.*

garrulous (ˈgarələs, ˈgaryə-) *a.* (frivolously) talkative —**garrulity** (gəˈrōōliti, ga-) *n.* loquacity

garter (ˈgärtər) *n.* band worn round leg to hold up sock or stocking —**garter stitch** knitting with all rows in knit stitch

gas (gas) *n.* **1.** airlike substance with the capacity to expand indefinitely and not liquefy or solidify at ordinary temperatures **2.** fossil fuel in form of gas, used for heating or lighting **3.** gaseous anesthetic **4.** poisonous or irritant substance dispersed through atmosphere in warfare *etc.* **5.** *inf.* gasoline **6.** *inf.* accelerator pedal in motor vehicle (*pl.* **-es,** ˈ**gasses**) —*vt.* **7.** project gas over **8.** poison with gas —*vi.* **9.** *inf.* talk idly, boastfully (**-ss-**) —ˈ**gaseous** *a.* of, like gas —ˈ**gassy** *a.* —ˈ**gasbag** *n. sl.* person who talks idly —**gas chamber** airtight room into which poison gas is introduced to kill people —**gas**

mask mask with chemical filter to guard against poisoning by gas —**gas meter** apparatus for measuring amount of gas passed through it —**ga'someter** *n.* laboratory apparatus for measuring gases —**gas plant** dittany —**gas range** cooking stove that uses gas as fuel —**gas station** place that sells gasoline, oil, tires *etc.* and provides other services for motor vehicles (*also* **filling station, service station**) —**gas tank** 1. tank for storing gas or gasoline 2. tank containing gasoline supply in a gasoline-engine vehicle —**'gasworks** *pl.n.* (*with sing. v.*) plant where gas, *esp.* coal gas, is made

gash (gash) *n.* 1. gaping wound, slash —*vt.* 2. cut deeply

gasket ('gaskit) *n.* rubber, asbestos *etc.* used as seal between metal faces, *esp.* in engines

gasohol (gasə'höl) *n.* mixture of small proportion of alcohol to gasoline used as fuel for internal-combustion engine

gasoline *or* **gasolene** ('gasəlēn, gasə'lēn) *n.* by-product of crude oil used mainly as fuel for internal-combustion engine

gasp (gasp) *vi.* 1. catch breath with open mouth, as in exhaustion or surprise —*n.* 2. convulsive catching of breath

gastric ('gastrik) *a.* of stomach —**gas'trectomy** *n.* partial or complete removal of the stomach —**gastroente'ritis** *n.* inflammation of stomach and intestines —**'gastronome** *or* **gas'tronomist** *n.* gourmet —**gastro'nomical** *a.* —**ga'stronomy** *n.* art of good eating —**gastric juice** digestive fluid secreted by stomach, containing hydrochloric acid *etc.* —**gastric ulcer** ulcer of stomach lining

gastro- *or oft. before vowel* **gastr-** (*comb. form*) stomach, as in *gastroenteritis, gastritis*

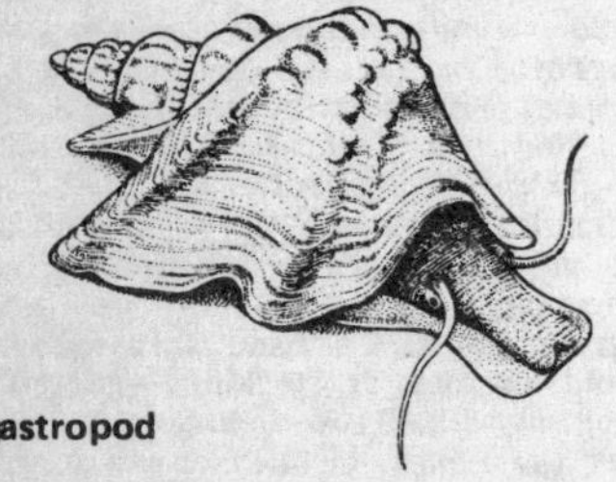

gastropod

gastropod ('gastrəpod) *n.* any mollusk with a single, sometimes vestigial, shell

gate (gāt) *n.* 1. opening in wall, fence *etc.* 2. barrier for closing it 3. sluice 4. any entrance or way out 5. (entrance money paid by) those attending sporting event —**gate-crash** *v.* enter (meeting, social function *etc.*) uninvited —**'gatehouse** *n.* house built at or over gateway —**gate-leg table** table with leaves supported by hinged leg swung out from frame —**'gateway** *n.* means of entrance and exit

gather ('gadhər) *v.* 1. (cause to) assemble 2. increase gradually 3. draw together —*vt.* 4. collect 5. learn, understand 6. draw (material) into small tucks or folds —**'gathering** *n.* assembly

GATT (gat) General Agreement on Tariffs and Trade

gauche (gōsh) *a.* tactless, blundering —**gaucherie** (gōshə'rē) *n.* awkwardness, clumsiness

gaucho ('gowchō) *n.* S Amer. cowboy (*pl.* **-s**) —**gaucho pants** mid-calf-length wide-bottomed culottes

gaudy ('gödi) *a.* showy in a tasteless way —**'gaudily** *adv.* —**'gaudiness** *n.*

gauge *or* **gage** (gāj) *n.* 1. standard measure, as of diameter of wire, thickness of sheet metal *etc.* 2. distance between rails of railroad 3. capacity, extent 4. instrument for measuring such things as wire, rainfall, height of water in boiler *etc.* —*vt.* 5. measure 6. estimate

Gaul (göl) *n.* 1. native of Gaul, region in Roman times stretching from N Italy to S Netherlands 2. Frenchman

gaunt (gönt) *a.* lean, haggard

gauntlet ('göntlit) *n.* 1. armored glove 2. glove covering part of arm —**run the gauntlet** 1. formerly, run as punishment between two lines of men striking at runner with sticks *etc.* 2. be exposed to criticism or unpleasant treatment 3. undergo ordeal —**throw down the gauntlet** offer challenge

gauss (gows) *n.* unit of density of magnetic field (*pl.* **gauss**)

gauze (göz) *n.* 1. thin transparent fabric of silk, wire *etc.* 2. cotton surgical dressing —**'gauzy** *a.*

gave (gāv) *pt. of* GIVE

gavel ('gavəl) *n.* mallet of presiding officer or auctioneer

gavotte (gə'vot) *n.* 1. lively dance 2. music for it

gawk (gök) *vi.* stare stupidly —**'gawky** *a.* clumsy, awkward

gawp (göp) *vi. sl.* 1. stare stupidly 2. gape

gay (gā) *a.* 1. merry 2. lively 3. cheerful 4. bright 5. light-hearted 6. showy 7. given to pleasure 8. *inf.* homosexual —**'gaiety** *n.* 1. state or condition of being gay 2. festivity; merrymaking —**'gaily** *adv.*

gaze (gāz) *vi.* 1. look fixedly —*n.* 2. fixed look

gazebo (gə'zābō, -'zēbō) *n.* summerhouse, turret on roof, with extensive view (*pl.* **-s, -es**)

gazelle (gə'zel) *n.* small graceful antelope

gazetteer (gazi'tēər) *n.* geographical dictionary

G.B. Great Britain

GCA ground-controlled approach

G clef *see* **treble clef** *at* TREBLE

Gd *Chem.* gadolinium

GDR German Democratic Republic

Ge *Chem.* germanium

gear (gēər) *n.* **1.** set of wheels working together, *esp.* by engaging cogs **2.** connection by which engine, motor *etc.* is brought into work **3.** arrangement by which driving wheel of cycle or motor vehicle performs more or fewer revolutions relative to pedals, pistons *etc.* **4.** equipment **5.** clothing **6.** goods, utensils **7.** apparatus, tackle, tools **8.** rigging **9.** harness —*vt.* **10.** adapt (one thing) so as to conform with another **11.** provide with gear **12.** put in gear —**'gearing** *n.* **1.** assembly of gears for transmitting motion **2.** act or technique of providing gears to transmit motion —**'gearbox** *n.* case protecting gearing of bicycle or motor vehicle —**gear lever** *or* **'gearshift** *n.* lever used to move gearwheels relative to each other in motor vehicle *etc.* —**'gearwheel** *n.* toothed wheel in system of gears (*also* **gear**) —**in gear** connected up and ready for work —**out of gear 1.** disconnected, out of working order **2.** upset

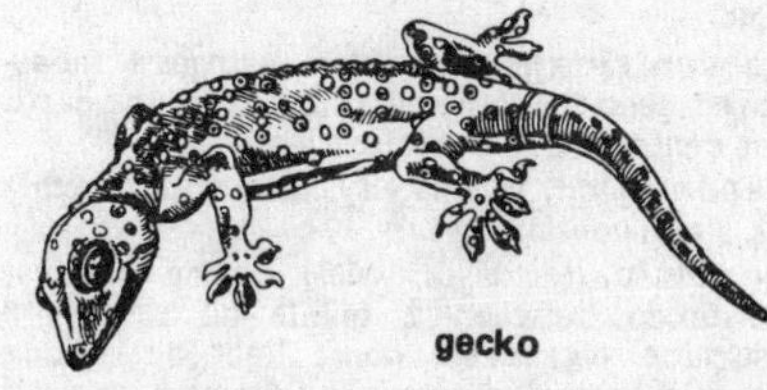

gecko

gecko ('gekō) *n.* insectivorous lizard of warm regions (*pl.* **-s, -es**)

gee (jē) *interj.* **1.** exclamation to horse *etc.* to encourage it to turn to right, go on or go faster (*also* **gee up**) —*vt.* **2.** (*usu. with* up) move (horse *etc.*) ahead; urge on

geese (gēs) *n., pl. of* GOOSE

geezer ('gēzər) *n. inf.* old (eccentric) man

Geiger counter ('gīgər) *or* **Geiger-Müller counter** (-'myōōlər, -'milər, -'mulər) instrument for detecting radioactivity, cosmic radiation and charged atomic particles

geisha ('gāshə, 'gē-) *n.* in Japan, professional female companion for men

gel (jel) *n.* **1.** jellylike substance —*vi.* **2.** form a gel (**-ll-**)

gelatin *or* **gelatine** ('jelətin) *n.* **1.** substance prepared from animal bones *etc.*, producing edible jelly **2.** anything resembling this —**ge'latinous** *a.* like gelatin or jelly

geld (geld) *vt.* castrate —**'gelding** *n.* castrated horse

gelid ('jelid) *a.* very cold

gelignite ('jelignīt) *n.* powerful explosive consisting of dynamite in gelatin form

gelt (gelt) *n. sl.* money

gem (jem) *n.* **1.** precious stone, *esp.* when cut and polished **2.** treasure —*vt.* **3.** adorn with gems (**-mm-**)

geminate ('jemināt) *v.* double, pair, repeat —**gemi'nation** *n.*

Gemini ('jeminē, -nī) *n.* (twins) 3rd sign of zodiac, operative May 21st–June 20th

gemma ('jemə) *n.* asexual reproductive structure in mosses *etc.* that becomes detached from parent and develops into new individual (*pl.* **-mae** (-mē))

gemsbok ('gemzbok) *n.* S Afr. oryx

gen. **1.** gender **2.** general **3.** genitive **4.** genus

Gen. **1.** General **2.** *Bible* Genesis

-gen (*comb. form*) **1.** producing; that which produces, as in *hydrogen* **2.** something produced, as in *antigen*

gendarme ('zhondärm) *n.* policeman in France

gender ('jendər) *n.* **1.** sex, male or female **2.** grammatical classification of nouns

gene (jēn) *n.* basic unit of heredity, segment of DNA molecule —**genetic** (ji'netik) *a.* —**ge'netics** *pl.n.* (*with sing. v.*) scientific study of heredity and variation in organisms —**genetic code** relationship between base-unit sequence in RNA, or DNA parents, and sequence of amino-acid residues in proteins —**genetic engineering** alteration of structure of chromosomes in living organisms

genealogy (jēni'aləji) *n.* **1.** account of descent from ancestors **2.** pedigree **3.** study of pedigrees —**genea'logical** *a.* —**gene'alogist** *n.*

genera ('jenərə) *n., pl. of* GENUS

general ('jenərəl, 'jenrəl) *a.* **1.** common, widespread **2.** not particular or specific **3.** applicable to all or most **4.** not restricted to one department **5.** usual, prevalent **6.** miscellaneous **7.** dealing with main element only **8.** vague, indefinite —*n.* **9.** army officer of rank above colonel —**gene'rality** *n.* **1.** general principle **2.** vague statement **3.** indefiniteness —**generali'zation** *n.* **1.** general conclusion from particular instance **2.** inference —**'generalize** *vt.* **1.** reduce to general laws —*vi.* **2.** draw general conclusions —**'generally** *adv.* —**General Assembly 1.** main deliberative body of the United Nations **2.** (**g- a-**) supreme governing body of many Protestant denominations, *esp.* the Presbyterian Church (U.S.) —**general election** any election for city, state or federal officials held at specified intervals —**general practitioner** nonspecialist physician —**general-purpose** *a.* having a variety of uses —**general strike** strike by all or most of workers of country *etc.*

generalissimo (jenərə'lisimō, jenrə-) *n.* supreme commander of combined military, naval and air forces in some countries (*pl.* **-s**)

generate ('jenərāt) *vt.* **1.** bring into being **2.** produce —**gene'ration** *n.* **1.** bringing into being **2.** all persons born about same time **3.** average time between two such generations (about 30 years) —**'generative** *a.* —**'genera-**

tor *n.* **1.** apparatus for producing steam, electricity *etc.* **2.** begetter —**generation gap** years separating one generation from next, *esp.* regarded as representing difference in outlook and lack of understanding between them

generic (ji'nerik) *a.* belonging to, characteristic of class or genus —**ge'nerically** *adv.*

generous ('jenərəs, 'jenrəs) *a.* **1.** liberal, free in giving **2.** abundant —**gene'rosity** *n.* —'**generously** *adv.*

genesis ('jenisis) *n.* **1.** origin **2.** mode of formation (*pl.* **-eses** (-isēz))

Genesis ('jenisis) *n. Bible* 1st book of the O.T., account of the creation of the world, the fall of man and the promise of redemption

-genesis (*comb. form*) genesis, development, generation, as in *biogenesis, parthenogenesis*

genet ('jenit) *n.* catlike mammal of Afr. and S Europe

Geneva Convention (ji'nēvə) **1.** international agreement, formulated in 1864, establishing code for wartime treatment of sick or wounded: revised to cover maritime warfare and prisoners of war **2.** *see* **Universal Copyright Convention** *at* UNIVERSAL

genial ('jēnyəl) *a.* **1.** cheerful, warm in behavior **2.** mild, conducive to growth —**geni'ality** *n.* —'**genially** *adv.*

genie ('jēni) *n.* in fairy tales, servant appearing by, and working, magic

genital ('jenitəl) *a.* relating to sexual organs or reproduction —'**genitals** *or* **genitalia** (jeni'tālyə) *pl.n.* the sexual organs

genitive ('jenitiv) *a./n.* possessive (case) —**genitival** (jeni'tīvəl) *a.*

genius ('jēnyəs, -niəs) *n.* **1.** (person with) exceptional power or ability, *esp.* of mind **2.** distinctive spirit or nature (of nation *etc.*)

genocide ('jenəsīd) *n.* murder of a nationality or ethnic group

-genous (*comb. form*) **1.** yielding; generating, as in *erogenous* **2.** generated by; issuing from, as in *endogenous*

genre ('zhänrə) *n.* **1.** kind **2.** sort **3.** style **4.** painting of homely scene

gent (jent) *inf. n.* **1.** gentleman —*pl.* **2.** men's public toilet

genteel (jen'tēl) *a.* **1.** well-bred **2.** stylish **3.** affectedly proper —**gen'teelly** *adv.*

gentian ('jenchən) *n.* plant, usu. with blue flowers —**gentian violet** violet dye used as antiseptic *etc.*

Gentile ('jentīl) *a.* **1.** of race other than Jewish **2.** heathen —*n.* **3.** person, *esp.* Christian, who is not a Jew **4.** (among Mormons) person who is not a Mormon

gentle ('jentəl) *a.* **1.** mild, quiet, not rough or severe **2.** soft and soothing **3.** courteous **4.** moderate **5.** gradual **6.** noble **7.** well-born —**gen'tility** *n.* **1.** noble birth **2.** respectability, politeness —'**gentleness** *n.* **1.** quality of being gentle **2.** tenderness —'**gently** *adv.* —'**gentlefolk** *or* '**gentlefolks** *pl.n.* persons regarded as being of good breeding —'**gentleman** *n.* **1.** chivalrous well-bred man **2.** man of good social position **3.** man (used as a mark of politeness) —'**gentlemanly** *or* '**gentlemanlike** *a.* —**gentlemen's agreement** agreement binding by honor but not valid in law —'**gentlewoman** *n.*

gentry ('jentri) *pl.n.* aristocracy —**gentrifi'cation** *n.* rise in amenity of decaying urban neighborhoods through the movement of middle-class families into the area

genuflect ('jenyəflekt) *vi.* bend knee, *esp.* in worship —**genu'flection** *n.*

genuine ('jenyōōin) *a.* **1.** real, true, not fake; authentic **2.** sincere **3.** pure

genus ('jēnəs) *n.* **1.** *Biol.* taxonomic division of plants and animals below family and above species **2.** the first word of a scientific name in binomial nomenclature class, order, group (*pl.* **-es,** '**genera**)

geo- (*comb. form*) earth, as in *geomorphology*

geocentric (jēō'sentrik) *a. Astron.* **1.** measured, seen from the earth **2.** having the earth as center —**geo'centrically** *adv.*

geode ('jēōd) *n.* **1.** cavity lined with crystals **2.** stone containing this

geodesic (jēə'desik, -'dē-) *n.* the shortest distance between 2 points on a curved surface —**geodesic dome** light but strong hemispherical construction formed from set of polygons

geodesy (ji'odisi) *n.* science of measuring the earth's surface

geog. **1.** geographer **2.** geographic(al) **3.** geography

geography (ji'ografi) *n.* science of earth's form, physical features, climate, population *etc.* —**ge'ographer** *n.* —**geo'graphic(al)** *a.* —**geo'graphically** *adv.* —**geographical mile** *see* MILE

geoid ('jēoid) *n.* **1.** hypothetical surface that corresponds to mean sea level, extending under continents **2.** shape of the earth

geol. **1.** geologic(al) **2.** geologist **3.** geology

geology (ji'oləji) *n.* science of earth's crust, rocks, strata *etc.* —**geo'logical** *a.* —**geo'logically** *adv.* —**ge'ologist** *n.*

geometry (ji'omitri) *n.* science of properties and relations of lines, surfaces, solids and angles —**geo'metric(al)** *a.* —**geo'metrically** *adv.* —**geome'trician** *n.* —**geometric mean** middle term of a geometric progression —**geometric progression** sequence of numbers, each of which differs from succeeding one by constant ratio, as 1, 2, 4, 8 —**geometric series** such numbers written as sum

geophysics (jēə'fiziks) *pl.n.* (*with sing. v.*) science dealing with the physics of the earth —**geo'physical** *a.* —**geo'physicist** *n.*

George Cross (jörj) British award for bravery

georgette (jör'jet) *n.* fine fabric with dull crepelike surface

Georgia ('jörjə) *n.* South Atlantic state of the U.S.: ratified the Constitution in 1788. Abbrev.: **GA** (with ZIP code)

Georgian ('jörjən) *a.* of the times of the four Georges (1714–1830) or of George V (1910–36)

georgic ('jörjik) *n.* poem on rural life, *esp.* one by Virgil

geostationary (jēō'stāshəneri) *a.* (of satellite) in orbit around earth so it remains over same point on surface

geotropism (ji'otrəpizəm) *n.* response of plant part to stimulus of gravity

Ger. 1. German **2.** Germany

geranium (ji'rāniəm) *n.* **1.** common cultivated plant with red, pink or white flowers, pelargonium **2.** strong pink color

gerbil

gerbil *or* **gerbille** ('jərbil) *n.* burrowing desert rodent of Asia and Afr. with long hind legs adapted for leaping

gerent ('jēərənt) *n.* ruler, governor, director

gerfalcon ('jərfalkən, -föl-) *n. see* GYRFALCON

geriatrics (jeri'atriks) *pl.n.* (*with sing. v.*) branch of medicine dealing with old age and its diseases —**geri'atric** *a./n.* old (person) —**geria'trician** *n.*

germ (jərm) *n.* **1.** microbe, *esp.* causing disease **2.** elementary thing **3.** rudiment of new organism, of animal or plant —**germi'cidal** *a.* —**'germicide** *n.* substance for destroying disease germs —**germ cell** sexual reproductive cell —**germ theory** theory that certain diseases are caused by specific microbes —**germ warfare** use of bacteria against enemy

german ('jərmən) *a.* **1.** of the same parents **2.** closely akin (*only in* **brother-, sister-, cousin-german**)

German ('jərmən) *n./a.* (language or native) of Germany —**Ger'manic** *n.* **1.** branch of Indo-European family of languages including Dutch, German *etc.* **2.** unrecorded language from which these languages developed (*also* **Proto-Germanic**) —*a.* **3.** of this group of languages **4.** of Germany, German language or any people that speaks Germanic language —**German measles** *see* RUBELLA —**German shepherd** large wolflike breed of dog

German Democratic Republic country in Europe bounded north by the Baltic Sea, east by Poland, south by Czechoslovakia and south and west by the Federal Republic of Germany (*also* **East Germany**)

germander (jər'mandər) *n.* European plant having two-lipped flowers with very small upper lip

germane (jər'mān) *a.* relevant, pertinent

germanium (jər'māniəm) *n. Chem.* metallic element *Symbol* Ge, at. wt. 72.6, at. no. 32

Germany ('jərməni) *n.* —**Federal Republic of Germany** country in Europe bounded north by the North Sea, Denmark and the Baltic Sea, east by the German Democratic Republic, Czechoslovakia and Austria, south by Austria and Switzerland and west by France, Luxembourg, Belgium and the Netherlands (*also* **West Germany**)

germinate ('jərmināt) *v.* (cause to) sprout or begin to grow —**germi'nation** *n.* —**'germinative** *a.*

gerontology (jerən'toləji) *n.* scientific study of ageing and problems of elderly people —**geron'tologist** *n.*

gerrymander (jeri'mandər, 'jerimandər) *vt.* **1.** divide constituencies of (voting area) so as to give one party unfair advantage **2.** manipulate or adapt to one's advantage —*n.* **3.** act or result of gerrymandering

gerund ('jerənd) *n.* noun formed from verb, *eg* living

gerundive (ji'rundiv) *n.* **1.** in Latin grammar, adjective formed from verb, expressing desirability *etc.* of activity denoted by verb —*a.* **2.** of gerund or gerundive

gesso ('jesō) *n.* **1.** white ground of plaster and size, used to prepare panels *etc.* for painting *etc.* **2.** any white substance, *esp.* plaster of Paris, that forms ground when mixed with water

Gestapo (ge'stäpō) *n.* secret state police in Nazi Germany

gestate ('jestāt) *v.* carry (developing young) in uterus during pregnancy —**ges'tation** *n.* period of pregnancy in mammals

gesticulate (je'stikyəlāt) *vi.* use expressive movements of hands and arms when speaking —**gesticu'lation** *n.*

gesture ('jeschər) *n.* **1.** movement to convey meaning **2.** indication of state of mind —*vi.* **3.** make such a movement

get (get) *vt.* **1.** obtain, procure **2.** contract **3.** catch **4.** earn **5.** cause to go or come **6.** bring into position or state **7.** induce **8.** engender **9.** *inf.* understand —*vi.* **10.** succeed in coming or going **11.** (*oft. with* to) reach, attain **12.** become (**got** *pt.*, **got** *or* **gotten** *pp.*, **'getting**

pr.p.) —**'getaway** *n.* escape —**get-together** *n. inf.* small informal social gathering —**get-up** *n. inf.* **1.** costume, outfit **2.** arrangement of book *etc.* —**get-up-and-go** *n. inf.* energy, drive —**get across** (cause to) be understood —**get at 1.** gain access to **2.** mean, intend **3.** annoy **4.** criticize **5.** influence —**get by** *inf.* manage, *esp.* in spite of difficulties —**get on 1.** grow late **2.** (of person) grow old **3.** make progress, manage, fare **4.** (*oft. with* with) establish friendly relationship **5.** (*with* with) continue to do —**get (one's) goat** *sl.* make (one) angry, annoyed —**get one's own back** *inf.* obtain one's revenge —**have got** possess —**have got to** must, have to

geum ('jēəm) *n.* garden plant with orange, yellow or white flowers

geyser ('gīzər) *n.* hot spring throwing up spout of water from time to time

Ghana ('gänə, 'gan-) *n.* country in Africa bounded south by Atlantic, west by Ivory Coast and Burkina-Faso, north by Burkina-Faso and east by Togo

ghastly ('gastli) *a.* **1.** *inf.* unpleasant **2.** deathlike, pallid **3.** *inf.* unwell **4.** horrible —*adv.* **5.** sickly

ghat (gôt) *n.* (in India) **1.** stairs leading down to river **2.** mountain pass

ghee (gē) *n.* clarified butter or vegetable fat used in cuisine of India, Pakistan and Bangladesh

gherkin ('gərkin) *n.* small cucumber used in pickling

ghetto ('getō) *n.* densely populated (*esp.* by one racial group) slum area (*pl.* **-s, -es**)

ghost (gōst) *n.* **1.** spirit, dead person appearing again **2.** specter **3.** semblance **4.** faint trace **5.** one who writes work to appear under another's name —*v.* **6.** ghostwrite —*vt.* **7.** haunt —**'ghostly** *a.* —**ghost town** deserted town, *esp.* one in western U.S.A. that was formerly a boom town —**'ghostwrite** *v.* write (article *etc.*) on behalf of person who is then credited as author (*also* **ghost**) —**'ghostwriter** *n.*

ghoul (gōōl) *n.* **1.** malevolent spirit **2.** person with morbid interests **3.** fiend —**'ghoulish** *a.* **1.** of or like ghoul **2.** horrible

G.H.Q. *Mil.* General Headquarters

GI (*short for* **Government Issue,** stamped on U.S. military equipment) *inf.* U.S. soldier

giant ('jīənt) *n.* **1.** mythical being of superhuman size **2.** very tall person, plant *etc.* —*a.* **3.** huge —**gi'gantic** *a.* enormous, huge —**gi'gantism** *n.* abnormal growth of the skeleton caused by disorder of the endocrine glands

giaour ('jowər) *n. derogatory* non-Muslim, *esp.* Christian

gib (gib) *n.* **1.** metal wedge, pad or thrust bearing let into steam engine crosshead —*vt.* **2.** fasten or supply with gib (**-bb-**)

Gib (jib) *n. inf.* Gibraltar

gibber ('jibər) *vi.* **1.** make meaningless sounds with mouth **2.** jabber, chatter —**'gibberish** *n.* meaningless speech or words

gibbet ('jibit) *n.* **1.** gallows **2.** post with arm on which executed criminals were formerly hung **3.** death by hanging —*vt.* **4.** hang on gibbet **5.** hold up to scorn

gibbon ('gibən) *n.* small tailless arboreal ape of E Indies and southern Asia

gibbous ('jibəs, 'gib-) *a.* **1.** (of moon *etc.*) more than half illuminated **2.** hunchbacked **3.** bulging —**'gibbousness** *or* **gibbosity** (ji'bositi, gi-) *n.*

gibe *or* **jibe** (jīb) *v.* **1.** utter taunts (at) **2.** mock **3.** jeer —*n.* **4.** provoking remark

giblets ('jiblits) *pl.n.* internal edible parts of fowl, as liver, gizzard *etc.*

Gibraltar (ji'brôltər) *n.* crown colony of United Kingdom with area of 2 $^1/_2$ sq. mi. at the extreme south of Spain and the western entrance to the Mediterranean

Gibson ('gibsən) *n.* drink made of gin and vermouth and garnished with a cocktail onion

giddy ('gidi) *a.* **1.** dizzy, feeling as if about to fall **2.** liable to cause this feeling **3.** flighty, frivolous —**'giddily** *adv.* —**'giddiness** *n.*

gift (gift) *n.* **1.** thing given, present **2.** faculty, power —*vt.* **3.** present, endow, bestow —**'gifted** *a.* talented —**gift certificate** voucher given as present which recipient can exchange for gift

gig (gig) *n.* **1.** light, two-wheeled carriage **2.** *inf.* single booking of musicians to play at concert *etc.* **3.** cluster of fish hooks

giga- ('jigə-, 'gigə-) (*comb. form*) 10^9, as in *gigavolt*

gigantic (jī'gantik) *a. see* GIANT

giggle ('gigəl) *vi.* **1.** laugh nervously, foolishly —*n.* **2.** such a laugh **3.** joke

GIGO ('gīgō) *Comp.* garbage in, garbage out

gigolo ('jigəlō, 'zhig-) *n.* **1.** man kept by (older) woman **2.** man paid to escort women

gigot ('jigət) *n.* **1.** leg of lamb or mutton **2.** leg-of-mutton sleeve

Gilchrist's disease ('gilkrists) *see* BLASTOMYCOSIS

gild[1] (gild) *vt.* **1.** put thin layer of gold on **2.** make falsely attractive (**'gilded** *pt.*, **gilt** *or* **'gilded** *pp.*) —**gilt** *a.* **1.** gilded —*n.* **2.** thin layer of gold applied in gilding **3.** superficial appearance —**gilt-edged** *a.* **1.** (of securities) dated over short, medium, or long term, and characterized by minimum risk and usu. issued by Government **2.** (of books *etc.*) having gilded edges

gild[2] (gild) *n. see* GUILD

gill[1] (gil) *n.* (*usu. pl.*) breathing organ in fish

gill[2] (jil) *n.* liquid measure comprising 4 fluid ounces, equal to 7.219 cubic inches or 118.291 milliliters

gillie, ghillie, *or* **gilly** ('gili) *n.* in Scotland, attendant for hunting or fishing

gill-over-the-ground (jil-) *n. see* **ground ivy** *at* GROUND[1]

gillyflower *or* **gilliflower** ('jiliflowər) *n.* fragrant flower

gilt (gilt) *n.* young female pig

gimbals ('jimbəlz, 'gim-) *pl.n.* pivoted rings, for keeping things, *eg* compass, horizontal at sea

gimcrack ('jimkrak) *a.* **1.** cheap; shoddy —*n.* **2.** cheap showy trifle

gimlet ('gimlit) *n.* boring tool, usu. with screw point —**gimlet-eyed** *a.* having a piercing glance

gimmick ('gimik) *n.* clever device, stratagem *etc.*, *esp.* designed to attract attention or publicity

gimp *or* **guimpe** (gimp) *n.* narrow fabric or braid used as edging or trimming

gin[1] (jin) *n.* spirit flavored with juniper berries —**gin rummy** form of rummy for two players in which 'gin' is called by player melding all ten cards

gin[2] (jin) *n.* **1.** primitive engine in which vertical shaft is turned to drive horizontal beam in a circle **2.** machine for separating cotton from seeds **3.** snare, trap

ginger ('jinjər) *n.* **1.** plant with hot-tasting spicy root used in cooking *etc.* **2.** the root **3.** *inf.* spirit, mettle **4.** light reddish-yellow color —'**gingery** *a.* **1.** of, like ginger **2.** hot **3.** high-spirited **4.** reddish —**ginger ale** ginger-flavored carbonated drink —**ginger beer** drink resembling ginger ale but with stronger ginger flavor —'**gingerbread** *n.* cake flavored with ginger —**ginger snap** crisp cookie flavored with ginger

gingerly ('jinjərli) *adv.* **1.** cautiously, warily, reluctantly —*a.* **2.** cautious, reluctant or timid

gingham ('gingəm) *n.* cotton cloth, usu. checked, woven from dyed yarn

gingivitis (jinji'vītis) *n.* inflammation of gums

ginkgo *or* **gingko** ('gingkō, 'gingkgō) *n.* ornamental Chinese tree (*pl.* **-es**)

ginseng ('jinsang, -seng) *n.* **1.** plant of China or of N Amer., whose roots are used medicinally **2.** root of this plant or substance obtained from root

gip (jip) *see* GYP

Gipsy ('jipsi) *n. see* GYPSY

giraffe (ji'raf) *n.* Afr. ruminant animal, with spotted coat and very long neck and legs

gird[1] (gərd) *vt.* **1.** put belt round **2.** fasten (clothing) thus **3.** equip with sword **4.** prepare (oneself) **5.** encircle (**girt,** '**girded** *pt./pp.*) —'**girder** *n.* large beam, *esp.* of steel

gird[2] (gərd) *dial. v.* **1.** jeer (at); mock —*n.* **2.** taunt; gibe

girdle ('gərdəl) *n.* **1.** corset **2.** waistband **3.** anything that surrounds, encircles —*vt.* **4.** surround, encircle

girl (gərl) *n.* **1.** female child **2.** young (unmarried) woman —'**girlhood** *n.* —'**girlie** *a. inf.* (of magazine) featuring nude or scantily dressed women —'**girlish** *a.* —**girl Friday** female employee with wide range of secretarial and clerical duties —'**girlfriend** *n.* **1.** female friend with whom male is romantically or sexually involved **2.** any female friend —**Girl Scout** member of U.S. organization for girls founded in 1912 to foster citizenship, character, health and skills

girt[1] (gərt) *pt./pp. of* GIRD[1]

girt[2] (gərt) *vt.* **1.** bind; encircle; gird **2.** measure girth of

girth (gərth) *n.* **1.** measurement around something **2.** leather or cloth band put around horse's belly to hold saddle *etc.* —*vt.* **3.** surround, secure with girth

gist (jist) *n.* substance, main point (of remarks *etc.*)

give (giv) *vt.* **1.** bestow, confer ownership of, make present of **2.** deliver **3.** impart **4.** assign **5.** yield, supply **6.** utter, emit **7.** be host of (party *etc.*) **8.** make over **9.** cause to have —*vi.* **10.** yield, give way, move (**gave,** '**given,** '**giving**) —*n.* **11.** yielding, elasticity —**give-and-take** *n.* **1.** mutual concessions, shared benefits and cooperation **2.** smoothly flowing exchange of ideas and talk —'**giveaway** *n.* **1.** betrayal or disclosure, *esp.* when unintentional —*a.* **2.** very cheap (*esp. in* **giveaway prices**) —**give and take** make mutual concessions —**give away 1.** donate or bestow as gift *etc.* **2.** sell very cheaply **3.** reveal, betray **4.** fail to use (opportunity) through neglect **5.** present (bride) formally to her husband in marriage ceremony —**give or take** plus or minus —**give up 1.** acknowledge defeat **2.** abandon

gizzard ('gizərd) *n.* part of bird's stomach

Gjetost ('yetōst) *n. see* MYSOST

glabrous ('glābrəs) *a. Biol.* without hairs or any unevenness; smooth

glacé (gla'sā) *a.* **1.** crystallized, candied, iced **2.** glossy

glacier ('glāshər, -zhər) *n.* river of ice, slow-moving mass of ice formed by accumulated snow in mountain valleys —**glacial** ('glāshəl) *a.* **1.** of ice, or of glaciers **2.** very cold —**glaciated** ('glāshiātid) *a.* —**glaciation** (glāshi'āshən, -si-) *n.* —**glacial period** time when large part of earth's surface was covered by ice

glad (glad) *a.* **1.** pleased **2.** happy, joyous **3.** giving joy —'**gladden** *vt.* make glad —'**gladly** *adv.* —'**gladness** *n.* —**glad eye** *inf.* inviting or seductive glance (*esp. in* **give (someone) the glad eye**) —'**gladrags** *pl.n. sl.* clothes for special occasions

glade (glād) *n.* clear, grassy space in wood or forest

gladiator ('gladiātər) *n.* trained fighter in Roman arena

gladiolus (gladi'ōləs) *n.* kind of iris, with sword-shaped leaves (*pl.* **-lus, -li** (-lī))

glair (glāər) *n.* **1.** white of egg **2.** sticky

substance —*vt.* **3.** smear with white of egg —'**glairy** *a.*

glamour *or* **glamor** ('glamər) *n.* alluring charm, fascination —'**glamorize** *or* '**glamourize** *vt.* make appear glamorous —'**glamorous** *or* '**glamourous** *a.*

glance (glans) *vi.* **1.** look rapidly or briefly **2.** allude briefly to or touch on subject **3.** (*usu. with* off) glide off (something struck) —*n.* **4.** brief look **5.** flash **6.** gleam **7.** sudden (deflected) blow

gland (gland) *n.* one of various small organs controlling different bodily functions by chemical means —'**glanders** *n.* contagious horse disease —'**glandular** *a.* —**glandular fever** acute disease characterized by fever, swollen lymph nodes *etc.* (*also* **infectious mononucleosis**)

glare (glāər) *vi.* **1.** look fiercely **2.** shine brightly, intensely **3.** be conspicuous —*n.* **4.** angry stare **5.** dazzling light —'**glaring** *a.*

glass (glas) *n.* **1.** hard transparent substance made by fusing sand, soda, potash *etc.* **2.** things made of it **3.** tumbler **4.** its contents **5.** lens **6.** mirror **7.** telescope **8.** barometer **9.** microscope —*pl.* **10.** eyeglasses —'**glassily** *adv.* —'**glassiness** *n.* —'**glassy** *a.* **1.** like glass **2.** expressionless —**glass-blower** *n.* —**glass-blowing** *n.* process of shaping molten glass by blowing air into it through tube —**glass harmonica** musical instrument consisting of series of graded glass disks which produces sound by rubbing the fingers against the wetted rims —'**glasshouse** *n.* **1.** greenhouse **2.** *inf.* army prison —**glass wool** spun glass in fluffy mass used for thermal insulation and filtering air

Glaswegian (glas'wējən) *a.* **1.** of Glasgow, city in Scotland —*n.* **2.** native or inhabitant of Glasgow

glaucoma (glow'kōmə, glŏ-) *n.* eye disorder in which there is an increase in the fluid pressure within the eye leading to progressive loss of vision and eventual blindness —**glau'comatous** *a.*

glaucous ('glŏkəs) *a.* **1.** *Bot.* covered with waxy or powdery bloom **2.** bluish-green

glaze (glāz) *vt.* **1.** furnish with glass **2.** cover with glassy substance —*vi.* **3.** become glassy —*n.* **4.** transparent coating **5.** substance used for this **6.** glossy surface —**glazier** ('glāzhər) *n.* person who glazes windows

gleam (glēm) *n.* **1.** slight or passing beam of light **2.** faint or momentary show —*vi.* **3.** give out gleams

glean (glēn) *v.* **1.** pick up (facts *etc.*) **2.** gather (useful remnants of crop) in cornfields after harvesting —'**gleaner** *n.* —'**gleanings** *pl.n.*

glebe (glēb) *n.* land belonging to parish church or benefice

glee (glē) *n.* **1.** mirth, merriment **2.** musical composition for three or more voices —'**gleeful** *a.* —'**gleefully** *adv.* —**glee club** choral society

glen (glen) *n.* narrow valley, usu. wooded and with a stream, *esp.* in Scotland

glengarry (glen'gari) *n.* Scottish woolen boat-shaped cap with ribbons hanging down back

glib (glib) *a.* **1.** fluent but insincere or superficial **2.** plausible —'**glibly** *adv.* —'**glibness** *n.*

glide (glīd) *vi.* **1.** pass smoothly and continuously **2.** (of airplane) move without use of engines —*n.* **3.** smooth, silent movement **4.** *Mus.* sounds made in passing from tone to tone —'**glider** *n.* aircraft without engine which moves in air currents —'**gliding** *n.* sport of flying gliders

glimmer ('glimər) *vi.* **1.** shine faintly, flicker —*n.* **2.** glow or twinkle of light —'**glimmering** *n.* **1.** faint gleam of light **2.** faint idea, notion

glimpse (glimps) *n.* **1.** brief or incomplete view —*vt.* **2.** catch glimpse of

glint (glint) *v.* **1.** flash —*vi.* **2.** glance, glitter **3.** reflect —*n.* **4.** bright gleam; flash

glissade (gli'säd, -'sād) *n.* **1.** gliding dance step **2.** slide, usu. on feet down slope of ice —*vi.* **3.** perform glissade

glisten ('glisən) *vi.* gleam by reflecting light

glister ('glistər) *vi./n. obs.* glitter

glitter ('glitər) *vi.* **1.** shine with bright quivering light, sparkle **2.** be showy —*n.* **3.** luster **4.** sparkle —**glitter ice C** ice formed from freezing rain

gloaming ('glōming) *n. Scot., poet.* evening twilight

gloat (glōt) *vi.* regard, dwell (on) with smugness or malicious satisfaction

glob (glob) *n. inf.* soft lump or mass

globe (glōb) *n.* **1.** sphere with map of earth or stars **2.** heavenly sphere, *esp.* the earth **3.** ball, sphere —'**global** *a.* —**globular** ('globyələr) *a.* globe-shaped —**globule** ('globyōōl) *n.* **1.** small round particle **2.** drop —'**globetrotter** *n.* (habitual) worldwide traveler —**the globe** the world; the earth

globulin ('globyəlin) *n.* class of proteins found in all living organisms

glockenspiel ('glokənspēl, -shpēl) *n.* percussion instrument of metal bars which are struck with hammers

glomerate ('glomərit) *a.* **1.** gathered into rounded mass **2.** *Anat.* (*esp.* of glands) conglomerate in structure

glomerulonephritis (gləmeryəlōni'frītis, -merə-) *n.* kidney infection affecting children and young adults

gloom (glōōm) *n.* **1.** darkness **2.** melancholy, depression —'**gloomily** *adv.* —'**gloomy** *a.*

glory ('glōri) *n.* **1.** renown, honorable fame **2.** splendor **3.** exalted or prosperous state **4.** heavenly bliss —*vi.* **5.** take pride ('**gloried,** '**glorying**) —**glorifi'cation** *n.* —'**glorify** *vt.* **1.** make glorious **2.** invest with glory (**-ified, -ifying**) —'**glorious** *a.* **1.** illustrious **2.** splendid **3.** excellent **4.** delightful —'**glori-**

ously *adv.* —**glory hole** *inf.* untidy cupboard, room or receptacle for storage

gloss[1] (glos) *n.* **1.** surface shine, luster —*vt.* **2.** put gloss on **3.** (*esp. with* over) (try to) cover up, pass over (fault, error) —'**glossiness** *n.* —'**glossy** *a.* **1.** smooth, shiny —*n.* **2.** photograph printed on shiny paper

gloss[2] (glos) *n.* **1.** marginal interpretation of word **2.** comment, explanation —*vt.* **3.** interpret **4.** comment **5.** (*oft. with* over) explain away —'**glossary** *n.* list of items peculiar to a field of knowledge with explanations

glossitis (glo'sītis) *n.* inflammation of the tongue

glottis ('glotis) *n.* human vocal apparatus, larynx (*pl.* **-es, -tides** (-tidēz)) —'**glottal** *or* '**glottic** *a.*

glove (gluv) *n.* **1.** (*oft. pl.*) covering for the hand —*vt.* **2.** cover with, or as with glove —**glove compartment** small storage area in dashboard of automobile —**the gloves 1.** boxing gloves **2.** boxing

glow (glō) *vi.* **1.** give out light and heat without flames **2.** shine **3.** experience feeling of wellbeing or satisfaction **4.** be or look hot **5.** burn with emotion —*n.* **6.** shining heat **7.** warmth of color **8.** feeling of wellbeing **9.** ardor —**glow-worm** *n.* female insect giving out green light

glower ('glowər) *vi.* **1.** scowl —*n.* **2.** sullen or angry stare

gloxinia (glok'siniə) *n.* tropical plant with large bell-shaped flowers

glucose ('gloo͞kōs, -kōz) *n.* **1.** type of sugar found in fruit *etc.* **2.** syrup made from cornstarch

glue (gloo͞) *n.* **1.** any natural or synthetic adhesive **2.** any sticky substance —*vt.* **3.** fasten with glue —'**gluey** *a.*

glum (glum) *a.* sullen, moody, gloomy

glut (glut) *n.* **1.** surfeit, excessive amount —*vt.* **2.** feed, gratify to the full or to excess **3.** overstock (market *etc.*) with commodity (**-tt-**)

gluten ('gloo͞tən) *n.* protein present in strong wheat flour —'**glutinous** *a.* sticky, gluey

glutton[1] ('glutən) *n.* **1.** greedy person **2.** one with great liking or capacity for something —'**gluttonous** *a.* like glutton, greedy —'**gluttony** *n.*

glutton[2] ('glutən) *n.* wolverine

glycerin, glycerine ('glisərin), *or* **glycerol** ('glisəröl) *n.* colorless sweet liquid with wide application in chemistry and industry

glycogen ('glīkəjən) *n.* polysaccharide consisting of glucose units: form in which carbohydrate is stored in animals —**glyco'genesis** *n.* —**glyco'genic** *a.*

glyptic ('gliptik) *a.* pert. to carving, *esp.* on precious stones

gm. gram

G-man *n.* **1.** FBI agent **2.** *Irish* political detective

GMT Greenwich Mean Time

gnarled (närld) *or* **gnarly** *a.* **1.** knobby, rugged **2.** (*esp.* of hands) twisted

gnash (nash) *vt.* grind (teeth) together as in anger or pain

gnat (nat) *n.* small, biting, two-winged fly

gnaw (nö) *v.* **1.** bite or chew steadily **2.** (*esp. with* at) cause distress (to)

gneiss (nīs) *n.* coarse-grained metamorphic rock

gnome (nōm) *n.* legendary creature like small old man —**Gnomes of Zürich** important Swiss financial institutions

gnomic ('nōmik) *a.* of or like an aphorism

gnomon ('nōmon) *n.* **1.** stationary arm that projects shadow on sundial **2.** geometric figure remaining after parallelogram has been removed from corner of larger parallelogram **3.** term of a certain kind of arithmetical progression

gnostic ('nostik) *a.* **1.** of, relating to knowledge, *esp.* spiritual knowledge —*n.* **2.** (**G-**) adherent of Gnosticism —'**Gnosticism** *n.* religious movement characterized by belief in intuitive spiritual knowledge: regarded as heresy by Christian Church

GNP Gross National Product

gnu (nyo͞o, no͞o) *n.* S Afr. antelope somewhat like ox (*pl.* **-s, gnu**)

go[1] (gō) *vi.* **1.** move along, make way **2.** be moving **3.** depart **4.** function **5.** make specified sound **6.** fail, give way, break down **7.** elapse **8.** be kept, put **9.** be able to be put **10.** result **11.** (*with* toward) contribute to (result) **12.** (*with* toward) tend to **13.** be accepted, have force **14.** become (**went** *pt.*, **gone** *pp.*) —*n.* **15.** going **16.** energy, vigor **17.** attempt **18.** turn —'**goer** *n.* **1.** person who attends something regularly, as in *moviegoer* **2.** person or thing that goes, *esp.* very fast —'**going** *n.* **1.** departure; farewell **2.** condition of road surface with regard to walking *etc.* **3.** *inf.* speed, progress *etc.* —*a.* **4.** thriving (*esp. in* **a going concern**) **5.** current; accepted **6.** available —**goner** ('gonər) *n.* person beyond help or recovery, *esp.* person about to die —**go-ahead** *n.* **1.** *inf.* permission to proceed —*a.* **2.** enterprising, ambitious —**go-between** *n.* person who acts as intermediary for two people or groups —**go-cart** *n.* **1.** baby stroller **2.** baby walker **3.** handcart, pushcart **4.** vehicle used in soapbox derby —**go-getter** *n. inf.* ambitious person —**go-go dancer** dancer, usu. scantily dressed, who performs rhythmic and oft. erotic modern dance routines in nightclubs *etc.* —**going-over** *n. inf.* **1.** check; examination; investigation **2.** castigation; thrashing (*pl.* **goings-over**) —**goings-on** *pl.n. inf.* **1.** actions or conduct, *esp.* regarded with disapproval **2.** happenings or events, *esp.* mysterious or suspicious —**go down 1.** move to lower place or level; sink, decline, decrease *etc.* **2.** be received or accepted **3.**

be remembered or recorded (*esp.* *in* **go down in history**) —**go down on** perform fellatio or cunnilingus on

go[2] (gō) *n.* board game for two players played with 181 stones each on a board with 19 equidistant lines parallel to one edge and 19 lines at right angles to them, the object of the game being to occupy the territory of the board —**go moku** (ˈmōkōō) *or* **bang** game played on go board whose object is to place five stones in a row

goad (gōd) *n.* **1.** spiked stick for driving cattle **2.** anything that urges to action **3.** incentive —*vt.* **4.** urge on **5.** torment

goal (gōl) *n.* **1.** end of race **2.** object of effort **3.** posts through which ball is to be driven in football *etc.* **4.** the score so made —ˈ**goalkeeper** *n. Sport* player in goal whose duty is to prevent ball from entering it

goat (gōt) *n.* four-footed animal with long hair, horns and beard —**goaˈtee** *n.* pointed tuftlike beard growing on chin —**goat-herd** *n.* —ˈ**goatsucker** *n.* nightjar —**get (someone's) goat** *sl.* annoy (someone)

gob (gob) *n.* **1.** lump **2.** (*usu. pl*) large amount *sl.* —ˈ**gobbet** *n.* lump (of food) —ˈ**gobble** *v.* eat hastily, noisily or greedily

gobble (ˈgobəl) *n.* **1.** throaty, gurgling cry of the turkey-cock —*vi.* **2.** make this sound —ˈ**gobbler** *n.* male turkey

gobbledygook *or* **gobbledegook** (gobəldiˈgŏŏk, -ˈgōōk) *n.* pretentious language, *esp.* as used by officials

goblet (ˈgoblit) *n.* drinking cup

goblin (ˈgoblin) *n. Folklore* small, usu. malevolent being

goby (ˈgōbi) *n.* small spiny-finned fish having ventral fins modified as sucker

god (god) *n.* **1.** superhuman being worshiped as having supernatural power **2.** object of worship, idol **3.** (G-) in monotheistic religions, the Supreme Being, creator and ruler of the universe (ˈ**goddess** *fem.*) —ˈ**godlike** *a.* —ˈ**godliness** *n.* —ˈ**godly** *a.* devout, pious —ˈ**godchild** *n.* person sponsored by adults at baptism (ˈ**godson** *or* ˈ**goddaughter**) —**god-fearing** *a.* religious, good —ˈ**godforsaken** *a.* hopeless, dismal —ˈ**godhead** *n.* divine nature or deity —ˈ**godparent** *n.* sponsor at baptism (ˈ**godfather** *or* ˈ**godmother**) —ˈ**godsend** *n.* something unexpected but welcome —**GodˈSpeed** *interj./n.* expression of good wishes for person's success and safety

godetia (gəˈdēshə) *n.* annual garden plant

godwit (ˈgodwit) *n.* large shore bird of N regions

gofer (ˈgōfər) *n.* person in office who runs errands

goffer (ˈgōfər) *vt.* **1.** press pleats into (frill) **2.** decorate (edges of book) —*n.* **3.** ornamental frill made by pressing pleats **4.** decoration formed by goffering books

goggle (ˈgogəl) *vi.* **1.** (of eyes) bulge **2.** stare —*pl.n.* **3.** protective eyeglasses —**goggle-eyed** *a.* having bulging eyes

Goidelic (goiˈdelik) *n.* **1.** N group of Celtic languages, consisting of Irish Gaelic, Scottish Gaelic and Manx —*a.* **2.** of or characteristic of this group of languages

goiter (ˈgoitər) *n.* enlargement of thyroid gland.

gold (gōld) *n.* **1.** *Chem.* yellow noble metal used for coins, jewelry and as a medium of exchange *Symbol* Au, at. wt. 197.0, at. no. 79 **2.** coins made of this **3.** wealth **4.** beautiful or precious thing **5.** color of gold —*a.* **6.** of, like gold —ˈ**golden** *a.* —ˈ**goldcrest** *n.* Eurasian songbird with yellow crown —**gold-digger** *n.* woman skillful in extracting money from men —**golden age 1.** *Class. myth.* first and best age of mankind, when existence was happy, prosperous and innocent **2.** most flourishing period, *esp.* in history of art or nation —**golden boy** *or* **girl** a popular or successful person —**golden eagle** large eagle of mountainous regions of N hemisphere —**Golden Fleece** *Gr. myth.* fleece of winged ram stolen by Jason and Argonauts —**golden hamster** tawny species of hamster, popular as pet and used as laboratory animal —**golden handshake** *inf.* money given to employee on retirement or for loss of employment —**golden mean** middle course between extremes —ˈ**goldenrod** *n.* tall plant with golden flower spikes —**golden rule** important principle of action —**golden wedding** fiftieth wedding anniversary —ˈ**goldfield** *n.* place where gold deposits are known to exist —ˈ**goldfish** *n.* any of various ornamental pond or aquarium fish —**gold mine 1.** place where gold is mined **2.** a source of great wealth —**gold plate 1.** thin coating of gold, usu. produced by electroplating **2.** vessels or utensils made of gold —**gold-plate** *vt.* —**gold reserve** gold held by central bank to guarantee value of a country's currency —**gold rush** large-scale migration of people to territory where gold has been found —ˈ**goldsmith** *n.* **1.** dealer in articles made of gold **2.** artisan who makes such articles —**gold standard** financial arrangement whereby currencies of countries accepting it are expressed in fixed terms of gold

Gold Coast *former name of* GHANA (*also* **Togoland**)

golf (golf) *n.* **1.** outdoor game in which player attempts to propel a small resilient ball with clubs around a turfed course with widely spaced holes in regular progression with the smallest number of strokes —*vi.* **2.** play this game —ˈ**golfer** *n.* —**golf club 1.** long-shafted club with wood or metal head used to strike golf ball **2.** (premises of) association of golf players, usu. having its own course and facilities —**golf course** area of open land on which golf is played —**golf links** golf course located by the sea

Golf (golf) *n.* word used in communications for the letter *g*

Goliath (gə'līəth) *n. Bible* Philistine giant killed by David with stone from sling

golly ('goli) *interj.* exclamation of mild surprise

-gon (*comb. form*) figure having specified number of angles, as in *pentagon*

gonad ('gōnad) *n.* gland producing gametes —**gonado'tropin** *n.* hormone which stimulates the gonads

gondola ('gondələ) *n.* Venetian canal boat —**gondo'lier** *n.* person who propels gondola

gone (gon) *pp. of* GO[1]

gonfalon ('gonfəlon, -lən) *n.* **1.** banner hanging from crossbar, used *esp.* by certain medieval Italian republics **2.** battle flag suspended crosswise on staff, usu. having serrated edge

gong (gong) *n.* **1.** orchestral percussion instrument consisting of large circular bronze disk with turned edge and struck with a heavy bass-drum beater **2.** anything used thus

gonorrhea (gonə'rēə) *n.* a venereal disease

good (go͝od) *a.* **1.** commendable **2.** right **3.** proper **4.** excellent **5.** beneficial **6.** well-behaved **7.** virtuous **8.** kind **9.** financially safe or secure **10.** adequate **11.** sound **12.** valid ('**better** *comp.*, **best** *sup.*) —*n.* **13.** benefit **14.** wellbeing **15.** profit —*pl.* **16.** property **17.** wares —'**goodly** *a.* large, considerable —'**goodness** *n.* —**Good Book** the Bible —**Good Conduct Medal** U.S. Army medal awarded to enlisted men for meritorious service —**Good Friday** *see* FRIDAY —**good-hearted** *a.* kind and generous —**Good Samaritan 1.** *N.T.* figure in one of Christ's parables who is example of compassion toward those in distress **2.** kindly person who helps another in difficulty —**good sort** *inf.* agreeable person —**good turn** helpful, friendly act; good deed; favor —**good will 1.** kindly feeling, heartiness **2.** value of a business in reputation *etc.* over and above its tangible assets —**goody-goody** *n.* **1.** *inf.* smugly virtuous or sanctimonious person —*a.* **2.** smug and sanctimonious

goodbye (go͝od'bī) *interj./n.* form of address on parting

gooey ('go͞oi) *a. inf.* sticky, soft —**goo** *n. inf.* **1.** sticky substance **2.** coy or sentimental language or ideas

goof (go͞of) *inf. n.* **1.** mistake **2.** stupid person —*vi.* **3.** make mistake —'**goofy** *a.* silly, sloppy

goon (go͞on) *n. inf.* stupid fellow

goosander (go͞o'sandər) *n.* type of duck

goose (go͞os) *n.* **1.** web-footed bird **2.** its flesh **3.** simpleton (*pl.* **geese**) —**goose flesh** bristling of skin due to cold, fright —**goose step** formal parade step

gooseberry ('go͞osberi, 'go͞oz-; -bri) *n.* **1.** thorny shrub **2.** its hairy fruit **3.** *inf.* unwelcome third party (*oft. in* **play gooseberry**)

gopher ('gōfər) *n.* various species of Amer. burrowing rodents

Gordian knot ('gördiən) **1.** in Greek legend, complicated knot, tied by King Gordius, that Alexander the Great cut with sword **2.** intricate problem (*esp. in* **cut the Gordian knot**)

gore[1] (gör) *n.* (dried) blood from wound —'**gorily** *adv.* —'**gory** *a.* **1.** horrific; bloodthirsty **2.** involving bloodshed and killing **3.** covered in gore

gore[2] (gör) *vt.* pierce with horns

gore[3] (gör) *n.* **1.** triangular piece inserted to shape garment —*vt.* **2.** shape thus

Gore-tex ('görteks) *n.* trade name for laminated fabric used for protection from rain

gorge (görj) *n.* **1.** ravine **2.** disgust, resentment —*vi.* **3.** eat greedily —'**gorget** *n.* armor, ornamentation or clothing for throat —**gorge oneself** stuff oneself with food

gorgeous ('görjəs) *a.* **1.** splendid, showy, dazzling **2.** *inf.* extremely pleasing

Gorgon ('görgən) *n.* terrifying or repulsive woman

Gorgonzola (görgən'zōlə) *n.* a semihard, blue-veined cheese made from cow's milk, with a rich, piquant flavor, orig. from Italy

gorilla (gə'rilə) *n.* largest anthropoid ape, found in Afr.

gormandize ('görməndīz) *v.* eat (food) hurriedly or like a glutton

gorse (görs) *n.* prickly shrub

gory ('göri) *a. see* GORE[1]

gosh (gosh) *interj.* exclamation of mild surprise or wonder

goshawk ('gos-hök) *n.* large hawk

gosling ('gozling) *n.* young goose

gospel ('gospəl) *n.* **1.** unquestionable truth **2.** (**G-**) any of first four books of New Testament

gossamer ('gosəmər) *n.* **1.** filmy substance like spider's web **2.** thin gauze or silk fabric

gossip ('gosip) *n.* **1.** idle (malicious) talk about other persons, *esp.* regardless of facts **2.** one who talks thus (*also* '**gossipmonger**) —*vi.* **3.** engage in gossip **4.** chatter —**gossip column** part of newspaper devoted to gossip about well-known people

got (got) *pt./pp. of* GET

Goth (goth) *n.* **1.** member of East Germanic people who invaded Roman Empire from 3rd to 5th cent. **2.** rude or barbaric person —'**Gothic** *a.* **1.** *Archit.* of the pointed arch style common in Europe from 12th–16th centuries **2.** of Goths **3.** (*sometimes* **g-**) barbarous **4.** (*sometimes* **g-**) of literary style characterized by gloom, the grotesque, and the supernatural —*n.* **5.** (of type) German black letter **6.** bold type style without serifs

gotten ('gotən) *pp. of* GET

gouache (gwäsh) *n.* **1.** painting technique

using opaque watercolor in which pigments are bound with glue (*also* **body color**) **2.** paint used in this technique **3.** painting done by this method

Gouda ('go͞odə) *n.* a firm cheese of mild flavor made from cow's milk, shaped like disk and covered with red wax, orig. from Holland

gouge (gowj) *vt.* (*usu. with* out) **1.** scoop out **2.** force out —*n.* **3.** chisel with curved cutting edge

goulash ('go͞oläsh, -lash) *n.* stew of meat and vegetables seasoned with paprika (*also* **Hungarian goulash**)

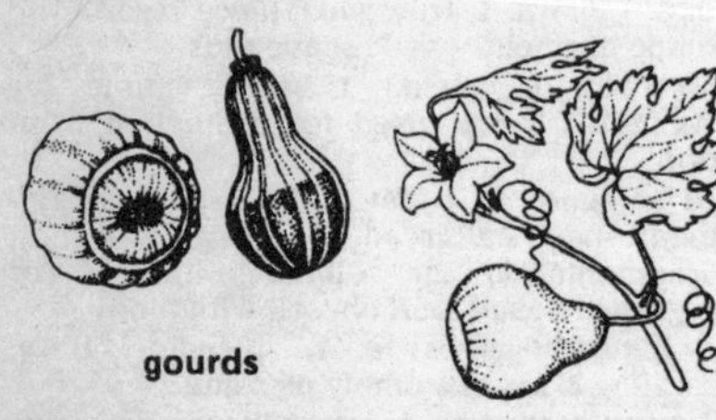

gourds

gourd (gōrd, go͞oərd) *n.* **1.** trailing or climbing plant **2.** its large fleshy fruit **3.** its rind as vessel

gourmand ('go͞oərmänd, -mənd) *n.* glutton —'**gourmandize** *v.*

gourmet ('go͞oərmā, go͞or'mā) *n.* **1.** connoisseur of wine, food **2.** epicure

gout (gowt) *n.* disease characterized by inflammation, *esp.* of joints —'**gouty** *a.*

Gov. *or* **gov. 1.** government **2.** governor

govern ('guvərn) *vt.* **1.** rule, direct, guide, control **2.** decide, determine **3.** be followed by (grammatical case *etc.*) —'**governable** *a.* —'**governance** *n.* act of governing —'**governess** *n.* woman teacher, *esp.* in private household —'**government** *n.* **1.** exercise of political authority in directing a people, state *etc.* **2.** system by which community is ruled **3.** body of people in charge of government of state **4.** ministry in a parliamentary system **5.** executive power **6.** control **7.** direction **8.** exercise of authority —**govern'mental** *a.* —**governor** ('guvnər, 'guvənər, 'guvərnər) *n.* **1.** one who governs, *esp.* one invested with supreme authority in state *etc.* **2.** chief administrator of an institution **3.** member of committee responsible for an organization or institution **4.** regulator for speed of engine

Govt. *or* **govt.** government

gown (gown) *n.* **1.** loose flowing outer garment **2.** woman's (long) dress **3.** official robe, as in university *etc.*

goy (goi) *n.* (among Jews) a non-Jew (*pl.* **goyim** ('goiim), **-s**)

G.P. General Practitioner

GPO 1. General Post Office **2.** Government Printing Office

Gr. 1. Grecian **2.** Greece **3.** Greek

gr. 1. grade **2.** grain **3.** gram **4.** gravity **5.** gross

grab (grab) *vt.* **1.** grasp suddenly **2.** snatch (**-bb-**) —*n.* **3.** sudden clutch **4.** quick attempt to seize **5.** device or implement for clutching —**grab bag** box or bag containing small prizes for which children search

grace (grās) *n.* **1.** charm, elegance **2.** accomplishment **3.** good will, favor **4.** sense of propriety **5.** postponement granted **6.** short thanksgiving before or after meal **7.** title of duke or archbishop —*pl.* **8.** affectation of manner (*esp. in* **airs and graces**) —*vt.* **9.** add grace to, honor —'**graceful** *a.* —'**gracefully** *adv.* —'**graceless** *a.* shameless, depraved —'**gracious** *a.* **1.** favorable **2.** kind **3.** pleasing **4.** indulgent, beneficent, condescending —'**graciously** *adv.* —**grace note** *Mus.* melodic ornament

Graces ('grāsiz) *pl.n. Gr. myth.* three sister goddesses, givers of charm and beauty

grade (grād) *n.* **1.** step, stage **2.** degree of rank *etc.* **3.** class **4.** mark, rating **5.** slope —*vt.* **6.** arrange in classes **7.** assign grade to **8.** level (ground), move (earth) with grader —**gradation** (grā'dāshən, grə-) *n.* **1.** series of degrees or steps **2.** each of them **3.** arrangement in steps **4.** in painting, gradual passing from one shade *etc.* to another —'**grader** *n.* **1.** person or thing that grades **2.** machine with wide blade used in road making —**make the grade** succeed

gradient ('grādiənt) *n.* (degree of) slope

gradual ('grajo͞oəl) *a.* **1.** taking place by degrees **2.** slow and steady **3.** not steep —'**gradually** *adv.*

graduate ('grajo͞oāt) *vi.* **1.** complete successful course of study, *esp.* university —*vt.* **2.** divide into degrees **3.** mark, arrange according to scale —*n.* ('grajo͞oit) **4.** holder of diploma, certificate or degree —**gradu'ation** *n.*

graffiti (gra'fētē) *pl.n.* (*oft.* obscene) writing, drawing on walls (*sing.* **graf'fito**)

graft (graft) *n.* **1.** shoot of plant set in stalk of another **2.** the process **3.** surgical transplant of skin to an area of body in need of tissue —*vt.* **4.** insert (shoot) in another stalk **5.** transplant (living tissue in surgery)

graham ('grāəm) *a. see* **whole-grain** *at* WHOLE

Grail (grāl) *n. see* **Holy Grail** *at* HOLY

grain (grān) *n.* **1.** seed, fruit of cereal plant **2.** wheat and allied plants **3.** small hard particle **4.** unit of weight, 0.002083 ounce (0.0648 gram) in avoirdupois, troy or apothecaries' system **5.** texture **6.** arrangement of fibers **7.** any very small amount **8.** natural temperament or disposition —'**grainy** *a.*

gram *or* **gramme** (gram) *n.* unit of weight in metric system, one thousandth of a kilogram, about the weight of one cubic centimeter of water at 4° Celsius

-gram (*comb. form*) drawing; something

written or recorded, as in *hexagram, telegram*

gramineous (grə'miniəs) *a.* **1.** of or belonging to grass family **2.** resembling grass; grasslike (*also* **graminaceous** (grami'nāshəs))

graminivorous (grami'nivərəs) *a.* (of animals) feeding on grass

grammar ('gramər) *n.* **1.** science of structure and usages of language **2.** book on this **3.** correct use of words —**grammarian** (grə'meriən, -'mar-) *n.* —**gram'matical** *a.* according to grammar —**gram'matically** *adv.* —**grammar school** elementary school

grampus ('grampəs) *n.* **1.** cetacean related to killer whale common in northern seas **2.** giant whip scorpion of southern U.S.

granary ('granəri) *n.* **1.** storehouse for grain **2.** rich grain growing region

grand (grand) *a.* **1.** imposing **2.** magnificent **3.** majestic **4.** noble **5.** splendid **6.** eminent **7.** lofty **8.** chief, of chief importance **9.** final (total) —**grandeur** ('granjər) *n.* **1.** nobility **2.** magnificence **3.** dignity —**gran'diloquence** *n.* —**gran'diloquent** *a.* pompous in speech —**gran'diloquently** *adv.* —**'grandiose** *a.* **1.** imposing **2.** affectedly grand **3.** striking —**grandchild** ('granchīld, 'grand-) *n.* child of one's child (**grandson** ('gransun, 'grand-) *or* **granddaughter** ('grandd ōtər, 'granddōtər)) —**grand duke 1.** prince or nobleman who rules territory, state or principality **2.** son or male descendant in male line of Russian czar —**grandfather clock** long-pendulum clock in tall standing wooden case —**grand jury** jury, comprising 12 to 33 persons, designated to inquire into accusations of crime and ascertain whether evidence is adequate to found indictment —**Grand National** annual steeplechase race at Aintree racecourse at Liverpool, England —**grand opera** opera with serious plot and fully composed text —**grandparent** ('granparənt, 'grand-; -per-) *n.* parent of parent (**grandfather** ('granfädhər, 'grand-) *or* **grandmother** ('granmudhər, 'grand-)) —**grand piano** large harp-shaped piano with horizontal strings —**grand slam** *Bridge* bidding for and winning all thirteen tricks —**Grand Slam 1.** *Tennis* winning of Australian, French, U.S. and Wimbledon championships within a calendar year **2.** *Golf* winning of a group of championships **3.** *Baseball* a home run with runners on all bases —**grandstand** ('granstand, 'grand-) *n.* structure with tiered seats for spectators

grande dame (grăd 'dam) *Fr.* woman regarded as most experienced or prominent member of her profession *etc.*

grandee (gran'dē) *n.* Spanish nobleman of highest rank

grand mal ('grănd 'măl) form of epilepsy characterized by convulsions and loss of consciousness

Grand Prix (*Fr.* grã 'prē) any of series of international formula motor races

grange (grānj) *n.* **1.** country house with farm buildings **2.** (**G-**) lodge or local branch of the "Patrons of Husbandry", an association founded in 1867 to promote the interests of agriculture

granite ('granit) *n.* hard crystalline igneous rock —**gra'nitic** *a.*

granivorous (grə'nivərəs, grā-) *a.* feeding on grain or seeds

granny ('grani) *n. inf.* grandmother —**granny glasses** eyeglasses with round lenses and thin wire frames —**granny knot** square knot with loops crossed wrongly and thus insecure

grant (grant) *vt.* **1.** consent to fulfill (request) **2.** permit **3.** bestow **4.** admit —*n.* **5.** something bestowed, *esp.* land or money for a special purpose —**gran'tee** *n.* —**'granter** *or (Law)* **'grantor** *n.* —**grant-in-aid** *n.* money granted by central to local government for program *etc.* (*pl.* **grants-in-aid**)

Grant (grant) *n.* **Ulysses Simpson.** the 18th President of the U.S. (1869-73)

granule ('granyōōl) *n.* small grain —**'granular** *a.* of or like grains —**'granulate** *vt.* **1.** form into grains —*vi.* **2.** take form of grains —**granu'lation** *n.*

granuloma (granyə'lōmə) *n.* tumorlike nodule which develops in response to infection or irritation

grape (grāp) *n.* fruit of vine —**grape hyacinth** plant with clusters of small, rounded blue flowers —**'grapeshot** *n.* bullets scattering when fired —**'grapevine** *n.* **1.** grape-bearing vine **2.** *inf.* unofficial means of conveying information

grapefruit ('grāpfrōōt) *n.* subtropical citrus fruit

graph (graf) *n.* drawing depicting relation of different numbers, quantities *etc.* (*also* **chart**)

-graph (*n. comb. form*) **1.** instrument that writes or records, as in *telegraph* **2.** writing, record; drawing, as in *autograph, lithograph* —**-grapher** (*n. comb. form*) **1.** person skilled in subject, as in *geographer, photographer* **2.** person who writes or draws in specified way, as in *stenographer, lithographer* —**-graphic(al)** (*a. comb. form*) —**-graphy** (*n. comb. form*) **1.** form of writing, representing *etc.*, as in *calligraphy, photography* **2.** art; descriptive science, as in *choreography, oceanography*

graphic ('grafik) *or* **graphical** *a.* **1.** vividly descriptive **2.** of, in, relating to, writing, drawing, painting *etc.* —**'graphically** *adv.* —**'graphics** *pl.n.* **1.** (*with sing. v.*) art of drawing in accordance with mathematical principles **2.** (*with sing. v.*) study of writing systems **3.** (*with pl. v.*) drawings *etc.* in layout of magazine or book —**'graphite** *n.* form of carbon (used in pencils) —**gra'phol-**

ogy *n.* study of handwriting —**graphic arts** fine or applied visual arts based on drawing or use of line, *esp.* illustration and printmaking —**graph paper** paper with intersecting lines for drawing graphs *etc.*

grapnel ('grapnəl) *n.* **1.** hooked iron instrument for seizing anything **2.** small anchor with several flukes

grapple ('grapəl) *v.* **1.** come to grips, wrestle **2.** cope, contend —*n.* **3.** grappling **4.** grapnel —**grappling iron** grapnel, *esp.* for securing ships

GRAS list (gras) the official Food and Drug Administration list of food additives which are *g*enerally *r*ecognized *a*s *s*afe

grasp (grasp) *v.* **1.** (try, struggle to) seize hold (of) —*vt.* **2.** understand —*n.* **3.** act of grasping **4.** grip **5.** comprehension —'**grasping** *a.* greedy, avaricious

grass (gras) *n.* **1.** common type of plant with jointed stems and long narrow leaves (including cereals, bamboo *etc.*) **2.** such plants grown as lawn **3.** pasture **4.** *sl.* marijuana —*vt.* **5.** cover with grass —**grass hockey C** hockey played on field —'**grasshopper** *n.* jumping, chirping insect —**grass roots** fundamentals —'**grassroots** *a.* coming from ordinary people, the rank and file —**grass widow** wife whose husband is absent

grate[1] (grāt) *vt.* **1.** rub into small bits on rough surface —*vi.* **2.** rub with harsh noise **3.** have irritating effect —'**grater** *n.* utensil with rough surface for reducing substance to small particles

grate[2] (grāt) *n.* framework of metal bars for holding fuel in fireplace —'**grating** *n.* framework of parallel or latticed bars covering opening

grateful ('grātfəl) *a.* **1.** thankful **2.** appreciative **3.** pleasing —'**gratefully** *adv.* —'**gratefulness** *n.* —**gratitude** ('gratityōōd, -tōōd) *n.* sense of being thankful for favor

gratify ('gratifī) *vt.* **1.** satisfy **2.** please **3.** indulge —**gratifi'cation** *n.*

gratin (*Fr.* gra'tē̃) **1.** method of cooking to form light crust **2.** dish so cooked

gratis ('gratis, 'grātis) *adv./a.* free, for nothing

gratuitous (grə'tyōōitəs, -'tōō-) *a.* **1.** given free **2.** uncalled-for —**gra'tuitously** *adv.* —**gra'tuity** *n.* **1.** gift of money for services rendered **2.** donation

gravamen (grə'vāmən) *n.* **1.** *Law* part of accusation weighing most heavily against accused **2.** *Law* substance of complaint **3.** *rare* grievance (*pl.* **-vamina** (-'vaminə))

grave[1] (grāv) *n.* **1.** hole dug to bury corpse **2.** *Poet.* death —'**gravestone** *n.* monument on grave —'**graveyard** *n.*

grave[2] (grāv) *a.* **1.** serious, weighty **2.** dignified, solemn **3.** plain, dark in color **4.** deep in note —'**gravely** *adv.*

grave[3] (grāv) *vt.* clean (ship's bottom) by scraping —**graving dock** dry dock

grave[4] (gräv) *n. Phonet.* accent (`) used to indicate quality of vowel, full pronunciation of syllable *etc.*

gravel ('gravəl) *n.* **1.** small stones **2.** coarse sand —*vt.* **3.** cover with gravel —'**gravelly** *a.*

graven ('grāvən) *a.* carved, engraved

Graves (gräv) *n.* **1.** (*sometimes* **g-**) white or red wine from district around Bordeaux, France **2.** dry or medium sweet white wine from any country

gravid ('gravid) *a.* pregnant

gravimetric (gravi'metrik) *a.* **1.** of measurement by weight **2.** *Chem.* of analysis of quantities by weight

gravitate ('gravitāt) *vi.* **1.** move by gravity **2.** tend (toward center of attraction) **3.** sink, settle down —**gravi'tation** *n.*

gravity ('graviti) *n.* **1.** force of attraction of one body for another, *esp.* of objects to the earth **2.** heaviness **3.** importance **4.** seriousness **5.** staidness

gravy ('grāvi) *n.* **1.** juices from meat in cooking **2.** sauce for food made from these —**gravy boat** small boat-shaped vessel for serving gravy

gray *or* **grey** (grā) *a.* **1.** of color between black and white, as ashes or lead **2.** clouded **3.** dismal **4.** turning white **5.** aged **6.** intermediate, indeterminate —*n.* **7.** gray color **8.** gray or whitish horse —'**grayling** *n.* fish of salmon family —**Gray Friar** Franciscan friar —'**grayhen** *n.* female of black grouse —'**grayhound** *n.* swift slender dog used in coursing and racing —'**graylag** *or* **graylag goose** *n.* large gray Eurasian goose —**gray matter 1.** grayish tissue of brain and spinal cord, containing nerve cell bodies and fibers **2.** *inf.* brains; intellect

graze[1] (grāz) *v.* feed on (grass, pasture) —**grazier** ('grāzhər) *n.* one who raises cattle for market —'**grazing** *n.* **1.** vegetation on ranges or pastures that is available for livestock to feed upon **2.** land on which this is growing

graze[2] (grāz) *vt.* **1.** touch lightly in passing, scratch, scrape —*n.* **2.** grazing **3.** abrasion

grease (grēs) *n.* **1.** soft melted fat of animals **2.** thick oil as lubricant —*vt.* (grēs, grēz) **3.** apply grease to —'**greaser** *n.* **1.** *offens.* native or inhabitant of Latin America, esp. Mexican **2.** swaggering aggressive white male of working-class background —'**greasily** *adv.* —'**greasiness** *n.* —'**greasy** *a.* —**grease gun** appliance for injecting oil or grease into machinery —**grease monkey** *inf.* mechanic —'**greasepaint** *n.* theatrical make-up —**grease pencil** crayon-like pencil used to mark glossy surfaces —**grease the palm** (*or* **hand**) **of** bribe

great (grāt) *a.* **1.** large, big **2.** important **3.** pre-eminent, distinguished **4.** *inf.* excellent —'**greatly** *adv.* —'**greatness** *n.* —**great circle** circular section of sphere with radius equal to that of sphere —'**greatcoat** *n.*

overcoat, *esp.* military —**Great Dane** breed of very large dog —**Great Russian** *n.* **1.** *Linguis.* Russian **2.** member of chief East Slavonic people of Russia —*a.* **3.** of this people or their language —**great seal** (*oft.* **G- S-**) principal seal of nation *etc.* used to authenticate documents of highest importance

great- (*comb. form*) indicates a degree further removed in relationship, as in *great-grandfather*

Great Lakes chain of five large lakes along U.S.-Canadian border

Great Plains region in central North America

Great Salt Lake strongly saline lake in Utah

Great White Father American Indian name for U.S. president

Great White Way theater section of New York City on Broadway

greave (grēv) *n.* (*oft. pl.*) armor for leg below knee

grebe (grēb) *n.* aquatic diving bird

Grecian (ˈgrēshən) *a.* of (ancient) Greece —**Grecian profile** profile in which nose and forehead form almost straight line

Greco- *or* **Graeco-** (*comb. form*) Greek, as in *Greco-Roman*

Greece (grēs) *n.* country in S Europe bounded north by Albania, Yugoslavia and Bulgaria, east by Turkey and the Aegean Sea, south by the Mediterranean and west by the Ionian Sea

greed (grēd) *n.* excessive consumption of, desire for, food, wealth —ˈ**greedily** *adv.* —ˈ**greediness** *n.* voracity of appetite —ˈ**greedy** *a.* **1.** gluttonous **2.** eagerly desirous **3.** voracious **4.** covetous

Greek (grēk) *n.* **1.** native language of Greece —*a.* **2.** of Greece, the Greeks or the Greek language —**Greek cross** cross with four arms of same length —**Greek gift** gift given with harmful intent —**Greek Orthodox Church 1.** established Church of Greece, in which Metropolitan of Athens has primacy of honor (*also* **Greek Church**) **2.** *see* **Orthodox Church** *at* ORTHODOX

green (grēn) *a.* **1.** of color between blue and yellow in the spectrum **2.** grass-colored **3.** emerald **4.** unripe **5.** inexperienced **6.** gullible **7.** envious —*n.* **8.** color **9.** area of grass —*pl.* **10.** green vegetables —ˈ**greenery** *n.* vegetation —**green bean** string bean —**green-eyed** *a.* jealous, envious —**green-eyed monster** jealousy, envy —ˈ**greenfinch** *n.* European finch with dull green plumage in male —ˈ**greenfly** *n.* aphid —ˈ**greengage** *n.* kind of plum —ˈ**greenhorn** *n.* inexperienced person, newcomer —ˈ**greenhouse** *n.* building mainly of glass, with heat and humidity regulated for raising plants —**greenhouse effect** the insulating action of an atmospheric substance, *esp.* carbon dioxide, which permits the heat of the sun to pass through to the earth and prevents the heat from leaving —**green light 1.** signal to go, *esp.* green traffic light **2.** permission to proceed with project *etc.* —**green manure** crop plowed into soil to fertilize it —**green pepper** green unripe fruit of sweet pepper —ˈ**greenroom** *n.* room for actors when offstage —ˈ**greenshank** *n.* large European sandpiper —**greens keeper** person responsible for golf course —**greenstick fracture** fracture in children in which bone is partly bent and splinters only on convex side of bend —ˈ**greenstone** *n.* New Zealand jade —ˈ**greensward** *n.* turf —**green thumb** unusual ability to raise plants

Greenland (ˈgrēnlənd) *n.* division of Denmark occupying an island in the N Atlantic separated from Canada by Baffin Bay, Davis Strait and the Labrador Sea

Greenwich Mean Time *or* **Greenwich Time** (ˈgrinij) local time of 0° meridian passing through Greenwich, England: standard time for Britain and basis for calculating times throughout world

greet (grēt) *vt.* **1.** meet with expressions of welcome **2.** accost, salute **3.** receive —ˈ**greeting** *n.*

gregarious (griˈgariəs, -ˈger-) *a.* **1.** fond of company, sociable **2.** living in flocks —**greˈgariousness** *n.*

Gregorian calendar (griˈgōriən) calendar introduced by Pope Gregory XIII in 1582 and still in use

Gregorian chant *see* PLAINSONG

gremlin (ˈgremlin) *n. sl.* imaginary being blamed for mechanical and other troubles

Grenada (grəˈnādə) *n.* country in the Caribbean Sea occupying the most southerly of the Windward Islands

grenade (griˈnād) *n.* explosive shell or bomb, thrown by hand or shot from rifle —**grenadier** (grenəˈdēər) *n.* formerly, grenade thrower

grenadine (grenəˈdēn, ˈgrenədēn) *n.* syrup made from pomegranate juice, for sweetening and coloring drinks

grew (grōō) *pt. of* GROW

grey (grā) *see* GRAY

grid (grid) *n.* **1.** network of horizontal and vertical lines, bars *etc.* **2.** any interconnecting system of links **3.** national network of electricity supply

griddle (ˈgridəl) *n.* flat iron plate for cooking

gridiron (ˈgridīərn) *n.* **1.** frame of metal bars for cooking on **2.** football field

grief (grēf) *n.* deep sorrow —ˈ**grievance** *n.* real or imaginary grounds for complaint —**grieve** *vi.* **1.** feel grief —*vt.* **2.** cause grief to —ˈ**grievous** *a.* **1.** painful, oppressive **2.** very serious —**grief-stricken** *a.* stricken with grief; sorrowful

griffin (ˈgrifin), **griffon,** *or* **gryphon** *n.*

fabulous monster with eagle's head and wings and lion's body

grill (gril) *n.* **1.** device on cooker to radiate heat downwards, broiler **2.** food cooked under it **3.** gridiron —*v.* **4.** cook (food) under broiler —*vt.* **5.** subject to severe questioning —**'grilling** *a.* **1.** very hot —*n.* **2.** severe cross-examination —**'grillroom** *n.* informal dining room in hotel

grille *or* **grill** (gril) *n.* grating, crosswork of bars over opening

grilse (grils) *n.* salmon at stage when it returns for first time from sea (*pl.* **-s, grilse**)

grim (grim) *a.* **1.** stern **2.** of stern or forbidding aspect, relentless **3.** joyless —**'grimly** *adv.*

grimace ('grimis, gri'mās) *n.* **1.** wry face —*vi.* **2.** pull wry face

grimalkin (gri'mŏlkin, -'mal-) *n.* **1.** old cat, *esp.* female cat **2.** crotchety or shrewish old woman

grime (grīm) *n.* **1.** ingrained dirt, soot —*vt.* **2.** soil, dirty, blacken —**'grimy** *a.*

grin (grin) *vi.* **1.** show teeth, as in laughter (**-nn-**) —*n.* **2.** grinning smile

grind (grīnd) *vt.* **1.** crush to powder **2.** oppress **3.** make sharp, smooth **4.** grate —*vi.* **5.** perform action of grinding **6.** *inf.* work, *esp.* study hard **7.** grate (**ground** *pt./pp.*) —*n.* **8.** *inf.* hard work **9.** act of grinding —**'grinder** *n.* —**'grindstone** *n.* stone used for grinding

gringo ('gringgō) *n. offens.* (among Spanish Americans) a foreigner, *esp.* North American (*pl.* **-s**)

grip (grip) *n.* **1.** firm hold, grasp **2.** grasping power **3.** mastery **4.** handle **5.** suitcase or traveling bag (*also* **'handgrip**) —*vt.* **6.** grasp or hold tightly **7.** hold interest or attention of (**-pp-**)

gripe (grīp) *vi.* **1.** *inf.* complain (persistently) —*n.* **2.** intestinal pain (*esp.* in infants) **3.** *inf.* complaint

grippe (grip) *n.* influenza

grisly ('grizli) *a.* grim, causing terror, ghastly

grist (grist) *n.* corn to be ground —**grist to** (*or* **for**) **the** (*or* **one's**) **mill** something which can be turned to advantage

gristle ('grisəl) *n.* cartilage, tough flexible tissue

grit (grit) *n.* **1.** rough particles of sand **2.** coarse sandstone **3.** courage —*n./a.* **4.** (**G-**) **C** *inf.* Liberal —*pl.* **5.** wheat *etc.* coarsely ground —*vt.* **6.** clench, grind (teeth) (**-tt-**) —**'grittiness** *n.* —**'gritty** *a.*

grizzle ('grizəl) *v.* make, become gray —**'grizzled** *a.* —**'grizzly** *a.* —**grizzly bear** large North Amer. bear

groan (grōn) *vi.* **1.** make low, deep sound of grief or pain **2.** be in pain or overburdened —*n.* **3.** groaning sound

groat (grōt) *n.* formerly, silver coin worth four pennies

groats (grōts) *pl.n.* hulled and crushed grain of oats, wheat or certain other cereals

grocer ('grōsər) *n.* dealer in foodstuffs —**'groceries** *pl.n.* commodities sold by grocer —**'grocery** *n.* trade, premises of grocer

grog (grog) *n.* spirit (*esp.* rum) and water —**'groggy** *a. inf.* unsteady, shaky, weak

groin (groin) *n.* **1.** fold where legs meet abdomen **2.** wall or jetty built out from river bank or shore to control erosion **3.** *Archit.* edge made by intersection of two vaults —*vt.* **4.** build with groins

groom (grōōm, grŏŏm) *n.* **1.** person caring for horses **2.** *see* **bridegroom** *at* BRIDE —*vt.* **3.** tend or look after **4.** brush or clean (*esp.* horse) **5.** train (someone for something) —**'groomsman** *n.* friend attending bridegroom —**well-groomed** *a.* neat, smart

groove (grōōv) *n.* **1.** narrow channel, hollow, *esp.* cut by tool **2.** rut, routine —*vt.* **3.** cut groove in —**'groovy** *a. sl.* fashionable, exciting

grope (grōp) *vi.* feel about, search blindly

grosbeak ('grōsbēk) *n.* finch with large powerful bill

grosgrain ('grōgrān) *n.* heavy ribbed silk or rayon fabric —**grosgrain ribbon** ribbon used for trimming and reinforcing clothes *etc.*

gros point (grō) **1.** needlepoint stitch covering two horizontal and two vertical threads **2.** work done in this stitch

gross (grōs) *a.* **1.** very fat **2.** total, not net **3.** coarse **4.** indecent **5.** flagrant **6.** thick, rank —*n.* **7.** twelve dozen —**'grossly** *adv.* —**gross national product** total value of final goods and services produced annually by nation

grotesque (grō'tesk) *a.* **1.** (horribly) distorted **2.** absurd —*n.* **3.** 16th-cent. decorative style using distorted human, animal and plant forms **4.** grotesque person, thing —**gro'tesquely** *adv.*

grotto ('grotō) *n.* cave

grotty ('groti) *a. inf.* dirty, untidy, unpleasant

grouch (growch) *inf. n.* **1.** persistent grumbler **2.** discontented mood —*vi.* **3.** grumble, be peevish

ground[1] (grownd) *n.* **1.** surface of earth **2.** soil, earth **3.** (*oft. pl.*) reason, motive **4.** coating to work on with paint **5.** background, main surface worked on in painting, embroidery *etc.* **6.** special area **7.** bottom of sea —*pl.* **8.** dregs, *esp.* from coffee **9.** enclosed land round house —*vt.* **10.** establish **11.** instruct (in elements) **12.** place on ground —*vi.* **13.** run ashore —**'grounded** *a.* (of aircraft) unable or not permitted to fly —**'grounding** *n.* basic general knowledge of a subject —**'groundless** *a.* without reason —**ground ball** a batted baseball that rolls or bounces along the ground —**ground cloth** waterproof sheet for spreading on the ground (*also* **'groundsheet**) —**ground cover** low-growing perennial plants used as grass substitutes or to control erosion —**ground crew** group of people in charge of maintenance and repair of aircraft —**ground-effect machine** vehicle supported above surface of ground or water by cushion of air, used for mowing grass or traveling short distances (*also* **air-cushion vehicle**) —**ground floor** floor of building level or almost level with ground —**'groundhog** *n.* *see* **woodchuck** *at* WOOD —**ground ivy** trailing herb of the mint family with blue flowers (*also* **creeping Charlie, gill-over-the-ground**) —**'groundspeed** *n.* aircraft's speed in relation to ground —**ground swell 1.** considerable swell of sea, oft. caused by distant storm **2.** rapidly developing general opinion —**'groundwork** *n.* **1.** preliminary work as foundation or basis **2.** ground or background of painting *etc.* —**get in on the ground floor** *inf.* be in project *etc.* from its inception

ground[2] (grownd) *pt./pp. of* GRIND

groundsel ('grownsəl) *n.* Eurasian yellow-flowered weed

group (gro͞op) *n.* **1.** number of persons or things considered as collective unit **2.** number of persons bound together by common interests *etc.* **3.** small musical band of players or singers **4.** class **5.** two or more figures forming one artistic design —*v.* **6.** place, fall into group —**group therapy** simultaneous treatment of number of individuals brought together to share their problems in group discussion

grouper ('gro͞opər) *n.* large bottom-feeding food fish of tropical seas (*pl.* **-s, grouper**)

grouse[1] (grows) *n.* **1.** game bird **2.** its flesh (*pl.* **grouse**)

grouse[2] (grows) *vi.* **1.** grumble, complain —*n.* **2.** complaint —**'grouser** *n.* grumbler

grout (growt) *n.* **1.** thin fluid mortar —*vt.* **2.** fill up with grout

grove (grōv) *n.* **1.** small group of trees **2.** road lined with trees

grovel ('grovəl, 'gruv-) *vi.* **1.** abase oneself **2.** lie face down

grow (grō) *vi.* **1.** develop naturally **2.** increase in size, height *etc.* **3.** be produced **4.** become by degrees —*vt.* **5.** produce by cultivation (**grew** *pt.*, **grown** *pp.*) —**growth** *n.* **1.** growing **2.** increase **3.** what has grown or is growing —**growing pains 1.** pains in joints sometimes experienced by growing children **2.** difficulties besetting new enterprise in early stages —**grown-up** *a./n.* adult

growl (growl) *vi.* **1.** make low guttural sound of anger **2.** rumble **3.** murmur, complain —*n.* **4.** act or sound of growling

grub (grub) *vt.* **1.** (*oft. with* up *or* out) dig superficially **2.** root up —*vi.* **3.** dig, rummage **4.** plod (**-bb-**) —*n.* **5.** larva of insect **6.** *sl.* food —**'grubby** *a.* dirty

grudge (gruj) *vt.* **1.** be unwilling to give, allow —*n.* **2.** ill will

gruel ('gro͞oəl) *n.* food of oatmeal *etc.*, boiled in milk or water —**'grueling** *or* **'gruelling** *a./n.* exhausting, severe (experience)

gruesome ('gro͞osəm) *a.* fearful, horrible, grisly —**'gruesomeness** *n.*

gruff (gruf) *a.* rough in manner or voice, surly —**'gruffly** *adv.*

grumble ('grumbəl) *vi.* **1.** complain **2.** rumble, murmur **3.** make growling sounds —*n.* **4.** complaint **5.** low growl —**'grumbler** *n.*

grumpy ('grumpi) *a.* ill-tempered, surly —**'grumpily** *adv.*

grunt (grunt) *vi.* **1.** make sound characteristic of pig —*n.* **2.** deep, hoarse sound of pig **3.** gruff noise

Gruyère (gro͞o'yāər) *n.* a cooked, hard cheese, pale yellow in color, honeycombed with holes, made from whole cow's milk, orig. from Switzerland

gryphon ('grifən) *n. see* GRIFFIN

G.S. 1. General Staff **2.** ground speed

GSA General Services Administration

G-string *n.* **1.** very small covering for genitals **2.** *Mus.* string tuned to G

G-suit *n.* close-fitting garment worn by crew of high-speed aircraft, pressurized to prevent blackout during maneuvers

Guam (gwäm) *n.* island in the western Pacific Ocean, a territory of the U.S.

guanaco (gwə'näkō) *n.* cud-chewing S Amer. mammal closely related to domesticated llama (*pl.* **-s**)

guano ('gwänō) *n.* sea bird manure (*pl.* **-s**)

Guarani (gwärə'nē) *n.* Amerindian language spoken in Paraguay

guarantee (garən'tē) *n.* **1.** formal assurance, *esp.* in writing, that product *etc.* will meet certain standards, last for given time *etc.* —*vt.* **2.** give guarantee of, for something **3.** secure (against risk *etc.*) (**guaran'teed, guaran'teeing**) —**guaran'tor** *n.* one who undertakes fulfillment of another's promises —**'guaranty** *n.* **1.** pledge of responsibility for fulfilling another person's obligations in case of default **2.** thing given or taken as security for guaranty **3.** act of providing security **4.** guarantor —*v.* **5.** guarantee

guard (gärd) *vt.* **1.** protect, defend —*vi.* **2.** be careful, take precautions —*n.* **3.** person, group that protects, supervises, keeps watch **4.** sentry **5.** soldiers protecting anything **6.** protection **7.** screen for enclosing anything dangerous **8.** protector **9.** posture of defense —*pl.* **10.** (**G-**) any of certain British regiments —**'guarded** *a.* **1.** kept under surveillance **2.** prudent, restrained or noncommittal —**'guardedly** *adv.* —**'guardian** *n.* **1.** keeper, protector **2.** person having custody of infant *etc.* —**'guardianship** *n.* care —**'guardhouse** *or* **'guardroom** *n.* place for stationing those on guard or for prisoners —**'guardsman** *n.* soldier in Guards

Guarnerius (gwär'nēəriəs, -'ner-) *n.* violin

made by member of the Guarnerius family, called 'dark Strad'

Guatemala (gwäti'mälə) *n.* country in Central America bounded on the north and west by Mexico, south by the Pacific Ocean and east by El Salvador, Honduras and Belize

guava ('gwävə) *n.* tropical tree with fruit used to make jelly

gubernatorial (go͞obərnə'tōriəl, gyo͞o-) *a.* of or relating to governor

gudgeon[1] ('gujən) *n.* small freshwater fish

gudgeon[2] ('gujən) *n.* **1.** pivot bearing **2.** socket for rudder **3.** kind of connecting pin

guelder-rose (geldər'rōz) *n.* shrub with clusters of white flowers

guerdon ('gərdən) *n.* reward

Guernsey ('gərnzi) *n.* **1.** breed of cattle **2.** close-fitting knitted sweater

guerrilla *or* **guerilla** (gə'rilə) *n.* member of irregular armed force, *esp.* fighting established force, government *etc.*

guess (ges) *vt.* **1.** estimate without calculation **2.** conjecture, suppose **3.** consider, think —*vi.* **4.** form conjectures —*n.* **5.** estimate —'**guesstimate** *n.* estimate based on guesswork and experience —'**guesswork** *n.* **1.** set of conclusions *etc.* arrived at by guessing **2.** process of making guesses

guest (gest) *n.* **1.** one entertained at another's house **2.** one living in hotel —**guest of honor** person honored by a social occasion —**guest room** room in house reserved for guest

guff (guf) *n. sl.* silly talk

guffaw (gu'fö) *n.* **1.** burst of boisterous laughter —*vi.* **2.** laugh in this way

guide (gīd) *n.* **1.** one who shows the way **2.** adviser **3.** book of instruction or information **4.** contrivance for directing motion —*vt.* **5.** lead, act as guide to **6.** arrange —'**guidance** *n.* —**guided missile** missile whose flight path is controlled by radio or preprogrammed homing mechanism —**guide dog** dog trained to lead blind person —'**guideline** *n.* principle put forward to determine course of action —**guide word** word at head of page of alphabetical reference book giving the first or last word on the page

guidon ('gīdon, -dən) *n.* **1.** pennant, used as marker, *esp.* by cavalry regiments **2.** man or vehicle that carries this

guild *or* **gild** (gild) *n.* **1.** organization, club **2.** society for mutual help, or with common object **3.** *Hist.* society of merchants or tradesmen —'**guildhall** *n.* meeting place of guild or corporation

guilder ('gildər) *or* **gulden** ('go͞oldən, 'go͞ol-) *n.* **1.** standard monetary unit of Netherlands (*also* '**gilder**) **2.** former gold or silver coin of Germany, Austria or Netherlands (*pl.* **-s, -der** *or* **-s, -den**)

guile (gīl) *n.* cunning, deceit —'**guileful** *a.* —'**guilefully** *adv.* —'**guileless** *a.*

guillemot ('gilimot) *n.* species of sea bird

guillotine ('gilətēn) *n.* **1.** device for beheading **2.** machine for cutting paper **3.** in legislature, method of restricting length of debate by fixing time for taking vote —*vt.* **4.** behead **5.** use guillotine on **6.** limit (debate) by guillotine

guilt (gilt) *n.* **1.** fact, state of having done wrong **2.** responsibility for criminal or moral offense —'**guiltily** *adv.* —'**guiltiness** *n.* —'**guiltless** *a.* innocent —'**guilty** *a.* having committed an offense

guinea pig

guinea ('gini) *n.* formerly, Brit. gold coin worth 21 shillings —**guinea fowl** bird allied to pheasant —**guinea pig 1.** rodent originating in S Amer. **2.** *inf.* person or animal used in experiments —**guinea worm** tropical roundworm parasite in humans

Guinea ('gini) *n.* country in W Africa bounded northwest by Guinea-Bissau and Senegal, northeast by Mali, southeast by the Ivory Coast, south by Liberia and Sierra Leone and west by the Atlantic Ocean

Guinea-Bissau (ginibi'sow) *n.* country in Africa bounded north by Senegal, west by the Atlantic Ocean and east and south by Guinea

guipure (gi'pyo͝oər, -'po͝oər) *n.* **1.** any of many types of lace that have their pattern connected by threads, rather than supported on net mesh (*also* **guipure lace**) **2.** heavy corded trimming; gimp

guise (gīz) *n.* external appearance, *esp.* one assumed

guitar (gi'tär) *n.* plucked, stringed musical instrument with a flat, waisted body, long fretted neck and six strings —**gui'tarist** *n.* —**bass guitar** guitar with 12 strings and lower register —**electric** *or* **steel guitar** guitar with solid body which merely supports the strings as sound is produced by an electric amplifying system —**Hawaiian guitar** ukulele

Gulag ('go͞olag) *n.* central administrative department of Soviet security service, responsible for prisons, labor camps *etc.*

gulch (gulch) *n.* **1.** ravine **2.** gully

gulf (gulf) *n.* **1.** large inlet of the sea **2.** chasm **3.** large gap —**Gulf Stream** warm ocean current flowing from Gulf of Mexico toward NW Europe (*also* **North Atlantic Drift**) —'**gulfweed** *n.* seaweed forming dense floating masses in tropical Atlantic waters, *esp.* Gulf Stream (*also* **sar'gasso, sargasso weed**)

gull[1] (gul) *n.* long-winged web-footed sea bird

gull[2] (gul) *n.* **1.** dupe, fool —*vt.* **2.** dupe, cheat —**gulli'bility** *n.* —**'gullible** *a.* easily imposed on, credulous

gullet ('gulit) *n.* food passage from mouth to stomach

gully ('guli) *n.* channel or ravine worn by water

gulp (gulp) *vt.* **1.** swallow eagerly —*vi.* **2.** gasp, choke —*n.* **3.** act of gulping

gum[1] (gum) *n.* firm flesh in which teeth are set —**'gummy** *a.* toothless —**'gumboil** *n.* abscess on gum

gum[2] (gum) *n.* **1.** sticky substance issuing from certain trees **2.** an adhesive **3.** chewing gum —*vt.* **4.** stick with gum (**-mm-**) —**'gummy** *a.* —**gum arabic** water-soluble gum obtained from some acacias used in manufacture of adhesives, confectionery and drugs —**gum resin** mixture of resin and gum obtained from various plants and trees —**'gumtree** *n.* any species of eucalyptus —**gum up the works** *inf.* impede progress —**up a gumtree** *sl.* in a difficult position

gumption ('gumpshən) *n.* **1.** resourcefulness **2.** shrewdness, sense

gun (gun) *n.* **1.** weapon with metal tube from which missiles are discharged by explosion **2.** cannon, pistol *etc.* —*vt.* **3.** (*oft. with* down) shoot **4.** race (engine of motor vehicle) —*vi.* **5.** hunt with gun (**-nn-**) —**'gunner** *n.* —**'gunnery** *n.* use or science of large guns —**'gunboat** *n.* small warship —**gunboat diplomacy** diplomacy conducted by threats of military intervention —**'guncotton** *n.* cellulose nitrate containing large amount of nitrogen: used as explosive —**gun dog** (breed of) dog used to find or retrieve game —**'gunman** *n.* armed criminal —**'gunmetal** *n.* **1.** alloy of copper and tin or zinc, formerly used for guns **2.** color of gunmetal: pewter gray —*a.* **3.** of this color —**'gunpoint** *n.* muzzle of gun —**'gunpowder** *n.* explosive mixture of saltpeter, sulfur and charcoal —**'gunrunner** *n.* —**'gunrunning** *n.* smuggling of guns and ammunition into country —**'gunshot** *n.* **1.** shot or range of gun —*a.* **2.** caused by missile from gun —**'gunstock** *n.* wooden handle or support to which is attached barrel of rifle —**gunwale** *or* **gunnel** ('gunəl) *n.* upper edge of ship's side —**at gunpoint** under threat of being shot

gunny ('guni) *n.* strong, coarse sacking made from jute

guppy ('gupi) *n.* small aquarium fish

gurgle ('gərgəl) *n.* **1.** bubbling noise —*vi.* **2.** utter, flow with gurgle

Gurkha ('gərkə) *n.* **1.** any of a warlike people in Nepal **2.** member of this people serving as soldier in British army

gurnard ('gərnərd) *n.* spiny armor-headed sea fish; sea robin

guru (gə'ro͞o, 'go͝oro͞o) *n.* **1.** Hindu spiritual teacher **2.** influential or revered teacher

gush (gush) *vi.* **1.** flow out suddenly and copiously, spurt —*n.* **2.** sudden and copious flow **3.** effusiveness —**'gusher** *n.* **1.** gushing person **2.** something, such as spurting oil well, that gushes

gusset ('gusit) *n.* triangle or diamond-shaped piece of material let into garment —**'gusseted** *a.*

gust (gust) *n.* **1.** sudden blast of wind **2.** burst of rain, anger, passion *etc.* —**'gusty** *a.*

gustation (gu'stāshən) *n.* act of tasting or faculty of taste —**'gustatory** *a.*

gusto ('gustō) *n.* enjoyment, zest

gut (gut) *n.* **1.** (*oft. pl.*) entrails, intestines **2.** material made from guts of animals, *eg* for violin strings *etc.* —*pl.* **3.** *inf.* essential, fundamental part **4.** courage —*vt.* **5.** remove guts from (fish *etc.*) **6.** remove, destroy contents of (house) (**-tt-**) —**'gutless** *a. inf.* lacking courage —**'gutsy** *a. inf.* **1.** greedy **2.** courageous

gutta-percha (gutə'pərchə) *n.* (tropical tree producing) whitish rubber substance

gutter ('gutər) *n.* **1.** shallow trough for carrying off water from roof or side of street —*vt.* **2.** make channels in —*vi.* **3.** flow in streams **4.** (of candle) melt away by wax forming channels and running down —**gutter press** journalism that relies on sensationalism —**'guttersnipe** *n.* **1.** neglected slum child **2.** mean vindictive person

guttural ('gutərəl) *a.* **1.** of, relating to, or produced in, the throat —*n.* **2.** guttural sound or letter

guy[1] (gī) *n. inf.* a man

guy[2] (gī) *n.* **1.** rope, chain to steady, secure something (*eg* tent) —*vt.* **2.** keep in position by guy —**'guyrope** *n.*

Guyana (gī'anə) *n.* country in South America bounded northeast by the Atlantic Ocean, east by Suriname, south and west by Brazil and west by Venezuela

guzzle ('guzəl) *v.* eat or drink greedily

gybe (jīb) *vi. see* JIBE[1]

gym (jim) *n.* **1.** gymnasium **2.** gymnastics —**gym shoes** rubber-soled shoes worn in gymnasium —**gym suit** clothing worn for gym class

gymnasium (jim'nāziəm) *n.* place equipped for muscular exercises, athletic training (*pl.* **-s, -nasia** (-'nāziə)) —**'gymnast** *n.* expert in gymnastics —**gym'nastics** *pl.n.* sport in which both prescribed and optional physical exercises must be performed in an artistic yet formally correct manner

gymnosperm ('jimnəspərm) *n.* seed-bearing plant in which ovules are borne naked on open scales: all conifers, sago palm, ginkgo, Mormon tea bush

gynecology (gīni'koləji) *n.* branch of medicine dealing with diseases and disorders of females, *esp.* the reproductive organs —**gy-**

neco'logical *or* **gyneco'logic** *a.* —**gyne'cologist** *n.*

gyp (jip) *sl. vt.* **1.** swindle, cheat, defraud (**-pp-**) —*n.* **2.** act of cheating **3.** person who gyps

gypsophila (jip'sofilə) *n.* garden plant with small white or pink flowers

gypsum ('jipsəm) *n.* crystalline sulfate of lime: source of plaster

Gypsy *or* **Gipsy** ('jipsi) *n.* one of wandering race originally from NW India, Romany

gyrate ('jīrāt) *vi.* move in circle, spirally, revolve —**gy'ration** *n.* —**gy'rational** *a.* —**gyratory** ('jīrətōri) *a.* revolving, spinning

gyrfalcon *or* **gerfalcon** ('jərfalkən, -föl-) *n.* large, rare falcon

gyro ('jīrō) *n.* **1.** *see* GYROCOMPASS **2.** *see* GYROSCOPE (*pl.* **-s**)

gyro- *or before vowel* **gyr-** (*comb. form*) **1.** rotating or gyrating motion, as in *gyroscope* **2.** gyroscope, as in *gyrocompass*

gyrocompass ('jīrōkumpəs) *n.* compass using gyroscope to indicate true north

gyroscope ('jīrəskōp) *n.* disk or wheel so mounted as to be able to rotate about any axis, *esp.* to keep disk (with compass *etc.*) level despite movement of ship *etc.* —**gyroscopic** (jīrə'skopik) *a.*

gyrostabilizer (jīrō'stābilīzər) *n.* gyroscopic device to prevent rolling of ship or airplane

gyve (jīv, gīv) *obs. vt.* **1.** shackle, fetter —*n.* **2.** (*usu. pl.*) fetter

H

h *or* **H 1.** eighth letter of English alphabet **2.** speech sound represented by this letter **3.** something shaped like an H

H 1. *Chem.* hydrogen **2.** (of pencils) hard

ha hectare

Habacuc (ˈhabəkuk) *n. Bible* Habakkuk in the Douay Version of the O.T.

Habakkuk (ˈhabəkuk) *n. Bible* 35th book of the O.T., written by the prophet Habakkuk, a group of psalms on the triumph of justice and divine mercy over evil

habeas corpus (ˈhābiəs ˈkörpəs) writ issued to produce prisoner in court

haberdasher (ˈhabərdashər) *n.* dealer in articles of dress, ribbons, pins, needles *etc.* —**ˈhaberdashery** *n.*

habiliments (həˈbilimənts) *pl.n.* dress

habit (ˈhabit) *n.* **1.** settled tendency or practice **2.** constitution **3.** customary apparel, *esp.* of nun or monk **4.** woman's riding dress —**haˈbitual** *a.* **1.** formed or acquired by habit **2.** usual, customary —**haˈbitually** *adv.* —**haˈbituate** *vt.* accustom —**habituˈation** *n.* —**habitué** (həˈbichōōā) *n.* constant visitor

habitable (ˈhabitəbəl) *a.* fit to live in —**ˈhabitant** *n.* **C** (descendant of) original French settler —**ˈhabitat** *n.* natural home (of animal *etc.*) —**habiˈtation** *n.* dwelling place

hachure (haˈshōōər) *n.* shading of short lines drawn on relief map to indicate gradients

hacienda (hasiˈendə, asiˈendə) *n.* ranch or large estate in Spanish Amer.

hack[1] (hak) *vt.* **1.** cut, chop (at) violently **2.** *Sport* foul by kicking the shins —*vi.* **3.** *inf.* utter harsh, dry cough —*n.* **4.** cut or gash **5.** any tool used for shallow digging

hack[2] (hak) *n.* **1.** horse hired out for ordinary riding **2.** drudge, *esp.* writer of inferior literary works —**hack work** dull, repetitive work

hackle

hackle (ˈhakəl) *n.* **1.** neck feathers of turkey *etc.* —*pl.* **2.** hairs on back of neck of dog and other animals, which are raised in anger

hackney (ˈhakni) *n.* carriage or coach kept for hire

hackneyed (ˈhaknid) *a.* (of words *etc.*) stale, trite because of overuse

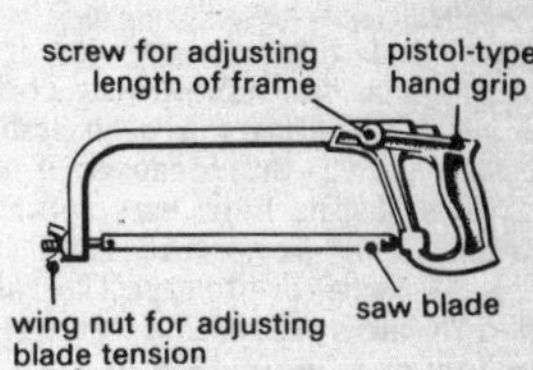

hacksaw

hacksaw (ˈhaksö) *n.* handsaw for cutting metal

had (had) *pt./pp. of* HAVE

haddock (ˈhadək) *n.* large, edible seafish

Hades (ˈhādēz) *n.* **1.** abode of the dead **2.** underworld **3.** hell

hadj (haj) *n. see* HAJJ

haemoglobin (ˈhēməglōbin) *n. see* HEMOGLOBIN

hafnium (ˈhafniəm) *n. Chem.* metallic element *Symbol* Hf, at. wt. 178.5, at. no. 72

haft (haft) *n.* **1.** handle (of knife *etc.*) —*vt.* **2.** provide with haft

hag (hag) *n.* **1.** ugly old woman **2.** witch —**hag-ridden** *a.* troubled, careworn

Haggadah (həˈgädə) *n. Judaism* reading at Passover Seder recounting Israel's bondage and flight from Egypt

Haggai (ˈhagiī, ˈhagī) *n. Bible* 37th book of the O.T., written by the prophet Haggai about 520 B.C. urging the renewal of work on restoring the temple after the Babylonian captivity

haggard (ˈhagərd) *a.* **1.** wild-looking **2.** anxious, careworn —*n.* **3.** *Falconry* untamed hawk

haggis (ˈhagis) *n.* Scottish dish made from sheep's heart, lungs, liver, chopped with oatmeal, suet, onion *etc.* and boiled in stomach-bag

haggle (ˈhagəl) *vi.* (*oft.* *with* over) bargain, wrangle (over price, terms *etc.*)

hagiology (hagiˈoləji) *n.* literature of the lives and legends of saints —**hagiˈographer** *n.* —**hagiˈography** *n.* writing of this

ha-ha[1] (ˈhäˈhä) *interj.* **1.** representation of the sound of laughter **2.** exclamation expressing derision, mockery *etc.*

ha-ha[2] (ˈhähä) *n.* sunken fence bordering garden *etc.*, that allows uninterrupted views from within

haiku (ˈhīkōō) *n.* epigrammatic Japanese verse form in 17 syllables (*pl.* **-ku**)

hail[1] (hāl) *n.* **1.** (shower of) pellets of ice **2.** intense shower, barrage —*v.* **3.** pour down as shower of hail —ˈ**hailstone** *n.*

hail[2] (hāl) *vt.* **1.** greet, *esp.* enthusiastically **2.** acclaim, acknowledge **3.** call —**hail from** come from —**Hail Mary** (ˈmāəri) *R.C.* prayer to the Virgin Mary consisting of salutation and plea for her intercession (*also* **Ave Maria**)

hair (hāər) *n.* **1.** filament growing from skin of mammals **2.** such filaments collectively —ˈ**hairiness** *n.* —ˈ**hairy** *a.* —ˈ**hairdo** *n.* way of dressing hair —ˈ**hairdresser** *n.* one who attends to and cuts hair, *esp.* women's hair —ˈ**hairline** *a./n.* very fine (line) —ˈ**hairpiece** *n.* **1.** wig or toupee **2.** false hair attached to one's real hair to give it greater bulk or length —ˈ**hairpin** *n.* pin for keeping hair in place —**hairpin bend** U-shaped turn of road —**hair-raising** *a.* terrifying —**hair's-breadth** *n.* very short margin or distance —**hair shirt** rough shirt worn as penance by religious ascetics —ˈ**hairsplitting** *n.* making of overfine distinctions —ˈ**hairspring** *n.* very fine, delicate spring in timepiece —ˈ**hairstyle** *n.* —**hair trigger** trigger operated by light touch

Haiti (ˈhāti) *n.* country in the Caribbean occupying the western portion of the island of Hispaniola —**Haitian** (ˈhāshən, ˈhātiən) *a./n.*

hajj *or* **hadj** (haj) *n.* pilgrimage to Mecca that every Muslim is required to make —ˈ**hajji** *or* ˈ**hadji** *n.* Muslim who has made pilgrimage to Mecca (*pl.* **-s**)

hake (hāk) *n.* edible fish of the cod family

Halakah (häˈläkə) *n.* codification of laws of the Talmud

halberd (ˈhalbərd) *or* **halbert** *n.* combined spear and battleax

halcyon (ˈhalsiən) *n.* bird fabled to calm the sea and to breed on floating nest, kingfisher —**halcyon days** time of peace and happiness

hale[1] (hāl) *a.* robust, healthy (*esp. in* **hale and hearty**)

hale[2] (hāl) *vt.* pull; drag —ˈ**haler** *n.*

half (haf, häf) *n.* **1.** either of two equal parts of something (*pl.* **halves**) —*a.* **2.** forming half —*adv.* **3.** to the extent of half —**half-and-half** *n.* mixture of half one thing and half another thing, *esp.* half milk and half cream —ˈ**halfback** *n.* **1.** in football, one of two backs who line up on each side of the fullback **2.** in field hockey, rugby and soccer, player behind forwards —**half-baked** *a.* **1.** underdone **2.** *inf.* immature, silly —**half-blood** *n.* **1.** relationship between individuals having only one parent in common; individual having such relationship **2.** half-breed —**half-breed** *or* **half-caste** *n.* person with parents of different races —**half-brother, -sister** *n.* brother (sister) by one parent only —**half-cock** *n.* halfway position of firearm's hammer when trigger is locked —**half-cocked** *a.* ill-prepared —**half-dollar** *n.* (coin representing) 50 cents —**half-hardy** *a.* (of plant) being able to withstand low but not freezing temperature —**half-hearted** *a.* unenthusiastic —**half-hitch** *n.* knot made by passing end of piece of rope around itself and through loop thus made —**half hour** thirty minutes —**half-life** *n.* time taken for half the atoms in radioactive material to decay —**half-mast** *n.* (of flag) halfway position to which flag is lowered on mast to mourn dead —**half measures** inadequate measures or actions —**half-moon** *n.* the moon when its disk is half illuminated —**half-nelson** *n.* hold in wrestling —**half shell** half of mollusk shell for serving shellfish on —**half-size** *n.* clothing size for the full-figured woman —**half sole** sole of boot or shoe from shank to toe —**half-timbered** *or* **half-timber** *a.* (of building) having exposed timber framework filled with brick —**half-time** *n. Sport* rest period between two halves of game —**half-title** *n.* title of book as printed on right-hand page preceding title page —ˈ**halftone** *n.* illustration printed from relief plate, showing light and shadow by means of minute dots —**half-track** *n.* vehicle with caterpillar tracks on wheels that supply motive power only —**half-true** *a.* —**half-truth** *n.* partially true statement intended to mislead —**half volley** striking of ball the moment it bounces —ˈ**half**ˈ**way** *adv./a.* at or to half distance —**halfway house 1.** place to rest midway on journey **2.** halfway point in any progression **3.** center or hostel to facilitate readjustment to private life of released prisoners *etc.* —ˈ**halfwit** *n.* **1.** mentally retarded person **2.** stupid person —**by halves** imperfectly —**go halves** share expenses *etc.* equally —**half seas over** *inf.* drunk —**meet halfway** compromise with

halibut (ˈhalibət) *n.* large edible flatfish

halitosis (haliˈtōsis) *n.* bad-smelling breath

hall (hôl) *n.* **1.** (entrance) passage **2.** large room or building belonging to particular group or used for particular purpose, *esp.* public assembly —ˈ**hallway** *n.* hall or corridor —**Hall of Fame 1.** national shrine commemorating outstanding Americans at New York University in New York City **2.** place set aside to honor outstanding persons in any profession or location **3.** persons acclaimed as outstanding

hallelujah (haliˈlōōyə) *or* **alleluia** *n./interj.* exclamation of praise to God

hallmark (ˈhôlmärk) *n.* **1.** mark used to indicate standard of tested gold and silver **2.** mark of excellence **3.** distinguishing feature

hallo (həˈlō) *or* **halloo** (həˈlōō) *n.* **1.** call to spur on hunting dogs —*vi.* **2.** shout loudly

hallow (ˈhalō) *vt.* make or honor as holy —**Hallowe'en** *or* **Halloween** (halōˈēn) *n.* the evening of Oct. 31st, the day before Allhallows or All Saints' Day

hallucinate (hə'lōōsināt) *vi.* suffer illusions —**halluci'nation** *n.* illusion —**hal'lucinatory** *a.* —**hal'lucinogen** *n.* usu. illicit substance taken to produce vivid mental imagery

hallux vulgus ('haləks 'vulgəs) bunion

halo ('hālō) *n.* **1.** circle of light round moon, sun *etc.* **2.** disk of light round saint's head in picture **3.** aura surrounding admired person, thing *etc.* (*pl.* **-es, -s**) —*vt.* **4.** surround with halo

halogen ('haləjən) *n.* group of elements comprising fluorine, chlorine, bromine, iodine, astatine (in ascending atomic no. order) —**ha'logenous** *a.*

halophyte ('haləfīt) *n.* plant which grows in soil or water containing a high proportion of salt

halothane ('haləthān) *n.* nonexplosive inhaled anesthetic

halt[1] (hölt) *n.* **1.** interruption or end to progress *etc., esp.* as command to stop marching **2.** minor railroad station without station buildings —*v.* **3.** (cause to) stop

halt[2] (hölt) *vi.* falter, fail —**'halting** *a.* hesitant, lame

halter ('höltər) *n.* **1.** rope or strap with headgear to fasten horses or cattle **2.** low-cut dress style with strap passing behind neck **3.** noose for hanging a person —*vt.* **4.** put halter on

halvah *or* **halva** ('hälvä, 'hälvə) *n.* a sweet, sticky confection from the Middle East and India made of honey and sesame seeds or semolina and fruit

halve (hav, häv) *vt.* **1.** cut in half **2.** reduce to half **3.** share

halyard ('halyərd) *n.* rope for raising sail, signal flags *etc.*

ham (ham) *n.* **1.** meat, *esp.* salted or smoked, from thigh of pig **2.** actor adopting exaggerated, unconvincing style **3.** amateur radio enthusiast —*v.* **4.** overact (**-mm-**) —**'hammy** *a. inf.* **1.** (of actor) tending to overact **2.** (of play, performance *etc.*) overacted —**ham-fisted** *or* **ham-handed** *a.* clumsy —**'hamstring** *n.* **1.** tendon at back of knee —*vt.* **2.** cripple by cutting this —**'hamstrung** *a.* **1.** crippled **2.** thwarted —**hamstring muscle** any of three muscles at back of thigh that flex and rotate the leg

hamadryad (hamə'drīəd) *n. Class. myth.* nymph which inhabits tree and dies with it

hamburger ('hambərgər) *n.* broiled or fried patty of ground beef, *esp.* served in bread roll

Hamitic (ha'mitik, hə-) *n.* **1.** group of N Afr. languages related to Semitic —*a.* **2.** denoting this group of languages **3.** denoting Hamites, group of peoples of N Afr., including ancient Egyptians, supposedly descended from Noah's son Ham

hamlet ('hamlit) *n.* small village

hammer ('hamər) *n.* **1.** tool usu. with heavy head at end of handle, for beating, driving nails *etc.* **2.** machine with similar function **3.** contrivance for exploding charge of gun **4.** auctioneer's mallet **5.** metal ball on wire thrown in sports —*v.* **6.** strike (blows) with, or as with, hammer —**'hammerhead** *n.* shark with wide, flattened head —**'hammertoe** *n.* deformed toe —**hammer and sickle** emblem on flag of Soviet Union, representing industrial workers and peasants respectively —**hammer out** solve problem by full investigation of difficulties

hammock ('hamək) *n.* bed of canvas *etc.*, hung on cords

Hammond organ ('hamənd) trade name of musical instrument shaped like small piano with two keyboards which generates tone electronically

hamper[1] ('hampər) *n.* **1.** large covered basket **2.** large parcel, box *etc.* of food, wines *etc., esp.* one sent as Christmas gift

hamper[2] ('hampər) *vt.* impede, obstruct movements of

hamster ('hamstər) *n.* rodent with cheek pouches for carrying grain, sometimes kept as pet

hand (hand) *n.* **1.** extremity of arm beyond wrist **2.** side, quarter, direction **3.** style of writing **4.** cards dealt to player **5.** measure of four inches **6.** manual worker **7.** sailor **8.** help, aid **9.** pointer on dial **10.** applause —*vt.* **11.** pass **12.** deliver **13.** hold out —**'handful** *n.* **1.** small quantity or number **2.** *inf.* person or thing causing problems (*pl.* **-s**) —**'handily** *adv.* —**'handiness** *n.* **1.** dexterity **2.** state of being near, available —**'handy** *a.* **1.** convenient **2.** clever with the hands —**'handbag** *n.* **1.** woman's bag for personal articles **2.** bag for carrying in hand —**'handball** *n.* indoor or outdoor court game for two or four players in which object is to hit a small hard ball with a gloved hand against a wall so that opponent cannot return the ball before it bounces twice —**'handbill** *n.* small printed notice —**'handbook** *n.* small reference or instruction book —**'handcart** *n.* cart drawn or pushed by hand —**'handcuff** *n.* **1.** fetter for wrist, usu. joined in pair —*vt.* **2.** secure thus —**'handicraft** *n.* manual occupation or skill —**'handiwork** *n.* thing done by particular person —**handkerchief** ('hangkərchif, -chēf) *n.* **1.** small square of fabric carried in pocket for wiping nose *etc.* **2.** neckerchief —**handkerchief linen** *see* **Irish linen** *at* IRELAND —**hand-me-down** *n. inf.* **1.** something, *esp.* outgrown garment, passed down from one person to another **2.** anything already used by another —**hand-out** *n.* **1.** money, food *etc.* given free **2.** pamphlet giving news, information *etc.* —**hand-pick** *vt.* select with great care —**hand-picked** *a.* —**'handset** *n.* telephone mouthpiece and earpiece mounted as single unit —**hands-on** *a.* involving active participation and operating experience —ˈ**handspring** *n.* gymnastic feat in which person leaps forward or backward into handstand and then on to his feet —ˈ**handstand** *n.* act of supporting body in upside-down position by hands alone —**hand-to-hand** *a./adv.* at close quarters —**hand-to-mouth** *a./adv.* with barely enough money or food to satisfy immediate needs —ˈ**handwriting** *n.* way person writes —ˈ**handyman** *n.* **1.** man employed to do various tasks **2.** man skilled in odd jobs —**hand in glove with** very intimate with

handicap (ˈhandikap) *n.* **1.** something that hampers or hinders **2.** race, contest in which chances are equalized by starts, weights carried *etc.* **3.** condition so imposed **4.** any physical disability —*vt.* **5.** hamper **6.** impose handicaps on (**-pp-**) —ˈ**handicapped** *a.* physically or mentally disabled

handle (ˈhandəl) *n.* **1.** part of utensil *etc.* which is to be held —*vt.* **2.** touch, feel with hands **3.** manage **4.** deal with **5.** trade —ˈ**handler** *n.* **1.** person who trains and controls animals **2.** trainer or second of boxer —ˈ**handlebars** *pl.n.* curved metal bar used to steer bicycle, motorcycle *etc.*

handsome (ˈhansəm) *a.* **1.** of fine appearance **2.** generous **3.** ample —ˈ**handsomely** *adv.*

hang (hang) *vt.* **1.** suspend **2.** kill by suspension by neck (**hanged** *pt./pp.*) **3.** attach, set up (wallpaper, doors *etc.*) —*vi.* **4.** be suspended (**hung** *pt./pp.*) —ˈ**hanger** *n.* frame on which garment *etc.* can be hung —ˈ**hangdog** *a.* sullen, dejected —**hanger-on** *n.* sycophantic follower or dependant (*pl.* **hangers-on**) —**hang-glider** *n.* glider like large kite, with pilot hanging in frame below —**hang-gliding** *n.* —ˈ**hangman** *n.* executioner —ˈ**hangnail** *n.* piece of skin hanging loose at base or side of fingernail —ˈ**hangover** *n.* aftereffects of too much drinking —**hang-up** *n. inf.* persistent emotional problem —**hang out** *inf.* reside, frequent

hangar (ˈhangər) *n.* building for aircraft

hank (hangk) *n.* coil, skein, length, *esp.* as measure of yarn

hanker (ˈhangkər) *vi.* (*with* for *or* after) have a yearning

hanky *or* **hankie** (ˈhangki) *n. inf.* handkerchief

hanky-panky (hangkiˈpangki) *n. inf.* **1.** trickery **2.** illicit sexual relations

Hansard (ˈhansərd, ˈhansärd) *n.* official printed record of speeches, debates *etc.* in Brit., Aust. and other parliaments

Hanseatic League (hansiˈatik) commercial organization of towns in N Germany formed to protect and control trade

Hansen's disease (ˈhansənz) leprosy

hansom (ˈhansəm) *n.* (*sometimes* **H-**) two-wheeled horse-drawn cab for two to ride inside with driver mounted up behind

haphazard (hapˈhazərd) *a.* **1.** random **2.** careless

hapless (ˈhaplis) *a.* unlucky

haploid (ˈhaploid) *n.* cell having half the basic number of chromosomes

happen (ˈhapən) *vi.* **1.** come about, occur **2.** chance (to do) —ˈ**happening** *n.* occurrence, event

happy (ˈhapi) *a.* **1.** glad **2.** content **3.** lucky, fortunate **4.** apt —ˈ**happily** *adv.* —ˈ**happiness** *n.* —**happy-go-lucky** *a.* casual, light-hearted

hara-kiri (hariˈkiri) *n.* in Japan, ritual suicide by disemboweling

harangue (həˈrang) *n.* **1.** vehement speech **2.** tirade —*v.* **3.** address (person or crowd) in angry, forceful or persuasive way

harass (həˈras, ˈharəs) *vt.* worry, trouble, torment —**haˈrassment** *n.*

harbinger (ˈhärbinjər) *n.* **1.** one who announces another's approach **2.** forerunner, herald

harbor (ˈhärbər) *n.* **1.** shelter for ships **2.** shelter —*vt.* **3.** give shelter or protection to **4.** maintain (secretly) (*esp.* grudge *etc.*)

hard (härd) *a.* **1.** firm, resisting pressure **2.** solid **3.** difficult to understand **4.** harsh, unfeeling **5.** difficult to bear **6.** practical, shrewd **7.** heavy **8.** strenuous **9.** (of water) not making lather well with soap **10.** (of drugs) highly addictive —*adv.* **11.** vigorously **12.** with difficulty **13.** close —ˈ**harden** *v.* —ˈ**hardly** *adv.* **1.** unkindly, harshly **2.** scarcely, not quite **3.** only just —ˈ**hardness** *n.* —ˈ**hardship** *n.* **1.** ill luck **2.** severe toil, suffering **3.** instance of this —ˈ**hardback** *n.* **1.** book bound in stiff covers —*a.* **2.** of or denoting hardback or publication of hardbacks (*also* ˈ**casebound,** ˈ**hardbound,** ˈ**hardcover**) —**hard-bitten** *a. inf.* tough and realistic —ˈ**hardboard** *n.* thin stiff sheet made of compressed sawdust and woodchips with one smooth face —**hard-boiled** *a.* **1.** (of egg) cooked sufficiently long to solidify white and yolk **2.** *inf.* (of person) experienced, unemotional, unsympathetic —**hard copy** *Comp.* output that can be read by eye —**hard core 1.** members of group who form intransigent nucleus resisting change **2.** material, such as broken stones, used to form foundation for road *etc.* —**hard-core** *a.* **1.** (of pornography) depicting sexual acts in explicit detail **2.** completely established in belief *etc.* —**hard court** tennis court with hard surface —**hard-headed** *a.* shrewd —**hardˈhearted** *a.* unkind or intolerant —**hardˈheartedness** *n.* —**hard labor** formerly, penalty of compulsory labor in addition to imprisonment —**hard line** uncompromising course or policy —ˈ**hardˈliner** *n.* —**hard palate** anterior bony portion of roof of mouth —**hard paste** basis of vitreous porcelain —**hard-pressed** *a.* **1.** in difficulties **2.** closely pursued —**hard sell** aggressive technique of selling or advertising —ˈ**hard-**

ware *n.* 1. tools, implements 2. necessary (parts of) machinery 3. *Comp.* mechanical and electronic parts —**hard water** water with large concentration of ions *esp.* calcium, magnesium and iron —**hard wheat** wheat high in gluten for making bread —ˈ**hardwood** *n.* heavy wood from certain deciduous trees, *eg* oak, teak —**hard of hearing** rather deaf —**hard up** very short of money

Harding (ˈhärding) *n.* **Warren Gamaliel.** the 29th President of the U.S. (1921-23)

hardy (ˈhärdi) *a.* 1. robust, vigorous 2. bold 3. (of plants) able to grow in the open all year round —ˈ**hardihood** *n.* extreme boldness, audacity —ˈ**hardily** *adv.* —ˈ**hardiness** *n.*

hare (hāər) *n.* animal like large rabbit, with longer legs and ears, noted for speed —ˈ**harebell** *n.* plant with slender stems and leaves and bell-shaped blue flowers —**hare-ˈbrained** *a.* rash, wild —**hareˈlip** *n.* fissure of upper lip (*also* **cleft lip**) —**hare and hounds** paper chase

Hare Krishna (ˈhäri ˈkrishnə) member of religious movement founded by Swami Prabhupada in the U.S. in 1965, based on the founder's transcription of the Bhagavad Gita

harem (ˈharəm, ˈher-) *n.* 1. women's part of Muslim dwelling 2. one man's wives collectively —**harem pants** full trousers for women gathered at ankles —**harem skirt** full straight-cut skirt gathered or pleated onto a band at knees or ankles

haricot (ˈharikō) *n.* type of French bean that can be dried and stored

hark (härk) *vi.* listen —**hark back** return (to previous subject of discussion)

harken (ˈhärkən) *vi. see* HEARKEN

harlequin (ˈhärlikwin) *n.* 1. stock comic character, *esp.* masked clown in diamond-patterned costume —*a.* 2. multicolored

Harley Street (ˈhärli) street in central London famous for its large number of medical specialists' consulting rooms

harlot (ˈhärlət) *n.* whore, prostitute —ˈ**harlotry** *n.*

harm (härm) *n.* 1. damage, injury —*vt.* 2. cause harm to —ˈ**harmful** *a.* —ˈ**harmfully** *adv.* —ˈ**harmless** *a.* unable or unlikely to hurt —ˈ**harmlessly** *adv.*

harmony (ˈhärməni) *n.* 1. agreement 2. concord 3. peace 4. *Mus.* combination of notes to make chords 5. melodious sound —**harmonic** (härˈmonik) *a.* 1. of harmony —*n.* 2. tone or note whose frequency is a multiple of its pitch —**harmonica** (härˈmonikə) *n.* small wind instrument played with mouth —**harmonics** (härˈmoniks) *pl.n.* 1. (*with sing. v.*) science of musical sounds 2. harmonious sounds —**harˈmonious** *a.* —**harˈmoniously** *adv.* —ˈ**harmonist** *n.* —**harˈmonium** *n.* keyboard musical instrument whose tones are produced by thin metal tongues or reeds set in motion by foot-operated bellows —**harmoniˈzation** *n.* —ˈ**harmonize** *vt.* 1. bring into harmony 2. cause to agree 3. reconcile —*vi.* 4. be in harmony 5. sing in harmony, as with other singers

harness (ˈhärnis) *n.* 1. equipment for attaching horse to cart, plow *etc.* 2. any such equipment —*vt.* 3. put on, in harness 4. utilize energy or power of (waterfall *etc.*) —**in harness** in or at one's routine work

harp (härp) *n.* 1. musical instrument of strings played by hand —*vi.* 2. play on harp 3. (*with* on *or* upon) dwell (on) continuously —ˈ**harper** *or* ˈ**harpist** *n.* —ˈ**harpsichord** *n.* stringed keyboard instrument resembling grand piano but differing from it as sound is produced by plucking, not striking, the strings

harpoon (härˈpo͞on) *n.* 1. barbed spear with rope attached for catching whales —*vt.* 2. catch, kill with or as if with a harpoon —**harˈpooner** *n.* —**harpoon gun** gun for firing harpoon in whaling

harpy (ˈhärpi) *n.* 1. monster with body of woman and wings and claws of bird 2. cruel, grasping person

harquebus (ˈhärkwibəs) *n.* heavy portable gun of 15th cent. usu. fired from support (*also* **arquebus**)

harridan (ˈharidən) *n.* shrewish old woman, hag

harrier (ˈhariər) *n.* 1. hound used in hunting hares 2. falcon 3. cross-country runner

Harrison[1] (ˈharisən) *n.* **Benjamin.** the 23rd President of the U.S. (1889-93)

Harrison[2] (ˈharisən) *n.* **William Henry.** the 9th President of the U.S. (Mar.-Apr. 1841)

Harrison Narcotic Act federal law of 1914 controlling the sale of certain drugs

Harris tweed (ˈharis) trade name for tweed spun, dyed and woven on the island of Lewis with Harris

harrow (ˈharō) *n.* 1. implement for smoothing, leveling, or stirring up soil —*vt.* 2. draw harrow over 3. distress greatly —ˈ**harrowing** *a.* 1. heart-rending 2. distressful

harry (ˈhari) *vt.* 1. harass 2. ravage (**-ried, -rying**)

harsh (härsh) *a.* 1. rough, discordant 2. severe 3. unfeeling —ˈ**harshly** *adv.*

hart (härt) *n.* male deer —**hartshorn** (ˈhärtshörn) *n.* material made from harts' horns, formerly chief source of ammonia

hartebeest (ˈhärtibēst) *n.* Afr. antelope

harum-scarum (harəmˈskarəm, herəmˈskerəm) *a.* 1. reckless, wild 2. giddy

harvest (ˈhärvist) *n.* 1. (season for) gathering in grain 2. gathering 3. crop 4. product of action —*v.* 5. reap and gather in (crop) —ˈ**harvester** *n.* —**harvest mite** chigger (*also* **red bug**)

has (haz) *third person sing. pres. indicative of* HAVE —**has-been** *n. inf.* person or thing that is no longer popular, successful *etc.*

hash (hash) *n.* **1.** dish of preserved or cooked meat mixed with potatoes and browned **2.** *inf.* hashish —*vt.* **3.** cut up into small pieces **4.** muddle, confuse —**hash browns** *or* **hash brown potatoes** diced boiled potatoes and onions formed into cake and fried —**hash-house** *n. sl.* cheap restaurant —**hash mark 1.** broken line on football field showing where ball may be returned to play **2.** service stripe on uniform of enlisted personnel —**make a hash of** mess up, bungle —**settle a person's hash** get rid of or subdue a person

hashish (ˈhashēsh, -ish) *n.* resinous extract of Indian hemp, *esp.* used as hallucinogen

Hasid (ˈhasid) *n.* sect of Jews holding fundamental, mystical, reactionary views identified by dress and customs (*pl.* **ˈHasidim**)

hasp (hasp) *n.* **1.** clasp passing over staple for fastening door *etc.* —*vt.* **2.** fasten, secure with hasp

hassle (ˈhasəl) *inf. n.* **1.** quarrel **2.** great deal of bother or trouble —*vi.* **3.** quarrel, fight —*vt.* **4.** harass (persistently)

hassock (ˈhasək) *n.* **1.** kneeling-cushion **2.** footstool for resting one's legs

hast (hast) *obs. second person sing. pres. indicative of* HAVE

haste (hāst) *n.* **1.** speed, quickness, hurry —*vi.* **2.** *Poet.* hasten —**hasten** (ˈhāsən) *v.* (cause to) hurry, increase speed —**ˈhastily** *adv.* —**ˈhasty** *a.*

hat (hat) *n.* head covering, usu. with brim —**ˈhatter** *n.* dealer in, maker of hats —**hat trick** any three successive achievements, *esp.* in sport

hatch[1] (hach) *v.* **1.** (of young, *esp.* of birds) (cause to) emerge from egg —*vt.* **2.** contrive, devise —**ˈhatchery** *n.*

hatch[2] (hach) *n.* **1.** hatchway **2.** trapdoor over it **3.** opening in wall or door, as service hatch, to facilitate service of meals *etc.* between two rooms **4.** lower half of divided door —**ˈhatchback** *n.* automobile with single lifting door in rear —**ˈhatchway** *n.* opening in deck of ship *etc.*

hatch[3] (hach) *vt.* **1.** engrave or draw lines on for shading **2.** shade with parallel lines

hatchet (ˈhachit) *n.* small ax —**hatchet job** *inf.* malicious verbal or written attack —**hatchet man** *inf.* person carrying out unpleasant assignments for another —**bury the hatchet** make peace

hate (hāt) *vt.* **1.** dislike strongly, bear malice toward —*n.* **2.** intense dislike **3.** that which is hated —**ˈhateful** *a.* detestable —**ˈhatefully** *adv.* —**hatred** (ˈhātrid) *n.* extreme dislike, active ill will

hauberk (ˈhöbərk) *n.* long coat of mail

haughty (ˈhöti) *a.* proud, arrogant —**ˈhaughtily** *adv.* —**ˈhaughtiness** *n.*

haul (höl) *vt.* **1.** pull, drag with effort —*vi.* **2.** (of wind) shift —*n.* **3.** hauling **4.** something that is hauled **5.** catch of fish **6.** acquisition **7.** distance (to be) covered —**ˈhaulage** *n.* **1.** carrying of loads **2.** charge for this —**ˈhaulier** *n.* firm, person that transports goods by road

haulm (höm) *n.* **1.** stalks of beans, potatoes, grasses *etc.* collectively **2.** single stem of such plant

haunch (hönch) *n.* **1.** human hip or fleshy hindquarter of animal **2.** leg and loin of venison

haunt (hönt) *vt.* **1.** visit regularly **2.** visit in form of ghost **3.** recur to —*n.* **4.** place frequently visited —**ˈhaunted** *a.* **1.** frequented by ghosts **2.** worried —**ˈhaunting** *a.* **1.** (of memories) poignant or persistent **2.** poignantly sentimental —**ˈhauntingly** *adv.*

hautbois *or* **hautboy** (ˈōboi) *n.* oboe

haute couture (ōt ko͞oˈtür) *Fr.* high fashion

hauteur (höˈtər, ōˈtər, hōˈtər) *n.* haughty spirit

Havana cigar (həˈvanə) fine quality of cigar (*also* **Haˈvana**)

have (hav) *vt.* **1.** hold, possess **2.** be possessed, affected with **3.** cheat, outwit **4.** engage in **5.** obtain **6.** contain **7.** allow **8.** cause to be (done) **9.** give birth to **10.** as auxiliary, forms perfect and other tenses (*pres. tense:* I *have,* thou *hast,* he *has,* we, you, they *have*) (**had, ˈhaving**) —**have to** be obliged to

haven (ˈhāvən) *n.* place of safety

Haverhill fever (ˈhāvəril) acute bacterial disease usu. transmitted by rat bites (*also* **streptobacillary fever**)

haversack (ˈhavərsak) *n.* canvas bag for provisions *etc.,* slung from shoulder when hiking

havoc (ˈhavək) *n.* **1.** devastation, ruin **2.** *inf.* confusion, chaos

haw (hö) *n.* **1.** fruit of hawthorn **2.** hawthorn

Hawaii (həˈwäyē) *n.* Pacific state of the U.S., admitted to the Union in 1960. Abbrev.: **HI** (with ZIP code)

hawfinch (ˈhöfinch) *n.* Eurasian finch

hawk[1] (hök) *n.* **1.** small-to-medium bird of prey with very short wings and long tail **2.** supporter, advocate of warlike policies —*vi.* **3.** hunt with hawks **4.** soar and swoop like hawk —**hawk-eyed** *a.* **1.** having extremely keen sight **2.** vigilant or observant

hawk[2] (hök) *vt.* offer (goods) for sale, as in street —**ˈhawker** *n.*

hawk[3] (hök) *vi.* clear throat noisily

hawse (höz) *n.* part of ship's bows with holes for cables

hawser (ˈhözər) *n.* large rope or cable

hawthorn (ˈhöthörn) *n.* thorny shrub or tree having pink or white flowers and reddish fruits (*also* **May, May tree**)

Hawthorne effect (ˈhöthörn) the change in output or results in a situation purely as an effect of applying different stimuli

hay (hā) *n.* grass mown and dried —**ˈhaybox** *n.* box filled with hay in which heated food is left to finish cooking —**hay fever** allergic reaction to pollen, dust *etc.* —'**haymaker** *n.* **1.** person who cuts or turns hay **2.** either of two machines, one designed to crush stems of hay, the other to break and bend them, in order to cause more rapid and even drying **3.** *Boxing sl.* wild swinging punch —'**haymaking** *a./n.* —'**haystack** *n.* large pile of hay —'**haywire** *a.* **1.** crazy **2.** disorganized

Hayes (hāz) *n.* **Rutherford Birchard.** the 19th President of the U.S. (1877-81)

hazard ('hazərd) *n.* **1.** chance **2.** risk, danger —*vt.* **3.** expose to risk **4.** run risk of —'**hazardous** *a.* risky

haze (hāz) *n.* **1.** mist, oft. due to heat **2.** obscurity —'**hazy** *a.* **1.** misty **2.** obscured **3.** vague

hazel ('hāzəl) *n.* **1.** bush bearing nuts **2.** yellowish-brown color of the nuts —*a.* **3.** light yellowish brown

Hb hemoglobin

H.B.C. Hudson's Bay Company

H-bomb hydrogen bomb

H.C.F. highest common factor

he (hē; *unstressed* ē) *pron.* **1.** (*third person masculine pronoun*) person, animal already referred to **2.** (*comb. form*) male, as in *he-goat* —**he-man** *n. inf.* strongly built muscular man

He *Chem.* helium

HE *or* **H.E. 1.** high explosive **2.** His Eminence **3.** His (*or* Her) Excellency

head (hed) *n.* **1.** upper part of person's or animal's body, containing mouth, sense organs and brain **2.** upper part of anything **3.** chief of organization, school *etc.* **4.** chief part **5.** aptitude, capacity **6.** culmination or crisis **7.** leader **8.** section of chapter **9.** title **10.** headland **11.** person, animal considered as unit **12.** white froth on beer *etc.* **13.** *inf.* headache —*a.* **14.** chief, principal **15.** (of wind) contrary —*vt.* **16.** be at the top, head of **17.** lead, direct **18.** provide with head **19.** hit (ball) with head —*vi.* **20.** (*with* for) make (for) **21.** form a head —'**header** *n.* **1.** *inf.* headlong fall or dive **2.** brick laid with end in face of wall **3.** action of striking ball with head —'**heading** *n.* **1.** direction **2.** title —**heads** *adv. inf.* with obverse side (of coin) uppermost —'**heady** *a.* apt to intoxicate or excite —'**headache** *n.* **1.** continuous pain in head **2.** *inf.* worrying circumstance —'**headboard** *n.* vertical board at head of bed —'**headdress** *n.* any head covering, *esp.* ornate one —'**headgear** *n.* **1.** hat, headdress *etc.* **2.** any part of horse's harness worn on head —**head-hunter** *n.* —**head-hunting** *n.* **1.** practice among certain peoples of removing heads of slain enemies and preserving them as trophies **2.** (of company or corporation) recruitment of, or drive to recruit, new high-level personnel —'**headland** *n.* promontory —'**headlight** *n.* powerful lamp carried on front of locomotive, motor vehicle *etc.* —'**headline** *n.* news summary, *usu.* in large type in newspaper —**head'long** *adv.* **1.** with head foremost **2.** with great haste —**head louse** louse that lives on the scalp of man —**head-on** *adv./a.* **1.** (of collision *etc.*) front foremost **2.** with directness —'**headphones** *pl.n.* two earphones held in position by strap over head (*also* (*inf.*) **cans**) —**head pin** foremost pin in arrangement of bowling pins —'**headquarters** *pl.n.* **1.** operational center of commander-in-chief **2.** center of administration —'**headroom** *or* '**headway** *n.* clear space between decks —'**headshrinker** *n.* **1.** *sl.* psychiatrist (*also* **shrink**) **2.** head-hunter who shrinks heads of his victims —'**headstall** *n.* part of bridle that fits round horse's head —**head start** initial advantage in competitive situation —'**headstone** *n.* gravestone —'**headstrong** *a.* self-willed —'**headwaters** *pl.n.* tributary streams of river —'**headway** *n.* advance, progress —'**headwind** *n.* wind blowing directly against course of aircraft or ship —'**headword** *n.* key word placed at beginning of line *etc.* as in dictionary entry —**come to a head** reach a crisis —**head and shoulders (above)** clearly superior (to) —**put heads together** pool ideas

heal (hēl) *v.* make or become well —**health** (helth) *n.* **1.** soundness of body **2.** condition of body **3.** toast drunk in person's honor —**healthily** ('helthili) *adv.* —**healthiness** ('helthinis) *n.* —**healthy** ('helthi) *a.* **1.** of strong constitution **2.** of or producing good health, wellbeing *etc.* **3.** vigorous

heap (hēp) *n.* **1.** pile of things lying one on another **2.** great quantity —*vt.* **3.** pile **4.** load (with)

hear (hēər) *vt.* **1.** perceive by ear **2.** listen to **3.** *Law* try (case) **4.** heed —*vi.* **5.** perceive sound **6.** (*with* of *or* about) learn (**heard** (hərd) *pt./pp.*) —'**hearer** *n.* —'**hearing** *n.* **1.** ability to hear **2.** earshot **3.** judicial examination —**hearing aid 1.** miniaturized amplifier designed to aid those with difficulty in hearing **2.** any device serving the same purpose, *eg* ear trumpet —'**hearsay** *n.* **1.** rumor —*a.* **2.** based on hearsay —**hear! hear!** exclamation of approval, agreement

hearken *or* **harken** ('härkən) *vi.* listen

hearse (hərs) *n.* funeral carriage for carrying coffin to grave

heart (härt) *n.* **1.** organ which makes blood circulate **2.** seat of emotions and affections **3.** mind, soul, courage **4.** central part **5.** playing card marked with symbol of heart **6.** one of these marks —*pl.* **7.** (*with sing. v.*) any of family of card games for two to six players each playing for himself, played with standard 52-card deck in which the object is to avoid taking certain cards or tricks —'**hearten** *v.* make, become cheerful —'**heartily** *adv.* —'**heartless** *a.* unfeeling —'**hearty** *a.* **1.** friendly **2.** vigorous **3.** in good health **4.** satisfying the appetite —'**heartache** *n.* intense anguish or mental suffering —**heart attack** sudden severe malfunction of heart —'**heartbreak** *n.* intense and overwhelming grief or disappointment —'**heartbreaking** *a.* —'**heartburn** *n.* burning sensation originating in the upper abdomen and moving behind the breastbone —**heart failure** **1.** inability of heart to pump adequate amount of blood to tissues **2.** sudden cessation of heartbeat, resulting in death —'**heartfelt** *a.* sincerely and strongly felt —'**heartfree** *a.* with the affections free or disengaged —**heart-lung machine** device which duplicates functions of heart and lungs —**heart-rending** *a.* **1.** overwhelming with grief **2.** agonizing —**heart-searching** *n.* examination of one's feelings or conscience —'**heartsease** *n.* wild pansy —**heart-throb** *n.* *sl.* object of infatuation —**heart-to-heart** *a.* **1.** (*esp.* of conversation) concerned with personal problems —*n.* **2.** intimate conversation —**heart-warming** *a.* **1.** pleasing; gratifying **2.** emotionally moving —'**heartwood** *n.* central core of dark hard wood in tree trunks —**by heart** memorized —**take to heart** be deeply troubled by —**wear one's heart on one's sleeve** let one's feelings show

hearth (härth) *n.* **1.** part of room where fire is made **2.** home

heat (hēt) *n.* **1.** hotness **2.** sensation of this **3.** hot weather or climate **4.** warmth of feeling, anger *etc.* **5.** sexual excitement caused by readiness to mate in female animals (*also* **estrus, estrum**) **6.** one of many races *etc.* to decide persons to compete in finals —*v.* **7.** make, become hot —'**heated** *a.* angry —'**heatedly** *adv.* —'**heater** *n.* any device for supplying heat, such as a convector —**heat cramp** painful contractions following heavy loss of body salts through perspiration —**heat exhaustion** inability of the circulatory system to adapt to additional demand of cooling the skin in a hot climate —**heat pump** device for extracting heat from substance that is at slightly higher temperature than its surroundings and delivering it to factory *etc.* at much higher temperature —**heat stroke** the breakdown of the heat-regulating mechanisms of the body, always fatal when untreated —**heat wave** continuous spell of abnormally hot weather

heath (hēth) *n.* **1.** tract of wasteland **2.** low-growing evergreen shrub

heathen ('hēdhən) *a.* **1.** not adhering to a religious system **2.** pagan **3.** barbarous **4.** unenlightened —*n.* **5.** heathen person (*pl.* **-s, 'heathen**) —'**heathendom** *n.* —'**heathenish** *a.* **1.** of or like heathen **2.** rough **3.** barbarous —'**heathenism** *n.*

heather ('hedhər) *n.* shrub growing on heaths and mountains —'**heathery** *a.*

heave (hēv) *vt.* **1.** lift with effort **2.** throw (something heavy) **3.** utter (sigh) —*vi.* **4.** swell, rise **5.** feel nausea —*n.* **6.** act or effort of heaving

heaven ('hevən) *n.* **1.** abode of God **2.** place of bliss **3.** (*also pl.*) sky —'**heavenly** *a.* **1.** lovely, delightful, divine **2.** beautiful **3.** of or like heaven

heavy ('hevi) *a.* **1.** weighty, striking, falling with force **2.** dense **3.** sluggish **4.** difficult, severe **5.** sorrowful **6.** serious **7.** dull —'**heavily** *adv.* —'**heaviness** *n.* —**heavy-duty** *a.* made to withstand hard wear, bad weather *etc.* —**heavy-handed** *a.* **1.** clumsy **2.** harsh and oppressive —**heavy-hearted** *a.* sad; melancholy —**heavy industry** basic, large-scale industry producing metal, machinery *etc.* —**heavy-metal** *a.* of type of rock music characterized by strong beat and amplified instrumental effects —**heavy water** deuterium oxide, water in which normal hydrogen content has been replaced by deuterium

Heb. **1.** Hebrew **2.** *Bible* Hebrews

hebdomadal (heb'domədəl) *a.* weekly

Hebrew ('hēbrōō) *n.* **1.** member of an ancient Semitic people **2.** their language **3.** its modern form, used in Israel —**He'braic(al)** *a.* of or characteristic of Hebrews, their language or culture

Hebrews ('hēbrōōz) *pl.n.* (*with sing. v.*) *Bible* 19th book of the N.T., epistle of disputed authorship espousing the perfection of Christ

heckle ('hekəl) *v.* interrupt or try to annoy (speaker) by questions, taunts *etc.*

hectare ('hektāər, -tär) *n.* metric unit of area: one hundred ares or 10 000 square meters, equal to 2.47 acres

hectic ('hektik) *a.* rushed, busy

hecto- *or before vowel* **hect-** (*comb. form*) one hundred, *esp.* in metric system, as in *hectoliter, hectometer*

hector ('hektər) *vt.* **1.** bully —*vi.* **2.** bluster —*n.* **3.** blusterer

heddle ('hedəl) *n.* *Weaving* one of set of frames of vertical wires

hedge (hej) *n.* **1.** fence of bushes —*vt.* **2.** surround with hedge **3.** obstruct **4.** hem in **5.** guard against risk of loss in (bet *etc.*), *esp.* by laying bets with other bookmakers —*vi.* **6.** make or trim hedges **7.** be evasive **8.** secure against loss —'**hedgehog** *n.* small Old World mammal covered with spines —'**hedgerow** *n.* bushes forming hedge —**hedge sparrow** small brownish songbird

hedonism ('hēdənizəm) *n.* **1.** doctrine that pleasure is the chief good **2.** indulgence in sensual pleasure —**he'donics** *pl.n.* (*with sing. v.*) **1.** branch of psychology concerned with the study of pleasant and unpleasant sensations **2.** in philosophy, study of pleasures —'**hedonist** *n.* —**hedo'nistic** *a.*

heed (hēd) *vt.* take notice of —'**heedful** *a.* —'**heedless** *a.* careless

heehaw ('hēhō, 'hē'hō) *interj.* imitation or representation of braying sound of donkey

heel[1] (hēl) *n.* **1.** hinder part of foot **2.** part of shoe supporting this **3.** *sl.* undesirable person —*vt.* **4.** supply with heel **5.** touch (ground, ball) with heel —'**heelball** *n.* mixture of beeswax and lampblack used by shoemakers and in taking rubbings, *esp.* brass rubbings —**heel spur** bony growth on the heel bone

heel[2] (hēl) *v.* **1.** (of ship) (cause to) lean to one side —*n.* **2.** heeling, list

hefty ('hefti) *a.* **1.** bulky **2.** weighty **3.** strong

hegemony (hi'jeməni, -'gem-) *n.* leadership, political domination —**hegemonic** (hejə-'monik, hegə-) *a.*

hegira *or* **hejira** (hi'jīrə, 'hejirə) *n.* **1.** flight of Mohammed from Mecca to Medina in 622 A.D. **2.** escape or flight

heifer ('hefər) *n.* young cow

height (hīt) *n.* **1.** measure from base to top **2.** quality of being high **3.** elevation **4.** highest degree **5.** (*oft. pl.*) hilltop —'**heighten** *vt.* **1.** make higher **2.** intensify

Heimlich maneuver ('hīmlik) applying manual pressure to the lower chest to dislodge a foreign object from the windpipe

heinous ('hānəs) *a.* atrocious, extremely wicked, detestable

heir (āər) *n.* person entitled to inherit property or rank ('**heiress** *fem.*) —'**heirloom** *n.* thing that has been in family for generations

Helanca (hə'langkə) *n.* trade name for nylon stretch yarn

held (held) *pt./pp. of* HOLD[1]

helical ('helikəl) *a.* spiral

helicopter ('helikoptər) *n.* aircraft made to rise vertically by pull of airscrew revolving horizontally —'**heliport** *n.* airport for helicopters

helio- *or before vowel* **heli-** (*comb. form*) sun, as in *heliocentric*

heliocentric (hēliō'sentrik) *a.* **1.** having sun at its center **2.** measured in relation to sun —**helio'centrically** *adv.*

heliograph ('hēliəgraf) *n.* signaling apparatus employing mirror to reflect sun's rays

heliostat ('hēliəstat) *n.* astronomical instrument used to reflect light of sun in constant direction

heliotherapy (hēliō'therəpi) *n.* therapeutic use of sunlight

heliotrope ('hēliətrōp, 'helyə-) *n.* **1.** plant with purple flowers **2.** bluish-violet to purple color —**heliotropic** (hēliə'trōpik, -'tropik) *a.* growing, turning toward source of light

helium ('hēliəm) *n. Chem.* noble gas present in the sun's atmosphere *Symbol* He, at. wt. 4.003, at. no. 2

helix ('hēliks) *n.* **1.** spiral **2.** incurving fold that forms margin of external ear **3.** *see* VOLUTE (sense 1) (*pl.* **helices** ('helisēz), **-es**)

hell (hel) *n.* **1.** abode of the damned **2.** abode of the dead generally **3.** place or state of wickedness, misery or torture —'**hellish** *a./adv.* —'**hellbent** *a.* (*with* on) *inf.* strongly or rashly intent —'**hellfire** *n.* **1.** torment of hell, envisaged as eternal fire —*a.* **2.** characterizing sermons that emphasize this —**Hell's Angel** member of motorcycle gang who typically dress in leather clothing, noted for their lawless behavior

hellebore ('helibōr) *n.* plant with white flowers that bloom in winter, Christmas rose

Hellenic (he'lenik, hə-) *a.* pert. to inhabitants of Greece —'**Hellenist** *n.*

hello (hə'lō, he-) *interj.* expression of greeting or surprise

helm (helm) *n.* tiller, wheel for turning ship's rudder

helmet ('helmit) *n.* defensive or protective covering for head (*also* **helm**)

helminth ('helminth) *n.* parasitic worm, *esp.* nematode or fluke —**hel'minthic** *a.*

Helot ('helət) *n.* **1.** in ancient Sparta, member of class of serfs owned by state **2.** (*usu.* **h-**) serf or slave —'**Helotism** *n.* —'**Helotry** *n.*

help (help) *vt.* **1.** aid, assist **2.** support **3.** succor **4.** remedy, prevent —*n.* **5.** act of helping or being helped **6.** person or thing that helps —'**helper** *n.* —'**helpful** *a.* —'**helping** *n.* single portion of food taken at meal —'**helpless** *a.* **1.** useless, incompetent **2.** unaided **3.** unable to help —'**helplessly** *adv.* —'**helpmate** *or* '**helpmeet** *n.* **1.** helpful companion **2.** husband or wife

helter-skelter (heltər'skeltər) *adv./a./n.* **1.** (in) hurry and confusion —*n.* **2.** high spiral slide at fairground

helve (helv) *n.* handle of hand tool such as ax or pick

hem[1] (hem) *n.* **1.** border of cloth, *esp.* one made by turning over edge and sewing it down —*vt.* **2.** sew thus **3.** (*usu. with* in) confine, shut in (**-mm-**) —'**hemstitch** *n.* **1.** ornamental stitch —*v.* **2.** decorate (hem *etc.*) with hemstitches

hem[2] (hem) *n./interj.* **1.** representation of sound of clearing throat, used to gain attention *etc.* —*vi.* **2.** utter this sound (**-mm-**) —**hem** (*or* **hum**) **and haw** hesitate in speaking

hematite ('hēmətīt) *n.* ore of iron

hematology (hēmə'toləji) *n.* branch of medicine concerned with diseases of blood

hematoma (hēmə'tōmə) *n.* tumorlike swelling resulting from the escape of blood from a ruptured vessel into the tissues

hemi- (*comb. form*) half, as in *hemisphere*

hemiplegia (hemi'plējiə) *n.* paralysis of one side of the body

hemisphere ('hemisfēər) *n.* **1.** half sphere **2.** half of celestial sphere **3.** half of the earth —**hemispheric(al)** (hemi'sfēərik(əl), -'sferik(əl)) *a.*

hemistich ('hemistik) *n.* half line of verse

hemlock ('hemlok) *n.* **1.** either of two native N Amer. trees of the pine family: one in the northwest, the other in the east **2.** poisonous European perennial herb naturalized sporadically in wet places throughout N Amer. **3.** native poisonous herb of wet habitats (*also* **water hemlock**) —**ground hemlock** low spreading yew of eastern N Amer.

hemo- (*comb. form*) blood

hemoglobin ('hēməglōbin) *n.* coloring and oxygen-bearing matter of red blood corpuscles

hemolytic streptococci (hēmə'litik) bacteria which cause several illnesses in humans

hemophilia (hēmə'filiə) *n.* hereditary tendency to intensive bleeding as blood fails to clot —**hemo'philiac** *a./n.*

hemorrhage ('hemərij) *n.* profuse bleeding

hemorrhoids ('hemərοidz) *pl.n.* swollen veins in rectum (*also* **piles**)

hemp (hemp) *n.* **1.** Indian plant **2.** its fiber used for rope *etc.* **3.** any of several narcotic drugs made from varieties of hemp —**'hempen** *a.* made of hemp or rope

hen (hen) *n.* female of domestic fowl and others —**'henpeck** *vt.* (of woman) harass (a man, *esp.* husband) by nagging

hence (hens) *adv.* **1.** from this point **2.** for this reason —**hence'forward** *or* **'henceforth** *adv.* from now onward

henchman ('henchmən) *n.* trusty follower

henge (henj) *n.* circular monument, *oft.* containing circle of stones

henna ('henə) *n.* **1.** flowering shrub **2.** reddish dye made from it

henotheism ('henəthēizəm) *n.* belief in one god (of several) as special god of one's family, tribe *etc.*

henry ('henri) *n.* unit of electrical inductance

heparin ('hepərin) *n.* compound produced by liver that inhibits clotting of the blood

hepatic (hi'patik) *a.* pert. to the liver —**hepa'titis** *n.* inflammation of the liver

hepta- *or before vowel* **hept-** (*comb. form*) seven, as in *heptameter*

heptagon ('heptəgon) *n.* figure with seven angles —**hep'tagonal** *a.*

heptarchy ('heptärki) *n.* rule by seven

her (hər; *unstressed* ər) *a.* objective and possessive case of SHE —**hers** *pron.* of her —**her'self** *pron.*

herald ('herəld) *n.* **1.** messenger, envoy **2.** officer who makes royal proclamations, arranges ceremonies, regulates armorial bearings *etc.* —*vt.* **3.** announce **4.** proclaim approach of —**he'raldic** *a.* —**'heraldry** *n.* study of (right to have) heraldic bearings

herb (ərb) *n.* **1.** plant with soft stem which dies down after flowering **2.** plant used in cooking or medicine —**her'baceous** *a.* **1.** of, like herbs **2.** flowering perennially —**'herbage** *n.* **1.** herbs **2.** grass **3.** pasture —**'herbal** *a.* **1.** of herbs —*n.* **2.** book on herbs —**'herbalist** *n.* **1.** writer on herbs **2.** dealer in medicinal herbs —**her'barium** *n.* collection of dried plants (*pl.* **-s, -ia** (-iə)) —**'herbicide** *n.* chemical which destroys plants —**her'bivorous** *a.* feeding on plants

Hercules ('hərkyəlēz) *n.* mythical hero noted for strength —**herculean** (hərkyə'lēən) *a.* requiring great strength, courage *etc.*

herd (hərd) *n.* **1.** company of animals, *usu.* of same species, feeding or traveling together **2.** herdsman —*v.* **3.** collect or be collected together —*vt.* **4.** tend (livestock) —**herd instinct** *Psychol.* inborn tendency to associate with others and follow group's behavior —**'herdsman** *n.*

here (hēər) *adv.* **1.** in this place **2.** at or to this point —**here'after** *adv.* **1.** in time to come —*n.* **2.** future existence —**here'by** *adv.* by means of or as result of this —**'heretofore** *adv.* before —**here'with** *adv.* together with this

heredity (hi'rediti) *n.* the transmission of physical traits from parent organisms to their offspring through genes —**here'ditament** *n.* property that can be inherited —**heredi'tarily** *adv.* —**he'reditary** *a.* **1.** descending by inheritance **2.** holding office by inheritance **3.** that can be transmitted from one generation to another

heresy ('herəsi) *n.* opinion contrary to orthodox opinion or belief —**'heretic** *n.* one holding opinions contrary to orthodox faith —**he'retical** *a.* —**he'retically** *adv.*

heritage ('heritij) *n.* **1.** what may be or is inherited **2.** anything from past, *esp.* owned or handed down by tradition —**'heritable** *a.* that can be inherited

hermaphrodite (hər'mafrədīt) *n.* **1.** animal or flower that has both male and female reproductive organs **2.** person having both male and female characteristics

hermetic (hər'metik) *or* **hermetical** *a.* sealed so as to be airtight —**her'metically** *adv.*

hermit ('hərmit) *n.* one living in solitude, *esp.* from religious motives —**'hermitage** *n.* his abode —**hermit crab** soft-bodied crustacean living in and carrying about empty shells of mollusks

hernia ('hərniə) *n.* projection of (part of) organ through lining encasing it (*pl.* **-s, -iae** (-iē)) —**'hernial** *a.*

hero ('hēərō) *n.* **1.** one greatly regarded for achievements or qualities **2.** principal character in play *etc.* **3.** illustrious warrior **4.** demigod (*pl.* **-es**) (**heroine** ('herōin) *fem.*) —**heroic** (hi'rōik) *a.* **1.** of, like hero **2.** courageous, daring —**heroically** (hi'rōikəli) *adv.* —**heroics** (hi'rōiks) *pl.n.* extravagant behavior —**heroism** ('herōizəm) *n.* **1.** qualities of hero **2.** courage, boldness —**heroic verse** type of verse suitable for epic or heroic subjects —**hero worship 1.** admiration of heroes or of great men **2.** excessive admiration of others —**hero-worship** *vt.* feel admiration or adulation for

heroin (ˈherōin) *n.* white crystalline derivative of morphine, a highly addictive narcotic

heron (ˈherən) *n.* long-legged wading bird —ˈ**heronry** *n.* place where herons breed

herpes (ˈhərpēz) *n.* any of several virus diseases characterized by blister formation on the skin or mucous membranes

Herr (*German* her) *n.* German man: used before name as title equivalent to *Mr* (*pl.* **Herren** (ˈherən))

herring (ˈhering) *n.* important food fish of northern hemisphere —ˈ**herringbone** *n.* stitch or pattern of zigzag lines —**herring gull** common gull that has white plumage with black-tipped wings

hertz (hərts) *n.* unit of frequency (*pl.* **hertz**)

hesitate (ˈhezitāt) *vi.* **1.** hold back **2.** feel or show indecision **3.** be reluctant —ˈ**hesitancy** *or* **hesiˈtation** *n.* **1.** wavering **2.** doubt **3.** stammering —ˈ**hesitant** *a.* undecided, pausing —ˈ**hesitantly** *adv.*

hessian (ˈhesiən) *n.* burlap

hest (hest) *n.* behest, command

hetaera (hiˈtēərə) *or* **hetaira** (hiˈtīrə) *n. esp.* in ancient Greece, prostitute, *esp.* educated courtesan (*pl.* **-taerae** (-ˈtēərē) *or* **-tairai** (-ˈtīrī))

hetero- (*comb. form*) other; different, as in *heterosexual*

heterodox (ˈhetərədoks) *a.* not orthodox —ˈ**heterodoxy** *n.*

heterodyne (ˈhetərədīn) *v.* **1.** *Electron.* mix (two alternating signals) to produce two signals having frequencies corresponding to sum and difference of original frequencies —*a.* **2.** produced by, operating by, or involved in heterodyning two signals

heterogeneous (hetərəˈjēniəs) *a.* composed of diverse elements —**heterogeˈneity** *n.*

heteromorphic (hetərəˈmörfik) *a. Biol.* **1.** differing from normal form **2.** (*esp.* of insects) having different forms at different stages of life cycle —**heteroˈmorphism** *n.*

heterosexual (hetərōˈsekshōōəl) *n.* person sexually attracted to members of the opposite sex —**heterosexuˈality** *n.*

heuchera (ˈhoikərə) *n.* genus of N Amer. plants of the saxifrage family; alumroot

heuristic (hyōōˈristik) *a.* **1.** (of methods of teaching) encouraging students to find out things for themselves **2.** (in solving problems by computer) proceeding by trial and error

hew (hyōō) *v.* chop, cut with ax (**hewn, hewed** *pp.*) —ˈ**hewer** *n.*

HEW Health, Education and Welfare: U.S. government agency

hexa- *or before vowel* **hex-** (*comb. form*) six, as in *hexachord*

hexagon (ˈheksəgon) *n.* figure with six angles —**hexˈagonal** *a.*

hexagram (ˈheksəgram) *n.* star-shaped figure formed by extending sides of regular hexagon to meet at six points

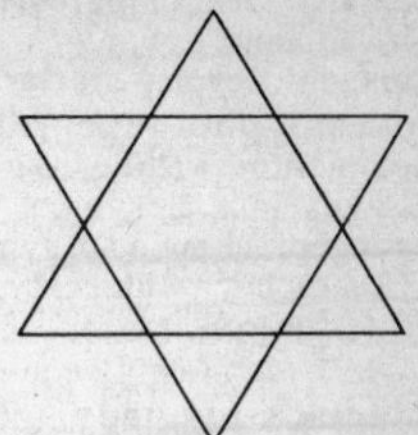

hexagram

hexameter (hekˈsamitər) *n.* line of verse of six feet

hexapod (ˈheksəpod) *n.* insect

hey (hā) *interj.* expression indicating surprise, dismay, discovery *etc.*—ˈ**heyday** *n.* bloom, prime —**hey presto** exclamation used by conjurers to herald climax of trick

Hf *Chem.* hafnium

HF, H.F., hf, *or* **h.f.** high frequency

hf. half

Hg *Chem.* mercury

H.H. 1. His (*or* Her) Highness **2.** His Holiness (title of Pope)

HI Hawaii

hiatus (hīˈātəs) *n.* break or gap where something is missing —**hiatus hernia** part of intestinal tract that slips in and out of gap in diaphragm (*pl.* **-es, hiˈatus**)

hibernate (ˈhībərnāt) *vi.* pass the winter, *esp.* in a torpid state —**hiberˈnation** *n.* —ˈ**hibernator** *n.*

Hibernian (hīˈbərniən) *a./n.* Irish (person)

hibiscus (hīˈbiskəs, hi-) *n.* **1.** flowering (sub)tropical shrub **2.** Rose of Sharon

hiccup (ˈhikup) *n.* **1.** spasm of the breathing organs with an abrupt coughlike sound —*vi.* **2.** make a hiccup or hiccups (*also* ˈ**hiccough**)

hick (hik) *inf. a.* **1.** rustic **2.** unsophisticated —*n.* **3.** person like this

hickory (ˈhikəri) *n.* **1.** N Amer. nut-bearing tree **2.** its tough wood

hide[1] (hīd) *vt.* **1.** put, keep out of sight **2.** conceal, keep secret —*vi.* **3.** conceal oneself (**hid** (hid) *pt.*, **hidden** (ˈhidən) *or* **hid** *pp.*, ˈ**hiding** *pr.p.*) —*n.* **4.** place of concealment, *eg* for birdwatcher —ˈ**hideaway** *n.* hiding place or secluded spot —**hide-out** *n.* hiding place

hide[2] (hīd) *n.* skin of animal —ˈ**hiding** *n. sl.* thrashing —ˈ**hidebound** *a.* **1.** restricted, *esp.* by petty rules *etc.* **2.** narrow-minded **3.** (of tree) having bark so close that it impedes growth

hideous (ˈhidiəs) *a.* repulsive, revolting —ˈ**hideously** *adv.*

hie (hī) *v. obs.* hasten (**hied** *pt./pp.*, ˈ**hying** *or* ˈ**hieing** *pr.p.*)

hierarchy (ˈhīərärki) *n.* system of persons or things arranged in graded order —**hierˈarchic(al)** *a.*

hieratic (hīəˈratik) *a.* **1.** of priests **2.** of

cursive form of hieroglyphics used by priests in ancient Egypt —*n.* **3.** hieratic script of ancient Egypt —**hier'atically** *adv.*

hieroglyphic (hīərə'glifik) *a.* **1.** of a system of picture writing, *esp.* as used in ancient Egypt —*n.* **2.** symbol representing object, concept, or sound **3.** symbol, picture, difficult to decipher —'**hieroglyph** *n.*

hi-fi ('hī'fī) *inf. a.* **1.** *see* **high-fidelity** *at* HIGH —*n.* **2.** high-fidelity equipment

higgledy-piggledy (higəldi'pigəldi) *adv./a. inf.* in confusion

high (hī) *a.* **1.** tall, lofty **2.** far up **3.** (of roads) main **4.** (of meat) tainted **5.** (of season) well advanced **6.** (of sound) acute in pitch **7.** expensive **8.** of great importance, quality, or rank **9.** *inf.* in state of euphoria, *esp.* induced by drugs **10.** *inf.* bad-smelling —*adv.* **11.** far up **12.** strongly, to a great extent **13.** at, to a high pitch **14.** at a high rate —'**highly** *adv.* —'**highness** *n.* **1.** quality of being high **2.** (**H-**) title of prince or princess —'**highball** *n.* long iced drink consisting of liquor base with soda water *etc.* —**high beam** headlight with a long range —'**highbrow** *sl. n.* **1.** intellectual, *esp.* intellectual snob —*a.* **2.** intellectual **3.** difficult **4.** serious —'**highchair** *n.* long-legged chair for child, *esp.* one with table-like tray —**High Church** party within Church of England emphasizing authority of bishops and importance of sacraments, rituals and ceremonies —**higher education** education and training at colleges, universities *etc.* —**high explosive** extremely powerful chemical explosive —**highfa'lutin** *or* **highfa'luting** *a. inf.* pompous or pretentious —**high-fidelity** *a.* of high-quality sound-reproducing equipment —**high-flier** *or* **high-flyer** *n.* **1.** person extreme in aims, ambition *etc.* **2.** person of great ability, *esp.* in career —**high-flown** *a.* extravagant, bombastic —**high frequency** radio frequency lying between 30 and 3 megahertz —**High German** standard German language, historically developed from the form of W Germanic spoken in S Germany —**high-handed** *a.* domineering, dogmatic —**high jump** athletic event in which competitor has to jump over high bar —**Highland** ('hīlənd) *a.* of, from the Highlands of Scotland —**highland(s)** ('hīlənd(z)) (*pl.*)*n.* relatively high ground —**high-level language** *Comp.* language suitable for problem solving where a single instruction can correspond to several instructions —'**highlight** *n.* **1.** lightest or brightest area in painting, photograph *etc.* **2.** outstanding feature —*vt.* **3.** bring into prominence —**highly strung** excitable, nervous —**High Mass** solemn and elaborate sung Mass —**high-minded** *a.* having or characterized by high moral principles —**high-mindedness** *n.* —**high-powered** *a.* **1.** (of optical instrument or lens) having high magnification **2.** dynamic and energetic —**high-pressure** *a.* **1.** having, using, or designed to withstand pressure above normal **2.** *inf.* (of selling) persuasive in aggressive and persistent manner —**high priest 1.** *Judaism* priest of highest rank **2.** head of cult —**high school** secondary school —**high seas** open seas, outside jurisdiction of any one nation —**high-sounding** *a.* pompous, imposing —**high-spirited** *a.* vivacious, bold or lively —**high-tension** *a.* carrying or operating at relatively high voltage —**high tide 1.** tide at its highest level **2.** culminating point —**high time** latest possible time —**high treason** act of treason directly affecting sovereign or state —**high water 1.** high tide **2.** state of any stretch of water at its highest level —'**highway** *n.* **1.** main road **2.** ordinary route —'**highwayman** *n.* formerly, robber on road, *esp.* mounted

hijack *or* **highjack** ('hījak) *vt.* **1.** divert or wrongfully take command of (vehicle or its contents) while in transit **2.** rob —'**hijacker** *or* '**highjacker** *n.*

hike (hīk) *vi.* **1.** walk a long way (for pleasure) in country —*vt.* **2.** pull (up), hitch —*n.* **3.** long walk —'**hiker** *n.*

hilarity (hi'lariti) *n.* cheerfulness, gaiety —**hilarious** (hi'lariəs, -'ler-) *a.*

hill (hil) *n.* **1.** natural elevation, small mountain **2.** mound —'**hillock** *n.* little hill —'**hilly** *a.* —'**hillbilly** *n.* unsophisticated (country) person

hilt (hilt) *n.* handle of sword *etc.* —**to the hilt** to the full

hilum ('hīləm) *n. Bot.* scar on seed marking its point of attachment to seed stalk (*pl.* **-la** (-lə))

him (him; *unstressed* im) *pron.* objective case of HE —**him'self** *pron.* emphatic form of HE

hind[1] (hīnd) *or* **hinder** ('hīndər) *a.* at the back, posterior —'**hindquarter** *n.* **1.** one of two back quarters of carcass of beef *etc.* —*pl.* **2.** rear, *esp.* of four-legged animal —'**hindsight** *n.* **1.** ability to understand, after something has happened, what should have been done **2.** firearm's rear sight

hind[2] (hīnd) *n.* female of deer

hinder ('hindər) *vt.* obstruct, impede, delay —'**hindrance** *n.*

Hindi ('hindi) *n.* language of N central India —'**Hindu** *or* '**Hindoo** *n.* person who adheres to **Hinduism,** the dominant religion of India —**Hindustani** *or* **Hindostani** (hindōō'stani, -'stäni) *n.* **1.** dialect of Hindi spoken in Delhi **2.** all spoken forms of Hindi and Urdu considered together —*a.* **3.** of or relating to these languages or Hindustan

hinge (hinj) *n.* **1.** movable joint, as that on which door hangs —*vt.* **2.** attach with, or as with, hinge —*vi.* **3.** turn, depend (on)

hinny ('hini) *n.* sterile hybrid offspring of male horse and female donkey

hint (hint) *n.* **1.** slight indication or suggestion —*v.* **2.** (*sometimes with* at) suggest indirectly

hinterland (ˈhintərland) *n.* district lying behind coast, or near city, port *etc.*

hip[1] (hip) *n.* **1.** (*oft. pl.*) either side of body below waist and above thigh **2.** angle formed where sloping sides of roof meet **3.** fruit of rose, *esp.* wild —ˈ**hipbone** *n.* large flaring bone forming half of pelvis in mammals composed of ilium, ischium and pubis which become consolidated in the adult (*also* **innominate bone**)

hip[2] (hip) *a. sl.* **1.** aware of or following latest trends **2.** informed

hippeastrum (hipiˈastrəm) *n.* genus of tropical and subtropical bulbs of lily family related to and often sold as amaryllis, with strap-shaped leaves and stout flower stems carrying funnel-shaped flowers, widely grown as house plant

hippie *or* **hippy** (ˈhipi) *n.* (young) person whose behavior, dress *etc.* implies rejection of conventional values

hippo (ˈhipō) *n. inf.* hippopotamus (*pl.* **-s**)

Hippocratic oath (hipəˈkratik) oath taken by doctor to observe code of medical ethics

hippodrome (ˈhipədrōm) *n.* arena for equestrian display

hippogriff (ˈhipəgrif) *n.* legendary griffinlike creature with horse's body

hippopotamus (hipəˈpotəməs) *n.* large Afr. animal living in rivers (*pl.* **-es, -mi** (-mī))

hire (ˈhīər) *vt.* **1.** obtain temporary use of by payment **2.** engage for wage —*n.* **3.** hiring or being hired **4.** payment for use of something —ˈ**hireling** *n.* one who serves for wages

hirsute (ˈhərsōōt) *a.* hairy —**hirsutism** (ˈhərsitizəm) *n.* unusual growth of hair on females

his (hiz; *unstressed* iz) *pron./a.* belonging to him

Hispanic (hiˈspanik) *a.* of or derived from Spain or the Spanish —**Hiˈspanicism** *n.*

hispid (ˈhispid) *a.* **1.** rough with bristles or minute spines **2.** bristly, shaggy —**hisˈpidity** *n.*

hiss (his) *vi.* **1.** make sharp sound of letter *s*, *esp.* in disapproval —*vt.* **2.** express disapproval of, deride thus —*n.* **3.** sound like that of prolonged *s* —ˈ**hissing** *n.*

hist. **1.** historian **2.** historical **3.** history

histamine (ˈhistəmēn) *n.* substance released by body tissues, sometimes creating allergic reactions

histogeny (hiˈstojəni) *n.* formation and development of organic tissues

histogram (ˈhistəgram) *n.* graph using vertical columns to illustrate frequency distribution

histology (hiˈstoləji) *n.* branch of biology concerned with the structure of tissues —**hisˈtologist** *n.*

histoplasmosis (histoplazˈmōsis) *n.* disease caused by infection with a soil fungus

history (ˈhistəri) *n.* **1.** record of past events **2.** study of these **3.** past events **4.** train of events, public or private **5.** course of life or existence **6.** systematic account of phenomena —**hisˈtorian** *n.* writer of history —**historic** (hiˈstorik) *a.* noted in history —**historical** (hiˈstorikəl) *a.* **1.** of, based on, history **2.** belonging to the past —**historically** (hiˈstorikəli) *adv.* —**histoˈricity** *n.* historical authenticity —**historiˈographer** *n.* **1.** official historian **2.** one who studies historical method

histrionic (histriˈonik) *a.* excessively theatrical, insincere, artificial in manner —**histriˈonics** *pl.n.* behavior like this

hit (hit) *vt.* **1.** strike with blow or missile **2.** affect injuriously **3.** reach —*vi.* **4.** strike a blow **5.** (*with* upon) light (upon) (**hit,** ˈ**hitting**) —*n.* **6.** blow **7.** *inf.* success —ˈ**hitter** *n.* —**hit-and-run** *a.* **1.** denoting motor-vehicle accident in which driver leaves scene without stopping **2.** (of attack *etc.*) relying on surprise allied to rapid departure from scene of operations —**hit-and-run play** baseball play in which base runner moves off as soon as the pitcher begins to pitch and the batter swings —**hit man** hired assassin —**hit parade** list of currently most popular songs, ranked in order of sales per record —**hit it off** get along (with person) —**hit or miss** casual; haphazard —**hit the hay** *sl.* go to bed —**hit the nail on the head** express the truth exactly —**hit the trail** *or* **road** *inf.* **1.** proceed on journey **2.** leave

hitch (hich) *vt.* **1.** fasten with loop *etc.* **2.** raise, move with jerk —*vi.* **3.** be caught or fastened —*n.* **4.** difficulty **5.** knot, fastening **6.** jerk —ˈ**hitchhike** *or* **hitch** *vi.* travel by begging free rides

hither (ˈhidhər) *adv.* **1.** to or toward this place (*esp. in* **come hither**) —*a.* **2.** *obs.* situated on this side —ˈ**hitherto** *adv.* up to now or to this time

hive (hīv) *n.* **1.** structure in which bees live or are housed **2.** *fig.* place swarming with busy occupants —*v.* **3.** gather, place bees, in hive —**hive away** store, keep —**hive off** **1.** transfer **2.** dispose of

hives (hīvz) *pl.n.* urticaria

H.M. His (*or* Her) Majesty

H.M.C.S. His (*or* Her) Majesty's Canadian Ship

H.M.S. His (*or* Her) Majesty's Service *or* Ship

H.M.S.O. **UK** His (*or* Her) Majesty's Stationery Office

ho (hō) *interj.* **1.** imitation or representation of sound of deep laugh (*also* **ho-ho**) **2.** exclamation used to attract attention *etc.*

Ho *Chem.* holmium

hoard (hörd) *n.* **1.** stock, store, *esp.* hidden away —*vt.* **2.** amass and hide away **3.** store

hoarding (ˈhörding) *n.* **1.** large board for displaying advertisements **2.** temporary wooden fence round building or piece of ground

hoarse (hörs) *a.* rough, harsh-sounding, husky —**'hoarsely** *adv.* —**'hoarseness** *n.*

hoary ('höri) *a.* **1.** gray with age **2.** grayish-white **3.** of great antiquity **4.** venerable —**'hoarfrost** *n.* frozen dew

hoax (hōks) *n.* **1.** practical joke **2.** deceptive trick —*vt.* **3.** play trick upon **4.** deceive —**'hoaxer** *n.*

hob (hob) *n.* **1.** flat-topped casing of fireplace **2.** top area of cooking stove —**'hobnail** *n.* large-headed nail for boot soles

hobble ('hobəl) *vi.* **1.** walk lamely —*vt.* **2.** tie legs of (horse *etc.*) together —*n.* **3.** straps or ropes put on an animal's legs to prevent it straying **4.** limping gait

hobbledehoy ('hobəldihoi) *n. obs.* rough, ill-mannered clumsy youth

hobby ('hobi) *n.* **1.** favorite occupation as pastime **2.** small falcon —**'hobbyhorse** *n.* **1.** toy horse **2.** favorite topic, preoccupation

hobgoblin ('hobgoblin) *n.* mischievous fairy

hobnob ('hobnob) *vi.* (*oft. with* with) **1.** be familiar **2.** *obs.* drink (**-bb-**)

hobo ('hōbō) *n.* shiftless, wandering person (*pl.* **-s, -es**)

Hobson's choice ('hobsənz) choice of taking what is offered or nothing at all

hock[1] (hok) *n.* **1.** backward-pointing joint on leg of horse *etc.*, corresponding to human ankle —*vt.* **2.** disable by cutting tendons of hock

hock[2] (hok) *n.* dry white wine

hock[3] (hok) *inf. vt.* **1.** pawn, pledge —*n.* **2.** state of being in pawn —**'hocker** *n.* —**in hock 1.** in prison **2.** in debt **3.** in pawn

hockey ('hoki) *n.* **1.** *see* **field hockey** *at* FIELD **2.** *see* **ice hockey** *at* ICE

hocus-pocus (hōkəs'pōkəs) *n.* **1.** trickery **2.** mystifying jargon

hod (hod) *n.* **1.** small trough on a staff for carrying mortar, bricks *etc.* **2.** tall, narrow coal scuttle

hodgepodge ('hojpoj) *n.* medley

Hodgkin's disease ('hojkinz) disease of unknown origin marked by enlargement of the lymph glands, considered by some to be a form of cancer

hoe (hō) *n.* **1.** tool for weeding, breaking ground *etc.* —*v.* **2.** dig, weed or till (surface soil) with hoe (**hoed, 'hoeing**)

hog (hog) *n.* **1.** pig, *esp.* castrated male for fattening **2.** greedy, dirty person —*vt.* **3.** *inf.* eat, use selfishly (**-gg-**) —**'hogback** *n.* **1.** narrow ridge with steep sides (*also* **hog's back**) **2.** *Archaeol.* tomb with sloping sides —**'hogshead** *n.* **1.** large cask **2.** liquid measure, having several values, used *esp.* for alcoholic beverages —**'hogwash** *n.* **1.** nonsense **2.** pig food

hogan ('hōgən) *n.* dwelling of logs and mud used by Navaho Indians

Hogmanay (hogmə'nā) *n.* in Scotland, last day of year

Hohokum (hō'hōkəm) *n.* Amerindian culture of Arizona of 800 A.D.

hoick (hoik) *vt.* raise abruptly and sharply

hoi polloi ('hoi pə'loi) **1.** the common mass of people **2.** the masses

hoist (hoist) *vt.* raise aloft, raise with tackle *etc.*

hoity-toity (hoiti'toiti) *a. inf.* arrogant, haughty

hokum ('hōkəm) *n. sl.* **1.** claptrap; bunk **2.** obvious or hackneyed material of a sentimental nature in motion picture *etc.*

hold[1] (hōld) *vt.* **1.** keep fast, grasp **2.** support in or with hands *etc.* **3.** maintain in position **4.** have capacity for **5.** own, occupy **6.** carry on **7.** detain **8.** celebrate **9.** keep back **10.** believe —*vi.* **11.** cling **12.** remain fast or unbroken **13.** (*with* to) abide (by) **14.** keep **15.** remain relevant, valid or true (**held** *pt./pp.*) —*n.* **16.** grasp **17.** influence —**'holder** *n.* —**'holding** *n.* (*oft. pl.*) property, such as land or stocks and shares —**'holdall** *n.* valise or case for carrying clothes *etc.* —**'holdfast** *n.* clamp —**holding company** company formed to hold stock of other companies, which it then controls —**holding pattern** circular route for aircraft awaiting landing —**'holdup** *n.* **1.** armed robbery **2.** delay

hold[2] (hōld) *n.* space in ship or aircraft for cargo

hole (hōl) *n.* **1.** hollow place, cavity **2.** perforation **3.** opening **4.** *inf.* unattractive place **5.** *inf.* difficult situation —*vt.* **6.** make holes in **7.** drive into a hole —*vi.* **8.** go into a hole —**'holey** *a.* —**hole-and-corner** *a. inf.* furtive or secretive

holiday ('holidā) *n.* day or other period of rest from work *etc.*, *esp.* spent away from home

Holland ('holənd) *n.* **1.** popular name for the Netherlands **2.** (**h-**) linen fabric —**'Hollands** *n.* spirit, gin

holler ('holər) *inf. v.* **1.** shout or yell (something) —*n.* **2.** shout; call

hollow ('holō) *a.* **1.** having a cavity, not solid **2.** empty **3.** false **4.** insincere **5.** not full-toned —*n.* **6.** cavity, hole, valley —*vt.* **7.** make hollow, make hole in **8.** excavate —**hollow back** *see* LORDOSIS —**'hollowware** *or* **'holloware** *n.* dishes, *esp.* silver serving dishes, having depth and volume

holly ('holi) *n.* evergreen shrub with prickly leaves and red berries

hollyhock ('holihok) *n.* tall plant bearing many large flowers

holmium ('hōlmiəm) *n. Chem.* metallic element *Symbol* Ho, at. wt. 164.9, at. no. 67

holm oak (hōm, hōlm) evergreen Mediterranean oak tree

holocaust ('hōləköst, 'holə-) *n.* **1.** great destruction of life, *esp.* by fire **2.** (*oft.* **H-**) murder of Jews by the Nazis during World War II

holograph ('hŏləgraf, 'holə-) *n.* document wholly written by the signer

holography (hŏ'logrəfi) *n.* science of using lasers to produce photographic record (**hologram**) which can reproduce a three-dimensional image

Holstein ('hŏlstīn) *n.* one of breed of large black-and-white dairy cattle

holster ('hŏlstər) *n.* leather case for pistol, hung from belt *etc.*

holt (hŏlt) *n. Poet.* wood, wooded hill

holy ('hŏli) *a.* **1.** belonging, devoted to God **2.** free from sin **3.** divine **4.** consecrated —'**holily** *adv.* —'**holiness** *n.* **1.** sanctity **2.** (**H-**) Pope's title —**holier-than-thou** *a.* offensively sanctimonious or self-righteous —**Holy Communion** service of the Eucharist —**holy day** day of religious festival —**Holy Ghost** *or* **Spirit** third person of Trinity —**Holy Grail** cup or dish used by Christ at the Last Supper —**holy orders 1.** sacrament whereby person is admitted to Christian ministry **2.** grades of Christian ministry **3.** status of ordained Christian minister —**Holy See** *R.C.Ch.* **1.** the see of the pope as bishop of Rome **2.** Roman curia —**Holy Week** week before Easter —**the Holy Land** Palestine

homage ('homij) *n.* **1.** tribute, respect, reverence **2.** formal acknowledgment of allegiance

homburg ('hombərg) *n.* man's hat of felt with dented crown and stiff upturned brim

home (hŏm) *n.* **1.** dwelling place **2.** residence **3.** native place **4.** institution for the elderly, infirm *etc.* —*a.* **5.** of one's home, country *etc.* —*adv.* **6.** to, at one's home **7.** to the point —*v.* **8.** direct or be directed on to a point or target —'**homeless** *a.* —'**homely** *a.* plain —'**homeward** *a./adv.* —'**homewards** *adv.* —'**homing** *a. Zool.* of ability to return home after traveling great distances —**home-brew** *n.* alcoholic drink made at home —**home economics** study of diet, budgeting and other subjects concerned with running a home —**home plate** baseball base at which batter stands: last of four a base runner must touch to score a run —**home rule 1.** self-government **2.** partial autonomy sometimes granted to national minority or colony —**home run** baseball hit that allows batter to make complete circuit of bases and score a run —'**homesick** *a.* depressed by absence from home —'**homesickness** *n.* —'**homespun** *a.* **1.** domestic **2.** simple —*n.* **3.** cloth made of homespun yarn —'**homestead** *n.* **1.** house with outbuildings, *esp.* on farm **2.** house and land occupied by owner and exempt from seizure and forced sale for debt —'**homesteader** *n.* —'**homework** *n.* school work to be done at home —**homing pigeon** domestic pigeon developed for its homing instinct, used for racing (*also* '**homer**) —**bring home to** impress deeply upon —**home and dry** safe or successful

homeo- *or* **homoio-** (*comb. form*) like, similar, as in *homeomorphism*

homeopathy (hŏmi'opəthi) *n.* treatment of disease by small doses of drug that produces, in healthy person, symptoms similar to those of disease being treated —'**homeopath** *n.* one who believes in or practices homeopathy —**homeo'pathic** *a.* —**homeo'pathically** *adv.*

homeostasis (hŏmiŏ'stāsis) *n.* the tendency of all living organisms to maintain a steady state for continued functioning

homicide ('homisīd) *n.* **1.** killing of human being **2.** killer —**homi'cidal** *a.*

homily ('homili) *n.* **1.** sermon **2.** religious discourse —**homi'letic** *a.* —**homi'letics** *pl.n.* (*with sing. v.*) art of preaching

hominid ('hominid) *n./a.* (of or relating to) man and his ancestors

hominoid ('hominoid) *a.* **1.** manlike **2.** of or belonging to primate family, which includes anthropoid apes and man —*n.* **3.** hominoid animal

Homo ('hŏmŏ) *n.* genus to which modern man belongs —**Homo sapiens** ('sapiənz, 'sāpiənz, -enz) specific name of modern man

homo- (*comb. form*) same, as in *homosexual.* Such words are not given here where the meaning may easily be inferred from the simple word

homogeneous (hŏmə'jēniəs, -nyəs) *a.* **1.** formed of uniform parts **2.** similar, uniform **3.** of the same nature —**homoge'neity** *n.* —**homogenize** (hŏ'mojinīz, hə-) *vt.* break up fat globules (in milk and cream) to distribute them evenly

homograph ('homəgraf) *n.* one of group of words spelt in the same way but having different meanings —**homo'graphic** *a.*

homologous (hŏ'moləgəs, hə-) *a.* having the same relation, relative position *etc.* —'**homologue** *or* '**homolog** *n.* homologous thing

homonym ('homənim) *n.* word of same form as another, but having different meaning —**homo'nymic** *or* **ho'monymous** *a.*

homophone ('hŏməfŏn) *n.* a word of the same sound as another, but having different spelling

homosexual (hŏmə'sekshōōəl) *n.* **1.** person sexually attracted to members of the same sex —*a.* **2.** of or relating to homosexuals or homosexuality —**homosexu'ality** *n.*

Hon *or* **Hon. 1.** Honorable **2.** (*also* **h-**) honorary

Honduras (hon'dyōōrəs, -'dōō-) *n.* country in Central America bounded north by the Caribbean, east and southeast by Nicaragua, west by Guatemala, southwest by El Salvador and south by the Pacific Ocean —**Hon'duran** *n./a.* (native or inhabitant) of Honduras

hone (hŏn) *n.* **1.** whetstone —*vt.* **2.** sharpen with hone

honest ('onist) *a.* **1.** not cheating, lying, stealing *etc.* **2.** genuine **3.** without pretension —'**honestly** *adv.* —'**honesty** *n.* **1.** quality of being honest **2.** plant with silvery seed pods

honey ('huni) *n.* sweet fluid made by bees —'**honeyed** *or* '**honied** *a. Poet.* **1.** flattering or soothing **2.** made sweet or agreeable **3.** full of honey —'**honeybee** *n.* any of various social bees widely domesticated as source of honey and beeswax —'**honeycomb** *n.* **1.** wax structure in hexagonal cells in which bees place honey, eggs *etc.* **2.** raised effect on cloth resembling honeycomb —*vt.* **3.** fill with cells or perforations —'**honeydew** *n.* **1.** sweet sticky substance found on plants **2.** type of sweet melon —'**honeymoon** *n.* journey taken by newly-wedded pair —'**honeysuckle** *n.* climbing plant

Hong Kong (hong kong) crown colony of the United Kingdom 20 miles east of the mouth of the Pearl River and 80 miles south of Canton

honk (hongk) *n.* **1.** call of wild goose **2.** any sound like this, *esp.* sound of automobile horn —*vi.* **3.** make this sound

honky ('hongki) *n.* (among Blacks) White person

honky-tonk ('hongkitongk) *n.* **1.** *sl.* cheap disreputable nightclub *etc.* **2.** style of ragtime piano-playing

honor ('onər) *n.* **1.** personal integrity **2.** renown **3.** reputation **4.** sense of what is right or due **5.** chastity **6.** high rank or position **7.** source, cause of honor **8.** pleasure, privilege —*pl.* **9.** mark of respect **10.** distinction in examination —*vt.* **11.** respect highly **12.** confer honor on **13.** accept or pay (bill *etc.*) when due —'**honorable** *a.* —'**honorably** *adv.* —**hono'rarium** *n.* a fee (*pl.* **-s, -ia** (-iə)) —'**honorary** *a.* **1.** conferred for the sake of honor only **2.** holding position without pay or usual requirements **3.** giving services without pay —**hono'rific** *a.* conferring honor —**honor roll 1.** list of names of persons deserving honor, *esp.* students **2.** public display of names of local citizens who have served in the armed forces —**honor society** society for recognition of academic achievement, *esp.* of undergraduates —**honor system** system whereby members of institution are trusted to abide by the rules without supervision

hooch *or* **hootch** (hōōch) *n. sl.* alcoholic drink, *esp.* when illicitly distilled

hood (hŏŏd) *n.* **1.** covering for head and neck, oft. part of cloak or gown **2.** hoodlike thing as (adjustable) top of automobile, baby carriage *etc.* **3.** metal cover of automobile engine —'**hooded** *a.* covered with or shaped like hood —**hooded crow** crow that has gray body and black head, wings, and tail —'**hoodwink** *vt.* deceive

hoodlum ('hōōdləm, 'hŏŏd-) *n.* gangster, bully —**hood** *n. sl.* hoodlum

hoodoo ('hōōdōō) *n.* **1.** voodoo **2.** cause of bad luck

hooey ('hōōi) *n./interj. sl.* nonsense

hoof (hōōf) *n.* horny casing of foot of horse *etc.* (*pl.* **-s, hooves**) —**on the hoof** (of livestock) alive

hoo-ha ('hōōhä) *n.* needless fuss, bother *etc.*

hook (hŏŏk) *n.* **1.** bent piece of metal used to suspend, hold, or pull something **2.** something resembling hook in shape or function **3.** curved cutting tool **4.** *Boxing* blow delivered with bent elbow —*vt.* **5.** grasp, catch, hold, as with hook **6.** fasten with hook **7.** *Golf* drive (ball) widely to the left —**hooked** *a.* **1.** shaped like hook **2.** caught **3.** *sl.* addicted —'**hooker** *n. sl.* prostitute —**hook-up** *n.* linking of radio, television stations —'**hookworm** *n.* infestation with intestinal roundworm

hookah ('hŏŏkə) *n.* oriental pipe in which smoke is drawn through water and long tube

hooligan ('hōōligən) *n.* violent, irresponsible (young) person —'**hooliganism** *n.*

hoop (hōōp) *n.* **1.** rigid circular band of metal, wood *etc.* **2.** such a band used for binding barrel *etc.*, for use as toy, or for jumping through as in circus acts —*vt.* **3.** bind with hoops **4.** encircle —**go through the hoop(s)** *inf.* go through an ordeal or test

hoopla ('hōōplä) *n.* **1.** commotion **2.** communication intended to confuse

hoopoe ('hōōpōō) *n.* bird with large crest

hooray (hōō'rā) *interj. see* HURRAH

Hoosier ('hōōzhər) *n.* native or resident of Indiana

hoot (hōōt) *n.* **1.** owl's cry or similar sound **2.** cry of disapproval or derision **3.** *inf.* funny person or thing —*vi.* **4.** utter hoot, *esp.* in derision

Hoover ('hōōvər) *n.* **Herbert Clark.** the 31st President of the U.S. (1929-33)

hooves (hōōvz) *n., pl. of* HOOF

hop[1] (hop) *vi.* **1.** spring on one foot **2.** *inf.* move quickly (**-pp-**) —*n.* **3.** leap, skip **4.** one stage of journey **5.** *inf.* dance —'**hopscotch** *n.* children's game of hopping in pattern drawn on ground

hop[2]

hop[2] (hop) *n.* **1.** climbing plant with bitter cones used to flavor beer *etc.* —*pl.* **2.** the cones

hope (hōp) *n.* **1.** expectation of something desired **2.** thing that gives, or object of, this feeling —*v.* **3.** feel hope —'**hopeful** *a.* —'**hopefully** *adv. inf.* it is hoped —'**hopeless** *a.* —**young hopeful** promising boy or girl

Hopi ('hōpi) *n.* **1.** (member of) Amerindian people of northeastern Arizona (*pl.* **Hopi, -s**) **2.** the Uto-Aztecan language of the Hopi

hopper ('hopər) *n.* **1.** one who hops **2.** device for feeding material into mill or machine, or grain into railroad truck *etc.* **3.** mechanical hop-picker

horal ('hörəl) *a.* **1.** pert. to an hour **2.** hourly

horde (hörd) *n.* large crowd, *esp.* moving together

horehound ('hörhownd) *n.* plant with bitter juice used to flavor candy

horizon (hə'rīzən) *n.* **1.** boundary of part of the earth seen from any given point **2.** line where earth and sky seem to meet **3.** boundary of mental outlook —**horizontal** (hori'zontəl) *a.* parallel with horizon, level —**horizontally** (hori'zontəli) *adv.*

hormone ('hörmōn) *n.* **1.** substance secreted by certain glands which stimulates organs of the body **2.** synthetic substance with same effect

horn (hörn) *n.* **1.** hard projection on heads of certain animals, *eg* cows **2.** substance of horns **3.** various things made of, or resembling it **4.** wind instrument *orig.* made of horn **5.** device, *esp.* in motor vehicle, emitting sound as warning *etc.* —**horned** *a.* having horns —'**horny** *a.* **1.** of, like or hard as horn **2.** having horn(s) **3.** *sl.* sexually aroused —'**hornbeam** *n.* tree with smooth gray bark —'**hornbill** *n.* type of bird with horny growth on large bill —'**hornbook** *n.* page bearing religious text or alphabet, held in frame with thin window of horn over it —**horn of plenty** *see* CORNUCOPIA —'**hornpipe** *n.* lively dance, *esp.* associated with sailors

hornblende ('hörnblend) *n.* mineral consisting of silica, with magnesia, lime or iron

hornet ('hörnit) *n.* any large social wasp

horologe ('horəlōj) *n.* *rare* any timepiece —**ho'rology** *n.* art or science of clock-making and measuring time

horoscope ('horəskōp) *n.* **1.** observation of, or scheme showing disposition of planets *etc.*, at given moment, *esp.* birth, by which character and abilities of individual are predicted **2.** telling of person's fortune by this method

horror ('horər) *n.* **1.** terror **2.** loathing, fear **3.** its cause —**hor'rendous** *a.* horrific —'**horrible** *a.* exciting horror, hideous, shocking —'**horribly** *adv.* —'**horrid** *a.* **1.** unpleasant, repulsive **2.** *inf.* unkind —**hor'rific** *a.* particularly horrible —'**horrify** *vt.* move to horror (**-ified, -ifying**)

hors d'oeuvre (ör 'dərv) small dish served before main meal

horse (hörs) *n.* **1.** four-legged herbivorous mammal with flowing mane and tail, ranging in size from 24 inches to 68 inches at the shoulders. Domesticated species are used to carry loads, to pull vehicles and for riding **2.** cavalry **3.** vaulting-block **4.** frame for support *etc.* —*vt.* **5.** provide with horse or horses —'**horsy** *or* '**horsey** *a.* **1.** having to do with horses **2.** devoted to horses or horse racing —**horse brass** decorative brass ornament, orig. attached to horse's harness —**horse chestnut** tree with conical clusters of white or pink flowers and large nuts —'**horseflesh** *n.* **1.** horses collectively **2.** flesh of horse, *esp.* edible horse meat —'**horsefly** *n.* large, bloodsucking fly —**horse laugh** harsh boisterous laugh —'**horseman** *n.* rider on horse ('**horsewoman** *fem.*) —'**horseplay** *n.* rough or rowdy play —'**horsepower** *n.* unit of power of engine *etc.* 550 foot-pounds per second —'**horseradish** *n.* plant with pungent root —**horse sense** *see* **common sense** *at* COMMON —'**horseshoe** *n.* **1.** protective U-shaped piece of iron nailed to horse's hoof **2.** thing so shaped —**horseshoe pitching** game played by two or four players in which horseshoes are thrown toward an iron stake at each end of a court —'**horsetail** *n.* primitive plant with erect jointed stems with whorls of small leaves around the joints: a garden weed —**horse about** *or* **around** *inf.* play roughly, boisterously

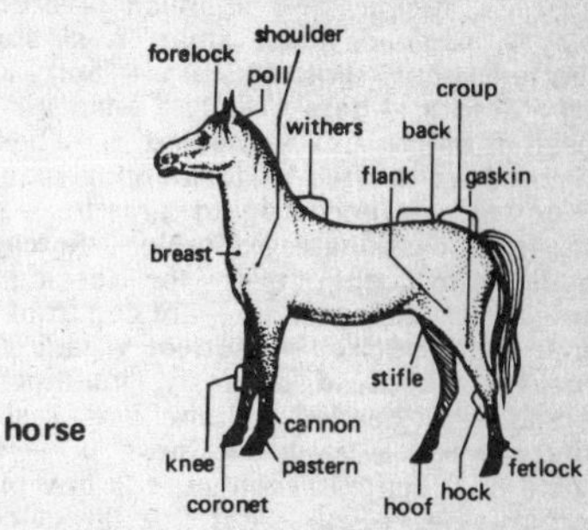

hortatory ('hörtətöri) *or* **hortative** ('hörtətiv) *a.* tending to exhort; encouraging —**hor'tation** *n.*

horticulture ('hörtikulchər) *n.* art or science of gardening —**horti'cultural** *a.* —**horti'culturist** *n.*

Hos. *Bible* Hosea

hosanna *or* **hosannah** (hō'zanə) *n./interj.* cry of praise, adoration

hose (hōz) *n.* **1.** flexible tube for conveying liquid or gas **2.** stockings —*vt.* **3.** water with hose —**hosier** ('hōzhər) *n.* dealer in stockings *etc.* —**hosiery** ('hōzhəri) *n.* stockings *etc.*

Hosea (hō'zāə, -'zēə) *n.* *Bible* 28th book of the O.T., written by the prophet Hosea in which he uses his domestic life as an analogy for the relationship between God and man

hospice ('hospis) *n.* *obs.* **1.** traveler's house of rest kept by religious order **2.** place for care of the dying

hospital ('hospitəl) *n.* institution for care of

sick —**hospitali'zation** *n.* —**'hospitalize** *vt.* place for care in hospital

hospitality (hospi'taliti) *n.* friendly and liberal reception of strangers or guests —**hos'pitable** *a.* welcoming, kindly —**hos'pitably** *adv.*

host[1] (hōst) *n.* **1.** one who entertains another (**'hostess** *fem.*) **2.** innkeeper **3.** compere of show **4.** animal, plant on which parasite lives —*v.* **5.** be host of (party, program *etc.*)

host[2] (hōst) *n.* large number

Host (hōst) *n.* consecrated bread of the Eucharist

hosta ('hōstə, 'hostə) *n.* plantain lily

hostage ('hostij) *n.* person taken or given as pledge or security

hostel ('hostəl) *n.* supervised lodging *esp.* for youth traveling by bicycle or on foot —**'hostelry** *n. obs.* inn

hostile ('hostil) *a.* **1.** opposed, antagonistic **2.** warlike **3.** of or relating to an enemy **4.** unfriendly —**hos'tility** *n.* **1.** enmity —*pl.* **2.** acts of warfare

hot (hot) *a.* **1.** of high temperature, very warm, giving or feeling heat **2.** angry **3.** severe **4.** recent, new **5.** much favored **6.** spicy **7.** *sl.* good, quick, smart **8.** *sl.* stolen (**'hotter** *comp.*, **'hottest** *sup.*) —**'hotly** *adv.* —**'hotness** *n.* —**hots** *n. sl.* lust —**hot air** *inf.* boastful, empty talk —**'hotbed** *n.* **1.** bed of enclosed soil heated by fermenting manure **2.** any place encouraging growth —**hot-blooded** *a.* passionate, excitable —**'hotcap** *n.* small translucent cover for forcing or protecting outdoor plants —**hot dog** frankfurter in long split roll —**'hotfoot** *vi./adv.* (go) quickly —**'hothead** *n.* hasty, intemperate person —**hot-headed** *a.* impetuous, rash or hot-tempered —**hot-headedness** *n.* —**'hothouse** *n.* **1.** heated greenhouse **2.** any place encouraging growth —**hot line** direct communication link between heads of government *etc.* —**hot money** capital that is transferred from one commercial center to another seeking best opportunity for short-term gain —**'hotplate** *n.* **1.** solid disk on electric stove **2.** portable device for cooking or keeping food warm —**hot potato** situation likely to cause trouble to person dealing with it —**hot rod** automobile with engine that has been modified to produce increased power —**hot seat 1.** *inf.* difficult or dangerous position **2.** *sl.* electric chair —**hot-foot it** go quickly —**in hot water** *inf.* in trouble —**make it hot for** cause trouble for —**sell like hot cakes** sell readily

hotchpotch ('hochpoch) *n.* **1.** dish of many ingredients **2.** hodgepodge

hotel (hō'tel, 'hōtel) *n.* **1.** commercial establishment providing lodging and meals **2.** (**H-**) word used in communications for the letter *h* —**hotel keeper** *or* **ho'telier** *n.*

Hottentot ('hotəntot) *n.* **1.** member of a people of southwest Africa related to the Bushmen (*pl.* **-tot, -s**) **2.** the 'click' language of the Khoisan family spoken by the Hottentot

hough (hok) *see* HOCK[1]

hound (hownd) *n.* **1.** any of class of purebred dogs defined by the American Kennel Club, typically with large drooping ears, which hunt by scent and are used in the chase —*vt.* **2.** chase, pursue **3.** urge on —**houndstooth check** *or* **hound's tooth check** ('howndz-'to͞oth, 'hownz-) medium-sized broken-check fabric pattern

hour ('owər) *n.* **1.** twenty-fourth part of day **2.** sixty minutes **3.** time of day **4.** appointed time —*pl.* **5.** fixed periods for work, prayers *etc.* **6.** book of prayers —**'hourly** *adv.* **1.** every hour **2.** frequently —*a.* **3.** frequent **4.** happening every hour —**'hourglass** *n.* **1.** device consisting of two transparent chambers linked by narrow channel, containing quantity of sand that takes specified time to trickle from one chamber to the other —*a.* **2.** well-proportioned with small waist

houri ('ho͞oəri) *n.* beautiful nymph of the Muslim paradise (*pl.* **-s**)

house (hows) *n.* **1.** building for human habitation **2.** building for other specified purpose **3.** legislative or other assembly **4.** (**H-**) family, *esp.* royal **5.** business firm **6.** theater audience —*v.* (howz) **7.** give or receive shelter, lodging or storage —*vt.* (howz) **8.** cover; contain —**housing** ('howzing) *n.* **1.** (providing of) houses **2.** part or structure designed to cover, protect, contain —**house arrest** confinement to one's own home rather than in prison —**'houseboat** *n.* boat for living in on river *etc.* —**'housebound** *a.* unable to leave one's house —**'housebreak** *vt.* teach acceptable behavior to (*esp.* pets) —**'housebreaker** *n.* burglar —**'housecoat** *n.* woman's long loose garment for casual wear at home —**'housefly** *n.* pestiferous two-winged insect found throughout the world —**'household** *n.* persons living in house collectively —**'householder** *n.* **1.** occupier of house as his dwelling **2.** head of household —**household name** *or* **word** person or thing that is very well known —**'househusband** *n.* married man who runs household while wife earns income —**'housekeeper** *n.* person managing affairs of household —**'housekeeping** *n.* running household —**housemaid's knee** inflammation and swelling of bursa in front of kneecap —**'houseman** *n.* man who performs general domestic duties —**House of Commons UK, C** lower chamber of Parliament —**House of Lords UK** upper chamber of Parliament, composed of the peers of the realm —**House of Representatives** the lower legislative branch of the U.S. Congress, of many states and of some other countries —**house organ** periodical published by business for its employees —**house plant** plant for growing indoors —**house-proud** *a.*

preoccupied with appearance of one's house —**'housetop** *n.* roof of house —**'housewarming** *n.* party to celebrate entry into new house or premises —**'housewife** *n.* **1.** married woman who runs a household **2.** ('huzif) small sewing kit for traveling —**'housework** *n.* work of running home, such as cleaning *etc.* —**on the house** at owner's expense —**put one's house in order** make the necessary reforms

hove (hōv) *chiefly Naut. pt./pp. of* HEAVE

hovel ('huvəl, 'hov-) *n.* small, wretched usu. dirty house

hover ('huvər, 'hov-) *vi.* **1.** (of bird *etc.*) hang in the air **2.** loiter **3.** be in state of indecision —**'Hovercraft** *n.* trade name for ground-effect machine used to cross short stretches of water

how (how) *adv.* **1.** in what way **2.** by what means **3.** in what condition **4.** to what degree —**howbeit** (how'bēit) *adv. obs.* nevertheless —**how'ever** *adv.* **1.** nevertheless **2.** in whatever way, degree **3.** all the same

howdah ('howdə) *n.* (canopied) seat on elephant's back

howitzer ('howitsər) *n.* short gun firing shells at high elevation

howl (howl) *vi.* **1.** utter long loud cry —*n.* **2.** such cry —**'howler** *n.* **1.** one that howls **2.** *inf.* stupid mistake —**'howling** *a. inf.* great

hoyden ('hoidən) *n.* wild, boisterous girl, tomboy —**'hoydenish** *a.*

hoyle (hoil) *n.* compendium of rules of indoor (*esp.* card) games —**according to hoyle** following the rules, correctly

H.P. **1.** half pay **2.** high pressure **3.** horsepower (*also* **hp**)

H.Q. *or* **h.q.** headquarters

hr. *or* **hr** hour

H.R.H. His (*or* Her) Royal Highness

HT *Phys.* high tension

huarache (wə'rächi, hə-) *n.* low-heeled sandal with upper made of interwoven leather thongs

hub (hub) *n.* **1.** middle part of wheel, from which spokes radiate **2.** central point of activity

hubble-bubble ('hubəlbubəl) *n.* **1.** *see* HOOKAH **2.** turmoil **3.** gargling sound

hubbub ('hubub) *n.* **1.** confused noise of many voices **2.** uproar

hubris ('hyōōbris) *or* **hybris** *n.* pride or arrogance —**hu'bristic** *or* **hy'bristic** *a.*

huckaback ('hukəbak) *n.* coarse absorbent linen or cotton fabric used for towels *etc.* (*also* **huck**)

huckster ('hukstər) *n.* **1.** person using aggressive or questionable methods of selling —*vt.* **2.** sell (goods) thus

huddle ('hudəl) *n.* **1.** crowded mass **2.** *inf.* impromptu conference —*v.* **3.** heap, crowd together **4.** hunch (oneself)

hue (hyōō) *n.* **1.** color or gradation of color **2.** aspect of color which permits classification

hue and cry **1.** public uproar, outcry **2.** formerly, loud outcry usu. in pursuit of wrongdoer

huff (huf) *n.* **1.** passing mood of anger —*v.* **2.** make or become angry, resentful —*vi.* **3.** blow, puff heavily —**'huffily** *adv.* —**'huffy** *a.*

hug (hug) *vt.* **1.** clasp tightly in the arms **2.** cling to **3.** keep close to (**-gg-**) —*n.* **4.** fond embrace

huge (hyōōj, yōōj) *a.* very big —**'hugely** *adv.* very much

hugger-mugger ('hugərmugər) *n.* **1.** confusion **2.** *rare* secrecy —*a./adv. obs.* **3.** with secrecy **4.** in confusion —*vt.* **5.** *obs.* keep secret —*vi.* **6.** *obs.* act secretly

Huguenot ('hyōōgənot) *n.* **1.** French Calvinist, *esp.* of 16th or 17th century —*a.* **2.** designating French Protestant Church

huh (*spelling pron.* hu) *interj.* exclamation of derision, bewilderment, inquiry *etc.*

hula ('hōōlə) *n.* native dance of Hawaii

Hula-Hoop *n.* trade name for hoop of plastic *etc.* swung round body by wriggling hips

hulk (hulk) *n.* **1.** body of abandoned vessel **2.** *offens.* large, unwieldy person or thing —**'hulking** *a.* unwieldy, bulky

hull (hul) *n.* **1.** frame, body of ship **2.** calyx of strawberry, raspberry or similar fruit **3.** shell, husk —*vt.* **4.** remove shell, hull from **5.** pierce hull of (vessel *etc.*)

hullabaloo ('huləbəlōō) *n.* uproar, clamor, row

hum (hum) *vi.* **1.** make low continuous sound as bee **2.** *sl.* be very active —*vt.* **3.** sing with closed lips (**-mm-**) —*n.* **4.** humming sound **5.** *sl.* great activity **6.** in radio, disturbance affecting reception —**'hummingbird** *n.* member of family of very small colorful New World birds found from Arctic N Amer. to tip of S Amer. which are notable for ability to hover while feeding on nectar

human ('hyōōmən, 'yōō-) *a.* of, relating to, or characteristic of mankind —**humane** (hyōō'mān, yōō-) *a.* **1.** benevolent, kind **2.** merciful —**'humanism** *n.* **1.** belief in human effort rather than religion **2.** interest in human welfare and affairs **3.** classical literary culture —**'humanist** *n.* —**humani'tarian** *n.* **1.** philanthropist —*a.* **2.** having the welfare of mankind at heart —**hu'manity** *n.* **1.** human nature **2.** human race **3.** kindliness —*pl.* **4.** study of literature, philosophy, the arts —**'humanize** *vt.* **1.** make human **2.** civilize —**'humanly** *adv.* —**'humanoid** *a.* **1.** like human being in appearance —*n.* **2.** being with human rather than anthropoid characteristics **3.** in science fiction, robot or creature resembling human being —**'humankind** *n.* whole race of man

humble ('humbəl) *a.* **1.** lowly, modest —*vt.* **2.** bring low, abase, humiliate —**'humbly** *adv.* —**humble pie** apology or retraction made under duress —**eat humble pie** be forced to submit to humiliation

humbug (ˈhumbug) *n.* **1.** impostor **2.** sham, nonsense, deception —*vt.* **3.** deceive; defraud (**-gg-**)

humdinger (ˈhumˈdingər) *n. sl.* excellent person or thing

humdrum (ˈhumdrum) *a.* commonplace, dull, monotonous

humeral (ˈhyōōmərəl) *a.* of shoulder —**ˈhumerus** *n.* long bone between elbow and shoulder (*pl.* **-meri** (-mərī))

humid (ˈhyōōmid, ˈyōō-) *a.* moist, damp —**huˈmidifier** *n.* device for increasing amount of water vapor in air in room *etc.* —**huˈmidify** *vt.* —**huˈmidity** *n.*

humiliate (hyōōˈmiliāt, yōō-) *vt.* lower dignity of, abase, mortify —**humiliˈation** *n.*

humility (hyōōˈmiliti, yōō-) *n.* **1.** state of being humble **2.** meekness

hummock (ˈhumək) *n.* **1.** low knoll, hillock **2.** ridge of ice

humor (ˈhyōōmər, ˈyōōmər) *n.* **1.** faculty of saying or perceiving what excites amusement **2.** state of mind, mood **3.** temperament **4.** *obs.* any of various fluids of body —*vt.* **5.** gratify, indulge —**ˈhumorist** *n.* person who acts, speaks, writes humorously —**ˈhumorous** *a.* funny, amusing —**ˈhumorously** *adv.*

hump (hump) *n.* **1.** normal or deforming lump, *esp.* on back **2.** hillock **3.** *inf.* dejection —*vt.* **4.** make hump-shaped **5.** *sl.* carry, heave —**ˈhumpback** *n.* person with hump —**ˈhumpˈbacked** *a.* having a hump

humph (*spelling pron.* humf) *interj.* exclamation of annoyance, indecision *etc.*

humus (ˈhyōōməs, ˈyōō-) *n.* decayed vegetable and animal matter

Hun (hun) *n.* **1.** member of Asiatic nomadic peoples who invaded Europe in 4th and 5th centuries A.D. **2.** *inf. derog.* German **3.** *inf.* vandal —**ˈHunlike** *a.* —**ˈHunnish** *a.*

hunch (hunch) *n.* **1.** intuition or premonition **2.** hump —*vt.* **3.** thrust, bend into hump —**ˈhunchback** *n.* **1.** curvature of the spine in which back is rounded (*also* **kyphosis**) **2.** person with this condition

hundred (ˈhundrəd) *n./a.* cardinal number, ten times ten —**ˈhundredfold** *a./adv.* —**ˈhundredth** *a./n.* ordinal number of a hundred —**ˈhundredweight** *n.* weight of 100 lbs. (45.4 kg.)

hung (hung) *v.* **1.** *pt./pp. of* HANG —*a.* **2.** (of jury *etc.*) unable to decide **3.** not having majority —**hung-over** *a. inf.* suffering from aftereffects of excessive drinking —**hung up** *inf.* **1.** delayed **2.** emotionally disturbed

Hungary (ˈhunggəri) *n.* country in Europe bounded north by Czechoslovakia, northeast by the U.S.S.R., east by Romania, south by Yugoslavia and west by Austria —**Hunˈgarian** *n./a.* **1.** (native or inhabitant) of Hungary —*n.* **2.** language of Hungary which is the major member of the Ugric branch of Finno-Ugrian

hunger (ˈhunggər) *n.* **1.** discomfort, exhaustion from lack of food **2.** strong desire —*vi.* **3.** (*usu. with* for *or* after) have great desire (for) —**ˈhungrily** *adv.* —**ˈhungry** *a.* having keen appetite —**hunger strike** refusal of all food, as protest

hunk (hungk) *n.* thick piece

hunker (ˈhungkər) *vi.* squat (down)

hunkers (ˈhungkərz) *pl.n. dial.* haunches

hunt (hunt) *v.* **1.** (seek out to) kill or capture for sport or food **2.** search (for) —*n.* **3.** chase, search **4.** (party organized for) hunting —**ˈhunter** *n.* **1.** one who hunts (**ˈhuntress** *fem.*) **2.** horse, dog bred for hunting —**ˈhuntsman** *n.* man in charge of pack of hounds

hurdle (ˈhərdəl) *n.* **1.** portable frame of bars for temporary fences or for jumping over **2.** obstacle —*pl.* **3.** race over hurdles —*vi.* **4.** race over hurdles —**ˈhurdler** *n.* one who races over hurdles

hurdy-gurdy (hərdiˈgərdi) *n.* mechanical (musical) instrument (*eg* barrel organ)

hurl (hərl) *vt.* throw violently —**hurly-burly** *n.* loud confusion

hurling (ˈhərling) *n.* traditional Irish game resembling field hockey but differing in that the ball may be struck with the hand and kicked when off the ground and may be balanced in the stick and hurled

Huron (ˈhyōōrən, ˈhōō-) *n.* **1.** confederacy of Amerindian peoples of St. Lawrence valley **2.** member of any of these peoples (*pl.* **-ron, -s**)

hurrah (hōōˈrö, -ˈrä) *or* **hooray** *interj.* exclamation of joy or applause

hurricane (ˈhurikān, ˈhurikən) *n.* very strong, potentially destructive wind or storm —**hurricane lamp** lamp with glass covering round flame

hurry (ˈhuri) *v.* **1.** (cause to) move or act in great haste (**ˈhurried, ˈhurrying**) —*n.* **2.** undue haste **3.** eagerness —**ˈhurriedly** *adv.*

hurst (hərst) *n. obs.* **1.** wood **2.** sandbank

hurt (hərt) *vt.* **1.** injure, damage, give pain to **2.** wound feelings of, distress —*vi.* **3.** *inf.* feel pain (**hurt** *pt./pp.*) —*n.* **4.** wound, injury, harm —**ˈhurtful** *a.*

hurtle (ˈhərtəl) *vi.* **1.** move rapidly **2.** rush violently **3.** whirl

husband (ˈhuzbənd) *n.* **1.** married man —*v.* **2.** economize, manage or use to best advantage —**ˈhusbandry** *n.* **1.** farming **2.** economy

hush (hush) *v.* **1.** make or be silent —*n.* **2.** stillness **3.** quietness —**hush-hush** *a. inf.* secret —**hush up** suppress (rumors, information), make secret

husk (husk) *n.* **1.** dry covering of certain seeds and fruits **2.** worthless outside part —*vt.* **3.** remove husk from —**ˈhusky** *a.* **1.** rough in tone, hoarse **2.** dry as husk, dry in the throat **3.** of, full of, husks **4.** *inf.* big and strong

husky (ˈhuski) *n.* **1.** Arctic sled dog **2.** **C** *sl.* Inuit

hussar (hə'zär, -'sär) *n.* lightly armed cavalry soldier

hussy ('husi, -zi) *n.* brazen girl or young woman

hustings ('hustingz) *pl.n.* **1.** platform from which political speeches are made **2.** political campaigning

hustle ('husəl) *v.* **1.** push about, jostle, hurry —*vi.* **2.** *sl.* solicit —*n.* **3.** instance of hustling —'**hustler** *n.*

hut (hut) *n.* any small house or shelter, usu. of wood or metal

hutch (huch) *n.* boxlike pen for rabbits *etc.*

hyacinth ('hīəsinth) *n.* **1.** bulbous plant with bell-shaped flowers, *esp.* purple-blue **2.** this blue **3.** orange gem jacinth

hyaena (hī'ēnə) *n. see* HYENA

hyaline ('hīəlin) *a.* clear, translucent

hyaluronidase (hīlyōō'ronidās) *n.* enzyme which breaks down tissue thus enabling therapeutic liquids to be absorbed efficiently

hybrid ('hībrid) *n.* **1.** offspring of two plants or animals of different species **2.** mongrel —*a.* **3.** crossbred —'**hybridism** *n.* —'**hybridize** *v.* (cause to) produce hybrids; crossbreed

hybris ('hībris, 'he-) *n. see* HUBRIS

hydatid ('hīdətid) *a./n.* (of) watery cyst, resulting from development of tapeworm larva causing serious disease (in man)

hydra ('hīdrə) *n.* **1.** fabulous many-headed water serpent **2.** any persistent problem **3.** freshwater polyp (*pl.* **-s, -drae** (-drē)) —**hydra-headed** *a.* hard to root out

hydrangea (hī'drānjə) *n.* ornamental shrub with pink, blue, or white flowers

hydrant ('hīdrənt) *n.* pipe with valve and spout at which water may be drawn from a main pipe

hydrate ('hīdrāt) *n.* **1.** chemical compound containing water that is chemically combined with substance —*v.* **2.** (cause to) undergo treatment or impregnation with water —**hy'dration** *n.* —'**hydrator** *n.*

hydraulic (hī'drölik) *a.* concerned with, operated by, pressure transmitted through liquid in pipe —**hy'draulics** *pl.n.* (*with sing. v.*) science of mechanical properties of liquid in motion

Hydro ('hīdrō) *n.* **C** hydroelectric power company

hydro- *or before vowel* **hydr-** (*comb. form*) **1.** water, as in *hydroelectric* **2.** presence of hydrogen, as in *hydrocarbon*

hydrocarbon (hīdrə'kärbən) *n.* compound of hydrogen and carbon

hydrocephalus (hīdrō'sefələs) *or* **hydrocephaly** (hīdrō'sefəli) *n.* accumulation of cerebrospinal fluid within ventricles of brain —**hydrocephalic** (hīdrōsə'falik) *or* **hydro'cephalous** *a.*

hydrochloric acid (hīdrə'klorik) strong colorless acid used in many industrial and laboratory processes

hydrocyanic acid (hīdrōsī'anik) *see* **hydrogen cyanide** *at* HYDROGEN

hydrodynamics (hīdrōdī'namiks) *pl.n.* (*with sing. v.*) science of the motions of system wholly or partly fluid

hydroelectric (hīdrōi'lektrik) *a.* pert. to generation of electricity by use of water

hydrofoil ('hīdrəfoil) *n.* fast, light vessel with hull raised out of water at speed by vanes in water

hydrogen ('hīdrijən) *n. Chem.* gaseous element *Symbol* H, at. wt. 1.0, at. no. 1 —**hy'drogenate** *v.* (cause to) undergo reaction with hydrogen —**hydrogen'ation** *n.* —**hydrogen bomb** atom bomb of enormous power —**hydrogen cyanide** colorless poisonous liquid with faint odor of bitter almonds, used for making plastics and as war gas —**hydrogen peroxide** colorless liquid used as antiseptic and bleach

hydrography (hī'drogrəfi) *n.* description of waters of the earth —**hy'drographer** *n.* —**hydro'graphic** *a.*

hydrology (hī'droləji) *n.* study of distribution, use *etc.* of the water of the earth and its atmosphere —**hydrologic** (hīdrə'lojik) *a.* —**hy'drologist** *n.*

hydrolysis (hī'drolisis) *n.* decomposition of chemical compound reacting with water

hydrometer (hī'dromitər) *n.* device for measuring relative density of liquid

hydronephrosis (hīdrōni'frōsis) *n.* dilation of parts of kidney by dammed-up urine

hydrophilic (hīdrə'filik) *a. Chem.* tending to dissolve in, mix with, or be wetted by water —'**hydrophile** *n.*

hydrophobia (hīdrə'fōbiə) *n.* rabies

hydrophone ('hīdrəfōn) *n.* instrument for detecting sound through water

hydroplane ('hīdrəplān) *n.* **1.** speedboat with hull raised partly out of water **2.** seaplane **3.** vane controlling motion of submarine *etc.*

hydroponics (hīdrə'poniks) *pl.n.* (*with sing. v.*) science of cultivating plants in water without using soil

hydrosphere ('hīdrəsfēər) *n.* watery part of earth's surface, including oceans, lakes, water vapor in atmosphere *etc.*

hydrostatics (hīdrə'statiks) *pl.n.* (*with sing. v.*) branch of science concerned with mechanical properties and behavior of fluids that are not in motion —**hydro'static** *a.*

hydrotherapy (hīdrə'therəpi) *n. Med.* treatment of disease by external application of water

hydrotropism (hī'drotrəpizəm) *n.* directional growth of plants in response to water

hydrous ('hīdrəs) *a.* containing water

hydroxide (hī'droksīd) *n. Chem.* any compound containing OH group, *eg* NaOH (sodium hydroxide)

hydrozoan (hīdrə'zōən) *n.* **1.** any coelenterate of the class *Hydrozoa,* which includes hydra and Portuguese man-of-war —*a.* **2.** of *Hydrozoa*

hyena

hyena *or* **hyaena** (hī'ēnə) *n.* nocturnal carnivorous mammal of Asia and Africa having howl like wild laughter

hygiene ('hījēn) *n.* **1.** principles and practice of health and cleanliness **2.** study of these principles —**hygienic** (hīji'enik) *a.* —**hygienically** (hīji'enikəli) *adv.* —**hy'gienist** *n.*

hygrometer (hī'gromitər) *n.* instrument for measuring humidity of air

hygroscopic (hīgrə'skopik) *a.* readily absorbing moisture from the atmosphere

hymen ('hīmən) *n.* **1.** membrane partly covering vagina of virgin **2.** (**H-**) Greek god of marriage

hymenopterous (hīmi'noptərəs) *a.* of large order of insects having two pairs of membranous wings —**hyme'nopteran** *n.* any hymenopterous insect (*pl.* **-tera** (-tərə))

hymn (him) *n.* **1.** song of praise, *esp.* to God —*vt.* **2.** praise in song —**hymnal** ('himnəl) *a.* **1.** of hymns —*n.* **2.** book of hymns (*also* **hymn book**) —**hymnodist** ('himnədist) *n.* —**hymnody** ('himnədl) *n.* singing or composition of hymns

hyoscyamine (hīə'sīəmēn) *n.* poisonous alkaloid occurring in belladonna and related plants and used like atropine

hype[1] (hīp) *sl.* *n.* **1.** hypodermic syringe **2.** drug addict —*vi.* **3.** (*with* up) inject oneself with drug

hype[2] (hīp) *sl.* *n.* **1.** deception; racket **2.** intensive or exaggerated publicity or sales promotion —*vt.* **3.** market or promote, using exaggerated or intensive publicity

hyper- (*comb. form*) over, above, excessively, as in *hyperactive.* Such words are not given here where the meaning may easily be inferred from the simple word

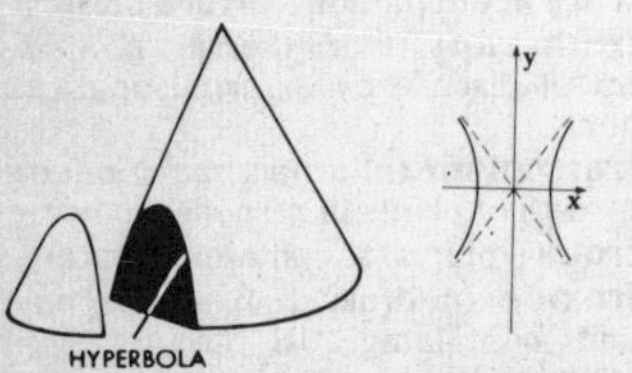

HYPERBOLA

hyperbola (hī'pərbələ) *n.* curve (in two parts) produced when double right circular cone is cut by plane making larger angle with the base than the side makes (*pl.* **-s, -le** (-lē))

hyperbole (hī'pərbəli) *n.* rhetorical exaggeration —**hyperbolic(al)** (hīpər'bolik(əl)) *a.*

Hyperborean (hīpər'bōriən) *a./n.* (inhabitant) of extreme north

hypercritical (hīpər'kritikəl) *a.* too critical —**hyper'criticism** *n.*

hyperglycemia (hīpərglī'sēmiə) *n.* abnormally large amount of sugar in blood —**hypergly'cemic** *a.*

hyperhidrosis (hīpərhi'drōsis, -hī-) *n.* excessive sweating

hyperinsulinism (hīpər'insəlinizəm) *n.* overproduction of insulin

hypermetropia (hīpərmi'trōpiə) *n.* condition in which images come to a focus behind the retina of the eye resulting in better vision for distant objects (*also* **hyperopia, farsightedness**) —**hypermetropic** (hīpərmi'tropik) *a.*

hyperon ('hīpəron) *n.* *Phys.* any baryon that is not a nucleon

hyperopia (hīpə'rōpiə) *n.* *see* HYPERMETROPIA —**hyperopic** (hīpə'rōpik, -'ropik) *a.*

hypersensitive (hīpər'sensitiv) *a.* unduly vulnerable emotionally or physically

hypersonic (hīpər'sonik) *a.* concerned with or having velocity of at least five times that of sound in same medium under the same conditions —**hyper'sonics** *n.*

hypertension ('hīpərtenchən) *n.* abnormally high blood pressure

hypertrophy (hī'pərtrəfi) *n.* **1.** enlargement of organ or part resulting from increase in size of cells —*v.* **2.** (cause to) undergo this condition

hyperventilation (hīpərventi'lāshən) *n.* increase in rate of breathing, sometimes resulting in cramp and dizziness

hyphen ('hīfən) *n.* short line (-) indicating that two words or syllables are to be connected or separated —**'hyphenate** *vt.* —**'hyphenated** *a.* joined by hyphen

hypno- *or before vowel* **hypn-** (*comb. form*) **1.** sleep, as in *hypnophobia* **2.** hypnosis, as in *hypnotherapy*

hypnosis (hip'nōsis) *n.* induced state like deep sleep in which subject acts on external suggestion (*pl.* **-ses** (-sēz)) —**hypnotic** (hip'notik) *a./n.* (of, relating to) drug which induces sleep —**'hypnotism** *n.* —**'hypnotist** *n.* —**'hypnotize** *vt.* affect with hypnosis —**hypno'therapy** *n.* use of hypnosis in treatment of physical or mental disorders

hypo ('hīpō) *n.* sodium thiosulfate, used as fixer in developing photographs

hypo- *or before vowel* **hyp-** (*comb. form*) under, below, less, as in *hypocrite, hyphen.* Such words are not given here where meaning may easily be inferred from simple word

hypocaust ('hīpəköst) *n.* ancient Roman underfloor heating system

hypochondria (hīpə'kondriə) *or* **hypochondriasis** (hīpəkən'drīəsis) *n.* morbid preoccupation about one's own health —**hypo'chondriac** *a./n.* —**hypochon'driacal** *a.*

hypocrisy (hi'pokrəsi) *n.* **1.** assuming of false appearance of virtue **2.** insincerity —**'hypocrite** *n.* —**hypo'critical** *a.* —**hypo'critically** *adv.*

hypodermic (hīpə'dərmik) *a.* **1.** introduced, injected beneath the skin —*n.* **2.** hypodermic syringe or needle

hypogastric (hīpə'gastrik) *a.* relating to, situated in, lower part of abdomen

hypoglycemia (hīpōglī'sēmiə) *n.* abnormally low concentration of sugar in the blood

hypogonadism (hīpō'gonədizəm) *n.* partial or complete lack of functioning of the sex glands

hypostasis (hī'postəsis) *n.* **1.** *Metaphys.* essential nature of anything **2.** *Christianity* any of the three persons of the Godhead **3.** accumulation of blood in organ or part as result of poor circulation (*pl.* **-ses** (-sēz)) —**hypostatic** (hīpə'statik) *or* **hypo'statical** *a.*

hypotension ('hīpōtenchən) *n.* abnormally low blood pressure —**hypo'tensive** *a.*

hypotenuse (hī'potinyōōs, -nōōs, -nyōōz, -nōōz) *n.* side of a right-angled triangle opposite the right angle

hypothecate (hī'pothikāt) *vt.* **1.** *see* **hypothesize** *at* HYPOTHESIS **2.** *Law* pledge (personal property) as security for debt without transferring possession —**hypothe'cation** *n.* —**hy'pothecator** *n.*

hypothermia (hīpō'thərmiə) *n.* condition of having body temperature reduced to dangerously low level

hypothesis (hī'pothisis) *n.* **1.** suggested explanation of something **2.** assumption as basis of reasoning (*pl.* **-eses** (-isēz)) —**hy'pothesize** *v.* —**hypo'thetical** *a.* —**hypo'thetically** *adv.*

hypso- *or before vowel* **hyps-** (*comb. form*) height, as in *hypsometry*

hypsography (hip'sogrəfi) *n.* branch of geography dealing with altitudes

hypsometer (hip'somitər) *n.* instrument for measuring altitudes —**hyp'sometry** *n.* science of measuring altitudes

hyrax ('hīraks) *n.* genus of hoofed but rodent-like animals (*pl.* **-es, hyraces** ('hīrəsēz))

hyssop ('hisəp) *n.* small aromatic herb

hysterectomy (histə'rektəmi) *n.* surgical operation for removing the uterus

hysteresis (histə'rēsis) *n. Phys.* lag or delay in changes in variable property of a system

hysteria (hi'steriə, -'stēəriə) *n.* **1.** mental disorder with emotional outbursts **2.** any frenzied emotional state **3.** fit of crying or laughing —**hys'terical** *a.* —**hys'terically** *adv.* —**hys'terics** *pl.n.* fits of hysteria

Hz hertz

I

i *or* **I** (ī) *n.* **1.** ninth letter of English alphabet **2.** any of several speech sounds represented by this letter **3.** something shaped like I (*pl.* **i's, I's** *or* **Is**) —**dot one's i's and cross one's t's** pay attention to detail

i 1. interest **2.** intransitive **3.** island(s) **4.** isle(s)

I (ī) *pron.* the pronoun of the first person singular

I 1. *Chem.* iodine **2.** *Phys.* current **3.** *Phys.* isospin **4.** Roman numeral, one

IA Iowa

-ia (*comb. form*) **1.** in place names, as in *Columbia* **2.** in names of diseases, as in *pneumonia* **3.** in words denoting condition or quality, as in *utopia* **4.** in names of botanical genera and zoological classes, as in *Reptilia* **5.** in collective nouns borrowed from Latin, as in *regalia*

IAEA International Atomic Energy Agency

-ial (*comb. form*) of or relating to, as in *managerial*

iamb ('īam, 'īamb) *or* **iambus** (ī'ambəs) *n.* metrical foot of short and long syllable (*pl.* **'iambs** *or* **-buses, -bi** (-bī)) —**i'ambic** *a.*

IATA (ī'ätə, ē'ätə) International Air Transport Association

-iatrics *or* **-iatry** (*n. comb. form*) medical care or treatment, as in *pediatrics, psychiatry* —**-iatric(al)** (*a. comb. form*)

iatrogenic (īatrə'jenik) *a.* (of a disease) induced inadvertently by a physician

Iberian (ī'bēəriən) *a.* of Iberia, *ie* Spain and Portugal

ibex ('ībeks) *n.* wild goat with large horns (*pl.* **-es, 'ibex**)

ibid. *or* **ib.** ibidem (*Lat.*, in the same place)

ibis ('ībis) *n.* storklike bird

-ible (*a. comb. form*) *see* -ABLE —**-ibly** (*adv. comb. form*) —**-ibility** (*n. comb. form*)

i/c 1. in charge (of) **2.** internal combustion

-ic (*comb. form*) **1.** of, relating to or resembling, as in *periodic* (*also* **-ical**) **2.** *Chem.* indicating that element is chemically combined in higher of two possible valence states, as in *ferric*

ICA International Cooperation Administration

-ical (*a. comb. form*) *see* -IC (sense 1) —**-ically** (*adv. comb. form*)

ICBM intercontinental ballistic missile

ICC 1. Interstate Commerce Commission **2.** Indian Claims Commission

ice (īs) *n.* **1.** frozen water **2.** frozen confection, ice cream —*v.* **3.** (*oft. with* up, over *etc.*) cover, become covered with ice —*vt.* **4.** cool with ice **5.** cover with icing —**'icicle** *n.* tapering spike of ice hanging where water has dripped —**'icily** *adv.* —**'iciness** *n.* —**'icing** *n.* semisolid flavored sweet mixture used to coat cakes and cookies (*also* **frosting**) —**'icy** *a.* **1.** covered with ice **2.** cold **3.** chilling —**ice age** *see* **glacial period** *at* GLACIER —**'iceberg** *n.* large floating mass of ice —**'icebox** *n.* **1.** refrigerator **2.** insulated cabinet packed with ice for storing food —**'icebreaker** *n.* **1.** vessel for breaking up ice in bodies of water (*also* **'iceboat**) **2.** device for breaking ice into smaller pieces —**'icecap** *n.* mass of glacial ice that permanently covers polar regions *etc.* —**ice cream** sweetened frozen dessert made from cream, eggs *etc.* —**ice floe** sheet of floating ice —**ice hockey** indoor or outdoor game played by two teams of six players wearing ice skates whose object is to score points by propelling a disk called a puck into the opponents' goal —**ice pack 1.** bag *etc.* containing ice, applied to part of body to reduce swelling *etc.* **2.** *see* **pack ice** *at* PACK —**ice skate** boot having steel blade fitted to sole to enable wearer to glide over ice —**ice-skate** *vi.* glide over ice on ice skates —**ice-skater** *n.* —**on thin ice** unsafe; vulnerable

Iceland ('īslənd, -land) *n.* country occupying a large island in the N Atlantic Ocean close to the Arctic Circle —**'Icelander** *n.* native or inhabitant of Iceland —**Ice'landic** *a.* **1.** of, or relating to Iceland —*n.* **2.** language of Iceland, which is a Scandinavian language

ichneumon (ik'nyōōmən, -'nōō-) *n.* grayish-brown mongoose

ichor ('īkôr) *n.* **1.** *Gr. myth.* fluid said to flow in veins of gods **2.** *Pathol.* foul-smelling watery discharge from wound or ulcer —**'ichorous** *a.*

ichthyology (ikthi'oləji) *n.* scientific study of fish —**ichthyosaurus** (ikthiə'sôrəs) *n.* prehistoric marine animal (*pl.* **-i** (-ī))

icicle ('īsikəl) *n. see* ICE

icon *or* **ikon** ('īkon) *n.* image, representation, *esp.* of religious figure —**i'conoclasm** *n.* —**i'conoclast** *n.* **1.** one who attacks established principles *etc.* **2.** breaker of icons —**icono'clastic** *a.* —**ico'nography** *n.* **1.** icons collectively **2.** study of icons —**ico'nostasis** *n.* icon-covered screen in Greek or Russian Orthodox Church that separates sanctuary from public areas

icono- *or before vowel* **icon-** (*comb. form*) image; likeness, as in *iconology*

ichthyosis (ikthi'ōsis) *n.* skin disease characterized by dry and scaly skin (*also* **fish skin**)

icterus ('iktərəs) *n.* condition in which bile pigments accumulate in body fluids tinting skin and whites of eyeballs a greenish yellow (*also* **jaundice**)

ictus ('iktəs) *n.* **1.** *Prosody* metrical or rhythmical stress in verse feet, as contrasted with stress accent on words **2.** *Med.* sudden attack or stroke (*pl.* **-es, -tus**) —'**ictal** *a.*

id (id) *n. Psychoanal.* the mind's instinctive energies

ID **1.** Idaho **2.** identification

-id (*comb. form*) member of zoological family, as in *cyprinid*

Idaho ('Īdəhō) *n.* Mountain state of the U.S., admitted to the Union in 1890. Abbrev.: **ID** (with ZIP code)

idea (ī'dēə) *n.* **1.** notion in the mind **2.** conception **3.** vague belief **4.** plan, aim —**i'deal** *n.* **1.** conception of something that is perfect **2.** perfect person or thing —*a.* **3.** perfect **4.** visionary **5.** existing only in idea —**i'dealism** *n.* **1.** tendency to seek perfection in everything **2.** philosophy that mind is the only reality —**i'dealist** *n.* **1.** one who holds doctrine of idealism **2.** one who strives after the ideal **3.** impractical person —**ideal'istic** *a.* —**ideali'zation** *n.* —**i'dealize** *vt.* portray as ideal —**i'deally** *adv.*

idée fixe (ēdā 'fēks) *Fr.* fixed idea; obsession (*pl.* ***idées fixes*** (ēdā 'fēks))

idem ('Īdem, 'idem) *Lat.,* the same

identity (ī'dentiti) *n.* **1.** individuality **2.** being the same, exactly alike —**i'dentical** *a.* very same —**i'dentically** *adv.* —**i'dentifiable** *a.* —**identifi'cation** *n.* —**i'dentify** *vt.* **1.** establish identity of **2.** treat as identical —*v.* **3.** associate (oneself) (**i'dentified, i'dentifying**) —**identification parade** group of persons assembled for purpose of discovering whether witness can identify suspect

ideo- (*comb. form*) idea; ideas, as in *ideology*

ideogram ('idiəgram) *or* **ideograph** ('idiəgraf) *n.* picture, symbol, figure *etc.* suggesting an object without naming it —**ide'ography** *n.* representation of things by ideograms

ideology (Īdi'oləji) *n.* body of ideas, beliefs of group, nation *etc.* —**ideo'logical** *a.*

ides (Īdz) *n.* the 15th of March, May, July and Oct. and the 13th of other months of the Ancient Roman calendar

id est (id est) *Lat.,* that is

idiocy ('idiəsi) *n. see* IDIOT

idiom ('idiəm) *n.* **1.** way of expression natural or peculiar to a language or group **2.** characteristic style of expression —**idio'matic** *a.* **1.** using idioms **2.** colloquial

idiosyncrasy (idiə'singkrəsi) *n.* peculiarity of mind, temper or disposition in a person

idiot ('idiət) *n.* **1.** mentally deficient person **2.** foolish, senseless person —'**idiocy** *n.* **1.** state of being an idiot **2.** foolish act or remark —**idi'otic** *a.* utterly senseless or stupid —**idi'otically** *adv.* —**idiot box** television —**idiot card** *sl.* card for prompting television performer

idle ('Īdəl) *a.* **1.** unemployed **2.** lazy **3.** useless; vain **4.** groundless —*vi.* **5.** be idle **6.** (of engine) run slowly with gears disengaged —*vt.* **7.** (*esp. with* away) waste —'**idleness** *n.* —'**idler** *n.* —'**idly** *adv.*

idol ('Īdəl) *n.* **1.** image of deity as object of worship **2.** object of excessive devotion —**i'dolater** *n.* worshiper of idols (**i'dolatress** *fem.*) —**i'dolatrous** *a.* —**i'dolatry** *n.* —'**idolize** *vt.* **1.** love or venerate to excess **2.** make an idol of

idyll *or* **idyl** ('Īdil) *n.* **1.** short descriptive poem of picturesque or charming scene or episode, *esp.* of rustic life **2.** charming or picturesque scene or event —**i'dyllic** *a.* **1.** of, like, idyll **2.** delightful —**i'dyllically** *adv.*

i.e. id est

if (if) *conj.* **1.** on condition or supposition that **2.** whether **3.** although —*n.* **4.** uncertainty, doubt (*esp. in* **ifs and buts**)

-iferous (*comb. form*) containing, yielding, as in *carboniferous*

igloo

igloo ('iglu:) *n.* Eskimo house built of soil, wood or stone or of snow and ice

igneous ('igniəs) *a.* (*esp.* of rocks) formed as molten rock cools and hardens

ignis fatuus ('ignis 'fachōōəs) will-o'-the-wisp (*pl.* **ignes fatui** ('ignēz 'fachōōī))

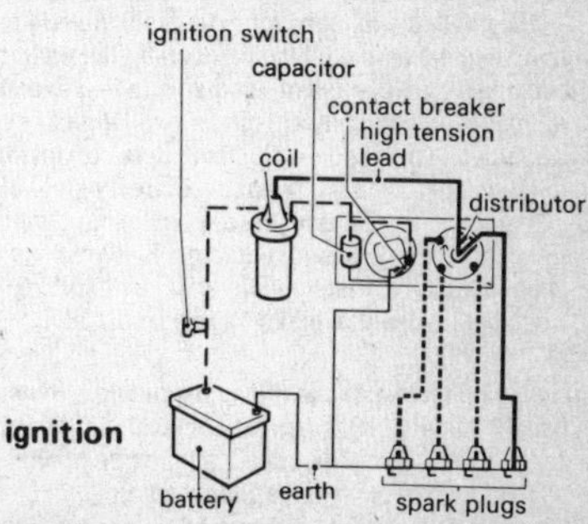

ignition

ignite (ig'nīt) *v.* (cause to) burn —**ignition** (ig'nishən) *n.* **1.** act of kindling or setting on fire **2.** in internal-combustion engine, means of firing explosive mixture, usu. electric spark

ignoble (ig'nōbəl) *a.* **1.** mean, base **2.** of low birth —**ig'nobly** *adv.*

ignominy ('ignəmini) *n.* **1.** dishonor, disgrace **2.** shameful act —**igno'minious** *a.*

ignore (ig'nör) *vt.* disregard; leave out of account —**ignoramus** (ignə'rāməs) *n.* ignorant person (*pl.* **-es**) —**'ignorance** *n.* lack of knowledge —**'ignorant** *a.* **1.** lacking knowledge **2.** uneducated **3.** unaware —**'ignorantly** *adv.*

iguana (i'gwänə) *n.* large tropical American tree-climbing lizard

ikebana (ikā'bänə) *n.* Japanese decorative art of flower arrangement

ikon ('īkon) *n. see* ICON

IL Illinois

il- (*comb. form*) *see* IN-[1], IN-[2]

ileum ('iliəm) *n.* lower part of small intestine (*pl.* **-ea** (-iə)) —**'ileac** *a.* —**'ileus** *n.* interference with normal flow of intestinal contents caused by mechanical obstruction or by disturbance of blood or nerve supply

ilex ('īleks) *n.* any of genus of trees or shrubs such as holly and inkberry

ilium ('iliəm) *n.* uppermost and widest of three sections of hipbone (*pl.* **-ia** (-iə)) —**'iliac** *a.*

ilk (ilk) *a.* same —**of that ilk 1.** of the same type or class **2.** *Scot.* of the place of the same name

ill (il) *a.* **1.** not in good health **2.** bad, evil **3.** faulty **4.** unfavorable —*n.* **5.** evil, harm **6.** mild disease —*adv.* **7.** badly **8.** hardly, with difficulty —**'illness** *n.* —**ill-advised** *a.* imprudent, injudicious —**ill-bred** *a.* badly brought up; lacking good manners —**ill-considered** *a.* done without due consideration; not thought out —**ill-disposed** *a.* (*oft. with* toward) not kindly disposed —**ill fame** bad reputation —**ill-fated** *a.* unfortunate —**ill-favored** *a.* ugly, deformed —**ill-founded** *a.* not founded on true or reliable premises; unsubstantiated —**ill-gotten** *a.* obtained dishonestly —**ill-mannered** *a.* boorish, uncivil —**ill-natured** *a.* naturally unpleasant and mean —**ill-omened** *a.* unlucky, inauspicious —**ill-starred** *a.* unlucky, ill-fated —**ill-timed** *a.* inopportune —**ill-treat** *vt.* treat cruelly —**ill-use** ('il'yōōz) *vt.* **1.** use badly or cruelly; abuse —*n.* ('il'yōōs), *also* **ill-usage 2.** harsh or cruel treatment; abuse —**ill will** unkind feeling, hostility —**house of ill fame** brothel

Ill. Illinois

illegal (i'lēgəl) *a.* **1.** forbidden by law; unlawful; illicit **2.** unauthorized or prohibited by code of official or accepted rules —**ille'gality** *n.* —**il'legally** *adv.*

illegible (i'lejibəl) *a.* unable to be read or deciphered —**illegi'bility** *n.*

illegitimate (ili'jitimit) *a.* **1.** born out of wedlock **2.** unlawful **3.** not regular —**ille'gitimacy** *n.*

illiberal (i'libərəl) *a.* **1.** narrow-minded; prejudiced; intolerant **2.** not generous; mean **3.** lacking in culture or refinement —**illiber'ality** *n.*

illicit (i'lisit) *a.* **1.** illegal **2.** prohibited, forbidden

illimitable (i'limitəbəl) *a.* that cannot be limited, boundless, unrestricted, infinite —**il'limitableness** *n.*

Illinois (ili'noi) *n.* **1.** East North Central state of the U.S., admitted to the Union in 1818. Abbrev.: **Ill., IL** (with ZIP code) **2.** confederacy of Algonquian-speaking Amerindian peoples of Illinois, Iowa and Wisconsin **3.** member of any of these peoples (*pl.* **-nois**)

illiterate (i'litərit) *a.* **1.** not literate, unable to read or write **2.** violating accepted standards in reading and writing **3.** uneducated, ignorant, uncultured —*n.* **4.** illiterate person —**il'literacy** *n.*

illogical (i'lojikəl) *a.* **1.** characterized by lack of logic, senseless; unreasonable **2.** disregarding logical principles —**illogi'cality** *or* **il'logicalness** *n.* —**il'logically** *adv.*

illuminate (i'lōōmināt) *vt.* **1.** light up **2.** clarify **3.** decorate with lights **4.** decorate with gold and colors —**il'luminant** *n.* agent of lighting —**illumi'nation** *n.* —**il'luminative** *a.*

illus. *or* **illust. 1.** illustrated **2.** illustration

illusion (i'lōōzhən) *n.* deceptive appearance or belief —**il'lusionist** *n.* conjurer —**il'lusory** *or* **il'lusive** *a.* false

illustrate ('iləstrāt) *vt.* **1.** provide with pictures or examples **2.** exemplify —**illus'tration** *n.* **1.** picture, diagram **2.** example **3.** act of illustrating —**'illustrative** *a.* providing explanation —**'illustrator** *n.*

illustrious (i'lustriəs) *a.* famous, distinguished, exalted

im- (*comb. form*) *see* IN-[1], IN-[2]

image ('imij) *n.* **1.** representation or likeness of person or thing **2.** optical counterpart, as in mirror **3.** double, copy **4.** general impression **5.** mental picture created by words, *esp.* in literature **6.** personality presented to the public by a person —*vt. rare* **7.** make image of **8.** reflect —**'imagery** *n.* images collectively, *esp.* in literature

imagine (i'majin) *vt.* **1.** picture to oneself **2.** think **3.** conjecture —**i'maginable** *a.* —**i'maginary** *a.* existing only in fancy —**imagi'nation** *n.* **1.** faculty of making mental images of things not present **2.** fancy —**im'aginative** *a.* —**im'aginatively** *adv.*

imago (i'māgō) *n.* **1.** last, perfected state of insect life **2.** image (*pl.* **-s, imagines** (i'māgənēz))

imam (i'mäm) *n.* **1.** leader of prayers in mosque **2.** (**I-**) title of any of various Muslim leaders

imbalance (im'baləns) *n.* lack of balance, proportion
imbecile ('imbisil) *n.* **1.** idiot —*a.* **2.** idiotic —**imbe'cility** *n.*
imbed (im'bed) *vt. see* EMBED
imbibe (im'bīb) *vt.* **1.** drink in **2.** absorb —*vi.* **3.** drink
imbricate ('imbrikit) *a.* lying over each other in regular order, like tiles or shingles on roof (*also* **'imbricated**) —**imbri'cation** *n.*
imbroglio (im'brōlyō) *n.* complicated situation, plot (*pl.* **-s**)
imbue (im'byo͞o) *vt.* inspire
IMF International Monetary Fund
imitate ('imitāt) *vt.* **1.** take as model **2.** mimic, copy —**'imitable** *a.* —**imi'tation** *n.* **1.** act of imitating **2.** copy of original **3.** likeness **4.** counterfeit —**'imitative** *a.* —**'imitator** *n.*
immaculate (i'makyo͝olit) *a.* **1.** spotless **2.** pure **3.** unsullied
immanent ('imənənt) *a.* existing within, inherent —**'immanence** *n.*
immaterial (imə'tēəriəl) *a.* **1.** unimportant, trifling **2.** not consisting of matter **3.** spiritual
immeasurable (i'mezhərəbəl) *a.* incapable of being measured, *esp.* by virtue of great size; limitless —**immeasura'bility** *or* **im'measurableness** *n.* —**im'measurably** *adv.*
immediate (i'mēdiət) *a.* **1.** occurring at once **2.** direct, not separated by others —**im'mediacy** *n.* —**im'mediately** *adv.*
immemorial (imi'möriəl) *a.* beyond memory
immense (i'mens) *a.* huge, vast —**im'mensely** *adv.* —**im'mensity** *n.* vastness
immerse (i'mərs) *vt.* **1.** dip, plunge into liquid **2.** involve, engross —**im'mersion** *n.* immersing —**immersion foot** circulatory disturbance arising from prolonged exposure to below-freezing cold and dampness (*also* **trench foot**)
immesh (i'mesh) *vt. see* ENMESH
immigrate ('imigrāt) *vi.* come into country as settler —**'immigrant** *n./a.* —**immi'gration** *n.*
imminent ('iminənt) *a.* **1.** liable to happen soon **2.** close at hand —**'imminence** *n.* —**'imminently** *adv.*
immobilize (i'mōbilīz) *vt.* **1.** make immobile **2.** *Fin.* convert (circulating capital) into fixed capital —**immobili'zation** *n.* —**im'mobilizer** *n.*
immolate ('imәlāt) *vt.* kill, sacrifice —**immo'lation** *n.*
immoral (i'morəl) *a.* **1.** corrupt **2.** promiscuous **3.** indecent **4.** unethical —**immo'rality** *n.*
immortal (i'mörtəl) *a.* **1.** deathless **2.** famed for all time —*n.* **3.** immortal being **4.** god **5.** one whose fame will last —**immor'tality** *n.* —**im'mortalize** *vt.*
immune (i'myo͞on) *a.* **1.** able to resist (disease *etc.*) **2.** secure **3.** exempt —**im'munity** *n.* **1.** state of being immune **2.** freedom from prosecution, tax *etc.* —**immuni'zation** *n.* process of making immune to disease —**'immunize** *vt.* make immune —**immu'nology** *n.* branch of biology concerned with study of immunity
immure (i'myo͞oər) *vt.* imprison, wall up
immutable (i'myo͞otəbəl) *a.* unchangeable
imp (imp) *n.* **1.** little devil **2.** mischievous child —**'impish** *a.* of or like an imp; mischievous
imp. 1. imperative **2.** imperfect
impact ('impakt) *n.* **1.** collision **2.** profound effect —*vt.* (im'pakt) **3.** drive, press —**im'pacted** *a.* **1.** (of tooth) wedged against another tooth below gum **2.** (of fracture) having jagged broken ends wedged into each other
impair (im'pāər) *vt.* weaken, damage —**im'pairment** *n.*

impala

impala (im'palə) *n.* antelope of southern Afr.
impale (im'pāl) *vt.* **1.** pierce with sharp instrument **2.** combine (two coats of arms) by placing them side by side with line between —**im'palement** *n.*
impanel (im'panəl) *vt. Law* **1.** enter on list (names of persons to be summoned for jury service) **2.** select (jury) from such list —**im'panelment** *n.*
impart (im'pärt) *vt.* **1.** communicate (information *etc.*) **2.** give
impartial (im'pärshəl) *a.* **1.** not biased or prejudiced **2.** fair —**imparti'ality** *n.*
impassable (im'pasəbəl) *a.* **1.** not capable of being passed **2.** blocked, as mountain pass
impasse ('impas, im'pas) *n.* **1.** deadlock **2.** place, situation, from which there is no outlet
impassible (im'pasəbəl) *a. rare* **1.** not susceptible to pain or injury **2.** impassive; unmoved —**impassi'bility** *or* **im'passibleness** *n.*
impassioned (im'pashənd) *a.* deeply moved, ardent
impassive (im'pasiv) *a.* **1.** showing no emotion **2.** calm —**impas'sivity** *n.*
impasto (im'pastō) *n.* **1.** paint applied thickly, so that brush marks are evident **2.** technique of painting in this way

impeach (im'pēch) *vt.* **1.** charge with crime **2.** call to account **3.** denounce —**im'peachable** *a.* —**im'peachment** *n.*

impeccable (im'pekəbəl) *a.* without flaw or error —**impecca'bility** *n.*

impecunious (impi'kyo͞onyəs, -niəs) *a.* poor —**impecuni'osity** *n.*

impede (im'pēd) *vt.* hinder —**im'pedance** *n.* *Elec.* measure of opposition offered to flow of alternating current —**impediment** (im'pedimənt) *n.* **1.** obstruction **2.** defect —**impedimenta** (impedi'mentə) *pl.n.* **1.** any objects that impede progress, *esp.* baggage and equipment carried by army **2.** *Law* obstructions to making of contract, *esp.* of marriage

impel (im'pel) *vt.* **1.** induce, incite **2.** drive, force (**-ll-**) —**im'peller** *n.*

impend (im'pend) *vi.* **1.** threaten, be imminent **2.** (*with* over) *rare* hang —**im'pending** *a.*

impenitent (im'penitənt) *a.* not sorry or penitent; unrepentant —**im'penitence** *n.*

imperative (im'perətiv) *a.* **1.** necessary **2.** peremptory **3.** expressing command —*n.* **4.** imperative mood —**im'peratively** *adv.*

imperceptible (impər'septibəl) *a.* too slight, subtle, gradual *etc.* to be perceived —**imperceptibility** *n.* —**imper'ceptibly** *adv.*

imperfect (im'pərfikt) *a.* **1.** exhibiting or characterized by faults, mistakes *etc.;* defective **2.** not complete or finished; deficient **3.** *Gram.* denoting tense of verbs usu. used to describe continuous or repeated past actions or events **4.** *Law* legally unenforceable **5.** *Mus.* proceeding to dominant from tonic, subdominant or any chord other than dominant **6.** *Mus.* of or relating to all intervals other than fourth, fifth and octave —*n.* **7.** *Gram.* (verb in) imperfect tense —**imper'fection** *n.* **1.** condition or quality of being imperfect **2.** fault, defect

imperial (im'pēəriəl) *a.* **1.** of empire or emperor **2.** majestic **3.** denoting weights and measures established by law, the customary system in U.S. —**im'perialism** *n.* **1.** extension of empire **2.** belief in colonial empire —**im'perialist** *a./n.* —**imperial'istic** *a.*

imperil (im'peril) *vt.* bring into peril, endanger

imperious (im'pēəriəs) *a.* domineering; haughty; dictatorial

impermeable (im'pərmiəbəl) *a.* (of substance) not allowing passage of fluid through interstices —**impermea'bility** *n.*

impersonal (im'pərsənəl) *a.* **1.** objective, having no personal significance **2.** devoid of human warmth, personality *etc.* **3.** (of verb) without personal subject —**imperson'ality** *n.*

impersonate (im'pərsənāt) *vt.* **1.** pretend to be (another person) **2.** imitate **3.** play the part of —**imperson'ation** *n.* —**im'personator** *n.*

impertinent (im'pərtinənt) *a.* insolent, rude —**im'pertinence** *n.* —**im'pertinently** *adv.*

imperturbable (impər'tərbəbəl) *a.* calm, not excitable —**imper'turbably** *adv.*

impervious (im'pərviəs) *a.* **1.** not affording passage **2.** (*oft. with* to) not receptive (to feeling, argument *etc.*) —**im'perviously** *adv.* —**im'perviousness** *n.*

impetigo (impi'tēgō, -'tīgō) *n.* contagious skin disease

impetuous (im'pecho͞oəs) *a.* likely to act without consideration, rash —**impetu'osity** *n.* —**im'petuously** *adv.*

impetus ('impitəs) *n.* **1.** force with which body moves **2.** impulse

impinge (im'pinj) *vi.* **1.** (*usu. with* on *or* upon) encroach **2.** (*usu. with* on, against *or* upon) collide (with) —**im'pingement** *n.*

impious ('impiəs) *a.* irreverent, profane, wicked —**impiety** (im'pīiti) *n.* **1.** lack of reverence or proper respect for a god **2.** any lack of proper respect **3.** impious act

implacable (im'plakəbəl) *a.* **1.** not to be appeased **2.** unyielding —**implaca'bility** *n.*

implant (im'plant) *vt.* **1.** insert, fix —*n.* ('implant) **2.** anything implanted, *esp.* surgically, such as tissue graft

implement ('implimənt) *n.* **1.** tool, instrument, utensil —*vt.* ('impliment) **2.** carry out (instructions *etc.*); put into effect

implicate ('implikāt) *vt.* **1.** involve, include **2.** imply **3.** *rare* entangle —**impli'cation** *n.* something implied —**im'plicit** *a.* **1.** implied but not expressed **2.** absolute and unreserved

implode (im'plōd) *v.* collapse inward

implore (im'plör) *vt.* entreat earnestly

imply (im'plī) *vt.* **1.** indicate by hint, suggest **2.** mean (**im'plied, im'plying**)

impolitic (im'politik) *a.* not politic or expedient —**im'politicly** *adv.*

imponderable (im'pondərəbəl, -drəbəl) *a.* **1.** unable to be weighed or assessed —*n.* **2.** something difficult or impossible to assess —**impondera'bility** *n.* —**im'ponderably** *adv.*

import (im'pört, 'impört) *vt.* **1.** bring in, introduce (*esp.* goods from foreign country) **2.** imply —*n.* ('impört) **3.** thing imported **4.** meaning **5.** importance **6.** **C** *sl.* sportsman not native to area where he plays —**im'portable** *a.* —**impor'tation** *n.* —**im'porter** *n.*

important (im'pörtənt) *a.* **1.** of great consequence **2.** momentous **3.** pompous —**im'portance** *n.* —**im'portantly** *adv.*

importune (impər'tyo͞on, -'to͞on, im'pörchən) *vt.* request, demand of (someone) persistently —**im'portunate** *a.* persistent —**im'portunately** *adv.* —**impor'tunity** *n.*

impose (im'pōz) *vt.* **1.** levy (tax, duty *etc.*) —*vi.* **2.** (*usu. with* on *or* upon) take advantage (of), practice deceit (on) —**im'posing** *a.* impressive —**impo'sition** *n.* **1.** that which is imposed **2.** tax **3.** burden **4.** deception —**'impost** *n.* duty, tax on imports

impossible (im'posəbəl) *a.* **1.** incapable of being done or experienced **2.** absurd **3.** unreasonable —**impossi'bility** *n.* —**im'possibly** *adv.*

impost ('impōst) *n. Archit.* member at top of column that supports arch

impostor *or* **imposter** (im'postər) *n.* deceiver, one who assumes false identity —**im'posture** *n.*

impotent ('impətənt) *a.* **1.** powerless **2.** (of males) incapable of sexual intercourse —'**impotence** *n.* —'**impotently** *adv.*

impound (im'pownd) *vt.* **1.** take legal possession of and, oft., place in a pound (automobiles, animals *etc.*) **2.** confiscate

impoverish (im'povərish) *vt.* make poor or weak —**im'poverishment** *n.*

impracticable (im'praktikəbəl) *a.* **1.** incapable of being put into practice or accomplished **2.** unsuitable for desired use —**impractica'bility** *n.* —**im'practicably** *adv.*

impractical (im'praktikəl) *a.* **1.** not practical or workable **2.** not gifted with practical skills —**impracti'cality** *n.* —**im'practically** *adv.*

imprecation (impri'kāshən) *n.* **1.** invoking of evil **2.** curse —'**imprecate** *v.*

impregnable (im'pregnəbəl) *a.* **1.** proof against attack **2.** unassailable **3.** unable to be broken into —**impregna'bility** *n.* —**im'pregnably** *adv.*

impregnate (im'pregnāt) *vt.* **1.** saturate, infuse **2.** make pregnant —**impreg'nation** *n.*

impresario (imprə'säriō) *n.* organizer of public entertainment; manager of opera, ballet *etc.* (*pl.* **-s**)

impress[1] (im'pres) *vt.* **1.** affect deeply, usu. favorably **2.** imprint, stamp **3.** fix —*n.* ('impres) **4.** act of impressing **5.** mark impressed —**impressi'bility** *n.* —**im'pressible** *a.* —**im'pression** *n.* **1.** effect produced, *esp.* on mind **2.** notion, belief **3.** imprint **4.** a printing **5.** total of copies printed at once **6.** printed copy —**impressiona'bility** *n.* —**im'pressionable** *a.* susceptible to external influences —**im'pressionism** *n.* art style that renders general effect without detail —**im'pressionist** *n.* —**impression'istic** *a.* —**im'pressive** *a.* making deep impression

impress[2] (im'pres) *vt.* press into service

imprest (im'prest) *vt.* **1.** advance on loan by government —*n.* **2.** money advanced by government

imprimatur (impri'mätŏŏər, im'primətyŏŏər, -tŏŏər) *n.* license to print book *etc.*

imprint ('imprint) *n.* **1.** mark made by pressure **2.** characteristic mark **3.** publisher's or printer's name and address in book *etc.* —*vt.* (im'print) **4.** produce (mark) on (surface) by pressure, printing or stamping **5.** fix in mind

imprison (im'prizən) *vt.* put in prison —**im'prisonment** *n.*

improbity (im'prōbiti) *n.* dishonesty, wickedness, unscrupulousness

impromptu (im'promptyōō, -tōō) *adv./a.* **1.** extempore; unrehearsed —*n.* **2.** improvisation

improper (im'propər) *a.* **1.** lacking propriety; not seemly or fitting **2.** unsuitable for certain use or occasion; inappropriate **3.** irregular; abnormal —**impropriety** (imprə'prīiti) *n.* **1.** lack of propriety; indecency **2.** improper act or use **3.** state of being improper —**improper fraction** fraction in which numerator is greater than denominator, as 7/6

improve (im'prōōv) *v.* make or become better in quality, standard, value *etc.* —**im'provable** *a.* —**im'provement** *n.* —**im'prover** *n.*

improvident (im'providənt) *a.* **1.** thriftless; imprudent **2.** negligent —**im'providence** *n.*

improvise ('imprəvīz) *v.* **1.** perform or make quickly from materials at hand **2.** perform (poem, piece of music *etc.*), composing as one goes along —**improvi'sation** *n.* —'**improviser** *or* '**improvisor** *n.*

impudent ('impyədənt) *a.* disrespectful, impertinent —'**impudence** *n.* —'**impudently** *adv.*

impugn (im'pyōōn) *vt.* call in question, challenge

impulse ('impuls) *n.* **1.** sudden inclination to act **2.** sudden application of force **3.** motion caused by it **4.** stimulation of nerve moving muscle —**im'pulsion** *n.* impulse —**im'pulsive** *a.* given to acting without reflection, rash

impunity (im'pyōōniti) *n.* freedom, exemption from injurious consequences or punishment

impurity (im'pyŏŏriti) *n.* **1.** quality of being impure **2.** impure thing or element **3.** *Electron.* small quantity of element added to pure semiconductor crystal to control its electrical conductivity

impute (im'pyōōt) *vt.* ascribe, attribute —**imputa'bility** *n.* —**impu'tation** *n.* **1.** that which is imputed as a charge or fault **2.** reproach, censure

in (in) *prep.* **1.** expresses inclusion within limits of space, time, circumstance, sphere *etc.* —*adv.* **2.** in or into some state, place *etc.* **3.** *inf.* in vogue *etc.* —*a.* **4.** *inf.* fashionable —**in for** about to be affected by —**ins and outs** intricacies, complications; details

In *Chem.* indium

IN Indiana

in. **1.** inch(es) **2.** inlet

in-[1], **il-**, **im-**, *or* **ir-** (*comb. form*) **1.** not; non-, as in *incredible, illegal, imperfect, irregular* **2.** lack of, as in *inexperience.* See the list below

in-[2], **il-**, **im-**, *or* **ir-** (*comb. form*) **1.** in; into; toward; within; on, as in *infiltrate, immigrate*

2. having intensive or causative function, as in *inflame, imperil*

in absentia (in abˈsenchə) *Lat.* in absence of (someone indicated)

inadvertent (inədˈvərtənt) *a.* **1.** not attentive **2.** negligent **3.** unintentional —**inadˈvertence** *or* **inadˈvertency** *n.* —**inadˈvertently** *adv.*

inalienable (inˈālyənəbəl) *a.* not able to be transferred to another —**inalienaˈbility** *n.*

inamorata (inaməˈrätə) *n.* woman with whom one is in love; lover (*pl.* **-s**)

inane (iˈnān) *a.* foolish, silly, vacant —**inanition** (inəˈnishən) *n.* **1.** exhaustion **2.** silliness —**inanity** (iˈnaniti) *n.*

inanimate (inˈanimit) *a.* **1.** lacking qualities of living beings **2.** appearing dead **3.** lacking vitality

inapposite (inˈapəzit) *a.* not appropriate or pertinent

inapt (inˈapt) *a.* **1.** not apt or fitting **2.** lacking skill; inept —**inˈaptitude** *or* **inˈaptness** *n.*

inasmuch as (inəzˈmuch) seeing that

inaugurate (inˈögyərāt, -gərāt) *vt.* **1.** begin, initiate the use of, *esp.* with ceremony **2.** admit to office —**inˈaugural** *a.* —**inˈaugurally** *adv.* —**inauguˈration** *n.* **1.** act of inaugurating **2.** ceremony to celebrate the initiation or admission of

inauspicious (inöˈspishəs) *a.* not auspicious; unlucky; unfavorable —**inausˈpiciously** *adv.*

inboard (ˈinbörd) *a.* inside hull or bulwarks

inborn (ˈinˈbörn) *a.* existing from birth; inherent

inbreed (ˈinˈbrēd) *v.* breed from union of closely related individuals (**ˈinˈbred** *pt./pp.*) —**ˈinˈbred** *a.* **1.** produced as result of inbreeding **2.** inborn, ingrained —**ˈinbreeding** *n.*

inc. 1. inclusive **2.** incorporated **3.** increase

incalculable (inˈkalkyələbəl) *a.* beyond calculation; very great

in camera in secret or private session

incandescent (inkanˈdesənt) *a.* **1.** glowing with heat, shining **2.** (of artificial light) produced by glowing filament —**incanˈdesce** *vi.* glow —**incanˈdescence** *n.*

incantation (inkanˈtāshən) *n.* magic spell or formula, charm

incapacitate (inkəˈpasitāt) *vt.* **1.** disable; make unfit **2.** disqualify —**incaˈpacity** *n.*

incarcerate (inˈkärsərāt) *vt.* imprison —**incarceˈration** *n.* —**inˈcarcerator** *n.*

incarnate (inˈkärnāt) *vt.* **1.** embody in flesh, *esp.* in human form —*a.* (inˈkärnit, -nāt) **2.** embodied in flesh, in human form **3.** typified —**incarˈnation** *n.*

incendiary (inˈsendieri) *a.* **1.** of malicious setting on fire of property **2.** creating strife, violence *etc.* **3.** designed to cause fires —*n.* **4.** fire raiser **5.** agitator **6.** bomb filled with flammable substance —**inˈcendiarism** *n.*

incense[1] (ˈinsens) *n.* **1.** gum, spice giving perfume when burned **2.** its smoke —*vt.* **3.** burn incense to **4.** perfume with it

incense[2] (inˈsens) *vt.* enrage

incentive (inˈsentiv) *n.* **1.** something that arouses to effort or action **2.** stimulus

inception (inˈsepshən) *n.* beginning

incessant (inˈsesənt) *a.* unceasing

incest (ˈinsest) *n.* sexual intercourse between two people too closely related to marry —**inˈcestuous** *a.*

inch[1] (inch) *n.* **1.** one twelfth of foot, or 0.0254 meter —*v.* **2.** move very slowly

inch[2] (inch) *n. Scot., Irish* small island

inchoate (inˈkōāt, ˈinkōāt) *a.* **1.** just begun **2.** undeveloped

incident (ˈinsidənt) *n.* **1.** event, occurrence —*a.* (*usu. with* to) **2.** naturally attaching (to) **3.** striking, falling (upon) —**ˈincidence** *n.* **1.** degree, extent or frequency of occurrence **2.** a falling on, or affecting —**inciˈdental** *a.* occurring as a minor part or an inevitable accompaniment or by chance —**inciˈdentally** *adv.* **1.** by chance **2.** by the way —**inciˈdentals** *pl.n.* accompanying items —**incidental music** background music for motion picture *etc.*

incinerate (inˈsinərāt) *vt.* burn up completely; reduce to ashes —**incinerˈation** *n.* —**inˈcinerator** *n.* furnace or apparatus for incinerating something, *esp.* refuse

incipient (inˈsipiənt) *a.* beginning

incise (inˈsīz) *vt.* produce (lines *etc.*) by cutting into surface of (something) with sharp tool —**incision** (inˈsizhən) *n.* **1.** act of incising **2.** cut, gash, notch **3.** cut made with knife during surgical operation —**incisive** (inˈsīsiv) *a.* **1.** (of remark *etc.*) keen, biting **2.** sharp —**inˈcisor** *n.* cutting tooth

immaˈture
imˈmiscible
imˈmobile
imˈmoderate
imˈmodest
imˈmov(e)able
imˈpalpable
imˈpatience
imˈpatient
imˈpenetrable
imˈpermanent
imperˈmissible
imˈplausible
impoˈlite
impreˈcise
imˈprobable
imˈprudent
imˈpure
inaˈbility
inacˈcessible
inˈaccurate
inˈadequate
inadˈmissible
inadˈvisable
inˈapplicable
inapˈpropriate
inarˈticulate
inarˈtistic
inatˈtentive
inˈaudible
inˈcapable
inˈcomparable
incomˈpatible
incomˈplete
incompreˈhensible
inconˈclusive
inconˈsiderable
inconˈsiderate
inconˈsistent
inconˈsolable
inconˈspicuous
inˈconstant
inconˈtestable
inˈcontinent
inconˈvenience
inconˈvenient
incorˈrect
incorˈruptible

incite (in'sīt) *vt.* stir up or provoke to action —**inci'tation** *or* **in'citement** *n.*

incl. **1.** including **2.** inclusive

inclement (in'klemənt) *a.* (of weather) stormy, severe, cold —**in'clemency** *n.*

incline (in'klīn) *v.* **1.** lean, slope **2.** (cause to) be disposed —*vt.* **3.** bend or lower (head *etc.*) —*n.* ('inklīn) **4.** slope —**inclination** (inkli'nāshən) *n.* **1.** liking, tendency, preference **2.** sloping surface **3.** degree of deviation —**inclined plane** plane whose angle to horizontal is oblique

inclose (in'klōz) *vt. see* ENCLOSE

include (in'klo͞od) *vt.* **1.** have as (part of) contents **2.** comprise **3.** add in **4.** take in —**in'clusion** *n.* —**in'clusive** *a.* including (everything) —**in'clusively** *adv.*

incognito (inkog'nētō) *or* (*fem.*) **incognita** *adv./a.* **1.** under assumed identity —*n.* **2.** assumed identity (*pl.* **-s**)

incognizant (in'kognizənt) *a.* unaware —**in'cognizance** *n.*

incoherent (inkō'hēərənt) *a.* **1.** lacking clarity, disorganized **2.** inarticulate —**inco'herence** *n.* —**inco'herently** *adv.*

income ('inkum) *n.* **1.** amount of money, *esp.* annual, from salary, investments *etc.* **2.** receipts —**income tax** personal tax levied on annual income

incoming ('inkuming) *a.* **1.** coming in **2.** about to come into office; next **3.** (of interest *etc.*) being received; accruing

incommensurable (inkə'mensərəbəl, -'mench-) *a.* **1.** incapable of being measured comparatively **2.** incommensurate **3.** *Math.* having no common factor other than 1 —*n.* **4.** something incommensurable —**incommensura'bility** *n.*

incommensurate (inkə'mensərit, -'mench-) *a.* **1.** disproportionate **2.** incommensurable

incommode (inkə'mōd) *vt.* trouble, inconvenience, disturb —**incom'modious** *a.* **1.** cramped **2.** inconvenient

incommunicado (inkəmyo͞oni'kädō) *a./adv.* deprived (by force or by choice) of communication with others

incomparable (in'kompərəbəl, -prəbəl) *a.* **1.** beyond or above comparison; matchless; unequaled **2.** lacking basis for comparison; not having qualities or features that can be compared —**incompara'bility** *or* **in'comparableness** *n.* —**in'comparably** *adv.*

incompetent (in'kompitənt) *a.* **1.** not possessing necessary ability, skill *etc.* to do or carry out task; incapable **2.** marked by lack of ability, skill *etc.* **3.** *Law* not legally qualified —*n.* **4.** incompetent person —**in'competence** *or* **in'competency** *n.*

incongruous (in'konggro͞oəs) *or* **incongruent** *a.* **1.** not appropriate **2.** inconsistent, absurd —**incon'gruity** *n.* —**in'congruously** *adv.*

inconsequential (inkonsi'kwenchəl) *or* **inconsequent** (in'konsikwənt) *a.* **1.** illogical **2.** irrelevant; trivial

incontrovertible (inkontrə'vərtəbəl) *a.* undeniable; indisputable

incorporate (in'körpərāt) *v.* **1.** include **2.** unite into one body **3.** form into corporation —**incorpo'ration** *n.*

incorporeal (inkör'pöriəl) *a.* **1.** without material form, body or substance **2.** spiritual, metaphysical **3.** *Law* having no material existence —**incorpo'reity** *or* **incorpore'ality** *n.*

incorrigible (in'korijəbəl) *a.* **1.** beyond correction or reform **2.** firmly rooted —**incorrigi'bility** *n.*

increase (in'krēs) *v.* **1.** make or become greater in size, number *etc.* —*n.* ('inkrēs) **2.** growth, enlargement —**in'creasingly** *adv.* more and more

incredible (in'kredəbəl) *a.* **1.** unbelievable **2.** *inf.* marvelous; amazing

incredulous (in'krejo͞oləs) *a.* unbelieving —**incre'dulity** *n.*

increment ('inkrimənt) *n.* increase, *esp.* one of a series

incriminate (in'kriminát) *vt.* **1.** imply guilt of **2.** charge with crime —**in'criminatory** *a.*

incrust (in'krust) *v. see* ENCRUST

incubate ('ingkyəbāt, 'inkyə-) *vt.* **1.** provide (eggs, embryos, bacteria *etc.*) with heat or other favorable condition for development —*vi.* **2.** develop in this way —**incu'bation** *n.* —**'incubator** *n.* apparatus for artificially hatching eggs, for rearing premature babies

incubus ('ingkyəbəs, 'inkyə-) *n.* **1.** nightmare; obsession **2.** (*orig.*) demon believed to afflict sleeping person (*pl.* **-bi** (-bī), **-es**)

inculcate (in'kulkāt, 'inkulkāt) *vt.* impress

in'curable
inde'cipherable
inde'cision
inde'cisive
inde'finable
in'definite
inde'structible
indis'cernible
indis'putable
indis'tinct
indis'tinguishable
inef'ficient
ine'lastic
in'elegant
in'equable
in'equitable
ines'sential
inex'act
inex'cusable
inex'pedient
inex'pensive
inex'perience
inex'perienced
in'expert
inex'tinguishable
in'fertile
infer'tility
in'formal
in'frequent
in'gratitude
inhos'pitable
inju'dicious
inof'fensive
in'sanitary
in'sensitive
in'separable
insig'nificant
insin'cere
in'soluble
in'solvent
insta'bility
insub'stantial
insuf'ficient
insur'mountable
in'tangible
in'tolerable
in'tolerant
in'variable

on the mind —**incul'cation** *n.* —**in'culcator** *n.*

inculpate (in'kulpāt, 'inkulpāt) *vt.* incriminate; cause blame to be imputed to —**incul'pation** *n.* —**in'culpatory** *a.*

incumbent (in'kumbənt) *a.* **1.** lying, resting —*n.* **2.** holder of office, *esp.* church benefice —**in'cumbency** *n.* **1.** obligation **2.** office or tenure of incumbent —**it is incumbent on** it is the duty of

incumber (in'kumbər) *vt. see* ENCUMBER

incur (in'kər) *vt.* **1.** fall into **2.** bring upon oneself (**-rr-**) —**in'cursion** *n.* **1.** invasion **2.** penetration

incus ('ingkəs) *n.* the middle bone in a chain of three bones in the ear of a mammal (*pl.* **incudes** (ing'kyōōdēz))

incuse (in'kyōōz, -'kyōōs) *vt.* **1.** impress by striking or stamping —*a.* **2.** hammered —*n.* **3.** impression made by stamping

ind. **1.** independent **2.** index **3.** indicative

Ind. **1.** Independent **2.** India **3.** Indian **4.** Indiana **5.** Indies

indebted (in'detid) *a.* **1.** owing gratitude (for help, favors *etc.*) **2.** owing money —**in'debtedness** *n.*

indecent (in'dēsənt) *a.* **1.** offensive to standards of decency, *esp.* in sexual matters **2.** unseemly, improper (*esp.* *in* **indecent haste**) —**in'decency** *n.* **1.** state or quality of being indecent **2.** indecent act *etc.* —**indecent exposure** offense of indecently exposing one's body, *esp.* genitals, in public

indeed (in'dēd) *adv.* **1.** in truth, really, in fact, certainly —*interj.* **2.** denoting surprise, doubt *etc.*

indefatigable (indi'fatigəbəl) *a.* untiring —**inde'fatigably** *adv.*

indefeasible (indi'fēzəbəl) *a.* that cannot be lost or annulled —**indefeasi'bility** *n.*

indefensible (indi'fensəbəl) *a.* not justifiable or defensible —**inde'fensibly** *adv.*

indelible (in'delibəl) *a.* **1.** that cannot be blotted out, effaced or erased **2.** producing such a mark —**indeli'bility** *n.* —**in'delibly** *adv.*

indelicate (in'delikit) *a.* **1.** coarse **2.** embarrassing, tasteless

indemnity (in'demniti) *n.* **1.** compensation for loss **2.** security against loss —**indemnifi'cation** *n.* —**in'demnify** *vt.* **1.** give indemnity to **2.** compensate (**in'demnified, in'demnifying**)

indent (in'dent) *v.* **1.** set (written matter *etc.*) in from margin *etc.* **2.** notch (edge, border *etc.*); make (something) jagged **3.** cut (document in duplicate) so that irregular lines may be matched **4.** make an order upon (someone) or for (something) —*n.* ('indent) **5.** notch **6.** order, requisition —**inden'tation** *n.* **1.** hollowed, notched or cut place, as an edge or coastline **2.** series of hollows, notches or cuts **3.** act of indenting; condition of being indented **4.** leaving of space or amount of space left between margin and start of indented line (*also* **in'dention, 'indent**) —**in'dention** *n.* indentation (on page) —**in'denture** *n.* **1.** indented document **2.** contract, *esp.* one binding apprentice to master —*vt.* **3.** bind thus

independent (indi'pendənt) *a.* **1.** not subject to others **2.** self-reliant **3.** free **4.** valid in itself **5.** politically of no party —**inde'pendence** *or* **inde'pendency** *n.* **1.** being independent **2.** self-reliance **3.** self-support —**inde'pendently** *adv.* —**Independence Day** July 4th, U.S. national holiday in commemoration of the adoption of the Declaration of Independence —**independent clause** *Gram.* main or coordinate clause

in-depth *a.* carefully worked out, detailed, thorough

indescribable (indi'skrībəbəl) *a.* **1.** beyond description **2.** too intense *etc.* for words —**inde'scribably** *adv.*

indeterminate (indi'tərminit) *a.* **1.** uncertain **2.** inconclusive **3.** incalculable **4.** *Math.* (of an equation) having more than one variable

index ('indeks) *n.* **1.** alphabetical list of references, usu. at end of book **2.** pointer, indicator **3.** *Math.* exponent (*pl.* **-es, 'indices**) —*vt.* **4.** provide (book) with index **5.** insert in index —**index finger** finger next to thumb (*also* **'forefinger**) —**index number** number used to compare some quantity, such as cost of living, at different times

India ('indiə) *n.* **1.** country in Asia bounded northwest by Pakistan, north by China, Tibet, Nepal and Bhutan, east by Burma, southeast, south and southwest by the Indian Ocean **2.** word used in communications for the letter *i* —**'Indian** *n./a.* **1.** (of, or relating to) Amerindian **2.** (native or inhabitant) of India —**'Indic** *a.* **1.** denoting, belonging to or relating to branch of Indo-European languages —*n.* **2.** this group of languages —**'Indiaman** *n.* formerly, merchant ship engaged in trade with India —**Indian club** bottle-shaped club, usu. used by gymnasts *etc.* —**Indian corn** maize —**Indian file** single file —**Indian giver** person who gives something and then takes it back —**Indian hemp** cannabis —**Indian ink** very dark black (drawing) ink —**Indian list C** *inf.* list of people to whom liquor may not be sold —**Indian Ocean** ocean south of Asia, east of Africa and west of Australia —**Indian pipe** white leafless saprophytic plant of U.S. and Asia —**Indian pudding** baked dessert made of cornmeal, milk and molasses —**Indian red** moderate-to-strong brownish red —**Indian summer** period of unusually warm weather in fall —**Indian wrestling** contest in which seated opponents clasp hands with elbows on the table and attempt to force each other's hand down —**India paper** extremely thin, opaque printing paper used *esp.* for Bibles and dictionaries —**India rubber** rubber, eraser

Indiana (indi'anə) *n.* East North central state of the U.S., admitted to the Union in 1816. Abbrev.: **Ind., IN** (with ZIP code)

indicate ('indikāt) *vt.* **1.** point out **2.** state briefly **3.** signify —**indi'cation** *n.* **1.** sign **2.** token **3.** explanation —**in'dicative** *a.* **1.** (*with* of) pointing (to) **2.** *Gram.* stating fact —*n.* **3.** *Gram.* (verb in) indicative mood —'**indicator** *n.* **1.** one who, that which, indicates **2.** on vehicle, flashing light showing driver's intention to turn

indices ('indisēz) *n., pl. of* INDEX

indict (in'dīt) *vt.* accuse, *esp.* by legal process —**in'dictable** *a.* —**in'dictment** *n.*

indifferent (in'difrənt, -fərənt) *a.* **1.** uninterested **2.** unimportant **3.** neither good nor bad **4.** inferior **5.** neutral —**in'difference** *n.*

indigenous (in'dijinəs) *a.* born in or natural to a country —**indigene** ('indijēn) *n.* **1.** aborigine **2.** native

indigent ('indijənt) *a.* poor; needy —'**indigence** *n.* poverty

indigestion (indī'jeschən, -di-) *n.* (discomfort, pain caused by) difficulty in digesting food —**indi'gestible** *a.*

indignant (in'dignənt) *a.* **1.** moved by anger and scorn **2.** angered by sense of injury or injustice —**in'dignantly** *adv.* —**indig'nation** *n.* —**in'dignity** *n.* humiliation; insult, slight

indigo ('indigō) *n.* **1.** blue dye obtained from plant **2.** the plant (*pl.* **-s, -es**) —*a.* **3.** deep blue

indirect (indi'rekt, -dī-) *a.* **1.** deviating from direct course or line **2.** not coming as direct effect or consequence **3.** not straightforward, open or fair —**indi'rectly** *adv.* —**indi'rectness** *n.* —**indirect discourse** reporting of something said by conveying what was meant rather than repeating exact words —**indirect object** *Gram.* noun, pronoun or noun phrase indicating recipient or beneficiary of action of verb and its direct object —**indirect tax** tax levied on goods or services rather than on individuals or companies

indiscreet (indi'skrēt) *a.* not discreet; imprudent; tactless —**indiscretion** (indi'skreshən) *n.* **1.** characteristic or state of being indiscreet **2.** indiscreet act, remark *etc.*

indiscrete (indi'skrēt, in'diskrēt) *a.* not divisible or divided into parts

indiscriminate (indi'skriminit) *a.* **1.** lacking discrimination **2.** jumbled

indispensable (indi'spensəbəl) *a.* necessary; essential

indisposition (indispə'zishən) *n.* **1.** sickness **2.** disinclination —**indis'pose** *vt.* —**indis'posed** *a.* **1.** unwell, not fit **2.** disinclined

indissoluble (indi'solyəbəl) *a.* permanent

indium ('indiəm) *n. Chem.* metallic element *Symbol* In, at. wt. 114.8, at. no. 49

individual (indi'vijōōəl) *a.* **1.** single **2.** characteristic of single person or thing **3.** distinctive —*n.* **4.** single person or thing, *esp.* when regarded as distinct from others —**indi'vidualism** *n.* principle of asserting one's independence —**indi'vidualist** *n.* —**individual'istic** *a.* —**individu'ality** *n.* **1.** distinctive character **2.** personality —**indi'vidualize** *vt.* make (or treat as) individual —**indi'vidually** *adv.* singly

Indo- ('indō-) (*comb. form*) India; Indian, as in *Indo-European*

indoctrinate (in'doktrināt) *vt.* implant beliefs in the mind of

Indo-European *a./n.* (denoting) the most geographically widespread and numerically important family of languages which includes English; a member of the Germanic branch

indolent ('indələnt) *a.* lazy —'**indolence** *n.*

indomitable (in'domitəbəl) *a.* unyielding

Indonesia (indō'nēzhə, -shə) *n.* **1.** country in southern Pacific consisting of the islands of Sumatra, Java and Madura, Celebes, Borneo, Lesser Sundas, Moluccas, the western half of New Guinea and some 3000 smaller islands and islets **2.** Malay archipelago —**Indo'nesian** *n./a.* **1.** (native or inhabitant) of Indonesia —*n.* **2.** language of Indonesia which is a member of the Malayo-Polynesian family, differing from Malay in its transcription

indoor ('indōr) *a.* **1.** within doors **2.** under cover —**in'doors** *adv.* inside or into house or other building

indorse (in'dōrs) *vt. see* ENDORSE

indubitable (in'dyōōbitəbəl, -'dōō-) *a.* beyond doubt; certain —**in'dubitably** *adv.*

induce (in'dyōōs, -'dōōs) *vt.* **1.** persuade **2.** bring on **3.** cause **4.** produce by induction —**in'ducement** *n.* incentive, attraction

induct (in'dukt) *vt.* install in office —**in'ductance** *n.* —**in'duction** *n.* **1.** an inducting **2.** general inference from particular instances **3.** production of electric or magnetic state in body by its being near (not touching) electrified or magnetized body **4.** in internal-combustion engine, part of the piston's action which draws gas from carburetor —**in'ductive** *a.* —**in'ductively** *adv.* —**in'ductor** *n.* —**induction coil** transformer for producing high voltage from low voltage

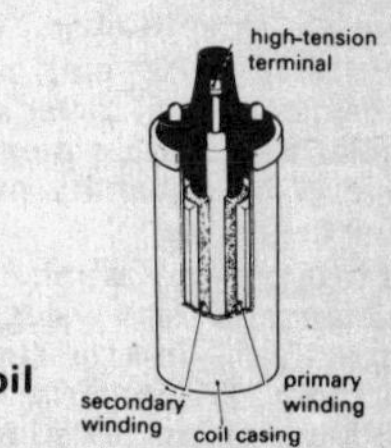

induction coil

indue (in'dyōō, -'dōō) *vt. see* ENDUE

indulge (in'dulj) *vt.* **1.** gratify **2.** give free course to **3.** pamper, spoil —**in'dulgence** *n.* **1.** an indulging **2.** extravagance **3.** something granted as a favor or privilege **4.** *R.C.Ch.* remission of temporal punishment due after absolution —**in'dulgent** *a.* —**in'dulgently** *adv.*

indurate ('indyərāt, -dә-) *v.* **1.** make or become hard or callous **2.** make or become hardy —*a.* ('indyərit, -dә-) **3.** hardened, callous, or unfeeling —'**indurative** *a.*

industry ('indəstri) *n.* **1.** manufacture, processing *etc.* of goods **2.** branch of this **3.** diligence, habitual hard work —**in'dustrial** *a.* of industries, trades —**in'dustrialist** *n.* person engaged in control of industrial enterprise —**in'dustrialize** *v.* —**in'dustrious** *a.* diligent —**industrial design** application of aesthetic principles to the design of machine-made articles, with standards independent of those for hand-made objects —**industrial medicine** branch of medicine dealing with medical care of workers (*also* **occupational medicine**) —**Industrial Revolution** transformation in 18th and 19th centuries of Brit. and other countries into industrial nations

-ine (*comb. form*) **1.** of, relating to or belonging to, as in *saturnine* **2.** consisting of; resembling, as in *crystalline* **3.** indicating any of various classes of chemical compounds, as in *chlorine, nicotine, glycerine* (*also* **-in**) **4.** indicating feminine form, as in *heroine*

inebriate (in'ēbriāt) *vt.* **1.** make drunk; intoxicate —*a.* (in'ēbriit) **2.** drunken —*n.* (in'ēbriit) **3.** habitual drunkard —**inebri'ation** *or* **inebriety** (ini'briiti) *n.* drunkenness

inedible (in'edibəl) *a.* **1.** not eatable **2.** unfit for food —**inedi'bility** *n.*

ineducable (in'ejəkəbəl) *a.* incapable of being educated, *esp.* through mental retardation

ineffable (in'efəbəl) *a.* **1.** too great or sacred for words **2.** unutterable —**ineffa'bility** *n.* —**in'effably** *adv.*

ineligible (in'elijəbəl) *a.* not fit or qualified (for something) —**ineligi'bility** *n.*

ineluctable (ini'luktəbəl) *a.* (*esp.* of fate) incapable of being avoided; inescapable

inept (in'ept) *a.* **1.** absurd **2.** out of place **3.** clumsy —**in'eptitude** *n.*

inequality (ini'kwoliti) *n.* **1.** state or quality of being unequal **2.** lack of smoothness or regularity **3.** *Math.* statement indicating that value of one quantity or expression is not equal to another

inert (in'ərt) *a.* **1.** without power of action or resistance **2.** slow, sluggish **3.** chemically unreactive —**inertia** (in'ərshə, -shiə) *n.* **1.** inactivity **2.** property by which matter continues in its existing state of rest or motion in straight line, unless that state is changed by external force —**in'ertly** *adv.* —**in'ertness** *n.* —**inertial guidance** guidance of aircraft or spacecraft by use of automatic instruments carried by craft

inescapable (ini'skāpəbəl) *a.* incapable of being escaped or avoided

inestimable (in'estiməbəl) *a.* too good, too great to be estimated

inevitable (in'evitəbəl) *a.* **1.** unavoidable **2.** sure to happen —**inevita'bility** *n.* —**in'evitably** *adv.*

inexorable (in'eksərəbəl) *a.* relentless —**in'exorably** *adv.*

inexpiable (in'ekspiəbəl) *a.* **1.** incapable of being expiated **2.** *obs.* implacable

inexplicable (inik'splikəbəl, in'eksplikəbəl) *a.* impossible to explain

in extenso (in ik'stensō) *Lat.* at full length

in extremis (in ik'strāmis, ik'strēmis) *Lat.* at the point of death

inextricable (iniks'trikəbəl, in'ekstrikəbəl) *a.* **1.** not able to be escaped from **2.** not able to be disentangled *etc.* **3.** extremely involved or intricate —**inextrica'bility** *or* **inex'tricableness** *n.* —**inex'tricably** *adv.*

inf. **1.** infinitive **2.** informal **3.** information

infallible (in'faləbəl) *a.* **1.** unerring **2.** not liable to fail **3.** certain, sure —**infalli'bility** *n.* —**in'fallibly** *adv.*

infamous ('infəməs) *a.* **1.** notorious **2.** shocking —'**infamously** *adv.* —'**infamy** *n.*

infant ('infənt) *n.* very young child —'**infancy** *n.* —**in'fanticide** *n.* **1.** murder of newborn child **2.** person guilty of this —'**infantile** *a.* childish —**infantile paralysis** poliomyelitis

infante (in'fanti) *n.* formerly, son of king of Spain or Portugal, *esp.* one not heir to throne —**infanta** (in'fantə) *n.* **1.** formerly, daughter of king of Spain or Portugal **2.** wife of infante

infantry ('infəntri) *n.* foot soldiers

infatuate (in'fachōōāt) *vt.* inspire with folly or foolish passion —**in'fatuated** *a.* foolishly enamored —**infatu'ation** *n.*

infect (in'fekt) *vt.* **1.** affect (with disease) **2.** contaminate —**in'fection** *n.* —**in'fectious** *a.* catching, spreading, pestilential —**infectious hepatitis** acute infectious viral disease, usu. benign, transmitted by food or water contaminated by fecal matter —**infectious mononucleosis** acute infectious disease characterized by fever, sore throat, swollen lymph nodes *etc.* (*also* **glandular fever**)

infelicitous (infi'lisitəs) *a.* unfortunate; unsuitable —**infe'licity** *n.* **1.** being infelicitous **2.** unsuitable or inapt remark *etc.*

infer (in'fər) *vt.* deduce, conclude (**-rr-**) —'**inference** *n.* —**infer'ential** *a.* deduced

inferior (in'fēəriər) *a.* **1.** of poor quality **2.** lower —*n.* **3.** one lower (in rank *etc.*) —**inferi'ority** *n.* —**inferiority complex** *Psychoanal.* sense of inferiority, lack of confidence

infernal (in'fərnəl) *a.* **1.** devilish **2.** hellish **3.** *inf.* irritating, confounded —**in'fernally** *adv.*

inferno (in'fərnō) *n.* **1.** region of hell **2.** conflagration (*pl.* **-s**)

infest (in'fest) *vt.* inhabit or overrun in dangerously or unpleasantly large numbers —**infes'tation** *n.*

infidelity (infi'deliti) *n.* **1.** unfaithfulness **2.** religious disbelief **3.** disloyalty **4.** treachery —**'infidel** *n.* **1.** unbeliever —*a.* **2.** rejecting a specific religion, *esp.* Christianity or Islam **3.** of unbelievers or unbelief

infield ('infēld) *n.* **1.** area of baseball field enclosed by base lines **2.** area inside running track or racetrack —**'infielder** *n.*

infighting ('infīting) *n.* **1.** *Boxing* combat at close quarters **2.** intense conflict, as between members of same organization —**'infighter** *n.*

infiltrate (in'filtrāt, 'infiltrāt) *v.* **1.** trickle through —*vt.* **2.** (cause to) gain access surreptitiously **3.** cause to pass through pores —**infil'tration** *n.*

infin. infinitive

infinite ('infinit) *a.* boundless —**'infinitely** *adv.* exceedingly —**infini'tesimal** *a.* extremely, infinitely small —**in'finitude** *n.* state or quality of being infinite —**in'finity** *n.* unlimited and endless extent

infinitive (in'finitiv) *a./n.* (denoting) verb form with characteristics of noun and verb and in English used with *to*

infirm (in'fərm) *a.* **1.** physically weak **2.** mentally weak **3.** irresolute —**in'firmary** *n.* hospital; sick quarters —**in'firmity** *n.*

infix ('infiks, in'fiks) *vt.* **1.** fix firmly in **2.** instill, inculcate **3.** *Gram.* insert (affix) into middle of word —*n.* ('infiks) **4.** *Gram.* affix inserted into middle of word

in flagrante delicto (in flə'granti di'liktō) while committing the offense

inflame (in'flām) *vt.* **1.** rouse to anger, excitement **2.** cause inflammation in —*vi* **3.** become inflamed —**inflammability** (inflamə'biliti) *n.* —**inflammable** (in'flaməbəl) *a.* **1.** flammable **2.** excitable —**inflammation** (inflə'māshən) *n.* reaction of body to irritant by pain, heat, swelling and redness —**inflammatory** (in'flamətōri) *a.*

inflate (in'flāt) *v.* **1.** blow up with air, gas **2.** swell —*vt.* **3.** cause economic inflation of (prices *etc.*) —*vi.* **4.** undergo economic inflation —**in'flatable** *a.* —**in'flation** *n.* increase in prices and fall in value of money —**in'flationary** *a.*

inflect (in'flekt) *vt.* **1.** modify (words) to show grammatical relationships **2.** bend inward —**in'flection** *n.* **1.** modification of word **2.** modulation of voice

inflexible (in'fleksəbəl) *a.* **1.** incapable of being bent **2.** stern —**inflexi'bility** *n.*

inflict (in'flikt) *vt.* **1.** impose **2.** deliver forcibly —**in'fliction** *n.* **1.** inflicting **2.** punishment

in-flight *a.* provided during flight in aircraft

inflorescence (inflə'resəns) *n.* **1.** flowering part of a plant **2.** *Bot.* arrangement of flowers on stem

inflow ('inflō) *n.* **1.** something, such as liquid or gas, that flows in **2.** act of flowing in; influx

influence ('inflo͞oəns) *n.* **1.** effect of one person or thing on another **2.** power of person or thing having an effect **3.** thing, person exercising this —*vt.* **4.** sway **5.** induce **6.** affect —**influ'ential** *a.*

influenza (inflo͞o'enzə) *n.* contagious feverish virus disease marked by muscular pain and inflammation of the respiratory system

influx ('influks) *n.* **1.** a flowing in **2.** inflow

info ('infō) *inf.* information

infold (in'fōld) *vt. see* ENFOLD

inform (in'fōrm) *vt.* **1.** tell **2.** animate —*vi.* **3.** (*oft. with* on *or* against) give information (about) —**in'formant** *n.* one who tells —**infor'mation** *n.* **1.** facts acquired through experience or study **2.** knowledge of specific and timely events or situations; news **3.** act of informing; condition of being informed **4.** office, agency *etc.* providing information **5.** charge or complaint made by prosecuting officer **6.** *Comp.* results derived from processing of data according to programmed instructions **7.** *Comp.* information operated on by computer program (*also* **'data**) —**infor'mational** *a.* —**in'formative** *a.* —**in'formed** *a.* having much knowledge of something —**in'former** *n.* **1.** person who informs against someone, *esp.* criminal **2.** person who provides information —**information retrieval** techniques of storing and recovering facts, *esp.* by the use of computerized systems —**information technology** technology concerned with collecting and storing information, *esp.* by computer or electronically —**information theory** theory that deals statistically with coding, transmitting, storing, retrieving and decoding information

infra ('infrə) *adv.* **1.** below **2.** under **3.** after —**infra dig** *inf.* beneath one's dignity —**infra'red** *a.* denoting rays below red end of visible spectrum —**infra'sonic** *a.* having frequency below that of sound

infraction (in'frakshən) *n.* infringement

infrangible (in'franjibəl) *a.* **1.** incapable of being broken **2.** not capable of being violated or infringed —**infrangi'bility** *or* **in'frangibleness** *n.*

infrastructure ('infrəstrukchər) *n.* basic structure or fixed-capital items of an organization or economic system

infringe (in'frinj) *vt.* transgress, break —**in'fraction** *n.* breach, violation —**in'fringement** *n.*

infuriate (in'fyo͝oriāt) *vt.* enrage

infuse (in'fyo͞oz) *v.* **1.** soak to extract flavor *etc.* —*vt.* **2.** instill, charge —**in'fusible** *a.* capable of being infused —**in'fusion** *n.* **1.** an infusing **2.** liquid extract obtained

infusible (in'fyo͞ozəbəl) *a.* not fusible; not

easily melted; having high melting point —**infusi'bility** *or* **in'fusibleness** *n.*

-ing[1] (*comb. form*) **1.** action of, process of, result of or something connected with verb, as in *meeting, wedding, winnings* **2.** something used in, consisting of, involving *etc.*, as in *tubing, soldiering*

-ing[2] (*comb. form*) **1.** forming present participle of verbs, as in *walking, believing* **2.** forming participial adjectives, as in *growing boy, sinking ship* **3.** forming adjectives not derived from verbs, as in *swashbuckling*

ingenious (in'jēnyəs) *a.* **1.** clever at contriving **2.** cleverly contrived —**in'geniously** *adv.* —**inge'nuity** *n.*

ingénue ('anjənōō, 'än-) *n.* **1.** artless girl or young woman **2.** actress playing such a part

ingenuous (in'jenyōōəs) *a.* **1.** frank **2.** naive, innocent —**in'genuously** *adv.*

ingest (in'jest) *vt.* take (food or liquid) into the body —**in'gestible** *a.* —**in'gestion** *n.*

inglenook ('inggəlnōōk) *n.* corner by a fireplace

inglorious (in'glōriəs) *a.* dishonorable, shameful, disgraceful

ingot ('inggət) *n.* brick of cast metal, *esp.* gold

ingrain *or* **engrain** (in'grān) *vt.* **1.** implant deeply **2.** *obs.* dye, infuse deeply —**in'grained** *or* **en'grained** *a.* **1.** deep-rooted **2.** inveterate **3.** (*esp.* of dirt) worked into or through fiber, grain, pores *etc.*

ingratiate (in'grāshiāt) *v. refl.* get (oneself) into favor —**in'gratiatingly** *adv.*

ingredient (in'grēdiənt) *n.* component part of a mixture

ingress ('in-gres) *n.* **1.** entry **2.** means or right of entrance

ingrown ('in-grōn) *a.* **1.** (*esp.* of toenail) grown abnormally into flesh **2.** grown within; native; innate

inhabit (in'habit) *vt.* dwell in —**in'habitable** *a.* —**in'habitant** *n.* —**inhabi'tation** *n.*

inhale (in'hāl) *v.* breathe in (air *etc.*) —**in'halant** *a.* **1.** (*esp.* of medicinal preparation) inhaled for its therapeutic effect **2.** inhaling —*n.* **3.** inhalant medicinal preparation —**inha'lation** *n.* —**in'haler** *n.* device producing and assisting inhalation of therapeutic vapors

inhere (in'hēər) *vi.* **1.** (of qualities) exist **2.** (of rights) be vested —**in'herence** *n.* —**in'herent** *a.* existing as an inseparable part

inherit (in'herit) *vt.* **1.** receive as heir **2.** derive from parents —*vi.* **3.** succeed as heir —**inherita'bility** *or* **in'heritableness** *n.* —**in'heritable** *a.* **1.** capable of being transmitted by heredity **2.** capable of being inherited —**in'heritance** *n.* —**in'heritor** *n.* (**in'heritress** *or* **in'heritrix** *fem.*)

inhesion (in'hēzhən) *n.* inherence

inhibit (in'hibit) *vt.* **1.** restrain (impulse, desire *etc.*) **2.** hinder (action) **3.** forbid —**inhibition** (ini'bishən, inhi-) *n.* **1.** repression of emotion, instinct **2.** a stopping or retarding —**in'hibitory** *a.*

inhuman (in'hyōōmən, -'yōō-) *a.* **1.** cruel, brutal **2.** not human —**inhu'manity** *n.*

inhume (in'hyōōm) *vt.* bury, inter —**inhu'mation** *n.*

inimical (i'nimikəl) *a.* **1.** unfavorable **2.** unfriendly; hostile

inimitable (i'nimitəbəl) *a.* defying imitation

iniquity (i'nikwiti) *n.* **1.** gross injustice **2.** wickedness, sin —**in'iquitous** *a.* **1.** unfair, unjust **2.** sinful **3.** *inf.* outrageous

initial (i'nishəl) *a.* **1.** of, occurring at the beginning —*n.* **2.** initial letter, *esp.* of person's name —*vt.* **3.** mark, sign with one's initials —**in'itialize** *vt. Comp.* set (program) to starting position or value —**in'itially** *adv.* —**initial teaching alphabet** alphabet of 44 characters for teaching beginners to read English

initiate (i'nishiāt) *vt.* **1.** originate, begin **2.** admit into closed society **3.** instruct in elements of something —*n.* (i'nishiit, -āt) **4.** initiated person —**initi'ation** *n.* —**in'itiative** *n.* **1.** first step, lead **2.** ability to act independently —*a.* **3.** originating —**in'itiatory** *a.*

inject (in'jekt) *vt.* introduce (*esp.* fluid, medicine *etc.* with syringe) —**in'jection** *n.*

injunction (in'jungkshən) *n.* **1.** judicial order to restrain **2.** authoritative order

injury ('injəri) *n.* **1.** physical damage or harm **2.** wrong —**'injurable** *a.* —**'injure** *vt.* **1.** do harm or damage to **2.** offend, *esp.* by injustice —**'injured** *a.* —**in'jurious** *a.* —**in'juriously** *adv.* —**injury time** *Soccer* extra time added on to compensate for time spent attending to injured players during match

injustice (in'justis) *n.* **1.** want of justice **2.** wrong **3.** injury **4.** unjust act

ink (ingk) *n.* **1.** fluid used for writing or printing —*vt.* **2.** mark with ink **3.** cover, smear with ink —**'inker** *n.* —**'inky** *a.* **1.** resembling ink, *esp.* in color; dark; black **2.** of, containing or stained with ink —**'inkstand** *n.* —**'inkwell** *n.* vessel for holding ink

inkling ('ingkling) *n.* hint, slight knowledge or suspicion

inlaid ('in'lād) *a.* decorated with inset pattern

inland ('inland, -lənd) *n.* **1.** interior of country —*a.* **2.** in interior of country **3.** away from the sea **4.** within a country —*adv.* **5.** in or toward the inland

in-law *n.* relative by marriage

inlay (in'lā) *vt.* **1.** embed **2.** decorate with inset pattern (**in'laid** *pt./pp.*) —*n.* ('inlā) **3.** inlaid piece or pattern

inlet ('inlet, -lət) *n.* **1.** entrance **2.** mouth of creek **3.** piece inserted

in loco parentis (in 'lōkō pə'rentis) *Lat.* in place of a parent

inmate ('inmāt) *n.* occupant, *esp.* of prison, hospital *etc.*

inmost ('inmōst) *a.* *sup. of* IN most inward, deepest

inn (in) *n.* **1.** tavern **2.** country hotel —'**innkeeper** *n.* —**Inns of Court 1.** four societies admitting to English Bar **2.** their buildings

innards ('inərdz) *pl.n. inf.* internal organs or working parts (*orig.* '**inwards**)

innate (i'nāt, 'ināt) *a.* **1.** inborn **2.** inherent

inner ('inər) *a.* **1.** lying within —*n.* **2.** ring next to bull's-eye on target —'**innermost** *a.* —**inner city** sections of a large city in or near its center —**inner man 1.** mind; soul **2.** *jocular* stomach; appetite (**inner woman** *fem.*) —**inner tube** rubber air tube of pneumatic tire

inning ('ining) *n.* **1.** division of baseball game in which a team is at bat until it has three outs —*pl.* **2.** similar division of cricket game

innocent ('inəsənt) *a.* **1.** pure **2.** guiltless **3.** harmless —*n.* **4.** innocent person, *esp.* young child —'**innocence** *n.* —'**innocently** *adv.*

innocuous (i'nokyōōəs) *a.* harmless

innominate bone (i'nominit) *see* **hipbone** *at* HIP[1]

innovate ('inəvāt) *vt.* introduce (changes, new things) —**inno'vation** *n.* —'**innovator** *n.*

innuendo (inyōō'endō) *n.* **1.** allusive remark, hint **2.** indirect accusation (*pl.* **-es**)

innumerable (i'nyōōmərəbəl, i'nyōōmrəbəl; -'nōō-) *or* **innumerous** *a.* countless; very numerous

inoculate (i'nokyōōlāt) *vt.* immunize by injecting vaccine —**inocu'lation** *n.*

inoperable (in'opərəbəl, -'oprə-) *a.* **1.** unworkable **2.** *Med.* that cannot be operated on —**in'operative** *a.* **1.** not operative **2.** ineffective

inopportune (inopər'tyōōn, -'tōōn) *a.* badly timed

inordinate (in'ördinit) *a.* excessive

inorganic (inör'ganik) *a.* **1.** not having structure or characteristics of living organisms **2.** of substances without carbon the study of which is a branch of chemistry

inpatient ('inpāshənt) *n.* patient that stays in hospital

in perpetuum (in pər'petyōōəm) *Lat.* for ever

input ('inpōōt) *n.* **1.** act of putting in **2.** that which is put in, as resource needed for industrial production *etc.* **3.** data *etc.* fed into a computer

inquest ('inkwest) *n.* **1.** legal or judicial inquiry presided over by a coroner **2.** detailed inquiry or discussion

inquietude (in'kwīityōōd, -tōōd) *n.* restlessness, uneasiness, anxiety —**in'quiet** *a.*

inquire (in'kwīər) *vi.* seek information —**in'quirer** *n.* —**in'quiry** *n.* **1.** question **2.** investigation

inquisition (inkwi'zishən) *n.* **1.** searching investigation, official inquiry **2.** (**I-**) *Hist.* tribunal for suppression of heresy —**in'quisitor** *n.* —**inquisi'torial** *a.*

inquisitive (in'kwizitiv) *a.* **1.** curious **2.** prying

in re (in 'rā, 'rē) in the matter of: used *esp.* in bankruptcy proceedings

inroad ('inrōd) *n.* incursion

inrush ('inrush) *n.* sudden, usu. overwhelming, inward flow or rush; influx

ins. 1. inches **2.** insurance

insane (in'sān) *a.* **1.** mentally deranged; crazy **2.** senseless —**in'sanely** *adv.* **1.** like a lunatic, madly **2.** excessively —**insanity** (in'saniti) *n.*

insatiable (in'sāshəbəl) *or* **insatiate** (in'sāshiit) *a.* incapable of being satisfied

inscribe (in'skrīb) *vt.* **1.** write, engrave (in or on something) **2.** mark **3.** dedicate **4.** trace (figure) within another —**inscription** (in'skripshən) *n.* **1.** inscribing **2.** words inscribed on monument *etc.*

inscrutable (in'skrōōtəbəl) *a.* **1.** mysterious, impenetrable **2.** affording no explanation —**inscruta'bility** *n.* —**in'scrutably** *adv.*

insect ('insekt) *n.* any of a class of small arthropods with three pairs of legs, head, thorax and abdomen and two or four wings —**in'secticide** *n.* substance for killing insects —**insec'tivorous** *a.* insect-eating

insecure (insi'kyōōər) *a.* **1.** not safe or firm **2.** anxious, not confident

inseminate (in'semināt) *vt.* implant semen into —**artificial insemination** impregnation of the female by artificial means

insensate (in'sensāt, -sit) *a.* **1.** without sensation, unconscious **2.** unfeeling

insensible (in'sensəbəl) *a.* **1.** unconscious **2.** without feeling **3.** not aware **4.** not perceptible —**insensi'bility** *n.* —**in'sensibly** *adv.* imperceptibly

insert (in'sərt) *vt.* **1.** introduce **2.** place or put in, into or between —*n.* ('insərt) **3.** something inserted —**in'sertion** *n.*

in-service *a.* denoting training that is given to employees during the course of employment

inset ('inset) *n.* **1.** something extra inserted, *esp.* as decoration —*vt.* ('inset, in'set) **2.** set or place in or within; insert

inshore ('in'shōr) *adv./a.* near shore

inside ('in'sīd) *n.* **1.** inner side, surface or part —*a.* ('insīd) **2.** of, in, or on inside —*adv.* (in'sīd) **3.** in or into the inside **4.** *sl.* in prison —*prep.* (in'sīd) **5.** within, on inner side of

insidious (in'sidiəs) *a.* **1.** stealthy, treacherous **2.** unseen but deadly —**in'sidiously** *adv.*

insight ('insīt) *n.* mental penetration, discernment

insignia (in'signiə) *pl.n.* badges, emblems of honor or office (*sing.* **in'signia**)

insinuate (in'sinyōōāt) *vt.* **1.** hint **2.** work

(oneself) into favor **3.** introduce gradually or subtly —**insinu'ation** *n.*

insipid (in'sipid) *a.* **1.** dull, spiritless **2.** tasteless —**insi'pidity** *n.*

insist (in'sist) *vi.* (*oft. with* on *or* upon) **1.** demand persistently **2.** maintain **3.** emphasize —**in'sistence** *n.* —**in'sistent** *a.*

in situ (in 'sītōō) *Lat.* in its original position

insofar (insō'fär) *adv.* (*usu. with* as) to the degree or extent (that)

insole ('insōl) *n.* **1.** inner sole of shoe or boot **2.** loose additional inner sole to give extra warmth or make shoe fit

insolent ('insələnt) *a.* arrogantly impudent —**'insolence** *n.* —**'insolently** *adv.*

insomnia (in'somniə) *n.* sleeplessness —**in'somniac** *a./n.*

insomuch (insə'much) *adv.* to such an extent

insouciant (in'sōōsiənt) *a.* indifferent, careless, unconcerned —**in'souciance** *n.*

inspect (in'spekt) *vt.* examine closely or officially —**in'spection** *n.* —**in'spector** *n.* —**in'spectorate** *n.* body of inspectors

inspire (in'spīər) *vt.* **1.** animate, invigorate **2.** arouse, create feeling, thought in **3.** give rise to —*vi.* **4.** breathe in, inhale —**inspiration** (inspi'rāshən) *n.* **1.** good idea **2.** creative influence or stimulus

inspirit (in'spirit) *vt.* animate, put spirit into, encourage

inst. (*instant*) of the current month

install *or* **instal** (in'stōl) *vt.* **1.** have (apparatus) put in **2.** establish **3.** place (person in office *etc.*) with ceremony —**installation** (instə'lāshən) *n.* **1.** act of installing **2.** that which is installed

installment (in'stōlmənt) *n.* **1.** payment of part of debt **2.** any of parts of a whole delivered in succession —**installment plan** arrangement for paying in installments

instance ('instəns) *n.* **1.** example, particular case **2.** request **3.** stage in proceedings —*vt.* **4.** cite —**for instance** for or as an example

instant ('instənt) *n.* **1.** moment, point of time —*a.* **2.** immediate **3.** urgent **4.** (of foods) requiring little preparation —**instan'taneous** *a.* happening in an instant —**instan'taneously** *adv.* —**in'stanter** *adv.* at once —**'instantly** *adv.* at once

instead (in'sted) *adv.* **1.** in place **2.** as a substitute

instep ('instep) *n.* arched part of foot between toes and ankle

instigate ('instigāt) *vt.* **1.** incite, urge **2.** bring about —**insti'gation** *n.* —**'instigator** *n.*

instill (in'stil) *vt.* implant; inculcate —**instil'lation** *n.* —**in'stillment** *n.*

instinct ('instingkt) *n.* **1.** inborn impulse or propensity **2.** unconscious skill **3.** intuition —**in'stinctive** *a.* —**in'stinctively** *adv.*

institute ('instityōōt, -tōōt) *vt.* **1.** establish, found **2.** appoint **3.** set going —*n.* **4.** society for promoting some public object, *esp.* scientific **5.** its building —**'instituter** *or* **'institutor** *n.* —**insti'tution** *n.* **1.** an instituting **2.** establishment for care or education, hospital, college *etc.* **3.** an established custom or law or (*inf.*) person —**insti'tutional** *a.* **1.** of institutions **2.** routine —**insti'tutionalize** *vt.* **1.** subject to (adverse) effects of confinement in institution **2.** place in an institution —*v.* **3.** make or become an institution

instruct (in'strukt) *vt.* **1.** teach **2.** inform **3.** order —**in'struction** *n.* **1.** teaching **2.** order —*pl.* **3.** directions —**in'structive** *a.* **1.** informative **2.** useful —**in'structively** *adv.* —**in'structor** *n.* (**in'structress** *fem.*)

instrument ('instrəmənt) *n.* **1.** tool, implement, means, person, thing used to make, do, measure *etc.* **2.** mechanism for producing musical sound **3.** legal document —**instru'mental** *a.* **1.** acting as instrument or means **2.** helpful **3.** belonging to, produced by musical instruments —**instru'mentalist** *n.* player of musical instrument —**instrumen'tality** *n.* agency, means —**instru'mentally** *adv.* —**instrumen'tation** *n.* arrangement of music for instruments

insubordinate (insə'bördinit) *a.* **1.** not submissive **2.** mutinous, rebellious —**insubordi'nation** *n.*

insufferable (in'sufərəbəl) *a.* intolerable; unendurable —**in'sufferably** *adv.*

insular ('insyələr, 'insələr) *a.* **1.** of an island **2.** remote, detached **3.** narrow-minded; prejudiced —**insu'larity** *n.*

insulate ('insəlāt) *vt.* **1.** prevent or reduce transfer of electricity, heat, sound *etc.* to or from (body or device) by surrounding with nonconducting material **2.** isolate, detach —**insu'lation** *n.* —**'insulator** *n.*

insulin ('insəlin) *n.* pancreatic hormone essential for using sugar —**insulin shock** state of collapse resulting from administration of too much insulin thus causing decrease in blood sugar

insult (in'sult) *vt.* **1.** behave rudely to **2.** offend —*n.* ('insult) **3.** offensive remark **4.** affront —**in'sulting** *a.* —**in'sultingly** *adv.*

insuperable (in'sōōpərəbəl, -prəbəl) *a.* **1.** that cannot be got over or surmounted **2.** unconquerable —**in'superably** *adv.*

insupportable (insə'pörtəbəl) *a.* **1.** incapable of being endured; intolerable; insufferable **2.** incapable of being supported or justified; indefensible

insure (in'shōōər) *vi.* **1.** contract for payment in event of loss, death *etc.* by payment of premiums —*vt.* **2.** obtain insurance for **3.** (*with* against) make safe (against) —**in'surable** *a.* —**in'surance** *n.* —**in'surer** *n.* —**insurance policy** contract of insurance

insurgent (in'sərjənt) *a.* **1.** in revolt —*n.* **2.** rebel —**in'surgence** *or* **insur'rection** *n.* revolt

int. **1.** interest **2.** interior **3.** internal **4.** international

intact (in'takt) *a.* **1.** untouched **2.** uninjured

intaglio (in'talyō) *n.* **1.** engraved design **2.** gem so cut (*pl.* **-s, -gli** (-lyē))

intake ('intāk) *n.* **1.** what is taken in **2.** quantity taken in **3.** opening for taking in **4.** in motor vehicle, air passage into carburetor

integer ('intijər) *n.* **1.** whole number **2.** whole of anything

integral ('intigrəl) *a.* constituting an essential part of a whole —**'integrate** *v.* **1.** combine into one whole **2.** unify diverse elements (of community *etc.*) —**inte'gration** *n.* —**integral calculus** branch of mathematics concerned with finding the limit of a sum of terms —**integrated circuit** tiny electronic circuit, usu. on silicon chip

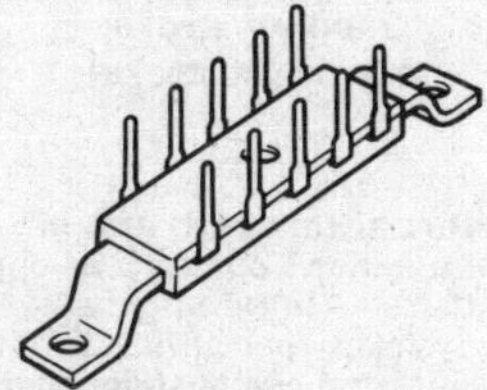

integrated circuit

integrity (in'tegriti) *n.* **1.** honesty **2.** original perfect state

integument (in'tegyəmənt) *n.* natural covering, skin, rind, husk

intellect ('intilekt) *n.* power of thinking and reasoning —**intel'lectual** *a.* **1.** of, appealing to intellect **2.** having good intellect —*n.* **3.** one endowed with intellect and attracted to intellectual things —**intellectu'ality** *n.*

intelligent (in'telijənt) *a.* **1.** having, showing good intellect **2.** quick at understanding **3.** informed —**in'telligence** *n.* **1.** quickness of understanding **2.** mental power or ability **3.** intellect **4.** information, news, *esp.* military information —**in'telligently** *adv.* —**intelli'gentsia** *n.* intellectual or cultured classes —**intelligi'bility** *n.* —**in'telligible** *a.* understandable —**in'telligibly** *adv.* —**intelligence quotient** range of numbers used to define relative mental ability as measured by standard tests of intelligence

intemperate (in'tempərit, -prit) *a.* **1.** drinking alcohol to excess **2.** immoderate **3.** unrestrained —**in'temperance** *n.*

intend (in'tend) *v.* propose, mean (to do, say *etc.*) —**in'tended** *a.* **1.** planned, future —*n.* **2.** *inf.* proposed spouse

intense (in'tens) *a.* **1.** very strong or acute **2.** emotional —**intensifi'cation** *n.* —**in'tensify** *v.* **1.** make or become stronger **2.** increase (**in'tensified, in'tensifying**) —**in'tensity** *n.* **1.** intense quality **2.** strength —**in'tensive** *a.* characterized by intensity or emphasis on specified factor —**in'tensively** *adv.*

intent (in'tent) *n.* **1.** purpose —*a.* **2.** concentrating **3.** resolved, bent **4.** preoccupied, absorbed —**in'tention** *n.* purpose, aim —**in'tentional** *a.* —**in'tently** *adv.* —**in'tentness** *n.*

inter (in'tər) *vt.* bury (**-rr-**) —**in'terment** *n.*

inter- (*comb. form*) between, among, mutually as in *interglacial, interrelation.* Such words are not given here where the meaning may easily be inferred from the simple word

intercol'legiate
intercom'municate
inter'company
intercon'nect
intercon'nection
interdenomi'national
interdepart'mental
interde'pend
interde'pendence
inter'flow
interga'lactic
intergovern'mental
inter'knit
inter'mesh
inter'mingle
inter'mix
inter'racial
interuni'versity
inter'war
inter'weave

interact (intər'akt) *vi.* act on each other —**inter'action** *n.*

inter alia ('intər 'āliə) *Lat.* among other things

interbreed (intər'brēd) *v.* breed within a related group

intercede (intər'sēd) *vi.* plead (in favor of), mediate —**intercession** (intər'seshən) *n.* —**intercessor** (intər'sesər) *n.*

intercept (intər'sept) *vt.* **1.** cut off **2.** seize, stop in transit —**inter'ception** *n.* —**inter'ceptor** *or* **inter'cepter** *n.* **1.** one who, that which intercepts **2.** fast fighter plane, missile *etc.*

interchange (intər'chānj) *v.* **1.** (cause to) exchange places —*n.* ('intərchānj) **2.** highway junction —**inter'changeable** *a.* able to be exchanged in position or use

intercom ('intərkom) *n.* internal telephonic system

intercommunion (intərkə'myōōnyən) *n.* association between Churches, involving *esp.* mutual reception of Holy Communion

intercontinental (intərkonti'nentəl) *a.* **1.** connecting continents **2.** (of missile) able to reach one continent from another

intercourse ('intərkörs) *n.* **1.** mutual dealings; communication **2.** copulation

interdict ('intərdikt) *n.* **1.** decree of Pope restraining clergy from performing divine service **2.** formal prohibition —*vt.* (intər'dikt) **3.** prohibit, forbid **4.** restrain —**inter'diction** *n.*

interdisciplinary (intər'disiplineri) *a.* involving two or more academic disciplines

interest ('intrist, -tərist) *n.* **1.** concern, curiosity **2.** thing exciting this **3.** sum paid for use of borrowed money **4.** (*oft. pl.*) benefit, advantage **5.** (*oft. pl.*) right, share —*vt.* **6.**

excite curiosity or concern of **7.** cause to become involved in something; concern —**'interested** *a.* **1.** showing or having interest **2.** personally involved or implicated —**'interesting** *a.* —**'interestingly** *adv.*

interface ('intərfās) *n.* area, surface, boundary linking two systems

interfere (intər'fēər) *vi.* **1.** meddle, intervene **2.** clash **3.** (*with* with) *euphemistic* assault sexually —**inter'ference** *n.* **1.** act of interfering **2.** *Rad.* interruption of reception by atmospherics or by unwanted signals

interferon (intər'fēəron) *n.* a protein produced by the body that stops the development of an invading virus

interim ('intərim) *n.* **1.** meantime —*a.* **2.** temporary, intervening

interior (in'tēəriər) *a.* **1.** inner **2.** inland **3.** indoors —*n.* **4.** inside **5.** inland region —**interior angle** angle of polygon contained between two adjacent sides —**interior design** colors, furniture *etc.* of interior of house *etc.*

interject (intər'jekt) *vt.* interpose (remark *etc.*) —**inter'jection** *n.* **1.** exclamation **2.** interjected remark

interlace (intər'lās) *vt.* unite, as by lacing together —**inter'lacement** *n.*

interlard (intər'lärd) *vt.* intersperse

interleave (intər'lēv) *vt.* insert, as blank leaves in book, between other leaves —**'interleaf** *n.* extra leaf

interlining ('intərlīning) *n.* material used between lining and outer fabric of *esp.* outdoor garment

interlock (intər'lok) *v.* **1.** lock together firmly —*n.* ('intərlok) **2.** fabric constructed by interlocking two ribbed fabrics

interlocutor (intər'lokyətər) *n.* one who takes part in conversation —**interlo'cution** *n.* dialogue —**inter'locutory** *a.*

interloper ('intərlōpər) *n.* one intruding in another's affairs

interlude ('intərlōōd) *n.* **1.** interval (in play *etc.*) **2.** something filling an interval

intermarry (intər'mari) *vi.* **1.** (of families, races, religions) become linked by marriage **2.** marry within one's family —**inter'marriage** *n.*

intermediate (intər'mēdiit) *a.* coming between; interposed —**inter'mediary** *n./a.*

intermezzo (intər'metsō) *n.* short performance between acts of play or opera (*pl.* **-s, -mezzi** (-'metsē))

interminable (in'tərminəbəl) *a.* endless

intermit (intər'mit) *v.* stop for a time (**-tt-**) —**inter'mission** *n.* **1.** short period between events or activities; pause **2.** act of intermitting; state of being intermitted —**inter'mittent** *a.* occurring at intervals

intern (in'tərn) *vt.* **1.** confine to special area or camp —*n.* ('intərn) **2.** internee **3.** advanced student or recent graduate undergoing supervised practical training, *esp.* in medicine (*also* **'interne**) —**inter'nee** *n.* person who is interned, *esp.* enemy citizen in wartime or terrorism suspect —**in'ternment** *n.*

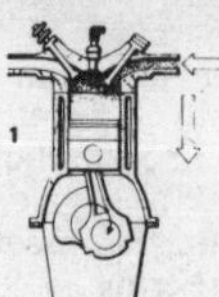

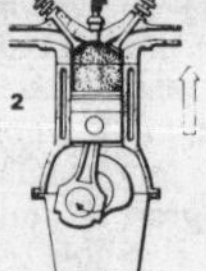

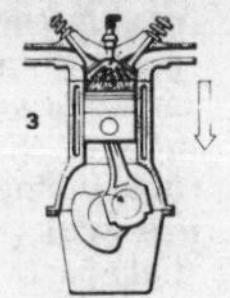

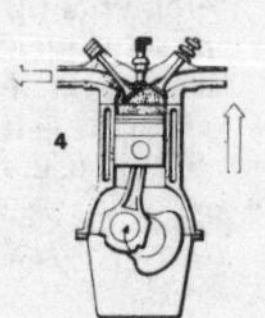

internal-combustion engine (1. induction stroke; 2. compression stroke; 3. power stroke; 4. exhaust stroke)

internal (in'tərnəl) *a.* **1.** inward **2.** interior **3.** of a nation's domestic as opposed to foreign affairs —**in'ternally** *adv.* —**'internist** *n.* physician specializing in internal medicine —**internal-combustion engine** heat engine in which combustion occurs within engine rather than in an external furnace —**internal medicine** branch of medicine concerned with treatment of diseases, *esp.* of adults, not requiring surgical intervention —**internal revenue** revenue of a government from any domestic source —**Internal Revenue Service** division of the U.S. Department of the Treasury that collects income and excise taxes and enforces revenue laws

international (intər'nashənəl) *a.* **1.** of relations between nations —*n.* **2.** game or match between teams of different countries —**inter'nationalism** *n.* ideal or practice of cooperation and understanding between nations —**inter'nationalist** *n.* —**inter'nationally** *adv.* —**international nautical mile** unit of distance in sea and air navigation equal to 6067.1033 feet or 1.852 kilometers (*also* **international air mile**) —**International Phonetic Alphabet** series of signs and letters for representation of human speech sounds —**international pitch** *Mus.* tuning standard of 440 vibrations per second for A above middle C

internecine (intər'nesēn, -'nēsīn) *a.* **1.** mutually destructive **2.** deadly

interplanetary (intər'planiteri) *a.* of, linking planets

interplay ('intərplā) *n.* **1.** action and reaction of two things, sides *etc.* upon each other **2.** interaction **3.** reciprocation

Interpol ('intərpol) International Criminal Police Organization

interpolate (in'tərpəlāt) *vt.* **1.** insert (new,

esp. misleading matter) in (book *etc.*) **2.** interject (remark) **3.** *Math.* estimate (a value) between known values —**interpo'lation** *n.*

interpose (intər'pōz) *vt.* **1.** insert **2.** say as interruption **3.** put in the way —*vi.* **4.** intervene —**interpo'sition** *n.*

interpret (in'tərprit) *vt.* **1.** explain **2.** *Art* render, represent —*vi.* **3.** translate, *esp.* orally —**interpre'tation** *n.* —**in'terpreter** *n.*

interregnum (intə'regnəm) *n.* **1.** interval between reigns **2.** gap in continuity (*pl.* **-na** (-nə), **-s**)

interrelate (intərri'lāt) *v.* place in or come into mutual or reciprocal relationship —**interre'lation** *n.*

interrogate (in'terəgāt) *vt.* question, *esp.* closely or officially —**interro'gation** *n.* —**inter'rogative** *a.* **1.** questioning —*n.* **2.** word used in asking question —**in'terrogator** *n.* —**inter'rogatory** *a.* **1.** of inquiry —*n.* **2.** question, set of questions —**interrogation point** *see* **question mark** *at* QUESTION

interrupt (intə'rupt) *v.* **1.** break in (upon) —*vt.* **2.** stop the course of **3.** block —**inter'ruption** *n.*

interscholastic (intərskə'lastik) *a.* **1.** (of sports events, competitions *etc.*) occurring between two or more schools **2.** representative of various schools

intersect (intər'sekt) *vt.* **1.** divide by passing across or through —*vi.* **2.** meet and cross —**inter'section** *n.* point where lines, roads cross

interspace (intər'spās) *vt.* **1.** make or occupy space between —*n.* ('intərspās) **2.** space between or among things —**interspatial** (intər'spāshəl) *a.*

intersperse (intər'spərs) *vt.* sprinkle (something) with or (something) among or in —**inter'spersion** *n.*

interstate (intər'stāt) *a.* **1.** between, involving two or more states —*n.* **2.** interstate highway —**interstate highway system** road system that links all states of the U.S.

interstellar (intər'stelər) *a.* (of the space) between stars

interstice (in'tərstis) *n.* chink, gap, crevice —**inter'stitial** *a.*

intertrigo (intər'trīgō) *n.* inflammation caused by repeated friction between two opposing skin surfaces

intertwine (intər'twīn) *v.* twist together, entwine

interurban (intər'ərbən) *a.* between or connecting cities

interval ('intərvəl) *n.* **1.** intervening time or space **2.** pause, break **3.** *Mus.* difference in pitch between two tones

intervene (intər'vēn) *vi.* **1.** come into a situation in order to change it **2.** (*with* on *or* between) be, come (between or among) **3.** occur in meantime **4.** interpose —**intervention** (intər'venchən) *n.*

interview ('intərvyōō) *n.* **1.** meeting, *esp.* formally arranged and involving questioning of a person —*vt.* **2.** have interview with —**interview'ee** *n.* —**'interviewer** *n.*

intestate (in'testāt, -tit) *a.* **1.** not having made a will **2.** (of property) not disposed of by will —**in'testacy** *n.*

intestine (in'testin) *n.* (*usu. pl.*) lower part of alimentary canal between stomach and anus —**in'testinal** *a.* —**intestinal obstruction** *see* **ileus** *at* ILEUM

intimate[1] ('intimit) *a.* **1.** closely acquainted, familiar **2.** private **3.** extensive **4.** having sexual relations —*n.* **5.** intimate friend —**'intimacy** *n.*

intimate[2] ('intimāt) *vt.* **1.** announce **2.** imply —**inti'mation** *n.* notice

intimidate (in'timidāt) *vt.* **1.** frighten into submission **2.** deter by threats —**intimi'dation** *n.* —**in'timidator** *n.*

into ('intōō; *unstressed* 'intə) *prep.* **1.** expresses motion to a point within **2.** indicates change of state **3.** indicates coming up against, encountering **4.** indicates arithmetical division

intone (in'tōn) *or* **intonate** *vt.* **1.** chant **2.** recite in monotone —**into'nation** *n.* **1.** modulation of voice **2.** quality of a musical sound, *esp.* regarding pitch **3.** intoning **4.** accent

in toto (in 'tōtō) *Lat.* totally, entirely, completely

intoxicate (in'toksikāt) *vt.* **1.** make drunk **2.** excite to excess —**in'toxicant** *a./n.* (anything) causing intoxication —**intoxi'cation** *n.*

intr. intransitive

intra- (*comb. form*) within, as in *intrastate*

intractable (in'traktəbəl) *a.* **1.** difficult to influence **2.** hard to control

intramural (intrə'myŏŏrəl) *a.* operating within or involving those within boundaries, *esp.* of school or college

intransigent (in'transijənt) *a.* uncompromising, obstinate

intransitive (in'transitiv) *a.* denoting a verb that does not require direct object —**intransi'tivity** *or* **in'transitiveness** *n.*

intrauterine (intrə'yōōtərin) *a.* within the womb (*see also* IUD)

intravenous (intrə'vēnəs) *a.* into a vein

in-tray *n.* tray for incoming papers *etc.* requiring attention

intrench (in'trench) *vt. see* ENTRENCH

intrepid (in'trepid) *a.* fearless, undaunted —**intre'pidity** *n.*

intricate ('intrikit) *a.* involved, puzzlingly entangled —**'intricacy** *n.* —**'intricately** *adv.*

intrigue ('intrēg, in'trēg) *n.* **1.** underhand plot **2.** secret love affair —*vi.* (in'trēg) **3.** carry on intrigue —*vt.* (in'trēg) **4.** interest, puzzle

intrinsic (in'trinzik, -sik) *a.* inherent; essential —**in'trinsically** *adv.*

intro. *or* **introd.** 1. introduction 2. introductory

intro- (*comb. form*) into, within, as in *introduce, introvert*

introduce (intrəˈdyōōs, -ˈdōōs) *vt.* 1. make acquainted 2. present 3. bring in 4. bring forward 5. bring into practice 6. insert —**introˈduction** *n.* 1. an introducing 2. presentation of one person to another 3. preliminary section or treatment 4. *Mus.* opening passage in movement or composition, that precedes main material —**introˈductory** *a.* preliminary

introit (ˈintrōit, -troit) *n. Eccles.* anthem sung as priest approaches altar

introspection (intrəˈspekshən) *n.* examination of one's own thoughts —**introˈspective** *a.*

introvert (ˈintrəvərt) *n. Psychoanal.* one who looks inward rather than at the external world —**introˈversible** *a.* —**introˈversion** *n.* —**introˈversive** *a.* —**ˈintroverted** *a.*

intrude (inˈtrōōd) *v.* thrust (oneself) in uninvited —**inˈtruder** *n.* —**inˈtrusion** *n.* —**inˈtrusive** *a.*

intrust (inˈtrust) *vt. see* ENTRUST

intuition (intyōōˈishən, intōō-) *n.* 1. immediate mental apprehension without reasoning 2. immediate insight —**inˈtuit** *vt.* —**inˈtuitive** *a.*

intussusception (intəsəˈsepshən) *n.* condition in which one segment of intestine is telescoped into another

Inuit (ˈinyōōit) *n.* Eskimo of N Amer. or Greenland

inundate (ˈinundāt) *vt.* 1. flood 2. overwhelm —**inunˈdation** *n.*

inure *or* **enure** (iˈnyōōər, iˈnōōər) *vt.* accustom, *esp.* to hardship, danger *etc.*

in vacuo (in ˈvakyōōō) *Lat.* in vacuum

invade (inˈvād) *v.* 1. enter (a country *etc.*) by force with hostile intent —*vt.* 2. overrun 3. pervade —**inˈvader** *n.* —**inˈvasion** *n.* 1. act of invading with armed forces 2. any encroachment or intrusion 3. onset of something harmful, *esp.* disease

invalid[1] (ˈinvəlid) *n.* 1. one suffering from chronic ill health —*a.* 2. ill, suffering from sickness or injury —*vt.* 3. cause to become an invalid

invalid[2] (inˈvalid) *a.* 1. not valid; having no cogency or legal force 2. *Logic* having conclusion that does not necessarily follow from its premises; not valid —**inˈvalidate** *vt.* 1. render weak or ineffective, as argument 2. take away legal force or effectiveness of; annul —**invaliˈdation** *n.* —**inˈvalidator** *n.*

invaluable (inˈvalyōōəbəl) *a.* priceless

Invar (inˈvär) *n.* trade name for steel containing 30 per cent nickel, with low coefficient of expansion

invasion (inˈvāzhən) *n. see* INVADE

inveigh (inˈvā) *vi.* speak violently —**invective** (inˈvektiv) *n.* abusive speech or writing, vituperation

inveigle (inˈvāgəl, -ˈvē-) *vt.* entice, seduce, wheedle —**inˈveiglement** *n.*

invent (inˈvent) *vt.* 1. devise, originate 2. fabricate (falsehoods *etc.*) —**inˈvention** *n.* 1. that which is invented 2. ability to invent 3. contrivance 4. deceit; lie —**inˈventive** *a.* resourceful; creative —**inˈventively** *adv.* —**inˈventor** *n.*

inventory (ˈinvəntōri) *n.* 1. detailed list of goods *etc.* —*vt.* 2. make list of

invert (inˈvərt) *vt.* 1. turn upside down 2. reverse position, relations of —**inverse** (inˈvərs, ˈinvərs) *a.* 1. inverted 2. opposite —**inˈversely** *adv.* —**inˈversion** *n.*

invertebrate (inˈvərtibrit, -brāt) *n.* animal without a backbone —**invertebrate biology** study of such animals

invest (inˈvest) *vt.* 1. lay out (money, time, effort *etc.*) for profit or advantage 2. install 3. endow 4. *obs.* clothe 5. *Poet.* cover, as with garment —**inˈvestiture** *n.* formal installation of person in office or rank —**inˈvestment** *n.* 1. investing 2. money invested 3. stocks and bonds bought —**inˈvestor** *n.* —**investment company** company that invests its funds in other companies and issues its own securities against these investments

investigate (inˈvestigāt) *vt.* inquire into; examine —**investiˈgation** *n.* —**inˈvestigator** *n.*

inveterate (inˈvetərit) *a.* 1. deep-rooted; long-established 2. confirmed —**inˈveteracy** *n.*

invidious (inˈvidiəs) *a.* likely to cause ill will or envy —**inˈvidiously** *adv.*

invigilate (inˈvijilāt) *vi.* supervise examination candidates —**inˈvigilator** *n.*

invigorate (inˈvigərāt) *vt.* give vigor to, strengthen

invincible (inˈvinsəbəl) *a.* unconquerable —**invinciˈbility** *n.*

inviolable (inˈvīələbəl) *a.* 1. not to be profaned; sacred 2. unalterable —**inˈviolate** *a.* 1. unhurt 2. unprofaned 3. unbroken

invisible (inˈvizəbəl) *a.* 1. not visible; not able to be perceived by eye 2. concealed from sight; hidden 3. not easily seen or noticed 4. kept hidden from public view; secret; clandestine 5. *Econ.* of services, such as insurance and freight, rather than goods —*n.* 6. *Econ.* invisible item of trade; service —**invisiˈbility** *or* **inˈvisibleness** *n.* —**inˈvisibly** *adv.*

invite (inˈvīt) *vt.* 1. request the company of 2. ask courteously 3. ask for 4. attract, call forth —*n.* (ˈinvīt) 5. *inf.* invitation —**invitation** (inviˈtāshən) *n.* —**inˈviting** *a.* tempting; alluring; attractive

invoice (ˈinvois) *n.* 1. a list of goods or services sold, with prices —*vt.* 2. present with an invoice 3. make an invoice of

invoke (in'vōk) *vt.* **1.** call on **2.** appeal to **3.** ask earnestly for **4.** summon —**invo'cation** *n.*

involuntary (in'volənteri) *a.* **1.** not done voluntarily **2.** unintentional **3.** instinctive

involute ('invəlōōt) *a.* **1.** complex **2.** coiled spirally **3.** rolled inward (*also* **invo'luted**) —*n.* **4.** *Math.* curve with inward spiral —**invo'lution** *n.*

involve (in'volv) *vt.* **1.** include **2.** entail **3.** implicate (person) **4.** concern **5.** entangle —**in'volved** *a.* **1.** complicated **2.** concerned —**in'volvement** *n.*

inward ('inwərd) *a.* **1.** internal **2.** situated within **3.** spiritual, mental —*adv.* **4.** toward the inside **5.** into the mind (*also* **'inwards**) —*pl.n.* **6.** *see* INNARDS —**'inwardly** *adv.* **1.** in the mind **2.** internally

iodine ('Iədīn, 'Iədin, 'Iədēn) *n. Chem.* nonmetallic element *Symbol* I, at. wt. 126.9, at. no. 53 —**iodide** ('Iədīd) *n.* **1.** salt of hydriodic acid, containing the iodide ion **2.** compound containing an iodine atom —**'iodize** *vt.* treat with iodine or iodide —**iodoform** (I'ōdəfōrm, I'od-) *n.* antiseptic

I.O.M. Isle of Man

ion ('Iən, -on) *n.* charged particle formed from an atom or group of atoms through the gain or loss of one or more electrons —**i'onic** *a.* —**ioni'zation** *n.* the loss of one or more outer electrons of an atom causing it to become electrically positively charged, or the gain of one or more extra electrons, causing the atom to become negatively charged —**'ionize** *v.* change or become changed into ions —**i'onosphere** *n.* region of atmosphere 60 to 100 km above earth's surface

-ion (*comb. form*) action, process, state, as in *creation, objection*

Ionic (I'onik) *a. Archit.* distinguished by scroll-like decoration on columns

iota (I'ōtə) *n.* **1.** ninth letter in Gr. alphabet (Ι, ι) **2.** (*usu. with* not one *or* an) very small amount

IOU *n.* signed paper acknowledging debt

-ious (*comb. form*) characterized by; full of, as in *ambitious, suspicious*

I.O.W. Isle of Wight

Iowa ('Iōə) *n.* West North Central state of the U.S., admitted to the Union in 1846. Abbrev.: IA (with ZIP code)

IPA International Phonetic Alphabet

ipecac ('ipikak) *or* **ipecacuanha** (ēpikakyōō'anyə) *n.* S Amer. plant yielding an emetic

ipso facto ('ipsō 'faktō) *Lat.* by that very fact

I.Q. intelligence quotient

Ir *Chem.* iridium

Ir. **1.** Ireland **2.** Irish

IR **1.** information retrieval **2.** internal revenue

ir- (*comb. form*) *see* IN-[1], IN-[2]

I.R.A. Irish Republican Army

Iran (i'rän, -'ran, I'ran) *n.* country in western Asia bounded north by the U.S.S.R. and the Caspian Sea, east by Afghanistan and Pakistan, south by the Gulf of Oman and the Persian Gulf, and west by Iraq and Turkey —**Iranian** (i'rāniən) *a./n.* **1.** (native or inhabitant) of Iran —*n.* **2.** branch of Indo-European languages to which Persian, the official language of Iran, belongs

Iraq (i'räk, -rak) *n.* country in Middle East bounded north by Turkey, east by Iran, southeast by the Persian Gulf, south by Kuwait and Saudi Arabia and west by Jordan and Syria —**I'raqi** *n.* **1.** native or inhabitant of Iraq (*pl.* **-s**) —*a.* **2.** of Iraq

irascible (i'rasibəl) *a.* hot-tempered —**irasci'bility** *n.* —**i'rascibly** *adv.*

IRBM intermediate-range ballistic missile

ire ('Iər) *n.* anger, wrath —**i'rate** *a.* angry

Ireland ('Iərlənd) *n.* **1. Republic of Ireland.** country lying in the N Atlantic in the smaller of the British Isles, separated from Great Britain by the Irish Sea to the east and bounded northeast by Northern Ireland **2.** island made up of Republic of Ireland and Northern Ireland —**'Irish** *a.* **1.** of Ireland, its people or their language —*n.* **2.** Irish Gaelic —**Irish coffee** coffee mixed with whiskey and topped with cream —**Irish Gaelic** Goidelic language of the Celts of Ireland; official language of Republic of Ireland since 1921 —**Irish linen** very fine lightweight fabric woven from Irish flax (*also* **handkerchief linen**) —**Irish moss** carrageen —**Irish stew** stew made of mutton, potatoes, onions *etc.* —**Irish tweed** tweed with white warp and colored weft threads

iridaceous (iri'dāshəs, I-) *a.* belonging to iris family

iridescent (iri'desənt) *a.* exhibiting changing colors like those of the rainbow —**iri'descence** *n.*

iridium (i'ridiəm) *n. Chem.* noble metallic element *Symbol* Ir, at. wt. 192.2, at. no. 77

iris

iris ('Iris) *n.* **1.** circular membrane of eye containing pupil **2.** (*also* **flag**) plant with sword-shaped leaves and showy flowers (*pl.* **-es, irides** ('īridēz, 'iri-))

irk (ərk) *vt.* irritate, vex —'**irksome** *a.* tiresome

iron ('īərn) *n.* **1.** *Chem.* metallic element *Symbol* Fe, at. wt. 55.9, at. no. 26 **2.** tool *etc.* of this metal **3.** appliance used, when heated, to smooth cloth **4.** metal-headed golf club **5.** splintlike support for malformed leg **6.** great hardness, strength or resolve —*pl.* **7.** fetters —*a.* **8.** of, like iron **9.** inflexible, unyielding **10.** robust —*v.* **11.** smooth, cover, fetter *etc.* with iron or an iron —'**irony** *a.* of, resembling, or containing iron —**Iron Age** era of iron implements beginning in central Europe from about the 7th cent. B.C. until the Christian era —**iron'clad** *a.* protected with or as with iron —**Iron Curtain 1.** guarded border between countries of Soviet bloc and the rest of Europe **2.** (**i- c-**) any barrier that separates communities or ideologies —**iron hand** harsh or rigorous control —**ironing board** board, usu. on legs, with suitable covering on which to iron clothes —**iron lung** apparatus for administering artificial respiration for a prolonged period —**iron maiden** medieval instrument of torture, consisting of enclosed space lined with iron spikes —**iron pyrites 1.** fool's gold **2.** marcasite —**iron rations** emergency food supplies —'**ironstone** *n.* **1.** any rock consisting mainly of iron-bearing ore **2.** tough durable earthenware —'**ironwood** *n.* **1.** the hop hornbeam, deciduous tree of the birch family of eastern N Amer. **2.** tough wood of this tree —'**ironwork** *n.* work done in iron, *esp.* decorative work —'**ironworks** *pl.n.* (*sometimes with sing. v.*) building in which iron is smelted, cast or wrought —**irons in the fire** projects, undertakings —**strike while the iron is hot** act when opportunity knocks

irony ('īrəni) *n.* **1.** (*usu.* humorous or mildly sarcastic) use of words to mean the opposite of what is said **2.** event, situation opposite of that expected —**i'ronic(al)** *a.* of, using irony

Iroquoian (irə'kwoiən) *n.* Amerindian language family spoken in upper New York state, Oklahoma and North Carolina

Iroquois ('irəkwoi, -kwä) *n.* **1.** Amerindian confederacy of New York comprising Cayuga, Mohawk, Oneida, Onondaga, Seneca and later Tuscaroro tribes **2.** any member of these peoples (*pl.* **-ois**)

irradiate (i'rādiāt) *vt.* **1.** treat by irradiation **2.** shine upon, throw light upon, light up —**irradi'ation** *n.* impregnation by x-rays, light rays

irrational (i'rashənəl) *a.* **1.** inconsistent with reason or logic **2.** incapable of reasoning **3.** *Math.* of real number which cannot be expressed as a ratio of two integers —**irration'ality** *n.*

irreconcilable (irekən'sīləbəl, i'rekənsī-) *a.* **1.** not able to be reconciled; incompatible —*n.* **2.** person or thing that is implacably hostile **3.** (*usu. pl.*) one of various principles *etc.* that are incapable of being brought into agreement —**irreconcila'bility** *n.* —**irrecon'cilably** *adv.*

irrecoverable (iri'kuvərəbəl, -'kuvrə-) *a.* **1.** not able to be recovered or regained **2.** not able to be remedied or rectified

irredeemable (iri'dēməbəl) *a.* **1.** (of bonds *etc.*) without date of redemption of capital; incapable of being bought back directly or paid off **2.** (of paper money) not convertible into specie **3.** (of loss) not able to be recovered; irretrievable **4.** not able to be improved or rectified; irreparable —**irre'deemably** *adv.*

irredentist (iri'dentist) *n.* **1.** (*sometimes* **I-**) person, *esp.* member of 19th-century It. association, who favored acquisition of territory that had once been part of his country —*a.* **2.** of irredentism —**irre'dentism** *n.*

irreducible (iri'dyōōsibəl, -'dōōs-) *a.* **1.** not able to be reduced or lessened **2.** not able to be brought to simpler or reduced form **3.** *Math.* (of polynomial) unable to be factorized into polynomials of lower degree —**irreduci'bility** *n.*

irrefrangible (iri'franjəbəl) *a.* **1.** inviolable **2.** in optics, not susceptible to refraction

irrefutable (iri'fyōōtəbəl, i'refyətəbəl) *a.* that cannot be refuted, disproved

irreg. irregular(ly)

irregular (i'regyələr) *a.* **1.** lacking uniformity or symmetry; uneven in shape, arrangement *etc.* **2.** not occurring at expected or equal intervals **3.** differing from normal or accepted practice or routine **4.** (of formation, inflections or derivations of word) not following usual pattern of formation in language **5.** (of troops) not belonging to regular forces —*n.* **6.** soldier not in regular army —**irregu'larity** *n.*

irrelevant (i'reləvənt) *a.* not relating or pertinent to matter at hand; not important —**ir'relevance** *or* **ir'relevancy** *n.*

irremissible (iri'misəbəl) *a.* **1.** unpardonable; inexcusable **2.** that must be done, as through duty or obligation —**irremissi'bility** *n.*

irreparable (i'repərəbəl, i'reprəbəl) *a.* not able to be repaired or remedied

irreplaceable (iri'plāsəbəl) *a.* not able to be replaced

irrepressible (iri'presəbəl) *a.* not capable of being repressed, controlled or restrained —**irrepressi'bility** *n.* —**irre'pressibly** *adv.*

irreproachable (iri'prōchəbəl) *a.* not deserving reproach; blameless

irresistible (iri'zistəbəl) *a.* **1.** not able to be resisted or refused; overpowering **2.** very fascinating or alluring —**irre'sistibly** *adv.*

irresolute (i'rezəlōōt) *a.* lacking resolution;

wavering; hesitating —**ir'resolutely** *adv.* —**ir'resoluteness** *or* **irreso'lution** *n.*

irrespective (iri'spektiv) *a.* —**irrespective of** without taking account of

irresponsible (iri'sponsəbəl) *a.* **1.** not showing or done with due care for consequences of one's actions or attitudes; reckless **2.** not capable of bearing responsibility —**irresponsi'bility** *or* **irre'sponsibleness** *n.* —**irre'sponsibly** *adv.*

irretrievable (iri'trēvəbəl) *a.* not able to be retrieved, recovered or repaired —**irretrieva'bility** *n.* —**irre'trievably** *adv.*

irreverence (i'revərəns) *n.* **1.** lack of due respect or veneration **2.** disrespectful remark or act —**ir'reverent** *a.*

irreversible (iri'vərsəbəl) *a.* **1.** not able to be reversed **2.** not able to be revoked or repealed **3.** *Chem., phys.* capable of changing or producing change in one direction only —**irreversi'bility** *n.* —**irre'versibly** *adv.*

irrevocable (i'revəkəbəl) *a.* not able to be changed, undone, altered

irrigate ('irigāt) *vt.* water by artificial channels, pipes *etc.* —**irri'gation** *n.* —**'irrigator** *n.*

irritate ('iritāt) *vt.* **1.** annoy **2.** inflame **3.** stimulate —**'irritable** *a.* easily annoyed —**'irritably** *adv.* —**'irritant** *a./n.* (person or thing) causing irritation —**irri'tation** *n.*

irrupt (i'rupt) *vi.* **1.** enter forcibly **2.** increase suddenly —**ir'ruption** *n.*

IRS Internal Revenue Service

is (iz) third person singular, *present indicative of* BE

is. 1. island **2.** isle

Isa. *Bible* Isaiah

Isaiah (ī'zāə) *n. Bible* 23rd book of the O.T., first of the prophetic books, written by Isaiah; oft. called the Old Testament Gospel as it is about the judgment of God and the deliverance of man

Isaias (ī'zāəs) *n. Bible* Isaiah in the Douay Version of the O.T.

I.S.B.N. *or* **ISBN** International Standard Book Number

ischium ('iskiəm) *n.* curved bone forming base of each half of pelvis

-ish (*comb. form*) **1.** of a nationality, as in *Scottish* **2.** *oft. derogatory* having manner or qualities of; resembling, as in *slavish, boyish* **3.** somewhat; approximately, as in *yellowish, sevenish* **4.** concerned or preoccupied with, as in *bookish*

isinglass ('īzin-glas, 'īzingglas) *n.* kind of gelatin obtained from some freshwater fishes

Islam (is'läm) *n.* Muslim faith or world —**Is'lamic** *a.* —**Islamic art** Muslim art, typically nonfigurative, highly ornamental, using texts from the Koran for decoration

island ('īlənd) *n.* **1.** piece of land surrounded by water **2.** anything like this, as raised piece for pedestrians in middle of road —**'islander** *n.* inhabitant of island

isle (īl) *n.* island —**'islet** *n.* little island

ism ('izəm) *n. inf., oft. derogatory* unspecified doctrine, system or practice

-ism (*comb. form*) **1.** action, process, result, as in *criticism* **2.** state; condition, as in *paganism* **3.** doctrine, system, body of principles and practices, as in *Leninism, spiritualism* **4.** behavior; characteristic quality, as in *heroism* **5.** characteristic usage, *esp.* of language, as in *Scotticism*

isobar ('īsəbär) *n.* line on map connecting places of equal mean barometric pressure —**iso'baric** *a.*

isochronal (ī'sokrənəl) *or* **isochronous** *a.* **1.** having same duration; equal in time **2.** occurring at equal time intervals; having uniform period of vibration —**i'sochronism** *n.*

isolate ('īsəlāt) *vt.* place apart or alone —**iso'lation** *n.* —**iso'lationism** *n.* policy of not participating in international affairs —**iso'lationist** *n./a.*

isomer ('īsəmər) *n.* substance with same molecules as another but different atomic arrangement —**iso'meric** *a.* —**i'somerism** *n.*

isometric (īsə'metrik) *a.* **1.** having equal dimensions **2.** relating to muscular contraction without external movement —**iso'metrics** *pl.n.* (*with sing. v.*) system of isometric exercises

isomorphism (īsə'mörfizəm) *n.* **1.** *Biol.* similarity of form **2.** *Chem.* existence of two or more substances of different composition in similar crystalline form **3.** *Math.* one-to-one correspondence between elements of two or more sets —**iso'morphic** *or* **iso'morphous** *a.*

isoniazid (īsō'nīəzid) *n.* drug for oral treatment of tuberculosis

isosceles (ī'sosilēz) *a.* (of triangle) having two sides equal

isotherm ('īsəthərm) *n.* line on map connecting points of equal mean temperature

isotope ('īsətōp) *n.* atom of element having a different nuclear mass and atomic weight from other atoms in same element —**isotopic** (īsə'topik, -'tōpik) *a.*

isotropic (īsə'trōpik, -'tropik) *or* **isotropous** (ī'sotrəpəs) *a.* **1.** having uniform physical properties in all directions **2.** *Biol.* not having predetermined axes —**i'sotropy** *n.*

Israel ('izriəl) *n.* **1.** country in Middle East bounded west by Egypt and the Mediterranean, north by Lebanon, east by Syria and Jordan **2.** ancient kingdom of Jews in this region —**Israeli** (iz'rāli) *n./a.* —**'Israelite** *n. Bible* member of ethnic group claiming descent from Jacob; Hebrew —**Children of Israel** the Jewish people or nation

issue ('ishyōō) *n.* **1.** sending or giving out officially or publicly **2.** number or amount so given out **3.** discharge **4.** offspring, children **5.** topic of discussion **6.** question, dispute **7.** outcome, result —*vi.* **8.** go out **9.** result (in) **10.** arise (from) —*vt.* **11.** emit, give out, send out **12.** distribute **13.** publish —**take issue** disagree

-ist (*comb. form*) **1.** person who performs certain action or is concerned with something specified, as in *soloist* **2.** person who practices in specific field, as in *physicist* **3.** person who advocates particular doctrine, system *etc.;* of doctrine advocated, as in *socialist* **4.** person characterized by specified trait, tendency *etc.;* of such a trait, as in *purist* —**-istic** (*a. comb. form*)

isthmus (ˈisməs) *n.* neck of land between two seas

it (it) *pron.* neuter pronoun of the third person —**its** *a.* belonging to it —**itˈself** *pron.* emphatic form of IT

It. 1. Italian **2.** Italy

i.t.a. *or* **I.T.A.** initial teaching alphabet

ital. *Print.* italic

italic (iˈtalik) *a.* (of type) sloping —**iˈtalicize** *vt.* put in italics —**iˈtalics** *pl.n.* italic type, now used for emphasis *etc.*

Italy (ˈitəli) *n.* country in southern Europe occupying a long peninsula extending into the Mediterranean, bounded east by Yugoslavia, north by Austria and Switzerland and west by France —**Italian** (iˈtalyən) *n./a.* **1.** (native or inhabitant) of Italy —*n.* **2.** language of Italy, which is a Romance language —**Iˈtalianate** *or* **Italiaˈnesque** *a.* Italian in style or character

itch (ich) *n.* **1.** irritation in the skin **2.** restless desire —*vi.* **3.** feel or produce irritating or tickling sensation **4.** have a restless desire (to do something) —**ˈitchy** *a.*

-ite (*comb. form*) **1.** native or inhabitant of, as in *Israelite* **2.** follower or advocate of; supporter of group, as in *Luddite, laborite* **3.** *Biol.* division of body or organ, as in *neurite* **4.** mineral; rock, as in *nephrite, peridotite* **5.** commercial product, as in *vulcanite*

item (ˈītəm) *n.* **1.** single thing in list, collection *etc.* **2.** piece of information **3.** entry in account *etc.* —*adv.* (ˈītem, ˈītəm) **4.** also —**ˈitemize** *vt.*

iterate (ˈitərāt) *vt.* repeat —**iterˈation** *n.* —**iterative** (ˈitərātiv, ˈitərətiv) *a.*

itinerant (īˈtinərənt, i-) *a.* **1.** traveling from place to place **2.** working for a short time in various places **3.** traveling on circuit —**iˈtineracy** *n.* —**iˈtinerary** *n.* **1.** record, line of travel **2.** route **3.** guidebook

-itis (*comb. form*) inflammation of specified part, as in *tonsillitis*

-ity (*comb. form*) state; condition, as in *technicality*

IUD intrauterine device (for contraception)

-ive (*comb. form*) tendency, inclination, character, quality, as in *divisive, festive, massive*

ivory (ˈīvəri, -vri) *n.* **1.** hard white substance of the tusks of elephants *etc.* **2.** yellowish-white color; cream —*a.* **3.** yellowish-white; cream —**ˈivories** *pl.n. sl.* **1.** piano keys **2.** teeth **3.** dice —**ivory tower** seclusion, remoteness

Ivory Coast country in Africa bounded west by Liberia and Guinea, north by Mali and Burkina-Faso, east by Ghana and south by the Gulf of Guinea —**Ivory Coaster**

ivy (ˈīvi) *n.* climbing evergreen plant —**ˈivied** *a.* covered with ivy

-ize (*comb. form*) **1.** cause to become, resemble or agree with, as in *legalize* **2.** become; change into, as in *crystallize* **3.** affect in specified way; subject to, as in *hypnotize* **4.** act according to some principle, policy *etc.*, as in *economize*

J

j *or* **J** (jā) *n.* **1.** tenth letter of English alphabet **2.** speech sound represented by this letter (*pl.* **j's, J's** *or* **Js**)

J 1. joule(s) **2.** *Cards* jack **3.** journal

JA joint account

J.A. judge advocate

jab (jab) *vt.* **1.** poke roughly **2.** thrust, stab abruptly (**-bb-**) —*n.* **3.** poke **4.** *inf.* injection

jabber (ˈjabər) *vi.* **1.** chatter **2.** talk rapidly, incoherently —ˈ**jabberwocky** *n.* nonsense, *esp.* in verse

jabot (zhaˈbō, ˈzhabō) *n.* frill, ruffle at throat or breast of garment

jacaranda (jakəˈrandə) *n.* S Amer. tree with fernlike leaves and pale purple flowers

jacinth (ˈjāsinth, ˈjas-) *n.* reddish-orange semi-precious stone

jack (jak) *n.* **1.** fellow, man **2.** *inf.* sailor **3.** male of some animals **4.** device for lifting heavy weight, *esp.* automobile **5.** various mechanical appliances **6.** lowest court card, with picture of page boy **7.** *Bowls* ball aimed at **8.** socket and plug connection in electronic equipment **9.** small flag, *esp.* national, at sea —*vt.* **10.** (*usu. with* up) lift (an object) with a jack —**Jack Frost** personification of frost —**jack-in-the-box** *n.* toy consisting of figure on tight spring in box, which springs out when lid is opened (*pl.* **jack-in-the-boxes, jacks-in-the-box**) —**jack of all trades** person who undertakes many kinds of work (*pl.* **jacks of all trades**) —**jack-o'-lantern** *n.* **1.** lantern made from hollowed pumpkin, cut to represent human face **2.** will-o'-the-wisp —**Jack Tar** *chiefly lit.* sailor

jackal (ˈjakəl, -ôl) *n.* wild, gregarious animal of Asia and Afr. closely allied to dog

jackanapes (ˈjakənāps) *n.* **1.** conceited impertinent person **2.** mischievous child **3.** *obs.* monkey

jackass (ˈjakas) *n.* **1.** the male of the ass **2.** blockhead —**laughing jackass** the Aust. kookaburra

jackboot (ˈjakbo͞ot) *n.* large riding boot coming above knee

jackdaw (ˈjakdô) *n.* European bird of crow family

jacket (ˈjakit) *n.* **1.** outer garment, short coat **2.** outer casing, cover —ˈ**jacketed** *a.*

jackhammer (ˈjak-hamər) *n.* pneumatic hammer

jackknife (ˈjaknīf) *n.* **1.** pocketknife **2.** dive with sharp bend at waist in midair —*vi.* **3.** (of trailer truck) go out of control in such a way that trailer forms right angle to tractor

jackpot (ˈjakpot) *n.* large prize, accumulated stake, as pool in poker —**hit the jackpot** win a jackpot; achieve great success, *esp.* through luck

jack rabbit hare

jacks (jaks) *pl.n.* game in which bone or metal pieces (**jackstones**) are thrown and picked up between bounces of small ball

Jackson (ˈjaksən) *n.* **Andrew.** the 7th President of the U.S. (1829-37)

Jacobean (jakəˈbēən) *a.* of the reign of James I (1603–25)

Jacobite (ˈjakəbīt) *n.* adherent of Stuarts after overthrow of James II

Jacquard (ˈjakärd) *n.* **1.** fabric in which design is incorporated into the weave **2.** loom for weaving such fabrics

Jacuzzi (jəˈko͞ozi) *n.* **1.** trade name for device which swirls water in bath **2.** bath containing such a device

jade[1] (jād) *n.* **1.** ornamental semiprecious stone, usu. dark green **2.** this color

jade[2] (jād) *n.* **1.** old worn-out horse **2.** *obs., offens.* woman considered to be disreputable —ˈ**jaded** *a.* **1.** tired **2.** off color

jag[1] (jag) *n.* sharp or ragged projection —**jagged** (ˈjagid) *a.*

jag[2] (jag) *n. sl.* **1.** intoxication from drugs or liquor **2.** bout of drinking, drug-taking *etc.*

J.A.G. judge advocate general

jaguar (ˈjagyo͞oär) *n.* medium-sized, black-marked feline of the New World (*also* **American leopard**)

jai alai (ˈhīlī, hī əˈlī) court game in which the ball is caught in a wicker racket and hurled against the walls of the enclosed arena

jail (jāl) *n.* **1.** building for confinement of criminals or suspects —*vt.* **2.** send to, confine in prison —ˈ**jailer** *or* ˈ**jailor** *n.* —ˈ**jailbird** *n.* hardened criminal

jalopy (jəˈlopi) *n. inf.* decrepit old automobile

jalousie (ˈjaləsē) *n.* **1.** adjustable blind or shutter constructed from angled slats to allow ventilation and to prevent the ingress of rain **2.** window made of angled slats of glass

jam (jam) *vt.* **1.** pack together **2.** (*oft. with* on) apply fiercely **3.** squeeze **4.** *Rad.* block (another station) with impulses of equal wavelength —*v.* **5.** (cause to) stick together and become unworkable —*vi.* **6.** *sl.* play in jam session (**-mm-**) —*n.* **7.** fruit preserved by boiling with sugar **8.** crush **9.** hold-up of traffic **10.** awkward situation —**jam-packed**

a. filled to capacity —**jam session** (improvised) jazz or pop music session

Jamaica (jə'mākə) *n.* country in Caribbean comprising an island in the Greater Antilles 90 miles south of the east end of Cuba —**Ja'maican** *n./a.*

jamb (jam) *n.* side and head lining of door, window *etc.*

jamboree (jambə'rē) *n.* **1.** celebration, spree **2.** national or international rally of Boy Scouts

James (jāmz) *n. Bible* 20th book of the N.T., epistle addressed to converted Jews living around the Mediterranean, written by a half-brother of Jesus

Jan. January

jangle ('janggəl) *v.* **1.** (cause to) sound harshly, as bell —*vt.* **2.** produce jarring effect on —*n.* **3.** harsh sound

janitor ('janitər) *n.* **1.** caretaker **2.** doorkeeper ('**janitress** *fem.*)

January ('janyōōeri) *n.* first month

japan (jə'pan) *n.* **1.** very hard, *usu.* black varnish —*vt.* **2.** cover with this (**-nn-**)

Japan (jə'pan) *n.* country lying in Pacific off the east coast of Asia comprising four main islands and many smaller islands, separated from Korea by the Korea Strait and from the U.S.S.R. by La Perouse Strait —**Japa'nese** *a.* **1.** of Japan —*n.* **2.** native or inhabitant of Japan (*pl.* **-ese**) **3.** the language of Japan, which is the only member of its family

jape (jāp) *n./vi.* joke

japonica (jə'ponikə) *n.* shrub with red flowers (*also* **Japanese quince**)

jar[1] (jär) *n.* usu. round vessel of glass, earthenware *etc.*

jar[2] (jär) *v.* **1.** (cause to) vibrate suddenly, violently —*vt.* **2.** have disturbing, painful effect on (**-rr-**) —*n.* **3.** jarring sound **4.** shock *etc.*

jardinière (järdi'nēər, zhärdi'nyāər) *n.* ornamental pot for growing plants

jargon ('järgən) *n.* **1.** specialized language concerned with particular subject **2.** pretentious or nonsensical language

Jas. James

jasmine ('jazmin) *n.* any of a genus of tender and hardy, deciduous and evergreen shrubs and climbers of the olive family grown for their white or yellow flowers, many of which are strongly fragrant

jasper ('jaspər) *n.* red, yellow, dark green or brown quartz used as gemstone

jaundice ('jöndis) *n.* **1.** symptom marked by yellowness of skin (*also* '**icterus**) **2.** bitterness, ill humor **3.** prejudice —*vt.* **4.** make prejudiced, bitter *etc.*

jaunt (jönt) *n.* **1.** short pleasurable excursion —*vi.* **2.** go on such an excursion —**jaunting car** formerly, light, two-wheeled, one-horse vehicle used in Ireland

jaunty ('jönti) *a.* **1.** sprightly **2.** brisk **3.** smart, trim —'**jauntily** *adv.*

Java ('javə) *n.* **1.** island of Indonesia **2.** (**j-**) *sl.* brewed coffee —**Java'nese** *a.* **1.** of Java —*n.* **2.** native or inhabitant of Java (*pl.* **-ese**) **3.** Malayan language of Java

javelin ('javlin) *n.* spear, *esp.* for throwing in sporting events

jaw (jö) *n.* **1.** one of bones in which teeth are set —*pl.* **2.** mouth **3.** gripping part of vise *etc.* **4.** *fig.* narrow opening of gorge or valley —*vi.* **5.** *sl.* talk lengthily

jay

jay (jā) *n.* woodland bird of Europe, N Afr. and N Asia with raucous voice —'**jaywalk** *vi.* walk in or across street carelessly or illegally —'**jaywalker** *n.*

jazz (jaz) *n.* syncopated music and dance —'**jazzy** *a.* flashy, showy —**jazz up 1.** play as jazz **2.** make more lively, appealing

JC junior college

JCS joint chiefs of staff

jct junction

JD 1. junior dean **2.** doctor of jurisprudence; doctor of law(s) **3.** justice department **4.** juvenile delinquent

JDL Jewish Defense League

jealous ('jeləs) *a.* **1.** distrustful of the faithfulness (of) **2.** envious **3.** suspiciously watchful —'**jealously** *adv.* —'**jealousy** *n.*

jeans (jēnz) *pl.n.* casual trousers with yoke at back, *esp.* made of denim

Jeep (jēp) *n.* trade name for light four-wheel-drive utility vehicle

jeer (jēər) *v.* **1.** scoff —*n.* **2.** scoff, taunt, gibe

Jefferson ('jefərsən) *n.* **Thomas.** the 3rd President of the U.S. (1801-09)

Jehovah (ji'hōvə) *n. O.T.* God —**Jehovah's Witness** member of Christian sect which believes end of world is near

jejune (ji'jōōn) *a.* **1.** simple, naive **2.** meager

Jekyll and Hyde ('jekəl; hīd) person with two distinct personalities, one good, the other evil

jell (jel) *v.* **1.** congeal —*vi.* **2.** *inf.* assume definite form

Jello ('jelō) *n.* trade name for gelatin dessert usu. flavored and colored like fruit

jelly ('jeli) *n.* **1.** semitransparent food made with gelatin, becoming softly stiff as it cools **2.** anything of the consistency of this —'**jellybean** *n.* bean-shaped candy with chewy filling and hard sugar coating —'**jellyfish** *n.* jellylike small sea animal

jenny ('jeni) *n.* **1.** female ass **2.** female wren

jeopardy ('jepərdi) *n.* (*usu. with* in) danger —'**jeopardize** *vt.* endanger

Jer. *Bible* Jeremiah

jerboa (jər'bōə) *n.* **1.** small Afr. burrowing rodent resembling a mouse **2.** desert rat

jeremiad (jeri'mīəd) *n.* lamentation; complaint

Jeremiah (jerə'mīə) *n. Bible* 24th book of the O.T., written by a major prophet who lived at the time of the fall of Jerusalem

Jeremias (jerə'mīəs) *n. Bible* Jeremiah in the Douay Version of the O.T.

jerk[1] (jərk) *n.* **1.** sharp, abruptly stopped movement **2.** twitch **3.** sharp pull **4.** *sl.* stupid person —*v.* **5.** move or throw with a jerk —'**jerkily** *adv.* —'**jerkiness** *n.* —'**jerky** *a.* uneven, spasmodic

jerk[2] (jərk) *vt.* **1.** preserve (beef *etc.*) by cutting into strips and drying in sun —*n.* **2.** jerked meat (*also* '**jerky**)

jerkin ('jərkin) *n.* sleeveless jacket, *esp.* of leather

jerry-built ('jeri-) *a.* of flimsy construction with cheap materials —**jerry-builder** *n.*

jerry can flat-sided can for storing or transporting motor fuel *etc.*

jersey ('jərzi) *n.* **1.** plain machine-knitted fabric of natural or man-made fibers **2.** circular-knitted sweater **3.** (**J-**) breed of cattle

jessamine ('jesəmin) *n.* jasmine

jest (jest) *n./vi.* joke —'**jester** *n.* joker, *esp.* employed by medieval ruler

Jesuit ('jezhŏŏit) *n.* member of Society of Jesus, order founded by Ignatius Loyola in 1534 —**Jesu'itical** *a.* of Jesuits

Jesus ('jēzəs) *n.* **1.** ?4 B.C.-?29 A.D., founder of Christianity, believed by Christians to be the Son of God (*also* **Jesus Christ, Jesus of Nazareth**) —*interj.* **2.** used to express intense surprise, dismay *etc.* (*also* **Jesus wept**)

jet[1] (jet) *n.* **1.** stream of liquid, gas *etc.*, *esp.* shot from small hole **2.** the small hole **3.** spout, nozzle **4.** aircraft driven by jet propulsion —*vt.* **5.** throw out —*vi.* **6.** shoot forth —*v.* **7.** transport or be transported by jet (**-tt-**) —**jet lag** fatigue caused by crossing time zones in jet aircraft —**jet-propelled** *a.* driven by jet propulsion —**jet propulsion** propulsion by thrust provided by jet of gas or liquid —**jet set** rich, fashionable social set, members of which travel widely for pleasure —'**jetsetter** *n.*

jet[2] (jet) *n.* hard black coal capable of brilliant polish —**jet-black** *a.* glossy black

jetsam ('jetsəm) *n.* cargo thrown overboard to lighten ship and later washed ashore —'**jettison** *vt.* **1.** abandon **2.** throw overboard

jetty ('jeti) *n.* small pier, wharf

Jew (jōō) *n.* **1.** person of Hebrew religion or ancestry **2.** *inf., offens.* miser ('**Jewess** *fem.*) —'**Jewish** *a.* —'**Jewry** *n.* the Jewish people —**jew's-harp** *n.* small musical instrument held between teeth and played by finger

jewel ('jōōəl) *n.* **1.** precious stone **2.** ornament containing one **3.** precious thing —'**jeweler** *n.* dealer in jewels —'**jewelry** *n.* items of bodily adornment other than clothing

jewfish ('jōōfish) *n.* large fish of tropical and temperate waters

Jezebel ('jezəbəl) *n.* **1.** *O.T.* wife of Ahab, king of Israel **2.** (*sometimes* **j-**) shameless or scheming woman

j.g. junior grade

jib (jib) *n.* **1.** triangular sail set forward of mast **2.** projecting arm of crane or derrick —*vi.* **3.** object to proceeding **4.** (of horse, person) stop and refuse to go on (**-bb-**) —'**jibber** *n.* —**jib boom** spar from end of bowsprit

jibe[1] (jīb) *or* **jib** (jib) *vi.* **1.** (of boom of fore-and-aft sail) swing over to other side with following wind **2.** alter course thus

jibe[2] (jīb) *vi. inf.* agree; accord; harmonize

jiffy ('jifi) *n. inf.* very short period of time

Jiffy bag ('jifi) trade name for padded envelope

jig[1] (jig) *n.* **1.** lively dance **2.** music for it **3.** small mechanical device **4.** mechanical device used as guide for cutting *etc.* **5.** *Angling* any of various lures —*vi.* **6.** dance jig **7.** make jerky up-and-down movements (**-gg-**) —'**jigger** *n.* —'**jigsaw** *n.* machine fretsaw —**jigsaw (puzzle)** picture stuck on board and cut into interlocking pieces with jigsaw —**in jig time** right away —**the jig is up** *sl.* success is hopeless

jig[2] (jig) *n. offens.* a Negro

jigger ('jigər) *n.* 1½ oz. glass for spirits

jiggery-pokery ('jigəri'pōkəri) *n. inf.* trickery, nonsense

jiggle ('jigəl) *v.* move (up and down *etc.*) with short jerky movements

jilt (jilt) *vt.* cast off (lover)

jim crow ('jim 'krō) (*oft.* **J- C-**) **1.** policy or practice of segregating Negroes **2.** *offens.* Negro

jimjams ('jimjamz) *pl.n.* **1.** *sl.* delirium tremens **2.** state of nervous tension or anxiety

jimmy ('jimi) *n.* short steel crowbar, pinchbar

jingle ('jinggəl) *n.* **1.** mixed metallic noise, as of shaken chain **2.** catchy, rhythmic verse, song *etc.* —*v.* **3.** (cause to) make jingling sound

jingo ('jinggō) *n.* **1.** loud, bellicose patriot **2.** jingoism (*pl.* **-es**) —'**jingoism** *n.* chauvinism —**jingo'istic** *a.* —**by jingo** exclamation of surprise

jinks (jingks) *pl.n.* boisterous merrymaking (*esp. in* **high jinks**)

jinni (ji'nē, 'jini) *or* **jinn** (jin) *n.* spirit in Muslim mythology who could assume human or animal form (*pl.* **jinn, jinns**) (*also* **djinni, djinn, djin**)

jinx (jingks) *n.* **1.** force, person, thing bringing bad luck —*vt.* **2.** be or put a jinx on

jitney ('jitni) *n.* small passenger bus following a regular route at varying hours —**jitney cab** automobile run as jitney

jitters ('jitərz) *pl.n.* worried nervousness, anxiety —'**jittery** *a.* nervous —'**jitterbug** *n.* **1.** fast jerky Amer. dance popular in 1940s **2.** person who dances jitterbug —*vi.* **3.** perform such dance

jiujitsu *or* **jiujutsu** (jōō'jitsōō) *n. see* JUJITSU

Jivaro ('hēvərō) *n.* Amerindian language spoken in Peru and Ecuador

jive (jīv) *n.* **1.** fast jazz music **2.** dancing to jazz music **3.** jargon of jazz musicians and jazz fans **4.** glib, deceptive talk

Jn *or* **Jno** John

JND just noticeable difference

job (job) *n.* **1.** piece of work, task **2.** post, office **3.** *inf.* difficult task **4.** *inf.* crime, *esp.* robbery —'**jobber** *n.* stockjobber —'**jobbing** *a.* doing single, particular jobs for payment —'**jobless** *a./pl.n.* unemployed (people) —**job lot 1.** assortment sold together **2.** miscellaneous collection

Job (jōb) *n. Bible* 18th book of the O.T., a poetical book of the Bible written by the man whose name has become synonymous with patience —**Job's comforter** person who adds to distress while purporting to give sympathy

jockey ('joki) *n.* **1.** professional rider in horse races (*pl.* **-s**) —*v.* **2.** (*esp. with* for) maneuver ('**jockeyed,** '**jockeying**)

jockstrap ('jokstrap) *n.* piece of elasticated material worn by men, *esp.* athletes, to support genitals (*also* **athletic supporter**)

jocose (jō'kōs) *a.* waggish, humorous —**jo'cosely** *adv.* —**jocosity** (jō'kositi) *n.* —**jocular** ('jokyələr) *a.* **1.** joking **2.** given to joking —**jocularity** (jokyə'lariti) *n.*

jocund ('jokənd) *a.* merry, cheerful —**jo'cundity** *n.*

jodhpurs ('jodpərz) *pl.n.* tight-legged riding breeches —**jodhpur boot** ankle-high shoe fastened with buckle at side

Joel ('jōəl) *n. Bible* 29th book of the O.T., a prophetic book built around the plague of locusts present at the time of its writing

jog (jog) *vi.* **1.** run slowly or move at a trot, *esp.* for physical exercise —*vt.* **2.** jar, nudge **3.** remind, stimulate (**-gg-**) —*n.* **4.** jogging —'**jogger** *n.* —'**jogging** *n.* —**jog trot** slow regular trot

joggle ('jogəl) *v.* **1.** move to and fro in jerks **2.** shake —*n.* **3.** act of joggling

john (jon) *n. sl.* toilet

John (jon) *n. Bible* **1.** the 4th book of the N.T., the Gospel of John **2.** the 23rd, 24th and 25th books of the N.T., epistles written by John **3.** the apostle, writer of the Gospel, the epistles and Revelation

John Bull personification of the English nation

Johnson[1] ('jonsən) *n.* **Andrew.** the 17th President of the U.S. (1865-69)

Johnson[2] ('jonsən) *n.* **Lyndon Baines.** the 36th President of the U.S. (1963-69)

Johnston and Sand Islands ('jonsən, -stən) a territory of the U.S. in the south Pacific Ocean

joie de vivre (zhwad 'vēvr) *Fr.* enjoyment of life, ebullience

join (join) *vt.* **1.** put together, fasten, unite **2.** become member of —*vi.* **3.** become united, connected **4.** (*with* up) enlist **5.** (*usu. with* in) take part —*n.* **6.** joining **7.** place of joining —'**joiner** *n.* **1.** maker of finished woodwork **2.** one who joins —'**joinery** *n.* joiner's work

joint (joint) *n.* **1.** arrangement by which two things fit together, rigidly or loosely **2.** place of this **3.** meat for roasting, oft. with bone **4.** *inf.* house, place *etc.* **5.** *sl.* disreputable bar or nightclub **6.** *sl.* marijuana cigarette —*a.* **7.** common **8.** shared by two or more —*vt.* **9.** connect by joints **10.** divide at the joints —'**jointly** *adv.* —**joint-stock company** business enterprise whose owners are issued shares of transferable stock —**out of joint 1.** dislocated **2.** disorganized

jointure ('joinchər) *n. Law* property settled on wife for her use after husband's death

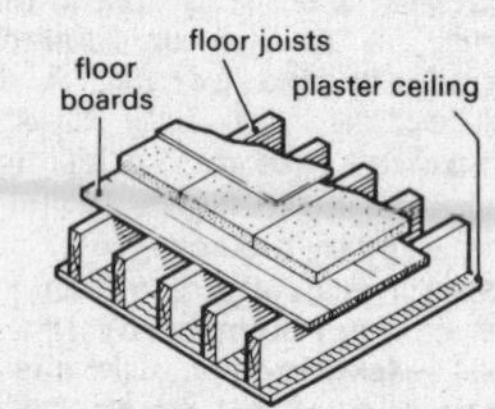

joist

joist (joist) *n.* one of the parallel beams stretched from wall to wall on which to fix floor or ceiling —'**joisted** *a.*

joke (jōk) *n.* **1.** thing said or done to cause laughter **2.** something said or done merely in fun **3.** ridiculous or humorous circumstance —*vi.* **4.** make jokes —'**joker** *n.* **1.** one who jokes **2.** *sl.* fellow **3.** extra card in pack, counting as highest or wild card in some games

jolly ('joli) *a.* **1.** jovial **2.** festive, merry —*vt.* **3.** (*esp. with* along) (try to) make (person, occasion *etc.*) happier ('**jollied,** '**jollying**) —**jollifi'cation** *n.* merrymaking —'**jollity** *n.*

Jolly Roger pirates' flag with white skull and crossbones on black field

jolt (jōlt) *n.* **1.** sudden jerk **2.** bump **3.** shock —*v.* **4.** move, shake with jolts —'**jolty** *a.*

Jon. *Bible* Jonah

Jonah ('jōnə) *n.* **1.** *Bible* 32nd book of the O.T., written by the prophet who was swallowed by a great fish **2.** person believed to bring bad luck to those around him

Jonas ('jōnəs) *n. Bible* Jonah in the Douay Version of the O.T.

jonquil (ˈjonkwil, ˈjong-) *n.* **1.** fragrant yellow or white narcissus —*a.* **2.** pale yellow

Jordan (ˈjördən) *n.* country in Middle East bounded south by Saudi Arabia, west by Israel, north by Syria and east by Iraq —**Jordanian** (jörˈdānIən) *n./a.*

Josh. *Bible* Joshua

Joshua (ˈjoshəwə, -shwə) *n. Bible* 6th book of the O.T., in which the successor to Moses describes the return to Palestine

joss (jos) *n.* Chinese idol —**joss house** Chinese temple —**joss stick** stick of Chinese incense

jostle (ˈjosəl) *v.* knock or push against (someone)

Josue (ˈjoshəwi, -shwi) *n. Bible* Joshua in the Douay Version of the O.T.

jot (jot) *n.* **1.** small amount, whit —*vt.* **2.** write briefly; make note of (**-tt-**) —ˈ**jotter** *n.* notebook

joule (jo͞ol) *n.* unit of energy equal to work done when a force of one newton acts over a distance of one meter

journal (ˈjərnəl) *n.* **1.** daily newspaper or other periodical **2.** daily record **3.** logbook **4.** part of axle or shaft resting on the bearings —**journaˈlese** *n.* **1.** journalists' jargon **2.** high-flown style, full of clichés —ˈ**journalism** *n.* editing, writing in periodicals —ˈ**journalist** *n.* —**journaˈlistic** *a.*

journey (ˈjərni) *n.* **1.** traveling from one place to another; excursion **2.** distance traveled —*vi.* **3.** travel

journeyman (ˈjərnimən) *n.* craftsman or artisan employed by another

joust (jowst) *Hist. n.* **1.** encounter with lances between two mounted knights —*vi.* **2.** engage in joust

Jove (jōv) *n. see* JUPITER (sense 1) —ˈ**Jovian** *a.* —**by Jove** exclamation of surprise

jovial (ˈjōviəl) *a.* convivial, merry, gay

jowl (jowl) *n.* **1.** cheek, jaw **2.** outside of throat when prominent

joy (joi) *n.* **1.** gladness, pleasure, delight **2.** cause of this —ˈ**joyful** *a.* —ˈ**joyless** *a.* —ˈ**joyous** *a.* **1.** having happy nature or mood **2.** joyful —ˈ**joyously** *adv.* —**joy ride** trip, *esp.* in stolen automobile —ˈ**joystick** *n. inf.* control column of aircraft

J.P. Justice of the Peace

Jr. Junior

Jth. *Bible* Judith

jubilate (ˈjo͞obilāt) *vi.* rejoice —ˈ**jubilant** *a.* exultant —ˈ**jubilantly** *adv.* —**jubiˈlation** *n.*

jubilee (ˈjo͞obilē) *n.* time of rejoicing, *esp.* 25th or 50th anniversary

Jud. *Bible* Judges

Judaic (jo͞oˈdāik) *a.* of the Jews or Judaism —ˈ**Judaism** *n.* **1.** religion of the Jews **2.** religious and cultural traditions of the Jews **3.** the Jews collectively —ˈ**Judaize** *vt.* **1.** make Jewish —*v.* **2.** conform or bring into conformity with Judaism

Judas (ˈjo͞odəs) *n.* **1.** *N.T.* apostle who betrayed Jesus to his enemies for 30 pieces of silver **2.** person who betrays a friend; traitor

judder (ˈjudər) *inf. vi.* **1.** shake, vibrate —*n.* **2.** a vibrating motion

Jude (jo͞od) *n. Bible* 26th book of the N.T., an epistle exhorting believers to guard against apostasy

Judesmo (jo͞oˈdezmō) *n. see* LADINO (sense 1)

judge (juj) *n.* **1.** officer appointed to try cases in court of law **2.** one who decides in dispute, contest *etc.* **3.** one able to form reliable opinion, arbiter **4.** umpire **5.** in Jewish history, ruler —*vi.* **6.** act as judge —*vt.* **7.** act as judge of **8.** try, estimate **9.** decide —ˈ**judgment** *or* ˈ**judgement** *n.* **1.** faculty of judging **2.** sentence of court **3.** opinion **4.** misfortune regarded as sign of divine displeasure —**Judgment Day** occasion of Last Judgment by God at end of world

Judges (ˈjujiz) *pl.n.* (*with sing. v.*) *Bible* 7th book of the O.T., describing a period of 400 years during which the people of Israel suffered repeated judgments by God for their sins

judicature (ˈjo͞odikəcho͞oər) *n.* **1.** administration of justice **2.** body of judges —**juˈdicial** *a.* **1.** of, or by, a court or judge **2.** having qualities proper to a judge **3.** discriminating —**juˈdicially** *adv.* —**juˈdiciary** *n.* system of courts and judges —**juˈdicious** *a.* well-judged, sensible, prudent

Judith (ˈjo͞odith) *n. Bible* 18th book in the Douay Version of the O.T.

judo (ˈjo͞odō) *n.* modern sport derived from jujitsu eliminating dangerous techniques

jug (jug) *n.* **1.** vessel for liquids, with handle and small spout **2.** its contents **3.** *sl.* prison —*vt.* **4.** stew (*esp.* hare) in jug (**-gg-**)

juggernaut (ˈjugərnöt) *n.* any irresistible, destructive force

juggle (ˈjugəl) *v.* **1.** throw and catch (several objects) so most are in the air simultaneously **2.** manage, manipulate (accounts *etc.*) to deceive —*n.* **3.** act of juggling —ˈ**juggler** *n.*

jugular vein (ˈjugyələr) one of three large veins of the neck returning blood from the head

juice (jo͞os) *n.* **1.** liquid part of vegetable, fruit or meat **2.** *inf.* electric current **3.** *inf.* gasoline **4.** vigor, vitality —ˈ**juicy** *a.* succulent

jujitsu, jujutsu, *or* **jiujutsu** (jo͞oˈjitso͞o) *n.* system of weaponless combat and self-defense

juju (ˈjo͞ojo͞o) *n.* **1.** object superstitiously revered by certain W Afr. peoples and used as charm or fetish **2.** power associated with juju

jujube (ˈjo͞ojo͞ob) *n.* **1.** any of several spiny trees that have yellowish flowers and dark red edible fruits **2.** fruit of any of these trees **3.** lozenge of gelatin, sugar *etc.*

jukebox ('jo͞okboks) *n.* automatic, coin-operated phonograph

Jul. July

julep ('jo͞olip) *n.* **1.** tall drink of liquor, sugar, crushed ice and flavoring, *esp.* mint **2.** sweet drink of syrup, flavoring and water

Julian ('jo͞olyən) *a.* of Julius Caesar —**Julian calendar** calendar as adjusted by Julius Caesar in 46 B.C., in which the year was made to consist of 365 days, 6 hours, instead of 365 days

julienne (jo͞oli'en) *a.* **1.** (of vegetables or meats) cut into thin strips —*n.* **2.** clear meat soup containing julienne vegetables

Juliett (jo͞oli'et) *n.* word used in communications for the letter *j*

July (jo͝o'lī) *n.* seventh month

jumble ('jumbəl) *v.* **1.** mingle, mix in confusion **2.** remember in confused form —*n.* **3.** confused heap, muddle **4.** sale

jumbo ('jumbō) *n. inf.* **1.** elephant **2.** anything very large (*pl.* **-s**) —**jumbo jet** *inf.* large jet-propelled airliner

jump (jump) *v.* **1.** (cause to) spring, leap (over) **2.** pass or skip (over) —*vi.* **3.** move hastily **4.** rise steeply **5.** parachute from aircraft **6.** start, jerk (with astonishment *etc.*) **7.** (of faulty film *etc.*) make abrupt movements —*vt.* **8.** come off (tracks, rails *etc.*) **9.** *inf.* attack without warning —*n.* **10.** act of jumping **11.** obstacle to be jumped **12.** distance, height jumped **13.** sudden nervous jerk or start **14.** sudden rise in prices —'**jumper** *n.* **1.** one who, that which jumps **2.** dress without sleeves or collar, usu. worn over blouse or sweater **3.** wire for making or breaking electrical circuit —'**jumpy** *a.* nervous —**jumper cables** cables for carrying current from one battery to another —**jump jet** *inf.* fixed-wing jet aircraft that can land and take off vertically —**jump rope** rope used in children's game in which player jumps over twirling rope —**jump suit** one-piece garment of trousers and top —**jump the gun** start before permitted time —**one jump ahead** one step ahead of one's rival

Jun. **1.** June **2.** junior (*also* **jun.**)

junction ('jungkshən) *n.* **1.** railroad station *etc.* where lines, routes join **2.** place of joining **3.** joining

juncture ('jungkchər) *n.* state of affairs

June (jo͞on) *n.* sixth month

jungle ('junggəl) *n.* **1.** tangled vegetation of equatorial forest **2.** land covered with it **3.** tangled mass **4.** condition of intense competition, struggle for survival —'**jungly** *a.*

junior ('jo͞onyər) *a.* **1.** younger **2.** of lower standing —*n.* **3.** junior person —**junior college** college offering two-year curriculum —**junior high school** school including usu. grades 7, 8 and 9 —**Junior League** organization of women under the age of 40 for voluntary civic and social service —**junior varsity** athletic team for those not eligible for the varsity

juniper ('jo͞onipər) *n.* evergreen shrub with berries yielding oil of juniper, used for medicine and gin making

junk[1] (jungk) *n.* **1.** discarded, useless objects **2.** *inf.* nonsense **3.** *sl.* narcotic drug —'**junkie** *or* '**junky** *n. sl.* drug addict —**junk food** food eaten in addition to or instead of regular meals, oft. with low nutritional value

junk[2] (jungk) *n.* Chinese sailing vessel

junket ('jungkit) *n.* **1.** curdled milk flavored and sweetened —*vi.* **2.** feast, picnic

junta ('ho͝ontə, 'jun-, 'hun-) *n.* group of military officers holding power in a country

Jupiter ('jo͞opitər) *n.* **1.** Roman chief of gods **2.** largest of the planets

Jurassic (jo͝o'rasik) *a.* **1.** of second period of Mesozoic era —*n.* **2.** Jurassic period or rock system

juridical (jo͝o'ridikəl) *a.* of law or administration of justice; legal

jurisdiction (jo͝oəris'dikshən) *n.* **1.** administration of justice **2.** authority **3.** territory covered by it —**juris'prudence** *n.* science of, skill in, law —'**jurist** *n.* one skilled in law —**ju'ristic(al)** *a.*

jury ('jo͝oəri) *n.* **1.** body of persons sworn to render verdict in court of law **2.** body of judges of competition —'**juror** *or* '**juryman** *n.* one of jury —**jury box** enclosure in court where jury sit

jury- (*comb. form*) *chiefly naut.* makeshift, as in *jury-rigged*

just (just) *a.* **1.** fair **2.** upright, honest **3.** proper, right, equitable —*adv.* **4.** exactly **5.** barely **6.** at this instant **7.** merely, only **8.** really —'**justice** *n.* **1.** quality of being just **2.** fairness **3.** judicial proceedings **4.** judge, magistrate —**jus'ticiary** *a.* **1.** of administration of justice —*n.* **2.** officer or administrator of justice; judge —'**justifiable** *a.* —'**justifiably** *adv.* —**justifi'cation** *n.* —'**justify** *vt.* **1.** prove right, true or innocent **2.** vindicate **3.** excuse (**-ified, -ifying**) —'**justly** *adv.* —**justice of the peace** lay magistrate whose function is to preserve peace in his area, try summarily minor cases, administer oaths and perform marriages

jut (jut) *vi.* **1.** (*oft. with* out) project, stick out (**-tt-**) —*n.* **2.** projection

jute (jo͞ot) *n.* fiber of certain plants, used for rope, canvas *etc.*

juvenile ('jo͞ovinil) *a.* **1.** young **2.** of, for young children **3.** immature —*n.* **4.** young person, child —**juve'nescence** *n.* —**juve'nescent** *a.* becoming young —'**juve'nilia** *pl.n.* works produced in author's youth —**juve'nility** *n.* —**juvenile court** court dealing with young offenders or children in need of care —**juvenile delinquent** young person guilty of some offense, antisocial behavior *etc.*

juxtapose ('jukstəpōz) *vt.* put side by side —**juxtapo'sition** *n.* contiguity, being side by side

JV junior varsity

K

k *or* **K** (kā) *n.* **1.** 11th letter of English alphabet **2.** speech sound represented by this letter, as in *kitten* (*pl.* **k's, K's** *or* **Ks**)

k 1. kilo **2.** *Math.* unit vector along *z*-axis **3.** knit

K 1. kelvin **2.** *Chess* king **3.** *Chem.* potassium **4.** *Phys.* kaon **5.** one thousand **6.** *Comp.* unit of 1024 words, bytes or bits

kabob (ˈkābob, kəˈbob) *or* **kebab** *n.* cubes of marinated meat or vegetables placed on a skewer and cooked with radiant heat

Kabuki (kəˈbo͞oki, ˈkäbo͝oki) *n.* traditional Japanese popular drama performed in highly conventional manner

kachina (kəˈchēnə) *n.* in Pueblo culture, doll symbolizing powers and manifestations of nature and ancestors

Kaddish (ˈkädish) *n. Judaism* **1.** prayer closing synagogue service **2.** prayer of mourners for the dead **3.** *inf.* son

Kaffir *or* **Kafir** (ˈkafər) *n.* **SA** *offens.* any Black African

Kaiser (ˈkīzər) *n.* (*sometimes* **k-**) *Hist.* **1.** any of three German emperors **2.** any Austro-Hungarian emperor

kalanchoe (kalənˈkōi) *n.* succulent plant with red, pink or yellow flowers

kale (kāl) *n.* type of cabbage

kaleidoscope (kəˈlīdəskōp) *n.* **1.** optical toy for producing changing symmetrical patterns by multiple reflections of colored glass chips *etc.*, in inclined mirrors enclosed in tube **2.** any complex, frequently changing pattern —**kaleidoscopic** (kəlīdəˈskopik) *a.* swiftly changing

Kamasutra (kāməˈso͞otrə) *n.* ancient Hindu text on erotic pleasure

kamikaze (kämiˈkäzi) *n.* (*oft.* **K-**) suicidal attack, *esp.* as in World War II, by Japanese pilots

Kampuchea (kampo͞oˈchēə) *n.* country in southeast Asia bounded north by Laos and Thailand, west by Thailand, east by Vietnam and south by the Gulf of Thailand

Kan. *or* **Kans.** Kansas

kangaroo (kanggəˈro͞o) *n.* **1.** Aust. marsupial with very strongly developed hind legs for jumping —*vi.* **2.** *inf.* (of motor vehicle) move forward with sudden jerks —**kangaroo court** irregular, illegal court

Kansas (ˈkanzəs) *n.* Central state of the U.S., admitted to the Union in 1861. Abbrev.: **Kan., Kans., KS** (with ZIP code)

kaolin (ˈkāəlin) *n.* fine white clay used for porcelain and medicinally

kaon (ˈkāon) *n.* meson that has rest mass of about 996 or 964 electron masses (*also* **K-meson**)

kapok

kapok (ˈkāpok) *n.* **1.** tropical tree **2.** fiber from its seed pods used to stuff cushions *etc.*

kappa (ˈkapə) *n.* tenth letter in Gr. alphabet (Κ, κ)

kaput (käˈpo͝ot) *a. inf.* ruined, broken, no good

karakul (ˈkarəkəl) *n.* **1.** tightly curled, lustrous coat of young lambs from Russia, SW Africa or China used for clothing (*also* **astrakhan, Persian lamb**) **2.** sheep of this breed —**karakul cloth** heavy woolen fabric resembling this

karat *or* **carat** (ˈkarət) *n.* measure of fineness for gold equal to $^1/_{24}$ part of pure gold in any alloy

karate (kəˈräti) *n.* system of self-defense using hands, arms, feet and legs as sole weapons

kart (kärt) *n.* light low-framed vehicle with small wheels and engine for recreational racing (**karting**) (*also* **go-cart, go-kart**)

kasbah (ˈkazbä) *n. see* CASBAH

katydid (ˈkātidid) *n.* green long-horned grasshopper living in trees in N Amer.

kauri (ˈkowri) *n.* large N.Z. pine giving valuable timber (*pl.* **-s**)

kava (ˈkävə) *n.* **1.** Polynesian shrub **2.** beverage prepared from the aromatic roots of this shrub

kayak (ˈkīak) *n.* **1.** Eskimo canoe made of sealskins stretched over frame **2.** any canoe of this design

kazoo (kəˈzo͞o) *n.* cigar-shaped toy musical instrument producing nasal sound

kc kilocycle

K.C. King's Counsel

kcal kilocalorie

kea (ˈkēə) *n.* large New Zealand parrot with brownish-green plumage

kebab ('kābăb, kə'băb) *n. see* KABOB

kedge (kej) *n.* **1.** small anchor —*vt.* **2.** move (ship) by cable attached to kedge

kedgeree (kejə'rē) *n.* dish of fish cooked with rice, eggs *etc.*

keel (kēl) *n.* lowest longitudinal support on which ship is built —'**keelhaul** *vt.* **1.** formerly, punish by hauling under keel of ship **2.** rebuke severely —**keelson** ('kelsən, 'kēl-) *n.* line of timbers or plates bolted to keel —**keel over 1.** turn upside down **2.** *inf.* collapse suddenly —**on an even keel** well-balanced; steady

keen[1] (kēn) *a.* **1.** sharp **2.** acute **3.** eager **4.** shrewd **5.** strong —'**keenly** *adv.* —'**keenness** *n.*

keen[2] (kēn) *n.* **1.** funeral lament —*vi.* **2.** wail over the dead

keep (kēp) *vt.* **1.** retain possession of, not lose **2.** store **3.** cause to continue **4.** take charge of **5.** maintain **6.** detain **7.** provide upkeep of **8.** reserve —*vi.* **9.** remain good **10.** remain **11.** continue (**kept** *pt./pp.*) —*n.* **12.** living or support **13.** charge or care **14.** central tower of castle, stronghold —'**keeper** *n.* —'**keeping** *n.* **1.** harmony, agreement **2.** care, charge, possession —'**keepsake** *n.* gift that evokes memories of person or event

keg (keg) *n.* **1.** small barrel **2.** metal container for beer

kelp (kelp) *n.* **1.** large seaweed **2.** its ashes, yielding iodine

kelt (kelt) *n.* salmon that has recently spawned

Keltic ('keltik) *n. see* CELTIC

kelvin ('kelvin) *n.* unit of temperature —**Kelvin temperature** temperature on a scale where absolute zero (-273.15° Celsius) is taken as zero degrees

ken (ken) *n.* **1.** range of knowledge —*v.* **2.** in Scotland, know (**kenned** *or* **kent** *pt./pp.*)

kendo ('kendō) *n.* Japanese form of fencing using wooden staves

Kennedy ('kenədi) *n.* **John Fitzgerald.** the 35th President of the U.S. (1961-63)

kennel ('kenəl) *n.* **1.** house, shelter for dog —*pl.* **2.** place for breeding, boarding dogs —*vt.* **3.** put into kennel

kentledge ('kentlij) *n. Naut.* scrap metal used as ballast

Kentucky (kən'tuki) *n.* East South Central state of the U.S., admitted to the Union in 1792. Abbrev.: **KY** (with ZIP code) —**Kentucky Derby** *see* DERBY (sense 1)

Kenya ('kenyə, 'kēn-) *n.* country in Africa bounded north by Ethiopia, west by Uganda, south by Tanzania and east by Somalia and the Indian Ocean —'**Kenyan** *n./a.*

kepi ('kāpē) *n.* military cap with circular top and visor (*pl.* **-s**)

kept (kept) *pt./pp. of* KEEP

keratitis (kerə'tītis) *n.* inflammation of the cornea

kerchief ('kərchif) *n.* **1.** head-cloth **2.** scarf

kermes ('kərmis) *n.* insect used for red dyestuff

kernel ('kərnəl) *n.* **1.** inner seed of nut or fruit stone **2.** central, essential part

kerosine *or* **kerosene** ('kerəsēn) *n.* fuel oil distilled from petrolatum, also used as solvent

kestrel ('kestrəl) *n.* small falcon

ketch (kech) *n.* two-masted sailing vessel

ketchup ('kechəp, 'kach-, 'kats-) *n. see* CATSUP

ketone ('kētōn) *n.* one of class of chemical compounds with the general formula R′COR, where R and R′ are organic groups, the simplest ketone being acetone —**ketonic** (kē'tonik) *a.* —**ke'tosis** *n.* disturbance of body chemistry produced by the use of fat as a source of energy

kettle ('ketəl) *n.* metal vessel with spout and handle, *esp.* for boiling water —'**kettledrum** *n.* musical instrument made of membrane stretched over copper hemisphere (*also* **timpani**) —**a fine kettle of fish** awkward situation, mess

key[1] (kē) *n.* **1.** instrument for operating lock, winding clock *etc.* **2.** something providing control, explanation, means of achieving an end *etc.* **3.** main note or tonal center of musical composition **4.** operating lever of typewriter, piano, flute *etc.* **5.** system of identifying characteristics **6.** means of solving encoded material —*vt.* **7.** provide symbols on (map *etc.*) to assist identification of positions on it **8.** scratch (plaster surface) to provide bond for plaster or paint **9.** insert (copy, information) by keystroke —*a.* **10.** vital **11.** most important —'**keyboard** *n.* set of keys on piano *etc.* —'**keyhole** *n.* aperture in lock case into which key is inserted —'**keynote** *n.* **1.** dominant idea **2.** basic note of musical key —**key punch** device having keyboard operated manually to transfer data onto punched cards *etc.* (*also* **card punch**) —**key-punch** *vt.* transfer (data) by key punch —**key signature** *Mus.* sharps or flats at beginning of each stave line to indicate key —'**keystone** *n.* **1.** central stone of arch **2.** something necessary to connect other related things —'**keystroke** *n.* depression of single key on keyboard of typewriter, computer *etc.* —**key word** significant word used to facilitate indexing of documents

key[2] (kē) *n. see* CAY

Keynesianism ('kānziənizəm) *n.* group of theories and programs of J.M. Keynes (1883-1946) and his followers, *esp.* advocacy of government intervention to maintain high employment —'**Keynesian** *n./a.* (denoting) one who supports the economic ideas propounded by Keynes

kg *or* **kg.** kilogram

K.G.B. Soviet secret police

khaki ('kaki, 'kä-) *a.* **1.** dull yellowish-brown —*n.* **2.** dull yellowish-brown color **3.** hard-wearing fabric of this color, used *esp.* for military uniforms (*pl.* **-s**)

khan (kän) *n.* **1.** formerly, (title borne by) medieval Chinese emperors and Mongol and Turkic rulers **2.** title of respect borne by important personages in Afghanistan and central Asia

Khmer (kmäər) *n.* member of a people of Kampuchea

kHz kilohertz

kibble (ˈkibəl) *vt.* grind into small pieces

kibbutz (kiˈbo͞ots) *n.* Jewish communal agricultural settlement in Israel (*pl.* **kibbutzim** (kibo͞otˈsēm)) —**kibˈbutznik** *n.* **1.** member of kibbutz **2.** enthusiast about kibbutzim

kibitzer (ˈkibitsər, kiˈbit-) *n.* **1.** *inf.* one who watches a game of cards without comment **2.** person giving unsolicited advice

kibosh (ˈkībosh) *n. sl.* —**put the kibosh on 1.** silence **2.** get rid of **3.** defeat

kick (kik) *vi.* **1.** strike out with foot **2.** (*sometimes with* against) be recalcitrant **3.** recoil —*vt.* **4.** strike or hit with foot **5.** score (goal) with a kick **6.** *inf.* free oneself of (habit *etc.*) —*n.* **7.** foot blow **8.** recoil **9.** excitement, thrill —**ˈkickback** *n.* **1.** strong reaction **2.** money paid illegally for favors done *etc.* —**ˈkickoff** *n.* **1.** place kick from center of field in football **2.** time at which first such kick is due to take place —**kick pleat** inverted pleat at back of narrow skirt —**ˈkickstand** *n.* short metal bar which when kicked into vertical position holds stationary cycle upright —**kick turn** skiing turn in stationary position used to change direction —**kick off 1.** start game of football **2.** *inf.* begin (discussion *etc.*) —**kick the bucket** *sl.* die —**kick the habit** give up a habit —**kick (someone) upstairs** promote (someone) to an apparently better position

kid (kid) *n.* **1.** young goat **2.** leather of its skin **3.** *inf.* child —*vt.* **4.** tease; deceive —*vi.* **5.** behave, speak in fun (**-dd-**) —**kid glove** glove made of kidskin —**ˈkidˈglove** *a.* **1.** overdelicate **2.** diplomatic; tactful —**handle with kid gloves** treat with great tact or caution

kidnap (ˈkidnap) *vt.* seize and hold to ransom (**-pp-**) —**ˈkidnapper** *n.*

kidney (ˈkidni) *n.* **1.** either of the pair of organs which secrete urine **2.** animal kidney used as food **3.** nature, kind (*esp. in* **of the same** *or* **a different kidney**) (*pl.* **-s**) —**kidney bean** any large bean seed of the cultivated plant, *esp.* a large dark red one —**kidney machine** machine carrying out functions of kidney (*also* **artificial kidney, dialysis machine**) —**kidney stones** calculi

kilim (kēˈlēm) *n.* type of pileless rug woven in Near East with identical pattern on both sides

kill (kil) *vt.* **1.** deprive of life **2.** destroy **3.** neutralize **4.** pass (time) **5.** weaken; dilute **6.** *inf.* exhaust **7.** *inf.* cause to suffer pain **8.** *inf.* quash, defeat, veto —*n.* **9.** act or time of killing **10.** animals *etc.* killed in hunt —**ˈkiller** *n.* one who, that which, kills —**ˈkilling** *inf. a.* **1.** very tiring **2.** very funny —*n.* **3.** sudden success, *esp.* on stock market —**killer whale** ferocious toothed whale most common in cold seas —**kill-joy** *n.* person who spoils other people's pleasure

kiln (kiln, kil) *n.* furnace, oven

kilo (ˈkēlō) *n.* kilogram (*pl.* **-s**)

Kilo (ˈkēlō) *n.* word used in communications for the letter *k*

kilo- (*comb. form*) one thousand, as in *kiloliter, kilometer*

kilocycle (ˈkiləsīkəl) *n. short for* kilocycle per second: former unit of frequency equal to 1 kilohertz

kilogram (ˈkēləgram, ˈkilə-) *n.* basic unit of mass in metric system equal to 1000 grams or 2.205 pounds

kilohertz (ˈkiləhərts, ˈkēlə-) *n.* one thousand cycles per second

kiloton (ˈkēlōtun, ˈkilō-) *n.* **1.** one thousand tons **2.** explosive power, *esp.* of nuclear weapon, equal to power of 1000 tons of TNT

kilowatt (ˈkiləwot) *n. Elec.* one thousand watts —**kilowatt-hour** *n.* unit of energy equal to work done by power of 1000 watts in one hour

kilt (kilt) *n.* usu. tartan knee-length skirt, deeply pleated, worn orig. by Scottish Highlanders

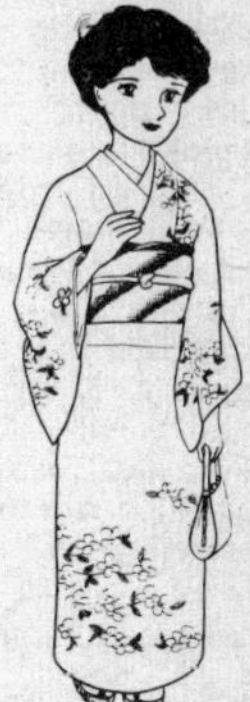

kimono

kimono (kiˈmōnə, -nō) *n.* **1.** loose, wide-sleeved Japanese robe, fastened with sash **2.** European garment like this (*pl.* **-s**)

kin (kin) *n.* **1.** family, relatives —*a.* **2.** related by blood —**kindred** (ˈkindrid) *n.* **1.** relationship by blood **2.** relatives collectively —*a.* **3.** similar **4.** related —**ˈkinsfolk** *pl.n.* —**ˈkinship** *n.*

-kin (*comb. form*) small, as in *lambkin*

kind (kīnd) *n.* **1.** genus, sort, class —*a.* **2.** sympathetic, considerate **3.** good, benevolent **4.** gentle —**ˈkindliness** *n.* —**ˈkindly** *a.* **1.** kind, genial —*adv.* **2.** in a considerate or humane way —'**kindness** *n.* —**kind-hearted** *a.* kindly, readily sympathetic —**in kind 1.** (of payment) in goods rather than money **2.** with something similar

kindergarten ('kındərgärtən) *n.* class, school for children of about four to six years old

kindle ('kindəl) *vt.* **1.** set on fire **2.** inspire, excite —*vi.* **3.** catch fire —'**kindling** *n.* wood, straw *etc.* to kindle fire

kinematic (kini'matik) *a.* of motion without reference to mass or force —**kine'matics** *pl.n.* (*with sing. v.*) science of this —**kine'matograph** *n.* *see* **cinematograph** *at* CINEMA

kinetic (ki'netik) *a.* of motion in relation to force —**ki'netics** *pl.n.* (*with sing. v.*) science of this —**kinetic art** art, *esp.* sculpture, that moves or has moving parts —**kinetic energy** energy created by movement

king (king) *n.* **1.** male sovereign ruler of independent state, monarch **2.** piece in game of chess whose capture loses the game **3.** highest face card, with picture of a king **4.** *Checkers* two pieces on top of one another, allowed freedom of movement —'**kingdom** *n.* **1.** state ruled by king **2.** realm **3.** sphere —'**kingly** *a.* **1.** royal **2.** appropriate to a king —**Kings** *pl.n.* (*with sing. v.*) *Bible* 11th and 12th books of the O.T., which record the reign of Solomon and division of the kingdom and the captivity of the northern tribes by Assyria —'**kingship** *n.* —**King Charles spaniel** toy breed of spaniel with very long ears —'**kingcup** *n.* any of several yellow-flowered plants, *esp.* buttercup —'**kingfisher** *n.* small bird of Europe or tropical regions with bright plumage which dives for fish —**King James Version** the Authorized Version of the Bible used by Protestants, published in 1611 in the reign of King James I —'**kingpin** *n.* **1.** swivel pin **2.** central or front pin in bowling **3.** *inf.* chief person or thing —**king post** beam in roof framework rising from tie beam to the ridge —**king-size** *or* **king-sized** *a.* **1.** large **2.** larger than standard size

kink (kingk) *n.* **1.** tight twist in rope, wire, hair *etc.* **2.** crick, as of neck **3.** *inf.* eccentricity —*v.* **4.** make, become kinked —'**kinky** *a.* **1.** full of kinks **2.** *inf.* eccentric, *esp.* given to deviant (sexual) practices

kiosk ('kēosk) *n.* **1.** small, sometimes movable booth selling drinks, cigarettes, newspapers *etc.* **2.** public telephone booth

Kiowa ('kīəwō, -wä) *n.* **1.** member of Amerindian people of Colorado, Kansas, New Mexico, Oklahoma and Texas (*pl.* **-wa, -s**) **2.** the Uto-Aztecan language of this people

kipper ('kipər) *vt.* **1.** cure (fish) by splitting open, rubbing with salt and drying or smoking —*n.* **2.** kippered fish

Kiribati (kiri'bas) *n.* country occupying a large expanse of the central Pacific comprising Banaba Island, the 16 Gilbert Islands, the 8 Phoenix Islands and 8 of the 11 Line Islands

kirk (kərk) *n.* in Scotland, church

Kirsch (kēərsh) *n.* brandy made from cherries

kismet ('kizmet, -mit) *n.* fate, destiny

kiss (kis) *n.* **1.** touch or caress with lips **2.** light touch —*vt.* **3.** touch with the lips as an expression of love, greeting *etc.* —*vi.* **4.** join lips with another person in act of love or desire —'**kisser** *n.* **1.** one who kisses **2.** *sl.* mouth; face —**kiss of life** mouth-to-mouth resuscitation

kist (kist) *n.* large wooden chest

kit (kit) *n.* **1.** outfit, equipment **2.** personal effects, *esp.* of traveler **3.** set of pieces of equipment sold ready to be assembled —'**kitbag** *n.* bag for holding soldier's or traveler's kit

kitchen ('kichin) *n.* room used for preparing and cooking food —**kitchen'ette** *n.* small room (or part of larger room) used for cooking —**kitchen garden** garden for raising vegetables, herbs *etc.*

kite (kīt) *n.* **1.** light papered frame flown in wind **2.** *sl.* airplane **3.** large hawk

kith (kith) *n.* acquaintance, kindred (*only in* **kith and kin**)

kithara ('kithərə) *n.* foremost stringed instrument of the ancient Greeks and legendary instrument of their god Apollo, with a U-shaped frame, a crossbar between the arms and at least five strings

kitsch (kich) *n.* vulgarized, pretentious art, literature *etc.*, usu. with popular, sentimental appeal

kitten ('kitən) *n.* young cat —'**kittenish** *a.* **1.** like kitten; lively **2.** (of woman) flirtatious, *esp.* coyly

kittiwake ('kitiwāk) *n.* type of seagull

kitty ('kiti) *n.* **1.** kitten or cat **2.** in some gambling games, pool **3.** communal fund

kiva ('kēvə) *n.* Pueblo Indian ceremonial structure, usu. round and partly underground

kiwi ('kēwē) *n.* **1.** N.Z. flightless bird having long beak, stout legs and weakly barbed feathers **2.** brown, hairy, oval fruit **3.** *inf.* New Zealander (*pl.* **-s**)

kl. kiloliter

klaxon ('klaksən) *n.* formerly, powerful electric motor horn

Klein bottle (klīn) bottle-shaped figure which is enclosed, but has no inside or outside, no edges and one surface, formed by inserting the end of a tapering tube through one side of the tube making the ends contiguous

kleptomania (kleptə'māniə) *n.* compulsive tendency to steal *esp.* when there is no obvious motivation —**klepto'maniac** *n.*

klipspringer ('klipspringər) *n.* small agile Afr. antelope

km *or* **km.** kilometer

knack (nak) *n.* **1.** acquired facility or dexterity **2.** trick **3.** habit

knacker (ˈnakər) *n.* buyer of worn-out horses *etc.*, for killing —ˈ**knackered** *a. sl.* exhausted

knapsack (ˈnapsak) *n.* soldier's or traveler's bag to strap to the back, rucksack

knapweed (ˈnapwēd) *n.* plant having purplish thistle-like flowers

knave (nāv) *n.* **1.** jack at cards **2.** *obs.* rogue —ˈ**knavery** *n.* villainy —ˈ**knavish** *a.*

knead (nēd) *vt.* **1.** work (flour) into dough **2.** work, massage —ˈ**kneader** *n.*

knee (nē) *n.* **1.** joint between thigh and lower leg **2.** part of garment covering knee **3.** lap —*vt.* **4.** strike, push with knee —ˈ**kneecap** *n.* bone in front of knee (*also* **patella**)

kneel (nēl) *vi.* fall, rest on knees (**knelt** *pt./pp.*)

knell (nel) *n.* **1.** sound of a bell, *esp.* at funeral or death **2.** portent of doom

knelt (nelt) *pt./pp. of* KNEEL

knew (nyōō, nōō) *pt. of* KNOW

knickerbocker (ˈnikərbokər) *n.* **1.** (**K-**) native or resident of New York City or New York state —*pl.* **2.** knickers

knickers (ˈnikərz) *pl.n.* loose-fitting breeches gathered at knees

knick-knack (ˈniknak) *n.* trifle, trinket

knife (nīf) *n.* **1.** cutting blade, *esp.* one in handle, used as implement or weapon (*pl.* **knives**) —*vt.* **2.** cut or stab with knife —**knife edge** critical, possibly dangerous situation

knight (nīt) *n.* **1.** man of rank below baronet, having right to prefix *Sir* to his name **2.** member of medieval order of chivalry **3.** champion **4.** piece in chess —*vt.* **5.** confer knighthood on —ˈ**knighthood** *n.* —ˈ**knightly** *a.*

knit (nit) *v.* **1.** form (garment *etc.*) by putting together series of loops with knitting needles **2.** draw together **3.** unite (ˈ**knitted, knit** *pt./pp.*, ˈ**knitting** *pr.p.*) —ˈ**knitter** *n.* —ˈ**knitting** *n.* **1.** knitted work **2.** act of knitting —ˈ**knitwear** *n.* knitted clothing, *esp.* sweaters

knives (nīvz) *n., pl. of* KNIFE

knob (nob) *n.* rounded lump, *esp.* at end or on surface of anything —ˈ**knobby** *or* ˈ**knobbly** *a.*

knock (nok) *vt.* **1.** strike, hit **2.** *inf.* disparage —*vi.* **3.** rap audibly **4.** (of engine) make metallic noise, pink —*n.* **5.** blow, rap —ˈ**knocker** *n.* **1.** metal appliance for knocking on door **2.** person or thing that knocks —**knock-kneed** *a.* having incurved legs —ˈ**knockout** *n.* **1.** blow *etc.* that renders unconscious, *esp.* in boxing **2.** *inf.* person or thing overwhelmingly attractive —**knock down 1.** strike to ground with blow, as in boxing **2.** in auctions, declare (article) sold **3.** demolish **4.** dismantle for ease of transport **5.** *inf.* reduce (price *etc.*) —**knocked up** *inf.* pregnant —**knock off** *inf.* **1.** cease work **2.** make hurriedly **3.** kill **4.** steal —**knock out 1.** render unconscious, *esp.* in boxing **2.** *inf.* overwhelm, amaze

knockwurst (ˈnokwərst) *n.* short thick smoked sausage

knoll (nōl) *n.* small rounded hill, mound

knot[1] (not) *n.* **1.** fastening of strands by looping and pulling tight **2.** cockade, cluster **3.** small closely knit group **4.** tie, bond **5.** hard lump, *esp.* of wood where branch joins or has joined **6.** unit of speed of one International Nautical Mile (6076.1155 feet or 1852 meters) per hour **7.** difficulty —*vt.* **8.** tie with knot, in knots (**-tt-**) —ˈ**knotty** *a.* **1.** full of knots **2.** puzzling, difficult —ˈ**knothole** *n.* hole in wood where knot has been

knot[2] (not) *n.* small northern sandpiper with gray plumage

know (nō) *vt.* **1.** be aware of **2.** have information about **3.** be acquainted with **4.** recognize **5.** have experience of, understand —*vi.* **6.** have information or understanding (**knew** *pt.*, **known** *pp.*) —ˈ**knowable** *a.* —ˈ**knowing** *a.* cunning, shrewd —ˈ**knowingly** *adv.* **1.** shrewdly **2.** deliberately —**knowledge** (ˈnolij) *n.* **1.** knowing **2.** what one knows **3.** learning —**knowledgeable** (ˈnolijəbəl) *a.* well-informed —**known** *a.* identified —**know-how** *n. inf.* practical knowledge, experience, aptitude —**know-it-all** *n. inf.* person who pretends or appears to know a great deal —**in the know** *inf.* informed

knuckle (ˈnukəl) *n.* **1.** bone at finger joint **2.** knee joint of calf or pig —*vt.* **3.** strike with knuckles —**knuckle-duster** *n.* metal appliance worn on knuckles to add force to blow —**knuckle down** *inf.* get down (to work) —**knuckle under** yield, submit —**near the knuckle** *inf.* approaching indecency

knur (nər) *n.* **1.** knot in wood **2.** hard lump

knurl (nərl) *vt.* **1.** impress with series of fine ridges or serrations —*n.* **2.** small ridge, *esp.* one of series —**knurled** *a.* **1.** serrated **2.** gnarled

koala (kōˈälə, kəˈwäl-) *n.* tailless arboreal Aust. marsupial mammal feeding almost exclusively on eucalyptus leaves (*also* **koala bear**)

kohl (kōl) *n.* black powder used *esp.* in Eastern countries for darkening the eyelids

kohlrabi (kōlˈrabi, -ˈräbi) *n.* type of cabbage with edible stem

koine (koiˈnā, kēˈnē) *n.* **1.** (**K-**) the Greek language consisting of an amalgamation of dialects spoken during the time of the Roman Empire (c. 31 B.C.-476 A.D.) **2.** a lingua franca

kokanee (kōˈkani) *n.* salmon of N Amer. lakes

kola (ˈkōlə) *n. see* COLA

kolinsky (kəˈlinski) *n.* **1.** any of various Asian minks **2.** rich tawny fur of this animal

Kol Nidre (kōl ˈnidrā, kōl; -rə) *Judaism* the

prayer chanted just before sunset on Yom Kippur eve

komatik (kō'matik) *n.* **C** Eskimo sledge with wooden runners

koodoo ('ko͞odo͞o) *n. see* KUDU

kook (ko͝ok) *n. inf.* eccentric or foolish person —'**kooky** *or* '**kookie** *a.*

kookaburra ('ko͝okəburə) *n.* large Aust. kingfisher with cackling cry (*also* **laughing jackass**)

kopeck *or* **kopek** ('kōpek) *n.* Soviet monetary unit, one hundredth of rouble

Koran (kə'ran, -'rän) *n.* sacred book of Muslims (*also* **Alkoran, Alcoran**)

Korea (kə'rēə) *n.* country in Asia bounded north by the demilitarized zone separating it from North Korea, east by the Sea of Japan, south by the Korea Strait separating it from Japan and west by the Yellow Sea —**Ko'rean** *n./a.* **1.** (native or inhabitant) of Korea —*n.* **2.** language of Korea, which is the only member of its branch

Korsakoff's psychosis ('körsəkofs) severe mental disturbance seen mainly in chronic alcoholics marked by loss of memory and degeneration of nervous tissue (*also* **amnestic confabulatory syndrome**)

kosher ('kōshər) *a.* **1.** permitted, clean, good, as of food *etc.*, conforming to the Jewish dietary law **2.** *inf.* legitimate, authentic —*n.* **3.** kosher food

kowtow (kow'tow) *n.* **1.** former Chinese custom of touching ground with head in respect **2.** submission —*vi.* (*esp. with* to) **3.** prostrate oneself **4.** be obsequious, fawn (on)

Kr *Chem.* krypton

kraal (kröl, kräl) *n.* **SA** **1.** hut village, *esp.* one surrounded by fence **2.** corral

kraken ('kräkən) *n.* mythical Norwegian sea monster

Kraut (krowt) *a./n. sl., offens.* German

Krebs cycle (krebz) series of chemical reactions occurring in the tissues of mammals by which food is made available for energy (*also* **citric acid cycle, tricarboxylic acid cycle**)

Kremlin ('kremlin) *n.* **1.** fortress within Russian town, *esp.* Moscow **2.** central government of Soviet Union

krill (kril) *n.* small shrimplike marine animal

kris (krēs) *n.* Malayan and Indonesian knife with scalloped edge

krona ('krōnə) *n.* standard monetary unit of Sweden and Iceland (*pl.* **-nor** (-nör, -nər))

krone ('krōnə) *n.* standard monetary unit of Norway and Denmark (*pl.* **-ner** (-nər))

krypton ('kripton) *n. Chem.* noble gaseous element *Symbol* Kr, at. wt. 83.80, at. no. 36

KS Kansas

Kt *Chess* knight (*also* **N**)

kudos ('kyo͞odos, 'ko͞odos) *n.* **1.** fame **2.** credit

kudu *or* **koodoo** ('ko͞odo͞o) *n.* Afr. antelope with spiral horns

Ku Klux Klan (ko͞o kluks 'klan, kyo͞o) **1.** secret organization of White Southerners formed after U.S. Civil War to fight Black emancipation **2.** secret organization of White Protestant Americans, mainly in South, who use violence against Blacks, Jews *etc.*

kukri ('ko͝okri) *n.* heavy, curved Gurkha knife

kulak (ko͞o'lak, kyo͞o-; 'ko͞olak, 'kyo͞o-) *n.* independent well-to-do Russian peasant

kümmel ('kiməl) *n.* cumin-flavored German liqueur

kumquat ('kumkwot) *n.* **1.** small Chinese tree **2.** its round orange fruit

kung fu ('ko͝ong 'fo͞o) Chinese martial art combining techniques of judo and karate

Kuwait (kə'wāt) *n.* country in Middle East situated on the northwestern coast of the Arabian Gulf —**Ku'waiti** *n./a.*

kvass (kə'väs, kfäs) *n.* Russian beer made from barley, malt and rye

kW *or* **kw** kilowatt

kwashiorkor (kwäshi'örkər) *n.* severe malnutrition of young children, resulting from dietary deficiency of protein

kWh, kwh, *or* **kw-h** kilowatt-hour

KWIC (kwik) *Comp.* key word in context (*esp. in* **KWIC index**)

KWOC (kwok) *Comp.* key word out of context

KY Kentucky

kymograph ('kīməgraf) *n.* instrument for recording on graph pressure, oscillations, sound waves

Kymric ('kimrik) *a. see* CYMRIC

kyphosis (kī'fōsis) *n. see* **hunchback** (sense 1) *at* HUNCH

L

l *or* **L** (el) *n.* **1.** 12th letter of English alphabet **2.** speech sound represented by this letter **3.** something shaped like L (*pl.* **l's, L's** *or* **Ls**)

L 1. lambert **2.** large **3.** Latin **4.** *Phys.* length **5.** pound (*usually written:* £) **6.** longitude **7.** *Electron.* inductor (in circuit diagrams) **8.** *Phys.* latent heat **9.** *Phys.* self-inductance **10.** Roman numeral, 50

L. *or* **l. 1.** lake **2.** left **3.** line (*pl.* **LL.** *or* **ll.**) **4.** liter

la (lä) *n. Mus.* **1.** in fixed system of solmization, the note A **2.** in movable do system, the sixth note of a major scale

La *Chem.* lanthanum

LA 1. Los Angeles **2.** Louisiana

laager ('lägər) *n.* **SA** encampment surrounded by wagons

lab (lab) *inf.* laboratory

Lab. Labrador

label ('lābəl) *n.* **1.** slip of paper, metal *etc.*, fixed to object to give information about it **2.** brief, descriptive phrase or term —*vt.* **3.** fasten label to **4.** mark with label **5** describe or classify in a word or phrase

labiate ('lābiit, -āt) *n.* **1.** plant of family *Labiatae,* having square stems, aromatic leaves and two-lipped corolla —*a.* **2.** of family *Labiatae*

labium ('lābiəm) *n.* **1.** lip; liplike structure **2.** any of four lip-shaped folds of vulva, comprising outer pair (**labia majora**) and inner pair (**labia minora**) (*pl.* **-bia** (-biə)) —'**labial** *a.* **1.** of the lips **2.** pronounced with the lips —*n.* **3.** speech sound pronounced thus

labor ('lābər) *n.* **1.** exertion of body or mind **2.** task **3.** workers collectively **4.** effort, pain of childbirth or time taken for this —*vi.* **5.** work hard **6.** strive **7.** maintain normal motion with difficulty **8.** (*esp.* of ship) be tossed heavily —*vt.* **9.** stress to excess —'**labored** *a.* uttered, done, with difficulty —'**laborer** *n.* one who labors, *esp.* man doing manual work for wages —**la'borious** *a* tedious —**la'boriously** *adv.* —**labor-saving** *a.* eliminating or lessening physical labor —**Labour Party 1.** Brit. political party, generally supporting interests of organized labor **2.** similar party in various other countries

laboratory ('labrətōri) *n.* place for scientific investigations or for manufacture of chemicals

Labrador ('labrədōr) *n.* breed of large, smooth-coated retriever dog (*also* **Labrador retriever**)

laburnum (lə'bərnəm) *n.* tree with yellow hanging flowers

labyrinth ('labərinth) *n.* **1.** network of tortuous passages, maze **2.** inexplicable difficulty **3.** perplexity **4.** inner ear —**laby'rinthine** *a.* —**labyrin'thitis** *n.* inflammation of the inner ear characterized by loss of balance and nausea

lac[1] (lak) *n.* resinous substance secreted by some insects

lac[2] (läk) *n.* one hundred thousand (of rupees)

lace (lās) *n.* **1.** fine patterned openwork fabric **2.** cord, usu. one of pair, to draw edges together, *eg* to tighten shoes *etc.* **3.** ornamental braid —*vt.* **4.** fasten with laces **5.** flavor with spirit —'**lacy** *a.* fine, like lace

lacerate ('lasərāt) *vt.* **1.** tear, mangle **2.** distress —'**lacerable** *a.* —**lacer'ation** *n.*

lachrymal *or* **lacrimal** ('lakriməl) *a.* of tears —'**lachrymatory** *or* '**lacrimatory** *a.* causing tears or inflammation of eyes —'**lachrymose** *a.* tearful —'**lachrymosely** *adv.*

lack (lak) *n.* **1.** deficiency, need —*vt.* **2.** need, be short of —'**lackluster** *a.* lacking brilliance or vitality

lackadaisical (lakə'dāzikəl) *a.* **1.** languid, listless **2.** lazy, careless

lackey ('laki) *n.* **1.** servile follower **2.** footman (*pl.* **-s**) —*vi.* **3.** be or play, the lackey **4.** (*with* for) wait (upon)

laconic (lə'konik) *a.* **1.** using, expressed in few words **2.** brief, terse **3.** offhand, not caring —**la'conically** *adv.* —**la'conicism** *n.*

lacquer ('lakər) *n.* **1.** hard varnish —*vt.* **2.** coat with this

lacrimal ('lakriməl) *a. see* LACHRYMAL

lacrosse (lə'kros) *n.* goal game played with crosse

lactic ('laktik) *a.* of milk —'**lactate** *vi.* secrete milk —**lac'tation** *n.* —**lac'tometer** *n.* instrument for measuring purity and density of milk —'**lactose** *n.* white crystalline substance occurring in milk —**lactic acid** colorless syrupy acid found in sour milk *etc.*

lacuna (lə'kyōōnə, -'kōōnə) *n.* gap, missing part, *esp.* in document or series (*pl.* **-nae** (-nē), **-s**)

lad (lad) *n.* boy, young fellow

ladder ('ladər) *n.* frame of two poles connected by rungs, used for climbing —**ladder back** type of chair in which back is constructed of horizontal slats between two uprights

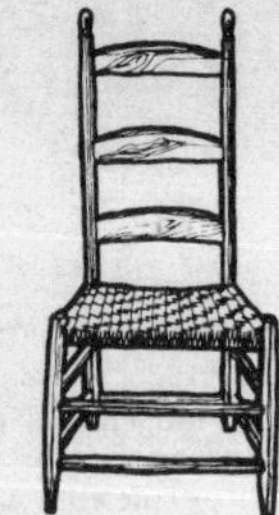

lade (lād) *vt.* **1.** load **2.** ship **3.** burden, weigh down (ˈ**laden** *pp.*) —ˈ**lading** *n.* cargo, freight

la-di-da *or* **la-de-da** (lädēˈdä) *a. inf.* affecting exaggeratedly genteel manners or speech

Ladino (ləˈdēnō) *n.* **1.** (*also* **Judesmo, Dzhudesmo**) a dialect of Spanish and Portuguese, the vernacular of Sephardic Jews **2.** (**l-**) Spanish-speaking Latin American person (*pl.* **-s**)

ladle (ˈlādəl) *n.* **1.** spoon with long handle and large bowl —*vt.* **2.** (*oft. with* out) serve out (as) with ladle

lady (ˈlādi) *n.* **1.** female counterpart of gentleman **2.** *polite term for* a woman **3.** title of some women of rank —ˈ**ladies** *or* **ladies' room** *n. inf.* women's public toilet —ˈ**ladyship** *n.* title of a lady —ˈ**ladybug** *n.* small beetle, usu. red with black spots —**Lady Day** Feast of the Annunciation, March 25th —ˈ**ladyfinger** *n.* small finger-shaped sponge cake —**lady-in-waiting** *n.* lady who attends queen or princess (*pl.* **ladies-in-waiting**) —**lady-killer** *n. inf.* man who believes he is irresistible to women —ˈ**ladylike** *a.* **1.** gracious **2.** well-mannered —**lady's-slipper** *n.* orchid with reddish or purple flowers —**Our Lady** the Virgin Mary

lag[1] (lag) *vi.* **1.** (*oft. with* behind) go too slowly, fall behind (**-gg-**) —*n.* **2.** lagging, interval of time between events —ˈ**laggard** *n.* one who lags —ˈ**lagging** *a.* loitering, slow

lag[2] (lag) *vt.* wrap (boiler, pipes *etc.*) with insulating material (**-gg-**) —ˈ**lagging** *n.* this material

lag[3] (lag) *n. sl.* convict (*esp. in* **old lag**)

lager (ˈlägər) *n.* light-bodied type of beer

lagoon (ləˈgo͞on) *n.* saltwater lake, enclosed by atoll, or separated by sandbank from sea

laic (ˈlāik) *a.* secular, lay —**laiciˈzation** *n.* —ˈ**laicize** *vt.* render secular or lay

laid (lād) *pt./pp. of* LAY[2] —**laid-back** *a.* relaxed in style or character; easy-going and unhurried —**laid paper** paper with regular mesh impressed upon it

lain (lān) *pp. of* LIE[1]

lair (lāər) *n.* resting place, den of animal

laird (lāərd) *n.* Scottish landowner —ˈ**lairdship** *n.* estate

laissez faire *or* ***laisser faire*** (lesā ˈfāər) *Fr.* **1.** principle of nonintervention, *esp.* by government in commercial affairs **2.** indifference

laity (ˈlāiti) *n.* laymen, the people as opposed to clergy

lake[1] (lāk) *n.* expanse of inland water —ˈ**lakelet** *n.*

lake[2] (lāk) *n.* red pigment

lam[1] (lam) *vt. sl.* beat, hit (**-mm-**) —ˈ**lamming** *n.* beating, thrashing

lam[2] (lam) *n. sl.* —**on the lam** making an escape

Lam. *Bible* Lamentations

lama (ˈlämə) *n.* Buddhist priest in Tibet or Mongolia —ˈ**Lamaism** *n.* form of Buddhism of Tibet and Mongolia —ˈ**Lamaist** *n./a.* —ˈ**lamasery** *n.* monastery of lamas

lamb (lam) *n.* **1.** young of the sheep **2.** its meat **3.** innocent or helpless creature —*vi.* **4.** (of sheep) give birth —ˈ**lambkin** *n.* **1.** small lamb **2.** term of affection for child —ˈ**lamblike** *a.* meek, gentle —**lamb's ears** hardy perennial garden plant with woolly leaves and small purple flowers in dense whorls —ˈ**lambskin** *n.* **1.** skin of lamb, *esp.* with wool still on **2.** material or garment prepared from this —**lamb's wool** soft, virgin wool from seven-month-old lamb having superior spinning qualities —**Lamb of God** (among Christians) Jesus

lambaste *or* **lambast** (lamˈbāst) *vt.* **1.** beat **2.** reprimand

lambda (ˈlamdə) *n.* 11th letter in Gr. alphabet (Λ, λ)

lambent (ˈlambənt) *a.* **1.** (of flame) flickering softly **2.** glowing

lambert (ˈlambərt) *n.* cgs unit of illumination

lame (lām) *a.* **1.** crippled in a limb, *esp.* leg **2.** limping **3.** (of excuse *etc.*) unconvincing —*vt.* **4.** cripple —**lame duck** **1.** disabled, weak person or thing **2.** elected official or body of officials remaining in office between election and inauguration of successor(s)

lamé (läˈmā) *n./a.* (fabric) interwoven with gold or silver thread

lamella (ləˈmelə) *n.* thin plate or scale *esp.* of mushroom gill or mollusk gill (*pl.* **-lae** (-lē), **-s**) —**laˈmellar** *or* **lamellate** (ləˈmelit, ˈlamilāt) *a.*

lament (ləˈment) *v.* **1.** feel, express sorrow (for) —*n.* **2.** passionate expression of grief **3.** song of grief —ˈ**lamentable** *a.* deplorable —**lamenˈtation** *n.*

Lamentations (lamənˈtāshənz) *pl.n.* (*with sing. v.*) *Bible* 25th book of the O.T., written by Jeremiah, describing the capture and destruction of Jerusalem by the Babylonians

lamina (ˈlaminə) *n.* thin plate, scale, flake (*pl.* **-nae** (-nē), **-s**) —**laminate** (ˈlamināt) *vt.* **1.** make (sheet of material) by bonding together two or more thin sheets **2.** split, beat, form into thin sheets **3.** cover with thin sheet of material *—n.* ('laminit, -nāt) **4.** laminated sheet **—lami'nation** *n.*

Lammas ('laməs) *n.* Aug. 1st, formerly a harvest festival

lammergeier *or* **lammergeyer** ('lamərgīər) *n.* type of rare vulture

lamp (lamp) *n.* **1.** any of various appliances (*esp.* electrical) that produce light, heat, radiation *etc.* **2.** formerly, vessel holding oil burned by wick for lighting **—'lampblack** *n.* pigment made from soot **—'lamplight** *n.* **—'lamppost** *n.* post supporting lamp in street **—'lampshade** *n.*

lampoon (lam'pōōn) *n.* **1.** satire ridiculing person, literary work *etc.* *—vt.* **2.** satirize, ridicule **—lam'pooner** *or* **lam'poonist** *n.*

lamprey ('lampri) *n.* fish like an eel with a sucker mouth

lanceolate

lance (lans) *n.* **1.** horseman's spear *—vt.* **2.** pierce with lance or lancet **—lanceolate** ('lansiəlāt) *a.* lance-shaped, tapering **—'lancer** *n.* formerly, cavalry soldier armed with lance **—'lancers** *pl.n.* (*with sing. v.*) **1.** quadrille for eight or sixteen couples **2.** music for this dance **—'lancet** *n.* pointed two-edged surgical knife

land (land) *n.* **1.** solid part of earth's surface **2.** ground, soil **3.** country **4.** property consisting of land *—pl.* **5.** estates *—vi.* **6.** come to land, disembark **7.** bring an aircraft or (of aircraft) come from air to land or water **8.** alight, step down **9.** arrive on ground **10.** **C** be legally admitted as immigrant *—vt.* **11.** bring to land **12.** bring to some point or condition **13.** *inf.* obtain **14.** catch **15.** *inf.* strike **—'landed** *a.* possessing, consisting of lands **—'landing** *n.* **1.** act of landing **2.** platform between flights of stairs **3.** a landing stage **—'landless** *a.* **—'landward** *a./adv.* **—'landfall** *n.* ship's approach to land at end of voyage **—land grant** tract of land given by government, usu. for colleges **—land-grant college** college or university in the U.S. entitled to federal government support under certain laws **—landing gear** undercarriage **—landing stage** floating wharf **—'landlocked** *a.* enclosed by land **—'landlord** *or* **'landlady** *n.* person who lets land, houses *etc.* **—'landlubber** *n.* person ignorant of the sea and ships **—'landmark** *n.* **1.** boundary mark, conspicuous object, as guide for direction *etc.* **2.** event, decision *etc.* considered as important stage in development of something **—'landmass** *n.* large continuous area of land **—land mine** *Mil.* explosive charge placed in ground, usu. detonated by stepping or driving on it **—land-poor** *a.* needing money while owning land **—land reform** program, *esp.* by national government, to redistribute large holdings of land to the landless **—'landscape** *n.* **1.** piece of inland scenery **2.** picture of it **3.** prospect *—v.* **4.** create, arrange (garden, park *etc.*) **—landscape gardener —landscape painter —'landslide** *n.* **1.** falling of soil, rock *etc.* down mountainside **2.** overwhelming electoral victory **—'landsman** *n.* fellow countryman **—land of milk and honey** land of natural fertility promised to Israelites by God **—land on one's feet** emerge safely from a risky situation **—see how the land lies** ascertain the facts before acting

landau ('landow, -dö) *n.* four-wheeled carriage with folding top

lane (lān) *n.* **1.** narrow road or street **2.** specified route followed by shipping or aircraft **3.** area of road for one stream of traffic

lang. language

language ('langgwij) *n.* **1.** system of sounds, symbols *etc.* for communicating thought **2.** specialized vocabulary used by a particular group **3.** style of speech or expression **—language laboratory** room equipped with tape recorders *etc.* for learning foreign languages

languish ('langgwish) *vi.* **1.** be or become weak or faint **2.** be in depressing or painful conditions **3.** droop, pine **—'languid** *a.* **1.** lacking energy, interest **2.** spiritless, dull **—'languidly** *adv.* **—languor** ('langgər) *n.* **1.** want of energy or interest **2.** faintness **3.** tender mood **4.** softness of atmosphere **—languorous** ('langgərəs) *a.*

lank (langk) *a.* **1.** lean and tall **2.** greasy and limp **—'lanky** *a.* tall, thin and ungainly

lanolin ('lanəlin) *n.* grease from wool used in ointments *etc.*

lantern ('lantərn) *n.* **1.** transparent case for lamp or candle **2.** erection on dome or roof to admit light **—lantern jaw** long hollow jaw that gives face drawn appearance **—lantern-jawed** *a.* **—lanthorn** ('lantərn) *n.* *obs.* lantern

lanthanum ('lanthənəm) *n.* *Chem.* metallic element *Symbol* La, at. wt. 138.9, at. no. 57 **—lanthanide series** class of 15 chemically related elements (**lanthanides**) with atomic numbers from 57 (lanthanum) to 71 (lutetium)

lanyard ('lanyərd) *n.* **1.** short cord for securing knife or whistle **2.** short nautical rope **3.** cord for firing cannon

Laos ('laōōs, 'lāos, 'läōs) *n.* country in Asia bounded in the north by China, east by Vietnam, south by Kampuchea and west by Thailand and Burma **—Laotian** (lā'ōshən) *a./n.*

lap[1] (lap) *n.* **1.** the part between waist and knees of a person when sitting **2.** *fig.* place where anything lies securely **3.** single circuit of racecourse, track **4.** stage or part of journey **5.** single turn of wound thread *etc.* —*vt.* **6.** enfold, wrap round **7.** overtake (opponent) to be one or more circuits ahead (**-pp-**) —**'lappet** *n.* flap, fold —**'lapdog** *n.* small pet dog —**lap joint** joint made by placing one member over another and fastening together (*also* **lapped joint**) —**lap of honor** ceremonial circuit of racing track *etc.* by winner of race

lap[2] (lap) *v.* **1.** (*oft. with* up) drink by scooping up with tongue **2.** (of waves *etc.*) beat softly (**-pp-**)

lapel (lə'pel) *n.* part of front of coat *etc.* folded back toward shoulders

lapidary ('lapideri) *a.* **1.** of stones **2.** engraved on stone —*n.* **3.** cutter, engraver of stones

lapis lazuli ('lapis 'lazyhəlē) bright blue stone or pigment

lapse (laps) *n.* **1.** fall (in standard, condition, virtue *etc.*) **2.** slip **3.** mistake **4.** passing (of time *etc.*) —*vi.* **5.** fall away **6.** end, *esp.* through disuse

lapwing ('lapwing) *n.* type of plover

larboard ('lärbərd) *n./a. obs.* port (side of ship)

larceny ('lärsini) *n.* theft

larch (lärch) *n.* deciduous coniferous tree

lard (lärd) *n.* **1.** prepared pig's fat —*vt.* **2.** insert strips of bacon in (meat) **3.** intersperse, decorate (speech) (with strange words *etc.*) —**'lardy** *a.*

larder ('lärdər) *n.* storeroom or cupboard for food

large (lärj) *a.* **1.** broad in range or area **2.** great in size, number *etc.* **3.** liberal **4.** generous —*adv.* **5.** in a big way —**'largely** *adv.* —**lar'gess** *or* **lar'gesse** *n.* **1.** bounty **2.** gift **3.** donation —**large-scale** *a.* **1.** wide-ranging, extensive **2.** (of maps and models) constructed or drawn to big scale —**at large** **1.** free, not confined **2.** in general **3.** fully

largo ('lärgō) *a./adv. Mus.* to be performed moderately slowly

lariat ('lariət) *n.* lasso

lark[1] (lärk) *n.* any of a family of ground-nesting songbirds of which the meadowlark and prairie horned lark are found in N Amer. —**'larkspur** *n.* plant with spikes of blue, pink or white flowers

lark[2] (lärk) *n.* **1.** frolic, spree —*vi.* **2.** indulge in lark —**'larky** *a.*

larrigan ('larigən) *n.* knee-high moccasin boot worn by trappers *etc.*

larva ('lärvə) *n.* insect in immature but active stage (*pl.* **-ae** (-ē)) —**'larval** *a.* —**'larviform** *a.*

larynx ('laringks) *n.* part of throat containing vocal cords (*pl.* **larynges** (lə'rinjēz), **-es**) —**laryn'geal** *a.* **1.** of larynx **2.** *Phonet.* articulated at larynx; glottal —**laryn'gitis** *n.* inflammation of larynx

lasagna *or* **lasagne** (lə'zänyə) *n.* pasta formed in wide, flat sheets

lascar ('laskər) *n.* E Indian seaman

lascivious (lə'siviəs) *a.* lustful

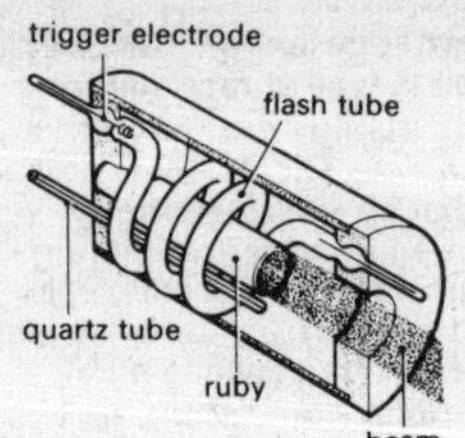

laser

laser ('lāzər) *n.* *l*ight *a*mplification by *s*timulated *e*mission of *r*adiation: device that amplifies focused coherent light waves and concentrates them in narrow intense beam

lash[1] (lash) *n.* **1.** stroke with whip **2.** flexible part of whip **3.** eyelash —*vt.* **4.** strike with whip, thong *etc.* **5.** dash against (as waves) **6.** attack verbally, ridicule **7.** flick, wave sharply to and fro —**'lashing** *n.* **1.** whipping, flogging **2.** scolding —**lash out** **1.** burst into or resort to verbal or physical attack **2.** *inf.* be extravagant, as in spending

lash[2] (lash) *vt.* fasten or bind tightly with cord *etc.* —**'lashing** *n.* rope *etc.* used for binding or securing —**lash-up** *n.* temporary connection of equipment for experimental or emergency use

lass (las) *n.* girl —**'lassie** *n. inf.* little lass; girl

Lassa fever ('lasə) serious viral disease of Central W Afr., characterized by high fever *etc.*

lassitude ('lasityo͞od, -to͞od) *n.* weariness

lasso ('lasō, la'so͞o) *n.* **1.** rope with noose for catching cattle *etc.* (*pl.* **-s, -es**) —*vt.* **2.** catch (as) with lasso (**'lassoed, 'lassoing**)

last[1] (last) *a./adv.* **1.** after all others, coming at the end **2.** most recent(ly) —*a.* **3.** *sup. of* LATE **4.** only remaining —*n.* **5.** last person or thing —**'lastly** *adv.* finally —**last-ditch** *a.* made or done as last desperate effort in face of opposition —**last name** family name —**last rites** *see* **extreme unction** *at* EXTREME —**on its last legs** at the end of its usefulness —**the Last Judgment** in Christian belief, the day God will judge all men, living and dead —**the last straw** final irritation or problem that stretches one's endurance or patience beyond limit —**the Last Supper** the meal eaten by Jesus and his disciples the night of his betrayal —**the last word** **1.** the final statement in a dispute **2.** a definitive statement **3.** the latest fashion

last[2] (last) *vi.* continue, hold out, remain alive or unexhausted, endure —**'lasting** *a.* permanent; enduring —**'lastingly** *adv.*

last[3] (last) *n.* model of foot on which shoes are made, repaired

Lastex ('lasteks) *n.* trade name for yarn made from combination of rubber with silk, cotton or rayon

lat. latitude

latch (lach) *n.* **1.** fastening for door, consisting of bar, catch for it, and lever to lift it **2.** small lock with spring action —*vt.* **3.** fasten with latch —**latchkey child** child who has to let himself in at home after school as his parents are out at work

late (lāt) *a.* **1.** coming after the appointed time **2.** delayed **3.** that was recently but now is not **4.** recently dead **5.** recent in date **6.** of late stage of development ('**later** *comp.*, '**latest, last** *sup.*) —*adv.* **7.** after proper time **8.** recently **9.** at, till late hour —'**lately** *adv.* not long since —'**latish** *a.* rather late —**Late Greek** Greek language from about 3rd to 8th century A.D. —**Late Latin** form of written Latin used from 3rd to 7th century A.D.

lateen sail (lə'tēn) triangular sail on long yard hoisted to head of mast

latent ('lātənt) *a.* **1.** existing but not developed **2.** hidden

lateral ('latərəl) *a.* of, at, from the side —'**laterally** *adv.*

laterite ('latərīt) *n.* dark red rock or clay formed by weathering of rock in tropical regions

latex ('lāteks) *n.* sap or fluid of plants, *esp.* of rubber tree (*pl.* **-es, latices** ('lātisēz, 'lat-)) —**laticiferous** (lati'sifərəs) *a.* bearing or containing latex or sap

lath (lath) *n.* thin strip of wood —'**lathing** *n.* —'**lathy** *a.* **1.** like a lath **2.** tall and thin

lathe (lādh) *n.* machine for turning object while it is being shaped

lather ('ladhər) *n.* **1.** froth of soap and water **2.** frothy sweat —*vi.* **3.** form lather —*vt.* **4.** *inf.* beat

Latin ('latin) *n.* **1.** language of ancient Romans —*a.* **2.** of ancient Romans **3.** of, in their language **4.** speaking a Romance language —'**Latinism** *n.* word, idiom imitating Latin —**La'tinity** *n.* **1.** manner of writing Latin **2.** Latin style —**Latin alphabet** alphabet used for writing Latin and adapted for writing many modern languages including English —**Latin America** those areas of Amer. whose official languages are Spanish and Portuguese: S Amer., Central Amer., Mexico and certain islands in the Caribbean —**Latin American**

latitude ('latityo͞od, -to͞od) *n.* **1.** angular distance on meridian reckoned N or S from equator **2.** deviation from a standard **3.** freedom from restriction **4.** scope —*pl.* **5.** regions —**lati'tudinal** *a.* —**latitudi'narian** *a.* claiming, showing latitude of thought, *esp.* in religion —**latitudi'narianism** *n.*

latrine (lə'trēn) *n.* in army *etc.*, toilet

latter ('latər) *a.* **1.** second of two **2.** later **3.** more recent —*n.* **4.** second or last-mentioned person or thing —'**latterly** *adv.* —**Latter-Day Saint** Mormon

lattice ('latis) *n.* **1.** structure of strips of wood, metal *etc.* crossing with spaces between **2.** window so made —'**latticed** *a.*

laud (lŏd) *Lit. n.* **1.** praise, song of praise —*vt.* **2.** praise, glorify —**lauda'bility** *n.* —'**laudable** *a.* praiseworthy —'**laudably** *adv.* —**lau'dation** *n.* **1.** praise **2.** honor paid —'**laudatory** *a.* expressing, containing praise

laudanum ('lŏdənəm) *n.* tincture of opium

laugh (laf, lăf) *vi.* **1.** make sounds instinctively expressing amusement, merriment or scorn —*n.* **2.** such sound —'**laughable** *a.* ludicrous —'**laughably** *adv.* —'**laughter** *n.* —**laughing gas** nitrous oxide as anesthetic —**laughing hyena** spotted hyena, so called from its cry —**laughing jackass** *see* KOOKABURRA —**laughing stock** object of general derision

launch[1] (lŏnch) *vt.* **1.** set afloat **2.** set in motion **3.** begin **4.** propel (missile, spacecraft) into space **5.** hurl, send —*vi.* **6.** enter on course —'**launcher** *n.* installation, vehicle, device for launching rockets, missiles *etc.* —**launch pad** platform from which spacecraft *etc.* is launched

launch[2] (lŏnch) *n.* large power-driven boat

Laundromat ('lŏndrəmat) *n.* trade name for launderette

laundry ('lŏndri) *n.* **1.** place for washing clothes, *esp.* as a business **2.** clothes *etc.* for washing —'**launder** *vt.* **1.** wash and iron **2.** legitimize (money obtained from criminal activity) —**launder'ette** *n.* place equipped with laundry equipment that customers may use for a fee

laureate ('lŏriit) *a.* crowned with laurels —'**laureateship** *n.* post of poet laureate —**poet laureate UK** poet with appointment to Royal Household, nominally to compose verses on important royal occasions

laurel ('lŏrəl) *n.* **1.** glossy-leaved shrub, bay tree —*pl.* **2.** its leaves, emblem of victory or merit

lava ('lăvə) *n.* molten matter thrown out by volcanoes, solidifying as it cools

lavatory ('lavətŏri) *n.* **1.** fixed washbowl with running water and drainpipe **2.** bathroom

lave (lāv) *vt. obs.* wash, bathe

lavender ('lavəndər) *n.* **1.** shrub with fragrant flowers **2.** color of the flowers, pale lilac —**lavender water** perfume or toilet water made from flowers of lavender plant

lavish ('lavish) *a.* **1.** giving or spending profusely **2.** very, too abundant —*vt.* **3.** spend, bestow profusely

law (lŏ) *n.* **1.** rule binding on community **2.** system of such rules **3.** legal science **4.** knowledge, administration of it **5.** *inf.* (member of) police force **6.** general principle deduced from facts **7.** invariable sequence of events in nature —'**lawful** *a.* allowed by law —'**lawfully** *adv.* —'**lawless** *a.* **1.** ignoring laws **2.** violent —'**lawlessly** *adv.* —'**lawyer** *n.* professional expert in law —**law-abiding** *a.* **1.** obedient to laws **2.** well-behaved —'**lawgiver** *n.* one who makes laws —'**lawsuit** *n.* prosecution of claim in court

lawn[1] (lôn) *n.* stretch of carefully tended grass, *esp.* around house —**lawn mower** hand- or power-operated machine for cutting grass —**lawn tennis** tennis played on grass court

lawn[2] (lôn) *n.* fine soft cotton fabric

lawrencium (lô'rensiəm) *n. Chem.* transuranic element *Symbol* Lr, at. wt. 257, at. no. 103

lawyer ('lôyər, 'loiər) *n. see* LAW

lax (laks) *a.* **1.** not strict **2.** lacking precision **3.** loose, slack —'**laxative** *a.* **1.** having loosening effect on bowels —*n.* **2.** agent stimulating evacuation of feces —'**laxity** *or* '**laxness** *n.* **1.** slackness **2.** looseness of (moral) standards —'**laxly** *adv.*

lay[1] (lā) *pt. of* LIE[1] —'**layabout** *n.* lazy person, loafer

lay[2] (lā) *vt.* **1.** deposit, set, cause to lie **2.** *sl.* have sexual intercourse with (**laid,** '**laying**) —*n. sl.* **3.** female sexual partner —'**layer** *n.* **1.** single thickness of some substance, as stratum or coating on surface **2.** laying hen **3.** shoot of plant pegged down or partly covered with earth to encourage root growth —*vt.* **4.** propagate (plants) by making layers —**lay-off** *n.* —'**layout** *n.* arrangement, *esp.* of matter for printing —**lay by** store for future use —**lay it on the line** *sl.* speak out without reserve —**lay off** dismiss (staff) during slack period —**lay on 1.** provide, supply **2.** apply **3.** strike —**lay out 1.** display **2.** expend **3.** prepare for burial **4.** *sl.* knock out —**lay waste** devastate

lay[3] (lā) *n.* minstrel's song

lay[4] (lā) *a.* **1.** not clerical or professional **2.** of or done by persons not clergymen —'**layman** *n.* ordinary person —**lay reader 1.** *Ch. of England* person licensed by bishop to conduct religious services other than Eucharist **2.** *R.C.Ch.* layman chosen to read epistle at Mass

layette (lā'et) *n.* clothing, accessories *etc.* for newborn child

lay figure 1. jointed figure of the body used by artists **2.** nonentity

lazy ('lāzi) *a.* averse to work, indolent —**laze** *vi.* indulge in laziness —'**lazily** *adv.* —'**laziness** *n.* —**lazy Susan** ('sōōzən) revolving circular tray

lb. pound

lbs. pounds

l.c. *Print.* lower case

L.C. Library of Congress

L/C letter of credit

LCD liquid crystal display

L.C.D. least common denominator

LCDR lieutenant commander

LCL less-than-carload lot

L.C.M. least common multiple

LD lethal dose

L-dopa ('el'dōpə) *n.* drug used to treat Parkinson's disease

L.D.S. 1. Latter-Day Saint **2.** *laus Deo semper* (*Lat.*, praise be to God for ever)

lea (lē, lā) *n. Poet.* piece of meadow or open ground

leach (lēch) *v.* **1.** remove or be removed from substance by percolating liquid **2.** (cause to) lose soluble substances by action of percolating liquid —*n.* **3.** act or process of leaching **4.** substance that is leached or constituents removed by leaching **5.** porous vessel for leaching

lead[1] (lēd) *vt.* **1.** guide, conduct **2.** persuade **3.** direct **4.** control —*vi.* **5.** be, go, play first **6.** (*with* to) result (in) **7.** give access (**led** (led), '**leading**) —*n.* **8.** leading **9.** that which leads or is used to lead **10.** example **11.** front or principal place, role *etc.* **12.** cable bringing current to electric instrument —'**leader** *n.* —'**leadership** *n.* —**leading light** *inf.* important or outstanding person, *esp.* in organization —**leading question** question worded to prompt answer desired —**leading tone** *Mus.* **1.** seventh degree of major or minor scale (*also* **sub'tonic**) **2.** *esp.* in cadences, note that tends most naturally to resolve to note lying one semitone above —**lead time** time between design of product and its production

lead[2] (led) *n.* **1.** *Chem.* metallic element *Symbol* Pb, at. wt. 207.2, at. no. 82 **2.** plummet, used for sounding depths of water **3.** graphite —*pl.* **4.** lead-covered piece of roof **5.** strips of lead used to widen spaces in printing *etc.* —*vt.* **6.** cover, weight or space with lead ('**leaded,** '**leading**) —'**leaden** *a.* **1.** of, like lead **2.** heavy **3.** dull —'**leadsman** *n.* sailor who heaves the lead —**lead poisoning 1.** acute or chronic poisoning by lead, characterized by abdominal pain *etc.* **2.** *sl.* death or injury resulting from being shot with bullets

leaf (lēf) *n.* **1.** organ of photosynthesis in plants, consisting of a flat, usu. green blade on stem **2.** two pages of book *etc.* **3.** thin sheet **4.** flap, movable part of table *etc.* (*pl.* **leaves** (lēvz)) —*v.* **5.** (*oft. with* through) turn through (pages *etc.*) cursorily —'**leafless** *a.* —'**leaflet** *n.* **1.** small leaf **2.** single sheet, often folded, of printed matter for distribution, handbill —'**leafy** *a.*

league[1] (lēg) *n.* **1.** agreement for mutual help **2.** parties to it **3.** federation of clubs *etc.* **4.** *inf.* class, level —*vi.* **5.** form an alliance; combine in an association —'**leaguer** *n.* member of league —**not in the same league** (as) inferior (to)

league[2] (lēg) *n. obs.* measure of distance varying from 2½ to 4½ miles

leak (lēk) *n.* **1.** hole, defect, that allows

escape or entrance of liquid, gas, radiation *etc.* **2.** disclosure **3.** *sl.* act of urinating —*vi.* **4.** let fluid *etc.* in or out **5.** (of fluid *etc.*) find its way through leak —*vt.* **6.** let escape —*v.* **7.** (*oft. with* out) (allow to) become known little by little —**'leakage** *n.* **1.** leaking **2.** gradual escape or loss —**'leaky** *a.*

lean[1] (lēn) *a.* **1.** lacking fat **2.** thin **3.** meager **4.** (of mixture of fuel and air) with too little fuel —*n.* **5.** lean part of meat, mainly muscular tissue

lean[2] (lēn) *v.* **1.** rest (against) **2.** bend, incline —*vi.* **3.** (*with* to *or* toward) tend (toward) **4.** (*with* on *or* upon) depend, rely (on) —**'leaning** *n.* tendency —**lean-to** *n.* room, shed built against existing wall

leap (lēp) *vi.* **1.** spring, jump —*vt.* **2.** spring over (**leapt** *or* **leaped** *pt./pp.*) —*n.* **3.** jump —**'leapfrog** *n.* **1.** game in which player vaults over another bending down —*v.* **2.** (cause to) advance by jumps or stages (**-gg-**) —**leap year** year with Feb. 29th as extra day, occurring every fourth year

learn (lərn) *vt.* **1.** gain knowledge of or acquire skill in (something) by study, practice or teaching —*vi.* **2.** gain knowledge **3.** be taught **4.** (*oft. with* of *or* about) find out —**learned** ('lərnid) *a.* **1.** erudite, deeply read **2.** showing much learning —**learnedly** ('lərnidli) *adv.* —**'learner** *n.* —**'learning** *n.* knowledge got by study

lease (lēs) *n.* **1.** contract by which land or property is rented for stated time by owner to tenant —*vt.* **2.** let, rent by, take on lease —**'leasehold** *n.* property held on lease

leash (lēsh) *n.* **1.** thong for holding a dog **2.** set of three animals held in leash —*vt.* **3.** hold in, secure by leash

least (lēst) *sup. of* LITTLE *a.* **1.** smallest —*n.* **2.** smallest one —*adv.* **3.** in smallest degree

leather ('ledhər) *n.* prepared skin of animal —**'leathery** *a.* like leather, tough —**'leatherback** *n.* largest existing sea turtle —**'leatherjacket** *n.* crane-fly grub —**'leatherwood** *n.* N Amer. shrub with tough, leathery bark formerly used as emergency fiber for thongs

leave[1] (lēv) *vt.* **1.** go away from **2.** deposit **3.** allow to remain **4.** entrust **5.** bequeath —*vi.* **6.** go away, set out (**left, 'leaving**)

leave[2] (lēv) *n.* **1.** permission **2.** permission to be absent from work, duty **3.** period of such absence **4.** formal parting —**leave of absence 1.** leave from work or duty, *esp.* for a long time **2.** this period of time —**leave-taking** *n.* act of departing; farewell —**by** *or* **with your leave** with your permission

leave[3] (lēv) *vi.* produce or grow leaves (**leaved, 'leaving**)

leaven ('levən) *n.* **1.** yeast **2.** *fig.* transforming influence —*vt.* **3.** raise with leaven **4.** taint; modify

Lebanon ('lebənən) *n.* country in Middle East bounded on the north and east by Syria, west by the Mediterranean and south by Israel —**Leba'nese** *n./a.*

lecher ('lechər) *n.* man given to lewdness —**lech** *vi. inf.* (*usu. with* after) behave lecherously (toward) —**'lecherous** *a.* **1.** lewd **2.** provoking lust **3.** lascivious —**'lecherously** *adv.* —**'lecherousness** *n.* —**'lechery** *n.*

lecithin ('lesithin) *n.* one of a class of phosphorus-containing fats found in animal tissues, egg yolk and soybeans used in the manufacture of pharmaceuticals, cosmetics, margarine and chocolate (*also* **phosphatidyl choline**)

lectern ('lektərn) *n.* reading desk, *esp.* in church

lection ('lekshən) *n.* **1.** difference in copies of manuscript or book **2.** reading —**'lectionary** *n.* book, list of scripture lessons for particular days —**'lector** *n.* reader

lecture ('lekchər) *n.* **1.** instructive discourse **2.** speech of reproof —*vi.* **3.** deliver discourse —*vt.* **4.** reprove —**'lecturer** *n.* —**'lectureship** *n.* appointment as lecturer

LED light-emitting diode

ledge (lej) *n.* **1.** narrow shelf sticking out from wall, cliff *etc.* **2.** ridge, rock below surface of sea

ledger ('lejər) *n.* **1.** book of debit and credit accounts, chief account book of firm **2.** flat stone —**ledger line** *Mus.* short line, above or below stave

lee (lē) *n.* **1.** shelter **2.** side of anything, *esp.* ship, away from wind —**'leeward** *a./n.* **1.** (on) lee side —*adv.* **2.** toward this side —**lee shore** shore toward which wind is blowing —**'leeway** *n.* **1.** leeward drift of ship **2.** room for free movement within limits **3.** loss of progress

leech[1] (lēch) *n.* **1.** species of bloodsucking worm **2.** *Hist.* physician —**'leechcraft** *n.*

leech[2] (lēch) *n.* edge of a sail

leek (lēk) *n.* **1.** plant like onion with long bulb and thick stem **2.** this as Welsh emblem

leer (lēər) *vi.* **1.** glance with malign, sly or lascivious expression —*n.* **2.** such glance —**'leery** *a.* **1.** *chiefly dial.* knowing, sly **2.** *sl.* (*with* of) suspicious, wary

lees (lēz) *pl.n.* **1.** sediment of wine *etc.* **2.** dregs of liquor

left[1] (left) *a.* **1.** denoting the side that faces west when the front faces north **2.** opposite to the right —*n.* **3.** the left hand or part **4.** *Pol.* reforming or radical party (*also* **left wing**) —*adv.* **5.** on or toward the left —**'leftist** *n./a.* (person) of the political left —**left-handed** *a.* **1.** using left hand with greater ease than right **2.** performed with left hand **3.** designed for use by left hand **4.** awkward, clumsy **5.** ironically ambiguous **6.** turning from right to left; anticlockwise —*adv.* **7.** with left hand —**left-hander** *n.*

left[2] (left) *pt./pp. of* LEAVE[1]

leg (leg) *n.* **1.** one of limbs on which person or animal walks, runs, stands **2.** part of garment covering leg **3.** anything which supports, as leg of table **4.** stage of journey —**'leggings** *pl.n.* covering of leather or other material for legs —**'leggy** *a.* **1.** long-legged **2.** (of plants) straggling —**'legroom** *n.* room to move legs comfortably, as in aircraft —**give someone a leg up** help someone to get over an obstacle or difficulty —**has not a leg to stand on** has no facts to support argument

legacy ('legəsi) *n.* **1.** anything left by will, bequest **2.** thing handed down to successor —**lega'tee** *n.* recipient of legacy

legal ('lēgəl) *a.* of, appointed or permitted by, or based on, law —**legal'ese** *n.* conventional language in which legal documents are written —**'legalism** *n.* strict adherence to law, *esp.* letter of law rather than its spirit —**legal'istic** *a.* —**le'gality** *n.* —**legali'zation** *n.* —**'legalize** *vt.* make legal —**'legally** *adv.* —**legal tender** currency that creditor must by law accept in redemption of debt

legate ('legit) *n.* ambassador, *esp.* papal —**'legateship** *n.* —**le'gation** *n.* **1.** diplomatic minister and his staff **2.** his residence

legato (li'gätō) *adv. Mus.* smoothly

legend ('lejənd) *n.* **1.** traditional story or myth **2.** traditional literature **3.** famous, renowned, person or event **4.** inscription —**'legendary** *a.*

legerdemain (lejərdə'mān) *n.* **1.** juggling, conjuring, sleight of hand **2.** trickery

leghorn ('leghörn, 'legörn, 'legərn) *n.* **1.** kind of straw **2.** hat made of it **3.** (**L-**) breed of fowls

legible ('lejəbəl) *a.* easily read —**legi'bility** *n.* —**'legibly** *adv.*

legion ('lējən) *n.* **1.** body of infantry in Roman army **2.** various modern military bodies **3.** association of veterans **4.** large number —*a.* **5.** very numerous —**'legionary** *a./n.* —**legion'naire** *n.* (*oft.* **L-**) member of military force or association —**Legionnaire's disease** bacterial infection of the lungs

legislator ('lejislātər) *n.* maker of laws —**'legislate** *vi.* make laws —**legis'lation** *n.* **1.** act of legislating **2.** laws which are made —**'legislative** *a.* —**'legislature** *n.* body that makes laws of a state —**legislative assembly** (*oft.* **L- A-**) single-chamber legislature in most Canad. provinces

legitimate (li'jitimit) *a.* **1.** born in wedlock **2.** lawful, regular **3.** fairly deduced —*vt.* (li'jitimāt) **4.** make legitimate —**le'gitimacy** *n.* —**le'gitimateness** *n.* —**legiti'mation** *n.* —**le'gitimism** *n.* —**le'gitimist** *n.* supporter of hereditary title to monarchy —**le'gitimize** *vt.* legitimate

leguan ('legōōän) *n.* large S Afr. lizard

legume ('legyōōm, li'gyōōm) *n.* **1.** any plant bearing capsules or pods with opposing sutures which can open to discharge its seeds **2.** the fruit, including table vegetables such as peas and beans, from such a plant —**le'guminous** *a.* (of plants) pod-bearing

lei (lā, 'lāē) *n.* garland of flowers

leishmaniasis (lēshmə'nīəsis) *n.* any of number of conditions caused by infection with parasites transmitted by blood-sucking sandflies which have bitten infected mammals

leisure ('lēzhər) *n.* **1.** freedom from occupation **2.** spare time —**'leisured** *a.* with plenty of spare time —**'leisurely** *a.* **1.** deliberate, unhurried —*adv.* **2.** slowly

leitmotiv *or* **leitmotif** ('lītmōtēf) *n. Mus.* recurring theme associated with some person, situation, thought

L.E.M. (lem) lunar excursion module

lemming ('leming) *n.* rodent of arctic regions

lemon ('lemən) *n.* **1.** pale yellow acid fruit **2.** tree bearing it **3.** its color **4.** *sl.* useless or defective person or thing —**lemon'ade** *n.* drink made from lemon juice —**lemon sole** European flatfish highly valued as food

lemur ('lēmər) *n.* nocturnal animal like monkey

lend (lend) *vt.* **1.** give temporary use of **2.** let out for hire or interest **3.** give, bestow (**lent, 'lending**) —**'lender** *n.* —**lends itself to** is suitable for

length (lengkth, length) *n.* **1.** quality of being long **2.** measurement from end to end **3.** duration **4.** extent **5.** piece of a certain length —**'lengthen** *v.* **1.** make, become longer **2.** draw out —**'lengthily** *adv.* —**'lengthwise** *adv./a.* in direction of length —**'lengthy** *a.* (over)long —**at length 1.** in full detail **2.** at last

lenient ('lēniənt) *a.* mild, tolerant, not strict —**'lenience** *or* **'leniency** *n.* —**'leniently** *adv.*

lenity ('leniti) *n.* **1.** mercy **2.** clemency

lens (lenz) *n.* piece of glass or similar material with one or both sides curved, used to converge or diverge light rays in cameras, eyeglasses, telescopes *etc.* (*pl.* **-es**)

lent (lent) *pt./pp. of* LEND

Lent (lent) *n.* period of fasting from Ash Wednesday to Easter Eve —**'Lenten** *a.* of, in or suitable to Lent

lentil ('lentil) *n.* edible seed of leguminous plant —**len'ticular** *a.* like lentil

lento ('lentō) *adv. Mus.* slowly

Leo ('lēō) *n.* (lion) 5th sign of zodiac, operative *c.* Jul. 22nd–Aug. 21st

leonine ('lēənīn) *a.* like a lion

leopard ('lepərd) *n.* large, tawny black-spotted feline of southern Asia and Africa (**'leopardess** *fem.*)

leotard ('lēətärd) *n.* tight-fitting garment covering most of body, worn by acrobats, dancers *etc.*

leper ('lepər) *n.* **1.** one suffering from leprosy **2.** person ignored or despised —**'leprosy** *n.* chronic infectious disease characterized by formation of painful inflamed nodules beneath skin and disfigurement and wasting of infected parts (*also* **Hansen's disease**) —ˈ**leprous** *a.*

Lepidoptera (lepiˈdoptərə) *pl.n.* order of insects with four wings covered with fine gossamer scales, as moths, butterflies —**lepiˈdopterist** *n.* person who studies or collects moths and butterflies —**lepiˈdopterous** *a.*

leprechaun (ˈleprəkon, -kōn) *n.* mischievous elf of Irish folklore

lepton (ˈlepton) *n. Phys.* any of group of elementary particles and their antiparticles, that participate in weak interactions

leptospiroses (leptōspīˈrōsēz) *pl.n.* group of diseases caused by strains of corkscrew-shaped microorganisms, found in bodies of wild rodents or domestic animals, which contaminate water and soil with urine

lesbian (ˈlezbiən) *n.* homosexual woman —ˈ**lesbianism** *n.*

lese-majesty (ˈlēzˈmajisti) *n.* **1.** treason **2.** taking of liberties

lesion (ˈlēzhən) *n.* **1.** injury **2.** injurious change in texture or action of an organ of the body

Lesotho (ləˈsōtō) *n.* country in Africa bounded west by the Orange Free State, north by the Orange Free State and Natal, east by Natal and East Griqualand and south by the Cape Province

less (les) *comp. of* LITTLE *a.* **1.** not so much —*n.* **2.** smaller part, quantity **3.** a lesser amount —*adv.* **4.** to a smaller extent or degree —*prep.* **5.** after deducting, minus —ˈ**lessen** *v.* diminish, reduce —ˈ**lesser** *a.* **1.** less **2.** smaller **3.** minor

-less (*comb. form*) **1.** without; lacking, as in *speechless* **2.** not able to (do something) or not able to be (done, performed *etc.*), as in *countless*

lessee (leˈsē) *n.* one to whom lease is granted

lesson (ˈlesən) *n.* **1.** installment of course of instruction **2.** content of this **3.** experience that teaches **4.** portion of Scripture read in church

lessor (ˈlesōr, leˈsōr) *n.* grantor of a lease

lest (lest) *conj.* **1.** in order that not **2.** for fear that

let[1] (let) *vt.* **1.** allow, enable, cause to **2.** allow to escape **3.** grant use of for rent, lease —*vi.* **4.** be leased —*v. aux.* **5.** used to express a proposal, command, threat, assumption (**let, ˈletting**) —ˈ**letdown** *n.* disappointment —**let-up** *n. inf.* lessening, abatement —**let down 1.** lower **2.** disappoint **3.** undo, shorten and resew (hem) **4.** untie (long hair that is bound up) and allow to fall loose **5.** deflate —**let off 1.** allow to disembark or leave **2.** explode or fire (bomb *etc.*) **3.** excuse from (work *etc*) **4.** *inf.* allow to get away without expected punishment *etc.* —**let's** let us: used to express suggestion *etc.* by speaker to himself and hearers

let[2] (let) *n.* **1.** hindrance **2.** in some games, minor infringement or obstruction of ball requiring replaying of point

lethal (ˈlēthəl) *a.* deadly

lethargy (ˈlethərji) *n.* **1.** apathy, want of energy or interest **2.** unnatural drowsiness —**leˈthargic** *a.* —**leˈthargically** *adv.*

letter (ˈletər) *n.* **1.** alphabetical symbol **2.** written message **3.** strict meaning, interpretation —*pl.* **4.** literature **5.** knowledge of books —*vt.* **6.** mark with, in, letters —ˈ**lettered** *a.* learned —**letter bomb** explosive device in envelope, detonated when envelope is opened —ˈ**letterhead** *n.* sheet of writing paper printed with one's address, name *etc.* —**letter-perfect** *a.* **1.** correct in every detail **2.** (of speaker *etc.*) knowing one's text perfectly —ˈ**letterpress** *n.* matter printed from a raised surface —**letter of credit** letter issued by bank entitling bearer to draw funds from that bank or its agencies —**letter of the law** exact requirements of law, in contrast to spirit or purpose of legislation

lettuce (ˈletis) *n.* plant grown for use in salad

leucocyte (ˈlo͞okəsīt) *n. see* LEUKOCYTE —**leucocyˈtosis** *n.* abnormal increase of white blood cells in the blood

leucoma (lo͞oˈkōmə) *n. see* LEUKOMA

leucotomy (lo͞oˈkotəmi) *n. see* **lobotomy** *at* LOBE

leukemia (lo͞oˈkēmiə) *n.* a progressive blood disease marked by the uncontrollable increase of leukocytes

leukocyte *or* **leucocyte** (ˈlo͞okəsīt) *n.* any white blood corpuscle

leukoma *or* **leucoma** (lo͞oˈkōmə) *n.* dense, white opacity of the cornea

leukopenia (lo͞okəˈpēniə) *n.* the abnormal decrease of white blood cells in the blood

leukoplakia (lo͞okōˈplākiə) *n.* whitish, thickened plaques of mucous membranes developed in response to irritation

leukorrhea (lo͞okəˈrēə) *n.* whitish discharge from female genital tract

Lev. *Bible* Leviticus

Levant (liˈvant) *n. old name for* area of E Mediterranean now occupied by Lebanon, Syria and Israel —**leˈvanter** *n.* (*sometimes* **L-**) **1.** easterly wind in W Mediterranean area **2.** inhabitant of the Levant —**Levantine** (ˈlevəntīn) *a./n.*

levee[1] (ˈlevi, ləˈvē, ləˈvā) *n.* **1.** Brit. sovereign's reception for men only **2.** *Hist.* reception held by sovereign on rising

levee[2] (ˈlevi) *n.* **1.** natural or artificial river embankment **2.** landing place

level (ˈlevəl) *a.* **1.** horizontal **2.** even in surface **3.** consistent in style, quality *etc.* —*n.* **4.** horizontal line or surface **5.** instrument for showing, testing horizontal plane **6.** position on scale **7.** standard, grade **8.** horizontal passage in mine —*vt.* **9.** make level **10.** bring to same level **11.** knock down **12.** aim (gun or accusation *etc.*) —*vi.* **13.** *inf.* (*esp. with* with) be honest, frank —'**leveler** *or* '**leveller** *n.* advocate of social equality —**level-headed** *a.* not apt to be carried away by emotion

lever ('levər) *n.* **1.** rigid bar pivoted about a fulcrum to transfer a force with mechanical advantage **2.** handle pressed, pulled *etc.* to operate something —*vt.* **3.** pry, move with lever —'**leverage** *n.* **1.** action, power of lever **2.** influence **3.** power to accomplish something **4.** advantage

leveret ('levərit, -vrit) *n.* young hare

leviathan (li'vīəthən) *n.* **1.** sea monster **2.** anything huge or formidable

levitation (levi'tāshən) *n.* the power of raising a solid body into the air supernaturally —'**levitate** *v.* (cause to) do this

Leviticus (li'vitikəs) *n. Bible* 3rd book of the O.T., setting out the feasts and codifying the rules of behavior for Jews

levity ('leviti) *n.* **1.** inclination to make a joke of serious matters, frivolity **2.** facetiousness

levulose ('levyəlōs) *n.* fructose

levy ('levi) *vt.* **1.** impose (tax) **2.** raise (troops) ('**levied,** '**levying**) —*n.* **3.** imposition or collection of taxes **4.** enrolling of troops **5.** amount, number levied

lewd (lōōd) *a.* **1.** lustful **2.** indecent —'**lewdly** *adv.* —'**lewdness** *n.*

lexicon ('leksikon, -kən) *n.* dictionary —'**lexical** *a.* —**lexi'cographer** *n.* writer of dictionaries —**lexi'cography** *n.*

ley (lē, lā) *n.* **1.** arable land temporarily under grass **2.** line joining two prominent points in landscape, thought to be line of prehistoric track (*also* **ley line**)

Leyden jar ('līdən) *Phys.* early type of capacitor consisting of glass jar with lower part of inside and outside coated with tinfoil

L.F. *Rad.* low frequency

LG *or* **L.G.** Low German

Lhasa apso ('läsə) small dog of Tibetan breed with long straight coat

Li *Chem.* lithium

liable ('līəbəl) *a.* **1.** answerable **2.** exposed **3.** subject **4.** likely —**lia'bility** *n.* **1.** state of being liable, obligation **2.** hindrance, disadvantage —*pl.* **3.** debts

liaison ('lēəzon, li'āzon) *n.* **1.** union **2.** connection **3.** intimacy, *esp.* secret —**li'aise** *vi.* communicate and maintain contact —**liaison officer** officer who keeps units of troops in touch

liana (li'änə) *n.* climbing plant of tropical forests

liar ('līər) *n. see* LIE[2]

lib (lib) *inf.* liberation

lib. 1. liber (*Lat.,* book) **2.** librarian **3.** library

Lib. Liberal

libation (lī'bāshən) *n.* drink poured as offering to the gods

libel ('lībəl) *n.* **1.** published statement falsely damaging person's reputation —*vt.* **2.** defame falsely —'**libelous** *or* '**libellous** *a.* defamatory

liberal ('libərəl, 'librəl) *a.* **1.** (*also* **L-**) of political party favoring democratic reforms or favoring individual freedom **2.** generous **3.** tolerant **4.** abundant **5.** (of education) designed to develop general cultural interests —*n.* **6.** one who has liberal ideas or opinions —'**liberalism** *n.* —**libe'rality** *n.* munificence —'**liberalize** *v.* —'**liberally** *adv.*

liberate ('libərāt) *vt.* set free —**libe'ration** *n.* —'**liberator** *n.*

Liberia (lī'bēəriə) *n.* country in Africa bounded south by the Atlantic, west by Sierra Leone, north by Guinea and east by the Ivory Coast —**Li'berian** *n./a.*

libertarian (libər'teriən) *n.* **1.** believer in freedom of thought *etc.,* or in free will —*a.* **2.** of, like a libertarian —**liber'tarianism** *n.*

libertine ('libərtēn) *n.* **1.** morally dissolute person —*a.* **2.** dissolute —'**libertinism** *n.*

liberty ('libərti) *n.* **1.** freedom —*pl.* **2.** rights, privileges —**at liberty 1.** free **2.** having the right —**take liberties** be presumptuous

libido (li'bēdō) *n.* **1.** life force **2.** emotional craving, *esp.* of sexual origin (*pl.* **-s**) —**libidinous** (li'bidinəs) *a.* lustful

Libra ('lībrə, 'lēbrə) *n.* **1.** (balance) 7th sign of zodiac, operative *c.* Sept. 22nd–Oct. 22nd **2.** (**l-**) *Hist.* a pound weight (*pl.* **librae** ('lībrē, 'lēbrī))

library ('lībreri) *n.* **1.** room, building where books are kept **2.** collection of books, phonograph records *etc.* **3.** reading, writing room in house —**li'brarian** *n.* keeper of library —**li'brarianship** *n.*

libretto (li'bretō) *n.* words of an opera (*pl.* **-s, -ti** (-tē)) —**li'brettist** *n.*

Libya ('libiə) *n.* country in Africa bounded north by the Mediterranean, west by Tunisia and Algeria, south by Niger and Chad and east by Sudan and Egypt —'**Libyan** *n./a.*

lice (līs) *n., pl. of* LOUSE

license ('līsəns) *n.* **1.** (document, certificate giving) leave, permission **2.** excessive liberty **3.** dissoluteness **4.** writer's, artist's transgression of rules of his art (*oft.* **poetic license**) —*vt.* **5.** grant license to —**licen'see** *n.* holder of license —**li'centiate** *n.* one licensed to practice art, profession

licentious (lī'senchəs) *a.* **1.** dissolute **2.** sexually immoral —**li'centiously** *adv.*

lichee ('līchē) *n. see* LITCHI

lichen ('līkən) *n.* plant organism formed by symbiotic association of an alga and a fungus —'**lichened** *a.* —**liche'nology** *n.* —**lichen planus** ('plānəs) skin disorder marked by flat-topped, violet-colored, pinhead-sized raised spots

lich-gate (lich-) *n. see* LYCH-GATE

licit ('lisit) *a. rare* lawful

lick (lik) *vt.* **1.** pass the tongue over **2.** touch lightly **3.** *sl.* defeat **4.** *sl.* flog, beat —*n.* **5.** act of licking **6.** small amount (*esp.* of paint *etc.*) **7.** block or natural deposit of salt or other chemical licked by cattle *etc.* **8.** *inf.* speed —ˈ**licking** *n. sl.* beating

licorice (ˈlikərish, ˈlikrish; -ris) *n.* **1.** leguminous plant of Europe and Asia **2.** sweet-tasting dried root of this plant used in confectionery, medicine *etc.* —**licorice stick** *sl.* clarinet

lid (lid) *n.* **1.** movable cover **2.** cover of the eye **3.** *sl.* hat

lido (ˈlēdō) *n.* pleasure center with swimming and boating (*pl.* **-s**)

lie[1] (lī) *vi.* **1.** be horizontal, at rest **2.** be situated **3.** remain, be in certain state or position **4.** exist, be found **5.** recline (**lay, lain,** ˈ**lying**) —*n.* **6.** state (of affairs *etc.*) **7.** direction

lie[2] (lī) *vi.* **1.** make false statement (**lied,** ˈ**lying**) —*n.* **2.** deliberate falsehood —ˈ**liar** *n.* person who tells lies —**give the lie to** disprove —**white lie** untruth said without evil intent

Liechtenstein (ˈliktənshtīn, -stīn) *n.* country in Europe bounded east by Austria and west by Switzerland —ˈ**Liechtensteiner** *n.*

Liederkranz (ˈlēdərkrants) *n.* trade name for creamy cheese with edible russet crust which develops a robust odor as it changes from white to cream

lief (lēv, lēf) *adv.* **1.** *rare* gladly, willingly —*a. obs.* **2.** ready; glad **3.** dear, beloved

liege (lēj) *a.* **1.** bound to render or receive feudal service **2.** faithful —*n.* **3.** lord **4.** vassal, subject

lien (lēn, ˈlēən) *n.* right to hold another's property until claim is met

lieu (lo͞o) *n.* place —**in lieu (of)** instead (of)

lieutenant (lo͞oˈtenənt) *n.* **1.** deputy **2.** fire- or police-department officer below captain **3.** commissioned officer in armed forces ranking below one specified, as in *lieutenant colonel, lieutenant commander, lieutenant general* **4.** navy or coastguard officer below lieutenant commander and above lieutenant junior grade —**first lieutenant** officer in army, air force or marine corps ranking below captain and above second lieutenant —**second lieutenant** commissioned officer of the lowest rank in army, air force or marine corps —**lieutenant governor 1.** elected U.S. state official substituting for governor when necessary **2. C** representative of Crown in province appointed by federal government —**lieutenant junior grade** navy or coastguard officer above ensign

life (līf) *n.* **1.** active principle of existence of animals and plants, animate existence **2.** time of its lasting **3.** history of such existence **4.** way of living **5.** vigor, vivacity (*pl.* **lives**) —ˈ**lifeless** *a.* **1.** dead **2.** inert **3.** dull —**life belt** buoyant device to keep afloat person in danger of drowning —ˈ**lifeblood** *n.* **1.** blood, considered as vital to life **2.** essential or animating force —ˈ**lifeboat** *n.* boat for rescuing people at sea, escaping from sinking ship *etc.* —**life buoy** buoyant device for keeping person afloat in emergency —ˈ**lifeguard** *n.* person at beach or pool to protect bathers —**life insurance** insurance providing for payment of specified sum to named beneficiary on death of policyholder —**life jacket** sleeveless jacket worn to keep person afloat —ˈ**lifelike** *a.* closely resembling life —ˈ**lifeline** *n.* **1.** line thrown or fired aboard vessel for hauling in hawser for breeches buoy **2.** line by which deep-sea diver is raised or lowered **3.** vital line of access or communication —ˈ**lifelong** *a.* lasting a lifetime —**life preserver** life belt; life jacket —**life-size** *or* **life-sized** *a.* representing actual size —**life style** particular attitudes, habits *etc.* of person or group —ˈ**lifetime** *n.* length of time person, animal or object lives or functions

lift (lift) *vt.* **1.** raise in position, status, mood, volume *etc.* **2.** take up and remove **3.** exalt spiritually **4.** *inf.* steal —*vi.* **5.** rise —*n.* **6.** raising apparatus **7.** act of lifting **8.** ride in automobile *etc.* as passenger **9.** air force acting at right angles on aircraft wing, so lifting it **10.** *inf.* feeling of cheerfulness, uplift —ˈ**liftoff** *n.* **1.** initial movement of rocket from launching pad **2.** instant at which this occurs —**lift off** (of rocket) leave launching pad

ligament (ˈligəmənt) *n.* band of tissue joining bones —ˈ**ligature** *n.* **1.** anything which binds **2.** thread for tying up artery **3.** *Print.* character of two or more joined letters

light[1] (līt) *a.* **1.** of, or bearing little weight **2.** not severe **3.** gentle **4.** easy, requiring little effort **5.** trivial **6.** (of industry) producing small, usu. consumer goods, using light machinery —*adv.* **7.** in light manner —*vi.* **8.** alight (from vehicle *etc.*) **9.** (*with* on *or* upon) come by chance (upon) (ˈ**lighted, lit** *pt./pp.*) —ˈ**lighten** *vt.* reduce, remove (load *etc.*) —ˈ**lightly** *adv.* —ˈ**lightness** *n.* —**lights** *pl.n.* lungs of butchered animals —**light-fingered** *a.* having nimble fingers, *esp.* for thieving or picking pockets —**light flyweight** amateur boxer weighing not more than 48 kg (106 lbs.) —**light-headed** *a.* **1.** dizzy, inclined to faint **2.** delirious —**light-hearted** *a.* carefree —**light heavyweight 1.** professional boxer weighing 72.5–79.5 kg (160–175 lbs.) **2.** amateur boxer weighing 75–81 kg (165–179 lbs.) **3.** wrestler weighing usu. 87–97 kg (192–214 lbs.) —**light middleweight** amateur boxer weighing 67–71 kg (148–157 lbs.) —**light-minded** *a.* frivolous —**light muscat** dry or semisweet white table wine —ˈ**lightweight** *n./a.* (person) of little weight or importance —**light welterweight** amateur boxer weighing 60–63.5 kg (132–140 lbs.)

light[2] (līt) *n.* **1.** electromagnetic radiation by which things are visible **2.** source of this, lamp **3.** window **4.** mental vision **5.** light part of anything **6.** means or act of setting fire to something **7.** understanding —*pl.* **8.** traffic lights —*a.* **9.** bright **10.** pale, not dark —*vt.* **11.** set burning **12.** give light to —*vi.* **13.** take fire **14.** brighten (**'lighted, lit** *pt./pp.*) —**'lighten** *vt.* give light to —**'lighting** *n.* apparatus for supplying artificial light —**'lightning** *n.* visible discharge of electricity in atmosphere —**'lighthouse** *n.* tower with a light to guide ships —**light year** *Astron.* distance light travels in one year, about six million million miles

lighter ('līt**ə**r) *n.* **1.** device for lighting cigarettes *etc.* **2.** flat-bottomed boat for unloading ships

ligneous ('ligniəs) *a.* of, or of the nature of, wood —**'lignite** *n.* woody or brown coal

lignin ('lignin) *n.* organic substance which forms characteristic part of all woody fibers

lignum vitae ('lignəm 'vīti) *Lat.* **1.** tropical tree **2.** its extremely hard wood

like[1] (līk) *a.* **1.** resembling **2.** similar to **3.** characteristic of —*adv.* **4.** in the manner of —*pron.* **5.** similar thing —**'likelihood** *n.* probability —**'likely** *a.* **1.** probable **2.** hopeful, promising —*adv.* **3.** probably —**'liken** *vt.* compare —**'likeness** *n.* **1.** resemblance **2.** portrait —**'likewise** *adv.* **1.** in addition; moreover; also **2.** in like manner

like[2] (līk) *vt.* find agreeable, enjoy, love —**'likable** *or* **'likeable** *a.* —**'liking** *n.* **1.** fondness **2.** inclination, taste

-like (*comb. form*) **1.** resembling, similar to, as in *lifelike* **2.** having characteristics of, as in *childlike*

lilac ('līlək) *n.* **1.** shrub of the olive family cultivated for its panicles of highly scented flowers in white, pink or pale purple **2.** a variable color ranging near pale purple —*a.* **3.** of this color

Lilliputian (lili'pyōōshən) *a.* **1.** diminutive —*n.* **2.** midget, pygmy

lilt (lilt) *vi.* **1.** (of melody) have a lilt **2.** move lightly —*n.* **3.** rhythmical effect in music, swing —**'lilting** *a.*

lily ('lili) *n.* any of a genus of the lily family, erect bulbous perennials with showy flowers in late summer that are native to the northern hemisphere and cultivated widely in a variety of sizes —**lily-livered** *a.* cowardly; timid —**lily pad** floating leaf of water lily —**lily-white** *a.* **1.** of a pure white **2.** *inf.* pure; irreproachable —**lily of the valley** low perennial plant with fragrant, white bell-like flowers

Lima ('lēmə) *n.* word used in communications for the letter *l*

limb[1] (lim) *n.* **1.** arm or leg **2.** wing **3.** branch of tree —**limbed** *a.* **1.** having limbs **2.** having specified number or kind of limbs

limb[2] (lim) *n.* **1.** edge of sun or moon **2.** edge of sextant

limber[1] ('limbər) *n.* detachable front of gun carriage

limber[2] ('limbər) *a.* pliant, lithe —**limber up** loosen stiff muscles by exercises

lily of the valley

limbo[1] ('limbō) *n.* **1.** (*oft.* **L-**) *R.C.Ch.* region intermediate between Heaven and Hell for the unbaptized **2.** intermediate, indeterminate place or state (*pl.* **-s**)

limbo[2] ('limbō) *n.* W Indian dance in which dancers pass under a bar (*pl.* **-s**)

Limburger ('limbərgər) *n.* a semihard, fermented, cow's-milk cheese with a full flavor orig. from Belgium

lime[1] (līm) *n.* **1.** any of certain calcium compounds used in making fertilizer, cement —*vt.* **2.** treat (land) with lime —**'limy** *a.* of, like or smeared with birdlime —**'limekiln** *n.* kiln in which calcium carbonate is calcined to produce quicklime —**'limelight** *n.* **1.** formerly, intense white light obtained by heating lime **2.** glare of publicity —**'limestone** *n.* sedimentary rock used in building

lime[2] (līm) *n.* small, greenish-yellow citrus fruit —**'limey** *n. sl.* Englishman —**'limy** *a.* —**lime juice** juice of lime prepared as drink

lime[3] (līm) *n.* tree, the linden

limerick ('limərik) *n.* self-contained, nonsensical, humorous verse of five lines

limit ('limit) *n.* **1.** utmost extent or duration **2.** boundary —*vt.* **3.** restrict, restrain, bound —**'limitable** *a.* —**limi'tation** *n.* —**'limited** *a.* **1.** restricted; confined **2.** without scope; narrow **3.** (of governing powers *etc.*) restricted or checked, by or as if by constitution, laws or assembly —**'limitless** *a.* —**limited liability** liability limited by law

limn (lim) *vt.* paint; depict; draw —**limner** ('limnər, 'limər) *n.*

limo ('limō) *n. inf.* limousine (*pl.* **-s**)

limousine ('liməzēn, limə'zēn) *n.* large, luxurious automobile

limp[1] (limp) *a.* without firmness or stiffness —**'limply** *adv.*

limp[2] (limp) *vi.* **1.** walk lamely —*n.* **2.** limping gait

limpet ('limpit) *n.* shellfish which sticks tightly to rocks

limpid ('limpid) *a.* **1.** clear **2.** translucent —**lim'pidity** *n.* —**'limpidly** *adv.*

linchpin ('linchpin) *n.* **1.** pin to hold wheel on its axle **2.** essential person or thing

Lincoln ('lingkən) *n.* **Abraham.** the 16th President of the U.S. (1861-65)

linden ('lindən) *n.* deciduous tree with fragrant flowers, the lime

line (līn) *n.* **1.** long narrow mark **2.** stroke made with pen *etc.* **3.** continuous length without breadth **4.** row **5.** series, course **6.** telephone connection **7.** progeny **8.** province of activity **9.** shipping company **10.** railroad track **11.** any class of goods **12.** cord **13.** string **14.** wire **15.** advice, guidance —*vt.* **16.** cover inside of **17.** mark with lines **18.** bring into line **19.** be, form border, edge of —'**linage** *n.* number of lines in piece of written or printed matter —**lineage** ('liniij) *n.* descent from, descendants of an ancestor —**lineal** ('liniəl) *a.* **1.** of lines **2.** in direct line of descent —**lineament** ('liniəmənt) *n.* feature —**linear** ('liniər) *a.* of, in lines —**lineation** (lini'āshən) *n.* **1.** marking with lines **2.** arrangement of or division into lines —'**liner** *n.* large ship or aircraft of passenger line —'**lining** *n.* covering for inside of garment *etc.* —**Linear B** form of writing employing syllabic characters used from the 15th to the 12th centuries B.C. for documents in the Mycenean language —**linear measure** system of units for measurement of length —'**linebacker** *n.* defensive football player immediately behind the line of scrimmage —**line drawing** drawing made with lines only —'**lineman** *n.* football player in the forward line —**line printer** electromechanical device that prints a line of characters at a time —**line score** score of baseball game showing hits, runs and errors of each team —'**linesman** *n.* in some sports, official who helps referee, umpire —**line-up** *n.* **1.** row or arrangement of people or things assembled for particular purpose **2.** members of team taking part in a game —**get a line on** obtain all relevant information about —**line of credit** maximum credit allowed to borrower or holder of charge card —**line of fire** flight path of missile discharged from firearm —**line up 1.** form, put into or organize line-up **2.** produce, organize and assemble **3.** align —**out of line** inappropriate

linen ('linin) *a.* **1.** made of flax —*n.* **2.** cloth made of flax **3.** linen articles collectively **4.** sheets, tablecloths *etc.*; shirts (orig. made of linen)

ling[1] (ling) *n.* slender food fish

ling[2] (ling) *n.* heather

-ling (*comb. form*) **1.** person or thing associated with group, activity or quality specified, as in *nestling, underling* **2.** diminutive, as in *duckling*

linger ('linggər) *vi.* delay, loiter, remain long

lingerie (länzhə'rä) *n.* women's underwear or nightwear

lingo ('linggō) *n. inf.* language, speech, *esp.* applied to dialects (*pl.* **-es**)

lingua franca ('linggwə 'frangkə) language used for communication between people of different mother tongues (*pl.* **lingua francas, linguae francae** ('linggwē 'frangkē))

lingual ('linggwəl) *a.* **1.** of the tongue or language —*n.* **2.** sound made by the tongue, as *d, l, t* —'**linguist** *n.* one skilled in languages or language study —**lin'guistic** *a.* of languages or their study —**lin'guistics** *pl.n.* (*with sing. v.*) study, science of language

liniment ('linimənt) *n.* embrocation

link (lingk) *n.* **1.** ring of a chain **2.** connection **3.** unit of measure, 7.92 in. —*vt.* **4.** join with, as with, link **5.** intertwine —*vi.* **6.** be so joined —'**linkage** *n.* —'**linkman** *n.* presenter of television or radio program consisting of number of outside broadcasts from different locations

links (lingks) *pl.n.* golf course

linnet ('linit) *n.* songbird of finch family

linoleum (li'nōliəm) *n.* floor covering of burlap with smooth, hard, decorative coating of powdered cork, linseed oil *etc.* —**linoleum block 1.** design carved in relief on mounted linoleum **2.** a print from this

linseed ('linsēd) *n.* seed of flax plant —**linseed oil** yellow oil extracted from it

linsey-woolsey (linzi'wo͝olzi) *n.* rough fabric of linen warp and coarse wool or cotton filling

lint (lint) *n.* **1.** shreds or bits of thread **2.** staple cotton fiber

lintel ('lintəl) *n.* top piece of door or window

lion ('līən) *n.* large social feline of Africa and S Asia with a shaggy mane in the adult male ('**lioness** *fem.*) —'**lionize** *vt.* treat as celebrity —**lion-hearted** *a.* brave —**the lion's share** largest portion

lip (lip) *n.* **1.** either edge of the mouth **2.** edge or margin **3.** *sl.* impudence —**lip-reading** *n.* method of understanding spoken words by interpreting movements of speaker's lips —**lip service** insincere tribute or respect —'**lipstick** *n.* cosmetic preparation in stick form, for coloring lips —**lip sync** (singk) synchronizing lip movements with recorded sound

lipoma (lī'pōmə) *n.* slow-growing tumor of fat tissue

lipotropic factors (līpō'trōpik) substances preventing or reversing abnormal accumulation of fat in the liver

liqueur (li'kyo͞oər -'ko͞oər; *Fr.* lē'kœr) *n.* alcoholic liquor flavored and sweetened

liquid ('likwid) *a.* **1.** fluid, not solid or gaseous **2.** flowing smoothly **3.** (of assets) in form of money or easily converted into money —*n.* **4.** matter in fluid phase in which surface is free, volume is definite, and shape determined by the container —**lique'faction** *n.* —'**liquefy** *v.* make or become liquid —**li'quescence** *n.* —**li'quescent** *a.* tending to become liquid —ˈ**liquidize** *v.* —ˈ**liquidizer** *n.* kitchen appliance with blades for puréeing vegetables, blending liquids *etc.* (*also* ˈ**blender**) —**liquid air** air reduced to liquid state on application of increased pressure at low temperature —**liquid crystal display** display of numbers, *esp.* in electronic calculator, using cells containing a liquid with crystalline properties, that change their reflectivity when an electric field is applied to them —**liquid gold** suspension of finely-divided gold particles in oil, used chiefly in gilding —**liquid measure** system of units for measuring volumes of liquids or their containers

liquidate (ˈlikwidāt) *vt.* **1.** pay (debt) **2.** arrange affairs of and dissolve (company) **3.** wipe out, kill —**liquiˈdation** *n.* **1.** process of clearing up financial affairs **2.** state of being bankrupt —ˈ**liquidator** *n.* official appointed to liquidate business —**liˈquidity** *n.* state of being able to meet financial obligations

liquor (ˈlikər) *n.* **1.** alcoholic drink **2.** juice produced by boiling food

liquorice (ˈlikərish, ˈlikrish; -ris) *n. see* LICORICE

lira (ˈlēərə; *It.* ˈlēra) *n.* monetary unit of Italy and Turkey (*pl.* **lire** (ˈlēəri; *It.* ˈlērā), **-s**)

lisle (līl) *n.* fine hand-twisted cotton thread

lisp (lisp) *vi.* **1.** speak with faulty pronunciation of 's' and 'z' **2.** speak falteringly —*n.* **3.** such pronunciation or speech

lissome *or* **lissom** (ˈlisəm) *a.* **1.** supple **2.** agile

list[1] (list) *n.* **1.** inventory, register **2.** catalog **3.** edge of cloth —*pl.* **4.** field for combat —*vt.* **5.** place on list —**list price** selling price of merchandise as quoted in catalog or advertisement

list[2] (list) *vi.* **1.** (of ship) lean to one side —*n.* **2.** inclination of ship

listen (ˈlisən) *vi.* try to hear, attend (to) —ˈ**listener** *n.*

listless (ˈlistlis) *a.* indifferent, languid —ˈ**listlessly** *adv.*

lit (lit) *pt./pp. of* LIGHT[1], LIGHT[2]

litany (ˈlitəni) *n.* prayer with responses from congregation

litchi

litchi, lichee, *or* **lychee** (ˈlīchē) *n.* **1.** Chinese tree with red edible fruits **2.** fruit of this tree, which has whitish juicy pulp (*also* **litchi nut**)

liter (ˈlētər) *n.* unit of volume in metric system, exactly 1000 cm^3, $1m^3$ or 10 deciliters or approximately 0.908 dry quart and 1.057 liquid quarts

literal (ˈlitərəl) *a.* **1.** according to sense of actual words, not figurative **2.** exact in wording **3.** of letters —ˈ**literalism** *n.* **1.** disposition to take words and statements in literal sense **2.** literal or realistic portrayal in art or literature —ˈ**literally** *adv.*

literate (ˈlitərit) *a.* **1.** able to read and write **2.** educated —*n.* **3.** literate person —ˈ**literacy** *n.* —**literati** (litəˈrätē) *pl.n.* scholarly, literary people

literature (ˈlitərichōōər, ˈlitri-; -chər) *n.* **1.** books and writings, *esp.* of particular country, period or subject **2.** *inf.* printed material —**liteˈrarily** *adv.* —ˈ**literary** *a.* of or learned in literature

lithe (līdh, lith) *a.* supple, pliant —ˈ**lithesome** *a.* lissome, supple

lithium (ˈlithiəm) *n. Chem.* metallic element *Symbol* Li, at. wt. 6.9, at. no. 3

litho (ˈlīthō) *n.* **1.** lithography **2.** lithograph (*pl.* **-s**) —*a.* **3.** lithographic —*adv.* **4.** lithographically

litho- *or before vowel* **lith-** (*comb. form*) stone, as in *lithograph*

lithography (liˈthogrəfi) *n.* method of printing from metal or stone block using the antipathy of grease and water —ˈ**lithograph** *n.* **1.** print so produced —*vt.* **2.** print thus —**liˈthographer** *n.* —**lithoˈgraphic** *a.*

lithotomy (lithˈotəmi) *n.* operation to remove stones from urinary bladder

litigate (ˈlitigāt) *vt.* **1.** contest in law —*vi.* **2.** carry on a lawsuit —ˈ**litigant** *n./a.* (person) conducting a lawsuit —**litiˈgation** *n.* lawsuit —**litigious** (liˈtijəs) *a.* **1.** given to engaging in lawsuits **2.** disputatious

litmus (ˈlitməs) *n.* blue dye turned red by acids and restored to blue by alkali —**litmus paper**

litotes (ˈlītətēz) *n.* ironical understatement for rhetorical effect (*pl.* **-tes**)

Litt.D. *or* **Lit.D.** **1.** Doctor of Letters **2.** Doctor of Literature

litter (ˈlitər) *n.* **1.** untidy refuse **2.** odds and ends **3.** young of animal produced at one birth **4.** straw *etc.* as bedding for animals **5.** portable couch **6.** kind of stretcher for wounded —*v.* **7.** strew (with) litter **8.** give birth to (young) —ˈ**litterbug** *n. sl.* person who drops refuse in public places

little (ˈlitəl) *a.* **1.** small, not much (**less, least**) —*n.* **2.** small quantity —*adv.* **3.** to a small extent **4.** not much or often **5.** not at all (**less, least**) —**Little Bear, Little Dipper** Ursa Minor —**little people** *Folklore* small supernatural beings, such as leprechauns —**little slam** *Bridge* bidding for and winning twelve tricks (*also* **small slam**)

littoral (ˈlitərəl) *a.* **1.** pert. to the seashore —*n.* **2.** coastal district

liturgy (ˈlitərji) *n.* prescribed form of public worship —**liˈturgical** *a.*

live[1] (liv) *v.* **1.** have life **2.** pass one's life **3.** continue in life **4.** continue, last **5.** dwell **6.** feed —ˈ**livable** *or* ˈ**liveable** *a.* **1.** suitable for living in **2.** tolerable —ˈ**liver** *n.* person who lives in specified way —ˈ**living** *n.* **1.** action of being in life **2.** people now alive **3.** way of life **4.** means of living **5.** church benefice —**living room** room in house used for relaxation and entertainment —**living wage** wage adequate to maintain person and his family in reasonable comfort —**live down** overcome (past misdeeds)

live[2] (līv) *a.* **1.** living, alive **2.** active, vital **3.** flaming **4.** (of rail *etc.*) carrying electric current **5.** (of broadcast) transmitted during the actual performance —ˈ**liveliness** *n.* —ˈ**lively** *a.* brisk, active, vivid —ˈ**liven** *vt.* (*esp. with* up) make (more) lively —**live oak** evergreen oak of southeastern U.S. —ˈ**livestock** *n.* domestic animals —**live wire 1.** wire carrying electric current **2.** able, very energetic person

livelihood (ˈlīvlihŏŏd) *n.* **1.** means of living **2.** subsistence, support

livelong (ˈlivˈlong) *a.* lasting throughout the whole day

liver (ˈlivər) *n.* **1.** organ secreting bile **2.** animal liver as food —ˈ**liverish** *a.* **1.** unwell, as from liver upset **2.** cross, touchy, irritable —**liver fluke** parasitic flatworm inhabiting bile ducts of sheep, cattle *etc.* —**liver sausage** sausage made of pork liver and seasonings —**liver spots** light brown spots on skin of usu. middle-aged or older persons —**liverwurst** (ˈlivərwərst) *n.* liver sausage

liverwort (ˈlivərwərt) *n.* simple land plant resembling moss but lacking radial symmetry

livery (ˈlivəri) *n.* **1.** distinctive dress of person or group, *esp.* servant(s) **2.** allowance of food for horses **3.** a livery stable —ˈ**liveried** *a.* (*esp.* of servants *etc.*) wearing livery —ˈ**liveryman** *n.* member of a London guild —**livery stable** stable where horses are kept at a charge or hired out

lives (līvz) *n., pl. of* LIFE

livid (ˈlivid) *a.* **1.** of a bluish pale color **2.** discolored, as by bruising **3.** *inf.* angry, furious

lizard (ˈlizərd) *n.* four-footed reptile

L.L. 1. Late Latin **2.** Low Latin

llama (ˈlămə) *n.* woolly animal used as beast of burden in S Amer.

LL.B. Bachelor of Laws

LL.D. Doctor of Laws

Lloyd's (loidz) *n.* association of London underwriters originally concerned with marine insurance and shipping information and now subscribing a variety of insurance policies and publishing daily list (**Lloyd's List**) of shipping data and news

loach (lōch) *n.* carplike freshwater fish

load (lōd) *n.* **1.** burden **2.** amount usu. carried at once **3.** actual load carried by vehicle **4.** resistance against which engine has to work **5.** amount of electrical energy drawn from a source —*vt.* **6.** put load on or into **7.** charge (gun) **8.** weigh down —ˈ**loaded** *a.* **1.** carrying a load **2.** (of dice) dishonestly weighted **3.** biased **4.** (of question) containing hidden trap or implication **5.** *sl.* wealthy **6.** *sl.* drunk

loadstar (ˈlōdstär) *n. see* **lodestar** *at* LODE

loadstone (ˈlōdstōn) *n. see* **lodestone** *at* LODE

loaf[1] (lōf) *n.* **1.** mass of bread as baked **2.** shaped mass of food (*pl.* **loaves**)

loaf[2] (lōf) *vi.* idle, loiter —ˈ**loafer** *n.* idler

Loafer (ˈlōfər) *n.* trade name for shoe resembling a moccasin

loam (lōm) *n.* fertile soil

loan (lōn) *n.* **1.** act of lending **2.** thing lent **3.** money borrowed at interest **4.** permission to use —*vt.* **5.** lend, grant loan of

loath *or* **loth** (lōth, lōdh) *a.* unwilling, reluctant —**loathe** (lōdh) *vt.* hate, abhor —**loathing** (ˈlōdhing) *n.* **1.** disgust **2.** repulsion —**loathsome** (ˈlōthsəm, ˈlōdhsəm) *a.* disgusting

loaves (lōvz) *n., pl. of* LOAF[1]

lob (lob) *n.* **1.** in tennis *etc.*, shot pitched high in air —*v.* **2.** throw, pitch (shot) thus (**-bb-**)

lobby (ˈlobi) *n.* **1.** corridor into which rooms open **2.** passage or room in legislative building, *esp.* houses of parliament of Britain and Aust., to which the public has access or one of two rooms where members indicate their vote **3.** group which tries to influence members of lawmaking assembly —ˈ**lobbying** *n.* frequenting lobby to collect news or influence members —ˈ**lobbyist** *n.* person employed by particular interest to lobby

lobe (lōb) *n.* **1.** any rounded projection **2.** subdivision of body organ **3.** soft, hanging part of ear —ˈ**lobar** *a.* of lobe —ˈ**lobate** *a.* **1.** having or resembling lobes **2.** (of birds) having separate toes each fringed with weblike lobe —**lobed** *a.* —**loˈbectomy** *n.* surgical removal of a lobe of an organ —**loˈbotomy** *n.* any of various surgical methods of treating certain mental disorders (*also* **prefrontal lobotomy, leucotomy**)

lobelia (lōˈbēlyə, -liə) *n.* garden plant with blue, red or white flowers

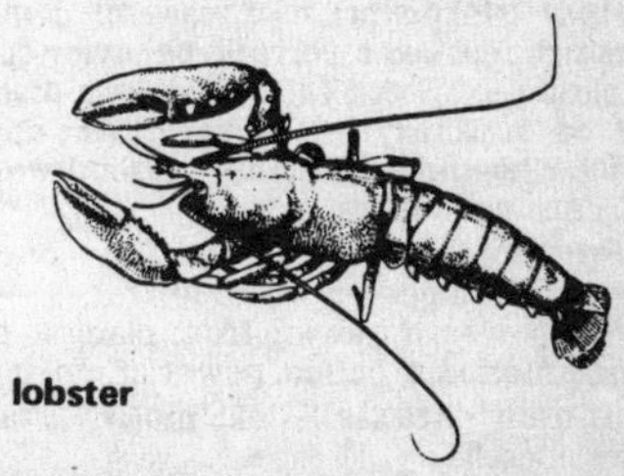
lobster

lobster (ˈlobstər) *n.* shellfish with long tail and claws, turning red when boiled

lobworm (ˈlobwərm) *n.* lugworm

local (ˈlōkəl) *a.* **1.** of, existing in particular place **2.** confined to a definite spot, district or part of the body **3.** of place —*n.* **4.** person belonging to a district **5.** *inf.* (nearby) pub —**locale** (lōˈkal) *n.* scene of event —**loˈcality** *n.* **1.** place, situation **2.** district —ˈ**localize** *vt.* assign, restrict to definite place —ˈ**locally** *adv.* —**local anesthetic** anesthetic which produces insensibility in one part of body —**local color** behavior *etc.* characteristic of a certain region or time, introduced into novel *etc.* to supply realism

locate (ˈlōkāt, lōˈkāt) *vt.* **1.** attribute to a place **2.** find the place of **3.** situate —**loˈcation** *n.* **1.** placing **2.** situation **3.** site of motion-picture production away from studio **4.** **SA** Black Afr. or Colored township —**locative** (ˈlokətiv) *a./n.* (of) grammatical case denoting 'place where'

loch (lok, lokh) *n.* Scottish lake or long narrow bay

loci (ˈlōsī) *n., pl. of* LOCUS

lock[1] (lok) *n.* **1.** appliance for fastening door, lid *etc.* **2.** mechanism for firing gun **3.** enclosure in river or canal for moving boats from one level to another **4.** extent to which vehicle's front wheels will turn **5.** appliance to check the revolution of a wheel **6.** interlocking **7.** block, jam —*vt.* **8.** fasten, make secure with lock **9.** join firmly **10.** cause to become immovable **11.** embrace closely —*vi.* **12.** become fixed or united **13.** become immovable —ˈ**locker** *n.* small cupboard with lock —ˈ**lockkeeper** *n.* person tending lock on river or canal —ˈ**locknut** *n.* second nut used on top of first on bolt to prevent it shaking loose —ˈ**lockout** *n.* exclusion of workmen by employers as means of coercion —ˈ**locksmith** *n.* one who makes and mends locks —ˈ**lockup** *n. sl.* prison —**lock, stock and barrel** completely

lock[2] (lok) *n.* tress of hair

locket (ˈlokit) *n.* small hinged pendant for portrait *etc.*

lockjaw (ˈlokjö) *n.* tetanus

loco (ˈlōkō) *inf.* locomotive

locoism (ˈlōkōizəm) *n.* disease of domestic livestock marked by erratic behavior caused by eating locoweed (*also* **loco, loco disease**) —ˈ**loco** *a.* crazy —ˈ**locoweed** *n.* any of various leguminous plants of southwestern U.S. causing locoism

locomotive (lōkəˈmōtiv) *n.* **1.** engine for pulling carriages on railroad tracks —*a.* **2.** having power of moving from place to place —**locoˈmotion** *n.* action, power of moving

locomotor ataxia (lōkəˈmōtər əˈtaksiə) tabes dorsalis

locum tenens (ˈlōkəm ˈtēnenz) *Lat.* substitute, *esp.* for doctor or clergyman during absence (*pl.* **locum tenentes** (təˈnentēz)) (*also* ˈ**locum**) —**locum tenency**

locus (ˈlōkəs) *n.* **1.** exact place or locality **2.** *Math.* any set of points that satisfy certain conditions and no points that do not **3.** position of gene in a chromosome (*pl.* **loci**)

locust (ˈlōkəst) *n.* destructive winged insect —**locust bean** bean-shaped fruit of locust tree —**locust tree 1.** N. Amer. leguminous tree having prickly branches, white flowers and reddish-brown seed pods **2.** the carob

locution (lōˈkyōōshən) *n.* **1.** a phrase **2.** speech **3.** mode or style of speaking

lode (lōd) *n.* a vein of ore —ˈ**lodestar** *or* ˈ**loadstar** *n.* Pole Star —ˈ**lodestone** *or* ˈ**loadstone** *n.* magnetic iron ore

loden (ˈlōdən) *n.* **1.** thick soft woolen cloth used for outer clothing **2.** dull grayish green

lodge (loj) *n.* **1.** house, cabin used seasonally or occasionally, *eg* for hunting, skiing **2.** gatekeeper's house **3.** meeting place of branch of Freemasons *etc.* **4.** the branch **5.** beaver's or otter's dwelling —*vt.* **6.** house **7.** deposit **8.** bring (a charge *etc.*) against someone —*vi.* **9.** live in another's house at fixed charge **10.** come to rest —ˈ**lodger** *n.* —ˈ**lodging** *n.* rented room(s) in another person's house —ˈ**lodgment** *or* ˈ**lodgement** *n.* lodging, being lodged

loft (loft) *n.* **1.** space between top story and roof **2.** gallery in church *etc.* —*vt.* **3.** send (golf ball *etc.*) high —ˈ**loftily** *adv.* haughtily —ˈ**loftiness** *n.* —ˈ**lofty** *a.* **1.** of great height, elevated **2.** haughty

log[1] (log) *n.* **1.** portion of felled tree stripped of branches **2.** detailed record of voyages, time traveled *etc.* of ship, aircraft *etc.* **3.** apparatus used formerly for measuring ship's speed —*vt.* **4.** keep a record of **5.** travel (specified distance, time) (**-gg-**) —ˈ**logger** *n.* lumberjack —ˈ**logging** *n.* cutting and transporting logs to river —ˈ**logbook** *n.*

log[2] (log) *n.* logarithm

logan (ˈlōgən) *n.* **C** *see* BOGAN

loganberry (ˈlōgənberi) *n.* **1.** trailing prickly plant, cross between raspberry and blackberry **2.** its purplish-red fruit

logarithm (ˈlogəridhəm) *n.* the exponent of the power to which a fixed number is to be raised to produce a given number —**logaˈrithmic** *a.*

loggerhead (ˈlogərhed) *n.* —**at loggerheads** quarreling, disputing

loggia (ˈlōjiə, ˈlōjä) *n.* covered, arcaded gallery (*pl.* **-s, loggie** (ˈlōjā))

logic (ˈlojik) *n.* **1.** art or philosophy of reasoning **2.** reasoned thought or argument **3.** coherence of various facts, events *etc.* —ˈ**logical** *a.* **1.** of logic **2.** according to reason **3.** reasonable **4.** apt to reason correctly —ˈ**logically** *adv.* —**loˈgician** *n.*

logistics (lōˈjistiks, lə-) *pl.n.* (*with sing. or pl. v.*) **1.** the transport, housing and feeding of troops **2.** organization of any project, operation —**lo'gistical** *a.*

logo ('logō) *n.* company emblem or motto (*pl.* **-s**)

Logos ('lōgos, -gōs) *n.* the Divine Word incarnate, Christ

-logue *or* **-log** (*comb. form*) **1.** speech or discourse of particular kind, as in *monologue* **2.** field of specialist study, as in *pedagogue, sinologue*

-logy (*n. comb. form*) **1.** science or study of, as in *musicology* **2.** writing, discourse or body of writings, as in *trilogy, phraseology, martyrology* —**-logical** *or* **-logic** (*a. comb. form*) —**-logist** (*n. comb. form*)

loin (loin) *n.* **1.** part of body between ribs and hip **2.** cut of meat from this —*pl.* **3.** hips and lower abdomen —'**loincloth** *n.* garment covering loins only

loiter ('loitər) *vi.* **1.** dawdle, hang about **2.** idle —'**loiterer** *n.*

loll (lol) *vi.* **1.** sit, lie lazily **2.** (*esp.* of the tongue) hang out —*vt.* **3.** hang out (tongue)

lollipop *or* **lollypop** ('lolipop) *n.* hard candy on small wooden stick

London ('lundən) *n.* the capital of England and of the United Kingdom —**London broil** broiled flank steak cut across the grain in thin slices

lone (lōn) *a.* solitary —'**loneliness** *n.* —'**lonely** *a.* **1.** sad because alone **2.** unfrequented **3.** solitary, alone —'**loner** *n. inf.* one who prefers to be alone —'**lonesome** *a.* lonely

long[1] (long) *a.* **1.** having length, *esp.* great length, in space or time **2.** extensive **3.** protracted —*adv.* **4.** for a long time —'**longbow** *n. esp.* in medieval England, large powerful hand-drawn bow —**long division** process of dividing one number by another and putting steps down in full —**long-drawn-out** *a.* overprolonged, extended —'**longhair** *a. inf.* of intellectuals or their tastes, *esp.* preferring classical music to jazz *etc.* (*also* **long-haired**) —'**longhand** *n.* writing of words, letters *etc.* in full —**long-headed** *a.* astute; shrewd; sagacious —**long johns** *inf.* underpants with long legs —**long jump** athletic contest in which competitors try to cover farthest distance possible with running jump from fixed board or mark —**long-playing** *a.* (of record) to be played at 33 $^{1}/_{3}$ revolutions per minute, a microgroove record —**long-range** *a.* **1.** of the future **2.** able to travel long distances without refueling **3.** (of weapons) designed to hit distant target —**long shot** competitor, undertaking, bet *etc.* with small chance of success —**long-standing** *a.* existing for a long time —**long-term** *a.* **1.** lasting or extending over a long time **2.** *Fin.* maturing after a long period —**long ton** the imperial ton (2240 lbs.) —**long wave** radio wave with wavelength greater than 1000 meters —**long-winded** *a.* tediously loquacious —**the long and the short of it** all that needs to be said

long[2] (long) *vi.* have keen desire, yearn —'**longing** *n.* yearning

long. longitude

longeron ('lonjəron) *n.* long spar running fore and aft in body of aircraft

longevity (lon'jeviti) *n.* long existence or life

longitude ('lonjityo͞od, -'to͞od) *n.* distance east or west from Greenwich meridian —**longi'tudinal** *a.* **1.** of length or longitude **2.** lengthwise

longshoreman ('longshōrmən) *n.* person who loads and unloads ships at a seaport

loofah ('lo͞ofə) *n.* **1.** pod of plant used as sponge **2.** the plant

look (lo͝ok) *vi.* **1.** direct, use eyes **2.** face **3.** seem **4.** (*with* for) search **5.** (*with* for) hope **6.** (*with* after) take care (of) —*n.* **7.** looking **8.** view **9.** search **10.** (*oft. pl.*) appearance —**looker-on** *n.* spectator —**looking glass** mirror —'**lookout** *n.* **1.** guard **2.** place for watching **3.** prospect **4.** watchman **5.** *inf.* worry, concern —**good looks** beauty —**look after** tend —**look down on** despise

loom[1] (lo͞om) *n.* **1.** machine for weaving **2.** middle part of oar

loom[2] (lo͞om) *vi.* **1.** appear dimly **2.** seem ominously close **3.** assume great importance

loon[1] (lo͞on) *n.* any of several large fish-eating diving birds of N Amer. best known for its haunting cry

loon[2] (lo͞on) *n. inf.* stupid, foolish person —'**loony** *a./n.* —**loony bin** *inf.* mental hospital

loop (lo͞op) *n.* **1.** figure made by curved line crossing itself **2.** similar rounded shape in cord, rope *etc.* crossed on itself **3.** contraceptive coil **4.** aerial maneuver in which aircraft describes complete circle **5.** *Figure skating* curve crossing itself made on single edge —*vt.* **6.** make loop in or of —**loop line** railroad line which leaves, then rejoins, main line

loophole ('lo͞ophōl) *n.* **1.** means of escape, of evading rule without infringing it **2.** vertical slit in wall, *esp.* for defense

loose (lo͞os) *a.* **1.** not tight, fastened, fixed or tense **2.** slack **3.** vague **4.** dissolute —*vt.* **5.** free **6.** unfasten **7.** slacken —*vi.* **8.** (*with* off) shoot, let fly (bullet *etc.*) —'**loosely** *adv.* —'**loosen** *v.* make or become loose —'**looseness** *n.* —**loose-jointed** *a.* **1.** supple and easy in movement **2.** loosely built; with ill-fitting joints —**loose-leaf** *a.* (of binder *etc.*) capable of being opened to allow removal and addition of pages —**on the loose 1.** free **2.** *inf.* on a spree

loot (lo͞ot) *n./v.* plunder

lop[1] (lop) *vt.* (*usu. with* off) **1.** cut away (twigs and branches) from tree **2.** chop (off) (**-pp-**)

lop[2] (lop) *vi.* hang limply (**-pp-**) —**lop-eared** *a.* having drooping ears —'**lop'sided** *a.* with one side lower than the other, badly balanced

lope (lōp) *vi.* run with long, easy strides

loquacious (lō'kwāshəs) *a.* talkative —**loquacity** (lō'kwasiti) *n.*

loquat ('lōkwot) *n.* **1.** Asian evergreen tree of rose family **2.** its yellow edible fruit

lor (lör) *interj. nonstandard* exclamation of surprise or dismay

loran ('lörən) *n.* radio navigation system operating over long distances

lord (lörd) *n.* **1.** British nobleman, peer of the realm **2.** feudal superior **3.** one ruling others **4.** owner **5.** God —*v.* **6.** be domineering (*esp. in* **lord it over someone**) —'**lordliness** *n.* —'**lordly** *a.* **1.** imperious, proud **2.** fit for a lord —'**lordship** *n.* **1.** rule, ownership **2.** domain **3.** title of some noblemen —**Lord Mayor** mayor in City of London and certain other boroughs —**Lord Spiritual** archbishop or bishop in the House of Lords (*pl.* **Lords Spiritual**) —**Lord Temporal** peer who is not archbishop or bishop in the House of Lords (*pl.* **Lords Temporal**) —**the Lord's Day** Christian Sabbath; Sunday —**the Lord's Prayer** prayer taught by Jesus Christ to his disciples (*also* **Our Father, Pater'noster**) —**the Lord's Supper** *see* **Holy Communion** *at* HOLY

lordosis (lör'dōsis) *n.* exaggeration of normal forward curve of lower spine (*also* **hollow back**)

lore (lör) *n.* **1.** learning **2.** body of facts and traditions

lorgnette (lör'nyet) *n.* pair of eyeglasses mounted on long handle

lorikeet ('lörikēt) *n.* small parrot

loris ('löris) *n.* tree-dwelling, nocturnal Asian animal (*pl.* **-ris**)

lorn (lörn) *a. poet.* **1.** abandoned **2.** desolate

lory ('löri), **lowry,** *or* **lowrie** *n.* small, brightly colored parrot of Aust. and Indonesia

lose (lōōz) *vt.* **1.** be deprived of, fail to retain or use **2.** let slip **3.** fail to get **4.** (of clock *etc.*) run slow by (specified amount) **5.** be defeated in —*vi.* **6.** suffer loss (**lost** *pt./pp.*, '**losing** *pr.p.*) —'**loser** *n.* **1.** person or thing that loses **2.** *inf.* person or thing that seems destined to fail *etc.* —**loss** (los) *n.* **1.** a losing **2.** what is lost **3.** harm or damage resulting from losing —**lost** (lost) *a.* **1.** unable to be found **2.** unable to find one's way **3.** bewildered **4.** not won **5.** not utilized

lot (lot) *pron.* **1.** great number —*n.* **2.** collection **3.** large quantity **4.** share **5.** fate **6.** destiny **7.** item at auction **8.** one of a set of objects used to decide something by chance (*esp. in* **to cast lots**) **9.** area of land —*pl.* **10.** *inf.* great numbers or quantity —*adv.* **11.** *inf.* a great deal

loth (lōth, lōdh) *a. see* LOATH

lotion ('lōshən) *n.* liquid for washing wounds, improving skin *etc.*

lotos ('lōtəs) *n. see* LOTUS

lottery ('lotəri) *n.* **1.** method of raising funds by selling tickets and prizes by chance **2.** gamble

lotto ('lotō) *n.* game of chance like bingo

lotus *or* **lotos** ('lōtəs) *n.* **1.** legendary plant whose fruits induce forgetfulness when eaten **2.** Egyptian water lily —**lotus-eater** *n. Gk myth.* one of people encountered by Odysseus in N Afr. who lived in indolent forgetfulness, drugged by fruit of legendary lotus —**lotus position** seated cross-legged position in yoga

loud (lowd) *a.* **1.** strongly audible **2.** noisy **3.** obtrusive —'**loudly** *adv.* —**loud'mouth** *n. inf.* person who brags or talks too loudly —**loud'mouthed** *a.* —'**loud'speaker** *n.* instrument for converting electrical signals into sound audible at a distance

lough (lok, lokh) *n.* in Ireland, lake

Louisiana (looēzi'anə) *n.* West South Central state of the U.S., admitted to the Union in 1812. Abbrev.: **LA** (with ZIP code)

lounge (lownj) *vi.* **1.** sit, lie, walk or stand in a relaxed manner —*n.* **2.** living room of house **3.** general waiting, relaxing area in airport, hotel *etc.* —'**lounger** *n.* loafer

loup cervier (lōō sər'vyā) *see* **Canada lynx** *at* CANADA

lour ('lowər) *see* LOWER

lourie ('lowri) *n.* S Afr. bird with bright plumage

louse (lows) *n.* parasitic insect (*pl.* **lice**) —**lousy** ('lowzi) *a.* **1.** *sl.* nasty, unpleasant **2.** (*with* with) *sl.* (too) generously provided, thickly populated (with) **3.** *sl.* bad, poor **4.** having lice

lout (lowt) *n.* crude, oafish person —'**loutish** *a.*

louver ('lōōvər) *n./a.* **1.** (of) one of a set of boards or panes set parallel and slanted to admit air but not rain —*n.* **2.** ventilating structure of these

lovage ('luvij) *n.* European umbelliferous plant used for flavoring food

love (luv) *n.* **1.** warm affection **2.** benevolence **3.** charity **4.** sexual passion **5.** sweetheart **6.** *Tennis etc.* score of nothing —*vt.* **7.** admire passionately **8.** delight in —*vi.* **9.** be in love —'**lovable** *or* '**loveable** *a.* —'**loveless** *a.* —'**loveliness** *n.* —'**lovely** *a.* beautiful, delightful —'**lover** *n.* —'**loving** *a.* **1.** affectionate **2.** tender —'**lovingly** *adv.* —'**lovebird** *n.* **1.** small parrot **2.** *inf.* lover (*usu. pl.*) —**love child** *euphemistic* illegitimate child, bastard —**love-in-a-mist** *n.* garden plant with pale blue flowers —**love letter** —'**lovelorn** *a.* forsaken by, pining for a lover —**love seat** armchair or sofa for two persons —'**lovesick** *a.* pining or languishing because of love —'**lovesickness** *n.* —**loving cup** bowl formerly passed round at banquet —**make love** (to) have sexual intercourse (with)

low[1] (lō) *a.* **1.** not tall, high or elevated **2.**

humble **3.** coarse, vulgar **4.** dejected **5.** ill **6.** not loud **7.** moderate **8.** cheap —**'lower** *vt.* **1.** cause, allow to descend **2.** move down **3.** degrade —*vi.* **4.** diminish —*a.* **5.** below in position or rank **6.** at an early stage, period of development —**'lowliness** *n.* —**'lowly** *a.* modest, humble —**low beam** short range of automobile headlight —**'low'born** *a. rare* of ignoble or common parentage —**low'bred** *a.* vulgar —**'lowbrow** *n./a.* (one) having no intellectual or cultural interests —**'lowdown** *n. inf.* inside information —**low-down** *a. inf.* base, shabby, dishonorable —**lower-case** *a.* **1.** of small letters —*vt.* **2.** print with lower-case letters —**lower class** social stratum having lowest position in social hierarchy —**lower-class** *a.* **1.** of lower class **2.** inferior; vulgar —**lower house** one of houses of bicameral legislature, usu. the larger and more representative (*also* **lower chamber**) —**lower plant** nonflowering plant —**low frequency** radio waveband with frequency between 30 and 300 kilohertz —**Low German** language of N Germany, spoken *esp.* in rural areas (*also* **'Plattdeutsch**) —**low-grade** *a.* of inferior quality —**low-key** *a.* subdued, restrained, not intense —**lowland** ('lōlənd) *n.* low-lying country —**lowlander** ('lōləndər) *n.* —**Low Mass** Mass that has simplified ceremonial form and is spoken rather than sung —**low-minded** *a.* having vulgar or crude mind and character —**low profile** position or attitude characterized by deliberate avoidance of prominence or publicity —**low season** period of low activity, *esp.* of resorts —**low-tension** *a.* carrying, operating at low voltage —**low tide 1.** tide at lowest level or time at which it reaches this **2.** lowest point —**low water 1.** low tide **2.** state of any stretch of water at its lowest level

low[2] (lō) *n.* **1.** cry of cattle, bellow —*vi.* **2.** (of cattle) utter their cry, bellow

lower *or* **lour** ('lowər) *vi.* **1.** look gloomy or threatening, as sky **2.** scowl —*n.* **3.** scowl, frown

lowrie ('lowri) *n. see* LORY

lox[1] (loks) *n.* smoked salmon

lox[2] (loks) *n. short for* liquid oxygen, *esp.* when used as oxidizer for rocket fuels

loyal ('loiəl) *a.* faithful, true to allegiance —**'loyalist** *n.* —**'Loyalist** *n.* **C** United Empire Loyalist —**'loyally** *adv.* —**'loyalty** *n.* —**loyal toast** toast drunk in pledging allegiance to sovereign, usu. after meal

lozenge ('lozinj) *n.* **1.** rhombus, diamond figure **2.** small medicated candy shaped like this

LP long-playing (record)

LPG *or* **LP gas** liquid petroleum gas

Lr *Chem.* lawrencium

LSD 1. lysergic acid diethylamide (hallu'cinogenic drug) **2.** librae, solidi, denarii (*Lat.*, pounds, shillings, pence)

Lt. Lieutenant

ltd. Limited

Lu *Chem.* lutetium

lubber ('lubər) *n.* **1.** clumsy fellow **2.** unskilled seaman

lubricate ('lo͞obrikāt) *vt.* **1.** oil, grease **2.** make slippery —**'lubricant** *n.* substance used for this —**lubri'cation** *n.* —**'lubricator** *n.* —**lu'bricity** *n.* **1.** slipperiness, smoothness **2.** lewdness

lucent ('lo͞osənt) *a.* bright, shining

lucerne (lo͞o'sərn) *n.* alfalfa

lucid ('lo͞osid) *a.* **1.** clear **2.** easily understood **3.** sane —**lu'cidity** *or* **'lucidness** *n.* —**'lucidly** *adv.*

Lucite ('lo͞osīt) *n.* trade name for acrylic resin that is used as a glass substitute in sheet form

luck (luk) *n.* **1.** fortune, good or bad **2.** good fortune **3.** chance —**'luckily** *adv.* fortunately —**'luckless** *a.* having bad luck —**'lucky** *a.* having good luck

lucre ('lo͞okər) *n. usu. facetious* money, wealth —**'lucrative** *a.* very profitable —**filthy lucre** *inf.* money

Luddite ('ludīt) *n.* **1.** orig. member of band of workmen organized to destroy machinery believing that its use led to unemployment **2.** person opposed to technological advance

ludicrous ('lo͞odikrəs) *a.* absurd, laughable, ridiculous

luff (luf) *n.* **1.** the part of fore-and-aft sail nearest mast —*v.* **2.** sail (ship) into wind so that sails flap —*vi.* **3.** (of sails) flap

lug[1] (lug) *v.* drag (something heavy) with effort (**-gg-**)

lug[2] (lug) *n.* **1.** projection, tag serving as handle or support **2.** *inf.* ear

luggage ('lugij) *n.* traveler's trunks and other baggage

lugger ('lugər) *n.* working boat (*eg* fishing, prawning lugger) orig. fitted with lugsail

lugsail ('lugsāl, -səl) *n.* oblong sail fixed on yard which hangs slanting on mast

lugubrious (lo͞o'go͞obriəs) *a.* mournful, doleful, gloomy —**lu'gubriously** *adv.*

lugworm ('lugwərm) *n.* large worm used as bait

Luke (lo͝ok) *n. Bible* 3rd book of the N.T.: synoptic gospel presenting Christ as a man among men in this account written by the author of Acts

lukewarm ('lo͞ok'wôrm) *a.* **1.** moderately warm, tepid **2.** unenthusiastic

lull (lul) *vt.* **1.** soothe, sing (to sleep) **2.** make quiet —*vi.* **3.** become quiet, subside —*n.* **4.** brief time of quiet in storm *etc.* —**lullaby** ('luləbī) *n.* lulling song, *esp.* for children

lumbar ('lumbər) *a.* relating to body between lower ribs and hips —**lumbago** (lum'bāgō) *n.* rheumatism in the lower part of the back

lumber ('lumbər) *n.* **1.** disused articles, useless rubbish **2.** sawn timber —*vi.* **3.** move heavily —*vt.* **4.** *inf.* burden with something unpleasant —**'lumberjack** *n.* man who fells trees and prepares logs for transport to mill —**'lumberyard** *n.* place where lumber and other building materials are sold

lumen ('lo͞omin) *n.* SI unit of luminous flux (*pl.* **-s, -mina** (-minə))

luminous ('lo͞ominəs) *a.* **1.** bright **2.** shedding light **3.** glowing **4.** lucid —**'luminary** *n.* **1.** learned person **2.** heavenly body giving light —**lumi'nescence** *n.* emission of light at low temperatures by process (*eg* chemical) not involving burning —**lumi'nosity** *n.*

lump (lump) *n.* **1.** shapeless piece or mass **2.** swelling **3.** large sum —*vt.* **4.** (*oft. with* together) throw (together) in one mass or sum —*vi.* **5.** move heavily —**'lumpish** *a.* **1.** clumsy **2.** stupid —**'lumpy** *a.* **1.** full of lumps **2.** uneven —**lump sum** relatively large sum of money, paid at one time —**lump it** *inf.* put up with something

lunar ('lo͞onər) *a.* relating to the moon —**lunar module** module used to carry astronauts from spacecraft to surface of moon and back

lunatic ('lo͞onətik) *a.* **1.** insane —*n.* **2.** insane person —**'lunacy** *n.* —**lunatic asylum** *old name for* institution for mentally ill —**lunatic fringe** extreme, radical section of group *etc.*

lunch (lunch) *n.* **1.** meal taken in the middle of the day —*v.* **2.** eat, entertain to lunch —**luncheon** ('lunchən) *n.* a lunch

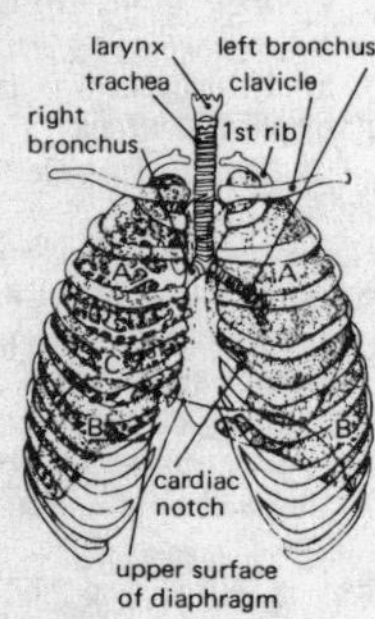

lungs

A upper lobes
B lower lobes
C middle lobe of right lung

lung (lung) *n.* one of the two organs of respiration in vertebrates —**'lungfish** *n.* type of fish with air-breathing lung —**'lungworm** *n.* parasitic worm infesting lungs of some animals —**'lungwort** *n.* flowering plant

lunge (lunj) *vi.* **1.** thrust with sword *etc.* —*n.* **2.** such thrust **3.** sudden movement of body, plunge

lupine[1] *or* **lupin** ('lo͞opin) *n.* leguminous plant with tall spikes of flowers

lupine[2] ('lo͞opīn) *a.* like a wolf

lupus ('lo͞opəs) *n.* skin disease characterized by skin lesions —**lupus erythematosus** (erithēmə'tōsəs) inflammatory disease of the connective or supporting tissues of the body —**lupus vulgaris** (vul'gäris) tuberculosis of the skin

lurch (lərch) *n.* **1.** sudden roll to one side —*vi.* **2.** stagger —**leave in the lurch** leave in difficulties

lurcher ('lərchər) *n.* crossbred dog trained to hunt silently

lure (lo͝oər) *n.* **1.** something which entices **2.** bait **3.** power to attract —*vt.* **4.** entice **5.** attract

Lurex ('lo͝oəreks, 'lo͞or-) *n.* trade name for metallic thread made from plastic-coated aluminum

lurid ('lo͞orid) *a.* **1.** vivid in shocking detail, sensational **2.** pale, wan **3.** lit with unnatural glare —**'luridly** *adv.*

lurk (lərk) *vi.* lie hidden —**'lurking** *a.* (of suspicion) not definite

luscious ('lushəs) *a.* **1.** sweet, juicy **2.** extremely pleasurable or attractive

lush[1] (lush) *a.* (of grass *etc.*) luxuriant and juicy, fresh

lush[2] (lush) *n. sl.* **1.** heavy drinker **2.** alcoholic —**'lushy** *a.*

lust (lust) *n.* **1.** strong desire for sexual gratification **2.** any strong desire —*vi.* **3.** have passionate desire —**'lustful** *a.* —**'lustily** *adv.* —**'lusty** *a.* vigorous, healthy

luster *or* **lustre** ('lustər) *n.* **1.** gloss, sheen **2.** splendor **3.** renown **4.** glory **5.** glossy material **6.** metallic pottery glaze —**'lustrous** *a.* shining, luminous

lustration (lus'trāshən) *n.* purification by sacrifice —**'lustral** *a.* used in lustration —**'lustrate** *vt.*

lute[1] (lo͞ot) *n.* plucked stringed musical instrument with body in the shape of a halved pear from which extends a fretted angled neck —**'lutenist** *or* **'lutist** *n.*

lute[2] (lo͞ot) *n.* **1.** composition to make joints airtight —*vt.* **2.** close with lute

lutetium (lo͞o'tēshiəm) *n. Chem.* metallic element *Symbol* Lu, at. wt. 175.0, at. no. 71

Lutheran ('lo͞othərən) *n.* **1.** member of Protestant Christian denomination believing that salvation is by faith alone through grace —*a.* **2.** of Lutheran Church —**'Lutheranism** *n.*

lutz (lo͞ots) *n. Ice-skating* jump from one skate with complete turn in air and return to other skate

lux (luks) *n.* SI unit of illumination (*pl.* **lux**)

luxe (lo͝oks, luks; *Fr.* lüks) *n. see* DE LUXE

Luxembourg *or* **Luxemburg** ('luksəmbərg) *n.* country in Europe bounded west by Belgium, south by France and east by West Germany —**'Luxembourger** *or* **'Luxemburger** *n.* —**Luxem'bourgian** *or* **Luxem'burgian** *a.*

luxury ('lukshəri, 'lugzhəri) *n.* **1.** possession

and use of costly, choice things for enjoyment **2.** enjoyable but not necessary thing **3.** comfortable surroundings —**luxuriance** (lug'zhŏŏriəns, luk'shŏŏr-) *n.* abundance, proliferation —**luxuriant** (lug'zhŏŏriənt, luk'shŏŏr-) *a.* **1.** growing thickly **2.** abundant —**luxuriantly** (lug'zhŏŏriəntli, luk'shŏŏr-) *adv.* —**luxuriate** (lug'zhŏŏriāt, luk'shŏŏr-) *vi.* **1.** indulge in luxury **2.** flourish profusely **3.** take delight —**luxurious** (lug'zhŏŏriəs, luk'shŏŏr-) *a.* **1.** fond of luxury **2.** self-indulgent **3.** sumptuous —**luxuriously** (lug'zhŏŏriəsli, luk'shŏŏr-) *adv.*

lyceum (lī'sēəm) *n.* public building for concerts *etc.*

lychee ('līchē) *n. see* LITCHI

lych-gate ('lichgāt) *n.* roofed gate of churchyard (*also* **lich-gate**)

Lycra ('līkrə) *n.* trade name for synthetic elastic polyurethane fiber

lyddite ('lidīt) *n.* powerful explosive used in shells

lye (lī) *n.* water made alkaline with wood ashes *etc.* for use as cleaning agent

lying ('līing) *pr.p. of* LIE[1], LIE[2] —**lying-in** *n.* confinement in childbirth (*pl.* **lyings-in**)

lymph (limf) *n.* colorless bodily fluid, mainly of white blood cells —**lym'phatic** *a.* **1.** of lymph **2.** flabby, sluggish —*n.* **3.** vessel in the body conveying lymph —**lymph node** any of numerous bean-shaped masses of tissue, situated along course of lymphatic vessels

lymphogranuloma venereum ('limfōgranyə'lōma və'nēəriəm) infectious venereal disease caused by virus-like organism

lynch (linch) *vt.* put to death without trial —**lynch law** procedure of self-appointed court trying and executing accused

lynx

lynx (lingks) *n.* animal of cat family —**lynx-eyed** *a.* having keen sight

lyre ('līər) *n* instrument like harp —**lyric** ('lirik) *n.* **1.** lyric poem —*pl.* **2.** words of popular song —**lyric(al)** ('lirik(əl)) *a.* **1.** of short personal poems expressing emotion **2.** of lyre **3.** meant to be sung —**lyricist** ('lirisist) *n.* —**lyrist** ('lirist) *n.* **1.** lyric poet **2.** ('līərist) player on lyre —'**lyrebird** *n.* Aust. bird, the male of which displays tail shaped like a lyre —**wax lyrical** express great enthusiasm

lysogeny (lī'sojəni) *n.* the coexistence between a virus and a bacterium

-lyte (*n. comb. form*) substance that can be decomposed or broken down, as in *electrolyte* —**-lytic** (*a. comb. form*) loosening, dissolving, as in *paralytic*

M

m *or* **M** (em) *n.* **1.** 13th letter of English alphabet **2.** speech sound represented by this letter (*pl.* **m's, M's** *or* **Ms**)

m meter(s)

M 1. Mach **2.** mega- **3.** *Currency* mark(s) **4.** million **5.** Roman numeral, 1000

m. 1. male **2.** married **3.** masculine **4.** mile **5.** minute

M. 1. Medieval **2.** Monsieur

ma (mä, mö) *n. inf.* mother

MA 1. Massachusetts **2.** Maritime Administration

M.A. Master of Arts

ma'am (mäm) *n.* madam

Mac *or* **Macc** Maccabees

Mac-, Mc- *or* **M'-** (*comb. form*) in surnames of Gaelic origin, son of, as in *MacDonald*

macabre (mə'käbər, -brə) *a.* gruesome, ghastly

macadam (mə'kadəm) *n.* road surface made of pressed layers of small broken stones —**ma'cadamize** *vt.* pave (road) with this

macaroni (makə'rōni) *n.* pasta in long, thin tubes (*pl.* **-s, -es**)

macaroon (makə'rōōn) *n.* cookie made of egg white, sugar and almonds or coconut

macaw (mə'kö) *n.* kind of parrot

Maccabees ('makəbēz) *pl.n.* (*with sing. v.*) *Bible* 45th and 46th books in the Douay Version of the O.T.

mace[1] (mās) *n.* **1.** staff with metal head **2.** staff of office

mace[2] (mās) *n.* spice made of the husk of the nutmeg

macerate ('masərāt) *v.* **1.** soften by soaking **2.** (cause to) waste away —**mace'ration** *n.*

Mach. *Bible* Machabees

Machabees ('makəbēz) *pl.n. see* MACCABEES

machete (mə'sheti, -'chēti, -'shet) *n.* broad, heavy knife used for cutting or as a weapon

Machiavellian (makiə'veliən) *a.* politically unprincipled, crafty, perfidious, subtle, deep-laid

machination (maki'nāshən) *n.* (*usu. pl.*) plotting, intrigue —**'machinate** *v.* lay or devise (plots)

machine (mə'shēn) *n.* **1.** apparatus combining action of several parts to apply mechanical force **2.** controlling organization **3.** mechanical appliance **4.** vehicle —*vt.* **5.** sew, print, shape *etc.* with machine —**ma'chinery** *n.* **1.** parts of machine collectively **2.** machines —**ma'chinist** *n.* one who makes or works machines —**machine gun** gun firing repeatedly and continuously with an automatic loading and firing mechanism —**machine-readable** *a.* (of data) in a form that can be directly fed into a computer —**machine shop** workshop in which machine tools are operated —**machine tool** power-driven machine, such as lathe, for cutting or shaping metals *etc.*

machismo (mä'chēzmō, -'chiz-) *n.* strong or exaggerated masculine pride or masculinity (*oft.* **macho** ('mächō))

Mach (number) (mäk) *n.* the ratio of the air speed of an aircraft to the velocity of sound under given conditions

mackerel ('makrəl) *n.* edible sea fish with blue and silver stripes —**mackerel shark** *see* PORBEAGLE

mackinaw ('makinö) *n.* **1.** heavy blanket cloth, usu. plaid with nap on both sides **2.** short coat made from this or similar fabric **3.** blanket formerly distributed to Indians by U.S. government **4.** flat-bottomed boat

macramé (makrə'mā) *n.* ornamental work of knotted cord

macro- *or before vowel* **macr-** (*comb. form*) **1.** large, long, or great in size or duration, as in *macroscopic* **2.** *Pathol.* abnormal enlargement, as in *macrocephaly*

macrobiotic (makrōbī'otik) *a.* of dietary system advocating whole grain and vegetables in belief that it will prolong life

macrocosm ('makrəkozəm) *n.* **1.** the universe **2.** any large, complete system

macron ('mākron, 'makron, -krən) *n.* diacritical mark (–) placed over letter to represent long vowel

macroscopic (makrə'skopik) *a.* **1.** visible to the naked eye **2.** concerned with large units —**macro'scopically** *adv.*

mad (mad) *a.* **1.** suffering from mental disease, insane **2.** wildly foolish **3.** very enthusiastic **4.** excited **5.** *inf.* furious, angry —**'madden** *vt.* make mad —**'madly** *adv.* —**'madness** *n.* **1.** insanity **2.** folly —**'madhouse** *n. inf.* **1.** mental hospital or asylum **2.** state of uproar or confusion —**'madman** *n.*

Madagascar (madə'gaskər) *n.* country lying off the southeast of Africa from which it is separated by the Mozambique channel by the least distance of 250 miles —**Mada'gascan** *n./a.*

madam ('madəm) *n.* polite form of address to a woman used without name, *esp.* in correspondence (*pl.* **mesdames**)

madame (məˈdam, maˈdam, ˈmadəm) *n.* married Frenchwoman (*pl.* **mesdames**)

madcap (ˈmadkap) *n.* **1.** reckless person —*a.* **2.** reckless

madder (ˈmadər) *n.* **1.** climbing plant **2.** its root **3.** red dye made from this

made (mād) *pt./pp. of* MAKE —**made-up** *a.* **1.** invented **2.** wearing make-up **3.** put together

Madeira (məˈdēərə, -ˈderə) *n.* rich sherry wine

madeleine (ˈmadələn) *n.* small rich cake shaped like a shell

mademoiselle (madmwəˈzel, mamˈzel) *n.* **1.** young unmarried French girl or woman **2.** French teacher or governess

Madison (ˈmadisən) *n.* **James.** the 4th President of the U.S. (1809-17)

Madonna (məˈdonə) *n.* **1.** the Virgin Mary **2.** picture or statue of her

madras (məˈdräs) *n.* woven cotton fabric available in varying weights and patterns, usu. stripes and plaids

madrepore (ˈmadripôr) *n.* kind of coral

madrigal (ˈmadrigəl) *n.* **1.** unaccompanied part song **2.** short love poem or song

maelstrom (ˈmālstrəm, -strom) *n.* **1.** great whirlpool **2.** turmoil

maenad (ˈmēnad) *n. Class. lit.* frenzied female worshiper of Dionysus

maestoso (mīˈstōsō) *adv. Mus.* grandly, in majestic manner

maestro (ˈmīstrō) *n.* **1.** outstanding musician, conductor **2.** man regarded as master of any art (*pl.* **-tri** (-trē), **-s**)

Mafia (ˈmäfiə, ˈmaf-) *n.* **1.** international secret criminal organization, *orig.* Italian **2.** (**m-**) clique, faction —**Mafiˈoso** *n.* member of the Mafia

magazine (ˈmagəzēn, magəˈzēn) *n.* **1.** periodical publication with stories and articles by different writers **2.** appliance for supplying cartridges automatically to gun **3.** storehouse for explosives or arms

magenta (məˈjentə) *a./n.* (of) deep purplish-red color

maggot (ˈmagət) *n.* grub, larva —ˈ**maggoty** *a.* infested with maggots

magi (ˈmājī) *pl.n.* **1.** priests of ancient Persia **2.** the wise men from the East at the Nativity (*sing.* **-gus** (-gəs))

magic (ˈmajik) *n.* **1.** art of supposedly invoking supernatural powers to influence events *etc.* **2.** any mysterious agency or power **3.** witchcraft, conjuring —*a.* **4.** magical, enchanting —ˈ**magical** *a.* —ˈ**magically** *adv.* —**maˈgician** *n.* one skilled in magic, wizard, conjurer, enchanter —**magic lantern** early form of projector using slides —**magic square** array of numbers in the form of a square characterized by the fact that every row and column and each diagonal has the same sum

magistrate (ˈmajistrāt, -strit) *n.* **1.** civil officer administering law **2.** justice of the peace —**magisˈterial** *a.* **1.** of, referring to magistrate **2.** dictatorial —ˈ**magistracy** *n.* **1.** office of magistrate **2.** magistrates collectively

magma (ˈmagmə) *n.* **1.** paste or suspension consisting of finely divided solid dispersed in liquid **2.** molten rock inside earth's crust

Magna Charta (ˈmagnə ˈkärtə) charter obtained from King John in 1215 establishing the English people's right to personal and political liberty

magna cum laude (ˈmägnə ko͞om ˈlowdə) *Lat.* (*esp.* of college or university degree) with great distinction

magnanimous (magˈnaniməs) *a.* noble, generous, not petty —**magnaˈnimity** *n.*

magnate (ˈmagnāt, -nit) *n.* influential or wealthy person

magnesium (magˈnēziəm) *n. Chem.* metallic element *Symbol* Mg, at. wt. 24.3, at. no. 12 —**magˈnesia** *n.* white powder compound of this, used in medicine

magnet (ˈmagnit) *n.* **1.** piece of iron, steel having properties of attracting iron, steel and pointing north and south when suspended **2.** lodestone —**magˈnetic** *a.* **1.** with properties of magnet **2.** exerting powerful attraction —**magˈnetically** *adv.* —ˈ**magnetism** *n.* **1.** magnetic phenomena **2.** science of magnetic phenomena **3.** personal charm or power of attracting others —ˈ**magnetite** *n.* black magnetizable mineral that is important source of iron —**magnetiˈzation** *n.* —ˈ**magnetize** *vt.* **1.** make into a magnet **2.** attract as if by magnet **3.** fascinate —**magneto** (magˈnētō) *n.* apparatus for ignition in internal-combustion engine (*pl.* **-s**) —**magneˈtometer** *n.* instrument used to measure magnetic force —ˈ**magnetron** *n.* two-electrode electronic valve used with applied magnetic field to generate high-power microwave oscillations —**magnetic field** field of force surrounding permanent magnet or moving charged particle —**magnetic mine** mine designed to activate when magnetic field is detected —**magnetic needle** magnetized rod used in certain instruments for indicating direction of magnetic field —**magnetic north** direction in which compass needle points, usu. at angle from direction of true north —**magnetic pole 1.** either of two places on the earth's surface in the polar regions toward which a compass will point **2.** either pole of a magnet —**magnetic storm** sudden severe disturbance of earth's magnetic field —**magnetic tape** long coated plastic strip for recording sound or video signals

Magnificat (magˈnifikat) *n.* hymn of Virgin Mary in Luke 1. 46–55

magnificent (magˈnifisənt) *a.* **1.** splendid **2.** stately, imposing **3.** excellent —**magˈnificence** *n.* —**magˈnificently** *adv.*

magnify (ˈmagnifī) *vt.* **1.** increase apparent

size of, as with lens **2.** exaggerate **3.** make greater (**-fied**; **-fying**) —**magnifi'cation** *n.*

magniloquent (mag'niləkwənt) *a.* **1.** speaking pompously **2.** grandiose —**mag'niloquence** *n.*

magnitude ('magnityōōd, -tōōd) *n.* **1.** importance **2.** greatness, size

magnolia (mag'nōlyə) *n.* shrub or tree with large white, sweet-scented flowers

magnum ('magnəm) *n.* large wine bottle (approx. 1½ quarts)

magnum opus great work of art or literature

magpie ('magpī) *n.* black-and-white bird

Magyar ('magyär) *n.* **1.** member of prevailing people in Hungary **2.** native speech of Hungary —*a.* **3.** pert. to Magyars

maharaja *or* **maharajah** (mähə'räjə) *n.* former title of some Hindu princes ranking above a raja

maharani *or* **maharanee** (mähə'ränē) *n.* **1.** wife of maharaja **2.** woman holding rank of maharaja

maharishi (mə'härishi) *n.* Hindu religious teacher or mystic

mahatma (mə'hätmə) *n.* **1.** *Hinduism* man of saintly life with supernatural powers **2.** one endowed with great wisdom and power

mah-jongg (mä'zhong, -'jong) *n.* game for four players played with 144 tiles comprising 108 suit tiles, 28 honors and 8 flowers or seasons, the object of which is to obtain sets of tiles

mahlstick ('mölstik) *n. see* MAULSTICK

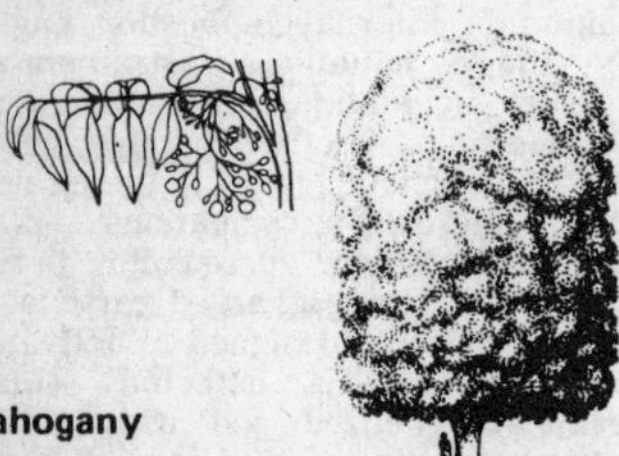

mahogany

mahogany (mə'hogəni) *n.* tree yielding reddish-brown wood

mahout (mə'howt) *n.* in India and E Indies, elephant driver or keeper

maiden ('mādən) *n.* **1.** *Lit.* young unmarried woman —*a.* **2.** unmarried **3.** of, suited to maiden **4.** first **5.** having blank record —**maid** *n.* **1.** *Lit.* young unmarried woman **2.** woman servant —'**maidenhood** *n.* —'**maidenly** *a.* modest —'**maidenhair** *n.* fern with delicate stalks and fronds —'**maidenhead** *n.* **1.** hymen **2.** virginity —**maiden name** woman's surname before marriage —**maid of honor 1.** principal unmarried attendant of bride **2.** unmarried lady attending queen or princess

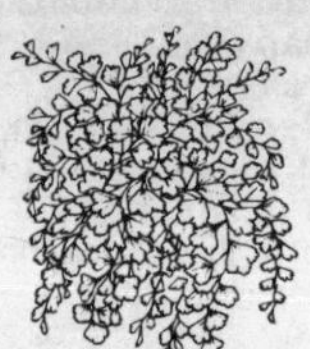

maidenhair

mail[1] (māl) *n.* **1.** letters *etc.* transported and delivered by the post office **2.** letters *etc.* conveyed at one time **3.** the postal system **4.** train, ship *etc.* carrying mail —*vt.* **5.** send by mail —**mail box 1.** public box for holding postal matter to be transmitted **2.** private box for holding letters *etc.* delivered by mailman —'**mailman** *n.* man who delivers, and sometimes collects, mail (*also* '**postman**) —**mail order 1.** order for merchandise sent by mail **2.** system of buying and selling merchandise through mail

mail[2] (māl) *n.* armor of interlaced rings or overlapping plates —**mailed** *a.* covered with mail

maillot (mī'ō, mä'yō) *n.* woman's one-piece bathing suit

maim (mām) *vt.* cripple, mutilate

main (mān) *a.* **1.** chief, principal, leading —*n.* **2.** principal pipe, line carrying water, electricity *etc.* **3.** chief part **4.** strength, power **5.** *obs.* open sea —'**mainly** *adv.* for the most part, chiefly —**main chance** one's own interests (*usu. in* **have an eye to the main chance**) —**main clause** *Gram.* clause that can stand alone as sentence —**main force** physical strength —**mainland** ('mānland, -lənd) *n.* stretch of land which forms main part of a country —**main line 1.** principal railroad line or highway **2.** *sl.* main vein into which narcotic drug can be injected —'**mainline** *vi. sl.* inject drug thus —'**mainmast** *n.* principal mast in ship —**mainsail** ('mānsāl; *Naut.* 'mānsəl) *n.* lowest sail of mainmast —'**mainspring** *n.* **1.** chief spring of watch or clock **2.** chief cause or motive —'**mainstay** *n.* **1.** rope from mainmast **2.** chief support —'**mainstream** *n.* **1.** main current (of river, cultural trend *etc.*) —*a.* **2.** of style of jazz that lies between traditional and modern

Maine (mān) *n.* New England state of the U.S., admitted to the Union in 1820. Abbrev.: **ME** (with ZIP code)

maintain (mān'tān) *vt.* **1.** carry on **2.** preserve **3.** support **4.** sustain **5.** keep up **6.** keep supplied **7.** affirm **8.** support by argument **9.** defend —**main'tainable** *a.* —'**maintenance** *n.* **1.** maintaining **2.** means of support **3.** upkeep of buildings *etc.* **4.** provision of money for separated or divorced spouse

maiolica (mə'yolikə) *n. see* MAJOLICA

maisonette (māzəˈnet) *n.* **1.** small house **2.** apartment occupying two floors

maître d'hôtel (mātrə dōˈtel, metrə) *Fr.* head waiter or waitress

maize (māz) *n.* Indian corn

Maj. Major

majesty (ˈmajisti) *n.* **1.** stateliness **2.** sovereignty **3.** grandeur —**maˈjestic** *a.* **1.** splendid **2.** regal —**maˈjestically** *adv.*

majolica (məˈjolikə) *or* **maiolica** *n.* type of ornamented Italian pottery

major (ˈmājər) *n.* **1.** army officer ranking next above captain **2.** major scale in music **3.** principal field of study at university *etc.* **4.** person of legal majority —*a.* **5.** greater in number, quality, extent **6.** significant, serious —*vi.* **7.** (*usu. with* in) do one's principal study (in particular subject) —**maˈjority** *n.* **1.** greater number **2.** larger party voting together **3.** excess of the vote on one side **4.** coming of age **5.** rank of major —**major-domo** (-ˈdōmō) *n.* house steward (*pl.* **-s**) —**major general** *Mil.* officer immediately junior to lieutenant general —**major scale** *Mus.* scale with semitones instead of whole tones after third and seventh notes

make (māk) *vt.* **1.** construct **2.** produce **3.** create **4.** establish **5.** appoint **6.** amount to **7.** cause to (do something) **8.** accomplish **9.** reach **10.** earn —*vi.* **11.** tend (**made, ˈmaking**) —*n.* **12.** brand, type, style —**ˈMaker** *n.* title given to God (as Creator) —**ˈmaking** *n.* **1.** creation —*pl.* **2.** necessary requirements or qualities —**make-believe** *n.* fantasy or pretense —**ˈmakeshift** *n.* temporary expedient —**make-up** *n.* **1.** cosmetics **2.** characteristics **3.** layout —**ˈmakeweight** *n.* trifle added to make something stronger or better —**(go to) meet one's Maker** die —**make believe** pretend; enact fantasy —**make up 1.** compose **2.** compile **3.** complete **4.** compensate **5.** apply cosmetics **6.** invent —**on the make** *sl.* **1.** intent on gain **2.** in search of sexual partner

mako (ˈmäkō) *n.* type of shark (*pl.* **-s**)

Mal *Bible* Malachi

mal- (*comb. form*) ill, badly, as in *malformation, malfunction*

malabsorption syndrome (maləbˈsörpshən) disease in which digestive tract is unable to absorb certain nutrients

malacca (məˈlakə) *a.* of brown cane used for walking stick or umbrella handle

Malachi (ˈmaləkī) *n. Bible* 39th book of the O.T., last book in the English Canon, written by the prophet Malachi, stating the final message from God to a rebellious people

Malachias (maləˈkīəs) *n. Bible* Malachi in the Douay Version of the O.T.

malachite (ˈmaləkīt) *n.* green mineral used as gemstone and to make ornaments

maladjusted (maləˈjustid) *a.* **1.** *Psychol.* unable to meet the demands of society **2.** badly adjusted —**maladˈjustment** *n.*

maladministration (malədminisˈtrāshən) *n.* inefficient or dishonest administration

maladroit (maləˈdroit) *a.* clumsy, awkward

malady (ˈmalədi) *n.* disease

Malagasy Republic (maləˈgasi) *former name for* MADAGASCAR

malaise (məˈlāz, maˈlāz) *n.* vague, unlocated feeling of discomfort

malapropism (ˈmaləpropizəm) *n.* ludicrous misuse of word

malapropos (malaprəˈpō) *a./adv.* inappropriate(ly)

malaria (məˈleriə) *n.* infectious disease caused by parasites transmitted by mosquitoes —**maˈlarial** *a.*

Malathion (maləˈthīən, -on) *n.* trade name for insecticide consisting of organic phosphate

Malawi (məˈläwi) *n.* country in Africa bounded north by Tanzania, south by Mozambique, west by Zambia and south and west by Lake Malawi —**Maˈlawian** *n./a.*

Malaysia (məˈlāzhə) *n.* country in the Indian Ocean occupying a peninsula in the Indian Ocean bounded north by Thailand and the northern part of the island of Borneo —**Malay** (məˈlā) *n./a.* **1.** (native or inhabitant) of Malaysia, eastern Sumatra and parts of Borneo —*n.* **2.** the language of the Malays which is a branch of the Malayo-Polynesian family —**Maˈlayan** *n./a.* —**Maˈlaysian** *n./a.*

malcontent (malkənˈtent) *a.* **1.** actively discontented —*n.* **2.** malcontent person

Maldives (ˈmöldēvz, ˈmal-; -dīvz, -divz) *pl.n.* —**Republic of Maldives** country lying in the Indian Ocean consisting of about 2000 low-lying coral islands 400 miles southwest of Sri Lanka —**Maldivian** (mölˈdiviən, mal-) *n./a.*

male (māl) *a.* **1.** of sex producing gametes which fertilize female gametes **2.** of men or male animals —*n.* **3.** male person or animal

malediction (maliˈdikshən) *n.* curse

malefactor (ˈmalifaktər) *n.* criminal

maleficent (məˈlefisənt) *a.* harmful, hurtful —**maˈleficence** *n.*

malevolent (məˈlevələnt) *a.* full of ill will —**maˈlevolence** *n.*

Mali (ˈmäli, ˈmali) *n.* country in Africa bounded west by Senegal, northwest by Mauritania, northeast by Algeria, east by Niger and south by Burkina-Faso, the Ivory Coast and Guinea —**ˈMalian** *n./a.*

malice (ˈmalis) *n.* **1.** ill will **2.** spite —**maˈlicious** *a.* **1.** intending evil or unkindness **2.** spiteful **3.** moved by hatred —**maˈliciously** *adv.*

malign (məˈlīn) *a.* **1.** evil in influence or effect —*vt.* **2.** slander, misrepresent —**malignancy** (məˈlignənsi) *n.* —**malignant** (məˈlignənt) *a.* **1.** feeling extreme ill will **2.** (of disease) resistant to therapy —**malignantly** (məˈlignəntli) *adv.* —**malignity** (məˈligniti) *n.* malignant disposition

malinger (mə'linggər) *vi.* feign illness to escape duty —**ma'lingerer** *n.*

mall (mōl) *n.* **1.** level, shaded walk **2.** street, shopping area closed to vehicles

mallard ('malərd) *n.* wild duck

malleable ('maliəbəl) *a.* **1.** capable of being hammered into shape **2.** adaptable —**malle-a'bility** *n.*

mallet ('malit) *n.* **1.** (wooden) hammer **2.** croquet or polo stick

mallow ('malō) *n.* wild plant with purple flowers

malmsey ('mämzi, 'mälm-) *n.* strong sweet wine

malnutrition (malnyōō'trishən, -nōō-) *n.* inadequate nutrition

malodorous (mal'ōdərəs) *a.* evil-smelling

malpractice (mal'praktis) *n.* negligent treatment by a professional, *esp.* doctor or dentist, resulting in injury

malt (mōlt) *n.* **1.** grain used for brewing —*v.* **2.** make into or become malt —**'maltster** *n.* maker of malt

Malta ('mōltə) *n.* country in the Mediterranean comprising the islands of Malta, Gozo and Comina and some islets about 60 miles south of Sicily —**Mal'tese** *n./a.* **1.** (native or inhabitant) of Malta —*n.* **2.** the Semitic language of the Maltese **3.** breed of toy dogs with long white silky coat (*pl.* **-tese**) —**Maltese cross** cross with triangular arms that taper toward center

maltreat (mal'trēt) *vt.* treat badly, handle roughly —**mal'treatment** *n.*

mama *or* **mamma** ('mämə) *n.* **1.** mother **2.** *sl.* wife, woman

mamba ('mämbə, 'mam-) *n.* deadly S Afr. snake

mambo ('mambō) *n.* Latin Amer. dance like rumba (*pl.* **-s**)

mamma ('mamə) *n.* milk-secreting organ of female mammals: breast in women, udder in cows *etc.* (*pl.* **-mae** (-mē)) —**'mammary** *a.*

mammal ('maməl) *n.* member of class of warm-blooded vertebrates which suckle their young with milk —**mammalian** (mə'māliən, ma-) *a.*

mammilla (ma'milə) *n.* **1.** nipple **2.** any nipple-shaped prominence (*pl.* **-lae** (-lē)) —**'mammillary** *a.*

mammon ('mamən) *n.* **1.** wealth regarded as source of evil **2.** (**M-**) false god of covetousness —**'mammonism** *n.* —**'mammonist** *n.*

mammoth ('maməth) *n.* **1.** extinct animal like an elephant —*a.* **2.** colossal

man (man) *n.* **1.** human being **2.** person **3.** human race **4.** adult male **5.** **SA** *sl.* any person **6.** manservant **7.** piece used in chess *etc.* (*pl.* **men**) —*vt.* **8.** supply (ship *etc.*) with necessary men **9.** fortify (**-nn-**) —**'manful** *a.* brave, vigorous —**'manfully** *adv.* —**'manhood** *n.* —**'manlike** *a.* —**'manliness** *n.* —**'manly** *a.* —**'mannish** *a.* like a man —**man Friday 1.** loyal male servant or assistant **2.** any factotum, *esp.* in office (*also* **girl Friday, person Friday**) —**'manhandle** *vt.* treat roughly —**'manhole** *n.* opening through which man may pass to a drain, sewer *etc.* —**man-hour** *n.* unit of work in industry, equal to work done by one man in one hour —**'manhunt** *n.* organized search for fugitive —**'man'kind** *n.* human beings in general —**man-of-war** *or* **man o' war** *n.* **1.** warship **2.** *see* **Portuguese man-of-war** *at* PORTUGAL —**'manpower** *n.* **1.** power of human effort **2.** available number of workers —**'manslaughter** *n.* culpable homicide without malice aforethought —**man in the street** typical person —**man of letters 1.** writer **2.** scholar —**man of the world** man of wide experience

mana ('mänə) *n.* **1.** generalized supernatural force or power in objects or persons **2.** moral authority

manacle ('manəkəl) *n.* **1.** fetter, handcuff —*vt.* **2.** shackle

manage ('manij) *v.* **1.** be in charge (of), administer **2.** succeed in (doing) —*vt.* **3.** control **4.** handle, cope with **5.** conduct, carry on —**'manageable** *a.* —**'management** *n.* **1.** those who manage, as board of directors *etc.* **2.** administration **3.** skillful use of means **4.** conduct —**'manager** *n.* **1.** one in charge of business, institution, actor *etc.* (**'manageress** *fem.*) **2.** one who manages efficiently —**mana'gerial** *a.* —**'managing** *a.* having administrative control

mañana (mə'nyänə) *Sp.* **1.** tomorrow **2.** some other and later time

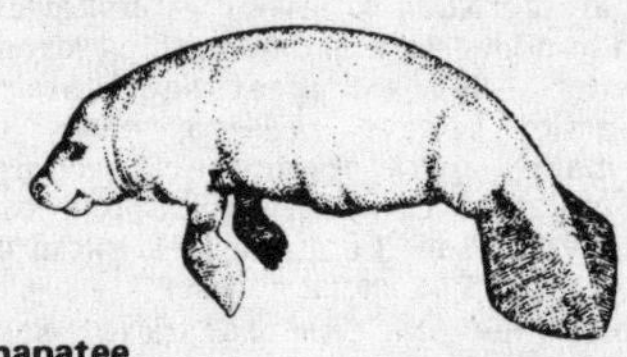

manatee

manatee ('manətē) *n.* large, plant-eating aquatic mammal

Manchu ('manchōō, man'chōō) *n.* **1.** member of Mongoloid people of Manchuria (*pl.* **-s, -chu**) **2.** language of this people

Mancunian (man'kyōōniən) *n.* **1.** native or inhabitant of Manchester, England —*a.* **2.** of Manchester, England

mandala ('mundələ) *n.* any of various designs, usu. circular, symbolizing the universe

mandamus (man'dāməs) *n.* writ from superior to lower court, officer, corporation *etc.* commanding that a specific thing be done

mandarin ('mandərin) *n.* **1.** *Hist.* Chinese high-ranking bureaucrat **2.** *fig.* any high government official **3.** Chinese variety of orange **4.** (**M-**) Beijing, formerly Peking, dialect which is the official pronunciation of the Chinese language —**mandarin duck** Asian duck, the male of which has brightly colored patterned plumage and crest

mandate ('mandāt) *n.* **1.** command of, or commission to act for, another **2.** commission from United Nations to govern a territory **3.** instruction from electorate to representative or government —'**mandated** *a.* committed to a mandate —**mandatory** ('mandətöri) *n.* **1.** holder of a mandate —*a.*, *also* '**mandatary 2.** compulsory

mandible ('mandibəl) *n.* **1.** lower jawbone **2.** either part of bird's beak —**man'dibular** *a.* of, like mandible

mandolin (mandə'lin) *n.* plucked musical instrument descended from the lute but with a smaller almost straight neck

mandrake ('mandrāk) *or* **mandragora** (man'dragərə) *n.* narcotic plant

mandrel *or* **mandril** ('mandrəl) *n.* **1.** axis on which material is supported in a lathe **2.** rod round which metal is cast or forged

mandrill ('mandril) *n.* large blue-faced baboon

mane (mān) *n.* long hair on neck of horse, lion *etc.* —**maned** *a.*

maneuver (mə'nōōvər, -'nyōōvər) *n.* **1.** contrived, complicated, perhaps deceptive plan or action **2.** skillful management —*vt.* **3.** contrive or accomplish with skill or cunning —*vi.* **4.** manipulate situations *etc.* in order to gain some end —*v.* **5.** (cause to) perform maneuvers

manganese ('mangganēz, -nēs) *n. Chem.* metallic element *Symbol* Mn, at. wt. 54.9, at. no. 25

mange (mānj) *n.* any of various contagious skin diseases caused by mites affecting humans and domestic animals —'**mangy** *or* '**mangey** *a.* scruffy, shabby

mangel ('manggəl) *n.* coarse beet grown for cattle (*also* **mangel-wurzel** (-wərzəl))

manger ('mānjər) *n.* eating trough in stable

mangle ('manggəl) *vt.* mutilate, spoil, hack

mango ('manggō) *n.* **1.** tropical fruit **2.** tree bearing it (*pl.* **-s, -es**)

mangrove

mangrove ('man-grōv, 'mang-) *n.* tropical tree which grows on muddy banks of estuaries

Manhattan (man'hatən) *n.* **1.** borough of New York City **2.** (*sometimes* **m-**) cocktail made of whiskey, sweet vermouth and sometimes bitters

mania ('māniə) *n.* **1.** madness **2.** prevailing craze —'**maniac, maniacal** (mə'nīəkəl) *or* **manic** ('manik) *a.* affected by mania —'**maniac** *n. inf.* **1.** mad person **2.** crazy enthusiast —**manic-depressive** *a. Psych.* **1.** pert. to mental disorder characterized by alternation between extreme confidence and deep depression —*n.* **2.** person afflicted with this disorder

manicure ('manikyōōər) *n.* **1.** treatment and care of fingernails and hands —*vt.* **2.** apply such treatment to —'**manicurist** *n.* one doing this professionally

manifest ('manifest) *a.* **1.** clearly revealed, visible, undoubted —*vt.* **2.** make manifest —*n.* **3.** list of cargo for customs —**manifes'tation** *n.* —'**manifestly** *adv.* clearly —**mani'festo** *n.* declaration of policy by political party, government, or movement (*pl.* **-s, -es**)

manifold ('manifōld) *a.* **1.** numerous and varied —*n.* **2.** in internal-combustion engine, pipe with several outlets —*vt.* **3.** make copies of (document)

Manila (mə'nilə) *n.* **1.** fiber used for ropes **2.** tough paper

manipulate (mə'nipyəlāt) *vt.* **1.** handle **2.** deal with skillfully **3.** manage **4.** falsify —**manipu'lation** *n.* **1.** act of manipulating, working by hand **2.** skilled use of hands —**ma'nipulative** *a.* —**ma'nipulator** *n.*

manitou *or* **manitu** ('manitōō) *n.* Algonquian concept denoting the supernatural force of the natural world

manna ('manə) *n.* **1.** food of Israelites in the wilderness **2.** any spiritual or divine nourishment

mannequin ('manikin) *n.* **1.** woman who wears clothing displayed at fashion show; model **2.** life-size dummy of human body used to fit or display clothes **3.** *Arts see* LAY FIGURE (sense 1)

manner ('manər) *n.* **1.** way thing happens or is done **2.** sort, kind **3.** custom **4.** style —*pl.* **5.** social behavior —'**mannered** *a.* having idiosyncrasies or mannerisms; affected —'**mannerism** *n.* person's distinctive habit, trait —'**mannerly** *a.* polite

manor ('manər) *n.* **1.** *Hist.* land belonging to a lord **2.** feudal unit of land —**ma'norial** *a.* —**manor house** residence of lord of manor

manqué (mong'kā) *Fr.* unfulfilled; would-be

mansard ('mansärd) *n.* roof with break in its slope, lower part being steeper than upper —'**mansarded** *a.*

manse (mans) *n.* **1.** house of minister in some religious denominations **2.** mansion

mansion ('manchən) *n.* large house

mantel ('mantəl) *n.* structure around fireplace —**mantel shelf** *or* '**mantelpiece** *n.* shelf at top of mantel

mantilla (man'tēya, man'tilə) *n.* in Spain, (lace) scarf worn as headdress

mantis (ˈmantis) *n.* genus of insects including the stick insects and leaf insects (*pl.* **mantes** (ˈmantēz))
mantissa (manˈtisə) *n.* decimal part of common logarithm
mantle (ˈmantəl) *n.* **1.** loose cloak **2.** covering **3.** incandescent gauze around gas jet —*vt.* **4.** cover **5.** conceal
mantra (ˈmantrə) *n.* *Hinduism* word or formula to be recited or sung as aid to meditation
manual (ˈmanyōōəl) *a.* **1.** of, or done with, the hands **2.** by human labor, not automatic —*n.* **3.** handbook **4.** textbook **5.** organ keyboard
manufacture (manyəˈfakchər) *vt.* **1.** process, make (materials) into finished articles **2.** produce (articles) **3.** invent, concoct —*n.* **4.** making of articles, materials, *esp.* in large quantities **5.** anything produced from raw materials —**manuˈfacturer** *n.* owner of factory
manumit (manyəˈmit) *vt.* free from slavery (**-tt-**) —**manuˈmission** *n.*
manure (məˈnyōōər, məˈnōōər) *vt.* **1.** enrich (land) —*n.* **2.** dung or chemical fertilizer used to enrich land
manuscript (ˈmanyəskript) *n.* **1.** book, document, written by hand **2.** copy for printing —*a.* **3.** handwritten
Manx (mangks) *a.* **1.** of Isle of Man —*n.* **2.** Manx language —**Manx cat** tailless breed of cat —ˈ**Manxman** *n.*
many (ˈmeni) *a.* **1.** numerous (**more** *comp.*, **most** *sup.*) —*n.* **2.** large number
Maoism (ˈmowizəm) *n.* form of Marxism advanced by Mao Tse-tung (in Pinyin, Mao Ze Dong) in China —ˈ**Maoist** *n./a.*
Maori (ˈmowri) *n.* **1.** member of New Zealand native race (*pl.* **-s, -ri**) **2.** their language
map (map) *n.* **1.** flat representation of the earth or some part of it, or of the heavens —*vt.* **2.** make a map of **3.** (*with* out) plan (**-pp-**)
maple (ˈmāpəl) *n.* **1.** any of family and genus of deciduous trees or shrubs of N temperate zone with green, purple or golden lobed leaves and winged seeds borne in pairs **2.** hard light-colored wood of a maple used for flooring and furniture —**maple leaf** national emblem of Canada —**maple sugar** sugar made by boiling maple syrup —**maple syrup** syrup made by boiling sap of maple, *esp.* sugar maple
maquis (maˈkē, mä-) *n.* **1.** scrubby undergrowth of Mediterranean countries **2.** (*oft.* **M-**) name adopted by French underground resistance movement in World War II
mar (mär) *vt.* spoil, impair (**-rr-**)
Mar. March
marabou (ˈmarəbōō) *n.* **1.** kind of stork **2.** its soft white lower tail feathers, used to trim hats *etc.* **3.** kind of silk
maraca (məˈräkə, -ˈrakə) *n.* percussion instrument of gourd containing dried seeds *etc.*
maraschino (marəˈskēnō) *n.* **1.** liqueur made from bitter wild cherries **2.** large red cherry preserved in syrup (*pl.* **-s**)
marathon (ˈmarəthon) *n.* **1.** long-distance race **2.** endurance contest
maraud (məˈröd) *vi.* **1.** make raid for plunder —*v.* **2.** pillage —**maˈrauder** *n.*
marble (ˈmärbəl) *n.* **1.** kind of limestone capable of taking polish **2.** slab of, sculpture in this **3.** small ball used in children's game —ˈ**marbled** *a.* having mottled appearance, like marble —ˈ**marbly** *a.*
marc (märk) *n.* **1.** remains of grapes *etc.* that have been pressed for wine-making **2.** brandy distilled from these
marcasite (ˈmärkəsīt) *n.* **1.** pale yellow crystallized iron pyrites **2.** polished form of steel or white metal used for making jewelry
march[1] (märch) *vi.* **1.** walk with military step **2.** go, progress —*vt.* **3.** cause to march —*n.* **4.** action of marching **5.** distance marched in day **6.** tune to accompany marching —**marching orders 1.** *Mil.* instructions about march, its destination *etc.* **2.** *inf.* any notice of dismissal, *esp.* from employment —**march-past** *n.* review of troops as they march past a saluting point
march[2] (märch) *n.* **1.** border or frontier —*vi.* **2.** (*oft. with* upon *or* with) share a common border (with)
March (märch) *n.* third month —**March hare** hare during its breeding season, noted for its excitable behavior
marchioness (ˈmärshənis) *n.* wife, ex-wife or widow of marquis
Mardi Gras (ˈmärdi grä) **1.** festival of Shrove Tuesday **2.** revelry celebrating this
mare[1] (māər) *n.* female horse —**mare's nest** supposed discovery which proves worthless
mare[2] (ˈmärā) *n.* (**M-** *when part of name*) huge dry plain on surface of moon (*pl.* **maria** (ˈmäriə))
margarine (ˈmärjərin, -rēn) *n.* butter substitute made from vegetable fats
margin (ˈmärjin) *n.* **1.** border, edge **2.** space round printed page **3.** amount allowed beyond what is necessary —ˈ**marginal** *a.*
marguerite (märgəˈrēt) *n.* large daisy
marigold (ˈmarigōld) *n.* plant with yellow flowers
marijuana *or* **marihuana** (mariˈwänə, -ˈhwänə) *n.* dried flowers and leaves of hemp plant, used as narcotic
marimba (məˈrimbə) *n.* a percussion instrument similar to but larger than the xylophone, used by bands
marina (məˈrēnə) *n.* mooring facility for yachts and pleasure boats
marinade (mariˈnād) *n.* seasoned, flavored liquid used to soak fish, meat *etc.* before cooking —ˈ**marinate** *v.*

marine (mə'rēn) *a.* **1.** of the sea or shipping **2.** used at, found in sea —*n.* **3.** shipping, fleet **4.** soldier trained for land or sea combat —**mariner** ('marinər) *n.* sailor

marionette (mariə'net) *n.* puppet worked with strings

marital ('maritəl) *a.* relating to a husband or to marriage

maritime ('maritīm) *a.* **1.** connected with seafaring, naval **2.** bordering on the sea **3.** (of climate) having small temperature differences between summer and winter —**Maritime Provinces** certain of the Canadian provinces with coasts facing the Gulf of St. Lawrence or Atlantic (*also* '**Maritimes**)

marjoram ('märjərəm) *n.* aromatic herb

mark[1] (märk) *n.* **1.** line, dot, scar *etc.* **2.** sign, token **3.** inscription **4.** letter, number showing evaluation of schoolwork *etc.* **5.** indication **6.** target —*vt.* **7.** make a mark on **8.** be distinguishing mark of **9.** indicate **10.** notice **11.** watch **12.** assess, *eg* examination paper **13.** stay close to (sporting opponent) to hamper his play —**marked** *a.* **1.** obvious, evident, or noticeable **2.** singled out, *esp.* as target of attack **3.** *Linguis.* distinguished by specific feature, as in phonology —**markedly** ('märkidli) *adv.* —'**marker** *n.* **1.** one who, that which keeps score at games **2.** counter used at card playing *etc.* —'**marksman** *n.* skilled shot

mark[2] (märk) *n.* German coin

Mark (märk) *n.* *Bible* 2nd book of the N.T., synoptic gospel presenting Jesus in the role of servant in the chronology of His life written by a disciple

market ('märkit) *n.* **1.** assembly, place for buying and selling **2.** demand for goods **3.** center for trade —*vt.* **4.** offer or produce for sale —'**marketable** *a.* —'**marketing** *n.* business of selling goods, including advertising, packaging *etc.* —**market research** analysis of data relating to demand for product

marl (märl) *n.* **1.** soil rich in calcium carbonate used as fertilizer —*vt.* **2.** fertilize with it

marline *or* **marlin** ('märlin) *n.* two-strand cord —'**marlinspike** *or* '**marlinespike** *n.* pointed tool, *esp.* for unraveling rope to be spliced

marmalade ('märməlād) *n.* sweet jelly usu. made of oranges, lemons *etc.* incorporating shreds of rind

marmoreal (mär'mōriəl) *or* **marmorean** *a.* of or like marble

marmoset ('märməset, -zet) *n.* small bushy-tailed monkey

marmot ('märmət) *n.* any of various N Amer. burrowing rodents living in colonies (*also* **rockchuck**)

maroon[1] (mə'rōōn) *n.* **1.** brownish crimson —*a.* **2.** of this color

maroon[2] (mə'rōōn) *vt.* **1.** leave (person) on deserted island or coast **2.** isolate, cut off by any means

marquee (mär'kē) *n.* large tent

marquetry *or* **marqueterie** ('märkitri) *n.* inlaid work, wood mosaic

marquis ('märkwis, mär'kē) *n.* nobleman of rank below duke —**marquisate** ('märkwizit) *n.*

marquise (mär'kēz) *n.* **1.** in various countries, marchioness **2.** gemstone cut in pointed oval shape

Marrano (mə'ränō) *n.* Spanish or Portuguese Jew forcibly converted to Christianity in the 15th cent. (*pl.* **-s**)

marrow ('marō) *n.* **1.** fatty substance inside bones **2.** vital part —'**marrowy** *a.* —'**marrowfat** *n.* large pea

marry ('mari) *v.* **1.** take (someone as husband or wife) in marriage **2.** unite closely —*vt.* **3.** join as husband and wife ('**married,** '**marrying**) —**marriage** ('marij) *n.* **1.** state of being married **2.** wedding —**marriageable** ('marijəbəl) *a.* —**marriage bureau** business concern set up to introduce people wishing to get married —**marriage guidance** advice given to couples who have problems in their married life

Mars (märz) *n.* **1.** Roman god of war **2.** planet nearest but one to earth —**Martian** ('märshən) *n.* **1.** supposed inhabitant of Mars —*a.* **2.** of Mars

marsala (mär'sälə) *n.* fortified dessert wine

Marseillaise (märsə'lāz) *n.* the French national anthem

marsh (märsh) *n.* low-lying wet land —'**marshy** *a.* —**marsh gas** gas composed of methane produced when vegetation decomposes under water —**marshmallow** ('märshmelō) *n.* confection orig. made from root of **marsh mallow,** shrubby plant growing near marshes

marshal *or* **marshall** ('märshəl) *n.* **1.** high officer of state **2.** law enforcement officer —*vt.* **3.** arrange in due order **4.** conduct with ceremony —**marshaling yard** railroad depot for freight trains

marsupial (mär'sōōpiəl) *n.* **1.** animal that carries its young in pouch, *eg* kangaroo —*a.* **2.** of marsupials —**mar'supium** *n.* external pouch in most female marsupials (*pl.* **-pia** (-piə))

mart (märt) *n.* **1.** place of trade **2.** market

Martello tower (mär'telō) round fort, for coast defense

marten ('märtin) *n.* **1.** weasel-like animal **2.** its fur

martial ('märshəl) *a.* **1.** relating to war **2.** warlike, brave —**court martial** *see* COURT —**martial law** law enforced by military authorities in times of danger or emergency

martin ('märtin) *n.* species of swallow

martinet (märti'net) *n.* strict disciplinarian

martingale ('märtin-gāl, 'märtinggāl) *n.*

strap to prevent horse from throwing up its head

martini (mär'tēni) *n.* **1.** cocktail containing gin and vermouth decorated with maraschino cherry **2.** (**M-**) trade name for Italian vermouth (*pl.* **-s**)

Martinique (märti'nēk) *n.* an overseas department of France situated in the Lesser Antilles between Dominica and St. Lucia —**Marti'nican** *n./a.*

Martinmas ('märtinməs) *n.* feast of St. Martin, Nov. 11th

martlet ('märtlit) *n. Her.* bird without feet

martyr ('märtər) *n.* **1.** one put to death for his beliefs **2.** one who suffers in some cause **3.** one in constant suffering —*vt.* **4.** make martyr of —'**martyrdom** *n.* —**martyr'ology** *n.* list, history of Christian martyrs

marvel ('märvəl) *vi.* **1.** wonder —*n.* **2.** wonderful thing —'**marvelous** *or* '**marvellous** *a.* **1.** amazing **2.** wonderful

Marxism ('märksizəm) *n.* state socialism as conceived by Karl Marx —'**Marxian** *a.* —'**Marxist** *n./a.*

Maryland ('merilənd) *n.* South Atlantic state of the U.S.: ratified the Constitution in 1788. Abbrev.: **MD** (with ZIP code)

marzipan ('märtsipän, -pan, 'märzipan) *n.* paste of almonds, sugar *etc.* used in candy, cakes *etc.*

Masai (mä'sī, 'mäsī) *n.* **1.** member of Negroid pastoral people living chiefly in Kenya and Tanzania (*pl.* **-s,** **-'sai**) **2.** language of this people

masc. masculine

mascara (ma'skarə) *n.* cosmetic for darkening eyelashes

mascot ('maskot, -kət) *n.* thing supposed to bring luck

masculine ('maskyəlin) *a.* **1.** relating to males **2.** manly **3.** of the grammatical gender of words referring to males or things conventionally regarded as male

maser ('māzər) *n.* device for amplifying microwaves

mash (mash) *n.* **1.** meal mixed with warm water **2.** warm food for horses *etc.* **3.** soft pulpy mass or consistency —*vt.* **4.** make into a mash **5.** crush into soft mass or pulp

mashie *or* **mashy** ('mashi) *n. Golf* iron club with deep sloping blade for lob shots

mask (mask) *n.* **1.** covering for face **2.** *Surg.* covering for nose and mouth **3.** disguise, pretense —*vt.* **4.** cover with mask **5.** hide, disguise —**masking tape** adhesive tape used to protect surfaces surrounding an area to be painted

maskanonge ('maskənonj), **maskelonge** ('maskəlonj), *or* **maskinonge** ('maskinonj) *n. see* MUSKELLUNGE

masochism ('masəkizəm) *n.* abnormal condition where pleasure (*esp.* sexual) is derived from pain, humiliation *etc.* —'**masochist** *n.* —**maso'chistic** *a.*

mason ('māsən) *n.* **1.** worker in stone **2.** (**M-**) Freemason —**Masonic** (mə'sonik) *a.* of Freemasonry —'**masonry** *n.* **1.** stonework **2.** (**M-**) Freemasonry

masque *or* **mask** (mask) *n. Hist.* form of theatrical performance —**masquerade** (maskə'rād) *n.* **1.** masked ball —*vi.* **2.** appear in disguise

mass (mas) *n.* **1.** quantity of matter **2.** dense collection of this **3.** large quantity or number —*v.* **4.** form into a mass —'**massive** *a.* large and heavy —'**massy** *a.* solid, weighty —**mass market** market for mass-produced goods —**mass-market** *a.* of mass market —**mass media** means of communication to large numbers of people, such as television, newspapers *etc.* —**mass-produce** *vt.* produce (standardized articles) in large quantities —**mass production** —**mass spectrometer** instrument in which ions are separated by electric or magnetic fields according to their ratios of charge to mass (*also* '**spectroscope**) —**the masses** the populace

Mass (mas) *n.* service of the Eucharist, *esp.* in R.C. Church

Massachusetts (masə'cho͞osits) *n.* New England state of the U.S.: ratified the Constitution in 1788. Abbrev.: **Mass., MA** (with ZIP code)

massacre ('masəkər) *n.* **1.** indiscriminate, large-scale killing, *esp.* of unresisting people —*vt.* **2.** kill indiscriminately

massage (mə'säzh, -'säj) *n.* **1.** rubbing and kneading of muscles *etc.* as curative treatment —*vt.* **2.** apply this treatment to **3.** manipulate (figures *etc.*) in order to deceive —**masseur** (ma'sər) *n.* one who practices massage (**masseuse** (ma'səz, -'sərz, -'so͞oz) *fem.*)

massé ('masi) *n. Billiards* stroke with cue upright

massif (ma'sēf) *n.* compact group of mountains

mast[1] (mast) *n.* **1.** pole for supporting ship's sails **2.** tall upright support for antenna *etc.* —'**masthead** *n.* **1.** *Naut.* head of mast **2.** name of newspaper, its proprietors, staff *etc.*, printed at top of front page —*vt.* **3.** raise (sail) to masthead

mast[2] (mast) *n.* fruit of beech, oak *etc.* used as pig fodder

mastectomy (ma'stektəmi) *n.* surgical removal of a breast

master ('mastər) *n.* **1.** one in control **2.** employer **3.** head of household **4.** owner **5.** document *etc.* from which copies are made **6.** captain of merchant ship **7.** expert **8.** great artist **9.** teacher —*vt.* **10.** overcome **11.** acquire knowledge of or skill in —'**masterful** *a.* imperious, domineering —'**masterly** *a.* showing great competence —'**mastery** *n.* **1.** full understanding **2.** expertise **3.** authority **4.** victory —**master key** key that opens many different locks —'**mastermind** *vt.* **1.** plan, direct —*n.* **2.** very intelligent person, *esp.* one who directs an undertaking —'**masterpiece** *n.* outstanding work, *orig.* the test piece by which a craftsman was admitted to his guild —'**masterstroke** *n.* outstanding piece of strategy *etc.* —**Master of Arts** (*or* **Science** *etc.*) **1.** degree given by university usu. to postgraduate **2.** person who has this degree —**master of ceremonies** person who presides over public ceremony *etc.*, introducing events *etc.*

mastic ('mastik) *n.* **1.** gum obtained from certain trees **2.** puttylike substance

masticate ('mastikāt) *v.* chew —**masti'cation** *n.* —'**masticatory** *a.*

mastiff

mastiff ('mastif) *n.* large dog

mastitis (ma'stītis) *n.* inflammation of breast or udder

mastodon ('mastədon) *n.* **1.** extinct elephantlike mammal **2.** anything unusually large

mastoid ('mastoid) *a.* **1.** nipple-shaped —*n.* **2.** prominence on bone behind human ear —**mastoid'ectomy** *n.* surgical removal of infected mastoid —**mastoi'ditis** *n.* inflammation of mastoid

masturbate ('mastərbāt) *v.* stimulate (one's own or one's partner's) genital organs —**mastur'bation** *n.*

mat[1] (mat) *n.* **1.** small rug **2.** piece of fabric to protect another surface or to wipe feet on *etc.* **3.** thick tangled mass —*v.* **4.** form into such mass (**-tt-**) —**on the mat** *inf.* called up for reprimand

mat[2] *or* **matt** (mat) *a.* dull, lusterless, not shiny

matador ('matədōr) *n.* man who slays bull in bullfights

match[1] (mach) *n.* **1.** contest, game **2.** equal **3.** person, thing exactly corresponding to another **4.** marriage **5.** person regarded as eligible for marriage —*vt.* **6.** get something corresponding to (color, pattern *etc.*) **7.** oppose, put in competition with **8.** join (in marriage) —*vi.* **9.** correspond —'**matchless** *a.* unequaled —'**matchboard** *n.* long, flimsy board tongued and grooved for lining work —'**matchmaker** *n.* one who tries to bring about a marriage —**match play** *Golf* scoring according to number of holes won and lost

match[2] (mach) *n.* **1.** small stick with head which ignites when rubbed **2.** fuse —'**matchbox** *n.* —'**matchlock** *n.* early musket fired by fuse —'**matchwood** *n.* small splinters

mate[1] (māt) *n.* **1.** comrade **2.** husband, wife **3.** one of pair **4.** officer in merchant ship **5.** *inf.* common Brit. and Aust. term of address, *esp.* between males —*v.* **6.** marry or join in marriage **7.** pair —'**matey** *a.* *inf.* friendly, sociable

mate[2] (māt) *n./vt.* *Chess* checkmate

maté *or* **mate** ('mätā) *n.* **1.** tealike beverage drunk in South America **2.** shrub or tree from which this drink is made **3.** leaves and shoots of this tree

mater ('mātər) *n.* **UK** *sl.* mother

material (mə'tēəriəl) *n.* **1.** substance from which thing is made **2.** cloth, fabric —*a.* **3.** of matter or body **4.** affecting physical wellbeing **5.** unspiritual **6.** important, essential —**ma'terialism** *n.* **1.** excessive interest in, desire for money and possessions **2.** doctrine that nothing but matter exists, denying independent existence of spirit —**ma'terialist** *a./n.* —**material'istic** *a.* —**ma'terialize** *vi.* **1.** come into existence or view —*vt.* **2.** make material —**ma'terially** *adv.* appreciably

matériel *or* **materiel** (mətēəri'el) *n.* equipment of organization, *esp.* of military force

maternal (mə'tərnəl) *a.* of, related through mother —**ma'ternity** *n.* motherhood

math (math) *n.* *inf.* mathematics

mathematics (mathə'matiks) *pl.n.* (*with sing. v.*) science of number, quantity, shape and space —**mathe'matical** *a.* —**mathe'matically** *adv.* —**mathema'tician** *n.*

matinée (mati'nā) *n.* afternoon performance in theater —**matinée coat** short coat for baby

matins ('matinz) *pl.n.* morning prayers

matriarch ('mātriärk) *n.* mother as head and ruler of family —**matri'archal** *a.* —'**matriarchy** *n.* society with matriarchal government and descent reckoned in female line

matricide ('matrisīd, 'mā-) *n.* **1.** the crime of killing one's mother **2.** one who does this

matriculate (mə'trikyəlāt) *v.* enroll, be enrolled in a college or university —**matricu'lation** *n.*

matrimony ('matrimōni) *n.* marriage —**matri'monial** *a.*

matrix ('mātriks) *n.* **1.** substance, situation in which something originates, takes form, or is enclosed **2.** intercellular substance of bone, cartilage *etc.* **3.** mold for casting **4.** *Math.* rectangular array of elements set out in rows and columns (*pl.* **matrices** ('mātrisēz, 'ma-))

matron ('mātrən) *n.* **1.** married woman **2.** woman who superintends domestic arrangements of public institution, boarding school *etc.* —'**matronly** *a.* sedate —**matron of honor** married woman serving as chief attendant to bride

matt (mat) *a. see* MAT[2]
Matt. *Bible* Matthew
matter ('matər) *n.* **1.** anything that has weight and occupies space **2.** physical or bodily substance **3.** affair, business **4.** cause of trouble **5.** substance of book *etc.* **6.** pus —*vi.* **7.** be of importance, signify —**matter-of-fact** *a.* unimaginative or emotionless —**matter of fact** fact that is undeniably true —**as a matter of fact** actually; in fact
Matthew ('mathyōō) *n. Bible* 1st book of the N.T., synoptic gospel presenting Jesus as fulfillment of the O.T. promises of Redeemer and King of Israel, written by a disciple
mattock ('matək) *n.* tool like pick with ends of blades flattened for cutting, hoeing
mattress ('matris) *n.* **1.** stuffed flat case, often with springs, or foam-rubber pad, used as part of bed **2.** underlay
mature (mə'tyŏŏər, -'tŏŏər, -'chŏŏər) *a.* **1.** ripe, completely developed **2.** grown-up —*v.* **3.** bring, come to maturity —*vi.* **4.** (of bill) fall due —**matu'ration** *n.* process of maturing —**ma'turity** *n.* full development
matutinal (machŏŏ'tīnəl) *a.* of, occurring in, or during morning
matzo ('mätsō) *n.* flat, unleavened bread resembling a soda cracker
maudlin ('mödlin) *a.* weakly or tearfully sentimental
maul (möl) *vt.* **1.** handle roughly **2.** beat; bruise —*n.* **3.** heavy wooden hammer
maulstick *or* **mahlstick** ('mölstik) *n.* light stick with ball at one end, held in left hand to support right hand while painting
maunder ('möndər) *vi.* talk, act aimlessly, dreamily
maundy ('möndi) *n.* **1.** foot-washing ceremony on Thursday before Easter **2.** royal alms given on that day
Mauritania (möri'tāniə, mor-; -nyə) *n.* country in Africa bounded west by the Atlantic Ocean, north by Western Sahara, northeast by Algeria, east and southeast by Mali, and south by Senegal —**Mauri'tanian** *n./a.*
Mauritius (mö'rishəs) *n.* country in the Indian Ocean about 500 miles east of Madagascar comprising two islands —**Mau'ritian** *n./a.*
mausoleum (mösə'lēəm) *n.* stately building as a tomb (*pl.* **-s, -lea** (-'lēə))
mauve (mōv) *a./n.* (of) pale purple color
maven ('māvən) *or* **mavin** *n. inf.* expert; connoisseur
maverick ('mavərik) *n.* **1.** unbranded steer, stray cow **2.** independent, unorthodox person
mavin ('māvin) *n. see* MAVEN
maw (mö) *n.* stomach, crop
mawkish ('mökish) *a.* **1.** weakly sentimental, maudlin **2.** sickly
max. maximum
maxi ('maksi) *n.* **1.** long skirt, dress, or coat —*a.* **2.** large, considerable
maxilla (mak'silə) *n.* jawbone (*pl.* **-lae** (-lē)) —**'maxillary** *a.* of the jaw
maxim ('maksim) *n.* **1.** general truth, proverb **2.** rule of conduct, principle
maximum ('maksiməm) *n.* **1.** greatest size or number **2.** highest point (*pl.* **-s, -ma** (-mə)) —*a.* **3.** greatest —**'maximize** *vt.*
maxwell ('makswel, 'makswəl) *n.* cgs unit of magnetic flux
may (mā) *v. aux.* expresses possibility, permission, opportunity *etc.* (**might** *pt.*) —**maybe** ('mābē) *adv.* perhaps; possibly
May (mā) *n.* **1.** fifth month **2.** hawthorn or its flowers —**'mayfly** *n.* short-lived flying insect, found near water —**'maypole** *n.* pole set up for dancing round on **May Day**, first day of May —**May queen** girl chosen to preside over May-Day celebrations
Maya ('mīə) *n.* **1.** member of Amerindian people of Yucatán, Belize and N Guatemala (*pl.* **-ya, -s**) **2.** language of this people
Mayday (mā'dā, 'mādā) *n.* international radiotelephone distress signal
mayhap ('māhap) *adv. obs.* perhaps
mayhem ('māhem) *n.* **1.** depriving person by violence of limb, member or organ, or causing mutilation of body **2.** any violent destruction **3.** confusion
mayonnaise ('māənāz, māə'nāz) *n.* creamy sauce of egg yolks, oil *etc., esp.* for salads
mayor (māər) *n.* head of municipality —**'mayoral** *a.* —**'mayoralty** *n.* (time of) office of mayor —**'mayoress** *n.* **1.** mayor's wife **2.** lady mayor
maze (māz) *n.* **1.** labyrinth **2.** network of paths, lines **3.** state of confusion
mazel ('mäzəl) *n. inf.* luck —**mazel tov** (töf) expression of felicitation or congratulations
mazurka *or* **mazourka** (mə'zərkə) *n.* **1.** lively Polish dance like polka **2.** music for it
MB Manitoba
M.B. Bachelor of Medicine
M.C. **1.** Master of Ceremonies **2.** Military Cross
M.C.C. Marylebone Cricket Club
McKinley (mə'kinli) *n.* **William.** the 25th President of the U.S. (1897-1901)
Md *Chem.* mendelevium
MD Maryland
M.D. Doctor of Medicine
me[1] (mē; *unstressed* mi) *pron.* objective case of pronoun I
me[2] (mē) *n. Mus. see* MI
ME Maine
ME *or* **M.E.** Middle English
M.E. **1.** Marine Engineer **2.** Mechanical Engineer **3.** Methodist Episcopal **4.** Mining Engineer **5.** in titles, Most Excellent
mea culpa ('māä 'kŏŏlpä) *Lat.* my fault
mead[1] (mēd) *n.* alcoholic drink made from honey

mead[2] (mēd) *n. obs., poet.* meadow

meadow ('medō) *n.* piece of grassland —'**meadowsweet** *n.* plant with dense heads of small fragrant flowers

meager ('mēgər) *a.* **1.** lean, thin **2.** scanty, insufficient

meal[1] (mēl) *n.* **1.** occasion when food is served and eaten **2.** the food —**meal ticket** person, situation *etc.* providing source of livelihood or income

meal[2] (mēl) *n.* grain ground to powder —'**mealy** *a.* —**mealy-mouthed** *a.* euphemistic, insincere in what one says

mealie ('mēli) *n.* **SA** maize

mean[1] (mēn) *vt.* **1.** intend **2.** signify —*vi.* **3.** have the intention of behaving (**meant** *pt./pp.*, '**meaning** *pr.p.*) —'**meaning** *n.* **1.** sense, significance —*a.* **2.** expressive —'**meaningful** *a.* of great meaning or significance —'**meaningless** *a.*

mean[2] (mēn) *a.* **1.** ungenerous, petty **2.** miserly, niggardly **3.** unpleasant **4.** callous **5.** shabby **6.** ashamed —'**meanly** *adv.* —'**meanness** *n.*

mean[3] (mēn) *n.* **1.** thing which is intermediate **2.** middle point —*pl.* **3.** that by which thing is done **4.** money **5.** resources —*a.* **6.** intermediate in time, quality *etc.* **7.** average —**means test** inquiry into person's means to decide eligibility for pension, grant *etc.* —'**meantime** *or* '**meanwhile** *adv./n.* (during) time between one happening and another —**by all means** certainly —**by no means** not at all

meander (mi'andər) *vi.* **1.** flow windingly **2.** wander aimlessly

meant (ment) *pt./pp. of* MEAN[1]

measles ('mēzəlz) *n.* highly contagious virus disease marked by eruptions of skin (*also* **rubeola**) —'**measly** *a.* **1.** *inf.* poor, wretched, stingy **2.** of measles

measure ('mezhər) *n.* **1.** size, quantity **2.** vessel, rod, line *etc.* for ascertaining size or quantity **3.** unit of size or quantity **4.** course, plan of action **5.** law **6.** poetical rhythm **7.** musical time **8.** *Poet.* tune **9.** *obs.* dance —*vt.* **10.** ascertain size, quantity of **11.** indicate measurement of **12.** estimate **13.** bring into competition against —*vi.* **14.** make measurement(s) **15.** be (so much) in size or quantity —'**measurable** *a.* —'**measured** *a.* **1.** determined by measure **2.** steady **3.** rhythmical **4.** carefully considered —'**measurement** *n.* **1.** measuring **2.** size —*pl.* **3.** dimensions

meat (mēt) *n.* **1.** animal flesh as food **2.** food —'**meaty** *a.* **1.** (tasting) of, like meat **2.** brawny **3.** full of import or interest

Mecca ('mekə) *n.* **1.** holy city of Islam **2.** place that attracts visitors

mechanic (mi'kanik) *n.* **1.** one employed in working with machinery **2.** skilled workman —*pl.* **3.** scientific theory of motion —**me'chanical** *a.* **1.** concerned with machines or operation of them **2.** worked, produced (as though) by machine **3.** acting without thought —**me'chanically** *adv.* —**mecha'nician** *n.* —**mechanical drawing** drawing done with T squares, scales *etc.*

mechanism ('mekənizəm) *n.* **1.** structure of machine **2.** piece of machinery —**mechani'zation** *n.* —'**mechanize** *vt.* **1.** equip with machinery **2.** make mechanical, automatic **3.** *Mil.* equip with armored vehicles —'**mechanized** *a.*

mechlorethamine (məklörə'thămin) *n. see* **nitrogen mustard** *at* NITROGEN

Med (med) *n. inf.* Mediterranean region

med. **1.** medical **2.** medicine **3.** medieval **4.** medium

M.Ed. Master of Education

medal ('medəl) *n.* piece of metal with inscription *etc.* used as reward or memento —'**medalist** *or* '**medallist** *n.* **1.** winner of a medal **2.** maker of medals —**me'dallion** *n.* **1.** large medal **2.** any of various things like this in decorative work

meddle ('medəl) *vi.* interfere, busy oneself unnecessarily —'**meddlesome** *a.*

media ('mēdiə) *n., pl. of* MEDIUM, used *esp.* of the mass media, radio, television *etc.* —**media event** event staged for or exploited by the mass media

mediaeval (mēdi'ēvəl, medi-) *a. see* MEDIEVAL

medial ('mēdiəl) *a.* **1.** in the middle **2.** pert. to a mean or average —'**median** *a./n.* middle (point or line) —**median strip** space, oft. landscaped, dividing opposing traffic on a highway

mediate ('mēdiāt) *vi.* **1.** intervene to reconcile —*vt.* **2.** bring about by mediation —*a.* ('mēdiit) **3.** depending on mediation —**medi'ation** *n.* **1.** intervention in behalf of another **2.** act of going between —'**mediator** *n.*

medicine ('medisin) *n.* **1.** drug or remedy for treating disease **2.** science of preventing, diagnosing, alleviating, or curing disease —'**medic** *n. inf.* **1.** doctor **2.** medical orderly **3.** medical student —'**medical** *a.* —'**medically** *adv.* —**me'dicament** *n.* remedy —'**medicate** *vt.* impregnate with medicinal substances —**medi'cation** *n.* —'**medicative** *a.* healing —**me'dicinal** *a.* curative —'**medico** *n. inf.* **1.** doctor **2.** medical student (*pl.* **-s**) —**medical electronics** use of technology in diagnosis and treatment of human disease —**medicine ball** heavy ball for physical training —**medicine man** witch doctor

medieval *or* **mediaeval** (mēdi'ēvəl, medi-) *a.* of Middle Ages —**medi'evalism** *or* **medi'aevalism** *n.* **1.** spirit of Middle Ages **2.** cult of medieval ideals —**medi'evalist** *or* **medi'aevalist** *n.* student of Middle Ages —**Medieval Greek** Greek language from 7th cent. A.D.–1204 —**Medieval Latin** Latin language as used throughout Europe in Middle Ages

mediocre (mēdi'ōkər) *a.* **1.** neither bad nor good, ordinary, middling **2.** second-rate —**mediocrity** (mēdi'okriti) *n.*

meditate ('meditāt) *vi.* **1.** be occupied in thought **2.** reflect deeply on spiritual matters —**medi'tation** *n.* **1.** thought **2.** absorption in thought **3.** religious contemplation —**'meditative** *a.* **1.** thoughtful **2.** reflective —**'meditatively** *adv.*

Mediterranean (meditə'rāniən) *n.* **1.** *short for* **Mediterranean Sea,** sea between S Europe, N Afr., and SW Asia **2.** native or inhabitant of Mediterranean country —*a.* **3.** of Mediterranean Sea

medium ('mēdiəm) *a.* **1.** between two qualities, degrees *etc.*, average —*n.* **2.** middle quality, degree **3.** intermediate substance conveying force **4.** means, agency of communicating news *etc.* to public, as radio, newspapers *etc.* **5.** person through whom communication can supposedly be held with spirit world **6.** surroundings, environment (*pl.* **-s, 'media**) —**medium waves** *Rad.* waves between 100 and 1000 meters

medlar ('medlər) *n.* **1.** tree with fruit like small apple **2.** the fruit, eaten when decayed

medley ('medli) *n.* miscellaneous mixture (*pl.* **-s**)

medulla (mi'dulə) *n.* **1.** marrow **2.** pith **3.** inner tissue —**medullary** ('medəleri) *a.*

Medusa (mi'dyōōsə, -'dōōsə; -zə) *n.* **1.** *Myth.* Gorgon whose head turned beholders into stone **2.** (**m-**) jellyfish (*pl.* **-sae** (-sē, -zē))

meek (mēk) *a.* submissive, humble —**'meekly** *adv.* —**'meekness** *n.*

meerkat ('mēərkat) *n.* S Afr. mongoose

meerschaum ('mēərshəm) *n.* **1.** white substance like clay **2.** tobacco pipe bowl made of this

meet[1] (mēt) *vt.* **1.** come face to face with, encounter **2.** satisfy **3.** pay —*vi.* **4.** come face to face **5.** converge at specified point **6.** assemble **7.** come into contact (**met** *pt./pp.*) —*n.* **8.** meeting, *esp.* for sports —**'meeting** *n.* **1.** assembly **2.** encounter

meet[2] (mēt) *a. obs.* fit, suitable

mega- (*comb. form*) **1.** denoting 10^6, as in *megawatt* **2.** in computer technology, denoting 2^{20} (1 048 576), as in *megabyte* **3.** large, great, as in *megalith*

megadeath ('megədeth) *n.* death of a million people, *esp.* in nuclear war

megahertz ('megəhərts) *n.* one million hertz (*pl.* **'megahertz**)

megalith ('megəlith) *n.* great stone —**mega'lithic** *a.*

megalomania (megəlō'māniə) *n.* desire for, delusions of grandeur, power *etc.* —**megalo'maniac** *a./n.*

megalopolis (megə'lopəlis) *n.* urban complex, usu. comprising several towns —**megalopolitan** (megəlō'politən) *a./n.*

megamouth ('megəmowth) *n.* plankton-feeding shark found in Pacific

megaphone ('megəfōn) *n.* cone-shaped instrument to amplify voice

megaton ('megətun) *n.* **1.** one million tons **2.** explosive power of 1 000 000 tons of TNT

megohm ('megōm) *n. Elec.* one million ohms

meiosis (mī'ōsis) *n.* cell division in which the chromosomes of sperm and egg are reduced from the number characteristic of the species to one half so that the resulting zygote will have the correct number of chromosomes (*pl.* **-ses** (-sēz)) —**meiotic** (mī'otik) *a.*

melamine ('meləmēn) *n.* colorless crystalline compound used in making synthetic resins —**melamine resin** resilient kind of plastic

melancholy ('melənkoli) *n.* **1.** sadness, dejection, gloom —*a.* **2.** gloomy, dejected —**melancholia** (melən'kōliə) *n.* mental disease accompanied by depression —**'melancholic** *n./a.*

Melanesian (melə'nēzhən) *a.* **1.** of Melanesia, its people, or their languages —*n.* **2.** native or inhabitant of Melanesia **3.** group or branch of languages spoken in Melanesia

mélange (mā'lāzh) *Fr.* mixture

melanin ('melənin) *n.* dark pigment found in hair, skin *etc.* of humans and other animals —**mela'noma** *n.* tumor containing melanin which may be benign or cancerous —**mela'nosis** *n.* excessive deposits of melanin in the tissues

Melba toast ('melbə) very thin crisp toast

meld (meld) *v.* **1.** (in card games) declare (cards, which then score points) —*n.* **2.** act of melding **3.** set of cards for melding

melee *or* **mêlée** ('mālā, mā'lā) *n.* confused, noisy fight or crowd

melioidosis (mēlioi'dōsis) *n.* disease of humans and animals caused by bacteria found in soil and water

meliorate ('mēlyərāt, -liə-) *v.* improve —**melio'ration** *n.* —**'meliorism** *n.* doctrine that the world may be improved by human effort —**'meliorist** *n.*

mellifluous (me'liflōōəs, mə-) *or* **mellifluent** *a.* (of sound) smooth, sweet —**mel'lifluence** *n.*

mellophone ('meləfōn) *n.* musical instrument played in a brass band resembling the French horn

mellow ('melō) *a.* **1.** ripe **2.** softened by age, experience **3.** soft, not harsh **4.** genial, gay —*v.* **5.** make, become mellow

melodeon (mi'lōdiən) *n. Mus.* **1.** small accordion **2.** keyboard instrument similar to harmonium

melodrama ('melədrämə) *n.* **1.** play full of sensational and startling situations, often highly emotional **2.** overdramatic behavior, emotion —**melodra'matic** *a.*

melody ('melədi) *n.* **1.** series of musical notes which make tune **2.** sweet sound —**melodic**

(mi'lodik) *a.* **1.** of or relating to melody **2.** of or relating to part in piece of music —**me'lodious** *a.* **1.** pleasing to the ear **2.** tuneful —**'melodist** *n.* **1.** singer **2.** composer

melon ('melən) *n.* large, fleshy, juicy fruit

melt (melt) *v.* **1.** (cause to) become liquid by heat **2.** dissolve **3.** soften **4.** (cause to) waste away **5.** blend —*vi.* **6.** disappear (**'melted** *pt./pp.*, **'molten** *pp.*) —**'melting** *a.* **1.** softening **2.** languishing **3.** tender —**melting point** temperature at which solid turns into liquid —**'meltwater** *n.* melted snow or ice

melton ('meltən) *n.* heavy smooth woolen fabric with short nap

mem. **1.** member **2.** memoir **3.** memorandum **4.** memorial

member ('membər) *n.* **1.** any of individuals making up body or society **2.** limb **3.** any part of complex whole —**'membership** *n.* —**Member of Parliament UK** member of House of Commons or similar legislative body

membrane ('membrān) *n.* thin flexible tissue in plant or animal body —**'membranous** *a.*

memento (mi'mentō) *n.* thing serving to remind, souvenir (*pl.* **-s, -es**) —**memento mori** ('mōrē) object intended to remind people of death

memo ('memō) *n.* memorandum (*pl.* **-s**)

memoir ('memwär) *n.* **1.** autobiography, personal history or biography **2.** record of events

memory ('meməri) *n.* **1.** faculty of recollecting, recalling to mind **2.** recollection **3.** thing remembered **4.** length of time one can remember **5.** commemoration **6.** part or faculty of computer which stores information —**memorabilia** (memərə'biliə) *pl.n.* memorable events or things (*sing.* **-rabile** (-'rabili)) —**'memorable** *a.* worthy of remembrance, noteworthy —**'memorably** *adv.* —**memo'randum** *n.* **1.** note to help the memory *etc.* **2.** informal letter **3.** note of contract (*pl.* **-s, -da** (-də)) —**me'morial** *a.* **1.** of, preserving memory —*n.* **2.** thing, *esp.* a monument, which serves to keep in memory —**me'morialist** *n.* —**me'morialize** *vt.* commemorate —**'memorize** *vt.* commit to memory

men (men) *n., pl. of* MAN

menace ('menis) *n.* **1.** threat —*v.* **2.** threaten

ménage (mā'näzh) *n.* persons of a household —***ménage à trois*** (mānazh a 'trwa) *Fr.* sexual arrangement involving married couple and lover of one of them (*pl.* ***ménages à trois*** (mānazh a 'trwa))

menagerie (mi'najəri) *n.* exhibition, collection of wild animals

mend (mend) *vt.* **1.** repair, patch **2.** reform, correct, put right —*vi.* **3.** improve, *esp.* in health —*n.* **4.** repaired breakage, hole —**on the mend** regaining health

mendacious (men'dāshəs) *a.* untruthful —**mendacity** (men'dasiti) *n.* (tendency to) untruthfulness

mendelevium (mendi'lēviəm) *n. Chem.* transuranic element *Symbol* Mv, at. wt. 256, at. no. 101

mendicant ('mendikənt) *a.* **1.** begging —*n.* **2.** beggar —**'mendicancy** *or* **men'dicity** *n.* begging

menhir ('menhēər) *n.* single, upright monumental stone, monolith

menial ('mēniəl) *a.* **1.** of work requiring little skill **2.** of household duties or servants **3.** servile —*n.* **4.** servant **5.** servile person

Ménière's disease (mən'yerz, 'menyərz) progressive disorder of the inner ear characterized by severe vertigo, tinnitus and deafness

meninges (mi'ninjēz) *pl.n.* three membranes that envelop brain and spinal cord (*sing.* **meninx** ('mēningks)) —**meningeal** (menin'jēəl) *a.* —**meningi'oma** *n.* tumor of the meninges —**meningitis** (menin'jītis) *n.* inflammation of the membranes of the brain

meniscus (mi'niskəs) *n.* **1.** curved surface of liquid **2.** curved lens

menopause ('menəpôz) *n.* period of gradual decline in activity of female reproductive organs

menorah (mi'nōrə) *n.* branched candelabrum used in Jewish celebrations

menses ('mensēz) *n.* **1.** menstruation **2.** matter discharged during menstruation (*pl.* **'menses**)

menstruation (menstrōō'āshən) *n.* approximately monthly discharge of blood and cellular debris from womb of nonpregnant woman —**'menstrual** *a.* —**'menstruate** *vi.*

mensuration (mensə'rāshən, menchə-) *n.* measuring, *esp.* of areas

-ment (*comb. form*) **1.** state; condition; quality, as in *enjoyment* **2.** result or product of action, as in *embankment* **3.** process; action, as in *management*

mental ('mentəl) *a.* **1.** of, done by the mind **2.** *inf.* feeble-minded, mad —**men'tality** *n.* state or quality of mind —**'mentally** *adv.*

menthol ('menthôl) *n.* organic compound found in peppermint, used medicinally

mention ('menchən) *vt.* **1.** refer to briefly, speak of —*n.* **2.** acknowledgment **3.** reference to or remark about person or thing —**'mentionable** *a.* fit or suitable to be mentioned

mentor ('mentôr) *n.* wise, trusted adviser, guide

menu ('menyōō) *n.* list of dishes to be served, or from which to order

meow, miaow (mi'ow), *or* **miaul** (mi'owl) *vi.* **1.** (of cat) make characteristic crying sound —*interj.* **2.** imitation of this sound

meperidine (mə'peridēn) *n.* synthetic pain-relieving drug with sedative and antispasmodic properties: a morphine substitute (*also* **Demerol**)

mercantile ('mərkəntēl, -tīl) *a.* of, engaged in trade, commerce

mercenary ('mərsineri) *a.* **1.** influenced by greed **2.** working merely for reward *—n.* **3.** hired soldier

mercer ('mərsər) *n. esp.* formerly, dealer in fabrics —'**mercery** *n.* his trade, goods

mercerize ('mərsərīz) *vt.* give luster to (cotton fabrics) by treating with chemicals —'**mercerized** *a.*

merchant ('mərchənt) *n.* **1.** one engaged in trade **2.** wholesale trader —**merchandise** ('mərchəndīz, -dīs) *n.* his wares —'**merchantman** *n.* trading ship —**merchant navy** ships engaged in a nation's commerce

Mercurochrome (mər'kyoorəkrōm) *n.* trade name for red organic compound used to disinfect skin and mucous membranes

mercury ('mərkyəri) *n.* **1.** *Chem.* metallic element *Symbol* Hg, at. wt. 200.8, at. no. 80 (*also* **quicksilver**) **2.** (**M-**) *Roman myth.* messenger of the gods **3.** (**M-**) planet nearest to sun —**mer'curial** *a.* **1.** relating to, containing mercury **2.** lively, changeable

mercy ('mərsi) *n.* refraining from infliction of suffering by one who has right, power to inflict it, compassion —'**merciful** *a.* —'**merciless** *a.* —**mercy killing** *see* EUTHANASIA

mere[1] (mēər) *a.* **1.** only **2.** not more than **3.** nothing but —'**merely** *adv.*

mere[2] (mēər) *n. obs.* lake

meretricious (meri'trishəs) *a.* **1.** superficially or garishly attractive **2.** insincere

merganser (mər'gansər) *n.* large, crested diving duck

merge (mərj) *v.* (cause to) lose identity or be absorbed —'**merger** *n.* **1.** combination of business firms into one **2.** absorption into something greater

meridian (mə'ridiən) *n.* **1.** circle of the earth passing through poles **2.** imaginary circle in sky passing through celestial poles **3.** highest point reached by star *etc.* **4.** period of greatest splendor *—a.* **5.** of meridian **6.** at peak of something

meringue (mə'rang) *n.* **1.** baked mixture of white of eggs and sugar **2.** cake of this

merino (mə'rēnō) *n.* **1.** breed of sheep originating in Spain (*pl.* **-s**) **2.** long, fine wool of this sheep **3.** yarn or cloth made from this wool

merit ('merit) *n.* **1.** excellence, worth **2.** quality of deserving reward *—pl.* **3.** excellence *—vt.* **4.** deserve —**meri'tocracy** *n.* **1.** rule by persons chosen for their superior talents or intellect **2.** persons constituting such group —**meri'torious** *a.* deserving praise

merlin ('mərlin) *n.* small falcon

merlot (mər'lō) *n.* dry red wine from grape grown in Bordeaux and California

mermaid ('mərmād) *n.* imaginary sea creature with upper part of woman and lower part of fish

merry ('meri) *a.* joyous, cheerful —'**merrily** *adv.* —'**merriment** *n.* —**merry-go-round** *n.* roundabout

mésalliance (māzal'yäns) *n.* marriage with person of lower social status

mescal (me'skal) *n.* small, bluish-green cactus native to southwest U.S. and Mexico (*also* **peyote**) —**mescaline** ('meskəlin, -lēn) *n.* psychedelic drug obtained from this plant —**mescal buttons** rounded parts of stem yielding mescaline

mesdames (mā'däm, -'dam) *n., pl. of* MADAM, MADAME

mesdemoiselles (mādmwə'zel) *n., pl. of* MADEMOISELLE

mesembryanthemum (mizembri'anthiməm) *n.* low-growing plant with daisylike flowers of various colors

mesh (mesh) *n.* **1.** (one of the open spaces of, or wires *etc.* forming) network, net *—v.* **2.** entangle, become entangled **3.** (of gears) engage *—vi.* **4.** coordinate

meshugge (mə'shoogə) *a. inf.* crazy, obsessed, phobic, bizarre —**meshugene** (mə'shoogənə) *n.* meshugge male —**meshugener** (mə'shoogənər) *n.* meshugge female

mesmerism ('mezmərizəm) *n. former term for* HYPNOTISM —**mes'meric** *a.* —'**mesmerist** *n.* —'**mesmerize** *vt.* **1.** hypnotize **2.** fascinate, hold spellbound

meso- *or before vowel* **mes-** (*comb. form*) middle or intermediate, as in *mesomorph*

Mesolithic (mezə'lithik, mēz-, mēs-, mes-) *n.* **1.** period between Paleolithic and Neolithic *—a.* **2.** of or relating to Mesolithic

meson ('mezon, 'mēz-, 'mēs-, 'mes-) *n.* elementary atomic particle of small mass and very short life

Mesozoic (mezə'zōik, mēz-, mēs-, mes-) *a.* of, denoting, or relating to era of geological time that began 225 000 000 years ago and lasted about 155 000 000 years

mess (mes) *n.* **1.** untidy confusion **2.** trouble, difficulty **3.** group in armed services who regularly eat together **4.** place where they eat *—vi.* **5.** make mess **6.** *Mil.* eat in a mess *—vt.* **7.** muddle —'**messy** *a.* —**mess about** *or* **around** potter about

message ('mesij) *n.* **1.** communication sent **2.** meaning, moral **3.** errand —'**messenger** *n.* bearer of message

Messiah (mi'sīə) *n.* **1.** Jews' promised deliverer **2.** Christ —**Messianic** (mesi'anik) *a.*

messieurs (mə'syə, mā'syə; mə'sēərz) *n., pl. of* MONSIEUR

Messrs. ('mesərz) *n., pl. of* MR.

mestizo (me'stēzō) *n.* person of mixed European and Amerindian ancestry (*pl.* **-s**)

met (met) *pt./pp. of* MEET[1]

met. **1.** meteorological **2.** meteorology **3.** metropolitan

meta- *or sometimes before vowel* **met-**

(*comb. form*) change, as in *metamorphose, metathesis*

metabolism (miˈtabəlizəm) *n.* chemical process of living organism *esp.* energy production, tissue synthesis, formation and excretion of waste products —**metaˈbolic** *a.* —**meˈtabolize** *v.*

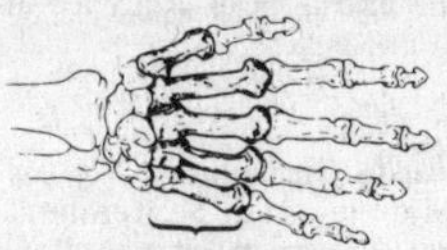

metacarpus

metacarpus (metəˈkärpəs) *n.* **1.** skeleton of hand between wrist and fingers **2.** corresponding bones in other vertebrates (*pl.* **-pi** (-pī)) —**metaˈcarpal** *a./n.*

metal (ˈmetəl) *n.* **1.** mineral substance, opaque, fusible and malleable, capable of conducting heat and electricity **2.** *Chem.* such a substance in a pure state, as distinguished from alloys —**meˈtallic** *a.* —**ˈmetalloid** *n.* **1.** nonmetallic element that has some of properties of metal —*a.* (*also* **metalˈloidal**) **2.** of or being metalloid **3.** resembling metal —**metalˈlurgic** *or* **metalˈlurgical** *a.* —**ˈmetallurgist** *n.* —**ˈmetallurgy** *n.* scientific study of extracting, refining metals, and their structure and properties

metamorphosis (metəˈmörfəsis) *n.* change of shape, character *etc.* (*pl.* **-phoses** (-fəsēz)) —**metaˈmorphic** *a.* (*esp.* of rocks) changed in texture, structure by heat, pressure *etc.* —**metaˈmorphose** *v.* transform

metaphor (ˈmetəför, -fər) *n.* **1.** figure of speech in which term is transferred to something it does not literally apply to **2.** instance of this —**metaˈphorical** *a.* figurative —**metaˈphorically** *adv.*

metaphysics (metəˈfiziks) *pl.n.* (*with sing. v.*) branch of philosophy concerned with being and knowing —**metaˈphysical** *a.* —**metaphyˈsician** *n.*

metastasis (miˈtastəsis) *n. Pathol.* spreading of disease, *esp.* cancer cells, from one part of body to another (*pl.* **-ses** (-sēz)) —**metastatic** (metəˈstatik) *a.*

metatarsus

metatarsus (metəˈtärsəs) *n.* **1.** skeleton of foot between toes and ankle **2.** corresponding bones in other vertebrates (*pl.* **-si** (-sī)) —**metaˈtarsal** *a./n.*

metate (məˈtäti) *n.* stone for grinding maize

metathesis (miˈtathəsis) *n.* transposition, *esp.* of letters in word, *eg* Old English *bridd* gives modern *bird* (*pl.* **-eses** (-əsēz))

metazoan (metəˈzōən) *n.* **1.** any animal having a body composed of many cells —*a.* (*also* **metaˈzoic**) **2.** of or relating to metazoans

mete (mēt) *vt.* measure —**mete out 1.** distribute **2.** allot as punishment

metempsychosis (mitemsiˈkōsis, mitempsi-; metəmsīˈkōsis) *n.* migration of soul from one body to another (*pl.* **-ses** (-sēz)) —**metempsyˈchosist** *n.*

meteor (ˈmētiər) *n.* small, fast-moving celestial body, visible as streak of incandescence if it enters earth's atmosphere —**meteˈoric** *a.* **1.** of, like meteor **2.** brilliant but short-lived —**ˈmeteorite** *n.* fallen meteor —**ˈmeteoroid** *n.* any of small celestial bodies that are thought to orbit sun —**meteorˈoidal** *a.*

meteorology (mētiəˈroləji) *n.* study of earth's atmosphere, *esp.* for weather forecasting —**meteoroˈlogical** *a.* —**meteorˈologist** *n.*

meter (ˈmētər) *n.* **1.** basic unit of length in metric system defined by path of speed of light during specific interval **2.** instrument for recording consumption of gas, electricity *etc.* **3.** *Mus.* basic scheme of beats within a measure —**ˈmetric** *a.* of system of weights and measures in which meter is a unit —**metrical** (ˈmetrikəl) *a.* of measurement of poetic meter —**metricate** (ˈmetrikāt) *v.* convert (measuring system *etc.*) from nonmetric to metric units —**metrication** (metriˈkāshən) *n.* —**metric ton** *see* TONNE

Meth. Methodist

methane (ˈmethān) *n.* flammable gas, compound of carbon and hydrogen

methanol (ˈmethənöl) *n.* colorless, poisonous liquid used as solvent and fuel (*also* **methyl alcohol**)

methinks (miˈthingks) *v. impers. obs.* it seems to me (**meˈthought** *pt.*)

method (ˈmethəd) *n.* **1.** way, manner **2.** technique **3.** orderliness, system —**meˈthodical** *a.* orderly —**ˈmethodize** *vt.* reduce to order —**methoˈdology** *n.* particular method or procedure

Methodist (ˈmethədist) *n./a.* (member) of Protestant Christian denomination derived from system of faith and practice initiated by John Wesley and his followers in 1738 —**ˈMethodism** *n.*

methyl (ˈmethil) *n.* (compound containing) a saturated hydrocarbon group of atoms —**ˈmethylate** *vt.* **1.** combine with methyl **2.** mix with methanol —**methyl alcohol** *see* METHANOL —**methylated spirits** ethyl alcohol contaminated with methyl alcohol to make it undrinkable

meticulous (miˈtikyələs) *a.* (over)particular about details

métier (ˈmetyā) *n.* **1.** profession, vocation **2.** forte

métis (māˈtēs) *n.* person of mixed blood

metonymy (miˈtonimi) *n.* figure of speech in which thing is replaced by another associated with it, *eg the Crown* for *the king* —**metoˈnymical** *a.*

metric (ˈmetrik) *a. see* METER

Metro (ˈmetrō) *n.* **C** metropolitan city administration

metronome (ˈmetrənōm) *n.* instrument which marks musical time by means of ticking pendulum

metropolis (miˈtropəlis) *n.* chief city of a country, region —**metroˈpolitan** *a.* **1.** of metropolis —*n.* **2.** bishop with authority over other bishops of a province

-metry (*n. comb. form*) process or science of measuring, as in *geometry* —**-metric** (*a. comb. form*)

mettle (ˈmetəl) *n.* courage, spirit —ˈ**mettlesome** *a.* high-spirited

mew[1] (myōō) *n.* **1.** cry of cat, gull —*vi.* **2.** utter this cry

mew[2] (myōō) *n.* any sea gull, *esp.* common gull

Mex. **1.** Mexican **2.** Mexico

Mexico (ˈmeksikō) *n.* country in Central America bounded north by the U.S.A., west and southwest by the Pacific, south by Guatemala and Belize and east by the Gulf of Mexico —ˈ**Mexican** *n./a.*

mezuza (məˈzōōzə) *n.* small oblong container holding printed verses from Deuteronomy fixed to door jamb, sometimes worn as ornament

mezzanine (ˈmezənēn) *n.* intermediate story, balcony between two main stories, *esp.* between first and second floors

mezzo (ˈmetsō) *adv. Mus.* moderately; quite —**mezzo-soprano** *n.* voice, singer between soprano and contralto (*pl.* **-s**)

mezzotint (ˈmetsōtint) *n.* **1.** method of engraving by scraping roughened surface **2.** print so made

mf *Mus.* mezzo forte

MF **1.** *Rad.* medium frequency. **2.** Middle French

mfr. **1.** manufacture **2.** manufacturer

mg *or* **mg.** milligram(s)

Mg *Chem.* magnesium

Mgr. **1.** manager **2.** Monseigneur **3.** Monsignor

MHG Middle High German

MHS Mohs' scale

MHz megahertz

mi (mē) *n. Mus.* **1.** in fixed system of solmization, the note E **2.** in movable do system, the third note of a major scale

MI Michigan

Miami (mīˈami) *n.* member of Algonquian-speaking Amerindian people orig. of Wisconsin and Indiana (*pl.* **Miami, -s**)

miaow (miˈow) *see* MEOW

miasma (mīˈazmə, mi-) *n.* unwholesome or foreboding atmosphere (*pl.* **-mata** (-mətə), **-s**) —**miasmatic** (mīəzˈmatik) *a.*

mica (ˈmīkə) *n.* mineral found as glittering scales, plates

Micah (ˈmīkə) *n. Bible* 33rd book of the O.T., written by the prophet Micah, displaying the character and acts of Jehovah in relation to the nation of Israel

mice (mīs) *n., pl. of* MOUSE

Mich. Michigan

Michaelmas (ˈmikəlməs) *n.* feast of Archangel St. Michael, 29th September —**Michaelmas daisy** common garden flower of aster family

Micheas (ˈmīkiəs) *n. Bible* Micah in the Douay Version of the O.T.

Michigan (ˈmishigən) *n.* East North Central state of the U.S., admitted to the Union in 1837. Abbrev.: **Mich., MI** (with ZIP code)

mick (mik) *n. offens.* Irishman

Mickey Finn (fin) *sl.* drink containing drug to make drinker unconscious

micro (ˈmīkrō) *n. inf.* **1.** microcomputer **2.** microprocessor (*pl.* **-s**)

micro- *or before vowel* **micr-** (*comb. form*) **1.** small or minute, as in *microdot* **2.** magnification or amplification, as in *microscope, microphone* **3.** involving use of microscope, as in *microscopy* **4.** one millionth, as in *microfarad* (millionth of a farad)

microbe (ˈmīkrōb) *n.* **1.** minute organism **2.** disease germ —**miˈcrobial** *a.*

microbiology (mīkrōbīˈoləji) *n.* branch of biology involving study of microorganisms —**microbioˈlogic(al)** *a.*

Microcard (ˈmīkrōkärd) *n.* trade name for card having microcopies of printed data

microcephaly (mīkrōˈsefəli) *n.* condition in which the brain is small and undeveloped

microchip (ˈmīkrōchip) *n.* small wafer of silicon *etc.* containing electronic circuits (*also* **chip**)

microcircuit (ˈmīkrōsərkit) *n.* miniature electronic circuit, *esp.* integrated circuit —ˈ**microcircuitry** *n.*

microcomputer (mīkrōkəmˈpyōōtər) *n.* computer in which central processing unit is contained in one or more silicon chips

microcopy (ˈmīkrōkopi) *n.* minute photographic replica useful for storage because of its small size

microcosm (ˈmīkrəkozəm) *or* **microcosmos** (mīkrəˈkozməs) *n.* **1.** miniature representation, model *etc.* of some larger system **2.** the microscopic or even smaller world —**microˈcosmic** *a.*

microdot (ˈmīkrōdot) *n.* extremely small microcopy

microelectronics (ˈmīkrōilekˈtroniks) *pl.n.* (*with sing. v.*) branch of electronics concerned with microcircuits

microfauna (ˈmīkrofōnə) *n.* minute animals living in sand and gravel below the sea's surface

microfiche (ˈmīkrōfēsh) *n.* microfilm in sheet form

microfilm (ˈmīkrəfilm) *n.* miniaturized recording of manuscript, book on roll of film

microgroove (ˈmīkrōgrōōv) *n.* **1.** narrow groove of long-playing phonograph record —*a.* **2.** (of a record) having such grooves

micrometer (mīˈkromitər) *n.* instrument for measuring very small distances or angles

microminiaturization (mīkrōminiəchōōriˈzāshən) *n.* production of small components and circuits and equipment in which they are used

micron (ˈmīkron) *n.* unit of length, one millionth of a meter

microorganism (mīkrōˈörgənizəm) *n.* smallest and simplest form of life, *eg* bacteria, yeasts, protozoa *etc.*

microphone (ˈmīkrəfōn) *n.* instrument for amplifying, transmitting sounds

microprint (ˈmīkrəprint) *n.* greatly reduced photographic copy of print, read by magnifying device

microprocessor (mīkrōˈprōsesər) *n.* integrated circuit acting as central processing unit in small computer

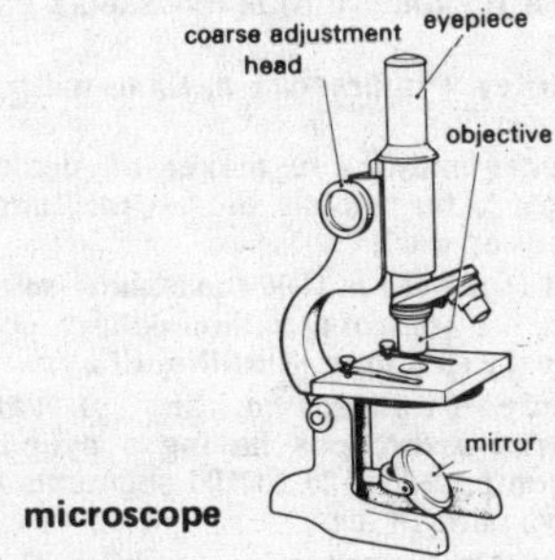

microscope

microscope (ˈmīkrəskōp) *n.* instrument by which very small body is magnified and made visible —**microscopic** (mīkrəˈskopik) *a.* **1.** of microscope **2.** very small —**microscopy** (mīˈkroskəpi) *n.* use of microscope

microstructure (ˈmīkrōstrukchər) *n.* structure on microscopic scale, *esp.* of alloy as observed by etching, polishing *etc.* under microscope

microsurgery (mīkrōˈsərjəri) *n.* minute surgical dissection or manipulation of individual cells under a microscope

microwave (ˈmīkrəwāv) *n.* electromagnetic wave with wavelength of a few centimeters, used in radar, cooking *etc.*

micturate (ˈmikchərāt) *vi.* urinate —**micturition** (mikchəˈrishən) *n.*

mid (mid) *a.* intermediate, in the middle of —ˈ**midday** *n.* noon —**midland** (ˈmidlənd) *n.* **1.** interior of a country —*pl.* **2.** central England —ˈ**midnight** *n.* twelve o'clock at night —**midnight sun** sun visible at midnight during summer inside Arctic and Antarctic circles —ˈ**midshipman** *n.* naval officer of lowest commissioned rank —ˈ**mid**ˈ**summer** *n.* **1.** summer solstice **2.** middle of summer —ˈ**midway** *a./adv.* halfway —ˈ**mid**ˈ**winter** *n.*

midden (ˈmidən) *n.* **1.** dunghill **2.** rubbish heap

middle (ˈmidəl) *a.* **1.** equidistant from two extremes **2.** medium, intermediate —*n.* **3.** middle point or part —ˈ**middling** *a.* **1.** mediocre **2.** moderate —*adv.* **3.** *inf.* moderately —**middle age** period of life between youth and old age, usu. considered to be between ages of 40 and 60 —**middle-aged** *a.* —**Middle Ages** period from end of Roman Empire to Renaissance, roughly A.D. 500–1500 —**middle C** *Mus.* note written on first ledger line below treble staff or first ledger line above bass staff —**middle class** social class of businessmen, professional people *etc.* —**middle-class** *a.* —**middle ear** sound-conducting part of ear —**Middle East** (loosely) area around E Mediterranean, *esp.* Israel and Arab countries from Turkey to N Afr. and eastward to Iran —**Middle Eastern** —**Middle English** English language from about 1100 to about 1450 —**Middle High German** High German from about 1200 to about 1500 —**Middle Low German** Low German from about 1200 to about 1500 —ˈ**middleman** *n.* trader between producer and consumer —**middle-of-the-road** *a.* not extreme; moderate —ˈ**middleweight** *n.* **1.** professional boxer weighing 154–160 lbs. (70–72.5 kg); amateur boxer weighing 157–165 lbs. (71–75 kg) **2.** wrestler weighing usu. 172–192 lbs. (78–87 kg)

midget (ˈmijit) *n.* very small person or thing

midi (ˈmidi) *a.* (of skirt *etc.*) reaching to below knee or midcalf

midriff (ˈmidrif) *n.* middle part of body

midst (midst) *prep.* **1.** in the middle of —*n.* **2.** middle —**in the midst of** surrounded by, among

Midway Islands (ˈmidwā) territory of the U.S. located in western Pacific Ocean

midwife (ˈmidwīf) *n.* trained person who assists at childbirth —**midwifery** (midˈwifəri) *n.* art, practice of this

mien (mēn) *n.* person's bearing, demeanor or appearance

might[1] (mīt) *pt.* *of* MAY

might[2] (mīt) *n.* power, strength —ˈ**mightily** *adv.* **1.** strongly **2.** powerfully —ˈ**mighty** *a.* **1.** of great power **2.** strong **3.** valiant **4.** important —*adv.* **5.** *inf.* very

mignonette (minyəˈnet) *n.* gray-green plant with sweet-smelling flowers

migraine (ˈmīgrān) *n.* severe recurring

headache marked by nausea and visual disturbances and usu. on one side of head

migrate (ˈmīgrāt, mīˈgrāt) *vi.* move from one place to another —ˈ**migrant** *n./a.* —**miˈgration** *n.* **1.** act of passing from one place, condition to another **2.** number migrating together —ˈ**migratory** *a.* **1.** of, capable of migration **2.** (of animals) changing from one place to another according to season

mikado (miˈkädō) *n.* (*oft.* **M-**) Japanese emperor

mike (mīk) *n. inf.* microphone

Mike (mīk) *n.* word used in communications for the letter *m*

milady (miˈlādi) *n.* formerly, continental title used for English gentlewoman

milch (milk, milch) *a.* giving, kept for milk

mild (mīld) *a.* **1.** not strongly flavored **2.** gentle, merciful **3.** calm or temperate —ˈ**mildly** *adv.* —ˈ**mildness** *n.* —**mild steel** any strong tough steel that contains low quantity of carbon

mildew (ˈmildyōō, -dōō) *n.* **1.** destructive fungus on plants or things exposed to damp —*v.* **2.** become tainted, affect with mildew

mile (mīl) *n.* measure of length, 1760 yards, 1.609 km —ˈ**mileage** *n.* **1.** distance in miles **2.** traveling expenses per mile **3.** miles traveled (per gallon of gasoline) **4.** *inf.* advantage, profit, use —ˈ**milestone** *n.* **1.** stone marker showing distance **2.** significant event, achievement —**nautical mile** *see* NAUTICAL

milfoil (ˈmilfoil) *n.* yarrow

milieu (mēlˈyə, -ˈyōō) *n.* environment, condition in life

military (ˈmiliteri) *a.* **1.** of, for, soldiers, armies or war **2.** of style of dress marked by severe cut, brass buttons, epaulettes *etc.* —*n.* **3.** armed services —ˈ**militancy** *n.* —ˈ**militant** *a.* **1.** aggressive, vigorous in support of cause **2.** prepared, willing to fight —ˈ**militarism** *n.* enthusiasm for military force and methods —ˈ**militarist** *n.* —ˈ**militarize** *vt.* convert to military use —**militia** (miˈlishə) *n.* military force of citizens for home service

militate (ˈmilitāt) *vi.* (*esp. with* against) have strong influence, effect (on)

milium (ˈmiliəm) *n.* whitish lump in the skin due to a blocked duct in an oil gland (*pl.* **-ia** (-iə))

Milium (ˈmiliəm) *n.* trade name for metal-insulated fabric used for lining outer clothing and curtains

milk (milk) *n.* **1.** white fluid with which mammals feed their young **2.** fluid in some plants —*vt.* **3.** draw milk from —ˈ**milky** *a.* **1.** containing, like milk **2.** (of liquids) opaque, clouded —**milk-and-water** *a.* weak, feeble, or insipid —ˈ**milkmaid** *n. esp.* formerly, woman working with cows or in dairy —**milk run** *Aeron. inf.* routine and uneventful flight —**milk shake** frothy drink made of milk, flavoring and ice cream —ˈ**milksop** *n.* effeminate fellow —**milk teeth** first set of teeth in young mammals —**Milky Way** luminous band of stars *etc.* stretching across sky, the galaxy —**milk of magnesia** suspension of magnesium hydroxide in water, used as laxative (*also* **magnesia magma**)

mill (mil) *n.* **1.** factory **2.** machine for grinding, pulverizing corn, paper *etc.* —*vt.* **3.** put through mill **4.** cut fine grooves across edges of (*eg* coins) —*vi.* **5.** move in confused manner, as cattle or crowds of people —ˈ**miller** *n.* —ˈ**millpond** *n.* pool formed by damming stream to provide water to turn mill wheel —ˈ**millrace** *n.* current of water driving mill wheel —ˈ**millstone** *n.* flat circular stone for grinding

millennium (miˈleniəm) *n.* **1.** period of a thousand years during which some claim Christ is to reign on earth **2.** period of a thousand years **3.** period of peace, happiness (*pl.* **-s, -ia** (-iə))

millet (ˈmilit) *n.* a cereal grass

milli- (*comb. form*) thousandth, as in *milliliter*

milliard (ˈmilyärd, ˈmiliärd) *n.* in England, France, and Germany, the name for one billion, the number one followed by nine zeros: 1 000 000 000

millibar (ˈmilibär) *n.* unit of atmospheric pressure

milligram (ˈmiligram) *n.* thousandth part of a gram

millimeter (ˈmilimētər) *n.* thousandth part of a meter

milliner (ˈmilinər) *n.* maker of, dealer in women's hats, ribbons *etc.* —ˈ**millinery** *n.* his goods or work

million (ˈmilyən) *n.* 1000 thousand —**millionˈaire** *n.* **1.** owner of a million dollars, pounds *etc.* **2.** very rich man —ˈ**millionth** *a./n.*

millipede (ˈmilipēd) *n.* any of various terrestrial arthropods having a cylindrical body composed of 20 to 100 segments each with two pairs of legs

milt (milt) *n.* reproductive secretion of male fish

mime (mīm) *n.* **1.** acting without the use of words —*v.* **2.** act in mime

mimic (ˈmimik) *vt.* **1.** imitate (person, manner *etc.*), *esp.* for satirical effect (ˈ**mimicked**, ˈ**mimicking**) —*n.* **2.** one who, or animal which does this, or is adept at it —*a.* **3.** imitative, simulated —**miˈmetic** *a.* **1.** of, resembling, or relating to imitation **2.** *Biol.* of or exhibiting protective resemblance to another species —ˈ**mimicry** *n.* mimicking

mimosa (miˈmōsə, mī-; -zə) *n.* genus of plants with fluffy, yellow flowers and sensitive leaves

min. **1.** minim **2.** minimum **3.** minute

mina (ˈmīnə) *n. see* MYNAH

minaret (minəˈret, ˈminəret) *n.* tall slender tower of mosque

minatory ('minətōri) *or* **minatorial** *a.* threatening or menacing

mince (mins) *vt.* **1.** cut, chop small **2.** soften or moderate (words *etc.*) —*vi.* **3.** walk, speak in affected manner —'**mincing** *a.* affected in manner —'**mincemeat** *n.* mixture of currants, spices, suet *etc.* —**mince pie** pie containing mincemeat

mind (mīnd) *n.* **1.** thinking faculties as distinguished from the body, intellectual faculties **2.** memory, attention **3.** intention **4.** opinion **5.** sanity —*vt.* **6.** take offense at **7.** care for **8.** attend to **9.** be cautious, careful about **10.** be concerned, troubled about —*vi.* **11.** be careful —'**mindful** *a.* **1.** heedful **2.** keeping in memory —'**mindless** *a.* stupid, careless —**mind-reader** *n.* person seemingly able to discern thoughts of another —**mind's eye** visual memory or imagination

mine[1] (mīn) *pron.* belonging to me

mine[2] (mīn) *n.* **1.** deep hole for digging out coal, metals *etc.* **2.** in war, hidden deposit of explosive to blow up ship *etc.* **3.** profitable source —*vt.* **4.** dig from mine **5.** make mine in or under **6.** place explosive mines in, on —*vi.* **7.** make, work in mine —'**miner** *n.* one who works in a mine —'**minefield** *n.* area of land or sea containing mines —'**minelayer** *n.* ship for laying mines —'**minesweeper** *n.* ship for clearing away mines

mineral ('minərəl, 'minrəl) *n.* **1.** chemical element or compound occurring naturally as a product of inorganic processes **2.** atom of substance other than carbon, hydrogen, oxygen and nitrogen in living system **3.** any of various homogeneous substances, *esp.* coal, salt, water or gas, obtained from the ground **4.** anything neither animal nor vegetable —'**mineralist** *n.* —**minera'logical** *a.* —**mine'ralogy** *n.* science of minerals —**mineral oil** oil of mineral origin, *esp.* refined petrolatum jelly, used as a laxative —**mineral water** water impregnated with minerals or gases

minestrone (mini'strōni) *n.* thick vegetable soup usu. containing beans and pasta

mingle ('minggəl) *v.* mix, blend, unite, merge

mingy ('minji) *a. inf.* miserly, stingy, or niggardly

mini ('mini) *n.* something small or miniature —'**miniskirt** *n.* very short skirt, one at least four inches above knee

mini- (*comb. form*) smaller or shorter than standard size

miniature ('miniəchŏŏər) *n.* **1.** small painted portrait **2.** anything on small scale —*a.* **3.** small-scale, minute —'**miniaturist** *n.* —'**miniaturize** *vt.* make or construct on a very small scale

minim ('minim) *n.* **1.** unit of fluid measure, one sixtieth of a fluid dram **2.** *Mus.* half note

minimize ('minimīz) *vt.* bring to, estimate at smallest possible amount —'**minimal** *a.* —'**minimum** *n.* **1.** lowest size or quantity (*pl.* **-s, -ma** (-mə)) —*a.* **2.** least possible —**minimum wage** lowest wage that employer is permitted to pay by law or union contract

minion ('minyən) *n.* **1.** favorite **2.** servile dependent

minister ('ministər) *n.* **1.** diplomatic representative **2.** clergyman —*vi.* **3.** (*oft. with* to) attend to needs (of), take care (of) —'**ministrant** *a./n.* —**minis'tration** *n.* rendering help, *esp.* to sick —'**ministry** *n.* **1.** office of clergyman **2.** period of service of minister **3.** act of ministering

miniver ('minivər) *n.* a white fur used in ceremonial costumes

mink (mingk) *n.* **1.** variety of weasel **2.** its (brown) fur

Minnesota (mini'sōtə) *n.* West North Central state of the U.S., admitted to the Union in 1858. Abbrev.: **Minn., MN** (with ZIP code)

minnow ('minō) *n.* small freshwater fish

Minoan (mi'nōən) *a.* **1.** of Bronze Age culture of Crete from about 3000 B.C. to about 1100 B.C. —*n.* **2.** Cretan belonging to Minoan culture

minor ('mīnər) *a.* **1.** lesser **2.** under age —*n.* **3.** person below age of legal majority **4.** minor scale in music —**minority** (mi'nōriti) *n.* **1.** lesser number **2.** smaller party voting together **3.** ethical or religious group in a minority in any state **4.** state of being a minor —**minor arts** generally all art forms not painting, sculpture or architecture —**minor scale** *Mus.* scale with semitones instead of whole tones after second and seventh notes

Minotaur ('minətōr) *n.* fabled monster, half bull, half man

minster ('minstər) *n.* **1.** *Hist.* monastery church **2.** cathedral, large church

minstrel ('minstrəl) *n.* **1.** medieval singer, musician, poet —*pl.* **2.** performers of Negro songs —'**minstrelsy** *n.* **1.** art, body of minstrels **2.** collection of songs

mint[1] (mint) *n.* **1.** place where money is coined —*vt.* **2.** coin, invent

mint[2] (mint) *n.* aromatic plant —**mint julep** tall drink of bourbon, ice, sugar and mint

minuet (minyōō'et) *n.* **1.** stately dance in moderate triple time **2.** music for it

minus ('mīnəs) *prep.* **1.** less, with the deduction of, deprived of —*a.* **2.** lacking **3.** negative —*n.* **4.** the sign of subtraction (-)

minuscule ('minəskyōōl) *n.* **1.** lower-case letter **2.** writing using such letters —*a.* **3.** relating to, printed in, or written in small letters **4.** very small —**minuscular** (mi'nuskyələr) *a.*

minute[1] (mī'nyōōt, -'nōōt) *a.* **1.** very small **2.** precise —**mi'nutely** *adv.* —**minutiae** (mi'nyōōshiē, -'nōō-) *pl.n.* trifles, precise details

minute[2] ('minit) *n.* **1.** 60th part of hour or degree **2.** moment **3.** memorandum —*pl.* **4.**

record of proceedings of meeting *etc.* —*vt.* **5.** make minute of **6.** record in minutes —**minute steak** small steak that can be cooked quickly

minx (mingks) *n.* bold, flirtatious woman

minyan (ˈminyən) *n. Judaism* the ten male Jews required for a religious service (*pl.* **minyanim** (minyəˈnēm))

Miocene (ˈmīəsēn) *a.* **1.** of or denoting fourth epoch of Tertiary period —*n.* **2.** this epoch or rock system

miracle (ˈmirəkəl) *n.* **1.** supernatural event **2.** marvel —**miˈraculous** *a.* —**miˈraculously** *adv.* —**miracle drug** newly discovered drug that has startling therapeutic effect (*also* **wonder drug**) —**miracle play** drama (*esp.* medieval) based on sacred subject

mirage (miˈräzh) *n.* deceptive image in atmosphere, *eg* of lake in desert

mire (ˈmīər) *n.* **1.** swampy ground, mud —*vt.* **2.** stick in, dirty with mud

mirror (ˈmirər) *n.* **1.** glass or polished surface reflecting images —*vt.* **2.** reflect —**mirror image 1.** image as observed in mirror **2.** object that corresponds to another in reverse as does image in mirror

mirth (mərth) *n.* merriment, gaiety —ˈ**mirthful** *a.* —ˈ**mirthless** *a.*

mis- (*comb. form*) wrong(ly), bad(ly). See the list below

misadventure (misədˈvenchər) *n.* unlucky chance

misalliance (misəˈlīəns) *n.* unsuitable alliance or marriage —**misalˈly** *v.*

misanthrope (ˈmisənthrōp) *n.* hater of mankind —**misanthropic** (misənˈthropik) *a.* —**miˈsanthropy** *n.*

misappropriate (misəˈprōpriāt) *vt.* **1.** put to dishonest use **2.** embezzle —**misappropriˈation** *n.*

misbegotten (misbiˈgotən) *a.* **1.** unlawfully obtained **2.** badly conceived or designed **3.** *Lit., dial.* illegitimate; bastard

miscarry (misˈkari) *vi.* **1.** bring forth young prematurely **2.** go wrong, fail —**misˈcarriage** *n.*

miscast (misˈkast) *v.* **1.** distribute (acting parts) wrongly —*vt.* **2.** assign to unsuitable role

miscegenation (misejiˈnāshən, misijiˈnā-) *n.* interbreeding of races

miscellaneous (misəˈlāniəs) *a.* mixed, assorted —**misˈcellany** *n.* **1.** collection of assorted writings in one book **2.** medley

mischance (misˈchans) *n.* unlucky event

mischief (ˈmischif) *n.* **1.** annoying behavior **2.** inclination to tease, disturb **3.** harm **4.** source of harm or annoyance —ˈ**mischievous** *a.* **1.** (of a child) full of pranks **2.** disposed to mischief **3.** having harmful effect

miscible (ˈmisibəl) *a.* capable of mixing

misconception (miskənˈsepshən) *n.* wrong idea, belief

miscreant (ˈmiskriənt) *n.* wicked person, evildoer, villain

misdemeanor (misdiˈmēnər) *n.* **1.** formerly, offense less grave than a felony **2.** minor offense

misdoubt (misˈdowt) *v. obs.* doubt or suspect

mise en scène (mēz ã ˈsen) *Fr.* **1.** arrangement of scenery *etc.* in play; stage setting **2.** environment of event

miser (ˈmīzər) *n.* **1.** hoarder of money **2.** stingy person —ˈ**miserliness** *n.* —ˈ**miserly** *a.* **1.** avaricious **2.** niggardly

miserable (ˈmizərəbəl) *a.* **1.** very unhappy, wretched **2.** causing misery **3.** worthless **4.** squalid —ˈ**miserableness** *n.* —ˈ**misery** *n.* **1.** great unhappiness **2.** distress **3.** poverty

misericord *or* **misericorde** (miˈzerikörd) *n.* ledge projecting from underside of hinged seat of choir stall in church, on which occupant can support himself while standing

misfire (misˈfīər) *vi.* fail to fire, start, function successfully

misfit (ˈmisfit) *n. esp.* person not suited to his environment or work

misgiving (misˈgiving) *n.* (*oft. pl.*) feeling of fear, doubt *etc.*

misguided (misˈgīdid) *a.* foolish, unreasonable

mishap (ˈmis-hap) *n.* minor accident

mishmash (ˈmishmash) *n.* confused collection or mixture

mislay (misˈlā) *vt.* put in place which cannot later be remembered

mislead (misˈlēd) *vt.* **1.** give false information to **2.** lead astray (**misˈled** *pt./pp.*) —**misˈleading** *a.* deceptive

misnomer (misˈnōmər) *n.* **1.** wrong name or term **2.** use of this

misogamy (miˈsogəmi) *n.* hatred of marriage —**miˈsogamist** *n.*

misogyny (miˈsojini) *n.* hatred of women —**miˈsogynist** *n.*

misrepresent (misrepriˈzent) *vt.* portray in wrong or misleading light

misrule (misˈrōōl) *vt.* **1.** govern inefficiently or without justice —*n.* **2.** inefficient or unjust government **3.** disorder

misadˈdress
misadminisˈtration
misaˈlignment
misapˈply
misbeˈhave
misˈcalculate
misconˈceive
misˈconduct
misˈcount
misˈdeed
misemˈploy
misˈfortune
misˈgovern
misˈgovernment
misˈhandle
misˈhear
misˈhit
misˈjudge
misˈmanage
misˈmanagement
misˈmarriage
misperˈception
misˈphrase
misˈread
misreˈport
misˈstate
misˈstatement
misˈtime
misˈtreat
misˈtype
misunderˈstand
misˈuse

miss (mis) *vt.* **1.** fail to hit, reach, find, catch, or notice **2.** not be in time for **3.** omit **4.** notice or regret absence of **5.** avoid —*vi.* **6.** (of engine) misfire —*n.* **7.** fact, instance of missing —**'missing** *a.* **1.** lost **2.** absent —**missing link 1.** hypothetical extinct animal intermediate between anthropoid apes and man **2.** any missing section or part in series

Miss (mis) *n.* **1.** title of unmarried woman **2.** (**m-**) girl

Miss. Mississippi

missal ('misəl) *n.* book containing prayers *etc.* of the Mass

missile ('misil) *n.* that which may be thrown, shot, homed to damage, destroy —**guided missile** *see* GUIDE

mission ('mishən) *n.* **1.** specific task or duty **2.** calling in life **3.** delegation **4.** sending or being sent on some service **5.** those sent —**'missionary** *n.* **1.** one sent to a place, society to spread religion —*a.* **2.** of, like missionary or religious mission

missis ('misiz, -is) *n. see* MISSUS

Mississippi (misi'sipi) *n.* East South Central state of the U.S., admitted to the Union in 1817. Abbrev.: **Miss., MS** (with ZIP code)

missive ('misiv) *n.* letter

Missouri (mi'zo͞ori, -'zo͞orə) *n.* West North Central state of the U.S., admitted to the Union in 1821. Abbrev.: **Mo., MO** (with ZIP code)

misspend (mis'spend) *v.* spend thoughtlessly or wastefully (**-'spending, -'spent**)

missus *or* **missis** ('misiz, -is) *n.* (*usu. with* the) one's wife or wife of person addressed or referred to

mist (mist) *n.* water vapor in fine drops —**'mistily** *adv.* —**'misty** *a.* **1.** full of mist **2.** dim **3.** obscure

mistake (mi'stāk) *n.* **1.** error, blunder —*vt.* **2.** fail to understand **3.** form wrong opinion about **4.** take (person or thing) for another —**mis'taken** *a.* **1.** wrong in opinion *etc.* **2.** arising from error in judgment *etc.*

mister ('mistər) *n.* title of courtesy to a man

mistle thrush ('misəl) European thrush with brown back and spotted breast

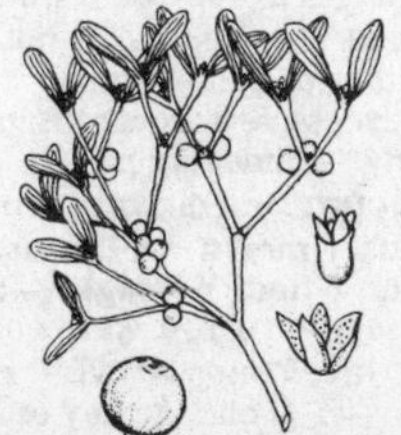

mistletoe

mistletoe ('misəltō) *n.* evergreen parasitic plant with white berries, which grows on trees

mistook (mi'sto͝ok) *pt. of* MISTAKE

mistral ('mistrəl, mi'sträl) *n.* strong, dry, N wind in France

mistress ('mistris) *n.* **1.** object of man's illicit love **2.** woman with mastery or control **3.** woman owner **4.** woman teacher **5.** *obs.* title given to married woman

mistrial (mis'trīəl) *n. Law* trial made void because of some error

mistrust (mis'trust) *vt.* **1.** have doubts or suspicions about —*n.* **2.** distrust —**mis'trustful** *a.*

misunderstanding (misundər'standing) *n.* **1.** failure to understand properly **2.** disagreement —**misunder'stood** *a.* not properly or sympathetically understood

mite (mīt) *n.* **1.** very small arachnid **2.** anything very small **3.** small but well-meant contribution

miter ('mītər) *n.* **1.** bishop's headdress **2.** joint between two pieces of wood *etc.* meeting at right angles —*vt.* **3.** join with, shape for a miter joint **4.** put miter on

mitigate ('mitigāt) *vt.* make less severe —**miti'gation** *n.* —**mitigating circumstances** circumstances which lessen the culpability of an offender

mitosis (mī'tōsis) *n.* cell division by which growth takes place in all living organisms in which nuclear genetic material is equally divided between two daughter cells —**mitotic** (mī'totik) *a.*

mitt (mit) *n.* **1.** glove leaving fingers bare **2.** baseball catcher's glove **3.** *sl.* hand

mitten ('mitən) *n.* glove with two compartments, one for thumb and one for fingers

mix (miks) *vt.* **1.** put together, combine, blend, mingle —*vi.* **2.** be mixed **3.** associate —**mixed** *a.* composed of different elements, races, sexes *etc.* —**'mixer** *n.* one who, that which mixes —**'mixture** *n.* —**mixed bag** *inf.* something composed of diverse elements, people *etc.* —**mixed blessing** situation *etc.* having advantages and disadvantages —**mixed doubles** *Tennis* game with man and woman as partners on each side —**mixed grill** dish of broiled chops, sausages, bacon *etc.* —**mixed marriage** marriage between persons of different races or religions —**mixed media 1.** the use of several different materials in a work of art **2.** performances combining song, dance, sound, light, speech *etc.* —**mixed-up** *a. inf.* confused —**mix-up** *n.* confused situation

mizzen *or* **mizen** ('mizən) *n.* lowest fore-and-aft sail on aftermost mast of ship —**mizzenmast** ('mizənmast; *Naut.* 'mizənməst) *n.* aftermost mast on full-rigged ship

mks units metric system of units based on the meter, kilogram and second

ml milliliter(s)

M.L. Medieval Latin

M.L.A. C Member of the Legislative Assembly

M.Litt. Master of Letters
Mlle *or* **Mlle.** Mademoiselle (*pl.* **Mlles, Mlles.**)
mm millimeter(s)
Mme *or* **Mme.** Madame (*pl.* **Mmes, Mmes.**)
Mn *Chem.* manganese
MN Minnesota
MNA *or* **M.N.A.** C Member of the National Assembly
mnemonic (ni'monik) *a.* **1.** helping the memory —*n.* **2.** something intended to help the memory
mo (mō) *n. inf.* moment
Mo *Chem.* molybdenum
MO *or* **Mo.** Missouri
M.O. Medical Officer
-mo (*comb. form*) in bookbinding, indicating book size by specifying number of leaves formed by folding one sheet of paper, as in *sixteenmo*
moa ('mōə) *n.* any of various extinct flightless birds of New Zealand
moan (mōn) *n.* **1.** low murmur, usually of pain —*v.* **2.** utter (words *etc.*) with moan —*vi.* **3.** lament
moat (mōt) *n.* **1.** deep wide ditch, *esp.* round castle —*vt.* **2.** surround with moat
mob (mob) *n.* **1.** disorderly crowd of people **2.** mixed assembly —*vt.* **3.** attack in mob, hustle or ill-treat (**-bb-**) —'**mobster** *n. sl.* gangster
mobcap ('mobkap) *n.* formerly, woman's large cotton cap with pouched crown
mobile ('mōbil) *a.* **1.** capable of movement **2.** easily moved or changed —*n.* **3.** hanging structure of card, plastic *etc.*, designed to move in air currents —**mo'bility** *n.*
mobilize ('mōbilīz) *vi.* **1.** (of armed services) prepare for military service —*vt.* **2.** organize for a purpose —**mobilization** (mōbili'zāshən) *n.* in war time, calling up of men and women for active service
Möbius strip ('mōbiəs) a surface with only one side and one edge made by putting a single twist in a long, rectangular strip of paper and pasting the ends together
moccasin ('mokəsin) *n.* **1.** flat shoe based on Amerindian footwear where leather is placed under foot, brought around side and pleated on to a U-shaped vamp **2.** *see* **water moccasin** *at* WATER **3.** snake resembling water moccasin —**moccasin flower** any of several lady's-slippers, *esp.* orchid found in N Amer. woodlands
mocha ('mōkə) *n.* **1.** type of strong, dark coffee **2.** this flavor
mock (mok) *vt.* **1.** make fun of, ridicule **2.** mimic —*vi.* **3.** scoff —*n.* **4.** act of mocking **5.** laughing stock —*a.* **6.** sham, imitation —'**mocker** *n.* —'**mockery** *n.* **1.** derision **2.** travesty —**mocking bird** N Amer. bird which imitates songs of others —**mock orange** shrub with white fragrant flowers —**mock turtle soup** imitation turtle soup made from calf's head —**mock-up** *n.* scale model —**put the mockers on** *inf.* ruin chances of success of
mod[1] (mod) *a.* of any fashion in dress regarded as stylish
mod[2] (mod) *n.* annual Highland Gaelic meeting with musical and literary competitions
mod. **1.** moderate **2.** modern
mod cons (konz) *inf.* modern conveniences
mode (mōd) *n.* **1.** method, manner **2.** prevailing fashion **3.** *Mus.* any of various scales of notes within one octave —'**modal** *a.* **1.** of or relating to mode or manner **2.** *Gram.* expressing distinction of mood **3.** *Metaphys.* of or relating to form of thing as opposed to its substance *etc.* **4.** *Mus.* of or relating to mode —**mo'dality** *n.* —'**modish** *a.* in the fashion —**modiste** (mō'dēst) *n.* fashionable dressmaker or milliner
model ('modəl) *n.* **1.** miniature representation **2.** pattern **3.** person or thing worthy of imitation **4.** person employed by artist to pose, or by dress designer to display clothing —*vt.* **5.** make model of **6.** mold —*v.* **7.** display (clothing) for dress designer
modem ('mōdem) *n. Comp.* coupler used with telephone or on direct line for transmitting information from one computer to another
moderate ('modərit) *a.* **1.** not going to extremes, temperate, medium —*n.* **2.** person of moderate views —*v.* ('modərāt) **3.** make, become less violent or excessive **4.** preside (over) —**mode'ration** *n.* —'**moderator** *n.* **1.** mediator **2.** president of Presbyterian body **3.** arbitrator
moderato (modə'rätō) *adv. Mus.* **1.** at moderate tempo **2.** direction indicating that tempo specified be used with restraint
modern ('modərn) *a.* **1.** of present or recent times **2.** in, of current fashion —*n.* **3.** person living in modern times —'**modernism** *n.* (support of) modern tendencies, thoughts *etc.* —'**modernist** *n.* —**mo'dernity** *n.* —**moderni'zation** *n.* —'**modernize** *vt.* bring up to date —**modern art** term for realist painting beginning in mid-19th century —**Modern English** English language since about 1450 —**modern languages** current European languages as subject of study
modest ('modist) *a.* **1.** not overrating one's qualities or achievements **2.** shy **3.** moderate, not excessive **4.** decorous, decent —'**modestly** *adv.* —'**modesty** *n.*
modicum ('modikəm) *n.* small quantity
modify ('modifī) *vt.* **1.** change slightly **2.** tone down (**-fied, -fying**) —**modifi'cation** *n.* —'**modifier** *n. esp.* word qualifying another
modulate ('mojəlāt) *vt.* **1.** regulate **2.** vary in tone —*vi.* **3.** change key of music —**modu'lation** *n.* **1.** modulating **2.** *Electron.* superimposing signals on to high-frequency carrier **3.** *Mus.* the change of key within a composition —'**modulator** *n.*

module (ˈmojo͞ol) *n.* (detachable) unit, section, component with specific function —ˈ**modular** *a.* designed or constructed to a standardized scale or to standard parts

modulus (ˈmojələs) *n.* **1.** *Phys.* coefficient expressing specified property of specified substance **2.** *Math.* number by which logarithm to one base is multiplied to give the corresponding logarithm to another base **3.** *Math.* integer that can be divided exactly into the difference between two other integers (*pl.* **-li** (-lī))

modus operandi (ˈmōdəs opəˈrandē) *Lat.* method of operating, tackling task (*pl.* ***modi operandi*** (ˈmōdē))

modus vivendi (viˈvendē) *Lat.* working arrangement between conflicting interests (*pl.* ***modi vivendi*** (ˈmōdē))

Mogen David (ˈmōgən ˈdōvid) double triangle forming the six-pointed star of David: a symbol of Jewry and of the state of Israel

mogul (ˈmōgul, mōˈgul) *n.* important or powerful person

mohair (ˈmōhāər) *n.* **1.** fine cloth of goat's hair **2.** hair of Angora goat

Mohammed (mōˈhamid) *n. see* MUHAMMAD

Mohawk (ˈmōhök) *n.* **1.** Amerindian people of Mohawk River valley, New York **2.** member of this people (*pl.* **-hawk, -s**) **3.** Iroquoian language of this people

Mohican (mōˈhēkən) *n.* member of Amerindian people of upper Hudson River valley, New York (*pl.* **-can, -s**)

Mohs' scale (mōz) a scale measuring the resistance of substances to being scratched ranging from 1 (talc) to 10 (diamond)

moiety (ˈmoiiti) *n.* a half

moire (ˈmoiər, mör, mwär) *n.* fabric, usu. silk, having watered effect —**moiré** (möˈrā, mwäˈrā) *a.* **1.** having watered or wavelike pattern —*n.* **2.** such pattern, impressed on fabrics by means of engraved rollers **3.** any fabric having such pattern, moire

moist (moist) *a.* damp, slightly wet —**moisten** (ˈmoisən) *v.* —ˈ**moisture** *n.* liquid, *esp.* diffused or in drops —ˈ**moisturize** *vt.* add, restore moisture to (skin *etc.*)

mol *Chem.* mole

molar (ˈmōlər) *a.* **1.** (of teeth) for grinding —*n.* **2.** molar tooth

molasses (məˈlasiz) *n.* syrup, by-product of process of sugar refining

mold[1] (mōld) *n.* **1.** hollow object in which metal *etc.* is cast **2.** pattern for shaping **3.** character **4.** shape, form —*vt.* **5.** shape or pattern —ˈ**molding** *n.* **1.** molded object **2.** ornamental edging **3.** decoration —ˈ**moldboard** *n.* curved blade of plow

mold[2] (mōld) *n.* fungoid growth caused by dampness —ˈ**moldy** *a.* stale, musty

mold[3] (mōld) *n.* loose or surface earth —ˈ**molder** *vi.* decay into dust

mole[1] (mōl) *n.* small dark protuberant spot on the skin

mole[2] (mōl) *n.* **1.** small burrowing animal **2.** spy, informer —ˈ**molehill** *n.* small mound of earth thrown up by burrowing mole —**make a mountain out of a molehill** exaggerate an unimportant matter out of all proportion

mole[3] (mōl) *n.* **1.** pier or breakwater **2.** causeway **3.** harbor within this

mole[4] (mōl) *n.* SI unit of amount of substance

molecule (ˈmolikyo͞ol) *n.* **1.** smallest particle of a substance, either element or compound, in ordinary existence **2.** very small particle —**moˈlecular** *a.* of, inherent in molecules —**molecular biology** science concerned with biological structure at the level of the molecule —**molecular weight** sum of all atomic weights of atoms in a molecule

molest (məˈlest) *vt.* pester, interfere with so as to annoy or injure —**molestation** (mōleˈstāshən) *n.*

moll (mol) *n. sl.* **1.** gangster's female accomplice **2.** prostitute

mollify (ˈmolifī) *vt.* calm down, placate, soften (**-fied, -fying**) —**mollifiˈcation** *n.*

mollusk *or* **mollusc** (ˈmoləsk) *n.* any member of a phylum (*Mollusca*) of invertebrate animals with a soft body and usu. external shell including oysters, snails, clams, squids and octopuses

mollycoddle (ˈmolikodəl) *vt.* pamper

Molotov cocktail (ˈmolətöf) primitive bomb made of bottle filled with usu. gasoline with a wick that is ignited at time of hurling

molt (mōlt) *v.* **1.** cast or shed (fur, feathers *etc.*) —*n.* **2.** molting

molten (ˈmōltən) *a.* **1.** liquefied; melted **2.** made by having been melted —*v.* **3.** *pp. of* MELT

molto (ˈmōltō) *adv. Mus.* very

molybdenum (məˈlibdinəm) *n. Chem.* metallic element *Symbol* Mo, at. wt. 95.9, at. no. 42

moment (ˈmōmənt) *n.* **1.** very short space of time **2.** (present) point in time —**momenˈtarily** *adv.* —ˈ**momentary** *a.* lasting only a moment —**moment of force** effective tendency of a force to rotate a body to which it is applied —**moment of truth** moment when person or thing is put to test

momentous (mōˈmentəs) *a.* of great importance

momentum (mōˈmentəm) *n.* **1.** force of a moving body **2.** impetus gained from motion (*pl.* **-ta** (-tə), **-s**)

Mon. Monday

Monaco (ˈmonəkō) *n.* country in Europe, an enclave in France, on the Mediterranean —**Monegasque** (moniˈgask) *n./a.*

monad (ˈmōnad) *n.* **1.** *Philos.* any fundamental singular metaphysical entity **2.** single-celled organism **3.** atom, ion, or radical with valency of one —**monadic** (mōˈnadik) *a.*

monandrous (məˈnandrəs, mo-) *a.* **1.** having only one male sexual partner over a period of time **2.** (of plants) having flowers with only one stamen —**mo'nandry** *n.*

monarch ('monərk) *n.* sovereign ruler of a state —**mon'archic** *a.* —**'monarchist** *n.* supporter of monarchy —**'monarchy** *n.* **1.** state ruled by sovereign **2.** his rule

monastery ('monəsterī) *n.* house occupied by a religious order —**mo'nastic** *a.* **1.** relating to monks, nuns, or monasteries —*n.* **2.** monk, recluse —**mo'nasticism** *n.*

monaural (mo'nōrəl) *a.* relating to, having, or hearing with only one ear

Monday ('mundi) *n.* second day of the week, or first of working week

money ('muni) *n.* bank notes, coin *etc.*, used as medium of exchange (*pl.* **-s, -ies**) —**monetarism** ('monitərizəm) *n.* theory that inflation is caused by increase in money supply —**monetarist** ('monitərist) *n./a.* —**monetary** ('moniteri) *a.* —**monetization** (moniti'zāshən) *n.* —**monetize** ('monitīz) *vt.* make into, recognize as money —**'moneyed** *or* **'monied** *a.* rich —**'moneybags** *n. sl.* very rich person —**money-grubbing** *a. inf.* seeking greedily to obtain money —**'moneylender** *n.* person who lends money at interest as a living —**money-spinner** *n. inf.* enterprise, idea *etc.* that is source of wealth

monger ('munggər) *n.* trader or dealer: usu. in compounds, as in *ironmonger*

Mongolia (mon'gōlyə, mong-; -'gōliə) *n.* country in Asia bounded north by the U.S.S.R., east, south and west by China —**Mon'golian** *n./a.* **1.** (native or inhabitant) of Mongolia —*n.* **2.** the Altaic language of the Mongolians

mongolism ('monggəlizəm) *or* **Mongolianism** (mong'gōliənizəm) *n.* Down's syndrome —**'mongol** *n./a.* (one) afflicted with this —**'mongoloid** *a.* relating to or characterized by mongolism

Mongoloid ('monggəloid) *a.* of major racial group of mankind, including most of peoples of Asia, Eskimos, and N Amer. Indians

mongoose ('mon-go͞os, 'monggo͞os) *n.* small animal of Asia and Afr. noted for killing snakes (*pl.* **-s**)

mongrel ('munggrəl, 'monggrəl) *n.* **1.** animal, *esp.* dog, of mixed breed, hybrid —*a.* **2.** of mixed breed

monitor ('monitər) *n.* **1.** person or device which checks, controls, warns or keeps record of something **2.** pupil assisting teacher with odd jobs in school **3.** television set used in a studio for checking program being transmitted **4.** type of large lizard —*vt.* **5.** watch, check on —**mo'nition** *n.* warning —**'monitory** *a.*

monk (mungk) *n.* one of a religious community of men bound by vows of poverty *etc.* —**'monkish** *a.* —**'monkshood** *n.* poisonous plant with hooded flowers

monkey ('mungki) *n.* **1.** long-tailed primate **2.** mischievous child —*vi.* **3.** meddle, fool —**monkey business** *inf.* mischievous or dishonest behavior or acts —**monkey puzzle** coniferous tree with sharp stiff leaves —**monkey wrench** spanner with movable jaws

mono ('monō) *a.* **1.** monophonic —*n.* **2.** monophonic sound

mono- *or before vowel* **mon-** (*comb. form*) single, as in *monosyllabic*

monochrome ('monəkrōm) *n.* **1.** representation in one color —*a.* **2.** of one color —**monochro'matic** *a.*

monocle ('monəkəl) *n.* single eyeglass

monocotyledon (monəkoti'lēdən) *n.* any of various flowering plants having single embryonic seed leaf and leaves with parallel veins —**monocoty'ledonous** *a.*

monocular (mo'nokyələr) *a.* one-eyed

monocyte ('monəsīt) *n.* large phagocytic leukocyte formed in bone marrow or spleen

monoecious (mə'nēshəs) *a.* (of plants) having male and female reproductive organs carried separately on the same plant

monogamy (mə'nogəmi) *n.* custom of being married to one person at a time

monogram ('monəgram) *n.* design of letters interwoven

monograph ('monəgraf) *n.* short book on single subject

monogyny (mə'nojini) *n.* having only one female sexual partner over a period of time —**mo'nogynous** *a.*

monolith ('monəlith) *n.* monument consisting of single standing stone

monologue ('monəlog) *n.* **1.** dramatic composition with only one speaker **2.** long speech by one person

monomania (monə'māniə) *n.* excessive preoccupation with one thing

monomial (mo'nōmiəl) *n.* **1.** *Math.* expression consisting of single term —*a.* **2.** consisting of single algebraic term

mononucleosis (monōnyo͞okli'ōsis, -no͞o-) *n.* **1.** *Pathol.* presence of large number of monocytes in blood **2.** *see* **infectious mononucleosis** *at* INFECT

monophonic (monə'fonik) *a.* **1.** (of reproduction of sound) using only one channel between source and loudspeaker (*also* **mo'naural**) **2.** *Mus.* of style of musical composition consisting of single melodic line

monoplane ('monəplān) *n.* airplane with one pair of wings

monopoly (mə'nopəli) *n.* **1.** exclusive possession of trade, privilege *etc.* **2.** (**M-**) trade name for board game for two to six players —**mo'nopolist** *n.* —**mo'nopolize** *vt.* claim, take exclusive possession of

monorail ('monərāl) *n.* railroad with cars running on or suspended from single rail

monosodium glutamate (monə'sōdiəm 'glo͞otəmāt) white crystalline substance used as food flavoring

monosyllable (ˈmonəsiləbəl) *n.* word of one syllable

monotheism (ˈmonəthēizəm) *n.* belief in only one God —**ˈmonotheist** *n.*

monotone (ˈmonətōn) *n.* continuing on one note —**moˈnotonous** *a.* lacking in variety, dull, wearisome —**moˈnotony** *n.*

monovalent (monəˈvālənt) *a. Chem.* **1.** having valency of one **2.** having only one valency (*also* **uniˈvalent**) —**monoˈvalence** *or* **monoˈvalency** *n.*

monoxide (məˈnoksīd) *n.* oxide that contains one oxygen atom per molecule

Monroe (mənˈrō) *n.* **James.** the 5th President of the U.S. (1821-25)

Monseigneur (mōseˈnyœr) *Fr.* title given to French bishops, prelates, and princes (*pl.* ***Messeigneurs*** (māseˈnyœr))

monsieur (məsˈyə) *n.* French title of address equivalent to *sir* when used alone or *Mr.* before name

Monsignor (monˈsēnyər) *n. R.C.Ch.* ecclesiastical title attached to certain offices and prefixed to surname

monsoon (monˈsōōn) *n.* **1.** seasonal wind of SE Asia **2.** very heavy rainfall season

monster (ˈmonstər) *n.* **1.** fantastic imaginary beast **2.** misshapen animal or plant **3.** very wicked person **4.** huge person, animal or thing —*a.* **5.** huge —**monˈstrosity** *n.* **1.** monstrous being **2.** deformity **3.** distortion —**ˈmonstrous** *a.* **1.** of, like monster **2.** unnatural **3.** enormous **4.** horrible —**ˈmonstrously** *adv.*

monstrance (ˈmonstrəns) *n. R.C.Ch.* vessel in which consecrated Host is exposed for adoration

Mont. Montana

montage (monˈtäzh) *n.* **1.** elements of two or more pictures imposed upon a single background to give a unified effect **2.** method of editing a motion picture

Montana (monˈtanə) *n.* Mountain state of the U.S., admitted to the Union in 1889. Abbrev.: **Mont., MT** (with ZIP code)

montbretia (monˈbrēshə) *n.* plant with orange flowers on long stems

Montezuma's revenge (montiˈzōōməz) diarrhea, *esp.* contracted in Mexico by tourist

month (munth) *n.* **1.** one of twelve periods into which the year is divided **2.** period of moon's revolution —**ˈmonthly** *a.* **1.** happening or payable once a month —*adv.* **2.** once a month —*n.* **3.** magazine published every month

Montserrat (montsəˈrat) *n.* crown colony of the United Kingdom lying in the Caribbean Sea 25 miles southwest of Antigua

monument (ˈmonyəmənt) *n.* anything that commemorates, *esp.* a building or statue —**monuˈmental** *a.* **1.** vast, lasting **2.** of or serving as monument —**monumental mason** maker and engraver of tombstones

moo (mōō) *n.* **1.** cry of cow —*vi.* **2.** make this noise, low

mooch (mōōch) *vi. sl.* loaf, slouch

mood[1] (mōōd) *n.* state of mind and feelings —**ˈmoody** *a.* **1.** gloomy, pensive **2.** changeable in mood

mood[2] (mōōd) *n. Gram.* form indicating function of verb

Moog synthesizer (mōōg, mōg) trade name for electrophonic instrument operated by keyboard and pedals

moon (mōōn) *n.* **1.** satellite which takes lunar month to revolve around earth **2.** any secondary planet —*vi.* **3.** (*oft. with* around) go about dreamily —**ˈmoony** *a.* **1.** *inf.* dreamy or listless **2.** of or like moon —**ˈmooncalf** *n.* **1.** born fool; dolt **2.** person who idles time away (*pl.* **-calves**) —**ˈmoonlight** *n.* **1.** light of moon —*vi.* **2.** hold two paid occupations —**moonlight flit** hurried departure by night to escape from one's creditors —**ˈmoonscape** *n.* general surface of moon or representation of it —**ˈmoonshine** *n.* **1.** whiskey illicitly distilled **2.** nonsense —**ˈmoonshot** *n.* launching of spacecraft *etc.* to moon —**ˈmoonstone** *n.* transparent semiprecious stone —**ˈmoonstruck** *a.* deranged

moor[1] (mōōər) *n.* tract of open uncultivated land, often hilly and heather-clad —**ˈmoorhen** *n.* water bird

moor[2] (mōōər) *v.* secure (ship) with chains or ropes —**ˈmoorage** *n.* place, charge for mooring —**ˈmoorings** *pl.n.* **1.** ropes *etc.* for mooring **2.** something providing stability, security

Moor (mōōər) *n.* member of race in Morocco and adjoining parts of N Afr.

moose (mōōs) *n.* N Amer. deer, like elk

moot (mōōt) *a.* **1.** that is open to argument, debatable —*vt.* **2.** bring for discussion —*n.* **3.** meeting

mop (mop) *n.* **1.** bundle of yarn, cloth *etc.* on end of stick, used for cleaning **2.** tangle (of hair *etc.*) —*vt.* **3.** clean, wipe with mop or other absorbent stuff (**-pp-**)

mope (mōp) *vi.* be gloomy, apathetic

moped (ˈmōped) *n.* light motorized bicycle

moquette (mōˈket) *n.* thick fabric used for upholstery *etc.*

moraine (məˈrān) *n.* accumulated mass of debris, earth, stones *etc.*, deposited by glacier

moral (ˈmŏrəl, ˈmorəl) *a.* **1.** pert. to right and wrong conduct **2.** of good conduct —*n.* **3.** practical lesson, *eg* of fable —*pl.* **4.** habits with respect to right and wrong, *esp.* in matters of sex —**ˈmoralist** *n.* teacher of morality —**moˈrality** *n.* **1.** good moral conduct **2.** moral goodness or badness **3.** kind of medieval drama, containing moral lesson —**ˈmoralize** *vi.* **1.** write, talk about moral aspect of things —*vt.* **2.** interpret morally —**ˈmorally** *adv.* —**moral philosophy** branch of philosophy dealing with ethics —**moral victory** triumph that is psychological rather than practical

morale (mə'ral) *n.* degree of confidence, hope of person or group

morass (mə'ras) *n.* **1.** marsh **2.** mess

moratorium (morə'töriəm) *n.* **1.** act authorizing postponement of payments *etc.* **2.** delay (*pl.* **-ria** (-riə))

moray

moray (mə'rā, 'mörā) *n.* large, voracious eel

morbid ('mörbid) *a.* **1.** unduly interested in death **2.** gruesome **3.** diseased

mordant ('mördənt) *a.* **1.** biting **2.** corrosive **3.** scathing —*n.* **4.** substance that fixes dyes

more (mör) *comp. of* MANY *and* MUCH *a.* **1.** greater in quantity or number —*adv.* **2.** to a greater extent **3.** in addition —*pron.* **4.** greater or additional amount or number —**more'over** *adv.* besides, further

morel (mə'rel, mö'rel) *n.* edible fungus in which mushroom has pitted cap

morello (mə'relō) *n.* variety of small dark sour cherry (*pl.* **-s**)

mores ('mörāz) *pl.n.* customs and conventions embodying fundamental values of society *etc.*

morganatic marriage (mörgə'natik) marriage of king or prince in which wife does not share husband's rank or possessions and children do not inherit from father

morgue (mörg) *n.* mortuary

moribund ('moribund) *a.* **1.** dying **2.** stagnant

Mormon ('mörmən) *n.* member of Church of Latter-Day Saints whose authority is the Bible, Book of Mormon, revelations to Joseph Smith by the Angel Moroni in 1827 and certain pronouncements of the 1st Presidency (*also* **Latter-Day Saint**) —'**Mormonism** *n.*

mornay (mör'nā) *a.* denoting cheese sauce used in various dishes

morning ('mörning) *n.* early part of day until noon —**morn** *n. Poet.* morning —**morning dress** formal day dress for men, comprising cutaway frock coat, usu. with gray trousers and top hat —**morning-glory** *n.* plant with trumpet-shaped flowers which close in late afternoon —**morning sickness** *inf.* nausea occurring shortly after rising during early months of pregnancy —**morning star** planet, usu. Venus, seen just before sunrise —**the morning after** *inf.* aftereffects of excess, *esp.* hangover

Morocco (mə'rokō) *n.* **1.** country in Africa bounded east and southeast by Algeria, southwest by Western Sahara, northwest by the Atlantic Ocean and north by the Mediterranean Sea **2.** (**m-**) fine goatskin leather —**Mo'roccan** *n./a.*

moron ('möron) *n.* **1.** mentally deficient person **2.** *inf.* fool —**mo'ronic** *a.*

morose (mə'rōs) *a.* sullen, moody

morphine ('mörfēn) *or* **morphia** ('mörfiə) *n.* narcotic extract of opium, drug used to induce sleep and relieve pain

morphology (mör'foləji) *n.* **1.** science of structure of organisms **2.** form and structure of words of a language —**morpho'logical** *a.*

morris dance ('moris) English folk dance

morrow ('morō) *n. Poet.* next day

Morse (mörs) *n.* system of telegraphic signaling in which letters of alphabet are represented by combinations of dots and dashes, or short and long flashes

morsel ('mörsəl) *n.* fragment, small piece

mortal ('mörtəl) *a.* **1.** subject to death **2.** causing death —*n.* **3.** mortal creature —**mor'tality** *n.* **1.** state of being mortal **2.** great loss of life **3.** death rate —'**mortally** *adv.* **1.** fatally **2.** deeply, intensely —**mortal sin** *R.C.Ch.* sin meriting damnation

mortar ('mörtər) *n.* **1.** mixture of lime, sand and water for holding bricks and stones together **2.** small cannon firing over short range **3.** vessel in which substances are pounded —'**mortarboard** *n.* **1.** board for holding mortar **2.** square academic cap

mortgage ('mörgij) *n.* **1.** conveyance of property as security for debt with provision that property be reconveyed on payment within agreed time —*vt.* **2.** convey by mortgage **3.** pledge as security —**mortga'gee** *n.* —**mortgagor** (mörgi'jör) *or* '**mortgager** *n.*

mortify ('mörtifī) *vt.* **1.** humiliate **2.** subdue by self-denial —*vi.* **3.** (of flesh) be affected with gangrene (**-fied, -fying**) —**mortifi'cation** *n.*

mortise *or* **mortice** ('mörtis) *n.* **1.** hole in piece of wood *etc.* to receive the tongue (tenon) and end of another piece —*vt.* **2.** make mortise in **3.** fasten by mortise and tenon —**mortise lock** lock embedded in door

mortuary ('mörchōōəri) *n.* **1.** building where corpses are kept before burial —*a.* **2.** of, for burial

mosaic (mō'zāik) *n.* **1.** picture or pattern of small bits of colored stone, glass *etc.* **2.** this process of decoration

Mosaic (mō'zāik) *a.* of Moses

Moselle (mō'zel) *n.* light white wine

Moslem ('mozləm) *see* MUSLIM

mosque (mosk) *n.* Muslim temple

mosquito (mə'skētō) *n.* any of various kinds of flying, biting insects of which the adult female sucks the blood of birds and mammals (*pl.* **-es**)

moss (mos) *n.* **1.** simple land plant without roots, reproducing by spores **2.** peat bog, swamp —**'mossy** *a.* covered with moss —**moss agate** agate with mosslike markings —**moss stitch** knitting stitch made up of alternate knit and purl stitches

most (mōst) *sup. of* MUCH *and* MANY *a.* **1.** greatest in size, number, or degree —*n.* **2.** greatest number, amount, or degree —*adv.* **3.** in the greatest degree **4.** almost —**'mostly** *adv.* for the most part, generally, on the whole —**Most Reverend** courtesy title applied to archbishops

M.O.T. Member of Our Tribe: used by Jews

mote (mōt) *n.* tiny speck

motel (mō'tel) *n.* roadside hotel with accommodation for motorists and vehicles

motet (mō'tet) *n.* short sacred vocal composition

moth (moth) *n.* **1.** usu. nocturnal insect like butterfly **2.** its grub —**'mothy** *a.* infested with moths —**'mothball** *n.* **1.** small ball of camphor or naphthalene to repel moths from stored clothing *etc.* —*vt.* **2.** put in mothballs **3.** store, postpone *etc.* —**'motheaten** *a.* **1.** eaten, damaged by grub of moth **2.** decayed, scruffy

mother ('mudhər) *n.* **1.** female parent **2.** head of religious community of women —*a.* **3.** natural, native, inborn —*vt.* **4.** act as mother to —**'motherhood** *n.* —**'motherly** *a.* —**Mother Carey's chicken** ('kariz, 'keriz) *see* **storm petrel** (sense 1) *at* STORM —**mother country 1.** original country of colonists or settlers **2.** person's native country —**mother earth 1.** earth as a mother, particularly in its fertility **2.** soil; ground —**mother-in-law** *n.* mother of one's husband or wife —**mother of pearl** iridescent lining of certain shells —**Mother's Day** day for honoring mothers, usu. the 2nd Sunday in May —**mother tongue 1.** language first learned by child **2.** language from which another has evolved

motif (mō'tēf) *n.* **1.** dominating theme **2.** recurring design

motion ('mōshən) *n.* **1.** process or action or way of moving **2.** proposal in meeting **3.** application to judge —*v.* **4.** signal or direct by sign —**'motionless** *a.* still, immobile —**motion sickness** disorder marked by headache, dizziness, sweating, nausea, pallor or cold sweats caused by reaction to movement (*also* **airsickness, carsickness, seasickness**)

motive ('mōtiv) *n.* **1.** that which makes person act in particular way **2.** inner impulse —*a.* **3.** causing motion —**'motivate** *vt.* **1.** instigate **2.** incite —**moti'vation** *n.* —**motive power 1.** any source of energy used to produce motion **2.** means of supplying power to engine *etc.*

mot juste (mō 'zhüst) *Fr.* appropriate word or expression (*pl.* ***mots justes*** (mō 'zhüst))

motley ('motli) *a.* **1.** miscellaneous, varied **2.** multicolored —*n.* **3.** motley color or mixture **4.** jester's particolored dress

motocross ('mōtōkros) *n.* motorcycle race over rough course

motor ('mōtər) *n.* **1.** that which imparts movement **2.** machine to supply motive power **3.** automobile —*vi.* **4.** travel by automobile —**'motoring** *n.* —**'motorist** *n.* user of automobile —**'motorize** *vt.* **1.** equip with motor **2.** provide with motor transport —**'motorboat, 'motorcar, 'motorcycle, motor scooter** *n.* vehicles driven by motor —**motorcade** ('mōtərkād) *n.* parade of motor vehicles —**motor nerve** nerve which controls muscular movement

mottle ('motəl) *vt.* **1.** mark with blotches, variegate —*n.* **2.** arrangement of blotches **3.** blotch on surface

motto ('motō) *n.* **1.** saying adopted as rule of conduct **2.** short inscribed sentence **3.** word or sentence on heraldic crest (*pl.* **-s, -es**)

moue (moo) *Fr.* pouting look

moufflon (moo'flon) *n.* wild mountain sheep

mound (mownd) *n.* **1.** heap of earth or stones **2.** small hill

mount (mownt) *vi.* **1.** rise **2.** increase **3.** get on horseback —*vt.* **4.** get up on **5.** frame (picture) **6.** fix, set up **7.** provide with horse —*n.* **8.** that on which thing is supported or fitted **9.** horse **10.** hill

mountain ('mowntin) *n.* **1.** hill of great size **2.** surplus —**mountain'eer** *n.* one who lives among or climbs mountains —**mountain'eering** *n.* technique of climbing high places of the earth —**'mountainous** *a.* very high, rugged —**mountain lion** cougar —**Mountain Standard Time** time as reckoned from the 105th to 120th meridians west of Greenwich

mountebank ('mowntibangk) *n.* charlatan, fake

Mountie ('mownti) *n. inf.* member of Royal Canadian Mounted Police

mourn (mörn) *v.* feel, show sorrow (for) —**'mourner** *n.* —**'mournful** *a.* sad, dismal —**'mournfully** *adv.* —**'mourning** *n.* **1.** grieving **2.** conventional signs of grief for death **3.** clothes of mourner —**mourning band** piece of black material, *esp.* armband, worn to indicate mourning

mouse (mows) *n.* **1.** small rodent (*pl.* **mice**) —*vi.* (mowz) **2.** catch, hunt mice **3.** prowl —**'mouser** *n.* cat used for catching mice —**'mousy** *or* **'mousey** *a.* **1.** like mouse, *esp.* in color **2.** meek, shy —**'mousetrap** *n.* **1.** any trap for catching mice **2.** *inf.* cheese of indifferent quality

mousse (moos) *n.* sweet dish of flavored cream whipped and chilled

mousseline (moosə'lēn) *n.* sheer fabric resembling muslin —**mousseline de laine** (də 'len) lightweight plain-weave woolen cloth, oft. printed —**mousseline de soie** (də 'swä) silk or rayon muslin, crisper and firmer than chiffon

moustache ('mustash, məs'tash) *n.* *see* MUSTACHE

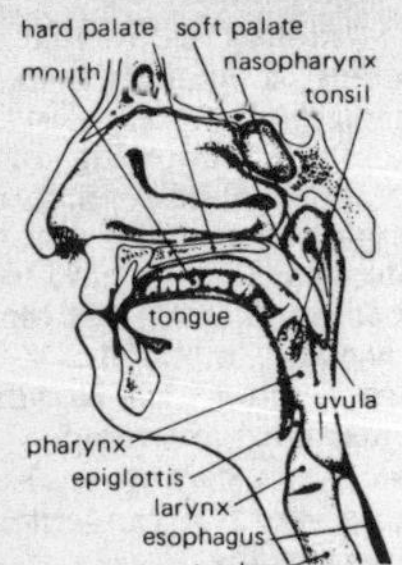

mouth

mouth (mowth) *n.* **1.** opening in head for eating, speaking *etc.* **2.** opening into anything hollow **3.** outfall of river **4.** entrance to harbor *etc.* —*vt.* (mowdh) **5.** declaim, *esp.* in public **6.** form (words) with lips without speaking **7.** take, move in mouth —'**mouthful** *n.* **1.** as much as is held in mouth at one time **2.** small quantity, as of food **3.** word *etc.* difficult to say —**mouth organ** harmonica —'**mouthpiece** *n.* **1.** end of anything placed between lips, *eg* pipe **2.** spokesman —'**mouthwash** *n.* solution for cleansing mouth

move (mo͞ov) *vt.* **1.** change position of **2.** stir emotions of **3.** incite **4.** propose for consideration —*vi.* **5.** change places **6.** change one's dwelling *etc.* **7.** take action —*n.* **8.** a moving **9.** motion toward some goal —'**movable** *or* '**moveable** *a./n.* —'**movement** *n.* **1.** process, action of moving **2.** moving parts of machine **3.** division of piece of music

movie ('mo͞ovi) *n.* **1.** motion picture —*pl.* **2.** place where motion picture is shown **3.** the motion-picture industry and medium —**movie star** popular motion-picture actor or actress

mow (mō) *v.* cut (grass *etc.*) (**mown** *pp.*) —'**mower** *n.* man or machine that mows

Mozambique (mōzəm'bēk) *n.* country in Africa bounded east by the Indian Ocean, south by South Africa, southwest by Swaziland, west by South Africa and Zimbabwe and north by Zambia, Malawi and Tanzania —**Mozam'bican** *n./a.*

Mozzarella (motsə'relə) *n.* a semisoft cheese from cow's milk, notable for its elasticity when melted, orig. from Italy

mp *or* **m.p.** *Mus.* mezzo piano

M.P. **1.** Member of Parliament **2.** Military Police **3.** Mounted Police

m.p.g. miles per gallon

m.p.h. miles per hour

M.Phil. *or* **M.Ph.** Master of Philosophy

Mr. ('mistər) mister

Mrs. ('misiz, -is) title of married woman

MS Mississippi

Ms. (miz) title used instead of Miss or Mrs.

MS. *or* **ms.** manuscript (*pl.* **MSS.** *or* **mss.**)

M.Sc. Master of Science

M.S.T. Mountain Standard Time

MT Montana

Mt. *or* **mt.** Mount

mu (myo͞o, mo͞o) *n.* 12th letter in Gr. alphabet (M, μ)

much (much) *a.* **1.** existing in quantity —*n.* **2.** large amount **3.** a great deal **4.** important matter —*adv.* **5.** in a great degree **6.** nearly (**more** *comp.*, **most** *sup.*)

mucilage ('myo͞osilij) *n.* glue

muck (muk) *n.* **1.** cattle dung **2.** unclean refuse —'**mucky** *a.* **1.** dirty **2.** messy **3.** unpleasant —'**muckamuck** *n.* arrogant person —'**muckrake** *vi.* seek out and expose scandal, *esp.* concerning public figures —'**muckraking** *n.* —**muck up** ruin, spoil

mucus ('myo͞okəs) *n.* viscid fluid secreted by mucous membrane —**mu'cosity** *n.* —'**mucous** *a.* **1.** resembling mucus **2.** secreting mucus **3.** slimy —**mucous membrane** lining of canals and cavities of the body

mud (mud) *n.* **1.** wet and soft earth **2.** *inf.* slander —'**muddy** *a.* —'**mudpack** *n.* cosmetic paste to improve complexion —'**mudslinger** *n.* —'**mudslinging** *n.* casting malicious slurs on an opponent, *esp.* in politics

muddle ('mudəl) *vt.* **1.** (*esp. with* up) confuse **2.** bewilder **3.** mismanage —*n.* **4.** confusion **5.** tangle

Muenster ('munstər, 'mo͞on-) *n.* a semihard, whole-milk cheese, cylindrical in shape with a brick-red rind, orig. from Alsace

muesli ('myo͞ozli) *n.* mixture of rolled oats, dried fruit *etc.* eaten with milk

muezzin (mo͞o'ezin) *n.* crier who summons Muslims to prayer

muff[1] (muf) *n.* tube-shaped covering to keep the hands warm

muff[2] (muf) *vt.* miss, bungle, fail in

muffin ('mufin) *n.* small cup-shaped sweet bread roll, usually eaten hot with butter

muffle ('mufəl) *vt.* wrap up, *esp.* to deaden sound —'**muffler** *n.* **1.** scarf **2.** device to reduce noise of engine exhaust *etc.*

mufti ('mufti) *n.* plain clothes as distinguished from uniform, *eg* of soldier

mug[1] (mug) *n.* drinking cup

mug[2] (mug) *n. sl.* **1.** face **2.** fool, simpleton, one easily imposed upon —*vt.* **3.** *inf.* rob violently (**-gg-**) —'**mugger** *n.*

muggy ('mugi) *a.* damp and stifling

mugwump ('mugwump) *n.* person who sits on the fence concerning party politics

Muhammad (mō'hamid) *n.* prophet, and founder of Islam —**Mu'hammadan** *a./n.* Muslim —**Mu'hammadanism** *n.* another word (not in Muslim use) for ISLAM

mukluk ('mukluk) *n.* **1.** Eskimo's soft

(sealskin) boot **2.** knitted boot with soft leather soles for indoor wear

mulatto (myo͞oˈlatō, mo͞o-) *n.* child of one White and one Black parent (*pl.* **-s, -es**)

mulberry (ˈmulberi, -bəri) *n.* **1.** tree whose leaves are used to feed silkworms **2.** its purplish fruit

mulch (mulch) *n.* **1.** straw, leaves *etc.*, spread as protection for roots of plants —*vt.* **2.** protect thus

mulct (mulkt) *vt.* **1.** defraud **2.** fine

mule[1] (myo͞ol) *n.* **1.** animal which is cross between horse and ass **2.** hybrid **3.** spinning machine —**muleteer** (myo͞oliˈtēər) *n.* mule driver —ˈ**mulish** *a.* obstinate

mule[2] (myo͞ol) *n.* backless shoe or slipper

mull[1] (mul) *vt.* heat (wine) with sugar and spices —**mull over** think over, ponder

mull[2] (mul) *n.* light muslin fabric of soft texture

mullah (ˈmulə, ˈmo͝olə) *n.* Muslim theologian

mullein (ˈmulin) *n.* plant with tall spikes of yellow flowers

mullet (ˈmulit) *n.* edible sea fish

mulligatawny (muligəˈtōni) *n.* vegetable or meat soup flavored with curry powder

mullion (ˈmulyən) *n.* upright dividing bar in window —ˈ**mullioned** *a.*

multangular (mulˈtanggyo͝olər) *or* **multiangular** *a.* having many angles

multi- (*comb. form*) many, as in *multiracial, multistory.* Such words are omitted where the meaning may easily be found from the simple word

multifarious (multiˈfariəs, -ˈfer-) *a.* of various kinds or parts —**multiˈfariously** *adv.*

multilateral (multiˈlatərəl, multī-; -ˈlatrəl) *a.* **1.** of or involving more than two nations or parties **2.** having many sides

multinational (multiˈnashənəl, multī-) *a.* (of large business company) operating in several countries

multiple (ˈmultipəl) *a.* **1.** having many parts —*n.* **2.** quantity which contains another an exact number of times —**multipliˈcand** *n. Math.* number to be multiplied —**multipliˈcation** *n.* —**multiˈplicity** *n.* variety, greatness in number —ˈ**multiplier** *n.* **1.** person or thing that multiplies **2.** number by which multiplicand is multiplied **3.** *Phys.* any instrument, as photomultiplier, for increasing effect —ˈ**multiply** *vt.* **1.** increase in number **2.** add (a number) to itself a given number of times —*vi.* **3.** increase in number or amount (**-plied, -plying**) —**multiple-choice** *a.* having a number of possible given answers out of which the correct one must be chosen —**multiple personality** condition in which individual leads two or more distinct and separate existences —**multiple sclerosis** disease of the human nervous system affecting persons between ages of 10 and 50 —**multiplication table** one of group of tables giving results of multiplying two numbers together

multiplex (ˈmultipleks) *a.* **1.** having many elements or parts **2.** capable of transmitting numerous messages over same wire or channel

multitude (ˈmultityo͞od, -to͞od) *n.* **1.** great number **2.** great crowd **3.** populace —**multiˈtudinous** *a.* very numerous

mum (mum) *n. inf.* **1.** mother **2.** large shaggy chrysanthemum flower

mumble (ˈmumbəl) *vi.* **1.** speak indistinctly —*v.* **2.** mutter

mumbo jumbo (ˈmumbō) **1.** foolish religious reverence or incantation **2.** meaningless or unnecessarily complicated language

mummer (ˈmumər) *n.* actor in dumb show —**mum** *a.* **1.** silent —*v.* **2.** act in mime (**-mm-**) —ˈ**mummery** *n.* dumb-show acting

mummy (ˈmumi) *n.* embalmed body, *esp.* as prepared for burial in ancient Egypt —ˈ**mummify** *v.* (**-fied, -fying**)

mumps (mumps) *pl.n.* infectious virus disease occurring chiefly in children usu. attacking salivary glands (*also* **epidemic parotitis**)

mun. municipal

munch (munch) *v.* **1.** chew noisily and vigorously **2.** crunch

mundane (munˈdān, ˈmundān) *a.* **1.** ordinary, everyday **2.** belonging to this world, earthly

mung bean (mung) **1.** E Asian bean plant grown for forage: source of bean sprouts **2.** seed of this plant

municipal (myo͞oˈnisipəl) *a.* belonging to affairs of city or town —**municiˈpality** *n.* **1.** city or town with local self-government **2.** its governing body

munificent (myo͞oˈnifisənt) *a.* very generous —**muˈnificence** *n.* bounty

muniments (ˈmyo͞onimənts) *pl.n.* title deeds, documents verifying ownership

munition (myo͞oˈnishən) *n.* (*usu. pl.*) military stores

muon (ˈmyo͞oon) *n.* positive or negative elementary particle with mass 207 times that of electron

mural (ˈmyo͝orəl) *n.* **1.** painting on a wall —*a.* **2.** of or on a wall

murder (ˈmərdər) *n.* **1.** unlawful premeditated killing of human being —*vt.* **2.** kill thus —ˈ**murderer** *n.* (ˈ**murderess** *fem.*) —ˈ**murderous** *a.*

murk *or* **mirk** (mərk) *n.* thick darkness —ˈ**murky** *or* ˈ**mirky** *a.* gloomy

murmur (ˈmərmər) *n.* **1.** low, indistinct sound —*vi.* **2.** make such a sound **3.** complain —*vt.* **4.** utter in a low voice

Murphy's law (ˈmərfiz) notion that if anything is liable to go wrong, it will

murrain (ˈmurin) *n.* cattle plague

mus. **1.** museum **2.** music(al)

Mus.B. *or* **Mus.Bac.** Bachelor of Music

muscat (ˈmuskat, -kət) *n.* **1.** musk-flavored grape **2.** raisin —**muscaˈtel** *n.* **1.** muscat **2.** strong wine made from it

muscle (ˈmusəl) *n.* **1.** specialized tissue in humans and other animals concerned with movement **2.** system of muscles —**muscular** (ˈmuskyələr) *a.* **1.** with well-developed muscles **2.** strong **3.** of, like muscle —**musculature** (ˈmuskyələchŏŏər) *n.* **1.** arrangement of muscles in organ or part **2.** total muscular system of organism —**muscle-bound** *a.* with muscles stiff through overdevelopment —**ˈmuscleman** *n.* **1.** man with highly developed muscles **2.** henchman employed by gangster *etc.* to intimidate or use violence upon victims —**muscular dystrophy** inherited disease of several types involving progressive degeneration of skeletal muscle —**muscle in** *inf.* force one's way in

Muscovy (musˈkōvi) *or* **musk duck** large crested widely domesticated S Amer. duck

Mus.D. *or* **Mus.Doc.** Doctor of Music

muse (myōōz) *vi.* **1.** ponder **2.** consider meditatively **3.** be lost in thought —*n.* **4.** state of musing or abstraction **5.** reverie

Muse (myōōz) *n.* one of the nine goddesses inspiring learning and the arts

museum (myōōˈzēəm) *n.* (place housing) collection of natural, artistic, historical or scientific objects —**museum piece 1.** object fit to be kept in museum **2.** *inf.* person or thing regarded as antiquated

mush (mush) *n.* **1.** soft pulpy mass **2.** *inf.* cloying sentimentality —**ˈmushy** *a.*

mushroom (ˈmushrōōm, -rōōm) *n.* **1.** any edible fungus with fruiting body consisting of stalked cap with gills —*vi.* **2.** shoot up rapidly **3.** expand —**mushroom cloud** mushroom-shaped cloud produced by nuclear explosion

music (ˈmyōōzik) *n.* **1.** art form using melodious and harmonious combination of notes **2.** laws of this **3.** composition in this art —**ˈmusical** *a.* **1.** of, like music **2.** interested in, or with instinct for, music **3.** pleasant to ear —*n.* **4.** show, motion picture in which music plays essential part —**ˈmusically** *adv.* —**muˈsician** *n.* —**musiˈcologist** *n.* —**musiˈcology** *n.* scientific study of music —**musical chairs** party game in which players walk around chairs to music, there being one fewer chairs than players: when music stops, player without a chair is eliminated —**musical comedy** light dramatic entertainment with songs, dances *etc.* —**music** *or* **musical box** mechanical instrument that plays tunes by means of pins on revolving cylinder striking tuned teeth of comblike metal plate —**music hall** vaudeville theater

musk (musk) *n.* **1.** scent obtained from gland of **musk deer 2.** any of various plants with similar scent —**ˈmusky** *a.* —**ˈmuskmelon** *n.* any of several varieties of melon, such as cantaloupe, having ribbed or warty rind and musky aroma —**musk ox** ox of Arctic Amer. —**ˈmuskrat** *n.* **1.** N Amer. rodent found near water **2.** its fur —**musk rose** rose cultivated for its white musk-scented flowers

muskeg (ˈmuskeg) *n.* **C** boggy hollow

muskellunge (ˈmuskəlunj) *or* **muskallonge** (ˈmuskəlonj) *n.* large game and food fish of pike family found in lakes and rivers of eastern and midwestern N Amer. (*also* **maskanonge, maskelonge, maskinonge**)

musket (ˈmuskit) *n. Hist.* infantryman's gun —**muskeˈteer** *n.* —**ˈmusketry** *n.* (use of) small firearms

Muskogean (musˈkōgiən) *n.* Amerindian language family spoken orig. in southeastern U.S., now in Oklahoma

Muslim (ˈmuzlim, ˈmŏŏs-, ˈmŏŏz-) *or* **Moslem** *n.* **1.** follower of religion of Islam —*a.* **2.** of religion, culture *etc.* of Islam

muslin (ˈmuzlin) *n.* fine cotton fabric —**ˈmuslined** *a.*

mussel (ˈmusəl) *n.* **1.** marine bivalve mollusk **2.** freshwater bivalve mollusk

must[1] (must; *unstressed* məst, məs) *v. aux.* **1.** be obliged to, or certain to —*n.* **2.** something one must do

must[2] (must) *n.* **1.** newly-pressed grape juice **2.** unfermented wine

mustache *or* **moustache** (ˈmustash, məsˈtash) *n.* hair on the upper lip —**mustache cup** cup with partial cover to protect drinker's mustache

mustang (ˈmustang) *n.* wild horse

mustard (ˈmustərd) *n.* **1.** powder made from the seeds of a plant, used in paste as a condiment **2.** the plant —**mustard gas** poisonous gas causing blistering —**mustard plaster** irritant preparation used to stimulate blood flow

mustargen (ˈmustərjən) *n. see* **nitrogen mustard** *at* NITROGEN

muster (ˈmustər) *v.* **1.** assemble —*n.* **2.** assembly, *esp.* for exercise, inspection

musty (ˈmusti) *a.* moldy, stale —**must** *or* **ˈmustiness** *n.*

mutate (ˈmyōōtāt, myōōˈtāt) *v.* (cause to) undergo mutation —**ˈmutable** *a.* liable to change —**ˈmutant** *n.* mutated animal, plant *etc.* —**muˈtation** *n.* change in the genetic material of a living organism which can be inherited

mute (myōōt) *a.* **1.** dumb **2.** silent —*n.* **3.** dumb person **4.** *Mus.* contrivance to soften tone of instruments —**ˈmuted** *a.* **1.** (of sound) muffled **2.** (of light) subdued —**ˈmutely** *adv.*

mutilate (ˈmyōōtilāt) *vt.* **1.** deprive of a limb or other part **2.** damage, deface —**mutiˈlation** *n.* —**ˈmutilator** *n.*

mutiny (ˈmyōōtini) *n.* **1.** rebellion against authority, esp. against officers of disciplined body —*vi.* **2.** commit mutiny (**ˈmutinied, ˈmutinying**) —**mutiˈneer** *n.* —**ˈmutinous** *a.* rebellious

mutt (mut) *n. inf.* **1.** stupid person **2.** dog

mutter (ˈmutər) *vi.* **1.** speak with mouth nearly closed, indistinctly **2.** grumble —*vt.* **3.** utter in such tones —*n.* **4.** act, sound of muttering

mutton (ˈmutən) *n.* flesh of sheep used as food —**mutton bird** migratory seabird —ˈ**muttonchops** *pl.n.* side whiskers trimmed in shape of chops —ˈ**muttonhead** *n. sl.* fool

mutual (ˈmyo͞ocho͞oəl) *a.* **1.** done, possessed *etc.* by each of two with respect to the other **2.** reciprocal **3.** *inf.* common to both or all —ˈ**mutually** *adv.*

muumuu (ˈmo͞omo͞o) *n.* loose dress in bright colors and patterns adapted from dresses orig. given to Hawaiian women by missionaries

Muzak (ˈmyo͞ozak) *n.* trade name for recorded light music played in shops *etc.*

muzzle (ˈmuzəl) *n.* **1.** mouth and nose of animal **2.** cover for these to prevent biting **3.** open end of gun —*vt.* **4.** put muzzle on **5.** silence, gag

muzzy (ˈmuzi) *a.* indistinct, confused, muddled

MV **1.** mean variation **2.** motor vessel

MVA Missouri Valley Authority

MW megawatt(s)

MWe megawatts electric

Mx *Phys.* maxwell

my (mī) *a.* belonging to me —**myˈself** *pron.* emphatic or reflexive form of I

myalgia (mīˈaljiə) *n.* pain in a muscle

myasthenia gravis (mīəsˈthēniə ˈgrävis) rare disease marked by muscle weakness and fatigue

mycelium (mīˈsēliəm) *n.* vegetative body of fungi (*pl.* **-lia** (-liə)) —**myˈcelial** *a.*

Mycenaean (mīsiˈnēən) *a.* **1.** of ancient Mycenae or its inhabitants **2.** of Aegean civilization of Mycenae (1400 to 1100 B.C.)

mycology (mīˈkoləji) *n.* science of fungi

mycorrhiza (mīkəˈrīzə) *n.* symbiosis between roots of a higher plant and a fungus

mynah *or* **myna** (ˈmīnə) *n.* Indian bird related to starling

myopia (mīˈōpiə) *n.* near-sightedness —**myopic** (mīˈopik) *a.*

myositis (mīəˈsītis) *n.* muscular pain or discomfort of unknown origin

myosotis (mīəˈsōtis) *n.* any of genus of plants of the borage family, *eg* forget-me-not

Myr million years

myriad (ˈmiriəd) *a.* **1.** innumerable —*n.* **2.** large indefinite number

myriapod (ˈmiriəpod) *n.* **1.** any of group of terrestrial arthropods having long segmented body, such as the centipede —*a.* **2.** of or belonging to this group

myrmidon (ˈmərmidon, -dən) *n.* follower or henchman

myrrh (mər) *n.* aromatic gum, formerly used as incense

myrtle (ˈmərtəl) *n.* **1.** flowering evergreen shrub **2.** periwinkle

myself (mīˈself) *pron. see* MY

Mysost (ˈmīsost) *n.* a hard cheese, oft. brown in color, from goat's milk, orig. produced in all Scandinavian countries (*also* **Gjetost, Primost**)

mystery (ˈmistəri, -tri) *n.* **1.** obscure or secret thing **2.** anything strange or inexplicable **3.** religious rite —**mysˈterious** *a.* —**mysˈteriously** *adv.* —**mystery play** medieval drama based on biblical incidents

mystic (ˈmistik) *n.* **1.** one who seeks divine, spiritual knowledge, *esp.* by prayer, contemplation *etc.* —*a.* **2.** of hidden meaning, *esp.* in religious sense —ˈ**mystical** *a.* —ˈ**mysticism** *n.*

mystify (ˈmistifī) *vt.* bewilder, puzzle (**-fied, -fying**) —**mystifiˈcation** *n.*

mystique (miˈstēk) *n.* aura of mystery, power *etc.*

myth (mith) *n.* **1.** tale with supernatural characters or events **2.** invented story **3.** imaginary person or object —ˈ**mythical** *a.* —**mythoˈlogical** *a.* —**myˈthologist** *n.* —**myˈthology** *n.* **1.** myths collectively **2.** study of them

myxedema (miksiˈdēmə) *n.* illness caused by severe thyroxine deficiency

myxomatosis (miksōməˈtōsis) *n.* contagious, fatal disease of rabbits caused by a virus sometimes introduced as biological control

N

n *or* **N** (en) *n.* **1.** 14th letter of English alphabet **2.** speech sound represented by this letter (*pl.* **n's, N's** *or* **Ns**)

n (en) *a.* indefinite number (of) —**nth** (enth) *a.* **1.** *Math.* of unspecified ordinal number, usu. greatest in series **2.** *inf.* being last or most extreme of long series —**to the nth degree** *inf.* to the utmost extreme

N 1. *Chess* knight **2.** *Chem.* nitrogen **3.** *Phys.* newton **4.** north(ern)

n. 1. neuter **2.** noun **3.** number

Na *Chem.* sodium

nab (nab) *vt. inf.* **1.** arrest (criminal) **2.** catch suddenly (**-bb-**)

nacre (ˈnākər) *n.* **1.** mother-of-pearl **2.** shellfish

nadir (ˈnādēər, ˈnādər) *n.* **1.** point opposite the zenith **2.** lowest point

nae (nā) *a. Scots word for* NO (sense 1)

nag[1] (nag) *v.* **1.** scold or annoy constantly **2.** cause pain to constantly (**-gg-**) —*n.* **3.** nagging **4.** one who nags

nag[2] (nag) *n.* **1.** *inf.* horse **2.** small horse for riding

Nahum (ˈnāhəm) *n. Bible* 34th book of the O.T., written by the prophet Nahum, dealing with the judgment upon the city of Nineveh

naiad (ˈnāəd, ˈnīəd, -ad) *n.* water nymph (*pl.* **-s, -ades** (-ədēz))

naïf *or* **naif** (näˈēf) *a. see* NAIVE

nail (nāl) *n.* **1.** horny shield at ends of fingers, toes **2.** claw **3.** small metal spike for fixing wood *etc.* —*vt.* **4.** fix, stud with nails **5.** *inf.* catch —ˈ**nailfile** *n.* small file used to trim nails —**nail set** punch for driving head of nail below or flush with surrounding surface

nainsook (ˈnānsŏŏk) *n.* soft fine cotton, oft. mercerized

naive, naïve (näˈēv), **naïf,** *or* **naif** *a.* simple, unaffected, ingenuous —**naiveté, naïveté** (nāēvəˈtā), *or* **naivety** (näˈēvəti) *n.*

naked (ˈnākid) *a.* **1.** without clothes **2.** exposed, bare **3.** undisguised —ˈ**nakedly** *adv.* —ˈ**nakedness** *n.* —**naked eye** the eye unassisted by any optical instrument

namby-pamby (nambiˈpambi) *a.* **1.** weakly **2.** sentimental **3.** insipid —*n.* **4.** namby-pamby person

name (nām) *n.* **1.** word by which person, thing *etc.* is denoted **2.** reputation **3.** title **4.** credit **5.** family **6.** famous person —*vt.* **7.** give name to **8.** call by name **9.** entitle **10.** appoint **11.** mention **12.** specify —ˈ**nameless** *a.* **1.** without a name **2.** indescribable **3.** too dreadful to be mentioned **4.** obscure —ˈ**namely** *adv.* that is to say —**name-calling** *n.* speaking abusively to or about a person —**name day** *R.C.Ch.* feast day of saint whose name one bears —**name-dropper** *n.* —**name-dropping** *n. inf.* referring frequently to famous people, *esp.* as though they were intimate friends, in order to impress others —ˈ**nameplate** *n.* small panel on door bearing occupant's name —ˈ**namesake** *n.* person with same name as another —**name of the game** object of the activity

Namibia (nəˈmibiə) *n.* country in Africa bounded north by Angola and Zambia, east by Botswana, Southeast by South Africa, and west by the Atlantic

nance (ˈnans) *n. offens.* effeminate or homosexual boy or man

nankeen (nanˈkēn) *or* **nankin** (ˈnanˈkin) *n.* **1.** buff-colored cotton fabric —*pl.* **2.** trousers made of this

nanny (ˈnani) *n.* **UK** child's nurse —**nanny goat** she-goat

nano- (*comb. form*) one billionth (10^{-9}), as in *nanosecond*

nap[1] (nap) *vi.* **1.** take short sleep, *esp.* in daytime (**-pp-**) —*n.* **2.** short sleep

nap[2] (nap) *n.* downy surface on cloth made by projecting fibers

nap[3] (nap) *n.* card game of the whist family

napalm (ˈnāpäm, ˈnāpälm) *n.* jellied gasoline, highly inflammable, used in bombs *etc.*

nape (nāp) *n.* back of neck

naphtha (ˈnafthə, ˈnap-) *n.* liquid distilled from crude petroleum used as solvent for cleaning and as raw material for gasoline —ˈ**naphthalene** *n.* white crystalline product distilled from coal tar or petroleum, used in disinfectants, mothballs *etc.*

napkin (ˈnapkin) *n.* cloth, paper for wiping fingers or lips at table

narcissus

narcissus (när'sisəs) *n.* genus of bulbous plants including daffodil, jonquil, *esp.* one with white flowers (*pl.* **-cissi** (-'sisī)) —**'narcissism** *n.* abnormal love and admiration of oneself —**'narcissist** *n.*

narcolepsy ('närkəlepsi) *n.* illness marked by sudden short spells of overpowering sleepiness (*also* **Friedman's disease**)

narcotic (när'kotik) *n.* **1.** any of a group of drugs, including morphine and opium, producing numbness and stupor, used medicinally but addictive —*a.* **2.** of narcotics or narcosis —**narcosis** (när'kōsis) *n.* effect of narcotic

nard (närd) *n.* **1.** *see* **spikenard** *at* SPIKE **2.** plant whose aromatic roots were formerly used in medicine

Narraganset (narə'gansit) *n.* member of Algonquian-speaking Amerindian people of Rhode Island (*pl.* **-set, -s**)

narrate ('narāt, na'rāt) *vt.* relate, recount, tell (story) —**nar'ration** *n.* —**'narrative** *n.* **1.** account, story —*a.* **2.** relating —**'narrator** *n.*

narrow ('narō) *a.* **1.** of little breadth, *esp.* in comparison to length **2.** limited **3.** barely adequate or successful —*v.* **4.** make, become narrow —**'narrowly** *adv.* —**'narrowness** *n.* —**'narrows** *pl.n.* narrow part of straits —**'narrowback** *n. inf.* (among Irish) recent immigrant to the U.S.A. from Ireland —**narrow-minded** *a.* **1.** illiberal **2.** bigoted —**narrow-mindedness** *n.* prejudice, bigotry

narwhal ('närwäl, -wəl) *or* **narwhale** ('närwāl) *n.* arctic whale with tusk developed from teeth

NASA ('nasə) National Aeronautics and Space Administration

nasal ('nāzəl) *a.* **1.** of nose —*n.* **2.** sound partly produced in nose —**'nasalize** *vt.* make nasal in sound —**'nasally** *adv.*

nascent ('nasənt, 'nā-) *a.* **1.** just coming into existence **2.** springing up

nasturtium

nasturtium (nə'stərshəm) *n.* **1.** genus of plants which includes the watercress **2.** trailing garden plant with red or orange flowers

nasty ('nasti) *a.* foul, disagreeable, unpleasant —**'nastily** *adv.* —**'nastiness** *n.*

nat. 1. national **2.** native **3.** natural

natal ('nātəl) *a.* of birth

natatory ('nātətōri) *or* **natatorial** (nātə'tōriəl, nat-) *a.* of swimming —**na'tation** *n.*

nation ('nāshən) *n.* people or race organized as a state —**national** ('nashənəl) *a.* **1.** belonging or pert. to a nation **2.** public, general —*n.* **3.** member of a nation —**nationalism** ('nashənəlizəm) *n.* **1.** loyalty, devotion to one's country **2.** movement for independence of state, people, ruled by another —**nationalist** ('nashənəlist) *n./a.* —**nationality** (nashə'naliti) *n.* **1.** national quality or feeling **2.** fact of belonging to particular nation —**nationalization** (nashənəli'zāshən) *n.* acquisition and management of industries by the State —**nationalize** ('nashənəlīz) *vt.* convert (private industry, resources *etc.*) to state control —**nationally** ('nashənəli) *adv.* —**national debt** total financial obligations incurred by nation's central government —**National Foundation** foundation established in 1938 to conduct research for prevention of poliomyelitis and care for sufferers. The program is now expanded to include prevention of birth defects and virus diseases —**National Guard** U.S. military reserve force maintained by the states but available for federal use —**national park** area of land controlled by the state to preserve its natural beauty *etc.* —**National Safety Council** nonprofit cooperative organization chartered by Congress which furnishes leadership to the national safety movement

native ('nātiv) *a.* **1.** inborn **2.** born in particular place **3.** found in pure state **4.** that was place of one's birth —*n.* **5.** one born in a place **6.** member of indigenous race of a country **7.** species of plant, animal *etc.* originating in a place —**Native American** American Indian, Amerindian

nativity (nə'tiviti) *n.* **1.** birth **2.** time, circumstances of birth **3.** (**N-**) birth of Christ

NATO ('nātō) North Atlantic Treaty Organization

natterjack ('natərjak) *n.* small European toad

natty ('nati) *a.* neat and smart; spruce —**'nattily** *adv.*

nature ('nāchər) *n.* **1.** innate or essential qualities of person or thing **2.** class, sort **3.** life force **4.** (*oft.* **N-**) power underlying all phenomena in material world **5.** material world as a whole **6.** natural unspoilt scenery or countryside, and plants and animals in it **7.** disposition, temperament —**natural** ('nachrəl) *a.* **1.** of, according to, occurring in, provided by, nature **2.** inborn **3.** normal **4.** unaffected **5.** illegitimate —*n.* **6.** something, somebody well suited for something **7.** *Mus.* character (♮) used to remove effect of a sharp or flat preceding it —**naturalism** ('nachrəlizəm) *n.* **1.** movement, *esp.* in art and literature, advocating realism **2.** belief that all religious truth is based on study of natural causes and processes —**naturalist**

('nachrəlist) *n.* student of natural history —**naturalistic** (nachrə'listik) *a.* of or imitating nature in effect or characteristics —**naturalization** (nachrəli'zāshən) *n.* —**naturalize** ('nachrəlīz) *vt.* **1.** admit to citizenship **2.** accustom to new climate —**naturally** ('nachrəli) *adv.* **1.** of or according to nature **2.** by nature **3.** of course —**natural childbirth** system of childbirth involving minimum use of drugs for which mother has undergone training —**natural gas** gaseous mixture, consisting mainly of methane, trapped below ground; used extensively as fuel —**natural history** study of animals and plants —**natural law** principle of law or action considered as derived from nature or right reason and binding in human society —**natural number** any of positive integers 1, 2, 3, 4,... —**natural resources** naturally occurring materials such as coal *etc.* —**natural science** any of sciences that are involved in study of physical world, including biology, physics *etc.* —**natural selection** process resulting in survival of those individuals from population of animals *etc.* that are best adapted to prevailing environmental conditions —**nature trail** path through countryside of particular interest to naturalists

Naugahyde ('nŏgəhīd) *n.* trade name for a vinyl material imitating leather, oft. used for upholstery

naught (nŏt) *n.* **1.** *obs.* nothing **2.** cipher 0 —**set at naught** defy, disregard

naughty ('nŏti) *a.* **1.** disobedient, not behaving well **2.** *inf.* mildly indecent —'**naughtily** *adv.*

Nauru (nä'ōōrōō) *n.* country lying in the south Pacific Ocean comprising an island lying at 0° 32' S latitude and 166° 56' E longitude

nausea ('nŏziə, -shə, -siə, -zhə) *n.* feeling that precedes vomiting —'**nauseate** *vt.* sicken —**nauseous** ('nŏshəs, 'nŏziəs) *a.* **1.** disgusting **2.** causing nausea

nautical ('nŏtikəl) *a.* **1.** of seamen or ships **2.** marine —**nautical mile** measure of length used in navigation, 1.852 km, 2022 yards

nautilus ('nŏtiləs) *n.* univalvular mollusk of warm seas (*pl.* **-es, -tili** (-tilī))

Navaho *or* **Navajo** ('navəhō) *n.* **1.** member of Amerindian people of northern New Mexico and Arizona (*pl.* **-ho** *or* **-jo, -s**) **2.** the Athapascan language of this people

naval ('nāvəl) *a.* *see* NAVY

nave[1] (nāv) *n.* main part of church

nave[2] (nāv) *n.* hub of wheel

navel ('nāvəl) *n.* small scar, depression in middle of abdomen where umbilical cord was attached (*also* **umbilicus**)

navigate ('navigāt) *v.* **1.** plan, direct, plot path or position of (ship *etc.*) **2.** travel —'**navigable** *a.* —**navi'gation** *n.* **1.** science of directing course of seagoing vessel, or of aircraft in flight **2.** shipping —'**navigator** *n.* one who navigates

navy ('nāvi) *n.* **1.** fleet **2.** warships of country with their crews and organization —*a.* **3.** navy-blue —'**naval** *a.* of the navy —**navy-blue** *a.* very dark blue

Nazi ('nätsi) *n.* **1.** member of the National Socialist political party in Germany, 1919-45 **2.** one who thinks, acts like a Nazi (*pl.* **-s**) —*a.* **3.** of Nazis —'**Nazism** *or* '**Naziism** *n.* Nazi doctrine

Nb *Chem.* niobium

NB **1.** Nebraska **2.** New Brunswick

NB, N.B., *or* **n.b.** nota bene

NBS National Bureau of Standards

NC North Carolina

N.C.O. noncommissioned officer

Nd *Chem.* neodymium

ND North Dakota

N.D.P. **C** New Democratic Party

Ne *Chem.* neon

NE **1.** northeast(ern) **2.** Nebraska

Neanderthal (ni'andərtŏl, -thŏl) *a.* of Middle Paleolithic man

neap (nēp) *a.* low —**neap tide** the low tide at the first and third quarters of the moon

Neapolitan (nēə'politən) *n.* **1.** native or inhabitant of Naples —*a.* **2.** of Naples —**Neapolitan ice cream** brick of ice cream with different flavors in layers

near (nēər) *prep.* **1.** close to —*adv.* **2.** at or to a short distance —*a.* **3.** close at hand **4.** closely related **5.** narrow, so as barely to escape **6.** stingy **7.** closer (of two); left (of pair) —*v.* **8.** approach —'**nearly** *adv.* **1.** closely **2.** almost —'**nearness** *n.* —**near'by** *a.* adjacent —**Near East** **1.** *see* **Middle East** *at* MIDDLE **2.** formerly, Balkan States and area of Ottoman Empire —'**near'sightedness** *n.* condition in which images come to a focus in front of the retina (*also* **myopia**)

neat (nēt) *a.* **1.** tidy, orderly **2.** efficient **3.** precise, deft **4.** cleverly worded **5.** undiluted **6.** simple and elegant **7.** *sl.* pleasing; admirable; excellent —'**neaten** *vt.* make neat; tidy —'**neatly** *adv.* —'**neatness** *n.*

neath (nēth) *prep. obs.* beneath

N.E.B. New English Bible

Nebraska (ni'braskə) *n.* West North Central state of the U.S., admitted to the U.S. in 1867. Abbrev.: **Nebr., NB** (with ZIP code)

nebula ('nebyələ) *n. Astron.* diffuse cloud of particles, gases (*pl.* **-s, -ulae** (-yəlē)) —'**nebulous** *a.* **1.** cloudy **2.** vague, indistinct

necessary ('nesiseri) *a.* **1.** needful, requisite, that must be done **2.** unavoidable, inevitable —**neces'sarily** *adv.* —**ne'cessitate** *vt.* make necessary —**ne'cessitous** *a.* poor, needy, destitute —**ne'cessity** *n.* **1.** something needed, requisite **2.** constraining power or state of affairs **3.** compulsion **4.** poverty

neck (nek) *n.* **1.** part of body joining head to shoulders **2.** narrower part of a bottle *etc.* **3.** narrow piece of anything between wider parts —*vi.* **4.** *sl.* embrace, cuddle —'**neckerchief** *n.* kerchief for the neck —'**necklet** *n.* neck ornament, piece of fur *etc.* —**necklace** ('neklis) *n.* ornament round the neck —'**necktie** *n.* long narrow piece of material worn knotted around collar of shirt

necro- *or before vowel* **necr-** (*comb. form*) death, dead body, dead tissue, as in *necrosis*

necromancy ('nekrəmansi) *n.* magic, *esp.* by communication with dead —'**necromancer** *n.* wizard

necrophilia (nekrə'filiə) *n.* sexual attraction for or intercourse with dead bodies (*also* **necro'mania, ne'crophilism**)

necropolis (nə'kropəlis, ne-) *n.* cemetery (*pl.* **-es, -oleis** (-əlās))

nectar ('nektər) *n.* **1.** honey of flowers **2.** drink of the gods —'**nectary** *n.* honey gland of flower

nectarine

nectarine (nektə'rēn) *n.* smooth-skinned peach

née *or* **nee** (nā) *a.* indicating maiden name of married woman

need (nēd) *vt.* **1.** want, require —*n.* **2.** (state, instance of) want **3.** requirement **4.** necessity **5.** poverty —'**needful** *a.* necessary, requisite —'**needless** *a.* unnecessary —**needs** *adv.* of necessity (*esp. in* **needs must** *or* **must needs**) —'**needy** *a.* poor, in want

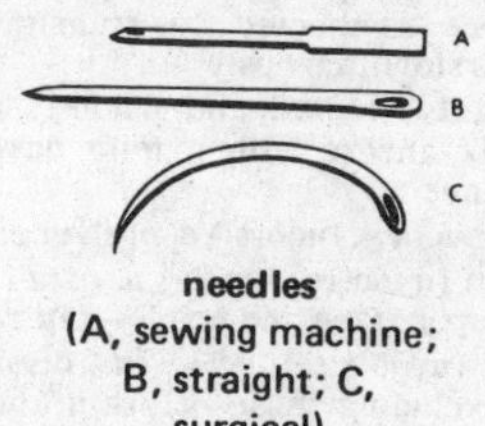

needles
(A, sewing machine; B, straight; C, surgical)

needle ('nēdəl) *n.* **1.** pointed pin with an eye and no head, for sewing **2.** long, pointed pin for knitting **3.** pointer of gauge, dial **4.** magnetized bar of compass **5.** stylus for phonograph **6.** leaf of fir or pine **7.** obelisk **8.** *inf.* hypodermic syringe —*vt.* **9.** *inf.* goad, provoke —'**needlecord** *n.* corduroy fabric with narrow ribs —'**needlepoint** *n.* **1.** embroidery done on canvas with various stitches so as to resemble tapestry **2.** point lace —'**needlework** *n.* embroidery, sewing

ne'er (nāər) *adv. Lit.* never —**ne'er-do-well** *n.* worthless person

nefarious (ni'fariəs, -'fer-) *a.* wicked

neg. negative(ly)

negate (ni'gāt) *vt.* deny, nullify —**ne'gation** *n.* contradiction, denial

negative ('negətiv) *a.* **1.** expressing denial or refusal **2.** lacking enthusiasm, energy, interest **3.** not positive **4.** (of electrical charge) having the same polarity as the charge of an electron —*n.* **5.** negative word or statement **6.** *Photog.* picture made by action of light on chemicals in which lights and shades are reversed —*vt.* **7.** disprove, reject —**negative feedback** *see* **feedback** *at* FEED

neglect (ni'glekt) *vt.* **1.** disregard, take no care of **2.** omit through carelessness —*vi.* **3.** fail (to do) —*n.* **4.** fact of neglecting or being neglected —**ne'glectful** *a.*

negligee *or* **negligé** (negli'zhā) *n.* **1.** woman's light, gauzy dressing gown **2.** easy, informal attire

negligence ('neglijəns) *n.* **1.** neglect **2.** carelessness —'**negligent** *a.* —'**negligible** *a.* **1.** able to be disregarded **2.** very small or unimportant

negotiate (ni'gōshiāt) *vi.* **1.** discuss with view to mutual settlement —*vt.* **2.** arrange by conference **3.** transfer (bill, check *etc.*) **4.** get over, past, around (obstacle) —**ne'gotiable** *a.* —**negoti'ation** *n.* **1.** treating with another on business **2.** discussion **3.** transference (of bill, check *etc.*) —**ne'gotiator** *n.*

Negro ('nēgrō) *n.* member of Black orig. Afr. race (*pl.* **-es**) ('**Negress** *fem.*) —**negritude** ('negritōōd, 'nē-; -tyōōd) *n.* **1.** fact of being a Negro **2.** awareness and cultivation of Negro culture *etc.* —'**Negroid** *a.* of or like a Negro

negus ('nēgəs) *n.* hot drink of port and lemon juice

Nehemiah (nēhə'mīə, nēə'mīə) *n. Bible* 16th book of the O.T., completing the story of the return to Palestine after the exile

neigh (nā) *n.* **1.** cry of horse —*vi.* **2.** utter this cry

neighbor ('nābər) *n.* one who lives near another —'**neighborhood** *n.* **1.** district **2.** people of a district **3.** region round about —'**neighboring** *a.* situated nearby —'**neighborly** *a.* **1.** as or befitting a good or friendly neighbor **2.** friendly **3.** sociable **4.** helpful

neither ('nēdhər, 'nīdhər) *a./pron.* **1.** not the one or the other —*adv.* **2.** not on the one hand **3.** not either —*conj.* **4.** not

nelson ('nelsən) *n.* wrestling hold in which wrestler places his arm(s) under his opponent's arm(s) from behind and exerts pressure with his palms on back of opponent's neck

nematode ('nemətōd) *n.* roundworm

nem. con. nemine contradicente (*Lat.,* without contradiction)

nem. diss. nemine dissentiente (*Lat.*, without dissent, unanimously)

nemesia (niˈmēzhə) *n.* garden plant with flowers of various colors

Nemesis (ˈnemisis) *n.* **1.** retribution **2.** the goddess of vengeance (*pl.* **-ses** (-sēz))

neo- *or sometimes before vowel* **ne-** (*comb. form*) new, later, revived in modified form, based upon

neodymium (nēōˈdimiəm) *n. Chem.* metallic element *Symbol* Nd, at. wt. 144.2, at. no. 60

Neolithic (nēəˈlithik) *a.* of the later Stone Age

neologism (niˈoləjizəm) *or* **neology** *n.* new-coined word or phrase —**neˈologize** *vi.*

neon (ˈnēon) *n. Chem.* element, noble gas *Symbol* Ne, at. wt. 83.80, at. no. 36 —**neon lamp** *or* **sign** illumination device containing neon and other gases

neophyte (ˈnēəfīt) *n.* **1.** new convert **2.** beginner, novice

Nepal (nəˈpōl, -ˈpol) *n.* country in Asia bounded north by Tibet, east by India and West Bengal, south and west by India —**Nepalese** (nepəˈlēz, -ˈlēs) *n./a.* (native or inhabitant) of Nepal

nephew (ˈnefyōō) *n.* brother's or sister's son

nephritis (niˈfrītis) *n.* inflammation of a kidney

nephrosis (niˈfrōsis) *n.* kidney condition marked by protein in the urine and edema

nepotism (ˈnepətizəm) *n.* undue favoritism toward one's relations

Neptune (ˈneptyōōn, -tōōn) *n.* **1.** god of the sea **2.** planet second farthest from sun

neptunium (nepˈtyōōniəm, -ˈtōōniəm) *n. Chem.* metallic element *Symbol* Np, at. wt. 237, at. no. 93

nerve (nərv) *n.* **1.** sinew, tendon **2.** fiber or bundle of fibers conveying feeling, impulses to motion *etc.* to and from brain and other parts of body **3.** assurance **4.** coolness in danger **5.** audacity —*pl.* **6.** irritability, unusual sensitiveness to fear, annoyance *etc.* —*vt.* **7.** give courage or strength to —**ˈnerveless** *a.* **1.** without nerves **2.** useless **3.** weak **4.** paralyzed —**ˈnervous** *a.* **1.** excitable, timid **2.** apprehensive, worried **3.** of the nerves —**ˈnervously** *adv.* —**ˈnervousness** *n.* —**ˈnervy** *a.* **1.** nervous **2.** jumpy **3.** irritable **4.** on edge —**nerve cell** *see* NEURON —**nerve center** **1.** group of nerve cells associated with specific function **2.** principal source of control over any complex activity —**nerve gas** poisonous gas that has paralyzing effect on central nervous system that can be fatal —**nerve-racking** *or* **nerve-wracking** *a.* very distressing, exhausting or harrowing —**nervous breakdown** condition of mental, emotional disturbance, disability —**nervous system** system of specialized tissue controlling internal activities of organism and regulating interaction with environment

ness (nes) *n.* headland, cape

-ness (*comb. form*) state, condition, quality, as in *greatness, selfishness*

nest (nest) *n.* **1.** place in which bird lays and hatches its eggs **2.** animal's breeding place **3.** snug retreat —*vi.* **4.** make, have a nest —**nest egg** (fund of) money in reserve

nestle (ˈnesəl) *vi.* settle comfortably, usu. pressing in or close to something

nestling (ˈnestling) *n.* bird too young to leave nest

net[1] (net) *n.* **1.** openwork fabric of meshes of cord *etc.* **2.** piece of it used to catch fish *etc.* —*vt.* **3.** cover with, or catch in, net (**-tt-**) —**ˈnetting** *n.* string or wire net

net[2] (net) *a.* **1.** left after all deductions **2.** free from deduction —*vt.* **3.** gain, yield as clear profit (**-tt-**) —**net profit** gross profit minus all operating costs not included in calculation of gross profit

nether (ˈnedhər) *a.* lower —**ˈnethermost** *a.* farthest down; lowest —**nether world** **1.** underworld **2.** hell (*also* **nether regions**)

Netherlands (ˈnedhərləndz) *pl.n.* (*with sing. v.*) —**the Netherlands** country in Europe bounded north and west by the North Sea, south by Belgium and east by West Germany —**ˈNetherland, ˈNetherlandic,** *or* **ˈNetherlandish** *a.* —**ˈNetherlander** *n.*

Netherlands Antilles (anˈtilēz) *pl.n.* (*with sing. v.*) —**the Netherlands Antilles** division of the Kingdom of the Netherlands comprising two groups of islands in the Caribbean

netsuke (ˈnetsəki) *n.* carved wooden or ivory toggle or button worn in Japan

nettle (ˈnetəl) *n.* **1.** plant with stinging hairs on the leaves —*vt.* **2.** irritate, provoke —**nettle rash** urticaria

network (ˈnetwərk) *n.* **1.** system of intersecting lines, roads *etc.* **2.** interconnecting group of people or things **3.** in broadcasting, group of stations connected to transmit same programs simultaneously

Neufchatel (nyōōshəˈtel, nōō-) *n.* soft cow's-milk cheese with a mild flavor orig. from France

neural (ˈnyōōrəl, ˈnōōrəl) *a.* of the nerves

neuralgia (nyōōˈraljə, nōō-) *n.* pain in, along nerves, *esp.* of face and head —**neuˈralgic** *a.*

neuritis (nyōōˈrītis, nōō-) *n.* disorder of nerves excluding those of brain and spinal cord caused by disease, mechanical pressure, vitamin deficiency *etc.*

neuro- *or before vowel* **neur-** (*comb. form*) nerve; nervous system, as in *neurology*

neurology (nyōōˈroləji, nōō-) *n.* science, study of nerves —**neuˈrologist** *n.*

neuron (ˈnyōōron, ˈnōōr-, ˈnyōōə-, ˈnōōə-) *or* **neurone** (ˈnyōōrōn, ˈnōō-, ˈnjōōə-, ˈnōōə-) *n.* cell specialized to conduct nerve impulses (*also* **nerve cell**) —**neuˈronic** *a.*

neurosis (nyōōˈrōsis, nōō-) *n.* relatively mild mental disorder (*pl.* **-ses** (-sēz)) —**neurotic** (nyōōˈrotik, nōō-) *a.* **1.** suffering from nervous disorder **2.** abnormally sensitive —*n.* **3.** neurotic person

neurosurgery (nyŏŏrō'sərjəri, nŏŏrō-) *n.* branch of surgery concerned with nervous system —**neuro'surgical** *a.*

neuter ('nyōōtər, 'nōōtər) *a.* **1.** neither masculine nor feminine —*n.* **2.** neuter word **3.** neuter gender —*vt.* **4.** castrate, spay (domestic animal)

neutral ('nyōōtrəl, 'nōōtrəl) *a.* **1.** taking neither side in war, dispute *etc.* **2.** without marked qualities **3.** belonging to neither of two classes —*n.* **4.** neutral nation or a subject of one **5.** neutral gear —**neu'trality** *n.* —**'neutralize** *vt.* **1.** make ineffective **2.** counterbalance —**neutral gear** in vehicle, position of gears that leaves transmission disengaged

neutrino (nyōō'trēnō, nōō-) *n. Phys.* stable elementary particle with zero rest mass (*pl.* **-s**)

neutron ('nyōōtron, 'nōō-) *n.* electrically neutral particle of the nucleus of an atom

Nevada (nə'vadə) *n.* Mountain state of the U.S., admitted to the Union in 1864. Abbrev.: **Nev., NV** (with ZIP code)

never ('nevər) *adv.* at no time —**never'more** *adv. Lit.* never again —**neverthe'less** *adv.* for all that, notwithstanding

nevus ('nēvəs) *n.* birthmark (*pl.* **nevi** ('nēvī))

new (nyōō, nōō) *a.* **1.** not existing before, fresh **2.** that has lately come into some state or existence **3.** unfamiliar, strange —*adv.* **4.** recently, fresh (*usu.* **'newly**) —**'newly** *adv.* —**'newness** *n.* —**'newcomer** *n.* recent arrival —**New Deal** policies for social reform and economic recovery in U.S. initiated by Franklin D. Roosevelt —**New English Bible** translation of Bible by British interdenominational committee first published in 1970 —**'new'fangled** *a.* of new fashion —**new math** approach to mathematics in which basic principles of set theory are introduced in elementary school —**new moon** moon when it appears as narrow waxing crescent —**'newspeak** *n.* language of bureaucrats and politicians, regarded as deliberately ambiguous and misleading —**New Testament** second part of the Bible concerned with the life and teaching of Jesus and the early Christian church —**New Year** first day or days of year —**New Year's Day** January 1st, U.S. national holiday —**the New World** the Americas; western hemisphere

newel ('nyōōəl, 'nōōəl) *n.* **1.** central pillar of winding staircase **2.** post at top or bottom of staircase rail

New Hampshire ('hampshər) New England state of the U.S.: ratified the Constitution in 1788. Abbrev.: **NH** (with ZIP code)

New Jersey ('jərzi) Middle Atlantic state of the U.S.: ratified the Constitution in 1787. Abbrev.: **NJ** (with ZIP code)

New Mexico ('meksikō) Mountain state of the U.S., admitted to the Union in 1912. Abbrev.: **N. Mex., NM** (with ZIP code)

news (nyōōz, nōōz) *n.* **1.** report of recent happenings, tidings **2.** interesting fact not previously known —**'newsy** *a.* full of news —**news agency** organization that provides news reports for subscribing newspapers *etc.* —**'newsboy** *n.* boy who delivers or sells newspapers —**'newscast** *n.* news broadcast —**'newscaster** *n.* —**news flash** brief item of important news, oft. interrupting radio or television program —**'newsletter** *n.* **1.** printed periodical bulletin circulated to members of group (*also* **news-sheet**) **2.** *Hist.* written or printed account of news —**'newspaper** *n.* periodical, usu. daily or weekly, publication containing news —**'newsprint** *n.* paper of the kind used for newspapers *etc.* —**'newsreel** *n.* short movie giving news —**'newsstand** *n.* stand from which newspapers are sold —**'newsworthy** *a.* sufficiently interesting or important to be reported as news

newt (nyōōt, nōōt) *n.* small, tailed amphibious creature

newton ('nyōōtən, 'nōōtən) *n.* SI unit of force

New York (yörk) Middle Atlantic state of the U.S.: ratified the Constitution in 1788. Abbrev.: **NY** (with ZIP code)

New Zealand ('zēlənd) country lying in the South Pacific southeast of Australia comprising North and South Islands, Stewart Island, Chatham Islands and other islands as well as territories overseas —**New Zealander** ('zēləndər)

next (nekst) *a./adv.* **1.** nearest **2.** immediately following —**next door** at or to adjacent house, apartment *etc.* —**next-of-kin** *n.* nearest relative

nexus ('neksəs) *n.* tie, connection, link (*pl.* **'nexus**)

Nez Percé (nez pərs, nes pāərs; *Fr.* nā per'sā) **1.** member of Amerindian people of Idaho, Washington and Oregon **2.** Penutian language of this people

NF Newfoundland

NH New Hampshire

Ni *Chem.* nickel

nib (nib) *n.* **1.** (split) pen point **2.** bird's beak —*pl.* **3.** crushed cocoa beans

nibble ('nibəl) *v.* **1.** take little bites (of) —*n.* **2.** little bite

nibs (nibz) *n.* mock title of respect, as in *his nibs*

Nicaragua (nikə'rägwə) *n.* country in Central America bounded east by the Atlantic, south by Costa Rica, west by the Pacific and north by El Salvador and Honduras —**Nica'raguan** *n./a.*

nice (nīs) *a.* **1.** pleasant **2.** friendly, kind **3.** attractive **4.** subtle, fine **5.** careful, exact **6.** difficult to decide —**'nicely** *adv.* —**nicety** ('nīsiti) *n.* **1.** minute distinction or detail **2.** subtlety **3.** precision

niche (nich) *n.* **1.** recess in wall **2.** suitable place in life, public estimation *etc.*

nick (nik) *vt.* **1.** make notch in, indent **2.** *sl.* steal —*n.* **3.** notch **4.** exact point of time —**in good nick** *inf.* in good condition

nickel (ˈnikəl) *n.* **1.** *Chem.* metallic element *Symbol* Ni, at. wt. 58.7, at. no. 28 **2.** five-cent piece —**nickel silver** white alloy containing copper, zinc and nickel (*also* **German silver**)

nicker (ˈnikər) *vi.* **1.** (of horse) neigh softly **2.** snigger

nicknack (ˈnikˌnak) *n. see* KNICK-KNACK

nickname (ˈniknām) *n.* familiar name added to or replacing an ordinary name

nicotine (ˈnikətēn) *n.* liquid alkaloid obtained from leaves of tobacco plant —ˈ**nicotinism** *n.* tobacco poisoning

nictitate (ˈniktitāt) *or* **nictate** (ˈniktāt) *v.* blink —**nictiˈtation** *or* **nicˈtation** *n.*

niece (nēs) *n.* brother's or sister's daughter

niello (nēˈelō) *n.* black alloy of lead, silver, copper and sulfur used to decorate metal objects

nifty (ˈnifti) *a. inf.* **1.** neat, smart **2.** quick

Niger (ˈnījər) *n.* country in Africa bounded north by Algeria and Libya, east by Chad, south by Nigeria, southwest by Benin and Burkina-Faso and west by Mali —**Nigerois** (nēzhərˈwä, -zher-) *n.*

Nigeria (nīˈjēəriə) *n.* country in Africa bounded north by Niger, northeast by Lake Chad, east by Cameroon, south by the Atlantic and west by Benin and Niger —**Niˈgerian** *n./a.*

niggard (ˈnigərd) *n.* mean, stingy person —ˈ**niggardly** *a./adv.*

nigger (ˈnigər) *n. offens.* Negro

niggle (ˈnigəl) *vi.* **1.** find fault continually —*vt.* **2.** annoy —ˈ**niggling** *a.* **1.** petty **2.** irritating and persistent

nigh (nī) *a./adv./prep. obs., poet.* near

night (nīt) *n.* **1.** time of darkness between sunset and sunrise **2.** end of daylight **3.** dark —ˈ**nightie** *n.* nightdress —ˈ**nightly** *a.* **1.** happening, done every night **2.** of the night —*adv.* **3.** every night **4.** by night —**nights** *adv. inf.* at night, *esp.* regularly —**night blindness** *Pathol.* inability to see normally in dim light (*also* **nyctalopia**) —ˈ**nightcap** *n.* **1.** cap worn in bed **2.** late-night (alcoholic) drink —ˈ**nightclub** *n.* establishment for dancing, music *etc.* opening late at night —ˈ**nightdress** *n.* woman's loose robe worn in bed —ˈ**nightfall** *n.* approach of darkness; dusk —ˈ**nightingale** *n.* any of various old world thrushes noted for sweet singing, *esp.* at night —ˈ**nightmare** *n.* **1.** very bad dream **2.** terrifying experience —**night school** educational institution that holds classes in evening —ˈ**nightshade** *n.* any of various plants of potato family, some of them with very poisonous berries —ˈ**nightspot** *n. inf.* nightclub —ˈ**nightstick** *n.* short club carried by uniformed member of police —**night-time** *n.* —**night watch 1.** guard kept at night, *esp.* for security **2.** period of time watch is kept

NIH National Institutes of Health

nihilism (ˈnīilizəm, ˈnīhilizəm) *n.* **1.** rejection of all religious and moral principles **2.** opposition to all constituted authority or government —ˈ**nihilist** *n.* —**nihilˈistic** *a.*

-nik (*comb. form*) *inf., oft. offens.* person associated with specified state or quality: *beatnik, jognik, richnik*

nil (nil) *n.* nothing, zero

nimble (ˈnimbəl) *a.* agile, active, quick, dexterous —ˈ**nimbly** *adv.*

nimbus (ˈnimbəs) *n.* **1.** rain or storm cloud **2.** cloud of glory, halo (*pl.* **-bi** (-bī), **-es**)

nincompoop (ˈninkəmpo͞op, ˈning-) *n.* fool, simpleton

nine (nīn) *a./n.* cardinal number next above eight —**nineˈteen** *a./n.* nine more than ten —**nineˈteenth** *a.* —ˈ**ninetieth** *a./n.* —ˈ**ninety** *a./n.* nine tens —**ninth** (nīnth) *a.* —**ninthly** (ˈnīnthli) *adv.* —**nine-days wonder** something that arouses great interest but only for short period —ˈ**ninepins** *pl.n.* (*with sing. v.*) game where wooden pins are set up to be knocked down by rolling ball, skittles —**nineteenth hole** *Golf sl.* bar in golf clubhouse

niobium (nīˈōbiəm) *n. Chem.* metallic element *Symbol* Nb, at. wt. 92.9, at. no. 41 (*formerly* **columbium**)

nip (nip) *vt.* **1.** pinch sharply **2.** detach by pinching, bite **3.** check growth of (plants) thus **4.** *sl.* steal —*vi.* **5.** *inf.* hurry (**-pp-**) —*n.* **6.** pinch **7.** check to growth **8.** sharp coldness of weather **9.** short drink —ˈ**nipper** *n.* **1.** thing (*eg* crab's claw) that nips **2.** *inf.* small child —*pl.* **3.** pincers —ˈ**nippy** *a. inf.* **1.** cold **2.** quick

nipple (ˈnipəl) *n.* **1.** point of a breast, teat **2.** anything like this

Nippon (ˈnipon) *n.* Japan —**Nippoˈnese** *a./n.*

nisei (nēˈsā, ˈnēsā) *n.* person whose parents immigrated to the U.S.A. from Japan (*pl.* **nisei, -s**)

nit (nit) *n.* **1.** egg of louse or other parasite **2.** *inf.* nitwit —**nitty-gritty** *n. inf.* basic facts, details —ˈ**nitwit** *n. inf.* fool

niter (ˈnītər) *n.* **1.** potassium nitrate **2.** sodium nitrate

nitrogen (ˈnītrəjən) *n. Chem.* gaseous element *Symbol* N, at. wt. 14.0, at. no. 7 —ˈ**nitrate** *n.* compound of nitric acid and an alkali —ˈ**nitric** *or* ˈ**nitrous** *a.* —ˈ**nitrify** *vt.* **1.** treat or cause to react with nitrogen **2.** treat (soil) with nitrates **3.** (of nitrobacteria) convert (ammonium compounds) into nitrates by oxidation —**niˈtrogenous** *a.* of, containing nitrogen —**nitric acid** corrosive liquid —**nitrobacˈteria** *pl.n.* soil bacteria involved in nitrification —**nitrogen cycle** natural circulation of nitrogen by living organisms —**nitrogen mustard** anticancer drug related to sulfur mustard gas used in warfare (*also* **mustargen, mechlorethamine**) —**nitroglycerin** *or* **nitroglycerine** (nītrə'glisərin) *n.* explosive liquid —**nitrous oxide** gas with sweet smell, used as anesthetic in dentistry (*also* **laughing gas**)

nix (niks) *sl. n.* **1.** nothing —*vt.* **2.** reject (proposal, plan)

Nixon ('niksən) *n.* **Richard Milhous.** the 37th President of the U.S. (1969-74)

NJ New Jersey

NLRB National Labor Relations Board

NM *or* **N. Mex.** New Mexico

NNE north-northeast

NNW north-northwest

no (nō) *a.* **1.** not any, not a **2.** not at all —*adv.* **3.** expresses negative reply to question or request —*n.* **4.** refusal **5.** denial **6.** negative vote or voter (*pl.* **-es**) —**no-go** *a. sl.* **1.** not functioning properly **2.** hopeless —**no-man's-land** *n.* **1.** waste or unclaimed land **2.** contested land between two opposing forces —**no-one** *or* **no one** *pron.* nobody —**no-trump** *Cards n.* **1.** bid or contract to play without trumps (*also* **no-trumps**) —*a.* **2.** (of hand) of balanced distribution suitable for playing without trumps (*also* **no-trumper**) —'**noway** *adv. sl.* not at all

No[1] *or* **Noh** (nō) *n.* traditional Japanese drama evolved from Shinto rites

No[2] *Chem.* nobelium

No. number (*pl.* **Nos.**)

nob (nob) *n. sl.* **1.** member of upper classes **2.** head

nobelium (nō'bēliəm) *n. Chem.* transuranic element *Symbol* No, at. wt. 254, at. no. 102

noble ('nōbəl) *a.* **1.** of the nobility **2.** showing, having high moral qualities **3.** impressive, excellent —*n.* **4.** member of the nobility —**no'bility** *n.* **1.** class holding special rank, usu. hereditary, in state **2.** quality of being noble —'**nobly** *adv.* —**noble gas** gaseous element that almost never combines with other elements (*also* **rare gas**) —'**nobleman** *n.* —**noble metal** metallic element not corroding or tarnishing in air or water and highly resistant to chemical action

noblesse oblige (nō'bles ə'blēzh) *oft. ironic* supposed obligation of nobility to be honorable and generous

nobody ('nōbədi) *pron.* **1.** no person —*n.* **2.** person of no importance

nock (nok) *n.* **1.** notch on arrow that fits on bowstring **2.** groove at either end of bow that holds bowstring —*vt.* **3.** fit (arrow) on bowstring

nocturnal (nok'tərnəl) *a.* **1.** of, in, by, night **2.** active by night

nocturne ('noktərn) *n.* **1.** dreamy piece of music **2.** night scene

nod (nod) *v.* **1.** bow (head) slightly and quickly in assent, command *etc.* —*vi.* **2.** let head droop with sleep (**-dd-**) —*n.* **3.** act of nodding —**nodding acquaintance** slight knowledge of person or subject —**nod off** *inf.* fall asleep

node (nōd) *n.* **1.** knot or knob **2.** point at which curve crosses itself —'**nodal** *a.* —'**nodical** *a.*

nodule ('nojo͞ol) *n.* **1.** little knot **2.** rounded irregular mineral mass

Noel (nō'el) *n.* **1.** Christmas **2.** (**n-**) Christmas carol

nog[1] (nog) *n.* beverage made with beaten eggs, usu. with alcoholic liquor, such as *eggnog*

nog[2] (nog) *n.* **1.** peg or block **2.** stump —'**nogging** *n.* horizontal timber member in framed construction

noggin ('nogin) *n.* **1.** small amount of liquor **2.** small mug **3.** *inf.* head

Noh (nō) *n. see* No[1]

noise (noiz) *n.* **1.** any sound, *esp.* disturbing one **2.** clamor, din **3.** loud outcry **4.** talk; interest —*vt.* **5.** (*usu. with* abroad *or* about) spread (gossip *etc.*) —'**noiseless** *a.* without noise, quiet, silent —'**noisily** *adv.* —'**noisy** *a.* **1.** making much noise **2.** clamorous

noisome ('noisəm) *a.* **1.** (*esp.* of smells) offensive **2.** harmful, noxious

nom. nominative

nomad ('nōmad) *n.* **1.** member of tribe with no fixed dwelling place **2.** wanderer —**no'madic** *a.*

nom de plume (nom də 'plo͞om) *Fr.* writer's assumed name, pen name, pseudonym (*pl.* **noms de plume**)

nomenclature ('nomənklāchər) *n.* terminology of particular science *etc.*

nominal ('nominəl) *a.* **1.** in name only **2.** (of fee *etc.*) small, insignificant **3.** of a name or names —'**nominalism** *n.* philosophical theory that general word, such as *dog,* is merely name and does not denote real object, the general idea 'dog' —'**nominalist** *n.* —'**nominally** *adv.* **1.** in name only **2.** not really

nominate ('nomindruck) *vt.* **1.** propose as candidate **2.** appoint to office —**nomi'nation** *n.* —'**nominative** *a./n.* (of) case of nouns, pronouns when subject of verb —'**nominator** *n.* —**nomi'nee** *n.* candidate

non- (*comb. form*) negatives the idea of the simple word. See the list below

nonage ('nonij, 'nōnij) *n.* **1.** *Law* state of being under any of various ages at which person may legally enter into certain transactions **2.** any period of immaturity

nonagenarian (nōnəji'neriən) *a.* **1.** aged between ninety and ninety-nine —*n.* **2.** person of such age

nonaligned (nonə'līnd) *a.* (of states *etc.*) not part of a major alliance or power bloc

nonce (nons) *n.* —**nonce word** word coined for single occasion —**for the nonce 1.** for the occasion only **2.** for the present

nonchalant (nonshə'länt, 'nonshəlänt, -lənt) *a.* casually unconcerned, indifferent, cool —**noncha'lance** *n.*

noncombatant (nonkəm'batənt, non'kombətənt) *n.* **1.** civilian during war **2.** member of army who does not fight, *eg* doctor, chaplain

noncommissioned officer (nonkə'mishənd) *Mil.* subordinate officer, risen from the ranks

noncommittal (nonkə'mitəl) *a.* avoiding definite preference or pledge

non compos mentis ('non 'kompəs 'mentis) *Lat.* of unsound mind

nondescript (nondi'skript) *a.* lacking distinctive characteristics, indeterminate

none (nun) *pron.* **1.** no-one, not any —*a.* **2.** no —*adv.* **3.** in no way —**nonesuch** *or* **nonsuch** ('nunsuch) *n. obs.* matchless person or thing; nonpareil —**nonethe'less** *adv.* despite that, however

nonentity (non'entiti) *n.* **1.** insignificant person, thing **2.** nonexistent thing

nonevent ('nonivent, noni'vent) *n.* disappointing or insignificant occurrence, *esp.* one predicted to be important

nonferrous (non'ferəs) *a.* **1.** denoting metal other than iron **2.** not containing iron

nonflammable (non'flaməbəl) *a.* **1.** incapable of burning **2.** not easily set on fire

nonintervention (nonintər'venchən) *n.* refusal to intervene, *esp.* abstention by state from intervening in affairs of other states

noniron (non'īərn) *a.* not requiring ironing

nonnuclear (non'nyo͞okliər, -'no͞o-) *a.* not operated by or using nuclear energy

nonpareil (nonpə'rel) *a.* **1.** unequaled, matchless —*n.* **2.** person or thing unequaled or unrivaled **3.** *Print.* 6-point type or 6-point space **4.** small chocolate disk covered with tiny beads of colored sugar **5.** one of the beads of sugar used to decorate cakes and cookies

nonpartisan (non'pärtizən) *a.* not supporting any single political party

nonplus ('non'plus) *vt.* disconcert, confound or bewilder completely (**-ss-**)

nonproliferation (nonprəlifər'āshən) *n.* limitation of production *esp.* of nuclear weapons

nonrepresentational (nonreprizen'tāshənəl) *a. Art* abstract

nonsectarian (nonsek'teriən) *a.* not sectarian; not confined to any specific religion

nonsense ('nonsens, -səns) *n.* **1.** lack of sense **2.** absurd language **3.** absurdity **4.** silly conduct —**non'sensical** *a.* **1.** ridiculous **2.** meaningless **3.** without sense

non sequitur ('non 'sekwitər) *Lat.* statement with little or no relation to what preceded it

nonstarter (non'stärtər) *n.* **1.** horse that fails to run in race for which it has been entered **2.** person or thing that has little chance of success

nonsuch ('nunsuch) *n. see* **nonesuch** *at* NONE

non-U *a.* (*esp.* of language) not characteristic of upper class

nonunion (non'yo͞onyən) *a.* **1.** not belonging to trade union **2.** not favoring or employing union labor **3.** not produced by union labor

noodle[1] ('no͞odəl) *n.* strip of pasta served in soup *etc.*

noodle[2] ('no͞odəl) *n.* simpleton, fool

nook (no͝ok) *n.* sheltered corner, retreat

noon (no͞on) *n.* midday, twelve o'clock —'**noonday** *n.* noon —'**noontide** *n.* the time about noon

noose (no͞os) *n.* **1.** running loop **2.** snare —*vt.* **3.** catch, ensnare in noose, lasso

nor (nör; *unstressed* nər) *conj.* and not

nor' *or* **nor** (nör) north (*esp.* in compounds)

Nor. 1. Norman **2.** north **3.** Norway **4.** Norwegian

Nordic ('nördik) *a.* pert. to peoples of Germanic stock

norm (nörm) *n.* **1.** average level of achievement **2.** rule or authoritative standard **3.** model **4.** standard type or pattern —'**normal** *a.* **1.** ordinary **2.** usual **3.** conforming to type —*n.* **4.** *Geom.* perpendicular —**nor'mality** *n.* —**normali'zation** *n.* —'**normalize** *vt.* **1.** bring or make into normal state **2.** bring into conformity with standard **3.** heat (steel) above critical temperature and allow it to cool in air to relieve internal stresses; anneal —'**normally**

nonac'ceptance
nonag'gression
nonalco'holic
nonap'pearance
nonbe'liever
nonbel'ligerent
non'breakable
non-Catholic
noncom'bustible
non'communist
noncom'petitive
noncom'pliance
noncon'secutive
noncon'tagious
noncon'tributory
noncontro'versial
noncooper'ation
nonde'livery
nondenomi'national
non'drinker
non'driver
nones'sential
nonex'istent
non'fiction
nonin'fectious
nonin'flammable
nonmag'netic
nonma'lignant
non'member
non'metal
non'militant
non-negotiable
nonob'servance
nonoper'ational
non'party
non'payment
non-playing
non'poisonous
non'porous
non-profit-making
non'racial
non'reader
non'registered
nonrepre'sentative
non'resident
nonre'sistant
nonre'turnable
nonse'lective
non'shrink(able)
non'slip
non'smoker
non'standard
non'stick
non'stop
non'swimmer
non'taxable
non'technical
non'toxic
nontrans'ferable
non'tropical
non'venomous
non'verbal
non'violent
non'voter

adv. —ˈ**normative** *a.* creating or prescribing norm or standard

Norman (ˈnōrmən) *n.* **1.** in Middle Ages, member of people of Normandy in N France, descended from 10th-century Scandinavian conquerors of the country and native French **2.** native of Normandy **3.** medieval Norman and English dialect of Old French (*also* **Norman French**) —*a.* **4.** of Normans or their dialect of French **5.** of Normandy **6.** denoting Romanesque architecture used in Britain from Norman Conquest until 12th century, characterized by massive masonry walls *etc.*

Norse (nōrs) *a.* **1.** of ancient and medieval Scandinavia **2.** of Norway —*n.* **3.** N group of Germanic languages, spoken in Scandinavia **4.** any of these languages, *esp.* in ancient or medieval forms —ˈ**Norseman** *n. see* VIKING —**the Norse 1.** Norwegians **2.** Vikings

north (nōrth) *n.* **1.** direction to the right of person facing the sunset **2.** part of the world, of country *etc.* toward this point **3.** person occupying this position in game —*adv.* **4.** toward or in the north —*a.* **5.** to, from or in the north —**northerly** (ˈnōrdhərli) *a.* **1.** of or situated in north —*n.* **2.** wind from the north —**northern** (ˈnōrdhərn) *a.* —**northerner** (ˈnōrdhərnər) *n.* person from the north —**northward** (ˈnōrthwərd; *Naut.* ˈnōrdhərd) *a./n./adv.* —**northwards** (ˈnōrthwərdz) *adv.* —**northeast** (nōrthˈēst; *Naut.* nōrˈēst) *n.* **1.** direction midway between north and east **2.** (*oft.* **N-**) area lying in or toward this direction —*a.* **3.** (*sometimes* **N-**) of northeastern part of specified country *etc.* **4.** in, toward or facing northeast **5.** (*esp.* of wind) from northeast (*also* **northˈeastern**) —*adv.* **6.** in, to, toward or (*esp.* of wind) from northeast —**Northˈeast** *n.* areas or regions lying to northeast of implied point of orientation —**northeaster** (nōrthˈēstər; *Naut.* nōrˈēstər) *n.* strong wind or storm from northeast —**northern hemisphere** (*oft.* **N-H-**) half of globe lying north of equator —**northern lights** aurora borealis —**north-northeast** *n.* **1.** direction midway between north and northeast —*a./adv.* **2.** in, from or toward this direction —**north-northwest** *n.* **1.** direction midway between northwest and north —*a./adv.* **2.** in, from or toward this direction —**North Pole 1.** northernmost point on earth's axis **2.** *Astron.* point of intersection of earth's extended axis and northern half of celestial sphere (*also* **north celestial pole**) —**northwest** (nōrthˈwest; *Naut.* nōrˈwest) *n.* **1.** direction midway between north and west **2.** (*oft.* **N-**) area lying in or toward this direction —*a.* **3.** (*sometimes* **N-**) of northwestern part of specified country *etc.* (*also* **northˈwestern**) —*a./adv.* **4.** in, to, toward or (*esp.* of wind) from northwest —**northwester** (nōrthˈwestər; *Naut.* nōrˈwestər) *n.* strong wind or storm from northwest —**the North Star** *see* **Pole Star** *at* POLE[2]

North Carolina (karəˈlīnə) South Atlantic state of the U.S.: ratified the Constitution in 1789. Abbrev.: **NC** (with ZIP code)

North Dakota (dəˈkōtə) West North Central state of the U.S., admitted to the Union in 1889. Abbrev.: **ND** (with ZIP code)

Northern Rhodesia *former name of* ZAMBIA

North Korea country in Asia bounded north by China, east by the Sea of Japan, west by the Yellow Sea and south by Korea from which it is separated by a demilitarized zone

Norw. 1. Norway **2.** Norwegian

Norway (ˈnōrwā) *n.* country in Europe bounded north by the Arctic Ocean, east by the U.S.S.R., Finland and Sweden, south by the Skagerrak Straits and west by the North Sea —**Norwegian** (nōrˈwējən) *n./a.* **1.** (native or inhabitant) of Norway —*n.* **2.** language of Norway which is a Scandinavian language

Nos. numbers

nose (nōz) *n.* **1.** organ of smell, used also in breathing, as opening to balance pressure on eardrum, and sounding board to form speech sounds **2.** any projection resembling a nose, as prow of ship, aircraft *etc.* —*v.* **3.** (cause to) move forward slowly and carefully —*vt.* **4.** touch with nose **5.** smell, sniff —*vi.* **6.** smell **7.** (*with* into, around, about *etc.*) pry —ˈ**nosy** *or* ˈ**nosey** *a. inf.* inquisitive —ˈ**nosebag** *n.* bag fastened around head of horse in which feed is placed —ˈ**noseband** *n.* detachable part of horse's bridle that goes around nose —**nose dive** downward sweep of aircraft —ˈ**nosegay** *n.* bunch of flowers

nosh (nosh) *n.* **1.** a snack **2.** anything eaten between meals —ˈ**nosher** *n.* **1.** one who eats between meals **2.** one with a sweet tooth —**nosh-up** *n.* **UK** large and satisfying meal

nostalgia (noˈstaljə) *n.* **1.** longing for return of past events **2.** homesickness —**nosˈtalgic** *a.*

nostril (ˈnostril) *n.* one of the two external openings of the nose

nostrum (ˈnostrəm) *n.* **1.** quack medicine **2.** secret remedy

not (not) *adv.* expressing negation, refusal, denial —**not proven** (ˈprōvən) a third verdict available to Scottish courts, returned when there is insufficient evidence to convict

nota bene (ˈnōtə ˈbēni) *Lat.* note well

notable (ˈnōtəbəl) *a.* **1.** worthy of note, remarkable —*n.* **2.** person of distinction —**notaˈbility** *n.* an eminent person —ˈ**notably** *adv.*

notary (ˈnōtəri) *n.* person authorized to draw up deeds, contracts

notation (nōˈtāshən) *n.* **1.** representation of numbers, quantities, by symbols **2.** set of such symbols **3. C** footnote, memorandum

notch (noch) *n.* **1.** V-shaped cut or indentation 2. *inf.* step, grade —*vt.* 3. make notches in

note (nōt) *n.* 1. brief comment or record 2. short letter 3. symbol for musical sound 4. single tone 5. sign 6. indication, hint 7. fame 8. notice 9. regard —*pl.* 10. brief jottings written down for future reference —*vt.* 11. observe, record 12. heed —**'noted** *a.* well-known —**'notelet** *n.* folded card with printed design on front, for writing short letter —**'notebook** *n.* small book with blank pages for writing —**'notepaper** *n.* paper for writing notes —**'noteworthy** *a.* 1. worth noting 2. remarkable

nothing ('nuthing) *pron.* 1. no thing 2. not anything, nought —*adv.* 3. not at all, in no way —**'nothingness** *n.*

notice ('nōtis) *n.* 1. observation 2. attention, consideration 3. warning, intimation, announcement 4. advance notification of intention to end a contract *etc.,* as of employment 5. review —*vt.* 6. observe, mention 7. give attention to —**'noticeable** *a.* 1. conspicuous 2. attracting attention 3. appreciable

notify ('nōtifī) *vt.* 1. report 2. give notice of or to (**-fied, -fying**) —**'notifiable** *a.* —**notifi'cation** *n.*

notion ('nōshən) *n.* 1. concept 2. opinion 3. whim —**'notional** *a.* speculative, imaginary, abstract

notorious (nō'tōriəs) *a.* 1. known for something bad 2. well-known —**notoriety** (nōtə'rīiti) *n.* discreditable publicity

notwithstanding (notwith'standing) *prep.* 1. in spite of —*adv.* 2. all the same —*conj.* 3. although

nougat ('nōōgət) *n.* chewy candy containing nuts, fruit *etc.*

nought (nōt) *n.* 1. nothing 2. cipher 0

noun (nown) *n.* word used as name of person, idea, or thing, substantive

nourish ('nurish) *vt.* 1. feed 2. nurture 3. tend 4. encourage —**'nourishment** *n.*

nouveau riche (nōōvo 'rēsh) *Fr.* person who has acquired wealth recently and is regarded as vulgarly ostentatious (*pl.* ***nouveaux riches*** (nōōvo 'rēsh))

Nov. November

nova ('nōvə) *n.* star that suddenly becomes brighter then loses brightness through months or years (*pl.* **-vae** (-vē), **-s**)

novel[1] ('novəl) *n.* fictitious tale in book form —**nove'lette** *n.* 1. short novel 2. trite, oversentimental novel —**'novelist** *n.* writer of novels

novel[2] ('novəl) *a.* 1. new, recent 2. strange —**'novelty** *n.* 1. newness 2. something new or unusual 3. small ornament, trinket

novella (nō'velə) *n.* 1. short narrative tale, *esp.* one having satirical point 2. short novel (*pl.* **-s, -le** (-li))

November (nō'vembər) *n.* 1. eleventh month 2. word used in communications for the letter *n*

novena (nō'vēnə) *n. R.C.Ch.* prayers, services, lasting nine consecutive days (*pl.* **-nae** (-nē))

novice ('novis) *n.* 1. one new to anything 2. beginner 3. candidate for admission to religious order —**novitiate** (nō'vishit) *n.* 1. probationary period 2. part of religious house for novices 3. novice

Novocain ('nōvəkān) *n.* trade name for procaine hydrochloride

now (now) *adv.* 1. at the present time 2. immediately 3. recently (*oft. with* just) —*conj.* 4. seeing that, since —**'nowadays** *adv.* in these times, at present

Nowel *or* **Nowell** (nō'el) *n. see* NOEL

nowhere ('nōwāər) *adv.* not in any place or state

nowise ('nōwīz) *adv.* not in any manner or degree

noxious ('nokshəs) *a.* poisonous, harmful

nozzle ('nozəl) *n.* pointed spout, *esp.* at end of hose

Np *Chem.* neptunium

NRA National Rifle Association

NS Nova Scotia

NSA National Shipping Authority

NSC National Security Council

NSF National Science Foundation

N.S.P.C.A. National Society for the Prevention of Cruelty to Animals

N.S.P.C.C. National Society for the Prevention of Cruelty to Children

N.S.T. Newfoundland Standard Time

N.T. 1. New Testament 2. no-trump

nt. wt. *or* **nt wt** net weight

nu (nyōō, nōō) *n.* 13th letter in Gr. alphabet (Ν, ν)

nuance ('nyōōäns, nōō'äns) *n.* delicate shade of difference, in color, tone of voice *etc.*

nub (nub) *n.* 1. small lump 2. main point (of story *etc.*)

nubile ('nyōōbil, 'nōō-) *a.* marriageable

nucleon ('nyōōklion, 'nōō-) *n.* proton or neutron

nucleus ('nyōōkliəs, 'nōō-) *n.* 1. center, kernel 2. beginning meant to receive additions 3. core of the atom (*pl.* **-lei** (-liī)) —**'nuclear** *a.* of, pert. to atomic nucleus —**nucle'onics** *pl.n.* (*with sing. v.*) branch of physics dealing with applications of nuclear energy —**nuclear bomb** bomb whose force is due to uncontrolled nuclear fusion or nuclear fission —**nuclear disarmament** elimination of nuclear weapons from country's armament —**nuclear energy** energy released by nuclear fission —**nuclear family** *Sociol., anthropol.* primary social unit consisting of parents and their offspring —**nuclear fission** disintegration of the atom —**nuclear fusion** reaction in which two nuclei combine to form nucleus with release of energy (*also* 'fusion) —**nuclear physics** branch of physics concerned with structure of nucleus and particles of which it consists —**nuclear reaction** change in structure and energy content of atomic nucleus by interaction with another nucleus, particle —**nuclear reactor** *see* REACT —**nucleic acid** (nyōō'klēik, nōō-; -'klā-) substance whose molecules contain information which guides the synthesis of proteins —**nucleo'protein** *n.* large complex combination of proteins and nucleic acids found in all living cells

nude (nyōōd, nōōd) *n.* **1.** state of being naked **2.** (picture, statue *etc.* of) naked person —*a.* **3.** naked —'**nudism** *n.* practice of nudity —'**nudist** *n.* —'**nudity** *n.*

nudge (nuj) *vt.* **1.** touch slightly with elbow —*n.* **2.** such touch

nugatory ('nyōōgətöri, 'nōō-) *a.* trifling, futile

nugget ('nugit) *n.* rough lump of native gold

nuisance ('nyōōsəns, 'nōō-) *n.* something or someone harmful, offensive, annoying or disagreeable

null (nul) *a.* of no effect, void —'**nullify** *vt.* **1.** cancel **2.** make useless or ineffective (**-fied, -fying**) —'**nullity** *n.* state of being null and void —**null set** *Math.* set having no members (*also* **empty set**)

num. 1. number **2.** numeral

Num. Numbers

numb (num) *a.* **1.** deprived of feeling, *esp.* by cold —*vt.* **2.** make numb **3.** deaden —'**numbskull** *n. see* NUMSKULL

number ('numbər) *n.* **1.** sum, aggregate **2.** word or symbol saying how many **3.** single issue of a paper *etc.* issued in regular series **4.** classification as to singular or plural **5.** song, piece of music **6.** performance **7.** company, collection **8.** identifying number, as of particular house, telephone *etc.* **9.** *sl.* measure, correct estimation —*vt.* **10.** count **11.** class, reckon **12.** give a number to **13.** amount to —'**numberless** *a.* countless —**number crunching** the performing of complicated calculations involving large numbers, *esp.* at high speed by computer —**number one** *n.* **1.** *inf.* oneself —*a.* **2.** first in importance, urgency *etc.* —**Number Ten** 10 Downing Street, British prime minister's official London residence

Numbers ('numbərz) *pl.n.* (*with sing. v.*) *Bible* 4th book of the O.T., continuing the story of the deliverance, describing the 40 years wandering in the desert

numeral ('nyōōmərəl, 'nōō-) *n.* sign or word denoting a number —'**numerable** *a.* able to be numbered or counted —'**numeracy** *n.* —**numerate** ('nyōōmərit, 'nōō-) *a.* **1.** able to use numbers, *esp.* in calculations —*vt.* ('nyōōmərāt, 'nōō-) **2.** count —**nume'ration** *n.* —'**numerator** *n.* top part of fraction, figure showing how many of the fractional units are taken —**nu'merical** *a.* of, in respect of, number or numbers —**nume'rology** *n.* study of numbers, and of their supposed influence on human affairs —'**numerous** *a.* many

numismatic (nyōōmiz'matik, nōō-) *a.* of coins —**numis'matics** *pl.n.* (*with sing. v.*) the study of coins —**nu'mismatist** *n.*

numskull *or* **numbskull** ('numskul) *n.* dolt, dunce

nun (nun) *n.* woman living (in convent) under religious vows —'**nunnery** *n.* convent of nuns —**nun's veiling** very lightweight worsted dress fabric

nuncio ('nunsiō, 'nōōn-) *n.* ambassador of the Pope (*pl.* **-s**)

nunny bag ('nuni) **C** small sealskin haversack

nuptial ('nupshəl, -chəl) *a.* of, relating to marriage —'**nuptials** *pl.n.* (*sometimes with sing. v.*) **1.** marriage **2.** wedding ceremony

nurse (nərs) *n.* **1.** person trained for care of sick or injured **2.** woman tending another's child —*vt.* **3.** act as nurse to **4.** suckle **5.** pay special attention to **6.** harbor (grudge *etc.*) —'**nursery** *n.* **1.** room for children **2.** rearing place for plants —'**nursemaid** *n.* woman employed to look after children (*also* **nurse**) —'**nurseryman** *n.* one who raises plants for sale —**nursery rhyme** short traditional verse or song for children —**nursery school** school for young children —**nursery slope** gentle slope for beginners in skiing —**nursing home** private hospital or residence for aged or infirm persons

nurture ('nərchər) *n.* **1.** bringing up **2.** education **3.** rearing **4.** nourishment —*vt.* **5.** bring up **6.** educate

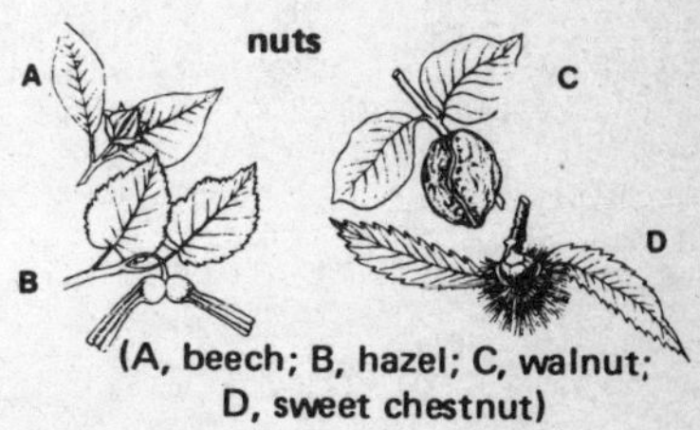

(A, beech; B, hazel; C, walnut; D, sweet chestnut)

nut (nut) *n.* **1.** seed consisting of hard shell and kernel **2.** hollow metal collar into which a screw fits **3.** *inf.* head **4.** *inf.* eccentric or crazy person —*vi.* **5.** gather nuts (**-tt-**) —'**nutty** *a.* **1.** of, like nut **2.** pleasant to taste and bite **3.** *sl.* insane, crazy (*also* **nuts**) —'**nutcase** *n. sl.* insane or foolish person —'**nutcracker** *n.* **1.** (*oft. pl.*) device for cracking shells of nuts **2.** Old World or North American bird having speckled plumage and feeding on nuts *etc.* —'**nuthatch** *n.* small songbird —'**nutmeg** *n.* aromatic seed of Indian tree —'**nutshell** *n.* shell around kernel of nut —**in a nutshell** in essence;

briefly —**nuts and bolts** *inf.* essential or practical details

nutria (ˈnyo͞otriə, ˈno͞o-) *n.* fur of coypu

nutrient (ˈnyo͞otriənt, ˈno͞o-) *a.* **1.** nourishing —*n.* **2.** something nutritious

nutriment (ˈnyo͞otrimənt, ˈno͞o-) *n.* nourishing food —**nuˈtrition** *n.* **1.** branch of biology concerned with relation of food substances to body function and health **2.** nutriment —**nuˈtritionist** *n.* —**nuˈtritious** *or* **ˈnutritive** *a.* **1.** nourishing **2.** promoting growth

nux vomica (ˈnuks ˈvomikə) seed of tree which yields strychnine

nuzzle (ˈnuzəl) *v.* **1.** burrow, press with nose —*vi.* **2.** nestle

NV Nevada

NW northwest(ern)

N.W.T. Northwest Territories (of Canada)

NY New York

Nyasaland (nīˈasəland) *n. former name of* MALAWI

nyctalopia (niktəˈlōpiə) *n. see* **night blindness** *at* NIGHT

nylon (ˈnīlon) *n.* **1.** synthetic material used for fabrics, bristles, ropes *etc.* —*pl.* **2.** stockings made of this

nymph (nimf) *n.* legendary semidivine maiden of sea, woods, mountains *etc.*

nymphomania (nimfəˈmāniə) *n.* abnormally intense sexual desire in women —**nymphoˈmaniac** *n.*

N.Z. *or* **N. Zeal.** New Zealand

o *or* **O** (ō) *n.* **1.** 15th letter of English alphabet **2.** any of several speech sounds represented by this letter, as in *code, pot, cow* or *form* **3.** something shaped like O; zero (*pl.* **o's, O's** *or* **Os**)

O[1] **1.** *Chem.* oxygen **2.** human blood type of ABO group **3.** Old

O[2] (ō) *interj.* **1.** *see* OH **2.** exclamation introducing invocation, entreaty, wish *etc.* —**O Canada** the Canadian national anthem

o' (ə) *prep. inf.* of

O'- (*comb. form*) in surnames of Irish Gaelic origin, descendant of, as in *O'Corrigan*

oaf (ōf) *n.* **1.** lout **2.** dolt

oak (ōk) *n.* **1.** common, deciduous forest tree —*pl.* **2.** (**O-**) horse race for fillies held annually at Epsom —'**oaken** *a.* of oak —**oak apple** round gall on oak trees —**oak wilt** fungal disease of oak trees

oakum ('ōkəm) *n.* loose fiber got by unraveling old rope

oar (ōr) *n.* **1.** wooden lever with broad blade worked by the hands to propel boat **2.** oarsman —*v.* **3.** row —'**oarsman** *n.* —'**oarsmanship** *n.* skill in rowing

OAS Organization of American States

oasis (ō'āsis) *n.* fertile spot in desert (*pl.* **oases** (ō'āsēz))

oast (ōst) *n.* kiln for drying hops

oat (ōt) *n.* **1.** (*usu. pl.*) grain of cereal plant **2.** the plant —'**oaten** *a.* —'**oatmeal** *n.*

oath (ōth) *n.* **1.** confirmation of truth of statement by naming something sacred **2.** curse (*pl.* **oaths** (ōdhz, oths))

OAU Organization of African Unity

ob. 1. (on tombstones *etc.*) obiit (*Lat.*, he or she died) **2.** obiter (*Lat.*, incidentally, in passing) **3.** oboe

ob- (*comb. form*) inverse; inversely, as in *obovate*

Obadiah (ōbə'dīə) *n. Bible* 31st book of the O.T., written by the prophet Obadiah to show judgment on the nation of Edom

obbligato (obli'gätō) *Mus. a.* **1.** not to be omitted —*n.* **2.** essential part in score (*pl.* **-s, -ti** (-tē))

obdurate ('obdyōōrit, 'obdərit) *a.* stubborn, unyielding —'**obduracy** *or* '**obdurateness** *n.*

obedience (ō'bēdiəns, ə-) *n.* submission to authority —**o'bedient** *a.* **1.** willing to obey **2.** compliant **3.** dutiful —**o'bediently** *adv.*

obeisance (ō'bēsəns, ə-; -'bā-) *n.* bow; curtsy

obelisk ('obilisk) *n.* tapering rectangular stone column with pyramidal apex

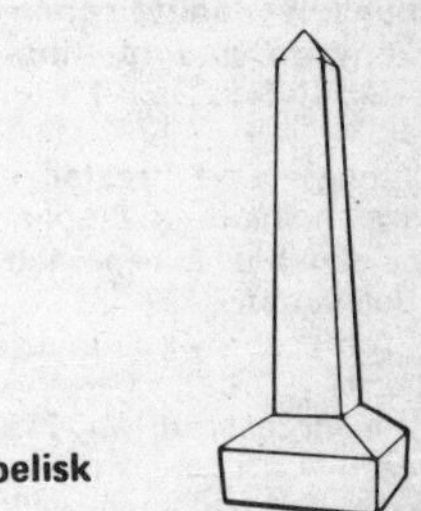
obelisk

obese (ō'bēs) *a.* very fat, corpulent —**o'besity** *n.* result of imbalance between food consumption and energy needs

obey (ō'bā, ə-) *vt.* **1.** do the bidding of **2.** act in accordance with —*vi.* **3.** do as ordered **4.** submit to authority

obfuscate ('obfuskāt) *vt.* **1.** perplex **2.** darken

obituary (ə'bichōōəri) *n.* **1.** notice, record of death **2.** biographical sketch of deceased person, *esp.* in newspaper (*also* (*inf.*) **o'bit**)

obj. 1. object **2.** objective

object[1] ('objikt) *n.* **1.** material thing **2.** that to which feeling or action is directed **3.** end, aim **4.** *Gram.* word dependent on verb or preposition —**object lesson** lesson with practical and concrete illustration —**no object** not an obstacle or hindrance

object[2] (əb'jekt) *vt.* **1.** state in opposition —*vi.* **2.** feel dislike or reluctance (to something) —**ob'jection** *n.* —**ob'jectionable** *a.* **1.** disagreeable **2.** justly liable to objection —**ob'jector** *n.*

objective (əb'jektiv) *a.* **1.** external to the mind **2.** impartial —*n.* **3.** thing or place aimed at —**objec'tivity** *n.*

objet d'art (obzhe 'dar) *Fr.* small object considered to be of artistic worth (*pl.* ***objets d'art*** (obzhe 'dar))

objet trouvé (obzhe trōō'vā) *Fr.* found object

oblate[1] (ob'lāt, 'oblāt) *a.* (of sphere) flattened at the poles

oblate[2] ('oblāt) *n.* person dedicated to religious work

oblation (ə'blāshən) *n.* offering —**ob'lational** *a.*

oblige (ə'blīj) *vt.* **1.** bind morally or legally to do service to **2.** compel —**obligate** ('obligāt) *vt.* **1.** bind, *esp.* by legal contract **2.** put under obligation —**obligation** (obli'gāshən) *n.* **1.** binding duty, promise **2.** debt of gratitude —**obligatory** (ə'bligətöri, o-) *a.* **1.** required **2.** binding —**o'bliging** *a.* ready to serve others, civil, helpful, courteous

oblique (ō'blēk, ə-) *a.* **1.** slanting **2.** indirect —**o'bliquely** *adv.* —**obliquity** (ō'blikwiti, ə-) *n.* **1.** slant **2.** dishonesty —**oblique angle** angle not a right angle

obliterate (ə'blitərāt) *vt.* blot out, efface, destroy completely —**oblite'ration** *n.*

oblivion (ə'bliviən) *n.* forgetting or being forgotten —**ob'livious** *a.* **1.** forgetful **2.** unaware

oblong ('oblong) *a.* **1.** rectangular, with adjacent sides unequal —*n.* **2.** oblong figure

obloquy ('obləkwi) *n.* **1.** reproach, abuse **2.** disgrace **3.** detraction

obnoxious (ob'nokshəs, əb-) *a.* offensive, disliked, odious

oboe ('ōbō) *n.* orchestral woodwind instrument formed like a conical pipe with holes closed by keys and a double-reeded mouthpiece —'**oboist** *n.* —**oboe d'amore** (dä'mörā) larger type of oboe used in 18th century

obs. 1. observation **2.** obsolete

obscene (ob'sēn, əb-) *a.* **1.** indecent, lewd **2.** repulsive —**obscenity** (ob'seniti, əb-) *n.*

obscure (ob'skyōōər, əb-) *a.* **1.** unclear, indistinct **2.** unexplained **3.** dark, dim **4.** humble —*vt.* **5.** make unintelligible **6.** dim **7.** conceal —**ob'scurant** *n.* one who opposes enlightenment or reform —**ob'scurantism** *n.* —**ob'scurity** *n.* **1.** indistinctness **2.** lack of intelligibility **3.** darkness **4.** obscure, *esp.* unrecognized, place or position **5.** retirement

obsequies ('obsikwiz) *pl.n.* funeral rites

obsequious (əb'sēkwiəs) *a.* servile, fawning

observe (əb'zərv) *vt.* **1.** notice, remark **2.** watch **3.** note systematically **4.** keep, follow —*vi.* **5.** make a remark —**ob'servable** *a.* —**ob'servably** *adv.* —**ob'servance** *n.* **1.** paying attention **2.** keeping —**ob'servant** *a.* quick to notice —**obser'vation** *n.* **1.** action, habit of observing **2.** noticing **3.** remark —**ob'servatory** *n.* place for watching stars *etc.* —**ob'server** *n.*

obsess (əb'ses) *vt.* haunt, fill the mind of —**ob'session** *n.* **1.** fixed idea **2.** domination of the mind by one idea —**ob'sessive** *a.*

obsidian (əb'sidiən) *n.* fused volcanic rock, forming hard, dark, natural glass

obsolete (obsə'lēt, 'obsəlēt) *a.* disused, out of date —**obso'lescent** *a.* going out of use

obstacle ('obstəkəl) *n.* **1.** hindrance **2.** impediment, barrier, obstruction

obstetrics (əb'stetriks, ob-) *pl.n.* (*with sing. v.*) branch of medicine concerned with childbirth and care of women before and after childbirth —**ob'stetric(al)** *a.* —**obste'trician** *n.*

obstinate ('obstinit) *a.* **1.** stubborn **2.** self-willed **3.** unyielding **4.** hard to overcome or cure —'**obstinacy** *n.* —'**obstinately** *adv.*

obstreperous (əb'strepərəs) *a.* unruly, noisy, boisterous

obstruct (əb'strukt) *vt.* **1.** block up **2.** hinder, impede —**ob'struction** *n.* —**ob'structionist** *n.* one who deliberately opposes transaction of business —**ob'structive** *a.*

obtain (əb'tān) *vt.* **1.** get **2.** acquire **3.** procure by effort —*vi.* **4.** be customary —**ob'tainable** *a.* procurable

obtrude (əb'trōōd) *v.* thrust forward unduly —**ob'trusion** *n.* —**ob'trusive** *a.* forward, pushing —**ob'trusively** *adv.*

obtuse (ob'tyōōs, əb-; -'tōōs) *a.* **1.** dull of perception **2.** stupid **3.** (of angle) greater than right angle **4.** not pointed —**ob'tusely** *adv.*

obverse ('obvərs, ob'vərs) *n.* **1.** fact, idea *etc.* which is the complement of another **2.** side of coin, medal *etc.* that has the principal design —*a.* **3.** facing the observer **4.** complementary, opposite

obviate ('obviāt) *vt.* remove, make unnecessary

obvious ('obviəs) *a.* **1.** clear, evident **2.** wanting in subtlety

ocarina (okə'rēnə) *n.* popular musical instrument in the shape of an egg, a bird, or a sweet potato with a protruding mouthpiece and a number of fingerholes

occasion (ə'kāzhən) *n.* **1.** time when thing happens **2.** reason, need **3.** opportunity **4.** special event —*vt.* **5.** cause —**oc'casional** *a.* **1.** happening, found now and then **2.** produced for some special event, as *occasional music* —**oc'casionally** *adv.* sometimes, now and then

Occident ('oksidənt) *n.* the West —**Occi'dental** *a.*

occlude (ə'klōōd) *vt.* shut in or out —**oc'clusion** *n.* —**oc'clusive** *a.* serving to occlude —**occluded front** *Met.* line occurring where cold front of depression has overtaken warm front, raising warm sector from ground level (*also* **oc'clusion**)

occult (ə'kult, o'kult, 'okult) *a.* **1.** secret, mysterious **2.** supernatural —*n.* **3.** esoteric knowledge —*vt.* (ə'kult, o'kult) **4.** hide from view —**occul'tation** *n.* eclipse —**oc'cultism** *n.* study of supernatural —**oc'cultness** *n.* mystery

occupy ('okyəpī) *vt.* **1.** inhabit, fill **2.** employ **3.** take possession of (**-pied, -pying**) —'**occupancy** *n.* **1.** fact of occupying **2.** residing —'**occupant** *n.* —**occu'pation** *n.* **1.** employment **2.** pursuit **3.** fact of occupying **4.** seizure —**occu'pational** *a.* **1.** pert. to occupation, *esp.* of diseases arising from a particular occupation **2.** pert. to use of occupations, *eg* craft, hobbies *etc.* as means of rehabilitation —'**occupier** *n.* tenant —**occupational medicine** *see* **industrial medicine** *at* INDUSTRY —**occupational therapy** *Med.* therapeutic use of crafts, hobbies *etc.*, *esp.* in rehabilitation of emotionally disturbed patients

occur (ə'kər) *vi.* **1.** happen **2.** come to find (**-rr-**) —**oc'currence** *n.* happening

OCDM Office of Civil and Defense Mobilization

ocean ('ōshən) *n.* **1.** great body of water **2.** large division of this **3.** the sea —**oceanic** (ōshi'anik) *a.* —**ocean'ographer** *n.* —**ocean'ography** *n.* study of physical and biological features of the sea —**ocean'ology** *n.* study of the sea, *esp.* of its economic geography —**ocean-going** *a.* (of ship, boat *etc.*) suited for travel on ocean

ocelot ('osilot, 'ō-) *n.* medium-sized feline with fawn, black-bordered spots on a yellow body of the southwest U.S. and western South America

oche ('oki) *n. Darts* mark on floor behind which player must stand to throw

ocher ('ōkər) *n.* various earths used as yellow or brown pigments —**ochreous** ('ōkərəs, 'ōkriəs), **'ocherous,** *or* **'ochery** *a.*

o'clock (ə'klok) *adv.* by the clock

OCR optical character reader *or* recognition

Oct. October

oct- (*comb. form*) eight

octagon ('oktəgon) *n.* plane figure with eight angles —**oc'tagonal** *a.*

octahedron (oktə'hēdrən) *n.* solid figure with eight sides (*pl.* **-s, -dra** (-drə))

octane ('oktān) *n.* ingredient of motor fuel —**octane number** a number usually between 0 and 100 which indicates the relative performance of a fuel in an internal-combustion engine

octave ('oktiv) *n.* **1.** *Mus.* eighth note above or below given note **2.** this space **3.** eight lines of verse

octavo (ok'tāvō) *n.* book in which each sheet is folded three times forming eight leaves (*pl.* **-s**)

octennial (ok'teniəl) *a.* lasting, happening every eight years

octet (ok'tet) *n.* **1.** group of eight **2.** music for eight instruments or singers

October (ok'tōbər) *n.* tenth month

octogenarian (oktəji'neriən) *or* **octogenary** (ok'tojineri) *n.* **1.** person aged between eighty and ninety —*a.* **2.** of an octogenarian

octopus

octopus ('oktəpəs) *n.* mollusk with eight arms covered with suckers —**'octopod** *n./a.* (mollusk) with eight arms

octoroon (oktə'rōōn) *n.* person of one-eighth Negro ancestry

octosyllable ('oktəsiləbəl) *n.* word, line of verse of eight syllables

ocular ('okyələr) *a.* of eye or sight —**'ocularly** *adv.*

oculist ('okyəlist) *n. Med. obs.* ophthalmologist

O.D. *Med.* overdose

odd (od) *a.* **1.** strange, queer **2.** incidental, random **3.** that is one in addition when the rest have been divided into equal groups **4.** not even **5.** not part of a set —**'oddity** *n.* **1.** odd person or thing **2.** quality of being odd —**'oddment** *n.* (*oft. pl.*) **1.** remnant **2.** trifle —**odds** *pl.n.* (*with* on *or* against) **1.** advantage conceded in betting **2.** likelihood —**odd-jobman** *or* **odd-jobber** *n.* person who does casual work, *esp.* domestic repairs —**odds-on** *a.* **1.** (of chance, horse *etc.*) rated at even money or less to win **2.** regarded as more or most likely to win, happen *etc.* —**odds and ends** odd fragments or scraps

ode (ōd) *n.* lyric poem on particular subject

odium ('ōdiəm) *n.* hatred, widespread dislike —**'odious** *a.* hateful, repulsive, obnoxious

odometer (ō'domitər) *n.* device for measuring distance traveled *esp.* in automobile

odor ('ōdər) *n.* smell —**odo'riferous** *a.* spreading an odor —**'odorless** *a.* —**'odorous** *a.* **1.** fragrant **2.** scented

Odyssey ('odisi) *n.* **1.** Homer's epic describing Odysseus' return from Troy **2.** any long adventurous journey

OE, O.E., *or* **OE.** Old English (language)

O.E.C.D. Organization for Economic Cooperation and Development

Oedipus complex ('edipəs, 'ēdipəs) *Psychoanal.* usu. unconscious desire of child to possess sexually parent of opposite sex —**'oedipal** *or* **oedi'pean** *a.*

o'er (ōər, ōr) *prep./adv. Poet.* over

oeuvre ('œvrə) *Fr.* total output of artist, musician or writer —***oeuvre* catalog** definitive list of artist's, musician's or writer's output

of (ov; *unstressed* əv) *prep.* removal, separation, ownership, attribute, material, quality

off (of) *adv.* **1.** away —*prep.* **2.** away from —*a.* **3.** not operative **4.** canceled or postponed **5.** bad, sour *etc.* **6.** more distant (of two); right (of pair) —**'offing** *n.* part of sea visible to observer on ship or shore —**'offbeat** *n.* **1.** *Mus.* any of normally unaccented beats in bar —*a.* **2.** unusual, unconventional or eccentric —**off chance** slight possibility —**off color** slightly ill —**off cut** piece of paper, wood *etc.* remaining after main pieces have been cut; remnant —**'off'hand** *a.* **1.** without previous thought **2.** curt (*also* **'off'handed**) —**off key 1.** *Mus.* not in correct key; out of tune **2.** out of keeping; discordant —**off line 1.** of or concerned with part of computer system not connected to central processing unit but controlled by computer storage device **2.** disconnected from computer —**off-peak** *a.* of or relating to services as used outside periods of intensive use —**offset** ('ofset) *n.* **1.** that which counterbalances, compensates **2.** method of printing **3.** narrow horizontal or sloping surface formed where wall is reduced in thickness toward top —*vt.* ('ofset, of'set) **4.** counterbalance, compensate for **5.** print (text *etc.*) using offset process **6.** construct offset in (wall) —'**offshoot** *n.* **1.** shoot or branch growing from main stem of plant **2.** something that develops from principal source —'**off'side** *a./adv. Sport* illegally forward —'**offspring** *n.* children, issue —**off-the-peg** *a.* (of clothing) ready to wear; not produced especially for person buying —**in the offing** likely to happen soon —**on the off chance** with the hope

off. 1. office **2.** officer **3.** official

offal ('ofəl) *n.* **1.** edible entrails of animal **2.** refuse

offend (ə'fend) *vt.* **1.** hurt feelings of, displease —*vi.* **2.** do wrong —**of'fender** *n.* —**of'fense** *n.* **1.** wrong **2.** crime **3.** insult —**of'fensive** *a.* **1.** causing displeasure **2.** aggressive —*n.* **3.** position or movement of attack

offer ('ofər) *vt.* **1.** present for acceptance or refusal **2.** tender **3.** propose **4.** attempt —*vi.* **5.** present itself —*n.* **6.** offering, bid —'**offerer** *or* '**offeror** *n.* —'**offering** *n.* **1.** something that is offered **2.** contribution **3.** sacrifice, as of animal, to deity —'**offertory** *n.* **1.** offering of the bread and wine at the Eucharist **2.** collection in church service

office ('ofis) *n.* **1.** room(s), building, in which business, clerical work *etc.* is done **2.** commercial or professional organization **3.** official position **4.** service **5.** duty **6.** form of worship —*pl.* **7.** task **8.** service —'**officer** *n.* **1.** one in command in army, navy, ship *etc.* **2.** official

official (ə'fishəl) *a.* **1.** with, by, authority —*n.* **2.** one holding office, *esp.* in public body —**of'ficialdom** *n.* officials collectively, or their attitudes, work, usu. in contemptuous sense —**officia'lese** *n.* language characteristic of official documents, *esp.* when verbose

officiate (ə'fishiāt) *vi.* **1.** perform duties of office **2.** perform ceremony

officious (ə'fishəs) *a.* **1.** importunate in offering service **2.** interfering

oft (oft) *adv.* often (*obs., poet.* except in combinations such as *oft-repeated* and *oft-recurring*)

often ('ofən) *adv.* many times, frequently

ogee arch ('ōjē) pointed arch with S-shaped curve on both sides

ogle ('ōgəl) *v.* **1.** stare, look (at) amorously —*n.* **2.** this look —'**ogler** *n.*

ogre ('ōgər) *n.* **1.** *Folklore* man-eating giant **2.** monster ('**ogress** *fem.*)

oh (ō) *interj.* exclamation of surprise, pain *etc.*

Ohio (ō'hīō) *n.* East North Central state of the U.S., admitted to the Union in 1803. Abbrev.: **Oh., OH** (with ZIP code)

ohm (ōm) *n.* unit of electrical resistance —'**ohmic** *a.* —'**ohmmeter** *n.*

O.H.M.S. UK On His (*or* Her) Majesty's Service

-oid (*comb. form*) likeness, resemblance, similarity, as in *anthropoid*

oil (oil) *n.* **1.** any of a number of viscous liquids with smooth, sticky feel and wide variety of uses **2.** petroleum **3.** any of variety of petroleum derivatives, *esp.* as fuel or lubricant —*vt.* **4.** lubricate with oil **5.** apply oil to —'**oily** *a.* **1.** soaked in or smeared with oil or grease **2.** consisting of, containing or resembling oil **3.** flatteringly servile or obsequious —**oil cake** stock feed consisting of compressed linseed —'**oilcloth** *n.* waterproof material made by treating cotton fabric with drying oil or synthetic resin —'**oilfield** *n.* area containing reserves of petroleum —'**oilfired** *a.* (of central heating *etc.*) using oil as fuel —**oil painting 1.** picture painted with oil paints **2.** art of painting with oil paints —**oil rig** *see* RIG (sense 6) —'**oilskin** *n.* cloth treated to make it waterproof —**oil slick** mass of floating oil covering area of water —**oil well** boring into earth or sea bed for extraction of petroleum —**well oiled** *sl.* drunk

ointment ('ointmənt) *n.* greasy preparation for healing or beautifying the skin

Ojibwa (ō'jibwā) *n.* **1.** member of Amerindian people of Michigan (*pl.* **-wa, -s**) **2.** Algonquian language of this people (*also* **Chippewa**)

OK Oklahoma

O.K. *inf. a./adv.* **1.** all right —*n.* **2.** approval —*vt.* **3.** approve (**O.K.ing** (ō'kāing), **O.K.ed** (ō'kād))

okapi (ō'käpi) *n.* Afr. animal like short-necked giraffe (*pl.* **-s, -pi**)

Oklahoma (ōklə'hōmə) *n.* West South Central state of the U.S., admitted to the Union in 1907. Abbrev.: **Okla., OK** (with ZIP code)

okra ('ōkrə) *n.* **1.** annual plant with yellow-and-red flowers and edible pods **2.** pod of this plant, eaten in soups, stews *etc.*

old (ōld) *a.* **1.** aged, having lived or existed long **2.** belonging to earlier period ('**older,** '**elder** *comp.,* '**oldest,** '**eldest** *sup.*) —'**olden** *a.* old —'**oldie** *n. inf.* old song, movie, person *etc.* —'**oldish** *a.* —**old age** period during which life cycle is drawing toward conclusion —**Old Bailey** Central Criminal Court of England —**old country** country of origin of immigrant or immigrant's ancestors —**Old**

English English language from time of earliest Saxon settlements in fifth century A.D. to about 1100 (*also* **Anglo-Saxon**) **—old-fashioned** *a.* **1.** in style of earlier period, out of date **2.** fond of old ways *—n.* **3.** cocktail containing spirit, bitters, fruit *etc.* **—Old Glory** the U.S. flag **—old guard 1.** group that works for long-established principles *etc.* **2.** conservative element in political party or other groups **—old hat** old-fashioned; trite **—old maid** elderly spinster **—old man 1.** *inf.* father; husband **2.** (*sometimes* **O- M-**) *inf.* man in command, such as employer, foreman *etc.* **3.** *jocular* affectionate term used in addressing man **—old master 1.** one of great European painters before 19th cent. **2.** painting by one of these **—Old Nick** *inf., jocular* Satan **—old school** group of people favoring traditional ideas *etc.* **—Old Testament** collection of books comprising sacred Scriptures of Hebrews; first part of Christian Bible **—old wives' tale** belief passed on as piece of traditional wisdom **—Old World** eastern hemisphere **—old-world** *a.* of former times, *esp.* quaint or traditional

oleaginous (ōli'ajinəs) *a.* **1.** oily, producing oil **2.** unctuous, fawning **—ole'aginousness** *n.*

oleander ('ōliandər, ōli'andər) *n.* poisonous evergreen flowering shrub

oleo- (*comb. form*) oil, as in *oleomargarine*

olfactory (ol'faktəri, ōl-) *a.* of smelling

oligarchy ('oligärki) *n.* government by a few **—'oligarch** *n.* **—oli'garchic(al)** *a.*

Oligocene ('oligōsēn, 'ōli-; ə'lig-) *a.* **1.** of third epoch of Tertiary period *—n.* **2.** Oligocene epoch or rock series

olive ('oliv) *n.* **1.** evergreen tree **2.** its oil-yielding fruit **3.** its wood *—a.* **4.** grayish-green **—olive branch** any offering of peace or conciliation **—olive oil** pale yellow oil extracted from olives, used in medicines *etc.*

Olympian (ə'limpiən) *a.* **1.** of Mount Olympus or classical Greek gods **2.** majestic in manner or bearing **3.** of ancient Olympia or its inhabitants *—n.* **4.** god of Mount Olympus **5.** inhabitant of ancient Olympia

Olympic (ə'limpik) *a.* **1.** of Olympic Games **2.** of ancient Olympia **—Olympic Games 1.** Panhellenic festival, held every fourth year in honor of Zeus at ancient Olympia **2.** series of competitive sports events held every four years for amateur athletes

Omaha ('ōməhō, -hä) *n.* member of Siouan-speaking Amerindian people of northeastern Nebraska (*pl.* **-ha, -s**)

Oman (ō'män, ō'man) *n.* country in the Middle East bounded south and east by the Arabian Sea, west by the People's Republic of Yemen and north by Saudi Arabia

omega (ō'megə) *n.* **1.** last letter in Gr. alphabet (Ω, ω) **2.** end

omelet *or* **omelette** ('omlit) *n.* dish of eggs beaten up and fried with seasoning

omen ('ōmən) *n.* prophetic object or happening **—ominous** ('ominəs) *a.* boding evil, threatening

omicron ('omikron, 'ōmikron) *n.* 15th letter in Gr. alphabet (Ο, ο)

omit (ō'mit) *vt.* **1.** leave out, neglect **2.** leave undone (**-tt-**) **—o'mission** *n.* **—o'missive** *a.*

omni- (*comb. form*) all

omnibus ('omnibus, -bəs) *n.* **1.** large road vehicle traveling on set route and taking passengers at any stage (*also* **bus**) **2.** book containing several works *—a.* **3.** serving, containing several objects

omnidirectional (omnidi'rekshənəl, omnī-; -dī-) *a.* in radio, denotes transmission, reception in all directions

omnipotent (om'nipətənt) *a.* all-powerful **—om'nipotence** *n.*

omnipresent (omni'prezənt) *a.* present everywhere **—omni'presence** *n.*

omniscient (om'nishənt) *a.* knowing everything **—om'niscience** *n.*

omnivorous (om'nivərəs) *a.* **1.** devouring all foods **2.** not fastidious

on (on) *prep.* **1.** above and touching, at, near, toward *etc.* **2.** attached to **3.** concerning **4.** performed upon **5.** during **6.** taking regularly *—a.* **7.** operating **8.** taking place *—adv.* **9.** so as to be on **10.** forward **11.** continuously **12.** in progress **—'oncoming** *a.* **1.** coming nearer in space or time; approaching *—n.* **2.** approach; onset **—'ongoing** *a.* **1.** actually in progress **2.** continually moving forward **—on line** of or concerned with peripheral device that is directly connected to and controlled by central processing unit of computer **—'onrush** *n.* forceful forward rush or flow **—'onset** *n.* **1.** violent attack **2.** assault **3.** beginning **—'onslaught** *n.* attack **—on stream** (of manufacturing process, equipment *etc.*) in or about to go into operation or production **—'onward** *a.* **1.** advanced or advancing *—adv.* **2.** in advance, ahead, forward **—'onwards** *adv.*

ON Ontario

on- (*comb. form*) on, as in *onlooker*

onager ('onəjər) *n.* wild ass

Onandaga (ōnən'dägə) *n.* member of Iroquoian-speaking Amerindian people of upper New York state (*pl.* **-ga, -s**)

onanism ('ōnənizəm) *n.* masturbation

once (wuns) *adv.* **1.** one time **2.** formerly **3.** ever **—once-over** *n. inf.* quick examination **—at once** immediately; simultaneously

onchocerciasis (ongkōsər'kīəsis) *n.* infection with a worm transmitted by black flies which bite humans, eventually resulting in blindness

one (wun) *a.* **1.** lowest cardinal number **2.** single **3.** united **4.** only, without others **5.** identical *—n.* **6.** number or figure 1 **7.** unity **8.** single specimen *—pron.* **9.** particular but not stated person **10.** any person **—'oneness** *n.* **1.** unity **2.** uniformity **3.** singleness **—one'self** *pron.* **—one-armed bandit** *inf.* slot machine operated by pulling down lever at one side —**one-horse** *a. inf.* small; obscure —**one-night stand 1.** performance given only once at any one place **2.** *inf.* sexual encounter lasting only one night —**one-sided** *a.* **1.** partial **2.** uneven —**one-track** *a.* **1.** *inf.* obsessed with one idea, subject *etc.* **2.** having or consisting of single track —**one-way** *a.* denoting system of traffic circulation in one direction only

onerous (ˈonərəs, ˈō-) *a.* burdensome

onion (ˈunyən) *n.* edible bulb of pungent flavor

only (ˈōnli) *a.* **1.** being the one specimen —*adv.* **2.** solely, merely, exclusively —*conj.* **3.** but then, excepting that

onomatopoeia (onəmatəˈpēə) *n.* formation of a word by using sounds that resemble or suggest the object or action to be named —**onomatoˈpoeic** *or* **onomatopoetic** (onəmatəpōˈetik) *a.*

onto *or* **on to** (ˈontōō; *unstressed* ˈontə) *prep.* **1.** on top of **2.** aware of

ontology (onˈtoləji) *n.* science of being or reality —**ontoˈlogical** *a.* —**onˈtologist** *n.*

onus (ˈōnəs) *n.* responsibility, burden

onyx (ˈoniks) *n.* variety of chalcedony with parallel regular color bands used as gemstone

oodles (ˈōōdəlz) *pl.n. inf.* abundance

oolite (ˈōəlīt) *n.* any sedimentary rock, *esp.* limestone, consisting of tiny spherical grains within fine matrix —**oolitic** (ōəˈlitik) *a.*

ooze (ōōz) *vi.* **1.** pass slowly out —*v.* **2.** exude (moisture *etc.*) —*n.* **3.** sluggish flow **4.** wet mud, slime —ˈ**oozy** *a.*

op. 1. opera **2.** operation **3.** opus

o.p. *or* **O.P.** out of print

opal (ˈōpəl) *n.* gemstone displaying variegated colors —**opaˈlescent** *a.*

opaque (ōˈpāk) *a.* not allowing the passage of light, not transparent —**opacity** (ōˈpasiti) *n.*

op. cit. opere citato (*Lat.*, in the work cited)

OPEC (ˈōpek) Organization of Petroleum Exporting Countries

open (ˈōpən) *a.* **1.** not shut or blocked up **2.** without lid or door **3.** bare **4.** undisguised **5.** not enclosed, covered or exclusive **6.** spread out, accessible **7.** frank, sincere —*vt.* **8.** set open, uncover, give access to **9.** disclose, lay bare **10.** begin **11.** make a hole in —*vi.* **12.** become open **13.** begin —*n.* **14.** clear space, unenclosed country **15.** *Sport* competition in which all may enter —ˈ**opening** *n.* **1.** hole, gap **2.** beginning **3.** opportunity —*a.* **4.** first **5.** initial —ˈ**openly** *adv.* without concealment —**open-and-shut** *a.* easily decided or solved —**open-ended** *a.* without definite limits, as of duration or amount —**open-handed** *a.* generous —**open-hearted** *a.* frank, magnanimous —**open-heart surgery** surgical repair of heart during which blood circulation is oft. maintained mechanically —**open-minded** *a.* unprejudiced —**open-plan** *a.* having no or few dividing walls between areas —**open prison** prison without restraints to prevent absconding —**open secret** something that is supposed to be secret but is widely known —**open verdict** coroner's verdict not stating cause (of death) —ˈ**openwork** *n.* pattern with interstices

opera (ˈopərə, ˈoprə) *n.* musical drama —**operˈatic** *a.* of opera —**opeˈretta** *n.* light, comic opera —**opera glasses** small binoculars used by audiences in theaters *etc.*

operation (opəˈrāshən) *n.* **1.** working, way things work **2.** scope **3.** act of surgery **4.** military action —**operaˈbility** *n.* —ˈ**operable** *a.* **1.** capable of being treated by surgical operation **2.** capable of being put into practice —ˈ**operate** *vt.* **1.** cause to function **2.** control functioning of —*vi.* **3.** work **4.** produce an effect **5.** perform act of surgery **6.** exert power —**opeˈrational** *a.* **1.** of operation(s) **2.** working —ˈ**operative** *a.* **1.** working —*n.* **2.** worker, *esp.* with a special skill —ˈ**operator** *n.* —**operating room** room in which surgical operations are performed —**operations research** analysis of problems in business involving quantitative techniques

operculum (ōˈpərkyələm) *n.* lid; cover (*pl.* **-s, -la** (-lə))

ophidian (ōˈfidiən) *a.* **1.** snakelike **2.** of suborder of reptiles which comprises snakes —*n.* **3.** any reptile of this suborder

ophthalmic (ofˈthalmik) *a.* of eyes —**ophˈthalmia** *n.* inflammation of eye —**ophthalˈmologist** *n.* medical practitioner specializing in diagnosis and treatment of eye diseases —**ophthalˈmology** *n.* study of eye and its diseases —**ophˈthalmoscope** *n.* instrument for examining interior of eye

opiate (ˈōpiit) *see* OPIUM

opinion (əˈpinyən) *n.* **1.** what one thinks about something **2.** belief, judgment —**opine** (ōˈpīn) *vt.* **1.** think —*vi.* **2.** utter opinion —**oˈpinionated** *a.* stubborn in one's opinions, dogmatic

opium (ˈōpiəm) *n.* addictive narcotic drug made from poppy —ˈ**opiate** *n.* **1.** drug containing opium **2.** narcotic —*a.* **3.** inducing sleep **4.** soothing

opossum (əˈposəm) *or* **possum** *n.* small Amer. and Aust. marsupial

opp. 1. opposed **2.** opposite

opponent (əˈpōnənt) *n.* adversary, antagonist

opportune (opərˈtyōōn, -ˈtōōn) *a.* seasonable, well-timed —**opporˈtunism** *n.* policy of doing what is expedient at the time regardless of principle —**opporˈtunist** *n./a.* —**opporˈtunity** *n.* **1.** favorable time or condition **2.** good chance

oppose (əˈpōz) *vt.* **1.** resist, withstand **2.** contrast **3.** set against —**opˈposer** *n.* —ˈ**opposite** *a.* **1.** contrary **2.** facing **3.** diametrically different **4.** adverse **5.** *Bot.* (of leaves) growing in pairs on either side of a

opposite (sense 5)

stem —*n.* **6.** the contrary —*prep./adv.* **7.** facing **8.** on the other side —**oppo'sition** *n.* **1.** antithesis **2.** resistance **3.** obstruction **4.** hostility **5.** group opposing another **6.** party opposing that in power —**opposite number** person holding corresponding position on another side or situation

oppress (ə'pres) *vt.* **1.** govern with tyranny **2.** weigh down —**op'pression** *n.* **1.** act of oppressing **2.** severity **3.** misery —**op'pressive** *a.* **1.** tyrannical **2.** hard to bear **3.** heavy **4.** (of weather) hot and tiring —**op'pressively** *adv.* —**op'pressor** *n.*

opprobrium (ə'prōbriəm) *n.* disgrace —**op'probrious** *a.* **1.** reproachful **2.** shameful **3.** abusive

oppugn (ə'pyo͞on) *vt.* call into question, dispute

opt (opt) *vi.* make a choice —**'optative** *a.* **1.** expressing wish or desire —*n.* **2.** mood of verb expressing wish

opt. **1.** optical **2.** optional

optic ('optik) *a.* **1.** of eye or sight —*n.* **2.** eye —*pl.* **3.** (*with sing. v.*) science of sight and light —**'optical** *a.* —**op'tician** *n.* maker of, dealer in spectacles, optical instruments —**optical character reader** computer device enabling characters, usu. printed on paper, to be optically scanned and input to storage device —**optic nerve** bundle of nerve fibers which conduct visual impulses from eye to brain

optimism ('optimizəm) *n.* **1.** disposition to look on the bright side **2.** doctrine that good must prevail in the end **3.** belief that the world is the best possible world —**'optimist** *n.* —**opti'mistic** *a.* —**opti'mistically** *adv.*

optimum ('optiməm) *a./n.* the best, the most favorable (*pl.* **-s, -ma** (-mə))

option ('opshən) *n.* **1.** choice **2.** preference **3.** thing chosen **4.** in business, purchased privilege of either buying or selling things at specified price within specified time —**'optional** *a.* leaving to choice

optometrist (op'tomitrist) *n.* person *usu.* not medically qualified, testing eyesight, prescribing corrective lenses *etc.* —**op'tometry** *n.* measurement of the visual power of the eye

opulent ('opyələnt) *a.* **1.** rich **2.** copious —**'opulence** *n.* riches, wealth

opus ('ōpəs) *n.* **1.** work **2.** musical composition (*pl.* **opera** ('ōpərə, 'op-), **-es**)

or (ŏr; *unstressed* ər) *conj.* **1.** introducing alternatives **2.** if not

OR Oregon

O.R. **1.** operating room **2.** operational research **3.** owner's risk

-or[1] (*comb. form*) person or thing that does what is expressed by verb, as in *actor, sailor*

-or[2] (*comb. form*) state, condition, activity, as in *terror, error, behavior, labor*

oracle ('orəkəl) *n.* **1.** divine utterance, prophecy, *oft.* ambiguous, given at shrine of god **2.** the shrine **3.** wise or mysterious adviser —**o'racular** *a.* **1.** of oracle **2.** prophetic **3.** authoritative **4.** ambiguous

oral ('ŏrəl, 'orəl) *a.* **1.** spoken **2.** by mouth —*n.* **3.** spoken examination —**'orally** *adv.*

orange ('orinj) *n.* **1.** bright reddish-yellow round fruit **2.** tree bearing it **3.** fruit's color —**orange'ade** *n.* effervescent orange-flavored drink —**'orangery** *n.* building, such as greenhouse, in which orange trees are grown —**orange pekoe** ('pēkō) black tea from smallest top leaves, grown in India and Sri Lanka

Orangeman ('orinjmən) *n.* member of society founded as secret order in Ireland to uphold Protestantism

orangutan (ə'rangətan) *n.* large Indonesian ape

orator ('orətər) *n.* **1.** maker of speech **2.** skillful speaker —**o'ration** *n.* formal speech —**ora'torical** *a.* of orator or oration —**'oratory** *n.* **1.** speeches **2.** eloquence **3.** small private chapel

oratorio (orə'tŏriō) *n.* semidramatic composition of sacred music (*pl.* **-s**)

orb (ŏrb) *n.* globe, sphere —**or'bicular** *a.*

orbit ('ŏrbit) *n.* **1.** track of planet, satellite, comet *etc.*, around another heavenly body **2.** field of influence, sphere **3.** eye socket —*v.* **4.** move in, or put into, an orbit

Orcadian (ŏr'kādiən) *n.* **1.** native or inhabitant of the Orkneys —*a.* **2.** of or relating to the Orkneys

orchard ('ŏrchərd) *n.* **1.** area for cultivation of fruit trees **2.** the trees

orchestra ('ŏrkistrə) *n.* **1.** band of musicians **2.** place for such a band in theater *etc.* (*also* **orchestra pit**) **3.** all seating for spectators on the main floor —**or'chestral** *a.* —**'orchestrate** *vt.* **1.** compose or arrange (music) for orchestra **2.** organize, arrange

orchid ('ŏrkid) *n.* genus of various flowering plants

orchitis (ŏr'kītis) *n.* inflammation of the testis

ordain (ŏr'dān) *vt.* **1.** admit to Christian ministry **2.** confer holy orders upon **3.** decree, enact **4.** destine —**ordi'nation** *n.*

ordeal (ŏr'dēl) *n.* **1.** severe, trying experience **2.** *Hist.* form of trial by which accused underwent severe physical test

order ('ŏrdər) *n.* **1.** regular or proper arrangement or condition **2.** sequence **3.**

peaceful condition of society **4.** rank, class **5.** group **6.** command **7.** request for something to be supplied **8.** mode of procedure **9.** instruction **10.** monastic society **11.** *Biol.* taxonomic division of plants and animals ranking above a family and below a class —*vt.* **12.** command **13.** request (something) to be supplied or made **14.** arrange —**'orderliness** *n.* —**'orderly** *a.* **1.** tidy **2.** methodical **3.** well-behaved —*n.* **4.** hospital attendant **5.** soldier following officer to carry orders —**'ordinal** *a.* **1.** showing position in a series —*n.* **2.** ordinal number —**ordinal number** number denoting order, quality or degree in group, such as *first, second, third*

ordinance ('ördnəns) *n.* **1.** decree, rule **2.** rite, ceremony

ordinary ('ördəneri) *a.* **1.** usual, normal **2.** common **3.** plain **4.** commonplace —*n.* **5.** bishop in his province —**ordi'narily** *adv.*

ordinate ('ördinit) *n.* vertical or *y*-coordinate of point in two-dimensional system of Cartesian coordinates

ordnance ('ördnəns) *n.* **1.** big guns, artillery **2.** military stores —**Ordnance Survey** official geographical survey of Britain

Ordovician (ördə'vishən) *a.* **1.** of, denoting or formed in second period of Paleozoic era —*n.* **2.** Ordovician period or rock system

ordure ('örjər) *n.* **1.** dung **2.** filth

ore (ör) *n.* naturally occurring mineral which yields metal

Oreg. Oregon

oregano (ə'regənō) *n.* herb, variety of marjoram

Oregon ('örigən, 'or-) *n.* Pacific state of the U.S., admitted to the Union in 1859. Abbrev.: **Oreg., OR** (with ZIP code)

organ ('örgən) *n.* **1.** large complex musical keyboard instrument in which sound is produced by means of a number of pipes arranged in sets or stops, supplied with air from a bellows **2.** structure of animal or plant carrying out particular function. **3.** means of action **4.** medium of information, *esp.* newspaper —**or'ganic** *a.* **1.** of, derived from, living organisms **2.** of bodily organs **3.** affecting bodily organs **4.** having vital organs **5.** *Chem.* of compounds formed from carbon **6.** grown with fertilizers derived from animal or vegetable matter **7.** organized, systematic —**or'ganically** *adv.* —**'organist** *n.* organ player —**organ loft** gallery in church *etc.* for an organ —**organ transplantation** transplantation of body's organs and tissues to replace or restore functions lost by injury, disease or old age

organdy *or* **organdie** ('örgəndi) *n.* light, transparent muslin with a crisp finish

organize ('örgənīz) *vt.* **1.** give definite structure to **2.** get up, arrange **3.** put into working order **4.** unite in a society —**'organism** *n.* **1.** organized body or system **2.** plant, animal —**organi'zation** *n.* **1.** act of organizing **2.** body of people, society —**'organizer** *n.*

organza (ör'ganzə) *n.* thin, stiff transparent fabric of silk or synthetic fiber

orgasm ('örgazəm) *n.* sexual climax

orgy ('örji) *n.* **1.** drunken or licentious revel, debauch **2.** act of immoderation, overindulgence

oriel ('öriəl) *n.* **1.** projecting part of an upper room with a window **2.** the window

orient ('öriənt) *n.* **1.** (**O-**) the East **2.** luster of best pearls —*a.* **3.** rising **4.** (**O-**) Eastern —*vt.* ('örient) **5.** place so as to face East **6.** adjust or align (oneself *etc.*) according to surroundings or circumstances **7.** position or set (map *etc.*) with reference to compass *etc.* —**ori'ental** *a./n.* —**ori'entalist** *n.* expert in Eastern languages and history —**'orientate** *vt.* orient —**orien'tation** *n.* —**orien'teering** *n.* competitive sport involving compass and map-reading skills

orifice ('orifis) *n.* opening, mouth of a cavity, *eg* pipe

orig. **1.** origin **2.** original(ly)

origami (öri'gämi) *n.* Japanese art of paper folding

origin ('orijin) *n.* **1.** beginning **2.** source **3.** parentage

original (ə'rijinəl) *a.* **1.** primitive, earliest **2.** new, not copied or derived **3.** thinking or acting for oneself **4.** eccentric —*n.* **5.** pattern, thing from which another is copied **6.** unconventional or strange person —**origi'nality** *n.* power of producing something individual to oneself —**o'riginally** *adv.* at first, in the beginning —**original sin** *Theol.* state of sin held to be innate in mankind as descendants of Adam

originate (ə'rijināt) *v.* come or bring into existence, begin —**origi'nation** *n.* —**o'riginator** *n.*

oriole ('öriōl) *n.* any of various New World birds of which the males are black and orange or yellow

orison ('örisən, 'or-; -zən) *n.* prayer

Orlon ('örlon) *n.* trade name for acrylic fabric used for clothing *etc.*

ormolu ('örməlōō) *n.* **1.** gilded bronze **2.** gold-colored alloy **3.** articles of these

ornament ('örnəmənt) *n.* **1.** any object used to adorn or decorate **2.** decoration —*vt.* ('örnəment) **3.** adorn —**orna'mental** *a.*

ornate (ör'nāt) *a.* highly decorated or elaborate

ornery ('örnəri) *a. dial., inf.* **1.** stubborn; vile-tempered **2.** low; treacherous **3.** ordinary

ornithology (örni'tholəji) *n.* science of birds —**ornitho'logical** *a.* —**orni'thologist** *n.*

orotund ('orətund) *a.* **1.** full, clear and musical **2.** pompous

orphan ('örfən) *n.* child bereaved of one or both parents —**'orphanage** *n.* institution for care of orphans —**'orphanhood** *n.*

orrery ('orəri) *n.* mechanical model of solar system to show revolutions, planets *etc.*
orris ('oris) *n.* any of various kinds of iris
ortho- *or before vowel* **orth-** (*comb. form*) right, correct
orthodontics (ŏrthə'dontiks) *or* **orthodontia** (ŏrthə'donchiə) *n.* branch of dentistry concerned with correcting irregularities of teeth —**ortho'dontic** *a.* —**ortho'dontist** *n.*
orthodox ('ŏrthədoks) *a.* **1.** holding accepted views **2.** conventional —**'orthodoxy** *n.* —**Orthodox Church 1.** collective body of Eastern Churches that were separated from western Church in 11th cent. and are in communion with either Patriarch of Moscow or Patriarch of Constantinople **2.** the Orthodox Church in America, which has been autonomous since 1970
orthography (ŏr'thogrəfi) *n.* correct spelling
orthopedics (ŏrthə'pēdiks) *pl.n.* (*with sing. v.*) branch of surgery concerned with disorders of spine and joints and repair of deformities of these parts —**ortho'pedic** *a.*
orthopterous (ŏr'thoptərəs) *a.* of large order of insects, including crickets, locusts and grasshoppers, having leathery forewings and membranous hind wings
ortolan ('ŏrtələn) *n.* a small bird, *esp.* as table delicacy
-ory[1] (*comb. form*) **1.** place for, as in *observatory* **2.** something having specified use, as in *directory*
-ory[2] (*comb. form*) of, relating to; characterized by; having effect of, as in *contributory*
oryx ('oriks) *n.* large Afr. antelope (*pl.* **-es, -yx**)
Os *Chem.* osmium
O.S. 1. Old Style **2.** Ordinary Seaman **3.** outsize **4.** (*also* **OS**) Old Saxon (language)
Osage (ō'sāj) *n.* **1.** member of Amerindian people of Missouri (*pl.* **-s, Osage**) **2.** Siouan language of this people
Oscar ('oskər) *n.* **1.** any of several small gold statuettes awarded annually in U.S.A. for outstanding achievements in the motion-picture industry **2.** word used in communications for the letter *o*
oscillate ('osilāt) *vi.* **1.** swing to and fro **2.** waver **3.** fluctuate (regularly) —**oscil'lation** *n.* —**'oscillator** *n.* —**'oscillatory** *a.* —**os'cilloscope** *n.* electronic instrument producing visible representation of rapidly changing quantity
osculate ('oskyəlāt) *v. jocular* kiss —**'oscular** *a.* —**oscu'lation** *n.* —**'osculatory** *a.*
Osee ('ōzē, ō'zāə) *n. Bible* Hosea in the Douay Version of the O.T.
osier ('ōzhər) *n.* species of willow used for basketwork
-osis (*comb. form*) **1.** process; state, as in *metamorphosis* **2.** diseased condition, as in *tuberculosis* **3.** formation or development of something, as in *fibrosis*
osmium ('ozmiəm) *n. Chem.* noble metal *Symbol* Os, at. wt. 192.2, at. no. 76
osmosis (oz'mōsis, os-) *n.* the passage of water through a permeable membrane from a low-to-high concentrate of solutions —**osmotic** (oz'motik, os-) *a.*
osprey ('ospri, -prā) *n.* **1.** fishing hawk **2.** plume
osseous ('osiəs) *a.* **1.** of, like bone **2.** bony —**ossifi'cation** *n.* —**'ossify** *v.* **1.** turn into bone —*vi.* **2.** grow rigid (**-fied, -fying**)
osteitis deformans (osti'ītis di'fŏrmənz) *see* PAGET'S DISEASE
ostensible (o'stensibəl) *a.* **1.** apparent **2.** professed —**os'tensibly** *adv.*
ostentation (ostən'tāshən) *n.* show, pretentious display —**osten'tatious** *a.* **1.** given to display **2.** showing off —**osten'tatiously** *adv.*
osteo- *or before vowel* **oste-** (*comb. form*) bone(s)
osteoarthritis (ostiōăr'thrītis) *n.* arthritis produced by degeneration of the cartilage found at the junction of bones and the overgrowth of bone at the margin
osteochondritis (ostiōkon'drītis) *n.* condition in which there is limited destruction of bone, usu. following injury
osteomalacia (ostiōmə'lāshiə) *n.* abnormal condition of bone marked by abundance of fibrous matrix and cartilage and mineral deficiency
osteomyelitis (ostiōmīi'lītis) *n.* infection of bone by microorganisms
osteopathy (osti'opəthi) *n.* art of treating disease by removing structural derangement by manipulation, *esp.* of spine —**'osteopath** *n.* one skilled in this art
osteoporosis (ostiōpə'rōsis) *n.* disorder of bone caused by decreased matrix and mineral portions
ostler ('oslər) *or* **hostler** *n. Hist.* stableman at an inn
ostracize ('ostrəsīz) *vt.* exclude, banish from society, exile —**'ostracism** *n.* social boycotting
ostrich ('ostrich) *n.* large swift-running flightless Afr. bird
O.T. 1. occupational therapy **2.** Old Testament **3.** overtime
other ('udhər) *a.* **1.** not this **2.** not the same **3.** alternative, different —*pron.* **4.** other person or thing —**'otherwise** *adv.* **1.** differently **2.** in another way —*conj.* **3.** or else, if not —**'otherworldly** *a.* **1.** of or relating to spiritual or imaginative world **2.** impractical, unworldly
otiose ('ōshiōs, 'ōtiōs) *a.* **1.** superfluous **2.** useless
otitis (ō'tītis) *n.* inflammation of ear
Oto-Manguean (ōtə'mänggāən) *n.* Amerindian language family spoken in southern Mexico
otosclerosis (ōtōskli'rōsis) *n.* disease of

unknown cause marked by deposits of bone in the ear resulting in progressive deafness

Ottawa ('otəwə) *n.* member of Siouan-speaking Amerindian people *orig.* of Michigan and southern Ontario and now of Oklahoma (*pl.* **-s, -wa**)

otter ('otər) *n.* furry aquatic fish-eating mammal

Ottoman ('otəmən) *a.* **1.** Turkish —*n.* **2.** Turk (*pl.* **-s**) **3.** (**o-**) cushioned, backless seat, storage box (*pl.* **-s**) **4.** (**o-**) heavy corded silk or synthetic fabric with flat crosswise ribs

oubliette (o͞obli'et) *n.* dungeon entered by trapdoor

ouch (owch) *interj.* exclamation of sudden pain

ought (öt) *v. aux.* **1.** expressing duty, obligation or advisability **2.** be bound

Ouija

Ouija ('wējə) *n.* trade name for board with letters and symbols used to obtain messages at seances

ounce (owns) *n.* a weight, sixteenth of avoirdupois pound (28.4 grams), twelfth of apothecaries' or troy pound (31.1 grams)

our ('owər) *a.* belonging to us —'**ours** *pron.* —**Our Father** *see* **the Lord's Prayer** *at* LORD —**our'self** *pron.* myself, used in regal or formal style —**our'selves** *pl. pron.* emphatic or reflexive form of WE

-ous (*comb. form*) **1.** having; full of, as in *dangerous, spacious* **2.** *Chem.* indicating that element is chemically combined in lower of two possible valency states, as in *ferrous*

ousel ('o͞ozəl) *n. see* OUZEL

oust (owst) *vt.* put out, expel

out (owt) *adv.* **1.** from within, away **2.** wrong **3.** on strike —*a.* **4.** not worth considering **5.** not allowed **6.** unfashionable **7.** unconscious **8.** not in use, operation *etc.* **9.** at an end **10.** not burning **11.** *Sport* dismissed —'**outer** *a.* away from the inside —'**outermost** *or* '**outmost** *a.* on extreme outside —'**outing** *n.* pleasure excursion —'**outward** *a./adv.* —'**outwardly** *adv.* —'**outwards** *adv.* —**out-and-out** *a.* thoroughgoing; complete —**outer space** any region of space beyond atmosphere of earth —**out-of-the-way** *a.* **1.** distant from more populous areas **2.** uncommon or unusual —**out of date** no longer valid, current, or fashionable —**out of pocket 1.** having lost money, as in a commercial enterprise **2.** without money to spend **3.** (of expenses) unbudgeted and paid for in cash

out- (*comb. form*) **1.** beyond, in excess, as in *outclass, outdistance, outsize* **2.** so as to surpass or defeat, as in *outfox, outmaneuver* **3.** outside, away from, as in *outpatient, outgrowth.* See the list below

outback ('owt'bak) *n.* A remote, sparsely populated country

outbalance (owt'baləns) *vt.* **1.** outweigh **2.** exceed in weight

outboard ('owtbörd) *a.* (of boat's engine) mounted outside stern

outbreak ('owtbrāk) *n.* sudden occurrence, *esp.* of disease or strife

outbuilding ('owtbilding) *n.* structure for storage *etc.* away from main premises of house or factory

outburst ('owtbərst) *n.* bursting out, *esp.* of violent emotion

outcast ('owtkast) *n.* **1.** someone rejected —*a.* **2.** rejected, cast out

outclass (owt'klas) *vt.* excel, surpass

outcome ('owtkum) *n.* result

outcrop ('owtkrop, owt'krop) *Geol. n.* **1.** rock coming out of stratum to the surface —*vi.* (owt'krop) **2.** come out to the surface (**-pp-**)

outcry ('owtkrī) *n.* **1.** widespread or vehement protest —*vt.* (owt'krī) **2.** cry louder or make more noise than

outdo (owt'do͞o) *vt.* surpass or exceed in performance (**-'doing, -'did, -'done**)

outdoors (owt'dörz) *adv.* in the open air —'**out'door** *a.*

outfall ('owtföl) *n.* mouth of river

outfit ('owtfit) *n.* **1.** equipment **2.** clothes and accessories **3.** *inf.* group or association regarded as a unit —'**outfitter** *n.* one who deals in outfits

outflank (owt'flangk) *vt.* **1.** get beyond the flank of (enemy army) **2.** circumvent

outgoing ('owtgōing) *a.* **1.** departing **2.** friendly, sociable

outgrow (owt'grō) *vt.* **1.** become too large or too old for **2.** surpass in growth (**-'grew, -'grown, -'growing**)

outhouse ('owt-hows) *n.* **1.** outbuilding **2.** outdoor privy

outlandish (owt'landish) *a.* queer, extravagantly strange

out'bid
out'box
out'distance
out'face
'outfield
out'fight
'outflow
out'fox
'outgrowth
out'last
out'live
outma'neuver
out'match
out'number
out'pace
out'play
'outpost
out'rank
out'reach
'outrider
out'rival
out'run
out'shine
'outsize
out'smart
'out'spread
out'stare
'outstation
out'stretch
out'value
out'vote
out'weigh

outlaw ('owtlö) *n.* **1.** one beyond protection of the law **2.** exile, bandit —*vt.* **3.** make (someone) an outlaw **4.** ban —'**outlawry** *n.*

outlay ('owtlā) *n.* expenditure

outlet ('owtlet, -lit) *n.* **1.** opening, vent **2.** means of release or escape **3.** market for product or service

outline ('owtlīn) *n.* **1.** rough sketch **2.** general plan **3.** lines enclosing visible figure —*vt.* **4.** sketch **5.** summarize

outlook ('owtlo͝ok) *n.* **1.** point of view **2.** probable outcome **3.** view

outlying ('owtlīing) *a.* distant, remote

outmoded (owt'mōdid) *a.* no longer fashionable or accepted

output ('owtpo͝ot) *n.* **1.** quantity produced **2.** *Comp.* information produced

outrage ('owtrāj) *n.* **1.** violation of others' rights **2.** gross or violent offense or indignity **3.** anger arising from this —*vt.* **4.** offend grossly **5.** insult **6.** injure, violate —**out'rageous** *a.*

outré (o͞o'trā) *a.* **1.** extravagantly odd **2.** bizarre

outrigger ('owtrigər) *n.* **1.** frame, *esp.* with float attached, outside boat's gunwale **2.** frame on rowing boat's side with rowlock **3.** boat equipped with such a framework

outright ('owtrīt) *a.* **1.** undisputed **2.** downright **3.** positive —*adv.* (owt'rīt) **4.** completely **5.** instantly **6.** openly

outset ('owtset) *n.* beginning

outside ('owt'sīd) *n.* **1.** exterior **2.** **C** settled parts of Canada —*adv.* (owt'sīd) **3.** not inside **4.** in the open air —*a.* ('owtsīd) **5.** on exterior **6.** remote, unlikely **7.** greatest possible, probable —**out'sider** *n.* **1.** person outside specific group **2.** contestant thought unlikely to win —**outside broadcast** *T.V., rad.* broadcast not made from studio

overa'bundance
over'act
overam'bitious
over'anxious
over'awe
over'book
over'burden
overca'pacity
over'cautious
over'charge
'overcoat
over'compensate
over'confident
overcon'sumption
over'cook
over'crowd
over'curious
overde'pendent
overde'velop
over'do
'overdose
over'due
over'eager
over'eat
over'emphasize
over'estimate
overex'cite
overex'ert
overex'pand
overex'penditure
over'fill
over'flow *v.*
'overflow *n.*
'overgarment
over'grow
over'hang
over'hasty
overin'dulge
overin'dulgence
overin'sistent
over'joy
'overlay
over'lie
over'load *v.*
'overload *n.*
'overlord

outskirts ('owtskərts) *pl.n.* outer areas, districts, *esp.* of city

outspan ('owtspan) *n.* **SA** **1.** unyoking of oxen **2.** area for rest

outspoken (owt'spōkən) *a.* frank, candid

outstanding (owt'standing) *a.* **1.** excellent **2.** remarkable **3.** unsettled, unpaid

outstrip (owt'strip) *vt.* outrun, surpass

outwit (owt'wit) *vt.* get the better of by cunning

outwork ('owtwərk) *n.* part of fortress outside main wall

ouzel *or* **ousel** ('o͞ozəl) *n.* **1.** type of thrush **2.** kind of diving bird

ouzo ('o͞ozō) *n.* strong aniseed-flavored spirit from Greece

ova ('ōvə) *n., pl. of* OVUM

oval ('ōvəl) *a.* **1.** egg-shaped, elliptical —*n.* **2.** something of this shape

ovary ('ōvəri) *n.* female egg-producing organ —**o'varian** *a.*

ovation (ō'vāshən) *n.* enthusiastic burst of applause

oven ('uvən) *n.* heated chamber for baking in

over ('ōvər) *adv.* **1.** above, above and beyond, going beyond, in excess, too much, past, finished, in repetition, across, downwards *etc.* —*prep.* **2.** above **3.** on, upon **4.** more than, in excess of, along *etc.* —*a.* **5.** upper, outer

over- (*comb. form*) too, too much, in excess, above, to a prostrate position. See the list below

overall ('ōvəröl) *n.* **1.** (*also pl.*) loose garment worn as protection against dirt *etc.* —*a.* (ōvər'öl, 'ōvəröl) **2.** total

overbalance (ōvər'baləns) *v.* **1.** lose or cause to lose balance —*n.* ('ōvərbaləns) **2.** excess of weight, value *etc.*

overbearing (ōvər'bāəring) *a.* domineering

over'many
over'modest
over'much
over'night
'overpass
over'pay
over'play
overpopu'lation
over'praise
over'price
overpro'duce
overpro'duction
over'rate
over'reach
overre'act
over'ripe
over'run
over'sensitive
over'shadow
'overshoe
over'shoot
oversimplifi'cation
over'simplify
over'size
over'sleep
over'specialize
over'spend
over'spill *v.*
'overspill *n.*
over'stay
over'steer *v.*
'oversteer *n.*
over'step
over'stock *v.*
'overstock *n.*
over'stretch
over'tire
over'top
over'trump
over'turn
over'use
over'value
over'weight
over'work *v.*
'overwork *n.*
over'zealous

overblown (ōvər'blōn) *a.* excessive, bombastic

overboard ('ōvərbörd) *adv.* from a vessel into the water

overcast ('ōvərkast) *a.* covered over, *esp.* by clouds

overcheck ('ōvərchek) *n.* (in textiles) checked pattern laid over another checked pattern

overcoat ('ōvərkōt) *n.* warm coat worn over outer clothing

overcome (ōvər'kum) *vt.* **1.** conquer **2.** surmount **3.** make incapable or powerless —*vi.* **4.** be victorious

overdrive ('ōvərdrīv) *n.* **1.** very high gear in motor vehicle used at high speeds to reduce wear —*vt.* (ōvər'drīv) **2.** drive too hard or too far; overwork (-'**driving,** -'**drove,** -'**driven**)

overhaul (ōvər'höl) *vt.* **1.** examine and set in order, repair **2.** overtake —*n.* ('ōvərhöl) **3.** thorough examination, *esp.* for repairs

overhead ('ōvərhed) *a.* **1.** over one's head, above —*adv.* (ōvər'hed) **2.** aloft, above —'**overheads** *pl.n.* expenses of running a business, over and above cost of manufacturing and of raw materials

overhear (ōvər'hēər) *vt.* hear (person, remark *etc.*) without knowledge of speaker (-'**hearing,** -'**heard**)

overkill ('ōvərkil) *n.* capacity, advantage greater than required

overland ('ōvərland) *a./adv.* by land

overlap (ōvər'lap) *v.* **1.** (of two things) extend or lie partly over (each other) **2.** cover and extend beyond (something) —*vi.* **3.** coincide partly in time, subject *etc.* (**-pp-**) —*n.* ('ōvərlap) **4.** part that overlaps or is overlapped **5.** amount, length *etc.* overlapping

overleaf ('ōvərlēf) *adv.* on other side of page

overlook (ōvər'lo͝ok) *vt.* **1.** fail to notice **2.** disregard **3.** look over

overpower (ōvər'powər) *vt.* **1.** conquer by superior force **2.** have such strong effect on as to make ineffective **3.** supply with more power than necessary —**over'powering** *a.*

override (ōvər'rīd) *vt.* **1.** set aside, disregard **2.** cancel **3.** trample down

overrule (ōvər'ro͞ol) *vt.* **1.** disallow arguments of (person) by use of authority **2.** rule or decide against (decision *etc.*) **3.** prevail over; influence **4.** exercise rule over

overseas (ōvər'sēz) *a.* **1.** foreign **2.** from or to a place over the sea (*also* **over'sea**) —*adv.* **3.** beyond the sea; abroad —**overseas cap** *see* **garrison cap** *at* GARRISON

overseer ('ōvərsēər) *n.* supervisor —**over'see** *vt.* supervise

oversight ('ōvərsīt) *n.* **1.** failure to notice **2.** mistake

overt (ō'vərt, 'ōvərt) *a.* open, unconcealed

overtake (ōvər'tāk) *vt.* **1.** come up with in pursuit **2.** catch up

overthrow (ōvər'thrō) *vt.* **1.** upset, overturn **2.** defeat (-'**threw,** -'**thrown,** -'**throwing**) —*n.* ('ōvərthrō) **3.** ruin **4.** defeat **5.** fall

overtime ('ōvərtīm) *n.* **1.** time at work, outside normal working hours **2.** payment for this time

overtone ('ōvərtōn) *n.* **1.** additional meaning, nuance **2.** *Mus., Acoustics* any tone in harmonic series produced by fundamental tone

overture ('ōvərcho͞oər) *n.* **1.** *Mus.* orchestral introduction **2.** opening of negotiations **3.** formal offer

overweening (ōvər'wēning) *a.* thinking too much of oneself

overwhelm (ōvər'welm) *vt.* **1.** crush **2.** submerge, engulf —**over'whelming** *a.* **1.** decisive **2.** irresistible —**over'whelmingly** *adv.*

overwrought (ōvər'röt) *a.* **1.** overexcited **2.** too elaborate

ovi- *or* **ovo-** (*comb. form*) egg; ovum, as in *oviform*

oviduct ('ōvidukt) *n.* tube through which ova are conveyed from ovary (*also* (in mammals) **Fallopian tube**) —**oviducal** (ōvi'dyo͞okəl, -'do͞okəl) *or* **ovi'ductal** *a.*

oviform ('ōviförm) *a.* egg-shaped

ovine ('ōvīn) *a.* of, like, sheep

oviparous ('ō'vipərəs) *a.* laying eggs

ovoid ('ōvoid) *a.* egg-shaped

ovoviviparous ('ōvōvī'vipərəs) *a.* (of certain reptiles, fishes *etc.*) producing eggs that hatch within body of mother —**ovovivi'parity** *n.*

ovule ('ovyo͞ol) *n.* unfertilized seed —'**ovulate** *vi.* produce, discharge egg from ovary —**ovu'lation** *n.*

ovum ('ōvəm) *n.* female egg cell, in which development of fetus takes place (*pl.* **ova**)

owe (ō) *vt.* be bound to repay, be indebted for —'**owing** *a.* owed, due —**owing to** caused by, as a result of

owl (owl) *n.* night bird of prey —'**owlet** *n.* young owl —'**owlish** *a.* solemn and dull

own (ōn) *a.* **1.** denoting possession —*vt.* **2.** possess **3.** acknowledge —*vi.* **4.** confess —'**owner** *n.* —'**ownership** *n.* possession

ox (oks) *n.* **1.** large cloven-footed and usu. horned farm animal **2.** bull or cow (*pl.* **oxen**) —'**oxbow** *n.* **1.** U-shaped harness collar of ox **2.** lake formed from deep bend of river —'**oxeye** *n.* daisylike plant —'**oxtail** *n.* skinned tail of ox, used *esp.* in soups and stews —'**oxtongue** *n.* **1.** any of various plants having bristly tongue-shaped leaves **2.** tongue of ox, braised or boiled as food

oxalis (ok'salis) *n.* genus of plants —**ox'alic** *a.* —**oxalic acid** poisonous acid derived from oxalis

Oxbridge ('oksbrij) *n.* Brit. universities of Oxford and Cambridge, *esp.* considered as prestigious academic institutions

oxen ('oksən) *n., pl. of* ox

Oxfam (ˈoksfam) Oxford Committee for Famine Relief

Oxford cloth (ˈoksfərd) heavy cotton cloth used for shirts

oxide (ˈoksīd) *n.* compound of oxygen and one other element —**oxidate** (ˈoksidāt) *v.* —**oxidation** (oksiˈdāshən) *n.* act or process of oxidizing —**oxidization** (oksidiˈzāshən) *n.* —**oxidize** (ˈoksidīz) *v.* (cause to) combine with oxide, rust

oxygen (ˈoksijən) *n. Chem.* gaseous element *Symbol* O, at. wt. 16.0, at. no. 8 —ˈ**oxygenate** *or* ˈ**oxygenize** *vt.* combine or treat with oxygen —**oxyaˈcetylene** *a.* denoting flame used for welding produced by mixture of oxygen and acetylene —**oxygen tent** *Med.* transparent enclosure covering patient, into which oxygen is released to help maintain respiration

oxymoron (oksiˈmöron) *n.* figure of speech in which two ideas of opposite meaning are combined to form an expressive phrase or epithet, as in *cruel kindness* (*pl.* **-mora** (-ˈmörə))

oxytocin (oksiˈtōsin) *n.* hormone secreted by pituitary gland which enables lactation

oyez (ōˈyā, ōˈyes) *n.* call, uttered three times by public crier or court official

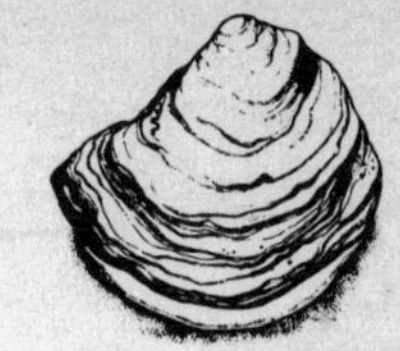

oyster

oyster (ˈoistər) *n.* edible bivalve mollusk —ˈ**oystercatcher** *n.* shore bird —**oyster plant** salsify

oyster catcher

oz *or* **oz.** ounce

ozone (ˈōzōn) *n.* form of oxygen with pungent odor —ˈ**ozonize** *vt.* —**ozone layer** layer of ozone in the upper atmosphere which absorbs harmful radiation from the sun

P

p *or* **P** (pē) *n.* **1.** 16th letter of English alphabet **2.** speech sound represented by this letter (*pl.* **p's, P's** *or* **Ps**) —**mind one's p's and q's** be careful to use polite language

p 1. page **2. UK** pence **3. UK** penny **4.** *Mus.* piano (softly)

P 1. *Chess* pawn **2.** *Chem.* phosphorus **3.** pressure

Pa *Chem.* protactinium

PA Pennsylvania

P.A. 1. personal assistant **2.** power of attorney **3.** press agent **4.** private account **5.** public-address system **6.** publicity agent **7.** Publishers Association **8.** purchasing agent

p.a. per annum

pace (pās) *n.* **1.** step **2.** its length **3.** rate of movement **4.** walk, gait —*vi.* **5.** step —*vt.* **6.** set speed for **7.** cross, measure with steps —ˈ**pacer** *n.* one who sets the pace for another —ˈ**pacemaker** *n. esp.* electronic device surgically implanted in those with heart disease

pachyderm (ˈpakidərm) *n.* thick-skinned animal, *eg* elephant —**pachyˈdermatous** *a.* thick-skinned, stolid

Pacific (pəˈsifik) *n.* (*short for* **Pacific Ocean**) world's largest ocean, bordered by America, Asia and Australia, divided by equator into North Pacific and South Pacific —**Pacific Standard Time** time as reckoned from the 120th meridian west of Greenwich

pacify (ˈpasifī) *vt.* **1.** calm **2.** restore to peace (**-ified, -ifying**) —**paˈcific** *a.* **1.** peaceable **2.** calm, tranquil —**pacifiˈcation** *n.* —**paˈcificatory** *a.* tending to make peace —ˈ**pacifier** *n.* **1.** person or thing that pacifies **2.** baby's dummy or teething ring —ˈ**pacifism** *n.* —ˈ**pacifist** *n.* **1.** advocate of abolition of war **2.** one who refuses to participate in war

pack (pak) *n.* **1.** bundle **2.** band of animals **3.** large set of people or things **4.** set of, container for, retail commodities **5.** set of playing cards **6.** mass of floating ice —*v.* **7.** put (articles) together in suitcase *etc.* **8.** press tightly together, cram —*vt.* **9.** make into a bundle **10.** fill with things **11.** fill (meeting *etc.*) with one's own supporters **12.** (*oft. with* off *or* away) order off —ˈ**package** *n.* **1.** parcel **2.** set of items offered together —*vt.* **3.** wrap in or put into package —ˈ**packet** *n.* **1.** small parcel **2.** small container (and contents) **3.** *sl.* large sum of money —**package store** store selling alcoholic beverages for consumption outside its premises —**packet (boat)** *n.* mail-boat —ˈ**packhorse** *n.* horse for carrying goods —**pack ice** loose floating ice which has been compacted together —**pack saddle** saddle for carrying goods

pact (pakt) *n.* covenant, agreement, compact

pad[1] (pad) *n.* **1.** piece of soft stuff used as a cushion, protection *etc.* **2.** block of sheets of paper **3.** foot or sole of various animals **4.** place for launching rockets **5.** *sl.* residence —*vt.* **6.** make soft, fill in, protect *etc.* with pad or padding (**-dd-**) —ˈ**padding** *n.* **1.** material used for stuffing **2.** literary matter put in simply to increase quantity —**padded cell** room, *esp.* in mental hospital, with padded surfaces, in which violent inmates are placed

pad[2] (pad) *vi.* **1.** walk with soft step **2.** travel slowly (**-dd-**) —*n.* **3.** sound of soft footstep

paddle[1] (ˈpadəl) *n.* **1.** short oar with broad blade at one or each end —*v.* **2.** move by, as with, paddles **3.** row gently —**paddle tennis** indoor or outdoor court game played by two or four persons using wooden or plastic paddles instead of standard tennis rackets —**paddle wheel** wheel with crosswise blades striking water successively to propel ship

paddle[2] (ˈpadəl) *vi.* **1.** walk with bare feet in shallow water —*n.* **2.** act of paddling

paddock (ˈpadək) *n.* small grass field or enclosure

paddy (ˈpadi) *n.* rice growing or in the husk —**paddy field** field where rice is grown

padlock (ˈpadlok) *n.* **1.** detachable lock with hinged hoop to go through staple or ring —*vt.* **2.** fasten thus

padre (ˈpädrā, -ri) *n.* **1.** priest, clergyman **2.** chaplain with the armed forces

paean (ˈpēən) *n.* song of triumph or thanksgiving

paella (päˈelə, -ˈālyə) *n.* Spanish dish of rice, shellfish and chicken cooked and served in a large shallow pan

pagan (ˈpāgən) *a./n.* heathen —ˈ**paganism** *n.*

page[1] (pāj) *n.* one side of leaf of book *etc.*

page[2] (pāj) *n.* **1.** boy servant or attendant —*vt.* **2.** summon by loudspeaker announcement —ˈ**pager** *n.* device carried on person so that he or she can be summoned —ˈ**pageboy** *n.* medium-length hair style with ends of hair curled under

pageant (ˈpajənt) *n.* **1.** show of persons in costume in procession, dramatic scenes *etc.*, usu. illustrating history **2.** brilliant show —ˈ**pageantry** *n.*

Paget's disease (ˈpajits) chronic bone

disease of unknown origin marked by thickening, enlargement and painful deformation (*also* **osteitis deformans**)

paginate (ˈpajināt) *vt.* number pages of —**pagiˈnation** *n.*

pagoda (pəˈgōdə) *n.* pyramidal temple or tower of Chinese or Indian type

paid (pād) *pt./pp. of* PAY —**put paid to** *inf.* end, destroy

pail (pāl) *n.* bucket —ˈ**pailful** *n.*

pain (pān) *n.* **1.** bodily or mental suffering **2.** penalty or punishment —*pl.* **3.** trouble, exertion —*vt.* **4.** inflict pain upon —**pained** *a.* having or expressing pain or distress, *esp.* mental or emotional —ˈ**painful** *a.* —ˈ**painfully** *adv.* —ˈ**painless** *a.* —ˈ**painlessly** *adv.* —ˈ**painkiller** *n.* drug, as aspirin, that reduces pain —ˈ**painstaking** *a.* diligent, careful

paint (pānt) *n.* **1.** coloring matter spread on a surface with brushes, roller, spray gun *etc.* —*vt.* **2.** portray, color, coat, or make picture of, with paint **3.** apply make-up to **4.** describe —ˈ**painter** *n.* —ˈ**painting** *n.* picture in paint

painter[1] (ˈpāntər) *n.* cougar

painter[2] (ˈpāntər) *n.* line at bow of boat for tying it up

pair (pāər) *n.* **1.** set of two, *esp.* existing or generally used together —*v.* **2.** (*oft. with* off) group or be grouped in twos

paisley (ˈpāzli) *n.* pattern of small curving shapes

Paiute (ˈpīyōōt, ˈpīōōt) *n.* **1.** member of Amerindian people of northeastern Arizona, southern Utah and southeastern Nevada **2.** Shoshonean language of this people

pajamas (pəˈjäməz) *pl.n.* sleeping or lounging suit

Pakistan (pakiˈstan, päkiˈstän) *n.* country in Asia bounded northwest by Afghanistan, north by the U.S.S.R. and China, east by India and south by the Arabian Sea —**Pakiˈstani** *n./a.*

pal (pal) *n. inf.* friend —ˈ**pally** *a. inf.* on friendly terms

palace (ˈpalis) *n.* **1.** residence of king, bishop *etc.* **2.** stately mansion —**paˈlatial** *a.* **1.** like a palace **2.** magnificent —ˈ**palatine** *a.* with royal privileges

paladin (ˈpalədin) *n. Hist.* knight errant

palanquin (palənˈkēn) *n.* covered litter, formerly used in Orient, carried on shoulders of four men

palate (ˈpalit) *n.* **1.** roof of mouth **2.** sense of taste —ˈ**palatable** *a.* agreeable to eat —ˈ**palatal** *or* ˈ**palatine** *a.* **1.** of the palate **2.** made by placing tongue against palate —*n.* **3.** palatal sound

palatial (pəˈlāshəl) *a. see* PALACE

palaver (pəˈlavər, -ˈlävər) *n.* **1.** fuss **2.** conference, discussion

pale[1] (pāl) *a.* **1.** wan, dim, whitish —*vi.* **2.** whiten **3.** lose superiority or importance —ˈ**paleface** *n.* derogatory term for White person, said to have been used by N Amer. Indians

pale[2] (pāl) *n.* stake, boundary —ˈ**paling** *n.* upright plank making up fence

paleo- *or before vowel* **pale-** (*comb. form*) old, ancient, prehistoric, as in *paleography*

Paleocene (ˈpaliōsēn) *a.* **1.** of first epoch of Tertiary period —*n.* **2.** Paleocene epoch or rock series

Paleolithic (paliōˈlithik) *a.* of the old Stone Age

paleontology (palionˈtoləji) *n.* study of past geological periods and fossils —**paleontoˈlogical** *a.*

Paleozoic (paliōˈzōik) *a.* **1.** of geological time that began with Cambrian period and lasted until end of Permian period —*n.* **2.** Paleozoic era

Palestinian (paliˈstiniən) *a.* **1.** of Palestine, former country in Middle East —*n.* **2.** native or inhabitant of this area **3.** descendant of inhabitant of this area, displaced when Israel became state

palette (ˈpalit) *n.* **1.** surface on which artist sets out and mixes pigments **2.** range of colors used by an artist —**palette knife** spatula with thin flexible blade, used in painting *etc.*

palindrome (ˈpalindrōm) *n.* word, verse or sentence that is the same when read backward or forward

palisade (paliˈsād) *n.* **1.** fence of stakes —*vt.* **2.** enclose or protect with one

pall[1] (pōl) *n.* **1.** cloth spread over a coffin **2.** depressing, oppressive atmosphere —ˈ**pallbearer** *n.* one carrying, attending coffin at funeral

pall[2] (pōl) *vi.* **1.** become tasteless or tiresome **2.** cloy

palladium (pəˈlādiəm) *n. Chem.* white noble metal *Symbol* Pd, at. wt. 106.4, at. no. 46

pallet[1] (ˈpalit) *n.* **1.** straw mattress **2.** small bed

pallet[2] (ˈpalit) *n.* portable platform for storing and moving goods

palliate (ˈpaliāt) *vt.* **1.** relieve without curing **2.** excuse —**palliˈation** *n.* —**palliative** (ˈpaliātiv, ˈpalyə-) *a.* **1.** giving temporary or partial relief —*n.* **2.** that which excuses, mitigates or alleviates

pallid (ˈpalid) *a.* pale, wan, colorless —ˈ**pallor** *n.* paleness

palmate

palm (päm, pälm) *n.* **1.** inner surface of hand **2.** tropical tree **3.** leaf of the tree as symbol of victory —*vt.* **4.** conceal in palm of hand **5.** pass off by trickery —**palmate** ('palmāt, 'pälmāt, 'pämāt) *or* **'palmated** *a.* **1.** shaped like open hand **2.** *Bot.* having five lobes that spread out from common point **3.** (of water birds) having three toes connected by web —**'palmist** *n.* —**'palmistry** *n.* fortune-telling from lines on palm of hand —**'palmy** *a.* flourishing, successful —**palm oil** oil obtained from fruit of certain palms —**Palm Sunday** Sunday before Easter —**palm off** (*oft. with* on) **1.** offer, sell or spend fraudulently **2.** divert in order to be rid of

palomino (palə'mēnō) *n.* golden horse with white mane and tail (*pl.* **-s**)

palpable ('palpəbəl) *a.* **1.** obvious **2.** certain **3.** that may be touched or felt —**'palpably** *adv.*

palpate ('palpāt) *vt. Med.* examine by touch

palpitate ('palpitāt) *vi.* **1.** throb **2.** pulsate violently —**palpi'tation** *n.* **1.** throbbing **2.** violent, irregular beating of heart

palsy ('pölzi) *n.* paralysis

paltry ('pöltri) *a.* worthless, contemptible, trifling

pampas ('pampəz, -pəs) *n.* (*oft. with pl. v.*) vast grassy treeless plains in S Amer.

pamper ('pampər) *vt.* overindulge, spoil by coddling

pamphlet ('pamflit) *n.* thin unbound book usu. on some topical subject

pan[1] (pan) *n.* **1.** broad, shallow vessel **2.** depression in ground, *esp.* where salt forms —*vt.* **3.** wash (gold ore) in pan **4.** *inf.* criticize harshly (**-nn-**) —**'pantile** *n.* curved roofing tile —**pan out** result

pan[2] (pan) *v.* move (motion-picture camera) slowly while filming to cover scene, follow moving object *etc.* (**-nn-**)

pan- (*comb. form*) all, as in *panacea, pantomime.* Such words are not given here where the meaning may easily be inferred from simple word

panacea (panə'sēə) *n.* universal remedy, cure for all ills

panache (pə'nash, -'näsh) *n.* dashing style

panama ('panəmä) *n.* **1.** fine straw from a palmlike plant from Ecuador **2.** cotton and wool cloth for summer suits

Panama ('panəmä) *n.* country in Central America bounded north by the Caribbean, east by Colombia, south by the Pacific and west by Costa Rica —**Panamanian** (panə'mānian) *n./a.* (native or inhabitant) of Panama

Pan-American *a.* of North, South and Central America collectively —**Pan-American games** series of sports events for amateur athletes of the western hemisphere held every four years

pancake ('pankāk) *n.* **1.** thin cake of batter fried in pan **2.** flat cake or stick of compressed make-up —*vi.* **3.** *Aviation* make flat landing by dropping in a level position

panchromatic (pankrō'matik) *a. Photog.* sensitive to light of all colors

pancreas ('pangkriəs) *n.* gland behind stomach and liver which secretes enzymes to aid digestion and hormones into the blood stream —**pancre'atic** *a.* —**pancrea'titis** *n.* inflammation of this gland

panda ('pandə) *n.* **1.** reddish-brown carnivore of the Himalayas resembling and related to raccoon, with long fur and bushy tail marked with pale rings (*also* **lesser panda**) **2.** large black-and-white herbivore of Tibet and western China resembling bear, but related to raccoon, and symbol of the World Wildlife Fund (*also* **giant panda**)

pandemic (pan'demik) *a.* (of disease) occurring over wide area

pandemonium (pandi'mōniəm) *n.* scene of din and uproar

pander ('pandər) *v.* **1.** (*esp. with* to) give gratification (to weakness or desires) —*n.* **2.** pimp

pandit ('pundit; *spelling pron.* 'pandit) *n. see* PUNDIT (sense 2)

P. & L. profit and loss

pane (pān) *n.* single piece of glass in window or door

panegyric (pani'jirik) *n.* speech of praise —**pane'gyrical** *a.* laudatory —**pane'gyrist** *n.*

panel ('panəl) *n.* **1.** compartment of surface, usu. raised or sunk, *eg* in door **2.** any distinct section of something, *eg* of body of automobile **3.** strip of material inserted in garment **4.** group of persons as team in quiz game *etc.* **5.** list of jurors, doctors *etc.* **6.** thin board with picture on it —*vt.* **7.** adorn with panels —**'paneling** *n.* paneled work —**'panelist** *n.* member of panel —**panel game** quiz *etc.* played by group of people, *esp.* on TV

pang (pang) *n.* **1.** sudden pain, sharp twinge **2.** compunction

pangolin ('panggəlin, pan'gōlin, pang'gōlin) *n.* mammal with scaly body and long snout for feeding on ants *etc.* (*also* **scaly anteater**)

panic ('panik) *n.* **1.** sudden and infectious fear **2.** extreme fright **3.** unreasoning terror —*a.* **4.** of fear *etc.* —*v.* **5.** feel or cause to feel panic (**-icked, -icking**) —**'panicky** *a.* **1.** inclined to panic **2.** nervous —**'panicmonger** *n.* one who starts panic —**panic-stricken** *or* **panic-struck** *a.*

panicle ('panikəl) *n.* compound raceme, as in oat

panjandrum (pan'jandrəm) *n.* pompous self-important man

pannier ('panyər, 'paniər) *n.* basket carried by beast of burden, bicycle, or on person's shoulders

panoply ('panəpli) *n.* complete, magnificent array —**'panoplied** *a.*

panorama (panə'ramə, -'rämə) *n.* **1.** unobstructed or complete view of a region **2.** continuous painting, usu. a landscape, around the walls of a room or rolled on a cylinder —**pano'ramic** *a.* —**panoramic sight** form of periscopic sight used by marksmen

panpipes ('panpīps) *pl.n.* primitive wind instrument comprising a number of graded pipes, made from bamboo canes or clay, bound together in the form of a raft

pansy ('panzi) *n.* **1.** flower, species of violet **2.** *inf.* effeminate man

pant (pant) *vi.* **1.** gasp for breath **2.** yearn, long **3.** throb —*n.* **4.** gasp

pantaloon (pantə'lo͞on) *n.* **1.** in pantomime, foolish old man who is the butt of clown —*pl.* **2.** *inf.* baggy trousers

pantechnicon (pan'teknikən) *n.* large van, *esp.* for carrying furniture

pantheism ('panthiizəm) *n.* identification of God with the universe —**'pantheist** *n.* —**panthe'istic** *a.* —**'pantheon** *n.* temple of all gods

panther ('panthər) *n.* variety of leopard

panties ('pantiz) *pl.n.* woman's or child's undergarment with closed crotch covering lower trunk —**panty hose** ('panti) garment for woman combining hosiery and panties

pantograph ('pantəgraf) *n.* instrument for copying maps *etc.* to any scale

pantomime ('pantəmīm) *n.* **1. UK** theatrical show, usu. produced at Christmastime, oft. founded on fairy tale **2.** dramatic entertainment in dumb show

pantry ('pantri) *n.* room for storing food or utensils

pants (pants) *pl.n.* **1.** undergarment for lower trunk **2.** trousers

panzer ('panzər; *Ger.* 'pantsər) *a.* **1.** of fast mechanized armored units employed by German army in World War II —*n.* **2.** vehicle belonging to panzer unit, *esp.* tank —*pl.* **3.** armored troops

pap[1] (pap) *n.* **1.** soft food for infants, invalids *etc.* **2.** pulp, mash **3. SA** maize porridge

pap[2] (pap) *n.* **1.** breast **2.** nipple

papa ('päpə) *n. inf.* father

Papa ('päpə) *n.* word used in communications for the letter *p*

papacy ('pāpəsi) *n.* **1.** office of Pope **2.** papal system —**'papal** *a.* of, relating to, the Pope

Papago ('päpəgō) *n.* **1.** member of Amerindian people of southern Arizona (*pl.* **-go, -s**) **2.** Uto-Aztecan language of the Papago

Papanicolaou's stain (päpə'nēkəlowz) *see* PAP SMEAR

papaw *or* **pawpaw** ('päpô, 'pôpô) *n.* **1.** tree bearing melon-shaped fruit **2.** its fruit

paper ('pāpər) *n.* **1.** material made by pressing pulp of rags, straw, wood *etc.* into thin, flat sheets **2.** printed sheet of paper **3.** newspaper **4.** article, essay **5.** set of examination questions —*pl.* **6.** documents *etc.* —*vt.* **7.** cover, decorate with paper —**'paperback** *n.* book with flexible covers —**'paperboy** *n.* boy employed to deliver newspapers (**'papergirl** *fem.*) —**paper chase** cross-country run in which runner lays trail of paper for others to follow —**'paperclip** *n.* clip for holding sheets of paper together, *esp.* one of bent wire —**'paperhanger** *n.* person who hangs wallpaper as occupation —**'paperknife** *n.* knife with comparatively blunt blade for opening sealed envelopes *etc.* —**paper money** paper currency issued by government or central bank as legal tender —**'paperweight** *n.* small heavy object to prevent loose papers from scattering —**'paperwork** *n.* clerical work, such as writing of reports or letters

papier-mâché (pāpərmə'shā, papyāmə'shā) *n.* pulp from rags or paper mixed with size, shaped by molding and dried hard

papilla (pə'pilə) *n.* **1.** small projection of tissue at base of hair *etc.* **2.** any similar protuberance (*pl.* **-lae** (-lē)) —**'papillary, 'papillate** *or* **'papillose** *a.*

papoose (pa'po͞os, pə-) *n.* N Amer. Indian child

paprika (pə'prēkə, pa-) *n.* (powdered seasoning prepared from) type of red pepper

Pap smear (pap) test for cancer of the womb by examining cells from its neck (*also* **Papanicolaou's stain**)

Papua New Guinea ('papyo͞oə, 'päpo͞oə) country lying in the South Pacific occupying the eastern part of the island of New Guinea, bordering the Netherlands Antilles

papyrus

papyrus (pə'pīrəs) *n.* **1.** species of reed **2.** (manuscript written on) kind of paper made from this plant (*pl.* **-ri** (-rī), **-es**)

par (pär) *n.* **1.** equality of value or standing **2.** face value (of stocks) **3.** *Golf* estimated standard score —**'parity** *n.* **1.** equality **2.** analogy —**par value** value imprinted on face of stock certificate or bond and used to assess dividend *etc.*

par. 1. paragraph **2.** parallel **3.** parenthesis

para- *or before vowel* **par-** (*comb. form*) beside, beyond, as in *paradigm, parallel, parody*

parable ('parəbəl) *n.* allegory, story with a moral lesson —**para'bolic(al)** *a.* of parable

parabola (pə'rabələ) *n.* section of cone cut by

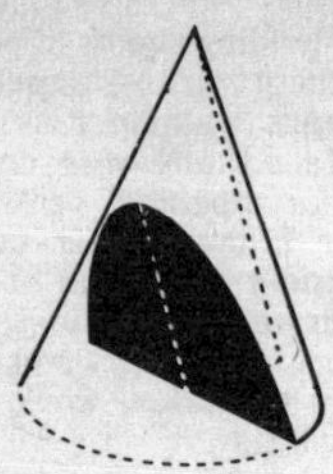

parabola

plane parallel to the cone's side —**para'bolic** *a.* of parabola

parachute ('parəshōōt) *n.* **1.** apparatus extending like umbrella used to retard the descent of a falling body —*v.* **2.** land or cause to land by parachute —**'parachutist** *n.*

parade (pə'rād) *n.* **1.** display **2.** muster of troops **3.** parade ground **4.** public walk —*vi.* **5.** march —*vt.* **6.** display

paradigm ('parədīm) *n.* example, model —**paradigmatic** (parədig'matik) *a.*

paradise ('parədīs) *n.* **1.** Heaven **2.** state of bliss **3.** Garden of Eden

paradox ('parədoks) *n.* **1.** antinomy **2.** self-contradictory or false statement —**para'doxical** *a.*

paraffin ('parəfin) *n.* waxlike or liquid hydrocarbon mixture used as fuel, solvent, in candles *etc.*

paragon ('parəgon, -gən) *n.* pattern or model of excellence

paragraph ('parəgraf) *n.* **1.** section of chapter or book **2.** short notice, as in newspaper —*vt.* **3.** arrange in paragraphs

Paraguay ('parəgwī, -gwā) *n.* country in South America bounded east by Brazil, east, south and west by Argentina and north by Bolivia —**Para'guayan** *n./a.* (native or inhabitant) of Paraguay

parakeet *or* **parrakeet** ('parəkēt) *n.* small long-tailed parrot

Paralipomenon (parəli'pomənon) *n. Bible* Chronicles in the Douay Version of the O.T.

parallax ('parəlaks) *n.* apparent difference in object's position or direction as viewed from different points

parallel ('parəlel) *a.* **1.** continuously at equal distances **2.** precisely corresponding —*n.* **3.** line equidistant from another at all points **4.** thing exactly like another **5.** comparison **6.** line of latitude —*vt.* **7.** represent as similar, compare —**'parallelism** *n.* —**paral'lelogram** *n.* four-sided plane figure with opposite sides parallel —**parallel bars** *Gymnastics* pair of wooden bars on uprights used for exercises

paralysis (pə'ralisis) *n.* incapacity to move or feel, due to damage to nervous system (*pl.* **-yses** (-isēz)) —**para'lytic** *a./n.* (person) afflicted with paralysis —**'paralyze** *vt.* **1.** afflict with paralysis **2.** cripple **3.** make useless or ineffectual —**infantile paralysis** poliomyelitis

paramedical (parə'medikəl) *a.* **1.** of persons working in various capacities in support of medical profession **2.** of professionals in allied fields, *eg* technicians, chiropodists, physiotherapists *etc.*

parameter (pə'ramitər) *n.* any constant limiting factor

paramilitary (parə'militeri) *a.* of civilian group organized on military lines or in support of the military

paramount ('parəmownt) *a.* supreme, eminent, pre-eminent, chief

paramour ('parəmōōər) *n. esp.* formerly, illicit lover, mistress

parang ('pärang) *n.* heavy Malay knife

paranoia (parə'noiə) *n.* mental disease with delusions of fame, grandeur, persecution —**paranoiac** (parə'noiak, -ik) *a./n.* —**'paranoid** *a.* **1.** of paranoia **2.** *inf.* exhibiting fear of persecution *etc.* —*n.* **3.** person afflicted with paranoia

parapet ('parəpit, -pet) *n.* low wall, railing along edge of balcony, bridge *etc.*

paraphernalia (parəfər'nālyə) *pl.n.* (*sometimes with sing. v.*) **1.** personal belongings **2.** odds and ends of equipment

paraphrase ('parəfrāz) *n.* **1.** expression of meaning of passage in other words **2.** free translation —*vt.* **3.** put into other words

paraplegia (parə'plējə) *n.* paralysis of lower half of body —**para'plegic** *n./a.*

parapsychology (parəsī'koləji) *n.* study of subjects pert. to extrasensory perception, *eg* telepathy

paraquat ('parəkwot) *n.* fast-acting herbicide which becomes inactive when in contact with soil

parasite ('parəsīt) *n.* **1.** animal or plant living in or on another **2.** self-interested hanger-on —**parasitic** (parə'sitik) *a.* of the nature of, living as, parasite —**'parasitism** *n.*

parasol ('parəsöl, -sol) *n.* sunshade

parataxis (parə'taksis) *n.* arrangement of sentences which omits connecting words

parathion (parə'thīən, -on) *n.* toxic oil used as insecticide

parathyroid gland (parə'thīroid) one of two bean-shaped structures in front of neck essential to life as they secrete hormones controlling bone development and maintain calcium and phosphate metabolism

paratroops ('parətrōōps) *pl.n.* troops trained to descend by parachute

paratyphoid fever (parə'tīfoid) infectious disease contracted by eating contaminated food with symptoms resembling typhoid fever

parboil ('pärboil) *vt.* boil until partly cooked

parcel ('pärsəl) *n.* **1.** packet of goods, *esp.* one enclosed in paper **2.** quantity dealt with at one time **3.** piece of land —*vt.* **4.** wrap up **5.** divide into parts

parch (pärch) *v.* **1.** dry by heating **2.** make, become hot and dry **3.** scorch **4.** roast slightly

parchment (ˈpärchmənt) *n.* **1.** sheep, goat, calf skin prepared for writing **2.** manuscript of this

pardon (ˈpärdən) *vt.* **1.** forgive, excuse —*n.* **2.** forgiveness **3.** release from punishment —**ˈpardonable** *a.* —**ˈpardonably** *adv.*

pare (pāər) *vt.* **1.** trim, cut edge or surface of **2.** decrease bit by bit —**ˈparing** *n.* piece pared off, rind

paregoric (parəˈgörik) *n.* narcotic preparation containing small amount of opium used to treat colic, earache, teething pain and diarrhea (*also* **camphorated opium tincture**)

parent (ˈparənt, ˈper-) *n.* father or mother —**ˈparentage** *n.* descent, extraction —**paˈrental** *a.* —**ˈparenthood** *n.* —**parent teacher association** group of parents of children at school and their teachers formed in order to foster better understanding between them *etc.*

parenthesis (pəˈrenthisis) *n.* word or sentence inserted in passage independently of grammatical sequence and usu. marked off by brackets, dashes, or commas —**paˈrentheses** *pl.n.* round brackets, ( ), used for this —**paˈrenthesize** *vt.* **1.** place in parentheses **2.** insert as parenthesis **3.** intersperse with parentheses —**parenˈthetical** *a.*

par excellence (par ekseˈläs) *Fr.* to degree of excellence; beyond comparison

pariah (pəˈrīə, ˈpariə) *n.* social outcast

parietal (pəˈrīitəl) *a.* of the walls of bodily cavities, *eg* skull

pari-mutuel (pariˈmyo͞ocho͞oəl) *n.* system of betting in which those who have bet on winners of race share in total amount wagered less percentage for management (*pl.* **pari-mutuels, paris-mutuels** (pariˈmyo͞ocho͞oəlz))

parish (ˈparish) *n.* **1.** district under one clergyman **2.** (in Louisiana) a county —**paˈrishioner** *n.* inhabitant of parish

parity (ˈpariti) *n. see* PAR

park (pärk) *n.* **1.** large area of land in natural state preserved for recreational use **2.** large enclosed piece of ground, usu. with grass or woodland, attached to country house or for public use **3.** space in camp for military supplies —*vt.* **4.** leave for a short time **5.** maneuver (vehicle) into a suitable space **6.** arrange or leave in a park —**parking lot** area where vehicles may be left for a time —**parking meter** timing device, usu. coin-operated, that indicates how long vehicle may be left parked —**parking ticket** summons served for parking offense —**ˈparkland** *n.* grassland with scattered trees

parka (ˈpärkə) *n.* warm waterproof coat, oft. with hood

Parkinson's disease (ˈpärkinsənz) progressive chronic disorder of central nervous system characterized by impaired muscular coordination and tremor (*also* **ˈparkinsonism**)

Parkinson's law notion, expressed facetiously as law of economics, that work expands to fill time available

parlance (ˈpärləns) *n.* **1.** way of speaking, conversation **2.** idiom

parley (ˈpärli) *n.* **1.** meeting between leaders or representatives of opposing forces to discuss terms —*vi.* **2.** hold discussion about terms

parliament (ˈpärləmənt) *n.* **1.** the legislature of the United Kingdom **2.** any similar legislative assembly —**parliamenˈtarian** *n.* member of parliament —**parliaˈmentary** *a.*

parlor (ˈpärlər) *n.* **1.** sitting room, room for receiving company in small house **2.** place for milking cows **3.** room or shop as business premises, *esp.* hairdresser *etc.*

Parmesan (ˈpärmizän, -zan, -zən) *n.* the hardest cheese, made of cow's milk, with mild flavor, best grated, orig. from Italy (*also* **Parmigiano** (pärmiˈjänō), **Reggiano Lodigiano**)

parochial (pəˈrōkiəl) *a.* **1.** narrow, provincial **2.** of a parish —**paˈrochialism** *n.*

parody (ˈparədi) *n.* **1.** composition in which author's style is made fun of by imitation **2.** travesty —*vt.* **3.** write parody of (**-odied, -odying**) —**ˈparodist** *n.*

parole (pəˈrōl) *n.* **1.** early freeing of prisoner on condition he is of good behavior **2.** word of honor —*vt.* **3.** place on parole

parotid (pəˈrotid) *a.* **1.** relating to or situated near parotid gland —*n.* **2.** parotid gland —**parotid gland** large salivary gland in front of and below each ear

-parous (*comb. form*) giving birth to, as in *oviparous*

paroxysm (ˈparəksizəm) *n.* sudden violent attack of pain, rage, laughter

parquet (ˈpärkā) *n.* **1.** flooring of wooden blocks arranged in pattern **2.** method of preventing warping of wood by reinforcement —**parquetry** (ˈpärkitri) *n.*

parr (pär) *n.* salmon up to two years of age (*pl.* **-s, parr**)

parrakeet (ˈparəkēt) *n. see* PARAKEET

parricide (ˈparisīd) *n.* murder or murderer of a parent

parrot (ˈparət) *n.* **1.** any of several related birds with short hooked beak, some varieties of which can imitate speaking **2.** unintelligent imitator —**parrot fever** *or* **disease** *see* **psittacosis** *at* PSITTACINE

parry (ˈpari) *vt.* **1.** ward off, turn aside (**ˈparried, ˈparrying**) —*n.* **2.** act of parrying, *esp.* in fencing

parse (pärs, pärz) *vt.* **1.** describe (word) **2.** analyze (sentence) in terms of grammar

parsec (ˈpärsek) *n.* unit of length used in expressing distance of stars

parsimony (ˈpärsimōni) *n.* **1.** stinginess **2.** undue economy —**parsiˈmonious** *a.* sparing

parsley (ˈpärsli) *n.* herb used for seasoning, garnish *etc.*

parsnip (ˈpärsnip) *n.* edible yellow root vegetable

parson (ˈpärsən) *n.* **1.** clergyman of parish or church **2.** clergyman —ˈ**parsonage** *n.* parson's house —**parson's nose** fatty extreme end portion of tail of fowl when cooked

part (pärt) *n.* **1.** portion, section, share **2.** division **3.** actor's role **4.** duty **5.** (*oft. pl.*) region **6.** interest **7.** division between sections of hair on head —*v.* **8.** divide **9.** separate —ˈ**parting** *n.* **1.** separation **2.** leave-taking —ˈ**partly** *adv.* in part —**part of speech** class of words sharing important syntactic or semantic features; group of words in language that may occur in similar positions or fulfill similar functions in sentence —**part song** song for several voices singing in harmony (*also* **canon, round**) —**part-time** *a.* **1.** for less than entire time appropriate to activity —*adv.* **2.** on part-time basis —**part-timer** *n.*

part. **1.** participle **2.** particular

partake (pärˈtāk) *vi.* **1.** (*with* of) take or have share (in) **2.** take food or drink (-ˈ**took,** -ˈ**taken,** -ˈ**taking**)

parterre (pärˈtāər) *n.* **1.** ornamental arrangement of beds in a flower garden **2.** the pit of a theater

parthenogenesis (pärthinōˈjenisis) *n.* the reproduction of an individual plant or animal from an unfertilized ovule or ovum —**parthenogeˈnetic** *a.*

Parthian shot (ˈpärthiən) hostile remark or gesture delivered while departing

partial (ˈpärshəl) *a.* **1.** not general or complete **2.** prejudiced **3.** (*with* to) fond (of) —**partiˈality** *n.* **1.** favoritism **2.** fondness —ˈ**partially** *adv.* partly

participate (pərˈtisipāt, pär-) *v.* (*with* in) **1.** share (in) **2.** take part (in) —**parˈticipant** *n.* —**particiˈpation** *n.* —**parˈticipator** *n.*

participle (ˈpärtisipəl) *n.* adjective made by inflection from verb and keeping verb's relation to dependent words —**partiˈcipial** *a.*

particle (ˈpärtikəl) *n.* **1.** minute portion of matter **2.** least possible amount **3.** minor part of speech in grammar, prefix, suffix —**particle accelerator** device to impart high velocity to an elementary particle, increasing its energy

parti-colored (pärtiˈkulərd) *a.* differently colored in different parts, variegated

particular (pərˈtikyələr) *a.* **1.** relating to one, not general **2.** distinct **3.** minute **4.** very exact **5.** fastidious —*n.* **6.** detail, item —*pl.* **7.** detailed account **8.** items of information —**particuˈlarity** *n.* —**parˈticularize** *vt.* mention in detail —**parˈticularly** *adv.*

partisan (ˈpärtizən, -sən) *n.* **1.** adherent of a party **2.** guerrilla, member of resistance movement —*a.* **3.** adhering to faction **4.** prejudiced

partition (pərˈtishən, pär-) *n.* **1.** division **2.** interior dividing wall —*vt.* **3.** divide, cut into sections

partitive (ˈpärtitiv) *a.* **1.** *Gram.* indicating that noun involved in construction refers only to part of what it otherwise refers to **2.** serving to separate or divide into parts —*n.* **3.** *Gram.* partitive linguistic element or feature

partner (ˈpärtnər) *n.* **1.** ally or companion **2.** a member of a partnership **3.** one that dances with another **4.** a husband or wife **5.** *Golf, Tennis etc.* one who plays with another against opponents —*vt.* **6.** (cause to) be a partner (of) —ˈ**partnership** *n.* association of persons for business *etc.*

partridge (ˈpärtrij) *n.* any of various game birds of the grouse family

parturition (pärtəˈrishən, pärchə-, pärtyōō-) *n.* **1.** act of bringing forth young **2.** childbirth —**parˈturient** *a.* **1.** of childbirth **2.** giving birth **3.** producing new idea *etc.*

party (ˈpärti) *n.* **1.** social assembly **2.** group of persons traveling or working together **3.** group of persons united in opinion **4.** side **5.** person —*a.* **6.** of, belonging to, a party or faction —**party line 1.** telephone line serving two or more subscribers **2.** policies of political party —**party wall** common wall separating adjoining premises

parulis (pəˈrōōlis) *n.* gumboil

parvenu *or* (*fem.*) **parvenue** (ˈpärvənyōō, -nōō) *n.* **1.** one newly risen into position of notice, power, wealth **2.** upstart

pas (pä) *n.* dance step or movement, *esp.* in ballet (*pl.* **pas**)

pascal (ˈpaskəl) *n.* SI unit of pressure

Paschal (ˈpaskəl) *a.* of the Passover or Easter

pasha (ˈpäshə, ˈpashə) *n.* formerly, high official of Ottoman Empire or modern Egyptian kingdom: placed after name when used as title

Pashto (ˈpushtō) *n.* the Iranian language of the Pathan people which is the chief vernacular of eastern Afghanistan and adjacent parts of Pakistan

pasqueflower (ˈpaskflowər) *n.* **1.** small purple-flowered plant of N and Central Europe and W Asia **2.** any of several related N Amer. plants

pass (pas) *vt.* **1.** go by, beyond, through *etc.* **2.** exceed **3.** be accepted by **4.** undergo successfully **5.** spend **6.** transfer **7.** exchange **8.** disregard **9.** undergo (examination) successfully **10.** bring into force, sanction (a parliamentary bill *etc.*) —*vi.* **11.** go **12.** be transferred from one state or person to another **13.** elapse —*n.* **14.** way, *esp.* a narrow and difficult way **15.** permit, license, authorization **16.** successful result from test **17.** condition **18.** *Sport* transfer of ball

—'**passable** *a.* (just) acceptable —'**passing** *a.* **1.** transitory **2.** cursory, casual —'**passbook** *n.* bankbook —**passer-by** *n.* person that is passing by, *esp.* on foot (*pl.* **passers-by**) —'**passkey** *n.* **1.** any of various keys, *esp.* latchkey **2.** master key **3.** skeleton key —**pass up** ignore, neglect; reject

passage ('pasij) *n.* **1.** channel, opening **2.** way through, corridor **3.** part of book *etc.* **4.** journey, voyage, fare **5.** enactment of law by parliament *etc.* **6.** *rare* conversation; dispute —'**passageway** *n.* way, *esp.* one in or between buildings; passage

Passamaquoddy (pasəmə'kwodi) *n.* (member of) Algonquian-speaking Amerindian people of Maine, which is a member of Abnaki confederacy (*pl.* **-dy, -s**)

passé (pa'sā) *a.* **1.** out of date **2.** past the prime

passenger ('pasinjər) *n.* **1.** traveler, *esp.* by public conveyance **2.** one of a team who does not pull his weight

passerine ('pasərīn) *a./n.* (member) of the order of perching birds

passim ('pasim) *Lat.* everywhere, throughout

passion ('pashən) *n.* **1.** ardent desire, *esp.* sexual **2.** any strongly felt emotion **3.** suffering (*esp.* that of Christ) —'**passionate** *a.* (easily) moved by strong emotions —'**passionflower** *n.* tropical Amer. plant —**passion fruit** edible fruit of passionflower —**Passion play** play depicting Passion of Christ

passive ('pasiv) *a.* **1.** unresisting **2.** submissive **3.** inactive **4.** denoting grammatical mood of verb in which the action is suffered by the subject —**pas'sivity** *n.* —**passive resistance** resistance to government *etc.* without violence, as by fasting, demonstrating or refusing to cooperate

Passover ('pasōvər) *n.* Jewish spring holiday commemorating the liberation of the Jews from slavery in Egypt (*also* **Pesach**)

passport ('paspōrt) *n.* official document granting permission to pass, travel abroad *etc.*

password ('paswərd) *n.* **1.** word, phrase, to distinguish friend from enemy **2.** countersign

past (past) *a.* **1.** ended **2.** gone by **3.** elapsed —*n.* **4.** bygone times —*adv.* **5.** by **6.** along —*prep.* **7.** beyond **8.** after —**past master 1.** person with talent for, or experience in a particular activity **2.** person who has held office of master in guild *etc.* —**past participle** participial form of verbs used to modify noun that is logically object of verb, also used in certain compound tenses and passive forms of verb —**past perfect** *Gram. a.* **1.** denoting tense of verbs used in relating past events where action had already occurred at time of action of main verb that is itself in past tense —*n.* **2.** past perfect tense **3.** verb in this tense

pasta ('pästə) *n.* any of several variously shaped edible preparations of dough, *eg* spaghetti

paste (pāst) *n.* **1.** soft composition, as toothpaste **2.** soft plastic mixture or adhesive **3.** fine glass to imitate gems —*vt.* **4.** fasten with paste —'**pasty** *a.* **1.** like paste **2.** white **3.** sickly —'**pasteboard** *n.* stiff thick paper

pastel (pa'stel) *n.* **1.** colored crayon **2.** art of drawing with crayons **3.** pale, delicate color —*a.* **4.** delicately tinted

pastern ('pastərn) *n.* part of horse's foot between fetlock and hoof

pasteurize ('paschərīz, 'pastə-) *vt.* sterilize by heat —**pasteuri'zation** *n.*

pastiche (pa'stēsh) *or* **pasticcio** (pa'stēchō) *n.* **1.** literary, musical, artistic work composed of parts borrowed from other works and loosely connected together **2.** work imitating another's style

pastille (pa'stēl) *or* **pastil** ('pastəl) *n.* **1.** lozenge **2.** aromatic substance burnt as fumigator

pastime ('pastīm) *n.* **1.** that which makes time pass agreeably **2.** recreation

pastor ('pastər) *n.* clergyman in charge of a congregation —'**pastoral** *a.* **1.** of, or like, shepherd's or rural life **2.** of office of pastor —*n.* **3.** poem describing rural life —**pastorale** (pastə'räl) *n. Mus.* **1.** composition evocative of rural life **2.** musical play based on rustic story (*pl.* **-s, -rali** (*It.* -'rälē)) —'**pastorate** *n.* office, jurisdiction of pastor

pastry ('pāstri) *n.* article of food made chiefly of flour, fat and water

pasture ('paschər) *n.* **1.** grass for food of cattle **2.** ground on which cattle graze —*v.* **3.** (cause to) graze —'**pasturage** *n.* (right to) pasture

pasty ('pasti) *n.* small pie of meat and crust, baked without a dish

pat[1] (pat) *vt.* **1.** tap (**-tt-**) —*n.* **2.** light, quick blow **3.** small mass, as of butter, beaten into shape

pat[2] (pat) *adv.* **1.** exactly **2.** fluently **3.** opportunely —*a.* **4.** glib **5.** exactly right

pat. patent(ed)

patch (pach) *n.* **1.** piece of cloth sewn on garment **2.** spot **3.** plot of ground **4.** protecting pad for the eye **5.** small contrasting area **6.** short period —*vt.* **7.** mend **8.** repair clumsily —'**patchy** *a.* **1.** of uneven quality **2.** full of patches —**patch test** test to detect skin sensitivity to contact with irritants or allergic agents —'**patchwork** *n.* **1.** work composed of pieces sewn together **2.** jumble

patchouli *or* **patchouly** ('pachəli, pə'chōōli) *n.* **1.** Indian herb **2.** perfume made from it

pate (pāt) *n.* **1.** head **2.** top of head

pâté (pä'tā, pa'tā) *n.* spread of finely minced liver *etc.* —**pâté de foie gras** (*Fr.* pätā də fwa 'grä) smooth rich paste made from liver of specially fattened goose (*pl.* **pâtés de foie gras** (*Fr.* pätä))

patella (pə'telə) *n.* kneecap (*pl.* **patellae** (pə'telē)) —**pa'tellar** *a.*

paten ('patən) *n.* plate for bread in the Eucharist

patent ('patənt) *n.* **1.** deed securing to person exclusive right to invention —*a.* **2.** open **3.** (*also* 'pātənt) evident; manifest **4.** open to public perusal, as in *letters patent* —*vt.* **5.** secure a patent for —**paten'tee** *n.* one that has a patent —**patently** ('patəntli, 'pātəntli) *adv.* obviously —**patent leather** (imitation) leather processed to give hard, glossy surface —**patent medicine** medicine with patent, available without prescription —**Patent Office** government department that issues patents

pater ('pātər) *n.* **UK** *sl.* father

paterfamilias (pātərfə'miliəs) *n.* father of a family (*pl.* **patresfamilias** (pātrēzfə'miliəs, pätrās-))

paternal (pə'tərnəl) *a.* **1.** fatherly **2.** of a father —**pa'ternalism** *n.* authority exercised in a way that limits individual responsibility —**paternal'istic** *a.* —**pa'ternity** *n.* **1.** relation of a father to his offspring **2.** fatherhood —**paternity test** blood or tissue test used to determine whether a man is the father of a particular child

paternoster ('patərnostər, pätər'nostər) *n.* **1.** (**P-**) Lord's Prayer **2.** beads of rosary **3.** type of elevator with platforms rising and falling in an endless moving chain

path (path, päth) *n.* **1.** way or track **2.** course of action —'**pathway** *n.* **1.** path **2.** *Biochem.* chain of reactions associated with particular metabolic process

-path (*comb. form*) **1.** person suffering from specified disease or disorder, as in *neuropath* **2.** practitioner of particular method of treatment, as in *osteopath*

pathetic (pə'thetik) *a.* **1.** affecting or moving tender emotions **2.** distressingly inadequate —**pa'thetically** *adv.* —**pathetic fallacy** *Lit.* presentation of nature *etc.* as possessing human feelings

pathogenic (pathə'jenik) *a.* producing disease —**pa'thogeny** *n.* mode of development of disease

pathology (pə'tholəji) *n.* science of diseases —**patho'logical** *a.* **1.** of the science of disease **2.** due to disease **3.** *inf.* compulsively motivated

pathos ('pāthos) *n.* power of exciting tender emotions

-pathy (*n. comb. form*) **1.** feeling, perception, as in *telepathy* **2.** disease, as in *psychopathy* **3.** method of treating disease, as in *osteopathy* —**-pathic** (*a. comb. form*)

patient ('pāshənt) *a.* **1.** bearing trials calmly —*n.* **2.** person under medical treatment —'**patience** *n.* quality of enduring

patina ('patinə) *n.* **1.** fine layer on a surface **2.** sheen of age on woodwork

patio ('patiō) *n.* paved area adjoining house (*pl.* **-s**)

patois ('patwä; *Fr.* pa'twa) *n.* regional dialect (*pl.* **patois** ('patwäz; *Fr.* pa'twa))

pat. pend. patent pending

patriarch ('pātriärk) *n.* father and ruler of family, *esp.* Biblical —**patri'archal** *a.* venerable —'**patriarchy** *n.* **1.** form of social organization in which male is head of family and descent, kinship and title are traced through male line **2.** society governed by such system

patrician (pə'trishən) *n.* **1.** noble of ancient Rome **2.** one of noble birth —*a.* **3.** of noble birth

patricide ('patrisīd) *n.* murder or murderer of father

patriot ('pātriət, -ot) *n.* one that loves his country and maintains its interests —**patri'otic** *a.* inspired by love of one's country —'**patriotism** *n.*

patrol (pə'trōl) *n.* **1.** regular circuit by guard **2.** person, small group patrolling **3.** unit of Scouts —*v.* **4.** go round on guard or reconnoitering (**-ll-**)

patron ('pātrən) *n.* **1.** one who sponsors or aids artists, charities *etc.* **2.** protector **3.** regular customer **4.** guardian saint **5.** one that has disposition of church living *etc.* —**patronage** ('patrənij) *n.* support given by, or position of, a patron —'**patronize** *vt.* **1.** assume air of superiority toward **2.** frequent as customer **3.** encourage —'**patronizing** *a.* condescending

patronymic (patrə'nimik) *n.* name derived from that of father or ancestor

patter ('patər) *vi.* **1.** make noise, as sound of quick, short steps **2.** tap in quick succession **3.** pray, talk rapidly —*n.* **4.** quick succession of taps **5.** *inf.* glib, rapid speech

pattern ('patərn) *n.* **1.** arrangement of repeated parts **2.** design **3.** shape to direct cutting of cloth *etc.* **4.** model **5.** specimen —*vt.* **6.** (*with* on, after) model **7.** decorate with pattern

paucity ('pösiti) *n.* **1.** scarcity **2.** smallness of quantity **3.** fewness

paunch (pönch) *n.* belly

pauper ('pöpər) *n.* poor person, *esp.*, formerly, one supported by the public —'**pauperism** *n.* **1.** destitution **2.** extreme poverty

pause (pöz) *vi.* **1.** cease for a time —*n.* **2.** stop or rest

pavane *or* **pavan** (pə'vän, -'van) *n.* **1.** slow, stately dance of 16th and 17th centuries **2.** music for this dance

pave (pāv) *vt.* **1.** form surface on with stone or brick **2.** prepare, make easier (*esp. in* **pave the way**) —'**pavement** *n.* **1.** paved floor, footpath **2.** material for paving

pavilion (pə'vilyən) *n.* **1.** clubhouse on

playing field *etc.* **2.** building for housing exhibition *etc.* **3.** large ornate tent

pavlova (pav'lōvə) *n.* meringue cake with whipped cream and fruit

paw (pö) *n.* **1.** foot of animal —*v.* **2.** scrape with forefoot —*vt.* **3.** handle roughly **4.** stroke with the hands

pawl (pöl) *n.* pivoted lever shaped to engage with ratchet wheel to prevent motion in particular direction

pawn[1] (pön) *vt.* **1.** deposit (article) as security for money borrowed —*n.* **2.** article deposited —'**pawnbroker** *n.* lender of money on goods pledged

pawn[2] (pön) *n.* **1.** piece in chess **2.** *fig.* person used as mere tool

Pawnee (pö'nē) *n.* member of Siouan-speaking Amerindian people orig. of Kansas and Nebraska, now of Oklahoma (*pl.* **-nee, -s**)

pawpaw ('popö, 'pö-) *n. see* PAPAW

pax (paks) *n. chiefly R.C.Ch.* **1.** kiss of peace **2.** small plate formerly used to convey kiss of peace from celebrant at Mass to those attending it

pay (pā) *vt.* **1.** give (money *etc.*) for goods or services rendered **2.** compensate **3.** give, bestow **4.** be profitable to **5.** (*with* out) release bit by bit, as rope **6.** (*with* out) spend —*vi.* **7.** be remunerative or profitable (**paid, 'paying**) —*n.* **8.** wages **9.** paid employment —'**payable** *a.* **1.** justly due **2.** profitable —**pay'ee** *n.* person to whom money is paid or due —'**payment** *n.* discharge of debt —**pay'ola** *n. inf.* **1.** bribe given to secure special treatment, *esp.* to disc jockey to promote commercial product **2.** practice of paying or receiving such bribes —**paying guest** boarder, lodger, *esp.* in private house —'**payload** *n.* **1.** part of cargo earning revenue **2.** explosive power of missile *etc.* —'**paymaster** *n.* official of government *etc.*, responsible for payment of wages and salaries —'**payoff** *n.* **1.** final settlement, *esp.* in retribution **2.** *inf.* climax, consequence or outcome of events *etc.* **3.** final payment of debt *etc.* **4.** time of such payment **5.** *inf.* bribe —**pay packet 1.** envelope containing employee's wages **2.** the wages —'**payroll** *n.* **1.** list of employees, specifying salary or wage of each **2.** total of these amounts or actual money equivalent —**pay off 1.** pay all that is due in wages *etc.* and discharge from employment **2.** pay complete amount of (debt *etc.*) **3.** turn out to be profitable **4.** take revenge on (person) or for (wrong done) **5.** *inf.* give bribe to

Pb *Chem.* lead

p.c. 1. per cent **2.** postcard

Pd *Chem.* palladium

pd. paid

PE Prince Edward Island

P.E. physical education

pea (pē) *n.* **1.** fruit, growing in pods, of climbing plant **2.** the plant —**pea-green** *a.* of shade of green like color of green peas —**pea jacket** *or* '**peacoat** *n.* sailor's short heavy woolen overcoat —**pea'souper** *n. inf.* thick fog

peace (pēs) *n.* **1.** freedom from war **2.** harmony **3.** quietness of mind **4.** calm **5.** repose —'**peaceable** *a.* disposed to peace —'**peaceably** *adv.* —'**peaceful** *a.* **1.** free from war, tumult **2.** mild **3.** undisturbed —'**peacefully** *adv.* —'**peacemaker** *n.* person who establishes peace, *esp.* between others —**peace offering 1.** something given to adversary in hope of procuring or maintaining peace **2.** *Judaism* sacrificial meal shared between offerer and Jehovah —**peace pipe** pipe smoked by N Amer. Indians, *esp.* as token of peace (*also* '**calumet**)

peach[1] (pēch) *n.* **1.** stone fruit of delicate flavor **2.** *inf.* anything very pleasant **3.** pinkish-yellow color —'**peachy** *a.* **1.** like peach **2.** *inf.* fine, excellent

peach[2] (pēch) *vi. sl.* become informer

peacock ('pēkok) *n.* **1.** male of bird ('**peafowl**) with fanlike tail, brilliantly colored ('**peahen** *fem.*) —*vi.* **2.** strut about or pose, like a peacock

peak (pēk) *n.* **1.** pointed end of anything, *esp.* hill's sharp top **2.** point of greatest development *etc.* **3.** sharp increase **4.** projecting piece on front of cap —*v.* **5.** (cause to) form, reach peaks —**peaked** *or* '**peaky** *a.* **1.** like, having a peak **2.** sickly, wan, drawn —**peak hour** time at which maximum occurs, either in amount of traffic or demand for gas *etc.* —**peak load** maximum load on electrical power-supply system

peal (pēl) *n.* **1.** loud sound or succession of loud sounds **2.** changes rung on set of bells **3.** chime —*v.* **4.** sound loudly

peanut ('pēnut) *n.* **1.** pea-shaped nut that ripens underground —*pl.* **2.** *inf.* trifling amount of money

pear (pāər) *n.* **1.** tree yielding sweet, juicy fruit **2.** the fruit —**pear-shaped** *a.* shaped like a pear, heavier at the bottom than the top

pearl (pərl) *n.* hard, lustrous structure found in several mollusks, *esp.* pearl oyster and used as jewel —'**pearly** *a.* like pearls —**pearl barley** barley with skin ground off —**pearl diver** *or* **fisher** person who dives for pearl-bearing mollusks

peasant ('pezənt) *n.* member of low social class, *esp.* in rural district —'**peasantry** *n.* peasants collectively

pease (pēz) *n. obs., dial.* pea (*pl.* **pease**)

peat (pēt) *n.* **1.** decomposed vegetable substance found in bogs **2.** turf of it used for fuel —**peat moss** any of various mosses, *esp.* sphagnum, that grow in wet places and decay to form peat (*see also* SPHAGNUM)

pebble ('pebəl) *n.* **1.** small roundish stone **2.** pale, transparent rock crystal **3.** grainy, irregular surface —*vt.* **4.** pave, cover with pebbles

pecan (pi'kän, -'kan; 'pēkan) *n.* **1.** N Amer. tree, species of hickory, allied to walnut **2.** its edible nut

peccadillo (pekə'dilō) *n.* **1.** slight offense **2.** petty crime (*pl.* **-es, -s**)

peccary

peccary ('pekəri) *n.* vicious Amer. animal allied to pig

peck[1] (pek) *n.* **1.** fourth part of bushel, 2 gallons **2.** great deal

peck[2] (pek) *v.* **1.** pick, strike with or as with beak **2.** nibble —*vt.* **3.** *inf.* kiss quickly —*n.* **4.** act, instance of pecking —'**peckish** *a. inf.* hungry

pectin ('pektin) *n.* gelatinizing substance obtained from ripe fruits —'**pectic** *a.* **1.** congealing **2.** denoting pectin

pectoral ('pektərəl) *a.* **1.** of the breast —*n.* **2.** chest medicine **3.** breastplate —**pectoral fin** either of pair of fins, situated just behind head in fishes —**pectoral girdle** bony arch supporting forelimbs of a vertebrate (*also* **shoulder girdle**)

peculate ('pekyəlāt) *v.* **1.** embezzle **2.** steal —**pecu'lation** *n.* —'**peculator** *n.*

peculiar (pi'kyōōlyər) *a.* **1.** strange **2.** particular **3.** (*with* to) belonging (to) —**peculi'arity** *n.* **1.** oddity **2.** characteristic **3.** distinguishing feature

pecuniary (pi'kyōōnieri) *a.* relating to, or consisting of, money

-ped *or* **-pede** (*comb. form*) foot or feet, as in *quadruped, centipede*

pedagogue *or* **pedagog** ('pedəgog) *n.* **1.** schoolmaster **2.** pedant —**pedagogic** (pedə'gojik, -'gōj-) *a.* —**pedagogy** ('pedəgōji, -goji) *n.* principles, practice or profession of teaching

pedal ('pedəl) *n.* **1.** something to transmit motion from foot **2.** foot lever to modify tone or swell of musical instrument **3.** *Mus.* note, usu. bass, held through successive harmonies —*a.* ('pēdəl) **4.** of a foot —*v.* **5.** propel (bicycle) by using pedals —*vi.* **6.** use pedals

pedalo ('pedəlō) *n.* small watercraft with paddle wheel propelled by foot pedals (*pl.* **-s, -es**)

pedant ('pedənt) *n.* one who overvalues, or insists on, petty details of book-learning, grammatical rules *etc.* —**pe'dantic** *a.*

peddle ('pedəl) *v.* go round selling (goods) —'**peddler** *n.* one who sells, *esp.* narcotic drugs

pederast ('pedərast) *n.* man who has homosexual relations with boy —'**pederasty** *n.*

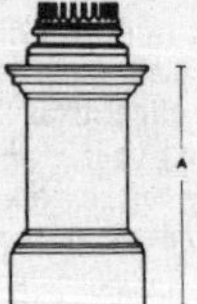

pedestal

pedestal ('pedistəl) *n.* base of column, pillar

pedestrian (pi'destriən) *n.* **1.** one who walks on foot —*a.* **2.** going on foot **3.** commonplace; dull, uninspiring —**pe'destrianism** *n.* the practice of walking —**pe'destrianize** *vt.* convert into area for use of pedestrians only —**pedestrian crossing UK** crosswalk —**pedestrian precinct** area for pedestrians only to shop *etc.*

pedi- (*comb. form*) foot, as in *pedicure*

pediatrics (pēdi'atriks) *n.* branch of medicine dealing with diseases and disorders of children —**pedia'trician** *n.*

pediculosis (pədikyə'lōsis) *n.* infestation by lice

pedicure ('pedikyōōər) *n.* medical or cosmetic treatment of feet

pedigree ('pedigrē) *n.* **1.** register of ancestors **2.** genealogy

pediment ('pedimənt) *n.* triangular part over Greek portico *etc.* —**pedi'mental** *a.*

pedo- *or before vowel* **ped-** (*comb. form*) child, children, as in *pedophilia*

pedophilia (pēdə'filiə) *n.* condition of being sexually attracted to children —**pedophile** ('pēdəfīl) *or* **pedo'philiac** *n./a.*

peduncle ('pēdungkəl, pi'dungkəl) *n.* **1.** flower stalk **2.** stalklike structure

peek (pēk) *vi./n.* peep, glance

peel (pēl) *vt.* **1.** strip off skin, rind or any form of covering from —*vi.* **2.** come off, as skin, rind —*n.* **3.** rind, skin —**peeled** *a. inf.* (of eyes) watchful

peen (pēn) *n.* **1.** end of hammer head opposite striking face, oft. rounded or wedge-shaped —*vt.* **2.** strike with peen of hammer or stream of metal shot

peep[1] (pēp) *vi.* **1.** look slyly or quickly —*n.* **2.** such a look —'**peeper** *n.* **1.** person who peeps **2.** (*oft. pl.*) *sl.* eye —**Peeping Tom** man who furtively observes women undressing; voyeur —'**peepshow** *n.* box with peephole through which series of pictures can be seen

peep[2] (pēp) *vi.* **1.** cry, as chick, chirp —*n.* **2.** such a cry

peer[1] (pēər) *n.* **1.** nobleman **2.** one of the same rank ('**peeress** *fem.*) —'**peerage** *n.* **1.** body of peers **2.** rank of peer —'**peerless** *a.* without match or equal —**peer group** social group composed of individuals of approximately same age

peer[2] (pēər) *vi.* look closely and intently

peevish (ˈpēvish) *a.* **1.** fretful **2.** irritable —**peeved** *a. inf.* sulky, irritated —ˈ**peevishly** *adv.* —ˈ**peevishness** *n.* annoyance

peewit *or* **pewit** (ˈpēwit) *n. see* LAPWING

peg (peg) *n.* **1.** nail or pin for joining, fastening, marking *etc.* **2.** (mark of) level, standard *etc.* —*vt.* **3.** fasten with pegs **4.** stabilize (prices) **5.** *inf.* throw —*vi.* **6.** (*with* away) persevere (**-gg-**) —ˈ**pegboard** *n.* **1.** board having pattern of holes into which small pegs can be fitted, used for playing certain games or keeping score **2.** *see* **solitaire** (sense 3) *at* SOLITARY **3.** hardboard perforated by pattern of holes in which articles may be hung, as for display —**peg leg** *inf.* **1.** artificial leg, *esp.* one made of wood **2.** person with artificial leg —**peg out** *sl.* die

peignoir (pānˈwär) *n.* lady's dressing gown, jacket, wrapper

pejorative (piˈjörətiv, -ˈjor-; ˈpējər-) *a.* (of words *etc.*) with unpleasant, disparaging connotation

Pekingese *or* **Pekinese** (pēkəˈnēz, pēkingˈēz) *n.* small Chinese dog (*also* **peke**) —**Peking man** (ˈpēˈking) extinct man of Pleistocene period

pelargonium (pelärˈgōniəm) *n.* any of a genus of tender perennials commonly referred to as geraniums when grown as houseplants, with red, white or pink flowers

pelf (pelf) *n. contemptuous* money; wealth

pelican (ˈpelikən) *n.* large, fish-eating waterfowl with large pouch beneath its bill

pelisse (pəˈlēs, pe-) *n.* **1.** fur-trimmed cloak **2.** loose coat, usu. fur-trimmed, worn *esp.* by women in early 19th cent.

pellagra (pəˈlagrə, -ˈlā-) *n.* disease caused by dietary deficiency of niacin, characterized by scaling of skin *etc.*

pellet (ˈpelit) *n.* little ball, pill

pellicle (ˈpelikəl) *n.* thin skin, film

pell-mell (ˈpelˈmel) *adv.* in utter confusion, headlong

pellucid (pəˈlo͞osid) *a.* **1.** translucent **2.** clear —**pelluˈcidity** *n.*

pelmet

pelmet (ˈpelmit) *n.* ornamental drapery or board, concealing curtain rail

pelt[1] (pelt) *vt.* **1.** strike with missiles —*vi.* **2.** throw missiles **3.** rush **4.** fall persistently, as rain

pelt[2] (pelt) *n.* raw hide or skin

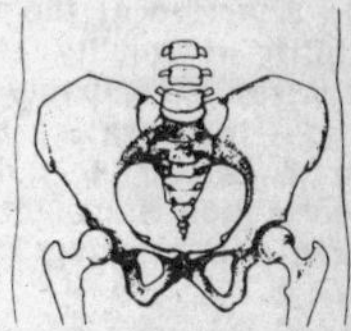

pelvis

pelvis (ˈpelvis) *n.* basin-shaped structure holding some abdominal organs in skeleton of vertebrate (*pl.* **-es, -ves** (-vēz)) —ˈ**pelvic** *a.* pert. to pelvis —**pelvic girdle** bony arch supporting hind or lower limbs of vertebrate

pemmican *or* **pemican** (ˈpemikən) *n.* **1.** concentrated food used by Amerindians made of pounded lean dried meat mixed with smelted fat **2.** similar preparation used for emergency rations

pemphigus vulgaris (ˈpemfigəs vulˈgäris) serious skin disorder of adult life of unknown origin

pen[1] (pen) *n.* **1.** instrument for writing —*vt.* **2.** compose **3.** write (**-nn-**) —ˈ**penknife** *n.* small knife with one or more blades that fold into handle —ˈ**penmanship** *n.* style or technique of writing by hand —**pen name** author's pseudonym —**pen pal** person with whom one exchanges letters, oft. person in another country whom one has not met —ˈ**penpusher** *n.* clerk involved with boring paperwork

pen[2] (pen) *n.* **1.** small enclosure, as for sheep —*vt.* **2.** put, keep in enclosure (**-nn-**)

pen[3] (pen) *n.* female swan

Pen. Peninsula

penal (ˈpēnəl) *a.* of, incurring, inflicting, punishment —ˈ**penalize** *vt.* **1.** impose penalty on **2.** handicap —**penalty** (ˈpenəlti) *n.* **1.** punishment for crime or offense **2.** forfeit **3.** *Sport* handicap or disadvantage imposed for infringement of rule *etc.* —**penal code** codified body of laws that relate to crime and punishment

penance (ˈpenəns) *n.* **1.** suffering submitted to as expression of penitence **2.** repentance

penchant (ˈpenchənt; *Fr.* pāˈshā) *n.* inclination, decided taste

pencil (ˈpensəl) *n.* **1.** instrument as of graphite, for writing *etc.* **2.** *Optics* narrow beam of light —*vt.* **3.** paint or draw **4.** mark with pencil

pendant (ˈpendənt) *n.* hanging ornament —ˈ**pendent** *a.* **1.** suspended, hanging **2.** projecting

pending (ˈpending) *prep.* **1.** during, until —*a.*

2. awaiting settlement 3. undecided 4. imminent

pendulous ('penjələs, 'pendyələs, 'pendələs) *a.* hanging, swinging —'**pendulum** *n.* suspended weight swinging to and fro, *esp.* as regulator for clock

penetrate ('penitrāt) *vt.* 1. enter into 2. pierce 3. arrive at the meaning of —**penetra'bility** *n.* quality of being penetrable —'**penetrable** *a.* capable of being entered or pierced —'**penetrating** *a.* 1. sharp 2. easily heard 3. subtle 4. quick to understand —**pene'tration** *n.* insight, acuteness —'**penetrative** *a.* 1. piercing 2. discerning —'**penetrator** *n.*

penguin ('penggwin) *n.* flightless, short-legged swimming bird

penicillin (peni'silin) *n.* antibiotic drug effective against a wide range of diseases, infections

peninsula (pi'ninsələ, -'ninchələ) *n.* portion of land nearly surrounded by water —**pe'ninsular** *a.*

penis ('pēnis) *n.* male organ of copulation (and of urination) in man and mammals (*pl.* **-es, penes** ('pēnēz))

penitent ('penitənt) *a.* 1. affected by sense of guilt —*n.* 2. one that repents of sin —'**penitence** *n.* 1. sorrow for sin 2. repentance —**peni'tential** *a.* of, or expressing, penitence —**peni'tentiary** *a.* 1. relating to penance, or to the rules of penance —*n.* 2. prison

Pennacook ('penəkŏŏk) *n.* (member of) Algonquian-speaking Amerindian people of New Hampshire (*pl.* **-cook, -s**)

pennant ('penənt) *n.* long narrow flag

pennon ('penən) *n.* small pointed or swallow-tailed flag

Pennsylvania (pensil'vānyə, -niə) *n.* Middle Atlantic state of the U.S.: ratified the Constitution in 1787. Abbrev.: **PA** (with ZIP code)

penny ('peni) *n.* bronze coin, 100th part of dollar (*pl.* '**pennies**) —'**penniless** *a.* 1. having no money 2. poor —**Penny Black** first postage stamp, issued in Brit. in 1840 —**penny-pincher** *n. inf.* person who is excessively careful with money —**penny-pinching** *n./a.* —**penny-wise** *a.* greatly concerned with saving small sums of money —**bad penny** someone or something unwanted —**penny-wise and pound-foolish** careful about trifles but wasteful in large ventures —**pretty penny** considerable sum of money

Penobscot (pə'nobskot) *n.* member of Algonquian-speaking Amerindian people of Maine, member of Abnaki confederacy (*pl.* **-scot, -s**)

penology (pi'noləji) *n.* study of punishment and prevention of crime

pension[1] ('penchən) *n.* 1. regular payment to old people, retired public officials, soldiers *etc.* —*vt.* 2. grant pension to —'**pensioner** *n.*

pension[2] (pã'syõ) *Fr.* 1. continental boarding house 2. (full) board

pensive ('pensiv) *a.* 1. thoughtful with sadness 2. wistful

penstemon (pen'stēmən) *n. see* PENTSTEMON

pent (pent) *a.* shut up, kept in —**pent-up** *a.* not released, repressed

penta- (*comb. form*) five, as in *pentagon, pentameter*

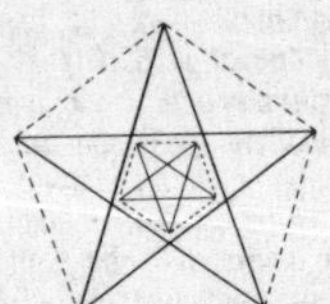

pentacle

pentacle ('pentəkəl) *n.* 1. star-shaped figure with five points 2. such figure used by Pythagoreans, black magicians *etc.* (*also* '**pentagram,** '**pentangle**)

pentagon ('pentəgon) *n.* 1. plane figure having five angles 2. (**P-**) building in Virginia containing the U.S. Department of Defense 3. (**P-**) the U.S. military establishment —**pen'tagonal** *a.*

pentameter (pen'tamitər) *n.* verse of five metrical feet

Pentateuch ('pentətyōōk, -tōōk) *n.* the first five books of the O.T. comprising Genesis, Exodus, Leviticus, Numbers and Deuteronomy

pentathlon (pen'tathlən, -lon) *n.* athletic contest of five events

pentatonic scale (pentə'tonik) *Mus.* scale consisting of five notes

Pentecost ('pentikost) *n.* 1. Whitsuntide 2. Jewish harvest festival on 50th day after Passover —**Pente'costal** *a.* 1. denoting a mainly Protestant Christian movement, now with various organized forms, emphasizing the immediate presence of God in the Holy Spirit 2. of Pentecost or influence of Holy Ghost —*n.* 3. member of a Pentecostal Church —**Pente'costalist** *n./a.*

penthouse ('pent-hows) *n.* apartment or other structure on top, or top floor, of building

pentode ('pentōd) *n. Electron.* five-electrode thermionic valve, having anode, cathode and three grids

pentothal sodium ('pentəthōl) barbiturate used for anesthesia and to produce relaxed state in psychotherapy (*also* **sodium pentothal**)

pentstemon (pent'stēmən) *or* **penstemon** *n.* bright-flowered garden plant

penult ('pēnult, pi'nult) *n.* last syllable but one of word —**pe'nultimate** *a.* next before the last

penumbra (pi'numbrə) *n.* 1. imperfect shadow 2. in an eclipse, the partially shadowed region which surrounds the full shadow

penury ('penyəri) *n.* **1.** extreme poverty **2.** extreme scarcity —**pe'nurious** *a.* **1.** niggardly, stingy **2.** poor, scanty

peony ('pēəni) *n.* any of genus of N Amer. plants with showy red, pink or white flowers

people ('pēpəl) *pl.n.* **1.** persons generally **2.** community, nation **3.** family —*n.* **4.** race —*vt.* **5.** stock with inhabitants, populate

pep (pep) *n.* **1.** vigor **2.** energy **3.** enthusiasm —*vt.* (*usu. with* up) **4.** impart energy to **5.** speed up (**-pp-**) —**pep pill** *inf.* tablet containing stimulant —**pep talk** *inf.* enthusiastic talk designed to increase confidence, production *etc.*

pepper ('pepər) *n.* **1.** fruit of climbing plant, which yields pungent aromatic spice **2.** various slightly pungent vegetables, *eg* capsicum —*vt.* **3.** season with pepper **4.** sprinkle, dot **5.** pelt with missiles —**'peppery** *a.* **1.** having the qualities of pepper **2.** irritable —**pepper-and-salt** *a.* **1.** (of cloth *etc.*) marked with fine mixture of black and white **2.** (of hair) streaked with gray —**'peppercorn** *n.* **1.** dried pepper berry **2.** something trifling —**pepper mill** hand mill used to grind peppercorns —**'peppermint** *n.* **1.** plant noted for aromatic pungent liquor distilled from it **2.** a sweet flavored with this

pepperidge ('pepərij) *n. see* **black gum** *at* BLACK

pepsin ('pepsin) *n.* enzyme produced in stomach, which, when activated by acid, breaks down proteins

peptic ('peptik) *a.* relating to digestion or digestive juices

peptide ('peptīd) *n.* **1.** chain of two or more amino acids **2.** antibiotic substance isolated from microorganisms

peptone ('peptōn) *n.* one of a group of compounds obtained by partial decomposition of proteins used commercially as food supplements

Pequot ('pēkwot) *n.* member of Algonquian-speaking Amerindian people of Connecticut

per (pər) *prep.* **1.** for each **2.** by **3.** in manner of

per- (*comb. form*) through, thoroughly, as in *perfect, perspicacious*

peradventure ('pərədvenchər) *obs. adv.* **1.** by chance; perhaps —*n.* **2.** chance; doubt

perambulate (pə'rambyəlāt) *vt.* **1.** walk through or over **2.** traverse —*vi.* **3.** walk about —**per'ambulator** *n.* baby carriage

per annum ('anəm) *Lat.* by the year

percale (pər'kāl) *n.* closely woven cotton fabric with smooth finish used for bedclothes

per capita ('kapitə) of or for each person

perceive (pər'sēv) *vt.* **1.** obtain knowledge of through senses **2.** observe **3.** understand —**per'ceivable** *a.* —**percepti'bility** *n.* —**per'ceptible** *a.* discernible, recognizable —**per'ception** *n.* **1.** faculty of perceiving **2.** intuitive judgment —**per'ceptive** *a.*

percentage (pər'sentij) *n.* proportion or rate per hundred —**per cent** in each hundred —**per'centile** *n.* one of 99 actual or notional values of a variable dividing its distribution into 100 groups with equal frequencies (*also* **'centile**)

perception (pər'sepshən) *n. see* PERCEIVE

perch[1] (pərch) *n.* any of a family of freshwater fishes

perch[2] (pərch) *n.* **1.** resting place, as for bird **2.** formerly, measure of 5½ yards —*vt.* **3.** place, as on perch —*vi.* **4.** alight, settle on fixed body **5.** roost **6.** balance

perchance (pər'chans) *adv. Poet.* perhaps

percipient (pər'sipiənt) *a.* **1.** having faculty of perception **2.** perceiving —*n.* **3.** one who perceives

percolate ('pərkəlāt) *v.* **1.** pass through fine mesh as liquor **2.** permeate **3.** filter —**perco'lation** *n.* —**'percolator** *n.* coffeepot with filter

percussion (pər'kushən) *n.* **1.** collision **2.** impact **3.** vibratory shock —**per'cussionist** *n. Mus.* person who plays percussion instrument —**percussion cap** detonator consisting of paper or thin metal cap containing material that explodes when struck —**percussion instrument** one played by being struck, *eg* drum, cymbals, piano

perdition (pər'dishən) *n.* spiritual ruin

peregrinate ('perigrināt) *vi.* travel about, roam —**peregri'nation** *n.*

peregrine ('perigrin) *n.* type of falcon

peremptory (pə'remptəri) *a.* **1.** authoritative, imperious **2.** forbidding debate **3.** decisive

perennial (pə'reniəl) *a.* **1.** lasting through the years **2.** perpetual, unfailing —*n.* **3.** plant living at least 3 years —**pe'rennially** *adv.*

perfect ('pərfikt) *a.* **1.** complete **2.** finished **3.** whole **4.** unspoilt **5.** faultless **6.** correct, precise **7.** excellent **8.** of highest quality —*n.* **9.** tense denoting a complete act —*vt.* (pər'fekt) **10.** improve **11.** finish **12.** make skillful —**per'fectable** *a.* capable of becoming perfect —**per'fection** *n.* **1.** state of being perfect **2.** faultlessness —**per'fectionism** *n.* **1.** *Philos.* doctrine that man can attain perfection in this life **2.** demand for highest standard of excellence —**per'fectionist** *n.* —**'perfectly** *adv.* —**perfect number** number that is the sum of all its divisors, *eg* 6 and 28 —**perfect participle** past participle

perfidy ('pərfidi) *n.* treachery, disloyalty —**per'fidious** *a.*

perforate ('pərfərāt) *vt.* make holes in, penetrate —**perfo'ration** *n.*

perforce (pər'fōrs) *adv.* of necessity

perform (pər'fōrm) *vt.* **1.** bring to completion **2.** accomplish; fulfill **3.** represent on stage —*vi.* **4.** function **5.** act part **6.** play, as on musical instrument —**per'formance** *n.* —**per'former** *n.*

perfume ('pərfyōōm) *n.* **1.** agreeable scent **2.** fragrance —*vt.* (pər'fyōōm) **3.** imbue with an agreeable odor, scent —**per'fumer** *n.* —**per'fumery** *n.* perfumes in general

perfunctory (pər'fungktəri) *a.* **1.** superficial **2.** hasty **3.** done indifferently

pergola ('pərgələ) *n.* **1.** area covered by plants growing on trellis **2.** the trellis

perhaps (pər'haps; *inf.* praps) *adv.* possibly

peri- (*comb. form*) round, as in *perimeter, period, periphrasis*

perianth ('perianth) *n.* outer part of flower, consisting of calyx and corolla

pericardium (peri'kärdiəm) *n.* membrane enclosing the heart (*pl.* **-dia** (-diə)) —**peri'cardiac** *or* **peri'cardial** *a.* —**pericar'ditis** *n.* inflammation of pericardium

peridot ('peridō) *n.* yellowish-green semiprecious stone, a variety of chrysolite

perigee ('perijē) *n.* point in its orbit around earth when moon or satellite is nearest earth

perihelion (peri'hēlyən) *n.* point in orbit of planet or comet when nearest to sun (*pl.* **-lia** (-lyə))

peril ('peril) *n.* **1.** danger **2.** exposure to injury —**'perilous** *a.* full of peril, hazardous

perimeter (pə'rimitər) *n.* **1.** the total outer boundary of a space or structure **2.** boundary of a figure —**perimeter fence** enclosure for the space bound

perineum (peri'nēəm) *n.* **1.** region of body between anus and genital organs **2.** surface of human trunk between thighs (*pl.* **-nea** (-'nēə))

period ('pēriəd) *n.* **1.** particular portion of time **2.** a series of years **3.** single occurrence of menstruation **4.** cycle **5.** conclusion **6.** full stop (.) at end of sentence **7.** complete sentence —*a.* **8.** (of furniture, dress, play *etc.*) belonging to particular time in history —**peri'odic** *a.* recurring at regular intervals —**peri'odical** *a./n.* **1.** (of) publication issued at regular intervals —*a.* **2.** of a period **3.** periodic —**perio'dicity** *n.* —**periodic law** principle that chemical properties of elements are periodic functions of their atomic numbers —**periodic table** tabular organization of the properties of elements in horizontal rows (periods) and vertical columns (groups)

peripatetic (peripə'tetik) *a.* itinerant, walking, traveling about

periphery (pə'rifəri) *n.* **1.** circumference **2.** surface, outside —**pe'ripheral** *a.* **1.** minor, unimportant **2.** of periphery

periphrasis (pə'rifrəsis) *n.* **1.** roundabout speech or phrase **2.** circumlocution (*pl.* **-rases** (-rəsēz)) —**peri'phrastic** *a.*

periscope ('periskōp) *n.* instrument, used *esp.* in submarines, for giving view of objects on different level —**periscopic** (peri'skopik) *a.*

perish ('perish) *vi.* **1.** die, waste away **2.** decay, rot —**perisha'bility** *n.* —**'perishable** *a.* **1.** that will not last long —*pl.n.* **2.** perishable food —**'perishing** *a.* **1.** *inf.* (of weather *etc.*) extremely cold **2.** *sl.* confounded

peristalsis (peri'stölsis, -'stolsis, -'stalsis) *n.* succession of waves of involuntary muscular contraction of various bodily tubes, *esp.* of alimentary tract (*pl.* **-ses** (-sēz))

peristyle ('peristīl) *n.* **1.** range of pillars surrounding building, square *etc.* **2.** court within this

peritoneum (peritə'nēəm) *n.* membrane lining internal surface of abdomen (*pl.* **-s, -nea** (-'nēə)) —**perito'nitis** *n.* inflammation of peritoneum

periwig ('periwig) *n. Hist.* wig

periwinkle ('periwingkəl) *n.* **1.** myrtle **2.** small edible shellfish (*also* **'winkle**)

perjure ('pərjər) *vt.* render (oneself) guilty of perjury —**'perjury** *n.* **1.** crime of false testimony on oath **2.** false swearing

perk[1] (pərk) *n. inf.* perquisite

perk[2] (pərk) *vi. inf.* (of coffee) percolate

perky ('pərki) *a.* lively, cheerful, jaunty, gay —**perk up** make, become cheerful

perm (pərm) *n. inf. see* PERMANENT (sense 3)

permafrost ('pərməfrost) *n.* permanently frozen ground

permanent ('pərmənənt) *a.* **1.** continuing in same state **2.** lasting —*n.* **3.** (treatment of hair producing) long-lasting style (*also* **permanent wave**) —**'permanence** *or* **'permanency** *n.* fixedness

permanganate (pər'manggənāt) *n.* salt of an acid of manganese

permeate ('pərmiāt) *vt.* **1.** pervade, saturate **2.** pass through pores of —**'permeable** *a.* admitting of passage of fluids

Permian ('pərmiən) *a.* **1.** of last period of Paleozoic era, between Carboniferous and Triassic periods —*n.* **2.** Permian period or rock system

permit (pər'mit) *vt.* **1.** allow **2.** give leave to (-tt-) —*n.* ('pərmit) **3.** warrant or license to do something **4.** written permission —**per'missible** *a.* allowable —**per'mission** *n.* authorization, leave, liberty —**per'missive** *a.* (too) tolerant, lenient, *esp.* sexually

permute (pər'myōōt) *vt.* change sequence of —**permu'tation** *n.* **1.** mutual transference **2.** *Math.* arrangement of a number of quantities in every possible order

pernicious (pər'nishəs) *a.* **1.** wicked or mischievous **2.** extremely hurtful **3.** having quality of destroying or injuring —**pernicious anemia** form of anemia characterized by lesions of spinal cord, weakness, diarrhea *etc.*

pernickety (pər'nikiti) *a. inf.* fussy, fastidious about trifles

pernio (ˈpərniō) *n.* chilblain (*pl.* **perniones** (pərniˈōnēz))

peroration (ˈperərāshən) *n.* concluding part of oration —ˈ**perorate** *vi.*

peroxide (pəˈroksīd) *n.* **1.** oxide of a given base containing greatest quantity of oxygen **2.** *see* **hydrogen peroxide** *at* HYDROGEN

perpendicular

perpendicular (pərpənˈdikyələr) *a.* **1.** at right angles to the plane of the horizon **2.** at right angles to given line or surface **3.** of style of English Gothic architecture characterized by vertical lines **4.** exactly upright —*n.* **5.** line falling at right angles on another line or plane

perpetrate (ˈpərpitrāt) *vt.* perform or be responsible for (deception, crime *etc.*) —**perpeˈtration** *n.* —ˈ**perpetrator** *n.*

perpetual (pərˈpechōōəl) *a.* **1.** continuous **2.** lasting for ever —**perˈpetually** *adv.* —**perˈpetuate** *vt.* **1.** make perpetual **2.** not allow to be forgotten —**perpetuˈation** *n.* —**perpetuity** (pərpəˈtyōōiti, -ˈtōō-) *n.* —**perpetual motion** motion of hypothetical mechanism that continues indefinitely without any external source of energy

perplex (pərˈpleks) *vt.* **1.** puzzle, bewilder **2.** make difficult to understand —**perˈplexity** *n.* puzzled or tangled state

perquisite (ˈpərkwizit) *n.* **1.** any incidental benefit from a certain type of employment **2.** casual payment in addition to salary

Perrier water (ˈperiā) trade name for mineral water, orig. from France

perry (ˈperi) *n.* fermented drink made from pears

per se (sā) *Lat.* by or in itself

persecute (ˈpərsikyōōt) *vt.* **1.** oppress because of race, religion *etc.* **2.** subject to persistent ill-treatment —**perseˈcution** *n.* —ˈ**persecutor** *n.*

persevere (pərsiˈvēər) *vi.* (*oft. with* in) persist, maintain effort —**perseˈverance** *n.* persistence

Persia (ˈpərzhə) *n. former name of* IRAN —ˈ**Persian** *a.* **1.** of ancient Persia or modern Iran —*n.* **2.** native or inhabitant of modern Iran; Iranian **3.** language of Iran or Persia in any of ancient or modern forms —**Persian cat** long-haired domestic cat —**Persian lamb** *see* KARAKUL

persimmon (pərˈsimən) *n.* **1.** any of several tropical trees typically having hard wood **2.** its fruit

persist (pərˈsist) *vi.* (*oft. with* in) continue in spite of obstacles or objections —**perˈsistence** *or* **perˈsistency** *n.* —**perˈsistent** *a.* **1.** persisting **2.** steady **3.** persevering **4.** lasting

person (ˈpərsən) *n.* **1.** individual (human) being **2.** body of human being **3.** *Gram.* classification, or one of the classes, of pronouns and verb forms according to the person speaking, spoken to, or spoken of —**perˈsona** *n.* assumed character (*pl.* **-nae** (-nē)) —ˈ**personable** *a.* good-looking —ˈ**personage** *n.* notable person —ˈ**personal** *a.* **1.** individual, private, or one's own **2.** of, relating to grammatical person —**persoˈnality** *n.* **1.** distinctive character **2.** a celebrity —ˈ**personalize** *vt.* **1.** endow with personal or individual qualities **2.** mark with person's initials, name *etc.* **3.** take personally **4.** personify —ˈ**personally** *adv.* in person —ˈ**personalty** *n.* personal property —ˈ**personate** *vt.* pass oneself off as —**persoˈnation** *n.* —**personal property** *Law* all property except land and interests in land that pass to heir —**in person** actually present

persona non grata (pərˈsōnə non ˈgratə, ˈgrätə) *Lat.* **1.** unacceptable or unwelcome person **2.** diplomat who is not acceptable to government to whom he is accredited (*pl.* ***personae non gratae*** (pərˈsōnē non ˈgratē, ˈgrätē))

personify (pərˈsonifī) *vt.* **1.** represent as person **2.** typify (**-ified, -ifying**) —**personifiˈcation** *n.*

personnel (pərsəˈnel) *n.* **1.** staff employed in a service or institution **2.** department that interviews or keeps records of employees

perspective (pərˈspektiv) *n.* **1.** mental view **2.** art of drawing on flat surface to give effect of solidity and relative distances and sizes **3.** drawing in perspective

perspicacious (pərspiˈkāshəs) *a.* having quick mental insight —**perspicacity** (pərspiˈkasiti) *n.*

perspicuous (pərˈspikyōōəs) *a.* **1.** clearly expressed **2.** lucid **3.** plain **4.** obvious —**perspiˈcuity** *n.*

perspire (pərˈspīər) *vi.* sweat —**perspiration** (pərspəˈrāshən) *n.* sweating

persuade (pərˈswād) *vt.* **1.** bring (one to do something) by argument, charm *etc.* **2.** convince —**perˈsuasion** *n.* **1.** art, act of persuading **2.** way of thinking or belief —**perˈsuasive** *a.*

pert (pərt) *a.* forward, saucy

pertain (pərˈtān) *vi.* (*oft. with* to) **1.** belong, relate, have reference (to) **2.** concern

pertinacious (pərtiˈnāshəs) *a.* obstinate, persistent —**pertinacity** (pərtiˈnasiti) *or* **pertiˈnaciousness** *n.* doggedness, resolution

pertinent (ˈpərtinənt) *a.* relating to the matter at hand —ˈ**pertinence** *or* ˈ**pertinency** *n.* relevance

perturb (pərˈtərb) *vt.* **1.** disturb greatly **2.**

alarm —**per'turbable** *a.* —**pertur'bation** *n.* agitation of mind

pertussis (pər'tusis) *n.* whooping cough

Peru (pə'ro͞o) *n.* country in South America bounded east by Brazil and Bolivia, south by Chile, west by the Atlantic Ocean and Ecuador and north by Colombia —**Pe'ruvian** *n./a.* (native or inhabitant) of Peru

peruke (pə'ro͞ok) *n. Hist.* wig

peruse (pə'ro͞oz) *vt.* read, *esp.* in slow and careful, or leisurely, manner —**pe'rusal** *n.*

pervade (pər'vād) *vt.* **1.** spread through **2.** be rife among —**per'vasion** *n.* —**per'vasive** *a.*

pervert (pər'vərt) *vt.* **1.** turn to wrong use **2.** lead astray —*n.* ('pərvərt) **3.** one who shows unhealthy abnormality, *esp.* in sexual matters —**per'verse** *a.* **1.** obstinately or unreasonably wrong **2.** self-willed **3.** headstrong **4.** wayward —**per'versely** *adv.* —**per'version** *n.*

pervious ('pərviəs) *a.* **1.** permeable **2.** penetrable, giving passage

Pesach ('pāsäk) *n. see* PASSOVER

peseta (pə'sātə; pā'sāta) *n.* monetary unit of Spain

peso ('pāsō) *n.* monetary unit of Mexico *etc.* (*pl.* **pesos** ('pāsōz; *Sp.* 'pāsos))

pessary ('pesəri) *n.* **1.** instrument used to support mouth and neck of uterus **2.** appliance to prevent conception **3.** vaginal suppository

pessimism ('pesimizəm) *n.* **1.** tendency to see the worst side of things **2.** theory that everything turns to evil —**'pessimist** *n.* —**pessi'mistic** *a.*

pest (pest) *n.* **1.** troublesome or harmful thing, person or insect **2.** *rare* plague —**'pesticide** *n.* chemical for killing pests, *esp.* insects —**pes'tiferous** *a.* **1.** troublesome **2.** bringing plague

pester ('pestər) *vt.* trouble or vex persistently, harass

pestilence ('pestiləns) *n.* epidemic disease, *esp.* bubonic plague —**'pestilent** *a.* **1.** troublesome **2.** deadly —**pesti'lential** *a.*

pestle ('pesəl) *n.* **1.** instrument with which things are pounded in a mortar —*v.* **2.** pound with pestle

pet[1] (pet) *n.* **1.** animal kept for companionship *etc.* **2.** person regarded with affection —*vt.* **3.** make pet of —*v.* **4.** *inf.* hug, embrace, fondle (**-tt-**)

pet[2] (pet) *n.* fit of sulkiness, *esp.* at what is felt to be a slight; pique —**'pettish** *a.* peevish, petulant

Pet. *Bible* Peter

petal ('petəl) *n.* white or colored leaflike part of flower —**'petaled** *a.*

petard (pi'tärd) *n.* formerly, an explosive device

peter ('pētər) *vi.* —**peter out** *inf.* disappear, lose power gradually

Peter ('pētər) *n. Bible* 21st and 22nd books of the N.T., epistles written by St. Peter to the Jews between 60 and 70 A.D.

Peter Pan youthful or immature man

Peter principle notion that in every hierarchy each employee tends to rise to his level of incompetence, thus every post tends to be filled by a person incompetent to execute its duties

pethidine ('pethidēn) *n.* water-soluble drug used as analgesic (*also* **me'peridine**)

petiole ('petiōl) *n.* **1.** stalk by which leaf is attached to plant **2.** *Zool.* slender stalk or stem, as between thorax and abdomen of ants —**'petiolate** *a.*

petit ('peti) *a. Law* small, petty —**petit bourgeois** *n.* **1.** section of middle class with lowest social status, as shopkeepers *etc.* **2.** member of this stratum (*pl.* **petits bourgeois** ('peti 'bo͞oərzhwäz)) (*also* **petite bourgeoisie, petty bourgeoisie**) —*a.* **3.** of petit bourgeois, *esp.* indicating sense of self-righteousness *etc.* —**petit four** any of various small fancy cakes and biscuits (*pl.* **petits fours** ('peti 'förz)) —**petit jury** jury of 12 persons impaneled to determine facts of case and decide issue pursuant to direction of court on points of law (*also* **petty jury**) —**petit mal** (mal) mild form of epilepsy characterized by periods of impairment or loss of consciousness for up to 30 seconds —**petit point 1.** small diagonal needlepoint stitch used for fine detail **2.** work done with such stitches

petite (pə'tēt) *a.* (of women) small, dainty

petition (pi'tishən) *n.* **1.** entreaty, request, *esp.* one presented to sovereign or parliament —*vt.* **2.** present petition to —**pe'titionary** *a.*

petrel ('petrəl) *n.* any of a family of sea birds

petrify ('petrifī) *vt.* **1.** turn to stone **2.** *fig.* make motionless with fear **3.** make dumb with amazement (**-ified, -ifying**) —**petri'faction** *or* **petrifi'cation** *n.*

petrochemical (petrō'kemikəl) *n.* **1.** any substance, such as acetone or ethanol, obtained from petroleum —*a.* **2.** of petrochemicals; related to petrochemistry —**petro'chemistry** *n.*

petrocurrency ('petrōkurənsi) *n.* currency oil-producing countries acquire as profit from oil sales to other countries

petrodollar ('petrōdolər) *n.* money earned by country by exporting of petroleum

petrolatum (petrə'lātəm) *n.* translucent gelatinous substance obtained from petroleum

petroleum (pə'trōliəm) *n.* mineral oil used as a lubricant, rust preventive in machinary, in manufacturing cosmetics and in medicine as a protective dressing —**petroleum jelly** *see* PETROLATUM

petrology (pe'troləji) *n.* study of rocks and their structure

petticoat ('petikōt) *n.* women's undergarment worn under skirts, dresses *etc.*

pettifogger ('petifogər) *n.* **1.** low-class lawyer **2.** one given to mean dealing in small matters

petty ('peti) *a.* **1.** unimportant, trivial **2.** small-minded, mean **3.** on a small scale —**petty cash** cash kept by firm to pay minor incidental expenses —**petty jury** *see* **petit jury** *at* PETIT —**petty officer** noncommissioned officer in Navy

petulant ('pechələnt) *a.* given to small fits of temper, peevish —'**petulance** *or* '**petulancy** *n.*

petunia (pi'tyōōnyə, -'tōōnyə) *n.* any plant of tropical Amer. genus with funnel-shaped purple or white flowers

pew (pyōō) *n.* **1.** fixed seat in church **2.** *inf.* chair, seat

pewit *or* **peewit** ('pēwit) *n. see* LAPWING

pewter ('pyōōtər) *n.* **1.** alloy of tin and lead **2.** ware made of this

peyote (pā'ōti) *or* **peyotl** (pā'ōtəl) *n. see* MESCAL

pH potential of hydrogen; measure of acidity or alkalinity of solution

PHA Public Housing Administration

phagocyte ('fagəsīt) *n.* blood cell that ingests and destroys foreign particles, bacteria and other cells —**phagocytic** (fagə'sitik) *a.*

phagocytosis (fagəsi'tōsis) *n.* ingestion of small particles by certain cells, *eg* leukocytes

phalanx ('fālangks) *n.* body of men formed in close array (*pl.* **-es, phalanges** (fa'lanjēz))

phalarope ('falərōp) *n.* any of a family of small wading birds

phallus ('faləs) *n.* **1.** penis **2.** symbol of it used in primitive rites (*pl.* **-es, -li** (-lī)) —'**phallic** *a.* —'**phallicism** *n.*

phantasm ('fantazəm) *n.* **1.** vision of absent person **2.** illusion —**phantasma'goria** *or* **phan'tasmagory** *n.* **1.** crowd of dim or unreal figures **2.** exhibition of illusions —**phan'tasmal** *a.* —'**phantasy** *n. see* FANTASY

phantom ('fantəm) *n.* **1.** apparition, specter, ghost **2.** fancied vision

Pharaoh ('fāərō) *n.* title of ancient Egyptian kings

Pharisee ('farisē) *n.* **1.** sanctimonious person **2.** hypocrite —**phari'saic(al)** *a.*

pharmaceutical (färmə'sōōtikəl) *or* **pharmaceutic** *a.* of pharmacy —**pharma'ceutics** *pl.n.* (*with sing. v.*) science of pharmacy —'**pharmacist** *n.* person qualified to dispense drugs —**pharma'cology** *n.* science concerned with the development of drugs, their use and the mechanism of their action —**pharmacopeia** (färməkə'pēə) *n.* official book with list and directions for use of drugs —'**pharmacy** *n.* **1.** preparation and dispensing of drugs **2.** dispensary

pharos ('fāəros) *n.* marine lighthouse or beacon

pharynx ('faringks) *n.* cavity forming back part of mouth and terminating in gullet (*pl.* **pharynges** (fə'rinjēz)) —**pharyn'geal** *or* **pha'ryngal** *a.* —**pharyn'gitis** *n.* inflammation of pharynx

phase (fāz) *n.* **1.** any distinct or characteristic period or stage in a development or chain of events —*vt.* **2.** arrange, execute in stages or to coincide with something else

Ph.D. Doctor of Philosophy (*also* **D.Phil.**)

pheasant ('fezənt) *n.* any of various game birds with bright plumage

pheno- *or before vowel* **phen-** (*comb. form*) **1.** showing, manifesting, as in *phenotype* **2.** indicating that molecule contains benzene rings, as in *phenobarbital*

phenobarbital (fēnō'bärbitōl) *n.* drug inducing sleep

phenol ('fēnōl) *n.* carbolic acid

phenomenon (fi'nominon) *n.* **1.** anything appearing or observed **2.** remarkable person or thing (*pl.* **phenomena** (fi'nominə)) —**phe'nomenal** *a.* **1.** relating to phenomena **2.** remarkable **3.** recognizable or evidenced by senses —**phe'nomenalism** *n.* **1.** theory that only phenomena are real and can be known **2.** tendency to think about things as phenomena only —**phe'nomenalist** *n./a.*

pheromone ('ferəmōn) *n.* substance secreted by one insect which affects the behavior of another insect of the same species

phew (fyōō, fōō) *interj.* exclamation of relief, surprise *etc.*

phi (fī) *n.* 21st letter in Gr. alphabet (Φ, φ) (*pl.* **-s**)

phial ('fīəl) *n.* small bottle for medicine *etc.*

Phil. **1.** *Bible* Philippians **2.** Philippines **3.** Philadelphia

philander (fi'landər) *vi.* (of man) flirt with women

philanthropy (fi'lanthrəpi) *n.* **1.** practice of doing good to one's fellow men **2.** love of mankind —**philan'thropic** *a.* loving mankind, benevolent —**phi'lanthropist** *or* '**philanthrope** *n.*

philately (fi'latəli) *n.* stamp collecting —**phila'telic** *a.* —**phi'latelist** *n.*

-phile *or* **-phil** (*comb. form*) person or thing having fondness for something specified, as in *bibliophile*

Philemon (fi'lēmən, fī-) *n. Bible* 18th book of the N.T., epistle written by St. Paul during his imprisonment addressed to Philemon

philharmonic (filər'monik, filhär-, filär-) *a.* **1.** fond of music **2.** (**P-** *when part of name*) denoting orchestra, choir *etc.* devoted to music

philhellene (fil'helēn) *n.* **1.** lover of Greece and Greek culture **2.** *European hist.* supporter of cause of Greek national independence —**philhel'lenic** *a.*

Philippians (fi'lipiənz) *pl.n.* (*with sing. v.*)

Bible 11th book of the N.T., epistle written by St. Paul to Christians of Philippi (Macedonia)

philippic (fi'lipik) *n.* bitter or impassioned speech of denunciation; invective

Philippines (fili'pēnz) *n.* country lying in the Pacific comprising 7100 islands and islets situated between 21° 25′ and 4° 23′ north latitude and between 116° and 127° east longitude —**Fili'pino** *a.* **1.** of the Philippines —*n.* **2.** native or inhabitant of the Philippines (*pl.* **-s**)

Philistine ('filistēn) *n.* **1.** ignorant, smug person **2.** member of non-Semitic people who inhabited ancient Philistia —*a.* **3.** (*sometimes* **p-**) boorishly uncultured **4.** of the ancient Philistines —'**philistinism** *n.*

Phillips ('filips) *n.* trade name for screw that has two slots crossing at center of head which can only be manipulated with a special screwdriver

philo- *or before vowel* **phil-** (*comb. form*) love of, as in *philology, philanthropic*

philology (fi'loləji) *n.* science of structure and development of languages —**philo'logical** *a.* —**phi'lologist** *or* **phi'lologer** *n.*

philos. **1.** philosopher **2.** philosophical

philosophy (fi'losəfi) *n.* **1.** pursuit of wisdom **2.** study of realities and general principles **3.** system of theories on nature of things or on conduct **4.** calmness of mind —**phi'losopher** *n.* one who studies, possesses or originates philosophy —**philo'sophic(al)** *a.* **1.** of, like philosophy **2.** wise, learned **3.** calm, stoical —**phi'losophize** *vi.* **1.** reason like philosopher **2.** theorize **3.** moralize

philter *or* **philtre** ('filtər) *n.* love potion

phlebitis (fli'bītis) *n.* inflammation of a vein

phlebotomy (fli'botəmi) *n.* the technique of withdrawing blood to treat disease (*also* **bloodletting**)

phlegm (flem) *n.* **1.** viscid substance formed by mucous membrane and ejected by coughing *etc.* **2.** calmness, sluggishness —**phlegmatic(al)** (fleg'matik(əl)) *a.* **1.** not easily agitated **2.** composed

phloem ('flōem) *n.* tissue in higher plants that conducts food substances to all parts of plant

phlogiston (flō'jistən) *n.* hypothetical substance formerly thought to be present in all combustible materials

phlox (floks) *n.* any of chiefly N Amer. genus of flowering plants (*pl.* **phlox, -es**)

phobia ('fōbiə) *n.* **1.** fear, aversion **2.** unreasoning dislike

-phobia (*n. comb. form*) extreme abnormal fear of or aversion to, as in *acrophobia, claustrophobia* —**-phobe** (*n. comb. form*) one that fears or hates, as in *xenophobe* —**-phobic** (*a. comb. form*)

Phoenician (fə'nishən, -'nēshən) *n.* **1.** member of ancient Semitic people of NW Syria **2.** extinct language of this people —*a.* **3.** of Phoenicia, Phoenicians or their language

phoenix ('fēniks) *n.* **1.** legendary bird **2.** unique thing

phone (fōn) *n./v. inf.* telephone —**phone-in** *n. Rad., T.V.* program in which listeners' or viewers' questions, comments *etc.* are telephoned to studio and broadcast live as part of discussion

-phone (*n. comb. form*) **1.** device giving off sound, as in *telephone* —(*a. comb. form*) **2.** speaking a particular language, as in *Francophone* —**-phonic** (*a. comb. form*)

phoneme ('fōnēm) *n. Linguis.* one of set of speech sounds in a language, that serve to distinguish one word from another —**pho'nemic** *a.* —**pho'nemics** *pl.n.* (*with sing. v.*) aspect of linguistics concerned with classification and analysis of phonemes of a language

phonetic (fə'netik) *a.* of vocal sounds —**phone'tician** *or* '**phonetist** *n.* —**pho'netics** *pl.n.* (*with sing. v.*) science of vocal sounds

phoney ('fōni) *a. see* PHONY

phono- *or before vowel* **phon-** (*comb. form*) sounds, as in *phonology*

phonograph ('fōnəgraf) *n.* instrument recording and reproducing sounds —**phono'graphic** *a.*

phonology (fə'noləji) *n.* **1.** study of speech sounds and their development **2.** system of sounds in a language —**phono'logic(al)** *a.* —**pho'nologist** *n.*

phony *or* **phoney** ('fōni) *a. inf.* **1.** counterfeit, sham, fraudulent **2.** suspect

phosphatidyl choline (fosfə'tīdil 'kōlēn) *see* LECITHIN

phosphorus ('fosfərəs) *n.* **1.** *Chem.* metalloid element *Symbol* P, at. wt. 31.0, at. no. 15 **2.** phosphorescent substance or body that shines in the dark —'**phosphate,** '**phosphide,** '**phosphite** *n.* compounds of phosphorus —'**phosphor** *n.* substance capable of emitting light when irradiated with particles of electromagnetic radiation —**phospho'resce** *vi.* exhibit phosphorescence —**phospho'rescence** *n.* faint glow in the dark —**phos'phoric** *a.* of or containing phosphorus with valence of five —'**phosphorous** *a.* of or containing phosphorus in trivalent state

photo ('fōtō) *n. inf.* photograph (*pl.* **-s**) —**photo finish** photo taken at end of race to show placing of contestants

photo- (*comb. form*) light, as in *photometer, photosynthesis*

photocell ('fōtəsel) *n.* device in which photoelectric or photovoltaic effect or photoconductivity is used to produce current or voltage when exposed to light or other electromagnetic radiation (*also* **photoelectric cell, electric eye**)

photochemistry (fōtō'kemistri) *n.* study of chemical action of light

photoconductivity (fōtōkonduk'tiviti) *n.* change in electrical conductivity of certain substances as a result of absorption of electromagnetic radiation

photocopy ('fōtəkopi) *n.* **1.** photographic reproduction —*vt.* **2.** make photocopy of —'**photocopier** *n.* instrument using light-sensitive photographic materials to reproduce written, printed or graphic work

photoelectricity (fōtōilek'trisiti) *n.* electricity produced or affected by action of light —**photoe'lectric** *a.* of electric or electronic effects caused by light or other electromagnetic radiation —**photoe'lectrically** *adv.* —**photoelectric cell** *see* PHOTOCELL

photoelectron (fōtōi'lektron) *n.* electron liberated from metallic surface by action of beam of light

photoflood ('fōtōflud) *n.* highly incandescent tungsten lamp used for indoor photography, television *etc.*

photogelatin (fōtō'jelətin) *n. see* COLLOTYPE

photogenic (fōtə'jenik) *a.* (*esp.* of person) capable of being photographed attractively

photograph ('fōtəgraf) *n.* **1.** picture made by chemical action of light on sensitive film —*vt.* **2.** take photograph of —**pho'tographer** *n.* —**photo'graphic** *a.* —**pho'tography** *n.*

photogravure (fōtəgrə'vyōōər, -'vōōər) *n.* **1.** process of etching, product of photography **2.** picture so reproduced

photolithography (fōtōli'thogrəfi) *n.* art of printing from photographs transferred to stone or metal plate —**photolitho'graphic** *a.*

photometer (fō'tomitər) *n.* instrument for measuring intensity of light —**pho'tometry** *n.*

photomontage (fōtōmon'täzh) *n.* **1.** technique of producing composite picture by combining several photographs **2.** composite picture so produced

photon ('fōton) *n.* pulse of light energy

photosensitive (fōtō'sensitiv) *a.* sensitive to electromagnetic radiation, *esp.* light —**photosensi'tivity** *n.* —**photo'sensitize** *vt.*

Photostat ('fōtəstat) *n.* **1.** trade name for apparatus for obtaining direct, facsimile, photographic reproductions of documents, manuscripts, drawings *etc.*, without printing from negatives —*vt.* **2.** take Photostat copy of

photosynthesis (fōtō'sinthisis) *n.* process by which green plant manufactures sugar from carbon dioxide and water in the presence of light

phototropism (fō'totrəpizəm) *n.* growth response of plant parts to stimulus of light

photovoltaic effect (fōtōvol'tāik) effect when electromagnetic radiation falls on thin film of one solid deposited on surface of dissimilar solid producing a difference in potential between the two materials

phrase (frāz) *n.* **1.** group of words **2.** pithy expression **3.** mode of expression —*vt.* **4.** express in words —**phraseology** (frāzi'oləji) *n.* manner of expression, choice of words —**phrasal verb** phrase consisting of verb and preposition, oft. with meaning different to the parts (*eg* take in)

phrenology (fri'noləji) *n.* **1.** formerly, study of skull's shape **2.** theory that character and mental powers are indicated by shape of skull —**phreno'logical** *a.* —**phre'nologist** *n.*

PHS Public Health Service

phthisis ('thīsis, 'thisis) *n. see* **tuberculosis** *at* TUBERCLE

phylactery (fi'laktəri) *n.* leather case containing religious texts worn by Jewish men

phylloxera (filok'sēərə, fi'loksərə) *n.* any of several plant lice which attack leaves and roots of grapevines

phylum ('fīləm) *n.* **1.** major taxonomic division of animals and plants that contain one or more classes **2.** group of related language families or linguistic stocks (*pl.* **-la** (-lə))

phys. 1. physical **2.** physician **3.** physics **4.** physiological **5.** physiology

physic ('fizik) *n.* **1.** *rare* medicine, *esp.* cathartic —*pl.* **2.** (*with sing. v.*) science of properties of matter and energy —'**physical** *a.* **1.** bodily, as opposed to mental or moral **2.** material **3.** of physics of body —'**physically** *adv.* —**phy'sician** *n.* qualified medical practitioner —'**physicist** *n.* one skilled in, or student of physics —**physical change** alteration that does not affect the molecular composition of a substance —**physical chemistry** chemistry concerned with way in which physical properties of substances depend on their chemical structure, properties and reactions —**physical education** training and practice in sports, gymnastics *etc.* —**physical geography** branch of geography that deals with natural features of earth's surface —**physical science** any science concerned with nonliving matter, such as physics, chemistry *etc.* —**physical training** method of keeping fit by following course of bodily exercises

physiognomy (fizi'onəmi, fizi'ognəmi) *n.* **1.** judging character by face **2.** face **3.** outward appearance of something

physiography (fizi'ogrəfi) *n.* science of the earth's surface —**physi'ographer** *n.*

physiology (fizi'oləji) *n.* science of normal function of living things —**physi'ologist** *n.*

physiotherapy (fiziō'therəpi) *n.* therapeutic use of physical means, as massage *etc.* —**physio'therapist** *n.*

physique (fi'zēk) *n.* bodily structure, constitution and development

pi[1] (pī) *n.* **1.** 16th letter in Gr. alphabet (Π, π) **2.** *Math.* ratio of circumference of circle to its diameter (*pl.* **-s**)

pi[2] *or* **pie** (pī) *n.* **1.** jumbled pile of printer's type **2.** jumbled mixture (*pl.* **pies**) —*vt.* **3.** spill and mix (set type) indiscriminately **4.** mix up (**pied** *pt./pp.*, '**piing,** '**pieing** *pr.p.*)

pia mater ('pīə 'mātər) innermost of three membranes that cover brain and spinal cord

pian (pi'an, pi'än, pyän) *n. see* YAWS

piano (pi'anō) *n.* **1.** (*orig.* **pianoforte** (pi'anəfört)) musical instrument with strings which are struck by hammers worked by keys (*pl.* **-s**) —*a./adv.* (pi'änō) **2.** *Mus.* to be performed softly —**pia'nissimo** *a./adv. Mus.* to be performed very quietly —**'pianist** *n.* performer on piano

piazza (pi'azə; *It.* 'pyattsa) *n.* square, marketplace

pibroch ('pēbrok, -brokh) *n.* form of bagpipe music

pica ('pīkə) *n.* **1.** printing type of 6 lines to the inch (*also* **em, pica em**) **2.** formerly, size of type equal to 12 point **3.** typewriter type size (10 letters to inch)

picador ('pikədör) *n.* mounted bullfighter with lance

picaresque (pikə'resk) *a.* (of fiction) episodic and dealing with adventures of rogues

piccalilli (pikə'lili) *n.* pickle of mixed vegetables in mustard sauce

piccaninny (pikə'nini) *n. see* PICKANINNY

piccolo ('pikəlō) *n.* woodwind instrument of flute family pitched an octave higher than flute (*pl.* **-s**)

pick[1] (pik) *vt.* **1.** choose, select carefully **2.** pluck, gather **3.** peck at **4.** pierce with something pointed **5.** find occasion for —*n.* **6.** act of picking **7.** choicest part —**picked** *a.* selected with care —**'pickings** *pl.n.* **1.** gleanings **2.** odds and ends of profit —**'picky** *a. inf.* fussy; finicky —**'picklock** *n.* instrument for opening locks —**pick-me-up** *n. inf.* **1.** tonic **2.** stimulating drink —**'pickpocket** *n.* one who steals from another's pocket —**pick-up** *n.* **1.** device for conversion of mechanical energy into electric signals, as in phonograph *etc.* **2.** small truck —**pick on** find fault with —**pick up 1.** raise, lift **2.** collect **3.** improve, get better **4.** accelerate

pick[2] (pik) *n.* tool with curved iron crossbar and wooden shaft, used for breaking up hard ground or masonry —**'pickax** *n.* pick

pickaback ('pikəbak) *n. see* PIGGYBACK

pickaninny *or* **piccaninny** (pikə'nini) *n. offens.* small Negro child

picket ('pikit) *n.* **1.** prong, pointed stake **2.** party of labor unionists posted to deter would-be workers during strike —*vt.* **3.** post as picket **4.** beset with pickets **5.** tether to peg —**picket fence** fence of pickets —**picket line** line of people acting as pickets

pickle ('pikəl) *n.* **1.** food preserved in brine, vinegar *etc.* **2.** liquid used for preserving **3.** awkward situation —*pl.* **4.** pickled vegetables —*vt.* **5.** preserve in pickle —**'pickled** *a. inf.* drunk

picnic ('piknik) *n.* **1.** pleasure excursion during which food is consumed outdoors —*vi.* **2.** take part in picnic (**'picnicked, 'picnicking**)

picot ('pēkō) *n.* any of pattern of small loops, as on lace

picric acid ('pikrik) powerful acid used in dyeing, medicine and as ingredient in certain explosives

Pict (pikt) *n.* member of ancient race of NE Scotland —**'Pictish** *a.*

pictograph ('piktəgraf) *n.* **1.** picture or symbol standing for word or group of words **2.** chart on which symbols are used to represent values (*also* **'pictogram**)

picture ('pikchər) *n.* **1.** drawing or painting **2.** mental image **3.** beautiful or picturesque object —*vt.* **4.** represent in, or as in, a picture —**pic'torial** *a.* **1.** of, in, with, painting or pictures **2.** graphic —*n.* **3.** newspaper with pictures —**pic'torially** *adv.* —**picturesque** (pikchə'resk) *a.* **1.** such as would be effective in picture **2.** striking, vivid —**picture card** *see* **face card** *at* FACE —**picture molding 1.** edge around framed picture **2.** molding or rail near top of wall from which pictures are hung (*also* **picture rail**) —**picture postcard** postcard with picture on one side —**picture window** large window having single pane of glass, usu. facing view

piddling ('pidling) *a. inf.* petty; trifling

pidgin ('pijin) *n.* lingua franca based on reduced English, French, Spanish or Portuguese vocabulary and smattering of native words —**Pidgin English 1.** language used by traders in Orient **2.** official language of Papua New Guinea

pie (pī) *n.* **1.** baked dish of meat or fruit *etc.*, usu. with pastry crust **2.** *obs.* magpie —**pie chart** circular graph divided into sectors proportional to magnitudes of quantities represented —**pie in the sky** *inf.* illusory hope of some future good

piebald ('pīböld) *a.* **1.** irregularly marked with black and white **2.** motley —*n.* **3.** piebald horse or other animal —**pied** *a.* **1.** piebald **2.** variegated

piece (pēs) *n.* **1.** bit, part, fragment **2.** single object **3.** literary or musical composition *etc.* **4.** *sl.* young woman **5.** small object used in checkers, chess *etc.* —*vt.* **6.** (*with* together) mend, put together —**piece goods** goods, *esp.* fabrics, made in standard widths and lengths —**'piecemeal** *adv.* by, in, or into pieces, a bit at a time —**'piecework** *n.* work paid for according to quantity produced

pièce de résistance (pyes də rāzēs'tās) *Fr.* principal item

pied-à-terre (pyāta'ter) *Fr.* apartment or other lodging for occasional use (*pl.* ***pieds-à-terre*** (pyāta'ter))

pier (pēər) *n.* **1.** structure running into sea as landing stage **2.** piece of solid upright masonry, *esp.* supporting bridge —**pier glass** tall narrow mirror designed to hang on wall between windows

pierce (pēərs) *vt.* **1.** make hole in **2.** make a

way through —'**piercing** *a.* keen, penetrating

Pierce (pēərs) *n.* **Franklin.** the 14th President of the U.S. (1853-57)

Pierrot ('pēərō; *Fr.* pye'rō) *n.* pantomime character, clown

piety ('pīiti) *n.* **1.** godliness **2.** devoutness, goodness **3.** dutifulness —'**pietism** *n.* exaggerated or affected piety

piezoelectricity (pēāzōilek'trisiti) *n. Phys.* **1.** production of electricity or electric polarity by applying mechanical stress to certain crystals **2.** converse effect in which stress is produced in crystal as result of applied potential difference

piffle ('pifəl) *n. inf.* rubbish, twaddle, nonsense

pig (pig) *n.* **1.** wild or domesticated mammal killed for pork, ham, bacon **2.** *inf.* greedy, dirty person **3.** *sl.* policeman **4.** oblong mass of smelted metal —*vi.* **5.** (of sow) produce litter (**-gg-**) —'**piggery** *n.* **1.** place for keeping, breeding pigs **2.** greediness —'**piggish** *a.* **1.** dirty **2.** greedy **3.** stubborn —'**piggy** *n.* child's word for a pig —'**piglet** *n.* young pig —**piggy bank** child's bank shaped like pig with slot for coins —**pig-headed** *a.* obstinate —**pig iron** crude iron produced in blast furnace and poured into molds —'**pigskin** *n.* **1.** skin of domestic pig **2.** leather made of this skin **3.** *inf.* football —*a.* **4.** made of pigskin —'**pigsty** *or* '**pigpen** *n.* **1.** pen for pigs; sty **2.** untidy place —'**pigswill** *n.* waste food *etc.* fed to pigs (*also* **pig's wash**) —'**pigtail** *n.* braid of hair hanging from back or either side of head

pigeon ('pijin) *n.* **1.** bird of many wild and domesticated varieties, oft. trained to carry messages **2.** *inf.* concern, responsibility (*oft. in* **it's his, her** *etc.* **pigeon**) —'**pigeonhole** *n.* **1.** compartment for papers in desk *etc.* —*vt.* **2.** defer **3.** classify —**pigeon-toed** *a.* with feet, toes turned inward

piggyback ('pigibak) *or* **pickaback** *n.* ride on back of man or animal, given to child

pigment ('pigmənt) *n.* coloring matter, paint or dye —**pigmen'tation** *n.* **1.** coloration in plants, animals or man caused by presence of pigments **2.** deposition of pigment in animals, plants or man

pigmy ('pigmi) *see* PYGMY

pike[1] (pīk) *n.* any of various types of large, predatory freshwater fishes

pike[2] (pīk) *n.* spear formerly used by infantry

pilaf *or* **pilaff** (pi'läf) *n.* any Turkish dish based on sautéed rice simmered in broth and seasonings

pilaster ('pīlastər, pi'lastər) *n.* square column, usu. set in wall

pilau *or* **pilaw** (pi'lō) *n. see* PILAF

pilchard ('pilchərd) *n.* small sea fish like the herring

pile[1] (pīl) *n.* **1.** heap **2.** great mass of building —*vt.* **3.** heap (up), stack (load) —*vi.* **4.** (*with in, out, off etc.*) move in a group —**pile-up** *n. inf.* multiple collision of vehicles —**atomic pile** nuclear reactor —**pile up 1.** gather or be gathered in pile **2.** *inf.* (cause to) crash

pile[2] (pīl) *n.* beam driven into the ground, *esp.* as foundation for building in water or wet ground —'**piledriver** *n.* machine for driving down piles

pile[3] (pīl) *n.* **1.** nap of cloth, *esp.* of velvet, carpet *etc.* **2.** down

piles (pīlz) *pl.n.* varicosed veins of rectum, hemorrhoids

pilfer ('pilfər) *v.* steal in small quantities

pilgrim ('pilgrim) *n.* **1.** one who journeys to sacred place **2.** wanderer, wayfarer —'**pilgrimage** *n.* —**the Pilgrim Fathers** *or* **Pilgrims** English Puritans who founded Plymouth Colony in Massachusetts

pill (pil) *n.* **1.** small ball of medicine swallowed whole **2.** anything disagreeable which has to be endured —'**pilling** *n.* the gathering of fibers into small balls on the surface of a fabric —'**pillbox** *n.* **1.** small box for pills **2.** small round hat —**the pill** oral contraceptive

pillage ('pilij) *v.* **1.** plunder, ravage, sack —*n.* **2.** seizure of goods, *esp.* in war **3.** plunder

pillar ('pilər) *n.* **1.** slender, upright structure, column **2.** prominent supporter

pillion ('pilyən) *n.* seat, cushion, for passenger behind rider of motorcycle or horse

pillory ('piləri) *n.* **1.** frame with holes for head and hands in which offender was formerly confined and exposed to public abuse and ridicule —*vt.* **2.** expose to ridicule and abuse **3.** set in pillory ('**pilloried,** '**pillorying**)

pillow ('pilō) *n.* **1.** cushion for the head, *esp.* in bed —*vt.* **2.** lay on, or as on, pillow —'**pillowcase** *or* '**pillowslip** *n.* removable washable cover for pillow

pilot ('pīlət) *n.* **1.** person qualified to fly an aircraft or spacecraft **2.** one qualified to take charge of ship entering or leaving harbor **3.** steersman **4.** guide —*a.* **5.** experimental and preliminary —*vt.* **6.** act as pilot to **7.** steer —'**pilotage** *n.* **1.** act of piloting ship or aircraft **2.** pilot's fee —**pilot fish** small fish of tropical and subtropical seas which oft. accompanies sharks —**pilot house** *Naut.* enclosed structure on bridge of vessel from which it can be navigated; wheelhouse —**pilot lamp** small light in electric circuit that lights when current is on —**pilot light 1.** small auxiliary flame lighting main burner in gas appliance *etc.* **2.** small electric light as indicator

pilpul ('pilpəl) *n. Judaism* **1.** intensive argument used in discussion of passages in the Talmud **2.** hairsplitting

pilule ('pilyōōl) *n.* small pill

Pima ('pēmə) *n.* **1.** (member of) Amerindian people of southern Arizona (*pl.* **-ma, -s**) **2.** the Uto-Aztecan language of the Pima —**Pima**

cotton variety of cotton grown in southwestern U.S. used *esp.* for clothing

pimento (pi'mentō) *n.* **1.** allspice **2.** sweet red pepper (*pl.* **-s**) (*also* **pimiento** (pi'mentō, -'myen-))

pi-meson ('pī'mezon) *n. see* PION

pimp (pimp) *n.* **1.** one who solicits for prostitute —*vi.* **2.** act as pimp

pimpernel ('pimpərnel, -nəl) *n.* any of several plants with small scarlet, blue or white flowers closing in dull weather

pimple ('pimpəl) *n.* small pus-filled spot on skin

pin (pin) *n.* **1.** short thin piece of stiff wire with point and head, for fastening **2.** wooden or metal peg or rivet —*vt.* **3.** fasten with pin **4.** seize and hold fast (**-nn-**) —**pinball machine** electrically operated table game, where small ball is shot through various obstacles —'**pincushion** *n.* small cushion in which pins are stuck ready for use —'**pinhead** *n.* **1.** head of pin **2.** something very small **3.** *sl.* stupid person —**pin money** trivial sum —'**pinpoint** *vt.* mark exactly —'**pinprick** *n.* **1.** slight puncture made (as if) by pin **2.** small irritation —*vt.* **3.** puncture (as if) with pin —'**pinstripe** *n.* in textiles, very narrow stripe in fabric or fabric itself —**pin tuck** narrow, ornamental fold, *esp.* on shirt fronts *etc.* —'**pinwheel** *n.* child's toy of paper or plastic mounted on stick designed to revolve when blown by wind —**on pins and needles** in a state of anxious suspense —**pins and needles** *inf.* tingling sensation in fingers *etc.* caused by return of normal blood circulation after its temporary impairment

pinafore ('pinəfōr) *n.* sleeveless garment fastened at back and worn as apron or dress

pince-nez (pans'nā; *Fr.* pēs'nā) *n.* eyeglasses kept on nose by spring (*pl.* **pince-nez**)

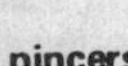

pincers

pincers ('pinsərz) *pl.n.* **1.** tool for gripping, composed of two limbs crossed and pivoted **2.** claws of lobster *etc.*

pinch (pinch) *vt.* **1.** nip, squeeze **2.** stint **3.** *inf.* steal **4.** *inf.* arrest —*n.* **5.** nip **6.** as much as can be taken up between finger and thumb **7.** stress **8.** emergency —'**pinchbar** *n.* crowbar that serves as fulcrum

pinchbeck ('pinchbek) *n.* **1.** zinc and copper alloy —*a.* **2.** counterfeit, flashy

pine[1] (pīn) *n.* **1.** any of a family of evergreen coniferous trees **2.** its wood —**pine cone** seed-producing structure of pine tree

pine[2] (pīn) *vi.* **1.** yearn **2.** waste away with grief

pineal ('pīniəl) *a.* shaped like pine cone —**pineal body** glandlike structure located in center of brain, function still unknown (*also* **epiphysis**)

pineapple ('pīnapəl) *n.* **1.** tropical plant with spiny leaves bearing large edible fruit **2.** the fruit

ping (ping) *n.* **1.** short high-pitched resonant sound, as of bullet striking metal or sonar echo —*vi.* **2.** make such noise

Ping-Pong ('pingpong) *n.* trade name for table tennis

pinion[1] ('pinyən) *n.* **1.** bird's wing —*vt.* **2.** disable or confine by binding wings, arms *etc.*

pinion[2] ('pinyən) *n.* small cogwheel

pink (pingk) *n.* **1.** pale reddish color **2.** garden plant **3.** best condition, fitness —*a.* **4.** of color pink —*vt.* **5.** pierce **6.** ornament with perforations or scalloped, indented edge —*vi.* **7.** (of engine) knock

pinkie *or* **pinky** ('pingki) *n.* little finger

pinnace ('pinis) *n.* ship's tender

pinnacle ('pinəkəl) *n.* **1.** highest pitch or point **2.** mountain peak **3.** pointed turret on buttress or roof

pinnate ('pināt) *a.* **1.** like feather **2.** (of compound leaves) having leaflets growing opposite each other in pairs on either side of stem

pinochle ('pēnukəl) *n.* card game usu. for four players in two partnerships played with deck of 48 cards comprising two each of ace, king, queen, jack, ten and nine in the four familiar suits the object of which is to score points by melding and taking tricks

piñon *or* **pinyon** ('pinyōn, -yon, -yən; pin'yōn) *n.* any of various low-growing pines of western N Amer. with edible seeds (*pl.* **-s, piñones** (pin'yōnēz)) —**piñon nuts** the edible seeds of the piñon

Pinot noir (pē'nō nwär) **1.** red table wine **2.** grape used to make this wine

pint (pīnt) *n.* liquid measure, half a quart, ⅛ gallon (.473 liter) —**pint-size** *or* **pint-sized** *a.* *inf.* very small

pintle ('pintəl) *n.* pivot pin

pinto ('pintō) *a.* **1.** marked with patches of white; piebald —*n.* **2.** pinto horse (*pl.* **-s**)

pin-up *n. inf.* picture of sexually attractive person, *esp.* (partly) naked

Pinyin ('pin'yin) *n.* official system of romanizing Chinese

pion ('pīon) *or* **pi-meson** *n. Phys.* meson having positive or negative charge and rest mass 273 times that of electron, or no charge and rest mass 264 times that of electron

pioneer (pīə'nēər) *n.* **1.** explorer **2.** early settler **3.** originator **4.** one of advance party preparing road for troops —*vi.* **5.** act as pioneer or leader

pious ('pīəs) *a.* **1.** devout **2.** righteous

pip[1] (pip) *n.* seed in fruit

pip[2] (pip) *n.* **1.** high-pitched sound used as time signal on radio **2.** spot on playing cards, dice or dominoes **3.** *inf.* star on junior officer's shoulder showing rank

pip[3] (pip) *n.* disease of fowl

pipe (pīp) *n.* **1.** tube of metal or other material **2.** tube with small bowl at end for smoking tobacco **3.** musical instrument, whistle **4.** wine cask —*pl.* **5.** bagpipe —*v.* **6.** play on pipe **7.** utter (something) shrilly —*vt.* **8.** convey by pipe **9.** ornament with a piping or fancy edging —**'piper** *n.* player of pipe or bagpipe —**'piping** *n.* **1.** system of pipes **2.** decoration of icing on cake **3.** fancy edging or trimming on clothing **4.** act or art of playing pipe, *esp.* bagpipe —**'pipeclay** *n.* **1.** white clay used in manufacture of tobacco pipes *etc.* and for whitening leather *etc.* —*vt.* **2.** whiten with pipeclay —**pipe cleaner** short length of thin wires twisted so as to hold tiny tufts of yarn: used to clean stem of tobacco pipe —**pipe dream** fanciful, impossible plan *etc.* —**'pipeline** *n.* **1.** long pipe for transporting oil, water *etc.* **2.** means of communication —**in the pipeline 1.** yet to come **2.** in process of completion *etc.* —**pipe down** *sl.* stop talking, making noise *etc.* —**pipe up 1.** commence singing or playing musical instrument **2.** speak up, *esp.* in shrill voice

pipette (pī'pet) *n.* slender glass tube to transfer fluids from one vessel to another

pipit ('pipit) *n.* any of various songbirds, *esp.* meadow pipit

pippin ('pipin) *n.* any of several kinds of apple

pipsqueak ('pipskwēk) *n.* *inf.* insignificant or contemptible person or thing

piquant ('pēkənt, -känt) *a.* **1.** pungent **2.** stimulating —**'piquancy** *or* **'piquantness** *n.*

pique (pēk) *n.* **1.** feeling of injury, baffled curiosity or resentment —*vt.* **2.** hurt pride of **3.** irritate **4.** stimulate

piqué (pi'kā, 'pēkā) *n.* firm cotton fabric with lengthwise corded effect

piranha (pi'ranyə, -'ränyə, -'ränə) *n.* any of various small voracious freshwater fishes of tropical Amer.

pirate ('pīrit) *n.* **1.** sea robber **2.** publisher *etc.* who infringes copyright —*n./a.* **3.** (person) broadcasting illegally —*vt.* **4.** use or reproduce (artistic work *etc.*) illicitly —**'piracy** *n.* —**piratic(al)** (pi'ratik(əl), pī-) *a.* —**piratically** (pi'ratikəli, pī-) *adv.*

piroshki *or* **pirozhki** (pirəsh'kē) *pl.n.* finger-sized, crescent-shaped pastries filled with savory mixture usu. served with Russian soups

pirouette (piro͞o'et) *n.* **1.** spinning round on the toe —*vi.* **2.** perform pirouette

Pisces ('pīsēz, 'pi-) *pl.n.* (fishes) 12th sign of zodiac, operative *c.* Feb. 19th-Mar. 20th —**piscatorial** (piskə'tōriəl) *or* **piscatory** ('piskətōri) *a.* of fishing or fishes —**piscine** ('pīsēn) *a.* of fish

pistachio (pi'stashiō, -'stäshiō) *n.* **1.** small hard-shelled, greenish, sweet-tasting nut **2.** tree producing it **3.** pale green color (*pl.* **-s**)

pistil ('pistil) *n.* seed-bearing organ of flower —**'pistillate** *a.* (of plants) **1.** having pistils but no anthers **2.** producing pistils

pistol ('pistəl) *n.* **1.** small firearm for one hand —*vt.* **2.** shoot with pistol

piston ('pistən) *n.* in internal-combustion engine, steam engine *etc.*, cylindrical part propelled to and fro in hollow cylinder by pressure of gas *etc.* to convert reciprocating motion to rotation

pit[1] (pit) *n.* **1.** deep hole in ground **2.** mine or its shaft **3.** depression **4.** part of theater occupied by orchestra (*also* **orchestra pit**) **5.** enclosure where animals were set to fight **6.** servicing, refueling area at auto racecourse —*vt.* **7.** set to fight, match **8.** mark with small dents or scars (**-tt-**) —**'pitfall** *n.* **1.** any hidden danger **2.** covered pit for catching animals or men —**'pithead** *n.* top of mine shaft and buildings *etc.* around it

pit[2] (pit) *n.* **1.** stone of cherry *etc.* —*vt.* **2.** extract stone from (fruit) (**-tt-**)

pit-a-pat (piti'pat) *adv.* **1.** with quick light taps —*vi.* **2.** make quick light taps (**-tt-**) —*n.* **3.** such taps

Pitcairn Island ('pitkāərn) administrative district of New Zealand lying in the South Pacific equidistant from New Zealand and Panama

pitch[1] (pich) *vt.* **1.** cast or throw **2.** set up **3.** set the key of (a tune) —*vi.* **4.** fall headlong **5.** (of ship) plunge lengthwise —*n.* **6.** act of pitching **7.** degree, height, intensity **8.** slope **9.** distance airscrew advances during one revolution **10.** distance between threads of screw, teeth of saw *etc.* **11.** acuteness of tone **12.** *Sport* field of play **13.** station of street vendor *etc.* **14.** *inf.* persuasive sales talk —**'pitcher** *n.* *Baseball* player who delivers ball to batter —**pitched battle 1.** battle ensuing from deliberate choice of time and place **2.** any fierce encounter, *esp.* one with large numbers —**'pitchfork** *n.* **1.** fork for lifting hay *etc.* —*vt.* **2.** throw with, as with, pitchfork —**pitch pipe** small pipe that sounds note or notes of standard frequency —**pitch in 1.** cooperate; contribute **2.** begin energetically —**pitch into 1.** assail physically or verbally **2.** get on with doing (something)

pitch[2] (pich) *n.* **1.** dark sticky substance obtained from tar or turpentine —*vt.* **2.** coat with this —**'pitchy** *a.* **1.** covered with pitch **2.** black as pitch —**pitch-black** *or* **pitch-dark** *a.* very dark —**pitch pine** any of various kinds of resinous pine

pitchblende ('pichblend) *n.* dark massive mineral yielding uranium and radium

pitcher ('pichər) *n.* large jug —**pitcher plant** insectivorous plant with leaves modified to form pitcher-like organs that attract and trap insects

pith (pith) *n.* **1.** soft innermost tissue in a

plant **2.** essential substance, most important part —**'pithily** *adv.* —**'pithless** *a.* —**'pithy** *a.* **1.** terse, cogent, concise **2.** consisting of pith —**pith helmet** lightweight hat made of pith that protects wearer from sun (*also* **to'pi**)

piton ('pēton) *n. Mountaineering* metal spike that may be driven into crevice and used to secure rope *etc.*

pitressin (pi'tresin) *n. see* VASOPRESSIN

pittance ('pitəns) *n.* **1.** small allowance **2.** inadequate wages

pitter-patter ('pitərpatər) *n.* **1.** sound of light rapid taps or pats, as of raindrops —*vi.* **2.** make such sound —*adv.* **3.** with such sound

pituitary (pi'tyōōiteri, -'tōō-) *a.* of, pert. to, endocrine gland at base of brain

pity ('piti) *n.* **1.** sympathy, sorrow for others' suffering **2.** regrettable fact —*vt.* **3.** feel pity for (**'pitied, 'pitying**) —**'piteous** *a.* **1.** deserving pity **2.** sad, wretched —**'pitiable** *a.* —**'pitiably** *adv.* —**'pitiful** *a.* **1.** woeful **2.** contemptible —**'pitiless** *a.* feeling no pity, hard, merciless

pityriasis rosea (piti'rīəsis rō'zēə) common skin disease of unknown origin marked by red scaly areas resembling ringworm

più (pyōō) *adv. Mus.* more (quickly *etc.*)

pivot ('pivət) *n.* **1.** shaft or pin on which thing turns —*vt.* **2.** furnish with pivot —*vi.* **3.** hinge on pivot —**'pivotal** *a.* **1.** of, acting as, pivot **2.** of crucial importance

pixie *or* **pixy** ('piksi) *n.* fairy

pizza ('pētsə) *n.* dish, *orig.* It., of baked disk of dough covered with wide variety of savory toppings —**pizzeria** (pētsə'rēə) *n.* place selling pizzas

pizzicato (pitsi'kätō) *a./n. Mus.* (note, passage) played by plucking string of violin *etc.* with finger

pl. **1.** place **2.** plate **3.** plural

placard ('plakärd) *n.* **1.** paper or card with notice on one side for posting up or carrying; poster —*vt.* **2.** post placards on **3.** advertise, display on placards

placate ('plākāt) *vt.* conciliate, pacify, appease —**'placatory** *a.*

place (plās) *n.* **1.** locality, spot **2.** position **3.** stead **4.** duty **5.** town, village, residence, buildings **6.** office, employment **7.** seat, space —*vt.* **8.** put in particular place **9.** set **10.** identify **11.** make (order, bet *etc.*) —**'placement** *n.* **1.** act of placing or state of being placed **2.** arrangement, position **3.** process of finding employment —**place kick** *Football* kick in which ball is placed in position before it is kicked —**place-kick** *v.* kick (ball) in this way —**place mat** small mat serving as individual table cover for person at meal —**place setting** flatware, tableware and glassware laid for one person at dining table

placebo (plə'sēbō) *n.* inactive substance given to unsuspecting patient as active drug (*pl.* **-s, -es**)

placenta (plə'sentə) *n.* organ formed in uterus during pregnancy, providing nutrients for fetus; afterbirth (*pl.* **-s, -tae** (-tē)) —**pla'cental** *a.*

placer ('plasər) *n.* surface sediment containing particles of gold or some other valuable mineral

placid ('plasid) *a.* **1.** calm **2.** equable —**pla'cidity** *n.* mildness, quiet

placket ('plakit) *n.* opening at top of skirt *etc.* fastened with buttons, zipper *etc.*

plagiarism ('plājərizəm) *n.* act of taking ideas, passages *etc.* from an author and presenting them as one's own —**'plagiarize** *v.*

plague (plāg) *n.* **1.** highly contagious disease, *esp.* bubonic plague **2.** *inf.* nuisance **3.** affliction —*vt.* **4.** trouble, annoy

plaice (plās) *n.* European flatfish

plaid (plad) *n.* **1.** long Highland cloak or shawl **2.** checked or tartan pattern

plain (plān) *a.* **1.** flat, level **2.** unobstructed, not intricate **3.** clear, obvious **4.** easily understood **5.** simple **6.** ordinary **7.** without decoration **8.** not beautiful —*n.* **9.** tract of level country —*adv.* **10.** clearly —**'plainly** *adv.* —**'plainness** *n.* —**plain chocolate** chocolate with slightly bitter flavor and dark color —**plain clothes** civilian dress, as opposed to uniform —**plain sailing** unobstructed course of action —**plain speaking** frankness, candor

plainsong ('plānsong) *n.* style of unison unaccompanied vocal music used in medieval Church

plaint (plānt) *n.* **1.** *Law* statement of complaint **2.** *obs.* lament —**'plaintiff** *n. Law* one who sues in court —**'plaintive** *a.* sad, mournful

plait (plāt, plat) *n.* **1.** braid of hair, straw *etc.* —*vt.* **2.** form or weave into plaits

plan (plan) *n.* **1.** scheme **2.** way of proceeding **3.** project, design **4.** drawing of horizontal section **5.** diagram, map —*vt.* **6.** make plan of **7.** arrange beforehand (**-nn-**)

planchette (plan'shet) *n.* small board used in spiritualism

plane

plane[1] (plān) *n.* **1.** smooth surface **2.** a level **3.** carpenter's tool for smoothing wood —*vt.* **4.** make smooth with plane —*a.* **5.** perfectly flat or level —**'planar** *a.* **1.** of plane **2.** lying in one plane; flat —**'planer** *n.* planing machine

plane[2] (plān) *vi.* **1.** (of airplane) glide **2.** (of boat) rise and partly skim over water —*n.* **3.** wing of airplane **4.** airplane

plane[3] (plān) *n.* sycamore

planet (ˈplanit) *n.* heavenly body revolving round the sun —ˈ**planetary** *a.* of planets

planetarium (planiˈteriəm) *n.* **1.** an apparatus that shows the movement of sun, moon, stars and planets by projecting lights on the inside of a dome **2.** building in which the apparatus is housed (*pl.* **-s, -ia** (-iə))

plangent (ˈplanjənt) *a.* resounding

plank (plangk) *n.* **1.** long flat piece of sawn timber —*vt.* **2.** cover with planks

plankton (ˈplangktən) *n.* minute animal and vegetable organisms floating in ocean

planography (plāˈnogrəfi) *n.* process of printing from a flat surface

plant (plant) *n.* **1.** any living organism feeding on inorganic substances and without power of locomotion **2.** such an organism that is smaller than tree or shrub **3.** equipment or machinery needed for manufacture **4.** building and equipment for manufacturing purposes **5.** heavy vehicles used for road building *etc.* —*vt.* **6.** set in ground to grow **7.** support, establish **8.** stock with plants **9.** *sl.* hide, *esp.* to deceive or observe —ˈ**planter** *n.* **1.** one who plants **2.** ornamental pot or stand for house plants —**plant kingdom** the plant species of the world collectively

plantain[1]

plantain[1] (ˈplantin) *n.* cosmopolitan weed with broad leaves and yellow flowers

plantain[2] (ˈplantin) *n.* **1.** tropical plant like banana **2.** its fruit

plantation (planˈtāshən) *n.* **1.** estate for cultivation of tea, tobacco *etc.* **2.** wood of planted trees **3.** formerly, colony

plantigrade (ˈplantigrād) *a.* walking on soles of feet

plaque (plak) *n.* **1.** ornamental plate, tablet **2.** plate of clasp or brooch **3.** filmy deposit on surfaces of teeth, conducive to decay

-plasm (*n. comb. form*) *Biol.* material forming cells, as in *protoplasm* —**-plasmic** (*a. comb. form*)

plasma (ˈplazmə) *or* **plasm** (ˈplazəm) *n.* clear yellowish fluid portion of blood —ˈ**plasmic** *a.* —**plasma expander** substance used as temporary substitute for whole blood to prevent loss of fluids

plaster (ˈplastər) *n.* **1.** mixture of lime, sand *etc.* for coating walls *etc.* **2.** piece of fabric spread with medicinal or adhesive substance —*vt.* **3.** apply plaster to **4.** apply like plaster —ˈ**plastered** *a. sl.* intoxicated; drunk —ˈ**plasterer** *n.* —ˈ**plasterboard** *n.* thin board in form of layer of plaster compressed between two layers of fiberboard, used to form or cover walls *etc.* —**plaster of Paris** (ˈparis) **1.** white powder that sets to hard solid when mixed with water, used for sculptures and casts *etc.* **2.** hard plaster produced when this powder is mixed with water

plastic (ˈplastik) *n.* **1.** any of a group of synthetic products derived from casein, cellulose *etc.*, which can be readily molded into any form and are extremely durable —*a.* **2.** made of plastic **3.** easily molded, pliant **4.** capable of being molded **5.** produced by molding **6.** *sl.* superficially attractive yet unoriginal or artificial —**plasticity** (plaˈstisiti) *n.* ability to be molded —**plasticizer** (ˈplastisīzər) *n.* any of number of substances added to materials to soften and improve flexibility *etc.* —**plastic surgery** repair or reconstruction of missing or malformed parts of the body for medical or cosmetic reasons

plate (plāt) *n.* **1.** shallow round dish **2.** flat thin sheet of metal, glass *etc.* **3.** utensils of gold or silver **4.** device for printing **5.** illustration in book **6.** device used by dentists to straighten children's teeth **7.** *inf.* set of false teeth —*vt.* **8.** cover with thin coating of gold, silver or other metal —ˈ**plateful** *n.* —ˈ**plater** *n.* —**plate glass** kind of thick glass used for mirrors, windows *etc.*

plateau (plaˈtō, ˈplatō) *n.* **1.** tract of level high land, tableland **2.** period of stability (*pl.* **-s, -eaux** (-ōz))

platelet (ˈplātlit) *n.* minute particle occurring in blood of vertebrates and involved in clotting of blood

platen (ˈplatən) *n.* **1.** *Print.* plate by which paper is pressed against type **2.** roller in typewriter

platform (ˈplatfōrm) *n.* **1.** raised level surface or floor, stage **2.** raised area in station from which passengers board trains **3.** political program

platinum (ˈplatinəm) *n. Chem.* grayish-white noble metal *Symbol* Pt., at. wt. 195.1, at. no. 78 —**platinum-blond** *or* **platinum-blonde** *a.* **1.** (of hair) of pale silver-blond color **2.** having hair of this color

platitude (ˈplatityo͞od, -to͞od) *n.* commonplace remark —**platiˈtudinous** *a.*

Platonic (pləˈtonik) *a.* **1.** of Plato or his philosophy **2.** (*oft.* **p-**) (of love) purely spiritual, friendly —**Platonism** (ˈplātənizəm) *n.* **1.** teachings of Plato, Gr. philosopher, and his followers **2.** philosophical theory that meanings of general words are real entities (forms) and describe particular objects *etc.* by virtue of some relationship of these to form —**Platonist** (ˈplātənist) *n.*

platoon (pləˈtōōn) *n.* body of soldiers employed as unit

platter (ˈplatər) *n.* flat dish

platypus (ˈplatipəs) *n. see* **duck-billed platypus** *at* DUCK[1]

plaudit (ˈplödit) *n.* act of applause, hand-clapping

plausible (ˈplözəbəl) *a.* **1.** apparently fair or reasonable **2.** fair-spoken —**plausiˈbility** *n.*

play (plā) *vi.* **1.** amuse oneself **2.** take part in game **3.** behave carelessly; trifle **4.** act a part on the stage **5.** perform on musical instrument **6.** move with light or irregular motion, flicker *etc.* —*vt.* **7.** contend with in game **8.** take part in (game) **9.** act the part of **10.** perform (music) **11.** perform on (instrument) **12.** use, work (instrument) —*n.* **13.** dramatic piece or performance **14.** sport **15.** amusement **16.** manner of action or conduct **17.** activity **18.** brisk or free movement **19.** gambling —ˈ**player** *n.* —ˈ**playful** *a.* lively —ˈ**playback** *n.* **1.** act or process of reproducing recording, *esp.* on magnetic tape **2.** part of tape recorder serving to or used for reproducing recorded material —ˈ**playbill** *n.* **1.** poster or bill advertising play **2.** program of play —ˈ**playboy** *n.* man, *esp.* of private means, who devotes himself to the pleasures of nightclubs, female company *etc.* —ˈ**playground** *n.* **1.** outdoor area for children's play, *esp.* one having swings *etc.* or adjoining school **2.** place popular as resort —ˈ**playgroup** *n.* group of young children playing regularly under adult supervision —ˈ**playhouse** *n.* theater —**playing card** one of set of 52 cards used in card games —ˈ**playmate** *or* ˈ**playfellow** *n.* friend or partner in play or recreation —**play-off** *n.* **1.** *Sport* extra contest to decide winner when competitors are tied **2.** contest or series of games to determine championship —ˈ**playpen** *n.* small enclosure, usu. portable, in which young child can be left to play in safety —ˈ**plaything** *n.* toy —ˈ**playwright** *n.* author of plays —**play back** reproduce (recorded material) on (magnetic tape) by means of tape recorder —**play off 1.** (*usu. with* against) manipulate as if playing game **2.** take part in play-off —**play on words** pun

plaza (ˈplazə, ˈpläzə) *n.* **1.** open space or square **2.** complex of shops *etc.*

plea (plē) *n.* **1.** entreaty **2.** statement of prisoner or defendant **3.** excuse —**plead** *vi.* **1.** make earnest appeal **2.** address court of law —*vt.* **3.** bring forward as excuse or plea (ˈ**pleaded** *or* **pled** (pled), ˈ**pleading**)

please (plēz) *vt.* **1.** be agreeable to **2.** gratify **3.** delight —*vi.* **4.** like, be willing —*adv.* **5.** word of request —**pleasance** (ˈplezəns) *n.* secluded part of garden —**pleasant** (ˈplezənt) *a.* pleasing, agreeable —**pleasantly** (ˈplezəntli) *adv.* —**pleasantry** (ˈplezəntri) *n.* joke, humor —**pleasurable** (ˈplezhərəbəl) *a.* giving pleasure —**pleasure** (ˈplezhər) *n.* **1.** enjoyment, satisfaction **2.** will, choice

pleat (plēt) *n.* **1.** any of various types of fold made by doubling material back on itself —*vt.* **2.** make, gather into pleats

plebeian (pləˈbēən) *a.* **1.** belonging to the common people **2.** low or rough —*n.* **3.** one of the common people (*also* (*offens. sl.*) **pleb** (pleb))

plebiscite (ˈplebisīt, -sit) *n.* decision by direct voting of the electorate

plectrum (ˈplektrəm) *or* **plectron** (ˈplektrən) *n.* small implement for plucking strings of guitar *etc.* (*pl.* **-tra** (-trə), **-s**)

pledge (plej) *n.* **1.** promise **2.** thing given over as security **3.** toast —*vt.* **4.** promise formally **5.** bind or secure by pledge **6.** give over as security

Pleiocene (ˈplīəsēn) *n. see* PLIOCENE

Pleistocene (ˈplīstəsēn) *a.* **1.** of glacial period of formation —*n.* **2.** Pleistocene epoch or rock series

plenary (ˈplēnəri, ˈplen-) *a.* **1.** complete, without limitations, absolute **2.** (of meeting *etc.*) with all members present

plenipotentiary (plenipəˈtenchəri) *a./n.* (envoy) having full powers

plenitude (ˈplenityōōd, -tōōd) *n.* **1.** completeness, entirety **2.** abundance

plenty (ˈplenti) *n.* **1.** abundance **2.** quite enough —ˈ**plenteous** *a.* **1.** ample **2.** rich **3.** copious —ˈ**plentiful** *a.* abundant

plenum (ˈplenəm, ˈplēnəm) *n.* **1.** space as considered to be full of matter (opposed to vacuum) **2.** condition of fullness (*pl.* **-s, -na** (-nə))

plethora (ˈplethərə) *n.* oversupply

pleura (ˈplōōrə) *n.* membrane lining the chest and covering the lungs (*pl.* **pleurae** (ˈplōōrē)) —ˈ**pleurisy** *n.* inflammation of the pleura

pliable (ˈplīəbəl) *a.* easily bent or influenced —**pliaˈbility** *n.* —ˈ**pliancy** *n.* —ˈ**pliant** *a.* pliable

pliers (ˈplīərz) *pl.n.* tool with hinged arms and jaws for gripping

plight[1] (plīt) *n.* **1.** distressing state **2.** predicament

plight[2] (plīt) *vt.* promise —**plight one's troth** make a promise, *esp.* of marriage

plinth (plinth) *n.* **1.** square slab at base of column **2.** narrow rectangular platform to form toe space on furniture and appliances

Pliocene *or* **Pleiocene** (ˈplīəsēn) *a.* **1.** of the most recent tertiary deposits —*n.* **2.** Pliocene epoch or rock series

plissé (pliˈsā) *n.* **1.** fabric with wrinkled finish, achieved by treatment involving caustic soda **2.** such finish on fabric

P.L.O. Palestine Liberation Organization

plod (plod) *vi.* walk or work doggedly (**-dd-**)

plop (plop) *n.* **1.** sound of object falling into

water without splash —*v.* **2.** (cause to) fall with such sound (**-pp-**)

plosion ('plōzhən) *n. Phonet.* sound of abrupt break or closure, *esp.* audible release of stop (*also* **ex'plosion**) —**'plosive** *Phonet. a.* **1.** accompanied by plosion —*n.* **2.** plosive consonant; stop

plot[1] (plot) *n.* **1.** secret plan, conspiracy **2.** essence of story, play *etc.* —*vt.* **3.** devise secretly **4.** mark position of **5.** make map of —*vi.* **6.** conspire (**-tt-**)

plot[2] (plot) *n.* small piece of land

plover ('pluvər) *n.* any of various shore birds, typically with round head, straight bill and long pointed wings

plow (plow) *n.* **1.** implement for turning up soil **2.** similar implement for clearing snow *etc.* —*vt.* **3.** turn up with plow, furrow —*vi.* **4.** (*with* through) work (at) slowly —**'plowman** *n.* —**'plowshare** *n.* blade of plow

ploy (ploi) *n.* **1.** stratagem **2.** occupation **3.** prank

pluck (pluk) *vt.* **1.** pull, pick off **2.** strip **3.** sound strings of (guitar *etc.*) with fingers, plectrum —*n.* **4.** courage **5.** sudden pull or tug —**'pluckily** *adv.* —**'plucky** *a.* courageous

plug (plug) *n.* **1.** thing fitting into and filling a hole **2.** *Elec.* device connecting appliance to electricity supply **3.** tobacco pressed hard **4.** *inf.* recommendation, advertisement —*vt.* **5.** stop with plug **6.** *inf.* advertise (product, show *etc.*) by constant repetition, as on television **7.** *sl.* punch **8.** *sl.* shoot —*vi.* **9.** *inf.* (*with* away) work hard (**-gg-**) —**plug in** connect (electrical appliance) with power source by means of plug

plum (plum) *n.* **1.** stone fruit **2.** tree bearing it **3.** choicest part, piece, position *etc.* —*a.* **4.** choice **5.** of dark reddish-purple color —**'plummy** *a.* of plums

plumage ('plo͞omij) *n. see* PLUME

plumb (plum) *n.* **1.** ball of lead (**plumb bob**) attached to string used for sounding, finding the perpendicular *etc.* —*a.* **2.** perpendicular —*adv.* **3.** perpendicularly **4.** exactly **5.** downright **6.** honestly **7.** exactly —*vt.* **8.** set exactly upright **9.** find depth of **10.** reach, undergo **11.** equip with, connect to plumbing system —**'plumber** *n.* worker who attends to water and sewage systems —**'plumbing** *n.* **1.** trade of plumber **2.** system of water and sewage pipes —**'plumbline** *n.* cord with plumb attached

plume (plo͞om) *n.* **1.** feather **2.** ornament of feathers or horsehair —*vt.* **3.** furnish with plumes **4.** pride (oneself) —**'plumage** *n.* bird's feathers collectively

plummet ('plumit) *vi.* **1.** plunge headlong —*n.* **2.** plumbline

plump[1] (plump) *a.* **1.** of rounded form, moderately fat, chubby —*v.* **2.** (*oft. with* up *or* out) make, become plump

plump[2] (plump) *vi.* **1.** sit, fall abruptly —*vt.* **2.** drop, throw abruptly —*adv.* **3.** suddenly **4.** heavily **5.** directly —**plump for** choose, vote only for

plunder ('plundər) *vt.* **1.** take by force **2.** rob systematically —*vi.* **3.** rob —*n.* **4.** pillage **5.** booty, spoils

plunge (plunj) *vt.* **1.** put forcibly —*vi.* **2.** throw oneself **3.** enter, rush with violence **4.** descend very suddenly —*n.* **5.** dive —**'plunger** *n.* **1.** rubber suction cap to unblock drains **2.** pump piston —**take the plunge** *inf.* **1.** embark on risky enterprise **2.** get married

plunk (plungk) *v.* **1.** pluck (string of banjo *etc.*) **2.** drop suddenly

pluperfect (plo͞o'pərfikt) *a./n.* (tense) expressing action completed before past point of time

plural ('plo͝orəl) *a.* **1.** of, denoting more than one person or thing —*n.* **2.** word in its plural form —**'pluralism** *n.* **1.** holding of more than one appointment, vote *etc.* **2.** coexistence of different social groups *etc.* in one society —**'pluralist** *n./a.* —**plu'rality** *n.* majority of votes *etc.*

plus (plus) *prep.* **1.** with addition of (*usu.* indicated by the sign +) —*a.* **2.** to be added **3.** positive —**plus fours** men's baggy knickerbockers reaching below knee

plush (plush) *n.* **1.** fabric with long nap, long-piled velvet —*a.* **2.** luxurious

Pluto[1] ('plo͞otō) *n. Gr. myth.* god of underworld; Hades —**Plu'tonian** *a.* pert. to Pluto or the infernal regions, dark —**plutonic** (plo͞o'tonik) *a.* (of igneous rocks) derived from magma that has cooled and solidified below surface of earth

Pluto[2] ('plo͞otō) *n.* second smallest planet and farthest known from sun

plutocracy (plo͞o'tokrəsi) *n.* **1.** government by the rich **2.** state ruled thus **3.** wealthy class —**'plutocrat** *n.* wealthy man —**pluto'cratic** *a.*

plutonium (plo͞o'tōniəm) *n. Chem.* transuranic element *Symbol* Pu, at. wt. 242, at. no. 94

pluvial ('plo͞oviəl) *a.* of, caused by the action of rain

ply[1] (plī) *vt.* **1.** wield **2.** work at **3.** supply pressingly **4.** urge **5.** keep busy —*vi.* **6.** go to and fro, run regularly (**plied, 'plying**)

ply[2] (plī) *n.* **1.** fold or thickness **2.** strand of yarn —**'plywood** *n.* board of thin layers of wood glued together with grains at right angles

Pm *Chem.* promethium

p.m. *or* **P.M.** **1.** post meridiem (*Lat.*, after noon) **2.** postmortem

PMS premenstrual syndrome

PMT premenstrual tension

pneumatic (nyo͞o'matik, no͞o-) *a.* of, worked by, inflated with wind or air —**pneu'matics** *pl.n.* (*with sing. v.*) branch of physics concerned with mechanical properties of gases, *esp.* air

pneumoconiosis ('nyo͞omōkōni'ōsis, 'no͞o-)

n. any lung disorder caused by inhaling dust particles

pneumonia (nyōō'mōnyə, nōō-) *n.* inflammation of the lungs

pneumothorax (nyōōmə'thōraks, nōōmə-) *n.* the presence of air between the lung and chest wall, formerly induced as treatment for tuberculosis

Po *Chem.* polonium

P.O. 1. Petty Officer **2.** Post Office

poach[1] (pōch) *vt.* **1.** catch (game) illegally **2.** trample, make swampy or soft —*vi.* **3.** trespass for purpose of poaching **4.** encroach

poach[2] (pōch) *vt.* simmer (eggs, fish *etc.*) gently in water *etc.* —**'poacher** *n.*

pock (pok) *n.* pustule, as in smallpox *etc.*

pocket ('pokit) *n.* **1.** small bag inserted in garment **2.** cavity filled with ore *etc.* **3.** socket, cavity, pouch or hollow **4.** mass of water or air differing from that surrounding it **5.** isolated group or area —*vt.* **6.** put into one's pocket **7.** appropriate, steal —*a.* **8.** small —**'pocketbook** *n.* **1.** small bag or case for money, papers *etc.* **2.** handbag —**'pocketknife** *n.* small knife with one or more blades that fold into handle —**pocket money** money for small, occasional expenses

poco ('pōkō; *It.* 'pōkō) *or* **un poco** *a./adv.* *Mus.* little; to a small degree

pod (pod) *n.* **1.** long seed vessel, as of peas, beans *etc.* —*vi.* **2.** form pods —*vt.* **3.** shell (**-dd-**)

-pod *or* **-pode** (*comb. form*) indicating certain type or number of feet, as in *arthropod, tripod*

podiatry (pə'dīətri) *n.* paramedical specialty dealing with diagnosis and treatment of disorders of the feet (*also* **chiropody**)

podium ('pōdiəm) *n.* small raised platform (*pl.* **-s, -dia** (-diə))

poem ('pōim) *n.* imaginative composition in rhythmic lines —**poesy** ('pōizi) *n.* poetry —**'poet** *n.* writer of poems —**poetaster** ('pōitastər) *n.* would-be or inferior poet —**po'etic(al)** *a.* —**po'etically** *adv.* —**'poetry** *n.* art or work of poet, verse —**poetic justice** fitting retribution —**poetic license** justifiable departure from conventional rules of form, fact *etc.*, as in poetry

pogey *or* **pogy** ('pōgi) *n.* **C** *sl.* **1.** unemployment insurance **2.** dole

pogo stick ('pōgō) stout pole with handle at top, steps for feet and spring at bottom, so that user can spring up, down and along on it

pogrom ('pōgrəm) *n.* organized persecution and massacre, *esp.* of Jews in Russia

poignant ('poinyənt, -nənt) *a.* **1.** moving **2.** biting, stinging **3.** vivid **4.** pungent —**'poignancy** *or* **'poignance** *n.*

poinciana (poinsi'anə) *n.* tropical tree with scarlet flowers

poinsettia (poin'setə, -'setiə) *n. orig.* Amer. shrub, widely cultivated for its clusters of scarlet bracts, resembling petals

point (point) *n.* **1.** dot, mark **2.** punctuation mark **3.** item, detail **4.** unit of value **5.** position, degree, stage **6.** moment **7.** gist of an argument **8.** purpose **9.** striking or effective part or quality **10.** essential object or thing **11.** sharp end **12.** single unit in scoring **13.** headland **14.** one of direction marks of compass **15.** movable rail changing train to other rails **16.** fine kind of lace **17.** act of pointing **18.** unit of academic credit **19.** printing unit, one twelfth of a pica —*pl.* **20.** electrical contacts in distributor of engine —*vi.* **21.** show direction or position by extending finger **22.** direct attention **23.** (of dog) indicate position of game by standing facing it —*vt.* **24.** aim, direct **25.** sharpen **26.** fill up joints of (brickwork *etc.*) with mortar **27.** give value to (words *etc.*) —**'pointed** *a.* **1.** sharp **2.** direct, telling —**'pointedly** *adv.* —**'pointer** *n.* **1.** index **2.** indicating rod *etc.* used for pointing **3.** indication **4.** dog trained to point —**'pointless** *a.* **1.** blunt **2.** futile, irrelevant —**point-blank** *a.* **1.** aimed horizontally **2.** plain, blunt —*adv.* **3.** with level aim (there being no necessity to elevate for distance) **4.** at short range —**point of no return 1.** point at which irreversible commitment must be made to action *etc.* **2.** point in journey at which, if one continues, supplies will be insufficient for return to starting place —**point of order** question raised in meeting as to whether rules governing procedures are being breached (*pl.* **points of order**) —**point of view 1.** position from which someone or something is observed **2.** mental viewpoint or attitude (*pl.* **points of view**)

pointillism ('pwantēizəm, 'pointilizəm) *n.* technique of painting elaborated from impressionism, in which dots of unmixed color are juxtaposed on white ground so that from distance they fuse in viewer's eye into appropriate intermediate tones —**pointillist** (pwantē'ēst, 'pointəlist) *n./a.*

poise (poiz) *n.* **1.** composure **2.** self-possession **3.** balance, equilibrium, carriage (of body *etc.*) —*v.* **4.** (cause to) be balanced or suspended —*vt.* **5.** hold in readiness

poison ('poizən) *n.* **1.** substance which kills or injures when introduced into living organism —*vt.* **2.** give poison to **3.** infect **4.** pervert, spoil —**'poisoner** *n.* —**'poisonous** *a.* —**poison control center** center, usu. in hospital, coordinating data on all aspects of poisoning and making such information available to physicians —**poison ivy** N Amer. shrub or climbing plant that causes itching rash on contact —**poison oak** either of two plants, vine found on west coast of U.S. and shrub in central and eastern U.S. with same effect as poison ivy —**poison-pen letter** malicious anonymous letter —**poison sumac** shrub found in swamps from Maine to Florida with same effect as poison ivy

poke[1] (pōk) *vt.* **1.** push, thrust with finger,

stick *etc.* **2.** thrust —*vi.* **3.** make thrusts **4.** pry —*n.* **5.** act of poking —**'poker** *n.* metal rod for poking fire —**'poky** *or* **'pokey** *a.* small, confined, cramped

poke[2] (pōk) *n.* —**pig in a poke** something bought *etc.* without previous inspection

poker ('pōkər) *n.* any of various card games in which player with highest card or hand wins the pool or kitty —**poker face** *inf.* face without expression, as of poker player concealing value of his cards —**poker-faced** *a.*

pol. **1.** political **2.** politics

Pol. **1.** Poland **2.** Polish

Poland ('pōlənd) *n.* country in Europe bounded north by the Baltic Sea, east by the U.S.S.R., south by Czechoslovakia and west by the German Democratic Republic —**Pole** *n.* native or inhabitant of Poland —**'Polish** *n./a.* **1.** (of) Polish language which is a branch of Balto-Slavic —*a.* **2.** of Poles and Poland

polar ('pōlər) *a. see* POLE[2]

Polaris (pə'laris, -'läris) *n.* **1.** brightest star in constellation Ursa Minor, situated slightly less than 1° from north celestial pole (*also* **Pole Star, North Star**) **2.** type of Amer. ballistic missile, usu. fired by submarine

Polaroid ('pōləroid) *n.* trade name for: **1.** type of material which polarizes light **2.** camera that develops print very quickly inside itself

polder ('pōldər, 'pol-) *n.* land reclaimed from the sea

pole[1] (pōl) *n.* **1.** long rounded piece of wood *etc.* —*vt.* **2.** propel with pole —**pole-vault** *vi.* perform or compete in the pole vault —**pole-vaulter** *n.* —**the pole vault** field event in which competitors attempt to clear high bar with aid of long flexible pole

pole[2] (pōl) *n.* **1.** either of the ends of axis of earth or celestial sphere **2.** either of opposite ends of magnet, electric cell *etc.* —**'polar** *a.* **1.** pert. to the N and S pole, or to magnetic poles **2.** directly opposite in tendency, character *etc.* —**po'larity** *n.* —**polari'zation** *n.* —**'polarize** *vt.* give polarity to —**polar bear** white Arctic bear —**polar circle** either Arctic Circle or Antarctic Circle —**the Pole Star** star closest to N celestial pole at any particular time, at present Polaris

poleax ('pōlaks) *n.* **1.** battle-ax —*vt.* **2.** hit, fell as with poleax

polecat ('pōlkat) *n.* small animal of weasel family

polemic (pə'lemik) *a.* **1.** controversial (*also* **po'lemical**) —*n.* **2.** war of words, argument —**po'lemics** *pl.n.* (*with sing. v.*) art or practice of dispute or argument

police (pə'lēs) *n.* **1.** the civil force which maintains public order —*vt.* **2.** keep in order —**police dog** dog trained to help police —**po'liceman** *n.* member of police force (**po'licewoman** *fem.*) —**police state** state or country in which repressive government maintains control through police —**police station** office or headquarters of police force of district

policy[1] ('polisi) *n.* **1.** course of action adopted, *esp.* in state affairs **2.** prudence

policy[2] ('polisi) *n.* insurance contract

poliomyelitis (pōliōmīə'lītis) *n.* disease of spinal cord characterized by fever and sometimes paralysis (*also* **infantile paralysis**)

polish ('polish) *vt.* **1.** make smooth and glossy **2.** refine —*n.* **3.** shine **4.** polishing **5.** substance for polishing **6.** refinement

Politburo ('politbyŏŏərō) *n.* **1.** executive committee of a Communist Party **2.** supreme policy-making authority in most Communist countries

polite (pə'līt) *a.* **1.** showing regard for others in manners, speech *etc.* **2.** refined, cultured —**po'litely** *adv.* —**po'liteness** *n.* courtesy

politic ('politik) *a.* **1.** wise **2.** shrewd **3.** expedient **4.** cunning —**po'litical** *a.* of the state or its affairs —**poli'tician** *n.* one engaged in politics —**'politics** *pl.n.* **1.** (*with sing. v.*) art of government **2.** political affairs or life —**'polity** *n.* **1.** form of government **2.** organized state **3.** civil government —**political asylum** refuge given to someone for political reasons —**political economy** *former name for* economics —**political prisoner** someone imprisoned for holding or expressing particular political beliefs —**political science** study of state, government and politics —**political scientist**

Polk (pōk) *n.* **James Knox.** the 11th President of the U.S. (1845-49)

polka ('pōlkə) *n.* **1.** lively dance in 2/4 time **2.** music for it —**polka dot** one of pattern of bold spots on fabric *etc.*

poll (pōl) *n.* **1.** voting **2.** counting of votes **3.** number of votes recorded **4.** canvassing of sample of population to determine general opinion **5.** (top of) head —*vt.* **6.** receive (votes) **7.** take votes of **8.** lop, shear **9.** cut horns from (animals) —*vi.* **10.** vote —**'pollster** *n.* one who conducts polls

pollard ('polərd) *n.* **1.** hornless animal of normally horned variety **2.** tree on which a close head of young branches has been made by polling —*vt.* **3.** make a pollard of

pollen ('polən) *n.* fertilizing dust of flower —**'pollinate** *vt.* —**pollen count** measure of pollen present in air over 24-hour period

pollute (pə'lōōt) *vt.* **1.** make foul **2.** corrupt **3.** desecrate —**pol'lutant** *n.* —**pol'lution** *n.*

polo ('pōlō) *n.* game in which two teams of players on horseback attempt to drive a ball through goals set up at each end of a turf field —**polo neck** **1.** collar on garment, worn rolled over to fit closely round neck **2.** sweater with such collar

polonaise (polə'nāz) *n.* **1.** Polish dance **2.** music for it

polonium (pə'lōniəm) *n. Chem.* transuranic element *Symbol* Po, at. wt. 210.0, at. no. 84

poltergeist ('pōltərgīst) *n.* noisy mischievous spirit

poltroon (pol'tro͞on) *n.* abject coward

poly- (*comb. form*) many, as in *polysyllabic*

polyandry ('poliandri) *n.* polygamy in which woman has more than one husband

polyanthus (poli'anthəs) *n.* cultivated primrose

polychrome ('polikrōm) *a.* **1.** having various colors —*n.* **2.** work of art in many colors —**polychro'matic** *a.*

polycythemia (polisī'thēmiə) *n.* the increase in number of red cells in the blood

polyester ('poliestər) *n.* any of large class of synthetic materials used as plastics, textile fibers *etc.*

polygamy (pə'ligəmi) *n.* custom of being married to several persons at same time —**po'lygamist** *n.*

polyglot ('poliglot) *a.* speaking, writing in several languages

polygon ('poligon) *n.* figure with many angles or sides —**po'lygonal** *a.*

polygraph ('poligraf) *n.* **1.** instrument for recording pulse rate and perspiration, used *esp.* as lie detector **2.** device for producing copies of written matter

polygyny (pə'lijəni) *n.* polygamy in which man has more than one wife

polyhedron (poli'hēdrən) *n.* solid figure contained by many faces (*pl.* **-s, -dra** (-drə))

polymath ('polimath) *n.* person of great and varied learning

polymer ('polimər) *n.* substance whose molecules are made up of many structural units held together by interatomic bonds —**poly'meric** *a.* of polymer —**polymeri'zation** *n.* —**'polymerize** *v.*

polymorphous (poli'môrfəs) *or* **polymorphic** *a.* **1.** having, taking or passing through many different forms or stages **2.** exhibiting or undergoing polymorphism

Polynesian (poli'nēzhən, -shən) *a.* **1.** of Polynesia, group of Pacific islands, its people or any of their languages —*n.* **2.** member of people of Polynesia, generally of Caucasoid features with light skin and wavy hair **3.** branch of Malayo-Polynesian family of languages, including Maori and Hawaiian

polynomial (poli'nōmiəl) *a.* **1.** of two or more names or terms —*n.* **2.** mathematical expression consisting of sum of terms each of which is product of constant and one or more variables raised to positive or zero integral power **3.** mathematical expression consisting of sum of a number of terms (*also* **multi'nomial**)

polyp ('polip) *n.* **1.** sea anemone or allied animal **2.** tumor with branched roots (*also* **'polypus**)

polyphase ('polifāz) *a.* (of alternating current of electricity) possessing number of regular sets of alternations

polyphony (pə'lifəni) *n.* polyphonic style of composition or piece of music utilizing it —**poly'phonic** *a.* **1.** *Mus.* composed of relatively independent parts; contrapuntal **2.** many-voiced

polysaccharide (poli'sakərīd) *n.* organic compound composed of monosaccharides found widely distributed in nature, *eg* cellulose, starch and glycogen

polystyrene (poli'stīrēn) *n.* synthetic material used *esp.* as white rigid foam for packing *etc.*

polytechnic (poli'teknik) *n.* **1.** college dealing mainly with various arts and crafts —*a.* **2.** of or relating to technical instruction

polytheism ('politheizəm) *n.* belief in many gods —**'polytheist** *n.*

polyunsaturated ('poliun'sachərātid) *a.* of group of fats that do not form cholesterol in blood

polyurethane (poli'yo͝orəthān) *n.* class of synthetic materials, oft. in foam or flexible form

polyvalent (poli'vālənt) *a.* having more than one valency

pomace ('pumis) *n.* **1.** pulpy residue of apples or similar fruit after crushing and pressing, as in cider-making **2.** any pulpy substance left after crushing *etc.*

pomade (pō'mād, -'mäd) *n.* **1.** perfumed oil or ointment applied to hair, to make it smooth and shiny —*vt.* **2.** put pomade on

pomander ('pōmandər, pō'mandər) *n.* (container for) mixture of sweet-smelling herbs *etc.*

pomegranate ('pomigranit, 'pomgranit) *n.* **1.** tree cultivated for its edible fruit **2.** its fruit with thick rind containing many seeds in red pulp

pomelo ('poməlō) *n. see* GRAPEFRUIT (*pl.* **-s**)

Pomeranian (pomə'rāniən) *n.* breed of toy dog

pommel ('puməl, 'pom-) *n.* **1.** front of saddle **2.** knob of sword hilt —*vt.* **3.** *see* PUMMEL

pommy ('pomi) *n.* (*sometimes* **P-**) **A, NZ** *sl.* British person (*also* **pom**)

pomp (pomp) *n.* splendid display or ceremony

pompon ('pompon) *or* **pompom** ('pompom) *n.* tuft of ribbon, wool, feathers *etc.* decorating hat, shoe *etc.*

pompous ('pompəs) *a.* **1.** self-important **2.** ostentatious **3.** (of language) inflated, stilted —**pom'posity** *n.*

poncho ('ponchō) *n.* **1.** square or oblong blanket-like fabric with opening in middle for head **2.** waterproof garment resembling poncho (*pl.* **-s**)

pond (pond) *n.* small body, pool or lake of still water

ponder ('pondər) *v.* **1.** muse, meditate, think over **2.** consider, deliberate (on)

ponderous ('pondərəs) *a.* **1.** heavy, unwieldy **2.** boring

pongee (pon'jē) *n.* soft unbleached washable silk woven from filaments of wild silkworms

pontiff ('pontif) *n.* **1.** Pope **2.** high priest **3.** bishop —**pon'tifical** *a.* —**pontificate** (pon'tifikit) *n.* **1.** dignity or office of pontiff —*vi.* (pon'tifikāt) **2.** speak bombastically (*also* **'pontify**) **3.** act as pontiff

pontoon (pon'tōōn) *n.* flat-bottomed boat or metal drum for use in supporting temporary bridge

pony ('pōni) *n.* **1.** horse of small breed **2.** very small glass, *esp.* for liqueurs —**'ponytail** *n.* long hair tied in one bunch at back of head

poodle ('pōōdəl) *n.* pet dog with long curly hair oft. clipped fancifully —**poodle cloth** fabric made of wool and mohair with loops on surface

Pooh-Bah ('pōōbä) *n.* pompous official

pooh-pooh ('pōōpōō) *vt.* express disdain or scorn for; dismiss, belittle

pool[1] (pōōl) *n.* **1.** small body of still water **2.** deep place in river or stream **3.** puddle **4.** swimming pool

pool[2] (pōōl) *n.* **1.** common fund or resources **2.** group of people, *eg* typists, any of whom can work for any of several employers **3.** aggregate of money or chips at stake in game of cards consisting usu. of contributions from each player (*also* **kitty, pot**) **4.** cartel **5.** variety of billiards —*vt.* **6.** put in common fund

poop (pōōp) *n.* ship's stern

poor (pōōər, pōr) *a.* **1.** having little money **2.** unproductive **3.** inadequate, insignificant **4.** needy **5.** miserable, pitiable **6.** feeble **7.** not fertile —**'poorly** *adv.* **1.** badly —*a.* **2.** *inf.* not in good health —**'poorness** *n.* —**poor box** box, *esp.* in church, used for collection of alms or money for poor —**'poorhouse** *n.* formerly, publicly maintained institution offering accommodation to the poor

pop[1] (pop) *vi.* **1.** make small explosive sound **2.** *inf.* go or come unexpectedly or suddenly —*vt.* **3.** cause to make small explosive sound **4.** put or place suddenly (**-pp-**) —*n.* **5.** small explosive sound **6.** *inf.* nonalcoholic fizzy drink —**'popper** *n.* **1.** person or thing that pops **2.** container for cooking popcorn in —**'popcorn** *n.* **1.** any kind of maize that puffs up when roasted **2.** the roasted product —**'popgun** *n.* toy gun that fires pellet or cork by means of compressed air

pop[2] (pop) *n. inf.* **1.** father **2.** old man

pop[3] (pop) *n.* **1.** music of general appeal, *esp.* to young people —*a.* **2.** *inf.* popular —**pop art** American art movement of 1960s which used commercial illustration techniques to portray imagery from popular culture and commercial art

pop. **1.** popular **2.** population

pope (pōp) *n.* (*oft.* **P-**) bishop of Rome and head of R.C. Church —**'popery** *n. offens.* papal system, doctrines —**'popish** *a. derogatory* belonging to or characteristic of Roman Catholicism

popeyed ('pop'īd) *a.* **1.** having bulging, prominent eyes **2.** staring in astonishment

popinjay ('popinjā) *n.* **1.** conceited or talkative person **2.** *obs.* parrot

poplar ('poplər) *n.* **1.** any of a genus of slender fast-growing trees of the willow family **2.** the wood from these trees **3.** the tulip tree or its wood

poplin ('poplin) *n.* corded fabric *usu.* of cotton

poppadom *or* **poppadum** ('popədəm) *n.* thin, round, crisp Indian bread

poppet ('popit) *n.* **1.** mushroom-shaped valve lifted from seating by applying axial force to stem (*also* **poppet valve**) **2.** *Naut.* temporary supporting brace for vessel hauled on land

poppy ('popi) *n.* bright-flowered plant yielding opium

poppycock ('popikok) *n. inf.* nonsense

Popsicle ('popsikəl) *n.* trade name for flavored colored water frozen onto two flat sticks

populace ('popyələs) *n.* (*sometimes with pl. v.*) the common people, the masses

popular ('popyələr) *a.* **1.** finding general favor **2.** of, by the people —**popu'larity** *n.* state or quality of being generally liked —**populari'zation** *n.* —**'popularize** *vt.* make popular —**'popularly** *adv.* —**popular front** (*oft.* **P- F-**) left-wing group or party that opposes spread of fascism

populate ('popyəlāt) *vt.* fill with inhabitants —**popu'lation** *n.* **1.** inhabitants **2.** the number of such inhabitants —**'populous** *a.* thickly populated or inhabited

porbeagle ('pōrbēgəl) *n.* any of several sharks of northern seas (*also* **mackerel shark**)

porcelain ('pōrslin) *n.* fine ceramic ware, china —**porcelain enamel** vitreous enamel

porch (pōrch) *n.* covered approach to entrance of building

porcine ('pōrsīn) *a.* of, like pigs

porcupine ('pōrkyəpīn) *n.* any of various rodents covered with long, pointed quills

pore[1] (pōr) *vi.* **1.** fix eye or mind **2.** (*with* over) study closely

pore[2] (pōr) *n.* minute opening, *esp.* in skin —**po'rosity** *n.* —**'porous** *a.* **1.** allowing liquid to soak through **2.** full of pores

pork (pōrk) *n.* pig's flesh used as food —**'porker** *n.* pig raised for food —**'porky** *a.* fleshy, fat —**porkpie hat** hat with round flat crown and brim that can be turned up or down

porn (pōrn) *or* **porno** *n. inf.* pornography

pornography (pōr'nogrəfi) *n.* indecent literature, pictures *etc.* —**por'nographer** *n.* —**porno'graphic** *a.* —**porno'graphically** *adv.*

porphyria (pōr'firiə) *n.* any of group of rare

inborn diseases which block hemoglobin formation

porphyry ('pörfiri) *n.* reddish stone with embedded crystals

porpoise ('pörpəs) *n.* blunt-nosed sea mammal like dolphin (*pl.* **-poise, -s**)

porridge ('porij) *n.* **1.** soft food of oatmeal *etc.* boiled in water **2.** *sl.* imprisonment

porringer ('porinjər) *n.* small dish, oft. with handle, for soup, porridge *etc.*

port[1] (pört) *n.* **1.** harbor, haven **2.** town with harbor

port[2] (pört) *n.* **1.** left side of ship or aircraft (*also* (*formerly*) **'larboard**) —*v.* **2.** turn to left side of ship

port[3] (pört) *n.* strong red wine

port[4] (pört) *n.* opening in side of ship —**'porthole** *n.* small opening or window in side of ship

port[5] (pört) *Mil.* *vt.* **1.** carry (rifle *etc.*) diagonally across body —*n.* **2.** this position

Port. **1.** Portugal **2.** Portuguese

portable ('pörtəbəl) *n./a.* (something) easily carried

portage ('pörtij) *n.* (cost of) transport

portal ('pörtəl) *n.* large doorway or imposing gate

portcullis (pört'kulis) *n.* defense grating to raise or lower in front of castle gateway

Port-du-Salut (pördəsəl'yōō, -sə'lōō) *or* **Port-Salut** *n.* a semihard, fermented and flat, round whole-milk cheese orig. from France

portend (pör'tend) *vt.* foretell, be an omen of —**'portent** *n.* **1.** omen, warning **2.** marvel —**por'tentous** *a.* **1.** ominous, threatening **2.** pompous

porter[1] ('pörtər) *n.* **1.** person employed to carry burden, *eg* on railroad **2.** doorkeeper —**'porterage** *n.* (charge for) carrying of supplies

porter[2] ('pörtər) *n.* dark sweet ale brewed from black malt —**'porterhouse** *n.* thick choice steak of beef cut from middle ribs or sirloin (*also* **porterhouse steak**)

portfolio (pört'fōliō) *n.* **1.** flat portable case for loose papers **2.** office of minister of state (*pl.* **-s**)

portico ('pörtikō) *n.* **1.** colonnade **2.** covered walk (*pl.* **-es, -s**)

portière (*Fr.* por'tyer) *n.* curtain hung in doorway

portion ('pörshən) *n.* **1.** part **2.** share **3.** helping **4.** destiny, lot —*vt.* **5.** divide into shares —**'portionless** *a.*

portly ('pörtli) *a.* bulky, stout

portmanteau (pört'mantō) *n.* leather suitcase, *esp.* one opening into two compartments (*pl.* **-s, -teaux** (-tōz)) —**portmanteau word** word formed by joining together beginning and end of two other words (*also* **blend**)

portray (pör'trā) *vt.* make pictures of, describe —**portrait** ('pörtrit, -trāt) *n.* likeness of (face of) individual —**portraiture** ('pörtrichōōər, -chər) *n.* —**por'trayal** *n.* act of portraying

Portugal ('pörchigəl) *n.* country in Europe bounded north and east by Spain and south and west by the Atlantic —**Portu'guese** *n./a.* **1.** (native or inhabitant) of Portugal —*n.* **2.** language of Portugal, which is a Romance language —**Portuguese man-of-war** sea animal with stinging tentacles

pose (pōz) *vt.* **1.** place in attitude **2.** put forward —*vi.* **3.** assume attitude, affect or pretend to be a certain character —*n.* **4.** attitude, *esp.* one assumed for effect —**'poser** *n.* one who poses —**poseur** (pō'zər) *n.* one who assumes affected attitude to create impression

poser ('pōzər) *n.* puzzling question

posh (posh) *a.* *inf.* **1.** smart, elegant, stylish **2.** upper-class or genteel

posit ('pozit) *vt.* lay down as principle

position (pə'zishən) *n.* **1.** place **2.** situation **3.** location, attitude **4.** status **5.** state of affairs **6.** employment **7.** strategic point **8.** *Mus.* vertical spacing or layout of written notes in chord —*vt.* **9.** place in position

positive ('pozitiv) *a.* **1.** certain, sure **2.** definite, absolute, unquestionable **3.** utter, downright **4.** confident **5.** not negative **6.** greater than zero **7.** *Elec.* having deficiency of electrons —*n.* **8.** something positive **9.** *Photog.* print in which lights and shadows are not reversed —**'positively** *adv.* —**'positivism** *n.* philosophy recognizing only matters of fact and experience —**'positivist** *a./n.* (one) believing in this —**positive discrimination** provision of special opportunities for disadvantaged group —**positive feedback** *see* **feedback** (sense 1) *at* FEED

positron ('pozitron) *n.* positive electron

poss. **1.** possession **2.** possessive **3.** possible **4.** possibly

posse ('posi) *n.* **1.** body of men, *esp.* for maintaining law and order **2.** **C** group of trained horsemen who perform at rodeos

possess (pə'zes) *vt.* **1.** own **2.** (of evil spirit *etc.*) have mastery of —**pos'session** *n.* **1.** act of possessing **2.** thing possessed **3.** ownership —**pos'sessive** *a.* **1.** of, indicating possession **2.** with excessive desire to possess, control —*n.* **3.** possessive case in grammar

possible ('posibəl) *a.* **1.** that can, or may, be, exist, happen or be done **2.** worthy of consideration —*n.* **3.** possible candidate —**possi'bility** *n.* —**'possibly** *adv.* perhaps

possum ('posəm) *n.* *see* OPOSSUM —**play possum** pretend to be dead, asleep *etc.* to deceive opponent

post[1] (pōst) *n.* **1.** upright pole of timber or metal fixed firmly, usu. to support or mark something —*vt.* **2.** display **3.** put up (notice *etc.*) on wall *etc.* —**'poster** *n.* **1.** large advertising bill **2.** one who posts bills

—**poster paints** *or* **colors** lusterless paints used for writing posters *etc.*

post[2] (pōst) *n.* **1.** official carrying of letters or parcels **2.** collection or delivery of these **3.** office **4.** situation **5.** point, station, place of duty **6.** place where soldier is stationed **7.** place held by body of troops **8.** fort —*vt.* **9.** put into official box for carriage by post **10.** supply with latest information **11.** station (soldiers *etc.*) in particular spot **12.** transfer (entries) to ledger —*adv.* **13.** in haste —'**postage** *n.* charge for mailing an item —'**postal** *a.* —**postage stamp** printed paper label with gummed back for attaching to mail as official indication that required postage has been paid —**postal card** preprinted card purchased at post office —**Postal Service** U.S. government corporation responsible for transportation and delivery of mail —'**postcard** *n.* **1.** message on illustrated card without envelope —*vt.* **2.** send postcard to —'**postman** *n.* mailman —**postman's knock** parlor game involving exchange of kisses —'**postmark** *n.* official mark with name of office *etc.* stamped on letters —'**postmaster** *or* '**postmistress** *n.* official in charge of local post office —**postmaster general** executive head of postal service in certain countries (*pl.* **postmasters general**) —**post office** place where postal business is conducted —'**post'paid** *adv./a.* with postage prepaid

post- (*comb. form*) after, behind, later than, as in *postwar.* Such compounds are not given here where the meaning can easily be found from the simple word

postdate (pōst'dāt) *vt.* assign date to (event *etc.*) that is later than actual date

posterior (pō'stēriər, po-) *a.* **1.** later **2.** hinder —*n.* **3.** the buttocks

posterity (po'steriti) *n.* **1.** later generations **2.** descendants

postern ('pōstərn, 'postərn) *n.* **1.** private entrance **2.** small door, gate

postexilic (pōstig'zilik) *a. O.T.* existing or occurring after Babylonian exile of Jews (587-539 B.C.)

postgraduate (pōst'grajōōit) *a.* **1.** carried on after graduation —*n.* **2.** student taking course of study after graduation

posthaste ('pōst'hāst) *adv.* **1.** with great haste —*n.* **2.** *obs.* great haste

posthumous ('poschəməs, 'postyəməs, 'postəməs) *a.* **1.** occurring after death **2.** born after father's death **3.** (of book *etc.*) published after author's death —'**posthumously** *adv.*

posthypnotic suggestion (pōst-hip'notik) suggestion made to subject while in hypnotic trance, to be acted upon some time after emerging from trance

postilion *or* **postillion** (pō'stilyən) *n. Hist.* man riding one of pair of horses drawing a carriage

postimpressionism (pōstim'preshənizəm) *n.* movement in painting at end of 19th cent. which rejected naturalism and momentary effects of impressionism but adapted its use of pure color to paint subjects with greater subjective emotion —**postim'pressionist** *a.* of Paul Cézanne, Vincent Van Gogh, Paul Gauguin and neoimpressionists

post meridiem (mə'ridiəm) *see* P.M. (sense 1)

postmortem (pōst'mörtəm) *n.* **1.** analysis of recent event —*a.* **2.** taking place after death —**postmortem examination** medical examination of dead body

postnasal drip (pōst'nāzəl) the discharge of fluid secretions into the back part of the nose and throat from nasal and sinus tissues

postnatal (pōst'nātəl) *a.* after birth

post-obit (pōst'ōbit) *a.* taking effect after death

postoperative (pōst'opərətiv) *a.* of period following surgical operation

postpartum depression (pōst'pärtəm) condition sometimes occurring after childbirth, marked by weeping, sensitivity and depression

postpone (pōst'pōn, pōs'pōn) *vt.* put off to later time, defer —**post'ponement** *n.*

postprandial (pōst'prandiəl) *a.* after-dinner

postscript ('pōsskript) *n.* **1.** note added at end of letter, after signature **2.** supplement added to book, document *etc.*

postulant ('poschələnt) *n.* candidate for admission to religious order

postulate ('poschəlāt) *vt.* **1.** take for granted **2.** lay down as self-evident **3.** stipulate —*n.* ('poschəlit) **4.** proposition assumed without proof **5.** prerequisite —**postu'lation** *n.*

posture ('poschər) *n.* **1.** attitude, position of body —*vi.* **2.** pose

posy ('pōzi) *n.* bunch of flowers

pot (pot) *n.* **1.** round vessel **2.** cooking vessel **3.** trap, *esp.* for crabs, lobsters **4.** *sl.* cannabis **5.** *see* POOL[2] (sense 3) —*pl.* **6.** *inf.* a lot —*vt.* **7.** put into, preserve in pot (**-tt-**) —'**potted** *a.* **1.** preserved in a pot **2.** *inf.* abridged —'**pot'bellied** *a.* —'**potbelly** *n.* **1.** enlarged protruding abdomen (*also* **beer belly**) **2.** one having such an abdomen —'**potboiler** *n. inf.* artistic work of little merit produced quickly to make money —**pot-bound** *a.* (of pot plant) having grown to fill all available root space and lacking room for continued growth —'**potherb** *n.* any plant having leaves, stems *etc.* that are used in cooking —'**pothole** *n.* **1.** pitlike cavity in rocks, usu. limestone, produced by faulting and water action **2.** hole worn in road —'**pothook** *n.* **1.** S-shaped hook for suspending pot over fire **2.** long hook for lifting hot pots *etc.* **3.** S-shaped mark, oft. made by children when learning to write —'**pothunter** *n.* **1.** person who hunts for profit without regard to rules of sport **2.** *inf.* person who enters competitions for sole purpose of winning prizes —'**pot'luck** *n.* **1.** whatever food is available without special preparation **2.** choice dictated by lack of alternative (*esp. in* **take potluck**) —**pot plant** plant grown in flowerpot —**pot roast** meat cooked slowly in covered pot with little water —'**potsherd** *n.* broken fragment of pottery —**pot shot** easy or random shot

potable ('pōtəbəl) *a.* drinkable

potage (po'tazh; *English* pō'täzh) *Fr.* thick soup

potash ('potash) *n.* **1.** alkali used in soap *etc.* **2.** crude potassium carbonate

potassium (pə'tasiəm) *n. Chem.* metallic element *Symbol* k, at. wt. 39.1, at. no. 19 —**potassium nitrate** crystalline compound used in gunpowders, fertilizers and as preservative (*also* **'salt'peter, 'niter**)

potato (pə'tātō) *n.* plant with tubers grown for food (*pl.* **-es**) —**potato chip** very thin fried slice of potato, eaten cold —**sweet potato 1.** trailing plant **2.** its edible sweetish tubers

potent ('pōtənt) *a.* **1.** powerful, influential **2.** (of male) capable of sexual intercourse —'**potency** *n.* **1.** physical or moral power **2.** efficacy

potentate ('pōtəntāt) *n.* ruler

potential (pə'tenchəl) *a.* **1.** latent, that may or might but does not now exist or act —*n.* **2.** possibility **3.** amount of potential energy **4.** *Elec.* level of electric pressure —**potenti'ality** *n.* —**potential difference** difference in electric potential between two points in electric field

pother ('podhər) *n.* **1.** commotion, fuss **2.** choking cloud of smoke *etc.*

potion ('pōshən) *n.* dose of medicine or poison

potpourri (pōpōō'rē) *n.* **1.** mixture of rose petals, spices *etc.* **2.** musical, literary medley (*pl.* **-s**)

pottage ('potij) *n.* thick soup containing vegetables and meat

potter ('potər) *n.* maker of ceramic ware —'**pottery** *n.* **1.** earthenware and stoneware **2.** place where it is made **3.** art of making it —**potter's wheel** device with horizontal rotating disk, on which clay is molded by hand —**the Potteries** region of W central England in which china industries are concentrated

pouch (powch) *n.* **1.** small bag **2.** *Anat.* any sac, pocket or pouchlike cavity —*vt.* **3.** put into pouch

poult-de-soie (pōōdə'swä) *n.* fine corded silk or rayon

poultice ('pōltis) *n.* soft composition of mustard, kaolin *etc.*, applied hot to sore or inflamed parts of body

poultry ('pōltri) *n.* domestic fowls collectively —'**poulterer** *n.* dealer in poultry

pounce (powns) *vi.* **1.** spring suddenly, swoop —*n.* **2.** swoop or sudden descent

pound[1] (pownd) *vt.* **1.** beat, thump **2.** crush to pieces or powder —*vi.* **3.** walk, run heavily

pound[2] (pownd) *n.* **1.** unit of troy and apothecaries' weight equal to 0.373 kg **2.** unit of avoirdupois weight equal to 0.454 kg **3.** monetary unit in U.K. —'**poundage** *n.* charge of so much per pound of weight

pound[3] (pownd) *n.* **1.** enclosure for stray animals or officially removed vehicles **2.** confined space —'**poundage** *n.* **1.** confinement within an enclosure or boundary **2.** fee required to free animal from pound

poundal ('powndəl) *n.* unit of force in the foot-pound-second system

pour (pōr) *vi.* **1.** come out in a stream, crowd *etc.* **2.** flow freely **3.** rain heavily —*vt.* **4.** give out in a stream, crowd *etc.* **5.** cause to run out

pourboire (pōōr'bwar) *Fr.* tip; gratuity

pout[1] (powt) *v.* **1.** thrust out (lips) —*vi.* **2.** look sulky —*n.* **3.** act of pouting —'**pouter** *n.* pigeon with power of inflating its crop

pout[2] (powt) *n.* type of food fish (*pl.* **pout, -s**)

poverty ('povərti) *n.* **1.** state of being poor **2.** poorness **3.** lack of means **4.** scarcity —**poverty line** level of income below which one is classified as poor by federal government standards —**poverty-stricken** *a.* suffering from extreme poverty

P.O.W. prisoner of war

powder ('powdər) *n.* **1.** solid matter in fine dry particles **2.** medicine in this form **3.** gunpowder **4.** face powder *etc.* —*vt.* **5.** apply powder to **6.** reduce to powder; pulverize —'**powdery** *a.* —**powder keg 1.** small barrel to hold gunpowder **2.** potential source of violence *etc.* —**powder puff** soft pad for applying cosmetic powder —**powder room** ladies' toilet

power ('powər) *n.* **1.** ability to do or act **2.** strength **3.** authority **4.** control **5.** person or thing having authority **6.** mechanical energy **7.** electricity supply **8.** rate of doing work **9.** product from continuous multiplication of number by itself —'**powered** *a.* having or operated by mechanical or electrical power —'**powerful** *a.* —'**powerless** *a.* —'**powerhouse** *or* **power station** *n.* installation for generating and distributing electric power —**power of attorney 1.** legal authority to act for another person in certain specified matters **2.** document conferring such authority

powwow ('powwow) *n.* **1.** Amerindian ceremony of celebration (cure of disease, success in hunting or war *etc.*) **2.** council or conference of or with Amerindians **3.** *inf.* any meeting —*vi.* **4.** hold a powwow

pox (poks) *n.* **1.** one of several diseases marked by pustular eruptions of skin **2.** *inf.* syphilis

pp *or* **pp.** pianissimo

pp. pages

p.p. 1. parcel post **2.** past participle **3.** prepaid

4. postpaid 5. by delegation to 6. on prescriptions, after meal

ppd. 1. postpaid 2. prepaid

P.P.S. *or* **p.p.s.** post postscriptum

PQ Quebec

Pr *Chem.* praseodymium

pr. 1. pair (*pl.* **prs.**) 2. present 3. price 4. pronoun

P.R. public relations

practical ('praktikəl) *a.* 1. given to action rather than theory 2. relating to action or real existence 3. useful 4. in effect though not in name 5. virtual —**practica'bility** *n.* —**'practicable** *a.* that can be done, used *etc.* —**'practically** *adv.* —**prac'titioner** *n.* one engaged in a profession —**practical joke** trick usu. intended to make victim appear foolish

practice *or* **practise** ('praktis) *n.* 1. habit 2. mastery, skill 3. exercise of art or profession 4. action, not theory —*vt.* 5. do repeatedly, work at to gain skill 6. do habitually 7. put into action —*vi.* 8. exercise oneself 9. exercise profession

praetor ('prētər) *n.* in ancient Rome, senior magistrate ranking just below consul

pragmatic (prag'matik) *a.* 1. concerned with practical consequence 2. of the affairs of state —**prag'matical** *a.* —**'pragmatism** *n.*

prairie dog

prairie ('prāəri) *n.* large treeless tract of grassland of Central U.S.A. and Canad. —**prairie dog** small N Amer. rodent inhabiting burrows in grasslands —**prairie schooner** canvas-covered wagon used by early Americans to cross the continent

praise (prāz) *n.* 1. commendation 2. fact, state of being praised —*vt.* 3. express approval, admiration of 4. speak well of 5. glorify —**'praiseworthy** *a.*

praline ('prälēn) *n.* sweet composed of nuts and sugar

prance (prans) *vi.* 1. swagger 2. caper 3. walk with bounds —*n.* 4. prancing

prank (prangk) *n.* mischievous trick or escapade, frolic

prase (prāz) *n.* light green translucent chalcedony

praseodymium (prāziō'dimiəm) *n. Chem.* metallic element *Symbol* Pr, at. wt. 140.9, at. no. 59

prate (prāt) *vi.* 1. talk idly, chatter —*n.* 2. idle or trivial talk

prattle ('pratəl) *vi.* 1. talk like child —*n.* 2. trifling, childish talk —**'prattler** *n.* babbler

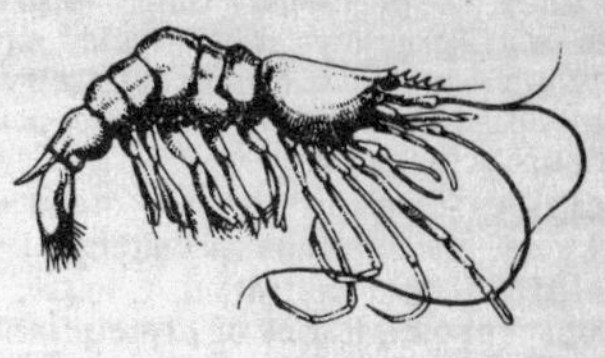

prawn

prawn (prön) *n.* edible sea crustacean like shrimp but larger

praxis ('praksis) *n.* practice, *esp.* as opposed to theory (*pl.* **-es, praxes** ('praksēz))

pray (prā) *vt.* 1. ask earnestly, entreat —*vi.* 2. offer prayers, *esp.* to God —**prayer** (prāər) *n.* 1. action, practice of praying to God 2. earnest entreaty —**prayer rug** small carpet on which Muslim kneels while saying prayers (*also* **prayer mat**) —**prayer wheel** *Buddhism esp.* in Tibet, wheel or cylinder inscribed with prayers, each revolution of which is counted as uttered prayer —**praying mantis** *or* **mantid** *see* MANTIS

pre- (*comb. form*) before, beforehand, as in *prenatal, prerecord, preshrunk.* Such compounds are not given here where the meaning can easily be found from the simple word

preach (prēch) *vi.* 1. deliver sermon 2. give moral, religious advice —*vt.* 3. set forth in religious discourse 4. advocate —**'preacher** *n.*

preamble ('prēambəl, prē'ambəl) *n.* introductory part of story *etc.*

prebend ('prebənd) *n.* stipend of canon or member of cathedral chapter —**pre'bendal** *a.* —**'prebendary** *n.* holder of this

Precambrian (prē'kambriən) *a.* 1. of earliest geological era, which lasted for about 4 000 000 000 years before Cambrian period —*n.* 2. Precambrian era

precarious (pri'kariəs, -'ker-) *a.* insecure, unstable, perilous

precaution (pri'köshən) *n.* 1. previous care to prevent evil or secure good 2. preventive measure —**pre'cautionary** *a.*

precede (pri'sēd) *vt.* go, come before in rank, order, time *etc.* —**precedence** ('presidəns) *n.* priority in position, rank, time *etc.* —**precedent** ('presidənt) *n.* previous example or occurrence taken as rule

precentor (pri'sentər) *n.* leader of singing choir or congregation

precept ('prēsept) *n.* rule for conduct, maxim —**pre'ceptor** *n.* instructor —**precep'torial** *a.*

precinct ('prēsingkt) *n.* 1. enclosed, limited area 2. area in town, oft. closed to traffic, reserved for particular activity 3. administrative area of city —*pl.* 4. environs

precious ('preshəs) *a.* **1.** beloved, cherished **2.** of great value, highly valued **3.** rare —**preci'osity** *n.* overrefinement in art or literature —**'preciously** *adv.* —**'preciousness** *n.* —**precious metal** gold, silver or platinum —**precious stone** (in jewelry trade) diamond, emerald, ruby, sapphire, pearl and sometimes black opal

precipice ('presipis) *n.* very steep cliff or rockface —**precipitous** (pri'sipitəs) *a.* sheer

precipitant (pri'sipitənt) *a.* **1.** hasty, rash **2.** abrupt —**pre'cipitance** *or* **pre'cipitancy** *n.*

precipitate (pri'sipitāt) *vt.* **1.** hasten happening of **2.** throw headlong **3.** *Chem.* cause to be deposited in solid form from solution —*a.* (pri'sipitit) **4.** too sudden **5.** rash, impetuous —*n.* (pri'sipitit) **6.** substance chemically precipitated —**pre'cipitately** *adv.* —**precipi'tation** *n.* rain, snow, sleet *etc.*

précis (prā'sē, 'prāsē) *n.* abstract, summary (*pl.* **précis** (prā'sēz, 'prāsēz))

precise (pri'sīs) *a.* **1.** definite **2.** particular **3.** exact, strictly worded **4.** careful in observance **5.** punctilious, formal —**pre'cisely** *adv.* —**precision** (pri'sizhən) *n.* accuracy

preclude (pri'klōōd) *vt.* **1.** prevent from happening **2.** shut out

precocious (pri'kōshəs) *a.* developed, matured early or too soon —**precocity** (pri'kositi) *or* **pre'cociousness** *n.*

precognition (prēkog'nishən) *n. Psychol.* alleged ability to foresee future events —**pre'cognitive** *a.*

pre-Columbian art (prēkə'lumbiən) the indigenous art of North, Central and South America before 1492

preconceive (prēkən'sēv) *vt.* form an idea of beforehand —**precon'ception** *n.*

precondition (prēkən'dishən) *n.* necessary or required condition

precursor (pri'kərsər) *n.* one who or that which precedes —**pre'cursive** *or* **pre'cursory** *a.*

pred. predicate

predate (prē'dāt) *vt.* **1.** affix date to (document *etc.*) that is earlier than actual date **2.** assign date to (event *etc.*) that is earlier than actual or previously assigned date of occurrence **3.** be or occur at earlier date than; precede in time

predatory ('predətōri) *a.* **1.** hunting, killing other animals *etc.* for food **2.** plundering —**'predator** *n.* predatory animal

predecease (prēdi'sēs) *vt.* die before (some other person)

predecessor ('prēdisesər) *n.* **1.** one who precedes another in an office or position **2.** ancestor

predestine (prē'destin) *vt.* decree beforehand, foreordain —**predesti'nation** *n.*

predetermine (prēdi'tərmin) *vt.* **1.** determine beforehand **2.** influence, bias —**predetermi'nation** *n.*

predicament (pri'dikəmənt) *n.* perplexing, embarrassing or difficult situation

predicant ('predikənt) *a.* **1.** of preaching —*n.* **2.** member of religious order founded for preaching, *esp.* Dominican

predicate ('predikāt) *vt.* **1.** affirm, assert **2.** (*with* on *or* upon) base (argument *etc.*) —*n.* ('predikit) **3.** that which is predicated **4.** *Gram.* statement made about a subject —**'predicable** *a.* **1.** capable of being predicated —*n.* **2.** quality that can be predicated **3.** *Logic* any of five general forms of attribution, namely genus, species, differentia, property and accident —**predi'cation** *n.* —**'predicative** *a.*

predict (pri'dikt) *vt.* foretell, prophesy —**pre'dictable** *a.* —**pre'diction** *n.*

predilection (predi'lekshən, prē-) *n.* preference, liking, partiality

predispose (prēdi'spōz) *vt.* **1.** incline, influence **2.** make susceptible

predominate (pri'domināt) *vi.* be main or controlling element —**pre'dominance** *n.* —**pre'dominant** *a.* chief

pre-eminent (pri'eminənt) *a.* excelling all others, outstanding —**pre-eminence** *n.* —**pre-eminently** *adv.*

pre-empt (pri'empt) *vt.* acquire in advance of or to exclusion of others —**pre-emption** *n.* —**pre-emptive** *a.*

preen (prēn) *vt.* **1.** (of birds) trim (feathers) with beak, plume **2.** smarten (oneself)

pref. **1.** preface **2.** preference **3.** prefix

prefabricate (prē'fabrikāt) *vt.* manufacture (buildings *etc.*) in shaped sections, for rapid assembly on site —**pre'fab** *n.* prefabricated building, *esp.* house

preface ('prefis) *n.* **1.** introduction to book *etc.* —*vt.* **2.** introduce —**'prefatory** *a.*

prefect ('prēfekt) *n.* person put in authority —**'prefecture** *n.* office, residence, district of a prefect

prefer (pri'fər) *vt.* **1.** like better **2.** promote (-rr-) —**preferable** ('prefərəbəl) *a.* more desirable —**preferably** ('prefərəbli) *adv.* —**preference** ('prefərəns, 'prefrəns) *n.* —**preferential** (prefə'renchəl) *a.* giving, receiving preference —**pre'ferment** *n.* promotion, advancement

prefigure (prē'figyər) *vt.* exhibit, suggest by previous types, foreshadow —**pre'figurative** *a.*

prefix ('prēfiks) *n.* **1.** preposition or particle put at beginning of word or title —*vt.* (prē'fiks, 'prēfiks) **2.** put as introduction **3.** put before word to make compound

prefrontal lobotomy (prē'fruntəl) *see* **lobotomy** *at* LOBE

pregnant ('pregnənt) *a.* **1.** carrying fetus in womb **2.** full of meaning, significance **3.** inventive —**'pregnancy** *n.*

prehensile (prē'hensil, -sīl) *a.* capable of grasping —**prehen'sility** *n.*

prehistoric (prēhi'storik) *or* **prehistorical**

a. before period in which written history begins —**pre'history** *n.*

prejudge (prē'juj) *vt.* judge beforehand, *esp.* without sufficient evidence

prejudice ('prejədis) *n.* **1.** preconceived opinion **2.** bias, partiality **3.** injury likely to happen to person or his rights as result of others' action or judgment —*vt.* **4.** influence **5.** bias **6.** injure —**preju'dicial** *a.* **1.** injurious **2.** disadvantageous

prelate ('prelit) *n.* bishop or other church dignitary of equal or higher rank —**'prelacy** *n.* his office —**prelatical** (pri'latikəl) *a.*

preliminary (pri'limineri) *a.* **1.** preparatory, introductory —*n.* **2.** introductory, preparatory statement, action **3.** eliminating contest held before main competition

prelims ('prēlimz, prə'limz) *pl.n.* pages of book, such as title page *etc.* before main text (*also* **front matter**)

prelude ('prelyōōd) *n.* **1.** *Mus.* introductory movement **2.** performance, event *etc.* serving as introduction —*v.* **3.** serve as prelude to (something) —*vt.* **4.** introduce

premarital (prē'maritəl) *a.* occurring before marriage

premature (premə'tyōōər, -'tōōər, -'chōōər) *a.* **1.** happening, done before proper time **2.** impulsive, hasty **3.** (of infant) born before end of full period of gestation

premeditate (pri'meditāt) *vt.* consider, plan beforehand —**premedi'tation** *n.*

premenstrual (prē'menstrōōəl) *a.* of period in menstrual cycle just before menstruation

premier (pri'mēər, 'premiər) *n.* **1.** prime minister **2.** head of government of Aust. state —*a.* **3.** chief, foremost **4.** first —**pre'miership** *n.*

premiere (pri'myāər, -'mēər; primi'āər) *n.* first public performance of a play, motion picture *etc.*

premise ('premis) *n.* **1.** *Logic* proposition from which inference is drawn (*also* **'premiss**) —*pl.* **2.** house, building with its belongings **3.** *Law* beginning of deed —*vt.* ('premis, pri'mīz) **4.** state by way of introduction

premium ('prēmiəm) *n.* **1.** bonus **2.** sum paid for insurance **3.** excess over nominal value **4.** great value or regard

premonition (premə'nishən) *n.* presentiment, foreboding

prenatal (prē'nātəl) *a.* occurring, existing or taking place before birth

preoccupy (prē'okyəpī) *vt.* occupy to the exclusion of other things (**-pying, -pied**) —**preoccu'pation** *n.* mental concentration or absorption

preordain (prēōr'dān) *vt.* ordain or decree beforehand

prep. **1.** preparation **2.** preparatory **3.** preposition

prepare (pri'pāər) *vt.* **1.** make ready **2.** make —*vi.* **3.** get ready —**preparation** (prepə'rāshən) *n.* **1.** making ready beforehand **2.** something that is prepared, as a medicine **3.** at school, (time spent) preparing work for lesson —**preparatory** (pri'parətōri) *a.* **1.** serving to prepare **2.** introductory —**preparedness** (pri'paridnis, -'per-) *n.* state of being prepared —**'preppie** *or* **'preppy** *n./a.* (denoting) one who apparently has a preparatory-school background —**preparatory school** private secondary school preparing students for college (*also* **prep school**)

prepay (prē'pā) *vt.* pay in advance

prepense (pri'pens) *a.* usu. in legal contexts, premeditated (*esp. in* **malice prepense**)

preponderate (pri'pondərāt) *vi.* be of greater weight or power —**pre'ponderance** *n.* superiority of power, numbers *etc.*

preposition (prepə'zishən) *n.* word marking relation between noun or pronoun and other words —**prepo'sitional** *a.*

prepossess (prēpə'zes) *vt.* **1.** preoccupy or engross mentally **2.** impress, *esp.* favorably, beforehand —**prepos'sessing** *a.* inviting favorable opinion, attractive, winning —**prepos'session** *n.*

preposterous (pri'postərəs) *a.* utterly absurd, foolish

prepuce ('prēpyōōs) *n.* **1.** retractable fold of skin covering tip of penis; foreskin **2.** similar fold of skin covering tip of clitoris

Pre-Raphaelite (prē'rafiəlīt) *n.* **1.** member of **Pre-Raphaelite Brotherhood,** association of painters and writers founded in 1848 to revive qualities of It. painting before Raphael —*a.* **2.** of Pre-Raphaelite painting and painters

prerequisite (prē'rekwizit) *n./a.* (something) required as prior condition

prerogative (pri'rogətiv) *n.* **1.** peculiar power or right, *esp.* as vested in sovereign —*a.* **2.** privileged

pres. **1.** present (time) **2.** presidential

Pres. President

presage ('presij) *n.* **1.** omen, indication of something to come —*vt.* ('presij, pri'sāj) **2.** foretell

presbyopia (prezbi'ōpiə) *n.* progressively diminishing ability of the eye to focus, *esp.* on near objects; long-sightedness

presbyter ('prezbitər) *n.* **1.** elder in early Christian church **2.** priest **3.** member of a presbytery —**Presby'terian** *a./n.* (member) of Protestant Christian church emphasizing sovereignty and justice of God in highly structured representational system of ministers and lay persons —**Presby'terianism** *n.* —**'presbytery** *n.* **1.** church court composed of all ministers within a certain district and one ruling elder from each church **2.** *R.C.Ch.* priest's house

prescience ('preshiəns, 'preshəns, 'presiəns) *n.* foreknowledge —**'prescient** *a.*

prescribe (pri'skrīb) *v.* **1.** set out rules (for) **2.** order **3.** ordain **4.** order use of (medicine)

—**prescription** (pri'skripshən) *n.* **1.** prescribing **2.** thing prescribed **3.** written statement of it —**prescriptive** (pri'skriptiv) *a.*

present[1] ('prezənt) *a.* **1.** that is here **2.** now existing or happening —*n.* **3.** present time or tense —'**presence** *n.* **1.** being present **2.** appearance, bearing —'**presently** *adv.* **1.** soon **2.** now —**presence of mind** ability to remain calm and act constructively during crises —**present-day** *a.* of modern day; current —**present participle** participial form of verbs used adjectivally when action it describes is contemporaneous with that of main verb of sentence and also used in formation of certain compound tenses —**present perfect** *Gram. see* PERFECT (sense 9)

present[2] (pri'zent) *vt.* **1.** introduce formally **2.** show **3.** give **4.** offer **5.** point, aim —*n.* ('prezənt) **6.** gift —**pre'sentable** *a.* fit to be seen —**presentation** (prēzen'tāshən, prezən-) *n.*

presentiment (pri'zentimənt) *n.* sense of something (*esp.* evil) about to happen

preserve (pri'zərv) *vt.* **1.** keep from harm, injury or decay **2.** maintain **3.** pickle —*n.* **4.** special area **5.** that which is preserved, as fruit *etc.* **6.** place where game is kept for private fishing, shooting —**preservation** (prezər'vāshən) *n.* —**pre'servative** *n.* **1.** chemical added to perishable foods, drinks *etc.* to prevent them from rotting —*a.* **2.** tending to preserve **3.** having quality of preserving

preside (pri'zīd) *vi.* **1.** be chairman **2.** (*with* over) superintend —**presidency** ('prezidənsi) *n.* —**president** ('prezidənt) *n.* head of society, company, republic *etc.* —**presidential** (prezi'denchəl) *a.*

presidium (pri'sidiəm) *n.* **1.** (*oft.* **P-**) in Communist countries, permanent committee of larger body, such as legislature, that acts for it when it is in recess **2.** collective presidency

press[1] (pres) *vt.* **1.** subject to push or squeeze **2.** smooth by pressure or heat **3.** urge steadily, earnestly —*vi.* **4.** bring weight to bear **5.** throng **6.** hasten —*n.* **7.** a pressing **8.** machine for pressing, *esp.* printing machine **9.** printing house **10.** art or process of printing **11.** newspapers collectively **12.** crowd **13.** stress **14.** large cupboard —'**pressing** *a.* **1.** urgent **2.** persistent —**press agent** person employed to secure publicity —**press conference** interview for press reporters given by politician *etc.* —**press gallery** area for newspaper reporters, *esp.* in legislative assembly —'**pressman** *n.* **1.** printer who attends to the press **2.** journalist —**press-up** *n.* exercise in which body is alternately raised and lowered by arms only, trunk being kept straight (*also* **push-up**)

press[2] (pres) *vt.* force to serve in navy or army —**press gang** formerly, body of men employed to press men into naval service

pressure ('preshər) *n.* **1.** act of pressing **2.** influence **3.** authority **4.** difficulties **5.** *Phys.* thrust per unit area —**pressuri'zation** *n.* in aircraft, maintenance of normal atmospheric pressure at high altitudes —'**pressurize** *vt.* —**pressure cooker** vessel like saucepan which cooks food rapidly by steam under pressure —**pressure group** organized group which exerts influence on policies, public opinion *etc.*

prestidigitation (prestidiji'tāshən) *n. see* **sleight of hand** *at* SLEIGHT —**presti'digitator** *n.*

prestige (pre'stēzh) *n.* **1.** reputation based on high achievement, character, wealth *etc.* **2.** power to impress or influence —**prestigious** (pre'stijəs) *a.*

presto ('prestō) *adv.* **1.** *Mus.* quickly **2.** immediately (*esp. in* **hey presto**)

prestressed (prē'strest) *a.* (of concrete) containing stretched steel cables for strengthening

presume (pri'zōōm) *vt.* **1.** take for granted —*vi.* **2.** take liberties —**pre'sumably** *adv.* **1.** probably **2.** doubtlessly —**presumption** (pri'zumpshən) *n.* **1.** forward, arrogant opinion or conduct **2.** strong probability —**presumptive** (pri'zumptiv) *a.* that may be assumed as true or valid until contrary is proved —**presumptuous** (pri'zumpchōōəs) *a.* forward, impudent, taking liberties —**presumptuously** (pri'zumpchōōəsli) *adv.* —**heir presumptive** heir whose right may be defeated by birth of nearer relative

presuppose (prēsə'pōz) *vt.* assume or take for granted beforehand —**presuppo'sition** *n.*

pretend (pri'tend) *vt.* **1.** claim or allege (something untrue) **2.** make believe, as in play —*vi.* **3.** lay claim (to) —**pre'tender** *n.* claimant (to throne) —'**pretense** *or* '**pretence** *n.* **1.** simulation **2.** pretext —**pre'tension** *n.* —**pre'tentious** *a.* **1.** making claim to special merit or importance **2.** given to outward show

preter- (*comb. form*) beyond, more than

preterit *or* **preterite** ('pretərit) *a.* **1.** past **2.** expressing past state or action —*n.* **3.** past tense

preternatural (prētər'nachrəl) *a.* **1.** out of ordinary way of nature **2.** abnormal, supernatural

pretext ('prētekst) *n.* excuse

pretty ('priti) *a.* **1.** having beauty that is attractive rather than imposing **2.** charming —*adv.* **3.** fairly, moderately —'**prettify** *vt.* make pretty, *esp.* in trivial way; embellish —'**prettily** *adv.* —'**prettiness** *n.*

pretzel ('pretsəl) *n.* brittle biscuit usu. in form of knot or stick

prevail (pri'vāl) *vi.* **1.** gain mastery **2.** triumph **3.** be in fashion, generally established —**pre'vailing** *a.* **1.** widespread **2.** predominant —**prevalence** ('prevələns) *n.*

—**prevalent** (ˈprevələnt) *a.* extensively existing, rife

prevaricate (priˈvarikāt) *vi.* **1.** make evasive or misleading statements **2.** tell lie(s) —**prevariˈcation** *n.* —**preˈvaricator** *n.*

prevent (priˈvent) *vt.* stop, hinder —**preˈventable** *a.* —**preˈvention** *n.* —**preˈventive** *a.* preventing, or serving to prevent, *esp.* disease (*also* **preˈventative**) —**preventive medicine** medical specialty dealing with prevention of disease

preview (ˈprēvyōō) *n.* **1.** advance showing **2.** showing of scenes from forthcoming motion picture

previous (ˈprēviəs) *a.* **1.** earlier **2.** preceding **3.** *inf.* hasty —ˈ**previously** *adv.* before

prey (prā) *n.* **1.** animal hunted and killed by another carnivorous animal **2.** victim —*vi.* (*oft. with* (up)on) **3.** seize for food **4.** treat as prey **5.** afflict, obsess

price (prīs) *n.* **1.** that for which thing is bought or sold **2.** cost **3.** value **4.** reward **5.** odds in betting —*vt.* **6.** fix, ask price for —ˈ**priceless** *a.* **1.** invaluable **2.** *inf.* very funny —ˈ**pricey** *or* ˈ**pricy** *a. inf.* expensive —**price control** establishment of maximum price levels for basic goods and services by government —**at any price** whatever the price or cost

prick (prik) *vt.* **1.** pierce slightly with sharp point **2.** cause to feel mental pain **3.** mark by prick —*v.* **4.** (*usu. with* up) erect (ears) —*n.* **5.** slight hole made by pricking **6.** pricking or being pricked **7.** sting **8.** remorse **9.** that which pricks **10.** sharp point —ˈ**prickle** *n.* **1.** thorn, spike —*vi.* **2.** feel tingling or pricking sensation —ˈ**prickly** *a.* —**prickly heat** inflammation of skin with stinging pains —**prickly pear 1.** tropical cactus having flattened or cylindrical spiny joints and oval fruit **2.** fruit of prickly pear

pride (prīd) *n.* **1.** too high an opinion of oneself, inordinate self-esteem **2.** worthy self-esteem **3.** feeling of elation or great satisfaction **4.** something causing this **5.** group (of lions) —*v.refl.* **6.** take pride

prie-dieu (prēˈdyə) *n.* piece of furniture consisting of low surface for kneeling upon and narrow front surmounted by rest, for use when praying

priest (prēst) *or* (*fem.*) **priestess** *n.* official minister of religion, clergyman —ˈ**priesthood** *n.* —ˈ**priestly** *a.*

prig (prig) *n.* self-righteous person who professes superior culture, morality *etc.* —ˈ**priggery** *n.* —ˈ**priggish** *a.*

prim (prim) *a.* very restrained, formally prudish

prima (ˈprēmə) *a.* first —**prima ballerina** leading female ballet dancer —**prima donna** (ˈprimə ˈdonə, ˈprēmə) **1.** principal female singer in opera **2.** *inf.* temperamental person (*pl.* **-s**)

primacy (ˈprīməsi) *n.* **1.** state of being first in rank, grade *etc.* **2.** office of archbishop

prima facie (ˈprīmə ˈfāshə, -ˈfāshi) *Lat.* at first sight

primal (ˈpraīməl) *a.* **1.** of earliest age **2.** first, original —**priˈmarily** *adv.* —ˈ**primary** *a.* **1.** chief **2.** of the first stage, decision *etc.* **3.** elementary —**primary accent** *or* **stress** *Linguis.* strongest accent in word or breath group —**primary colors** red, yellow and blue, which can produce all other colors, but cannot themselves be made from any combination of other colors —**primary election 1.** election in which voters directly nominate the candidate of their own party for office **2.** election where voters of the same political party select delegates to a nominating convention

primate (ˈprīmāt) *n.* **1.** one of order of mammals comprising man, apes, monkeys, marmosets and lemurs **2.** archbishop or the highest ranking bishop of a province

prime[1] (prīm) *a.* **1.** fundamental **2.** original **3.** chief **4.** best —*n.* **5.** first, best part of anything **6.** youth **7.** full health and vigor —*vt.* **8.** prepare (gun, engine, pump *etc.*) for use **9.** fill up, *eg* with information, liquor —ˈ**priming** *n.* powder mixture used for priming gun —**prime meridian** the 0° meridian from which other meridians are calculated, usu. taken to pass through Greenwich —**Prime Minister 1.** the chief executive of a parliamentary government **2.** chief minister of ruler or state —**prime number** integer that cannot be divided into other integers but is only divisible by itself or 1

prime[2] (prīm) *vt.* prepare for paint with preliminary coating of oil, size *etc.* —ˈ**primer** *or* ˈ**priming** *n.* paint *etc.* for priming

primer (ˈprimər) *n.* elementary school book or manual

primeval (prīˈmēvəl) *a.* of the earliest age of the world

primitive (ˈprimitiv) *a.* **1.** of an early undeveloped kind, ancient **2.** crude, rough

primogeniture (prīmōˈjenichōōər, -chər) *n.* the exclusive right of inheritance by the first-born, usu. son —**primoˈgenital** *a.* —**primoˈgenitor** *n.* **1.** forefather; ancestor **2.** earliest parent or ancestor, as of race

primordial (prīˈmördiəl) *a.* existing at or from the beginning

Primost (ˈprēmöst) *n. see* MYSOST

primp (primp) *v.* dress (oneself), *esp.* in fine clothes; prink

primrose (ˈprimrōz) *n.* **1.** any of various pale yellow spring flowers of the genus *Primula* **2.** this color —*a.* **3.** of this color —**primrose path** pleasurable way of life

primula (ˈprimyələ) *n.* genus of plants of cosmopolitan distribution of over 500 species and countless hybrids, all with 5-petaled flowers

prince (prins) *n.* **1.** male member of royal or

noble family **2.** ruler, chief **3.** person of high standing or privilege, as in *prince of the church* (**'princess** *fem.*) —**'princely** *a.* **1.** generous, lavish **2.** stately **3.** magnificent —**'princess** *a.* (of dress) cut to follow curves of body with no seam at waistline —**Prince of Darkness** the devil —**Prince of Peace** Jesus Christ —**Prince of Wales** title usu. conferred on heir to British throne —**Prince-of-Wales check** woven fabric with large, open-check pattern with colored overcheck

principal ('prinsipəl) *a.* **1.** chief in importance —*n.* **2.** person for whom another is agent **3.** head of institution, *esp.* school or college **4.** sum of money lent and yielding interest **5.** chief actor —**princi'pality** *n.* country ruled by a prince —**principal parts** *Gram.* main inflected forms of verb, from which all other inflections may be deduced

principle ('prinsipəl) *n.* **1.** moral rule **2.** settled reason of action **3.** uprightness **4.** fundamental truth or element

prink (pringk) *v.* **1.** dress (oneself *etc.*) finely; deck out —*vi.* **2.** preen oneself

print (print) *vt.* **1.** reproduce (words, pictures *etc.*) by pressing inked types on blocks to paper *etc.* **2.** produce thus **3.** write in imitation of this **4.** impress **5.** *Photog.* produce (pictures) from negatives **6.** stamp (fabric) with colored design —*n.* **7.** printed matter **8.** printed lettering **9.** written imitation of printed type **10.** photograph **11.** impression, mark left on surface by thing that has pressed against it **12.** printed cotton fabric —**'printer** *n.* one engaged in printing —**'printing** *n.* **1.** business or art of producing printed matter **2.** printed text **3.** copies of book *etc.* printed at one time (*also* **im'pression**) **4.** form of writing in which letters resemble printed letters —**printed circuit** electronic circuit with wiring printed on an insulating base —**printed matter** printed material eligible for special postage rates —**printer's devil** apprentice or errand boy in printing establishment —**printing press** machine for printing —**print-out** *n.* printed information from computer, teleprinter *etc.* —**out of print** no longer available from publisher

prior ('prīər) *a.* **1.** earlier —*n.* **2.** chief of religious house or order (**-ess** *fem.*) —**pri'ority** *n.* **1.** precedence **2.** something given special attention —**'priory** *n.* monastery, nunnery under prior, prioress

prise (prīz) *vt. see* PRIZE[1] (senses 6, 7)

prism ('prizəm) *n.* **1.** transparent body bounded in part by two plane faces which are not parallel **2.** something which refracts light **3.** in geometry, polyhedron two of whose faces are polygons that lie on parallel planes and whose other faces are parallelograms intersecting on parallel lines —**pris'matic** *a.* **1.** of prism shape **2.** (of color) such as is produced by refraction through prism, rainbow-like, brilliant

prison ('prizən) *n.* jail —**'prisoner** *n.* **1.** one kept in prison **2.** captive —**prisoner of war** person, *esp.* serviceman, captured by enemy in time of war —**prisoner's base** children's game where members of opposing sides are captured and can only be freed in specified ways

prissy ('prisi) *a. inf.* fussy, prim

pristine ('pristēn, pris'tēn) *a.* **1.** original **2.** primitive **3.** unspoiled, good

private ('prīvit) *a.* **1.** secret, not public **2.** reserved for, belonging to, or concerning, an individual only **3.** personal **4.** secluded **5.** denoting soldier of lowest rank —*n.* **6.** soldier or marine one grade above a recruit —**'privacy** *n.* —**'privately** *adv.* —**privati'zation** *n.* —**'privatize** *vt.* take into or return to private ownership (a company or concern previously owned by the State) —**private eye** *inf.* private detective —**private first class** enlisted man in the army or marines above the rank of private and below the rank of corporal —**private parts** *or* **'privates** *pl.n.* genitals —**private school** school under financial and managerial control of private body or charitable trust

privateer (prīvə'tēər) *n. Hist.* **1.** privately owned armed vessel authorized by government to take part in war **2.** captain of such ship

privation (prī'vāshən) *n.* **1.** loss or lack of comforts or necessities **2.** hardship **3.** act of depriving —**privative** ('privətiv) *a.*

privet ('privit) *n.* any of various ornamental shrubs with half-evergreen leaves and white flowers

privilege ('privilij) *n.* **1.** advantage or favor that only a few obtain **2.** right, advantage belonging to person or class —**'privileged** *a.* enjoying special right or immunity

privy ('privi) *a.* **1.** admitted to knowledge of secret —*n.* **2.** toilet, *esp.* outhouse **3.** *Law* person having interest in an action —**'privily** *adv.* —**privy council** council of state of monarch or governor

prize[1] (prīz) *n.* **1.** reward given for success in competition **2.** thing striven for **3.** thing won, *eg* in lottery *etc.* —*a.* **4.** winning or likely to win a prize —*vt.* **5.** value highly **6.** force open by levering **7.** obtain with difficulty —**'prizefight** *n.* boxing match for money —**'prizefighter** *n.*

prize[2] (prīz) *n.* ship, property captured in (naval) warfare

pro[1] (prō) *adv./prep.* in favor (of)

pro[2] (prō) *n.* **1.** professional **2.** prostitute (*pl.* **-s**) —*a.* **3.** professional

pro- (*comb. form*) for, instead of, before, in front, as in *proconsul, pronoun, project.* Such compounds are not given here where the meaning may easily be found from the simple word

probable ('probəbəl) *a.* likely —**proba'bility** *n.* **1.** ratio of number of ways in which an event can occur in a specified form to the total ways in which the event can occur **2.** anything that has appearance of truth **3.** branch of mathematics —'**probably** *adv.*

probate ('prōbāt) *n.* **1.** proving of authenticity of will **2.** certificate of this —**probate court** court for the probate of wills, administration of estates, and related matters

probation (prō'bāshən) *n.* **1.** system of dealing with lawbreakers, *esp.* juvenile ones, by placing them under supervision of probation officer for stated period **2.** testing of candidate before admission to full membership —**pro'bationer** *n.* person on probation —**probation officer** officer of court who supervises offenders placed on probation

probe (prōb) *vt.* **1.** search into, examine, question closely —*n.* **2.** that which probes, or is used to probe **3.** thorough inquiry

probity ('prōbiti) *n.* honesty, uprightness, integrity

problem ('probləm) *n.* **1.** matter *etc.* difficult to deal with or solve **2.** question set for solution **3.** puzzle —**proble'matic(al)** *a.* **1.** questionable; uncertain **2.** disputable

proboscis (prə'bosis) *n.* trunk or long snout, *eg* of elephant (*pl.* **-es, proboscides** (prə'bosidēz))

procaine hydrochloride ('prōkān) local or general anesthetic administered by injection or intravenously in conjunction with adrenaline

proceed (prə'sēd) *vi.* **1.** go forward, continue **2.** be carried on **3.** go to law —**pro'cedural** *a.* —**pro'cedure** *n.* **1.** act, manner of proceeding **2.** conduct —**pro'ceeding** *n.* **1.** act or course of action **2.** transaction —*pl.* **3.** minutes of meeting **4.** methods of prosecuting charge, claim *etc.* —'**proceeds** *pl.n.* price or profit

process ('prōses) *n.* **1.** series of actions or changes **2.** method of operation **3.** state of going on **4.** action of law **5.** outgrowth —*vt.* **6.** handle, treat, prepare by special method of manufacture *etc.* —**pro'cession** *n.* **1.** regular, orderly progress **2.** train of persons in formal order

proclaim (prə'klām) *vt.* announce publicly, declare —**proclamation** (proklə'māshən) *n.*

proclivity (prō'kliviti) *n.* inclination, tendency

proconsul (prō'konsəl) *n. Hist.* governor of province

procrastinate (prə'krastināt, prō-) *vi.* put off (an action) until later, delay —**procrasti'nation** *n.* —**pro'crastinator** *n.*

procreate ('prōkriāt) *v.* produce (offspring) —**procre'ation** *n.*

Procrustean (prə'krustiən, prō-) *a.* compelling uniformity by violence

proctology (prok'toləji) *n.* branch of medicine concerned with anus and rectum

proctor ('proktər) *n.* **1.** steward, proxy **2.** university official with disciplinary powers

procure (prə'kyŏŏər) *vt.* **1.** obtain, acquire **2.** provide **3.** bring about —*vi.* **4.** act as pimp —**pro'curable** *a.* —**procuration** (prokyə'rāshən) *n.* —**procurator** ('prokyŏŏrātər) *n.* one who manages another's affairs —**pro'curement** *n.* —**pro'curer** *n.* **1.** one who procures **2.** pimp

prod (prod) *vt.* **1.** poke with something pointed (**-dd-**) —*n.* **2.** prodding **3.** goad **4.** pointed instrument

prodigal ('prodigəl) *a.* **1.** wasteful **2.** extravagant —*n.* **3.** spendthrift —**prodi'gality** *n.* reckless extravagance

prodigy ('prodiji) *n.* **1.** person with some marvelous gift **2.** thing causing wonder —**pro'digious** *a.* **1.** very great, immense **2.** extraordinary —**pro'digiously** *adv.*

produce (prə'dyōōs, -'dōōs) *vt.* **1.** bring into existence **2.** yield **3.** make **4.** bring forward **5.** manufacture **6.** exhibit **7.** present on stage, screen, television **8.** *Geom.* extend in length —*n.* ('prodōōs, 'prō-; -dyōōs) **9.** that which is yielded or made —**pro'ducer** *n.* person who produces, *esp.* play, motion picture *etc.* —**product** ('produkt) *n.* **1.** result of process of manufacture **2.** number resulting from multiplication —**pro'duction** *n.* **1.** producing **2.** things produced —**pro'ductive** *a.* **1.** fertile **2.** creative **3.** efficient —**productivity** (produk'tiviti) *n.*

proem ('prōem) *n.* introduction or preface, such as to work of literature

Prof. Professor

profane (prō'fān, prə-) *a.* **1.** irreverent, blasphemous **2.** not sacred —*vt.* **3.** pollute, desecrate —**profanation** (profə'nāshən) *n.* —**profanity** (prō'faniti, prə-) *n.* profane talk or behavior, blasphemy

profess (prə'fes) *vt.* **1.** affirm, acknowledge **2.** confess publicly **3.** assert **4.** claim, pretend —**professedly** (prə'fesidli) *adv.* avowedly —**pro'fession** *n.* **1.** calling or occupation, *esp.* learned, scientific or artistic **2.** a professing **3.** vow of religious faith on entering religious order —**pro'fessional** *a.* **1.** engaged in a profession **2.** engaged in a game or sport for money —*n.* **3.** paid player —**pro'fessor** *n.* **1.** teacher of highest rank in university **2.** *inf.* one who teaches or professes special knowledge in any art, sport or occupation requiring skill —**professorial** (prōfi'sōriəl, profi-) *a.* —**professoriate** (prōfi'sōriit, profi-) *n.* body of university professors —**pro'fessorship** *n.*

proffer ('profər) *vt./n.* offer

proficient (prə'fishənt) *a.* skilled; expert —**pro'ficiency** *n.*

profile ('prōfīl) *n.* **1.** outline, *esp.* of face, as seen from side **2.** brief biographical sketch **3.**

verbal, numerical or graphical summary or analysis

profit ('profit) *n.* **1.** (*oft. pl.*) money gained **2.** benefit obtained —*v.* **3.** benefit —'**profitable** *a.* yielding profit —**profi'teer** *n.* **1.** one who makes excessive profits at the expense of the public —*vi.* **2.** make excessive profits —'**profitless** *a.* —**profit-sharing** *n.* system in which portion of net profit of business is distributed to employees, usu. in proportion to wages or length of service

profligate ('profligit) *a.* **1.** dissolute **2.** reckless, wasteful —*n.* **3.** dissolute person —'**profligacy** *n.*

pro forma ('prō 'fōrmə) *Lat.* for the sake of, as a matter of form —***pro forma* invoice** invoice presented at time of payment

profound (prə'fownd) *a.* **1.** very learned **2.** deep —**profundity** (prə'funditi) *n.*

profuse (prə'fyōōs) *a.* abundant, prodigal —**pro'fusion** *n.*

progeny ('projini) *n.* children —**progenitor** (prō'jenitər) *n.* ancestor

progesterone (prō'jestərōn) *n.* hormone which prepares uterus for pregnancy and prevents further ovulation

prognathous ('prognəthəs, prog'nāthəs) *or* **prognathic** (prog'nathik) *a.* with projecting lower jaw

prognosis (prog'nōsis) *n.* **1.** art of foretelling course of disease by symptoms **2.** forecast (*pl.* **-noses** (-'nōsēz)) —**prognostic** (prog'nostik) *a.* **1.** of, serving as prognosis —*n.* **2.** *Med.* any symptom used in making prognosis **3.** sign of some future occurrence —**prognosticate** (prog'nostikāt) *vt.* foretell —**prognostication** (prognosti'kāshən) *n.*

program ('prōgram) *n.* **1.** plan, detailed notes of intended proceedings **2.** broadcast on radio or television **3.** syllabus or curriculum **4.** detailed instructions for computer —*vt.* **5.** feed program into (computer) **6.** arrange detailed instructions for (computer) (**-mm-**) —'**programmer** *n.*

progress ('progris, -gres) *n.* **1.** onward movement **2.** development —*vi.* (prə'gres) **3.** go forward **4.** improve —**pro'gression** *n.* **1.** moving forward **2.** advance, improvement **3.** increase or decrease of numbers or magnitudes according to fixed law **4.** *Mus.* regular succession of chords —**pro'gressive** *a.* **1.** progressing by degrees **2.** favoring political or social reform **3.** *Gram.* designating form of verb expressing action or state

prohibit (prō'hibit, prə-) *vt.* forbid —**prohibition** (prōi'bishən) *n.* **1.** act of forbidding **2.** interdict **3.** interdiction of supply and consumption of alcoholic drinks —**pro'hibitive** *a.* **1.** tending to forbid or exclude **2.** (of prices) very high —**pro'hibitory** *a.*

project ('projekt) *n.* **1.** plan, scheme **2.** design —*vt.* (prə'jekt) **3.** plan **4.** throw **5.** cause to appear on distant background —*vi.* (prə'jekt) **6.** stick out, protrude —**projectile** (prə'jektil) *n.* **1.** heavy missile, *esp.* shell or ball —*a.* **2.** designed for throwing —**projection** (prə'jekshən) *n.* —**projectionist** (prə'jekshənist) *n.* operator of motion-picture projector —**projector** (prə'jektər) *n.* **1.** apparatus for projecting photographic images, motion pictures, slides on screen **2.** one that forms scheme or design

prolapse (prō'laps, 'prōlaps) *n.* falling, slipping down of internal part of body from normal position (*also* **pro'lapsus**)

prolate ('prōlāt) *a.* having polar diameter greater than the equatorial diameter

prolegomena (prōle'gominə) *pl.n.* introductory remarks prefixed to book; preface

proletariat (prōli'teriit, -'tar-; -iat) *n.* **1.** all wage earners collectively **2.** lowest class of community, working class —**prole'tarian** *a./n.*

proliferate (prə'lifərāt) *v.* grow or reproduce rapidly —**prolifer'ation** *n.*

prolific (prə'lifik) *a.* **1.** producing fruit, offspring *etc.* in abundance **2.** producing constant or successful results **3.** fruitful

prolix (prō'liks, 'prōliks) *a.* (of speech *etc.*) wordy, long-winded —**pro'lixity** *n.*

prologue ('prōlog) *n.* introductory act or event

prolong (prə'long) *vt.* lengthen, protract —**prolongation** (prōlong'gāshən) *n.*

prom (prom) *n. inf.* dance at school or college

promenade (promə'nād, -'näd) *n.* **1.** leisurely walk **2.** place made or used for this —*vi.* **3.** take leisurely walk **4.** go up and down

promethium (prə'mēthiəm) *n. Chem.* metallic element *Symbol* Pm, at. wt. 147, at. no. 61

prominent ('prominənt) *a.* **1.** sticking out **2.** conspicuous **3.** distinguished —'**prominence** *n.*

promiscuous (prə'miskyōōəs) *a.* **1.** indiscriminate, *esp.* in sexual relations **2.** mixed without distinction —**promiscuity** (promi'skyōōiti) *n.*

promise ('promis) *v.* **1.** give undertaking or assurance (of) —*vi.* **2.** be likely —*n.* **3.** undertaking to do or not to do something **4.** potential —'**promising** *a.* showing good signs, hopeful —'**promissory** *a.* containing promise —**Promised Land 1.** *O.T.* land of Canaan, promised by God to Abraham and his descendants as their heritage **2.** *Christianity* heaven **3.** place where one expects to find greater happiness —**promissory note** written promise to pay sum to person named

promontory ('proməntōri) *n.* point of high land jutting out into the sea, headland

promote (prə'mōt) *vt.* **1.** help forward **2.** move up to higher rank or position **3.** work for **4.** encourage sale of —**pro'moter** *n.* —**pro'motion** *n.* **1.** advancement **2.** preferment

prompt (prompt) *a.* **1.** done at once **2.** acting with alacrity **3.** punctual **4.** ready —*vt.* **5.**

urge, suggest —*v.* **6.** help out (actor or speaker) by reading or suggesting next words —**'prompter** *n.* —**'promptitude** *or* **'promptness** *n.* —**'promptly** *adv.*

promulgate ('proməlgāt) *vt.* proclaim, publish —**promul'gation** *n.* —**'promulgator** *n.*

pron. **1.** pronoun **2.** pronunciation

prone (prōn) *a.* **1.** lying face or front downward **2.** inclined —**'proneness** *n.*

prong (prong) *n.* single spike of fork or similar instrument

pronghorn ('pronghörn) *n.* deerlike antelope found in treeless country in W North America from southern Canada to northern Mexico

pronoun ('prōnown) *n.* word used to replace noun —**pro'nominal** *a.* pert. to, like pronoun

pronounce (prə'nowns) *vt.* **1.** utter formally **2.** form with organs of speech **3.** say distinctly **4.** declare —*vi.* **5.** give opinion or decision —**pro'nounceable** *a.* —**pro'nounced** *a.* strongly marked, decided —**pro'nouncement** *n.* declaration —**pronunci'ation** *n.* **1.** manner in which word *etc.* is pronounced **2.** articulation **3.** phonetic transcription of a word

pronto ('prontō) *adv. inf.* at once, immediately, quickly

proof (proōf) *n.* **1.** evidence **2.** thing which proves **3.** test, demonstration **4.** trial impression from type or engraved plate **5.** *Photog.* print from a negative **6.** standard of strength of alcoholic drink —*a.* **7.** giving impenetrable defense **8.** of proved strength —**'proofread** *v.* read and correct (proofs) —**'proofreader** *n.* —**'proofreading** *n.*

-proof (*comb. form*) impervious to; resisting effects of, as in *waterproof*

prop[1] (prop) *vt.* **1.** support, sustain, hold up (**-pp-**) —*n.* **2.** pole, beam *etc.* used as support

prop[2] (prop) *n.* propeller —**'prop'jet** *n. see* TURBOPROP

prop[3] (prop) *n.* (theatrical) property

prop. **1.** proper(ly) **2.** property **3.** proposition **4.** proprietor

propaganda (propə'gandə) *n.* organized dissemination of information to spread particular doctrines, principles, information *etc.* —**propa'gandist** *a./n.*

propagate ('propəgāt) *vt.* **1.** reproduce, breed, spread by sowing, breeding *etc.* **2.** transmit —*vi.* **3.** breed, multiply —**propa'gation** *n.* —**'propagative** *a.*

propane ('prōpān) *n.* colorless, flammable gas occurring naturally in crude petroleum

propel (prə'pel) *vt.* cause to move forward (**-ll-**) —**pro'pellant** *or* **pro'pellent** *n.* something causing propulsion, *eg* rocket fuel —**pro'peller** *n.* revolving shaft with blades for driving ship or aircraft —**pro'pulsion** *n.* act of driving forward —**pro'pulsive** *or* **pro'pulsory** *a.* **1.** tending, having power to propel **2.** urging on

propensity (prə'pensiti) *n.* **1.** inclination or bent **2.** tendency **3.** disposition

proper ('propər) *a.* **1.** appropriate **2.** correct **3.** conforming to etiquette, decorous **4.** strict **5.** (of noun) denoting individual person or place —**'properly** *adv.* —**proper fraction** fraction in which numerator is greater than denominator

property ('propərti) *n.* **1.** that which is owned **2.** estate whether in lands, goods or money **3.** quality, attribute of something **4.** article used on stage in play *etc.*

prophet ('profit) *n.* **1.** inspired teacher or revealer of Divine Will **2.** foreteller of future (**-ess** *fem.*) —**prophecy** ('profisi) *n.* prediction, prophetic utterance —**prophesy** ('profisī) *v.* foretell —**prophetic** (prə'fetik) *a.*

prophylactic (prōfi'laktik, profi-) *n./a.* **1.** (something) done or used to ward off disease —*n.* **2.** condom —**prophy'laxis** *n.*

propinquity (prə'pingkwiti) *n.* nearness, proximity, close kinship

propitiate (prō'pishiāt) *vt.* appease, gain favor of —**propiti'ation** *n.* —**pro'pitiatory** *a.* —**pro'pitious** *a.* favorable, auspicious

proponent (prə'pōnənt) *n.* one who advocates something

proportion (prə'pörshən) *n.* **1.** part of whole **2.** the equality of 2 ratios, *eg* 1 is to 2 as 4 is to 8 **3.** correct relation in size and/or amount of degree between one thing and another —*pl.* **4.** dimensions —*vt.* **5.** arrange proportions of —**pro'portionable** *a.* —**pro'portional** *or* **pro'portionate** *a.* **1.** having a due proportion **2.** corresponding in size, number *etc.* —**pro'portionally** *adv.* —**proportional representation** representation of parties in elective body in proportion to votes they win

propose (prə'pōz) *vt.* **1.** put forward for consideration **2.** nominate **3.** intend —*vi.* **4.** offer marriage —**pro'posal** *n.* —**pro'poser** *n.* —**proposition** (propə'zishən) *n.* **1.** offer **2.** statement, assertion **3.** theorem **4.** suggestion of terms **5.** *inf.* thing to be dealt with

propound (prə'pownd) *vt.* put forward for consideration or solution

proprietor (prə'prīətər) *n.* owner (**-tress, -trix** *fem.*) —**pro'prietary** *a.* **1.** belonging to owner **2.** made by firm with exclusive rights of manufacture

propriety (prə'prīəti) *n.* properness, correct conduct, fitness

propulsion (prə'pulshən) *n. see* PROPEL

pro rata ('rātə, 'rätə) *Lat.* in proportion

prorate (prō'rāt) *vt.* divide proportionately

prorogue (prə'rōg) *vt.* dismiss (parliament) at end of session without dissolution

prosaic (prō'zāik) *a.* commonplace, unromantic

pros and cons various arguments in favor of and against motion, course of action *etc.*

proscenium (prō'sēniəm) *n.* arch or opening framing stage (*pl.* **-nia** (-niə))

proscribe (prōˈskrīb) *vt.* outlaw, condemn —**proscription** (prōˈskripshən) *n.*

prose (prōz) *n.* speech or writing without rhyme or meter —ˈ**prosily** *adv.* —ˈ**prosiness** *n.* —ˈ**prosy** *a.* tedious, dull

prosecute (ˈprosikyōōt) *vt.* carry on, bring legal proceedings against —**proseˈcution** *n.* —ˈ**prosecutor** *n.* (-**trix** *fem.*)

proselyte (ˈprosilīt) *n.* convert —**proselytism** (ˈprosilītizəm, -lit-) *n.* —**proselytize** (ˈprosilitīz) *v.*

prosody (ˈprosədi) *n.* system, study of versification —ˈ**prosodist** *n.*

prospect (ˈprospekt) *n.* **1.** (*sometimes pl.*) expectation, chance for success **2.** view, outlook **3.** likely customer or subscriber **4.** mental view —*v.* **5.** explore, *esp.* for gold —**proˈspective** *a.* **1.** anticipated **2.** future —**proˈspectively** *adv.* —ˈ**prospector** *n.* —**proˈspectus** *n.* circular describing company, school *etc.*

prosper (ˈprospər) *v.* (cause to) do well —**prosˈperity** *n.* good fortune, wellbeing —ˈ**prosperous** *a.* **1.** doing well, successful **2.** flourishing, rich, well-off —ˈ**prosperously** *adv.*

prostaglandin (prostəˈglandin) *n.* any of group of biological compounds which act on smooth muscle of the vascular and reproductive systems

prostate (ˈprostāt) *n.* gland accessory to male generative organs

prosthesis (prosˈthēsis, ˈprosthisis) *n.* (replacement of part of body with) artificial substitute (*pl.* **-ses** (-sēz))

prostitute (ˈprostityōōt, -tōōt) *n.* **1.** one who offers sexual intercourse in return for payment —*vt.* **2.** make a prostitute of **3.** put to unworthy use —**prostiˈtution** *n.*

prostrate (ˈprostrāt) *a.* **1.** lying flat **2.** crushed, submissive, overcome —*vt.* **3.** throw flat on ground **4.** reduce to exhaustion —**prosˈtration** *n.*

Prot. Protestant

protactinium (prōtakˈtiniəm) *n. Chem.* metallic element *Symbol* Pa, at. wt. 231.0, at. no. 91

protagonist (prōˈtagənist) *n.* **1.** leading character **2.** principal actor **3.** champion of a cause

protasis (ˈprotəsis) *n.* introductory clause of conditional sentence (*pl.* **-ses** (-sēz))

protean (ˈprōtiən, prōˈtēən) *a.* **1.** variable **2.** versatile

protect (prəˈtekt) *vt.* defend, guard, keep from harm —**proˈtection** *n.* —**proˈtectionist** *n.* one who advocates protecting industries by taxing competing imports —**proˈtective** *a.* —**proˈtector** *n.* **1.** one who protects **2.** regent —**proˈtectorate** *n.* **1.** relation of state to territory it protects and controls **2.** such territory **3.** office, period of protector of a state

protégé *or* (*fem.*) **protégée** (ˈprōtizhā) *n.* one under another's care, protection or patronage

protein (ˈprōtēn) *n.* any of various kinds of organic compound which form most essential part of food of living creatures —**proteinuria** (prōtənˈyōōriə, -ˈōōriə) *n.* protein in the urine, usu. indicating kidney disease

pro tempore (ˈprō ˈtempəri) *Lat.* for the time being (*also* **pro tem**)

protest (ˈprōtest) *n.* **1.** declaration or demonstration of objection —*vi.* (prəˈtest) **2.** object —*v.* (prəˈtest) **3.** make declaration (against) **4.** assert formally —**protesˈtation** *n.* strong declaration

Protestant (ˈprotistənt) *a.* **1.** belonging to any branch of the Western Church outside the Roman Catholic Church —*n.* **2.** member of such a church —ˈ**Protestantism** *n.*

prothrombin (prōˈthrombin) *n.* substance important in blood clotting

proto- *or sometimes before vowel* **prot-** (*comb. form*) first, as in *prototype*

protocol (ˈprōtəkol) *n.* **1.** diplomatic etiquette **2.** draft of terms signed by parties as basis of formal treaty **3.** plan for medical or scientific experiment

proton (ˈprōton) *n.* positively charged particle in nucleus of atom

protoplasm (ˈprōtəplazəm) *n.* substance that is living matter of all animal and plant cells —**protoˈplasmic** *a.*

prototype (ˈprōtətīp) *n.* **1.** original or model after which thing is copied **2.** pattern

protozoan (prōtəˈzōən) *n.* minute animal of lowest and simplest class (*pl.* **-zoa** (-ˈzōə))

protract (prōˈtrakt, prə-) *vt.* **1.** lengthen **2.** prolong **3.** delay **4.** draw to scale —**proˈtracted** *a.* **1.** long-drawn-out **2.** tedious —**proˈtraction** *n.* —**proˈtractor** *n.* instrument for measuring angles on paper

protrude (prōˈtrōōd) *v.* stick out, (cause to) project —**proˈtrusile** *a. Zool.* capable of being thrust forward —**proˈtrusion** *n.* —**proˈtrusive** *a.* thrusting forward —**proˈtrusively** *adv.*

protuberant (prōˈtyōōbərənt, -ˈtōō-) *a.* bulging out —**proˈtuberance** *or* **proˈtuberancy** *n.* bulge, swelling

proud (prowd) *a.* **1.** feeling or displaying pride **2.** arrogant **3.** gratified **4.** noble **5.** self-respecting **6.** stately —ˈ**proudly** *adv.* —**proud flesh** flesh growing around healing wound

Prov. **1.** Provençal **2.** *Bible* Proverbs **3.** Province **4.** Provost

prove (prōōv) *vt.* **1.** establish validity of **2.** demonstrate, test —*vi.* **3.** turn out (to be *etc.*) **4.** (of dough) rise in warm place before baking (**proved,** ˈ**proven** *pp.*) —**proving ground** place for testing new equipment *etc.*

provenance (ˈprovinəns) *n.* place of origin, source

Provençal (provənˈsäl; *Fr.* provãˈsal) *a.* **1.** of Provence, former province of SE France, its dialect of French or its Romance language —*n.* **2.** language of Provence, closely related to French and Italian, belonging to Romance group of Indo-European family **3.** native or inhabitant of Provence

provender (ˈprovindər) *n.* fodder

proverb (ˈprovərb) *n.* short, pithy, traditional saying in common use —**proˈverbial** *a.*

Proverbs (ˈprovərbz) *pl.n.* (*with sing. v.*) *Bible* 20th book of the O.T., written by Solomon, a guide for moral practice outside of the place of worship

provide (prəˈvīd) *vi.* **1.** make preparation —*vt.* **2.** supply, equip, prepare, furnish, give —**proˈvider** *n.* —**proˈviding** *or* **proˈvided** *conj.* (*sometimes with* that) on condition or understanding (that)

provident (ˈprovidənt) *a.* **1.** thrifty **2.** showing foresight —**ˈprovidence** *n.* **1.** kindly care of God or nature **2.** foresight **3.** economy —**proviˈdential** *a.* strikingly fortunate, lucky —**proviˈdentially** *adv.*

province (ˈprovins) *n.* **1.** division of a country, district **2.** sphere of action —*pl.* **3.** any part of country outside capital —**proˈvincial** *a.* **1.** of a province **2.** unsophisticated **3.** narrow in outlook —*n.* **4.** unsophisticated person **5.** inhabitant of province —**proˈvincialism** *n.* **1.** narrowness of outlook **2.** lack of refinement **3.** idiom peculiar to province

provision (prəˈvizhən) *n.* **1.** a providing, *esp.* for the future **2.** thing provided —*pl.* **3.** food **4.** *Law* articles of instrument or statute —*vt.* **5.** supply with food —**proˈvisional** *a.* **1.** temporary **2.** conditional

proviso (prəˈvīzō) *n.* condition (*pl.* **-s, -es**)

provoke (prəˈvōk) *vt.* **1.** irritate **2.** incense **3.** arouse **4.** excite **5.** cause —**provocation** (provəˈkāshən) *n.* —**provocative** (prəˈvokətiv) *a.*

Provolone (prōvəˈlōni) *n.* a hard, mellow cheese, usu. smoked after drying, orig. from Italy

provost (ˈprōvōst, ˈprovəst) *n.* **1.** one who superintends or presides **2.** head of certain colleges

prow (prow) *n.* bow of vessel

prowess (ˈprowis) *n.* **1.** bravery, fighting capacity **2.** skill

prowl (prowl) *vi.* **1.** roam stealthily, *esp.* in search of prey or booty —*n.* **2.** act of prowling —**ˈprowler** *n.* —**on the prowl 1.** moving about stealthily **2.** pursuing members of opposite sex

prox. proximo

proximate (ˈproksimit) *a.* nearest, next, immediate —**proxˈimity** *n.* —**ˈproximo** *adv.* in the next month

proxy (ˈproksi) *n.* **1.** authorized agent or substitute **2.** writing authorizing one to act as this

prude (proo͞d) *n.* one who affects excessive modesty or propriety —**ˈprudery** *n.* —**ˈprudish** *a.*

prudent (ˈproo͞dənt) *a.* **1.** careful, discreet **2.** sensible —**ˈprudence** *n.* **1.** habit of acting with careful deliberation **2.** wisdom applied to practice —**pruˈdential** *a.*

prune[1] (proo͞n) *n.* dried plum

prune[2] (proo͞n) *vt.* **1.** cut out (dead parts, excessive branches *etc.*) from **2.** shorten, reduce —**pruning hook** tool with curved blade terminating in hook, used for pruning

prurient (ˈproo͝riənt) *a.* **1.** given to, springing from lewd thoughts **2.** having unhealthy curiosity or desire —**ˈprurience** *or* **ˈpruriency** *n.*

pruritus (proo͞ˈrītəs) *n.* intense itching —**pruritic** (proo͞ˈritik) *a.*

prussic acid (ˈprusik) extremely poisonous aqueous solution of hydrogen cyanide

pry (prī) *vi.* **1.** make furtive or impertinent inquiries **2.** look curiously —*vt.* **3.** force open (**pried, ˈprying**)

P.S. postscript (*also* **p.s.**)

Ps. *or* **Psa.** *Bible* Psalm(s)

psalm (säm, sälm) *n.* **1.** sacred song **2.** (**P-**) any of the sacred songs making up the Book of Psalms in the Bible —**ˈpsalmist** *n.* writer of psalms —**ˈpsalmody** *n.* art, act of singing sacred music —**Psalter** (ˈsöltər) *n.* **1.** book of psalms **2.** copy of the Psalms as separate book —**psaltery** (ˈsöltəri) *n.* obsolete stringed instrument like lyre

Psalms (sämz, sälmz) *pl.n.* (*with sing. v.*) *Bible* 19th book of the O.T., collection of 150 psalms, many of which were written by David for worship

psephology (sēˈfoləji) *n.* statistical and sociological study of elections

pseud (soo͞d) *inf. n.* **1.** false or pretentious person —*a.* **2.** sham, fake (*also* **ˈpseudo**)

pseudo- *or sometimes before vowel* **pseud-** (*comb. form*) sham, as in *pseudo-Gothic, pseudomodern.* Such compounds are not given here where the meaning may easily be inferred from the simple word

pseudonym (ˈsoo͞dənim) *n.* false, fictitious name —**pseudonymous** (soo͞ˈdoniməs) *a.*

psi (sī, psī) *n.* 23rd letter in Gr. alphabet (Ψ, ψ), transliterated as *ps*

psittacine (ˈsitəsīn) *a.* pert. to, like parrots —**psittaˈcosis** *n.* dangerous infectious disease, virus of which is carried by parrots

psoriasis (səˈrīəsis) *n.* skin disease characterized by formation of reddish spots and patches covered with silvery scales

psst (pst) *interj.* exclamation of beckoning, *esp.* made surreptitiously

P.S.T. Pacific Standard Time

psyche (ˈsīki) *n.* human mind or soul

psychedelic (sīkiˈdelik) *a.* **1.** of or causing hallucinations **2.** like intense colors *etc.* experienced during hallucinations

psychic (ˈsīkik) *a.* **1.** sensitive to phenomena lying outside range of normal experience **2.** of soul or mind **3.** that appears to be outside region of physical law (*also* **ˈpsychical**)

—**psychiatry** (si'kīətri, sī-) *n.* medical treatment of mental diseases —**psychoa'nalysis** *n.* method of studying and treating mental disorders —**psycho'analyst** *n.* —**psycho'analyze** *vt.* treat by psychoanalysis —**psychogenic** (sīkə'jenik) *a. Psychol.* (*esp.* of disorders or symptoms) of mental, rather than organic origin —**psychoki'nesis** *n.* (in parapsychology) alteration of state of object supposedly by mental influence alone —**psycho'logical** *a.* **1.** of psychology **2.** of the mind —**psy'chologist** *n.* —**psy'chology** *n.* **1.** study of mind **2.** *inf.* person's mental make-up —**psy'chometry** *n.* **1.** measurement, testing of psychological processes **2.** supposed ability to divine unknown person's qualities by handling object used or worn by him —'**psychopath** *n.* person afflicted with severe mental disorder causing him to commit antisocial, oft. violent acts —**psycho'pathic** *a.* —'**psychopharma'cology** *n.* study of effect of drugs on the mind —**psy'chosis** *n.* severe mental disorder in which person's contact with reality becomes distorted (*pl.* **-choses** (-'kōsēz)) —**psychoso'matic** *a.* of physical disorders thought to have psychological causes —**psycho'therapy** *n.* treatment of disease by psychological, rather than by physical, means —**psychological moment** most appropriate time for producing desired effect —**psychological warfare** military application of psychology, *esp.* to manipulation of morale in time of war —**psychosomatic medicine** branch of psychiatry dealing with physical illnesses that result from emotional conflicts

psycho ('sīkō) *sl. n.* **1.** psychopath (*pl.* **-s**) —*a.* **2.** psychopathic

psycho- *or sometimes before vowel* **psych-** (*comb. form*) mind, psychological or mental processes, as in *psychology, psychosomatic*

Pt *Chem.* platinum

pt. **1.** part **2.** pint **3.** point

Pt. **1.** Point **2.** Port

P.T. **1.** physical therapy **2.** physical training

P.T.A. parent teacher association

ptarmigan ('tärmigən) *n.* bird of grouse family which turns white in winter (*pl.* **-s, -gan**)

Pte. Private (soldier)

pteridophyte (tə'ridəfīt) *n.* any of phylum of plants comprising ferns, club mosses, horsetails and quillworts

ptero- (*comb. form*) wing, as in *pterodactyl*

pterodactyl (terə'daktil) *n.* extinct flying reptile with batlike wings

P.T.O. *or* **p.t.o.** please turn over

ptomaine ('tōmān) *n.* any of group of poisonous alkaloids found in decaying matter

ptyalin ('tīəlin) *n.* enzyme found in saliva which breaks down starch

Pu *Chem.* plutonium

pub (pub) *n.* **UK** public house, building with bar(s) and license to sell alcoholic drinks —**pub-crawl** *sl. n.* **1.** drinking tour of number of pubs or bars —*vi.* **2.** make such tour

pub. **1.** public **2.** publication **3.** published **4.** publisher **5.** publishing

puberty ('pyo͞obərti) *n.* sexual maturity —'**pubertal** *a.*

pubes ('pyo͞obēz) *n.* **1.** region above external genital organs, covered with hair from time of puberty **2.** pubic hair (*pl.* '**pubes**) **3.** *pl. of* PUBIS

pubescent (pyo͞o'besənt) *a.* **1.** arriving or arrived at puberty **2.** (of certain plants and animals or their parts) covered with fine short hairs or down —**pu'bescence** *n.*

pubic ('pyo͞obik) *a.* of the pubes or pubis

pubis ('pyo͞obis) *n.* bone forming front of each half of pelvis (*pl.* **-bes** (-bēz))

public ('publik) *a.* **1.** of or concerning the public as a whole **2.** not private **3.** open to general observation or knowledge **4.** accessible to all **5.** serving the people —*n.* **6.** the community or its members —'**publican** *n.* keeper of public house —'**publicly** *adv.* —**public-address system** system of microphones, amplifiers and loudspeakers for increasing sound level, used in auditoriums *etc.* (*also* **P.A. system**) —**public enemy** notorious person, such as criminal, regarded as menace to public —**public health** organized efforts of community to protect its members against disease —**Public Health Service** chief health agency of U.S. government, which works closely with states, sets standards for sanitation, maintains quarantine services *etc.* —**public house UK** pub —**public relations** promotion of good relations of an organization or authority with the general public —**public school 1.** in England and Wales, private independent fee-paying school **2.** in some Canad. provinces, a local elementary school —**public servant** elected or appointed holder of public office —**public spirit** interest in and devotion to welfare of community —**public-spirited** *a.* having or showing active interest in good of community —**public transport** trains, buses *etc.* that have fixed routes and are available to general public

publicist ('publisist) *n.* **1.** writer on public concerns **2.** journalist —**pub'licity** *n.* **1.** process of attracting public attention **2.** attention thus gained —*a.* **3.** pert. to advertisement —'**publicize** *vt.* advertise

publish ('publish) *vt.* **1.** prepare and issue for sale (books, music *etc.*) **2.** make generally known **3.** proclaim —**publi'cation** *n.* —'**publisher** *n.*

puce (pyo͞os) *a./n.* purplish-brown (color)

puck[1] (puk) *n.* rubber disk used instead of ball in ice hockey

puck[2] (puk) *n.* mischievous sprite —'**puckish** *a.*

pucka ('pukə) *a. see* PUKKA

pucker (ˈpukər) *v.* **1.** gather into wrinkles —*n.* **2.** crease, fold

pudding (ˈpŏŏding) *n.* **1.** sweet, usu. cooked dessert, oft. made from flour or other cereal **2.** soft savory dish with pastry or batter **3.** kind of sausage

puddle (ˈpudəl) *n.* **1.** small muddy pool **2.** rough cement for lining ponds *etc.* —*vt.* **3.** line with puddle **4.** make muddy

pudendum (pyŏŏˈdendəm) *n.* (*oft. pl.*) human external genital organs, *esp.* of female (*pl.* **-da** (-də)) —**puˈdendal** *or* **ˈpudic** *a.*

pudgy (ˈpuji) *a.* plump and short

pueblo (pōōˈeblō, ˈpweblō) *n.* **1.** communal dwelling consisting of continuous flat-roofed houses in groups occupied by Amerindians of southwestern U.S. **2.** Amerindian village of southwestern U.S. **3.** (**P-**) (member of) group of Amerindian peoples of southwestern U.S. (*pl.* **-s**)

puerile (ˈpyŏŏəril) *a.* **1.** childish **2.** foolish **3.** trivial

puerperium (pyōōərˈpēəriəm) *n.* period of about six weeks after childbirth —**puerperal** (pyōōˈərpərəl) *a.* —**puerperal fever** blood poisoning caused by infection during childbirth

Puerto Rico (ˈpörtə ˈrēkō, ˈpwertō) island in the West Indies, Commonwealth of the U.S. —**Puerto Rican** (native or inhabitant) of Puerto Rico

puff (puf) *n.* **1.** short blast of breath, wind *etc.* **2.** its sound **3.** type of pastry **4.** laudatory notice or advertisement —*vi.* **5.** blow abruptly **6.** breathe hard —*vt.* **7.** send out in a puff **8.** blow out, inflate **9.** advertise **10.** smoke hard —**puffed** *a.* **1.** breathless; winded **2.** puffy —ˈ**puffy** *a.* **1.** short-winded **2.** swollen —**puff adder 1.** large venomous Afr. viper that inflates its body when alarmed **2.** N Amer. nonvenomous snake that inflates its body when alarmed (*also* **hognose snake**) —ˈ**puffball** *n.* ball-shaped fungus —**puff paste** dough for making a rich flaky pastry

puffin (ˈpufin) *n.* any of various sea birds with large brightly colored beaks

pug (pug) *n.* **1.** small snub-nosed dog **2.** *sl.* boxer —**pug nose** snub nose

pugilism (ˈpyōōjilizəm) *n.* art, practice or profession of fighting with fists; boxing —ˈ**pugilist** *n.* —**pugiˈlistic** *a.*

pugnacious (pugˈnāshəs) *a.* given to fighting —**pugnacity** (pugˈnasiti) *n.*

puissant (ˈpwisənt, ˈpyōōisənt) *a. Poet.* powerful, mighty —ˈ**puissance** *n.* show-jumping competition over very high fences

puke (pyōōk) *sl. vi.* **1.** vomit —*n.* **2.** act of vomiting

pukka *or* **pucka** (ˈpukə) *a. Anglo-Indian* properly or perfectly done, constructed *etc.*; good; genuine

pulchritude (ˈpulkrityōōd, -tōōd) *n. Lit.* beauty

pule (pyōōl) *vi.* whine; whimper

Pulitzer Prize (ˈpŏŏlitsər) any of annual prizes awarded for achievements in American journalism, letters and music

pull (pŏŏl) *vt.* **1.** exert force on (object) to move it toward source of force **2.** strain, stretch **3.** tear **4.** propel by rowing —*n.* **5.** act of pulling **6.** force exerted by it **7.** draft of liquor **8.** *inf.* power, influence —**pull in 1.** (of train) arrive **2.** (of automobile *etc.*) draw in to side of road, stop **3.** attract **4.** *sl.* arrest —**pull off** *inf.* carry through to successful issue —**pull out 1.** withdraw **2.** extract **3.** (of train) depart **4.** (of automobile *etc.*) move away from side of road; move out to overtake —**pull (someone's) leg** *inf.* make fun of (someone) —**pull up 1.** tear up **2.** recover lost ground **3.** improve **4.** come to a stop **5.** halt **6.** reprimand

pullet (ˈpŏŏlit) *n.* young hen

pulley (ˈpŏŏli) *n.* wheel with groove in rim for cord, used to raise weights by downward pull

Pullman (ˈpŏŏlmən) *n.* railroad saloon car (*pl.* **-s**) (*also* **Pullman car**)

pullover (ˈpŏŏlōvər) *n.* sweater without fastening, to be pulled over head

pulmonary (ˈpŏŏlməneri, ˈpul-) *a.* **1.** of lungs **2.** having lungs or lunglike organs —**pulmonary embolism** obstruction of artery in lung by embolus or foreign substance

pulp (pulp) *n.* **1.** soft, moist, vegetable or animal matter **2.** flesh of fruit **3.** any soft soggy mass —*vt.* **4.** reduce to pulp

pulpit (ˈpŏŏlpit) *n.* raised (enclosed) platform for preacher

pulsar (ˈpulsär) *n.* small dense star emitting radio waves

pulse[1] (puls) *n.* **1.** movement of blood in arteries corresponding to heartbeat, discernible to touch, *eg* in wrist **2.** any regular beat or vibration —ˈ**pulsate** *vi.* throb, quiver —**pulˈsation** *n.*

pulse[2] (puls) *n.* edible seeds of pod-bearing plants, *eg* beans

pulverize (ˈpulvərīz) *vt.* **1.** reduce to powder **2.** smash, demolish —**pulveriˈzation** *n.*

puma (ˈpyōōmə, ˈpōōmə) *n.* cougar

pumice (ˈpumis) *n.* light porous variety of volcanic rock used to scour, smooth and polish (*also* **pumice stone**)

pummel (ˈpuməl) *vt.* strike repeatedly

pump[1] (pump) *n.* **1.** appliance in which piston and handle are used for raising water, or putting in or taking out air, liquid *etc.* —*vt.* **2.** raise, put in, take out *etc.* with pump **3.** empty by means of pump **4.** extract information from —*vi.* **5.** work pump **6.** work like pump

pump[2] (pump) *n.* low-cut shoe without laces or straps

pumpernickel (ˈpumpərnikəl) *n.* sour black bread made of coarse rye flour

pumpkin ('pumpkin) *n.* any of several varieties of gourd, eaten *esp.* as vegetable

pun (pun) *n.* **1.** humorous use of words that have the same sound, but have different meanings —*vi.* **2.** make pun (**-nn-**) —'**punster** *n.*

punch[1] (punch) *n.* **1.** tool for perforating or stamping **2.** blow with fist **3.** *inf.* vigor —*vt.* **4.** stamp, perforate with punch **5.** strike with fist —'**punchball** *n.* stuffed or inflated ball or bag, either suspended or supported by flexible rod, that is punched for exercise, *esp.* boxing training —**punch card** *or* **punched card** card on which data can be coded in form of punched holes —**punch-drunk** *or* (*inf.*) '**punchy** *a.* dazed, as by repeated blows —**punch line** culminating part of joke *etc.*, that gives it its point —**punch tape** strip of paper used in computers *etc.* for recording information in form of punched holes

punch[2] (punch) *n.* drink of spirits or wine with fruit juice, spice *etc.* —**punch bowl** bowl in which punch is mixed and served

punctilious (pungk'tiliəs) *a.* **1.** making much of details of etiquette **2.** very exact, particular

punctual ('pungkchōōəl) *a.* in good time, not late, prompt —**punctu'ality** *n.* —'**punctually** *adv.*

punctuate ('pungkchōōāt) *vt.* **1.** insert punctuation marks into **2.** interrupt at intervals —**punctu'ation** *n.* marks, *eg* commas, colons *etc.*, put in writing to assist in making sense clear

puncture ('pungkchər) *n.* **1.** small hole made by sharp object, *esp.* in tire **2.** act of puncturing —*vt.* **3.** prick hole in, perforate

pundit *or* **pandit** ('pundit) *n.* **1.** self-appointed expert **2.** Brahman learned in Sanskrit and, *esp.* in Hindu religion, philosophy or law

pungent ('punjənt) *a.* **1.** biting **2.** irritant **3.** piercing **4.** tart **5.** caustic —'**pungency** *n.*

punish ('punish) *vt.* **1.** cause (someone) to suffer for offense **2.** inflict penalty on **3.** use or treat roughly —'**punishable** *a.* —'**punishment** *n.* —**punitive** ('pyōōnitiv) *a.* inflicting or intending to inflict punishment

punk[1] (pungk) *a./n.* **1.** inferior, rotten, worthless (person or thing) **2.** petty (hoodlum) **3.** (of) style of rock music

punk[2] (pungk) *n.* **1.** sticklike or coiled substance that smolders when lit **2.** dried decayed wood or other substance that smolders when ignited: used as tinder

punkah *or* **punka** ('pungkə) *n.* **1.** fan made of palm leaf or leaves **2.** large fan made of palm leaves *etc.* worked mechanically to cool room

punt[1] (punt) *n.* **1.** flat-bottomed, square-ended boat, propelled by pushing with pole —*vt.* **2.** propel thus

punt[2] (punt) *Sport vt.* **1.** kick (ball) before it touches ground, when let fall from hands —*n.* **2.** such a kick

punt[3] (punt) *vi.* gamble, bet —'**punter** *n.* **1.** one who punts **2.** professional gambler **3.** *inf.* customer or client, *esp.* prostitute's client

puny ('pyōōni) *a.* small and feeble

pup (pup) *n.* young of certain animals, *eg* dog

pupa ('pyōōpə) *n.* stage between larva and adult in metamorphosis of insect, chrysalis (*pl.* **pupae** ('pyōōpē)) —'**pupal** *a.*

pupil ('pyōōpəl) *n.* **1.** person being taught **2.** opening in iris of eye

puppet ('pupit) *n.* small doll or figure of person *etc.* controlled by operator's hand —**puppe'teer** *n.* —'**puppetry** *n.* —**puppet show** show with puppets worked by hidden showman —**puppet state** state that appears independent but is controlled by another

puppy ('pupi) *n.* young dog —**puppy fat** fatty tissue in child or adolescent, usu. disappearing with age

purblind ('pərblīnd) *a.* **1.** partly or nearly blind **2.** lacking in insight or understanding

purchase ('pərchis) *vt.* **1.** buy —*n.* **2.** act of buying **3.** what is bought **4.** leverage, grip

purdah ('pərdə) *n.* **1.** Muslim, Hindu custom of keeping women in seclusion **2.** screen, veil to achieve this

pure (pyōōər) *a.* **1.** unmixed, untainted **2.** simple **3.** spotless **4.** faultless **5.** innocent **6.** concerned with theory only —'**purely** *adv.* —**purifi'cation** *n.* —**pu'rificatory** *a.* —'**purify** *v.* make, become pure, clear or clean (**-ified, -ifying**) —'**purism** *n.* excessive insistence on correctness of language —'**purist** *n.* —'**purity** *n.* state of being pure —**purebred** ('pyōōər'bred) *a.* **1.** denoting pure strain obtained through many generations of controlled breeding —*n.* ('pyōōər-bred) **2.** purebred animal

purée (pyōō'rā) *n.* **1.** pulp of cooked fruit or vegetables —*vt.* **2.** make (cooked foods) into purée

purgatory ('pərgətōri) *n.* place or state of torment, pain or distress, *esp.* temporary —**purga'torial** *a.*

purge (pərj) *vt.* **1.** make clean, purify **2.** remove, get rid of **3.** clear out —*n.* **4.** act, process of purging **5.** removal of undesirable members from political party, army *etc.* —**purgation** (pər'gāshən) *n.* —**purgative** ('pərgətiv) *a./n.*

Purim ('pōōrim) *n. Judaism* Feast of Lots commemorating the rescue of the Persian Jews from Haman's plot to exterminate them

purine ('pyōōərēn) *n.* ring-structured compound, building block of DNA and RNA

Puritan ('pyōōritən) *n.* **1.** *Hist.* member of extreme Protestant party **2.** (**p-**) person of extreme strictness in morals or religion —**puri'tanic(al)** *a.* **1.** strict in the observance of religious and moral duties **2.** overscrupulous —'**puritanism** *n.*

purl[1] (pərl) *n.* **1.** stitch that forms ridge in knitting —*v.* **2.** knit in purl

purl[2] (pərl) *vi.* flow with burbling sound, swirl, babble

purlieus (ˈpərlyōōz, -lōōz) *pl.n.* outlying parts, outskirts

purlin (ˈpərlin) *n.* horizontal beam that provides support for rafters of roof

purloin (pərˈloin) *vt.* **1.** steal **2.** pilfer

purple (ˈpərpəl) *n./a.* (of) color between blue and red —**Purple Heart 1.** decoration awarded to members of U.S. Armed Forces for wound received in action **2.** *sl.* amphetamine pill

purport (pərˈpört) *vt.* **1.** claim to be (true *etc.*) **2.** signify, imply —*n.* (ˈpərpört) **3.** meaning **4.** apparent meaning **5.** significance

purpose (ˈpərpəs) *n.* **1.** reason, object **2.** design **3.** aim, intention —*vt.* **4.** intend —ˈ**purposely** *adv.* —**purpose-built** *a.* made to serve specific purpose —**on purpose** intentionally

purr (pər) *n.* **1.** (*esp.* of cats) make low vibrant sound, usu. considered as expressing pleasure *etc.* —*vi.* **2.** utter this sound

purse (pərs) *n.* **1.** pocketbook, small bag for money **2.** resources **3.** money as prize —*vt.* **4.** pucker (mouth, lips *etc.*) in wrinkles —*vi.* **5.** become wrinkled and drawn in —ˈ**purser** *n.* ship's officer who keeps accounts —**purse strings** control of expenditure (*esp. in* **hold** *or* **control the purse strings**)

purslane (ˈpərslin) *n.* plant used (*esp.* formerly) in salads and as potherb

pursue (pərˈsōō) *vt.* **1.** run after **2.** chase **3.** aim at **4.** engage in **5.** continue **6.** follow —*vi.* **7.** go in pursuit **8.** continue —**purˈsuance** *n.* carrying out —**purˈsuant** *adj. chiefly law* in agreement or conformity —**purˈsuer** *n.* —**purˈsuit** *n.* **1.** running after, attempt to catch **2.** occupation

purulent (ˈpyŏŏryələnt, ˈpyŏŏrələnt) *a. see at* PUS

purvey (pərˈvā) *vt.* supply (provisions) —**purˈveyance** *n.* —**purˈveyor** *n.*

purview (ˈpərvyōō) *n.* scope, range

pus (pus) *n.* yellowish discharge produced by suppuration —**purulence** (ˈpyŏŏryələns, ˈpyŏŏrələns) *n.* —ˈ**purulent** *a.* **1.** forming, discharging pus **2.** septic

push (pŏŏsh) *vt.* **1.** move, try to move away by pressure **2.** drive, impel **3.** *inf.* sell (*esp.* narcotic drugs) illegally —*vi.* **4.** make thrust **5.** advance with steady effort —*n.* **6.** thrust **7.** persevering self-assertion **8.** big military advance **9.** *sl.* dismissal —ˈ**pusher** *n.* —ˈ**pushing** *or* (*inf.*) ˈ**pushy** *a.* given to pushing oneself —**push button** electrical switch operated by pressing button, which closes or opens circuit —**push-button** *a.* **1.** operated by push button **2.** initiated as simply as by pressing button —ˈ**pushchair** *n. esp.* **UK** (collapsible) chair-shaped carriage for baby —ˈ**pushover** *n. sl.* **1.** something easily achieved **2.** person *etc.* easily taken advantage of or defeated —**push-start** *vt.* **1.** start (motor vehicle) by pushing while in gear, thus turning engine —*n.* **2.** this process

pusillanimous (pyōōsiˈlaniməs) *a.* cowardly —**pusillaˈnimity** *n.*

puss (pŏŏs) *n.* cat (*also* ˈ**pussy**) —**pussy willow** willow tree with silvery silky catkins

pussyfoot (ˈpŏŏsifŏŏt) *vi. inf.* **1.** move stealthily **2.** act indecisively, procrastinate

pustule (ˈpuschōōl, -tyōōl, -tōōl) *n.* pimple containing pus —ˈ**pustular** *a.* —**pustulate** (ˈpuschəlāt, ˈpustyə-, ˈpustə-) *v.* **1.** (cause to) form into pustules —*a.* (ˈpuschəlit, ˈpustyə-, ˈpustə-) **2.** covered with pustules

put (pŏŏt) *vt.* **1.** place **2.** set **3.** express **4.** throw (*esp.* shot) (**put,** ˈ**putting**) —*n.* **5.** throw —**put-down** *n.* cruelly critical remark —**put-up** *a.* dishonestly or craftily prearranged (*esp. in* **put-up job**) —**put across** express successfully —**put down 1.** make written record of **2.** repress **3.** consider **4.** attribute **5.** put (animal) to death because of old age or illness **6.** table on agenda **7.** *sl.* reject, humiliate —**put off 1.** postpone **2.** disconcert **3.** repel —**put up 1.** erect **2.** accommodate **3.** nominate

putative (ˈpyōōtətiv) *a.* reputed, supposed —ˈ**putatively** *adv.*

putrid (ˈpyōōtrid) *a.* **1.** decomposed **2.** rotten —ˈ**putrefy** *v.* make or become rotten (**-efied, -efying**) —**putreˈfaction** *n.* —**puˈtrescence** *n.* —**puˈtrescent** *a.* becoming rotten —**puˈtridity** *n.*

Putsch (pŏŏch) *n.* surprise attempt to overthrow the existing power, political revolt

putt (put) *vt.* strike (golf ball) along ground in direction of hole —ˈ**putter** *n.* golf club for putting —**putting green 1.** on golf course, area of closely mown grass at end of fairway where hole is **2.** area of smooth grass with several holes for putting games

puttee (ˈputi) *n.* strip of cloth wound round leg like bandage, serving as gaiter

putto (ˈpŏŏtō) *n.* figure of naked baby boy, sometimes with wings, common in Renaissance art (*pl.* **putti** (ˈpŏŏtē))

putty (ˈputi) *n.* **1.** paste of whiting and oil as used by glaziers **2.** jeweler's polishing powder —*vt.* **3.** fix, fill with putty (**-ied, -ying**)

puzzle (ˈpuzəl) *v.* **1.** perplex or be perplexed —*n.* **2.** bewildering, perplexing question, problem or toy —ˈ**puzzlement** *n.*

PVC polyvinyl chloride (synthetic thermoplastic material used in insulation, shoes *etc.*)

pye-dog (ˈpīdog) *n.* ownerless half-wild Asian dog

pyelonephritis (pīəlōniˈfrītis) *n.* infection of the kidney

pyemia (pīˈēmiə) *n.* form of blood poisoning —**pyˈemic** *a.*

pygmy *or* **pigmy** (ˈpigmi) *n.* **1.** abnormally

undersized person **2.** (**P-**) member of one of dwarf peoples of Equatorial Afr. —*a.* **3.** undersized

pylon (ˈpīlon, -lən) *n.* towerlike erection, *esp.* to carry electric cables

pyo- *or before vowel* **py-** (*comb. form*) pus, as in *pyosis*

pyorrhea (pīəˈrēə) *n.* inflammation of the gums with discharge of pus and loosening of teeth

pyramid (ˈpirəmid) *n.* **1.** massive structure with square base and four triangular faces meeting at apex **2.** solid geometrical figure having a polygon as base whose sides are triangles sharing a common apex —*vt.* **3.** build up in the form of a pyramid **4.** increase rapidly on a broadening base —**pyˈramidal** *a.*

pyre (ˈpīər) *n.* pile of wood for burning a dead body

pyrethrum (pīˈrēthrəm) *n.* **1.** any of several types of cultivated chrysanthemums **2.** insecticide made from it

pyretic (pīˈretik) *a.* of fever

Pyrex (ˈpīreks) *n.* trade name for glassware resistant to heat and chemicals

pyridoxine (piriˈdoksēn) *n.* vitamin B_6

pyrite (ˈpīrīt) *n.* yellow mineral consisting of iron sulfide in cubic crystalline form

pyrites (piˈrītēz, pī-) *n.* **1.** *see* PYRITE **2.** any of a number of other disulfides of metals, *esp.* of copper and tin (*pl.* **pyˈrites**)

pyro- *or before vowel* **pyr-** (*comb. form*) **1.** fire or heat, as in *pyromania, pyrometer* **2.** *Chem.* new substance obtained by heating another, as in *pyroboric acid* **3.** *Min.* having property that changes upon application of heat; having flame-colored appearance, as in *pyroxylin*

pyrogenic (pīrōˈjenik) *or* **pyrogenous** (pīˈrojinəs) *a.* **1.** produced by or producing heat **2.** causing or resulting from fever

pyrography (pīˈrogrəfi) *n.* **1.** art of burning designs on wood or leather with heated tools **2.** design made by this process

pyromania (pīrōˈmāniə) *n.* uncontrollable impulse and practice of setting things on fire —**pyroˈmaniac** *n.*

pyrometer (pīˈromitər) *n.* instrument for measuring very high temperature —**pyˈrometry** *n.*

pyrotechnics (pīrəˈtekniks) *pl.n.* **1.** (*with sing. v.*) manufacture of fireworks **2.** (*with sing. or pl. v.*) firework display —**pyroˈtechnist** *n.*

Pyrrhic victory (ˈpirik) victory won at excessive cost

Pythagorean theorem (pithagəˈrēən, pī-) proposition that in right-angled triangle square of length of hypotenuse equals sum of squares of other two sides

python (ˈpīthon, -thən) *n.* large snake that crushes its prey

pyx (piks) *n.* **1.** vessel in which consecrated Host is preserved **2.** (*also* **pyx chest**) box in Brit. Royal Mint holding specimen coins kept to be tested for weight

Q

q *or* **Q** (kyo͞o) *n.* **1.** 17th letter of English alphabet **2.** speech sound represented by this letter (*pl.* **q's, Q's** *or* **Qs**)

Q 1. *Chess* Queen **2.** Question **3.** Quebec

q. 1. quart **2.** quarter **3.** quarto (*pl.* **qq., Qq.**) (*also* **Q.**) **4.** question

Qatar (ˈkätər, ˈgät-) *n.* country in Middle East occupying a peninsula in the Persian Gulf, bounded by Saudi Arabia to the south

Q.E.D. quod erat demonstrandum (*Lat.*, which was to be proved)

Qld. Queensland

Q.M. Quartermaster

qr. 1. quarter **2.** quire (*pl.* **qrs.**)

qt. 1. quart (*pl.* **qt., qts.**) **2.** quantity

q.t. *inf.* quiet —**on the q.t.** secretly

qto quarto

qua (kwā̆, kwā) *prep.* in the capacity of

quack (kwak) *n.* **1.** harsh cry of duck **2.** pretender to medical or other skill —*vi.* **3.** (of duck) utter cry

quack grass perennial grass, a garden weed which spreads very rapidly by means of trailing underground stems which root at every node (*also* **quick grass, twitch grass, witch grass**)

quad (kwod) *n.* **1.** quadrant **2.** *inf.* quadruplet **3.** quadrangle **4.** quadraphonic

quadrangle (ˈkwodranggəl) *n.* **1.** four-sided figure **2.** four-sided courtyard in a building —**quadˈrangular** *a.*

quadrant (ˈkwodrənt) *n.* **1.** quarter of circle **2.** instrument for taking angular measurements —**ˈquadrate** *vt.* make square —**quadratic** (kwoˈdratik) *a.* (of equation) involving square of unknown quantity

quadraphonic (kwodrəˈfonik) *a.* (of a sound system) using four independent speakers

quadrennial (kwoˈdreniəl) *a.* **1.** lasting four years **2.** occurring every four years —*n.* **3.** period of four years

quadri- *or before vowel* **quadr-** (*comb. form*) four

quadrilateral (kwodriˈlatərəl) *a.* **1.** four-sided —*n.* **2.** four-sided figure

quadrille (kwoˈdril, kwə-) *n.* **1.** square dance **2.** music played for it

quadrillion (kwoˈdrilyən) *n.* **1.** in Amer. and France, number represented as one followed by 15 zeros (10^{15}) **2.** in Brit. and Germany, number represented as one followed by 24 zeros (10^{24})

quadriplegia (kwodriˈplējiə) *n.* paralysis of all four limbs (*also* **tetraˈplegia**) —**quadriˈplegic** *a.*

quadrivalent (kwodriˈvāl ənt) *a. Chem.* having four valencies (*also* **tetraˈvalent**) —**quadriˈvalency** *or* **quadriˈvalence** *n.*

quadroon (kwoˈdro͞on) *n.* person of one quarter Negro ancestry

quadruped (ˈkwodrəped) *n.* four-footed animal —**quadˈrupedal** *a.*

quadruple (kwoˈdro͞opəl, ˈkwodrəpəl) *a.* **1.** fourfold **2.** consisting of four parts —*v.* **3.** make, become four times as much —*n.* **4.** quantity or number four times as great as another —**quadˈruplicate** *a.* fourfold

quadruplet (kwoˈdro͞oplit, -ˈdrup-; ˈkwodro͞oplit) *n.* one of four offspring born at one birth

quaff (kwof) *v.* drink heartily or in one draft

quag (kwag) *n.* bog, swamp

quagga (ˈkwagə) *n.* recently extinct member of horse family

quail[1] (kwāl) *vi.* flinch; cower

quail²

quail[2] (kwāl) *n.* small game bird resembling domestic fowl (**bobwhite quail** sometimes considered a songbird, **California quail** sometimes pet, **Gambrel's quail** protected by law)

quaint (kwānt) *a.* **1.** interestingly old-fashioned or odd **2.** curious **3.** whimsical —**ˈquaintly** *adv.* —**ˈquaintness** *n.*

quake (kwāk) *vi.* shake, tremble

Quaker (ˈkwākər) *n.* member of Christian sect, the **Society of Friends** (**ˈQuakeress** *fem.*)

qualify (ˈkwolifī) *vi.* **1.** make oneself competent —*vt.* **2.** moderate **3.** limit **4.** make competent **5.** ascribe quality to **6.** describe (**-fied, -fying**) —**qualifiˈcation** *n.* **1.** thing that qualifies, attribute **2.** restriction **3.** qualifying

quality (ˈkwoliti) *n.* **1.** attribute, characteristic, property **2.** degree of excellence **3.** rank —**ˈqualitative** *a.* depending on quality —**qualitative analysis** *Chem.* decomposition of substance to determine kinds of constituents present; result obtained by such determination —**quality control** control of relative quality of manufactured product, usu. by statistical sampling techniques

qualm (kwăm, kwălm) *n.* **1.** misgiving **2.** sudden feeling of sickness —**'qualmish** *a.*

quandary ('kwondri) *n.* state of perplexity; puzzling situation; dilemma

quantity ('kwontiti) *n.* **1.** size, number, amount **2.** specified or considerable amount —**'quantify** *vt.* discover, express quantity of —**'quantitative** *a.* **1.** involving considerations of amount or size **2.** capable of being measured **3.** *Prosody* of metrical system based on length of syllables —**'quantum** *n.* desired or required amount (*pl.* **-ta**) —**quantitative analysis** *Chem.* decomposition of substance to determine amount of each constituent; result obtained by such determination —**quantum theory** theory that, in radiation, energy of electrons is discharged not continuously but in discrete units or quanta

quarantine ('kworəntēn) *n.* **1.** isolation to prevent spreading of infection —*vt.* **2.** put, keep in quarantine

quark (kwörk, kwärk) *n.* *Phys.* any of several hypothetical particles thought to be fundamental units of matter

quarrel[1] ('kworəl) *n.* **1.** angry dispute **2.** argument —*vi.* **3.** argue **4.** find fault —**'quarrelsome** *a.*

quarrel[2] ('kworəl) *n.* **1.** crossbow arrow **2.** diamond-shaped pane

quarry[1] ('kwori) *n.* **1.** object of hunt or pursuit **2.** prey

quarry[2] ('kwori) *n.* **1.** excavation where stone *etc.* is got from ground for building *etc.* —*v.* **2.** get (stone *etc.*) from quarry (**'quarried, 'quarrying**)

quart (kwört) *n.* **1.** measure of liquid capacity equal to two pints or one quarter of a gallon, measuring 57.75 cubic inches, and equivalent to .946 liter **2.** measure of dry capacity equal to two pints or one eighth of a peck, measuring 67.201 cubic inches and equivalent to 1.101 liters

quarter ('kwörtər) *n.* **1.** fourth part **2.** 25 cents **3.** region, district **4.** mercy —*pl.* **5.** lodgings —*vt.* **6.** divide into quarters —*v.* **7.** billet or be billeted in lodgings —**'quarterly** *a.* **1.** happening, due *etc.* each quarter of year —*n.* **2.** quarterly periodical —**quar'tet** *n.* **1.** group of four musicians **2.** music for four performers —**'quarto** *n.* **1.** size of book in which sheets are folded into four leaves (*pl.* **-s**) —*a.* **2.** of this size —**'quarterback** *n.* member of football team who calls the signals —**'quarterdeck** *n.* after part of upper deck used *esp.* for official, ceremonial purposes —**quarter'final** *n.* round before semifinal in competition —**quarter horse** small, powerful breed of horse —**'quartermaster** *n.* officer responsible for stores —**quarter note** *Mus.* one fourth of time value of whole note —**quarter rest** pause in music lasting as long as quarter note —**'quarterstaff** *n.* long staff for fighting (*pl.* **-staves**)

quartz (kwörts) *n.* stone of pure crystalline silica —**'quartzite** *n.* quartz rock

quasar ('kwāzär, -sär) *n.* extremely distant starlike object emitting powerful radio waves

quash (kwosh) *vt.* **1.** annul **2.** reject **3.** subdue forcibly

quasi- ('kwāzī-) (*comb. form*) seemingly, resembling but not actually being, as in *quasi-scientific*

quassia ('kwoshə) *n.* tropical Amer. tree

quaternary ('kwotərneri, kwə'tərnəri) *a.* **1.** of the number four **2.** having four parts **3.** (**Q-**) *Geol.* of most recent period, after Tertiary —*n.* **4.** (**Q-**) Quaternary period or rock system

quatrain ('kwotrān) *n.* four-line stanza, *esp.* rhymed alternately

quatrefoil ('katərfoil) *n.* **1.** leaf composed of four leaflets **2.** *Archit.* carved ornament having four arcs arranged about common center

quattrocento (kwätrō'chentō) *n.* the 15th century., *esp.* when referring to Italian art and literature

quaver ('kwāvər) *vt.* **1.** say or sing in tremulous tones —*vi.* **2.** tremble, shake, vibrate

quay (kē) *n.* **1.** solid, fixed landing stage **2.** wharf

queasy ('kwēzi) *a.* inclined to, or causing, sickness

Quebec (kwi'bek) *n.* word used in communications for the letter *q*

Quechua ('kechōōə, kə'chōōə) *n.* Amerindian language spoken in Peru, Bolivia and Ecuador

queen (kwēn) *n.* **1.** king's wife **2.** female sovereign **3.** piece in chess **4.** fertile female bee, wasp *etc.* **5.** face card with picture of a queen, ranking between king and jack **6.** *inf.* male homosexual **7.** female domestic cat —**'queenly** *a./adv.* —**Queen Anne** (an) **1.** of architecture, furniture and silver ware in the reign of Queen Anne of England (1702-14) **2.** of American architectural style of late 19th cent. combining many materials and styles —**Queen Anne's lace** wild carrot —**queen consort** wife of reigning king —**queen dowager** widow of king —**queen mother** widow of former king who is also mother of reigning sovereign —**Queen's Counsel** in Canad., honorary title which may be bestowed by government on lawyers with long experience —**queen's highway** in Canad., main road maintained by provincial government —**queen-size** *a.* smaller than king-size

Queens (kwēnz) *n.* borough of New York City

Queen Anne (sense 1)

Queensberry rules (ˈkwēnzberi) **1.** code of rules followed in modern boxing **2.** *inf.* gentlemanly conduct, *esp.* in dispute

queer (kwēər) *a.* **1.** odd, strange **2.** *inf.* homosexual —*n.* **3.** *inf.* homosexual —*vt. inf.* **4.** spoil **5.** interfere with

quell (kwel) *vt.* **1.** crush, put down **2.** allay **3.** pacify

quench (kwench) *vt.* **1.** slake **2.** extinguish, put out **3.** suppress

quern (kwərn) *n.* stone hand mill

querulous (ˈkweryələs, ˈkwerələs) *a.* **1.** fretful **2.** peevish, whining

query (ˈkwēəri) *n.* **1.** question **2.** mark of interrogation —*vt.* **3.** question (ˈ**queried,** ˈ**querying**)

quest (kwest) *n./vi.* search

question (ˈkweschən) *n.* **1.** sentence seeking for answer **2.** that which is asked **3.** interrogation **4.** inquiry **5.** problem **6.** point for debate **7.** debate, strife —*vt.* **8.** ask questions of, interrogate **9.** dispute **10.** doubt —ˈ**questionable** *a.* doubtful, *esp.* not clearly true or honest —**questionnaire** (kweschəˈnāər) *n.* list of questions drawn up for formal answer —**question mark 1.** punctuation mark **?**, used at end of questions *etc.* where doubt or ignorance is implied **2.** this mark used for any other purpose, as to draw attention to possible mistake (*also* **interrogation point**)

queue (kyōō) *n.* **1.** line of waiting persons, vehicles **2.** pigtail worn by Chinese males under order of Manchus —*vi.* **3.** (*with* up) wait in queue

quibble (ˈkwibəl) *n.* **1.** trivial objection —*vi.* **2.** make this

quiche (kēsh) *n.* open unsweetened pastry shell filled with rich custard flavored with cheese, onion, bacon *etc.*

quick (kwik) *a.* **1.** rapid, swift **2.** keen **3.** brisk **4.** hasty —*n.* **5.** sensitive flesh **6.** innermost feelings (*esp. in* **cut to the quick**) —*adv.* **7.** *inf.* rapidly —ˈ**quicken** *v.* make, become faster or more lively —ˈ**quickie** *n. inf.* anything made, done *etc.* rapidly or in haste —ˈ**quickly** *adv.* —**quick bread** any biscuit, bread, cake, doughnut, pancake or waffle leavened with baking powder —**quick-freeze** *vt.* freeze (food) rapidly enough so that ice crystals formed are too small to rupture cells —**quick grass** *see* QUACK GRASS —ˈ**quicklime** *n.* calcium oxide —ˈ**quicksand** *n.* loose wet sand easily yielding to pressure and engulfing persons, animals *etc.* —ˈ**quicksilver** *n.* mercury —ˈ**quickstep** *n.* **1.** ballroom dance —*vi.* **2.** perform this dance —**quick-tempered** *a.* irascible —**quick time** rate of marching in which 120 steps are taken in one minute —**quick-witted** *a.* having keenly alert mind —**quick-wittedness** *n.* —**the quick** *obs.* living people

quid (kwid) *n.* piece of tobacco suitable for chewing

quiddity (ˈkwiditi) *n.* **1.** essential nature **2.** petty or trifling distinction; quibble

quid pro quo (kwid prō ˈkwō) *Lat.* something given in exchange

quiescent (kwīˈesənt, kwi-) *a.* **1.** at rest, inactive, inert **2.** silent —**quiˈescence** *or* **quiˈescency** *n.*

quiet (ˈkwīət) *a.* **1.** with little or no motion or noise **2.** undisturbed **3.** not showy or obtrusive —*n.* **4.** state of peacefulness, absence of noise or disturbance —*v.* **5.** make, become quiet —ˈ**quieten** *v.* make, become quiet —ˈ**quietly** *adv.* —ˈ**quietness** *or* ˈ**quietude** *n.*

quietism (ˈkwīətizəm) *n.* passive attitude to life, *esp.* as form of religion —ˈ**quietist** *n.*

quietus (kwīˈētəs) *n.* **1.** anything that serves to quash, eliminate or kill **2.** release from life; death **3.** discharge or settlement of debts, duties *etc.*

quill (kwil) *n.* **1.** large feather **2.** hollow stem of this **3.** pen, plectrum made from feather **4.** spine of porcupine —ˈ**quillwort** *n.* lower plant resembling a tuft of grass found in eastern U.S.

quilt (kwilt) *n.* **1.** padded coverlet —*vt.* **2.** stitch (two pieces of cloth) with pad between

quince (kwins) *n.* **1.** acid pear-shaped fruit **2.** tree bearing it

quincunx (ˈkwinkungks) *n.* group of five objects arranged in shape of rectangle with one at each corner and fifth in center

quindecillion (kwindiˈsilyən) *n.* **1.** in Amer. and France, number represented as one followed by 48 zeros **2.** in Brit. and Germany, number represented as one followed by 90 zeros

quinine (ˈkwīnīn) *n.* bitter drug made from bark of tree, used to treat fever, and as tonic

Quinquagesima (kwingkəˈjesimə) *n.* Sunday 50 days before Easter

quinquennial (kwinˈkweniəl) *a.* **1.** lasting five years **2.** occurring every five years —*n.* **3.** period of five years

quinquereme (ˈkwingkwirēm) *n.* ancient Roman galley with five banks of oars

quinsy (ˈkwinzi) *n.* inflammation of throat or tonsils

quint (kwint) *n. inf.* quintuplet

quintessence (kwin'tesəns) *n.* **1.** purest form, essential feature **2.** embodiment —**quintes'sential** *a.*
quintet (kwin'tet) *n.* **1.** set of five singers or players **2.** composition for five voices or instruments
quintillion (kwin'tilyən) *n.* **1.** in Amer. and France, number represented as one followed by 18 zeros (10^{18}) **2.** in Brit. and Germany, number represented as one followed by 30 zeros (10^{30})
quintuple (kwin'tyōōpəl, -'tōō-; 'kwintəpəl) *v.* **1.** multiply by five —*a.* **2.** five times as much or as many; fivefold **3.** consisting of five parts —*n.* **4.** quantity or number five times as great as another —**quin'tuplicate** *a.*
quintuplet (kwin'tuplit, -'tyōō-, -'tōō-; 'kwintəplit) *n.* one of five offspring born at one birth
quip (kwip) *n.* **1.** witty saying —*vi.* **2.** make quip (**-pp-**)
quipu ('kēpōō) *n.* device consisting of cord with attached strings of various colors used by ancient Peruvians for recording events and for calculating
quire ('kwīər) *n.* 24 sheets of paper of the same size and quality
quirk (kwərk) *n.* **1.** individual peculiarity of character **2.** unexpected twist or turn
quisling ('kwizling) *n.* traitor who aids occupying enemy force
quit (kwit) *vi.* **1.** stop doing a thing **2.** depart —*vt.* **3.** leave, go away from **4.** cease from (**quit** *or* '**quitted** *pt./pp.*) —*a.* **5.** free, rid —**quits** *a.* on equal or even terms by repayment *etc.* —'**quittance** *n.* **1.** discharge **2.** receipt —'**quitter** *n.* one lacking perseverance
quite (kwīt) *adv.* **1.** wholly, completely **2.** very considerably **3.** somewhat, rather —*interj.* **4.** exactly, just so
quiver[1] ('kwivər) *vi.* **1.** shake, tremble —*n.* **2.** quivering **3.** vibration
quiver[2] ('kwivər) *n.* carrying case for arrows
quixotic (kwik'sotik) *a.* unrealistically and impractically optimistic, idealistic, chivalrous
quiz (kwiz) *n.* **1.** short written or oral test **2.** entertainment in which general or specific knowledge of players is tested by questions —*vt.* **3.** question, interrogate (**-zz-**) —'**quizzical** *a.* **1.** questioning **2.** mocking
quod (kwod) *n. sl.* prison
quoin (koin, kwoin) *n.* **1.** external corner of building **2.** small wedge for locking printing type into form
quoit (kwāt, koit, kwoit) *n.* **1.** ring for throwing at peg as a game —*pl.* **2.** (*with sing. v.*) the game
quondam ('kwondəm, -dam) *a.* of an earlier time; former
quorum ('kwörəm) *n.* number that must be present in meeting to make its transactions valid
quota ('kwōtə) *n.* **1.** share to be contributed or received **2.** specified number, quantity, which may be imported or admitted
quote (kwōt) *vt.* **1.** copy or repeat passages from **2.** refer to, *esp.* to confirm view **3.** state price for (commodity, stock or bond) —'**quotable** *a.* —**quo'tation** *n.* —**quotation mark** either of punctuation marks used to begin or end quotation, respectively " and " or ' and '
quoth (kwōth) *v. obs.* said
quotidian (kwō'tidiən) *a.* **1.** daily **2.** everyday, commonplace
quotient ('kwōshənt) *n.* number resulting from dividing one number by another
q.v. quod vide (*Lat.*, which see)
qwerty *or* **QWERTY** ('kwərti) *n. inf.* standard typewriter keyboard

R

r[1] *or* **R** (är) *n.* **1.** 18th letter of English alphabet **2.** speech sound represented by this letter (*pl.* **r's, R's** *or* **Rs**) **—the three Rs** three skills regarded as fundamentals of education: reading, writing and arithmetic

r[2] *or* **R** **1.** rabbi **2.** radius **3.** rare **4.** Republican **5.** *Phys., electron.* resistance **6.** right **7.** river **8.** roentgen *or* röntgen **9.** *Chess* rook **10.** run

R **1.** *Chem.* radical **2.** rand **3.** rupee **4.** Réaumur (scale) **5.** Royal **6.** *Chem.* gas constant

R. **1.** Regina (*Lat.,* Queen) **2.** Rex (*Lat.,* King) **3.** *Chem.* any organic group

Ra *Chem.* radium

R.A. **1.** Royal Academy **2.** Royal Artillery

rabbet ('rabit) *see* REBATE[2]

rabbi ('rabī) *n.* Jewish learned man, spiritual leader (*pl.* **-s**) **—rabbinical** (rə'binikəl) *or* **rab'binic** *a.*

rabbit ('rabit) *n.* **1.** small burrowing rodent like hare *—vi.* **2.** hunt rabbits **—rabbit fever** *see* TULAREMIA **–rabbit punch** sharp blow to back of neck

rabble ('rabəl) *n.* **1.** crowd of vulgar, noisy people **2.** mob **—rabble-rouser** *n.* person who manipulates passions of mob; demagogue

Rabelaisian (rabə'lāzhən, -ziən) *a.* **1.** of or resembling work of François Rabelais, Fr. writer, characterized by broad, oft. bawdy humor and sharp satire *—n.* **2.** student or admirer of Rabelais

rabid ('rabid, 'rā-) *a.* **1.** relating to or having rabies **2.** furious **3.** mad **4.** fanatical **—'rabidly** *adv.* **—'rabidness** *n.*

rabies ('rābēz) *n.* fatal virus disease of central nervous system transmitted by the bite of an infected warm-blooded animal

raccoon (ra'kōōn, rə-) *n.* nocturnal tree-dwelling N Amer. omnivorous mammal with grayish-brown fur, sharp snout and bushy ringed tail

race[1] (rās) *n.* **1.** contest of speed, as in running, swimming *etc.* **2.** contest, rivalry **3.** strong current of water, *esp.* leading to waterwheel *—pl.* **4.** meeting for horse racing *—vt.* **5.** cause to run rapidly *—vi.* **6.** run swiftly **7.** (of engine, pedal *etc.*) move rapidly and erratically, *esp.* on removal of resistance **—'racer** *n.* **1.** person, vehicle, animal that races **2.** any of various Amer. snakes **—'racetrack** *n.* long broad track, over which horses are raced

race[2] (rās) *n.* **1.** group of people of common ancestry with distinguishing physical features, skin color *etc.* **2.** species **3.** type **—'racial** *a.* **—'racialism** *or* **'racism** *n.* **1.** belief in innate superiority of particular race **2.** antagonism toward members of different race based on this belief **—'racialist** *or* **'racist** *a./n.* **—race riot** riot caused by racial animosity

raceme (rā'sēm, rə-) *n.* cluster of flowers along a central stem, as in foxglove

rack[1] (rak) *n.* **1.** framework for displaying or holding baggage, books, hats, bottles *etc.* **2.** *Mech.* straight bar with teeth on its edge, to work with pinion **3.** instrument of torture by stretching *—vt.* **4.** stretch on rack or wheel **5.** torture **6.** stretch, strain **—'racking** *a.* agonizing **—rack-and-pinion** *n.* **1.** device for converting rotary into linear motion and vice versa, in which gearwheel (pinion) engages with flat toothed bar (rack) *—a.* **2.** (of type of steering gear in motor vehicles) having track rod with rack along part of its length that engages with pinion attached to steering column **—rack railway** mountain railway having middle rail fitted with rack that engages pinion on locomotive (*also* **cog railway**)

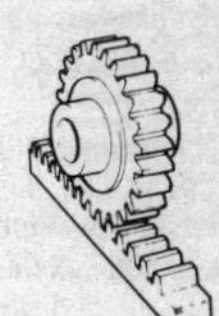

rack-and-pinion

rack[2] (rak) *n.* destruction (*esp. in* **rack and ruin**)

racket[1] ('rakit) *n.* **1.** loud noise, uproar **2.** occupation by which money is made illegally **—racket'eer** *n.* one making illegal profits **—racket'eering** *n.* **—'rackety** *a.* noisy

racket[2] *or* **racquet** ('rakit) *n.* **1.** bat used in tennis *etc.* *—pl.n.* **2.** (*with sing. v.*) racket game played by two players in which points are scored by server (*also* **hard rackets**) **—racket games** indoor racket-and-ball games played in walled enclosures having surfaces of cement or boards including court tennis, rackets and squash rackets

raconteur (rakon'tər) *n.* skilled storyteller

racy ('rāsi) *a.* **1.** spirited **2.** lively **3.** having strong flavor **4.** spicy **5.** piquant **—'racily** *adv.* **—'raciness** *n.*

radar ('rādär) *n.* *ra*dio *d*etecting and

ranging, system for detecting the presence, position or movement of objects by sending out radio waves that they reflect

raddled ('radəld) *a.* (*esp.* of person) unkempt or run-down in appearance

radial ('rādiəl) *a. see* RADIUS

radiate ('rādiāt) *v.* **1.** emit, be emitted in rays —*vi.* **2.** spread out from center —'**radiance** *n.* **1.** brightness **2.** splendor —'**radiant** *a.* **1.** beaming **2.** shining **3.** emitting rays —*n.* **4.** point or object that emits radiation, *esp.* part of heater that gives out heat **5.** *Astron.* the point in space from which a meteor shower appears to emanate —**radi'ation** *n.* **1.** transmission of heat, light *etc.* from one body to another **2.** particles, rays, emitted in nuclear decay **3.** act of radiating —'**radiator** *n.* **1.** that which radiates, *esp.* heating apparatus for rooms **2.** cooling apparatus of automobile engine —**radiant energy** energy emitted or propagated in form of particles or electromagnetic radiation —**radiation sickness** illness caused by overexposure of body to ionizing radiations from radioactive material *etc.* —**radiation therapy** use of x-ray apparatus and other sources of high-energy radiation in treatment of human and animal diseases

radical ('radikəl) *a.* **1.** fundamental, thorough **2.** extreme **3.** *Math.* of roots of numbers or quantities —*n.* **4.** person of extreme (political) views **5.** radicle **6.** *Math.* number expressed as root of another **7.** group of atoms of several elements which remain unchanged in a series of chemical compounds —'**radicalism** *n.* —**radical sign** symbol $\sqrt{}$ placed before number or quantity to indicate extraction of root, *esp.* square root

radicle ('radikəl) *n. Bot.* root

radio ('rādiō) *n.* **1.** use of electromagnetic waves for broadcasting, communication *etc.* **2.** device for receiving, amplifying radio signals **3.** broadcasting, content of radio program —*vt.* **4.** transmit (message *etc.*) by radio —**radio'active** *a.* emitting invisible rays that penetrate matter —**radioac'tivity** *n.* disintegration of the nuclei of the atoms of certain elements during which rays and elementary particles are emitted —**radio astronomy** astronomy in which radio telescope is used to detect and analyze radio signals received on earth from radio sources in space —**radiocarbon dating** technique for determining age of organic materials based on their content of radioisotope ^{14}C acquired from atmosphere when they formed part of living plant (*see also* **carbon dating** *at* CARBON) —**radio'chemical** *a.* —**radio'chemist** *n.* —**radio'chemistry** *n.* chemistry of radioactive elements and their compounds —**radio frequency** **1.** any frequency that lies in range 10 kilohertz to 300 000 megahertz and can be used for broadcasting **2.** frequency transmitted by particular radio station —'**radiograph** *n.* image produced on sensitized film or plate by radiation —**radi'ographer** *n.* —**radi'ography** *n.* production of image on film or plate by radiation —**radio'isotope** *n.* radioactive isotope —**radi'ologist** *n.* —**radi'ology** *n.* science of use of rays in medicine —**radioscopic** (rādiō'skopik) *a.* —**radi'oscopy** *n. see* **fluoroscopy** *at* FLUORESCENCE —**radiosonde** ('rādiōsond) *n.* airborne instrument to send meteorological information back to earth by radio —**radio'telegraph** *v./n.* —**radiote'legraphy** *n.* telegraphy in which messages (usu. in Morse code) are transmitted by radio waves —**radio'telephone** *n.* **1.** device for communications by means of radio waves —*v.* **2.** telephone (person) by radiotelephone —**radiote'lephony** *n.* —**radio telescope** instrument used in radio astronomy to pick up and analyze radio waves from space and to transmit radio waves —**radio'therapy** *n.* diagnosis and treatment of disease by x-rays

radio- (*comb. form*) **1.** denoting radio, broadcasting or radio frequency, as in *radiotelegraphy* **2.** indicating radioactivity or radiation, as in *radiochemistry*

radish ('radish) *n.* pungent root vegetable

radium ('rādiəm) *n. Chem.* metallic element *Symbol* Ra, at. wt. 226.1, at. no. 88

radius ('rādiəs) *n.* **1.** straight line from center to circumference of circle **2.** bone on the thumb side of a human forearm (*pl.* **radii** ('rādiī), **-es**) —'**radial** *a.* **1.** arranged like radii of circle **2.** of ray or rays **3.** of radius —'**radian** *n.* SI unit of plane angle; angle between two radii of circle that cut off on circumference arc equal in length to radius —**radial-ply** *a.* (of pneumatic tire) having fabric cords in outer casing running radially, enabling sidewalls to be flexible

radon ('rādon) *n. Chem.* gaseous element *Symbol* Rn, at. wt. 222.0 at. no. 86

RAF (*nonstandard* raf) *or* **R.A.F.** Royal Air Force

raffia *or* **raphia** ('rafiə) *n.* prepared palm fiber for making mats *etc.*

raffish ('rafish) *a.* disreputable

raffle ('rafəl) *n.* **1.** lottery in which an article is assigned by lot to one of those buying tickets —*vt.* **2.** dispose of by raffle

raft (raft) *n.* floating structure of logs, planks *etc.*

rafter ('raftər) *n.* one of main beams of roof

rag[1] (rag) *n.* **1.** fragment of cloth **2.** torn piece **3.** *inf.* newspaper *etc., esp.* one considered worthless **4.** piece of ragtime music —*pl.* **5.** tattered clothing —**ragged** ('ragid) *a.* **1.** shaggy **2.** torn **3.** clothed in torn clothes **4.** lacking smoothness —'**ragbag** *n.* confused assortment —'**ragtag** *n. derogatory* common people; rabble (*esp. in* **ragtag and bobtail**) —'**ragtime** *n.* style of jazz piano music —**rag trade** *inf.* clothing industry, trade —'**ragwort**

n. European plant with yellow daisylike flowers (*see also* GROUNDSEL)

rag[2] (rag) *vt.* **1.** tease **2.** torment **3.** play practical jokes on (**-gg-**) —*n.* **4.** period of carnival with procession *etc.* organized by students to raise money for charities

rag[3] (rag) *Jazz n.* **1.** piece of ragtime music —*vt.* **2.** compose or perform in ragtime (**-gg-**)

ragamuffin (ˈragəmufin) *n.* ragged, dirty person

rage (rāj) *n.* **1.** violent anger or passion **2.** fury —*vi.* **3.** speak, act with fury **4.** proceed violently and without check (as storm, battle *etc.*) **5.** be widely and violently prevalent —**all the rage** very popular

raglan (ˈraglən) *a.* (of sleeve) cut in two sections, with point at neckline and seam down the center of the arm, used mainly in suits and overcoats

ragout (raˈgo͞o) *n.* highly seasoned stew of meat and vegetables

raid (rād) *n.* **1.** rush, attack **2.** foray —*vt.* **3.** make raid on —ˈ**raider** *n.*

rail[1] (rāl) *n.* horizontal bar, *esp.* as part of fence, track *etc.* —ˈ**railing** *n.* fence, barrier made of rails supported by posts —ˈ**railhead** *n.* farthest point to which railroad line extends —ˈ**railroad** *n.* **1.** track of iron rails on which trains run **2.** company operating railroad —**off the rails** *inf.* **1.** astray **2.** on wrong track **3.** in error **4.** leading reckless, dissipated life

rail[2] (rāl) *vi.* (*with* at *or* against) **1.** utter abuse **2.** scoff **3.** scold **4.** reproach —ˈ**raillery** *n.* banter

rail[3] (rāl) *n.* any of various kinds of marsh bird

raiment (ˈrāmənt) *n. obs.* clothing

rain (rān) *n.* **1.** moisture falling in drops from clouds **2.** fall of such drops —*vi.* **3.** fall as rain —*vt.* **4.** pour down like rain —ˈ**rainy** *a.* —ˈ**rainbow** *n.* arch of prismatic colors in sky —ˈ**raincoat** *n.* light water-resistant overcoat —ˈ**rainfall** *n.* **1.** precipitation in form of raindrops **2.** *Met.* amount of precipitation in specified place and time —ˈ**rainforest** *n.* dense forest found in tropical areas of heavy rainfall —**rain gauge** instrument for measuring rainfall —**rainy day** future time of need, *esp.* financial

raise (rāz) *vt.* **1.** lift up **2.** set up **3.** build **4.** increase **5.** elevate **6.** promote **7.** heighten, as pitch of voice **8.** breed into existence **9.** levy, collect **10.** end (siege)

raisin (ˈrāzən) *n.* dried grape

raison d'être (rezō ˈdetr) *Fr.* reason or justification for existence (*pl.* ***raisons d'être*** (rezō ˈdetr))

raj (räj) *n.* rule, sway, *esp.* in India —ˈ**raja** *or* ˈ**rajah** *n.* Indian prince or ruler

rake[1] (rāk) *n.* **1.** tool with long handle and crosspiece with teeth for gathering hay, leaves *etc.* —*vt.* **2.** gather, smooth with rake **3.** sweep, search over **4.** sweep with shot —**rake-off** *n. inf.* monetary commission, *esp.* illegal

rake[2] (rāk) *n.* dissolute or dissipated man —ˈ**rakish** *a.* dissolute; profligate

rake[3] (rāk) *n.* **1.** slope, *esp.* backward, of ship's funnel *etc.* —*v.* **2.** incline from perpendicular —ˈ**rakish** *a.* appearing dashing or speedy

raku (ˈräko͞o) *n.* coarse-grained Japanese pottery notable for its refined rusticity

rally[1] (ˈrali) *vt.* **1.** bring together, *esp.* what has been scattered, as routed army or dispersed troops —*vi.* **2.** come together **3.** regain health or strength, revive (ˈ**rallied,** ˈ**rallying**) —*n.* **4.** act of rallying **5.** assembly, *esp.* outdoor, of any organization **6.** *Tennis* lively exchange of strokes

rally[2] (ˈrali) *v.* mock or ridicule (someone) in good-natured way; chaff; tease

ram (ram) *n.* **1.** male sheep **2.** hydraulic machine **3.** battering engine —*vt.* **4.** force, drive **5.** strike against with force **6.** stuff **7.** strike with ram (**-mm-**) —ˈ**ramrod** *n.* **1.** rod for cleaning barrel of rifle *etc.* **2.** rod for ramming in charge of muzzle-loading firearm

RAM (ram) *Comp.* random access memory

ramada (rəˈmädə) *n.* shelter with open sides

Ramadan (ˈramədän) *n.* **1.** 9th Islamic month **2.** strict fasting observed during this time

ramble (ˈrambəl) *vi.* **1.** walk without definite route **2.** wander **3.** talk incoherently **4.** spread in random fashion —*n.* **5.** rambling walk —ˈ**rambler** *n.* **1.** climbing rose **2.** one who rambles

rambutan (ramˈbo͞otən) *n.* **1.** SE Asian tree **2.** its bright red edible fruit

ramekin *or* **ramequin** (ˈramikin) *n.* **1.** small fireproof dish **2.** savory food baked in it

ramify (ˈramifī) *v.* **1.** spread in branches, subdivide —*vi.* **2.** become complex (**-ified, -ifying**) —**ramifiˈcation** *n.* **1.** branch, subdivision **2.** process of branching out **3.** consequence

ramp (ramp) *n.* gradual slope joining two level surfaces

rampage (ˈrampāj, ramˈpāj) *vi.* **1.** dash about violently —*n.* (ramˈpāj) **2.** angry or destructive behavior —**ramˈpageous** *a.* —**on the rampage** behaving violently or destructively

rampant (ˈrampənt) *a.* **1.** violent **2.** rife **3.** rearing

rampart (ˈrampärt) *n.* **1.** mound, wall for defense —*vt.* **2.** defend with rampart

rampike (ˈrampīk) *n.* **C** tall tree, burnt or bare of branches

ramshackle (ˈramshakəl) *a.* tumbledown, rickety, makeshift

ran (ran) *pt. of* RUN

ranch (ranch) *n.* **1.** Amer. cattle farm —*vi.* **2.** live or work on a ranch —ˈ**rancher** *n.*

rancherie (ˈranchəri) *n.* **C** Indian reservation
rancid (ˈransid) *a.* (of food) having unpleasant smell or taste —**ranˈcidity** *n.*
rancor (ˈrangkər) *n.* bitter, inveterate hate —**ˈrancorous** *a.* **1.** malignant **2.** virulent
rand (rand, rond, ront) *n.* monetary unit of S Afr.
R & B rhythm-and-blues
R & D research and development
random (ˈrandəm) *a.* made or done by chance, without plan —**at random** haphazard(ly)
randy (ˈrandi) *a. sl.* sexually aroused
rang (rang) *pt. of* RING[2]
range (rānj) *n.* **1.** limits **2.** row **3.** scope, sphere **4.** distance missile can travel **5.** distance of mark shot at **6.** place for shooting practice or rocket testing **7.** rank **8.** kitchen stove —*vt.* **9.** set in row **10.** classify **11.** roam —*vi.* **12.** extend **13.** roam **14.** pass from one point to another **15.** fluctuate (as prices) —**ˈranger** *n.* official in charge of or patrolling park *etc.* —**ˈrangy** *a.* **1.** with long, slender limbs **2.** spacious —**ˈrangefinder** *n.* instrument for finding distance away of given object
rani *or* **ranee** (räˈnē, ˈräni) *n.* queen or princess; wife of raja
rank[1] (rangk) *n.* **1.** line **2.** place where taxis wait **3.** order **4.** social class **5.** status **6.** relative place or position —*pl.* **7.** common soldiers **8.** great mass or majority of people (*also* **rank and file**) —*vt.* **9.** draw up in rank, classify —*vi.* **10.** have rank, place **11.** have certain distinctions
rank[2] (rangk) *a.* **1.** growing too thickly, coarse **2.** offensively strong **3.** rancid **4.** vile **5.** flagrant —**ˈrankly** *adv.*
rankle (ˈrangkəl) *vi.* fester, continue to cause anger, resentment or bitterness
ransack (ˈransak) *vt.* **1.** search thoroughly **2.** pillage, plunder
ransom (ˈransəm) *n.* **1.** release from captivity by payment **2.** amount paid —*vt.* **3.** pay ransom for —**ˈransomer** *n.*
rant (rant) *vi.* **1.** rave in violent, high-sounding language —*n.* **2.** noisy, boisterous speech **3.** wild gaiety —**ˈranter** *n.*
ranunculus (rəˈnungkyələs) *n.* any of a genus of plants that includes buttercup, crowfoot and spearwort
rap[1] (rap) *n.* **1.** smart slight blow —*vt.* **2.** give rap to (**-pp-**) —**take the rap** *sl.* suffer punishment, whether guilty or not
rap[2] (rap) *n.* the least amount (*esp. in* **not care a rap**)
rapacious (rəˈpāshəs) *a.* **1.** greedy **2.** grasping —**rapacity** (rəˈpasiti) *n.*
rape[1] (rāp) *vt.* **1.** force (woman) to submit unwillingly to sexual intercourse —*n.* **2.** act of raping **3.** any violation or abuse
rape[2] (rāp) *n.* plant with oil-yielding seeds, also used as fodder (*also* **ˈcolza, cole**)
rapid (ˈrapid) *a.* **1.** quick, swift —*pl.n.* **2.** part of river with fast, turbulent current —**raˈpidity** *or* **ˈrapidness** *n.* —**ˈrapidly** *adv.* —**rapid eye movement** movement of eyeballs during sleep, while sleeper is dreaming
rapier (ˈrāpiər) *n.* fine-bladed sword used as thrusting weapon
rapine (ˈrapin, -pīn) *n.* plunder
rapport (raˈpör) *n.* harmony, agreement
rapprochement (raproshˈmā) *Fr.* re-establishment of friendly relations between nations
rapscallion (rapˈskalyən) *n.* rascal, rogue
rapt (rapt) *a.* engrossed, spellbound —**ˈrapture** *n.* ecstasy —**ˈrapturous** *a.*
raptorial (rapˈtöriəl) *a.* **1.** predatory **2.** of the order of birds of prey
rare[1] (rāər) *a.* **1.** uncommon **2.** infrequent **3.** of uncommon quality **4.** (of atmosphere) having low density, thin —**ˈrarely** *adv.* seldom —**ˈrareness** *n.* —**rarity** (ˈrariti, ˈrer-) *n.* **1.** anything rare **2.** rareness —**rare earth** **1.** any oxide of lanthanide **2.** any element of lanthanide series (*also* **rare-earth element**) —**rare gas** *see* **noble gas** *at* NOBLE
rare[2] (rāər) *a.* (of meat) lightly cooked
rarebit (ˈrāərbit) *n. see* **Welsh rabbit** *at* WALES
rarefy (ˈrāərifī) *v.* **1.** make, become thin, rare or less dense —*vt.* **2.** refine (**-fied, -fying**) —**rareˈfaction** *or* **rarefiˈcation** *n.*
raring (ˈrāəring) *a.* enthusiastically willing, ready
rascal (ˈraskəl) *n.* **1.** rogue **2.** naughty (young) person —**rasˈcality** *n.* roguery, baseness —**ˈrascally** *a./adv.*
raschel (räˈshel) *n.* **1.** type of knitting machine producing ribbed jersey **2.** the fabric produced
rase (rāz) *vt. see* RAZE
rash[1] (rash) *a.* hasty, reckless, incautious —**ˈrashly** *adv.*
rash[2] (rash) *n.* **1.** skin eruption **2.** outbreak, series of (unpleasant) occurrences
rasp (rasp) *n.* **1.** harsh, grating noise **2.** coarse file —*vt.* **3.** scrape with rasp —*vi.* **4.** grate upon **5.** irritate **6.** make scraping noise **7.** speak in grating voice
raspberry (ˈrazberi, -bəri) *n.* **1.** red, juicy, edible berry **2.** plant which bears it **3.** *inf.* spluttering noise with tongue and lips to show contempt
Rastafarian (rastəˈfariən) *n.* **1.** member of Jamaican cult that regards Ras Tafari, former emperor of Ethiopia, Haile Selassie, as God —*a.* **2.** of Rastafarians —**ˈRasta** *a./n.*
rat (rat) *n.* **1.** small rodent **2.** *inf.* contemptible person, *esp.* deserter, informer *etc.* —*vi.* **3.** inform **4.** (*with* on) betray **5.** (*with* on) desert, abandon **6.** hunt rats (**-tt-**) —**ˈratter** *n.* **1.** dog or cat that catches and kills rats **2.** *inf.* worker who works during strike; blackleg; scab (*also* **rat**) —**ˈratty** *a. sl.* **1.** mean, ill-tempered, irritable **2.** (of hair)

straggly, unkempt, greasy —**rat-bite fever 1.** *see* HAVERHILL FEVER **2.** acute infectious febrile disease caused by bite of rat infected with *Spirillum minus* bacterium —**rat-catcher** *n.* one whose job is to drive away or destroy vermin, *esp.* rats —**rat race** continual hectic competitive activity —ˈ**ratsbane** *n.* rat poison, *esp.* arsenic oxide —**smell a rat** have suspicions of some treacherous practice

ratchet (ˈrachit) *n.* set of teeth on bar or wheel allowing motion in one direction only

rate[1] (rāt) *n.* **1.** proportion between two things **2.** charge **3.** degree of speed *etc.* —*pl.* **4. UK** local tax on property —*vt.* **5.** value **6.** estimate value of **7. UK** assess for local taxation —ˈ**ratable** *or* ˈ**rateable** *a.* **1.** that can be rated **2. UK** liable to pay rates —ˈ**ratepayer** *n.*

rate[2] (rāt) *vt.* scold, chide

rather (ˈradhər, ˈrä-) *adv.* **1.** to some extent **2.** preferably **3.** more willingly

ratify (ˈratifī) *vt.* confirm (**-ified, -ifying**) —**ratifiˈcation** *n.*

rating (ˈrāting) *n.* **1.** valuing or assessing **2.** fixing a rate **3.** classification, *esp.* of ship **4.** angry rebuke

ratio (ˈrāshō, -shiō) *n.* **1.** proportion **2.** quantitative relation

ratiocinate (ratiˈosināt) *vi.* reason —**ratiociˈnation** *n.*

ration (ˈrashən) *n.* **1.** fixed allowance of food *etc.* —*vt.* **2.** supply with, limit to certain amount

rational (ˈrashnəl, -shənəl) *a.* **1.** reasonable, sensible **2.** capable of thinking, reasoning —**rationale** (rashəˈnal) *n.* reasons given for actions *etc.* —ˈ**rationalism** *n.* philosophy which regards reason as only guide or authority —ˈ**rationalist** *n.* —**ratioˈnality** *n.* —**rationaliˈzation** *n.* —ˈ**rationalize** *vt.* **1.** justify by plausible reasoning **2.** reorganize to improve efficiency *etc.* —ˈ**rationally** *adv.*

ratline (ˈratlin) *n. Naut.* any of light lines tied across shrouds of sailing vessel for climbing aloft

rattan (raˈtan) *n.* **1.** climbing palm with jointed stems **2.** cane made of this

rattle (ˈratəl) *vi.* **1.** give out succession of short sharp sounds **2.** clatter —*vt.* **3.** shake briskly causing a sharp clatter of sounds **4.** *inf.* confuse, fluster —*n.* **5.** succession of short sharp sounds **6.** baby's toy filled with small pellets for making this sound **7.** set of horny rings in rattlesnake's tail —ˈ**rattling** *adv. inf.* very —ˈ**rattlesnake** *n.* poisonous snake —ˈ**rattletrap** *n. inf.* broken-down old vehicle, *esp.* automobile

raucous (ˈrökəs) *a.* **1.** hoarse **2.** harsh

raunchy (ˈrönchi) *a.* **1.** lecherous, smutty **2.** slovenly; dirty

ravage (ˈravij) *vt.* **1.** lay waste, plunder —*n.* **2.** destruction

rave (rāv) *vi.* **1.** talk wildly, as in delirium **2.** write or speak (about) enthusiastically —*n.* **3.** enthusiastic or extravagant praise —ˈ**raving** *a.* **1.** delirious; frenzied **2.** *inf.* exciting admiration —*adv.* **3.** so as to cause raving —**rave-up** *n. sl.* party

ravel (ˈravəl) *vt.* **1.** entangle **2.** fray out **3.** disentangle

raven[1] (ˈrāvən) *n.* **1.** black bird like crow —*a.* **2.** jet-black

raven[2] (ˈravən) *v.* seek (prey, plunder) —ˈ**ravening** *a.* (of animals) voracious; predatory —ˈ**ravenous** *a.* very hungry

ravine (rəˈvēn) *n.* narrow steep-sided valley worn by stream, gorge

ravioli (raviˈōli) *n.* small cases of pasta filled with highly seasoned chopped meat or vegetables

ravish (ˈravish) *vt.* **1.** enrapture **2.** commit rape upon —ˈ**ravishing** *a.* lovely, entrancing

raw (rö) *a.* **1.** uncooked **2.** not manufactured or refined **3.** skinned **4.** inexperienced, unpracticed, as recruits **5.** sensitive **6.** chilly —ˈ**rawˈboned** *a.* having lean bony physique —**raw deal** unfair or dishonest treatment —ˈ**rawhide** *n.* **1.** untanned hide **2.** whip made of this —**in the raw 1.** *inf.* without clothing; naked **2.** in natural or unmodified state

ray[1] (rā) *n.* **1.** single line or narrow beam of light, heat *etc.* **2.** any of set of radiating lines —*vi.* **3.** come out in rays **4.** radiate

ray[2] (rā) *n.* marine fish, oft. very large, with winglike pectoral fins and whiplike tail

rayon (ˈrāon) *n.* (fabric made of) synthetic fiber

raze *or* **rase** (rāz) *vt.* **1.** destroy completely **2.** wipe out, delete **3.** level

razor (ˈrāzər) *n.* sharp instrument for shaving or for cutting hair —ˈ**razorbill** *n.* N Atlantic auk

razzle-dazzle (razəlˈdazəl) *or* **razzmatazz** (razməˈtaz) *n. sl.* **1.** noisy or showy fuss or activity **2.** spree; frolic

Rb *Chem.* rubidium

R.C. 1. Red Cross **2.** Roman Catholic

R.C.A.F. Royal Canadian Air Force

R.C.M.P. Royal Canadian Mounted Police

R.C.N. Royal Canadian Navy

Rd. Road

re[1] (rā) *n. Mus.* **1.** in fixed system of solmization, the note D **2.** in movable do system, the second note of a major scale

re[2] (rā, rē) *prep.* with reference to, concerning

Re *Chem.* rhenium

re- (*comb. form*) again. See the list below

REA Rural Electrification Administration

reach (rēch) *vt.* **1.** arrive at **2.** extend as far as **3.** succeed in touching **4.** attain to —*vi.* **5.** stretch out hand **6.** extend —*n.* **7.** act of reaching **8.** power of touching **9.** grasp, scope **10.** range **11.** stretch of river between two bends —**'reachable** *a.* —**reach-me-down** *n.* **1.** *see* **hand-me-down** *at* HAND **2.** ready-made garment

react (ri'akt) *vi.* act in return, opposition or toward former state —**re'actance** *n. Elec.* resistance in coil, apart from ohmic resistance, due to current reacting on itself —**re'action** *n.* **1.** any action resisting another **2.** counter or backward tendency **3.** mental depression following overexertion **4.** *inf.* response **5.** chemical or nuclear change —**re'actionary** *n./a.* (person) opposed to change, *esp.* in politics *etc.* —**re'active** *a.* chemically active —**nuclear reactor** apparatus in which nuclear reaction is maintained and controlled to produce nuclear energy

read (rēd) *vt.* **1.** look at and understand (written or printed matter) **2.** learn by reading **3.** interpret mentally **4.** read and utter **5.** interpret **6.** study **7.** understand (any indicating instrument) **8.** (of instrument) register —*vi.* **9.** be occupied in reading **10.** find mentioned in reading (**read** (red) *pt./pp.*) —**reada'bility** *n.* —**'readable** *a.* that can be read, or read with pleasure —**'reader** *n.* **1.** one who reads **2.** school textbook **3.** one who reads manuscripts submitted to publisher **4.** one who reads printer's proofs —**'readership** *n.* all readers of particular publication or author —**'reading** *n.* —**readout** *n.* **1.** retrieving of information from computer memory or storage device **2.** information retrieved —**read between the lines** *inf.* deduce a meaning that is implied —**read out 1.** read aloud **2.** expel from political party *etc.* **3.** retrieve information from computer memory or storage device

ready ('redi) *a.* **1.** prepared for use or action **2.** willing, prompt —**'readily** *adv.* **1.** promptly **2.** willingly —**'readiness** *n.* —**ready-made** *a.* **1.** made for purchase and immediate use by customer **2.** extremely convenient; ideally suited **3.** unoriginal, conventional —*n.* **4.** ready-made article, *esp.* garment —**ready reckoner** table of numbers used to facilitate simple calculations, *esp.* for working out interest *etc.*

Reagan ('rāgən) *n.* **Ronald Wilson.** the 40th President of the U.S. from 1981

reagent (rē'ājənt) *n.* chemical substance that reacts with another and is used to detect presence of the other —**re'agency** *n.*

real (rēəl) *a.* **1.** existing in fact **2.** happening **3.** actual **4.** genuine **5.** (of property) consisting of land and houses —**'realism** *n.* **1.** regarding things as they are **2.** artistic treatment with this outlook —**'realist** *n.* —**rea'listic** *a.* —**reality** (rē'aliti) *n.* real existence —**'really** *adv.* —**'realty** *n.* real estate —**real estate** landed property —**real tennis** *see* **court tennis** *at* COURT

realize ('rēəlīz) *vt.* **1.** apprehend, grasp significance of **2.** make real **3.** convert into money —**reali'zation** *n.*

realm (relm) *n.* **1.** kingdom, domain **2.** province, sphere

ream[1] (rēm) *n.* **1.** twenty quires of paper: 480, 500 or 516 sheets —*pl.* **2.** *inf.* large quantity of written matter

ream[2] (rēm) *vt.* enlarge, bevel out, as hole in metal —**'reamer** *n.* tool for this

reap (rēp) *v.* **1.** cut and gather (harvest) —*vt.* **2.** receive as fruit of previous activity —**'reaper** *n.*

rear[1] (rēər) *n.* **1.** back part **2.** part of army, procession *etc.* behind others —**'rearmost** *a.* —**rear admiral** lowest flag rank in certain navies —**'rearguard** *n.* troops protecting rear of army —**rear-view mirror** mirror on motor vehicle enabling driver to see traffic behind —**'rearward** *a.* **1.** toward or in rear —*adv.* **2.** toward or in rear (*also* **'rearwards**) —*n.* **3.** position in rear, *esp.* rear division of military formation

rear[2] (rēər) *vt.* **1.** care for and educate (children) **2.** breed **3.** erect —*vi.* **4.** rise, *esp.* on hind feet

reason ('rēzən) *n.* **1.** ground, motive **2.**

re'activate
read'dress
read'just
read'mission
read'mit
reaf'firm
reaffir'mation
rea'lign
rea'lignment
re'allocate
reap'pear
reap'pearance
reap'praisal
reap'praise
rear'range
rear'rangement
reas'semble
reas'sert
reas'sertion
reas'sess
reas'sessment
rea'waken
re'bid *v.*
'rebid *n.*
re'born
re'build
re'calculate
re'capture
re'cast
re'charge
recom'mence
recon'nect
recon'nection
recon'sider
recon'struct
recon'struction
recon'vene
re-cover
re-create
re'decorate
rede'ploy
rede'sign
rede'velop
rede'velopment
redi'rect
redi'rection
redis'cover
redis'tribute
redistri'bution
re'do
re'draft
re'draw
re-echo
re-educate
re-elect
re-election
re-emerge
re-emergence
re-emphasize
re-employ
re-enact
re-enactment
re-enforce
re-enforcement

faculty of thinking **3.** sanity **4.** sensible or logical thought or view —*vi.* **5.** think logically in forming conclusions **6.** (*usu. with* with) persuade by logical argument into doing *etc.* —**'reasonable** *a.* **1.** sensible, not excessive **2.** suitable **3.** logical —**'reasoning** *n.* **1.** drawing of conclusions from facts *etc.* **2.** arguments, proofs *etc.* so adduced

reassure (rēə'shōōər) *vt.* restore confidence to

rebate[1] ('rēbāt) *n.* **1.** discount, refund —*vt.* ('rēbāt, ri'bāt) **2.** deduct

rebate[2] ('rabit, 'rēbāt) *or* **rabbet** *n.* **1.** recess, groove cut into piece of timber to join with matching piece —*vt.* **2.** cut rebate in

rebel (ri'bel) *vi.* **1.** revolt, resist lawful authority, take arms against ruling power (**-ll-**) —*n.* ('rebəl) **2.** one who rebels **3.** insurgent —*a.* ('rebəl) **4.** in rebellion —**re'bellion** *n.* organized open resistance to authority —**re'bellious** *a.* —**re'belliously** *adv.*

rebirth (rē'bərth) *n.* **1.** revival, renaissance **2.** second or new birth

rebore ('rēbör) *n.* boring of cylinder to regain true shape

rebound ('rē'bownd, ri'bownd) *vi.* **1.** spring back **2.** misfire, *esp.* so as to hurt perpetrator (of plan, deed *etc.*) —*n.* ('rēbownd, ri'bownd) **3.** act of springing back or recoiling **4.** return

rebuff (ri'buf) *n.* **1.** blunt refusal **2.** check —*vt.* **3.** snub

rebuke (ri'byōōk) *vt.* **1.** reprove, reprimand, find fault with —*n.* **2.** reprimand, scolding

rebus ('rēbəs) *n.* riddle in which names of things *etc.* are represented by pictures standing for syllables *etc.* (*pl.* **-es**)

rebut (ri'but) *vt.* refute, disprove (**-tt-**) —**re'buttal** *n.*

rec. **1.** receipt **2.** recipe **3.** record

recalcitrant (ri'kalsitrənt) *a./n.* willfully disobedient (person) —**re'calcitrance** *n.*

recall (ri'köl) *vt.* **1.** recollect, remember **2.** call, summon, order back **3.** annul, cancel **4.** revive, restore —*n.* **5.** summons to return **6.** ability to remember

recant (ri'kant) *v.* withdraw (statement, opinion *etc.*) —**recan'tation** *n.*

recap ('rēkap, ri'kap) *v.* **1.** recapitulate (**-pp-**) —*n.* ('rēkap) **2.** recapitulation

recapitulate (rēkə'pichəlāt) *vt.* **1.** state again briefly **2.** repeat —**recapitu'lation** *n.*

recce ('reki) *sl. n.* **1.** reconnaissance —*v.* **2.** reconnoiter

recd. *or* **rec'd.** received

recede (ri'sēd) *vi.* **1.** go back **2.** become distant **3.** slope backward **4.** start balding

receipt (ri'sēt) *n.* **1.** written acknowledgment of money received **2.** receiving or being received —*vt.* **3.** acknowledge payment of in writing

receive (ri'sēv) *vt.* **1.** take, accept, get **2.** experience **3.** greet (guests) —**re'ceivable** *a.* —**re'ceiver** *n.* **1.** officer appointed to take public money **2.** one who takes stolen goods knowing them to have been stolen **3.** equipment in telephone, radio or television that converts electrical signals into sound and light

recent ('rēsənt) *a.* **1.** that has lately happened **2.** new **3.** (**R-**) of second and most recent epoch of Quaternary period, which began 10 000 years ago (*also* **'Holocene**) —*n.* **4.** (**R-**) Recent epoch or rock series (*also* **'Holocene**) —**'recently** *adv.*

receptacle (ri'septəkəl) *n.* vessel, place or space to contain anything

reception (ri'sepshən) *n.* **1.** receiving **2.** manner of receiving **3.** welcome **4.** formal party **5.** area for receiving guests, clients *etc.* **6.** in broadcasting, quality of signals received —**re'ceptionist** *n.* person who receives guests, clients *etc.* —**reception room** **1.** room in house suitable for entertaining guests **2.** room in hotel suitable for receptions *etc.*

receptive (ri'septiv) *a.* able, quick, willing to receive new ideas, suggestions *etc.* —**receptivity** (rēsep'tiviti) *or* **re'ceptiveness** *n.*

recess ('rēses, ri'ses) *n.* **1.** niche, alcove **2.** hollow **3.** secret, hidden place **4.** remission or suspension of business **5.** vacation

recession (ri'seshən) *n.* **1.** period of reduc-

re-enter
re-equip
re-examine
re'fill *v.*
'refill *n.*
re'float
re'forest
re-form
re'fuel
re'furnish
re'gain
re'gather
re'grow
re'harden
re'heat
re'house
reim'pose
rein'terpret
reinterpre'tation
reintro'duce
reintro'duction
re'kindle
re'lay *v.*
'relay *n.*
re'light
re'load
relo'cate
relo'cation
re'marriage
re'marry
re'match *v.*
'rematch *n.*
re'model
re'number
re'occupy
re'open
re'order
reorgani'zation
re'organize
re'pack
re'paint
re'paper
re'phrase
re'plant
re'print *v.*
'reprint *n.*
re'route
re'set
re'settle
re'shuffle
re'spray *v.*
'respray *n.*
re'start
re'stock
re'surface
re'think *v.*
'rethink *n.*
re'trial
re'try
re'type
reu'nite
re'use
re'visit
re'wind

tion in trade **2.** act of receding —**re'cessive** *a.* receding

recessional (ri'seshənəl) *n.* hymn sung while clergy retire

recherché (rəsher'shā, rə'shāərshā) *a.* **1.** of studied elegance **2.** exquisite **3.** choice

recidivism (ri'sidivizəm) *n.* habitual relapse into crime —**re'cidivist** *n./a.*

recipe ('resipē) *n.* **1.** directions for cooking a dish **2.** prescription **3.** expedient

recipient (ri'sipiənt) *a.* **1.** that can or does receive —*n.* **2.** one who, that which receives —**re'cipience** *or* **re'cipiency** *n.*

reciprocal (ri'siprəkəl) *a.* **1.** complementary **2.** mutual **3.** moving backward and forward **4.** alternating —**re'ciprocally** *adv.* —**re'ciprocate** *vt.* **1.** give and receive mutually **2.** return —*vi.* **3.** move backward and forward —**recipro'cation** *n.* —**reciprocity** (resi'prositi) *n.*

recite (ri'sīt) *vt.* repeat aloud, *esp.* to audience —**re'cital** *n.* **1.** musical performance, usu. by one person **2.** act of reciting **3.** narration of facts *etc.* **4.** story **5.** public entertainment of recitations *etc.* —**recitation** (resi'tāshən) *n.* **1.** recital, usu. from memory, of poetry or prose **2.** recountal —**recitative** (resitə'tēv) *n.* musical declamation —**re'citer** *n.*

reckless ('reklis) *a.* heedless, incautious —'**recklessness** *n.*

reckon ('rekən) *v.* **1.** count —*vt.* **2.** include **3.** consider **4.** think, deem —*vi.* **5.** make calculations —'**reckoner** *n.* —'**reckoning** *n.* **1.** counting, calculating **2.** settlement of account *etc.* **3.** bill, account **4.** retribution for one's actions (*esp. in* **day of reckoning**) **5.** *Navigation see* **dead reckoning** *at* DEAD

reclaim (ri'klām) *vt.* **1.** make fit for cultivation **2.** bring back **3.** reform **4.** demand the return of —**re'claimable** *a.*

recline (ri'klīn) *vi.* sit, lie back or on one's side

recluse ('reklo͞os, ri'klo͞os) *n.* **1.** hermit —*a.* **2.** living in complete retirement —**re'clusion** *n.* —**re'clusive** *a.*

recognize ('rekəgnīz) *vt.* **1.** know again **2.** treat as valid **3.** notice, show appreciation of —**recognition** (rekəg'nishən) *n.* —'**recognizable** *a.* —**recognizance** (ri'kognizəns) *n.* **1.** avowal **2.** bond by which person undertakes before court to observe some condition **3.** *obs.* recognition

recoil (ri'koil) *vi.* **1.** draw back in horror *etc.* **2.** go wrong so as to hurt the perpetrator **3.** (*esp.* of gun when fired) rebound —*n.* ('rēkoil, ri'koil) **4.** backward spring **5.** retreat **6.** recoiling

recollect (rekə'lekt) *vt.* call back to mind, remember —**recol'lection** *n.*

recommend (rekə'mend) *vt.* **1.** advise, counsel **2.** praise, commend **3.** make acceptable —**recommen'dation** *n.*

recompense ('rekəmpens) *vt.* **1.** reward **2.** compensate, make up for —*n.* **3.** compensation **4.** reward **5.** requital

reconcile ('rekənsīl) *vt.* **1.** bring back into friendship **2.** adjust, settle, harmonize —'**reconcilable** *a.* —'**reconcilement** *n.* —**reconciliation** (rekənsili'āshən) *n.*

recondite ('rekəndīt, ri'kondīt) *a.* obscure, abstruse, little known

recondition (rēkən'dishən) *vt.* restore to good condition or working order

reconnoiter *or* **reconnoitre** (rekə'noitər) *vt.* **1.** make preliminary survey of **2.** survey position of (enemy) —*vi.* **3.** make reconnaissance —**reconnaissance** (ri'konizəns, -səns) *n.* **1.** examination or survey for military or engineering purposes **2.** scouting

reconstitute (rē'konstityo͞ot, -to͞ot) *vt.* restore (food) to former state, *esp.* by addition of water to a concentrate

record ('rekərd, -körd) *n.* **1.** being recorded **2.** document or other thing that records **3.** disk with indentations which phonograph transforms into sound **4.** best recorded achievement **5.** known facts about person's past —*vt.* (ri'körd) **6.** put in writing **7.** register —*v.* (ri'körd) **8.** preserve (sound, TV programs *etc.*) on plastic disk, magnetic tape *etc.* for reproduction on playback device —**re'corder** *n.* **1.** one who, that which records **2.** type of flute which is held vertically and blown through mouthpiece containing fipple which leaves only a narrow slit for passage of breath, usu. made in soprano (descant), treble (alto), tenor and bass sizes **3.** judge in certain courts —**re'cording** *n.* **1.** process of making records from sound **2.** something recorded, *eg* radio or TV program —**record-player** *n.* machine for playing phonograph records —**for the record** for the sake of strict factual accuracy —**off the record** confidential or confidentially

recorder (sense 2)

recount[1] (ri'kownt) *vt.* tell in detail

recount[2] (rē'kownt) *v.* **1.** count (votes *etc.*) again —*n.* ('rēkownt) **2.** second or further count, *esp.* of votes

recoup (ri'ko͞op) *vt.* **1.** recompense, compensate **2.** recover (what has been expended or lost)

recourse ('rēkörs, ri'körs) *n.* **1.** (resorting to) source of help **2.** *Law* right of action or appeal

recover (ri'kuvər) *vt.* **1.** regain, get back —*vi.* **2.** get back health —**re'coverable** *a.* —**re'covery** *n.*

recreant ('rekriənt) *a.* **1.** cowardly, disloyal —*n.* **2.** recreant person **3.** renegade —'**recreance** *or* '**recreancy** *n.*

recreation (rekri'āshən) *n.* agreeable or refreshing occupation, relaxation, amusement —**'recreative** *a.*

recriminate (ri'kriminăt) *vi.* make countercharge or mutual accusation —**recrimi'nation** *n.* mutual abuse and blame —**re'criminative** *or* **re'criminatory** *a.*

recrudesce (rēkrōō'des) *vi.* break out again —**recru'descence** *n.* —**recru'descent** *a.*

recruit (ri'krōōt) *n.* **1.** newly enlisted soldier **2.** one newly joining society *etc.* —*vt.* **3.** enlist (fresh soldiers *etc.*) —**re'cruitment** *n.*

rectangle ('rektanggəl) *n.* oblong four-sided figure with four right angles —**rec'tangular** *a.* shaped thus

rectify ('rektifī) *vt.* **1.** put right, correct, remedy **2.** purify (**-fied, -fying**) —**rectifi'cation** *n.* **1.** act of setting right **2.** refining by repeated distillation **3.** *Elec.* conversion of alternating current into direct current —**'rectifier** *n.* thing that rectifies

rectilinear (rekti'liniər) *or* **rectilineal** *a.* **1.** in straight line **2.** characterized by straight lines

rectitude ('rektityōōd, -tōōd) *n.* **1.** moral uprightness **2.** honesty of purpose

recto ('rektō) *n.* right-hand page of book, front of leaf (*pl.* **-s**)

rector ('rektər) *n.* **1.** clergyman with care of parish **2.** head of certain institutions, chiefly academic —**'rectorship** *n.* —**'rectory** *n.* rector's house

rectum ('rektəm) *n.* final section of large intestine (*pl.* **-s, -ta** (-tə)) —**'rectal** *a.*

recumbent (ri'kumbənt) *a.* lying down —**re'cumbence** *or* **re'cumbency** *n.*

recuperate (ri'kyōōpərāt, -'kōō-) *vi.* **1.** recover from illness, convalesce —*v.* **2.** restore, be restored from losses *etc.* —**recuper'ation** *n.*

recur (ri'kər) *vi.* **1.** happen again **2.** return again and again **3.** go or come back in mind (**-rr-**) —**re'currence** *n.* repetition —**re'current** *a.*

recusant ('rekyəzənt) *n.* **1.** one who refused to conform to rites of Established Anglican Church —*a.* **2.** obstinate in refusal

recycle (rē'sīkəl) *vt.* **1.** reprocess (manufactured substance) for use again **2.** reuse

red (red) *a.* **1.** of color varying from crimson to orange and seen in blood, rubies, glowing fire *etc.* —*n.* **2.** the color **3.** *inf.* communist —**'redden** *vt.* **1.** make red —*vi.* **2.** become red **3.** flush —**'reddish** *a.* —**red blood cell** *see* ERYTHROCYTE —**red-blooded** *a.* **1.** vigorous **2.** virile —**'redbreast** *n.* robin —**red bug** chigger —**red carpet 1.** strip of red carpeting laid for important dignitaries to walk on **2.** deferential treatment accorded to person of importance —**'redcoat** *n.* **1.** *obs.* soldier **2.** C *inf.* Mountie —**Red Crescent** emblem of Red Cross Society in Muslim country —**Red Cross** international humanitarian organization providing medical care for war casualties, famine relief *etc.* —**red deer** large deer formerly widely distributed in woodlands of Europe and Asia —**Red Ensign** national flag of Canad. until 1965 —**'redfish** *n.* any of various types of fish —**red flag 1.** emblem of communist party **2.** (**R- F-**) their song **3.** danger signal —**red-handed** *a. inf.* (caught) in the act —**red hat** broad-brimmed crimson hat given to cardinals as symbol of rank —**'redhead** *n.* person with red hair —**'redheaded** *a.* —**red herring** topic introduced to divert attention from main issue —**red-hot** *a.* **1.** (*esp.* of metal) heated to temperature at which it glows red **2.** extremely hot **3.** keen, excited, eager **4.** furious; violent **5.** very recent or topical —**red-hot poker** garden plant with tall spikes of red or orange flowers —**red lead** (led) red poisonous insoluble oxide of lead —**red-letter day** memorably important or happy occasion —**red light 1.** signal to stop, *esp.* traffic signal **2.** danger signal **3.** red lamp hanging outside house indicating it is a brothel —**red-light district** district containing many brothels —**red pepper 1.** pepper plant cultivated for its hot pungent red podlike fruits **2.** this fruit **3.** ripe red fruit of sweet pepper **4.** *see* CAYENNE PEPPER —**red rag** provocation; something that infuriates —**'redshank** *n.* large European sandpiper —**red shift** shift in spectral lines of stellar spectrum toward red end of visible region relative to wavelength of these lines in terrestrial spectrum —**'redskin** *n. inf.* Amer. Indian —**'redstart** *n.* **1.** European songbird of thrush family **2.** N Amer. warbler —**red tape** excessive adherence to official rules —**'redwing** *n.* small European thrush having speckled breast and reddish flanks —**'redwood** *n.* giant coniferous tree of California —**in the red** *inf.* in debt —**see red** *inf.* be angry

redeem (ri'dēm) *vt.* **1.** buy back **2.** set free **3.** free from sin **4.** make up for —**re'deemable** *a.* —**redemption** (ri'dempshən) *n.* —**The Redeemer** Jesus Christ

redeploy (rēdi'ploi) *v.* assign new positions or tasks to (labor *etc.*) —**rede'ployment** *n.*

redolent ('redələnt) *a.* **1.** smelling strongly, fragrant **2.** reminiscent —**'redolence** *n.*

redouble (rē'dubəl) *v.* **1.** increase, multiply, intensify **2.** *Bridge* double a second time

redoubt (ri'dowt) *n.* detached outwork in fortifications

redoubtable (ri'dowtəbəl) *a.* dreaded, formidable

redound (ri'downd) *vi.* **1.** contribute **2.** recoil

redress (ri'dres) *vt.* **1.** set right **2.** make amends for —*n.* **3.** compensation, amends

reduce (ri'dyōōs, -'dōōs) *vt.* **1.** bring down, lower **2.** lessen, weaken **3.** bring by force or necessity to some state or action **4.** slim **5.** simplify **6.** dilute —*vi.* **7.** *Chem.* separate substance from others with which it is combined —**re'ducible** *a.* —**reduction**

(ri'dukshən) *n.* —**reducing agent** substance used to deoxidize or lessen density of another substance

redundant (ri'dundənt) *a.* **1.** superfluous **2.** (of worker) deprived of job because it is no longer needed —**re'dundancy** *n.*

reduplicate (ri'dyo͞oplikāt, -'do͞o-) *v.* **1.** make or become double; repeat **2.** repeat (sound or syllable) in word or (of sound or syllable) be repeated —*a.* (ri'dyo͞oplikit, -'do͞o-) **3.** doubled; repeated **4.** (of petals or sepals) having margins curving outward —**redupli'cation** *n.*

reed (rēd) *n.* **1.** any of various marsh or water plants **2.** tall straight stem of one **3.** *Mus.* vibrating cane or metal strip of certain wind instruments —**'reedy** *a.* **1.** full of reeds **2.** like reed instrument **3.** harsh and thin in tone —**'reedbuck** *n.* S Afr. antelope with buff coat —**reed bunting** common European bunting that has brown streaked plumage —**reed organ** *see* **harmonium** *at* HARMONY

reef (rēf) *n.* **1.** ridge of rock or coral near surface of sea **2.** vein of ore **3.** part of sail which can be rolled up to reduce area —*vt.* **4.** take in a reef of —**'reefer** *n.* **1.** sailor's jacket **2.** *sl.* hand-rolled cigarette, *esp.* containing cannabis —**reef knot** knot consisting of two overhand knots turned opposite ways (*also* **square knot**)

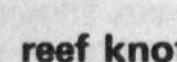
reef knot

reek (rēk) *n.* **1.** strong (unpleasant) smell —*vi.* **2.** emit fumes **3.** smell

reel (rēl, rēəl) *n.* **1.** spool on which film is wound **2.** *Cine.* portion of motion picture **3.** winding apparatus **4.** bobbin **5.** thread wound on this **6.** lively dance **7.** music for it **8.** act of staggering —*vt.* **9.** wind on to reel **10.** draw (in) by means of reel —*vi.* **11.** stagger, sway, rock —**reel off** recite, write fluently, quickly

re-entry (rē'entri) *n.* **1.** retaking possession of land *etc.* **2.** return of spacecraft into earth's atmosphere

reeve[1] (rēv) *n.* **1.** *Hist.* manorial steward or official **2. C** president of local (rural) council

reeve[2] (rēv) *vt.* pass (rope) through hole, in block *etc.*

reeve[3] (rēv) *n.* female of ruff (bird)

ref. 1. referee 2. reference 3. reformed

refectory (ri'fektəri, -tri) *n.* room for meals in college *etc.* —**re'fection** *n.* meal —**refectory table** long narrow dining table supported by two trestles

refer (ri'fər) *vi.* **1.** relate, allude —*vt.* **2.** send for information **3.** trace, ascribe **4.** submit for decision (**-rr-**) —**referable** ('refərəbəl) *or* **re'ferrable** *a.* —**referee** (refə'rē) *n.* **1.** arbitrator **2.** person willing to testify to someone's character *etc.* **3.** umpire —*v.* **4.** act as referee (in) —**reference** ('refərəns, 'refrəns) *n.* **1.** act of referring **2.** citation or direction in book **3.** appeal to judgment of another **4.** testimonial **5.** one to whom inquiries as to character *etc.* may be made —**referendum** (refə'rendəm) *n.* submitting of question to electorate (*pl.* **-s, -da** (-də)) —**referent** ('refərənt) *n.* object or idea to which word or phrase refers —**re'ferral** *n.* act, instance of referring —**reference library** library where books may be consulted but not taken away by readers

refine (ri'fīn) *vt.* purify —**re'fined** *a.* **1.** not coarse or vulgar; genteel, elegant, polite **2.** freed from impurities; purified —**re'finement** *n.* **1.** subtlety **2.** improvement, elaboration **3.** fineness of feeling, taste or manners —**re'finer** *n.* —**re'finery** *n.* place where sugar, oil *etc.* is refined

refit (rē'fit) *v.* **1.** make or be made ready for use again by repairing *etc.* (**-tt-**) —*n.* ('rēfit) **2.** repair or re-equipping, as of ship, for further use

reflation (rē'flāshən) *n.* (steps taken to produce) increase in economic activity of country *etc.*

reflect (ri'flekt) *vt.* **1.** throw back, *esp.* rays of light **2.** cast (discredit *etc.*) upon —*vi.* **3.** meditate —**re'flection** *n.* **1.** act of reflecting **2.** return of rays of heat, light or waves of sound from surface **3.** image of object given back by mirror *etc.* **4.** conscious thought **5.** meditation **6.** expression of thought —**re'flective** *a.* **1.** meditative, quiet, contemplative **2.** throwing back images —**re'flector** *n.* polished surface for reflecting light *etc.*

reflex ('rēfleks) *n.* **1.** reflex action **2.** reflected image **3.** reflected light, color *etc.* —*a.* **4.** (of muscular action) involuntary **5.** reflected **6.** bent back —**re'flexive** *a. Gram.* denoting agent's action on himself —**reflex action** involuntary response to (nerve) stimulation

reflux ('rēfluks) *n.* flowing back, ebb —**refluence** ('reflo͞oəns) *n.* —**refluent** ('reflo͞oənt) *a.* returning, ebbing

reform (ri'fôrm) *vt.* **1.** improve **2.** reconstruct —*vi.* **3.** abandon evil practices —*n.* **4.** improvement —**reformation** (refər'māshən) *n.* —**re'formatory** *n.* **1.** institution for reforming juvenile offenders —*a.* **2.** reforming —**re'former** *n.*

refract (ri'frakt) *vt.* change course of (light *etc.*) passing from one medium to another —**re'fraction** *n.* —**re'fractive** *a.*

refractory (ri'fraktəri) *a.* **1.** unmanageable **2.** difficult to treat or work **3.** *Med.* resistant to treatment **4.** resistant to heat

refrain[1] (ri'frān) *vi.* abstain

refrain[2] (ri'frān) *n.* chorus

refresh (ri'fresh) *vt.* **1.** give freshness to **2.** revive **3.** renew **4.** brighten **5.** provide with refreshment —**re'fresher** *n.* that which refreshes —**re'freshment** *n.* **1.** that which refreshes, *esp.* food, drink **2.** restorative

refrigerate (ri'frijərāt) *vt.* **1.** freeze **2.** cool —**re'frigerant** *n.* **1.** refrigerating substance —*a.* **2.** causing cooling or freezing —**refriger'ation** *n.* —**re'frigerator** *n.* apparatus in which foods, drinks are kept cool

refuge ('refyōōj) *n.* shelter, protection, sanctuary —**refu'gee** *n.* one who seeks refuge, *esp.* in foreign country

refulgent (ri'fōōljənt, -'ful-) *a.* shining, radiant —**re'fulgence** *n.* —**re'fulgency** *n.* splendor

refund (ri'fund) *vt.* **1.** pay back —*n.* ('rēfund) **2.** return of money to purchaser or amount so returned

refurbish (ri'fərbish) *vt.* furbish, furnish or polish anew

refuse[1] (ri'fyōōz) *v.* decline, deny, reject —**re'fusal** *n.* **1.** denial of anything demanded or offered **2.** option

refuse[2] ('refyōōs) *n.* rubbish, useless matter

refute (ri'fyōōt) *vt.* disprove —**re'futable** *a.* —**refutation** (refyōō'tāshən) *n.*

regal ('rēgəl) *a.* of, like a king —**regalia** (ri'gālyə) *pl.n.* (*sometimes with sing. v.*) **1.** insignia of royalty, as used at coronation *etc.* **2.** emblems of high office, an order *etc.* —**re'gality** *n.* —**'regally** *adv.*

regale (ri'gāl) *vt.* **1.** give pleasure to **2.** feast —**re'galement** *n.*

regard (ri'gärd) *vt.* **1.** look at **2.** consider **3.** relate to **4.** heed —*n.* **5.** look **6.** attention **7.** particular respect **8.** esteem —*pl.* **9.** expression of good will —**re'gardful** *a.* heedful, careful —**re'garding** *prep.* in respect of; on the subject of —**re'gardless** *a.* **1.** heedless —*adv.* **2.** in spite of everything

regatta (ri'gätə, -'gatə) *n.* meeting for yacht or boat races

regenerate (ri'jenərāt) *v.* **1.** (cause to) undergo spiritual rebirth **2.** reform morally **3.** reproduce, re-create **4.** reorganize —*a.* (ri'jenərit) **5.** born anew —**regener'ation** *n.* —**re'generative** *a.* —**re'generator** *n.*

regent ('rējənt) *n.* **1.** ruler of kingdom during absence, minority *etc.* of its monarch —*a.* **2.** ruling —**'regency** *n.* status of, (period of) office of regent —**regency style** eclectic architectural and decorative style named for Prince Regent (later George IV) seen from late 18th cent. to about 1830

reggae ('regā) *n.* style of popular West Indian music with strong beat

Reggiano Lodigiano (re'jänō lōdē'jänō) *see* PARMESAN

regicide ('rejisīd) *n.* **1.** one who kills a king **2.** this crime

regime *or* **régime** (rā'zhēm) *n.* **1.** system of government, administration **2.** *see* REGIMEN (sense 1)

regimen ('rejimən) *n.* **1.** prescribed system of diet *etc.* (*also* **re'gime**) **2.** rule

regiment ('rejimənt) *n.* **1.** organized body of troops as unit of army —*vt.* ('rejiment) **2.** discipline, organize rigidly or too strictly —**regi'mental** *a.* of regiment —**regi'mentals** *pl.n.* uniform

region ('rējən) *n.* **1.** area, district **2.** stretch of country **3.** part of the body **4.** sphere, realm **5.** (*oft.* **R-**) administrative division of a country —**'regional** *a.* —**regional enteritis** *see* CROHN'S DISEASE

register ('rejistər) *n.* **1.** list **2.** catalog **3.** roll **4.** device for registering **5.** written record **6.** range of voice or instrument —*v.* **7.** show, be shown on meter, face *etc.* —*vt.* **8.** enter in register **9.** record **10.** show **11.** set down in writing **12.** *Print., photog.* cause to correspond precisely —**'registrar** *n.* keeper of a register —**regis'tration** *n.* —**'registry** *n.* **1.** registering **2.** place where registers are kept, *esp.* of births, marriages, deaths —**registered mail 1.** Postal Service facility by which compensation is paid for loss of or damage to mail for which registration fee has been paid **2.** mail sent by this service

regorge (ri'görj) *vt.* vomit up

regress (ri'gres) *vi.* **1.** return, revert to former place, condition *etc.* —*n.* ('rēgres) **2.** movement in backward direction —**re'gression** *n.* **1.** act of returning **2.** retrogression —**re'gressive** *a.* falling back —**re'gressively** *adv.*

regret (ri'gret) *vt.* **1.** feel sorry, distressed for loss of or on account of (-tt-) —*n.* **2.** sorrow, distress for thing done or left undone or lost —**re'gretful** *a.* —**re'grettable** *a.*

regular ('regyələr) *a.* **1.** normal **2.** habitual **3.** done, occurring, according to rule **4.** periodical **5.** straight, level **6.** living under rule **7.** belonging to standing army —*n.* **8.** regular soldier **9.** *inf.* regular customer —**regu'larity** *n.* —**'regularize** *v.*

regulate ('regyəlāt) *vt.* **1.** adjust **2.** arrange **3.** direct **4.** govern **5.** put under rule —**regu'lation** *n.* —**'regulator** *n.* contrivance to produce uniformity of motion, as flywheel, governor valve *etc.*

regurgitate (rē'gərjitāt) *v.* **1.** vomit **2.** bring back (swallowed food) into mouth —**regurgi'tation** *n.*

rehabilitate (rēə'bilitāt) *vt.* **1.** help (person) to readjust to society after period of illness, imprisonment *etc.* **2.** restore to reputation or former position **3.** make fit again **4.** reinstate —**rehabili'tation** *n.*

rehash (rē'hash) *vt.* **1.** rework, reuse —*n.* **2.** old materials presented in new form

rehearse (ri'hərs) *vt.* **1.** practice (play *etc.*) **2.** repeat aloud **3.** say over again **4.** train, drill —**re'hearsal** *n.*

Reich (rīk) *n.* **1.** Holy Roman Empire (962-1806) (**First Reich**) **2.** Hohenzollern empire in Germany from 1871 to 1918 (**Second Reich**) **3.** Nazi dictatorship in Germany from 1933-45 (**Third Reich**)

reign (rān) *n.* **1.** period of sovereign's rule —*vi.* **2.** be sovereign **3.** be supreme

reimburse (rēim'bərs) *vt.* **1.** refund **2.** pay back —**reim'bursement** *n.*

rein (rān) *n.* **1.** (*oft. pl.*) narrow strap attached to bit to guide horse **2.** instrument for governing —*vt.* **3.** check, manage with reins **4.** control —**give (a) free rein** remove restraints

reincarnation (rēinkär'nāshən) *n.* **1.** rebirth of soul in successive bodies **2.** one of series of such transmigrations —**rein'carnate** *vt.*

reindeer

reindeer ('rāndēər) *n.* large deer of northern regions of America, Asia and Europe, oft. domesticated and used as food source (*pl.* **-deer, -s**)

reinforce (rēin'fōrs) *vt.* **1.** strengthen with new support, material, force **2.** strengthen with additional troops, ships *etc.* —**rein'forcement** *n.* —**reinforced concrete 1.** concrete strengthened internally by steel bars **2.** ferroconcrete

reinstate (rēin'stāt) *vt.* replace, restore, re-establish —**rein'statement** *n.*

reiterate (rē'itərāt) *vt.* repeat again and again —**reiter'ation** *n.* repetition

reject (ri'jekt) *vt.* **1.** refuse to accept **2.** put aside **3.** discard **4.** renounce —*n.* ('rējekt) **5.** person or thing rejected as not up to standard —**re'jection** *n.* refusal

rejig (rē'jig) *vt.* **1.** re-equip (factory, plant) **2.** *inf.* rearrange (**-gg-**)

rejoice (ri'jois) *v.* **1.** make or be joyful, merry —*vt.* **2.** exult **3.** gladden

rejoin (ri'join) *vt.* **1.** reply **2.** (rē'join) join again —**re'joinder** *n.* answer, retort

rejuvenate (ri'jōōvināt) *vt.* restore to youth —**rejuve'nation** *n.* —**rejuve'nescence** *n.* process of growing young again

relapse (ri'laps) *vi.* **1.** fall back (into evil, illness *etc.*) —*n.* **2.** act or instance of relapsing

relate (ri'lāt) *vt.* **1.** narrate, recount **2.** establish relation between —*vi.* (*with* to) **3.** have reference or relation **4.** form sympathetic relationship —**re'lated** *a.* **1.** connected; associated **2.** connected by kinship or marriage

relation (ri'lāshən) *n.* **1.** relative quality or condition **2.** connection by blood or marriage **3.** connection (between things) **4.** act of relating **5.** narrative —**re'lationship** *n.* —**relative** ('relətiv) *a.* **1.** dependent on relation to something else, not absolute **2.** having reference or relation —*n.* **3.** one connected by blood or marriage **4.** relative word or thing —**relatively** ('relətivli) *adv.* —**relativity** (relə'tiviti) *n.* **1.** state of being relative **2.** subject of two theories of Albert Einstein, dealing with relationships of space, time and motion and acceleration and gravity

relax (ri'laks) *vt.* **1.** make loose or slack —*vi.* **2.** become loosened or slack **3.** ease up from effort or attention **4.** become more friendly, less strict —**relax'ation** *n.* **1.** relaxing recreation **2.** alleviation **3.** abatement

relay ('rēlā) *n.* **1.** fresh set of people or animals relieving others **2.** *Elec.* device for making or breaking local circuit **3.** *Rad., T.V.* broadcasting station receiving programs from another station —*vt.* ('rēlā, ri'lā) **4.** pass on, as message (**'relayed, 'relaying**) —**relay race** race between teams of which each runner races part of distance

release (ri'lēs) *vt.* **1.** give up, surrender, set free **2.** permit public showing of (motion picture *etc.*) —*n.* **3.** setting free **4.** releasing **5.** written discharge **6.** permission to show publicly **7.** motion picture, record *etc.* newly issued

relegate ('religāt) *vt.* **1.** banish, consign **2.** demote —**rele'gation** *n.*

relent (ri'lent) *vi.* give up harsh intention, become less severe —**re'lentless** *a.* **1.** pitiless **2.** merciless

relevant ('relivənt) *a.* having to do with the matter in hand, to the point —**'relevance** *n.*

reliable (ri'līəbəl) *a. see* RELY

relic ('relik) *n.* **1.** thing remaining, *esp.* as memorial of saint **2.** memento —*pl.* **3.** remains, traces **4.** *obs.* dead body —**'relict** *n.* *obs.* widow

relief (ri'lēf) *n.* **1.** alleviation, end of pain, distress *etc.* **2.** money, food given to victims of disaster, poverty *etc.* **3.** release from duty **4.** one who relieves another from work or duty **5.** bus, plane *etc.* that carries passengers when a scheduled service is full **6.** freeing of besieged city *etc.* **7.** projection of carved design from surface **8.** distinctness, prominence —**re'lieve** *vt.* bring or give relief to —**relief map** map showing elevations and depressions of country in relief

religion (ri'lijən) *n.* system of belief in, worship of a supernatural power or god —**religiose** (ri'lijiōs) *a.* affectedly or extremely pious; sanctimoniously religious —**religiosity** (riliji'ositi) *n.* —**re'ligious** *a.* **1.** pert. to religion **2.** pious **3.** conscientious —**re'ligiously** *adv.* **1.** in religious manner **2.** scrupulously **3.** conscientiously

relinquish (ri'lingkwish) *vt.* **1.** give up,

abandon **2.** surrender or renounce (claim, right *etc.*) —**re'linquishment** *n.*

reliquary ('relikweri) *n.* case or shrine for holy relics

relish ('relish) *vt.* **1.** enjoy, like —*n.* **2.** liking, gusto **3.** savory taste **4.** taste, flavor

relive (rē'liv) *vt.* experience (sensation *etc.*) again, *esp.* in imagination —**re'livable** *a.*

reluctant (ri'luktənt) *a.* unwilling, disinclined —**re'luctance** *n.*

rely (ri'lī) *vi.* **1.** depend **2.** (*with* on) trust (**re'lied, re'lying**) —**relia'bility** *n.* —**re'liable** *a.* trustworthy, dependable —**re'liance** *n.* **1.** trust **2.** confidence **3.** dependence —**re'liant** *a.* confident

REM rapid eye movement

remain (ri'mān) *vi.* **1.** stay, be left behind **2.** continue **3.** abide **4.** last —**re'mainder** *n.* **1.** what is left after subtraction —*vt.* **2.** offer (end of consignment of goods, material *etc.*) at reduced prices —**re'mains** *pl.n.* **1.** relics, *esp.* of ancient buildings **2.** dead body

remand (ri'mand) *vt.* send back, *esp.* into custody —**remand home** *or* **center** place of detention for young delinquents

remark (ri'märk) *vi.* **1.** make casual comment —*vt.* **2.** comment, observe **3.** say **4.** take notice of —*n.* **5.** observation, comment —**re'markable** *a.* noteworthy, unusual —**re'markably** *adv.* **1.** exceedingly **2.** unusually

remedy ('remidi) *n.* **1.** means of curing, counteracting or relieving disease, trouble *etc.* —*vt.* **2.** put right (**-edied, -edying**) —**remediable** (ri'mēdiəbəl) *a.* —**remedial** (ri'mēdiəl) *a.* designed, intended to correct specific disability, handicap *etc.*

remember (ri'membər) *vt.* **1.** retain in, recall to memory **2.** have in mind —**re'membrance** *n.* **1.** memory **2.** token **3.** souvenir **4.** reminiscence —**Remembrance Day C** statutory holiday observed on Nov. 11th in memory of the dead of both World Wars

remind (ri'mīnd) *vt.* **1.** cause to remember **2.** put in mind —**re'minder** *n.*

reminisce (remi'nis) *vi.* talk, write of past times, experiences *etc.* —**remi'niscence** *n.* **1.** remembering **2.** thing recollected —*pl.* **3.** memoirs —**remi'niscent** *a.* reminding, suggestive

remiss (ri'mis) *a.* negligent, careless —**re'missly** *adv.*

remit (ri'mit) *v.* **1.** send (money) for goods, services *etc.*, *esp.* by mail **2.** refrain from exacting (penalty) —*vt.* **3.** give up **4.** restore, return **5.** slacken **6.** *obs.* forgive (**-tt-**) —*n.* (ri'mit, 'rēmit) **7.** area of competence, authority —**re'missible** *a.* —**re'mission** *n.* **1.** abatement **2.** reduction in length of prison term **3.** pardon, forgiveness —**re'mittance** *n.* **1.** sending of money **2.** money sent —**re'mittence** *n.* —**re'mittent** *a.* (of symptoms of disease) characterized by periods of diminished severity —**re'mittently** *adv.*

remnant ('remnənt) *n.* **1.** (*oft. pl.*) fragment or small piece remaining **2.** oddment

remonstrate (ri'monstrāt, 'remənstrāt) *vi.* protest, reason, argue —**re'monstrance** *n.*

remorse (ri'mörs) *n.* regret and repentance —**re'morseful** *a.* —**re'morsefully** *adv.* —**re'morseless** *a.* pitiless

remote (ri'mōt) *a.* **1.** far away, distant **2.** aloof **3.** slight —**re'motely** *adv.* —**remote control** control of apparatus from a distance by electrical device

remove (ri'mo͞ov) *vt.* **1.** take away or off **2.** transfer **3.** withdraw —*vi.* **4.** go away, change residence —*n.* **5.** degree of difference —**re'movable** *a.* —**re'moval** *n.*

remunerate (ri'myo͞onərāt) *vt.* reward, pay —**remuner'ation** *n.* —**re'munerative** *a.*

renaissance (renə'sons, -'zons) *or* **renascence** (ri'nasəns, -'nā-) *n.* revival, rebirth, *esp.* (**R-**) revival of learning in 14th-16th centuries

renal ('rēnəl) *a.* of the kidneys

renascent (ri'nasənt, -'nā-) *a.* springing up again into being

rend (rend) *v.* **1.** tear, wrench apart **2.** burst, break, split (**rent, 'rending**)

render ('rendər) *vt.* **1.** submit, present **2.** give in return, deliver up **3.** cause to become **4.** portray, represent **5.** melt down **6.** cover with plaster

rendezvous ('rondivo͞o) *n.* **1.** meeting place **2.** appointment **3.** haunt **4.** assignation (*pl.* **-vous** (-vo͞oz)) —*vi.* **5.** meet, come together

rendition (ren'dishən) *n.* **1.** performance **2.** translation

renegade ('renigād) *n.* **1.** deserter **2.** outlaw **3.** rebel

renege (ri'nēg) *vi.* go back (on promise *etc.*)

renew (ri'nyo͞o, -'no͞o) *vt.* **1.** begin again **2.** reaffirm **3.** make valid again **4.** make new **5.** revive **6.** restore to former state **7.** replenish —*vi.* **8.** be made new **9.** grow again —**renewa'bility** *n.* —**re'newable** *a.* —**re'newal** *n.* **1.** revival, restoration **2.** regeneration

rennet ('renit) *n.* preparation for curdling milk

renounce (ri'nowns) *vt.* **1.** give up, cast off, disown **2.** abjure **3.** resign, as title or claim —**renunci'ation** *n.* **1.** act or instance of renouncing **2.** formal declaration renouncing something

renovate ('renəvāt) *vt.* restore, repair, renew, do up —**reno'vation** *n.*

renown (ri'nown) *n.* fame —**re'nowned** *a.*

rent[1] (rent) *n.* **1.** payment for use of land, buildings, machines *etc.* —*vt.* **2.** hold by lease **3.** hire **4.** let —**'rental** *n.* sum payable as rent

rent[2] (rent) *n.* **1.** tear **2.** fissure —*v.* **3.** *pt./pp. of* REND

renunciation (rinunsi'āshən) *n.* *see* RENOUNCE

rep[1] (rep) *a./n.* repertory (company, theater, group)

rep[2] (rep) *n.* representative
repaid (rē'pād) *pt./pp. of* REPAY
repair[1] (ri'pāər) *vt.* **1.** make whole, sound again **2.** mend **3.** patch **4.** restore —*n.* **5.** act or process of repairing —**re'pairable** *a.* —**reparation** (repə'rāshən) *n.* **1.** repairing **2.** amends, compensation
repair[2] (ri'pāər) *vi.* (*usu. with* to) resort, go
repartee (repər'tē, -pär-) *n.* **1.** witty retort **2.** interchange of witty retorts
repast (ri'past) *n.* meal
repatriate (rē'pātriāt, -'pat-) *vt.* send (someone) back to his own country —**repatri'ation** *n.*
repay (rē'pā) *vt.* **1.** pay back, refund **2.** make return for (**re'paid, re'paying**) —**re'payable** *a.* —**re'payment** *n.*
repeal (ri'pēl) *vt.* **1.** revoke, annul, cancel —*n.* **2.** act of repealing
repeat (ri'pēt) *vt.* **1.** say, do again **2.** reproduce —*vi.* **3.** recur —*n.* **4.** act, instance of repeating, *esp.* TV show broadcast again —**re'peatedly** *adv.* **1.** again and again **2.** frequently —**re'peater** *n.* **1.** firearm that may be discharged many times without reloading **2.** timepiece that strikes hours —**repe'tition** *n.* **1.** act of repeating **2.** thing repeated **3.** piece learnt by heart and repeated —**repetitious** (repi'tishəs) *a.* repeated unnecessarily —**repetitive** (ri'petitiv) *a.* repeated
repel (ri'pel) *vt.* **1.** drive back, ward off, refuse **2.** be repulsive to (**-ll-**) —**re'pellent** *a.* **1.** distasteful **2.** resisting (water *etc.*) —*n.* **3.** that which repels, *esp.* chemical to repel insects
repent (ri'pent) *vi.* **1.** wish one had not done something **2.** feel regret for deed or omission —*vt.* **3.** feel regret for —**re'pentance** *n.* contrition —**re'pentant** *a.*
repercussion (rēpər'kushən) *n.* **1.** (*oft. pl.*) indirect effect, oft. unpleasant **2.** recoil **3.** echo
repertory ('repərtöri) *n.* **1.** repertoire, collection **2.** store —**repertoire** ('repərtwär) *n.* stock of plays, songs *etc.* that player or company can give —**repertory company** *or* **theater** (theater with) permanent company producing succession of plays
repetition (repi'tishən) *n. see* REPEAT
repine (ri'pīn) *vi.* fret, complain
replace (ri'plās) *vt.* **1.** substitute for **2.** put back —**re'placement** *n.*
replay ('rēplā) *n.* **1.** immediate reshowing on TV of incident in sport, *esp.* in slow motion (*also* **action replay**) **2.** replaying of a match —*vt.* (rē'plā) **3.** play again
replenish (ri'plenish) *vt.* fill up again —**re'plenishment** *n.*
replete (ri'plēt) *a.* filled, gorged —**re'pletion** *n.* complete fullness
replica ('replikə) *n.* **1.** exact copy **2.** facsimile, duplicate —**'replicate** *vt.* make, be a copy of
reply (ri'plī) *v.* **1.** answer (**re'plied, re'plying**) —*n.* **2.** an answer; response
report (ri'pört) *n.* **1.** account, statement **2.** written statement of child's progress at school **3.** rumor **4.** repute **5.** bang —*vt.* **6.** announce, relate **7.** make, give account of **8.** take down in writing **9.** complain about —*vi.* **10.** make report **11.** act as reporter **12.** present oneself (to) —**re'porter** *n.* one who reports, *esp.* for newspaper
repose (ri'pōz) *n.* **1.** peace **2.** composure **3.** sleep —*vi.* **4.** rest —*vt.* **5.** lay at rest **6.** place **7.** rely, lean (on) —**repository** (ri'pozitöri) *n.* **1.** place where valuables are deposited for safety **2.** store
repossess (rēpə'zes) *vt.* take back possession of (property), *esp.* for nonpayment of money due on installment plan —**repos'session** *n.*
repoussé (rəpōō'sā, rə'pōōsā) *a.* **1.** embossed **2.** hammered into relief from reverse side —*n.* **3.** metal work so produced
reprehend (repri'hend) *vt.* find fault with —**repre'hensible** *a.* **1.** deserving censure **2.** unworthy —**repre'hension** *n.* censure
represent (repri'zent) *vt.* **1.** stand for **2.** deputize for **3.** act, play **4.** symbolize **5.** make out to be **6.** call up by description or portrait —**represen'tation** *n.* —**repre'sentative** *n.* **1.** one chosen to stand for group **2.** traveling salesman —*a.* **3.** typical
repress (ri'pres) *vt.* keep down or under, quell, check —**re'pression** *n.* restraint —**re'pressive** *a.*
reprieve (ri'prēv) *vt.* **1.** suspend execution of (condemned person) **2.** give temporary relief to —*n.* **3.** postponement or cancellation of punishment **4.** respite **5.** last-minute intervention
reprimand ('reprimand) *n.* **1.** formal admonition —*vt.* **2.** admonish formally
reprisal (ri'prīzəl) *n.* retaliation
reproach (ri'prōch) *vt.* **1.** blame, rebuke —*n.* **2.** scolding, upbraiding **3.** expression of this **4.** thing bringing discredit —**re'proachful** *a.*
reprobate ('reprəbāt) *a.* **1.** depraved **2.** cast off by God —*n.* **3.** depraved or disreputable person —*vt.* **4.** disapprove of, reject —**repro'bation** *n.*
reproduce (rēprə'dyōōs, -'dōōs) *vt.* **1.** produce copy of **2.** bring (new individuals) into existence **3.** re-create, produce anew —*vi.* **4.** propagate **5.** generate —**repro'ducible** *a.* —**repro'duction** *n.* **1.** process of reproducing **2.** that which is reproduced **3.** facsimile, as of painting *etc.* —**repro'ductive** *a.*
reprove (ri'prōōv) *vt.* censure —**re'proof** *n.*
reptile ('reptil, -tīl) *n.* cold-blooded, air-breathing vertebrate with horny scales or plates, as snake, tortoise *etc.* —**reptilian** (rep'tiliən) *a.*
republic (ri'publik) *n.* state without monarch in which supremacy of people or their elected representatives is formally acknowl-

edged —**re'publican** *a./n.* —**re'publicanism** *n.*

repudiate (ri'pyōōdiāt) *vt.* **1.** reject authority or validity of **2.** cast off, disown

repugnant (ri'pugnənt) *a.* **1.** offensive **2.** distasteful **3.** contrary —**re'pugnance** *n.* **1.** dislike, aversion **2.** incompatibility

repulse (ri'puls) *vt.* **1.** drive back **2.** rebuff **3.** repel —*n.* **4.** driving back, rejection, rebuff —**re'pulsion** *n.* **1.** distaste, aversion **2.** *Phys.* force separating two objects —**re'pulsive** *a.* loathsome, disgusting

repute (ri'pyōōt) *vt.* **1.** reckon, consider —*n.* **2.** reputation, credit —**reputable** ('repyətəbəl) *a.* **1.** of good repute **2.** respectable —**reputation** (repyə'tāshən) *n.* **1.** estimation in which person is held **2.** character **3.** good name —**re'puted** *a.* generally reckoned or considered; supposed —**re'putedly** *adv.*

request (ri'kwest) *n.* **1.** asking **2.** thing asked for —*vt.* **3.** ask

Requiem ('rekwiəm) *n.* **1.** Mass for the dead **2.** music for this

requiescat in pace (rekwi'eskat in 'päke) *Lat.* may he (or she) rest in peace

require (ri'kwīər) *vt.* **1.** want, need **2.** demand —**re'quirement** *n.* **1.** essential condition **2.** specific need **3.** want

requisite ('rekwizit) *a.* **1.** necessary **2.** essential —*n.* **3.** something indispensable; necessity

requisition (rekwi'zishən) *n.* **1.** formal demand, *eg* for materials or supplies —*vt.* **2.** demand (supplies) **3.** press into service

requite (ri'kwīt) *vt.* repay —**re'quital** *n.*

reredos ('rerədos, 'rēərədos, 'rēərdos) *n.* ornamental screen behind altar

rerun (rē'run) *vt.* **1.** broadcast or put on (motion picture *etc.*) again **2.** run (race *etc.*) again —*n.* ('rērun) **3.** motion picture *etc.* that is broadcast again; repeat **4.** race that is run again

rescind (ri'sind) *vt.* cancel, annul —**re'scindment** *or* **rescission** (ri'sizhən) *n.*

rescue ('reskyōō) *vt.* **1.** bring out of danger *etc.*, deliver, extricate (**-cuing, -cued**) —*n.* **2.** act or instance of rescuing —**'rescuer** *n.* —**'rescuing** *n.*

research (ri'sərch) *n.* **1.** investigation, *esp.* scientific study to discover facts —*v.* **2.** carry out investigations (on, into) —**re'searcher** *n.*

resemble (ri'zembəl) *vt.* **1.** be like **2.** look like —**re'semblance** *n.*

resent (ri'zent) *vt.* **1.** show, feel indignation at **2.** retain bitterness about —**re'sentful** *a.* —**re'sentment** *n.*

reserve (ri'zərv) *vt.* **1.** hold back, set aside, keep for future use —*n.* **2.** (*also pl.*) something, *esp.* money, troops *etc.*, kept for emergencies **3.** area of land reserved for particular purpose or for use by particular group of people *etc.* (*also* **reser'vation**) **4.** reticence, concealment of feelings or friendliness —**reservation** (rezər'vāshən) *n.* **1.** reserving **2.** thing reserved **3.** doubt **4.** exception; limitation —**re'served** *a.* not showing feelings, lacking cordiality —**re'servist** *n.* one serving in reserve —**reserve price** minimum price acceptable to owner of property being auctioned

reservoir ('rezərvwär) *n.* **1.** enclosed area for storage of water, *esp.* for community supplies **2.** receptacle for liquid, gas *etc.* **3.** place where anything is kept in store

reside (ri'zīd) *vi.* dwell permanently —**residence** ('rezidəns) *n.* **1.** home **2.** house —**resident** ('rezidənt) *a./n.* —**residential** (rezi'denchəl) *a.* **1.** (of part of town) consisting mainly of residences **2.** of, connected with residence **3.** providing living accommodation

residue ('rezidyōō, -dōō) *n.* what is left, remainder —**residual** (ri'zijōōəl) *a.* —**residuary** (ri'zijōōeri) *a.* —**residuum** (ri'zijōōəm) *n. formal* residue (*pl.* **-ua** (-ōōə))

resign (ri'zīn) *vt.* **1.** give up **2.** reconcile (oneself) —*vi.* **3.** give up office, employment *etc.* —**resignation** (rezig'nāshən) *n.* **1.** resigning **2.** being resigned, submission —**re'signed** *a.* content to endure

resilient (ri'zilyənt) *a.* **1.** (of an object) capable of returning to normal after stretching *etc.*; elastic **2.** (of a person) recovering quickly from shock *etc.* —**re'silience** *or* **re'siliency** *n.*

resin ('rezin) *n.* sticky substance formed in and oozing from plants, *esp.* firs and pines (*also* **'rosin**) —**'resinous** *a.* of, like resin

resist (ri'zist) *v.* **1.** withstand **2.** oppose —**re'sistance** *n.* **1.** act of resisting **2.** opposition **3.** hindrance **4.** *Elec.* opposition offered by circuit to passage of current through it —**re'sistant** *a.* —**re'sistible** *a.* —**resis'tivity** *n.* measure of electrical resistance —**re'sistor** *n.* component of electrical circuit producing resistance

resit (rē'sit) *vt.* **1.** sit (examination) again —*n.* ('rēsit) **2.** examination one must sit again

resolute ('rezəlōōt) *a.* determined —**'resolutely** *adv.* —**reso'lution** *n.* **1.** resolving **2.** firmness **3.** purpose or thing resolved upon **4.** decision of court or vote of assembly

resolve (ri'zolv) *vi.* **1.** make up one's mind **2.** decide with effort of will —*vt.* **3.** form by resolution of vote **4.** separate component parts of **5.** make clear —*n.* **6.** resolution **7.** fixed purpose —**resoluble** (ri'zolyəbəl) *or* **re'solvable** *a.* able to be resolved or analyzed —**re'solved** *a.* fixed in purpose or intention; determined —**resolvedly** (ri'zolvidli) *adv.* —**re'solvent** *a./n.* —**re'solver** *n.*

resonance ('rezənəns) *n.* **1.** echoing, *esp.* in deep tone **2.** sound produced by body vibrating in sympathy with neighboring source of sound —**'resonant** *a.* —**'resonate** *v.* —**'resonator** *n.*

resort (ri'zört) *vi.* **1.** have recourse **2.** (*with*

to) frequent —*n.* **3.** place of recreation, *eg* beach **4.** recourse **5.** frequented place, haunt
resound (ri'zownd) *vi.* echo, go on sounding —**re'sounding** *a.* **1.** echoing **2.** thorough
resource (ri'sörs, -'zörs) *n.* **1.** capability, ingenuity **2.** that to which one resorts for support **3.** expedient —*pl.* **4.** source of economic wealth **5.** stock that can be drawn on **6.** means of support, funds —**re'sourceful** *a.* —**re'sourcefully** *adv.* —**re'sourcefulness** *n.*
respect (ri'spekt) *n.* **1.** deference, esteem **2.** point, aspect **3.** reference, relation —*vt.* **4.** treat with esteem **5.** show consideration for —**respecta'bility** *n.* —**re'spectable** *a.* **1.** worthy of respect, decent **2.** fairly good —**re'specter** *n.* —**re'spectful** *a.* —**re'specting** *prep.* concerning —**re'spective** *a.* **1.** relating separately to each of those in question **2.** several, separate —**re'spectively** *adv.*
respire (ri'spīər) *v.* breathe —**respirable** ('respirəbəl) *a.* —**respiration** (respə'rāshən) *n.* —**respirator** ('respərātər) *n.* apparatus worn over mouth and breathed through as protection against dust, poison gas *etc.* or to provide artificial respiration —**respiratory** ('respərətöri) *a.*
respite ('respit, ri'spīt) *n.* **1.** pause **2.** interval **3.** suspension of labor **4.** delay **5.** reprieve
resplendent (ri'splendənt) *a.* **1.** brilliant, splendid **2.** shining —**re'splendence** *or* **re'splendency** *n.*
respond (ri'spond) *vi.* **1.** answer **2.** act in answer to any stimulus **3.** react —**re'spondent** *a.* **1.** replying —*n.* **2.** one who answers **3.** defendant —**re'sponse** *n.* answer —**re'sponsive** *a.* readily reacting to some influence —**re'sponsiveness** *n.*
responsible (ri'sponsəbəl) *a.* **1.** liable to answer (for) **2.** accountable **3.** dependable **4.** involving responsibility **5.** of good credit or position —**responsi'bility** *n.* **1.** state of being answerable **2.** duty **3.** charge **4.** obligation
rest[1] (rest) *n.* **1.** repose **2.** freedom from exertion *etc.* **3.** that on which anything rests or leans **4.** pause, *esp.* in music **5.** support —*vi.* **6.** take rest **7.** be supported —*vt.* **8.** give rest to **9.** place on support —**'restful** *a.* —**'restless** *a.*
rest[2] (rest) *n.* **1.** remainder **2.** others —*vi.* **3.** remain **4.** continue to be
restaurant ('restərənt, 'restəront, -tront) *n.* commercial establishment serving food —**restaurateur** (restərə'tər) *n.* keeper of restaurant
restitution (resti'tyōōshən, -'tōō-) *n.* **1.** giving back or making up **2.** reparation, compensation
restive ('restiv) *a.* **1.** restless **2.** resisting control, impatient
restore (ri'stör) *vt.* **1.** build up again, renew **2.** re-establish **3.** give back —**restoration** (restə'rāshən) *n.* —**re'storative** *a.* **1.** restoring —*n.* **2.** medicine to strengthen *etc.* —**re'storer** *n.*
restrain (ri'strān) *vt.* **1.** check, hold back **2.** prevent **3.** confine —**re'straint** *n.* restraining, control, *esp.* self-control
restrict (ri'strikt) *vt.* limit, bound —**re'striction** *n.* **1.** limitation **2.** restraint **3.** rule —**re'strictive** *a.* —**restrictive clause** *Gram.* relative clause that restricts the number of possible referents of its antecedent —**restrictive practices** agreements to limit competition or output in industry
result (ri'zult) *vi.* **1.** follow as consequence **2.** happen **3.** end —*n.* **4.** effect, outcome —**re'sultant** *a.* arising as result
resume (ri'zōōm) *v.* begin again —**résumé** ('rezəmā) *n.* **1.** curriculum vitae **2.** summary, abstract —**resumption** (ri'zumpshən) *n.* **1.** resuming **2.** fresh start —**resumptive** (ri'zumptiv) *a.*
resurgence (ri'sərjəns) *n.* rising again —**re'surgent** *a.*
resurrect (rezə'rekt) *vt.* **1.** restore to life, resuscitate **2.** use once more (something discarded *etc.*) —**resur'rection** *n.* **1.** rising again (*esp.* from dead) **2.** revival
resuscitate (ri'susitāt) *vt.* revive to life, consciousness —**resusci'tation** *n.*
retail ('rētāl) *n.* **1.** sale of goods in small quantities —*adv.* **2.** by retail —*v.* **3.** sell, be sold, retail **4.** (ri'tāl) recount —**'retailer** *n.*
retain (ri'tān) *vt.* **1.** keep **2.** engage services of —**re'tainer** *n.* **1.** fee to retain professional adviser, *esp.* barrister **2.** *Hist.* follower of nobleman *etc.* —**retention** (ri'tenchən) *n.* —**retentive** (ri'tentiv) *a.* capable of retaining, remembering —**retaining wall** wall constructed to hold back earth *etc.* (*also* **re'vetment**)
retake (rē'tāk) *vt.* **1.** take back, capture again **2.** *Cine.* shoot (scene) again **3.** tape (recording) again —*n.* ('rētāk) **4.** *Cine.* rephotographed scene **5.** retaped recording
retaliate (ri'taliāt) *vi.* **1.** repay someone in kind **2.** revenge oneself —**retali'ation** *n.* —**re'taliative** *or* **re'taliatory** *a.*
retard (ri'tärd) *vt.* **1.** make slow or late **2.** keep back **3.** impede development of —**retar'dation** *n.* —**re'tarded** *a.* underdeveloped, *esp.* mentally
retch (rech) *vi.* try to vomit
reticent ('retisənt) *a.* **1.** reserved in speech **2.** uncommunicative —**'reticence** *n.*
reticulate (ri'tikyəlit) *a.* **1.** made or arranged like a net (*also* **re'ticular**) —*v.* (ri'tikyəlāt) **2.** make, be like net —**reticu'lation** *n.* —**reticuloendothelial system** (ri'tikyəlōendə'thēliəl) vast widely distributed network of cells which form a major link in body defense against infection
retina ('retinə) *n.* light-sensitive membrane at back of eye (*pl.* **-s, -nae** (-nē)) —**retinal detachment** partial or complete separation of the retina from its attachment

retinue (ˈretinyōō, -nōō) *n.* band of followers or attendants

retire (riˈtīər) *vi.* **1.** give up office or work **2.** go away **3.** withdraw **4.** go to bed —*vt.* **5.** cause to retire —**reˈtired** *a.* that has retired from office *etc.* —**reˈtirement** *n.* —**reˈtiring** *a.* unobtrusive, shy

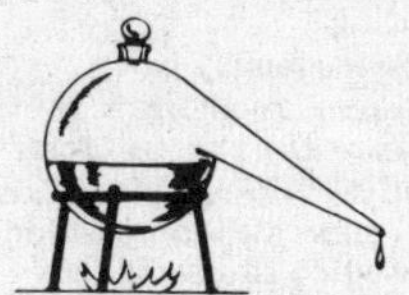
retort

retort (riˈtört) *vt.* **1.** reply **2.** repay in kind, retaliate **3.** hurl back (charge *etc.*) —*vi.* **4.** reply with countercharge —*n.* **5.** vigorous reply or repartee **6.** vessel with bent neck used for distilling

retouch (rēˈtuch) *vt.* touch up, improve by new touches, *esp.* of paint *etc.*

retrace (rēˈtrās) *vt.* go back over (a route *etc.*) again

retract (riˈtrakt) *v.* draw back, recant —**reˈtractable** *or* **reˈtractible** *a.* —**reˈtractile** *a.* capable of being drawn in —**reˈtraction** *n.* drawing or taking back, *esp.* of statement *etc.* —**reˈtractor** *n.* **1.** muscle **2.** surgical instrument

retread (rēˈtred) *vt.* **1.** renovate (worn rubber tire) (**-ˈtreaded, -ˈtreading**) —*n.* (ˈrētred) **2.** renovated tire

retreat (riˈtrēt) *vi.* **1.** move back from any position **2.** retire —*n.* **3.** act of, or military signal for, retiring, withdrawal **4.** place to which anyone retires, *esp.* for religious contemplation **5.** period of seclusion, *esp.* for religious contemplation **6.** refuge **7.** sunset call on bugle

retrench (riˈtrench) *v.* **1.** reduce (expenditure), *esp.* by dismissing staff —*vt.* **2.** cut down —**reˈtrenchment** *n.*

retribution (retriˈbyōōshən) *n.* **1.** recompense, *esp.* for evil deeds **2.** vengeance —**retributive** (riˈtribyətiv) *a.*

retrieve (riˈtrēv) *vt.* **1.** fetch back again **2.** restore **3.** rescue from ruin **4.** recover (*esp.* information) from computer **5.** regain —**reˈtrievable** *a.* —**reˈtrieval** *n.* —**reˈtriever** *n.* dog trained to retrieve game

retro- (*comb. form*) **1.** back; backward, as in *retroactive* **2.** located behind, as in *retrochoir*

retroact (ˈretrōakt) *vi.* **1.** react **2.** act in opposite direction —**retroˈactive** *a.* applying or referring to the past —**retroˈactively** *adv.*

retrochoir (ˈretrōkwīər) *n.* space in large church or cathedral behind high altar

retrograde (ˈretrəgrād) *a.* **1.** going backward, reverting **2.** reactionary —**retroˈgress** *vi.* **1.** go back to earlier, *esp.* worse, condition; degenerate, deteriorate **2.** move backward; recede —**retroˈgression** *n.* —**retroˈgressive** *a.*

retrolental fibroplasia (retrōˈlentəl fībrəˈplāzhə) eye disease formerly causing blindness in infants subjected to excess oxygen supply

retrorocket (ˈretrōrokit) *n.* rocket engine to slow or reverse spacecraft *etc.*

retrospect (ˈretrəspekt) *n.* looking back, survey of past —**retroˈspection** *n.* —**retroˈspective** *a.*

retroussé (rətrōōˈsā, rəˈtrōōsā) *a.* (of nose) turned upward, pug

retsina (retˈsēnə) *n.* Greek wine

return (riˈtərn) *vi.* **1.** go, come back —*vt.* **2.** give, send back **3.** report officially **4.** elect —*n.* **5.** returning, being returned **6.** profit **7.** official report **8.** return ticket —**return ticket** ticket allowing passenger to travel to and from a place

reunion (rēˈyōōnyən) *n.* gathering of people who have been apart

rev (rev) *inf. n.* **1.** revolution (of engine) —*v.* **2.** (*oft. with* up) increase speed of revolution (of) (**-vv-**)

Rev. 1. *Bible* Revelation **2.** Reverend

revaluate (rēˈvalyōōāt) *v.* adjust exchange value of (currency) upward —**revaluˈation** *n.*

revamp (rēˈvamp) *vt.* renovate, restore

reveal (riˈvēl) *vt.* **1.** make known **2.** show —**revelation** (revəˈlāshən) *n.*

reveille (ˈrevəli) *n.* morning bugle call *etc.* to waken soldiers

revel (ˈrevəl) *vi.* **1.** take pleasure (in) **2.** make merry —*n.* **3.** (*usu. pl.*) merrymaking —**ˈreveler** *n.* —**ˈrevelry** *n.* festivity

Revelation (revəˈlāshən) *n. Bible* 27th book of the N.T., the last book of the Bible, written by St. John the Divine, considered a book on prophecy about the world to come

revenge (riˈvenj) *n.* **1.** retaliation for wrong done **2.** act that satisfies this **3.** desire for this —*vt.* **4.** avenge **5.** make retaliation for —*v.refl.* **6.** avenge oneself —**reˈvengeful** *a.* **1.** vindictive **2.** resentful

revenue (ˈrevinyōō, -nōō) *n.* income, *esp.* of state, as taxes *etc.* —**Internal Revenue Service** *see at* INTERNAL

reverberate (riˈvərbərāt) *v.* echo, resound, throw back (sound *etc.*) —**reverberˈation** *n.*

revere (riˈvēər) *vt.* hold in great regard or religious respect —**reverence** (ˈrevərəns) *n.* **1.** revering **2.** awe mingled with respect and esteem **3.** veneration —**reverend** (ˈrevərənd) *a.* (*esp.* as prefix to clergyman's name) worthy of reverence —**reverent** (ˈrevərənt, ˈrevrənt) *a.* showing reverence —**reverential** (revəˈrenchəl) *a.* marked by reverence

reverie (ˈrevəri) *n.* daydream, absent-minded state

revers (riˈvēər) *n.* part of garment which is turned back, *eg* lapel (*pl.* **-vers** (-ˈvēərz))

reverse (riˈvərs) *v.* **1.** (of vehicle) (cause to)

move backward —*vt.* **2.** turn upside down or other way round **3.** change completely —*n.* **4.** opposite, contrary **5.** side opposite, obverse **6.** defeat **7.** reverse gear —*a.* **8.** opposite, contrary —**re'versal** *n.* —**re'versible** *a.* —**reverse gear** mechanism enabling vehicle to move backward —**reversing light** light on rear of motor vehicle to provide illumination when reversing

revert (ri'vərt) *vi.* **1.** return to former state **2.** come back to subject **3.** refer (to) a second time **4.** turn backward —**re'version** *n.* (of property) rightful passing to owner or designated heir *etc.* —**re'verted** *a.* —**re'vertible** *a.*

review (ri'vyo͞o) *vt.* **1.** examine **2.** look back on **3.** reconsider **4.** hold, make, write review of —*n.* **5.** general survey **6.** critical notice of book *etc.* **7.** periodical with critical articles **8.** inspection of troops **9.** *see* REVUE —**re'viewer** *n.* writer of reviews

revile (ri'vīl) *vt.* be viciously scornful of, abuse —**re'viler** *n.*

revise (ri'vīz) *vt.* **1.** look over and correct **2.** restudy (work done previously) in preparation for examination **3.** change, alter —**re'viser** *n.* —**revision** (ri'vizhən) *n.* **1.** reexamination for purpose of correcting **2.** revising of notes, subject for examination **3.** revised copy —**revisionism** (ri'vizhənizəm) *n.* **1.** (*sometimes* **R-**) moderate, nonrevolutionary version of Marxism developed in Germany around 1900 **2.** (*sometimes* **R-**) in Marxist-Leninist ideology, dangerous departure from true interpretation of Marx's teachings **3.** advocacy of revision of some political theory *etc.* —**revisionist** (ri'vizhənist) *n./a.* —**re'visory** *a.* of revision

revive (ri'vīv) *v.* bring, come back to life, vigor, use *etc.* —**re'vival** *n.* reviving, *esp.* of religious fervor —**re'vivalist** *n./a.*

revoke (ri'vōk) *vt.* **1.** take back, withdraw **2.** cancel —**revocable** ('revəkəbəl) *a.* —**revocation** (revə'kāshən) *n.* repeal

revolt (ri'vōlt) *n.* **1.** rebellion —*vi.* **2.** rise in rebellion **3.** feel disgust —*vt.* **4.** affect with disgust —**re'volting** *a.* disgusting, horrible

revolve (ri'volv) *vi.* **1.** turn round, rotate **2.** be centered (on) —*vt.* **3.** rotate —**revolution** (revə'lo͞oshən) *n.* **1.** violent overthrow of government **2.** great change **3.** complete rotation, turning or spinning round —**revolutionary** (revə'lo͞oshəneri) *a./n.* —**revolutionize** (revə'lo͞oshənīz) *vt.* **1.** change considerably **2.** bring about revolution in —**revolving door** door that rotates about vertical axis, *esp.* with four leaves at right angles to each other

revolver (ri'volvər) *n.* repeating pistol with revolving magazine

revue *or* **review** (ri'vyo͞o) *n.* theatrical entertainment with topical sketches and songs

revulsion (ri'vulshən) *n.* **1.** sudden violent change of feeling **2.** marked repugnance or abhorrence

reward (ri'wōrd) *vt.* **1.** pay, make return to (someone) for service, conduct *etc.* —*n.* **2.** something given in return for a deed or service rendered —**re'warding** *a.* giving personal satisfaction, worthwhile

rewire (rē'wīər) *vt.* provide (house *etc.*) with new wiring

RF radio frequency

Rh 1. *Chem.* rhodium **2.** rhesus (*esp. in* **Rh factor** (*see also* **rhesus factor** *at* RHESUS))

rhapsody ('rapsədi) *n.* enthusiastic or high-flown (musical) composition or utterance —**rhapsodic** (rap'sodik) *a.* —**'rhapsodist** *n.* —**rhapsodize** ('rapsədīz) *v.*

rhea ('rēə) *n.* S Amer. three-toed ostrich

rhebok ('rēbok) *n.* brownish-gray S Afr. antelope

rhenium ('rēniəm) *n. Chem.* metallic element *Symbol* Re, at. wt. 186.2, at. no. 75

rheostat ('rēəstat) *n.* instrument for regulating the value of the resistance in an electric circuit

rhesus ('rēsəs) *n.* small, long-tailed monkey of S Asia —**rhesus factor** feature distinguishing different types of human blood (*also* **Rh factor**)

rhetoric ('retərik) *n.* **1.** art of effective speaking or writing **2.** artificial or exaggerated language —**rhe'torical** *a.* (of question) not requiring an answer —**rheto'rician** *n.*

rheum (ro͞om) *n.* **1.** watery discharge, mucus **2.** catarrh —**'rheumy** *a.*

rheumatism ('ro͞omətizəm) *n.* painful inflammation of joints or muscles —**rheu'matic** *a./n.* —**'rheumatoid** *a.* of, like rheumatism —**rheumatic fever** disease characterized by inflammation and pain in joints —**rheumatoid arthritis** chronic disease characterized by inflammation and swelling of joints

Rh factor *see* **rhesus factor** *at* RHESUS

rhinestone ('rīnstōn) *n.* imitation gem made of paste

Rhine wine (rīn) dry wine, usu. white, from the vineyards bordering the River Rhine in Germany

rhinitis (rī'nītis) *n.* inflammation of the mucous membranes lining the nasal passages

rhino ('rīnō) *n.* rhinoceros (*pl.* **-s, 'rhino**)

rhino- *or before vowel* **rhin-** (*comb. form*) nose, as in *rhinology*

rhinoceros (rī'nosərəs, ri-) *n.* large thick-skinned animal with one or two horns on nose (*pl.* **-es, -ros**)

rhizome ('rīzōm) *n.* thick horizontal underground stem whose buds develop into new plants (*also* **'rootstock, 'rootstalk**)

rho (rō) *n.* 17th letter in Gr. alphabet (Ρ, ρ) (*pl.* **-s**)

Rhode Island (rōd) New England state of the U.S.: ratified the Constitution in 1790.

rhizome

Abbrev.: **RI** (with ZIP code)

Rhodes scholar (rōdz) person holding a Rhodes scholarship, endowed by Cecil J. Rhodes, to study at Oxford University, England

rhodium (ˈrōdiəm) *n. Chem.* grayish-white noble metal *Symbol* Rh, at. wt. 102.9, at. no. 45 —**ˈrhodic** *a.*

rhododendron (rōdəˈdendrən) *n.* any of various evergreen flowering shrubs

rhombus (ˈrombəs) *n.* equilateral but not right-angled parallelogram, diamond-shaped figure (*pl.* **-es, -bi** (-bī)) —**rhombohedron** (rombōˈhēdrən) *n.* six-sided prism whose sides are parallelograms —**ˈrhomboid** *n./a.* —**rhomˈboidal** *a.*

rhubarb (ˈro͞obärb) *n.* **1.** garden plant of which the fleshy stalks are cooked and used as fruit **2.** laxative from root of allied Chinese plant

rhumb line (rum) **1.** imaginary line on surface of sphere that intersects all meridians at same angle **2.** course navigated by vessel or aircraft that maintains uniform compass heading (*also* **rhumb**)

rhyme (rīm) *n.* **1.** identity of sounds at ends of lines of verse, or in words **2.** word or syllable identical in sound to another **3.** verse marked by rhyme —*vt.* **4.** use (word) to make rhymes —**rhymester** (ˈrīmstər) *or* **ˈrhymer** *n.* poet, *esp.* one considered mediocre; poetaster, versifier —**rhyme scheme** pattern of rhymes used in piece of verse, usu. indicated by letters —**rhyming slang** slang in which word is replaced by word or phrase that rhymes with it

rhythm (ˈridhəm) *n.* measured beat or flow, *esp.* of words, music *etc.* —**ˈrhythmic(al)** *a.* —**ˈrhythmically** *adv.* —**rhythm-and-blues** *n.* kind of popular music derived from or influenced by blues —**rhythm method** method of contraception by restricting sexual intercourse to days in woman's menstrual cycle when conception is considered least likely to occur

RI Rhode Island

R.I. **1.** Regina et Imperatrix (*Lat.*, Queen and Empress) **2.** Rex et Imperator (*Lat.*, King and Emperor) **3** Royal Institution

ria (ˈrēə) *n.* long narrow inlet of sea coast, being former valley submerged by sea

rib[1] (rib) *n.* **1.** one of paired curved bony rods stiffening the body of most vertebrates protecting heart, lungs *etc.* **2.** cut of meat including rib(s) **3.** curved timber of framework of boat **4.** raised series of rows in knitting *etc.* —*vt.* **5.** furnish, mark with ribs **6.** knit to form rib pattern (**-bb-**) —**ˈribbing** *n.* —**ˈribcage** *n.* wall of chest consisting of ribs and connective tissue

rib[2] (rib) *vt. inf.* tease, ridicule (**-bb-**)

ribald (ˈribəld) *a.* **1.** irreverent, scurrilous **2.** indecent —*n.* **3.** ribald person —**ˈribaldry** *n.* vulgar, indecent talk

ribbon (ˈribən) *n.* **1.** narrow band of fabric used for trimming, tying *etc.* **2.** long strip or line of anything

riboflavin (rībəˈflāvin) *n.* form of vitamin B

ribonucleic acid (rībōnyo͞oˈklēik, -no͞o-; -ˈklā-) *see* RNA

rice (rīs) *n.* **1.** cereal plant **2.** its seeds as food —**rice paper** fine, edible paper

rich (rich) *a.* **1.** wealthy **2.** fertile **3.** abounding **4.** valuable **5.** (of food) containing much fat or sugar **6.** mellow **7.** amusing —*n.* **8.** the wealthy classes —**ˈriches** *pl.n.* wealth —**ˈrichly** *adv.*

Richmond (ˈrichmənd) *n.* borough of New York City

Richter scale (ˈriktər) logarithmic scale ranging from one to ten for expressing intensity of earthquake

rick[1] (rik) *n.* stack of hay *etc.*

rick[2] (rik) *vt./n.* sprain, wrench

rickets (ˈrikits) *n.* disease of children marked by softening of bones, bandy legs *etc.*, caused by vitamin D deficiency —**ˈrickety** *a.* **1.** shaky, insecure, unstable **2.** suffering from rickets

rickettsia (riˈketsiə) *n.* any of group of microorganisms between bacteria and viruses in size activated only in presence of living cells —**rickettsial diseases** diseases transmitted by lice, fleas *etc.*, including typhus and spotted fever —**rickettsial pox** infectious disease resembling chickenpox transmitted by mites

ricksha *or* **rickshaw** (ˈrikshō) *n.* light two-wheeled man-drawn Asian vehicle

ricochet (ˈrikəshā) *vi.* **1.** (of bullet) rebound or be deflected by solid surface or water —*n.* **2.** bullet or shot to which this happens

Ricotta (riˈkotə) *n.* creamy, soft cheese with mild flavor orig. from Italy

rid (rid) *vt.* **1.** clear, relieve **2.** free **3.** deliver (**rid, ˈridding**) —**ˈriddance** *n.* **1.** clearance **2.** act of ridding **3.** deliverance **4.** relief

ridden (ˈridən) *pp. of* RIDE

-ridden (*comb. form*) afflicted by, affected by, as in *disease-ridden*

riddle[1] (ˈridəl) *n.* **1.** question made puzzling to test one's ingenuity **2.** enigma **3.** puzzling thing, person —*vi.* **4.** speak in, make riddles

riddle[2] (ˈridəl) *vt.* **1.** pierce with many holes —*n.* **2.** coarse sieve for gravel *etc.* —**riddled with** full of, *esp.* holes

ride (rīd) *v.* **1.** sit on and control or propel

(horse, bicycle *etc.*) —*vi.* **2.** go on horseback or in vehicle **3.** lie at anchor **4.** be carried on or across —*vt.* **5.** travel over (**rode, 'ridden, 'riding**) —*n.* **6.** journey on horse *etc.*, or in any vehicle **7.** riding track —**'rider** *n.* **1.** one who rides **2.** supplementary clause **3.** addition to a document **4.** mathematical problem on given proposition —**'riderless** *a.* —**riding crop** short whip with handle at one end for opening gates —**riding lamp** *or* **light** light on vessel showing it is at anchor

ridge (rij) *n.* **1.** long, narrow hill **2.** long, narrow elevation on surface **3.** line of meeting of two sloping surfaces —*v.* **4.** form into ridges —**'ridgepole** *n.* **1.** timber along ridge of roof, to which rafters are attached **2.** horizontal pole at apex of tent

ridiculous (ri'dikyələs) *a.* deserving to be laughed at; absurd, foolish —**'ridicule** *n.* **1.** language or behavior intended to humiliate or mock —*vt.* **2.** laugh at, deride

riding ('rīding) *n.* **1.** (**R-** *when part of name*) former administrative district of Yorkshire **2.** C parliamentary constituency

riesling ('rēzling) *n.* **1.** dry white wine **2.** type of grape used to make this wine

rife (rīf) *a.* prevalent, common

riffle ('rifəl) *v.* flick through (pages *etc.*) quickly

riffraff ('rifraf) *n.* disreputable people, *esp.* collectively; rabble

rifle ('rīfəl) *vt.* **1.** search and rob **2.** ransack **3.** make spiral grooves in (gun barrel *etc.*) —*n.* **4.** firearm with long barrel —**'rifling** *n.* **1.** arrangement of grooves in gun barrel **2.** pillaging

rift (rift) *n.* crack, split, cleft —**rift valley** long narrow valley resulting from subsidence of land between two faults

rig (rig) *vt.* **1.** provide (ship) with spars, ropes *etc.* **2.** equip **3.** set up, *esp.* as makeshift **4.** arrange in dishonest way (**-gg-**) —*n.* **5.** way ship's masts and sails are arranged **6.** apparatus for drilling for oil and gas **7.** horse-drawn vehicle —**'rigger** *n.* —**'rigging** *n.* ship's spars and ropes —**'rigout** *n. inf.* person's clothing or costume, *esp.* bizarre outfit —**rig out 1.** (*oft. with* with) equip or fit out (with) **2.** dress or be dressed

rigamarole ('rigəmərōl) *n. see* RIGMAROLE

right (rīt) *a.* **1.** just **2.** in accordance with truth and duty **3.** true **4.** correct **5.** proper **6.** of side that faces east when front is turned to north **7.** *Pol.* conservative or reactionary (*also* **right-wing**) **8.** straight **9.** upright **10.** of outer or more finished side of fabric —*vt.* **11.** bring back to vertical position **12.** do justice to —*vi.* **13.** come back to vertical position —*n.* **14.** claim, title *etc.* allowed or due **15.** what is right, just or due **16.** conservative political party **17.** *Boxing* punch, blow with right hand —*adv.* **18.** straight **19.** properly **20.** very **21.** on or to right side —**'rightful** *a.* —**'rightly** *adv.* —**right angle** angle of 90° —**right-hand** *a.* **1.** of, located on or moving toward the right **2.** for use by right hand —**right-handed** *a.* **1.** using right hand with greater skill than left **2.** performed with right hand **3.** for use by right hand **4.** turning from left to right —**right-minded** *a.* holding opinions or principles that accord with what is right or with opinions of speaker —**Right Reverend** title of high ecclesiastical official —**right triangle** triangle one angle of which is right angle —**right whale** large gray or black whalebone whale with large head and no dorsal fin —**right-hand man** most valuable assistant —**right of way** *Law* **1.** right to pass over someone's land **2.** path used (*pl.* **rights of way**)

righteous ('rīchəs) *a.* **1.** just, upright **2.** godly **3.** virtuous **4.** good **5.** honest —**'righteousness** *n.*

rigid ('rijid) *a.* **1.** inflexible **2.** harsh, stiff —**ri'gidity** *n.*

rigmarole ('rigmərōl) *or* **rigamarole** *n.* **1.** meaningless string of words **2.** long, complicated procedure

Rigmel shrunk ('rigməl) trade name for shrinking process which limits subsequent shrinking to 1 per cent in any dimension

rigor[1] ('rigər) *n.* sudden coldness attended by shivering —**rigor mortis** ('mŏrtis) stiffening of body after death

rigor[2] ('rigər) *n.* **1.** harshness, severity, strictness **2.** hardship —**'rigorous** *a.* stern, harsh, severe

rile (rīl) *vt. inf.* anger, annoy

rill (ril) *n.* small stream

rim (rim) *n.* **1.** edge, border, margin **2.** outer ring of wheel —**rimmed** *a.* bordered, edged

rime (rīm) *n.* hoarfrost —**'rimy** *a.*

rind (rīnd) *n.* outer coating of fruits *etc.*

rinderpest ('rindərpest) *n.* malignant infectious disease of cattle

ring[1] (ring) *n.* **1.** circle of gold *etc.*, *esp.* for finger **2.** any circular band, coil, rim *etc.* **3.** people or things arranged so as to form circle **4.** group of people working together to advance their own interests **5.** enclosed area, *esp.* roped-in square for boxing —*vt.* **6.** put ring round **7.** mark (bird *etc.*) with ring —**'ringer** *n.* **1.** one who rings bells **2.** *sl.* person, thing apparently identical to another (*esp. in* **dead ringer**) —**'ringlet** *n.* curly lock of hair —**'ringbark** *v.* kill (tree) by cutting bark round trunk —**ring finger** third finger, *esp.* of left hand, on which wedding ring is worn —**'ringleader** *n.* instigator of mutiny, riot *etc.* —**'ringmaster** *n.* master of ceremonies in circus —**ring road** main road that bypasses a town (center) —**'ringside** *n.* **1.** row of seats nearest boxing or wrestling ring **2.** any place affording close uninterrupted view —**'ringworm** *n.* fungal skin disease in circular patches

ring[2] (ring) *vi.* **1.** give out clear resonant sound, as bell **2.** resound —*vt.* **3.** cause (bell) to sound **4.** call (person) by telephone (**rang** *pt.*, **rung** *pp.*) —*n.* **5.** a ringing **6.** telephone call

rink (ringk) *n.* **1.** sheet of ice for skating or curling **2.** floor for roller skating

rinkhals ('ringk-hows) *n.* S Afr. ring-necked cobra

rinse (rins) *vt.* **1.** remove detergent from (washed clothing, hair *etc.*) by applying clean water **2.** wash lightly —*n.* **3.** a rinsing **4.** liquid to tint hair

riot ('rīət) *n.* **1.** tumult, disorder **2.** loud revelry **3.** disorderly, unrestrained disturbance **4.** profusion —*vi.* **5.** make, engage in riot —'**riotous** *a.* unruly, rebellious, wanton

rip[1] (rip) *vt.* **1.** cut, tear away, slash, rend (**-pp-**) —*n.* **2.** rent, tear —'**ripcord** *n.* cord pulled to open parachute —**rip-roaring** *a. inf.* characterized by excitement, intensity or boisterous behavior —'**ripsaw** *n.* saw with coarse teeth (used for cutting wood along grain) —**rip-off** *n. sl.* act of stealing, overcharging *etc.* —**rip off** *sl.* **1.** steal **2.** overcharge

rip[2] (rip) *n.* strong current, *esp.* one moving away from the shore

R.I.P. *requiescat in pace*

riparian (ri'periən, rī-) *a.* of, on banks of river

ripe (rīp) *a.* **1.** ready to be reaped, eaten *etc.* **2.** matured **3.** (of judgment *etc.*) sound —'**ripen** *v.* **1.** make or grow ripe —*vi.* **2.** mature

riposte (ri'pōst) *n.* **1.** verbal retort **2.** counterstroke **3.** *Fencing* quick lunge after parry

ripple ('ripəl) *n.* **1.** slight wave, ruffling of surface **2.** sound like ripples of water —*vi.* **3.** flow, form into little waves **4.** (of sounds) rise and fall gently —*vt.* **5.** form ripples on

rise (rīz) *vi.* **1.** get up **2.** move upward **3.** appear above horizon **4.** reach higher level **5.** increase in value or price **6.** rebel **7.** adjourn **8.** originate; begin (**rose, risen** ('rizən), '**rising**) —*n.* **9.** rising **10.** slope upward **11.** increase, *esp.* of wages —'**riser** *n.* **1.** one who rises, *esp.* from bed **2.** vertical part of step —'**rising** *n.* **1.** revolt —*a.* **2.** increasing in rank, maturity

risible ('rizibəl) *a.* **1.** inclined to laugh **2.** laughable —**risi'bility** *n.*

risk (risk) *n.* **1.** chance of disaster or loss —*vt.* **2.** venture **3.** put in jeopardy **4.** take chance of —'**riskily** *adv.* —'**risky** *a.* **1.** dangerous **2.** hazardous —**take** *or* **run a risk** proceed in an action regardless of danger involved

risotto (ri'sotō, -'zotō) *n.* dish of rice cooked in stock and served with various other ingredients

risqué (ri'skā) *a.* suggestive of indecency

rite (rīt) *n.* formal practice or custom, *esp.* religious —**ritual** ('richōōəl) *n.* **1.** prescribed order or book of rites **2.** regular, stereotyped action or behavior —*a.* **3.** concerning rites —**ritualism** ('richōōəlizəm) *n.* practice of ritual —**ritualist** ('richōōəlist) *n.*

ritzy ('ritsi) *a. sl.* luxurious; elegant

rival ('rīvəl) *n.* **1.** one that competes with another for favor, success *etc.* —*vt.* **2.** vie with —*a.* **3.** in position of rival —'**rivalry** *n.* keen competition

rive (rīv) *v.* (*usu. as pp./a.* **riven**) **1.** split asunder **2.** tear apart (**rived** *pt.*, **rived, 'riven** *pp.*, '**riving** *pr.p.*) —**riven** ('rivən) *a.* split

river ('rivər) *n.* **1.** large natural stream of water **2.** copious flow —**river basin** area drained by river and its tributaries —'**riverbed** *n.* channel in which river flows or has flowed

rivet ('rivit) *n.* **1.** bolt for fastening metal plates, the end being put through holes and then beaten flat —*vt.* **2.** fasten with rivets **3.** cause to be fixed or held firmly, *esp.* (*fig.*) in surprise, horror *etc.* —'**riveter** *n.*

Riviera (rivi'erə) *n.* **1.** resort area along northern Mediterranean coast in France and Italy **2.** any opulent seaside resort area

rivulet ('rivyəlit, 'rivəlit) *n.* small stream

R.M. C Rural Municipality

rms *or* **r.m.s.** root mean square

Rn *Chem.* radon

RNA *Biochem.* ribonucleic acid; any of group of nucleic acids, present in all living cells, that play essential role in synthesis of proteins

roach (rōch) *n.* European freshwater fish (*pl.* **roach, -es**)

road (rōd) *n.* **1.** track, way prepared for passengers, vehicles *etc.* **2.** direction, way **3.** street —'**roadster** *n.* **1.** *obs.* touring car **2.** kind of bicycle —'**roadblock** *n.* barricade across road to stop traffic for inspection *etc.* —**road hog** selfish, aggressive driver —'**roadholding** *n.* extent to which motor vehicle is stable and does not skid, *esp.* on sharp bends *etc.* —'**roadhouse** *n.* public house, restaurant on country route —**road metal** broken stones used in macadamizing roads —**road sense** sound judgment in driving road vehicles —**road show** **1.** *Rad.* live program, usu. with audience participation, transmitted from radio van taking particular show on the road **2.** group of entertainers on tour —'**roadside** *n./a.* —'**roadstead** *n. Naut.* partly sheltered anchorage (*also* **roads**) —**road test** test to ensure that vehicle is roadworthy, *esp.* after repair *etc.*, by driving it on roads —**road-test** *vt.* test (vehicle) in this way —'**roadway** *n.* **1.** surface of road **2.** part of road used by vehicles —'**roadworks** *pl.n.* repairs to road, *esp.* blocking part of road —'**roadworthy** *a.* (of vehicle) mechanically sound —**hit the road** *sl.* start or resume traveling —**one for the road** a last alcoholic drink before leaving

roam (rōm) *v.* wander about —'**roamer** *n.*

roan (rōn) *a.* **1.** (of horses) having coat in

which main color is thickly interspersed with another, *esp.* bay, sorrel or chestnut mixed with white or gray —*n.* **2.** horse having such a coat

roar (rŏr) *vi.* **1.** make or utter loud, deep, hoarse sound, as of lion —*v.* **2.** (of people) utter (something) with loud deep cry, as in anger or triumph —*n.* **3.** such a sound —**'roaring** *a.* **1.** *inf.* brisk and profitable —*adv.* **2.** noisily

roast (rōst) *v.* **1.** bake, cook in closed oven **2.** cook by exposure to open fire **3.** make, be very hot —*n.* **4.** roasted joint —*a.* **5.** roasted —**'roaster** *n.* **1.** oven *etc.* for roasting meat **2.** chicken *etc.* suitable for roasting —**'roasting** *n. esp. inf.* severe criticism, scolding

rob (rob) *vt.* **1.** plunder, steal from **2.** pillage, defraud (**-bb-**) —**'robber** *n.* —**'robbery** *n.*

robe (rōb) *n.* **1.** any long outer garment, oft. denoting rank or office —*vt.* **2.** dress —*vi.* **3.** put on robes, vestments

robin ('robin) *n.* small brown bird with red breast (*also* (**robin**) **redbreast**)

robot ('rōbot) *n.* **1.** automated machine, *esp.* performing functions in human manner **2.** person of machine-like efficiency —**ro'botic** *a.* of or like robot —**ro'botics** *pl.n.* (*with sing. v.*) study of use of robots —**'robotize** *vt.* **1.** equip (factory) with robots **2.** turn (human) into robot

Rob Roy (rob roi) a Manhattan made with Scotch whisky

robust (rō'bust, 'rōbust) *a.* sturdy, strong —**ro'bustious** *a. obs.* **1.** rough; boisterous **2.** strong, robust, stout —**ro'bustness** *n.*

roc (rok) *n.* monstrous bird of Arabian mythology

rock[1] (rok) *n.* **1.** stone **2.** large rugged mass of stone **3.** hard candy in sticks —**'rockery** *n.* mound or grotto of stones or rocks for plants in garden —**'rocky** *a.* **1.** having many rocks **2.** rugged —**rock bottom** lowest possible level —**rock-bound** *a.* hemmed in or encircled by rocks (*also* (*poet.*) **rock-girt**) —**'rockchuck** *n. see* MARMOT —**rock crystal** transparent colorless quartz —**rock garden** garden featuring rocks or rockeries —**rock plant** plant that grows on rocks or in rocky ground —**rock rabbit SA** hyrax —**rock salmon** various food fishes, *esp.* dogfish —**rock salt** mineral consisting of sodium chloride in crystalline form, occurring in sedimentary beds *etc.*: important source of table salt (*also* **'halite**)

rock[2] (rok) *v.* **1.** (cause to) sway to and fro **2.** reel or sway or cause (someone) to reel or sway, as with shock or emotion —*vi.* **3.** dance in rock-and-roll style —*n.* **4.** rocking motion **5.** rock-and-roll —**'rocker** *n.* curved piece of wood *etc.* on which thing may rock —**'rocky** *a.* **1.** weak, unstable **2.** *inf.* (of person) dizzy; nauseated —**rock-and-roll** *or* **rock-'n'-roll** *n.* **1.** type of pop music of 1950s as blend of rhythm-and-blues and country-and-western **2.** dancing performed to such music —**rocking horse** toy horse mounted on rockers, on which child can rock to and fro in seesaw movement —**off one's rocker** *inf.* insane

rocket[1] ('rokit) *n.* **1.** self-propelling device powered by burning of explosive contents, used as firework, for display, signaling, line carrying, weapon *etc.* **2.** vehicle propelled by rocket engine, as weapon or carrying spacecraft —*vi.* **3.** move fast, *esp.* upward, as rocket —**'rocketry** *n.*

rocket[2] ('rokit) *n.* any of several kinds of flowering plant

Rocky Mountain spotted fever ('roki) severe rickettsial disease transmitted by ticks

rococo (rə'kōkō) *a.* (*oft.* **R-**) **1.** of furniture, architecture *etc.* having much conventional decoration in style of early 18th-cent. work in Europe **2.** tastelessly florid

rod (rod) *n.* **1.** slender cylinder of metal, wood *etc.* **2.** cane **3.** unit of length equal to 5½ yards

rode (rōd) *pt. of* RIDE

rodent ('rōdənt) *n.* any gnawing animal, *eg* rat

rodeo ('rōdiō, rə'dāō) *n.* public performance of competitive games and skills of the cowboy (*pl.* **-s**)

rodomontade (rodəmən'tād, rōdə-; -'täd) *Lit. n.* **1.** boastful words or behavior —*vi.* **2.** boast; rant

roe[1] (rō) *n.* small species of deer

roe[2] (rō) *n.* mass of eggs in fish

roentgen *or* **röntgen** ('rentgən, 'rənt-; -jən) *n.* measuring unit of radiation dose

rogation (rō'gāshən) *n.* (*usu. pl.*) *Christianity* solemn supplication, *esp.* in form of ceremony prescribed by Church —**Rogation Days** three days preceding Ascension Day

roger ('rojər) *interj.* **1.** *Telecomm. etc.* message received and understood **2.** expression of agreement

rogue (rōg) *n.* **1.** scoundrel **2.** mischief-loving person, *oft.* child **3.** wild beast of savage temper, living apart from herd —**'roguery** *n.* —**'roguish** *a.* —**rogues' gallery** collection of portraits of known criminals kept by police for identification purposes

roister ('roistər) *vi.* **1.** be noisy or boisterous **2.** brag, bluster or swagger —**'roisterer** *n.* reveler

role *or* **rôle** (rōl) *n.* **1.** actor's part **2.** specific task or function

roll (rōl) *v.* **1.** move by turning over and over —*vt.* **2.** wind round **3.** smooth out with roller —*vi.* **4.** move, sweep along **5.** undulate **6.** (of ship) swing from side to side **7.** (of aircraft) turn about a line from nose to tail in flight —*n.* **8.** act of lying down and turning over and over or from side to side **9.** piece of paper *etc.* rolled up **10.** any object thus shaped, as in *meat roll* **11.** official list or register, *esp.* of names **12.** bread baked into small oval or round **13.** continuous sound, as of drums, thunder *etc.* —**ˈroller** *n.* **1.** cylinder of wood, stone, metal *etc.* used for pressing, crushing, smoothing, supporting thing to be moved, winding thing on *etc.* **2.** long wave of sea **3.** any of various Old World birds that have blue, green and brown plumage and erratic flight —**ˈrolling** *a.* **1.** having gentle rising and falling slopes **2.** reverberating **3.** that may be turned up or down **4.** *sl.* extremely rich —*adv.* **5.** *sl.* swaying, staggering (*esp. in* **rolling drunk**) —**roll call** act, time of calling over list of names, as in schools or army —**rolled gold** metal coated with thin layer of gold —**roller bearings** bearings of hardened steel rollers —**roller coaster** (in amusement parks) narrow railway with open carriages that run swiftly over route of sharp curves and steep inclines —**roller skate** skate with wheels instead of runner —**roller skating** —**roller towel** loop of towel on roller —**rolling mill 1.** mill or factory where ingots of heated metal are passed between rollers to produce sheets or bars of a required cross section and form **2.** machine used for this purpose —**rolling pin** cylindrical roller for dough —**rolling stock** locomotives, carriages *etc.* of railroad —**rolling stone** restless or wandering person —**roll-on** *a.* **1.** (of deodorant *etc.*) dispensed by means of revolving ball fitted into neck of container —*n.* **2.** woman's foundation garment —**roll-top** *a.* (of desk) with flexible lid sliding in grooves —**roll up** *inf.* appear, turn up

rollick (ˈrolik) *vi.* **1.** behave in carefree or boisterous manner —*n.* **2.** boisterous or carefree escapade —**ˈrollicking** *a.*

roly-poly (rōliˈpōli) *a.* round, plump

ROM (rom) *Comp.* read only memory

rom. *Print.* roman (type)

Rom. *Bible* Romans

romaine (rōˈmān) *n.* lettuce with long slender leaves (*also* **cos lettuce**)

Roman (ˈrōmən) *a.* of Rome or Church of Rome —**Roman alphabet** alphabet evolved by ancient Romans for writing of Latin and still used for writing most of languages of Western Europe —**Roman candle** firework that produces continuous shower of sparks punctuated by colored balls of fire —**Roman Catholic** member of Christian Church traditionally founded by Jesus who named St. Peter the first Vicar and whose authority is the Pope and tradition as recorded in scripture and expressed in Church councils —**Roman nose** nose having high prominent bridge —**Roman numerals** letters I, V, X, L, C, D, M used to represent numbers in manner of Romans —**roman type** plain upright letters, ordinary style of printing

romance (rōˈmans, rɚ-; ˈrōmans) *n.* **1.** love affair, *esp.* intense and happy one **2.** mysterious or exciting quality **3.** tale of chivalry **4.** tale with scenes remote from ordinary life **5.** literature like this **6.** picturesque falsehood —*vi.* **7.** exaggerate, fantasize —**roˈmancer** *n.* —**roˈmantic** *a.* **1.** characterized by romance **2.** of or dealing with love **3.** (of literature *etc.*) preferring passion and imagination to proportion and finish —*n.* **4.** romantic person **5.** person whose tastes in art, literature *etc.* lie mainly in romanticism —**roˈmanticism** *n.* —**roˈmanticist** *n.* —**roˈmanticize** *v.*

Romance (rōˈmans, rɚ-; ˈrōmans) *a.* **1.** of vernacular language of certain countries, developed from Latin, as French, Spanish *etc.* —*n.* **2.** this group of languages

Romanesque (rōməˈnesk) *a./n.* (in) style of round-arched vaulted architecture of period between Classical and Gothic

Romania (rōˈmāniə) *n.* country in eastern Europe bounded north by the U.S.S.R., east by the U.S.S.R. and the Black Sea, south by Bulgaria and west by Yugoslavia and Hungary —**Roˈmanian** *n./a.* **1.** (native or inhabitant) of Romania —*n.* **2.** language of Romania, which is a Romance language

Romans (ˈrōmənz) *pl.n.* (*with sing. v.*) *Bible* 6th book of the N.T., epistle written by St. Paul to Christians of Rome and considered the foundation of Christian theology

Romany (ˈroməni, ˈrō-) *n.* **1.** Gypsy **2.** Gypsy language —*a.* **3.** of the Gypsies or their language

Romeo (ˈrōmiō) *n.* word used in communications for the letter *r*

romp (romp) *vi.* **1.** run, play wildly, joyfully —*n.* **2.** spell of romping —**ˈrompers** *pl.n.* child's one-piece garment consisting of trousers and bib with straps —**romp home** win easily

rondavel (ronˈdävəl) *n.* **SA** circular building, oft. thatched

rondo (ˈrondō) *n.* piece of music with leading theme to which return is continually made (*pl.* **-s**)

röntgen (ˈrentgən, ˈrənt-; -jən) *n. see* ROENTGEN

rood (ro͞od) *n.* **1.** the Cross **2.** crucifix **3.** quarter of acre —**rood screen** screen separating nave from choir

roof (ro͞of) *n.* **1.** outside upper covering of building **2.** top, covering part of anything —*vt.* **3.** put roof on, over —**ˈroofing** *n.* **1.** material used to construct roof **2.** act of constructing roof —**roof rack** rack attached to roof of motor vehicle for carrying luggage *etc.* —**ˈrooftree** *n. see* **ridgepole** *at* RIDGE —**hit** (*or* **raise** *or* **go through**) **the roof** *inf.* become extremely angry

rook[1] (ro͝ok) *n.* **1.** bird of crow family —*vt.* **2.** *sl.* swindle, cheat —**ˈrookery** *n.* colony of rooks

rook[2] (ro͝ok) *n.* chessman (*also* **ˈcastle**)

rookie (ˈro͝oki) *n. inf.* recruit, *esp.* in army

room (ro͞om, ro͝om) *n.* **1.** space **2.** space enough **3.** division of house **4.** scope, opportunity —*pl.* **5.** lodging —ˈ**roomy** *a.* spacious —ˈ**roommate** *n.* person with whom one shares room or lodging —**room service** service in hotel providing meals *etc.* in guests' rooms

Roosevelt[1] (ˈrōzəvəlt) *n.* **Franklin Delano.** the 32nd President of the U.S. (1933-45)

Roosevelt[2] (ˈrōzəvəlt) *n.* **Theodore.** the 26th President of the U.S. (1901-09)

roost (ro͞ost) *n.* **1.** perch for fowls —*vi.* **2.** perch —ˈ**rooster** *n.* domestic cock —**come home to roost** have unfavorable repercussions

root (ro͞ot) *n.* **1.** part of plant that grows down into earth and conveys nourishment to plant **2.** plant with edible root, *eg* carrot **3.** vital part **4.** source, origin, original cause of anything **5.** *Anat.* embedded portion of tooth, nail, hair *etc.* **6.** primitive word from which other words are derived **7.** *Math.* factor of a quantity which, when multiplied by itself the number of times indicated, gives the quantity —*v.* **8.** (cause to) take root —*vt.* **9.** pull by roots —*vi.* **10.** dig, burrow —ˈ**rootless** *a.* having no roots or ties —**root mean square** square root of average of squares of set of numbers —ˈ**rootstock** *n.* **1.** *see* RHIZOME **2.** *see* STOCK (sense 6) **3.** *Biol.* basic structure from which offshoots have developed —**root out** remove or eliminate completely

root for *inf.* cheer, applaud, encourage —ˈ**rooter** *n.*

rope (rōp) *n.* **1.** thick cord —*vt.* **2.** secure, mark off with rope —ˈ**ropiness** *n.* —ˈ**ropy** *a.* **1.** *inf.* inferior, inadequate **2.** *inf.* not well **3.** (of liquid) sticky and stringy —ˈ**ropewalk** *n.* long narrow shed where ropes are made —**know the ropes** know details or procedures, as of job

Roquefort (ˈrōkfərt) *n.* semisoft sheep's-milk cheese with blue-green mold veining imported from France

rorqual (ˈrörkwəl) *n.* whalebone whale with dorsal fin and series of grooves along throat and chest (*also* ˈ**finback**)

rosacea (rōˈzāshə) *n.* skin disease of adults marked by redness, pus pimples and swollen blood vessels of the face

rosaceous (rōˈzāshəs) *a.* **1.** of *Rosaceae,* family of plants typically having five-petaled flowers, including rose, strawberry *etc.* **2.** like rose, esp. rose-colored

rosary (ˈrōzəri) *n.* **1.** *R.C.Ch.* series of prayers **2.** string of beads for counting these prayers as they are recited **3.** rose garden

rose[1] (rōz) *n.* **1.** shrub, climbing plant *usu.* with prickly stems and fragrant flowers **2.** the flower, national floral emblem of U.S. **3.** perforated flat nozzle for hose *etc.* **4.** pink color —*a.* **5.** of this color —**roseate** (ˈrōziit, -āt) *a.* rose-colored, rosy —**roˈsette** *n.* **1.** rose-shaped bunch of ribbon **2.** rose-shaped architectural ornament —ˈ**rosy** *a.* **1.** flushed **2.** hopeful, promising —**rose-colored** *a.* **1.**

rosette

having color of rose **2.** unwarrantably optimistic —**rose-water** *n.* **1.** scented water made by distillation of rose petals or by impregnation with oil of roses —*a.* **2.** elegant or delicate, *esp.* excessively so —**rose window** circular window with series of mullions branching from center —ˈ**rosewood** *n.* fragrant wood —**rose of Sharon** (ˈsharən, ˈsher-) **1.** creeping shrub native to SE Europe but widely cultivated, with large yellow flowers **2.** hardy hibiscus

rose[2] (rōz) *pt. of* RISE

rosé (rōˈzā) *n.* pink wine

rosemary (ˈrōzmeri) *n.* evergreen fragrant flowering shrub

Rosh Hashanah (rōsh həˈshōnə, rosh həˈshänə; *Hebrew* ˈrosh hashaˈna) Jewish New Year

Rosicrucian (rōziˈkro͞oshən) *n.* **1.** member of secret order devoted to occult beliefs —*a.* **2.** of the Rosicrucians or Rosicrucianism —**Rosiˈcrucianism** *n.*

rosin (ˈrozin) *n.* resin

roster (ˈrostər) *n.* **1.** list or plan showing turns of duty —*vt.* **2.** place on roster

rostrum (ˈrostrəm) *n.* **1.** platform, stage, pulpit **2.** beak or bill of bird (*pl.* **-s, -tra** (-trə))

rot (rot) *v.* **1.** (cause to) decompose naturally —*vt.* **2.** corrupt (**-tt-**) —*n.* **3.** decay, putrefaction **4.** any disease producing decomposition of tissue **5.** *inf.* nonsense —ˈ**rotten** *a.* **1.** decomposed, putrid **2.** corrupt

rota (ˈrōtə) *n.* roster, list

rotary (ˈrōtəri) *a.* **1.** (of movement) circular **2.** operated by rotary movement —**Roˈtarian** *n.* member of Rotary Club —ˈ**rotate** *v.* (cause to) move round center or on pivot —**roˈtation** *n.* **1.** rotating **2.** regular succession —ˈ**rotatory** *a.* —ˈ**rototill** *vt.* —ˈ**Rototiller** *n.* trade name for a mechanical cultivator with rotary blades —**Rotary Club** one of international association of businessmen's clubs

ROTC Reserve Officer Training Corps

rote (rōt) *n.* —**rote learning** method of learning by repetition —**by rote** from memory

rotisserie (rōˈtisəri) *n.* (electrically driven) rotating spit for cooking meat

rotor (ˈrōtər) *n.* revolving portion of a dynamo motor or turbine

rotten (ˈrotən) *a. see* ROT

rotund (rō'tund) *a.* **1.** round **2.** plump **3.** sonorous —**ro'tundity** *n.*

rotunda (rō'tundə) *n.* circular building or room, *esp.* with dome

rouble ('ro͞obəl) *n. see* RUBLE

roué (ro͞o'ā) *n.* debauched or lecherous man; rake

rouge (ro͞ozh) *n.* **1.** red powder, cream used to color cheeks —*vt.* **2.** color with rouge

rough (ruf) *a.* **1.** not smooth, of irregular surface **2.** violent, stormy, boisterous **3.** rude **4.** uncivil **5.** lacking refinement **6.** approximate **7.** in preliminary form —*vt.* **8.** make rough **9.** plan out approximately **10.** (*with* it) live without usual comforts *etc.* —*n.* **11.** rough state or area **12.** sketch —**'roughage** *n.* unassimilated portion of food promoting proper intestinal action —**'roughen** *v.* —**'roughly** *adv.* —**rough-and-ready** *a.* **1.** crude, unpolished or hastily prepared, but sufficient for purpose **2.** (of person) without formality or refinement —**rough-and-tumble** *n.* **1.** fight or scuffle without rules —*a.* **2.** characterized by disorderliness and disregard for rules —**rough diamond** trustworthy but unsophisticated person —**rough-dry** *a.* **1.** (of clothing or linen) dried ready for pressing —*vt.* **2.** dry (clothing *etc.*) without ironing —**rough-hew** *vt.* shape roughly —**'roughhouse** *n. sl.* fight, row —**'roughneck** *n. inf.* **1.** tough, coarse male **2.** skilled worker other than driller in oilfield —**rough'shod** *a.* (of horse) shod with rough-bottomed shoes to prevent sliding —**ride roughshod over** treat harshly and without consideration

roulette (ro͞o'let) *n.* game of chance played with revolving wheel and ball

round (rownd) *a.* **1.** spherical **2.** cylindrical **3.** circular **4.** curved **5.** full, complete **6.** roughly correct **7.** large, considerable **8.** plump **9.** positive —*adv.* **10.** with circular or circuitous course —*n.* **11.** thing round in shape **12.** recurrent duties **13.** stage in competition **14.** customary course, as of mailman **15.** game (of golf) **16.** one of several periods in boxing match *etc.* **17.** cartridge for firearm **18.** rung **19.** movement in circle —*prep.* **20.** about **21.** on all sides of —*v.* **22.** make, become round —*vt.* **23.** move round —**'roundly** *adv.* **1.** plainly **2.** thoroughly —**'roundabout** *a.* indirect; devious —**round dance 1.** dance in which dancers form circle **2.** ballroom dance in which couples revolve —**round figure** *or* **number** whole number, usu. multiple of ten —**'Roundhead** *n. English hist.* supporter of Parliament against Charles I during Civil War —**round lot** unit of trading on the stock exchange —**round robin** tournament in which each competitor plays against every other participant —**round-shouldered** *a.* denoting faulty posture characterized by drooping shoulders and slight forward bending of back —**round table** meeting of parties or people on equal terms for discussion —**round-the-clock** *a.* throughout day and night —**round trip** trip to place and back again —**'roundup** *n.* **1.** act of gathering together cattle *etc.* for branding, counting or selling **2.** *inf.* any similar act of bringing together —**'roundworm** *n.* any member of a phylum of invertebrate animals with cylindrical, elongated bodies parasitic in plants or animals or free-living in soil or water, such as hookworm and filiaria (*also* **nematode**) —**round up 1.** drive (cattle) together **2.** collect and arrest (criminals)

roundel ('rowndəl) *n.* **1.** poem consisting of three stanzas each of three lines with refrain after first and third **2.** small disk —**'roundelay** *n.* simple song with refrain

rouse (rowz) *vt.* **1.** wake up, stir up, excite to action **2.** cause to rise —*vi.* **3.** waken

rout[1] (rowt) *n.* **1.** overwhelming defeat, disorderly retreat **2.** noisy rabble —*vt.* **3.** scatter and put to flight

rout[2] (rowt) *v.* **1.** dig over or turn up (something), *esp.* (of animal) with snout; root —*vt.* **2.** (*usu. with* out *or* up) find by searching **3.** (*usu. with* out) drive out **4.** (*oft. with* out) hollow or gouge out —*vi.* **5.** search, poke, rummage

route (ro͞ot, rowt) *n.* road, chosen way

routine (ro͞o'tēn) *n.* **1.** regularity of procedure, unvarying round **2.** regular course —*a.* **3.** ordinary, regular

rove (rōv) *v.* wander, roam —**'rover** *n.* **1.** one who roves **2.** pirate

row[1] (rō) *n.* **1.** number of things in a straight line **2.** rank **3.** file **4.** line

row[2] (rō) *v.* **1.** propel (boat) by oars —*n.* **2.** spell of rowing —**'rowboat** *n.*

row[3] (row) *inf. n.* **1.** dispute **2.** disturbance —*vi.* **3.** quarrel noisily

rowan ('rowən, 'rōən) *n.* small deciduous tree, native to Europe, producing bright red berries (*also* **(European) mountain ash**)

rowdy ('rowdi) *a.* **1.** disorderly, noisy and rough —*n.* **2.** person like this

rowel ('rowəl) *n.* small wheel with points on spur

rowlock ('rolək) *n.* appliance on gunwale of boat serving as point of leverage for oar

royal ('roiəl) *a.* **1.** of, worthy of, befitting, patronized by, king or queen **2.** splendid —**'royalist** *n.* supporter of monarchy —**'royalty** *n.* **1.** royal dignity or power **2.** royal persons **3.** payment to owner of land for right to work minerals, or to inventor for use of his invention **4.** payment to author depending on sales —**Royal Air Force** air force of Great Britain —**royal blue** (of) deep blue color —**royal jelly** substance secreted by pharyngeal glands of worker bees and fed to all larvae when very young and to larvae destined to become queens throughout their development —**Royal Marines UK** corps of soldiers trained in amphibious warfare —**Royal Navy** navy of Great Britain —**royal**

palm palm tree of tropical Amer. having tall trunk with tuft of feathery pinnate leaves

r.p.m. revolutions per minute

R.R. 1. Right Reverend 2. C Rural Route

R.S. UK Royal Society

R.S.A. Republic of South Africa

RSFSR Russian Soviet Federated Socialist Republic

R.S.V. Revised Standard Version (of the Bible)

R.S.V.P. répondez s'il vous plaît (*Fr.*, please reply)

Ru *Chem.* ruthenium

rub (rub) *vt.* **1.** apply pressure to with circular or backward and forward movement **2.** clean, polish, dry, thus **3.** pass hand over **4.** abrade, chafe **5.** remove by friction —*vi.* **6.** come into contact accompanied by friction **7.** become frayed or worn by friction (**-bb-**) —*n.* **8.** rubbing **9.** impediment —**'rubbing** *n.* impression taken of incised or raised surface by laying paper over it and rubbing with wax *etc.*

rubato (rōō'bätō) *Mus. n.* **1.** flexibility of tempo in performance (*pl.* **-s**) —*a./adv.* **2.** to be played with flexible tempo

rubber[1] ('rubər) *n.* **1.** coagulated sap of rough, elastic consistency, of certain tropical trees (*also* **India rubber, gum elastic, 'caoutchouc**) **2.** piece of rubber *etc.* used for erasing **3.** thing for rubbing **4.** person who rubs **5.** condom —*a.* **6.** made of rubber —**'rubberize** *vt.* coat, impregnate, treat with rubber —**'rubbery** *a.* —**rubber band** continuous loop of thin rubber, used to hold papers *etc.* together —**'rubberneck** *sl. n.* **1.** person who gapes inquisitively **2.** sightseer, tourist —*vi.* **3.** stare in naive or foolish manner —**rubber plant 1.** plant with glossy leathery leaves, cultivated as house plant in Europe and N Amer. **2.** any of several tropical trees, sap of which yields crude rubber —**rubber-sheet geometry** *see* TOPOLOGY (sense 1) —**rubber stamp 1.** device for imprinting dates *etc.* **2.** automatic authorization

rubber[2] ('rubər) *n.* **1.** series of odd number of games or contests at various games **2.** two out of three games won

rubbish ('rubish) *n.* **1.** waste material **2.** anything worthless **3.** trash, nonsense —**'rubbishy** *a.* valueless

rubble ('rubəl) *n.* **1.** fragments of stone *etc.* **2.** builders' rubbish

rubella (rōō'belə) *n.* mild contagious virus disease which may cause severe damage to an unborn child (*also* **German measles**)

rubeola (rōōbi'ōlə) *n. see* MEASLES

rubicund ('rōōbikənd) *a.* of reddish color; ruddy

rubidium (rōō'bidiəm) *n. Chem.* metallic element *Symbol* Rb, at. wt. 85.5, at. no. 37

ruble *or* **rouble** ('rōōbəl) *n.* monetary unit of Soviet Union

rubric ('rōōbrik) *n.* **1.** title, heading **2.** direction in liturgy **3.** instruction

ruby ('rōōbi) *n.* **1.** precious red gem **2.** its color —*a.* **3.** of this color —**ruby wedding** fortieth wedding anniversary

ruche (rōōsh) *n.* strip of pleated or frilled lace *etc.* used to decorate blouses *etc.*

ruck[1] (ruk) *n.* **1.** crowd **2.** common herd **3.** rank and file

ruck[2] (ruk) *n.* **1.** crease —*v.* **2.** make, become wrinkled

rucksack ('ruksak) *n.* pack carried on back (*also* **back pack**)

ruction ('rukshən) *n. inf.* noisy disturbance

rudder ('rudər) *n.* flat piece hinged to boat's stern or rear of aircraft used to steer

ruddy ('rudi) *a.* **1.** of fresh or healthy red color **2.** rosy **3.** florid

rude (rōōd) *a.* **1.** impolite **2.** coarse **3.** vulgar **4.** primitive **5.** roughly made **6.** uneducated **7.** sudden, violent —**'rudely** *adv.*

rudiments ('rōōdimənts) *pl.n.* elements, first principles —**rudi'mentary** *a.*

rue[1] (rōō) *v.* **1.** grieve (for) —*vt.* **2.** regret **3.** deplore —*vi.* **4.** repent —*n.* **5.** *obs.* repentance —**'rueful** *a.* **1.** sorry **2.** regretful **3.** dejected **4.** deplorable —**'ruefully** *adv.*

rue[2] (rōō) *n.* plant with evergreen bitter leaves

ruff[1] (ruf) *n.* **1.** starched and frilled collar **2.** natural collar of feathers, fur *etc.* on some birds and animals **3.** type of shore bird —**'ruffle** *vt.* **1.** rumple, disorder **2.** annoy, put out **3.** frill, pleat —*n.* **4.** frilled trimming

ruff[2] (ruf) *n./v. Cards* trump

ruffian ('rufiən) *n.* violent, lawless person —**'ruffianism** *n.* —**'ruffianly** *a.*

rufous ('rōōfəs) *a.* reddish-brown

rug (rug) *n.* **1.** small, *oft.* shaggy or thick-piled floor mat **2.** thick woolen wrap, coverlet

rugby ('rugbi) *n.* game of the football family played by two teams of 15 players in which the object is to score points by carrying the oval, leather-covered ball over the opponent's goal line or kicking it over the crossbar and between uprights on the goal line

rugged ('rugid) *a.* **1.** rough **2.** broken **3.** unpolished **4.** harsh, austere

ruin ('rōōin) *n.* **1.** decay, destruction **2.** downfall **3.** fallen or broken state **4.** loss of wealth, position *etc.* —*pl.* **5.** ruined buildings *etc.* —*vt.* **6.** reduce to ruins **7.** bring to decay or destruction **8.** spoil **9.** impoverish —**rui'nation** *n.* —**'ruinous** *a.* causing or characterized by ruin or destruction —**'ruinously** *adv.*

rule (rōōl) *n.* **1.** principle **2.** precept **3.** authority **4.** government **5.** what is usual **6.** control **7.** measuring stick —*vt.* **8.** govern **9.** decide **10.** mark with straight lines **11.** draw (line) —**'ruler** *n.* **1.** one who governs **2.** stick for measuring or ruling lines —**'ruling** *n.* **1.**

decision of someone in authority, such as judge **2.** one or more parallel ruled lines —*a.* **3.** controlling or exercising authority **4.** predominant —**rule of thumb** rough and practical approach, based on experience, rather than theory

rum (rum) *n.* spirit distilled from sugar cane

rumba (ˈrumbə, ˈro͞om-) *n.* **1.** rhythmic dance, *orig.* Cuban **2.** music for it

rumble (ˈrumbəl) *vi.* **1.** make noise as of distant thunder, heavy vehicle *etc.* —*n.* **2.** such noise

rumbustious (rumˈbuschəs) *a.* boisterous, unruly

ruminate (ˈro͞omināt) *vi.* **1.** chew cud **2.** ponder, meditate —**ˈruminant** *a./n.* cud-chewing (animal) —**rumiˈnation** *n.* quiet meditation and reflection —**ˈruminative** *a.*

rummage (ˈrumij) *v.* **1.** search thoroughly —*n.* **2.** act of rummaging

rummy (ˈrumi) *n.* any of family of card games played with one or two standard decks of 52 cards in which the object is to form matched sets or sequences, the deduction of which will bring the value of the unmatched cards to a lower total than that of the opponent(s)

rumor (ˈro͞omər) *n.* **1.** hearsay, common talk, unproved statement —*vt.* **2.** put round as, by way of, rumor

rump (rump) *n.* **1.** hindquarters of mammal, not including legs **2.** person's buttocks

rumple (ˈrumpəl) *v./n.* crease, wrinkle

rumpus (ˈrumpəs) *n.* **1.** disturbance **2.** noise and confusion

run (run) *vi.* **1.** move with more rapid gait than walking **2.** go quickly **3.** flow **4.** flee **5.** compete in race, contest, election **6.** revolve **7.** continue **8.** function **9.** travel according to schedule **10.** fuse **11.** melt **12.** spread **13.** have certain meaning —*vt.* **14.** cross by running **15.** expose oneself to (risk *etc.*) **16.** cause to run **17.** (of newspaper) print, publish **18.** land and dispose of (smuggled goods) **19.** manage **20.** operate (**ran** *pt.*, **run** *pp.*, **ˈrunning** *pr.p.*) —*n.* **21.** act, spell of running **22.** rush **23.** tendency, course **24.** period **25.** sequence **26.** heavy demand **27.** enclosure for domestic fowls, animals **28.** ride in automobile **29.** series of unraveled stitches **30.** score of one at baseball **31.** steep snow-covered course for skiing *etc.* —**ˈrunner** *n.* **1.** racer **2.** messenger **3.** curved piece of wood on which sledge slides **4.** blade of ice skate **5.** slender stem of plant running along ground forming new roots at intervals **6.** strip of lace *etc.* placed on table for decoration **7.** strip of carpet —**ˈrunning** *a.* **1.** continuous **2.** consecutive **3.** flowing **4.** discharging **5.** effortless **6.** entered for race **7.** used for running —*n.* **8.** act of moving or flowing quickly **9.** management —**ˈrunny** *a.* tending to flow or exude moisture —**ˈrunabout** *n.* small light vehicle or aircraft —**ˈrunaway** *n.* **1.** person or animal that runs away **2.** act or instance of running away —*a.* **3.** rising rapidly, as prices **4.** (of race *etc.*) easily won —**ˈrundown** *n.* summary —**run-down** *a.* exhausted —**runner-up** *n.* contestant finishing race or competition in second place (*pl.* **runners-up**) —**running board** ledge beneath doors of some automobiles and other conveyances —**running head** *Print.* heading printed at top of every page of book —**running knot** knot that moves or slips easily —**running repairs** repairs that do not (greatly) interrupt operations —**run-of-the-mill** *a.* ordinary —**run-up** *n.* **1.** approach run by athlete for long jump, pole vault *etc.* **2.** preliminary or preparatory period —**ˈrunway** *n.* level stretch where aircraft take off and land —**run about** move busily from place to place —**run away 1.** take flight; escape **2.** go away; depart **3.** (of horse) gallop away uncontrollably —**run away with 1.** abscond or elope with **2.** make off with; steal **3.** escape from control of **4.** win easily or be assured of victory in (competition) —**run down 1.** stop working **2.** reduce **3.** exhaust **4.** denigrate —**run up 1.** amass; incur **2.** make by sewing together quickly **3.** hoist —**in the running** having a fair chance in a competition

rune (ro͞on) *n.* **1.** character of earliest Germanic alphabet **2.** magic sign —**ˈrunic** *a.*

rung[1] (rung) *n.* crossbar or spoke, *esp.* in ladder

rung[2] (rung) *pp. of* RING[2]

runnel (ˈrunəl) *n.* **1.** gutter **2.** small brook or rivulet

running (ˈruning) *see* RUN

Runnymede (ˈrunimēd) *n.* place where Magna Charta was granted

runt (runt) *n.* **1.** smallest young animal in litter **2.** *offens.* undersized person

rupee (ro͞oˈpē) *n.* monetary unit of India, Pakistan, Sri Lanka *etc.*

rupture (ˈrupchər) *n.* **1.** breaking, breach **2.** hernia —*v.* **3.** break **4.** burst, sever

rural (ˈro͝orəl) *a.* of the country —**ˈruralize** *v.* —**rural route** mail service in rural area

ruse (ro͞os, ro͞oz) *n.* stratagem, trick

rush[1] (rush) *vt.* **1.** impel, carry along violently and rapidly **2.** take by sudden assault —*vi.* **3.** cause to hurry **4.** move violently or rapidly —*n.* **5.** rushing, charge **6.** hurry **7.** eager demand **8.** heavy current (of air, water *etc.*) —*a.* **9.** done with speed **10.** characterized by speed —**rush hour** period at beginning and end of day when many people are traveling to and from work

rush[2] (rush) *n.* **1.** marsh plant with slender pithy stem **2.** the stems used as material for baskets —**ˈrushy** *a.* full of rushes

rusk (rusk) *n.* slice of sweet, dried bread cooked again in oven, zwieback

Russ. Russia(n)

russet (ˈrusit) *a.* **1.** reddish-brown —*n.* **2.** the color

Russian (ˈrushən) *n.* **1.** official language of Soviet Union: Indo-European language belonging to East Slavonic branch **2.** native or inhabitant of Russia or Soviet Union —*a.* **3.** of Russia or Soviet Union —**Russian Revolution** uprising in Russia in March 1917 in which the czar's government collapsed —**Russian roulette 1.** act of bravado in which person spins cylinder of revolver loaded with only one cartridge and presses trigger with barrel against his own head **2.** any foolish or potentially suicidal undertaking —**Russian wolfhound** *see* BORZOI

rust (rust) *n.* **1.** reddish-brown coating formed on iron by oxidation **2.** disease of plants —*v.* **3.** contract, affect with rust —ˈ**rusty** *a.* **1.** coated with, affected by, or consisting of rust **2.** of rust color **3.** out of practice —ˈ**rustproof** *a.*

rustic (ˈrustik) *a.* **1.** of or as of country people **2.** rural **3.** of rude manufacture **4.** made of untrimmed branches —*n.* **5.** countryman, peasant —ˈ**rusticate** *vi.* live a country life —**rustiˈcation** *n.* —**rusˈticity** *n.*

rustle (ˈrusəl) *vi.* **1.** make sound as of blown dead leaves *etc.* —*vt.* **2.** steal (cattle) —*n.* **3.** soft fluttering or crackling sound —ˈ**rustler** *n.* cattle thief

rut[1] (rut) *n.* **1.** furrow made by wheel **2.** settled habit or way of living **3.** groove —ˈ**rutty** *a.*

rut[2] (rut) *n.* **1.** periodic sexual excitement among animals —*vi.* **2.** be under influence of this (**-tt-**)

Ruth (ro͞oth) *n. Bible* 8th book of the O.T., story of Moabite woman who remained loyal to her mother-in-law, Naomi, after death of her husband

ruthenium (ro͞oˈthēniəm) *n. Chem.* rare white noble metal *Symbol* Ru, at. wt. 101.1, at. no. 44

ruthless (ˈro͞othlis) *a.* pitiless, merciless —ˈ**ruthlessly** *adv.*

R.V. Revised Version (of the Bible)

Rwanda (ro͝oˈändə) *n.* country in Africa bounded south by Burundi, west by Zaïre, north by Uganda and east by Tanzania —**Rwˈandan** *n./a.*

-ry (*comb. form*) *see* -ERY

rye (rī) *n.* **1.** grain used for fodder and bread **2.** plant bearing it **3.** whiskey made from rye —**rye bread** bread made entirely or partly from rye flour

rye-grass *n.* any of various kinds of grasses cultivated for fodder

S

s *or* **S** (es) *n.* **1.** 19th letter of English alphabet **2.** speech sound represented by this letter, either voiceless, as in *sit*, or voiced, as in *dogs* **3.** something shaped like S (*pl.* **s's, S's** *or* **Ss**)

S 1. Society **2.** South(ern) **3.** *Chem.* sulfur **4.** *Phys.* entropy **5.** *Phys.* siemens **6.** *Phys.* strangeness

s. 1. second (of time) **2.** shilling **3.** singular **4.** son **5.** succeeded

-'s (*comb. form*) **1.** forming possessive singular of nouns and some pronouns, as in *man's* **2.** forming possessive plural of nouns whose plurals do not end in *-s*, as in *children's* **3.** forming plural of numbers, letters, or symbols, as in *20's*

-s' (*comb. form*) forming possessive of plural nouns and some singular nouns ending in sounded *s*, as in *girls'; for goodness' sake*

S.A. 1. Salvation Army **2.** South Africa **3.** South Australia **4.** *Sturmabteilung*: Nazi terrorist militia

Sabbath (ˈsabəth) *n.* **1.** Jewish and Christian day of worship and rest **2.** Sunday —**sabˈbatical** *a./n.* (denoting) leave granted to university staff *etc.* for study

saber *or* **sabre** (ˈsābər) *n.* curved cavalry sword —**saber rattling** display of armed force —**saber-toothed tiger** extinct cat with curved swordlike upper canine teeth

sable (ˈsābəl) *n.* **1.** small weasel-like Arctic animal **2.** its fur **3.** black (*pl.* **-s, ˈsable**) —*a.* **4.** black, *esp.* in heraldry

sabot (saˈbō, ˈsabō) *n.* shoe made of wood, or with wooden sole

sabotage (ˈsabətäzh) *n.* **1.** intentional damage done to roads, machines *etc., esp.* secretly in war —*vt.* **2.** carry out sabotage on **3.** destroy, disrupt —**saboteur** (sabəˈtər) *n.*

sac (sak) *n.* pouchlike structure in an animal or vegetable body

saccharin (ˈsakərin) *n.* artificial sweetener —**saccharine** (ˈsakərin, -rēn, -rīn) *a. lit., fig.* excessively sweet

sacerdotal (sasərˈdōtəl) *a.* of priests

sachet (saˈshā) *n.* small envelope or bag, *esp.* one holding liquid, as shampoo

sack[1] (sak) *n.* **1.** large bag, *orig.* of coarse material **2.** pillaging **3.** *inf.* dismissal **4.** *sl.* bed **5.** loose straight dress tapering to below knees —*vt.* **6.** pillage (captured town) **7.** *inf.* dismiss —ˈ**sacking** *n.* material for sacks —ˈ**sackcloth** *n.* coarse fabric used for sacks —**sackcloth and ashes** public display of extreme grief

sack[2] (sak) *n. obs.* dry white wine from SW Europe

sacrament (ˈsakrəmənt) *n.* one of certain ceremonies of Christian Church, *esp.* Eucharist —**sacraˈmental** *a.*

sacred (ˈsākrid) *a.* **1.** dedicated, regarded as holy **2.** set apart, reserved **3.** inviolable **4.** connected with, intended for religious use —ˈ**sacredly** *adv.* —ˈ**sacredness** *n.* —**sacred cow** *inf.* person *etc.* held to be beyond criticism

sacrifice (ˈsakrifīs) *n.* **1.** giving something up for sake of something else **2.** act of giving up **3.** thing so given up **4.** making of offering to a god **5.** thing offered —*vt.* **6.** offer as sacrifice **7.** give up **8.** sell at very cheap price —**sacrificial** (sakriˈfishəl) *a.*

sacrilege (ˈsakrilij) *n.* misuse, desecration of something sacred —**sacrilegious** (sakriˈlijəs) *a.* **1.** profane **2.** desecrating

sacristan (ˈsakristən) *or* **sacrist** (ˈsakrist, ˈsā-) *n.* official in charge of vestments and sacred vessels of church —ˈ**sacristy** *n.* room where sacred vessels *etc.* are kept

sacrosanct (ˈsakrōsangkt) *a.* **1.** preserved by religious fear against desecration or violence **2.** inviolable —**sacroˈsanctity** *n.*

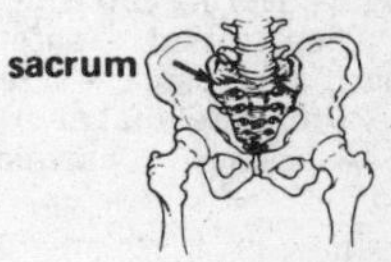

sacrum (ˈsakrəm, ˈsākrəm) *n.* five vertebrae forming compound bone at base of spinal column (*pl.* **-cra** (-krə)) —**sacroˈiliac** *a./n.* (of) joint of lower back above largest bone of pelvis

sad (sad) *a.* **1.** sorrowful **2.** unsatisfactory, deplorable —ˈ**sadden** *vt.* make sad

saddle (ˈsadəl) *n.* **1.** rider's seat to fasten on horse, bicycle *etc.* **2.** anything resembling a saddle, *esp.* marking on backs of various animals **3.** cut of meat including the two loins **4.** ridge of hill —*vt.* **5.** put saddle on **6.** lay burden, responsibility on —ˈ**saddler** *n.* maker of saddles *etc.* —ˈ**saddlery** *n.* —ˈ**saddlebag** *n.* small bag attached to saddle of bicycle *etc.* —**saddle shoe** lace-up shoe with contrasting band of leather across instep —**saddle soap** soft soap for preserving and cleaning leather —**saddle stitch** decorative running stitch made with thick thread —ˈ**saddletree** *n.* frame of saddle

Sadducee (ˈsajəsē, ˈsadyəsē) *n. Judaism* member of ancient Jewish sect, denying resurrection of dead and validity of oral tradition

sadism (ˈsādizəm) *n.* form of (sexual) perversion marked by love of inflicting pain —ˈ**sadist** *n.* —**sadistic** (səˈdistik) *a.* —**sado**ˈ**masochism** *n.* sadistic and masochistic elements in one person —**sadomaso**ˈ**chistic** *a.*

s.a.e. stamped addressed envelope

safari (səˈfäri) *n.* **1.** (party making) overland (hunting) journey, *esp.* in Afr. (*pl.* **-s**) —*a.* **2.** denoting style of dress marked by belted vented jackets and pleated pockets with buttoned flaps

safe (sāf) *a.* **1.** protected **2.** uninjured, out of danger **3.** not involving risk **4.** trustworthy **5.** sure, reliable **6.** cautious —*n.* **7.** strong lockable container **8.** ventilated cupboard for meat *etc.* —ˈ**safely** *adv.* —ˈ**safety** *n.* —**safe-conduct** *n.* passport, permit to pass somewhere —**safe-cracker** *n.* person who breaks open and robs safes —**safe-deposit** *or* **safety-deposit box** box in bank vault for safe storage of money *etc.* —ˈ**safeguard** *n.* **1.** protection —*vt.* **2.** protect —**safety belt** belt worn by person and attached to object, worn to prevent injury —**safety glass** glass made unsplinterable by lamination with plastic —**safety lamp** miner's oil lamp in which flame is surrounded by metal gauze to prevent it igniting combustible gas —**safety match** match that will light only when struck against prepared surface —**safety pin** spring clasp with covering catch, designed to shield point when closed —**safety razor** razor with guard over blade —**safety valve** **1.** valve in pressure vessel that allows fluid to escape at excess pressure **2.** harmless outlet for emotion *etc.*

safflower (ˈsaflowər) *n.* thistle-like plant with flowers used for dye, oil

saffron (ˈsafrən) *n.* **1.** crocus **2.** orange-colored flavoring obtained from it **3.** the color —*a.* **4.** orange

sag (sag) *vi.* **1.** sink in middle **2.** hang sideways **3.** curve downward under pressure **4.** give way **5.** tire **6.** (of clothing) hang loosely (**-gg-**) —*n.* **7.** droop

saga (ˈsägə) *n.* **1.** legend of Norse heroes **2.** any long (heroic) story

sagacious (səˈgāshəs) *a.* wise —**sa**ˈ**gaciously** *adv.* —**sagacity** (səˈgasiti) *n.*

sage[1] (sāj) *n.* **1.** very wise man —*a.* **2.** wise —ˈ**sagely** *adv.*

sage[2] (sāj) *n.* **1.** any of various shrubs of the mint family **2.** their aromatic grayish-green leaves used in cooking

sagebrush (ˈsājbrush) *n.* aromatic plant of West N Amer.

Sagittarius (sajiˈteriəs) *n.* (archer) 9th sign of zodiac, operative *c.* Nov. 22nd-Dec. 20th

sago (ˈsāgō) *n.* starchy cereal from powdered pith of palm (**sago palm**), used for puddings and as thickening agent

said (sed) *pt./pp. of* SAY

sail (sāl) *n.* **1.** piece of fabric stretched to catch wind for propelling ship *etc.* **2.** act of sailing **3.** journey upon the water **4.** ships collectively **5.** arm of windmill —*vi.* **6.** travel by water **7.** move smoothly **8.** begin voyage —*vt.* **9.** navigate —ˈ**sailor** *n.* **1.** member of ship's crew, *esp.* of rank below officer **2.** one who sails —ˈ**sailcloth** *n.* **1.** fabric from which sails are made **2.** canvas-like cloth used for clothing *etc.*

saint (sānt) *n.* **1.** (title of) person formally recognized (*esp.* by R.C. Church) after death as having gained by holy deeds a special place in heaven **2.** exceptionally good person —ˈ**sainted** *a.* **1.** canonized **2.** sacred —ˈ**saintliness** *n.* holiness —ˈ**saintly** *a.* —**Saint Andrew's Cross** (ˈandrōōz) X-shaped cross —**Saint Bernard** (bərˈnärd) breed of large working dog orig. from Swiss Alps —**Saint Patrick's Day** (ˈpatriks) March 17th, in honor of the patron saint of Ireland —**Saint Valentine's Day** Feb. 14th; observed as day for sending valentines —**Saint Vitus's dance** (ˈvītəsiz) *see* CHOREA

Saint Christopher Nevis (ˈkristəfərˈnēvis) *n.* country lying in Caribbean forming part of the Lesser Antilles (*also* **St. Kitts-Nevis**)

Saint Helena (əlˈēnə, həˈlēnə) crown colony of United Kingdom lying in the south Atlantic 1200 miles from the west coast of Africa at about 5° W longitude and 15° S latitude

Saint Lucia (ˈlōōshə) country lying in east Caribbean comprising a small island in the Lesser Antilles

Saint Vincent and the Grenadines (ˈvinsənt; grenəˈdēnz) country lying in the eastern Caribbean comprising the island of St. Vincent and the Northern Grenadines

saithe (sāth) *n.* coalfish

sake[1] (sāk) *n.* **1.** cause, account **2.** end, purpose —**for the sake of 1.** in behalf of **2.** to please or benefit

sake[2], **saké,** *or* **saki** (ˈsäki) *n.* Japanese alcoholic drink made of fermented rice

salaam (səˈläm) *n.* **1.** bow of salutation, mark of respect in East —*vt.* **2.** salute

salacious (səˈlāshəs) *a.* excessively concerned with sex, lewd —**salacity** (səˈlasiti) *n.*

salad (ˈsaləd) *n.* mixed vegetables, or fruit, used as food usu. without cooking —**salad days** period of youth and inexperience —**salad dressing** oil, vinegar, herbs *etc.* mixed together as sauce for salad

salamander (ˈsaləmandər) *n.* **1.** variety of lizard **2.** mythical lizard-like fire spirit

salami (səˈlämi) *n.* highly-spiced sausage of pork or beef

salary (ˈsaləri) *n.* fixed regular payment to persons employed usu. in nonmanual work —ˈ**salaried** *a.*

salchow (ˈsölkō) *n.* *Figure skating* jump from inner backward edge of one foot with full turn in air, returning to outer backward edge of opposite foot

sale (sāl) *n.* **1.** selling **2.** selling of goods at unusually low prices **3.** auction —ˈ**salable** *or* ˈ**saleable** *a.* capable of being sold —ˈ**salesman** *n.* man employed to sell goods or services in a store or in a defined territory —ˈ**salesmanship** *n.* art of selling or presenting goods in most effective way —**sales talk** persuasion used in selling —**sales tax** tax paid by buyer and collected by seller for city or state

salicin (ˈsalisin) *n.* substance obtained from poplars and used in medicine —**saliˈcylic** *a.* —**salicylic acid** white crystalline substance used in manufacture of aspirin, and as fungicide

salient (ˈsālyənt, -liənt) *a.* **1.** prominent, noticeable **2.** jutting out —*n.* **3.** salient angle, *esp.* in fortification —ˈ**salience** *or* ˈ**saliency** *n.*

saline (ˈsālēn, -līn) *a.* **1.** containing, consisting of a chemical salt, *esp.* common salt **2.** salty —**salinity** (sāˈliniti, sə-) *n.*

Salish (ˈsalish) *n.* Amerindian language family spoken in Pacific Northwest, Montana and Wyoming

saliva (səˈlīvə) *n.* liquid which forms in mouth —**salivary** (ˈsaliveri) *a.* —**salivate** (ˈsalivāt) *v.* —**salivary glands** in humans, three pairs of glands in lower jaw: parotid, submaxillary, and sublingual —**saliva test** test for use of drugs in athletes, race horses *etc.*

Salk vaccine (sölk, sök) vaccine against poliomyelitis made from killed viruses

sallow[1] (ˈsalō) *a.* of unhealthy pale or yellowish color

sallow[2] (ˈsalō) *n.* tree or low shrub allied to the willow

sally (ˈsali) *n.* **1.** rushing out, *esp.* by troops **2.** outburst **3.** witty remark —*vi.* **4.** rush **5.** set out (ˈ**sallied,** ˈ**sallying**)

salmagundi (salməˈgundi) *n.* **1.** mixed salad dish of cooked meats, eggs, beetroot *etc.* **2.** miscellany

salmon (ˈsamən) *n.* **1.** large silvery fish with orange-pink flesh valued as food **2.** color of its flesh, a yellowish pink —*a.* **3.** of this color —ˈ**salmonberry** *n.* salmon-colored raspberry of Pacific coast

salmonella (salməˈnelə) *n.* any of genus of bacteria causing disease, *esp.* food poisoning (*pl.* **-lae** (-lē))

salon (səˈlon, ˈsalon) *n.* **1.** (reception room for) guests in fashionable household **2.** commercial premises of hairdressers, beauticians *etc.*

saloon (səˈlo͞on) *n.* **1.** principal cabin or public room in passenger ship **2.** public room for buying and consuming alcoholic beverages

salpiglossis (salpiˈglosis) *n.* any of small genus of plants of the nightshade family with bright funnel-shaped flowers

salsify (ˈsalsifi) *n.* purple-flowered plant with edible root (*also* **oyster plant, vegetable oyster**)

salt (sölt) *n.* **1.** white powdery or granular crystalline substance consisting mainly of sodium chloride, used to season or preserve food **2.** chemical compound of acid and metal **3.** wit —*vt.* **4.** season, sprinkle with, preserve with salt —ˈ**saltless** *a.* —ˈ**saltness** *n.* —ˈ**salty** *a.* of, like salt —ˈ**saltbush** *n.* shrub that grows in alkaline desert regions —ˈ**saltcellar** *n.* small vessel for salt at table —**salt lick** deposit, block of salt licked by game, cattle *etc.* —ˈ**saltpan** *n.* depression encrusted with salt after draining away of water —ˈ**saltˈpeter** *n.* **1.** sodium nitrate used as meat preservative **2.** potassium nitrate used in gunpowder —ˈ**saltˈwater** *a.* —**old salt** sailor —**salt away** *or* **down** hoard or save (money, valuables *etc.*) —**with a pinch, grain, of salt** allowing for exaggeration —**worth one's salt** efficient

SALT (sölt) Strategic Arms Limitation Talks

saltant (ˈsaltənt) *a.* **1.** leaping **2.** dancing —**salˈtation** *n.* —ˈ**saltatory** *a.*

salubrious (səˈlo͞obriəs) *a.* favorable to health, beneficial —**saˈlubrity** *n.*

Saluki (səˈlo͞oki) *n.* tall hound with silky coat

salutary (ˈsalyəteri) *a.* wholesome, resulting in good —**saluˈtarily** *adv.*

salute (səˈlo͞ot) *vt.* **1.** greet with words or sign **2.** acknowledge with praise —*vi.* **3.** perform military salute —*n.* **4.** word, sign by which one person greets another **5.** motion of arm as mark of respect to superior *etc.* in military usage **6.** firing of guns as military greeting of honor —**salutation** (salyəˈtāshən) *n.*

Salvadoran (salvəˈdörən), **Salvadorean,** *or* **Salvadorian** (salvəˈdöriən) *see* EL SALVADOR

salvage (ˈsalvij) *n.* **1.** act of saving ship or other property from danger of loss **2.** property so saved —*vt.* **3.** rescue, save from wreck or ruin

salvation (salˈvāshən) *n.* (*esp.* of soul) fact or state of being saved —**Salvation Army** Christian body organized for evangelism and social work among poor

salve (sav, säv, salv) *n.* **1.** healing ointment —*vt.* **2.** anoint with salve **3.** soothe

salver (ˈsalvər) *n.* (silver) tray for presentation of food, letters *etc.*

salvia (ˈsalviə) *n.* any of a large, widely distributed plant of the mint family grown for ornament

salvo (ˈsalvō) *n.* simultaneous discharge of guns *etc.* (*pl.* **-s, -es**)

sal volatile (sal vəˈlatili) preparation of

ammonia used to revive persons who faint *etc.*

SAM (sam) surface-to-air missile

Sam. *Bible* Samuel

Samaritan (sə'maritən) *n.* **1.** native of ancient Samaria **2.** benevolent person

samarium (sə'meriəm, -'mar-) *n. Chem.* metallic element *Symbol* Sm, at. wt. 150.4, at. no. 62

samba ('sambə) *n.* **1.** dance of S Amer. origin **2.** music for it

Sam Browne belt (sam brown) leather belt having supporting belt over right shoulder, formerly used to support sword, now part of dress uniform of many military or civil forces

same (sām) *a.* (*usu. with* the) **1.** identical, not different, unchanged **2.** uniform **3.** just mentioned previously —**'sameness** *n.* **1.** similarity **2.** monotony

samite ('samīt) *n.* rich silk cloth

Samoa (sə'mōə) *n.* group of islands in south Pacific Ocean of which the eastern part is a territory of the U.S. —**Sa'moan** *n./a.*

samovar ('saməvär) *n.* Russian tea urn

Samoyed ('saməyed, 'samoied) *n.* dog with thick white coat and tightly curled tail

sampan ('sampan) *n.* small oriental boat

samphire ('samfīər) *n.* herb found on rocks by sea shore

sample ('sampəl) *n.* **1.** specimen —*vt.* **2.** take, give sample of **3.** try **4.** test **5.** select —**'sampler** *n.* beginner's exercise in embroidery —**'sampling** *n.* **1.** the taking of samples **2.** sample

Samson ('samsən) *n.* **1.** *O.T.* judge of Israel, who performed herculean feats of strength until he was betrayed by his mistress Delilah **2.** any man of outstanding physical strength

Samuel ('samyōōəl) *n. Bible* 9th and 10th books of the O.T.: accounts of the reunification of the people of Israel and Samuel's yielding to their demand for a king. As a result Saul was established on the throne and David anointed as a future king

samurai ('samərī, 'samyərī) *n.* member of ancient Japanese warrior caste (*pl.* **-rai**)

sanatorium (sanə'tōriəm) *n. see* **sanitarium** *at* SANITARY

sanctify ('sangktifī) *vt.* **1.** set apart as holy **2.** free from sin (**-fied, -fying**) —**sanctifi'cation** *n.* —**'sanctity** *n.* **1.** saintliness **2.** sacredness **3.** inviolability —**'sanctuary** *n.* **1.** holy place **2.** part of church nearest altar **3.** formerly, place where fugitive was safe from arrest or violence **4.** place protected by law where animals *etc.* can live without interference —**'sanctum** *n.* **1.** sacred place or shrine **2.** person's private room (*pl.* **-s, -ta**)

sanctimonious (sangkti'mōniəs) *a.* making a show of piety, holiness —**'sanctimony** *or* **sancti'moniousness** *n.*

sanction ('sangkshən) *n.* **1.** permission, authorization **2.** penalty for breaking law —*pl.* **3.** boycott or other coercive measure, *esp.* by one state against another regarded as having violated a law, right *etc.* —*vt.* **4.** allow, authorize, permit

sand (sand) *n.* **1.** substance consisting of small grains of rock or mineral, *esp.* on beach or in desert —*pl.* **2.** stretches or banks of this, usu. forming sea shore —*vt.* **3.** polish, smooth with sandpaper **4.** cover, mix with sand —**'sander** *n.* **1.** vehicle equipped to sand roads **2.** power tool for smoothing surfaces —**'sandy** *a.* **1.** like sand **2.** sand-colored **3.** consisting of, covered with sand —**'sandbag** *n.* bag filled with sand or earth, used as protection against gunfire *etc.* and as weapon —**sand bar** ridge of sand in lake, river or sea, built up by action of water —**'sandblast** *n.* **1.** jet of sand blown from a nozzle under pressure for cleaning, grinding *etc.* —*vt.* **2.** clean or decorate (surface) with sandblast —**sand box** receptacle containing sand for children to play in —**'sandman** *n.* in folklore, magical person supposed to put children to sleep by sprinkling sand in their eyes —**sand martin** small brown European songbird with white underparts —**'sandpaper** *n.* paper with sand stuck on it for scraping or polishing wood *etc.* —**'sandpiper** *n.* shore bird resembling plover —**'sandstone** *n.* sedimentary rock composed of sand consolidated with such materials as quartz, hematite and clay minerals —**'sandstorm** *n.* strong wind that whips up clouds of sand —**sand yacht** wheeled boat with sails, built to be propelled over sand

sandal ('sandəl) *n.* shoe consisting of sole attached by straps

sandalwood ('sandəlwōōd) *n.* sweet-scented wood of S Asia

sanderling ('sandərling) *n.* small sandpiper that frequents sandy shores

sandwich ('sanwich, 'sandwich) *n.* **1.** two slices of bread with meat or other substance between —*vt.* **2.** insert between two other things —**sandwich board** one of two connected boards hung over shoulders in front of and behind person to display advertisements —**sandwich man** man who carries sandwich board

sane (sān) *a.* **1.** of sound mind **2.** sensible, rational —**sanity** ('saniti) *n.*

Sanforizing ('sanfərīzing) *n.* trade name for method of preshrinking fabric using a patented process

sang (sang) *pt. of* SING

sang-froid (*Fr.* sā'frwa) *n.* composure; self-possession

Sangreal ('san'grāəl, 'sang-) *n. see* **Holy Grail** *at* HOLY

sangria (sang'grēə) *n.* Sp. drink of red wine and fruit juice, sometimes laced with brandy

sanguine ('sanggwin) *a.* **1.** cheerful, confident **2.** ruddy in complexion —**'sanguinary**

a. **1.** accompanied by bloodshed **2.** bloodthirsty

Sanhedrin (san'hedrin, sän-; san'hēdrin; 'sanidrin) *n. Judaism* supreme judicial, ecclesiastical, and administrative council of Jews in New Testament times

sanitary ('saniteri) *a.* helping protection of health against dirt *etc.* —**'sanatory** *or* **'sanative** *a.* curative —**sani'tarium** *or* **sana'torium** *n.* health resort (*pl.* **-s, -ria** (-riə)) —**sani'tation** *n.* measures, apparatus for preservation of public health —**sanitary napkin** absorbent pad worn externally by women during menstruation

sank (sangk) *pt. of* SINK

San Marino (san mə'rēnō) country of Europe landlocked in central Italy, 12 miles from the Adriatic Sea —**San Marinese** (san mari'nēz)

sans (sanz) *prep.* without —**sans-culotte** (sanskyōō'lot, -kōō-) *n.* **1.** revolutionary of poorer class during French Revolution **2.** any revolutionary extremist

sansei (sän'sā) *n.* person whose grandparents immigrated to the U.S.A. from Japan (*pl.* **sansei, -s**)

Sanskrit ('sanskrit) *n.* ancient language of inhabitants of N India, Pakistan and part of Ceylon

Santa Claus ('santi klöz, 'santə) legendary patron saint of children, who brings presents at Christmas

São Tomé e Principe (sown tə'mā ā 'prinsipə) country lying in Atlantic Ocean about 120 miles off the west coast of Gabon

sap[1] (sap) *n.* **1.** moisture which circulates in plants **2.** energy —*vt.* **3.** drain of sap (**-pp-**) —**'sapless** *a.* —**'sapling** *n.* young tree

sap[2] (sap) *vt.* **1.** undermine **2.** destroy insidiously **3.** weaken (**-pp-**) —*n.* **4.** trench dug in order to approach or undermine enemy position

sap[3] (sap) *n. inf.* gullible person —**'sappy** *a.*

sapid ('sapid) *a.* **1.** having pleasant taste **2.** agreeable or engaging —**sa'pidity** *n.*

sapient ('sāpiənt) *a.* (*usu. ironical*) wise, discerning, shrewd, knowing —**'sapience** *n.*

saponify (sə'ponifī) *Chem. v.* **1.** convert (fat) into soap by treatment with alkali —*vi.* **2.** undergo reaction in which ester is hydrolyzed to acid and alcohol as result of treatment with alkali —**saponifi'cation** *n.*

Sapphic ('safik) *a.* **1.** of Sappho, 6th-cent. B.C. Grecian poetess **2.** of meter associated with Sappho —*n.* **3.** Sapphic verse —**'sapphism** *n.* lesbianism

sapphire ('safīər) *n.* **1.** blue precious stone **2.** deep blue —*a.* **3.** of sapphire (blue) **4.** denoting 45th anniversary

saprophyte ('saprəfīt) *n.* plant that lives on dead organic matter —**saprophytic** (saprō'fitik) *a.*

saraband *or* **sarabande** ('sarəband) *n.* **1.** slow, stately Sp. dance **2.** music for it

Saracen ('sarəsən) *n.* **1.** Arabian **2.** adherent of Islam in Syria and Palestine **3.** infidel —**Saracenic** (sarə'senik) *a.*

sarcasm ('särkazəm) *n.* **1.** bitter or wounding ironic remark **2.** such remarks **3.** taunt; sneer **4.** irony **5.** use of such expressions —**sar'castic** *a.* —**sar'castically** *adv.*

sarcoidosis (särkoi'dōsis) *n.* disease of adults marked by formation of nodules and scar tissue in lungs and many other parts of the body

sarcoma (sär'kōmə) *n.* malignant tumor arising from connective tissue (*pl.* **-s, -mata** (-mətə)) —**sar'comatous** *a.*

sarcophagus (sär'kofəgəs) *n.* stone coffin (*pl.* **-gi** (-gī), **-es**)

sard (särd) *or* **sardius** ('särdiəs) *n.* precious stone, variety of chalcedony

sardine (sär'dēn) *n.* small fish of herring family, usu. preserved in oil

sardonic (sär'donik) *a.* characterized by irony, mockery or derision

sardonyx (sär'doniks, 'särdəniks) *n.* variety of onyx with deep orange-red layers used as gemstone

Sargasso Sea (sär'gasō) calm area of water in N Atlantic, northeast of the West Indies —**sargasso** *or* **sargasso weed** *n. see* **gulfweed** *at* GULF

sargassum (sär'gasəm) *n.* gulfweed, type of floating seaweed

saris

sari ('säri) *n.* length of fabric wound around the body worn by Southern Asian women (*pl.* **-s**)

sarong (sə'rong) *n.* skirtlike garment worn in Asian and Pacific countries

sarsaparilla (sasəpə'rilə, saspə-; särs-) *n.* (flavor of) drink, *orig.* made from aromatic root of tropical Amer. prickly climbing plant

sartorial (sär'töriəl) *a.* of tailor, tailoring or men's clothing

sash[1] (sash) *n.* decorative belt or ribbon, wound around the body

sash[2] (sash) *n.* wooden window frame opened by moving up and down in grooves

saskatoon (saskə'to͞on) *n.* Canad. shrub with purplish berries

sassafras ('sasəfras) *n.* laurel-like tree with aromatic bark used medicinally

Sassenach ('sasənak, -nakh) *n. Scot.* English person

sat (sat) *pt./pp. of* SIT

SAT Standard Achievement Test

Sat. **1.** Saturday **2.** Saturn

Satan ('sātən) *n.* the devil —**satanic(al)** (sə'tanik(əl)) *a.* devilish, fiendish —**satanically** (sə'tanikəli) *adv.* —'**Satanism** *n.* **1.** worship of Satan **2.** satanic disposition —'**Satanist** *n./a.*

satchel ('sachəl) *n.* small bag, *esp.* for school books

sate (sāt) *vt.* satisfy (a desire or appetite) fully or excessively

sateen (sa'tēn) *n.* glossy linen or cotton fabric that resembles satin

satellite ('satəlīt) *n.* **1.** celestial body or man-made projectile orbiting planet **2.** person, country *etc.* dependent on another

satiate ('sāshiāt) *vt.* **1.** satisfy to the full **2.** surfeit —'**satiable** *a.* —**sati'ation** *n.* —**satiety** (sə'tīiti) *n.* feeling of having had too much

satin ('satin) *n.* fabric (of silk, rayon *etc.*) with glossy surface on one side —'**satiny** *a.* of, like satin —'**satinwood** *n.* any of various tropical trees that yield hard satiny wood

satire ('satīər) *n.* **1.** composition in which vice, folly or foolish person is held up to ridicule **2.** use of ridicule or sarcasm to expose vice and folly —**satiric(al)** (sə'tirik(əl)) *a.* **1.** of nature of satire **2.** sarcastic **3.** bitter —**satirist** ('satərist) *n.* —**satirize** ('satərīz) *vt.* **1.** make object of satire **2.** censure thus

satisfy ('satisfī) *vt.* **1.** content, meet wishes of **2.** pay **3.** fulfill, supply adequately **4.** convince (**-fied, -fying**) —**satis'faction** *n.* —**satis'factory** *a.*

saturate ('sachərāt) *vt.* **1.** soak thoroughly **2.** cause to absorb maximum amount **3.** *Chem.* cause (substance) to combine to its full capacity with another **4.** shell or bomb heavily —**satu'ration** *n.* act, result of saturating

Saturday ('satərdi) *n.* seventh day of week

Saturn ('satərn) *n.* **1.** Roman god **2.** one of planets —**Saturnalia** (satər'nālyə, -liə) *n.* **1.** ancient festival of Saturn **2.** (*also* **s-**) noisy revelry, orgy —'**saturnine** *a.* **1.** gloomy **2.** sluggish in temperament, dull, morose

satyr ('sātər, 'satər) *n.* **1.** woodland deity, part man, part goat **2.** lustful man —**satyric** (sā'tirik, sə-) *a.*

sauce (sös) *n.* **1.** liquid added to food to enhance flavor **2.** *inf.* impudence —*vt.* **3.** add sauce to **4.** *inf.* be cheeky, impudent to —'**saucily** *adv.* —'**saucy** *a.* impudent —'**saucepan** *n.* cooking pot with long handle

saucer ('sösər) *n.* **1.** curved plate put under cup **2.** shallow depression

Saudi Arabia ('sowdi) country in Middle East bounded west by the Red Sea, south by Yemen and the People's Republic of Yemen, east by the People's Republic of Yemen and Oman, and north by the United Arab Emirates, the Persian Gulf, Kuwait, Iraq and Jordan —'**Saudi** *n./a.* —**Saudi Arabian**

sauerkraut ('sowərkrowt) *n.* Ger. dish of finely shredded and pickled cabbage

sauna ('sownə, 'sönə) *n.* kind of steam bath, *orig.* Finnish

saunter ('söntər) *vi.* **1.** walk in leisurely manner, stroll —*n.* **2.** leisurely walk or stroll

-saur *or* **-saurus** (*comb. form*) lizard, as in *dinosaur*

saurian ('söriən) *n.* one of the order of reptiles including the alligator, lizard *etc.*

sausage ('sösij) *n.* ground and seasoned meat enclosed in thin tube of animal intestine or synthetic material

sauté (sö'tā, sō-) *a.* fried quickly with little fat

Sauternes (sō'tərn) *n.* sweet white Fr. wine

savage ('savij) *a.* **1.** wild **2.** ferocious **3.** brutal **4.** uncivilized, primitive —*n.* **5.** member of savage tribe, barbarian —*vt.* **6.** attack ferociously —'**savagely** *adv.* —'**savagery** *n.*

savanna *or* **savannah** (sə'vanə) *n.* extensive open grassy plain

savant (sa'vänt, sə-; sə'vant, 'savənt) *n.* man of learning

save (sāv) *vt.* **1.** rescue, preserve **2.** protect **3.** secure **4.** keep for future, lay by **5.** prevent need of **6.** spare **7.** except —*vi.* **8.** lay by money —*prep.* **9.** *obs.* except —*conj.* **10.** *obs.* but —'**saving** *a.* **1.** frugal **2.** thrifty **3.** delivering from sin **4.** excepting **5.** compensating —*prep.* **6.** excepting —*n.* **7.** economy —*pl.* **8.** money, earnings put by for future use —**savings bank** bank that accepts savings of depositors and pays interest on the deposits —**savings bond** a nontransferable registered bond issued by the U.S. government

savior ('sāvyər) *n.* **1.** person who rescues another **2.** (**S-**) Christ

savoir-faire (savwär'fāər; *Fr.* savwar'fer) ability to do, say, the right thing in any situation

savor ('sāvər) *n.* **1.** characteristic taste **2.** flavor **3.** odor **4.** distinctive quality —*vi.* **5.** have particular smell or taste **6.** (*with* of) have suggestion (of) —*vt.* **7.** give flavor to **8.** have flavor of **9.** enjoy, appreciate —'**savory** *a.* **1.** attractive to taste or smell **2.** not sweet

savory ('sāvəri) *n.* aromatic herb used in cooking

savoy cabbage (sə'voi) variety of cabbage with wrinkled leaves

savvy ('savi) *sl. v.* **1.** understand —*n.* **2.** wits, intelligence

saw[1] (sö) *n.* **1.** tool for cutting wood *etc.* by tearing it with toothed edge —*vt.* **2.** cut with saw —*vi.* **3.** make movements of sawing (**sawed, sawn, 'sawing**) —**'sawyer** *n.* **1.** one who saws timber **2.** felled tree projecting from stream bed —**'sawbones** *n. sl.* surgeon or doctor —**'sawdust** *n.* fine wood fragments made in sawing —**'sawfish** *n.* fish of tropical waters armed with toothed snout —**'sawhorse** *n.* stand for supporting timber during sawing —**'sawmill** *n.* apparatus for sawing logs

saw[2] (sö) *pt. of* SEE[1]

saw[3] (sö) *n.* wise saying, proverb

sawn (sön) *pp. of* SAW[1]

sax (saks) *inf.* saxophone

saxhorn ('saks-hörn) *n.* any of family of brass instruments, developed by Adolphe Sax, upright with three pistons standing on top of the tube —**sax tuba** bass saxhorn

saxifrage ('saksifrij, -frāj) *n.* any of genus of low, spreading perennials with basal leaves grown in Alpine or rock gardens

Saxon ('saksən) *n.* **1.** member of West Germanic people who settled widely in Europe in the early Middle Ages —*a.* **2.** of this people or their language

saxophone ('saksəfōn) *n.* metal woodwind instrument with a conical bore, using a single reed, available in six sizes, played in bands

say (sā) *vt.* **1.** speak **2.** pronounce **3.** state **4.** express **5.** take as example or as near enough **6.** make a case for (**said** *pt./pp.*, **'saying** *pr.p.*, **says** (sez) *3rd pers. sing. pres. ind.*) —*n.* **7.** what one has to say **8.** chance of saying it **9.** share in decision —**'saying** *n.* maxim, proverb

Sb *Chem.* antimony

SBA Small Business Administration

Sc *Chem.* scandium

SC South Carolina

sc. **1.** scale **2.** scene **3.** science **4.** screw **5.** scruple (unit of weight)

s.c. *Print.* small capital letters

S.C. **1.** Signal Corps **2.** C Social Credit

scab (skab) *n.* **1.** crust formed over wound **2.** skin disease **3.** disease of plants **4.** *offens.* one who works during strike —**'scabby** *a.*

scabbard ('skabərd) *n.* sheath for sword or dagger

scabies ('skābēz) *n.* contagious skin disease —**'scabious** *a.* having scabies, scabby

scabrous ('skabrəs, 'skā-) *a.* **1.** having rough surface **2.** thorny **3.** indecent **4.** risky

scaffold ('skafəld) *n.* **1.** temporary platform for workmen **2.** gallows —**'scaffolding** *n.* (material for building) scaffold

scalar ('skālər) *n./a.* (variable quantity, *eg* time) having magnitude but no direction

scalawag ('skaliwag) *n. inf.* scamp, rascal

scald (sköld) *vt.* **1.** burn with hot liquid or steam **2.** clean, sterilize with boiling water **3.** heat (liquid) almost to boiling point —*n.* **4.** injury by scalding

scale[1] (skāl) *n.* **1.** one of the thin, overlapping plates covering fishes and reptiles **2.** thin flake **3.** incrustation which forms in boilers *etc.* —*vt.* **4.** remove scales from —*vi.* **5.** come off in scales —**'scaly** *a.* resembling or covered in scales

scale[2] (skāl) *n.* **1.** (*chiefly in pl.*) weighing instrument —*vt.* **2.** weigh in scales **3.** have weight of

scale[3] (skāl) *n.* **1.** graduated table or sequence of marks at regular intervals used as reference or for fixing standards, as in making measurements, in music *etc.* **2.** ratio of size between a thing and a model or map of it **3.** (relative) degree, extent —*vt.* **4.** climb —*a.* **5.** proportionate —**scale up** *or* **down** increase or decrease proportionately in size

scalene ('skālēn) *a.* (of triangle) with three unequal sides

scallion ('skalyən) *n.* young onion before enlargement of the bulb

scallop ('skoləp, 'skal-) *or* **scollop** ('skoləp) *n.* **1.** any of various marine mollusks **2.** the edible muscle of the scallop **3.** edging in small curves like edge of scallop shell —*vt.* **4.** shape like scallop shell **5.** cook in scallop shell or dish like one

scalp (skalp) *n.* **1.** skin and hair of top of head —*vt.* **2.** cut off scalp of

scalpel ('skalpəl) *n.* small surgical knife

scam (skam) *n.* confidence game, swindle

scamp (skamp) *n.* **1.** mischievous person or child —*vt.* **2.** skimp

scamper ('skampər) *vi.* **1.** run about **2.** run hastily from place to place —*n.* **3.** act of scampering

scan (skan) *vt.* **1.** look at carefully, scrutinize **2.** measure or read (verse) by metrical feet **3.** examine, search by systematically varying the direction of a radar or sonar beam **4.** glance over quickly —*vi.* **5.** (of verse) conform to metrical rules (**-nn-**) —*n.* **6.** scanning —**'scanner** *n.* device, *esp.* electronic, which scans —**'scansion** *n.* analysis of metrical structure of verse

Scand. Scandinavia(n)

scandal ('skandəl) *n.* **1.** action, event generally considered disgraceful **2.** malicious gossip —**'scandalize** *vt.* shock —**'scandalous** *a.* outrageous, disgraceful —**'scandalmonger** *n.* person who spreads gossip *etc.*

Scandinavian (skandi'nāviən) *a.* **1.** of Scandinavia, its inhabitants or their languages which are mutually intelligible Germanic languages —*n.* **2.** native or inhabitant of Denmark, Iceland, Norway or Sweden

scandium ('skandiəm) *n. Chem.* metallic element *Symbol* Sc, at. wt. 45.0, at. no. 21

scant (skant) *a.* barely sufficient or not sufficient —**'scantily** *adv.* —**'scanty** *a.*

scapegoat ('skāpgōt) *n.* person bearing blame due to others

scapegrace ('skāpgrās) *n.* mischievous person

scapula ('skapyələ) *n.* shoulder blade (*pl.* **-lae** (-lē), **-s**) —'**scapular** *a.* **1.** of scapula —*n.* **2.** part of habit of certain religious orders in R.C. Church

scar[1] (skär) *n.* **1.** mark left by healed wound, burn or sore **2.** change resulting from emotional distress —*v.* **3.** mark, heal with scar (**-rr-**)

scar[2] (skär) *n.* bare craggy rock formation

scarab ('skarəb) *n.* **1.** sacred beetle of ancient Egypt **2.** gem cut in shape of this

scarce (skāərs) *a.* **1.** hard to find **2.** existing or available in insufficient quantity **3.** uncommon —'**scarcely** *adv.* **1.** only just **2.** not quite **3.** definitely or probably not —'**scarceness** *or* '**scarcity** *n.*

scare (skāər) *vt.* **1.** frighten —*n.* **2.** fright, sudden panic —'**scary** *a.* —'**scarecrow** *n.* **1.** thing set up to frighten birds from crops **2.** badly dressed or miserable-looking person —'**scaremonger** *n.* one who spreads alarming rumors

scarf[1] (skärf) *n.* long narrow strip, large piece of material to put round neck, head *etc.* (*pl.* **-s, scarves**)

scarf[2] (skärf) *n.* **1.** part cut away from each of two pieces of timber to be jointed longitudinally **2.** joint so made (*pl.* **-s**) —*vt.* **3.** cut or join in this way —'**scarfing** *n.*

scarify ('skarifī, 'skeri-) *vt.* **1.** scratch, cut slightly all over **2.** lacerate **3.** stir surface soil of **4.** criticize mercilessly (**-fied, -fying**) —**scarifi'cation** *n.*

scarlatina (skärlə'tēnə) *n.* scarlet fever

scarlet ('skärlit) *n.* **1.** brilliant red color **2.** cloth or clothing of this color, *esp.* military uniform —*a.* **3.** of this color **4.** immoral, *esp.* unchaste —**scarlet fever** infectious bacterial disease, formerly major cause of death in children, now controlled by antibiotics (*also* **scarlatina**)

scarp (skärp) *n.* **1.** steep slope **2.** inside slope of ditch in fortifications

scarves (skärvz) *n., pl. of* SCARF[1]

scat[1] (skat) *vi. inf.* (*usu. imp.*) go away (**-tt-**)

scat[2] (skat) *n. Jazz* singing characterized by improvised vocal sounds instead of words

scathe (skādh) (*usu. now as pp./a.* **scathed** & **un'scathed**) *n.* **1.** injury, harm, damage —*vt.* **2.** injure, damage —'**scathing** *a.* **1.** harshly critical **2.** cutting **3.** damaging

Scaticook ('skatikŏŏk) *n.* Algonquian-speaking Amerindian people of Connecticut

scatology (ska'toləji) *n.* **1.** scientific study of excrement, *esp.* in medicine and paleontology **2.** preoccupation with obscenity, *esp.* in form of references to excrement —**scato'logical** *a.*

scatter ('skatər) *vt.* **1.** throw in various directions **2.** put here and there —*vi.* **3.** separate and move in various directions —*n.* **4.** sprinkling —'**scatty** *a. inf.* silly, useless —'**scatterbrain** *n.* silly, careless person

scavenge ('skavinj) *v.* search for (anything usable), *usu.* among discarded material —'**scavenger** *n.* **1.** person who scavenges **2.** animal, bird which feeds on refuse

scene (sēn) *n.* **1.** place of action of novel, play *etc.* **2.** place of any action **3.** subdivision of play **4.** view **5.** episode **6.** display of strong emotion —**scenario** (si'nariō, -'ner-) *n.* summary of plot (of play *etc.*) or plan (*pl.* **-s**) —'**scenery** *n.* **1.** natural features of district **2.** constructions of wood, canvas *etc.* used on stage to represent a place where action is happening —'**scenic** *a.* **1.** picturesque **2.** of or on the stage

scent (sent) *n.* **1.** distinctive smell, *esp.* pleasant one **2.** trail, clue **3.** perfume —*vt.* **4.** detect or track by or as if by smell **5.** suspect, sense **6.** fill with fragrance

scepter ('septər) *n.* **1.** ornamental staff as symbol of royal power **2.** royal dignity

schedule ('skejŏŏəl, -jŏŏl) *n.* **1.** plan of procedure for a project **2.** list **3.** timetable —*vt.* **4.** enter in schedule **5.** plan to occur at certain time —**on schedule** on time

schema ('skēmə) *n.* overall plan or diagram (*pl.* **-mata** (-mətə)) —**sche'matic** *a.* presented as plan or diagram —'**schematize** *vt.*

scheme (skēm) *n.* **1.** plan, design **2.** project **3.** outline —*v.* **4.** devise, plan, *esp.* in underhand manner —'**schemer** *n.*

scherzo ('skāərtsō) *n. Mus.* light playful composition (*pl.* **-s, -zi** (-tsē))

Schick test (shik) test for susceptibility to diphtheria

schism ('sizəm, 'skiz-) *n.* (group resulting from) division in political party, church *etc.* —**schis'matic** *n./a.*

schist (shist) *n.* crystalline rock which splits into layers —'**schistose** *a.*

schistosomiasis (shistəsō'mīəsis) *n.* severe infectious disease caused by flatworm infestation transmitted to humans by snails (*also* **bilharzia, snail fever**)

schizo ('skitsō) *inf. a.* **1.** schizophrenic —*n.* **2.** schizophrenic person (*pl.* **-s**)

schizo- *or before vowel* **schiz-** (*comb. form*) indicating cleavage, split, or division, as in *schizophrenia*

schizophrenia (skitsə'frēniə) *n.* mental disorder involving deterioration of, confusion about personality —'**schizoid** *a.* of schizophrenia —**schizophrenic** (skitsə'frenik) *a./n.*

schmaltz *or* **schmalz** (shmölts, shmolts) see SHMALZ

schnapps (shnaps) *n.* **1.** spirit distilled from potatoes **2.** *inf.* any strong spirit

schnitzel ('shnitsəl) *n.* thin slice of meat, *esp.* veal

scholar ('skolər) *n. see* SCHOOL[1]

scholium ('skōliəm) *n.* **1.** marginal annotation **2.** note **3.** comment (*pl.* **-lia** (-liə)) —'**scholiast** *n.* **1.** commentator **2.** annotator

school[1] (skōōl) *n.* **1.** institution for teaching children or for giving instruction in any subject **2.** buildings of such institution **3.** group of thinkers, writers, artists *etc.* with principles or methods in common —*vt.* **4.** educate **5.** bring under control, train —'**scholar** *n.* **1.** learned person **2.** one taught in school **3.** one quick to learn —**scholarly** ('skolərli) *a.* learned, erudite —**scholarship** ('skolərship) *n.* **1.** learning **2.** prize, grant to student for payment of school or college fees —**scholastic** (skə'lastik) *a.* **1.** of schools or scholars, or education **2.** pedantic —'**schooling** *n.* **1.** education **2.** training of animal, *esp.* of horse for dressage —'**schoolhouse** *n.* **1.** building used as school **2.** house attached to school —'**schoolman** *n.* medieval philosopher —'**schoolmarm** *n. inf.* **1.** woman schoolteacher **2.** woman considered old-fashioned or prim —'**schoolmaster** *n.* **1.** man who teaches school **2.** edible snapper of Gulf of Mexico and tropical Atlantic —'**schoolmistress** *n.* woman who teaches school —'**schoolteacher** *n.* person who teaches school

school[2] (skōōl) *n.* shoal (of fish, whales *etc.*)

schooner ('skōōnər) *n.* **1.** fore-and-aft rigged vessel with two or more masts **2.** tall glass

schottische ('shotish, sho'tēsh) *n.* **1.** 19th-century German dance **2.** music for this

schwa (shwä) *n.* **1.** central vowel represented in International Phonetic Alphabet by (ə), *eg* 'a' in *around* **2.** symbol (ə) used to represent this sound

sciatica (sī'atikə) *n.* **1.** neuralgia of hip and thigh **2.** pain in sciatic nerve —**sci'atic** *a.* **1.** of the hip **2.** of sciatica

science ('sīəns) *n.* **1.** systematic study and knowledge of natural or physical phenomena **2.** any branch of study concerned with observed material facts —**scien'tific** *a.* **1.** of the principles of science **2.** systematic —**scien'tifically** *adv.* —'**scientist** *n.* person versed in natural sciences —**science fiction** stories set in a fantasy world making imaginative use of scientific knowledge

Scientology (sīən'toləji) *n.* religious cult based on belief that self-awareness is paramount

sci-fi ('sī'fī) *n. inf.* science fiction

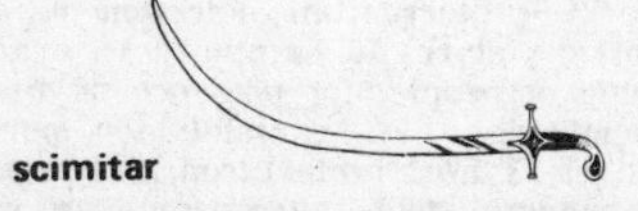
scimitar

scimitar ('simitər) *n.* oriental curved sword

scintilla (sin'tilə) *n. rare* minute amount

scintillate ('sintilāt) *vi.* **1.** give off sparks **2.** be animated, witty, clever —**scintil'lation** *n.* —**scintillation counter** instrument for detecting and measuring intensity of high-energy radiation

scion ('sīən) *n.* **1.** descendant, heir **2.** slip for grafting

scission ('sizhən) *n.* act of cutting, dividing, splitting —'**scissile** *a.*

scissors ('sizərz) *pl.n.* **1.** cutting instrument of two blades pivoted together (*also* **pair of scissors**) —*n./a.* **2.** (with) scissor-like action of limbs in swimming, athletics *etc.* —**scissor-like** *a.*

scleroderma (sklerə'dərmə) *n.* progressive disease of the connective tissues of the body

sclerosis (skli'rōsis) *n.* a hardening of bodily organs, tissues *etc.* (*pl.* **-ses** (-sēz)) —**sclera** ('sklerə) *n.* firm white fibrous membrane that forms outer covering of eyeball —**sclerotic** (skli'rotik) *a.* **1.** of sclera **2.** of or having sclerosis —*n.* **3.** sclera

scoff[1] (skof) *vi.* **1.** (*oft. with* at) express derision (for) —*n.* **2.** derision **3.** mocking words —'**scoffer** *n.*

scoff[2] (skof) *v. sl.* eat rapidly

scold (skōld) *v.* **1.** find fault (with) —*vt.* **2.** reprimand, be angry with —*n.* **3.** one who does this

scoliosis (skōli'ōsis) *n.* lateral curvature of the spine

scollop ('skoləp) *see* SCALLOP

sconce[1] (skons) *n.* bracket candlestick on wall

sconce[2] (skons) *n.* small protective fortification

scone (skōn, skon) *n.* small plain cake baked on griddle or in oven

scoop (skōōp) *n.* **1.** small shovel-like tool for ladling, hollowing out *etc.* **2.** *sl.* profitable deal **3.** *Journalism* exclusive news item —*vt.* **4.** ladle out **5.** hollow out, rake in with scoop **6.** make sudden profit **7.** beat (rival newspaper *etc.*)

scoot (skōōt) *vi. sl.* move off quickly —'**scooter** *n.* **1.** child's vehicle propelled by pushing on ground with one foot **2.** light motorcycle (*also* **motor scooter**)

scope (skōp) *n.* **1.** range of activity or application **2.** opportunity

-scope (*n. comb. form*) indicating instrument for observing or detecting, as in *microscope* —**-scopic** (*a. comb. form*)

scopolamine (skō'poləmēn) *n.* drug obtained from plants of nightshade family used as preanesthetic and as 'truth drug'

scorbutic (skör'byōōtik) *a.* of or having scurvy —**scor'butically** *adv.*

scorch (skörch) *v.* **1.** burn, be burnt, on surface **2.** parch **3.** shrivel **4.** wither —*n.* **5.** slight burn —'**scorcher** *n. inf.* very hot day

score (skör) *n.* **1.** points gained in game, competition **2.** group of 20 **3.** (*esp. pl.*) a lot **4.** copy of musical composition **5.** mark or notch, *esp.* to keep tally **6.** reason, account **7.** grievance —*v.* **8.** gain (points) in game —*vt.* **9.** mark **10.** (*with* out) cross out **11.** arrange music for —*vi.* **12.** keep tally of points **13.** succeed —'**scorecard** *n.* **1.** card on which scores are recorded **2.** card identifying players in sports match

scoria (ˈsköriə) *n.* **1.** solidified lava containing many cavities **2.** refuse obtained from smelted ore (*pl.* **-riae** (-riē))

scorn (skörn) *n.* **1.** contempt, derision —*vt.* **2.** despise —ˈ**scorner** *n.* —ˈ**scornful** *a.* derisive —ˈ**scornfully** *adv.*

Scorpio (ˈsköрpiō) *n.* (scorpion) 8th sign of zodiac, operative *c.* Oct. 23rd-Nov. 21st

scorpion (ˈsköрpiən) *n.* small lobster-shaped animal with sting at end of jointed tail

Scot. **1.** Scotland **2.** Scottish

scotch (skoch) *vt.* **1.** put an end to **2.** *obs.* wound

scoter (ˈskōtər) *n.* sea duck of northern regions

scot-free *a.* without harm or loss

Scotland (ˈskotlənd) *n.* division of the United Kingdom in N Great Britain —**Scot** *n.* native of Scotland —**Scotch** (skoch) *n.* whisky made in Scotland —ˈ**Scottie** *or* ˈ**Scotty** *n.* **1.** Scottish terrier **2.** *inf.* Scotsman —ˈ**Scottish** *or* **Scots** *a.* —**Scotland Yard** headquarters of police force of metropolitan London —ˈ**Scotsman** *n.* —**Scots** *or* **Scotch pine** **1.** coniferous tree of Europe and W and N Asia **2.** its wood —**Scottish terrier** small long-haired breed of terrier

scoundrel (ˈskowndrəl) *n.* villain, blackguard —ˈ**scoundrelly** *a.*

scour[1] (ˈskowər) *vt.* **1.** clean, polish by rubbing **2.** clear or flush out —**scouring rush** primitive plant resembling horsetail but taller, used for cleaning as stems contain embedded silica

scour[2] (ˈskowər) *v.* move rapidly along or over (territory) in search of something

scourge (skərj) *n.* **1.** whip, lash **2.** severe affliction **3.** pest **4.** calamity —*vt.* **5.** flog **6.** punish severely

scout (skowt) *n.* **1.** one sent out to reconnoiter **2.** Boy Scout; Girl Scout —*vi.* **3.** go out, act as scout **4.** reconnoiter

scow (skow) *n.* unpowered barge

scowl (skowl) *vi.* **1.** frown gloomily or sullenly —*n.* **2.** angry or gloomy expression

scrabble (ˈskrabəl) *vi.* **1.** scrape with hands, claws in disorderly manner —*n.* **2.** (**S-**) trade name for word game where object is to form interlocking words by using letters with designated values

scrag (skrag) *n.* **1.** lean person or animal **2.** lean end of a neck of mutton —ˈ**scraggy** *a.* thin, bony

scraggly (ˈskragli) *a.* untidy

scram (skram) *vi. inf.* (*oft. imp.*) go away hastily, get out (**-mm-**)

scramble (ˈskrambəl) *vi.* **1.** move along or up by crawling, climbing *etc.* **2.** struggle with others **3.** run with football after protection has been broken down —*vt.* **4.** mix up **5.** cook (eggs) beaten up with milk **6.** render (speech) unintelligible by electronic device —*n.* **7.** scrambling **8.** rough climb **9.** disorderly proceeding —ˈ**scrambler** *n.* electronic device that renders speech unintelligible during transmission

scrap (skrap) *n.* **1.** small piece or fragment **2.** waste material **3.** *inf.* fight —*vt.* **4.** break up, discard as useless —*vi.* **5.** *inf.* fight (**-pp-**) —ˈ**scrappy** *a.* **1.** unequal in quality **2.** badly finished —ˈ**scrapbook** *n.* book in which newspaper cuttings *etc.* are kept —**scrap heap** pile of waste material

scrape (skrāp) *vt.* **1.** rub with something sharp **2.** clean, smooth thus **3.** grate **4.** scratch **5.** rub with harsh noise —*n.* **6.** act, sound of scraping **7.** *inf.* awkward situation, *esp.* as result of escapade —ˈ**scraper** *n.* **1.** instrument for scraping **2.** contrivance on which mud is scraped from shoes *etc.*

scratch (skrach) *vt.* **1.** score, make narrow surface wound on with claws, nails, or anything pointed **2.** make marks on with pointed instruments **3.** scrape (skin) with nails to relieve itching **4.** remove, withdraw from list, race *etc.* —*vi.* **5.** use claws or nails, *esp.* to relieve itching —*n.* **6.** wound, mark or sound made by scratching **7.** line or starting point —*a.* **8.** got together at short notice **9.** impromptu —ˈ**scratchy** *a.*

scrawl (skröl) *vt.* **1.** write, draw untidily —*n.* **2.** thing scrawled **3.** careless writing

scrawny (ˈskröni) *a.* thin, bony

scream (skrēm) *vi.* **1.** utter piercing cry, *esp.* of fear, pain *etc.* **2.** be very obvious —*vt.* **3.** utter in a scream —*n.* **4.** shrill, piercing cry **5.** *inf.* very funny person or thing

scree (skrē) *n.* **1.** loose shifting stones **2.** slope covered with these

screech (skrēch) *vi./n.* scream —**screech owl** **1.** small N Amer. owl having reddish-brown or gray plumage **2.** **UK** any owl that utters screeching cry

screed (skrēd) *n.* **1.** long (tedious) letter, passage or speech **2.** thin layer of cement

screen (skrēn) *n.* **1.** device to shelter from heat, light, draft, observation *etc.* **2.** anything used for such purpose **3.** mesh over doors, windows to keep out insects **4.** white or silvered surface on which photographic images are projected **5.** maneuver in some sports to impede opponent legally **6.** wooden or stone partition in church —*vt.* **7.** shelter, hide **8.** protect from detection **9.** show (motion picture) **10.** scrutinize **11.** examine (group of people) for presence of disease, weapons *etc.* **12.** examine for political motives **13.** *Elec.* protect from stray electric or magnetic fields —ˈ**screenplay** *n.* script for motion picture, including instructions for sets and camera work —**screen process** *see* **silk-screen** *at* SILK —**the screen** the motion-picture industry

screw (skroo͞) *n.* **1.** (nail-like device or cylinder with) spiral thread cut to engage similar thread or to bore into material (wood *etc.*) to pin or fasten **2.** anything resembling a screw in shape, *esp.* in spiral form **3.** propeller **4.** twist —*vt.* **5.** fasten with screw **6.** twist around **7.** *inf.* extort —'**screwy** *a. inf.* crazy, eccentric —'**screwball** *sl. n.* **1.** eccentric person —*a.* **2.** odd; eccentric —'**screwdriver** *n.* tool for turning screws —**put the screws on** compel by applying pressure on (debtor) —**screw up 1.** distort **2.** *inf.* bungle

scribble ('skribəl) *v.* **1.** write, draw carelessly —*vi.* **2.** make meaningless marks with pen or pencil —*n.* **3.** something scribbled —'**scribbly** *a.*

scribe (skrīb) *n.* **1.** writer **2.** copyist —*v.* **3.** scratch a line on (a surface) with pointed instrument

scrimmage ('skrimij) *n.* scuffle

scrimp (skrimp) *vt.* **1.** make too small or short **2.** treat meanly —'**scrimpy** *a.*

script (skript) *n.* **1.** (system or style of) handwriting **2.** written characters **3.** written text of motion picture, play or radio or television program **4.** answer paper in examination

scripture ('skripchər) *n.* **1.** sacred writings **2.** the Bible —'**scriptural** *a.*

scrofula ('skrofyələ) *n.* tuberculosis of lymphatic glands of neck —'**scrofulous** *a.*

scroll (skrōl) *n.* **1.** roll of parchment or paper **2.** list **3.** ornament shaped thus

Scrooge (skrōōj) *n.* miserly person

scrotum ('skrōtəm) *n.* pouch containing testicles (*pl.* **-ta** (-tə)) —'**scrotal** *a.*

scrounge (skrownj) *v. inf.* get (something) without cost, by begging —'**scrounger** *n.*

scrub[1] (skrub) *vt.* **1.** clean with hard brush and water **2.** scour **3.** *inf.* cancel, get rid of (**-bb-**) —*n.* **4.** scrubbing —'**scrubber** *n.* **1.** person or thing that scrubs **2.** apparatus for purifying gas

scrub[2] (skrub) *n.* **1.** stunted trees **2.** brushwood —'**scrubby** *a.* **1.** covered with scrub **2.** stunted **3.** *inf.* messy

scrub typhus infectious disease caused by rickettsia transmitted to humans by mites

scruff (skruf) *n.* nape (of neck)

scruffy ('skrufi) *a.* unkempt or shabby

scrumptious ('skrumpshəs) *a. inf.* very pleasing; delicious —'**scrumptiously** *adv.*

scrumpy ('skrumpi) *n.* rough dry cider

scrunch (skrunch) *v.* **1.** crumple or crunch or be crumpled or crunched —*n.* **2.** act or sound of scrunching

scruple ('skrōōpəl) *n.* **1.** doubt or hesitation about what is morally right **2.** apothecaries' weight of 20 grains —*vi.* **3.** hesitate —'**scrupulous** *a.* **1.** extremely conscientious **2.** thorough, attentive to small points

scrutiny ('skrōōtini) *n.* **1.** close examination **2.** critical investigation **3.** official examination of votes *etc.* **4.** searching look —**scruti'neer** *n.* person who examines —'**scrutinize** *vt.* examine closely

scuba ('skyōōbə, 'skōōbə) *n./a.* (relating to) self-contained underwater breathing apparatus

scud (skud) *vi.* **1.** run fast **2.** run before the wind (**-dd-**)

scuff (skuf) *vi.* **1.** drag, scrape with feet in walking —*vt.* **2.** scrape with feet **3.** graze —*n.* **4.** act, sound of scuffing —*pl.* **5.** thong sandals —**scuffed** *a.* (of shoes) scraped or slightly grazed

scuffle ('skufəl) *vi.* **1.** fight in disorderly manner **2.** shuffle —*n.* **3.** disorderly struggle

scull (skul) *n.* **1.** oar used in stern of boat **2.** short oar used in pairs —*v.* **3.** propel, move by means of scull(s)

scullery ('skuləri) *n.* place for washing dishes *etc.* —'**scullion** *n.* helper in kitchen

sculpture ('skulpchər) *n.* **1.** art of forming figures in relief or solid **2.** product of this art —*vt.* **3.** represent by sculpture —**sculpt** *v.* —'**sculptor** *n.* —'**sculptural** *a.* with qualities proper to sculpture

scum (skum) *n.* **1.** froth or other floating matter on liquid **2.** waste part of anything **3.** vile person(s) or thing(s) —'**scummy** *a.*

scupper ('skupər) *n.* **1.** hole in ship's side level with deck to carry off water —*vt.* **2.** *inf.* ruin, destroy, kill

scurf (skərf) *n.* flaky matter on scalp, dandruff

scurrilous ('skuriləs) *a.* coarse, indecently abusive —**scur'rility** *n.*

scurry ('skuri) *vi.* **1.** run hastily ('**scurried,** '**scurrying**) —*n.* **2.** bustling haste **3.** flurry

scurvy ('skərvi) *n.* **1.** disease caused by lack of vitamin C —*a.* **2.** mean, contemptible

scut (skut) *n.* short tail of hare or other animal

scuttle[1] ('skutəl) *n.* fireside container for coal

scuttle[2] ('skutəl) *vi.* **1.** rush away —*n.* **2.** hurried pace, run

scuttle[3] ('skutəl) *vt.* cause (ship) to sink by making holes in bottom

scythe (sīdh) *n.* **1.** manual implement with long curved blade for cutting grass —*vt.* **2.** cut with scythe

SD South Dakota

Se *Chem.* selenium

SE southeast(ern)

sea anemone

sea (sē) *n.* **1.** mass of salt water covering greater part of earth **2.** broad tract of this **3.**

waves **4.** swell **5.** large quantity **6.** vast expanse —**sea anchor** *Naut.* device dragged in water to slow vessel —**sea anemone** sea animal with suckers like petals —'**seaboard** *n.* territory bordering sea coast —**sea cow 1.** dugong or manatee **2.** *obs.* walrus —**sea cucumber** echinoderm with elongated body covered with leathery skin and cluster of tentacles at oral end —**sea dog** experienced or old sailor —'**seafaring** *a.* occupied in sea voyages —'**seafood** *n.* edible saltwater fish or shellfish —**sea-girt** *a. Lit.* surrounded by sea —**sea gull** gull —**sea horse** fish with bony plated body and horselike head —**sea kale** European coastal plant with edible asparagus-like shoots —**sea legs** *inf.* **1.** ability to maintain one's balance on board ship **2.** ability to resist seasickness —**sea level** level of surface of sea, taken to be mean level between high and low tide —**sea lion** any of large-eared seals of Pacific —'**seaman** *n.* sailor —'**seamanship** *n.* skill in navigating, maintaining and operating vessel —**sea mile** *see* **nautical mile** *at* NAUTICAL —'**seaplane** *n.* aircraft that lands on and takes off from water —**Sea Scout** member of Scouting program teaching seamanship —'**seashell** *n.* empty shell of marine mollusk —'**seasick** *a.* —'**seasickness** *n. see* **motion sickness** *at* MOTION —'**seaside** *n.* place, *esp.* resort, on coast —**sea urchin** marine animal with globular body enclosed in rigid, spiny test —'**seaweed** *n.* **1.** mass of marine or freshwater plants **2.** marine alga, *esp.* kelp —'**seaworthy** *a.* in fit condition to put to sea

sea horse

seal[1] (sēl) *n.* **1.** device impressed on piece of wax *etc.*, fixed to letter *etc.* as mark of authentication **2.** impression thus made **3.** device, material preventing passage of water, air, oil *etc.* (*also* '**sealer**) —*vt.* **4.** affix seal to **5.** ratify, authorize **6.** mark with stamp as evidence of some quality **7.** keep close or secret **8.** settle **9.** make watertight, airtight *etc.* —**sealing wax** hard material made of shellac and turpentine that softens when heated

seal[2] (sēl) *n.* **1.** amphibious furred carnivorous mammal with flippers as limbs —*vi.* **2.** hunt seals —'**sealer** *n.* person or ship engaged in sealing —'**sealskin** *n.* skin, fur of seals

seam (sēm) *n.* **1.** line of junction of two edges, *eg* of two pieces of cloth, or two planks **2.** thin layer, stratum —*vt.* **3.** mark with furrows or wrinkles —'**seamless** *a.* —**seamstress** ('sēmstris, 'sem-) *or* **sempstress** ('sempstris, 'semstris) *n.* woman who sews and makes clothing, *esp.* professionally —'**seamy** *a.* **1.** sordid **2.** marked with seams

seance ('sāons) *n.* meeting of spiritualists

sear (sēər) *vt.* **1.** scorch, brand with hot iron **2.** deaden

search (sərch) *v.* **1.** look over or through (a place *etc.*) to find something —*vt.* **2.** probe into, examine —*n.* **3.** act of searching **4.** quest —'**searcher** *n.* —'**searching** *a.* **1.** keen **2.** thorough **3.** severe —'**searchlight** *n.* powerful electric light with concentrated beam —**search warrant** legal document authorizing search of premises for stolen goods *etc.*

season ('sēzən) *n.* **1.** one of four divisions of year (spring, summer, fall and winter), which have characteristic weather conditions **2.** period during which thing takes place, grows, is active *etc.* **3.** proper time —*vt.* **4.** flavor with salt, herbs *etc.* **5.** make reliable or ready for use **6.** make experienced —'**seasonable** *a.* **1.** appropriate for the season **2.** opportune **3.** fit —'**seasonal** *a.* depending on, varying with seasons —'**seasoning** *n.* flavoring —**season ticket** ticket for series of journeys, events *etc.* within a certain time

seat (sēt) *n.* **1.** thing for sitting on **2.** buttocks **3.** base **4.** right to sit (*eg* in council *etc.*) **5.** place where something is located, centered **6.** locality of disease, trouble *etc.* **7.** country house —*vt.* **8.** bring to or place on seat **9.** provide sitting accommodation for **10.** install firmly —**seat belt** belt worn in automobile, aircraft *etc.* to secure seated passenger

SEATO ('sētō) South East Asia Treaty Organization

sebaceous (si'bāshəs) *a.* **1.** of, pert. to fat **2.** secreting fat, oil —**sebaceous cyst** round or oval swelling caused by blocking of oil glands of skin (*also* **wen**)

sec[1] (sek) *a.* **1.** (of wines) dry **2.** (of champagne) of medium sweetness

sec[2] (sek) *inf.* second (of time)

sec[3] (sek) secant

sec. **1.** second (of time) **2.** secondary **3.** secretary **4.** section **5.** sector

S.E.C. Securities and Exchange Commission

secant ('sēkant, -kənt) *n. Math.* **1.** (of angle) the reciprocal of its cosine **2.** line that intersects a curve

secede (si'sēd) *vi.* withdraw formally from federation, Church *etc.* —**secession** (si'seshən) *n.* —**secessionist** (si'seshənist) *n.*

seclude (si'klo͞od) *vt.* guard from, remove from sight, view, contact with others —**se'cluded** *a.* **1.** remote **2.** private —**se'clusion** *n.*

second[1] ('sekənd) *a.* **1.** next after first **2.** alternate **3.** additional **4.** of lower quality —*n.* **5.** person or thing coming second **6.**

attendant **7.** sixtieth part of minute **8.** unit of time **9.** moment **10.** (*esp. pl.*) inferior goods —*vt.* **11.** support **12.** support (motion in meeting) so that discussion may be in order —**'seconder** *n.* —**'secondly** *adv.* —**second-best** *a.* next to best —**second chamber** upper house of bicameral legislative assembly —**second class** class next in value *etc.* to first —**second-class** *a.* **1.** of grade next to best in quality *etc.* **2.** shoddy or inferior **3.** (of accommodations in hotel, on aircraft *etc.*) next in quality to first-class **4.** of mail that consists mainly of newspapers *etc.* —*adv.* **5.** by second-class mail *etc.* —**Second Coming** *or* **Advent** *Christian theol.* prophesied return of Christ to earth at Last Judgment —**second cousin** child of first cousin of either of one's parents —**second fiddle** *inf.* **1.** second violin in string quartet **2.** person who has secondary status —**second hand** pointer on face of timepiece that indicates seconds —**second-hand** *a.* **1.** bought after use by another **2.** not original **3.** dealing in goods that are not new —*adv.* **4.** not directly —**second lieutenant** commissioned officer of lowest rank in army, air force and marine corps, below first lieutenant —**second nature** habit *etc.* long practiced so as to seem innate —**second person** grammatical category of pronouns and verbs used when referring to individual(s) being addressed —**second-rate** *a.* **1.** mediocre **2.** second in importance *etc.* —**second sight** faculty of seeing events before they occur —**second thought** revised opinion on matter already considered —**second wind** (wind) **1.** return of breath at normal rate, *esp.* following exertion **2.** renewed ability to continue in effort —**come off second-best** *inf.* be defeated in competition

second[2] ('sekənd) *vt.* transfer (employee, officer) temporarily

secondary ('sekənderi) *a.* **1.** of less importance **2.** developed from, or dependent on, something else —**secon'darily** *adv.* —**secondary color** color formed by mixing two primary colors in equal parts: orange, green or violet —**secondary road 1.** road not of primary importance **2.** feeder road

secret ('sēkrit) *a.* **1.** kept, meant to be kept from knowledge of others **2.** hidden **3.** private —*n.* **4.** thing kept secret —**'secrecy** *n.* keeping or being kept secret —**'secretive** *a.* given to having secrets; uncommunicative, reticent —**'secretiveness** *n.* —**'secretly** *adv.* —**secret agent** person employed in espionage —**secret police** police force that operates secretly to check subversion —**secret service** government department that conducts intelligence or counterintelligence operations

secretary ('sekrəteri) *n.* **1.** person employed by individual or organization to deal with papers and correspondence, keep records, prepare business *etc.* **2.** head of a U.S. government department —**secre'tarial** *a.* —**secre'tariat** *n.* **1.** body of secretaries **2.** building occupied by secretarial staff —**'secretaryship** *n.* —**secretary bird** large Afr. bird of prey

secretary bird

secrete (si'krēt) *vt.* **1.** hide, conceal **2.** (of gland *etc.*) collect and supply (particular substance in body) —**se'cretion** *n.* —**se'cretory** *a.*

sect (sekt) *n.* **1.** group of people (within religious body *etc.*) with common interest **2.** faction —**sec'tarian** *a.* **1.** of a sect **2.** narrow-minded

section ('sekshən) *n.* **1.** part cut off **2.** division **3.** portion **4.** distinct part of city, country, people *etc.* **5.** cutting **6.** drawing of anything as if cut through —**'sectional** *a.*

sector ('sektər) *n.* **1.** part, subdivision **2.** part of circle enclosed by two radii and the arc which they cut off

secular ('sekyələr) *a.* **1.** worldly **2.** lay, not religious **3.** not monastic **4.** lasting for, or occurring once in, an age **5.** centuries old —**'secularism** *n.* —**'secularist** *n.* one who believes that religion should have no place in civil affairs —**seculari'zation** *n.* —**'secularize** *vt.* transfer from religious to lay possession or use

secure (si'kyŏŏər) *a.* **1.** safe **2.** free from fear, anxiety **3.** firmly fixed **4.** certain **5.** sure, confident —*vt.* **6.** gain possession of **7.** make safe **8.** free (creditor) from risk of loss **9.** make firm —**se'curely** *adv.* —**se'curity** *n.* **1.** state of safety **2.** protection **3.** that which secures **4.** assurance **5.** anything given as bond, caution or pledge **6.** one that becomes surety for another —**security risk** person deemed to be threat to state security

sedan (si'dan) *n.* enclosed automobile for four or more persons including the driver —**sedan chair** *Hist.* closed chair for one person, carried on poles by bearers

sedate[1] (si'dāt) *a.* **1.** calm, collected **2.** serious

sedate[2] (si'dāt) *vt.* make calm by sedative —**se'dation** *n.* —**sedative** ('sedətiv) *a.* **1.** having soothing or calming effect —*n.* **2.** sedative drug

sedentary ('sedənteri) *a.* **1.** done sitting down **2.** sitting much **3.** (of birds) not migratory

sedge (sej) *n.* plant like coarse grass growing

in swampy ground —**sedge warbler** European songbird having streaked brownish plumage with white eye stripes

sedilia (sə'dēlyə) *pl.n.* (*with sing. v.*) stone seats on south side of altar for priests

sediment ('sedimənt) *n.* **1.** matter which settles to the bottom of liquid **2.** matter deposited from water, ice or wind —**sedi'mentary** *a.*

sedition (si'dishən) *n.* speech or action threatening authority of a state —**se'ditious** *a.*

seduce (si'dyōōs, -'dōōs) *vt.* **1.** persuade to commit some (wrong) deed, *esp.* sexual intercourse **2.** tempt **3.** attract —**se'ducer** *n.* (**seductress** (si'duktris) *fem.*) —**seduction** (si'dukshən) *n.* —**seductive** (si'duktiv) *a.* **1.** alluring **2.** winning

sedulous ('sejələs) *a.* **1.** diligent **2.** industrious **3.** persevering, persistent —**se'dulity** *n.*

sedum ('sēdəm) *n.* rock plant

see[1] (sē) *vt.* **1.** perceive with eyes or mentally **2.** observe **3.** watch **4.** find out **5.** consider **6.** have experience of **7.** interview **8.** make sure **9.** accompany —*vi.* **10.** have power of sight **11.** consider **12.** understand (**saw, seen, 'seeing**) —**'seeing** *conj.* since, in view of the fact that

see[2] (sē) *n.* diocese, office or jurisdiction of bishop

seed (sēd) *n.* **1.** reproductive germs of plants **2.** one grain of this **3.** such grains saved or used for sowing **4.** origin **5.** sperm **6.** *obs.* offspring —*vt.* **7.** sow with seed **8.** arrange (draw for lawn tennis or other tournament) so that best players do not meet in early rounds —*vi.* **9.** produce seed —**'seedling** *n.* young plant raised from seed —**'seedy** *a.* **1.** shabby **2.** (of plant) at seed-producing stage **3.** *inf.* unwell, ill —**seed pearl** tiny pearl weighing less than a quarter of a grain

seek (sēk) *vt.* **1.** make search or inquiry for —*vi.* **2.** search (**sought, 'seeking**)

seem (sēm) *vi.* **1.** appear (to be or to do) **2.** look **3.** appear to one's judgment —**'seeming** *a.* apparent but not real —**'seemingly** *adv.*

seemly ('sēmli) *a.* becoming and proper —**'seemliness** *n.*

seen (sēn) *pp. of* SEE[1]

seep (sēp) *vi.* trickle through slowly, as water, ooze

seer (sēər) *n.* prophet

seersucker ('sēərsukər) *n.* light cotton fabric with slightly crinkled surface

seesaw ('sēsö) *n.* **1.** game in which children sit at opposite ends of plank supported in middle and swing up and down **2.** plank used for this —*vi.* **3.** move up and down

seethe (sēdh) *vi.* **1.** boil, foam **2.** be very agitated **3.** be in constant movement (as large crowd *etc.*) (**seethed, 'seething**)

segment ('segmənt) *n.* **1.** piece cut off **2.** section —*v.* ('segment) **3.** divide into segments —**seg'mental** *a.* —**segmen'tation** *n.*

segregate ('segrigāt) *vt.* set apart from the rest —**segre'gation** *n.*

seigneur (sā'nyər; *Fr.* se'nyœr) *n.* **1.** member of landed gentry in Canada **2.** feudal lord of the manor —**sei'gneurial** *a.*

seine (sān) *n.* type of large fishing net

seismic ('sīzmik) *a.* pert. to earthquakes —**'seismograph** *n.* instrument that records earthquakes (*also* **seis'mometer**) —**seismo'logic(al)** *a.* pert. to seismology —**seis'mologist** *n.* person versed in seismology —**seis'mology** *n.* science of earthquakes

seismo- *or before vowel* **seism-** (*comb. form*) earthquake, as in *seismology*

seize (sēz) *vt.* **1.** grasp **2.** lay hold of **3.** capture —*vi.* **4.** (of mechanical parts) stick tightly through overheating —**'seizable** *a.* —**'seizure** *n.* **1.** act of taking, *esp.* by warrant, as goods **2.** sudden onset of disease

seldom ('seldəm) *adv.* not often, rarely

select (si'lekt) *vt.* **1.** pick out, choose —*a.* **2.** choice, picked **3.** exclusive —**se'lection** *n.* —**se'lective** *a.* —**selec'tivity** *n.* —**se'lector** *n.*

selenium (si'lēniəm) *n. Chem.* metalloid element *Symbol* Se, at. wt. 79.0, at. no. 34 —**se'lenic** *a.*

self (self) *pron.* **1.** used reflexively or to express emphasis (*pl.* **selves**) —*a.* **2.** (of color) same throughout, uniform —*n.* **3.** one's own person or individuality (*pl.* **selves**) —**'selfish** *a.* **1.** concerned unduly over personal profit or pleasure **2.** lacking consideration for others **3.** greedy —**'selfishly** *adv.* —**'selfless** *a.* **1.** having no regard to self **2.** unselfish

self-abasement
self-absorbed
self-absorption
self-addressed
self-adhesive
self-appointed
self-appraisal
self-approbation
self-catering
self-centered
self-complacent
self-confessed
self-confidence
self-confident
self-contained
self-control
self-deception
self-defeating
self-defense
self-delusion
self-denial
self-doubt
self-engrossed
self-esteem
self-evident
self-explanatory
self-help
self-indulgence
self-indulgent
self-inflicted
self-instructed
self-justification
self-knowledge
self-pity
self-portrait
self-preservation
self-raised
self-realization
self-regard
self-reliance
self-reliant
self-reproach
self-restraint
self-righting
self-selection
self-set
self-supporting
self-taught

self- (*comb. form*) of oneself or itself. See the list above

self-abnegation *n.* denial of one's own interests

self-abuse *n.* **1.** misuse of one's own abilities *etc.* **2.** *euphemism for* **masturbation** (*see at* MASTURBATE)

self-aggrandizement *n.* act of increasing one's own power *etc.* —**self-aggrandizing** *a.*

self-assertion *n.* act of putting forward one's own opinions *etc., esp.* in aggressive manner —**self-asserting** *a.* —**self-assertive** *a.*

self-assurance *n.* confidence in validity *etc.* of one's own opinions *etc.* —**self-assured** *a.*

self-conscious *a.* **1.** unduly aware of oneself **2.** conscious of one's acts or states

self-determination *n.* the right of person or nation to decide for himself or itself

self-discipline *n.* disciplining of one's own feelings, desires *etc.* —**self-disciplined** *a.*

self-educated *a.* educated through one's own efforts without formal instruction

self-effacement *n.* act of making oneself, one's actions *etc.* inconspicuous —**self-effacing** *a.*

self-employed *a.* earning one's living in one's own business —**self-employment** *n.*

self-expression *n.* expression of one's own personality *etc.* as in painting *etc.* —**self-expressive** *a.*

self-government *n.* government of country *etc.* by its own people —**self-governed** *a.* —**self-governing** *a.*

selfheal (ˈselfhēl) *n.* any of several European herbaceous plants reputedly having healing powers

self-important *a.* having unduly high opinion of one's own importance *etc.* —**self-importance** *n.*

self-improvement *n.* improvement of one's status, education *etc.* by one's own efforts

self-induced *a.* induced by oneself or itself

self-interest *n.* **1.** one's personal interest or advantage **2.** act of pursuing one's own interest

self-made *a.* having achieved wealth, status *etc.* by one's own efforts

self-opinionated *a.* **1.** having unduly high regard for oneself or one's own opinions **2.** clinging stubbornly to one's own opinions

self-possessed *a.* calm, composed —**self-possession** *n.*

self-propelled *a.* (of vehicle) provided with its own source of tractive power

self-respect *n.* proper sense of one's own dignity and integrity

self-righteous *a.* smugly sure of one's own virtue

self-rising *a.* (of flour) having leavening agent and salt already added

self-sacrifice *n.* sacrifice of one's own desires *etc.* for sake of wellbeing of others —**self-sacrificing** *a.*

selfsame (ˈselfsām) *a.* very same

self-satisfied *a.* having or showing complacent satisfaction with oneself, one's own actions *etc.* —**self-satisfaction** *n.*

self-sealing *a.* **1.** (*esp.* of envelope) designed to become sealed by pressure only **2.** (of tire) capable of sealing itself after being pierced

self-seeking *n.* **1.** act of seeking one's own profit or interest —*a.* **2.** having exclusive preoccupation with one's own profit or interest —**self-seeker** *n.*

self-service *a./n.* (of) restaurant *etc.* where customers serve themselves

self-starter *n.* **1.** electric motor used to start internal-combustion engine **2.** switch that operates this motor

self-styled *a.* claiming to be of specified nature, profession *etc.*

self-sufficient *or* **self-sufficing** *a.* **1.** sufficient in itself **2.** relying on one's own powers

self-will *n.* **1.** obstinacy **2.** willfulness —**self-willed** *a.* headstrong

self-winding *a.* (of wrist watch) winding automatically

sell (sel) *vt.* **1.** hand over for a price **2.** stock, have for sale **3.** make (someone) accept **4.** *inf.* betray, cheat —*vi.* **5.** find purchasers (**sold, ˈselling**) —*n.* **6.** *inf.* hoax —**ˈseller** *n.* —**ˈsellout** *n.* **1.** disposing of completely by selling **2.** betrayal

seltzer (ˈseltsər) *n.* aerated mineral water

selvage *or* **selvedge** (ˈselvij) *n.* finished, nonfraying edge of cloth

selves (selvz) *n., pl. of* SELF

semantic (siˈmantik) *a.* relating to meaning of words or symbols —**seˈmantics** *pl.n.* (*with sing. v.*) study of linguistic meaning

semaphore (ˈseməfōr) *n.* **1.** post with movable arms for signaling **2.** system of signaling by human or mechanical arms

semblance (ˈsembləns) *n.* **1.** (false) appearance **2.** image, likeness

semen (ˈsēmən) *n.* fluid carrying sperm of male animals

semester (siˈmestər) *n.* **1.** period of six months **2.** either of two usu. 18-week periods of academic instruction —**semester hour** unit of academic credit

semi- (*comb. form*) half, partly, not completely, as in *semicircle*

semiannual (semiˈanyo͞oəl, semī-) *a.* **1.** occurring every half-year **2.** lasting for half a year —**semiˈannually** *adv.*

semicircle (ˈsemisərkəl) *n.* half of circle —**semiˈcircular** *a.* —**semicircular canal** *Anat.* any of three looped fluid-filled membranous tubes that comprise labyrinth of ear

semicolon (ˈsemikōlən) *n.* punctuation mark (;)

semiconductor (semikənˈduktər, semī-) *n.* **1.**

substance, as silicon, having electrical conductivity that increases with temperature 2. device, as transistor, dependent on properties of such substance

semidetached (semidi'tacht, semī-) *a./n.* (of) house joined to another on one side only

semifinal (semi'fīnəl) *n.* match, round *etc.* before final

Semillon (sāmi'yon) *n.* **1.** semisweet white wine **2.** grape used to make this wine

seminal ('seminəl) *a.* **1.** capable of developing **2.** influential, important **3.** rudimentary **4.** of semen or seed

seminar ('seminär) *n.* meeting of group (of students) for discussion

seminary ('semineri) *n.* **1.** college for priests **2.** finishing school for young women

Seminole ('seminōl) *n.* member of Amerindian people of Florida (*pl.* **-s, -nole**)

semiprecious (semi'preshəs, semī-) *a.* (of gemstones) having less value than precious stones

semiprofessional (semiprə'feshnəl, -shənəl; semī-) *a.* **1.** (of person) engaged in activity or sport part time but for pay **2.** (of activity or sport) engaged in by semiprofessionals **3.** of person whose activities are professional in some respects —*n.* **4.** semiprofessional person

semiskilled (semi'skild, semī-) *a.* partly skilled, trained but not for specialized work

Semite ('semīt) *n.* member of group of people now inhabiting the Middle East including Arabs and Jews —**Semitic** (si'mitik) *a.* **1.** of languages including Amharic, Arabic and Hebrew and speakers of these languages **2.** Jewish

semitone ('semitōn, 'semī-) *n. Mus.* difference in pitch between any two immediately adjacent keys on piano

semitrailer ('semitrālər, 'semī-) *n.* type of trailer that has wheels only at rear, front end being supported by towing vehicle

semivowel ('semivowəl) *n. Phonet.* vowel-like sound that acts like consonant, as (w) in *well* and (j), represented as *y*, in *yell* (*also* **glide**)

semolina (semə'lēnə) *n.* milled product of hard wheat used *esp.* for pasta

sempervivum (sempər'vīvəm) *n.* plant with ornamental rosettes of leaves

sempre ('semprā) *adv. Mus.* always; consistently

Sen. *or* **sen. 1.** senate **2.** senator **3.** senior

senate ('senit) *n.* **1.** upper council of state, university *etc.* **2.** (**S-**) upper house of U.S. Congress —'**senator** *n.* —**sena'torial** *a.*

send (send) *vt.* **1.** cause to go or be conveyed **2.** dispatch **3.** transmit (by radio) (**sent, 'sending**) —'**sendoff** *n. inf.* demonstration of good wishes to person about to set off on journey *etc.* —**send-up** *n.* parody or imitation —**send off 1.** cause to depart **2.** *Soccer, rugby etc.* (of referee) dismiss (player) from field of play for some offense —**send up** *sl.* **1.** send to prison **2.** make fun of, *esp.* by doing parody of

Seneca ('senikə) *n.* (member of) Iroquoian-speaking Amerindian people of upper New York state (*pl.* **Seneca, -s**)

Senegal (seni'gōl) *n.* country in Africa bounded north and northeast by Mauritania, east by Mali, south by Guinea and Guinea-Bissau and west by the Atlantic Ocean with The Gambia forming an enclave on that shore —**Senegalese** (senigə'lēz) *n./a.*

senescent (si'nesənt) *a.* **1.** growing old **2.** characteristic of old age —**se'nescence** *n.*

senile ('sēnīl) *a.* showing weakness of old age —**senility** (si'niliti) *n.*

senior ('sēnyər) *a.* **1.** superior in rank or standing **2.** older —*n.* **3.** superior **4.** elder person —**seni'ority** *n.*

senna ('senə) *n.* **1.** tropical plant **2.** its dried leaves or pods, used as laxative

señor (sā'nyōr; *Sp.* sā'nyor) *n.* Sp. title of respect, like Mr. (*pl.* **-s, -ñores** (*Sp.* -'nyorās)) —**se'ñora** *n.* Mrs. —**seño'rita** *n.* Miss

sensation (sen'sāshən) *n.* **1.** operation of sense, feeling, awareness **2.** excited feeling, state of excitement **3.** exciting event **4.** strong impression **5.** commotion —**sen'sational** *a.* **1.** producing great excitement **2.** melodramatic **3.** of perception by senses —**sen'sationalism** *n.* **1.** use of sensational language *etc.* to arouse intense emotional excitement **2.** doctrine that sensations are basis of all knowledge

sense (sens) *n.* **1.** any of bodily faculties of perception or feeling **2.** sensitiveness of any or all of these faculties **3.** ability to perceive, mental alertness **4.** consciousness **5.** meaning **6.** coherence, intelligible meaning **7.** sound practical judgment —*vt.* **8.** perceive **9.** understand —'**senseless** *a.* —'**senselessly** *adv.* —**sense organ** structure in animals that is specialized for receiving external stimuli and transmitting them to brain

sensible ('sensibəl) *a.* **1.** reasonable **2.** perceptible by senses **3.** aware, mindful **4.** considerable, appreciable —**sensi'bility** *n.* ability to feel, *esp.* emotional or moral feelings —'**sensibly** *adv.*

sensitive ('sensitiv) *a.* **1.** open to, acutely affected by, external impressions **2.** easily affected or altered **3.** easily upset by criticism **4.** responsive to slight changes —'**sensitively** *adv.* —**sensi'tivity** *or* '**sensitiveness** *n.* —'**sensitize** *vt.* make sensitive, *esp.* make (photographic film *etc.*) sensitive to light

sensor ('sensōr, 'sensər) *n.* device that responds to stimulus

sensory ('sensəri) *or* **sensorial** (sen'sōriəl) *a.* relating to organs, operation, of senses —**sensory deprivation** extended isolation accompanied by exclusion of sensory input such as light, sound and tactile impulses

sensual ('senchōōəl) *a.* **1.** of senses only and not of mind **2.** given to pursuit of pleasures of sense **3.** self-indulgent **4.** licentious —'**sensualism** *n.* —'**sensualist** *n.* —**sensu'ality** *n.*

sensuous ('senchōōəs) *a.* stimulating, or apprehended by senses, *esp.* in aesthetic manner

sent (sent) *pt./pp. of* SEND

sentence ('sentəns) *n.* **1.** combination of words, which is complete as expressing a thought **2.** judgment passed on criminal by court or judge —*vt.* **3.** pass sentence on, condemn —**sen'tential** *a.* of sentence —**sen'tentious** *a.* **1.** full of axioms and maxims **2.** pithy **3.** pompously moralizing —**sen'tentiously** *adv.* —**sen'tentiousness** *n.*

sentient ('senchiənt, -chənt; 'sentiənt) *a.* **1.** capable of feeling **2.** feeling **3.** thinking —'**sentience** *or* '**sentiency** *n.*

sentiment ('sentimənt) *n.* **1.** tendency to be moved by feeling rather than reason **2.** verbal expression of feeling **3.** mental feeling, emotion **4.** opinion —**senti'mental** *a.* **1.** given to indulgence in sentiment and in its expression **2.** weak **3.** of sentiment —**senti'mentalist** *n.* —**sentimen'tality** *n.* —**senti'mentalize** *v.*

sentinel ('sentinəl) *n.* sentry

sentry ('sentri) *n.* soldier on watch —**sentry box** small shelter in which sentry may stand to be sheltered from weather

sepal ('sēpəl, 'sepəl) *n.* leaf or division of the calyx of a flower

separate ('sepərāt) *vt.* **1.** part **2.** divide **3.** sever **4.** put apart **5.** occupy place between —*vi.* **6.** withdraw, become parted —*a.* ('seprit, 'sepərit) **7.** disconnected, apart **8.** distinct, individual —'**separable** *a.* —**separately** ('sepritli, 'sepəritli) *adv.* —**sepa'ration** *n.* **1.** disconnection **2.** *Law* living apart of married people without divorce —'**separatism** *n.* —'**separatist** *n.* person who advocates secession from organization, union *etc.* —'**separator** *n.* **1.** that which separates **2.** apparatus for separating cream from milk —**separate school C** school for a large religious minority

Sephardi (sə'fārdi) *n.* **1.** Spanish or Portuguese Jew or descendant of Sephardim **2.** member of Ashkenazic Hasidim who use part of the Sephardic liturgy (*pl.* **Se'phardim**)

sepia ('sēpiə) *n.* **1.** reddish-brown pigment made from a fluid secreted by the cuttlefish —*a.* **2.** of this color

sepoy ('sēpoi) *n.* formerly, Indian soldier in service of Brit.

sepsis ('sepsis) *n.* presence of pus-forming bacteria in body

Sept. September

September (sep'tembər) *n.* 9th month

septennial (sep'teniəl) *a.* lasting, occurring every seven years

septet (sep'tet) *n.* **1.** music for seven instruments or voices **2.** group of seven performers

septic ('septik) *a.* **1.** of, caused by, sepsis **2.** (of wound) infected —**septicemia** (septi'sēmiə) *n.* blood poisoning —**septic tank** tank for containing sewage to be decomposed by anaerobic bacteria

septuagenarian (septyōōəji'neriən, septōōə-) *a.* **1.** aged between seventy and seventy-nine —*n.* **2.** person of this age

Septuagesima (septōōə'jesimə) *n.* third Sunday before Lent

septum ('septəm) *n. Biol., anat.* dividing partition between two tissues or cavities (*pl.* **-ta** (-tə))

septuple (sep'tyōō'pəl, -'tōō-; 'septəpəl) *a.* **1.** seven times as much or many **2.** consisting of seven parts or members —*vt.* **3.** multiply by seven —**sep'tuplicate** *n./a.*

sepulcher ('sepəlkər) *n.* tomb, burial vault —**se'pulchral** *a.* **1.** of burial, or the grave **2.** mournful **3.** gloomy —'**sepulture** *n.* burial

sequel ('sēkwəl) *n.* **1.** consequence **2.** continuation, *eg* of story

sequence ('sēkwəns) *n.* **1.** arrangement of things in successive order **2.** section, episode of film story —'**sequent** *or* **se'quential** *a.*

sequester (si'kwestər) *vt.* **1.** separate **2.** seclude **3.** put aside —**sequestrate** ('sēkwəstrāt, 'sek-; si'kwes-) *vt.* **1.** confiscate **2.** divert or appropriate income of (property) to satisfy claims against its owner —**seques'tration** *n.*

sequin ('sēkwin) *n.* **1.** small ornamental shiny disk on dresses *etc.* **2.** formerly, Venetian gold coin

sequoia (si'kwoiə) *n.* giant Californian coniferous tree

seraglio (se'ralyō, -'räl-) *or* **serail** (sə'rī) *n.* harem, palace, of Turkish sultan (*pl.* **-s**)

seraph ('serəf) *n.* member of highest order of angels (*pl.* **-s, -aphim** (-əfim)) —**se'raphic** *a.*

Serbian ('sərbiən) *a.* **1.** of Serbia, its people or their dialect of Serbo-Croatian —*n.* **2.** dialect of Serbo-Croatian spoken in Serbia **3.** native or inhabitant of Serbia (*also* **Serb**) —**Serbo-Croatian** *or* **Serbo-Croat** (-'krōat) *n.* **1.** chief official language of Yugoslavia —*a.* **2.** of this language which is written in the Cyrillic alphabet

serenade (seri'nād) *n.* **1.** sentimental piece of music or song of type addressed to woman by lover, *esp.* at evening —*v.* **2.** sing serenade (to)

serendipity (serən'dipiti) *n.* faculty of making fortunate discoveries by accident

serene (si'rēn) *a.* **1.** calm, tranquil **2.** unclouded **3.** quiet, placid —**se'renely** *adv.* —**serenity** (si'reniti) *n.*

serf (sərf) *n.* one of class of medieval laborers bound to, and transferred with, land —'**serfdom** *or* '**serfhood** *n.*

serge (sərj) *n.* strong hard-wearing twilled worsted fabric

sergeant (ˈsärjənt) *n.* **1.** noncommissioned officer in army, air force or marine corps **2.** police officer below captain —**sergeant major** title of three highest noncommissioned officers in army, air force and marine corps: sergeant major of the army *etc.* command sergeant major and sergeant major

series (ˈsēərēz) *n.* **1.** sequence **2.** set (*eg* of radio, TV programs with same characters, setting, but different stories) (*pl.* **-ries**) —ˈ**serial** *n.* **1.** story or play produced in successive episodes or installments **2.** periodical publication —*a.* **3.** of, in or forming a series —ˈ**serialize** *vt.* publish, present as serial —**seriatim** (sēəriˈātim, -ˈatim) *adv.* one after another

serif (ˈserif) *n. Print.* small line finishing off stroke of letter

seriocomic (sēəriōˈkomik) *a.* mixing serious and comic elements —**serioˈcomically** *adv.*

serious (ˈsēəriəs) *a.* **1.** thoughtful **2.** earnest, sincere **3.** of importance **4.** giving cause for concern —ˈ**seriously** *adv.*

sermon (ˈsərmən) *n.* **1.** discourse of religious instruction or exhortation spoken or read from pulpit **2.** any similar discourse —ˈ**sermonize** *vi.* **1.** talk like preacher **2.** compose sermons

serotonin (sēərəˈtōnin) *n.* compound found in many venoms and many tissues of the human body

serpent (ˈsərpənt) *n. Lit.* snake —ˈ**serpentine** *a.* **1.** like, shaped like, serpent —*n.* **2.** any of several kinds of green-to-black rock

serrate (ˈserāt, səˈrāt) *a.* having notched, sawlike edge —**serˈrated** *a.* —**serˈration** *n.*

serried (ˈserid) *a.* in close order, shoulder to shoulder

serum (ˈsēərəm) *n.* watery animal fluid, *esp.* thin part of blood as used for inoculation or vaccination (*pl.* **-s, -ra** (-rə)) —**seˈrosity** *n.* —ˈ**serous** *a.* of or producing serum —**serum sickness** allergic reaction to injected animal serums used for treatment or immunization

serval (ˈsərvəl) *n.* feline Afr. mammal

serve (sərv) *vt.* **1.** work for, under **2.** attend to (customers) in store *etc.* **3.** provide **4.** provide (guests) with (food *etc.*) **5.** present (food *etc.*) in particular way **6.** provide with regular supply of **7.** pay homage to **8.** go through (period of service *etc.*) **9.** suit **10.** *Tennis etc.* put (ball) into play —*vi.* **11.** be member of military unit —*n.* **12.** *Tennis etc.* act of serving ball —ˈ**servant** *n.* personal or domestic attendant —ˈ**service** *n.* **1.** the act of serving, helping, assisting **2.** system organized to provide for needs of public **3.** maintenance of vehicle **4.** use **5.** readiness, availability for use **6.** set of dishes *etc.* **7.** form, session, of public worship —*pl.* **8.** armed forces —*vt.* **9.** overhaul —ˈ**serviceable** *a.* **1.** in working order, usable **2.** durable —ˈ**serving** *n.* portion of food or drink —**service charge** *or* **fee** percentage of bill added to total to pay for service —ˈ**serviceman** *n.* **1.** member of the armed forces **2.** service-station attendant —ˈ**serviceperson** *n.* —**service station** place supplying fuel, oil, maintenance for motor vehicles (*also* **filling station, gas station**) —**service tree** Eurasian rosaceous tree with white flowers and brown edible apple-like fruits

servile (ˈsərvil, -vīl) *a.* **1.** without independence **2.** cringing, fawning **3.** menial —**serˈvility** *n.*

servitude (ˈsərvityōōd, -tōōd) *n.* bondage, slavery

servomechanism (ˈsərvōmekənizəm) *n.* device for converting small mechanical force into larger force, *esp.* in steering mechanisms

servomotor (ˈsərvōmōtər) *n.* motor that supplies power to servomechanism

sesame (ˈsesəmi) *n.* E Indian annual plant with seeds used as flavoring and for making oil

sesqui- (*comb. form*) one and a half, as in *sesquicentennial*

sessile (ˈsesīl) *a.* **1.** (of flowers or leaves) having no stalk **2.** (of animals such as barnacle) permanently attached —**sessility** (seˈsiliti) *n.*

session (ˈseshən) *n.* **1.** meeting of court *etc.* **2.** assembly **3.** continuous series of such meetings **4.** any period devoted to an activity

sestet (seˈstet) *n.* **1.** *Prosody* last six lines of sonnet **2.** *see* SEXTET (sense 1)

set (set) *vt.* **1.** put or place in specified position or condition **2.** cause to sit **3.** fix **4.** point **5.** put up **6.** make ready **7.** establish **8.** prescribe, allot **9.** put to music **10.** (of hair) arrange while wet, so that it dries in position —*vi.* **11.** become firm or fixed **12.** (of sun) go down **13.** have direction (**set, ˈsetting**) —*a.* **14.** fixed, established **15.** deliberate **16.** formal **17.** arranged beforehand **18.** unvarying —*n.* **19.** act or state of being set **20.** bearing, posture **21.** *Rad., T.V.* complete apparatus for reception or transmission **22.** *Theat., cine.* organized settings and equipment to form ensemble of scene **23.** number of things, persons associated as being similar, complementary or used together **24.** *Math.* group of numbers, objects *etc.* with at least one common property —ˈ**setback** *n.* anything that hinders or impedes —**set piece 1.** work of literature *etc.* intended to create impressive effect **2.** display of fireworks —ˈ**setscrew** *n.* screw that fits into coupling, cam *etc.* and prevents motion of part relative to shaft on which it is mounted —**set-to** *n. inf.* brief disagreement or fight —ˈ**setup** *n.* **1.** position **2.** organization —**set to 1.** begin working **2.** start fighting —**set up** establish

sett *or* **set** (set) *n.* badger's burrow

settee (seˈtē) *n.* **1.** long seat with back support **2.** sofa

setter (ˈsetər) *n.* any of various breeds of sporting dog

setting (ˈseting) *n.* **1.** background **2.** surroundings **3.** scenery and other stage accessories **4.** act of fixing **5.** decorative metalwork holding precious stone *etc.* in position **6.** tableware and flatware for (single place at) table **7.** descending below horizon of sun **8.** music for song

settle[1] (ˈsetəl) *vt.* **1.** arrange, put in order **2.** establish, make firm or secure **3.** make quiet or calm **4.** decide upon **5.** end (dispute *etc.*) **6.** pay **7.** bestow (property) by legal deed —*vi.* **8.** come to rest **9.** subside and become firm or compact **10.** become clear **11.** take up residence **12.** sink to bottom **13.** come to agreement —ˈ**settlement** *n.* **1.** act of settling **2.** place newly inhabited **3.** money bestowed legally **4.** subsidence (of building) —ˈ**settler** *n.* colonist

settle[2] (ˈsetəl) *n.* seat, usu. made of wood with high back and arms

seven (ˈsevən) *a./n.* cardinal number, next after six —**sevenˈteen** *a./n.* ten and seven —ˈ**seventh** *a.* ordinal number of seven —ˈ**seventy** *a./n.* ten times seven —**seven seas** all the oceans of the world —**seventh heaven** **1.** final state of eternal bliss **2.** state of supreme happiness

sever (ˈsevər) *v.* **1.** divide —*vt.* **2.** cut off —ˈ**severance** *n.* —**severance pay** compensation paid by a firm to employee for loss of employment

several (ˈsevrəl) *a.* **1.** some, a few **2.** separate; individual **3.** various **4.** different —*pron.* **5.** indefinite small number —ˈ**severally** *adv.* apart from others

severe (siˈvēər) *a.* **1.** strict; rigorous **2.** hard to do **3.** harsh **4.** austere **5.** extreme —**seˈverely** *adv.* —**severity** (siˈveriti) *n.*

seviche (səˈvēchā) *n.* cubes of fish marinated in lime or lemon juice served as accompaniment or appetizer to main course or snack

sew (sō) *v.* **1.** join (pieces of fabric *etc.*) with needle and thread —*vt.* **2.** make by sewing (**sewed** *pt.*, **sewed, sewn** *pp.*, ˈ**sewing** *pr.p.*) —ˈ**sewing** *n.*

sewage (ˈso͞oij) *n.* refuse, waste matter, excrement conveyed in sewer —ˈ**sewer** *n.* underground drain to remove waste water and refuse —ˈ**sewerage** *n.* **1.** arrangement of sewers **2.** sewage —**sewage farm** place where sewage is treated, *esp.* for use as manure

sex (seks) *n.* **1.** state of being male or female **2.** males or females collectively **3.** sexual intercourse —*a.* **4.** concerning sex —*vt.* **5.** ascertain sex of —ˈ**sexism** *n.* discrimination on basis of sex —ˈ**sexist** *n./a.* —ˈ**sexless** *a.* **1.** having no sexual differentiation **2.** having no sexual appeal or desires —ˈ**sexual** *a.* —ˈ**sexually** *adv.* —ˈ**sexy** *a. inf.* provoking or intended to provoke sexual interest —**sex appeal** quality of attracting opposite sex —**sex change** change of sex, *esp.* involving medical or surgical treatment to alter sexual characteristics to those of opposite sex —**sex chromosome** chromosome determining sex of animals —**sexual intercourse** act in which male's penis is inserted into female's vagina

sex- (*comb. form*) six, as in *sextet*

sexagenarian (seksəjiˈneriən) *a.* **1.** aged between sixty and sixty-nine —*n.* **2.** person of this age

Sexagesima (seksəˈjesimə) *n.* second Sunday before Lent

sextant (ˈsekstənt) *n.* navigator's instrument for measuring elevations of heavenly body *etc.*

sextet (seksˈtet) *n.* **1.** music for six instruments or voices **2.** group of six performers

sexton (ˈsekstən) *n.* official in charge of a church, oft. acting as grave digger

sextuple (seksˈtyo͞opəl, -ˈto͞o-; ˈsekstəpəl) *n.* **1.** quantity or number six times as great as another —*a.* **2.** six times as much or as many **3.** consisting of six parts or members —**sexˈtuplet** *n.* **1.** one of six offspring born at one birth **2.** *Mus.* group of six notes played in time value of four

Seychelles (sāˈshelz, sāˈshel) *pl.n.* country lying in the Indian Ocean north of Madagascar comprising 112 islands and islets

SF *or* **sf** science fiction

sforzando (sförˈtsändō) *Mus. a./adv.* **1.** to be played with emphasis —*n.* **2.** symbol, mark *etc.* indicating this

Sgt. Sergeant

sh (sh) *interj.* exclamation to request silence or quiet

shabby (ˈshabi) *a.* **1.** faded, worn, ragged **2.** poorly dressed **3.** mean, dishonorable **4.** dirty —ˈ**shabbily** *adv.* —ˈ**shabbiness** *n.*

shack (shak) *n.* rough hut —**shack up** (*usu. with* with) *sl.* live (*esp.* with lover)

shackle (ˈshakəl) *n.* (*oft. pl.*) **1.** metal ring or fastening for prisoner's wrist or ankle **2.** anything that confines —*vt.* **3.** fasten with shackles **4.** hamper

shad (shad) *n.* any of several important food fishes of N Amer. and Europe resembling herring

shade (shād) *n.* **1.** partial darkness **2.** shelter, place sheltered from light, heat *etc.* **3.** darker part of anything **4.** depth of color **5.** tinge **6.** ghost **7.** screen **8.** anything used to screen **9.** window blind —*pl.* **10.** *sl.* sunglasses —*vt.* **11.** screen from light, darken **12.** represent (shades) in (drawing) —ˈ**shady** *a.* **1.** shielded from sun **2.** dim **3.** dubious **4.** dishonest **5.** dishonorable

shadow (ˈshadō) *n.* **1.** dark figure projected

by anything that intercepts rays of light **2.** patch of shade **3.** slight trace **4.** indistinct image **5.** gloom **6.** inseparable companion —*vt.* **7.** cast shadow over **8.** follow and watch closely —**'shadowy** *a.*

shaft (shaft) *n.* **1.** straight rod, stem **2.** handle **3.** arrow **4.** ray, beam (of light) **5.** revolving rod for transmitting power **6.** one of the bars between which horse is harnessed **7.** entrance boring of mine

shag[1] (shag) *n.* **1.** matted wool or hair **2.** long-napped cloth **3.** coarse shredded tobacco —**'shaggy** *a.* **1.** covered with rough hair or wool **2.** tousled, unkempt

shag[2] (shag) *n.* any of various varieties of cormorant

shagreen (sha'grēn) *n.* **1.** rough skin of certain sharks and rays **2.** rough grainy leather made from certain animal hides

shah (shä) *n.* formerly, ruler of Iran

Shahaptian (shə'haptiən) *n.* Amerindian linguistic family of Oregon, Washington and Idaho

shake (shāk) *v.* **1.** (cause to) move with quick vibrations **2.** grasp the hand (of another) in greeting —*vi.* **3.** sway; totter —*vt.* **4.** upset **5.** wave, brandish (**shook, 'shaken**) —*n.* **6.** act of shaking **7.** vibration **8.** jolt **9.** *inf.* short period of time, jiffy —**'shaker** *n.* **1.** person or thing that shakes **2.** container from which condiment is shaken **3.** container in which ingredients of alcoholic drinks are shaken together —**'shakily** *adv.* —**'shaky** *a.* unsteady, insecure

shale (shāl) *n.* flaky, sedimentary rock

shall (shal; *unstressed* shəl) *v. aux.* makes compound tenses or moods to express obligation, command, condition or intention (**should** *pt.*)

shallot (shə'lot) *n.* kind of small onion

shallow ('shalō) *a.* **1.** not deep **2.** having little depth of water **3.** superficial **4.** not sincere —*n.* **5.** shallow place —**'shallowness** *n.*

shalom aleichem ('shōləm ə'lākəm) *Hebrew* peace be to you: used by Jews as greeting or farewell (*oft. also* **shalom** (shä'lōm))

sham (sham) *a./n.* **1.** imitation, counterfeit —*vi.* **2.** pretend —*v.* **3.** feign (**-mm-**)

shaman ('shämən) *n.* **1.** priest of shamanism **2.** medicine man of similar religion (*pl.* **-s**) —**'shamanism** *n.* religion of certain peoples of northern Asia, based on belief in good and evil spirits who can be controlled only by shamans

shamble ('shambəl) *vi.* walk in shuffling, awkward way

shambles ('shambəlz) *pl.n.* (*with sing. v.*) messy, disorderly thing or place

shame (shām) *n.* **1.** emotion caused by consciousness of guilt or dishonor in one's conduct or state **2.** cause of disgrace **3.** ignominy **4.** pity, hard luck —*vt.* **5.** cause to feel shame **6.** disgrace **7.** force by shame —**'shameful** *a.* disgraceful —**'shamefully** *adv.* —**'shameless** *a.* **1.** with no sense of shame **2.** indecent —**'shame'faced** *a.* ashamed

shammy ('shami) *n. see* CHAMOIS (sense 2)

shampoo (sham'pōō) *n.* **1.** any of various preparations of liquid detergent for washing hair, carpets *etc.* **2.** this process —*vt.* **3.** use shampoo to wash

shamrock ('shamrok) *n.* any three-leaved plant used as an Irish emblem

shamus ('shäməs, 'shāməs) *n. inf.* **1.** private detective **2.** caretaker of a synagogue

shandygaff ('shandigaf) *n.* mixed drink, *esp.* beer diluted with soft drink

shanghai (shang'hī) *vt.* force, trick (someone) into doing something

Shangri La ('shranggri 'lä) a place where life approaches perfection

shank (shangk) *n.* **1.** lower leg **2.** tibia **3.** stem of thing

shantung (shan'tung) *n.* soft, natural Chinese silk

shanty[1] ('shanti) *n.* **1.** temporary wooden building **2.** crude dwelling

shanty[2] ('shanti) *n.* sailor's song with chorus

shape (shāp) *n.* **1.** external form or appearance **2.** mold, pattern **3.** *inf.* condition, *esp.* of physical fitness —*vt.* **4.** form, mold, fashion, make —*vi.* **5.** develop (**shaped, 'shaping**) —**'shapeless** *a.* —**'shapely** *a.* well-proportioned

SHAPE (shāp) Supreme Headquarters Allied Powers Europe

shard (shärd) *or* **sherd** *n.* broken fragment, *esp.* of earthenware

share[1] (shāər) *n.* **1.** portion, quota, lot **2.** unit of ownership in public company —*v.* **3.** give, take a share (of) **4.** join with others in doing, using (something)

share[2] (shāər) *n.* blade of plow

shark (shärk) *n.* **1.** large usu. predatory sea fish **2.** person who cheats others

sharkskin ('shärkskin) *n.* stiff rayon fabric

sharp (shärp) *a.* **1.** having keen cutting edge or fine point **2.** keen **3.** not gradual or gentle **4.** brisk **5.** clever **6.** harsh **7.** dealing cleverly but unfairly **8.** shrill **9.** strongly marked, *esp.* in outline —*adv.* **10.** promptly —*n.* **11.** *Mus.* note half a tone above natural pitch **12.** *sl.* cheat, swindler —**'sharpen** *vt.* make sharp —**'sharper** *n.* person who cheats or swindles —**'sharply** *adv.* —**'sharpness** *n.* —**sharp practice** dishonest dealings —**sharp-set** *a.* **1.** set to give acute cutting angle **2.** keenly hungry —**'sharpshooter** *n.* marksman —**sharp-witted** *a.* having or showing keen intelligence

shatter ('shatər) *v.* **1.** break in pieces —*vt.* **2.** ruin (plans *etc.*) **3.** disturb (person) greatly

shave (shāv) *v.* **1.** cut close (*esp.* hair of face or head) —*vt.* **2.** pare away **3.** graze **4.** reduce (**shaved, 'shaven, 'shaving**) —*n.* **5.** shaving —**'shaver** *n.* **1.** person or thing that shaves **2.**

electrical implement for shaving —**'shavings** *pl.n.* parings —**close** *or* **near shave** narrow escape

Shavian ('shāviən) *a.* **1.** of or like George Bernard Shaw, his works, ideas *etc.* —*n.* **2.** admirer of Shaw or his works

shawl (shöl) *n.* piece of fabric to cover woman's shoulders or wrap baby

Shawnee (shö'nē) *n.* **1.** member of Amerindian people orig. of the central Ohio valley (*pl.* **-ee, -s**) **2.** language of this people

she (shē) *pron.* 3rd person singular feminine pronoun

sheaf (shēf) *n.* **1.** bundle, *esp.* corn **2.** loose leaves of paper (*pl.* **sheaves**)

shear (shēər) *vt.* **1.** clip hair, wool from **2.** cut (through) **3.** fracture (**sheared** *pt.*, **shorn, sheared** *pp.*, **'shearing** *pr.p.*) —**'shearer** *n.* —**shears** *pl.n.* **1.** large pair of scissors **2.** any of various analogous cutting instruments

shearwater ('shēərwötər) *n.* any of various sea birds having long wings and a hooked bill

sheath (shēth) *n.* **1.** close-fitting cover, *esp.* for knife or sword **2.** enclosing structure of body or plant part **3.** close-fitting dress (*pl.* **sheaths** (shēdhz)) —**sheathe** *vt.* put into sheath

sheave (shēv) *n.* wheel with grooved rim, *esp.* one used as pulley

sheaves (shēvz) *n., pl. of* SHEAF

shebang (shi'bang) *n. sl.* situation, matter (*esp. in* **the whole shebang**)

shebeen *or* **shebean** (shə'bēn) *n.* **1.** *Irish, Scot.*, **SA** place where alcohol is sold illegally **2.** in S Afr., place where Black Afr. men engage in social drinking

shed[1] (shed) *n.* roofed shelter used as store or workshop

shed[2] (shed) *v.* **1.** (cause to) pour forth (*eg* tears, blood) —*vt.* **2.** cast off (**shed, 'shedding**)

sheen (shēn) *n.* gloss —**'sheeny** *a.*

sheep (shēp) *n.* ruminant animal bred for wool and meat (*pl.* **sheep**) —**'sheepish** *a.* embarrassed, shy —**sheep-dip** *n.* (deep trough containing) solution in which sheep are immersed to kill vermin and germs in fleece —**'sheepdog** *n.* any of various breeds of dog, *orig.* for herding sheep —**'sheepfold** *n.* pen or enclosure for sheep —**'sheepshank** *n.* knot *etc.* made in rope to shorten it temporarily

sheer[1] (shēər) *a.* **1.** perpendicular **2.** (of material) very fine, transparent **3.** absolute, unmitigated

sheer[2] (shēər) *vi.* deviate from course, swerve, turn aside

sheet[1] (shēt) *n.* **1.** broad length of fabric to cover bed **2.** broad piece of any thin material **3.** large expanse —*vt.* **4.** cover with sheet —**sheet music** printed copy of short composition or piece

sheet[2] (shēt) *n.* rope fastened in corner of sail —**sheet anchor** large anchor for emergency

Sheffield plate ('shefēld) objects made by fusing a thin sheet of silver to a thin sheet of copper

shegetz ('shāgits) *n.* a male goy

sheikh *or* **sheik** (shēk, shāk) *n.* Arab chief

shekel ('shekəl) *n.* **1.** Hebrew weight and silver coin **2.** (*oft. pl.*) *inf.* money, cash

shelf (shelf) *n.* **1.** board fixed horizontally (on wall *etc.*) for holding things **2.** ledge (*pl.* **shelves**) —**shelf life** length of time packaged food *etc.* will last without deteriorating

shell (shel) *n.* **1.** hard outer case (*esp.* of egg, nut *etc.*) **2.** husk **3.** explosive projectile **4.** outer part of structure left when interior is removed —*vt.* **5.** take shell from **6.** take out of shell **7.** fire at with shells —**'shellfish** *n.* any edible water animal with a shell —**shell shock** *see* **combat fatigue** *at* COMBAT —**shell out** *inf.* pay up

shellac (shə'lak) *n.* **1.** resin usu. produced in thin plates for use as varnish —*vt.* **2.** coat with shellac (**-'lacked, -'lacking**)

shelter ('sheltər) *n.* **1.** place, structure giving protection **2.** protection **3.** refuge; haven —*vt.* **4.** give protection to **5.** act as shelter for —*vi.* **6.** take shelter

shelve (shelv) *vt.* **1.** put on a shelf **2.** put off, defer indefinitely **3.** cease to employ —*vi.* **4.** slope gradually —**'shelving** *n.* **1.** material for making shelves **2.** set of shelves

shelves (shelvz) *n., pl. of* SHELF

shenanigan (shi'nanigən) *n. sl.* **1.** frolicking **2.** act of playing tricks *etc.*

shepherd ('shepərd) *n.* **1.** man who tends sheep (**'shepherdess** *fem.*) —*vt.* **2.** guide, watch over —**shepherd's-purse** *n.* plant with white flowers

sherbet ('shərbət) *n.* fruit-flavored frozen dessert

sherd (shərd) *n. see* SHARD

sheriff ('sherif) *n.* **1.** law enforcement officer **2.** **C** municipal officer who enforces court orders *etc.* —**'sheriffdom** *n.*

Sherpa ('shərpə) *n.* member of a Tibetan people (*pl.* **-s, 'Sherpa**)

sherry ('sheri) *n.* fortified wine

Shetland pony ('shetlənd) very small sturdy breed of pony

shewbread *or* **showbread** ('shōbred) *n.* consecrated unleavened bread formerly placed in Tabernacle on Sabbath

shield (shēld) *n.* **1.** piece of armor carried on arm **2.** any protection used to stop blows, missiles *etc.* **3.** any protective device **4.** sports trophy —*vt.* **5.** cover, protect

shift (shift) *v.* **1.** (cause to) move, change position —*n.* **2.** relay of workers **3.** time of their working **4.** evasion **5.** expedient **6.** removal **7.** woman's underskirt or dress —**'shiftiness** *n.* —**'shiftless** *a.* lacking in resource or character —**'shifty** *a.* **1.** evasive **2.** of dubious character

shikse (ˈshiksə) *n.* a female goy

shillelagh *or* **shillala** (shəˈlāli) *n.* in Ireland, cudgel

shilling (ˈshiling) *n.* **1.** former Brit. coin, now 5p **2.** monetary unit in various countries

shilly-shally (ˈshilishali) *vi.* **1.** waver —*n.* **2.** wavering, indecision

shim (shim) *n.* **1.** thin washer used to adjust clearance for gears *etc.* —*vt.* **2.** modify clearance on (gear *etc.*) by use of shims (**-mm-**)

shimmer (ˈshimər) *vi.* **1.** shine with quivering light —*n.* **2.** such light **3.** glimmer

shimmy (ˈshimi) *n.* **1.** Amer. ragtime dance with much shaking of hips and shoulders **2.** abnormal wobbling motion in motor vehicle

shin (shin) *n.* **1.** front of lower leg —*v.* **2.** climb with arms and legs —*vt.* **3.** kick on shin (**-nn-**) —ˈ**shinˈbone** *n.* tibia

shindig (ˈshindig) *or* **shindy** (ˈshindi) *n. inf.* row; noisy disturbance

shine (shīn) *vi.* **1.** give out, reflect light **2.** perform very well, excel —*vt.* **3.** cause to shine by polishing (**shone, ˈshining**) —*n.* **4.** brightness, luster **5.** polishing —ˈ**shiner** *n.* **1.** something that shines, such as polishing device **2.** small N Amer. freshwater cyprinid fish **3.** *inf.* black eye —ˈ**shiny** *a.*

shingle[1] (ˈshinggəl) *n.* **1.** wooden roof tile —*vt.* **2.** cover with shingles

shingle[2] (ˈshinggəl) *n.* mass of pebbles

shingles (ˈshinggəlz) *n.* disease causing inflammation along a nerve

Shinto (ˈshintō) *n.* native Japanese religion characterized by the veneration of nature and of ancestors —ˈ**Shintoism** *n.*

ship (ship) *n.* **1.** large sea-going vessel —*vt.* **2.** put on or send by ship —*vi.* **3.** embark **4.** take service in ship (**-pp-**) —ˈ**shipment** *n.* **1.** act of shipping **2.** goods shipped —ˈ**shipper** *n.* company *etc.* in business of shipping freight —ˈ**shipping** *n.* **1.** freight transport business **2.** ships collectively —ˈ**shipboard** *a.* taking place, used, or intended for use aboard ship —ˈ**shipmate** *n.* sailor who serves on same ship as another —ˈ**shipˈshape** *a.* orderly, trim —ˈ**shipwreck** *n.* **1.** destruction of ship through storm, collision *etc.* —*vt.* **2.** cause to undergo shipwreck —ˈ**shipwright** *n.* artisan skilled in tasks required to build vessels —ˈ**shipyard** *n.* place for building and repair of ships

-ship (*comb. form*) **1.** state, condition, as in *fellowship* **2.** rank, office, position, as in *lordship* **3.** craft, skill, as in *scholarship*

shire horse (ˈshīər) large heavy breed of carthorse

shirk (shərk) *vt.* evade, try to avoid (duty *etc.*)

shirr (shər) *vt.* **1.** gather (fabric) into parallel rows —*n.* **2.** series of gathered rows decorating dress *etc.*

shirt (shərt) *n.* garment for upper part of body —ˈ**shirty** *a. sl.* annoyed —**shirt-tail** *n.* part of shirt that extends below waist —ˈ**shirtwaist** *n.* woman's garment with bodice resembling shirt

shish kebab (shish) *see* KABOB

shiver[1] (ˈshivər) *vi.* **1.** tremble, usu. with cold or fear; shudder; vibrate —*n.* **2.** act, state of shivering

shiver[2] (ˈshivər) *v.* **1.** break in pieces —*n.* **2.** splinter

shlemiel (shləˈmēl) *n. inf.* clumsy or unlucky person

shlep (shlep) *vt.* **1.** drag, carry (**-pp-**) —*n.* **2.** unkempt person **3.** petty thief **4.** hobo, bum

shlock (shlok) *n. inf.* poor-quality article, junk, trash

shmalz (shmōlts, shmolts) *inf. n.* **1.** excessive sentimentality **2.** rendered chicken fat —*vi.* **3.** convey inappropriate emotion —*a.* **4.** corny, mawkish, trite

shmeer (shmēər) *inf. n.* **1.** bribe **2.** the entire deal —*vt.* **3.** spread, smear **4.** bribe

shmoos (shmo͞os) *inf. n.* **1.** aimless, friendly chat —*vi.* **2.** engage in a heart-to-heart talk

shnook (shno͝ok) *n. inf.* **1.** *see* SHLEMIEL **2.** timid, unassertive person

shnorer (ˈshnōrər) *n. inf.* **1.** cadger **2.** chiseler, compulsive haggler —**shnor** *vi.* beg

shoal[1] (shōl) *n.* **1.** stretch of shallow water **2.** sandbank, sandbar —*v.* **3.** make, become shallow

shoal[2] (shōl) *n.* **1.** large number of fish swimming together —*vi.* **2.** form shoal

shock[1] (shok) *vt.* **1.** horrify —*n.* **2.** violent or damaging blow **3.** emotional disturbance **4.** state of weakness, illness, caused by physical or mental shock **5.** paralytical stroke **6.** collision **7.** effect on sensory nerves of electric discharge —ˈ**shocker** *n.* person or thing that shocks or distresses —ˈ**shocking** *a.* **1.** causing shock, disgust *etc.* **2.** *inf.* very bad or terrible —**shock absorber** device, *esp.* in automobiles, to absorb shocks —**shock therapy** *or* **treatment** treatment of certain psychotic conditions by injecting drugs or by passing electric current through brain

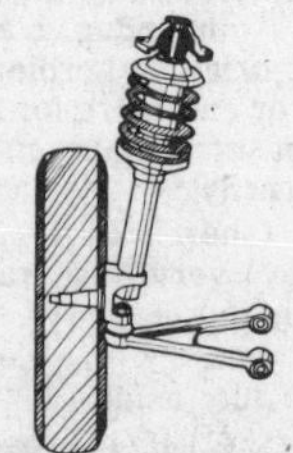

shock absorber

shock[2] (shok) *n.* group of corn sheaves placed together

shock[3] (shok) *n.* **1.** mass of hair —*a.* **2.** shaggy —ˈ**shockheaded** *a.*

shod (shod) *pt./pp. of* SHOE

shoddy (ˈshodi) *a.* **1.** worthless, trashy **2.** second-rate **3.** made of poor material

shoe (sho͞o) *n.* **1.** covering for foot, not enclosing ankle **2.** metal rim or curved bar put on horse's hoof **3.** any of various protective plates or undercoverings —*vt.* **4.** protect, furnish with shoe or shoes (**shod** *pt./pp.,* **ˈshoeing** *pr.p.*) —**ˈshoehorn** *n.* curved plastic or metal implement, inserted at back of shoe, used to ease in heel —**ˈshoestring** *a./n.* very small (amount of money *etc.*) —**ˈshoetree** *n.* wooden or metal block inserted into shoe to preserve shape

shofar (ˈshōfär, -fər) *n.* *Judaism* trumpet made from ram's horn, used by Jews throughout history to mark important occasions

shogun (ˈshōgən) *n.* Japanese hereditary military dictator and virtual ruler before 1868

shone (shōn) *pt./pp. of* SHINE

shoo (sho͞o) *interj.* **1.** go away —*vt.* **2.** drive away

shook (sho͝ok) *pt. of* SHAKE

shoot (sho͞ot) *vt.* **1.** hit, wound, kill with missile fired from weapon **2.** send, slide, push rapidly —*v.* **3.** discharge (weapon) **4.** photograph, film —*vi.* **5.** hunt **6.** sprout (**shot, ˈshooting**) —*n.* **7.** young branch **8.** shooting competition **9.** hunting expedition —**ˈshooter** *n.* **1.** person that shoots **2.** revolver —**ˈshooting** *n.* sport in which small arms are fired for accuracy at stationary targets —**shooting star** *inf.* meteor —**shooting stick** device resembling walking stick, having spike at one end and folding seat at other

shop (shop) *n.* **1.** place for retail sale of goods and services **2.** workshop, works building —*vi.* **3.** visit stores to buy (**-pp-**) —**ˈshopkeeper** *n.* person who owns or manages shop —**ˈshoplifter** *n.* one who steals from shop —**shopping center 1.** area of town where most of shops are situated **2.** complex of stores, restaurants *etc.* with adjoining parking lot —**ˈshopsoiled** *a.* faded *etc.* from being displayed in shop —**shop steward** labor union representative of workers in factory *etc.* —**ˈshoptalk** *n.* conversation concerning one's work, *esp.* outside business hours —**ˈshopwalker** *n.* overseer who directs customers *etc.* —**talk shop** talk of one's business *etc.* at unsuitable moments

shore[1] (shör) *n.* edge of sea or lake

shore[2] (shör) *vt.* (*oft. with* up) prop (up)

shorn (shörn) *pp. of* SHEAR

short (shört) *a.* **1.** not long **2.** not tall **3.** brief, hasty **4.** not reaching quantity or standard required **5.** wanting, lacking **6.** abrupt, rude **7.** friable —*adv.* **8.** suddenly, abruptly **9.** without reaching end —*n.* **10.** short circuit **11.** shortstop —*pl.* **12.** short trousers —**ˈshortage** *n.* deficiency —**ˈshorten** *v.* —**ˈshortening** *n.* butter, lard or other fat, used in cake mixture *etc.* to make pastry light —**ˈshortly** *adv.* **1.** soon **2.** briefly —**ˈshortbread** *n.* sweet, brittle cake made of butter, flour and sugar —**ˈshortcake** *n.* quick bread —**short-change** *vt.* **1.** give less than correct change to **2.** *sl.* cheat, swindle —**short circuit** faulty connection between two points in electric circuit, establishing path of low resistance through which excessive current can flow —**short-circuit** *v.* **1.** develop or cause to develop short circuit —*vt.* **2.** bypass (procedure *etc.*) —**ˈshortcoming** *n.* failing, defect —**short cut 1.** shorter route than usual one **2.** means of saving time or effort —**short-cut** *vi.* use short cut —**ˈshortfall** *n.* failure to meet requirement —**ˈshorthair** *n.* domestic cat with short dense coat —**ˈshorthand** *n.* method of rapid writing by signs or contractions —**short-handed** *a.* lacking the usual or necessary number of workers, helpers —**ˈshorthorn** *n.* short-horned breed of cattle with several regional varieties —**short-lived** *a.* living or lasting only for a short time —**short-range** *a.* of limited extent in time or distance —**short shrift** summary treatment —**short-sighted** *a.* **1.** relating to or suffering from myopia **2.** lacking foresight —**ˈshortstop** *n.* baseball player defending infield —**short-tempered** *a.* easily moved to anger —**short-term** *a.* **1.** extending over limited period **2.** *Fin.* extending over or maturing within short period of time —**short ton** ton (2000 lbs.) —**short wave** radio wave between 10 and 100 meters —**short-winded** *a.* **1.** tending to run out of breath, *esp.* after exertion **2.** (of speech or writing) abrupt —**have by the short hairs** *sl.* have at one's mercy

Shoshone (shəˈshōni, shəˈshōn, ˈshōshōn) *or* **Shoshoni** (shəˈshōni) *n.* **1.** group of Amerindian peoples orig. ranging through California, Colorado, Utah, Nebraska and Kansas **2.** member of any of these peoples (*pl.* **-s, -ne** *or* **-ni**) —**Shoˈshonean** *n.* language family of Uto-Aztecan phylum

shot (shot) *n.* **1.** act of shooting **2.** missile **3.** lead in small pellets **4.** marksman, shooter **5.** try, attempt **6.** photograph **7.** short film sequence **8.** dose **9.** *inf.* injection —*a.* **10.** woven so that color is different, according to angle of light —*v.* **11.** *pt./pp. of* SHOOT —**ˈshotgun** *n.* **1.** firearm with unrifled bore used mainly for hunting small game —*a.* **2.** involving coercion or duress —**shot put** athletic event in which contestants hurl heavy metal ball as far as possible

should (sho͝od) *pt. of* SHALL

shoulder (ˈshōldər) *n.* **1.** part of body to which arm or foreleg is attached **2.** anything resembling shoulder **3.** side of road —*vt.* **4.** undertake **5.** bear (burden) **6.** accept (responsibility) **7.** put on one's shoulder —*vi.* **8.** make way by pushing —**shoulder blade** either of pair of large triangular bones lying at upper back of body (*also* **scapula**) —**shoulder girdle** pectoral girdle

shout (showt) *n.* **1.** loud cry —*v.* **2.** utter (cry *etc.*) with loud voice

shove (shuv) *vt.* **1.** push **2.** *inf.* put —*n.* **3.** push —**shove off** *inf.* go away

shovel ('shuvəl) *n.* **1.** instrument for scooping, lifting earth *etc.* —*vt.* **2.** lift, move (as) with shovel —'**shoveler** *n.* duck with spoon-shaped bill

show (shō) *vt.* **1.** expose to view **2.** point out **3.** display, exhibit **4.** explain; prove **5.** guide **6.** accord (favor *etc.*) —*vi.* **7.** appear **8.** be noticeable (**showed, shown,** '**showing**) —*n.* **9.** display, exhibition **10.** public spectacle **11.** theatrical or other entertainment **12.** indication **13.** competitive event **14.** ostentation **15.** semblance **16.** pretense —'**showily** *adv.* —'**showy** *a.* **1.** gaudy **2.** ostentatious —**show business** entertainment industry (*also* (*inf.*) **show biz**) —'**showcase** *n.* **1.** glass case used for displaying and protecting objects in museum *etc.* **2.** setting in which anything may be displayed to best advantage —'**showdown** *n.* **1.** confrontation **2.** final test —'**showman** *n.* **1.** one employed in, or owning, show at fair *etc.* **2.** one skilled at presenting anything in effective way —**show-off** *n.* —'**showpiece** *n.* **1.** anything exhibited **2.** anything prized as fine example of its type —**show off 1.** exhibit to invite admiration **2.** behave in such a way as to make an impression —**show up 1.** reveal **2.** expose **3.** *inf.* embarrass **4.** *inf.* arrive

shower ('showər) *n.* **1.** short fall of rain **2.** anything coming down like rain **3.** kind of bath in which person stands while being sprayed with water **4.** party to present gifts to a person —*vt.* **5.** bestow liberally —*vi.* **6.** take bath in shower —'**showery** *a.*

shrank (shrangk) *pt. of* SHRINK

shrapnel ('shrapnəl) *n.* **1.** shell filled with pellets which scatter on bursting **2.** shell splinters

shred (shred) *n.* **1.** fragment, torn strip **2.** small amount —*vt.* **3.** cut, tear to shreds (**shred** *or* '**shredded,** '**shredding**)

shrew

shrew (shrōō) *n.* **1.** any of various small, insectivorous rodents having long, pointed nose and sometimes poor eyesight **2.** bad-tempered woman **3.** scold —'**shrewish** *a.* nagging

shrewd (shrōōd) *a.* **1.** astute, intelligent **2.** crafty

shriek (shrēk) *n.* **1.** shrill cry **2.** piercing scream —*v.* **3.** screech

shrift (shrift) *n.* **1.** confession **2.** absolution

shrike (shrīk) *n.* bird of prey

shrill (shril) *a.* **1.** piercing, sharp in tone —*v.* **2.** utter (words *etc.*) in such tone —'**shrilly** *adv.*

shrimp (shrimp) *n.* **1.** small edible crustacean **2.** *inf.* undersized person —*vi.* **3.** fish for shrimps

shrine (shrīn) *n.* place (building, tomb, alcove) of worship, usu. associated with saint

shrink (shringk) *vi.* **1.** become smaller **2.** retire, flinch, recoil —*vt.* **3.** make smaller (**shrank** *pt.*, '**shrunken, shrunk** *pp.*, '**shrinking** *pr.p.*) —*n.* **4.** *sl.* psychiatrist —'**shrinkage** *n.* —**shrink-wrap** *vt.* package (product) in flexible plastic wrapping designed to shrink about its contours

shrivel ('shrivəl) *vi.* shrink and wither

shroud (shrowd) *n.* **1.** sheet, wrapping, for corpse **2.** anything which covers, envelops like shroud —*pl.* **3.** set of ropes to masthead —*vt.* **4.** put shroud on **5.** screen, veil **6.** wrap up

Shrovetide ('shrōvtīd) *n.* the three days preceding Lent —**Shrove Tuesday** day before Ash Wednesday

shrub (shrub) *n.* bushy plant —'**shrubbery** *n.* plantation, part of garden, filled with shrubs

shrug (shrug) *vi.* **1.** raise shoulders, as sign of indifference, ignorance *etc.* —*vt.* **2.** move (shoulders) thus **3.** (*with* off) dismiss as unimportant (**-gg-**) —*n.* **4.** shrugging

shrunk (shrungk) *pp. of* SHRINK

shtetl ('shtetl) *n.* any of the former Jewish village communities of Eastern Europe, *esp.* in czarist Russia (*pl.* **shtetlach** ('shtetläk))

shuck (shuk) *n.* shell, husk, pod

shudder ('shudər) *vi.* **1.** shake, tremble violently, *esp.* with horror —*n.* **2.** shuddering, tremor

shuffle ('shufəl) *vi.* **1.** move feet without lifting them **2.** act evasively —*vt.* **3.** mix (cards) **4.** (*with* off) evade, pass to another —*n.* **5.** shuffling **6.** rearrangement —'**shuffler** *n.*

shul (shōōl) *n. inf.* synagogue

shun (shun) *vt.* **1.** avoid **2.** keep away from (**-nn-**)

shunt (shunt) *vt.* **1.** push aside **2.** divert **3.** move (train) from one line to another

shush (shush, shōōsh) *interj.* **1.** be quiet, hush —*vt.* **2.** silence or calm by saying "shush"

shut (shut) *v.* **1.** close —*vt.* **2.** bar **3.** forbid entrance to (**shut,** '**shutting**) —'**shutter** *n.* **1.** movable window screen, usu. hinged to frame **2.** device in camera admitting light as required to film or plate —'**shuteye** *n. sl.*

sleep —**shut down** close or stop (factory, machine *etc.*)

shuttle (ˈshutəl) *n.* **1.** instrument which threads weft between threads of warp in weaving **2.** similar appliance in sewing machine **3.** plane, bus *etc.* traveling to and fro over short distance —ˈ**shuttlecock** *n.* small, light cone with cork stub and fan of feathers used in badminton

shy[1] (shī) *a.* **1.** awkward in company **2.** timid, bashful **3.** reluctant **4.** scarce, lacking (*esp.* in card games, not having enough money for bet *etc.*) —*vi.* **5.** start back in fear **6.** show sudden reluctance (**shied,** ˈ**shying**) —*n.* **7.** start of fear by horse —ˈ**shyly** *adv.* —ˈ**shyness** *n.*

shy[2] (shī) *vt./n.* throw (**shied,** ˈ**shying**)

Shylock (ˈshīlok) *n.* heartless or demanding creditor

shyster (ˈshīstər) *n. sl.* dishonest, deceitful person *esp.* lawyer

si (sē) *or* **ti** *n. Mus.* **1.** in fixed system of solmization, the note B **2.** in movable do system, the seventh note of a major scale

Si *Chem.* silicon

SI *Fr.* Système International (d'Unités): the 1960 revision of the International Metric System where the basic units of length, volume and mass are the meter, cubic meter and kilogram

Siam (sīˈam) *n. former name of* THAILAND –**Siaˈmese** *n./a.* —**Siamese cat** breed of cat with blue eyes —**Siamese twins** twins born joined to each other by some part of body

sibilant (ˈsibilənt) *a.* **1.** hissing —*n.* **2.** speech sound with hissing effect

sibling (ˈsibling) *n.* person's brother or sister

sibyl (ˈsibil) *n.* woman endowed with spirit of prophecy —**sibylline** (ˈsibilīn) *a.* occult

sic (sik) *Lat.* thus: used to indicate that something has been quoted exactly

sick (sik) *a.* **1.** inclined to vomit **2.** not well or healthy, physically or mentally **3.** *inf.* macabre, sadistic, morbid **4.** *inf.* bored, tired **5.** *inf.* disgusted —ˈ**sicken** *v.* **1.** make, become sick —*vt.* **2.** disgust; nauseate —ˈ**sickening** *a.* **1.** causing sickness or revulsion **2.** *inf.* extremely annoying —ˈ**sickly** *a.* **1.** unhealthy **2.** inducing nausea —ˈ**sickness** *n.* —ˈ**sickbay** *n.* place set aside for treating sick people, *esp.* in ships

sickle (ˈsikəl) *n.* reaping hook —**sickle cell anemia** inherited form of anemia in which large number of red blood cells become sickle-shaped

side (sīd) *n.* **1.** one of the surfaces of object, *esp.* upright inner or outer surface **2.** either surface of thing having only two **3.** part of body that is to right or left **4.** region nearer or farther than, or right or left of, dividing line *etc.* **5.** region **6.** aspect or part **7.** one of two parties or sets of opponents **8.** sect, faction **9.** line of descent traced through one parent **10.** *sl.* insolence, arrogance, pretentiousness —*a.* **11.** at, in the side **12.** subordinate, incidental —*vi.* **13.** (*usu. with* with) take up cause (of) —ˈ**siding** *n.* short line of rails on which trains or wagons are shunted from main line —**side arms** weapons carried on person, by belt or holster, such as sword, pistol *etc.* —ˈ**sideboard** *n.* piece of furniture for holding dishes *etc.* in dining room —ˈ**sideburns** *pl.n.* man's whiskers grown down either side of face in front of ears —ˈ**sidecar** *n.* small car attached to side of motorcycle —ˈ**sidekick** *n. sl.* close friend or follower —ˈ**sidelight** *n.* light displayed by ships under weigh at night —ˈ**sideline** *n.* **1.** *Sport* boundary of playing area **2.** subsidiary interest or activity —**sideˈlong** *a.* **1.** lateral, not directly forward —*adv.* **2.** obliquely —**side-saddle** *n.* riding saddle orig. designed for women riders in skirts, who sit with both legs on same side of horse —ˈ**sideshow** *n.* **1.** small show offered in conjunction with larger attraction, as at circus **2.** subordinate event —ˈ**sideslip** *n.* skid —ˈ**sidesman** *n. Anglican Ch.* man elected to help parish churchwarden —**side-splitting** *a.* **1.** producing great mirth **2.** (of laughter) very hearty —ˈ**sidestep** *v.* **1.** step aside from or out of way of (something) —*vt.* **2.** dodge —**side step** movement to one side, as in boxing *etc.* —ˈ**sidetrack** *v.* **1.** distract or be distracted from main topic —*n.* **2.** digression —ˈ**sidewalk** *n.* paved walk alongside street —ˈ**sideways** *adv.* **1.** to or from the side **2.** laterally (*also* ˈ**sidewise**)

sidereal (sīˈdēəriəl) *a.* relating to, fixed by, stars

sidle (ˈsīdəl) *vi.* **1.** move in furtive or stealthy manner **2.** move sideways

SIDS sudden infant death syndrome

siege (sēj) *n.* besieging of town or fortified place

siemens (ˈsēmənz) *n.* derived SI unit of electrical conductance

sienna (siˈenə) *n.* (pigment of) brownish-yellow color

sierra (siˈerə) *n.* range of mountains with jagged peaks

Sierra (siˈerə) *n.* word used in communications for the letter *s*

Sierra Leone (lēˈōn) country in Africa bounded northwest, north and northeast by Guinea, southeast by Liberia and southwest by the Atlantic Ocean —**Sierra Leonean** (lēˈōniən)

siesta (siˈestə) *n.* rest, sleep in afternoon

sieve (siv) *n.* **1.** device with network or perforated bottom for sifting —*vt.* **2.** sift **3.** strain

sift (sift) *vt.* **1.** separate (*eg* with sieve) coarser portion from finer **2.** examine closely

sigh (sī) *vi./n.* (utter) long audible breath —**sigh for** yearn for, grieve for

sight (sīt) *n.* **1.** faculty of seeing **2.** seeing **3.**

thing seen **4.** view **5.** glimpse **6.** device for guiding eye **7.** spectacle **8.** *inf.* pitiful or ridiculous object **9.** *inf.* large number, great deal —*vt.* **10.** catch sight of **11.** adjust sights of (gun *etc.*) —**'sightless** *a.* —**sight-read** *v.* play, sing (music) at first sight —**'sightsee** *v.* visit (place) to look at interesting sights —**'sightseeing** *n.*

sigma ('sigmə) *n.* **1.** 18th letter in Gr. alphabet (Σ, σ or, when final, ς), consonant, transliterated as *S* **2.** *Math.* symbol Σ, indicating summation

sign (sīn) *n.* **1.** mark, gesture *etc.* to convey some meaning **2.** (board, placard bearing) notice, warning *etc.* **3.** symbol **4.** omen **5.** evidence —*vt.* **6.** put one's signature to **7.** ratify —*vi.* **8.** make sign or gesture **9.** affix signature —**sign language** any system of communication by signs, *esp.* used by deaf —**'signpost** *n.* **1.** post bearing sign that shows way, as at roadside **2.** something that serves as indication —*vt.* **3.** mark with signposts

signal ('signəl) *n.* **1.** sign to convey order or information, *esp.* on railroad **2.** that which in first place impels any action **3.** *Rad. etc.* sequence of electrical impulses transmitted or received —*a.* **4.** remarkable, striking —*vt.* **5.** make signals to —*vi.* **6.** give orders *etc.* by signals —**'signalize** *vt.* make notable —**'signally** *adv.* —**signal box 1.** building containing signal levers for railroad lines **2.** control point for large area of railroad system —**'signalman** *n.* railroad employee in charge of signals

signatory ('signətōri) *n.* one of those who sign agreements, treaties

signature ('signichōōər, -chər) *n.* **1.** person's name written by himself **2.** act of writing it —**signature tune** tune associated with particular program, person *etc.*

signet ('signit) *n.* small seal —**signet ring** finger ring bearing signet

significant (sig'nifikənt) *a.* **1.** revealing **2.** designed to make something known **3.** important —**sig'nificance** *n.* **1.** import, weight **2.** meaning —**sig'nificantly** *adv.* —**signifi'cation** *n.* meaning —**significant figures 1.** figures of number that express magnitude to specified degree of accuracy **2.** number of such figures

signify ('signifī) *vt.* **1.** mean **2.** indicate **3.** denote **4.** imply —*vi.* **5.** be of importance (**'signified, 'signifying**)

signor *or* **signior** (sēn'yōr; *It.* sēny'nyōr) *n.* It. title of respect, like Mr. (*pl.* **-s, -gnori** (*It.* -'nyōrē)) —**signora** (sēn'yōrə; *It.* sēny'nyōra) *n.* Mrs. (*pl.* **-s, -re** (*It.* -rā)) —**signorina** (sēnyə'rēnə; *It.* sēnynyo'rēna) *n.* Miss (*pl.* **-s, -ne** (*It.* -nā))

Sikh (sēk) *n.* member of Indian religious sect

silage ('sīlij) *n.* fodder crop harvested while green and stored in state of partial fermentation

silence ('sīləns) *n.* **1.** absence of noise **2.** refraining from speech —*vt.* **3.** make silent **4.** put a stop to —**'silencer** *n.* device to reduce noise of firearm —**'silent** *a.*

silhouette (silōō'et) *n.* **1.** outline of object seen against light **2.** profile portrait in black

silica ('silikə) *n.* naturally occurring dioxide of silicon —**siliceous** *or* **silicious** (si'lishəs) *a.* —**sili'cosis** *n.* lung disease caused by inhaling silica dust over a long period —**silica gel** form of silica with property of great absorbency used to dry atmosphere and articles

silicon ('silikən) *n. Chem.* metalloid element *Symbol* Si, at. wt. 28.1, at. no. 14 —**'silicone** *n.* large class of synthetic substances, related to silicon and used in chemistry, industry and medicine —**silicon chip** *see* CHIP (sense 4)

silk (silk) *n.* **1.** fiber made by larvae (**silkworm**) of certain moth **2.** thread, fabric made from this —**'silken** *a.* **1.** made of, like silk **2.** soft **3.** smooth **4.** dressed in silk —**'silkily** *adv.* —**'silkiness** *n.* —**'silky** *a.* —**silk hat** man's top hat covered with silk —**silk-screen** *n.* stencil process of printing a design through screen of fine mesh cloth

sill (sil) *n.* **1.** ledge beneath window **2.** bottom part of door or window frame

sillabub ('siləbub) *n. see* SYLLABUB

silly ('sili) *a.* **1.** foolish **2.** trivial **3.** feeble-minded —**'silliness** *n.*

silo ('sīlō) *n.* **1.** pit, tower for storing fodder or grain **2.** underground missile launching site (*pl.* **-s**)

silt (silt) *n.* **1.** mud deposited by water —*v.* **2.** fill, be choked with silt —**sil'tation** *n.* —**'silty** *a.*

Silurian (sī'lōōriən) *a.* **1.** of or formed in third period of Paleozoic era, during which fishes first appeared —*n.* **2.** Silurian period or rock system

silvan ('silvən) *a. see* SYLVAN

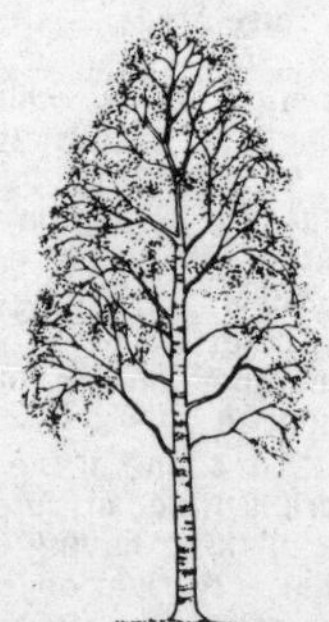

silver birch

silver ('silvər) *n.* **1.** *Chem.* metallic element *Symbol* Ag, at. wt. 107.9, at. no. 47 **2.** things made of it **3.** silver coins **4.** flatware —*a.* **5.**

made of silver **6.** resembling silver or its color **7.** having pale luster, as moon **8.** soft, melodious, as sound **9.** bright *—vt.* **10.** coat with silver **—'silvery** *a.* **—silver birch** tree having silvery-white peeling bark **—silver jubilee** 25th anniversary **—silver lining** hopeful aspect of otherwise desperate situation **—silver plate 1.** thin layer of silver deposited on base metal **2.** articles, *esp.* tableware, made of silver plate **—silver-plate** *vt.* coat (metal *etc.*) with silver **—silver point** method of drawing in which great delicacy is achieved by using a silver-tipped drawing implement **—silver screen** *inf.* **1.** motion-picture industry **2.** screen on to which movies are projected **—'silversmith** *n.* craftsman who makes articles of silver **—silver wedding** 25th wedding anniversary

silviculture ('silvikulchər) *n.* branch of forestry concerned with cultivation of trees

simian ('simiən) *a.* of, like apes

similar ('similər) *a.* resembling, like **—simi'larity** *n.* likeness, close resemblance

simile ('simili) *n.* comparison of one thing with another, using *as* or *like*, *esp.* in poetry

similitude (si'milityōōd, -tōōd) *n.* **1.** outward appearance, likeness **2.** guise

simmer ('simər) *v.* **1.** keep or be just bubbling or just below boiling point *—vi.* **2.** be in state of suppressed anger or laughter

simper ('simpər) *v.* **1.** smile, utter in silly or affected way *—n.* **2.** simpering smile

simple ('simpəl) *a.* **1.** not complicated **2.** plain **3.** not combined or complex **4.** ordinary, mere **5.** guileless **6.** stupid **—'simpleness** *n.* **—'simpleton** *n.* foolish person **—sim'plicity** *n.* **1.** simpleness **2.** clearness **3.** artlessness **—simplifi'cation** *n.* **—'simplify** *vt.* make simple, plain or easy (**-plified, -plifying**) **—sim'plistic** *a.* very simple, naive **—'simply** *adv.* **—simple fracture** fracture in which broken bone does not pierce skin **—simple interest** interest paid on principal alone **—simple-minded** *a.* **1.** stupid; feeble-minded **2.** mentally defective **3.** unsophisticated **—simple-mindedness** *n.* **—simple sentence** sentence consisting of single main clause

simulate ('simyəlāt) *vt.* **1.** make pretense of **2.** reproduce, copy (*esp.* conditions of particular situation) **—simu'lation** *n.* **—'simulator** *n.*

simultaneous (sīməl'tāniəs) *a.* occurring at the same time **—simultaneity** (sīməltə'nēiti) *or* **simul'taneousness** *n.* **—simul'taneously** *adv.*

sin[1] (sin) *n.* **1.** transgression of divine or moral law, *esp.* committed consciously **2.** offense against principle or standard *—vi.* **3.** commit sin (**-nn-**) **—'sinful** *a.* **1.** of nature of sin **2.** guilty of sin **—'sinfully** *adv.* **—'sinner** *n.* **—sin bin C** *sl.* penalty box used in ice hockey **—Sin City** Las Vegas, Nevada

sin[2] *Math.* sine

SIN C Social Insurance Number

since (sins) *prep.* **1.** during or throughout period of time after *—conj.* **2.** from time when **3.** because *—adv.* **4.** from that time

sincere (sin'sēər) *a.* **1.** not hypocritical, actually moved by or feeling apparent emotions **2.** true, genuine **3.** unaffected **—sin'cerely** *adv.* **—sincerity** (sin'seriti) *n.*

sine (sīn) *n.* mathematical function, *esp.* ratio of length of hypotenuse to opposite side in right-angled triangle

sinecure ('sīnikyōōər) *n.* office with pay but minimal duties

sine die ('sīni 'dīi) *Lat.* with no date, indefinitely postponed

sine qua non ('sini kwä 'non, 'sīni kwā 'non) *Lat.* essential condition or requirement

sinew ('sinyōō) *n.* **1.** tough, fibrous cord joining muscle to bone *—pl.* **2.** muscles, strength **—'sinewy** *a.* **1.** stringy **2.** muscular

sing (sing) *vi.* **1.** utter musical sounds **2.** hum, whistle, ring *—vt.* **3.** utter (words) with musical modulation **4.** celebrate in song or poetry (**sang, sung, 'singing**) **—'singer** *n.* **—'singsong** *n.* **1.** informal singing session *—a.* **2.** monotonously regular in tone, rhythm

Singapore ('singgəpōr) *n.* country in Indian Ocean consisting of Singapore Island and 54 islets lying at southern tip of Malaysia **—Singaporean** (singgə'pōriən) *n./a.*

singe (sinj) *vt.* **1.** burn surface of (**singed, 'singeing**) *—n.* **2.** act or effect of singeing

Singh (sing) *n.* title assumed by Sikh on becoming full member of community

single ('singgəl) *a.* **1.** one only **2.** alone, separate **3.** unmarried **4.** for one **5.** formed of only one part, fold *etc.* **6.** denoting ticket for train *etc.* valid for outward journey only **7.** wholehearted, straightforward *—n.* **8.** single thing **9.** phonograph record with one short item on each side **10.** single ticket *—vt.* **11.** (*with* out) pick (out) **—'singleton** *n.* **1.** *Bridge etc.* original holding of one card only in suit **2.** single object as distinguished from pair or group **3.** *Math.* set containing only one member **—'singly** *adv.* **—single-breasted** *a.* (of garment) overlapping only slightly and with one row of fastenings **—single entry** *Book-keeping* entered in one account only **—single file** persons, things arranged in one line **—single-handed** *a./adv.* without assistance **—single-minded** *a.* having but one aim or purpose **—single-mindedness** *n.*

singular ('singgyələr) *a.* **1.** remarkable **2.** unusual **3.** unique **4.** denoting one person or thing **—singu'larity** *n.* something unusual **—'singularly** *adv.* **1.** particularly **2.** peculiarly

Sinhalese (singgə'lēz, sinhə-, sinə-) *n.* **1.** member of people living chiefly in Sri Lanka **2.** language of this people which is descended from Sanskrit *—a.* **3.** of this people or their language

sinister ('sinistər) *a.* **1.** threatening **2.** evil-looking **3.** wicked **4.** unlucky **5.** *Her.* on left-hand side

sink (singk) *vi.* **1.** become submerged (in water) **2.** drop, give way **3.** decline in value, health *etc.* **4.** penetrate —*vt.* **5.** cause to sink **6.** make by digging out **7.** invest (**sank** *pt.*, **sunk, 'sunken** *pp.*, **'sinking** *pr.p.*) —*n.* **8.** receptacle with pipe for carrying away waste water **9.** cesspool **10.** place of corruption, vice —**'sinker** *n.* weight for fishing line —**sinking fund** money set aside at intervals for payment of particular liability at fixed date

Sinn Fein ('shin 'fān) the movement for Irish independence —**Sinn Feiner** ('fānər) —**Sinn Feinism** ('fānizəm)

Sino- (*comb. form*) Chinese, of China, as in *Sino-Tibetan*

Sinology (sī'noləji) *n.* study of Chinese history, language, culture *etc.* —**Sinological** (sīnə'lojikəl) *a.* —**Si'nologist** *n.*

sinuous ('sinyōōəs) *a.* **1.** curving **2.** devious **3.** lithe —**'sinuate** *a.* —**sinu'osity** *n.*

sinus ('sīnəs) *n.* cavity, *esp.* any of air passages in bones of skull —**sinu'sitis** *n.* infection of air cavities of bones of skull connecting with nasal passages

Sion ('sīən) *n. see* ZION

Siouan ('sōōən) *n.* Amerindian language family spoken in northern Midwest, Montana and Oklahoma

Sioux (sōō) *n. see* DAKOTA

sip (sip) *v.* **1.** drink in very small portions (**-pp-**) —*n.* **2.** small drink

siphon ('sīfən) *n.* **1.** device, *esp.* bent tube, which uses atmospheric or gaseous pressure to draw liquid from container —*vt.* **2.** draw off thus **3.** draw off in small amounts

sir (sər) *n.* **1.** polite term of address for a man **2.** (**S-**) title of knight or baronet

sire ('sīər) *n.* **1.** male parent, *esp.* of horse or domestic animal **2.** term of address to king —*vt.* **3.** beget

siren ('sīərən) *n.* **1.** device making loud wailing noise, *esp.* giving warning of danger **2.** legendary sea nymph who lured sailors to destruction **3.** alluring woman

Sirius ('siriəs) *n.* brightest star in sky, lying in constellation Canis Major (*also* **Dog Star**)

sirloin ('sərloin) *n.* prime cut of loin of beef

sirocco (si'rokō) *n.* hot oppressive wind beginning in N Afr. and reaching S Europe (*pl.* **-s**)

sisal ('sīsəl) *n.* (fiber of) plant used in making ropes

siskin ('siskin) *n.* small olive-green bird of finch family

sissy ('sisi) *a./n.* weak, cowardly (person)

sister ('sistər) *n.* **1.** daughter of same parents **2.** woman fellow-member, *esp.* of religious body —*a.* **3.** closely related, similar —**'sisterhood** *n.* **1.** relation of sister **2.** order, band of women —**'sisterly** *a.* —**sister-in-law** *n.* **1.** sister of husband or wife **2.** brother's wife

sit (sit) *vi.* **1.** adopt posture or rest on buttocks, thighs **2.** perch **3.** (of bird) cover eggs to hatch them **4.** pose for portrait **5.** occupy official position **6.** hold session **7.** remain **8.** keep watch over baby *etc.* —*vt.* **9.** take (examination) (**sat, 'sitting**) —**'sitter** *n.* **1.** person or animal that sits **2.** person who is posing for portrait **3.** *see* **baby-sitter** *at* BABY —**'sitting** *n.* **1.** continuous period of being seated **2.** in canteen *etc.*, such period during which one of two or more meals is served **3.** meeting, *esp.* of official body **4.** incubation period of bird's eggs during which mother sits on them —**sit-down** *a.* (of meal *etc.*) eaten while sitting down at table —**sit-down strike** strike in which employees refuse to leave their place of employment —**sit-in** *n.* protest involving refusal to move from place —**sitting duck** *inf.* person or thing in defenseless position —**sit down 1.** adopt sitting posture **2.** (*with* under) suffer (insults *etc.*) without protest —**sit in** protest by sit-in

sitar (si'tär) *n.* stringed musical instrument, *esp.* of India

site (sīt) *n.* **1.** place, location **2.** space for, with, a building —*vt.* **3.** locate in specific place

situate ('sichōōāt) *vt.* place, locate —**situ'ation** *n.* **1.** place, position **2.** state of affairs **3.** employment, post —**situation comedy** comedy based on humorous situations that could arise in day-to-day life

six (siks) *a./n.* cardinal number one more than five —**six'teen** *n./a.* six and ten —**sixth** *a.* **1.** ordinal number of six —*n.* **2.** sixth part —**'sixty** *n./a.* six times ten —**Six Counties** Northern Ireland —**six-shooter** *n. inf.* revolver with six chambers —**sixth sense** any supposed means of perception, such as intuition

size[1] (sīz) *n.* **1.** bigness, dimensions **2.** one of series of standard measurements of clothing *etc.* **3.** *inf.* state of affairs —*vt.* **4.** arrange according to size —**'sizable** *or* **'sizeable** *a.* quite large —**size up** *inf.* assess (person, situation *etc.*)

size[2] (sīz) *n.* **1.** gluelike sealer, filler —*vt.* **2.** coat, treat with size

skate[2]

sizzle ('sizəl) *vi./n.* (make) hissing, spluttering sound, as of frying —'**sizzler** *n. inf.* hot day

SK Saskatchewan

skat (skät, skat) *n.* card game of the euchre family for three, four or five players but with only three actually playing

skate[1] (skāt) *n.* **1.** steel blade attached to boot, for gliding over ice —*vi.* **2.** glide as on skates —'**skateboard** *n.* small board mounted on roller-skate wheels

skate[2] (skāt) *n.* large marine ray

skedaddle (ski'dadəl) *vi. inf.* scamper off

skein (skān) *n.* **1.** quantity of yarn, wool *etc.* in loose knot **2.** flight of wildfowl

skeleton ('skelitən) *n.* **1.** bones of animal **2.** bones separated from flesh and preserved in their natural position **3.** very thin person **4.** outline, draft, framework **5.** nucleus —*a.* **6.** reduced to a minimum **7.** drawn in outline **8.** not in detail —'**skeletal** *a.* —**skeleton key** key filed down so as to open many different locks

skeptic ('skeptik) *n.* **1.** one who maintains doubt or disbelief **2.** agnostic **3.** unbeliever —'**skeptical** *a.* —'**skepticism** *n.*

skerry ('skeri) *n.* rocky island or reef

sketch (skech) *n.* **1.** rough drawing **2.** brief account **3.** essay **4.** short humorous play —*v.* **5.** make sketch (of) —'**sketchy** *a.* **1.** omitting detail **2.** incomplete **3.** inadequate

skew (skyōō) *vi.* **1.** move obliquely —*a.* **2.** slanting **3.** crooked —'**skew'whiff** *a. inf.* **1.** aslant **2.** crooked

skewbald ('skyōōbōld) *a.* (*esp.* of horse) white and any other color (except black) in patches

skewer ('skyōōər, skyōōər) *n.* **1.** pin to fasten meat together —*vt.* **2.** pierce or fasten with skewer

ski (skē) *n.* **1.** long runner fastened to foot for sliding over snow or water (*pl.* **-s, ski**) —*vi.* **2.** slide on skis (**skied, 'skiing**) —**ski jump** ramp overhanging slope from which skiers compete to make longest jump —**ski-jump** *vi.*

skid (skid) *v.* **1.** (cause (*esp.* vehicle) to) slide (sideways) out of control with wheels not revolving (**-dd-**) —*n.* **2.** instance of this **3.** device to facilitate sliding, *eg* in moving heavy objects —**skid row** *sl.* dilapidated section of city inhabited by vagrants *etc.*

skiddoo *or* **skidoo** (ski'dōō) *vi.* go away, leave

skidoo (ski'dōō) *n.* **C** snowmobile

skiff (skif) *n.* small boat

skill (skil) *n.* practical ability, cleverness, dexterity —**skilled** *a.* having, requiring knowledge, united with readiness and dexterity —'**skillful** *a.* expert, masterly, adroit —'**skillfully** *adv.*

skillet ('skilit) *n.* small frying pan

skim (skim) *vt.* **1.** remove floating matter from surface of (liquid) **2.** glide over lightly and rapidly **3.** read thus —*vi.* **4.** move thus (**-mm-**) —**skim** *or* **skimmed milk** milk from which cream has been removed

skimp (skimp) *v.* **1.** give short measure (on) **2.** do (thing) imperfectly —'**skimpy** *a.* **1.** meager **2.** scanty

skin (skin) *n.* **1.** outer covering of vertebrate body, lower animal or fruit **2.** animal skin used as material or container **3.** film on surface of cooling liquid *etc.* **4.** complexion —*vt.* **5.** remove skin of (**-nn-**) —'**skinless** *a.* —**skinned** *a.* **1.** stripped of skin **2.** having skin of specified kind —'**skinner** *n.* **1.** dealer in hides **2.** furrier —'**skinny** *a.* thin —**skin-deep** *a.* **1.** superficial **2.** slight —**skin diving** underwater swimming using breathing apparatus —**skin flick** motion picture containing much nudity and explicit sex scenes —'**skinflint** *n.* miser, niggard —**skin graft** transplant of piece of healthy skin to wound to form new skin —'**skin'tight** *a.* fitting close to skin —**keep one's eyes skinned** watch carefully

skip[1] (skip) *vi.* **1.** leap lightly **2.** jump a rope as it is swung under one —*vt.* **3.** pass over, omit (**-pp-**) —*n.* **4.** act of skipping

skip[2] (skip) *n.* **1.** large open container for builders' rubbish *etc.* **2.** large bucket, container for transporting men, materials in mines *etc.*

skipper ('skipər) *n.* **1.** captain of ship, plane or team —*vt.* **2.** captain

skirl (skərl) *n.* sound of bagpipes

skirmish ('skərmish) *n.* **1.** fight between small parties, small battle —*vi.* **2.** fight briefly or irregularly

skirt (skərt) *n.* **1.** woman's garment hanging from waist **2.** lower part of woman's dress, coat *etc.* **3.** outlying part **4.** *sl.* woman —*vt.* **5.** border **6.** go round —'**skirting** *n.* material for women's skirts

skit (skit) *n.* satire, *esp.* theatrical burlesque

skittish ('skitish) *a.* frisky, frivolous

skittles ('skitəlz) *pl.n.* ninepins

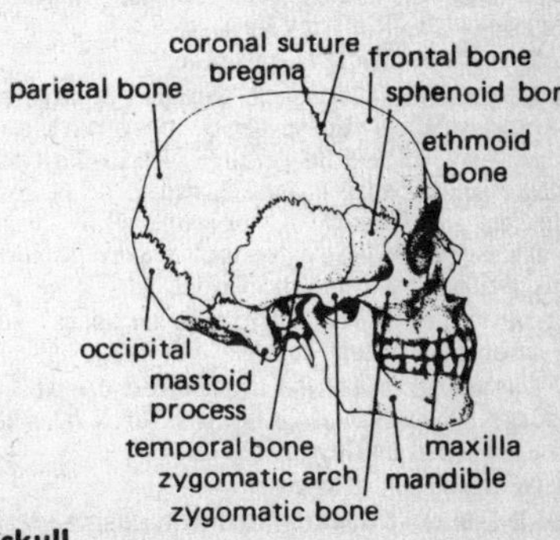

skull

skivvy (ˈskivi) *n.* female servant who does menial work

skua (ˈskyōōə) *n.* large predatory gull

skulk (skulk) *vi.* **1.** sneak out of the way **2.** lurk

skull (skul) *n.* skeleton of head of vertebrate forming bony case protecting brain and chief sense organs and supporting jaw —**skull and crossbones** picture of human skull above two crossed thighbones, used as warning of danger or death —ˈ**skullcap** *n.* close-fitting cap

skullduggery (skulˈdugəri) *n. inf.* trickery

skunk

skunk (skungk) *n.* **1.** small N Amer. animal which emits evil-smelling fluid **2.** *sl.* contemptible person

sky (skī) *n.* **1.** apparently dome-shaped expanse extending upward from the horizon **2.** outer space **3.** heavenly regions (*pl.* **skies**) —*vt.* **4.** hit (cricket ball) high —ˈ**skydiving** *n.* parachute jumping with delayed opening of parachute —**sky-high** *a./adv.* **1.** at or to unprecedented level —*adv.* **2.** high into air —ˈ**skyjack** *vt.* hijack (an aircraft) —ˈ**skylark** *n.* **1.** lark, noted for singing while hovering at great height —*vi.* **2.** *inf.* romp or play jokes —ˈ**skylight** *n.* window in roof or ceiling —ˈ**skyline** *n.* **1.** line at which earth and sky appear to meet **2.** outline of trees *etc.* seen against sky —ˈ**skyscraper** *n.* very tall building —**blow sky-high** destroy

Skye terrier (skī) short-legged breed of terrier with long wiry hair

slab (slab) *n.* thick, broad piece

slack (slak) *a.* **1.** loose **2.** sluggish **3.** careless, negligent **4.** not busy —*n.* **5.** loose part, as of rope —*vi.* **6.** be idle or lazy —ˈ**slacken** *v.* **1.** make or become looser **2.** make or become slower —ˈ**slacker** *n.* person who evades work —ˈ**slackly** *adv.* —**slack water** period of still water around turn of tide

slacks (slaks) *pl.n.* informal trousers worn by men or women

slag (slag) *n.* **1.** refuse of smelted metal **2.** *sl.* coarse woman —**slag heap** hillock of waste matter from coal-mining *etc.*

slain (slān) *pp. of* SLAY

slake (slāk) *vt.* **1.** satisfy (thirst, desire *etc.*) **2.** combine (lime) with water to produce calcium hydroxide

slalom (ˈslāləm) *n.* race over winding course in skiing *etc.*

slam (slam) *v.* **1.** shut noisily **2.** bang —*vt.* **3.** hit **4.** dash down **5.** *inf.* criticize harshly (**-mm-**) —*n.* **6.** (noise of) this action **7.** *sl.* jail (*also* ˈ**slammer**) **8.** *Bridge* winning of all tricks by one side

slander (ˈslandər) *n.* **1.** false or malicious statement about person —*v.* **2.** utter such statement (about) —ˈ**slanderer** *n.* —ˈ**slanderous** *a.*

slang (slang) *n.* **1.** colloquial language —*vt.* **2.** *sl.* scold, abuse violently

slant (slant) *v.* **1.** slope —*vt.* **2.** put at angle **3.** write, present (news *etc.*) with bias —*n.* **4.** slope **5.** point of view **6.** idea —*a.* **7.** sloping, oblique —ˈ**slantwise** *or* ˈ**slantways** *adv.*

slap (slap) *n.* **1.** blow with open hand or flat instrument —*vt.* **2.** strike thus **3.** *inf.* put (on, down) carelessly or messily (**-pp-**) —ˈ**slap-ˈdash** *a.* careless and abrupt —ˈ**slaphappy** *a. inf.* **1.** cheerfully irresponsible **2.** dazed as if from repeated blows —ˈ**slapstick** *n.* boisterous knockabout comedy

slash (slash) *vt.* **1.** gash **2.** lash **3.** cut, slit **4.** criticize unmercifully —*n.* **5.** gash **6.** cutting stroke

slat (slat) *n.* narrow strip of wood or metal as in blinds *etc.*

slate (slāt) *n.* **1.** kind of stone which splits easily in flat sheets **2.** piece of this for covering roof or, formerly, for writing on —*vt.* **3.** cover with slates **4.** abuse —ˈ**slating** *n.* severe reprimand

slater (ˈslātər) *n.* woodlouse

slattern (ˈslatərn) *n.* slut —ˈ**slatternly** *a.* slovenly, untidy

slaughter (ˈslötər) *n.* **1.** killing —*vt.* **2.** kill —ˈ**slaughterous** *a.* —ˈ**slaughterhouse** *n.* place for killing animals for food

Slav (släv) *n.* member of any of peoples of E Europe or Soviet Asia who speak Slavonic language —**Slaˈvonic** *or* ˈ**Slavic** *n.* **1.** branch of Indo-European family of languages, including Bulgarian, Russian, Polish, Czech *etc.* —*a.* **2.** of this group of languages

slave (slāv) *n.* **1.** captive, person without freedom or personal rights **2.** one dominated by another or by a habit *etc.* —*vi.* **3.** work like slave —ˈ**slaver** *n.* person, ship engaged in slave traffic —ˈ**slavery** *n.* —ˈ**slavish** *a.* servile —**slave-driver** *n.* **1.** *esp.* formerly, person forcing slaves to work **2.** employer demanding excessively hard work from employees

slaver (ˈslavər) *vi.* **1.** dribble saliva from mouth **2.** fawn —*n.* **3.** saliva running from mouth

slaw (slö) *n.* coleslaw

slay (slā) *vt.* **1.** kill **2.** *inf.* impress, *esp.* by being very funny (**slew, slain,** ˈ**slaying**)

sleazy (ˈslēzi) *a.* sordid

sled (sled) *n.* **1.** vehicle on runners for sliding

on snow **2.** toboggan —*v.* **3.** convey, travel by sled (**-dd-**)

sledge (slej) *n.* heavy hammer with long handle (*also* ˈ**sledgehammer**)

sleek (slēk) *a.* glossy, smooth, shiny

sleep (slēp) *n.* **1.** unconscious state regularly occurring in man and animals **2.** period spend sleeping —*vi.* **3.** take rest in sleep (**slept,** ˈ**sleeping**) —ˈ**sleeper** *n.* **1.** one who sleeps **2.** railroad sleeping car —ˈ**sleepily** *adv.* —ˈ**sleepiness** *n.* —ˈ**sleepless** *a.* —ˈ**sleepy** *a.* —**sleeping bag** large well-padded bag for sleeping in, *esp.* outdoors —**sleeping car** railroad car fitted with compartments containing bunks for sleeping in —**sleeping partner** partner in business who does not play active role (*also* **silent partner**) —**sleeping pill** drug used to induce sleep —**sleeping sickness** Afr. disease spread by tsetse fly —ˈ**sleepwalk** *vi.* walk while asleep

sleet (slēt) *n.* rain and snow or hail falling together

sleeve (slēv) *n.* **1.** part of garment which covers arm **2.** case surrounding shaft **3.** phonograph record cover —*vt.* **4.** furnish with sleeves —**sleeved** *a.* —ˈ**sleeveless** *a.* —**have (something) up one's sleeve** have (something) prepared secretly for emergency

sleight (slīt) *n.* **1.** dexterity **2.** trickery **3.** deviousness —**sleight of hand 1.** (manual dexterity in) conjuring, juggling **2.** legerdemain

slender (ˈslendər) *a.* **1.** of small width relative to length or height **2.** feeble

slept (slept) *pt./pp. of* SLEEP

sleuth (slōōth) *n.* **1.** detective **2.** tracking dog (*also* ˈ**sleuthhound**) —*vt.* **3.** track

slew (slōō) *pt. of* SLAY

slice (slīs) *n.* **1.** thin flat piece cut off **2.** share **3.** flat culinary tool —*vt.* **4.** cut into slices **5.** cut cleanly **6.** hit (ball) with bat *etc.* at angle

slick (slik) *a.* **1.** smooth **2.** smooth-tongued **3.** flattering **4.** superficially attractive **5.** sly —*vt.* **6.** make glossy, smooth —*n.* **7.** slippery area **8.** patch of oil on water

slide (slīd) *vi.* **1.** slip smoothly along **2.** glide, as over ice **3.** deteriorate morally —*v.* **4.** pass imperceptibly (**slid** (slid) *pt.,* **slid, slidden** (ˈslidən) *pp.,* ˈ**sliding** *pr.p.*) —*n.* **5.** sliding **6.** surface, track for sliding **7.** sliding part of mechanism **8.** piece of glass holding object to be viewed under microscope **9.** photographic transparency **10.** ornamental clip to hold hair in place, hair slide —**slide rule** instrument of two parts, one of which slides upon the other, for rapid calculations —**sliding scale** schedule for automatically varying one thing (*eg* wages) according to fluctuations of another (*eg* cost of living)

slight (slīt) *a.* **1.** small, trifling **2.** not substantial, fragile **3.** slender —*vt.* **4.** disregard **5.** neglect —*n.* **6.** indifference **7.** act of discourtesy —ˈ**slightly** *adv.*

slim (slim) *a.* **1.** small in width relative to height or length **2.** small in amount or quality —*v.* **3.** make or become slim by diet and exercise (**-mm-**)

slime (slīm) *n.* greasy, thick, liquid mud or similar substance —ˈ**slimy** *a.* **1.** like slime **2.** fawning

sling (sling) *n.* **1.** strap, loop with string attached at each end for hurling stone **2.** bandage for supporting wounded limb **3.** rope, belt *etc.* for hoisting, carrying weights —*vt.* **4.** throw **5.** hoist, swing by rope (**slung,** ˈ**slinging**) —ˈ**slingback** *n.* shoe with strap instead of full covering for heel

slink (slingk) *vi.* move stealthily (**slunk,** ˈ**slinking**) —ˈ**slinky** *a.* **1.** sinuously graceful **2.** (of clothing *etc.*) figure-hugging

slip[1] (slip) *v.* **1.** (cause to) move smoothly, easily, quietly **2.** pass out of (mind *etc.*) **3.** (of motor vehicle clutch) engage partially, fail —*vi.* **4.** lose balance by sliding **5.** fall from person's grasp **6.** (*usu. with* up) make mistake **7.** decline in health, morals —*vt.* **8.** put on or take off easily, quickly **9.** let go (anchor *etc.*) **10.** dislocate (bone) (**-pp-**) —*n.* **11.** act or occasion of slipping **12.** mistake **13.** petticoat **14.** small piece of paper **15.** plant cutting **16.** launching slope on which ships are built **17.** covering for pillow —ˈ**slippy** *a. see* SLIPPERY (sense 1) —ˈ**slipknot** *n.* knot tied so that it will slip along rope round which it is made (*also* **running knot**) —**slip-on** *a.* **1.** (of garment or shoe) easily put on or removed —*n.* **2.** slip-on garment or shoe —**slipped disk** herniated intervertebral disk, oft. resulting in pain due to pressure on spinal nerves —ˈ**slipshod** *a.* slovenly, careless —ˈ**slipstream** *n. Aviation* stream of air driven astern by engine —**slip-up** *n. inf.* mistake or mishap —ˈ**slipway** *n.* incline for launching ships —**slip up** *inf.* blunder

slip[2] (slip) *n.* clay mixed with water to creamy consistency, used for decorating ceramic ware

slipper (ˈslipər) *n.* light shoe for indoor use

slippery (ˈslipəri, -pri) *a.* **1.** so smooth as to cause slipping or to be difficult to hold or catch **2.** changeable **3.** unreliable **4.** crafty, wily

slit (slit) *vt.* **1.** make long straight cut in **2.** cut in strips (**slit,** ˈ**slitting**) —*n.* **3.** long narrow cut or opening

slither (ˈslidhər) *vi.* slide unsteadily (down slope *etc.*)

sliver (ˈslivər) *n.* **1.** thin small piece torn off something **2.** splinter

slivovitz (ˈslivəvits, ˈslē-) *n.* plum brandy

slob (slob) *n. inf.* stupid, coarse person

slobber (ˈslobər) *or* **slabber** (ˈslabər) *vi.* **1.** slaver **2.** be weakly and excessively demonstrative —*n.* **3.** running saliva **4.** maudlin speech —ˈ**slobbery** *or* ˈ**slabbery** *a.*

slob ice C sludgy masses of floating ice

sloe (slō) *n.* blue-black, sour fruit of blackthorn —**sloe-eyed** *a.* having dark slanted or almond-shaped eyes

slog (slog) *vt.* **1.** hit vigorously, *esp.* at cricket —*vi.* **2.** work or study with dogged determination **3.** move, work with difficulty (**-gg-**) —*n.* **4.** tiring walk **5.** long exhausting work **6.** heavy blow

slogan (ˈslōgən) *n.* distinctive phrase (in advertising *etc.*)

sloop (sloo͞p) *n.* **1.** small one-masted vessel **2.** *Hist.* small warship

slop (slop) *vi.* **1.** spill —*vt.* **2.** spill, splash (**-pp-**) —*n.* **3.** liquid spilt **4.** liquid food **5.** dirty liquid —*pl.* **6.** liquid refuse —ˈ**sloppy** *a.* **1.** careless, untidy **2.** sentimental **3.** wet, muddy

slope (slōp) *vt.* **1.** place slanting —*vi.* **2.** lie in, follow an inclined course **3.** go furtively —*n.* **4.** inclined portion of ground **5.** upward, downward inclination

slosh (slosh) *n.* **1.** watery mud, snow *etc.* **2.** *sl.* heavy blow —*v.* **3.** splash —*vt.* **4.** hit —**sloshed** *a. sl.* drunk

slot (slot) *n.* **1.** narrow hole or depression **2.** slit for coins —*vt.* **3.** put in slot **4.** sort **5.** *inf.* place in series, organization (**-tt-**) —**slot machine** automatic machine worked by insertion of coin

sloth (slōth, slōth) *n.* **1.** sluggish S Amer. animal **2.** sluggishness —ˈ**slothful** *a.* lazy, idle

slouch (slowch) *vi.* **1.** walk, sit *etc.* in lazy or ungainly, drooping manner —*n.* **2.** drooping bearing **3.** incompetent or slovenly person —*a.* **4.** (of hat) with wide, flexible brim

slough[1] (sloo͞) *n.* **1.** bog **2.** (sloo͞, slow) C hole where water collects

slough[2] (sluf) *n.* **1.** skin shed by snake —*v.* **2.** shed (skin) —**slough off** cast off (cares *etc.*)

sloven (ˈsluvən) *n.* dirty, untidy person —ˈ**slovenly** *a.* **1.** untidy **2.** careless **3.** disorderly —*adv.* **4.** in slovenly manner

slow (slō) *a.* **1.** lasting a long time **2.** moving at low speed **3.** behind the true time **4.** dull —*v.* **5.** (cause to) decrease in speed —ˈ**slowly** *adv.* —ˈ**slowness** *n.* —ˈ**slowcoach** *n.* person slow in moving, acting, deciding *etc.* —**slow-motion** *a.* (of motion-picture or television image) showing movement greatly slowed down

slowworm (ˈslōwərm) *n.* small legless lizard, blindworm

sludge (sluj) *n.* **1.** slush, ooze **2.** sewage

slue (sloo͞) *n. see* SLOUGH[1] (sense 2)

slug[1] (slug) *n.* **1.** land snail with no shell **2.** bullet —ˈ**sluggard** *n.* lazy, idle person —ˈ**sluggish** *a.* **1.** slow **2.** lazy, inert **3.** not functioning well —ˈ**sluggishness** *n.*

slug[2] (slug) *vt.* **1.** hit, slog (**-gg-**) —*n.* **2.** heavy blow **3.** portion of spirits —ˈ**slugger** *n.* hard-hitting boxer, slogger

sluice (sloo͞s) *n.* **1.** gate, door to control flow of water —*vt.* **2.** pour water over, through

slum (slum) *n.* **1.** squalid street or neighborhood —*vi.* **2.** visit slums (**-mm-**)

slumber (ˈslumbər) *vi./n.* sleep —ˈ**slumberer** *n.*

slump (slump) *vi.* **1.** fall heavily **2.** relax ungracefully **3.** decline suddenly in value, volume or esteem —*n.* **4.** sudden decline **5.** (of prices *etc.*) sharp fall **6.** depression

slung (slung) *pt./pp. of* SLING

slunk (slungk) *pt./pp. of* SLINK

slur (slər) *vt.* **1.** pass over lightly **2.** run together (words, musical notes) **3.** disparage (**-rr-**) —*n.* **4.** slight, stigma **5.** *Mus.* curved line above or below notes to be slurred

slurp (slərp) *v. inf.* eat, drink noisily

slurry (ˈsluri) *n.* muddy liquid mixture, such as cement, mud *etc.*

slush (slush) *n.* **1.** watery, muddy substance **2.** excess sentimentality —**slush fund** fund for financing bribery, corruption

slut (slut) *n.* dirty (immoral) woman —ˈ**sluttish** *a.* —ˈ**sluttishness** *n.*

sly (slī) *a.* **1.** wily, knowing **2.** secret, deceitful —ˈ**slyly** *or* ˈ**slily** *adv.* —ˈ**slyness** *n.*

Sm *Chem.* samarium

smack[1] (smak) *n.* **1.** taste, flavor **2.** *sl.* heroin —*vi.* (*with* of) **3.** have taste (of) **4.** be suggestive (of)

smack[2] (smak) *vt.* **1.** slap **2.** open and close (lips) with loud sound —*n.* **3.** smacking slap **4.** crack **5.** such sound **6.** loud kiss —*adv.* **7.** *inf.* squarely; directly —ˈ**smacker** *n. sl.* **1.** loud kiss **2.** pound note or dollar bill

smack[3] (smak) *n.* small sailing vessel, usu. for fishing

small (smöl) *a.* **1.** little **2.** unimportant; petty **3.** short **4.** weak **5.** mean —*n.* **6.** small slender part, *esp.* of the back —*pl.* **7.** *inf.* personal laundry, underwear —ˈ**smallness** *n.* —**small change 1.** coins, *esp.* those of low value **2.** *rare* person or thing of little importance —**small hours** hours just after midnight —**small-minded** *a.* having narrow views; petty —ˈ**smallpox** *n.* contagious disease —**small-scale** *a.* **1.** of limited size **2.** (of map *etc.*) giving small representation of something —**small slam** *Bridge* bidding for and winning twelve tricks (*also* **little slam**) —**small talk** light, polite conversation —**small-time** *a. inf.* insignificant; petty —**small-timer** *n.*

smarm (smärm) *vi. inf.* fawn —ˈ**smarmy** *a. inf.* unpleasantly suave; fawning

smart (smärt) *a.* **1.** astute **2.** brisk **3.** clever, witty **4.** impertinent **5.** well dressed **6.** fashionable **7.** causing stinging pain —*v.* **8.** feel, cause pain —*n.* **9.** sharp pain —ˈ**smarten** *v.* —ˈ**smartly** *adv.* —ˈ**smartness** *n.* —**smart aleck** (ˈalik) *or* **ass** *inf.* conceited person, know-it-all

smash (smash) *vt.* **1.** break violently **2.** strike hard **3.** ruin **4.** destroy —*vi.* **5.** break **6.** dash violently —*n.* **7.** heavy blow **8.** collision (of vehicles *etc.*) **9.** total financial failure **10.** *inf.*

popular success —**smashed** *a. sl.* very drunk or affected by drugs —'**smasher** *n. inf.* attractive person, thing —'**smashing** *a.* excellent

smattering ('smatəring) *n.* slight superficial knowledge

smear (smēər) *vt.* **1.** rub with grease *etc.* **2.** smudge, spread with dirt, grease *etc.* —*n.* **3.** mark made thus **4.** sample of secretion for medical examination **5.** slander

smell (smel) *vt.* **1.** perceive by nose **2.** *fig.* suspect —*vi.* **3.** give out odor **4.** use nose (**smelt** *or* **smelled,** '**smelling**) —*n.* **5.** faculty of perceiving odors by nose **6.** anything detected by sense of smell —'**smelly** *a.* with strong (unpleasant) smell —**smelling salts** preparation of ammonium carbonate that has stimulant action when sniffed in cases of faintness *etc.*

smelt[1] (smelt) *vt.* extract (metal) from (ore) —'**smeltery** *n.*

smelt[2] (smelt) *n.* fish of salmon family

smew (smyo͞o) *n.* type of duck

smilax ('smīlaks) *n.* **1.** climbing shrub having slightly lobed leaves and berry-like fruits **2.** much branched vine of S Afr. with glossy green foliage

smile (smīl) *n.* **1.** curving or parting of lips in pleased or amused expression —*vi.* **2.** wear, assume a smile **3.** (*with* on) approve, favor

smirch (smərch) *vt.* **1.** dirty, sully **2.** disgrace, discredit —*n.* **3.** stain **4.** disgrace

smirk (smərk) *n.* **1.** smile expressing scorn, smugness —*vi.* **2.** give such smile

smite (smīt) *vt.* **1.** strike **2.** attack **3.** afflict **4.** affect, *esp.* with love or fear (**smote,** '**smitten,** '**smiting**)

smith (smith) *n.* worker in iron, gold *etc.* —**smithy** ('smithi, 'smidhi) *n.* blacksmith's workshop

smithereens (smidhə'rēnz) *pl.n.* small bits

smitten ('smitən) *pp. of* SMITE

smock (smok) *n.* **1.** loose outer garment —*vt.* **2.** gather by sewing in honeycomb pattern

smog (smog) *n.* mixture of smoke and fog

smoke (smōk) *n.* **1.** cloudy mass of suspended particles that rises from fire or anything burning **2.** spell of tobacco smoking —*vi.* **3.** give off smoke **4.** inhale and expel tobacco smoke —*vt.* **5.** use (tobacco) by smoking **6.** expose to smoke (*esp.* in curing fish *etc.*) —'**smoker** *n.* —'**smokily** *adv.* —'**smoky** *a.* —**smoke screen 1.** *Mil.* cloud of smoke produced to obscure movements **2.** something said or done to conceal truth —'**smokestack** *n.* chimney that conveys smoke into air

smolder ('smōldər) *vi.* **1.** burn slowly without flame **2.** (of feelings) exist in suppressed state

smolt (smōlt) *n.* young salmon at stage when it migrates from fresh water to sea

smooch (smo͞och) *vi./n. inf.* kiss, cuddle

smooth (smo͞odh) *a.* **1.** not rough, even of surface or texture **2.** sinuous **3.** flowing **4.** calm, soft, soothing **5.** suave, plausible **6.** free from jolts —*vt.* **7.** make smooth **8.** quieten —'**smoothly** *adv.* —**smooth-spoken** *a.* speaking in gently persuasive manner —**smooth-tongued** *a.* suave or persuasive in speech

smorgasbord ('smörgəsbörd) *n.* buffet meal of assorted dishes

smote (smōt) *pt. of* SMITE

smother ('smudhər) *vt.* **1.** suffocate by cutting off from air **2.** envelop **3.** suppress —*vi.* **4.** be suffocated by being cut off from air

smudge (smuj) *vt.* **1.** make smear, stain, dirty mark on —*n.* **2.** smear or dirty mark

smug (smug) *a.* self-satisfied, complacent

smuggle ('smugəl) *vt.* **1.** import, export without paying customs duties **2.** conceal, take secretly

smut (smut) *n.* **1.** piece of soot, particle of dirt **2.** lewd or obscene talk *etc.* **3.** disease of grain —*vt.* **4.** blacken, smudge (**-tt-**) —'**smutty** *a.* **1.** soiled with smut, soot **2.** obscene, lewd

Sn *Chem.* tin

snack (snak) *n.* light, hasty meal —**snack bar** bar at which snacks are served

snaffle ('snafəl) *n.* **1.** jointed bit for bridle —*vt.* **2.** put snaffle on

snag (snag) *n.* **1.** difficulty **2.** sharp protuberance **3.** hole, loop in fabric caused by sharp object **4.** obstacle (*eg* tree branch *etc.* in river bed) —*vt.* **5.** catch, damage on snag (**-gg-**)

snail (snāl) *n.* **1.** slow-moving mollusk with shell **2.** slow, sluggish person —**snail-like** *a.* —**snail fever** *see* SCHISTOSOMIASIS —**snail's pace** very slow rate

snake (snāk) *n.* **1.** long scaly limbless reptile —*vi.* **2.** move like snake —'**snaky** *a.* of, like snakes —**snake charmer** entertainer who appears to charm snakes by playing music —**snakes and ladders** obstacle game governed by throw of dice and instructions printed on the board on which it is played

snap (snap) *v.* **1.** break suddenly **2.** (cause to) make cracking sound **3.** bite (at) suddenly **4.** speak (words) suddenly, angrily (**-pp-**) —*n.* **5.** act of snapping **6.** fastener **7.** *inf.* snapshot **8.** *inf.* easy task **9.** brief period, *esp.* of cold weather —*a.* **10.** sudden, unplanned, arranged quickly —'**snapper** *n.* **1.** perchlike fish **2.** decorated paper tube filled with party favors which pops when pulled apart —'**snappy** *a.* **1.** irritable **2.** *sl.* quick **3.** *sl.* well-dressed, fashionable —'**snapdragon** *n.* plant with flowers that can be opened like a mouth —**snap fastener** fastening device with projecting knob on one part that snaps into hole on other part —'**snapshot** *n.* photograph

snare[1] (snāər) *n.* **1.** (noose used as) trap —*vt.* **2.** catch with one

snare[2] (snāər) *n. Mus.* set of gut strings

wound with wire fitted across bottom of drum to increase vibration —**snare drum** cylindrical double-headed drum with snares

snarl (snärl) *n.* **1.** growl of angry dog **2.** tangle, knot —*vi.* **3.** utter snarl **4.** grumble —**snarl-up** *n. inf.* confusion, obstruction, *esp.* traffic jam

snatch (snach) *vt.* **1.** make quick grab or bite at **2.** seize, catch —*n.* **3.** grab **4.** fragment **5.** short spell

snazzy ('snazi) *a. inf.* stylish, flashy

sneak (snēk) *vi.* **1.** slink **2.** move about furtively **3.** act in mean, underhand manner —*n.* **4.** mean, treacherous person **5.** petty informer —'**sneaking** *a.* secret but persistent —**sneak thief** person who steals articles from premises which he enters through open windows *etc.*

sneakers ('snēkərz) *pl.n.* canvas shoes with flexible soles

sneer (snēər) *n.* **1.** scornful, contemptuous expression or remark —*vi.* **2.** assume scornful expression —*v.* **3.** speak or utter contemptuously

sneeze (snēz) *vi.* **1.** emit breath through nose with sudden involuntary spasm and noise —*n.* **2.** sound or act of sneezing

snicker ('snikər) *see* SNIGGER

snide (snīd) *a.* malicious, supercilious

sniff (snif) *vi.* **1.** inhale through nose with sharp hiss **2.** (*with* at) express disapproval *etc.* by sniffing —*vt.* **3.** take up through nose **4.** smell —*n.* **5.** act or sound of sniffing —'**sniffle** *vi.* sniff noisily through nose, *esp.* when suffering from a cold in the head, snuffle

snifter ('sniftər) *n.* **1.** pear-shaped glass with bowl that narrows toward the top so that aroma of brandy *etc.* is retained **2.** *inf.* small alcoholic drink

snigger ('snigər) *n.* **1.** sly, disrespectful laugh, *esp.* partly stifled —*vi.* **2.** utter such laugh

snip (snip) *v.* **1.** cut (bits off) (**-pp-**) —*n.* **2.** act, sound of snipping **3.** bit cut off **4.** *inf.* bargain **5.** *inf.* certainty —'**snippet** *n.* shred, fragment, clipping —**snips** *pl.n.* tool for cutting

snipe (snīp) *n.* **1.** wading bird —*v.* **2.** shoot at (enemy) from cover **3.** (*with* at) criticize, attack (person) slyly —'**sniper** *n.*

snitch (snich) *inf. vt.* **1.** steal —*vi.* **2.** inform on someone —*n.* **3.** telltale

snivel ('snivəl) *vi.* **1.** sniffle to show distress **2.** whine

snob (snob) *n.* one who offensively judges others by social rank *etc.* —'**snobbery** *n.* —'**snobbish** *a.* of, like snob —'**snobbishly** *adv.*

snood (snōōd) *n.* pouchlike hat, worn at back of head to hold woman's hair

snook (snōōk) *n.* rude gesture, made by putting one thumb to nose with fingers outstretched (*esp. in* **cock a snook at**)

snooker ('snōōkər) *n.* **1.** variety of pool played with 15 red balls and 6 balls of other colors —*vt.* **2.** hoodwink

snoop (snōōp) *vi.* **1.** pry, meddle **2.** peer —*n.* **3.** one who acts thus **4.** act or instance of snooping

snooty ('snōōti) *a. sl.* haughty

snooze (snōōz) *vi.* **1.** take short sleep, be half asleep —*n.* **2.** nap

snore (snōr) *vi.* **1.** breathe noisily when asleep —*n.* **2.** noise of snoring

snorkel ('snōrkəl) *n.* **1.** tube for breathing underwater —*vi.* **2.** swim, fish using this

snort (snōrt) *vi.* **1.** make (contemptuous) noise by driving breath through nostrils —*n.* **2.** such noise

snot (snot) *n. vulg.* mucus from nose —'**snotty** *a.* spitefully unpleasant

snout (snowt) *n.* animal's nose

snow (snō) *n.* **1.** frozen vapor which falls in flakes **2.** *sl.* cocaine —*v.* **3.** fall, sprinkle as snow —*vt.* **4.** let fall, throw down like snow **5.** cover with snow **6.** *inf.* mislead, charm insincerely, persuade —'**snowy** *a.* **1.** of, like snow **2.** covered with snow **3.** very white —'**snowball** *n.* **1.** snow pressed into hard ball for throwing —*vi.* **2.** increase rapidly in importance *etc.* **3.** play, fight with snowballs —'**snowberry** *n.* shrub with small pink flowers and white berries —**snow blindness** temporary blindness due to brightness of snow —'**snowdrift** *n.* bank of deep snow —'**snowdrop** *n.* small, white, bell-shaped spring flower —'**snowfall** *n.* **1.** fall of snow **2.** *Met.* amount of snow received in specified place and time —**snow fence** fence erected in winter to protect from drifting snow —'**snowflake** *n.* **1.** one of mass of ice crystals that fall as snow **2.** any of various European plants that have white bell-shaped flowers —**snow goose** white N Amer. goose —**snow-in-summer** *n.* rock plant with white flowers —**snow line** elevation above which snow does not melt —'**snowman** *n.* figure shaped out of snow —'**snowmobile** *n.* any automotive vehicle for traveling on snow —'**snowplow** *n.* **1.** implement or vehicle for clearing away snow **2.** stemming with both skis to slow or stop —'**snowshoe** *n.* light wooden frame with strips of leather stretched across it for walking or running on deep snow —**snow under 1.** cover and block with snow **2.** *fig.* overwhelm

snub (snub) *vt.* **1.** insult (*esp.* by ignoring) intentionally (**-bb-**) —*n.* **2.** snubbing, rebuff —*a.* **3.** short and blunt

snuff[1] (snuf) *n.* powdered tobacco for inhaling through nose

snuff[2] (snuf) *vt.* extinguish (*esp.* light from candle) —'**snuffer** *n.* **1.** cone-shaped implement for extinguishing candles —*pl.* **2.** instrument resembling scissors for trimming wick of candle —**snuff it** *sl.* die

snuffle ('snufəl) *vi.* breathe noisily or with difficulty

snug (snug) *a.* warm, comfortable —**'snuggle** *v.* lie close to, for warmth or affection —**'snugly** *adv.*

snye (snī) *n.* C side channel of river

so[1] (sō) *adv.* **1.** to such an extent **2.** in such a manner **3.** very **4.** the case being such **5.** accordingly —*conj.* **6.** therefore **7.** in order that **8.** with the result that —*interj.* **9.** well —**so-and-so** *n. inf.* **1.** person whose name is forgotten or ignored **2.** *euphemistic* person or thing regarded as unpleasant —**so-called** *a.* called by but doubtfully deserving the name —**so long** *inf.* farewell; goodbye

so[2] (sō) *n. Mus. see* SOL

So. south(ern)

soak (sōk) *v.* **1.** make, become or be thoroughly wet, *esp.* by immersion in liquid —*vt.* **2.** absorb **3.** drench —*vi.* **4.** lie in liquid —*n.* **5.** soaking **6.** *sl.* habitual drunkard

soap (sōp) *n.* **1.** compound of alkali and oil used in washing —*vt.* **2.** apply soap to —**'soapy** *a.* —**'soapbox** *n.* crate used as platform for speech-making —**soapbox derby** race for children down ramped course on hand-made motorless vehicles made by drivers —**soap opera** radio or television serial of domestic life —**'soapstone** *n.* massive compact variety of talc, used for making hearths *etc.* (*also* **steatite**)

soar (sōr) *vi.* **1.** fly high **2.** increase, rise (in price *etc.*)

sob (sob) *vi.* **1.** catch breath, *esp.* in weeping (**-bb-**) —*n.* **2.** sobbing —**sob story** tale of personal distress told to arouse sympathy

sober ('sōbər) *a.* **1.** not drunk **2.** temperate **3.** subdued **4.** dull, plain **5.** solemn —*v.* **6.** make, become sober —**'soberly** *adv.* —**so'briety** *n.* state of being sober

sobriquet ('sōbrikā) *n.* **1.** nickname **2.** assumed name

Soc. *or* **soc.** Society

soccer ('sokər) *n.* football game played by two teams of 11 players each of which attempts to score points by propelling a round ball into the other's goal (*also* **association football**)

sociable ('sōshəbəl) *a.* **1.** friendly **2.** convivial —**socia'bility** *n.* —**'sociably** *adv.*

social ('sōshəl) *a.* **1.** living in communities **2.** relating to society **3.** sociable —*n.* **4.** informal gathering —**'socialite** *n.* member of fashionable society —**sociali'zation** *n.* —**'socialize** *v.* —**'socially** *adv.* —**social contract** *or* **compact** agreement entered into by individuals, that results in formation of state and entails surrender of some personal liberties —**Social Register** trade name for directory of eminent persons in a community —**social science** study of society and of relationship of individual members within society, including economics, history, psychology *etc.* —**social security** state provision for the unemployed, aged *etc.* —**social services** welfare activities organized by state —**social studies** (*with sing. v.*) study of how people live and organize themselves in society, embracing geography, economics *etc.* —**social work** work to improve welfare of others

socialism ('sōshəlizəm) *n.* political system which advocates public ownership of means of production, distribution and exchange —**'socialist** *n./a.* —**socia'listic** *a.*

society (sə'sīəti) *n.* **1.** living associated with others **2.** those so living **3.** companionship **4.** company **5.** association **6.** club **7.** fashionable people collectively

socio- (*comb. form*) denoting social or society, as in *socioeconomic*

socioeconomic (sōsiōekə'nomik, -ēkə-) *a.* of or involving both economic and social factors

sociology (sōsi'oləji) *n.* study of societies

sociopolitical (sōsiōpə'litikəl) *a.* of or involving both political and social factors

sock[1] (sok) *n.* cloth covering for foot

sock[2] (sok) *sl. vt.* **1.** hit —*n.* **2.** blow

socket ('sokit) *n.* hole or recess for something to fit into

Socratic (sə'kratik) *a.* of, like Gr. philosopher Socrates

sod (sod) *n.* **1.** lump of earth with grass **2.** *sl.* person considered obnoxious **3.** *sl.* person, as specified

soda ('sōdə) *n.* **1.** compound of sodium **2.** soda water —**soda fountain 1.** counter that serves drinks, snacks *etc.* **2.** apparatus dispensing soda water —**soda water** water charged with carbon dioxide

sodden ('sodən) *a.* **1.** soaked **2.** drunk **3.** heavy and doughy

sodium ('sōdiəm) *n. Chem.* metallic element *Symbol* Na, at. wt. 23.0, at. no. 11 —**sodium bicarbonate** *or* **sodium hydrogen carbonate** chemical compound used in baking powder *etc.* (*also* **bicarbonate of soda**) —**sodium carbonate** soluble crystalline compound used in manufacture of glass, ceramics, soap and paper, and as cleansing agent —**sodium chloride** common table salt —**sodium hydroxide** white strongly alkaline solid used in manufacture of rayon, paper, aluminum, soap and sodium compounds —**sodium pentothal** *see* PENTOTHAL SODIUM

Sodom ('sodəm) *n.* **1.** *O.T.* city that, with Gomorrah, traditionally typifies depravity **2.** this city as representing homosexuality **3.** any place notorious for depravity

sodomy ('sodəmi) *n.* anal intercourse —**'sodomite** *n.*

sofa ('sōfə) *n.* upholstered seat with back and arms, for two or more people

soft (soft) *a.* **1.** yielding easily to pressure **2.** mild **3.** easy **4.** subdued **5.** quiet, gentle **6.** (too) lenient **7.** oversentimental **8.** feebleminded **9.** (of water) containing few mineral salts **10.** (of drugs) not liable to cause addiction —**soften** ('sofən) *v.* **1.** make, become soft or softer —*vt.* **2.** mollify **3.**

lighten **4.** mitigate **5.** make less loud —**'softly** *adv.* gently, quietly —**'softy** *or* **'softie** *n. inf.* person who is sentimental, weakly foolish or lacking in physical endurance —**'softball** *n.* bat-and-ball game resembling baseball, but played on a smaller field, with a smaller bat and a larger ball, and consisting of seven innings. Pitching must be underhand —**soft-boiled** *a.* (of egg) boiled for a short time so that yolk remains soft —**soft drink** drink that is nonalcoholic —**soft'hearted** *a.* easily moved to pity —**soft palate** posterior fleshy portion of roof of mouth —**soft-pedal** *vt.* **1.** mute tone of (piano) **2.** *inf.* make (something) less obvious by deliberately failing to emphasize it —**soft pedal** foot-operated lever on piano that causes fewer of strings to sound —**soft sell** method of selling based on indirect suggestion or inducement —**soft-shoe** *a.* (of tap-dancing) done without metal pieces on shoes —**soft soap** flattery —**soft spot** sentimental fondness —**'software** *n.* computer programs, tapes *etc.* for a particular computer system —**'softwood** *n.* wood of coniferous tree

soggy ('sogi) *a.* **1.** soaked with liquid **2.** damp and heavy

soigné *or* (*fem.*) **soignée** (swä'nyā) *a.* well-groomed

soil[1] (soil) *n.* **1.** earth, ground **2.** country, territory

soil[2] (soil) *v.* **1.** make, become dirty —*vt.* **2.** tarnish, defile —*n.* **3.** dirt **4.** sewage **5.** stain

soiree (swä'rā) *n.* private evening party, *esp.* with music

sojourn ('sōjərn, sō'jərn) *vi.* **1.** stay for a time —*n.* **2.** short stay —**'sojourner** *n.*

sol (sōl) *n. Mus.* **1.** in fixed system of solmization, the note G **2.** in movable do system, the fifth note of a major scale

solace ('solis) *n./vt.* comfort in distress

solar ('sōlər) *a.* of the sun —**solari'zation** *n.* —**'solarize** *vt.* affect by sunlight —**solar cell** cell that produces electricity from sun's rays —**solar plexus** ('pleksəs) network of nerves at pit of stomach —**solar system** system containing sun and heavenly bodies held in its gravitational field

solarium (sō'lariəm, sə-; -'ler-) *n.* **1.** room built mainly of glass to give exposure to sun **2.** (place with) bed for acquiring suntan by artificial means

sold (sōld) *pt./pp. of* SELL

solder ('sodər) *n.* **1.** easily melted alloy used for joining metal —*vt.* **2.** join with solder —**soldering iron**

soldier ('sōljər) *n.* **1.** one serving in army —*vi.* **2.** serve in army **3.** (*with* on) persist doggedly —**'soldierly** *a.* —**'soldiery** *n.* troops —**soldier of fortune** man who seeks money or adventure as soldier

sole[1] (sōl) *a.* **1.** one and only, unique **2.** solitary —**'solely** *adv.* **1.** alone **2.** only **3.** entirely

sole[2] (sōl) *n.* **1.** underside of foot **2.** underpart of boot *etc.* —*vt.* **3.** fit with sole

sole[3] (sōl) *n.* small edible flatfish

solecism ('solisizəm) *n.* breach of grammar or etiquette

solemn ('soləm) *a.* **1.** serious **2.** formal **3.** impressive —**solemnity** (sə'lemniti) *n.* —**solemnization** ('soləmni'zāshən) *n.* —**solemnize** ('sōləmnīz) *vt.* **1.** celebrate, perform **2.** make solemn —**'solemnly** *adv.*

solenoid ('sōlinoid) *n.* coil of wire as part of electrical apparatus used to control doors

sol-fa ('sōl'fä) *n. Mus.* system of syllables sol, fa *etc.* sung in scale

solicit (sə'lisit) *vt.* **1.** request **2.** accost **3.** urge **4.** entice —**solici'tation** *n.* —**so'licitor** *n.* —**so'licitous** *a.* **1.** anxious **2.** eager **3.** earnest —**so'licitude** *n.*

solid ('solid) *a.* **1.** not hollow **2.** compact **3.** composed of one substance **4.** firm **5.** massive **6.** reliable —*n.* **7.** body of three dimensions **8.** substance not liquid or gas —**soli'darity** *n.* **1.** unity of interests **2.** united state —**solidifi'cation** *n.* —**so'lidify** *v.* **1.** make, become solid or firm **2.** harden (**-ified, -ifying**) —**so'lidity** *n.* —**'solidly** *adv.* —**solid geometry** branch of geometry concerned with solid geometric figures —**solid-state** *a.* (of electronic device) consisting chiefly of semiconductor materials and controlled by means of their electrical properties

solidus ('solidəs) *n.* short stroke (/) used in text to separate items (*pl.* **-di** (-dī)) (*also* **diagonal, virgule**)

soliloquy (sə'liləkwi) *n. esp.* in drama, thoughts spoken by person while alone —**so'liloquize** *v.*

solipsism ('sōlipsizəm, 'sol-) *n.* doctrine that self is the only thing known to exist —**'solipsist** *n.*

solitary ('soliteri) *a.* **1.** alone, single —*n.* **2.** hermit —**'solitaire** *n.* **1.** precious stone, *esp.* diamond, set alone in a ring **2.** card game for one person in which cards have to be played in a prescribed manner **3.** board game for one person in which pegs have to be brought to a particular arrangement —**'solitude** *n.* **1.** state of being alone **2.** loneliness —**solitary confinement** isolation imposed on prisoner —**double solitaire** solitaire game adapted for two persons

solo ('sōlō) *n.* **1.** music for one performer (*pl.* **-s, -li** (-lē)) **2.** card game like whist (*pl.* **-s**) —*a.* **3.** not concerted **4.** unaccompanied, alone **5.** piloting airplane alone —**'soloist** *n.*

Solomon Islands ('soləmən) country lying in south Pacific comprising an archipelago east of New Guinea within the area 5° to 12°30' S latitude and 155°30' to 169°45' E longitude

solstice ('solstis) *n.* either shortest (winter) or longest (summer) day of year —**solstitial** (sol'stishəl) *a.*

solve (solv) *vt.* **1.** work out answer to **2.** find answer to —**solubility** (solyə'biliti) *n.* —**soluble** ('solyəbəl) *a.* **1.** capable of being dissolved in liquid **2.** able to be solved or explained —**solute** ('solyōōt) *n.* **1.** substance dissolved in solution —*a.* **2.** *Bot.* unattached —**solution** (sə'lōōshən) *n.* **1.** answer to problem **2.** dissolving **3.** liquid with something dissolved in it —'**solvable** *a.* —'**solvency** *n.* —'**solvent** *a.* **1.** able to meet financial obligations —*n.* **2.** liquid with power of dissolving

Somalia (sō'mäliə) *n.* country in Africa bounded north by the Gulf of Aden, east and south by the Indian Ocean and west by Kenya —**So'malian** *n./a.*

somatic (sō'matik) *a.* **1.** of the body, as distinct from the mind **2.** of animal body or body wall as distinct from viscera, limbs and head

somber ('sombər) *a.* dark, gloomy

sombrero (səm'brāərō, som-) *n.* wide-brimmed hat (*pl.* **-s**)

some (sum; *unstressed* səm) *a.* **1.** denoting an indefinite number, amount or extent **2.** one or other **3.** amount of **4.** certain **5.** approximately —*pron.* **6.** portion, quantity —'**somebody** *pron.* **1.** some person —*n.* **2.** important person —'**somehow** *adv.* by some means unknown —'**someone** *pron.* some person —'**something** *pron.* **1.** thing not clearly defined **2.** indefinite amount, quantity or degree —'**sometime** *adv.* **1.** formerly **2.** at some (past or future) time —*a.* **3.** former —'**sometimes** *adv.* **1.** occasionally **2.** now and then —'**somewhat** *adv.* to some extent, rather —'**somewhere** *adv.*

somersault ('sumərsölt) *n.* tumbling head over heels

somnambulist (som'nambyəlist) *n.* sleepwalker —**som'nambulism** *n.* —**somnambu'listic** *a.*

somnolent ('somnələnt) *a.* **1.** drowsy **2.** causing sleep —'**somnolence** *or* '**somnolency** *n.*

son (sun) *n.* male child —'**sonny** *n.* familiar term of address to boy or man —**son-in-law** *n.* daughter's husband

sonar ('sōnär) *n.* *so*und *na*vigating *r*anging device that detects submerged objects by reflected vibrations

sonata (sə'nätə) *n.* piece of music in several movements —**sonatina** (sonə'tēnə) *n.* short sonata

son et lumière (sōn ā lōō'myāər) *Fr.* entertainment staged at night at famous place, building, giving dramatic history of it with lighting and sound effects

song (song) *n.* **1.** singing **2.** poem *etc.* for singing —'**songster** *n.* **1.** singer **2.** songbird ('**songstress** *fem.*) —'**songbird** *n.* **1.** passerine bird with highly developed vocal organs and *usu.* musical call **2.** any bird with musical call —**Song of Solomon** *Bible* 22nd book of the O.T., written by Solomon, delineating the perfect picture of true love

sonic ('sonik) *a.* pert. to sound waves —**sonic barrier** *see* **sound barrier** *at* SOUND[1] —**sonic boom** explosive sound caused by aircraft traveling at supersonic speed

sonnet ('sonit) *n.* fourteen-line poem with definite rhyme scheme —**sonne'teer** *n.* writer of this

sonorous (sə'nörəs, 'sonərəs) *a.* giving out (deep) sound, resonant —**sonority** (sə'nöriti) *n.* —**so'norously** *adv.*

soon (sōōn) *adv.* **1.** in a short time **2.** before long **3.** early, quickly

soot (sŏŏt) *n.* black powdery substance formed by burning of coal *etc.* —'**sooty** *a.* of, like soot

sooth (sōōth) *n.* truth —'**soothsayer** *n.* one who foretells future, diviner

soothe (sōōdh) *vt.* **1.** make calm, tranquil **2.** relieve (pain *etc.*)

sop (sop) *n.* **1.** piece of bread *etc.* soaked in liquid **2.** concession, bribe —*vt.* **3.** steep in water *etc.* **4.** soak (up) (**-pp-**) —'**sopping** *a.* completely soaked —'**soppy** *a. inf.* oversentimental

sophist ('sofist) *n.* fallacious reasoner, quibbler —'**sophism** *n.* specious argument —**so'phistical** *a.* —'**sophistry** *n.*

sophisticate (sə'fistikāt) *vt.* **1.** make artificial, spoil, falsify, corrupt —*n.* (sə'fistikit, -kāt) **2.** sophisticated person —**so'phisticated** *a.* **1.** having refined or cultured tastes, habits **2.** worldly **3.** superficially clever **4.** complex —**sophisti'cation** *n.*

sophomore ('sofmör) *n.* student in second year at college or high school

Sophonias (sofə'nīəs) *n.* *Bible* Zephaniah in the Douay Version of the O.T.

-sophy (*n. comb. form*) indicating knowledge or intellectual system, as in *philosophy* —**-sophic** *or* **-sophical** (*a. comb. form*)

soporific (sopə'rifik) *a.* **1.** causing sleep (*esp.* by drugs) —*n.* **2.** drug or other agent that induces sleep

soprano (sə'pranō, -'pränō) *n.* **1.** highest voice in women and boys **2.** singer with this voice **3.** musical part for it (*pl.* **-s**)

sorbet ('sörbit) *n.* (fruit-flavored) water ice

sorcerer ('sörsərər) *or* (*fem.*) **sorceress** ('sörsəris) *n.* magician —'**sorcery** *n.* witchcraft, magic

sordid ('sördid) *a.* **1.** mean, squalid **2.** ignoble, base —'**sordidly** *adv.* —'**sordidness** *n.*

sore (sör) *a.* **1.** painful **2.** causing annoyance **3.** severe **4.** distressed **5.** annoyed —*adv.* **6.** *obs.* grievously, intensely —*n.* **7.** sore place, ulcer, boil *etc.* —'**sorely** *adv.* **1.** grievously **2.** greatly

sorghum ('sörgəm) *n.* kind of grass cultivated for fodder, smother crop and production of syrup

sorority (sə'röriti) *n.* social club or society for women

sorrel ('sörəl) *n.* **1.** plant **2.** reddish-brown color **3.** horse of this color —*a.* **4.** of this color

sorrow ('sorō) *n.* **1.** pain of mind, grief, sadness —*vi.* **2.** grieve —'**sorrowful** *a.*

sorry ('sori) *a.* **1.** feeling pity or regret **2.** distressed **3.** miserable, wretched **4.** mean, poor —'**sorrily** *adv.* —'**sorriness** *n.*

sort (sört) *n.* **1.** kind or class —*vt.* **2.** classify

sortie ('sörti) *n.* sally by besieged forces

SOS **1.** international code signal of distress **2.** call for help

so-so *a. inf.* mediocre

sostenuto (sōstə'nōōtō, sōs-) *a./adv. Mus.* in smooth sustained manner

sot (sot) *n.* habitual drunkard

sotto voce ('sotō 'vōchi) *It.* in an undertone

sou (sōō) *n.* **1.** former French coin **2.** small amount of money

soubrette (sōō'bret) *n.* **1.** minor female role in comedy **2.** any flirtatious girl

soufflé (sōō'flā, 'sōōflā) *n.* dish of eggs beaten to froth, flavored and baked

sough (sow) *n.* low murmuring sound as of wind in trees

sought (sōt) *pt./pp. of* SEEK

souk (sōōk) *n.* open-air market place, *esp.* in N Afr. and Middle East

soul (sōl) *n.* **1.** spiritual and immortal part of human being **2.** example, pattern **3.** person —'**soulful** *a.* full of emotion or sentiment —'**soulless** *a.* **1.** mechanical **2.** lacking sensitivity or nobility **3.** heartless, cruel —**soul-destroying** *a.* (of occupation *etc.*) monotonous —**soul food** *inf.* food, as yams *etc.*, traditionally eaten by Blacks —**soul mate** person for whom one has deep affinity —**soul music** type of Black music resulting from addition of jazz and gospel to urban blues style —**soul-searching** *n.* deep or critical examination of one's motives, actions *etc.*

sound[1] (sownd) *n.* **1.** what is heard **2.** noise —*vi.* **3.** make sound **4.** seem **5.** resonate with a certain quality —*vt.* **6.** cause to sound **7.** utter —**sound barrier** large increase in resistance encountered by aircraft approaching speed of sound —**sound effect** sound artificially produced to create theatrical effect, as in plays, motion pictures *etc.* —**sounding board** **1.** thin wooden board in violin *etc.* designed to reflect sound **2.** person *etc.* used to test new idea *etc.* —**sound track** recorded sound accompaniment of motion picture *etc.* —**sound wave** wave that propagates sound

sound[2] (sownd) *a.* **1.** in good condition **2.** solid **3.** of good judgment **4.** legal **5.** solvent **6.** thorough **7.** effective **8.** watertight **9.** deep —'**soundly** *adv.* thoroughly

sound[3] (sownd) *vt.* **1.** measure depth of (well, sea *etc.*) **2.** probe —'**soundings** *pl.n.* measurements taken by sounding —**sound out** ascertain views of

sound[4] (sownd) *n.* channel, strait

soup (sōōp) *n.* liquid food made by boiling meat, vegetables *etc.* —'**soupy** *a.* **1.** like soup **2.** murky **3.** sentimental —**soup kitchen** place where food, *esp.* soup, is served to destitute people —**soup up** *inf.* **1.** enliven **2.** increase power of (an engine)

soupçon (sōōp'sō) *Fr.* small amount

sour ('sowər) *a.* **1.** acid **2.** gone bad **3.** rancid **4.** peevish **5.** disagreeable —*v.* **6.** make, become sour —'**sourly** *adv.* —'**sourness** *n.* —**sour ball** hard round candy with tart flavor —**sour cream** commercially fermented cream —'**sourdough** *n.* **1.** dough leavened by culture of mild yeast **2.** pioneer, *esp.* old-timer in Alaska —**sour grapes** attitude of despising something because one cannot have it oneself —**sour gum** *see* **black gum** *at* BLACK —'**sourpuss** *n.* sullen, sour-faced person —**sour salt** citric acid crystals used for flavoring

source (sörs) *n.* **1.** origin, starting point **2.** spring

sousaphone ('sōōzəfōn) *n.* brass musical instrument, largest of those resembling the cornet, carried over the shoulder, with a wide, conspicuous bell, used in a brass band

souse (sows) *v.* **1.** plunge, drench or be drenched **2.** pickle —*n.* **3.** sousing **4.** brine for pickling

soutane (sōō'tän, -'tan) *n.* cassock

south (sowth) *n.* **1.** cardinal point opposite north **2.** region, part of country *etc.* lying to that side —*a./adv.* **3.** (that is) toward south —**southerly** ('sudhərli) *a.* **1.** toward south —*n.* **2.** wind from the south —**southern** ('sudhərn) *a.* in south —**Southerner** ('sudhərnər) *n.* (*sometimes* **s-**) native or inhabitant of south of any specified region —'**southward** *adv.* —'**Southdown** *n.* breed of sheep —**south'east** *n.* **1.** point of compass midway between south and east —*a.* **2.** (*sometimes* **S-**) denoting southeastern part of specified country *etc.* **3.** in, toward or facing southeast —*adv.* **4.** in, to, toward or (*esp.* of wind) from southeast —**Southern Cross** small constellation in S hemisphere whose four brightest stars form cross —**southern hemisphere** (*oft.* **S- H-**) that half of earth lying south of equator —**southern lights** aurora australis —'**southpaw** *inf. n.* **1.** any left-handed person —*a.* **2.** of or relating to southpaw —**South Pole** southernmost point on earth's axis —**South Seas** seas south of equator —**south-southeast** *n.* **1.** point on compass midway between southeast and south —*a./adv.* **2.** in, from or toward this direction —**south-southwest** *n.* **1.** point on compass midway between south and southwest —*a./adv.* **2.** in, from or toward this direction —**south'west** *n.* **1.** point on compass midway between west and south —*a.* **2.** (*sometimes* **S-**) of or denoting southwestern part of specified country *etc.* **3.** in or toward southwest —*adv.* **4.** in, to, toward or (*esp.* of wind) from southwest —**South'west** *n.* (*usu. with* the) southwestern part of the U.S.

South Africa —**Republic of South Africa** country in Africa bounded north by Botswana and Zimbabwe, northeast by Mozambique and Swaziland, east by the Indian Ocean, south and west by the Atlantic and northwest by Namibia

South Carolina (karə'līnə) South Atlantic state of the U.S.: ratified the Constitution in 1788. Abbrev.: **SC** (with ZIP code)

South Dakota (də'kōtə) West North Central state of the U.S., admitted to the Union in 1889. Abbrev.: **SD** (with ZIP code)

South West Africa *see* NAMIBIA

souvenir ('so͞ovənēər, so͞ovə'nēər) *n.* keepsake, memento

sou'wester (sow'westər) *n.* waterproof hat

sovereign ('sovrin) *n.* **1.** king, queen **2.** former Brit. gold coin worth 20 shillings —*a.* **3.** supreme **4.** efficacious —'**sovereignty** *n.* **1.** supreme power and right to exercise it **2.** dominion **3.** independent state

soviet ('sōviət, 'sov-) *n.* **1.** elected council at various levels of government in U.S.S.R. **2.** (**S-**) citizen of U.S.S.R. —*a.* **3.** (**S-**) of U.S.S.R., its people or its government —'**sovietism** *n.*

Soviet Union Russia; U.S.S.R.

sow[1] (sō) *vi.* **1.** scatter, plant seed —*vt.* **2.** scatter, deposit (seed) **3.** spread abroad (**sowed** *pt.*, **sown** *or* **sowed** *pp.*, '**sowing** *pr.p.*)

soybean ('soi'bēn) *n.* edible bean used as meat substitute, in making soy sauce *etc.* —**soy sauce** (soi) salty, dark brown sauce made from fermented soybeans, used *esp.* in Oriental cookery (*also* **soya sauce** ('soiə))

sp. **1.** special **2.** species (*pl.* **spp.**) **3.** specific **4.** specimen **5.** spelling

spa (spä) *n.* **1.** medicinal spring **2.** place or resort with such a spring

space (spās) *n.* **1.** extent **2.** room **3.** period **4.** empty place **5.** area **6.** expanse **7.** region beyond earth's atmosphere —*vt.* **8.** place at intervals —**spacious** ('spāshəs) *a.* roomy, extensive —**space age** period in which exploration of space has become possible —**space-age** *a.* ultramodern —'**spacecraft** *or* '**spaceship** *n.* vehicle for travel beyond earth's atmosphere —'**spaceman** *n.* —**space shuttle** vehicle designed to carry men and materials to space stations *etc.* —**space station** any manned artificial satellite designed to orbit earth and provide base for scientific research in space —'**spacesuit** *n.* sealed, pressurized suit worn by astronaut —**space-time** *n. Phys.* continuum having three spatial coordinates and one time coordinate that together specify location of particle or event (*also* **space-time continuum**)

spade[1] (spād) *n.* tool for digging —'**spadework** *n.* arduous preparatory work

spade[2] (spād) *n.* leaf-shaped black symbol on playing card

spadix ('spādiks) *n.* spike of small flowers on fleshy stem, whole being enclosed in spathe (*pl.* **spadices** ('spādisēz))

spaghetti (spə'geti) *n.* pasta in form of long strings

Spain (spān) *n.* country in Europe bounded north by the Bay of Biscay and the Pyrenees, east and south by the Mediterranean and the Straits of Gibraltar, southwest by the Atlantic and west by Portugal and the Atlantic —**Spaniard** ('spanyərd) *n.* native or inhabitant of Spain —**Spanish** ('spanish) *a.* **1.** of Spain —*n.* **2.** language of Spain and most of Central and South America: the Romance language with the largest number of speakers —**Spanish America** parts of America colonized by Spaniards and now chiefly Spanish-speaking —**Spanish fly** **1.** European blister beetle, the dried bodies of which yield cantharides **2.** cantharides —**Spanish Main** **1.** mainland of Spanish America **2.** Caribbean Sea

span (span) *n.* **1.** space from thumb to little finger as measure **2.** extent, space **3.** stretch of arch *etc.* **4.** distance from wingtip to wingtip (*also* '**wingspan**) —*vt.* **5.** stretch over **6.** measure with hand (**-nn-**)

spandex ('spandeks) *n.* synthetic elastomeric fiber

spangle ('spanggəl) *n.* **1.** small shiny metallic ornament —*vt.* **2.** decorate with spangles

spaniel ('spanyəl) *n.* any of several breeds of dog with long ears and silky hair

spank (spangk) *vt.* **1.** slap with flat of hand, *esp.* on buttocks —*n.* **2.** one or series of these slaps —'**spanking** *n.* **1.** series of spanks —*a.* **2.** quick, lively **3.** large, fine

spar[1] (spär) *n.* pole, beam, *esp.* as part of ship's rigging

spar[2] (spär) *vi.* **1.** box **2.** dispute, *esp.* in fun (**-rr-**) —*n.* **3.** sparring —**sparring partner** person who practices with boxer during training

spar[3] (spär) *n.* any of various kinds of crystalline mineral

spare (spāər) *vt.* **1.** leave unhurt **2.** show mercy **3.** abstain from using **4.** do without **5.** give away —*a.* **6.** additional **7.** in reserve **8.** thin, lean **9.** scanty —*n.* **10.** spare part (for machine) —'**sparing** *a.* economical, careful —'**sparerib** *n.* cut of pork ribs with most of meat trimmed off

spark (spärk) *n.* **1.** small glowing or burning particle **2.** flash of light produced by electrical discharge **3.** vivacity, humor **4.** trace **5.** in internal-combustion engines, electric spark (in spark plug) which ignites explosive mixture in cylinder —*vi.* **6.** emit sparks —*vt.* **7.** (*oft. with* off) kindle, excite

—**spark plug** device screwed into cylinder head of internal-combustion engine to ignite explosive mixture by means of electric spark

sparkle (ˈspärkəl) *vi.* **1.** glitter **2.** effervesce **3.** scintillate —*n.* **4.** small spark **5.** glitter **6.** flash **7.** luster —ˈ**sparkler** *n. inf.* sparkling gem

sparrow (ˈsparō) *n.* small brownish bird —**sparrow grass** *inf.* asparagus —**sparrow hawk** hawk that hunts small birds

sparse (spärs) *a.* thinly scattered

Spartan (ˈspärtən) *a.* **1.** of ancient Gk. city of Sparta, its inhabitants or their culture **2.** (*sometimes* **s-**) very strict or austere **3.** (*sometimes* **s-**) possessing courage and resolve

spasm (ˈspazəm) *n.* **1.** sudden convulsive (muscular) contraction **2.** sudden burst of activity *etc.* —**spasˈmodic** *a.* occurring in spasms

spastic (ˈspastik) *a.* **1.** affected by spasms, suffering cerebral palsy —*n.* **2.** person who has cerebral palsy

spat[1] (spat) *pt./pp. of* SPIT[1]

spat[2] (spat) *n.* short gaiter

spat[3] (spat) *n.* petty quarrel

spate (spāt) *n.* **1.** rush, outpouring **2.** flood

spathe (spādh) *n.* large sheathlike leaf enclosing flower cluster

spatial (ˈspāshəl) *a.* of, in space

spatter (ˈspatər) *vt.* **1.** splash, cast drops over —*vi.* **2.** be scattered in drops —*n.* **3.** slight splash **4.** sprinkling

spatula (ˈspachələ) *n.* utensil with broad, flat blade used for various purposes

spawn (spön) *n.* **1.** eggs of fish or frog **2.** fragments of mycelia used to propagate mushrooms —*vi.* **3.** (of fish or frog) cast eggs —*vt.* **4.** produce, engender

spay (spā) *vt.* remove ovaries from (animal)

speak (spēk) *vi.* **1.** utter words **2.** converse **3.** deliver discourse —*vt.* **4.** utter **5.** pronounce **6.** express **7.** communicate in (**spoke, ˈspoken, ˈspeaking**) —ˈ**speakable** *a.* —ˈ**speaker** *n.* **1.** one who speaks **2.** one who specializes in speech-making **3.** (*oft.* **S-**) official chairman of many legislative bodies **4.** loudspeaker —ˈ**speakeasy** *n.* place where alcoholic drink was sold illicitly during Prohibition

spear (spēər) *n.* **1.** long pointed weapon **2.** slender shoot, as of asparagus —*vt.* **3.** transfix, pierce, wound with spear —ˈ**spearhead** *n.* **1.** leading force in attack, campaign —*vt.* **2.** lead, initiate (attack, campaign *etc.*)

spearmint (ˈspēərmint) *n.* type of mint

spec. 1. special **2.** specification **3.** speculation

special (ˈspeshəl) *a.* **1.** beyond the usual **2.** particular, individual **3.** distinct **4.** limited —ˈ**specialism** *n.* —ˈ**specialist** *n.* one who devotes himself to special subject or branch of subject —**specialiˈzation** *n.* —ˈ**specialize** *vi.* **1.** be specialist —*vt.* **2.** make special —ˈ**specially** *adv.* —ˈ**specialty** *n.* special product, skill, characteristic *etc.* —**special delivery** delivery of mail outside time of scheduled delivery

specie (ˈspēshē) *n.* coined, as distinct from paper, money

species (ˈspēshēz; *Lat.* ˈspēshiēz) *n.* **1.** sort, kind, *esp.* of animals *etc.* **2.** class **3.** subdivision **4.** *Biol.* group of plants or animals able to reproduce among themselves (*pl.* **-cies**)

specific (spiˈsifik) *a.* **1.** definite **2.** exact in detail **3.** characteristic of a thing or kind —**speˈcifically** *adv.* —**specifiˈcation** *n.* detailed description of something to be made, done —ˈ**specify** *vt.* state definitely or in detail (**-ified, -ifying**) —**specific gravity** ratio of density of substance to that of water

specimen (ˈspesimin) *n.* **1.** part typifying whole **2.** individual example **3.** *Med.* sample of tissue, urine *etc.* taken for diagnostic examination

specious (ˈspēshəs) *a.* deceptively plausible, but false —ˈ**speciously** *adv.* —ˈ**speciousness** *n.*

speck (spek) *n.* **1.** small spot, particle —*vt.* **2.** spot —ˈ**speckle** *n./vt.* speck

spectacle (ˈspektəkəl) *n.* **1.** public display or performance **2.** thing exhibited **3.** ridiculous sight —*pl.* **4.** pair of lenses for correcting defective sight —**specˈtacular** *a.* **1.** impressive **2.** showy **3.** grand **4.** magnificent —*n.* **5.** lavishly produced performance —**specˈtator** *n.* one who looks on

specter (ˈspektər) *n.* **1.** ghost **2.** image of something unpleasant —ˈ**spectral** *a.* ghostly

spectrum (ˈspektrəm) *n.* **1.** image formed by light or sound in which the parts are arranged according to wavelength or frequency **2.** continuous sequence or range (*pl.* **-tra**) —ˈ**spectroscope** *n.* instrument for producing, examining spectra —**specˈtroscopist** *n.* —**specˈtroscopy** *n.* study of spectra by use of spectroscopes *etc.*

speculate (ˈspekyəlāt) *vi.* **1.** guess, conjecture **2.** engage in (risky) commercial transactions —**specuˈlation** *n.* —ˈ**speculative** *a.* given to, characterized by speculation —ˈ**speculator** *n.*

speculum (ˈspekyələm) *n.* **1.** mirror **2.** reflector of polished metal, *esp.* in reflecting telescopes **3.** instrument for dilating body passages (*pl.* **-la** (-lə), **-s**) —ˈ**specular** *a.*

sped (sped) *pt./pp. of* SPEED

speech (spēch) *n.* **1.** act, faculty of speaking **2.** words, language **3.** conversation **4.** discourse **5.** (formal) talk given before audience —ˈ**speechify** *vi.* make speech, *esp.* long and tedious one (**-ified, -ifying**) —ˈ**speechless** *a.* **1.** dumb **2.** at a loss for words

speed (spēd) *n.* **1.** swiftness **2.** rate of progress **3.** degree of sensitivity of photographic film **4.** *sl.* amphetamine —*vi.* **5.**

move quickly **6.** drive vehicle at high speed **7.** *obs.* succeed —*vt.* **8.** further **9.** expedite (**sped** *or* **'speeded** *pt./pp.*) —**'speedily** *adv.* —**'speeding** *n.* driving (vehicle) at high speed, *esp.* over legal limit —**'speedo** *n. inf.* speedometer (*pl.* **-s**) —**'speedy** *a.* **1.** quick **2.** rapid **3.** nimble **4.** prompt —**'speedball** *n.* game combining features of soccer and basketball with elements of Amer. football played on standard field by two teams of 11 players whose object is to move the round ball in the direction of the opponents' goal —**'speedboat** *n.* light, fast motorboat —**speed limit** maximum permitted speed at which vehicle may travel on certain roads —**speed'ometer** *n.* instrument to show speed of vehicle —**'speedway** *n.* track for motorcycle racing —**'speedwell** *n.* any plant of the genus *Veronica* with small, *usu.* blue flowers

speleology (spēli'oləji) *n.* study, exploring of caves —**speleo'logical** *a.*

spell[1] (spel) *vt.* **1.** give letters of in order **2.** read letter by letter **3.** indicate, result in (**spelled** *or* **spelt** *pt./pp.*, **'spelling** *pr.p.*) —**'spelling** *n.* —**spell out** make explicit

spell[2] (spel) *n.* **1.** magic formula **2.** enchantment —**'spellbound** *a.* enchanted, entranced

spell[3] (spel) *n.* (short) period of time, work

spelt (spelt) *pt./pp. of* SPELL[1]

spend (spend) *vt.* **1.** pay out **2.** pass (time) on activity *etc.* **3.** use up completely (**spent** *pt./pp.*, **'spending** *pr.p.*) —**'spender** *n.* —**spent** *a.* used up, exhausted —**'spendthrift** *n.* wasteful person

sperm (spərm) *n.* **1.** male reproductive cell **2.** semen —**spermaceti** (spərmə'sēti, -'seti) *n.* white, waxy substance obtained from oil from head of sperm whale —**sper'matic** *a.* of sperm —**spermatozoon** (spərmatə'zōon) *n.* any of male reproductive cells released in semen during ejaculation (*pl.* **-zoa** (-'zōə)) (*also* **sperm, 'zoosperm**) —**'spermicide** *n.* drug *etc.* that kills sperm —**sperm whale** large, toothed whale hunted for sperm oil, spermaceti and ambergris (*also* **'cachalot**)

spew (spyōō) *v.* vomit

sphagnum ('sfagnəm) *n.* moss that grows in bogs

sphere (sfēər) *n.* **1.** ball, globe **2.** range **3.** field of action **4.** status **5.** position **6.** province —**spherical** ('sfēərikəl, 'sfer-) *a.* —**'spheroid** *n.* **1.** geometric surface produced by rotating ellipse about one of its two axes —*a.* **2.** shaped like but not exactly a sphere

sphincter ('sfingktər) *n.* ring of muscle surrounding opening of hollow bodily organ

sphinx (sfingks) *n.* **1.** statue in Egypt with lion's body and human head **2.** (**S-**) monster with woman's head and lion's body **3.** enigmatic person (*pl.* **-es, sphinges** ('sfinjēz))

sphygmomanometer (sfigmōmə'nomitər) *n.* instrument for measuring blood pressure

spice (spīs) *n.* **1.** aromatic or pungent vegetable substance **2.** spices collectively **3.** anything that adds flavor, relish, piquancy, interest *etc.* —*vt.* **4.** season with spices, flavor —**'spicily** *adv.* —**'spicy** *a.* **1.** flavored with spices **2.** *inf.* slightly indecent, risqué

spick-and-span *or* **spic-and-span** (spikən-'span) *a.* **1.** neat, smart **2.** new-looking

spider ('spīdər) *n.* small eight-legged creature which spins web to catch prey —**'spidery** *a.* —**spider plant** hardy house plant with long thin leaves

spiel (spēl) *inf. n.* **1.** glib (sales) talk —*vi.* **2.** deliver spiel, recite —**'spieler** *n.*

spigot ('spigət) *n.* peg, plug

spike (spīk) *n.* **1.** sharp point **2.** sharp pointed object **3.** long flower cluster with flowers attached directly to the stalk —*vt.* **4.** pierce, fasten with spike **5.** render ineffective **6.** add alcohol to (drink) —**'spiky** *a.* —**'spikenard** *n.* **1.** aromatic Indian plant with rose-purple flowers **2.** aromatic ointment obtained from this plant

spill[1] (spil) *v.* **1.** (cause to) pour, flow over, fall out, *esp.* unintentionally **2.** upset —*vi.* **3.** be lost or wasted (**spilt** (spilt) *or* **spilled** *pt./pp.*) —*n.* **4.** fall **5.** amount spilt —**'spillage** *n.*

spill[2] (spil) *n.* thin strip of wood, twisted paper *etc.* for lighting fires *etc.*

spin (spin) *v.* **1.** (cause to) revolve rapidly **2.** whirl —*vt.* **3.** twist into thread **4.** (*with* out) prolong **5.** *inf.* tell (a story) —*vi.* **6.** fish with lure (**spun,** *obs.* **span** (span) *pt.*, **spun** *pp.*, **'spinning** *pr.p.*) —*n.* **7.** spinning **8.** (of aircraft) descent in dive with continued rotation **9.** rapid run or ride **10.** in skating, rapid turning on the spot **11.** angular momentum of elementary particle —**'spinner** *n.* **1.** person or thing that spins **2.** fishing lure with fin or wing that revolves —**spinne'ret** *n.* any of several organs in spiders *etc.* through which silk threads are exuded —**'spinning** *n.* act, process of drawing out and twisting into threads, as wool, cotton, flax *etc.* —**spinning jenny** early type of spinning frame with several spindles —**spinning wheel** household machine with large wheel turned by treadle for spinning wool *etc.* into thread —**spin-off** *n.* any product or development derived incidentally from application of existing knowledge or enterprise

spina bifida ('spīnə 'bīfidə) congenital condition in which meninges of spinal cord protrude through gap in backbone

spinach ('spinich) *n.* **1.** annual plant with edible leaves **2.** the leaves, eaten boiled as vegetable

spindle ('spindəl) *n.* rod, axis for spinning —**'spindly** *a.* **1.** long and slender **2.** attenuated —**'spindlelegs** *or* **'spindleshanks** *pl.n.* **1.** long thin legs **2.** person who has such legs

spindrift ('spindrift) *n.* spray blown along surface of sea

spine (spīn) *n.* **1.** backbone **2.** thin spike, *esp.* on fish *etc.* **3.** ridge **4.** back of book —**'spinal** *a.* —**'spineless** *a.* **1.** lacking spine **2.** cowardly —**'spiny** *a.* **1.** (of animals) having or covered with quills or spines **2.** (of plants) covered with spines **3.** troublesome —**spinal column** structure in vertebrates consisting of vertebrae protecting the spinal cord and uniting skull, rib cage, shoulder and pelvic girdles into skeleton (*also* **backbone**) —**spinal cord** cord of nerve tissue within spinal canal, which together with brain forms central nervous system —**spine-chiller** *n.* motion picture *etc.* that arouses terror

spinel *or* **spinelle** (spi'nel) *n.* hard crystalline mineral of various colors used as gemstone

spinet ('spinit, spi'net) *n.* **1.** small modern piano **2.** oblong pianoforte of 19th cent. **3.** harpsicord with one manual

spinnaker ('spinəkər; *Naut.* 'spangkər) *n.* large yacht sail

spinney ('spini) *n.* small wood

spinster ('spinstər) *n.* unmarried woman

spiracle ('spirəkəl, 'spīrə-) *n. Zool.* opening for breathing

spiral ('spīrəl) *n.* **1.** continuous curve drawn at ever-increasing distance from fixed point **2.** anything resembling this —*a.* **3.** having shape of spiral —**'spirally** *adv.*

spirant ('spīrənt) *a.* **1.** *Phonet. see* FRICATIVE —*n.* **2.** fricative consonant

spire ('spīər) *n.* **1.** pointed part of steeple **2.** pointed stem

spirea *or* **spiraea** (spī'rēə) *n.* any of various plants with small white or pink flower sprays

spirit ('spirit) *n.* **1.** life principle animating body **2.** disposition **3.** liveliness **4.** courage **5.** frame of mind **6.** essential character or meaning **7.** soul **8.** ghost **9.** liquid got by distillation, alcohol —*pl.* **10.** emotional state **11.** strong alcoholic drink, *eg* whiskey —*vt.* **12.** (*usu. with* away *or* off) carry away mysteriously —**'spirited** *a.* lively —**'spiritless** *a.* listless, apathetic —**'spiritual** *a.* **1.** given to, interested in things of the spirit —*n.* **2.** Negro sacred song, hymn —**'spiritualism** *n.* belief that spirits of the dead communicate with the living —**'spiritualist** *n.* —**spiritu'ality** *n.* —**'spiritually** *adv.* —**'spirituous** *a.* alcoholic —**spirit gum** glue made from gum dissolved in ether —**spirit lamp** lamp that burns methylated or other spirits —**spirit level** glass tube containing bubble in liquid, used to check horizontal, vertical surfaces —**spirits of salts** hydrochloric acid

spirochete ('spirəkēt) *n.* spiral bacterium with flexible cell wall found in mud and water and as parasite in animals producing diseases, *eg* syphilis, yaws, leptospirosis

spirt (spərt) *see* SPURT

spit[1] (spit) *vi.* **1.** eject saliva —*vt.* **2.** eject

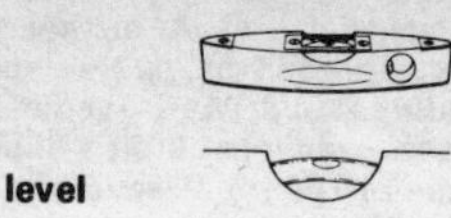

spirit level

from mouth (**spat, spit** *pt./pp.*, **'spitting** *pr.p.*) —*n.* **3.** spitting, saliva —**'spittle** *n.* saliva —**spit'toon** *n.* vessel to spit into —**'spitfire** *n.* person with fiery temper —**spitting image** *inf.* person who bears physical resemblance to another —**spit and polish** *inf.* punctilious attention to neatness, discipline *etc., esp.* in armed forces

spit[2] (spit) *n.* **1.** sharp rod to put through meat for roasting **2.** sandy point projecting into the sea —*vt.* **3.** thrust through (**-tt-**)

spite (spīt) *n.* **1.** malice —*vt.* **2.** thwart spitefully —**'spiteful** *a.* —**'spitefully** *adv.* —**in spite of** regardless of; notwithstanding

splake (splāk) *n.* type of hybrid Canad. trout

splash (splash) *v.* **1.** scatter (liquid) about, on or over (something) —*vt.* **2.** print, display prominently —*n.* **3.** sound of water being scattered **4.** patch, *esp.* of color **5.** (effect of) extravagant display **6.** small amount —**'splashdown** *n.* **1.** controlled landing of spacecraft on water **2.** time scheduled for this event —**splash down**

splat (splat) *n.* wet, slapping sound

splatter ('splatər) *v./n.* spatter

splay (splā) *a.* **1.** spread out **2.** slanting **3.** turned outward —*v.* **4.** spread out **5.** twist outward —*n.* **6.** slant surface **7.** spread —**splay'footed** *a.* flat and broad (of foot)

spleen (splēn) *n.* **1.** organ in abdomen **2.** anger **3.** irritable or morose temper —**splenetic** (spli'netik) *a.* —**'spleenwort** *n.* any of various ferns

splendid ('splendid) *a.* **1.** magnificent **2.** brilliant **3.** excellent —**'splendidly** *adv.* —**'splendor** *n.*

splice (splīs) *vt.* **1.** join by interweaving strands **2.** join (wood) by overlapping **3.** *sl.* join in marriage —*n.* **4.** spliced joint

spline (splīn) *n.* narrow groove, ridge, strip, *esp.* joining wood *etc.*

splint (splint) *n.* rigid support for broken limb *etc.*

splinter ('splintər) *n.* **1.** thin fragment of glass, wood *etc.* —*v.* **2.** break into fragments, shiver —**splinter group** group that separates from main party, organization, *oft.* after disagreement

split (split) *v.* **1.** break asunder **2.** separate **3.** divide —*vi.* **4.** *sl.* depart; leave (**split, 'splitting**) —*n.* **5.** crack, fissure **6.** dessert of fruit and ice cream —**'splitting** *a.* **1.** (of headache) acute **2.** (of head) assailed by overpowering unbearable pain —**split infinitive** in English grammar, infinitive used with another word between *to* and verb —**split-level** *a.* (of house *etc.*) having floor level of one part about half story above floor level of adjoining part —**split personality** 1. tendency to change rapidly in mood or temperament 2. schizophrenia —**split second** infinitely small period of time —**split-second** *a.* made or arrived at in infinitely short time

splotch (sploch) *n./vt.* splash, daub —**'splotchy** *a.*

splurge (splərj) *v.* 1. spend (money) extravagantly —*n.* 2. ostentatious display, *esp.* of wealth 3. bout of unrestrained extravagance

splutter ('splutər) *vi.* 1. make hissing, spitting sounds —*vt.* 2. utter incoherently with spitting sounds —*n.* 3. process or noise of spluttering 4. spluttering incoherent speech

spode (spōd) *n.* (*sometimes* **S-**) china or porcelain manufactured by Josiah Spode, English potter, or his company

spoil (spoil) *vt.* 1. damage, injure 2. damage manners or behavior of (*esp.* child) by indulgence 3. pillage —*vi.* 4. go bad (**spoiled** *or* **spoilt** *pt./pp.*, **'spoiling** *pr.p.*) —*n.* 5. booty 6. waste material, *esp.* in mining (*also* **'spoilage**) —**'spoiler** *n.* slowing device on aircraft wing *etc.* —**'spoilsport** *n. inf.* one who spoils pleasure of other people —**spoiling for** eager for

spoke[1] (spōk) *pt. of* SPEAK —**'spoken** *pp. of* SPEAK —**'spokesman** *n.* one deputed to speak for others

spoke[2] (spōk) *n.* radial bar of wheel

spoliation (spōli'āshən) *n.* 1. act of spoiling 2. robbery 3. destruction

spondee ('spondē) *n.* metrical foot consisting of two long syllables (¯ ¯)

sponge (spunj) *n.* 1. freshwater or marine invertebrate 2. its skeleton, or a synthetic substance like it, used to absorb liquids 3. raised yeast dough 4. pad used in surgery to absorb fluid —*vt.* 5. wipe with sponge —*vi.* 6. live at expense of others —*v.* 7. cadge —**'sponger** *n. sl.* one who cadges or lives at expense of others —**'spongy** *a.* 1. spongelike 2. wet and soft —**sponge cake** type of light cake

sponsor ('sponsər) *n.* 1. one promoting, advertising something 2. one who agrees to give money to a charity on completion of specified activity by another 3. one taking responsibility (*esp.* for welfare of child at baptism, *ie* godparent) 4. guarantor —*vt.* 5. act as sponsor for —**'sponsorship** *n.*

spontaneous (spon'tāniəs) *a.* 1. voluntary 2. natural 3. not forced 4. produced without external force —**spontaneity** (spontə'nēiti, -'nā-) *n.* —**spon'taneously** *adv.* —**spon'taneousness** *n.* —**spontaneous combustion** ignition of substance as result of internal oxidation processes

spoof (spo͞of) *n.* 1. mild satirical mockery 2. trick, hoax

spook (spo͞ok) *n.* ghost —**'spooky** *a.*

spool (spo͞ol) *n.* reel, bobbin

spoon (spo͞on) *n.* 1. implement with shallow bowl at end of handle for eating or serving food *etc.* —*vt.* 2. lift with spoon —**'spoonful** *n.* —**'spoonbill** *n.* any of several wading birds having long horizontally flattened bill —**spoon-feed** *vt.* 1. feed with spoon 2. spoil 3. provide (person) with ready-made opinions *etc.*

spoonerism ('spo͞onərizəm) *n.* amusing transposition of initial consonants, *eg* 'half-warmed fish' for 'half-formed wish'

spoor (spo͞oər, spōr) *n.* 1. trail of animal, *esp.* wild animals —*v.* 2. follow spoor (of)

sporadic (spə'radik) *or* **sporadical** *a.* 1. intermittent 2. scattered —**spo'radically** *adv.*

spore (spōr) *n.* minute reproductive body of flowerless plant or protozoan

sporran ('sporən) *n.* pouch worn in front of kilt

sport (spōrt) *n.* 1. game, activity for pleasure, competition, exercise 2. enjoyment 3. mockery 4. cheerful person, good loser —*vt.* 5. wear, *esp.* ostentatiously —*vi.* 6. frolic 7. play (sport) —**'sporting** *a.* 1. of sport 2. behaving with fairness, generosity —**'sportive** *a.* playful —**'sporty** *a.* 1. stylish, loud or gay 2. relating to or appropriate to sportsman —**sporting chance** sufficient prospect of success to justify the attempt —**sports car** fast (open) car —**sports jacket** man's casual jacket —**'sportsman** *n.* 1. one who engages in sport 2. good loser

spot (spot) *n.* 1. small mark 2. blemish 3. pimple 4. place 5. (difficult) situation 6. *inf.* small quantity —*vt.* 7. mark with spots 8. detect 9. observe (**-tt-**) —**'spotless** *a.* 1. unblemished 2. pure —**'spotlessly** *adv.* —**'spotty** *a.* 1. with spots 2. uneven —**spot check** random examination —**'spotlight** *n.* 1. powerful light illuminating small area 2. center of attention —**spot-weld** *vt.* 1. join (two pieces of metal) by electrically generated heat —*n.* 2. weld so formed

spouse (spows, spowz) *n.* husband or wife —**spousal** ('spowzəl) *n.* marriage

spout (spowt) *v.* 1. pour out —*vi.* 2. *sl.* speechify —*n.* 3. projecting tube or lip for pouring liquids 4. copious discharge

sprain (sprān) *n./vt.* wrench or twist (of muscle *etc.*)

sprang (sprang) *pt. of* SPRING

sprat (sprat) *n.* small sea fish

sprawl (sprōl) *vi.* 1. lie or sit about awkwardly —*v.* 2. spread in rambling, unplanned way —*n.* 3. sprawling

spray[1] (sprā) *n.* 1. (device for producing) fine drops of liquid —*vt.* 2. sprinkle with shower of fine drops —**spray gun** device that sprays fluid in finely divided form by atomizing it in air jet

spray[2] (sprā) *n.* 1. branch, twig with buds, flowers *etc.* 2. floral ornament, brooch *etc.* like this

spread (spred) *v.* **1.** extend **2.** stretch out **3.** open out **4.** scatter **5.** distribute or be distributed **6.** unfold —*vt.* **7.** cover (**spread, ˈspreading**) —*n.* **8.** extent **9.** increase **10.** ample meal **11.** food which can be spread on bread *etc.* —**spread-eagle** *a.* with arms and legs outstretched (*also* **spread-eagled**)

spree (sprē) *n.* **1.** session of overindulgence **2.** romp

sprig (sprig) *n.* **1.** small twig **2.** ornamental design like this **3.** small nail

sprightly (ˈsprītli) *a.* lively, brisk —**ˈsprightliness** *n.*

spring (spring) *vi.* **1.** leap **2.** shoot up or forth **3.** come into being **4.** appear **5.** grow **6.** become bent or split —*vt.* **7.** produce unexpectedly **8.** set off (trap) (**sprang, sprung, ˈspringing**) —*n.* **9.** leap **10.** recoil **11.** piece of coiled or bent metal with much resilience **12.** flow of water from earth **13.** first season of year —**ˈspringy** *a.* elastic —**ˈspringboard** *n.* flexible board for diving —**spring-clean** *v.* clean (house) thoroughly —**spring-cleaning** *n.* —**springer spaniel** breed of spaniel with silky coat, used for flushing or springing game —**spring tide** high tide at new or full moon

springbok

springbok (ˈspringbok) *n.* **1.** S Afr. antelope **2.** (**S-**) South African national sportsman

sprinkle (ˈspringkəl) *vt.* scatter small drops on, strew —**ˈsprinkler** *n.* —**ˈsprinkling** *n.* small quantity or number

sprint (sprint) *vi.* **1.** run short distance at great speed —*n.* **2.** such run, race

sprit (sprit) *n.* small spar set diagonally across fore-and-aft sail in order to extend it —**spritsail** (ˈspritsāl; *Naut.* ˈspritsəl) *n.* sail extended by sprit

sprite (sprīt) *n.* fairy, elf

sprocket (ˈsprokit) *n.* **1.** projection on wheel or capstan for engaging chain **2.** wheel with sprockets (*also* **sprocket wheel**)

sprout (sprowt) *v.* **1.** put forth (shoots) —*vi.* **2.** spring up —*n.* **3.** shoot

spruce[1] (sproōs) *n.* variety of fir

spruce[2] (sproōs) *a.* neat in dress

sprue (sproō) *n.* disease of the small intestine marked by impaired absorption of nutrients

sprung (sprung) *pp. of* SPRING

spry (sprī) *a.* nimble, vigorous

spud (spud) *n. inf.* potato

spume (spyoōm) *n./vi.* foam, froth

spun (spun) *pt./pp. of* SPIN

spunk (spungk) *n.* courage, spirit

spur (spər) *n.* **1.** pricking instrument attached to horseman's heel **2.** incitement **3.** stimulus **4.** projection on cock's leg **5.** projecting mountain range **6.** railroad branch line or siding —*vt.* **7.** ride hard (**-rr-**)

spurious (ˈspyoŏriəs) *a.* not genuine

spurn (spərn) *vt.* reject with scorn, thrust aside

spurt *or* **spirt** (spərt) *v.* **1.** send, come out in jet —*vi.* **2.** rush suddenly —*n.* **3.** jet **4.** short sudden effort, *esp.* in race

sputnik (ˈspoŏtnik, ˈsput-) *n.* any of series of Russian satellites

sputter (ˈsputər) *v.* splutter

sputum (ˈspyoōtəm, ˈspoōtəm) *n.* spittle (*pl.* **-ta** (-tə))

spy (spī) *n.* **1.** one who watches (*esp.* in rival countries, companies *etc.*) and reports secretly —*vi.* **2.** act as spy —*vt.* **3.** catch sight of (**spied, ˈspying**) —**ˈspyglass** *n.* small telescope

Sq. **1.** Square **2.** Squadron

squab (skwob) *n.* **1.** young unfledged bird, *esp.* pigeon **2.** short fat person **3.** well-stuffed cushion —*a.* **4.** (of birds) unfledged **5.** short and fat

squabble (ˈskwobəl) *vi.* **1.** engage in petty, noisy quarrel, bicker —*n.* **2.** petty quarrel

squad (skwod) *n.* small party, *esp.* of soldiers —**ˈsquadron** *n.* basic unit of air force fighting group

squalid (ˈskwolid) *a.* mean and dirty —**ˈsqualor** *n.*

squall (skwŏl) *n.* **1.** harsh cry **2.** sudden gust of wind **3.** short storm —*vi.* **4.** yell

squander (ˈskwondər) *vt.* spend wastefully, dissipate

square (skwāər) *n.* **1.** equilateral rectangle **2.** area of this shape **3.** in town, open space (of this shape) **4.** product of a number multiplied by itself **5.** instrument for drawing right angles —*a.* **6.** square in form **7.** honest **8.** straight, even **9.** level, equal **10.** denoting a measure of area **11.** *inf.* old-fashioned, conservative —*vt.* **12.** make square **13.** find square of **14.** pay **15.** bribe —*vi.* **16.** fit, suit —**ˈsquarely** *adv.* —**square dance** any of various formation dances in which couples form squares —**square-dance** *vi.* perform such dance —**square deal** any transaction *etc.* that is honest and fair —**square measure** unit or system of units for measuring areas —**square meter** *etc.* area equal to that of square with sides one meter *etc.* long —**square root** number that, multiplied by itself, gives number of which it is factor

squash (skwosh) *vt.* **1.** crush flat **2.** pulp **3.** suppress **4.** humiliate —*n.* **5.** juice of crushed fruit **6.** crowd **7.** any of various edible gourds —**squash rackets** (*with sing. v.*) indoor racket-and-ball game for (usually) two players in which ball is struck off wall(s) of court and in which only the server can score points

squat (skwot) *vi.* **1.** sit on heels **2.** act as squatter (**-tt-**) —*a.* **3.** short and thick —**'squatter** *n.* one who settles on land or occupies house without permission

squaw (skwō) *n.* N Amer. Indian woman

squawk (skwōk) *n.* **1.** short harsh cry, *esp.* of bird —*vi.* **2.** utter this cry

squeak (skwēk) *vi./n.* (make) short shrill sound

squeal (skwēl) *n.* **1.** long piercing squeak —*vi.* **2.** make one **3.** *sl.* confess information (about another)

squeamish ('skwēmish) *a.* **1.** easily made sick **2.** easily shocked **3.** overscrupulous

squeegee ('skwējē) *or* **squilgee** ('skwējē, 'skwiljē) *n.* **1.** tool with rubber blade for clearing water (from glass *etc.*), spreading wet paper *etc.* —*vt.* **2.** press, smooth with squeegee

squeeze (skwēz) *vt.* **1.** press **2.** wring **3.** force **4.** hug **5.** subject to extortion —*n.* **6.** act of squeezing **7.** period of hardship, difficulty caused by financial weakness

squelch (skwelch) *vi.* **1.** make, walk with wet sucking sound, as in walking through mud —*n.* **2.** squelching sound

squib (skwib) *n.* **1.** small firework that hisses before exploding **2.** insignificant person

squid (skwid) *n.* type of cuttlefish

squiggle ('skwigəl) *n.* **1.** wavy, wriggling mark —*vi.* **2.** wriggle **3.** draw squiggle

squill (skwil) *n.* **1.** Mediterranean plant of lily family **2.** its bulb, used medicinally as expectorant

squint (skwint) *vi.* **1.** have the eyes turned in different directions **2.** glance sideways —*n.* **3.** this eye disorder **4.** glance —*a.* **5.** having a squint

squire ('skwīər) *n.* country gentleman

squirm (skwərm) *vi.* **1.** wriggle **2.** be embarrassed —*n.* **3.** squirming movement

squirrel ('skwirəl) *n.* **1.** any of various arboreal rodents with gray or reddish-brown fur and bushy tail. **2.** its bushy pelt

squirt (skwərt) *v.* **1.** force (liquid) or (of liquid) be forced through narrow opening —*n.* **2.** jet **3.** *inf.* short or insignificant person

Sr *Chem.* strontium

Sr. *or* **Sr 1.** Senior **2.** Sister

Sri Lanka (srē 'längkə) country lying off the southeast coast of India in the Indian Ocean —**Sri Lankan** ('längkən)

SS 1. Saints **2.** paramilitary organization within Nazi party that provided Hitler's bodyguard, security forces, concentration camp guards *etc.* **3.** (*also* **S.S.**) steamship

SSA Social Security Administration

SSE south-southeast

SSR Soviet Socialist Republic

SSS Selective Service System

SSW south-southwest

St. *or* **St 1.** Saint **2.** Strait **3.** Street

stab (stab) *v.* **1.** pierce, strike (at) with pointed weapon (**-bb-**) —*n.* **2.** blow, wound so inflicted **3.** sudden sensation, *eg* of fear **4.** attempt

stabilize ('stābilīz) *vt.* make steady, restore to equilibrium, *esp.* of money values, prices and wages —**stabili'zation** *n.* —**'stabilizer** *n.* device to maintain equilibrium of ship, aircraft *etc.*

stable[1] ('stābəl) *n.* **1.** building for horses **2.** race horses of particular owner, establishment **3.** such establishment —*vt.* **4.** put into stable

stable[2] ('stābəl) *a.* **1.** firmly fixed **2.** steadfast, resolute —**stability** (stə'biliti) *n.* **1.** steadiness **2.** ability to resist change of any kind —**'stably** *adv.*

staccato (stə'kätō) *a.* **1.** *Mus.* with notes sharply separated **2.** abrupt

stack (stak) *n.* **1.** ordered pile, heap **2.** chimney —*vt.* **3.** pile in stack **4.** control (aircraft waiting to land) so that they fly at different altitudes

stadium ('stādiəm) *n.* open-air arena for athletics *etc.* (*pl.* **-s, -dia** (-diə))

staff (staf) *n.* **1.** body of officers or workers employed by a company *etc.*; personnel (*pl.* **-s**) **2.** pole (*pl.* **-s, staves**) **3.** set of five lines on which music is written (*pl.* **-s, staves**) —*vt.* **4.** supply with personnel —**staff sergeant** noncommissioned officer who ranks: in Army, above sergeant and below sergeant first class; in Air Force, above airman first class and below technical sergeant; in Marine Corps, above sergeant and below gunnery sergeant

stag (stag) *n.* **1.** male deer —*a.* **2.** for men only

stage (stāj) *n.* **1.** period, division of development **2.** raised floor or platform **3.** (platform of) theater **4.** scene of action **5.** stopping place on road, distance between two of them **6.** separate unit of space rocket that can be jettisoned —*vt.* **7.** put (play) on stage **8.** arrange, bring about —**'staging** *n.* any temporary structure used in building, *esp.* platforms supported by scaffolding —**'stagy** *a.* theatrical —**'stagecoach** *n.* formerly, four-wheeled horse-drawn vehicle used to carry passengers *etc.* on regular route —**stage fright** panic that may beset person about to appear in front of audience —**'stagehand** *n.* person who sets stage, moves props *etc.* in theatrical production —**stage-manage** *v.* **1.** work as stage manager for (play *etc.*) —*vt.* **2.** arrange or supervise from behind the scenes —**stage manager** person who supervises stage arrangements of theatrical production —**stage-struck** *a.* infatuated with glamor of theatrical life —**stage whisper** loud whisper intended to be heard by audience

stagger (ˈstagər) *vi.* **1.** walk unsteadily —*vt.* **2.** astound **3.** arrange in overlapping or alternating positions, times **4.** distribute over a period —*n.* **5.** act of staggering —*pl.* **6.** form of vertigo **7.** disease of horses —**ˈstaggering** *a.* astounding

stagnate (ˈstagnāt) *vi.* cease to flow or develop —**ˈstagnant** *a.* **1.** sluggish **2.** not flowing **3.** foul, impure —**stagˈnation** *n.*

staid (stād) *a.* of sober and quiet character, sedate —**ˈstaidly** *adv.* —**ˈstaidness** *n.*

stain (stān) *vt.* **1.** spot, mark **2.** apply liquid coloring to (wood *etc.*) **3.** bring disgrace upon —*n.* **4.** spot, mark, discoloration **5.** moral taint —**ˈstainless** *a.* —**stained glass** glass colored with metallic oxides and joined with lead strips to form design —**stainless steel** rustless steel alloy

stairs (stāərz) *pl.n.* set of steps, *esp.* as part of house —**ˈstaircase** *n.* structure enclosing stairs —**ˈstairway** *n.* stairs —**ˈstairwell** *n.* vertical shaft that contains stairs

stake (stāk) *n.* **1.** sharpened stick or post **2.** money wagered or contended for —*vt.* **3.** secure, mark out with stakes **4.** wager, risk —**stake out** *sl.* keep under surveillance

stalactite (stəˈlaktīt, ˈstaləktīt) *n.* lime deposit like icicle on roof of cave

stalagmite (stəˈlagmīt, ˈstaləgmīt) *n.* lime deposit like pillar on floor of cave

stale (stāl) *a.* **1.** old, lacking freshness **2.** hackneyed **3.** lacking energy, interest through monotony —**ˈstalemate** *n.* **1.** *Chess* position in chess when neither player can win as the player to move can only move his king into check **2.** deadlock, impasse

stalk[1] (stök) *n.* **1.** plant's stem **2.** anything like this

stalk[2] (stök) *v.* **1.** follow, approach (game *etc.*) stealthily —*vi.* **2.** walk in stiff and stately manner —*n.* **3.** stalking —**stalking-horse** *n.* pretext

stall (stöl) *n.* **1.** compartment in stable *etc.* **2.** erection for display and sale of goods **3.** seat in chancel of church **4.** finger sheath —*vt.* **5.** put in stall **6.** hinder **7.** stick fast —*v.* **8.** delay **9.** stop unintentionally (motor engine) **10.** lose flying speed (of aircraft) —*vi.* **11.** prevaricate

stallion (ˈstalyən) *n.* male horse, *esp.* one used for breeding

stalwart (ˈstölwərt) *a.* **1.** strong **2.** brave **3.** staunch —*n.* **4.** stalwart person

stamen (ˈstāmən) *n.* male organ of flowering plant (*pl.* **-s, stamina** (ˈstāminə, ˈstaminə))

stamina (ˈstaminə) *n.* power of endurance, vitality

stammer (ˈstamər) *v.* **1.** speak, say with repetition of syllables —*n.* **2.** habit of so speaking —**ˈstammerer** *n.*

stamp (stamp) *vi.* **1.** put down foot with force —*vt.* **2.** impress mark on **3.** affix postage stamp to **4.** fix (in memory) **5.** reveal, characterize —*n.* **6.** stamping with foot **7.** imprinted mark **8.** appliance for marking **9.** piece of gummed paper printed with device as evidence of postage *etc.* **10.** character —**stamping ground** habitual meeting or gathering place

stampede (stamˈpēd) *n.* **1.** sudden frightened rush, *esp.* of herd of cattle **2.** headlong rush of a crowd **3.** C rodeo —*vi.* **4.** cause, take part in stampede

stance (stans) *n.* **1.** manner, position of standing **2.** attitude **3.** point of view

stanch (stönch, stänch) *vt.* *see* STAUNCH (sense 1)

stanchion (ˈstanchən) *n.* **1.** upright bar, support —*vt.* **2.** support

stand (stand) *v.* **1.** have, take, set in upright position —*vi.* **2.** remain **3.** be situated **4.** remain firm or stationary **5.** cease to move **6.** adhere to principles **7.** offer oneself as a candidate **8.** (*with* for) be symbol *etc.* (of) —*vt.* **9.** endure **10.** *inf.* provide free, treat to (**stood, ˈstanding**) —*n.* **11.** holding firm **12.** position **13.** halt **14.** something on which thing may be placed **15.** structure from which spectators watch sport *etc.* **16.** stop made by pop group *etc.* —**ˈstanding** *n.* **1.** reputation, status **2.** duration —*a.* **3.** erect **4.** permanent, lasting **5.** stagnant **6.** performed from stationary position, as in *standing jump* —**stand-by** *n.* person or thing that is ready for use or can be relied on in emergency —**stand-in** *n.* person, thing that acts as substitute —**standˈoffish** *a.* reserved or aloof —**ˈstandstill** *n.* complete cessation of movement —**stand by 1.** be available and ready to act if needed **2.** be present as onlooker **3.** be faithful to —**stand in** deputize —**stand over 1.** watch closely **2.** postpone

standard (ˈstandərd) *n.* **1.** accepted example of something against which others are judged **2.** degree, quality **3.** flag **4.** weight or measure to which others must conform **5.** post —*a.* **6.** usual, regular **7.** average **8.** of recognized authority, competence **9.** accepted as correct —**standardiˈzation** *n.* —**ˈstandardize** *vt.* regulate by a standard —**standard-bearer** *n.* **1.** man who carries a standard **2.** leader of party *etc.* —**standard gauge** railroad track with distance of 56½ inches between lines —**standard time** official local time of region or country determined by distance from Greenwich of line of longitude passing through area —**standard of living** level of subsistence or material welfare of community, person *etc.*

standpoint (ˈstandpoint) *n.* **1.** point of view, opinion **2.** mental attitude

stank (stangk) *pt. of* STINK

stannary ('stanəri) *n.* place or region where tin is mined or worked

stannous ('stanəs) *a.* of, containing tin

stanza ('stanzə) *n.* group of lines of verse

staphylococcus (stafilō'kokəs) *n.* spherical bacterium usu. growing in grapelike clusters, a major cause of common infections (*pl.* **-cocci** (-'koksī))

staple ('stāpəl) *n.* **1.** U-shaped piece of wire used to fasten papers, cloth *etc.* **2.** short length of stiff wire formed into U-shape with pointed ends, used for holding hasp to post, securing electrical cables *etc.* **3.** main product **4.** fiber **5.** pile of wool *etc.* —*a.* **6.** principal **7.** regularly produced or made for market —*vt.* **8.** fasten with staple **9.** sort, classify (wool *etc.*) according to length of fiber —'**stapler** *n.* small device for fastening papers together

star (stär) *n.* **1.** celestial body, seen as twinkling point of light **2.** asterisk (*) **3.** celebrated player, actor *etc.* **4.** medal, jewel *etc.* of apparent shape of star —*vt.* **5.** adorn with stars **6.** mark (with asterisk) **7.** feature as star performer —*vi.* **8.** play leading role (in motion picture *etc.*) (**-rr-**) —*a.* **9.** leading, most important, famous —'**stardom** *n.* —'**starlet** *n.* young actress who is projected as potential star —'**starry** *a.* covered with stars —**star-crossed** *a.* dogged by ill luck —'**starfish** *n.* small star-shaped sea creature —'**stargaze** *vi.* **1.** observe stars **2.** daydream —'**stargazing** *n./a.* —**starry-eyed** *a.* given to naive wishes, judgments *etc.* —**Star-Spangled Banner 1.** national anthem of the United States **2.** Stars and Stripes —**star-studded** *a.* featuring large proportion of well-known performers —**Star of David** Mogen David —**Stars and Stripes** the U.S. flag

starboard ('stärbərd) *n.* **1.** right-hand side of ship, looking forward —*a.* **2.** of, on this side

starch (stärch) *n.* **1.** substance forming the main food element in bread, potatoes *etc.*, and used mixed with water, for stiffening certain fabrics —*vt.* **2.** stiffen thus —'**starchy** *a.* **1.** containing starch **2.** stiff **3.** formal **4.** prim

stare (stāər) *vi.* **1.** look fixedly **2.** gaze with wide-open eyes —*n.* **3.** staring, fixed gaze —**stare one in the face** be obvious or visible to one —**stare out** abash by staring at

stark (stärk) *a.* **1.** blunt, bare **2.** desolate **3.** absolute —*adv.* **4.** completely

starling ('stärling) *n.* glossy black speckled songbird

start (stärt) *vt.* **1.** begin **2.** set going —*vi.* **3.** begin, *esp.* journey **4.** make sudden movement —*n.* **5.** beginning **6.** abrupt movement **7.** advantage of a lead in a race —'**starter** *n.* **1.** electric motor starting automobile engine **2.** competitor in, supervisor of, start of race

startle ('stärtəl) *vt.* surprise, frighten or alarm suddenly

starve (stärv) *v.* (cause to) suffer or die from hunger —**star'vation** *n.*

stash (stash) *vt. inf.* put away, hide

-stat (*comb. form*) device that causes something to remain stationary or constant, as in *thermostat*

state (stāt) *n.* **1.** condition **2.** place, situation **3.** politically organized people **4.** government **5.** rank **6.** pomp —*vt.* **7.** express in words —'**stated** *a.* **1.** fixed **2.** regular **3.** settled —'**stateless** *a.* **1.** without nationality **2.** without state or states —'**stately** *a.* dignified, lofty —'**statement** *n.* **1.** expression in words **2.** account —**state attorney** *or* **state's attorney** legal officer representing a state in court proceedings —**state-of-the-art** *a.* (of hi-fi equipment *etc.*) up-to-the-minute —'**stateroom** *n.* **1.** private cabin on ship **2.** large room in palace, mansion, used for ceremonial occasions —'**stateside** *a.* denoting continental U.S. —'**statesman** *n.* respected political leader —**states' rights** all rights not vested in the federal government by the Constitution of the U.S. —**state tree** tree selected as emblem for a state

static ('statik) *a.* **1.** motionless, inactive **2.** pert. to bodies at rest or in equilibrium **3.** *Comp.* (of a memory) not needing its contents refreshed periodically —*n.* **4.** electrical interference in radio reception —*pl.* **5.** (*with sing. v.*) branch of physics —'**statically** *adv.*

station ('stāshən) *n.* **1.** place where thing stops or is placed **2.** stopping place for railroad trains **3.** local office for police force, fire brigade *etc.* **4.** place equipped for radio or television transmission **5.** bus garage **6.** post, employment **7.** status **8.** position in life —*vt.* **9.** put in position —'**stationary** *a.* **1.** not moving, fixed **2.** not changing —**Stations of the Cross** series of 14 images representing the events of Christ's Passion —**station wagon** automobile longer than sedan with open trunk area

stationer ('stāshənər) *n.* dealer in writing materials *etc.* —'**stationery** *n.*

statistics (stə'tistiks) *pl.n.* **1.** numerical facts collected systematically and arranged **2.** (*with sing. v.*) the study of them —**sta'tistical** *a.* —**sta'tistically** *adv.* —**statis'tician** *n.* one who compiles and studies statistics

statue ('stachōō) *n.* solid carved or cast image of person, animal *etc.* —'**statuary** *n.* statues collectively —**statuesque** (stachōō'esk) *a.* **1.** like statue **2.** dignified —**statu'ette** *n.* small statue

stature ('stachər) *n.* **1.** bodily height **2.** greatness

status ('stātəs) *n.* **1.** position, rank **2.** prestige **3.** relation to others —**status quo** (kwō) existing state of affairs —**status symbol** possession regarded as proof of owner's wealth *etc.*

statute ('stachōōt) *n.* written law —'**statu-**

tory *a.* enacted, defined or authorized by statute

staunch (stönch) *vt.* **1.** stop flow of (blood) (*also* **stanch**) —*a.* **2.** trustworthy, loyal

Staunton (ˈstöntən) *a.* denoting pattern of chessmen used in tournament and club play

stave (stāv) *n.* **1.** one of the pieces forming barrel **2.** verse, stanza **3.** *Mus.* staff —*vt.* **4.** (*usu. with* in) burst or force (hole in something) **5.** (*with* off) ward (off) (**stove, staved** *pt./pp.*, **ˈstaving** *pr.p.*)

staves (stāvz) *n., pl. of* STAFF, STAVE

stay[1] (stā) *vi.* **1.** remain **2.** sojourn **3.** pause **4.** wait **5.** endure —*vt.* **6.** stop **7.** hinder **8.** postpone (**stayed, ˈstaying**) —*n.* **9.** remaining, sojourning **10.** check **11.** restraint **12.** deterrent **13.** postponement —**stay-at-home** *a./n.* (person) enjoying quiet and unadventurous use of leisure —**staying power** endurance

stay[2] (stā) *n.* **1.** support, prop **2.** rope supporting mast *etc.* —*pl.* **3.** formerly, laced corsets

stead (sted) *n. rare* place —**stand (someone) in good stead** be useful or of good service to (someone)

steady (ˈstedi) *a.* **1.** firm **2.** regular **3.** temperate **4.** industrious **5.** reliable —*vt.* **6.** make steady —**ˈsteadily** *adv.* —**ˈsteadiness** *n.* —**ˈsteadfast** *a.* firm, fixed, unyielding —**ˈsteadfastly** *adv.* —**steady state** *Phys.* condition of system when some or all of quantities describing it are independent of time —**steady (on)** be careful

steak (stāk) *n.* **1.** thick slice of meat **2.** slice of fish

steal (stēl) *v.* **1.** take (something) without right or leave —*vi.* **2.** move silently (**stole, ˈstolen, ˈstealing**)

stealth (stelth) *n.* secret or underhand procedure, behavior —**ˈstealthily** *adv.* —**ˈstealthy** *a.*

steam (stēm) *n.* **1.** vapor of boiling water **2.** *inf.* power, energy —*vi.* **3.** give off steam **4.** rise in vapor **5.** move by steam power —*vt.* **6.** cook or treat with steam —**ˈsteamer** *n.* **1.** steam-propelled ship **2.** vessel for cooking or treating with steam —**ˈsteamy** *a.* **1.** of, full of, or covered with steam **2.** *inf.* lustful —**steam bath** room or enclosure that can be filled with steam in which people bathe to induce sweating and refresh or cleanse themselves —**steam-engine** *n.* engine worked or propelled by steam —**steam iron** electric iron that emits steam to facilitate pressing and ironing —**ˈsteamˈroller** *n.* **1.** large roller, *orig.* moved by steam, for leveling road surfaces *etc.* **2.** any great power used to crush opposition —*vt.* **3.** crush —**ˈsteamship** *n.*

stearin (ˈstēərin) *n.* **1.** colorless crystalline ester, present in fats and used in soap and candles (*also* **triˈstearin**) **2.** fat in its solid form

steatite (ˈstēətīt) *n.* soapstone

steatopygia (stēatəˈpījiə) *n.* hereditary condition of overdevelopment of the buttocks

steatorrhea (stēatəˈrēə) *n.* excessive secretion of fat in the stool

steed (stēd) *n. Poet.* horse

steel (stēl) *n.* **1.** hard and malleable metal made by mixing carbon in iron **2.** tool, weapon of steel **3.** C railroad track, line —*vt.* **4.** harden —**ˈsteely** *a.* —**steel band** type of band consisting mainly of percussion instruments made from oildrums —**steel guitar** *see* GUITAR —**steel wool** woven mass of fine steel fibers, used for cleaning or polishing

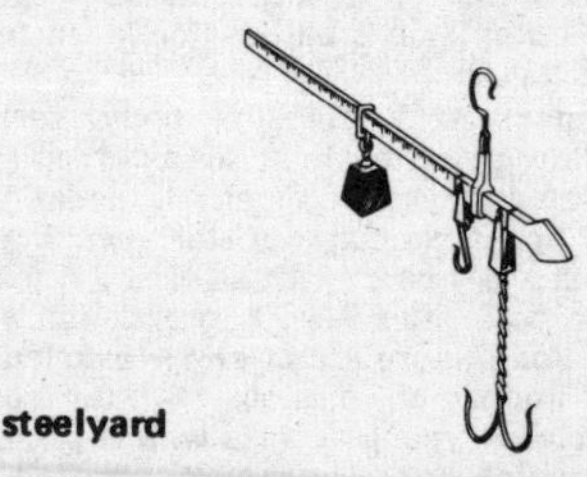

steelyard

steelyard (ˈstēlyärd) *n.* kind of balance with unequal arms

steep[1] (stēp) *a.* **1.** rising, sloping abruptly **2.** precipitous **3.** *inf.* difficult **4.** (of prices) very high or exorbitant **5.** *inf.* unreasonable —**ˈsteepen** *v.* —**ˈsteeply** *adv.*

steep[2] (stēp) *vt.* **1.** soak, saturate —*vi.* **2.** be soaked —*n.* **3.** act or process of steeping **4.** the liquid used for this purpose

steeple (ˈstēpəl) *n.* church tower with spire —**ˈsteeplechase** *n.* **1.** horse race with ditches and fences to jump **2.** foot race with hurdles *etc.* to jump —**ˈsteeplejack** *n.* one who builds, repairs chimneys, steeples *etc.*

steer[1] (stēər) *vt.* **1.** guide, direct course of (vessel, motor vehicle *etc.*) —*vi.* **2.** direct one's course —**ˈsteerage** *n.* **1.** effect of a helm **2.** formerly, cheapest accommodation on ship —**steering committee** committee set up to prepare topics to be discussed, order of business *etc.* for legislative assembly *etc.* —**steering gear, wheel** *etc.* mechanism for steering —**ˈsteersman** *n.* helmsman of vessel

steer[2] (stēər) *n.* castrated male ox

stein (stīn) *n.* earthenware beer mug

stele (stēl, ˈstēli) *n.* ancient carved stone pillar or slab (*pl.* **stelae** (ˈstēlē), **steles** (ˈstēliz, stēlz))

stellar (ˈstelər) *a.* of stars

stem[1] (stem) *n.* **1.** stalk, trunk **2.** long slender part, as in tobacco pipe **3.** part of word to which inflections are added **4.** foremost part of ship

stem[2] (stem) *vt.* check, stop, dam up (**-mm-**)

stench (stench) *n.* offensive smell

stencil (ˈstensəl) *n.* **1.** thin sheet of plastic or metal pierced with pattern, which is brushed over with paint or ink, leaving pattern on surface under it **2.** pattern produced by this process —*vt.* **3.** mark (surface) with stencil

Sten gun (sten) light sub-machine-gun

stenography (stəˈnogrəfi) *n.* shorthand writing —**steˈnographer** *n.* —**stenoˈgraphic** *a.*

stentorian (stenˈtōriən) *a.* (of voice) very loud

step (step) *vi.* **1.** move and set down foot **2.** proceed (in this way) —*vt.* **3.** measure in paces (**-pp-**) —*n.* **4.** act of stepping **5.** sound made by stepping **6.** mark made by foot **7.** manner of walking **8.** series of foot movements forming part of dance **9.** gait **10.** pace **11.** measure, act, stage in proceeding **12.** board, rung *etc.* to put foot on **13.** degree in scale **14.** mast socket **15.** promotion —*pl.* **16.** stepladder —**ˈstepladder** *n.* four-legged ladder having broad flat steps —**stepping stone 1.** one of series of stones acting as footrests for crossing streams *etc.* **2.** circumstance that assists progress toward some goal

stepchild (ˈstepchīld) *n.* child of husband or wife by former marriage —**ˈstepbrother** *n.* —**ˈstepfather** *n.* —**ˈstepmother** *n.* —**ˈstepsister** *n.*

stephanotis (stefəˈnōtis) *n.* climbing shrub with fragrant waxy flowers

steppe (step) *n.* (*oft. pl.*) extensive treeless plain in European and Asiatic Russia

-ster (*comb. form*) **1.** indicating person who is engaged in certain activity, as in *prankster* **2.** indicating person associated with or being something specified, as in *mobster, youngster*

stere (stēər) *n.* cubic meter

stereo- *or sometimes before vowel* **stere-** (*comb. form*) three-dimensional quality or solidity, as in *stereoscope*

stereophonic (sterīəˈfonik, stēər-) *a.* (of sound reproduction) using two or more separate microphones to feed two or more loudspeakers through separate channels in order to give spatial effect to sound —**ˈstereo** *a./n.* (of, for) stereophonic phonograph *etc.*

stereoscope (ˈsteriəskōp, ˈstēər-) *n.* optical instrument for viewing two-dimensional pictures, giving illusion of depth and relief —**stereoscopic** (steriəˈskopik, stēər-) *a.*

stereotype (ˈsteriətīp, ˈstēər-) *n.* **1.** metal plate for printing cast from set-up type **2.** something (monotonously) familiar, conventional, predictable —*vt.* **3.** make stereotype of —**ˈstereotyped** *a.* **1.** lacking originality or individuality **2.** reproduced from or on stereotype printing plate

sterile (ˈsteril) *a.* **1.** unable to produce fruit, crops, young *etc.* **2.** free from (harmful) germs —**steˈrility** *n.* —**steriliˈzation** *n.* process or act of making sterile —**ˈsterilize** *vt.* render sterile

sterling (ˈstərling) *a.* **1.** genuine, true **2.** of solid worth, dependable **3.** in British money —*n.* **4.** British money —**sterling silver** alloy of 925 parts silver to 75 parts base metal

stern[1] (stərn) *a.* severe, strict

stern[2] (stərn) *n.* rear part of ship

sternum (ˈstərnəm) *n.* breastbone (*pl.* **-na** (-nə), **-s**)

steroid (ˈstēəroid) *n.* any of group of naturally occurring substances, *eg* sex hormones, cholesterol, digitalis, cortisone, with basic structure of 17 carbon atoms in four fused ring systems, producing variety of physiological effects on human body

stertorous (ˈstərtərəs) *a.* **1.** with sound of heavy snoring **2.** breathing in this way

stet (stet) *Lat.,* let it stand (proofreader's direction to cancel alteration previously made)

stethoscope (ˈstethəskōp) *n.* instrument for listening to action of heart, lungs *etc.*

stetson (ˈstetsən) *n.* type of broad-brimmed felt hat

stevedore (ˈstēvidōr) *n.* one who loads or unloads ships

stew (styo͞o, sto͞o) *n.* **1.** food cooked slowly in closed vessel **2.** state of excitement, agitation or worry —*v.* **3.** cook by stewing —**stewed** *a.* **1.** (of fish *etc.*) cooked by stewing **2.** *sl.* drunk

steward (ˈstyo͞oərd, ˈsto͞oərd) *n.* **1.** one who manages another's property **2.** official managing race meeting, assembly *etc.* **3.** attendant on ship's or aircraft's passengers (**ˈstewardess** *fem.*)

stick (stik) *n.* **1.** long, thin piece of wood **2.** anything shaped like a stick **3.** *inf.* person, as in *good stick* —*vt.* **4.** pierce, stab **5.** place, fasten, as by pins, glue **6.** *inf.* tolerate, abide —*vi.* **7.** adhere **8.** come to stop, jam **9.** remain **10.** be fastened (**stuck** *pt./pp.*) —**ˈsticker** *n.* adhesive label, poster —**ˈsticky** *a.* **1.** covered with, like adhesive substance **2.** (of weather) warm, humid **3.** *inf.* difficult, unpleasant —**stick insect** insect that resembles a twig —**stick-in-the-mud** *n. inf.* person who lacks initiative or imagination —**stick-up** *n. sl.* robbery at gunpoint —**stick out** protrude —**stick up** *sl.* rob, *esp.* at gunpoint —**stick up for** *inf.* support or defend

stickleback (ˈstikəlbak) *n.* small fish with sharp spines on back

stickler (ˈstiklər) *n.* (*usu. with* for) person who insists on something

stiff (stif) *a.* **1.** not easily bent or moved **2.** rigid **3.** awkward **4.** difficult **5.** thick, not fluid **6.** formal **7.** stubborn **8.** unnatural **9.** strong or fresh, as breeze **10.** *inf.* excessive —*n.* **11.** *sl.* corpse —**ˈstiffen** *v.* —**ˈstiffly** *adv.* —**ˈstiffness** *n.* —**stiff-necked** *a.* obstinate, stubborn

stifle (ˈstīfəl) *vt.* smother, suppress

stigma (ˈstigmə) *n.* distinguishing mark, *esp.* of disgrace (*pl.* **-s, stigmata** (stigˈmätə, ˈstigmətə)) —**ˈstigmatism** *n.* —**ˈstigmatize** *vt.* mark with stigma

stile (stīl) *n.* arrangement of steps for climbing a fence

stiletto (stiˈletō) *n.* **1.** small dagger **2.** small boring tool **3.** very high heel on woman's shoe, tapering to very narrow tip (*pl.* **-s**) —*a.* **4.** thin, pointed like stiletto

still[1] (stil) *a.* **1.** motionless **2.** noiseless **3.** at rest —*vt.* **4.** quiet —*adv.* **5.** to this time **6.** yet **7.** even —*n.* **8.** photograph, *esp.* of motion-picture scene —**ˈstillness** *n.* —**stillˈborn** *a.* born dead —**still life** painting of inanimate objects

still[2] (stil) *n.* apparatus for distilling —**still room** pantry, store room in large house

stilt (stilt) *n.* **1.** pole with footrests for walking raised from ground **2.** long post supporting building *etc.* **3.** shore bird similar to avocet but having straight bill —**ˈstilted** *a.* stiff in manner, pompous —**ˈstiltedly** *adv.*

Stilton (ˈstiltən) *n.* semihard, double cream, inoculated blue-mold cheese, *orig.* from England

stimulus (ˈstimyələs) *n.* **1.** something that rouses to activity **2.** incentive (*pl.* **-uli** (-yəlī, -yəlē)) —**ˈstimulant** *n.* drug *etc.* acting as a stimulus —**ˈstimulate** *vt.* rouse up, spur —**ˈstimulating** *a.* acting as stimulus —**stimuˈlation** *n.* —**ˈstimulative** *a./n.*

sting (sting) *vt.* **1.** thrust sting into **2.** cause sharp pain to **3.** *sl.* impose upon by asking for money **4.** overcharge —*vi.* **5.** feel sharp pain (**stung, ˈstinging**) —*n.* **6.** (wound, pain, caused by) sharp pointed organ, oft. poisonous, of certain insects and animals —**ˈstingray** *n.* ray having whiplike tail bearing serrated venomous spine capable of inflicting painful weals

stingy (ˈstinji) *a.* **1.** niggardly **2.** avaricious —**ˈstingily** *adv.* —**ˈstinginess** *n.*

stink (stingk) *vi.* **1.** give out strongly offensive smell **2.** *sl.* be abhorrent (**stank, stunk, ˈstinking**) —*n.* **3.** such smell, stench **4.** *inf.* fuss, bother —**ˈstinker** *n. sl.* **1.** difficult or unpleasant person or thing **2.** something of very poor quality —**stink bomb** small bomb containing liquid with offensive smell

stint (stint) *v.* **1.** be frugal, miserly to (someone) with (something) —*n.* **2.** allotted amount of work or time **3.** limitation, restriction

stipend (ˈstīpend) *n.* salary, *esp.* of clergyman —**stiˈpendiary** *a.* receiving stipend

stipple (ˈstipəl) *vt.* **1.** engrave, paint in dots —*n.* **2.** this process

stipulate (ˈstipyəlāt) *vt.* specify in making a bargain —**stipuˈlation** *n.* proviso, condition —**ˈstipulator** *n.*

stipule (ˈstipyo͞ol) *n.* small paired outgrowth occurring at base of leaf or its stalk —**ˈstipular** *a.*

stir[1] (stər) *v.* **1.** (begin to) move —*vt.* **2.** set, keep in motion **3.** excite; rouse **4.** (*with* up) cause (trouble) (**-rr-**) —*n.* **5.** commotion, disturbance —**ˈstirring** *a.* **1.** exciting emotions; stimulating **2.** active or busy

stir[2] (stər) *n. sl.* prison —**stir-crazy** *a. sl.* mentally disturbed as result of being in prison

stirrup (ˈstirəp) *n.* metal loop hung from strap for supporting foot of rider on horse (*also* **stirrup iron**) —**stirrup pump** hand-operated pump, base of cylinder of which is placed in bucket of water: used in fighting fires

stitch (stich) *n.* **1.** movement of needle in sewing *etc.* **2.** its result in the work **3.** sharp pain in side **4.** least fragment (of clothing) —*vt.* **5.** sew, fasten *etc.* with stitches

stoat (stōt) *n.* the ermine in its brown summer coat

stock (stok) *n.* **1.** goods, material stored, *esp.* for sale or later use **2.** reserve, fund **3.** financial shares in, or capital of, company *etc.* **4.** standing, reputation **5.** farm animals, livestock **6.** plant, stem from which cuttings are taken **7.** handle of gun, tool *etc.* **8.** liquid broth produced by boiling meat *etc.* **9.** flowering plant **10.** lineage —*pl.* **11.** *Hist.* frame to secure feet, hands (of offender) **12.** frame to support ship during construction —*a.* **13.** kept in stock **14.** standard, hackneyed —*vt.* **15.** keep (goods) for sale **16.** supply with livestock, fish *etc.* —**ˈstocky** *a.* thickset —**ˈstockbreeder** *n.* person who breeds livestock as occupation —**ˈstockbroker** *n.* agent for buying, selling shares in companies —**stock car** ordinary car strengthened and modified for a form of racing in which cars often collide —**stock certificate** certificate signifying ownership of one or more shares in a corporation —**stock exchange** institution for buying and selling shares —**ˈstockman** *n.* man experienced in driving, handling cattle, sheep —**stock market** stock exchange —**ˈstockpile** *v.* acquire and store large quantity of (something) —**stock-still** *a.* motionless —**ˈstocktaking** *n.* examination, counting and valuing of goods in shop *etc.* —**ˈstockyard** *n.* yard with pens or covered buildings where farm animals are assembled, sold *etc.* —**stock in trade 1.** goods necessary for carrying on business **2.** anything constantly used by someone as part of his occupation, trade *etc.*

stockade (stoˈkād) *n.* enclosure of stakes, barrier

stockinet (stokiˈnet) *n.* machine-knitted elastic fabric

stocking (ˈstoking) *n.* one of pair of close-fitting coverings for legs and feet —**ˈstockinged** *a.*

stodgy ('stoji) *a.* (*esp.* of food) heavy, dull —**stodge** *n.* heavy, solid food

stoic ('stōik) *a.* **1.** capable of much self-control, great endurance without complaint —*n.* **2.** stoical person —'**stoical** *a.* —**stoicism** ('stōisizəm) *n.*

stoke (stōk) *v.* feed, tend (fire or furnace) —'**stoker** *n.* —'**stokehold** *n. Naut.* **1.** coal bunker for ship's furnace **2.** hold for ship's boilers; fire room —'**stokehole** *n.* **1.** stokehold **2.** hole in furnace through which it is stoked

stole[1] (stōl) *pt. of* STEAL —'**stolen** *pp. of* STEAL

stole[2] (stōl) *n.* long scarf or shawl

stolid ('stolid) *a.* **1.** hard to excite **2.** heavy, slow, apathetic —**sto'lidity** *n.* —'**stolidly** *adv.*

stoma ('stōmə) *n.* **1.** *Bot.* epidermal pore in plant leaves, that controls passage of gases through plant **2.** *Zool., anat.* mouth or mouthlike part (*pl.* '**stomata**)

stomach ('stumək) *n.* **1.** sac forming chief digestive organ in any animal **2.** appetite **3.** desire, inclination —*vt.* **4.** put up with —**stomach pump** suction device for removing stomach contents —**stomach ache** pain in stomach or abdomen

stomp (stomp) *vi. inf.* stamp

stone (stōn) *n.* **1.** (piece of) rock **2.** gem **3.** hard seed of fruit **4.** hard deposit formed in kidneys, bladder **5.** grindstone, millstone —*vt.* **6.** throw stones at **7.** free (fruit) from stones —**stoned** *a. sl.* stupefied by alcohol or drugs —'**stonily** *adv.* —'**stony** *or* '**stoney** *a.* **1.** of, like stone **2.** hard **3.** cold —**Stone Age** period in human culture identified by use of stone implements —**stone-blind** *a.* completely blind —'**stonechat** *n.* common European songbird —**stone-cold** *a.* completely cold —**stone-cold sober** completely sober —'**stonecrop** *n.* any of the sedums *esp.* useful as rock and wall plants —**stone deaf** completely deaf —'**stonemason** *n.* person skilled in preparing stone for building —**stone's throw** short distance —'**stoneware** *n.* hard, opaque vitrified ceramic ware —**stony-broke** *a. sl.* with no money left

stood (stŏŏd) *pt./pp. of* STAND

stooge (stōōj) *n.* **1.** *Theat. etc.* performer who is always the butt of another's jokes **2.** *sl.* one taken advantage of by another

stook (stōōk) *n.* group of sheaves set upright in field to dry

stool (stōōl) *n.* **1.** backless chair **2.** excrement —**stool pigeon 1.** living or dummy pigeon used as decoy **2.** police informer

stoop (stōōp) *vi.* **1.** lean forward or down, bend **2.** swoop **3.** abase, degrade oneself —*n.* **4.** stooping carriage of the body

stop (stop) *vt.* **1.** check, bring to halt **2.** prevent **3.** interrupt **4.** suspend **5.** desist from **6.** fill up (an opening) —*vi.* **7.** cease, come to a halt **8.** stay (**-pp-**) —*n.* **9.** stopping or becoming stopped **10.** punctuation mark, *esp.* full stop **11.** any device for altering or regulating pitch **12.** set of pipes in organ having tones of a distinct quality —'**stoppage** *n.* —'**stopper** *n.* plug for closing bottle *etc.* —'**stopgap** *n.* temporary substitute —'**stoplight** *n.* taillight of a vehicle that lights up as the driver steps on the brake pedal to slow down or stop —'**stopoff** *or* '**stopover** *n.* short break in journey —'**stopwatch** *n.* watch which can be stopped for exact timing of race

store (stōr) *vt.* **1.** stock, furnish, keep —*n.* **2.** shop **3.** abundance **4.** stock **5.** department store **6.** place for keeping goods **7.** warehouse —*pl.* **8.** stocks of goods, provisions —'**storage** *n.* —**storage battery** accumulator —'**storehouse** *n.*

stork (stōrk) *n.* large wading bird

storm (stōrm) *n.* **1.** violent weather with wind, rain, hail, sand, snow *etc.* **2.** assault on fortress **3.** violent outbreak, discharge —*vt.* **4.** assault **5.** take by storm —*vi.* **6.** rage —'**stormy** *a.* **1.** like storm **2.** (emotionally) violent —**storm center 1.** center of cyclonic storm *etc.* where pressure is lowest **2.** center of disturbance or trouble —**storm door** additional door outside ordinary door, providing extra insulation against wind *etc.* —**storm petrel** *or* **stormy petrel 1.** any of various small sea birds typically having dark plumage and paler underparts **2.** person who brings trouble —**storm-trooper** *n.* **1.** member of Nazi S.A. **2.** member of force of shock troops

story ('stōri) *n.* **1.** (book, piece of prose *etc.*) telling about events, happenings **2.** *inf.* lie **3.** horizontal division of a building (*also* '**storey**) —'**storybook** *n.* book containing stories, *esp.* for children —'**storyteller** *n.*

stoup (stōōp) *n.* small basin near church door for holy water

stout (stowt) *a.* **1.** fat **2.** sturdy **3.** resolute —*n.* **4.** kind of beer —'**stoutly** *adv.* —'**stoutness** *n.* —'**stout'hearted** *a.* brave

stove[1] (stōv) *n.* apparatus for cooking, heating *etc.* —'**stovepipe** *n.* **1.** pipe that serves as flue to stove **2.** man's tall silk hat

stove[2] (stōv) *pt./pp. of* STAVE

stow (stō) *vt.* pack away —'**stowage** *n.* —'**stowaway** *n.* one who hides in ship to obtain free passage

strabismus (strə'bizməs) *n.* abnormal parallel alignment of one or both eyes, characterized by turning inward or outward from nose (*also* **squint**)

straddle ('stradəl) *vt.* **1.** bestride —*vi.* **2.** spread legs wide —*n.* **3.** act or position of straddling

Stradivarius (stradi'variəs, -'ver-) *n.* **1.** violin or cello made by member of the Stradivarius family (*also* **Strad**) **2. Antonius.** 1644-1737, violin-maker of Cremona, pupil of Nicolò Amati

strafe (strāf) *vt.* attack (*esp.* with bullets, rockets) from air

straggle (ˈstragəl) *vi.* stray, get dispersed, linger —ˈ**straggler** *n.*

straight (strāt) *a.* **1.** without bend **2.** honest **3.** level **4.** in order **5.** (of spirits) undiluted, neat **6.** expressionless **7.** (of drama, actor *etc.*) serious **8.** *sl.* heterosexual —*n.* **9.** straight state or part —*adv.* **10.** direct —ˈ**straighten** *v.* —**straightaˈway** *adv.* immediately (*also* **straight away**) —**straight face** serious facial expression, *esp.* one that conceals impulse to laugh —**straight-faced** *a.* —**straightˈforward** *a.* **1.** open, frank **2.** simple **3.** honest —**straightˈforwardly** *adv.* —**straight man** subsidiary actor who acts as stooge to comedian

strain[1] (strān) *vt.* **1.** stretch tightly **2.** stretch to full or to excess **3.** filter —*vi.* **4.** make great effort —*n.* **5.** stretching force **6.** violent effort **7.** injury from being strained **8.** burst of music or poetry **9.** great demand **10.** (condition caused by) overwork, worry *etc.* **11.** tone of speaking or writing —**strained** *a.* —ˈ**strainer** *n.* **1.** filter, sieve **2.** stretcher, tightener

strain[2] (strān) *n.* **1.** breed or race **2.** *esp. Biol.* type **3.** trace, streak

strait (strāt) *n.* **1.** channel of water connecting two larger areas of water —*pl.* **2.** position of difficulty or distress —*a.* **3.** narrow **4.** strict —ˈ**straiten** *vt.* **1.** make strait, narrow **2.** press with poverty —ˈ**straitjacket** *n.* jacket to confine arms of violent person —**strait-laced** *a.* **1.** austere, strict **2.** puritanical

strand[1] (strand) *v.* **1.** run aground **2.** leave, be left helpless or in difficulties —*n.* **3.** *Poet.* shore

strand[2] (strand) *n.* one of individual fibers or threads of string, wire *etc.*

strange (strānj) *a.* **1.** odd, queer **2.** unaccustomed **3.** foreign **4.** uncommon **5.** wonderful **6.** singular —ˈ**strangely** *adv.* —ˈ**strangeness** *n.* —ˈ**stranger** *n.* **1.** unknown person **2.** foreigner **3.** (*with* to) one unaccustomed (to)

strangle (ˈstranggəl) *vt.* **1.** kill by squeezing windpipe **2.** suppress —**stranguˈlation** *n.* strangling —ˈ**stranglehold** *n.* **1.** wrestling hold in which wrestler's arms are pressed against opponent's windpipe **2.** complete control over person or situation

strap (strap) *n.* **1.** strip, *esp.* of leather —*vt.* **2.** fasten, beat with strap (**-pp-**) —ˈ**strapping** *a.* tall and well-made —ˈ**straphanger** *n.* in bus, train, one who has to stand, steadying himself with strap provided for this

strata (ˈstrātə, ˈstratə) *n., pl. of* STRATUM

stratagem (ˈstratijəm) *n.* plan, trick —**strategic(al)** (strəˈtējik(əl)) *a.* —ˈ**strategist** *n.* —ˈ**strategy** *n.* **1.** art of war **2.** overall plan

strathspey (strathˈspā) *n.* type of Scottish dance with gliding steps

stratosphere (ˈstratəsfēər) *n.* upper part of the atmosphere, approx. 15 miles above earth's surface

stratum (ˈstrātəm, ˈstratəm) *n.* **1.** layer, *esp.* of rock **2.** class in society (*pl.* **-s, -ta**) —**stratification** (stratifiˈkāshən) *n.* —**stratify** (ˈstratifī) *v.* form, deposit in layers (**-ified, -ifying**)

stratus (ˈstrātəs, ˈstratəs) *n.* gray layer cloud (*pl.* **-ti** (-tī))

straw (strö) *n.* **1.** stalks of grain **2.** single stalk **3.** long, narrow tube used to suck up liquid —**strawberry** (ˈtröberi, -bəri) *n.* **1.** any of various temperature zone plants bearing a soft juicy fruit with seeds on the surface **2.** the usu. red conical fruit —**strawberry blonde** (of hair) reddish blonde —**strawberry mark** soft vascular red birthmark

stray (strā) *vi.* **1.** wander **2.** digress **3.** get lost —*a.* **4.** strayed **5.** occasional, scattered —*n.* **6.** stray animal

streak (strēk) *n.* **1.** long line or band **2.** element, trace —*vt.* **3.** mark with streaks —*vi.* **4.** move fast —ˈ**streaky** *a.* **1.** having streaks **2.** striped

stream (strēm) *n.* **1.** flowing body of water or other liquid **2.** steady flow **3.** current or flow of air —*vi.* **4.** flow **5.** run with liquid **6.** float, wave in the air —ˈ**streamer** *n.* **1.** (paper) ribbon **2.** narrow flag —**stream of consciousness** **1.** *Psychol.* continuous flow of ideas, feelings *etc.* forming content of individual's consciousness **2.** literary technique that reveals flow of thoughts and feelings of characters through long passages of soliloquy

streamlined (ˈstrēmlīnd) *a.* (of automobile, plane *etc.*) built so as to offer least resistance to air

street (strēt) *n.* public thoroughfare in town or village, usu. lined with houses —ˈ**streetwalker** *n.* prostitute

strength (strength) *n.* **1.** quality of being strong **2.** power **3.** capacity for exertion or endurance **4.** vehemence **5.** force **6.** full or necessary number of people —ˈ**strengthen** *v.* make or become stronger —**on the strength of** **1.** relying on **2.** because of

strenuous (ˈstrenyōōəs) *a.* **1.** energetic **2.** earnest —ˈ**strenuously** *adv.*

streptobacillary fever (streptōbəˈsiləri) *see* HAVERHILL FEVER

streptococcus (streptōˈkokəs) *n.* any of genus of bacteria that produces lactic acid from the fermentation of sugars, producing cheese and butter and causing disease, *eg* pneumonia, erysipelas (*pl.* **-cocci** (-ˈkoksī))

streptomycin (streptəˈmīsin) *n.* antibiotic drug produced by soil microorganism

stress (stres) *n.* **1.** emphasis **2.** strain **3.** impelling force **4.** effort **5.** tension —*vt.* **6.** emphasize **7.** accent **8.** put mechanical stress on

stretch (strech) *vt.* **1.** extend **2.** exert to

utmost **3.** tighten, pull out **4.** reach out *—vi.* **5.** reach **6.** have elasticity *—n.* **7.** stretching, being stretched, expanse **8.** spell **—'stretcher** *n.* **1.** person, thing that stretches **2.** appliance on which ill, wounded or dead person is carried **3.** wooden frame on which canvas for a painting is stretched

strew (strōō) *vt.* scatter over surface, spread (**strewed** *pt.,* **strewed** *or* **strewn** *pp.,* **'strewing** *pr.p.*)

strewth (strōōth) *interj.* expression of surprise or dismay

stria ('strīə) *n.* small channel or threadlike line in surface of shell or other object (*pl.* **striae** ('strīē)) **—striate** ('strīit) *a.* **1.** streaked, furrowed, grooved (*also* **'striated**) *—vt.* ('strīāt) **2.** mark with streaks **3.** score **—stri'ation** *n.*

stricken ('strikən) *a.* **1.** seriously affected by disease, grief, famine **2.** afflicted *—v.* **3.** *pp. of* STRIKE

strict (strikt) *a.* **1.** not lax or indulgent **2.** defined **3.** without exception **—'strictly** *adv.*

stricture ('strikchər) *n.* **1.** critical remark **2.** constriction

stride (strīd) *vi.* **1.** walk with long steps (**strode, stridden** ('stridən), **'striding**) *—n.* **2.** single step **3.** its length **4.** regular pace

strident ('strīdənt) *a.* **1.** harsh in tone **2.** loud **3.** urgent

strife (strīf) *n.* **1.** conflict **2.** quarreling

strike (strīk) *v.* **1.** hit (against) **2.** ignite **3.** (of snake) bite **4.** (of plants) (cause to) take root **5.** attack **6.** hook (fish) **7.** sound (time) as bell in clock *etc.* *—vt.* **8.** affect **9.** arrive at, come upon **10.** enter mind of **11.** discover (gold, oil *etc.*) **12.** dismantle, remove **13.** make (coin) *—vi.* **14.** cease work as protest or to make demands (**struck** *pt.,* **'stricken, struck** *pp.,* **'striking** *pr.p.*) *—n.* **15.** act of striking **—'striker** *n.* **—'striking** *a.* noteworthy, impressive **—'strikebreaker** *n.* person who tries to make strike ineffectual by working **—'strikebreaking** *n./a.* **—strike pay** *or* **benefit** allowance paid by labor union to members on strike **—strike off** remove

Strine (strīn) *n.* humorous transliteration of Australian pronunciation

string (string) *n.* **1.** (length of) thin cord or other material **2.** strand, row **3.** series **4.** fiber in plants *—pl.* **5.** conditions *—vt.* **6.** provide with, thread on string **7.** form in line, series (**strung, 'stringing**) **—stringed** *a.* (of musical instruments) furnished with strings **—'stringer** *n.* **1.** *Archit.* horizontal timber beam used for structural purposes **2.** *Naut.* longitudinal structural brace for strengthening hull of vessel **3.** part-time journalist retained by newspaper to cover particular area **—'stringy** *a.* **1.** like string **2.** fibrous **—string course** *Archit.* ornamental projecting band or continuous molding along wall (*also* **'cordon**)

stringent ('strinjənt) *a.* strict, rigid, binding **—'stringency** *n.* severity **—'stringently** *adv.*

strip (strip) *vt.* **1.** lay bare, take covering off **2.** dismantle **3.** deprive *—vi.* **4.** undress (**-pp-**) *—n.* **5.** long, narrow piece **6.** act of undressing or performing striptease **—'stripper** *n.* **—strip poker** game of poker in which loser of a hand removes an article of clothing **—'striptease** *n.* cabaret or theater act in which person undresses

stripe (strīp) *n.* **1.** narrow mark, band **2.** chevron as symbol of military rank **—'stripy** *a.*

stripling ('stripling) *n.* youth

strive (strīv) *vi.* try hard, struggle, contend (**strove, striven** ('strivən), **'striving**)

strobe (strōb) *n.* apparatus which produces high-intensity flashing light

stroboscope ('strōbəskōp) *n.* **1.** instrument producing intense flashing light **2.** similar device synchronized with shutter of camera so that series of still photographs can be taken of moving object **—stroboscopic(al)** (strōbə'skopik(əl)) *a.*

strode (strōd) *pt. of* STRIDE

stroke (strōk) *n.* **1.** blow **2.** sudden action, occurrence **3.** apoplexy **4.** mark of pen, pencil, brush *etc.* **5.** chime of clock **6.** completed movement in series **7.** act, manner of striking (ball *etc.*) **8.** style, method of swimming **9.** rower sitting nearest stern setting the rate of rowing **10.** act of stroking *—vt.* **11.** set stroke for (rowing crew) **12.** pass hand lightly over

stroll (strōl) *vi.* **1.** walk in leisurely or idle manner *—n.* **2.** leisurely walk

strong (strong) *a.* **1.** powerful **2.** robust **3.** healthy **4.** difficult to break **5.** noticeable **6.** intense **7.** emphatic **8.** not diluted **9.** having a certain number **—'strongly** *adv.* **—strong-arm** *inf. a.* **1.** of or involving physical force or violence *—vt.* **2.** show violence toward **—'strongbox** *n.* box or safe in which valuables are locked for safety **—'stronghold** *n.* fortress **—strong language** swearing

strontium ('stronchiəm, -chəm; 'strontiəm) *n. Chem.* metallic element *Symbol* Sr, at. wt. 87.6, at. no. 38 **—strontium 90** radioactive isotope of strontium present in fallout of nuclear explosions

strop (strop) *n.* **1.** leather for sharpening razors *—vt.* **2.** sharpen on strop (**-pp-**) **—'stroppy** *a. sl.* angry, awkward

strophe ('strōfi) *n.* division of ode **—strophic** ('strōfik, 'strof-) *a.*

strove (strōv) *pt. of* STRIVE

struck (struk) *pt./pp. of* STRIKE

structure ('strukchər) *n.* **1.** (arrangement of parts in) construction, building *etc.* **2.** form **3.** organization *—vt.* **4.** give structure to **—'structural** *a.*

strudel ('strōōdəl) *n.* thin sheet of dough usu. filled with apple and baked

struggle ('strugəl) *vi.* **1.** contend **2.** fight **3.**

proceed, work, move with difficulty and effort —*n.* **4.** act of struggling

strum (strum) *v.* stroke strings of (guitar *etc.*) (**-mm-**)

strumpet (ˈstrumpit) *n. obs.* promiscuous woman

strung (strung) *pt./pp. of* STRING

strut (strut) *vi.* **1.** walk affectedly or pompously (**-tt-**) —*n.* **2.** brace **3.** rigid support, usu. set obliquely **4.** strutting gait

strychnine (ˈstriknīn, -nin, -nēn) *n.* poison obtained from nux vomica seeds —ˈ**strychnic** *a.*

stub (stub) *n.* **1.** remnant of anything, *eg* pencil, cigarette *etc.* **2.** counterfoil of check *etc.* —*vt.* **3.** strike (toes) against fixed object **4.** extinguish by pressing against surface (**-bb-**) —ˈ**stubby** *a.* short, broad

stubble (ˈstubəl) *n.* **1.** stumps of cut grain after reaping **2.** short growth of beard

stubborn (ˈstubərn) *a.* unyielding, obstinate

stucco (ˈstukō) *n.* plaster (*pl.* **-s, -es**) —ˈ**stuccoed** *a.*

stuck (stuk) *pt./pp. of* STICK —**stuck-up** *a. inf.* conceited; snobbish

stud[1] (stud) *n.* **1.** nail with large head **2.** removable double-headed button **3.** vertical wall support —*vt.* **4.** set with studs (**-dd-**)

stud[2] (stud) *n.* set of animals, *esp.* horses, kept for breeding —ˈ**studbook** *n.* book giving pedigree of horses —**stud farm**

studio (ˈstyōōdiō, ˈstōōdiō) *n.* **1.** workroom of artist, photographer *etc.* **2.** building, room where motion pictures, television or radio shows are made, broadcast (*pl.* **-s**) —**studio couch** upholstered couch that can be converted into double bed

study (ˈstudi) *vi.* **1.** be engaged in learning —*vt.* **2.** make study of **3.** try constantly to do **4.** consider **5.** scrutinize (ˈ**studied,** ˈ**studying**) —*n.* **6.** effort to acquire knowledge **7.** subject of this **8.** room to study in **9.** book, report *etc.* produced as result of study **10.** carefully worked-out detail in drawing, painting or clay model for proposed work of art —**student** (ˈstyōōdənt, ˈstōō-) *n.* one who studies —ˈ**studied** *a.* carefully designed, premeditated —**studious** (ˈstyōōdiəs, ˈstōō-) *a.* **1.** fond of study **2.** thoughtful **3.** painstaking **4.** deliberate

stuff (stuf) *vi.* **1.** eat (large amount) —*vt.* **2.** pack, cram, fill (completely) **3.** fill with seasoned mixture **4.** fill (animal's skin) with material to preserve lifelike form —*n.* **5.** material, fabric **6.** any substance —ˈ**stuffing** *n.* material for stuffing, *esp.* seasoned mixture for inserting in poultry *etc.* before cooking —ˈ**stuffy** *a.* **1.** lacking fresh air **2.** *inf.* dull, conventional —**do your stuff** *inf.* do what is required or expected of you

stultify (ˈstultifī) *vt.* make ineffectual (**-ified, -ifying**) —**stultifiˈcation** *n.*

stumble (ˈstumbəl) *vi.* **1.** trip and nearly fall **2.** falter —*n.* **3.** act of stumbling —**stumbling block** obstacle

stump (stump) *n.* **1.** remnant of tree, tooth *etc.* when main part has been cut away **2.** one of uprights of wicket in cricket —*vt.* **3.** confuse, puzzle —*vi.* **4.** walk heavily, noisily —ˈ**stumpy** *a.* short and thickset

stun (stun) *vt.* **1.** knock senseless **2.** amaze (**-nn-**) —ˈ**stunner** *n. inf.* person or thing of great beauty, quality *etc.* —ˈ**stunning** *a.*

stung (stung) *pt./pp. of* STING

stunk (stungk) *pp. of* STINK

stunt[1] (stunt) *vt.* check growth of, dwarf —ˈ**stunted** *a.* **1.** underdeveloped **2.** undersized

stunt[2] (stunt) *n.* **1.** feat of dexterity or daring **2.** anything spectacular, unusual, done to gain publicity —**stunt man** professional acrobat substituted for actor when dangerous scenes are filmed

stupefy (ˈstyōōpifī, ˈstōō-) *vt.* **1.** make insensitive, lethargic **2.** astound (**-efied, -efying**) —**stupeˈfaction** *n.*

stupendous (styōōˈpendəs, stōō-) *a.* **1.** astonishing, amazing **2.** huge

stupid (ˈstyōōpid, ˈstōō-) *a.* **1.** slow-witted **2.** silly **3.** dazed or stupefied

stupor (ˈstyōōpər, ˈstōō-) *n.* **1.** dazed state **2.** insensibility

sturdy (ˈstərdi) *a.* **1.** robust **2.** strongly built **3.** vigorous —ˈ**sturdily** *adv.* —ˈ**sturdiness** *n.*

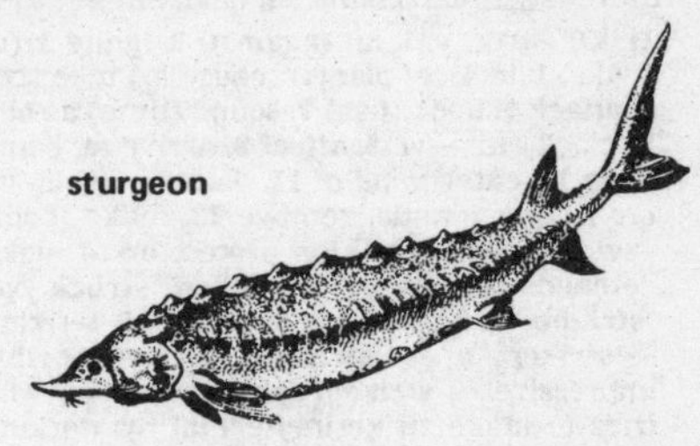
sturgeon

sturgeon (ˈstərjən) *n.* fish yielding caviar and isinglass

stutter (ˈstutər) *v.* **1.** speak (word *etc.*) with difficulty **2.** stammer —*n.* **3.** act or habit of stuttering

sty[1] (stī) *n.* **1.** place in which pigs are kept **2.** hovel, dirty place

sty[2] *or* **stye** (stī) *n.* inflammation on edge of eyelid

Stygian (ˈstijiən) *a.* **1.** of river Styx in Hades **2.** gloomy **3.** infernal

style (stīl) *n.* **1.** manner of writing, doing *etc.* **2.** designation **3.** sort **4.** elegance, refinement **5.** superior manner, quality **6.** design —*vt.* **7.** shape, design **8.** adapt **9.** designate —ˈ**stylish** *a.* fashionable —ˈ**stylishly** *adv.* —ˈ**stylist** *n.* **1.** one cultivating style in literary or other execution **2.** designer **3.** hairdresser —**sty-**

'listic *a.* —'**stylize** *vt.* give conventional stylistic form to

stylus ('stīləs) *n.* **1.** writing instrument **2.** in phonograph, tiny point running in groove of record (*pl.* **-li** (-lī), **-es**)

stymie ('stīmi) *vt.* hinder, thwart

styptic ('stiptik) *a./n.* (designating) a substance that stops bleeding

styrene ('stīrēn) *n.* colorless liquid used in making synthetic rubber, plastics

suave (swäv) *a.* smoothly polite, affable, bland —'**suavity** *n.*

sub (sub) *n.* **1.** subeditor **2.** submarine **3.** subscription **4.** substitute **5.** *inf.* advance payment of wages, salary —*vi.* **6.** *inf.* serve as substitute —*v.* **7.** *inf.* grant or receive (advance payment) —*vt.* **8.** subedit (**-bb-**)

sub- (*comb. form*) under, less than, in lower position, subordinate, forming subdivision, as in *subaqua, subeditor, subheading, subnormal, subsoil.* Such words are not given here where the meaning may be easily inferred from the simple word

subcommittee ('subkəmiti, subkə'miti) *n.* section of committee functioning separately from main body

subconscious (sub'konchəs) *a.* **1.** acting, existing without one's awareness —*n.* **2.** *Psychol.* that part of human mind unknown, or only partly known, to possessor

subcontinent ('sub'kontinənt) *n.* large land mass that is distinct part of continent —**subconti'nental** *a.*

subcontract ('sub'kontrakt) *n.* **1.** subordinate contract under which supply of materials or labor is let out to someone other than party to main contract —*vi.* (sub'kontrakt, subkən'trakt) **2.** (*oft. with* for) enter into subcontract —*vt.* (sub'kontrakt, subkən'trakt) **3.** let out (work) on subcontract —**sub'contractor** *n.*

subculture ('subkulchər) *n.* subdivision of national culture with distinct integrated network of behavior, beliefs and attitudes

subcutaneous (subkyōō'tāniəs) *a.* under the skin

subdivide (subdi'vīd, 'subdivīd) *vt.* divide again —**subdivision** (subdi'vizhən, 'subdivizhən) *n.*

subdominant (sub'dominənt) *Mus. n.* **1.** fourth degree of major or minor scale **2.** key or chord based on this —*a.* **3.** of the subdominant

subdue (səb'dyōō, -'dōō) *vt.* **1.** win control over; conquer **2.** overcome **3.** render less intense or less conspicuous (**-'dued, -'duing**)

subedit (sub'edit) *v.* edit and correct (written or printed material) —**sub'editor** *n.* person who checks and edits copy, *esp.* on newspaper

subfusc (sub'fusk, 'subfusk) *a.* devoid of brightness; drab, dull or dark

subject ('subjikt) *n.* **1.** theme, topic **2.** that about which something is predicated **3.** conscious self **4.** one under power of another —*a.* **5.** owing allegiance **6.** subordinate **7.** dependent **8.** liable —*vt.* (səb'jekt) **9.** cause to undergo **10.** make liable **11.** subdue —**sub'jection** *n.* act of bringing, or state of being, under control —**sub'jective** *a.* **1.** based on personal feelings, not impartial **2.** of the self **3.** existing in the mind **4.** displaying artist's individuality —**subjec'tivity** *n.*

subjoin (sub'join) *vt.* add to end of something written *etc.*

sub judice (sōōb 'yōōdikā, sub 'jōōdisi) *Lat.* under judicial consideration

subjugate ('subjigāt) *vt.* **1.** force to submit **2.** conquer —**subju'gation** *n.* —'**subjugator** *n.*

subjunctive (səb'jungktiv) *Gram. n.* **1.** mood used mainly in subordinate clauses expressing wish, possibility —*a.* **2.** in, of that mood

sublease ('sub'lēs, 'sublēs) *n.* **1.** lease of property made by lessee of that property —*v.* **2.** grant sublease of (property); sublet

sublet ('sub'let) *vt.* (of tenant) let whole or part of what he has rented to another

sublimate ('sublimāt) *vt.* **1.** *Psychol.* direct energy (*esp.* sexual) into activities considered more socially acceptable **2.** refine —*n.* **3.** *Chem.* material obtained when substance is sublimed —**subli'mation** *n.*

sublime (sə'blīm) *a.* **1.** elevated **2.** eminent **3.** majestic **4.** inspiring awe **5.** exalted —*v.* **6.** *Chem.* (cause to) change from solid to vapor —**sub'limely** *adv.* —**sublimity** (sə'blimiti) *or* **su'blimeness** *n.*

subliminal (sub'liminəl) *a.* resulting from processes of which the individual is not aware

sub-machine-gun *n.* portable automatic gun with short barrel

submarine ('submərēn, submə'rēn) *n.* **1.** (war)ship which can travel (and attack from) below surface of sea and remain submerged for long periods —*a.* **2.** below surface of sea

submerge (səb'mərj) *or* **submerse** (səb'mərs) *v.* place, go under water —**sub'mergence** *or* **sub'mersion** *n.* —**sub'mersible** *or* **sub'mergible** *a.* **1.** able to be submerged **2.** capable of operating under water *etc.* —*n.* **3.** warship designed to operate under water

submit (səb'mit) *vt.* **1.** surrender **2.** put forward for consideration —*vi.* **3.** surrender **4.** defer (**-tt-**) —**sub'mission** *n.* —**sub'missive** *a.* meek, obedient

subordinate (sə'bördinit) *a.* **1.** of lower rank or less importance —*n.* **2.** inferior **3.** one under order of another —*vt.* (sə'bördināt) **4.** make, treat as subordinate —**sub'ordinately** *adv.* —**subordi'nation** *n.* —**subordinate clause** *Gram.* clause with adjectival, adverbial or nominal function, rather than one that functions as separate sentence in its own right

suborn (sə'börn) *vt.* bribe to do evil

—**subornation** (subör'nāshən) *n.* —**sub'orner** *n.*

subplot ('subplot) *n.* subordinate plot in novel, motion picture *etc.*

subpoena (sə'pēnə) *n.* **1.** writ requiring attendance at court of law —*vt.* **2.** summon by such order (**-naed, -naing**)

sub rosa ('rōzə) in secret

subscribe (səb'skrīb) *vt.* **1.** pay, promise to pay (contribution) —*v.* **2.** write (one's name) at end of document —**sub'scriber** *n.* —**subscription** (səb'skripshən) *n.* **1.** subscribing **2.** money paid

subscript ('subskript) *a.* **1.** *Print.* (of character) printed below base line —*n.* **2.** subscript character (*also* **sub'index**)

subsection ('subsekshən) *n.* division of a section

subsequent ('subsikwənt) *a.* later, following or coming after in time —'**subsequence** *n.*

subservient (səb'sərviənt) *a.* submissive, servile —**sub'servience** *n.*

subset ('subset) *n.* mathematical set contained within larger set

subside (səb'sīd) *vi.* **1.** abate, come to an end **2.** sink **3.** settle **4.** collapse —**subsidence** (səb'sīdəns, 'subsidəns) *n.*

subsidiary (səb'sidieri) *a.* **1.** supplementing **2.** secondary **3.** auxiliary —*n.* **4.** subsidiary person or thing

subsidize ('subsidīz) *vt.* **1.** help financially **2.** pay grant to —'**subsidy** *n.* money granted

subsist (səb'sist) *vi.* exist, sustain life —**sub'sistence** *n.* **1.** the means by which one supports life **2.** livelihood

subsonic (sub'sonik) *a.* concerning speeds less than that of sound

substance ('substəns) *n.* **1.** matter with uniform properties **2.** particular kind of matter **3.** chief part, essence **4.** wealth —**sub'stantial** *a.* **1.** considerable **2.** of real value **3.** solid, big **4.** important **5.** really existing —**substanti'ality** *n.* —**sub'stantially** *adv.* —**sub'stantiate** *vt.* bring evidence for, confirm, prove —**substanti'ation** *n.* —'**substantive** *a.* **1.** having independent existence **2.** real, fixed —*n.* **3.** noun

substitute ('substityo͞ot, -to͞ot) *v.* **1.** put, serve in exchange (for) —*n.* **2.** thing, person put in place of another **3.** deputy —**substi'tution** *n.*

substratum ('substrātəm, -stratəm) *n.* **1.** that which is laid or spread under **2.** layer of earth lying under another **3.** basis (*pl.* **-ta** (-tə), **-s**)

subsume (səb'so͞om) *vt.* incorporate (idea, case *etc.*) under comprehensive heading, classification

subtenant (sub'tenənt) *n.* person who rents property from tenant —**sub'tenancy** *n.*

subtend (səb'tend) *vt. Geom.* be opposite to and delimit

subterfuge ('subtərfyo͞oj) *n.* trick, lying excuse used to evade something

subterranean (subtə'rāniən) *a.* underground (*also* **subter'restrial**)

subtitle ('subtītəl) *n.* **1.** secondary title of book **2.** (*oft. pl.*) *Cine.* text or fragment of translation appearing at the bottom of the screen

subtle ('sutəl) *a.* **1.** not immediately obvious **2.** ingenious, acute **3.** crafty **4.** intricate **5.** delicate **6.** making fine distinctions —'**subtlety** *n.* —'**subtly** *adv.*

subtonic (sub'tonik) *n. Mus.* seventh degree of major or minor scale

subtract (səb'trakt) *vt.* take away, deduct —**sub'traction** *n.*

subtrahend ('subtrəhend) *n.* number to be subtracted from another number (**minuend**)

subtropical (sub'tropikəl) *a.* of regions bordering on the tropics

suburb ('subərb) *n.* residential area on outskirts of city —**su'burban** *a./n.* —**su'burbia** *n.* **1.** suburbs or people living in them considered as an identifiable community or class in society **2.** life, customs *etc.* of suburban people

subvention (səb'venchən) *n.* subsidy

subvert (səb'vərt) *vt.* **1.** overthrow **2.** corrupt —**sub'version** *n.* —**sub'versive** *a.*

subway ('subwā) *n.* **1.** underground passage **2.** underground railway

succeed (sək'sēd) *vi.* **1.** accomplish purpose **2.** turn out satisfactorily **3.** follow —*vt.* **4.** follow, take place of —**success** (sək'ses) *n.* **1.** favorable accomplishment, attainment, issue or outcome **2.** successful person or thing —**successful** (sək'sesfəl) *a.* —**successfully** (sək'sesfəli) *adv.* —**succession** (sək'seshən) *n.* **1.** following **2.** series **3.** succeeding —**successive** (sək'sesiv) *a.* following in order, consecutive —**successively** (sək'sesivli) *adv.* —**successor** (sək'sesər) *n.*

succinct (sək'singkt) *a.* terse, concise

succor ('sukər) *vt./n.* help in distress

succubus ('sukyəbəs) *n.* female demon fabled to have sexual intercourse with sleeping men (*pl.* **-bi** (-bī))

succulent ('sukyələnt) *a.* **1.** juicy, full of juice **2.** (of plant) having thick, fleshy leaves —*n.* **3.** such plant —'**succulence** *or* '**succulency** *n.*

succumb (sə'kum) *vi.* **1.** yield, give way **2.** die

such (such) *a.* **1.** of the kind or degree mentioned **2.** so great, so much **3.** so made *etc.* **4.** of the same kind —**such and such** particular thing that is unspecified —'**suchlike** *inf. a.* **1.** such —*pron.* **2.** other such things

suck (suk) *vt.* **1.** draw into mouth **2.** hold, dissolve in mouth **3.** draw in —*n.* **4.** sucking —'**sucker** *n.* **1.** person, thing that sucks **2.** organ, appliance which adheres by suction **3.** shoot coming from root or base of stem of plant **4.** *inf.* person easily deceived or taken in

suckle (ˈsukəl) *v.* feed from the breast —ˈ**suckling** *n.* unweaned infant

sucrose (ˈsōōkrōs, -krōz) *n.* sugar

suction (ˈsukshən) *n.* **1.** drawing or sucking of air or fluid **2.** force produced by difference in pressure

Sudan (sōōˈdan) *n.* —**Democratic Republic of Sudan** country in Africa bounded north by Egypt, northeast by the Red Sea, east by Eritrea and Ethiopia, south by Kenya, Uganda and Zaïre, west by the Central African Republic and Chad and northwest by Libya —**Sudaˈnese** *n./a.*

sudden (ˈsudən) *a.* **1.** done, occurring unexpectedly **2.** abrupt, hurried —ˈ**suddenly** *adv.* —ˈ**suddenness** *n.* —**sudden infant death syndrome** unexplained death of infant during sleep (*also* **crib death**)

sudorific (sōōdəˈrifik) *a.* **1.** causing perspiration —*n.* **2.** medicine that produces sweat

suds (sudz) *pl.n.* froth of soap and water, lather

sue (sōō) *vt.* **1.** prosecute **2.** seek justice from **3.** beseech —*vi.* **4.** make application or entreaty (**sued, ˈsuing**)

suede (swād) *n.* leather with soft, velvety finish

suet (ˈsōōit) *n.* hard animal fat from around the kidney

suffer (ˈsufər) *v.* **1.** undergo, endure, experience (pain *etc.*) —*vt.* **2.** *obs.* allow —ˈ**sufferable** *a.* —ˈ**sufferance** *n.* toleration —ˈ**sufferer** *n.*

suffice (səˈfīs) *v.* be adequate, satisfactory (for) —**sufficiency** (səˈfishənsi) *n.* adequate amount —**sufficient** (səˈfishənt) *a.* enough, adequate

suffix (ˈsufiks) *n.* **1.** letter or word added to end of word —*vt.* (ˈsufiks, səˈfiks) **2.** add, annex to the end

suffocate (ˈsufəkāt) *v.* **1.** kill, be killed by deprivation of oxygen **2.** smother —**suffoˈcation** *n.*

suffrage (ˈsufrij) *n.* vote or right of voting —ˈ**suffragist** *n.* one claiming a right of voting (**suffraˈgette** *fem.*)

suffuse (səˈfyōōz) *vt.* well up and spread over —**sufˈfusion** *n.*

sugar (ˈshōōgər) *n.* **1.** sweet crystalline vegetable substance —*vt.* **2.** sweeten, make pleasant (with sugar) —ˈ**sugary** *a.* —**sugar candy** confection made by boiling pure sugar until it hardens —**sugar cane** plant from whose juice sugar is obtained —**sugar daddy** *sl.* wealthy (elderly) man who pays for (*esp.* sexual) favors of younger person —**sugar loaf** conical mass of hard refined sugar

suggest (səˈjest) *vt.* **1.** propose **2.** call up the idea of —**suggestiˈbility** *n.* —**sugˈgestible** *a.* easily influenced —**sugˈgestion** *n.* **1.** hint **2.** proposal **3.** insinuation of impression, belief *etc.* into mind —**sugˈgestive** *a.* containing, open to suggestion, *esp.* of something indecent

suicide (ˈsōōisīd) *n.* **1.** act or instance of killing oneself intentionally **2.** person who does this —**suiˈcidal** *a.*

suit (sōōt) *n.* **1.** set of clothing **2.** garment worn for particular event, purpose **3.** one of four sets in deck of cards **4.** action at law —*v.* **5.** make, be fit or appropriate (for) **6.** be acceptable (to) —**suitaˈbility** *n.* —ˈ**suitable** *a.* **1.** fitting, proper **2.** convenient **3.** becoming —ˈ**suitably** *adv.* —ˈ**suitcase** *n.* flat rectangular traveling case

suite (swēt) *n.* **1.** matched set, *esp.* of furniture **2.** set of rooms **3.** retinue

suitor (ˈsōōtər) *n.* **1.** man who courts woman **2.** one who sues **3.** petitioner

sukiyaki (skiˈyäki, sōōkiˈyäki) *n.* dish of thin slices of meat and vegetables cooked in soy sauce, sake and sugar in a chafing dish

sulfa drug (ˈsulfə) sulfonamide used to treat bacterial infections

sulfate (ˈsulfāt) *n.* salt formed by sulfuric acid in combination with any base

sulfonamide (sulˈfonəmīd) *n.* any of group of drugs used as internal germicides in treatment of many bacterial diseases

sulfone (ˈsulfōn) *n.* any of group of drugs used to treat leprosy

sulfur (ˈsulfər) *n. Chem.* nonmetallic element *Symbol* S, at. wt. 32.1, at. no. 16 —ˈ**sulfide** *n.* compound of sulfur with more electropositive element —ˈ**sulfite** *n.* salt or ester of acid —**sulfitic** (sulˈfitik) *a.* —**sulfuric** (sulˈfyōōərik) *a.* —**sulfurous** (ˈsulfyərəs, -fərəs) *a.* —**sulfur dioxide** colorless soluble pungent gas used in manufacture of sulfuric acid, preservation of foodstuffs, bleaching and disinfecting —**sulfuric acid** colorless oily corrosive liquid used in manufacture of fertilizers, dyes and explosives

sulk (sulk) *vi.* **1.** be silent, resentful, *esp.* to draw attention to oneself —*n.* **2.** sulky mood —ˈ**sulkily** *adv.* —ˈ**sulky** *a.*

sullen (ˈsulən) *a.* **1.** unwilling to talk or be sociable; morose **2.** dismal, dull —ˈ**sullenly** *adv.*

sully (ˈsuli) *vt.* stain, tarnish, disgrace (ˈ**sullied, ˈsullying**)

sultan (ˈsultən) *n.* ruler of Muslim country —**sulˈtana** *n.* **1.** sultan's wife **2.** kind of raisin —ˈ**sultanate** *n.* **1.** territory or country ruled by sultan **2.** office, rank or jurisdiction of sultan

sultry (ˈsultri) *a.* **1.** (of weather) hot, humid **2.** (of person) looking sensual

sum (sum) *n.* **1.** amount **2.** problem in arithmetic —*v.* **3.** add up **4.** (*with* up) make summary of (**-mm-**) —**summing-up** *n.* summary of main points of speech *etc.* —**sum total 1.** total obtained by adding up sum or sums **2.** everything included

sumac (ˈsōōmak, ˈshōō-) *n.* shrub with clusters of green flowers and red hairy fruits

summa cum laude (ˈsōōmə kōōm ˈlowdə) *Lat.* with the greatest distinction, *esp.* of college or university degree

summary (ˈsuməri) *n.* **1.** abridgment or statement of chief points of longer document, speech *etc.* **2.** abstract —*a.* **3.** done quickly —**sumˈmarily** *adv.* **1.** speedily **2.** abruptly —**ˈsummarize** *vt.* **1.** make summary of **2.** present briefly and concisely —**sumˈmation** *n.* adding up

summer (ˈsumər) *n.* **1.** second, warmest season —*vi.* **2.** pass the summer —**ˈsummery** *a.* —**summer camp** camp providing recreational or educational activities for children in residence —**ˈsummerhouse** *n.* small building in garden or park, used for shade in summer —**summer school** academic course *etc.* held during summer —**summer solstice** **1.** time at which sun is at its northernmost point in sky; June 21st **2.** *Astron.* point on celestial sphere at which ecliptic is furthest north from celestial equator —**ˈsummertime** *n.* the season of summer or period resembling it

summit (ˈsumit) *n.* **1.** highest point or part **2.** peak —**summit conference** meeting of heads of governments

summon (ˈsumən) *vt.* **1.** demand attendance of **2.** call on **3.** bid (witness) appear in court **4.** gather up (energies *etc.*) —**ˈsummons** *n.* **1.** call **2.** authoritative demand

sumptuous (ˈsumpchōōəs) *a.* **1.** lavish, magnificent **2.** costly —**ˈsumptuary** *a.* pert. to or regulating expenditure —**ˈsumptuously** *adv.* —**ˈsumptuousness** *n.*

sunflower

sun (sun) *n.* **1.** luminous body round which earth and other planets revolve **2.** its rays —*vt.* **3.** expose to sun's rays (**-nn-**) —**ˈsunless** *a.* —**ˈsunny** *a.* **1.** like the sun **2.** warm **3.** cheerful —**ˈsunbathing** *n.* exposure of whole or part of body to sun's rays —**ˈsunbeam** *n.* ray of sun —**ˈsunburn** *n.* inflammation of skin due to excessive exposure to sun —**ˈsundial** *n.* device indicating time during hours of sunlight by means of pointer that casts shadow on to surface marked in hours —**ˈsundown** *n.* sunset —**ˈsunfish** *n.* sea fish with large rounded body —**ˈsunflower** *n.* plant with large golden flowers —**ˈsunglasses** *pl.n.* glasses with darkened or polarizing lenses that protect eyes from sun's glare —**sun-god** *n.* sun considered as personal deity —**sun lamp** lamp that generates infrared-to-ultraviolet rays —**ˈsunrise** *n.* **1.** daily appearance of sun above horizon **2.** atmospheric phenomena accompanying this appearance **3.** time at which sun rises at particular locality —**ˈsunset** *n.* **1.** daily disappearance of sun below horizon **2.** atmospheric phenomena accompanying this disappearance **3.** time at which sun sets at particular locality —**ˈsunshade** *n.* device, *esp.* parasol or awning, serving to shade from sun —**ˈsunshine** *n.* **1.** light or warmth received directly from sun **2.** light-hearted term of affection —**ˈsunshiny** *a.* —**ˈsunspot** *n.* dark patch appearing temporarily on sun's surface —**ˈsunstroke** *n.* frequently fatal condition caused by prolonged exposure to intensely hot sun —**ˈsuntan** *n.* browning of skin by exposure to sun

Sun. Sunday

sundae (ˈsundi) *n.* ice cream topped with syrup and chopped nuts

Sunday (ˈsundi) *n.* **1.** first day of week **2.** Christian Sabbath —**Sunday best** one's best clothes —**Sunday school** school for religious instruction of children

sunder (ˈsundər) *vt.* separate, sever

sundry (ˈsundri) *a.* several, various —**ˈsundries** *pl.n.* odd items not mentioned in detail

sung (sung) *pp. of* SING

sunk (sungk) *pp. of* SINK

sup (sup) *vt.* **1.** take by sips —*vi.* **2.** take supper (**-pp-**) —*n.* **3.** mouthful of liquid

sup. 1. above **2.** superior **3.** *Gram.* superlative **4.** supplement **5.** supplementary **6.** supply

super (ˈsōōpər) *a. inf.* very good

super- (*comb. form*) above, greater, exceeding(ly), as in *superhuman, superman, superstore, supertanker.* Such compounds are not given here where the meaning may be inferred from the simple word

superable (ˈsōōpərəbəl) *a.* **1.** capable of being overcome **2.** surmountable

superannuate (sōōpərˈanyōōāt) *vt.* **1.** pension off **2.** discharge or dismiss as too old —**superˈannuated** *a.* —**superannuˈation** *n.* **1.** pension given on retirement **2.** contribution by employee to pension

superb (sōōˈpərb) *a.* **1.** splendid **2.** grand **3.** impressive —**suˈperbly** *adv.*

supercargo (sōōpərˈkärgō, ˈsōōpərkärgō) *n.* officer on merchant ship in charge of cargo

supercharge (ˈsōōpərchärj) *vt.* charge, fill to excess —**ˈsupercharged** *a.* —**ˈsupercharger** *n.* in internal-combustion engine, device to ensure complete filling of cylinder with explosive mixture when running at high speed

supercilious (sōōpərˈsiliəs) *a.* displaying arrogant pride, scorn, indifference

superconductivity (sōōpərkondukˈtiviti) *n.*

Phys. property of certain substances that have almost no electrical resistance at temperatures close to absolute zero —**supercon'ductive** *or* **supercon'ducting** *a.* —**supercon'ductor** *n.*

supercool (soopər'kool) *v. Chem.* cool without freezing or crystallization to temperature below that at which freezing or crystallization should occur

superego (soopər'ēgō, -'egō) *n. Psychoanal.* that part of the unconscious mind that acts as conscience for the ego

supererogation (soopərerə'gāshən) *n.* **1.** performance of work in excess of that required **2.** *R.C.Ch.* prayers, devotions *etc.* beyond those prescribed as obligatory

superficial (soopər'fishəl) *a.* **1.** of or on surface **2.** not careful or thorough **3.** without depth —**superfici'ality** *n.*

superfluous (soo'pərflooəs) *a.* **1.** extra, unnecessary **2.** excessive **3.** left over —**super'fluity** *n.* **1.** superabundance **2.** unnecessary amount —**su'perfluously** *adv.*

superheat (soopər'hēt) *vt.* **1.** heat (vapor, *esp.* steam) to temperature above its saturation point for given pressure **2.** heat (liquid) to temperature above its boiling point without boiling occurring **3.** overheat —**super'heater** *n.*

superheterodyne receiver (soopər'hetərədīn) radio receiver that combines two radio-frequency signals by heterodyne action to produce signal above audible frequency limit

superimpose (soopərim'pōz) *vt.* **1.** set or place on or over something else **2.** (*usu. with* on *or* upon) add (to) —**superimpo'sition** *n.*

superintend (soopərin'tend) *vt.* **1.** have charge of **2.** overlook **3.** manage —**superin'tendence** *n.* —**superin'tendent** *n.*

superior (soo'pēəriər) *a.* **1.** greater in quality or quantity **2.** upper, higher in position, rank or quality **3.** showing consciousness of being so —**superi'ority** *n.* quality of being higher, greater or more excellent

superlative (soo'pərlətiv) *a.* **1.** of, in highest degree or quality **2.** surpassing **3.** *Gram.* denoting form of adjective, adverb meaning 'most' —*n.* **4.** *Gram.* superlative degree of adjective or adverb

supermarket ('soopərmärkit) *n.* large self-service store selling chiefly food and household goods

supernatural (soopər'nachərəl) *a.* **1.** being beyond the powers or laws of nature **2.** miraculous —**super'naturally** *adv.*

supernova (soopər'nōvə) *n.* star that explodes and is for a few days up to one hundred million times brighter than sun (*pl.* **-vae** (-vē), **-s**)

supernumerary (soopər'nyoomərerі, -'noo-) *a.* **1.** in excess of normal number, extra —*n.* **2.** extra person or thing **3.** person hired for walk-on part in drama or opera

superphosphate (soopər'fosfāt) *n.* chemical fertilizer

superpose (soopər'pōz) *vt. Geom.* place (one figure) upon another so that their perimeters coincide

superpower ('soopərpowər) *n.* an extremely powerful state

superscribe ('soopərskrīb, soopər'skrīb) *vt.* write (inscription *etc.*) above, on top of or outside —**superscription** (soopər'skripshən) *n.*

superscript ('soopərskript) *n./a.* (character) printed, written above the line

supersede (soopər'sēd) *vt.* **1.** take the place of **2.** set aside, discard, supplant —**supersession** (soopər'seshən) *n.*

supersonic (soopər'sonik) *a.* denoting speed greater than that of sound

superstition (soopər'stishən) *n.* religion, opinion or practice based on belief in luck or magic —**super'stitious** *a.* —**super'stitiously** *adv.*

superstructure ('soopərstrukchər) *n.* **1.** structure above foundations **2.** part of ship above deck

supervene (soopər'vēn) *vi.* happen, as an interruption or change —**supervention** (soopər'venchən) *n.*

supervise ('soopərvīz) *vt.* **1.** oversee **2.** direct **3.** inspect and control **4.** superintend —**supervision** (soopər'vizhən) *n.* —**'supervisor** *n.* —**super'visory** *a.*

supine (soo'pīn) *a.* **1.** lying on back with face upward **2.** indolent —*n.* ('soopīn) **3.** Latin verbal noun

supper ('supər) *n.* **1.** (light) evening meal, *esp.* when main meal is at midday **2.** social event featuring supper

supplant (sə'plant) *vt.* **1.** take the place of, *esp.* unfairly **2.** oust —**sup'planter** *n.*

supple ('supəl) *a.* **1.** pliable **2.** flexible **3.** compliant —**'supply** *or* **'supplely** *adv.*

supplement ('supliмənt) *n.* **1.** thing added to fill up, supply deficiency, *esp.* extra part added to book *etc.* **2.** additional number of periodical, usu. on special subject **3.** separate, oft. illustrated section published periodically with newspaper —*vt.* ('supliment) **4.** add to **5.** remedy deficiency of —**supple'mentary** *a.* additional —**supplementary angle** either of two angles whose sum is 180°

suppliant ('supliənt) *a.* **1.** petitioning —*n.* **2.** petitioner

supplicate ('suplikāt) *v.* **1.** beg humbly —*vt.* **2.** entreat —**suppli'cation** *n.* —**'supplicatory** *a.*

supply (sə'plī) *vt.* **1.** furnish **2.** make available **3.** provide (**sup'plied, sup'plying**) —*n.* **4.** supplying, substitute **5.** stock, store

support (sə'pört) *vt.* **1.** hold up **2.** sustain **3.** assist —*n.* **4.** supporting, being supported **5.** means of support —**sup'portable** *a.* —**sup'porter** *n.* adherent —**sup'porting** *a.* (of motion-picture *etc.* role) less important —**sup'portive** *a.*

suppose (sə'pōz) *vt.* **1.** assume as theory **2.** take for granted **3.** accept as likely **4.** (in passive) be expected, obliged **5.** (in passive) ought —**supposed** (sə'pōzid, -'pōzd) *a.* —**supposedly** (sə'pōzidli) *adv.* —**suppo'sition** *n.* **1.** assumption **2.** belief without proof **3.** conjecture —**suppo'sitious** *or* **supposititious** (səpozi'tishəs) *a.* sham, spurious, counterfeit

suppository (sə'pozitōri) *n.* medication (in capsule) for insertion in orifice of body

suppress (sə'pres) *vt.* **1.** put down, restrain **2.** crush **3.** keep or withdraw from publication —**sup'pression** *n.*

suppurate ('supyərāt) *vi.* fester, form pus —**suppu'ration** *n.*

supra- (*comb. form*) above, over, as in *supranational.* Such words are not given here where the meaning may easily be inferred from the simple word

supreme (sə'prēm, sōō-) *a.* **1.** highest in authority or rank **2.** utmost —**supremacy** (sə'preməsi, sōō-) *n.* position of being supreme —**su'premely** *adv.* —**Supreme Being** God —**Supreme Commander** military commander of all allied forces —**Supreme Court** the highest court in the U.S. and of most states

Supt. *or* **supt.** superintendent

sur-[1] (*comb. form*) over, above; beyond, as in *surcharge*

sur-[2] (*comb. form*) *see* SUB-

surcease ('sərsēs, sər'sēs) *v.* **1.** (cause to) cease —*n.* **2.** cessation

surcharge ('sərchärj) *n.* **1.** additional charge —*vt.* **2.** subject to additional charge

surd (sərd) *n.* **1.** *Math.* sum containing one or more irrational roots of numbers **2.** *Phonet.* voiceless consonant —*a.* **3.** of or relating to surd

sure (shōōər, shōr) *a.* **1.** certain **2.** trustworthy **3.** without doubt —*adv.* **4.** *inf.* certainly —'**surely** *adv.* —**surety** ('shōōəriti, 'shōōərti) *n.* one who makes himself responsible for another's obligations —**sure-fire** *a. inf.* certain to succeed or meet expectations —**sure-footed** *a.* **1.** unlikely to fall, slip or stumble **2.** not likely to err or fall

surf (sərf) *n.* **1.** waves breaking on shore —*vi.* **2.** swim in, ride surf —'**surfer** *n.* —'**surfboard** *n.* board used in sport of riding over surf —'**surfboarding** *n.* sport of riding a board on the fast-moving incline of a wave (*also* '**surfing**)

surface ('sərfis) *n.* **1.** outside face of body **2.** exterior **3.** plane **4.** top, visible side **5.** superficial appearance, outward impression —*a.* **6.** involving the surface only **7.** going no deeper than surface —*v.* **8.** (cause to) come to surface —*vt.* **9.** put a surface on —**surface tension** property of liquids caused by intermolecular forces near surface leading to apparent presence of surface film

surfeit ('sərfit) *n.* **1.** excess **2.** disgust caused by excess —*vt.* **3.** feed to excess

surge (sərj) *n.* **1.** wave **2.** sudden increase **3.** *Elec.* sudden rush of current in circuit —*vi.* **4.** move in large waves **5.** swell, billow

surgeon ('sərjən) *n.* medical practitioner who specializes in surgery —'**surgery** *n.* branch of medicine concerned with the treatment of disease or disorder by physical intervention —'**surgical** *a.* —'**surgically** *adv.* —**surgeon general 1.** chief medical officer of any of the armed forces (*pl.* **surgeons general**) **2.** (**S- G-**) head of U.S. Bureau of Public Health or a state health agency

Suriname (sōōri'nämə) *n.* country in South America bounded north by the Atlantic, east by French Guiana, west by Guyana and south by Brazil

surly ('sərli) *a.* **1.** gloomily morose **2.** ill-natured **3.** cross and rude —'**surlily** *adv.* —'**surliness** *n.*

surmise (sər'mīz) *v./n.* guess, conjecture

surmount (sər'mownt) *vt.* get over, overcome —**sur'mountable** *a.*

surname ('sərnām) *n.* family name

surpass (sər'pas) *vt.* **1.** go beyond **2.** excel **3.** outstrip —**sur'passable** *a.* —**sur'passing** *a.* **1.** excellent **2.** exceeding others

surplice ('sərplis) *n.* loose white vestment worn by clergy and choristers

surplus ('sərpləs) *n.* what remains over in excess

surprise (sər'prīz) *vt.* **1.** cause surprise to **2.** astonish **3.** take, come upon unexpectedly **4.** startle (someone) into action thus —*n.* **5.** what takes unawares **6.** something unexpected **7.** emotion aroused by being taken unawares

surrealism (sə'rēəlizəm) *n.* movement in art and literature emphasizing expression of the unconscious —**sur'real** *a.* —**sur'realist** *n./a.*

surrender (sə'rendər) *vt.* **1.** hand over, give up —*vi.* **2.** allow oneself to yield **3.** cease resistance **4.** capitulate —*n.* **5.** act of surrendering

surreptitious (surəp'tishəs) *a.* **1.** done secretly or stealthily **2.** furtive —**surrep'titiously** *adv.*

surrogate ('surəgāt, -git) *n.* **1.** deputy, *esp.* of bishop **2.** substitute

surround (sə'rownd) *vt.* **1.** be, come all round, encompass **2.** encircle **3.** hem in —*n.* **4.** border, edging —**sur'roundings** *pl.n.* conditions, scenery *etc.* around a person, place, environment

surtax ('sərtaks) *n.* additional tax

surveillance (sər'vāləns) *n.* close watch, supervision —**sur'veillant** *a./n.*

survey (sər'vā, 'sərvā) *vt.* **1.** scrutinize **2.** inspect, examine **3.** measure, map (land) —*n.* ('sərvā, sər'vā) **4.** a surveying **5.** inspection **6.** report incorporating results of survey —**sur'veyor** *n.*

survive (sər'vīv) *vt.* **1.** outlive **2.** come through alive —*vi.* **3.** continue to live or exist —**sur'vival** *n.* continuation of existence of persons, things *etc.* —**sur'vivor** *n.* one left alive when others have died —**survival of the fittest** natural selection

susceptible (sə'septəbəl) *a.* **1.** yielding readily **2.** capable **3.** impressionable —**suscepti'bility** *n.*

suspect (sə'spekt) *vt.* **1.** doubt innocence of **2.** have impression of existence or presence of **3.** be inclined to believe **4.** mistrust —*a.* ('suspekt) **5.** of suspected character —*n.* ('suspekt) **6.** suspected person

suspend (sə'spend) *vt.* **1.** hang up **2.** cause to cease for a time **3.** debar from an office or privilege **4.** keep inoperative **5.** sustain in fluid —**sus'penders** *pl.n.* straps worn over shoulders to hold up trousers —**suspended animation** temporary cessation of vital functions —**suspended sentence** prison sentence that is not served by offender unless he commits further offense during its currency

suspense (sə'spens) *n.* **1.** state of uncertainty, *esp.* while awaiting news, an event *etc.* **2.** anxiety, worry —**sus'pension** *n.* **1.** state of being suspended **2.** springs on axle of body of vehicle **3.** dispersion of liquid or solid in liquid in which the dispersed substance does not dissolve —**sus'pensory** *a.* —**suspension bridge** bridge suspended from cables that hang between two towers and are anchored at both ends

suspicion (sə'spishən) *n.* **1.** suspecting, being suspected **2.** slight trace —**sus'picious** *a.*

sustain (sə'stān) *vt.* **1.** keep, hold up **2.** endure **3.** keep alive **4.** confirm —**sus'tainable** *a.* —**sustenance** ('sustənəns) *n.* food

suture ('so͞ochər) *n.* **1.** act of sewing **2.** sewing up of a wound **3.** material used for this **4.** a joining of the bones of the skull —**'sutural** *a.*

suzerain ('so͞ozərən, -rān) *n.* **1.** sovereign with rights over autonomous state **2.** feudal lord —**suzerainty** ('so͞ozərənti, -rānti) *n.*

svelte (sfelt) *a.* **1.** lightly built, slender **2.** sophisticated

SW *or* **S.W.** southwest(ern)

Sw. 1. Sweden **2.** Swedish

swab (swob) *n.* **1.** mop **2.** pad of surgical wool *etc.* for cleaning, taking specimen *etc.* **3.** *sl.* low or unmannerly fellow —*vt.* **4.** clean with swab (**-bb-**) —**'swabber** *n.*

swaddle ('swodəl) *vt.* swathe —**swaddling clothes** long strips of cloth for wrapping newborn baby

swag (swag) *n.* **1.** garland or drapery suspended between two points and hanging in an arc **2.** *sl.* stolen property **3. A** *inf.* bag carried by swagman —**'swagman** *n.* **A** itinerant vagrant worker

swagger ('swagər) *vi.* **1.** strut **2.** boast —*n.* **3.** strutting gait **4.** boastful, overconfident manner —**swagger stick** short cane or stick carried on occasion by army officers

Swahili (swä'hēli) *n.* **1.** Bantu language widely used as lingua franca throughout E and central Afr. **2.** member of people speaking this language (*pl.* **-s, -li**) —**Swa'hilian** *a.*

swain (swān) *n.* rustic lover

swallow[1] ('swolō) *vt.* **1.** cause, allow to pass down gullet **2.** engulf **3.** suppress, keep back **4.** *inf.* believe gullibly —*n.* **5.** act of swallowing

swallow[2] ('swolō) *n.* migratory bird with forked tail and skimming manner of flight —**'swallowtail** *n.* **1.** butterfly having tail-like extension of each hind wing **2.** forked tail of swallow or similar bird

swam (swam) *pt. of* SWIM

swami ('swämi) *n.* in India, title of respect for Hindu saint or religious teacher (*pl.* **-es, -s**)

swamp (swomp) *n.* **1.** bog —*vt.* **2.** entangle in swamp **3.** overwhelm **4.** flood —**'swampy** *a.*

swan (swon) *n.* **1.** large, web-footed water bird with graceful curved neck —*vi.* **2.** *inf.* stroll idly (**-nn-**) —**'swannery** *n.* —**swan dive** dive in which diver arches back and stretches arms sideways —**swan's-down** *n.* **1.** fine soft down feathers of swan, used to trim clothing *etc.* **2.** thick soft fabric of wool with silk, cotton or rayon **3.** cotton fabric with heavy nap —**swan song 1.** fabled song of a swan before death **2.** last act *etc.* before death

swank (swangk) *vi. sl.* **1.** swagger **2.** show off —**'swanky** *a. sl.* **1.** smart **2.** showy

swap (swop) *n./v. inf.* **1.** exchange **2.** barter (**-pp-**)

sward (swörd) *or* **swarth** (swörth) *n.* green turf

swarm[1] (swörm) *n.* **1.** large cluster of insects **2.** vast crowd —*vi.* **3.** (of bees) be on the move in swarm **4.** gather in large numbers

swarm[2] (swörm) *v.* climb (rope *etc.*) by grasping with hands and knees

swarthy ('swördhi) *a.* dark-complexioned

swashbuckler ('swoshbuklər) *n.* swaggering daredevil person —**'swashbuckling** *a.*

swastika ('swostikə) *n.* form of cross with arms bent at right angles: form with counterclockwise arms used as emblem by Amerindians and in Orient; form with clockwise arms official symbol of Nazi Party and the Third Reich

swat (swot) *vt.* **1.** hit smartly **2.** kill, *esp.* insects (**-tt-**)

swatch (swoch) *n.* sample of cloth or other material

swathe (swādh) *vt.* cover with wraps or bandages

sway (swā) *v.* **1.** swing unsteadily **2.** (cause to) vacillate in opinion *etc.* —*vt.* **3.** influence opinion *etc.* of —*n.* **4.** control **5.** power **6.** swaying motion

Swaziland ('swäziland) *n.* country in Africa bounded north, west and south by South Africa and east by Mozambique

swear (swāər) *vt.* **1.** promise on oath **2.** cause to take an oath —*vi.* **3.** declare **4.** curse (**swore, sworn, 'swearing**) —**'swearword** *n.* socially taboo word of a profane, obscene or insulting character

sweat (swet) *n.* **1.** moisture oozing from, forming on skin, *esp.* in humans —*v.* **2.** (cause to) exude sweat —*vi.* **3.** toil **4.** *inf.* worry —*vt.* **5.** employ at wrongfully low wages (**sweat** *or* **'sweated** *pt./pp.*, **'sweating** *pr.p.*) —**'sweaty** *a.* —**'sweatband** *n.* **1.** band of material set in hat to protect it from sweat **2.** piece of cloth tied around forehead to keep sweat out of eyes or around wrist to keep hands dry, as in sports —**sweat shirt** long-sleeved knitted cotton sweater —**'sweatshop** *n.* workshop where employees work long hours for low wages

sweater ('swetər) *n.* knitted or crocheted jacket or pullover

Sweden ('swēdən) *n.* country in Europe bounded east by the Gulf of Bothnia, south by the Baltic Sea, west and northwest by Norway and northeast by Finland —**Swede** *n.* —**'Swedish** *a.* **1.** of Sweden —*n.* **2.** language of Sweden which is a Scandinavian language

sweep (swēp) *vi.* **1.** effect cleaning with broom **2.** pass quickly or magnificently **3.** extend in continuous curve —*vt.* **4.** clean with broom **5.** carry impetuously (**swept, 'sweeping**) —*n.* **6.** act of cleaning with broom **7.** sweeping motion **8.** wide curve **9.** range **10.** long oar **11.** one who cleans chimneys —**'sweeping** *a.* **1.** wide-ranging **2.** without limitations, reservations —**sweep** *or* **'sweepstake** *n.* gamble in which winner takes stakes contributed by all

sweet (swēt) *a.* **1.** tasting like sugar **2.** agreeable **3.** kind, charming **4.** fresh, fragrant **5.** in good condition **6.** tuneful **7.** gentle, dear, beloved —*n.* **8.** small piece of sweet food —**'sweeten** *v.* —**'sweetener** *n.* **1.** sweetening agent, *esp.* one that is sugar-free **2.** *sl.* bribe —**'sweetish** *a.* —**'sweetly** *adv.* —**'sweetbread** *n.* animal's pancreas used as food —**'sweetbrier** *n.* wild rose —**sweet corn** variety of maize —**'sweetheart** *n.* lover —**'sweetmeat** *n.* sweetened delicacy, *eg* small cake, candy —**sweet pea** plant of pea family with bright flowers —**sweet potato 1.** trailing plant **2.** its edible, sweetish, starchy tubers —**sweet-talk** *vt. inf.* coax, flatter —**sweet tooth** strong liking for sweet foods —**sweet william** ('wilyəm) garden plant with flat flower clusters

swell (swel) *v.* **1.** expand —*vi.* **2.** be greatly filled with pride, emotion (**swelled, 'swollen, 'swelling**) —*n.* **3.** act of swelling or being swollen **4.** wave of sea **5.** mechanism in organ to vary volume of sound **6.** *sl.* person of high social standing —*a.* **7.** *sl.* smart, fine —**swell'headed** *a. inf.* having inflated view of one's own worth

swelter ('sweltər) *vi.* be oppressed with heat

swept (swept) *pt./pp. of* SWEEP

swerve (swərv) *vi.* **1.** swing round, change direction during motion **2.** turn aside (from duty *etc.*) —*n.* **3.** swerving

swift (swift) *a.* **1.** rapid, quick, ready —*n.* **2.** bird like a swallow —**'swiftly** *adv.*

swig (swig) *n.* **1.** large swallow of drink —*v.* **2.** drink thus (**-gg-**)

swill (swil) *v.* **1.** drink greedily —*vt.* **2.** pour water over or through —*n.* **3.** liquid pig food **4.** greedy drinking **5.** rinsing

swim (swim) *vi.* **1.** support and move oneself in water **2.** float **3.** be flooded **4.** have feeling of dizziness —*vt.* **5.** cross by swimming **6.** compete in by swimming (**swam, swum, 'swimming**) —*n.* **7.** spell of swimming —**'swimmer** *n.* —**'swimming** *n.* act of propelling the body through water with arm and leg motion without artificial aid —**'swimmingly** *adv.* successfully, effortlessly —**swimming pool** artificial pool for swimming —**'swimsuit** *n.* swimming garment

swindle ('swindəl) *n./v.* cheat —**'swindler** *n.*

swine (swīn) *n.* **1.** pig **2.** contemptible person (*pl.* **swine**) —**'swinish** *a.* —**swine fever** infectious viral disease of pigs —**'swineherd** *n.*

swing (swing) *v.* **1.** (cause to) move to and fro **2.** (cause to) pivot, turn **3.** hang **4.** arrange, play (music) with (jazz) rhythm —*vi.* **5.** be hanged **6.** hit out (at) (**swung** *pt./pp.*) —*n.* **7.** act, instance of swinging **8.** seat hung to swing on **9.** fluctuation (*esp.* in voting pattern) **10. C** train of freight sleds, canoes —**'swinger** *n. inf.* **1.** person regarded as modern, lively **2.** one who indulges freely in sex

swingeing ('swinjing) *a. esp.* **UK 1.** severe **2.** huge

swingletree ('swingg əltrē) *n.* crossbar in horse's harness to which ends of traces are attached (*also* **'whiffletree**)

swipe (swīp) *v.* **1.** (*sometimes with* at) strike with wide, sweeping or glancing blow —*vt.* **2.** *sl.* steal

swirl (swərl) *v.* **1.** (cause to) move with eddying motion —*n.* **2.** such motion

swish (swish) *v.* **1.** (cause to) move with audible hissing sound —*n.* **2.** the sound —*a.* **3.** *inf.* fashionable, smart

Swiss (swis) *see* SWITZERLAND

switch (swich) *n.* **1.** mechanism to complete or interrupt electric circuit *etc.* **2.** abrupt change **3.** flexible stick or twig **4.** tufted end of animal's tail **5.** tress of false hair —*vi.* **6.** shift, change **7.** swing —*vt.* **8.** affect (current *etc.*) with switch **9.** change abruptly **10.** strike with switch —**'switchback** *n.* road, railroad with steep rises and descents —**'switchboard** *n.* installation for establishing or varying connections in telephone and electric circuits

Switzerland (ˈswitsərlənd) *n.* country in Europe bounded south by Italy, east by France, north by West Germany and west by Austria —**Swiss** *n./a.* (native or inhabitant) of Switzerland —**Swiss chard** *see* CHARD –**Swiss cheese** hard, yellow cheese with many holes made from half-skimmed cow's milk

swivel (ˈswivəl) *n.* **1.** mechanism of two parts which can revolve the one on the other —*v.* **2.** turn (on swivel)

swizzle (ˈswizəl) *n.* an alcoholic drink containing gin or rum —**swizzle stick** small rod used to agitate effervescent drink to facilitate escape of carbon dioxide

swollen (ˈswōlən) *pp. of* SWELL

swoon (swōōn) *vi./n.* faint

swoop (swōōp) *vi.* **1.** dive, as hawk —*n.* **2.** act of swooping **3.** sudden attack

swoosh (swŏŏsh) *vi.* **1.** make rustling, swirling sound, *esp.* when moving, pouring out —*n.* **2.** swirling, rustling sound or movement

sword (sörd) *n.* weapon with long blade for cutting or thrusting —**sword dance** dance in which performers dance nimbly over swords on ground or brandish them in the air —ˈ**swordfish** *n.* fish with elongated sharp upper jaw, like sword —ˈ**swordplay** *n.* **1.** action or art of fighting with sword **2.** verbal sparring —**sword swallower** person who swallows or appears to swallow swords, in a circus *etc.*

swore (swör) *pt. of* SWEAR —**sworn** *pp. of* SWEAR

swum (swum) *pp. of* SWIM

swung (swung) *pt./pp. of* SWING

sybarite (ˈsibərīt) *n.* person who loves luxury —**sybaritic** (sibəˈritik) *a.*

sycamore (ˈsikəmör) *n.* family of plane trees native to eastern U.S., California and southern Arizona grown widely throughout U.S. as street trees

sycophant (ˈsikəfənt) *n.* one using flattery to gain favors —ˈ**sycophancy** *n.* —**sycoˈphantic** *a.*

Sydenham's chorea (ˈsidənəmz) *see* CHOREA

syllable (ˈsiləbəl) *n.* division of word as unit for pronunciation —**sylˈlabic** *a.* —**sylˈlabify** *vt.*

syllabub *or* **sillabub** (ˈsiləbub) *n.* **1.** sweet frothy dish of cream, sugar and wine **2.** something insubstantial

syllabus (ˈsiləbəs) *n.* **1.** outline of a course of study **2.** program, list of subjects studied on course (*pl.* **-es, -bi** (-bī))

syllogism (ˈsiləjizəm) *n.* form of logical reasoning consisting of two premises and conclusion —**sylloˈgistic** *a.*

sylph (silf) *n.* **1.** slender, graceful woman **2.** sprite —ˈ**sylphlike** *a.*

sylvan *or* **silvan** (ˈsilvən) *a.* of forests, trees

Sylvaner (silˈvanər) *n.* **1.** semisweet white table wine **2.** grape used to make this wine

sym- *see* SYN-

symbiosis (simbīˈōsis, -bi-) *n.* living together of two organisms of different kinds, *esp.* to their mutual benefit —**symbiotic** (simbīˈotik, -bi-) *a.*

symbol (ˈsimbəl) *n.* **1.** thing representing or typifying something **2.** letter, figure or sign used in mathematics *etc.* to represent a quantity *etc.* —**symˈbolic** *a.* —**symˈbolically** *adv.* —ˈ**symbolism** *n.* **1.** use of, representation by symbols **2.** movement in art holding that work of art should express idea in symbolic form —ˈ**symbolist** *n./a.* —ˈ**symbolize** *v.*

symmetry (ˈsimitri) *n.* **1.** proportion between parts **2.** balance of arrangement between two sides **3.** order —**symˈmetrical** *a.* **1.** having due proportion in parts **2.** harmonious **3.** regular

sympathy (ˈsimpəthi) *n.* **1.** feeling for another in pain *etc.* **2.** compassion, pity **3.** sharing of emotion, interest, desire *etc.* **4.** fellow feeling —**sympaˈthectomy** *n.* operation to sever fibers of sympathetic nervous system —**sympaˈthetic** *a.* —**sympaˈthetically** *adv.* —ˈ**sympathize** *vi.* —**sympathetic magic** type of magic in which it is sought to produce large-scale effect by performing some small-scale ceremony resembling it, as pouring of water on altar to induce rainfall —**sympathetic nervous system** part of nervous system controlling secretion, contraction of smooth muscle and blood vessels *etc.*

symphony (ˈsimfəni) *n.* **1.** composition for full orchestra **2.** harmony of sounds —**symphonic** (simˈfonik) *a.* —**symphonious** (simˈfōniəs) *a.* harmonious —**symphonic poem** extended orchestral composition, based on nonmusical material, such as work of literature or folk tale —**symphony orchestra** large orchestra comprising strings, brass, woodwind, harp and percussion

symposium (simˈpōziəm) *n.* **1.** conference, meeting **2.** discussion, writings on a given topic (*pl.* **-s, -sia** (-ziə))

symptom (ˈsimptəm) *n.* **1.** change in body indicating its state of health or disease **2.** sign, token —**symptoˈmatic** *a.*

syn- *or* **sym-** (*comb. form*) with, together, alike

synagogue (ˈsinəgog) *n.* (place of worship of) Jewish congregation

synchromesh (ˈsingkrōmesh) *a.* (of gearbox) having device that synchronizes speeds of gears before they engage

synchronize (ˈsingkrənīz) *vt.* **1.** make agree in time —*vi.* **2.** happen at same time —ˈ**synchronism** *n.* —**synchroniˈzation** *n.* —ˈ**synchronous** *a.* simultaneous

synchrotron (ˈsingkrətron) *n.* device for acceleration of stream of electrons

syncopate (ˈsingkəpāt) *vt.* accentuate (weak beat in bar of music) —**syncoˈpation** *n.*

syncope (ˈsingkəpi) *n.* **1.** fainting **2.** elision of letter(s) from middle of word

syncretize (ˈsingkritīz) *v.* attempt to combine characteristic teachings, beliefs, or practices of (differing systems of religion or philosophy) —**syncretiˈzation** *n.*

syndicate (ˈsindikit) *n.* **1.** body of people, delegates associated for some enterprise —*vt.* (ˈsindikāt) **2.** form into syndicate **3.** publish in many newspapers at the same time —ˈ**syndicalism** *n.* economic movement aiming at combination of workers in all trades to enforce demands of labor

syndrome (ˈsindrōm) *n.* **1.** combination of several symptoms in disease **2.** symptom, set of symptoms or characteristics

synecdoche (sinˈekdəki) *n.* figure of speech by which whole of thing is put for part or part for whole, *eg sail* for *ship*

synod (ˈsinəd, ˈsinod) *n.* **1.** church council **2.** convention

synonym (ˈsinənim) *n.* word with same meaning as another —**synoˈnymity** *n.* —**synonymous** (siˈnonimәs) *a.*

synopsis (siˈnopsis) *n.* summary, outline (*pl.* **-ses** (-sēz)) —**synˈoptic** *a.* **1.** of, like synopsis **2.** having same viewpoint

syntax (ˈsintaks) *n.* part of grammar treating of arrangement of words in sentence —**synˈtactic** *a.* —**synˈtactically** *adv.*

synthesis (ˈsinthisis) *n.* putting together, combination (*pl.* **-theses** (-thisēz)) —ˈ**synthesize** *v.* (cause to) combine into a whole —ˈ**synthesizer** *n.* **1.** *see* MOOG SYNTHESIZER **2.** person or thing that synthesizes —**synthetic** (sinˈthetik) *a.* **1.** artificial **2.** of synthesis —**synthetic detergent** synthetic substance other than soap cabable of soaplike cleaning action

syphilis (ˈsifilis) *n.* contagious venereal disease —**syphiˈlitic** *a.*

syphon (ˈsīfən) *n.* bottle for holding carbonated water

Syria (ˈsiriə) *n.* country in Middle East bounded west by the Mediterranean and Lebanon, south by Israel and Jordan, east by Iraq and north by Turkey —ˈ**Syrian** *n./a.*

syringe (siˈrinj, ˈsirinj) *n.* **1.** instrument for drawing in liquid by piston and forcing it out in fine stream or spray **2.** squirt —*vt.* **3.** spray, cleanse with syringe

syrup (ˈsirəp) *n.* **1.** thick solution obtained in process of refining sugar **2.** any liquid like this, *esp.* in consistency —ˈ**syrupy** *a.*

system (ˈsistəm) *n.* **1.** complex whole, organization **2.** method **3.** classification —**systeˈmatic** *a.* methodical —**systeˈmatically** *adv.* —ˈ**systematize** *vt.* **1.** reduce to system **2.** arrange methodically —**systemic** (siˈstemik) *a.* affecting entire body or organism —**systems analysis** analysis of methods involved in scientific and industrial operations, usu. with computer, so that improved system can be designed

systole (ˈsistəli) *n.* contraction of heart and arteries for expelling blood and carrying on circulation —**systolic** (siˈstolik) *a.* **1.** contracting **2.** of systole

T

t *or* **T** (tē) *n.* **1.** 20th letter of English alphabet **2.** speech sound represented by this letter **3.** something shaped like T (*pl.* **t's, T's** *or* **Ts**) —**to a T** in every detail; perfectly

t 1. tense **2.** ton

T 1. absolute temperature **2.** *Chem.* tritium **3.** surface tension **4.** tablespoon

ta (tä) *interj.* **UK** *inf.* thank you

Ta *Chem.* tantalum

Taal (täl) *n.* **SA** language, *esp.* Afrikaans

tab[1] (tab) *n.* tag, label, short strap —**keep tabs on** *inf.* keep watchful eye on

tab[2] (tab) **1.** tabulator **2.** tablet

tabard ('tabərd) *n.* (herald's) short tunic open at sides

tabby ('tabi) *n./a.* (cat) with markings of stripes *etc.* on lighter background

tabernacle ('tabərnakəl) *n.* **1.** portable shrine of Israelites **2.** *R.C.Ch.* receptacle containing consecrated Host **3.** place of worship not called a church

tabes dorsalis ('tābēz dör'salis) late manifestation of syphilis involving spinal cord resulting in progressive failure of lower limbs

table ('tābəl) *n.* **1.** piece of furniture consisting of flat board supported by legs **2.** food **3.** set of facts, figures arranged in lines or columns —*vt.* **4.** lay on table **5.** suspend discussion of (bill *etc.*) indefinitely **6. UK** submit (motion *etc.*) for consideration by meeting —**'tablecloth** *n.* cloth for covering table —**'tableland** *n.* plateau, high flat area —**'tablespoon** *n.* spoon used for serving food *etc.* —**table tennis** ball game played on table with small bats and light hollow ball

tableau ('tablō) *n.* **1.** group of persons, silent and motionless, arranged to represent some scene **2.** dramatic scene (*pl.* **-leaux** (-lōz))

table d'hôte ('täbəl 'dōt) *Fr.* (meal) with limited choice of dishes, at a fixed price

tablet ('tablit) *n.* **1.** pill of compressed powdered medicinal substance **2.** flattish cake of soap *etc.* **3.** slab of stone, wood *etc.*, *esp.* used formerly for writing on

tabloid ('tabloid) *n.* illustrated popular small-sized newspaper with terse, sensational headlines

taboo *or* **tabu** (tə'bōō) *a.* **1.** forbidden; disapproved of —*n.* **2.** prohibition resulting from social conventions *etc.* **3.** thing prohibited —*vt.* **4.** place under taboo

tabor *or* **tabour** ('tābər) *n.* small drum, used *esp.* in Middle Ages, struck with one hand while other held pipe

tabular ('tabyələr) *a.* shaped, arranged like a table —**'tabulate** *vt.* arrange (figures, facts *etc.*) in tables —**tabu'lation** *n.* —**'tabulator** *n.* **1.** device for setting stops that locate column margins on typewriter **2.** *Comp.* machine that reads data from punched cards *etc.*, producing lists, tabulations or totals

tachism ('tashizəm) *n.* action painting

tacho- (*comb. form*) speed, as in *tachometer*

tachometer (ta'komitər) *n.* device for measuring speed, *esp.* of revolving shaft (in automobile) and hence revolutions per minute

tacit ('tasit) *a.* **1.** implied but not spoken **2.** silent —**'tacitly** *adv.* —**'taciturn** *a.* **1.** talking little **2.** habitually silent —**taci'turnity** *n.*

tack[1] (tak) *n.* **1.** small nail **2.** long, loose, temporary stitch **3.** *Naut.* course of ship obliquely to windward **4.** course, direction **5.** *inf.* food —*vt.* **6.** nail with tacks **7.** stitch (garment) with long, loose temporary stitches, baste **8.** append, attach —*v.* **9.** sail to windward

tack[2] (tak) *n.* riding harness for horses

tackle ('takəl) *n.* **1.** equipment, apparatus, *esp.* lifting appliances with ropes **2.** *Sport* physical challenge of opponent —*vt.* **3.** take in hand **4.** grapple with **5.** challenge

tacky[1] ('taki) *a.* sticky, not quite dry —**'tackiness** *n.*

tacky[2] ('taki) *a. inf.* **1.** shabby, shoddy **2.** ostentatious and vulgar

tact (takt) *n.* **1.** skill in dealing with people or situations **2.** delicate perception of the feelings of others —**'tactful** *a.* —**'tactfully** *adv.* —**'tactless** *a.* —**'tactlessly** *adv.*

tactics ('taktiks) *pl.n.* **1.** (*with sing. v.*) art of handling troops, ships in battle **2.** adroit management of a situation **3.** plans for this —**'tactical** *a.* —**tac'tician** *n.*

tactile ('taktil) *a.* of the sense of touch

tadpole ('tadpōl) *n.* immature frog, in its first state before gills and tail are absorbed

taffeta ('tafitə) *n.* smooth, stiff fabric of silk, rayon *etc.*

taffrail ('tafrāl) *n.* **1.** rail at stern of ship **2.** flat ornamental part of stern

Taffy ('tafi) *n. sl.* Welshman

Taft (taft) *n.* **William Howard.** the 27th President of the U.S. (1909-13)

tag[1] (tag) *n.* **1.** label identifying or showing price of something **2.** ragged, hanging end **3.** pointed end of shoelace *etc.* **4.** trite quotation **5.** any appendage —*vt.* **6.** append, add (on)

—*vi.* **7.** (*usu. with* on *or* along) trail behind (**-gg-**)

tag[2] (tag) *n.* **1.** children's game where one being chased becomes chaser upon being touched by chaser —*vt.* **2.** touch (**-gg-**) —**tag wrestling** wrestling match for teams of two, where one partner may replace the other upon being touched on hand

tagetes (ta'jētēz) *n.* plant with yellow or orange flowers

t'ai chi ch'uan *or* **tai chi chuan** (tī jē chōō'än, tī chē) Chinese system of disciplined movements practiced as aid to meditation or for exercise (*also* **t'ai chi**)

tail (tāl) *n.* **1.** flexible prolongation of animal's spine **2.** lower or inferior part of anything **3.** appendage **4.** rear part of aircraft **5.** *inf.* person employed to follow and spy on another —*pl.* **6.** reverse side of coin **7.** *inf.* tail coat —*vt.* **8.** remove tail of **9.** *inf.* follow closely, trail —**tailed** *a.* —**'tailings** *pl.n.* waste left over from some (*eg* industrial) process —**'tailless** *a.* —**'tailboard** *n.* removable or hinged rear board on vehicle —**tail coat** man's evening dress jacket —**tail end** last part —**'tailgate** *n.* **1.** gate used to control flow of water at lower end of lock **2.** tailboard —*v.* **3.** drive very close behind (vehicle) —**'taillight** *n.* light, *usu.* red, at rear of vehicle —**'tailpiece** *n.* **1.** extension or appendage that lengthens or completes something **2.** decorative design at foot of page *etc.* **3.** piece of wood to which strings of violin *etc.* are attached at lower end **4.** short beam or rafter with one end embedded in wall —**'tailpipe** *n.* pipe from which exhaust gases are discharged, *esp.* at rear of motor vehicle —**'tailplane** *n.* stabilizing surface at rear of aircraft —**'tailspin** *n.* spinning dive of aircraft —**'tailwind** *n.* wind blowing in same direction as course of aircraft or ship —**tail off** diminish gradually, dwindle —**turn tail** run away

tailor ('tālər) *n.* maker of outer clothing, *esp.* for men —**'tailored** *a.* **1.** having simple lines, as some women's garments **2.** specially fitted —**'tailorbird** *n.* tropical Asian warbler that builds nest by sewing together large leaves using plant fibers —**tailor-made** *a.* **1.** made by tailor **2.** well-fitting **3.** appropriate —*n.* **4.** *inf.* factory-made cigarette

taint (tānt) *v.* **1.** affect or be affected by pollution *etc.* —*n.* **2.** defect, flaw **3.** infection, contamination

Taiwan ('tī'wän) *n.* country in Asia situated on an island between the East and South China Seas (*also* **Republic of China**) —**Taiwa'nese** *n./a.*

take (tāk) *vt.* **1.** grasp, get hold of **2.** get, receive **3.** assume **4.** adopt **5.** accept **6.** understand **7.** consider **8.** carry, conduct **9.** use **10.** capture **11.** consume **12.** require —*vi.* **13.** be effective **14.** please (**took, 'taken, 'taking**) —*n.* **15.** *esp. Cine.* (recording of) scene, sequence photographed without interruption —**'taking** *a.* charming —**'takings** *pl.n.* earnings, receipts —**'takeaway UK, A, NZ** *a.* **1.** sold for consumption away from premises **2.** selling food for consumption away from premises —*n.* **3.** shop or restaurant that sells such food —**take-off** *n.* **1.** instant at which aircraft becomes airborne **2.** commencement of flight **3.** *inf.* act of mimicry —**'takeover** *n.* act of assuming power, control *etc.* —**take after** resemble in appearance or character —**take down 1.** write down **2.** dismantle **3.** humiliate —**take in 1.** understand **2.** make (garment *etc.*) smaller **3.** deceive —**take in vain 1.** blaspheme **2.** mention (person's name) —**take off 1.** (of aircraft) leave ground **2.** *inf.* go away **3.** *inf.* mimic —**take over 1.** assume control or management (of) **2.** *Print.* move (copy) to next line —**take to** become fond of

talc (talk) *n.* **1.** soft mineral of magnesium silicate **2.** talcum powder —**talcum powder** powder, *usu.* scented, to absorb body moisture, deodorize *etc.*

tale (tāl) *n.* **1.** story, narrative, report **2.** fictitious story —**tell tales 1.** tell fanciful lies **2.** report malicious stories *etc., esp.* to someone in authority

talent ('talənt) *n.* **1.** natural ability or power **2.** ancient weight or money **3.** *inf.* (*esp.* attractive) members of opposite sex —**'talented** *a.* gifted —**talent scout** person whose occupation is searching for talented sportsmen, performers *etc.* for engagement as professionals

talis ('tälis) *n. Judaism* prayer shawl used by Jewish males at certain religious services (*pl.* **taleysem** (tä'lāsəm))

talisman ('talismən, 'talizmən) *n.* **1.** object supposed to have magic power **2.** amulet (*pl.* **-s**) —**talis'manic** *a.*

talk (tök) *vi.* **1.** express, exchange ideas *etc.* in words **2.** spread rumors or gossip —*vt.* **3.** express in speech **4.** discuss —*n.* **5.** speech, lecture **6.** conversation **7.** rumor —**'talkative** *a.* fond of talking —**'talker** *n.* —**talking book** recording of book, designed to be used by the blind —**talking-to** *n. inf.* reproof —**talk back** answer boldly or impudently —**talk into** persuade to by talking —**talk out of** dissuade from by talking

tall (töl) *a.* **1.** high, of great stature **2.** incredible, untrue (*esp. in* **tall story**) —**'tallboy** *n.* high chest of drawers —**tall order** demand which is difficult to accomplish

tallow ('talō) *n.* **1.** melted and clarified animal fat —*vt.* **2.** smear with this

tally ('tali) *vi.* **1.** correspond one with the other **2.** keep score (**-lied, -lying**) —*n.* **3.** record, account, total number —**'tallier** *n.*

tally-ho (tali'hō) *interj.* huntsman's cry to urge on hounds

Talmud ('tälmŏŏd) *n.* body of Jewish law —**Tal'mudic** *a.*

talon ('talən) *n.* claw

tamarind ('tamərind) *n.* **1.** tropical tree **2.** its pods containing sour brownish pulp

tamarisk ('tamərisk) *n.* ornamental, evergreen tree or shrub with slender branches, very small leaves and spiky flowers

tambour ('tambŏŏər) *n.* **1.** *Real tennis* sloping buttress on one side of receiver's end of court **2.** embroidery frame consisting of two hoops over which fabric is stretched while being worked **3.** embroidered work done on such frame **4.** sliding door on desks *etc.*, made of thin strips of wood glued on to canvas backing **5.** *Archit.* wall that is circular in plan, *esp.* supporting dome or surrounded by colonnade **6.** drum —*v.* **7.** embroider on tambour

tambourine (tambə'rēn) *n.* flat half-drum with jingling disks of metal attached

tame (tām) *a.* **1.** not wild, domesticated **2.** subdued **3.** uninteresting —*vt.* **4.** make tame —'**tamely** *adv.* **1.** in a tame manner **2.** without resisting —'**tamer** *n.*

Tamil ('tamil) *n.* **1.** member of a people of S India and Sri Lanka **2.** language of this people (*pl.* **-s, 'Tamil**) —*a.* **3.** of this people

tam-o'-shanter ('taməshantər) *n.* Scottish brimless wool cap with bobble in center

tamp (tamp) *vt.* pack, force down by repeated blows

tamper ('tampər) *vi.* (*usu. with* with) interfere improperly, meddle

tampon ('tampon) *n.* **1.** plug of lint, cotton *etc.* inserted in wound, body cavity, to stop flow of blood, absorb secretions *etc.* **2.** two-headed drumstick

tan[1] (tan) *a./n.* **1.** (of) brown color of skin after long exposure to rays of sun *etc.* —*v.* **2.** (cause to) go brown —*vt.* **3.** (of animal hide) convert to leather by chemical treatment **4.** *inf.* beat, flog (**-nn-**) —'**tanner** *n.* —'**tannery** *n.* place where hides are tanned —'**tannic** *a.* of tan, tannin or tannic acid —'**tannin** *n.* vegetable substance used as tanning agent —'**tanbark** *n.* bark of certain trees, yielding tannin —**tannic acid** astringent derived from oak bark *etc.*, used in tanning *etc.*

tan[2] (tan) *Trig.* tangent

tanager ('tanəjər) *n.* any of family of Amer. songbirds having short thick bill and, in male, brilliantly colored plumage

tandem ('tandəm) *n.* bicycle for two riders, one behind the other

tandoor (tän'dŏŏər) *n.* clay oven in which food is cooked, usu. over charcoal (*pl.* **tan'doori**) —**tan'doori** *a.* cooked in a tandoor

tang (tang) *n.* **1.** strong pungent taste or smell **2.** trace, hint **3.** spike, barb —'**tangy** *a.*

Tanganyika and Zanzibar (tanggə'nyēkə; 'zanzibär) *former name of* TANZANIA —**Tanga'nyikan** *n./a.*

tangent ('tanjənt) *n.* **1.** line that touches a curve without cutting **2.** divergent course **3.** *Trig.* ratio of side opposite given acute angle in right-angled triangle to adjacent side —*a.* **4.** touching, meeting without cutting —**tan'gential** *a.* —**tan'gentially** *adv.*

tangerine ('tanjərēn, tanjə'rēn) *n.* **1.** Asian citrus tree **2.** its fruit, a variety of orange **3.** reddish-orange color

tangible ('tanjəbəl) *a.* **1.** that can be touched **2.** definite **3.** palpable; concrete —**tangi'bility** *n.*

tangle ('tanggəl) *n.* **1.** confused mass or situation —*vt.* **2.** twist together in muddle —*vi.* **3.** contend

tango ('tanggō) *n.* dance of S Amer. origin (*pl.* **-s**)

Tango ('tanggō) *n.* word used in communications for the letter *t*

tangram ('tanggrəm, 'tan-grəm) *n.* Chinese puzzle comprising square cut in five triangles, a square and a rhomboid capable of being recombined to represent many figures

tank (tangk) *n.* **1.** storage vessel for liquids or gas **2.** armored motor vehicle moving on tracks **3.** cistern **4.** reservoir —'**tanker** *n.* ship, plane or truck for carrying liquid in bulk —**tank farming** *see* HYDROPONICS —**tank up** *sl.* imbibe large quantity of alcoholic drink

tankard ('tangkərd) *n.* large drinking cup of metal or glass, usu. with hinged lid

tanner ('tanər) *n.* **UK** *inf.* sixpence

tannin ('tanin) *n. see* TAN[1]

tansy ('tanzi) *n.* yellow-flowered aromatic herb

tantalize ('tantəlīz) *vt.* torment by appearing to offer something desired —'**tantalus** *n.* **UK** case in which bottles may be locked with their contents visible

tantalum ('tantələm) *n.* *Chem.* metallic element *Symbol* Ta, at. wt. 181.0, at. no. 73

tantamount ('tantəmownt) *a.* **1.** equivalent in value or signification **2.** equal, amounting

tantrum ('tantrəm) *n.* childish outburst of temper

Tanzania (tanzə'nēə) *n.* country in Africa bounded northeast by Kenya, north by Lake Victoria and Uganda, northwest by Rwanda and Burundi, west by Lake Tanganyika, southwest by Zambia and Malawi and south by Mozambique —**Tanza'nian** *n./a.*

Taoism ('dowizəm, 'tow-) *n.* system of religion and philosophy based on teachings of Lao-tse, Chinese philosopher, and advocating simple, honest life and noninterference with course of natural events —'**Taoist** *n./a.* —**Tao'istic** *a.*

tap[1] (tap) *v.* **1.** strike lightly but with some noise (**-pp-**) —*n.* **2.** slight blow, rap —**tap dance** step dance in which performer wears shoes equipped with metal pieces that make rhythmic sound on stage as he dances —**tap-**

dance *vi.* perform tap dance —**tap-dancer** *n.* —**tap-dancing** *n.*

tap[2] (tap) *n.* **1.** valve with handle to regulate or stop flow of fluid in pipe *etc.* **2.** stopper, plug permitting liquid to be drawn from cask *etc.* **3.** steel tool for forming internal screw threads —*vt.* **4.** put tap in **5.** draw off (as) with tap **6.** make secret connection to (telephone wire) to overhear conversation on it **7.** make connection to (pipe, drain *etc.*) **8.** form internal threads in **9.** ask (someone) for money; obtain (money) from someone (**-pp-**) —ˈ**taproom** *n.* bar or bar room

tape (tāp) *n.* **1.** narrow long strip of fabric, paper *etc.* **2.** magnetic recording of music *etc.* —*vt.* **3.** record (speech, music *etc.*) —**tape deck** platform supporting spools *etc.* of tape recorder, incorporating motor and playback, recording and erasing heads —**tape machine** telegraphic device that records current stock quotations electronically or on ticker tape —**tape measure** tape of fabric or metal, marked off in centimeters, inches *etc.* —**tape recorder** apparatus for recording sound on magnetized tape and playing it back —**tape recording 1.** act of recording on magnetic tape **2.** magnetized tape used for this **3.** music *etc.* so recorded —ˈ**tapeworm** *n.* long flat worm parasitic in animals and man —**have (someone) taped** *inf.* have (someone) sized up, have measure of (someone)

taper (ˈtāpər) *vi.* **1.** become gradually thinner toward one end —*n.* **2.** thin candle **3.** long wick covered with wax; spill **4.** a narrowing

tapestry (ˈtapistri) *n.* fabric decorated with designs in colors woven by needles, not in shuttles —ˈ**tapestried** *a.*

tapioca (tapiˈōkə) *n.* beadlike starch made from cassava root, used *esp.* in puddings and as a thickening agent

tapir (ˈtāpər) *n.* Amer. animal with elongated snout, allied to pig

tappet (ˈtapit) *n.* in internal-combustion engine, short steel rod conveying movement imparted by the lift of a cam to the valve stem

taproot (ˈtaproo͞t) *n.* large single root growing straight down

tar[1] (tär) *n.* **1.** thick black liquid distilled from coal *etc.* —*vt.* **2.** coat, treat with tar (**-rr-**)

tar[2] (tär) *n. inf.* sailor

tarantella (tarənˈtelə) *n.* **1.** lively It. dance **2.** music for it

tarantula (təˈranchələ) *n.* any of various large (poisonous) hairy spiders (*pl.* **-s, -lae** (-lē))

tarboosh (tärˈbo͞osh) *n.* felt brimless cap, usu. red and oft. with silk tassel, worn by Muslim men

tardy (ˈtärdi) *a.* **1.** slow **2.** late —ˈ**tardily** *adv.*

tare[1] (tāər) *n.* **1.** weight of wrapping or container for goods **2.** unladen weight of vehicle

tare[2] (tāər) *n.* **1.** vetch **2.** weed

target (ˈtärgit) *n.* **1.** mark to aim at in shooting *etc.* **2.** thing aimed at **3.** object of criticism **4.** butt —**target language** language into which text *etc.* is translated

Tarheel (ˈtärhēl) *n.* nickname for native or resident of North Carolina

tariff (ˈtarif) *n.* **1.** tax levied on imports *etc.* **2.** list of charges **3.** method of charging for supply of services, *eg* electricity

Tarmac (ˈtärmak) *n.* trade name for mixture of tar, bitumen and crushed stones rolled to give hard, smooth surface

tarn (tärn) *n.* small mountain lake

tarnish (ˈtärnish) *v.* **1.** (cause to) become stained, lose shine or become dimmed or sullied —*n.* **2.** discoloration, blemish

taro (ˈtärō) *n.* **1.** widely cultivated tropical plant with broad leaves and edible rootstock **2.** its edible rootstock

tarot (ˈtarō) *n.* one of special set of cards now used mainly by fortune-tellers

tarpaulin (tärˈpōlin) *n.* (sheet of) heavy hard-wearing waterproof fabric

tarragon (ˈtarəgən) *n.* aromatic herb

tarry (ˈtari) *vi.* **1.** linger, delay **2.** stay behind (**-ried, -rying**)

tarsier (ˈtärsiā, -siər) *n.* nocturnal tree-dwelling mammal of Indonesia *etc.*

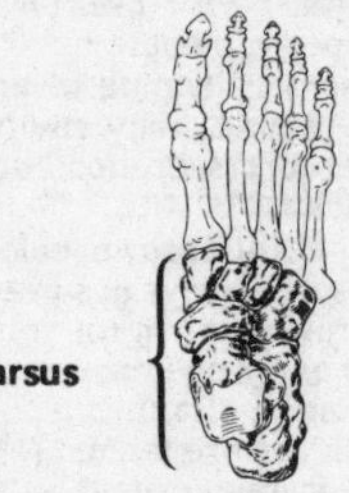

tarsus (ˈtärsəs) *n.* **1.** bones of ankle and heel collectively **2.** corresponding part in other mammals *etc.* **3.** connective tissue supporting free edge of each eyelid (*pl.* **-si** (-sī)) —ˈ**tarsal** *a.* **1.** of tarsus or tarsi —*n.* **2.** tarsal bone

tart[1] (tärt) *n.* **1.** pie or flan filled with fruit, jam *etc.* **2.** *inf., offens.* promiscuous woman, *esp.* prostitute

tart[2] (tärt) *a.* **1.** sour, bitter **2.** sharp

tartan (ˈtärtən) *n.* **1.** woolen cloth woven in pattern of colored checks, *esp.* in colors, patterns associated with Scottish clans **2.** such pattern

tartar[1] (ˈtärtər) *n.* **1.** crust deposited on teeth **2.** deposit formed during fermentation of wine —**tarˈtaric** *a.* —**tartaric acid** colorless crystalline acid found in many fruits

tartar[2] ('tärtər) *n.* vicious-tempered person, difficult to deal with

Tartar ('tärtər) *see* TATAR

tartar sauce mayonnaise sauce mixed with chopped herbs, capers *etc.*

Tas. Tasmania

task (task) *n.* **1.** piece of work (*esp.* unpleasant or difficult) set or undertaken —*vt.* **2.** assign task to **3.** exact —**task force** naval or military unit dispatched to carry out specific undertaking —'**taskmaster** *n.* overseer —**take to task** reprove

Taslan ('taslən) *n.* trade name for bulking process which makes loops in yarn

Tasmanian devil (taz'mānion) small, ferocious, carnivorous marsupial of Tasmania

Tass (tas) *n.* principal news agency of Soviet Union

tassel ('tasəl) *n.* **1.** ornament of fringed knot of threads *etc.* **2.** tuft

taste (tāst) *n.* **1.** sense by which flavor, quality of substance is detected by the tongue **2.** this act or sensation **3.** (brief) experience of something **4.** small amount **5.** preference, liking **6.** power of discerning, judging **7.** discretion, delicacy —*v.* **8.** observe or distinguish the taste of (a substance) **9.** take small amount of (food *etc.*) into mouth —*vt.* **10.** experience —*vi.* **11.** have specific flavor —'**tasteful** *a.* **1.** in good style **2.** with, showing good taste —'**tastefully** *adv.* —'**tasteless** *a.* —'**taster** *n.* **1.** person who samples food or drink for quality **2.** device used in tasting or sampling **3.** *esp.* formerly, person employed to taste food and drink prepared for king *etc.* to test for poison —'**tasty** *a.* pleasantly or highly flavored —**taste bud** small organ of taste on tongue

tat[1] (tat) *v.* make (something) by tatting (**-tt-**) —'**tatter** *n.* —'**tatting** *n.* type of handmade lace

tat[2] (tat) *n.* **1.** ragged, shoddy article **2.** tattiness

Tatar ('tätər) *or* **Tartar** *n.* **1.** member of Mongoloid people who established powerful state in central Asia in 13th century **2.** descendant of this people, now scattered throughout Soviet Union **3.** Turkic language or dialect spoken by this people —*a.* **4.** of Tatars

tatter ('tatər) *v.* **1.** make or become ragged, worn to shreds —*n.* **2.** ragged piece

tattle ('tatəl) *vi./n.* gossip, chatter —'**tattletale** *n.* **1.** scandalmonger, gossip —*a.* **2.** telltale

tattoo[1] (ta'to͞o) *n.* **1.** formerly, beat of drum and bugle call **2.** military spectacle or pageant

tattoo[2] (ta'to͞o) *vt.* **1.** mark (skin) in patterns *etc.* by pricking and filling punctures with indelible colored inks (**-'tooed, -'tooing**) —*n.* **2.** mark so made

tatty ('tati) *a.* shabby, worn-out —'**tattiness** *n.*

tau (tow, tö) *n.* 19th letter in Gr. alphabet (T, τ)

taught (töt) *pt./pp. of* TEACH

taunt (tönt) *vt.* **1.** provoke, deride with insulting words *etc.* **2.** tease; tantalize —*n.* **3.** instance of this

taupe (tōp) *n.* brownish-gray color

Taurus ('törəs) *n.* (bull) 2nd sign of zodiac, operative *c.* Apr. 21st-May 20th

taut (töt) *a.* **1.** drawn tight **2.** under strain —'**tauten** *vt.* make tight or tense

tauto- *or before vowel* **taut-** (*comb. form*) identical, same, as in *tautology*

tautology (tö'toləji) *n.* repetition of same thing in other words in same sentence —**tauto'logical** *a.*

tavern ('tavərn) *n.* **1.** premises licensed to sell alcoholic beverages **2.** inn

tawdry ('tödri) *a.* showy, but cheap and without taste, flashy —'**tawdrily** *adv.* —'**tawdriness** *n.*

tawny ('töni) *a./n.* (of) light (yellowish) brown —**tawny owl** European owl having reddish-brown plumage and round head

tax (taks) *n.* **1.** compulsory payments by wage earners, companies *etc.* imposed by government to raise revenue **2.** heavy demand (on something) —*vt.* **3.** impose tax on **4.** strain **5.** accuse, blame —'**taxable** *a.* —**tax'ation** *n.* levying of taxes —**tax-deductible** *a.* legally deductible from income before tax assessment —**tax-free** *a.* exempt from taxation —'**taxpayer** *n.* —**tax return** statement of personal income for tax purposes

taxi ('taksi) *n.* **1.** taxicab (*pl.* **-s**) —*vi.* **2.** (of aircraft) run along ground under its own power **3.** go in taxicab ('**taxied** *pt./pp.*, '**taxying,** '**taxiing** *pr.p.*) —'**taxicab** *n.* motor vehicle for hire with driver —'**taximeter** *n.* meter fitted to taxicab to register fare, based on length of journey —**taxi stand** place where taxicabs wait to be hired

taxidermy ('taksidərmi) *n.* art of stuffing, mounting animal skins to give them lifelike appearance —**taxi'dermal** *or* **taxi'dermic** *a.* —'**taxidermist** *n.*

taxonomy (tak'sonəmi) *n.* science, practice of classifying by structure, *esp.* living organisms —**taxo'nomic** *a.*

taxoplasmosis (taksōplaz'mōsis) *n.* infectious disease affecting humans, dogs, cats, chickens and other animals whose method of transmission is unknown and which may be congenital

Taylor ('tālər) *n.* **Zachary.** the 12th President of the U.S. (1849-50)

Tb *Chem.* terbium

T.B. *or* **t.b.** tuberculosis

T-bone steak steak cut from sirloin of beef, containing T-shaped bone

tbs. *or* **tbsp.** tablespoon(ful)

Tc *Chem.* technetium

tch *interj./n.* **1.** clicking sound made with

tongue, to express disapproval *etc.* —*vi.* **2.** utter tch's

Te *Chem.* tellurium

tea (tē) *n.* **1.** dried leaves of plant cultivated *esp.* in (sub)tropical Asia **2.** infusion of it as beverage **3.** any of various herbal infusions **4.** tea, cakes *etc.* as light afternoon meal **5.** main evening meal —**tea bag** small porous bag of paper containing tea leaves —**tea ball** perforated metal ball filled with tea leaves and used to make tea —**'teacup** *n.* **1.** cup out of which tea may be drunk **2.** amount teacup will hold, usu. six fluid ounces (*also* **'teacupful**) —**'teahouse** *n.* restaurant where tea and light refreshments are served —**tea leaf 1.** dried leaf of tea shrub, used to make tea **2.** (*usu. pl.*) shredded parts of these leaves, *esp.* after infusion —**tea party** social gathering at which tea is served —**'teapot** *n.* container with lid, spout and handle, in which tea is made —**'teaspoon** *n.* **1.** small spoon for stirring tea *etc.* **2.** cooking measure equal to five milliliters or ⅓ of a tablespoon —**tea tree** Aust., N.Z. tree —**tea wagon** small table on wheels for serving tea or holding dishes

teach (tēch) *vt.* **1.** instruct **2.** educate **3.** train **4.** impart knowledge of —*vi.* **5.** act as teacher (**taught, 'teaching**) —**'teacher** *n.* —**'teaching** *n.* —**teaching machine** machine that presents information and questions to user, registers answers, and indicates whether these are correct or acceptable

teak (tēk) *n.* **1.** tall evergreen tree of SE Asia **2.** very hard wood obtained from it

teal (tēl) *n.* **1.** type of small duck **2.** greenish-blue color

team (tēm) *n.* **1.** set of animals, players of game *etc.* associated in activity —*v.* **2.** (*usu. with* up) (cause to) make a team —**'teamster** *n.* driver of team of draft animals —**team-mate** *n.* fellow member of team —**team spirit** subordination of individual desire for good of team —**'teamwork** *n.* cooperative work by team acting as unit

tear[1] (tēər) *n.* drop of fluid appearing in and falling from eye —**'tearful** *a.* **1.** inclined to weep **2.** involving tears —**'tearless** *a.* —**'teardrop** *n.* —**tear gas** irritant gas causing abnormal watering of eyes and temporary blindness —**tear-jerker** *n. inf.* excessively sentimental motion picture *etc.*

tear[2] (tāər) *vt.* **1.** pull apart, rend —*vi.* **2.** become torn **3.** rush (**tore, torn, 'tearing**) —*n.* **4.** hole, cut; split —**tear away** persuade (oneself or someone else) to leave

tease (tēz) *vt.* **1.** tantalize, irritate, bait **2.** pull apart fibers of —*n.* **3.** one who teases —**'teaser** *n.* annoying or puzzling problem —**'teasing** *a.*

teasel ('tēzəl) *n.* plant with prickly leaves and head

teat (tēt) *n.* mammary gland; nipple

tech (tek) *a./n. inf.* technical (school, college or institute)

tech. 1. technical **2.** technology

technetium (tek'nēshiəm) *n. Chem.* metallic element *Symbol* Tc, at. wt. 99, at. no. 43

technical ('teknikəl) *a.* **1.** of, specializing in industrial, practical or mechanical arts and applied sciences **2.** skilled in practical and mechanical arts **3.** belonging to particular art or science **4.** according to letter of the law —**techni'cality** *n.* **1.** point of procedure **2.** state of being technical —**'technically** *adv.* —**tech'nician** *n.* one skilled in technique of an art —**technique** (tek'nēk) *n.* **1.** method of performance in an art **2.** skill required for mastery of subject —**technical knockout** *Boxing* judgment of knockout given when boxer is in referee's opinion too badly beaten to continue

Technicolor ('teknikulər) *n.* trade name for color process in motion pictures

techno- (*comb. form*) **1.** craft; art, as in *technology, technography* **2.** technological; technical, as in *technocracy*

technocracy (tek'nokrəsi) *n.* **1.** government by technical experts **2.** group of these experts

technology (tek'noləji) *n.* **1.** application of practical, mechanical sciences to industry, commerce **2.** technical methods, skills, knowledge —**techno'logical** *a.* —**tech'nologist** *n.*

tectonic (tek'tonik) *a.* of construction or building —**tec'tonics** *pl.n.* (*with sing. v.*) art, science of building

teddy bear ('tedi) child's soft toy bear (*also* **'teddy**)

Te Deum (tā 'dāəm, tē 'dēəm) **1.** ancient Latin hymn in rhythmic prose **2.** musical setting of this hymn **3.** service of thanksgiving in which recital of this hymn forms central part

tedious ('tēdiəs) *a.* causing fatigue or boredom, monotonous —**'tedium** *n.* monotony

tee (tē) *n.* **1.** *Golf* slightly raised ground from which first stroke of hole is made **2.** small peg supporting ball for this stroke **3.** target in some games (*eg* quoits) —**tee off** make first stroke of hole in golf

teem (tēm) *vi.* **1.** abound, swarm, be prolific **2.** pour, rain heavily

teens (tēnz) *pl.n.* years of life from 13 to 19 —**'teenage** *a.* —**'teenager** *n.* young person between 13 and 19 —**'teenybopper** *n. sl.* young teenager, usu. girl, who avidly follows fashions

teeny ('tēni) *a.* extremely small; tiny (*also* **teeny-weeny** (tēni'wēni), **teensy-weensy** (tēnsi'wēnsi))

tee shirt *see* T-SHIRT

teeter ('tētər) *vi.* **1.** seesaw or make similar movements **2.** vacillate

teeth (tēth) *n., pl. of* TOOTH —**teethe** (tēdh) *vi.*

(of baby) grow first teeth —**teething** ('tēdhing) *n.* eruption of the "milk" or deciduous teeth in infancy —**teething ring** hard ring on which babies may bite while teething —**teething troubles** problems, difficulties at first stage of something

teetotal ('tē'tōtəl) *a.* pledged to abstain from alcohol —**tee'totaler** *n.* —**tee'totalism** *n.*

Teflon ('teflon) *n.* trade name for polymer used to make nonstick coatings on cooking utensils

tel. 1. telegram 2. telegraph(ic) 3. telephone

tele- *or before vowel* **tel-** (*comb. form*) at a distance, from far off, as in *telescope*

telecast ('telikast) *vi./n.* (broadcast) television program

telecommunications (telikəmyōōni'kāshənz) *pl.n.* (*with sing. v.*) science and technology of communications by telephony, radio, television *etc.*

telegram ('teligram) *n.* message sent by telegraph

telegraph ('teligraf) *n.* **1.** electrical apparatus for transmitting messages to a distance **2.** any signaling device for transmitting messages —*v.* **3.** communicate by telegraph —*vt.* **4.** C cast (votes) illegally by impersonating registered voters —**tele'graphic** *a.* —**tele'graphically** *adv.* —**te'legraphist** *n.* one who works telegraph —**te'legraphy** *n.* **1.** science of telegraph **2.** use of telegraph

telekinesis (teliki'nēsis, -kī-) *n.* **1.** movement of a body caused by thought or willpower **2.** ability to cause such movement —**telekinetic** (teliki'netik, -kī-) *a.*

teleology (teli'oləji, tēli-) *n.* **1.** doctrine of final causes **2.** belief that things happen because of the purpose or design that will be fulfilled by them —**teleo'logic(al)** *a.*

telepathy (ti'lepəthi) *n.* action of one mind on another at a distance —**tele'pathic** *a.* —**tele'pathically** *adv.*

telephone ('telifōn) *n.* **1.** apparatus for communicating sound to hearer at a distance —*v.* **2.** communicate, speak by telephone —**telephonic** (teli'fonik) *a.* —**te'lephony** *n.* —**telephone booth** soundproof enclosure having public telephone —**telephone directory** book listing names, addresses and telephone numbers of subscribers in particular area

telephoto (teli'fōtō) *a.* (of lens) producing magnified image of distant object —**telepho'tography** *n.* process or technique of photographing distant objects using telephoto lens

teleprinter ('teliprintər) *n.* *see* TELETYPEWRITER

TelePrompTer ('telipromptər) *n.* *T.V.* trade name for device to enable speaker to refer to his script out of sight of the cameras

telescope ('teliskōp) *n.* **1.** optical instrument for magnifying distant objects —*v.* **2.** slide or drive together, *esp.* parts designed to fit one inside the other **3.** make smaller, shorter —**telescopic** (teli'skopik) *a.*

teletypewriter (teli'tīpwrītər) *n.* apparatus capable of being used over telephone networks to send and receive signals and to produce hard copy

television ('telivizhən) *n.* **1.** system of producing on screen images of distant objects, events *etc.* by electromagnetic radiation **2.** device for receiving this transmission and converting it to optical images **3.** program *etc.* viewed on television set —**'televise** *vt.* **1.** transmit by television **2.** make, produce as television program

telex ('teleks) *n.* **1.** international communication service by means of teletypewriters connected through automatic exchanges —*vt.* **2.** transmit (message) by telex

tell (tel) *vt.* **1.** let know **2.** order, direct **3.** narrate, make known **4.** discern **5.** distinguish **6.** count —*vi.* **7.** give account **8.** be of weight, importance **9.** *inf.* reveal secrets (**told, 'telling**) —**'teller** *n.* **1.** narrator **2.** bank cashier —**'telling** *a.* effective, striking —**'telltale** *n.* **1.** sneak **2.** automatic indicator —*a.* **3.** revealing

tellurian (tə'lōōriən, te-) *a.* of the earth —**tel'luric** *a.* —**tel'lurium** *n.* *Chem.* metalloid element *Symbol* Te, at. wt. 127.6, at. no. 52 —**tellurous** ('telyərəs; tə'lōōrəs, te-) *a.*

temerity (ti'meriti) *n.* boldness, audacity

temp (temp) *inf.* *n.* **1.** one employed on temporary basis —*vi.* **2.** work as temp

temp. 1. temperature 2. temporary

temper ('tempər) *n.* **1.** frame of mind **2.** anger, oft. noisy **3.** mental constitution **4.** degree of hardness of steel *etc.* —*vt.* **5.** restrain, qualify, moderate **6.** harden **7.** bring to proper condition —**'tempered** *a.* having temper or temperament as specified, as in *ill-tempered*

tempera ('tempərə) *n.* painting medium in which pigment is dissolved with egg white and combined with egg yolk

temperament ('tempərəmənt) *n.* **1.** natural disposition **2.** excitability; moodiness; anger —**tempera'mental** *a.* **1.** given to extremes of temperament, moody **2.** of, occasioned by temperament **3.** *inf.* working erratically and inconsistently; unreliable —**tempera'mentally** *adv.*

temperate ('tempərit) *a.* **1.** not extreme **2.** showing, practicing moderation —**'temperance** *n.* **1.** moderation **2.** abstinence, *esp.* from alcohol —**'temperately** *adv.* —**Temperate Zone** parts of earth's surface lying between Arctic Circle and tropic of Cancer and between Antarctic Circle and tropic of Capricorn

temperature ('tempərchōōər, 'tempri-; -chər) *n.* **1.** degree of heat or coldness **2.** *inf.* (abnormally) high body temperature

tempest ('tempist) *n.* violent storm —**tem-**

'**pestuous** *a.* **1.** turbulent **2.** violent, stormy —**tem'pestuously** *adv.*

template *or* **templet** ('templit) *n.* mold, pattern to help shape something accurately

temple[1] ('tempəl) *n.* **1.** building for worship **2.** shrine

temple[2] ('tempəl) *n.* flat part on either side of forehead

tempo ('tempō) *n.* rate, rhythm, *esp.* in music (*pl.* **-s, -pi** (-pē))

temporal[1] ('tempərəl) *a.* **1.** of time **2.** of this life or world, secular **3.** *Gram.* of tense or linguistic expression of time —**tempo'rality** *n.*

temporal[2] ('tempərəl) *a.* *Anat.* of temple or temples —**temporal bone** either of two compound bones forming sides of skull

temporary ('tempəreri) *a.* lasting, used only for a time —**tempo'rarily** *adv.*

temporize ('tempərīz) *vi.* **1.** use evasive action; hedge; gain time by negotiation *etc.* **2.** conform to circumstances —'**temporizer** *n.*

tempt (tempt) *vt.* **1.** try to persuade, entice, *esp.* to something wrong or unwise **2.** dispose, cause to be inclined —**temp'tation** *n.* **1.** act of tempting **2.** thing that tempts —'**tempter** *n.* ('**temptress** *fem.*) —'**tempting** *a.* attractive, inviting

tempus fugit ('tempəs 'fyo͞ojit) *Lat.* time flies

ten (ten) *n./a.* cardinal number next after nine —**tenth** *a./n.* ordinal number —**ten-gallon hat** cowboy's broad-brimmed felt hat with high crown —**tenpins** ('tenpinz) *pl.n.* (*with sing. v.*) bowling game in which bowls are rolled down lane to knock over ten target pins —**the Ten Commandments** *O.T.* commandments summarizing basic obligations of man toward God and his fellow men

ten. *Mus.* **1.** tenor **2.** tenuto

tenable ('tenəbəl) *a.* able to be held, defended, maintained

tenacious (ti'nāshəs) *a.* **1.** holding fast **2.** retentive **3.** stubborn —**tenacity** (ti'nasiti) *n.*

tenant ('tenənt) *n.* one who holds lands, house *etc.* on rent or lease —'**tenancy** *n.* —'**tenantry** *n.* body of tenants —**tenant farmer** person who farms land rented from another, rent usu. taking form of crops *etc.*

tench (tench) *n.* freshwater game fish

tend[1] (tend) *vi.* **1.** be inclined **2.** be conducive **3.** go or move (in particular direction) —'**tendency** *n.* inclination, bent —**ten'dentious** *or* **ten'dencious** *a.* having, showing tendency or bias, controversial

tend[2] (tend) *vt.* take care of, watch over —'**tender** *n.* **1.** small boat carried by yacht or ship **2.** carriage for fuel and water attached to steam locomotive **3.** one who tends, *eg* bar tender

tender[1] ('tendər) *a.* **1.** not tough or hard **2.** easily injured **3.** gentle, loving, affectionate **4.** delicate, soft —'**tenderize** *vt.* soften (meat) by pounding or by treating with substance made for this purpose —'**tenderly** *adv.* —'**tenderness** *n.* —'**tenderfoot** *n.* newcomer, *esp.* to ranch *etc.* —'**tenderloin** *n.* tenderest muscle of loin of pork *etc.*

tender[2] ('tendər) *vt.* **1.** offer —*vi.* **2.** make offer or estimate —*n.* **3.** offer **4.** offer or estimate for contract to undertake specific work **5.** what may legally be offered in payment

tendon ('tendən) *n.* sinew attaching muscle to bone *etc.*

tendril ('tendril) *n.* **1.** slender curling stem by which climbing plant clings to anything **2.** curl, as of hair

tenement ('tenəmənt) *n.* building divided into separate apartments (*also* **tenement building**)

tenet ('tenit, 'tēnit) *n.* doctrine, belief

Tennessee (tenə'sē) *n.* East South Central state of the U.S., admitted to the Union in 1796. Abbrev.: **Tenn., TN** (with ZIP code)

tennis ('tenis) *n.* game in which ball is struck with racket by players on opposite sides of net, lawn tennis —**tennis elbow** strained muscle as a result of playing tennis —**tennis shoe** sneaker

tenon ('tenən) *n.* tongue put on end of piece of wood *etc.* to fit into a mortise —**tenon saw**

tenor ('tenər) *n.* **1.** male voice between alto and bass **2.** music for, singer with this **3.** saxophone *etc.* intermediate between alto and baritone or bass **4.** general course, meaning

tenosynovitis ('tenōsinə'vītis) *n.* inflammation of sheath enveloping certain tendons

tense[1] (tens) *n.* modification of verb to show time of action

tense[2] (tens) *a.* **1.** stretched tight, strained; taut **2.** emotionally strained —*v.* **3.** make, become tense —'**tensile** *a.* **1.** of tension **2.** capable of being stretched —'**tension** *n.* **1.** stretching **2.** strain when stretched **3.** emotional strain or excitement **4.** hostility **5.** suspense **6.** *Elec.* voltage —**tensile strength** measure of ability of material to withstand longitudinal stress

tent (tent) *n.* portable shelter of canvas —**tent dress** dress widening from shoulders in shape of tent —**tent stitch** *see* **petit point** *at* PETIT

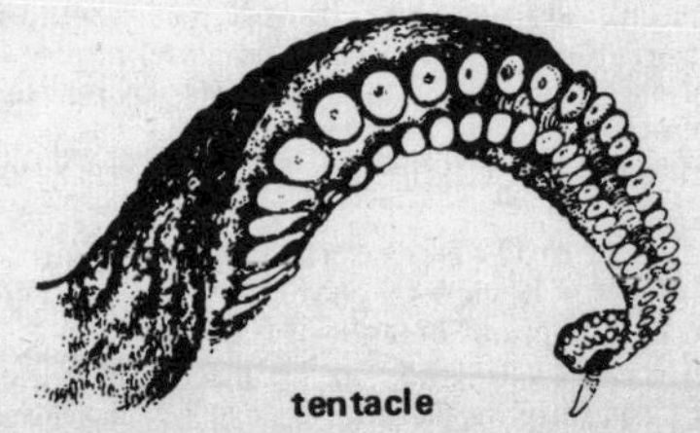

tentacle

tentacle (ˈtentəkəl) *n.* elongated, flexible organ of some animals (*eg* octopus) used for grasping, feeding *etc.*

tentative (ˈtentətiv) *a.* **1.** done as a trial **2.** experimental, cautious —ˈ**tentatively** *adv.*

tenterhooks (ˈtentərhŏŏks) *pl.n.* —**on tenterhooks** in anxious suspense

tenuous (ˈtenyŏŏəs) *a.* **1.** flimsy, uncertain **2.** thin, fine, slender —**te**ˈ**nuity** *n.*

tenure (ˈtenyər, ˈtenyŏŏər) *n.* (length of time of) possession, holding of office, position *etc.*

tenuto (tāˈnōōtō) *a./adv. Mus.* (of note) to be held for or beyond its full time value

tepee (ˈtēpē) *n.* Amerindian cone-shaped tent of animal skins

tepid (ˈtepid) *a.* **1.** moderately warm, lukewarm **2.** half-hearted

tequila (tiˈkēlə) *n.* Mexican alcoholic spirit

ter. 1. terrace **2.** territory

terbium (ˈtərbiəm) *n. Chem.* metallic element *Symbol* Tb, at. wt. 158.9, at no. 65

tercel (ˈtərsəl) *or* **tiercel** *n.* male falcon or hawk, *esp.* as used in falconry

tercentenary (tərsenˈtenəri) *or* **tercentennial** *a./n.* (of) three hundredth anniversary

tergiversate (tərˈjivərsāt) *vi.* **1.** change sides or loyalties **2.** be evasive or ambiguous —**tergiver**ˈ**sation** *n.*

term (tərm) *n.* **1.** expression **2.** limited period of time **3.** period during which courts sit, schools are open *etc.* **4.** limit, end —*pl.* **5.** conditions **6.** mutual relationship —*vt.* **7.** name, designate —**terms of reference** specific limits of responsibility that determine activities of investigating body *etc.*

termagant (ˈtərməgənt) *n.* shrewish woman; scold

terminal (ˈtərminəl) *a.* **1.** at, forming an end **2.** pert. to, forming a terminus **3.** (of disease) ending in death —*n.* **4.** terminal part or structure **5.** extremity **6.** point where current enters, leaves electrical device (*eg* battery) **7.** device permitting operation of computer at some distance from it —**terminal velocity 1.** constant maximum velocity reached by body falling under gravity through fluid, *esp.* atmosphere **2.** velocity of missile or projectile when it reaches target **3.** maximum velocity attained by rocket *etc.* flying in parabolic flight path **4.** maximum velocity that aircraft can attain

terminate (ˈtərmināt) *v.* bring, come to an end —ˈ**terminable** *a.* —**termi**ˈ**nation** *n.*

terminology (tərmiˈnoləji) *n.* **1.** set of technical terms or vocabulary **2.** study of terms —**termino**ˈ**logical** *a.*

terminus (ˈtərminəs) *n.* **1.** finishing point **2.** farthest limit **3.** railroad station, bus station *etc.* at end of long-distance line (*pl.* **-ni** (-nī), **-es**)

termite (ˈtərmīt) *n.* insect, many species of which feed on and damage living trees and wooden structures (*also* **white ant**)

tern (tərn) *n.* sea bird like gull

ternary (ˈtərnəri) *a.* **1.** consisting of three **2.** proceeding in threes

Terpsichore (tərpˈsikəri) *n.* Muse of dance and choral song —**Terpsichorean** (tərpsikəˈrēən, -ˈkōriən) *oft. jocular a.* **1.** of dancing (*also* **Terpsichoˈreal**) —*n.* **2.** dancer

Terr. 1. Terrace **2.** Territory

terrace (ˈterəs) *n.* **1.** raised level place **2.** level cut out of hill **3.** row, street of houses built on raised or sloping ground or as one block **4.** (*oft. pl.*) unroofed tier for spectators at football stadium —*vt.* **5.** form into, furnish with terrace

terra cotta (ˈterə ˈkotə) **1.** hard unglazed pottery **2.** its color, brownish red

terra firma (ˈfərmə) *Lat.* firm ground; dry land

terrain (təˈrān) *n.* area of ground, *esp.* with reference to its physical character

terra incognita (inkogˈnētə, inˈkognitə) *Lat.* unexplored or unknown area

terrapin

terrapin (ˈterəpin) *n.* type of aquatic turtle

terrazzo (teˈrazō, -ˈrätsō) *n.* floor, wall finish of chips of stone set in mortar and polished

terrene (teˈrēn) *a.* **1.** of earth; worldly; mundane **2.** *rare* of earth; earthy —*n.* **3.** land **4.** *rare* earth

terrestrial (təˈrestriəl) *a.* **1.** of the earth **2.** of, living on land

terrible (ˈterəbəl) *a.* **1.** serious **2.** dreadful, frightful **3.** excessive **4.** causing fear —ˈ**terribly** *adv.*

terrier (ˈteriər) *n.* small dog of various breeds, *orig.* for following quarry into burrow

terrific (təˈrifik) *a.* **1.** very great **2.** *inf.* good, excellent **3.** terrible, awe-inspiring

terrify (ˈterifī) *vt.* fill with fear, dread

terrine (təˈrēn, te-) *n.* **1.** oval earthenware cooking dish **2.** food cooked or served in such dish, *esp.* pâté

territory (ˈteritōri) *n.* **1.** region **2.** geographical area under control of a political unit, *esp.* a sovereign state **3.** area of knowledge —**terri**ˈ**torial** *a.* of territory —**territorial waters** waters over which nation exercises jurisdiction

terror (ˈterər) *n.* **1.** great fear **2.** *inf.* troublesome person or thing —ˈ**terrorism** *n.* **1.** use of violence, intimidation to achieve ends **2.** state of terror —ˈ**terrorist** *n./a.* —ˈ**terrorize** *vt.* force, oppress by fear, violence

terry (ˈteri) *n./a.* (pile fabric) with the loops uncut (used to make towels, curtains and clothing)

terse (tərs) *a.* **1.** expressed in few words, concise **2.** abrupt

tertiary (ˈtərshieri, -shəri) *a.* **1.** third in degree, order *etc.* **2.** (T-) of Tertiary period or rock system —*n.* **3.** (T-) geological period before Quaternary —**tertiary colors** colors produced by mixing secondary colors

tessellate (ˈtesilāt) *vt.* **1.** make, pave, inlay with mosaic of small tiles **2.** (of identical shapes) fit together exactly —ˈ**tessellated** *a.* —**tesselˈlation** *n.* —**tessera** (ˈtesərə) *n.* small cube of glass, marble or stone used in mosaic (*pl.* **-ae** (-ē))

test (test) *vt.* **1.** put to the proof **2.** carry out test(s) on —*n.* **3.** critical examination **4.** means of trial —ˈ**testing** *a.* difficult —**test case** lawsuit viewed as means of establishing precedent —**test match** one of series of international sports contests, *esp.* cricket —**test paper 1.** *Chem.* paper impregnated with indicator for chemical tests **2.** question sheet of test **3.** paper completed by test candidate —**test pilot** pilot who flies aircraft of new design to test performance in air —**test tube** narrow cylindrical glass vessel used in scientific experiments —**test-tube baby** baby conceived outside womb and subsequently implanted in womb

testament (ˈtestəmənt) *n.* **1.** *Law* will **2.** declaration **3.** (T-) one of the two main divisions of the Bible —**testaˈmentary** *a.*

testate (ˈtestāt, ˈtestit) *a.* having left a valid will —ˈ**testacy** *n.* state of being testate —ˈ**testator** *n.* maker of will (ˈ**testatrix** *fem.*)

testicle (ˈtestikəl) *n.* either of two male reproductive glands

testify (ˈtestifī) *v.* **1.** declare **2.** bear witness (to) (**-fied, -fying**)

testimony (ˈtestimōni) *n.* **1.** affirmation **2.** evidence —**testiˈmonial** *n.* **1.** certificate of character, ability *etc.* **2.** tribute given by person expressing regard for recipient —*a.* **3.** of testimony or testimonial

testis (ˈtestis) *n.* testicle (*pl.* **testes** (ˈtestēz)) —**tesˈtosterone** *n.* male sex hormone

testy (ˈtesti) *a.* irritable, short-tempered —ˈ**testily** *adv.*

tetanus (ˈtetənəs) *n.* serious bacterial disease producing muscular spasms, contractions (*also* ˈ**lockjaw**)

tetchy (ˈtechi) *a.* cross, irritable, touchy —ˈ**tetchiness** *n.*

tête-à-tête (ˈtātətāt) *n.* **1.** private conversation between two people **2.** small sofa for two people, *esp.* S-shaped (*pl.* **-s, -tête**) —*adv.* (tātəˈtāt) **3.** intimately; in private

tether (ˈtedhər) *n.* **1.** rope or chain for fastening (grazing) animal —*vt.* **2.** tie up with rope —**be at the end of one's tether** have reached limit of one's endurance

tetra- *or before vowel* **tetr-** (*comb. form*) four, as in *tetrameter*

tetracycline (tetrəˈsīklēn) *n.* any of group of antibiotic drugs used to treat wide range of diseases

tetrad (ˈtetrad) *n.* group or series of four

tetraethyl lead (tetrəˈethil led) colorless oily insoluble liquid used in gasoline to prevent knocking

tetragon (ˈtetrəgon) *n.* figure with four angles and four sides —**teˈtragonal** *a.* —**tetraˈhedron** *n.* solid contained by four plane faces

tetralogy (teˈtraləji) *n.* series of four related works, as in drama or opera

tetrameter (teˈtramitər) *n. Prosody* **1.** line of verse consisting of four metrical feet **2.** verse composed of such lines

Teuton (ˈtyōōtən, ˈtōōtən) *n.* **1.** member of ancient Germanic people from Jutland who migrated to S Gaul in 2nd century B.C. **2.** member of any Germanic-speaking people, *esp.* German —*a.* **3.** Teutonic —**Teuˈtonic** *a.* **1.** German **2.** of ancient Teutons

Texas (ˈteksəs) *n.* West South Central state of the U.S., admitted to the Union in 1845. Abbrev.: **Tex., TX** (with ZIP code)

text (tekst) *n.* **1.** (actual words of) book, passage *etc.* **2.** passage of Scriptures *etc.*, *esp.* as subject of discourse —ˈ**textual** *a.* of, in a text —ˈ**textbook** *n.* book of instruction on particular subject —**textual criticism 1.** scholarly study of manuscripts, *esp.* of Bible, to establish original text **2.** literary criticism emphasizing close analysis of text

textile (ˈtekstīl) *n.* **1.** any fabric or cloth, *esp.* woven —*a.* **2.** of (the making of) fabrics

Textralizing (ˈtekstrəlīzing) *n.* trade name for texturing process applied to yarns

texture (ˈtekschər) *n.* **1.** surface of material, *esp.* as perceived by sense of touch **2.** character, structure **3.** consistency —*vt.* **4.** give distinctive texture to

Th *Chem.* thorium

-th[1] (*comb. form*) **1.** action or its consequence, as in *growth* **2.** quality, as in *width*

-th[2] *or* **-eth** (*comb. form*) forming ordinal numbers, as in *fourth, thousandth*

Thailand (ˈtīland) *n.* country in Asia bounded west by Burma and the Indian Ocean, east by the Gulf of Thailand and Kampuchea and east and north by Laos —**Thai** *n./a.* **1.** (native or inhabitant) of Thailand (*pl.* **Thai**) —*n.* **2.** language of Thailand which is probably a Sino-Tibetan language

thalidomide (thəˈlidəmīd) *n.* drug formerly used as sedative, but found to cause abnormalities in developing fetus

thallium (ˈthaliəm) *n. Chem.* metallic element *Symbol* Tl, at. wt. 204.4, at. no. 81 —ˈ**thallic** *a.*

thallophyte (ˈthaləfīt) *n.* any of phylum of plants comprising algae and fungi

than (dhan; *unstressed* dhən) *conj.* introduces second part of comparison

thane *or* **thegn** (thān) *n. Hist.* nobleman holding lands in return for certain services

thank (thangk) *vt.* **1.** express gratitude to **2.** say thanks to **3.** hold responsible —**'thankful** *a.* grateful, appreciative —**'thankless** *a.* **1.** having, bringing no thanks **2.** unprofitable —**thanks** *pl.n.* words of gratitude —**Thanksgiving Day** national public holiday in Canad. and U.S.: fourth Thursday in November in U.S., second Monday in October in Canad.

that (dhat; *unstressed* dhət) *a.* **1.** demonstrates or particularizes (*pl.* **those**) —*demonstrative pron.* **2.** particular thing meant (*pl.* **those**) —*adv.* **3.** as —*relative pron.* **4.** which, who —*conj.* **5.** introduces noun or adverbial clauses

thatch (thach) *n.* **1.** reeds, straw *etc.* used as roofing material —*vt.* **2.** roof (a house) with reeds, straw *etc.* —**'thatcher** *n.*

thaw (thö) *v.* **1.** melt **2.** (cause to) unfreeze **3.** defrost —*vi.* **4.** become warmer or more genial —*n.* **5.** a melting (of frost *etc.*)

the (*stressed or emphatic* dhē; *unstressed before consonant* dhə; *unstressed before vowel* dhi) the definite article

theater ('thēətər) *n.* **1.** place where plays *etc.* are performed **2.** drama, dramatic works generally **3.** large room with (tiered) seats, used for lectures *etc.* —**theatrical** (thi'atrikəl) *a.* **1.** of, for the theater **2.** exaggerated, affected —**theatrically** (thi'atrikəli) *adv.* —**theatricals** (thi'atrikəlz) *pl.n.* amateur dramatic performances

thee (dhē) *pron. obs.* objective and dative of THOU[1]

theft (theft) *n.* stealing

their (dhāər) *a.* belonging to them —**theirs** *pron.* something or someone belonging to them

theism ('thēizəm) *n.* belief in creation of universe by one god —**'theist** *n.* —**the'istic(al)** *a.*

them (dhem; *unstressed* dhəm) *pron.* **1.** objective case of THEY **2.** those persons or things —**them'selves** *pron.* emphatic and reflexive form of THEY

theme (thēm) *n.* **1.** main idea or topic of conversation, book *etc.* **2.** subject of composition **3.** recurring melody in music —**the'matic** *a.*

then (dhen) *adv.* **1.** at that time **2.** next **3.** that being so

thence (dhens) *adv.* from that place, point of reasoning *etc.*

theo- *or before vowel* **the-** (*comb. form*) God; gods, as in *theology*

theocracy (thi'okrəsi) *n.* government by a deity or a priesthood —**theo'cratic** *a.*

theodolite (thi'odəlīt) *n.* surveying instrument for measuring angles

theology (thi'oləji) *n.* systematic study of religion(s) and religious belief(s) —**theologian** (thēə'lōjən) *n.* —**theo'logical** *a.* —**theo'logically** *adv.*

theorem ('thēərəm) *n.* proposition which can be demonstrated by argument —**theore'matic** *or* **theo'remic** *a.*

theory ('thēəri) *n.* **1.** supposition to account for something **2.** system of rules and principles **3.** rules and reasoning *etc.* as distinguished from practice —**theo'retic(al)** *a.* **1.** based on theory **2.** speculative, as opposed to practical —**theo'retically** *adv.* —**theore'tician** *n.* student or user of theory rather than practical aspects of subject —**'theorist** *n.* —**'theorize** *vi.* form theories, speculate

theosophy (thi'osəfi) *n.* any of various religious, philosophical systems claiming possibility of intuitive insight into divine nature

therapy ('therəpi) *n.* healing treatment (*usu.* in *comb. forms* as *radiotherapy*) —**therapeutic** (therə'pyōōtik) *a.* **1.** of healing **2.** serving to improve or maintain health —**therapeutics** (therə'pyōōtiks) *pl.n.* (*with sing. v.*) art of healing —**'therapist** *n.*

there (dhāər) *adv.* **1.** in that place **2.** to that point —**therea'bouts** *or* **therea'bout** *adv.* near that place, time *etc.* —**there'after** *adv.* from that time on; after that time —**there'by** *adv.* by that means —**'therefore** *adv.* in consequence, that being so —**there'in** *adv. Formal, law* in or into that place *etc.* —**there'of** *adv. Formal, law* **1.** of or concerning that or it **2.** from or because of that —**there'to** *adv.* **1.** *Formal, law* to that or it **2.** *obs.* in addition to that —**there'under** *adv. Formal, law* **1.** in documents *etc.*, below that or it; subsequently in that; thereafter **2.** under terms or authority of that —**'thereupon** *adv.* at that point, immediately afterward —**there'with** *or* **'therewithal** *adv.* **1.** *Formal, law* with or in addition to that **2.** *rare* thereupon **3.** *obs.* by means of or on account of that

therm (thərm) *n.* unit of measurement of heat —**'thermal** *a.* **1.** of, pert. to heat **2.** hot, warm (*esp.* of spring *etc.*) **3.** (of garments) specially made so as to have exceptional heat-retaining qualities —**'thermic** *a.*

thermion ('thərmīən) *n. Phys.* ion emitted by incandescent body —**thermi'onic** *a.* pert. to thermion —**thermionic valve** electronic valve in which electrons are emitted from a heated rather than a cold cathode

thermo- *or before vowel* **therm-** (*comb. form*) related to, caused by or producing heat, as in *thermometer*

thermocouple ('thərməkupəl) *n.* **1.** device for measuring temperature consisting of pair of wires of different metals joined at both ends **2.** similar device with only one junction between two dissimilar metals

thermodynamics (thərmōdī'namiks) *pl.n.* (*with sing. v.*) the science that deals with the interrelationship and interconversion of different forms of energy

thermoelectricity (thərmōilek'trisiti) *n.* electricity developed by the action of heat —**thermoe'lectric(al)** *a.* **1.** of conversion of heat energy to electrical energy **2.** of conversion of electrical energy

thermometer (thər'momitər) *n.* instrument to measure temperature —**thermo'metric** *a.*

thermonuclear (thərmō'nyo͞okliər, -'no͞okliər) *a.* involving nuclear fusion

thermoplastic (thərmə'plastik) *n.* **1.** plastic that retains its properties after being melted and solidified —*a.* **2.** (of plastic *etc.*) becoming soft when heated and rehardening on cooling without appreciable change of properties

thermos ('thərməs) *n.* vacuum bottle

thermosetting ('thərmōseting) *a.* (of material, *esp.* synthetic plastic) hardening permanently after one application of heat and pressure

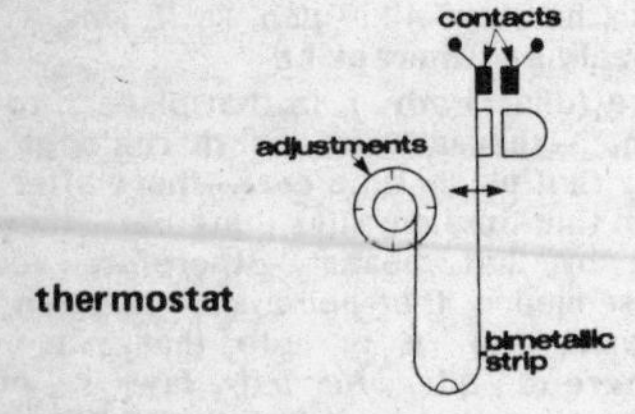

thermostat

thermostat ('thərməstat) *n.* apparatus for automatically regulating temperature —**thermo'static** *a.*

thesaurus (thi'sōrəs) *n.* **1.** book containing lists of synonyms and sometimes antonyms **2.** dictionary of selected words, topics (*pl.* **-es, -ri** (-rī))

these (dhēz) *pron., pl. of* THIS

thesis ('thēsis) *n.* **1.** written work submitted for degree, diploma **2.** theory maintained in argument (*pl.* **theses** ('thēsēz))

Thespian ('thespiən) *a.* **1.** theatrical —*n.* **2.** actor, actress

Thess. *Bible* Thessalonians

Thessalonians (thesə'lōnyənz) *pl.n.* (*with sing. v.*) *Bible* 13th and 14th books of the N.T., epistles written by St. Paul to the church at Thessalonica

theta ('thātə, 'thētə) *n.* eighth letter in Gr. alphabet (Θ, θ)

they (dhā) *pron.* the third person plural pronoun

thick (thik) *a.* **1.** having great thickness, not thin **2.** dense, crowded **3.** having dense consistency **4.** (of voice) throaty **5.** *inf.* stupid, insensitive **6.** *inf.* friendly (*esp. in* **thick as thieves**) —*n.* **7.** busiest, most intense part —'**thicken** *v.* **1.** make, become thick —*vi.* **2.** become more involved, complicated —'**thickening** *n.* **1.** something added to liquid to thicken it **2.** thickened part or piece —'**thicket** *n.* thick growth of small trees —'**thickly** *adv.* —'**thickness** *n.* **1.** dimensions of anything measured through it, at right angles to length and breadth **2.** state of being thick **3.** layer —'**thickhead** *n.* **1.** stupid or ignorant person; fool **2.** Aust. or SE Asian songbird —**thick'headed** *a.* —**thick'headedness** *n.* —**thick'set** *a.* **1.** sturdy and solid of body **2.** set closely together —**thick-skinned** *a.* insensitive to criticism or hints; not easily upset or affected

thief (thēf) *n.* one who steals (*pl.* **thieves** (thēvz)) —**thieve** *v.* steal —'**thievish** *a.*

thigh (thī) *n.* upper part of leg —'**thigh'bone** *n.* bone of hind or lower limb (*also* **femur**)

thimble ('thimbəl) *n.* cap protecting end of finger when sewing

thin (thin) *a.* **1.** of little thickness **2.** slim, lean **3.** of little density **4.** sparse; fine **5.** loose, not close-packed **6.** *inf.* unlikely —*v.* **7.** make, become thin (**-nn-**) —'**thinner** *n.* —'**thinness** *n.* —**thin-skinned** *a.* sensitive to criticism or hints; easily upset or affected

thine (dhīn) *pron./a.* (thing) belonging to thee

thing (thing) *n.* **1.** material object **2.** any possible object of thought **3.** preoccupation, obsession (*esp. in* **have a thing about**) —**thingumabob** ('thingəməbob), **thingamajig** *or* **thingumajig** ('thingəməjig) *n. inf.* person or thing the name of which is unknown, temporarily forgotten or deliberately overlooked

think (thingk) *vi.* **1.** have one's mind at work **2.** reflect, meditate **3.** reason **4.** deliberate **5.** imagine **6.** hold opinion —*vt.* **7.** conceive, consider in the mind **8.** believe **9.** esteem (**thought, 'thinking**) —'**thinkable** *a.* able to be conceived, considered, possible, feasible —'**thinker** *n.* —'**thinking** *a.* reflecting —**think-tank** *n.* group of experts studying specific problems

thio- *or before vowel* **thi-** (*comb. form*) sulfur, *esp.* denoting replacement of oxygen atom with sulfur atom, as in *thiol, thiosulfate*

thiopentone sodium (thīō'pentōn) *or* **thiopental sodium** (thīō'pental) barbiturate drug used as intravenous general anesthetic (*also* **sodium pentothal**)

third (thərd) *a.* **1.** ordinal number corresponding to *three* —*n.* **2.** third part —**third degree** *see* DEGREE —**third dimension** dimension of depth by which solid object may be distinguished from two-dimensional drawing or picture of it —**third party** *Law, insurance etc.* person involved by chance or only incidentally in legal proceedings *etc.* —**third person** grammatical category of pronouns and verbs used when referring to objects or individuals other than speaker or his addressee(s) —**third-rate** *a.* mediocre, inferior —**Third World** developing countries of Afr., Asia, Latin Amer.

thirst (thərst) *n.* **1.** desire to drink **2.** feeling caused by lack of drink **3.** craving, yearning —*vi.* **4.** feel lack of drink —'**thirstily** *adv.* —'**thirsty** *a.*

thirteen (thər'tēn) *n./a.* three plus ten —**Thirteen Colonies** the colonies of British North America that joined in the American Revolution and became the United States

thirty ('thərti) *n./a.* three times ten

this (dhis) *demonstrative a./pron.* denotes thing, person near, or just mentioned (*pl.* **these**)

thistle ('thisəl) *n.* prickly plant with dense flower heads —'**thistledown** *n.* mass of feathery plumed seeds produced by thistle

thither ('thidhər, 'dhidhər) *or* **thitherward** *adv. obs.* to or toward that place

thixotropic (thiksə'trōpik, -'tropik) *a.* (of certain liquids, as paints) having property of thickening if left undisturbed but becoming less viscous when stirred

tho *or* **tho'** (dhō) *poet. see* THOUGH

thole[1] (thōl) *or* **tholepin** ('thōlpin) *n.* wooden pin set upright in gunwale of rowing boat to serve as fulcrum in rowing

thole[2] (thōl) *vt.* **1.** *dial.* put up with; bear **2.** suffer

thong (thong) *n.* **1.** narrow strip of leather, strap **2.** rubber-soled sandal attached to foot by thong between big toe and next toe

thorax ('thōraks) *n.* part of body between neck and belly —**thoracic** (thə'rasik) *a.*

Thorazine ('thōrəzēn) *n.* trade name for chlorpromazine

thorium ('thōriəm) *n. Chem.* metallic element *Symbol* Th, at. wt. 232.0, at. no. 90

thorn (thōrn) *n.* **1.** prickle on plant **2.** spine **3.** bush noted for its thorns **4.** *fig.* anything which causes trouble or annoyance (*esp. in* **thorn in one's side** *or* **flesh**) —'**thorny** *a.*

thorough ('thərō) *a.* **1.** careful, methodical **2.** complete, entire —'**thoroughly** *adv.* —'**thoroughbred** *a.* **1.** of pure breed —*n.* **2.** purebred animal, *esp.* horse —'**thoroughfare** *n.* **1.** road or passage open at both ends **2.** right of way —**thorough'going** *a.* **1.** extremely thorough **2.** absolute; complete

those (dhōz) *pron., pl. of* THAT

thou[1] (dhow) *pron. obs.* the second person singular pronoun (*pl.* **ye, you**)

thou[2] (thow) *n.* **1.** thousandth of inch **2.** *inf.* thousand (*pl.* **-s, thou**)

though (dhō) *conj.* **1.** in spite of the fact that, even if —*adv.* **2.** nevertheless

thought (thōt) *n.* **1.** process of thinking **2.** what one thinks **3.** product of thinking **4.** meditation —*v.* **5.** *pt./pp. of* THINK —'**thoughtful** *a.* **1.** considerate **2.** showing careful thought **3.** engaged in meditation **4.** attentive —'**thoughtless** *a.* inconsiderate, careless, heedless —**thought transference** *Psychol. see* TELEPATHY

thousand ('thowzənd) *n./a.* cardinal number, ten hundred

thrall (thrōl) *n.* **1.** slavery **2.** slave, bondsman —*vt.* **3.** enslave —'**thralldom** *or* '**thraldom** *n.* bondage

thrash (thrash) *vt.* **1.** beat, whip soundly **2.** defeat soundly —*v.* **3.** *see* THRESH (sense 1) —*vi.* **4.** move, plunge, *esp.* arms, legs in wild manner —**thrash out 1.** argue about from every angle **2.** solve by exhaustive discussion

thread (thred) *n.* **1.** fine cord **2.** fine strand, filament or fiber of some material **3.** ridge cut spirally on screw **4.** theme, meaning —*vt.* **5.** put thread into **6.** fit film, magnetic tape *etc.* into (machine) **7.** put on thread **8.** pick (one's way *etc.*) —'**threadbare** *a.* **1.** worn, with nap rubbed off **2.** meager **3.** shabby

threat (thret) *n.* **1.** declaration of intention to harm, injure *etc.* **2.** person or thing regarded as dangerous —'**threaten** *vt.* **1.** utter threats against **2.** menace

three (thrē) *n./a.* cardinal number, one more than two —'**threesome** *n.* group of three —**three-D** *or* **3-D** *n.* three-dimensional effect —**three-dimensional** *a.* **1.** having three dimensions **2.** simulating the effect of depth —**three-legged race** race in which pairs of competitors run with adjacent legs tied together —**threepenny bit** *or* **thrupenny bit** ('threpni, -əni; 'thrip-, 'thrup-) former twelve-sided Brit. coin valued at three old pence —**three-ply** *a.* having three layers (as wood) or strands (as wool) —**three-quarter** *a.* **1.** being three quarters of something **2.** being of three quarters the normal length —'**three'score** *n./a. obs.* sixty

threnody ('threnədi) *or* **threnode** ('thrēnōd, 'thren-) *n.* ode, song or speech of lamentation, *esp.* for dead —'**threnodist** *n.*

thresh (thrash, thresh) *v.* **1.** beat, rub (wheat, *etc.*) to separate grain from husks and straw —*vi.* **2.** toss and turn; thrash

threshold ('threshōld, 'threshhōld) *n.* **1.** bar of stone or wood forming bottom of doorway **2.** entrance **3.** starting point **4.** point at which a stimulus is perceived, or produces a response

threw (thro͞o) *pt. of* THROW

thrice (thrīs) *adv.* three times

thrift (thrift) *n.* **1.** saving, economy **2.** genus of plant, sea pink —'**thrifty** *a.* economical, frugal, sparing

thrill (thril) *n.* **1.** sudden sensation of excitement and pleasure —*v.* **2.** (cause to) feel a thrill —*vi.* **3.** vibrate, tremble —'**thriller** *n.* book, motion picture *etc.* with story of mystery, suspense —'**thrilling** *a.* exciting

thrips (thrips) *n.* small slender-bodied insect that feeds on plant sap (*pl.* **thrips**)

thrive (thrīv) *vi.* **1.** grow well **2.** flourish, prosper (**throve, thrived** *pt.*, **thriven** ('thrivən), **thrived** *pp.*, '**thriving** *pr.p.*)

thro' *or* **thro** (thro͞o) *Poet. see* THROUGH

throat (thrōt) *n.* **1.** front of neck **2.** either or both of passages through it —ˈ**throaty** *a.* (of voice) hoarse

throb (throb) *vi.* **1.** beat, quiver strongly, pulsate (**-bb-**) —*n.* **2.** pulsation, beat; vibration

throes (thrōz) *pl.n.* condition of violent pangs, pain *etc.* —**in the throes of** *inf.* in the process of

thrombin (ˈthrombin) *n.* substance important in blood clotting

thromboangiitis obliterans (thrombōanjiˈītis ōˈblitəranz) *see* BUERGER'S DISEASE

thrombophlebitis (thrombōfliˈbītis) *n.* formation of blood clot in wall of inflamed vein

thrombosis (thromˈbōsis) *n.* formation of clot of coagulated blood in blood vessel or heart

throne (thrōn) *n.* **1.** ceremonial seat, powers and duties of king or queen —*vt.* **2.** place on throne, declare king *etc.*

throng (throng) *n./v.* crowd

throstle (ˈthrosəl) *n. see* THRUSH[1]

throttle (ˈthrotəl) *n.* **1.** device controlling amount of fuel entering engine and thereby its speed —*vt.* **2.** strangle **3.** suppress **4.** restrict (flow of liquid *etc.*)

through (throō) *prep.* **1.** from end to end, from side to side of **2.** between the sides of **3.** in consequence of **4.** by means or fault of —*adv.* **5.** from end to end **6.** to the end —*a.* **7.** completed **8.** *inf.* finished **9.** continuous **10.** (of transport, traffic) not stopping —**through**ˈ**out** *adv./prep.* in every part (of) —ˈ**throughput** *n.* quantity of material processed, *esp.* by computer —**through ticket** ticket for whole of journey —**through train, bus** *etc.* train, bus *etc.* which travels whole (unbroken) length of long journey —**carry through** accomplish

throve (thrōv) *pt. of* THRIVE

throw (thrō) *vt.* **1.** fling, cast **2.** move, put abruptly, carelessly **3.** give, hold (party *etc.*) **4.** cause to fall **5.** shape on potter's wheel **6.** move (switch, lever *etc.*) **7.** *inf.* baffle, disconcert (**threw, thrown,** ˈ**throwing**) —*n.* **8.** act or distance of throwing —ˈ**throwaway** *a.* **1.** said incidentally, *esp.* for rhetorical effect; casual —*n.* **2.** anything that can be thrown away or discarded **3.** handbill —**throw away 1.** get rid of; discard **2.** fail to make good use of; waste —ˈ**throwback** *n.* **1.** one who, that which reverts to character of an ancestor **2.** this process

thrum (thrum) *v.* **1.** strum rhythmically but without expression on (musical instrument) —*vi.* **2.** drum incessantly (**-mm-**) —*n.* **3.** repetitive strumming

thrush[1] (thrush) *n.* songbird

thrush[2] (thrush) *n.* **1.** fungal disease of mouth, *esp.* in infants **2.** vaginal infection caused by same fungus **3.** foot disease of horses

thrust (thrust) *vt.* **1.** push, drive —*v.* **2.** (make a) stab —*vi.* **3.** push one's way (**thrust,** ˈ**thrusting**) —*n.* **4.** lunge, stab with pointed weapon *etc.* **5.** cutting remark **6.** propulsive force or power

thud (thud) *n.* **1.** dull heavy sound —*vi.* **2.** make thud (**-dd-**)

thug (thug) *n.* brutal, violent person —ˈ**thuggery** *n.* —ˈ**thuggish** *a.*

thuja (ˈthyoōjə, ˈthoōjə) *n.* any of various coniferous trees of N Amer. and E Asia

thulium (ˈthyoōliəm, ˈthoō-) *n. Chem.* metallic element *Symbol* Tm, at. wt. 168.9, at. no. 69

thumb (thum) *n.* **1.** first, shortest, thickest finger of hand —*vt.* **2.** handle, dirty with thumb **3.** signal for (ride in vehicle) **4.** flick through (pages of book *etc.*) —**thumb index** series of indentations cut into fore-edge of book to facilitate quick reference —**thumb-index** *vt.* furnish with thumb index —ˈ**thumbnail** *n.* **1.** nail of thumb —*a.* **2.** concise and brief —ˈ**thumbscrew** *n.* **1.** instrument of torture that pinches or crushes thumbs **2.** screw with projections on head enabling it to be turned by thumb and forefinger

thump (thump) *n.* **1.** dull heavy blow **2.** sound of one —*vt.* **3.** strike heavily —*vi.* **4.** throb, beat or pound violently —ˈ**thumping** *a. sl.* huge; excessive

thunder (ˈthundər) *n.* **1.** loud noise accompanying lightning —*vi.* **2.** rumble with thunder **3.** make noise like thunder —*vt.* **4.** utter loudly —ˈ**thundering** *a. sl.* very great; excessive —ˈ**thunderous** *a.* —ˈ**thundery** *a.* sultry —ˈ**thunderbolt** *or* ˈ**thunderclap** *n.* **1.** lightning flash followed by peal of thunder **2.** anything totally unexpected and unpleasant —ˈ**thundercloud** *n.* electrically charged cumulonimbus cloud associated with thunderstorms —ˈ**thunderstorm** *n.* storm with thunder and lightning and usu. heavy rain or hail —ˈ**thunderstruck** *a.* amazed

thurible (ˈthyoōribəl, ˈthoōr-) *n. see* CENSER

Thurs. Thursday

Thursday (ˈthərzdi) *n.* fifth day of week

thus (dhus) *adv.* **1.** in this way **2.** therefore

thwack (thwak) *vt./n.* whack

thwart (thwört) *vt.* **1.** foil, frustrate —*adv.* **2.** *obs.* across —*n.* **3.** seat across a boat

thy (dhī) *a.* belonging to thee —**thy**ˈ**self** *pron.* emphatic form of THOU[1]

thyme (tīm) *n.* aromatic herb

thymol (ˈthīmöl) *n.* white crystalline substance obtained from thyme and used as antiseptic *etc.*

thymus (ˈthīməs) *n.* small ductless gland in upper part of chest (*pl.* **-es, -mi** (-mī))

thyroid (ˈthīroid) *a.* **1.** of thyroid gland **2.** of largest cartilage of larynx —*n.* **3.** thyroid gland **4.** preparation of thyroid gland of certain animals, used to treat hypothyroidism —**thyroid-blocking drug** any of group of compounds inhibiting manufacture or release of hormones from thyroid gland (*also* **antithyroid drug**) —**thyroid gland** endocrine gland controlling body growth, situated in humans at base of throat

thyroxine (thī'roksēn) *n.* iodine containing hormone of the thyroid gland

ti (tē) *n. see* SI

Ti *Chem.* titanium

tiara (ti'arə) *n.* jeweled head ornament, coronet

tibia ('tibiə) *n.* inner and thicker of two bones of the leg below the knee (*also* **shinbone**) (*pl.* **-biae** (-biē), **-s**) —'**tibial** *a.*

tic (tik) *n.* spasmodic twitch in muscles, *esp.* of face —**tic douloureux** (do͞olə'ro͞o) *see* TRIGEMINAL NEURALGIA

tick[1] (tik) *n.* **1.** slight tapping sound, as of watch movement **2.** small mark (✓) —*vt.* **3.** mark with tick —*vi.* **4.** make ticking sound —'**ticker** *n.* **1.** *sl.* heart **2.** *sl.* watch **3.** person or thing that ticks **4.** tape machine —**ticker tape** continuous paper ribbon —'**ticktock** *n.* **1.** ticking sound as made by clock —*vi.* **2.** make ticking sound

tick[2] (tik) *n.* arachnid related to and larger than mite, parasitic at all stages of development

tick[3] (tik) *n.* mattress case —'**ticking** *n.* strong material for mattress covers

tick[4] (tik) *n. inf.* credit, account

ticket ('tikit) *n.* **1.** card, paper entitling holder to admission, travel *etc.* **2.** label **3.** summons served for parking or traffic offense **4.** list of candidates of one party for election —*vt.* **5.** attach label to **6.** issue tickets to

tickle ('tikəl) *vt.* **1.** touch, stroke, poke (person, part of body *etc.*) to produce laughter *etc.* **2.** please, amuse (*oft. in* **tickle one's fancy**) —*vi.* **3.** be irritated, itch —*n.* **4.** act, instance of this **5. C** narrow strait —'**ticklish** *a.* **1.** sensitive to tickling **2.** requiring care or tact

tidbit ('tidbit) *n.* **1.** tasty morsel of food **2.** pleasing scrap (of scandal *etc.*)

tiddlywinks ('tidliwingks) *pl.n.* game of trying to flip small plastic disks into cup

tide (tīd) *n.* **1.** rise and fall of sea happening twice each lunar day **2.** stream **3.** season, time —'**tidal** *a.* of, like tide —**tidal wave** great wave, *esp.* produced by earthquake —'**tidemark** *n.* mark left by highest or lowest point of tide —**tide someone over** help someone for a while, *esp.* by loan *etc.*

tidings ('tīdingz) *pl.n.* news

tidy ('tīdi) *a.* **1.** orderly, neat **2.** *inf.* of fair size —*vt.* **3.** put in order

tie (tī) *vi.* **1.** make an equal score —*vt.* **2.** fasten, bind, secure **3.** restrict (**tied,** '**tying**) —*n.* **4.** that with which anything is bound **5.** restriction, restraint **6.** bond, link **7.** drawn game, contest **8.** match, game in eliminating competition —**tie-dyeing** *n.* way of dyeing cloth in patterns by tying sections tightly so they will not absorb dye —'**tiepin** *n.* ornamental pin used to pin ends of tie to shirt —**tie-up** *n.* **1.** link, connection **2.** standstill **3.** *inf.* traffic jam —**tie up 1.** bind securely (as if) with string *etc.* **2.** moor (vessel) **3.** engage attentions of **4.** conclude (organization of something) **5.** come or bring to complete standstill **6.** commit (funds *etc.*) and so make unavailable for other uses **7.** subject (property) to conditions that prevent sale *etc.*

tier (tēər) *n.* row, rank, layer

tiercel ('tēərsəl) *n. see* TERCEL

tiff (tif) *n.* petty quarrel

tiffin ('tifin) *n.* in India, light meal, *esp.* at midday

tiger ('tīgər) *n.* large, tawny, black-striped feline of Asia —'**tigress** *n.* **1.** female tiger **2.** fierce, cruel or wildly passionate woman —**tiger lily** lily plant cultivated for its flowers, which have black-spotted orange petals —**tiger moth** moth with wings conspicuously marked with stripes and spots —**tiger's-eye** *or* '**tigereye** *n.* semiprecious golden-brown stone

tight (tīt) *a.* **1.** taut, tense **2.** closely fitting **3.** secure, firm **4.** not allowing passage of water *etc.* **5.** cramped **6.** *inf.* miserly **7.** *inf.* drunk —'**tighten** *v.* —'**tightly** *adv.* —**tights** *pl.n.* one-piece clinging garment covering body from waist to feet —'**tight'fisted** *a.* miserly —**tight'knit** *a.* **1.** closely integrated **2.** organized carefully —**tight-lipped** *a.* **1.** secretive; taciturn **2.** with lips pressed tightly together, as through anger —'**tightrope** *n.* rope stretched taut above the ground, on which acrobats perform

tigon ('tīgən) *or* **tiglon** ('tiglən) *n.* offspring of tiger and lioness

tike (tīk) *n. see* TYKE

tiki ('tēkē) *n.* amulet, figurine of Maori cultures

tilde ('tildə) *n.* diacritical mark (˜) placed over letter to indicate nasal sound, as in Sp. *señor*

tile (tīl) *n.* **1.** flat piece of ceramic, plastic *etc.* material used for roofs, walls, floors, fireplaces *etc.* —*vt.* **2.** cover with tiles —**tiled** *a.* —'**tiling** *n.* —**on the tiles** *inf.* on a spree, *esp.* of drinking or debauchery

till[1] (til) *prep.* **1.** up to the time of —*conj.* **2.** to the time that

till[2] (til) *vt.* cultivate —'**tillage** *n.* —'**tiller** *n.*

till[3] (til) *n.* **1.** drawer for money in shop counter **2.** cash register

tiller ('tilər) *n.* lever to move rudder of boat

tilt (tilt) *v.* **1.** incline, slope, slant **2.** tip up —*vi.* **3.** take part in medieval combat with lances **4.** thrust, aim —*n.* **5.** slope, incline **6.** *Hist.* combat for mounted men with lances, joust

tilth (tilth) *n.* **1.** tilled land **2.** condition of soil

Tim. *Bible* Timothy

timber ('timbər) *n.* **1.** wood for building *etc.*

2. trees suitable for the sawmill —'**timbered** *a.* 1. made of wood 2. covered with trees —**timber limit** 1. C area to which rights of cutting trees are limited 2. timber line —**timber line** geographical limit beyond which trees will not grow

timbre *or* **timber** ('tambər, 'timbər) *n.* 1. *Mus.* quality of sound 2. *Phonet.* tone differentiating one vowel *etc.* from another

time (tīm) *n.* 1. existence as a succession of states 2. hour 3. duration 4. period 5. point in duration 6. opportunity 7. occasion 8. leisure 9. tempo —*vt.* 10. choose time for 11. note time taken by —'**timeless** *a.* 1. unaffected or unchanged by time; ageless 2. eternal —'**timely** *a.* at opportune or appropriate time —'**timer** *n.* person, device for recording or indicating time —'**timing** *n.* regulation of actions or remarks in relation to others to produce best effect, as in theater *etc.* —**time and motion study** analysis of industrial or work procedures to determine most efficient methods of operation (*also* **time and motion, time study, motion study**) —**time bomb** bomb designed to explode at prearranged time —**time clock** clock which records, by punching or stamping **timecards** inserted into it, time of arrival or departure of employees —**time exposure** 1. exposure of photographic film for a relatively long period, usu. a few seconds 2. photograph produced by such exposure —**time-honored** *a.* respectable because old —**time-lag** *n.* period of time between cause and effect —**time off** period when one is absent from work for vacation, through sickness *etc.* —**time-out** *n.* 1. *Sport* interruption in play during which players rest, discuss tactics *etc.* 2. period of rest; break —'**timepiece** *n.* device, such as watch or clock, which measures and indicates time —'**timeserver** *n.* person who compromises and changes his opinions *etc.* to suit current fashions —**time sharing** 1. system by which users at different terminals of computer can apparently communicate with it at same time 2. system of part-ownership of vacation home, whereby each participant owns property for particular period every year —**time signature** *Mus.* sign, usu. consisting of two figures, one above other, after key signature, indicating tempo —'**timetable** *n.* plan showing hours of work, times of arrival and departure *etc.* —'**timeworn** *a.* 1. showing adverse effects of overlong use or of old age 2. hackneyed; trite —**time zone** region throughout which same standard time is used —**on time** 1. at the expected or scheduled time 2. payable in installments —**time and a half** rate of pay equaling one and a half times normal rate, oft. for overtime

timid ('timid) *a.* 1. easily frightened 2. lacking self-confidence —**ti'midity** *or* '**timidness** *n.* —'**timidly** *adv.* —'**timorous** *a.* 1. timid 2. indicating fear

Timothy ('timəthi) *n. Bible* 15th and 16th books of the N.T., epistles written by St. Paul to the minister in charge of the churches at Ephesus

timpani ('timpəni) *pl.n.* set of kettledrums —'**timpanist** *n.*

tin (tin) *n.* 1. *Chem.* metallic element *Symbol* Sn, at. wt. 118.7 at. no. 50 2. container made of tin or tinned iron —*vt.* 3. put in tin, *esp.* for preserving (food); can 4. coat with tin (**-nn-**) —'**tinny** *a.* 1. (of sound) thin, metallic 2. cheap, shoddy —'**tinfoil** *n.* 1. thin foil made of tin or alloy of tin and lead 2. thin foil made of aluminum; used for wrapping foodstuffs —**tin god** 1. self-important person 2. person erroneously regarded as holy or venerable —**tin lizzie** ('lizi) *inf.* old or decrepit automobile —**tin plate** thin steel sheet coated with layer of tin that protects steel from corrosion —**tin-plate** *vt.* coat with layer of tin —'**tinpot** *a. inf.* inferior, worthless —'**tinsmith** *n.* person who works with tin or tin plate

tincture ('tingkchər) *n.* 1. solution of medicinal substance in alcohol 2. color, stain —*vt.* 3. color, tint

tinder ('tindər) *n.* dry, easily burning material used to start fire —'**tinderbox** *n.* 1. formerly, box for holding tinder, *esp.* one fitted with flint and steel 2. touchy or explosive person or thing

tine (tīn) *n.* tooth, spike of fork, antler, harrow *etc.*

tinea ('tiniə) *n.* ringworm —**tinea pedis** ('pedis) athlete's foot —**tinea capitis** ('kapitis) ringworm of the scalp —**tinea corporis** ('kôrpəris) ringworm of the body —**tinea cruris** ('kro͝oris) ringworm of the body creases, *esp.* groin

ting (ting) *n.* 1. sharp sound, as of bell 2. tinkling —*vi.* 3. tinkle —**ting-a-ling** *n.* sound of small bell

tinge (tinj) *n.* 1. slight trace, flavor —*vt.* 2. color, flavor slightly

tingle ('tinggəl) *vi.* 1. feel thrill or pricking sensation —*n.* 2. sensation of tingling

tinker ('tingkər) *n.* 1. formerly, traveling mender of pots and pans —*vi.* 2. fiddle, meddle (*eg* with machinery), oft. inexpertly —**tinker's damn** *or* **cuss** *sl.* slightest heed (*esp. in* **not give a tinker's damn** *or* **cuss**)

tinkle ('tingkəl) *v.* 1. (cause to) give out series of light sounds like small bell —*n.* 2. this sound or action

tinnitus ('tinitəs) *n.* noises in the ear

tinsel ('tinsəl) *n.* 1. glittering, metallic substance for decoration 2. anything sham and showy

tint (tint) *n.* 1. color 2. shade of color 3. tinge —*vt.* 4. dye, give tint to

tintinnabulation (tintinabyə'lāshən) *n.* act or instance of ringing or pealing of bells

tiny ('tīni) *a.* very small, minute

-tion (*comb. form*) state, condition, action, process, result, as in *election, prohibition*

tip[1] (tip) *n.* **1.** slender or pointed end of anything **2.** piece of metal, leather *etc.* protecting an extremity —*vt.* **3.** put a tip on (**-pp-**)

tip[2] (tip) *n.* **1.** small present of money given for service rendered **2.** helpful piece of information **3.** warning, hint —*vt.* **4.** give tip to (**-pp-**) —'**tipster** *n.* one who sells tips about races —**tip-off** *n.* warning or hint, *esp.* given confidentially and based on inside information —**tip off**

tip[3] (tip) *vt.* **1.** tilt, upset **2.** touch lightly —*vi.* **3.** topple over (**-pp-**) —*n.* **4. UK** place where rubbish is dumped

tippet ('tipit) *n.* covering for the neck and shoulders

tipple ('tipəl) *v.* **1.** drink (alcohol) habitually, *esp.* in small quantities —*n.* **2.** alcoholic drink —'**tippler** *n.*

tipsy ('tipsi) *a.* (slightly) drunk

tiptoe ('tiptō) *vi.* **1.** walk on ball of foot and toes **2.** walk softly

tiptop ('tip'top) *a.* of the best quality or highest degree

tirade (tī'rād) *n.* long speech, generally vigorous and hostile, denunciation

tire[1] ('tīər) *vt.* **1.** reduce energy of, *esp.* by exertion **2.** bore **3.** irritate —*vi.* **4.** become tired, wearied, bored —**tired** a. **1.** fatigued **2.** no longer fresh; hackneyed —'**tireless** *a.* unable to be tired —'**tirelessly** *adv.* —'**tiresome** *a.* wearisome, irritating, tedious —'**tiring** *a.*

tire[2] ('tīər) *n.* **1.** (inflated) rubber ring over rim of wheel of road vehicle **2.** metal band on rim of cartwheel

tissue ('tishōō) *n.* **1.** substance of animal body, plant *etc.* **2.** fine, soft paper, *esp.* used as handkerchief *etc.* **3.** fine woven fabric

tit[1] (tit) *n.* any of numerous small, active Old World songbirds *esp.* bluetit *etc.*

tit[2] (tit) *n.* **1.** *vulgar sl.* female breast **2.** *sl.* despicable, stupid person

Tit. *Bible* Titus

titan ('tītən) *n.* person of great strength or size —**ti'tanic** *a.* huge, epic

titanium (tī'tāniəm) *n.* *Chem.* metallic element *Symbol* Ti, at. wt. 47.9, at. no. 22

tit for tat blow for blow, retaliation

tithe (tīdh) *n.* **1.** *esp. Hist.* tenth part of agricultural produce paid for the upkeep of the clergy or as tax —*vt.* **2.** exact tithes from —**tithe barn** formerly, large barn where agricultural tithe of parish was stored

Titian ('tishən) *a.* of reddish-gold color, auburn

titillate ('titilāt) *vt.* tickle, stimulate agreeably —**titil'lation** *n.* —'**titillator** *n.*

titivate *or* **tittivate** ('titivāt) *v.* dress or smarten up —**titi'vation** *or* **titti'vation** *n.*

title ('tītəl) *n.* **1.** name of book **2.** heading **3.** name **4.** appellation denoting rank **5.** legal right or document proving it **6.** *Sport* championship —'**titled** *a.* of the aristocracy —**title deed** legal document as proof of ownership —'**titleholder** *n.* person who holds title, *esp.* sporting championship —**title page** page in book that gives title, author, publisher *etc.* —**title role** role of character after whom play *etc.* is named

titration (tī'trāshən) *n.* operation in which measured amount of one solution is added to known quantity of another solution until reaction between the two is complete —'**titrate** *vt.* measure volume or concentration of (solution) by titration

titter ('titər) *vi.* **1.** laugh in suppressed way —*n.* **2.** such laugh

tittle ('titəl) *n.* whit, detail

tittle-tattle *n./vi.* gossip

titular ('tichələr) *a.* **1.** pert. to title **2.** nominal **3.** held by virtue of a title

Titus ('tītəs) *n.* *Bible* 17th book of the N.T., epistle written by St. Paul to Titus while Titus was ministering on the isle of Crete

tizzy ('tizi) *n.* *inf.* state of confusion, anxiety

Tl *Chem.* thallium

Tm *Chem.* thulium

TN Tennessee

tn. ton(s)

TNT trinitrotoluene

to (tōō; *unstressed* tŏŏ, tə) *prep.* **1.** toward, in the direction of **2.** as far as **3.** used to introduce a comparison, ratio, indirect object, infinitive mood *etc.* —*adv.* **4.** to the required or normal state or position —**to and fro 1.** back and forth **2.** here and there —**toing and froing**

toad (tōd) *n.* animal like large frog

toadflax ('tōdflaks) *n.* perennial plant having yellow-orange flowers (*also* **butter-and-eggs**)

toadstool ('tōdstōōl) *n.* poisonous fungus resembling mushroom

toady ('tōdi) *n.* **1.** one who flatters, ingratiates himself —*vi.* **2.** do this ('**toadied**, '**toadying**)

toast (tōst) *n.* **1.** slice of bread crisped and browned on both sides by heat **2.** tribute, proposal of health, success *etc.* made by company of people and marked by drinking together **3.** person toasted —*vt.* **4.** crisp and brown (as bread) **5.** drink toast to **6.** dry or warm at fire —'**toaster** *n.* electrical device for toasting bread —'**toastmaster** *n.* person who introduces speakers, proposes toasts *etc.* at public dinners ('**toastmistress** *fem.*)

Tob. *Bible* Tobias

tobacco (tə'bakō) *n.* **1.** plant with leaves used for smoking or chewing or in snuff **2.** the prepared leaves (*pl.* **-s, -es**) —**to'bacconist** *n.* one who sells tobacco products

Tobias (tə'bīəs) *n.* *Bible* 17th book in the Douay Version of the O.T.

toboggan (tə'bogən) *n.* **1.** sled of thin boards curving up at front end with handrails at side **2.** sharp decline —*vi.* **3.** slide on toboggan **4.** decline suddenly and sharply (in value)

toby jug ('tōbi) mug in form of stout, seated man

toccata (tə'kätə) *n.* rapid piece of music for keyboard instrument

tocsin ('toksin) *n.* alarm signal, bell

today (tə'dā) *n.* **1.** this day —*adv.* **2.** on this day **3.** nowadays

toddle ('todəl) *vi.* **1.** walk with unsteady, short steps **2.** *inf.* stroll —*n.* **3.** toddling —'**toddler** *n.* child beginning to walk

toddy ('todi) *n.* sweetened mixture of liquor, hot water *etc.*

to-do *n. inf.* fuss, commotion (*pl.* **-s**)

toe (tō) *n.* **1.** digit of foot **2.** anything resembling toe in shape or position —*vt.* **3.** reach, touch or kick with toe —'**toecap** *n.* reinforced covering for toe of shoe —'**toe-hold** *n.* **1.** small foothold to facilitate climbing **2.** any means of gaining access, support *etc.* **3.** wrestling hold in which opponent's toe is held and leg twisted —**toe the line** conform

toffee ('tofi) *n.* chewy candy made of boiled sugar *etc.* —**toffee-apple** *n.* apple fixed on stick and coated with toffee

tofu ('tōfōō) *n.* soybean curd

toga ('tōgə) *n.* loose outer garment worn by ancient Romans

together (tə'gedhər) *adv.* **1.** in company **2.** simultaneously —*a./adv.* **3.** *inf.* (well) organized —**to'getherness** *n.* feeling of closeness or affection from being united with other people

toggle ('togəl) *n.* **1.** small wooden, metal peg fixed crosswise on cord, wire *etc.* and used for fastening as button **2.** any similar device —**toggle joint** device consisting of two arms pivoted at common joint and at outer ends, and used to apply pressure by straightening angle between two arms —**toggle switch** electric switch having projecting lever that is manipulated in particular way to open or close circuit

Togo ('tōgō) *n.* country in Africa bounded west by Ghana, north by Burkina-Faso, east by Benin and south by the Bight of Benin —'**Togolander** *n.* —**Togo'lese** *n./a.*

Togoland ('tōgōland) *n. former name of* GHANA (*also* **Gold Coast**)

togs (togz) *pl.n. inf.* clothing

toil (toil) *n.* **1.** heavy work or task —*vi.* **2.** labor —'**toilsome** *or* '**toilful** *a.* laborious —'**toilworn** *a.* **1.** weary with toil **2.** hard and lined

toilet ('toilit) *n.* **1.** fixture usu. consisting of water-flushed bowl used for defecation and urination **2.** process of washing, dressing **3.** articles used for this —'**toiletry** *n.* object or cosmetic used in making up *etc.* —**toilet paper** thin absorbent paper, oft. wound in roll round cardboard cylinder (**toilet roll**), used for cleaning oneself after defecation or urination —**toilet training** training of young child to use toilet when he needs to discharge bodily waste —**toilet water** form of liquid perfume lighter than cologne

Tokay (tō'kā) *n.* dessert wine made by blending angelica, port and sherry

token ('tōkən) *n.* **1.** sign or object used as evidence **2.** symbol **3.** piece used as money —*a.* **4.** nominal, slight —'**tokenism** *n.* practice of making only token effort or doing no more than minimum, *esp.* to comply with law

told (tōld) *pt./pp. of* TELL

tolerate ('tolərāt) *vt.* **1.** put up with **2.** permit —'**tolerable** *a.* **1.** bearable **2.** fair, moderate —'**tolerably** *adv.* —'**tolerance** *n.* (degree of) ability to endure stress, pain, radiation *etc.* —'**tolerant** *a.* **1.** disinclined to interfere with others' ways or opinions **2.** forbearing **3.** broad-minded —'**tolerantly** *adv.* —**tole'ration** *n.*

toll[1] (tōl) *vt.* **1.** make (bell) ring slowly at regular intervals **2.** announce (death) thus —*vi.* **3.** ring thus —*n.* **4.** tolling sound

toll[2] (tōl) *n.* **1.** tax, *esp.* for the use of bridge or road **2.** loss, damage incurred through accident, disaster *etc.* —'**tollgate** *n.* gate across toll road or bridge at which travelers must stop and pay

toluene ('tolyōōēn) *n.* volatile flammable liquid obtained from petroleum and coal tar

tolulosis (tōlə'lōsis) *n. see* CRYPTOCOCCOSIS

tom (tom) *n.* male of some animals, *esp.* cat

tomahawk ('tomihök) *n.* **1.** fighting axe of N Amer. Indians —*vt.* **2.** strike, kill with tomahawk

tomato (tə'mātō) *n.* **1.** plant with red or yellow fruit **2.** the fruit, used in salads *etc.* (*pl.* **-es**)

tomb (tōōm) *n.* **1.** grave **2.** monument over grave —'**tombstone** *n.* gravestone

tomboy ('tomboi) *n.* girl who acts, dresses in boyish way

Tom, Dick, and (or) Harry ordinary, undistinguished or common person (*esp. in* **every Tom, Dick, and Harry; any Tom, Dick, or Harry**)

tome (tōm) *n.* large book or volume

tomfoolery (tom'fōōləri) *n.* nonsense, silly behavior

tommy ('tomi) *n. sl.* private soldier in Brit. army —**Tommy gun** type of sub-machine-gun —'**tommyrot** *n.* utter nonsense

tomorrow (tə'morō) *adv./n.* (on) the day after today

tom-tom *n.* any long and narrow small-headed drum beaten with the hands

ton (tun) *n.* **1.** measure of weight, 1016 kg (2240 lbs.) (*also* **long ton**) **2.** measure of weight, 907 kg (2000 lbs.) (*also* **short ton**) **3.** metric ton **4.** *inf.* any large quantity

—'**tonnage** *n.* **1.** carrying capacity **2.** charge per ton **3.** ships collectively

tondo ('tondō) *n.* circular painting or sculptured medallion (*pl.* **tondi** ('tondē))

tone (tōn) *n.* **1.** quality of musical sound **2.** quality of hue **3.** general character, style **4.** healthy condition —*vt.* **5.** give tone to —*v.* **6.** blend, harmonize —'**tonal** *a.* —**to'nality** *n.* —**tone-deaf** *a.* unable to distinguish differences in musical pitch —**tone deafness** —**tone poem** orchestral work based on story, legend *etc.*

tong (tong) *n.* formerly, secret society of Chinese Americans

Tonga ('tonggə) *n.* protectorate of the United Kingdom lying in the South Pacific and comprising about 169 islands lying between 15° and 23°30' S latitude and 173° and 177° W longitude —'**Tongan** *a./n.*

tongs (tongz) *pl.n.* large pincers, *esp.* for handling coal, sugar

tongue-and-groove joint

tongue (tung) *n.* **1.** muscular organ inside mouth, used for speech, taste *etc.* **2.** various things shaped like this **3.** language; speech; voice —**tongue-and-groove joint** joint made by means of tongue along edge of one board that fits into groove along edge of another board —**tongue-lash** *vt.* reprimand severely; scold —**tongue-lashing** *n./a.* —**tongue-tie** *n.* congenital condition in which tongue has restricted mobility as result of abnormally short fold of skin under tongue —**tongue-tied** *a.* **1.** speechless, *esp.* with embarrassment or shyness **2.** having condition of tongue-tie —**tongue twister** sentence or phrase difficult to articulate clearly and quickly

tonic ('tonik) *n.* **1.** medicine to improve bodily tone or condition **2.** *Mus.* first keynote of scale —*a.* **3.** invigorating, restorative **4.** of tone —**tonic sol-fa** method of teaching music, by which syllables are used as names for notes of major scale in any key —**tonic water** *or* **tonic** mineral water oft. containing quinine

tonight (tə'nīt) *n.* **1.** this night **2.** the coming night —*adv.* **3.** on this night

tonne (tun) *n.* metric ton, 1000 kg

tonsil ('tonsəl) *n.* gland in throat —'**tonsillar** *a.* —**tonsil'lectomy** *n.* surgical removal of tonsils —**tonsil'litis** *n.* inflammation of tonsils

tonsorial (ton'sōriəl) *a.* *oft. jocular* of barbering or hairdressing

tonsure ('tonchər) *n.* **1.** shaving of part of head as religious or monastic practice **2.** part shaved —*vt.* **3.** shave thus

too (tōō) *adv.* **1.** also, in addition **2.** in excess, overmuch

took (tŏŏk) *pt. of* TAKE

tool (tōōl) *n.* **1.** implement or appliance for mechanical operations **2.** servile helper **3.** means to an end —*vt.* **4.** work on with tool **5.** indent design on (leather book cover *etc.*) —'**tooling** *n.* **1.** decorative work **2.** setting up *etc.* of tools, *esp.* for machine operation

toot (tōōt) *v.* **1.** (cause to) give short blast, hoot or whistle —*n.* **2.** short sound of horn, trumpet *etc.*

tooth (tōōth) *n.* **1.** bonelike projection in gums of upper and lower jaws of vertebrates **2.** any of various pointed things like this **3.** prong, cog (*pl.* **teeth**) —'**toothsome** *a.* of delicious or appetizing appearance, flavor or smell —'**toothy** *a.* having or showing numerous, large or projecting teeth —'**toothache** *n.* pain in or about tooth —'**toothbrush** *n.* small brush, usu. with long handle, for cleaning teeth —**tooth-comb** *n.* small comb with teeth close together —'**toothpaste** *n.* paste for cleaning teeth, applied with toothbrush —'**toothpick** *n.* small sharp sliver of wood *etc.* for extracting pieces of food from between teeth

tootle ('tōōtəl) *inf. v.* **1.** toot —*n.* **2.** soft hoot or series of hoots

top[1] (top) *n.* **1.** highest part, summit **2.** highest rank **3.** first in merit **4.** garment for upper part of body **5.** lid, stopper of bottle *etc.* **6.** platform on ship's mast —*vt.* **7.** cut off, pass, reach, surpass top of **8.** provide top for (**-pp-**) —'**topless** *a.* (of costume or woman) with no covering for breasts —'**topmost** *a.* **1.** supreme **2.** highest —'**topping** *n.* **1.** something that tops something else, *esp.* sauce or garnish for food —*a.* **2.** high or superior in rank, degree *etc.* —**top brass** *inf.* **1.** high-ranking army officers **2.** important officials —'**topcoat** *n.* outdoor coat worn over suit *etc.* —**top dog** *inf.* leader or chief of group —**top-drawer** *a.* of highest standing, *esp.* socially —**top-dress** *vt.* spread soil, fertilizer *etc.* on surface of (land) —**top dressing** —**top-flight** *a.* of superior or excellent quality —**topgallant** (top'galənt; *Naut.* tə'galənt) *n.* **1.** mast on square-rigger above topmast or extension of topmast **2.** sail set on yard of topgallant mast —*a.* **3.** of topgallant —**top gear 1.** highest forward ratio of gearbox in motor vehicle **2.** highest speed, greatest energy *etc.* (*also* **top**) —**top hat** man's hat with tall cylindrical crown —**top-heavy** *a.* **1.** unbalanced **2.** with top too heavy for base —'**topknot** *n.* **1.** crest, tuft, chignon *etc.* on top of head **2.** European flatfish —**top-level** *a.* of those on highest level of influence or authority —**topmast** ('topmast; *Naut.* 'topməst) *n.* mast next above lower mast on sailing vessel —**top'notch** *a.* excellent, first-class —**topsail** ('topsāl; *Naut.*

'topsəl) *n.* square sail carried on yard set on topmast —**top-secret** *a.* needing highest level of secrecy, security —**'top'side** *n.* **1.** uppermost side **2.** (*oft. pl.*) part of ship's sides above water line **3.** (*oft. pl.*) part of ship above decks —**Top Sider** trade name for shoe worn for sailing —**'topsoil** *n.* surface layer of soil

top[2] (top) *n.* toy which spins on tapering point

topaz ('tōpaz) *n.* **1.** gemstone of any of various colors, *esp.* yellow —*a.* **2.** of color of yellow topaz

tope[1] (tōp) *v.* consume (liquor) as regular habit, usu. in large quantities —**'toper** *n.*

tope[2] (tōp) *n.* small gray shark of European coastal waters

topi (tō'pē, 'tōpē; -pi) *n.* lightweight hat made of pith (*pl.* **-s**)

topiary ('tōpieri) *a.* **1.** (of shrubs) shaped by cutting or pruning, made ornamental by trimming or training —*n.* **2.** topiary work **3.** topiary garden —**'topiarist** *n.*

topic ('topik) *n.* subject of discourse, conversation *etc.* —**'topical** *a.* **1.** up-to-date, having news value **2.** of topic

topography (tə'pogrəfi) *n.* (description of) surface features of a place —**to'pographer** *n.* —**topo'graphic** *a.* —**topo'graphically** *adv.*

topology (tə'poləji) *n.* **1.** branch of mathematics concerned with the properties of geometric figures that remain unchanged even when distorted (*also* **rubber-sheet geometry**) **2.** study of topography of given place **3.** anatomy of any specific bodily area, structure or part —**topo'logic(al)** *a.* —**to'pologist** *n.*

topple ('topəl) *v.* (cause to) fall over, collapse

topsy-turvy (topsi'tərvi) *a.* **1.** upside down **2.** in confusion

toque (tōk) *n.* **1.** small round hat **2.** **C** knitted cap

tor (tör) *n.* high, rocky hill

Torah ('tōrə) *n.* **1.** the Pentateuch **2.** scroll on which this is written **3.** whole body of Jewish sacred writings and tradition, including oral expositions of the Law

torch (törch) *n.* **1.** burning brand *etc.* **2.** any apparatus burning with hot flame (*eg* for welding) —**'torchbearer** *n.* —**torch singer** —**torch song** sentimental song, usu. sung by woman —**carry a torch for** be in love with, *esp.* unrequitedly

tore (tör) *pt. of* TEAR[2] —**torn** *pp. of* TEAR[2]

toreador ('toriədör) *n.* bullfighter

torment (tör'ment) *vt.* **1.** torture in body or mind **2.** afflict **3.** tease —*n.* ('törment) **4.** suffering, torture, agony of body or mind —**tor'mentor** *n.*

tornado (tör'nādō) *n.* **1.** whirlwind **2.** violent storm (*pl.* **-es, -s**)

torpedo (tör'pēdō) *n.* **1.** cylindrical, self-propelled underwater missile with explosive warhead, fired *esp.* from submarine (*pl.* **-es**) —*vt.* **2.** strike, sink with, as with, torpedo

torpid ('törpid) *a.* sluggish, apathetic —**tor'pidity** *or* **'torpidness** *n.* —**'torpor** *n.* torpid state

torque (törk) *n.* **1.** collar, similar ornament of twisted gold or other metal **2.** *Mech.* any rotating or twisting force

torr (tör) *n.* unit of pressure equal to one millimeter of mercury (133.322 newtons per square meter)

torrent ('torənt) *n.* **1.** rushing stream **2.** downpour —**tor'rential** *a.* **1.** resembling a torrent **2.** overwhelming

torrid ('torid) *a.* **1.** parched, dried with heat **2.** highly emotional —**tor'ridity** *or* **'torridness** *n.* —**Torrid Zone** land between tropics

torsion ('törshən) *n.* twist, twisting

torso ('törsō) *n.* **1.** (statue of) body without head or limbs **2.** trunk (*pl.* **-s, -si** (-si))

tort (tört) *n.* *Law* private or civil wrong

torticollis (törti'kolis) *n.* condition in which neck is twisted and head tilted

tortilla (tör'tēə) *n.* thin Mexican pancake

tortoise ('törtəs) *n.* four-footed reptile covered with shell of horny plates —**tortoiseshell** ('törtəshel) *n.* **1.** mottled brown shell of hawksbill turtle used commercially —*a.* **2.** of yellowish-brown mottled color **3.** made of tortoiseshell

tortuous ('törchōōəs) *a.* **1.** winding, twisting **2.** involved, not straightforward —**tortu'osity** *n.*

torture ('törchər) *n.* **1.** infliction of severe pain —*vt.* **2.** subject to torture —**'torturer** *n.* —**torture chamber**

Tory ('töri) *n.* **1.** member of Brit., Canad. conservative party **2.** politically reactionary person

toss (tos) *vt.* **1.** throw up, about —*vi.* **2.** be thrown, fling oneself about —*n.* **3.** act of tossing —**toss-up** *n.* **1.** instance of tossing up coin **2.** *inf.* even chance or risk —**toss up** spin (coin) in air to decide between alternatives by guessing which side will fall uppermost

tot[1] (tot) *n.* **1.** very small child **2.** small quantity, *esp.* of drink

tot[2] (tot) *v.* (*with* up) total; add (**-tt-**)

total ('tōtəl) *n.* **1.** whole amount **2.** sum, aggregate —*a.* **3.** complete, entire, full, absolute —*v.* **4.** (*sometimes with* to) amount —*vt.* **5.** add up —**to'tality** *n.* —**'totalizator** *or* **'totalizer** *n.* machine to operate system of betting on racecourse in which money is paid out to winners in proportion to their stakes

totalitarian (tōtali'teriən) *a.* of dictatorial, one-party government

tote[1] (tōt) totalizator

tote[2] (tōt) *vt.* haul, carry —**tote bag** large handbag or shopping bag

totem ('tōtəm) *n.* tribal badge or emblem

—to'temic *a.* —**totem pole** post carved, painted with totems, *esp.* by Amer. Indians

totter ('totər) *vi.* **1.** walk unsteadily **2.** begin to fall

toucan ('to͞okan) *n.* tropical Amer. bird with large bill

touch (tuch) *n.* **1.** sense by which qualities of object *etc.* are perceived by touching **2.** characteristic manner or ability **3.** touching **4.** slight blow, stroke, contact, amount *etc.* —*vt.* **5.** come into contact with **6.** put hand on **7.** reach **8.** affect emotions of **9.** deal with, handle **10.** eat, drink **11.** *inf.* (try to) borrow from —*vi.* **12.** be in contact **13.** (*with* on) refer (to) —**touched** *a.* **1.** moved to sympathy or emotion **2.** showing slight insanity —'**touching** *a.* **1.** emotionally moving —*prep.* **2.** concerning —'**touchy** *a.* easily offended, sensitive —'**touchdown** *n.* **1.** moment at which landing aircraft or spacecraft comes into contact with landing surface **2.** *American football* scoring play for six points achieved by being in possession of ball in opponents' end zone —'**touchline** *n.* side line of pitch in some games —'**touchstone** *n.* criterion —**touch-type** *vi.* type without looking at keyboard —**touch-typist** *n.* —'**touchwood** *n.* tinder —**touch and go** precarious (situation) —**touch down 1.** (of aircraft *etc.*) land **2.** *Rugby* place ball behind goal line, as when scoring try

touché (to͞o'shā) *interj. orig.* in fencing, acknowledgment that blow, witty remark *etc.* has been successful

tough (tuf) *a.* **1.** strong, resilient, not brittle **2.** sturdy **3.** able to bear hardship, strain **4.** difficult **5.** needing effort to chew **6.** *sl.* rough, uncivilized, violent **7.** *inf.* unlucky, unfair —*n.* **8.** *inf.* rough, violent person —'**toughen** *v.* —'**toughness** *n.*

toupee (to͞o'pā) *n.* wig or piece of false hair that covers bald patch

tour (to͞oər) *n.* **1.** traveling round **2.** journey to one place after another **3.** excursion —*v.* **4.** make tour (of) —'**tourism** *n.* **1.** tourist travel **2.** this as an industry —'**tourist** *n.* one who travels for pleasure —'**touristy** *a. inf., oft. derogatory* abounding in or designed for tourists —**touring car** large open automobile, usu. seating driver and four passengers

tour de force (to͞or də 'fors) *Fr.* brilliant stroke, achievement

tourmaline ('to͞orməlin, -lēn) *n.* gemstone of variable color

tournament ('to͞ornəmənt) *n.* **1.** competition, contest usu. with several stages to decide overall winner **2.** *Hist.* contest between knights on horseback —'**tourney** *n. Hist.* knightly tournament

tourniquet ('to͞ornikət) *n.* bandage, surgical instrument to constrict artery and stop bleeding

tousle ('towzəl) *vt.* **1.** tangle, ruffle **2.** treat roughly —*n.* **3.** disorderly, tangled or rumpled state **4.** disheveled or disordered mass, *esp.* of hair

tout (towt) *vi.* **1.** solicit custom (usu. in undesirable fashion) **2.** obtain and sell information about race horses —*n.* **3.** one who touts

tow[1] (tō) *vt.* **1.** drag along behind, *esp.* at end of rope —*n.* **2.** towing or being towed **3.** vessel, vehicle in tow —'**towage** *n.* —'**towbar** *n.* metal bar attached to automobile for towing trailer *etc.* —'**towpath** *n.* path beside canal, river, orig. for towing —'**towrope** *n.* rope or cable used for towing vehicle or vessel (*also* '**towline**)

tow[2] (tō) *n.* fiber of hemp, flax —**tow-headed** *a.* with pale-colored or rumpled hair

toward (tōrd, tə'wōrd) *prep.* **1.** in direction of **2.** with regard to **3.** as contribution to (*also* **towards**)

towel ('towəl) *n.* **1.** cloth or paper for wiping off moisture after washing —*vt.* **2.** dry or wipe with towel —'**toweling** *n.* material used for making towels —**throw in the towel** give up completely

tower ('towər) *n.* **1.** tall strong structure oft. forming part of church or other large building **2.** fortress —*vi.* **3.** stand very high **4.** loom —'**towering** *a.* **1.** very tall; lofty **2.** outstanding, as in importance or stature **3.** (of rage) intense

town (town) *n.* collection of dwellings *etc.*, larger than village and smaller than city —'**township** *n.* **1.** small town **2. C** land-survey area —**town clerk** chief administrative officer of town —**town crier** formerly, person employed to make public announcements in streets —**town hall** chief building in which municipal business is transacted, oft. with hall for public meetings —**town planning** comprehensive planning of physical and social development of town —'**townspeople** *pl.n.*

toxic ('toksik) *a.* **1.** poisonous **2.** due to poison —**tox'emia** *n.* blood poisoning —**tox'icity** *n.* strength of a poison —**toxi'cology** *n.* study of poisons —'**toxin** *n.* poison of bacterial origin —'**toxoid** *n.* bacterial poison that has been made harmless without removing its ability to stimulate the production of antibodies

toxophily (tok'sofili) *n.* archery —**tox'ophilite** *n.*

toy (toi) *n.* **1.** something designed to be played with **2.** (miniature) replica —*a.* **3.** very small —*vi.* **4.** act idly —**toy dog** purebred dog characterized by diminutiveness

trace[1] (trās) *n.* **1.** track left by anything **2.** indication **3.** minute quantity —*vt.* **4.** follow course, track of **5.** find out **6.** make plan of **7.** draw or copy exactly, *esp.* using tracing paper —'**tracer** *n.* **1.** person or thing that traces **2.** ammunition that can be observed when in flight by burning of chemical substances in base of projectile **3.** *Med.*

radioactive isotope introduced into body to study metabolic processes *etc.* by following its progress with Geiger counter or other detector **4.** investigation to trace missing cargo *etc.* —ˈ**tracery** *n.* interlaced ornament, *esp.* stonework of Gothic window —ˈ**tracing** *n.* traced copy of drawing —**trace element** chemical element needed by all living organisms in minute quantities —**tracer bullet** bullet which leaves visible trail so that aim can be checked —**tracing paper** transparent paper placed over drawing, map *etc.* to enable exact copy to be taken

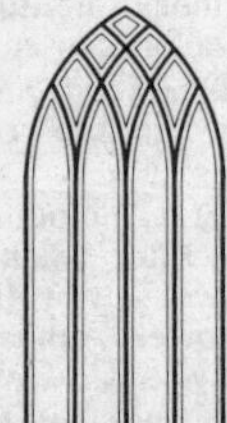

tracery

trace² (trās) *n.* **1.** chain, strap by which horse pulls vehicle **2.** *Angling* short piece of gut, nylon attaching hook or fly to line

trachea (ˈtrākiə) *n.* windpipe (*pl.* **tracheae** (ˈtrākiē)) —ˈ**tracheal** *or* ˈ**tracheate** *a.* —**tracheˈotomy** *n.* surgical incision into trachea

trachoma (trəˈkōmə) *n.* highly contagious virus disease of the eyes

track (trak) *n.* **1.** mark, line of marks, left by passage of anything **2.** path, rough road **3.** course **4.** railroad line **5.** distance between two road wheels on one axle **6.** circular jointed metal band driven by wheels as on tank, bulldozer *etc.* **7.** course for running or racing **8.** separate section on phonograph record —*vt.* **9.** follow trail or path of **10.** (*with* down) find thus —**track-and-field** *a.* of series of competitive events comprising running for speed, jumping for height or distance and throwing for distance —**track events** athletic sports held on a track —**track record** past accomplishments of person, company *etc.* —**track shoe** light running shoe fitted with steel spikes for better grip —ˈ**tracksuit** *n.* warm, two-piece garment worn *esp.* by athletes

Tracrium (ˈtrākriəm) *n.* trade name for atracurium

tract¹ (trakt) *n.* **1.** wide expanse, area **2.** *Anat.* system of organs *etc.* with particular function

tract² (trakt) *n.* treatise or pamphlet, *esp.* religious one —ˈ**tractate** *n.* short tract

tractable (ˈtraktəbəl) *a.* easy to manage, docile, amenable

traction (ˈtrakshən) *n.* **1.** action of drawing, pulling **2.** force applied to produce tension on part of body by various means in medical treatment —**traction engine** steam-powered locomotive used, *esp.* formerly, for drawing heavy loads along roads or over rough ground

tractor (ˈtraktər) *n.* motor vehicle for hauling, pulling *etc.*

trade (trād) *n.* **1.** commerce, business **2.** buying and selling **3.** any profitable pursuit **4.** those engaged in trade —*vi.* **5.** engage in trade —*vt.* **6.** buy and sell **7.** barter **8.** exchange (one thing) for another —ˈ**trader** *n.* —**trade-in** *n.* used article given in part payment for new —ˈ**trademark** *or* **trade name** *n.* name, symbol or other mark registered and legally restricted to use by owner —**trade price** price of commodities as sold by wholesalers to retailers —**trade secret** secret formula, process *etc.* known and used to advantage by only one manufacturer —ˈ**tradesman** *n.* **1.** shopkeeper **2.** skilled worker —**trade union** society of workers for protection of their interests —**trade wind** wind blowing constantly toward equator in certain parts of globe —**trading stamp** stamp given by some retail organizations to customers, redeemable for merchandise or cash

tradescantia (tradisˈkanchiə) *n.* widely cultivated plant with striped variegated leaves

tradition (trəˈdishən) *n.* **1.** unwritten body of beliefs, facts *etc.* handed down from generation to generation **2.** custom, practice of long standing **3.** process of handing down —**traˈditional** *a.* —**traˈditionally** *adv.*

traduce (trəˈdyōōs, -ˈdōōs) *vt.* slander

traffic (ˈtrafik) *n.* **1.** vehicles passing to and fro in street, town *etc.* **2.** (illicit) trade —*vi.* **3.** trade, *esp.* in illicit goods (*eg* drugs) (ˈ**trafficked,** ˈ**trafficking**) —ˈ**trafficker** *n.* trader —**traffic lights** set of colored lights at road junctions *etc.* to control flow of traffic

tragedy (ˈtrajidi) *n.* **1.** sad or calamitous event **2.** dramatic, literary work dealing with serious, sad topic and with ending marked by (inevitable) disaster —**traˈgedian** *n.* actor in, writer of tragedies (**tragediˈenne** *fem.*) —ˈ**tragic** *a.* **1.** of, in manner of tragedy **2.** disastrous **3.** appalling —ˈ**tragically** *adv.* —**tragiˈcomedy** *n.* play with both tragic and comic elements

trail (trāl) *vt.* **1.** drag behind one **2.** follow or hunt (animal or person) by following marks or tracks —*vi.* **3.** be drawn behind **4.** hang, grow loosely —*n.* **5.** track, trace **6.** thing that trails **7.** rough, ill-defined track in wild country —ˈ**trailer** *n.* **1.** vehicle towed by another vehicle **2.** large enclosed vehicle for living in, pulled by automobile **3.** *Cine.* advertisement of forthcoming motion picture **4.** trailing plant —ˈ**trailblazer** *n.* **1.** pioneer in particular field **2.** person who blazes trail

train (trān) *vt.* **1.** educate, instruct, exercise

2. cause to grow in particular way 3. aim (gun *etc.*) —*vi.* 4. follow course of training, *esp.* to achieve physical fitness for athletics —*n.* 5. line of railroad vehicles joined to locomotive 6. succession, *esp.* of thoughts, events *etc.* 7. procession of animals, vehicles *etc.* traveling together 8. trailing part of dress 9. body of attendants —**trai'nee** *n.* one training to be skilled worker, *esp.* in industry —**'trainer** *n.* 1. person who trains athletes 2. piece of equipment employed in training, such as simulated aircraft cockpit 3. person who schools race horses —**'training** *n.* —**'trainbearer** *n.* attendant who holds up train of dignitary's robe —**train spotter** person who collects numbers of railroad locomotives

traipse (trāps) *vi. inf.* walk wearily

trait (trāt) *n.* characteristic feature

traitor ('trātər) *n.* one who betrays or is guilty of treason —**'traitorous** *a.* 1. disloyal 2. guilty of treachery —**'traitorously** *adv.*

trajectory (trə'jektəri) *n.* line of flight, (curved) path of projectile

trammel ('traməl) *n.* 1. anything that restrains or holds captive 2. type of compasses —*vt.* 3. restrain, hinder

tramp (tramp) *vi.* 1. travel on foot, *esp.* as vagabond or for pleasure 2. walk heavily —*n.* 3. (homeless) person who travels about on foot 4. walk 5. tramping 6. vessel that takes cargo wherever shippers desire 7. *sl.* prostitute; promiscuous woman

trample ('trampəl) *v.* tread (on) and crush under foot

trampoline (trampə'lēn, 'trampəlēn) *n.* tough canvas sheet stretched horizontally with elastic cords *etc.* to frame, for gymnastic, acrobatic use

trance (trans) *n.* 1. unconscious or dazed state 2. state of ecstasy or total absorption

tranquil ('trangkwil) *a.* calm, quiet —**'tranquilize** *vt.* make calm —**'tranquilizer** *n.* drug which induces calm, tranquil state —**tran'quillity** *or* **tran'quility** *n.* —**'tranquilly** *adv.*

trans. 1. transaction 2. transferred 3. transitive 4. translated 5. translator 6. transport(ation) 7. transverse

trans- (*comb. form*) across, through, beyond, on the other side, as in *transatlantic*

transact (trans'akt, tranz-) *vt.* 1. carry through 2. negotiate 3. conduct (affair *etc.*) —**trans'action** *n.* 1. performing of any business 2. that which is performed 3. single sale or purchase —*pl.* 4. proceedings 5. reports of a society

transatlantic (transət'lantik, tranz-) *a.* 1. on or from the other side of the Atlantic 2. crossing the Atlantic

transceiver (tran'sēvər) *n.* combined radio transmitter and receiver

transcend (tran'send) *vt.* 1. rise above 2. exceed, surpass —**tran'scendence** *n.* —**tran'scendent** *a.* —**transcen'dental** *a.* 1. surpassing experience 2. supernatural 3. abstruse —**transcen'dentalism** *n.* —**transcendental meditation** technique, based on Hindu traditions, for relaxing and refreshing mind and body through silent repetition of mantra

transcribe (tran'skrīb) *vt.* 1. copy out 2. transliterate, translate 3. record for later broadcast 4. arrange (music) for different instrument —**'transcript** *n.* copy —**tran'scription** *n.* 1. act or instance of transcribing or state of being transcribed 2. something transcribed 3. representation in writing of actual pronunciation of word *etc.* using phonetic symbols

transducer (trans'dyo͞osər, tranz-; -'do͞osər) *n.* any device that converts one form of energy into another

transept ('transept) *n.* 1. transverse part of cruciform church 2. either of its arms

transfer (trans'fər) *v.* 1. move, send from one person, place *etc.* to another (**-rr-**) —*n.* ('transfər) 2. removal of person or thing from one place to another 3. design which can be transferred from one surface to another by pressure, heat *etc.* —**trans'ferable** *or* **trans'ferrable** *a.* —**transference** (trans'fərəns, 'transfərəns) *n.* transfer

transfigure (trans'figyər) *vt.* alter appearance of —**transfiguration** (transfigyə'rāshən, -figə-) *n.*

transfix (trans'fiks) *vt.* 1. astound, stun 2. pierce

transform (trans'fōrm) *vt.* change shape, character of —**transfor'mation** *n.* —**trans'former** *n. Elec.* apparatus for changing voltage of alternating current

transfuse (trans'fyo͞oz) *vt.* convey from one vessel to another, *esp.* blood from healthy person to one injured or ill —**trans'fusion** *n.*

transgress (trans'gres, tranz-) *vt.* 1. break (law) —*vi.* 2. sin —**trans'gression** *n.* —**trans'gressor** *n.*

tranship (tran'ship) *v. see* TRANSSHIP

transient ('tranchənt, 'tranziənt) *a.* fleeting, not permanent —**'transience** *n.*

transistor (tran'zistər) *n.* 1. *Electron.* small, semiconducting device used to amplify electric currents 2. portable radio using transistors —**tran'sistorize** *v.* 1. convert to use or manufacture of transistors and other solid-state components —*vt.* 2. equip with transistors and other solid-state components

transit ('transit, 'tranz-) *n.* passage, crossing —**transition** (tran'sishən, tran'zishən) *n.* change from one state to another —**transitional** (tran'sishnəl, tran'zishnəl; -ənəl) *a.* —**'transitive** *a.* (of verb) requiring direct object —**'transitory** *a.* not lasting long, transient —**transit camp** camp in which refugees *etc.* live temporarily

translate (trans'lāt, tranz-) *vt.* 1. turn from one language into another 2. interpret 3.

transfer (a bishop) to another see —**trans'lation** *n.* —**trans'lator** *n.*

transliterate (trans'litərāt, tranz-) *vt.* write in the letters of another alphabet —**translit-er'ation** *n.*

translucent (trans'lo͞osənt, tranz-) *a.* letting light pass through, semitransparent —**trans'lucence** *n.*

transmigrate (trans'mīgrāt, tranz-) *vi.* (of soul) pass into another body —**transmi'gration** *n.*

transmit (trans'mit, tranz-) *vt.* **1.** send, cause to pass to another place, person *etc.* **2.** communicate **3.** send out (signals) by means of radio waves **4.** broadcast (radio, television program) (-tt-) —**trans'mission** *n.* **1.** transference **2.** gear by which power is communicated from engine to road wheels —**trans'mitter** *n.* **1.** person or thing that transmits **2.** equipment used for generating and amplifying radio-frequency carrier, modulating carrier with information and feeding it to antenna for transmission **3.** microphone in telephone that converts sound waves into audio-frequency electrical signals **4.** device that converts mechanical movements into coded electrical signals transmitted along telegraph circuit

transmogrify (trans'mogrifī, tranz-) *vt. inf.* change completely *esp.* into bizarre form

transmute (trans'myo͞ot, tranz-) *vt.* change in form, properties or nature —**transmu'tation** *n.*

transom ('transəm) *n.* **1.** crosspiece **2.** lintel

transparent (trans'parənt, -'per-) *a.* **1.** letting light pass without distortion **2.** that can be seen through distinctly **3.** obvious —**trans'parence** *n.* —**trans'parency** *n.* **1.** quality of being transparent **2.** photographic slide **3.** picture made visible by light behind it —**trans'parently** *adv.*

transpire (tran'spīər) *vi.* **1.** become known **2.** *inf.* happen **3.** (of plants) give off water vapor through leaves —**transpiration** (transpə'rāshən) *n.*

transplant (trans'plant) *vt.* **1.** move and plant again in another place **2.** transfer (organ) surgically from one body to another —*n.* ('transplant) **3.** surgical transplanting of organ **4.** anything transplanted —**transplan'tation** *n.*

transponder (tran'spondər) *n.* radio or radar transmitter-receiver that transmits signals automatically when it receives predetermined signals

transport (trans'pōrt) *vt.* **1.** convey from one place to another **2.** *Hist.* banish, as criminal, to penal colony **3.** enrapture —*n.* ('transpōrt) **4.** means of conveyance **5.** ships, aircraft *etc.* used in transporting stores, troops *etc.* **6.** a ship *etc.* so used **7.** ecstasy, rapture or any powerful emotion —**transpor'tation** *n.* **1.** transporting **2.** *Hist.* deportation to penal colony

transpose (trans'pōz) *vt.* **1.** change order of, interchange **2.** put (music) into different key —**trans'posal** *n.* —**transpo'sition** *n.*

transsexual (trans'sekshoo͞əl) *n.* **1.** person who is completely identified with opposite sex **2.** person who has undergone medical procedures to alter sexual characteristics to those of opposite sex

transship (tran'ship, trans'ship) *or* **tranship** *v.* move from one ship, train *etc.* to another

transubstantiation (transəbstanchi'āshən) *n.* doctrine that substance of bread and wine changes into substance of Christ's body when consecrated in Eucharist

transuranic (transhə'ranik), **transuranian** (transhə'rāniən), *or* **transuranium** *a.* **1.** (of element) having atomic number greater than that of uranium **2.** of behavior of transuranic elements

transverse (trans'vərs, tranz-) *a.* **1.** lying across **2.** at right angles

transvestite (trans'vestīt, tranz-) *n.* person seeking sexual pleasure by wearing clothing normally worn by opposite sex

trap[1] (trap) *n.* **1.** snare, device for catching game *etc.* **2.** anything planned to deceive, betray *etc.* **3.** arrangement of pipes to prevent escape of gas **4.** movable opening, *esp.* through ceiling *etc.* **5.** *Hist.* two-wheeled carriage **6.** *sl.* mouth —*vt.* **7.** catch, ensnare (-pp-) —**'trapper** *n.* one who traps animals for their fur —**trap door** door in floor or roof

trap[2] (trap) *vt.* (*oft. with* out) dress, adorn (-pp-)

trapeze (tra'pēz, trə-) *n.* horizontal bar suspended from two ropes for use in gymnastics, acrobatic exhibitions *etc.* —**trapeze dress** tent-shaped dress with stiff full skirt molding body to high bust and falling free from shoulders at back

trapezoid ('trapəzoid) *n.* quadrilateral figure with only two sides parallel —**trapezium** (trə'pēziəm) *n.* quadrilateral with no parallel sides (*pl.* **-s, -zia** (-ziə))

trappings ('trapingz) *pl.n.* equipment, ornaments

Trappist ('trapist) *n.* member of Cistercian order of monks who observe strict silence

trash (trash) *n.* **1.** anything without value **2.** worthless person(s) —*vt.* **3.** destroy (a person's character) —**'trashy** *a.*

trauma ('trowmə, 'trōmə) *n.* **1.** nervous shock **2.** injury (*pl.* **-ta** (-tə), **-s**) —**trau'matic** *a.* of, causing, caused by trauma

travail (trə'vāl, 'travāl) *vi./n.* labor, toil

travel ('travəl) *vi.* **1.** go, move from one place to another —*n.* **2.** act of traveling, *esp.* as tourist **3.** *Machinery* distance component is permitted to move —*pl.* **4.** (account of) traveling —**'traveler** *n.* —**'travelogue** *or* **'travelog** *n.* motion picture *etc.* about travels —**travel agency** agency that arranges and negotiates vacations *etc.* for travelers

—**travel agent** —**traveler's check** check sold by bank *etc.* to bearer, who signs it on purchase and can cash it abroad by signing it again —**traveling fellowship** fellowship which requires recipient to pursue study or research away from his or her normal place of study or research —**traveling salesman** salesman who travels within assigned territory to sell merchandise or solicit orders for commercial enterprise he represents by direct personal contact with (potential) customers

traverse (trəˈvərs, tra-; ˈtravərs) *vt.* **1.** cross, go through or over —*vi.* **2.** (of gun) move laterally —*n.* (ˈtravərs) **3.** anything set across **4.** partition **5.** *Mountaineering* face, steep slope to be crossed from side to side —*a.* (ˈtravərs; trəˈvərs, tra-) **6.** being, lying across

travesty (ˈtravisti) *n.* **1.** farcical, grotesque imitation **2.** mockery —*vt.* **3.** make, be a travesty of **(-estied, -estying)**

travois (trəˈvoi, ˈtravoi) *n.* vehicle used by Plains Indians comprising two trailing poles bearing a platform or net for the load

trawl (trōl) *n.* **1.** net dragged at deep levels behind special boat, to catch fish —*vi.* **2.** fish with one —ˈ**trawler** *n.* trawling vessel

tray (trā) *n.* **1.** flat board, usu. with rim, for carrying things **2.** any similar utensil

treachery (ˈtrechəri) *n.* deceit, betrayal —ˈ**treacherous** *a.* **1.** disloyal **2.** unreliable, dangerous —ˈ**treacherously** *adv.*

tread (tred) *vt.* **1.** set foot on **2.** trample —*vi.* **3.** walk **4.** (*sometimes with* on) repress (**trod** *pt.*, ˈ**trodden** *or* **trod** *pp.*, ˈ**treading** *pr.p.*) —*n.* **5.** treading **6.** fashion of walking **7.** upper surface of step **8.** part of rubber tire in contact with ground —ˈ**treadmill** *n.* **1.** *Hist.* cylinder turned by treading on steps projecting from it **2.** dreary routine *etc.*

treadle (ˈtredəl) *n.* lever worked by foot to turn wheel

treason (ˈtrēzən) *n.* **1.** violation by subject of allegiance to sovereign or state **2.** treachery; disloyalty —ˈ**treasonable** *or* ˈ**treasonous** *a.* constituting treason —ˈ**treasonably** *adv.*

treasure (ˈtrezhər) *n.* **1.** riches **2.** stored wealth or valuables —*vt.* **3.** prize, cherish **4.** store up —ˈ**treasurer** *n.* official in charge of funds —ˈ**treasury** *n.* **1.** place for treasure **2.** (**T-**) government department in charge of finance —**treasure-trove** *n.* treasure found hidden with no evidence of ownership

treat (trēt) *n.* **1.** pleasure, entertainment given —*vt.* **2.** deal with, act toward **3.** give medical treatment to **4.** give (someone) gift, food *etc.* at one's own expense —*vi.* **5.** negotiate **6.** (*with* of) discourse (on) —ˈ**treatment** *n.* **1.** method of counteracting a disease **2.** act or mode of treating **3.** manner of handling an artistic medium

treatise (ˈtrētis, -iz) *n.* book discussing a subject, formal essay

treaty (ˈtrēti) *n.* signed contract between states *etc.*

treble (ˈtrebəl) *a.* **1.** threefold, triple **2.** *Mus.* high-pitched —*n.* **3.** soprano voice **4.** part of music for it **5.** singer with such voice —*v.* **6.** increase threefold —ˈ**trebly** *adv.* —**treble clef** *Mus.* clef that establishes G fifth above middle C as being on second line of staff

tree (trē) *n.* **1.** large perennial plant with woody trunk **2.** beam **3.** anything (*eg* genealogical chart) resembling tree or tree's structure —*vt.* **4.** force, drive up tree —**tree creeper** small songbird

trefoil (sense 2)

trefoil (ˈtrēfoil, ˈtref-) *n.* **1.** plant with three-lobed leaf, clover **2.** carved ornament like this

trek (trek) *n.* **1.** long difficult journey, *esp.* on foot **2.** migration by ox wagon —*vi.* **3.** make a trek (**-kk-**) —ˈ**trekker** *n.*

trellis (ˈtrelis) *n.* **1.** lattice or grating of light bars fixed crosswise —*vt.* **2.** screen, supply with one

tremble (ˈtrembəl) *vi.* **1.** quiver, shake **2.** feel fear, anxiety —*n.* **3.** involuntary shaking, quiver, tremor —ˈ**trembler** *n.* trembling spring that makes electrical contact when shaken

tremendous (triˈmendəs) *a.* **1.** vast, immense **2.** *inf.* exciting, unusual **3.** *inf.* excellent

tremolo (ˈtreməlō) *n.* quivering or vibrating effect in singing or playing (*pl.* **-s**)

tremor (ˈtremər) *n.* **1.** quiver **2.** shaking **3.** minor earthquake

tremulous (ˈtremyələs) *a.* **1.** quivering slightly **2.** timorous, agitated

trench (trench) *n.* **1.** long narrow ditch, *esp.* as shelter in war —*vt.* **2.** cut grooves or ditches in —**trench coat** double-breasted waterproof coat —**trench foot** *see* **immersion foot** *at* IMMERSE

trenchant (ˈtrenchənt) *a.* cutting, incisive, biting

trencher (ˈtrenchər) *n. Hist.* wooden plate on which food was served —ˈ**trencherman** *n.* person who enjoys food; hearty eater

trend (trend) *n.* **1.** direction, tendency, inclination, drift **2.** fashion; mode —ˈ**trendiness** *n.* —ˈ**trendy** *a./n. inf.* consciously fashionable (person) —ˈ**trendsetter** *n.* person or thing that creates or may create new fashion —ˈ**trendsetting** *a.*

trephine (ˈtrēfīn) *n.* **1.** instrument for cutting circular pieces, *esp.* from skull —*vt.* **2.** remove circular section of bone, *esp.* from skull, of (someone)

trepidation (trepiˈdāshən) *n.* fear, anxiety

trespass (ˈtrespəs, -pas) *vi.* **1.** intrude (on property *etc.* of another) **2.** transgress, sin —*n.* **3.** wrongful entering on another's land **4.** wrongdoing —ˈ**trespasser** *n.*

tress (tres) *n.* long lock of hair

trestle (ˈtresəl) *n.* board fixed on pairs of spreading legs and used as support

Trevira (trəˈvēərə) *n.* trade name for polyester fiber

tri- (*comb. form*) three, as in *trisect*

triad (ˈtrīad) *n.* **1.** group of three **2.** *Chem.* element, radical with valency of three

trial (ˈtrīəl, trīl) *n.* **1.** act of trying, testing **2.** experimental examination **3.** *Law* investigation of case before judge **4.** thing, person that strains endurance or patience —**trial and error** method of discovery *etc.* based on practical experiment and experience rather than theory —**trial balance** *Book-keeping* statement of all debit and credit balances in ledger of double-entry system

triangle (ˈtrīanggəl) *n.* **1.** figure with three angles **2.** percussion musical instrument —**triˈangular** *a.* —**triangulate** (trīˈanggyəlāt) *vt.* **1.** survey by method of triangulation **2.** calculate trigonometrically **3.** divide into triangles **4.** make triangular —*a.* (trīˈanggyəlit) **5.** marked with or composed of triangles —**trianguˈlation** *n.* method of surveying in which area is divided into triangles, one side and all angles of which are measured and lengths of other lines calculated trigonometrically

Triassic (trīˈasik) *a.* **1.** of first period of Mesozoic era —*n.* **2.** Triassic period or rock system (*also* ˈ**Trias**)

triathlon (trīˈathlən, -lon) *n.* athletic event comprising swimming, cycling and running

tribe (trīb) *n.* **1.** race **2.** subdivision of race of people —ˈ**tribal** *a.*

tribulation (tribyəˈlāshən) *n.* **1.** misery, trouble, affliction, distress **2.** cause of this

tribune (ˈtribyōōn) *n.* person or institution upholding public rights —**tribunal** (trīˈbyōōnəl, tri-) *n.* **1.** lawcourt **2.** body appointed to inquire into and decide specific matter **3.** seat of judge

tributary (ˈtribyəteri) *n.* **1.** stream flowing into another —*a.* **2.** auxiliary **3.** contributory **4.** paying tribute

tribute (ˈtribyōōt) *n.* **1.** sign of honor or recognition **2.** tax paid by one state to another

trice (trīs) *n.* moment —**in a trice** instantly

triceps (ˈtrīseps) *n.* muscle having three heads, *esp.* one that extends forearm (*pl.* **-es, -ceps**)

trichina (triˈkīnə) *n.* minute parasitic worm (*pl.* **-nae** (-nē)) —**trichinosis** (trikiˈnōsis) *n.* infestation by trichinae transmitted by eating contaminated pork

trichomonas (trikəˈmōnəs) *n.* single-celled organism causing disease in reproductive organs of cattle and humans

trichromatic (trīkrōˈmatik) *or* **trichromic** (trīˈkrōmik) *a.* **1.** involving combination of three primary colors **2.** of normal color vision **3.** having three colors —**triˈchromatism** *n.*

trick (trik) *n.* **1.** deception **2.** prank **3.** mannerism **4.** illusion **5.** feat of skill or cunning **6.** knack **7.** cards played in one round **8.** spell of duty —*vt.* **9.** cheat, hoax, deceive —ˈ**trickery** *n.* —ˈ**trickster** *n.* —ˈ**tricky** *a.* **1.** difficult, needing careful handling **2.** crafty

trickle (ˈtrikəl) *v.* (cause to) run, flow, move in thin stream or drops

tricolor (ˈtrīkulər) *a.* **1.** three-colored —*n.* **2.** tricolor flag (*eg* of France)

tricot (ˈtrēkō) *n.* thin rayon or nylon fabric knitted or resembling knitting

tricycle (ˈtrīsikəl) *n.* three-wheeled vehicle operated by pedals

trident (ˈtrīdənt) *n.* three-pronged fork or spear

triennial (trīˈeniəl) *a.* happening every, or lasting, three years

trifle (ˈtrīfəl) *n.* **1.** insignificant thing or matter **2.** small amount **3.** dessert of sponge cake, whipped cream *etc.* —*vi.* **4.** toy **5.** act, speak idly —ˈ**trifler** *n.* —ˈ**trifling** *a.* **1.** insignificant, petty **2.** frivolous; idle

trig. **1.** trigonometry **2.** trigonometrical —**trig station** *or* **point** landmark which surveyor uses

trigeminal neuralgia (trīˈjeminəl) nerve disorder marked by attacks of severe stabbing pains of the face (*also* **tic douloureux**)

trigger (ˈtrigər) *n.* **1.** catch which releases spring, *esp.* to fire gun —*vt.* **2.** (*oft. with* off) start, set in action *etc.* —**trigger-happy** *a.* tending to irresponsible, ill-considered behavior, *esp.* in use of firearms

trigonometry (trigəˈnomitri) *n.* branch of mathematics dealing with relations of sides and angles of triangles —**trigonoˈmetrical** *a.*

trike (trīk) tricycle

trilateral (trīˈlatərəl) *a.* having three sides —**triˈlaterally** *adv.*

trilby (ˈtrilbi) *n.* man's soft felt hat

trill (tril) *vi.* **1.** sing with quavering voice **2.** sing lightly —*n.* **3.** such singing or sound

trillion (ˈtrilyən) *n.* in the U.S. and France, 10^{12}: the numeral 1 followed by 12 zeros; in Britain and Germany, 10^{18}: the numeral 1 followed by 18 zeros

trilobite (ˈtrīləbīt) *n.* extinct marine arthropod abundant in Paleozoic times, having segmented exoskeleton divided into three parts —**trilobitic** (trīləˈbitik) *a.*

trilogy (ˈtriləji) *n.* series of three related (literary) works

trim (trim) *a.* **1.** neat, smart **2.** slender **3.** in good order —*vt.* **4.** shorten slightly by cutting, prune **5.** decorate **6.** adjust **7.** put in good order **8.** adjust balance of (ship, aircraft) (**-mm-**) —*n.* **9.** decoration **10.** order, state of being trim **11.** haircut that neatens existing style **12.** upholstery, accessories in automobile **13.** edging material, as inside woodwork round doors, windows *etc.* —**'trimming** *n.* (*oft. pl.*) decoration, addition

trimaran ('trīməran) *n.* three-hulled vessel

Trinidad and Tobago ('trinidad; tə'bāgō) country lying in the Caribbean off the coast of Venezuela comprising the islands of Trinidad and Tobago —**Trinidadian** (trini'dādiən, -'dadiən) *n./a.*

trinitrotoluene (trīnītrō'tolyōōēn) *or* **trinitrotoluol** (trīnītrō'tolyōōol) *n.* a high explosive derived from toluene

trinity ('triniti) *n.* **1.** the state of being threefold **2.** (**T-**) the three persons of the Godhead —**trini'tarian** *n./a.* —**Trinity Sunday** Sunday after Whit Sunday

trinket ('tringkit) *n.* small ornament, trifle —**'trinketry** *n.*

trio ('trēō) *n.* **1.** group of three **2.** music for three parts (*pl.* **-s**)

triode ('trīōd) *n. Electron.* three-electrode valve

trip (trip) *n.* **1.** (short) journey for pleasure **2.** stumble **3.** switch **4.** *inf.* hallucinatory experience caused by drug —*v.* **5.** (*oft. with* up) (cause to) stumble **6.** (cause to) make false step, mistake —*vi.* **7.** run lightly; skip; dance **8.** *inf.* take hallucinatory drugs —*vt.* **9.** operate (switch) (**-pp-**) —**'tripper** *n.* tourist

tripartite (trī'pärtīt) *a.* having, divided into three parts

tripe (trīp) *n.* **1.** stomach of cow *etc.* prepared for food **2.** *inf.* nonsense

triphosphopyridine nucleotide (trīfosfō'pīridēn 'nyōōkliətīd, 'nōōkliətīd) coenzyme found in tissues of body where it participates in energy-producing reactions

triplane ('trīplān) *n.* airplane with three wings one above another

triple ('tripəl) *a.* **1.** threefold —*v.* **2.** treble —**'triplet** *n.* **1.** three of a kind **2.** one of three offspring born at one birth —**'triply** *adv.* —**triple jump** athletic event in which competitor has to perform hop, step and jump in continuous movement —**triple point** *Chem.* temperature and pressure at which three phases of substance are in equilibrium

triplicate ('triplikit) *a.* **1.** threefold —*vt.* ('triplikāt) **2.** make threefold —*n.* **3.** state of being triplicate **4.** one of set of three copies —**tripli'cation** *n.*

tripod ('trīpod) *n.* stool, stand *etc.* with three feet

tripos ('trīpos) *n.* degree examination at Cambridge University, England

triptych ('triptik) *n.* carving, set of pictures, *esp.* altarpiece, on three panels hinged side by side

trireme ('trīrēm) *n.* ancient Gr. galley with three banks of oars on each side

trisect ('trīsekt, trī'sekt) *vt.* divide into three (equal) parts —**tri'section** *n.*

trite (trīt) *a.* hackneyed, banal

tritium ('tritiəm) *n.* radioactive isotope of hydrogen

triumph ('trīəmf) *n.* **1.** great success **2.** victory **3.** exultation —*vi.* **4.** achieve great success or victory **5.** exult —**tri'umphal** *a.* celebrating triumph —**tri'umphant** *a.* experiencing or displaying triumph

triumvirate (trī'umvirit) *n.* joint rule by three persons

trivalent (trī'vāIənt) *a. Chem.* **1.** having valency of three **2.** having three valencies (*also* **ter'valent**) —**tri'valency** *n.*

trivet ('trivit) *n.* metal bracket or stand for pot or kettle

trivia ('triviə) *pl.n.* petty, unimportant things, details —**'trivial** *a.* **1.** of little consequence **2.** commonplace —**trivi'ality** *n.*

trochee ('trōkē) *n.* in verse, foot of two syllables, first long and second short —**tro'chaic** *a.*

trod (trod) *pt. of* TREAD —**'trodden** *or* **trod** *pp. of* TREAD

troglodyte ('trogləd̄īt) *n.* cave dweller

troika ('troikə) *n.* **1.** Russian vehicle drawn by three horses abreast **2.** three horses harnessed abreast **3.** triumvirate

Trojan ('trōjən) *n./a.* **1.** (inhabitant) of ancient Troy **2.** steadfast or persevering (person) —**Trojan Horse 1.** *Gr. myth.* hollow wooden figure of horse left outside Troy by Greeks and dragged inside by Trojans. Men concealed inside opened city to final Greek assault **2.** trap intended to undermine enemy

troll[1] (trōl) *vt.* fish for by dragging baited hook or lure through water

troll[2] (trōl) *n.* supernatural being in Scandinavian mythology and folklore

trolley bus ('troli) bus deriving power from overhead electric wire but not running on rails

trollop ('troləp) *n.* promiscuous or slovenly woman

trombone (trom'bōn) *n.* deep-toned brass wind instrument with sliding tube —**trom'bonist** *n.*

trompe l'oeil (trömp'ləi) painting that creates the illusion of being that which is depicted

troop (trōōp) *n.* **1.** group or crowd of persons or animals **2.** unit of cavalry —*pl.* **3.** soldiers —*vi.* **4.** move in a troop, flock —**'trooper** *n.* **1.** mounted policeman **2.** state policeman

trope (trōp) *n.* figure of speech

trophy ('trōfi) *n.* **1.** prize, award, as shield, cup **2.** memorial of victory, hunt *etc.*

-trophy (*n. comb. form*) certain type of nourishment or growth, as in *dystrophy* —**-trophic** (*a. comb. form*)

tropic ('tropik) *n.* **1.** either of two lines of latitude at 23½° N (**tropic of Cancer**) or 23½° S (**tropic of Capricorn**) —*pl.* **2.** area of earth's surface between these lines —'**tropical** *a.* **1.** pert. to, within tropics **2.** (of climate) very hot —**tropical medicine** branch of medicine dealing with diseases of tropics and subtropics —'**tropicbird** *n.* tropical aquatic bird having long tail feathers and white plumage with black markings

tropism ('trōpizəm) *n.* response of organism, *esp.* plant, to external stimulus by growth in direction determined by stimulus

troposphere ('trōpəsfēər, 'trop-) *n.* lowest atmospheric layer, in which air temperature decreases normally with height at about 6.5°C per km

trot (trot) *vi.* **1.** (of horse) move at medium pace, lifting feet in diagonal pairs **2.** (of person) run easily with short strides (**-tt-**) —*n.* **3.** trotting, jog —'**trotter** *n.* **1.** horse trained to trot in race **2.** foot of certain animals, *esp.* pig

troth (troth, trōth, trōth) *n. obs.* fidelity, truth

Trotskyism ('trotskiizəm) *n.* theory of communism of Leon Trotsky, Russian revolutionary and writer, in which he called for immediate worldwide revolution by proletariat —'**Trotskyite** *or* '**Trotskyist** *n./a.*

troubadour ('trōōbədōr, -dōōər) *n.* one of school of early poets and singers

trouble ('trubəl) *n.* **1.** state or cause of mental distress, pain, inconvenience *etc.* **2.** care, effort —*vt.* **3.** be trouble to —*vi.* **4.** be inconvenienced, concerned **5.** be agitated **6.** take pains; exert oneself —'**troublesome** *a.* —'**troubleshooter** *n.* person who locates cause of trouble and removes or treats it, as in running of machine —'**troubleshooting** *n./a.*

trough (trof) *n.* **1.** long open vessel, *esp.* for animals' food or water **2.** hollow between two waves **3.** *Met.* area of low pressure

trounce (trowns) *vt.* beat thoroughly, thrash

troupe (trōōp) *n.* company of performers —'**trouper** *n.* **1.** member of troupe **2.** dependable worker or associate

trousers ('trowzərz) *pl.n.* two-legged outer garment with legs reaching to the ankles

trousseau ('trōōsō) *n.* bride's outfit of clothing (*pl.* **-seaux** (-sōz), **-s**)

trout (trowt) *n.* freshwater sport and food fish

trowel ('trowəl) *n.* small tool like spade for spreading mortar, lifting plants *etc.*

troy weight (troi) system of weights based on ounce of 20 pennyweights or 480 grains to the ounce and 12 ounces to the pound

truant ('trōōənt) *n.* **1.** one absent without leave, *esp.* child so absenting himself or herself from school —*a.* **2.** being or relating to truant —'**truancy** *n.*

Trubenizing ('trōōbənīzing) *n.* (formerly, trade name for) process for making collars and cuffs on shirts permanently stiff

truce (trōōs) *n.* **1.** temporary cessation of fighting **2.** respite, lull

truck[1] (truk) *n.* wheeled (motor) vehicle for moving goods

truck[2] (truk) *n.* **1.** barter **2.** dealing (*esp. in* **have no truck with**) **3.** payment of workmen in goods **4.** *inf.* rubbish

truckle ('trukəl) *vi.* yield weakly

truckle bed low bed on wheels, stored under larger bed

truculent ('trukyələnt) *a.* aggressive, defiant

trudge (truj) *vi.* **1.** walk laboriously —*n.* **2.** laborious or wearisome walk

true (trōō) *a.* **1.** in accordance with facts **2.** faithful **3.** exact, correct **4.** genuine —'**truism** *n.* self-evident truth —'**truly** *adv.* **1.** exactly **2.** really **3.** sincerely —**truth** *n.* **1.** state of being true **2.** something that is true —'**truthful** *a.* **1.** accustomed to speak the truth **2.** accurate, exact —'**truthfully** *adv.* —**true-blue** *a.* unwaveringly or staunchly loyal —**true blue** one who is true-blue

truffle ('trufəl) *n.* **1.** edible fungus growing underground **2.** soft candy made of a chocolate mixture

truism ('trōōizəm) *n. see* TRUE

Truman ('trōōmən) *n.* **Harry S** the 33rd President of the U.S. (1945-53)

trump[1] (trump) *n.* **1.** card of suit temporarily ranking above others —*v.* **2.** play trump card on (plain suit) —**trump up** invent, concoct —**turn up** *or* **out trumps** turn out (unexpectedly) well, successfully

trump[2] (trump) *n.* **1.** trumpet **2.** blast on trumpet —**the last trump** final trumpet call on Day of Judgment

trumpery ('trumpəri) *a.* **1.** showy but worthless —*n.* **2.** worthless finery **3.** trash, rubbish

trumpet ('trumpit) *n.* **1.** metal wind instrument like horn —*vi.* **2.** blow trumpet **3.** make sound like one, as elephant —*vt.* **4.** proclaim, make widely known

truncate ('trungkāt, trung'kāt) *vt.* cut short —'**truncated** *a.* **1.** (of cone *etc.*) having apex or end removed by plane intersection **2.** shortened (as if) by cutting off (*also* '**truncate**)

truncheon ('trunchən) *n.* **1.** short thick club or baton **2.** staff of office or authority —*vt.* **3.** cudgel

trundle ('trundəl) *vt.* roll, as a thing on little wheels

trunk (trungk) *n.* **1.** main stem of tree **2.** person's body without or excluding head and limbs **3.** box for clothing *etc.* **4.** elephant's proboscis —*pl.* **5.** man's swimsuit —**trunk line** main line of railroad, canal, telephone *etc.*

truss (trus) *vt.* **1.** (*oft. with* up) fasten, tie —*n.* **2.** support **3.** medical device of belt *etc.* to hold hernia in place **4.** package, bundle (of hay *etc.*) **5.** cluster of flowers at end of single stalk

trust (trust) *n.* **1.** confidence **2.** firm belief **3.** reliance **4.** combination of producers to reduce competition and keep up prices **5.** care, responsibility **6.** property held for another —*vt.* **7.** rely on **8.** believe in **9.** consign for care —*v.* **10.** expect, hope —**trus'tee** *n.* one legally holding property on another's behalf —**trus'teeship** *n.* —**'trustful** *a.* **1.** inclined to trust **2.** credulous —**'trustworthy** *a.* **1.** reliable, dependable, honest **2.** safe —**'trusty** *a.* **1.** faithful **2.** reliable —**trust fund** money, securities *etc.* held in trust

Trust Territory of the Pacific islands and atolls including the Carolines, the Marshalls and Marianas in the Pacific Ocean, a UN trust territory administered by the U.S.

truth (trōōth) *n. see* TRUE

try (trī) *vi.* **1.** attempt, endeavor —*vt.* **2.** attempt **3.** test **4.** make demands upon **5.** investigate (case) **6.** examine (person) in court of law **7.** purify; refine (as metals) (**tried, 'trying**) —*n.* **8.** attempt, effort **9.** *Rugby* score gained by touching ball down over opponent's goal line —**tried** *a.* **1.** proved **2.** afflicted —**'trying** *a.* **1.** upsetting, annoying **2.** difficult —**'tryout** *n.* —**trysail** ('trīsāl; *Naut.* 'trīsəl) *n.* small fore-and-aft sail set on sailing vessel in foul weather to help keep her head to wind —**try on 1.** put on (garment) to find out whether it fits *etc.* **2.** *inf.* attempt to deceive or fool (*esp. in* **try it on**) —**try out 1.** test; put to experimental use **2.** (*usu. with* for) (of actor *etc.*) undergo test; submit (actor *etc.*) to test to determine suitability for role *etc.*

trypanosome (tri'panəsōm) *n.* protozoon with spindle-shaped body and single flagellum, blood parasite of vertebrates causing disease, *eg* sleeping sickness —**African trypanosomiasis** (tripanəsə'mīəsis) sleeping sickness transmitted by tsetse fly

tryst (trist) *n.* **1.** appointment to meet **2.** place appointed

tsar (zär) *n. see* CZAR

tsetse fly ('tsetsi) Afr. bloodsucking fly whose bite transmits various diseases to man and animals

T-shirt *or* **tee shirt** *n.* informal (short-sleeved) sweater, *usu.* of cotton

tsimmes ('tsimis) *n.* **1.** a fruit or vegetable stew **2.** a state of confusion **3.** a complicated or overelaborated procedure

tsores *or* **tsuris** ('tsorəs) *pl.n.* (*sometimes with sing. v.*) *inf.* troubles, worries, afflictions

tsp. teaspoon

T square T-shaped ruler for drawing parallel lines, right angles *etc.*

tub (tub) *n.* **1.** open wooden vessel like bottom half of barrel **2.** small round container **3.** bath **4.** *inf.* old, slow ship *etc.* —**'tubby** *a.* **1.** plump **2.** shaped like tub

tuba ('tyōōbə, 'tōōbə) *n.* valved brass wind instrument of low pitch

tube (tyōōb, tōōb) *n.* **1.** long, narrow, hollow cylinder **2.** flexible cylinder with cap to hold liquids, pastes **3.** **UK** (*sometimes* **T-**) underground electric railway, *esp.* in London **4.** *sl.* television set —**'tubing** *n.* **1.** tubes collectively **2.** length of tube **3.** system of tubes **4.** fabric in form of tube —**'tubular** *a.* like tube

tuber ('tyōōbər, 'tōōbər) *n.* swollen stem or root, usu. underground, of plant —**'tuberous** *a.*

tubercle ('tyōōbərkəl, 'tōōbərkəl) *n.* **1.** any small rounded nodule on skin *etc.* **2.** small lesion of tissue, *esp.* produced by tuberculosis —**tu'bercular** *a.* —**tu'berculin** *n.* extraction from bacillus used to test for and treat tuberculosis —**tubercu'losis** *n.* bacterial disease affecting lungs, skin, lymph glands, brain and blood stream (*also* **consumption, phthisis**)

tuck (tuk) *vt.* **1.** push, fold into small space **2.** gather, stitch in folds **3.** draw, roll together —*n.* **4.** stitched fold **5.** *inf.* food —**'tucker** *n.* strip of linen or lace formerly worn across bosom by women —**tuck in 1.** put to bed and make snug **2.** thrust loose ends or sides of (something) into confining space **3.** *inf.* eat, *esp.* heartily

Tudor ('tyōōdər, 'tōōdər) *a.* **1.** of the English royal house ruling 1485-1603 **2.** in, resembling style of this period, *esp.* of architecture

Tues. Tuesday

Tuesday ('tyōōzdi, 'tōōzdi) *n.* third day of week

tufa ('tyōōfə, 'tōōfə) *n.* porous rock formed as deposit from springs *etc.*

tuff (tuf) *n.* hard volcanic rock consisting of consolidated fragments of lava

tuffet ('tufit) *n.* small mound or seat

tuft (tuft) *n.* bunch of feathers, threads *etc.*

tug (tug) *vt.* **1.** pull hard or violently **2.** haul **3.** jerk forward (**-gg-**) —*n.* **4.** violent pull **5.** ship used to tow other vessels —**tug of war** contest in which two teams pull against one another on a rope

tuition (tyōō'ishən, tōō-) *n.* **1.** teaching, instruction **2.** private coaching —**tu'itional** *a.*

tularemia (tyōōlə'rēmiə, tōōlə-) *n.* bacterial disease transmitted to humans by contact, ingestion and insects from infected rabbits, rodents and other wild animals

tulip ('tyōōlip, 'tōōlip) *n.* any of several bulbous plants native to Asia with bright cup-shaped flowers —**tulip tree** N Amer. forest tree with tulip-shaped greenish-yellow flowers and long conelike fruits

tulle (tōōl) *n.* kind of fine thin silk or lace

tullibee ('tuləbē) *n.* Canad. whitefish

tumble ('tumbəl) *v.* **1.** (cause to) fall, roll, twist *etc.*, *esp.* in play —*vt.* **2.** rumple, disturb

—*n.* **3.** fall **4.** somersault —**'tumbler** *n.* **1.** stemless drinking glass **2.** acrobat **3.** spring catch in lock —**tumble-down** *a.* dilapidated —**tumble to** *inf.* realize, understand

tumbril *or* **tumbrel** ('tumbrəl) *n.* open cart for taking victims of French Revolution to guillotine

tumefy ('tyo͞omifī, 'to͞o-) *v.* (cause to) swell —**tu'mescence** *n.* —**tu'mescent** *a.* (becoming) swollen

tummy ('tumi) *n. inf.* stomach

tumor ('tyo͞omər, 'to͞omər) *n.* abnormal growth in or on body

tumult ('tyo͞omult) *n.* violent uproar, commotion —**tu'multuous** *a.*

tumulus ('tyo͞omyələs, 'to͞o-) *n.* burial mound, barrow (*pl.* **-li** (-lī))

tun (tun) *n.* **1.** large cask **2.** measure of liquid

tuna

tuna ('tyo͞onə, 'to͞onə) *n.* any of various large marine food fishes

tundra ('tundrə) *n.* vast treeless zone between icecap and timber line of N Amer. and Eurasia

tune (tyo͞on, to͞on) *n.* **1.** melody **2.** quality of being in pitch **3.** adjustment of musical instrument **4.** concord **5.** frame of mind —*vt.* **6.** put in tune **7.** adjust (machine) to obtain most efficient running **8.** adjust (radio circuit) —**'tuneful** *a.* —**'tunefully** *adv.* —**'tuner** *n.* —**tune-up** *n.* adjustments to engine to improve performance —**tuning fork** two-pronged metal fork that when struck produces pure note of constant specified pitch —**tune in** adjust (radio, television) to receive (a station, program) —**tune up 1.** adjust (musical instrument) to particular pitch **2.** tune (instruments) to common pitch **3.** adjust (engine) in (motor vehicle) to improve performance

tungsten ('tungstən) *n. Chem.* metallic element *Symbol* W, at. wt. 183.9, at. no. 74

tunic ('tyo͞onik, 'to͞onik) *n.* **1.** close-fitting jacket forming part of uniform **2.** loose hiplength or kneelength garment

Tunisia (tyo͞o'nēzhiə, to͞o-) *n.* country in Africa bounded north and east by the Mediterranean Sea, west by Algeria and south by Libya —**Tu'nisian** *n./a.*

tunnel ('tunəl) *n.* **1.** underground passage, *esp.* as track for railroad line **2.** burrow of a mole *etc.* —*vt.* **3.** make tunnel through —*vi.* **4.** (*with* through, under *etc.*) make or force a way (through or under something) —**'tunneler** *n.*

tup (tup) *n.* male sheep, ram

tupik ('to͞opək) *n.* **C** tent used as summer shelter by Eskimos

turban ('tərbən) *n.* **1.** in certain countries, man's headdress, made by coiling length of cloth round head or a cap **2.** woman's hat like this

turbid ('tərbid) *a.* **1.** muddy, not clear **2.** disturbed —**tur'bidity** *or* **'turbidness** *n.*

turbine ('tərbin, -bīn) *n.* rotary engine driven by steam, gas, water or air playing on blades

turbo- (*comb. form*) of, relating to, or driven by a turbine, as in *turbofan*

turbofan ('tərbōfan) *n.* **1.** bypass engine in which large fan driven by turbine forces air rearward around exhaust gases to increase propulsive thrust **2.** aircraft driven by turbofans **3.** fan in such engine

turbojet ('tərbōjet) *n.* **1.** turbojet engine **2.** aircraft powered by turbojet engines —**turbojet engine** gas turbine in which exhaust gases provide propulsive thrust to drive aircraft

turboprop ('tərbōprop) *n.* **1.** gas turbine for driving aircraft propeller **2.** aircraft powered by turboprops

turbot ('tərbət) *n.* large European flatfish

turbulent ('tərbyələnt) *a.* **1.** in commotion **2.** swirling **3.** riotous —**'turbulence** *n. Met.* instability of atmosphere causing gusty air currents *etc.*

tureen (tə'rēn) *n.* serving dish for soup

turf (tərf) *n.* **1.** short grass with earth bound to it by matted roots **2.** grass, *esp.* as lawn (*pl.* **-s, turves**) **3.** territory, *esp.* area claimed by juvenile gang —*vt.* **4.** lay with turf —**turf accountant** bookmaker —**the turf 1.** horse racing **2.** racecourse —**turf out** *inf.* dismiss, throw out

turgid ('tərjid) *a.* **1.** swollen, inflated **2.** bombastic —**tur'gescent** *a.* —**tur'gidity** *n.*

turkey ('tərki) *n.* **1.** large bird reared for its flesh **2.** *inf.* unsuccessful theatrical performance. **3.** *sl.* stupid, incompetent or unappealing person

Turkey ('tərki) *n.* country in Europe and Asia bounded west by the Aegean Sea and Greece, north by Bulgaria and the Black Sea, east by the U.S.S.R. and Iran and south by Iraq, Syria and the Mediterranean —**Turk** *n.* —**'Turkic** *a.* of the branch of Altaic stretching from northern Siberia to Turkey —**'Turkish** *n./a.* **1.** of Turkey —*n.* **2.** language of Turkey which is a Turkic language —**Turkish bath** steam bath —**Turkish coffee** very strong black coffee —**Turkish delight** gelatin flavored and coated with powdered sugar —**Turkish towel** towel made of terry cloth

Turkoman *or* **Turcoman** ('tərkəmən) *n.* member of group of peoples living in the Turkmen, Uzbek and Kazakh republics of the U.S.S.R. (*pl.* **-s**)

Turks and Caicos Islands ('kākəs) crown

colony of the United Kingdom forming an archipelago southeast of the Bahamas

turmeric ('tərmərik) *n.* **1.** Asian plant **2.** powdered root of this used as dye, medicine and condiment

turmoil ('tərmoil) *n.* confusion and bustle, commotion

turn (tərn) *v.* **1.** move around, rotate **2.** change, reverse, alter position or direction (of) —*vi.* **3.** (*oft. with* into) change in nature, character *etc.* **4.** (of milk) become rancid or sour —*vt.* **5.** make, shape on lathe —*n.* **6.** act of turning **7.** inclination **8.** period, spell **9.** turning **10.** short walk **11.** (part of) rotation **12.** performance —'**turner** *n.* —'**turning** *n.* road, path leading off main route —'**turnabout** *n.* **1.** act of turning so as to face different direction **2.** reversal of opinion *etc.* —'**turncoat** *n.* one who forsakes his party or principles —**turning circle** smallest circle in which vehicle can turn —**turning point 1.** moment when course of events is changed **2.** point at which there is change in direction or motion —'**turnkey** *n. obs.* keeper of keys, *esp.* in prison; warder, jailer —**turn-off** *n.* **1.** road *etc.* branching off from main thoroughfare **2.** something or someone that turns one off —**turn-on** *n.* something or someone that turns one on —'**turnout** *n.* **1.** number of people appearing for some purpose, occasion **2.** way in which person is dressed, equipped —'**turnover** *n.* **1.** total sales made by business over certain period **2.** rate at which staff leave and are replaced **3.** small pasty —'**turnpike** *n.* highway with tollgates —'**turnstile** *n.* revolving gate for controlling admission of people —'**turnstone** *n.* shore bird that lifts up stones in search of food —'**turntable** *n.* revolving platform, *esp.* of phonograph —**turn-up** *n.* unexpected or chance occurrence —**turn down** refuse —**turn off 1.** leave (road *etc.*) **2.** (of road *etc.*) deviate from (another road *etc.*) **3.** cause (something) to cease operating by turning knob *etc.* **4.** *inf.* cause (person *etc.*) to feel dislike or distaste for (something) —**turn on 1.** cause (something) to operate by turning knob *etc.* **2.** depend or hinge on **3.** become hostile; retaliate **4.** *inf.* produce (charm *etc.*) suddenly or automatically **5.** *sl.* arouse emotionally or sexually **6.** *sl.* take or become intoxicated by drugs **7.** *sl.* introduce to drugs —**turn up 1.** appear **2.** be found **3.** increase (flow, volume)

turnip ('tərnip) *n.* plant with globular root used as food

turpentine ('tərpəntīn) *n.* **1.** resin got from certain trees **2.** oil, spirits made from this

turpitude ('tərpityōōd, -tōōd) *n.* depravity

turps (tərps) turpentine

turquoise *or* **turquois** ('tərkwoiz, -koiz) *n.* **1.** bluish-green or greenish-gray gemstone **2.** variable color averaging light greenish blue —**turquoise blue** color of the stone turquoise —**turquoise green** color averaging light bluish green

turret ('turit) *n.* **1.** small tower **2.** revolving armored tower for guns on warship, tank *etc.*

turtle ('tərtəl) *n.* sea tortoise —'**turtleneck** *n.* **1.** round high close-fitting neck on sweater **2.** sweater itself

turtledove ('tərtəlduv) *n.* **1.** Old World dove having brown plumage with speckled wings and long dark tail **2.** gentle or loving person

tusk (tusk) *n.* long pointed side tooth of certain animals (*eg* elephant, wild boar *etc.*) —'**tusker** *n.* animal with tusks fully developed

tussle ('tusəl) *n./vi.* fight, struggle

tussock ('tusək) *n.* **1.** clump of grass **2.** tuft —'**tussocky** *a.*

tutelage ('tyōōtilij, 'tōō-) *n.* act, office of tutor or guardian —'**tutelary** *or* '**tutelar** *a.*

tutor ('tyōōtər, 'tōōtər) *n.* **1.** one teaching individuals or small groups —*v.* **2.** teach thus —**tu'torial** *n.* period of instruction with tutor

tutti ('tōōti, 'tŏŏti) *a./adv. Mus.* to be performed by whole orchestra, choir *etc.*

tutti-frutti (tōōti'frōōti) *n.* ice cream containing small pieces of candied fruits

tutu ('tōōtōō) *n.* short, stiff skirt worn by ballerinas

Tuvalu (tōō'välōō) *n.* country lying in South Pacific comprising nine islands lying between 5°30' and 11° S latitude and 180° E longitude —**Tuva'luan** *a./n.*

tu-whit tu-whoo (tə'wit tə'wōō) imitation of sound made by owl

tuxedo (tuk'sēdō) *n.* semiformal evening suit for men (*pl.* **-s**)

TV 1. television **2.** *sl.* transvestite

TVA Tennessee Valley Authority

twaddle ('twodəl) *n.* silly talk

twain (twān) *n. obs.* two —**in twain** asunder

twang (twang) *n.* **1.** vibrating metallic sound **2.** nasal speech —*v.* **3.** (cause to) make such sounds

tweak (twēk) *vt.* **1.** pinch and twist or pull —*n.* **2.** a tweaking

twee (twē) *a. inf.* excessively sentimental, sweet, pretty

tweed (twēd) *n.* **1.** rough-surfaced cloth used for clothing —*pl.* **2.** suit of tweed —'**tweedy** *a.* **1.** of tweed **2.** showing fondness for hearty outdoor life, usu. associated with wearers of tweeds

tweet (twēt) *n./vi.* chirp —'**tweeter** *n.* loudspeaker reproducing high-frequency sounds

tweezers ('twēzərz) *pl.n.* small forceps or tongs

twelve (twelv) *n./a.* cardinal number two more than ten —**twelfth** *a./n.* ordinal number —**Twelfth Day** Jan. 6th, twelfth day after Christmas; feast of Epiphany —**twelve-tone** *a.* of type of serial music which uses as musical material tone row formed by 12 semitones of chromatic scale

twenty ('twenti) *n./a.* cardinal number, twice ten —'**twentieth** *a./n.* ordinal number —**twenty-four-hour time** measuring day beginning at midnight expressed as 0000 used widely in scientific work, in operations of the armed forces and in all travel timetables in Europe —**twenty questions** word-guessing parlor game in which guesser attempts to discover word selected by other players within 20 questions —**twenty-twenty** *or* **20/20 vision** normal standard of vision

twerp *or* **twirp** (twərp) *n. inf.* silly person

twice (twīs) *adv.* two times

twiddle ('twidəl) *v.* **1.** fiddle —*vt.* **2.** twist

twig[1] (twig) *n.* small branch, shoot

twig[2] (twig) *v. inf.* notice; understand (**-gg-**)

twilight ('twīlīt) *n.* soft light after sunset —'**twilit** *a.* —**twilight zone 1.** inner-city area where houses have become dilapidated **2.** any indefinite or transitional condition or area

twill (twil) *n.* fabric woven so as to have surface of parallel ridges

twin (twin) *n.* **1.** one of pair, *esp.* of two children born together —*a.* **2.** being a twin —*v.* **3.** pair, be paired

twine (twīn) *v.* **1.** twist, coil round —*n.* **2.** string, cord

twinge (twinj) *n.* **1.** momentary sharp, shooting pain **2.** qualm

twinkle ('twingkəl) *vi.* **1.** shine with dancing or quivering light, sparkle —*n.* **2.** twinkling **3.** flash **4.** gleam of amusement in eyes —'**twinkling** *n.* very brief time

twirl (twərl) *v.* **1.** turn or twist round quickly **2.** whirl —*vt.* **3.** twiddle —*n.* **4.** rotating; being rotated; whirl, twist **5.** something wound around or twisted; coil **6.** written flourish

twist (twist) *v.* **1.** make, become spiral, by turning with one end fast **2.** distort, change **3.** wind —*n.* **4.** thing twisted **5.** dance popular in 1960s, in which dancers vigorously twist the hips —'**twister** *n. inf.* swindler —'**twisty** *a.*

twit (twit) *n.* **1.** *inf.* foolish person —*vt.* **2.** taunt (**-tt-**)

twitch (twich) *v.* **1.** give momentary sharp pull or jerk (to) —*n.* **2.** such pull or jerk **3.** spasmodic jerk, spasm

twitch grass *see* QUACK GRASS

twitter ('twitər) *vi.* **1.** (of birds) utter succession of tremulous sounds —*n.* **2.** such succession of notes

two (tōō) *n./a.* cardinal number, one more than one —'**twofold** *a./adv.* —'**twosome** *n.* **1.** two together, *esp.* two people **2.** match between two people —**two-edged** *a.* **1.** having two cutting edges **2.** (*esp.* of remark) having two interpretations —**two-faced** *a.* **1.** double-dealing, deceitful **2.** with two faces —**two-ply** *a.* **1.** made of two layers, strands *etc.* —*n.* **2.** two-ply knitting yarn *etc.* —**two-step** *n.* **1.** ballroom dance in duple time **2.** music for such dance —**two-stroke** *a.* (of internal-combustion engine) making one explosion to every two strokes of piston —**two-time** *v. inf.* deceive (someone, *esp.* lover) by carrying on relationship with another —**two-timer** *n.*

TX Texas

-ty[1] (*comb. form*) multiple of ten, as in *sixty, seventy*

-ty[2] (*comb. form*) state, condition, quality, as in *cruelty*

tycoon (tī'kōōn) *n.* powerful, influential businessman

tyke *or* **tike** (tīk) *n.* **1.** *inf.* small, cheeky child **2.** small (mongrel) dog

Tyler ('tīlər) *n.* **John.** the 10th President of the U.S. (1841-45)

tympani ('timpəni) *pl.n. see* TIMPANI

tympanum ('timpənəm) *n.* **1.** cavity of middle ear **2.** tympanic membrane **3.** any diaphragm resembling that in middle ear in function **4.** *Archit.* recessed space, *esp.* triangular, bounded by cornices of pediment **5.** recessed space bounded by arch and lintel of doorway or window below it **6.** *Mus.* drum **7.** scoop wheel for raising water (*pl.* **-s, -na** (-nə)) —**tym'panic** *a.* —**tympanic membrane** thin membrane separating external ear from middle ear

Tynwald ('tinwəld, 'tīn-) *n.* Parliament of Isle of Man

type (tīp) *n.* **1.** class, sort **2.** model; pattern **3.** characteristic build **4.** specimen **5.** block bearing letter used for printing **6.** such pieces collectively —*vt.* **7.** print with typewriter **8.** typify **9.** classify —'**typist** *n.* one who operates typewriter —'**typo** *n. inf.* error in typing —'**typecast** *vt.* cast (actor) in same kind of role continually —'**typeface** *n.* **1.** printing surface of any type character **2.** style or design of character on type (*also* **face**) —'**typescript** *n.* typewritten document or copy —'**typesetter** *n.* **1.** person who sets type; compositor **2.** typesetting machine —'**typewrite** *v.* —'**typewriter** *n.* keyed writing machine

-type (*comb. form*) **1.** type, form, as in *archetype* **2.** printing type; photographic process, as in *collotype*

typhoid ('tīfoid) *n.* **1.** acute infectious disease, affecting *esp.* intestines —*a., also* **ty'phoidal 2.** resembling typhus —'**typhus** *n.* rickettsial disease occurring in epidemic (louse-borne) and endemic (flea-borne from mice and rats) forms —**Typhoid Mary** ('māəri) person who is an unknowing source of contamination

typhoon (tī'fōōn) *n.* violent tropical storm or cyclone —**typhonic** (tī'fonik) *a.*

typical ('tipikəl) *or* **typic** *a.* **1.** true to type **2.** characteristic —'**typically** *adv.*

typify ('tipifī) *vt.* serve as type or model of (**-ified, -ifying**)

typography (tī'pogrəfi) *n.* **1.** art of printing

2. style of printing —**ty'pographer** *n.* —**typo'graphical** *a.*

tyrannosaur (ti'ranəsör) *or* **tyrannosaurus** (tiranə'sörəs) *n.* large carnivorous two-footed dinosaur common in N Amer. in Upper Jurassic and Cretaceous times

tyrant ('tīrənt) *n.* **1.** oppressive or cruel ruler **2.** one who forces his will on others cruelly and arbitrarily —**tyrannical** (ti'ranikəl) *a.* **1.** despotic **2.** ruthless —**tyrannically** (ti'ranikəli) *adv.* —**tyrannicide** (ti'ranisīd) *n.* **1.** slayer of tyrant **2.** his deed —**tyrannize** ('tirənīz) *v.* exert ruthless or tyrannical authority (over) —**tyrannous** ('tirənəs) *a.* —**tyranny** ('tirəni) *n.* despotism

Tyrian ('tiriən) *n.* **1.** native of ancient Tyre, port in S Lebanon and center of ancient Phoenician culture —*a.* **2.** of ancient Tyre

tyro ('tīrō) *n.* novice, beginner (*pl.* **-s**)

tzar (zär) *n. see* CZAR

U

u *or* **U** (yōō) *n.* **1.** 21st letter of English alphabet **2.** any of several speech sounds represented by this letter, as in *mute, cut* or *minus* **3.** something shaped like U (*pl.* **u's, U's** *or* **Us**)

U **1.** united **2.** unionist **3.** university **4.** **UK** universal (used to describe category of film certified as suitable for viewing by anyone) **5.** *Chem.* uranium

U.A.E. United Arab Emirates

ubiquitous (yōō'bikwitəs) *a.* **1.** everywhere at once **2.** omnipresent —**u'biquity** *n.*

U-boat *n.* German submarine

u.c. *Print.* upper case

udder ('udər) *n.* milk-secreting organ of cow *etc.*

UFO unidentified flying object

Uganda (yōō'gandə, ōō'gandə; -'gän-) *n.* country in Africa bounded north by Sudan, east by Kenya, south by Tanzania and west by Zaïre —**U'gandan** *n./a.*

ugh (ug, əkh, ə) *interj.* exclamation of disgust, annoyance *etc.*

ugly ('ugli) *a.* **1.** unpleasant or repulsive to the sight, hideous **2.** ill-omened **3.** threatening —**'uglify** *v.* —**'ugliness** *n.* —**ugly duckling** person or thing, initially ugly or unpromising, that changes into something beautiful or admirable

UHF ultrahigh frequency

U.K. United Kingdom

ukase (yōō'kās, -'kāz) *n.* in imperial Russia, edict of czar

Ukrainian (yōō'krāniən) *a.* **1.** of Ukraine —*n.* **2.** East Slavonic language of Ukrainians **3.** native or inhabitant of Ukraine

ukulele (yōōkə'lāli) *n.* small four-stringed guitar, *esp.* of Hawaii

ulcer ('ulsər) *n.* open sore on skin, mucous membrane that is slow to heal —**'ulcerate** *v.* make, form ulcer(s) —**'ulcerated** *a.* —**ulce'ration** *n.* —**'ulcerative** *a.* —**'ulcerous** *a.* —**ulcerative colitis** inflammation of colon resulting in formation of ulcers

ulna ('ulnə) *n.* bone of the human forearm on the little finger side (*pl.* **ulnae** ('ulnē), **-s**)

Ulster ('ulstər) *n.* **1.** Northern Ireland **2.** (**u-**) man's heavy double-breasted overcoat —**'Ulsterite** *n.* —**'Ulsterman** *n.*

ult. **1.** ultimate **2.** ultimo

ulterior (ul'tēəriər) *a.* **1.** lying beneath, beyond what is revealed or evident (*eg* motives) **2.** situated beyond

ultimate ('ultimit) *a.* **1.** last **2.** highest **3.** most significant **4.** fundamental —**'ultimately** *adv.* —**ultimatum** (ulti'mātəm) *n.* **1.** final proposition **2.** final terms offered (*pl.* **-s, -ta** (-tə)) —**'ultimo** *adv.* in last month

ultra ('ultrə) *a.* **1.** extreme, *esp.* in beliefs or opinions —*n.* **2.** extremist

ultra- (*comb. form*) beyond, excessive(ly), extreme(ly) as in *ultramodern*

ultrahigh frequency (ultrə'hī) (band of) radio waves of very short wavelength

ultramarine (ultrəmə'rēn) *n.* blue pigment

ultrasonic (ultrə'sonik) *a.* of sound waves beyond the range of human ear —**ultra'sonics** *pl.n.* (*with sing. v.*) branch of physics concerned with ultrasonic waves (*also* **super'sonics**)

ultrasound ('ultrəsownd) *n.* ultrasonic waves, used in cleaning metallic parts, echo sounding, medical diagnosis *etc.*

ultraviolet (ultrə'vīəlit) *a.* of electromagnetic radiation, *eg* of sun *etc.*, beyond limit of visibility at violet end of spectrum

ululate ('ulyəlāt) *vi.* howl, wail —**'ululant** *a.* —**ulu'lation** *n.*

umbel ('umbəl) *n.* umbrella-like flower cluster with stalks springing from central point —**umbel'liferous** *a.*

umber ('umbər) *n.* dark brown pigment

umbilical (um'bilikəl) *a.* of (region of) navel —**umbilicus** (umbi'līkəs, um'bilikəs) *n.* **1.** *Biol.* hollow structure, such as cavity at base of gastropod shell **2.** *Anat.* navel (*pl.* **-bilici** (-bi'līkī, -sī; -'bilikī, -sī)) —**umbilical cord** **1.** cordlike structure connecting fetus with placenta of mother **2.** cord joining astronaut to spacecraft *etc.*

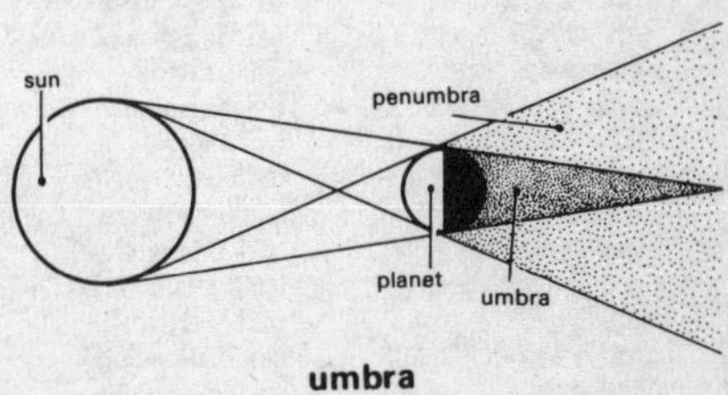

umbra

umbra ('umbrə) *n.* **1.** region of complete shadow due to obstruction of light by opaque object, *esp.* shadow cast by moon onto earth during solar eclipse **2.** darker inner region of sunspot (*pl.* **-brae** (-brē), **-s**) —**'umbral** *a.*

umbrage ('umbrij) *n.* offense, resentment (*esp. in* **give** *or* **take umbrage**)

umbrella (um'brelə) *n.* **1.** folding circular cover of nylon *etc.* on stick, carried in hand to protect against rain, heat of sun **2.** anything shaped or functioning like an umbrella

umiak ('o͞omiak) *n.* Eskimo boat made of skins, usu. propelled by paddles

umlaut ('o͝omlowt) *n.* **1.** mark (¨) placed over vowel in some languages, such as German **2.** *esp.* in Germanic languages, change of vowel within word caused by assimilating influence of vowel or semivowel in preceding or following syllable

umpire ('umpīər) *n.* **1.** person chosen to decide question, or to decide disputes and enforce rules in a game —*v.* **2.** act as umpire in or for (game *etc.*)

umpteen ('ump'tēn) *a. inf.* many —**ump'teenth** *n./a.*

UN United Nations

un- (*comb. form*) not, contrary to, opposite of, reversal of an action, removal from, release, deprivation. See the list below

unaccountable (unə'kowntəbəl) *a.* that cannot be explained

unaffected[1] (unə'fektid) *a.* unpretentious, natural —**unaf'fectedly** *adv.*

unaffected[2] (unə'fektid) *a.* not affected

unanimous (yo͞o'nanimәs) *a.* **1.** in complete agreement **2.** agreed by all —**una'nimity** *n.* —**u'nanimously** *adv.*

unassailable (unə'sāləbəl) *a.* **1.** able to withstand attack **2.** irrefutable —**unas'sailably** *adv.*

unassuming (unə'so͞oming) *a.* not pretentious, modest

unattached (unə'tacht) *a.* **1.** not connected with any specific thing, group *etc.* **2.** not engaged or married

unavailing (unə'vāling) *a.* useless, futile

unaware (unə'wāər) *a.* not aware, uninformed —**una'wares** *adv.* **1.** without previous warning **2.** unexpectedly

una'bated
una'bridged
unac'ceptable
unac'companied
unac'customed
unac'knowledged
unac'quainted
una'dorned
una'dulterated
unad'venturous
una'fraid
un'aided
unal'loyed
un'alterable
unam'biguous
un'answerable
unap'pealing
un'appetizing
unap'preciated
unap'proachable
un'armed
una'shamed
un'asked
unat'tainable
unat'tended
unat'tractive
un'authorized
una'vailable
un'balanced
un'bearable
un'beaten
unbe'coming
unbe'lievable
unbe'liever
unbe'lieving
un'biased

unbend (un'bend) *v.* **1.** release or be released from restraints of formality **2.** *inf.* relax (mind) or (of mind) become relaxed **3.** make or become straight from original bent shape (**-'bent, -'bending**) —**un'bending** *a.* **1.** rigid, inflexible **2.** characterized by sternness or severity

unbidden (un'bidən) *a.* **1.** not commanded; voluntary, spontaneous **2.** not invited

unbosom (un'bo͝ozəm) *vt.* tell or reveal (one's secrets *etc.*)

unbounded (un'bowndid) *a.* having no boundaries or limits —**un'boundedly** *adv.*

unbridled (un'brīdəld) *a.* **1.** with all restraints removed **2.** (of horse *etc.*) wearing no bridle

unburden (un'bərdən) *vt.* **1.** remove load or burden from **2.** relieve, make free (one's mind, oneself *etc.*) of worry *etc.* by revelation or confession

uncalled-for *a.* unnecessary; unwarranted

uncanny (un'kani) *a.* **1.** characterized by apparently supernatural wonder *etc.* **2.** beyond what is normal or expected

UNCIAL

uncial ('unshəl) *a.* **1.** of large letters, as used in Greek and Latin manuscripts of third to ninth centuries, that resemble modern capitals but are more rounded —*n.* **2.** uncial letter or manuscript —**'uncially** *adv.*

uncle ('ungkəl) *n.* **1.** brother of father or mother **2.** husband of aunt —**Uncle Sam** personification of American nation

uncompromising (un'komprəmīzing) *a.* not prepared to compromise —**un'compromisingly** *adv.*

unconscionable (un'konchənəbəl) *a.* **1.** unscrupulous, unprincipled **2.** excessive

unconscious (un'konchəs) *a.* **1.** insensible **2.** not aware **3.** not knowing **4.** of thoughts, memories *etc.* of which one is not normally

un'bind
un'blemished
un'blinking
un'block
un'bolt
un'born
un'breakable
un'broken
un'buckle
uncared-for
un'ceasing
un'censored
un'censured
un'certain
un'challenged
uncharacte'ristic
un'charitable
un'checked
un'christian
un'circumcised
un'civil
un'claimed
un'clear
un'clothe
un'cluttered
un'coil
un'combed
un'comfortable
uncom'mitted
un'common
uncom'municative
uncom'plaining
un'complicated
uncompli'mentary
uncon'cerned
uncon'ditional

aware —*n.* **5.** these thoughts —**un'consciously** *adv.* —**un'consciousness** *n.*

uncounted (un'kowntid) *a.* **1.** innumerable **2.** not counted

uncouth (un'ko͞oth) *a.* **1.** clumsy, boorish **2.** without ease or polish

uncover (un'kuvər) *vt.* **1.** remove cover, top *etc.* from **2.** reveal, disclose —*v.* **3.** take off (one's head covering), *esp.* as mark of respect

unction ('ungkshən) *n.* **1.** anointing **2.** excessive politeness **3.** soothing words or thoughts —'**unctuous** *a.* **1.** slippery, greasy **2.** oily in manner, ingratiating

undeceive (undi'sēv) *vt.* reveal truth to (someone mistaken, misled)

under ('undər) *prep.* **1.** below, beneath **2.** bound by, included in **3.** less than **4.** subjected to **5.** known by **6.** in the time of —*adv.* **7.** in lower place or condition —*a.* **8.** lower —**under way 1.** in progress **2.** *Naut.* in motion in direction headed

under- (*comb. form*) beneath, below, lower, too little, as in *underground, underbid.* See the list below

undera'chieve
under'bid *v.*
'underbid *n.*
'underclothes
under'do
under'done
underem'ployed
under'foot
'undergarment
under'lie
under'manned
under'nourish
under'paid
'underpants
'underpart
under'priced
under'sea
under'sexed
under'shoot
under'sized
'underskirt
under'staffed
under'state
under'value
under'water
under'weight

underage (undər'āj) *a.* below required age, *esp.* below legal age for voting or drinking

undercarriage ('undərkarij) *n.* landing gear of aircraft

uncon'firmed
uncon'nected
un'conquered
uncon'trollable
uncon'trolled
uncontro'versial
uncon'ventional
uncon'vincing
unco'operative
unco'ordinated
un'cork
uncor'roborated
un'couple
un'critical
un'crowned
un'cultivated
un'cultured
un'curbed
un'curl
un'damaged
un'daunted
unde'cided
unde'feated
unde'fended
unde'manding
undemo'cratic
unde'monstrative
unde'niable
unde'served
unde'serving
unde'sirable
unde'tected
unde'terred
unde'veloped
undi'minished
un'disciplined

undercoat ('undərkōt) *n.* coat of paint applied before top coat

undercover ('undərkuvər) *a.* done or acting in secret

undercurrent ('undərkurənt) *n.* **1.** current that lies beneath another current **2.** opinion, emotion *etc.* lying beneath apparent feeling or meaning

undercut (undər'kut) *v.* **1.** charge less than (competitor) in order to obtain trade **2.** cut away under part of (something) **3.** *Sport* hit (ball) in such a way as to impart backspin —*n.* ('undərkut) **4.** act of cutting underneath **5.** *Sport* stroke that imparts backspin to ball

underdeveloped (undərdi'veləpt) *a.* **1.** immature; undersized **2.** relating to societies lacking economical and industrial development necessary to advance **3.** *Photog.* (of film *etc.*) processed in developer for less than required time

underdog ('undərdog) *n.* **1.** losing competitor in contest *etc.* **2.** person in position of inferiority

underestimate (undər'estimāt) *vt.* **1.** make too low an estimate of **2.** think insufficiently highly of —*n.* (undər'estimit) **3.** too low an estimate —**underesti'mation** *n.*

underexpose (undərik'spōz) *vt.* **1.** *Photog.* expose (film *etc.*) for too short a period or with insufficient light **2.** fail to subject to appropriate publicity —**underex'posure** *n.*

undergo (undər'gō) *vt.* experience, endure, sustain (-'**went,** -'**gone,** -'**going**)

undergraduate (undər'grajo͞oit) *n.* student member of university or college who has not taken degree

underground ('undərgrownd) *a.* **1.** under the ground **2.** secret —*adv.* (undər'grownd) **3.** under earth's surface **4.** secretly —*n.* **5.** secret but organized resistance to government in power **6.** railway system under the ground

undergrowth ('undərgrōth) *n.* small trees, bushes *etc.* growing beneath taller trees in wood or forest

undis'covered
undis'puted
undis'turbed
un'drinkable
un'dying
un'earned
un'eatable
uneco'nomic
un'educated
une'motional
un'ending
un'equal
un'equaled
une'quivocal
un'ethical
un'even
une'ventful
unex'pected
unex'plained
un'failing
un'fair
un'faithful
unfa'miliar
un'fashionable
un'fasten
un'fathomable
un'favorable
un'feeling
un'feigned
un'finished
un'fit
un'flinching
un'fold
unfore'seen
unfor'gettable
unfor'givable

underhand (ˈundərhand) *a.* **1.** secret, sly **2.** *Sport* of style of throwing, bowling or serving in which hand is swung below shoulder level

underlay (undərˈlā) *vt.* **1.** place (something) under or beneath **2.** support by something laid beneath (**-ˈlaid, -ˈlaying**) —*n.* (ˈundərlā) **3.** lining, support *etc.* laid underneath something else **4.** felt, rubber *etc.* laid beneath carpet to increase insulation

underline (ˈundərlīn, undərˈlīn) *vt.* **1.** put line under **2.** emphasize

underling (ˈundərling) *n.* subordinate

underlying (undərˈlīing) *a.* **1.** concealed but detectable **2.** fundamental; basic **3.** lying under

undermine (undərˈmīn) *vt.* **1.** wear away base, support of **2.** weaken insidiously

underneath (undərˈnēth) *adv.* **1.** below —*prep.* **2.** under —*a.* **3.** lower —*n.* **4.** lower part, surface *etc.*

underpass (ˈundərpas) *n.* section of road passing under another road, railroad line *etc.*

underpin (undərˈpin) *vt.* **1.** support from beneath, *esp.* by prop **2.** give corroboration or support to (**-nn-**)

underprivileged (undərˈprivilijd) *a.* lacking rights and advantages of other members of society

undershirt (ˈundərshərt) *n.* upper undergarment for males, usu. with short sleeves, worn between skin and shirt

underside (ˈundərsīd) *n.* bottom or lower surface

understand (undərˈstand) *v.* **1.** know and comprehend **2.** realize —*vt.* **3.** infer **4.** take for granted (**-ˈstood, -ˈstanding**) —**underˈstandable** *a.* —**underˈstandably** *adv.* —**underˈstanding** *n.* **1.** intelligence **2.** opinion **3.** agreement —*a.* **4.** sympathetic

understudy (ˈundərstudi) *n.* **1.** one prepared to take over theatrical part from performer if necessary —*vt.* **2.** act as understudy (to) or learn (part) thus

undertake (undərˈtāk) *vt.* **1.** make oneself responsible for **2.** enter upon **3.** promise (**-ˈtook, -ˈtaken, -ˈtaking**) —**ˈundertaker** *n.* one who arranges funerals —**ˈundertaking** *n.* **1.** that which is undertaken **2.** project **3.** guarantee

undertone (ˈundərtōn) *n.* **1.** quiet, dropped tone of voice **2.** underlying tone or suggestion

undertow (ˈundərtō) *n.* **1.** backwash of wave **2.** current beneath surface moving in different direction from surface current

underwear (ˈundərwāər) *n.* garments worn next to skin (*also* **ˈunderclothes**)

underworld (ˈundərwərld) *n.* **1.** criminals and their associates **2.** *Myth.* abode of the dead

underwrite (ˈundərrīt, undərˈrīt) *vt.* **1.** agree to pay **2.** accept liability in (insurance policy) (**-ˈwrote, -ˈwritten, -ˈwriting**) —**ˈunderwriter** *n.* **1.** one that underwrites **2.** agent for insurance company who assesses risks

undies (ˈundiz) *pl.n. inf.* women's underwear

undo (unˈdōō) *vt.* **1.** untie, unfasten **2.** reverse **3.** cause downfall of (**-ˈdid, -ˈdone, -ˈdoing**) —**unˈdoing** *n.* —**unˈdone** *a.* **1.** ruined **2.** not performed

undoubted (unˈdowtid) *a.* certain; indisputable —**unˈdoubtedly** *adv.*

undue (unˈdyōō, -ˈdōō) *a.* **1.** excessive **2.** improper; illegal —**unˈduly** *adv.* immoderately

undulate (ˈunjəlāt) *v.* move up and down like waves —**ˈundulant** *a.* —**unduˈlation** *n.* —**ˈundulatory** *a.* —**undulant fever** *see* BRUCELLOSIS

unearth (unˈərth) *vt.* **1.** dig up **2.** discover

unearthly (unˈərthli) *a.* **1.** ghostly; eerie **2.** heavenly; sublime **3.** ridiculous or unreasonable (*esp. in* **unearthly hour**) —**unˈearthliness** *n.*

uneasy (unˈēzi) *a.* **1.** anxious **2.** uncomfortable

unemployed (unimˈploid) *a.* having no paid employment, out of work —**unemˈployment** *n.*

unˈfreeze
unˈfurl
unˈgodly
unˈgovernable
unˈgracious
ungramˈmatical
unˈgrateful
unˈhallowed
unˈhappy
unˈharmed
unˈhealthy
unˈheard
unheard-of
unˈheated
unˈheeded
unˈhelpful
unˈhurried
unˈhurt
unhyˈgienic
uniˈdentified
uniˈmaginable
uniˈmaginative
unimˈpaired
unimˈportant
unimˈpressed
uninˈformed
uninˈhabited
uninˈhibited
unˈinjured
uninˈspired
uninˈsured
uninˈtelligent
uninˈtelligible
uninˈtended
uninˈtentional
unˈinteresting
uninterˈrupted
uninˈvited
uninˈviting
unˈjustified
unˈkind
unˈknown
unˈlabeled
unˈladylike
unˈlawful
unˈlearned
unˈleash
unˈlettered
unˈlike
unˈlikely
unˈlimited
unˈlined
unˈload
unˈlock
unlooked-for
unˈlucky
unˈmade
unˈmake
unˈmanageable
unˈmanned
unˈmannerly
unˈmarked
unˈmarried
unˈmask
unˈmentionable
unˈmerciful
unˈmerited
unmisˈtakable
unˈmoved
unˈmusical
unˈnamed
unnecesˈsarily

unerring (un'ering) *a.* **1.** not missing the mark **2.** consistently accurate

UNESCO (yōō'neskō) United Nations Educational, Scientific and Cultural Organization

unexceptionable (unik'sepshnəbəl, -shənəbəl) *a.* beyond criticism or objection —**unex'ceptionably** *adv.*

unexceptional (unik'sepshnəl, -shənəl) *a.* **1.** ordinary or normal **2.** subject to or allowing no exceptions —**unex'ceptionally** *adv.*

unfortunate (un'fōrchənit) *a.* **1.** causing or attended by misfortune **2.** unlucky or unhappy **3.** regrettable; unsuitable —*n.* **4.** unlucky person —**un'fortunately** *adv.*

unfounded (un'fowndid) *a.* **1.** (of ideas, allegations *etc.*) baseless **2.** not yet established —**un'foundedly** *adv.*

unfrock (un'frok) *vt.* deprive (person in holy orders) of ecclesiastical status

ungainly (un'gānli) *a.* awkward, clumsy

unguarded (un'gärdid) *a.* **1.** unprotected; vulnerable **2.** open; frank **3.** incautious

unguent ('unggwənt) *n.* ointment

ungulate ('unggyəlit, 'un-gyəlit, -lāt) *n.* any of large group of mammals all of which have hooves

unhinge (un'hinj) *vt.* **1.** remove (door *etc.*) from its hinges **2.** unbalance (person, his mind *etc.*)

unholy (un'hōli) *a.* **1.** not holy or sacred **2.** immoral or depraved **3.** *inf.* outrageous; unnatural

uni- (*comb. form*) one, as in *unicorn, uniform.* Such words are not given here where the meanings may easily be inferred from the simple word

UNICEF ('yōōnisef) United Nations International Children's Emergency Fund

unicellular (yōōni'selyələr) *a.* (of organisms and certain algae) consisting of single cell —**unicellu'larity** *n.*

unicorn ('yōōnikōrn) *n.* mythical horselike animal with single long horn

uniform ('yōōnifōrm) *n.* **1.** identifying clothing worn by members of same group, *eg* soldiers, nurses *etc.* —*a.* **2.** not changing, unvarying **3.** regular, consistent **4.** conforming to same standard or rule —**uni'formity** *n.* sameness —**'uniformly** *adv.*

Uniform ('yōōnifōrm) *n.* word used in communications for the letter *u*

unify ('yōōnifī) *v.* make or become one (**-ified, -ifying**) —**unifi'cation** *n.* —**Unification Church** religious sect founded by Rev. Sun Myung Moon, S Korean industrialist and religious leader

unilateral (yōōni'latərəl) *a.* **1.** one-sided **2.** (of contract) binding one party only —**uni'laterally** *adv.*

unimpeachable (unim'pēchəbəl) *a.* unquestionable as to honesty, truth *etc.*

union ('yōōnyən) *n.* **1.** joining into one **2.** state of being joined **3.** result of being joined **4.** federation, combination of societies *etc.* **5.** labor union **6.** in set theory, the set containing all the members of two given sets only —**'unionism** *n.* —**'unionist** *n.* supporter of union —**'unionize** *v.* organize (workers) into labor union —**Union Jack** national flag of United Kingdom

Union of Soviet Socialist Republics country in Europe and Asia bounded north by the Arctic Ocean, east by the Pacific Ocean, south by China, Mongolia, Afghanistan, Iran, Turkey, the Black Sea, Romania and Hungary and west by Czechoslovakia, Poland, the Baltic Sea, Finland and Norway

unique (yōō'nēk) *a.* **1.** being only one of its kind **2.** unparalleled

unisex ('yōōniseks) *a.* of clothing, hairstyle, hairdressers *etc.* that can be worn or used by either sex

unison ('yōōnisən) *n.* **1.** *Mus.* singing *etc.* of same note as others **2.** agreement, harmony, concord

unit ('yōōnit) *n.* **1.** single thing or person **2.** standard quantity **3.** group of people or things with one purpose —**Uni'tarian** *n.* member of Christian body that denies

un'necessary
un'noticed
unob'servant
unob'served
unob'tainable
unob'trusive
un'occupied
unof'ficial
un'opened
unop'posed
un'organized
un'orthodox
un'pack
un'paid
un'pardonable
un'pick
un'pin
un'playable
un'pleasant
un'pleasing
un'plumbed
un'popular
un'practiced
un'precedented
unpre'dictable
unpre'pared
unprepos'sessing
unpre'tentious
un'printable
unpro'ductive
unpro'fessional
un'profitable
un'promising
unpro'pitious
unpro'tected
unpro'voked
un'qualified
un'questionable
un'real
unrea'listic
un'reasonable
un'registered
unre'lenting
unre'liable
unre'pentant
unrepre'sentative
unre'quited
unre'served
unre'solved
unre'strained
un'righteous
un'ripe
un'rivaled
un'ruffled
un'saddle
un'safe
un'said
un'salable
unsatis'factory
un'scathed
un'scheduled
unscien'tific
un'scramble
un'screw
un'scrupulous
un'seasonable
un'seat
un'seemly
unself'conscious
un'selfish
un'settle
un'shakable

doctrine of the Trinity —**Uni'tarianism** *n.* —**'unitary** *a.*

unite (yŏŏ'nIt) *vt.* **1.** join into one, connect **2.** associate **3.** cause to adhere —*vi.* **4.** become one **5.** combine —**'unity** *n.* **1.** state of being one **2.** harmony **3.** agreement, uniformity **4.** combination of separate parts into connected whole **5.** *Math.* the number one —**United Church of Christ** Protestant Christian denomination created by ecumenical union in 1957 of Congregationalist, Evangelical and Reformed Churches representing both Calvinist and Lutheran traditions —**United Empire Loyalist** American colonist who settled in Canada during American Revolution from loyalty to Britain —**United Nations Organization** organization formed in 1945 to promote peace and international cooperation

United Arab Emirates (i'mēərits, ā'mēərits) country in Middle East bounded north by the Persian Gulf, east by Oman, south and west by Saudi Arabia and northwest by Qatar

United Kingdom of Great Britain and Northern Ireland country lying in N Atlantic comprising England, Scotland and Wales occupying the island of Great Britain and the northeast portion of the smaller of the British Isles in which is located Northern Ireland, bounded south and west by the Republic of Ireland

United States of America country in North America bounded north by Canada, east by the Atlantic, south by the Gulf of Mexico, the Rio Grande and Mexico and west by the Pacific

Univ. University

univalent (yōōni'vālənt) *a.* **1.** (of chromosome during meiosis) not paired with its homologue **2.** *Chem. see* MONOVALENT —**uni'valency** *n.*

universe ('yōōnivərs) *n.* **1.** all existing things considered as constituting systematic whole **2.** human beings collectively —**uni'versal** *a.* **1.** relating to all things or all people **2.** applying to all members of a community —**univer'sality** *n.* —**uni'versally** *adv.* —**Universal Copyright Convention** agreement formulated in 1952 under auspices of UNESCO for reciprocal protection of copyright among contracting states. The symbol © is used to indicate that the work concerned is protected (*also* **Geneva Convention, UNESCO Convention**) —**universal joint** *or* **coupling** form of coupling between two rotating shafts allowing freedom of movement in all directions

university (yōōni'vərsiti) *n.* educational institution with teaching and research facilities comprising graduate and professional schools awarding master's degrees and doctorates and an undergraduate division awarding bachelor's degrees

unjust (un'just) *a.* not in accordance with accepted standards of justice; unfair —**un'justly** *adv.*

unkempt (un'kempt) *a.* of rough or uncared-for appearance

unless (un'les) *conj.* except under the circumstances that

unloose (un'lōōs) *or* **unloosen** *vt.* **1.** release **2.** loosen (hold, grip *etc.*) **3.** unfasten, untie

unman (un'man) *vt.* **1.** cause to lose nerve *etc.* **2.** make effeminate **3.** remove men from (**-nn-**)

unmitigated (un'mitigātid) *a.* not diminished in intensity, severity *etc.*

unnatural (un'nachərəl) *a.* **1.** abnormal **2.** not in accordance with accepted standards of behavior **3.** uncanny; supernatural **4.** affected, forced **5.** inhuman, monstrous —**un'naturally** *adv.*

unnerve (un'nərv) *vt.* cause to lose courage, confidence *etc.*

unparalleled (un'parələld) *a.* unequaled

unprincipled (un'prinsipəld) *a.* lacking moral precepts

unquote (un'kwōt) *interj.* expression used parenthetically to indicate that preceding quotation is finished

un'sheathe
un'skilled
un'skillful
un'sociable
un'social
unso'licited
un'solved
unso'phisticated
un'sound
un'sparing
un'specified
un'spoken
un'sporting
un'stable
un'steady
un'stinted
un'string
un'stuffy
unsub'stantiated
unsuc'cessful
un'suitable
un'sure
unsur'passed
unsus'pected
unsus'pecting
un'sweetened
unsympa'thetic
unsyste'matic
un'tainted
un'tamed
un'tangle
un'tapped
un'taught
un'taxed
un'thinking
un'throne
un'tidy
un'timely
un'trained
un'troubled
un'true
un'trustworthy
un'truthful
un'tutored
un'twist
un'typical
un'usable
un'used
un'usual
un'utilized
un'veil
un'verified
un'voiced
un'wanted
un'warranted
un'wary
un'washed
un'wavering
un'welcome
un'wept
un'wholesome
un'willing
un'wind
un'wise
un'workable
un'worldly
un'worn
un'worthy
un'wrap
un'written
un'yielding
un'zip

unravel (un'ravəl) *vt.* undo, untangle
unread (un'red) *a.* **1.** (of book *etc.*) not yet read **2.** (of person) having read little
unregenerate (unri'jenərit) *a.* **1.** unrepentant **2.** obstinately adhering to one's own views —**unre'generacy** *n.* —**unre'generately** *adv.*
unremitting (unri'miting) *a.* never slackening or stopping
unrest (un'rest) *n.* troubled or rebellious state of discontent
unroll (un'rōl) *v.* **1.** open out (something rolled or folded) or (of something rolled *etc.*) become unwound —*vi.* **2.** become visible or apparent, *esp.* gradually
unruly (un'ro͞oli) *a.* badly behaved, ungovernable, disorderly
unsaturated (un'sachərātid) *a.* **1.** not saturated **2.** (of chemical compound, *esp.* organic compound) containing one or more double or triple bonds and thus capable of undergoing addition reactions —**unsatu'ration** *n.*
unsavory (un'sāvəri) *a.* distasteful, disagreeable
unsightly (un'sītli) *a.* ugly
unspeakable (un'spēkəbəl) *a.* **1.** incapable of expression in words **2.** indescribably bad or evil **3.** not to be uttered —**un'speakably** *adv.*
unstructured (un'strukchərd) *a.* without formal or systematic organization
unstrung (un'strung) *a.* **1.** emotionally distressed **2.** (of stringed instrument) with strings detached
unstudied (un'studid) *a.* **1.** natural **2.** (*with* in) without knowledge or training
unsung (un'sung) *a.* **1.** not acclaimed or honored **2.** not yet sung
untenable (un'tenəbəl) *a.* (of theories *etc.*) incapable of being maintained, defended
unthinkable (un'thingkəbəl) *a.* **1.** out of the question **2.** inconceivable **3.** unreasonable
untie (un'tī) *v.* **1.** unfasten or free (knot or something that is tied) or (of knot *etc.*) become unfastened —*vt.* **2.** free from restriction (**-'tied, -'tying**)
until (un'til) *conj.* **1.** to the time that **2.** (with a negative) before —*prep.* **3.** up to the time of
unto ('untə, 'unto͞o) *prep. obs.* to
untold (un'tōld) *a.* **1.** incapable of description **2.** incalculably great in number or quantity **3.** not told
untouched (un'tucht) *a.* **1.** not touched **2.** not harmed —**un'touchable** *a.* **1.** not able to be touched —*n.* **2.** *esp.* formerly, noncaste Hindu, forbidden to be touched by one of caste
untoward (un'tōrd, 'untōrd, untə'wōrd) *a.* awkward, inconvenient
unutterable (un'utərəbəl) *a.* incapable of being expressed in words —**un'utterably** *adv.*
unwell (un'wel) *a.* not well, ill
unwieldy (un'wēldi) *a.* **1.** awkward, big, heavy to handle **2.** clumsy
unwitting (un'witing) *a.* **1.** not knowing **2.** not intentional
up (up) *prep.* **1.** from lower to higher position **2.** along —*adv.* **3.** in or to higher position, source, activity *etc.* **4.** indicating completion ('**upper** *comp.*, '**uppermost** *sup.*) —'**upward** *a./adv.* —'**upwards** *or* '**upward** *adv.* —**up-and-coming** *a.* promising continued or future success; enterprising —'**uphill** *a.* **1.** inclining; sloping **2.** requiring protracted effort —*adv.* **3.** up incline or slope **4.** against difficulties —*n.* **5.** rising incline —**up-to-date** *a.* modern; fashionable —**up against** confronted with
up- (*comb. form*) up, upper, upward, as in *uproot, upgrade.* Such words are not given here where the meaning may easily be inferred from the simple word
upbeat ('upbēt) *n.* **1.** *Mus.* unaccented beat; upward gesture of conductor's baton indicating this —*a.* **2.** *inf.* cheerful; optimistic
upbraid (up'brād) *vt.* scold, reproach
upbringing ('upbringing) *n.* rearing and education of children
update (up'dāt) *vt.* bring up to date
upgrade ('upgrād, up'grād) *vt.* **1.** promote to higher position **2.** improve — *n.* ('upgrād) **3.** upward slope
upheaval (up'hēvəl) *n.* sudden or violent disturbance
uphold (up'hōld) *vt.* **1.** maintain **2.** support (**up'held, up'holding**)
upholster (up'hōlstər) *vt.* fit springs, padding and coverings on (chairs *etc.*) —**up'holsterer** *n.* —**up'holstery** *n.*
upkeep ('upkēp) *n.* act, process or cost of keeping something in good repair
upland ('uplənd) *n.* high land
uplift (up'lift) *vt.* **1.** raise aloft —*n.* ('uplift) **2.** a lifting up **3.** mental, social or emotional improvement —*a.* ('uplift) **4.** designating brassiere for lifting and supporting breasts
upon (ə'pon) *prep.* on
upper ('upər) *a. comp. of* UP **1.** higher, situated above —*n.* **2.** upper part of boot or shoe —'**uppermost** *a. sup. of* UP —**uppercase** *a.* of or relating to capital letters used in setting or production of printed or typed matter —'**uppercut** *n.* short-arm upward blow —**the upper hand** position of control
uppish ('upish) *a. inf.* **1.** self-assertive **2.** arrogant **3.** affectedly superior
upright ('uprīt) *a.* **1.** erect **2.** honest, just —*adv.* **3.** vertically —*n.* **4.** thing standing upright, *eg* post in framework **5.** upright piano —**upright piano** piano with rectangular vertical case
uprising ('uprīzing) *n.* rebellion, revolt
uproar ('uprōr) *n.* tumult, disturbance —**up'roarious** *a.* rowdy —**up'roariously** *adv.*
uproot (up'ro͞ot) *vt.* **1.** pull up by or as if by

the roots **2.** displace (person or persons) from native or habitual surroundings

upset (up'set) *vt.* **1.** overturn **2.** distress **3.** disrupt **4.** make ill (**up'set, up'setting**) —*n.* ('upset) **5.** unexpected defeat **6.** confusion **7.** trouble **8.** overturning

upshot ('upshot) *n.* outcome, end

upside down ('upsīd) **1.** turned over completely; inverted **2.** in disorder or chaos

upsilon ('yo͞opsilon, 'upsilon) *n.* 20th letter in Gr. alphabet (Υ, υ), vowel transliterated as *y* or *u*

upstage ('up'stāj) *a.* **1.** of back of stage —*vt.* (up'stāj) **2.** *inf.* draw attention away from (another) to oneself

upstanding (up'standing) *a.* **1.** of good character **2.** upright and vigorous in build

upstart ('upstärt) *n.* one suddenly raised to wealth, power *etc.*

uptake ('uptāk) *n.* **1.** shaft *etc.* used to convey smoke or gases, *esp.* one that connects furnace to chimney **2.** lifting up —**quick** (*or* **slow**) **on the uptake** *inf.* quick (or slow) to understand or learn

uptight ('up'tīt) *a.* *inf.* **1.** displaying tense nervousness, irritability **2.** repressed

upturn ('uptərn, up'tərn) *v.* **1.** turn or cause to turn over or upside down —*vt.* **2.** create disorder in **3.** direct upward —*n.* ('uptərn) **4.** upward trend or improvement

uranium (yo͝o'rāniəm) *n.* *Chem.* metallic element *Symbol* U, at. wt. 238.0, at. no. 92

urban ('ərbən) *a.* relating to town or city —'**urbanize** *vt.* change (countryside) to residential or industrial area

urbane (ər'bān) *a.* elegant, sophisticated —**urbanity** (ər'baniti) *n.*

urchin ('ərchin) *n.* mischievous, unkempt child

Urdu ('o͝oərdo͞o, 'ər-) *n.* official language of Pakistan, belonging to Indic branch of Indo-European family of languages, closely related to Hindi

urea (yo͝o'rēə) *n.* product of animal (including human) metabolism excreted in urine

ureter ('yo͝oritər) *n.* tube that conveys urine from kidney to urinary bladder or cloaca —**ureteral** (yo͝o'rētərəl) *or* **ureteric** (yo͝ori'terik) *a.*

urethra (yo͝o'rēthrə) *n.* canal conveying urine from bladder out of body (*pl.* **-thrae** (-thrē), **-s**)

urge (ərj) *vt.* **1.** exhort earnestly **2.** entreat **3.** drive on —*n.* **4.** strong desire —'**urgency** *n.* —'**urgent** *a.* **1.** pressing **2.** needing attention at once —'**urgently** *adv.*

urine ('yo͝orin) *n.* fluid excreted by kidneys to bladder and passed as waste from body —**u'remia** *n.* urine in the blood —'**uric** *a.* —'**urinal** *n.* (place with) sanitary fitting(s) used by men for urination —'**urinary** *a.* —'**urinate** *vi.* discharge urine —**uri'nation** *n.* —**uric acid** compound manufactured in tissues from proteins and purines and excreted by most vertebrates and some lower animals —**urinary bladder** muscular sac located in lower part of abdomen which collects and stores urine

urn (ərn) *n.* **1.** vessel like vase, *esp.* for ashes of the dead **2.** large container with tap for making and dispensing tea, coffee *etc.*

urogenital (yo͝orō'jenitəl) *a.* of urinary and genital organs and their functions (*also* **genito'urinary**)

Ursa Major ('ərsə 'mājər) extensive conspicuous constellation in N hemisphere. The seven brightest stars form Great Bear or Big Dipper

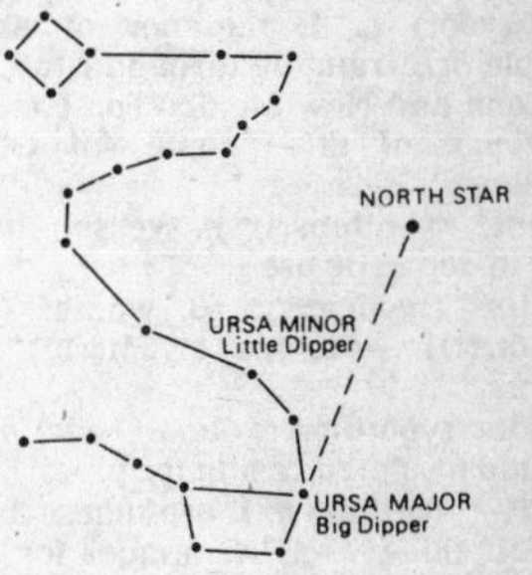

Ursa Minor ('ərsə 'mīnər) small faint constellation, brightest star of which is Pole Star (*also* **Little Bear, Little Dipper**)

ursine ('ərsīn) *a.* of, like a bear

Uruguay ('yo͝orəgwī, -gwā; 'o͝orəgwī) *n.* country in South America bounded northeast by Brazil, southeast by the Atlantic, south by the Río de la Plata and west by Argentina —**Uru'guayan** *n./a.*

Urundi (o͝o'ro͞ondi) *n.* *former name of* BURUNDI

us (us) *pron. pl.* the objective case of WE

U.S. United States

U.S.A. United States of America

U.S.C.G. United States Coast Guard

use (yo͞oz) *vt.* **1.** employ, avail oneself of **2.** exercise **3.** exploit **4.** consume —*n.* (yo͞os) **5.** employment, application to a purpose **6.** need to employ **7.** serviceableness **8.** profit **9.** habit —'**usable** *or* '**useable** *a.* fit for use —**usage** ('yo͞osij, -zij) *n.* **1.** act of using **2.** custom **3.** customary way of using —**used** *a.* second-hand, not new —**useful** ('yo͞osfəl) *a.* **1.** of use **2.** helpful **3.** serviceable —**usefully** ('yo͞osfəli) *adv.* —**usefulness** ('yo͞osfəlnis) *n.* —**useless** ('yo͞oslis) *a.* —**uselessly** ('yo͞oslisli) *adv.* —**uselessness** ('yo͞oslisnis) *n.* —**user-friendly** *a.* (of computers) easy to operate —**used to** (yo͞ost) *a.* **1.** accustomed to —*vt.* **2.** did so formerly

usher ('ushər) *n.* **1.** doorkeeper, one showing people to seats *etc.* (**ushe'rette** *fem.*) —*vt.* **2.** introduce, announce **3.** inaugurate

U.S.I.A. United States Information Agency
U.S.M.C. United States Marine Corps
U.S.S.R. Union of Soviet Socialist Republics
usual ('yo͞ozho͞oəl) *a.* habitual, ordinary —'**usually** *adv.* **1.** as a rule **2.** generally, commonly

usurp (yo͞o'sərp, -'zərp) *vt.* seize wrongfully —**usur'pation** *n.* violent or unlawful seizing of power —**u'surper** *n.*

usury ('yo͞ozhəri) *n.* **1.** lending of money at excessive interest **2.** such interest —'**usurer** *n.* moneylender —**u'surious** *a.*

Utah ('yo͞otô) *n.* Mountain state of the U.S., admitted to the Union in 1896. Abbrev.: **UT** (with ZIP code)

Ute (yo͞ot) *n.* **1.** member of Amerindian people *orig.* ranging through Utah, Colorado, Arizona and New Mexico (*pl.* **Ute, -s**) **2.** the language of this people (of Uto-Aztecan phylum)

utensil (yo͞o'tensəl) *n.* vessel, implement, *esp.* in domestic use

uterus ('yo͞otərəs) *n.* womb (*pl.* **uteri** ('yo͞otərī)) —**uterine** ('yo͞otərīn) *a.* of the uterus

utilidor (yo͞o'tilədər; *Canad.* -dôr) *n.* **C** aboveground insulated casing for pipes

utility (yo͞o'tiliti) *n.* **1.** usefulness **2.** benefit **3.** useful thing —*a.* **4.** made for practical purposes —**utili'tarian** *a.* **1.** useful rather than beautiful **2.** of utilitarianism —*n.* **3.** believer in utilitarianism —**utili'tarianism** *n.* doctrine that morality of actions is to be tested by their utility, *esp.* that the greatest good of the greatest number should be the sole end of public action —**utili'zation** *n.* —'**utilize** *vt.* make use of —**utility room** room used for storage, laundry *etc.*

utmost ('utmōst) *or* **uttermost** *a.* **1.** to the highest degree **2.** extreme, furthest —*n.* **3.** greatest possible amount

Uto-Aztecan (yo͞otō'aztekən) *n.* Amerindian language family spoken throughout the Amer. southwest and Mexico

Utopia (yo͞o'tōpiə) *n.* (*sometimes* **u-**) imaginary state with perfect political and social conditions or constitution —**U'topian** *a.* (*sometimes* **u-**) ideally perfect but impracticable

utter[1] ('utər) *vt.* **1.** express, emit audibly, say **2.** put in circulation (forged bank notes, counterfeit coin) —'**utterance** *n.* **1.** act of speaking **2.** expression in words **3.** spoken words

utter[2] ('utər) *a.* complete, total, absolute —'**utterly** *adv.*

uttermost ('utərmōst) *see* UTMOST

U-turn *n.* **1.** U-shaped turn by vehicle in order to go in opposite direction **2.** reversal of political policy

U.V. ultraviolet

uvula ('yo͞ovyələ) *n.* pendent fleshy part of soft palate (*pl.* **-lae** (-lē), **-s**) —'**uvular** *a.*

uxorious (uk'sôriəs) *a.* excessively fond of one's wife

V

v *or* **V** (vē) *n.* **1.** 22nd letter of English alphabet **2.** speech sound represented by this letter, as in *vote* **3.** something shaped like V (*pl.* **v's, V's** *or* **Vs**)

v volt

V *Chem.* vanadium

v. 1. verb **2.** verso **3.** versus **4.** very **5.** vide

V-1 *n.* flying robot bomb invented by Germans in World War II (*also* **'doodlebug, 'buzzbomb**)

VA 1. Veterans Administration **2.** Virginia

vacant ('vākənt) *a.* **1.** without thought, empty **2.** unoccupied —**'vacancy** *n.* **1.** state of being unoccupied **2.** unfilled post, accommodation *etc.* —**'vacantly** *adv.*

vacate ('vākāt, vā'kāt) *vt.* quit, leave empty —**va'cation** *n.* **1.** time when universities and law courts are closed **2.** period in which break is taken from work or studies, for rest, travel or recreation **3.** act of vacating — *vi.* **4.** take or spend vacation

vaccinate ('vaksināt) *vt.* inoculate with vaccine as protection against a specific disease —**vacci'nation** *n.* —**'vaccinator** *n.* —**vaccine** (vak'sēn, 'vaksēn) *n.* treated microorganisms used for immunization

vacillate ('vasilāt) *vi.* **1.** fluctuate in opinion **2.** waver **3.** move to and fro —**vacil'lation** *n.* **1.** indecision **2.** wavering **3.** unsteadiness

vacuum ('vakyōōəm) *n.* **1.** place, region containing no matter and from which all or most air, gas has been removed (*pl.* **-s, -ua** (-yōōə)) —*v.* **2.** clean with vacuum cleaner —**va'cuity** *n.* —**'vacuous** *a.* **1.** vacant **2.** expressionless **3.** unintelligent —**vacuum bottle** double-walled cylinder with vacuum between walls, for keeping contents of inner flask at temperature at which they were inserted —**vacuum cleaner** apparatus for removing dust by suction —**vacuum-packed** *a.* packed in airtight container to maintain freshness *etc.* —**vacuum pump** pump for producing low gas pressure —**vacuum tube** *or* **valve** part of radio or television which controls flow of current

vade mecum ('vādi 'mēkəm, 'vādi 'mākəm) handbook *etc.* carried on person for immediate use when needed

vagabond ('vagəbond) *n.* **1.** person with no fixed home **2.** wandering beggar or thief —*a.* **3.** like a vagabond

vagary ('vāgəri, və'gāəri) *n.* **1.** something unusual, erratic **2.** whim

vagina (və'jīnə) *n.* passage from womb to exterior —**vaginal** ('vajinəl) *a.*

vagrant ('vāgrənt) *n.* **1.** vagabond —*a.* **2.** wandering, *esp.* without purpose —**'vagrancy** *n.*

vague (vāg) *a.* **1.** indefinite, uncertain **2.** indistinct **3.** not clearly expressed **4.** absent-minded

vain (vān) *a.* **1.** conceited **2.** worthless, useless **3.** unavailing **4.** foolish —**'vainly** *adv.*

vainglory ('vān-glōri, vān'glōri) *n.* boastfulness, vanity —**vain'glorious** *a.*

valance ('valəns) *n.* **1.** short curtain round base of bed *etc.* **2.** short frame or piece of fabric used to conceal curtain fixtures

vale (vāl) *n. Poet.* valley

valediction (vali'dikshən) *n.* farewell —**valedic'torian** *n.* student, usu. one ranking highest in the graduating class, who delivers the valedictory at commencement exercises —**vale'dictory** *n.* **1.** farewell address —*a.* **2.** parting, farewell

valency ('vālənsi) *or* **valence** ('vāləns) *n. Chem.* combining power of element or atom

valentine ('valəntīn) *n.* (one receiving) card, gift, expressing affection on Saint Valentine's Day, Feb. 14th

valet ('valit, 'valā) *n.* gentleman's personal servant

valetudinarian (valityōōdi'neriən, -tōō-) *or* **valetudinary** (vali'tyōōdineri, -'tōō-) *a.* **1.** sickly **2.** infirm —*n.* **3.** person obliged or disposed to live the life of an invalid

valiant ('valyənt) *a.* brave, courageous

valid ('valid) *a.* **1.** sound **2.** capable of being justified **3.** of binding force in law —**va'lidity** *n.* **1.** soundness **2.** power to convince **3.** legal force —**'validate** *vt.* make valid

valise (və'lēs) *n.* traveling bag

valley ('vali) *n.* **1.** low area between hills **2.** river basin

valor ('valər) *n.* bravery —**'valorous** *a.*

value ('valyōō) *n.* **1.** desirability of a thing, oft. in respect of usefulness, exchangeability *etc.* **2.** utility **3.** equivalent **4.** importance —*pl.* **5.** principles, standards —*vt.* **6.** estimate value of **7.** hold in respect **8.** prize —**'valuable** *a.* **1.** precious **2.** worthy **3.** capable of being valued —*n.* **4.** (*usu. pl.*) valuable thing —**valu'ation** *n.* estimated worth —**'valued** *a.* **1.** estimated; appraised **2.** highly thought of —**'valueless** *a.* —**'valuer** *n.* —**value judgment** subjective assessment based on one's own values or those of one's class

valve (valv) *n.* **1.** device to control passage of fluid *etc.* through pipe **2.** *Anat.* part of body allowing one-way passage of fluids **3.** any of separable parts of shell of mollusk **4.** *Mus.* device on brass instrument for lengthening tube —**'valvular** *a.* of, like valves

vamoose (və'mo͞os) *vi. sl.* depart quickly

vamp[1] (vamp) *inf. n.* **1.** woman who deliberately allures men —*v.* **2.** exploit (man) as vamp

vamp[2] (vamp) *n.* **1.** something patched up **2.** front part of shoe upper —*vt.* **3.** patch up, rework

vampire ('vampīər) *n.* **1.** in folklore, corpse that rises from dead to drink blood of the living **2.** bat that sucks blood of animals

van[1] (van) *n.* **1.** covered vehicle, *esp.* for goods **2.** detachable, transportable structure; passenger cabin

van[2] (van) *n.* vanguard

vanadium (və'nādiəm) *n. Chem.* metallic element *Symbol* V, at. wt. 51.0, at. no. 23

Van Buren (van 'byo͞orən) **Martin.** the 8th President of the U.S. (1837-41)

vandal ('vandəl) *n.* one who wantonly and deliberately damages or destroys —**'vandalism** *n.* —**'vandalize** *vt.*

Vandyke beard (van'dīk) short pointed beard (*also* **Van'dyke**)

vane (vān) *n.* **1.** flate plate or blade of metal mounted on vertical axis in exposed position to indicate wind direction **2.** blade of propeller **3.** fin on bomb *etc.* **4.** sight on quadrant

vanguard ('van-gärd) *n.* leading, foremost group, position *etc.*

vanilla (və'nilə) *n.* **1.** tropical climbing orchid **2.** its seed (pod) **3.** essence of this for flavoring

vanish ('vanish) *vi.* **1.** disappear **2.** fade away —**vanishing act 1.** unannounced or unauthorized disappearance **2.** illusion by magician —**vanishing cream** cosmetic cream that is colorless once applied, used as foundation or cleansing cream —**vanishing point 1.** point to which parallel lines appear to converge **2.** point at which something disappears

vanity ('vaniti) *n.* **1.** excessive pride or conceit **2.** ostentation —**vanity case** woman's small hand case for carrying cosmetics *etc.* —**vanity plate** *inf.* automobile license plate bearing owner's name or other distinctive word —**vanity press** publishing house that publishes books at the author's expense

vanquish ('vangkwish) *vt.* **1.** subdue in battle **2.** conquer, overcome —**'vanquishable** *a.* —**'vanquisher** *n.*

vantage ('vantij) *n.* advantage

Vanuatu (vano͞o'äto͞o) *n.* country lying in S Pacific roughly 500 miles west of Fiji and 1100 miles east of Australia

vapid ('vapid) *a.* flat, dull, insipid —**va'pidity** *n.*

vapor ('vāpər) *n.* **1.** gaseous form of a substance more familiar as liquid or solid **2.** steam, mist **3.** invisible moisture in air —**'vaporize** *v.* convert into, pass off in, vapor —**'vaporizer** *n.* —**'vaporous** *a.*

variable ('veriəbəl, 'var-) *see* VARY

varicella (vari'selə) *n. see* **chickenpox** *at* CHICK

varicose ('varikōs) *a.* (of vein) denoting dilation caused by failure of valves in the vein

variegate ('veriəgāt, 'verigāt, 'var-) *vt.* diversify by patches of different colors —**'variegated** *a.* streaked, spotted, dappled —**varie'gation** *n.*

variety (və'rīiti) *n.* **1.** state of being varied or various **2.** diversity **3.** varied assortment **4.** sort, kind

variola (veri'ōlə, vari-; və'rīələ) *n.* smallpox or cowpox

various ('veriəs, 'var-) *a.* manifold, diverse, of several kinds

varlet ('värlit) *n.* formerly, menial servant, rascal

varmint ('värmint) *n. inf.* obnoxious person or animal

varnish ('värnish) *n.* **1.** resinous solution put on a surface to make it hard and shiny —*vt.* **2.** apply varnish to

varsity ('värsiti) *n.* main athletic team of school, college or university

vary ('vāəri) *v.* (cause to) change, diversify, differ, deviate (**'varied, 'varying**) —**varia'bility** *n.* —**'variable** *a.* **1.** changeable **2.** unsteady; fickle —*n.* **3.** something subject to variation —**'variance** *n.* state of discord, discrepancy —**'variant** *a.* **1.** different —*n.* **2.** difference in form **3.** alternative form or reading —**vari'ation** *n.* **1.** alteration **2.** extent to which thing varies **3.** modification —**vari'ational** *a.* —**'varied** *a.* **1.** diverse **2.** modified **3.** variegated

vas (vas) *n. Anat.* vessel, tube carrying bodily fluid (*pl.* **vasa** ('vāzə)) —**vas deferens** ('defərənz, -renz) duct within each testis that conveys spermatozoa to ejaculatory duct (*pl.* **vasa deferentia** (defə'renchiə))

vascular ('vaskyələr) *a.* of, with vessels for conveying sap, blood *etc.*

vase (vās) *n.* vessel, jar as ornament or for holding flowers

vasectomy (və'sektəmi) *n.* surgical removal of part of vas bearing sperm from testicle

Vaseline ('vasilēn) *n.* trade name for jelly-like petroleum product

vasoconstrictor (vāzōkən'striktər) *n.* drug which constricts the blood vessels

vasodilator (vāzōdī'lātər, -di-) *n.* drug that expands blood vessels

vasopressin (vāzō'presin) *n.* hormone of pituitary gland which helps control volume of urine production (*also* **pitressin**)

vassal ('vasəl) *n.* **1.** holder of land by feudal tenure **2.** dependent —**'vassalage** *n.*

vast (vast) *a.* very large —**'vastly** *adv.* —**'vastness** *n.*

vat (vat) *n.* large tub, tank

Vatican City State (ˈvatikən) sovereign state forming an enclave in Rome under the absolute powers of the Pope —ˈ**Vatican** *n.* **1.** Pope's palace **2.** papal authority

vaudeville (ˈvōdəvil, ˈvōdvil; ˈvod-, ˈvōd-) *n.* theatrical entertainment with songs, juggling acts, dance *etc.*

vault

vault[1] (vōlt) *n.* **1.** arched roof **2.** arched apartment **3.** cellar **4.** burial chamber **5.** place for storing valuables —*vt.* **6.** build with arched roof —ˈ**vaulting** *n.* one or more vaults in building or such structures collectively

vault[2] (vōlt) *v.* **1.** spring, jump over (object) with the hands resting on something —*n.* **2.** such jump —ˈ**vaulting** *a.* **1.** excessively confident **2.** used to vault

vaunt (vönt) *v./n.* boast

vb. verb

VC Vietcong

VCR video cassette recorder

VD venereal disease

V Day day of victory

VDU visual display unit

veal (vēl) *n.* calf flesh as food

vector (ˈvektər) *n.* **1.** quantity (*eg* force) having both magnitude and direction **2.** disease-carrying organism, *esp.* insect **3.** compass direction, course

veer (vēər) *vi.* **1.** change direction **2.** change one's mind

vegan (ˈvejən, -an; ˈvēgən) *n.* strict vegetarian, who does not eat animal products

vegetable (ˈvejtəbəl) *n.* **1.** plant, *esp.* edible one **2.** *inf.* person who has lost use of his mental faculties, limbs *etc.* **3.** *inf.* dull person —*a.* **4.** of, from, concerned with plants —**vegetable oil** any of group of oils obtained from plants —**vegetable oyster** salsify

vegetarian (vejiˈteriən) *n.* **1.** one who does not eat meat —*a.* **2.** not eating meat; without meat —**vegeˈtarianism** *n.*

vegetate (ˈvejitāt) *vi.* **1.** (of plants) grow, develop **2.** (of person) live dull, unproductive life —**vegeˈtation** *n.* **1.** plants collectively **2.** plants growing in a place **3.** process of plant growth —ˈ**vegetative** *a.*

vehement (ˈvēimənt) *a.* **1.** marked by intensity of feeling **2.** vigorous **3.** forcible —ˈ**vehemence** *n.* —ˈ**vehemently** *adv.*

vehicle (ˈvēikəl, ˈvēhikəl) *n.* **1.** means of conveying **2.** means of expression **3.** medium —**vehicular** (vēˈhikyələr) *a.*

veil (vāl) *n.* **1.** light material to cover face or head **2.** mask, cover —*vt.* **3.** cover with, as with, veil —**veiled** *a.* disguised —**take the veil** become a nun

vein (vān) *n.* **1.** tube in body taking blood to heart **2.** rib of leaf or insect's wing **3.** fissure in rock filled with ore **4.** streak **5.** distinctive trait, strain *etc.* **6.** mood —*vt.* **7.** mark with streaks —ˈ**veiny** *a.* —**venation** (veˈnāshən, vē-) *n.* **1.** arrangement of veins in leaf *etc.* **2.** such veins collectively —ˈ**venous** *a.* of veins

Velcro (ˈvelkrō) *n.* trade name for fastening consisting of two strips of nylon fabric, one having tiny hooked threads and the other a coarse surface, that form strong bond when pressed together

veld *or* **veldt** (velt, felt) *n.* elevated grassland in S Afr. —**veldskoen** (ˈveltsko͝on, ˈfelt-) *n.* **SA** ankle-length boot *orig.* of raw hide

vellum (ˈveləm) *n.* **1.** parchment of calfskin used for manuscripts or bindings **2.** paper resembling this

velocipede (viˈlosipēd) *n.* early form of bicycle

velocity (viˈlositi) *n.* **1.** rate of motion in given direction **2.** speed

velodrome (ˈvēlədrōm, ˈvel-) *n.* area with banked track for cycle racing

velour *or* **velours** (vəˈlo͝oər) *n.* **1.** fabric with velvety finish **2.** fur felt with long nap, used *esp.* for hats

velum (ˈvēləm) *n.* **1.** membranous covering or organ **2.** soft palate (*pl.* **vela** (ˈvēlə))

velvet (ˈvelvit) *n.* silk or cotton fabric with thick, short pile —**velveˈteen** *n.* cotton fabric resembling velvet —ˈ**velvety** *a.* **1.** of, like velvet **2.** soft and smooth

vena cava (ˈvēnə ˈkāvə) either of two large veins that convey oxygen-depleted blood to heart (*pl.* **venae cavae** (ˈvēnē ˈkāvē))

venal (ˈvēnəl) *a.* **1.** guilty of taking, prepared to take, bribes **2.** corrupt —**veˈnality** *n.*

vend (vend) *vt.* sell —ˈ**vendible** *a.* **1.** salable, marketable —*n.* **2.** (*usu. pl.*) *rare* salable object —ˈ**vendor** *n.* —**vending machine** machine that automatically dispenses goods when money is inserted

vendetta (venˈdetə) *n.* bitter, prolonged feud

veneer (viˈnēər) *n.* **1.** thin layer of fine wood **2.** superficial appearance —*vt.* **3.** cover with veneer

venerable (ˈvenərəbəl) *a.* worthy of reverence —ˈ**venerate** *vt.* look up to, respect, reverence —**venerˈation** *n.*

venereal (viˈnēəriəl) *a.* **1.** (of disease) transmitted by sexual intercourse **2.** infected with venereal disease **3.** of genitals or sexual intercourse

venery[1] ('venəri) *n. obs.* pursuit of sexual gratification

venery[2] ('venəri) *n. Hist.* art, practice of hunting

Venetian (vi'nēshən) *a.* **1.** of Venice, port in NE Italy —*n.* **2.** native or inhabitant of Venice —**Venetian blind** window blind made of thin horizontal slats arranged to turn so as to admit or exclude light

Venezuela (veni'zwālə) *n.* country in South America bounded north by the Caribbean, east by Guyana, south by Brazil and south and southwest by Colombia —**Vene'zuelan** *n./a.*

vengeance ('venjəns) *n.* **1.** revenge **2.** retribution for wrong done —**'vengeful** *a.*

venial ('vēniəl) *a.* pardonable

venison ('venisən, -zən) *n.* flesh of deer as food

Venn diagrams (ven) diagrams using overlapping circles to show relationships between sets

venom ('venəm) *n.* **1.** poison **2.** spite —**'venomous** *a.* poisonous

venous ('vēnəs) *a. see* VEIN

vent[1] (vent) *n.* **1.** small hole or outlet —*vt.* **2.** give outlet to **3.** utter **4.** pour forth

vent[2] (vent) *n.* vertical slit in garment, *esp.* at back of jacket

ventilate ('ventilāt) *vt.* **1.** supply with fresh air **2.** bring into discussion —**venti'lation** *n.* —**'ventilator** *n.*

ventral ('ventrəl) *a.* abdominal

ventricle ('ventrikəl) *n.* cavity, hollow in body, *esp.* in heart or brain —**ven'tricular** *a.*

ventriloquist (ven'triləkwist) *n.* one who can so speak that the sounds seem to come from some other person or place —**ven'triloquism** *n.*

venture ('venchər) *vt.* **1.** expose to hazard **2.** risk —*vi.* **3.** dare **4.** have courage (to do something or go somewhere) —*n.* **5.** risky undertaking **6.** speculative commercial undertaking —**'venturesome** *or* **'venturous** *a.*

venue ('venyōō) *n.* **1.** *Law* district in which case is tried **2.** meeting place **3.** location

Venus ('vēnəs) *n.* **1.** Roman goddess of love **2.** planet between earth and Mercury —**Venus's flytrap** insect-eating plant

veracious (və'rāshəs) *a.* **1.** truthful **2.** true —**veracity** (və'rasiti) *n.*

veranda *or* **verandah** (və'randə) *n.* open or partly enclosed porch on outside of house

verb (vərb) *n.* part of speech used to express action or being —**'verbal** *a.* **1.** of, by, or relating to words spoken rather than written **2.** of, like a verb —**'verbalism** *n.* **1.** verbal expression; phrase; word **2.** exaggerated emphasis on importance of words **3.** statement lacking real content —**'verbalize** *vt.* **1.** put into words —*vi.* **2.** speak —**'verbally** *adv.* —**verbatim** (vər'bātim) *adv./a.* word for word, literal(ly) —**verbal noun** noun derived from verb

verbascum (vər'baskəm) *n.* perennial garden plant

verbena (vər'bēnə) *n.* **1.** genus of fragrant, beautiful plants **2.** their characteristic scent

verbiage ('vərbiij) *n.* excess of words —**verbose** (vər'bōs) *a.* long-winded —**verbosity** (vər'bositi) *n.*

verdant ('vərdənt) *a.* green and fresh —**'verdure** *n.* **1.** greenery **2.** freshness —**'verdurous** *a.*

verdict ('vərdikt) *n.* **1.** decision of a jury **2.** opinion reached after examination of facts

verdigris ('vərdigrēs, -gris) *n.* green film on copper

verdure ('vərjər) *n. see* VERDANT

verge (vərj) *n.* **1.** edge **2.** brink **3.** tiling projected over gable of building —*vi.* **4.** (*with* on) come close (to) **5.** (*sometimes with* on) be on the border (of)

verger ('vərjər) *n.* **1.** caretaker and attendant in church **2.** bearer of wand of office

verify ('verifī) *vt.* **1.** prove, confirm truth of **2.** test accuracy of (**-ified, -ifying**) —**'verifiable** *a.* —**verifi'cation** *n.*

verily ('verili) *adv. obs.* **1.** truly **2.** in truth

verisimilitude (verisi'milityōōd, -tōōd) *n.* **1.** appearance of truth **2.** likelihood —**veri'similar** *a.* probable; likely

veritable ('veritəbəl) *a.* actual, true, genuine —**'veritably** *adv.*

verity ('veriti) *n.* **1.** truth **2.** reality **3.** true assertion

vermi- (*comb. form*) worm, as in *vermicide, vermiform, vermifuge*

vermicelli (vərmi'cheli, -'seli) *n.* pasta in fine strands

vermicide ('vərmisīd) *n.* substance to destroy worms —**ver'micular** *a.* **1.** resembling form, motion or tracks of worms **2.** of worms —**'vermiform** *a.* shaped like a worm (*eg* **vermiform appendix**)

vermiculite (vər'mikyəlīt) *n.* granular substance formed by subjecting mica to heat, used in horticulture for its water-retaining property

vermilion (vər'milyən) *a./n.* (of) bright red color or pigment

vermin ('vərmin) *n.* (*with pl. v.*) injurious animals, parasites *etc.* —**'verminous** *a.*

Vermont (vər'mont) *n.* New England state of the U.S., admitted to the Union in 1791. Abbrev.: **Vt., VT** (with ZIP code)

vermouth (vər'mōōth) *n.* wine flavored with aromatic herbs *etc.*

vernacular (vər'nakyələr) *n.* **1.** commonly spoken language or dialect of particular country or place —*a.* **2.** of vernacular **3.** native

vernal ('vərnəl) *a.* of spring

vernier ('vərniər) *n.* sliding scale for obtaining fractional parts of subdivision of graduated scale

veronica (vəˈronikə) *n.* genus of plants including speedwell

verruca (vəˈro͞okə) *n.* wart

versatile (ˈvərsətil) *a.* **1.** capable of or adapted to many different uses, skills *etc.* **2.** liable to change —**versaˈtility** *n.*

verse (vərs) *n.* **1.** stanza or short subdivision of poem or the Bible **2.** poetry **3.** line of poetry —**versifiˈcation** *n.* —ˈ**versifier** *n.* —ˈ**versify** *v.* turn (something) into verse (**-ified, -ifying**) —**versed in** skilled in

version (ˈvərzhən, -shən) *n.* **1.** description from certain point of view **2.** translation **3.** adaptation

verso (ˈvərsō) *n.* back of sheet of printed paper, left-hand page (*pl.* **-s**)

versus (ˈvərsəs) *prep.* against

vertebra (ˈvərtibrə) *n.* single section of backbone (*pl.* **-brae** (-brē), **-s**) —ˈ**vertebral** *a.* of the spine —ˈ**vertebrate** *n./a.* (of) animal with backbone, such as fish, amphibians, reptiles, birds and mammals —**vertebrate biology** the study of this phylum (*Chordata*)

vertex (ˈvərteks) *n.* summit (*pl.* **-es, vertices** (ˈvərtisēz))

vertical (ˈvərtikəl) *a.* **1.** at right angles to the horizon **2.** upright **3.** overhead —ˈ**vertically** *adv.*

vertigo (ˈvərtigō) *n.* giddiness (*pl.* **-es, vertigines** (vərˈtijinēz)) —**vertiginous** (vərˈtijinəs) *a.* dizzy

vertu (vərˈto͞o) *n. see* VIRTU

verve (vərv) *n.* **1.** enthusiasm **2.** spirit **3.** energy, vigor

very (ˈveri) *a.* **1.** exact, ideal **2.** same **3.** complete **4.** actual —*adv.* **5.** extremely, to great extent —**very high frequency** radio frequency or band lying between 300 and 30 megahertz —**very low frequency** radio frequency band or radio frequency lying between 30 and 3 kilohertz

vesicle (ˈvesikəl) *n.* small blister, bubble or cavity —**veˈsicular** *a.*

vespers (ˈvespərz) *n.* **1.** evening church service **2.** evensong

vessel (ˈvesəl) *n.* **1.** any object used as container, *esp.* for liquids **2.** ship, large boat **3.** tubular structure conveying liquids (*eg* blood) in body

vest (vest) *n.* **1.** sleeveless garment worn under jacket or coat —*vt.* **2.** place **3.** bestow **4.** confer **5.** clothe —ˈ**vestment** *n.* robe or official garment —**vested interest** strong personal interest in particular state of affairs

vestal (ˈvestəl) *a.* pure, chaste —**vestal virgin** in ancient Rome, one of virgin priestesses whose lives were dedicated to Vesta and to maintaining sacred fire in her temple

vestibule (ˈvestibyo͞ol) *n.* entrance hall, lobby

vestige (ˈvestij) *n.* small trace, amount —**vesˈtigial** *a.*

vestry (ˈvestri) *n.* room in church for keeping vestments, holding meetings *etc.*

vet (vet) *n.* **1.** veterinarian —*vt.* **2.** examine **3.** check (**-tt-**)

vet. 1. veteran **2.** veterinarian

vetch (vech) *n.* plant of bean family

veteran (ˈvetərən) *n.* **1.** one who has served a long time, *esp.* in fighting services —*a.* **2.** long-serving

veterinarian (vetəriˈneriən) *n.* person qualified and licensed to treat disorders and diseases of animals, *esp.* livestock and pets (*also* **vet**) —ˈ**veterinary** *a.* of, relating to the science of treating injured and diseased animals

veto (ˈvētō) *n.* **1.** power of rejecting piece of legislation or preventing it from coming into effect **2.** any prohibition (*pl.* **-es**) —*vt.* **3.** enforce veto against **4.** forbid with authority

vex (veks) *vt.* **1.** annoy **2.** distress —**vexˈation** *n.* **1.** cause of irritation **2.** state of distress —**vexˈatious** *a.* —**vexed** *a.* **1.** cross, annoyed **2.** much discussed

VHF *or* **vhf** very high frequency

V.I. Vancouver Island

via (ˈvīə, ˈvēə) *prep.* by way of

viable (ˈvīəbəl) *a.* **1.** practicable **2.** able to live and grow independently —**viaˈbility** *n.*

viaduct (ˈvīədukt) *n.* bridge over valley for a road or railroad

vial (ˈvīəl) *n. see* PHIAL

viands (ˈvīəndz) *pl.n.* food

viaticum (vīˈatikəm) *n.* **1.** Holy Communion as administered to person dying or in danger of death **2.** *rare* provisions or travel allowance for journey (*pl.* **-ca** (-kə), **-s**)

vibes (vībz) *pl.n. inf.* **1.** vibrations **2.** vibraphone

vibraphone

vibraphone (ˈvībrəfōn) *n.* musical instrument like xylophone, but with electronic resonators, that produces a gentle vibrato

vibrate (ˈvībrāt) *v.* **1.** (cause to) move to and fro rapidly and continuously **2.** give off (light or sound) by vibration —*vi.* **3.** oscillate **4.** quiver —ˈ**vibrant** *a.* **1.** throbbing **2.** vibrating **3.** appearing vigorous, lively —**viˈbration** *n.* **1.** a vibrating —*pl.* **2.** *inf.* instinctive feelings about a place, person *etc.* —**vibrato** (viˈbrätō) *n.* vibrating effect in music (*pl.* **-s**) —ˈ**vibrator** *n.* **1.** device for producing vibratory motion, as in massage **2.** such a device with vibrating part or tip, used as dildo —ˈ**vibratory** *a.*

viburnum (vīˈbərnəm) *n.* subtropical shrub with white flowers and berry-like fruits

vicar (ˈvikər) *n.* clergyman in charge of parish —ˈ**vicarage** *n.* vicar's house —**vicarial** (vīˈkeriəl, vi-; -ˈkar-) *a.* of vicar —**vicar apostolic** *R.C. Ch.* titular bishop having jurisdiction in missionary countries (*pl.* **vicars apostolic**) —**vicar general** official appointed to assist bishop of diocese in administrative or judicial duties (*pl.* **vicars general**) —**Vicar of Christ** *R.C.Ch.* the Pope

vicarious (vīˈkeriəs, vi-; -ˈkar-) *a.* **1.** obtained, enjoyed or undergone at second hand through sympathetic participation in another's experiences **2.** suffered, done *etc.* as substitute for another —**viˈcariously** *adv.*

vice[1] (vīs) *n.* **1.** evil or immoral habit or practice **2.** criminal immorality, *esp.* prostitution **3.** fault, imperfection —**vice squad** police division which deals with enforcement of gaming and prostitution laws

vice[2] (vīs) *n. inf.* **1.** person who serves as deputy to another **2.** person succeeding another

vice- (*comb. form*) in place of, second to, as in *vice-chairman, viceroy.* Such compounds are not given here where meaning may be inferred from simple word

vice admiral commissioned officer in navy or coastguard ranking above a rear admiral and whose insignia is three stars

vicegerent (vīsˈjēərənt) *n.* **1.** person appointed to exercise all or some of authority of another **2.** *R.C.Ch.* representative of God or Christ on earth, such as pope —*a.* **3.** invested with or characterized by delegated authority —**viceˈgerency** *n.*

vice president officer ranking immediately below president and serving as his deputy —**vice-presidency** *n.*

viceroy (ˈvīsroi) *n.* ruler acting for king in province or dependency (**vicereine** (ˈvīsrān) *fem.*) —**viceˈregal** *a.* of viceroy —ˈ**viceroyalty** *n.*

vice versa (ˈvīsi ˈvərsə) *Lat.* conversely, the other way round

vichy water (ˈvishi) **1.** (*sometimes* **V- w-**) mineral water from Vichy in France, reputed to be beneficial to health **2.** any sparkling mineral water resembling this

vicinage (ˈvisənij) *n. rare* **1.** residents of particular neighborhood **2.** vicinity

vicinity (viˈsiniti) *n.* neighborhood

vicious (ˈvishəs) *a.* **1.** wicked, cruel **2.** ferocious, dangerous **3.** leading to vice —ˈ**viciously** *adv.* —**vicious circle 1.** situation in which attempt to resolve one problem creates new problems that lead back to original situation **2.** *Logic* invalid form of reasoning in which conclusion is derived from premise orig. deduced from same conclusion **3.** *Logic* circular definition

vicissitude (viˈsisityōōd, -tōōd) *n.* **1.** change of fortune —*pl.* **2.** ups and downs of fortune —**vicissiˈtudinous** *a.*

victim (ˈviktim) *n.* **1.** person or thing killed, injured *etc.* as result of another's deed, or accident, circumstances *etc.* **2.** person cheated **3.** sacrifice —**victimiˈzation** *n.* —ˈ**victimize** *vt.* **1.** punish unfairly **2.** make victim of

victor (ˈviktər) *n.* **1.** conqueror **2.** winner —**vicˈtorious** *a.* having defeated an adversary —ˈ**victory** *n.* winning of battle *etc.*

Victor (ˈviktər) *n.* word used in communications for the letter *v*

victoria (vikˈtōriə) *n.* four-wheeled horse-drawn carriage with folding hood

Victorian (vikˈtōriən) *a.* **1.** of Victoria, queen of Great Brit. and Ireland, or period of her reign (1837–1901) **2.** exhibiting characteristics popularly attributed to Victorians, *esp.* prudery *etc.* **3.** of Victoria (state in Aust. or any of the cities) —*n.* **4.** person who lived during reign of Queen Victoria **5.** inhabitant of Victoria (state or any of the cities) —**Victoria Day** Monday preceding May 24th: national holiday in Canad. in commemoration of Queen Victoria's birthday

victual (ˈvitəl) *n.* **1.** (*usu. pl.*) food —*v.* **2.** supply with or obtain food —ˈ**victualler** *or* ˈ**victualer** *n.*

vicuña (viˈkōōnyə, vī-; -ˈkyōōnə, -ˈkōōnə) *n.* **1.** S Amer. animal like llama **2.** fine, light cloth made from its wool

vide (ˈvīdi) *Lat.* see —**vide infra** see below —**vide supra** see above

videlicet (viˈdeliset) *Lat.* namely

video (ˈvidiō) *a.* **1.** relating to or used in transmission or production of television image —*n.* **2.** apparatus for recording television programs *etc.* —**video cassette** cassette containing video tape —**video cassette recorder** tape recorder for vision and sound signals using magnetic tape in closed plastic cassettes, for recording and playing back television programs and motion pictures (*also* **video**) —ˈ**videodisc** *or* ˈ**videodisk** *n.* disk stored with information, which one plays like a phonograph record, the result being translated, in sound and vision, on to TV set —ˈ**videophone** *n.* telephonic device in which there is both verbal and visual communication between parties —**video tape** magnetic tape on which to record television program —**video tape recorder**

vie (vī) *vi.* (*with* with *or* for) contend, compete (against or for someone, something) (**vied, ˈvying**)

Vietnam (vēˈetˈnäm, vyet-) *n.* country in Asia bounded north by China, east and south by the South China Sea and west by Kampuchea and Laos —**Viˈetˈcong** *n.* in Vietnam War, (member of) Communist-led guerrilla force and revolutionary army of South Vietnam —**Vietnaˈmese** *n./a.* **1.**

(native or inhabitant) of Vietnam —*n.* **2.** language of Vietnam whose linguistic affiliation is uncertain

view (vyo͞o) *n.* **1.** survey by eyes or mind **2.** range of vision **3.** picture **4.** scene **5.** opinion **6.** purpose —*vt.* **7.** look at **8.** survey **9.** consider —ˈ**viewer** *n.* **1.** one who views **2.** one who watches television **3.** optical device to assist viewing of photographic slides —ˈ**viewfinder** *n.* device on camera enabling user to see what will be included in photograph —ˈ**viewpoint** *n.* **1.** way of regarding a subject **2.** position commanding view of landscape

vigil (ˈvijil) *n.* **1.** a keeping awake, watch **2.** eve of feast day —ˈ**vigilance** *n.* —ˈ**vigilant** *a.* watchful, alert —**vigilance committee** self-appointed body of citizens organized to maintain order *etc.*

vigilante (vijiˈlanti) *n.* one, *esp.* as member of group, who unofficially takes it upon himself to enforce law

vignette (viˈnyet) *n.* **1.** short literary essay, sketch **2.** photograph or portrait with the background shaded off

vigor (ˈvigər) *n.* **1.** force, strength **2.** energy, activity —ˈ**vigorous** *a.* **1.** strong **2.** energetic **3.** flourishing —ˈ**vigorously** *adv.*

Viking (ˈvīking) *n.* medieval Scandinavian seafarer, raider, settler

vile (vīl) *a.* **1.** very wicked, shameful **2.** disgusting **3.** despicable —ˈ**vilely** *adv.* —ˈ**vileness** *n.* —**vilification** (vilifiˈkāshən) *n.* —**vilify** (ˈvilifī) *vt.* **1.** speak ill of **2.** slander (**-ified, -ifying**)

villa (ˈvilə) *n.* **1.** large, luxurious, country house **2.** detached or semidetached suburban house

village (ˈvilij) *n.* small group of houses in country area —ˈ**villager** *n.*

villain (ˈvilən) *n.* **1.** wicked person **2.** *inf.* mischievous person —ˈ**villainous** *a.* **1.** wicked **2.** vile —ˈ**villainy** *n.*

villein (ˈvilən) *n.* in medieval Europe, peasant personally bound to his lord, to whom he paid dues and services in return for land —ˈ**villeinage** *n.*

vim (vim) *n. inf.* force, energy

vinaigrette (viniˈgret) *n.* **1.** small bottle of smelling salts **2.** type of salad dressing

Vincent's disease *or* **angina** (ˈvinsənts) ulcerative condition of mouth, throat and gums with thick membrane-like coating

vinculum (ˈvingkyələm) *n.* **1.** line drawn above group of mathematical terms, used as equivalent to parentheses or brackets around them **2.** *Anat.* bandlike structure, *esp.* uniting two or more parts (*pl.* **-la** (-lə))

vindicate (ˈvindikāt) *vt.* **1.** clear of charges **2.** justify **3.** establish the truth or merit of —ˈ**vindicable** *a.* capable of being vindicated; justifiable —**vindiˈcation** *n.* —ˈ**vindicator** *n.* —ˈ**vindicatory** *a.*

vindictive (vinˈdiktiv) *a.* **1.** revengeful **2.** inspired by resentment

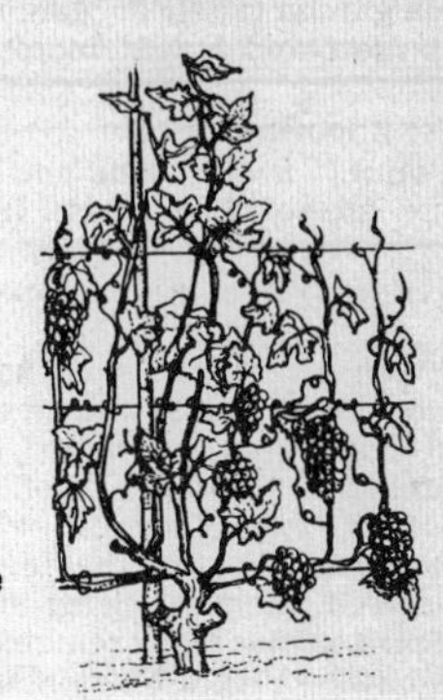

vine

vine (vīn) *n.* climbing plant bearing grapes —ˈ**vinery** *n.* **1.** hothouse for growing grapes **2.** vineyard **3.** vines collectively —**viˈnosity** *n.* distinctive and essential quality and flavor of wine —**vintage** (ˈvintij) *n.* **1.** gathering of the grapes **2.** the yield **3.** wine of particular year **4.** time of origin —*a.* **5.** best and most typical —**vintner** (ˈvintnər) *n.* dealer in wine —**vineyard** (ˈvinyərd) *n.* plantation of vines

vinegar (ˈvinigər) *n.* sour liquid usu. obtained from alcoholic liquors —ˈ**vinegary** *a.* **1.** like vinegar **2.** sour **3.** bad-tempered

vini- *or before vowel* **vin-** (*comb. form*) wine, as in *viniculture*

viniculture (ˈvinikulchər) *n.* process or business of growing grapes and making wine

Vinland (ˈvinlənd) *n.* region in eastern N Amer. visited and described by Norsemen about 1000 A.D.

vinyl (ˈvīnil) *n.* plastic material with variety of domestic and industrial uses

vinyon (ˈvinyon) *n.* any of various polyvinyl fibers

viol (ˈvīəl) *n.* early stringed instrument preceding violin —ˈ**violist** *n.* person who plays viola or viol

viola[1] (viˈōlə) *n. see* VIOLIN

viola[2] (vīˈōlə, vi-; ˈvīələ) *n.* single-colored variety of pansy

violate (ˈvīəlāt) *vt.* **1.** break (law, agreement *etc.*), infringe **2.** rape **3.** outrage, desecrate —ˈ**violable** *a.* —**vioˈlation** *n.* —ˈ**violator** *n.*

violent (ˈvīələnt) *a.* **1.** marked by, due to, extreme force, passion or fierceness **2.** of great force **3.** intense —ˈ**violence** *n.* —ˈ**violently** *adv.*

violet (ˈvīəlit) *n.* **1.** plant with small bluish-purple or white flowers **2.** the flower **3.** bluish-purple color —*a.* **4.** of this color

violin (vīəˈlin) *n.* **1.** small four-stringed musical instrument — *a.* **2.** denoting family of string instruments constructed on same principles of producing sound —**vi'ola** *n.* large violin with lower range —**vio'linist** *n.* —**violoncello** (vīələn'chelō) *n. see* CELLO —**viola da gamba** (vi'ōlə də 'gämbə, 'gambə) second largest and lowest member of viol family

V.I.P. very important person

viper ('vīpər) *n.* **1.** common European venomous snake **2.** vicious, treacherous person

virago (vi'rägō) *n.* abusive woman (*pl.* **-es, -s**)

virgin ('vərjin) *n.* **1.** one who has not had sexual intercourse —*a.* **2.** without experience of sexual intercourse **3.** unsullied, fresh **4.** (of land) untilled —**'virginal** *a.* **1.** of, like virgin —*n.* **2.** (*oft. pl.*) type of spinet —**vir'ginity** *n.* —**Virgin Birth** doctrine that Jesus Christ was conceived solely by direct intervention of Holy Spirit so that Mary remained a virgin after his birth —**Virgin Mary** Mary, mother of Christ (*also* **the Virgin**)

Virginia (vər'jinyə) *n.* South Atlantic state of the U.S.: ratified the Constitution in 1788. Abbrev.: **VA** (with ZIP code) —**Virginia creeper** N Amer. deciduous climbing vine having palmate leaves and bluish-black berries (*also* **woodbine**)

Virgin Islands territory of the U.S. in the Caribbean

Virgo ('vərgō) *n.* (virgin) 6th sign of the zodiac operative c. Aug. 22nd-Sept. 21st

virgule ('vərgyōōl) *n.* solidus

virile ('viril) *a.* **1.** (of male) capable of copulation or procreation **2.** strong, forceful —**vi'rility** *n.*

virology (vī'roləji) *n. see* VIRUS

virtu *or* **vertu** (vər'tōō) *n.* **1.** taste or love for curios or works of fine art **2.** such objects collectively **3.** quality of being appealing to connoisseur (*esp. in* **articles of virtu, objects of virtu**)

virtual ('vərchōōəl) *a.* so in effect, though not in appearance or name —**'virtually** *adv.* practically, almost

virtue ('vərchōō) *n.* **1.** moral goodness **2.** good quality **3.** merit **4.** inherent power —**'virtuous** *a.* **1.** morally good **2.** chaste —**'virtuously** *adv.*

virtuoso (vərchōō'ōsō, -'ōzō) *n.* one with special skill, *esp.* in a fine art (*pl.* **-s, -si** (-sē, -zē)) —**virtuosity** (vərchōō'ositi) *n.* great technical skill, *esp.* in a fine art, as music

virulent ('viryələnt, 'virələnt) *a.* **1.** very infectious, poisonous *etc.* **2.** malicious

virus ('vīrəs) *n.* any single-celled disease-causing organic structure distinct from and oft. smaller than bacteria that can only reproduce in a living organism —**'viral** *a.* of virus —**vi'rology** *n.* study of viruses

visa ('vēzə) *n.* endorsement on passport permitting the bearer to travel into country of issuing government —**'visaed** *a.*

visage ('vizij) *n.* face

vis-à-vis ('vēzə'vē) *Fr.* **1.** in relation to, regarding **2.** opposite to

viscera ('visərə) *pl.n.* large internal organs of body, *esp.* of abdomen (*sing.* **viscus** ('viskəs)) —**'visceral** *a.*

viscid ('visid) *a.* sticky, of a consistency like molasses —**vi'scidity** *n.*

viscose ('viskōs) *n.* (substance used to produce) synthetic fabric

viscount ('vīkownt) *n.* Brit. nobleman ranking below earl and above baron —**'viscountess** *n.* **1.** wife, ex-wife or widow of viscount **2.** noblewoman ranking below countess and above baroness

viscous ('viskəs) *a.* thick and sticky —**vis'cosity** *n.*

vise (vīs) *n.* fixed appliance with screw to apply controlled pressure to object held in jaws of vise

visible ('vizibəl) *a.* that can be seen —**visi'bility** *n.* degree of clarity of atmosphere, *esp.* for navigation —**'visibly** *adv.*

vision ('vizhən) *n.* **1.** sight **2.** insight **3.** dream **4.** phantom **5.** imagination —**'visionary** *a.* **1.** marked by vision **2.** impractical —*n.* **3.** mystic **4.** impractical person

visit ('vizit) *v.* **1.** go, come and see, stay temporarily with (someone) —*n.* **2.** stay **3.** call at person's home *etc.* **4.** official call —**'visitant** *n.* **1.** ghost; apparition **2.** visitor or guest, usu. from far away **3.** migratory bird that is present in particular region only at certain times (*also* **'visitor**) —**visi'tation** *n.* **1.** formal visit or inspection **2.** affliction or plague —**'visitor** *n.*

visor *or* **vizor** ('vīzər) *n.* **1.** front part of helmet made to move up and down before face **2.** eyeshade, *esp.* on automobile **3.** peak on cap

vista ('vistə) *n.* view, *esp.* distant view

visual ('vizhōōəl) *a.* **1.** of sight **2.** visible —**visuali'zation** *n.* —**'visualize** *vt.* form mental image of —**visual aids** devices, such as motion pictures, slides *etc.*, that display in visual form material to be understood or remembered

vital ('vītəl) *a.* **1.** necessary to, affecting life **2.** lively, animated **3.** essential **4.** highly important —**vi'tality** *n.* life, vigor —**'vitalize** *vt.* **1.** give life to **2.** lend vigor to —**'vitally** *adv.* —**'vitals** *pl.n.* vital organs of body —**vital statistics 1.** data concerning human life or conditions affecting it, such as death rate **2.** *inf.* measurements of woman's bust, waist and hips

vitamin ('vītəmin) *n.* any of group of substances occurring in foodstuffs and essential to health

vitiate ('vishiāt) *vt.* **1.** spoil **2.** deprive of efficacy **3.** invalidate —**viti'ation** *n.*

viticulture ('vitikulchər) *n.* **1.** science, art or process of cultivating grapevines **2.** study of (growing of) grapes —**viti'culturist** *n.*

vitreous ('vitriəs) *a.* **1.** of glass **2.** glassy

—vitrifi'cation *n.* —'vitrify *v.* convert or be converted into glass, or glassy substance (-ified, -ifying) —vitreous humor transparent gelatinous substance that fills eyeball between lens and retina

vitriol ('vitriəl) *n.* **1.** sulfuric acid **2.** caustic speech —**vitri'olic** *a.*

vituperate (vī'tyōōpərāt, vi-; -'tōō-) *vt.* abuse in words, revile —**vituper'ation** *n.* —**vi'tuperative** *a.*

viva ('vēvə) *interj.* long live; up with (specified person or thing)

vivace (vē'vächā, -chi) *a./adv. Mus.* to be performed in brisk lively manner

vivacious (vi'vāshəs) *a.* lively, gay, sprightly —**vivacity** (vi'vasiti) *n.*

vivarium (vī'variəm, -'ver-) *n.* place where animals are kept under natural conditions for study *etc.* (*pl.* **-s, -ia** (-iə))

viva voce ('vīvə 'vōsi) *Lat. adv.* **1.** by word of mouth —*n.* **2.** oral examination (*oft.* '**viva**)

vivid ('vivid) *a.* **1.** bright, intense **2.** clear **3.** lively, animated **4.** graphic —'**vividly** *adv.*

vivify ('vivifī) *vt.* animate, inspire (**-ified, -ifying**)

viviparous (vī'vipərəs, vi-) *a.* bringing forth young alive

vivisection (vivi'sekshən) *n.* dissection of, or operating on, living animals —'**vivisect** *v.* subject (animal) to vivisection —**vivi'sectionist** *n.* —'**vivisector** *n.*

vixen ('viksən) *n.* **1.** female fox **2.** spiteful woman —'**vixenish** *a.*

Viyella (vī'yelə) *n.* trade name for twill-weave cloth made of cotton and wool

viz. videlicet

vizier (vi'zēər) *n.* high official in some Muslim countries

vizor ('vīzər) *n. see* VISOR

V-J Day day marking Allied victory over Japan in World War II (Aug. 15th, 1945)

V.L. Vulgar Latin

VLF *or* **vlf** *Rad.* very low frequency

V neck neck on garment resembling shape of letter V —**V-neck** *or* **V-necked** *a.*

voc. *or* **vocat.** vocative

vocable ('vōkəbəl) *n.* word regarded as sequence of letters or spoken sounds

vocabulary (vō'kabyəleri, və-) *n.* **1.** list of words, usu. in alphabetical order **2.** stock of words used in particular language *etc.*

vocal ('vōkəl) *a.* **1.** of, with, or giving out voice **2.** outspoken, articulate —*n.* **3.** piece of popular music that is sung —'**vocalist** *n.* singer —'**vocalize** *vt.* utter with voice —'**vocally** *adv.* —**vocal cords** either of two pairs of membranous folds in larynx.

vocalic (vō'kalik) *a.* of vowel(s)

vocation (vō'kāshən) *n.* (urge, inclination, predisposition to) particular career, profession *etc.* —**vo'cational** *a.*

vocative ('vokətiv) *n.* in some languages, case of nouns used in addressing a person

vociferate (vō'sifərāt) *v.* exclaim, cry out —**vocifer'ation** *n.* —**vo'ciferous** *a.* shouting, noisy

vodka ('vodkə) *n.* colorless alcoholic liquor distilled from rye, corn or potatoes

vogue (vōg) *n.* **1.** fashion, style **2.** popularity

voice (vois) *n.* **1.** sound given out by person in speaking, singing *etc.* **2.** quality of the sound **3.** expressed opinion **4.** (right to) share in discussion **5.** verbal form proper to relation of subject and action —*vt.* **6.** give utterance to, express —'**voiceless** *a.* —**voice-over** *n.* voice of unseen commentator heard during television broadcast —'**voiceprint** *n.* graphic representation of person's voice recorded electronically

void (void) *a.* **1.** empty **2.** destitute **3.** not legally binding —*n.* **4.** empty space —*vt.* **5.** make ineffectual or invalid **6.** empty out

voile (voil) *n.* light semitransparent fabric

vol. volume

volatile ('volətil) *a.* **1.** evaporating quickly **2.** lively **3.** fickle, changeable —**vola'tility** *n.* —**volatili'zation** *n.* —**vo'latilize** *v.* (cause to) evaporate

vol-au-vent (*Fr.* volō'vä) *n.* small, light pastry case with savory filling

volcano (vol'kānō) *n.* **1.** hole in earth's crust through which lava, ashes, smoke *etc.* are discharged **2.** mountain so formed (*pl.* **-es, -s**) —**volcanic** (vol'kanik) *a.* —**volcanology** (volkə'noləji) *or* **vulcanology** *n.* study of volcanoes and volcanic phenomena

vole (vōl) *n.* any of various small rodents resembling mice but with a short tail

volition (vō'lishən, və-) *n.* **1.** act, power of willing **2.** exercise of the will —**vo'litional** *a.*

Volk (folk) *n.* **SA** Afrikaner people

volley ('voli) *n.* **1.** simultaneous discharge of weapons or missiles **2.** rush of oaths, questions *etc.* **3.** *Sport* kick, stroke *etc.* at moving ball before it touches ground —*v.* **4.** discharge or be discharged —*vt.* **5.** utter **6.** fly, strike *etc.* in volley —'**volleyball** *n.* game played indoors or outdoors by two teams of six players each who seek to score points by hitting a ball back and forth across a net

volt (vōlt) *n.* unit of electric potential —'**voltage** *n.* electric potential difference expressed in volts —'**voltmeter** *n.*

voltaic (vol'tāik) *a. see* GALVANIC (sense 1)

volte-face (volt'fäs) *Fr. n.* complete reversal of opinion or direction (*pl.* **volte-face**)

voluble ('volyəbəl) *a.* talking easily, readily and at length —**volu'bility** *n.* —'**volubly** *adv.*

volume ('volyəm, -yōōm) *n.* **1.** space occupied **2.** bulk, mass **3.** amount **4.** power, fullness of voice or sound **5.** control on radio *etc.* for adjusting this **6.** book **7.** part of book bound in one cover —**volu'metric** *a.* pert. to measurement by volume —**voluminous** (və'lōōminəs) *a.* bulky, copious

voluntary ('volənteri) *a.* **1.** having, done by free will **2.** done without payment **3.**

supported by freewill contributions **4.** spontaneous *—n.* **5.** organ solo in church service **—volun'tarily** *adv.* **—volun'teer** *n.* **1.** one who offers service, joins force *etc.* of his own free will *—v.* **2.** offer oneself or one's services

voluptuous (və'lupchōōəs) *a.* of, contributing to pleasures of the senses **—vo'luptuary** *n.* one given to luxury and sensual pleasures

volute (və'lōōt) *n.* spiral or twisting turn, form or object

vomit ('vomit) *v.* **1.** eject (contents of stomach) through mouth *—n.* **2.** matter vomited

voodoo ('vōōdōō) *n.* **1.** practice of black magic, *esp.* in W Indies, witchcraft *—vt.* **2.** affect by voodoo

voracious (vŏ'rāshəs) *a.* greedy, ravenous **—vo'raciously** *adv.* **—voracity** (vŏ'rasiti) *n.*

-vorous (*a. comb. form*) feeding on; devouring, as in *carnivorous* **—-vore** (*n. comb. form*)

vortex ('vŏrteks) *n.* **1.** whirlpool **2.** whirling motion (*pl.* **-es, vortices** ('vŏrtisēz))

votary ('vōtəri) *n.* one vowed to service or pursuit (**'votaress** *fem.*) **—'votive** *a.* given, consecrated by vow

vote (vōt) *n.* **1.** formal expression of choice **2.** individual pronouncement **3.** right to give it, in question or election **4.** result of voting **5.** that which is given or allowed by vote *—v.* **6.** express, declare opinion, choice, preference *etc.* by vote **7.** authorize, enact *etc.* by vote **—'voter** *n.*

vouch (vowch) *vi.* (*usu. with* for) guarantee, make oneself responsible (for) **—'voucher** *n.* **1.** document proving correctness of item in accounts, or to establish facts **2.** ticket as substitute for cash **—vouch'safe** *vt.* condescend to grant or do

vow (vow) *n.* **1.** solemn promise, *esp.* religious one *—vt.* **2.** promise, threaten by vow

vowel ('vowəl) *n.* **1.** any speech sound pronounced without stoppage or friction of the breath **2.** letter standing for such sound, as *a, e, i, o, u*

vox (voks) *n.* voice; sound (*pl.* **voces** ('vōsēz)) **—vox populi** ('popyəlī) voice of the people; popular or public opinion

voyage ('voiij) *n.* **1.** journey, *esp.* long one, by sea or air *—vi.* **2.** make voyage **—'voyager** *n.* **—voyageur** (voiə'zhər, vwäyä'zhər; *Fr.* vwaya'zhœr) *n.* **C** guide, trapper in N regions

voyeur (vwä'yər) *n.* one obtaining sexual pleasure by watching sexual activities of others

vs. versus

V-sign *n.* gesture made by raising index and middle fingers with palm outward meaning victory or peace

V.S.O. very superior old (brandy)

V.S.O.P. very superior old pale (brandy)

VT *or* **Vt.** Vermont

VTOL ('vētol) vertical takeoff and landing

VTR video tape recorder

vulcanize ('vulkənīz) *vt.* treat (rubber) with sulfur at high temperature to increase its durability **—'vulcanite** *n.* rubber so hardened **—vulcani'zation** *n.* **—vulca'nology** *n.* *see* **volcanology** *at* VOLCANO

Vulg. Vulgate

vulgar ('vulgər) *a.* **1.** offending against good taste **2.** coarse **3.** common **—vulgarian** (vul'gariən, -'ger-) *n.* vulgar (rich) person **—'vulgarism** *n.* coarse, obscene word, phrase **—vulgarity** (vul'gariti) *n.* **—vulgari'zation** *n.* **—'vulgarize** *vt.* make vulgar or too common **—'vulgarly** *adv.* **—vulgar fraction** *see* **common fraction** *at* COMMON **—Vulgar Latin** any of dialects of Latin spoken in Roman Empire other than classical Latin

Vulgate ('vulgāt, -git) *n.* fourth-century Latin version of the Bible

vulnerable ('vulnərəbəl) *a.* **1.** capable of being physically or emotionally wounded or hurt **2.** exposed, open to attack, persuasion *etc.* **—vulnera'bility** *n.*

vulpine ('vulpīn) *a.* **1.** of foxes **2.** foxy

vulture ('vulchər) *n.* large bird which feeds on carrion **—'vulturine** *or* **'vulturous** *a.* **1.** of vulture **2.** rapacious

vulva ('vulvə) *n.* external genitals of human female

vv. **1.** versus **2.** *Mus.* volumes

v.v. vice versa

vying ('vīing) *pr.p. of* VIE

Vyrene ('vīrēn, vī'rēn) *n.* trade name for stretch fiber

W

w *or* **W** ('dubəlyōō) *n.* **1.** 23rd letter of English alphabet **2.** speech sound represented by this letter, usu. semivowel, as in *web* (*pl.* **w's, W's** *or* **Ws**)

W 1. *Chem.* tungsten **2.** energy

w. 1. warden **2.** water **3.** watt **4.** week **5.** weight **6.** west(ern) **7.** white **8.** wide **9.** width **10.** wife

W. 1. Wales **2.** Welsh

WA Washington

WAC Women's Army Corps

wacky ('waki) *a. sl.* eccentric or unpredictable

wad (wod) *n.* **1.** small pad of fibrous material **2.** thick roll of bank notes **3.** sum of money —*vt.* **4.** line, pad, stuff *etc.* with wad (**-dd-**) —'**wadding** *n.* stuffing

waddle ('wodəl) *vi.* **1.** walk like duck —*n.* **2.** this gait

wade (wād) *vi.* **1.** walk through something that hampers movement, *esp.* water **2.** proceed with difficulty —'**wader** *n.* **1.** person or bird that wades —*pl.* **2.** angler's high waterproof boots

Wade-Giles ('wād'jīlz) *n./a.* (of) system of transliterating the Chinese language into the Roman alphabet, superseded by Pinyin in some countries

Waf (waf) *n.* member of women's component of U.S. Air Force formed after World War II

wafer ('wāfər) *n.* **1.** thin, crisp biscuit **2.** thin slice of anything

waffle ('wofəl) *n.* kind of pancake with deep indentations on both sides —**waffle iron** utensil for cooking waffles, having two flat, studded plates hinged together

waft (woft, waft) *vt.* **1.** convey smoothly through air or water —*n.* **2.** breath of wind **3.** odor, whiff

wag (wag) *v.* **1.** (cause to) move rapidly from side to side (**-gg-**) —*n.* **2.** instance of wagging **3.** *inf.* humorous, witty person —'**waggish** *a.* —'**wagtail** *n.* small bird with wagging tail

wage (wāj) *n.* **1.** (*oft. pl.*) payment for work done —*vt.* **2.** engage in

wager ('wājər) *n./v.* bet

waggle ('wagəl) *v.* wag —'**waggly** *a.*

Wagnerian (väg'nēəriən) *a.* pert. to German composer Richard Wagner, his music or his theories

wagon ('wagən) *n.* **1.** four-wheeled vehicle for heavy loads **2.** railway freight truck —'**wagoner** *n.* —**wago'nette** *n.* four-wheeled horse-drawn vehicle with two lengthwise seats facing each other behind driver's seat

waif (wāf) *n.* homeless person, *esp.* child

wail (wāl) *v.* **1.** cry out —*vt.* **2.** lament —*n.* **3.** mournful cry

wainscot ('wānskət) *n.* **1.** wooden lining of walls of room —*vt.* **2.** line thus

waist (wāst) *n.* **1.** part of body between hips and ribs **2.** various narrow central parts —'**waistband** *n.* fabric or ribbon fitting around the waist of trousers or skirt —'**waistline** *n.* line, size of waist (of person, garment)

wait (wāt) *v.* **1.** stay in one place, remain inactive in expectation (of something) **2.** be prepared (for something) **3.** delay —*vi.* **4.** serve in restaurant *etc.* —*n.* **5.** act or period of waiting —*pl.* **6.** street musicians, carol singers —'**waiter** *n.* **1.** attendant on guests at hotel, restaurant *etc.* ('**waitress** *fem.*) **2.** one who waits —**waiting game** postponement of action in order to gain advantage —**waiting list** list of people waiting to obtain some object, treatment *etc.*

waive (wāv) *vt.* **1.** forgo **2.** not insist on —'**waiver** *n.* (written statement of) this act

wake[1] (wāk) *v.* **1.** rouse from sleep **2.** stir (up) (**woke, 'woken, 'waking**) —*n.* **3.** vigil **4.** watch beside corpse **5.** (*oft. pl.*) annual holiday in parts of N England —'**wakeful** *a.* —'**waken** *v.* wake

wake[2] (wāk) *n.* track or path left by anything that has passed, as track of turbulent water behind ship

Wake Island (wāk) territory of the U.S. in the western Pacific Ocean

Waldorf salad ('wöldörf) salad made usu. of diced apples, celery, nuts and mayonnaise

wale (wāl) *n.* **1.** raised mark left on skin after stroke of whip **2.** weave of fabric, such as ribs in corduroy **3.** *Naut.* ridge of planking along rail of ship —*v.* **4.** raise wales (on) by striking **5.** weave with wale

Wales (wālz) *n.* division of the United Kingdom in southwest Great Britain —**Welsh** *a./n.* —'**Welshman** *n.* —**Welsh rabbit** *or* **rarebit** savory dish of melted cheese on toast —**Welsh terrier** wire-haired breed of terrier with black-and-tan coat

walk (wök) *v.* **1.** (cause, assist to) move, travel on foot at ordinary pace —*vt.* **2.** cross, pass through by walking **3.** escort, conduct by walking —*n.* **4.** act, instance of walking **5.** path or other place or route for walking **6.** manner of walking **7.** occupation, career

—ˈ**walker** *n.* **1.** person who walks **2.** framework used as aid to walking, *esp.* for baby or crippled person **3.** escort, usu. male —ˈ**walkabout** *n.* **1.** informal stroll by a public figure **2.** (of Aust. Aborigine) wandering —**walkie-talkie** *n.* portable radio set containing both transmission and receiver units —**walking stick** stick, cane carried to assist walking —**walk-on** *n.* small part in play —ˈ**walkout** *n.* **1.** strike **2.** act of leaving as a protest —ˈ**walkover** *n.* unopposed or easy victory

wall (wŏl) *n.* **1.** structure of brick, stone *etc.* serving as fence, side of building *etc.* **2.** surface of one **3.** anything resembling this —*vt.* **4.** enclose with wall **5.** block up with wall —ˈ**wallboard** *n.* thin board made of materials, such as compressed wood fibers or gypsum plaster, used to cover walls *etc.* —ˈ**wallflower** *n.* **1.** hardy perennial or subshrub of the cabbage family, oft. scented, grown as ornamental **2.** woman who remains seated at dance *etc.* for lack of partner —ˈ**wallpaper** *n.* **1.** paper, usu. patterned, to cover interior walls —*v.* **2.** cover (surface) with wallpaper

wallaby

wallaby (ˈwoləbi) *n.* any of various small species of kangaroo

wallet (ˈwolit) *n.* small folding case, *esp.* for paper money, documents *etc.*

walleyed (ˈwŏlīd) *a.* **1.** squinting **2.** having eyes with pale irises

Walloon (woˈlo͞on) *n.* **1.** member of French-speaking people living chiefly in S and SE Belgium **2.** French dialect of Belgium —*a.* **3.** of Walloons or their dialect

wallop (ˈwoləp) *inf. vt.* **1.** beat soundly **2.** strike hard —*n.* **3.** stroke or blow —ˈ**walloper** *n. inf.* one who wallops —ˈ**walloping** *inf. n.* **1.** thrashing —*adv.* **2.** very, greatly —*a.* **3.** great

wallow (ˈwolō) *vi.* **1.** roll (in liquid or mud) **2.** revel —*n.* **3.** act or instance of wallowing **4.** muddy place where animals wallow

Wall Street dominant financial interests of the U.S. economy

walnut (ˈwŏlnut) *n.* **1.** edible nut of north temperature zone tree **2.** the tree **3.** its wood **4.** the hickory nut **5.** any fruit or tree resembling the walnut

walrus (ˈwŏlrəs, ˈwol-) *n.* either of two large marine mammals related to seals and found in Arctic seas (*pl.* **-es, -rus**)

waltz (wŏlts, wŏls) *n.* **1.** ballroom dance **2.** music in triple time —*v.* **3.** dance or lead (someone) in or as in a waltz

wampum (ˈwompəm) *n.* **1.** beads made of shells, formerly used by N Amer. Indians as money and for ornament **2.** *sl.* money

wan (won) *a.* pale, sickly complexioned, pallid

wand (wond) *n.* stick, usu. straight and slender, *esp.* as carried by magician *etc.*

wander (ˈwondər) *v.* **1.** roam, ramble —*vi.* **2.** go astray, deviate —*n.* **3.** stroll —ˈ**wanderer** *n.* —ˈ**wanderlust** *n.* irrepressible urge to wander or travel

wane (wān) *vi./n.* **1.** decline **2.** (of moon) decrease in size

wangle (ˈwanggəl) *inf. vt.* **1.** manipulate, manage in skillful way —*n.* **2.** intrigue, trickery, something obtained by craft

Wankel engine (ˈvängkəl, ˈwängkəl) type of rotary four-stroke internal-combustion engine without reciprocating parts

want (wont) *v.* **1.** desire —*vt.* **2.** lack —*n.* **3.** desire **4.** need **5.** deficiency —ˈ**wanted** *a.* being sought, *esp.* by the police —ˈ**wanting** *a.* **1.** lacking **2.** below standard

wanton (ˈwontən) *a.* **1.** dissolute **2.** without motive, thoughtless **3.** unrestrained —*n.* **4.** wanton person, *esp.* woman

wapiti (ˈwopiti) *n. see* ELK (sense 1) (*pl.* **wapiti, -s**)

war[1] (wŏr) *n.* **1.** fighting between nations **2.** state of hostility **3.** conflict, contest —*vi.* **4.** make war (**-rr-**) —ˈ**warlike** *a.* **1.** of, for war **2.** fond of war —ˈ**warrior** *n.* fighter —ˈ**warbonnet** *n.* Amerindian ceremonial headdress with feathered extension down back —**war crime** crime committed in wartime in violation of accepted customs of war —**war cry 1.** cry used by attacking troops in war **2.** distinctive word, phrase used by political party *etc.* —ˈ**warfare** *n.* hostilities —**war game 1.** notional tactical exercise for training military commanders, in which no military units are actually deployed **2.** game in which model soldiers are used to create battles in order to study tactics —ˈ**warhead** *n.* part of missile *etc.* containing explosives —ˈ**warhorse** *n.* **1.** horse used in battle **2.** *inf.* veteran soldier or politician —**war memorial** monument to those who die in war —ˈ**warmonger** *n.* one fostering, encouraging war —**war paint 1.** painted decoration of face and body applied by certain N Amer. Indians before battle **2.** *inf.* cosmetics —ˈ**warpath** *n.* route taken by N Amer. Indians on warlike expedition —ˈ**warship** *n.* vessel armed, armored for naval warfare —**'wartime** *n./a.* —**on the warpath** *inf.* in a state of anger

war[2] warrant

warble ('wörbəl) *v.* sing with trills —**'warbler** *n.* **1.** person or bird that warbles **2.** kind of small songbird

ward (wörd) *n.* **1.** division of city **2.** minor under care of guardian **3.** guardianship **4.** bar in lock, groove in key that prevents incorrectly cut key opening lock —**'warder** *n.* jailer (**'wardress** *fem.*) —**'wardship** *n.* **1.** office of guardian **2.** state of being under guardian —**'wardroom** *n.* officers' mess on warship —**ward off** avert, repel

-ward *or* **-wards** (*comb. form*) indicating direction toward, as in *backward step*

warden ('wördən) *n.* person, officer in charge of building, institution, college *etc.*

wardrobe ('wördrōb) *n.* **1.** piece of furniture for hanging clothes in **2.** person's supply of clothing **3.** costumes of theatrical company

ware (wāər) *n.* **1.** goods **2.** articles collectively —*pl.* **3.** goods for sale **4.** commodities **5.** merchandise —**'warehouse** *n.* storehouse for goods prior to distribution and sale

warlock ('wörlok) *n.* man who practices black magic

warm (wörm) *a.* **1.** moderately hot **2.** serving to maintain heat **3.** affectionate **4.** ardent **5.** earnest **6.** hearty **7.** (of color) having yellow or red base —*v.* **8.** make, become warm —**'warmly** *adv.* —**warmth** *n.* **1.** mild heat **2.** cordiality **3.** vehemence, anger —**warm-blooded** *a.* **1.** having constant body temperature independent of surroundings **2.** ardent —**warm-bloodedness** *n.* —**warm front** *Met.* advancing edge of warm air mass —**warming pan** metal container holding hot liquid or hot coals with a cover and long handle used to warm a bed

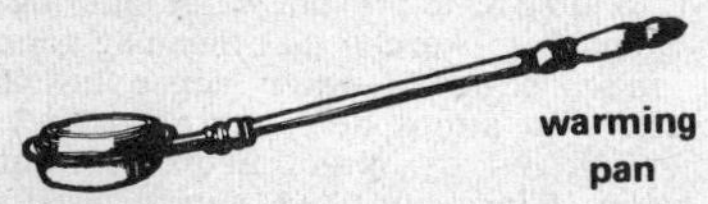

warming pan

warn (wörn) *vt.* **1.** put on guard **2.** caution, admonish **3.** give advance information to **4.** notify authoritatively —**'warning** *n.* **1.** hint of harm *etc.* **2.** admonition **3.** advance notice

warp (wörp) *v.* **1.** (cause to) twist (out of shape) **2.** pervert or be perverted —*n.* **3.** state, condition of being warped **4.** lengthwise threads on loom

warrant ('worənt) *n.* **1.** authority **2.** document giving authority —*vt.* **3.** guarantee **4.** authorize, justify —**warran'tee** *n.* person given warranty —**warran'tor** *n.* person, company giving warranty —**'warranty** *n.* **1.** guarantee of quality of goods **2.** security —**warrant officer 1.** officer in armed services who holds a rank between those of commissioned and noncommissioned officers **2.** commissioned officer ranking below ensign in the navy or coast guard and below a second lieutenant in the marine corps

warren ('worən) *n.* **1.** (burrows inhabited by) colony of rabbits **2.** crowded tenement or district **3.** maze of passageways or cubicles

wart (wört) *n.* small hard growth on skin caused by virus —**wart hog** kind of Afr. wild pig

wary ('wāəri) *a.* watchful, cautious, alert

was (woz; *unstressed* wəz) *pt.* first and third person sing. of BE

wash (wosh) *v.* **1.** clean (oneself, clothing *etc.*), *esp.* with water, soap *etc.* **2.** move, be moved by water —*vi.* **3.** be washable **4.** *inf.* be able to be proved true —*vt.* **5.** flow, sweep over, against —*n.* **6.** act of washing **7.** clothing washed at one time **8.** sweep of water, *esp.* set up by moving ship **9.** thin coat of color —**'washable** *a.* capable of being washed without damage *etc.* —**'washer** *n.* **1.** one who, that which, washes **2.** ring put under a nut —**'washing** *n.* clothing to be washed —**'washy** *a.* **1.** dilute **2.** watery **3.** insipid —**wash-and-wear** *a.* of or relating to fabric or clothing needing little or no ironing after washing —**'washboard** *n.* **1.** corrugated rectangular surface used for scrubbing clothes **2.** *Naut.* planklike shield fastened to gunwales of boat to prevent water from splashing over side —**wash drawing** pen-and-ink drawing that has been lightly brushed over with water —**washing soda** common name for sodium carbonate —**'washout** *n. inf.* complete failure —**washed out 1.** faded or colorless **2.** exhausted, pale

Washington[1] ('wöshingtən, 'wosh-) *n.* Pacific state of the U.S., admitted to the Union in 1889. Abbrev.: **Wash., WA** (with ZIP code)

Washington[2] ('wöshingtən, 'wosh-) *n.* **George.** the 1st President of the U.S. (1789-97)

wasp (wosp) *n.* striped stinging insect resembling bee —**'waspish** *a.* irritable, snappish —**wasp waist** very small waist

WASP *or* **Wasp** (wosp) *n.* White Anglo-Saxon Protestant: person descended from N European Protestant stock, *esp.* member of most privileged class of people in the U.S.

wassail ('wosəl, wo'sāl) *n.* **1.** formerly, toast made to person at festivities **2.** festivity when much drinking takes place **3.** alcoholic liquor drunk at such festivity, *esp.* spiced beer —*v.* **4.** drink health of (person) at wassail —*vi.* **5.** go from house to house singing carols at Christmas

Wassermann test ('wosərmən) diagnostic procedure used to detect syphilis

waste (wāst) *vt.* **1.** expend uselessly, use extravagantly **2.** fail to take advantage of **3.** lay desolate **4.** kill; injure severely —*vi.* **5.** dwindle **6.** pine away —*n.* **7.** act of wasting **8.** what is wasted **9.** desert —*a.* **10.** useless **11.** desert **12.** wasted —**'wastage** *n.* **1.** loss by use or decay **2.** reduction in numbers, *esp.* of work force —**'wasteful** *a.* extravagant —**'wastefully** *adv.* —**'wasting** *a.* reducing vitality, strength or robustness of body —**'wastrel** *n.* wasteful person, idler —**'wasteland** *n.* barren or desolate area of land

watch (woch) *vt.* **1.** observe closely **2.** guard —*vi.* **3.** wait expectantly **4.** be on watch —*n.* **5.** portable timepiece for wrist, pocket *etc.* **6.** state of being on the lookout **7.** guard **8.** spell of duty, *esp.* on shipboard where 24 hours is divided into six watches beginning at 12.30 a.m. —**'watchful** *a.* —**'watchfully** *adv.* —**'watchdog** *n.* **1.** dog trained to guard property **2.** person or group that acts as protector against inefficiency *etc.* —**'watchmaker** *n.* one skilled in making and repairing watches —**'watchman** *n.* man guarding building *etc.*, *esp.* at night —**watch night** in Protestant churches, service held on night of Dec. 31st, to mark passing of old year —**'watchword** *n.* **1.** password **2.** rallying cry

water ('wôtər) *n.* **1.** liquid form of compound of hydrogen and oxygen descending as rain, forming rivers, lakes and seas **2.** body of water **3.** river **4.** lake **5.** sea **6.** tear **7.** urine —*vt.* **8.** put water on or into **9.** irrigate, provide with water —*vi.* **10.** salivate **11.** (of eyes) fill with tears **12.** take in or obtain water —**'watery** *a.* —**water bed** waterproof mattress filled with water —**water biscuit** cracker made mainly of flour and water —**water boy** person who keeps group supplied with water —**'waterbuck** *n.* Afr. antelope —**water buffalo** domesticated Asian buffalo —**water bug** any of various aquatic insects with grasping forelimbs and partially thickened wings —**water cannon** device for directing stream of water used to control crowds —**water chestnut 1.** tuber of a Chinese sedge **2.** fruit of aquatic plant of primrose family —**'watercolor** *n.* **1.** paint in which water is the solvent of the binding material **2.** painting in this medium —**water cooler** device for supplying refrigerated drinking water —**'watercourse** *n.* natural or man-made channel through which water flows —**'waterfall** *n.* perpendicular descent of waters of a stream —**'waterfowl** *n.* **1.** any aquatic freshwater bird, *esp.* duck, goose or swan **2.** such birds collectively —**'waterfront** *n.* area of town abutting on a body of water —**water gauge** instrument that measures volume of water in tank —**water glass 1.** glass vessel for holding drinking water **2.** device with glass bottom for examining objects in or under water **3.** silicate of sodium used in commerce as cement, protective coating and fireproofing agent **4.** water gauge —**water ice** frozen dessert of water, sugar and flavoring —**watering place 1.** place where animals, *esp.* livestock, come to drink **2.** health or recreational resort featuring mineral springs **3.** nightclub, bar or lounge where drink is available —**water jump** obstacle in race consisting of pool, stream or ditch —**water lily** any of genus of aquatic plants with showy flowers —**'waterline** *n.* any of several lines marked on outside of ship to correspond with surface of the water —**'waterlogged** *a.* saturated, filled with water —**water main** pipe or conduit for conveying water —**'watermark** *n.* **1.** mark indicating height to which water has risen **2.** marking in paper produced by projecting design during manufacture **3.** design or pattern of the marking —*vt.* **4.** mark (paper) with watermark **5.** impress in the manner of a watermark —**'watermelon** *n.* **1.** large edible fruit with hard green rind and sweet watery reddish flesh **2.** any vine of the gourd family bearing watermelons —**water moccasin 1.** venomous semiaquatic pit viper related to copperhead (*also* **cottonmouth, cottonmouth moccasin**) **2.** Amer. snake living in or near water —**water ouzel** *see* DIPPER (sense 2) —**water pistol** toy pistol that squirts stream of water —**water polo** goal-type game played in water —**water power 1.** power latent in dynamic or static head of water as used to drive machinery **2.** source of such power, such as dam —**'waterproof** *a.* **1.** not letting water through —*vt.* **2.** make waterproof —**water-repellent** *a.* (of fabric) having a finish that resists absorption of water —**'watershed** *n.* **1.** drainage area **2.** the point of change between two conditions, phases *etc.* —**'waterskiing** *n.* sport in which person on skis is towed by boat —**'waterspout** *n.* **1.** pipe from which water is spouted **2.** the water lifted from a body of water by a tornado —**water table** level below which ground is saturated with water —**'watertight** *a.* **1.** so fitted as to prevent water entering or escaping **2.** so worded that meaning cannot be misconstrued —**water vapor** invisible moisture in atmosphere —**'waterwheel** *n.* wheel driven by direct action of water —**water wings** air-filled device used to support body of swimmer —**'waterworks** *pl.n.* **1.** (*with sing. v.*) system for storing, purifying and distributing water for community supply **2.** (*with pl. v.*) crying, tears **3.** (*with pl. v.*) urinary system

water wheel

Watergate ('wŏtərgāt) *n.* political scandal, usu. involving abuse of power of office and concealment

Waterloo (wŏtər'lōō) *n.* **1.** town in Belgium, site of battle where Napoleon met his final defeat **2.** total or crushing defeat (*esp. in* **meet one's Waterloo**)

watt (wot) *n.* unit of electric power —'**wattage** *n.* electric power expressed in watts —**watt-hour** *n.* unit of energy equal to one watt used for one hour —'**wattmeter** *n.* meter for measuring electric power in watts

wattle ('wotəl) *n.* **1.** frame of woven branches *etc.* as fence **2.** fleshy pendant lobe of neck of certain birds, *eg* turkey —**wattle and daub** form of wall construction consisting of interwoven twigs plastered with mixture of clay and water

waul *or* **wawl** (wŏl) *vi.* cry or wail plaintively like cat

wave (wāv) *v.* **1.** move to and fro, as hand in greeting or farewell **2.** signal by waving **3.** give, take shape of waves (as hair *etc.*) —*n.* **4.** ridge and trough on water *etc.* **5.** act, gesture of waving **6.** vibration, as in radio waves, of electric and magnetic forces alternating in direction **7.** prolonged spell of something **8.** upsurge **9.** wavelike shape in the hair *etc.* —'**wavy** *a.* —'**waveband** *n.* range of wavelengths or frequencies used for particular type of radio transmission —'**wavelength** *n.* distance between same points of two successive sound waves

waver ('wāvər) *vi.* **1.** hesitate, be irresolute **2.** be, become unsteady —'**waverer** *n.*

WAVES (wāvz) Women Accepted for Volunteer Emergency Service (Women's Reserve, U.S. Naval Reserve)

wax[1] (waks) *n.* **1.** yellow, soft, pliable material made by bees **2.** this or similar substance used for sealing, making candles *etc.* **3.** waxy secretion of ear —*vt.* **4.** put wax on —'**waxen** *a.* **1.** made of, treated with, or covered with wax **2.** resembling wax in color or texture —'**waxy** *a.* like wax —**wax bean** yellowish string bean with waxy pod —'**waxbill** *n.* Afr. finchlike weaverbird —**waxed** *or* **wax paper** paper coated with wax to make it resist water and oil, used as wrapping —'**waxwing** *n.* small songbird —'**waxwork** *n.* lifelike figure, *esp.* of famous person, reproduced in wax

wax[2] (waks) *vi.* grow, increase

way (wā) *n.* **1.** manner **2.** method, means **3.** track **4.** direction **5.** path **6.** passage **7.** course **8.** route **9.** progress **10.** state or condition —'**waybill** *n.* document attached to goods in transit specifying their nature, point of origin, destination and rate to be charged —'**wayfarer** *n.* traveler, *esp.* on foot —'**waylay** *vt.* lie in wait for and accost, attack (**-laid, -laying**) —**way-out** *a. inf.* **1.** extremely unconventional or experimental **2.** excellent or amazing —'**wayside** *n.* **1.** side or edge of a road —*a.* **2.** situated by the wayside —'**wayward** *a.* capricious, perverse, willful —'**waywardly** *adv.* —'**waywardness** *n.* —**ways and means 1.** revenues and methods of raising revenues needed for functioning of state *etc.* **2.** (**W- a- M-**) committee of legislature concerned with this purpose —**Way of the Cross** *see* **Stations of the Cross** *at* STATION

-ways (*comb. form*) indicating direction or manner, as in *sideways*

Wb *Phys.* weber

W.C. *or* **WC** without charge

WCTU Women's Christian Temperance Union

wd 1. wood **2.** word **3.** would

W.D. War Department

we (wē) *pron.* first person plural pronoun

weak (wēk) *a.* **1.** lacking strength **2.** feeble **3.** fragile **4.** defenseless **5.** easily influenced **6.** faint —'**weaken** *v.* —'**weakling** *n.* feeble creature —'**weakly** *a.* **1.** weak **2.** sickly —*adv.* **3.** in a weak or feeble manner —'**weakness** *n.* —**weak-kneed** *a. inf.* yielding readily to force, intimidation *etc.*

weal[1] (wēl) *n.* streak left on flesh by blow of stick or whip

weal[2] (wēl) *n. obs.* prosperity or wellbeing (*esp. in* **the public weal, common weal**)

weald (wēld) *n. obs.* forested country

wealth (welth) *n.* **1.** riches **2.** abundance —'**wealthiness** *n.* —'**wealthy** *a.*

wean (wēn) *vt.* **1.** accustom to food other than mother's milk **2.** coax away

weapon ('wepən) *n.* **1.** implement to fight with **2.** anything used to get the better of an opponent

wear (wāər) *vt.* **1.** have on the body **2.** show **3.** produce (hole *etc.*) by rubbing *etc.* **4.** harass; weaken **5.** *inf.* allow, tolerate —*vi.* **6.** last **7.** become impaired by use **8.** (*with* on) (of time) pass slowly (**wore, worn, 'wearing**) —*n.* **9.** act of wearing **10.** things to wear **11.** damage caused by use **12.** ability to resist effects of constant use —'**wearer** *n.* —**wear and tear** depreciation or loss resulting from ordinary use

weary ('wēəri) *a.* **1.** tired, exhausted, jaded **2.** tiring **3.** tedious —*v.* **4.** make, become weary ('**wearied, 'wearying**) —'**wearily** *adv.* —'**weariness** *n.* —'**wearisome** *a.* causing weariness

weasel ('wēzəl) *n.* **1.** any of various small, fierce carnivores with long slender bodies **2.** cunning person **3.** tracked vehicle resembling tractor used in snow **4.** *sl.* informer —*vi.* **5.** evade an obligation, renege —**weasel words** ambiguous words intended to mislead

weather ('wedhər) *n.* **1.** day-to-day meteorological conditions, *esp.* temperature, cloudiness *etc.* of a place —*a.* **2.** toward the wind —*v.* **3.** affect or be affected by weather —*vt.* **4.** endure **5.** resist **6.** come safely through **7.** sail to windward of —'**weathering** *n.*

mechanical and chemical breakdown of rocks by action of rain, cold *etc.* —**weather-beaten** *a.* showing signs of exposure to weather —ˈ**weatherboard** *n.* timber boards used as external cladding of house; clapboard —**weather-bound** *a.* (of vessel, aircraft *etc.*) delayed by bad weather —ˈ**weathercock** *n.* revolving vane to show which way wind blows —**weather eye 1.** vision of person trained to observe changes in weather **2.** *inf.* alert or observant gaze —**weather house** model house, usu. with two human figures, one that enters to foretell bad weather and one that enters to foretell good weather —**weather strip** thin strip of metal, felt *etc.* fitted between frame of door or window and opening part to exclude drafts and rain —**weather vane** vane designed to indicate direction in which wind is blowing

weave (wēv) *vt.* **1.** form into texture or fabric by interlacing, *esp.* on loom **2.** fashion, construct —*vi.* **3.** practice weaving **4.** make one's way, *esp.* with side-to-side motion (**wove** *or* **weaved**, ˈ**woven** *or* **weaved**, ˈ**weaving**) —ˈ**weaver** *n.* **1.** person who weaves **2.** weaverbird —ˈ**weaverbird** *n.* small Old World passerine songbird with short thick bill and dull plumage which builds covered nests

web (web) *n.* **1.** woven fabric **2.** net spun by spider **3.** membrane between toes of waterfowl, frogs *etc.* —ˈ**webbing** *n.* strong fabric woven in strips

weber (ˈwebər, ˈvābər) *n.* SI unit of magnetic flux

wed (wed) *v.* **1.** marry —*vt.* **2.** unite closely (ˈ**wedded, wed** *pt./pp.*, ˈ**wedding**) —ˈ**wedding** *n.* act of marrying, nuptial ceremony —ˈ**wedlock** *n.* marriage

Wed. Wednesday

wedge (wej) *n.* **1.** piece of wood, metal *etc.*, thick at one end, tapering to a thin edge —*vt.* **2.** fasten, split with wedge **3.** stick by compression or crowding

Wedgwood (ˈwejwŏŏd) *n.* trade name for dinner ware and ornamental ceramic objects

Wednesday (ˈwenzdi) *n.* fourth day of week

wee (wē) *a.* small, little

weed (wēd) *n.* **1.** plant growing where undesired **2.** *inf.* tobacco **3.** *inf.* marijuana **4.** *inf.* thin, sickly person, animal —*vt.* **5.** clear of weeds —ˈ**weedy** *a.* **1.** full of weeds **2.** *inf.* thin, weakly —**weed out** remove, eliminate what is unwanted

weeds (wēdz) *pl.n.* (widow's) mourning clothes

week (wēk) *n.* **1.** period of seven days, *esp.* one beginning on Sunday and ending on Saturday **2.** hours, days of work in seven-day period —ˈ**weekly** *a./adv.* **1.** (happening, done, published *etc.*) once a week —*n.* **2.** newspaper or magazine issued every week —ˈ**weekday** *n.* any day of week except Sunday and *usu.* Saturday —ˈ**weekend** *n.* Saturday and Sunday, *esp.* considered as rest period

weep (wēp) *v.* **1.** shed (tears) —*vi.* **2.** grieve **3.** excude fluid (**wept,** ˈ**weeping**) —ˈ**weepy** *a.* —**weeping willow** willow with drooping branches

weevil (ˈwēvil) *n.* any of numerous beetles with head prolonged to a snout, destructive to nuts, grain, fruit *etc.*

weft (weft) *n. see* WOOF[1]

weigh (wā) *vt.* **1.** find weight of **2.** consider **3.** raise (anchor) —*vi.* **4.** have weight **5.** be burdensome —**weight** *n.* **1.** force exerted on a quantity of matter by the gravity of the earth **2.** quality of heaviness **3.** heavy mass **4.** object of known mass for weighing **5.** unit of measurement of weight **6.** importance, influence —*vt.* **7.** add weight to —ˈ**weightily** *adv.* —ˈ**weighting** *n.* additional allowance payable in particular circumstances —ˈ**weightlessness** *n.* having little or no weight, experienced *esp.* at great distances from earth because of reduced gravitational attraction (*also* **zero gravity**) —ˈ**weighty** *a.* **1.** heavy **2.** onerous **3.** important **4.** momentous —ˈ**weighbridge** *n.* machine for weighing vehicles *etc.* by means of metal plate set into road —ˈ**weightlifting** *n.* sport of lifting barbells of specified weights in prescribed manner

weir (wēər) *n.* river dam

weird (wēərd) *a.* **1.** unearthly, uncanny **2.** strange, bizarre

welch (welch) *vi. see* WELSH

welcome (ˈwelkəm) *a.* **1.** received gladly **2.** freely permitted —*n.* **3.** kindly greeting —*vt.* **4.** greet with pleasure **5.** receive gladly (**-comed, -coming**)

weld (weld) *vt.* **1.** unite (metal) by softening with heat **2.** unite closely —*n.* **3.** welded joint —ˈ**welder** *n.* **1.** tradesman who welds **2.** machine used in welding

welfare (ˈwelfāər) *n.* **1.** well-being **2.** government aid, *esp.* financial, for the needy —**welfare state** system in which the government takes responsibility for the social, economic *etc.* security of its citizens

well[1] (wel) *adv.* **1.** in good manner or degree **2.** suitably **3.** intimately **4.** fully **5.** favorably, kindly **6.** to a considerable degree —*a.* **7.** in good health **8.** suitable (ˈ**better** *comp.*, **best** *sup.*) —*interj.* **9.** exclamation of surprise, interrogation *etc.* —**well-appointed** *a.* equipped or furnished well —**well-balanced** *a.* **1.** sane; sensible **2.** equally matched —**well-being** *n.* state of being well, happy or prosperous —**well-connected** *a.* having influential relatives —**well-disposed** *a.* having kindly or favorable feelings (toward) —**well-done** *a.* **1.** accomplished satisfactorily **2.** (of meat) cooked thoroughly —**well-earned** *a.* fully deserved —**well-grounded** *a.* **1.** thoroughly trained in rudiments of a subject **2.**

based on good reasons —**well-heeled** *a. sl.* rich —**well-informed** *a.* knowledgeable —**well-intentioned** *a.* having benevolent intentions, usu. with unfortunate results —**well-kept** *a.* **1.** (of person) having a tidy, pleasing appearance **2.** (of room *etc.*) neat **3.** (of secret) not divulged —**well-nigh** *adv. poet.* almost —**well-off** *a.* **1.** in satisfactory state **2.** rich —**well-read** *a.* having read much —**well-rounded** *a.* **1.** varied and complete **2.** (of person) having developed many abilities **3.** symmetrical **4.** (of sentence) expressed well —**well-spoken** *a.* speaking fluently, graciously, aptly —**well-to-do** *a.* moderately wealthy —**well tried** proven to be satisfactory by long experience —**well-wisher** *n.* person who shows benevolence toward person, cause *etc.* —**well-wishing** *a./n.* —**well-worn** *a.* **1.** so much used as to be affected by wear **2.** hackneyed

well[2] (wel) *n.* **1.** hole sunk into the earth to reach water, gas, oil *etc.* **2.** spring **3.** any shaft like a well **4.** lowered floor forming seating area —*vi.* **5.** spring, gush —**'wellhead** *n.* **1.** source of well or stream **2.** source, fountainhead or origin —**'wellspring** *n.* **1.** source of spring or stream **2.** source of abundant supply

welsh (welsh) *or* **welch** *vi.* fail to pay debt or fulfill obligation —**'welsher** *or* **'welcher** *n.*

Welsh (welsh) *a./n. see* WALES

welt (welt) *n.* **1.** raised, strengthened seam **2.** weal —*vt.* **3.** provide with welt **4.** thrash

welter ('weltər) *vi.* **1.** roll or tumble —*n.* **2.** turmoil, disorder

welterweight ('weltərwāt) *n.* **1.** professional boxer weighing 140-147 lbs (63.5-66.5 kg); amateur boxer weighing 140-148 lbs (63.5-67 kg) **2.** wrestler weighing usu. 154-172 lbs (70-78 kg)

wen (wen) *n.* cyst, *esp.* on scalp

wench (wench) *n. now oft. facetious* young woman

wend (wend) *v.* go, travel

wendigo ('wendigo) *n.* **C** *see* SPLAKE

went (went) *pt. of* GO[1]

wept (wept) *pt./pp. of* WEEP

were (wər) imperfect indicative plural and subjunctive sing. and pl. of BE

werewolf ('wēərwŏŏlf, 'wāər-) *n.* in folklore, human being turned into wolf

weskit ('weskit) *n.* woman's sleeveless garment for the upper body

Wesleyan ('wesliən, 'wez-) *a.* **1.** pert. to English preacher, John Wesley (1703-91), who founded Methodism **2.** of Methodism, *esp.* in its original form —*n.* **3.** follower of John Wesley **4.** member of Methodist Church —**'Wesleyanism** *n.*

west (west) *n.* **1.** part of sky where sun sets **2.** part of country *etc.* lying to this side **3.** occident —*a.* **4.** that is toward or in this region —*adv.* **5.** to the west —**'westerly** *a.* —**'western** *a.* **1.** of, in the west **2.** of dress based on clothes of working cowboys, *eg* jeans, high-heeled boots —*n.* **3.** motion picture, story *etc.* about cowboys or frontiersmen in western U.S. —**'westernize** *vt.* influence with customs, practices *etc.* of West —**'westward** *a./adv.* —**'westwards** *adv.* toward the west —**western hemisphere** (*oft.* **W- H-**) that half of the globe containing N and S Amer. —**go west** *inf.* **1.** disappear **2.** die **3.** be lost

West Germany *see* (Federal Republic of) GERMANY

Westminster ('westminstər) *n.* British Houses of Parliament

West Virginia East Central state of the U.S., admitted to the Union in 1863. Abbrev.: **W.Va., WV** (with ZIP code)

wet (wet) *a.* **1.** having water or other liquid on a surface or being soaked in it **2.** rainy **3.** (of paint, ink *etc.*) not yet dry **4.** permitting manufacture and sale of alcoholic liquors (**'wetter** *comp.*, **'wettest** *sup.*) —*vt.* **5.** make wet (**wet, 'wetted** *pt./pp.*, **'wetting** *pr.p.*) —*n.* **6.** moisture, rain —**'wetback** *n.* Mexican who enters U.S. illegally —**wet blanket** *inf.* one depressing spirits of others —**wet dream** erotic dream accompanied by emission of semen —**wet nurse** woman suckling another's child —**wet suit** close-fitting rubber suit worn by divers *etc.*

wether ('wedhər) *n.* castrated ram

WFTU World Federation of Trade Unions

wh **1.** which **2.** white

WH watt-hour

whack (wak) *vt.* **1.** strike with sharp resounding blow —*n.* **2.** such blow **3.** *inf.* share **4.** *inf.* attempt —**whacked** *a.* exhausted —**'whacking** *a. inf.* big, enormous

whale (wāl) *n.* **1.** any of order of large marine mammals with fishlike bodies and flattened heads **2.** thing or idea with great magnitude **3.** *Astron.* the constellation *Cetus* —**'whaler** *n.* man, ship employed in hunting whales —**'whaling** *n.* work or industry of hunting and processing whales for food, oil *etc.* —**'whalebone** *n.* **1.** horny elastic substance from projections of upper jaw of certain whales **2.** thin strip of this substance, or imitation in metal or plastic, used to stiffen bodices

wham (wam) *n.* **1.** forceful blow or sound produced by it —*v.* **2.** strike or cause to strike with great force (**-mm-**)

wharf (wörf) *n.* platform at harbor, on river *etc.* for loading and unloading ships (*pl.* **wharves** (wörvz), **-s**)

what (wot; *unstressed* wət) *pron.* **1.** which thing **2.** that which **3.** request for statement to be repeated —*a.* **4.** which **5.** as much as **6.** how great, surprising *etc.* —*interj.* **7.** exclamation of surprise, anger *etc.* —**what'ever** *pron.* **1.** anything which **2.** of what kind it may be —**whatso'ever** *a.* **1.** at all: used as intensifier with indefinite pronouns and determiners such as *none, anybody* —*pron.* **2.** *rare* whatever —**'whatnot** *n.* **1.** *inf.* person, thing whose name is unknown, forgotten *etc.* **2.** small stand with shelves

wheat (wēt) *n.* **1.** grain of a cereal plant that yields flour for bread, cakes, pasta *etc.* **2.** plant with dense spikes bearing the edible grain —**'wheaten** *a.* —**wheat bread** bread made from combined whole-grain and white flours —**wheat cake** pancake made of wheat flour —**'wheatear** *n.* any of various Old World thrushes —**wheat germ** embryo of wheat kernel

wheedle ('wēdəl) *v.* coax, cajole

wheel (wēl) *n.* **1.** circular frame or disk (with spokes) revolving on axle **2.** anything like a wheel in shape or function **3.** act of turning **4.** steering wheel —*v.* **5.** (cause to) turn as if on axis **6.** (cause to) move on or as if on wheels **7.** (cause to) change course, *esp.* in opposite direction —**'wheelbarrow** *n.* barrow with one wheel —**'wheelbase** *n.* distance between front and rear hubs of vehicle —**'wheelchair** *n.* chair mounted on large wheels, used by people who cannot walk —**wheeler-dealer** *n.* manipulative person, *esp.* in business or politics —**'wheelhorse** *n.* **1.** horse nearest the wheels (in a team) **2.** reliable and effective person, *esp.* in politics —**'wheelhouse** *n.* enclosed structure on vessel's bridge for steersman —**'wheelspin** *n.* revolution of wheels without full grip of road —**'wheelwright** *n.* person who makes or mends wheels as trade

wheeze (wēz) *vi.* **1.** breathe with difficulty and whistling noise —*n.* **2.** this sound **3.** *inf.* trick, idea, plan —**'wheezy** *a.*

whelk (welk) *n.* any of several large spiral-shelled marine snails

whelp (welp) *n.* **1.** young of certain animals, *esp.* of wolf or dog **2.** *disparaging* youth **3.** *jocular* child —*v.* **4.** give birth to (whelps)

when (wen) *adv.* **1.** at what time —*conj.* **2.** at the time that **3.** although **4.** since —*pron.* **5.** at which (time) —**when'ever** *adv./conj.* at whatever time —**'whensoever** *conj./adv.* *rare* whenever

whence (wens) *adv./conj.* *formal* **1.** from what place or source **2.** how

where (wāər) *adv./conj.* **1.** at what place **2.** at or to the place in which —**'whereabouts** *adv./conj.* **1.** in what, which place —*n.* **2.** present position —**where'as** *conj.* **1.** considering that **2.** while, on the contrary —**where'by** *conj.* by which —**'wherefore** *adv. obs.* **1.** why **2.** consequently —**where'of** *obs., formal adv.* **1.** of what or which person or thing? —*pron.* **2.** of which (person or thing) —**'whereupon** *conj.* at which point —**wher'ever** *adv./conj.* **1.** where in the world **2.** in what or which place **3.** in any circumstances in which —**'wherewithal** *n.* necessary funds, resources *etc.*

whet (wet) *vt.* **1.** sharpen **2.** stimulate (**-tt-**) —**'whetstone** *n.* stone for sharpening tools

whether ('wedhər) *conj.* introduces the first of two alternatives, of which the second may be expressed or implied

whew (hwōō) *interj.* exclamation expressing relief, delight *etc.*

whey (wā) *n.* watery part of milk left after separation of curd, *esp.* in cheese making

which (wich) *a.* **1.** used in requests for a selection from alternatives —*pron.* **2.** which person or thing **3.** the thing 'who' —**which'ever** *pron.*

whiff (wif) *n.* **1.** brief smell or suggestion of **2.** puff of air —*vt.* **3.** smell

Whig (wig) *n.* **1.** member of the Amer. political party supporting the Revolution **2.** UK member of 18th-cent. political party that sought to increase parliamentary power by limiting royal authority

while (wīl) *conj.* **1.** in the time that **2.** in spite of the fact that, although **3.** whereas —*vt.* **4.** pass (time, usu. idly) —*n.* **5.** period of time —**whilst** *conj.* while

whim (wim) *n.* sudden, passing fancy —**'whimsical** *a.* **1.** fanciful **2.** full of whims —**whimsi'cality** *n.* —**'whimsy** *or* **'whimsey** *n.* **1.** whim **2.** caprice —*a.* **3.** quaint, comical or unusual, oft. in tasteless way

whimper ('wimpər) *vi.* **1.** cry or whine softly **2.** complain in this way —*n.* **3.** such cry or complaint

whin (win) *n.* gorse

whine (wīn) *n.* **1.** high-pitched plaintive cry **2.** peevish complaint —*vi.* **3.** utter this

whinny ('wini) *vi.* **1.** neigh softly (**'whinnied, 'whinnying**) —*n.* **2.** gentle neigh

whip (wip) *vt.* **1.** strike with whip **2.** thrash **3.** beat (cream, eggs) to a froth **4.** lash **5.** *inf.* pull, remove, insert *etc.* quickly **6.** *inf.* steal —*vi.* **7.** dart (**-pp-**) —*n.* **8.** lash attached to handle for urging or punishing **9.** member of legislature appointed by a political party to enforce party discipline, *esp.* to secure attendance at important sessions **10.** elastic quality permitting bending in mast, fishing rod *etc.* **11.** whipped dessert —**'whipping** *n.* **1.** thrashing with whip or similar implement **2.** cord used for binding or lashing **3.** binding formed by wrapping rope *etc.* with cord or twine —**'whipcord** *n.* **1.** strong worsted fabric with diagonally ribbed surface **2.** hard twisted cord used for lashes of whips *etc.* —**whip hand** (*usu. with* the) **1.** in driving horses *etc.*, hand holding whip **2.** advantage or dominating position —**'whiplash** *n.* quick lash of whip or like that of whip —**whiplash injury** injury to neck as result of sudden jerking of unsupported head —**'whippersnapper** *n.* insignificant but pretentious or cheeky person, oft. young one. (*also* **'whipster**) —**whipping boy** scapegoat —**whip-round** *n. inf.* collection of money

whippet ('wipit) *n.* **1.** small, swift purebred

hound used for hunting rabbits and coursing **2.** fast, light tank used in World War I

whir *or* **whirr** (wɔr) *v.* **1.** (cause to) fly, spin *etc.* with buzzing or whizzing sound —*vi.* **2.** bustle —*n.* **3.** this sound **4.** bustle

whirl (wɔrl) *v.* **1.** swing rapidly round **2.** drive or be driven at high speed —*vi.* **3.** move rapidly in a circular course —*n.* **4.** whirling movement **5.** confusion, bustle, giddiness —**'whirligig** *n.* **1.** spinning toy **2.** merry-go-round —**'whirlpool** *n.* circular current, eddy —**'whirlwind** *n.* **1.** wind whirling round while moving forward —*a.* **2.** rapid or sudden —**'whirlybird** *n. inf.* helicopter

whisk (wisk) *vt.* **1.** brush, sweep, beat lightly **2.** beat to a froth —*v.* **3.** move, remove, quickly —*n.* **4.** light brush **5.** egg-beating implement

whisker ('wiskɔr) *n.* **1.** long stiff hair at side of mouth of cat or other animal **2.** any of hairs on a man's face —**by a whisker** *inf.* only just

whiskey ('wiski) *n.* spirit distilled from fermented cereals (*Scot.*, **C 'whisky**)

Whiskey ('wiski) *n.* word used in communications for the letter *w*

whisper ('wispɔr) *v.* **1.** speak in soft, hushed tones, without vibration of vocal cords **2.** rustle —*n.* **3.** such speech **4.** trace or suspicion **5.** rustle

whist (wist) *n.* any of family of card games for four players in two partnerships played with standard 52-card deck in which the object is to win at least seven tricks out of 13 in play

whistle ('wisəl) *vi.* **1.** produce shrill sound by forcing breath through rounded, nearly closed lips —*vt.* **2.** utter, summon *etc.* by whistle —*n.* **3.** such sound **4.** any similar sound **5.** instrument to make it —**'whistler** *n.* —**whistle stop 1.** minor railroad station where trains stop only on signal; small town having such a station **2.** brief appearance in town, *esp.* by political candidate

whit (wit) *n.* jot, particle (*esp. in* **not a whit**)

white (wīt) *a.* **1.** of the color of milk or table salt **2.** pale **3.** light in color **4.** (**W-**) having a light-colored skin —*n.* **5.** color of milk or table salt **6.** white pigment **7.** white part **8.** clear fluid round yolk of egg **9.** (**W-**) White person —**'whiten** *v.* —**'whiteness** *n.* —**'whiting** *n.* form of chalk used in polishing silver, whitewashing and making putty —**'whitish** *a.* —**white ant** termite —**'whitebait** *n.* young herring —**white blood cell** *see* LEUKOCYTE —**'whitecap** *n.* wave with white broken crest —**white-collar** *a.* denoting nonmanual salaried workers —**white dwarf** one of class of small faint stars of enormous density —**white elephant** useless, unwanted, gift or possession —**white feather** symbol or mark of cowardice —**'whitefish** *n.* any freshwater food fish related to salmon and trout —**white flag** white banner or cloth used as signal of surrender or truce —**'whitefly** *n.* very small, whitish fly with four wings, usu. found on the under surface of leaves —**white friar** Carmelite friar, so called because of white cloak that forms part of habit of this order —**white gold** pale alloy of gold resembling silver or platinum —**white goods 1.** household linen such as sheets, tablecloths *etc.* **2.** large household appliances, such as refrigerators *etc.* —**'whitehead** *n. see* MILIUM —**white heat 1.** intense heat characterized by emission of white light **2.** *inf.* state of intense excitement or activity —**white hope** one expected to bring honor or glory to his group, team *etc.* —**white horse** whitecap —**white-hot** *a.* **1.** at such high temperature that white light is emitted **2.** *inf.* in state of intense emotion —**white lead** (led) any of various lead-containing pigments used chiefly as exterior paints —**white lie** minor, unimportant lie —**white matter** whitish tissue of brain and spinal cord, consisting mainly of nerve fibers —**white meat** any meat that is light in color, such as chicken or turkey breast —**white noise** sound or electrical noise that has relatively wide continuous range of frequencies of uniform intensity —**'whiteout** *n.* condition of severely reduced visibility in snowy regions —**white pepper** condiment made from husked dried beans of pepper plant —**white sale** sale of white goods —**white sauce** thick sauce made from flour, butter, seasonings, and milk or stock —**white slave** woman, child forced or enticed away for purposes of prostitution —**white tie 1.** white bow tie worn as part of man's full evening dress **2.** full evening dress for men —**'whitewash** *n.* **1.** substance for whitening walls *etc.* —*vt.* **2.** apply this to **3.** cover up, gloss over, suppress —**white whale** small white toothed whale of northern waters (*also* **be'luga**) —**'whitewood** *n.* **1.** tree with light-colored wood, such as the tulip tree **2.** its wood —**show the white feather** act in cowardly manner —**the White House 1.** official Washington residence of president of U.S. **2.** U.S. presidency —**White man's burden** supposed duty of White race to bring education and Western culture to non-White inhabitants of their colonies

Whitehall ('wīt-hōl) *n.* **1.** street in London where main government offices are situated **2.** British Government

whither ('widhɔr) *adv. Poet.* **1.** to what place **2.** to which

whiting ('wīting) *n.* **1.** any of various marine food fishes found in seas around U.S. **2.** hake **3.** European food fish related to cod

whitlow ('witlō) *n.* abscess on finger, *esp.* round nail

Whitsun ('witsən) *n.* week following **Whit Sunday**, seventh Sunday after Easter (*also* **Pentecost**)

whittle ('witəl) *vt.* **1.** cut, carve with knife **2.**

pare away —**whittle down** reduce gradually, wear (away)

whiz *or* **whizz** (wiz) *n.* **1.** loud hissing sound **2.** *inf.* person skillful at something —*vi.* **3.** move with or make loud hissing sound **4.** *inf.* move quickly —**whiz** *or* **whizz kid** *inf.* person who is outstandingly successful for his or her age

who (hōō) *pron.* relative and interrogative pronoun, always referring to persons —**who-dunit** (hōō'dunit) *n.* *inf.* detective story —**who'ever** *pron.* who, any one or every one that —**whoso'ever** *pron. formal* whoever

W.H.O. World Health Organization

whoa (wō) *interj.* command used, *esp.* to horses, to stop or slow down

whole (hōl) *a.* **1.** complete **2.** containing all elements or parts **3.** entire **4.** not defective or imperfect **5.** healthy —*n.* **6.** complete thing or system —'**wholly** *adv.* —'**wholesome** *a.* producing good effect, physically or morally —**whole-grain** *a.* of, pert. to flour which contains the whole of the grain (*also* **graham**) —'**whole'hearted** *a.* **1.** sincere **2.** enthusiastic —**whole number 1.** integer **2.** natural number —'**wholesale** *n.* **1.** sale of goods by large quantities to retailers —*a.* **2.** dealing by wholesale **3.** extensive —'**whole-saler** *n.* —**on the whole 1.** taking everything into consideration **2.** in general

whom (hōōm) *pron.* objective case of WHO

whoop (hōōp) *n.* shout or cry expressing excitement *etc.*

whoopee ('wōōpē) *n. inf.* gay, riotous time —**make whoopee 1.** participate in wild noisy party **2.** make love

whooping cough ('hōōping) infectious disease of mucous membrane lining air passages, marked by convulsive coughing with shrill crowing sound on breathing in (*also* **pertussis**)

whoops (wōōps) *interj.* exclamation of surprise or of apology

whopper ('wopər) *n. inf.* **1.** anything unusually large **2.** monstrous lie —'**whopping** *a.*

whore (hōr) *n.* prostitute —'**whorehouse** *n.* brothel

whorl (wörl, wərl) *n.* **1.** ring of leaves or petals **2.** turn of spiral **3.** anything forming part of circular pattern, *eg* lines of human fingerprint

whortleberry ('wərtəlberi) *n.* small Eurasian shrub of erica genus with edible sweet blackish berries

whose (hōōz) *pron.* possessive case of WHO and WHICH

whs *or* **whse** warehouse

whsle wholesale

why (wī) *adv.* for what cause or reason

WI Wisconsin

W.I. **1.** West Indies **2.** wrought iron **3. UK** Women's Institute

WIA wounded in action

wick (wik) *n.* strip of thread feeding flame of lamp or candle with oil, grease *etc.*

wicked ('wikid) *a.* **1.** evil, sinful **2.** very bad **3.** mischievous —'**wickedly** *adv.* —'**wickedness** *n.*

wicker(work) ('wikər(wərk)) *n.* woven cane *etc.*, basketwork

wicket ('wikit) *n.* **1.** small gate **2.** *Cricket* set of three stumps and bails **3.** cricket pitch

wid widow *or* widower

wide (wīd) *a.* **1.** having a great extent from side to side, broad **2.** having considerable distance between **3.** spacious **4.** liberal **5.** vast **6.** far from the mark **7.** opened fully —*adv.* **8.** to the full extent **9.** far from the intended target —'**widely** *adv.* —'**widen** *v.* —**width** (width) *or* '**wideness** *n.* breadth —**wide-angle lens** lens system on camera that can cover angle of view of 60° or more —**wide-eyed** *a.* innocent or credulous —'**wide-'spread** *a.* **1.** extending over a wide area **2.** common

widow ('widō) *n.* **1.** woman whose husband is dead and who has not married again **2.** *fig.* woman temporarily abandoned by husband, as in *golf widow* —*vt.* **3.** make a widow of —'**widower** *n.* man whose wife is dead and who has not married again —'**widowhood** *n.*

wield (wēld) *vt.* **1.** hold and use **2.** brandish **3.** manage

wife (wīf) *n.* a man's partner in marriage, married woman (*pl.* **wives**) —'**wifely** *a.*

wig (wig) *n.* artificial hair for the head

wigeon *or* **widgeon** ('wijən) *n.* Eurasian duck of marshes, swamps *etc.*

wiggle ('wigəl) *v.* **1.** (cause to) move jerkily from side to side —*n.* **2.** such movement —'**wiggly** *a.*

wigwam ('wigwam) *n.* N Amer. Indian's hut of Great Lakes region and eastward

wild (wīld) *a.* **1.** not tamed or domesticated **2.** not cultivated **3.** savage **4.** stormy **5.** uncontrolled **6.** random **7.** excited **8.** rash **9.** frantic **10.** *inf.* (of party *etc.*) rowdy, exciting **11.** (of card, *esp.* joker or deuce, in some games) able to be given any value the holder pleases —'**wildly** *adv.* —'**wildness** *n.* —'**wildcat** *n.* **1.** bobcat —*a.* **2.** of sudden occurrence, *esp.* oil- or gas-well strike —**wild-goose chase** futile pursuit —'**wildlife** *n.* wild animals and plants collectively —**wild oats** *sl.* indiscretions of youth, *esp.* dissoluteness before settling down (*esp. in* **sow one's wild oats**) —**wild rice** tall aquatic N Amer. perennial grass or its edible grain —**Wild West** western U.S., *esp.* with reference to its frontier lawlessness

wildebeest ('wildibēst) *n.* gnu

wilderness ('wildərnis) *n.* **1.** desert, waste place **2.** state of desolation or confusion

wildfire ('wīldfīər) *n.* **1.** raging, uncontrollable fire **2.** anything spreading, moving fast

wile (wīl) *n.* trick —'**wily** *a.*

will (wil) *v. aux.* **1.** forms moods and tenses

indicating intention or conditional result (**would** *pt.*) —*vi.* **2.** have a wish —*vt.* **3.** wish **4.** intend **5.** leave as legacy —*n.* **6.** faculty of deciding what one will do **7.** purpose **8.** volition **9.** determination **10.** wish **11.** directions written for disposal of property after death —**'willful** *a.* **1.** obstinate, self-willed **2.** intentional —**'willfully** *adv.* —**'willfulness** *n.* —**'willing** *a.* **1.** ready **2.** given cheerfully —**'willingly** *adv.* —**'willingness** *n.* —**'willpower** *n.* ability to control oneself, one's actions, impulses

willies ('wiliz) *pl.n. sl.* nervousness, jitters, or fright (*esp. in* **give** (*or* **get**) **the willies**)

williwaw ('wiliwō) *n.* sudden violent gust of cold land air

will-o'-the-wisp (wilədhə'wisp) *n.* **1.** brief pale flame or phosphorescence sometimes seen over marshes **2.** elusive person or hope

willow ('wilō) *n.* **1.** tree, such as the weeping willow with long thin flexible branches **2.** its wood —**'willowy** *a.* lithe, slender, supple —**'willowherb** *n.* tall plant with mauve flowers

willy-nilly (wili'nili) *adv./a.* (occurring) whether desired or not

Wilson ('wilsən) *n.* **Woodrow.** the 28th President of the U.S. (1913-17)

wilt (wilt) *v.* (cause to) become limp, drooping or lose strength *etc.*

Wimbledon ('wimbəldən) *n.* residential area and shopping center in south London, location of All-England Lawn Tennis Championships

wimp (wimp) *n. inf.* feeble, ineffective person

wimple ('wimpəl) *n.* cloth wound around head to frame the face, now worn by some nuns

win (win) *vi.* **1.** be successful, victorious —*vt.* **2.** get by labor or effort **3.** reach **4.** allure **5.** be successful in **6.** gain the support, consent *etc.* of (**won, 'winning**) —*n.* **7.** victory, *esp.* in games —**'winner** *n.* —**'winning** *a.* charming —**'winnings** *pl.n.* sum won in game, betting *etc.*

wince (wins) *vi.* **1.** flinch, draw back, as from pain *etc.* —*n.* **2.** this act

winch (winch) *n.* **1.** machine for hoisting or hauling using cable wound round drum —*vt.* **2.** move (something) by using a winch

wind[1] (wind) *n.* **1.** air in motion **2.** breath **3.** flatulence **4.** idle talk **5.** hint or suggestion **6.** scent borne by air —*vt.* **7.** render short of breath, *esp.* by blow *etc.* **8.** get the scent of —**'windward** *n.* side against which wind is blowing —**'windy** *a.* **1.** exposed to wind **2.** flatulent **3.** *inf.* talking too much —**'windbag** *n. sl.* voluble person who has little of interest to communicate —**'windbreak** *n.* fence, line of trees *etc.* serving as protection from wind —**'windfall** *n.* **1.** unexpected good luck **2.** fallen fruit —**wind gauge** anemometer —**wind instrument** musical instrument played by blowing or air pressure —**'windjammer** *n.* large merchant sailing ship —**windmill** ('windmil, 'winmil) *n.* **1.** wind-driven apparatus with fanlike sails for raising water, crushing grain *etc.* **2.** imaginary opponent or evil —**'windpipe** *n.* passage from throat to lungs —**'windshield** *n.* protective sheet of glass *etc.* in front of driver or pilot —**'windsock** *n.* cone of material flown on mast at airfield to indicate wind direction (*also* **wind sleeve**) —**wind tunnel** chamber for testing aerodynamic properties of aircraft *etc.* in which current of air can be maintained at constant velocity

windjammer

wind[2] (wīnd) *vi.* **1.** twine **2.** meander —*vt.* **3.** turn or coil around some object or point **4.** wrap **5.** make ready for working by tightening spring (**wound, 'winding**) —*n.* **6.** act of winding **7.** single turn of something wound **8.** a turn, curve —**winding sheet** sheet in which corpse is wrapped for burial; shroud —**wind-up** *n. inf.* **1.** act of concluding **2.** end —**wind down 1.** lower or move down by cranking **2.** (of clock spring) become slack **3.** diminish gradually in force or power —**wind up 1.** bring to or reach a conclusion **2.** tighten spring of (clockwork mechanism) **3.** *inf.* make nervous, tense *etc.* **4.** *inf. see* LIQUIDATE (sense 2) **5.** *inf.* end up (in specified state)

windlass ('windləs) *n.* winch, *esp.* simple one worked by a crank

window ('windō) *n.* **1.** hole in wall (with glass) to admit light, air *etc.* **2.** anything similar in appearance or function **3.** area for display of goods behind glass of shop front —**window box** long narrow box, placed on windowsill, in which plants are grown —**window-dressing** *n.* **1.** arrangement of goods in a shop window **2.** deceptive display —**'windowpane** *n.* sheet of glass in window —**window-shop** *vi.* look at goods in shop windows without buying them (**-pp-**) —**'windowsill** *n.* sill below window

Windsor chair ('winzər) simple wooden chair, usu. having shaped seat, splayed legs, and back of many spindles

wine (wīn) *n.* fermented juice of grape *etc.* —**'wino** *n.* person who habitually drinks wine as means of getting drunk —**'wine-**

press *n.* apparatus for extracting juice from grape —'**wineskin** *n.* skin of sheep or goat sewn up and used as holder for wine

wing (wing) *n.* **1.** feathered limb a bird uses in flying **2.** one of organs of flight of insect or some animals **3.** main lifting surface of aircraft **4.** lateral extension **5.** side portion of building projecting from main central portion **6.** one of sides of a stage **7.** flank corps of army on either left or right side **8.** *inf.* arm of human being **9.** *Sport* (player on) either side of pitch **10.** faction, *esp.* of political party —*pl.* **11.** insignia worn by qualified aircraft pilot **12.** sides of stage —*vi.* **13.** fly **14.** move, go very fast —*vt.* **15.** disable, wound slightly —**winged** *a.* having wings —**wing chair** chair having wings on each side of back —'**wingspan** *n. see* SPAN (sense 4)

wink (wingk) *v.* **1.** close and open (an eye) rapidly, *esp.* to indicate friendliness or as signal —*vi.* **2.** twinkle —*n.* **3.** act of winking

winkle ('wingkəl) *n.* shellfish, periwinkle

winnow ('winō) *vt.* **1.** blow free of chaff **2.** sift, examine

winsome ('winsəm) *a.* charming, winning

winter ('wintər) *n.* **1.** the coldest season —*vi.* **2.** pass, spend the winter —'**wintry** *or* '**wintery** *a.* **1.** of, like winter **2.** cold —'**wintergreen** *n.* evergreen shrub, *esp.* subshrub of eastern N Amer., which has white, bell-shaped flowers and edible red berries —**winter solstice** time at which sun is at its southernmost point in sky appearing at noon at its lowest altitude above horizon. It occurs about Dec. 22nd —**winter sports** sports held in open air on snow or ice —**oil of wintergreen** aromatic compound, formerly made from the shrub but now synthesized: used medicinally and for flavoring

wipe (wīp) *vt.* **1.** rub so as to clean —*n.* **2.** wiping —'**wiper** *n.* **1.** one that wipes **2.** automatic wiping apparatus (*esp.* **windshield wiper**) —**wipe out 1.** erase **2.** annihilate **3.** *sl.* kill

wire ('wīər) *n.* **1.** metal drawn into thin, flexible strand **2.** something made of wire, *eg* fence **3.** telegram —*vt.* **4.** provide, fasten with wire **5.** send by telegraph —'**wiring** *n.* system of wires —'**wiry** *a.* **1.** like wire **2.** lean and tough —**wire-gauge** *n.* **1.** flat plate with slots in which standard wire sizes can be measured **2.** standard system of sizes for measuring diameters of wires —**wire-haired** *a.* (of various breeds of dog) with short stiff hair —'**wiretap** *v.* tap (telephone wire *etc.*) to obtain information secretly

wireless ('wīərlis) *n.* **1.** *old-fashioned term for* radio, radio set —*a.* **2.** of or for radio

Wisconsin (wis'konsin) *n.* East North Central state of the U.S., admitted to the Union in 1848. Abbrev.: **Wis., WI** (with ZIP code)

Wisd. *Bible* Wisdom of Solomon

wise[1] (wīz) *a.* **1.** having intelligence and knowledge **2.** sensible —**wisdom** ('wizdəm) *n.* **1.** (accumulated) knowledge, learning **2.** erudition —'**wisely** *adv.* —'**wiseacre** *n.* one who wishes to seem wise —**wisdom tooth** third molar usu. cut about 20th year

wise[2] (wīz) *n. obs.* manner

-wise (*comb. form*) **1.** indicating direction or manner, as in *clockwise, likewise* **2.** with reference to, as in *businesswise*

wisecrack ('wīzkrak) *n. inf.* flippant, (would-be) clever remark

wish (wish) *vi.* **1.** have a desire —*vt.* **2.** desire —*n.* **3.** desire **4.** thing desired —'**wishful** *a.* **1.** desirous **2.** too optimistic —'**wishbone** *n.* V-shaped bone above breastbone of fowl —**wishful thinking** erroneous belief that one's wishes are in accordance with reality

wishy-washy ('wishiwoshi) *a. inf.* **1.** lacking in substance, force, color *etc.* **2.** watery; thin

wisp (wisp) *n.* **1.** light, delicate streak, as of smoke **2.** twisted handful, usu. of straw *etc.* **3.** stray lock of hair —'**wispy** *a.*

wisteria (wi'stēəriə) *or* **wistaria** (wis'tēəriə, -'ter-) *n.* climbing shrub with usu. mauve flowers

wistful ('wistfəl) *a.* **1.** longing, yearning **2.** sadly pensive —'**wistfully** *adv.*

wit[1] (wit) *n.* **1.** ingenuity in connecting amusingly incongruous ideas **2.** person gifted with this power **3.** sense **4.** intellect **5.** understanding **6.** ingenuity **7.** humor —'**witless** *a.* foolish —'**witticism** *n.* witty remark —'**wittily** *adv.* —'**wittingly** *adv.* **1.** on purpose **2.** knowingly —'**witty** *a.*

wit[2] (wit) *v. obs.* be or become aware of (something) —**to wit** that is to say; namely

witch (wich) *n.* **1.** person, usu. female, believed to practice, practicing, or professing to practice (black) magic, sorcery **2.** ugly, wicked woman **3.** fascinating woman —'**witchery** *n.* —'**witchcraft** *n.* —**witch doctor** in certain societies, man appearing to cure or cause injury, disease by magic —**witch grass** *see* QUACK GRASS —**witch-hunt** *n.* rigorous campaign to expose dissenters on pretext of safeguarding public welfare —**witch-hunting** *n./a.*

witch- (*comb. form*) *see* WYCH-

witch hazel 1. any of genus of trees and shrubs of N Amer. having medicinal properties **2.** astringent medicinal solution containing extract of bark and leaves of one of these shrubs, applied to treat bruises *etc.*

with (widh, with) *prep.* **1.** in company or possession of **2.** against **3.** in relation to **4.** through **5.** by means of —**withal** (wi'dhōl) *adv.* also, likewise —**within** (wi'dhin) *prep./adv.* in, inside —**without** (wi'dhowt) *prep.* **1.** lacking **2.** *obs.* outside

withdraw (widh'drō) *v.* draw back or out (-'**drew,** -'**drawn,** -'**drawing**) —**with'drawal** *n.* —**with'drawn** *a.* reserved, unsociable

withe (with, widh, wīdh) *n.* **1.** strong flexible

twig, *esp.* of willow, suitable for binding things together —*vt.* **2.** bind with withes

wither (ˈwidhər) *v.* (cause to) wilt, dry up, decline —**ˈwithering** *a.* (of glance *etc.*) scornful

withers (ˈwidhərz) *pl.n.* ridge between a horse's shoulder blades

withhold (withˈhōld, widh-) *vt.* **1.** restrain **2.** keep back **3.** refrain from giving (**-ˈheld, -ˈholding**) —**withˈholder** *n.*

withstand (withˈstand, widh-) *vt.* oppose, resist, *esp.* successfully (**-ˈstood, -ˈstanding**)

withy (ˈwidhi) *n.* **1.** *see* WITHE (sense 1) **2.** willow tree

witness (ˈwitnis) *n.* **1.** one who sees something **2.** testimony **3.** one who gives testimony —*vi.* **4.** give testimony —*vt.* **5.** see **6.** attest to genuineness of **7.** see and sign as having seen —**witness stand** place in court of law in which witnesses stand to give evidence

wives (wīvz) *n., pl. of* WIFE —**old wives' tale** superstitious tradition

wizard (ˈwizərd) *n.* **1.** sorcerer, magician **2.** expert —**ˈwizardry** *n.*

wizened (ˈwizənd) *or* **wizen** *a.* shriveled, wrinkled

wk. 1. week (*pl.* **wks.**) **2.** work

wkly weekly

WL 1. waterline **2.** wavelength

wm wattmeter

WNW west-northwest

W.O. warrant officer

w/o without

woad (wōd) *n.* **1.** biennial plant of British Isles formerly grown for dye yielded by its leaves **2.** blue dye from this plant

wobble (ˈwobəl) *vi.* **1.** move unsteadily, sway —*n.* **2.** an unsteady movement —**ˈwobbly** *a.*

WOC without compensation

woe (wō) *n.* grief —**ˈwoebegone** *a.* looking sorrowful —**ˈwoeful** *a.* **1.** sorrowful **2.** pitiful **3.** wretched —**ˈwoefully** *adv.*

wold (wōld) *n.* open downs, moorland

wolf (wŏŏlf) *n.* **1.** wild predatory doglike animal of northern countries **2.** *inf.* man who habitually tries to seduce women (*pl.* **wolves** (wŏŏlvz)) —*vt.* **3.** eat ravenously —**ˈwolfhound** *n.* largest breed of dog, used formerly to hunt wolves —**wolf whistle** whistle by man expressing admiration for a woman —**cry wolf** raise false alarm

wolfram (ˈwŏŏlfrəm) *n.* tungsten

wolverine (wŏŏlvəˈrēn) *n.* carnivorous mammal inhabiting Arctic regions

woman (ˈwŏŏmən) *n.* **1.** adult human female **2.** women collectively (*pl.* **women** (ˈwimin)) —**ˈwomanhood** *n.* —**ˈwomanish** *a.* effeminate —**ˈwomanize** *vi. inf.* (of a man) indulge in many casual affairs with women —**ˈwomanizer** *n.* —**ˈwomankind** *n.* —**ˈwomanly** *a.* of, proper to woman —**Women's Liberation** movement for removal of attitudes, practices that preserve social, economic *etc.* inequalities between women and men (*also* **women's lib**)

womb (wōōm) *n.* female organ of conception and gestation

wombat (ˈwombat) *n.* Aust. burrowing marsupial with heavy body, short legs and dense fur

won (wun) *pt./pp. of* WIN

wonder (ˈwundər) *n.* **1.** emotion excited by amazing or unusual thing **2.** marvel, miracle —*vi.* **3.** be curious **4.** feel amazement —**ˈwonderful** *a.* **1.** remarkable **2.** very fine —**ˈwonderfully** *adv.* —**ˈwonderment** *n.* surprise —**ˈwondrous** *a.* **1.** inspiring wonder **2.** strange —**wonder drug** *see* **miracle drug** *at* MIRACLE

wonky (ˈwongki) *a. inf.* **1.** shaky, unsteady **2.** groggy **3.** askew **4.** unreliable

wont (wŏnt, wōnt) *n.* **1.** custom —*a.* **2.** accustomed —**ˈwonted** *a.* habitual, established

woo (wōō) *vt.* court, seek to marry —**ˈwooer** *n.* suitor

wood (wŏŏd) *n.* **1.** substance of trees, timber **2.** firewood **3.** tract of land with growing trees —**ˈwooded** *a.* having (many) trees —**ˈwooden** *a.* **1.** made of wood **2.** obstinate **3.** without expression —**ˈwoody** *a.* —**ˈwoodbine** *n.* Virginia creeper —**ˈwoodcarver** *n.* —**ˈwoodcarving** *n.* **1.** act of carving wood **2.** work of art produced by carving wood —**ˈwoodchuck** *n.* thickset marmot found east of Rockies from northern Canada to southern U.S. (*also* **groundhog**) —**ˈwoodcock** *n.* game bird —**ˈwoodcut** *n.* **1.** engraving on wood **2.** impression from this —**woodland** (ˈwŏŏdlənd) *n.* woods, forest —**ˈwoodlark** *n.* Old World lark similar to skylark —**ˈwoodlouse** *n.* small gray land crustacean with flattened elliptical body (*pl.* **-lice**) —**ˈwoodpecker** *n.* climbing bird usu. with brightly colored plumage and strong chisel-like bill with which it bores into trees for insects —**ˈwoodpile** *n.* heap of firewood —**wood pulp** finely pulped wood that has been digested by chemical, such as caustic soda, used in making paper and rayon —**ˈwoodruff** *n.* plant, *esp.* sweet woodruff, which has small sweet-scented white flowers, used to flavor wine and in perfumery —**wood screw** screw with slotted head and gimlet point permitting it to be driven into wood with a screwdriver —**wood sorrel** Eurasian plant having compound leaves, underground creeping stem and white purple-veined flowers —**woodwind** (ˈwŏŏdwind) *a./n.* (of) wind instruments of orchestra whose tones are produced by opening and closing holes —**ˈwoodwork** *n.* components made of wood, such as doors *etc.*

woof[1] (wŏŏf, wōōf) *n.* the threads that cross the warp in weaving

woof[2] (wo͞of) *interj.* **1.** imitation of bark of dog —*vi.* **2.** (of dog) bark

woofer (ˈwo͞ofər) *n.* loudspeaker for reproducing low-frequency sounds

wool (wo͝ol) *n.* **1.** soft hair of sheep, goat *etc.* **2.** yarn spun from this —ˈ**woolen** *or* ˈ**woollen** *a.* —ˈ**woolly** *or* ˈ**wooly** *a.* **1.** of wool **2.** vague, muddled —*n.* **3.** knitted woolen garment —ˈ**woolgathering** *a./n.* daydreaming —ˈ**woolsack** *n.* Lord Chancellor's seat in British House of Lords

woomera (ˈwoomərə) *n.* **1.** throwing stick used by Aust. Aborigines for propelling dart or spear **2.** short club used as missile

woozy (ˈwo͞ozi) *a. inf.* **1.** dazed or confused **2.** experiencing dizziness, nausea *etc.* as result of drink —ˈ**woozily** *adv.* —ˈ**wooziness** *n.*

word (wərd) *n.* **1.** unit of speech or writing regarded by users of a language as the smallest separate meaningful unit **2.** term **3.** message **4.** brief remark **5.** information **6.** promise **7.** command —*vt.* **8.** express in words, *esp.* in particular way —ˈ**wordily** *adv.* —ˈ**wording** *n.* choice and arrangement of words —ˈ**wordy** *a.* using more words than necessary, verbose —**word blindness 1.** alexia **2.** dyslexia —**word processing** production of documents by electronic system including typing, text editing and storage —**word processor** installation for word processing, typically consisting of keyboard and VDU incorporating microprocessor, storage and processing capabilities

wore (wôr) *pt. of* WEAR

work (wərk) *n.* **1.** labor **2.** employment **3.** occupation **4.** task **5.** toil **6.** something made or accomplished **7.** production of art or science **8.** book **9.** needlework —*pl.* **10.** factory **11.** total of person's deeds, writings *etc.* **12.** *inf.* everything, full or extreme treatment **13.** mechanism of clock *etc.* —*vt.* **14.** cause to operate **15.** make, shape —*vi.* **16.** apply effort **17.** labor **18.** operate **19.** be engaged in trade, profession *etc.* **20.** turn out successfully **21.** ferment —ˈ**workable** *a.* —ˈ**worker** *n.* —ˈ**working** *n.* **1.** operation or mode of operation of something **2.** act or process of molding something pliable **3.** (*oft. pl.*) part of mine or quarry that is being or has been worked —*a.* **4.** of or concerned with person or thing that works **5.** concerned with, used in, or suitable for work **6.** capable of being operated or used —ˈ**workaday** *a.* **1.** ordinary **2.** suitable for working days —**workaˈholic** *n.* person obsessively addicted to work —**work force 1.** total number of workers employed by company on specific project *etc.* **2.** total number of people who could be employed —ˈ**workhouse** *n. Hist.* institution offering food, lodgings for unpaid menial work —**working class** social class consisting of wage earners, *esp.* manual —**working-class** *a.* —**working party** advisory committee studying specific problem, question —ˈ**workman** *n.* manual worker —ˈ**workmanlike** *or* ˈ**workmanly** *a.* appropriate to or befitting a good workman —ˈ**workmanship** *n.* **1.** skill of workman **2.** way thing is finished **3.** style —**work-out** *n.* session of physical exercise, *esp.* for training or practice —ˈ**workroom** *n.* —ˈ**workshop** *n.* place where things are made —ˈ**workshy** *a.* not inclined to work —**work station** area in office *etc.* where one person works —**work in 1.** insert or become inserted **2.** find space for —**work of art 1.** piece of fine art, as painting, sculpture **2.** something that may be likened to piece of fine art, *esp.* in beauty *etc.* —**work out 1.** accomplish by effort **2.** solve by reasoning or calculation **3.** devise or formulate **4.** prove satisfactory **5.** happen as specified **6.** take part in physical exercise, as in training **7.** remove all mineral in (mine *etc.*) that can be profitably exploited

world (wərld) *n.* **1.** the universe **2.** the planet earth **3.** sphere of existence **4.** mankind, people generally **5.** society —ˈ**worldly** *a.* **1.** earthly **2.** mundane **3.** absorbed in the pursuit of material gain, advantage **4.** carnal —**World Bank** popular name for International Bank for Reconstruction and Development, established in 1945 —**world-beater** *n.* person or thing that surpasses all others in his, her or its category; champion —**World Court** the Permanent Court of International Justice at the Hague, Netherlands —**World Cup** international association football championship competition held every four years between national teams —**World Series** annual series of baseball games between pennant winners of major leagues to decide U.S. professional championship —**world-shaking** *a.* of enormous significance; momentous —**world war** war involving many countries

worm (wərm) *n.* **1.** small limbless creeping snakelike creature **2.** anything resembling worm in shape or movement **3.** *inf.* weak, despised person —*pl.* **4.** (disorder caused by) infestation of worms, *esp.* in intestines —*vi.* **5.** crawl —*vt.* **6.** work (oneself) in insidiously **7.** extract (secret) craftily **8.** rid of worms —ˈ**wormy** *a.* —ˈ**wormcast** *n.* coil of earth excreted by earthworm —**worm-eaten** *a.* **1.** full of holes gnawed by worms **2.** old, antiquated —**worm gear 1.** device consisting of threaded shaft (**worm**) that mates with gear wheel (**worm wheel**) so that rotary motion can be transferred between two

worm gear

shafts at right angles to each other **2.** gear wheel driven by threaded shaft or worm (*also* **worm wheel**) —**worm's-eye** *a.* seen from below

wormwood ('wərmwŏŏd) *n.* **1.** bitter herb **2.** bitterness

worn (wŏrn) *pp. of* WEAR —**worn-out** *a.* **1.** worn or used until threadbare, valueless or useless **2.** exhausted

worry ('wuri) *vi.* **1.** be (unduly) concerned —*vt.* **2.** trouble, pester, harass **3.** (of dog) seize, shake with teeth (**'worried, 'worrying**) —*n.* **4.** (cause of) anxiety, concern —**'worrier** *n.* —**'worrisome** *a.* **1.** causing worry **2.** tending to worry —**worry beads** string of beads that when played with supposedly relieves nervous tension

worse (wərs) *a./adv.* **1.** *comp. of* BAD *or* BADLY —*n.* **2.** inferior or less good person, thing or state —**'worsen** *v.* **1.** make, grow worse —*vt.* **2.** impair —*vi.* **3.** deteriorate —**worst** *a./adv.* **1.** *sup. of* BAD *or* BADLY —*n.* **2.** least good or most inferior person, part or thing

worship ('wərship) *vt.* **1.** show religious devotion to **2.** adore **3.** love and admire —*n.* **4.** act of worshiping **5.** title used to address mayor, magistrate *etc.* —**'worshiper** *n.* —**'worshipful** *a.*

worsted ('wŏŏstid) *n.* **1.** smooth, twisted woolen yarn —*a.* **2.** made of woolen yarn **3.** spun from wool

wort (wərt) *n.* **1.** *obs.* plant, herb **2.** infusion of malt before fermentation

worth (wərth) *a.* **1.** having or deserving to have value specified **2.** meriting —*n.* **3.** excellence **4.** merit, value **5.** virtue **6.** usefulness **7.** price **8.** quantity to be had for a given sum —**worthily** ('wərdhili) *adv.* —**worthiness** ('wərdhinis) *n.* —**'worthless** *a.* useless —**worthy** ('wərdhi) *a.* **1.** virtuous **2.** meriting —*n.* **3.** one of eminent worth —**worth'while** *a.* worth the time, effort *etc.* involved

would (wŏŏd; *unstressed* wəd) *v. aux.* **1.** expressing wish, intention, probability —*v.* **2.** *pt. of* WILL —**would-be** *a.* wishing, pretending to be

wound[1] (wōōnd) *n.* **1.** injury, hurt from cut, stab *etc.* —*vt.* **2.** inflict wound on, injure **3.** pain

wound[2] (wownd) *pt./pp. of* WIND[2]

wove (wōv) *pt. of* WEAVE

woven ('wōvən) *pp. of* WEAVE

wow (wow) *interj.* **1.** exclamation of astonishment, admiration *etc.* —*n.* **2.** *inf.* object of astonishment, admiration *etc.* **3.** variation, distortion in pitch in phonograph *etc.*

WP **1.** weather permitting **2.** without prejudice **3.** word processing **4.** word processor

WPA Works Progress Administration

WPC watts per candle

w.p.m. *or* **WPM** words per minute

wpn weapon

W.R. warehouse receipt

wrack (rak) *n.* kelp

wrack

wraith (rāth) *n.* **1.** apparition of a person seen shortly before or after death **2.** specter

wrangle ('ranggəl) *vi.* **1.** quarrel (noisily) **2.** dispute **3.** herd cattle —*n.* **4.** noisy quarrel **5.** dispute —**'wrangler** *n.* cowboy

wrap (rap) *vt.* **1.** cover, *esp.* by putting something round **2.** put round (**-pp-**) —**wrap** *or* **'wrapper** *n.* **1.** loose garment **2.** covering —**'wrapping** *n.* material used to wrap —**'wrapover, 'wraparound** *or* **'wrapround** *a.* (of garment, *esp.* skirt) not sewn up at one side, but worn wrapped round body and fastened so that open edges overlap

wrasse (ras) *n.* any of several edible marine fishes of warm seas

wrath (rath) *n.* anger —**'wrathful** *a.*

wreak (rēk) *vt.* **1.** inflict (vengeance) **2.** cause

wreath (rēth) *n.* something twisted into ring form, *esp.* band of flowers *etc.* as memorial or tribute on grave *etc.* —**wreathe** *vt.* **1.** form into wreath **2.** surround **3.** wind round

wreck (rek) *n.* **1.** destruction of ship **2.** wrecked ship **3.** ruin **4.** something ruined —*vt.* **5.** cause the wreck of —**'wreckage** *n.* —**'wrecker** *n.* **1.** person or thing that destroys, ruins **2.** person whose job is to demolish houses, dismantle old automobiles *etc.*

wren (ren) *n.* any of numerous small N Amer. songbirds distributed throughout the U.S. of which one species has spread to Europe and Asia

wrench (rench) *vt.* **1.** twist **2.** distort **3.** seize forcibly **4.** sprain —*n.* **5.** violent twist **6.** tool for twisting, screwing or holding **7.** sudden pain caused *esp.* by separation

wrest (rest) *vt.* **1.** take by force **2.** twist violently

wrestle ('resəl, 'rasəl) *vi.* **1.** fight (*esp.* as sport) by grappling and trying to throw down **2.** strive **3.** struggle —*n.* **4.** struggle, tussle —**'wrestler** *n.* —**'wrestling** *n.*

wretch (rech) *n.* **1.** despicable person **2.** miserable creature —**wretched** ('rechid) *a.* **1.** miserable, unhappy **2.** worthless —**wretchedly** ('rechidli) *adv.* —**wretchedness** ('rechidnis) *n.*

wriggle ('rigəl) *vi.* **1.** move with twisting action, as worm **2.** squirm —*n.* **3.** this action

wright (rīt) *n. obs.* workman; maker; builder

wring (ring) *vt.* **1.** twist **2.** extort **3.** pain **4.** squeeze out (**wrung, 'wringing**) —**'wringer** *n.* machine consisting of two rollers between which wet clothes are run to squeeze out the water

wrinkle ('ringkəl) *n.* **1.** slight ridge or furrow on surface **2.** crease in the skin **3.** fold **4.** pucker **5.** *inf.* (useful) trick, hint —*v.* **6.** make, become wrinkled, pucker

wrist (rist) *n.* joint between hand and arm —'**wristlet** *n.* band worn on wrist — **wrist watch**

writ (rit) *n.* written command from law court or other authority

write (rīt) *vi.* **1.** mark paper *etc.* with the symbols which are used to represent words or sounds **2.** compose **3.** send a letter —*vt.* **4.** set down in words **5.** compose **6.** communicate in writing **7.** *Comp.* transcribe (data) on an output medium **8.** *Comp.* transfer (data) into a section of memory (**wrote, written** ('ritən), '**writing**) —'**writer** *n.* **1.** one who writes **2.** author —**write-off** *n.* **1.** the deletion of an item from assets of a business **2.** reduction in book value of an asset **3.** *inf.* something damaged beyond repair —**write-up** *n.* written (published) account of something

writhe (rīdh) *vi.* **1.** twist, squirm in or as in pain *etc.* **2.** be acutely embarrassed (**writhed** *pt.*, **writhed,** *Poet.* **writhen** ('ridhən) *pp.*, '**writhing** *pr.p.*)

wrnt warrant

wrong (rong) *a.* **1.** not right or good **2.** not suitable **3.** wicked **4.** incorrect **5.** mistaken **6.** not functioning properly —*n.* **7.** that which is wrong **8.** harm **9.** evil —*vt.* **10.** do wrong to **11.** think badly of without justification —'**wrongful** *a.* —'**wrongfully** *adv.* —'**wrongly** *adv.* —'**wrong'doer** *n.* one who acts immorally or illegally —'**wrong'doing** *n.* —**wrong font** error of using the wrong kind of type —**wrong-headed** *a.* **1.** constantly wrong in judgment **2.** foolishly stubborn

wrote (rōt) *pt. of* WRITE

wrought (rôt) *v.* **1.** *pt./pp. of* WORK —*a.* **2.** (of metals) shaped by hammering or beating —**wrought iron** form of iron that is tough, malleable and relatively soft

wrung (rung) *pt./pp. of* WRING

wry (rī) *a.* **1.** turned to one side, contorted, askew **2.** sardonic, dryly humorous —'**wryneck** *n.* migratory woodpecker

WSW west-southwest

WT 1. watertight **2.** wireless telegraphy

wt. weight

wunderkind ('voondərkint) *n.* **1.** child prodigy **2.** person who succeeds in highly competitive field at an early age

WV *or* **W.Va.** West Virginia

WW 1. warehouse warrant **2.** with warrants

w/w wall-to-wall

WY Wyoming

wych- *or* **witch-** (*comb. form*) (of tree) with pliant branches

wynd (wīnd) *n.* in Scotland, narrow lane, alley

Wyoming (wī'ōming) *n.* Mountain state of the U.S., admitted to the Union in 1890. Abbrev.: **Wyo., WY** (with ZIP code)

wyvern ('wīvərn) *n.* mythical creature usu. represented as two-legged winged dragon with a barbed tail

x *or* **X** (eks) *n.* **1.** 24th letter of English alphabet **2.** speech sound sequence represented by this letter, pronounced as *ks* or *gz* or, in initial position, *z*, as in *xylophone* (*pl.* **x's, X's** *or* **Xs**)

x[1] **1.** first in order of class including *x, y, z* **2.** *Math.* unknown quantity

x[2] **1.** cross **2.** ex **3.** experimental **4.** extra

X **1.** Christ **2.** Christian **3.** Cross **4.** Roman numeral, 10 **5.** mark indicating error, a choice, a kiss, signature, position **6.** unknown, mysterious person, factor **7.** power of magnification **8.** multiplication symbol **9.** symbol indicating dimension

xanthine (ˈzanthēn) *n.* **1.** crystalline compound found in urine, blood and certain plants **2.** any of three derivatives of xanthine, which act as stimulants and diuretics

Xanthippe *or* **Xantippe** (zanˈtipi) *n.* wife of the Greek philosopher Socrates, of proverbially shrewish nature

x-axis *n.* **1.** in a plane Cartesian coordinate system, the horizontal axis along which the abscissa is measured **2.** in a 3-dimensional Cartesian coordinate, the axis along which values of *x* are measured and at which both *y* and *z* equal zero

XC *Fin.* ex coupon

X chromosome chromosome for femaleness, usu. occurring paired in female cells and single in male cells of many animals

xcp *Fin.* ex coupon

XD *or* **x div** *Fin.* ex dividend

Xe *Chem.* xenon

xebec (ˈzēbek) *n.* Mediterranean sailing ship with long overhanging bow and stern

xeno- *or before vowel* **xen-** (*comb. form*) something strange or foreign, as in *xenogamy*

xenogamy (zeˈnogəmi) *n.* **1.** pollination from another plant **2.** cross-fertilization

xenograft (ˈzenəgraft) *n.* tissue graft carried out between members of different species

xenon (ˈzēnon, ˈzenon) *n. Chem.* noble gas present in the atmosphere (about one part in 170 million by volume) used for filling television and other luminescent tubes *Symbol* Xe, at. wt. 131.3, at. no. 54

xenophobia (zenəˈfōbiə) *n.* dislike, hatred, fear, of strangers or aliens —ˈ**xenophobe** *n.* person who is hostile to what is foreign

xerography (ziˈrogrəfi) *n.* photocopying process —**xeroˈgraphic** *a.* —**Xerox** (ˈzēəroks) *n.* trade name for xerographic copying process, machine

xerophyte (ˈzēərəfīt) *n.* plant able to grow in dry conditions —ˈ**xeric** *a.*

x height height of lower-case letter x used to represent the main body of a lower-case letter

xi (zī, ksī) *n.* 14th letter in Gr. alphabet (Ξ, ξ) (*pl.* **-s**)

XI, x in, *or* **x int.** *Fin.* ex interest

XL **1.** extra large **2.** extra long

Xmas (ˈkrisməs, ˈeksməs) Christmas

Xn Christian

Xnty Christianity

XR *Fin.* ex rights

x-ray *or* **X-ray** *n.* **1.** radiation of very short wavelengths, capable of penetrating solid bodies, and printing on photographic plate shadow picture of objects not permeable by rays —*vt.* **2.** photograph by x-rays —**x-ray astronomy** astronomy dealing with heavenly bodies by means of x-rays they emit —**x-ray crystallography** study and practice of determining the structure of a crystal by using x-rays —**x-ray diffraction** scattering of x-rays by atoms of a crystal that produces an interference effect so that the diffraction pattern gives information on the structure of the crystal —**x-ray star** luminous heavenly object emitting major part of its radiation in form of x-rays —**x-ray therapy** medical treatment using x-rays —**x-ray tube** vacuum tube in which concentrated stream of electrons strikes a metal target and produces x-rays

X ray word used in communications for the letter *x*

XS extra small

XW *Fin.* ex warrants

xylem (ˈzīləm, -lem) *n.* plant tissue that conducts water and mineral salts from roots to other parts

xylene (ˈzīlēn) *n.* aromatic hydrocarbon existing in three isomeric forms, all three being colorless flammable volatile liquids used as solvents *etc.*

xylograph (ˈzīləgraf) *n.* **1.** wood engraving **2.** impression from wood block

xyloid (ˈzīloid) *a.* **1.** pert. to wood **2.** woody

xylophone (ˈzīləfōn) *n.* orchestral percussion instrument consisting of graded hardwood bars tuned in chromatic scale mounted on a horizontal frame struck with hammers

xylose (ˈzīlōs, -lōz) *n.* white crystalline sugar found in wood and straw and used in dyeing, tanning, diabetic food *etc.*

Y

y *or* **Y** (wī) *n.* **1.** 25th letter of English alphabet **2.** speech sound represented by this letter, usu. semivowel, as in *yawn,* or vowel, as in *symbol, shy* **3.** something shaped like Y (*pl.* **y's, Y's** *or* **Ys**)

y 1. yard(s) **2.** year(s) **3.** yen **4.** *Math.* y-axis or coordinate measured along y-axis in Cartesian coordinate system **5.** *Math.* algebraic variable

Y *Chem.* yttrium

-y[1] *or* **-ey** (*comb. form*) **1.** characterized by; consisting of; filled with; resembling, as in *sunny, sandy, smoky, classy* **2.** tending to; acting or existing as specified, as in *leaky, shiny*

-y[2], **-ie,** *or* **-ey** (*comb. form*) *inf.* **1.** denoting smallness and expressing affection and familiarity, as in *doggy, Jamie* **2.** person or thing concerned with or characterized by being, as in *groupie, goalie, fatty*

-y[3] (*comb. form*) **1.** act of doing what is indicated by verbal element, as in *inquiry* **2.** state, condition, quality, as in *geography, jealousy*

YA young adult

yacht (yot) *n.* vessel propelled by sail or power, used for racing, pleasure *etc.* —**'yachtsman** *n.*

yahoo ('yāhōō, 'yähōō) *n.* crude, coarse person

Yahweh ('yäwā, -vā) *n.* the God of the Hebrews

yak

yak[1] (yak) *n.* shaggy-haired, long-horned ox of Central Asia

yak[2] (yak) *sl. n.* **1.** noisy, continuous, trivial talk —*vi.* **2.** chatter or talk in this way (**-kk-**)

Yakima ('yakimō) *n.* **1.** member of group of Shahaptian peoples, of lower Yakima valley in south central Washington (*pl.* **Yakima, -s**) **2.** language of this people

yam (yam) *n.* **1.** moist-fleshed and usu. orange-fleshed sweet potato **2.** edible starchy tuberous root of various plants used as staple food in tropical areas

Yang (yang) *n. see* YIN AND YANG

yank (yangk) *vt.* **1.** jerk, tug; pull quickly —*n.* **2.** quick tug

Yankee ('yangki) *n.* **1.** native or inhabitant of New England **2.** native or inhabitant of northern U.S. **3.** native or inhabitant of U.S. **4.** word used in communications for the letter *y*

yanqui ('yängki) *n.* citizen of U.S. who is not a Hispano-American

yap (yap) *vi.* **1.** bark (as small dog) **2.** talk idly; gossip (**-pp-**) —*n.* **3.** sharp bark

Yaqui ('yäkē) *n.* (member of) Amerindian people of southern Arizona orig. from Sonora, Mexico (*pl.* **-qui, -s**)

yarborough ('yärbərə, -brə) *n. Bridge, whist* hand of 13 cards with no card higher than nine

yard[1] (yärd) *n.* **1.** unit of length, 0.915 meter, three feet **2.** (*usu. pl.*) great length or quantity **3.** *sl.* one hundred dollars **4.** spar slung across ship's mast to extend sails —**'yardage** *n.* **1.** aggregate number of yards **2.** length, extent or volume of goods measured in yards —**yard goods** fabrics sold by yard —**'yardstick** *n.* **1.** graduated measuring stick **2.** formula or standard of measurement or comparison

yard[2] (yärd) *n.* piece of enclosed ground, oft. attached to or adjoining building and used for some specific purpose, as garden, storage, holding livestock *etc.* —**'yardage** *n.* **1.** use of yard **2.** charge made for this —**'yardbird** *n.* **1.** soldier assigned to menial task or restricted to limited area as punishment **2.** untrained or inept enlisted man

yarmulke ('yäməkə, 'yärməlkə) *n. Judaism* man's skullcap worn at prayer, and by strongly religious Jews at all times

yarn (yärn) *n.* **1.** continuous strand of twisted fibers or filaments **2.** tale —*vi.* **3.** tell a tale

yarrow ('yarō) *n.* large genus of hardy herbaceous perennials of the daisy family with many forms and colors

yashmak *or* **yasmac** ('yashmak) *n.* face veil worn by Muslim women

yaup (yōp) *see* YAWP

yaw (yō) *vi.* **1.** (of aircraft *etc.*) turn about vertical axis **2.** (of ship *etc.*) deviate temporarily from course

yawl (yōl) *n.* two-masted sailing vessel

yawn (yŏn) *vi.* **1.** open mouth wide, *esp.* in sleepiness **2.** gape —*n.* **3.** a yawning
yawp *or* **yaup** (yŏp) *n./vi.* (make) raucous noise
yaws (yŏz) *pl.n.* contagious bacterial disease prevalent in tropics
y-axis *n.* reference axis of graph or two- or three-dimensional Cartesian coordinate system along which y-coordinate is measured
Yb *Chem.* ytterbium
YB yearbook
Y chromosome sex chromosome that occurs as one of pair with X chromosome in paired cells of males of many animals
yclept (iˈklept) *a. obs.* called (by the name of)
yd yard (measure)
ye (yē) *pron. obs.* you
yea (yā) *interj. obs.* yes
yeah (ˈyeə, yāə) *interj.* yes
year (yēər) *n.* **1.** time taken by one revolution of earth round sun, about 365 days **2.** twelve months —ˈ**yearling** *n.* animal one year old —ˈ**yearly** *adv.* **1.** every year, once a year —*a.* **2.** happening *etc.* once a year —ˈ**yearbook** *n.* **1.** school publication, usu. compiled by graduating class, that records the year's activities **2.** reference book published annually and containing details of events of previous year —**Yearly Meeting** organization uniting several Quarterly Meetings of the Society of Friends
yearn (yərn) *vi.* **1.** feel longing, desire **2.** be filled with pity, tenderness —ˈ**yearning** *n./a.*
yeast (yēst) *n.* **1.** frothy yellowish substance consisting of cells of a fungus reproducing in a saccharin liquid to produce an alcoholic fermentation used in leavening dough and making alcoholic beverages **2.** dried form of this **3.** wild airborne cells of this fungus —ˈ**yeasty** *a.* **1.** frothy, foamy **2.** exuberant
yegg (yeg) *n. inf.* **1.** safe-cracker **2.** robber
yell (yel) *v.* **1.** cry out in loud shrill tone **2.** *inf.* call —*n.* **3.** loud shrill cry **4.** *inf.* call
yellow (ˈyelō) *a.* **1.** of the color of lemons, gold *etc.* **2.** *inf.* cowardly —*n.* **3.** portion of spectrum lying between green and orange —**yellow fever** acute infectious viral disease transmitted by mosquitoes (*also* **yellow jack**) —ˈ**yellowhammer** *n.* small European bunting —**yellow jack 1.** flag raised by ship in quarantine **2.** yellow fever —**yellow jacket** any of various small ground-nesting wasps —**yellow pages** classified telephone directory or section of directory that lists subscribers by business or service provided —**yellow peril** supposed danger from Oriental peoples —**yellow streak** cowardly trait —ˈ**yellowwood** *n.* **1.** any of various trees having yellowish wood or yielding a yellowish extract **2.** the wood of such a tree
yelp (yelp) *vi./n.* (produce) quick, shrill cry
Yemen (ˈyemən) *n.* —**People's Democratic Republic of Yemen.** country in western Asia bounded north by Yemen Arab Republic and Saudi Arabia, east by Oman, south by the Gulf of Aden and west by the Yemen Arab Republic
Yemen Arab Republic country in western Asia bounded north by Saudi Arabia, south and east by the People's Democratic Republic of Yemen and west by the Red Sea
yen[1] (yen) *n.* Japanese monetary unit (*pl.* **yen**)
yen[2] (yen) *n. inf.* longing, craving
yenta (ˈyentə) *n.* vulgar, ill-tempered woman who gossips
yeoman (ˈyōmən) *n.* **1.** *Hist.* farmer cultivating his own land **2.** assistant, subordinate —ˈ**yeomanry** *n.* **1.** yeomen collectively **2.** Brit. volunteer cavalry force, organized in 1761 for home defense —**yeoman of the guard** member of ceremonial bodyguard (**Yeomen of the Guard**) of British monarch
yerba maté (ˈyerbə ˈmätā, ˈyərbə) *see* MATÉ
yes (yes) *interj.* affirms or consents, gives an affirmative answer —**yes man** weak person willing to agree to anything
yeshiva (yəˈshēvə) *n.* **1.** rabbinical seminary **2.** Hebrew secondary school (*pl.* **-s, yeshivoth** (yəshēˈvōt))
yesterday (ˈyestərdi, -dā) *n.* **1.** day before today **2.** recent time —*adv.* **3.** on the day before today
yet (yet) *adv.* **1.** now **2.** still **3.** besides **4.** hitherto **5.** nevertheless —*conj.* **6.** but, at the same time, nevertheless
yeti (ˈyeti) *n. see* **abominable snowman** *at* ABOMINATE
yew (yōō) *n.* **1.** genus of evergreen trees with dark leaves **2.** wood of any of these
Yggdrasil *or* **Ygdrasil** (ˈigdrəsil) *n.* in Norse legend, the great ash tree that supported the universe
Yiddish (ˈyidish) *a./n.* (of, in) dialect of mixed German and Hebrew, the vernacular of Ashkenazic Jews —**yid** *n. sl. offens.* Jew
yield (yēld) *vt.* **1.** give or return as food **2.** produce **3.** provide **4.** concede **5.** give up, surrender —*vi.* **6.** submit **7.** (*with* to) comply (with) **8.** surrender, give way —*n.* **9.** amount produced, result **10.** return, profit

yin and yang: the traditional Chinese symbol

Yin and Yang (yin) two complementary principles of Chinese philosophy: Yin is negative, dark and feminine; Yang is positive, bright and masculine
Y.M.C.A. Young Men's Christian Association
Y.M.H.A. Young Men's Hebrew Association
YO year old

y.o. year(s) old

YOB year of birth

yodel ('yōdəl) *n.* **1.** type of vocalization indigenous to mountain people of Switzerland and Tyrol marked by frequent and quick passing from low chest voice to high falsetto —*v.* **2.** sing in a yodel

Yoga ('yōgə) *n.* **1.** Hindu philosophical system aiming at spiritual, mental and physical well-being by means of certain physical and mental exercises **2.** (**y-**) system of exercises for attaining bodily well-being (**Hatha yoga**) —**yogi** ('yōgi) *n.* one who practices yoga (*pl.* **-s, -gin** (-gin))

yogurt *or* **yoghurt** ('yōgərt) *n.* semisolid food, oft. flavored, made of whole or skimmed milk fermented by cultures of certain bacteria

yoicks (yoiks) *interj.* cry used in fox-hunting to urge on hounds

yoke (yōk) *n.* **1.** wooden bar put across necks of two animals to hold them together and to which plow *etc.* may be attached **2.** various objects like a yoke in shape or use **3.** fitted part of garment, *esp.* round neck, shoulders **4.** bond, tie **5.** domination —*vt.* **6.** put a yoke on **7.** couple, unite

yokel ('yōkəl) *n.* naive or gullible inhabitant of small town or rural area

yolk (yōk) *n.* **1.** yellow central part of egg **2.** oily secretion of skin of sheep

Yom Kippur (yōm ki'pŏŏər; *Hebrew* yom kē'pōōr) Jewish holiday celebrated as day of fasting, when prayers of penitence are recited in synagogue (*also* **Day of Atonement**)

yon (yon) *a. obs., dial.* that or those over there —'**yonder** *a.* **1.** yon —*adv.* **2.** over there, in that direction

yoo-hoo ('yōōhōō) *interj.* call to attract attention

yore (yōr) *n. Poet.* the distant past

Yorkshire pudding ('yōrkshēər) batter consisting of eggs, flour and milk baked in meat drippings

Yorkshire terrier purebred toy dog with long straight silky coat mostly bluish-gray but tan on head and chest

you (yōō; *unstressed* yŏŏ) *pron.* referring to person(s) addressed, or to unspecified person(s) —**you-all** *pron.* (*used chiefly in southern U.S.*) **1.** in addressing two or more persons **2.** addressing one person as representing another or others

young (yung) *a.* **1.** not far advanced in growth, life or existence **2.** not yet old **3.** immature **4.** junior **5.** recently formed **6.** vigorous —*n.* **7.** offspring —'**youngster** *n.* child

younker ('yungkər) *n.* **1.** young man **2.** youngster

your (yōr, yŏŏər; *unstressed* yər) *a.* belonging to you —**yours** *pron.* —**your'self** *pron.* (*pl.* **your'selves**)

youth (yōōth) *n.* **1.** state or time of being young **2.** state before adult age **3.** young man **4.** young people —'**youthful** *a.* —**youth hostel** supervised lodging for young travelers

yowl (yowl) *vi./n.* (produce) mournful cry

yo-yo ('yōyō) *n.* toy consisting of a spool attached to a string, by which it can be spun out and reeled in while attached to the finger (*pl.* **-s**)

yr **1.** year **2.** younger **3.** your

yrs **1.** years **2.** yours

Y.S.T. Yukon Standard Time

Y.T. C Yukon Territory

ytterbium (i'terbiəm) *n. Chem.* metallic element *Symbol* Yb, at. wt. 173.0, at. no. 70

yttrium ('itriəm) *n. Chem.* metallic element *Symbol* Y, at. wt. 88.9, at. no. 39

yuan (yōō'än) *n.* Chinese monetary unit (*pl.* **yuan**)

yucca ('yukə) *n.* genus of hardy and tender evergreen shrubs and small trees of the lily family with long leaves and flowers borne on an erect stem

Yugoslavia (yōōgō'slāviə) *n.* country in Europe bounded north by Austria and Hungary, northeast by Romania, east by Bulgaria, south by Greece, and west by Albania, the Adriatic Sea, and Italy —**Yugo'slavian** *n./a.*

yule (yōōl) *n.* (*sometimes* **Y-**) the Christmas festival or season

Yuma ('yōōmə) *n.* Amerindian language family of southwest U.S. and northern Mexico —'**Yuman** *a./n.*

Yuppie ('yupi) *n.* young urban (usu. upwardly mobile) professional

yurt (yŏŏərt) *n.* circular domed tent consisting of collapsible lattice framework covered with skins or felt used as dwelling by Mongol nomads in Siberia

Y.W.C.A. Young Women's Christian Association

Y.W.H.A. Young Women's Hebrew Association

Z

z *or* **Z** (zē) *n.* **1.** 26th letter of English alphabet **2.** speech sound represented by this letter **3.** something shaped like Z (*pl.* **z's, Z's** *or* **Zs**)

z 1. zero **2.** zone **3.** *Math.* z-axis or coordinate measured along z-axis in Cartesian or cylindrical coordinate system **4.** *Math.* algebraic variable

Z *or* **ZD** zenith distance

Zach. *Bible* Zacharias

Zacharias (zakə'rīəs) *n. Bible* Zechariah in the Douay Version of the O.T.

Zaïre (zä'ēər) *n.* country in Africa bounded north by the Central African Republic, northeast by Sudan, east by Uganda, Rwanda, Burundi and Lake Tanganyika, south by Zambia, southwest by Angola, northwest by Congo —**Za'ïrian** *a./n.*

Zambia ('zambiə) *n.* country in Africa bounded north by Zaïre and Tanzania, east by Malawi, southeast by Mozambique, south by Zimbabwe and Namibia —**'Zambian** *a./n.*

zany ('zāni) *a.* comical, funny in unusual way

zarzuela (zär'zwālə) *n.* national type of Spanish opera, usu. light one-act comedy but occasionally dealing with serious dramatic subjects in two or three acts

ZD *see* Z

zeal (zēl) *n.* **1.** fervor **2.** keenness, enthusiasm —**zealot** ('zelət) *n.* **1.** fanatic **2.** enthusiast —**zealous** ('zeləs) *a.* **1.** ardent **2.** enthusiastic **3.** earnest —**zealously** ('zeləsli) *adv.*

zebra ('zēbrə) *n.* any of several fleet African mammals related to the horse but conspicuously striped

zebu ('zēbōō) *n.* humped Indian ox or cow

Zech. *Bible* Zechariah

Zechariah (zekə'rīə) *n. Bible* 38th book of the O.T., written by the prophet Zechariah in the 5th cent. B.C. about the coming of Christ

Zemstvo ('zemstvō) *n.* in czarist Russia, council composed of local elected officials

Zen (zen) *n.* form of Buddhism emphasizing meditation and physical work as means to enlightenment

zenana (zə'nänə) *n.* **1.** in India and Pakistan, women's part of high-caste dwelling **2.** lightweight quilted fabric used mainly for housecoats

zenith ('zēnith) *n.* **1.** point of the heavens directly above an observer **2.** point opposite nadir **3.** summit, peak **4.** climax —**'zenithal** *a.*

Zeph. *Bible* Zephaniah

Zephaniah (zefə'nīə) *n. Bible* 36th book of the O.T., written by the prophet Zephaniah about 5th cent. B.C. concerning the Day of the Lord

zephyr ('zefər) *n.* soft, gentle breeze

zeppelin ('zepəlin) *n.* large, cylindrical, rigid airship

zero ('zēərō) *n.* **1.** nothing **2.** figure 0 **3.** point on graduated instrument from which positive and negative quantities are reckoned **4.** the lowest point (*pl.* **-s, -es**) —**zero hour 1.** *Mil.* time set for start of attack *etc.* **2.** *inf.* critical time —**zero population growth** replacing of present population without increasing it

zest (zest) *n.* **1.** enjoyment **2.** excitement, interest, flavor **3.** peel of orange or lemon

zeta ('zātə, 'zētə) *n.* sixth letter in Gr. alphabet (Z, ζ)

Zeus (zōōs) *n.* supreme god of the ancient Greeks

ZI zone of interior

zibeline *or* **zibelline** ('zibəlēn) *n.* strongly colored cloth made from alpaca, mohair and camel's hair with lustrous long-napped finish

zigzag ('zigzag) *n.* **1.** line or course characterized by sharp turns in alternating directions —*vi.* **2.** move along in zigzag course (**-zagged** *pt./pp.*, **-zagging** *pr.p.*)

zilch (zilch) *inf. n.* **1.** nothing, zero —*a.* **2.** no

zillion ('zilyən) *n. inf.* extremely large, indeterminate number

Zimbabwe (zim'bäbwi) *n.* country in Africa located between northern border of Transvaal and the Zambesi River bordered on the east by Mozambique, on the west b[illegible] Botswana —**Zim'babwean** *a./n.*

zinc (zingk) *n. Chem.* metallic elem[illegible] *Symbol* Zn, at. wt. 65.4, at. no. 30 —**'zin[illegible] graph** *n.* —**zin'cographer** *n.* —**zin'cograp[illegible]** *n.* art or process of engraving zinc to for[illegible] printing plate —**zinc ointment** medicina[illegible] ointment of zinc oxide, petrolatum and paraffin —**zinc oxide** white insoluble powder used as pigment in paints, cosmetics, glass *etc.* (*also* **flowers of zinc**)

Zinfandel ('zinfəndel) *n.* **1.** red, medium-bodied table wine **2.** grape used to make this wine

zing (zing) *inf. n.* **1.** short high-pitched buzzing sound **2.** vitality; zest —*vi.* **3.** make or move with high-pitched buzzing sound

zinjanthropus (zin'janthrəpəs) *n.* fossil hominid characterized by very low brow and large molars

zinnia ('ziniə) *n.* genus of annual and

perennial plants and subshrubs of the daisy family grown for ornament

Zion ('zīən) *or* **Sion** *n.* **1.** hill on which Jerusalem stands **2.** Judaism **3.** Christian Church **4.** heaven —'**Zionism** *n.* movement to found, support Jewish homeland in Palestine —'**Zionist** *n./a.*

zip (zip) *n.* **1.** energy and vigor **2.** sharp whizzing sound —*vi.* **3.** move with zip —*vt.* **4.** add speed and force to (**-pp-**)

zip code system combining 2-letter abbreviation for a State and 5-figure number identifying postal delivery areas in the U.S. —**zip-code** *vt.* furnish with a zip code

zipper ('zipər) *n.* device for fastening with two rows of flexible metal or nylon teeth, interlocked and opened by a sliding clip —'**zippered** *a.* equipped with zipper —**zip up** close with zipper (**-pp-**)

zircon ('zərkon) *n.* mineral used as gemstone and in industry —**zir'conium** *n. Chem.* metallic element *Symbol* Zr, at. wt. 91.2, at. no. 40

zither ('zidhər) *n.* stringed instrument of ancient origin consisting of flat wooden box over which are stretched 30 to 45 strings. Four or five melody strings can be stopped on a fretted fingerboard and are played with a plectrum while other strings are plucked for the accompaniment

zloty ('zloti) *n.* Polish monetary unit (*pl.* **-s, zloty**)

Zn 1. *Chem.* zinc **2.** azimuth

zodiac ('zōdiak) *n.* imaginary belt of the heavens along which the sun, moon, and chief planets appear to move, divided crosswise into twelve equal areas, called **signs of the zodiac,** each named after a constellation —**zodiacal** (zō'dīəkəl) *a.*

zombie *or* **zombi** ('zombi) *n.* **1.** person appearing lifeless, apathetic *etc.* **2.** corpse supposedly brought to life by supernatural spirit

zone (zōn) *n.* **1.** region with particular characteristics or use **2.** any of the five belts into which tropics and arctic and antarctic circles divide the earth —'**zonal** *a.* —**zone defense** *Sport* system of defense in which each defensive player has an assigned zone

zonked (zongkt) *a. sl.* **1.** intoxicated by alcohol **2.** stupefied by drug

zoo (zo͞o) *n.* place where wild animals are kept, studied, bred and exhibited (*in full* **zoological gardens**)

zoo- *or before vowel* **zo-** (*comb. form*) animals, as in *zooplankton*

zoogeography (zōəji'ogrəfi) *n.* science of geographical distribution of animals

zoography (zō'ogrəfi) *n.* descriptive zoology —**zo'ographer** *or* **zo'ographist** *n.*

zooid ('zōoid) *n.* **1.** independent animal body, such as individual of coelenterate colony **2.** cell or body capable of spontaneous motion, produced by organism

zool. 1. zoological **2.** zoology

zoology (zō'oləji, zo͞o-) *n.* **1.** scientific study of animals **2.** characteristics of particular animals or of fauna of particular area —**zoo'logical** *a.* —**zo'ologist** *n.*

zoom (zo͞om) *v.* **1.** (cause to) make loud buzzing, humming sound **2.** (cause to) go fast or rise, increase sharply —*vi.* **3.** (*with* in *or* out) use camera lens of adjustable focal length to make subject appear closer or further away —**zoom lens** lens used in this way

zoonosis (zō'onəsis) *n.* disease transmissible from lower animals to man in natural conditions (*pl.* **-ses** (-sēz))

zoophyte ('zōəfīt) *n.* plantlike animal, *eg* sponge —**zoophytic** (zōə'fitik) *a.*

zori ('zōri) *n.* flat sandal with thong between big and second toe, usu. made of rubber (*pl.* **zori**)

Zoroastrianism (zōrō'astriənizəm) *or* **Zoroastrism** *n.* dualistic religion founded by Persian prophet Zoroaster, based on concept of continuous struggle between Ahura Mazda, god of creation, light and goodness, and his archenemy, Angra Mainyu, spirit of evil and darkness

Zouave (zo͞o'äv) *n.* member of French infantry unit orig. composed of Algerians wearing brilliant uniform and conducting spirited drill

zoysia ('zoishə) *n.* any of a genus of creeping perennial grasses with fine wiry leaves including some used for lawns in warm regions

ZPG zero population growth

Zr *Chem.* zirconium

zucchetto (zo͞o'ketō) *n. R.C.Ch.* ecclesiastical skullcap, black for priest, purple for bishop, red for cardinal, white for the pope (*pl.* **-es**)

zucchini (zo͞o'kēni) *n.* **1.** cylindrical dark green summer squash **2.** the bushy plant bearing this fruit (*pl.* **zucchini, -s**)

Zulu ('zo͞olo͞o) *n.* **1.** member of Bantu-speaking people of Natal **2.** Bantu language of the Zulus **3.** word used in communications for the letter *z*

Zuni ('zo͞onē) *or* **Zuñi** ('zo͞onyē) *n.* **1.** Amerindian people of western New Mexico **2.** member of this people (*pl.* **-i, -is**) **3.** language of this people —'**Zunian** *or* '**Zuñian** *a./n.*

zuppa inglese ('tso͞opə ing'glāzi) dessert made of sponge cake, rum-flavored custard, fruit and whipped cream

zwieback ('zwībak, 'zwē-) *n.* rich sweet bread that is sliced and baked again until it is dry and crisp

zygote ('zīgōt) *n.* fertilized egg cell

zymurgy ('zīmərji) *n.* chemistry of fermentation processes

For Gift Giving

WEDDING ANNIVERSARY SYMBOLS

	TRADITIONAL	MODERN
1st	paper	clocks
2nd	cotton	china
3rd	leather	crystal, glass
4th	books	electrical appliances
5th	wood	silverware
6th	sugar, candy	wood
7th	wool, copper	desk sets
8th	bronze, pottery	linens, laces
9th	pottery, willow	leather
10th	tin, aluminum	diamond jewelry
11th	steel	fashion jewelry
12th	silk, linen	pearls, colored gems
13th	lace	textiles, furs
14th	ivory	gold jewelry
15th	crystal	watches
20th	china	platinum
25th	silver	silver
30th	pearl	diamond
35th	coral	jade
40th	ruby	ruby
45th	sapphire	sapphire
50th	gold	gold
55th	emerald	emerald
60th	diamond	diamond
75th	diamond	diamond

BIRTHSTONES

January	Garnet
February	Amethyst
March	Bloodstone or Aquamarine
April	Diamond
May	Emerald
June	Pearl or Alexandrite
July	Ruby
August	Sardonyx or Peridot
September	Sapphire
October	Opal or Tourmaline
November	Topaz
December	Turquoise or Zircon